WHITAKER'S CONCISE ALMANACK 1997

CW00369191

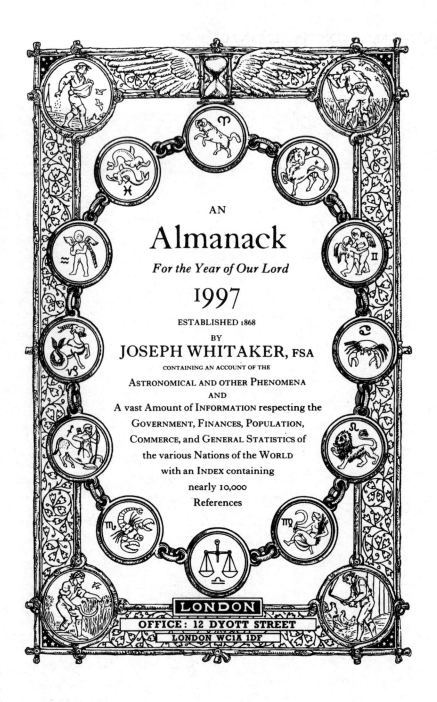

AN

Almanack

For the Year of Our Lord

1997

ESTABLISHED 1868

BY

JOSEPH WHITAKER, FSA

CONTAINING AN ACCOUNT OF THE

ASTRONOMICAL AND OTHER PHENOMENA

AND

A vast Amount of INFORMATION respecting the
GOVERNMENT, FINANCES, POPULATION,
COMMERCE, and GENERAL STATISTICS of
the various Nations of the WORLD
with an INDEX containing
nearly 10,000
References

LONDON

OFFICE: 12 DYOTT STREET
LONDON WC1A 1DF

The traditional design of the title page for Whitaker's Almanack which has appeared in each edition since 1868

Whitaker's Concise Almanack

1997

J. WHITAKER & SONS LTD

12 DYOTT STREET · LONDON WC1A 1DF

J. WHITAKER AND SONS LTD
12 Dyott Street, London WCIA IDF

Whitaker's Almanack published annually since 1868
© 129th edition J. Whitaker and Sons Ltd 1996
Concise Almanack (672 pages)
0 85021 262 6

Designed by Douglas Martin
Typeset by Page Bros (Norwich) Ltd
Printed and bound in Great Britain by
Clays Ltd, part of St Ives PLC, Bungay, Suffolk

Contents

Preface

TO THE 129TH ANNUAL VOLUME 1997

As the last edition of Whitaker was published, the future of the peace process in the Middle East looked uncertain following the assassination of Yitzhak Rabin, the prime minister of Israel. Progress towards peace has indeed faltered in the past year, and as this edition of Whitaker goes to press, violence between Israeli and Palestinian has left over 50 dead. Nearer home, the Northern Ireland peace process has also failed to live up to the hopes invested in it, expressed in the reception accorded President Clinton when he visited Ireland at the end of 1995, and this year has seen the return of terrorism and sectarian violence. However, the year has also seen an end to fighting in Bosnia-Hercegovina, where the establishment of stable government continues. Developments throughout the year in these areas are recorded in this edition.

By the time Whitaker 1997 is published, the National Lottery will have reached its second anniversary. Its impact on the social and cultural life of Britain has been phenomenal. Details of the amounts spent on the Lottery and of the grants made with the proceeds are summarized in this edition. Statistics about other forms of gambling provide a wider context, and the articles on the year in the arts, conservation, etc., record the effect of the grants.

A summer of high-profile sporting events included the Olympic Games and Euro '96; the highlights of both are recorded and illustrated. Coverage of local government and education reflects the local government changes in Wales, Scotland and parts of England in April 1996, and details are included of proposed changes in England in 1997 and 1998.

A significant revision is the rewriting of the Legal Notes in less legalistic language. We hope readers will find the information more clearly presented and easier to use.

As ever, I must thank my staff and our specialist contributors, and the many individuals and organizations who provide us with information; without their efforts, Whitaker's Almanack could not sustain its high standards of accuracy, comprehensiveness and topicality each year.

12 DYOTT STREET
LONDON WC1A 1DF
TEL 0171-420 6000

OCTOBER 1996

HILARY MARSDEN
Editor

The Year 1997

CHRONOLOGICAL CYCLES AND ERAS

Dominical Letter	E
Epact	21
Golden Number (Lunar Cycle)	III
Julian Period	6710
Roman Indiction	5
Solar Cycle	18

	Beginning
Japanese year Heisei 9	1 January
Regnal year 46	6 February
Chinese year of the Ox	7 February
Indian (Saka) year 1919	22 March
Hindu new year	8 April
Sikh new year	13 April
Muslim year AH 1418	9 May
Jewish year AM 5758	2 October
Roman year 2750 AUC	

RELIGIOUS CALENDARS

Epiphany	6 January
Ramadan, first day	10 January
Makara Sankranti	14 January
Birthday of Guru Gobind Singh Ji	15 January
Vasant Panchami (Sarasvati-puja)	11 February
Ash Wednesday	12 February
Mahashivaratri	7 March
Holi	23 March
Good Friday	28 March
Easter Day (western churches)	30 March
Baisakhi Mela (Sikh new year)	13 April
Ramanavami	16 April
Idu-l-adha	18 April
Passover, first day	22 April
Easter Day (Greek Orthodox)	27 April
Rogation Sunday	4 May
Ascension Day	8 May
Pentecost (Whit Sunday)	18 May
Trinity Sunday	25 May
Corpus Christi	29 May
Martyrdom of Guru Arjan Dev Ji	9 June
Feast of Weeks, first day	11 June
Raksha-bandhan	18 August
Janmashtami	24 August
Ganesh Chaturthi, first day	6 September
Ganesh festival, last day	15 September
Navaratri festival, first day	2 October
Durga-puja	2 October
Sarasvati-puja	9 October
Dasara	11 October
Yom Kippur (Day of Atonement)	11 October
Feast of Tabernacles, first day	16 October
Diwali (Hindu), first day	28 October
Diwali (Hindu), last day	2 November
Birthday of Guru Nanak Dev Ji	14 November
First Sunday in Advent	30 November
Martyrdom of Guru Tegh Bahadur Ji	4 December
Chanucah, first day	24 December
Christmas Day	25 December
Ramadan	31 December

CIVIL CALENDAR

Accession of Queen Elizabeth II	6 February
Duke of York's birthday	19 February
St David's Day	1 March
Prince Edward's birthday	10 March
Commonwealth Day	10 March
St Patrick's Day	17 March
Birthday of Queen Elizabeth II	21 April
St George's Day	23 April
Coronation of Queen Elizabeth II	2 June
Duke of Edinburgh's birthday	10 June
The Queen's Official Birthday	14 June
Diana, Princess of Wales' birthday	1 July
Queen Elizabeth the Queen Mother's birthday	4 August
Princess Royal's birthday	15 August
Princess Margaret's birthday	21 August
Lord Mayor's Day	8 November
Remembrance Sunday	9 November
Prince of Wales's birthday	14 November
Wedding Day of Queen Elizabeth II	20 November
St Andrew's Day	30 November

LEGAL CALENDAR

LAW TERMS

Hilary Term	11 January to 26 March
Easter Term	8 April to 23 May
Trinity Term	3 June to 31 July
Michaelmas Term	1 October to 20 December

QUARTER DAYS

England, Wales and Northern Ireland

Lady	25 March
Midsummer	24 June
Michaelmas	29 September
Christmas	25 December

TERM DAYS

Scotland

Candlemas	28 February
Whitsunday	28 May
Lammas	28 August
Martinmas	28 November
Removal Terms	28 May, 28 November

1997

JANUARY

Sunday		5	12	19	26
Monday		6	13	20	27
Tuesday		7	14	21	28
Wednesday	1	8	15	22	29
Thursday	2	9	16	23	30
Friday	3	10	17	24	31
Saturday	4	11	18	25	

FEBRUARY

Sunday		2	9	16	23
Monday		3	10	17	24
Tuesday		4	11	18	25
Wednesday		5	12	19	26
Thursday		6	13	20	27
Friday		7	14	21	28
Saturday	1	8	15	22	

MARCH

Sunday		2	9	16	23	30
Monday		3	10	17	24	31
Tuesday		4	11	18	25	
Wednesday		5	12	19	26	
Thursday		6	13	20	27	
Friday		7	14	21	28	
Saturday	1	8	15	22	29	

APRIL

Sunday		6	13	20	27
Monday		7	14	21	28
Tuesday	1	8	15	22	29
Wednesday	2	9	16	23	30
Thursday	3	10	17	24	
Friday	4	11	18	25	
Saturday	5	12	19	26	

MAY

Sunday		4	11	18	25
Monday		5	12	19	26
Tuesday		6	13	20	27
Wednesday		7	14	21	28
Thursday	1	8	15	22	29
Friday	2	9	16	23	30
Saturday	3	10	17	24	31

JUNE

Sunday	1	8	15	22	29
Monday	2	9	16	23	30
Tuesday	3	10	17	24	
Wednesday	4	11	18	25	
Thursday	5	12	19	26	
Friday	6	13	20	27	
Saturday	7	14	21	28	

JULY

Sunday		6	13	20	27
Monday		7	14	21	28
Tuesday	1	8	15	22	29
Wednesday	2	9	16	23	30
Thursday	3	10	17	24	31
Friday	4	11	18	25	
Saturday	5	12	19	26	

AUGUST

Sunday		3	10	17	24	31
Monday		4	11	18	25	
Tuesday		5	12	19	26	
Wednesday		6	13	20	27	
Thursday		7	14	21	28	
Friday	1	8	15	22	29	
Saturday	2	9	16	23	30	

SEPTEMBER

Sunday		7	14	21	28
Monday	1	8	15	22	29
Tuesday	2	9	16	23	30
Wednesday	3	10	17	24	
Thursday	4	11	18	25	
Friday	5	12	19	26	
Saturday	6	13	20	27	

OCTOBER

Sunday		5	12	19	26
Monday		6	13	20	27
Tuesday		7	14	21	28
Wednesday	1	8	15	22	29
Thursday	2	9	16	23	30
Friday	3	10	17	24	31
Saturday	4	11	18	25	

NOVEMBER

Sunday		2	9	16	23	30
Monday		3	10	17	24	
Tuesday		4	11	18	25	
Wednesday		5	12	19	26	
Thursday		6	13	20	27	
Friday		7	14	21	28	
Saturday	1	8	15	22	29	

DECEMBER

Sunday		7	14	21	28
Monday	1	8	15	22	29
Tuesday	2	9	16	23	30
Wednesday	3	10	17	24	31
Thursday	4	11	18	25	
Friday	5	12	19	26	
Saturday	6	13	20	27	

PUBLIC HOLIDAYS

	England and Wales	Scotland	Northern Ireland
New Year	1 January	1, 2 January	1 January
St Patrick's Day	—	—	17 March
*Good Friday	28 March	28 March	28 March
Easter Monday	31 March	—	31 March
May Day	5 May	26 May	5 May
Spring	26 May	5 May	26 May
Battle of the Boyne	—	—	14 July
Summer	25 August	4 August	25 August
*Christmas	25, 26 December	25, 26 December	25, 26 December

* In England, Wales, and Northern Ireland, Christmas Day and Good Friday are common law holidays
In the Channel Islands, Liberation Day (9 May) is a bank and public holiday

1998

JANUARY

Sunday		4	11	18	25
Monday		5	12	19	26
Tuesday		6	13	20	27
Wednesday		7	14	21	28
Thursday	1	8	15	22	29
Friday	2	9	16	23	30
Saturday	3	10	17	24	31

FEBRUARY

Sunday	1	8	15	22
Monday	2	9	16	23
Tuesday	3	10	17	24
Wednesday	4	11	18	25
Thursday	5	12	19	26
Friday	6	13	20	27
Saturday	7	14	21	28

MARCH

Sunday	1	8	15	22	29
Monday	2	9	16	23	30
Tuesday	3	10	17	24	31
Wednesday	4	11	18	25
Thursday	5	12	19	26
Friday	6	13	20	27
Saturday	7	14	21	28

APRIL

Sunday		5	12	19	26
Monday		6	13	20	27
Tuesday		7	14	21	28
Wednesday	1	8	15	22	29
Thursday	2	9	16	23	30
Friday	3	10	17	24
Saturday	4	11	18	25

MAY

Sunday		3	10	17	24	31
Monday		4	11	18	25
Tuesday		5	12	19	26
Wednesday		6	13	20	27
Thursday		7	14	21	28
Friday	1	8	15	22	29
Saturday	2	9	16	23	30

JUNE

Sunday		7	14	21	28
Monday	1	8	15	22	29
Tuesday	2	9	16	23	30
Wednesday	3	10	17	24
Thursday	4	11	18	25
Friday	5	12	19	26
Saturday	6	13	20	27

JULY

Sunday		5	12	19	26
Monday		6	13	20	27
Tuesday		7	14	21	28
Wednesday	1	8	15	22	29
Thursday	2	9	16	23	30
Friday	3	10	17	24	31
Saturday	4	11	18	25

AUGUST

Sunday		2	9	16	23	30
Monday		3	10	17	24	31
Tuesday		4	11	18	25
Wednesday		5	12	19	26
Thursday		6	13	20	27
Friday		7	14	21	28
Saturday	1	8	15	22	29

SEPTEMBER

Sunday		6	13	20	27
Monday		7	14	21	28
Tuesday	1	8	15	22	29
Wednesday	2	9	16	23	30
Thursday	3	10	17	24
Friday	4	11	18	25
Saturday	5	12	19	26

OCTOBER

Sunday		4	11	18	25
Monday		5	12	19	26
Tuesday		6	13	20	27
Wednesday		7	14	21	28
Thursday	1	8	15	22	29
Friday	2	9	16	23	30
Saturday	3	10	17	24	31

NOVEMBER

Sunday	1	8	15	22	29
Monday	2	9	16	23	30
Tuesday	3	10	17	24
Wednesday	4	11	18	25
Thursday	5	12	19	26
Friday	6	13	20	27
Saturday	7	14	21	28

DECEMBER

Sunday		6	13	20	27
Monday		7	14	21	28
Tuesday	1	8	15	22	29
Wednesday	2	9	16	23	30
Thursday	3	10	17	24	31
Friday	4	11	18	25
Saturday	5	12	19	26

PUBLIC HOLIDAYS

	England and Wales	Scotland	Northern Ireland
New Year	1 January	1, 2 January	1 January
St Patrick's Day	—	—	17 March
*Good Friday	10 April	10 April	10 April
Easter Monday	13 April	—	13 April
May Day	4 May	25 May	4 May
Spring	25 May	4 May	25 May
Battle of the Boyne	—	—	13 July†
Summer	31 August	3 August	31 August
*Christmas	25, 28 December	25, 28 December	25, 28 December

†provisional date

FORTHCOMING EVENTS 1997

This is the European Year Against Racism, and the Arts Council Year for Opera and Musical Theatre
The European City of Culture is Thessaloniki
* Provisional dates

3 – 12 January	London International Boat Show Earls Court, London
6 – 9 March	Cruft's Dog Show National Exhibition Centre, Birmingham
13 March – 6 April	Ideal Home Exhibition Earls Court, London
16 – 18 March	London International Book Fair Olympia, London
April – October	Chichester Festival Theatre season
*1 – 24 May	Mayfest 1997 Glasgow
2 May – 11 October	Pitlochry Festival Theatre season Tayside
16 May – 1 June	Bath International Music Festival
18 May – 24 August	Glyndebourne Festival Opera season Lewes, E. Sussex
22 – 23 May	Chelsea Flower Show Royal Hospital, Chelsea
23 May – 1 June	Hay Festival of Literature Hay-on-Wye, Hereford
*1 June – 10 August	Royal Academy Summer Exhibition Piccadilly, London
13 – 29 June	Aldeburgh Festival of Music and Arts Suffolk
14 June	Trooping the Colour Horse Guards Parade, London
30 June – 3 July	The Royal Show Stoneleigh Park, Kenilworth, Warks
4 – 13 July	York Early Music Festival
5 – 20 July	Cheltenham International Festival of Music
10 – 13 July	Hampton Court Palace Flower Show East Molesey, Surrey
*11 – 27 July	Buxton Festival Derbyshire
15 – 26 July	Royal Tournament Earls Court, London
17 – 26 July	Welsh Proms 1997 St David's Hall, Cardiff
17 July – 3 August	Buxton Festival Derbyshire
18 July – 13 September	Promenade Concerts season Royal Albert Hall, London
1 – 23 August	Edinburgh Military Tattoo Edinburgh Castle
2 – 9 August	Royal National Eisteddfod of Wales Bala
10 – 30 August	Edinburgh International Festival
14 – 15 August	Wisley Flower Show RHS Garden, Wisley, Surrey
14 – 15 August	Battle of the Flowers Jersey
17 – 22 August	Three Choirs Festival Hereford
24 – 25 August	Notting Hill Carnival Notting Hill, London
29 August – 2 November	Blackpool Illuminations
6 September	Braemar Royal Highland Gathering Aberdeenshire
8 – 12 September	TUC Annual Congress Blackpool
13 – 21 September	Southampton International Boat Show, Western Esplanade, Southampton
21 – 25 September	Liberal Democrat Party Conference Eastbourne
29 September – 3 October	Labour Party Conference Brighton
7 – 10 October	Conservative Party Conference Blackpool
24 – 27 October	Commonwealth Heads of Government meeting Edinburgh
November	London International Film Festival
2 November	London to Brighton Veteran Car Run
8 November	Lord Mayor's Procession and Show City of London
9 – 11 November	CBI Annual Conference Birmingham
19 – 30 November	Huddersfield Contemporary Music Festival

SPORTS EVENTS

18 January	Rugby Union: Ireland v. France Lansdowne Road, Dublin Scotland v. Wales Murrayfield, Edinburgh
1 February	Rugby Union: England v. Scotland Twickenham, London Wales v. Ireland Cardiff Arms Park
15 February	Rugby Union: Ireland v. England Lansdowne Road, Dublin France v. Wales Parc des Princes, Paris
1 March	Rugby Union: England v. France Twickenham, London Scotland v. Ireland Murrayfield, Edinburgh
7 – 9 March	Athletics: World Indoor Championships Paris
15 March	Rugby Union: Wales v. England Cardiff Arms Park France v. Scotland Parc des Princes
29 March	Oxford and Cambridge Boat Race Putney to Mortlake, London
*13 April	Athletics: London Marathon
19 April	Rugby Union: County Championship finals Twickenham, London
*19 April – 5 May	Snooker: World Professional Championship Crucible Theatre, Sheffield
3 May	Rugby League: Challenge Cup final Wembley Stadium, London
8 – 11 May	Badminton Horse Trials Badminton
*10 May	Rugby Union: Pilkington Cup final Twickenham, London
14 – 18 May	Royal Windsor Horse Show Home Park, Windsor

17 May	Football: FA Cup final
	Wembley Stadium, London
*17 May	Football: Welsh FA Cup final
	Cardiff Arms Park
*22 May	Cricket: One-day International
	England v. Australia
	Headingley, Leeds
24 May	Football: Scottish FA Cup final
	Hampden Park, Glasgow
*24 May	Cricket: One-day International
	England v. Australia
	The Oval, London
*25 May	Cricket: One-day International
	England v. Australia
	Lord's, London
1 June	TT Motorcycle Races
	Isle of Man
2 – 7 June	Golf: British Amateur Championship
	Royal St George's, Sandwich
*5 – 9 June	Cricket: 1st Test Match
	England v. Australia
	Edgbaston, Birmingham
*19 – 23 June	Cricket: 2nd Test Match
	England v. Australia
	Lord's, London
23 June – 6 July	Lawn Tennis Championships
	Wimbledon, London
2 – 6 July	Henley Royal Regatta
	Henley-on-Thames
*3 – 8 July	Cricket: 3rd Test Match
	England v. Australia
	Old Trafford, Manchester
13 July	British Formula 1 Grand Prix
	Silverstone, Northants
*12 July	Cricket: Benson and Hedges Cup
	final
	Lord's, London
12 – 26 July	Shooting: NRA Imperial Meeting
	Bisley Camp, Woking, Surrey
*24 – 28 July	Cricket: 4th Test Match
	England v. Australia
	Headingley, Leeds
28 July –	Yachting: Admiral's Cup
14 August	Cowes, Isle of Wight
1 – 10 August	Athletics: World Championships
	Athens
2 – 9 August	Yachting: Cowes Week
	Isle of Wight
*7 – 11 August	Cricket: 5th Test Match
	England v. Australia
	Trent Bridge, Nottingham
9 August	Yachting: Fastnet Race
	Cowes/Plymouth
9 – 10 August	Golf: Walker Cup
	Quaker Ridge, NY State, USA
14 – 24 August	Swimming: European
	Championships
	Seville
*21 – 25 August	Cricket: 6th Test Match
	England v. Australia
	The Oval, London
27 – 31 August	Show Jumping: European
	Championships
	Mannheim, Germany
*6 September	Cricket: NatWest Trophy Final
	Lord's, London
11 – 14 September	Eventing: Burghley Horse Trials
	Burghley, Lincs

26 – 28 September	Golf: Ryder Cup
	Valderrama, Sotogrande, Spain
October	Rugby League: World Cup
	Wembley Stadium, London
1 – 5 October	Horse of the Year Show
	Wembley Arena, London

HORSE RACING

*13 March	Cheltenham Gold Cup
*22 March	Lincoln Handicap
	Doncaster
*5 April	Grand National
	Aintree
*3 May	Two Thousand Guineas
	Newmarket
*4 May	One Thousand Guineas
	Newmarket
*6 June	The Oaks
	Epsom
*7 June	The Derby
	Epsom
*7 June	Coronation Cup
	Epsom
*17 – 20 June	Royal Ascot
*26 July	King George VI and Queen
	Elizabeth Diamond Stakes
	Ascot
*13 September	St Leger
	Doncaster
*4 October	Cambridgeshire Handicap
	Newmarket
*18 October	Cesarewitch
	Newmarket

The horse-racing fixtures are the copyright of the British Horse-racing Board

CENTENARIES OF 1997

597
*
    St Augustine landed in England and converted the kingdom of Kent to Christianity

1497
24 June   John Cabot, Italian explorer, discovered Newfoundland

1697
18 October   Antonio Canaletto, Venetian artist, born
10 November   William Hogarth, painter and pictorial satirist, born
2 December   The rebuilt St Paul's Cathedral opened

1797
31 January   Franz Schubert, Austrian composer, born
14 February   Battle of Cape St Vincent
2 March   Horace Walpole, politician and man of letters, died
27 March   Alfred, Comte de Vigny, French poet, born
8 July   Edmund Burke, statesman and political writer, died
30 August   Mary Wollstonecraft Shelley, novelist, born
10 September   Mary Wollstonecraft Godwin, writer, died
11 October   Battle of Camperdown
16 October   Earl of Cardigan, commander of the charge of the Light Brigade in the Crimean War, born

* exact date not known

13 December   Heinrich Heine, German poet and journalist, born

1897
8 January   Dennis Wheatley, novelist, born
12 January   Sir Isaac Pitman, inventor of phonetic shorthand system, died
19 February   Charles Blondin, tightrope walker famous for crossing Niagara Falls, died
3 April   Johannes Brahms, German composer, died
17 April   Thornton Wilder, American novelist and playwright, born
22 May   Blackwall Tunnel opened in London
27 May   Sir John Cockcroft, nuclear physicist and Nobel Prize winner, born
12 June   Leon Goossens, musician, born
12 June   Anthony Eden, Prime Minister 1955–7, born
21 July   Tate Gallery opened on Millbank
11 August   Enid Blyton, children's author and educationalist, born
3 September   Cecil Parker, film actor, born
25 September   William Faulkner, American novelist and Nobel Prize winner, born
29 October   Joseph Goebbels, Nazi leader, born
15 November   Aneurin Bevan, politician and Labour party leader, born
12 December   Royal Automobile Club founded under the name The Automobile Club of Great Britain

CENTENARIES OF 1998

1498
23 May   Girolamo Savonarola, Italian religious and political reformer, martyred

1598
13 April   Edict of Nantes, ending civil war in France
19 July   Gilbert Sheldon, Archbishop of Canterbury 1663–78, born

1798
19 January   Auguste Comte, French philosopher, born
26 April   Eugène Delacroix, French romantic painter, born
10 May   George Vancouver, British explorer, died
4 June   Giovanni Casanova, Italian adventurer and spy, died
1 August   Battle of The Nile
4 December   Luigi Galvani, Italian scientist and anatomist, died

1898
9 January   Dame Gracie Fields, singer and comedienne, born
14 January   Lewis Carroll, novelist, died
15 January   Uffa Fox, yachtsman, born
15 March   Sir Henry Bessemer, inventor and engineer, died

16 March   Aubrey Beardsley, illustrator, died
9 April   Paul Robeson, American singer and black activist, born
3 May   Golda Meir, Prime Minister of Israel 1969–74, born
19 May   William Gladstone, statesman and Prime Minister 1868–74, 1880–5, 1886 and 1892–4, died
3 June   Samuel Plimsoll, social reformer and inventor of the 'Plimsoll line' for the safe loading of ships, died
6 June   Dame Ninette de Valois, Irish dancer and choreographer, founder of the Royal Ballet, born
9 June   Hong Kong leased by Britain from China for 99 years
17 June   Sir Edward Burne-Jones, painter, died
30 July   Otto von Bismarck, Prusso-German statesman, died
    Henry Moore, sculptor, born
8 August   Waterloo and City Line on London Underground opened
2 September   Battle of Omdurman
26 September   George Gershwin, American composer, born
20 November   Sir John Fowler, civil engineer and co-designer of the Forth Bridge, died
26 December   Radium discovered by Pierre and Marie Curie

Astronomy

The following pages give astronomical data for each month of the year 1997. There are four pages of data for each month. All data are given for 0h Greenwich Mean Time (GMT), i.e. at the midnight at the beginning of the day named. This applies also to data for the months when British Summer Time is in operation (for dates, *see* below).

The astronomical data are given in a form suitable for observation with the naked eye or with a small telescope. These data do not attempt to replace the *Astronomical Almanac* for professional astronomers.

A fuller explanation of how to use the astronomical data is given on pages 71–3.

CALENDAR FOR EACH MONTH

The calendar for each month shows dates of religious, civil and legal significance for the year 1997.

The days in bold type are the principal holy days and the festivals and greater holy days of the Church of England as set out in the calendar of the Alternative Service Book 1980, and the calendar of Sundays set out in the Book of Common Prayer. Observance of certain festivals and greater holy days is transferred if the day falls on a principal holy day. The calendar shows the date on which holy days and festivals are to be observed in 1997.

The days in small capitals are dates of significance in the calendars of non-Anglican denominations and non-Christian religions.

The days in italic type are dates of civil and legal significance. The royal anniversaries shown in italic type are the days on which the Union flag is to be flown.

The rest of the calendar comprises days of general interest and the dates of birth or death of well-known people.

Fuller explanations of the various calendars can be found under Time Measurement and Calendars (pages 81–9).

The zodiacal signs through which the Sun is passing during each month are illustrated. The date of transition from one sign to the next, to the nearest hour, is given under Astronomical Phenomena.

JULIAN DATE

The Julian date on 1997 January 0.0 is 2450448.5. To find the Julian date for any other date in 1997 (at 0h GMT), add the day-of-the-year number on the extreme right of the calendar for each month to the Julian date for January 0.0.

SEASONS

The seasons are defined astronomically as follows:

Spring from the vernal equinox to the summer solstice
Summer from the summer solstice to the autumnal equinox
Autumn from the autumnal equinox to the winter solstice
Winter from the winter solstice to the vernal equinox

The seasons in 1997 are:

Northern hemisphere

Vernal equinox	March 20d 14h GMT
Summer solstice	June 21d 08h GMT
Autumnal equinox	September 23d 00h GMT
Winter solstice	December 21d 20h GMT

Southern hemisphere

Autumnal equinox	March 20d 14h GMT
Winter solstice	June 21d 08h GMT
Vernal equinox	September 23d 00h GMT
Summer solstice	December 21d 20h GMT

The longest day of the year, measured from sunrise to sunset, is at the summer solstice. For the remainder of this century the longest day in the United Kingdom will fall each year on 21 June. *See also* page 81.

The shortest day of the year is at the winter solstice. For the remainder of this century the shortest day in the United Kingdom will fall on 21 December in 1997 and 2000, and on 22 December in 1998 and 1999. *See also* page 81.

The equinox is the point at which day and night are of equal length all over the world. *See also* page 81.

In popular parlance, the seasons in the northern hemisphere comprise the following months:

Spring	March, April, May
Summer	June, July, August
Autumn	September, October, November
Winter	December, January, February

BRITISH SUMMER TIME

British Summer Time is the legal time for general purposes during the period in which it is in operation (*see also* page 75). During this period, clocks are kept one hour ahead of Greenwich Mean Time. The hour of changeover is 01h Greenwich Mean Time. The duration of Summer Time in 1997 is:

March 30 01h GMT to October 26 01h GMT

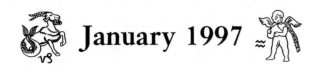

January 1997

FIRST MONTH, 31 DAYS. *Janus*, god of the portal, facing two ways, past and future

1	*Wednesday*	**The Naming of Jesus.** *Bank Holiday in the UK*	*week* 52 *day* 1
2	*Thursday*	*Bank Holiday in Scotland.* Sir Michael Tippett b. 1905	2
3	*Friday*	J. R. R. Tolkien b. 1892. Marshal Joffre d. 1931	3
4	*Saturday*	Augustus John b. 1878. Donald Campbell d. 1967	4
5	*Sunday*	**2nd S. after Christmas.** Twelfth Night	*week* 1 *day* 5
6	*Monday*	**The Epiphany.** Fanny Burney d. 1840	6
7	*Tuesday*	Francis Poulenc b. 1899. Trevor Howard d. 1988	7
8	*Wednesday*	Sir Lawrence Alma-Tadema b. 1836	8
9	*Thursday*	Simone de Beauvoir b. 1908. Ruskin Spear d. 1990	9
10	*Friday*	RAMADAN begins. Dashiell Hammett d. 1961	10
11	*Saturday*	*Hilary Law Sittings begin.* Fred Archer b. 1857	11
12	*Sunday*	**1st S. after Epiphany.** Charles Perrault b. 1628	*week* 2 *day* 12
13	*Monday*	Jan van Goyen b. 1596. James Joyce d. 1941.	13
14	*Tuesday*	Fantin-Latour b. 1836. Harold Abrahams d. 1978	14
15	*Wednesday*	British Museum opened 1759. Karl Liebknecht d. 1919	15
16	*Thursday*	Amilcare Ponchielli d. 1886. Laura Riding b. 1901	16
17	*Friday*	Gen. Thomas Fairfax b. 1612. David Lloyd George b. 1863	17
18	*Saturday*	Capt. Scott reaches the South Pole 1912	18
19	*Sunday*	**2nd S. after Epiphany.** Paul Cézanne b. 1839	*week* 3 *day* 19
20	*Monday*	David Garrick d. 1779. Audrey Hepburn d. 1993	20
21	*Tuesday*	Christian Dior b. 1905. Lytton Strachey d. 1932	21
22	*Wednesday*	Lord Byron b. 1788. Walter Sickert d. 1942	22
23	*Thursday*	Thomas Peacock d. 1866. Charles Kingsley d. 1875	23
24	*Friday*	Pierre de Beaumarchais b. 1732. ⚔ Battle of Dogger Bank 1915	24
25	*Saturday*	**Conversion of St Paul.** Somerset Maugham b. 1874	25
26	*Sunday*	**9th S. before Easter/Septuagesima**	*week* 4 *day* 26
27	*Monday*	Samuel Palmer b. 1805. Jerome Kern b. 1885	27
28	*Tuesday*	Gen. Charles Gordon b. 1833. W. B. Yeats d. 1939	28
29	*Wednesday*	Emanuel Swedenborg b. 1688. Fritz Kreisler d. 1962	29
30	*Thursday*	Walter Savage Landor b. 1775. Stanley Holloway d. 1982	30
31	*Friday*	Bonnie Prince Charlie d. 1788. A. A. Milne d. 1956	31

ASTRONOMICAL PHENOMENA

d	h	
1	01	Mars in conjunction with Moon. Mars 3° N.
2	00	Earth at perihelion (147 million km)
2	01	Mercury in inferior conjunction
7	17	Venus in conjunction with Moon. Venus 5° S.
8	05	Mercury in conjunction with Moon. Mercury 2° S.
9	18	Jupiter in conjunction with Moon. Jupiter 5° S.
12	15	Venus in conjunction with Mercury. Venus 3° S.
12	21	Mercury at stationary point
14	03	Saturn in conjunction with Moon. Saturn 2° S.
17	13	Neptune in conjunction
19	13	Jupiter in conjunction
20	01	Sun's longitude 300° ♒
24	05	Mercury at greatest elongation W.25°
24	14	Uranus in conjunction
28	20	Mars in conjunction with Moon. Mars 3° N.

MINIMA OF ALGOL

d	h	d	h	d	h
1	12.1	12	23.4	24	10.7
4	09.0	15	20.2	27	07.5
7	05.8	18	17.1	30	04.3
10	02.6	21	13.9		

CONSTELLATIONS

The following constellations are near the meridian at

d	h		d	h
December	1	24	January	16	21
December	16	23	February	1	20
January	1	22	February	15	19

Draco (below the Pole), Ursa Minor (below the Pole), Cameleopardus, Perseus, Auriga, Taurus, Orion, Eridanus and Lepus

THE MOON

Phases, Apsides and Node	d	h	m
☾ Last Quarter	2	01	45
● New Moon	9	04	26
☽ First Quarter	15	20	02
○ Full Moon	23	15	11
☾ Last Quarter	31	19	40
Perigee (359,227 km)	10	08	43
Apogee (406,218 km)	25	16	31

Mean longitude of ascending node on January 1, 183°

THE SUN

s.d. 16'.3

Day	Right Ascension	Dec.	Equation of time	Rise 52°	Rise 56°	Transit	Set 52°	Set 56°	Sidereal time	Transit of First Point of Aries
	h m s	° '	m s	h m	h m	h m	h m	h m	h m s	h m s
1	18 46 09	23 01	− 3 24	8 08	8 31	12 04	15 59	15 36	6 42 44	17 14 26
2	18 50 33	22 56	− 3 53	8 08	8 31	12 04	16 00	15 38	6 46 41	17 10 30
3	18 54 58	22 50	− 4 21	8 08	8 31	12 05	16 02	15 39	6 50 37	17 06 34
4	18 59 22	22 44	− 4 48	8 08	8 30	12 05	16 03	15 40	6 54 34	17 02 38
5	19 03 46	22 38	− 5 15	8 07	8 30	12 05	16 04	15 42	6 58 30	16 58 42
6	19 08 09	22 31	− 5 42	8 07	8 29	12 06	16 05	15 43	7 02 27	16 54 46
7	19 12 32	22 23	− 6 08	8 06	8 28	12 06	16 07	15 45	7 06 24	16 50 50
8	19 16 54	22 16	− 6 34	8 06	8 28	12 07	16 08	15 46	7 10 20	16 46 55
9	19 21 16	22 07	− 7 00	8 05	8 27	12 07	16 09	15 48	7 14 17	16 42 59
10	19 25 38	21 59	− 7 24	8 05	8 26	12 08	16 11	15 49	7 18 13	16 39 03
11	19 29 58	21 50	− 7 49	8 04	8 25	12 08	16 12	15 51	7 22 10	16 35 07
12	19 34 18	21 40	− 8 12	8 04	8 24	12 08	16 14	15 53	7 26 06	16 31 11
13	19 38 38	21 30	− 8 35	8 03	8 23	12 09	16 15	15 55	7 30 03	16 27 15
14	19 42 57	21 20	− 8 58	8 02	8 22	12 09	16 17	15 56	7 33 59	16 23 19
15	19 47 15	21 09	− 9 19	8 01	8 21	12 09	16 18	15 58	7 37 56	16 19 23
16	19 51 33	20 58	− 9 40	8 00	8 20	12 10	16 20	16 00	7 41 53	16 15 27
17	19 55 50	20 46	−10 00	7 59	8 19	12 10	16 22	16 02	7 45 49	16 11 31
18	20 00 06	20 34	−10 20	7 58	8 18	12 10	16 23	16 04	7 49 46	16 07 35
19	20 04 21	20 22	−10 39	7 57	8 16	12 11	16 25	16 06	7 53 42	16 03 39
20	20 08 36	20 09	−10 57	7 56	8 15	12 11	16 27	16 08	7 57 39	15 59 44
21	20 12 50	19 56	−11 14	7 55	8 13	12 11	16 28	16 10	8 01 35	15 55 48
22	20 17 03	19 43	−11 31	7 54	8 12	12 12	16 30	16 12	8 05 32	15 51 52
23	20 21 15	19 29	−11 47	7 53	8 10	12 12	16 32	16 14	8 09 28	15 47 56
24	20 25 27	19 15	−12 02	7 51	8 09	12 12	16 33	16 16	8 13 25	15 44 00
25	20 29 37	19 00	−12 16	7 50	8 07	12 12	16 35	16 18	8 17 22	15 40 04
26	20 33 47	18 45	−12 29	7 49	8 06	12 13	16 37	16 20	8 21 18	15 36 08
27	20 37 57	18 30	−12 42	7 47	8 04	12 13	16 39	16 22	8 25 15	15 32 12
28	20 42 05	18 14	−12 54	7 46	8 02	12 13	16 41	16 24	8 29 11	15 28 16
29	20 46 13	17 58	−13 05	7 45	8 00	12 13	16 42	16 27	8 33 08	15 24 20
30	20 50 19	17 42	−13 15	7 43	7 59	12 13	16 44	16 29	8 37 04	15 20 24
31	20 54 25	17 26	−13 24	7 42	7 57	12 13	16 46	16 31	8 41 01	15 16 29

DURATION OF TWILIGHT (in minutes)

Latitude	52°	56°	52°	56°	52°	56°	52°	56°
	1 January		11 January		21 January		31 January	
Civil	41	47	40	45	38	43	37	41
Nautical	84	96	82	93	80	90	78	87
Astronomical	125	141	123	138	120	134	117	130

THE NIGHT SKY

Mercury is visible in the mornings around the middle of the month, as it reaches greatest western elongation (25°) on the 24th. Even from England and Wales it will be difficult to detect, low above the south-eastern horizon around the beginning of morning civil twilight, between about the 12th to the 23rd. On the morning of the 13th Venus could be a useful guide to finding Mercury as Mercury will then be seen 3° above Venus. During its period of visibility its magnitude ranges from +0.6 to −0.1. Because of its considerable southerly declination, observers in Scotland are unlikely to see Mercury at all.

Venus is a brilliant object in the morning sky, magnitude −3.9, and at the beginning of the month is visible low in the east-south-eastern sky for nearly an hour before dawn. On the morning of the 7th the old crescent Moon, only two days before New, will be seen about 6° above the planet. For the last week of the month Venus is too close to the Sun for observation.

Mars, although technically a morning object, is becoming visible low in the eastern sky shortly before midnight. During January its magnitude increases in brightness from +0.5 to −0.2. Mars is moving slowly eastwards in the western part of Virgo. The Moon, near Last Quarter, passes about 3° S. of Mars on the mornings of the 1st and 29th.

Jupiter passes through conjunction on the 19th and is therefore too close to the Sun for observation.

Saturn magnitude +1.0, is an evening object in the south-western sky. Saturn is in the southern part of the constellation of Pisces. With a minor axis of only three arcseconds, the rings will be very difficult to detect with small telescopes.

THE MOON

Day	RA	Dec.	Hor. par.	Semi-diam.	Sun's co-long.	PA of Bright Limb	Phase	Age	Rise 52°	Rise 56°	Transit	Set 52°	Set 56°
	h m	°	'	'	°	°	%	d	h m	h m	h m	h m	h m
1	11 55	+ 0.2	54.7	14.9	173	113	60	21.3	—	—	5 21	11 23	11 22
2	12 41	− 3.6	55.2	15.0	185	113	51	22.3	0 14	0 17	6 05	11 47	11 42
3	13 28	− 7.3	55.9	15.2	197	112	41	23.3	1 20	1 27	6 51	12 12	12 04
4	14 18	−10.8	56.7	15.4	209	110	31	24.3	2 28	2 38	7 38	12 42	12 30
5	15 10	−13.9	57.6	15.7	221	108	22	25.3	3 37	3 50	8 30	13 16	13 02
6	16 06	−16.4	58.5	15.9	234	106	14	26.3	4 46	5 02	9 24	13 59	13 42
7	17 04	−17.9	59.4	16.2	246	104	7	27.3	5 52	6 10	10 22	14 51	14 33
8	18 05	−18.4	60.2	16.4	258	106	2	28.3	6 53	7 11	11 23	15 54	15 36
9	19 08	−17.6	60.7	16.6	270	145	0	29.3	7 46	8 03	12 24	17 06	16 50
10	20 10	−15.6	61.0	16.6	282	237	1	0.8	8 31	8 45	13 24	18 24	18 11
11	21 11	−12.5	61.0	16.6	295	245	5	1.8	9 09	9 19	14 22	19 44	19 36
12	22 10	− 8.6	60.6	16.5	307	246	12	2.8	9 42	9 48	15 18	21 04	21 00
13	23 06	− 4.3	60.1	16.4	319	246	20	3.8	10 11	10 13	16 11	22 22	22 22
14	0 01	+ 0.2	59.4	16.2	331	247	30	4.8	10 39	10 37	17 02	23 38	23 42
15	0 55	+ 4.6	58.6	16.0	343	247	41	5.8	11 07	11 01	17 53	—	—
16	1 47	+ 8.6	57.8	15.8	355	249	52	6.8	11 35	11 26	18 43	0 51	0 59
17	2 39	+12.1	57.1	15.6	8	251	62	7.8	12 07	11 55	19 33	2 02	2 13
18	3 31	+14.9	56.4	15.4	20	254	72	8.8	12 42	12 27	20 23	3 09	3 23
19	4 24	+16.9	55.8	15.2	32	257	81	9.8	13 21	13 05	21 13	4 11	4 27
20	5 16	+18.1	55.3	15.1	44	260	88	10.8	14 07	13 49	22 02	5 07	5 25
21	6 08	+18.4	54.9	15.0	56	262	94	11.8	14 57	14 40	22 51	5 57	6 15
22	6 59	+17.8	54.6	14.9	68	261	97	12.8	15 52	15 36	23 39	6 41	6 57
23	7 49	+16.4	54.3	14.8	80	247	99	13.8	16 51	16 37	—	7 18	7 32
24	8 38	+14.4	54.1	14.7	93	150	100	14.8	17 52	17 41	0 25	7 50	8 02
25	9 25	+11.7	54.0	14.7	105	120	98	15.8	18 54	18 45	1 10	8 18	8 27
26	10 12	+ 8.6	54.0	14.7	117	116	95	16.8	19 56	19 51	1 54	8 43	8 49
27	10 57	+ 5.1	54.1	14.7	129	114	90	17.8	20 59	20 57	2 36	9 06	9 09
28	11 42	+ 1.5	54.3	14.8	141	114	84	18.8	22 02	22 04	3 19	9 29	9 29
29	12 28	− 2.3	54.6	14.9	153	113	76	19.8	23 06	23 11	4 02	9 52	9 49
30	13 14	− 6.0	55.1	15.0	165	112	68	20.8	—	—	4 46	10 16	10 10
31	14 02	− 9.5	55.7	15.2	178	110	58	21.8	0 11	0 20	5 31	10 43	10 33

MERCURY

Day	RA	Dec.	Diam.	Phase	Transit	5° high 52°	5° high 56°
	h m	°	″	%	h m	h m	h m
1	18 56	−20.5	10	1	12 08	15 32	15 04
3	18 44	−20.2	10	1	11 49	8 24	8 52
5	18 33	−20.1	10	4	11 31	8 05	8 32
7	18 24	−20.0	10	10	11 14	7 48	8 15
9	18 18	−20.1	9	17	11 00	7 34	8 02
11	18 14	−20.2	9	24	10 49	7 24	7 52
13	18 13	−20.5	8	32	10 41	7 18	7 46
15	18 14	−20.7	8	39	10 35	7 13	7 42
17	18 17	−21.0	8	45	10 31	7 11	7 41
19	18 23	−21.3	7	51	10 28	7 11	7 42
21	18 29	−21.5	7	56	10 27	7 12	7 43
23	18 37	−21.8	7	61	10 27	7 14	7 46
25	18 46	−22.0	7	65	10 28	7 17	7 49
27	18 55	−22.1	6	68	10 30	7 19	7 52
29	19 05	−22.2	6	71	10 33	7 22	7 55
31	19 16	−22.2	6	74	10 35	7 25	7 58

VENUS

Day	RA	Dec.	Diam.	Phase	Transit	5° high 52°	5° high 56°
	h m	°	″	%	h m	h m	h m
1	17 10	−22.2	11	93	10 28	7 18	7 50
6	17 37	−22.8	11	94	10 35	7 30	8 05
11	18 04	−23.1	11	94	10 43	7 40	8 16
16	18 31	−23.1	11	95	10 50	7 48	8 23
21	18 59	−22.8	10	96	10 58	7 53	8 27
26	19 26	−22.3	10	96	11 05	7 55	8 28
31	19 52	−21.4	10	97	11 12	7 55	8 25

MARS

Day	RA	Dec.	Diam.	Phase	Transit	5° high 52°	5° high 56°
1	12 01	+ 2.7	8	91	5 18	23 35	23 36
6	12 07	+ 2.2	8	91	5 04	23 24	23 26
11	12 13	+ 1.7	9	91	4 50	23 12	23 14
16	12 17	+ 1.4	9	92	4 35	22 58	23 01
21	12 21	+ 1.1	10	92	4 19	22 44	22 46
26	12 24	+ 0.9	10	93	4 02	22 28	22 30
31	12 26	+ 0.8	11	94	3 45	22 10	22 13

SUNRISE AND SUNSET

	London		Bristol		Birmingham		Manchester		Newcastle		Glasgow		Belfast	
	0°05′	51°30′	2°35′	51°28′	1°55′	52°28′	2°15′	53°28′	1°37′	54°59′	4°14′	55°52′	5°56′	54°35′
	h m	h m	h m	h m	h m	h m	h m	h m	h m	h m	h m	h m	h m	h m
1	8 06	16 02	8 16	16 12	8 18	16 05	8 25	16 01	8 31	15 49	8 47	15 54	8 46	16 09
2	8 06	16 03	8 16	16 13	8 18	16 06	8 25	16 02	8 31	15 50	8 47	15 55	8 46	16 10
3	8 06	16 04	8 16	16 15	8 18	16 07	8 24	16 03	8 31	15 52	8 47	15 57	8 46	16 11
4	8 05	16 06	8 15	16 16	8 18	16 08	8 24	16 04	8 30	15 53	8 46	15 58	8 45	16 13
5	8 05	16 07	8 15	16 17	8 17	16 09	8 24	16 05	8 30	15 54	8 46	15 59	8 45	16 14
6	8 05	16 08	8 15	16 18	8 17	16 11	8 23	16 07	8 29	15 56	8 45	16 01	8 44	16 15
7	8 04	16 09	8 14	16 19	8 16	16 12	8 23	16 08	8 29	15 57	8 45	16 02	8 44	16 17
8	8 04	16 11	8 14	16 21	8 16	16 13	8 22	16 10	8 28	15 59	8 44	16 04	8 43	16 18
9	8 03	16 12	8 13	16 22	8 15	16 15	8 22	16 11	8 27	16 00	8 43	16 06	8 42	16 20
10	8 03	16 13	8 13	16 24	8 15	16 16	8 21	16 13	8 27	16 02	8 42	16 07	8 42	16 21
11	8 02	16 15	8 12	16 25	8 14	16 18	8 20	16 14	8 26	16 03	8 41	16 09	8 41	16 23
12	8 02	16 16	8 11	16 26	8 13	16 19	8 20	16 16	8 25	16 05	8 41	16 11	8 40	16 25
13	8 01	16 18	8 11	16 28	8 13	16 21	8 19	16 17	8 24	16 07	8 40	16 12	8 39	16 26
14	8 00	16 19	8 10	16 29	8 12	16 22	8 18	16 19	8 23	16 09	8 38	16 14	8 38	16 28
15	7 59	16 21	8 09	16 31	8 11	16 24	8 17	16 21	8 22	16 10	8 37	16 16	8 37	16 30
16	7 58	16 22	8 08	16 33	8 10	16 25	8 16	16 22	8 21	16 12	8 36	16 18	8 36	16 31
17	7 57	16 24	8 07	16 34	8 09	16 27	8 15	16 24	8 20	16 14	8 35	16 20	8 35	16 33
18	7 57	16 26	8 06	16 36	8 08	16 29	8 14	16 26	8 19	16 16	8 34	16 22	8 34	16 35
19	7 56	16 27	8 05	16 37	8 07	16 31	8 13	16 27	8 17	16 18	8 32	16 24	8 33	16 37
20	7 54	16 29	8 04	16 39	8 06	16 32	8 12	16 29	8 16	16 20	8 31	16 26	8 31	16 39
21	7 53	16 31	8 03	16 41	8 05	16 34	8 10	16 31	8 15	16 21	8 30	16 28	8 30	16 41
22	7 52	16 32	8 02	16 42	8 03	16 36	8 09	16 33	8 13	16 23	8 28	16 30	8 29	16 43
23	7 51	16 34	8 01	16 44	8 02	16 37	8 08	16 35	8 12	16 25	8 27	16 32	8 27	16 44
24	7 50	16 36	8 00	16 46	8 01	16 39	8 06	16 37	8 10	16 27	8 25	16 34	8 26	16 46
25	7 49	16 37	7 58	16 48	8 00	16 41	8 05	16 38	8 09	16 29	8 24	16 36	8 24	16 48
26	7 47	16 39	7 57	16 49	7 58	16 43	8 03	16 40	8 07	16 31	8 22	16 38	8 23	16 50
27	7 46	16 41	7 56	16 51	7 57	16 45	8 02	16 42	8 06	16 33	8 20	16 40	8 21	16 52
28	7 45	16 43	7 54	16 53	7 55	16 47	8 00	16 44	8 04	16 35	8 18	16 42	8 20	16 54
29	7 43	16 45	7 53	16 55	7 54	16 48	7 59	16 46	8 02	16 37	8 17	16 44	8 18	16 56
30	7 42	16 46	7 52	16 56	7 52	16 50	7 57	16 48	8 01	16 40	8 15	16 46	8 16	16 58
31	7 40	16 48	7 50	16 58	7 51	16 52	7 56	16 50	7 59	16 42	8 13	16 48	8 15	17 00

JUPITER

Day	RA	Dec.	Transit	5° high	
				52°	56°
	h m	° ′	h m	h m	h m
1	19 48.7	−21 25	13 04	16 21	15 50
11	19 58.6	−21 00	12 35	15 55	15 25
21	20 08.4	−20 32	12 05	15 29	15 01
31	20 18.2	−20 02	11 36	15 03	14 36

Diameters – equatorial 32″ polar 30″

SATURN

Day	RA	Dec.	Transit	5° high	
				52°	56°
	h m	° ′	h m	h m	h m
1	0 08.7	− 1 38	17 23	22 41	22 37
11	0 10.7	− 1 22	16 46	22 06	22 01
21	0 13.4	− 1 03	16 09	21 31	21 27
31	0 16.5	− 0 41	15 33	20 56	20 53

Diameters – equatorial 17″ polar 15″
Rings – major axis 38″ minor axis 3″

URANUS

Day	RA	Dec.	Transit	10° high	
				52°	56°
	h m	° ′	h m	h m	h m
1	20 22.8	−19 59	13 38	16 18	15 36
11	20 25.2	−19 51	13 01	15 42	15 01
21	20 27.6	−19 42	12 24	15 07	14 26
31	20 30.0	−19 34	11 47	14 31	13 51

Diameter 4″

NEPTUNE

Day	RA	Dec.	Transit	10° high	
				52°	56°
	h m	° ′	h m	h m	h m
1	19 55.1	−20 22	13 10	10 34	11 18
11	19 56.7	−20 18	12 33	9 56	10 39
21	19 58.3	−20 14	11 55	9 17	10 00
31	19 59.8	−20 09	11 17	8 39	9 21

Diameter 2″

February 1997

SECOND MONTH, 28 or 29 DAYS. *Februa*, Roman festival of Purification

1	*Saturday*	Clark Gable b. 1901. Piet Mondrian d. 1944	*week* 4 *day* 32
2	*Sunday*	**Presentation of Christ. 8th S. before Easter/Sexagesima**	*week* 5 *day* 33
3	*Monday*	Felix Mendelssohn b. 1809. Marquess of Salisbury b. 1830	34
4	*Tuesday*	Thomas Carlyle d. 1881. Charles Lindbergh b.1902	35
5	*Wednesday*	Sir Robert Peel b. 1788. Sir John Pritchard b. 1921	36
6	*Thursday*	*Queen's Accession 1952.* Charles II d. 1685	37
7	*Friday*	Sir Thomas More b. 1478. Charles Dickens b. 1812	38
8	*Saturday*	*Chinese Year of the Ox.* Sir Giles Gilbert Scott d. 1960	39
9	*Sunday*	**7th S. before Easter/Quinquagesima**	*week* 6 *day* 40
10	*Monday*	Charles Lamb b. 1775. Boris Pasternak b. 1890 (NS)	41
11	*Tuesday*	Shrove Tuesday. Thomas Edison b. 1847	42
12	*Wednesday*	**Ash Wednesday.** Lady Jane Grey exec. 1554	43
13	*Thursday*	Dame Christabel Pankhurst d. 1958	44
14	*Friday*	St Valentine's Day. Benvenuto Cellini d. 1571	45
15	*Saturday*	Galileo Galilei b. 1564. Mikhail Glinka d. 1857 (NS)	46
16	*Sunday*	**1st S. in Lent.** Angela Carter d. 1992	*week* 7 *day* 47
17	*Monday*	Johann Pestalozzi d. 1827. Heinrich Heine d. 1856	48
18	*Tuesday*	Martin Luther d. 1546. Dame Ngaio Marsh d. 1982	49
19	*Wednesday*	*Duke of York b. 1960.* Nicolas Copernicus b. 1473	50
20	*Thursday*	Dame Marie Rambert b. 1888. Ferruccio Lamborghini d. 1993	51
21	*Friday*	Léo Delibes b. 1836. Dame Margot Fonteyn d. 1991	52
22	*Saturday*	Arthur Schopenhauer b. 1788. Hugo Wolf d. 1903	53
23	*Sunday*	**2nd S. in Lent.** Samuel Pepys b. 1633	*week* 8 *day* 54
24	*Monday*	Wilhelm Grimm b. 1786. Dinah Shore d. 1994	55
25	*Tuesday*	Sir Christopher Wren d. 1723	56
26	*Wednesday*	Maj.-Gen. Orde Wingate b. 1903	57
27	*Thursday*	John Evelyn d. 1706. Henry Longfellow b. 1807	58
28	*Friday*	Sir Stephen Spender b. 1909. Sir Peter Medawar b. 1915	59

ASTRONOMICAL PHENOMENA

d	h	
6	01	Mars at stationary point
6	02	Jupiter in conjunction with Venus. Jupiter 0°.3 N.
6	02	Mercury in conjunction with Moon. Mercury 5° S.
6	15	Jupiter in conjunction with Moon. Jupiter 5° S.
6	16	Venus in conjunction with Moon. Venus 5° S.
10	16	Saturn in conjunction with Moon. Saturn 2° S.
12	18	Jupiter in conjunction with Mercury. Jupiter 1° N.
18	15	Sun's longitude 330° ♓
24	23	Mars in conjunction with Moon. Mars 3° N.

MINIMA OF ALGOL

d	h	d	h	d	h
2	01.2	13	12.5	24	23.7
4	22.0	16	09.3	27	20.6
7	18.8	19	06.1		
10	15.6	22	02.9		

CONSTELLATIONS

The following constellations are near the meridian at

	d	h		d	h
January	1	24	February	15	21
January	16	23	March	1	20
February	1	22	March	16	19

Draco (below the Pole), Camelopardus, Auriga, Taurus, Gemini, Orion, Canis Minor, Monoceros, Lepus, Canis Major and Puppis

THE MOON

Phases, Apsides and Node	d	h	m
● New Moon	7	15	06
☽ First Quarter	14	08	58
○ Full Moon	22	10	27
Perigee (356,848 km)	7	20	33
Apogee (406,395 km)	21	16	51

Mean longitude of ascending node on February 1, 181°

THE SUN

s.d. 16′.2

Day	Right Ascension	Dec. —	Equation of time	Rise 52°	Rise 56°	Transit	Set 52°	Set 56°	Sidereal time	Transit of First Point of Aries
	h m s	° ′	m s	h m	h m	h m	h m	h m	h m s	h m s
1	20 58 30	17 09	−13 33	7 40	7 55	12 14	16 48	16 33	8 44 57	15 12 33
2	21 02 35	16 52	−13 41	7 38	7 53	12 14	16 50	16 35	8 48 54	15 08 37
3	21 06 38	16 34	−13 48	7 37	7 51	12 14	16 52	16 37	8 52 51	15 04 41
4	21 10 41	16 16	−13 54	7 35	7 49	12 14	16 53	16 40	8 56 47	15 00 45
5	21 14 43	15 58	−14 00	7 33	7 47	12 14	16 55	16 42	9 00 44	14 56 49
6	21 18 45	15 40	−14 04	7 32	7 45	12 14	16 57	16 44	9 04 40	14 52 53
7	21 22 45	15 21	−14 08	7 30	7 43	12 14	16 59	16 46	9 08 37	14 48 57
8	21 26 45	15 03	−14 11	7 28	7 41	12 14	17 01	16 48	9 12 33	14 45 01
9	21 30 43	14 44	−14 14	7 26	7 39	12 14	17 03	16 51	9 16 30	14 41 05
10	21 34 41	14 24	−14 15	7 25	7 36	12 14	17 05	16 53	9 20 26	14 37 09
11	21 38 39	14 05	−14 16	7 23	7 34	12 14	17 07	16 55	9 24 23	14 33 14
12	21 42 35	13 45	−14 16	7 21	7 32	12 14	17 08	16 57	9 28 20	14 29 18
13	21 46 31	13 25	−14 15	7 19	7 30	12 14	17 10	16 59	9 32 16	14 25 22
14	21 50 26	13 04	−14 13	7 17	7 28	12 14	17 12	17 02	9 36 13	14 21 26
15	21 54 20	12 44	−14 11	7 15	7 25	12 14	17 14	17 04	9 40 09	14 17 30
16	21 58 13	12 23	−14 08	7 13	7 23	12 14	17 16	17 06	9 44 06	14 13 34
17	22 02 06	12 02	−14 04	7 11	7 21	12 14	17 18	17 08	9 48 02	14 09 38
18	22 05 58	11 41	−13 59	7 09	7 18	12 14	17 20	17 10	9 51 59	14 05 42
19	22 09 49	11 20	−13 54	7 07	7 16	12 14	17 21	17 13	9 55 55	14 01 46
20	22 13 40	10 59	−13 48	7 05	7 14	12 14	17 23	17 15	9 59 52	13 57 50
21	22 17 30	10 37	−13 41	7 03	7 11	12 14	17 25	17 17	10 03 48	13 53 55
22	22 21 19	10 15	−13 34	7 01	7 09	12 14	17 27	17 19	10 07 45	13 49 59
23	22 25 08	9 53	−13 26	6 59	7 06	12 13	17 29	17 21	10 11 42	13 46 03
24	22 28 56	9 31	−13 17	6 57	7 04	12 13	17 31	17 23	10 15 38	13 42 07
25	22 32 43	9 09	−13 08	6 55	7 02	12 13	17 32	17 26	10 19 35	13 38 11
26	22 36 30	8 47	−12 59	6 52	6 59	12 13	17 34	17 28	10 23 31	13 34 15
27	22 40 16	8 24	−12 48	6 50	6 57	12 13	17 36	17 30	10 27 28	13 30 19
28	22 44 02	8 02	−12 38	6 48	6 54	12 13	17 38	17 32	10 31 24	13 26 23

DURATION OF TWILIGHT (in minutes)

Latitude	52°	56°	52°	56°	52°	56°	52°	56°
	1 February		11 February		21 February		28 February	
Civil	37	41	35	39	34	38	34	38
Nautical	77	86	75	83	74	81	73	81
Astronomical	117	130	114	126	113	125	112	124

THE NIGHT SKY

Mercury is unsuitably placed for observation.

Venus is also unsuitably placed for observation.

Mars, its magnitude brightening during the month from −0.2 to −0.9, becomes an increasingly conspicuous object in the night sky, visible low in the eastern sky shortly after 22h at the beginning of February and shortly before 20h at the end. The gibbous Moon passes about 4°S. of the planet in the early hours of the 25th. Mars is in Virgo, reaching its first stationary point on the 6th, whereupon its motion becomes retrograde.

Jupiter is unsuitably placed for observation.

Saturn continues to be visible as an evening object in the south-western sky, magnitude +1.0, though by the end of the month it will be a difficult object to detect in the gathering twilight. On the evening of the 10th the thin crescent Moon, only three days old, will be seen only 1° above the planet .

Zodiacal Light. The evening cone may be observed stretching up from the western horizon, along the ecliptic after the end of twilight, from the beginning of the month to the 8th and again after the 22nd. This faint phenomenon is only visible under good conditions and in the absence of both moonlight and artificial lighting.

THE MOON

Day	RA	Dec.	Hor. par.	Semi-diam.	Sun's co-long.	PA of Bright Limb	Phase	Age	Rise 52°	Rise 56°	Transit	Set 52°	Set 56°
	h m	°	'	'	°	°	%	d	h m	h m	h m	h m	h m
1	14 52	−12.7	56.5	15.4	190	107	48	22.8	1 18	1 30	6 19	11 14	11 01
2	15 44	−15.3	57.3	15.6	202	104	38	23.8	2 25	2 40	7 10	11 51	11 36
3	16 40	−17.2	58.3	15.9	214	100	28	24.8	3 31	3 48	8 05	12 37	12 19
4	17 38	−18.2	59.3	16.1	226	96	18	25.8	4 33	4 51	9 02	13 32	13 14
5	18 39	−18.0	60.2	16.4	238	93	10	26.8	5 30	5 47	10 02	14 38	14 21
6	19 41	−16.7	60.9	16.6	251	91	4	27.8	6 19	6 34	11 03	15 52	15 38
7	20 42	−14.1	61.3	16.7	263	99	1	28.8	7 02	7 13	12 03	17 13	17 02
8	21 43	−10.6	61.4	16.7	275	222	0	0.4	7 38	7 46	13 01	18 35	18 28
9	22 43	− 6.3	61.2	16.7	287	243	3	1.4	8 10	8 14	13 58	19 57	19 55
10	23 40	− 1.7	60.7	16.5	299	246	8	2.4	8 40	8 40	14 52	21 17	21 19
11	0 36	+ 2.9	59.9	16.3	312	248	16	3.4	9 09	9 05	15 45	22 34	22 40
12	1 31	+ 7.2	59.0	16.1	324	250	25	4.4	9 38	9 31	16 37	23 48	23 58
13	2 25	+10.9	58.1	15.8	336	252	36	5.4	10 09	9 59	17 28	—	—
14	3 18	+14.0	57.2	15.6	348	255	46	6.4	10 44	10 30	18 19	0 58	1 11
15	4 11	+16.3	56.4	15.4	0	259	57	7.4	11 22	11 06	19 10	2 03	2 18
16	5 03	+17.7	55.7	15.2	12	263	66	8.4	12 06	11 48	19 59	3 02	3 19
17	5 55	+18.2	55.1	15.0	25	266	75	9.4	12 54	12 37	20 48	3 54	4 12
18	6 46	+17.9	54.6	14.9	37	270	83	10.4	13 47	13 31	21 36	4 39	4 56
19	7 36	+16.8	54.3	14.8	49	273	90	11.4	14 44	14 30	22 22	5 18	5 34
20	8 25	+14.9	54.1	14.7	61	275	95	12.4	15 44	15 32	23 08	5 52	6 05
21	9 13	+12.4	54.0	14.7	73	275	98	13.4	16 45	16 36	23 52	6 21	6 32
22	10 00	+ 9.5	54.0	14.7	85	261	100	14.4	17 47	17 42	—	6 48	6 55
23	10 46	+ 6.1	54.0	14.7	97	127	100	15.4	18 50	18 47	0 35	7 12	7 16
24	11 31	+ 2.5	54.2	14.8	110	115	98	16.4	19 53	19 54	1 18	7 35	7 36
25	12 17	− 1.2	54.4	14.8	122	112	94	17.4	20 57	21 01	2 00	7 58	7 55
26	13 03	− 4.9	54.7	14.9	134	111	89	18.4	22 02	22 09	2 44	8 21	8 16
27	13 50	− 8.5	55.2	15.0	146	109	82	19.4	23 07	23 17	3 29	8 47	8 39
28	14 38	−11.7	55.7	15.2	158	106	74	20.4	—	—	4 15	9 16	9 05

MERCURY

Day	RA	Dec.	Diam.	Phase	Transit	5° high 52°	5° high 56°
	h m	°	"	%	h m	h m	h m
1	19 21	−22.2	6	75	10 37	7 26	7 59
3	19 33	−22.0	6	77	10 41	7 29	8 01
5	19 44	−21.9	6	80	10 44	7 31	8 02
7	19 56	−21.6	6	82	10 48	7 32	8 03
9	20 08	−21.2	5	83	10 53	7 34	8 04
11	20 21	−20.8	5	85	10 57	7 35	8 04
13	20 33	−20.3	5	86	11 02	7 35	8 03
15	20 46	−19.7	5	88	11 07	7 35	8 02
17	20 58	−19.0	5	89	11 12	7 35	8 00
19	21 11	−18.2	5	91	11 17	7 34	7 58
21	21 24	−17.3	5	92	11 22	7 33	7 55
23	21 37	−16.4	5	93	11 27	7 32	7 52
25	21 50	−15.3	5	94	11 32	7 30	7 49
27	22 04	−14.2	5	95	11 38	7 28	7 45
29	22 17	−13.0	5	96	11 43	7 26	7 41
31	22 30	−11.6	5	97	11 49	7 23	7 37

VENUS

Day	RA	Dec.	Diam.	Phase	Transit	5° high 52°	5° high 56°
	h m	°	"	%	h m	h m	h m
1	19 58	−21.2	10	97	11 13	7 54	8 24
6	20 24	−20.1	10	97	11 20	7 52	8 19
11	20 50	−18.6	10	98	11 26	7 47	8 12
16	21 15	−17.0	10	98	11 32	7 41	8 03
21	21 40	−15.2	10	99	11 37	7 34	7 53
26	22 05	−13.2	10	99	11 41	7 26	7 42
31	22 29	−11.0	10	99	11 46	7 17	7 31

MARS

Day	RA	Dec.	Diam.	Phase	Transit	5° high 52°	5° high 56°
1	12 26	+ 0.8	11	94	3 41	22 07	22 09
6	12 27	+ 0.8	11	95	3 22	21 47	21 50
11	12 27	+ 1.0	12	96	3 02	21 26	21 29
16	12 25	+ 1.2	12	97	2 41	21 03	21 05
21	12 22	+ 1.6	13	97	2 18	20 38	20 40
26	12 18	+ 2.1	13	98	1 54	20 12	20 13
31	12 13	+ 2.7	13	99	1 30	19 44	19 45

SUNRISE AND SUNSET

	London		Bristol		Birmingham		Manchester		Newcastle		Glasgow		Belfast	
	0°05′	51°30′	2°35′	51°28′	1°55′	52°28′	2°15′	53°28′	1°37′	54°59′	4°14′	55°52′	5°56′	54°35′
	h m	h m	h m	h m	h m	h m	h m	h m	h m	h m	h m	h m	h m	h m
1	7 39	16 50	7 49	17 00	7 49	16 54	7 54	16 52	7 57	16 44	8 11	16 51	8 13	17 03
2	7 37	16 52	7 47	17 02	7 48	16 56	7 52	16 54	7 55	16 46	8 09	16 53	8 11	17 05
3	7 35	16 54	7 45	17 04	7 46	16 58	7 51	16 56	7 54	16 48	8 07	16 55	8 09	17 07
4	7 34	16 55	7 44	17 05	7 44	17 00	7 49	16 58	7 52	16 50	8 05	16 57	8 07	17 09
5	7 32	16 57	7 42	17 07	7 42	17 02	7 47	17 00	7 50	16 52	8 03	16 59	8 06	17 11
6	7 31	16 59	7 40	17 09	7 41	17 04	7 45	17 02	7 48	16 54	8 01	17 02	8 04	17 13
7	7 29	17 01	7 39	17 11	7 39	17 05	7 43	17 04	7 46	16 56	7 59	17 04	8 02	17 15
8	7 27	17 03	7 37	17 13	7 37	17 07	7 41	17 06	7 44	16 58	7 57	17 06	8 00	17 17
9	7 25	17 05	7 35	17 15	7 35	17 09	7 40	17 08	7 42	17 01	7 55	17 08	7 58	17 19
10	7 24	17 06	7 33	17 16	7 33	17 11	7 38	17 10	7 40	17 03	7 53	17 10	7 56	17 21
11	7 22	17 08	7 32	17 18	7 32	17 13	7 36	17 12	7 38	17 05	7 51	17 12	7 54	17 23
12	7 20	17 10	7 30	17 20	7 30	17 15	7 34	17 14	7 35	17 07	7 49	17 15	7 52	17 25
13	7 18	17 12	7 28	17 22	7 28	17 17	7 32	17 16	7 33	17 09	7 46	17 17	7 49	17 27
14	7 16	17 14	7 26	17 24	7 26	17 19	7 30	17 18	7 31	17 11	7 44	17 19	7 47	17 29
15	7 14	17 16	7 24	17 26	7 24	17 21	7 28	17 20	7 29	17 13	7 42	17 21	7 45	17 31
16	7 12	17 17	7 22	17 27	7 22	17 23	7 25	17 22	7 27	17 15	7 40	17 23	7 43	17 34
17	7 10	17 19	7 20	17 29	7 20	17 24	7 23	17 24	7 25	17 17	7 37	17 26	7 41	17 36
18	7 08	17 21	7 18	17 31	7 18	17 26	7 21	17 25	7 22	17 19	7 35	17 28	7 39	17 38
19	7 06	17 23	7 16	17 33	7 16	17 28	7 19	17 27	7 20	17 22	7 33	17 30	7 36	17 40
20	7 04	17 25	7 14	17 35	7 14	17 30	7 17	17 29	7 18	17 24	7 30	17 32	7 34	17 42
21	7 02	17 26	7 12	17 36	7 12	17 32	7 15	17 31	7 15	17 26	7 28	17 34	7 32	17 44
22	7 00	17 28	7 10	17 38	7 09	17 34	7 13	17 33	7 13	17 28	7 25	17 36	7 30	17 46
23	6 58	17 30	7 08	17 40	7 07	17 36	7 10	17 35	7 11	17 30	7 23	17 39	7 27	17 48
24	6 56	17 32	7 06	17 42	7 05	17 38	7 08	17 37	7 08	17 32	7 21	17 41	7 25	17 50
25	6 54	17 34	7 04	17 44	7 03	17 39	7 06	17 39	7 06	17 34	7 18	17 43	7 23	17 52
26	6 52	17 35	7 02	17 45	7 01	17 41	7 04	17 41	7 04	17 36	7 16	17 45	7 20	17 54
27	6 50	17 37	7 00	17 47	6 59	17 43	7 01	17 43	7 01	17 38	7 13	17 47	7 18	17 56
28	6 48	17 39	6 58	17 49	6 56	17 45	6 59	17 45	6 59	17 40	7 11	17 49	7 15	17 58

JUPITER

Day	RA	Dec.	Transit	5° high	
				52°	56°
	h m	° ′	h m	h m	h m
1	20 19.2	−19 59	11 33	8 05	8 32
11	20 28.8	−19 27	11 03	7 32	7 57
21	20 38.2	−18 55	10 33	6 57	7 22
31	20 47.2	−18 22	10 03	6 23	6 47

Diameters – equatorial 33″ polar 31″

SATURN

Day	RA	Dec.	Transit	5° high	
				52°	56°
	h m	° ′	h m	h m	h m
1	0 16.8	− 0 39	15 30	20 53	20 49
11	0 20.4	− 0 14	14 54	20 19	20 16
21	0 24.3	+ 0 13	14 18	19 46	19 43
31	0 28.5	+ 0 41	13 43	19 14	19 11

Diameters – equatorial 16″ polar 15″
Rings – major axis 37″ minor axis 3″

URANUS

Day	RA	Dec.	Transit	10° high	
				52°	56°
	h m	° ′	h m	h m	h m
1	20 30.2	−19 33	11 43	9 00	9 39
11	20 32.6	−19 25	11 07	8 21	9 00
21	20 34.9	−19 17	10 29	7 43	8 22
31	20 37.0	−19 09	9 52	7 05	7 43

Diameter 4″

NEPTUNE

Day	RA	Dec.	Transit	10° high	
				52°	56°
	h m	° ′	h m	h m	h m
1	20 00.0	−20 09	11 13	8 35	9 18
11	20 01.5	−20 05	10 35	7 57	8 39
21	20 02.9	−20 00	9 58	7 18	8 00
31	20 04.2	−19 57	9 20	6 39	7 21

Diameter 2″

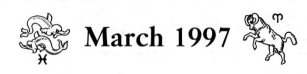

March 1997

THIRD MONTH, 31 DAYS. *Mars*, Roman god of battle

1	*Saturday*	St David's Day. Robert Lowell b. 1917	*week 8 day* 60
2	*Sunday*	**3rd S. in Lent.** Cardinal Archbishop Hume b. 1923	*week 9 day* 61
3	*Monday*	Alexander Graham Bell b. 1847. Jean Harlow b. 1911	62
4	*Tuesday*	Opening of the Forth Railway Bridge 1890	63
5	*Wednesday*	Gerardus Mercator b. 1512. Flora Macdonald d. 1790	64
6	*Thursday*	Valentina Tereshkova b. 1937. Zoltán Kodály d. 1967	65
7	*Friday*	Maurice Ravel b. 1875. Viv Richards b. 1952	66
8	*Saturday*	William III d. 1702. Sir William Walton d. 1983	67
9	*Sunday*	**4th S. in Lent.** Mothering Sunday	*week 10 day* 68
10	*Monday*	*Prince Edward b. 1964.* Commonwealth Day	69
11	*Tuesday*	Harold Wilson b. 1916. Haydn Wood d. 1959	70
12	*Wednesday*	Bishop George Berkeley b. 1685	71
13	*Thursday*	Angela Brazil d. 1947. Sir Frank Worrell d. 1967	72
14	*Friday*	Johann Strauss (the elder) b. 1804. Sir Huw Wheldon d. 1986	73
15	*Saturday*	Salvator Rosa d. 1673. Dame Rebecca West d. 1983	74
16	*Sunday*	**5th S. in Lent.** Georg Ohm b. 1787	*week 11 day* 75
17	*Monday*	St Patrick's Day. *Bank Holiday in Northern Ireland*	76
18	*Tuesday*	Grover Cleveland b. 1837. Rudolf Diesel b. 1858	77
19	*Wednesday*	**St Joseph of Nazareth.** A. J. Balfour d. 1930	78
20	*Thursday*	Sir Isaac Newton d. 1727. Dame Vera Lynn b. 1917.	79
21	*Friday*	Modest Mussorgsky b. 1839 (NS). Paul Tortelier b. 1914	80
22	*Saturday*	Johann Wolfgang von Goethe d. 1832	81
23	*Sunday*	**Palm Sunday.** Princess Eugenie of York b. 1990	*week 12 day* 82
24	*Monday*	Walter Bagehot d. 1877. J. M. Synge d. 1909	83
25	*Tuesday*	Joachim Murat b. 1767. Treaty of Rome signed 1957	84
26	*Wednesday*	*Hilary Law Sittings end.* Ludwig van Beethoven d. 1827	85
27	*Thursday*	**Maundy Thursday.** Alfred, Comte de Vigny b. 1797	86
28	*Friday*	**Good Friday.** *Public Holiday in the UK*	87
29	*Saturday*	**Easter Eve.** John Major b. 1943	88
30	*Sunday*	**Easter Day** (Western churches)	*week 13 day* 89
31	*Monday*	*Bank Holiday in England, Wales and Northern Ireland*	90

ASTRONOMICAL PHENOMENA

d	h	
2	15	Venus in conjunction with Mercury. Venus 0°.8 N.
6	12	Jupiter in conjunction with Moon. Jupiter 4° S.
8	13	Pluto at stationary point
8	15	Venus in conjunction with Moon. Venus 3° S.
8	21	Mercury in conjunction with Moon. Mercury 3° S.
9	01	Total eclipse of Sun (*see* page 66).
10	08	Saturn in conjunction with Moon. Saturn 1° S.
11	16	Mercury in superior conjunction
17	08	Mars at opposition
20	14	Sun's longitude 0° ♈
20	16	Saturn in conjunction with Mercury. Saturn 2° S.
23	10	Mars in conjunction with Moon. Mars 4° N.
24	05	Partial eclipse of Moon (*see* page 66).
30	22	Saturn in conjunction
31	13	Saturn in conjunction with Venus. Saturn 0°.9 S.

MINIMA OF ALGOL

d	h	d	h	d	h
2	17.4	14	04.7	25	16.0
5	14.2	17	01.5	28	12.8
8	11.0	19	22.3	31	09.6
11	07.9	22	19.1		

CONSTELLATIONS

The following constellations are near the meridian at

	d	h		d	h
February	1	24	March	16	21
February	15	23	April	1	20
March	1	22	April	15	19

Cepheus (below the Pole), Camelopardus, Lynx, Gemini, Cancer, Leo, Canis Minor, Hydra, Monoceros, Canis Major and Puppis

THE MOON

Phases, Apsides and Node	d	h	m
☾ Last Quarter	2	09	38
● New Moon	9	01	15
☽ First Quarter	16	00	06
○ Full Moon	24	04	45
☾ Last Quarter	31	19	38

Perigee (357,763 km)	8	08	54
Apogee (405,964 km)	20	23	29

Mean longitude of ascending node on March 1, 180°

THE SUN   s.d. 16'.1

Day	Right Ascension	Dec.	Equation of time	Rise 52°	Rise 56°	Transit	Set 52°	Set 56°	Sidereal time	Transit of First Point of Aries
	h m s	° '	m s	h m	h m	h m	h m	h m	h m s	h m s
1	22 47 47	−7 39	−12 26	6 46	6 52	12 12	17 40	17 34	10 35 21	13 22 27
2	22 51 32	−7 16	−12 15	6 44	6 49	12 12	17 41	17 36	10 39 17	13 18 31
3	22 55 16	−6 53	−12 02	6 41	6 47	12 12	17 43	17 38	10 43 14	13 14 35
4	22 59 00	−6 30	−11 50	6 39	6 44	12 12	17 45	17 41	10 47 11	13 10 40
5	23 02 44	−6 07	−11 36	6 37	6 41	12 11	17 47	17 43	10 51 07	13 06 44
6	23 06 26	−5 44	−11 23	6 35	6 39	12 11	17 49	17 45	10 55 04	13 02 48
7	23 10 09	−5 21	−11 09	6 33	6 36	12 11	17 50	17 47	10 59 00	12 58 52
8	23 13 51	−4 57	−10 54	6 30	6 34	12 11	17 52	17 49	11 02 57	12 54 56
9	23 17 33	−4 34	−10 40	6 28	6 31	12 11	17 54	17 51	11 06 53	12 51 00
10	23 21 15	−4 10	−10 25	6 26	6 29	12 10	17 56	17 53	11 10 50	12 47 04
11	23 24 56	−3 47	−10 09	6 24	6 26	12 10	17 57	17 55	11 14 46	12 43 08
12	23 28 36	−3 23	− 9 53	6 21	6 23	12 10	17 59	17 57	11 18 43	12 39 12
13	23 32 17	−3 00	− 9 37	6 19	6 21	12 09	18 01	17 59	11 22 40	12 35 16
14	23 35 57	−2 36	− 9 21	6 17	6 18	12 09	18 03	18 01	11 26 36	12 31 20
15	23 39 37	−2 12	− 9 04	6 14	6 16	12 09	18 05	18 03	11 30 33	12 27 25
16	23 43 17	−1 49	− 8 47	6 12	6 13	12 09	18 06	18 06	11 34 29	12 23 29
17	23 46 56	−1 25	− 8 30	6 10	6 10	12 08	18 08	18 08	11 38 26	12 19 33
18	23 50 35	−1 01	− 8 13	6 07	6 08	12 08	18 10	18 10	11 42 22	12 15 37
19	23 54 14	−0 37	− 7 55	6 05	6 05	12 08	18 11	18 12	11 46 19	12 11 41
20	23 57 53	−0 14	− 7 38	6 03	6 02	12 07	18 13	18 14	11 50 15	12 07 45
21	0 01 32	+0 10	− 7 20	6 00	6 00	12 07	18 15	18 16	11 54 12	12 03 49
22	0 05 10	+0 34	− 7 02	5 58	5 57	12 07	18 17	18 18	11 58 09	11 59 53
23	0 08 49	+0 57	− 6 44	5 56	5 54	12 07	18 18	18 20	12 02 05	11 55 57
24	0 12 27	+1 21	− 6 26	5 54	5 52	12 06	18 20	18 22	12 06 02	11 52 01
25	0 16 05	+1 45	− 6 07	5 51	5 49	12 06	18 22	18 24	12 09 58	11 48 06
26	0 19 44	+2 08	− 5 49	5 49	5 47	12 06	18 23	18 26	12 13 55	11 44 10
27	0 23 22	+2 32	− 5 31	5 47	5 44	12 05	18 25	18 28	12 17 51	11 40 14
28	0 27 00	+2 55	− 5 13	5 44	5 41	12 05	18 27	18 30	12 21 48	11 36 18
29	0 30 39	+3 18	− 4 54	5 42	5 39	12 05	18 29	18 32	12 25 44	11 32 22
30	0 34 17	+3 42	− 4 36	5 40	5 36	12 04	18 30	18 34	12 29 41	11 28 26
31	0 37 56	+4 05	− 4 18	5 37	5 33	12 04	18 32	18 36	12 33 37	11 24 30

DURATION OF TWILIGHT (in minutes)

Latitude	52°	56°	52°	56°	52°	56°	52°	56°
	1 March		11 March		21 March		31 March	
Civil	34	38	34	37	34	37	34	38
Nautical	73	81	73	80	74	82	76	84
Astronomical	112	124	113	125	116	129	120	136

THE NIGHT SKY

Mercury is unsuitably placed for observation at first, superior conjunction occurring on the 11th. It then moves rapidly eastwards from the Sun and for the last week of the month it is an evening object, magnitude − 1.2 to − 0.7. It is visible low above the western horizon about the end of evening civil twilight. This is the most favourable apparition of the year for observers in the northern hemisphere.

Venus continues to be unsuitably placed for observation.

Mars, magnitude − 1.3, is at opposition on the 17th and therefore visible throughout the hours of darkness. It is a prominent object with a slightly reddish tinge, which is a useful aid to identification. Mars is retrograding in Virgo and moves back into Leo at the end of the month. The Full Moon will be seen about 6° below Mars on the evening of the 23rd.

Jupiter is too close to the Sun for observation at first but shortly after the middle of March it should be possible to see it as a morning object, low above the south-eastern horizon for a short time before dawn. Its magnitude is − 2.0.

Saturn, magnitude +0.8 is only visible for a short time, low in the west-south-western sky in the early evenings for the early part of the month. Thereafter it is lost in the gathering twilight.

Zodiacal Light. The evening cone may be observed stretching up from the western horizon, after the end of twilight, from the beginning of the month to the 10th and again after the 24th.

THE MOON

Day	RA	Dec.	Hor. par.	Semi- diam.	Sun's co- long.	PA of Bright Limb	Phase	Age	Rise 52°	Rise 56°	Transit	Set 52°	Set 56°
	h m	°	'	'	°	°	%	d	h m	h m	h m	h m	h m
1	15 29	−14.5	56.4	15.4	170	103	65	21.4	0 12	0 26	5 04	9 50	9 36
2	16 22	−16.6	57.1	15.6	183	99	54	22.4	1 17	1 33	5 55	10 31	10 14
3	17 18	−17.9	58.0	15.8	195	95	44	23.4	2 18	2 36	6 50	11 20	11 02
4	18 15	−18.1	58.8	16.0	207	90	33	24.4	3 16	3 33	7 46	12 18	12 01
5	19 15	−17.3	59.7	16.3	219	86	23	25.4	4 07	4 23	8 44	13 26	13 10
6	20 15	−15.3	60.4	16.5	231	82	14	26.4	4 52	5 05	9 43	14 41	14 29
7	21 15	−12.3	61.0	16.6	244	79	6	27.4	5 30	5 40	10 41	16 01	15 53
8	22 15	− 8.4	61.3	16.7	256	78	2	28.4	6 05	6 11	11 38	17 24	17 19
9	23 13	− 3.9	61.2	16.7	268	121	0	29.4	6 36	6 38	12 35	18 46	18 46
10	0 11	+ 0.8	60.9	16.6	280	248	1	0.9	7 06	7 04	13 30	20 07	20 11
11	1 07	+ 5.3	60.2	16.4	292	251	6	1.9	7 36	7 30	14 24	21 25	21 33
12	2 03	+ 9.4	59.4	16.2	305	253	12	2.9	8 07	7 58	15 18	22 39	22 51
13	2 59	+12.9	58.4	15.9	317	256	20	3.9	8 41	8 29	16 10	23 49	—
14	3 53	+15.5	57.5	15.7	329	260	30	4.9	9 19	9 04	17 03	—	0 03
15	4 48	+17.3	56.5	15.4	341	264	40	5.9	10 02	9 45	17 54	0 52	1 09
16	5 41	+18.1	55.8	15.2	353	268	50	6.9	10 50	10 32	18 44	1 48	2 05
17	6 33	+18.0	55.1	15.0	6	272	60	7.9	11 42	11 25	19 32	2 36	2 54
18	7 23	+17.1	54.6	14.9	18	276	69	8.9	12 38	12 23	20 19	3 18	3 34
19	8 13	+15.4	54.3	14.8	30	280	78	9.9	13 37	13 24	21 05	3 53	4 07
20	9 01	+13.1	54.1	14.7	42	283	85	10.9	14 37	14 27	21 49	4 24	4 35
21	9 47	+10.3	54.0	14.7	54	285	91	11.9	15 39	15 32	22 33	4 51	4 59
22	10 33	+ 7.0	54.1	14.7	66	287	96	12.9	16 42	16 38	23 16	5 16	5 21
23	11 19	+ 3.4	54.2	14.8	78	289	99	13.9	17 45	17 44	23 59	5 39	5 41
24	12 05	− 0.3	54.5	14.8	91	299	100	14.9	18 49	18 52	—	6 02	6 01
25	12 51	− 4.0	54.8	14.9	103	104	99	15.9	19 54	20 00	0 42	6 26	6 22
26	13 38	− 7.6	55.1	15.0	115	105	97	16.9	20 59	21 09	1 27	6 51	6 44
27	14 27	−11.0	55.6	15.1	127	103	93	17.9	22 05	22 17	2 13	7 19	7 09
28	15 17	−13.9	56.1	15.3	139	101	86	18.9	23 09	23 25	3 01	7 52	7 38
29	16 09	−16.1	56.6	15.4	151	97	79	19.9	—	—	3 52	8 30	8 14
30	17 04	−17.6	57.2	15.6	164	93	69	20.9	0 11	0 29	4 44	9 15	8 57
31	18 00	−18.2	57.9	15.8	176	89	59	21.9	1 09	1 27	5 39	10 09	9 51

MERCURY

Day	RA	Dec.	Diam.	Phase	Transit	5° high 52°	5° high 56°
	h m	°	"	%	h m	h m	h m
1	22 17	−13.0	5	96	11 43	7 26	7 41
3	22 30	−11.6	5	97	11 49	7 23	7 37
5	22 44	−10.2	5	98	11 54	7 21	7 33
7	22 58	− 8.7	5	99	12 00	16 44	16 33
9	23 11	− 7.2	5	100	12 06	16 59	16 50
11	23 25	− 5.5	5	100	12 12	17 14	17 07
13	23 39	− 3.8	5	100	12 18	17 30	17 24
15	23 53	− 2.0	5	99	12 24	17 46	17 41
17	0 07	− 0.2	5	98	12 31	18 01	17 59
19	0 22	+ 1.7	5	96	12 37	18 17	18 16
21	0 36	+ 3.6	5	93	12 43	18 33	18 33
23	0 50	+ 5.4	5	89	12 49	18 49	18 51
25	1 03	+ 7.3	6	84	12 55	19 04	19 07
27	1 16	+ 9.0	6	78	13 00	19 18	19 22
29	1 29	+10.7	6	72	13 04	19 30	19 36
31	1 40	+12.2	6	64	13 08	19 41	19 49

VENUS

Day	RA	Dec.	Diam.	Phase	Transit	5° high 52°	5° high 56°
	h m	°	"	%	h m	h m	h m
1	22 19	−11.9	10	99	11 44	7 21	7 35
6	22 43	− 9.7	10	99	11 48	7 12	7 24
11	23 06	− 7.3	10	100	11 52	7 02	7 12
16	23 29	− 4.9	10	100	11 55	6 52	7 00
21	23 52	− 2.4	10	100	11 58	6 42	6 48
26	0 15	+ 0.1	10	100	12 01	6 32	6 36
31	0 38	+ 2.6	10	100	12 04	6 23	6 24

MARS

Day	RA	Dec.	Diam.	Phase	Transit	5° high 52°	5° high 56°
1	12 15	+ 2.5	13	99	1 40	19 55	19 56
6	12 10	+ 3.1	14	99	1 14	19 26	19 27
11	12 03	+ 3.8	14	100	0 48	18 57	18 57
16	11 56	+ 4.5	14	100	0 21	18 26	18 26
21	11 49	+ 5.2	14	100	23 49	17 56	17 55
26	11 41	+ 5.8	14	100	23 22	17 26	17 24
31	11 35	+ 6.4	14	99	22 56	16 57	16 55

SUNRISE AND SUNSET

	London		Bristol		Birmingham		Manchester		Newcastle		Glasgow		Belfast	
	0°05'	51°30'	2°35'	51°28'	1°55'	52°28'	2°15'	53°28'	1°37'	54°59'	4°14'	55°52'	5°56'	54°35'
	h m	h m	h m	h m	h m	h m	h m	h m	h m	h m	h m	h m	h m	h m
1	6 46	17 41	6 56	17 51	6 54	17 47	6 57	17 47	6 56	17 42	7 08	17 51	7 13	18 00
2	6 43	17 42	6 53	17 52	6 52	17 49	6 55	17 49	6 54	17 44	7 06	17 53	7 11	18 02
3	6 41	17 44	6 51	17 54	6 50	17 50	6 52	17 51	6 52	17 46	7 03	17 56	7 08	18 04
4	6 39	17 46	6 49	17 56	6 47	17 52	6 50	17 53	6 49	17 48	7 01	17 58	7 06	18 06
5	6 37	17 48	6 47	17 58	6 45	17 54	6 48	17 54	6 47	17 50	6 58	18 00	7 03	18 08
6	6 35	17 49	6 45	17 59	6 43	17 56	6 45	17 56	6 44	17 52	6 56	18 02	7 01	18 10
7	6 32	17 51	6 42	18 01	6 41	17 58	6 43	17 58	6 42	17 54	6 53	18 04	6 59	18 12
8	6 30	17 53	6 40	18 03	6 38	18 00	6 40	18 00	6 39	17 56	6 51	18 06	6 56	18 14
9	6 28	17 55	6 38	18 05	6 36	18 01	6 38	18 02	6 37	17 58	6 48	18 08	6 54	18 16
10	6 26	17 56	6 36	18 06	6 34	18 03	6 36	18 04	6 34	18 00	6 45	18 10	6 51	18 18
11	6 24	17 58	6 34	18 08	6 31	18 05	6 33	18 06	6 32	18 02	6 43	18 12	6 49	18 20
12	6 21	18 00	6 31	18 10	6 29	18 07	6 31	18 08	6 29	18 04	6 40	18 14	6 46	18 22
13	6 19	18 02	6 29	18 12	6 27	18 09	6 29	18 09	6 27	18 06	6 38	18 16	6 44	18 24
14	6 17	18 03	6 27	18 13	6 24	18 10	6 26	18 11	6 24	18 08	6 35	18 18	6 41	18 26
15	6 15	18 05	6 25	18 15	6 22	18 12	6 24	18 13	6 22	18 10	6 32	18 20	6 39	18 28
16	6 12	18 07	6 22	18 17	6 20	18 14	6 21	18 15	6 19	18 12	6 30	18 23	6 36	18 30
17	6 10	18 08	6 20	18 18	6 17	18 16	6 19	18 17	6 17	18 14	6 27	18 25	6 34	18 32
18	6 08	18 10	6 18	18 20	6 15	18 17	6 16	18 19	6 14	18 16	6 25	18 27	6 31	18 33
19	6 05	18 12	6 15	18 22	6 13	18 19	6 14	18 21	6 11	18 18	6 22	18 29	6 29	18 35
20	6 03	18 13	6 13	18 23	6 10	18 21	6 12	18 22	6 09	18 20	6 19	18 31	6 26	18 37
21	6 01	18 15	6 11	18 25	6 08	18 23	6 09	18 24	6 06	18 22	6 17	18 33	6 24	18 39
22	5 59	18 17	6 09	18 27	6 06	18 24	6 07	18 26	6 04	18 24	6 14	18 35	6 21	18 41
23	5 56	18 19	6 06	18 29	6 03	18 26	6 04	18 28	6 01	18 26	6 11	18 37	6 19	18 43
24	5 54	18 20	6 04	18 30	6 01	18 28	6 02	18 30	5 59	18 28	6 09	18 39	6 16	18 45
25	5 52	18 22	6 02	18 32	5 59	18 30	5 59	18 32	5 56	18 30	6 06	18 41	6 14	18 47
26	5 49	18 24	5 59	18 34	5 56	18 31	5 57	18 33	5 54	18 32	6 04	18 43	6 11	18 49
27	5 47	18 25	5 57	18 35	5 54	18 33	5 55	18 35	5 51	18 34	6 01	18 45	6 09	18 51
28	5 45	18 27	5 55	18 37	5 52	18 35	5 52	18 37	5 49	18 36	5 58	18 47	6 06	18 53
29	5 43	18 29	5 53	18 39	5 49	18 37	5 50	18 39	5 46	18 38	5 56	18 49	6 04	18 55
30	5 40	18 30	5 50	18 40	5 47	18 38	5 47	18 41	5 43	18 40	5 53	18 51	6 01	18 56
31	5 38	18 32	5 48	18 42	5 45	18 40	5 45	18 42	5 41	18 42	5 50	18 53	5 59	18 58

JUPITER

Day	RA	Dec.	Transit	5° high	
				52°	56°
	h m	° '	h m	h m	h m
1	20 45.4	−18 28	10 09	6 30	6 54
11	20 54.1	−17 55	9 38	5 55	6 19
21	21 02.2	−17 23	9 07	5 20	5 43
31	21 09.8	−16 52	8 35	4 45	5 06

Diameters – equatorial 34″ polar 32″

SATURN

Day	RA	Dec.	Transit	5° high	
				52°	56°
	h m	° '	h m	h m	h m
1	0 27.6	+ 0 35	13 50	19 20	19 17
11	0 32.0	+ 1 04	13 15	18 48	18 45
21	0 36.5	+ 1 34	12 41	18 15	18 13
31	0 41.1	+ 2 03	12 06	17 43	17 42

Diameters – equatorial 16″ polar 14″
Rings – major axis 36″ minor axis 4″

URANUS

Day	RA	Dec.	Transit	10° high	
				52°	56°
	h m	° '	h m	h m	h m
1	20 36.6	−19 11	10 00	7 12	7 50
11	20 38.6	−19 03	9 22	6 34	7 12
21	20 40.4	−18 57	8 45	5 55	6 33
31	20 42.0	−18 51	8 07	5 17	5 54

Diameter 4″

NEPTUNE

Day	RA	Dec.	Transit	10° high	
				52°	56°
	h m	° '	h m	h m	h m
1	20 04.0	−19 57	9 27	6 47	7 29
11	20 05.2	−19 54	8 49	6 08	6 50
21	20 06.2	−19 51	8 11	5 30	6 11
31	20 07.0	−19 48	7 32	4 51	5 32

Diameter 2″

April 1997

FOURTH MONTH, 30 DAYS. *Asperire*, to open; Earth opens to receive seed

1	Tuesday	Ferruccio Busoni b. 1866. Cosima Wagner d. 1930	*week* 13 *day* 91
2	Wednesday	Hans Christian Andersen b. 1805	92
3	Thursday	Richard D'Oyly Carte d. 1901. Kurt Weill d. 1950	93
4	Friday	Oliver Goldsmith d. 1774. Gloria Swanson d. 1983	94
5	Saturday	Joseph Lister b. 1827. A. C. Swinburne b. 1837	95
6	Sunday	**1st. S. after Easter.** Raphael d. 1520	*week* 14 *day* 96
7	Monday	**The Annunciation.** Henry Ford d. 1947	97
8	Tuesday	HINDU NEW YEAR. *Easter Law Sittings begin*	98
9	Wednesday	Sir Francis Bacon d. 1626. Sir Robert Helpmann b. 1909	99
10	Thursday	Joseph Pulitzer b. 1847. A. C. Swinburne d. 1909	100
11	Friday	Treaty of Utrecht 1713. Sir Charles Hallé b. 1819	101
12	Saturday	Feodor Chaliapin d. 1938. Alan Paton d. 1988	102
13	Sunday	**2nd S. after Easter.** SIKH NEW YEAR	*week* 15 *day* 103
14	Monday	Sir John Gielgud b. 1904. Ernest Bevin d. 1951	104
15	Tuesday	Henry James b. 1843. Matthew Arnold d. 1888	105
16	Wednesday	Anatole France b. 1844. Wilbur Wright b. 1867	106
17	Thursday	Benjamin Franklin d. 1790. Nikita Khrushchev b. 1894 (NS)	107
18	Friday	Judge Jeffreys d. 1689. Albert Einstein d. 1955	108
19	Saturday	Benjamin Disraeli d. 1881. Charles Darwin d. 1882	109
20	Sunday	**3rd S. after Easter.** Joan Miró b. 1893	*week* 16 *day* 110
21	Monday	*Queen Elizabeth II b. 1926.* Charlotte Brontë b. 1816	111
22	Tuesday	PASSOVER begins. Henry Fielding b. 1707	112
23	Wednesday	St George's Day. Viscount Allenby b. 1861	113
24	Thursday	Anthony Trollope b. 1815. Sir Stafford Cripps b. 1889	114
25	Friday	**St Mark.** Oliver Cromwell b. 1599	115
26	Saturday	David Hume b. 1711. Eugene Delacroix b. 1798	116
27	Sunday	**4th S. after Easter.** EASTER DAY (Greek Orthodox)	*week* 17 *day* 117
28	Monday	Lionel Barrymore b. 1878. Olivier Messiaen d. 1992	118
29	Tuesday	Sir Thomas Beecham b. 1879	119
30	Wednesday	Mary II b. 1662. Franz Lehár b. 1870	120

ASTRONOMICAL PHENOMENA

d h
2 14 Venus in superior conjunction
3 06 Jupiter in conjunction with Moon. Jupiter 4° S.
6 01 Mercury at greatest elongation E.19°
7 00 Saturn in conjunction with Moon. Saturn 1° S.
7 13 Venus in conjunction with Moon. Venus 0°.7 N.
8 20 Mercury in conjunction with Moon. Mercury 6° N.
15 00 Mercury at stationary point
19 03 Mars in conjunction with Moon. Mars 4° N.
20 01 Sun's longitude 30° ♉
22 07 Venus in conjunction with Mercury. Venus 3° S.
25 11 Mercury in inferior conjunction
27 19 Mars at stationary point
30 19 Jupiter in conjunction with Moon. Jupiter 4° S.

MINIMA OF ALGOL

d	h	d	h	d	h
3	06.4	14	17.7	26	05.0
6	03.2	17	14.5	29	01.8
9	00.1	20	11.3		
11	20.9	23	08.2		

CONSTELLATIONS
The following constellations are near the meridian at

	d	h		d	h
March	1	24	April	15	21
March	16	23	May	1	20
April	1	22	May	16	19

Cepheus (below the Pole), Cassiopeia (below the Pole), Ursa Major, Leo Minor, Leo, Sextans, Hydra and Crater

THE MOON

Phases, Apsides and Node	d	h	m
● New Moon	7	11	02
☽ First Quarter	14	17	00
○ Full Moon	22	20	33
☾ Last Quarter	30	02	37
Perigee (361,497 km)	5	16	42
Apogee (405,003 km)	17	15	20

Mean longitude of ascending node on April 1, 178°

THE SUN   s.d. 16′.0

Day	Right Ascension	Dec. +	Equation of time	Rise 52°	Rise 56°	Transit	Set 52°	Set 56°	Sidereal time	Transit of First Point of Aries
	h m s	° ′	m s	h m	h m	h m	h m	h m	h m s	h m s
1	0 41 34	4 28	−4 00	5 35	5 31	12 04	18 34	18 38	12 37 34	11 20 34
2	0 45 13	4 51	−3 42	5 33	5 28	12 04	18 35	18 40	12 41 31	11 16 38
3	0 48 52	5 14	−3 25	5 30	5 25	12 03	18 37	18 42	12 45 27	11 12 42
4	0 52 31	5 37	−3 07	5 28	5 23	12 03	18 39	18 44	12 49 24	11 08 46
5	0 56 10	6 00	−2 50	5 26	5 20	12 03	18 41	18 46	12 53 20	11 04 51
6	0 59 49	6 23	−2 33	5 24	5 18	12 02	18 42	18 48	12 57 17	11 00 55
7	1 03 29	6 46	−2 16	5 21	5 15	12 02	18 44	18 50	13 01 13	10 56 59
8	1 07 09	7 08	−1 59	5 19	5 13	12 02	18 46	18 52	13 05 10	10 53 03
9	1 10 49	7 31	−1 42	5 17	5 10	12 02	18 47	18 55	13 09 06	10 49 07
10	1 14 29	7 53	−1 26	5 15	5 07	12 01	18 49	18 57	13 13 03	10 45 11
11	1 18 10	8 15	−1 10	5 12	5 05	12 01	18 51	18 59	13 17 00	10 41 15
12	1 21 51	8 37	−0 54	5 10	5 02	12 01	18 53	19 01	13 20 56	10 37 19
13	1 25 32	8 59	−0 39	5 08	5 00	12 01	18 54	19 03	13 24 53	10 33 23
14	1 29 13	9 21	−0 24	5 06	4 57	12 00	18 56	19 05	13 28 49	10 29 27
15	1 32 55	9 42	−0 09	5 03	4 55	12 00	18 58	19 07	13 32 46	10 25 31
16	1 36 37	10 04	+0 05	5 01	4 52	12 00	18 59	19 09	13 36 42	10 21 36
17	1 40 19	10 25	+0 20	4 59	4 50	12 00	19 01	19 11	13 40 39	10 17 40
18	1 44 02	10 46	+0 33	4 57	4 47	11 59	19 03	19 13	13 44 35	10 13 44
19	1 47 45	11 07	+0 47	4 55	4 45	11 59	19 05	19 15	13 48 32	10 09 48
20	1 51 29	11 27	+1 00	4 53	4 42	11 59	19 06	19 17	13 52 29	10 05 52
21	1 55 13	11 48	+1 12	4 51	4 40	11 59	19 08	19 19	13 56 25	10 01 56
22	1 58 57	12 08	+1 25	4 48	4 37	11 58	19 10	19 21	14 00 22	9 58 00
23	2 02 42	12 28	+1 36	4 46	4 35	11 58	19 11	19 23	14 04 18	9 54 04
24	2 06 27	12 48	+1 48	4 44	4 32	11 58	19 13	19 25	14 08 15	9 50 08
25	2 10 13	13 08	+1 58	4 42	4 30	11 58	19 15	19 27	14 12 11	9 46 12
26	2 13 59	13 27	+2 09	4 40	4 28	11 58	19 16	19 29	14 16 08	9 42 17
27	2 17 46	13 47	+2 19	4 38	4 25	11 58	19 18	19 31	14 20 04	9 38 21
28	2 21 33	14 06	+2 28	4 36	4 23	11 57	19 20	19 33	14 24 01	9 34 25
29	2 25 21	14 24	+2 37	4 34	4 21	11 57	19 21	19 35	14 27 57	9 30 29
30	2 29 09	14 43	+2 45	4 32	4 18	11 57	19 23	19 37	14 31 54	9 26 33

DURATION OF TWILIGHT (in minutes)

Latitude	52°	56°	52°	56°	52°	56°	52°	56°
	1 April		11 April		21 April		30 April	
Civil	34	38	35	40	37	42	39	44
Nautical	76	85	79	90	84	96	89	105
Astronomical	121	137	128	148	138	167	152	200

THE NIGHT SKY

Mercury continues to be visible in the evenings, magnitude −0.6 to +1.0, for the first ten days of the month. It may be detected low above the western horizon around the end of evening civil twilight. Mercury passes through inferior conjunction on the 25th.

Venus passes through superior conjunction on the 2nd and is therefore too close to the Sun for observation throughout April.

Mars is just past opposition and therefore still available for observation during the greater part of the night, though by the end of the month it has sunk too low in the western sky to be visible after 03h. Its magnitude fades from −1.1 to −0.5 during April. On the 29th Mars reaches its second stationary point in the eastern part of Leo and then resumes its direct motion. The gibbous Moon will be seen 4° below Mars in the early hours of the 19th.

Jupiter, magnitude −2.1, is a brilliant object in the south-eastern sky for a short time in the mornings before dawn, though being so far south of the equator its altitude is always less than 20°. On the morning of the 3rd the old crescent Moon will be seen about 4° above the planet about an hour before sunrise.

Saturn is unsuitably placed for observation.

THE MOON

Day	RA h m	Dec. °	Hor. par. '	Semi-diam. '	Sun's co-long. °	PA of Bright Limb °	Phase %	Age d	Rise 52° h m	Rise 56° h m	Transit h m	Set 52° h m	Set 56° h m
1	18 57	−17.7	58.6	16.0	188	85	48	22.9	2 01	2 18	6 34	11 11	10 54
2	19 55	−16.1	59.2	16.1	200	80	37	23.9	2 46	3 01	7 31	12 21	12 07
3	20 53	−13.5	59.8	16.3	212	76	26	24.9	3 26	3 37	8 27	13 36	13 26
4	21 51	−10.0	60.3	16.4	225	73	16	25.9	4 01	4 09	9 23	14 55	14 48
5	22 48	− 5.9	60.6	16.5	237	70	9	26.9	4 32	4 36	10 18	16 15	16 13
6	23 45	− 1.3	60.6	16.5	249	67	3	27.9	5 02	5 02	11 13	17 36	17 38
7	0 42	+ 3.3	60.4	16.5	261	57	0	28.9	5 32	5 28	12 07	18 56	19 02
8	1 38	+ 7.7	60.0	16.3	273	267	0	0.5	6 02	5 55	13 02	20 14	20 23
9	2 35	+11.5	59.3	16.1	286	261	3	1.5	6 35	6 25	13 56	21 27	21 41
10	3 31	+14.6	58.4	15.9	298	262	9	2.5	7 12	6 58	14 50	22 36	22 52
11	4 27	+16.7	57.6	15.7	310	266	16	3.5	7 54	7 38	15 43	23 37	23 54
12	5 22	+17.9	56.7	15.4	322	269	24	4.5	8 41	8 23	16 35	—	—
13	6 15	+18.2	55.9	15.2	335	273	34	5.5	9 32	9 15	17 26	0 30	0 47
14	7 07	+17.5	55.2	15.0	347	277	43	6.5	10 28	10 12	18 14	1 15	1 32
15	7 58	+16.0	54.7	14.9	359	281	53	7.5	11 27	11 13	19 01	1 53	2 08
16	8 47	+13.9	54.3	14.8	11	284	62	8.5	12 27	12 16	19 46	2 26	2 38
17	9 34	+11.2	54.2	14.8	23	287	71	9.5	13 28	13 20	20 29	2 54	3 04
18	10 20	+ 8.0	54.1	14.8	36	290	79	10.5	14 31	14 26	21 12	3 20	3 26
19	11 06	+ 4.5	54.3	14.8	48	292	86	11.5	15 34	15 32	21 55	3 44	3 47
20	11 51	+ 0.8	54.5	14.9	60	293	92	12.5	16 38	16 39	22 39	4 06	4 07
21	12 38	− 2.9	54.9	14.9	72	296	97	13.5	17 43	17 48	23 23	4 30	4 27
22	13 25	− 6.7	55.3	15.1	84	304	99	14.5	18 49	18 57	—	4 54	4 48
23	14 13	−10.1	55.7	15.2	96	48	100	15.5	19 56	20 07	0 09	5 22	5 12
24	15 04	−13.2	56.2	15.3	109	90	99	16.5	21 02	21 16	0 57	5 53	5 40
25	15 56	−15.7	56.7	15.5	121	92	95	17.5	22 06	22 23	1 48	6 29	6 14
26	16 51	−17.4	57.2	15.6	133	90	89	18.5	23 05	23 23	2 40	7 12	6 55
27	17 47	−18.2	57.7	15.7	145	87	82	19.5	23 59	—	3 35	8 04	7 46
28	18 44	−18.0	58.2	15.8	157	83	73	20.5	—	0 17	4 30	9 03	8 46
29	19 41	−16.7	58.6	16.0	170	79	63	21.5	0 46	1 02	5 25	10 10	9 55
30	20 38	−14.4	59.0	16.1	182	75	51	22.5	1 26	1 39	6 21	11 22	11 10

MERCURY

Day	RA h m	Dec. °	Diam. "	Phase %	Transit h m	5° high 52° h m	5° high 56° h m
1	1 46	+12.9	7	60	13 09	19 46	19 54
3	1 56	+14.2	7	52	13 11	19 54	20 03
5	2 04	+15.3	7	45	13 11	20 00	20 10
7	2 12	+16.2	8	37	13 10	20 03	20 14
9	2 17	+16.9	8	30	13 07	20 04	20 15
11	2 22	+17.3	9	24	13 03	20 01	20 13
13	2 24	+17.6	9	18	12 57	19 56	20 08
15	2 25	+17.6	10	13	12 50	19 48	20 00
17	2 24	+17.4	10	9	12 41	19 37	19 49
19	2 22	+16.9	11	5	12 31	19 24	19 35
21	2 19	+16.3	11	3	12 20	19 09	19 19
23	2 16	+15.5	12	1	12 08	18 53	19 02
25	2 11	+14.6	12	0	11 56	5 15	5 06
27	2 07	+13.7	12	0	11 44	5 08	5 00
29	2 02	+12.7	12	1	11 32	5 01	4 54
31	1 59	+11.7	12	3	11 20	4 54	4 48

VENUS

Day	RA h m	Dec. °	Diam. "	Phase %	Transit h m	5° high 52° h m	5° high 56° h m
1	0 42	+ 3.1	10	100	12 05	17 50	17 50
6	1 05	+ 5.6	10	100	12 08	18 06	18 08
11	1 28	+ 8.0	10	100	12 11	18 22	18 26
16	1 51	+10.4	10	100	12 15	18 38	18 43
21	2 15	+12.7	10	100	12 19	18 53	19 01
26	2 38	+14.8	10	100	12 23	19 09	19 18
31	3 03	+16.8	10	99	12 27	19 24	19 36

MARS

Day	RA h m	Dec. °	Diam. "	Phase %	Transit h m	5° high 52° h m	5° high 56° h m
1	11 33	+ 6.5	14	99	22 51	4 55	4 57
6	11 27	+ 6.9	14	98	22 25	4 32	4 34
11	11 22	+ 7.2	13	97	22 01	4 09	4 11
16	11 19	+ 7.3	13	96	21 38	3 46	3 49
21	11 16	+ 7.4	12	95	21 16	3 24	3 27
26	11 15	+ 7.3	12	94	20 55	3 03	3 05
31	11 15	+ 7.1	12	93	20 35	2 42	2 44

SUNRISE AND SUNSET

	London		Bristol		Birmingham		Manchester		Newcastle		Glasgow		Belfast	
	0°05'	51°30'	2°35'	51°28'	1°55'	52°28'	2°15'	53°28'	1°37'	54°59'	4°14'	55°52'	5°56'	54°35'
	h m	h m	h m	h m	h m	h m	h m	h m	h m	h m	h m	h m	h m	h m
1	5 36	18 34	5 46	18 44	5 42	18 42	5 43	18 44	5 38	18 43	5 48	18 55	5 56	19 00
2	5 34	18 35	5 44	18 45	5 40	18 44	5 40	18 46	5 36	18 45	5 45	18 57	5 54	19 02
3	5 31	18 37	5 41	18 47	5 38	18 45	5 38	18 48	5 33	18 47	5 43	18 59	5 51	19 04
4	5 29	18 39	5 39	18 49	5 35	18 47	5 35	18 50	5 31	18 49	5 40	19 01	5 49	19 06
5	5 27	18 40	5 37	18 50	5 33	18 49	5 33	18 52	5 28	18 51	5 37	19 03	5 46	19 08
6	5 25	18 42	5 35	18 52	5 31	18 51	5 31	18 53	5 26	18 53	5 35	19 05	5 44	19 10
7	5 22	18 44	5 32	18 54	5 28	18 52	5 28	18 55	5 23	18 55	5 32	19 07	5 41	19 12
8	5 20	18 45	5 30	18 55	5 26	18 54	5 26	18 57	5 21	18 57	5 30	19 09	5 39	19 14
9	5 18	18 47	5 28	18 57	5 24	18 56	5 23	18 59	5 18	18 59	5 27	19 11	5 36	19 16
10	5 16	18 49	5 26	18 59	5 21	18 58	5 21	19 01	5 16	19 01	5 25	19 13	5 34	19 18
11	5 13	18 50	5 24	19 00	5 19	18 59	5 19	19 03	5 13	19 03	5 22	19 15	5 31	19 19
12	5 11	18 52	5 21	19 02	5 17	19 01	5 16	19 04	5 11	19 05	5 19	19 17	5 29	19 21
13	5 09	18 54	5 19	19 04	5 15	19 03	5 14	19 06	5 08	19 07	5 17	19 19	5 26	19 23
14	5 07	18 55	5 17	19 05	5 12	19 05	5 12	19 08	5 06	19 09	5 14	19 21	5 24	19 25
15	5 05	18 57	5 15	19 07	5 10	19 06	5 09	19 10	5 04	19 11	5 12	19 23	5 22	19 27
16	5 03	18 59	5 13	19 09	5 08	19 08	5 07	19 12	5 01	19 13	5 09	19 25	5 19	19 29
17	5 01	19 00	5 11	19 10	5 06	19 10	5 05	19 13	4 59	19 15	5 07	19 27	5 17	19 31
18	4 58	19 02	5 08	19 12	5 04	19 12	5 03	19 15	4 56	19 17	5 04	19 29	5 15	19 33
19	4 56	19 04	5 06	19 14	5 01	19 13	5 00	19 17	4 54	19 19	5 02	19 32	5 12	19 35
20	4 54	19 05	5 04	19 15	4 59	19 15	4 58	19 19	4 52	19 21	4 59	19 34	5 10	19 37
21	4 52	19 07	5 02	19 17	4 57	19 17	4 56	19 21	4 49	19 22	4 57	19 36	5 08	19 39
22	4 50	19 09	5 00	19 19	4 55	19 19	4 54	19 23	4 47	19 24	4 55	19 38	5 05	19 40
23	4 48	19 10	4 58	19 20	4 53	19 20	4 51	19 24	4 44	19 26	4 52	19 40	5 03	19 42
24	4 46	19 12	4 56	19 22	4 51	19 22	4 49	19 26	4 42	19 28	4 50	19 42	5 01	19 44
25	4 44	19 14	4 54	19 24	4 49	19 24	4 47	19 28	4 40	19 30	4 47	19 44	4 58	19 46
26	4 42	19 15	4 52	19 25	4 47	19 25	4 45	19 30	4 38	19 32	4 45	19 46	4 56	19 48
27	4 40	19 17	4 50	19 27	4 45	19 27	4 43	19 32	4 35	19 34	4 43	19 48	4 54	19 50
28	4 38	19 19	4 48	19 29	4 43	19 29	4 41	19 33	4 33	19 36	4 40	19 50	4 52	19 52
29	4 36	19 20	4 46	19 30	4 41	19 31	4 39	19 35	4 31	19 38	4 38	19 52	4 50	19 54
30	4 34	19 22	4 44	19 32	4 39	19 32	4 37	19 37	4 29	19 40	4 36	19 54	4 47	19 56

JUPITER

Day	RA	Dec.	Transit	5° high	
				52°	56°
	h m	° '	h m	h m	h m
1	21 10.5	−16 49	8 32	4 42	5 03
11	21 17.3	−16 20	7 59	4 06	4 26
21	21 23.3	−15 55	7 26	3 30	3 49
31	21 28.5	−15 32	6 52	2 53	3 12

Diameters – equatorial 37″ polar 34″

SATURN

Day	RA	Dec.	Transit	5° high	
				52°	56°
	h m	° '	h m	h m	h m
1	0 41.6	+ 2 06	12 02	6 25	6 26
11	0 46.2	+ 2 35	11 28	5 48	5 49
21	0 50.8	+ 3 03	10 53	5 10	5 11
31	0 55.2	+ 3 30	10 18	4 33	4 34

Diameters – equatorial 16″ polar 14″
Rings – major axis 36″ minor axis 5″

URANUS

Day	RA	Dec.	Transit	10° high	
				52°	56°
	h m	° '	h m	h m	h m
1	20 42.1	−18 51	8 03	5 13	5 50
11	20 43.3	−18 47	7 25	4 34	5 11
21	20 44.2	−18 44	6 47	3 55	4 32
31	20 44.8	−18 42	6 08	3 16	3 53

Diameter 4″

NEPTUNE

Day	RA	Dec.	Transit	10° high	
				52°	56°
	h m	° '	h m	h m	h m
1	20 07.1	−19 48	7 28	4 47	5 28
11	20 07.7	−19 46	6 50	4 08	4 48
21	20 08.0	−19 45	6 11	3 29	4 09
31	20 08.2	−19 45	5 31	2 49	3 30

Diameter 2″

May 1997

♉ ♊

FIFTH MONTH, 31 DAYS. *Maia*, goddess of growth and increase

1	*Thursday*	**SS Philip and James.** Joseph Addison b. 1672	*week* 17 *day* 121
2	*Friday*	Joseph McCarthy d. 1957. Nancy Astor d. 1964	122
3	*Saturday*	Niccolò Machiavelli b. 1469. Dodie Smith b. 1896	123
4	*Sunday*	**5th S. after Easter.** Audrey Hepburn b. 1929	*week* 18 *day* 124
5	*Monday*	*Bank Holiday in the UK.* Søren Kierkegaard b. 1813	125
6	*Tuesday*	Sigmund Freud b. 1856. Tony Blair b. 1953	126
7	*Wednesday*	Antonio Salieri d. 1825. Earl of Rosebery b. 1847	127
8	*Thursday*	**Ascension Day.** Harry Gordon Selfridge d. 1947	128
9	*Friday*	MUSLIM NEW YEAR (1418). Sir James Barrie b. 1860	129
10	*Saturday*	Karl Barth b. 1886. Sir Henry Stanley d. 1904	130
11	*Sunday*	**S. after Ascension Day.** Salvador Dali b. 1904	*week* 19 *day* 131
12	*Monday*	Sir Lennox Berkeley b. 1903. John Masefield d. 1967	132
13	*Tuesday*	Fridtjof Nansen d. 1930. Gary Cooper d. 1961	133
14	*Wednesday*	**St Matthias.** August Strindberg d. 1912	134
15	*Thursday*	Daniel O'Connell d. 1847. Edwin Muir b. 1887	135
16	*Friday*	Sir John Hare b. 1844. H. E. Bates b. 1905	136
17	*Saturday*	Sandro Botticelli d. 1510. Paul Dukas d. 1935	137
18	*Sunday*	**Pentecost/Whit Sunday.** Pope John Paul II b. 1920	*week* 20 *day* 138
19	*Monday*	Dame Nellie Melba b. 1861. Nathaniel Hawthorne d. 1864	139
20	*Tuesday*	John Stuart Mill b. 1806. Dame Barbara Hepworth d. 1975	140
21	*Wednesday*	Alexander Pope b. 1688. Elizabeth Fry b. 1780	141
22	*Thursday*	Blackwall Tunnel opened 1897	142
23	*Friday*	*Easter Law Sittings end.* Carl Linnaeus b. 1707	143
24	*Saturday*	George III b. 1738. Jean-Paul Marat b. 1743	144
25	*Sunday*	**Trinity Sunday.** Lord Beaverbrook b. 1879	*week* 21 *day* 145
26	*Monday*	*Bank Holiday in the UK.* Sir Matt Busby b. 1909	146
27	*Tuesday*	John Calvin d. 1564. Arnold Bennett b. 1867	147
28	*Wednesday*	William Pitt (the younger) b. 1759	148
29	*Thursday*	**Corpus Christi.** John F. Kennedy b. 1917	149
30	*Friday*	Rubens d. 1640. Alexander Pope d. 1744	150
31	*Saturday*	Joseph Grimaldi d. 1837. Walter Sickert b. 1860	151

ASTRONOMICAL PHENOMENA

d	h	
1	23	Neptune at stationary point
4	15	Saturn in conjunction with Moon. Saturn 0°.8 S.
5	17	Mercury in conjunction with Moon. Mercury 1° N.
7	14	Venus in conjunction with Moon. Venus 4° N.
8	18	Mercury at stationary point
13	04	Uranus at stationary point
16	14	Mars in conjunction with Moon. Mars 2° N.
21	00	Sun's longitude 60° ♊
22	23	Mercury at greatest elongation W. 25°
25	10	Pluto at opposition
28	04	Jupiter in conjunction with Moon. Jupiter 4° S.

MINIMA OF ALGOL

Algol is inconveniently situated for observation during May.

CONSTELLATIONS

The following constellations are near the meridian at

	d	h		d	h
April	1	24	May	16	21
April	15	23	June	1	20
May	1	22	June	15	19

Cepheus (below the Pole), Cassiopeia (below the Pole), Ursa Minor, Ursa Major, Canes Venatici, Coma Berenices, Bootes, Leo, Virgo, Crater, Corvus and Hydra

THE MOON

Phases, Apsides and Node	d	h	m
● New Moon	6	20	47
☽ First Quarter	14	10	55
○ Full Moon	22	09	13
☾ Last Quarter	29	07	51
Perigee (366,619 km)	3	11	06
Apogee (404,216 km)	15	10	09
Perigee (369,791 km)	29	06	58

Mean longitude of ascending node on May 1, 177°

THE SUN

s.d. 15′.8

Day	Right Ascension	Dec. +	Equation of time	Rise 52°	Rise 56°	Transit	Set 52°	Set 56°	Sidereal time	Transit of First Point of Aries
	h m s	° ′	m s	h m	h m	h m	h m	h m	h m s	h m s
1	2 32 58	15 01	+2 52	4 30	4 16	11 57	19 25	19 39	14 35 51	9 22 37
2	2 36 48	15 19	+3 00	4 29	4 14	11 57	19 26	19 41	14 39 47	9 18 41
3	2 40 38	15 37	+3 06	4 27	4 12	11 57	19 28	19 43	14 43 44	9 14 45
4	2 44 28	15 55	+3 12	4 25	4 10	11 57	19 30	19 45	14 47 40	9 10 49
5	2 48 19	16 12	+3 18	4 23	4 07	11 57	19 31	19 47	14 51 37	9 06 53
6	2 52 11	16 29	+3 22	4 21	4 05	11 57	19 33	19 49	14 55 33	9 02 57
7	2 56 03	16 46	+3 27	4 19	4 03	11 57	19 35	19 51	14 59 30	8 59 02
8	2 59 56	17 02	+3 30	4 18	4 01	11 56	19 36	19 53	15 03 26	8 55 06
9	3 03 49	17 18	+3 34	4 16	3 59	11 56	19 38	19 55	15 07 23	8 51 10
10	3 07 43	17 34	+3 36	4 14	3 57	11 56	19 40	19 57	15 11 20	8 47 14
11	3 11 38	17 50	+3 38	4 13	3 55	11 56	19 41	19 59	15 15 16	8 43 18
12	3 15 33	18 05	+3 40	4 11	3 53	11 56	19 43	20 01	15 19 13	8 39 22
13	3 19 29	18 20	+3 41	4 09	3 51	11 56	19 44	20 03	15 23 09	8 35 26
14	3 23 25	18 35	+3 41	4 08	3 49	11 56	19 46	20 05	15 27 06	8 31 30
15	3 27 22	18 49	+3 41	4 06	3 47	11 56	19 47	20 07	15 31 02	8 27 34
16	3 31 19	19 03	+3 40	4 05	3 45	11 56	19 49	20 09	15 34 59	8 23 38
17	3 35 17	19 17	+3 39	4 03	3 44	11 56	19 50	20 10	15 38 55	8 19 42
18	3 39 15	19 31	+3 37	4 02	3 42	11 56	19 52	20 12	15 42 52	8 15 47
19	3 43 14	19 44	+3 35	4 00	3 40	11 56	19 53	20 14	15 46 49	8 11 51
20	3 47 13	19 56	+3 32	3 59	3 38	11 57	19 55	20 16	15 50 45	8 07 55
21	3 51 13	20 09	+3 28	3 58	3 37	11 57	19 56	20 17	15 54 42	8 03 59
22	3 55 14	20 21	+3 24	3 56	3 35	11 57	19 58	20 19	15 58 38	8 00 03
23	3 59 15	20 33	+3 20	3 55	3 34	11 57	19 59	20 21	16 02 35	7 56 07
24	4 03 17	20 44	+3 15	3 54	3 32	11 57	20 00	20 22	16 06 31	7 52 11
25	4 07 19	20 55	+3 09	3 53	3 31	11 57	20 02	20 24	16 10 28	7 48 15
26	4 11 21	21 06	+3 03	3 52	3 29	11 57	20 03	20 26	16 14 24	7 44 19
27	4 15 24	21 16	+2 57	3 51	3 28	11 57	20 04	20 27	16 18 21	7 40 23
28	4 19 28	21 26	+2 50	3 50	3 27	11 57	20 06	20 29	16 22 18	7 36 27
29	4 23 32	21 35	+2 42	3 49	3 25	11 57	20 07	20 30	16 26 14	7 32 32
30	4 27 36	21 44	+2 34	3 48	3 24	11 57	20 08	20 32	16 30 11	7 28 36
31	4 31 41	21 53	+2 26	3 47	3 23	11 58	20 09	20 33	16 34 07	7 24 40

DURATION OF TWILIGHT (in minutes)

Latitude	52°	56°	52°	56°	52°	56°	52°	56°
	1 May		11 May		21 May		31 May	
Civil	39	45	41	49	44	53	46	57
Nautical	90	106	97	121	106	143	116	TAN
Astronomical	154	209	179	TAN	TAN	TAN	TAN	TAN

THE NIGHT SKY

Mercury, although at greatest western elongation on the 22nd, is unsuitably placed for observation.

Venus is beginning to move out of the long evening twilight, becoming a brilliant object in the evening sky, magnitude −3.9. It may be seen low above the western horizon for a short time after sunset.

Mars continues to move away from opposition and its magnitude fades during the month from −0.4 to +0.2. Mars is moving slowly eastwards in Virgo and is still a conspicuous object in the south-western skies in the evenings, though by the end of May it is not observable for long after midnight. During the evening of the 16th the waxing gibbous Moon will be seen about 5° to the left of Mars.

Jupiter continues to be visible as a brilliant object in the south-eastern sky in the mornings, magnitude −2.3. Jupiter is in the constellation of Capricornus. The Moon, near Last Quarter, will be seen to the left of Jupiter on the morning of the 1st, while on the morning of the 28th it will be seen 4° above the planet. The four Galilean satellites are readily observable with a small telescope, or a good pair of binoculars provided that they are held rigidly. Times of eclipses and shadow transits of these satellites are given on page 70.

Saturn remains too close to the Sun for observation.

THE MOON

Day	RA	Dec.	Hor. par.	Semi-diam.	Sun's co-long.	PA of Bright Limb	Phase	Age	Rise 52°	Rise 56°	Transit	Set 52°	Set 56°
	h m	°	'	'	°	°	%	d	h m	h m	h m	h m	h m
1	21 35	−11.2	59.4	16.2	194	72	40	23.5	2 02	2 11	7 15	12 37	12 29
2	22 31	− 7.3	59.6	16.3	206	69	29	24.5	2 33	2 39	8 08	13 55	13 50
3	23 26	− 3.0	59.8	16.3	218	67	19	25.5	3 02	3 04	9 01	15 13	15 13
4	0 21	+ 1.5	59.8	16.3	231	66	11	26.5	3 30	3 29	9 54	16 31	16 35
5	1 16	+ 6.0	59.6	16.2	243	64	5	27.5	4 00	3 54	10 48	17 49	17 56
6	2 12	+10.0	59.2	16.1	255	56	1	28.5	4 31	4 22	11 41	19 04	19 16
7	3 08	+13.4	58.7	16.0	267	320	0	0.1	5 05	4 53	12 36	20 16	20 30
8	4 04	+16.0	58.0	15.8	280	276	2	1.1	5 45	5 29	13 30	21 21	21 38
9	5 00	+17.7	57.3	15.6	292	274	6	2.1	6 29	6 12	14 23	22 19	22 37
10	5 55	+18.3	56.6	15.4	304	276	12	3.1	7 20	7 02	15 15	23 09	23 27
11	6 49	+18.0	55.8	15.2	316	279	19	4.1	8 15	7 58	16 06	23 51	—
12	7 41	+16.8	55.2	15.0	328	282	27	5.1	9 13	8 58	16 54	—	0 07
13	8 31	+14.8	54.7	14.9	341	285	36	6.1	10 14	10 01	17 40	0 27	0 40
14	9 19	+12.3	54.4	14.8	353	288	46	7.1	11 15	11 06	18 25	0 57	1 07
15	10 06	+ 9.2	54.3	14.8	5	290	55	8.1	12 18	12 11	19 08	1 23	1 31
16	10 51	+ 5.8	54.3	14.8	17	292	65	9.1	13 20	13 17	19 51	1 48	1 52
17	11 37	+ 2.2	54.4	14.8	30	293	73	10.1	14 24	14 24	20 34	2 10	2 12
18	12 22	− 1.6	54.8	14.9	42	294	81	11.1	15 28	15 32	21 17	2 33	2 32
19	13 09	− 5.4	55.2	15.0	54	294	88	12.1	16 34	16 41	22 03	2 57	2 52
20	13 57	− 9.0	55.8	15.2	66	295	94	13.1	17 41	17 52	22 50	3 23	3 15
21	14 47	−12.3	56.4	15.4	78	299	98	14.1	18 49	19 02	23 41	3 52	3 41
22	15 40	−15.1	57.0	15.5	90	326	100	15.1	19 55	20 12	—	4 26	4 12
23	16 35	−17.1	57.5	15.7	103	66	99	16.1	20 58	21 16	0 33	5 08	4 51
24	17 31	−18.2	58.1	15.8	115	79	97	17.1	21 56	22 14	1 28	5 57	5 39
25	18 29	−18.3	58.5	15.9	127	80	92	18.1	22 46	23 03	2 24	6 55	6 37
26	19 28	−17.3	58.8	16.0	139	77	85	19.1	23 29	23 43	3 21	8 00	7 44
27	20 26	−15.2	59.1	16.1	151	74	76	20.1	—	—	4 17	9 12	8 58
28	21 23	−12.2	59.2	16.1	164	71	65	21.1	0 06	0 17	5 12	10 26	10 17
29	22 18	− 8.5	59.3	16.2	176	69	54	22.1	0 38	0 45	6 05	11 42	11 37
30	23 13	− 4.3	59.3	16.2	188	67	42	23.1	1 07	1 10	6 57	12 59	12 57
31	0 07	+ 0.2	59.2	16.1	200	66	31	24.1	1 34	1 34	7 49	14 15	14 18

MERCURY

Day	RA	Dec.	Diam.	Phase	Transit	5° high 52°	5° high 56°
	h m	°	"	%	h m	h m	h m
1	1 59	+11.7	12	3	11 20	4 54	4 48
3	1 56	+10.9	12	5	11 10	4 48	4 42
5	1 54	+10.2	11	8	11 00	4 42	4 37
7	1 53	+ 9.6	11	11	10 51	4 36	4 32
9	1 53	+ 9.1	11	15	10 44	4 31	4 27
11	1 54	+ 8.9	10	18	10 38	4 25	4 21
13	1 56	+ 8.8	10	22	10 32	4 20	4 16
15	2 00	+ 8.9	10	25	10 28	4 15	4 12
17	2 04	+ 9.1	9	29	10 25	4 11	4 07
19	2 09	+ 9.4	9	32	10 22	4 06	4 02
21	2 15	+ 9.9	9	36	10 20	4 02	3 57
23	2 22	+10.5	8	39	10 20	3 58	3 53
25	2 30	+11.2	8	43	10 20	3 54	3 48
27	2 39	+12.0	8	47	10 20	3 51	3 44
29	2 48	+12.9	7	50	10 22	3 48	3 40
31	2 58	+13.8	7	54	10 24	3 45	3 37

VENUS

Day	RA	Dec.	Diam.	Phase	Transit	5° high 52°	5° high 56°
	h m	°	"	%	h m	h m	h m
1	3 03	+16.8	10	99	12 27	19 24	19 36
6	3 28	+18.6	10	99	12 33	19 40	19 53
11	3 53	+20.2	10	99	12 38	19 54	20 09
16	4 18	+21.5	10	98	12 44	20 08	20 25
21	4 44	+22.7	10	98	12 50	20 21	20 39
26	5 11	+23.5	10	97	12 57	20 33	20 52
31	5 38	+24.1	10	96	13 04	20 44	21 03

MARS

Day	RA	Dec.	Diam.	Phase	Transit	5° high 52°	5° high 56°
1	11 15	+ 7.1	12	93	20 35	2 42	2 44
6	11 16	+ 6.7	11	92	20 17	2 22	2 24
11	11 18	+ 6.3	11	92	19 59	2 02	2 04
16	11 20	+ 5.8	10	91	19 43	1 42	1 44
21	11 24	+ 5.2	10	90	19 27	1 24	1 24
26	11 29	+ 4.5	9	90	19 12	1 05	1 05
31	11 34	+ 3.8	9	89	18 58	0 47	0 47

SUNRISE AND SUNSET

	London		Bristol		Birmingham		Manchester		Newcastle		Glasgow		Belfast	
	0°05'	51°30'	2°35'	51°28'	1°55'	52°28'	2°15'	53°28'	1°37'	54°59'	4°14'	55°52'	5°56'	54°35'
	h m	h m	h m	h m	h m	h m	h m	h m	h m	h m	h m	h m	h m	h m
1	4 32	19 24	4 42	19 33	4 37	19 34	4 35	19 39	4 27	19 42	4 34	19 56	4 45	19 58
2	4 30	19 25	4 41	19 35	4 35	19 36	4 33	19 41	4 24	19 44	4 31	19 58	4 43	19 59
3	4 29	19 27	4 39	19 37	4 33	19 37	4 31	19 42	4 22	19 46	4 29	20 00	4 41	20 01
4	4 27	19 28	4 37	19 38	4 31	19 39	4 29	19 44	4 20	19 48	4 27	20 02	4 39	20 03
5	4 25	19 30	4 35	19 40	4 29	19 41	4 27	19 46	4 18	19 49	4 25	20 04	4 37	20 05
6	4 23	19 32	4 33	19 42	4 27	19 43	4 25	19 48	4 16	19 51	4 23	20 06	4 35	20 07
7	4 21	19 33	4 32	19 43	4 25	19 44	4 23	19 49	4 14	19 53	4 21	20 08	4 33	20 09
8	4 20	19 35	4 30	19 45	4 24	19 46	4 21	19 51	4 12	19 55	4 19	20 10	4 31	20 11
9	4 18	19 36	4 28	19 46	4 22	19 47	4 19	19 53	4 10	19 57	4 16	20 12	4 29	20 12
10	4 16	19 38	4 27	19 48	4 20	19 49	4 17	19 55	4 08	19 59	4 14	20 13	4 27	20 14
11	4 15	19 40	4 25	19 49	4 18	19 51	4 16	19 56	4 06	20 01	4 12	20 15	4 25	20 16
12	4 13	19 41	4 23	19 51	4 17	19 52	4 14	19 58	4 04	20 02	4 11	20 17	4 23	20 18
13	4 12	19 43	4 22	19 53	4 15	19 54	4 12	20 00	4 03	20 04	4 09	20 19	4 22	20 20
14	4 10	19 44	4 20	19 54	4 13	19 56	4 10	20 01	4 01	20 06	4 07	20 21	4 20	20 21
15	4 09	19 46	4 19	19 56	4 12	19 57	4 09	20 03	3 59	20 08	4 05	20 23	4 18	20 23
16	4 07	19 47	4 17	19 57	4 10	19 59	4 07	20 05	3 57	20 10	4 03	20 25	4 17	20 25
17	4 06	19 49	4 16	19 59	4 09	20 00	4 06	20 06	3 56	20 11	4 01	20 27	4 15	20 26
18	4 04	19 50	4 14	20 00	4 07	20 02	4 04	20 08	3 54	20 13	4 00	20 28	4 13	20 28
19	4 03	19 52	4 13	20 01	4 06	20 03	4 03	20 09	3 52	20 15	3 58	20 30	4 12	20 30
20	4 02	19 53	4 12	20 03	4 05	20 05	4 01	20 11	3 51	20 16	3 56	20 32	4 10	20 31
21	4 00	19 54	4 10	20 04	4 03	20 06	4 00	20 12	3 49	20 18	3 55	20 34	4 09	20 33
22	3 59	19 56	4 09	20 06	4 02	20 08	3 58	20 14	3 48	20 20	3 53	20 35	4 07	20 35
23	3 58	19 57	4 08	20 07	4 01	20 09	3 57	20 15	3 46	20 21	3 51	20 37	4 06	20 36
24	3 57	19 58	4 07	20 08	3 59	20 10	3 56	20 17	3 45	20 23	3 50	20 39	4 04	20 38
25	3 56	20 00	4 06	20 10	3 58	20 12	3 54	20 18	3 43	20 24	3 49	20 40	4 03	20 39
26	3 54	20 01	4 05	20 11	3 57	20 13	3 53	20 20	3 42	20 26	3 47	20 42	4 02	20 41
27	3 53	20 02	4 04	20 12	3 56	20 14	3 52	20 21	3 41	20 27	3 46	20 43	4 00	20 42
28	3 52	20 03	4 03	20 13	3 55	20 16	3 51	20 22	3 40	20 29	3 44	20 45	3 59	20 44
29	3 51	20 05	4 02	20 14	3 54	20 17	3 50	20 24	3 38	20 30	3 43	20 46	3 58	20 45
30	3 51	20 06	4 01	20 16	3 53	20 18	3 49	20 25	3 37	20 32	3 42	20 48	3 57	20 46
31	3 50	20 07	4 00	20 17	3 52	20 19	3 48	20 26	3 36	20 33	3 41	20 49	3 56	20 48

JUPITER

Day	RA	Dec.	Transit	5° high	
				52°	56°
	h m	° '	h m	h m	h m
1	21 28.5	−15 32	6 52	2 53	3 12
11	21 32.6	−15 15	6 16	2 16	2 35
21	21 35.7	−15 02	5 40	1 38	1 57
31	21 37.6	−14 55	5 03	1 00	1 18

Diameters – equatorial 40″ polar 38″

SATURN

Day	RA	Dec.	Transit	5° high	
				52°	56°
	h m	° '	h m	h m	h m
1	0 55.2	+ 3 30	10 18	4 33	4 34
11	0 59.4	+ 3 55	9 43	3 56	3 56
21	1 03.4	+ 4 18	9 07	3 19	3 18
31	1 07.1	+ 4 39	8 32	2 41	2 41

Diameters – equatorial 16″ polar 15″
Rings – major axis 37″ minor axis 6″

URANUS

Day	RA	Dec.	Transit	10° high	
				52°	56°
	h m	° '	h m	h m	h m
1	20 44.8	−18 42	6 08	3 16	3 53
11	20 45.1	−18 41	5 29	2 37	3 13
21	20 45.0	−18 42	4 49	1 58	2 34
31	20 44.6	−18 44	4 10	1 18	1 55

Diameter 4″

NEPTUNE

Day	RA	Dec.	Transit	10° high	
				52°	56°
	h m	° '	h m	h m	h m
1	20 08.2	−19 45	5 31	2 49	3 30
11	20 08.1	−19 45	4 52	2 10	2 51
21	20 07.8	−19 46	4 12	1 31	2 11
31	20 07.3	−19 47	3 33	0 51	1 32

Diameter 2″

June 1997

SIXTH MONTH, 30 DAYS. *Junius*, Roman *gens* (family)

1	*Sunday*	**2nd S. after Pentecost/1st S. after Trinity**	*week 22 day* 152
2	*Monday*	*Coronation Day 1953.* Sir Edward Elgar b. 1857	153
3	*Tuesday*	*Trinity Law Sittings begin.* Arthur Ransome d. 1967	154
4	*Wednesday*	⚔ Battle of Magenta 1859. Lord Thorneycroft d. 1994	155
5	*Thursday*	Sir Robert Mayer b. 1879. John Maynard Keynes b. 1883	156
6	*Friday*	Pierre Corneille b. 1606. Thomas Mann b. 1875	157
7	*Saturday*	Beau Brummell b. 1778. Jean Harlow d. 1937	158
8	*Sunday*	**3rd S. after Pentecost/2nd S. after Trinity**	*week 23 day* 159
9	*Monday*	Charles Dickens d. 1870. Robert Donat d. 1958	160
10	*Tuesday*	*Duke of Edinburgh b. 1921.* Frederick Loewe b. 1901	161
11	*Wednesday*	**St Barnabas.** FEAST OF WEEKS begins	162
12	*Thursday*	Leon Goossens b. 1897. John Ireland d. 1962	163
13	*Friday*	Dorothy L. Sayers b. 1893. Sir Henry Segrave d. 1930	164
14	*Saturday*	*Queen's Official Birthday.* Jerome K. Jerome d. 1927	165
15	*Sunday*	**4th S. after Pentecost/3rd S. after Trinity**	*week 24 day* 166
16	*Monday*	Margaret Bondfield d. 1953. Lord Reith d. 1971	167
17	*Tuesday*	John Wesley b. 1703. ⚔ Battle of Bunker Hill 1775	168
18	*Wednesday*	⚔ Battle of Waterloo 1815. Douglas Jardine d. 1958	169
19	*Thursday*	James I b. 1566. Walter Hammond b. 1903	170
20	*Friday*	Jacques Offenbach b. 1819. William IV d. 1837	171
21	*Saturday*	Prince William of Wales b. 1982.	172
22	*Sunday*	**5th S. after Pentecost/4th S. after Trinity**	*week 25 day* 173
23	*Monday*	Jean Anouilh b. 1910. Cecil James Sharp d. 1924	174
24	*Tuesday*	**St John the Baptist.** Grover Cleveland d. 1908	175
25	*Wednesday*	Col. George Custer d. 1876. Lady Baden-Powell d. 1977	176
26	*Thursday*	Samuel Crompton d. 1827. George IV d. 1830	177
27	*Friday*	Charles Stewart Parnell b. 1846	178
28	*Saturday*	Henry VIII b. 1491. Luigi Pirandello b. 1867	179
29	*Sunday*	**St Peter. 6th S. after Pentecost/5th S. after Trinity**	*week 26 day* 180
30	*Monday*	Tower Bridge opened 1894. Margery Allingham d. 1966	181

ASTRONOMICAL PHENOMENA

d h
1 03 Saturn in conjunction with Moon. Saturn 0°.4 S.
3 13 Mercury in conjunction with Moon. Mercury 2° N.
6 17 Venus in conjunction with Moon. Venus 6° N.
10 00 Jupiter at stationary point
13 16 Mars in conjunction with Moon. Mars 0°.3 N.
21 08 Sun's longitude 90° ♋.
24 10 Jupiter in conjunction with Moon. Jupiter 3° S.
25 19 Mercury in superior conjunction
28 12 Saturn in conjunction with Moon. Saturn 0°.2 S.

MINIMA OF ALGOL

Algol is inconveniently situated for observation during June.

CONSTELLATIONS

The following constellations are near the meridian at

	d	h		d	h
May	1	24	June	15	21
May	16	23	July	1	20
June	1	22	July	16	19

Cassiopeia (below the Pole), Ursa Minor, Draco, Ursa Major, Canes Venatici, Bootes, Corona, Serpens, Virgo and Libra

THE MOON

Phases, Apsides and Node	d	h	m
● New Moon	5	07	04
☽ First Quarter	13	04	51
○ Full Moon	20	19	09
☾ Last Quarter	27	12	42
Apogee (404,186 km)	12	05	07
Perigee (366,490 km)	24	05	07

Mean longitude of ascending node on June 1, 175°

THE SUN   s.d. 15′.8

Day	Right Ascension	Dec. +	Equation of time	Rise 52°	Rise 56°	Transit	Set 52°	Set 56°	Sidereal time	Transit of First Point of Aries
	h m s	° ′	m s	h m	h m	h m	h m	h m	h m s	h m s
1	4 35 47	22 02	+ 2 17	3 46	3 22	11 58	20 10	20 34	16 38 04	7 20 44
2	4 39 53	22 10	+ 2 08	3 45	3 21	11 58	20 11	20 36	16 42 00	7 16 48
3	4 43 59	22 17	+ 1 58	3 44	3 20	11 58	20 12	20 37	16 45 57	7 12 52
4	4 48 06	22 24	+ 1 48	3 44	3 19	11 58	20 13	20 38	16 49 53	7 08 56
5	4 52 12	22 31	+ 1 38	3 43	3 18	11 58	20 14	20 39	16 53 50	7 05 00
6	4 56 20	22 38	+ 1 27	3 42	3 17	11 59	20 15	20 41	16 57 47	7 01 04
7	5 00 27	22 44	+ 1 16	3 42	3 17	11 59	20 16	20 42	17 01 43	6 57 08
8	5 04 35	22 50	+ 1 04	3 41	3 16	11 59	20 17	20 43	17 05 40	6 53 12
9	5 08 43	22 55	+ 0 53	3 41	3 15	11 59	20 18	20 44	17 09 36	6 49 16
10	5 12 52	23 00	+ 0 41	3 41	3 15	11 59	20 19	20 44	17 13 33	6 45 21
11	5 17 00	23 04	+ 0 29	3 40	3 14	12 00	20 19	20 45	17 17 29	6 41 25
12	5 21 09	23 08	+ 0 17	3 40	3 14	12 00	20 20	20 46	17 21 26	6 37 29
13	5 25 18	23 12	+ 0 04	3 40	3 14	12 00	20 21	20 47	17 25 22	6 33 33
14	5 29 27	23 15	− 0 08	3 40	3 13	12 00	20 21	20 48	17 29 19	6 29 37
15	5 33 36	23 18	− 0 21	3 39	3 13	12 00	20 22	20 48	17 33 16	6 25 41
16	5 37 46	23 20	− 0 34	3 39	3 13	12 01	20 22	20 49	17 37 12	6 21 45
17	5 41 55	23 22	− 0 46	3 39	3 13	12 01	20 23	20 49	17 41 09	6 17 49
18	5 46 05	23 24	− 0 59	3 39	3 13	12 01	20 23	20 50	17 45 05	6 13 53
19	5 50 14	23 25	− 1 12	3 39	3 13	12 01	20 23	20 50	17 49 02	6 09 57
20	5 54 24	23 26	− 1 25	3 40	3 13	12 02	20 24	20 50	17 52 58	6 06 01
21	5 58 33	23 26	− 1 38	3 40	3 13	12 02	20 24	20 50	17 56 55	6 02 06
22	6 02 43	23 26	− 1 51	3 40	3 13	12 02	20 24	20 51	18 00 52	5 58 10
23	6 06 52	23 26	− 2 04	3 40	3 14	12 02	20 24	20 51	18 04 48	5 54 14
24	6 11 02	23 25	− 2 17	3 41	3 14	12 02	20 24	20 51	18 08 45	5 50 18
25	6 15 11	23 23	− 2 30	3 41	3 14	12 03	20 24	20 51	18 12 41	5 46 22
26	6 19 20	23 22	− 2 42	3 41	3 15	12 03	20 24	20 50	18 16 38	5 42 26
27	6 23 29	23 20	− 2 55	3 42	3 15	12 03	20 24	20 50	18 20 34	5 38 30
28	6 27 38	23 17	− 3 07	3 42	3 16	12 03	20 24	20 50	18 24 31	5 34 34
29	6 31 47	23 14	− 3 19	3 43	3 17	12 03	20 24	20 50	18 28 27	5 30 38
30	6 35 55	23 11	− 3 31	3 44	3 17	12 04	20 23	20 49	18 32 24	5 26 42

DURATION OF TWILIGHT (in minutes)

Latitude	52°	56°	52°	56°	52°	56°	52°	56°
	1 June		11 June		21 June		30 June	
Civil	47	58	48	61	49	63	49	62
Nautical	117	TAN	125	TAN	128	TAN	125	TAN
Astronomical	TAN	TAN	TAN	TAN	TAN	TAN	TAN	TAN

THE NIGHT SKY

Mercury is too close to the Sun for observation, superior conjunction occurring on the 25th.

Venus is a brilliant object in the evening skies, magnitude −3.9, but only visible low above the west-north-west horizon for about half an hour after sunset.

Mars is an evening object in the south-western skies, in Virgo, though by the end of June it is no longer observable after 23h. During the month its magnitude fades from +0.2 to +0.6. The Moon, at First Quarter, will be seen about 3° to the left of Mars on the evening of the 13th.

Jupiter, magnitude −2.6, is a brilliant object in the south-eastern sky in the mornings and becomes visible before midnight towards the end of the month. On the morning of the 24th the waning gibbous Moon will be seen about 6° to the right of Jupiter.

Saturn, magnitude +0.7, becomes a morning object early in the month, low above the east-south-east horizon before twilight inhibits observation. On the morning of the 28th the Moon, at Last Quarter, will be seen about 6° to the right of Jupiter.

Twilight. Reference to the section above shows that astronomical twilight lasts all night for a period around the summer solstice (i.e. in June and July), even in southern England. Under these conditions the sky never gets completely dark since the Sun is always less than 18° below the horizon.

THE MOON

Day	RA	Dec.	Hor. par.	Semi-diam.	Sun's co-long.	PA of Bright Limb	Phase	Age	Rise 52°	Rise 56°	Transit	Set 52°	Set 56°
	h m	°	'	'	°	°	%	d	h m	h m	h m	h m	h m
1	1 00	+ 4.6	59.0	16.1	213	66	21	25.1	2 02	1 58	8 40	15 31	15 37
2	1 54	+ 8.7	58.7	16.0	225	66	13	26.1	2 31	2 23	9 32	16 46	16 56
3	2 49	+12.3	58.3	15.9	237	66	6	27.1	3 03	2 52	10 25	17 58	18 11
4	3 44	+15.2	57.9	15.8	249	62	2	28.1	3 39	3 25	11 18	19 06	19 22
5	4 39	+17.2	57.3	15.6	262	29	0	29.1	4 21	4 04	12 12	20 07	20 25
6	5 35	+18.3	56.7	15.5	274	297	1	0.7	5 08	4 50	13 05	21 01	21 19
7	6 29	+18.4	56.1	15.3	286	286	3	1.7	6 01	5 44	13 56	21 47	22 04
8	7 22	+17.5	55.6	15.1	298	285	8	2.7	6 59	6 43	14 46	22 26	22 41
9	8 14	+15.8	55.0	15.0	311	287	14	3.7	7 59	7 45	15 34	22 59	23 11
10	9 03	+13.4	54.6	14.9	323	289	21	4.7	9 01	8 50	16 19	23 27	23 36
11	9 50	+10.5	54.4	14.8	335	291	30	5.7	10 04	9 56	17 03	23 52	23 58
12	10 37	+ 7.2	54.2	14.8	347	292	39	6.7	11 06	11 01	17 46	—	—
13	11 22	+ 3.7	54.3	14.8	359	293	48	7.7	12 09	12 08	18 28	0 15	0 18
14	12 07	− 0.1	54.5	14.9	12	294	58	8.7	13 13	13 14	19 11	0 37	0 37
15	12 53	− 3.9	54.9	15.0	24	293	67	9.7	14 17	14 22	19 55	1 00	0 57
16	13 40	− 7.5	55.4	15.1	36	293	76	10.7	15 23	15 32	20 41	1 25	1 18
17	14 29	−11.0	56.1	15.3	48	292	84	11.7	16 30	16 43	21 30	1 52	1 42
18	15 20	−14.0	56.8	15.5	60	291	91	12.7	17 38	17 53	22 22	2 23	2 10
19	16 14	−16.4	57.6	15.7	73	291	96	13.7	18 44	19 01	23 16	3 01	2 45
20	17 11	−18.0	58.3	15.9	85	300	99	14.7	19 45	20 04	—	3 47	3 29
21	18 10	−18.5	58.9	16.1	97	27	100	15.7	20 40	20 58	0 13	4 42	4 23
22	19 10	−17.8	59.4	16.2	109	67	98	16.7	21 28	21 43	1 11	5 46	5 29
23	20 09	−16.0	59.7	16.3	121	71	93	17.7	22 08	22 20	2 09	6 57	6 43
24	21 08	−13.2	59.8	16.3	134	70	87	18.7	22 42	22 51	3 06	8 13	8 02
25	22 05	− 9.6	59.8	16.3	146	68	78	19.7	23 12	23 17	4 01	9 30	9 23
26	23 01	− 5.5	59.6	16.2	158	67	67	20.7	23 40	23 41	4 54	10 48	10 45
27	23 55	− 1.1	59.3	16.2	170	67	56	21.7	—	—	5 46	12 05	12 05
28	0 49	+ 3.4	58.9	16.1	182	67	45	22.7	0 08	0 05	6 38	13 20	13 25
29	1 42	+ 7.6	58.5	15.9	195	68	34	23.7	0 36	0 29	7 29	14 34	14 43
30	2 35	+11.3	58.0	15.8	207	70	24	24.7	1 06	0 56	8 20	15 46	15 58

MERCURY

Day	RA	Dec.	Diam.	Phase	Transit	5° high 52°	5° high 56°
	h m	°	"	%	h m	h m	h m
1	3 03	+14.3	7	56	10 26	3 44	3 35
3	3 14	+15.3	7	60	10 29	3 41	3 32
5	3 26	+16.3	6	64	10 34	3 40	3 29
7	3 39	+17.4	6	69	10 39	3 39	3 27
9	3 53	+18.5	6	73	10 45	3 39	3 26
11	4 08	+19.5	6	78	10 52	3 39	3 26
13	4 23	+20.5	6	82	10 59	3 41	3 26
15	4 39	+21.5	5	87	11 08	3 44	3 28
17	4 56	+22.4	5	91	11 18	3 48	3 31
19	5 14	+23.1	5	94	11 28	3 53	3 35
21	5 33	+23.7	5	97	11 39	4 00	3 41
23	5 52	+24.2	5	99	11 50	4 08	3 49
25	6 11	+24.5	5	100	12 01	19 45	20 05
27	6 30	+24.6	5	100	12 13	19 56	20 16
29	6 49	+24.5	5	99	12 24	20 06	20 26
31	7 08	+24.2	5	97	12 34	20 14	20 34

VENUS

Day	RA	Dec.	Diam.	Phase	Transit	5° high 52°	5° high 56°
	h m	°	"	%	h m	h m	h m
1	5 43	+24.2	10	96	13 06	20 46	21 05
6	6 10	+24.4	10	96	13 13	20 54	21 14
11	6 37	+24.3	10	95	13 20	21 00	21 20
16	7 03	+23.9	11	94	13 27	21 04	21 23
21	7 30	+23.3	11	93	13 34	21 06	21 24
26	7 56	+22.3	11	92	13 40	21 06	21 23
31	8 21	+21.1	11	91	13 46	21 05	21 20

MARS

Day	RA	Dec.	Diam.	Phase	Transit	5° high 52°	5° high 56°
1	11 35	+ 3.6	9	89	18 55	0 43	0 43
6	11 42	+ 2.8	9	89	18 42	0 26	0 25
11	11 48	+ 1.9	8	89	18 29	0 08	0 07
16	11 56	+ 1.0	8	88	18 16	23 48	23 45
21	12 03	+ 0.1	8	88	18 05	23 31	23 27
26	12 11	− 1.0	8	88	17 53	23 14	23 10
31	12 20	− 2.0	7	88	17 42	22 57	22 52

SUNRISE AND SUNSET

	London		Bristol		Birmingham		Manchester		Newcastle		Glasgow		Belfast	
	0°05′	51°30′	2°35′	51°28′	1°55′	52°28′	2°15′	53°28′	1°37′	54°59′	4°14′	55°52′	5°56′	54°35′
	h m	h m	h m	h m	h m	h m	h m	h m	h m	h m	h m	h m	h m	h m
1	3 49	20 08	3 59	20 18	3 51	20 20	3 47	20 27	3 35	20 34	3 40	20 50	3 55	20 49
2	3 48	20 09	3 58	20 19	3 50	20 22	3 46	20 29	3 34	20 35	3 39	20 52	3 54	20 50
3	3 47	20 10	3 58	20 20	3 50	20 23	3 45	20 30	3 33	20 37	3 38	20 53	3 53	20 51
4	3 47	20 11	3 57	20 21	3 49	20 24	3 44	20 31	3 32	20 38	3 37	20 54	3 52	20 52
5	3 46	20 12	3 56	20 22	3 48	20 25	3 44	20 32	3 32	20 39	3 36	20 55	3 52	20 53
6	3 45	20 13	3 56	20 23	3 48	20 26	3 43	20 33	3 31	20 40	3 35	20 57	3 51	20 55
7	3 45	20 14	3 55	20 24	3 47	20 27	3 42	20 34	3 30	20 41	3 35	20 58	3 50	20 56
8	3 45	20 15	3 55	20 24	3 46	20 27	3 42	20 35	3 30	20 42	3 34	20 59	3 50	20 56
9	3 44	20 15	3 54	20 25	3 46	20 28	3 41	20 35	3 29	20 43	3 33	21 00	3 49	20 57
10	3 44	20 16	3 54	20 26	3 46	20 29	3 41	20 36	3 29	20 44	3 33	21 00	3 49	20 58
11	3 43	20 17	3 54	20 27	3 45	20 30	3 41	20 37	3 28	20 44	3 32	21 01	3 48	20 59
12	3 43	20 18	3 53	20 27	3 45	20 30	3 40	20 38	3 28	20 45	3 32	21 02	3 48	21 00
13	3 43	20 18	3 53	20 28	3 45	20 31	3 40	20 38	3 27	20 46	3 31	21 03	3 47	21 00
14	3 43	20 19	3 53	20 29	3 44	20 32	3 40	20 39	3 27	20 47	3 31	21 03	3 47	21 01
15	3 43	20 19	3 53	20 29	3 44	20 32	3 40	20 40	3 27	20 47	3 31	21 04	3 47	21 02
16	3 42	20 20	3 53	20 29	3 44	20 33	3 39	20 40	3 27	20 48	3 31	21 05	3 47	21 02
17	3 42	20 20	3 53	20 30	3 44	20 33	3 39	20 40	3 27	20 48	3 31	21 05	3 47	21 03
18	3 42	20 20	3 53	20 30	3 44	20 33	3 39	20 41	3 27	20 49	3 31	21 05	3 47	21 03
19	3 43	20 21	3 53	20 31	3 44	20 34	3 40	20 41	3 27	20 49	3 31	21 06	3 47	21 03
20	3 43	20 21	3 53	20 31	3 44	20 34	3 40	20 41	3 27	20 49	3 31	21 06	3 47	21 04
21	3 43	20 21	3 53	20 31	3 45	20 34	3 40	20 42	3 27	20 49	3 31	21 06	3 47	21 04
22	3 43	20 21	3 53	20 31	3 45	20 34	3 40	20 42	3 27	20 49	3 31	21 06	3 47	21 04
23	3 43	20 22	3 54	20 31	3 45	20 34	3 40	20 42	3 28	20 50	3 32	21 07	3 48	21 04
24	3 44	20 22	3 54	20 31	3 45	20 35	3 41	20 42	3 28	20 50	3 32	21 07	3 48	21 04
25	3 44	20 22	3 54	20 31	3 46	20 35	3 41	20 42	3 28	20 50	3 32	21 07	3 48	21 04
26	3 45	20 22	3 55	20 31	3 46	20 34	3 42	20 42	3 29	20 49	3 33	21 06	3 49	21 04
27	3 45	20 21	3 55	20 31	3 47	20 34	3 42	20 42	3 29	20 49	3 33	21 06	3 49	21 04
28	3 46	20 21	3 56	20 31	3 47	20 34	3 43	20 42	3 30	20 49	3 34	21 06	3 50	21 04
29	3 46	20 21	3 56	20 31	3 48	20 34	3 43	20 41	3 31	20 49	3 35	21 06	3 51	21 03
30	3 47	20 21	3 57	20 31	3 49	20 34	3 44	20 41	3 31	20 48	3 35	21 05	3 51	21 03

JUPITER

Day	RA	Dec.	Transit	5° high	
				52°	56°
	h m	° ′	h m	h m	h m
1	21 37.7	−14 55	4 59	0 56	1 15
11	21 38.2	−14 55	4 20	0 17	0 36
21	21 37.6	−15 01	3 40	23 34	23 53
31	21 35.6	−15 13	2 59	22 54	23 13

Diameters – equatorial 44″ polar 42″

SATURN

Day	RA	Dec.	Transit	5° high	
				52°	56°
	h m	° ′	h m	h m	h m
1	1 07.4	+ 4 41	8 28	2 38	2 37
11	1 10.6	+ 4 58	7 52	2 00	1 59
21	1 13.4	+ 5 13	7 15	1 22	1 21
31	1 15.7	+ 5 24	6 38	0 44	0 43

Diameters – equatorial 17″ polar 15″
Rings – major axis 38″ minor axis 7″

URANUS

Day	RA	Dec.	Transit	10° high	
				52°	56°
	h m	° ′	h m	h m	h m
1	20 44.5	−18 44	4 06	1 14	1 51
11	20 43.8	−18 47	3 26	0 35	1 11
21	20 42.7	−18 51	2 45	23 51	0 32
31	20 41.5	−18 56	2 05	23 11	23 49

Diameter 4″

NEPTUNE

Day	RA	Dec.	Transit	10° high	
				52°	56°
	h m	° ′	h m	h m	h m
1	20 07.2	−19 48	3 29	0 47	1 28
11	20 06.5	−19 50	2 49	0 07	0 48
21	20 05.6	−19 52	2 08	23 24	0 09
31	20 04.6	−19 55	1 28	22 44	23 25

Diameter 2″

July 1997

SEVENTH MONTH, 31 DAYS. *Julius* Caesar, formerly *Quintilis*, fifth month of Roman pre-Julian calendar

1	Tuesday	*Princess of Wales b. 1961.* George Sand b. 1804	*week 26 day* 182
2	Wednesday	Hermann Hesse b. 1877. Sir Herbert Beerbohm Tree d. 1917	183
3	Thursday	**St Thomas.** Tom Stoppard b. 1937	184
4	Friday	Alec Bedser b. 1918. Suzanne Lenglen d. 1938	185
5	Saturday	Mrs Sarah Siddons b. 1755. George Borrow b. 1803	186
6	Sunday	**7th S. after Pentecost/6th S. after Trinity**	*week 27 day* 187
7	Monday	Joseph Jacquard b. 1752. Marc Chagall b. 1887	188
8	Tuesday	Joseph Chamberlain b. 1836. Vivien Leigh d. 1967	189
9	Wednesday	Mrs Ann Radcliffe b. 1764. David Hockney b. 1937	190
10	Thursday	George Stubbs d. 1806. Camille Pissarro b. 1830	191
11	Friday	George Gershwin d. 1937. Paul Nash d. 1946	192
12	Saturday	Josiah Wedgwood bapt. 1730. Kirsten Flagstad b. 1895	193
13	Sunday	**8th S. after Pentecost/7th S. after Trinity**	*week 28 day* 194
14	Monday	*Bank Holiday in Northern Ireland*	195
15	Tuesday	St Swithin's Day. Ernest Bloch d. 1959	196
16	Wednesday	Sir Joshua Reynolds b. 1723. Hilaire Belloc d. 1953	197
17	Thursday	James Whistler d. 1903. Jules Henri Poincaré d. 1912	198
18	Friday	Jane Austen d. 1817. Thomas Sturge Moore d. 1944	199
19	Saturday	*Mary Rose* sank 1545. Edgar Degas b. 1834	200
20	Sunday	**9th S. after Pentecost/8th S. after Trinity**	*week 29 day* 201
21	Monday	Robert Burns d. 1796. Henry Longhurst d. 1978	202
22	Tuesday	**St Mary Magdalen.** Tate Gallery opened 1897	203
23	Wednesday	Raymond Chandler b. 1888. Olivia Manning d. 1980	204
24	Thursday	John Sell Cotman d. 1842. E. F. Benson b. 1867	205
25	Friday	**St James.** A. J. Balfour b. 1848	206
26	Saturday	George Bernard Shaw b. 1856. Carl Jung b. 1875	207
27	Sunday	**10th S. after Pentecost/9th S. after Trinity**	*week 30 day* 208
28	Monday	Thomas Cromwell exec. 1540. Sir Garfield Sobers b. 1936	209
29	Tuesday	Defeat of the Spanish Armada 1588	210
30	Wednesday	William Penn d. 1718. Henry Ford b. 1863	211
31	Thursday	*Trinity Law Sittings end.* Franz Liszt d. 1886	212

ASTRONOMICAL PHENOMENA

d	h	
4	19	Earth at aphelion (152 milion km)
5	18	Mercury in conjunction with Moon. Mercury 6° N.
6	23	Venus in conjunction with Moon. Venus 5° N.
12	03	Mars in conjunction with Moon. Mars 2° S.
21	07	Neptune at opposition
21	15	Jupiter in conjunction with Moon. Jupiter 4° S.
22	19	Sun's longitude 120° ♌
25	19	Saturn in conjunction with Moon. Saturn 0°.08 N.
29	19	Uranus at opposition

MINIMA OF ALGOL

d	h	d	h	d	h
1	03.7	12	14.9	24	02.2
4	00.5	15	11.8	26	23.0
6	21.3	18	08.6	29	19.8
9	18.1	21	05.4		

CONSTELLATIONS

The following constellations are near the meridian at

	d	h		d	h
June	1	24	July	16	21
June	15	23	August	1	20
July	1	22	August	16	19

Ursa Minor, Draco, Corona, Hercules, Lyra, Serpens, Ophiuchus, Libra, Scorpius and Sagittarius

THE MOON

Phases, Apsides and Node	d	h	m
● New Moon	4	18	40
☽ First Quarter	12	21	44
○ Full Moon	20	03	20
☾ Last Quarter	26	18	28
Apogee (404,947 km)	9	22	55
Perigee (361,577 km)	21	23	07

Mean longitude of ascending node on July 1, 173°

THE SUN
s.d. 15′.8

Day	Right Ascension	Dec. +	Equation of time	Rise 52°	Rise 56°	Transit	Set 52°	Set 56°	Sidereal time	Transit of First Point of Aries
	h m s	° ′	m s	h m	h m	h m	h m	h m	h m s	h m s
1	6 40 04	23 07	−3 43	3 44	3 18	12 04	20 23	20 49	18 36 21	5 22 46
2	6 44 12	23 03	−3 55	3 45	3 19	12 04	20 23	20 48	18 40 17	5 18 51
3	6 48 20	22 58	−4 06	3 46	3 20	12 04	20 22	20 48	18 44 14	5 14 55
4	6 52 27	22 53	−4 17	3 47	3 21	12 04	20 22	20 47	18 48 10	5 10 59
5	6 56 35	22 48	−4 28	3 47	3 22	12 05	20 21	20 46	18 52 07	5 07 03
6	7 00 42	22 42	−4 38	3 48	3 23	12 05	20 21	20 46	18 56 03	5 03 07
7	7 04 48	22 36	−4 48	3 49	3 24	12 05	20 20	20 45	19 00 00	4 59 11
8	7 08 55	22 30	−4 58	3 50	3 25	12 05	20 19	20 44	19 03 56	4 55 15
9	7 13 00	22 23	−5 07	3 51	3 27	12 05	20 19	20 43	19 07 53	4 51 19
10	7 17 06	22 15	−5 16	3 52	3 28	12 05	20 18	20 42	19 11 50	4 47 23
11	7 21 11	22 08	−5 25	3 53	3 29	12 05	20 17	20 41	19 15 46	4 43 27
12	7 25 15	22 00	−5 32	3 54	3 30	12 06	20 16	20 40	19 19 43	4 39 31
13	7 29 19	21 51	−5 40	3 55	3 32	12 06	20 15	20 39	19 23 39	4 35 36
14	7 33 23	21 42	−5 47	3 57	3 33	12 06	20 14	20 37	19 27 36	4 31 40
15	7 37 26	21 33	−5 53	3 58	3 35	12 06	20 13	20 36	19 31 32	4 27 44
16	7 41 28	21 23	−5 59	3 59	3 36	12 06	20 12	20 35	19 35 29	4 23 48
17	7 45 30	21 14	−6 05	4 00	3 38	12 06	20 11	20 33	19 39 25	4 19 52
18	7 49 32	21 03	−6 10	4 02	3 39	12 06	20 10	20 32	19 43 22	4 15 56
19	7 53 32	20 53	−6 14	4 03	3 41	12 06	20 09	20 31	19 47 19	4 12 00
20	7 57 33	20 42	−6 18	4 04	3 43	12 06	20 08	20 29	19 51 15	4 08 04
21	8 01 32	20 30	−6 21	4 06	3 44	12 06	20 06	20 27	19 55 12	4 04 08
22	8 05 32	20 19	−6 23	4 07	3 46	12 06	20 05	20 26	19 59 08	4 00 12
23	8 09 30	20 07	−6 26	4 08	3 48	12 06	20 04	20 24	20 03 05	3 56 16
24	8 13 28	19 54	−6 27	4 10	3 49	12 06	20 02	20 22	20 07 01	3 52 21
25	8 17 26	19 41	−6 28	4 11	3 51	12 06	20 01	20 21	20 10 58	3 48 25
26	8 21 23	19 28	−6 28	4 13	3 53	12 06	19 59	20 19	20 14 54	3 44 29
27	8 25 19	19 15	−6 28	4 14	3 55	12 06	19 58	20 17	20 18 51	3 40 33
28	8 29 15	19 01	−6 27	4 16	3 56	12 06	19 56	20 15	20 22 48	3 36 37
29	8 33 10	18 47	−6 26	4 17	3 58	12 06	19 55	20 13	20 26 44	3 32 41
30	8 37 05	18 33	−6 24	4 19	4 00	12 06	19 53	20 11	20 30 41	3 28 45
31	8 40 59	18 19	−6 22	4 20	4 02	12 06	19 52	20 09	20 34 37	3 24 49

DURATION OF TWILIGHT (in minutes)

Latitude	52°	56°	52°	56°	52°	56°	52°	56°
	1 July		11 July		21 July		31 July	
Civil	48	61	46	58	44	53	41	49
Nautical	124	TAN	116	TAN	107	144	98	122
Astronomical	TAN	TAN	TAN	TAN	TAN	TAN	180	TAN

THE NIGHT SKY

Mercury is still unsuitably placed for observation.

Venus, magnitude −3.9, is a brilliant object in the evening sky, but only visible low above the western horizon for about half an hour after sunset.

Mars, magnitude +0.7, is still visible in the evenings but no longer the prominent object that it was during the spring. It is moving rapidly towards the Sun and by the end of the month is only visible for a short time low in the west-south-western sky. The Moon, approaching First Quarter, is near the planet on the evening of the 11th.

Jupiter is now visible low above the south-eastern horizon well before midnight. Its magnitude is −2.8. On the evening of the 21st the Moon, just after Full, will be seen about 6° to the left of the planet.

Saturn is a morning object, magnitude +0.6, visible low in the south-eastern sky before it pales to invisibility in the morning twilight. By the end of the month it is visible well before midnight. On the morning of the 26th the waning gibbous Moon will be seen moving eastwards from the planet.

Uranus is at opposition on the 29th, in Capricornus. It is barely visible to the naked eye as its magnitude is only +5.7 but it is readily located with only small optical aid.

Neptune is at opposition on the 21st, on the borders of Sagittarius and Capricornus. It is not visible to the naked eye as its magnitude is +7.8.

THE MOON

Day	RA	Dec.	Hor. par.	Semi- diam.	Sun's co- long.	PA of Bright Limb	Phase	Age	Rise		Transit	Set	
									52°	56°		52°	56°
	h m	°	'	'	°	°	%	d	h m	h m	h m	h m	h m
1	3 29	+14.4	57.5	15.7	219	72	15	25.7	1 39	1 26	9 12	16 54	17 09
2	4 23	+16.7	57.0	15.5	231	73	8	26.7	2 18	2 02	10 04	17 57	18 14
3	5 18	+18.0	56.5	15.4	244	73	4	27.7	3 02	2 44	10 57	18 54	19 12
4	6 12	+18.5	56.0	15.3	256	63	1	28.7	3 52	3 34	11 48	19 43	20 00
5	7 05	+17.9	55.6	15.1	268	337	0	0.2	4 47	4 30	12 39	20 24	20 40
6	7 57	+16.5	55.1	15.0	280	297	2	1.2	5 47	5 31	13 27	20 59	21 13
7	8 47	+14.4	54.7	14.9	293	292	5	2.2	6 48	6 36	14 14	21 30	21 40
8	9 36	+11.7	54.4	14.8	305	292	10	3.2	7 50	7 41	14 58	21 56	22 03
9	10 22	+ 8.5	54.2	14.8	317	293	16	4.2	8 53	8 47	15 42	22 20	22 24
10	11 08	+ 5.0	54.1	14.8	329	293	24	5.2	9 56	9 53	16 24	22 42	22 44
11	11 53	+ 1.4	54.2	14.8	342	293	32	6.2	10 58	10 59	17 07	23 05	23 03
12	12 38	− 2.4	54.5	14.8	354	293	41	7.2	12 02	12 05	17 49	23 28	23 23
13	13 24	− 6.1	54.9	15.0	6	292	51	8.2	13 06	13 13	18 34	23 53	23 45
14	14 11	− 9.6	55.5	15.1	18	290	61	9.2	14 12	14 22	19 20	—	—
15	15 01	−12.8	56.2	15.3	31	288	70	10.2	15 18	15 32	20 10	0 22	0 10
16	15 53	−15.4	57.0	15.5	43	286	79	11.2	16 24	16 40	21 02	0 56	0 41
17	16 48	−17.3	57.9	15.8	55	283	87	12.2	17 28	17 46	21 58	1 36	1 20
18	17 46	−18.3	58.7	16.0	67	281	94	13.2	18 27	18 45	22 56	2 26	2 08
19	18 46	−18.2	59.5	16.2	79	282	98	14.2	19 19	19 35	23 55	3 26	3 08
20	19 46	−16.9	60.1	16.4	92	325	100	15.2	20 03	20 17	—	4 35	4 19
21	20 47	−14.5	60.5	16.5	104	59	99	16.2	20 42	20 52	0 54	5 51	5 38
22	21 46	−11.1	60.6	16.5	116	66	95	17.2	21 15	21 21	1 51	7 11	7 02
23	22 44	− 7.0	60.5	16.5	128	67	89	18.2	21 45	21 47	2 47	8 31	8 26
24	23 40	− 2.5	60.2	16.4	140	67	80	19.2	22 13	22 11	3 41	9 50	9 50
25	0 35	+ 2.1	59.6	16.2	153	68	70	20.2	22 41	22 36	4 34	11 08	11 11
26	1 30	+ 6.4	59.0	16.1	165	69	59	21.2	23 11	23 02	5 26	12 24	12 31
27	2 23	+10.3	58.3	15.9	177	71	48	22.2	23 43	23 31	6 18	13 36	13 47
28	3 17	+13.6	57.7	15.7	189	74	37	23.2	—	—	7 09	14 46	15 00
29	4 11	+16.1	57.0	15.5	201	77	27	24.2	0 19	0 04	8 01	15 50	16 06
30	5 05	+17.7	56.4	15.4	214	80	18	25.2	1 01	0 44	8 53	16 48	17 06
31	5 59	+18.3	55.9	15.2	226	83	11	26.2	1 48	1 30	9 44	17 39	17 57

MERCURY

Day	RA	Dec.	Diam.	Phase	Transit	5° high	
						52°	56°
	h m	°	"	%	h m	h m	h m
1	7 08	+24.2	5	97	12 34	20 14	20 34
3	7 26	+23.8	5	94	12 45	20 21	20 40
5	7 44	+23.2	5	92	12 54	20 26	20 44
7	8 00	+22.5	5	89	13 03	20 30	20 47
9	8 17	+21.6	5	86	13 11	20 33	20 48
11	8 32	+20.7	6	83	13 18	20 34	20 49
13	8 46	+19.7	6	80	13 24	20 34	20 48
15	9 00	+18.6	6	77	13 30	20 33	20 46
17	9 13	+17.5	6	74	13 35	20 32	20 43
19	9 26	+16.3	6	71	13 39	20 29	20 39
21	9 37	+15.1	6	68	13 43	20 26	20 35
23	9 48	+13.9	6	65	13 46	20 23	20 30
25	9 58	+12.7	7	62	13 48	20 18	20 25
27	10 08	+11.4	7	60	13 50	20 14	20 19
29	10 17	+10.3	7	57	13 51	20 08	20 13
31	10 25	+ 9.1	7	54	13 51	20 02	20 06

VENUS

Day	RA	Dec.	Diam.	Phase	Transit	5° high	
						52°	56°
	h m	°	"	%	h m	h m	h m
1	8 21	+21.1	11	91	13 46	21 05	21 20
6	8 47	+19.6	11	90	13 51	21 01	21 15
11	9 11	+18.0	11	89	13 56	20 56	21 08
16	9 35	+16.1	12	88	14 00	20 50	21 00
21	9 59	+14.0	12	87	14 04	20 42	20 50
26	10 22	+11.8	12	86	14 07	20 34	20 40
31	10 44	+ 9.5	12	84	14 10	20 24	20 28

MARS

Day	RA	Dec.	Diam.	Phase	Transit	5° high	
						52°	56°
1	12 20	− 2.0	7	88	17 42	22 57	22 52
6	12 29	− 3.1	7	88	17 31	22 41	22 35
11	12 38	− 4.2	7	88	17 21	22 25	22 18
16	12 48	− 5.3	7	88	17 11	22 09	22 01
21	12 58	− 6.4	7	88	17 01	21 53	21 44
26	13 08	− 7.6	7	88	16 52	21 37	21 27
31	13 19	− 8.7	6	88	16 43	21 22	21 10

SUNRISE AND SUNSET

	London		Bristol		Birmingham		Manchester		Newcastle		Glasgow		Belfast	
	0°05′	51°30′	2°35′	51°28′	1°55′	52°28′	2°15′	53°28′	1°37′	54°59′	4°14′	55°52′	5°56′	54°35′
	h m	h m	h m	h m	h m	h m	h m	h m	h m	h m	h m	h m	h m	h m
1	3 47	20 21	3 58	20 30	3 49	20 33	3 45	20 41	3 32	20 48	3 36	21 05	3 52	21 03
2	3 48	20 20	3 58	20 30	3 50	20 33	3 45	20 40	3 33	20 48	3 37	21 04	3 53	21 02
3	3 49	20 20	3 59	20 30	3 51	20 33	3 46	20 40	3 34	20 47	3 38	21 04	3 54	21 02
4	3 50	20 19	4 00	20 29	3 52	20 32	3 47	20 39	3 35	20 46	3 39	21 03	3 55	21 01
5	3 50	20 19	4 01	20 29	3 52	20 32	3 48	20 39	3 36	20 46	3 40	21 02	3 56	21 00
6	3 51	20 18	4 01	20 28	3 53	20 31	3 49	20 38	3 37	20 45	3 41	21 02	3 57	21 00
7	3 52	20 18	4 02	20 28	3 54	20 30	3 50	20 37	3 38	20 44	3 42	21 01	3 58	20 59
8	3 53	20 17	4 03	20 27	3 55	20 30	3 51	20 37	3 39	20 44	3 43	21 00	3 59	20 58
9	3 54	20 16	4 04	20 26	3 56	20 29	3 52	20 36	3 40	20 43	3 44	20 59	4 00	20 57
10	3 55	20 16	4 05	20 25	3 57	20 28	3 53	20 35	3 41	20 42	3 46	20 58	4 01	20 56
11	3 56	20 15	4 06	20 25	3 58	20 27	3 54	20 34	3 42	20 41	3 47	20 57	4 02	20 55
12	3 57	20 14	4 07	20 24	4 00	20 26	3 55	20 33	3 44	20 40	3 48	20 56	4 03	20 54
13	3 58	20 13	4 09	20 23	4 01	20 25	3 57	20 32	3 45	20 39	3 50	20 55	4 05	20 53
14	4 00	20 12	4 10	20 22	4 02	20 24	3 58	20 31	3 46	20 37	3 51	20 53	4 06	20 52
15	4 01	20 11	4 11	20 21	4 03	20 23	3 59	20 30	3 48	20 36	3 53	20 52	4 07	20 51
16	4 02	20 10	4 12	20 20	4 04	20 22	4 00	20 29	3 49	20 35	3 54	20 51	4 09	20 50
17	4 03	20 09	4 13	20 19	4 06	20 21	4 02	20 28	3 51	20 34	3 56	20 50	4 10	20 49
18	4 04	20 08	4 14	20 18	4 07	20 20	4 03	20 26	3 52	20 32	3 57	20 48	4 12	20 47
19	4 06	20 07	4 16	20 17	4 08	20 19	4 04	20 25	3 54	20 31	3 59	20 47	4 13	20 46
20	4 07	20 06	4 17	20 15	4 10	20 17	4 06	20 24	3 55	20 29	4 00	20 45	4 15	20 44
21	4 08	20 04	4 18	20 14	4 11	20 16	4 07	20 22	3 57	20 28	4 02	20 44	4 16	20 43
22	4 10	20 03	4 20	20 13	4 12	20 15	4 09	20 21	3 58	20 26	4 04	20 42	4 18	20 42
23	4 11	20 02	4 21	20 12	4 14	20 13	4 10	20 20	4 00	20 25	4 05	20 40	4 19	20 40
24	4 12	20 00	4 22	20 10	4 15	20 12	4 12	20 18	4 01	20 23	4 07	20 39	4 21	20 38
25	4 14	19 59	4 24	20 09	4 17	20 11	4 13	20 17	4 03	20 22	4 09	20 37	4 23	20 37
26	4 15	19 58	4 25	20 07	4 18	20 09	4 15	20 15	4 05	20 20	4 11	20 35	4 24	20 35
27	4 17	19 56	4 27	20 06	4 20	20 08	4 16	20 13	4 06	20 18	4 12	20 33	4 26	20 33
28	4 18	19 55	4 28	20 04	4 21	20 06	4 18	20 12	4 08	20 16	4 14	20 31	4 27	20 32
29	4 19	19 53	4 30	20 03	4 23	20 04	4 20	20 10	4 10	20 15	4 16	20 30	4 29	20 30
30	4 21	19 52	4 31	20 01	4 24	20 03	4 21	20 08	4 12	20 13	4 18	20 28	4 31	20 28
31	4 22	19 50	4 33	20 00	4 26	20 01	4 23	20 07	4 13	20 11	4 20	20 26	4 33	20 26

JUPITER

Day	RA	Dec.	Transit	5° high	
				52°	56°
	h m	° ′	h m	h m	h m
1	21 35.6	−15 13	2 59	22 54	23 13
11	21 32.6	−15 30	2 16	22 14	22 33
21	21 28.6	−15 52	1 33	21 33	21 52
31	21 23.9	−16 16	0 49	20 51	21 12

Diameters – equatorial 48″ polar 45″

SATURN

Day	RA	Dec.	Transit	5° high	
				52°	56°
	h m	° ′	h m	h m	h m
1	1 15.7	+ 5 24	6 38	0 44	0 43
11	1 17.4	+ 5 32	6 01	0 06	0 05
21	1 18.6	+ 5 35	5 23	23 23	23 22
31	1 19.1	+ 5 35	4 44	22 45	22 43

Diameters – equatorial 18″ polar 16″
Rings – major axis 41″ minor axis 8″

URANUS

Day	RA	Dec.	Transit	10° high	
				52°	56°
	h m	° ′	h m	h m	h m
1	20 41.5	−18 56	2 05	23 11	23 49
11	20 40.0	−19 02	1 24	22 31	23 09
21	20 38.5	−19 08	0 43	21 51	22 29
31	20 36.8	−19 14	0 02	21 11	21 50

Diameter 4″

NEPTUNE

Day	RA	Dec.	Transit	10° high	
				52°	56°
	h m	° ′	h m	h m	h m
1	20 04.6	−19 55	1 28	22 44	23 25
11	20 03.5	−19 59	0 48	22 04	22 46
21	20 02.4	−20 02	0 07	21 24	22 06
31	20 01.3	−20 05	23 23	20 44	21 26

Diameter 2″

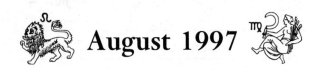

August 1997

EIGHTH MONTH, 31 DAYS. Julius, Caesar *Augustus*, formerly *Sextilis*, sixth month of Roman pre-Julian calendar

1	*Friday*	Queen Anne d. 1714. Herman Melville b. 1819	*week* 30 *day* 213
2	*Saturday*	William II d. 1100. Gen. von Hindenburg d. 1934	214
3	*Sunday*	**11th S. after Pentecost/10th S. after Trinity**	*week* 31 *day* 215
4	*Monday*	*Bank Holiday in Scotland. Queen Elizabeth the Queen Mother b. 1900*	216
5	*Tuesday*	Guy de Maupassant b. 1850. Marilyn Monroe d. 1962	217
6	*Wednesday*	**The Transfiguration.** Anne Hathaway d. 1623	218
7	*Thursday*	Joseph Jacquard d. 1834. Oliver Hardy d. 1957	219
8	*Friday*	Princess Beatrice of York b. 1988	220
9	*Saturday*	Thomas Telford b. 1757. Capt. Frederick Marryat d. 1848	221
10	*Sunday*	**12th S. after Pentecost/11th S. after Trinity**	*week* 32 *day* 222
11	*Monday*	Charlotte Yonge b. 1823. Edith Wharton d. 1937	223
12	*Tuesday*	George IV b. 1762. William Blake d. 1827	224
13	*Wednesday*	Sir Basil Spence b. 1907. Ben Hogan b. 1912	225
14	*Thursday*	Ira Sankey d. 1908. William Randolph Hearst d. 1951	226
15	*Friday*	*Princess Royal b. 1950.* Sir Walter Scott b. 1771	227
16	*Saturday*	Ted Hughes b. 1930. Stewart Granger d. 1993	228
17	*Sunday*	**13th S. after Pentecost/12th S. after Trinity**	*week* 33 *day* 229
18	*Monday*	Earl Russell b. 1792. Sir Frederick Ashton d. 1988	230
19	*Tuesday*	President Bill Clinton b. 1946. Groucho Marx d. 1977	231
20	*Wednesday*	Raymond Poincaré b. 1860. Gen. William Booth d. 1912	232
21	*Thursday*	*Princess Margaret b. 1930.* Elie Halévy d. 1937	233
22	*Friday*	⚔Battle of Bosworth Field 1485. Dr Jacob Bronowski d. 1974	234
23	*Saturday*	William Wallace exec. 1305. Rudolf Valentino d. 1926	235
24	*Sunday*	**St Bartholomew. 14th S. after Pentecost/13th S. after Trinity**	*week* 34 *day* 236
25	*Monday*	*Bank Holiday in England, Wales and Northern Ireland*	237
26	*Tuesday*	Sir Robert Walpole b. 1676. William James d. 1910	238
27	*Wednesday*	Umberto Giordano b. 1867. Eric Coates b. 1886	239
28	*Thursday*	Count Leo Tolstoy b. 1828 (os). Leigh Hunt d. 1859	240
29	*Friday*	Edward Carpenter b. 1844. Lady Diana Cooper b. 1892	241
30	*Saturday*	Mary Wollstonecraft Shelley b. 1797. Denis Healey b. 1917	242
31	*Sunday*	**15th S. after Pentecost/14th S. after Trinity**	*week* 35 *day* 243

ASTRONOMICAL PHENOMENA

d	h	
1	17	Saturn at stationary point
4	00	Mercury at greatest elongation E.27°
5	20	Mercury in conjunction with Moon. Mercury 1° S.
6	08	Venus in conjunction with Moon. Venus 2° N.
9	14	Jupiter at opposition
9	18	Mars in conjunction with Moon. Mars 4° S.
13	09	Pluto at stationary point
17	20	Jupiter in conjunction with Moon. Jupiter 4° S.
17	20	Mercury at stationary point
22	02	Saturn in conjunction with Moon. Saturn 0°.09 N.
23	02	Sun's longitude 150° ♍
31	14	Mercury in inferior conjunction

MINIMA OF ALGOL

d	h	d	h	d	h
1	16.6	13	03.9	24	15.1
4	13.4	16	00.7	27	11.9
7	10.2	18	21.5	30	08.7
10	07.0	21	18.3		

CONSTELLATIONS

The following constellations are near the meridian at

	d	h		d	h
July	1	24	August	16	21
July	16	23	September	1	20
August	1	22	September	15	19

Draco, Hercules, Lyra, Cygnus, Sagitta, Ophiuchus, Serpens, Aquila and Sagittarius

THE MOON

Phases, Apsides and Node	d	h	m
● New Moon	3	08	14
☽ First Quarter	11	12	42
○ Full Moon	18	10	55
☾ Last Quarter	25	02	24
Apogee (405,935 km)	6	13	42
Perigee (358,017 km)	19	05	09

Mean longitude of ascending node on August 1, 172°

THE SUN   s.d. 15'.8

Day	Right Ascension	Dec. +	Equation of time	Rise 52°	Rise 56°	Transit	Set 52°	Set 56°	Sidereal time	Transit of First Point of Aries
	h m s	° '	m s	h m	h m	h m	h m	h m	h m s	h m s
1	8 44 52	18 04	−6 19	4 22	4 04	12 06	19 50	20 07	20 38 34	3 20 53
2	8 48 45	17 48	−6 15	4 23	4 06	12 06	19 48	20 05	20 42 30	3 16 57
3	8 52 37	17 33	−6 10	4 25	4 08	12 06	19 46	20 03	20 46 27	3 13 01
4	8 56 29	17 17	−6 06	4 26	4 09	12 06	19 45	20 01	20 50 23	3 09 06
5	9 00 20	17 01	−6 00	4 28	4 11	12 06	19 43	19 59	20 54 20	3 05 10
6	9 04 10	16 45	−5 54	4 29	4 13	12 06	19 41	19 57	20 58 17	3 01 14
7	9 08 00	16 28	−5 47	4 31	4 15	12 06	19 39	19 55	21 02 13	2 57 18
8	9 11 49	16 11	−5 40	4 33	4 17	12 06	19 37	19 53	21 06 10	2 53 22
9	9 15 38	15 54	−5 32	4 34	4 19	12 05	19 36	19 51	21 10 06	2 49 26
10	9 19 26	15 37	−5 23	4 36	4 21	12 05	19 34	19 48	21 14 03	2 45 30
11	9 23 13	15 19	−5 14	4 37	4 23	12 05	19 32	19 46	21 17 59	2 41 34
12	9 27 00	15 01	−5 04	4 39	4 25	12 05	19 30	19 44	21 21 56	2 37 38
13	9 30 47	14 43	−4 54	4 41	4 27	12 05	19 28	19 41	21 25 52	2 33 42
14	9 34 32	14 25	−4 43	4 42	4 29	12 05	19 26	19 39	21 29 49	2 29 46
15	9 38 17	14 06	−4 32	4 44	4 31	12 04	19 24	19 37	21 33 46	2 25 51
16	9 42 02	13 48	−4 20	4 45	4 33	12 04	19 22	19 34	21 37 42	2 21 55
17	9 45 46	13 29	−4 07	4 47	4 35	12 04	19 20	19 32	21 41 39	2 17 59
18	9 49 30	13 09	−3 54	4 49	4 37	12 04	19 18	19 30	21 45 35	2 14 03
19	9 53 13	12 50	−3 41	4 50	4 39	12 04	19 16	19 27	21 49 32	2 10 07
20	9 56 55	12 30	−3 27	4 52	4 41	12 03	19 14	19 25	21 53 28	2 06 11
21	10 00 37	12 10	−3 12	4 54	4 43	12 03	19 11	19 22	21 57 25	2 02 15
22	10 04 19	11 50	−2 57	4 55	4 44	12 03	19 09	19 20	22 01 21	1 58 19
23	10 08 00	11 30	−2 42	4 57	4 46	12 03	19 07	19 17	22 05 18	1 54 23
24	10 11 41	11 10	−2 26	4 59	4 48	12 02	19 05	19 15	22 09 15	1 50 27
25	10 15 21	10 49	−2 10	5 00	4 50	12 02	19 03	19 12	22 13 11	1 46 31
26	10 19 01	10 29	−1 53	5 02	4 52	12 02	19 01	19 10	22 17 08	1 42 36
27	10 22 40	10 08	−1 36	5 03	4 54	12 01	18 58	19 07	22 21 04	1 38 40
28	10 26 20	9 47	−1 19	5 05	4 56	12 01	18 56	19 05	22 25 01	1 34 44
29	10 29 59	9 25	−1 01	5 07	4 58	12 01	18 54	19 02	22 28 57	1 30 48
30	10 33 37	9 04	−0 43	5 08	5 00	12 01	18 52	19 00	22 32 54	1 26 52
31	10 37 15	8 42	−0 25	5 10	5 02	12 00	18 49	18 57	22 36 50	1 22 56

DURATION OF TWILIGHT (in minutes)

Latitude	52°	56°	52°	56°	52°	56°	52°	56°
	1 August		11 August		21 August		31 August	
Civil	41	48	39	45	37	42	35	40
Nautical	97	120	89	106	83	96	79	89
Astronomical	177	TAN	153	205	138	166	127	147

THE NIGHT SKY

Mercury is at greatest eastern elongation on the 4th and at inferior conjunction on the last day of the month, but remains too close to the Sun for observation.

Venus continues to be visible as a brilliant object in the evening skies, magnitude −4.0, but only visible for about half an hour after sunset, low above the western horizon.

Mars, magnitude +0.9, passes 2° N. of Spica, magnitude +1.0, on the evening of the 2nd, but is not visible after the middle of the month as it moves closer to the Sun. The crescent Moon will be seen 4° above Mars on the evening of the 9th. Mars has the longest period of invisibility of any of the major planets as seen from the Earth. It will be almost a year before it reappears in the morning skies again.

Jupiter, magnitude −2.8, is at opposition on the 9th, and thus visible throughout the hours of darkness. Jupiter is in Capricornus. On the evening of the 17th the Full Moon passes 3° N. of the planet. An unusual event occurs on the evening of the 27th: none of the Galilean satellites is visible between 21h 39m and 21h 59m.

Saturn, magnitude +0.5, is becoming a more prominent object in the night sky and by the end of the month is rising in the eastern sky as soon as the sky is really dark. Saturn is in Pisces. On the night of the 21st to 22nd, the waning gibbous Moon passes 1° S. of the planet.

Meteors. The maximum of the famous Perseid meteor shower occurs on the 12th. A gibbous Moon will interfere with observations before midnight.

THE MOON

Day	RA h m	Dec. °	Hor. par. '	Semi-diam. '	Sun's co-long. °	PA of Bright Limb °	Phase %	Age d	Rise 52° h m	Rise 56° h m	Transit h m	Set 52° h m	Set 56° h m
1	6 51	+18.1	55.4	15.1	238	86	5	27.2	2 41	2 23	10 34	18 23	18 39
2	7 43	+17.0	55.0	15.0	250	85	2	28.2	3 38	3 22	11 23	19 00	19 14
3	8 33	+15.1	54.6	14.9	263	62	0	29.2	4 38	4 25	12 10	19 32	19 44
4	9 22	+12.6	54.4	14.8	275	308	0	0.7	5 40	5 29	12 55	20 00	20 08
5	10 09	+ 9.6	54.1	14.8	287	296	3	1.7	6 42	6 35	13 39	20 25	20 30
6	10 55	+ 6.2	54.0	14.7	299	294	6	2.7	7 45	7 41	14 22	20 48	20 50
7	11 40	+ 2.6	54.0	14.7	312	293	12	3.7	8 47	8 46	15 04	21 10	21 09
8	12 25	− 1.1	54.1	14.8	324	292	18	4.7	9 50	9 52	15 46	21 33	21 29
9	13 10	− 4.8	54.4	14.8	336	291	26	5.7	10 53	10 59	16 29	21 57	21 50
10	13 57	− 8.3	54.8	14.9	348	289	35	6.7	11 57	12 06	17 14	22 23	22 13
11	14 45	−11.6	55.4	15.1	1	287	45	7.7	13 02	13 14	18 01	22 54	22 41
12	15 35	−14.4	56.1	15.3	13	284	55	8.7	14 06	14 21	18 51	23 30	23 15
13	16 27	−16.5	56.9	15.5	25	281	65	9.7	15 10	15 27	19 43	—	23 57
14	17 22	−17.9	57.9	15.8	37	277	75	10.7	16 10	16 28	20 39	0 14	—
15	18 20	−18.3	58.8	16.0	49	273	84	11.7	17 05	17 22	21 37	1 08	0 50
16	19 20	−17.5	59.7	16.3	62	269	91	12.7	17 53	18 08	22 35	2 11	1 54
17	20 20	−15.6	60.5	16.5	74	267	97	13.7	18 35	18 47	23 34	3 24	3 09
18	21 21	−12.6	61.0	16.6	86	275	100	14.7	19 11	19 19	—	4 42	4 31
19	22 21	− 8.8	61.2	16.7	98	58	100	15.7	19 43	19 48	0 32	6 04	5 57
20	23 19	− 4.3	61.1	16.7	110	67	96	16.7	20 14	20 14	1 29	7 26	7 24
21	0 16	+ 0.4	60.8	16.6	122	68	91	17.7	20 43	20 39	2 24	8 48	8 49
22	1 13	+ 4.9	60.1	16.4	135	70	82	18.7	21 13	21 06	3 18	10 07	10 13
23	2 08	+ 9.1	59.3	16.2	147	72	73	19.7	21 45	21 34	4 12	11 23	11 33
24	3 03	+12.7	58.5	15.9	159	75	62	20.7	22 21	22 07	5 05	12 35	12 48
25	3 58	+15.4	57.6	15.7	171	78	51	21.7	23 01	22 45	5 57	13 42	13 58
26	4 52	+17.2	56.8	15.5	183	82	41	22.7	23 46	23 29	6 50	14 43	15 00
27	5 46	+18.2	56.1	15.3	196	86	31	23.7	—	—	7 41	15 36	15 54
28	6 39	+18.1	55.5	15.1	208	90	22	24.7	0 37	0 19	8 31	16 22	16 39
29	7 31	+17.3	55.0	15.0	220	94	14	25.7	1 32	1 16	9 20	17 01	17 16
30	8 21	+15.6	54.6	14.9	232	97	8	26.7	2 31	2 17	10 07	17 35	17 47
31	9 10	+13.3	54.3	14.8	245	100	4	27.7	3 32	3 21	10 53	18 03	18 13

MERCURY

Day	RA h m	Dec. °	Diam. "	Phase %	Transit h m	5° high 52° h m	56° h m
1	10 29	+ 8.5	7	52	13 51	19 59	20 03
3	10 37	+ 7.4	8	49	13 50	19 53	19 55
5	10 43	+ 6.3	8	46	13 48	19 46	19 47
7	10 49	+ 5.3	8	43	13 46	19 38	19 39
9	10 54	+ 4.4	8	40	13 43	19 31	19 31
11	10 58	+ 3.6	9	36	13 38	19 22	19 22
13	11 01	+ 2.9	9	32	13 33	19 13	19 12
15	11 03	+ 2.3	9	28	13 27	19 04	19 03
17	11 03	+ 1.9	10	24	13 19	18 55	18 53
19	11 03	+ 1.6	10	20	13 11	18 45	18 43
21	11 01	+ 1.6	10	16	13 00	18 35	18 33
23	10 58	+ 1.7	10	12	12 49	18 25	18 23
25	10 53	+ 2.1	11	8	12 37	18 14	18 13
27	10 48	+ 2.7	11	5	12 23	18 04	18 03
29	10 42	+ 3.5	11	2	12 09	17 55	17 54
31	10 35	+ 4.5	11	1	11 55	6 05	6 05

VENUS

Day	RA h m	Dec. °	Diam. "	Phase %	Transit h m	5° high 52° h m	56° h m
1	10 49	+ 9.0	12	84	14 11	20 22	20 26
6	11 11	+ 6.6	13	83	14 13	20 12	20 14
11	11 33	+ 4.1	13	81	14 15	20 01	20 01
16	11 54	+ 1.5	13	80	14 17	19 50	19 48
21	12 16	− 1.1	14	79	14 19	19 38	19 34
26	12 37	− 3.6	14	77	14 20	19 26	19 20
31	12 58	− 6.2	14	76	14 22	19 14	19 05

MARS

Day	RA h m	Dec. °	Diam. "	Phase %	Transit h m	5° high 52° h m	56° h m
1	13 21	− 8.9	6	89	16 41	21 19	21 07
6	13 32	−10.1	6	89	16 32	21 03	20 51
11	13 43	−11.3	6	89	16 24	20 48	20 34
16	13 55	−12.4	6	89	16 16	20 33	20 18
21	14 07	−13.5	6	89	16 08	20 19	20 02
26	14 19	−14.6	6	90	16 01	20 04	19 46
31	14 31	−15.7	6	90	15 54	19 50	19 30

SUNRISE AND SUNSET

	London		Bristol		Birmingham		Manchester		Newcastle		Glasgow		Belfast	
	0°05'	51°30'	2°35'	51°28'	1°55'	52°28'	2°15'	53°28'	1°37'	54°59'	4°14'	55°52'	5°56'	54°35'
	h m	h m	h m	h m	h m	h m	h m	h m	h m	h m	h m	h m	h m	h m
1	4 24	19 48	4 34	19 58	4 27	19 59	4 25	20 05	4 15	20 09	4 21	20 24	4 34	20 24
2	4 25	19 47	4 36	19 57	4 29	19 58	4 26	20 03	4 17	20 07	4 23	20 22	4 36	20 23
3	4 27	19 45	4 37	19 55	4 31	19 56	4 28	20 01	4 19	20 05	4 25	20 20	4 38	20 21
4	4 28	19 43	4 39	19 53	4 32	19 54	4 30	19 59	4 21	20 03	4 27	20 18	4 40	20 19
5	4 30	19 42	4 40	19 51	4 34	19 52	4 31	19 58	4 22	20 01	4 29	20 16	4 41	20 17
6	4 32	19 40	4 42	19 50	4 35	19 51	4 33	19 56	4 24	19 59	4 31	20 13	4 43	20 15
7	4 33	19 38	4 43	19 48	4 37	19 49	4 35	19 54	4 26	19 57	4 33	20 11	4 45	20 13
8	4 35	19 36	4 45	19 46	4 39	19 47	4 36	19 52	4 28	19 55	4 35	20 09	4 47	20 11
9	4 36	19 34	4 46	19 44	4 40	19 45	4 38	19 50	4 30	19 53	4 37	20 07	4 49	20 09
10	4 38	19 32	4 48	19 42	4 42	19 43	4 40	19 48	4 32	19 51	4 38	20 05	4 50	20 06
11	4 39	19 31	4 49	19 40	4 44	19 41	4 41	19 46	4 33	19 49	4 40	20 02	4 52	20 04
12	4 41	19 29	4 51	19 39	4 45	19 39	4 43	19 44	4 35	19 46	4 42	20 00	4 54	20 02
13	4 43	19 27	4 53	19 37	4 47	19 37	4 45	19 41	4 37	19 44	4 44	19 58	4 56	20 00
14	4 44	19 25	4 54	19 35	4 49	19 35	4 47	19 39	4 39	19 42	4 46	19 56	4 58	19 58
15	4 46	19 23	4 56	19 33	4 50	19 33	4 48	19 37	4 41	19 40	4 48	19 53	5 00	19 56
16	4 47	19 21	4 57	19 31	4 52	19 31	4 50	19 35	4 43	19 37	4 50	19 51	5 01	19 53
17	4 49	19 19	4 59	19 29	4 53	19 29	4 52	19 33	4 45	19 35	4 52	19 48	5 03	19 51
18	4 50	19 17	5 01	19 27	4 55	19 27	4 54	19 31	4 46	19 33	4 54	19 46	5 05	19 49
19	4 52	19 15	5 02	19 25	4 57	19 25	4 55	19 29	4 48	19 30	4 56	19 44	5 07	19 46
20	4 54	19 13	5 04	19 23	4 58	19 22	4 57	19 26	4 50	19 28	4 58	19 41	5 09	19 44
21	4 55	19 11	5 05	19 20	5 00	19 20	4 59	19 24	4 52	19 26	5 00	19 39	5 10	19 42
22	4 57	19 08	5 07	19 18	5 02	19 18	5 01	19 22	4 54	19 23	5 02	19 36	5 12	19 40
23	4 58	19 06	5 08	19 16	5 03	19 16	5 02	19 20	4 56	19 21	5 04	19 34	5 14	19 37
24	5 00	19 04	5 10	19 14	5 05	19 14	5 04	19 17	4 58	19 19	5 06	19 31	5 16	19 35
25	5 02	19 02	5 12	19 12	5 07	19 11	5 06	19 15	5 00	19 16	5 08	19 29	5 18	19 32
26	5 03	19 00	5 13	19 10	5 08	19 09	5 08	19 13	5 01	19 14	5 10	19 26	5 20	19 30
27	5 05	18 58	5 15	19 08	5 10	19 07	5 09	19 10	5 03	19 11	5 12	19 24	5 21	19 28
28	5 06	18 56	5 16	19 05	5 12	19 05	5 11	19 08	5 05	19 09	5 14	19 21	5 23	19 25
29	5 08	18 53	5 18	19 03	5 13	19 02	5 13	19 06	5 07	19 06	5 15	19 19	5 25	19 23
30	5 10	18 51	5 20	19 01	5 15	19 00	5 15	19 03	5 09	19 04	5 17	19 16	5 27	19 20
31	5 11	18 49	5 21	18 59	5 17	18 58	5 16	19 01	5 11	19 01	5 19	19 14	5 29	19 18

JUPITER

Day	RA	Dec.	Transit	5° high	
				52°	56°
	h m	° '	h m	h m	h m
1	21 23.4	−16 18	0 45	4 38	4 18
11	21 18.3	−16 43	0 00	3 51	3 30
21	21 13.2	−17 07	23 12	3 04	2 42
31	21 08.5	−17 29	22 28	2 17	1 55

Diameters – equatorial 49″ polar 46″

SATURN

Day	RA	Dec.	Transit	5° high	
				52°	56°
	h m	° '	h m	h m	h m
1	1 19.1	+ 5 35	4 40	22 41	22 39
11	1 18.9	+ 5 31	4 00	22 02	22 00
21	1 18.0	+ 5 23	3 20	21 22	21 21
31	1 16.6	+ 5 12	2 39	20 42	20 41

Diameters – equatorial 19″ polar 17″
Rings – major axis 43″ minor axis 9″

URANUS

Day	RA	Dec.	Transit	10° high	
				52°	56°
	h m	° '	h m	h m	h m
1	20 36.7	−19 15	23 54	2 45	2 06
11	20 35.1	−19 21	23 13	2 03	1 24
21	20 33.5	−19 26	22 32	1 21	0 42
31	20 32.1	−19 31	21 52	0 40	0 00

Diameter 4″

NEPTUNE

Day	RA	Dec.	Transit	10° high	
				52°	56°
	h m	° '	h m	h m	h m
1	20 01.2	−20 06	23 19	2 01	1 19
11	20 00.1	−20 09	22 38	1 20	0 38
21	19 59.1	−20 12	21 58	0 40	23 53
31	19 58.3	−20 15	21 18	23 55	23 12

Diameter 2″

September 1997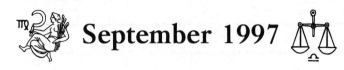

NINTH MONTH, 30 DAYS. *Septem* (seven), seventh month of Roman pre-Julian calendar

1	*Monday*	Amilcare Ponchielli b. 1834. Siegfried Sassoon d. 1967	*week* 35 *day* 244
2	*Tuesday*	Thomas Telford d. 1834. Frederick Soddy b. 1877	245
3	*Wednesday*	✗Battle of Dunbar 1650. Oliver Cromwell d. 1658	246
4	*Thursday*	Darius Milhaud b. 1892. Albert Schweitzer d. 1965	247
5	*Friday*	Jesse James b. 1847. Arthur Koestler b. 1905	248
6	*Saturday*	Marquis de Lafayette b. 1757. Austin Reed b. 1873	249
7	*Sunday*	**16th S. after Pentecost/15th S. after Trinity**	*week* 36 *day* 250
8	*Monday*	**Blessed Virgin Mary.** Antonin Dvořák b. 1841	251
9	*Tuesday*	Capt. William Bligh b. 1754. Mao Tse-tung d. 1976	252
10	*Wednesday*	Treaty of St Germain signed 1919. Arnold Palmer b. 1929	253
11	*Thursday*	✗Battle of Malplaquet 1709. David Ricardo d. 1823	254
12	*Friday*	Jean-Philippe Rameau d. 1764. Marshal von Blücher d. 1819	255
13	*Saturday*	Andrea Mantegna d. 1506. Leopold Stokowski d. 1977	256
14	*Sunday*	**17th S. after Pentecost/16th S. after Trinity**	*week* 37 *day* 257
15	*Monday*	Prince Henry of Wales b. 1984. Battle of Britain Day	258
16	*Tuesday*	Gabriel Fahrenheit d. 1736. John McCormack d. 1945	259
17	*Wednesday*	Comte de Vigny d. 1863. Fox Talbot d. 1877	260
18	*Thursday*	Dr Samuel Johnson d. 1709. Sean O'Casey d. 1964	261
19	*Friday*	Sir William Golding b. 1911. Sir Geraint Evans d. 1992	262
20	*Saturday*	✗Battle of the Alma 1854. Jean Sibelius d. 1957	263
21	*Sunday*	**St Matthew. 18th S. after Pentecost/17th S. after Trinity**	*week* 38 *day* 264
22	*Monday*	Michael Faraday b. 1791. Irving Berlin d. 1989	265
23	*Tuesday*	Vincenzo Bellini d. 1835. Baroness Orczy b. 1865	266
24	*Wednesday*	George Cross introduced 1940. Dame Isobel Baillie d. 1983	267
25	*Thursday*	William Faulkner b. 1897. Erich Maria Remarque d. 1970	268
26	*Friday*	Daniel Boone d. 1820. Charles Bradlaugh b. 1833	269
27	*Saturday*	Edgar Degas d. 1917. Adelina Patti d. 1919	270
28	*Sunday*	**19th S. after Pentecost/18th S. after Trinity**	*week* 39 *day* 271
29	*Monday*	**St Michael and All Angels.** Lord Nelson b. 1758	272
30	*Tuesday*	Truman Capote b. 1924. Storm Jameson d. 1986	273

ASTRONOMICAL PHENOMENA

d	h	
1	19	Mercury in conjunction with Moon. Mercury 3° S.
2	00	Partial eclipse of Sun (*see* page 66)
5	15	Venus in conjunction with Moon. Venus 3° S.
7	13	Mars in conjunction with Moon. Mars 5° S.
10	02	Mercury at stationary point
14	02	Jupiter in conjunction with Moon. Jupiter 4° S.
16	19	Total eclipse of Moon (*see* page 66)
16	22	Mercury at geatest elongation W.18°
18	10	Saturn in conjunction with Moon. Saturn 0°.2 S.
23	00	Sun's longitude 180° ♎
30	18	Mercury in conjunction with Moon. Mercury 1° N.

MINIMA OF ALGOL

d	h	d	h	d	h
2	05.5	13	16.8	25	04.0
5	02.3	16	13.6	28	00.8
7	23.1	19	10.4	30	21.6
10	19.9	22	07.2		

CONSTELLATIONS

The following constellations are near the meridian at

	d	h		d	h
August	1	24	September	15	21
August	16	23	October	1	20
September	1	22	October	16	19

Draco, Cepheus, Lyra, Cygnus, Vulpecula, Sagitta, Delphinus, Equuleus, Aquila, Aquarius and Capricornus

THE MOON

Phases, Apsides and Node	d	h	m
● New Moon	1	23	52
☽ First Quarter	10	01	31
○ Full Moon	16	18	50
☾ Last Quarter	23	13	35
Apogee (406,476 km)	2	21	33
Perigee (356,964 km)	16	15	28
Apogee (406,323 km)	29	23	44

Mean longitude of ascending node on September 1, 170°

THE SUN   s.d. 15'.9

Day	Right Ascension	Dec.	Equation of time	Rise 52°	Rise 56°	Transit	Set 52°	Set 56°	Sidereal time	Transit of First Point of Aries
	h m s	° '	m s	h m	h m	h m	h m	h m	h m s	h m s
1	10 40 53	+8 21	−0 06	5 12	5 04	12 00	18 47	18 54	22 40 47	1 19 00
2	10 44 31	+7 59	+0 13	5 13	5 06	12 00	18 45	18 52	22 44 43	1 15 04
3	10 48 08	+7 37	+0 32	5 15	5 08	11 59	18 43	18 49	22 48 40	1 11 08
4	10 51 45	+7 15	+0 52	5 16	5 10	11 59	18 40	18 47	22 52 37	1 07 12
5	10 55 22	+6 53	+1 11	5 18	5 12	11 59	18 38	18 44	22 56 33	1 03 16
6	10 58 58	+6 30	+1 31	5 20	5 14	11 58	18 36	18 41	23 00 30	0 59 21
7	11 02 35	+6 08	+1 52	5 21	5 16	11 58	18 33	18 39	23 04 26	0 55 25
8	11 06 11	+5 46	+2 12	5 23	5 18	11 58	18 31	18 36	23 08 23	0 51 29
9	11 09 47	+5 23	+2 33	5 25	5 20	11 57	18 29	18 34	23 12 19	0 47 33
10	11 13 22	+5 00	+2 54	5 26	5 22	11 57	18 27	18 31	23 16 16	0 43 37
11	11 16 58	+4 38	+3 15	5 28	5 24	11 57	18 24	18 28	23 20 12	0 39 41
12	11 20 33	+4 15	+3 36	5 29	5 26	11 56	18 22	18 26	23 24 09	0 35 45
13	11 24 09	+3 52	+3 57	5 31	5 27	11 56	18 20	18 23	23 28 06	0 31 49
14	11 27 44	+3 29	+4 18	5 33	5 29	11 56	18 17	18 20	23 32 02	0 27 53
15	11 31 19	+3 06	+4 40	5 34	5 31	11 55	18 15	18 18	23 35 59	0 23 57
16	11 34 54	+2 43	+5 01	5 36	5 33	11 55	18 13	18 15	23 39 55	0 20 02
17	11 38 29	+2 20	+5 23	5 38	5 35	11 54	18 10	18 12	23 43 52	0 16 06
18	11 42 04	+1 56	+5 44	5 39	5 37	11 54	18 08	18 10	23 47 48	0 12 10
19	11 45 39	+1 33	+6 05	5 41	5 39	11 54	18 05	18 07	23 51 45	0 08 14
20	11 49 14	+1 10	+6 27	5 43	5 41	11 53	18 03	18 04	23 55 41	0 04 18
21	11 52 50	+0 47	+6 48	5 44	5 43	11 53	18 01	18 02	23 59 38	{ 0 00 22 / 23 56 26
22	11 56 25	+0 23	+7 09	5 46	5 45	11 53	17 58	17 59	0 03 35	23 52 30
23	12 00 00	0 00	+7 31	5 47	5 47	11 52	17 56	17 56	0 07 31	23 48 34
24	12 03 36	−0 23	+7 52	5 49	5 49	11 52	17 54	17 54	0 11 28	23 44 38
25	12 07 12	−0 47	+8 12	5 51	5 51	11 52	17 51	17 51	0 15 24	23 40 42
26	12 10 48	−1 10	+8 33	5 52	5 53	11 51	17 49	17 49	0 19 21	23 36 47
27	12 14 24	−1 34	+8 53	5 54	5 55	11 51	17 47	17 46	0 23 17	23 32 51
28	12 18 00	−1 57	+9 14	5 56	5 57	11 51	17 44	17 43	0 27 14	23 28 55
29	12 21 37	−2 20	+9 34	5 57	5 59	11 50	17 42	17 41	0 31 10	23 24 59
30	12 25 13	−2 44	+9 53	5 59	6 01	11 50	17 40	17 38	0 35 07	23 21 03

DURATION OF TWILIGHT (in minutes)

Latitude	52°	56°	52°	56°	52°	56°	52°	56°
	1 September		11 September		21 September		30 September	
Civil	35	39	34	38	34	37	34	37
Nautical	79	89	76	84	74	82	73	80
Astronomical	127	146	120	135	115	129	113	126

THE NIGHT SKY

Mercury is too close to the Sun to be observed early in the month but after the first twelve days of the month it is visible low above the eastern horizon about the beginning of morning civil twilight. Mercury is then visible until almost the end of the month. This is the most favourable morning apparition of the year for observers in the northern hemisphere. During its period of visibility its magnitude ranges from +0.8 to −1.2.

Venus, magnitude −4.1, is a brilliant object in the early evening sky but only visible for about half an hour after sunset, low above the south-western horizon.

Mars is unsuitably placed for observation.

Jupiter continues to be visible as a brilliant object in the night sky, magnitude −2.7, though by the end of the month it is no longer visible after midnight. On the evening of the 13th the waxing gibbous Moon will be seen above and to the right of the planet.

Saturn continues to be visible in the southern skies during the greater part of the night, magnitude +0.3. On the morning of the 18th the gibbous Moon will be seen approaching the planet.

Zodiacal Light. The morning cone may be seen stretching up from the eastern horizon before the beginning of twilight from the beginning of the month until the 15th.

THE MOON

Day	RA	Dec.	Hor. par.	Semi- diam.	Sun's co- long.	PA of Bright Limb	Phase	Age	Rise 52°	Rise 56°	Transit	Set 52°	Set 56°
	h m	°	′	′	°	°	%	d	h m	h m	h m	h m	h m
1	9 57	+10.4	54.1	14.7	257	100	1	28.7	4 34	4 26	11 37	18 29	18 36
2	10 43	+ 7.1	54.0	14.7	269	19	0	0.0	5 36	5 31	12 20	18 53	18 56
3	11 29	+ 3.6	53.9	14.7	281	292	1	1.0	6 39	6 37	13 02	19 15	19 16
4	12 14	− 0.1	54.0	14.7	294	290	4	2.0	7 42	7 43	13 45	19 38	19 35
5	12 59	− 3.8	54.2	14.8	306	289	8	3.0	8 44	8 49	14 27	20 01	19 56
6	13 45	− 7.4	54.4	14.8	318	288	14	4.0	9 48	9 55	15 11	20 27	20 18
7	14 32	−10.7	54.8	14.9	330	285	21	5.0	10 51	11 02	15 57	20 55	20 43
8	15 20	−13.6	55.3	15.1	342	283	30	6.0	11 54	12 08	16 44	21 29	21 14
9	16 11	−15.9	56.0	15.3	355	279	39	7.0	12 57	13 13	17 34	22 08	21 51
10	17 04	−17.5	56.8	15.5	7	275	49	8.0	13 57	14 14	18 27	22 56	22 38
11	17 59	−18.2	57.6	15.7	19	271	60	9.0	14 52	15 10	19 22	23 53	23 35
12	18 56	−17.9	58.6	16.0	31	267	70	10.0	15 42	15 58	20 18	—	—
13	19 55	−16.5	59.5	16.2	43	262	80	11.0	16 26	16 40	21 16	0 59	0 43
14	20 54	−14.1	60.3	16.4	56	258	89	12.0	17 04	17 15	22 13	2 13	2 00
15	21 53	−10.6	61.0	16.6	68	255	95	13.0	17 38	17 45	23 11	3 32	3 23
16	22 52	− 6.4	61.4	16.7	80	251	99	14.0	18 10	18 12	—	4 54	4 49
17	23 51	− 1.7	61.4	16.7	92	79	100	15.0	18 40	18 38	0 07	6 17	6 17
18	0 49	+ 3.0	61.1	16.7	104	74	98	16.0	19 10	19 05	1 03	7 40	7 44
19	1 46	+ 7.5	60.5	16.5	116	74	93	17.0	19 43	19 34	1 59	9 00	9 08
20	2 43	+11.4	59.7	16.3	129	77	85	18.0	20 18	20 05	2 54	10 17	10 29
21	3 40	+14.6	58.8	16.0	141	80	76	19.0	20 58	20 42	3 49	11 29	11 44
22	4 36	+16.8	57.9	15.8	153	84	66	20.0	21 42	21 25	4 43	12 34	12 51
23	5 32	+18.0	56.9	15.5	165	88	56	21.0	22 32	22 15	5 36	13 31	13 49
24	6 26	+18.2	56.1	15.3	177	92	46	22.0	23 27	23 10	6 27	14 20	14 38
25	7 18	+17.5	55.4	15.1	190	96	36	23.0	—	—	7 17	15 02	15 17
26	8 09	+16.1	54.9	14.9	202	100	27	24.0	0 25	0 10	8 05	15 37	15 50
27	8 58	+13.9	54.5	14.8	214	104	19	25.0	1 25	1 12	8 51	16 07	16 18
28	9 45	+11.1	54.2	14.8	226	107	12	26.0	2 27	2 17	9 35	16 34	16 41
29	10 32	+ 8.0	54.0	14.7	238	109	6	27.0	3 29	3 22	10 18	16 58	17 02
30	11 17	+ 4.5	54.0	14.7	251	113	3	28.0	4 31	4 28	11 01	17 21	17 22

MERCURY

Day	RA	Dec.	Diam.	Phase	Transit	5° high 52°	5° high 56°
	h m	°	″	%	h m	h m	h m
1	10 32	+ 5.0	11	1	11 48	5 56	5 55
3	10 26	+ 6.1	10	2	11 34	5 37	5 35
5	10 21	+ 7.2	10	5	11 22	5 19	5 16
7	10 18	+ 8.1	10	9	11 11	5 03	4 59
9	10 17	+ 9.0	9	15	11 02	4 50	4 46
11	10 17	+ 9.6	9	22	10 56	4 40	4 35
13	10 21	+ 9.9	8	30	10 52	4 34	4 29
15	10 26	+10.0	8	39	10 50	4 31	4 26
17	10 33	+ 9.8	7	48	10 49	4 32	4 27
19	10 42	+ 9.3	7	57	10 51	4 35	4 31
21	10 52	+ 8.6	6	66	10 54	4 42	4 38
23	11 04	+ 7.7	6	73	10 57	4 50	4 47
25	11 16	+ 6.6	6	80	11 02	5 00	4 58
27	11 29	+ 5.4	6	85	11 07	5 12	5 11
29	11 42	+ 4.0	5	90	11 12	5 24	5 24
31	11 55	+ 2.6	5	93	11 17	5 36	5 38

VENUS

Day	RA	Dec.	Diam.	Phase	Transit	5° high 52°	5° high 56°
	h m	°	″	%	h m	h m	h m
1	13 03	− 6.7	14	75	14 22	19 12	19 02
6	13 24	− 9.2	15	74	14 24	19 00	18 48
11	13 46	−11.6	15	72	14 26	18 48	18 33
16	14 08	−13.9	16	70	14 28	18 36	18 18
21	14 30	−16.1	16	69	14 31	18 24	18 03
26	14 52	−18.2	17	67	14 33	18 12	17 48
31	15 15	−20.1	18	65	14 36	18 02	17 34

MARS

Day	RA	Dec.	Diam.	Phase	Transit	5° high 52°	5° high 56°
1	14 34	−15.9	6	90	15 52	19 47	19 27
6	14 47	−17.0	6	90	15 45	19 34	19 12
11	15 00	−18.0	6	90	15 39	19 20	18 57
16	15 14	−19.0	5	91	15 33	19 07	18 42
21	15 28	−19.9	5	91	15 27	18 55	18 28
26	15 42	−20.7	5	91	15 22	18 43	18 14
31	15 56	−21.5	5	92	15 17	18 32	18 01

SUNRISE AND SUNSET

	London		Bristol		Birmingham		Manchester		Newcastle		Glasgow		Belfast	
	0°05'	51°30'	2°35'	51°28'	1°55'	52°28'	2°15'	53°28'	1°37'	54°59'	4°14'	55°52'	5°56'	54°35'
	h m	h m	h m	h m	h m	h m	h m	h m	h m	h m	h m	h m	h m	h m
1	5 13	18 47	5 23	18 57	5 18	18 56	5 18	18 59	5 13	18 59	5 21	19 11	5 31	19 15
2	5 14	18 44	5 24	18 54	5 20	18 53	5 20	18 56	5 14	18 56	5 23	19 09	5 33	19 13
3	5 16	18 42	5 26	18 52	5 22	18 51	5 21	18 54	5 16	18 54	5 25	19 06	5 34	19 10
4	5 18	18 40	5 28	18 50	5 23	18 49	5 23	18 52	5 18	18 51	5 27	19 03	5 36	19 08
5	5 19	18 38	5 29	18 48	5 25	18 46	5 25	18 49	5 20	18 49	5 29	19 01	5 38	19 06
6	5 21	18 35	5 31	18 45	5 27	18 44	5 27	18 47	5 22	18 46	5 31	18 58	5 40	19 03
7	5 22	18 33	5 32	18 43	5 28	18 42	5 28	18 44	5 24	18 44	5 33	18 56	5 42	19 01
8	5 24	18 31	5 34	18 41	5 30	18 39	5 30	18 42	5 26	18 41	5 35	18 53	5 43	18 58
9	5 25	18 29	5 36	18 39	5 32	18 37	5 32	18 39	5 28	18 39	5 37	18 50	5 45	18 55
10	5 27	18 26	5 37	18 36	5 33	18 35	5 34	18 37	5 29	18 36	5 39	18 48	5 47	18 53
11	5 29	18 24	5 39	18 34	5 35	18 32	5 35	18 35	5 31	18 34	5 41	18 45	5 49	18 50
12	5 30	18 22	5 40	18 32	5 37	18 30	5 37	18 32	5 33	18 31	5 43	18 42	5 51	18 48
13	5 32	18 19	5 42	18 29	5 38	18 28	5 39	18 30	5 35	18 29	5 45	18 40	5 53	18 45
14	5 33	18 17	5 43	18 27	5 40	18 25	5 41	18 27	5 37	18 26	5 47	18 37	5 54	18 43
15	5 35	18 15	5 45	18 25	5 42	18 23	5 42	18 25	5 39	18 23	5 48	18 35	5 56	18 40
16	5 37	18 13	5 47	18 23	5 43	18 20	5 44	18 22	5 41	18 21	5 50	18 32	5 58	18 38
17	5 38	18 10	5 48	18 20	5 45	18 18	5 46	18 20	5 42	18 18	5 52	18 29	6 00	18 35
18	5 40	18 08	5 50	18 18	5 47	18 16	5 48	18 17	5 44	18 16	5 54	18 27	6 02	18 33
19	5 41	18 06	5 51	18 16	5 48	18 13	5 49	18 15	5 46	18 13	5 56	18 24	6 04	18 30
20	5 43	18 03	5 53	18 13	5 50	18 11	5 51	18 13	5 48	18 11	5 58	18 21	6 05	18 28
21	5 45	18 01	5 55	18 11	5 52	18 09	5 53	18 10	5 50	18 08	6 00	18 19	6 07	18 25
22	5 46	17 59	5 56	18 09	5 53	18 06	5 55	18 08	5 52	18 05	6 02	18 16	6 09	18 23
23	5 48	17 56	5 58	18 06	5 55	18 04	5 56	18 05	5 54	18 03	6 04	18 13	6 11	18 20
24	5 49	17 54	5 59	18 04	5 57	18 01	5 58	18 03	5 55	18 00	6 06	18 11	6 13	18 17
25	5 51	17 52	6 01	18 02	5 58	17 59	6 00	18 00	5 57	17 58	6 08	18 08	6 15	18 15
26	5 53	17 50	6 03	18 00	6 00	17 57	6 02	17 58	5 59	17 55	6 10	18 05	6 17	18 12
27	5 54	17 47	6 04	17 57	6 02	17 54	6 03	17 55	6 01	17 53	6 12	18 03	6 18	18 10
28	5 56	17 45	6 06	17 55	6 04	17 52	6 05	17 53	6 03	17 50	6 14	18 00	6 20	18 07
29	5 58	17 43	6 08	17 53	6 05	17 50	6 07	17 51	6 05	17 47	6 16	17 58	6 22	18 05
30	5 59	17 40	6 09	17 50	6 07	17 47	6 09	17 48	6 07	17 45	6 18	17 55	6 24	18 02

JUPITER

Day	RA		Dec.		Transit		5° high	
							52°	56°
	h	m	°	'	h	m	h m	h m
1	21	08.1	−17	31	22	23	2 13	1 50
11	21	04.2	−17	47	21	40	1 28	1 05
21	21	01.3	−17	59	20	58	0 44	0 21
31	20	59.7	−18	05	20	17	0 03	23 35

Diameters – equatorial 46″ polar 44″

SATURN

Day	RA		Dec.		Transit		5° high	
							52°	56°
	h	m	°	'	h	m	h m	h m
1	1	16.4	+ 5	11	2	35	20 38	20 37
11	1	14.4	+ 4	56	1	54	19 58	19 57
21	1	12.0	+ 4	40	1	12	19 18	19 17
31	1	09.2	+ 4	22	0	30	18 37	18 37

Diameters – equatorial 20″ polar 18″
Rings – major axis 44″ minor axis 8″

URANUS

Day	RA		Dec.		Transit		10° high	
							52°	56°
	h	m	°	'	h	m	h m	h m
1	20	32.0	−19	32	21	48	0 36	23 52
11	20	30.8	−19	36	21	07	23 50	23 11
21	20	29.9	−19	39	20	27	23 10	22 30
31	20	29.3	−19	41	19	47	22 30	21 49

Diameter 4″

NEPTUNE

Day	RA		Dec.		Transit		10° high	
							52°	56°
	h	m	°	'	h	m	h m	h m
1	19	58.2	−20	15	21	14	23 51	23 08
11	19	57.5	−20	17	20	34	23 11	22 27
21	19	57.0	−20	19	19	54	22 31	21 47
31	19	56.7	−20	20	19	14	21 51	21 07

Diameter 2″

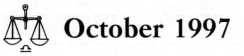 # October 1997

TENTH MONTH, 31 DAYS. *Octo* (eight), eighth month of Roman pre-Julian calendar

1	Wednesday	*Michaelmas Law Sittings begin.* Stanley Holloway b. 1890	*week 39 day* 274
2	Thursday	JEWISH NEW YEAR (5758). Gen. von Hindenberg b. 1847	275
3	Friday	Sir Malcolm Sargent d. 1967. Jean Anouilh d. 1987	276
4	Saturday	*Sputnik I* launched 1957. Max Planck d. 1947	277
5	Sunday	**20th S. after Pentecost/19th S. after Trinity**	*week 40 day* 278
6	Monday	Charles Stewart Parnell d. 1891. Helen Wills-Moody b. 1905	279
7	Tuesday	Archbishop William Laud b. 1573. Marie Lloyd d. 1922	280
8	Wednesday	Henry Fielding d. 1754. Clement Attlee d. 1967	281
9	Thursday	John Lennon b. 1940. André Maurois d. 1967	282
10	Friday	Jean Watteau b. 1684. Viscount Nuffield b. 1877	283
11	Saturday	YOM KIPPUR. Anton Bruckner d. 1896	284
12	Sunday	**21st S. after Pentecost/20th S. after Trinity**	*week 41 day* 285
13	Monday	Joachim Murat d. 1815. Lady Thatcher b. 1925	286
14	Tuesday	George Grenville b. 1712. Eamon de Valera b. 1882	287
15	Wednesday	Friedrich Nietzsche b. 1844. Dr Marie Stopes b. 1880	288
16	Thursday	FEAST OF TABERNACLES begins. Earl of Cardigan b. 1797	289
17	Friday	Sir Philip Sidney d. 1586. Arthur Miller b. 1915	290
18	Saturday	**St Luke.** Viscount Palmerston d. 1865	291
19	Sunday	**22nd S. after Pentecost/21st S. after Trinity**	*week 42 day* 292
20	Monday	Sir Christopher Wren b. 1632. Jack Buchanan d. 1957	293
21	Tuesday	Samuel Taylor Coleridge b. 1772. Sir Georg Solti b. 1912	294
22	Wednesday	Paul Cézanne b. 1906. Pablo Casals d. 1973	295
23	Thursday	Earl of Derby d. 1869. Pélé b. 1940	296
24	Friday	Alessandro Scarlatti d. 1725. Franz Lehár d. 1948	297
25	Saturday	Lord Grenville b. 1759. George II d. 1760	298
26	Sunday	**9th S. before Christmas/22nd S. after Trinity**	*week 43 day* 299
27	Monday	Theodore Roosevelt b. 1858. Dylan Thomas b. 1914	300
28	Tuesday	**SS Simon and Jude.** John Locke b. 1704	301
29	Wednesday	James Boswell b. 1740. Wilfred Rhodes b. 1877	302
30	Thursday	R. B. Sheridan bapt. 1751. Ezra Pound b. 1885	303
31	Friday	Hallowmass Eve. Jan Vermeer b. 1632	304

ASTRONOMICAL PHENOMENA

d	h	
5	17	Venus in conjunction with Moon. Venus 7° S.
6	09	Mars in conjunction with Moon. Mars 6° S.
8	05	Jupiter at stationary point
9	01	Neptune at stationary point
10	04	Saturn at opposition
11	09	Jupiter in conjunction with Moon. Jupiter 4° S.
13	21	Mercury in superior conjunction
14	11	Uranus at stationary point
15	18	Saturn in conjunction with Moon. Saturn 0°.4 S.
23	09	Sun's longitude 210° ♏
26	12	Mars in conjunction with Venus. Mars 2° N.

MINIMA OF ALGOL

d	h	d	h	d	h
3	18.4	15	05.7	26	16.9
6	15.2	18	02.5	29	13.7
9	12.1	20	23.3		
12	08.9	23	20.1		

CONSTELLATIONS

The following constellations are near the meridian at

	d	h		d	h
September	1	24	October	16	21
September	15	23	November	1	20
October	1	22	November	15	19

Ursa Major (below the Pole), Cepheus, Cassiopeia, Cygnus, Lacerta, Andromeda, Pegasus, Capricornus, Aquarius and Piscis Austrinus

THE MOON

Phases, Apsides and Node		d	h	m
● New Moon		1	16	52
☽ First Quarter		9	12	22
○ Full Moon		16	03	46
☾ Last Quarter		23	04	48
● New Moon		31	10	01
Perigee (358,864 km)		15	02	09
Apogee (405,597 km)		27	09	12

Mean longitude of ascending node on October 1, 169°

THE SUN   s.d. 16′.1

Day	Right Ascension	Dec. −	Equation of time	Rise 52°	Rise 56°	Transit	Set 52°	Set 56°	Sidereal time	Transit of First Point of Aries
	h m s	° ′	m s	h m	h m	h m	h m	h m	h m s	h m s
1	12 28 51	3 07	+10 13	6 01	6 03	11 50	17 38	17 35	0 39 03	23 17 07
2	12 32 28	3 30	+10 32	6 02	6 05	11 49	17 35	17 33	0 43 00	23 13 11
3	12 36 06	3 53	+10 51	6 04	6 07	11 49	17 33	17 30	0 46 57	23 09 15
4	12 39 43	4 17	+11 10	6 06	6 09	11 49	17 31	17 27	0 50 53	23 05 19
5	12 43 22	4 40	+11 28	6 07	6 11	11 48	17 28	17 25	0 54 50	23 01 23
6	12 47 00	5 03	+11 46	6 09	6 13	11 48	17 26	17 22	0 58 46	22 57 27
7	12 50 40	5 26	+12 03	6 11	6 15	11 48	17 24	17 20	1 02 43	22 53 32
8	12 54 19	5 49	+12 20	6 13	6 17	11 48	17 22	17 17	1 06 39	22 49 36
9	12 57 59	6 12	+12 37	6 14	6 19	11 47	17 19	17 15	1 10 36	22 45 40
10	13 01 39	6 34	+12 53	6 16	6 21	11 47	17 17	17 12	1 14 32	22 41 44
11	13 05 20	6 57	+13 09	6 18	6 23	11 47	17 15	17 09	1 18 29	22 37 48
12	13 09 01	7 20	+13 25	6 19	6 25	11 46	17 13	17 07	1 22 26	22 33 52
13	13 12 43	7 42	+13 39	6 21	6 27	11 46	17 10	17 04	1 26 22	22 29 56
14	13 16 25	8 05	+13 54	6 23	6 29	11 46	17 08	17 02	1 30 19	22 26 00
15	13 20 07	8 27	+14 08	6 25	6 31	11 46	17 06	16 59	1 34 15	22 22 04
16	13 23 51	8 49	+14 21	6 26	6 33	11 46	17 04	16 57	1 38 12	22 18 08
17	13 27 34	9 11	+14 34	6 28	6 35	11 45	17 02	16 54	1 42 08	22 14 13
18	13 31 19	9 33	+14 46	6 30	6 37	11 45	17 00	16 52	1 46 05	22 10 17
19	13 35 04	9 55	+14 58	6 32	6 39	11 45	16 57	16 50	1 50 01	22 06 21
20	13 38 50	10 16	+15 08	6 33	6 42	11 45	16 55	16 47	1 53 58	22 02 25
21	13 42 36	10 38	+15 19	6 35	6 44	11 45	16 53	16 45	1 57 55	21 58 29
22	13 46 23	10 59	+15 28	6 37	6 46	11 44	16 51	16 42	2 01 51	21 54 33
23	13 50 11	11 20	+15 37	6 39	6 48	11 44	16 49	16 40	2 05 48	21 50 37
24	13 53 59	11 41	+15 45	6 40	6 50	11 44	16 47	16 38	2 09 44	21 46 41
25	13 57 48	12 02	+15 53	6 42	6 52	11 44	16 45	16 35	2 13 41	21 42 45
26	14 01 38	12 23	+15 59	6 44	6 54	11 44	16 43	16 33	2 17 37	21 38 49
27	14 05 28	12 43	+16 05	6 46	6 56	11 44	16 41	16 31	2 21 34	21 34 53
28	14 09 20	13 03	+16 11	6 48	6 58	11 44	16 39	16 28	2 25 30	21 30 58
29	14 13 12	13 23	+16 15	6 49	7 00	11 44	16 37	16 26	2 29 27	21 27 02
30	14 17 05	13 43	+16 19	6 51	7 03	11 44	16 35	16 24	2 33 24	21 23 06
31	14 20 58	14 03	+16 22	6 53	7 05	11 44	16 34	16 22	2 37 20	21 19 10

DURATION OF TWILIGHT (in minutes)

Latitude	52°	56°	52°	56°	52°	56°	52°	56°
	1 October		11 October		21 October		31 October	
Civil	34	37	34	37	34	38	36	40
Nautical	73	80	73	80	74	81	75	83
Astronomical	113	125	112	124	113	124	114	126

THE NIGHT SKY

Mercury is unsuitably placed for observation, superior conjunction occurring on the 13th.

Venus continues to be visible as a brilliant object in the early evenings, magnitude −4.2, low above the south-western horizon after sunset. Although not visible for long after sunset, this interval increases slightly during October so that by the end of the month Venus is visible for nearly an hour. On the early evening of the 5th the waxing crescent Moon will be seen about 7° above Venus.

Mars is too close to the Sun for observation.

Jupiter, magnitude −2.5, is a splendid evening object in the south-western sky in the evenings. On the evenings of the 10th and 11th the gibbous Moon will be seen in the vicinity of the planet.

Saturn, magnitude +0.2, reaches opposition on the 10th and is therefore visible throughout the hours of darkness. On the evening of the 15th the Full Moon will be seen a few degrees to the left of Saturn. Titan, Saturn's largest satellite is of magnitude +8.5, visible in small telescopes. The rings of Saturn present a beautiful spectacle to the observer, even with only a small telescope. However, the minor axis is only 8 arcseconds, as compared with Saturn's polar diameter of 18 arcseconds.

THE MOON

Day	RA	Dec.	Hor. par.	Semi-diam.	Sun's co-long.	PA of Bright Limb	Phase	Age	Rise 52°	Rise 56°	Transit	Set 52°	Set 56°
	h m	°	′	′	°	°	%	d	h m	h m	h m	h m	h m
1	12 02	+ 0.8	54.0	14.7	263	121	0	29.0	5 34	5 34	11 43	17 43	17 41
2	12 48	− 2.9	54.1	14.8	275	261	0	0.3	6 37	6 40	12 26	18 06	18 01
3	13 33	− 6.6	54.4	14.8	287	280	2	1.3	7 40	7 47	13 10	18 31	18 23
4	14 20	− 9.9	54.7	14.9	300	281	5	2.3	8 44	8 54	13 55	18 58	18 47
5	15 08	−13.0	55.0	15.0	312	280	10	3.3	9 47	10 00	14 41	19 30	19 16
6	15 58	−15.4	55.5	15.1	324	277	17	4.3	10 50	11 05	15 30	20 07	19 51
7	16 50	−17.2	56.1	15.3	336	274	25	5.3	11 50	12 07	16 21	20 51	20 33
8	17 44	−18.2	56.7	15.5	348	270	34	6.3	12 45	13 04	17 14	21 43	21 25
9	18 39	−18.2	57.5	15.7	1	266	45	7.3	13 36	13 53	18 08	22 43	22 27
10	19 36	−17.2	58.2	15.9	13	261	55	8.3	14 20	14 36	19 03	23 52	23 37
11	20 33	−15.1	59.1	16.1	25	257	66	9.3	14 59	15 12	19 59	—	—
12	21 30	−12.1	59.8	16.3	37	253	77	10.3	15 34	15 43	20 54	1 06	0 55
13	22 27	− 8.3	60.5	16.5	49	250	86	11.3	16 06	16 10	21 49	2 24	2 17
14	23 25	− 3.9	60.9	16.6	61	247	93	12.3	16 36	16 36	22 45	3 45	3 42
15	0 22	+ 0.8	61.1	16.6	74	242	98	13.3	17 06	17 02	23 41	5 07	5 09
16	1 20	+ 5.5	61.0	16.6	86	197	100	14.3	17 37	17 30	—	6 30	6 35
17	2 18	+ 9.8	60.5	16.5	98	88	99	15.3	18 11	18 00	0 37	7 50	8 00
18	3 16	+13.4	59.9	16.3	110	84	95	16.3	18 50	18 35	1 33	9 07	9 20
19	4 14	+16.1	59.0	16.1	122	86	89	17.3	19 33	19 17	2 29	10 18	10 34
20	5 11	+17.8	58.1	15.8	134	89	81	18.3	20 22	20 05	3 25	11 21	11 38
21	6 07	+18.4	57.1	15.6	147	93	72	19.3	21 17	20 59	4 19	12 15	12 32
22	7 02	+18.0	56.3	15.3	159	97	62	20.3	22 15	21 59	5 11	13 00	13 17
23	7 54	+16.7	55.5	15.1	171	101	52	21.3	23 15	23 02	6 00	13 38	13 52
24	8 44	+14.7	54.9	15.0	183	105	42	22.3	—	—	6 47	14 10	14 22
25	9 33	+12.0	54.5	14.8	195	108	33	23.3	0 17	0 06	7 33	14 38	14 47
26	10 19	+ 8.9	54.2	14.8	207	110	24	24.3	1 19	1 12	8 16	15 03	15 08
27	11 05	+ 5.5	54.1	14.7	220	112	17	25.3	2 22	2 17	8 59	15 26	15 28
28	11 50	+ 1.9	54.1	14.7	232	114	10	26.3	3 24	3 23	9 41	15 48	15 47
29	12 35	− 1.9	54.2	14.8	244	117	5	27.3	4 27	4 30	10 24	16 11	16 07
30	13 21	− 5.6	54.4	14.8	256	121	2	28.3	5 31	5 37	11 07	16 35	16 28
31	14 08	− 9.1	54.8	14.9	268	147	0	29.3	6 35	6 44	11 52	17 01	16 51

MERCURY

Day	RA	Dec.	Diam.	Phase	Transit	5° high 52°	5° high 56°
	h m	°	″	%	h m	h m	h m
1	11 55	+ 2.6	5	93	11 17	5 36	5 38
3	12 08	+ 1.1	5	95	11 22	5 49	5 52
5	12 21	− 0.4	5	97	11 27	6 02	6 06
7	12 34	− 1.9	5	98	11 32	6 16	6 21
9	12 47	− 3.5	5	99	11 37	6 29	6 35
11	12 59	− 5.0	5	100	11 42	6 42	6 49
13	13 12	− 6.5	5	100	11 47	6 54	7 04
15	13 24	− 8.0	5	100	11 51	7 07	7 18
17	13 37	− 9.4	5	100	11 56	7 20	7 32
19	13 49	−10.8	5	100	12 00	16 26	16 13
21	14 01	−12.1	5	99	12 04	16 23	16 07
23	14 13	−13.4	5	99	12 09	16 19	16 02
25	14 26	−14.7	5	98	12 13	16 15	15 57
27	14 38	−15.9	5	97	12 17	16 12	15 51
29	14 50	−17.1	5	97	12 22	16 08	15 46
31	15 02	−18.2	5	96	12 26	16 05	15 41

VENUS

Day	RA	Dec.	Diam.	Phase	Transit	5° high 52°	5° high 56°
	h m	°	″	%	h m	h m	h m
1	15 15	−20.1	18	65	14 36	18 02	17 34
6	15 38	−21.8	18	63	14 40	17 52	17 20
11	16 01	−23.2	19	61	14 43	17 43	17 06
16	16 25	−24.5	20	59	14 47	17 35	16 54
21	16 49	−25.5	21	57	14 51	17 29	16 43
26	17 12	−26.3	22	55	14 55	17 25	16 34
31	17 35	−26.8	23	53	14 59	17 24	16 29

MARS

Day	RA	Dec.	Diam.	Phase	Transit	5° high 52°	5° high 56°
1	15 56	−21.5	5	92	15 17	18 32	18 01
6	16 11	−22.2	5	92	15 12	18 21	17 48
11	16 26	−22.8	5	92	15 07	18 11	17 36
16	16 42	−23.4	5	92	15 03	18 02	17 25
21	16 58	−23.9	5	93	14 59	17 54	17 16
26	17 14	−24.2	5	93	14 55	17 47	17 07
31	17 30	−24.5	5	93	14 52	17 41	17 00

SUNRISE AND SUNSET

	London		Bristol		Birmingham		Manchester		Newcastle		Glasgow		Belfast	
	0°05′	51°30′	2°35′	51°28′	1°55′	52°28′	2°15′	53°28′	1°37′	54°59′	4°14′	55°52′	5°56′	54°35′
	h m	h m	h m	h m	h m	h m	h m	h m	h m	h m	h m	h m	h m	h m
1	6 01	17 38	6 11	17 48	6 09	17 45	6 10	17 46	6 09	17 42	6 20	17 52	6 26	18 00
2	6 02	17 36	6 12	17 46	6 10	17 43	6 12	17 43	6 11	17 40	6 22	17 50	6 28	17 57
3	6 04	17 34	6 14	17 44	6 12	17 40	6 14	17 41	6 13	17 37	6 24	17 47	6 30	17 55
4	6 06	17 31	6 16	17 41	6 14	17 38	6 16	17 39	6 14	17 35	6 26	17 45	6 31	17 52
5	6 07	17 29	6 17	17 39	6 16	17 36	6 18	17 36	6 16	17 32	6 28	17 42	6 33	17 50
6	6 09	17 27	6 19	17 37	6 17	17 33	6 19	17 34	6 18	17 30	6 30	17 39	6 35	17 47
7	6 11	17 25	6 21	17 35	6 19	17 31	6 21	17 31	6 20	17 27	6 32	17 37	6 37	17 45
8	6 12	17 22	6 22	17 32	6 21	17 29	6 23	17 29	6 22	17 25	6 34	17 34	6 39	17 42
9	6 14	17 20	6 24	17 30	6 22	17 26	6 25	17 27	6 24	17 22	6 36	17 32	6 41	17 40
10	6 16	17 18	6 26	17 28	6 24	17 24	6 27	17 24	6 26	17 20	6 38	17 29	6 43	17 38
11	6 17	17 16	6 27	17 26	6 26	17 22	6 29	17 22	6 28	17 17	6 40	17 27	6 45	17 35
12	6 19	17 14	6 29	17 24	6 28	17 20	6 30	17 20	6 30	17 15	6 42	17 24	6 47	17 33
13	6 21	17 11	6 31	17 21	6 29	17 17	6 32	17 17	6 32	17 13	6 44	17 22	6 49	17 30
14	6 22	17 09	6 32	17 19	6 31	17 15	6 34	17 15	6 34	17 10	6 46	17 19	6 50	17 28
15	6 24	17 07	6 34	17 17	6 33	17 13	6 36	17 13	6 36	17 08	6 48	17 17	6 52	17 26
16	6 26	17 05	6 36	17 15	6 35	17 11	6 38	17 10	6 38	17 05	6 50	17 14	6 54	17 23
17	6 28	17 03	6 38	17 13	6 37	17 09	6 40	17 08	6 40	17 03	6 52	17 12	6 56	17 21
18	6 29	17 01	6 39	17 11	6 38	17 06	6 41	17 06	6 42	17 01	6 54	17 09	6 58	17 19
19	6 31	16 59	6 41	17 09	6 40	17 04	6 43	17 04	6 44	16 58	6 56	17 07	7 00	17 16
20	6 33	16 57	6 43	17 07	6 42	17 02	6 45	17 02	6 46	16 56	6 58	17 04	7 02	17 14
21	6 34	16 55	6 44	17 05	6 44	17 00	6 47	16 59	6 48	16 53	7 00	17 02	7 04	17 12
22	6 36	16 53	6 46	17 03	6 45	16 58	6 49	16 57	6 50	16 51	7 02	17 00	7 06	17 09
23	6 38	16 51	6 48	17 01	6 47	16 56	6 51	16 55	6 52	16 49	7 04	16 57	7 08	17 07
24	6 40	16 49	6 50	16 59	6 49	16 54	6 53	16 53	6 54	16 47	7 07	16 55	7 10	17 05
25	6 41	16 47	6 51	16 57	6 51	16 52	6 55	16 51	6 56	16 44	7 09	16 52	7 12	17 03
26	6 43	16 45	6 53	16 55	6 53	16 50	6 56	16 49	6 58	16 42	7 11	16 50	7 14	17 00
27	6 45	16 43	6 55	16 53	6 55	16 48	6 58	16 47	7 00	16 40	7 13	16 48	7 16	16 58
28	6 47	16 41	6 57	16 51	6 56	16 46	7 00	16 44	7 02	16 38	7 15	16 46	7 18	16 56
29	6 48	16 39	6 58	16 49	6 58	16 44	7 02	16 42	7 04	16 36	7 17	16 43	7 20	16 54
30	6 50	16 37	7 00	16 47	7 00	16 42	7 04	16 40	7 06	16 33	7 19	16 41	7 22	16 52
31	6 52	16 35	7 02	16 45	7 02	16 40	7 06	16 38	7 08	16 31	7 21	16 39	7 24	16 50

JUPITER

Day	RA	Dec.	Transit	5° high	
				52°	56°
	h m	° ′	h m	h m	h m
1	20 59.7	− 18 05	20 17	0 03	23 35
11	20 59.4	− 18 06	19 38	23 19	22 56
21	21 00.4	− 18 00	19 00	22 41	22 18
31	21 02.7	− 17 50	18 23	22 06	21 43

Diameters – equatorial 43″ polar 40″

SATURN

Day	RA	Dec.	Transit	5° high	
				52°	56°
	h m	° ′	h m	h m	h m
1	1 09.2	+ 4 22	0 30	6 19	6 19
11	1 06.3	+ 4 04	23 44	5 35	5 35
21	1 03.4	+ 3 46	23 02	4 52	4 51
31	1 00.7	+ 3 30	22 19	4 08	4 08

Diameters – equatorial 20″ polar 18″
Rings – major axis 45″ minor axis 8″

URANUS

Day	RA	Dec.	Transit	10° high	
				52°	56°
	h m	° ′	h m	h m	h m
1	20 29.3	− 19 41	19 47	22 30	21 49
11	20 29.0	− 19 41	19 07	21 50	21 10
21	20 29.0	− 19 41	18 28	21 11	20 30
31	20 29.4	− 19 39	17 49	20 32	19 52

Diameter 4″

NEPTUNE

Day	RA	Dec.	Transit	10° high	
				52°	56°
	h m	° ′	h m	h m	h m
1	19 56.7	− 20 20	19 14	21 51	21 07
11	19 56.6	− 20 20	18 35	21 11	20 28
21	19 56.8	− 20 20	17 56	20 32	19 49
31	19 57.2	− 20 19	17 17	19 54	19 10

Diameter 2″

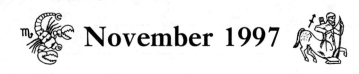

November 1997

ELEVENTH MONTH, 30 DAYS. *Novem* (nine), ninth month of Roman pre-Julian calendar

1	Saturday	**All Saints.** L. S. Lowry b. 1887. Gary Player b. 1935	*week* 43 *day* 305
2	Sunday	**8th S. before Christmas/23rd S. after Trinity**	*week* 44 *day* 306
3	Monday	Vincenzo Bellini b. 1801. Henri Matisse d. 1954	307
4	Tuesday	William III b. 1650. Wilfred Owen d. 1918	308
5	Wednesday	✕Battle of Inkerman 1854. Vladimir Horowitz d. 1989	309
6	Thursday	Colley Cibber b. 1671. Sir John Alcock b. 1892	310
7	Friday	Marie Curie b. 1867. Alexander Dubcek d. 1992	311
8	Saturday	John Milton d. 1674. Thomas Bewick d. 1828	312
9	Sunday	**7th S. before Christmas/24th S. after Trinity**	*week* 45 *day* 313
10	Monday	William Hogarth b. 1697. Kamâl Atatürk d. 1938	314
11	Tuesday	Armistice Day 1918. Sir Edward German d. 1936	315
12	Wednesday	Harry Haldeman d. 1993. Umberto Giordano d. 1948	316
13	Thursday	Robert Louis Stevenson b. 1850. Archbishop Carey b. 1935	317
14	Friday	*Prince of Wales b. 1948.* Claude Monet b. 1840	318
15	Saturday	Johann Kepler d. 1630. Aneurin Bevan b. 1897	319
16	Sunday	**6th S. before Christmas/25th S. after Trinity**	*week* 46 *day* 320
17	Monday	Robert Owen d. 1858. Heitor Villa-Lobos d. 1959	321
18	Tuesday	Francis Thompson d. 1907. Niels Bohr d. 1962	322
19	Wednesday	Gettysburg address 1863. Indira Gandhi b. 1917	323
20	Thursday	*Queen's Wedding Day 1947.* Thomas Chatterton b. 1752	324
21	Friday	Sir Arthur Quiller Couch b. 1863	325
22	Saturday	Martin Frobisher d. 1594. Benjamin Britten b. 1913	326
23	Sunday	**5th S. before Christmas/26th S. after Trinity**	*week* 47 *day* 327
24	Monday	John Knox d. 1572. Frances Hodgson Burnett b. 1849	328
25	Tuesday	Harley Granville-Barker b. 1877. Lilian Baylis d. 1937	329
26	Wednesday	William Cowper b. 1731. John McAdam d. 1836	330
27	Thursday	Anders Celsius b. 1701. Eugene O'Neill d. 1953	331
28	Friday	William Blake b. 1757. Friedrich Engels b. 1820	332
29	Saturday	Christian Doppler b. 1803. Giacomo Puccini d. 1924	333
30	Sunday	**Advent Sunday.** Sir Philip Sidney b. 1554	*week* 48 *day* 334

ASTRONOMICAL PHENOMENA

d	h	
1	10	Mercury in conjunction with Moon. Mercury 6° S.
4	06	Mars in conjunction with Moon. Mars 6° S.
4	11	Venus in conjunction with Moon. Venus 9° S.
6	07	Venus at greatest elongation E.47°
7	18	Jupiter in conjunction with Moon. Jupiter 4° S.
12	01	Saturn in conjunction with Moon. Saturn 0°.4 S.
22	07	Sun's longitude 240° ♐
27	17	Pluto in conjunction
28	16	Mercury at greatest elongation E.22°

MINIMA OF ALGOL

d	h	d	h	d	h
1	10.6	12	21.8	24	09.1
4	07.4	15	18.6	27	05.9
7	04.2	18	15.4	30	02.7
10	01.0	21	12.3		

CONSTELLATIONS

The following constellations are near the meridian at

	d	h		d	h
October	1	24	November	15	21
October	16	23	December	1	20
November	1	22	December	16	19

Ursa Major (below the Pole), Cepheus, Cassiopeia, Andromeda, Pegasus, Pisces, Aquarius and Cetus

THE MOON

Phases, Apsides and Node	d	h	m
☽ First Quarter	7	21	43
○ Full Moon	14	14	12
☾ Last Quarter	21	23	58
● New Moon	30	02	14
Perigee (363,384 km)	12	08	02
Apogee (404,699 km)	24	02	30

Mean longitude of ascending node on November 1, 167°

THE SUN

s.d. 16′.2

Day	Right Ascension	Dec.	Equation of time	Rise 52°	Rise 56°	Transit	Set 52°	Set 56°	Sidereal time	Transit of First Point of Aries
	h m s	° ′	m s	h m	h m	h m	h m	h m	h m s	h m s
1	14 24 53	14 22	+16 24	6 55	7 07	11 44	16 32	16 19	2 41 17	21 15 14
2	14 28 48	14 41	+16 25	6 57	7 09	11 44	16 30	16 17	2 45 13	21 11 18
3	14 32 44	15 00	+16 26	6 58	7 11	11 44	16 28	16 15	2 49 10	21 07 22
4	14 36 41	15 19	+16 25	7 00	7 13	11 44	16 26	16 13	2 53 06	21 03 26
5	14 40 38	15 37	+16 24	7 02	7 15	11 44	16 25	16 11	2 57 03	20 59 30
6	14 44 37	15 55	+16 22	7 04	7 18	11 44	16 23	16 09	3 00 59	20 55 34
7	14 48 36	16 13	+16 20	7 06	7 20	11 44	16 21	16 07	3 04 56	20 51 38
8	14 52 36	16 31	+16 16	7 07	7 22	11 44	16 19	16 05	3 08 52	20 47 43
9	14 56 37	16 48	+16 12	7 09	7 24	11 44	16 18	16 03	3 12 49	20 43 47
10	15 00 39	17 05	+16 07	7 11	7 26	11 44	16 16	16 01	3 16 46	20 39 51
11	15 04 41	17 22	+16 01	7 13	7 28	11 44	16 15	15 59	3 20 42	20 35 55
12	15 08 45	17 38	+15 54	7 15	7 30	11 44	16 13	15 57	3 24 39	20 31 59
13	15 12 49	17 55	+15 46	7 16	7 32	11 44	16 12	15 56	3 28 35	20 28 03
14	15 16 54	18 10	+15 38	7 18	7 34	11 44	16 10	15 54	3 32 32	20 24 07
15	15 21 00	18 26	+15 28	7 20	7 36	11 45	16 09	15 52	3 36 28	20 20 11
16	15 25 07	18 41	+15 18	7 22	7 39	11 45	16 07	15 50	3 40 25	20 16 15
17	15 29 14	18 56	+15 07	7 23	7 41	11 45	16 06	15 49	3 44 21	20 12 19
18	15 33 23	19 11	+14 55	7 25	7 43	11 45	16 05	15 47	3 48 18	20 08 23
19	15 37 32	19 25	+14 42	7 27	7 45	11 45	16 04	15 46	3 52 15	20 04 28
20	15 41 42	19 39	+14 29	7 28	7 47	11 46	16 02	15 44	3 56 11	20 00 32
21	15 45 53	19 52	+14 15	7 30	7 49	11 46	16 01	15 43	4 00 08	19 56 36
22	15 50 05	20 05	+13 59	7 32	7 51	11 46	16 00	15 41	4 04 04	19 52 40
23	15 54 18	20 18	+13 43	7 33	7 52	11 46	15 59	15 40	4 08 01	19 48 44
24	15 58 31	20 30	+13 26	7 35	7 54	11 47	15 58	15 39	4 11 57	19 44 48
25	16 02 45	20 42	+13 09	7 37	7 56	11 47	15 57	15 37	4 15 54	19 40 52
26	16 07 00	20 54	+12 50	7 38	7 58	11 47	15 56	15 36	4 19 50	19 36 56
27	16 11 16	21 05	+12 31	7 40	8 00	11 48	15 55	15 35	4 23 47	19 33 00
28	16 15 32	21 16	+12 11	7 41	8 02	11 48	15 54	15 34	4 27 44	19 29 04
29	16 19 50	21 27	+11 51	7 43	8 03	11 48	15 54	15 33	4 31 40	19 25 08
30	16 24 07	21 37	+11 29	7 44	8 05	11 49	15 53	15 32	4 35 37	19 21 13

DURATION OF TWILIGHT (in minutes)

Latitude	52°	56°	52°	56°	52°	56°	52°	56°
	1 November		11 November		21 November		30 November	
Civil	36	40	37	41	38	43	39	45
Nautical	75	84	78	87	80	90	82	93
Astronomical	115	127	117	130	120	134	123	137

THE NIGHT SKY

Mercury, although at greatest eastern elongation on the 28th, is not suitably placed for observation.

Venus, magnitude −4.5, is still visible as a brilliant object in the early evenings, low above the south-western horizon. The planet is at greatest eastern elongation (47°) on the 6th and during the month is gradually becoming visible for a little longer each evening, until by the end of November it may be seen for almost two hours after sunset. On the early evening of the 4th the crescent Moon will be seen about 9° N. of the planet.

Mars remains too close to the Sun for observation.

Jupiter continues to be visible as a splendid evening object, magnitude −2.3, low in the south-western sky. By the end of the month it is unlikely to be visible for long after 20h. On the evening of the 7th the Moon, at First Quarter, passes 3° N. of the planet.

Saturn is still visible for the greater part of the night, magnitude +0.4, but by the end of the month it is not visible after 02h. The waxing gibbous Moon occults the planet in the early hours of the 12th (see page 67 for details).

THE MOON

Day	RA h m	Dec. °	Hor. par. '	Semi-diam. '	Sun's co-long. °	PA of Bright Limb °	Phase %	Age d	Rise 52° h m	Rise 56° h m	Transit h m	Set 52° h m	Set 56° h m
1	14 56	−12.3	55.1	15.0	281	254	0	0.6	7 40	7 52	12 39	17 31	17 18
2	15 46	−15.0	55.5	15.1	293	268	3	1.6	8 44	8 59	13 27	18 06	17 51
3	16 38	−17.0	56.0	15.3	305	269	7	2.6	9 45	10 02	14 18	18 48	18 31
4	17 31	−18.2	56.5	15.4	317	267	13	3.6	10 43	11 01	15 10	19 38	19 20
5	18 26	−18.4	57.0	15.5	329	264	21	4.6	11 35	11 53	16 04	20 35	20 18
6	19 22	−17.7	57.6	15.7	342	260	30	5.6	12 20	12 37	16 58	21 40	21 24
7	20 18	−16.0	58.2	15.8	354	256	40	6.6	13 00	13 14	17 52	22 50	22 38
8	21 14	−13.3	58.7	16.0	6	253	51	7.6	13 35	13 45	18 45	—	23 56
9	22 09	− 9.8	59.3	16.2	18	250	62	8.6	14 06	14 12	19 39	0 05	—
10	23 05	− 5.6	59.8	16.3	30	247	73	9.6	14 35	14 38	20 32	1 22	1 17
11	0 00	− 1.1	60.1	16.4	42	246	83	10.6	15 04	15 02	21 25	2 41	2 40
12	0 56	+ 3.5	60.3	16.4	55	244	91	11.6	15 33	15 28	22 20	4 01	4 04
13	1 52	+ 8.0	60.3	16.4	67	241	96	12.6	16 05	15 56	23 16	5 21	5 28
14	2 50	+11.9	60.0	16.3	79	225	99	13.6	16 40	16 28	—	6 39	6 51
15	3 48	+15.1	59.5	16.2	91	118	100	14.6	17 21	17 06	0 12	7 54	8 09
16	4 46	+17.3	58.8	16.0	103	97	97	15.6	18 08	17 51	1 09	9 03	9 20
17	5 44	+18.4	58.0	15.8	115	96	92	16.6	19 01	18 43	2 05	10 03	10 21
18	6 41	+18.4	57.2	15.6	127	99	86	17.6	19 59	19 42	2 59	10 54	11 11
19	7 36	+17.5	56.3	15.4	140	102	78	18.6	21 01	20 46	3 51	11 36	11 52
20	8 28	+15.7	55.6	15.2	152	105	69	19.6	22 03	21 51	4 41	12 11	12 24
21	9 17	+13.2	55.0	15.0	164	108	60	20.6	23 06	22 57	5 27	12 41	12 51
22	10 05	+10.2	54.6	14.9	176	110	50	21.6	—	—	6 12	13 07	13 14
23	10 51	+ 6.8	54.3	14.8	188	112	41	22.6	0 09	0 03	6 55	13 31	13 34
24	11 37	+ 3.2	54.2	14.8	200	114	32	23.6	1 12	1 09	7 38	13 53	13 54
25	12 22	− 0.6	54.2	14.8	213	114	23	24.6	2 15	2 16	8 20	14 15	14 13
26	13 07	− 4.3	54.5	14.8	225	115	16	25.6	3 18	3 23	9 03	14 38	14 32
27	13 53	− 8.0	54.8	14.9	237	115	9	26.6	4 23	4 30	9 47	15 03	14 54
28	14 41	−11.3	55.2	15.0	249	117	5	27.6	5 28	5 39	10 33	15 32	15 20
29	15 31	−14.3	55.7	15.2	261	123	1	28.6	6 33	6 47	11 22	16 05	15 50
30	16 23	−16.6	56.2	15.3	274	177	0	29.6	7 37	7 53	12 12	16 45	16 28

MERCURY

Day	RA h m	Dec. °	Diam. "	Phase %	Transit h m	5° high 52° h m	5° high 56° h m
1	15 08	−18.7	5	96	12 28	16 04	15 38
3	15 21	−19.7	5	95	12 33	16 01	15 33
5	15 33	−20.6	5	94	12 37	15 58	15 29
7	15 45	−21.5	5	92	12 41	15 55	15 24
9	15 58	−22.3	5	91	12 46	15 53	15 20
11	16 10	−23.0	5	90	12 50	15 52	15 16
13	16 22	−23.7	5	88	12 55	15 50	15 12
15	16 34	−24.3	5	86	12 59	15 50	15 09
17	16 47	−24.7	5	84	13 03	15 49	15 07
19	16 59	−25.1	6	82	13 08	15 50	15 05
21	17 10	−25.5	6	79	13 11	15 51	15 04
23	17 22	−25.7	6	76	13 15	15 52	15 05
25	17 33	−25.8	6	72	13 18	15 54	15 06
27	17 43	−25.8	6	67	13 20	15 56	15 08
29	17 53	−25.8	7	62	13 21	15 58	15 11
31	18 01	−25.6	7	56	13 21	16 00	15 14

VENUS

Day	RA h m	Dec. °	Diam. "	Phase %	Transit h m	5° high 52° h m	5° high 56° h m
1	17 40	−26.8	24	52	14 59	17 24	16 28
6	18 03	−27.0	25	50	15 02	17 25	16 28
11	18 25	−26.9	26	47	15 05	17 29	16 33
16	18 46	−26.6	28	44	15 06	17 34	16 41
21	19 06	−26.1	30	41	15 06	17 41	16 52
26	19 25	−25.3	32	38	15 04	17 47	17 03
31	19 41	−24.4	35	35	15 01	17 53	17 13

MARS

Day	RA h m	Dec. °	Diam. "	Phase %	Transit h m	5° high 52° h m	5° high 56° h m
1	17 33	−24.5	5	93	14 51	17 40	16 59
6	17 49	−24.7	5	94	14 48	17 36	16 54
11	18 06	−24.7	5	94	14 45	17 33	16 51
16	18 22	−24.6	5	94	14 42	17 30	16 49
21	18 39	−24.4	5	95	14 39	17 29	16 49
26	18 56	−24.1	5	95	14 36	17 30	16 51
31	19 13	−23.7	5	95	14 33	17 31	16 53

SUNRISE AND SUNSET

	London		Bristol		Birmingham		Manchester		Newcastle		Glasgow		Belfast	
	0°05′	51°30′	2°35′	51°28′	1°55′	52°28′	2°15′	53°28′	1°37′	54°59′	4°14′	55°52′	5°56′	54°35′
	h m	h m	h m	h m	h m	h m	h m	h m	h m	h m	h m	h m	h m	h m
1	6 54	16 33	7 04	16 43	7 04	16 38	7 08	16 36	7 10	16 29	7 23	16 37	7 26	16 48
2	6 56	16 32	7 05	16 42	7 06	16 36	7 10	16 35	7 12	16 27	7 26	16 35	7 28	16 46
3	6 57	16 30	7 07	16 40	7 07	16 34	7 12	16 33	7 14	16 25	7 28	16 33	7 30	16 44
4	6 59	16 28	7 09	16 38	7 09	16 33	7 14	16 31	7 16	16 23	7 30	16 30	7 32	16 42
5	7 01	16 26	7 11	16 36	7 11	16 31	7 16	16 29	7 18	16 21	7 32	16 28	7 34	16 40
6	7 03	16 25	7 13	16 35	7 13	16 29	7 18	16 27	7 20	16 19	7 34	16 26	7 36	16 38
7	7 04	16 23	7 14	16 33	7 15	16 27	7 19	16 25	7 22	16 17	7 36	16 24	7 38	16 36
8	7 06	16 21	7 16	16 32	7 17	16 26	7 21	16 24	7 24	16 15	7 38	16 22	7 40	16 34
9	7 08	16 20	7 18	16 30	7 18	16 24	7 23	16 22	7 26	16 14	7 40	16 20	7 42	16 32
10	7 10	16 18	7 20	16 28	7 20	16 22	7 25	16 20	7 28	16 12	7 42	16 19	7 44	16 31
11	7 11	16 17	7 21	16 27	7 22	16 21	7 27	16 18	7 30	16 10	7 45	16 17	7 46	16 29
12	7 13	16 15	7 23	16 25	7 24	16 19	7 29	16 17	7 32	16 08	7 47	16 15	7 48	16 27
13	7 15	16 14	7 25	16 24	7 26	16 18	7 31	16 15	7 34	16 07	7 49	16 13	7 50	16 25
14	7 17	16 12	7 26	16 23	7 27	16 16	7 33	16 14	7 36	16 05	7 51	16 11	7 52	16 24
15	7 18	16 11	7 28	16 21	7 29	16 15	7 34	16 12	7 38	16 03	7 53	16 10	7 54	16 22
16	7 20	16 10	7 30	16 20	7 31	16 13	7 36	16 11	7 40	16 02	7 55	16 08	7 56	16 21
17	7 22	16 08	7 32	16 19	7 33	16 12	7 38	16 09	7 42	16 00	7 57	16 06	7 58	16 19
18	7 23	16 07	7 33	16 17	7 35	16 11	7 40	16 08	7 44	15 59	7 59	16 05	8 00	16 18
19	7 25	16 06	7 35	16 16	7 36	16 09	7 42	16 06	7 46	15 57	8 01	16 03	8 02	16 16
20	7 27	16 05	7 37	16 15	7 38	16 08	7 44	16 05	7 48	15 56	8 03	16 02	8 03	16 15
21	7 28	16 04	7 38	16 14	7 40	16 07	7 45	16 04	7 50	15 54	8 05	16 00	8 05	16 13
22	7 30	16 03	7 40	16 13	7 41	16 06	7 47	16 03	7 52	15 53	8 07	15 59	8 07	16 12
23	7 32	16 01	7 41	16 12	7 43	16 05	7 49	16 02	7 54	15 52	8 09	15 58	8 09	16 11
24	7 33	16 00	7 43	16 11	7 45	16 04	7 51	16 00	7 55	15 50	8 11	15 56	8 11	16 10
25	7 35	16 00	7 45	16 10	7 46	16 03	7 52	15 59	7 57	15 49	8 12	15 55	8 12	16 09
26	7 36	15 59	7 46	16 09	7 48	16 02	7 54	15 58	7 59	15 48	8 14	15 54	8 14	16 07
27	7 38	15 58	7 48	16 08	7 49	16 01	7 56	15 57	8 01	15 47	8 16	15 53	8 16	16 06
28	7 39	15 57	7 49	16 07	7 51	16 00	7 57	15 56	8 02	15 46	8 18	15 52	8 18	16 05
29	7 41	15 56	7 51	16 06	7 52	15 59	7 59	15 56	8 04	15 45	8 20	15 51	8 19	16 04
30	7 42	15 56	7 52	16 06	7 54	15 58	8 00	15 55	8 06	15 44	8 21	15 50	8 21	16 04

JUPITER

Day	RA	Dec.	Transit	5° high	
				52°	56°
	h m	° ′	h m	h m	h m
1	21 03.0	−17 48	18 19	22 02	21 40
11	21 06.7	−17 32	17 43	21 29	21 06
21	21 11.4	−17 10	17 09	20 57	20 35
31	21 17.1	−16 44	16 35	20 26	20 05

Diameters – equatorial 39″ polar 36″

SATURN

Day	RA	Dec.	Transit	5° high	
				52°	56°
	h m	° ′	h m	h m	h m
1	1 00.4	+ 3 29	22 15	4 04	4 03
11	0 58.1	+ 3 15	21 34	3 21	3 20
21	0 56.1	+ 3 05	20 52	2 39	2 38
31	0 54.7	+ 2 59	20 12	1 58	1 57

Diameters – equatorial 19″ polar 17″
Rings – major axis 44″ minor axis 7″

URANUS

Day	RA	Dec.	Transit	10° high	
				52°	56°
	h m	° ′	h m	h m	h m
1	20 29.5	−19 39	17 45	20 28	19 48
11	20 30.3	−19 36	17 07	19 50	19 10
21	20 31.4	−19 32	16 29	19 13	18 33
31	20 32.8	−19 27	15 51	18 36	17 57

Diameter 4″

NEPTUNE

Day	RA	Dec.	Transit	10° high	
				52°	56°
	h m	° ′	h m	h m	h m
1	19 57.2	−20 19	17 13	19 50	19 06
11	19 57.9	−20 17	16 35	19 11	18 28
21	19 58.7	−20 15	15 56	18 33	17 50
31	19 59.8	−20 12	15 18	17 55	17 13

Diameter 2″

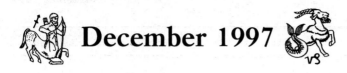

December 1997

TWELFTH MONTH, 31 DAYS. *Decem* (ten), tenth month of Roman pre-Julian calendar

1	*Monday*	**St Andrew.** Edmund Campion exec. 1581	*week* 48 *day* 335
2	*Tuesday*	Hernando Cortés d. 1547. ✕ Battle of Austerlitz 1805	336
3	*Wednesday*	Robert Louis Stephenson d. 1894. Renoir d. 1919	337
4	*Thursday*	Thomas Hobbes d. 1679. Edith Cavell b. 1865	338
5	*Friday*	Christina Rossetti b. 1830. Earl Jellicoe b. 1859	339
6	*Saturday*	Finland declared its independence 1917	340
7	*Sunday*	**2nd S. in Advent.** Ferdinand de Lesseps d. 1894	*week* 49 *day* 341
8	*Monday*	Jean Sibelius b. 1865. Golda Meir d. 1978	342
9	*Tuesday*	Sir Anthony van Dyck d. 1641. R. A. Butler b. 1902	343
10	*Wednesday*	Royal Academy of Arts founded 1768. Melvil Dewey b. 1851	344
11	*Thursday*	Hector Berlioz b. 1803. Alexander Solzhenitsyn b. 1918	345
12	*Friday*	Edward G. Robinson b. 1893. Frank Sinatra b. 1915	346
13	*Saturday*	Glen Byam Shaw b. 1904. Vassily Kandinsky d. 1944	347
14	*Sunday*	**3rd S. in Advent.** Stanley Baldwin d. 1947	*week* 50 *day* 348
15	*Monday*	Jan Vermeer d. 1675. Walt Disney d. 1966	349
16	*Tuesday*	Sir Jack Hobbs b. 1882. Zoltán Kodály b. 1882	350
17	*Wednesday*	Simón Bolívar d. 1830. Ford Madox Ford b. 1873	351
18	*Thursday*	Christopher Fry b. 1907. Sir John Alcock d. 1919	352
19	*Friday*	J. M. W. Turner d. 1851. Leonid Brezhnev b. 1906	353
20	*Saturday*	*Michaelmas Law Sittings end.* Artur Rubinstein d. 1982	354
21	*Sunday*	**4th S. in Advent.** Boccaccio d. 1375. Heinrich Böll b. 1917	*week* 51 *day* 355
22	*Monday*	Dame Peggy Ashcroft b. 1907. Beatrix Potter d. 1943	356
23	*Tuesday*	Richard Arkwright b. 1732. Thomas Malthus d. 1834	357
24	*Wednesday*	CHANUCAH begins. Vasco de Gama d. 1524	358
25	*Thursday*	**Christmas Day.** *Public Holiday in the UK*	359
26	*Friday*	**St Stephen.** *Bank Holiday in the UK*	360
27	*Saturday*	**St John the Evangelist.** Louis Pasteur b. 1822	361
28	*Sunday*	**1st S. after Christmas.** Paul Hindemith d. 1963	*week* 52 *day* 362
29	*Monday*	**Holy Innocents.** William Gladstone b. 1809	363
30	*Tuesday*	Amelia Bloomer d. 1894. L. P. Hartley b. 1895	364
31	*Wednesday*	RAMADAN begins. John Flamsteed d. 1719	365

ASTRONOMICAL PHENOMENA

d	h	
1	20	Mercury in conjunction with Moon. Mercury 7° S.
3	03	Mars in conjunction with Moon. Mars 5° S.
3	15	Venus in conjunction with Moon. Venus 7° S.
5	06	Jupiter in conjunction with Moon. Jupiter 3° S.
7	17	Mercury at stationary point
9	06	Saturn in conjunction with Moon. Saturn 0°.2 S.
11	23	Venus at greatest brilliancy
16	10	Saturn at stationary point
17	08	Mercury in inferior conjunction
21	20	Sun's longitude 270° ♑
22	22	Mars in conjunction with Venus. Mars 1° S.
26	21	Venus at stationary point
27	12	Mercury at stationary point
28	04	Mercury in conjunction with Moon. Mercury 2° S.
31	13	Venus in conjunction with Moon. Venus 1° S.

MINIMA OF ALGOL

d	h	d	h	d	h
2	23.5	14	10.8	25	22.1
5	20.3	17	07.6	28	18.9
8	17.2	20	04.4	31	15.7
11	14.0	23	01.3		

CONSTELLATIONS

The following constellations are near the meridian at

	d	h		d	h
November	1	24	December	16	21
November	15	23	January	1	20
December	1	22	January	16	19

Ursa Major (below the Pole), Ursa Minor (below the Pole), Cassiopeia, Andromeda, Perseus, Triangulum, Aries, Taurus, Cetus and Eridanus

THE MOON

Phases, Apsides and Node	d	h	m
☽ First Quarter	7	06	09
○ Full Moon	14	02	37
☾ Last Quarter	21	21	43
● New Moon	29	16	57
Perigee (368,878 km)	9	17	03
Apogee (404,259 km)	21	23	24

Mean longitude of ascending node on December 1, 165°

THE SUN   s.d. 16′.3

Day	Right Ascension	Dec. −	Equation of time	Rise 52°	Rise 56°	Transit	Set 52°	Set 56°	Sidereal time	Transit of First Point of Aries
	h m s	° ′	m s	h m	h m	h m	h m	h m	h m s	h m s
1	16 28 26	21 46	+11 07	7 46	8 07	11 49	15 52	15 31	4 39 33	19 17 17
2	16 32 45	21 55	+10 45	7 47	8 08	11 49	15 52	15 30	4 43 30	19 13 21
3	16 37 05	22 04	+10 21	7 48	8 10	11 50	15 51	15 29	4 47 26	19 09 25
4	16 41 25	22 13	+ 9 58	7 50	8 12	11 50	15 50	15 29	4 51 23	19 05 29
5	16 45 46	22 20	+ 9 33	7 51	8 13	11 51	15 50	15 28	4 55 19	19 01 33
6	16 50 08	22 28	+ 9 08	7 52	8 15	11 51	15 50	15 27	4 59 16	18 57 37
7	16 54 30	22 35	+ 8 43	7 54	8 16	11 52	15 49	15 27	5 03 13	18 53 41
8	16 58 52	22 42	+ 8 17	7 55	8 17	11 52	15 49	15 26	5 07 09	18 49 45
9	17 03 15	22 48	+ 7 50	7 56	8 19	11 52	15 49	15 26	5 11 06	18 45 49
10	17 07 39	22 54	+ 7 24	7 57	8 20	11 53	15 49	15 26	5 15 02	18 41 53
11	17 12 02	22 59	+ 6 56	7 58	8 21	11 53	15 48	15 25	5 18 59	18 37 58
12	17 16 27	23 04	+ 6 29	7 59	8 22	11 54	15 48	15 25	5 22 55	18 34 02
13	17 20 51	23 08	+ 6 01	8 00	8 23	11 54	15 48	15 25	5 26 52	18 30 06
14	17 25 16	23 12	+ 5 33	8 01	8 24	11 55	15 48	15 25	5 30 49	18 26 10
15	17 29 41	23 15	+ 5 04	8 02	8 25	11 55	15 49	15 25	5 34 45	18 22 14
16	17 34 07	23 18	+ 4 35	8 03	8 26	11 56	15 49	15 25	5 38 42	18 18 18
17	17 38 32	23 21	+ 4 06	8 03	8 27	11 56	15 49	15 25	5 42 38	18 14 22
18	17 42 58	23 23	+ 3 37	8 04	8 28	11 57	15 49	15 25	5 46 35	18 10 26
19	17 47 24	23 24	+ 3 07	8 05	8 28	11 57	15 50	15 26	5 50 31	18 06 30
20	17 51 50	23 25	+ 2 38	8 05	8 29	11 58	15 50	15 26	5 54 28	18 02 34
21	17 56 17	23 26	+ 2 08	8 06	8 30	11 58	15 50	15 27	5 58 24	17 58 38
22	18 00 43	23 26	+ 1 38	8 06	8 30	11 59	15 51	15 27	6 02 21	17 54 42
23	18 05 09	23 26	+ 1 08	8 07	8 31	11 59	15 52	15 28	6 06 18	17 50 47
24	18 09 36	23 25	+ 0 38	8 07	8 31	12 00	15 52	15 28	6 10 14	17 46 51
25	18 14 02	23 24	+ 0 08	8 07	8 31	12 00	15 53	15 29	6 14 11	17 42 55
26	18 18 29	23 22	− 0 21	8 08	8 31	12 01	15 54	15 30	6 18 07	17 38 59
27	18 22 55	23 20	− 0 51	8 08	8 32	12 01	15 54	15 31	6 22 04	17 35 03
28	18 27 21	23 17	− 1 21	8 08	8 32	12 02	15 55	15 32	6 26 00	17 31 07
29	18 31 47	23 14	− 1 50	8 08	8 32	12 02	15 56	15 33	6 29 57	17 27 11
30	18 36 13	23 11	− 2 19	8 08	8 32	12 03	15 57	15 34	6 33 53	17 23 15
31	18 40 38	23 06	− 2 48	8 08	8 31	12 03	15 58	15 35	6 37 50	17 19 19

DURATION OF TWILIGHT (in minutes)

Latitude	52°	56°	52°	56°	52°	56°	52°	56°
	1 December		11 December		21 December		31 December	
Civil	40	45	41	47	41	47	41	47
Nautical	82	93	84	96	85	97	84	96
Astronomical	123	138	125	141	126	142	125	141

THE NIGHT SKY

Mercury is unsuitably placed for observation at first, inferior conjunction occurring on the 17th. For the last week of the month Mercury is visible as a morning object, magnitude +0.9 to 0.0, low above the south-eastern horizon around the beginning of morning civil twilight. On the morning of the 28th the thin sliver of the crescent Moon, little more than one day before New, may be detected with Mercury about 1° below and to the right.

Venus is still a magnificent object in the early evening sky, attaining its greatest brilliancy (magnitude −4.7) on the 11th. It is visible low above the south-western horizon for about two hours after sunset. Observers with telescopes can witness the decreasing crescent phase during the month (falling from 35 per cent to 9 per cent illuminated) while the diameter increases from 35″ to 55″. On the evening of the 3rd the crescent Moon is near Venus, but some 6° higher in altitude.

Mars continues to be too close to the Sun for observation.

Jupiter, magnitude −2.2, is still visible as a splendid early evening object, low in the south-western sky. On the evenings of the 4th and 5th the crescent Moon will be seen in the vicinity of the planet.

Saturn, magnitude +0.6, is an evening object in the south-western sky. The Moon, just after First Quarter, is in the vicinity of the planet on the evenings of the 8th and 9th.

Meteors. The maximum of the well-known Geminid meteor showers occurs on the night of the 13th to 14th. The Full Moon will cause serious interference with observations.

THE MOON

Day	RA	Dec.	Hor. par.	Semi- diam.	Sun's co- long.	PA of Bright Limb	Phase	Age	Rise 52°	Rise 56°	Transit	Set 52°	Set 56°
	h m	°	'	'	°	°	%	d	h m	h m	h m	h m	h m
1	17 17	−18.1	56.8	15.5	286	250	1	0.9	8 37	8 56	13 05	17 32	17 14
2	18 12	−18.6	57.2	15.6	298	258	4	1.9	9 33	9 51	14 00	18 28	18 10
3	19 09	−18.2	57.7	15.7	310	257	9	2.9	10 21	10 38	14 54	19 31	19 15
4	20 06	−16.7	58.1	15.8	322	255	17	3.9	11 03	11 18	15 49	20 40	20 27
5	21 02	−14.2	58.5	15.9	334	252	26	4.9	11 39	11 51	16 42	21 54	21 43
6	21 57	−10.9	58.8	16.0	347	250	36	5.9	12 11	12 19	17 35	23 09	23 03
7	22 51	− 6.9	59.1	16.1	359	248	47	6.9	12 40	12 44	18 27	—	—
8	23 45	− 2.6	59.3	16.2	11	246	59	7.9	13 07	13 07	19 18	0 25	0 23
9	0 39	+ 1.9	59.4	16.2	23	246	70	8.9	13 35	13 31	20 11	1 42	1 44
10	1 34	+ 6.4	59.4	16.2	35	246	79	9.9	14 04	13 56	21 04	3 00	3 06
11	2 29	+10.5	59.3	16.2	47	247	88	10.9	14 36	14 25	21 58	4 17	4 27
12	3 25	+13.9	59.1	16.1	60	247	94	11.9	15 13	14 59	22 54	5 32	5 45
13	4 23	+16.5	58.7	16.0	72	242	98	12.9	15 56	15 39	23 49	6 43	6 59
14	5 21	+18.1	58.2	15.8	84	192	100	13.9	16 46	16 28	—	7 47	8 05
15	6 18	+18.7	57.5	15.7	96	114	99	14.9	17 42	17 24	0 45	8 43	9 01
16	7 14	+18.1	56.9	15.5	108	107	96	15.9	18 43	18 26	1 39	9 31	9 47
17	8 08	+16.7	56.2	15.3	120	107	91	16.9	19 46	19 32	2 30	10 10	10 24
18	8 59	+14.4	55.5	15.1	132	109	84	17.9	20 50	20 39	3 19	10 42	10 54
19	9 49	+11.5	55.0	15.0	144	111	76	18.9	21 54	21 47	4 06	11 10	11 19
20	10 36	+ 8.3	54.6	14.9	157	112	68	19.9	22 57	22 53	4 50	11 35	11 40
21	11 22	+ 4.7	54.3	14.8	169	113	59	20.9	—	23 59	5 33	11 58	12 00
22	12 07	+ 0.9	54.2	14.8	181	113	49	21.9	0 00	—	6 15	12 20	12 19
23	12 52	− 2.8	54.3	14.8	193	113	40	22.9	1 03	1 06	6 57	12 42	12 38
24	13 37	− 6.5	54.6	14.9	205	113	31	23.9	2 07	2 13	7 41	13 06	12 58
25	14 24	−10.0	55.0	15.0	217	112	22	24.9	3 11	3 20	8 25	13 32	13 22
26	15 13	−13.1	55.6	15.1	230	110	15	25.9	4 16	4 29	9 13	14 03	13 49
27	16 04	−15.7	56.2	15.3	242	109	8	26.9	5 21	5 36	10 02	14 39	14 23
28	16 58	−17.6	56.9	15.5	254	109	4	27.9	6 24	6 42	10 55	15 23	15 05
29	17 53	−18.6	57.5	15.7	266	119	1	28.9	7 23	7 42	11 50	16 16	15 58
30	18 51	−18.5	58.1	15.8	278	215	0	0.3	8 16	8 34	12 46	17 18	17 00
31	19 49	−17.3	58.7	16.0	291	247	2	1.3	9 02	9 18	13 42	18 27	18 12

MERCURY

Day	RA	Dec.	Diam.	Phase	Transit	5° high 52°	5° high 56°
	h m	°	"	%	h m	h m	h m
1	18 01	−25.6	7	56	13 21	16 00	15 14
3	18 07	−25.4	7	49	13 19	16 01	15 17
5	18 12	−25.0	8	42	13 16	16 01	15 18
7	18 15	−24.6	8	33	13 09	15 59	15 18
9	18 14	−24.1	9	24	13 00	15 54	15 16
11	18 10	−23.5	9	16	12 48	15 47	15 11
13	18 03	−22.9	9	8	12 32	15 37	15 03
15	17 54	−22.2	10	3	12 14	15 25	14 53
17	17 42	−21.5	10	0	11 55	8 40	9 10
19	17 31	−20.9	10	2	11 36	8 15	8 44
21	17 20	−20.4	10	6	11 18	7 54	8 21
23	17 12	−20.0	9	13	11 03	7 36	8 03
25	17 07	−19.8	9	21	10 51	7 22	7 49
27	17 05	−19.8	8	29	10 41	7 13	7 40
29	17 06	−20.0	8	38	10 34	7 07	7 34
31	17 09	−20.2	8	45	10 30	7 05	7 33

VENUS

Day	RA	Dec.	Diam.	Phase	Transit	5° high 52°	5° high 56°
	h m	°	"	%	h m	h m	h m
1	19 41	−24.4	35	35	15 01	17 53	17 13
6	19 56	−23.4	37	31	14 56	17 57	17 21
11	20 08	−22.2	40	27	14 48	17 59	17 27
16	20 17	−21.0	44	22	14 37	17 58	17 29
21	20 23	−19.8	48	18	14 22	17 52	17 26
26	20 24	−18.7	52	13	14 04	17 42	17 18
31	20 22	−17.6	55	9	13 41	17 27	17 04

MARS

Day	RA	Dec.	Diam.	Phase	Transit	5° high 52°	5° high 56°
1	19 13	−23.7	5	95	14 33	17 31	16 53
6	19 29	−23.1	5	95	14 30	17 33	16 57
11	19 46	−22.5	5	96	14 27	17 35	17 02
16	20 02	−21.7	4	96	14 23	17 38	17 07
21	20 19	−20.9	4	96	14 20	17 42	17 13
26	20 35	−19.9	4	96	14 16	17 46	17 19
31	20 51	−18.9	4	97	14 13	17 50	17 25

SUNRISE AND SUNSET

	London		Bristol		Birmingham		Manchester		Newcastle		Glasgow		Belfast	
	0°05'	51°30'	2°35'	51°28'	1°55'	52°28'	2°15'	53°28'	1°37'	54°59'	4°14'	55°52'	5°56'	54°35'
	h m	h m	h m	h m	h m	h m	h m	h m	h m	h m	h m	h m	h m	h m
1	7 44	15 55	7 53	16 05	7 55	15 58	8 02	15 54	8 07	15 43	8 23	15 49	8 22	16 03
2	7 45	15 54	7 55	16 04	7 57	15 57	8 03	15 53	8 09	15 43	8 25	15 48	8 24	16 02
3	7 46	15 54	7 56	16 04	7 58	15 56	8 05	15 53	8 10	15 42	8 26	15 47	8 25	16 01
4	7 48	15 53	7 57	16 03	8 00	15 56	8 06	15 52	8 12	15 41	8 28	15 46	8 27	16 01
5	7 49	15 53	7 59	16 03	8 01	15 55	8 07	15 52	8 13	15 41	8 29	15 46	8 28	16 00
6	7 50	15 52	8 00	16 03	8 02	15 55	8 09	15 51	8 15	15 40	8 31	15 45	8 30	16 00
7	7 51	15 52	8 01	16 02	8 04	15 55	8 10	15 51	8 16	15 40	8 32	15 45	8 31	15 59
8	7 53	15 52	8 02	16 02	8 05	15 54	8 11	15 50	8 17	15 39	8 33	15 44	8 32	15 59
9	7 54	15 52	8 04	16 02	8 06	15 54	8 13	15 50	8 19	15 39	8 35	15 44	8 34	15 58
10	7 55	15 51	8 05	16 02	8 07	15 54	8 14	15 50	8 20	15 38	8 36	15 43	8 35	15 58
11	7 56	15 51	8 06	16 01	8 08	15 54	8 15	15 50	8 21	15 38	8 37	15 43	8 36	15 58
12	7 57	15 51	8 07	16 01	8 09	15 54	8 16	15 50	8 22	15 38	8 38	15 43	8 37	15 58
13	7 58	15 51	8 08	16 01	8 10	15 54	8 17	15 49	8 23	15 38	8 39	15 43	8 38	15 58
14	7 59	15 51	8 08	16 01	8 11	15 54	8 18	15 49	8 24	15 38	8 40	15 43	8 39	15 58
15	7 59	15 51	8 09	16 02	8 12	15 54	8 19	15 50	8 25	15 38	8 41	15 43	8 40	15 58
16	8 00	15 52	8 10	16 02	8 13	15 54	8 19	15 50	8 26	15 38	8 42	15 43	8 41	15 58
17	8 01	15 52	8 11	16 02	8 13	15 54	8 20	15 50	8 27	15 38	8 43	15 43	8 42	15 58
18	8 02	15 52	8 12	16 02	8 14	15 54	8 21	15 50	8 28	15 39	8 44	15 43	8 42	15 58
19	8 02	15 52	8 12	16 03	8 15	15 55	8 22	15 51	8 28	15 39	8 45	15 44	8 43	15 59
20	8 03	15 53	8 13	16 03	8 15	15 55	8 22	15 51	8 29	15 39	8 45	15 44	8 44	15 59
21	8 04	15 53	8 13	16 03	8 16	15 56	8 23	15 51	8 29	15 40	8 46	15 44	8 44	15 59
22	8 04	15 54	8 14	16 04	8 16	15 56	8 23	15 52	8 30	15 40	8 46	15 45	8 45	16 00
23	8 05	15 54	8 14	16 05	8 17	15 57	8 24	15 52	8 30	15 41	8 47	15 46	8 45	16 01
24	8 05	15 55	8 15	16 05	8 17	15 57	8 24	15 53	8 31	15 41	8 47	15 46	8 45	16 01
25	8 05	15 56	8 15	16 06	8 18	15 58	8 24	15 54	8 31	15 42	8 47	15 47	8 46	16 02
26	8 06	15 56	8 15	16 07	8 18	15 59	8 25	15 55	8 31	15 43	8 47	15 48	8 46	16 03
27	8 06	15 57	8 16	16 07	8 18	16 00	8 25	15 55	8 31	15 44	8 48	15 49	8 46	16 04
28	8 06	15 58	8 16	16 08	8 18	16 00	8 25	15 56	8 32	15 45	8 48	15 49	8 46	16 04
29	8 06	15 59	8 16	16 09	8 18	16 01	8 25	15 57	8 32	15 46	8 48	15 50	8 46	16 05
30	8 06	16 00	8 16	16 10	8 18	16 02	8 25	15 58	8 32	15 47	8 48	15 52	8 46	16 06
31	8 06	16 01	8 16	16 11	8 18	16 03	8 25	15 59	8 31	15 48	8 47	15 53	8 46	16 07

JUPITER

Day	RA	Dec.	Transit	5° high	
				52°	56°
	h m	° '	h m	h m	h m
1	21 17.1	−16 44	16 35	20 26	20 05
11	21 23.7	−16 13	16 03	19 57	19 37
21	21 30.9	−15 38	15 30	19 29	19 10
31	21 38.8	−14 59	14 59	19 02	18 43

Diameters – equatorial 36″ polar 33″

SATURN

Day	RA	Dec.	Transit	5° high	
				52°	56°
	h m	° '	h m	h m	h m
1	0 54.7	+ 2 59	20 12	1 58	1 57
11	0 54.0	+ 2 57	19 32	1 17	1 17
21	0 53.9	+ 2 59	18 52	0 38	0 37
31	0 54.4	+ 3 06	18 14	0 00	23 55

Diameters – equatorial 18″ polar 17″
Rings – major axis 42″ minor axis 6″

URANUS

Day	RA	Dec.	Transit	10° high	
				52°	56°
	h m	° '	h m	h m	h m
1	20 32.8	−19 27	15 51	18 36	17 57
11	20 34.5	−19 20	15 13	17 59	17 20
21	20 36.4	−19 13	14 36	17 23	16 45
31	20 38.5	−19 05	13 59	16 47	16 09

Diameter 4″

NEPTUNE

Day	RA	Dec.	Transit	10° high	
				52°	56°
	h m	° '	h m	h m	h m
1	19 59.8	−20 12	15 18	17 55	17 13
11	20 01.0	−20 09	14 40	17 18	16 35
21	20 02.4	−20 05	14 02	16 41	15 58
31	20 03.8	−20 01	13 24	16 03	15 22

Diameter 2″

RISING AND SETTING TIMES

Table 1. Semi-diurnal Arcs (Hour Angles at Rising/Setting)

Dec.	Latitude 0°	10°	20°	30°	40°	45°	50°	52°	54°	56°	58°	60°	Dec.
	h m	h m	h m	h m	h m	h m	h m	h m	h m	h m	h m	h m	
0°	6 00	6 00	6 00	6 00	6 00	6 00	6 00	6 00	6 00	6 00	6 00	6 00	0°
1°	6 00	6 01	6 01	6 02	6 03	6 04	6 05	6 05	6 06	6 06	6 06	6 07	1°
2°	6 00	6 01	6 03	6 05	6 07	6 08	6 10	6 10	6 11	6 12	6 13	6 14	2°
3°	6 00	6 02	6 04	6 07	6 10	6 12	6 14	6 15	6 17	6 18	6 19	6 21	3°
4°	6 00	6 03	6 06	6 09	6 13	6 16	6 19	6 21	6 22	6 24	6 26	6 28	4°
5°	6 00	6 04	6 07	6 12	6 17	6 20	6 24	6 26	6 28	6 30	6 32	6 35	5°
6°	6 00	6 04	6 09	6 14	6 20	6 24	6 29	6 31	6 33	6 36	6 39	6 42	6°
7°	6 00	6 05	6 10	6 16	6 24	6 28	6 34	6 36	6 39	6 42	6 45	6 49	7°
8°	6 00	6 06	6 12	6 19	6 27	6 32	6 39	6 41	6 45	6 48	6 52	6 56	8°
9°	6 00	6 06	6 13	6 21	6 31	6 36	6 44	6 47	6 50	6 54	6 59	7 04	9°
10°	6 00	6 07	6 15	6 23	6 34	6 41	6 49	6 52	6 56	7 01	7 06	7 11	10°
11°	6 00	6 08	6 16	6 26	6 38	6 45	6 54	6 58	7 02	7 07	7 12	7 19	11°
12°	6 00	6 09	6 18	6 28	6 41	6 49	6 59	7 03	7 08	7 13	7 20	7 26	12°
13°	6 00	6 09	6 19	6 31	6 45	6 53	7 04	7 09	7 14	7 20	7 27	7 34	13°
14°	6 00	6 10	6 21	6 33	6 48	6 58	7 09	7 14	7 20	7 27	7 34	7 42	14°
15°	6 00	6 11	6 22	6 36	6 52	7 02	7 14	7 20	7 27	7 34	7 42	7 51	15°
16°	6 00	6 12	6 24	6 38	6 56	7 07	7 20	7 26	7 33	7 41	7 49	7 59	16°
17°	6 00	6 12	6 26	6 41	6 59	7 11	7 25	7 32	7 40	7 48	7 57	8 08	17°
18°	6 00	6 13	6 27	6 43	7 03	7 16	7 31	7 38	7 46	7 55	8 05	8 17	18°
19°	6 00	6 14	6 29	6 46	7 07	7 21	7 37	7 45	7 53	8 03	8 14	8 26	19°
20°	6 00	6 15	6 30	6 49	7 11	7 25	7 43	7 51	8 00	8 11	8 22	8 36	20°
21°	6 00	6 16	6 32	6 51	7 15	7 30	7 49	7 58	8 08	8 19	8 32	8 47	21°
22°	6 00	6 16	6 34	6 54	7 19	7 35	7 55	8 05	8 15	8 27	8 41	8 58	22°
23°	6 00	6 17	6 36	6 57	7 23	7 40	8 02	8 12	8 23	8 36	8 51	9 09	23°
24°	6 00	6 18	6 37	7 00	7 28	7 46	8 08	8 19	8 31	8 45	9 02	9 22	24°
25°	6 00	6 19	6 39	7 02	7 32	7 51	8 15	8 27	8 40	8 55	9 13	9 35	25°
26°	6 00	6 20	6 41	7 05	7 37	7 57	8 22	8 35	8 49	9 05	9 25	9 51	26°
27°	6 00	6 21	6 43	7 08	7 41	8 03	8 30	8 43	8 58	9 16	9 39	10 08	27°
28°	6 00	6 22	6 45	7 12	7 46	8 08	8 37	8 52	9 08	9 28	9 53	10 28	28°
29°	6 00	6 22	6 47	7 15	7 51	8 15	8 45	9 01	9 19	9 41	10 10	10 55	29°
30°	6 00	6 23	6 49	7 18	7 56	8 21	8 54	9 11	9 30	9 55	10 30	12 00	30°
35°	6 00	6 28	6 59	7 35	8 24	8 58	9 46	10 15	10 58	12 00	12 00	12 00	35°
40°	6 00	6 34	7 11	7 56	8 59	9 48	12 00	12 00	12 00	12 00	12 00	12 00	40°
45°	6 00	6 41	7 25	8 21	9 48	12 00	12 00	12 00	12 00	12 00	12 00	12 00	45°
50°	6 00	6 49	7 43	8 54	12 00	12 00	12 00	12 00	12 00	12 00	12 00	12 00	50°
55°	6 00	6 58	8 05	9 42	12 00	12 00	12 00	12 00	12 00	12 00	12 00	12 00	55°
60°	6 00	7 11	8 36	12 00	12 00	12 00	12 00	12 00	12 00	12 00	12 00	12 00	60°
65°	6 00	7 29	9 25	12 00	12 00	12 00	12 00	12 00	12 00	12 00	12 00	12 00	65°
70°	6 00	7 56	12 00	12 00	12 00	12 00	12 00	12 00	12 00	12 00	12 00	12 00	70°
75°	6 00	8 45	12 00	12 00	12 00	12 00	12 00	12 00	12 00	12 00	12 00	12 00	75°
80°	6 00	12 00	12 00	12 00	12 00	12 00	12 00	12 00	12 00	12 00	12 00	12 00	80°

Table 2. Correction for Refraction and Semi-diameter

	m	m	m	m	m	m	m	m	m	m	m	m	
0°	3	3	4	4	4	5	5	5	6	6	6	7	0°
10°	3	3	4	4	4	5	5	6	6	6	7	7	10°
20°	4	4	4	4	5	5	6	7	7	8	8	9	20°
25°	4	4	4	4	5	6	7	8	8	9	11	13	25°
30°	4	4	4	5	6	7	8	9	11	14	21	—	30°

NB: Regarding Table 1. If latitude and declination are of
the same sign, take out the respondent directly. If they are
of opposite signs, subtract the respondent from 12h.
Example:

Lat.	Dec.	Semi-diurnal arc
+52°	+20°	7h 51m
+52°	−20°	4h 09m

SUNRISE AND SUNSET

The local mean time of sunrise or sunset may be found by obtaining the hour angle from Table 1 and applying it to the time of transit. The hour angle is negative for sunrise and positive for sunset. A small correction to the hour angle, which always has the effect of increasing it numerically, is necessary to allow for the Sun's semi-diameter (16′) and for refraction (34′); it is obtained from Table 2. The resulting local mean time may be converted into the standard time of the country by taking the difference between the longitude of the standard meridian of the country and that of the place, adding it to the local mean time if the place is west of the standard meridian, and subtracting it if the place is east.

Example – Required the New Zealand Mean Time (12h fast on GMT) of sunset on May 23 at Auckland, latitude 36° 50′ S. (or minus), longitude 11h 39m E. Taking the declination as + 20°.6 (page 33), we find

	h	m
Tabular entry for 30° Lat. and Dec. 20°, opposite signs	+ 5	11
Proportional part for 6° 50′ of Lat.	−	15
Proportional part for 0°.6 of Dec.	−	2
Correction (Table 2)	+	4
Hour angle	4	58
Sun transits (page 33)	11	57
Longitudinal correction	+	21
New Zealand Mean Time	17	16

MOONRISE AND MOONSET

It is possible to calculate the times of moonrise and moonset using Table 1, though the method is more complicated because the apparent motion of the Moon is much more rapid and also more variable than that of the Sun.

The parallax of the Moon, about 57′, is near to the sum of the semi-diameter and refraction but has the opposite effect on these times. It is thus convenient to neglect all three quantities in the method outlined below.

TABLE 3. LONGITUDE CORRECTION

X	40m	45m	50m	55m	60m	65m	70m
A							
h	m	m	m	m	m	m	m
1	2	2	2	2	3	3	3
2	3	4	4	5	5	5	6
3	5	6	6	7	8	8	9
4	7	8	8	9	10	11	12
5	8	9	10	11	13	14	15
6	10	11	13	14	15	16	18
7	12	13	15	16	18	19	20
8	13	15	17	18	20	22	23
9	15	17	19	21	23	24	26
10	17	19	21	23	25	27	29
11	18	21	23	25	28	30	32
12	20	23	25	28	30	33	35
13	22	24	27	30	33	35	38
14	23	26	29	32	35	38	41
15	25	28	31	34	38	41	44
16	27	30	33	37	40	43	47
17	28	32	35	39	43	46	50
18	30	34	38	41	45	49	53
19	32	36	40	44	48	51	55
20	33	38	42	46	50	54	58
21	35	39	44	48	53	57	61
22	37	41	46	50	55	60	64
23	38	43	48	53	58	62	67
24	40	45	50	55	60	65	70

Notation

φ = latitude of observer
λ = longitude of observer (measured positively towards the west)
T_{-1} = time of transit of Moon on previous day
T_0 = time of transit of Moon on day in question
T_1 = time of transit of Moon on following day
δ_0 = approximate declination of Moon
δ_R = declination of Moon at moonrise
δ_S = declination of Moon at moonset
h_0 = approximate hour angle of Moon
h_R = hour angle of Moon at moonrise
h_S = hour angle of Moon at moonset
t_R = time of moonrise
t_S = time of moonset

Method

1. With arguments φ, δ_0 enter Table 1 on page 64 to determine h_0 where h_0 is negative for moonrise and positive for moonset.

2. Form approximate times from
$$t_R = T_0 + \lambda + h_0$$
$$t_S = T_0 + \lambda + h_0$$

3. Determine δ_R, δ_S for times t_R, t_S respectively.

4. Re-enter Table 1 on page 64 with
   (*a*) arguments φ, δ_R to determine h_R
   (*b*) arguments φ, δ_S to determine h_S

5. Form $t_R = T_0 + \lambda + h_R + AX$
$$t_S = T_0 + \lambda + h_S + AX$$

where $A = (\lambda + h)$

and $\quad X = (T_0 - T_{-1}) \quad$ if $(\lambda + h)$ is negative
$\qquad X = (T_1 - T_0) \quad$ if $(\lambda + h)$ is positive

AX is the respondent in Table 3.

Example – To find the times of moonrise and moonset at Vancouver ($\varphi = +49°$, $\lambda = +8h\ 12m$) on 1997 January 7. The starting data (page 18) are

$T_{-1} = 9h\ 24m$
$T_0 = 10h\ 22m$
$T_1 = 11h\ 23m$
$\delta_0 = -18°$

1. $h_0 = 4h\ 32m$
2. Approximate values
   $t_R = 7d\ 10h\ 22m + 8h\ 12m + (-4h\ 32m)$
   $\quad = 7d\ 14h\ 02m$
   $t_S = 7d\ 10h\ 22m + 8h\ 12m + (+4h\ 32m)$
   $\quad = 7d\ 23h\ 06m$
3. $\delta_R = -18°.2$
   $\delta_S = -18°.4$
4. $h_R = -4h\ 31m$
   $h_S = +4h\ 30m$
5. $t_R = 7d\ 10h\ 22m + 8h\ 12m + (-4h\ 31m) + 9m$
   $\quad = 7d\ 14h\ 12m$
   $t_S = 7d\ 10h\ 22m + 8h\ 12m + (+4h\ 30m) + 32m$
   $\quad = 7d\ 23h\ 36m$

To get the LMT of the phenomenon the longitude is subtracted from the GMT thus:
Moonrise = 7d 14h 12m − 8h 12m = 7d 06h 00m
Moonset = 7d 23h 36m − 8h 12m = 7d 15h 24m

ECLIPSES AND OCCULTATIONS 1997

ECLIPSES

There will be four eclipses in 1997, two of the Sun and two of the Moon. (Penumbral eclipses are not mentioned in this section as they are too difficult to observe.)

1. A total eclipse of the Sun on March 8–9 is visible as a partial eclipse from Asia, the Philippine Islands, the north-western part of the Pacific Ocean, Alaska, north-western Canada and the Arctic Ocean. The eclipse begins at 8d 23h 17m and ends at 9d 03h 31m. The track of the total phase starts on the borders of the CIS, Sinkiang (China) and Mongolia and then sweeps north-eastwards through the eastern part of the CIS before ending in the Arctic Ocean. The total phase begins at 9d 00h 41m and ends at 9d 02h 06m: the maximum duration is 2m 50s.

2. A partial eclipse of the Moon on March 24 is visible from Africa, the western part of Madagascar, western Asia Minor and western Asia, Europe, the Atlantic Ocean, Iceland, Greenland, the Americas, the eastern Pacific Ocean, and part of Antarctica. The eclipse begins at 2h 58m and ends at 6h 21m. At maximum eclipse 92 per cent of the Moon's diameter is obscured.

3. A partial eclipse of the Sun on September 1–2 is visible from Australasia, the south Pacific Ocean (including New Caledonia and Vanuatu), and part of Antarctica. The eclipse begins at 1d 21h 44m and ends at 2d 2h 23m.

4. A total eclipse of the Moon on September 16 is visible from the western Pacific Ocean, Australasia, Asia, the Indian Ocean, Africa, Europe, Iceland, eastern Greenland, the Atlantic Ocean, the eastern part of South America and Antarctica. The eclipse begins at 17h 08m and ends at 20h 25m. Totality begins at 18h 16m and ends at 19h 18m.

LUNAR OCCULTATIONS

Observations of the times of occultations are made by both amateur and professional astronomers. Such observations are later analysed to yield accurate positions of the Moon; this is one method of determining the difference between ephemeris time and universal time.

Many of the observations made by amateurs are obtained with the use of a stop-watch which is compared with a time-signal immediately after the observation. Thus an accuracy of about one-fifth of a second is obtainable, though the observer's personal equation may amount to one-third or one-half of a second.

The list on page 67 includes most of the occultations visible under favourable conditions in the British Isles. No occultation is included unless the star is at least 10° above the horizon and the Sun sufficiently far below the horizon to permit the star to be seen with the naked eye or with a small telescope. The altitude limit is reduced from 10° to 2° for stars and planets brighter than magnitude 2.0 and such occultations are also predicted in daylight.

The column Phase shows (i) whether a disappearance (D) or reappearance (R) is to be observed; and (ii) whether it is at the dark limb (D) or bright limb (B). The column headed 'El. of Moon' gives the elongation of the Moon from the Sun, in degrees. The elongation increases from 0° at New Moon to 180° at Full Moon and on to 360° (or 0°) at New Moon again. Times and position angles (P), reckoned from the north point in the direction north, east, south, west, are given for Greenwich (lat. 51° 30′, long. 0°) and Edinburgh (lat. 56° 00′, long. 3° 12′ west).

The coefficients a and b are the variations in the GMT for each degree of longitude (positive to the west) and latitude (positive to the north) respectively; they enable approximate times (to within about 1m generally) to be found for any point in the British Isles. If the point of observation is $\Delta\lambda$ degrees west and $\Delta\phi$ degrees north, the approximate time is found by adding $a.\Delta\lambda + b.\Delta\phi$ to the given GMT.

Example: the reappearance of ZC 692 on May 8 at Liverpool, found from both Greenwich and Edinburgh.

	Greenwich	Edinburgh
	°	°
Longitude	0.0	+ 3.2
Long. of Liverpool	+ 3.0	+ 3.0
$\Delta\lambda$	+ 3.0	− 0.2
Latitude	+ 51.5	+ 56.0
Lat. of Liverpool	+ 53.4	+ 53.4
$\Delta\phi$	+ 1.9	− 2.6
	h m	h m
GMT	14 19.0	14 15.0
$a.\Delta\lambda$	− 4.5	+ 0.3
$b.\Delta\phi$	+ 0.6	+ 0.3
	14 15.1	14 15.6

If the occultation is given for one station but not the other, the reason for the suppression is given by the following code:

N = star not occulted
A = star's altitude less than 10° (2° for bright stars and planets)
S = Sun not sufficiently below the horizon
G = occultation is of very short duration

In some cases the coefficients a and b are not given; this is because the occultation is so short that prediction for other places by means of these coefficients would not be reliable.

Observers may like to note that ZC 692 = *Aldebaran* (occulted on March 14, May 8, July 2, July 29 and December 13).

LUNAR OCCULTATIONS 1997

Date		ZC No.	Mag.	Phase	El. of Moon	GREENWICH				EDINBURGH			
						UT	a	b	P	UT	a	b	P
					°				°				°
						h m	m	m		h m	m	m	
January	11	3205	6.8	D.D.	36	17 14.8	−0.9	−0.8	74	17 9.4	−0.8	−0.5	61
	11	3208	6.5	D.D.	36	17 46.0	−0.4	0.2	35	17 47.4	−0.1	0.9	16
	12	3357	6.8	D.D.	50	18 41.9	−0.8	−0.8	72	18 36.8	−0.6	−0.5	58
	16	360	6.8	D.D.	101	17 14.6	−1.5	0.8	87	17 15.2	−1.1	1.2	75
	18	627	6.8	D.D.	126	20 19.8	−1.5	0.8	68	20 20.5	−1.2	1.4	53
	18	636	6.9	D.D.	127	22 52.3	G		2	N			
	19	667	5.3	D.D.	129	2 46.5	0.1	−1.5	95	2 39.6	0.0	−1.5	87
	19	672	6.6	D.D.	129	A				3 6.0	0.5	−2.9	142
	19	677	4.8	D.D.	130	A				3 45.2	0.5	−2.4	136
	20	806	5.1	D.D.	141	A				4 26.0	0.3	−1.6	102
February	12	344	8.4	D.D.	72	A				22 43.8	−0.1	−1.5	87
	13	464	6.4	D.D.	84	21 22.4	−0.7	−1.7	96	21 13.5	−0.8	−1.2	83
	15	741	5.7	D.D.	108	21 18.8	−1.4	0.0	63	21 15.9	−1.3	0.7	48
	16	878	5.5	D.D.	118	19 43.4	−1.6	0.5	80	19 42.4	−1.4	1.2	66
	17	1029	5.1	D.D.	131	22 13.3	G		30	N			
	20	1271	5.9	D.D.	154	2 4.2	−1.2	−0.9	66	1 57.0	−1.2	−0.6	59
March	14	692	1.1	D.D.	76	18 43.2	−1.4	0.0	69	18 40.1	−1.3	0.6	54
	14	692	1.1	R.B.	76	19 55.8	−1.0	−1.6	281	19 44.5	−1.0	−2.0	294
	16	975	6.8	D.D.	99	18 53.0	−1.7	0.0	88	S			
	17	1106	3.7	D.D.	111	21 32.0	−1.2	−1.9	117	21 21.0	−1.2	−1.4	108
	18	1234	6.1	D.D.	123	23 43.7	−0.4	−2.8	144	23 30.4	−0.6	−2.5	137
	20	1428	3.8	D.D.	143	20 7.1	G		170	19 54.1	−0.9	−1.3	151
April	10	635	3.9	D.D.	46	21 42.2	0.6	−2.8	143	21 32.0	0.3	−2.4	130
	13	1073	6.0	D.D.	81	22 33.0	G		162	22 19.0	0.1	−3.1	151
May	8	692	1.1	D.D.	22	13 3.1	−1.6	0.2	92	13 0.7	−1.3	0.7	78
	8	692	1.1	R.B.	23	14 19.0	−1.5	0.3	250	14 15.0	−1.3	−0.1	264
	9	878	5.5	D.D.	38	21 18.5	−0.1	−0.6	51	21 15.6	−0.2	−0.5	42
	12	1271	5.9	D.D.	74	23 35.2	0.1	−1.3	80	23 29.2	0.0	−1.4	76
June	16	2060	6.3	D.D.	131	21 18.1	−0.8	−2.0	164	S			
	16	2064	6.5	D.D.	131	21 45.2	−1.4	−1.1	124	S			
July	2	692	1.1	D.B.	328	4 3.9	0.4	2.5	28	4 18.4	G		12
	2	692	1.1	R.D.	329	4 41.3	−0.6	0.6	308	4 40.8	G		325
	29	635	3.9	R.D.	299	3 14.9	−0.4	1.7	257	S			
	29	692	1.1	D.B.	304	11 26.6	−1.1	−0.1	53	11 24.3	−1.1	0.6	37
	29	692	1.1	R.D.	304	12 23.4	−0.4	−2.4	299	12 10.0	−0.4	−3.0	313
August	5	Mercury	0.4	D.D.	27	A				19 38.2	0.0	−2.3	133
	23	327	4.5	R.D.	244	1 55.2	−1.5	0.4	291	1 51.5	−1.6	0.0	307
September	8	2291	5.5	D.D.	75	19 27.6	−1.3	−2.2	144	19 15.0	−1.2	−1.7	137
	11	2733	6.4	D.D.	113	21 35.8	G		162	21 16.0	−1.6	−1.8	141
	22	699	5.8	R.D.	251	0 13.2	−0.4	1.9	246	0 20.3	−0.4	1.8	256
	22	704	4.9	R.D.	251	0 27.5	0.2	3.4	200	0 40.5	−0.1	2.6	216
October	9	2846	6.9	D.D.	95	21 7.7	−1.4	−2.2	124	A			
	13	3430	5.7	D.D.	148	21 9.6	−1.2	0.9	59	21 10.6	−1.0	1.1	49
	19	635	3.9	R.D.	221	2 54.8	−1.4	1.1	234	2 54.2	−1.2	0.6	249
November	5	2787	6.4	D.D.	63	17 30.0	−1.2	−0.1	56	17 26.3	−1.1	0.0	47
	5	2794	6.7	D.D.	63	18 22.6	−1.5	−1.7	118	18 11.8	−1.3	−1.2	108
	9	3353	3.8	D.D.	114	17 43.5	−1.3	1.0	87	17 44.4	−1.1	1.1	79
	9	3360	6.3	D.D.	115	19 0.7	−1.2	1.0	52	19 2.2	−0.9	1.1	42
	9	3383	6.5	D.D.	117	23 26.9	−0.8	−1.6	97	23 18.1	−0.7	−1.2	82
	12	Saturn	0.4	D.D.	145	1 28.2	−0.5	0.0	43	1 28.0	−0.4	0.7	25
	12	Saturn	0.4	R.B.	146	2 21.2	−0.4	−1.7	278	2 10.4	−0.5	−2.5	295
December	4	3029	6.9	D.D.	57	16 38.2	−1.3	0.1	63	16 35.1	−1.1	0.2	55
	6	3333	6.9	D.D.	85	20 27.1	−1.0	−0.9	79	20 20.9	−0.8	−0.6	65
	8	55	6.4	D.D.	109	17 15.4	−1.2	1.1	82	17 17.4	−1.0	1.3	73
	12	635	3.9	D.D.	164	22 4.2	−1.9	−1.4	128	21 56.1	−1.4	−0.1	110
	13	692	1.1	D.D.	168	A				6 11.3	G		13
	22	1772	4.0	R.D.	274	7 7.9	G		10	N			

MEAN PLACES OF STARS 1997.5

Name	Mag.	RA h m	Dec. ° '	Spectrum	Name	Mag.	RA h m	Dec. ° '	Spectrum
α And *Alpheratz*	2.1	0 08.3	+29 05	A0p	γ Corvi	2.6	12 15.7	−17 32	B8
β Cassiopeiae *Caph*	2.3	0 09.0	+59 08	F5	α Crucis	1.0	12 26.5	−63 05	B1
γ Pegasi *Algenib*	2.8	0 13.1	+15 10	B2	γ Crucis	1.6	12 31.0	−57 06	M3
β Mensae	2.9	0 25.7	−77 16	G0	γ Centauri	2.2	12 41.4	−48 57	A0
α Phoenicis	2.4	0 26.2	−42 19	K0	γ Virginis	2.7	12 41.5	− 1 26	F0
α Cassiopeiae *Schedar*	2.2	0 40.4	+56 31	K0	β Crucis	1.3	12 47.6	−59 41	B1
β Ceti *Diphda*	2.0	0 43.5	−18 00	K0	ε Ursae Majoris *Alioth*	1.8	12 53.9	+55 58	A0p
γ Cassiopeiae*	Var.	0 56.6	+60 42	B0p	α Canum Venaticorum	2.9	12 55.9	+38 20	A0p
β Andromedae *Mirach*	2.1	1 09.6	+35 36	M0	ζ Ursae Majoris *Mizar*	2.1	13 23.8	+54 56	A2p
δ Cassiopeiae	2.7	1 25.7	+60 13	A5	α Virginis *Spica*	1.0	13 25.1	−11 09	B2
α Eridani *Achernar*	0.5	1 37.6	−57 15	B5	ε Centauri	2.6	13 39.7	−53 27	B1
β Arietis *Sheratan*	2.6	1 54.5	+20 48	A5	η Ursae Majoris *Alkaid*	1.9	13 47.4	+49 20	B3
γ Andromedae *Almak*	2.3	2 03.7	+42 19	K0	β Centauri *Hadar*	0.6	14 03.6	−60 22	B1
α Arietis *Hamal*	2.0	2 07.0	+23 27	K2	θ Centauri	2.1	14 06.5	−36 21	K0
α Ursae Minoris *Polaris*	2.0	2 29.1	+89 15	F8	α Bootis *Arcturus*	0.0	14 15.5	+19 12	K0
β Persei *Algol**	Var.	3 08.0	+40 57	B8	α Centauri *Rigil Kent*	0.1	14 39.4	−60 49	G0
α Persei *Mirfak*	1.8	3 24.1	+49 51	F5	ε Bootis	2.4	14 44.9	+27 05	K0
η Tauri *Alcyone*	2.9	3 47.3	+24 06	B5p	β UMi *Kochab*	2.1	14 50.7	+74 10	K5
α Tauri *Aldebaran*	0.9	4 35.8	+16 30	K5	γ Ursae Minoris	3.1	15 20.7	+71 51	A2
β Orionis *Rigel*	0.1	5 14.4	− 8 12	B8p	α CrB *Alphecca*	2.2	15 34.6	+26 43	A0
α Aurigae *Capella*	0.1	5 16.5	+46 00	G0	β Trianguli Australis	3.0	15 54.9	−63 25	F0
γ Orionis *Bellatrix*	1.6	5 25.0	+ 6 21	B2	δ Scorpii	2.3	16 00.2	−22 37	B0
β Tauri *Elnath*	1.7	5 26.1	+28 36	B8	β Scorpii	2.6	16 05.3	−19 48	B1
δ Orionis	2.2	5 31.9	− 0 18	B0	α Scorpii *Antares*	1.0	16 29.3	−26 26	M0
α Leporis	2.6	5 32.6	−17 49	F0	α Trianguli Australis	1.9	16 48.4	−69 01	K2
ε Orionis	1.7	5 36.1	− 1 12	B0	ε Scorpii	2.3	16 50.0	−34 17	K0
ζ Orionis	1.8	5 40.6	− 1 57	B0	α Herculis†	Var.	17 14.5	+14 24	M3
κ Orionis	2.1	5 47.6	− 9 40	B0	λ Scorpii	1.6	17 33.4	−37 06	B2
α Orionis *Betelgeuse**	Var.	5 55.0	+ 7 24	M0	α Ophiuchi *Rasalhague*	2.1	17 34.8	+12 34	A5
β Aurigae *Menkalinan*	1.9	5 59.3	+44 57	A0p	θ Scorpii	1.9	17 37.1	−43 00	F0
β CMa *Mirzam*	2.0	6 22.6	−17 57	B1	κ Scorpii	2.4	17 42.3	−39 02	B2
α Carinae *Canopus*	−0.7	6 23.9	−52 42	F0	γ Draconis	2.2	17 56.5	+51 29	K5
γ Geminorum *Alhena*	1.9	6 37.6	+16 24	A0	ε Sgr *Kaus Australis*	1.9	18 24.0	−34 23	A0
α Canis Majoris *Sirius*	−1.5	6 45.0	−16 43	A0	α Lyrae *Vega*	0.0	18 36.9	+38 47	A0
ε Canis Majoris	1.5	6 58.5	−28 58	B1	σ Sagittarii	2.0	18 55.1	−26 18	B3
δ Canis Majoris	1.9	7 08.3	−26 23	F8p	β Cygni *Albireo*	3.1	19 30.6	+27 57	K0
α Geminorum *Castor*	1.6	7 34.4	+31 54	A0	α Aquilae *Altair*	0.8	19 50.7	+ 8 52	A5
α CMi *Procyon*	0.4	7 39.2	+ 5 14	F5	α Capricorni	3.8	20 17.9	−12 33	G5
β Geminorum *Pollux*	1.1	7 45.2	+28 02	K0	γ Cygni	2.2	20 22.1	+40 15	F8p
ζ Puppis	2.3	8 03.5	−40 00	Od	α Pavonis	1.9	20 25.5	−56 45	B3
γ Velorum	1.8	8 09.5	−47 20	Oap	α Cygni *Deneb*	1.3	20 41.3	+45 16	A2p
ε Carinae	1.9	8 22.5	−59 30	K0	α Cephei *Alderamin*	2.4	21 18.5	+62 35	A5
δ Velorum	2.0	8 44.6	−54 42	A0	ε Pegasi	2.4	21 44.1	+ 9 52	K0
λ Velorum *Suhail*	2.2	9 07.9	−43 25	K5	δ Capricorni	2.9	21 46.9	−16 08	A5
β Carinae	1.7	9 13.2	−69 42	A0	α Gruis	1.7	22 08.1	−46 58	B5
ι Carinae	2.2	9 17.0	−59 16	F0	δ Cephei†	3.7	22 29.1	+58 24	†
κ Velorum	2.6	9 22.0	−55 00	B3	β Gruis	2.1	22 42.5	−46 54	M3
α Hydrae *Alphard*	2.0	9 27.5	− 8 39	K2	α PsA *Fomalhaut*	1.2	22 57.5	−29 38	A3
α Leonis *Regulus*	1.3	10 08.2	+11 59	B8	β Pegasi *Scheat*	2.4	23 03.7	+28 04	M0
γ Leonis *Algeiba*	1.9	10 19.8	+19 51	K0	α Pegasi *Markab*	2.5	23 04.6	+15 12	A0
β Ursae Majoris *Merak*	2.4	11 01.7	+56 24	A0					
α Ursae Majoris *Dubhe*	1.8	11 03.6	+61 46	K0					
δ Leonis	2.6	11 14.0	+20 32	A3					
β Leonis *Denebola*	2.1	11 48.9	+14 35	A2					
γ Ursae Majoris *Phecda*	2.4	11 53.7	+53 43	A0					

*γ Cassiopeiae, 1996 mag. 2.5. β Persei, mag. 2.1 to 3.4.
 α Orionis, mag. 0.1 to 1.2.
†α Herculis, mag. 3.1 to 3.9. δ Cephei, mag. 3.7 to 4.4,
 Spectrum F5 to G0.

The positions of heavenly bodies on the celestial sphere are defined by two co-ordinates, right ascension and declination, which are analogous to longitude and latitude on the surface of the Earth. If we imagine the plane of the terrestrial equator extended indefinitely, it will cut the celestial sphere in a great circle known as the celestial equator. Similarly the plane of the Earth's orbit, when extended, cuts in the great circle called the ecliptic. The two intersections of these circles are known as the First Point of Aries and the First Point of Libra. If from any star a perpendicular be drawn to the celestial equator, the length of this perpendicular is the star's declination. The arc, measured eastwards along the equator from the First Point of Aries to the foot of this perpendicular, is the right ascension. An alternative definition of right ascension is that it is the angle at the celestial pole (where the Earth's axis, if prolonged, would meet the sphere) between the great circles to the First Point of Aries and to the star.

The plane of the Earth's equator has a slow movement, so that our reference system for right ascension and declination is not fixed. The consequent alteration in these quantities from year to year is called precession. In right ascension it is an increase of about 3 seconds a year for equatorial stars, and larger or smaller changes in either direction for stars near the poles, depending on the right ascension of the star. In declination it varies between $+20''$ and $-20''$ according to the right ascension of the star.

A star or other body crosses the meridian when the sidereal time is equal to its right ascension. The altitude is then a maximum, and may be deduced by remembering that the altitude of the elevated pole is numerically equal to the latitude, while that of the equator at its intersection with the meridian is equal to the co-latitude, or complement of the latitude.

Thus in London (lat. 51° 30′) the meridian altitude of Sirius is found as follows:

	°	′
Altitude of equator	38	30
Declination south	16	43
Difference	21	47

The altitude of Capella (Dec. $+46°\ 00'$) at lower transit is:

	°	′
Altitude of pole	51	30
Polar distance of star	44	00
Difference	7	30

The brightness of a heavenly body is denoted by its magnitude. Omitting the exceptionally bright stars Sirius and Canopus, the twenty brightest stars are of the first magnitude, while the faintest stars visible to the naked eye are of the sixth magnitude. The magnitude scale is a precise one, as a difference of five magnitudes represents a ratio of 100 to 1 in brightness. Typical second magnitude stars are Polaris and the stars in the belt of Orion. The scale is most easily fixed in memory by comparing the stars with Norton's *Star Atlas* (*see* page 71). The stars Sirius and Canopus and the planets Venus and Jupiter are so bright that their magnitudes are expressed by negative numbers. A small telescope will show stars down to the ninth or tenth magnitude, while stars fainter than the twentieth magnitude may be photographed by long exposures with the largest telescopes.

MEAN AND SIDEREAL TIME

Acceleration					Retardation				
h	m s	m	s	s	h	m s	m	s	s
1	0 10	0	00		1	0 10	0	00	
2	0 20	3	02	0	2	0 20	3	03	0
3	0 30	9	07	1	3	0 29	9	09	1
4	0 39	15	13	2	4	0 39	15	15	2
5	0 49	21	18	3	5	0 49	21	21	3
6	0 59	27	23	4	6	0 59	27	28	4
7	1 09	33	28	5	7	1 09	33	34	5
8	1 19	39	34	6	8	1 19	39	40	6
9	1 29	45	39	7	9	1 28	45	46	7
10	1 39	51	44	8	10	1 38	51	53	8
11	1 48	57	49	9	11	1 48	57	59	9
12	1 58	60	00	10	12	1 58	60	00	10
13	2 08				13	2 08			
14	2 18				14	2 18			
15	2 28				15	2 27			
16	2 38				16	2 37			
17	2 48				17	2 47			
18	2 57				18	2 57			
19	3 07				19	3 07			
20	3 17				20	3 17			
21	3 27				21	3 26			
22	3 37				22	3 36			
23	3 47				23	3 46			
24	3 57				24	3 56			

The length of a sidereal day in mean time is 23h 56m 04s.09. Hence 1h MT = 1h + 9s.86 ST and 1h ST = 1h − 9s.83 MT.

To convert an interval of mean time to the corresponding interval of sidereal time, enter the acceleration table with the given mean time (taking the hours and the minutes and seconds separately) and add the acceleration obtained to the given mean time. To convert an interval of sidereal time to the corresponding interval of mean time, take out the retardation for the given sidereal time and subtract.

The columns for the minutes and seconds of the argument are in the form known as critical tables. To use these tables, find in the appropriate left-hand column the two entries between which the given number of minutes and seconds lies; the quantity in the right-hand column between these two entries is the required acceleration or retardation. Thus the acceleration for 11m 26s (which lies between the entries 9m 07s and 15m 13s) is 2s. If the given number of minutes and seconds is a tabular entry, the required acceleration or retardation is the entry in the right-hand column above the given tabular entry, e.g. the retardation for 45m 46s is 7s.

Example − Convert 14h 27m 35s from ST to MT

	h	m	s
Given ST	14	27	35
Retardation for 14h		2	18
Retardation for 27m 35s			5
Corresponding MT	14	25	12

For further explanation, *see* pages 73–4.

ECLIPSES AND SHADOW TRANSITS OF JUPITER'S SATELLITES 1997

GMT — d h m	Sat.	Phen.
APRIL		
9 05 17	I	Sh.I
20 03 58	II	Ec.D
24 04 42	IV	Sh.E
25 03 33	I	Sh.I
28 04 17	III	Ec.R
29 04 35	II	Sh.E
MAY		
6 04 19	II	Sh.I
11 04 05	I	Sh.E
16 02 16	III	Sh.E
18 03 42	I	Sh.I
22 03 35	II	Ec.D
23 02 42	III	Sh.I
26 02 55	I	Ec.D
27 02 20	I	Sh.E
31 01 21	II	Sh.I
JUNE		
3 01 57	I	Sh.I
5 03 15	IV	Ec.R
11 01 10	I	Ec.D
12 00 37	I	Sh.E
16 00 40	II	Ec.D
18 03 04	I	Ec.D
19 00 13	I	Sh.I
19 02 31	I	Sh.E
23 03 16	II	Ec.D
25 01 14	II	Sh.E
26 02 07	I	Sh.E
28 02 15	III	Sh.E
30 00 28	IV	Sh.I
JULY		
2 00 57	II	Sh.I
4 01 20	I	Ec.D
5 00 47	I	Sh.E
5 02 38	III	Sh.I
9 03 32	II	Sh.I
11 03 14	I	Ec.D
12 00 24	I	Sh.I
12 02 42	I	Sh.E
16 23 28	IV	Sh.E
18 00 24	II	Ec.D
19 02 18	I	Sh.I
19 22 15	II	Sh.E
19 23 36	I	Ec.D
20 23 05	I	Sh.E
23 00 33	III	Ec.D
25 03 01	II	Ec.D
26 04 13	I	Sh.I
26 21 58	I	Sh.I
27 00 49	II	Sh.E
27 01 30	I	Ec.D
27 22 41	I	Sh.I
28 00 59	I	Sh.E
AUGUST		
2 22 17	III	Sh.E
3 00 32	II	Sh.I
3 03 24	II	Sh.E

GMT — d h m	Sat.	Phen.
AUGUST		
3 03 24	I	Ec.D
4 00 36	I	Sh.I
4 02 54	I	Sh.E
4 21 53	I	Ec.D
5 21 23	I	Sh.E
9 22 39	III	Sh.I
10 02 18	III	Sh.E
10 03 07	II	Sh.I
11 02 31	I	Sh.I
11 03 46	IV	Ec.R
12 00 30	II	Ec.R
12 02 05	I	Ec.R
12 20 59	I	Sh.I
12 23 18	I	Sh.E
13 20 33	I	Ec.R
17 02 39	III	Sh.I
19 03 08	II	Ec.R
19 22 55	I	Sh.I
20 01 13	I	Sh.E
20 20 14	III	Ec.R
20 21 51	II	Sh.E
20 22 28	I	Ec.R
21 19 42	I	Sh.E
27 00 50	I	Sh.I
27 21 34	II	Sh.I
27 21 55	IV	Ec.R
28 00 14	III	Ec.R
28 00 22	I	Ec.R
28 00 25	II	Sh.E
28 21 37	I	Sh.E
SEPTEMBER		
4 00 09	II	Sh.I
4 21 14	I	Sh.I
4 23 32	I	Sh.E
5 01 10	IV	Sh.I
5 20 46	I	Ec.R
5 21 43	II	Ec.R
11 23 09	I	Sh.I
12 01 27	I	Sh.E
12 22 40	I	Ec.R
13 00 21	II	Ec.R
13 19 56	I	Sh.E
14 18 45	III	Sh.I
14 18 53	II	Sh.E
14 22 23	III	Sh.E
19 01 05	I	Sh.I
20 00 35	I	Ec.R
20 19 34	I	Sh.I
20 21 52	I	Sh.E
21 18 38	II	Sh.I
21 19 04	I	Ec.R
21 19 24	IV	Sh.I
21 21 28	II	Sh.I
21 22 46	III	Sh.I
22 00 12	IV	Sh.E
27 21 30	I	Sh.I
27 23 47	I	Sh.E
28 20 59	I	Ec.R
28 21 13	II	Sh.I
29 00 03	II	Sh.E
29 18 16	I	Sh.E
30 18 57	II	Ec.R

GMT — d h m	Sat.	Phen.
OCTOBER		
2 20 19	III	Ec.R
4 23 25	I	Sh.I
5 22 54	I	Ec.R
5 23 49	II	Sh.I
6 20 11	I	Sh.E
7 21 35	II	Ec.R
8 18 25	IV	Sh.E
9 20 41	III	Ec.D
13 19 50	I	Sh.I
13 22 07	I	Sh.E
14 19 18	I	Ec.R
16 18 32	II	Sh.E
20 18 30	III	Sh.E
20 21 46	I	Sh.I
21 21 13	I	Ec.R
22 18 32	I	Sh.E
23 18 19	II	Sh.I
23 21 08	II	Sh.E
27 18 55	III	Sh.I
27 22 32	III	Sh.E
29 18 11	I	Sh.I
29 20 27	I	Sh.E
30 17 38	I	Ec.R
30 20 55	II	Sh.I
NOVEMBER		
1 18 48	II	Ec.R
2 17 53	IV	Ec.D
5 20 06	I	Sh.I
6 19 33	I	Ec.R
8 21 26	II	Ec.R
13 21 28	I	Ec.R

GMT — d h m	Sat.	Phen.
NOVEMBER		
14 16 49	III	Ec.D
14 18 48	I	Sh.E
14 20 28	III	Ec.R
17 18 15	II	Sh.E
19 16 48	IV	Ec.R
21 18 27	I	Sh.I
21 20 44	I	Sh.E
21 20 50	III	Ec.D
22 17 53	I	Ec.R
24 18 02	II	Sh.I
24 20 52	II	Sh.E
27 20 25	IV	Sh.I
28 20 23	I	Sh.I
29 19 48	I	Ec.R
30 17 08	I	Sh.E
DECEMBER		
1 20 39	II	Sh.I
2 18 40	III	Sh.E
3 18 38	II	Ec.R
7 16 47	I	Sh.I
7 19 04	I	Sh.E
9 19 06	III	Sh.I
14 18 43	I	Sh.I
14 19 18	IV	Sh.E
15 18 08	I	Ec.R
19 18 01	II	Sh.E
20 16 34	III	Ec.R
23 17 24	I	Sh.E
26 17 49	II	Sh.I
27 16 58	III	Ec.D
30 17 02	I	Sh.I

Jupiter's satellites transit across the disk from east to west, and pass behind the disk from west to east. The shadows that they cast also transit across the disk. With the exception at times of Satellite IV, the satellites also pass through the shadow of the planet, i.e. they are eclipsed. Just before opposition the satellite disappears in the shadow to the west of the planet and reappears from occultation on the east limb. Immediately after opposition the satellite is occulted at the west limb and reappears from eclipse to the east of the planet. At times approximately two to four months before and after opposition, both phases of eclipses of Satellite III may be seen. When Satellite IV is eclipsed, both phases may be seen.

The times given refer to the centre of the satellite. As the satellite is of considerable size, the immersion and emersion phases are not instantaneous. Even when the satellite enters or leaves the shadow along a radius of the shadow, the phase can last for several minutes. With Satellite IV, grazing phenomena can occur so that the light from the satellite may fade and brighten again without a complete eclipse taking place.

The list of phenomena gives most of the eclipses and shadow transits visible in the British Isles under favourable conditions.

Ec. = Eclipse   R. = Reappearance
Sh. = Shadow transit   I. = Ingress
D. = Disappearance   E. = Egress

EXPLANATION OF ASTRONOMICAL DATA

Positions of the heavenly bodies are given only to the degree of accuracy required by amateur astronomers for setting telescopes, or for plotting on celestial globes or star atlases. Where intermediate positions are required, linear interpolation may be employed.

Definitions of the terms used cannot be given here. They must be sought in astronomical literature and textbooks. Probably the best source for the amateur is Norton's *Star Atlas and Reference Handbook* (Longman, 18th edition, 1989; £25.00), which contains an introduction to observational astronomy, and a series of star maps for showing stars visible to the naked eye. Certain more extended ephemerides are available in the British Astronomical Association Handbook, an annual popular among amateur astronomers (Secretary: Burlington House, Piccadilly, London wiv 9AG).

A special feature has been made of the times when the various heavenly bodies are visible in the British Isles. Since two columns, calculated for latitudes 52° and 56°, are devoted to risings and settings, the range 50° to 58° can be covered by interpolation and extrapolation. The times given in these columns are Greenwich Mean Times for the meridian of Greenwich. An observer west of this meridian must add his/her longitude (in time) and vice versa.

In accordance with the usual convention in astronomy, + and − indicate respectively north and south latitudes or declinations.

All data are, unless otherwise stated, for 0h Greenwich Mean Time (GMT), i.e. at the midnight at the beginning of the day named. Allowance must be made for British Summer Time during the period that this is in operation (*see* pages 15 and 75).

PAGE ONE OF EACH MONTH

The calendar for each month is explained on page 15.

Under the heading Astronomical Phenomena will be found particulars of the more important conjunctions of the Sun, Moon and planets with each other, and also the dates of other astronomical phenomena of special interest.

Times of Minima of Algol are approximate times of the middle of the period of diminished light.

The Constellations listed each month are those that are near the meridian at the beginning of the month at 22h local mean time. Allowance must be made for British Summer Time if necessary. The fact that any star crosses the meridian 4m earlier each night or 2h earlier each month may be used, in conjunction with the lists given each month, to find what constellations are favourably placed at any moment. The table preceding the list of constellations may be extended indefinitely at the rate just quoted.

The principal phases of the Moon are the GMTs when the difference between the longitude of the Moon and that of the Sun is 0°, 90°, 180° or 270°. The times of perigee and apogee are those when the Moon is nearest to, and farthest from, the Earth, respectively. The nodes or points of intersection of the Moon's orbit and the ecliptic make a complete retrograde circuit of the ecliptic in about 19 years. From a knowledge of the longitude of the ascending node and the inclination, whose value does not vary much from 5°, the path of the Moon among the stars may be plotted on a celestial globe or star atlas.

PAGE TWO OF EACH MONTH

The Sun's semi-diameter, in arc, is given once a month.

The right ascension and declination (Dec.) is that of the true Sun. The right ascension of the mean Sun is obtained by applying the equation of time, with the sign given, to the right ascension of the true Sun, or, more easily, by applying 12h to the Sidereal Time. The direction in which the equation of time has to be applied in different problems is a frequent source of confusion and error. Apparent Solar Time is equal to the Mean Solar Time plus the Equation of Time. For example at noon on August 8 the Equation of Time is −5m 36s and thus at 12h Mean Time on that day the Apparent Time is 12h − 5m 36s = 11h 54m 24s.

The Greenwich Sidereal Time at 0h and the Transit of the First Point of Aries (which is really the mean time when the sidereal time is 0h) are used for converting mean time to sidereal time and vice versa.

The GMT of transit of the Sun at Greenwich may also be taken as the local mean time (LMT) of transit in any longitude. It is independent of latitude. The GMT of transit in any longitude is obtained by adding the longitude to the time given if west, and vice versa.

LIGHTING-UP TIME

The legal importance of sunrise and sunset is that the Road Vehicles Lighting Regulations 1989 (SI 1989 No. 1796) make the use of front and rear position lamps on vehicles compulsory during the period between sunset and sunrise. Headlamps on vehicles are required to be used during the hours of darkness on unlit roads or whenever visibility is seriously reduced. The hours of darkness are defined in these regulations as the period between half an hour after sunset and half an hour before sunrise.

In all laws and regulations 'sunset' refers to the local sunset, i.e. the time at which the Sun sets at the place in question. This common-sense interpretation has been upheld by legal tribunals. Thus the necessity for providing for different latitudes and longitudes, as already described, is evident.

SUNRISE AND SUNSET

The times of sunrise and sunset are those when the Sun's upper limb, as affected by refraction, is on the true horizon of an observer at sea-level. Assuming the mean refraction to be 34′, and the Sun's semi-diameter to be 16′, the time given is that when the true zenith distance of the Sun's centre is 90° + 34′ + 16′ or 90° 50′, or, in other words, when the depression of the Sun's centre below the true horizon is 50′. The upper limb is then 34′ below the true horizon, but is brought there by refraction. It is true, of course, that an observer on a ship might see the Sun for a minute or so longer, because of the dip of the horizon, while another viewing the sunset over hills or mountains would record an earlier time. Nevertheless, the moment when the true zenith distance of the Sun's centre is 90° 50′ is a precise time dependent only on the latitude and longitude of the place, and independent of its altitude above sea-level, the contour of its horizon, the vagaries of refraction or the small seasonal change in the Sun's semi-diameter; this moment is suitable in every way as a definition of sunset (or sunrise) for all statutory purposes. (For further information, *see* footnote on page 72.)

TWILIGHT

Light reaches us before sunrise and continues to reach us for some time after sunset. The interval between darkness and sunrise or sunset and darkness is called twilight. Astronomically speaking, twilight is considered to begin or end when the Sun's centre is 18° below the horizon, as no light from the Sun can then reach the observer. As thus defined twilight may last several hours; in high latitudes at the summer solstice the depression of 18° is not reached, and twilight lasts from sunset to sunrise.

The need for some sub-division of twilight is met by dividing the gathering darkness into four stages.

(1) *Sunrise or Sunset*, defined as above
(2) *Civil twilight*, which begins or ends when the Sun's centre is 6° below the horizon. This marks the time when operations requiring daylight may commence or must cease. In England it varies from about 30 to 60 minutes after sunset and the same interval before sunrise
(3) *Nautical twilight*, which begins or ends when the Sun's centre is 12° below the horizon. This marks the time when it is, to all intents and purposes, completely dark
(4) *Astronomical twilight*, which begins or ends when the Sun's centre is 18° below the horizon. This marks theoretical perfect darkness. It is of little practical importance, especially if nautical twilight is tabulated

To assist observers the durations of civil, nautical and astronomical twilights are given at intervals of ten days. The beginning of a particular twilight is found by subtracting the duration from the time of sunrise, while the end is found by adding the duration to the time of sunset. Thus the beginning of astronomical twilight in latitude 52°, on the Greenwich meridian, on March 11 is found as 06h 24m − 113m = 04h 31m and similarly the end of civil twilight as 17h 57m + 34m = 18h 31m. The letters TAN (twilight all night) are printed when twilight lasts all night.

Under the heading The Night Sky will be found notes describing the position and visibility of the planets and other phenomena.

PAGE THREE OF EACH MONTH

The Moon moves so rapidly among the stars that its position is given only to the degree of accuracy that permits linear interpolation. The right ascension (RA) and declination (Dec.) are geocentric, i.e. for an imaginary observer at the centre of the Earth. To an observer on the surface of the Earth the position is always different, as the altitude is always less on account of parallax, which may reach 1°.

The lunar terminator is the line separating the bright from the dark part of the Moon's disk. Apart from irregularities of the lunar surface, the terminator is elliptical, because it is a circle seen in projection. It becomes the full circle forming the limb, or edge, of the Moon at New and Full Moon. The selenographic longitude of the terminator is measured from the mean centre of the visible disk, which may differ from the visible centre by as much as 8°, because of libration.

Instead of the longitude of the terminator the Sun's selenographic co-longitude (Sun's co-long.) is tabulated. It is numerically equal to the selenographic longitude of the morning terminator, measured eastwards from the mean centre of the disk. Thus its value is approximately 270° at New Moon, 360° at First Quarter, 90° at Full Moon and 180° at Last Quarter.

The Position Angle (PA) of the Bright Limb is the position angle of the midpoint of the illuminated limb, measured eastwards from the north point on the disk. The Phase column shows the percentage of the area of the Moon's disk illuminated; this is also the illuminated percentage of the diameter at right angles to the line of cusps. The terminator is a semi-ellipse whose major axis is the line of cusps, and whose semi-minor axis is determined by the tabulated percentage; from New Moon to Full Moon the east limb is dark, and vice versa.

The times given as moonrise and moonset are those when the upper limb of the Moon is on the horizon of an observer at sea-level. The Sun's horizontal parallax (Hor. par.) is about 9″, and is negligible when considering sunrise and sunset, but that of the Moon averages about 57′. Hence the computed time represents the moment when the true zenith distance of the Moon is 90° 50′ (as for the Sun) minus the horizontal parallax. The time required for the Sun or Moon to rise or set is about four minutes (except in high latitudes). *See also* page 65 and footnote below.

The GMT of transit of the Moon over the meridian of Greenwich is given; these times are independent of latitude but must be corrected for longitude. For places in the British Isles it suffices to add the longitude if west, and vice versa. For other places a further correction is necessary because of the rapid movement of the Moon relative to the stars. The entire correction is conveniently determined by first finding the west longitude λ of the place. If the place is in west longitude, λ is the ordinary west longitude; if the place is in east longitude λ is the complement to 24h (or 360°) of the longitude and will be greater than 12h (or 180°). The correction then consists of two positive portions, namely λ and the fraction $\lambda/24$ (or $\lambda/360$) multiplied by the difference between consecutive transits. Thus for Sydney, New South Wales, the longitude is 10h 05m east, so λ=13h 55m and the fraction $\lambda/24$ is 0.58. The transit on the local date 1997 January 15 is found as follows:

	d	h	m
GMT of transit at Greenwich　Jan.	15	17	53
λ		13	55
0.58×(18h 43m − 17h 53m)			29
GMT of transit at Sydney	16	08	17
Corr. to NSW Standard Time		10	00
Local standard time of transit	16	18	17

As is evident, for any given place the quantities λ and the correction to local standard time may be combined permanently, being here 23h 55m.

Positions of Mercury are given for every second day, and those of Venus and Mars for every fifth day; they may be interpolated linearly. The diameter (Diam.) is given in seconds of arc. The phase is the illuminated percentage of the disk. In the case of the inner planets this approaches 100 at superior conjunction and 0 at inferior conjunction. When the phase is less than 50 the planet is crescent-shaped or horned; for greater phases it is gibbous. In the case of the exterior planet Mars, the phase approaches 100 at conjunction and opposition, and is a minimum at the quadratures.

Since the planets cannot be seen when on the horizon, the actual times of rising and setting are not given; instead, the time when the planet has an apparent altitude of 5° has

---

SUNRISE, SUNSET AND MOONRISE, MOONSET

The tables have been constructed for the meridian of Greenwich, and for latitudes 52° and 56°. They give Greenwich Mean Time (GMT) throughout the year. To obtain the GMT of the phenomenon as seen from any other latitude and longitude in the British Isles, first interpolate or extrapolate for latitude by the usual rules of proportion. To the time thus found, the longitude (expressed in time) is to be added if west (as it usually is in Great Britain) or subtracted if east. If the longitude is expressed in degrees and minutes of arc, it must be converted to time at the rate of 1° = 4m and 15′ = 1m.

A method of calculating rise and set times for other places in the world is given on pages 64 and 65.

been tabulated. If the time of transit is between 00h and 12h the time refers to an altitude of 5° above the eastern horizon; if between 12h and 24h, to the western horizon. The phenomenon tabulated is the one that occurs between sunset and sunrise. The times given may be interpolated for latitude and corrected for longitude, as in the case of the Sun and Moon.

The GMT at which the planet transits the Greenwich meridian is also given. The times of transit are to be corrected to local meridians in the usual way, as already described.

PAGE FOUR OF EACH MONTH

The GMTs of sunrise and sunset for seven cities, whose adopted positions in longitude (W.) and latitude (N.) are given immediately below the name, may be used not only for these phenomena, but also for lighting-up times (*see* page 71 for a fuller explanation).

page 71 for a fuller explanation

The particulars for the four outer planets resemble those for the planets on Page Three of each month, except that, under Uranus and Neptune, times when the planet is 10° high instead of 5° high are given; this is because of the inferior brightness of these planets. The diameters given for the rings of Saturn are those of the major axis (in the plane of the planet's equator) and the minor axis respectively. The former has a small seasonal change due to the slightly varying distance of the Earth from Saturn, but the latter varies from zero when the Earth passes through the ring plane every 15 years to its maximum opening half-way between these periods. The rings were last open at their widest extent in 1988.

TIME

From the earliest ages, the natural division of time into recurring periods of day and night has provided the practical time-scale for the everyday activities of the human race. Indeed, if any alternative means of time measurement is adopted, it must be capable of adjustment so as to remain in general agreement with the natural time-scale defined by the diurnal rotation of the Earth on its axis. Ideally the rotation should be measured against a fixed frame of reference; in practice it must be measured against the background provided by the celestial bodies. If the Sun is chosen as the reference point, we obtain Apparent Solar Time, which is the time indicated by a sundial. It is not a uniform time but is subject to variations which amount to as much as a quarter of an hour in each direction. Such wide variations cannot be tolerated in a practical time-scale, and this has led to the concept of Mean Solar Time in which all the days are exactly the same length and equal to the average length of the Apparent Solar Day.

The positions of the stars in the sky are specified in relation to a fictitious reference point in the sky known as the First Point of Aries (or the Vernal Equinox). It is therefore convenient to adopt this same reference point when considering the rotation of the Earth against the background of the stars. The time-scale so obtained is known as Apparent Sidereal Time.

GREENWICH MEAN TIME

The daily rotation of the Earth on its axis causes the Sun and the other heavenly bodies to appear to cross the sky from east to west. It is convenient to represent this relative motion as if the Sun really performed a daily circuit around a fixed Earth. Noon in Apparent Solar Time may then be defined as the time at which the Sun transits across the observer's meridian. In Mean Solar Time, noon is similarly defined by the meridian transit of a fictitious Mean Sun moving uniformly in the sky with the same average speed as the true Sun. Mean Solar Time observed on the meridian of the transit circle telescope of the Old Royal Observatory at Greenwich is called Greenwich Mean Time (GMT). The mean solar day is divided into 24 hours and, for astronomical and other scientific purposes, these are numbered 0 to 23, commencing at midnight. Civil time is usually reckoned in two periods of 12 hours, designated a.m. (*ante meridiem*, i.e. before noon) and p.m. (*post meridiem*, i.e. after noon).

UNIVERSAL TIME

Before 1925 January 1, GMT was reckoned in 24 hours commencing at noon; since that date it has been reckoned from midnight. To avoid confusion in the use of the designation GMT before and after 1925, since 1928 astronomers have tended to use the term Universal Time (UT) or Weltzeit (WZ) to denote GMT measured from Greenwich Mean Midnight.

In precision work it is necessary to take account of small variations in Universal Time. These arise from small irregularities in the rotation of the Earth. Observed astronomical time is designated UT0. Observed time corrected for the effects of the motion of the poles (giving rise to a 'wandering' in longitude) is designated UT1. There is also a seasonal fluctuation in the rate of rotation of the Earth arising from meteorological causes, often called the annual fluctuation. UT1 corrected for this effect is designated UT2 and provides a time-scale free from short-period fluctuations. It is still subject to small secular and irregular changes.

APPARENT SOLAR TIME

As mentioned above, the time shown by a sundial is called Apparent Solar Time. It differs from Mean Solar Time by an amount known as the Equation of Time, which is the total effect of two causes which make the length of the apparent solar day non-uniform. One cause of variation is that the orbit of the Earth is not a circle but an ellipse, having the Sun at one focus. As a consequence, the angular speed of the Earth in its orbit is not constant; it is greatest at the beginning of January when the Earth is nearest the Sun.

The other cause is due to the obliquity of the ecliptic; the plane of the equator (which is at right angles to the axis of rotation of the Earth) does not coincide with the ecliptic (the plane defined by the apparent annual motion of the Sun around the celestial sphere) but is inclined to it at an angle of 23° 26'. As a result, the apparent solar day is shorter than average at the equinoxes and longer at the solstices. From the combined effects of the components due to obliquity and eccentricity, the equation of time reaches its maximum values in February (−14 minutes) and early November (+16 minutes). It has a zero value on four dates during the year, and it is only on these dates (approximately April 15, June 14, September 1, and December 25) that a sundial shows Mean Solar Time.

SIDEREAL TIME

A sidereal day is the duration of a complete rotation of the Earth with reference to the First Point of Aries. The term sidereal (or 'star') time is a little misleading since the time-scale so defined is not exactly the same as that which would be defined by successive transits of a selected star, as there is a small progressive motion between the stars and the First Point of Aries due to the precession of the Earth's axis. This makes the length of the sidereal day shorter than the true period of rotation by 0.008 seconds. Superimposed on this steady precessional motion are small oscillations (nutation), giving rise to fluctuations in apparent sidereal time amounting to as much as 1.2 seconds. It is therefore customary to employ Mean Sidereal Time, from which these fluctuations have been removed. The conversion of GMT to Greenwich sidereal time (GST) may be performed by adding the value of the GST at 0h on the day in question (Page Two of each month) to the GMT converted to sidereal time using the table on page 69.

Example – To find the GST at August 8d 02h 41m 11s GMT

	h	m	s
GST at 0h	21	07	07
GMT	2	41	11
Acceleration for 2h			20
Acceleration for 41m 11s			7
Sum = GST =	23	48	45

If the observer is not on the Greenwich meridian then his/her longitude, measured positively westwards from Greenwich, must be subtracted from the GST to obtain Local Sidereal Time (LST). Thus, in the above example, an observer 5h east of Greenwich, or 19h west, would find the LST as 4h 48m 45s.

Ephemeris Time

An analysis of observations of the positions of the Sun, Moon and planets taken over an extended period is used in preparing ephemerides. (An ephemeris is a table giving the apparent position of a heavenly body at regular intervals of time, e.g. one day or ten days, and may be used to compare current observations with tabulated positions.) Discrepancies between the positions of heavenly bodies observed over a 300-year period and their predicted positions arose because the time-scale to which the observations were related was based on the assumption that the rate of rotation of the Earth is uniform. It is now known that this rate of rotation is variable. A revised time-scale, Ephemeris Time (ET), was devised to bring the ephemerides into agreement with the observations.

The second of ET is defined in terms of the annual motion of the Earth in its orbit around the Sun (1/31556925.9747 of the tropical year for 1900 January 0d 12h ET). The precise determination of ET from astronomical observations is a lengthy process as the requisite standard of accuracy can only be achieved by averaging over a number of years.

In 1976 the International Astronomical Union adopted a new dynamical time-scale for general use whose scale unit is the SI second (*see* Atomic Time). ET is now of little more than historical interest.

Terrestrial Dynamical Time

The uniform time system used in computing the ephemerides of the solar system is Terrestrial Dynamical Time (TDT), which has replaced ET for this purpose. Except for the most rigorous astronomical calculations, it may be assumed to be the same as ET. During 1997 the estimated difference TDT – UT is about 63 seconds.

Atomic Time

The fundamental standards of time and frequency must be defined in terms of a periodic motion adequately uniform, enduring and measurable. Progress has made it possible to use natural standards, such as atomic or molecular oscillations. Continuous oscillations are generated in an electrical circuit, the frequency of which is then compared or brought into coincidence with the frequency characteristic of the absorption or emission by the atoms or molecules when they change between two selected energy levels. The

National Physical Laboratory (NPL) routinely uses clocks of high stability produced by locking a quartz oscillator to the frequencies defined by caesium or hydrogen atoms.

International Atomic Time (TAI), established through international collaboration, is formed by combining the readings of many caesium clocks and was set close to the astronomically-based Universal Time (UT) near the beginning of 1958. It was formally recognized in 1971 and since 1988 January 1 has been maintained by the International Bureau of Weights and Measures (BIPM). The second markers are generated according to the International System (SI) definition adopted in 1967 at the 13th General Conference of Weights and Measures: 'The second is the duration of 9 192 631 770 periods of the radiation corresponding to the transition between the two hyperfine levels of the ground state of the caesium-133 atom.'

Civil time in almost all countries is now based on Co-ordinated Universal Time (UTC), which was adopted for scientific purposes on 1972 January 1. UTC differs from TAI by an integer number of seconds (determined from studies of the rate of rotation of the Earth) and was designed to make both atomic time and UT accessible with accuracies appropriate for most users. The UTC time-scale is adjusted by the insertion (or, in principle, omission) of leap seconds in order to keep it within ±0.9 s of UT. These leap seconds are introduced, when necessary, at the same instant throughout the world, either at the end of December or at the end of June. So, for example, the 20th leap second occurred at 0h GMT on 1996 January 1. All leap seconds so far have been positive, with 61 seconds in the final minute of the UTC month. The time 23h 59m 60s UTC is followed one second later by 0h 0m 00s of the first day of the following month. Notices concerning the insertion of leap seconds are issued by the International Earth Rotation Service (IERS) at the Observatoire de Paris.

Radio Time-Signals

UTC is made generally available through time-signals and standard frequency broadcasts such as MSF in the UK, CHU in Canada and WWV and WWVH in the USA. These are based on national time-scales that are maintained in close agreement with UTC and provide traceability to the national time-scale and to UTC. The markers of seconds in the UTC scale coincide with those of TAI.

To disseminate the national time-scale in the UK, special signals are broadcast on behalf of the National Physical Laboratory from the BT (British Telecom) radio station at Rugby (call-sign MSF). The signals are controlled from a caesium beam atomic frequency standard and consist of a precise frequency carrier of 60 kHz which is switched off, after being on for at least half a second, to mark every second. In part of the first second of each minute the carrier may be switched on and off to carry data at 100 bits/second. In the other seconds the carrier is always off for at least one tenth of a second at the start and then it carries an on-off code giving similar information for British clock time and date, together with information identifying the start of the next minute. Changes to and from summer time are made following government announcements. Leap seconds are inserted as announced by the IERS and information provided by them on the difference between UTC and UT is also signalled. Other broadcast signals in the UK include the BBC six pips signal, the BT Timeline ('speaking clock'), the NPL Truetime service for computers, and a coded time-signal on the BBC 198 kHz transmitters which is used for timing in the electricity supply industry. From 1972 January 1 the six pips on the BBC have consisted of five short pips from second 55 to second 59 (six pips in the case of a leap second) followed by one lengthened pip, the start of which indicates the exact minute. From 1990 February 5 these signals have been controlled by the BBC with seconds markers referenced to the satellite-based US navigation system GPS (Global Positioning System) and time and day referenced to the MSF transmitter. Formerly they were generated by the Royal Greenwich Observatory. The BT Timeline is compared daily with the National Physical Laboratory caesium beam atomic frequency standard at the Rugby radio station. The NPL Truetime service is directly connected to the national time scale.

Accurate timing may also be obtained from the signals of international navigation systems such as the ground-based Loran-C or Omega, or the satellite-based American GPS or Russian GLONASS systems.

STANDARD TIME

Since 1880 the standard time in Britain has been Greenwich Mean Time (GMT); a statute that year enacted that the word 'time' when used in any legal document relating to Britain meant, unless otherwise specifically stated, the mean time of the Greenwich meridian. Greenwich was adopted as the universal meridian on 13 October 1884. A system of standard time by zones is used world-wide, standard time in each zone differing from that of the Greenwich meridian by an integral number of hours, either fast or slow. The large territories of the USA and Canada are divided into zones approximately 7.5° on either side of central meridians. (For time zones of countries of the world, see Index.)

Variations from the standard time of some countries occur during part of the year; they are decided annually and are usually referred to as Summer Time or Daylight Saving Time.

At the 180th meridian the time can be either 12 hours fast on Greenwich Mean Time or 12 hours slow, and a change of date occurs. The internationally-recognized date or calendar line is a modification of the 180th meridian, drawn so as to include islands of any one group on the same side of the line, or for political reasons. The line is indicated by joining up the following co-ordinates:

Lat.	Long.	Lat.	Long.
60° S.	180°	48° N.	180°
51° S.	180°	53° N.	170° E.
45° S.	172.5° W.	65.5° N.	169° W.
15° S.	172.5° W.	75° N.	180°
5° S.	180°		

BRITISH SUMMER TIME

In 1916 an Act ordained that during a defined period of that year the legal time for general purposes in Great Britain should be one hour in advance of Greenwich Mean Time. The Summer Time Acts 1922 to 1925 defined the period during which Summer Time was to be in force, stabilizing practice until the Second World War.

During the war the duration of Summer Time was extended and in the years 1941 to 1945 and in 1947 Double Summer Time (two hours in advance of Greenwich Mean Time) was in force. After the war, Summer Time was extended each year in 1948–52 and 1961–4 by Order in Council.

Between 1968 October 27 and 1971 October 31 clocks were kept one hour ahead of Greenwich Mean Time throughout the year. This was known as British Standard Time.

The most recent legislation is the Summer Time Act 1972, which enacted that 'the period of summer time for the purposes of this Act is the period beginning at two o'clock, Greenwich mean time, in the morning of the day after the third Saturday in March or, if that day is Easter Day, the day

after the second Saturday in March, and ending at two o'clock, Greenwich mean time, in the morning of the day after the fourth Saturday in October.'

The duration of Summer Time can be varied by Order in Council and in recent years alterations have been made to bring the operation of Summer Time in Britain closer to similar provisions in other countries of the European Union; for instance, since 1981 the hour of changeover has been 01h Greenwich Mean Time.

The duration of Summer Time in 1997 will be 30 March to 26 October.

MEAN REFRACTION

Alt.	Ref.	Alt.	Ref.	Alt.	Ref.
° '	'	° '	'	° '	'
1 20	21	3 12	13	7 54	6
1 30	20	3 34	12	9 27	5
1 41	19	4 00	11	11 39	4
1 52	18	4 30	10	15 00	3
2 05	17	5 06	9	20 42	2
2 19	16	5 50	8	32 20	1
2 35	15	6 44	7	62 17	0
2 52	14	7 54		90 00	
3 12					

The refraction table is in the form of a critical table (see page 69)

ASTRONOMICAL CONSTANTS

Solar parallax	8".794
Astronomical unit	149597870 km
Precession for the year 1997	50".291
Precession in right ascension	3s.075
Precession in declination	20".043
Constant of nutation	9".202
Constant of aberration	20".496
Mean obliquity of ecliptic (1997)	23° 26' 23"
Moon's equatorial hor. parallax	57' 02".70
Velocity of light in vacuo per second	299792.5 km
Solar motion per second	20.0 km
Equatorial radius of the Earth	6378.140 km
Polar radius of the Earth	6356.755 km
North galactic pole (IAU standard)	
	RA 12h 49m (1950.0). Dec. 27°.4 N.
Solar apex	RA 18h 06m Dec. + 30°

Length of year (in mean solar days)

Tropical	365.24219
Sidereal	365.25636
Anomalistic (perihelion to perihelion)	365.25964
Eclipse	346.6200

Length of month (mean values)	d	h	m	s
New Moon to New	29	12	44	02.9
Sidereal	27	07	43	11.5
Anomalistic (perigee to perigee)	27	13	18	33.2

ELEMENTS OF THE SOLAR SYSTEM

Orb	Mean distance from Sun (Earth = 1)	km 10⁶	Sidereal period days	Synodic period days	Incl. of orbit to ecliptic ° '	Diameter km	Mass (Earth = 1)	Period of rotation on axis days
Sun	—	—	—	—	—	1,392,530	332,946	25–35*
Mercury	0.39	58	88.0	116	7 00	4,879	0.0553	58.646
Venus	0.72	108	224.7	584	3 24	12,104	0.8150	243.017r
Earth	1.00	150	365.3	—	—	12,756e	1.0000	0.997
Mars	1.52	228	687.0	780	1 51	6,794e	0.1074	1.026
Jupiter	5.20	778	4,332.6	399	1 18	{142,984e 133,708p}	317.89	{0.410e}
Saturn	9.54	1427	10,759.2	378	2 29	{120,536e 108,728p}	95.18	{0.426e}
Uranus	19.18	2870	30,684.6	370	0 46	51,118e	14.54	0.718r
Neptune	30.06	4497	60,191.0	367	1 46	49,528e	17.15	0.671
Pluto	39.80	5954	91,708.2	367	17 09	2,302	0.002	6.387

e equatorial, p polar, r retrograde, * depending on latitude

THE SATELLITES

Name	Star mag.	Mean distance from primary km	Sidereal period of revolution d
EARTH			
I Moon	—	384,400	27.322
MARS			
I Phobos	12	9,380	0.319
II Deimos	13	23,460	1.262
JUPITER			
XVI Metis	17	127,960	0.295
XV Adrastea	19	128,980	0.298
V Amalthea	14	181,300	0.498
XIV Thebe	16	221,900	0.675
I Io	5	421,600	1.769
II Europa	5	670,900	3.551
III Ganymede	5	1,070,000	7.155
IV Callisto	6	1,880,000	16.689
XIII Leda	20	11,094,000	239
VI Himalia	15	11,480,000	251
X Lysithea	18	11,720,000	259
VII Elara	17	11,737,000	260
XII Ananke	19	21,200,000	631r
XI Carme	18	22,600,000	692r
VIII Pasiphae	17	23,500,000	735r
IX Sinope	18	23,700,000	758r
SATURN			
XVIII Pan	—	133,600	0.575
XV Atlas	18	137,640	0.602
XVI Prometheus	16	139,350	0.613
XVII Pandora	16	141,700	0.629
XI Epimetheus	15	151,420	0.694
X Janus	14	151,470	0.695
I Mimas	13	185,520	0.942
II Enceladus	12	238,020	1.370
III Tethys	10	294,660	1.888
XIII Telesto	19	294,660	1.888
XIV Calypso	19	294,660	1.888
IV Dione	10	377,400	2.737
XII Helene	18	377,400	2.737
V Rhea	10	527,040	4.518
VI Titan	8	1,221,850	15.945

Name	Star mag.	Mean distance from primary km	Sidereal period of revolution d
SATURN			
VII Hyperion	14	1,481,000	21.277
VIII Iapetus	11	3,561,300	79.330
IX Phoebe	16	12,952,000	550.5r
URANUS			
VI Cordelia	—	49,770	0.335
VII Ophelia	—	53,790	0.376
VIII Bianca	—	59,170	0.435
IX Cressida	—	61,780	0.464
X Desdemona	—	62,660	0.474
XI Juliet	—	64,350	0.493
XII Portia	—	66,090	0.513
XIII Rosalind	—	69,940	0.558
XIV Belinda	—	75,260	0.624
XV Puck	—	86,010	0.762
V Miranda	17	129,390	1.413
I Ariel	14	191,020	2.520
II Umbriel	15	266,300	4.144
III Titania	14	435,910	8.706
IV Oberon	14	583,520	13.463
NEPTUNE			
III Naiad	25	48,230	0.294
IV Thalassa	24	50,070	0.311
V Despina	23	52,530	0.335
VI Galatea	22	61,950	0.429
VII Larissa	22	73,550	0.555
VIII Proteus	20	117,650	1.122
I Triton	13	354,760	5.877
II Nereid	19	5,513,400	360.136
PLUTO			
I Charon	17	19,700	6.387

THE EARTH

The shape of the Earth is that of an oblate spheroid or solid of revolution whose meridian sections are ellipses not differing much from circles, whilst the sections at right angles are circles. The length of the equatorial axis is about 12,756 km, and that of the polar axis is 12,714 km. The mean density of the Earth is 5.5 times that of water, although that of the surface layer is less. The Earth and Moon revolve about their common centre of gravity in a lunar month; this centre in turn revolves round the Sun in a plane known as the ecliptic, that passes through the Sun's centre. The Earth's equator is inclined to this plane at an angle of 23.4°. This tilt is the cause of the seasons. In mid-latitudes, and when the Sun is high above the Equator, not only does the high noon altitude make the days longer, but the Sun's rays fall more directly on the Earth's surface; these effects combine to produce summer. In equatorial regions the noon altitude is large throughout the year, and there is little variation in the length of the day. In higher latitudes the noon altitude is lower, and the days in summer are appreciably longer than those in winter.

The average velocity of the Earth in its orbit is 30 km a second. It makes a complete rotation on its axis in about 23 h 56 m of mean time, which is the sidereal day. Because of its annual revolution round the Sun, the rotation with respect to the Sun, or the solar day, is more than this by about four minutes (see page 73). The extremity of the axis of rotation, or the North Pole of the Earth, is not rigidly fixed, but wanders over an area roughly 20 metres in diameter.

TERRESTRIAL MAGNETISM

A magnetic compass points along the horizontal component of a magnetic line of force. These lines of force converge on the 'magnetic dip-poles', the places where a freely suspended magnetized needle would become vertical. Not only do these poles move with time, but their exact locations are ill-defined, particularly so in the case of the north dip-pole where the lines of force on the north side of it, instead of converging radially, tend to bunch into a channel. Although it is therefore unrealistic to attempt to specify the locations of the dip-poles exactly, the present approximate adopted positions are 79°.0 N., 105°.1 W. and 64°.7 S., 138°.6 E. The two magnetic dip-poles are thus not antipodal, the line joining them passing through the centre of the Earth at a distance of about 1,250 km. The distances of the magnetic dip-poles from the north and south geographical poles are about 1,200 km and 2,800 km respectively.

There is also a 'magnetic equator', at all points of which the vertical component of the Earth's magnetic field is zero and a magnetized needle remains horizontal. This line runs between 2° and 10° north of the geographical equator in Asia and Africa, turns sharply south off the west African coast, and crosses South America through Brazil, Bolivia and Peru; it recrosses the geographical equator in mid-Pacific.

Reference has already been made to secular changes in the Earth's field. The following table indicates the changes in magnetic declination (or variation of the compass). Declination is the angle in the horizontal plane between the direction of true north and that in which a magnetic compass points. Similar, though much smaller, changes have occurred in 'dip' or magnetic inclination. Secular changes differ throughout the world. Although the London

observations strongly suggest a cycle with a period of several hundred years, an exact repetition is unlikely.

London		Greenwich	
1580	11° 15′ E.	1850	22° 24′ W.
1622	5° 56′ E.	1900	16° 29′ W.
1665	1° 22′ W.	1925	13° 10′ W.
1730	13° 00′ W.	1950	9° 07′ W.
1773	21° 09′ W.	1975	6° 39′ W.

In order that up-to-date information on declination may be available, many governments publish magnetic charts on which there are lines (isogonic lines) passing through all places at which specified values of declination will be found at the date of the chart.

In the British Isles, isogonic lines now run approximately north-east to south-west. Though there are considerable local deviations due to geological causes, a rough value of magnetic declination may be obtained by assuming that at 50° N. on the meridian of Greenwich, the value in 1997 is 3° 06′ west and allowing an increase of 15′ for each degree of latitude northwards and one of 28′ for each degree of longitude westwards. For example, at 53° N., 5° W., declination will be about 3° 06′ + 45′ + 140′, i.e. 6° 11′ west. The average annual change at the present time is about 9′ decrease.

The number of magnetic observatories is about 200, irregularly distributed over the globe. There are three in Great Britain, run by the British Geological Survey: at Hartland, north Devon; at Eskdalemuir, Dumfriesshire; and at Lerwick, Shetland Islands. The following are some recent annual mean values of the magnetic elements for Hartland.

Year	Declination West ° ′	Dip or inclination ° ′	Horizontal force gauss	Vertical force gauss
1955	10 30	66 49	0.1859	0.4340
1960	9 59	66 44	0.1871	0.4350
1965	9 30	66 34	0.1887	0.4354
1970	9 06	66 26	0.1903	0.4364
1975	8 32	66 17	0.1921	0.4373
1980	7 44	66 10	0.1933	0.4377
1985	6 56	66 08	0.1938	0.4380
1990	6 15	66 10	0.1939	0.4388
1995	5 33	66 07	0.1946	0.4395

The normal world-wide terrestrial magnetic field corresponds approximately to that of a very strong small bar magnet near the centre of the Earth, but with appreciable smooth spatial departures. The origin and the slow secular change of the normal field are not fully understood but are generally ascribed to electric currents associated with fluid motions in the Earth's core. Superimposed on the normal field are local and regional anomalies whose magnitudes may in places approach that of the normal field; these are due to the influence of mineral deposits in the Earth's crust. A small proportion of the field is of external origin, mostly associated with electric currents in the ionosphere. The configuration of the external field and the ionization of the atmosphere depend on the incident particle and radiation flux from the Sun. There are, therefore, short-term and non-periodic as well as diurnal, 27-day, seasonal and 11-year periodic changes in the magnetic field, dependent upon the position of the Sun and the degree of solar activity.

MAGNETIC STORMS

Occasionally, sometimes with great suddenness, the Earth's magnetic field is subject for several hours to marked disturbance. During a severe storm in 1989 the declination at Lerwick changed by almost 8° in less than an hour. In many instances such disturbances are accompanied by widespread displays of aurorae, marked changes in the incidence of cosmic rays, an increase in the reception of 'noise' from the Sun at radio frequencies, and rapid changes in the ionosphere and induced electric currents within the Earth which adversely affect radio and telegraphic communications. The disturbances are caused by changes in the stream of ionized particles which emanates from the Sun and through which the Earth is continuously passing. Some of these changes are associated with visible eruptions on the Sun, usually in the region of sun-spots. There is a marked tendency for disturbances to recur after intervals of about 27 days, the apparent period of rotation of the Sun on its axis, which is consistent with the sources being located on particular areas of the Sun.

ARTIFICIAL SATELLITES

To consider the orbit of an artificial satellite, it is best to imagine that one is looking at the Earth from a distant point in space. The Earth would then be seen to be rotating about its axis inside the orbit described by the rapidly revolving satellite. The inclination of a satellite orbit to the Earth's equator (which generally remains almost constant throughout the satellite's lifetime) gives at once the maximum range of latitudes over which the satellite passes. Thus a satellite whose orbit has an inclination of 53° will pass overhead all latitudes between 53° S. and 53° N., but would never be seen in the zenith of any place nearer the poles than these latitudes. If we consider a particular place on the earth, whose latitude is less than the inclination of the satellite's orbit, then the Earth's rotation carries this place first under the northbound part of the orbit and then under the southbound portion of the orbit, these two occurrences being always less than 12 hours apart for satellites moving in direct orbits (i.e. to the east). (For satellites in retrograde orbits, the words 'northbound' and 'southbound' should be interchanged in the preceding statement.) As the value of the latitude of the observer increases and approaches the value of the inclination of the orbit, so this interval gets shorter until (when the latitude is equal to the inclination) only one overhead passage occurs each day.

Observation of Satellites

The regression of the orbit around the Earth causes alternate periods of visibility and invisibility, though this is of little concern to the radio or radar observer. To the visual observer the following cycle of events normally occurs (though the cycle may start in any position): invisibility, morning observations before dawn, invisibility, evening observations after dusk, invisibility, morning observations before dawn, and so on. With reasonably high satellites and for observers in high latitudes around the summer solstice, the evening observations follow the morning observations without interruption as sunlight passing over the polar regions can still illuminate satellites which are passing over temperate latitudes at local midnight. At the moment all satellites rely on sunlight to make them visible, though a satellite with a flashing light has been suggested for a future launching. The observer must be in darkness or twilight in order to make any useful observations and the durations of twilight and the sunrise, sunset times given on Page Two of each month will be a useful guide.

Some of the satellites are visible to the naked eye and much interest has been aroused by the spectacle of a bright satellite disappearing into the Earth's shadow. The event is even more interesting telescopically as the disappearance occurs gradually as the satellite traverses the Earth's penumbral shadow, and during the last few seconds before the eclipse is complete the satellite may change colour (in suitable atmospheric conditions) from yellow to red. This is because the last rays of sunlight are refracted through the denser layers of our atmosphere before striking the satellite.

Some satellites rotate about one or more axes so that a periodic variation in brightness is observed. This was particularly noticeable in several of the Soviet satellites.

Satellite research has provided some interesting results, including a revised value of the Earth's oblateness (1/298.2), and the discovery of the Van Allen radiation belts.

Launchings

Apart from their names, e.g. Cosmos 6 Rocket, the satellites are also classified according to their date of launch. Thus 1961 α refers to the first satellite launching of 1961. A number following the Greek letter indicated the relative brightness of the satellites put in orbit. From the beginning of 1963 the Greek letters were replaced by numbers and the numbers by roman letters e.g. 1963–01A. For all satellites successfully injected into orbit the following table gives the designation and names of the main objects, the launch date and some initial orbital data. These are the inclination to the equator (i), the nodal period of revolution (P), eccentricity (e), and the perigee height.

Although most of the satellites launched are injected into orbits less than 1,000 km high, there are an increasing number of satellites in geostationary orbits, i.e. where the orbital inclination is zero, the eccentricity close to zero, and the period of revolution is 1436.1 minutes. Thus the satellite is permanently situated over the equator at one selected longitude at a mean height of 35,786 km. This geostationary band is crowded. In one case there are four television satellites (Astra 1A, Astra 1B, Astra 1C and Astra 1D) orbiting within a few tens of kilometres of each other. In the sky they appear to be separated by only a few arc minutes.

ARTIFICIAL SATELLITE LAUNCHES 1995–6

Designation	Satellite	Launch date	i	P	e	Perigee height
1995–			°	m		km
011	Himawari 5, GMS 5	March 18	0.6	1436.1	0.000	35786
012	Cosmos 2310, rocket	March 22	82.9	104.5	0.002	987
013	Intelsat 7-05	March 22	26.5	720.0	0.727	333
014	Cosmos 2311, Hotbird 1, rocket	March 22	67.0	88.8	0.001	190
015	DMSP 2-08	March 24	98.8	102.0	0.001	845
016	Brazilsat B2, Hotbird 1 Eutelsat	March 28	0.0	1436.0	0.000	35782
017	Orbcomm 1 & 2, Microlab 1	April 3	70.0	91.0	0.002	450
018	Offeq 3, rocket	April 5	143.0	102.7	0.095	200
019	AMSC 1	April 8	0.0	1436.0	0.000	35781
020	Progress M27, rocket	April 9	51.6	88.5	0.001	190
021	ERS2, rocket	April 20	98.7	102.0	0.002	860
022	USA 110	May 14	–	–	–	–
023	ARIANE	May 17	0.0	1436.0	0.000	35774
024	Spektr	May 20	51.6	89.4	0.001	190
025	GOES 9	May 23	0.1	1439.7	0.001	35807
026	Cosmos 2312, rocket	May 24	62.7	91.0	0.017	222
027	UHF5	May 31	4.8	1435.9	0.000	35774
028	Cosmos 2313	May 31	65.0	89.0	0.001	190
029	DBS3	May 31	0.0	1436.0	0.000	35765
030	STS71	June 23	51.6	91.5	0.161	302
031	Cosmos 2314	June 28	67.0	89.5	0.002	200
032	Cosmos 2315	July 5	82.9	104.0	0.001	987
033	Helios 1A, UPM LBSAT 1	July 7	98.0	100.0	0.001	833
034	USA112, Sigint	July 10	–	–	–	–
035	Shuttle 70, TDRS7	July 13	0.3	1436.1	0.000	35774
036	Progress M28	July 20	–	–	–	–
037	Cosmos 2317, 2316, rocket	July 24	65.0	674.0	0.002	19010
038	DSCS3	July 31	–	–	–	–
039	Interball 1, Magion 4	August 3	67.1	5463.0	0.881	5833
040	PAS 4	August 3	7.0	700.0	0.711	768
041	Muhungha	August 5	0.0	1436.1	0.000	35778
042	Molniya 3-47, platform	August 9	63.0	710.0	0.745	400
043	JCSAT 3	August 29	0.0	1436.0	0.000	35780
044	NSTAR 1	August 29	0.0	1436.0	0.007	36000
045	Cosmos 2319	August 30	0.0	1436.0	0.007	36000
046	SICH-1 Okean, rocket	August 31	82.5	97.8	0.003	632
047	Soyuz TM22	September 3	51.6	88.9	0.002	170
048	Spartan 201	September 7	28.5	90.0	0.001	290
049	Telstar 402	September 24	4.0	1436.0	0.004	36666
050	Resurs F2	September 26	82.2	89.0	0.000	230
051	Cosmos 2320	September 29	64.9	89.9	0.008	179
052	Cosmos 2321	October 6	82.9	95.1	0.039	257
053	Progress M29	October 8	51.6	91.5	0.004	194
054	Luch 1, platform	October 11	2.8	1436.0	0.001	35750
055	Astra 1E	October 19	0.1	1436.0	0.000	35777
056	STS73	October 20	39.0	90.0	0.001	267
057	UHF F6	October 22	5.0	1436.0	0.000	35779
058	Cosmos 2322	October 31	71.0	102.0	0.000	800
059	Radarsat	November 4	100.5	109.9	0.037	935
060	USA 115	November 6	–	–	–	–
061	STS74	November 12	51.6	90.9	0.108	300
062	ISO	November 17	4.8	1436.0	0.823	1097
063	GALS 2, rocket	November 17	0.1	1436.0	0.000	35771
064	Asiasat LMRB	November 28	0.2	1435.9	0.000	35780
065	Soho	December 2	–	–	–	–

Desig-nation	Satellite	Launch date	i	P	e	Perigee height
066	USA 116	December 5	–	–	–	–
067	Telecom 2C, rocket	December 6	0.0	1436.0	0.001	35666
068	Cosmos 2324, rocket	December 14	64.7	675.0	0.000	19111
069	GALAXY 3R	December 15	26.8	690.0	0.728	250
070	Progress M30	December 18	51.6	88.4	0.001	180
071	Cosmos 2326	December 20	65.0	88.4	0.001	180
072	Skipper	December 28	98.5	101.2	0.001	806
073	Echostar 1	December 28	0.1	1436.0	0.001	35764
074	XTE	December 30	23.0	95.9	0.001	562
1996–						
001	STS 72, OAST	January 11	28.5	90.4	0.000	310
002	Panamsat 3R, Measat 1	January 12	0.1	1435.4	0.000	35886
003	KOREASAT 2, rocket	January 14	0.2	1448.5	0.000	36343
004	COSMOS 2327, rocket	January 16	83.0	104.9	0.005	952
005	Gorizont, rocket	January 25	1.5	1477.5	0.002	36524
006	PALAPA C-1, rocket	February 1	0.1	1436.1	0.000	36000
007	N-STAR B	February 5	0.1	1436.0	0.001	35753
008	NEAR	February 17	(Heliocentric	orbit)		
009	Cosmos 2328-2330, rocket	February 19	82.5	113.9	0.001	1400
010	Raduga 33, rocket	February 19	48.6	645.5	0.733	241
011	SOYUZ TM23, rocket	February 21	51.6	88.7	0.001	180
012	STS75, TSS 1R	February 22	28.5	91.0	0.001	280
013	POLAR, rocket	February 24	86.0	937.2	0.793	186
014	REX II, rocket	March 9	89.9	100.0	0.000	768
015	Intelsat 707	March 14	0.0	1436.1	0.000	35780
016	Cosmos 2331, rocket	March 14	67.0	88.5	0.001	180
017	PSLV D3, rocket	March 21	98.7	101.4	0.003	802
018	STS76	March 22	51.6	92.3	0.001	388
019	GPS NAVSTAR, rocket	March 28	54.7	726.8	0.006	20252
020	Inmarsat 3	April 3	0.1	1436.0	0.001	35600

Time Measurement and Calendars

MEASUREMENTS OF TIME

Measurements of time are based on the time taken by the earth to rotate on its axis (day); by the moon to revolve round the earth (month); and by the earth to revolve round the sun (year). From these, which are not commensurable, certain average or mean intervals have been adopted for ordinary use.

THE DAY

The day begins at midnight and is divided into 24 hours of 60 minutes, each of 60 seconds. The hours are counted from midnight up to 12 noon (when the sun crosses the meridian), and these hours are designated a.m. (*ante meridiem*); and again from noon up to 12 midnight, which hours are designated p.m. (*post meridiem*), except when the 24-hour reckoning is employed. The 24-hour reckoning ignores a.m. and p.m., numbering the hours 0 to 23 from midnight.

Colloquially the 24 hours are divided into day and night, day being the time while the sun is above the horizon (including the four stages of twilight defined on page 72). Day is subdivided into morning, the early part of daytime, ending at noon; afternoon, from noon to about 6 p.m.; and evening, which may be said to extend from 6 p.m. until midnight. Night, the dark period between day and day, begins at the close of astronomical twilight (*see* page 72) and extends beyond midnight to sunrise the next day.

The names of the days are derived from Old English translations or adaptations of the Roman titles.

Sunday	Sun	Sol
Monday	Moon	Luna
Tuesday	Tiw/Tyr (god of war)	Mars
Wednesday	Woden/Odin	Mercury
Thursday	Thor	Jupiter
Friday	Frigga/Freyja	
	(goddess of love)	Venus
Saturday	Saeternes	Saturn

THE MONTH

The month in the ordinary calendar is approximately the twelfth part of a year, but the lengths of the different months vary from 28 (or 29) days to 31.

THE YEAR

The equinoctial or tropical year is the time that the earth takes to revolve round the sun from equinox to equinox, i.e. 365.24219 mean solar days, or 365 days 5 hours 48 minutes and 45 seconds.

The calendar year usually consists of 365 days but a year containing 366 days is called bissextile (*see* Roman calendar, page 89) or leap year, one day being added to the month of February so that a date 'leaps over' a day of the week. In the Roman calendar the day that was repeated was the sixth day before the beginning of March, the equivalent of 24 February.

A year is a leap year if the date of the year is divisible by four without remainder, unless it is the last year of the century. The last year of a century is a leap year only if its number is divisible by 400 without remainder, e.g. the years 1800 and 1900 had only 365 days but the year 2000 will have 366 days.

THE SOLSTICE

A solstice is the point in the tropical year at which the sun attains its greatest distance, north or south, from the Equator. In the northern hemisphere the furthest point north of the Equator marks the summer solstice and the furthest point south the winter solstice.

The date of the solstice varies according to locality. For example, if the summer solstice falls on 21 June late in the day by Greenwich time, that day will be the longest of the year at Greenwich though it may be by only a second, but it will fall on 22 June, local date, in Japan, and so 22 June will be the longest day there. The date of the solstice is also affected by the length of the tropical year, which is 365 days 6 hours less about 11 minutes 15 seconds. If a solstice happens late on 21 June in one year, it will be nearly six hours later in the next (unless the next year is a leap year), i.e. early on 22 June, and that will be the longest day.

This delay of the solstice does not continue because the extra day in leap year brings it back a day in the calendar. However, because of the 11 minutes 15 seconds mentioned above, the additional day in leap year brings the solstice back too far by 45 minutes, and the time of the solstice in the calendar is earlier, in a four-year pattern, as the century progresses. The last year of a century is in most cases not a leap year, and the omission of the extra day puts the date of the solstice later by about six hours too much. Compensation for this is made by the fourth centennial year being a leap year. The solstice has become earlier in date throughout this century and, because the year 2000 is a leap year, the solstice will get earlier still throughout the 21st century.

The date of the winter solstice, the shortest day of the year, is affected by the same factors as the longest day.

At Greenwich the sun sets at its earliest by the clock about ten days before the shortest day. The daily change in the time of sunset is due in the first place to the sun's movement southwards at this time of the year, which diminishes the interval between the sun's transit and its setting. However, the daily decrease of the Equation of Time causes the time of apparent noon to be continuously later day by day, which to some extent counteracts the first effect. The rates of the change of these two quantities are not equal or uniform; their combination causes the date of earliest sunset to be 12 or 13 December at Greenwich. In more southerly latitudes the effect of the movement of the sun is less, and the change in the time of sunset depends on that of the Equation of Time to a greater degree, and the date of earliest sunset is earlier than it is at Greenwich, e.g. on the Equator it is about 1 November.

THE EQUINOX

The equinox is the point at which the sun crosses the Equator and day and night are of equal length all over the world. This occurs in March and September.

DOG DAYS

The days about the heliacal rising of the Dog Star, noted from ancient times as the hottest period of the year in the northern hemisphere, are called the Dog Days. Their incidence has been variously calculated as depending on the Greater or Lesser Dog Star (Sirius or Procyon) and their duration has been reckoned as from 30 to 54 days. A generally accepted period is from 3 July to 15 August.

CHRISTIAN CALENDAR

In the Christian chronological system the years are distinguished by cardinal numbers before or after the birth of Christ, the period being denoted by the letters BC (Before Christ) or, more rarely, AC (*Ante Christum*), and AD (*Anno Domini* – In the Year of Our Lord). The correlative dates of the epoch are the fourth year of the 194th Olympiad, the 753rd year from the foundation of Rome, AM 3761 (Jewish chronology), and the 4714th year of the Julian period. The actual date of the birth of Christ is somewhat uncertain.

The system was introduced into Italy in the sixth century. Though first used in France in the seventh century, it was not universally established there until about the eighth century. It has been said that the system was introduced into England by St Augustine (AD 596), but it was probably not generally used until some centuries later. It was ordered to be used by the Bishops at the Council of Chelsea (AD 816).

THE JULIAN CALENDAR

In the Julian calendar (adopted by the Roman Empire in 45 BC, *see* page 89) all the centennial years were leap years, and for this reason towards the close of the 16th century there was a difference of ten days between the tropical and calendar years; the equinox fell on 11 March of the calendar, whereas at the time of the Council of Nicaea (AD 325), it had fallen on 21 March. In 1582 Pope Gregory ordained that 5 October should be called 15 October and that of the end-century years only the fourth should be a leap year (*see* page 81).

THE GREGORIAN CALENDAR

The Gregorian calendar was adopted by Italy, France, Spain and Portugal in 1582, by Prussia, the Roman Catholic German states, Switzerland, Holland and Flanders on 1 January 1583, by Poland in 1586, Hungary in 1587, the Protestant German and Netherland states and Denmark in 1700, and by Great Britain and Dominions (including the North American colonies) in 1752, by the omission of eleven days (3 September being reckoned as 14 September). Sweden omitted the leap day in 1700 but observed leap days in 1704 and 1708, and reverted to Julian calendar by having two leap days in 1712; the Gregorian calendar was adopted in 1753 by the omission of eleven days (18 February being reckoned as 1 March). Japan adopted the calendar in 1872, China in 1912, Bulgaria in 1915, Turkey and Soviet Russia in 1918, Yugoslavia and Romania in 1919, and Greece in 1923.

In the same year that the change was made in England from the Julian to the Gregorian calendar, the beginning of the new year was also changed from 25 March to 1 January (*see* page 86).

THE ORTHODOX CHURCHES

Some Orthodox Churches still use the Julian reckoning but the majority of Greek Orthodox Churches and the Romanian Orthodox Church have adopted a modified 'New Calendar', observing the Gregorian calendar for fixed feasts and the Julian for movable feasts.

The Orthodox Church year begins on 1 September. There are four fast periods and, in addition to Pascha (Easter), twelve great feasts, as well as numerous commemorations of the saints of the Old and New Testaments throughout the year.

THE DOMINICAL LETTER

The dominical letter is one of the letters A–G which are used to denote the Sundays in successive years. If the first day of the year is a Sunday the letter is A; if the second, B; the third, C; and so on. A leap year requires two letters, the first for 1 January to 29 February, the second for 1 March to 31 December (*see* page 84).

EPIPHANY

The feast of the Epiphany, commemorating the manifestation of Christ, later became associated with the offering of gifts by the Magi. The day was of great importance from the time of the Council of Nicaea (AD 325), as the primate of Alexandria was charged at every Epiphany feast with the announcement in a letter to the churches of the date of the forthcoming Easter. The day was also of importance in Britain as it influenced dates, ecclesiastical and lay, e.g. Plough Monday, when work was resumed in the fields, fell on the Monday in the first full week after Epiphany.

LENT

The Teutonic word *Lent*, which denotes the fast preceding Easter, originally meant no more than the spring season; but from Anglo-Saxon times at least it has been used as the equivalent of the more significant Latin term Quadragesima, meaning the 'forty days' or, more literally, the fortieth day. Ash Wednesday is the first day of Lent, which ends at midnight before Easter Day.

PALM SUNDAY

Palm Sunday, the Sunday before Easter and the beginning of Holy Week, commemorates the triumphal entry of Christ into Jerusalem and is celebrated in Britain (when palm is not available) by branches of willow gathered for use in the decoration of churches on that day.

MAUNDY THURSDAY

Maundy Thursday is the day before Good Friday, the name itself being a corruption of *dies mandati* (day of the mandate) when Christ washed the feet of the disciples and gave them the mandate to love one another.

EASTER DAY

Easter Day is the first Sunday after the full moon which happens on, or next after, the 21st day of March; if the full moon happens on a Sunday, Easter Day is the Sunday after.

This definition is contained in an Act of Parliament (24 Geo. II c. 23) and explanation is given in the preamble to the Act that the day of full moon depends on certain tables that have been prepared. These tables are summarized in the early pages of the Book of Common Prayer. The moon referred to is not the real moon of the heavens, but a hypothetical moon on whose 'full' the date of Easter depends, and the lunations of this 'calendar' moon consist of twenty-nine and thirty days alternately, with certain necessary modifications to make the date of its full agree as nearly as possible with that of the real moon, which is known as the Paschal Full Moon. At present, Easter falls on one of 35 days (22 March to 25 April).

A FIXED EASTER

In 1928 the House of Commons agreed to a motion for the third reading of a bill proposing that Easter Day shall, in the calendar year next but one after the commencement of the Act and in all subsequent years, be the first Sunday after the second Saturday in April. Easter would thus fall on the second or third Sunday in April, i.e. between 9 and 15 April (inclusive). A clause in the Bill provided that before it shall come into operation, regard shall be had to any opinion expressed officially by the various Christian churches.

Efforts by the World Council of Churches to secure a unanimous choice of date for Easter by its member churches have so far been unsuccessful.

ROGATION DAYS

Rogation Days are the Monday, Tuesday and Wednesday preceding Ascension Day and from the fifth century were observed as public fasts with solemn processions and supplications. The processions were discontinued as religious observances at the Reformation, but survive in the ceremony known as 'beating the parish bounds'. Rogation Sunday is the Sunday before Ascension Day.

EMBER DAYS

The Ember Days at the four seasons are the Wednesday, Friday and Saturday (*a*) before the third Sunday in Advent,

(*b*) before the second Sunday in Lent, and (*c*) before the Sundays nearest to the festivals of St Peter and of St Michael and All Angels.

TRINITY SUNDAY

Trinity Sunday is eight weeks after Easter Day, on the Sunday following Pentecost (Whit Sunday). Subsequent Sundays are reckoned in the Book of Common Prayer calendar of the Church of England as 'after Trinity'.

Thomas Becket (1118–70) was consecrated Archbishop of Canterbury on the Sunday after Whit Sunday and his first act was to ordain that the day of his consecration should be held as a new festival in honour of the Holy Trinity. This observance spread from Canterbury throughout the whole of Christendom.

MOVABLE FEASTS TO THE YEAR 2029

Year	Ash Wednesday	Easter	Ascension	Pentecost (Whit Sunday)	Sundays after Pentecost	Advent Sunday
1997	12 February	30 March	8 May	18 May	22	30 November
1998	25 February	12 April	21 May	31 May	20	29 November
1999	17 February	4 April	13 May	23 May	21	28 November
2000	8 March	23 April	1 June	11 June	19	3 December
2001	28 February	15 April	24 May	3 June	20	2 December
2002	13 February	31 March	9 May	19 May	22	1 December
2003	5 March	20 April	29 May	8 June	19	30 November
2004	25 February	11 April	20 May	30 May	20	28 November
2005	9 February	27 March	5 May	15 May	22	27 November
2006	1 March	16 April	25 May	4 June	20	3 December
2007	21 February	8 April	17 May	27 May	21	2 December
2008	6 February	23 March	1 May	11 May	23	30 November
2009	25 February	12 April	21 May	31 May	20	29 November
2010	17 February	4 April	13 May	23 May	21	28 November
2011	9 March	24 April	2 June	12 June	18	27 November
2012	22 February	8 April	17 May	27 May	21	2 December
2013	13 February	31 March	9 May	19 May	22	1 December
2014	5 March	20 April	29 May	8 June	19	30 November
2015	18 February	5 April	14 May	24 May	21	29 November
2016	10 February	27 March	5 May	15 May	22	27 November
2017	1 March	16 April	25 May	4 June	20	3 December
2018	14 February	1 April	10 May	20 May	22	2 December
2019	6 March	21 April	30 May	9 June	19	1 December
2020	26 February	12 April	21 May	31 May	20	29 November
2021	17 February	4 April	13 May	23 May	21	28 November
2022	2 March	17 April	26 May	5 June	19	27 November
2023	22 February	9 April	18 May	28 May	21	3 December
2024	14 February	31 March	9 May	19 May	22	1 December
2025	5 March	20 April	29 May	8 June	19	30 November
2026	18 February	5 April	14 May	24 May	21	29 November
2027	10 February	28 March	6 May	16 May	22	28 November
2028	1 March	16 April	25 May	4 June	20	3 December
2029	14 February	1 April	10 May	20 May	22	2 December

NOTES

Ash Wednesday (first day in Lent) can fall at earliest on 4 February and at latest on 10 March

Mothering Sunday (fourth Sunday in Lent) can fall at earliest on 1 March and at latest on 4 April

Easter Day can fall at earliest on 22 March and at latest on 25 April

Ascension Day is forty days after Easter Day and can fall at earliest on 30 April and at latest on 3 June

Pentecost (Whit Sunday) is seven weeks after Easter and can fall at earliest on 10 May and at latest on 13 June

Trinity Sunday is the Sunday after Whit Sunday

Corpus Christi falls on the Thursday after Trinity Sunday

Sundays after Pentecost – there are not less than 18 and not more than 23

Advent Sunday is the Sunday nearest to 30 November

EASTER DAYS AND DOMINICAL LETTERS 1500 to 2033

Dates up to and including 1752 are according to the Julian calendar

	1500–1599	1600–1699	1700–1799	1800–1899	1900–1999	2000–2033
March						
d 22	1573	1668	1761	1818		
e 23	1505/16	1600	1788	1845/56	1913	2008
f 24		1611/95	1706/99		1940	
g 25	1543/54	1627/38/49	1722/33/44	1883/94	1951	
A 26	1559/70/81/92	1654/65/76	1749/58/69/80	1815/26/37	1967/78/89	
b 27	1502/13/24/97	1608/87/92	1785/96	1842/53/64	1910/21/32	2005/16
c 28	1529/35/40	1619/24/30	1703/14/25	1869/75/80	1937/48	2027/32
d 29	1551/62	1635/46/57	1719/30/41/52	1807/12/91	1959/64/70	
e 30	1567/78/89	1651/62/73/84	1746/55/66/77	1823/34	1902/75/86/97	
f 31	1510/21/32/83/94	1605/16/78/89	1700/71/82/93	1839/50/61/72	1907/18/29/91	2002/13/24
April						
g 1	1526/37/48	1621/32	1711/16	1804/66/77/88	1923/34/45/56	2018/29
A 2	1553/64	1643/48	1727/38	1809/20/93/99	1961/72	
b 3	1575/80/86	1659/70/81	1743/63/68/74	1825/31/36	1904/83/88/94	
c 4	1507/18/91	1602/13/75/86/97	1708/79/90	1847/58	1915/20/26/99	2010/21
d 5	1523/34/45/56	1607/18/29/40	1702/13/24/95	1801/63/74/85/96	1931/42/53	2015/26
e 6	1539/50/61/72	1634/45/56	1729/35/40/60	1806/17/28/90	1947/58/69/80	
f 7	1504/77/88	1667/72	1751/65/76	1822/33/44	1901/12/85/96	
g 8	1509/15/20/99	1604/10/83/94	1705/87/92/98	1849/55/60	1917/28	2007/12
A 9	1531/42	1615/26/37/99	1710/21/32	1871/82	1939/44/50	2023
b 10	1547/58/69	1631/42/53/64	1726/37/48/57	1803/14/87/98	1955/66/77	
c 11	1501/12/63/74/85/96	1658/69/80	1762/73/84	1819/30/41/52	1909/71/82/93	2004
d 12	1506/17/28	1601/12/91/96	1789	1846/57/68	1903/14/25/36/98	2009/20
e 13	1533/44	1623/28	1707/18	1800/73/79/84	1941/52	2031
f 14	1555/60/66	1639/50/61	1723/34/45/54	1805/11/16/95	1963/68/74	
g 15	1571/82/93	1655/66/77/88	1750/59/70/81	1827/38	1900/06/79/90	2001
A 16	1503/14/25/36/87/98	1609/20/82/93	1704/75/86/97	1843/54/65/76	1911/22/33/95	2006/17/28
b 17	1530/41/52	1625/36	1715/20	1808/70/81/92	1927/38/49/60	2022/33
c 18	1557/68	1647/52	1731/42/56	1802/13/24/97	1954/65/76	
d 19	1500/79/84/90	1663/74/85	1747/67/72/78	1829/35/40	1908/81/87/92	
e 20	1511/22/95	1606/17/79/90	1701/12/83/94	1851/62	1919/24/30	2003/14/25
f 21	1527/38/49	1622/33/44	1717/28	1867/78/89	1935/46/57	2019/30
g 22	1565/76	1660	1739/53/64	1810/21/32	1962/73/84	
A 23	1508	1671		1848	1905/16	2000
b 24	1519	1603/14/98	1709/91	1859		2011
c 25	1546	1641	1736	1886	1943	

HINDU CALENDAR

The Hindu calendar is a luni-solar calendar of twelve months, each containing 29 days, 12 hours. Each month is divided into a light fortnight (Shukla or Shuddha) and a dark fortnight (Krishna or Vadya) based on the waxing and waning of the moon. In most parts of India the month starts with the light fortnight, i.e. the day after the new moon, although in some regions it begins with the dark fortnight, i.e. the day after the full moon.

The new year begins in the month of Chaitra (March/April) and ends in the month of Phalgun (March). The twelve months, Chaitra, Vaishakh, Jyeshtha, Ashadh, Shravan, Bhadrapad, Ashvin, Kartik, Margashirsh, Paush, Magh and Phalgun, have Sanskrit names derived from twelve asterisms (constellations). There are regional variations to the names of the months but the Sanskrit names are understood throughout India.

Every lunar month must have a solar transit and is termed pure (shuddha). The lunar month without a solar transit is impure (mala) and called an intercalary month. An intercalary month occurs approximately every 32 lunar months, whenever the difference between the Hindu year of 360 lunar days (354 days 8 hours solar time) and the 365 days 6 hours of the solar year reaches the length of one Hindu lunar month (29 days 12 hours).

The leap month may be added at any point in the Hindu year. The name given to the month varies according to when it occurs but is taken from the month immediately following it. Leap months occur in 1996–7 (Ashadh) and 1999–2000 (Jyeshtha).

The days of the week are called Raviwar (Sunday), Somawar (Monday), Mangalwar (Tuesday), Budhawar (Wednesday), Guruwar (Thursday), Shukrawar (Friday) and Shaniwar (Saturday). The names are derived from the Sanskrit names of the Sun, the Moon and five planets, Mars, Mercury, Jupiter, Venus and Saturn.

Most fasts and festivals are based on the lunar calendar but a few are determined by the apparent movement of the Sun, e.g. Sankranti, which is celebrated on 14/15 January to mark the start of the Sun's apparent journey northwards and a change of season.

Festivals celebrated throughout India are Chaitra (the New Year), Raksha-bandhan (the renewal of the kinship bond between brothers and sisters), Navaratri (a nine-night festival dedicated to the goddess Parvati), Dasara (the victory of Rama over the demon army), Diwali (a festival of lights), Makara Sankranti, Shivaratri (dedicated to Shiva), and Holi (a spring festival).

Regional festivals are Durga-puja (dedicated to the goddess Durga (Parvati)), Sarasvati-puja (dedicated to the goddess Sarasvati), Ganesh Chaturthi (worship of Ganesh on the fourth day (Chaturthi) of the light half of Bhadrapad), Ramanavami (the birth festival of the god Rama) and Janmashtami (the birth festival of the god Krishna).

The main festivals celebrated in Britain are Navaratri, Dasara, Durga-puja, Diwali, Holi, Sarasvati-puja, Ganesh Chaturthi, Raksha-bandhan, Ramanavami and Janmashtami.

The dates of the main festivals in 1997 are given on page 9.

JEWISH CALENDAR

The story of the Flood in the Book of Genesis indicates the use of a calendar of some kind and that the writers recognized thirty days as the length of a lunation. However, after the diaspora, Jewish communities were left in considerable doubt as to the times of fasts and festivals. This led to the formation of the Jewish calendar as used today. It is said that this was done in AD 358 by Rabbi Hillel II, though some assert that it did not happen until much later.

The calendar is luni-solar, and is based on the lengths of the lunation and of the tropical year as found by Hipparchus (c.120 BC), which differ little from those adopted at the present day. The year AM 5757 (1996–7) is the 19th year of the 303rd Metonic (Minor or Lunar) cycle of 19 years and the 17th year of the 206th Solar (or Major) cycle of 28 years since the Era of the Creation. Jews hold that the Creation occurred at the time of the autumnal equinox in the year known in the Christian calendar as 3760 BC (954 of the Julian period). The epoch or starting point of Jewish chronology corresponds to 7 October 3761 BC. At the beginning of each solar cycle, the Tekufah of Nisan (the vernal equinox) returns to the same day and to the same hour.

The hour is divided into 1080 minims, and the month between one new moon and the next is reckoned as 29 days, 12 hours, 793 minims. The normal calendar year, called a Regular Common year, consists of 12 months of 30 days and 29 days alternately. Since twelve months such as these comprise only 354 days, in order that each of them shall not diverge greatly from an average place in the solar year, a thirteenth month is occasionally added after the fifth month of the civil year (which commences on the first day of the month Tishri), or as the penultimate month of the ecclesiastical year (which commences on the first day of the month Nisan). The years when this happens are called Embolismic or leap years.

Of the 19 years that form a Metonic cycle, seven are leap years; they occur at places in the cycle indicated by the numbers 3, 6, 8, 11, 14, 17 and 19, these places being chosen so that the accumulated excesses of the solar years should be as small as possible.

A Jewish year is of one of the following six types:

Minimal Common	353 days
Regular Common	354 days
Full Common	355 days
Minimal Leap	383 days
Regular Leap	384 days
Full Leap	385 days.

The Regular year has alternate months of 30 and 29 days. In a Full year, whether common or leap, Marcheshvan, the second month of the civil year, has 30 days instead of 29; in Minimal years Kislev, the third month, has 29 instead of 30. The additional month in leap years is called Adar I and precedes the month called Adar in Common years. Adar II is called Adar Sheni in leap years, and the usual Adar festivals are kept in Adar Sheni. Adar I and Adar II always have 30 days, but neither this, nor the other variations mentioned, is allowed to change the number of days in the other months, which still follow the alternation of the normal twelve.

These are the main features of the Jewish calendar, which must be considered permanent because as a Jewish law it cannot be altered except by a great Sanhedrin.

The Jewish day begins between sunset and nightfall. The time used is that of the meridian of Jerusalem, which is 2h 21m in advance of Greenwich Mean Time. Rules for the beginning of sabbaths and festivals were laid down for the latitude of London in the 18th century and hours for nightfall are now fixed annually by the Chief Rabbi.

JEWISH CALENDAR 5757–8

AM 5757 (757) is a Minimal Leap year of 13 months, 55 sabbaths and 383 days. AM 5758 (758) is a Regular Common year of 12 months, 51 sabbaths and 354 days.

Jewish Month	AM 5757	AM 5758
Tishri 1	14 September 1996	2 October 1997
Marcheshvan 1	14 October	1 November
Kislev 1	12 November	30 November
Tebet 1	11 December	30 December
Shebat 1	9 January 1997	28 January 1998
*Adar 1	8 February	27 February
†*Adar* II	10 March	
Nisan 1	8 April	28 March
Iyar 1	8 May	27 April
Sivan 1	6 June	26 May
Tammuz 1	6 July	25 June
Ab 1	4 August	24 July
Elul 1	3 September	23 August

*Known as Adar Rishon in leap years
†Known as Adar Sheni in leap years

JEWISH FASTS AND FESTIVALS

For dates of principal festivals in 1997, *see* page 9

Tishri 1–2	Rosh Hashanah (New Year)
Tishri 3	*Fast of Gedaliah
Tishri 10	Yom Kippur (Day of Atonement)
Tishri 15–21	Succoth (Feast of Tabernacles)
Tishri 21	Hoshana Rabba
Tishri 22	Shemini Atseret (Solemn Assembly)
Tishri 23	Simchat Torah (Rejoicing of the Law)
Kislev 25	Chanucah (Dedication of the Temple) begins
Tebet 10	Fast of Tebet
†*Adar* 13	§Fast of Esther
†*Adar* 14	Purim
†*Adar* 15	Shushan Purim
Nisan 15–22	Pesach (Passover)
Sivan 6–7	Shavuot (Feast of Weeks)
Tammuz 17	*Fast of Tammuz
Ab 9	*Fast of Ab

*If these dates fall on the sabbath the fast is kept on the following day
†Adar Sheni in leap years
§This fast is observed on Adar 11 (or Adar Sheni 11 in leap years) if Adar 13 falls on a sabbath

THE MUSLIM CALENDAR

The Muslim era is dated from the *Hijrah*, or flight of the Prophet Muhammad from Mecca to Medina, the corresponding date of which in the Julian calendar is 16 July AD 622. Hijrah years (AH) are used principally in Iran, Turkey, Egypt, Malaysia, various Arab states and certain parts of India. The dating system was adopted about AD 639, commencing with the first day of the month Muharram. Muharram precedes the month in which the Hijrah took place and was recognized as the beginning of the year because it followed the month of pilgrimage.

The calendar is a lunar calendar and consists of twelve months containing an alternate sequence of 30 and 29 days, with the intercalation of one day at the end of the twelfth month at stated intervals in each cycle of 30 years. The object of the intercalation is to reconcile the date of the first day of the month with the date of the actual new moon.

Some adherents still take the date of the evening of the first physical sighting of the crescent of the new moon as that of the first of the month. For this reason, the beginning of a new month and the date of religious festivals can vary by a few days from the published calendars.

In each cycle of 30 years, 19 years are common and contain 354 days, and 11 years are intercalary (leap years) of 355 days, the latter being called *kabishah*. The mean length of the Hijrah years is 354 days 8 hours 48 minutes and the period of mean lunation is 29 days 12 hours 44 minutes.

To ascertain if a year is common or kabishah, divide it by 30: the quotient gives the number of completed cycles and the remainder shows the place of the year in the current cycle. If the remainder is 2, 5, 7, 10, 13, 16, 18, 21, 24, 26 or 29, the year is kabishah and consists of 355 days.

MUSLIM CALENDAR 1417–18

Hijrah year 1417 AH (remainder 7) is a kabishah year; 1418 AH (remainder 8) is a common year.

Month (length)	1417 AH	1418 AH
Muharram (30)	19 May 1996	9 May 1997
Safar (29)	18 June	8 June
Rabi' I (30)	17 July	7 July
Rabi' II (29)	16 August	6 August
Jumada I (30)	14 September	4 September
Jumada II (29)	14 October	4 October
Rajab (30)	12 November	2 November
Shaabân (29)	12 December	2 December
Ramadân (30)	10 January 1997	31 December
Shawwâl (29)	9 February	30 January 1998
Dhû'l-Qa'da (30)	10 March	28 February
Dhû'l-Hijjah (29 or 30)	9 April	30 March

MUSLIM FESTIVALS

Ramadan is a month of fasting for all Muslims because it is the month in which the revelation of the *Qur'an* (Koran) began. During Ramadan Muslims abstain from food, drink and sexual pleasure from dawn until after sunset throughout the month.

The two major festivals are *Idu-l-fitr* and *Idu-l-adha*. Idu-l-fitr marks the end of the Ramadan fast and is celebrated on the day after the sighting of the new moon of the following month. Idu-l-adha, the festival of sacrifice (also known as the great festival), celebrates the submission of the Prophet

Ibrahim (Abraham) to Allah. Idu-l-adha falls on the tenth day of Dhul-Hijjah, coinciding with the day when those on *hajj* (pilgrimage to Mecca) sacrifice animals.

Other days accorded special recognition are:

Muharram 1	New Year's Day
Muharram 10	Ashura (the day Prophet Nuh left the Ark and Prophet Musa was saved from Pharaoh (Sunni), the death of the Prophet's grandson Husain (Shi'ite))
Rabi'u-l-Awwal (Rabi' I) 12	Mawlidu-n-Nabiyy (birthday of the Prophet Muhammad)
Rajab 27	Laylatu-l-Isra wa l-Miraj (Night of the Journey and Ascension)
Ramadân Odd-numbered nights in the last 10 of the month	Laylatu-l-Qadr (Night of Power)
Dhû'l-Hijjah 10	Idu-l-adha (Festival of Sacrifice)

THE SIKH CALENDAR

The Sikh calendar is a lunar calendar of 365 days divided into 12 months. The length of the months varies between 29 and 32 days.

There are no prescribed feast days and no fasting periods. The main celebrations are Baisakhi Mela (the new year and the anniversary of the founding of the Khalsa), Diwali Mela (festival of light), Hola Mohalla Mela (a spring festival held in the Punjab), and the Gurpurbs (anniversaries associated with the ten Gurus).

The dates of the major celebrations in 1997 are given on page 9.

CIVIL AND LEGAL CALENDAR

THE HISTORICAL YEAR

Before the year 1752, two calendar systems were in use in England. The civil or legal year began on 25 March and the historical year on 1 January. Thus the civil or legal date 24 March 1658 was the same day as the historical date 24 March 1659; and a date in that portion of the year is written as 24 March 165⅝ the lower figure showing the historical year.

THE NEW YEAR

In England in the seventh century, and as late as the 13th, the year was reckoned from Christmas Day, but in the 12th century the Church in England began the year with the feast of the Annunciation of the Blessed Virgin ('Lady Day') on 25 March and this practice was adopted generally in the 14th century. The civil or legal year in the British Dominions (exclusive of Scotland) began with Lady Day until 1751. But in and since 1752 the civil year has begun with 1 January. New Year's Day in Scotland was changed from 25 March to 1 January in 1600.

Elsewhere in Europe, 1 January was adopted as the first day of the year by Venice in 1522, German states in 1544, Spain, Portugal, and the Roman Catholic Netherlands in 1556, Prussia, Denmark and Sweden in 1559, France in 1564, Lorraine in 1579, the Protestant Netherlands in 1583, Russia in 1725, and Tuscany in 1751.

REGNAL YEARS

Regnal years are the years of a sovereign's reign and each begins on the anniversary of his or her accession, e.g. regnal year 46 of the present Queen begins on 6 February 1997.

The system was used for dating Acts of Parliament until 1962. The Summer Time Act 1925, for example, is quoted as 15 and 16 Geo. V c. 64, because it became law in the parliamentary session which extended over part of both of these regnal years. Acts of a parliamentary session during which a sovereign died were usually given two year numbers, the regnal year of the deceased sovereign and the regnal year of his or her successor, e.g. those passed in 1952 were dated 16 Geo. VI and 1 Elizabeth II. Since 1962 Acts of Parliament have been dated by the calendar year.

QUARTER AND TERM DAYS

Holy days and saints days were the usual means in early times for setting the dates of future and recurrent appointments. The quarter days in England and Wales are the feast of the Nativity (25 December), the feast of the Annunciation (25 March), the feast of St John the Baptist (24 June) and the feast of St Michael and All Angels (29 September).

The term days in Scotland are Candlemas (the feast of the Purification), Whitsunday, Lammas (Loaf Mass), and Martinmas (St Martin's Day). These fell on 2 February, 15 May, 1 August and 11 November respectively. However, by the Term and Quarter Days (Scotland) Act 1990, the dates of the term days were changed to 28 February (Candlemas), 28 May (Whitsunday), 28 August (Lammas) and 28 November (Martinmas).

RED-LETTER DAYS

Red-letter days were originally the holy days and saints days indicated in early ecclesiastical calendars by letters printed in red ink. The days to be distinguished in this way were approved at the Council of Nicaea in AD 325.

These days still have a legal significance, as judges of the Queen's Bench Division wear scarlet robes on red-letter days falling during the law sittings. The days designated as red-letter days for this purpose are:

Holy and saints days
The Conversion of St Paul, the Purification, Ash Wednesday, the Annunciation, the Ascension, the feasts of St Mark, SS Philip and James, St Matthias, St Barnabas, St John the Baptist, St Peter, St Thomas, St James, St Luke, SS Simon and Jude, All Saints, St Andrew

Civil calendar
The anniversaries of The Queen's accession, The Queen's birthday and The Queen's coronation, The Queen's official birthday, the birthday of the Duke of Edinburgh, the birthday of Queen Elizabeth the Queen Mother, the birthday of the Prince of Wales, St David's Day and Lord Mayor's Day

PUBLIC HOLIDAYS

Public holidays are divided into two categories, common law and statutory. Common law holidays are holidays 'by habit and custom'; in England, Wales and Northern Ireland these are Good Friday and Christmas Day.

Statutory public holidays, known as bank holidays, were first established by the Bank Holidays Act 1871. They were, literally, days on which the banks (and other public institutions) were closed and financial obligations due on that day were payable the following day. The legislation currently governing public holidays in the United Kingdom is the Banking and Financial Dealings Act 1971. It stipulates which days are to be public holidays in England, Wales, Scotland and Northern Ireland.

Certain holidays (indicated by * below) are granted annually by royal proclamation, either throughout the United Kingdom or in any place in the United Kingdom. The public holidays are:

England and Wales
*New Year's Day
Easter Monday
*The first Monday in May
The last Monday in May
The last Monday in August
26 December, if it is not a Sunday
27 December when 25 or 26 December is a Sunday

Scotland
New Year's Day, or if it is a Sunday, 2 January
2 January, or if it is a Sunday, 3 January
Good Friday
The first Monday in May
*The last Monday in May
The first Monday in August
Christmas Day, or if it is a Sunday, 26 December
*Boxing Day – if Christmas Day falls on a Sunday, 26 December is given in lieu and an alternative day is given for Boxing Day

Northern Ireland
*New Year's Day
17 March, or if it is a Sunday, 18 March
Easter Monday
*The first Monday in May
The last Monday in May
*12 July, or if it is a Sunday, 13 July
The last Monday in August
26 December, if it is not a Sunday
27 December if 25 or 26 December is a Sunday

For dates of public holidays in 1997 and 1998, *see* pages 10–11.

CHRONOLOGICAL CYCLES AND ERAS

SOLAR (OR MAJOR) CYCLE
The solar cycle is a period of twenty-eight years in any corresponding year of which the days of the week recur on the same day of the month.

METONIC (LUNAR, OR MINOR) CYCLE
In 432 BC, Meton, an Athenian astronomer, found that 235 lunations are very nearly, though not exactly, equal in duration to 19 solar years and so after 19 years the phases of the Moon recur on the same days of the month (nearly). The dates of full moon in a cycle of 19 years were inscribed in figures of gold on public monuments in Athens, and the number showing the position of a year in the cycle is called the golden number of that year.

JULIAN PERIOD
The Julian period was proposed by Joseph Scaliger in 1582. The period is 7980 Julian years, and its first year coincides with the year 4713 BC. The figure of 7980 is the product of the number of years in the solar cycle, the Metonic cycle and the cycle of the Roman indiction (28 × 19 × 15).

ROMAN INDICTION

The Roman indiction is a period of fifteen years, instituted for fiscal purposes about AD 300.

EPACT

The epact is the age of the calendar Moon, diminished by one day, on 1 January, in the ecclesiastical lunar calendar.

CHINESE CALENDAR

A lunar calendar was the sole calendar in use in China until 1911, when the government adopted the new (Gregorian) calendar for official and most business activities. The Chinese tend to follow both calendars, the lunar calendar playing an important part in personal life, e.g. birth celebrations, festivals, marriages; and in rural villages the lunar calendar dictates the cycle of activities, denoting the change of weather and farming activities.

The lunar calendar is used in Hong Kong, Singapore, Malaysia, Tibet and elsewhere in south-east Asia. The calendar has a cycle of 60 years. The new year begins at the first new moon after the sun enters the sign of Aquarius, i.e. the new year falls between 21 January and 19 February in the Gregorian calendar.

Each year in the Chinese calendar is associated with one of 12 animals: the rat, the ox, the tiger, the rabbit, the dragon, the snake, the horse, the goat or sheep, the monkey, the chicken or rooster, the dog, and the pig.

The date of the Chinese new year and the astrological sign for the years 1997–2000 are:

1997	7 February	Ox
1998	28 January	Tiger
1999	16 February	Rabbit
2000	5 February	Dragon

COPTIC CALENDAR

In the Coptic calendar, which is used by part of the population of Egypt and Ethiopia, the year is made up of 12 months of 30 days each, followed, in general, by five complementary days. Every fourth year is an intercalary or leap year and in these years there are six complementary days. The intercalary year of the Coptic calendar immediately precedes the leap year of the Julian calendar. The era is that of Diocletian or the Martyrs, the origin of which is fixed at 29 August AD 284 (Julian date).

INDIAN ERAS

In addition to the Muslim reckoning, other eras are used in India. The Saka era of southern India, dating from 3 March AD 78, was declared the national calendar of the Republic of India with effect from 22 March 1957, to be used con-currently with the Gregorian calendar. As revised, the year of the new Saka era begins at the spring equinox, with five successive months of 31 days and seven of 30 days in ordinary years, and six months of each length in leap years. The year AD 1997 is 1919 of the revised Saka era.

The year AD 1997 corresponds to the following years in other eras:

Year 2054 of the Vikram Samvat era
Year 1404 of the Bengali San era
Year 1173 of the Kollam era
Jovian year (Barhaspatya varsa or 60-year cycle of Jupiter) 25 Vikrta (North Indian usage) and 11 Dhatri (South Indian usage)
Vedanga Jyotisa year 3 Parivatsara of the five-yearly cycle (384th cycle of Paitamah Siddhanta)
Year 5098 of the Kaliyuga era
Year 2541 of the Buddha Nirvana era

JAPANESE CALENDAR

The Japanese calendar is essentially the same as the Gregorian calendar, the years, months and weeks being of the same length and beginning on the same days as those of the Gregorian calendar. The numeration of the years is different, for Japanese chronology is based on a system of epochs or periods, each of which begins at the accession of an Emperor or other important occurrence. The method is not unlike the former British system of regnal years, except that each year of a period closes on 31 December. The Japanese chronology begins about AD 650 and the three latest epochs are defined by the reigns of Emperors, whose actual names are not necessarily used:

Epoch

Taishō   1 August 1912 to 25 December 1926
Shōwa   26 December 1926 to 7 January 1989
Heisei   8 January 1989

The year Heisei 9 begins on 1 January 1997.

The months are not named. They are known as First Month, Second Month, etc., First Month being equivalent to January. The days of the week are Nichiyōbi (Sun-day), Getsuyōbi (Moon-day), Kayōbi (Fire-day), Suiyōbi (Water-day), Mokuyōbi (Wood-day), Kinyōbi (Metal-day), Doyōbi (Earth-day).

THE MASONIC YEAR

Two dates are quoted in warrants, dispensations, etc., issued by the United Grand Lodge of England, those for the current year being expressed as *Anno Domini* 1997 – *Anno Lucis* 5997. This *Anno Lucis* (year of light) is based on the Book of Genesis 1:3, the 4000-year difference being derived, in modified form, from *Ussher's Notation*, published in 1654, which places the Creation of the World in 4004 BC.

OLYMPIADS

Ancient Greek chronology was reckoned in Olympiads, cycles of four years corresponding with the periodic Olympic Games held on the plain of Olympia in Elis once every four years. The intervening years were the first, second, etc., of the Olympiad, which received the name of the victor at the Games. The first recorded Olympiad is that of Choroebus, 776 BC.

ZOROASTRIAN CALENDAR

Zoroastrians, followers of the Iranian prophet Zarathushtra (known to the Greeks as Zoroaster) are mostly to be found in Iran and in India, where they are known as Parsees.

The Zoroastrian era dates from the coronation of the last Zoroastrian Sasanian king in AD 631. The Zoroastrian calendar is divided into twelve months, each comprising 30 days, followed by five holy days of the Gathas at the end of each year to make the year consist of 365 days.

In order to synchronize the calendar with the solar year of 365 days, an extra month was intercalated once every 120 years. However, this intercalation ceased in the 12th century and the New Year, which had fallen in the spring, slipped back until it now falls in August. Because intercalation ceased at different times in Iran and India, there was one month's difference between the calendar followed in Iran (Kadmi calendar) and by the Parsees (Shenshai calendar).

In 1906 a group of Zoroastrians decided to bring the calendar back in line with the seasons again and restore the New Year to 21 March each year (Fasli calendar).

The Shenshai calendar (New Year in August) is mainly used by Parsees. The Fasli calendar (New Year, 21 March) is mainly used by Zoroastrians living in Iran, in the Indian subcontinent, or away from Iran.

THE ROMAN CALENDAR

Roman historians adopted as an epoch the foundation of Rome, which is believed to have happened in the year 753 BC. The ordinal number of the years in Roman reckoning is followed by the letters AUC (*ab urbe condita*), so that the year 1997 is 2750 AUC (MMDCCL). The calendar that we know has developed from one said to have been established by Romulus using a year of 304 days divided into ten months, beginning with March. To this Numa added January and February, making the year consist of 12 months of 30 and 29 days alternately, with an additional day so that the total was 355. It is also said that Numa ordered an intercalary month of 22 or 23 days in alternate years, making 90 days in eight years, to be inserted after 23 February.

However, there is some doubt as to the origination and the details of the intercalation in the Roman calendar. It is certain that some scheme of this kind was inaugurated and not fully carried out, for in the year 46 BC Julius Caesar found that the calendar had been allowed to fall into some confusion. He sought the help of the Egyptian astronomer Sosigenes, which led to the construction and adoption (45 BC) of the Julian calendar, and, by a slight alteration, to the Gregorian calendar now in use. The year 46 BC was made to consist of 445 days and is called the Year of Confusion.

In the Roman (Julian) calendar the days of the month were counted backwards from three fixed points, or days, and an intervening day was said to be so many days before the next coming point, the first and last being counted. These three points were the Kalends, the Nones, and the Ides. Their positions in the months and the method of counting from them will be seen in the table below. The year containing 366 days was called *bissextilis annus*, as it had a doubled sixth day (*bissextus dies*) before the March Kalends on 24 February – *ante diem sextum Kalendas Martias*, or a.d. VI Kal. Mart.

Present days of the month	March, May, July, October have thirty-one days		January, August, December have thirty-one days		April, June, September, November have thirty days		February has twenty-eight days, and in leap year twenty-nine	
1	Kalendis		Kalendis		Kalendis		Kalendis	
2	VI ⎫		IV ⎫ ante		IV ⎫ ante		IV ⎫ ante	
3	V ⎪ ante		III ⎭ Nonas		III ⎭ Nonas		III ⎭ Nonas	
4	IV ⎬ Nonas		pridie Nonas		pridie Nonas		pridie Nonas	
5	III ⎭		Nonis		Nonis		Nonis	
6	pridie Nonas		VIII ⎫		VIII ⎫		VIII ⎫	
7	Nonis		VII ⎪		VII ⎪		VII ⎪	
8	VIII ⎫		VI ⎬ ante		VI ⎬ ante		VI ⎬ ante	
9	VII ⎪		V ⎪ Idus		V ⎪ Idus		V ⎪ Idus	
10	VI ⎬ ante		IV ⎪		IV ⎪		IV ⎪	
11	V ⎪ Idus		III ⎭		III ⎭		III ⎭	
12	IV ⎪		pridie Idus		pridie Idus		pridie Idus	
13	III ⎭		Idibus		Idibus		Idibus	
14	pridie Idus		XIX ⎫		XVIII ⎫		XVI ⎫	
15	Idibus		XVIII		XVII		XV	
16	XVII ⎫		XVII		XVI		XIV	
17	XVI ⎪		XVI		XV		XIII	
18	XV ⎪		XV		XIV		XII	
19	XIV ⎪		XIV		XIII		XI	
20	XIII ⎪		XIII		XII ⎫ ante Kalendas		X ⎫ ante Kalendas	
21	XII ⎪		XII ⎫ ante Kalendas		XI ⎪ (of the month		IX ⎬ Martias	
22	XI ⎬ ante Kalendas		XI ⎪ (of the month		X ⎭ following)		VIII	
23	X ⎪ (of the month		X ⎭ following)		IX		VII	
24	IX ⎪ following)		IX		VIII		*VI	
25	VIII ⎪		VIII		VII		V	
26	VII ⎪		VII		VI		IV	
27	VI ⎪		VI		V		III ⎭	
28	V ⎪		V		IV		pridie Kalendas	
29	IV ⎭		IV ⎭		III ⎭		Martias	
30	III ⎭		III ⎭		pridie Kalendas			
31	pridie Kalendas (Aprilis, Iunias, Sextilis, Novembris)		pridie Kalendas (Februarias, Septembris, Ianuarias)		(Maias, Quintilis, Octobris, Decembris)		* (repeated in leap year)	

Calendar for Any Year 1780–2040

To select the correct calendar for any year between 1780 and 2040, consult the index below
* leap year

Year		Year		Year		Year		Year		Year		Year		Year	
1780	N*	1813	K	1846	I	1879	G	1912	D*	1945	C	1978	A	2011	M
1781	C	1814	M	1847	K	1880	J*	1913	G	1946	E	1979	C	2012	B*
1782	E	1815	A	1848	N*	1881	M	1914	I	1947	G	1980	F*	2013	E
1783	G	1816	D*	1849	C	1882	A	1915	K	1948	J*	1981	I	2014	G
1784	J*	1817	G	1850	E	1883	C	1916	N*	1949	M	1982	K	2015	I
1785	M	1818	I	1851	G	1884	F*	1917	C	1950	A	1983	M	2016	L*
1786	A	1819	K	1852	J*	1885	I	1918	E	1951	C	1984	B*	2017	A
1787	C	1820	N*	1853	M	1886	K	1919	G	1952	F*	1985	E	2018	C
1788	F*	1821	C	1854	A	1887	M	1920	J*	1953	I	1986	G	2019	E
1789	I	1822	E	1855	C	1888	B*	1921	M	1954	K	1987	I	2020	H*
1790	K	1823	G	1856	F*	1889	E	1922	A	1955	M	1988	L*	2021	K
1791	M	1824	J*	1857	I	1890	G	1923	C	1956	B*	1989	A	2022	M
1792	B*	1825	M	1858	K	1891	I	1924	F*	1957	E	1990	C	2023	A
1793	E	1826	A	1859	M	1892	L*	1925	I	1958	G	1991	E	2024	D*
1794	G	1827	C	1860	B*	1893	A	1926	K	1959	I	1992	H*	2025	G
1795	I	1828	F*	1861	E	1894	C	1927	M	1960	L*	1993	K	2026	I
1796	L*	1829	I	1862	G	1895	E	1928	B*	1961	A	1994	M	2027	K
1797	A	1830	K	1863	I	1896	H*	1929	E	1962	C	1995	A	2028	N*
1798	C	1831	M	1864	L*	1897	K	1930	G	1963	E	1996	D*	2029	C
1799	E	1832	B*	1865	A	1898	M	1931	I	1964	H*	1997	G	2030	E
1800	G	1833	E	1866	C	1899	A	1932	L*	1965	K	1998	I	2031	G
1801	I	1834	G	1867	E	1900	C	1933	A	1966	M	1999	K	2032	J*
1802	K	1835	I	1868	H*	1901	E	1934	C	1967	A	2000	N*	2033	M
1803	M	1836	L*	1869	K	1902	G	1935	E	1968	D*	2001	C	2034	A
1804	B*	1837	A	1870	M	1903	I	1936	H*	1969	G	2002	E	2035	C
1805	E	1838	C	1871	A	1904	L*	1937	K	1970	I	2003	G	2036	G
1806	G	1839	E	1872	D*	1905	A	1938	M	1971	K	2004	J*	2037	I
1807	I	1840	H*	1873	G	1906	C	1939	A	1972	N*	2005	M	2038	K
1808	L*	1841	K	1874	I	1907	E	1940	D*	1973	C	2006	A	2039	M
1809	A	1842	M	1875	K	1908	H*	1941	G	1974	E	2007	C	2040	B*
1810	C	1843	A	1876	N*	1909	K	1942	I	1975	G	2008	F*		
1811	E	1844	D*	1877	C	1910	M	1943	K	1976	J*	2009	I		
1812	H*	1845	G	1878	E	1911	A	1944	N*	1977	M	2010	K		

A

	January	February	March
Sun.	1 8 15 22 29	5 12 19 26	5 12 19 26
Mon.	2 9 16 23 30	6 13 20 27	6 13 20 27
Tue.	3 10 17 24 31	7 14 21 28	7 14 21 28
Wed.	4 11 18 25	1 8 15 22	1 8 15 22 29
Thur.	5 12 19 26	2 9 16 23	2 9 16 23 30
Fri.	6 13 20 27	3 10 17 24	3 10 17 24 31
Sat.	7 14 21 28	4 11 18 25	4 11 18 25

	April	May	June
Sun.	2 9 16 23 30	7 14 21 28	4 11 18 25
Mon.	3 10 17 24	1 8 15 22 29	5 12 19 26
Tue.	4 11 18 25	2 9 16 23 30	6 13 20 27
Wed.	5 12 19 26	3 10 17 24 31	7 14 21 28
Thur.	6 13 20 27	4 11 18 25	1 8 15 22 29
Fri.	7 14 21 28	5 12 19 26	2 9 16 23 30
Sat.	1 8 15 22 29	6 13 20 27	3 10 17 24

	July	August	September
Sun.	2 9 16 23 30	6 13 20 27	3 10 17 24
Mon.	3 10 17 24 31	7 14 21 28	4 11 18 25
Tue.	4 11 18 25	1 8 15 22 29	5 12 19 26
Wed.	5 12 19 26	2 9 16 23 30	6 13 20 27
Thur.	6 13 20 27	3 10 17 24 31	7 14 21 28
Fri.	7 14 21 28	4 11 18 25	1 8 15 22 29
Sat.	1 8 15 22 29	5 12 19 26	2 9 16 23 30

	October	November	December
Sun.	1 8 15 22 29	5 12 19 26	3 10 17 24 31
Mon.	2 9 16 23 30	6 13 20 27	4 11 18 25
Tue.	3 10 17 24 31	7 14 21 28	5 12 19 26
Wed.	4 11 18 25	1 8 15 22 29	6 13 20 27
Thur.	5 12 19 26	2 9 16 23 30	7 14 21 28
Fri.	6 13 20 27	3 10 17 24	1 8 15 22 29
Sat.	7 14 21 28	4 11 18 25	2 9 16 23 30

EASTER DAYS

March 26	1815, 1826, 1837, 1967, 1978, 1989
April 2	1809, 1893, 1899, 1961
April 9	1871, 1882, 1939, 1950, 2023, 2034
April 16	1786, 1797, 1843, 1854, 1865, 1911, 1922, 1933, 1995, 2006, 2017
April 23	1905

B (LEAP YEAR)

	January	February	March
Sun.	1 8 15 22 29	5 12 19 26	4 11 18 25
Mon.	2 9 16 23 30	6 13 20 27	5 12 19 26
Tue.	3 10 17 24 31	7 14 21 28	6 13 20 27
Wed.	4 11 18 25	1 8 15 22 29	7 14 21 28
Thur.	5 12 19 26	2 9 16 23	1 8 15 22 29
Fri.	6 13 20 27	3 10 17 24	2 9 16 23 30
Sat.	7 14 21 28	4 11 18 25	3 10 17 24 31

	April	May	June
Sun.	1 8 15 22 29	6 13 20 27	3 10 17 24
Mon.	2 9 16 23 30	7 14 21 28	4 11 18 25
Tue.	3 10 17 24	1 8 15 22 29	5 12 19 26
Wed.	4 11 18 25	2 9 16 23 30	6 13 20 27
Thur.	5 12 19 26	3 10 17 24 31	7 14 21 28
Fri.	6 13 20 27	4 11 18 25	1 8 15 22 29
Sat.	7 14 21 28	5 12 19 26	2 9 16 23 30

	July	August	September
Sun.	1 8 15 22 29	5 12 19 26	2 9 16 23 30
Mon.	2 9 16 23 30	6 13 20 27	3 10 17 24
Tue.	3 10 17 24 31	7 14 21 28	4 11 18 25
Wed.	4 11 18 25	1 8 15 22 29	5 12 19 26
Thur.	5 12 19 26	2 9 16 23 30	6 13 20 27
Fri.	6 13 20 27	3 10 17 24 31	7 14 21 28
Sat.	7 14 21 28	4 11 18 25	1 8 15 22 29

	October	November	December
Sun.	7 14 21 28	4 11 18 25	2 9 16 23 30
Mon.	1 8 15 22 29	5 12 19 26	3 10 17 24 31
Tue.	2 9 16 23 30	6 13 20 27	4 11 18 25
Wed.	3 10 17 24 31	7 14 21 28	5 12 19 26
Thur.	4 11 18 25	1 8 15 22 29	6 13 20 27
Fri.	5 12 19 26	2 9 16 23 30	7 14 21 28
Sat.	6 13 20 27	3 10 17 24	1 8 15 22 29

EASTER DAYS

April 1	1804, 1888, 1956, 2040
April 8	1792, 1860, 1928, 2012
April 22	1832, 1984

C

Day	January	February	March
Sun.	7 14 21 28	4 11 18 25	4 11 18 25
Mon.	1 8 15 22 29	5 12 19 26	5 12 19 26
Tue.	2 9 16 23 30	6 13 20 27	6 13 20 27
Wed.	3 10 17 24 31	7 14 21 28	7 14 21 28
Thur.	4 11 18 25	1 8 15 22	1 8 15 22 29
Fri.	5 12 19 26	2 9 16 23	2 9 16 23 30
Sat.	6 13 20 27	3 10 17 24	3 10 17 24 31

Day	April	May	June
Sun.	1 8 15 22 29	6 13 20 27	3 10 17 24
Mon.	2 9 16 23 30	7 14 21 28	4 11 18 25
Tue.	3 10 17 24	1 8 15 22 29	5 12 19 26
Wed.	4 11 18 25	2 9 16 23 30	6 13 20 27
Thur.	5 12 19 26	3 10 17 24 31	7 14 21 28
Fri.	6 13 20 27	4 11 18 25	1 8 15 22 29
Sat.	7 14 21 28	5 12 19 26	2 9 16 23 30

Day	July	August	September
Sun.	1 8 15 22 29	5 12 19 26	2 9 16 23 30
Mon.	2 9 16 23 30	6 13 20 27	3 10 17 24
Tue.	3 10 17 24 31	7 14 21 28	4 11 18 25
Wed.	4 11 18 25	1 8 15 22 29	5 12 19 26
Thur.	5 12 19 26	2 9 16 23 30	6 13 20 27
Fri.	6 13 20 27	3 10 17 24 31	7 14 21 28
Sat.	7 14 21 28	4 11 18 25	1 8 15 22 29

Day	October	November	December
Sun.	7 14 21 28	4 11 18 25	2 9 16 23 30
Mon.	1 8 15 22 29	5 12 19 26	3 10 17 24 31
Tue.	2 9 16 23 30	6 13 20 27	4 11 18 25
Wed.	3 10 17 24 31	7 14 21 28	5 12 19 26
Thur.	4 11 18 25	1 8 15 22 29	6 13 20 27
Fri.	5 12 19 26	2 9 16 23 30	7 14 21 28
Sat.	6 13 20 27	3 10 17 24	1 8 15 22 29

EASTER DAYS

March 25	1883, 1894, 1951, 2035
April 1	1866, 1877, 1923, 1934, 1945, 2018, 2029
April 8	1787, 1798, 1849, 1855, 1917, 2007
April 15	1781, 1827, 1838, 1900, 1906, 1979, 1990, 2001
April 22	1810, 1821, 1962, 1973

E

Day	January	February	March
Sun.	6 13 20 27	3 10 17 24	3 10 17 24 31
Mon.	7 14 21 28	4 11 18 25	4 11 18 25
Tue.	1 8 15 22 29	5 12 19 26	5 12 19 26
Wed.	2 9 16 23 30	6 13 20 27	6 13 20 27
Thur.	3 10 17 24 31	7 14 21 28	7 14 21 28
Fri.	4 11 18 25	1 8 15 22	1 8 15 22 29
Sat.	5 12 19 26	2 9 16 23	2 9 16 23 30

Day	April	May	June
Sun.	7 14 21 28	5 12 19 26	2 9 16 23 30
Mon.	1 8 15 22 29	6 13 20 27	3 10 17 24
Tue.	2 9 16 23 30	7 14 21 28	4 11 18 25
Wed.	3 10 17 24	1 8 15 22 29	5 12 19 26
Thur.	4 11 18 25	2 9 16 23 30	6 13 20 27
Fri.	5 12 19 26	3 10 17 24 31	7 14 21 28
Sat.	6 13 20 27	4 11 18 25	1 8 15 22 29

Day	July	August	September
Sun.	7 14 21 28	4 11 18 25	1 8 15 22 29
Mon.	1 8 15 22 29	5 12 19 26	2 9 16 23 30
Tue.	2 9 16 23 30	6 13 20 27	3 10 17 24
Wed.	3 10 17 24 31	7 14 21 28	4 11 18 25
Thur.	4 11 18 25	1 8 15 22 29	5 12 19 26
Fri.	5 12 19 26	2 9 16 23 30	6 13 20 27
Sat.	6 13 20 27	3 10 17 24 31	7 14 21 28

Day	October	November	December
Sun.	6 13 20 27	3 10 17 24	1 8 15 22 29
Mon.	7 14 21 28	4 11 18 25	2 9 16 23 30
Tue.	1 8 15 22 29	5 12 19 26	3 10 17 24 31
Wed.	2 9 16 23 30	6 13 20 27	4 11 18 25
Thur.	3 10 17 24 31	7 14 21 28	5 12 19 26
Fri.	4 11 18 25	1 8 15 22 29	6 13 20 27
Sat.	5 12 19 26	2 9 16 23 30	7 14 21 28

EASTER DAYS

March 24	1799
March 31	1782, 1793, 1839, 1850, 1861, 1907
	1918, 1929, 1991, 2002, 2013
April 7	1822, 1833, 1901, 1985
April 14	1805, 1811, 1895, 1963, 1974
April 21	1867, 1878, 1889, 1935, 1946, 1957, 2019, 2030

D (LEAP YEAR)

Day	January	February	March
Sun.	7 14 21 28	4 11 18 25	3 10 17 24 31
Mon.	1 8 15 22 29	5 12 19 26	4 11 18 25
Tue.	2 9 16 23 30	6 13 20 27	5 12 19 26
Wed.	3 10 17 24 31	7 14 21 28	6 13 20 27
Thur.	4 11 18 25	1 8 15 22 29	7 14 21 28
Fri.	5 12 19 26	2 9 16 23	1 8 15 22 29
Sat.	6 13 20 27	3 10 17 24	2 9 16 23 30

Day	April	May	June
Sun.	7 14 21 28	5 12 19 26	2 9 16 23 30
Mon.	1 8 15 22 29	6 13 20 27	3 10 17 24
Tue.	2 9 16 23 30	7 14 21 28	4 11 18 25
Wed.	3 10 17 24	1 8 15 22 29	5 12 19 26
Thur.	4 11 18 25	2 9 16 23 30	6 13 20 27
Fri.	5 12 19 26	3 10 17 24 31	7 14 21 28
Sat.	6 13 20 27	4 11 18 25	1 8 15 22 29

Day	July	August	September
Sun.	7 14 21 28	4 11 18 25	1 8 15 22 29
Mon.	1 8 15 22 29	5 12 19 26	2 9 16 23 30
Tue.	2 9 16 23 30	6 13 20 27	3 10 17 24
Wed.	3 10 17 24 31	7 14 21 28	4 11 18 25
Thur.	4 11 18 25	1 8 15 22 29	5 12 19 26
Fri.	5 12 19 26	2 9 16 23 30	6 13 20 27
Sat.	6 13 20 27	3 10 17 24 31	7 14 21 28

Day	October	November	December
Sun.	6 13 20 27	3 10 17 24	1 8 15 22 29
Mon.	7 14 21 28	4 11 18 25	2 9 16 23 30
Tue.	1 8 15 22 29	5 12 19 26	3 10 17 24 31
Wed.	2 9 16 23 30	6 13 20 27	4 11 18 25
Thur.	3 10 17 24 31	7 14 21 28	5 12 19 26
Fri.	4 11 18 25	1 8 15 22 29	6 13 20 27
Sat.	5 12 19 26	2 9 16 23 30	7 14 21 28

EASTER DAYS

March 24	1940
March 31	1872, 2024
April 7	1844, 1912, 1996
April 14	1816, 1968

F (LEAP YEAR)

Day	January	February	March
Sun.	6 13 20 27	3 10 17 24	2 9 16 23 30
Mon.	7 14 21 28	4 11 18 25	3 10 17 24 31
Tue.	1 8 15 22 29	5 12 19 26	4 11 18 25
Wed.	2 9 16 23 30	6 13 20 27	5 12 19 26
Thur.	3 10 17 24 31	7 14 21 28	6 13 20 27
Fri.	4 11 18 25	1 8 15 22 29	7 14 21 28
Sat.	5 12 19 26	2 9 16 23	1 8 15 22 29

Day	April	May	June
Sun.	6 13 20 27	4 11 18 25	1 8 15 22 29
Mon.	7 14 21 28	5 12 19 26	2 9 16 23 30
Tue.	1 8 15 22 29	6 13 20 27	3 10 17 24
Wed.	2 9 16 23 30	7 14 21 28	4 11 18 25
Thur.	3 10 17 24	1 8 15 22 29	5 12 19 26
Fri.	4 11 18 25	2 9 16 23 30	6 13 20 27
Sat.	5 12 19 26	3 10 17 24 31	7 14 21 28

Day	July	August	September
Sun.	6 13 20 27	3 10 17 24 31	7 14 21 28
Mon.	7 14 21 28	4 11 18 25	1 8 15 22 29
Tue.	1 8 15 22 29	5 12 19 26	2 9 16 23 30
Wed.	2 9 16 23 30	6 13 20 27	3 10 17 24
Thur.	3 10 17 24 31	7 14 21 28	4 11 18 25
Fri.	4 11 18 25	1 8 15 22 29	5 12 19 26
Sat.	5 12 19 26	2 9 16 23 30	6 13 20 27

Day	October	November	December
Sun.	5 12 19 26	2 9 16 23 30	7 14 21 28
Mon.	6 13 20 27	3 10 17 24	1 8 15 22 29
Tue.	7 14 21 28	4 11 18 25	2 9 16 23 30
Wed.	1 8 15 22 29	5 12 19 26	3 10 17 24 31
Thur.	2 9 16 23 30	6 13 20 27	4 11 18 25
Fri.	3 10 17 24 31	7 14 21 28	5 12 19 26
Sat.	4 11 18 25	1 8 15 22 29	6 13 20 27

EASTER DAYS

March 23	1788, 1856, 2008
April 6	1828, 1980
April 13	1884, 1952, 2036
April 20	1924

G

	January	February	March
Sun.	5 12 19 26	2 9 16 23	2 9 16 23 30
Mon.	6 13 20 27	3 10 17 24	3 10 17 24 31
Tue.	7 14 21 28	4 11 18 25	4 11 18 25
Wed.	1 8 15 22 29	5 12 19 26	5 12 19 26
Thur.	2 9 16 23 30	6 13 20 27	6 13 20 27
Fri.	3 10 17 24 31	7 14 21 28	7 14 21 28
Sat.	4 11 18 25	1 8 15 22	1 8 15 22 29

	April	May	June
Sun.	6 13 20 27	4 11 18 25	1 8 15 22 29
Mon.	7 14 21 28	5 12 19 26	2 9 16 23 30
Tue.	1 8 15 22 29	6 13 20 27	3 10 17 24
Wed.	2 9 16 23 30	7 14 21 28	4 11 18 25
Thur.	3 10 17 24	1 8 15 22 29	5 12 19 26
Fri.	4 11 18 25	2 9 16 23 30	6 13 20 27
Sat.	5 12 19 26	3 10 17 24 31	7 14 21 28

	July	August	September
Sun.	6 13 20 27	3 10 17 24 31	7 14 21 28
Mon.	7 14 21 28	4 11 18 25	1 8 15 22 29
Tue.	1 8 15 22 29	5 12 19 26	2 9 16 23 30
Wed.	2 9 16 23 30	6 13 20 27	3 10 17 24
Thur.	3 10 17 24 31	7 14 21 28	4 11 18 25
Fri.	4 11 18 25	1 8 15 22 29	5 12 19 26
Sat.	5 12 19 26	2 9 16 23 30	6 13 20 27

	October	November	December
Sun.	5 12 19 26	2 9 16 23 30	7 14 21 28
Mon.	6 13 20 27	3 10 17 24	1 8 15 22 29
Tue.	7 14 21 28	4 11 18 25	2 9 16 23 30
Wed.	1 8 15 22 29	5 12 19 26	3 10 17 24 31
Thur.	2 9 16 23 30	6 13 20 27	4 11 18 25
Fri.	3 10 17 24 31	7 14 21 28	5 12 19 26
Sat.	4 11 18 25	1 8 15 22 29	6 13 20 27

EASTER DAYS

March 23	1845, 1913
March 30	1823, 1834, 1902, 1975, 1986, 1997
April 6	1806, 1817, 1890, 1947, 1958, 1969
April 13	1800, 1873, 1879, 1941, 2031
April 20	1783, 1794, 1851, 1862, 1919, 1930, 2003, 2014, 2025

I

	January	February	March
Sun.	4 11 18 25	1 8 15 22	1 8 15 22 29
Mon.	5 12 19 26	2 9 16 23	2 9 16 23 30
Tue.	6 13 20 27	3 10 17 24	3 10 17 24 31
Wed.	7 14 21 28	4 11 18 25	4 11 18 25
Thur.	1 8 15 22 29	5 12 19 26	5 12 19 26
Fri.	2 9 16 23 30	6 13 20 27	6 13 20 27
Sat.	3 10 17 24 31	7 14 21 28	7 14 21 28

	April	May	June
Sun.	5 12 19 26	3 10 17 24 31	7 14 21 28
Mon.	6 13 20 27	4 11 18 25	1 8 15 22 29
Tue.	7 14 21 28	5 12 19 26	2 9 16 23 30
Wed.	1 8 15 22 29	6 13 20 27	3 10 17 24
Thur.	2 9 16 23 30	7 14 21 28	4 11 18 25
Fri.	3 10 17 24	1 8 15 22 29	5 12 19 26
Sat.	4 11 18 25	2 9 16 23 30	6 13 20 27

	July	August	September
Sun.	5 12 19 26	2 9 16 23 30	6 13 20 27
Mon.	6 13 20 27	3 10 17 24 31	7 14 21 28
Tue.	7 14 21 28	4 11 18 25	1 8 15 22 29
Wed.	1 8 15 22 29	5 12 19 26	2 9 16 23 30
Thur.	2 9 16 23 30	6 13 20 27	3 10 17 24
Fri.	3 10 17 24 31	7 14 21 28	4 11 18 25
Sat.	4 11 18 25	1 8 15 22 29	5 12 19 26

	October	November	December
Sun.	4 11 18 25	1 8 15 22 29	6 13 20 27
Mon.	5 12 19 26	2 9 16 23 30	7 14 21 28
Tue.	6 13 20 27	3 10 17 24	1 8 15 22 29
Wed.	7 14 21 28	4 11 18 25	2 9 16 23 30
Thur.	1 8 15 22 29	5 12 19 26	3 10 17 24 31
Fri.	2 9 16 23 30	6 13 20 27	4 11 18 25
Sat.	3 10 17 24 31	7 14 21 28	5 12 19 26

EASTER DAYS

March 22	1818
March 29	1807, 1891, 1959, 1970
April 5	1795, 1801, 1863, 1874, 1885, 1931, 1942, 1953, 2015, 2026, 2037
April 12	1789, 1846, 1857, 1903, 1914, 1925, 1998, 2009
April 19	1829, 1835, 1981, 1987

H (LEAP YEAR)

	January	February	March
Sun.	5 12 19 26	2 9 16 23	1 8 15 22 29
Mon.	6 13 20 27	3 10 17 24	2 9 16 23 30
Tue.	7 14 21 28	4 11 18 25	3 10 17 24 31
Wed.	1 8 15 22 29	5 12 19 26	4 11 18 25
Thur.	2 9 16 23 30	6 13 20 27	5 12 19 26
Fri.	3 10 17 24 31	7 14 21 28	6 13 20 27
Sat.	4 11 18 25	1 8 15 22 29	7 14 21 28

	April	May	June
Sun.	5 12 19 26	3 10 17 24 31	7 14 21 28
Mon.	6 13 20 27	4 11 18 25	1 8 15 22 29
Tue.	7 14 21 28	5 12 19 26	2 9 16 23 30
Wed.	1 8 15 22 29	6 13 20 27	3 10 17 24
Thur.	2 9 16 23 30	7 14 21 28	4 11 18 25
Fri.	3 10 17 24	1 8 15 22 29	5 12 19 26
Sat.	4 11 18 25	2 9 16 23 30	6 13 20 27

	July	August	September
Sun.	5 12 19 26	2 9 16 23 30	6 13 20 27
Mon.	6 13 20 27	3 10 17 24 31	7 14 21 28
Tue.	7 14 21 28	4 11 18 25	1 8 15 22 29
Wed.	1 8 15 22 29	5 12 19 26	2 9 16 23 30
Thur.	2 9 16 23 30	6 13 20 27	3 10 17 24
Fri.	3 10 17 24 31	7 14 21 28	4 11 18 25
Sat.	4 11 18 25	1 8 15 22 29	5 12 19 26

	October	November	December
Sun.	4 11 18 25	1 8 15 22 29	6 13 20 27
Mon.	5 12 19 26	2 9 16 23 30	7 14 21 28
Tue.	6 13 20 27	3 10 17 24	1 8 15 22 29
Wed.	7 14 21 28	4 11 18 25	2 9 16 23 30
Thur.	1 8 15 22 29	5 12 19 26	3 10 17 24 31
Fri.	2 9 16 23 30	6 13 20 27	4 11 18 25
Sat.	3 10 17 24 31	7 14 21 28	5 12 19 26

EASTER DAYS

March 29	1812, 1964
April 5	1896
April 12	1868, 1936, 2020
April 19	1840, 1908, 1992

J (LEAP YEAR)

	January	February	March
Sun.	4 11 18 25	1 8 15 22 29	7 14 21 28
Mon.	5 12 19 26	2 9 16 23	1 8 15 22 29
Tue.	6 13 20 27	3 10 17 24	2 9 16 23 30
Wed.	7 14 21 28	4 11 18 25	3 10 17 24 31
Thur.	1 8 15 22 29	5 12 19 26	4 11 18 25
Fri.	2 9 16 23 30	6 13 20 27	5 12 19 26
Sat.	3 10 17 24 31	7 14 21 28	6 13 20 27

	April	May	June
Sun.	4 11 18 25	2 9 16 23 30	6 13 20 27
Mon.	5 12 19 26	3 10 17 24 31	7 14 21 28
Tue.	6 13 20 27	4 11 18 25	1 8 15 22 29
Wed.	7 14 21 28	5 12 19 26	2 9 16 23 30
Thur.	1 8 15 22 29	6 13 20 27	3 10 17 24
Fri.	2 9 16 23 30	7 14 21 28	4 11 18 25
Sat.	3 10 17 24	1 8 15 22 29	5 12 19 26

	July	August	September
Sun.	4 11 18 25	1 8 15 22 29	5 12 19 26
Mon.	5 12 19 26	2 9 16 23 30	6 13 20 27
Tue.	6 13 20 27	3 10 17 24 31	7 14 21 28
Wed.	7 14 21 28	4 11 18 25	1 8 15 22 29
Thur.	1 8 15 22 29	5 12 19 26	2 9 16 23 30
Fri.	2 9 16 23 30	6 13 20 27	3 10 17 24 31
Sat.	3 10 17 24 31	7 14 21 28	4 11 18 25

	October	November	December
Sun.	3 10 17 24 31	7 14 21 28	5 12 19 26
Mon.	4 11 18 25	1 8 15 22 29	6 13 20 27
Tue.	5 12 19 26	2 9 16 23 30	7 14 21 28
Wed.	6 13 20 27	3 10 17 24	1 8 15 22 29
Thur.	7 14 21 28	4 11 18 25	2 9 16 23 30
Fri.	1 8 15 22 29	5 12 19 26	3 10 17 24 31
Sat.	2 9 16 23 30	6 13 20 27	4 11 18 25

EASTER DAYS

March 28	1880, 1948, 2032
April 4	1920
April 11	1784, 1852, 2004
April 18	1824, 1976

K

	January	February	March
Sun.	3 10 17 24 31	7 14 21 28	7 14 21 28
Mon.	4 11 18 25	1 8 15 22	1 8 15 22 29
Tue.	5 12 19 26	2 9 16 23	2 9 16 23 30
Wed.	6 13 20 27	3 10 17 24	3 10 17 24 31
Thur.	7 14 21 28	4 11 18 25	4 11 18 25
Fri.	1 8 15 22 29	5 12 19 26	5 12 19 26
Sat.	2 9 16 23 30	6 13 20 27	6 13 20 27
	April	**May**	**June**
Sun.	4 11 18 25	2 9 16 23 30	6 13 20 27
Mon.	5 12 19 26	3 10 17 24 31	7 14 21 28
Tue.	6 13 20 27	4 11 18 25	1 8 15 22 29
Wed.	7 14 21 28	5 12 19 26	2 9 16 23 30
Thur.	1 8 15 22 29	6 13 20 27	3 10 17 24
Fri.	2 9 16 23 30	7 14 21 28	4 11 18 25
Sat.	3 10 17 24	1 8 15 22 29	5 12 19 26
	July	**August**	**September**
Sun.	4 11 18 25	1 8 15 22 29	5 12 19 26
Mon.	5 12 19 26	2 9 16 23 30	6 13 20 27
Tue.	6 13 20 27	3 10 17 24 31	7 14 21 28
Wed.	7 14 21 28	4 11 18 25	1 8 15 22 29
Thur.	1 8 15 22 29	5 12 19 26	2 9 16 23 30
Fri.	2 9 16 23 30	6 13 20 27	3 10 17 24
Sat.	3 10 17 24 31	7 14 21 28	4 11 18 25
	October	**November**	**December**
Sun.	3 10 17 24 31	7 14 21 28	5 12 19 26
Mon.	4 11 18 25	1 8 15 22 29	6 13 20 27
Tue.	5 12 19 26	2 9 16 23 30	7 14 21 28
Wed.	6 13 20 27	3 10 17 24	1 8 15 22 29
Thur.	7 14 21 28	4 11 18 25	2 9 16 23 30
Fri.	1 8 15 22 29	5 12 19 26	3 10 17 24 31
Sat.	2 9 16 23 30	6 13 20 27	4 11 18 25

EASTER DAYS

March 28	1869, 1875, 1937, 2027
April 4	1790, 1847, 1858, 1915, 1926, 1999, 2010, 2021
April 11	1819, 1830, 1841, 1909, 1971, 1982, 1993
April 18	1802, 1813, 1897, 1954, 1965
April 25	1886, 1943, 2038

M

	January	February	March
Sun.	2 9 16 23 30	6 13 20 27	6 13 20 27
Mon.	3 10 17 24 31	7 14 21 28	7 14 21 28
Tue.	4 11 18 25	1 8 15 22	1 8 15 22 29
Wed.	5 12 19 26	2 9 16 23	2 9 16 23 30
Thur.	6 13 20 27	3 10 17 24	3 10 17 24 31
Fri.	7 14 21 28	4 11 18 25	4 11 18 25
Sat.	1 8 15 22 29	5 12 19 26	5 12 19 26
	April	**May**	**June**
Sun.	3 10 17 24	1 8 15 22 29	5 12 19 26
Mon.	4 11 18 25	2 9 16 23 30	6 13 20 27
Tue.	5 12 19 26	3 10 17 24 31	7 14 21 28
Wed.	6 13 20 27	4 11 18 25	1 8 15 22 29
Thur.	7 14 21 28	5 12 19 26	2 9 16 23 30
Fri.	1 8 15 22 29	6 13 20 27	3 10 17 24
Sat.	2 9 16 23 30	7 14 21 28	4 11 18 25
	July	**August**	**September**
Sun.	3 10 17 24 31	7 14 21 28	4 11 18 25
Mon.	4 11 18 25	1 8 15 22 29	5 12 19 26
Tue.	5 12 19 26	2 9 16 23 30	6 13 20 27
Wed.	6 13 20 27	3 10 17 24 31	7 14 21 28
Thur.	7 14 21 28	4 11 18 25	1 8 15 22 29
Fri.	1 8 15 22 29	5 12 19 26	2 9 16 23 30
Sat.	2 9 16 23 30	6 13 20 27	3 10 17 24
	October	**November**	**December**
Sun.	2 9 16 23 30	6 13 20 27	4 11 18 25
Mon.	3 10 17 24 31	7 14 21 28	5 12 19 26
Tue.	4 11 18 25	1 8 15 22 29	6 13 20 27
Wed.	5 12 19 26	2 9 16 23 30	7 14 21 28
Thur.	6 13 20 27	3 10 17 24	1 8 15 22 29
Fri.	7 14 21 28	4 11 18 25	2 9 16 23 30
Sat.	1 8 15 22 29	5 12 19 26	3 10 17 24 31

EASTER DAYS

March 27	1785, 1842, 1853, 1910, 1921, 2005
April 3	1825, 1831, 1983, 1994
April 10	1803, 1814, 1887, 1898, 1955, 1966, 1977, 2039
April 17	1870, 1881, 1927, 1938, 1949, 2022, 2033
April 24	1791, 1859, 2011

L (LEAP YEAR)

	January	February	March
Sun.	3 10 17 24 31	7 14 21 28	6 13 20 27
Mon.	4 11 18 25	1 8 15 22 29	7 14 21 28
Tue.	5 12 19 26	2 9 16 23	1 8 15 22 29
Wed.	6 13 20 27	3 10 17 24	2 9 16 23 30
Thur.	7 14 21 28	4 11 18 25	3 10 17 24 31
Fri.	1 8 15 22 29	5 12 19 26	4 11 18 25
Sat.	2 9 16 23 30	6 13 20 27	5 12 19 26
	April	**May**	**June**
Sun.	3 10 17 24	1 8 15 22 29	5 12 19 26
Mon.	4 11 18 25	2 9 16 23 30	6 13 20 27
Tue.	5 12 19 26	3 10 17 24 31	7 14 21 28
Wed.	6 13 20 27	4 11 18 25	1 8 15 22 29
Thur.	7 14 21 28	5 12 19 26	2 9 16 23 30
Fri.	1 8 15 22 29	6 13 20 27	3 10 17 24
Sat.	2 9 16 23 30	7 14 21 28	4 11 18 25
	July	**August**	**September**
Sun.	3 10 17 24 31	7 14 21 28	4 11 18 25
Mon.	4 11 18 25	1 8 15 22 29	5 12 19 26
Tue.	5 12 19 26	2 9 16 23 30	6 13 20 27
Wed.	6 13 20 27	3 10 17 24 31	7 14 21 28
Thur.	7 14 21 28	4 11 18 25	1 8 15 22 29
Fri.	1 8 15 22 29	5 12 19 26	2 9 16 23 30
Sat.	2 9 16 23 30	6 13 20 27	3 10 17 24
	October	**November**	**December**
Sun.	2 9 16 23 30	6 13 20 27	4 11 18 25
Mon.	3 10 17 24 31	7 14 21 28	5 12 19 26
Tue.	4 11 18 25	1 8 15 22 29	6 13 20 27
Wed.	5 12 19 26	2 9 16 23 30	7 14 21 28
Thur.	6 13 20 27	3 10 17 24	1 8 15 22 29
Fri.	7 14 21 28	4 11 18 25	2 9 16 23 30
Sat.	1 8 15 22 29	5 12 19 26	3 10 17 24 31

EASTER DAYS

March 27	1796, 1864, 1932, 2016
April 3	1836, 1904, 1988
April 17	1808, 1892, 1960

N (LEAP YEAR)

	January	February	March
Sun.	2 9 16 23 30	6 13 20 27	5 12 19 26
Mon.	3 10 17 24 31	7 14 21 28	6 13 20 27
Tue.	4 11 18 25	1 8 15 22 29	7 14 21 28
Wed.	5 12 19 26	2 9 16 23	1 8 15 22 29
Thur.	6 13 20 27	3 10 17 24	2 9 16 23 30
Fri.	7 14 21 28	4 11 18 25	3 10 17 24 31
Sat.	1 8 15 22 29	5 12 19 26	4 11 18 25
	April	**May**	**June**
Sun.	2 9 16 23 30	7 14 21 28	4 11 18 25
Mon.	3 10 17 24	1 8 15 22 29	5 12 19 26
Tue.	4 11 18 25	2 9 16 23 30	6 13 20 27
Wed.	5 12 19 26	3 10 17 24 31	7 14 21 28
Thur.	6 13 20 27	4 11 18 25	1 8 15 22 29
Fri.	7 14 21 28	5 12 19 26	2 9 16 23 30
Sat.	1 8 15 22 29	6 13 20 27	3 10 17 24
	July	**August**	**September**
Sun.	2 9 16 23 30	6 13 20 27	3 10 17 24
Mon.	3 10 17 24 31	7 14 21 28	4 11 18 25
Tue.	4 11 18 25	1 8 15 22 29	5 12 19 26
Wed.	5 12 19 26	2 9 16 23 30	6 13 20 27
Thur.	6 13 20 27	3 10 17 24 31	7 14 21 28
Fri.	7 14 21 28	4 11 18 25	1 8 15 22 29
Sat.	1 8 15 22 29	5 12 19 26	2 9 16 23 30
	October	**November**	**December**
Sun.	1 8 15 22 29	5 12 19 26	3 10 17 24 31
Mon.	2 9 16 23 30	6 13 20 27	4 11 18 25
Tue.	3 10 17 24 31	7 14 21 28	5 12 19 26
Wed.	4 11 18 25	1 8 15 22 29	6 13 20 27
Thur.	5 12 19 26	2 9 16 23 30	7 14 21 28
Fri.	6 13 20 27	3 10 17 24	1 8 15 22 29
Sat.	7 14 21 28	4 11 18 25	2 9 16 23 30

EASTER DAYS

March 26	1780
April 2	1820, 1972
April 9	1944
April 16	2028
April 23	1848, 1916, 2000

GEOLOGICAL TIME

The earth is thought to have come into existence approximately 4,600 million years ago, but for nearly half this time, the Archean era, it was uninhabited. Life is generally believed to have emerged in the succeeding Proterozoic era. The Archean and the Proterozoic eras are often together referred to as the Precambrian.

Although primitive forms of life, e.g. algae and bacteria, existed during the Proterozoic era, it is not until the strata of Palaeozoic rocks is reached that abundant fossilized remains appear.

Since the Precambrian, there have been three great geological eras:

PALAEOZOIC ('ancient life')
c.570–c.245 million years ago

Cambrian – Mainly sandstones, slate and shales; limestones in Scotland. Shelled fossils and invertebrates, e.g. trilobites and brachiopods appear

Ordovician – Mainly shales and mudstones, e.g. in north Wales; limestones in Scotland. First fishes

Silurian – Shales, mudstones and some limestones, found mostly in Wales and southern Scotland

Devonian – Old red sandstone, shale, limestone and slate, e.g. in south Wales and the West Country

Carboniferous – Coal-bearing rocks, millstone grit, limestone and shale. First traces of land-living life

Permian – Marls, sandstones and clays. First reptile fossils

There were two great phases of mountain building in the Palaeozoic era: the Caledonian, characterized in Britain by NE–SW lines of hills and valleys; and the later Hercyian, widespread in west Germany and adjacent areas, and in Britain exemplified in E.–W. lines of hills and valleys.

The end of the Palaeozoic era was marked by the extensive glaciations of the Permian period in the southern continents and the decline of amphibians. It was succeeded by an era of warm conditions.

MESOZOIC ('middle forms of life')
c.245–c.65 million years ago

Triassic – Mostly sandstone, e.g. in the West Midlands

Jurassic – Mainly limestones and clays, typically displayed in the Jura mountains, and in England in a NE–SW belt from Lincolnshire and the Wash to the Severn and the Dorset coast

Cretaceous – Mainly chalk, clay and sands, e.g. in Kent and Sussex

Giant reptiles were dominant during the Mesozoic era, but it was at this time that marsupial mammals first appeared, as well as *Archaeopteryx lithographica*, the earliest known species of bird. Coniferous trees and flowering plants also developed during the era and, with the birds and the mammals, were the main species to survive into the Cenozoic era. The giant reptiles became extinct.

CENOZOIC ('recent life')
from c.65 million years ago

Palaeocene ⎫ The emergence of new forms of life, includ-
Eocene   ⎬ ing existing species
Oligocene – Fossils of a few still existing species
Miocene – Fossil remains show a balance of existing and extinct species
Pliocene – Fossil remains show a majority of still existing species
Pleistocene – The majority of remains are those of still existing species

Holocene – The present, post-glacial period. Existing species only, except for a few exterminated by man

In the last 25 million years, from the Miocene through the Pliocene periods, the Alpine-Himalayan and the circum-Pacific phases of mountain building reached their climax. During the Pleistocene period ice-sheets repeatedly locked up masses of water as land ice; its weight depressed the land, but the locking-up of the water lowered the sea-level by 100–200 metres. The glaciations and interglacials of the Ice Age are difficult to date and classify, but recent scientific opinion considers the Pleistocene period to have begun approximately 1.64 million years ago. The last glacial retreat, merging into the Holocene period, was 10,000 years ago.

HUMAN DEVELOPMENT

Any consideration of the history of mankind must start with the fact that all members of the human race belong to one species of animal, i.e. *Homo sapiens*, the definition of a species being in biological terms that all its members can interbreed. As a species of mammal it is possible to group man with other similar types, known as the primates. Amongst these is found a sub-group, the apes, which includes, in addition to man, the chimpanzees, gorillas, orang-utans and gibbons. All lack a tail, have shoulder blades at the back, and a Y-shaped chewing pattern on the surface of their molars, as well as showing the more general primate characteristics of four incisors, a thumb which is able to touch the fingers of the same hand, and finger and toe nails instead of claws. The factors available to scientific study suggest that human beings have chimpanzees and gorillas as their nearest relatives in the animal world. However, there remains the possibility that there once lived creatures, now extinct, which were closer to modern man than the chimpanzees and gorillas, and which shared with modern man the characteristics of having flat faces (i.e. the absence of a pronounced muzzle), being bipedal, and possessing large brains.

There are two broad groups of extinct apes recognized by specialists. The ramapithecines, the remains of which, mainly jaw fragments, have been found in east Africa, Asia, and Turkey. They lived about 14 to 8 million years ago, and from the evidence of their teeth it seems they chewed more in the manner of modern man than the other presently living apes. The second group, the australopithecines, have left more numerous remains amongst which sub-groups may be detected, although the geographic spread is limited to south and east Africa. Living between 5 and 1.5 million years ago, they were closer relatives of modern man to the extent that they walked upright, did not have an extensive muzzle and had similar types of pre-molars. The first australopithecine remains were recognized at Taung in South Africa in 1924 and subsequent discoveries include those at the Olduvai Gorge in Tanzania. The most impressive discovery was made at Hadar, Ethiopia, in 1974 when about half a skeleton, known as 'Lucy', was found.

Also in east Africa, between 2 million and 1.5 million years ago, lived a hominid group which not only walked upright, had a flat face, and a large brain case, but also made simple pebble and flake stone tools. On present evidence these habilines seem to have been the first people to make tools, however crude. This facility is related to the larger brain size and human beings are the only animals to make implements to be used in other processes. These early pebble tool users, because of their distinctive

GEOLOGICAL TIME

Era	Period	Epoch	Date began*	Evolutionary stages
Cenozoic	Quaternary	Holocene	0.01	Man
Cenozoic	Quaternary	Pleistocene	1.64	Man
Cenozoic	Tertiary	Pliocene	5.2	Man
Cenozoic	Tertiary	Miocene	23.3	Man
Cenozoic	Tertiary	Oligocene	35.4	Man
Cenozoic	Tertiary	Eocene	56.5	Man
Cenozoic	Tertiary	Palaeocene	65.0	Man
Mesozoic	Cretaceous		145.6	
Mesozoic	Jurassic		208.0	First birds
Mesozoic	Triassic		245.0	First mammals
Palaeozoic	Permian		290.0	First reptiles
Palaeozoic	Carboniferous		362.5	First amphibians and insects
Palaeozoic	Devonian		408.5	
Palaeozoic	Silurian		439.0	
Palaeozoic	Ordovician		510.0	First fishes
Palaeozoic	Cambrian		570.0	First invertebrates
Precambrian			4,600.0	First primitive life forms, e.g. algae and bacteria

*millions of years ago

characteristics, have been grouped as a separate sub-species, now extinct, of the genus *Homo* and are known as *Homo habilis*.

The use of fire, again a human characteristic, is associated with another group of extinct hominids whose remains, about a million years old, are found in south and east Africa, China, Indonesia, north Africa and Europe. Mastery of the techniques of making fire probably helped the colonization of the colder northern areas and in this respect the site of Vertesszollos in Hungary is of particular importance. *Homo erectus* is the name given to this group of fossils and it includes a number of famous individual discoveries, e.g. Solo Man, Heidelberg Man, and especially Peking Man who lived at the cave site at Choukoutien which has yielded evidence of fire and burnt bone.

The well-known group Neanderthal Man, or *Homo sapiens neandertalensis*, is an extinct form of modern man who lived between about 100,000 and 40,000 years ago, thus spanning the last Ice Age. Indeed, its ability to adapt to the cold climate on the edge of the ice-sheets is one of its characteristic features, the remains being found only in Europe, Asia and the Middle East. Complete neanderthal skeletons were found during excavations at Tabun in Israel, together with evidence of tool-making and the use of fire. Distinguished by very large brains, it seems that neanderthal man was the first to develop recognizable social customs, especially deliberate burial rites. Why the neanderthalers became extinct is not clear but it may be connected with the climatic changes at the end of the Ice Ages, which would have seriously affected their food supplies; possibly they became too specialized for their own good.

The Swanscombe skull is the only known human fossil remains found in England. Some specialists see Swan-scombe Man (or, more probably, woman) as a neander-thaler. Others group these remains together with the Steinheim skull from Germany, seeing both as a separate sub-species. There is too little evidence as yet on which to form a final judgement.

Modern Man, *Homo sapiens sapiens*, the surviving sub-species of *Homo sapiens*, had evolved to our present physical condition and had colonized much of the world by about 30,000 years ago. There are many previously distin-guished individual specimens, e.g. Cromagnon Man, which may now be grouped together as *Homo sapiens sapiens*. It was modern man who spread to the American continent by crossing the landbridge between Siberia and Alaska and thence moved south through North America and into South America. Equally it is modern man who over the last 30,000 years has been responsible for the major develop-ments in technology, art and civilization generally.

One of the problems for those studying fossil man is the lack in many cases of sufficient quantities of fossil bone for analysis. It is important that theories should be tested against evidence, rather than the evidence being made to fit the theory. The Piltdown hoax is a well-known example of 'fossils' being forged to fit what was seen in some quarters as the correct theory of man's evolution.

CULTURAL DEVELOPMENT

The Eurocentric bias of early archaeologists meant that the search for a starting point for the development and transmission of cultural ideas, especially by migration, trade and warfare, concentrated unduly on Europe and the Near East. The Three Age system, whereby pre-history was divided into a Stone Age, a Bronze Age and an Iron Age, was devised by Christian Thomsen, curator of the National Museum of Denmark in the early 19th century, to facilitate the classification of the museum's collections.

The descriptive adjectives referred to the materials from which the implements and weapons were made and came to be regarded as the dominant features of the societies to which they related. The refinement of the Three Age system once dominated archaeological thought and remains a generally accepted concept in the popular mind. However, it is now seen by archaeologists as an inadequate model for human development.

Common sense suggests that there were no complete breaks between one so-called Age and another, any more than contemporaries would have regarded 1485 as a complete break between medieval and modern English history. Nor can the Three Age system be applied universally. In some areas it is necessary to insert a Copper Age, while in Africa south of the Sahara there would seem to be no Bronze Age at all; in Australia, Old Stone Age societies survived, while in South America, New Stone Age communities existed into modern times. The civiliza-tions in other parts of the world clearly invalidate a Eurocentric theory of human development.

The concept of the 'Neolithic revolution', associated with the domestication of plants and animals, was a development of particular importance in the human cultural pattern. It reflected change from the primitive hunter/gatherer economies to a more settled agricultural way of life and therefore, so the argument goes, made possible the development of urban civilization. However, it can no longer be argued that this 'revolution' took place only in one area from which all development stemmed. Though it appears that the cultivation of wheat and barley was first undertaken, together with the domestication of cattle and goats/sheep in the Fertile Crescent (the area bounded by the rivers Tigris and Euphrates), there is evidence that rice was first deliberately planted and pigs domesticated in south-east Asia, maize first cultivated in Central America and llamas first domesticated in South America. It has been recognized in recent years that cultural changes can take place independently of each other in different parts of the world at different rates and different times. There is no need for a general diffusionist theory.

Although scholars will continue to study the particular societies which interest them, it may be possible to obtain a reliable chronological framework, in absolute terms of years, against which the cultural development of any particular area may be set. The development and refine-ment of radio-carbon dating and other scientific methods of producing absolute chronologies is enabling the cross-referencing of societies to be undertaken. As the techniques of dating become more rigorous in application and the number of scientifically obtained dates increases, the attainment of an absolute chronology for prehistoric societies throughout the world comes closer to being achieved.

Tidal Tables

CONSTANTS

The constant tidal difference may be used in conjunction with the time of high water at a standard port shown in the predictions data (pages 98–103) to find the time of high water at any of the ports or places listed below.

These tidal differences are very approximate and should be used only as a guide to the time of high water at the places below. More precise local data should be obtained for navigational and other nautical purposes.

All data allow high water time to be found in Greenwich Mean Time; this applies also to data for the months when British Summer Time is in operation and the hour's time difference should also be allowed for. Ports marked * are in a different time zone and the standard time zone difference also needs to be added/subtracted to give local time.

EXAMPLE

Required time of high water at Stranraer at 2 January 1997
Appropriate time of high water at Greenock

Morning tide 2 January	0556 hrs
Tidal difference	−0020 hrs
High water at Stranraer	0536 hrs

The columns headed 'Springs' and 'Neaps' show the height, in metres, of the tide above datum for mean high water springs and mean high water neaps respectively.

Port	Diff.		Springs	Neaps
		h m	m	m
Aberdeen	Leith	−1 19	4.3	3.4
*Antwerp (Prosperpolder)	London	+0 50	5.8	4.8
Ardrossan	Greenock	−0 15	3.2	2.6
Avonmouth	London	−6 45	13.2	9.8
Ayr	Greenock	−0 25	3.0	2.5
Barrow (Docks)	Liverpool	0 00	9.3	7.1
Belfast	London	−2 47	3.5	3.0
Blackpool	Liverpool	−0 10	8.9	7.0
*Boulogne	London	−2 44	8.9	7.2
*Calais	London	−2 04	7.2	5.9
*Cherbourg	London	−6 00	6.4	5.0
Cobh	Liverpool	−5 55	4.2	3.2
Cowes	London	−2 38	4.2	3.5
Dartmouth	London	+4 25	4.9	3.8
*Dieppe	London	−3 03	9.3	7.3
Douglas, IOM	Liverpool	−0 04	6.9	5.4
Dover	London	−2 52	6.7	5.3
Dublin	London	−2 05	4.1	3.4
Dun Laoghaire	London	−2 10	4.1	3.4
*Dunkirk	London	−1 54	6.0	4.9
Fishguard	Liverpool	−4 01	4.8	3.4
Fleetwood	Liverpool	0 00	9.2	7.3
*Flushing	London	−0 15	4.7	3.9
Folkestone	London	−3 04	7.1	5.7
Galway	Liverpool	−6 08	5.1	3.9
Glasgow	Greenock	+0 26	4.7	4.0
Harwich	London	−2 06	4.0	3.4
*Havre, Le	London	−3 55	7.9	6.6
Heysham	Liverpool	+0 05	9.4	7.4
Holyhead	Liverpool	−0 50	5.6	4.4
*Hook of Holland	London	−0 01	2.1	1.7
Hull (Albert Dock)	London	−7 40	7.5	5.8
Immingham	London	−8 00	7.3	5.8
Larne	London	−2 40	2.8	2.5

Lerwick	Leith	−3 48	2.2	1.6
Londonderry	London	−5 37	2.7	2.1
Lowestoft	London	−4 25	2.4	2.1
Margate	London	−1 53	4.8	3.9
Milford Haven	Liverpool	−5 08	7.0	5.2
Morecambe	Liverpool	+0 07	9.5	7.4
Newhaven	London	−2 46	6.7	5.1
Oban	Greenock	+5 43	4.0	2.9
*Ostend	London	−1 32	5.1	4.2
Plymouth (Devonport)	London	+4 05	5.5	4.4
Portland	London	+5 09	2.1	1.4
Portsmouth	London	−2 38	4.7	3.8
Ramsgate	London	−2 32	5.2	4.1
Richmond Lock	London	+1 00	4.9	3.7
Rosslare Harbour	Liverpool	−5 24	1.9	1.4
Rosyth	Leith	+0 09	5.8	4.7
*Rotterdam	London	+1 45	2.0	1.7
St Helier	London	+4 48	11.0	8.1
St Malo	London	+4 27	12.2	9.2
St Peter Port	London	+4 54	9.3	7.0
Scrabster	Leith	−6 06	5.0	4.0
Sheerness	London	−1 19	5.8	4.7
Shoreham	London	−2 44	6.3	4.9
Southampton (1st high water)	London	−2 54	4.5	3.7
Spurn Head	London	−8 25	6.9	5.5
Stornoway	Liverpool	−4 16	4.8	3.7
Stranraer	Greenock	−0 20	3.0	2.4
Stromness	Leith	−5 26	3.6	2.7
Swansea	London	−7 35	9.5	7.2
Tees, River Entrance	Leith	+1 09	5.5	4.3
Tilbury	London	−0 49	6.4	5.4
Tobermory	Liverpool	−5 11	4.4	3.3
Tyne River (North Shields)	London	−1030	5.0	3.9
Ullapool	Leith	−7 40	5.2	3.9
Walton-on-the-Naze	London	−2 10	4.2	3.4
Wick	Leith	−3 26	3.5	2.8
*Zeebrugge	London	−0 55	4.8	3.9

PREDICTIONS

The tidal predictions for London Bridge, Liverpool, Greenock and Leith on pages 98–103 are reproduced with the permission of the UK Hydrographic Office and the Controller of HMSO. Crown copyright reserved.
*Datum of predictions for each port shows the difference of height, in metres, from Ordnance data (Newlyn).

JANUARY 1997   High water   GMT

		LONDON BRIDGE				LIVERPOOL				GREENOCK				LEITH			
		*Datum of predictions 3.20 m below				*Datum of predictions 4.93 m below				*Datum of predictions 1.62 m below				*Datum of predictions 2.90 m below			
		hr	ht m	hr	ht m	hr	ht m	hr	ht m	hr	ht m	hr	ht m	hr	ht m	hr	ht m
1	Wednesday	05 50	6.3	18 31	6.4	03 27	8.0	15 47	8.1	05 08	3.1	17 04	3.3	07 15	4.7	19 29	4.7
2	Thursday	06 37	6.2	19 20	6.2	04 17	7.7	16 41	7.8	05 56	3.0	17 53	3.2	08 05	4.6	20 23	4.6
3	Friday	07 32	6.0	20 17	6.1	05 18	7.5	17 43	7.7	06 50	2.9	18 49	3.1	09 01	4.5	21 24	4.5
4	Saturday	08 36	5.9	21 21	6.1	06 28	7.5	18 50	7.7	07 52	2.9	19 53	3.0	10 03	4.6	22 31	4.6
5	Sunday	09 47	6.0	22 29	6.2	07 36	7.8	19 56	8.1	09 06	2.9	21 07	3.0	11 07	4.7	23 38	4.8
6	Monday	10 57	6.2	23 34	6.5	08 36	8.4	20 56	8.5	10 14	3.1	22 14	3.2	12 09	5.0	—	—
7	Tuesday	12 01	6.5	—	—	09 28	8.9	21 50	9.0	11 05	3.3	23 10	3.3	00 38	5.1	13 04	5.2
8	Wednesday	00 32	6.8	12 59	6.9	10 17	9.4	22 40	9.4	11 50	3.5	—	—	01 31	5.3	13 51	5.5
9	Thursday	01 24	7.0	13 51	7.2	11 04	9.8	23 29	9.7	00 02	3.4	12 35	3.6	02 18	5.6	14 35	5.7
10	Friday	02 13	7.2	14 40	7.4	11 52	10.0	—	—	00 52	3.4	13 18	3.7	03 03	5.8	15 18	5.9
11	Saturday	02 59	7.3	15 28	7.5	00 17	9.8	12 40	10.2	01 42	3.5	14 02	3.8	03 49	5.9	16 03	5.9
12	Sunday	03 43	7.3	16 14	7.5	01 06	9.8	13 29	10.1	02 29	3.5	14 45	3.9	04 36	5.9	16 50	5.9
13	Monday	04 27	7.3	17 00	7.4	01 54	9.7	14 17	9.9	03 15	3.5	15 29	3.9	05 25	5.7	17 40	5.7
14	Tuesday	05 10	7.1	17 47	7.1	02 42	9.3	15 06	9.6	04 00	3.5	16 14	3.8	06 17	5.5	18 34	5.5
15	Wednesday	05 56	6.9	18 38	6.8	03 32	8.9	15 57	9.0	04 46	3.4	17 02	3.6	07 12	5.2	19 33	5.3
16	Thursday	06 47	6.6	19 35	6.5	04 26	8.4	16 55	8.5	05 35	3.3	17 55	3.4	08 12	5.0	20 38	5.0
17	Friday	07 51	6.3	20 40	6.2	05 31	7.9	18 03	8.0	06 28	3.1	18 59	3.2	09 16	4.8	21 47	4.9
18	Saturday	09 06	6.1	21 47	6.2	06 47	7.7	19 18	7.9	07 33	3.0	20 37	3.0	10 24	4.8	22 57	4.8
19	Sunday	10 16	6.2	22 50	6.3	07 59	7.9	20 27	8.0	09 09	3.0	21 59	3.1	11 33	4.8	—	—
20	Monday	11 19	6.4	23 47	6.5	08 59	8.2	21 23	8.4	10 17	3.2	22 58	3.1	00 05	4.8	12 37	5.0
21	Tuesday	12 16	6.6	—	—	09 48	8.6	22 11	8.7	11 07	3.3	23 47	3.2	01 04	5.0	13 28	5.1
22	Wednesday	00 40	6.7	13 08	6.8	10 31	9.0	22 52	8.9	11 51	3.4	—	—	01 52	5.1	14 12	5.3
23	Thursday	01 28	6.8	13 54	6.9	11 09	9.1	23 29	9.0	00 31	3.2	12 31	3.5	02 32	5.2	14 49	5.3
24	Friday	02 10	6.8	14 35	6.9	11 44	9.2	—	—	01 11	3.2	13 07	3.5	03 07	5.3	15 23	5.4
25	Saturday	02 46	6.7	15 10	6.7	00 03	9.0	12 18	9.2	01 46	3.2	13 40	3.6	03 39	5.3	15 54	5.4
26	Sunday	03 15	6.6	15 40	6.6	00 36	9.0	12 51	9.2	02 18	3.1	14 11	3.6	04 11	5.3	16 26	5.3
27	Monday	03 42	6.5	16 09	6.6	01 09	8.9	13 24	9.1	02 48	3.2	14 43	3.6	04 44	5.2	16 58	5.3
28	Tuesday	04 12	6.5	16 42	6.7	01 42	8.8	13 58	9.0	03 19	3.2	15 17	3.5	05 20	5.1	17 32	5.2
29	Wednesday	04 46	6.6	17 19	6.7	02 17	8.6	14 34	8.8	03 53	3.1	15 53	3.5	05 57	5.0	18 07	5.0
30	Thursday	05 24	6.5	18 00	6.6	02 53	8.4	15 13	8.5	04 29	3.1	16 32	3.4	06 37	4.8	18 47	4.8
31	Friday	06 07	6.4	18 46	6.5	03 36	8.1	15 59	8.1	05 10	3.0	17 15	3.2	07 22	4.7	19 34	4.7

FEBRUARY 1997   High water   GMT

		LONDON BRIDGE				LIVERPOOL				GREENOCK				LEITH			
1	Saturday	06 57	6.2	19 39	6.3	04 29	7.7	16 58	7.8	05 57	2.9	18 05	3.0	08 14	4.6	20 33	4.5
2	Sunday	07 56	6.0	20 39	6.1	05 37	7.5	18 07	7.6	06 55	2.8	19 05	2.9	09 15	4.5	21 44	4.5
3	Monday	09 04	5.9	21 48	6.1	06 51	7.6	19 20	7.8	08 12	2.8	20 25	2.9	10 25	4.6	23 02	4.6
4	Tuesday	10 19	6.0	23 01	6.2	08 04	8.1	20 31	8.3	09 37	2.9	21 48	3.0	11 37	4.8	—	—
5	Wednesday	11 35	6.3	—	—	09 06	8.8	21 33	8.9	10 41	3.1	22 54	3.1	00 13	4.9	12 39	5.1
6	Thursday	00 07	6.6	12 40	6.7	10 00	9.4	22 26	9.4	11 31	3.4	23 49	3.3	01 12	5.3	13 31	5.4
7	Friday	01 04	6.9	13 35	7.1	10 49	9.9	23 15	9.8	12 18	3.6	—	—	02 01	5.6	14 16	5.7
8	Saturday	01 55	7.2	14 25	7.4	11 37	10.3	—	—	00 40	3.4	13 04	3.7	02 47	5.9	15 00	6.0
9	Sunday	02 42	7.4	15 12	7.6	00 03	10.0	12 25	10.4	01 29	3.4	13 49	3.8	03 32	6.0	15 45	6.1
10	Monday	03 27	7.5	15 57	7.7	00 50	10.1	13 11	10.4	02 15	3.5	14 32	3.9	04 18	5.9	16 32	6.1
11	Tuesday	04 09	7.5	16 41	7.6	01 35	9.9	13 57	10.2	02 57	3.5	15 14	3.9	05 05	5.8	17 21	5.9
12	Wednesday	04 51	7.4	17 24	7.3	02 20	9.6	14 42	9.7	03 37	3.5	15 55	3.8	05 54	5.5	18 13	5.6
13	Thursday	05 32	7.2	18 08	6.9	03 04	9.1	15 28	9.1	04 18	3.4	16 38	3.6	06 45	5.2	19 07	5.3
14	Friday	06 17	6.8	18 55	6.5	03 51	8.5	16 20	8.6	05 00	3.3	17 24	3.4	07 40	4.9	20 08	4.9
15	Saturday	07 10	6.3	19 55	6.0	04 49	7.8	17 25	7.7	05 47	3.2	18 17	3.1	08 40	4.7	21 15	4.7
16	Sunday	08 27	5.9	21 12	5.8	06 06	7.4	18 49	7.4	06 41	3.0	19 31	2.8	09 48	4.5	22 28	4.5
17	Monday	09 50	5.8	22 22	5.8	07 31	7.5	20 05	7.6	07 58	2.9	21 44	2.8	11 03	4.6	23 45	4.6
18	Tuesday	10 58	6.0	23 23	6.1	08 37	7.9	21 04	8.0	09 51	3.0	22 45	2.9	12 15	4.7	—	—
19	Wednesday	11 56	6.3	—	—	09 29	8.4	21 52	8.4	10 47	3.2	23 32	3.0	00 49	4.8	13 12	4.9
20	Thursday	00 17	6.4	12 48	6.7	10 12	8.8	22 34	8.7	11 32	3.3	—	—	01 37	5.0	13 55	5.1
21	Friday	01 06	6.7	13 33	6.8	10 51	9.1	23 10	8.9	00 14	3.1	12 13	3.4	02 15	5.1	14 31	5.3
22	Saturday	01 49	6.8	14 13	6.8	11 25	9.2	23 43	9.0	00 53	3.1	12 48	3.4	02 47	5.2	15 03	5.3
23	Sunday	02 26	6.7	14 48	6.8	11 58	9.2	—	—	01 27	3.1	13 19	3.4	03 16	5.3	15 33	5.4
24	Monday	02 56	6.6	15 17	6.7	00 15	9.0	12 29	9.2	01 56	3.1	13 48	3.4	03 47	5.3	16 03	5.4
25	Tuesday	03 24	6.6	15 46	6.7	00 46	9.0	13 01	9.1	02 22	3.1	14 18	3.4	04 19	5.3	16 34	5.3
26	Wednesday	03 52	6.6	16 17	6.8	01 17	9.0	13 33	9.1	02 49	3.1	14 52	3.4	04 53	5.2	17 06	5.2
27	Thursday	04 24	6.7	16 52	6.8	01 49	8.9	14 07	8.9	03 20	3.1	15 27	3.4	05 27	5.1	17 39	5.1
28	Friday	05 00	6.7	17 31	6.7	02 23	8.7	14 43	8.6	03 53	3.1	16 04	3.3	06 05	5.0	18 17	4.9

MARCH 1997   *High water*   GMT

		LONDON BRIDGE *Datum of predictions 3.20 m below				LIVERPOOL *Datum of predictions 4.93 m below				GREENOCK *Datum of predictions 1.62 m below				LEITH *Datum of predictions 2.90 m below			
		hr	ht m	hr	ht m	hr	ht m	hr	ht m	hr	ht m	hr	ht m	hr	ht m	hr	ht m
1	Saturday	05 42	6.6	18 16	6.5	03 02	8.4	15 27	8.3	04 30	3.0	16 44	3.2	06 46	4.8	19 03	4.8
2	Sunday	06 31	6.4	19 06	6.3	03 51	8.0	16 23	7.8	05 11	2.9	17 30	3.0	07 35	4.6	19 59	4.6
3	Monday	07 28	6.1	20 05	6.0	04 57	7.6	17 34	7.5	06 04	2.7	18 28	2.8	08 36	4.5	21 11	4.5
4	Tuesday	08 34	5.9	21 14	5.9	06 16	7.5	18 53	7.6	07 22	2.7	19 49	2.8	09 49	4.5	22 33	4.6
5	Wednesday	09 52	5.9	22 32	6.0	07 37	7.9	20 12	8.1	09 05	2.8	21 28	2.8	11 07	4.7	23 51	4.9
6	Thursday	11 15	6.2	23 44	6.4	08 45	8.6	21 17	8.8	10 18	3.0	22 40	3.0	12 15	5.0	—	—
7	Friday	12 22	6.7	—	—	09 42	9.3	22 10	9.4	11 11	3.3	23 36	3.2	00 52	5.3	13 10	5.4
8	Saturday	00 43	6.8	13 17	7.1	10 32	9.9	22 58	9.9	12 00	3.5	—	—	01 42	5.6	13 56	5.7
9	Sunday	01 35	7.2	14 07	7.5	11 19	10.3	23 44	10.1	00 25	3.3	12 47	3.7	02 27	5.8	14 41	6.0
10	Monday	02 22	7.5	14 53	7.7	12 05	10.5	—	—	01 12	3.4	13 32	3.8	03 12	6.0	15 26	6.1
11	Tuesday	03 06	7.6	15 36	7.7	00 28	10.1	12 50	10.4	01 54	3.5	14 15	3.8	03 56	5.9	16 13	6.1
12	Wednesday	03 48	7.7	16 18	7.6	01 12	10.0	13 34	10.1	02 33	3.5	14 56	3.8	04 42	5.8	17 01	5.9
13	Thursday	04 29	7.6	16 57	7.3	01 54	9.6	14 17	9.6	03 11	3.6	15 35	3.7	05 29	5.5	17 50	5.6
14	Friday	05 09	7.3	17 36	6.9	02 35	9.1	15 00	9.0	03 49	3.5	16 16	3.5	06 17	5.2	18 43	5.2
15	Saturday	05 50	6.9	18 16	6.5	03 18	8.5	15 47	8.2	04 29	3.4	16 59	3.3	07 08	4.9	19 39	4.8
16	Sunday	06 36	6.4	19 01	6.0	04 08	7.8	16 46	7.5	05 13	3.2	17 48	3.0	08 04	4.6	20 41	4.5
17	Monday	07 41	5.8	20 14	5.6	05 20	7.3	18 13	7.1	06 04	3.0	18 50	2.7	09 09	4.4	21 51	4.4
18	Tuesday	09 20	5.6	21 47	5.5	06 54	7.2	19 36	7.2	07 08	2.8	21 19	2.6	10 23	4.3	23 11	4.4
19	Wednesday	10 31	5.8	22 52	5.8	08 07	7.6	20 37	7.7	09 07	2.8	22 22	2.8	11 42	4.5	—	—
20	Thursday	11 29	6.1	23 48	6.2	09 01	8.1	21 26	8.2	10 19	3.0	23 08	2.9	00 22	4.6	12 44	4.7
21	Friday	12 20	6.5	—	—	09 46	8.5	22 07	8.6	11 06	3.2	23 49	3.0	01 11	4.8	13 28	4.9
22	Saturday	00 37	6.5	13 06	6.7	10 25	8.9	22 44	8.8	11 46	3.2	—	—	01 49	5.0	14 04	5.1
23	Sunday	01 21	6.7	13 46	6.8	11 00	9.0	23 17	9.0	00 26	3.1	12 22	3.2	02 20	5.1	14 36	5.3
24	Monday	01 59	6.7	14 20	6.8	11 33	9.1	23 49	9.0	01 00	3.1	12 52	3.2	02 49	5.2	15 07	5.4
25	Tuesday	02 32	6.7	14 51	6.8	12 04	9.1	—	—	01 28	3.1	13 20	3.3	03 20	5.3	15 39	5.4
26	Wednesday	03 03	6.7	15 22	6.8	00 19	9.1	12 35	9.1	01 52	3.1	13 52	3.3	03 53	5.3	16 10	5.4
27	Thursday	03 32	6.7	15 53	6.8	00 51	9.0	13 08	9.0	02 31	3.1	14 27	3.3	04 26	5.3	16 43	5.3
28	Friday	04 05	6.8	16 28	6.8	01 23	9.0	13 43	8.9	02 49	3.2	15 03	3.3	05 01	5.2	17 18	5.2
29	Saturday	04 41	6.8	17 07	6.7	01 58	8.8	14 21	8.7	03 23	3.2	15 41	3.3	05 37	5.1	17 57	5.0
30	Sunday	05 24	6.7	17 50	6.5	02 38	8.5	15 05	8.3	03 58	3.1	16 21	3.1	06 19	4.9	18 44	4.8
31	Monday	06 13	6.4	18 40	6.2	03 27	8.1	16 02	7.9	04 37	3.0	17 08	3.0	07 08	4.7	19 41	4.6

APRIL 1997   *High water*   GMT

		LONDON BRIDGE				LIVERPOOL				GREENOCK				LEITH			
1	Tuesday	07 09	6.1	19 38	6.0	04 32	7.8	17 13	7.5	05 29	2.8	18 08	2.8	08 08	4.5	20 52	4.5
2	Wednesday	08 16	5.9	20 49	5.8	05 52	7.6	18 35	7.6	06 47	2.7	19 31	2.7	09 22	4.5	22 13	4.6
3	Thursday	09 36	5.9	22 09	6.0	07 14	7.9	19 54	8.0	08 36	2.8	21 12	2.8	10 42	4.7	23 29	4.9
4	Friday	10 57	6.3	23 20	6.3	08 24	8.6	20 58	8.7	09 54	3.0	22 24	3.0	11 51	5.0	—	—
5	Saturday	12 01	6.8	—	—	09 22	9.2	21 51	9.3	10 50	3.3	23 18	3.2	00 31	5.2	12 47	5.4
6	Sunday	00 20	6.8	12 57	7.2	10 12	9.8	22 38	9.8	11 39	3.5	—	—	01 22	5.5	13 35	5.7
7	Monday	01 12	7.2	13 46	7.5	10 59	10.1	23 22	10.0	00 06	3.3	12 26	3.6	02 07	5.8	14 20	5.9
8	Tuesday	02 00	7.4	14 31	7.6	11 44	10.2	—	—	00 50	3.4	13 12	3.7	02 50	5.8	15 06	6.0
9	Wednesday	02 44	7.6	15 14	7.6	00 05	9.9	12 28	10.1	01 30	3.5	13 55	3.7	03 34	5.8	15 53	5.9
10	Thursday	03 27	7.6	15 54	7.5	00 47	9.8	13 10	9.8	02 08	3.6	14 36	3.7	04 19	5.7	16 41	5.7
11	Friday	04 08	7.5	16 32	7.2	01 28	9.4	13 52	9.3	02 45	3.6	15 16	3.6	05 04	5.4	17 29	5.4
12	Saturday	04 48	7.2	17 07	6.9	02 07	9.0	14 33	8.8	03 22	3.6	15 56	3.4	05 50	5.2	18 18	5.1
13	Sunday	05 28	6.8	17 43	6.5	02 48	8.5	15 17	8.1	04 02	3.4	16 39	3.2	06 38	4.9	19 10	4.8
14	Monday	06 12	6.4	18 23	6.1	03 34	7.9	16 09	7.5	04 45	3.3	17 27	2.9	07 30	4.6	20 06	4.5
15	Tuesday	07 06	5.9	19 15	5.7	04 33	7.4	17 23	7.0	05 34	3.1	18 26	2.7	08 30	4.4	21 09	4.3
16	Wednesday	08 32	5.6	20 49	5.4	06 02	7.1	18 52	7.0	06 33	2.9	19 51	2.6	09 38	4.3	22 20	4.3
17	Thursday	09 52	5.6	22 10	5.6	07 24	7.3	19 59	7.4	07 50	2.8	21 43	2.7	10 52	4.3	23 33	4.4
18	Friday	10 52	5.9	23 09	5.9	08 23	7.8	20 50	7.9	09 32	2.9	22 33	2.9	11 59	4.5	—	—
19	Saturday	11 44	6.3	—	—	09 11	8.2	21 33	8.3	10 28	3.0	23 15	3.0	00 29	4.6	12 49	4.8
20	Sunday	00 00	6.3	12 31	6.6	09 52	8.6	22 11	8.7	11 10	3.1	23 53	3.0	01 10	4.9	13 29	5.0
21	Monday	00 46	6.5	13 12	6.8	10 29	8.8	22 46	8.9	11 45	3.1	—	—	01 45	5.0	14 04	5.1
22	Tuesday	01 27	6.7	13 49	6.9	11 03	8.9	23 19	9.0	00 27	3.1	12 17	3.1	02 18	5.2	14 38	5.3
23	Wednesday	02 04	6.8	14 24	6.9	11 36	9.0	23 52	9.1	00 57	3.1	12 49	3.2	02 52	5.3	15 12	5.3
24	Thursday	02 39	6.8	14 58	6.9	12 09	9.0	—	—	01 23	3.1	13 25	3.2	03 27	5.3	15 47	5.3
25	Friday	03 13	6.8	15 32	6.9	00 25	9.1	12 46	9.0	01 52	3.2	14 04	3.3	04 02	5.3	16 22	5.3
26	Saturday	03 49	6.9	16 09	6.9	01 01	9.1	13 24	8.9	02 25	3.3	14 43	3.3	04 38	5.3	17 00	5.2
27	Sunday	04 28	6.8	16 48	6.7	01 40	8.9	14 06	8.7	03 00	3.3	15 24	3.2	05 16	5.1	17 43	5.1
28	Monday	05 12	6.7	17 32	6.5	02 24	8.7	14 54	8.4	03 37	3.2	16 08	3.1	05 59	5.0	18 32	4.9
29	Tuesday	06 01	6.5	18 21	6.2	03 15	8.4	15 50	8.0	04 18	3.1	16 58	2.9	06 50	4.8	19 30	4.8
30	Wednesday	06 59	6.2	19 20	6.0	04 19	8.0	16 59	7.7	05 12	2.9	18 02	2.8	07 50	4.7	20 38	4.7

MAY 1997   *High water*   GMT

		LONDON BRIDGE *Datum of predictions 3.20 m below				LIVERPOOL *Datum of predictions 4.93 m below				GREENOCK *Datum of predictions 1.62 m below				LEITH *Datum of predictions 2.90 m below			
		hr	ht m	hr	ht m	hr	ht m	hr	ht m	hr	ht m	hr	ht m	hr	ht m	hr	ht m
1	Thursday	08 07	6.1	20 32	5.9	05 34	7.9	18 17	7.7	06 30	2.8	19 23	2.8	09 03	4.6	21 54	4.7
2	Friday	09 25	6.2	21 49	6.1	06 51	8.1	19 32	8.1	08 10	2.8	20 52	2.8	10 19	4.7	23 06	4.9
3	Saturday	10 36	6.5	22 55	6.4	08 00	8.5	20 35	8.6	09 28	3.0	22 02	3.0	11 27	5.0	———	
4	Sunday	11 38	6.9	23 54	6.8	08 59	9.1	21 28	9.1	10 26	3.3	22 56	3.1	00 08	5.2	12 25	5.3
5	Monday	12 32	7.2	———		09 51	9.5	22 16	9.5	11 17	3.4	23 43	3.3	01 00	5.4	13 15	5.5
6	Tuesday	00 48	7.1	13 22	7.4	10 38	9.7	23 00	9.6	12 05	3.5	———		01 46	5.6	14 02	5.7
7	Wednesday	01 37	7.4	14 09	7.5	11 23	9.8	23 42	9.6	00 26	3.4	12 52	3.5	02 30	5.7	14 49	5.7
8	Thursday	02 24	7.5	14 52	7.5	12 06	9.7	———		01 07	3.4	13 36	3.5	03 14	5.7	15 36	5.7
9	Friday	03 08	7.4	15 32	7.3	00 23	9.5	12 49	9.4	01 45	3.5	14 18	3.5	03 58	5.5	16 23	5.5
10	Saturday	03 50	7.3	16 08	7.0	01 03	9.2	13 29	9.1	02 22	3.6	14 58	3.4	04 42	5.4	17 09	5.3
11	Sunday	04 30	7.1	16 42	6.8	01 42	8.9	14 09	8.6	03 00	3.6	15 39	3.3	05 25	5.1	17 54	5.0
12	Monday	05 10	6.7	17 16	6.5	02 22	8.5	14 50	8.2	03 39	3.5	16 21	3.1	06 10	4.9	18 41	4.8
13	Tuesday	05 51	6.4	17 55	6.2	03 05	8.1	15 36	7.7	04 20	3.3	17 09	2.9	06 58	4.6	19 31	4.5
14	Wednesday	06 37	6.0	18 42	5.9	03 35	7.7	16 33	7.3	05 06	3.1	18 03	2.8	07 51	4.4	20 25	4.4
15	Thursday	07 35	5.8	19 43	5.7	05 00	7.3	17 49	7.1	06 00	3.0	19 04	2.7	08 50	4.3	21 24	4.3
16	Friday	08 47	5.7	21 01	5.6	06 20	7.3	19 04	7.2	07 02	2.8	20 19	2.7	09 54	4.3	22 27	4.3
17	Saturday	09 56	5.8	22 13	5.8	07 31	7.5	20 03	7.6	08 13	2.8	21 40	2.8	10 59	4.4	23 28	4.5
18	Sunday	10 54	6.1	23 12	6.1	08 26	7.9	20 52	8.1	09 27	2.9	22 32	2.9	11 57	4.6	———	
19	Monday	11 46	6.4	———		09 12	8.2	21 34	8.5	10 21	3.0	23 15	3.0	00 20	4.7	12 46	4.8
20	Tuesday	00 03	6.4	12 33	6.7	09 52	8.6	22 12	8.8	11 02	3.0	23 52	3.0	01 05	4.9	13 28	5.0
21	Wednesday	00 51	6.6	13 16	6.9	10 30	8.8	22 48	9.0	11 40	3.1	———		01 45	5.1	14 08	5.2
22	Thursday	01 34	6.8	13 56	7.0	11 07	8.9	23 25	9.1	00 24	3.1	12 20	3.1	02 24	5.3	14 47	5.3
23	Friday	02 15	6.9	14 36	7.0	11 46	9.0	———		00 57	3.2	13 02	3.2	03 02	5.4	15 25	5.4
24	Saturday	02 55	7.0	15 15	7.0	00 03	9.2	12 28	9.1	01 31	3.3	13 45	3.2	03 40	5.4	16 04	5.4
25	Sunday	03 36	7.0	15 54	6.9	00 44	9.2	13 11	9.0	02 07	3.3	14 29	3.2	04 18	5.4	16 46	5.4
26	Monday	04 19	7.0	16 36	6.8	01 28	9.1	13 57	8.9	02 45	3.4	15 14	3.2	05 00	5.3	17 31	5.3
27	Tuesday	05 04	6.9	17 20	6.6	02 16	9.0	14 46	8.7	03 25	3.3	16 01	3.1	05 45	5.2	18 22	5.1
28	Wednesday	05 55	6.7	18 10	6.4	03 08	8.7	15 41	8.4	04 10	3.2	16 55	3.0	06 36	5.0	19 18	5.0
29	Thursday	06 51	6.5	19 08	6.2	04 08	8.4	16 44	8.1	05 05	3.1	17 57	2.9	07 36	4.9	20 23	4.9
30	Friday	07 57	6.3	20 17	6.2	05 16	8.2	17 55	8.0	06 15	3.0	19 07	2.9	08 45	4.8	21 33	4.8
31	Saturday	09 07	6.4	21 26	6.3	06 26	8.3	19 05	8.1	07 41	3.0	20 23	2.9	09 57	4.9	22 41	4.9

JUNE 1997   *High water*   GMT

		LONDON BRIDGE				LIVERPOOL				GREENOCK				LEITH			
1	Sunday	10 13	6.6	22 31	6.5	07 34	8.5	20 10	8.4	09 01	3.1	21 35	3.0	11 04	5.0	23 44	5.1
2	Monday	11 13	6.8	23 30	6.8	08 36	8.8	21 06	8.8	10 04	3.2	22 32	3.1	12 04	5.2	———	
3	Tuesday	12 08	7.1	———		09 31	9.1	21 55	9.1	10 58	3.3	23 22	3.2	00 39	5.3	12 59	5.3
4	Wednesday	00 26	7.0	13 00	7.3	10 20	9.3	22 40	9.3	11 47	3.3	———		01 28	5.4	13 49	5.4
5	Thursday	01 18	7.2	13 48	7.3	11 06	9.3	23 22	9.3	00 06	3.3	12 35	3.3	02 14	5.5	14 36	5.5
6	Friday	02 06	7.3	14 32	7.3	11 48	9.3	———		00 47	3.4	13 20	3.3	02 58	5.5	15 22	5.5
7	Saturday	02 52	7.2	15 12	7.1	00 02	9.2	12 30	9.1	01 26	3.5	14 03	3.2	03 41	5.4	16 06	5.4
8	Sunday	03 34	7.1	15 48	6.9	00 42	9.1	13 09	8.9	02 03	3.5	14 43	3.2	04 23	5.3	16 48	5.2
9	Monday	04 14	6.9	16 21	6.7	01 20	8.9	13 47	8.6	02 40	3.5	15 22	3.1	05 03	5.1	17 29	5.1
10	Tuesday	04 50	6.7	16 53	6.5	01 59	8.7	14 25	8.4	03 18	3.5	16 03	3.1	05 43	5.0	18 11	4.9
11	Wednesday	05 28	6.4	17 31	6.3	02 39	8.4	15 06	8.0	03 56	3.4	16 47	3.0	06 26	4.8	18 55	4.7
12	Thursday	06 09	6.2	18 14	6.2	03 22	8.1	15 52	7.7	04 38	3.2	17 34	2.9	07 12	4.6	19 42	4.5
13	Friday	06 55	6.1	19 05	6.0	04 12	7.7	16 47	7.4	05 25	3.1	18 24	2.8	08 04	4.5	20 34	4.4
14	Saturday	07 49	5.9	20 05	5.9	05 11	7.5	17 54	7.5	06 17	2.9	19 18	2.7	08 59	4.4	21 30	4.4
15	Sunday	08 50	5.9	21 10	5.8	06 19	7.4	19 03	7.5	07 16	2.8	20 21	2.7	09 59	4.4	22 28	4.4
16	Monday	09 54	6.0	22 16	6.0	07 25	7.6	20 02	7.8	08 21	2.8	21 32	2.8	11 00	4.5	23 28	4.6
17	Tuesday	10 56	6.3	23 17	6.2	08 23	7.9	20 53	8.3	09 25	2.9	22 30	2.9	11 59	4.7	———	
18	Wednesday	11 52	6.6	———		09 13	8.3	21 37	8.7	10 21	3.0	23 16	3.0	00 23	4.8	12 52	4.9
19	Thursday	00 13	6.5	12 43	6.8	09 58	8.7	22 19	9.0	11 10	3.1	23 55	3.1	01 13	5.1	13 39	5.1
20	Friday	01 04	6.8	13 31	7.0	10 42	8.9	23 01	9.3	11 55	3.1	———		01 58	5.3	14 23	5.3
21	Saturday	01 52	7.0	14 16	7.1	11 27	9.1	23 45	9.4	00 34	3.2	12 42	3.2	02 40	5.4	15 05	5.5
22	Sunday	02 38	7.2	14 59	7.1	12 12	9.2	———		01 14	3.4	13 30	3.2	03 20	5.5	15 47	5.5
23	Monday	03 23	7.2	15 42	7.1	00 30	9.5	13 00	9.3	01 54	3.4	14 18	3.2	04 01	5.6	16 31	5.6
24	Tuesday	04 09	7.2	16 25	7.0	01 18	9.5	13 48	9.2	02 35	3.5	15 06	3.2	04 45	5.5	17 18	5.5
25	Wednesday	04 55	7.1	17 09	6.9	02 07	9.4	14 37	9.1	03 17	3.5	15 55	3.2	05 32	5.5	18 09	5.4
26	Thursday	05 44	7.0	17 57	6.7	02 58	9.2	15 28	8.8	04 03	3.4	16 46	3.1	06 23	5.3	19 03	5.2
27	Friday	06 38	6.7	18 51	6.5	03 53	8.9	16 24	8.4	04 54	3.3	17 41	3.0	07 21	5.2	20 04	5.0
28	Saturday	07 38	6.5	19 54	6.4	04 53	8.6	17 28	8.2	05 54	3.2	18 39	3.0	08 26	5.0	21 08	4.9
29	Sunday	08 43	6.4	21 01	6.3	05 59	8.3	18 37	8.0	07 07	3.0	19 45	2.9	09 34	4.9	22 15	4.9
30	Monday	09 48	6.5	22 06	6.4	07 08	8.3	19 45	8.2	08 32	3.0	21 03	2.9	10 43	4.9	23 21	5.0

JULY 1997 *High water* GMT

	London Bridge *Datum of predictions 3.20 m below				Liverpool *Datum of predictions 4.93 m below				Greenock *Datum of predictions 1.62 m below				Leith *Datum of predictions 2.90 m below			
	hr	ht m	hr	ht m	hr	ht m	hr	ht m	hr	ht m	hr	ht m	hr	ht m	hr	ht m
1 Tuesday	10 49	6.6	23 09	6.6	08 15	8.4	20 46	8.4	09 44	3.1	22 09	3.0	11 48	5.0	——	—
2 Wednesday	11 46	6.9	——	—	09 14	8.6	21 39	8.8	10 44	3.1	23 02	3.1	00 21	5.1	12 48	5.1
3 Thursday	00 07	6.8	12 40	7.0	10 05	8.8	22 25	9.0	11 35	3.2	23 49	3.3	01 15	5.2	13 40	5.2
4 Friday	01 01	7.0	13 29	7.1	10 51	9.0	23 07	9.1	12 24	3.2	——	—	02 03	5.3	14 26	5.3
5 Saturday	01 51	7.1	14 14	7.1	11 33	9.0	23 46	9.1	00 30	3.3	13 09	3.1	02 46	5.4	15 09	5.3
6 Sunday	02 37	7.1	14 55	7.0	12 12	8.9	——	—	01 10	3.4	13 50	3.1	03 26	5.4	15 48	5.3
7 Monday	03 19	7.0	15 30	6.8	00 23	9.1	12 49	8.8	01 46	3.4	14 28	3.1	04 04	5.3	16 25	5.2
8 Tuesday	03 55	6.8	16 01	6.6	00 59	9.0	13 25	8.7	02 22	3.5	15 04	3.1	04 40	5.2	17 02	5.1
9 Wednesday	04 28	6.7	16 31	6.5	01 35	8.8	14 00	8.6	02 56	3.5	15 41	3.0	05 16	5.1	17 40	5.0
10 Thursday	05 01	6.6	17 06	6.5	02 12	8.7	14 37	8.3	03 32	3.4	16 19	3.0	05 54	5.0	18 20	4.9
11 Friday	05 38	6.5	17 45	6.4	02 50	8.4	15 16	8.1	04 09	3.3	16 59	3.0	06 35	4.8	19 03	4.7
12 Saturday	06 20	6.4	18 30	6.3	03 32	8.1	16 01	7.8	04 49	3.2	17 43	2.9	07 18	4.7	19 49	4.6
13 Sunday	07 07	6.2	19 21	6.1	04 21	7.8	16 55	7.5	05 36	3.0	18 31	2.8	08 08	4.5	20 40	4.5
14 Monday	08 02	6.1	20 20	6.0	05 19	7.6	18 00	7.4	06 29	2.9	19 25	2.7	09 04	4.4	21 38	4.5
15 Tuesday	09 04	6.1	21 25	6.0	06 24	7.5	19 08	7.6	07 31	2.8	20 30	2.7	10 07	4.4	22 40	4.5
16 Wednesday	10 10	6.2	22 32	6.1	07 32	7.7	20 11	8.0	08 40	2.8	21 43	2.8	11 14	4.6	23 44	4.7
17 Thursday	11 15	6.4	23 38	6.4	08 35	8.1	21 06	8.6	09 48	2.9	22 43	3.0	12 18	4.8	——	—
18 Friday	12 13	6.7	——	—	09 30	8.5	21 55	9.0	10 46	3.0	23 31	3.2	00 42	5.0	13 13	5.1
19 Saturday	00 38	6.7	13 07	7.0	10 21	9.0	22 41	9.4	11 38	3.1	——	—	01 33	5.3	14 01	5.4
20 Sunday	01 32	7.1	13 56	7.2	11 09	9.3	23 28	9.7	00 15	3.3	12 28	3.2	02 18	5.5	14 45	5.6
21 Monday	02 21	7.3	14 43	7.3	11 57	9.5	——	—	00 58	3.4	13 18	3.2	03 00	5.7	15 29	5.8
22 Tuesday	03 09	7.4	15 27	7.3	00 15	9.9	12 46	9.6	01 41	3.6	14 08	3.3	03 43	5.8	16 14	5.8
23 Wednesday	03 55	7.5	16 10	7.3	01 04	9.9	13 33	9.6	02 24	3.6	14 55	3.3	04 28	5.8	17 01	5.7
24 Thursday	04 40	7.4	16 53	7.2	01 52	9.8	14 21	9.4	03 07	3.7	15 41	3.3	05 18	5.8	17 51	5.6
25 Friday	05 27	7.2	17 38	7.1	02 41	9.6	15 08	9.1	03 50	3.6	16 27	3.3	06 07	5.6	18 43	5.3
26 Saturday	06 15	6.9	18 26	6.8	03 31	9.2	15 59	8.7	04 37	3.5	17 13	3.2	07 02	5.4	19 40	5.1
27 Sunday	07 10	6.6	19 23	6.5	04 26	8.7	16 58	8.2	05 28	3.3	18 04	3.1	08 04	5.1	20 42	4.9
28 Monday	08 13	6.3	20 31	6.3	05 31	8.2	18 08	7.8	06 29	3.1	19 00	3.0	09 11	4.9	21 48	4.8
29 Tuesday	09 21	6.2	21 42	6.2	06 44	7.9	19 22	7.8	07 57	2.9	20 19	2.9	10 22	4.8	22 58	4.8
30 Wednesday	10 25	6.3	22 50	6.3	07 57	8.0	20 29	8.1	09 31	2.9	21 47	3.0	11 33	4.8	——	—
31 Thursday	11 25	6.5	23 50	6.6	08 59	8.2	21 24	8.5	10 35	3.0	22 45	3.1	00 05	4.9	12 38	4.9

AUGUST 1997 *High water* GMT

	London Bridge				Liverpool				Greenock				Leith			
1 Friday	12 20	6.8	——	—	09 51	8.5	22 11	8.8	11 27	3.1	23 33	3.2	01 04	5.1	13 32	5.1
2 Saturday	00 45	6.9	13 10	7.0	10 37	8.8	22 52	9.0	12 14	3.1	——	—	01 52	5.2	14 16	5.2
3 Sunday	01 36	7.1	13 56	7.0	11 17	8.9	23 30	9.1	00 15	3.3	12 57	3.1	02 33	5.3	14 54	5.3
4 Monday	02 20	7.1	14 36	6.9	11 54	8.9	——	—	00 54	3.4	13 35	3.1	03 10	5.4	15 28	5.3
5 Tuesday	03 00	7.0	15 11	6.8	00 04	9.1	12 28	8.9	01 29	3.4	14 10	3.1	03 44	5.4	16 01	5.3
6 Wednesday	03 33	6.8	15 39	6.6	00 37	9.1	13 00	8.8	02 01	3.4	14 41	3.1	04 16	5.3	16 34	5.2
7 Thursday	04 02	6.7	16 08	6.6	01 10	9.0	13 33	8.7	02 32	3.4	15 12	3.1	04 48	5.3	17 09	5.1
8 Friday	04 32	6.7	16 39	6.6	01 44	8.8	14 07	8.6	03 05	3.4	15 45	3.1	05 23	5.2	17 46	5.0
9 Saturday	05 06	6.7	17 15	6.5	02 18	8.6	14 42	8.4	03 39	3.4	16 20	3.0	05 59	5.0	18 25	4.9
10 Sunday	05 44	6.6	17 55	6.4	02 56	8.4	15 21	8.1	04 17	3.3	17 00	3.0	06 38	4.8	19 08	4.7
11 Monday	06 28	6.4	18 42	6.2	03 40	8.0	16 09	7.8	04 58	3.1	17 44	2.9	07 22	4.7	19 56	4.6
12 Tuesday	07 19	6.2	19 37	6.1	04 34	7.7	17 09	7.5	05 47	2.9	18 37	2.8	08 16	4.5	20 53	4.5
13 Wednesday	08 18	6.0	20 41	5.9	05 39	7.5	18 21	7.5	06 48	2.8	19 42	2.7	09 21	4.4	21 58	4.5
14 Thursday	09 27	6.0	21 52	6.0	06 51	7.5	19 33	7.9	08 02	2.8	21 02	2.8	10 34	4.5	23 08	4.7
15 Friday	10 40	6.2	23 07	6.2	08 04	7.9	20 38	8.4	09 22	2.9	22 15	3.0	11 48	4.8	——	—
16 Saturday	11 46	6.5	——	—	09 08	8.5	21 33	9.1	10 30	3.0	23 09	3.2	00 14	5.0	12 50	5.1
17 Sunday	00 15	6.6	12 44	6.9	10 02	9.0	22 23	9.6	11 25	3.2	23 56	3.4	01 09	5.3	13 40	5.5
18 Monday	01 12	7.0	13 35	7.2	10 52	9.5	23 10	10.0	12 16	3.3	——	—	01 55	5.6	14 26	5.8
19 Tuesday	02 03	7.4	14 23	7.4	11 40	9.8	23 57	10.2	00 41	3.6	13 05	3.4	02 38	5.9	15 10	5.9
20 Wednesday	02 51	7.6	15 07	7.5	12 27	9.9	——	—	01 26	3.7	13 52	3.4	03 22	6.1	15 54	6.0
21 Thursday	03 36	7.7	15 50	7.5	00 44	10.2	13 13	9.8	02 09	3.8	14 37	3.5	04 08	6.1	16 41	5.9
22 Friday	04 20	7.6	16 32	7.5	01 31	10.1	13 58	9.6	02 52	3.8	15 18	3.5	04 55	6.0	17 29	5.7
23 Saturday	05 03	7.4	17 14	7.3	02 18	9.7	14 44	9.2	03 33	3.7	15 59	3.5	05 46	5.8	18 19	5.4
24 Sunday	05 47	7.0	17 58	7.0	03 05	9.2	15 31	8.7	04 15	3.6	16 41	3.4	06 40	5.5	19 14	5.1
25 Monday	06 34	6.6	18 49	6.5	03 57	8.5	16 25	8.1	05 01	3.4	17 27	3.2	07 41	5.1	20 14	4.9
26 Tuesday	07 34	6.1	19 57	6.1	05 00	7.9	17 36	7.6	05 54	3.1	18 19	3.1	08 48	4.8	21 20	4.7
27 Wednesday	08 50	5.9	21 19	5.9	06 21	7.5	19 00	7.5	07 09	2.8	19 26	2.9	10 00	4.7	22 32	4.7
28 Thursday	10 00	5.9	22 30	6.0	07 40	7.6	20 11	7.8	09 22	2.8	21 21	3.0	11 16	4.7	23 46	4.8
29 Friday	11 02	6.2	23 32	6.4	08 42	7.9	21 06	8.3	10 26	3.0	22 25	3.1	12 25	4.8	——	—
30 Saturday	11 58	6.6	——	—	09 34	8.3	21 53	8.7	11 15	3.1	23 14	3.3	00 47	5.0	13 18	5.0
31 Sunday	00 26	6.8	12 48	6.9	10 17	8.7	22 33	9.0	11 58	3.2	23 56	3.4	01 35	5.2	14 00	5.2

SEPTEMBER 1997   High water   GMT

| | | LONDON BRIDGE | | | LIVERPOOL | | | GREENOCK | | | LEITH | | |
| | | *Datum of predictions 3.20 m below | | | *Datum of predictions 4.93 m below | | | *Datum of predictions 1.62 m below | | | *Datum of predictions 2.90 m below | | |
		hr	m	hr	ht m	hr	m	hr	ht m	hr	m	hr	ht m	hr	m	hr	ht m
1	Monday	01 15	7.0	13 33	7.0	10 56	8.9	23 09	9.1	12 37	3.2	—	—	02 14	5.3	14 34	5.3
2	Tuesday	01 58	7.1	14 13	7.0	11 31	8.9	23 42	9.2	00 33	3.4	13 13	3.2	02 48	5.4	15 04	5.3
3	Wednesday	02 36	7.0	14 47	6.8	12 03	8.9	—	—	01 07	3.4	13 45	3.1	03 19	5.4	15 34	5.3
4	Thursday	03 07	6.9	15 16	6.7	00 12	9.1	12 34	8.9	01 37	3.4	14 13	3.1	03 49	5.4	16 05	5.3
5	Friday	03 35	6.8	15 43	6.6	00 43	9.0	13 04	8.8	02 06	3.4	14 40	3.2	04 20	5.4	16 39	5.3
6	Saturday	04 03	6.8	16 12	6.6	01 14	8.9	13 36	8.7	02 37	3.4	15 09	3.2	04 53	5.3	17 14	5.2
7	Sunday	04 35	6.8	16 46	6.6	01 47	8.7	14 09	8.6	03 11	3.4	15 43	3.2	05 27	5.1	17 51	5.0
8	Monday	05 11	6.7	17 25	6.5	02 23	8.5	14 46	8.3	03 47	3.3	16 19	3.1	06 05	5.0	18 31	4.9
9	Tuesday	05 52	6.5	18 10	6.3	03 05	8.1	15 31	8.0	04 26	3.2	17 00	3.0	06 48	4.8	19 18	4.7
10	Wednesday	06 40	6.3	19 04	6.1	03 57	7.7	16 30	7.6	05 12	3.0	17 51	2.9	07 41	4.6	20 14	4.6
11	Thursday	07 37	6.0	20 07	5.9	05 05	7.4	17 44	7.5	06 11	2.8	18 59	2.8	08 47	4.5	21 21	4.6
12	Friday	08 46	5.8	21 19	5.9	06 22	7.4	19 02	7.8	07 30	2.8	20 27	2.8	10 04	4.5	22 36	4.7
13	Saturday	10 05	6.0	22 40	6.1	07 41	7.8	20 14	8.4	09 02	2.9	21 48	3.0	11 22	4.8	23 46	5.0
14	Sunday	11 19	6.3	23 52	6.6	08 49	8.5	21 13	9.1	10 16	3.1	22 46	3.3	12 27	5.2	—	—
15	Monday	12 19	6.8	—	—	09 44	9.1	22 03	9.7	11 12	3.3	23 35	3.5	00 43	5.4	13 19	5.6
16	Tuesday	00 51	7.1	13 11	7.1	10 32	9.6	22 51	10.2	12 00	3.4	—	—	01 31	5.7	14 04	5.9
17	Wednesday	01 42	7.4	13 59	7.4	11 19	9.9	23 37	10.4	00 21	3.7	12 47	3.5	02 15	6.0	14 48	6.0
18	Thursday	02 29	7.7	14 43	7.6	12 04	10.0	—	—	01 07	3.8	13 31	3.6	03 00	6.2	15 32	6.1
19	Friday	03 13	7.8	15 26	7.7	00 22	10.3	12 49	9.9	01 51	3.9	14 12	3.6	03 46	6.2	16 17	6.0
20	Saturday	03 56	7.7	16 08	7.6	01 08	10.1	13 33	9.7	02 33	3.9	14 51	3.7	04 34	6.1	17 05	5.8
21	Sunday	04 36	7.4	16 49	7.4	01 53	9.7	14 16	9.2	03 13	3.8	15 30	3.6	05 25	5.8	17 54	5.5
22	Monday	05 17	7.1	17 32	7.0	02 38	9.1	15 00	8.7	03 54	3.6	16 10	3.6	06 18	5.4	18 47	5.1
23	Tuesday	05 57	6.6	18 19	6.5	03 27	8.4	15 51	8.0	04 37	3.4	16 54	3.4	07 17	5.0	19 44	4.8
24	Wednesday	06 44	6.1	19 21	6.0	04 28	7.7	16 59	7.5	05 28	3.1	17 45	3.2	08 21	4.7	20 50	4.6
25	Thursday	08 05	5.7	20 52	5.8	05 54	7.2	18 30	7.3	06 34	2.8	18 47	3.0	09 31	4.5	22 01	4.6
26	Friday	09 31	5.7	22 05	5.9	07 16	7.3	19 44	7.6	09 05	2.8	20 32	3.0	10 48	4.5	23 17	4.7
27	Saturday	10 34	6.0	23 06	6.2	08 18	7.7	20 41	8.1	10 08	3.0	21 57	3.1	12 00	4.7	—	—
28	Sunday	11 30	6.3	23 59	6.6	09 09	8.2	21 27	8.6	10 53	3.1	22 47	3.3	00 21	4.9	12 54	4.9
29	Monday	12 20	6.7	—	—	09 51	8.6	22 07	8.9	11 33	3.2	23 30	3.4	01 09	5.1	13 34	5.1
30	Tuesday	00 47	6.9	13 05	6.9	10 29	8.8	22 43	9.1	12 10	3.3	—	—	01 47	5.3	14 06	5.3

OCTOBER 1997   High water   GMT

		LONDON BRIDGE			LIVERPOOL			GREENOCK			LEITH		
1	Wednesday	01 30	7.0	13 45	6.9	11 03	9.0	23 15	9.1	00 07	3.4	12 45	3.3	02 20	5.4	14 35	5.4
2	Thursday	02 06	7.0	14 20	6.9	11 34	9.0	23 45	9.1	00 40	3.4	13 16	3.3	02 51	5.5	15 05	5.4
3	Friday	02 38	6.9	14 50	6.7	12 05	9.0	—	—	01 08	3.4	13 43	3.3	03 21	5.5	15 37	5.4
4	Saturday	03 06	6.9	15 19	6.7	00 15	9.0	12 35	8.9	01 37	3.4	14 08	3.3	03 54	5.4	16 11	5.4
5	Sunday	03 35	6.9	15 48	6.7	00 47	8.9	13 07	8.8	02 10	3.4	14 37	3.4	04 27	5.3	16 45	5.3
6	Monday	04 06	6.8	16 22	6.7	01 20	8.8	13 40	8.7	02 46	3.4	15 10	3.3	05 02	5.2	17 21	5.2
7	Tuesday	04 42	6.8	17 01	6.6	01 57	8.6	14 18	8.5	03 23	3.4	15 46	3.3	05 40	5.1	18 01	5.0
8	Wednesday	05 22	6.6	17 47	6.4	02 39	8.2	15 03	8.1	04 02	3.2	16 24	3.2	06 25	4.9	18 47	4.8
9	Thursday	06 09	6.3	18 41	6.2	03 32	7.8	16 02	7.8	04 43	3.1	17 12	3.0	07 18	4.7	19 44	4.7
10	Friday	07 04	6.0	19 43	6.0	04 40	7.5	17 16	7.6	05 44	2.9	18 21	2.9	08 24	4.6	20 52	4.6
11	Saturday	08 12	5.8	20 56	5.9	05 59	7.4	18 36	7.8	07 07	2.8	19 55	2.9	09 40	4.6	22 09	4.8
12	Sunday	09 35	5.9	22 18	6.2	07 20	7.8	19 50	8.4	08 49	2.9	21 21	3.1	10 58	4.9	23 20	5.1
13	Monday	10 50	6.3	23 28	6.6	08 28	8.5	20 50	9.1	09 59	3.1	22 22	3.4	12 03	5.3	—	—
14	Tuesday	11 52	6.7	—	—	09 23	9.2	21 42	9.7	10 54	3.3	23 13	3.6	00 18	5.4	12 56	5.6
15	Wednesday	00 26	7.1	12 45	7.1	10 11	9.7	22 30	10.1	11 41	3.5	—	—	01 08	5.8	13 41	5.9
16	Thursday	01 18	7.5	13 34	7.4	10 56	10.0	23 15	10.3	00 00	3.7	12 25	3.6	01 53	6.0	14 25	6.0
17	Friday	02 05	7.7	14 19	7.6	11 40	10.0	—	—	00 47	3.8	13 07	3.7	02 39	6.2	15 09	6.0
18	Saturday	02 49	7.7	15 03	7.7	00 00	10.2	12 24	9.9	01 31	3.9	13 47	3.8	03 26	6.1	15 55	5.9
19	Sunday	03 31	7.6	15 46	7.6	00 45	9.9	13 07	9.6	02 13	3.8	14 25	3.8	04 14	6.0	16 41	5.7
20	Monday	04 11	7.4	16 28	7.4	01 29	9.5	13 49	9.2	02 54	3.8	15 04	3.8	05 05	5.7	17 29	5.4
21	Tuesday	04 48	7.0	17 10	7.0	02 13	8.9	14 32	8.7	03 35	3.6	15 44	3.7	05 57	5.3	18 19	5.1
22	Wednesday	05 25	6.6	17 55	6.6	02 59	8.3	15 19	8.1	04 18	3.4	16 27	3.6	06 52	5.0	19 15	4.8
23	Thursday	06 02	6.2	18 49	6.1	03 53	7.6	16 17	7.6	05 08	3.1	17 16	3.4	07 51	4.7	20 16	4.6
24	Friday	06 52	5.7	20 12	5.7	05 10	7.2	17 42	7.3	06 09	2.9	18 15	3.2	08 54	4.5	21 22	4.5
25	Saturday	08 46	5.5	21 29	5.8	06 37	7.1	19 03	7.4	07 56	2.8	19 27	3.1	10 04	4.5	22 33	4.6
26	Sunday	09 57	5.7	22 30	6.0	07 43	7.5	20 05	7.8	09 32	3.0	21 09	3.1	11 16	4.6	23 40	4.7
27	Monday	10 54	6.1	23 24	6.3	08 35	7.9	20 54	8.3	10 20	3.1	22 11	3.3	12 14	4.8	—	—
28	Tuesday	11 45	6.4	—	—	09 19	8.4	21 36	8.6	11 01	3.3	22 56	3.3	00 32	4.9	12 57	5.0
29	Wednesday	00 12	6.6	12 31	6.7	09 57	8.7	22 13	8.9	11 39	3.4	23 35	3.4	01 13	5.1	13 32	5.2
30	Thursday	00 55	6.9	13 13	6.8	10 32	9.0	22 46	9.0	12 14	3.4	—	—	01 48	5.3	14 04	5.3
31	Friday	01 33	6.9	13 50	6.8	11 05	9.0	23 17	9.0	00 07	3.4	12 46	3.4	02 22	5.4	14 37	5.4

NOVEMBER 1997   *High water*   GMT

		LONDON BRIDGE				LIVERPOOL				GREENOCK				LEITH			
		*Datum of predictions 3.20 m below				*Datum of predictions 4.93 m below				*Datum of predictions 1.62 m below				*Datum of predictions 2.90 m below			
		hr	ht m	hr	ht m	hr	ht m	hr	ht m	hr	ht m	hr	ht m	hr	ht m	hr	ht m
1	Saturday	02 07	7.0	14 23	6.8	11 36	9.1	23 49	9.0	00 38	3.4	13 13	3.4	02 55	5.5	15 11	5.5
2	Sunday	02 39	6.9	14 56	6.8	12 08	9.1	—	—	01 10	3.4	13 40	3.5	03 30	5.5	15 45	5.4
3	Monday	03 11	6.9	15 29	6.8	00 23	9.0	12 43	9.0	01 46	3.4	14 11	3.5	04 05	5.4	16 20	5.4
4	Tuesday	03 44	6.9	16 05	6.8	01 00	8.9	13 19	8.9	02 24	3.4	14 45	3.5	04 42	5.3	16 57	5.3
5	Wednesday	04 20	6.8	16 46	6.7	01 39	8.7	14 00	8.7	03 04	3.4	15 22	3.5	05 22	5.2	17 37	5.1
6	Thursday	05 00	6.6	17 32	6.5	02 24	8.4	14 48	8.4	03 45	3.3	16 01	3.3	06 08	5.0	18 25	5.0
7	Friday	05 46	6.3	18 25	6.3	03 17	8.0	15 45	8.1	04 31	3.1	16 49	3.2	07 02	4.9	19 21	4.8
8	Saturday	06 40	6.1	19 27	6.1	04 22	7.7	16 55	7.9	05 30	3.0	17 54	3.1	08 05	4.8	20 28	4.8
9	Sunday	07 46	5.9	20 39	6.1	05 38	7.6	18 11	8.0	06 48	2.9	19 23	3.1	09 18	4.8	21 43	4.8
10	Monday	09 08	6.0	21 55	6.3	06 56	7.9	19 23	8.4	08 17	3.0	20 51	3.2	10 32	5.0	22 54	5.1
11	Tuesday	10 22	6.3	23 02	6.7	08 04	8.5	20 26	9.0	09 34	3.2	21 57	3.4	11 37	5.3	23 54	5.4
12	Wednesday	11 24	6.7	—	—	09 00	9.1	21 20	9.5	10 31	3.4	22 50	3.6	12 32	5.5	—	—
13	Thursday	00 01	7.0	12 20	7.1	09 49	9.5	22 10	9.8	11 19	3.5	23 40	3.7	00 46	5.7	13 20	5.7
14	Friday	00 53	7.4	13 10	7.4	10 35	9.8	22 56	10.0	12 03	3.6	—	—	01 35	5.9	14 05	5.9
15	Saturday	01 42	7.5	13 58	7.5	11 19	9.8	23 41	9.9	00 27	3.8	12 45	3.7	02 22	6.0	14 49	5.9
16	Sunday	02 27	7.6	14 44	7.6	12 02	9.7	—	—	01 13	3.8	13 25	3.8	03 09	5.9	15 34	5.8
17	Monday	03 09	7.4	15 28	7.5	00 24	9.7	12 44	9.5	01 57	3.7	14 04	3.9	03 58	5.8	16 20	5.6
18	Tuesday	03 49	7.2	16 11	7.3	01 08	9.3	13 26	9.2	02 38	3.7	14 43	3.9	04 46	5.6	17 06	5.4
19	Wednesday	04 25	6.9	16 53	7.0	01 50	8.8	14 07	8.8	03 19	3.5	15 22	3.8	05 35	5.3	17 53	5.2
20	Thursday	04 59	6.6	17 35	6.6	02 33	8.4	14 50	8.4	04 02	3.4	16 04	3.7	06 24	5.0	18 43	4.9
21	Friday	05 34	6.3	18 21	6.2	03 19	7.8	15 39	7.9	04 49	3.2	16 50	3.5	07 16	4.7	19 38	4.7
22	Saturday	06 17	6.0	19 16	5.9	04 16	7.4	16 40	7.5	05 44	3.0	17 42	3.3	08 11	4.6	20 37	4.5
23	Sunday	07 15	5.7	20 27	5.7	05 31	7.1	17 58	7.4	06 46	2.9	18 41	3.2	09 10	4.5	21 40	4.5
24	Monday	08 31	5.6	21 37	5.8	06 49	7.2	19 11	7.5	08 08	2.9	19 50	3.1	10 12	4.5	22 43	4.6
25	Tuesday	10 02	5.7	22 35	6.0	07 50	7.6	20 10	7.9	09 29	3.0	21 10	3.1	11 14	4.6	23 42	4.7
26	Wednesday	11 00	6.0	23 27	6.3	08 40	8.1	20 57	8.3	10 21	3.2	22 11	3.2	12 08	4.8	—	—
27	Thursday	11 50	6.3	—	—	09 22	8.5	21 38	8.6	11 04	3.3	22 55	3.3	00 32	4.9	12 52	5.0
28	Friday	00 14	6.6	12 36	6.6	10 00	8.8	22 15	8.8	11 42	3.4	23 32	3.3	01 14	5.1	13 32	5.2
29	Saturday	00 57	6.8	13 18	6.8	10 36	9.0	22 50	9.0	12 15	3.4	—	—	01 53	5.3	14 10	5.4
30	Sunday	01 37	6.9	13 57	6.9	11 11	9.2	23 26	9.1	00 08	3.3	12 46	3.5	02 31	5.4	14 47	5.5

DECEMBER 1997   *High water*   GMT

		LONDON BRIDGE				LIVERPOOL				GREENOCK				LEITH			
1	Monday	02 15	7.0	14 35	6.9	11 47	9.2	—	—	00 46	3.4	13 17	3.5	03 09	5.4	15 23	5.5
2	Tuesday	02 51	7.0	15 13	6.9	00 04	9.1	12 25	9.2	01 26	3.4	13 51	3.6	03 46	5.5	16 00	5.5
3	Wednesday	03 28	6.9	15 53	6.9	00 45	9.0	13 06	9.2	02 08	3.4	14 28	3.6	04 25	5.4	16 38	5.4
4	Thursday	04 06	6.8	16 36	6.9	01 28	8.9	13 50	9.0	02 50	3.4	15 07	3.6	05 07	5.3	17 20	5.3
5	Friday	04 46	6.7	17 23	6.7	02 15	8.7	14 39	8.9	03 34	3.3	15 48	3.5	05 54	5.2	18 08	5.2
6	Saturday	05 32	6.5	18 15	6.5	03 06	8.4	15 33	8.6	04 22	3.2	16 36	3.4	06 47	5.1	19 02	5.1
7	Sunday	06 23	6.3	19 13	6.4	04 05	8.1	16 35	8.4	05 18	3.1	17 35	3.3	07 47	5.0	20 06	5.0
8	Monday	07 26	6.1	20 21	6.3	05 14	7.9	17 44	8.3	06 25	3.0	18 49	3.2	08 54	4.9	21 17	5.0
9	Tuesday	08 42	6.1	21 31	6.4	06 27	8.0	18 54	8.4	07 41	3.0	20 16	3.2	10 05	5.0	22 28	5.1
10	Wednesday	09 55	6.3	22 37	6.6	07 37	8.3	20 01	8.7	09 01	3.1	21 30	3.3	11 11	5.1	23 32	5.2
11	Thursday	10 59	6.6	23 36	6.9	08 38	8.7	21 01	9.1	10 05	3.3	22 30	3.4	12 10	5.3	—	—
12	Friday	11 57	6.9	—	—	09 31	9.2	21 53	9.4	10 57	3.4	23 23	3.5	00 29	5.4	13 02	5.5
13	Saturday	00 30	7.1	12 52	7.2	10 19	9.5	22 41	9.5	11 43	3.5	—	—	01 26	5.6	13 50	5.6
14	Sunday	01 21	7.3	13 42	7.3	11 03	9.6	23 26	9.6	00 12	3.6	12 26	3.7	02 11	5.7	14 35	5.7
15	Monday	02 08	7.3	14 29	7.4	11 45	9.6	—	—	01 00	3.6	13 07	3.8	02 58	5.7	15 19	5.7
16	Tuesday	02 51	7.2	15 14	7.3	00 09	9.4	12 27	9.5	01 44	3.5	13 46	3.8	03 44	5.6	16 03	5.6
17	Wednesday	03 30	7.0	15 56	7.1	00 50	9.2	13 06	9.3	02 25	3.5	14 25	3.8	04 28	5.5	16 45	5.4
18	Thursday	04 05	6.8	16 35	6.9	01 29	8.9	13 46	9.0	03 05	3.4	15 04	3.8	05 12	5.3	17 27	5.2
19	Friday	04 37	6.6	17 13	6.6	02 08	8.6	14 25	8.7	03 45	3.3	15 43	3.7	05 55	5.1	18 10	5.0
20	Saturday	05 10	6.4	17 51	6.4	02 49	8.2	15 06	8.4	04 28	3.2	16 24	3.6	06 39	4.9	18 57	4.8
21	Sunday	05 50	6.2	18 34	6.2	03 33	7.8	15 53	8.0	05 13	3.1	17 08	3.4	07 26	4.7	19 47	4.7
22	Monday	06 36	6.0	19 23	6.0	04 25	7.5	16 47	7.7	06 03	3.0	17 57	3.3	08 17	4.5	20 43	4.5
23	Tuesday	07 33	5.8	20 20	5.9	05 31	7.3	17 54	7.5	06 57	3.0	18 51	3.1	09 12	4.5	21 41	4.5
24	Wednesday	08 41	5.7	21 24	5.9	06 45	7.3	19 05	7.5	08 02	2.9	19 53	3.0	10 10	4.5	22 43	4.5
25	Thursday	09 54	5.7	22 29	6.0	07 50	7.7	20 08	7.8	09 21	3.0	21 03	3.0	11 11	4.6	23 44	4.7
26	Friday	10 59	6.0	23 28	6.3	08 43	8.1	21 00	8.2	10 22	3.1	22 08	3.1	12 08	4.8	—	—
27	Saturday	11 56	6.3	—	—	09 28	8.6	21 45	8.6	11 08	3.3	22 58	3.2	00 38	4.9	12 59	5.1
28	Sunday	00 21	6.6	12 47	6.6	10 09	8.9	22 26	8.9	11 46	3.4	23 43	3.3	01 26	5.1	13 44	5.3
29	Monday	01 09	6.8	13 33	6.8	10 49	9.2	23 07	9.1	12 22	3.5	—	—	02 09	5.3	14 25	5.4
30	Tuesday	01 53	7.0	14 17	7.0	11 29	9.4	23 50	9.3	00 26	3.3	12 58	3.5	02 49	5.4	15 04	5.6
31	Wednesday	02 35	7.0	15 00	7.1	12 11	9.5	—	—	01 11	3.3	13 36	3.6	03 29	5.5	15 42	5.6

World Geographical Statistics

THE EARTH

The shape of the Earth is that of an oblate spheroid or solid of revolution whose meridian sections are ellipses, whilst the sections at right angles are circles.

DIMENSIONS

Equatorial diameter = 12,756.27 km (7,926.38 miles)
Polar diameter = 12,713.50 km (7,899.80 miles)
Equatorial circumference = 40,075.01 km (24,901.46 miles)
Polar circumference = 40,007.86 km (24,859.73 miles)

The equatorial circumference is divided into 360 degrees of longitude, which is measured in degrees, minutes and seconds east or west of the Greenwich meridian (0°) to 180°, the meridian 180° E. coinciding with 180° W. This was internationally ratified in 1884.

Distance north and south of the Equator is measured in degrees, minutes and seconds of latitude. The Equator is 0°, the North Pole is 90° N. and the South Pole is 90° S. The Tropics lie at 23° 26′ N. (Tropic of Cancer) and 23° 26′ S. (Tropic of Capricorn). The Arctic Circle lies at 66° 34′ N. and the Antarctic Circle at 66° 34′ S. (NB The Tropics and the Arctic and Antarctic circles are of variable latitude due to the mean obliquity of the Ecliptic; the values given are for 1997.5.)

AREA, ETC.

The surface area of the Earth is 510,069,120 km^2 (196,938,800 miles^2), of which the water area is 70.92 per cent and the land area is 29.08 per cent.

The velocity of a given point of the Earth's surface at the Equator exceeds 1,000 miles an hour (24,901.45 miles in 24 hours, viz 1,037.56 m.p.h.); the Earth's velocity in its orbit round the Sun averages 66,629 m.p.h. (584,081.400 miles in 365.256363 days). The Earth is distant from the Sun 92,955,900 miles, on average.

Source: Royal Greenwich Observatory

OCEANS

AREA

	km^2	miles^2
Pacific	166,240,000	64,186,300
Atlantic	86,550,000	33,420,000
Indian	73,427,000	28,350,500
Arctic	13,223,700	5,105,700

GREATEST DEPTHS

Greatest depth location	metres	feet
Mariana Trench (Pacific)	10,924	35,840
Puerto Rico Trench (Atlantic)	8,605	28,232
Java Trench (Indian)	7,125	23,376
Eurasian Basin (Arctic)	5,450	17,880

SEAS

AREA

	km^2	miles^2
South China	2,974,600	1,148,500
Caribbean	2,515,900	971,400
Mediterranean	2,509,900	969,100
Bering	2,226,100	873,000
Gulf of Mexico	1,507,600	582,100
Okhotsk	1,392,000	537,500
Japan	1,015,000	391,100
Hudson Bay	730,100	281,900
East China	664,600	256,600
Andaman	564,880	218,100
Black Sea	507,900	196,100
Red Sea	453,000	174,900
North Sea	427,100	164,900
Baltic Sea	382,000	147,500
Yellow Sea	294,000	113,500
Persian Gulf	230,000	88,800

GREATEST DEPTHS

	Maximum depth metres	feet
Caribbean	8,605	28,232
East China	7,507	24,629
South China	7,258	23,812
Mediterranean	5,150	16,896
Andaman	4,267	14,000
Bering	3,936	12,913
Gulf of Mexico	3,504	11,496
Okhotsk	3,365	11,040
Japan	3,053	10,016
Red Sea	2,266	7,434
Black Sea	2,212	7,257
North Sea	439	1,440
Hudson Bay	111	364
Baltic Sea	90	295
Yellow Sea	73	240
Persian Gulf	73	240

THE CONTINENTS

There are six geographic continents, though America is often divided politically into North and Central America, and South America.

AFRICA is surrounded by sea except for the narrow isthmus of Suez in the north-east, through which is cut the Suez Canal. Its extreme longitudes are 17° 20′ W. at Cape Verde, Senegal, and 51° 24′ E. at Ras Hafun, Somalia. The extreme latitudes are 37° 20′ N. at Cape Blanc, Tunisia, and 34° 50′ S. at Cape Agulhas, South Africa, about 4,400 miles apart. The Equator passes through the middle of the continent.

NORTH AMERICA, including Mexico, is surrounded by ocean except in the south, where the isthmian states of CENTRAL AMERICA link North America with South America. Its extreme longitudes are 168° 5′ W. at Cape Prince of Wales, Alaska, and 55° 40′ W. at Cape Charles,

Newfoundland. The extreme continental latitudes are the tip of the Boothia peninsula, NW Territories, Canada (71° 51' N.) and 14° 22' N. at Ocós in the south of Mexico.

SOUTH AMERICA lies mostly in the southern hemisphere; the Equator passes through the north of the continent. It is surrounded by ocean except where it is joined to Central America in the north by the narrow isthmus through which is cut the Panama Canal. Its extreme longitudes are 34° 47' W. at Cape Branco in Brazil and 81° 20' W. at Punta Pariña, Peru. The extreme continental latitudes are 12° 25' N. at Punta Gallinas, Colombia, and 53° 54' S. at the southernmost tip of the Brunswick peninsula, Chile. Cape Horn, on Cape Island, Chile, lies at 55° 59' S.

ANTARCTICA lies almost entirely within the Antarctic Circle (66° 34' S.) and is the largest of the world's glaciated areas. The continent has an area of about 5.5 million square miles, 99 per cent of which is permanently ice-covered. The ice amounts to some 7.2 million cubic miles and represents more than 90 per cent of the world's fresh water. The environment is too hostile for unsupported human habitation. See also pages 782–3

ASIA is the largest continent and occupies 30 per cent of the world's land surface. The extreme longitudes are 26° 05' E. at Baba Buran, Turkey and 169° 40' W. at Mys Dežneva (East Cape), Russia, a distance of about 6,000 miles. Its extreme northern latitude is 77° 45' N. at Cape Čeljuskin, Russia, and it extends over 5,000 miles south to about 1° 15' N. of the Equator.

AUSTRALIA is the smallest of the continents and lies in the southern hemisphere. It is entirely surrounded by ocean. Its extreme longitudes are 113° 11' E. at Steep Point and 153° 11' E. at Cape Byron. The extreme latitudes are 10° 42' S. at Cape York and 39° S. at South East Point, Tasmania.

EUROPE, including European Russia, is the smallest continent in the northern hemisphere. Its extreme latitudes are 71° 11' N. at North Cape in Norway, and 36° 23' N. at Cape Matapan in southern Greece, a distance of about 2,400 miles. Its breadth from Cabo Carvoeiro in Portugal (9° 34' W.) in the west to the Kara River, north of the Urals (66° 30' E.) in the east is about 3,300 miles. The division between Europe and Asia is generally regarded as the watershed of the Ural Mountains; down the Ural river to Gur'yev, Kazakhstan; across the Caspian Sea to Apsheronskiy Poluostrov, near Baku; along the watershed of the Caucasus Mountains to Anapa and thence across the Black Sea to the Bosporus in Turkey; across the Sea of Marmara to Çanakkale Boğazi (Dardanelles).

	Area km²	miles²
Asia	43,998,000	16,988,000
*America	41,918,000	16,185,000
Africa	29,800,000	11,506,000
Antarctica	c.13,600,000	c.5,500,000
†Europe	9,699,000	3,745,000
Australia	7,618,493	2,941,526

*North and Central America has an area of 24,255,000 km² (9,365,000 miles²)
†Includes 5,571,000 km² (2,151,000 miles²) of former USSR territory, including the Baltic states, Belarus, Moldova, the Ukraine, that part of Russia west of the Ural Mountains and Kazakhstan west of the Ural river. European Turkey (24,378 km²/9,412 miles²) comprises territory to the west and north of the Bosporus and the Dardanelles

GLACIATED AREAS

It is estimated that 15,600,000 km² (6,020,000 miles²) or 10.51 per cent of the world's land surface is permanently covered with ice.

	Area km²	miles²
South Polar regions	13,597,000	5,250,000
North Polar regions (incl. Greenland or Kalaallit Nunaat)	1,965,000	758,500
Alaska-Canada	58,800	22,700
Asia	37,800	14,600
South America	11,900	4,600
Europe	10,700	4,128
New Zealand	984	380
Africa	238	92

PENINSULAS

	Area km²	miles²
Arabian	3,250,000	1,250,000
Southern Indian	2,072,000	800,000
Alaskan	1,500,000	580,000
Labradorian	1,300,000	500,000
Scandinavian	800,300	309,000
Iberian	584,000	225,500

LARGEST ISLANDS

Island (and Ocean)	Area km²	miles²
Greenland (Kalaallit Nunaat) (Arctic)	2,175,500	840,000
New Guinea (Pacific)	792,500	306,000
Borneo (Pacific)	725,450	280,100
Madagascar (Indian)	587,040	226,658
Baffin Island (Arctic)	507,451	195,928
Sumatra (Indian)	427,350	165,000
Honshu (Pacific)	227,413	87,805
*Great Britain (Atlantic)	218,040	84,186
Victoria Island (Arctic)	217,292	83,897
Ellesmere Island (Arctic)	196,236	75,767
Sulawesi (Celebes) (Indian)	178,700	69,000
South Island, NZ (Pacific)	151,010	58,305
Java (Indian)	126,650	48,900
Cuba (Atlantic)	114,525	44,218
North Island, NZ (Pacific)	114,050	44,035
Newfoundland (Atlantic)	108,855	42,030
Luzon (Pacific)	105,880	40,880
Iceland (Atlantic)	103,000	39,770
Mindanao (Pacific)	95,247	36,775
Ireland (Atlantic)	82,462	31,839

*Mainland only

LARGEST DESERTS

	Area (approx.) km²	miles²
The Sahara (N. Africa)	9,000,000	3,500,000
Australian Desert	1,550,000	600,000
Arabian Desert	1,300,000	500,000
*The Gobi (Mongolia/China)	1,300,000	500,000
Kalahari Desert (Botswana/ Namibia/S. Africa)	583,000	225,000
Sonoran Desert (USA/ Mexico)	310,000	120,000
Namib Desert (Namibia)	310,000	120,000
†Kara Kum (Turkmenistan)	310,000	120,000
Thar Desert (India/ Pakistan)	260,000	100,000
Somali Desert (Somalia)	260,000	100,000
†Kyzyl Kum (Kazakhstan/ Uzbekistan)	260,000	100,000
Atacama Desert (Chile)	180,000	70,000
Dasht-e Lut (Iran)	52,000	20,000
Mojave Desert (USA)	35,000	13,500
Desierto de Sechura (Peru)	26,000	10,000

*Including the Takla Makan – 320,000 km² (125,000 miles²)
†Together known as the Turkestan Desert

DEEPEST DEPRESSIONS

	Maximum depth below sea level metres	feet
Dead Sea (Jordan/Israel)	395	1,296
Turfan Depression (Sinkiang, China)	153	505
Qattara Depression (Egypt)	132	436
Mangyshlak peninsula (Kazakhstan)	131	433
Danakil Depression (Ethiopia)	116	383
Death Valley (California, USA)	86	282
Salton Sink (California, USA)	71	235
W. of Ustyurt plateau (Kazakhstan)	70	230
Prikaspiyskaya Nizmennost' (Russia/Kazakhstan)	67	220
Lake Sarykamysh (Uzbekistan/ Turkmenistan)	45	148
El Faiyûm (Egypt)	44	147
Valdies peninsula, Lago Enriquillo (Dominican Republic)	40	131

The world's largest exposed depression is the Prikaspiyskaya Nizmennost' covering the hinterland of the northern third of the Caspian Sea, which is itself 28 m (92 ft) below sea level

Western Antarctica and Central Greenland largely comprise crypto-depressions under ice burdens. The Antarctic Wilkes subglacial basin has a bedrock 2,341 m (7,680 ft) below sea-level. In Greenland (lat. 73° N., long. 39° W.) the bedrock is 365 m (1,197 ft) below sea-level

LONGEST MOUNTAIN RANGES

Range (location)	Length km	miles
Cordillera de Los Andes (W. South America)	7,200	4,500
Rocky Mountains (W. North America)	4,800	3,000
Himalaya-Karakoram-Hindu Kush (S. Central Asia)	3,800	2,400
Great Dividing Range (E. Australia)	3,600	2,250
Trans-Antarctic Mts (Antarctica)	3,500	2,200
Atlantic Coast Range (E. Brazil)	3,000	1,900
West Sumatran-Javan Range (Indonesia)	2,900	1,800
Aleutian Range (Alaska and NW Pacific)	2,650	1,650
Tien Shan (S. Central Asia)	2,250	1,400
Central New Guinea Range (Irian Jaya/Papua New Guinea)	2,000	1,250

HIGHEST MOUNTAINS

The world's 8,000-metre mountains (with six subsidiary peaks) are all in the Himalaya-Karakoram-Hindu Kush range.

Mountain	Height metres	feet
Mt Everest*	8,848	29,028
K2 (Chogori)†	8,607	28,238
Kangchenjunga	8,597	28,208
Lhotse	8,511	27,923
Makalu I	8,481	27,824
Lhotse Shar (II)	8,400	27,560
Dhaulagiri I	8,171	26,810
Manaslu I (Kutang I)	8,156	26,760
Cho Oyu	8,153	26,750
Nanga Parbat (Diamir)	8,125	26,660
Annapurna I	8,078	26,504
Gasherbrum I (Hidden Peak)	8,068	26,470
Broad Peak I	8,046	26,400
Gasherbrum II	8,034	26,360
Shisha Pangma (Gosainthan)	8,012	26,287
Makalu South-East	8,010	26,280
Broad Peak Central	8,000	26,246

*Named after Sir George Everest (1790–1866), Surveyor-General of India 1830–43, in 1863. He pronounced his name Eve-rest
†Formerly Godwin-Austin

The culminating summits in the other major mountain ranges are:

Mountain (by range or country)	Height metres	feet
Pik Pobedy (Tien Shan)	7,439	24,406
Cerro Aconcagua (Cordillera de Los Andes)	6,960	22,834
Mt McKinley, S. Peak (Alaska Range)	6,194	20,320
Kilimanjaro (Kibo) (Tanzania)	5,894	19,340
Hkakabo Razi (Myanmar)	5,881	19,296
Citlaltépetl (Orizaba) (Sierra Madre Oriental, Mexico)	5,699	18,700

Mountain (by range or country)	Height metres	feet	Volcano (last major eruption) and location	Height metres	feet
El'brus, W. Peak (Caucasus)	5,641	18,510	Koryakskaya (1957), Kamchatka,		
Vinson Massif (E. Antarctica)	4,897	16,067	Russia	3,456	11,339
Puncak Jaya (Central New Guinea			Irazú (1992), Costa Rica	3,432	11,260
Range)	4,884	16,023	Slamet (1988), Java, Indonesia	3,428	11,247
Mt Blanc (Alps)	4,807	15,771	Spurr (1953), Alaska, USA	3,374	11,069
Klyuchevskaya Sopka (Kamchatka			Mt Etna (1169, 1669, 1993, 1995),		
peninsula, Russia)	4,750	15,584	Sicily, Italy	3,369	11,053
Ras Dashan (Ethiopian Highlands)	4,620	15,158	Raung, Java, Indonesia (1993)	3,322	10,932
Zard Kūh (Zagros Mts, Iran)	4,547	14,921	Shiveluch (1964), Kamchatka, Russia	3,283	10,771
Mt Kirkpatrick (Trans Antarctic)	4,529	14,860	Turrialba (1992), Costa Rica	3,246	10,650
Mt Belukha (Altai Mts, Russia/			Agung (1964), Bali, Indonesia	3,142	10,308
Kazakhstan)	4,505	14,783	Llaima (1990), Chile	3,128	10,239
Mt Elbert (Rocky Mountains)	4,400	14,433	Redoubt (1991), Alaska, USA	3,108	10,197
Mt Rainier (Cascade Range, N.			Tjareme (1938), Java, Indonesia	3,078	10,098
America)	4,392	14,410	On-Taka (1991), Japan	3,063	10,049
Nevado de Colima (Sierra Madre			Nyamuragira (1991), Zaïre	3,056	10,028
Occidental, Mexico)	4,268	14,003	Iliamna (1978), Alaska, USA	3,052	10,016
Jebel Toubkal (Atlas Mts, N. Africa)	4,165	13,665			
Kinabalu (Crocker Range, Borneo)	4,101	13,455	OTHER NOTABLE VOLCANOES		
Kerinci (West Sumatran-Javan					
Range, Indonesia)	3,800	12,467		Height	
Jabal an Nabī Shu'ayb (N. Tihāmat,				metres	feet
Yemen)	3,760	12,336	Tambora (1815), Sumbawa,		
Teotepec (Sierra Madre del Sur,			Indonesia	2,850	9,353
Mexico)	3,703	12,149	Mt St Helens (1980, 1986, 1991),		
Thaban Ntlenyana (Drakensberg,			Washington State, USA	2,530	8,300
South Africa)	3,482	11,425	Pinatubo (1991), Philippines	1,758	5,770
Pico de Bandeira (Atlantic Coast			Hekla (1981, 1991), Iceland	1,491	4,892
Range)	2,890	9,482	Mt Pelée (1902), Martinique	1,397	4,583
Shishaldin (Aleutian Range)	2,861	9,387	Mt Unzen (1792, 1991), Kyushu,		
Kosciusko (Great Dividing Range)	2,228	7,310	Japan	1,360	4,462
			Vesuvius (AD 79, 1944), Italy	1,280	4,198
			Kilauea (1995), Hawaii, USA	1,242	4,077

HIGHEST VOLCANOES

Volcano (last major eruption) and location	Height metres	feet
Guallatiri (1993), Andes, Chile	6,060	19,882
Lascar (1991), Andes, Chile	5,990	19,652
Cotopaxi (1975), Andes, Ecuador	5,897	19,347
Tupungatito (1986), Andes, Chile	5,640	18,504
Nevado del Ruiz (1985, 1992),		
Colombia	5,400	17,716
Sangay (1988), Andes, Ecuador	5,230	17,159
Guagua Pichincha (1988), Andes,		
Ecuador	4,784	15,696
Purace (1977), Colombia	4,756	15,601
Klyuchevskaya Sopka (1995),		
Kamchatka peninsula, Russia	4,750	15,584
Nevado de Colima (1991), Mexico	4,268	14,003
Galeras (1991), Colombia	4,266	13,996
Mauna Loa (1987), Hawaii Is.	4,170	13,680
Cameroon (1982), Cameroon	4,070	13,354
Acatenango (1972), Guatemala	3,960	12,992
Fuego (1988), Guatemala	3,835	12,582
Kerinci (1987), Sumatra, Indonesia	3,800	12,467
Erebus (1995), Ross Island,		
Antarctica	3,794	12,450
Tacana (1988), Guatemala	3,780	12,400
Fuji (1708), Honshu, Japan	3,775	12,388
Santiaguito (1902, 1991), Guatemala	3,768	12,362
Rindjani (1966), Lombok, Indonesia	3,726	12,224
Semeru (1995), Java, Indonesia	3,675	12,060
Nyirongo (1994), Zaïre	3,475	11,400

	Height metres	feet
Stromboli (1995), Lipari Is., Italy	926	3,038
Krakatau (1883, 1995), Sunda Strait,		
Indonesia	813	2,667
Santorini (Thíra) (1628 BC), Aegean		
Sea, Greece	566	1,857
Vulcano (Monte Aria), Lipari Is.,		
Italy	499	1,637
Tristan da Cunha (1961), South		
Atlantic	243	800
Surtsey (1963–7), off Iceland	173	568

LARGEST LAKES

The areas of some of these lakes are subject to seasonal variation.

	Area km^2	miles^2	Length km	miles
Caspian Sea, Iran/ Azerbaijan/Russia/ Turkmenistan/ Kazakhstan	371,000	143,000	1,171	728
*Michigan–Huron, USA/Canada	117,610	45,300	1,010	627
Superior, Canada/ USA	82,100	31,700	563	350

*Lakes Michigan and Huron are regarded as lobes of the same lake. The Michigan lobe has an area of 57,750 km^2 (22,300 miles^2) and the Huron lobe an area of 59,570 km^2 (23,000 miles^2)

	Area km²	miles²	Length km	miles
Victoria, Uganda/ Tanzania/Kenya	69,500	26,828	362	225
Aral Sea, Kazakhstan/ Uzbekistan	40,400	15,600	331	235
Tanganyika, Zaïre/ Tanzania/Zambia/ Burundi	32,900	12,700	675	420
†Baykal (*Baikal*), Russia	31,500	12,162	635	395
Great Bear, Canada	31,328	12,096	309	192
Malawi (Nyasa), Tanzania/Malawi/ Mozambique	28,880	11,150	580	360
Great Slave, Canada	28,570	11,031	480	298
Erie, Canada/USA	25,670	9,910	388	241
Winnipeg, Canada	24,390	9,417	428	266
Ontario, Canada/USA	19,550	7,550	310	193
Balkhash, Kazakhstan	18,427	7,115	605	376
Ladozhskoye (*Ladoga*), Russia	17,700	6,835	200	124

†World's deepest lake (1,940 m/6,365 ft)

UNITED KINGDOM (BY COUNTRY)

Lough Neagh, Northern Ireland	381.73	147.39	28.90	18.00
Loch Lomond, Scotland	71.12	27.46	36.44	22.64
Windermere, England	14.74	5.69	16.90	10.50
Lake Vyrnwy, Wales (artificial)	4.53	1.75	7.56	4.70
Llyn Tegid (*Bala*), Wales (natural)	4.38	1.69	5.80	3.65

LONGEST RIVERS

River (source and outflow)	Length km	miles
Nile (*Bahr-el-Nil*) (R. Luvironza, Burundi – E. Mediterranean Sea)	6,670	4,145
Amazon (*Amazonas*) (Lago Villafro, Peru – S. Atlantic Ocean)	6,448	4,007
Mississippi-Missouri-Red Rock (Montana – Gulf of Mexico)	5,970	3,710
Yenisey-Angara (W. Mongolia – Kara Sea)	5,540	3,442
Yangtze-Kiang (*Chang Jiang*) (Kunlun Mts, W. China – Yellow Sea)	5,530	3,436
Huang He (*Yellow River*) (Bayan Har Shan range, central China – Yellow Sea)	5,463	3,395
Ob'-Irtysh (W. Mongolia – Kara Sea)	5,410	3,362
Zaïre (*Congo*) (R. Lualaba, Zaïre-Zambia – S. Atlantic Ocean)	4,700	2,920
Amur-Argun (R. Argun, Khingan Mts, N. China – Sea of Okhotsk)	4,670	2,903
Lena-Kirenga (R. Kirenga, W. of Lake Baykal – Arctic Ocean)	4,400	2,734
Mackenzie-Peace (Tatlatui Lake, British Columbia – Beaufort Sea)	4,240	2,635
Mekong (Lants'ang, Tibet – South China Sea)	4,184	2,600
Niger (Loma Mts, Guinea – Gulf of Guinea, E. Atlantic Ocean)	4,168	2,590

River (source and outflow)	Length km	miles
Río de la Plata-Paraná (R. Paranáiba, central Brazil – S. Atlantic Ocean)	4,000	2,485
Murray-Darling (SE Queensland – Lake Alexandrina, S. Australia)	3,750	2,330
Volga (Valdai plateau – Caspian Sea)	3,690	2,293
Zambezi (NW Zambia – S. Indian Ocean)	3,540	2,200

OTHER NOTABLE RIVERS

St Lawrence (Minnesota, USA – Gulf of St Lawrence)	3,130	1,945
Ganges-Brahmaputra (R. Matsang, SW Tibet – Bay of Bengal)	2,900	1,800
Indus (R. Sengge, SW Tibet – N. Arabian Sea)	2,880	1,790
Danube (*Donau*) (Black Forest, SW Germany – Black Sea)	2,856	1,775
Tigris-Euphrates (R. Murat, E. Turkey – Persian Gulf)	2,740	1,700
Irrawaddy (R. Mali Hka, Myanmar – Andaman Sea)	2,151	1,337
Don (SE of Novomoskovsk – Sea of Azov)	1,969	1,224

BRITISH ISLES

Shannon (Co. Cavan, Rep. of Ireland – Atlantic Ocean)	386	240
Severn (Powys, Wales – Bristol Channel)	354	220
Thames (Gloucestershire, England – North Sea)	346	215
Tay (Perthshire, Scotland – North Sea)	188	117
Clyde (Lanarkshire, Scotland – Firth of Clyde)	158	98½
Tweed (Peeblesshire, Scotland – North Sea)	155	96½
Bann (Upper and Lower) (Co. Down, N. Ireland – Atlantic Ocean)	122	76

GREATEST WATERFALLS – BY HEIGHT

Waterfall (river and location)	Total drop metres	feet	Greatest single leap metres	feet
Angel (Carrao, Venezuela)	979	3,212	807	2,648
Tugela (Tugela, S. Africa)	947	3,110	410	1,350
Utigård (Jostedal Glacier, Norway)	800	2,625	600	1,970
Mongefossen (Monge, Norway)	774	2,540	—	—
Yosemite (Yosemite Creek, USA)	739	2,425	435	1,430
Østre Mardøla Foss (Mardals, Norway)	656	2,154	296	974
Tyssestrengane (Tysso, Norway)	646	2,120	289	948
Cuquenán (Arabopó, Venezuela)	610	2,000	—	—
Sutherland (Arthur, NZ)	580	1,904	248	815
*Kjellfossen (Naeröfjord, Norway)	561	1,841	149	490

*Volume often so low the fall atomizes into a 'bridal veil'

Waterfall (river and location)	Total drop		Greatest single leap	
	metres	feet	metres	feet
BRITISH ISLES (BY COUNTRY)				
Eas a' Chuàl Aluinn (Glas Bheinn, Sutherland, Scotland)	200	658		
Powerscourt Falls (Dargle, Co. Wicklow, Rep. of Ireland)	106	350		
Pistyll-y-Llyn (Powys/ Dyfed border, Wales)	c.73	240		(cascades)
Pistyll Rhyadr (Clwyd/ Powys border, Wales)	71.5	235		(single leap)
Caldron Snout (R. Tees, Cumbria/Durham, England)	61	200		(cascades)

GREATEST WATERFALLS – BY VOLUME

Waterfall (river and location)	Mean annual flow	
	m³/sec	galls/sec
Boyoma (R. Lualaba, Zaïre)	c.3,750,000	c.17,000
(Mekong, Laos) Khône	11,500	2,530,000
Niagara (Horseshoe) (R. Niagara/Lake Erie–Lake Ontario)	3,000	670,000
Paulo Afonso (R. São Francisco, Brazil)	2,800	625,000
Urubupunga (Alto Paraná, Brazil)	2,800	625,000
Cataratas del Iguazú (R. Iguaçu, Brazil/Argentina)	1,725	380,000
Patos-Maribando (Rio Grande, Brazil)	1,500	330,000
Victoria (Mosi-oa-tunya) (R. Zambezi, Zambia/ Zimbabwe)	1,000	220,000
Churchill (R. Churchill, Canada)	975	215,000
Kaieteur (R. Potaro, Guyana)	660	145,000

TALLEST DAMS

	metres	feet
Rogun, Tajikistan	335	1,098
Nurek, Russia	300	984
Grand Dixance, Switzerland	285	935
*Longtan, China	285	935
Inguri, Russia	272	892
Chicoasén, Mexico	261	856
*Tehri, India	261	856

*Under construction

The world's most massive dam is the Syncrude Tailings dam in Alberta, Canada, which will have a volume of 540 million cubic metres/706 million cubic yards

TALLEST INHABITED BUILDINGS

Building and city	Height	
	metres	feet
Petronas Towers I and II, Kuala Lumpur	450	1,476
Sears Tower, Chicago[1]	443	1,454
One World Trade Center Tower, New York[2]	417	1,368
Empire State Building, New York[3]	381	1,250
Amoco Building, Chicago	346	1,136
John Hancock Center, Chicago	343	1,127
Chrysler Building, New York	319	1,046
Bank of China, Hong Kong[4]	315	1,033
Nation's Bank Tower, Atlanta	312	1,023
First Interstate World Center, Los Angeles	310	1,017
Vegas World Tower	308	1,012
Central Plaza, Hong Kong[5]	306.5	1,005
Texas Commerce Tower, Houston	305	1,002

[1] With TV antennae 520 m/1,707 ft
[2] With TV antennae, 521.2 m/1,710 ft; Two World Trade Center Tower, 415 m/1,362 ft
[3] With TV tower (added 1950–1), 430.9 m/1,414 ft
[4] With steel mast, 367.4 m/1,205 ft
[5] With steel mast, 374 m/1,227 ft

TALLEST STRUCTURES

Structure and location	Height	
	metres	feet
*Warszawa Radio Mast, Konstantynow, Poland	646	2,120
KTHI-TV Mast, Fargo, North Dakota (guyed)	629	2,063
CN Tower, Metro Centre, Toronto, Canada	555	1,822
Ostankino Tower, Moscow	537	1,762

*Collapsed during renovation, August 1991

LONGEST BRIDGES – BY SPAN

Bridge and location	Length	
	metres	feet
SUSPENSION SPANS		
Humber Estuary, Humberside, England	1,410	4,626
Verrazano Narrows, Brooklyn–Staten I, USA	1,298	4,260
Golden Gate, San Francisco Bay, USA	1,280	4,200
Mackinac Straits, Michigan, USA	1,158	3,800
Minami Bisan-Seto, Japan	1,100	3,609
Bosporus I, Istanbul, Turkey	1,089	3,576
Bosporus II, Istanbul, Turkey	1,074	3,524
George Washington, Hudson River, New York City, USA	1,067	3,500
Ponte 25 Abril (Tagus), Lisbon, Portugal	1,013	3,323
Firth of Forth (road), nr Edinburgh, Scotland	1,006	3,300
Severn River, Severn Estuary, England	988	3,240

The Akashi-Kaikyo road bridge (1988–98) will have a main span of 1,990 m/6,528 ft and the Store Baelt East Bridge, Denmark (due for completion 1997) will have a span of 1,624 m/5,328 ft

Bridge and location	Length	
	metres	feet
CANTILEVER SPANS		
Pont de Québec (rail-road), St Lawrence, Canada	548.6	1,800
Ravenswood, W. Virginia, USA	525.1	1,723
Firth of Forth (rail), nr Edinburgh, Scotland	521.2	1,710
Nanko, Osaka, Japan	510.0	1,673
Commodore Barry, Chester, Pennsylvania, USA	494.3	1,622
Greater New Orleans, Louisiana, USA	480.0	1,575
Howrah (rail-road), Calcutta, India	457.2	1,500

STEEL ARCH SPANS

	metres	feet
New River Gorge, Fayetteville, W. Virginia, USA	553.8	1,817
Bayonne (Kill van Kull), Bayonne, NJ – Staten I, USA	503.5	1,652
Sydney Harbour, Sydney, Australia	502.9	1,650

The 'floating' bridging at Evergreen, Seattle, Washington State, USA, is 3,839 m/12,596 ft long
The longest stretch of bridgings of any kind are those between Mandeville and Jefferson, Louisiana, USA; the Lake Pontchartrain Causeway II 38.422 km/23.87 miles and Causeway I 38.352 km/23.83 miles

LONGEST VEHICULAR TUNNELS

Tunnel and location	Length	
	km	miles
*Seikan (rail), Tsugaru Channel, Japan	53.90	33.49
*Channel Tunnel, Cheriton, Kent – Sangatte, Calais	49.94	31.03
Moscow metro, Belyaevo – Bittsevsky, Moscow, Russia	37.90	23.50
Northern line tube, East Finchley – Morden, London	27.84	17.30
Oshimizu, Honshū, Japan	22.17	13.78
Simplon II (rail), Brigue, Switzerland – Iselle, Italy	19.82	12.31
Simplon I (rail), Brigue, Switzerland – Iselle, Italy	19.80	12.30
*Shin-Kanmon (rail), Kanmon Strait, Japan	18.68	11.61
Great Appennine (rail), Vernio, Italy	18.49	11.49
St Gotthard (road), Göschenen – Airolo, Switzerland	16.32	10.14
Rokko (rail), Ōsaka – Kōbe, Japan	16.09	10.00
*Sub-aqueous		

The longest non-vehicular tunnelling in the world is the Delaware Aqueduct in New York State, USA, constructed in 1937–44 to a length of 168.9 km/105 miles

BRITAIN – RAIL TUNNELS

	miles	yards
Severn, Bristol – Newport	4	484
Totley, Manchester – Sheffield	3	950
Standedge, Manchester – Huddersfield	3	66
Sodbury, Swindon – Bristol	2	924
Disley, Stockport – Sheffield	2	346

	miles	yards
Ffestiniog, Llandudno – Blaenau Ffestiniog	2	338
Bramhope, Leeds – Harrogate	2	241
Cowburn, Manchester – Sheffield	2	182

The longest road tunnel in Britain is the Mersey Road Tunnel, 2 miles 228 yards long. The longest canal tunnel, at Standedge, W. Yorks, is 3 miles 330 yards long; it was closed in 1944 but is currently being restored

LONGEST SHIP CANALS

Canal (opening date)	Length		Min. depth	
	km	miles	metres	feet
White Sea-Baltic (formerly Stalin) (1933) Canalized river; canal 51.5 km/32 miles	227	141.00	5.0	16.5
*Suez (1869) Links Red and Mediterranean Seas	162	100.60	12.9	42.3
V. I. Lenin Volga-Don (1952) Links Black and Caspian Seas	100	62.20	n/a	n/a
Kiel (or North Sea) (1895) Links North and Baltic Seas	98	60.90	13.7	45.0
*Houston (1940) Links inland city with sea	91	56.70	10.4	34.0
Alphonse XIII (1926) Gives Seville access to sea	85	53.00	7.6	25.0
Panama (1914) Links Pacific Ocean and Caribbean Sea; lake chain, 78.9 km/49 miles dug	82	50.71	12.5	41.0
Manchester Ship (1894) Links city with Irish Channel	64	39.70	8.5	28.0
Welland (1931) Circumvents Niagara Falls and Rapids	45	28.00	8.8	29.0
Brussels (Rupel Sea) (1922) Renders Brussels an inland port	32	19.80	6.4	21.0
*Has no locks				

The first section of China's Grand Canal, running 1,780 km/1,107 miles from Beijing to Hangchou, was opened AD 610
The longest boat canal in the world is the Volga-Baltic canal from Astrakhan to St Petersburg with 2,300 route km/1,850 miles

Distances from London by Air

The list of the distances in statute miles from London, Heathrow, to various cities (airport) abroad has been supplied by the publishers of *IATA/Serco-IAL Ltd Air Distances Manual*, Southall, Middx.

To	Miles
Abidjan	3,197
Abu Dhabi (International)	3,425
Addis Ababa	3,675
Adelaide (International)	10,111
Aden	3,670
Algiers	1,035
Amman (Queen Alia)	2,287
Amsterdam	230
Ankara (Esenboga)	1,770
Athens	1,500
Atlanta	4,198
Auckland	11,404
Baghdad (Saddam)	2,551
Bahrain	3,163
Baku	2,485
Bangkok	5,928
Barbados	4,193
Barcelona (Muntadas)	712
Basle	447
Beijing (Capital)	5,063
Beirut	2,161
Belfast (Aldergrove)	325
Belgrade	1,056
Berlin (Tegel)	588
Bermuda	3,428
Berne	476
Bogota	5,262
Bombay (Mumbai)	4,478
Boston	3,255
Brasilia	5,452
Bratislava	817
Brisbane (Eagle Farm)	10,273
Brussels	217
Bucharest (Otopeni)	1,307
Budapest	923
Buenos Aires	6,915
Cairo (International)	2,194
Calcutta	4,958
Calgary	4,357
Canberra	10,563
Cape Town	6,011
Caracas	4,639
Casablanca (Mohamed V)	1,300
Chicago (O'Hare)	3,941
Cologne	331
Colombo (Katunayake)	5,411
Copenhagen	608
Dakar	2,706
Dallas (Fort Worth)	4,736
Dallas (Lovefield)	4,732
Damascus (International)	2,223
Dar-es-Salaam	4,662
Darwin	8,613
Delhi	4,180
Denver	4,655

To	Miles
Detroit (Metropolitan)	3,754
Dhahran	3,143
Dhaka	4,976
Doha	3,253
Dubai	3,414
Dublin	279
Durban	5,937
Düsseldorf	310
Entebbe	4,033
Frankfurt (Main)	406
Freetown	3,046
Geneva	468
Gibraltar	1,084
Gothenburg (Landvetter)	664
Hamburg	463
Harare	5,156
Havana	4,647
Helsinki (Vantaa)	1,148
Hobart	10,826
Ho Chi Minh City	6,345
Hong Kong	5,990
Honolulu	7,220
Houston (Intercontinental)	4,821
Houston (William P. Hobby)	4,837
Islamabad	3,767
Istanbul	1,560
Jakarta (Halim Perdanakusuma)	7,295
Jeddah	2,947
Johannesburg	5,634
Kabul	3,558
Karachi	3,935
Kathmandu	4,570
Khartoum	3,071
Kiev (Borispol)	1,357
Kiev (Julyany)	1,337
Kingston, Jamaica	4,668
Kuala Lumpur (Subang)	6,557
Kuwait	2,903
Lagos	3,107
Larnaca	2,036
Lima	6,303
Lisbon	972
Lomé	3,129
Los Angeles (International)	5,439
Madras	5,113
Madrid	773
Malta	1,305
Manila	6,685
Marseille	614
Mauritius	6,075
Melbourne (Essendon)	10,504
Melbourne (Tullamarine)	10,499
Mexico City	5,529
Miami	4,414
Milan (Linate)	609
Minsk	1,176
Montego Bay	4,687
Montevideo	6,841
Montreal (Mirabel)	3,241
Moscow (Sheremetievo)	1,557
Munich (Franz Josef Strauss)	584

To	Miles
Muscat	3,621
Nairobi (Jomo Kenyatta)	4,248
Naples	1,011
Nassau	4,333
New York (J. F. Kennedy)	3,440
Nice	645
Oporto	806
Oslo (Fornebu)	722
Ottawa	3,321
Palma, Majorca (Son San Juan)	836
Paris (Charles de Gaulle)	215
Paris (Le Bourget)	215
Paris (Orly)	227
Perth, Australia	9,008
Port of Spain	4,404
Prague	649
Pretoria	5,602
Reykjavik (Domestic)	1,167
Reykjavik (Keflavik)	1,177
Rhodes	1,743
Rio de Janeiro	5,745
Riyadh	3,067
Rome (Fiumicino)	895
St John's, Newfoundland	2,308
St Petersburg	1,314
Salzburg	651
San Francisco	5,351
São Paulo	5,892
Sarajevo	1,017
Seoul (Kimpo)	5,507
Shanghai	5,725
Shannon	369
Singapore (Changi)	6,756
Sofia	1,266
Stockholm (Arlanda)	908
Suva	10,119
Sydney (Kingsford Smith)	10,568
Tangier	1,120
Tehran	2,741
Tel Aviv	2,227
Tokyo (Narita)	5,956
Toronto	3,544
Tripoli (International)	1,468
Tunis	1,137
Turin (Caselle)	570
Ulan Bator	4,340
Valencia	826
Vancouver	4,707
Venice (Tessera)	715
Vienna (Schwechat)	790
Vladivostok	5,298
Warsaw	912
Washington (Dulles)	3,665
Wellington	11,692
Yangon/Rangoon	5,582
Yokohama (Aomori)	5,647
Zagreb	848
Zürich	490

The United Kingdom

The United Kingdom comprises Great Britain (England, Wales and Scotland) and Northern Ireland. The Isle of Man and the Channel Islands are Crown dependencies with their own legislative systems, and not a part of the United Kingdom.

AREA AS AT 31 MARCH 1981

	Land miles²	km²	*Inland water miles²	km²	Total miles²	km²
United Kingdom	93,006	240,883	1,242	3,218	94,248	244,101
England	50,058	129,652	293	758	50,351	130,410
Wales	7,965	20,628	50	130	8,015	20,758
Scotland	29,767	77,097	653	1,692	30,420	78,789
†Northern Ireland	5,215	13,506	246	638	5,461	14,144
Isle of Man	221	572	—	—	221	572
Channel Islands	75	194	—	—	75	194

*Excluding tidal water
†Excluding certain tidal waters that are parts of statutory areas in Northern Ireland

POPULATION

The first official census of population in England, Wales and Scotland was taken in 1801 and a census has been taken every ten years since, except in 1941 when there was no census because of war. The last official census in the United Kingdom was taken on 21 April 1991 and the next is due in April 2001.

The first official census of population in Ireland was taken in 1841. However, all figures given below refer only to the area which is now Northern Ireland. Figures for Northern Ireland in 1921 and 1931 are estimates based on the censuses taken in 1926 and 1937 respectively.

Estimates of the population of England before 1801, calculated from the number of baptisms, burials and marriages, are:

1570	4,160,221	1670	5,773,646
1600	4,811,718	1700	6,045,008
1630	5,600,517	1750	6,517,035

	United Kingdom			England and Wales			Scotland			Northern Ireland		
Thousands	Total	Male	Female	Total	Male	Female	Total	Male	Female	Total	Male	Female
CENSUS RESULTS 1801–1991												
1801	—	—	—	8,893	4,255	4,638	1,608	739	869	—	—	—
1811	13,368	6,368	7,000	10,165	4,874	5,291	1,806	826	980	—	—	—
1821	15,472	7,498	7,974	12,000	5,850	6,150	2,092	983	1,109	—	—	—
1831	17,835	8,647	9,188	13,897	6,771	7,126	2,364	1,114	1,250	—	—	—
1841	20,183	9,819	10,364	15,914	7,778	8,137	2,620	1,242	1,378	1,649	800	849
1851	22,259	10,855	11,404	17,928	8,781	9,146	2,889	1,376	1,513	1,443	698	745
1861	24,525	11,894	12,631	20,066	9,776	10,290	3,062	1,450	1,612	1,396	668	728
1871	27,431	13,309	14,122	22,712	11,059	11,653	3,360	1,603	1,757	1,359	647	712
1881	31,015	15,060	15,955	25,974	12,640	13,335	3,736	1,799	1,936	1,305	621	684
1891	34,264	16,593	17,671	29,003	14,060	14,942	4,026	1,943	2,083	1,236	590	646
1901	38,237	18,492	19,745	32,528	15,729	16,799	4,472	2,174	2,298	1,237	590	647
1911	42,082	20,357	21,725	36,070	17,446	18,625	4,761	2,309	2,452	1,251	603	648
1921	44,027	21,033	22,994	37,887	18,075	19,811	4,882	2,348	2,535	1,258	610	648
1931	46,038	22,060	23,978	39,952	19,133	20,819	4,843	2,326	2,517	1,243	601	642
1951	50,225	24,118	26,107	43,758	21,016	22,742	5,096	2,434	2,662	1,371	668	703
1961	52,709	25,481	27,228	46,105	22,304	23,801	5,179	2,483	2,697	1,425	694	731
1971	55,515	26,952	28,562	48,750	23,683	25,067	5,229	2,515	2,714	1,536	755	781
1981	55,848	27,104	28,742	49,155	23,873	25,281	5,131	2,466	2,664	*1,533	750	783
1991	56,467	27,344	29,123	49,890	24,182	25,707	4,999	2,392	2,606	1,578	769	809
†RESIDENT POPULATION: PROJECTIONS (MID-YEAR)												
2001	59,800	29,475	30,325	52,989	26,148	26,841	5,143	2,508	2,636	1,667	819	848
2011	61,257	30,380	30,878	54,471	27,045	27,426	5,077	2,490	2,587	1,709	844	865
2021	62,146	30,883	31,263	55,320	27,518	27,802	5,051	2,486	2,565	1,775	879	896
2031	62,241	30,900	31,341	55,412	27,530	27,882	4,998	2,462	2,536	1,831	908	923

*Figures include 44,500 non-enumerated persons
† Projections are 1992 based

Source: HMSO – *Annual Abstract 1996*; OPCS – Census reports

ISLANDS: Census Results 1901–91

	Isle of Man			Jersey			*Guernsey		
	Total	Male	Female	Total	Male	Female	Total	Male	Female
1901	54,752	25,496	29,256	52,576	23,940	28,636	40,446	19,652	20,794
1911	52,016	23,937	28,079	51,898	24,014	27,884	41,858	20,661	21,197
1921	60,284	27,329	32,955	49,701	22,438	27,263	38,315	18,246	20,069
1931	49,308	22,443	26,865	50,462	23,424	27,038	40,643	19,659	20,984
1951	55,123	25,749	29,464	57,296	27,282	30,014	43,652	21,221	22,431
1961	48,151	22,060	26,091	57,200	27,200	30,000	45,068	21,671	23,397
1971	56,289	26,461	29,828	72,532	35,423	37,109	51,458	24,792	26,666
1981	64,679	30,901	33,778	77,000	37,000	40,000	53,313	25,701	27,612
1991	69,788	33,693	36,095	84,082	40,862	43,220	58,867	28,297	30,570

* Population of Guernsey, Herm, Jethou and Lithou. Figures for 1901–71 record all persons present on census night; census figures for 1981 and 1991 record all persons resident in the islands on census night
Source: 1991 Census

RESIDENT POPULATION

MID-YEAR ESTIMATE

	1984	1994
United Kingdom	56,506,000	58,395,000
England	47,004,000	48,708,000
Wales	2,806,000	2,913,000
Scotland	5,146,000	5,132,000
Northern Ireland	1,550,000	1,642,000

Source: HMSO – *Annual Abstract of Statistics 1996*

BY AGE AND SEX 1994

Males	Under 16	65 and over
United Kingdom	6,194,000	3,710,000
England	5,137,000	3,119,000
Wales	311,000	204,000
Scotland	531,000	304,000
Northern Ireland	214,000	83,000

Females	Under 16	60 and over
United Kingdom	5,881,000	6,920,000
England	4,874,000	5,774,000
Wales	295,000	376,000
Scotland	507,000	607,000
Northern Ireland	205,000	163,000

Source: HMSO – *Population Trends 84*

BY ETHNIC GROUP (1991 CENSUS (GREAT BRITAIN))

Ethnic group	Estimated population	Percentage
Caribbean	500,000	16.6
African	212,000	7
Other black	178,000	5.9
Indian	840,000	27.9
Pakistani	477,000	15.8
Bangladeshi	163,000	5.4
Chinese	157,000	5.2
Other Asian	198,000	6.6
Other	290,000	9.6
Total ethnic minority groups	3,015,000	100
White	51,874,000	—
All ethnic groups	54,889,000	—

Source: HMSO – *Population Trends 72*

AVERAGE DENSITY *Persons per hectare*

	1981	1991
England	3.55	3.61
Wales	1.34	1.36
Scotland	0.66	0.65
Northern Ireland	1.12	1.11

Sources: OPCS – Census reports

IMMIGRATION 1994
Acceptances for settlement in the UK by nationality

Region	Number of persons
Europe: total	4,650
European Economic Area	620
Remainder of Europe	4,040
Americas: total	7,890
USA	3,990
Canada	810
Africa: total	11,920
Asia: total	25,900
Indian sub-continent	14,070
Middle East	2,620
Oceania: total	2,850
British Overseas Citizens	710
Stateless	1,180
Total	55,110

Source: HMSO – *Annual Abstract of Statistics 1996*

LIVE BIRTHS AND BIRTH RATES 1994

	Live births	Birth rate*
United Kingdom	751,000	12.9
England and Wales	665,000	12.9
Scotland	62,000	12.0
Northern Ireland	24,000	14.9

*Live births per 1,000 population
Source: HMSO – *Annual Abstract of Statistics 1996*

LEGAL ABORTIONS 1994 (ENGLAND AND WALES)

Age group	Number
Under 16	3,250
16–19	25,200
20–34	108,500
35–44	19,200
45 and over	440
Age not stated	10
Total	156,500

Source: HMSO – Population Trends 84

BIRTHS OUTSIDE MARRIAGE (UK)

Age group	1981	1994
Under 20	30,000	41,000
20–24	33,000	80,000
25–29	16,000	65,000
Over 30	13,000	55,000
Total	91,000	240,000

Source: HMSO – Annual Abstract of Statistics 1996

MARRIAGE AND DIVORCE 1993

	Marriages	Divorces*
United Kingdom	341,246	—
England and Wales	299,197	165,018
Scotland	33,366	12,787
Northern Ireland	8,683	2,206

*Decrees absolute granted
Source: HMSO – Annual Abstract of Statistics 1996; Annual Report of the Registrar-General for Northern Ireland 1994

DEATHS AND DEATH RATES 1994

Males	Deaths	Death rate*
United Kingdom	303,333	10.6
England and Wales	267,555	—
Scotland	28,416	—
Northern Ireland	7,362	—
Females		
United Kingdom	324,303	10.9
England and Wales	285,639	—
Scotland	30,912	—
Northern Ireland	7,752	—

* Deaths per 1,000 population
Sources: OPCS; Annual Report of the Registrar-General for Scotland 1994; Annual Report of the Registrar-General for Northern Ireland 1994

INFANT MORTALITY 1994
Deaths of infants under 1 year of age per 1,000 live births

	Number
United Kingdom	6.2
England and Wales	6.2
Scotland	6.2
Northern Ireland	6.1

Source: HMSO – Annual Abstract of Statistics 1996

EXPECTATION OF LIFE LIFE TABLES 1991–93 (INTERIM FIGURES)

	England and Wales		Scotland		Northern Ireland	
Age	Male	Female	Male	Female	Male	Female
0	73.7	79.1	71.5	77.1	72.5	78.3
5	69.3	74.6	67.2	72.6	68.2	73.9
10	64.4	69.7	62.3	67.7	63.2	68.9
15	59.4	64.7	57.3	62.8	58.3	64.0
20	54.6	59.8	52.5	57.9	53.6	59.1
25	49.8	54.9	47.8	52.9	48.9	54.2
30	45.0	50.0	43.1	48.1	44.1	49.3
35	40.2	45.1	38.3	43.2	39.3	44.4
40	35.5	40.3	33.6	38.4	34.6	39.6
45	30.8	35.5	29.0	33.7	29.9	34.8
50	26.3	30.9	24.6	29.1	25.4	30.2
55	22.0	26.4	20.5	24.8	21.2	25.7
60	18.0	22.1	16.7	20.6	17.2	21.5
65	14.3	18.1	13.3	16.8	13.7	17.6
70	11.2	14.5	10.4	13.4	10.7	13.9
75	8.6	11.2	8.0	10.3	8.2	10.7
80	6.5	8.4	6.0	7.7	6.1	8.0
85	4.8	6.1	4.5	5.6	4.5	5.7

Source: HMSO – Annual Abstract of Statistics 1996

DEATHS ANALYSED BY CAUSE 1994

	England & Wales	Scotland	N. Ireland
TOTAL DEATHS	553,194	59,328	15,114
Infectious and parasitic diseases	3,318	306	39
Neoplasms	141,747	15,394	3,665
Malignant neoplasm of stomach	7,590	754	201
Malignant neoplasm of colon	10,899	1,139	324
Malignant neoplasm of rectum, rectosigmoid junction and anus	5,022	602	114
Malignant neoplasm of trachea, bronchus and lung	32,143	4,237	768
Malignant neoplasm of female breast	12,830	1,275	338
Leukaemia	3,507	290	94
Endocrine, nutritional and metabolic diseases and immunity disorders	7,430	754	73
Diabetes mellitus	5,938	503	45
Diseases of blood and blood-forming organs	1,898	121	29
Mental disorders	8,042	1,306	91
Diseases of the nervous system and sense organs	9,010	853	187
Meningitis	170	24	21
Diseases of the circulatory system	242,213	27,138	7,011
Chronic rheumatic heart disease	1,719	175	30
Hypertensive disease	2,800	312	79
Ischaemic heart disease	135,440	15,234	4,168
Diseases of pulmonary circulation and other forms of heart disease	25,795	2,200	633
Cerebrovascular disease	58,768	7,684	1,738
Atherosclerosis	2,480	281	49
Diseases of the respiratory system	81,484	6,981	2,398
Pneumonia	48,917	3,757	1,595
Diseases of the digestive system	18,635	2,192	424
Ulcer of stomach and duodenum	4,111	380	100
Chronic liver disease and cirrhosis	3,244	555	66
Diseases of the genitourinary system	6,812	816	220
Complications of pregnancy, childbirth and the puerperium	50	9	—
Diseases of the skin, musculoskeletal system and connective tissue	4,513	380	58
Congenital anomalies	1,301	170	131
Certain conditions originating in the perinatal period	147	191	69
Signs, symptoms and ill-defined conditions	7,754	331	44
Injury and Poisoning	16,091	2,372	688
Motor vehicle traffic accidents	3,232	352	158
Suicide and self-inflicted injury	3,619	624	138

Sources: OPCS; General Register Office for Scotland; *Annual Report of the Registrar-General for Northern Ireland 1994*

The National Flag

The national flag of the United Kingdom is the Union Flag, generally known as the Union Jack. (The name 'Union Jack' derives from the use of the Union Flag on the jack-staff of naval vessels.)

The Union Flag is a combination of the cross of St George, patron saint of England, the cross of St Andrew, patron saint of Scotland, and a cross similar to that of St Patrick, patron saint of Ireland.

Cross of St George: cross Gules in a field Argent (red cross on a white ground).

Cross of St Andrew: saltire Argent in a field Azure (white diagonal cross on a blue ground).

Cross of St Patrick: saltire Gules in a field Argent (red diagonal cross on a white ground).

The Union Flag was first introduced in 1606 after the union of the kingdoms of England and Scotland under one sovereign. The cross of St Patrick was added in 1801 after the union of Great Britain and Ireland.

DAYS FOR FLYING FLAGS

The correct orientation of the Union Flag when flying is with the broader diagonal band of white uppermost in the hoist (i.e. near the pole) and the narrower diagonal band of white uppermost in the fly (i.e. furthest from the pole).

It is the practice to fly the Union Flag daily on some customs houses. In all other cases, flags are flown on government buildings by command of The Queen.

Days for hoisting the Union Flag are notified to the Department of National Heritage by The Queen's command and communicated by the department to the other government departments. On the days appointed, the Union Flag is flown on government buildings in the United Kingdom from 8 a.m. to sunset.

The Queen's Accession	6 February
Birthday of The Duke of York	19 February
*St David's Day (in Wales only)	1 March
Birthday of The Prince Edward	10 March
Commonwealth Day (1997)	10 March
Birthday of The Queen	21 April
*St George's Day (in England only)	23 April
Coronation Day	2 June
Birthday of The Duke of Edinburgh	10 June
The Queen's Official Birthday (1997)	14 June
Birthday of Diana, Princess of Wales	1 July
Birthday of Queen Elizabeth the Queen Mother	4 August
Birthday of The Princess Royal	15 August
Birthday of The Princess Margaret	21 August
Remembrance Sunday (1997)	9 November
Birthday of The Prince of Wales	14 November
The Queen's Wedding Day	20 November
*St Andrew's Day (in Scotland only)	30 November
†The opening of Parliament by The Queen	
†The prorogation of Parliament by The Queen	

*Where a building has two or more flagstaffs, the appropriate national flag may be flown in addition to the Union Flag, but not in a superior position
†Flags are flown whether or not The Queen performs the ceremony in person. Flags are flown only in the Greater London area

FLAGS AT HALF-MAST

Flags are flown at half-mast on the following occasions:

(a) From the announcement of the death up to the funeral of the Sovereign, except on Proclamation Day, when flags are hoisted right up from 11 a.m. to sunset
(b) The funerals of members of the Royal Family, subject to special commands from The Queen in each case
(c) The funerals of foreign rulers, subject to special commands from The Queen in each case
(d) The funerals of Prime Ministers and ex-Prime Ministers of the United Kingdom, subject to special commands from The Queen in each case
(e) Other occasions by special command of The Queen

On occasions when days for flying flags coincide with days for flying flags at half-mast, the following rules are observed. Flags are flown:

(a) although a member of the Royal Family, or a near relative of the Royal Family, may be lying dead, unless special commands be received from The Queen to the contrary
(b) although it may be the day of the funeral of a foreign ruler

If the body of a very distinguished subject is lying at a government office, the flag may fly at half-mast on that office until the body has left (provided it is a day on which the flag would fly) and then the flag is to be hoisted right up. On all other government buildings the flag will fly as usual.

THE ROYAL STANDARD

The Royal Standard is hoisted only when The Queen is actually present in the building, and never when Her Majesty is passing in procession.

The Royal Family

ELIZABETH II, by the Grace of God, of the United Kingdom of Great Britain and Northern Ireland and of her other Realms and Territories Queen, Head of the Commonwealth, Defender of the Faith

Her Majesty Elizabeth Alexandra Mary of Windsor, elder daughter of King George VI and of HM Queen Elizabeth the Queen Mother
Born 21 April 1926, at 17 Bruton Street, London W1
Ascended the throne 6 February 1952
Crowned 2 June 1953, at Westminster Abbey
Married 20 November 1947, in Westminster Abbey, HRH The Duke of Edinburgh
Official residences: Buckingham Palace, London SW1; Windsor Castle, Berks; Palace of Holyroodhouse, Edinburgh
Private residences: Sandringham, Norfolk; Balmoral Castle, Aberdeenshire
Office: Buckingham Palace, London SW1A 1AA. Tel: 0171-930 4832

HUSBAND OF HM THE QUEEN

HRH THE PRINCE PHILIP, DUKE OF EDINBURGH, KG, KT, OM, GBE, AC, QSO, PC, Ranger of Windsor Park
Born 10 June 1921, son of Prince and Princess Andrew of Greece and Denmark (*see* page 129), naturalized a British subject 1947, created Duke of Edinburgh, Earl of Merioneth and Baron Greenwich 1947

CHILDREN OF HM THE QUEEN

HRH THE PRINCE OF WALES (Prince Charles Philip Arthur George), KG, KT, GCB and Great Master of the Order of the Bath, AK, QSO, PC, ADC(P)
Born 14 November 1948, created Prince of Wales and Earl of Chester 1958, succeeded as Duke of Cornwall, Duke of Rothesay, Earl of Carrick and Baron Renfrew, Lord of the Isles and Prince and Great Steward of Scotland 1952
Married 29 July 1981 Lady Diana Frances Spencer, now Diana, Princess of Wales (*born* 1 July 1961, youngest daughter of the 8th Earl Spencer and the Hon. Mrs Shand Kydd), marriage dissolved 1996
Issue:
(1) HRH Prince William of Wales (Prince William Arthur Philip Louis), *born* 21 June 1982
(2) HRH Prince Henry of Wales (Prince Henry Charles Albert David), *born* 15 September 1984
Residences of the Prince of Wales: St James's Palace, London SW1A 1BS; Highgrove, Doughton, Tetbury, Glos.
Office of the Prince of Wales: St James's Palace, London SW1A 1BS. Tel: 0171-930 4832
Residence of Diana, Princess of Wales: Kensington Palace, London W8 4PU
Office of Diana, Princess of Wales, St James's Palace, London SW1A 1BS. Tel: 0171-930 4832

HRH THE PRINCESS ROYAL (Princess Anne Elizabeth Alice Louise), KG, GCVO

Born 15 August 1950, declared The Princess Royal 1987
Married (1) 14 November 1973 Captain Mark Anthony Peter Phillips, CVO (*born* 22 September 1948); marriage dissolved 1992; (2) 12 December 1992 Captain Timothy James Hamilton Laurence, MVO (*born* 1 March 1955)
Issue:
(1) Peter Mark Andrew Phillips, *born* 15 November 1977
(2) Zara Anne Elizabeth Phillips, *born* 15 May 1981
Residence: Gatcombe Park, Minchinhampton, Glos.
Office: Buckingham Palace, London SW1A 1AA. Tel: 0171-930 4832

HRH THE DUKE OF YORK (Prince Andrew Albert Christian Edward), CVO, ADC(P)
Born 19 February 1960, created Duke of York, Earl of Inverness and Baron Killyleagh 1986
Married 23 July 1986 Sarah Margaret Ferguson, now The Duchess of York (*born* 15 October 1959, younger daughter of Major Ronald Ferguson and Mrs Hector Barrantes), marriage dissolved 1996
Issue:
(1) HRH Princess Beatrice of York (Princess Beatrice Elizabeth Mary), *born* 8 August 1988
(2) HRH Princess Eugenie of York (Princess Eugenie Victoria Helena), *born* 23 March 1990
Residences: Buckingham Palace, London SW1; Sunninghill Park, Ascot, Berks.
Office: Buckingham Palace, London SW1 1AA. Tel: 0171-930 4832

HRH THE PRINCE EDWARD (Prince Edward Antony Richard Louis), CVO
Born 10 March 1964
Residence and Office: Buckingham Palace, London SW1A 1AA. Tel: 0171-930 4832

SISTER OF HM THE QUEEN

HRH THE PRINCESS MARGARET, COUNTESS OF SNOWDON, CI, GCVO, Royal Victorian Chain, Dame Grand Cross of the Order of St John of Jerusalem
Born 21 August 1930, younger daughter of King George VI and HM Queen Elizabeth the Queen Mother
Married 6 May 1960 Antony Charles Robert Armstrong-Jones, GCVO (*born* 7 March 1930, created Earl of Snowdon 1961, Constable of Caernarvon Castle); marriage dissolved 1978
Issue:
(1) David Albert Charles, Viscount Linley, *born* 3 November 1961, *married* 8 October 1993 the Hon. Serena Stanhope
(2) Lady Sarah Chatto (Sarah Frances Elizabeth), *born* 1 May 1964, *married* 14 July 1994 Daniel Chatto, and has issue, Samuel David Benedict Chatto, *born* 28 July 1996
Residence and Office: Kensington Palace, London W8 4PU. Tel: 0171-930 3141

MOTHER OF HM THE QUEEN

HM QUEEN ELIZABETH THE QUEEN MOTHER (Elizabeth Angela Marguerite), Lady of the Garter, Lady of the Thistle, CI, GCVO, GBE, Dame Grand Cross of the Order of

St John, Royal Victorian Chain, Lord Warden and Admiral of the Cinque Ports and Constable of Dover Castle
Born 4 August 1900, youngest daughter of the 14th Earl of Strathmore and Kinghorne
Married 26 April 1923 (as Lady Elizabeth Bowes-Lyon) Prince Albert, Duke of York, afterwards King George VI (*see* page 128)
Residences: Clarence House, St James's Palace, London SW1; Royal Lodge, Windsor Great Park, Berks; Castle of Mey, Caithness
Office: Clarence House, St James's Palace, London SW1A 1BA. Tel: 0171-930 3141

AUNT OF HM THE QUEEN

HRH PRINCESS ALICE, DUCHESS OF GLOUCESTER (Alice Christabel), GCB, CI, GCVO, GBE, Grand Cordon of Al Kamal
Born 25 December 1901, third daughter of the 7th Duke of Buccleuch and Queensberry
Married 6 November 1935 (as Lady Alice Montagu-Douglas-Scott) Prince Henry, Duke of Gloucester, third son of King George V (*see* page 128)
Residence and Office: Kensington Palace, London W8 4PU. Tel: 0171-937 6374

COUSINS OF HM THE QUEEN

HRH THE DUKE OF GLOUCESTER (Prince Richard Alexander Walter George), GCVO, Grand Prior of the Order of St John of Jerusalem
Born 26 August 1944
Married 8 July 1972 Birgitte Eva van Deurs, now HRH The Duchess of Gloucester, GCVO (*born* 20 June 1946, daughter of Asger Henriksen and Vivian van Deurs)
Issue:
(1)   Earl of Ulster (Alexander Patrick Gregers Richard), *born* 24 October 1974
(2)   Lady Davina Windsor (Davina Elizabeth Alice Benedikte), *born* 19 November 1977
(3)   Lady Rose Windsor (Rose Victoria Birgitte Louise), *born* 1 March 1980
Residence and Office: Kensington Palace, London W8 4PU. Tel: 0171-937 6374

HRH THE DUKE OF KENT (Prince Edward George Nicholas Paul Patrick), KG, GCMG, GCVO, ADC(P)
Born 9 October 1935
Married 8 June 1961 Katharine Lucy Mary Worsley, now HRH The Duchess of Kent, GCVO (*born* 22 February 1933, daughter of Sir William Worsley, Bt.)
Issue:
(1)   Earl of St Andrews (George Philip Nicholas), *born* 26 June 1962, *married* 9 January 1988 Sylvana Tomaselli, and has issue, Edward Edmund Maximilian George, Baron Downpatrick, *born* 2 December 1988; Lady Marina Charlotte Alexandra Katharine Windsor, *born* 30 September 1992; Lady Amelia Sophia Theodora Mary Margaret Windsor, *born* 24 August 1995
(2)   Lady Helen Taylor (Helen Marina Lucy), *born* 28 April 1964, *married* 18 July 1992 Timothy Taylor, and has issue, Columbus George Donald Taylor, *born* 6 August 1994
(3)   Lord Nicholas Windsor (Nicholas Charles Edward Jonathan), *born* 25 July 1970
Residence and Office: York House, St James's Palace, London SW1 1BQ. Tel: 0171-930 4872

HRH PRINCESS ALEXANDRA, THE HON. LADY OGILVY (Princess Alexandra Helen Elizabeth Olga Christabel), GCVO *Born* 25 December 1936
Married 24 April 1963 The Hon. Sir Angus Ogilvy, KCVO (*born* 14 September 1928, second son of 12th Earl of Airlie)
Issue:
(1)   James Robert Bruce Ogilvy, *born* 29 February 1964, *married* 30 July 1988 Julia Rawlinson, and has issue, Flora Alexandra Ogilvy, *born* 15 December 1994
(2)   Marina Victoria Alexandra, Mrs Mowatt, *born* 31 July 1966, *married* 2 February 1990 Paul Mowatt (separated 1996), and has issue, Zenouska May Mowatt, *born* 26 May 1990; Christian Alexander Mowatt, *born* 4 June 1993
Residence: Thatched House Lodge, Richmond Park, Surrey
Office: Buckingham Palace, London SW1A 1AA. Tel: 0171-930 1860

HRH PRINCE MICHAEL OF KENT (Prince Michael George Charles Franklin), KCVO
Born 4 July 1942
Married 30 June 1978 Baroness Marie-Christine Agnes Hedwig Ida von Reibnitz, now HRH Princess Michael of Kent (*born* 15 January 1945, daughter of Baron Gunther von Reibnitz)
Issue:
(1)   Lord Frederick Windsor (Frederick Michael George David Louis), *born* 6 April 1979
(2)   Lady Gabriella Windsor (Gabriella Marina Alexandra Ophelia), *born* 23 April 1981
Residences: Kensington Palace, London W8 4PU; Nether Lypiatt Manor, Stroud, Glos.
Office: Kensington Palace, London W8 4PU. Tel: 0171-938 3519

ORDER OF SUCCESSION

1   HRH The Prince of Wales
2   HRH Prince William of Wales
3   HRH Prince Henry of Wales
4   HRH The Duke of York
5   HRH Princess Beatrice of York
6   HRH Princess Eugenie of York
7   HRH The Prince Edward
8   HRH The Princess Royal
9   Peter Phillips
10   Zara Phillips
11   HRH The Princess Margaret, Countess of Snowdon
12   Viscount Linley
13   Lady Sarah Chatto
14   Samuel Chatto
15   HRH The Duke of Gloucester
16   Earl of Ulster
17   Lady Davina Windsor
18   Lady Rose Windsor
19   HRH The Duke of Kent
20   Baron Downpatrick
21   Lady Marina Charlotte Windsor
22   Lady Amelia Windsor
23   Lord Nicholas Windsor
24   Lady Helen Taylor
25   Columbus Taylor
26   Lord Frederick Windsor
27   Lady Gabriella Windsor
28   HRH Princess Alexandra, the Hon. Lady Ogilvy
29   James Ogilvy
30   Flora Ogilvy
31   Marina, Mrs Paul Mowatt

Royal Households

THE QUEEN'S HOUSEHOLD

Lord Chamberlain, The Earl of Airlie, KT, GCVO, PC
Lord Steward, The Viscount Ridley, KG, GCVO, TD
Master of the Horse, The Lord Somerleyton, KCVO
Treasurer of the Household, A. Mackay, MP
Comptroller of the Household, T. Wood, MP
Vice-Chamberlain, D. Conway, MP

Gold Sticks, Maj.-Gen. Lord Michael Fitzalan-Howard,
GCVO, CB, CBE, MC; Gen. Sir Desmond Fitzpatrick, GCB,
DSO, MBE, MC
Vice-Adm. of the United Kingdom, Adm. Sir James Eberle, GCB
Rear-Adm. of the United Kingdom, Adm. Sir Nicholas Hunt,
GCB, LVO
First and Principal Naval Aide-de-Camp, Adm. Sir Jock Slater,
GCB, LVO
Flag Aide-de-Camp, Adm. Sir Michael Boyce, KCB, OBE
Aides-de-Camp-General, Gen. Sir Charles Guthrie, GCB,
LVO, OBE; Gen. Sir John Wilsey, GCB, CBE; Gen. Sir
Michael Rose, KCB, CBE, DSO, QGM
Air Aides-de-Camp, Air Chief Marshal Sir Michael
Graydon, GCB, CBE; Air Chief Marshal Sir William
Wratten, KBE, CB, AFC

Mistress of the Robes, The Duchess of Grafton, GCVO
Ladies of the Bedchamber, The Countess of Airlie, DCVO; The
Lady Farnham
Extra Lady of the Bedchamber, The Marchioness of
Abergavenny, DCVO
Women of the Bedchamber, Hon. Mary Morrison, DCVO; Lady
Susan Hussey, DCVO; Lady Dugdale, DCVO; The Lady
Elton
Extra Women of the Bedchamber, The Hon. Mrs Van der
Woude, CVO; Mrs John Woodroffe, CVO; Mrs Michael
Wall, DCVO; Lady Abel Smith, DCVO; Mrs Robert de Pass
Equerries, Lt.-Col. Sir Guy Acland, Bt., MVO; Lt.-Cdr. T.
Williamson; Capt. C. Winter (temp.)
Extra Equerries, Vice-Adm. Sir Peter Ashmore, KCB, KCVO,
DSC; Maj. Sir Shane Blewitt, GCVO; Lt.-Col. The Lord
Charteris of Amisfield, GCB, GCVO,QSO, OBE, PC; Maj.-
Gen. Sir Simon Cooper, KCVO; Air Cdre the Hon. T.
Elworthy, CVO, CBE; The Rt Hon. Sir Robert Fellowes,
GCVO, KCB; Sir Edward Ford, KCB, KCVO, ERD; Rear-
Adm. Sir John Garnier, KCVO, CBE; Rear-Adm. Sir Paul
Greening, GCVO; Brig. Sir Geoffrey Hardy-Roberts,
KCVO, CB, CBE; The Rt. Hon. Sir William Heseltine,
GCB, GCVO, AC, QSO; Lt.-Col. Sir John Johnston, GCVO,
MC; Lt.-Col. A. Mather, OBE; Sir Peter Miles, KCVO; Lt.-
Col. Sir John Miller, GCVO, DSO, MC; Air Cdre Sir
Dennis Mitchell, KBE, CVO, DFC, AFC; The Lord Moore
of Wolvercote, GCB, GCVO, CMG, QSO; Lt.-Gen. Sir John
Richards, KCB, KCVO; Lt.-Col. W. H. M. Ross, CVO, OBE;
Sir Kenneth Scott, KCVO, CMG; Air Vice-Marshal Sir
John Severne, KCVO, OBE, AFC; Lt.-Col. Sir Blair
Stewart-Wilson, KCVO; Rear-Adm. Sir Richard
Trowbridge, KCVO; Lt.-Col. G. West, CVO; Air Cdre Sir
Archie Winskill, KCVO, CBE, DFC, AE; Rear-Adm. Sir
Robert Woodard, KCVO

THE PRIVATE SECRETARY'S OFFICE

Buckingham Palace, London SW1A 1AA
Private Secretary to The Queen, The Rt Hon. Sir Robert
Fellowes, GCVO, KCB

Deputy Private Secretary, R. B. Janvrin, CVO
Assistant Private Secretary, Mrs M. Francis
Special Assistant to the Private Secretary, S. Gimson
Press Secretary, C. V. Anson, CVO
Deputy Press Secretary, G. Crawford, LVO
Assistant Press Secretary, Miss P. Russell-Smith
Chief Clerk, Mrs G. S. Coulson, LVO
Secretary to the Private Secretary, Miss E. Ash

THE QUEEN'S ARCHIVES
Round Tower, Windsor Castle, Berks
Keeper of The Queen's Archives, The Rt Hon. Sir Robert
Fellowes, GCVO, KCB
Assistant Keeper, O. Everett, CVO
Registrar, Lady de Bellaigue, MVO

THE PRIVY PURSE AND TREASURER'S OFFICE

Buckingham Palace, London SW1A 1AA
Keeper of the Privy Purse and Treasurer to The Queen, M. Peat,
CVO
Deputy Keeper of the Privy Purse and Deputy Treasurer,
J. Parsons, LVO
Chief Accountant and Paymaster, I. McGregor
Personnel Officer, Miss P. Lloyd
Land Agent, Sandringham, J. Major, FRICS
Resident Factor, Balmoral, P. Ord, FRICS
Master of The Queen's Music, M. Williamson, CBE, AO
Poet Laureate, Ted Hughes, OBE
Keeper of the Royal Philatelic Collection, C. Goodwyn

PROPERTY SERVICES
Director of Property Services, J. Tiltman
Superintending Architect, G. Sharpe

ROYAL ALMONRY
High Almoner, The Rt. Revd John Taylor
Hereditary Grand Almoner, The Marquess of Exeter
Sub-Almoner, Revd W. Booth
Secretary, C. Williams, RVM
Assistant Secretary, P. Hartley, LVO

THE LORD CHAMBERLAIN'S OFFICE

Buckingham Palace, London SW1A 1AA
Comptroller, Lt.-Col. W. H. M. Ross, CVO, OBE
Assistant Comptroller, Lt.-Col. A. Mather, OBE
Secretary, J. Spencer, MVO
State Invitations Assistant, J. O. Hope
Permanent Lords-in-Waiting, Lt.-Col. the Lord Charteris of
Amisfield, GCB, GCVO, OBE, QSO, PC; The Lord Moore of
Wolvercote, GCB, GCVO, CMG, QSO
Lords-in-Waiting, The Lord Camoys; The Viscount Long,
CBE; The Lord Lucas of Crudwell; The Earl of
Courtown
Baronesses-in-Waiting, The Baroness Trumpington; The
Baroness Miller of Hendon, MBE
Gentlemen Ushers, Maj. N. Chamberlayne-Macdonald, LVO,
OBE; Capt. M. Barrow, DSO, RN; Capt. M. Fulford-
Dobson, RN; Lt.-Gen. Sir Richard Vickers, KCB, LVO,
OBE; Air Vice-Marshal B. Newton, CB, OBE; Col.
M. Havergal, OBE; Rear Adm. C. H. D. Cooke-Priest, CB;
Air Vice-Marshal D. Hawkins, CB, MBE; Maj.-Gen. B.
Pennicott, CVO; Gp Capt. H. Rolfe, CVO, CBE

Extra Gentlemen Ushers, Maj. T. Harvey, CVO, DSO, ERD; Lt.-Col. Sir John Hugo, KCVO, OBE; Vice-Adm. Sir Ronald Brockman, KCB, CSI, CIE, CVO, CBE; Air Marshal Sir Maurice Heath, KBE, CB, CVO; Sir James Scholtens, KCVO; Sir Patrick O'Dea, KCVO; Adm. Sir David Williams, GCB; H. Davis, CVO, CM; Maj.-Gen. R. Reid, CVO, MC, CD; Lt.-Cdr. J. Holdsworth, CVO, OBE, RN; Col. G. Leigh, CVO, CBE; Lt.-Cdr. Sir Russell Wood, KCVO, VRD; Maj.-Gen. Sir Desmond Rice, KCVO, CBE; Lt.-Col. Sir Julian Paget, Bt., CVO; S. W. F. Martin, CVO; J. Haslam, CVO; Prof. Sir Norman Blacklock, KCVO, OBE, FRCS; Air Marshal Sir Roy Austen-Smith, KBE, CB, CVO, DFC; Vice-Adm. Sir David Loram, KCB, CVO; Sir Carron Greig, KCVO, CBE; Gp Capt J. Slessor, CVO
Gentleman Usher to the Sword of State, Gen. Sir Edward Burgess, KCB, OBE
Gentleman Usher of the Black Rod, Gen. Sir Edward Jones, KCB, CBE
Serjeants-at-Arms, Maj. B. Eastwood, LVO, MBE; M. Jephson, MVO
Marshal of the Diplomatic Corps, Vice-Adm. Sir James Weatherall, KBE
Vice-Marshal, P. Astley, LVO
Constable and Governor of Windsor Castle, Gen. Sir Patrick Palmer, KBE
Bargemaster, R. Crouch
Swan Warden, Prof. C. Perrins, LVO
Swan Marker, D. Barber
Superintendent of the State Apartments, St James's Palace, B. Andrews, BEM

ECCLESIASTICAL HOUSEHOLD

THE COLLEGE OF CHAPLAINS

Clerk of the Closet, Rt. Revd J. Waine
Deputy Clerk of the Closet, Revd W. Booth
Chaplains to The Queen, Ven. D. N. Griffiths, RD; Revd Canon J. V. Bean; Revd K. Huxley; Ven. P. Ashford; Revd Canon D. C. Gray, TD; Revd Canon J. Hester; Revd S. Pedley; Revd Canon M. A. Moxon; Revd Canon G. Murphy, LVO; Revd D. J. Burgess; Revd E. R. Ayerst; Revd R. S. Clarke; Revd Canon K. Pound; Revd J. Haslam; Revd Canon G. Hall; Revd Canon A. C. Hill; Revd J. C. Priestley; Revd Canon J. O. Colling; Revd Canon G. Jones; Revd Canon D. G. Palmer; Revd Canon D. H. Wheaton; Revd Canon P. Boulton; Revd Canon R. A. Bowden; Revd Canon E. Buchanan; Revd J. Robson; Revd Canon J. Stanley; Revd Canon I. Hardaker; Revd Canon L. F. Webber; Ven. F. Bentley; Revd D. Adams; Revd Canon J. Sykes; Revd Canon I. Smith-Cameron; Revd Canon A. Craig; Ven. D. Fleming; Revd Canon R. Gilbert; Ven. D. Bartles-Smith; Revd Canon I. Knox; Revd Canon M. Mingins
Extra Chaplains, Preb. S. A. Williams, CVO; Ven. E. J. G. Ward, LVO; Revd J. R W. Stott; Revd Canon A. D. Caesar, CVO; Revd Canon E. James; Revd Canon J. G. M. W. Murphy, LVO

CHAPELS ROYAL

Dean of the Chapels Royal, The Bishop of London
Sub-Dean of Chapels Royal, Revd W. Booth
Priests in Ordinary, Revd S. E. Young; Revd R. Bolton; Revd P. Hunt
Organist, Choirmaster and Composer, R. J. Popplewell, MVO, FRCO, FRCM
Domestic Chaplain, Buckingham Palace, Revd W. Booth
Domestic Chaplain, Windsor Castle, The Dean of Windsor
Domestic Chaplain, Sandringham, Revd Canon G. R. Hall

Chaplain, Royal Chapel, Windsor Great Park, Revd Canon M. Moxon
Chaplain, Hampton Court Palace, Revd Canon M. Moore
Chaplain, Tower of London, Revd P. Abram
Organist and Choirmaster, Hampton Court Palace, C. Jackson

MEDICAL HOUSEHOLD

Head of the Medical Household and Physician to The Queen, R. Thompson, DM, FRCP
Physician, R. W. Davey, MB, BS
Serjeant Surgeon, B. T. Jackson, MS, FRCS
Surgeon Oculist, P. Holmes Sellors, LVO, FRCS, FRCophth.
Surgeon Gynaecologist, M. E. Setchell, FRCS, FRCOG
Surgeon Dentist, N. A. Sturridge, CVO, LDS, BDS, DDS
Orthopaedic Surgeon, R. H. Vickers, BM, B.ch., FRCS
Physician to the Household, J. Cunningham, DM, FRCP
Surgeon to the Household, A. A. M. Lewis, MB, FRCS
Surgeon Oculist to the Household, T. J. ffytche, MB, FRCS, FRCophth.
Apothecary to The Queen and to the Household, N. R. Southward, CVO, MB, B.chir.
Apothecary to the Household at Windsor, J. H. D. Briscoe, MB, B.chir., D.obst., FRCGP
Apothecary to the Household at Sandringham, I. K. Campbell, MB, BS, D.obst., FRCGP
Coroner of The Queen's Household, J. Burton, CBE, MB, BS

CENTRAL CHANCERY OF THE ORDERS OF KNIGHTHOOD
St James's Palace, London SWIA IBS
Secretary, Lt.-Col. A. Mather, OBE
Assistant Secretary, Miss R. Wells, MVO

THE HONOURABLE CORPS OF GENTLEMEN-AT-ARMS
St James's Palace, London SWIA IBS
Captain, The Lord Strathclyde, PC
Lieutenant, Col. T. A. Hall, OBE
Standard Bearer, Maj. Sir Fergus Matheson of Matheson, Bt.
Clerk of the Cheque and Adjutant, Lt.-Col. R. Mayfield, DSO
Harbinger, Maj. Sir Philip Duncombe, Bt.

Gentlemen of the Corps

Colonels, Sir Piers Bengough, KCVO, OBE; Hon. N. Crossley, TD; T. Wilson; D. Fanshawe, OBE; J. Baker; R. ffrench Blake; Sir William Mahon, Bt.; Sir Brian Barttelot, Bt., OBE; M. J. C. Robertson, MC
Lieutenant-Colonels, Hon. P. H. Lewis; R. Macfarlane; Hon. G. B. Norrie; J. H. Fisher, OBE; R. Ker, MC; P. Chamberlin
Majors, J. A. J. Nunn; I. B. Ramsden, MBE; M. J. Drummond-Brady; A. Arkwright; G. M. B. Colenso-Jones; T. Gooch, MBE; J. B. B. Cockcroft; C. J. H. Gurney; P. D. Johnson; R. M. O. Webster; Maj. J. Warren; Maj. E. Crofton

THE QUEEN'S BODY GUARD OF THE YEOMEN OF THE GUARD
St James's Palace, London SWIA IBS
Captain, The Lord Chesham
Lieutenant, Col. G. W. Tufnell
Clerk of the Cheque and Adjutant, Col. S. Longsdon
Ensign, Maj. C. Marriott
Exons, Maj. C. Enderby; Maj. M. T. N. H. Wills

MASTER OF THE HOUSEHOLD'S DEPARTMENT

BOARD OF GREEN CLOTH
Buckingham Palace, London SW1A 1AA
Master of the Household, Maj.-Gen. Sir Simon Cooper, KCVO
Deputy Master of the Household, Lt.-Col. Sir Guy Acland, Bt., MVO
Assistants to the Master of the Household, M. T. Parker, MVO; A. Jarman
Chief Clerk, M. C. W. N. Jephson, MVO
Chief Housekeeper, Miss H. Colebrook, MVO
Palace Steward, P. S. Croasdale, RVM
Royal Chef, L. Mann, RVM
Superintendent, Windsor Castle, Maj. B. Eastwood, LVO, MBE
Superintendent, The Palace of Holyroodhouse, Lt.-Col. D. Anderson, OBE

ROYAL MEWS DEPARTMENT
Buckingham Palace, London SW1W 0QH
Crown Equerry, Lt.-Col. S. Gilbart-Denham, CVO
Veterinary Surgeon, P. Scott Dunn, LVO, MRCVS
Superintendent Royal Mews, Buckingham Palace, Maj. A. Smith, MVO, MBE

THE ROYAL COLLECTION TRUST
St James's Palace, London SW1A 1BS
Director of Royal Collection and Surveyor of The Queen's Works of Art, H. Roberts, LVO, FSA
Surveyor of The Queen's Pictures, C. Lloyd, LVO
Surveyor Emeritus of The Queen's Pictures, Sir Oliver Millar, GCVO, FBA, FSA
Surveyor Emeritus of The Queen's Works of Art, Sir Geoffrey de Bellaigue, GCVO, FBA, FSA
Librarian, The Royal Library, Windsor Castle, O. Everett, CVO
Deputy Surveyor of The Queen's Works of Art, J. Marsden
Librarian Emeritus, Sir Robin Mackworth-Young, GCVO, FSA
Director of Media Affairs, R. Arbiter, LVO
Curator of the Print Room, The Hon. Mrs Roberts, LVO
Financial Director, M. Stevens
Financial Controller, Mrs G. Johnson
Administrator and Assistant to The Surveyors, D. Rankin-Hunt, MVO, TD
Senior Picture Restorer, Miss V. Pemberton-Pigott, MVO
Chief Picture Restorer, Old Master Drawings, A. Donnithorne
Senior Furniture Restorer, E. Fancourt, MVO, RVM
Armourer, J. Jackson, RVM
Chief Binder, R. Day, MVO, RVM

ROYAL COLLECTION ENTERPRISES LTD
Managing Director, M. E. K. Hewlett, LVO

ASCOT OFFICE
St James's Palace, London SW1A 1BS
Tel 0171-930 9882
Her Majesty's Representative at Ascot, Col. Sir Piers Bengough, KCVO, OBE
Secretary, Miss L. Thompson-Royds, MVO

THE QUEEN'S HOUSEHOLD IN SCOTLAND

Hereditary Lord High Constable, The Earl of Erroll
Hereditary Master of the Household, The Duke of Argyll
Lord Lyon King of Arms, Sir Malcolm Innes of Edingight, KCVO, WS

Hereditary Bearer of the Royal Banner of Scotland, The Earl of Dundee
Hereditary Bearer of the Scottish National Flag, The Earl of Lauderdale
Hereditary Keepers:
Palace of Holyroodhouse, The Duke of Hamilton and Brandon
Falkland Palace, N. Crichton-Stuart
Stirling Castle, The Earl of Mar and Kellie
Dunstaffnage Castle, The Duke of Argyll
Dunconnel Castle, Sir Charles Maclean, Bt.
Hereditary Carver, Maj. Sir Ralph Anstruther, Bt., GCVO, MC
Keeper of Dumbarton Castle, vacant
Governor of Edinburgh Castle, Maj.-Gen. J. Hall, OBE
Historiographer, Prof. T. C. Smout, CBE, FBA, FRSE, FSA SCOT.
Botanist, Prof. D. Henderson, CBE, FRSE
Painter and Limner, vacant
Sculptor in Ordinary, Prof. Sir Eduardo Paolozzi, CBE, RA
Astronomer, Prof. J. Brown, PH.D., FRSE
Heralds and Pursuivants, see page 281

ECCLESIASTICAL HOUSEHOLD
Dean of the Chapel Royal, Very Revd J. Harkness, CB, OBE
Dean of the Order of the Thistle, Very Revd G. I. Macmillan
Chaplains in Ordinary, Very Revd J. Harkness, CB, OBE; Revd J. McLeod; Very Revd G. I. Macmillan; Revd M. D. Craig; Very Revd W. B. R. Macmillan, LL.D, DD.; Very Revd J. L. Weatherhead, DD; Revd C. Robertson; Very Revd J. A. Simpson; Revd N. W. Drummond; Revd J. Paterson; Revd A. Symington
Extra Chaplains, Very Revd W. R. Sanderson, DD; Revd T. J. T. Nicol, LVO, MBE, MC, TD; Very Revd Prof. J. McIntyre, CVO, DD, FRSE; Revd C. Forrester-Paton; Revd H. W. M. Cant; Very Revd R. A. S. Barbour, KCVO, MC, DD; Revd K. MacVicar, MBE, DFC, TD; Very Revd W. B. Johnston, DD; Revd A. J. C. Macfarlane; Revd M. I. Levison, DD; Revd J. K. Angus, LVO, TD; Revd J. McLeod; Very Revd W. J. Morris, KCVO, DD; Revd A. S. Todd, DD
Domestic Chaplain, Balmoral, Revd R. P. Sloan

MEDICAL HOUSEHOLD
Physicians in Scotland, P. Brunt, OBE, MD, FRCP; A. Toft, CBE, FRCPE
Surgeons in Scotland, J. Engeset, CH.M., FRCS; Prof. Sir David Carter MD, FRCS
Apothecary to the Household at Balmoral, D. J. A. Glass, MB, CH.B.
Apothecary to the Household at the Palace of Holyroodhouse, Dr J. Cormack, MD, FRCPE, FRCGP

THE QUEEN'S BODY GUARD FOR SCOTLAND

ROYAL COMPANY OF ARCHERS
Archers' Hall, Buccleuch Street, Edinburgh EH8 9LR
Captain-General and Gold Stick for Scotland, Maj. Sir Hew Hamilton-Dalrymple, Bt., KCVO
Captains, The Duke of Buccleuch and Queensberry, KT, VRD; Maj. the Earl of Wemyss and March, KT; The Earl of Airlie, KT, GCVO
Lieutenants, Capt. Sir Iain Tennant, KT; The Marquess of Lothian, KCVO; Cdre Sir John Clerk of Penicuik, Bt., CBE, VRD; The Earl of Elgin and Kincardine, KT
Ensigns, Col. G. R. Simpson, DSO, LVO, TD; Maj. Sir David Butter, KCVO, MC; The Earl of Minto, OBE; Maj.-Gen. Sir John Swinton, KCVO, OBE

Brigadiers, Gen. Sir Michael Gow, GCB; The Hon. Lord Elliott, MC; Maj. the Hon. Sir Lachlan Maclean, Bt.; The Rt. Hon. Lord Younger of Prestwick, KT, KCVO, TD; Capt. G. Burnet, LVO; The Duke of Montrose; Lt.-Gen. Sir Norman Arthur, KCB; The Hon. Sir William Macpherson of Cluny, TD; The Lord Nickson, KBE; Maj. the Lord Glenarthur; Earl of Dalkeith; Maj. R. Y. Henderson, TD; H. F. O. Bewsher, LVO, OBE
Adjutant, Maj. the Hon. Sir Lachlan Maclean, Bt.
Surgeon, Dr P. A. P. Mackenzie, TD
Chaplain, Very Revd W. J. Morris, KCVO, DD
President of the Council and Silver Stick for Scotland, vacant
Vice-President, Capt. Sir Iain Tennant, KT
Secretary, Capt. J. D. B. Younger
Treasurer, J. M. Haldane of Gleneagles

HOUSEHOLD OF THE PRINCE PHILIP, DUKE OF EDINBURGH

Treasurer, Sir Brian McGrath, KCVO
Private Secretary, Brig. M. G. Hunt-Davis, CBE
Equerry, Lt.-Col. A. C. Richards
Extra Equerries, J. B. V. Orr, CVO; The Lord Buxton of Alsa; Brig. C. Robertson, CVO; Sir Brian McGrath, KCVO
Temporary Equerries, Maj. J. Cosby; Capt. R. Goodfellow; Capt. the Hon. J. Geddes
Chief Clerk and Accountant, G. D. Partington

HOUSEHOLD OF QUEEN ELIZABETH THE QUEEN MOTHER

Lord Chamberlain, The Earl of Crawford and Balcarres, PC
Private Secretary, Comptroller and Equerry, Capt. Sir Alastair Aird, KCVO
Assistant Private Secretary and Equerry, Maj. R. Seymour, CVO
Treasurer and Equerry, Maj. Sir Ralph Anstruther, Bt., GCVO, MC
Equerry, Maj. A. C. B. MacEwan (*temp.*)
Extra Equerries, Maj. Sir John Griffin, KCVO; The Lord Sinclair, CVO; Maj. W. Richardson, LVO; Maj. D. McMicking, LVO; Capt. A. Windham, LVO
Apothecary to the Household, Dr N. Southward, CVO, MB, B.chir.
Surgeon-Apothecary to the Household (Royal Lodge, Windsor), Dr J. Briscoe, D.obst.
Mistress of the Robes, vacant
Ladies of the Bedchamber, The Lady Grimthorpe, DCVO; The Countess of Scarbrough
Women of the Bedchamber, Dame Frances Campbell-Preston, DCVO; Lady Angela Oswald, LVO; The Hon. Mrs Rhodes; Mrs Michael Gordon-Lennox
Extra Women of the Bedchamber, Lady Jean Rankin, DCVO; Miss Jane Walker-Okeover, LVO; Lady Margaret Colville, CVO; Lady Elizabeth Basset, DCVO
Clerk Comptroller, M. Blanch, CVO
Information Officer, Mrs R. Murphy, LVO
Clerks, Miss F. Fletcher, LVO; Mrs W. Stevens

HOUSEHOLD OF THE PRINCE OF WALES

Private Secretary and Treasurer to the Prince of Wales, Cdr. R. J. Aylard, CVO, RN
Deputy Private Secretary to the Prince of Wales, S. Lamport

Assistant Private Secretaries to the Prince of Wales, Dr M. Williams; J. Skan
Press Secretary to the Prince of Wales, Miss S. Henney
Assistant Press Secretary to the Prince of Wales, M. Bolland
Equerry to the Prince of Wales, Lt. Cdr. J. Lavery, RN
Extra Equerries to the Prince of Wales, The Hon. Edward Adeane, CVO; Maj.-Gen. Sir Christopher Airy, KCVO, CBE; Sqn. Ldr. Sir David Checketts, KCVO; Sir David Landale, KCVO; Sir John Riddell, Bt., CVO; G. J. Ward, CBE; Brig. J. Q. Winter, LVO; M. Butler
Secretary to the Duchy of Cornwall and Keeper of the Records, J. N. C. James, CBE

HOUSEHOLD OF DIANA, PRINCESS OF WALES

Private Secretary, M. Gibbins
Ladies-in-Waiting, Miss Anne Beckwith-Smith, LVO; Viscountess Campden, LVO; Mrs Max Pike; Mrs Duncan Byatt; Mrs James Lonsdale
Extra Lady-in-Waiting, Lady Sarah McCorquodale

HOUSEHOLD OF THE DUKE OF YORK

Private Secretary, Treasurer and Extra Equerry to the Duke of York, Capt. R. N. Blair, RN
Comptroller and Assistant Private Secretary to the Duke of York, Cdr. C. Manley, OBE
Equerry to The Duke of York, Capt. T. E. D. Allan

HOUSEHOLD OF THE PRINCE EDWARD

Private Secretary, Lt.-Col. S. G. O'Dwyer, LVO
Assistant Private Secretary, Mrs R. Warburton, MVO
Clerk, Miss L. Buggé

HOUSEHOLD OF THE PRINCESS ROYAL

Private Secretary, Lt.-Col. P. Gibbs, CVO
Assistant Private Secretary, The Hon. Mrs Louloudis
Ladies-in-Waiting, Lady Carew Pole, LVO; Mrs Andrew Feilden, LVO; The Hon. Mrs Legge-Bourke, LVO; Mrs William Nunneley; Mrs Timothy Holderness-Roddam; Mrs Charles Ritchie; Mrs David Bowes Lyon
Extra Ladies-in-Waiting, Miss Victoria Legge-Bourke, LVO; Mrs Malcolm Innes, LVO; The Countess of Lichfield

HOUSEHOLD OF THE PRINCESS MARGARET, COUNTESS OF SNOWDON

Private Secretary and Comptroller, The Lord Napier and Ettrick, KCVO
Lady-in-Waiting, The Hon. Mrs Whitehead, LVO
Extra Ladies-in-Waiting, Lady Elizabeth Cavendish, LVO; Lady Aird, LVO; Mrs Robin Benson, LVO, OBE; Lady Juliet Townsend, LVO; Mrs Jane Stevens, LVO; The Hon. Mrs Wills, LVO; The Lady Glenconner, LVO; The Countess Alexander of Tunis, LVO; Mrs Charles Vyvyan

HOUSEHOLD OF THE DUKE AND DUCHESS OF GLOUCESTER

Private Secretary, Comptroller and Equerry, Maj.
N. M. L. Barne, LVO
Assistant Private Secretary to the Duchess of Gloucester, Miss S.
Marland, LVO
Extra Equerry, Lt.-Col. Sir Simon Bland, KCVO
Ladies-in-Waiting, Mrs Michael Wigley, CVO; Mrs Euan
McCorquodale, LVO; Mrs Howard Page, LVO
Extra Ladies-in-Waiting, Miss Jennifer Thomson; The
Lady Camoys

HOUSEHOLD OF PRINCESS ALICE, DUCHESS OF GLOUCESTER

Private Secretary, Comptroller and Equerry, Maj.
N. M. L. Barne, LVO
Extra Equerry, Lt.-Col. Sir Simon Bland, KCVO
Ladies-in-Waiting, Dame Jean Maxwell-Scott, DCVO; Mrs
Michael Harvey, LVO
Extra Ladies-in-Waiting, Miss Diana Harrison; The Hon.
Jane Walsh, LVO; Miss Jane Egerton-Warburton, LVO

HOUSEHOLD OF THE DUKE AND DUCHESS OF KENT

Private Secretary, N. C. Adamson, OBE
Extra Equerries, Lt.-Cdr. Sir Richard Buckley, KCVO; Maj. J.
Stewart; A. Palmer, CVO, CMG
Temporary Equerry, Capt. M. Barnett
Ladies-in-Waiting, Mrs Fiona Henderson, CVO; Mrs Colin
Marsh, LVO; Mrs Julian Tomkins; Mrs Peter Troughton;
Mrs Richard Beckett

HOUSEHOLD OF PRINCE AND PRINCESS MICHAEL OF KENT

Personal Secretary, Ms P. Goldspink
Ladies-in-Waiting, The Hon. Mrs Sanders; Miss Anne
Frost; Mrs J. Fellowes

HOUSEHOLD OF PRINCESS ALEXANDRA, THE HON. LADY OGILVY

Comptroller and Private Secretary, Capt. N. Blair, RN
Extra Equerry, Maj. Sir Peter Clarke, KCVO
Lady-in-Waiting, Lady Mary Mumford, DCVO
Extra Ladies-in-Waiting, Mrs Peter Afia; Lady Mary
Colman; Lady Nicholas Gordon Lennox; The Hon.
Lady Rowley; Dame Mona Mitchell, DCVO

Royal Salutes

ENGLAND
A salute of 62 guns is fired on the wharf at the Tower of
London on the following occasions:
(a) the anniversaries of the birth, accession and
coronation of the Sovereign
(b) the anniversary of the birth of HM Queen Elizabeth
the Queen Mother
(c) the anniversary of the birth of HRH Prince Philip,
Duke of Edinburgh
A salute of 41 guns only is fired on extraordinary and
triumphal occasions, e.g. on the occasion of the Sovereign
opening, proroguing or dissolving Parliament in person, or
when passing through London in procession, except when
otherwise ordered.
A salute of 41 guns is fired from the two saluting stations
in London (the Tower of London and Hyde Park) on the
occasion of the birth of a Royal infant.
Constable of the Royal Palace and Fortress of London, Field
Marshal Sir Peter Inge, GCB
Lieutenant of the Tower of London, Lt.-Gen. Sir Michael Gray,
KCB, OBE
Resident Governor and Keeper of the Jewel House, Maj.-Gen. G.
Field, CB, OBE

Master Gunner of St James's Park, Gen. Sir Martin Farndale,
KCB
Master Gunner within the Tower, Col. S. Lalor

SCOTLAND
Royal salutes are authorized at Edinburgh Castle and
Stirling Castle, although in practice Edinburgh Castle is
the only operating saluting station in Scotland.
A salute of 21 guns is fired on the following occasions:
(a) the anniversaries of the birth, accession and coronation
of the Sovereign
(b) the anniversary of the birth of HM Queen Elizabeth
the Queen Mother
(c) the anniversary of the birth of HRH Prince Philip,
Duke of Edinburgh
A salute of 21 guns is fired in Edinburgh on the occasion
of the opening of the General Assembly of the Church of
Scotland.
A salute of 21 guns may also be fired in Edinburgh on the
arrival of HM The Queen, HM Queen Elizabeth the
Queen Mother, or a member of the Royal Family who is a
Royal Highness on an official visit.

Royal Finances

FUNDING

THE CIVIL LIST

The Civil List dates back to the late 17th century. It was originally used by the sovereign to pay the salaries of judges, ambassadors and other government offices as well as the expenses of the royal household. In 1760 on the accession of George III it was decided that the Civil List would be provided by Parliament in return for the King surrendering the hereditary revenues of the Crown. At that time Parliament undertook to pay the salaries of judges, ambassadors, etc. In 1831 Parliament agreed also to meet the costs of the royal palaces. Each sovereign has agreed to continue this arrangement.

The Civil List paid to The Queen is charged on the Consolidated Fund. Until 1972, the amount of money allocated annually under the Civil List was set for the duration of a reign. The system was then altered to a fixed annual payment for ten years but from 1975 high inflation made an annual review necessary. The system of payments reverted to the practice of a fixed annual payment for ten years from 1 January 1991.

The Civil List Acts provide for other members of the royal family to receive parliamentary annuities from government funds to meet the expenses of carrying out their official duties. Since 1975 The Queen has reimbursed the Treasury for the annuities paid to the Duke of Gloucester, the Duke of Kent and Princess Alexandra. Since April 1993 The Queen has reimbursed all the annuities except those paid to herself, Queen Elizabeth the Queen Mother and the Duke of Edinburgh.

The Prince of Wales does not receive a parliamentary annuity. He derives his income from the revenues of the Duchy of Cornwall and these monies meet the official and private expenses of the Prince of Wales and his family.

The annual payments for the years 1991–2000 are:

The Queen	£7,900,000
Queen Elizabeth the Queen Mother	643,000
The Duke of Edinburgh	359,000
*The Duke of York	249,000
*The Prince Edward	96,000
*The Princess Royal	228,000
*The Princess Margaret, Countess of Snowdon	219,000
*Princess Alice, Duchess of Gloucester	87,000
*The Duke of Gloucester	175,000
*The Duke of Kent	236,000
*Princess Alexandra	225,000
	10,417,000
*Refunded to the Treasury	1,515,000
Total	8,902,000

GRANT-IN-AID

Grant-in-aid from the Department of National Heritage is voted annually by Parliament to pay for the upkeep of the occupied royal palaces which are used as royal residences or for official or ceremonial purposes.

THE PRIVY PURSE

The funds received by the Privy Purse pay for official expenses incurred by The Queen as head of state and for some of The Queen's private expenditure. The revenues of the Duchy of Lancaster are the principal source of income for the Privy Purse. The revenues of the Duchy were retained by George III in 1760 when the hereditary revenues were surrendered in exchange for the Civil List.

PERSONAL INCOME

The Queen's personal income derives mostly from investments, and is used to meet private expenditure.

DEPARTMENTAL VOTES

Items of expenditure connected with the official duties of the royal family which fall on votes of government departments include:

Ministry of Defence – The Royal Yacht; The Queen's Flight
Foreign and Commonwealth Office – Marshal of the Diplomatic Corps; overseas visits at the request of government departments
Department of National Heritage – Royal palaces
Department of Transport – The Royal Train
HM Treasury – Central Chancery of the Orders of Knighthood

TAXATION

The sovereign is not legally liable to pay income tax, capital gains tax or inheritance tax. After income tax was reintroduced in 1842 some income tax was paid voluntarily by the sovereign but over a long period these payments were phased out. In 1992 the Prime Minister announced that The Queen had offered to pay tax on a voluntary basis from 6 April 1993, and that the Prince of Wales also wished to pay tax on a voluntary basis on his income from the Duchy of Cornwall. (He was already taxed in all other respects.)

The provisions for The Queen and the Prince of Wales to pay tax were set out in a Memorandum of Understanding on Royal Taxation presented to Parliament on 11 February 1993. The main provisions are that The Queen will pay income tax and capital gains tax in respect of her private income and assets, and on the proportion of the income and capital gains of the Privy Purse used for private purposes. Inheritance tax will be paid on The Queen's assets, except for those which pass to the next sovereign, whether automatically or by gift or bequest. The Prince of Wales will pay income tax on income from the Duchy of Cornwall used for private purposes.

The Prince of Wales has confirmed that he intends to pay tax on the same basis following his accession to the throne.

Other members of the royal family are subject to tax as for any taxpayer.

Military Ranks and Titles

THE QUEEN

Lord High Admiral of the United Kingdom

Colonel-in-Chief
The Life Guards; The Blues and Royals (Royal Horse Guards and 1st Dragoons); The Royal Scots Dragoon Guards (Carabiniers and Greys); The Queen's Royal Lancers; Royal Tank Regiment; Corps of Royal Engineers; Grenadier Guards; Coldstream Guards; Scots Guards; Irish Guards; Welsh Guards; The Royal Welch Fusiliers; The Queen's Lancashire Regiment; The Argyll and Sutherland Highlanders (Princess Louise's); The Royal Green Jackets; Adjutant General's Corps; The Royal Mercian and Lancastrian Yeomanry; The Governor General's Horse Guards (of Canada); The King's Own Calgary Regiment; Canadian Forces Military Engineers Branch; Royal 22e Regiment (of Canada); Governor-General's Foot Guards (of Canada); The Canadian Grenadier Guards; Le Regiment de la Chaudiere (of Canada); 2nd Bn Royal New Brunswick Regiment (North Shore); The 48th Highlanders of Canada; The Argyll and Sutherland Highlanders of Canada (Princess Louise's); The Calgary Highlanders; Royal Australian Engineers; Royal Australian Infantry Corps; Royal Australian Army Ordnance Corps; Royal Australian Army Nursing Corps; The Corps of Royal New Zealand Engineers; Royal New Zealand Infantry Regiment; Royal New Zealand Army Ordnance Corps; Royal Malta Artillery; The Malawi Rifles

Affiliated Colonel-in-Chief
The Queen's Gurkha Engineers

Captain-General
Royal Regiment of Artillery; The Honourable Artillery Company; Combined Cadet Force; Royal Regiment of Canadian Artillery; Royal Regiment of Australian Artillery; Royal Regiment of New Zealand Artillery; Royal New Zealand Armoured Corps

Patron
Royal Army Chaplains' Department

Air Commodore-in-Chief
Royal Auxiliary Air Force; Royal Air Force Regiment; Royal Observer Corps; Air Reserve (of Canada); Royal Australian Air Force Reserve; Territorial Air Force (of New Zealand)

Commandant-in-Chief
Royal Air Force College, Cranwell

Hon. Air Commodore
RAF Marham

HM QUEEN ELIZABETH THE QUEEN MOTHER

Colonel-in-Chief
1st The Queen's Dragoon Guards; The Queen's Royal Hussars (Queen's Own and Royal Irish); 9th/12th Royal Lancers (Prince of Wales's); The King's Regiment; The Royal Anglian Regiment; The Light Infantry; The Black Watch (Royal Highland Regiment); Royal Army Medical Corps; The Black Watch (Royal Highland Regiment) of Canada; The Toronto Scottish Regiment; Canadian Forces Medical Services; Royal Australian Army Medical Corps; Royal New Zealand Army Medical Corps

Hon. Colonel
The Royal Yeomanry; The London Scottish; Inns of Court and City Yeomanry

Commandant-in-Chief
Women in the Royal Navy; Women, Royal Air Force; Royal Air Force Central Flying School

HRH THE PRINCE PHILIP, DUKE OF EDINBURGH

Admiral of the Fleet
Field Marshal
Marshal of the Royal Air Force

Admiral of the Fleet, Royal Australian Navy
Field Marshal, Australian Military Forces
Marshal of the Royal Australian Air Force

Admiral of the Fleet, Royal New Zealand Navy
Field Marshal, New Zealand Army
Marshal of the Royal New Zealand Air Force

Captain-General, Royal Marines

Admiral
Royal Canadian Sea Cadets

Colonel-in-Chief
The Royal Gloucestershire, Berkshire and Wiltshire Regiment; The Highlanders (Seaforth, Gordons and Camerons); Corps of Royal Electrical and Mechanical Engineers; Intelligence Corps; Army Cadet Force; The Royal Canadian Regiment; The Royal Hamilton Light Infantry (Wentworth Regiment) (of Canada); The Cameron Highlanders of Ottawa; The Queen's Own Cameron Highlanders of Canada; The Seaforth Highlanders of Canada; The Royal Canadian Army Cadets; The Royal Australian Electrical and Mechanical Engineers; The Australian Cadet Corps; The Royal New Zealand Corps of Electrical and Mechanical Engineers

Deputy Colonel-in-Chief
The Queen's Royal Hussars (Queen's Own and Royal Irish)

Colonel
Grenadier Guards

Hon. Colonel
The King's Own Yorkshire Yeomanry (Light Infantry); City of Edinburgh Universities Officers' Training Corps; The Trinidad and Tobago Regiment

Air Commodore-in-Chief
Air Training Corps; Royal Canadian Air Cadets

Hon. Air Commodore
RAF Kinloss

HRH THE PRINCE OF WALES

Captain, Royal Navy
Group Captain, Royal Air Force

Colonel-in-Chief
The Royal Dragoon Guards; The Cheshire Regiment;
The Royal Regiment of Wales (24th/41st Foot); The
Parachute Regiment; The Royal Gurkha Rifles; Army
Air Corps; The Royal Canadian Dragoons; Lord
Strathcona's Horse (Royal Canadians); Royal Regiment
of Canada; Royal Winnipeg Rifles; Air Reserve Group
of Air Command (of Canada); Royal Australian
Armoured Corps; The Royal Pacific Islands Regiment

Deputy Colonel-in-Chief
The Highlanders (Seaforth, Gordons and Camerons)

Colonel
Welsh Guards

Air Commodore-in-Chief
Royal New Zealand Air Force

Hon. Air Commodore
RAF Valley

HRH THE DUKE OF YORK

Lieutenant-Commander, Royal Navy

Admiral
Sea Cadet Corps

Colonel-in-Chief
The Staffordshire Regiment (The Prince of Wales's);
The Royal Irish Regiment (27th (Inniskilling), 83rd,
87th and The Ulster Defence Regiment)

HRH THE PRINCESS ROYAL

Rear Admiral
Chief Commandant for Women in the Royal Navy

Colonel-in-Chief
The King's Royal Hussars; Royal Corps of Signals; The
Royal Scots (The Royal Regiment); The
Worcestershire and Sherwood Foresters Regiment
(29th/45th Foot); The Royal Logistic Corps; 8th
Canadian Hussars (Princess Louise's); Canadian Forces
Communications and Electronics Branch; The Grey
and Simcoe Foresters; The Royal Regina Rifle
Regiment; Royal Newfoundland Regiment; Royal
Australian Corps of Signals; Royal New Zealand Corps
of Signals; Royal New Zealand Nursing Corps

Affiliated Colonel-in-Chief
The Queen's Gurkha Signals; The Queen's Own
Gurkha Transport Regiment

Hon. Colonel
University of London Officers' Training Corps

Hon. Air Commodore
RAF Lyneham; University of London Air Squadron

Commandant-in-Chief
Women's Transport Service (FANY)

HRH THE PRINCESS MARGARET, COUNTESS OF SNOWDON

Colonel-in-Chief
The Royal Highland Fusiliers (Princess Margaret's
Own Glasgow and Ayrshire Regiment); Queen
Alexandra's Royal Army Nursing Corps; The Highland
Fusiliers of Canada; The Princess Louise Fusiliers (of
Canada); The Bermuda Regiment

Deputy Colonel-in-Chief
The Royal Anglian Regiment

Hon. Air Commodore
RAF Coningsby

HRH PRINCESS ALICE, DUCHESS OF GLOUCESTER

Air Chief Marshal

Colonel-in-Chief
The King's Own Scottish Borderers; Royal Australian
Corps of Transport; Royal New Zealand Corps of
Transport

Deputy Colonel-in-Chief
The King's Royal Hussars; The Royal Anglian
Regiment

Air Chief Commandant
Women, Royal Air Force

HRH THE DUKE OF GLOUCESTER

Deputy Colonel-in-Chief
The Royal Gloucestershire, Berkshire and Wiltshire
Regiment; The Royal Logistic Corps

Hon. Colonel
Royal Monmouthshire Royal Engineers (Militia)

Hon. Air Commodore
RAF Odiham

HRH THE DUCHESS OF GLOUCESTER

Colonel-in-Chief
Royal Australian Army Educational Corps; Royal New
Zealand Army Educational Corps

Deputy Colonel-in-Chief
Adjutant-General's Corps

HRH THE DUKE OF KENT

Field Marshal
Hon. Air Vice-Marshal

Colonel-in-Chief
The Royal Regiment of Fusiliers; The Devonshire and
Dorset Regiment; The Lorne Scots (Peel, Dufferin and
Hamilton Regiment)

Deputy Colonel-in-Chief
    The Royal Scots Dragoon Guards (Carabiniers and
    Greys)

Colonel
    Scots Guards

Hon. Air Commodore
    RAF Leuchars

HRH THE DUCHESS OF KENT

Hon. Major-General

Colonel-in-Chief
    The Prince of Wales's Own Regiment of Yorkshire

Deputy Colonel-in-Chief
    The Royal Dragoon Guards; Adjutant-General's Corps;
    The Royal Logistic Corps

HRH PRINCE MICHAEL OF KENT

Major (retd), The Royal Hussars (Prince of Wales's Own)

Hon. Commodore
    Royal Naval Reserve

HRH PRINCESS ALEXANDRA, THE HON. LADY OGILVY

Patron
    Queen Alexandra's Royal Naval Nursing Service

Colonel-in-Chief
    The King's Own Royal Border Regiment; The Queen's
    Own Rifles of Canada; The Canadian Scottish
    Regiment (Princess Mary's)

Deputy Colonel-in-Chief
    The Queen's Royal Lancers; The Light Infantry

Deputy Hon. Colonel
    The Royal Yeomanry

Patron and Air Chief Commandant
    Princess Mary's Royal Air Force Nursing Service

The Royal Arms

ENGLAND

1st and 4th quarters (representing England) – Gules, three
    lions passant guardant in pale Or
2nd quarter (representing Scotland) – Or, a lion rampant
    within a double tressure flory counterflory Gules
3rd quarter (representing Ireland) – Azure, a harp Or,
    stringed Argent
The whole shield is encircled with the Garter

SCOTLAND

The Royal Arms shown with the Lion of Scotland in the 1st
and 4th quarters, and the Lions of England in the 2nd
quarter
The whole shield is encircled with the Thistle

SUPPORTERS (ENGLAND)

Dexter (right) – a lion rampant guardant Or, imperially
    crowned (shown in Scotland on the sinister)
Sinister (left) – a unicorn Argent, armed, crined, and
    unguled Or, gorged with a coronet composed of crosses
    patées and fleurs-de-lis, a chain affixed, passing
    between the forelegs, and reflexed over the back (shown
    in Scotland on the dexter and imperially crowned)

CRESTS

England – the Royal Crown Proper thereon a lion statant
    guardant Or imperially crowned also Proper
Scotland – upon an imperial crown Proper a lion sejant
    affrontée Gules imperially crowned Or, holding in the
    dexter paw a sword and in the sinister a sceptre erect,
    also Proper
Ireland – a tower triple-towered of the First, from the
    portal a hart springing Argent, attired and hooved Or

BADGES

England – the red and white rose united, slipped and
    leaved proper
Scotland – a thistle, slipped and leaved proper
Ireland – a shamrock leaf slipped Vert; also a harp Or,
    stringed Argent
United Kingdom – the rose of England, the thistle of
    Scotland, and the shamrock of Ireland engrafted on the
    same stem proper, and an escutcheon charged as the
    Union Flag (all ensigned with the Royal Crown)
Wales – upon a mount Vert a dragon passant, wings
    elevated Gules

The House of Windsor

King George V assumed by royal proclamation (17 June 1917) for his House and family, as well as for all descendants in the male line of Queen Victoria who are subjects of these realms, the name of Windsor.

KING GEORGE V (George Frederick Ernest Albert), second son of King Edward VII, *born* 3 June 1865; *married* 6 July 1893 HSH Princess Victoria Mary Augusta Louise Olga Pauline Claudine Agnes of Teck (Queen Mary, *born* 26 May 1867; *died* 24 March 1953); *succeeded* to the throne 6 May 1910; *died* 20 January 1936. *Issue:*

1. HRH PRINCE EDWARD Albert Christian George Andrew Patrick David, *born* 23 June 1894, *succeeded* to the throne as King Edward VIII, 20 January 1936; *abdicated* 11 December 1936; created *Duke of Windsor*, 1937; *married* 3 June 1937, Mrs Wallis Warfield (Her Grace The Duchess of Windsor, *born* 19 June 1896; *died* 24 April 1986), *died* 28 May 1972

2. HRH PRINCE ALBERT Frederick Arthur George, *born* 14 December 1895, *created* Duke of York 1920; *married* 26 April 1923, Lady Elizabeth Bowes-Lyon, youngest daughter of the 14th Earl of Strathmore and Kinghorne (HM Queen Elizabeth the Queen Mother, *see* pages 117–8), *succeeded* to the throne as King George VI, 11 December 1936; *died* 6 February 1952, having had issue (*see* page 117)

3. HRH PRINCESS (Victoria Alexandra Alice) MARY (*Princess Royal*), *born* 25 April 1897, *married* 28 February 1922, Viscount Lascelles, later the 6th Earl of Harewood (1882–1947), *died* 28 March 1965. *Issue:*
   (1) George Henry Hubert Lascelles, 7th Earl of Harewood, KBE, *born* 7 February 1923; *married* (1) 1949, Maria (Marion) Stein (marriage dissolved 1967); *issue, (a)* David Henry George, Viscount Lascelles, *born* 1950; (*b*) James Edward, *born* 1953; (*c*)

(Robert) Jeremy Hugh, *born* 1955; (2) 1967, Mrs Patricia Tuckwell; *issue,* (*d*) Mark Hubert, *born* 1964
   (2) Gerald David Lascelles, *born* 21 August 1924, *married* (1) 1952, Miss Angela Dowding (marriage dissolved 1978); *issue,* (*a*) Henry Ulick, *born* 1953; (2) 1978, Mrs Elizabeth Colvin; *issue,* (*b*) Martin David, *born* 1962

4. HRH PRINCE HENRY William Frederick Albert, *born* 31 March 1900, *created* Duke of Gloucester, Earl of Ulster and Baron Culloden 1928, *married* 6 November 1935, Lady Alice Christabel Montagu-Douglas-Scott, daughter of the 7th Duke of Buccleuch (HRH Princess Alice, Duchess of Gloucester, *see* page 118); *died* 10 June 1974. *Issue:*
   (1) HRH Prince William Henry Andrew Frederick, *born* 18 December 1941; *accidentally killed* 28 August 1972
   (2) HRH Prince Richard Alexander Walter George (HRH The Duke of Gloucester), *see* page 118

5. HRH PRINCE GEORGE Edward Alexander Edmund, *born* 20 December 1902, *created* Duke of Kent, Earl of St Andrews and Baron Downpatrick 1934, *married* 29 November 1934, HRH Princess Marina of Greece and Denmark (*born* 30 November os, 1906; *died* 27 August 1968); *killed on active service,* 25 August 1942. *Issue:*
   (1) HRH Prince Edward George Nicholas Paul Patrick (HRH The Duke of Kent), *see* page 118
   (2) HRH Princess Alexandra Helen Elizabeth Olga Christabel (HRH Princess Alexandra, the Hon. Lady Ogilvy), *see* page 118
   (3) HRH Prince Michael George Charles Franklin (HRH Prince Michael of Kent), *see* page 118

6. HRH PRINCE JOHN Charles Francis, *born* 12 July 1905; *died* 18 January 1919

Descendants of Queen Victoria

QUEEN VICTORIA (Alexandrina Victoria), *born* 24 May 1819; *succeeded* to the throne 20 June 1837; *married* 10 February 1840 (Francis) Albert Augustus Charles Emmanuel, Duke of Saxony, Prince of Saxe-Coburg and Gotha (HRH Albert, Prince Consort, *born* 26 August 1819, *died* 14 December 1861); *died* 22 January 1901. *Issue:*

1. HRH PRINCESS VICTORIA Adelaide Mary Louisa (Princess Royal) (1840–1901), *m.* 1858, Frederic (1831–88), Emperor of Germany March–June 1888. *Issue:*
   (1) HIM Wilhelm II (1859–1941), Emperor of Germany 1888–1918, *m.* (1) 1881 Princess Augusta Victoria of Schleswig-Holstein-Sonderburg-Augustenburg (1858–1921); (2) 1922 Princess Hermine of Reuss (1887–1947). *Issue:*
      (*a*) Prince Wilhelm (1882–1951), *Crown Prince* 1888–1918, *m.* 1905 Duchess Cecilie of Mecklenburg-Schwerin; *issue:* Prince Wilhelm (1906–40); Prince Louis Ferdinand (1907–94), *m.* 1938 Grand Duchess Kira (*see* page 129); Prince Hubertus (1909–50); Prince Friedrich Georg (1911–66); Princess Alexandrine Irene (1915–80); Princess Cecilie (1917–75)
      (*b*) Prince Eitel-Friedrich (1883–1942), *m.* 1906 Duchess Sophie of Oldenburg (marriage dissolved 1926)
      (*c*) Prince Adalbert (1884–1948), *m.* 1914 Duchess Adelheid of Saxe-Meiningen; *issue:* Princess Victoria Marina (1917–81); Prince Wilhelm Victor (1919–89)
      (*d*) Prince August Wilhelm (1887–1949), *m.* 1908 Princess Alexandra of Schleswig-Holstein-Sonderburg-Glücksburg (marriage dissolved 1920); *issue:* Prince Alexander (1912–85)
      (*e*) Prince Oskar (1888–1958), *m.* 1914 Countess von Ruppin; *issue:* Prince Oskar (1915–39); Prince Burchard (1917–88); Princess Herzeleide (1918–89); Prince Wilhelm (*b.* 1922)
      (*f*) Prince Joachim (1890–1920), *m.* 1916 Princess Marie of Anhalt; *issue:* Prince Karl Franz Joseph (1916–75)

   (*g*) Princess Viktoria Luise (1892–1980), *m.* 1913 Ernst, Duke of Brunswick 1913–18 (1887–1953); *issue:* Prince Ernst (1914–87); Prince Georg (*b.* 1915), *m.* 1946 Princess Sophie of Greece (*see* page 129) and has issue (two sons, one daughter); Princess Frederika (1917–81), *m.* 1938 Paul I, King of the Hellenes (*see* page 129); Prince Christian (1919–81); Prince Welf Heinrich (*b.* 1923)
   (2) Princess Charlotte (1860–1919), *m.* 1878 Bernhard, Duke of Saxe-Meiningen 1914 (1851–1914). *Issue:*
      Princess Feodora (1879–1945), *m.* 1898 Prince Heinrich XXX of Reuss
   (3) Prince Heinrich (1862–1929), *m.* 1888 Princess Irene of Hesse (*see* page 129). *Issue:*
      (*a*) Prince Waldemar (1889–1945), *m.* Princess Calixsta of Lippe
      (*b*) Prince Sigismund (1896–1978), *m.* 1919 Princess Charlotte of Saxe-Altenburg; *issue:* Princess Barbara (*b.* 1920); Prince Alfred (*b.* 1924)
      (*c*) Prince Heinrich (1900–4)
   (4) Prince Sigismund (1864–6)
   (5) Princess Victoria (1866–1929), *m.* (1) 1890, Prince Adolf of Schaumburg-Lippe (1859–1916); (2) 1927 Alexander Zubkov
   (6) Prince Joachim Waldemar (1868–79)
   (7) Princess Sophie (1870–1932), *m.* 1889 Constantine I (1868–1923), King of the Hellenes 1913–17, 1920–3. *Issue:*
      (*a*) George II (1890–1947), King of the Hellenes 1923–4 and 1935–47, *m.* 1921 Princess Elisabeth of Roumania (marriage dissolved 1935) (*see* page 129)
      (*b*) Alexander I (1893–1920), King of the Hellenes 1917–20, *m.* 1919 Aspasia Manos; *issue:* Princess Alexandra (1921–93), *m.* 1944 King Petar II of Yugoslavia (*see* page 129)
      (*c*) Princess Helena (1896–1982), *m.* 1921 King Carol of Roumania (*see* page 129), (marriage dissolved 1928)

(d) Paul I (1901–64), King of the Hellenes 1947–64, m. 1938 Princess Frederika of Brunswick (see page 128); issue: King Constantine II (b. 1940), m. 1964 Princess Anne-Marie of Denmark (see page 130), and has issue (three sons, two daughters); Princess Sophie (b. 1938), m. 1962 Juan Carlos I of Spain (see page 130); Princess Irene (b. 1942)
(e) Princess Irene (1904–74), m. 1939 4th Duke of Aosta; issue: Prince Amedeo (b. 1943)
(f) Princess Katherine (Lady Katherine Brandram) (b. 1913), m. 1947 Major R. C. A. Brandram, MC, TD; issue: R. Paul G. A. Brandram (b. 1948)
(8) Princess Margarethe (1872–1954), m. 1893 Prince Friedrich Karl of Hesse (1868–1940). Issue:
(a) Prince Friedrich Wilhelm (1893–1916)
(b) Prince Maximilian (1894–1914)
(c) Prince Philipp (1896–1980), m. 1925 Princess Mafalda of Italy; issue: Prince Moritz (b. 1926); Prince Heinrich (b. 1927); Prince Otto (b. 1937); Princess Elisabeth (b. 1940)
(d) Prince Wolfgang (b. 1896), m. (1) 1924 Princess Marie Alexandra of Baden; (2) 1948 Ottilie Möller
(e) Prince Richard (1901–69)
(f) Prince Christoph (1901–43), m. 1930 Princess Sophie of Greece (see below) and has issue (two sons, three daughters)

2. HRH PRINCE ALBERT EDWARD (HM KING EDWARD VII), b. 9 November 1841, m. 1863 HRH Princess Alexandra of Denmark (1844–1925), succeeded to the throne 22 January 1901, d. 6 May 1910. Issue:
(1) Albert Victor, Duke of Clarence and Avondale (1864–92)
(2) George (HM KING GEORGE V) (see page 128)
(3) Louise (1867–1931) Princess Royal 1905–31, m. 1889 1st Duke of Fife (1849–1912). Issue:
(a) Princess Alexandra, Duchess of Fife (1891–1959), m. 1913 Prince Arthur of Connaught (see page 130)
(b) Princess Maud (1893–1945), m. 1923 11th Earl of Southesk (1893–1992); issue: The Duke of Fife (b. 1929)
(4) Victoria (1868–1935)
(5) Maud (1869–1938), m. 1896 Prince Carl of Denmark (1872–1957), later King Haakon VII of Norway 1905–57. Issue:
(a) Olav V (1903–91), King of Norway 1957–91, m. 1929 Princess Märtha of Sweden (1901–54); issue: Princess Ragnhild (b. 1930); Princess Astrid (b. 1932); Harald V, King of Norway (b. 1937)
(6) Alexander (6–7 April 1871)

3. HRH PRINCESS ALICE Maud Mary (1843–78), m. 1862 Prince Ludwig (1837–92), Grand Duke of Hesse 1877–92. Issue:
(1) Victoria (1863–1950), m. 1884 Admiral of the Fleet Prince Louis of Battenberg (1854–1921), cr. 1st Marquess of Milford Haven 1917. Issue:
(a) Alice (1885–1969), m. 1903 Prince Andrew of Greece (1882–1944); issue: Princess Margarita (1905–81) m. 1931 Prince Gottfried of Hohenlohe-Langenburg (see below); Princess Theodora (1906–69), m. Prince Berthold of Baden (1906–63) and has issue (two sons, one daughter); Princess Cecilie (1911–37), m. George, Grand Duke of Hesse (see below); Princess Sophie (b. 1914), m. (1) 1930 Prince Christoph of Hesse (see above); (2) 1946 Prince Georg of Hanover (see page 128); Prince Philip, Duke of Edinburgh (b. 1921) (see page 117)
(b) Louise (1889–1965), m. 1923 Gustaf VI Adolf (1882–1973), King of Sweden 1950–73
(c) George, 2nd Marquess of Milford Haven (1892–1938), m. 1916 Countess Nadejda, daughter of Grand Duke Michael of Russia; issue: Lady Tatiana (1917–88); David Michael, 3rd Marquess (1919–70)
(d) Louis, 1st Earl Mountbatten of Burma (1900–79), m. 1922 Edwina Ashley, daughter of Lord Mount Temple; issue: Patricia, Countess Mountbatten of Burma (b. 1924), Pamela (b. 1929)
(2) Elizabeth (1864–1918), m. 1884 Grand Duke Sergius of Russia (1857–1905)
(3) Irene (1866–1953), m. 1888 Prince Heinrich of Prussia (see page 128)
(4) Ernst Ludwig (1868–1937), Grand Duke of Hesse 1892–1918, m. (1) 1894 Princess Victoria Melita of Saxe-Coburg (see below) (marriage dissolved 1901); (2) 1905 Princess Eleonore of Solms-Hohensolmslich. Issue:
(a) Princess Elizabeth (1895–1903)

(b) George, Grand Duke of Hesse (1906–37), m. Princess Cecilie of Greece (see above), and had issue, two sons, accidentally killed with parents 1937
(c) Ludwig, Grand Duke of Hesse (1908–68), m. 1937 Margaret, daughter of 1st Lord Geddes
(5) Frederick William (1870–3)
(6) Alix (Tsaritsa of Russia) (1872–1918), m. 1894 Nicholas II (1868–1918) Tsar of All the Russias 1894–1917, assassinated 16 July 1918. Issue:
(a) Grand Duchess Olga (1895–1918)
(b) Grand Duchess Tatiana (1897–1918)
(c) Grand Duchess Marie (1899–1918)
(d) Grand Duchess Anastasia (1901–18)
(e) Alexis, Tsarevich of Russia (1904–18)
(7) Marie (1874–8)

4. HRH PRINCE ALFRED Ernest Albert, Duke of Edinburgh, Admiral of the Fleet (1844–1900), m. 1874 Grand Duchess Marie Alexandrovna of Russia (1853–1920); succeeded as Duke of Saxe-Coburg and Gotha 22 August 1893. Issue:
(1) Alfred (Prince of Saxe-Coburg) (1874–99)
(2) Marie (1875–1938), m. 1893 Ferdinand (1865–1927), King of Roumania 1914–27. Issue:
(a) Carol II (1893–1953), King of Roumania 1930–40, m. (2) 1921 Princess Helena of Greece (see page 128) (marriage dissolved 1928); issue: Michael (b. 1921), King of Roumania 1927–30, 1940–7, m. 1948 Princess Anne of Bourbon-Parma, and has issue (five daughters)
(b) Elisabeth (1894–1956), m. 1921 George II, King of the Hellenes (see page 128)
(c) Marie (1900–61), m. 1922 Alexander (1888–1934), King of Yugoslavia 1921–34; issue: Petar II (1923–70), King of Yugoslavia 1934–45, m. 1944 Princess Alexandra of Greece (see page 128) and has issue (Crown Prince Alexander, b. 1945); Prince Tomislav (b. 1928), m. (1) 1957 Princess Margarita of Baden (daughter of Princess Theodora of Greece and Prince Berthold of Baden, see above); (2) 1982 Linda Bonney; and has issue (three sons, one daughter); Prince Andrej (1929–90), m. (1) 1956 Princess Christina of Hesse (daughter of Prince Christoph of Hesse and Princess Sophie of Greece, see above); (2) 1963 Princess Kira-Melita of Leiningen (see below); and has issue (three sons, two daughters)
(d) Prince Nicolas (1903–78)
(e) Princess Ileana (1909–91), m. (1) 1931 Archduke Anton of Austria; (2) 1931 Dr Stefan Issarescu; issue: Archduke Stefan (b. 1932); Archduchess Maria Ileana (1933–59); Archduchess Alexandra (b. 1935); Archduke Dominic (b. 1937); Archduchess Maria Magdalena (b. 1939); Archduchess Elisabeth (b. 1942)
(f) Prince Mircea (1913–16)
(3) Victoria Melita (1876–1936), m. (1) 1894 Grand Duke Ernst Ludwig of Hesse (see above) (marriage dissolved 1901); (2) 1905 the Grand Duke Kirill of Russia (1876–1938). Issue:
(a) Marie Kirillovna (1907–51), m. 1925 Prince Friedrich Karl of Leiningen; issue: Prince Emich (b. 1926); Prince Karl (b. 1928); Princess Kira-Melita (b. 1930), m. Prince Andrej of Yugoslavia (see above); Princess Margarita (b. 1932); Princess Mechtilde (b. 1936); Prince Friedrich (b. 1938)
(b) Kira Kirillovna (1909–67), m. 1938 Prince Louis Ferdinand of Prussia (see page 128); issue: Prince Friedrich Wilhelm (b. 1939); Prince Michael (b. 1940); Princess Marie (b. 1942); Princess Kira (b. 1943); Prince Louis Ferdinand (1944–77); Prince Christian (b. 1946); Princess Xenia (1949–92)
(c) Vladimir Kirillovich (1917–92), m. 1948 Princess Leonida Bagration-Mukhransky; issue: Grand Duchess Maria (b. 1953), and has issue
(4) Alexandra (1878–1942), m. 1896 Ernst, Prince of Hohenlohe Langenburg. Issue:
(a) Gottfried (1897–1960), m. 1931 Princess Margarita of Greece (see above); issue: Prince Kraft (b. 1935), Princess Beatrix (b. 1936), Prince Georg Andreas (b. 1938), Prince Ruprecht (1944–); Prince Albrecht (1944–92)
(b) Maria (1899–1967), m. 1916 Prince Friedrich of Schleswig-Holstein-Sonderburg-Glücksburg; issue: Prince Peter (1922–80); Princess Marie (b. 1927)
(c) Princess Alexandra (1901–63)
(d) Princess Irma (1902–86)
(5) Princess Beatrice (1884–1966), m. 1909 Alfonso of Orleans, Infante of Spain. Issue:

(*a*) Prince Alvaro (*b*. 1910), *m*. 1937 Carla Parodi-Delfino;
issue: Doña Gerarda (*b*. 1939); Don Alonso (1941–75); Doña
Beatriz (*b*. 1943); Don Alvaro (*b*. 1947)
(*b*) Prince Alonso (1912–36)
(*c*) Prince Ataulfo (1913–74)

5. HRH PRINCESS HELENA Augusta Victoria (1846–1923), *m*. 1866
Prince Christian of Schleswig-Holstein-Sonderburg-Augustenburg (1831–1917). *Issue:*
(1) Prince Christian Victor (1867–1900)
(2) Prince Albert (1869–1931), Duke of Schleswig-Holstein
1921–31
(3) Princess Helena (1870–1948)
(4) Princess Marie Louise (1872–1956), *m*. 1891 Prince Aribert
of Anhalt (marriage dissolved 1900)
(5) Prince Harold (12–20 May 1876)

6. HRH PRINCESS LOUISE Caroline Alberta (1848–1939), *m*. 1871
the Marquess of Lorne, afterwards 9th Duke of Argyll (1845–1914);
without issue

7. HRH PRINCE ARTHUR William Patrick Albert, Duke of
Connaught, *Field Marshal* (1850–1942), *m*. 1879 Princess Louisa of
Prussia (1860–1917). *Issue:*
(1) Margaret (1882–1920), *m*. 1905 Crown Prince Gustaf Adolf
(1882–1973), afterwards King of Sweden 1950–73. *Issue:*
(*a*) Gustaf Adolf, Duke of Västerbotten (1906–47), *m*. 1932
Princess Sibylla of Saxe-Coburg-Gotha (*see* below); *issue:*
Princess Margaretha (*b*. 1934); Princess Birgitta (*b*. 1937);
Princess Désirée (*b*. 1938); Princess Christina (*b*. 1943); Carl
XVI Gustaf, King of Sweden (*b*. 1946)
(*b*) Count Sigvard Bernadotte (*b*. 1907), *m*.; *issue:* Count
Michael (*b*. 1944)
(*c*) Princess Ingrid (Queen Mother of Denmark) (*b*. 1910), *m*.
1935 Frederick IX (1899–72), King of Denmark 1947–72;
issue: Margrethe II, Queen of Denmark (*b*. 1940); Princess
Benedikte (*b*. 1944); Princess Anne-Marie (*b*. 1946), *m*. 1964
Constantine II of Greece (*see* page 129)
(*d*) Prince Bertil, Duke of Halland (*b*. 1912), *m*. 1976 Mrs
Lilian Craig
(*e*) Count Carl Bernadotte (*b*. 1916), *m*. (1) 1946 Mrs Kerstin
Johnson; (2) 1988 Countess Gunnila Bussler
(2) Arthur (1883–1938), *m*. 1913 HH the Duchess of Fife (*see*
page 129). *Issue:*
Alastair Arthur, 2nd Duke of Connaught (1914–43)
(3) (Victoria) Patricia (1886–1974), *m*. 1919 Adm. Hon. Sir
Alexander Ramsay. *Issue:*

Alexander Ramsay of Mar (*b*. 1919), *m*. 1956 Hon. Flora
Fraser (Lady Saltoun)

8. HRH PRINCE LEOPOLD George Duncan Albert, Duke of Albany
(1853–84), *m*. 1882 Princess Helena of Waldeck (1861–1922). *Issue:*
(1) Alice (1883–1981), *m*. 1904 Prince Alexander of Teck
(1874–1957), *cr*. 1st Earl of Athlone 1917. *Issue:*
(*a*) Lady May (1906–94), *m*. 1931 Sir Henry Abel-Smith,
KCMG, KCVO, DSO; *issue:* Anne (*b*. 1932); Richard (*b*. 1933);
Elizabeth (*b*. 1936)
(*b*) Rupert, Viscount Trematon (1907–28)
(*c*) Prince Maurice (March–September 1910)
(2) Charles Edward (1884–1954), Duke of Albany 1884 until
title suspended 1917, Duke of Saxe-Coburg-Gotha 1900–18, *m*.
1905 Princess Victoria Adelheid of Schleswig-Holstein-
Sonderburg-Glücksburg. *Issue:*
(*a*) Prince Johann Leopold (1906–72), and has issue, including Ernst-Leopold (*b*. 1935) in whom is vested the right to
petition for restoration of the Dukedom of Albany
(*b*) Princess Sibylla (1908–72) *m*. 1932 Prince Gustav Adolf
of Sweden (*see* above)
(*c*) Prince Dietmar Hubertus (1909–43)
(*d*) Princess Caroline (1912–83), and has issue
(*e*) Prince Friedrich Josias (*b*. 1918), and has issue

9. HRH PRINCESS BEATRICE Mary Victoria Feodore (1857–1944),
m. 1885 Prince Henry of Battenberg (1858–96). *Issue:*
(1) Alexander, 1st Marquess of Carisbrooke (1886–1960), *m*.
1917 Lady Irene Denison. *Issue:*
Lady Iris Mountbatten (1920–82), *m*.; *issue:* Robin A. Bryan (*b*.
1957)
(2) Victoria Eugénie (1887–1969), *m*. 1906 Alfonso XIII
(1886–1941) King of Spain 1886–1931. *Issue:*
(*a*) Prince Alfonso (1907–38)
(*b*) Prince Jaime (1908–75), and has issue
(*c*) Princess Beatrice (*b*. 1909), and has issue
(*d*) Princess Maria (*b*. 1911), and has issue
(*e*) Prince Juan (1913–93), Count of Barcelona, and has *issue:*
Princess Maria (*b*. 1936); Juan Carlos I, King of Spain (*b*.
1938), *m*. 1962 Princess Sophie of Greece (*see* page 129)
and has issue (one son, two daughters); Princess Margarita
(*b*. 1939)
(*f*) Prince Gonzalo (1914–34)
(3) Major Lord Leopold Mountbatten (1889–1922)
(4) Maurice (1891–1914), died of wounds received in action

Kings and Queens

HOUSES OF CERDIC AND DENMARK

Reign

927–939 ÆTHELSTAN
Son of Edward the Elder, by Ecgwynn, and
grandson of Alfred
Acceded to Wessex and Mercia *c*.924, established
direct rule over Northumbria 927, effectively
creating the Kingdom of England
Reigned 15 years

939–946 EDMUND I
Born 921, son of Edward the Elder, by Eadgifu
Married (1) Ælfgifu (2) Æthelflæd
Killed aged 25, *reigned* 6 years

946–955 EADRED
Son of Edward the Elder, by Eadgifu
Reigned 9 years

955–959 EADWIG
Born before 943, son of Edmund and Ælfgifu
Married Ælfgifu
Reigned 3 years

959–975 EDGAR I
Born 943, son of Edmund and Ælfgifu
Married (1) Æthelflæd (2) Wulfthryth (3) Ælfthryth
Died aged 32, *reigned* 15 years

975–978 EDWARD I (the Martyr)
Born c.962, son of Edgar and Æthelflæd
Assassinated aged *c*.16, *reigned* 2 years

978–1016 ÆTHELRED (the Unready)
Born c.968/969, son of Edgar and Ælfthryth
Married (1) Ælfgifu (2) Emma, daughter of
Richard I, count of Normandy
1013–14 dispossessed of kingdom by Swegn
Forkbeard (king of Denmark 987–1014)
Died aged *c*.47, *reigned* 38 years

1016 EDMUND II (Ironside)
Born before 993, son of Æthelred and Ælfgifu
Married Ealdgyth
Died aged over 23, *reigned* 7 months
(April–November)

1016–1035 CNUT (Canute)
Born c.995, son of Swegn Forkbeard, king of
Denmark, and Gunhild
Married (1) Ælfgifu (2) Emma, widow of
Æthelred the Unready
Gained submission of West Saxons 1015,
Northumbrians 1016, Mercia 1016, king of all
England after Edmund's death

King of Denmark 1019–35, king of Norway 1028–35
Died aged *c*.40, *reigned* 19 years

1035–1040   HAROLD I (Harefoot)
*Born c.*1016/17, son of Cnut and Ælfgifu
Married Ælfgifu
1035 recognized as regent for himself and his brother Harthacnut; 1037 recognized as king
Died aged *c*.23, *reigned* 4 years

1040–1042   HARTHACNUT
*Born c.*1018, son of Cnut and Emma
Titular king of Denmark from 1028
Acknowledged king of England 1035–7 with Harold I as regent; effective king after Harold's death
Died aged *c*.24, *reigned* 2 years

1042–1066   EDWARD II (the Confessor)
Born between 1002 and 1005, son of Æthelred the Unready and Emma
Married Eadgyth, daughter of Godwine, earl of Wessex
Died aged over 60, *reigned* 23 years

1066   HAROLD II (Godwinesson)
*Born c.*1020, son of Godwine, earl of Wessex, and Gytha
Married (1) Eadgyth (2) Ealdgyth
Killed in battle aged *c*.46, *reigned* 10 months (January–October)

THE HOUSE OF NORMANDY

1066–1087   WILLIAM I (the Conqueror)
Born 1027/8, son of Robert I, duke of Normandy; obtained the Crown by conquest
Married Matilda, daughter of Baldwin, count of Flanders
Died aged *c*.60, *reigned* 20 years

1087–1100   WILLIAM II (Rufus)
Born between 1056 and 1060, third son of William I; succeeded his father in England only
Killed aged *c*.40, *reigned* 12 years

1100–1135   HENRY I (Beauclerk)
Born 1068, fourth son of William I
Married (1) Edith or Matilda, daughter of Malcolm III of Scotland (2) Adela, daughter of Godfrey, count of Louvain
Died aged 67, *reigned* 35 years

1135–1154   STEPHEN
Born not later than 1100, third son of Adela, daughter of William I, and Stephen, count of Blois
Married Matilda, daughter of Eustace, count of Boulogne
1141 (February–November) held captive by adherents of Matilda, daughter of Henry I, who contested the crown until 1153
Died aged over 53, *reigned* 18 years

THE HOUSE OF ANJOU (PLANTAGENETS)

1154–1189   HENRY II (Curtmantle)
Born 1133, son of Matilda, daughter of Henry I, and Geoffrey, count of Anjou
Married Eleanor, daughter of William, duke of Aquitaine, and divorced queen of Louis VII of France
Died aged 56, *reigned* 34 years

1189–1199   RICHARD I (Coeur de Lion)
Born 1157, third son of Henry II
Married Berengaria, daughter of Sancho VI, king of Navarre
Died aged 42, *reigned* 9 years

1199–1216   JOHN (Lackland)
Born 1167, fifth son of Henry II
Married (1) Isabella or Avisa, daughter of William, earl of Gloucester (divorced) (2) Isabella, daughter of Aymer, count of Angoulême
Died aged 48, *reigned* 17 years

1216–1272   HENRY III
Born 1207, son of John and Isabella of Angoulême
Married Eleanor, daughter of Raymond, count of Provence
Died aged 65, *reigned* 56 years

1272–1307   EDWARD I (Longshanks)
Born 1239, eldest son of Henry III
Married (1) Eleanor, daughter of Ferdinand III, king of Castile (2) Margaret, daughter of Philip III of France
Died aged 68, *reigned* 34 years

1307–1327   EDWARD II
Born 1284, eldest surviving son of Edward I and Eleanor
Married Isabella, daughter of Philip IV of France
Deposed January 1327, *killed* September 1327 aged 43, *reigned* 19 years

1327–1377   EDWARD III
Born 1312, eldest son of Edward II
Married Philippa, daughter of William, count of Hainault
Died aged 64, *reigned* 50 years

1377–1399   RICHARD II
Born 1367, son of Edward (the Black Prince), eldest son of Edward III
Married (1) Anne, daughter of Emperor Charles IV (2) Isabelle, daughter of Charles VI of France
Deposed September 1399, *killed* February 1400 aged 33, *reigned* 22 years

THE HOUSE OF LANCASTER

1399–1413   HENRY IV
Born 1366, son of John of Gaunt, fourth son of Edward III, and Blanche, daughter of Henry, duke of Lancaster
Married (1) Mary, daughter of Humphrey, earl of Hereford (2) Joan, daughter of Charles, king of Navarre, and widow of John, duke of Brittany
Died aged *c*.47, *reigned* 13 years

1413–1422   HENRY V
Born 1387, eldest surviving son of Henry IV and Mary
Married Catherine, daughter of Charles VI of France
Died aged 34, *reigned* 9 years

1422–1471   HENRY VI
Born 1421, son of Henry V
Married Margaret, daughter of René, duke of Anjou and count of Provence
Deposed March 1461, *restored* October 1470
Deposed April 1471, *killed* May 1471 aged 49, *reigned* 39 years

THE HOUSE OF YORK

1461–1483   EDWARD IV
Born 1442, eldest son of Richard of York, who was the grandson of Edmund, fifth son of Edward III, and the son of Anne, great-granddaughter of Lionel, third son of Edward III
Married Elizabeth Woodville, daughter of Richard, Lord Rivers, and widow of Sir John Grey
Acceded March 1461, *deposed* October 1470, *restored* April 1471
Died aged 40, *reigned* 21 years

1483   EDWARD V
Born 1470, eldest son of Edward IV
Deposed June 1483, *died* probably July–September 1483, aged 12, *reigned* 2 months (April–June)

1483–1485   RICHARD III
Born 1452, fourth son of Richard of York and brother of Edward IV
Married Anne Neville, daughter of Richard, earl of Warwick, and widow of Edward, Prince of Wales, son of Henry VI
Killed in battle aged 32, *reigned* 2 years

THE HOUSE OF TUDOR

1485–1509   HENRY VII
Born 1457, son of Margaret Beaufort, great-granddaughter of John of Gaunt, fourth son of Edward III, and Edmund Tudor, earl of Richmond
Married Elizabeth, daughter of Edward IV
Died aged 52, reigned 23 years

1509–1547   HENRY VIII
Born 1491, second son of Henry VII
Married (1) Catherine, daughter of Ferdinand II, king of Aragon, and widow of his elder brother Arthur (divorced) (2) Anne, daughter of Sir Thomas Boleyn (executed) (3) Jane, daughter of Sir John Seymour (died in childbirth) (4) Anne, daughter of John, duke of Cleves (divorced) (5) Catherine Howard, niece of the Duke of Norfolk (executed) (6) Catherine, daughter of Sir Thomas Parr and widow of Lord Latimer
Died aged 55, reigned 37 years

1547–1553   EDWARD VI
Born 1537, son of Henry VIII and Jane Seymour
Died aged 15, reigned 6 years

1553   JANE
Born 1537, daughter of Frances, daughter of Mary Tudor, the younger sister of Henry VIII, and Henry Grey, duke of Suffolk
Married Lord Guildford Dudley, son of the Duke of Northumberland
Deposed July 1553, executed February 1554 aged 16, reigned 14 days

1553–1558   MARY I
Born 1516, daughter of Henry VIII and Catherine of Aragon
Married Philip II of Spain
Died aged 42, reigned 5 years

1558–1603   ELIZABETH I
Born 1533, daughter of Henry VIII and Anne Boleyn
Died aged 69, reigned 44 years

BRITISH KINGS AND QUEENS SINCE 1603

THE HOUSE OF STUART

Reign
1603–1625   JAMES I (VI OF SCOTLAND)
Born 1566, son of Mary, queen of Scots and granddaughter of Margaret Tudor, elder daughter of Henry VII, and Henry Stewart, Lord Darnley
Married Anne, daughter of Frederick II of Denmark
Died aged 58, reigned 22 years
(see also page 134)

1625–1649   CHARLES I
Born 1600, second son of James I
Married Henrietta Maria, daughter of Henry IV of France
Executed 1649 aged 48, reigned 23 years

COMMONWEALTH DECLARED 19 May 1649
1649–53 Government by a council of state
1653–8 Oliver Cromwell, Lord Protector
1658–9 Richard Cromwell, Lord Protector

1660–1685   CHARLES II
Born 1630, eldest son of Charles I
Married Catherine, daughter of John IV of Portugal
Died aged 54, reigned 24 years

1685–1688   JAMES II (VII of Scotland)
Born 1633, second son of Charles I
Married (1) Lady Anne Hyde, daughter of Edward, earl of Clarendon (2) Mary, daughter of Alphonso, duke of Modena
Reign ended with flight from kingdom December 1688
Died 1701 aged 67, reigned 3 years

INTERREGNUM 11 December 1688 to 12 February 1689

1689–1702   WILLIAM III
Born 1650, son of William II, prince of Orange, and Mary Stuart, daughter of Charles I
Married Mary, elder daughter of James II
Died aged 51, reigned 13 years

and
1689–1694   MARY II
Born 1662, elder daughter of James II and Anne
Died aged 32, reigned 5 years

1702–1714   ANNE
Born 1665, younger daughter of James II and Anne
Married Prince George of Denmark, son of Frederick III of Denmark
Died aged 49, reigned 12 years

THE HOUSE OF HANOVER

1714–1727   GEORGE I (Elector of Hanover)
Born 1660, son of Sophia (daughter of Frederick, elector palatine, and Elizabeth Stuart, daughter of James I) and Ernest Augustus, elector of Hanover
Married Sophia Dorothea, daughter of George William, duke of Lüneburg-Celle
Died aged 67, reigned 12 years

1727–1760   GEORGE II
Born 1683, son of George I
Married Caroline, daughter of John Frederick, margrave of Brandenburg-Anspach
Died aged 76, reigned 33 years

1760–1820   GEORGE III
Born 1738, son of Frederick, eldest son of George II
Married Charlotte, daughter of Charles Louis, duke of Mecklenburg-Strelitz
Died aged 81, reigned 59 years

REGENCY 1811–20
Prince of Wales regent owing to the insanity of George III

1820–1830   GEORGE IV
Born 1762, eldest son of George III
Married Caroline, daughter of Charles, duke of Brunswick-Wolfenbüttel
Died aged 67, reigned 10 years

1830–1837   WILLIAM IV
Born 1765, third son of George III
Married Adelaide, daughter of George, duke of Saxe-Meiningen
Died aged 71, reigned 7 years

1837–1901   VICTORIA
Born 1819, daughter of Edward, fourth son of George III
Married Prince Albert of Saxe-Coburg and Gotha
Died aged 81, reigned 63 years

THE HOUSE OF SAXE-COBURG AND GOTHA

1901–1910   EDWARD VII
Born 1841, eldest son of Victoria and Albert
Married Alexandra, daughter of Christian IX of Denmark
Died aged 68, reigned 9 years

THE HOUSE OF WINDSOR

1910–1936   GEORGE V
Born 1865, second son of Edward VII
Married Victoria Mary, daughter of Francis, duke of Teck
Died aged 70, reigned 25 years

1936   EDWARD VIII
Born 1894, eldest son of George V
Married (1937) Mrs Wallis Warfield
Abdicated 1936, died 1972 aged 77, reigned 10 months (20 January to 11 December)

1936–1952   GEORGE VI
Born 1895, second son of George V
Married Lady Elizabeth Bowes-Lyon, daughter of 14th Earl of Strathmore and Kinghorne (see also pages 117–8)
Died aged 56, reigned 15 years

1952–   ELIZABETH II
Born 1926, elder daughter of George VI
Married Philip, son of Prince Andrew of Greece
(see also page 117)
WHOM GOD PRESERVE

KINGS AND QUEENS OF SCOTS 1016 TO 1603

Reign
1016–1034   MALCOLM II
Born c.954, son of Kenneth II
Acceded to Alba 1005, secured Lothian c.1016,
obtained Strathclyde for his grandson Duncan
c.1016, thus forming the Kingdom of Scotland
Died aged c.80, reigned 18 years
1034–1040   DUNCAN I
Son of Bethoc, daughter of Malcolm II, and
Crinan
Married a cousin of Siward, earl of Northumbria
Reigned 5 years
1040–1057   MACBETH
Born c.1005, son of a daughter of Malcolm II and
Finlaec, mormaer of Moray
Married Gruoch, granddaughter of Kenneth III
Killed aged c.52, reigned 17 years
1057–1058   LULACH
Born c. 1032, son of Gillacomgan, mormaer of
Moray, and Gruoch (and stepson of Macbeth)
Died aged c.26, reigned 7 months (August–March)
1058–1093   MALCOLM III (Canmore)
Born c.1031, elder son of Duncan I
Married (1) Ingibiorg (2) Margaret (St Margaret),
granddaughter of Edmund II of England
Killed in battle aged c.62, reigned 35 years
1093–1097   DONALD III BÁN
Born c. 1033, second son of Duncan I
Deposed May 1094, restored November 1094, deposed
October 1097, reigned 3 years
1094   DUNCAN II
Born c.1060, elder son of Malcolm III and Ingibiorg
Married Octreda of Dunbar
Killed aged c.34, reigned 6 months
(May–November)
1097–1107   EDGAR
Born c.1074, second son of Malcolm III and
Margaret
Died aged c.32, reigned 9 years
1107–1124   ALEXANDER I (The Fierce)
Born c.1077, fifth son of Malcolm III and Margaret
Married Sybilla, illegitimate daughter of Henry I
of England
Died aged c.47, reigned 17 years
1124–1153   DAVID I (The Saint)
Born c.1085, sixth son of Malcolm III and Margaret
Married Matilda, daughter of Waltheof, earl of
Huntingdon
Died aged c.68, reigned 29 years
1153–1165   MALCOLM IV (The Maiden)
Born c.1141, son of Henry, earl of Huntingdon,
second son of David I
Died aged c.24, reigned 12 years
1165–1214   WILLIAM I (The Lion)
Born c.1142, brother of Malcolm IV
Married Ermengarde, daughter of Richard,
viscount of Beaumont
Died aged c.72, reigned 49 years
1214–1249   ALEXANDER II
Born 1198, son of William I
Married (1) Joan, daughter of John, king of
England (2) Marie, daughter of Ingelram de Coucy
Died aged 50, reigned 34 years

1249–1286   ALEXANDER III
Born 1241, son of Alexander II and Marie
Married (1) Margaret, daughter of Henry III of
England (2) Yolande, daughter of the Count of
Dreux
Killed accidentally aged 44, reigned 36 years
1286–1290   MARGARET (The Maid of Norway)
Born 1283, daughter of Margaret (daughter of
Alexander III) and Eric II of Norway
Died aged 7, reigned 4 years

FIRST INTERREGNUM 1290–2
Throne disputed by 13 competitors. Crown
awarded to John Balliol by adjudication of Edward
I of England

THE HOUSE OF BALLIOL

1292–1296   JOHN (Balliol)
Born c.1250, son of Dervorguilla, great-great-
granddaughter of David I, and John de Balliol
Married Isabella, daughter of John, earl of Surrey
Abdicated 1296, died 1313 aged c.63, reigned 3 years

SECOND INTERREGNUM 1296–1306
Edward I of England declared John Balliol to have
forfeited the throne for contumacy in 1296 and
took the government of Scotland into his own
hands

THE HOUSE OF BRUCE

1306–1329   ROBERT I (Bruce)
Born 1274, son of Robert Bruce and Marjorie,
countess of Carrick, and great-grandson of the
second daughter of David, earl of Huntingdon,
brother of William I
Married (1) Isabella, daughter of Donald, earl of
Mar (2) Elizabeth, daughter of Richard, earl of
Ulster
Died aged 54, reigned 23 years
1329–1371   DAVID II
Born 1324, son of Robert I and Elizabeth
Married (1) Joanna, daughter of Edward II of
England (2) Margaret Drummond, widow of Sir
John Logie (divorced)
Died aged 46, reigned 41 years

1332 Edward Balliol, son of John Balliol, crowned
King of Scots September, expelled December
1333–6 Edward Balliol restored as King of Scots

THE HOUSE OF STEWART

1371–1390   ROBERT II (Stewart)
Born 1316, son of Marjorie, daughter of Robert I,
and Walter, High Steward of Scotland
Married (1) Elizabeth, daughter of Sir Robert
Mure of Rowallan (2) Euphemia, daughter of
Hugh, earl of Ross
Died aged 74, reigned 19 years
1390–1406   ROBERT III
Born c.1337, son of Robert II and Elizabeth
Married Annabella, daughter of Sir John
Drummond of Stobhall
Died aged c.69, reigned 16 years
1406–1437   JAMES I
Born 1394, son of Robert III
Married Joan Beaufort, daughter of John, earl of
Somerset
Assassinated aged 42, reigned 30 years
1437–1460   JAMES II
Born 1430, son of James I
Married Mary, daughter of Arnold, duke of
Gueldres
Killed accidentally aged 29, reigned 23 years
1460–1488   JAMES III
Born 1452, son of James II
Married Margaret, daughter of Christian I of
Denmark
Assassinated aged 36, reigned 27 years

1488–1513	JAMES IV *Born* 1473, son of James III *Married* Margaret Tudor, daughter of Henry VII of England *Killed* in battle aged 40, *reigned* 25 years
1513–1542	JAMES V *Born* 1512, son of James IV *Married* (1) Madeleine, daughter of Francis I of France (2) Mary of Lorraine, daughter of the Duc de Guise *Died* aged 30, *reigned* 29 years
1542–1567	MARY *Born* 1542, daughter of James V and Mary *Married* (1) the Dauphin, afterwards Francis II of France (2) Henry Stewart, Lord Darnley (3) James Hepburn, earl of Bothwell *Abdicated* 1567, prisoner in England from 1568, *executed* 1587, *reigned* 24 years
1567–1625	JAMES VI (and I of England) *Born* 1566, son of Mary, queen of Scots, and Henry, Lord Darnley Acceded 1567 to the Scottish throne, *reigned* 58 years Succeeded 1603 to the English throne, so joining the English and Scottish crowns in one person. The two kingdoms remained distinct until 1707 when the parliaments of the kingdoms became conjoined For British Kings and Queens since 1603, *see* pages 132–3

WELSH SOVEREIGNS AND PRINCES

Wales was ruled by sovereign princes from the earliest times until the death of Llywelyn in 1282. The first English Prince of Wales was the son of Edward I, who was born in Caernarvon town on 25 April 1284. According to a discredited legend, he was presented to the Welsh chieftains as their prince, in fulfilment of a promise that they should have a prince who 'could not speak a word of English' and should be native born. This son, who afterwards became Edward II, was created 'Prince of Wales and Earl of Chester' at the Lincoln Parliament on 7 February 1301.

The title Prince of Wales is borne after individual conferment and is not inherited at birth, though some Princes have been declared and styled Prince of Wales but never formally so created (*s.*). The title was conferred on Prince Charles by The Queen on 26 July 1958. He was invested at Caernarvon on 1 July 1969.

INDEPENDENT PRINCES AD 844 TO 1282

844–878	Rhodri the Great
878–916	Anarawd, son of Rhodri
916–950	Hywel Dda, the Good
950–979	Iago ab Idwal (or Ieuaf)
979–985	Hywel ab Ieuaf, the Bad
985–986	Cadwallon, his brother
986–999	Maredudd ab Owain ap Hywel Dda
999–1008	Cynan ap Hywel ab Ieuaf
1018–1023	Llywelyn ap Seisyll
1023–1039	Iago ab Idwal ap Meurig
1039–1063	Gruffydd ap Llywelyn ap Seisyll
1063–1075	Bleddyn ap Cynfyn
1075–1081	Trahaern ap Caradog
1081–1137	Gruffydd ap Cynan ab Iago
1137–1170	Owain Gwynedd
1170–1194	Dafydd ab Owain Gwynedd
1194–1240	Llywelyn Fawr, the Great
1240–1246	Dafydd ap Llywelyn
1246–1282	Llywelyn ap Gruffydd ap Llywelyn

ENGLISH PRINCES SINCE 1301

1301	Edward (Edward II)
1343	Edward the Black Prince, s. of Edward III
1376	Richard (Richard II), s. of the Black Prince
1399	Henry of Monmouth (Henry V)
1454	Edward of Westminster, son of Henry VI

1471	Edward of Westminster (Edward V)
1483	Edward, son of Richard III (d. 1484)
1489	Arthur Tudor, son of Henry VII
1504	Henry Tudor (Henry VIII)
1610	Henry Stuart, son of James I (d. 1612)
1616	Charles Stuart (Charles I)
*c.*1638 (*s.*)	Charles (Charles II)
1688 (*s.*)	James Francis Edward (The Old Pretender) (d. 1766)
1714	George Augustus (George II)
1729	Frederick Lewis, s. of George II (d. 1751)
1751	George William Frederick (George III)
1762	George Augustus Frederick (George IV)
1841	Albert Edward (Edward VII)
1901	George (George V)
1910	Edward (Edward VIII)
1958	Charles Philip Arthur George

PRINCESSES ROYAL

The style Princess Royal is conferred at the Sovereign's discretion on his or her eldest daughter. It is an honorary title, held for life, and cannot be inherited or passed on. It was first conferred on Princess Mary, daughter of Charles I, in approximately 1642.

*c.*1642	Princess Mary (1631–60), daughter of Charles I
1727	Princess Anne (1709–59), daughter of George II
1766	Princess Charlotte (1766–1828), daughter of George III
1840	Princess Victoria (1840–1901), daughter of Victoria
1905	Princess Louise (1867–1931), daughter of Edward VII
1932	Princess Mary (1897–1965), daughter of George V
1987	Princess Anne (b. 1950), daughter of Elizabeth II

Precedence

ENGLAND AND WALES

The Sovereign
The Prince Philip, Duke of
Edinburgh
The Prince of Wales
The Sovereign's younger sons
The Sovereign's grandsons
The Sovereign's cousins
Archbishop of Canterbury
Lord High Chancellor
Archbishop of York
The Prime Minister
Lord President of the Council
Speaker of the House of Commons
Lord Privy Seal
Ambassadors and High
Commissioners
Lord Great Chamberlain
Earl Marshal
Lord Steward of the Household
Lord Chamberlain of the Household
Master of the Horse
Dukes, according to their patent of
creation:
(1) of England
(2) of Scotland
(3) of Great Britain
(4) of Ireland
(5) those created since the Union
Ministers and Envoys
Eldest sons of Dukes of Blood Royal
Marquesses, according to their
patent of creation:
(1) of England
(2) of Scotland
(3) of Great Britain
(4) of Ireland
(5) those created since the Union
Dukes' eldest sons
Earls, according to their patent of
creation:
(1) of England
(2) of Scotland
(3) of Great Britain
(4) of Ireland
(5) those created since the Union
Younger sons of Dukes of Blood
Royal
Marquesses' eldest sons
Dukes' younger sons
Viscounts, according to their patent
of creation:
(1) of England
(2) of Scotland
(3) of Great Britain
(4) of Ireland
(5) those created since the Union
Earls' eldest sons
Marquesses' younger sons
Bishops of London, Durham and
Winchester

Other English Diocesan Bishops,
according to seniority of
consecration
Suffragan Bishops, according to
seniority of consecration
Secretaries of State, if of the degree
of a Baron
Barons, according to their patent of
creation:
(1) of England
(2) of Scotland
(3) of Great Britain
(4) of Ireland
(5) those created since the Union
Treasurer of the Household
Comptroller of the Household
Vice-Chamberlain of the Household
Secretaries of State under the degree
of Baron
Viscounts' eldest sons
Earls' younger sons
Barons' eldest sons
Knights of the Garter
Privy Counsellors
Chancellor of the Exchequer
Chancellor of the Duchy of
Lancaster
Lord Chief Justice of England
Master of the Rolls
President of the Family Division
Vice-Chancellor
Lords Justices of Appeal
Judges of the High Court
Viscounts' younger sons
Barons' younger sons
Sons of Life Peers
Baronets, according to date of patent
Knights of the Thistle
Knights Grand Cross of the Bath
Members of the Order of Merit
Knights Grand Commanders of the
Star of India
Knights Grand Cross of St Michael
and St George
Knights Grand Commanders of the
Indian Empire
Knights Grand Cross of the Royal
Victorian Order
Knights Grand Cross of the British
Empire
Companions of Honour
Knights Commanders of the Bath
Knights Commanders of the Star of
India
Knights Commanders of St Michael
and St George
Knights Commanders of the Indian
Empire
Knights Commanders of the Royal
Victorian Order
Knights Commanders of the British
Empire
Knights Bachelor
Vice-Chancellor of the County
Palatine of Lancaster

Official Referees of the Supreme
Court
Circuit judges and judges of the
Mayor's and City of London
Court
Companions of the Bath
Companions of the Star of India
Companions of St Michael and St
George
Companions of the Indian Empire
Commanders of the Royal Victorian
Order
Commanders of the British Empire
Companions of the Distinguished
Service Order
Lieutenants of the Royal Victorian
Order
Officers of the British Empire
Companions of the Imperial Service
Order
Eldest sons of younger sons of Peers
Baronets' eldest sons
Eldest sons of Knights, in the same
order as their fathers
Members of the Royal Victorian
Order
Members of the British Empire
Younger sons of the younger sons of
Peers
Baronets' younger sons
Younger sons of Knights, in the same
order as their fathers
Naval, Military, Air, and other
Esquires by office

WOMEN

Women take the same rank as their
husbands or as their brothers; but the
daughter of a peer marrying a commoner retains her title as Lady or
Honourable. Daughters of peers rank
next immediately after the wives of
their elder brothers, and before their
younger brothers' wives. Daughters
of peers marrying peers of lower
degree take the same order of precedence as that of their husbands;
thus the daughter of a Duke marrying
a Baron becomes of the rank of
Baroness only, while her sisters
married to commoners retain their
rank and take precedence of the
Baroness. Merely official rank on the
husband's part does not give any
similar precedence to the wife.

Peeresses in their own right take
the same precedence as peers of the
same rank, i.e. from their date of
creation.

Forms of address

It is only possible to cover here the forms of address for peers, baronets and knights, their wife and children, and Privy Counsellors. Greater detail should be sought in one of the publications devoted to the subject.

Both formal and social forms of address are given where usage differs; nowadays, the social form is generally preferred to the formal, which increasingly is used only for official documents and on very formal occasions.

F— represents forename
S— represents surname

BARON – *Envelope (formal),* The Right Hon. Lord —; *(social),* The Lord —. *Letter (formal),* My Lord; *(social),* Dear Lord —. *Spoken,* Lord —.

BARON'S WIFE – *Envelope (formal),* The Right Hon. Lady —; *(social),* The Lady —. *Letter (formal),* My Lady; *(social),* Dear Lady —. *Spoken,* Lady —.

BARON'S CHILDREN – *Envelope,* The Hon. F—S—. *Letter,* Dear Mr/Miss/Mrs S—. *Spoken,* Mr/Miss/Mrs S—.

BARONESS IN OWN RIGHT – *Envelope,* may be addressed in same way as a Baron's wife or, if she prefers *(formal),* The Right Hon. the Baroness —; *(social),* The Baroness —. Otherwise as for a Baron's wife.

BARONET – *Envelope,* Sir F—S—, Bt. *Letter (formal),* Dear Sir; *(social),* Dear Sir F—. *Spoken,* Sir F—.

BARONET'S WIFE – *Envelope,* Lady S—. *Letter (formal),* Dear Madam; *(social),* Dear Lady S—. *Spoken,* Lady S—.

COUNTESS IN OWN RIGHT – As for an Earl's wife.

COURTESY TITLES – The heir apparent to a Duke, Marquess or Earl uses the highest of his father's other titles as a courtesy title. (For list, *see* pages 165–6.) The holder of a courtesy title is not styled The Most Hon. or The Right Hon., and in correspondence 'The' is omitted before the title. The heir apparent to a Scottish title may use the title 'Master' (*see* below).

DAME – *Envelope,* Dame F—S—, followed by appropriate post-nominal letters. *Letter (formal),* Dear Madam; *(social),* Dear Dame F—. *Spoken,* Dame F—.

DUKE – *Envelope (formal),* His Grace the Duke of —; *(social),* The Duke of —. *Letter (formal),* My Lord Duke; *(social),* Dear Duke. *Spoken (formal),* Your Grace; *(social),* Duke.

DUKE'S WIFE – *Envelope (formal),* Her Grace the Duchess of —; *(social),* The Duchess of —. *Letter (formal),* Dear Madam; *(social),* Dear Duchess. *Spoken,* Duchess.

DUKE'S ELDEST SON – *see* Courtesy titles.

DUKE'S YOUNGER SONS – *Envelope,* Lord F—S—. *Letter (formal),* My Lord; *(social),* Dear Lord F—. *Spoken (formal),* My Lord; *(social),* Lord F—.

DUKE'S DAUGHTER – *Envelope,* Lady F—S—. *Letter (formal),* Dear Madam; *(social),* Dear Lady F—. *Spoken,* Lady F—.

EARL – *Envelope (formal),* The Right Hon. the Earl (of) —; *(social),* The Earl (of) —. *Letter (formal),* My Lord; *(social),* Dear Lord —. *Spoken (formal),* My Lord; *(social),* Lord —.

EARL'S WIFE – *Envelope (formal),* The Right Hon. the Countess (of) —; *(social),* The Countess (of) —. *Letter (formal),* Madam; *(social),* Lady —. *Spoken (formal),* Madam; *(social),* Lady —.

EARL'S CHILDREN – *Eldest son, see* Courtesy titles. *Younger sons,* The Hon. F—S— (for forms of address, *see* Baron's children). *Daughters,* Lady F—S— (for forms of address, *see* Duke's daughter).

KNIGHT (BACHELOR) – *Envelope,* Sir F—S—. *Letter (formal),* Dear Sir; *(social),* Dear Sir F—. *Spoken,* Sir F—.

KNIGHT (ORDERS OF CHIVALRY) – *Envelope,* Sir F—S—, followed by appropriate post-nominal letters. Otherwise as for Knight Bachelor.

KNIGHT'S WIFE – As for Baronet's wife.

LIFE PEER – As for Baron or for Baroness in own right.

LIFE PEER'S WIFE – As for Baron's wife.

LIFE PEER'S CHILDREN – As for Baron's children.

MARQUESS – *Envelope (formal),* The Most Hon. the Marquess of —; *(social),* The Marquess of —. *Letter (formal),* My Lord; *(social),* Dear Lord —. *Spoken (formal),* My Lord; *(social),* Lord —.

MARQUESS'S WIFE – *Envelope (formal),* The Most Hon. the Marchioness of —; *(social),* The Marchioness of —. *Letter (formal),* Madam; *(social),* Dear Lady —. *Spoken,* Lady —.

MARQUESS'S CHILDREN – *Eldest son, see* Courtesy titles. *Younger sons,* Lord F—S— (for forms of address, *see* Duke's younger sons). *Daughters,* Lady F—S— (for forms of address, *see* Duke's daughter).

MASTER – The title is used by the heir apparent to a Scottish peerage, though usually the heir apparent to a Duke, Marquess or Earl uses his courtesy title rather than 'Master'. *Envelope,* The Master of —. *Letter (formal),* Dear Sir; *(social),* Dear Master of —. *Spoken (formal),* Master, or Sir; *(social),* Master, or Mr S—.

MASTER'S WIFE – Addressed as for the wife of the appropriate peerage style, otherwise as Mrs S—.

PRIVY COUNSELLOR – *Envelope,* The Right (or Rt.) Hon. F—S—. *Letter,* Dear Mr/Miss/Mrs S—. *Spoken,* Mr/Miss/Mrs S—. It is incorrect to use the letters PC after the name in conjunction with the prefix The Right Hon., unless the Privy Counsellor is a peer below the rank of Marquess and so is styled The Right Hon. because of his rank. In this case only, the post-nominal letters may be used in conjunction with the prefix The Right Hon.

VISCOUNT – *Envelope (formal),* The Right Hon. the Viscount —; *(social),* The Viscount —. *Letter (formal),* My Lord; *(social),* Dear Lord —. *Spoken,* Lord —.

VISCOUNT'S WIFE – *Envelope (formal),* The Right Hon. the Viscountess —; *(social),* The Viscountess —. *Letter (formal),* Madam; *(social),* Dear Lady —. *Spoken,* Lady —.

VISCOUNT'S CHILDREN – As for Baron's children.

The Peerage

and Members of the House of Lords

The rules which govern the creation and succession of peerages are extremely complicated. There are, technically, five separate peerages, the Peerage of England, of Scotland, of Ireland, of Great Britain, and of the United Kingdom. The Peerage of Great Britain dates from 1707 when an Act of Union combined the two kingdoms of England and Scotland and separate peerages were discontinued. The Peerage of the United Kingdom dates from 1801 when Great Britain and Ireland were combined under an Act of Union. Some Scottish peers have received additional peerages of Great Britain or of the United Kingdom since 1707, and some Irish peers additional peerages of the United Kingdom since 1801.

The Peerage of Ireland was not entirely discontinued from 1801 but holders of Irish peerages, whether predating or created subsequent to the Union of 1801, are not entitled to sit in the House of Lords if they have no additional English, Scottish, Great Britain or United Kingdom peerage. However, they are eligible for election to the House of Commons and to vote in parliamentary elections, which other peers are not. An Irish peer holding a peerage of a lower grade which enables him to sit in the House of Lords is introduced there by the title which enables him to sit, though for all other purposes he is known by his higher title.

In the Peerage of Scotland there is no rank of Baron; the equivalent rank is Lord of Parliament, abbreviated to 'Lord' (the female equivalent is 'Lady'). All peers of England, Scotland, Great Britain or the United Kingdom who are 21 years or over, and of British, Irish or Commonwealth nationality are entitled to sit in the House of Lords.

No fees for dignities have been payable since 1937. The House of Lords surrendered the ancient right of peers to be tried for treason or felony by their peers in 1948.

HEREDITARY WOMEN PEERS

Most hereditary peerages pass on death to the nearest male heir, but there are exceptions, and several are held by women (see pages 145 and 157–8).

A woman peer in her own right retains her title after marriage, and if her husband's rank is the superior she is designated by the two titles jointly, the inferior one second. Her hereditary claim still holds good in spite of any marriage whether higher or lower. No rank held by a woman can confer any title or even precedence upon her husband but the rank of a hereditary woman peer in her own right is inherited by her eldest son (or in some cases daughter).

Since the Peerage Act 1963, hereditary women peers in their own right have been entitled to sit in the House of Lords, subject to the same qualifications as men.

LIFE PEERS

Since 1876 non-hereditary or life peerages have been conferred on certain eminent judges to enable the judicial functions of the House of Lords to be carried out. These Lords are known as Lords of Appeal or law lords and, to date, such appointments have all been male.

Since 1958 life peerages have been conferred upon distinguished men and women from all walks of life, giving them seats in the House of Lords in the degree of Baron or Baroness. They are addressed in the same way as heredi-

tary Lords and Barons, and their children have similar courtesy titles.

PEERAGES EXTINCT SINCE THE LAST EDITION

VISCOUNTCIES: Watkinson (cr. 1964)
BARONIES: Airedale (cr. 1907)
LIFE PEERAGES: Bottomley (cr. 1984), Collison (cr. 1964), Faithfull (cr. 1975), Fraser of Kilmorack (cr. 1974), Home of the Hirsel (cr. 1974), Houghton of Sowerby (cr. 1974), Jacques (cr. 1968), Jay (cr. 1987), McFadzean (cr. 1966), Marshall of Goring (cr. 1985), Matthews (cr. 1980), O'Brien of Lothbury (cr. 1973), Pritchard (cr. 1975), Stedman (cr. 1974)

DISCLAIMER OF PEERAGES

The Peerage Act 1963 enables peers to disclaim their peerages for life. Peers alive in 1963 could disclaim within twelve months after the passing of the Act (31 July 1963); a person subsequently succeeding to a peerage may disclaim within twelve months (one month if an MP) after the date of succession, or of reaching 21, if later. The disclaimer is irrevocable but does not affect the descent of the peerage after the disclaimant's death, and children of a disclaimed peer may, if they wish, retain their precedence and any courtesy titles and styles borne as children of a peer. The disclaimer permits the disclaimant to sit in the House of Commons if elected as an MP.

The following peerages are currently disclaimed:

EARLDOMS: Durham (1970); Selkirk (1994)
VISCOUNTCIES: Camrose (1995); Hailsham (1963); Stansgate (1963)
BARONIES: Altrincham (1963); Archibald (1975); Merthyr (1977); Reith (1972); Sanderson of Ayot (1971); Silkin (1972)

PEERS WHO ARE MINORS (i.e. under 21 years of age)
EARLS: Craven (b. 1989)
BARONS: Elphinstone (b. 1980); Lovat (b. 1977)

CONTRACTIONS AND SYMBOLS

s. Scottish title
I. Irish title
*   The peer holds also an Imperial title, specified after the name by Engl., Brit. or UK
o   there is no 'of' in the title
b. born
s. succeeded
m. married
w. widower or widow
M. minor
†   heir not ascertained at time of going to press

Hereditary Peers

ROYAL DUKES

Style, His Royal Highness The Duke of ___
Style of address (formal) May it please your Royal Highness; *(informal)* Sir

Created	Title, order of succession, name, etc.	Heir
1947	*Edinburgh* (1st), The Prince Philip, Duke of Edinburgh, *(see* page 117)	The Prince of Wales
1337	*Cornwall,* Charles, Prince of Wales, *s.* 1952 *(see* page 117)	‡
1398	*Rothesay,* Charles, Prince of Wales, *s.* 1952 *(see* page 117)	‡
1986	*York* (1st), The Prince Andrew, Duke of York *(see* page 117)	None
1928	*Gloucester* (2nd), Prince Richard, Duke of Gloucester, *s.* 1974 *(see* page 118)	Earl of Ulster *(see* page 118)
1934	*Kent* (2nd), Prince Edward, Duke of Kent, *s.* 1942 *(see* page 118)	Earl of St Andrews *(see* page 118)

‡ The title is not hereditary but is held by the Sovereign's eldest son from the moment of his birth or the Sovereign's accession

DUKES

Coronet, Eight strawberry leaves
Style, His Grace the Duke of ___
Wife's style, Her Grace the Duchess of ___
Eldest son's style, Takes his father's second title as a courtesy title
Younger sons' style, 'Lord' before forename and family name
Daughters' style, 'Lady' before forename and family name
For forms of address, *see* page 136

Created	Title, order of succession, name, etc.	Heir
1868 I.*	*Abercorn* (5th), James Hamilton (6th *Brit. Marq.,* 1790, and 14th *Scott. Earl,* 1606, both *Abercorn*), *b.* 1934, *s.* 1979, *m.*	Marquess of Hamilton, *b.* 1969.
1701 s.*	*Argyll* (12th), Ian Campbell (5th *UK Duke Argyll,* 1892), *b.* 1937, *s.* 1973, *m.*	Marquess of Lorne, *b.* 1968.
1703 s.	*Atholl* (11th), John Murray, *b.* 1929, *s.* 1996, *m.*	Marquess of Tullibardine, *b.* 1960.
1682	*Beaufort* (11th), David Robert Somerset, *b.* 1928, *s.* 1984, *w.*	Marquess of Worcester, *b.* 1952.
1694	*Bedford* (13th), John Robert Russell, *b.* 1917, *s.* 1953, *m.*	Marquess of Tavistock, *b.* 1940.
1663 s.*	*Buccleuch* (9th) & *Queensberry* (11th) (1684), Walter Francis John Montagu Douglas Scott, KT, VRD (8th *Engl. Earl, Doncaster,* 1662), *b.* 1923, *s.* 1973, *m.*	Earl of Dalkeith, *b.* 1954.
1694	*Devonshire* (11th), Andrew Robert Buxton Cavendish, KG, MC, PC, *b.* 1920, *s.* 1950, *m.*	Marquess of Hartington, *b.* 1944.
1900	*Fife* (3rd), James George Alexander Bannerman Carnegie (12th *Scott. Earl, Southesk,* 1633, *s.* 1992), *b.* 1929, *s.* 1959. *(see* page 129)	Earl of Southesk, *b.* 1961.
1675	*Grafton* (11th), Hugh Denis Charles FitzRoy, KG, *b.* 1919, *s.* 1970, *m.*	Earl of Euston, *b.* 1947.
1643 s.*	*Hamilton* (15th) & *Brandon* (12th) (*Brit.* 1711), Angus Alan Douglas Douglas-Hamilton (*Premier Peer of Scotland*), *b.* 1938, *s.* 1973	Marquess of Douglas and Clydesdale, *b.* 1978.
1766 I.*	*Leinster* (8th), Gerald FitzGerald (*Premier Duke and Marquess of Ireland*; 8th *Brit. Visct., Leinster,* 1747), *b.* 1914, *s.* 1976, *m.*	Marquess of Kildare, *b.* 1948.
1719	*Manchester* (12th), Angus Charles Drogo Montagu, *b.* 1938, *s.* 1985, *m.*	Viscount Mandeville, *b.* 1962.
1702	*Marlborough* (11th), John George Vanderbilt Henry Spencer-Churchill, *b.* 1926, *s.* 1972, *m.*	Marquess of Blandford, *b.* 1955.
1707 s.*	*Montrose* (8th), James Graham (6th *Brit. Earl, Graham,* 1722), *b.* 1935, *s.* 1992, *m.*	Marquess of Graham, *b.* 1973.
1483	*Norfolk* (17th), Miles Francis Stapleton Fitzalan-Howard, KG, GCVO, CB, CBE, MC (*Premier Duke*; 12th *Eng. Baron Beaumont,* 1309, *s.* 1971; 4th *UK Baron Howard of Glossop,* 1869, *s.* 1972), *b.* 1915, *s.* 1975, *m. Earl Marshal*	Earl of Arundel and Surrey, *b.* 1956.
1766	*Northumberland* (12th), Ralph George Algernon Percy, *b.* 1956, *s.* 1995, *m.*	Earl Percy, *b.* 1984.
1675	*Richmond* (10th) & *Gordon* (5th) (*UK* 1876), Charles Henry Gordon Lennox (10th *Scott. Duke, Lennox,* 1675), *b.* 1929, *s.* 1989, *m.*	Earl of March and Kinrara, *b.* 1955.

Created	Title, order of succession, name, etc.	Heir
1707 s.*	*Roxburghe* (10th), Guy David Innes-Ker (5th *UK Earl, Innes,* 1837), *b.* 1954, *s.* 1974, *m.* (*Premier Baronet of Scotland*)	Marquess of Bowmont and Cessford, *b.* 1981.
1703	*Rutland* (10th), Charles John Robert Manners, CBE, *b.* 1919, *s.* 1940, *m.*	Marquess of Granby, *b.* 1959.
1684	*St Albans* (14th), Murray de Vere Beauclerk, *b.* 1939, *s.* 1988, *m.*	Earl of Burford, *b.* 1965.
1547	*Somerset* (19th), John Michael Edward Seymour, *b.* 1952, *s.* 1984, *m.*	Lord Seymour, *b.* 1982.
1833	*Sutherland* (6th), John Sutherland Egerton, TD (5th *UK Earl, Ellesmere,* 1846, *s.* 1944), *b.* 1915, *s.* 1963, *m.*	Francis R. E., *b.* 1940.
1814	*Wellington* (8th), Arthur Valerian Wellesley, KG, LVO, OBE, MC (9th *Irish Earl, Mornington,* 1760), *b.* 1915, *s.* 1972, *m.*	Marquess of Douro, *b.* 1945.
1874	*Westminster* (6th), Gerald Cavendish Grosvenor, OBE, *b.* 1951, *s.* 1979, *m.*	Earl Grosvenor, *b.* 1991.

MARQUESSES

Coronet, Four strawberry leaves alternating with four silver balls
Style, The Most Hon. the Marquess (of) ___ . In Scotland the spelling 'Marquis' is preferred for pre-Union creations
Wife's style, The Most Hon. the Marchioness (of) ___
Eldest son's style, Takes his father's second title as a courtesy title
Younger sons' style, 'Lord' before forename and family name
Daughters' style, 'Lady' before forename and family name
For forms of address, *see* page 136

Created	Title, order of succession, name, etc.	Heir
1916	*Aberdeen and Temair* (6th), Alastair Ninian John Gordon (12th *Scott. Earl, Aberdeen,* 1682), *b.* 1920, *s.* 1984, *m.*	Earl of Haddo, *b.* 1955.
1876	*Abergavenny* (5th), John Henry Guy Nevill, KG, OBE, *b.* 1914, *s.* 1954, *m.*	Christopher G. C. N., *b.* 1955.
1821	*Ailesbury* (8th), Michael Sidney Cedric Brudenell-Bruce, *b.* 1926, *s.* 1974	Earl of Cardigan, *b.* 1952.
1831	*Ailsa* (8th), Archibald Angus Charles Kennedy (20th *Scott. Earl, Cassillis,* 1509), *b.* 1956, *s.* 1994	Lord David Kennedy, *b.* 1958.
1815	*Anglesey* (7th), George Charles Henry Victor Paget, *b.* 1922, *s.* 1947, *m.*	Earl of Uxbridge, *b.* 1950.
1789	*Bath* (7th), Alexander George Thynn, *b.* 1932, *s.* 1992, *m.*	Viscount Weymouth, *b.* 1974.
1826	*Bristol* (7th), (Frederick William) John Augustus Hervey, *b.* 1954, *s.* 1985	Lord F. W. C. Nicholas W. H., *b.* 1961.
1796	*Bute* (7th), John Colum Crichton-Stuart (12th *Scott. Earl, Dumfries,* 1633), *b.* 1958, *s.* 1993, *m.*	Earl of Dumfries, *b.* 1989.
1812	°*Camden* (6th), David George Edward Henry Pratt, *b.* 1930, *s.* 1983	Earl of Brecknock, *b.* 1965.
1815	*Cholmondeley* (7th), David George Philip Cholmondeley (11th *Irish Viscount, Cholmondeley,* 1661), *b.* 1960, *s.* 1990. *Lord Great Chamberlain*	Charles G. C., *b.* 1959.
1816 I.*	°*Conyngham* (7th), Frederick William Henry Francis Conyngham (7th *UK Baron, Minster,* 1821), *b.* 1924, *s.* 1974, *m.*	Earl of Mount Charles, *b.* 1951.
1791 I.*	*Donegall* (7th), Dermot Richard Claud Chichester, LVO (7th *Brit. Baron, Fisherwick,* 1790, 6th *Brit. Baron, Templemore,* 1831, *s.* 1953), *b.* 1916, *s.* 1975, *m.*	Earl of Belfast, *b.* 1952.
1789 I.*	*Downshire* (8th), (Arthur) Robin Ian Hill (8th *Brit. Earl, Hillsborough,* 1772), *b.* 1929, *s.* 1989, *m.*	Earl of Hillsborough, *b.* 1959.
1801 I.*	*Ely* (8th) Charles John Tottenham (8th *UK Baron, Loftus,* 1801), *b.* 1913, *s.* 1969, *m.*	Viscount Loftus, *b.* 1943.
1801	*Exeter* (8th), (William) Michael Anthony Cecil, *b.* 1935, *s.* 1988, *m.*	Lord Burghley, *b.* 1970.
1800 I.*	*Headfort* (6th), Thomas Geoffrey Charles Michael Taylour (4th *UK Baron, Kenlis,* 1831), *b.* 1932, *s.* 1960, *m.*	Earl of Bective, *b.* 1959.
1793	*Hertford* (8th), Hugh Edward Conway Seymour (9th *Irish Baron, Conway,* 1712), *b.* 1930, *s.* 1940, *m.*	Earl of Yarmouth, *b.* 1958.
1599 s.*	*Huntly* (13th), Granville Charles Gomer Gordon (*Premier Marquess of Scotland*) (5th *UK Baron, Meldrum,* 1815), *b.* 1944, *s.* 1987, *m.*	Earl of Aboyne, *b.* 1973.
1784	*Lansdowne* (8th), George John Charles Mercer Nairne Petty-Fitzmaurice, PC (8th *Irish Earl, Kerry,* 1723), *b.* 1912, *s.* 1944, *m.*	Earl of Shelburne, *b.* 1941.
1902	*Linlithgow* (4th), Adrian John Charles Hope (10th *Scott. Earl, Hopetoun,* 1703), *b.* 1946, *s.* 1987, *m.*	Earl of Hopetoun, *b.* 1969.
1816 I.*	*Londonderry* (9th), Alexander Charles Robert Vane-Tempest-Stewart (6th *UK Earl, Vane,* 1823), *b.* 1937, *s.* 1955, *m.*	Viscount Castlereagh, *b.* 1972.
1701 s.*	*Lothian* (12th), Peter Francis Walter Kerr, KCVO (6th *UK Baron, Kerr,* 1821), *b.* 1922, *s.* 1940, *m.*	Earl of Ancram, PC, MP, *b.* 1945.

Created	Title, order of succession, name, etc.	Heir
1917	*Milford Haven* (4th), George Ivar Louis Mountbatten, *b.* 1961, *s.* 1970, *m.*	Earl of Medina, *b.* 1991.
1838	*Normanby* (5th), Constantine Edmund Walter Phipps, (9th *Irish Baron, Mulgrave,* 1767), *b.* 1954, *s.* 1994, *m.*	Lord Justin, C. P., *b.* 1958.
1812	*Northampton* (7th), Spencer Douglas David Compton, *b.* 1946, *s.* 1978, *m.*	Earl Compton, *b.* 1973.
1825 I.*	*Ormonde* (7th), James Hubert Theobald Charles Butler, MBE (7th *UK Baron, Ormonde,* 1821), *b.* 1899, *s.* 1971, *w.*	None to Marquessate. To Earldoms of Ormonde and Ossory, Viscount Mountgarret, *b.* 1936 (*see* page 147).
1682 S.	*Queensberry* (12th), David Harrington Angus Douglas, *b.* 1929, *s.* 1954	Viscount Drumlanrig, *b.* 1967.
1926	*Reading* (4th), Simon Charles Henry Rufus Isaacs, *b.* 1942, *s.* 1980, *m.*	Viscount Erleigh, *b.* 1986.
1789	*Salisbury* (6th), Robert Edward Peter Cecil, *b.* 1916, *s.* 1972, *m.*	Viscount Cranborne, PC, *b.* 1946 (*see also* Baron Cecil, page 150).
1800 I.*	*Sligo* (11th), Jeremy Ulick Browne (11th *UK Baron, Monteagle,* 1806), *b.* 1939, *s.* 1991, *m.*	Sebastian U. B., *b.* 1964.
1787	° *Townshend* (7th), George John Patrick Dominic Townshend, *b.* 1916, *s.* 1921, *w.*	Viscount Raynham, *b.* 1945.
1694 S.*	*Tweeddale* (13th), Edward Douglas John Hay (4th *UK Baron, Tweeddale,* 1881), *b.* 1947, *s.* 1979	Lord Charles D. M. H., *b.* 1947.
1789 I.*	*Waterford* (8th), John Hubert de la Poer Beresford (8th *Brit. Baron, Tyrone,* 1786), *b.* 1933, *s.* 1934, *m.*	Earl of Tyrone, *b.* 1958.
1551	*Winchester* (18th), Nigel George Paulet (*Premier Marquess of England*), *b.* 1941, *s.* 1968, *m.*	Earl of Wiltshire, *b.* 1969.
1892	*Zetland* (4th), Lawrence Mark Dundas (6th *UK Earl of Zetland,* 1838, 7th *Brit. Baron Dundas,* 1794), *b.* 1937, *s.* 1989, *m.*	Earl of Ronaldshay, *b.* 1965.

EARLS

Coronet, Eight silver balls on stalks alternating with eight gold strawberry leaves
Style, The Right Hon. the Earl (of) —
Wife's style, The Right Hon. the Countess (of) —
Eldest son's style, Takes his father's second title as a courtesy title
Younger sons' style, 'The Hon.' before forename and family name
Daughters' style, 'Lady' before forename and family name
For forms of address, *see* page 136

Created	Title, order of succession, name, etc.	Heir
1639 S.	*Airlie* (13th), David George Coke Patrick Ogilvy, KT, GCVO, PC, *b.* 1926, *s.* 1968, *m. Lord Chamberlain*	Lord Ogilvy, *b.* 1958.
1696	*Albemarle* (10th), Rufus Arnold Alexis Keppel, *b.* 1965, *s.* 1979	Crispian W. J. K., *b.* 1948.
1952	° *Alexander of Tunis* (2nd), Shane William Desmond Alexander, *b.* 1935, *s.* 1969, *m.*	Hon. Brian J. A., *b.* 1939.
1662 S.	*Annandale and Hartfell* (11th), Patrick Andrew Wentworth Hope Johnstone, *b.* 1941, *claim established* 1985, *m.*	Lord Johnstone, *b.* 1971.
1789 I.	° *Annesley* (10th), Patrick Annesley, *b.* 1924, *s.* 1979, *m.*	Hon. Philip H. A., *b.* 1927.
1785 I.	*Antrim* (9th), Alexander Randal Mark McDonnell, *b.* 1935, *s.* 1977, *m.* (*Viscount Dunluce*)	Hon. Randal A. St J. M., *b.* 1967.
1762 I.*	*Arran* (9th), Arthur Desmond Colquhoun Gore (5th *UK Baron Sudley,* 1884), *b.* 1938, *s.* 1983, *m.*	Paul A. G., CMG, CVO, *b.* 1921.
1955	° *Attlee* (3rd), John Richard Attlee, *b.* 1956, *s.* 1991, *m.*	None.
1714	*Aylesford* (11th), Charles Ian Finch-Knightley, *b.* 1918, *s.* 1958, *w.*	Lord Guernsey, *b.* 1947.
1937	° *Baldwin of Bewdley* (4th), Edward Alfred Alexander Baldwin, *b.* 1938, *s.* 1976, *m.*	Viscount Corvedale, *b.* 1973.
1922	*Balfour* (4th), Gerald Arthur James Balfour, *b.* 1925, *s.* 1968, *m.*	Eustace A. G. B., *b.* 1921.
1772	° *Bathurst* (8th), Henry Allen John Bathurst, *b.* 1927, *s.* 1943, *m.*	Lord Apsley, *b.* 1961.
1919	° *Beatty* (3rd), David Beatty, *b.* 1946, *s.* 1972, *m.*	Viscount Borodale, *b.* 1973.
1797 I.	*Belmore* (8th), John Armar Lowry-Corry, *b.* 1951, *s.* 1960, *m.*	Viscount Corry, *b.* 1985.
1739 I.*	*Bessborough* (11th), Arthur Mountifort Longfield Ponsonby (8th *UK Baron, Duncannon,* 1834), *b.* 1912, *s.* 1993, *m.*	Hon. Myles F. L. P., *b.* 1941.
1815	*Bradford* (7th), Richard Thomas Orlando Bridgeman, *b.* 1947, *s.* 1981, *m.*	Viscount Newport, *b.* 1980.
1677 S.	*Breadalbane and Holland* (10th), John Romer Boreland Campbell, *b.* 1919, *s.* 1959	None.

Created	Title, order of succession, name, etc.	Heir
1469 s.*	*Buchan* (17th), Malcolm Harry Erskine, (8th *UK Baron Erskine* 1806), *b.* 1930, *s.* 1984, *m.*	Lord Cardross, *b.* 1960.
1746	*Buckinghamshire* (10th), (George) Miles Hobart-Hampden, *b.* 1944, *s.* 1983, *m.*	Sir John Hobart, Bt., *b.* 1945.
1800	°*Cadogan* (7th), William Gerald Charles Cadogan, MC, *b.* 1914, *s.* 1933, *m.*	Viscount Chelsea, *b.* 1937.
1878	°*Cairns* (6th), Simon Dallas Cairns, CBE, *b.* 1939, *s.* 1989, *m.*	Viscount Garmoyle, *b.* 1965.
1455 s.	*Caithness* (20th), Malcolm Ian Sinclair, PC, *b.* 1948, *s.* 1965, *w.*	Lord Berriedale, *b.* 1981.
1800 I.	*Caledon* (7th), Nicholas James Alexander, *b.* 1955, *s.* 1980, *m.*	Viscount Alexander, *b.* 1990.
1661	*Carlisle* (13th), George William Beaumont Howard (13th *Scott. Baron, Ruthven of Freeland*, 1651), *b.* 1949, *s.* 1994	Hon. Philip C. W. *H.*, *b.* 1963.
1793	*Carnarvon* (7th), Henry George Reginald Molyneux Herbert, KCVO, KBE, *b.* 1924, *s.* 1987, *m.*	Lord Porchester, *b.* 1956.
1748 I.*	*Carrick* (10th), David James Theobald Somerset Butler (4th *UK Baron, Butler*, 1912), *b.* 1953, *s.* 1992, *m.*	Viscount Ikerrin, *b.* 1975.
1800 I.	°*Castle Stewart* (8th), Arthur Patrick Avondale Stuart, *b.* 1928, *s.* 1961, *m.*	Viscount Stuart, *b.* 1953.
1814	°*Cathcart* (6th), Alan Cathcart, CB, DSO, MC (15th *Scott. Baron, Cathcart*, 1447), *b.* 1919, *s.* 1927, *m.*	Lord Greenock, *b.* 1952.
1647 I.	*Cavan.* The 12th Earl died in 1988. Heir had not established his claim to the title at the time of going to press	Roger C. Lambart, *b.* 1944.
1827	°*Cawdor* (7th), Colin Robert Vaughan Campbell, *b.* 1962, *s.* 1993, *m.*	Hon. Frederick W. *C.*, *b.* 1965.
1801	*Chichester* (9th), John Nicholas Pelham, *b.* 1944, *s.* 1944, *m.*	Richard A. H. *P.*, *b.* 1952.
1803 I.*	*Clancarty* (9th), Nicholas Power Richard Le Poer Trench (8th *UK Visct. Clancarty*, 1823), *b.* 1952, *s.* 1995	None.
1776 I.*	*Clanwilliam* (7th), John Herbert Meade (5th *UK Baron Clanwilliam*, 1828), *b.* 1919, *s.* 1989, *m.*	Lord Gillford, *b.* 1960.
1776	*Clarendon* (7th), George Frederick Laurence Hyde Villiers, *b.* 1933, *s.* 1955, *m.*	Lord Hyde, *b.* 1976.
1620 I.*	*Cork* (14th) & *Orrery* (14th) (I. 1660), John William Boyle, DSC (10th *Brit. Baron, Boyle of Marston*, 1711), *b.* 1916, *s.* 1995, *m.*	Hon. John R. *B.*, *b.* 1945.
1850	*Cottenham* (8th), Kenelm Charles Everard Digby Pepys, *b.* 1948, *s.* 1968, *m.*	Viscount Crowhurst, *b.* 1983.
1762 I.*	*Courtown* (9th), James Patrick Montagu Burgoyne Winthrop Stopford (8th *Brit. Baron, Saltersford*, 1796), *b.* 1954, *s.* 1975, *m.*	Viscount Stopford, *b.* 1988.
1697	*Coventry* (11th), George William Coventry, *b.* 1934, *s.* 1940, *m.*	Viscount Deerhurst, *b.* 1957.
1857	°*Cowley* (7th), Garret Graham Wellesley, *b.* 1934, *s.* 1975, *m.*	Viscount Dangan, *b.* 1965.
1892	*Cranbrook* (5th), Gathorne Gathorne-Hardy, *b.* 1933, *s.* 1978, *m.*	Lord Medway, *b.* 1968.
1801	*Craven* (9th), Benjamin Robert Joseph Craven, *b.* 1989, *s.* 1990, *M.*	Rupert J. E. *C.*, *b.* 1926.
1398 s.*	*Crawford* (29th) & *Balcarres* (12th) (s. 1651), Robert Alexander Lindsay, PC (*Premier Earl on Union Roll*, 5th *UK Baron, Wigan*, 1826, and *Baron Balniel* (life peerage), 1974, *b.* 1927, *s.* 1975, *m.*	Lord Balniel, *b.* 1958.
1861	*Cromartie* (5th), John Ruaridh Blunt Grant Mackenzie, *b.* 1948, *s.* 1989, *m.*	Viscount Tarbat, *b.* 1987.
1901	*Cromer* (4th), Evelyn Rowland Esmond Baring, *b.* 1946, *s.* 1991, *m.*	Viscount Errington, *b* 1994.
1633 s.*	*Dalhousie* (16th), Simon Ramsay, KT, GCVO, GBE, MC (4th *UK Baron, Ramsay*, 1875), *b.* 1914, *s.* 1950, *m.*	Lord Ramsay, *b.* 1948.
1725 I.*	*Darnley* (11th), Adam Ivo Stuart Bligh (20th *Engl. Baron, Clifton of Leighton Bromswold*, 1608), *b.* 1941, *s.* 1980, *m.*	Lord Clifton, *b.* 1968.
1711	*Dartmouth* (9th), Gerald Humphry Legge, *b.* 1924, *s.* 1962, *m.*	Viscount Lewisham, *b.* 1949.
1761	°*De La Warr* (11th), William Herbrand Sackville, *b.* 1948, *s.* 1988, *m.*	Lord Buckhurst, *b.* 1979.
1622	*Denbigh* (12th) & *Desmond* (11th) (I. 1622), Alexander Stephen Rudolph Feilding, *b.* 1970, *s.* 1995, *m.*	William D. *F,* *b.* 1939.
1485	*Derby* (19th), Edward Richard William Stanley, *b.* 1962, *s.* 1994, *m.*	Hon. Peter H. C. *S.,* *b.* 1964.
1553	*Devon* (17th), Charles Christopher Courtenay, *b.* 1916, *s.* 1935, *m.*	Lord Courtenay, *b.* 1942.
1800 I.*	*Donoughmore* (8th), Richard Michael John Hely-Hutchinson (8th *UK Visct., Hutchinson*, 1821), *b.* 1927, *s.* 1981, *m.*	Viscount Suirdale, *b.* 1952.
1661 I.*	*Drogheda* (12th), Henry Dermot Ponsonby Moore (3rd *UK Baron, Moore*, 1954), *b.* 1937, *s.* 1989, *m.*	Viscount Moore, *b.* 1983.
1837	*Ducie* (7th), David Leslie Moreton, *b.* 1951, *s.* 1991, *m.*	Lord Moreton, *b.* 1981.
1860	*Dudley* (4th), William Humble David Ward, *b.* 1920, *s.* 1969, *m.*	Viscount Ednam, *b.* 1947.
1660 s.*	*Dundee* (12th), Alexander Henry Scrymgeour (2nd *UK Baron, Glassary*, 1954), *b.* 1949, *s.* 1983, *m.*	Lord Scrymgeour, *b.* 1982.
1669 s.	*Dundonald* (15th), Iain Alexander Douglas Blair Cochrane, *b.* 1961, *s.* 1986, *m.*	Lord Cochrane, *b.* 1991.
1686 s.	*Dunmore* (12th), Malcolm Kenneth Murray, *b.* 1946, *s.* 1995, *m.*	†
1822 I.	*Dunraven and Mount-Earl* (7th), Thady Windham Thomas Wyndham-Quin, *b.* 1939, *s.* 1965, *m.*	None.

Created	Title, order of succession, name, etc.	Heir
1833	*Durham.* Disclaimed for life 1970 (*Antony Claud Frederick Lambton, b.* 1922, *s.* 1970, *m.*)	Hon. Edward R. *L.* (Baron Durham), *b.* 1961.
1837	*Effingham* (7th), David Mowbray Algernon Howard (17th *Engl. Baron, Howard of Effingham,* 1554), *b.* 1939, *s.* 1996, *m.*	Lord Howard of Effingham, *b.* 1971.
1507 s.*	*Eglinton* (18th) & *Winton* (9th) (1600), Archibald George Montgomerie (6th *UK Earl, Winton,* 1859), *b.* 1939, *s.* 1966, *m.*	Lord Montgomerie, *b.* 1966.
1733 I.*	*Egmont* (11th), Frederick George Moore Perceval (9th *Brit. Baron, Lovel* & *Holland,* 1762), *b.* 1914, *s.* 1932, *m.*	Viscount Perceval, *b.* 1934.
1821	*Eldon* (5th), John Joseph Nicholas Scott, *b.* 1937, *s.* 1976, *m.*	Viscount Encombe, *b.* 1962.
1633 s.*	*Elgin* (11th), & *Kincardine* (15th) (s. 1647), Andrew Douglas Alexander Thomas Bruce (4th *UK Baron, Elgin,* 1849), KT, *b.* 1924, *s.* 1968, *m.*	Lord Bruce, *b.* 1961.
1789 I.*	*Enniskillen* (7th), Andrew John Galbraith Cole (5th *UK Baron, Grinstead,* 1815) *b.* 1942, *s.* 1989, *m.*	Arthur G. *C., b.* 1920.
1789 I.*	*Erne* (6th), Henry George Victor John Crichton (3rd *UK Baron, Fermanagh,* 1876), *b.* 1937, *s.* 1940, *m.*	Viscount Crichton, *b.* 1971.
1452 s.	*Erroll* (24th), Merlin Sereld Victor Gilbert Hay, *b.* 1948, *s.* 1978, *m. Hereditary Lord High Constable and Knight Marischal of Scotland*	Lord Hay, *b.* 1984.
1661	*Essex* (10th), Robert Edward de Vere Capell, *b.* 1920, *s.* 1981, *m.*	Viscount Malden, *b.* 1944.
1711	°*Ferrers* (13th), Robert Washington Shirley, PC, *b.* 1929, *s.* 1954, *m.*	Viscount Tamworth, *b.* 1952.
1789	°*Fortescue* (8th), Charles Hugh Richard Fortescue, *b.* 1951, *s.* 1993, *m.*	Hon. Martin D. *F., b.* 1924.
1841	*Gainsborough* (5th), Anthony Gerard Edward Noel, *b.* 1923, *s.* 1927, *m.*	Viscount Campden, *b.* 1950.
1623 s.*	*Galloway* (13th), Randolph Keith Reginald Stewart (6th *Brit. Baron, Stewart of Garlies,* 1796), *b.* 1928, *s.* 1978, *m.*	Andrew C. *S., b.* 1949.
1703 s.*	*Glasgow* (10th), Patrick Robin Archibald Boyle (4th *UK Baron, Fairlie,* 1897), *b.* 1939, *s.* 1984, *m.*	Viscount of Kelburn, *b.* 1978.
1806 I.*	*Gosford* (7th), Charles David Nicholas Alexander John Sparrow Acheson (5th *UK Baron, Worlingham,* 1835), *b.* 1942, *s.* 1966, *m.*	Hon. Patrick B. V. M. *A., b.* 1915.
1945	*Gowrie* (2nd), Alexander Patric Greysteil Hore-Ruthven, PC (3rd *UK Baron, Ruthven of Gowrie,* 1919), *b.* 1939, *s.* 1955, *m.*	Viscount Ruthven of Canberra, *b.* 1964.
1684 I.*	*Granard* (10th), Peter Arthur Edward Hastings Forbes, (5th *UK Baron, Granard,* 1806), *b.* 1957, *s.* 1992, *m.*	Viscount Forbes, *b.* 1981.
1833	°*Granville* (5th), Granville James Leveson-Gower, MC, *b.* 1918, *s.* 1953, *m.*	Lord Leveson, *b.* 1959.
1806	°*Grey* (6th), Richard Fleming George Charles Grey, *b.* 1939, *s.* 1963, *m.*	Philip K. *G., b.* 1940.
1752	*Guilford* (9th), Edward Francis North, *b.* 1933, *s.* 1949, *w.*	Lord North, *b.* 1971.
1619 s.	*Haddington* (13th), John George Baillie-Hamilton, *b.* 1941, *s.* 1986, *m.*	Lord Binning, *b.* 1985.
1919	°*Haig* (2nd), George Alexander Eugene Douglas Haig, OBE, *b.* 1918, *s.* 1928, *m.*	Viscount Dawick, *b.* 1961.
1944	*Halifax* (3rd), Charles Edward Peter Neil Wood (5th *UK Viscount, Halifax,* 1866), *b.* 1944, *s.* 1980, *m.*	Lord Irwin, *b.* 1977.
1898	*Halsbury* (3rd), John Anthony Hardinge Giffard, FRS, FENG., *b.* 1908, *s.* 1943, *w.*	Adam E. *G., b.* 1934.
1754	*Hardwicke* (10th), Joseph Philip Sebastian Yorke, *b.* 1971, *s.* 1974	Richard C. J. *Y., b.* 1916.
1812	*Harewood* (7th), George Henry Hubert Lascelles, KBE, *b.* 1923, *s.* 1947, *m.* (*see also* page 128)	Viscount Lascelles, *b.* 1950.
1742	*Harrington* (11th), William Henry Leicester Stanhope (8th *Brit. Viscount, Stanhope of Mahon,* 1717), *b.* 1922, *s.* 1929, *m.*	Viscount Petersham, *b.* 1945.
1809	*Harrowby* (7th), Dudley Danvers Granville Coutts Ryder, TD, *b.* 1922, *s.* 1987, *m.*	Viscount Sandon, *b.* 1951.
1605 s.	*Home* (15th) David Alexander Cospatrick Douglas-Home, *b.* 1943, *s.* 1995, *m.*	Lord Dunglass, *b.* 1987.
1821	°*Howe* (7th), Frederick Richard Penn Curzon, *b.* 1951, *s.* 1984, *m.*	Viscount Curzon, *b.* 1994.
1529	*Huntingdon* (16th), William Edward Robin Hood Hastings Bass, *b.* 1948, *s.* 1990, *m.*	Hon. Simon A. R. H. *H. B., b.* 1950.
1885	*Iddesleigh* (4th), Stafford Henry Northcote, *b.* 1932, *s.* 1970, *m.*	Viscount St Cyres, *b.* 1957.
1756	*Ilchester* (9th), Maurice Vivian de Touffreville Fox-Strangways, *b.* 1920, *s.* 1970, *m.*	Hon. Raymond G. *F.-S., b.* 1921.
1929	*Inchcape* (4th), (Kenneth) Peter (Lyle) Mackay, *b.* 1943, *s.* 1994, *m.*	Viscount Glenapp, *b.* 1979.
1919	*Iveagh* (4th), Arthur Edward Rory Guinness, *b.* 1969, *s.* 1992	Hon. Rory M. B. *G., b.* 1974.
1925	°*Jellicoe* (2nd), George Patrick John Rushworth Jellicoe, KBE, DSO, MC, PC, FRS, *b.* 1918, *s.* 1935, *m.*	Viscount Brocas, *b.* 1950.
1697	*Jersey* (9th), George Francis Child Villiers (12th *Irish Visct., Grandison,* 1620), *b.* 1910, *s.* 1923, *m.*	Viscount Villiers, *b.* 1948.
1822 I.	*Kilmorey* (6th), Richard Francis Needham, PC, MP, *b.* 1942, *s.* 1977, *m.*	Viscount Newry and Morne, *b.* 1966.
1866	*Kimberley* (4th), John Wodehouse, *b.* 1924, *s.* 1941, *m.*	Lord Wodehouse, *b.* 1951.
1768 I.	*Kingston* (11th), Barclay Robert Edwin King-Tenison, *b.* 1943, *s.* 1948, *m.*	Viscount Kingsborough, *b.* 1969.

Created	Title, order of succession, name, etc.	Heir
1633 s.*	Kinnoull (15th), Arthur William George Patrick Hay (9th Brit. Baron, Hay of Pedwardine, 1711), b. 1935, s. 1938, m.	Viscount Dupplin, b. 1962.
1677 s.*	Kintore (13th), Michael Canning William John Keith (3rd UK Viscount Stonehaven, 1938), b. 1939, s. 1989, m.	Lord Inverurie, b. 1976.
1914	°Kitchener of Khartoum (3rd), Henry Herbert Kitchener, TD, b. 1919, s. 1937	None.
1756 I.	Lanesborough (9th), Denis Anthony Brian Butler, TD, b. 1918, s. 1950, m.	None.
1624 s.	Lauderdale (17th), Patrick Francis Maitland, b. 1911, s. 1968, m.	Viscount Maitland, b. 1937.
1837	Leicester (7th), Edward Douglas Coke, b. 1936, s. 1994, m.	Viscount Coke, b. 1965.
1641 s.	Leven (14th) & Melville (13th) (s. 1690), Alexander Robert Leslie Melville, b. 1924, s. 1947, m.	Lord Balgonie, b. 1954.
1831	Lichfield (5th), Thomas Patrick John Anson, b. 1939, s. 1960	Viscount Anson, b. 1978.
1803 I.*	Limerick (6th), Patrick Edmund Pery, KBE (6th UK Baron, Foxford, 1815), b. 1930, s. 1967, m.	Viscount Glentworth, b. 1963.
1572	Lincoln (18th), Edward Horace Fiennes-Clinton, b. 1913, s. 1988, m.	Hon. Edward G. F.-C., b. 1943.
1633 s.	Lindsay (16th), James Randolph Lindesay-Bethune, b. 1955, s. 1989, m.	Viscount Garnock, b. 1990.
1626	Lindsey (14th) and Abingdon (9th) (1682), Richard Henry Rupert Bertie, b. 1931, s. 1963, m.	Lord Norreys, b. 1958.
1776 I.	Lisburne (8th), John David Malet Vaughan, b. 1918, s. 1965, m.	Viscount Vaughan, b. 1945.
1822 I.*	Listowel (5th), William Francis Hare, GCMG, PC, (3rd UK Baron, Hare, 1869), b. 1906, s. 1931, m.	Viscount Ennismore, b. 1964.
1905	Liverpool (5th), Edward Peter Bertram Savile Foljambe, b. 1944, s. 1969	Viscount Hawkesbury, b. 1972.
1945	°Lloyd George of Dwyfor (3rd), Owen Lloyd George, b. 1924, s. 1968, m.	Viscount Gwynedd, b. 1951.
1785 I.*	Longford (7th), Francis Aungier Pakenham, KG, PC (6th UK Baron, Silchester, 1821; 1st UK Baron, Pakenham, 1945), b. 1905, s. 1961, m.	Thomas F. D. P., b. 1933.
1807	Lonsdale (7th), James Hugh William Lowther, b. 1922, s. 1953, m.	Viscount Lowther, b. 1949.
1838	Lovelace (5th), Peter Axel William Locke King (12th Brit. Baron, King, 1725), b. 1951, s. 1964, m.	None.
1795 I.*	Lucan (7th), Richard John Bingham (3rd UK Baron, Bingham, 1934), b. 1934, s. 1964, m.	Lord Bingham, b. 1967.
1880	Lytton (5th), John Peter Michael Scawen Lytton (18th Engl. Baron, Wentworth, 1529), b. 1950, s. 1985, m.	Viscount Knebworth, b. 1989.
1721	Macclesfield (9th), Richard Timothy George Mansfield Parker, b. 1943, s. 1992, m.	Hon. J. David G. P., b. 1945.
1800	Malmesbury (6th), William James Harris, TD, b. 1907, s. 1950, w.	Viscount FitzHarris, b. 1946.
1776 & 1792	Mansfield and Mansfield (8th), William David Mungo James Murray (14th Scott. Visct., Stormont, 1621), b. 1930, s. 1971, m.	Viscount Stormont, b. 1956.
1565 s.	Mar (14th) & Kellie (16th) (s. 1616), James Thorne Erskine, b. 1949, s. 1994, m.	Hon. Alexander D. E., b. 1952.
1785 I.	Mayo (10th), Terence Patrick Bourke, b. 1929, s. 1962	Lord Naas, b. 1953.
1627 I.*	Meath (14th), Anthony Windham Normand Brabazon (5th UK Baron, Chaworth, 1831), b. 1910, s. 1949, m.	Lord Ardee, b. 1941.
1766 I.	Mexborough (8th), John Christopher George Savile, b. 1931, s. 1980, m.	Viscount Pollington, b. 1959.
1813	Minto (6th), Gilbert Edward George Lariston Elliot-Murray-Kynynmound, OBE, b. 1928, s. 1975, m.	Viscount Melgund, b. 1953.
1562 s.*	Moray (20th) Douglas John Moray Stuart (12th Brit. Baron, Stuart of Castle Stuart, 1796), b. 1928, s. 1974, m.	Lord Doune, b. 1966.
1815	Morley (6th), John St Aubyn Parker, b. 1923, s. 1962, m.	Viscount Boringdon, b. 1956.
1458 s.	Morton (22nd), John Charles Sholto Douglas, b. 1927, s. 1976, m.	Lord Aberdour, b. 1952.
1789	Mount Edgcumbe (8th), Robert Charles Edgcumbe, b. 1939, s. 1982	Piers V. E., b. 1946.
1831	Munster (7th), Anthony Charles FitzClarence, b. 1926, s. 1983, w.	None.
1805	°Nelson (9th), Peter John Horatio Nelson, b. 1941, s. 1981, m.	Viscount Merton, b. 1971.
1660 s.	Newburgh (12th), Don Filippo Giambattista Camillo Francesco Aldo Maria Rospigliosi, b. 1942, s. 1986, m.	Princess Donna Benedetta F. M. R., b. 1974.
1827 I.	Norbury (6th), Noel Terence Graham-Toler, b. 1939, s. 1955, m.	Viscount Glandine, b. 1967.
1806 I.*	Normanton (6th), Shaun James Christian Welbore Ellis Agar (9th Brit. Baron, Mendip, 1794, 4th UK Baron, Somerton, 1873), b. 1945, s. 1967, m.	Viscount Somerton, b. 1982.
1647 s.	Northesk (14th), David John MacRae Carnegie, b. 1954, s. 1994, m.	Lord Rosehill, b. 1980.
1801	Onslow (7th), Michael William Coplestone Dillon Onslow, b. 1938, s. 1971, m.	Viscount Cranley, b. 1967.
1696 s.	Orkney (8th), Cecil O'Bryen Fitz-Maurice, b. 1919, s. 1951, w.	O. Peter St John, b. 1938.
1925	Oxford and Asquith (2nd), Julian Edward George Asquith, KCMG, b. 1916, s. 1928, m.	Viscount Asquith, OBE, b. 1952.
1929	°Peel (3rd), William James Robert Peel (4th UK Viscount Peel, 1895), b. 1947, s. 1969, m.	Viscount Clanfield, b. 1976.

Created	Title, order of succession, name, etc.	Heir
1551	Pembroke (17th) & Montgomery (14th) (1605), Henry George Charles Alexander Herbert, b. 1939, s. 1969	Lord Herbert, b. 1978.
1605 s.	Perth (17th), John David Drummond, PC, b. 1907, s. 1951, w.	Viscount Strathallan, b. 1935.
1905	Plymouth (3rd), Other Robert Ivor Windsor-Clive (15th Engl. Baron, Windsor, 1529), b. 1923, s. 1943, m.	Viscount Windsor, b. 1951.
1785 I.	Portarlington (7th), George Lionel Yuill Seymour Dawson-Damer, b. 1938, s. 1959, m.	Viscount Carlow, b. 1965.
1689	Portland (11th), Count Henry Noel Bentinck, b. 1919, s. 1990, m.	Viscount Woodstock, b. 1953.
1743	Portsmouth (10th), Quentin Gerard Carew Wallop, b. 1954, s. 1984, m.	Viscount Lymington, b. 1981.
1804	Powis (8th), John George Herbert (9th Irish Baron, Clive, 1762), b. 1952, s. 1993, m.	Viscount Clive, b. 1979.
1765	Radnor (8th), Jacob Pleydell-Bouverie, b. 1927, s. 1968, m.	Viscount Folkestone, b. 1955.
1831 I.*	Ranfurly (7th), Gerald Françoys Needham Knox (8th UK Baron, Ranfurly, 1826), b. 1929, s. 1988, m.	Edward J. K., b. 1957.
1771 I.	Roden (10th), Robert John Jocelyn, b. 1938, s. 1993, m.	Viscount Jocelyn, b. 1989.
1801	Romney (7th), Michael Henry Marsham, b. 1910, s. 1975, m.	Julian C. M., b. 1948.
1703 s.*	Rosebery (7th), Neil Archibald Primrose (3rd UK Earl, Midlothian, 1911), b. 1929, s. 1974, m.	Lord Dalmeny, b. 1967.
1806 I.	Rosse (7th), William Brendan Parsons, b. 1936, s. 1979, m.	Lord Oxmantown, b. 1969.
1801	Rosslyn (7th), Peter St Clair-Erskine, b. 1958, s. 1977, m.	Lord Loughborough, b. 1986.
1457 s.	Rothes (21st), Ian Lionel Malcolm Leslie, b. 1932, s. 1975, m.	Lord Leslie, b. 1958.
1861	°Russell (5th), Conrad Sebastian Robert Russell, FBA, b. 1937, s. 1987, m.	Viscount Amberley, b. 1968.
1915	°St Aldwyn (3rd), Michael Henry Hicks Beach, b. 1950, s. 1992, m.	Hon. David S. H. B., b. 1955.
1815	St Germans (10th), Peregrine Nicholas Eliot, b. 1941, s. 1988	Lord Eliot, b. 1966.
1660	Sandwich (11th), John Edward Hollister Montagu, b. 1943, s. 1995, m.	Viscount Hinchingbrooke, b. 1969.
1690	Scarbrough (12th), Richard Aldred Lumley (13th Irish Visct., Lumley, 1628), b. 1932, s. 1969, m.	Viscount Lumley, b. 1973.
1701 s.	Seafield (13th), Ian Derek Francis Ogilvie-Grant, b. 1939, s. 1969, m.	Viscount Reidhaven, b. 1963.
1882	Selborne (4th), John Roundell Palmer, KBE, FRS, b. 1940, s. 1971, m.	Viscount Wolmer, b. 1971.
1646 s.	Selkirk. Disclaimed for life 1994. (Rt. Hon. Lord James Douglas-Hamilton, MP, b. 1942, succession decided in his favour 1996, m.)	Hon. John A. D.-H., b. 1978
1672	Shaftesbury (10th), Anthony Ashley-Cooper, b. 1938, s. 1961, m.	Lord Ashley, b. 1977.
1756 I.*	Shannon (9th), Richard Bentinck Boyle (8th Brit. Baron Carleton, 1786), b. 1924, s. 1963	Viscount Boyle, b. 1960.
1442	Shrewsbury & Waterford (22nd), (I. 1446), Charles Henry John Benedict Crofton Chetwynd Chetwynd-Talbot (Premier Earl of England and Ireland; 7th Earl Talbot, 1784), b. 1952, s. 1980, m.	Viscount Ingestre, b. 1978.
1961	Snowdon (1st), Antony Charles Robert Armstrong-Jones, GCVO, b. 1930, m. (see also page 117)	Viscount Linley, b. 1961 (see also page 117).
1880	°Sondes (5th), Henry George Herbert Milles-Lade, b. 1940, s. 1970, m.	None.
1765	°Spencer (9th), Charles Edward Maurice Spencer, b. 1964, s. 1992, m.	Viscount Althorp, b. 1994.
1703 s.*	Stair (14th), John David James Dalrymple (7th UK Baron, Oxenfoord, 1841), b. 1961, s. 1996	Hon. David H. D., b. 1963
1984	Stockton (2nd), Alexander Daniel Alan Macmillan, b. 1943, s. 1986, m.	Viscount Macmillan of Ovenden, b. 1974.
1821	Stradbroke (6th), Robert Keith Rous, b. 1937, s. 1983, m.	Viscount Dunwich, b. 1961.
1847	Strafford (8th), Thomas Edmund Byng, b. 1936, s. 1984, m.	Viscount Enfield, b. 1964.
1606 s.*	Strathmore & Kinghorne (18th), Michael Fergus Bowes Lyon (16th Scottish Earl, Strathmore, 1677, & 18th Kinghorne, 1606; 5th UK Earl, Strathmore & Kinghorne, 1937), b. 1957, s. 1987, m.	Lord Glamis, b. 1986.
1603	Suffolk (21st) & Berkshire (14th) (1626), Michael John James George Robert Howard, b. 1935, s. 1941, m.	Viscount Andover, b. 1974.
1955	Swinton (2nd), David Yarburgh Cunliffe-Lister, b. 1937, s. 1972, m.	Hon. Nicholas J. C.-L., b. 1939.
1714	Tankerville (10th), Peter Grey Bennet, b. 1956, s. 1980	Revd the Hon. George A. G. B., b. 1925.
1822	°Temple of Stowe (8th), (Walter) Grenville Algernon Temple-Gore-Langton, b. 1924, s. 1988, m.	Lord Langton, b. 1955.
1815	Verulam (7th), John Duncan Grimston (11th Irish Visct., Grimston, 1719; 16th Scott. Baron, Forrester of Corstorphine, 1633), b. 1951, s. 1973, m.	Viscount Grimston, b. 1978.
1729	°Waldegrave (13th), James Sherbrooke Waldegrave, b. 1940, s. 1995, m.	Viscount Chewton, b. 1986.
1759	Warwick (9th) & °Brooke (9th) (Brit. 1746), Guy David Greville, b. 1957, s. 1996, m.	Lord Brooke, b. 1982.
1633 s.*	Wemyss (12th) & March (8th) (s. 1697), Francis David Charteris, KT (5th UK Baron, Wemyss, 1821), b. 1912, s. 1937, m.	Lord Neidpath, b. 1948.
1621 I.	Westmeath (13th), William Anthony Nugent, b. 1928, s. 1971, m.	Hon. Sean C. W. N., b. 1965.
1624	Westmorland (16th), Anthony David Francis Henry Fane, b. 1951, s. 1993, m.	Hon. Harry St C. F., b. 1953.

Created	Title, order of succession, name, etc.	Heir
1876	Wharncliffe (5th), Richard Alan Montagu Stuart Wortley, b. 1953, s. 1987, m.	Viscount Carlton, b. 1980.
1801	Wilton (7th), Seymour William Arthur John Egerton, b. 1921, s. 1927, m.	Baron Ebury, b. 1934 (see page 151).
1628	Winchilsea (16th) & Nottingham (11th) (1681), Christopher Denys Stormont Finch Hatton, b. 1936, s. 1950, m.	Viscount Maidstone, b. 1967.
1766 I.	° Winterton (8th), (Donald) David Turnour, b. 1943, s. 1991, m.	Robert C. T., b. 1950.
1956	Woolton (3rd), Simon Frederick Marquis, b. 1958, s. 1969, m.	None.
1837	Yarborough (8th), Charles John Pelham, b. 1963, s. 1991, m.	Lord Worsley, b. 1990.

COUNTESSES IN THEIR OWN RIGHT

Style, The Right Hon. the Countess (of) —
Husband, Untitled
Children's style, As for children of an Earl
For forms of address, *see* page 136

Created	Title, order of succession, name, etc.	Heir
1643 s.	Dysart (11th in line), Rosamund Agnes Greaves, b. 1914, s. 1975	Lady Katherine Grant of Rothiemurchus, b. 1918.
1633 s.	Loudoun (13th in line), Barbara Huddleston Abney-Hastings, b. 1919, s. 1960, m.	Lord Mauchline, b. 1942.
c.1115 s.	Mar (31st in line), Margaret of Mar (Premier Earldom of Scotland), b. 1940, s. 1975, m.	Mistress of Mar, b. 1963.
1947	° Mountbatten of Burma (2nd in line), Patricia Edwina Victoria Knatchbull, CBE, b. 1924, s. 1979, m.	Lord Romsey, b. 1947 (see also page 149).
c.1235 s.	Sutherland (24th in line), Elizabeth Millicent Sutherland, b. 1921, s. 1963, m.	Lord Strathnaver, b. 1947.

VISCOUNTS

Coronet, Sixteen silver balls
Style, The Right Hon. the Viscount —
Wife's style, The Right Hon. the Viscountess —
Children's style, 'The Hon.' before forename and family name
In Scotland, the heir apparent to a Viscount may be styled 'The Master of — (title of peer)'
For forms of address, *see* page 136

Created	Title, order of succession, name, etc.	Heir
1945	Addison (4th), William Matthew Wand Addison, b. 1945, s. 1992, m.	Hon. Paul W. A., b. 1973.
1946	Alanbrooke (3rd), Alan Victor Harold Brooke, b. 1932, s. 1972	None.
1919	Allenby (3rd), Lt.-Col. Michael Jaffray Hynman Allenby, b. 1931, s. 1984, m.	Hon. Henry J. H. A., b. 1968.
1911	Allendale (3rd), Wentworth Hubert Charles Beaumont, b. 1922, s. 1956	Hon. Wentworth P. I. B., b. 1948.
1642 s.	of Arbuthnott (16th), John Campbell Arbuthnott, CBE, DSC, FRSE, b. 1924, s. 1966, m.	Master of Arbuthnott, b. 1950.
1751 I.	Ashbrook (11th), Michael Llowarch Warburton Flower, b. 1935, s. 1995, m.	Hon. Rowland F. W. F., b. 1975.
1917	Astor (4th), William Waldorf Astor, b. 1951, s. 1966, m.	Hon. William W. A., b. 1979.
1781 I.	Bangor (8th), William Maxwell David Ward, b. 1948, s. 1993, m.	Hon. E. Nicholas W., b. 1953.
1925	Bearsted (5th), Nicholas Alan Samuel, b. 1950, s. 1996, m.	Hon. Harry R. S., b. 1988.
1963	Blakenham (2nd), Michael John Hare, b. 1938, s. 1982, m.	Hon. Caspar J. H., b. 1972.
1935	Bledisloe (3rd), Christopher Hiley Ludlow Bathurst, QC, b. 1934, s. 1979	Hon. Rupert E. L. B., b. 1964.
1712	Bolingbroke (7th) & St John (8th) (1716), Kenneth Oliver Musgrave St John, b. 1927, s. 1974	Hon. Henry F. St J., b. 1957.
1960	Boyd of Merton (2nd), Simon Donald Rupert Neville Lennox-Boyd, b. 1939, s. 1983, m.	Hon. Benjamin A. L.-B., b. 1964.

Created	Title, order of succession, name, etc.	Heir
1717 I.*	*Boyne* (11th), Gustavus Michael Stucley Hamilton-Russell (5th *UK Baron, Brancepeth,* 1866), *b.* 1965, *s.* 1995, *m.*	Hon. Richard G. *H.-R.,* DSO, LVO, *b.* 1909.
1929	*Brentford* (4th), Crispin William Joynson-Hicks, *b.* 1933, *s.* 1983, *m.*	Hon. Paul W. *J.-H., b.* 1971.
1929	*Bridgeman* (3rd), Robin John Orlando Bridgeman, *b.* 1930, *s.* 1982, *m.*	Hon. William O. C. *B., b.* 1968.
1868	*Bridport* (4th), Alexander Nelson Hood (7th *Duke of Brontë in Sicily,* 1799, *and* 6th *Irish Baron Bridport,* 1794), *b.* 1948, *s.* 1969, *m.*	Hon. Peregrine A. N. *H., b.* 1974.
1952	*Brookeborough* (3rd), Alan Henry Brooke, *b.* 1952, *s.* 1987, *m.*	Hon. Christopher A. *B., b.* 1954.
1933	*Buckmaster* (3rd), Martin Stanley Buckmaster, OBE, *b.* 1921, *s.* 1974	Hon. Colin J. *B., b.* 1923.
1939	*Caldecote* (2nd), Robert Andrew Inskip, KBE, DSC, FE ng., *b.* 1917, *s.* 1947, *m.*	Hon. Piers J. H. *I., b.* 1947.
1941	*Camrose.* Disclaimed for life 1995 (*see* Baron Hartwell, page 160)	Hon. Adrian M. *Berry, b.* 1937.
1954	*Chandos* (3rd), Thomas Orlando Lyttelton, *b.* 1953, *s.* 1980, *m.*	Hon. Oliver A. *L., b.* 1986.
1665 I.	*Charlemont* (14th), John Day Caulfeild (18th *Irish Baron, Caulfeild of Charlemont,* 1620), *b.* 1934, *s.* 1985, *m.*	Hon. John D. *C., b.* 1966.
1921	*Chelmsford* (3rd), Frederic Jan Thesiger, *b.* 1931, *s.* 1970, *m.*	Hon. Frederic C. P. *T., b.* 1962.
1717 I.	*Chetwynd* (10th), Adam Richard John Casson Chetwynd, *b.* 1935, *s.* 1965, *m.*	Hon. Adam D. *C., b.* 1969.
1911	*Chilston* (4th), Alastair George Akers-Douglas, *b.* 1946, *s.* 1982, *m.*	Hon. Oliver I. *A.-D., b.* 1973.
1902	*Churchill* (3rd), Victor George Spencer (5th *UK Baron Churchill,* 1815), *b.* 1934, *s.* 1973	None to Viscountcy. To Barony, Richard H. R. *S., b.* 1926.
1718	*Cobham* (11th), John William Leonard Lyttelton (8th *Irish Baron, Westcote,* 1776), *b.* 1943, *s.* 1977	Hon. Christopher C. *L., b.* 1947.
1902	*Colville of Culross* (4th), John Mark Alexander Colville, QC (13th *Scott. Baron, Colville of Culross,* 1604), *b.* 1933, *s.* 1945, *m.*	Master of Colville, *b.* 1959.
1826	*Combermere* (5th), Michael Wellington Stapleton-Cotton, *b.* 1929, *s.* 1969, *m.*	Hon. Thomas R. W. *S.-C., b.* 1969.
1917	*Cowdray* (4th), Michael Orlando Weetman Pearson (4th *UK Baron, Cowdray,* 1910), *b.* 1944, *s.* 1995, *m.*	Hon. Charles A. *P., b.* 1956.
1927	*Craigavon* (3rd), Janric Fraser Craig, *b.* 1944, *s.* 1974	None.
1886	*Cross* (3rd), Assheton Henry Cross, *b.* 1920, *s.* 1932	None.
1943	*Daventry* (3rd), Francis Humphrey Maurice FitzRoy Newdegate, *b.* 1921, *s.* 1986, *m.*	Hon. James E. *F. N., b.* 1960.
1937	*Davidson* (2nd), John Andrew Davidson, *b.* 1928, *s.* 1970, *m.*	Hon. Malcolm W. M. *D., b.* 1934.
1956	*De L'Isle* (2nd), Philip John Algernon Sidney, MBE, (7th *Baron De L'Isle and Dudley,* 1835), *b.* 1945, *s.* 1991, *m.*	Hon. Philip W. E. *S., b.* 1985.
1776 I.	*De Vesci* (7th), Thomas Eustace Vesey (8th *Irish Baron, Knapton,* 1750), *b.* 1955, *s.* 1983, *m.*	Hon. Oliver I. *V., b.* 1991.
1917	*Devonport* (3rd), Terence Kearley, *b.* 1944, *s.* 1973	Chester D. H. *K., b.* 1932.
1964	*Dilhorne* (2nd), John Mervyn Manningham-Buller, *b.* 1932, *s.* 1980, *m.*	Hon. James E. *M.-B., b.* 1956.
1622 I.	*Dillon* (22nd), Henry Benedict Charles Dillon, *b.* 1973, *s.* 1982	Hon. Richard A. L. *D., b.* 1948.
1785 I.	*Doneraile* (10th), Richard Allen St Leger, *b.* 1946, *s.* 1983, *m.*	Hon. Nathaniel W. R. St J. *St L., b.* 1971.
1680 I.*	*Downe* (11th), John Christian George Dawnay (4th *UK Baron, Dawnay,* 1897), *b.* 1935, *s.* 1965, *m.*	Hon. Richard H. *D., b.* 1967.
1959	*Dunrossil* (2nd), John William Morrison, CMG, *b.* 1926, *s.* 1961, *m.*	Hon. Andrew W. R. *M., b.* 1953.
1964	*Eccles* (1st), David McAdam Eccles, CH, KCVO, PC, *b.* 1904, *m.*	Hon. John D. *E.,* CBE, *b.* 1931.
1897	*Esher* (4th), Lionel Gordon Baliol Brett, CBE, *b.* 1913. *s.* 1963, *m.*	Hon. Christopher L. B. *B., b.* 1936.
1816	*Exmouth* (10th), Paul Edward Pellew, *b.* 1940, *s.* 1970, *m.*	Hon. Edward F. *P., b.* 1978.
1620 S.	*Falkland* (15th), Lucius Edward William Plantagenet Cary (*Premier Scottish Viscount on the Roll*), *b.* 1935, *s.* 1984, *m.*	Master of Falkland, *b.* 1963.
1720	*Falmouth* (9th), George Hugh Boscawen (26th *Eng. Baron, Le Despencer,* 1264), *b.* 1919, *s.* 1962, *m.*	Hon. Evelyn A. H. *B., b.* 1955.
1720 I.*	*Gage* (8th), (Henry) Nicolas Gage, (7th *Brit. Baron, Gage,* 1790), *b.* 1934. *s.* 1993, *m.*	Hon. Henry W. *G., b.* 1975.
1727 I.	*Galway* (12th), George Rupert Monckton-Arundell, *b.* 1922, *s.* 1980, *m.*	Hon. J. Philip *M., b.* 1952.
1478 I.*	*Gormanston* (17th), Jenico Nicholas Dudley Preston (*Premier Viscount of Ireland;* 5th *UK Baron, Gormanston,* 1868), *b.* 1939, *s.* 1940, *w.*	Hon. Jenico F. T. *P., b.* 1974.
1816 I.	*Gort* (9th), Foley Robert Standish Prendergast Vereker, *b.* 1951, *s.* 1995, *m.*	Hon. Nicholas L. P. *V., b.* 1954.
1900	*Goschen* (4th), Giles John Harry Goschen, *b.* 1965, *s.* 1977, *m.*	None.
1849	*Gough* (5th), Shane Hugh Maryon Gough, *b.* 1941, *s.* 1951	None.
1937	*Greenwood* (2nd), David Henry Hamar Greenwood, *b.* 1914, *s.* 1948	Hon. Michael G. H. *G., b.* 1923.
1929	*Hailsham.* Disclaimed for life 1963 (*see* Lord Hailsham of St Marylebone, page 160)	Rt. Hon. Douglas M. *Hogg,* QC, MP, *b.* 1945.
1891	*Hambleden* (4th), William Herbert Smith, *b.* 1930, *s.* 1948, *m.*	Hon. William H. B. *S., b.* 1955.
1884	*Hampden* (6th), Anthony David Brand, *b.* 1937, *s.* 1975, *m.*	Hon. Francis A. *B., b.* 1970.
1936	*Hanworth* (2nd), David Bertram Pollock, *b.* 1916, *s.* 1936, *m.*	Hon. David S. G. *P., b.* 1946.
1791 I.	*Harberton* (10th), Thomas de Vautort Pomeroy, *b.* 1910, *s.* 1980, *m.*	Hon. Robert W. *P., b.* 1916.

Created	Title, order of succession, name, etc.	Heir
1846	Hardinge (6th), Charles Henry Nicholas Hardinge, b. 1956, s. 1984, m.	Hon. Andrew H. H., b. 1960.
1791 I.	Hawarden (9th), (Robert) Connan Wyndham Leslie Maude, b. 1961, s. 1991, m.	Hon. Thomas P. C. M., b. 1964.
1960	Head (2nd), Richard Antony Head, b. 1937, s. 1983, m.	Hon. Henry J. H., b. 1980.
1550	Hereford (18th), Robert Milo Leicester Devereux (Premier Viscount of England), b. 1932, s. 1952	Hon. Charles R. de B. D., b. 1975.
1842	Hill (8th), Antony Rowland Clegg-Hill, b. 1931, s. 1974, m.	Peter D. R. C. C.-H., b. 1945.
1796	Hood (7th), Alexander Lambert Hood (7th Irish Baron, Hood, 1782), b. 1914, s. 1981, m.	Hon. Henry L. A. H., b. 1958.
1956	Ingleby (2nd), Martin Raymond Peake, b. 1926, s. 1966, w.	None.
1945	Kemsley (2nd), (Geoffrey) Lionel Berry, b. 1909, s. 1968, m.	Richard G. B., b. 1951.
1911	Knollys (3rd), David Francis Dudley Knollys, b. 1931, s. 1966, m.	Hon. Patrick N. M. K., b. 1962.
1895	Knutsford (6th), Michael Holland-Hibbert, b. 1926, s. 1986, m.	Hon. Henry T. H.-H., b. 1959.
1945	Lambert (3rd), Michael John Lambert, b. 1912, s. 1989, m.	None.
1954	Leathers (3rd), Christopher Graeme Leathers, b. 1941, s. 1996, m.	Hon. James F. L., b. 1969.
1922	Leverhulme (3rd), Philip William Bryce Lever, KG, TD, b. 1915, s. 1949, w.	None.
1781 I.	Lifford (9th), (Edward) James Wingfield Hewitt, b. 1949, s. 1987, m.	Hon. James T. W. H., b. 1979.
1921	Long (4th), Richard Gerard Long, CBE, b. 1929, s. 1967, m.	Hon. James R. L., b. 1960.
1957	Mackintosh of Halifax (3rd), (John) Clive Mackintosh, b. 1958, s. 1980, m.	Hon. Thomas H. G. M., b. 1985.
1955	Malvern (3rd), Ashley Kevin Godfrey Huggins, b. 1949, s. 1978	Hon. M. James H., b. 1928.
1945	Marchwood (3rd), David George Staveley Penny, b. 1936, s. 1979, m.	Hon. Peter G. W. P., b. 1965.
1942	Margesson (2nd), Francis Vere Hampden Margesson, b. 1922, s. 1965, m.	Capt. Hon. Richard F. D. M., b. 1960.
1660 I.*	Massereene (14th) & Ferrard (7th) (1797), John David Clotworthy Whyte-Melville Foster Skeffington (7th UK Baron, Oriel, 1821), b. 1940, s. 1992, m.	Hon. Charles J. C. W.-M. F. S., b. 1973.
1802	Melville (9th), Robert David Ross Dundas, b. 1937, s. 1971, m.	Hon. Robert H. K. D., b. 1984.
1916	Mersey (4th), Richard Maurice Clive Bigham (13th Scott. Lord Nairne, 1681, s. 1995), b. 1934, s. 1979, m.	Hon. Edward J. H. B., b. 1966.
1717 I.*	Midleton (12th), Alan Henry Brodrick (9th Brit. Baron, Brodrick of Peper Harow, 1796), b. 1949, s. 1988, m.	Hon. Ashley R. B., b. 1980.
1962	Mills (3rd), Christopher Philip Roger Mills, b. 1956, s. 1988, m.	None.
1716 I.	Molesworth (11th), Richard Gosset Molesworth, b. 1907, s. 1961, w.	Hon. Robert B. K. M., b. 1959.
1801 I.*	Monck (7th), Charles Stanley Monck (4th UK Baron, Monck, 1866), b. 1953, s. 1982 (does not use title)	Hon. George S. M., b. 1957.
1957	Monckton of Brenchley (2nd), Maj.-Gen. Gilbert Walter Riversdale Monckton, CB, OBE, MC, b. 1915, s. 1965, m.	Hon Christopher W. M., b. 1952.
1946	Montgomery of Alamein (2nd), David Bernard Montgomery, CBE, b. 1928, s. 1976, m.	Hon. Henry D. M., b. 1954.
1550 I.*	Mountgarret (17th), Richard Henry Piers Butler (4th UK Baron, Mountgarret, 1911), b. 1936, s. 1966, m.	Hon. Piers J. R. B., b. 1961.
1952	Norwich (2nd), John Julius Cooper, CVO, b. 1929, s. 1954, m.	Hon. Jason C. D. B. C., b. 1959.
1651 S.	of Oxfuird (13th), George Hubbard Makgill, b. 1934, s. 1986, m.	Master of Oxfuird, b. 1969.
1873	Portman, (9th), Edward Henry Berkeley Portman, b. 1934, s. 1967, m.	Hon. Christopher E. B. P., b. 1958.
1743 I.*	Powerscourt (10th), Mervyn Niall Wingfield (4th UK Baron, Powerscourt, 1885), b. 1935, s. 1973, m.	Hon. Mervyn A. W., b. 1963.
1900	Ridley (4th), Matthew White Ridley, KG, GCVO, TD, b. 1925, s. 1964, m. Lord Steward	Hon. Matthew W. R., b. 1958.
1960	Rochdale (2nd), St John Durival Kemp, b. 1938, s. 1993, m.	Hon. Jonathan H. D. K., b. 1961.
1919	Rothermere (3rd), Vere Harold Esmond Harmsworth, b. 1925, s. 1978, m.	Hon. H. Jonathan E. V. H., b. 1967.
1937	Runciman of Doxford (3rd), Walter Garrison Runciman (Garry), CBE, FBA (4th UK Baron, Runciman, 1933), b. 1934, s. 1989, m.	Hon. David W. R., b. 1967.
1918	St Davids (3rd), Colwyn Jestyn John Philipps (20th Engl. Baron Strange of Knokin, 1299, 8th Engl. Baron Hungerford, 1426, and De Moleyns, 1445), b. 1939, s. 1991, m.	Hon. Rhodri C. P., b. 1966.
1801	St Vincent (7th), Ronald George James Jervis, b. 1905, s. 1940, m.	Hon. Edward R. J. J., b. 1951.
1937	Samuel (3rd), David Herbert Samuel, OBE, PH.D., b. 1922, s. 1978, m.	Hon. Dan J. S., b. 1925.
1911	Scarsdale (3rd), Francis John Nathaniel Curzon (7th Brit. Baron, Scarsdale, 1761), b. 1924, s. 1977, m.	Hon. Peter G. N. C., b. 1949.
1905	Selby (4th), Michael Guy John Gully, b. 1942, s. 1959, m.	Hon. Edward T. W. G., b. 1967.
1805	Sidmouth (7th), John Tonge Anthony Pellew Addington, b. 1914, s. 1976, m.	Hon. Jeremy F. A., b. 1947.
1940	Simon (3rd), Jan David Simon, b. 1940, s. 1993, m.	None.
1960	Slim (2nd), John Douglas Slim, OBE, b. 1927, s. 1970, m.	Hon. Mark W. R. S., b. 1960.

Created	Title, order of succession, name, etc.	Heir
1954	*Soulbury* (2nd), James Herwald Ramsbotham, *b.* 1915, *s.* 1971, *w.*	Hon. Sir Peter E. R., GCMG, GCVO, *b.* 1919.
1776 I.	*Southwell* (7th), Pyers Anthony Joseph Southwell, *b.* 1930, *s.* 1960, *m.*	Hon. Richard A. P. S., *b.* 1956.
1942	*Stansgate.* Disclaimed for life 1963 (*Rt. Hon. Anthony Neil Wedgwood Benn*, MP, *b.* 1925, *s.* 1960, *m.*)	Stephen M. W. B., *b.* 1951.
1959	*Stuart of Findhorn* (2nd), David Randolph Moray Stuart, *b.* 1924, *s.* 1971, *m.*	Hon. J. Dominic S., *b.* 1948.
1957	*Tenby* (3rd), William Lloyd George, *b.* 1927, *s.* 1983, *m.*	Hon. Timothy II. G. L. G., *b.* 1962.
1952	*Thurso* (3rd), John Archibald Sinclair, *b.* 1953, *s.* 1995, *m.*	Hon. James A. R. S., *b.* 1984.
1983	*Tonypandy* (1st), (Thomas) George Thomas, PC, *b.* 1909	None.
1721	*Torrington* (11th), Timothy Howard St George Byng, *b.* 1943, *s.* 1961, *m.*	John L. B., MC, *b.* 1919.
1936	*Trenchard* (3rd), Hugh Trenchard, *b.* 1951, *s.* 1987, *m.*	Hon. Alexander T. T., *b.* 1978.
1921	*Ullswater* (2nd), Nicholas James Christopher Lowther, PC, *b.* 1942, *s.* 1949, *m.*	Hon. Benjamin J. L., *b.* 1975.
1621 I.	*Valentia* (15th), Richard John Dighton Annesley, *b.* 1929, *s.* 1983, *m.*	Hon. Francis W. D. A., *b.* 1959.
1952	*Waverley* (3rd), John Desmond Forbes Anderson, *b.* 1949, *s.* 1990	None.
1938	*Weir* (3rd), William Kenneth James Weir, *b.* 1933, *s.* 1975, *m.*	Hon. James W. H. W., *b.* 1965.
1983	*Whitelaw* (1st), William Stephen Ian Whitelaw, KT, CH, MC, PC, *b.* 1918, *m.*	None.
1918	*Wimborne* (4th), Ivor Mervyn Vigors Guest (5th *UK Baron, Wimborne*, 1880), *b.* 1968, *s.* 1993	Hon. Julian J. G., *b.* 1945.
1923	*Younger of Leckie* (3rd), Edward George Younger, OBE, TD, *b.* 1906, *s.* 1946, *w.*	Baron Younger of Prestwick, KT, KCVO, TD, PC, *b.* 1931 (*see* page 162).

BARONS/LORDS

Coronet, Six silver balls
Style, The Right Hon. the Lord ___. In the Peerage of Scotland there is no rank of Baron; the equivalent rank is Lord of Parliament (*see* page 137) and Scottish peers should always be styled 'Lord', never 'Baron'
Wife's style, The Right Hon. the Lady ___
Children's style, 'The Hon.' before forename and family name
In Scotland, the heir apparent to a Lord may be styled 'The Master of ___ (title of peer)'
For forms of address, *see* page 136

Created	Title, order of succession, name, etc.	Heir
1911	*Aberconway* (3rd), Charles Melville McLaren, *b.* 1913, *s.* 1953, *m.*	Hon. H. Charles M., *b.* 1948.
1873	*Aberdare* (4th), Morys George Lyndhurst Bruce, KBE, PC, *b.* 1919, *s.* 1957, *m.*	Hon. Alastair J. L. B., *b.* 1947.
1835	*Abinger* (8th), James Richard Scarlett, *b.* 1914, *s.* 1943, *m.*	Hon. James H. S., *b.* 1959.
1869	*Acton* (4th), Richard Gerald Lyon-Dalberg-Acton, *b.* 1941, *s.* 1989, *m.*	Hon. John C. F. H. L.-D.-A., *b.* 1966.
1887	*Addington* (6th), Dominic Bryce Hubbard, *b.* 1963, *s.* 1982	Hon. Michael W. L. H., *b.* 1965.
1896	*Aldenham* (6th), and *Hunsdon of Hunsdon* (4th) (1923), Vicary Tyser Gibbs, *b.* 1948, *s.* 1986, *m.*	Hon. Humphrey W. F. G., *b.* 1989.
1962	*Aldington* (1st), Toby Austin Richard William Low, KCMG, CBE, DSO, TD, PC, *b.* 1914, *m.*	Hon Charles H. S. L., *b.* 1948.
1945	*Altrincham.* Disclaimed for life 1963 (*John Edward Poynder Grigg*, *b.* 1924, *s.* 1955, *m.*)	Hon. Anthony U. D. D. G.., *b.* 1934.
1929	*Alvingham* (2nd), Maj.-Gen. Robert Guy Eardley Yerburgh, CBE, *b.* 1926, *s.* 1955, *m.*	Capt. Hon. Robert R. G. Y., *b.* 1956.
1892	*Amherst of Hackney* (4th), William Hugh Amherst Cecil, *b.* 1940, *s.* 1980, *m.*	Hon. H. William A. C., *b.* 1968.
1881	*Ampthill* (4th), Geoffrey Denis Erskine Russell, CBE, PC, *b.* 1921, *s.* 1973	Hon. David W. E. R., *b.* 1947.
1947	*Amwell* (3rd), Keith Norman Montague, *b.* 1943, *s.* 1990, *m.*	Hon. Ian K. M., *b.* 1973.
1863	*Annaly* (6th), Luke Richard White, *b.* 1954, *s.* 1990, *m.*	Hon. Luke H. W., *b.* 1990.
1949	*Archibald.* Disclaimed for life 1975 (*George Christopher Archibald*, *b.* 1926, *s.* 1975, *m.*)	None.
1885	*Ashbourne* (4th), Edward Barry Greynville Gibson, *b.* 1933, *s.* 1983, *m.*	Hon. Edward C. d'O. G., *b.* 1967.

Created	Title, order of succession, name, etc.	Heir
1835	*Ashburton* (7th), John Francis Harcourt Baring, KG, KCVO, b. 1928, s. 1991, m.	Hon. Mark F. R. B., b. 1958.
1892	*Ashcombe* (4th), Henry Edward Cubitt, b. 1924, s. 1962, m.	Mark E. C., b. 1964.
1911	*Ashton of Hyde* (3rd), Thomas John Ashton, TD, b. 1926, s. 1983, m.	Hon. Thomas H. A., b. 1958.
1800 I.	*Ashtown* (7th), Nigel Clive Crosby Trench, KCMG, b. 1916, s. 1990, w.	Hon. Roderick N. G. T., b. 1944.
1956	*Astor of Hever* (3rd), John Jacob Astor, b. 1946, s. 1984, m.	Hon. Charles G. J. A., b. 1990.
1789 I.*	*Auckland* (9th), Ian George Eden (9th Brit. Baron, Auckland, 1793), b. 1926, s. 1957, m.	Hon. Robert I. B. E., b. 1962.
1313	*Audley* (25th), Richard Michael Thomas Souter, b. 1914, s. 1973, m.	Three co-heiresses.
1900	*Avebury* (4th), Eric Reginald Lubbock, b. 1928, s. 1971, m.	Hon. Lyulph A. J. L., b. 1954.
1718 I.	*Aylmer* (13th), Michael Anthony Aylmer, b. 1923, s. 1982, m.	Hon. A. Julian A., b. 1951.
1929	*Baden-Powell* (3rd), Robert Crause Baden-Powell, b. 1936, s. 1962, m.	Hon. David M. B.-P., b. 1940.
1780	*Bagot* (9th), Heneage Charles Bagot, b. 1914, s. 1979, m.	Hon. C. H. Shaun B., b. 1944.
1953	*Baillieu* (3rd), James William Latham Baillieu, b. 1950, s. 1973, m.	Hon. Robert L. B., b. 1979.
1607 S.	*Balfour of Burleigh* (8th), Robert Bruce, FRSE, b. 1927, s. 1967, m.	Hon. Victoria B., b. 1973.
1945	*Balfour of Inchrye* (2nd), Ian George Balfour, b. 1924, s. 1988, m.	None.
1924	*Banbury of Southam* (3rd), Charles William Banbury, b. 1953, s. 1981, m.	None.
1698	*Barnard* (11th), Harry John Neville Vane, TD, b. 1923, s. 1964	Hon. Henry F. C. V., b. 1959.
1887	*Basing* (5th), Neil Lutley Sclater-Booth, b. 1939, s. 1983, m.	Hon. Stuart W. S.-B., b. 1969.
1917	*Beaverbrook* (3rd), Maxwell William Humphrey Aitken, b. 1951, s. 1985, m.	Hon. Maxwell F. A, b. 1977.
1647 S.	*Belhaven and Stenton* (13th), Robert Anthony Carmichael Hamilton, b. 1927, s. 1961, m.	Master of Belhaven, b. 1953.
1848 I.	*Bellew* (7th), James Bryan Bellew, b. 1920, s. 1981, m.	Hon. Bryan E. B., b. 1943.
1856	*Belper* (4th), (Alexander) Ronald George Strutt, b. 1912, s. 1956	Hon. Richard H. S., b. 1941.
1938	*Belstead* (2nd), John Julian Ganzoni, PC, b. 1932, s. 1958	None.
1421	*Berkeley* (18th), Anthony Fitzhardinge Gueterbock, OBE, b. 1939, s. 1992, m.	Hon. Thomas F. G., b. 1969.
1922	*Bethell* (4th), Nicholas William Bethell, b. 1938, s. 1967, m.	Hon. James N. B., b. 1967.
1938	*Bicester* (3rd), Angus Edward Vivian Smith, b. 1932, s. 1968	Hugh C. V. S., b. 1934.
1903	*Biddulph* (5th), (Anthony) Nicholas Colin Maitland Biddulph, b. 1959, s. 1988, m.	Hon. William I. R. M. B., b. 1963.
1938	*Birdwood* (3rd), Mark William Ogilvie Birdwood, b. 1938, s. 1962, m.	None.
1958	*Birkett* (2nd), Michael Birkett, b. 1929, s. 1962, m.	Hon. Thomas B., b. 1982.
1907	*Blyth* (4th), Anthony Audley Rupert Blyth, b. 1931, s. 1977, m.	Hon. Riley A. J. B., b. 1955.
1797	*Bolton* (7th), Richard William Algar Orde-Powlett, b. 1929, s. 1963, m.	Hon. Harry A. N. O.-P., b. 1954.
1452 S.	*Borthwick* (23rd), John Henry Stuart Borthwick, TD, b. 1905, claim succeeded 1986, w.	Master of Borthwick, b. 1940.
1922	*Borwick* (4th), James Hugh Myles Borwick, MC, b. 1917, s. 1961, m.	Hon. George S. B., b. 1922.
1761	*Boston* (10th), Timothy George Frank Boteler Irby, b. 1939, s. 1978, m.	Hon. George W. E. B. I., b. 1971.
1942	*Brabazon of Tara* (3rd), Ivon Anthony Moore-Brabazon, b. 1946, s. 1974, m.	Hon. Benjamin M.-B., b. 1983.
1880	*Brabourne* (7th), John Ulick Knatchbull, CBE, b. 1924, s. 1943, m.	Lord Romsey, b. 1947 (*see* page 145).
1925	*Bradbury* (3rd), John Bradbury, b. 1940, s. 1994, m.	Hon. John B., b. 1973.
1962	*Brain* (2nd), Christopher Langdon Brain, b. 1926, s. 1966, m.	Hon. Michael C. B., DM, FRCP, b. 1928.
1938	*Brassey of Apethorpe* (3rd), David Henry Brassey, OBE, b. 1932, s. 1967, m.	Hon. Edward B., b. 1964.
1788	*Braybrooke* (10th), Robin Henry Charles Neville, b. 1932, s. 1990, m.	George N., b. 1943.
1957	*Bridges* (2nd), Thomas Edward Bridges, GCMG, b. 1927, s. 1969, m.	Hon. Mark T. B., b. 1954.
1945	*Broadbridge* (3rd), Peter Hewett Broadbridge, b. 1938, s. 1972, m.	Martin H. B., b. 1929.
1933	*Brocket* (3rd), Charles Ronald George Nall-Cain, b. 1952, s. 1967, m.	Hon. Alexander C. C. N.-C., b. 1984.
1860	*Brougham and Vaux* (5th), Michael John Brougham, CBE, b. 1938, s. 1967	Hon. Charles W. B., b. 1971.
1945	*Broughshane* (3rd), (William) Kensington Davison, DSO, DFC, b. 1914, s. 1995	None.
1776	*Brownlow* (7th), Edward John Peregrine Cust, b. 1936, s. 1978, m.	Hon. Peregrine E. Q. C., b. 1974.
1942	*Bruntisfield* (2nd), John Robert Warrender, OBE, MC, TD, b. 1921, s. 1993, m.	Hon. Michael J. V. W., b. 1949.
1950	*Burden* (3rd), Andrew Philip Burden, b. 1959, s. 1995	Hon. Fraser W. E. B., b. 1964.
1529	*Burgh* (7th), Alexander Peter Willoughby Leith, b. 1935, s. 1959, m.	Hon. A. Gregory D. L., b. 1958.
1903	*Burnham* (6th), Hugh John Frederick Lawson, b. 1931, s. 1993, m.	Hon. Harry F. A. L., b. 1968.
1897	*Burton* (3rd), Michael Evan Victor Baillie, b. 1924, s. 1962, m.	Hon. Evan M. R. B., b. 1949.
1643	*Byron* (13th), Robert James Byron, b. 1950, s. 1989, m.	Hon. Charles R. G. B., b. 1990.
1937	*Cadman* (3rd), John Anthony Cadman, b. 1938, s. 1966, m.	Hon. Nicholas A. J. C., b. 1977.
1796	*Calthorpe* (10th), Peter Waldo Somerset Gough-Calthorpe, b. 1927, s. 1945, m.	None.
1945	*Calverley* (3rd), Charles Rodney Muff, b. 1946, s. 1971, m.	Hon. Jonathan E. M., b. 1975.

Created	Title, order of succession, name, etc.	Heir
1383	*Camoys* (7th), (Ralph) Thomas Campion George Sherman Stonor, *b.* 1940, *s.* 1976, *m.*	Hon. R. William R. T. *S.*, *b.* 1974.
1715 I.	*Carbery* (11th), Peter Ralfe Harrington Evans-Freke, *b.* 1920, *s.* 1970, *m.*	Hon. Michael P. *E.-F.*, *b.* 1942.
1834 I.*	*Carew* (7th), Patrick Thomas Conolly-Carew (7th *UK Baron, Carew*, 1838), *b.* 1938, *s.* 1994, *m.*	Hon. William P. *C.-C.*, *b.* 1973.
1916	*Carnock* (4th), David Henry Arthur Nicolson, *b.* 1920, *s.* 1982	Nigel *N.*, MBE, *b.* 1917.
1796 I.*	*Carrington* (6th), Peter Alexander Rupert Carington, KG, GCMG, CH, MC, PC (6th *Brit. Baron, Carrington*, 1797), *b.* 1919, *s.* 1938, *m.*	Hon. Rupert F. J *C.*, *b* 1948.
1812 I.	*Castlemaine* (8th), Roland Thomas John Handcock, MBE, *b.* 1943, *s.* 1973, *m.*	Hon. Ronan M. E. *H.*, *b.* 1989.
1936	*Catto* (2nd), Stephen Gordon Catto, *b.* 1923, *s.* 1959, *m.*	Hon. Innes G. *C.*, *b.* 1950.
1918	*Cawley* (3rd), Frederick Lee Cawley, *b.* 1913, *s.* 1954, *m.*	Hon. John F. *C.*, *b.* 1946.
1603	*Cecil*, a subsidiary title of the Marquess of Salisbury. His heir Viscount Cranborne, PC, was given a Writ in Acceleration in this title to enable him to sit in the House of Lords whilst his father is still alive (*see also* page 140)	
1937	*Chatfield* (2nd), Ernle David Lewis Chatfield, *b.* 1917, *s.* 1967, *m.*	None.
1858	*Chesham* (6th), Nicholas Charles Cavendish, *b.* 1941, *s.* 1989, *m.*	Hon. Charles G. C. *C.*, *b.* 1974.
1945	*Chetwode* (2nd), Philip Chetwode, *b.* 1937, *s.* 1950, *m.*	Hon. Roger *C.*, *b.* 1968.
1945	*Chorley* (2nd), Roger Richard Edward Chorley, *b.* 1930, *s.* 1978, *m.*	Hon. Nicholas R. D. *C.*, *b.* 1966.
1858	*Churston* (5th), John Francis Yarde-Buller, *b.* 1934, *s.* 1991, *m.*	Hon. Benjamin F. A. *Y.-B.*, *b.* 1974.
1946	*Citrine* (2nd), Norman Arthur Citrine, *b.* 1914, *s.* 1983, *w.*	Hon. Ronald E. *C.*, *b.* 1919.
1800 I.	*Clanmorris* (8th), Simon John Ward Bingham, *b.* 1937, *s.* 1988, *m.*	Robert D. de B. *B.*, *b.* 1942.
1672	*Clifford of Chudleigh* (14th), Thomas Hugh Clifford, *b.* 1948, *s.* 1988, *m.*	Hon. Alexander T. H. *C.*, *b.* 1985.
1299	*Clinton* (22nd), Gerard Nevile Mark Fane Trefusis, *b.* 1934, *title called out of abeyance* 1965, *m.*	Hon. Charles P. R. F. *T.*, *b.* 1962.
1955	*Clitheroe* (2nd), Ralph John Assheton, *b.* 1929, *s.* 1984, *m.*	Hon. Ralph C. *A.*, *b.* 1962.
1919	*Clwyd* (3rd), (John) Anthony Roberts, *b.* 1935, *s.* 1987, *m.*	Hon. J. Murray *R.*, *b.* 1971.
1948	*Clydesmuir* (2nd), Ronald John Bilsland Colville, KT, CB, MBE, TD, *b.* 1917, *s.* 1954, *m.*	Hon. David R. *C.*, *b.* 1949.
1960	*Cobbold* (2nd), David Antony Fromanteel Lytton Cobbold, *b.* 1937, *s.* 1987, *m.*	Hon. Henry F. L. *C.*, *b.* 1962.
1919	*Cochrane of Cults* (4th), (Ralph Henry) Vere Cochrane, *b.* 1926, *s.* 1990, *m.*	Hon. Thomas H. V. *C.*, *b.* 1957.
1954	*Coleraine* (2nd), (James) Martin (Bonar) Law, *b.* 1931, *s.* 1980, *w.*	Hon. James P. B. *L.*, *b.* 1975.
1873	*Coleridge* (5th), William Duke Coleridge, *b.* 1937, *s.* 1984, *m.*	Hon. James D. *C.*, *b.* 1967.
1946	*Colgrain* (3rd), David Colin Campbell, *b.* 1920, *s.* 1973, *m.*	Hon. Alastair C. L. *C.*, *b.* 1951.
1917	*Colwyn* (3rd), (Ian) Anthony Hamilton-Smith, CBE, *b.* 1942, *s.* 1966, *m.*	Hon. Craig P. *H.-S.*, *b.* 1968.
1956	*Colyton* (2nd), Alisdair John Munro Hopkinson, *b.* 1958, *s.* 1996, *m.*	Hon. James P. M. *H.*, *b.* 1983.
1841	*Congleton* (8th), Christopher Patrick Parnell, *b.* 1930, *s.* 1967, *m.*	Hon. John P. C. *P.*, *b.* 1959.
1927	*Cornwallis* (3rd), Fiennes Neil Wykeham Cornwallis, OBE, *b.* 1921, *s.* 1982, *m.*	Hon. F. W. Jeremy *C.*, *b.* 1946.
1874	*Cottesloe* (5th), Cdr. John Tapling Fremantle, *b.* 1927, *s.* 1994, *m.*	Hon. Thomas F. H. *F.*, *b.* 1966.
1929	*Craigmyle* (3rd), Thomas Donald Mackay Shaw, *b.* 1923, *s.* 1944, *m.*	Hon. Thomas C. *S.*, *b.* 1960.
1899	*Cranworth* (3rd), Philip Bertram Gurdon, *b.* 1940, *s.* 1964, *m.*	Hon. Sacha W. R. *G.*, *b.* 1970.
1959	*Crathorne* (2nd), Charles James Dugdale, *b.* 1939, *s.* 1977, *m.*	Hon. Thomas A. J. *D.*, *b.* 1977.
1892	*Crawshaw* (4th), William Michael Clifton Brooks, *b.* 1933, *s.* 1946	Hon. David G. *B.*, *b.* 1934.
1940	*Croft* (2nd), Michael Henry Glendower Page Croft, *b.* 1916, *s.* 1947, *w.*	Hon. Bernard W. H. P. *C.*, *b.* 1949.
1797 I.	*Crofton* (7th), Guy Patrick Gilbert Crofton, *b.* 1951, *s.* 1989, *m.*	Hon. E. Harry P. *C.*, *b.* 1988.
1375	*Cromwell* (7th), Godfrey John Bewicke-Copley, *b.* 1960, *s.* 1982, *m.*	Hon. Thomas D. *B.-C.*, *b.* 1964.
1947	*Crook* (2nd), Douglas Edwin Crook, *b.* 1926, *s* 1989, *m.*	Hon. Robert D. E. *C.*, *b.* 1955.
1920	*Cullen of Ashbourne* (2nd), Charles Borlase Marsham Cokayne, MBE, *b.* 1912, *s.* 1932, *w.*	Hon. Edmund W. M. *C.*, *b.* 1916.
1914	*Cunliffe* (3rd), Roger Cunliffe, *b.* 1932, *s.* 1963, *m.*	Hon. Henry *C.*, *b.* 1962.
1927	*Daresbury* (3rd), Edward Gilbert Greenall, *b.* 1928, *s.* 1990, *m.*	Hon. Peter G. *G.*, *b.* 1953.
1924	*Darling* (2nd), Robert Charles Henry Darling, *b.* 1919, *s.* 1936, *m.*	Hon. R. Julian H. *D.*, *b.* 1944.
1946	*Darwen* (3rd), Roger Michael Davies, *b.* 1938, *s.* 1988, *m.*	Hon. Paul *D.*, *b.* 1962.
1932	*Davies* (3rd), David Davies, *b.* 1940, *s.* 1944, *m.*	Hon. David D. *D.*, *b.* 1975.
1812 I.	*Decies* (7th), Marcus Hugh Tristram de la Poer Beresford, *b.* 1948, *s.* 1992, *m.*	Hon. Robert M. D. *de la P. B.*, *b.* 1988.
1299	*de Clifford* (27th), John Edward Southwell Russell, *b.* 1928, *s.* 1982, *m.*	Hon. William S. *R.*, *b.* 1930.
1851	*De Freyne* (7th), Francis Arthur John French, *b.* 1927, *s.* 1935, *m.*	Hon. Fulke C. A. J. *F.*, *b.* 1957.
1821	*Delamere* (5th), Hugh George Cholmondeley, *b.* 1934, *s.* 1979, *m.*	Hon. Thomas P. G. *C.*, *b.* 1968.
1838	*de Mauley* (6th), Gerald John Ponsonby, *b.* 1921, *s.* 1962, *m.*	Col. Hon. Thomas M. *P.*, TD, *b.* 1930.
1937	*Denham* (2nd), Bertram Stanley Mitford Bowyer, KBE, PC, *b.* 1927, *s.* 1948, *m.*	Hon. Richard G. G. *B.*, *b.* 1959.

Created	Title, order of succession, name, etc.	Heir
1834	*Denman* (5th), Charles Spencer Denman, CBE, MC, TD, *b.* 1916, *s.* 1971, *w.*	Hon. Richard T. S. *D.*, *b.* 1946.
1885	*Deramore* (6th), Richard Arthur de Yarburgh-Bateson, *b.* 1911, *s.* 1964, *m.*	None.
1887	*De Ramsey* (4th), John Ailwyn Fellowes, *b.* 1942, *s.* 1993, *m.*	Hon. Freddie J. *F.*, *b.* 1978.
1264	*de Ros* (28th), Peter Trevor Maxwell, *b.* 1958, *s.* 1983, *m.* (*Premier Baron of England*)	Hon. Finbar J. *M.*, *b.* 1988.
1881	*Derwent* (5th), Robin Evelyn Leo Vanden-Bempde-Johnstone, LVO, *b.* 1930, *s.* 1986, *m.*	Hon. Francis P. H. *V.-B.-J.*, *b.* 1965.
1831	*de Saumarez* (7th), Eric Douglas Saumarez, *b.* 1956, *s.* 1991, *m.*	Hon. Victor T. *S.*, *b.* 1956.
1910	*de Villiers* (3rd), Arthur Percy de Villiers, *b.* 1911, *s.* 1934	Hon. Alexander C. *de V.*, *b.* 1940.
1930	*Dickinson* (2nd), Richard Clavering Hyett Dickinson, *b.* 1926, *s.* 1943, *m.*	Hon. Martin H. *D.*, *b.* 1961.
1620 I.*	*Digby* (12th), Edward Henry Kenelm Digby (6th *Brit. Baron, Digby,* 1765), *b.* 1924, *s.* 1964, *m.*	Hon. Henry N. K. *D.*, *b.* 1954.
1615	*Dormer* (17th), Geoffrey Henry Dormer, *b.* 1920, *s.* 1995, *m.*	Hon. William R. *D.*, *b.* 1960.
1943	*Dowding* (3rd), Piers Hugh Tremenheere Dowding, *b.* 1948, *s.* 1992	Hon. Mark D. J. *D.*, *b.* 1949.
1800 I.	*Dufferin and Clandeboye.* The 10th Baron died in 1991. Heir had not established his claim to the title at the time of going to press	Sir John Blackwood, Bt., *b.* 1944.
1929	*Dulverton* (3rd), (Gilbert) Michael Hamilton Wills, *b.* 1944, *s.* 1992, *m.*	Hon. Robert A. H. *W.*, *b.* 1983.
1800 I.	*Dunalley* (7th), Henry Francis Cornelius Prittie, *b.* 1948, *s.* 1992, *m.*	Hon. Joel H. *P.*, *b.* 1981.
1324 I.	*Dunboyne* (28th), Patrick Theobald Tower Butler, VRD, *b.* 1917, *s.* 1945, *m.*	Hon. John F. *B.*, *b.* 1951.
1802	*Dunleath* (5th), Michael Henry Mulholland, *b.* 1915, *s.* 1993, *w.*	Hon. Brian H. *M.*, *b.* 1950.
1439 I.	*Dunsany* (19th), Randal Arthur Henry Plunkett, *b.* 1906, *s.* 1957, *m.*	Hon. Edward J. C. *P.*, *b.* 1939.
1780	*Dynevor* (9th), Richard Charles Uryan Rhys, *b.* 1935, *s.* 1962	Hon. Hugo G. U. *R.*, *b.* 1966.
1857	*Ebury* (6th), Francis Egerton Grosvenor, *b.* 1934, *s.* 1957, *m.*	Hon. Julian F. M. *G.*, *b.* 1959.
1963	*Egremont* (2nd), & *Leconfield* (7th) (1859), John Max Henry Scawen Wyndham, *b.* 1948, *s.* 1972, *m.*	Hon. George R. V. *W.*, *b.* 1983.
1643	*Elibank* (14th), Alan D'Ardis Erskine-Murray, *b.* 1923, *s.* 1973, *m.*	Master of Elibank, *b.* 1964.
1802	*Ellenborough* (8th), Richard Edward Cecil Law, *b.* 1926, *s.* 1945, *m.*	Maj. Hon. Rupert E. H. *L.*, *b.* 1955.
1509 S.*	*Elphinstone* (19th), Alexander Mountstuart Elphinstone (5th *UK Baron Elphinstone,* 1885), *b.* 1980, *s.* 1994, *M.*	Hon. Angus J. *E.*, *b.* 1982.
1934	*Elton* (2nd), Rodney Elton, TD, *b.* 1930, *s.* 1973, *m.*	Hon. Edward P. *E.*, *b.* 1966.
1964	*Erroll of Hale* (1st), Frederick James Erroll, TD, PC, *b.* 1914, *m.*	None.
1627 S.	*Fairfax of Cameron* (14th), Nicholas John Albert Fairfax, *b.* 1956, *s.* 1964, *m.*	Hon. Edward N. T. *F.*, *b.* 1984.
1961	*Fairhaven* (3rd), Ailwyn Henry George Broughton, *b.* 1936, *s.* 1973, *m.*	Maj. Hon. James H. A. *B.*, *b.* 1963.
1916	*Faringdon* (3rd), Charles Michael Henderson, *b.* 1937, *s.* 1977, *m.*	Hon. James H. *H.*, *b.* 1961.
1756 I.	*Farnham* (12th), Barry Owen Somerset Maxwell, *b.* 1931, *s.* 1957, *m.*	Hon. Simon K. *M.*, *b.* 1933.
1856 I.	*Fermoy* (6th), Patrick Maurice Burke Roche, *b.* 1967, *s.* 1984	Hon. E. Hugh B. *R.*, *b.* 1972.
1826	*Feversham* (6th), Charles Antony Peter Duncombe, *b.* 1945, *s.* 1963, *m.*	Hon. Jasper O. S. *D.*, *b.* 1968.
1798 I.	*ffrench* (8th), Robuck John Peter Charles Mario ffrench, *b.* 1956, *s.* 1986, *m.*	Hon. John C. M. J. F. *ff.*, *b.* 1928.
1909	*Fisher* (3rd), John Vavasseur Fisher, DSC, *b.* 1921, *s.* 1955, *m.*	Hon. Patrick V. *F.*, *b.* 1953.
1295	*Fitzwalter* (21st), (Fitzwalter) Brook Plumptre, *b.* 1914, *title called out of abeyance,* 1953, *m.*	Hon. Julian B. *P.*, *b.* 1952.
1776	*Foley* (8th), Adrian Gerald Foley, *b.* 1923, *s.* 1927, *m.*	Hon. Thomas H. *F.*, *b.* 1961.
1445 S.	*Forbes* (22nd), Nigel Ivan Forbes, KBE (*Premier Lord of Scotland*), *b.* 1918, *s.* 1953, *m.*	Master of Forbes, *b.* 1946.
1821	*Forester* (8th), (George Cecil) Brooke Weld-Forester, *b.* 1938, *s.* 1977, *m.*	Hon. C. R. George *W.-F.*, *b.* 1975.
1922	*Forres* (4th), Alastair Stephen Grant Williamson, *b.* 1946, *s.* 1978, *m.*	Hon. George A. M. *W.*, *b.* 1972.
1917	*Forteviot* (4th), John James Evelyn Dewar, *b.* 1938, *s.* 1993, *m.*	Hon. Alexander J. E. *D.*, *b.* 1971.
1951	*Freyberg* (3rd), Valerian Bernard Freyberg, *b.* 1970, *s.* 1993	None.
1917	*Gainford* (3rd), Joseph Edward Pease, *b.* 1921, *s.* 1971, *m.*	Hon. George *P.*, *b.* 1926.
1818 I.	*Garvagh* (5th), (Alexander Leopold Ivor) George Canning, *b.* 1920, *s.* 1956, *m.*	Hon. Spencer G. S. de R. *C.*, *b.* 1953.
1942	*Geddes* (3rd), Euan Michael Ross Geddes, *b.* 1937, *s.* 1975, *m.*	Hon. James G. N. *G.*, *b.* 1969.
1876	*Gerard* (5th), Anthony Robert Hugo Gerard, *b.* 1949, *s.* 1992, *m.*	Hon. Rupert B. C. *G.*, *b.* 1981.
1824	*Gifford* (6th), Anthony Maurice Gifford, QC, *b.* 1940, *s.* 1961, *m.*	Hon. Thomas A. *G.*, *b.* 1967.
1917	*Gisborough* (3rd), Thomas Richard John Long Chaloner, *b.* 1927, *s.* 1951, *m.*	Hon. T. Peregrine L. *C.*, *b.* 1961.
1960	*Gladwyn* (1st), (Hubert Miles) Gladwyn Jebb, GCMG, GCVO, CB, *b.* 1900, *w.*	Hon. Miles A. G. *J.*, *b.* 1930.
1899	*Glanusk* (4th), David Russell Bailey, *b.* 1917, *s.* 1948, *m.*	Hon. Christopher R. *B.*, *b.* 1942.
1918	*Glenarthur* (4th), Simon Mark Arthur, *b.* 1944, *s.* 1976, *m.*	Hon. Edward A. *A.*, *b.* 1973.
1911	*Glenconner* (3rd), Colin Christopher Paget Tennant, *b.* 1926, *s.* 1983, *m.*	Hon. Charles E. P. *T.*, *b.* 1957.

Created	Title, order of succession, name, etc.	Heir
1964	*Glendevon* (2nd), Julian John Somerset Hope, *b.* 1950, *s.* 1996	Hon. Jonathan C. *H., b.* 1952.
1922	*Glendyne* (3rd), Robert Nivison, *b.* 1926, *s.* 1967, *m.*	Hon. John *N., b.* 1960.
1939	*Glentoran* (3rd), (Thomas) Robin (Valerian) Dixon, CBE, *b.* 1935, *s.* 1995, *m.*	Hon. Daniel G. *D., b.* 1959.
1909	*Gorell* (4th), Timothy John Radcliffe Barnes, *b.* 1927, *s.* 1963, *m.*	Hon. Ronald A. H. *B., b.* 1931.
1953	*Grantchester* (3rd), Christopher John Suenson-Taylor, *b.* 1951, *s.* 1995, *m.*	Hon. Jesse D. *S.-T., b.* 1977.
1782	*Grantley* (8th), Richard William Brinsley Norton, *b.* 1956, *s.* 1995	Hon. Francis J *H. N., b.* 1960.
1794 I.	*Graves* (9th), Evelyn Paget Graves, *b.* 1926, *s.* 1994, *m.*	Hon. Timothy E. *G., b.* 1960.
1445 S.	*Gray* (22nd), Angus Diarmid Ian Campbell-Gray, *b.* 1931, *s.* 1946, *m.*	Master of Gray, *b.* 1964.
1950	*Greenhill* (3rd), Malcolm Greenhill, *b.* 1924, *s.* 1989	None.
1927	*Greenway* (4th), Ambrose Charles Drexel Greenway, *b.* 1941, *s.* 1975, *m.*	Hon. Mervyn S. K. *G., b.* 1942.
1902	*Grenfell* (3rd), Julian Pascoe Francis St Leger Grenfell, *b.* 1935, *s.* 1976, *m.*	Francis P. J. *G., b.* 1938.
1944	*Gretton* (4th), John Lysander Gretton, *b.* 1975, *s.* 1989	None.
1397	*Grey of Codnor* (5th), Charles Legh Shuldham Cornwall-Legh, CBE, AE, *b.* 1903, *title called out of abeyance* 1989, *w.*	Hon. Richard H. *C.-L., b.* 1936.
1955	*Gridley* (3rd), Richard David Arnold Gridley, *b.* 1956, *s.* 1996, *m.*	Hon. Carl R. *G., b.* 1981.
1964	*Grimston of Westbury* (2nd), Robert Walter Sigismund Grimston, *b.* 1925, *s.* 1979, *m.*	Hon. Robert J. S. *G., b.* 1951.
1886	*Grimthorpe* (4th), Christopher John Beckett, OBE, *b.* 1915, *s.* 1963, *m.*	Hon. Edward J. *B., b.* 1954.
1945	*Hacking* (3rd), Douglas David Hacking, *b.* 1938, *s.* 1971, *m.*	Hon. Douglas F. *H., b.* 1968.
1950	*Haden-Guest* (5th), Christopher Haden-Guest, *b.* 1948, *s.* 1996, *m.*	Hon. Nicholas *H.-G., b.* 1951.
1886	*Hamilton of Dalzell* (4th), James Leslie Hamilton, *b.* 1938, *s.* 1990, *m.*	Hon. Gavin G. *H., b.* 1968.
1874	*Hampton* (6th), Richard Humphrey Russell Pakington, *b.* 1925, *s.* 1974, *m.*	Hon. John H. A. *P., b.* 1964.
1939	*Hankey* (2nd), Robert Maurice Alers Hankey, KCMG, KCVO, *b.* 1905, *s.* 1963, *m.*	Hon. Donald R. A. *H., b.* 1938.
1958	*Harding of Petherton* (2nd), John Charles Harding, *b.* 1928, *s.* 1989, *m.*	Hon. William A. J. *H., b.* 1969.
1910	*Hardinge of Penshurst* (3rd), George Edward Charles Hardinge, *b.* 1921, *s.* 1960, *m.*	Hon. Julian A. *H., b.* 1945.
1876	*Harlech* (6th), Francis David Ormsby-Gore, *b.* 1954, *s.* 1985, *m.*	Hon. Jasset D. C. *O.-G., b.* 1986.
1939	*Harmsworth* (3rd), Thomas Harold Raymond Harmsworth, *b.* 1939, *s.* 1990, *m.*	Hon. Dominic M. E. *H., b.* 1973.
1815	*Harris* (8th), Anthony Harris, *b.* 1942, *s.* 1996, *m.*	†
1954	*Harvey of Tasburgh* (2nd), Peter Charles Oliver Harvey, *b.* 1921, *s.* 1968, *w.*	Charles J. G. *H., b.* 1951.
1295	*Hastings* (22nd), Edward Delaval Henry Astley, *b.* 1912, *s.* 1956, *m.*	Hon. Delaval T. H. *A., b.* 1960.
1835	*Hatherton* (8th), Edward Charles Littleton, *b.* 1950, *s.* 1985, *m.*	Hon. Thomas E. *L., b.* 1977.
1776	*Hawke* (11th), Edward George Hawke, TD, *b.* 1950, *s.* 1992, *m.*	None.
1927	*Hayter* (3rd), George Charles Hayter Chubb, KCVO, CBE, *b.* 1911, *s.* 1967, *m.*	Hon. G. William M. *C., b.* 1943.
1945	*Hazlerigg* (2nd), Arthur Grey Hazlerigg, MC, TD, *b.* 1910, *s.* 1949, *w.*	Hon. Arthur G. *H., b.* 1951.
1943	*Hemingford* (3rd), (Dennis) Nicholas Herbert, *b.* 1934, *s.* 1982, *m.*	Hon. Christopher D. C. *H., b.* 1973.
1906	*Hemphill* (5th), Peter Patrick Fitzroy Martyn Martyn-Hemphill, *b.* 1928, *s.* 1957, *m.*	Hon. Charles A. M. *M.-H., b.* 1954.
1799 I.*	*Henley* (8th), Oliver Michael Robert Eden (6th *UK Baron, Northington,* 1885), *b.* 1953, *s.* 1977, *m.*	Hon. John W. O. *E., b.* 1988.
1800 I.*	*Henniker* (8th), John Patrick Edward Chandos Henniker-Major, KCMG, CVO, MC (4th *UK Baron, Hartismere,* 1866), *b.* 1916, *s.* 1980, *m.*	Hon. Mark I. P. C. *H.-M., b.* 1947.
1886	*Herschell* (3rd), Rognvald Richard Farrer Herschell, *b.* 1923, *s.* 1929, *m.*	None.
1935	*Hesketh* (3rd), Thomas Alexander Fermor-Hesketh, PC, *b.* 1950, *s.* 1955, *m.*	Hon. Frederick H. *F.-H., b.* 1988.
1828	*Heytesbury* (6th), Francis William Holmes à Court, *b.* 1931, *s.* 1971, *m.*	Hon. James W. *H. à C., b.* 1967.
1886	*Hindlip* (6th), Charles Henry Allsopp, *b.* 1940, *s.* 1993, *m.*	Hon. Henry W. *A., b.* 1973.
1950	*Hives* (2nd), John Warwick Hives, CBE, *b.* 1913, *s.* 1965, *m.*	Matthew P. *H., b.* 1971.
1912	*Hollenden* (3rd), Gordon Hope Hope-Morley, *b.* 1914, *s.* 1977, *m.*	Hon. Ian H. *H.-M., b.* 1946.
1897	*HolmPatrick* (4th), Hans James David Hamilton, *b.* 1955, *s.* 1991, *m.*	Hon. Ion H. J. *H., b.* 1956.
1933	*Horder* (2nd), Thomas Mervyn Horder, *b.* 1910, *s.* 1955	None.
1797 I.	*Hotham* (8th), Henry Durand Hotham, *b.* 1940, *s.* 1967, *m.*	Hon. William B. *H., b.* 1972.
1881	*Hothfield* (6th), Anthony Charles Sackville Tufton, *b.* 1939, *s.* 1991, *m.*	Hon. William S. *T., b.* 1977.
1597	*Howard de Walden* (9th), John Osmael Scott-Ellis, TD (5th *UK Baron, Seaford,* 1826), *b.* 1912, *s.* 1946, *m.*	To Barony of Howard de Walden, four co-heiresses. To Barony of Seaford, Colin H. F. *Ellis, b.* 1946.
1930	*Howard of Penrith* (2nd), Francis Philip Howard, *b.* 1905, *s.* 1939, *m.*	Hon. Philip E. *H., b.* 1945.
1960	*Howick of Glendale* (2nd), Charles Evelyn Baring, *b.* 1937, *s.* 1973, *m.*	Hon. David E. C. *B., b.* 1975.
1796 I.	*Huntingfield* (7th), Joshua Charles Vanneck, *b.* 1954, *s.* 1994, *m.*	Hon. Gerard C. A. *V., b.* 1985.

Created	Title, order of succession, name, etc.	Heir
1866	Hylton (5th), Raymond Hervey Jolliffe, b. 1932, s. 1967, m.	Hon. William H. M. J., b. 1967.
1933	Iliffe (3rd), Robert Peter Richard Iliffe, b. 1944, s. 1996, m.	Hon. Edward R. I., b. 1968.
1543 I.	Inchiquin (18th), Conor Myles John O'Brien, b. 1943, s. 1982, m.	Murrough R. O'B., b. 1910.
1962	Inchyra (2nd), Robert Charles Reneke Hoyer Millar, b. 1935, s. 1989, m.	Hon. C. James C. H. M., b. 1962.
1964	Inglewood (2nd), (William) Richard Fletcher-Vane, b. 1951, s. 1989, m.	Hon. Henry W. F. F.-V., b. 1990.
1919	Inverforth (4th), Andrew Peter Weir, b. 1966, s. 1982	Hon. John V. W., b. 1935.
1941	Ironside (2nd), Edmund Oslac Ironside, b. 1924, s. 1959, m.	Hon. Charles E. G. I., b. 1956.
1952	Jeffreys (3rd), Christopher Henry Mark Jeffreys, b. 1957, s. 1986, m.	Hon. Arthur M. H. J., b. 1989.
1906	Joicey (5th), James Michael Joicey, b. 1953, s. 1993, m.	Hon. William J. J., b. 1990.
1937	Kenilworth (4th), (John) Randle Siddeley, b. 1954, s. 1981, m.	Hon. William R. J. S., b. 1992.
1935	Kennet (2nd), Wayland Hilton Young, b. 1923, s. 1960, m.	Hon. W. A. Thoby Y., b. 1957.
1776 I.*	Kensington (8th), Hugh Ivor Edwardes (5th UK Baron, Kensington, 1886), b. 1933, s. 1981, m.	Hon. W. Owen A. E., b. 1964.
1951	Kenswood (2nd), John Michael Howard Whitfield, b. 1930, s. 1963, m.	Hon. Michael C. W., b. 1955.
1788	Kenyon (6th), Lloyd Tyrell-Kenyon, b. 1947, s. 1993, m.	Hon. Lloyd N. T.-K., b. 1972.
1947	Kershaw (4th), Edward John Kershaw, b. 1936, s. 1962, m.	Hon. John C. E. K., b. 1971.
1943	Keyes (2nd), Roger George Bowlby Keyes, b. 1919, s. 1945, m.	Hon. Charles W. P. K., b. 1951.
1909	Kilbracken (3rd), John Raymond Godley, DSC, b. 1920, s. 1950	Hon. Christopher J. G., b. 1945.
1900	Killanin (3rd), Michael Morris, MBE, TD, b. 1914, s. 1927, m.	Hon. G. Redmond F. M., b. 1947.
1943	Killearn (3rd), Victor Miles George Aldous Lampson, b. 1941, s. 1996, m.	Hon. Miles H. M. L., b. 1977.
1789 I.	Kilmaine (7th), John David Henry Browne, b. 1948, s. 1978, m.	Hon. John F. S. B., b. 1983.
1831	Kilmarnock (7th), Alastair Ivor Gilbert Boyd, b. 1927, s. 1975, m.	Hon. Robin J. B., b. 1941.
1941	Kindersley (3rd), Robert Hugh Molesworth Kindersley, b. 1929, s. 1976, m.	Hon. Rupert J. M. K., b. 1955.
1223 I.	Kingsale (35th), John de Courcy (Premier Baron of Ireland), b. 1941, s. 1969	Nevinson R. de C., b. 1920.
1682 S.*	Kinnaird (13th), Graham Charles Kinnaird (5th UK Baron, Kinnaird, 1860), b. 1912, s. 1972, m.	None.
1902	Kinross (5th), Christopher Patrick Balfour, b. 1949, s. 1985, m.	Hon. Alan I. B., b. 1978.
1951	Kirkwood (3rd), David Harvie Kirkwood, PH.D., b. 1931, s. 1970, m.	Hon. James S. K., b. 1937.
1800 I.	Langford (9th), Col. Geoffrey Alexander Rowley-Conwy, OBE, b. 1912, s. 1953, m.	Hon. Owain G. R.-C., b. 1958.
1942	Latham (2nd), Dominic Charles Latham, b. 1954, s. 1970	Anthony M. L., b. 1954.
1431	Latymer (8th), Hugo Nevill Money-Coutts, b. 1926, s. 1987, m.	Hon. Crispin J. A. N. M.-C., b. 1955.
1869	Lawrence (5th), David John Downer Lawrence, b. 1937, s. 1968	None.
1947	Layton (3rd), Geoffrey Michael Layton, b. 1947, s. 1989, m.	Hon. David L., MBE, b. 1914.
1839	Leigh (5th), John Piers Leigh, b. 1935, s. 1979, m.	Hon. Christopher D. P. L., b. 1960.
1962	Leighton of St Mellons (2nd), (John) Leighton Seager, b. 1922, s. 1963, m.	Hon. Robert W. H. L. S., b. 1955.
1797	Lilford (7th), George Vernon Powys, b. 1931, s. 1949, m.	Hon. Mark V. P., b. 1975.
1945	Lindsay of Birker (3rd), James Francis Lindsay, b. 1945, s. 1994, m.	Hon. Thomas M. L., b. 1915.
1758 I.	Lisle (7th), John Nicholas Horace Lysaght, b. 1903, s. 1919, m.	Patrick J. L., b. 1931.
1850	Londesborough (9th), Richard John Denison, b. 1959, s. 1968, m.	Hon. James F. D., b. 1990.
1541 I.	Louth (16th), Otway Michael James Oliver Plunkett, b. 1929, s. 1950, m.	Hon. Jonathan O. P., b. 1952.
1458 S.*	Lovat (16th), Simon Fraser (5th UK Baron, Lovat, 1837), b. 1977, s. 1995, M.	Jack F., b. 1984.
1946	Lucas of Chilworth (2nd), Michael William George Lucas, b. 1926, s. 1967, m.	Hon. Simon W. L., b. 1957.
1663	Lucas (11th) & Dingwall (8th) (Scottish Lordship, 1609), Ralph Matthew Palmer, b. 1951, s. 1991, m.	Hon. Lewis E. P., b. 1987
1929	Luke (3rd), Arthur Charles St John Lawson-Johnston, b. 1933, s. 1996, m.	Hon. Ian J. St J. L.-J., b. 1963.
1914	Lyell (3rd), Charles Lyell, b. 1939, s. 1943	None.
1859	Lyveden (6th), Ronald Cecil Vernon, b. 1915, s. 1973, m.	Hon. Jack L. V., b. 1938.
1959	MacAndrew (3rd), Christopher Anthony Colin MacAndrew, b. 1945, s. 1989, m.	Hon. Oliver C. J. M., b. 1983.
1776 I.	Macdonald (8th), Godfrey James Macdonald of Macdonald, b. 1947, s. 1970, m.	Hon. Godfrey E. H. T. M., b. 1982.
1949	Macdonald of Gwaenysgor (2nd), Gordon Ramsay Macdonald, b. 1915, s. 1966, m.	None.
1937	McGowan (3rd), Harry Duncan Cory McGowan, b. 1938, s. 1966, m.	Hon. Harry J. C. M., b. 1971.
1922	Maclay (3rd), Joseph Paton Maclay, b. 1942, s. 1969, m.	Hon. Joseph P. M., b. 1977.
1955	McNair (3rd), Duncan James McNair, b. 1947, s. 1989, m.	Hon. Thomas J. M., b. 1990.
1951	Macpherson of Drumochter (2nd), (James) Gordon Macpherson, b. 1924, s. 1965, m.	Hon. James A. M., b. 1979.

Created	Title, order of succession, name, etc.	Heir
1937	*Mancroft* (3rd), Benjamin Lloyd Stormont Mancroft, *b.* 1957, *s.* 1987, *m.*	None.
1807	*Manners* (5th), John Robert Cecil Manners, *b.* 1923, *s.* 1972, *m.*	Hon. John H. R. *M.*, *b.* 1956.
1922	*Manton* (3rd), Joseph Rupert Eric Robert Watson, *b.* 1924, *s.* 1968, *m.*	Maj. Hon. Miles R. M. *W.*, *b.* 1958.
1908	*Marchamley* (4th), William Francis Whiteley, *b.* 1968, *s.* 1994	None.
1964	*Margadale* (2nd), James Ian Morrison, TD, *b.* 1930, *s.* 1996, *m.*	Hon. Alastair J. *M.*, *b.* 1958.
1961	*Marks of Broughton* (2nd), Michael Marks, *b.* 1920, *s.* 1964	Hon. Simon R. *M.*, *b.* 1950.
1964	*Martonmere* (2nd), John Stephen Robinson, *b.* 1963, *s.* 1989	David A. *R.*, *b.* 1965.
1776 I.	*Massy* (9th), Hugh Hamon John Somerset Massy, *b.* 1921, *s.* 1958, *m.*	Hon. David H. S. *M.*, *b.* 1947.
1935	*May* (3rd), Michael St John May, *b.* 1931, *s.* 1950, *m.*	Hon. Jasper B. St J. *M.*, *b.* 1965.
1928	*Melchett* (4th), Peter Robert Henry Mond, *b.* 1948, *s.* 1973	None.
1925	*Merrivale* (3rd), Jack Henry Edmond Duke, *b.* 1917, *s.* 1951, *m.*	Hon. Derek J. P. *D.*, *b.* 1948.
1911	*Merthyr.* Disclaimed for life 1977 (*Trevor Oswin Lewis, Bt.*, CBE, *b.* 1935, *s.* 1977, *m.*)	David T. *L.*, *b.* 1977.
1919	*Meston* (3rd), James Meston, *b.* 1950, *s.* 1984, *m.*	Hon. Thomas J. D. *M.*, *b.* 1977.
1838	*Methuen* (7th), Robert Alexander Holt Methuen, *b.* 1931, *s.* 1994, *m.*	Christopher P. M. C. *Methuen-Campbell*, *b.* 1928.
1711	*Middleton* (12th), (Digby) Michael Godfrey John Willoughby, MC, *b.* 1921, *s.* 1970, *m.*	Hon. Michael C. J. *W.*, *b.* 1948.
1939	*Milford* (3rd), Hugo John Laurence Philipps, *b.* 1929, *s.* 1993, *m.*	Hon. Guy W. *P.*, *b.* 1961.
1933	*Milne* (2nd), George Douglass Milne, TD, *b.* 1909, *s.* 1948, *m.*	Hon. George A. *M.*, *b.* 1941.
1951	*Milner of Leeds* (2nd), Arthur James Michael Milner, AE, *b.* 1923, *s.* 1967, *m.*	Hon. Richard J. *M.*, *b.* 1959.
1947	*Milverton* (2nd), Revd Fraser Arthur Richard Richards, *b.* 1930, *s.* 1978, *m.*	Hon. Michael H. *R.*, *b.* 1936.
1873	*Moncreiff* (5th), Harry Robert Wellwood Moncreiff, *b.* 1915, *s.* 1942, *w.*	Hon. Rhoderick H. W. *M.*, *b.* 1954.
1884	*Monk Bretton* (3rd), John Charles Dodson, *b.* 1924, *s.* 1933, *m.*	Hon. Christopher M. *D.*, *b.* 1958.
1885	*Monkswell* (5th), Gerard Collier, *b.* 1947, *s.* 1984, *m.*	Hon. James A. *C.*, *b.* 1977.
1728	*Monson* (11th), John Monson, *b.* 1932, *s.* 1958, *m.*	Hon. Nicholas J. *M.*, *b.* 1955.
1885	*Montagu of Beaulieu* (3rd), Edward John Barrington Douglas-Scott-Montagu, *b.* 1926, *s.* 1929, *m.*	Hon. Ralph *D.-S.-M.*, *b.* 1961.
1839	*Monteagle of Brandon* (6th), Gerald Spring Rice, *b.* 1926, *s.* 1946, *m.*	Hon. Charles J. S. *R.*, *b.* 1953.
1943	*Moran* (2nd), (Richard) John (McMoran) Wilson, KCMG, *b.* 1924, *s.* 1977, *m.*	Hon. James M. *W.*, *b.* 1952.
1918	*Morris* (3rd), Michael David Morris, *b.* 1937, *s.* 1975, *m.*	Hon. Thomas A. S. *M.*, *b.* 1982.
1950	*Morris of Kenwood* (2nd), Philip Geoffrey Morris, *b.* 1928, *s.* 1954, *m.*	Hon. Jonathan D. *M.*, *b.* 1968.
1945	*Morrison* (2nd), Dennis Morrison, *b.* 1914, *s.* 1953	None.
1831	*Mostyn* (5th), Roger Edward Lloyd Lloyd-Mostyn, MC, *b.* 1920, *s.* 1965, *m.*	Hon. Llewellyn R. L. *L.-M.*, *b.* 1948.
1933	*Mottistone* (4th), David Peter Seely, CBE, *b.* 1920, *s.* 1966, *m.*	Hon. Peter J. P. *S.*, *b.* 1949.
1945	*Mountevans* (3rd), Edward Patrick Broke Evans, *b.* 1943, *s.* 1974, *m.*	Hon. Jeffrey de C. R. *E.*, *b.* 1948.
1283	*Mowbray* (26th), *Segrave* (27th) (1283), & *Stourton* (23rd) (1448), Charles Edward Stourton, CBE, *b.* 1923, *s.* 1965, *m.*	Hon. Edward W. S. *S.*, *b.* 1953.
1932	*Moyne* (3rd), Jonathan Bryan Guinness, *b.* 1930, *s.* 1992, *m.*	Hon. Jasper J. R. *G.*, *b.* 1954.
1929	*Moynihan.* Barony dormant since the 3rd Baron died in November 1991. A High Court case in July 1996 cleared the way for the 3rd Baron's half-brother Colin Moynihan to petition the House of Lords to consider his claim to the title. At the time of going to press a petition had not been submitted	
1781 I.	*Muskerry* (9th), Robert Fitzmaurice Deane, *b.* 1948, *s.* 1988, *m.*	Hon. Jonathan F. *D.*, *b.* 1986.
1627 S.	*Napier* (14th) & *Ettrick* (5th) (*UK* 1872), Francis Nigel Napier, KCVO, *b.* 1930, *s.* 1954, *m.*	Master of Napier, *b.* 1962.
1868	*Napier of Magdala* (6th), Robert Alan Napier, *b.* 1940, *s.* 1987, *m.*	Hon. James R. *N.*, *b.* 1966.
1940	*Nathan* (2nd), Roger Carol Michael Nathan, *b.* 1922, *s.* 1963, *m.*	Hon. Rupert H. B. *N.*, *b.* 1957.
1960	*Nelson of Stafford* (3rd), Henry Roy George Nelson, *b.* 1943, *s.* 1995, *m.*	Hon. Alistair W. H. *N.*, *b.* 1973.
1959	*Netherthorpe* (3rd), James Frederick Turner, *b.* 1964, *s.* 1982, *m.*	Hon. Andrew J. E. *T.*, *b.* 1993.
1946	*Newall* (2nd), Francis Storer Eaton Newall, *b.* 1930, *s.* 1963, *m.*	Hon. Richard H. E. *N.*, *b.* 1961.
1776 I.	*Newborough* (7th), Robert Charles Michael Vaughan Wynn, DSC, *b.* 1917, *s.* 1965, *m.*	Hon. Robert V. *W.*, *b.* 1949.
1892	*Newton* (5th), Richard Thomas Legh, *b.* 1950, *s.* 1992, *m.*	Hon. Piers R. *L.*, *b.* 1979.
1930	*Noel-Buxton* (3rd), Martin Connal Noel-Buxton, *b.* 1940, *s.* 1980, *m.*	Hon. Charles C. *N.-B.*, *b.* 1975.
1957	*Norrie* (2nd), (George) Willoughby Moke Norrie, *b.* 1936, *s.* 1977, *m.*	Hon. Mark W. J. *N.*, *b.* 1972.
1884	*Northbourne* (5th), Christopher George Walter James, *b.* 1926, *s.* 1982, *m.*	Hon. Charles W. H. *J.*, *b.* 1960.
1866	*Northbrook* (6th), Francis Thomas Baring, *b.* 1954, *s.* 1990, *m.*	None.
1878	*Norton* (8th), James Nigel Arden Adderley, *b.* 1947, *s.* 1993, *m.*	Hon. Edward J. A. *A.*, *b.* 1982.
1906	*Nunburnholme* (4th), Ben Charles Wilson, *b.* 1928, *s.* 1974	Hon. Charles T. *W.*, *b.* 1935.
	Oaksey, see *Trevethin and Oaksey*	

Created	Title, order of succession, name, etc.	Heir
1950	Ogmore (2nd), Gwilym Rees Rees-Williams, b. 1931, s. 1976, m.	Hon. Morgan R.-W., b. 1937.
1870	O'Hagan (4th), Charles Towneley Strachey, b. 1945, s. 1961	Hon. Richard T. S., b. 1950.
1868	O'Neill (4th), Raymond Arthur Clanaboy O'Neill, TD, b. 1933, s. 1944, m.	Hon. Shane S. C. O'N., b. 1965.
1836 I.*	Oranmore and Browne (4th), Dominick Geoffrey Edward Browne (2nd UK Baron Mereworth, 1926), b. 1901, s. 1927, m.	Hon. Dominick G. T. B., b. 1929.
1933	Palmer (4th), Adrian Bailie Nottage Palmer, b. 1951, s. 1990, m.	Hon. Hugo B. R. P., b. 1980.
1914	Parmoor (4th), (Frederick Alfred) Milo Cripps, b. 1929, s. 1977	M. Anthony L. C., CBE, DSO, TD, QC, b. 1913.
1937	Pender (3rd), John Willoughby Denison-Pender, b. 1933, s. 1965, m.	Hon. Henry J. R. D.-P., b. 1968.
1866	Penrhyn (6th), Malcolm Frank Douglas-Pennant, DSO, MBE, b. 1908, s. 1967, m.	Hon. Nigel D.-P., b. 1909.
1603	Petre (18th), John Patrick Lionel Petre, b. 1942, s. 1989, m.	Hon. Dominic W. P., b. 1966.
1918	Phillimore (5th), Francis Stephen Phillimore, b. 1944, s. 1994, m.	Hon. Tristan A. S. P., b. 1977.
1945	Piercy (3rd), James William Piercy, b. 1946, s. 1981	Hon. Mark E. P. P., b. 1953.
1827	Plunket (8th), Robin Rathmore Plunket, b. 1925, s. 1975, m.	Hon. Shaun A. F. S. P., b. 1931.
1831	Poltimore (7th), Mark Coplestone Bampfylde, b. 1957, s. 1978, m.	Hon. Henry A. W. B., b. 1985.
1690 s.	Polwarth (10th), Henry Alexander Hepburne-Scott, TD, b. 1916, s. 1944, m.	Master of Polwarth, b. 1947.
1930	Ponsonby of Shulbrede (4th), Frederick Matthew Thomas Ponsonby, b. 1958, s. 1990	None.
1958	Poole (2nd), David Charles Poole, b. 1945, s. 1993, m.	Hon. Oliver J. P., b. 1972.
1852	Raglan (5th), FitzRoy John Somerset, b. 1927, s. 1964	Hon. Geoffrey S., b. 1932.
1932	Rankeillour (4th), Peter St Thomas More Henry Hope, b. 1935, s. 1967	Michael R. H., b. 1940.
1953	Rathcavan (3rd), Hugh Detmar Torrens O'Neill, b. 1939, s. 1994, m.	Hon. François H. N. O'N., b. 1984.
1916	Rathcreedan (3rd), Christopher John Norton, b. 1949, s. 1990, m.	Hon. Adam G. N., b. 1952.
1868 I.	Rathdonnell (5th), Thomas Benjamin McClintock-Bunbury, b. 1938, s. 1959, m.	Hon. William L. M.-B., b. 1966.
1911	Ravensdale (3rd), Nicholas Mosley, MC, b. 1923, s. 1966, m.	Hon. Shaun N. M., b. 1949.
1821	Ravensworth (8th), Arthur Waller Liddell, b. 1924, s. 1950, m.	Hon. Thomas A. H. L., b. 1954.
1821	Rayleigh (6th), John Gerald Strutt, b. 1960, s. 1988, m.	Hon. John F. S., b. 1993.
1937	Rea (3rd), John Nicolas Rea, MD, b. 1928, s. 1981, m.	Hon. Matthew J. R., b. 1956.
1628 s.	Reay (14th), Hugh William Mackay, b. 1937, s. 1963, m.	Master of Reay, b. 1965.
1902	Redesdale (6th), Rupert Bertram Mitford, b. 1967, s. 1991	None.
1940	Reith. Disclaimed for life 1972 (Christopher John Reith, b. 1928, s. 1971, m.)	Hon. James H. J. R., b. 1971.
1928	Remnant (3rd), James Wogan Remnant, CVO, b. 1930, s. 1967, m.	Hon. Philip J. R., b. 1954.
1806 I.	Rendlesham (8th), Charles Anthony Hugh Thellusson, b. 1915, s. 1943, w.	Hon. Charles W. B. T., b. 1954.
1933	Rennell (3rd), (John Adrian) Tremayne Rodd, b. 1935, s. 1978, m.	Hon. James R. D. T. R., b. 1978.
1964	Renwick (2nd), Harry Andrew Renwick, b. 1935, s. 1973, m.	Hon. Robert J. R., b. 1966.
1885	Revelstoke (5th), John Baring, b. 1934, s. 1994	Hon. James C. B., b. 1938.
1905	Ritchie of Dundee (5th), (Harold) Malcolm Ritchie, b. 1919, s. 1978, m.	Hon. C. Rupert R. R., b. 1958.
1935	Riverdale (2nd), Robert Arthur Balfour, b. 1901, s. 1957, w.	Hon. Mark R. B., b. 1927.
1961	Robertson of Oakridge (2nd), William Ronald Robertson, b. 1930, s. 1974, m.	Hon. William B. E. R., b. 1975.
1938	Roborough (3rd), Henry Massey Lopes, b. 1940, s. 1992, m.	Hon. Massey J. H. L., b. 1969.
1931	Rochester (2nd), Foster Charles Lowry Lamb, b. 1916, s. 1955, m.	Hon. David C. L., b. 1944.
1934	Rockley (3rd), James Hugh Cecil, b. 1934, s. 1976, m.	Hon. Anthony R. C., b. 1961.
1782	Rodney (10th), George Brydges Rodney, b. 1953, s. 1992, m.	Nicholas S. H. R., b. 1947.
1651 s.*	Rollo (13th), Eric John Stapylton Rollo (4th UK Baron, Dunning, 1869), b. 1915, s. 1947, m.	Master of Rollo, b. 1943.
1959	Rootes (3rd), Nicholas Geoffrey Rootes, b. 1951, s. 1992, m.	William B. R., b. 1944.
1796 I.*	Rossmore (7th), William Warner Westenra (6th UK Baron, Rossmore, 1838), b. 1931, s. 1958, m.	Hon. Benedict W. W., b. 1983.
1939	Rotherwick (3rd), (Herbert) Robin Cayzer, b. 1954, s. 1996, m.	Hon. H. Robin C., b. 1989.
1885	Rothschild (4th), (Nathaniel Charles) Jacob Rothschild, b. 1936, s. 1990, m.	Hon. Nathaniel P. V. J. R., b. 1971.
1911	Rowallan (4th), John Polson Cameron Corbett, b. 1947, s. 1993, m.	Hon. Jason W. P. C. C., b. 1972.
1947	Rugby (3rd), Robert Charles Maffey, b. 1951, s. 1990, m.	Hon. Timothy J. H. M., b. 1975.
1919	Russell of Liverpool (3rd), Simon Gordon Jared Russell, b. 1952, s. 1981, m.	Hon. Edward C. S. R., b. 1985.
1876	Sackville (6th), Lionel Bertrand Sackville-West, b. 1913, s. 1965, m.	Hugh R. I. S.-W., MC, b. 1919.
1964	St Helens (2nd), Richard Francis Hughes-Young, b. 1945, s. 1980, m.	Hon. Henry T. H.-Y., b. 1986.
1559	St John of Bletso (21st), Anthony Tudor St John, b. 1957, s. 1978, m.	Hon. Oliver B. St J., b. 1995.
1887	St Levan (4th), John Francis Arthur St Aubyn, DSC, b. 1919, s. 1978, m.	Hon. O. Piers St A., MC, b. 1920.
1885	St Oswald (5th), Derek Edward Anthony Winn, b. 1919, s. 1984, m.	Hon. Charles R. A. W., b. 1959.

Created	Title, order of succession, name, etc.	Heir
1960	Sanderson of Ayot. Disclaimed for life 1971 (Alan Lindsay Sanderson, b. 1931, s. 1971, m.)	Hon. Michael S., b. 1959.
1945	Sandford (2nd), Revd John Cyril Edmondson, DSC, b. 1920, s. 1959, m.	Hon. James J. M. E., b. 1949.
1871	Sandhurst (5th), (John Edward) Terence Mansfield, DFC, b. 1920, s. 1964, m.	Hon. Guy R. J. M., b. 1949.
1802	Sandys (7th), Richard Michael Oliver Hill, b. 1931, s. 1961, m.	The Marquess of Downshire (see page 139).
1888	Savile (3rd), George Halifax Lumley-Savile, b. 1919, s. 1931	Hon. Henry L. T. L.-S., b. 1923.
1447	Saye and Sele (21st), Nathaniel Thomas Allen Fiennes, b. 1920, s. 1968, m.	Hon. Richard I. F., b. 1959.
1932	Selsdon (3rd), Malcolm McEacharn Mitchell-Thomson, b. 1937, s. 1963, m.	Hon. Callum M. M. M.-T., b. 1969.
1489 s.	Sempill (21st), James William Stuart Whitemore Sempill, b. 1949, s. 1995, m.	Master of Sempill, b. 1979.
1916	Shaughnessy (3rd), William Graham Shaughnessy, b. 1922, s. 1938, m.	Hon. Michael J. S., b. 1946.
1946	Shepherd (2nd), Malcolm Newton Shepherd, PC, b. 1918, s. 1954, m.	Hon. Graeme G. S., b. 1949.
1964	Sherfield (1st), Roger Mellor Makins, GCB, GCMG, FRS, b. 1904, w.	Hon. Christopher J. M., b. 1942.
1902	Shuttleworth (5th), Charles Geoffrey Nicholas Kay-Shuttleworth, b. 1948, s. 1975, m.	Hon. Thomas E. K.-S., b. 1976.
1950	Silkin. Disclaimed for life 1972 (Arthur Silkin, b. 1916, s. 1972, m.)	Hon. Christopher L. S., b. 1947.
1963	Silsoe (2nd), David Malcolm Trustram Eve, QC, b. 1930, s. 1976, m.	Hon. Simon R. T. E., b. 1966.
1947	Simon of Wythenshawe (2nd), Roger Simon, b. 1913, s. 1960, m.	Hon. Matthew S., b. 1955.
1449 s.	Sinclair (17th), Charles Murray Kennedy St Clair, CVO, b. 1914, s. 1957, m.	Master of Sinclair, b. 1968.
1957	Sinclair of Cleeve (3rd), John Lawrence Robert Sinclair, b. 1953, s. 1985	None.
1919	Sinha (5th), Anindo Kumar Sinha, b. 1930, s. 1992	†
1828	Skelmersdale (7th), Roger Bootle-Wilbraham, b. 1945, s. 1973, m.	Hon. Andrew B.-W., b. 1977.
1916	Somerleyton (3rd), Savile William Francis Crossley, KCVO, b. 1928, s. 1959, m. Master of the Horse	Hon. Hugh F. S. C., b. 1971.
1784	Somers (9th), Philip Sebastian Somers Cocks, b. 1948, s. 1995	Alan B. C., b. 1930
1780	Southampton (6th), Charles James FitzRoy, b. 1928, s. 1989, m.	Hon. Edward C. F., b. 1955.
1959	Spens (3rd), Patrick Michael Rex Spens, b. 1942, s. 1984, m.	Hon. Patrick N. G. S., b. 1968.
1640	Stafford (15th), Francis Melfort William Fitzherbert, b. 1954, s. 1986, m.	Hon. Benjamin J. B. F., b. 1983.
1938	Stamp (4th), Trevor Charles Bosworth Stamp, MD, FRCP, b. 1935, s. 1987, m.	Hon. Nicholas C. T. S., b. 1978.
1839	Stanley of Alderley (8th) & Sheffield (8th) (1738 I.), Thomas Henry Oliver Stanley (7th UK Baron Eddisbury, 1848), b. 1927, s. 1971, m.	Hon. Richard O. S., b. 1956.
1318	Strabolgi (11th), David Montague de Burgh Kenworthy, b. 1914, s. 1953, m.	Andrew D. W. K., b. 1967.
1954	Strang (2nd), Colin Strang, b. 1922, s. 1978, m.	None.
1955	Strathalmond (3rd), William Roberton Fraser, b. 1947, s. 1976, m.	Hon. William G. F., b. 1976.
1936	Strathcarron (2nd), David William Anthony Blyth Macpherson, b. 1924, s. 1937, m.	Hon. Ian D. P. M., b. 1949.
1955	Strathclyde (2nd), Thomas Galloway Dunlop du Roy de Blicquy Galbraith, PC, b. 1960, s. 1985, m.	Hon. Charles W. du R. de B. G., b. 1962.
1900	Strathcona and Mount Royal (4th), Donald Euan Palmer Howard, b. 1923, s. 1959, m.	Hon. D. Alexander S. H., b. 1961.
1836	Stratheden (6th) & Campbell (6th) (1841), Donald Campbell, b. 1934, s. 1987, m.	Hon. David A. C., b. 1963.
1884	Strathspey (6th), James Patrick Trevor Grant of Grant, b. 1943, s. 1992, m.	Hon. Michael P. F. G., b. 1953.
1838	Sudeley (7th), Merlin Charles Sainthill Hanbury-Tracy, b. 1939, s. 1941	D. Andrew J. H.-T., b. 1928.
1786	Suffield (11th), Anthony Philip Harbord-Hamond, MC, b. 1922, s. 1951, m.	Hon. Charles A. A. H.-H., b. 1953.
1893	Swansea (4th), John Hussey Hamilton Vivian, b. 1925, s. 1934, m.	Hon. Richard A. H. V., b. 1957.
1907	Swaythling (4th), David Charles Samuel Montagu, b. 1928, s. 1990, m.	Hon. Charles E. S. M., b. 1954.
1919	Swinfen (3rd), Roger Mynors Swinfen Eady, b. 1938, s. 1977, m.	Hon. Charles R. P. S. E., b. 1971.
1935	Sysonby (3rd), John Frederick Ponsonby, b. 1945, s. 1956	None.
1831 I.	Talbot of Malahide (10th), Reginald John Richard Arundell, b. 1931, s. 1987, m.	Hon. Richard J. T. A., b. 1957.
1946	Tedder (3rd), Robin John Tedder, b. 1955, s. 1994, m.	Hon. Benjamin J. T., b. 1985.
1884	Tennyson (5th), Cdr. Mark Aubrey Tennyson, DSC, b. 1920, s. 1991, m.	Lt.-Cdr. James A. T., DSC, b. 1913.
1918	Terrington (4th), (James Allen) David Woodhouse, b. 1915, s. 1961, m.	Hon. C. Montague W., DSO, OBE, b. 1917.
1940	Teviot (2nd), Charles John Kerr, b. 1934, s. 1968, m.	Hon. Charles R. K., b. 1971.

Created	Title, order of succession, name, etc.	Heir
1616	Teynham (20th), John Christopher Ingham Roper-Curzon, b. 1928, s. 1972, m.	Hon. David J. H. I. R.-C., b. 1965.
1964	Thomson of Fleet (2nd), Kenneth Roy Thomson, b. 1923, s. 1976, m.	Hon. David K. R. T., b. 1957.
1792	Thurlow (8th), Francis Edward Hovell-Thurlow-Cumming-Bruce, KCMG, b. 1912, s. 1971, w.	Hon. Roualeyn R. H.-T.-C.-B., b. 1952.
1876	Tollemache (5th), Timothy John Edward Tollemache, b. 1939, s. 1975, m.	Hon. Edward J. H. T., b. 1976.
1564 s.	Torphichen (15th), James Andrew Douglas Sandilands, b. 1946, s. 1975, m.	Douglas R. A. S., b. 1926.
1947	Trefgarne (2nd), David Garro Trefgarne, PC, b. 1941, s. 1960, m.	Hon. George G. T., b. 1970.
1921	Trevethin (4th), and Oaksey (2nd) (1947), John Geoffrey Tristram Lawrence, OBE, b. 1929, s. 1971, m.	Hon. Patrick J. T. L., b. 1960.
1880	Trevor (4th), Charles Edwin Hill-Trevor, b. 1928, s. 1950, m.	Hon. Marke C. H.-T., b. 1970.
1461 I.	Trimlestown (20th), Anthony Edward Barnewall, b. 1928, s. 1990, m.	Hon. Raymond C. B., b. 1930.
1940	Tryon (3rd), Anthony George Merrik Tryon, b. 1940, s. 1976, m.	Hon. Charles G. B. T., b. 1976.
1935	Tweedsmuir (3rd), William de l'Aigle Buchan, b. 1916, s. 1996, m.	Hon. John W. H. de l'A. B., b. 1950.
1523	Vaux of Harrowden (10th), John Hugh Philip Gilbey, b. 1915, s. 1977, m.	Hon. Anthony W. G., b. 1940.
1800 I.	Ventry (8th), Andrew Wesley Daubeny de Moleyns, b. 1943, s. 1987, m.	Hon. Francis W. D. de M., b. 1965.
1762	Vernon (10th), John Lawrance Vernon, b. 1923, s. 1963, m.	Col. William R. D. Vernon-Harcourt, OBE, b. 1909.
1922	Vestey (3rd), Samuel George Armstrong Vestey, b. 1941, s. 1954, m.	Hon. William G. V., b. 1983.
1841	Vivian (6th), Nicholas Crespigny Laurence Vivian, b. 1935, s. 1991, m.	Hon. Charles H. C. V., b. 1966.
1934	Wakehurst (3rd), (John) Christopher Loder, b. 1925, s. 1970, m.	Hon. Timothy W. L., b. 1958.
1723	Walpole (10th), Robert Horatio Walpole (8th Brit. Baron Walpole of Wolterton, 1756), b. 1938, s. 1989, m.	Hon. Jonathan R. H. W., b. 1967.
1780	Walsingham (9th), John de Grey, MC, b. 1925, s. 1965, m.	Hon. Robert de G., b. 1969.
1936	Wardington (2nd), Christopher Henry Beaumont Pease, b. 1924, s. 1950, m.	Hon. William S. P., b. 1925.
1792 I.	Waterpark (7th), Frederick Caryll Philip Cavendish, b. 1926, s. 1948, m.	Hon. Roderick A. C., b. 1959.
1942	Wedgwood (4th), Piers Anthony Weymouth Wedgwood, b. 1954, s. 1970, m.	John W, CBE, MD, FRCP, b. 1919.
1861	Westbury (5th), David Alan Bethell, CBE, MC, b. 1922, s. 1961, m.	Hon. Richard N. B., MBE, b. 1950.
1944	Westwood (3rd), (William) Gavin Westwood, b. 1944, s. 1991, m.	Hon. W. Fergus W, b. 1972.
1935	Wigram (2nd), (George) Neville (Clive) Wigram, MC, b. 1915, s. 1960, w.	Maj. Hon. Andrew F. C. W, MVO, b. 1949.
1491	Willoughby de Broke (21st), Leopold David Verney, b. 1938, s. 1986, m.	Hon. Rupert G. V., b. 1966.
1946	Wilson (2nd), Patrick Maitland Wilson, b. 1915, s. 1964, w.	None.
1937	Windlesham (3rd), David James George Hennessy, CVO, PC, b. 1932, s. 1962, w.	Hon. James R. H., b. 1968.
1951	Wise (2nd), John Clayton Wise, b. 1923, s. 1968, m.	Hon. Christopher J. C. W, PH.D., b. 1949.
1869	Wolverton (7th), Christopher Richard Glyn, b. 1938, s. 1988	Hon. Andrew J. G., b. 1943.
1928	Wraxall (2nd), George Richard Lawley Gibbs, b. 1928, s. 1931	Hon. Sir Eustace H. B. G., KCVO, CMG, b. 1929.
1915	Wrenbury (3rd), Revd John Burton Buckley, b. 1927, s. 1940, m.	Hon. William E. B., b. 1966.
1838	Wrottesley (6th), Clifton Hugh Lancelot de Verdon Wrottesley, b. 1968, s. 1977	Hon. Stephen J. W, b. 1955.
1919	Wyfold (3rd), Hermon Robert Fleming Hermon-Hodge, ERD, b. 1915, s. 1942	None.
1829	Wynford (8th), Robert Samuel Best, MBE, b. 1917, s. 1943, m.	Hon. John P. R. B., b. 1950.
1308	Zouche (18th), James Assheton Frankland, b. 1943, s. 1965, m.	Hon. William T. A. F., b. 1984.

BARONESSES/LADIES IN THEIR OWN RIGHT

Style, The Right Hon. the Lady ___ , *or* The Right Hon. the Baroness ___ , according to her preference. Either style may be used, except in the case of Scottish titles (indicated by s.), which are not baronies (*see* page 137) and whose holders are always addressed as Lady
Husband, Untitled
Children's style, As for children of a Baron
For forms of address, *see* page 136

Created	Title, order of succession, name, etc.	Heir
1455	*Berners* (16th in line), Pamela Vivien Kirkham, *b.* 1929, *title called out of* *abeyance* 1995, *m.*	Hon. Rupert W. T. *K.*, *b.* 1953.
1529	*Braye* (8th in line), Mary Penelope Aubrey-Fletcher, *b.* 1941, *s.* 1985, *m.*	Two co-heiresses.
1321	*Dacre* (27th in line), Rachel Leila Douglas-Home, *b.* 1929, *title called out of abeyance,* 1970, *w.*	Hon. James T. A. *D.-H.*, *b.* 1952.
1332	*Darcy de Knayth* (18th in line), Davina Marcia Ingrams, DBE, *b.* 1938, *s.* 1943, *w.*	Hon. Caspar D. *I.*, *b.* 1962.
1439	*Dudley* (14th in line), Barbara Amy Felicity Hamilton, *b.* 1907, *s.* 1972, *m.*	Hon. Jim A. H. *Wallace*, *b.* 1930.
1490 s.	*Herries of Terregles* (14th in line), Anne Elizabeth Fitzalan-Howard, *b.* 1938, *s.* 1975, *m.*	Lady Mary *Mumford*, CVO, *b.* 1940.
1602 s.	*Kinloss* (12th in line), Beatrice Mary Grenville Freeman-Grenville, *b.* 1922, *s.* 1944, *m.*	Master of Kinloss, *b.* 1953.
1445 s.	*Saltoun* (20th in line), Flora Marjory Fraser, *b.* 1930, *s.* 1979, *m.*	Hon. Katharine I. M. I. *F.*, *b.* 1957.
1628	*Strange* (16th in line), (Jean) Cherry Drummond of Megginch, *b.* 1928, *title called out of abeyance,* 1986, *m.*	Hon. Adam H. *D. of M.*, *b.* 1953.
1544/5	*Wharton* (11th in line), Myrtle Olive Felix Robertson, *b.* 1934, *title called out of abeyance,* 1990, *m.*	Hon. Myles C. D. *R.*, *b.* 1964.
1313	*Willoughby de Eresby* (27th in line), (Nancy) Jane Marie Heathcote-Drummond-Willoughby, *b.* 1934, *s.* 1983	Two co-heiresses.

Life Peers

Between 1 September 1995 and 31 August 1996, the conferment of 33 life peerages was announced:

LAW LORDS: (27 November 1995) the Rt. Hon. Sir Robin Cook, KBE; (4 June 1996) the Rt. Hon. Sir Thomas Bingham
'WORKING' PEERS (17 November 1995): Sir Gordon Borrie, QC; Sir Peter Bowness, CBE; Sir Basil Feldman; Sir Philip Harris; Helene Hayman; Tom McNally; Canon Peter Pilkington; John Sewel; Dr William Wallace; Lady Wilcox; Prof. Robert Winston; (21 August 1996) *John Alderdice; *Dame Joyce Anelay, DBE; *Dame Hazel Byford, DBE; *Prof. David Currie; *Peter Gummer; *Sir Ian MacLaurin; *Swraj Paul; *Ms Meta Ramsay; *Sir Richard Rogers, RA; *Maurice Saatchi; *Ms Elizabeth Symonds; *John Taylor; *Martin Thomas; *Larry Whitty
NEW YEAR'S HONOURS (29 December 1995): Sir David Gillmore, GCMG; Sir Robert Kilpatrick, CBE; Dick Taverne, QC
QUEEN'S BIRTHDAY HONOURS (7 June 1996): Prof. Dame June Lloyd, DBE; *Marmaduke Hussey; *Field Marshal Sir Richard Vincent, GBE, DSO

*No title gazetted at time of going to press

CREATED UNDER THE APPELLATE JURISDICTION ACT 1876 (AS AMENDED)

BARONS

Created	
1986	*Ackner,* Desmond James Conrad Ackner, PC, *b.* 1920, *m.*
1981	*Brandon of Oakbrook,* Henry Vivian Brandon, MC, PC, *b.* 1920, *m.*
1980	*Bridge of Harwich,* Nigel Cyprian Bridge, PC, *b.* 1917, *m.*
1982	*Brightman,* John Anson Brightman, PC, *b.* 1911, *m.*
1991	*Browne-Wilkinson,* Nicolas Christopher Henry Browne-Wilkinson, PC, *b.* 1930, *m.* Lord of Appeal in Ordinary
1957	*Denning,* Alfred Thompson Denning, PC, *b.* 1899, *w.*
1986	*Goff of Chieveley,* Robert Lionel Archibald Goff, PC, *b.* 1926, *m.* Lord of Appeal in Ordinary
1985	*Griffiths,* (William) Hugh Griffiths, MC, PC, *b.* 1923, *m.*
1995	*Hoffmann,* Leonard Hubert Hoffmann, PC, *b.* 1934, *m.*
1988	*Jauncey of Tullichettle,* Charles Eliot Jauncey, PC, *b.* 1925, *m.* Lord of Appeal in Ordinary

1977   *Keith of Kinkel*, Henry Shanks Keith, PC, *b*. 1922, *m*. Lord of Appeal in Ordinary

1979   *Lane*, Geoffrey Dawson Lane, AFC, PC, *b*. 1918, *m*.

1993   *Lloyd of Berwick*, Anthony John Leslie Lloyd, PC, *b*. 1929, *m*. Lord of Appeal in Ordinary

1992   *Mustill*, Michael John Mustill, PC, *b*. 1931, *m*. Lord of Appeal in Ordinary

1994   *Nicholls of Birkenhead*, Donald James Nicholls, PC, *b*. 1933, *m*.

1994   *Nolan*, Michael Patrick Nolan, PC, *b*. 1928, *m*. Lord of Appeal in Ordinary

1986   *Oliver of Aylmerton*, Peter Raymond Oliver, PC, *b*. 1921, *m*.

1980   *Roskill*, Eustace Wentworth Roskill, PC, *b*. 1911, *m*.

1977   *Scarman*, Leslie George Scarman, OBE, PC, *b*. 1911, *m*.

1992   *Slynn of Hadley*, Gordon Slynn, PC, *b*. 1930, *m*. Lord of Appeal in Ordinary

1995   *Steyn*, Johan van Zyl Steyn, PC, *b*. 1932, *m*.

1982   *Templeman*, Sydney William Templeman, MBE, PC, *b*. 1920, *w*.

1964   *Wilberforce*, Richard Orme Wilberforce, CMG, OBE, PC, *b*. 1907, *m*.

1992   *Woolf*, Harry Kenneth Woolf, PC, *b*. 1933, *m*. Master of the Rolls

CREATED UNDER THE LIFE PEERAGES ACT 1958

BARONS

Created

1988   *Alexander of Weedon*, Robert Scott Alexander, QC, *b*. 1936, *m*.

1976   *Allen of Abbeydale*, Philip Allen, GCB, *b*. 1912, *m*.

1961   *Alport*, Cuthbert James McCall Alport, TD, PC, *b*. 1912, *w*.

1992   *Amery of Lustleigh*, Julian Amery, PC, *b*. 1919, *w*.

1965   *Annan*, Noël Gilroy Annan, OBE, *b*. 1916, *m*.

1992   *Archer of Sandwell*, Peter Kingsley Archer, PC, QC, *b*. 1926, *m*.

1992   *Archer of Weston-super-Mare*, Jeffrey Howard Archer, *b*. 1940, *m*.

1988   *Armstrong of Ilminster*, Robert Temple Armstrong, GCB, CVO, *b*. 1927, *m*.

1992   *Ashley of Stoke*, Jack Ashley, CH, PC, *b*. 1922, *m*.

1993   *Attenborough*, Richard Samuel Attenborough, CBE, *b*. 1923, *m*.

1974   *Balniel*, The Earl of Crawford and Balcarres, *see* page 141

1982   *Bancroft*, Ian Powell Bancroft, GCB, *b*. 1922, *m*.

1974   *Banks*, Desmond Anderson Harvie Banks, CBE, *b*. 1918, *m*.

1974   *Barber*, Anthony Perrinott Lysberg Barber, TD, PC, *b*. 1920, *m*.

1992   *Barber of Tewkesbury*, Derek Coates Barber, *b*. 1918, *m*.

1983   *Barnett*, Joel Barnett, PC, *b*. 1923, *m*.

1982   *Bauer*, Prof. Peter Thomas Bauer, D.SC., FBA, *b*. 1915

1967   *Beaumont of Whitley*, Revd Timothy Wentworth Beaumont, *b*. 1928, *m*.

1979   *Bellwin*, Irwin Norman Bellow, *b*. 1923, *m*.

1981   *Beloff*, Max Beloff, FBA, *b*. 1913, *m*.

1996   *Bingham of Cornhill*, Thomas Henry Bingham, PC, *b*. 1933, *m*., *Lord Chief Justice of England*

1971   *Blake*, Robert Norman William Blake, FBA, *b*. 1916, *w*.

1994   *Blaker*, Peter Allan Renshaw Blaker, KCMG, PC, *b*. 1922, *m*.

1978   *Blease*, William John Blease, *b*. 1914, *m*.

1995   *Blyth of Rowington*, James Blyth, *b*. 1940, *m*.

1980   *Boardman*, Thomas Gray Boardman, MC, TD, *b*. 1919, *m*.

1996   *Borrie*, Gordon Johnson Borrie, QC, *b*. 1931, *m*.

1976   *Boston of Faversham*, Terence George Boston, QC, *b*. 1930, *m*.

1996   *Bowness*, Peter Spencer Bowness, CBE, *b*. 1943, *m*.

1972   *Boyd-Carpenter*, John Archibald Boyd-Carpenter, PC, *b*. 1908, *m*.

1992   *Braine of Wheatley*, Bernard Richard Braine, PC, *b*. 1914, *w*.

1987   *Bramall*, Edwin Noel Westby Bramall, KG, GCB, OBE, MC, *Field Marshal*, *b*. 1923, *m*.

1976   *Briggs*, Asa Briggs, FBA, *b*. 1921, *m*.

1975   *Brookes*, Raymond Percival Brookes, *b*. 1909, *m*.

1979   *Brooks of Tremorfa*, John Edward Brooks, *b*. 1927, *m*.

1974   *Bruce of Donington*, Donald William Trevor Bruce, *b*. 1912, *m*.

1976   *Bullock*, Alan Louis Charles Bullock, FBA, *b*. 1914, *m*.

1988   *Butterfield*, (William) John (Hughes) Butterfield, OBE, DM, FRCP, *b*. 1920, *m*.

1985   *Butterworth*, John Blackstock Butterworth, CBE, *b*. 1918, *m*.

1978   *Buxton of Alsa*, Aubrey Leland Oakes Buxton, MC, *b*. 1918, *m*.

1987   *Callaghan of Cardiff*, (Leonard) James Callaghan, KG, PC, *b*. 1912, *m*.

1979   *Dacre of Glanton*, Hugh Redwald Trevor-Roper, *b*. 1914, *m*.

1993   *Dahrendorf*, Ralf Dahrendorf, KBE, ph.D., D.phil., FBA, *b*. 1929, *m*.

1986   *Dainton*, Frederick Sydney Dainton, ph.D., SC.D., FRS, *b*. 1914, *m*.

1983   *Dean of Beswick*, Joseph Jabez Dean, *b*. 1922

1993   *Dean of Harptree*, (Arthur) Paul Dean, PC, *b*. 1924, *m*.

1986   *Deedes*, William Francis Deedes, MC, PC, *b*. 1913, *m*.

1991   *Desai*, Prof. Meghnad Jagdishchandra Desai, PH.D., *b*. 1940, *m*.

1970   *Diamond*, John Diamond, PC, *b*. 1907, *m*.

1993   *Dixon-Smith*, Robert William Dixon-Smith, *b*. 1934, *m*.

1967   *Donaldson of Kingsbridge*, John George Stuart Donaldson, OBE, *b*. 1907, *w*.

1988   *Donaldson of Lymington*, John Francis Donaldson, PC, *b*. 1920, *m*.

1985   *Donoughue*, Bernard Donoughue, D.phil., *b*. 1934.

1987   *Dormand of Easington*, John Donkin Dormand, *b*. 1919, *m*.

1994   *Dubs*, Alfred Dubs, *b*. 1932, *m*.

1995   *Eames*, Robert Henry Alexander Eames, ph.D., *b*. 1937, *m*.

1992   *Eatwell*, John Leonard Eatwell, *b*. 1945, *m*.

1983   *Eden of Winton*, John Benedict Eden, PC, *b*. 1925, *m*.

1992   *Elis-Thomas*, Dafydd Elis Elis-Thomas, *b*. 1946, *m*.

1985   *Elliott of Morpeth*, Robert William Elliott, *b*. 1920, *m*.

1981   *Elystan-Morgan*, Dafydd Elystan Elystan-Morgan, *b*. 1932, *m*.

1980   *Emslie*, George Carlyle Emslie, MBE, PC, FRSE, *b*. 1919, *m*.

1992   *Ewing of Kirkford,* Harry Ewing, *b.* 1931, *m.*
1983   *Ezra,* Derek Ezra, MBE, *b.* 1919, *m.*
1983   *Fanshawe of Richmond,* Anthony Henry Fanshawe Royle, KCMG, *b.* 1927, *m.*
1996   *Feldman,* Basil Feldman, *b.* 1926, *m.*
1992   *Finsberg,* Geoffrey Finsberg, MBE, *b.* 1926, *w.*
1983   *Fitt,* Gerard Fitt, *b.* 1926, *w.*
1979   *Flowers,* Brian Hilton Flowers, FRS, *b.* 1924, *m.*
1967   *Foot,* John Mackintosh Foot, *b.* 1909, *m.*
1982   *Forte,* Charles Forte, *b.* 1908, *m.*
1989   *Fraser of Carmyllie,* Peter Lovat Fraser, PC, QC, *b.* 1945, *m.*
1982   *Gallacher,* John Gallacher, *b.* 1920, *m.*
1992   *Geraint,* Geraint Wyn Howells, *b.* 1925, *m.*
1975   *Gibson,* (Richard) Patrick (Tallentyre) Gibson, *b.* 1916, *m.*
1979   *Gibson-Watt,* (James) David Gibson-Watt, MC, PC, *b.* 1918, *m.*
1996   *Gillmore of Thamesfield,* David Howe Gillmore, GCMG, *b.* 1934, *m.*
1992   *Gilmour of Craigmillar,* Ian Hedworth John Little Gilmour, PC, *b.* 1926, *m.*
1994   *Gladwin of Clee,* Derek Oliver Gladwin, CBE, *b.* 1930, *m.*
1977   *Glenamara,* Edward Watson Short, CH, PC, *b.* 1912, *m.*
1987   *Goold,* James Duncan Goold, *b.* 1934, *w.*
1976   *Grade,* Lew Grade, *b.* 1906, *m.*
1983   *Graham of Edmonton,* (Thomas) Edward Graham, *b.* 1925, *m.*
1967   *Granville of Eye,* Edgar Louis Granville, *b.* 1899, *m.*
1983   *Gray of Contin,* James (Hamish) Hector Northey Gray, PC, *b.* 1927, *m.*
1974   *Greene of Harrow Weald,* Sidney Francis Greene, CBE, *b.* 1910, *m.*
1974   *Greenhill of Harrow,* Denis Arthur Greenhill, GCMG, OBE, *b.* 1913, *m.*
1975   *Gregson,* John Gregson, *b.* 1924
1968   *Grey of Naunton,* Ralph Francis Alnwick Grey, GCMG, GCVO, OBE, *b.* 1910, *w.*
1991   *Griffiths of Fforestfach,* Brian Griffiths, *b.* 1941, *m.*
1995   *Habgood,* Rt. Revd John Stapylton Habgood, PC, PH.D., *b.* 1927, *m.*
1970   *Hailsham of St Marylebone,* Quintin McGarel Hogg, KG, CH, PC, FRS, *b.* 1907, *m.*
1994   *Hambro,* Charles Eric Alexander Hambro, *b.* 1930, *m.*
1983   *Hanson,* James Edward Hanson, *b.* 1922, *m.*
1974   *Harmar-Nicholls,* Harmar Harmar-Nicholls, *b.* 1912, *m.*
1974   *Harris of Greenwich,* John Henry Harris, *b.* 1930, *m.*
1979   *Harris of High Cross,* Ralph Harris, *b.* 1924, *m.*
1996   *Harris of Peckham,* Philip Charles Harris, *b.* 1942, *m.*
1968   *Hartwell,* (William) Michael Berry, MBE, TD, *b.* 1911, *w.*
1974   *Harvington,* Robert Grant Grant-Ferris, AE, PC, *b.* 1907, *m.*
1993   *Haskel,* Simon Haskel, *b.* 1934, *m.*
1990   *Haslam,* Robert Haslam, *b.* 1923, *m.*
1992   *Hayhoe,* Bernard John (Barney) Hayhoe, PC, *b.* 1925, *m.*
1992   *Healey,* Denis Winston Healey, CH, MBE, PC, *b.* 1917, *m.*
1984   *Henderson of Brompton,* Peter Gordon Henderson, KCB, *b.* 1922, *m.*
1979   *Hill-Norton,* Peter John Hill-Norton, GCB, *Admiral of the Fleet, b.* 1915, *m.*

1979   *Holderness,* Richard Frederick Wood, PC, *b.* 1920, *m.*
1991   *Hollick,* Clive Richard Hollick, *b.* 1945, *m.*
1990   *Holme of Cheltenham,* Richard Gordon Holme, CBE, *b.* 1936, *m.*
1979   *Hooson,* (Hugh) Emlyn Hooson, QC, *b.* 1925, *m.*
1995   *Hope of Craighead,* (James Arthur) David Hope, PC, *b.* 1938, *m.*
1992   *Howe of Aberavon,* (Richard Edward) Geoffrey Howe, CH, PC, QC, *b.* 1926, *m.*
1992   *Howell,* Denis Herbert Howell, PC, *b.* 1923, *m.*
1978   *Howie of Troon,* William Howie, *b.* 1924, *m.*
1961   *Hughes,* William Hughes, CBE, PC, *b.* 1911, *w.*
1966   *Hunt,* (Henry Cecil) John Hunt, KG, CBE, DSO, *b.* 1910, *m.*
1980   *Hunt of Tanworth,* John Joseph Benedict Hunt, GCB, *b.* 1919, *m.*
1978   *Hutchinson of Lullington,* Jeremy Nicolas Hutchinson, QC, *b.* 1915, *m.*
1982   *Ingrow,* John Aked Taylor, OBE, TD, *b.* 1917, *m.*
1987   *Irvine of Lairg,* Alexander Andrew Mackay Irvine, QC, *b.* 1940, *m.*
1988   *Jakobovits,* Immanuel Jakobovits, *b.* 1921, *m.*
1987   *Jenkin of Roding,* (Charles) Patrick (Fleeming) Jenkin, PC, *b.* 1926, *m.*
1987   *Jenkins of Hillhead,* Roy Harris Jenkins, OM, PC, *b.* 1920, *m.*
1981   *Jenkins of Putney,* Hugh Gater Jenkins, *b.* 1908, *w.*
1987   *Johnston of Rockport,* Charles Collier Johnston, TD, *b.* 1915, *m.*
1991   *Judd,* Frank Ashcroft Judd, *b.* 1935, *m.*
1980   *Keith of Castleacre,* Kenneth Alexander Keith, *b.* 1916, *m.*
1996   *Kilpatrick of Kincraig,* Robert Kilpatrick, CBE, *b.* 1926, *m.*
1985   *Kimball,* Marcus Richard Kimball, *b.* 1928, *m.*
1983   *King of Wartnaby,* John Leonard King, *b.* 1918, *m.*
1993   *Kingsdown,* Robert (Robin) Leigh-Pemberton, KG, PC, *b.* 1927, *m.*
1994   *Kingsland,* Christopher James Prout, TD, PC, QC, *b.* 1942
1965   *Kings Norton,* Harold Roxbee Cox, PH.D., FENG., *b.* 1902, *m.*
1975   *Kirkhill,* John Farquharson Smith, *b.* 1930, *m.*
1974   *Kissin,* Harry Kissin, *b.* 1912, *m.*
1987   *Knights,* Philip Douglas Knights, CBE, QPM, *b.* 1920, *m.*
1991   *Laing of Dunphail,* Hector Laing, *b.* 1923, *m.*
1990   *Lane of Horsell,* Peter Stewart Lane, *b.* 1925, *w.*
1992   *Lawson of Blaby,* Nigel Lawson, PC, *b.* 1932, *m.*
1993   *Lester of Herne Hill,* Anthony Paul Lester, QC, *b.* 1936, *m.*
1982   *Lewin,* Terence Thornton Lewin, KG, GCB, LVO, DSC, *Admiral of the Fleet, b.* 1920, *m.*
1989   *Lewis of Newnham,* Jack Lewis, FRS, *b.* 1928, *m.*
1974   *Lovell-Davis,* Peter Lovell Lovell-Davis, *b.* 1924, *m.*
1979   *Lowry,* Robert Lynd Erskine Lowry, PC, PC (NI), *b.* 1919, *m.*
1984   *McAlpine of West Green,* (Robert) Alistair McAlpine, *b.* 1942, *m.*
1988   *Macaulay of Bragar,* Donald Macaulay, QC, *b.* 1933, *m.*
1975   *McCarthy,* William Edward John McCarthy, D.PHIL., *b.* 1925, *m.*
1976   *McCluskey,* John Herbert McCluskey, *b.* 1929, *m.*
1989   *McColl of Dulwich,* Ian McColl, FRCS, FRCSE, *b.* 1933, *m.*
1995   *McConnell,* Robert William Brian McConnell, PC (NI), *b.* 1922, *m.*

1991   *Macfarlane of Bearsden*, Norman Somerville
       Macfarlane, FRSE, *b.* 1926, *m.*
1978   *McGregor of Durris*, Oliver Ross McGregor, *b.*
       1921, *m.*
1982   *McIntosh of Haringey*, Andrew Robert McIntosh, *b.*
       1933, *m.*
1991   *Mackay of Ardbrecknish*, John Jackson Mackay, PC,
       b. 1938, *m.*
1979   *Mackay of Clashfern*, James Peter Hymers
       Mackay, PC, FRSE, *b.* 1927, *m. Lord High
       Chancellor*
1995   *Mackay of Drumadoon*, Donald Sage Mackay, *b.*
       1946, *m.*
1988   *Mackenzie-Stuart*, Alexander John Mackenzie
       Stuart, *b.* 1924, *m.*
1974   *Mackie of Benshie*, George Yull Mackie, CBE, DSO,
       DFC, *b.* 1919, *m.*
1982   *MacLehose of Beoch*, (Crawford) Murray
       MacLehose, KT, GBE, KCMG, KCVO, *b.* 1917, *m.*
1995   *McNally*, Tom McNally, *b.* 1943, *m.*
1991   *Marlesford*, Mark Shuldham Schreiber, *b.* 1931, *m.*
1981   *Marsh*, Richard William Marsh, PC, *b.* 1928, *m.*
1987   *Mason of Barnsley*, Roy Mason, PC, *b.* 1924, *m.*
1981   *Mayhew*, Christopher Paget Mayhew, *b.* 1915, *m.*
1985   *Mellish*, Robert Joseph Mellish, PC, *b.* 1913, *m.*
1993   *Menuhin*, Yehudi Menuhin, OM, KBE, *b.* 1916, *m.*
1992   *Merlyn-Rees*, Merlyn Merlyn-Rees, PC, *b.* 1920, *m.*
1978   *Mishcon*, Victor Mishcon, *b.* 1915, *m.*
1981   *Molloy*, William John Molloy, *b.* 1918
1992   *Moore of Lower Marsh*, John Edward Michael
       Moore, PC, *b.* 1937, *m.*
1986   *Moore of Wolvercote*, Philip Brian Cecil Moore,
       GCB, GCVO, CMG, PC, *b.* 1921, *m.*
1990   *Morris of Castle Morris*, Brian Robert Morris,
       D.Phil., *b.* 1930, *m.*
1971   *Moyola*, James Dawson Chichester-Clark, PC
       (NI), *b.* 1923, *m.*
1985   *Murray of Epping Forest*, Lionel Murray, OBE, PC, *b.*
       1922, *m.*
1979   *Murton of Lindisfarne*, (Henry) Oscar Murton,
       OBE, TD, PC, *b.* 1914, *m.*
1994   *Nickson*, David Wigley Nickson, KBE, FRSE, *b.*
       1929, *m.*
1975   *Northfield*, (William) Donald Chapman, *b.* 1923
1976   *Oram*, Albert Edward Oram, *b.* 1913, *m.*
1971   *Orr-Ewing*, (Charles) Ian Orr-Ewing, OBE, *b.* 1912,
       m.
1992   *Owen*, David Anthony Llewellyn Owen, CH, PC,
       b. 1938, *m.*
1991   *Palumbo*, Peter Garth Palumbo, *b.* 1935, *m.*
1992   *Parkinson*, Cecil Edward Parkinson, PC, *b.* 1931, *m.*
1975   *Parry*, Gordon Samuel David Parry, *b.* 1925, *m.*
1990   *Pearson of Rannoch*, Malcolm Everard MacLaren
       Pearson, *b.* 1942, *m.*
1979   *Perry of Walton*, Walter Laing Macdonald Perry,
       OBE, FRS, FRSE, *b.* 1921, *m.*
1987   *Peston*, Maurice Harry Peston, *b.* 1931, *m.*
1983   *Peyton of Yeovil*, John Wynne William Peyton,
       PC, *b.* 1919, *m.*
1994   *Phillips of Ellesmere*, Prof. David Chilton Phillips,
       KBE, FRS, *b.* 1924, *m.*
1996   *Pilkington of Oxenford*, Revd Canon Peter
       Pilkington, *b.* 1933, *m.*
1992   *Plant of Highfield*, Prof. Raymond Plant, PH.D., *b.*
       1945, *m.*
1959   *Plowden*, Edwin Noel Plowden, GBE, KCB, *b.* 1907,
       m.
1987   *Plumb*, (Charles) Henry Plumb, MEP, *b.* 1925, *m.*
1981   *Plummer of St Marylebone*, (Arthur) Desmond
       (Herne) Plummer, TD, *b.* 1914, *m.*

1990   *Porter of Luddenham*, George Porter, OM, FRS, *b.*
       1920, *m.*
1992   *Prentice*, Reginald Ernest Prentice, PC, *b.* 1923, *m.*
1987   *Prior*, James Michael Leathes Prior, PC, *b.* 1927,
       m.
1982   *Prys-Davies*, Gwilym Prys Prys-Davies, *b.* 1923,
       m.
1987   *Pym*, Francis Leslie Pym, MC, PC, *b.* 1922, *m.*
1982   *Quinton*, Anthony Meredith Quinton, FBA, *b.*
       1925, *m.*
1994   *Quirk*, Prof. (Charles) Randolph Quirk, CBE, FBA,
       b. 1920, *m.*
1978   *Rawlinson of Ewell*, Peter Anthony Grayson
       Rawlinson, PC, QC, *b.* 1919, *m.*
1976   *Rayne*, Max Rayne, *b.* 1918, *m.*
1983   *Rayner*, Derek George Rayner, *b.* 1926
1987   *Rees*, Peter Wynford Innes Rees, PC, QC, *b.* 1926,
       m.
1988   *Rees-Mogg*, William Rees-Mogg, *b.* 1928, *m.*
1991   *Renfrew of Kaimsthorn*, (Andrew) Colin Renfrew,
       FBA, *b.* 1937, *m.*
1979   *Renton*, David Lockhart-Mure Renton, KBE, TD,
       PC, QC, *b.* 1908, *w.*
1990   *Richard*, Ivor Seward Richard, PC, QC, *b.* 1932, *m.*
1979   *Richardson*, John Samuel Richardson, LVO, MD,
       FRCP, *b.* 1910, *w.*
1983   *Richardson of Duntisbourne*, Gordon William
       Humphreys Richardson, KG, MBE, TD, PC, *b.*
       1915, *m.*
1987   *Rippon of Hexham*, (Aubrey) Geoffrey (Frederick)
       Rippon, PC, QC, *b.* 1924, *m.*
1992   *Rix*, Brian Norman Roger Rix, CBE, *b.* 1924, *m.*
1961   *Robens of Woldingham*, Alfred Robens, PC, *b.* 1910,
       m.
1992   *Rodger of Earlsferry*, Alan Ferguson Rodger, PC,
       QC, FBA, *b.* 1944, *Lord Advocate*
1992   *Rodgers of Quarry Bank*, William Thomas
       Rodgers, PC, *b.* 1928, *m.*
1977   *Roll of Ipsden*, Eric Roll, KCMG, CB, *b.* 1907, *m.*
1991   *Runcie*, Rt Revd Robert Alexander Kennedy
       Runcie, MC, PC, Royal Victoria Chain, *b.* 1921,
       m.
1975   *Ryder of Eaton Hastings*, Sydney Thomas Franklin
       (Don) Ryder, *b.* 1916, *m.*
1962   *Sainsbury*, Alan John Sainsbury, *b.* 1902, *w.*
1989   *Sainsbury of Preston Candover*, John Davan
       Sainsbury, KG, *b.* 1927, *m.*
1987   *St John of Fawsley*, Norman Antony Francis
       St John-Stevas, PC, *b.* 1929
1985   *Sanderson of Bowden*, Charles Russell Sanderson,
       b. 1933, *m.*
1979   *Scanlon*, Hugh Parr Scanlon, *b.* 1913, *m.*
1978   *Sefton of Garston*, William Henry Sefton, *b.* 1915,
       m.
1996   *Sewel*, John Buttifant Sewel, CBE, *b.* 19−
1994   *Shaw of Northstead*, Michael Norman Shaw, *b.*
       1920, *m.*
1959   *Shawcross*, Hartley William Shawcross, GBE, PC,
       QC, *b.* 1902, *w.*
1994   *Sheppard of Didgemere*, Allan John George
       Sheppard, *b.* 1932, *m.*
1980   *Sieff of Brimpton*, Marcus Joseph Sieff, OBE, *b.*
       1913, *m.*
1971   *Simon of Glaisdale*, Jocelyn Edward Salis Simon,
       PC, *b.* 1911, *m.*
1991   *Skidelsky*, Robert Jacob Alexander Skidelsky,
       D.Phil., *b.* 1939, *m.*
1978   *Smith*, Rodney Smith, KBE, FRCS, *b.* 1914, *m.*
1965   *Soper*, Revd Donald Oliver Soper, PH.D., *b.* 1903,
       m.

1990 *Soulsby of Swaffham Prior,* Ernest Jackson Lawson Soulsby, PH.D., *b.* 1926, *m.*

1983 *Stallard,* Albert William Stallard, *b.* 1921, *m.*

1991 *Sterling of Plaistow,* Jeffrey Maurice Sterling, CBE, *b.* 1934, *m.*

1987 *Stevens of Ludgate,* David Robert Stevens, *b.* 1936, *m.*

1992 *Stewartby,* (Bernard Harold) Ian (Halley) Stewart, RD, PC, FBA, FRSE, *b.* 1935, *m.*

1981 *Stodart of Leaston,* James Anthony Stodart, PC, *b.* 1916, *w.*

1983 *Stoddart of Swindon,* David Leonard Stoddart, *b.* 1926, *m.*

1969 *Stokes,* Donald Gresham Stokes, TD, FEng., *b.* 1914, *w.*

1971 *Tanlaw,* Simon Brooke Mackay, *b.* 1934, *m.*

1996 *Taverne,* Dick Taverne, QC, *b.* 1928, *m.*

1978 *Taylor of Blackburn,* Thomas Taylor, CBE, *b.* 1929, *m.*

1992 *Taylor of Gosforth,* Peter Murray Taylor, PC, *b.* 1930, *w.*

1968 *Taylor of Gryfe,* Thomas Johnston Taylor, FRSE, *b.* 1912, *m.*

1992 *Tebbit,* Norman Beresford Tebbit, CH, PC, *b.* 1931, *m.*

1987 *Thomas of Gwydir,* Peter John Mitchell Thomas, PC, QC, *b.* 1920, *w.*

1981 *Thomas of Swynnerton,* Hugh Swynnerton Thomas, *b.* 1931, *m.*

1977 *Thomson of Monifieth,* George Morgan Thomson, KT, PC, *b.* 1921, *m.*

1962 *Todd,* Alexander Robertus Todd, OM, D.SC., D.Phil., FRS, *b.* 1907, *w.*

1990 *Tombs,* Francis Leonard Tombs, FEng., *b.* 1924, *m.*

1994 *Tope,* Graham Norman Tope, CBE, *b.* 1943, *m.*

1981 *Tordoff,* Geoffrey Johnson Tordoff, *b.* 1928, *m*

1993 *Tugendhat,* Christopher Samuel Tugendhat, *b.* 1937, *m.*

1990 *Varley,* Eric Graham Varley, PC, *b.* 1932, *m.*

1985 *Vinson,* Nigel Vinson, LVO, *b.* 1931, *m.*

1990 *Waddington,* David Charles Waddington, GCVO, PC, QC, *b.* 1929, *m.*

1990 *Wade of Chorlton,* (William) Oulton Wade, *b.* 1932, *m.*

1992 *Wakeham,* John Wakeham, PC, *b.* 1932, *m.*

1992 *Walker of Worcester,* Peter Edward Walker, MBE, PC, *b.* 1932, *m.*

1974 *Wallace of Campsie,* George Wallace, *b.* 1915, *m.*

1974 *Wallace of Coslany,* George Douglas Wallace, *b.* 1906, *m.*

1995 *Wallace of Saltaire,* William John Lawrence Wallace, PH.D., *b.* 1941, *m.*

1989 *Walton of Detchant,* John Nicholas Walton, TD, FRCP, *b.* 1922, *m.*

1992 *Weatherill,* (Bruce) Bernard Weatherill, PC, *b.* 1920, *m.*

1977 *Wedderburn of Charlton,* (Kenneth) William Wedderburn, FBA, QC, *b.* 1927, *m.*

1976 *Weidenfeld,* (Arthur) George Weidenfeld, *b.* 1919, *m.*

1980 *Weinstock,* Arnold Weinstock, *b.* 1924, *m.*

1978 *Whaddon,* (John) Derek Page, *b.* 1927, *m.*

1974 *Wigoder,* Basil Thomas Wigoder, QC, *b.* 1921, *m.*

1985 *Williams of Elvel,* Charles Cuthbert Powell Williams, CBE, *b.* 1933, *m.*

1992 *Williams of Mostyn,* Gareth Wyn Williams, QC, *b.* 1941, *m.*

1969 *Wilson of Langside,* Henry Stephen Wilson, PC, QC, *b.* 1916, *m.*

1992 *Wilson of Tillyorn,* David Clive Wilson, GCMG, PH.D., *b.* 1935, *m.*

1995 *Winston,* Robert Maurice Lipson Winston, FRCOG, *b.* 1940, *m.*

1985 *Wolfson,* Leonard Gordon Wolfson, *b.* 1927, *m.*

1991 *Wolfson of Sunningdale,* David Wolfson, *b.* 1935, *m.*

1994 *Wright of Richmond,* Patrick Richard Henry Wright, GCMG, *b.* 1931, *m.*

1987 *Wyatt of Weeford,* Woodrow Lyle Wyatt, *b.* 1918, *m.*

1978 *Young of Dartington,* Michael Young, PH.D., *b.* 1915, *m.*

1984 *Young of Graffham,* David Ivor Young, PC, *b.* 1932, *m.*

1992 *Younger of Prestwick,* George Kenneth Hotson Younger, KT, KCVO, TD, PC, *b.* 1931, *m.*

BARONESSES

Created

1967 *Birk,* Alma Birk, *b.* 1921, *m.*

1987 *Blackstone,* Tessa Ann Vosper Blackstone, PH.D., *b.* 1942

1987 *Blatch,* Emily May Blatch, CBE, PC, *b.* 1937, *m.*

1990 *Brigstocke,* Heather Renwick Brigstocke, *b.* 1929, *w.*

1964 *Brooke of Ystradfellte,* Barbara Muriel Brooke, DBE, *b.* 1908, *w.*

1982 *Carnegy of Lour,* Elizabeth Patricia Carnegy of Lour, *b.* 1925

1990 *Castle of Blackburn,* Barbara Anne Castle, PC, *b.* 1910, *w.*

1992 *Chalker of Wallasey,* Lynda Chalker, PC, *b.* 1942, *m.*

1982 *Cox,* Caroline Anne Cox, *b.* 1937, *m.*

1990 *Cumberlege,* Julia Frances Cumberlege, CBE, *b.* 1943, *m.*

1978 *David,* Nora Ratcliff David, *b.* 1913, *w.*

1993 *Dean of Thornton-le-Fylde,* Brenda Dean, *b.* 1943, *m.*

1974 *Delacourt-Smith of Alteryn,* Margaret Rosalind Delacourt-Smith, *b.* 1916, *m.*

1978 *Denington,* Evelyn Joyce Denington, DBE, *b.* 1907, *m.*

1991 *Denton of Wakefield,* Jean Denton, CBE, *b.* 1935

1990 *Dunn,* Lydia Selina Dunn, DBE, *b.* 1940, *m.*

1990 *Eccles of Moulton,* Diana Catherine Eccles, *b.* 1933, *m.*

1972 *Elles,* Diana Louie Elles, *b.* 1921, *m.*

1974 *Falkender,* Marcia Matilda Falkender, CBE, *b.* 1932

1994 *Farrington of Ribbleton,* Josephine Farrington, *b.* 19–, *m.*

1974 *Fisher of Rednal,* Doris Mary Gertrude Fisher, *b.* 1919, *w.*

1990 *Flather,* Shreela Flather, *b.* 19–, *m.*

1981 *Gardner of Parkes,* (Rachel) Trixie (Anne) Gardner, *b.* 1927, *m.*

1993 *Gould of Potternewton,* Joyce Brenda Gould, *b.* 1932, *m.*

1991 *Hamwee,* Sally Rachel Hamwee, *b.* 1947

1996 *Hayman,* Helene Valerie Hayman, *b.* 1949, *m.*

1991 *Hilton of Eggardon,* Jennifer Hilton, QPM, *b.* 1936

1995 *Hogg,* Sarah Elizabeth Mary Hogg, *b.* 1946, *m.*

1990 *Hollis of Heigham,* Patricia Lesley Hollis, D.Phil., *b.* 1941, *m.*

1985 *Hooper,* Gloria Dorothy Hooper, *b.* 1939

1965 *Hylton-Foster,* Audrey Pellew Hylton-Foster, DBE, *b.* 1908, *w.*

1991 *James of Holland Park,* Phyllis Dorothy White (P. D. James), OBE, *b.* 1920, *w.*

1992 *Jay of Paddington,* Margaret Ann Jay, *b.* 1939

1979   *Jeger*, Lena May Jeger, *b.* 1915, *w.*
1967   *Llewelyn-Davies of Hastoe*, (Annie) Patricia
       Llewelyn-Davies, PC, *b.* 1915, *w.*
1996   *Lloyd of Highbury*, Prof. June Kathleen Lloyd, DBE,
       FRCP, FRCPE, FRCGP, *b.* 1928
1978   *Lockwood*, Betty Lockwood, *b.* 1924, *w.*
1979   *McFarlane of Llandaff*, Jean Kennedy McFarlane,
       b. 1926
1971   *Macleod of Borve*, Evelyn Hester Macleod, *b.* 1915,
       w.
1991   *Mallalieu*, Ann Mallalieu, QC, *b.* 1945, *m.*
1970   *Masham of Ilton*, Susan Lilian Primrose Cunliffe-
       Lister, *b.* 1935, *m.* (*Countess of Swinton*)
1993   *Miller of Hendon*, Doreen Miller, MBE, *b.* 1933, *m.*
1982   *Nicol*, Olive Mary Wendy Nicol, *b.* 1923, *m.*
1991   *O'Cathain*, Detta O'Cathain, OBE, *b.* 1938, *m.*
1989   *Oppenheim-Barnes*, Sally Oppenheim-Barnes, PC,
       b. 1930, *m.*
1990   *Park of Monmouth*, Daphne Margaret Sybil
       Désirée Park, CMG, OBE, *b.* 1921
1991   *Perry of Southwark*, Pauline Perry, *b.* 1931, *m.*
1974   *Pike*, (Irene) Mervyn (Parnicott) Pike, DBE, *b.*
       1918
1981   *Platt of Writtle*, Beryl Catherine Platt, CBE, FEng.,
       b. 1923, *m.*
1994   *Rawlings*, Patricia Elizabeth Rawlings, *b.* 1939

1974   *Robson of Kiddington*, Inga-Stina Robson, *b.* 1919,
       w.
1979   *Ryder of Warsaw*, Margaret Susan Cheshire (Sue
       Ryder), CMG, OBE, *b.* 1923, *w.*
1991   *Seccombe*, Joan Anna Dalziel Seccombe, DBE, *b.*
       1930, *m.*
1971   *Seear*, (Beatrice) Nancy Seear, PC, *b.* 1913
1967   *Serota*, Beatrice Serota, DBE, *b.* 1919, *m.*
1973   *Sharples*, Pamela Sharples, *b.* 1923, *m.*
1995   *Smith of Gilmorehill*, Elizabeth Margaret Smith, *b.*
       19 –, *w.*
1992   *Thatcher*, Margaret Hilda Thatcher, OM, PC, FRS,
       b. 1925, *m.*
1994   *Thomas of Walliswood*, Susan Petronella Thomas,
       OBE, *b.* 19 –, *m.*
1980   *Trumpington*, Jean Alys Barker, PC, *b.* 1922, *w.*
1985   *Turner of Camden*, Muriel Winifred Turner, *b.*
       1927, *m.*
1985   *Warnock*, Helen Mary Warnock, DBE, *b.* 1924, *w.*
1970   *White*, Eirene Lloyd White, *b.* 1909, *w.*
1996   *Wilcox*, Judith Ann Wilcox, *b.* 19 –, *w.*
1993   *Williams of Crosby*, Shirley Vivien Teresa Brittain
       Williams, PC, *b.* 1930, *m.*
1971   *Young*, Janet Mary Young, PC, *b.* 1926, *m.*

Lords Spiritual

The Lords Spiritual are the Archbishops of Canterbury
and York and 24 diocesan bishops of the Church of
England. The Bishops of London, Durham and Winchester
always have seats in the House of Lords; the other 21 seats
are filled by the remaining diocesan bishops in order of
seniority. The Bishop of Sodor and Man and the Bishop of
Gibraltar are not eligible to sit in the House of Lords.

ARCHBISHOPS

Style, The Most Revd and Right Hon. the Lord Archbishop
of ___
Addressed as Archbishop, *or* Your Grace

Introduced to House of Lords
1991   *Canterbury* (103rd), George Leonard Carey, PC,
       PH.D., *b.* 1935, *m.* Consecrated Bishop of Bath and
       Wells 1987, *trans.* 1991
1990   *York* (96th), David Michael Hope, KCVO, PC,
       D.Phil., *b.* 1940, *cons.* 1985, *elected* 1985, *trans.*
       1991, 1995

BISHOPS

Style, The Right Revd the Lord Bishop of ___
Addressed as My Lord
elected = date of election as diocesan bishop

Introduced to House of Lords
1995   *London* (132nd), Richard John Carew Chartres, *b.*
       1947, *m.*, *cons.* 1992

1994   *Durham* (93rd), (Anthony) Michael (Arnold)
       Turnbull, *b.* 1935, *m.*, *cons.* 1988, *elected* 1988,
       trans. 1994
1995   *Winchester* (96th), Michael Charles Scott-Joynt, *b.*
       1943, *m.*, *cons.* 1987
1979   *Chichester* (102nd), Eric Waldram Kemp, DD, *b.*
       1915, *m.*, *cons.* 1974, *elected* 1974
1980   *Liverpool* (6th), David Stuart Sheppard, *b.* 1929,
       m., *cons.* 1969, *elected* 1975
1984   *Ripon* (11th), David Nigel de Lorentz Young, *b.*
       1931, *m.*, *cons.* 1977, *elected* 1977
1985   *Sheffield* (5th), David Ramsay Lunn, *b.* 1930, *cons.*
       1980, *elected* 1980
1985   *Newcastle* (10th), Andrew Alexander Kenny
       Graham, *b.* 1929, *cons.* 1977, *elected* 1981
1988   *Southwark* (7th), Robert Kerr Williamson, *b.* 1932,
       m., *cons.* 1984, *elected* 1984, *trans.* 1991
1989   *Lichfield* (97th), Keith Norman Sutton, *b.* 1934,
       m., *cons.* 1978, *elected* 1984
1989   *Exeter* (69th), (Geoffrey) Hewlett Thompson, *b.*
       1929, *m.*, *cons.* 1974, *elected* 1985
1990   *Bristol* (54th), Barry Rogerson, *b.* 1936, *m.*, *cons.*
       1979, *elected* 1985
1991   *Coventry* (7th), Simon Barrington-Ward, *b.* 1930,
       m., *cons.* 1985, *elected* 1985
1991   *Norwich* (70th), Peter John Nott, *b.* 1933, *m.*, *cons.*
       1977, *elected* 1985
1993   *Lincoln* (70th), Robert Maynard Hardy, *b.* 1936,
       m., *cons.* 1980, *elected* 1986
1993   *Oxford* (41st), Richard Douglas Harries, *b.* 1936,
       m., *cons.* 1987, *elected* 1987
1994   *Birmingham* (7th), Mark Santer, *b.* 1936, *w.*, *cons.*
       1981, *elected* 1987
1995   *Southwell* (9th), Patrick Burnet Harris, *b.* 1934, *m.*,
       cons. 1973, *elected* 1988

1995   Blackburn (7th), Alan David Chesters, b. 1937, m.,
        cons. 1989, elected 1989
1996   Carlisle (65th), Ian Harland, b. 1932, m., cons. 1985,
        elected 1989

Bishops awaiting seats, in order of seniority
        Truro (13th), Michael Thomas Ball, b. 1932, cons.
        1980, elected 1990
        Ely (67th), Stephen Whitefield Sykes, b. 1939, m.,
        cons. 1990, elected 1990
        Hereford (103rd), John Keith Oliver, b. 1935, m.,
        cons. 1990, elected 1990
        Leicester (5th), Thomas Frederick Butler, b. 1940,
        m., cons. 1985, elected 1991
        Bath and Wells (77th), James Lawton Thompson,
        b. 1936, m., cons. 1978, elected 1991
        Wakefield (11th), Nigel Simeon McCulloch, b.
        1942, m., cons. 1986, elected 1992
        Bradford (8th), David James Smith, b. 1935, m.,
        cons. 1987, elected 1992
        Manchester (10th), Christopher John Mayfield, b.
        1935, m., cons. 1985, elected 1993

        Salisbury (77th), David Staffurth Stancliffe, b.
        1942, m., cons. 1993, elected 1993
        Gloucester (39th), David Edward Bentley, b. 1935,
        m., cons. 1986, elected 1993
        Rochester (106th), Michael James Nazir-Ali, PH.D.,
        b. 1949, m., cons. 1984, elected 1995
        Guildford (8th), John Warren Gladwin, b. 1942, m.,
        cons. 1994, elected 1994
        Derby (6th), Jonathan Sansbury Bailey, b. 1940,
        m., cons. 1992, elected 1995
        St Albans (9th), Christopher William Herbert, b.
        1944, m., cons. 1995, elected 1995
        Portsmouth (8th), Kenneth William Stevenson, b.
        1949, m., cons. 1995, elected 1995
        Peterborough (37th), Ian Cundy, b. 1945, m., cons.
        1992, elected 1996
        Chelmsford (8th), John Freeman Perry, b. 1935, m.,
        cons. 1989, elected 1996
        Chester (40th), Peter Robert Forster, PH.D., b.
        1950, cons. 1996, elected 1996
The sees of St Edmundsbury and Ipswich and Worcester
were vacant at the time of going to press

The Order of St John

THE MOST VENERABLE ORDER OF THE HOSPITAL OF ST JOHN OF JERUSALEM (1888)

GCStJ   Bailiff/Dame Grand Cross
KStJ   Knight of Justice/Grace
DStJ   Dame of Justice/Grace
ChStJ   Chaplain
CStJ   Commander
OStJ,   Officer
SBStJ   Serving Brother
SSStJ   Serving Sister
EsqStJ   Esquire

Mottoes, Pro Fide and Pro Utilitate Hominum

The Order of St John, founded in the early 12th century in
Jerusalem, was a religious order with a particular duty to
care for the sick. In Britain the Order was dissolved by
Henry VIII in 1540 but the British branch was revived in
the early 19th century. The branch was not accepted by
the Grand Magistracy of the Order in Rome but its search
for a role in the tradition of the Hospitallers led to the
founding of the St John Ambulance Association in 1877
and later the St John Ambulance Brigade; in 1882 the St

John Ophthalmic Hospital was founded in Jerusalem. A
royal charter was granted in 1888 establishing the British
Order of St John as a British Order of Chivalry with the
Sovereign as its head.
    Admission to the Order is conferred in recognition of
service, usually in St John Ambulance. Membership does
not confer any rank, style, title or precedence on a
recipient.

SOVEREIGN HEAD OF THE ORDER
HM The Queen

GRAND PRIOR
HRH The Duke of Gloucester, GCVO

Lord Prior, The Lord Vestey
Prelate, The Rt. Revd M. A. Mann, KCVO
Chancellor, Prof. A. R. Mellows, TD
Bailiff of Egle, The Lord Remnant
Headquarters, St John's Gate, Clerkenwell, London ECIM
    4DA. Tel: 0171-253 6644

COURTESY TITLES

From this list it will be seen that, for example, the Marquess of Blandford is heir to the Dukedom of Marlborough, and Viscount Amberley to the Earldom of Russell. Titles of second heirs are also given, and the courtesy title of the father of a second heir is indicated by *; e.g. Earl of Burlington, eldest son of *Marquess of Hartington
For forms of address, *see* page 136

MARQUESSES

*Blandford – *Marlborough, D.*
Bowmont and Cessford – *Roxburghe, D.*
Douglas and Clydesdale – *Hamilton, D.*
*Douro – *Wellington, D.*
Graham – *Montrose, D.*
Granby – *Rutland, D.*
Hamilton – *Abercorn, D.*
*Hartington – *Devonshire, D.*
*Kildare – *Leinster, D.*
Lorne – *Argyll, D.*
*Tavistock – *Bedford, D.*
Tullibardine – *Atholl, D.*
*Worcester – *Beaufort, D.*

EARLS

Aboyne – *Huntly, M.*
Altamont – *Sligo, M.*
Ancram – *Lothian, M.*
Arundel and Surrey – *Norfolk, D.*
*Bective – *Headfort, M.*
*Belfast – *Donegall, M.*
Brecknock – *Camden, M.*
Burford – *St Albans, D.*
Burlington – *Hartington, M.*
*Cardigan – *Ailesbury, M.*
Compton – *Northampton, M.*
*Dalkeith – *Buccleuch, D.*
Dumfries – *Bute, M.*
*Euston – *Grafton, D.*
Glamorgan – *Worcester, M.*
Grosvenor – *Westminster, D.*
*Haddo – *Aberdeen and Temair, M.*
*Hillsborough – *Downshire, M.*
Hopetoun – *Linlithgow, M.*
March and Kinrara – *Richmond, D.*
*Mount Charles – *Conyngham, M.*
Mornington – *Douro, M.*
Offaly – *Kildare, M.*
Percy – *Northumberland, D.*
Ronaldshay – *Zetland, M.*
*St Andrews – *Kent, D.*
*Shelburne – *Lansdowne, M.*
*Southesk – *Fife, D.*

Sunderland – *Blandford, M.*
*Tyrone – *Waterford, M.*
Ulster – *Gloucester, D.*
*Uxbridge – *Anglesey, M.*
Wiltshire – *Winchester, M.*
Yarmouth – *Hertford, M.*

VISCOUNTS

Althorp – *Spencer, E.*
Amberley – *Russell, E.*
Andover – *Suffolk and Berkshire, E.*
Anson – *Lichfield, E.*
Asquith – *Oxford & Asquith, E.*
Boringdon – *Morley, E.*
Borodale – *Beatty, E.*
Boyle – *Shannon, E.*
Brocas – *Jellicoe, E.*
Calne and Calstone – *Shelburne, E.*
Campden – *Gainsborough, E.*
Carlow – *Portarlington, E.*
Carlton – *Wharncliffe, E.*
Castlereagh – *Londonderry, M.*
Chelsea – *Cadogan, E.*
Chewton – *Waldegrave, E.*
Chichester – *Belfast, E.*
Clanfield – *Peel, E.*
Clive – *Powis, E.*
Coke – *Leicester, E.*
Corry – *Belmore, E.*
Corvedale – *Baldwin of Bewdley, E.*
Cranborne – *Salisbury, M.*
Cranley – *Onslow, E.*
Crichton – *Erne, E.*
Crowhurst – *Cottenham, E.*
Curzon – *Howe, E.*
Dangan – *Cowley, E.*
Dawick – *Haig, E.*
Deerhurst – *Coventry, E.*
Drumlanrig – *Queensberry, M.*
Dunwich – *Stradbroke, E.*
Dupplin – *Kinnoull, E.*
Ebrington – *Fortescue, E.*
Ednam – *Dudley, E.*
Emlyn – *Cawdor, E.*
Encombe – *Eldon, E.*
Ennismore – *Listowel, E.*
Enfield – *Strafford, E.*
Erleigh – *Reading, M.*
Errington – *Cromer, E.*

FitzHarris – *Malmesbury, E.*
Folkestone – *Radnor, E.*
Forbes – *Granard, E.*
Garmoyle – *Cairns, E.*
Garnock – *Lindsay, E.*
Glandine – *Norbury, E.*
Glenapp – *Inchcape, E.*
Glentworth – *Limerick, E.*
Grimstone – *Verulam, E.*
Gwynedd – *Lloyd George of Dwyfor, E.*
Hawkesbury – *Liverpool, E.*
Hinchingbrooke – *Sandwich, E.*
Ikerrin – *Carrick, E.*
Ingestre – *Shrewsbury, E.*
Ipswich – *Euston, E.*
Jocelyn – *Roden, E.*
Kelburn – *Glasgow, E.*
Kilwarlin – *Hillsborough, E.*
Kingsborough – *Kingston, E.*
Knebworth – *Lytton, E.*
Lascelles – *Harewood, E.*
Lewisham – *Dartmouth, E.*
Linley – *Snowdon, E.*
Loftus – *Ely, M.*
Lowther – *Lonsdale, E.*
Lumley – *Scarbrough, E.*
Lymington – *Portsmouth, E.*
Macmillan of Ovenden – *Stockton, E.*
Maidstone – *Winchilsea and Nottingham, E.*
Maitland – *Lauderdale, E.*
Malden – *Essex, E.*
Mandeville – *Manchester, D.*
Medina – *Milford Haven, M.*
Melgund – *Minto, E.*
Merton – *Nelson, E.*
Moore – *Drogheda, E.*
Newport – *Bradford, E.*
Newry and Mourne – *Kilmorey, E.*
Parker – *Macclesfield, E.*
Perceval – *Egmont, E.*
Petersham – *Harrington, E.*
Pollington – *Mexborough, E.*
Raynham – *Townshend, M.*
Reidhaven – *Seafield, E.*
Ruthven of Canberra – *Gowrie, E.*
St Cyres – *Iddesleigh, E.*
Sandon – *Harrowby, E.*
Savernake – *Cardigan, E.*
Slane – *Mount Charles, E.*
Somerton – *Normanton, E.*

Stopford – *Courtown, E.*
Stormont – *Mansfield, E.*
Strathallan – *Perth, E.*
Stuart – *Castle Stewart, E.*
Suirdale – *Donoughmore, E.*
Tamworth – *Ferrers, E.*
Tarbat – *Cromartie, E.*
Vaughan – *Lisburne, E.*
Villiers – *Jersey, E.*
Weymouth – *Bath, M.*
Windsor – *Plymouth, E.*
Wolmer – *Selborne, E.*
Woodstock – *Portland, E.*

BARONS (LORD __)

Aberdour – *Morton, E.*
Apsley – *Bathurst, E.*
Ardee – *Meath, E.*
Ashley – *Shaftesbury, E.*
Balgonie – *Leven & Melville, E.*
Balniel – *Crawford and Balcarres, E.*
Berriedale – *Caithness, E.*
Bingham – *Lucan, E.*
Binning – *Haddington, E.*
Brooke – *Warwick, E.*
Bruce – *Elgin, E.*
Buckhurst – *De La Warr, E.*
Burghley – *Exeter, M.*
Cardross – *Buchan, E.*
Carnegie – *Southesk, E.*
Clifton – *Darnley, E.*
Cochrane – *Dundonald, E.*
Courtenay – *Devon, E.*
Dalmeny – *Rosebery, E.*
Doune – *Moray, E.*
Downpatrick – *St Andrews, E.*
Dunglass – *Home, E.*
Eliot – *St Germans, E.*
Eskdail – *Dalkeith, E.*
Formartine – *Haddo, E.*
Gillford – *Clanwilliam, E.*
Glamis – *Strathmore, E.*
Greenock – *Cathcart, E.*
Guernsey – *Aylesford, E.*
Hay – *Erroll, E.*
Herbert – *Pembroke, E.*
Howard of Effingham – *Effingham, E.*
Howland – *Tavistock, M.*
Hyde – *Clarendon, E.*
Inverurie – *Kintore, E.*
Irwin – *Halifax, E.*
Johnstone – *Annandale and Hartfell, E.*
Kenlis – *Bective, E.*
Langton – *Temple of Stowe, E.*
La Poer – *Tyrone, E.*

Leslie – *Rothes, E.*
Leveson – *Granville, E.*
Loughborough – *Rosslyn, E.*
Maltravers – *Arundel and*
　Surrey, E.
Mauchline – *Loudoun, C.*
Medway – *Cranbrook, E.*
Montgomerie – *Eglinton*
　and Winton, E.

Moreton – *Ducie, E.*
Naas – *Mayo, E.*
Neidpath – *Wemyss &*
　March, E.
Norreys – *Lindsey &*
　Abingdon, E.
North – *Guilford, E.*
Ogilvy – *Airlie, E.*
Oxmantown – *Rosse, E.*

Paget de Beaudesert –
　Uxbridge, E.
Porchester – *Carnarvon, E.*
Ramsay – *Dalhousie, E.*
Romsey – *Mountbatten of*
　Burma, C.
Rosehill – *Northesk, E.*
Scrymgeour – *Dundee, E.*
Seymour – *Somerset, D.*

Strathnaver – *Sutherland,*
　C.
Wodehouse – *Kimberley,*
　E.
Worsley – *Yarborough, E.*

PEERS' SURNAMES WHICH DIFFER FROM THEIR TITLES

The following symbols
indicate the rank of the peer
holding each title:

C.　Countess
D.　Duke
E.　Earl
M.　Marquess
V.　Viscount
*　Life Peer

Where no designation is
given, the title is that of an
hereditary Baron or
Baroness

Abney-Hastings – *Loudoun,*
　C.
Acheson – *Gosford, E.*
Adderley – *Norton*
Addington – *Sidmouth, V.*
Agar – *Normanton, E.*
Aitken – *Beaverbrook*
Akers-Douglas – *Chilston,*
　V.
Alexander – *A. of Tunis, E.*
Alexander – *A. of Weedon**
Alexander – *A. of Caledon, E.*
Allen – *A. of Abbeydale**
Allen – *Croham**
Allsopp – *Hindlip*
Amery – *A. of Lustleigh**
Anderson – *Waverley, V.*
Annesley – *Valentia, V.*
Anson – *Lichfield, E.*
Archer – *A. of Sandwell**
Archer – *A. of Weston-super-*
　*Mare**
Armstrong – *A. of Ilminster**
Armstrong-Jones –
　Snowdon, E.
Arthur – *Glenarthur*
Arundell – *Talbot of*
　Malahide
Ashley – *A. of Stoke**
Ashley-Cooper –
　Shaftesbury, E.
Ashton – *A. of Hyde*
Asquith – *Oxford & Asquith,*
　E.
Assheton – *Clitheroe*
Astley – *Hastings*
Astor – *A. of Hever*
Atkins – *Colnbrook**
Aubrey-Fletcher – *Braye*
Bailey – *Glanusk*
Baillie – *Burton*

Baillie Hamilton –
　Haddington, E.
Baldwin – *B. of Bewdley, E.*
Balfour – *B. of Inchrye*
Balfour – *Kinross*
Balfour – *Riverdale*
Bampfylde – *Poltimore*
Banbury – *B. of Southam*
Barber – *B. of Tewkesbury**
Baring – *Ashburton*
Baring – *Cromer, E.*
Baring – *Howick of Glendale*
Baring – *Northbrook*
Baring – *Revelstoke*
Barker – *Trumpington**
Barnes – *Gorell*
Barnewall – *Trimlestown*
Bathurst – *Bledisloe, V.*
Beauclerk – *St Albans, D.*
Beaumont – *Allendale, V.*
Beaumont – *B. of Whitley**
Beckett – *Grimthorpe*
Bellow – *Bellwin**
Benn – *Stansgate, V.*
Bennet – *Tankerville, E.*
Bentinck – *Portland, E.*
Beresford – *Decies*
Beresford – *Waterford, M.*
Berry – *Camrose, V.*
Berry – *Hartwell**
Berry – *Kemsley, V.*
Bertie – *Lindsey, E.*
Best – *Wynford*
Bethell – *Westbury*
Bewicke-Copley –
　Cromwell
Bigham – *Mersey, V.*
Bingham – *Clanmorris*
Bingham – *Lucan, E.*
Bingham – *B. of Cornhill**
Blackwood – *Dufferin &*
　Clandeboye
Bligh – *Darnley, E.*
Blyth – *B. of Rowington**
Bootle-Wilbraham –
　Skelmersdale
Boscawen – *Falmouth, V.*
Boston – *B. of Faversham**
Bourke – *Mayo, E.*
Bowes Lyon – *Strathmore,*
　E.
Bowyer – *Denham*
Boyd – *Kilmarnock*
Boyle – *Cork & Orrery, E.*
Boyle – *Glasgow, E.*
Boyle – *Shannon, E.*

Brabazon – *Meath, E.*
Braine – *B. of Wheatley**
Brand – *Hampden, V.*
Brandon – *B. of Oakbrook**
Brassey – *B. of Apethorpe*
Brett – *Esher, V.*
Bridge – *B. of Harwich**
Bridgeman – *Bradford, E.*
Brodrick – *Midleton, V.*
Brooke – *Alanbrooke, V.*
Brooke – *Brookeborough, V.*
Brooke – *B. of Ystradfellte**
Brooks – *B. of Tremorfa**
Brooks – *Crawshaw*
Brougham – *Brougham and*
　Vaux
Broughton – *Fairhaven*
Browne – *Kilmaine*
Browne – *Oranmore and*
　Browne
Browne – *Sligo, M.*
Bruce – *Aberdare*
Bruce – *Balfour of Burleigh*
Bruce – *B. of Donington**
Bruce – *Elgin and*
　Kincardine, E.
Brudenell-Bruce –
　Ailesbury, M.
Buchan – *Tweedsmuir*
Buckley – *Wrenbury*
Butler – *Carrick, E.*
Butler – *Dunboyne*
Butler – *Lanesborough, E.*
Butler – *Mountgarret, V.*
Butler – *Ormonde, M.*
Buxton – *B. of Alsa**
Byng – *Strafford, E.*
Byng – *Torrington, V.*
Callaghan – *C. of Cardiff**
Cameron – *C. of Lochbroom**
Campbell – *Argyll, D.*
Campbell – *Breadalbane and*
　Holland, E.
Campbell – *C. of Alloway**
Campbell – *C. of Croy**
Campbell – *Cawdor, E.*
Campbell – *Colgrain*
Campbell – *Stratheden and*
　Campbell
Campbell-Gray – *Gray*
Canning – *Garvagh*
Capell – *Essex, E.*
Carington – *Carrington*
Carlisle – *C. of Bucklow**
Carmichael – *C. of*
　*Kelvingrove**

Carnegie – *Fife, D.*
Carnegie – *Northesk, E.*
Carr – *C. of Hadley**
Cary – *Falkland, V.*
Castle – *C. of Blackburn**
Caulfeild – *Charlemont, V.*
Cavendish – *C. of Furness**
Cavendish – *Chesham*
Cavendish – *Devonshire, D.*
Cavendish – *Waterpark*
Cayzer – *Rotherwick*
Cecil – *Amherst of Hackney*
Cecil – *Exeter, M.*
Cecil – *Rockley*
Cecil – *Salisbury, M.*
Chalker – *C. of Wallasey**
Chaloner – *Gisborough*
Chapman – *Northfield**
Charteris – *C. of Amisfield**
Charteris – *Wemyss and*
　March, E.
Cheshire – *Ryder of*
　*Warsaw**
Chetwynd-Talbot –
　Shrewsbury, E.
Chichester – *Donegall, M.*
Chichester-Clark –
　*Moyola**
Child Villiers – *Jersey, E.*
Cholmondeley – *Delamere*
Chubb – *Hayter*
Clark – *C. of Kempston**
Clegg-Hill – *Hill, V.*
Clifford – *C. of Chudleigh*
Cochrane – *C. of Cults*
Cochrane – *Dundonald, E.*
Cocks – *C. of Hartcliffe**
Cocks – *Somers*
Cokayne – *Cullen of*
　Ashbourne
Coke – *Leicester, E.*
Cole – *Enniskillen, E.*
Collier – *Monkswell*
Colville – *Clydesmuir*
Colville – *C. of Culross, V.*
Compton – *Northampton,*
　M.
Conolly-Carew – *Carew*
Constantine – *C. of*
　*Stanmore**
Cooke – *C. of Islandreagh**
Cooke – *C. of Thorndon**
Cooper – *Norwich, V.*
Corbett – *Rowallan*
Courtenay – *Devon, E.*
Cox – *Kings Norton**

Craig – *C. of Radley*[*]
Craig – *Craigavon*, V.
Crichton – *Erne*, E.
Crichton-Stuart – *Bute*, M.
Cripps – *Parmoor*
Crossley – *Somerleyton*
Cubitt – *Ashcombe*
Cunliffe-Lister – *Masham of Ilton*[*]
Cunliffe-Lister – *Swinton*, E.
Curzon – *Howe*, E.
Curzon – *Scarsdale*, V.
Cust – *Brownlow*
Dalrymple – *Stair*, E.
Daubeny de Moleyns – *Ventry*
Davies – *Darwen*
Davison – *Broughshane*
Dawnay – *Downe*, V.
Dawson-Damer – *Portarlington*, E.
Dean – *D. of Beswick*[*]
Dean – *D. of Harptree*[*]
Dean – *D. of Thornton-le-Fylde*[*]
Deane – *Muskerry*
de Courcy – *Kingsale*
de Grey – *Walsingham*
Delacourt-Smith – *Delacourt Smith of Alteryn*[*]
Denison – *Londesborough*
Denison-Pender – *Pender*
Denton – *D. of Wakefield*[*]
Devereux – *Hereford*, V.
Dewar – *Forteviot*
De Yarburgh-Bateson – *Deramore*
Dixon – *Glentoran*
Dodson – *Monk Bretton*
Donaldson – *D. of Kingsbridge*[*]
Donaldson – *D. of Lymington*[*]
Dormand – *D. of Easington*[*]
Douglas – *Morton*, E.
Douglas – *Queensberry*, M.
Douglas-Hamilton – *Hamilton*, D.
Douglas-Hamilton – *Selkirk*, E.
Douglas-Home – *Dacre*
Douglas-Home – *Home*, E.
Douglas-Pennant – *Penrhyn*
Douglas-Scott-Montagu – *Montagu of Beaulieu*
Drummond – *Perth*, E.
Drummond of Megginch – *Strange*
Dugdale – *Crathorne*
Duke – *Merrivale*
Duncombe – *Feversham*
Dundas – *Melville*, V.
Dundas – *Zetland*, M.
Eady – *Swinfen*
Eccles – *E. of Moulton*[*]
Eden – *Auckland*
Eden – *E. of Winton*[*]
Eden – *Henley*

Edgcumbe – *Mount Edgcumbe*, E.
Edmondson – *Sandford*
Edwardes – *Kensington*
Edwards – *Chelmer*[*]
Edwards – *Crickhowell*[*]
Egerton – *Sutherland*, D.
Egerton – *Wilton*, E.
Eliot – *St Germans*, E.
Elliot-Murray-Kynynmound – *Minto*, E.
Elliott – *E. of Morpeth*[*]
Erroll – *E. of Hale*
Erskine – *Buchan*, E.
Erskine – *Mar* & *Kellie*, E.
Erskine-Murray – *Elibank*
Evans – *Mountevans*
Evans-Freke – *Carbery*
Eve – *Silsoe*
Ewing – *E. of Kirkford*[*]
Fairfax – *F. of Cameron*
Fane – *Westmorland*, E.
Farrington – *F. of Ribbleton*[*]
Feilding – *Denbigh*, E.
Fellowes – *De Ramsey*
Fermor-Hesketh – *Hesketh*
Fiennes – *Saye* & *Sele*
Fiennes-Clinton – *Lincoln*, E.
Finch Hatton – *Winchilsea*, E.
Finch-Knightley – *Aylesford*, E.
Fisher – *F. of Rednal*[*]
Fitzalan-Howard – *Herries of Terregles*
Fitzalan-Howard – *Norfolk*, D.
FitzClarence – *Munster*, E.
FitzGerald – *Leinster*, D.
Fitzherbert – *Stafford*
Fitz-Maurice – *Orkney*, E.
FitzRoy – *Grafton*, D.
FitzRoy – *Southampton*
FitzRoy Newdegate – *Daventry*, V.
Fletcher-Vane – *Inglewood*
Flower – *Ashbrook*, V.
Foljambe – *Liverpool*, E.
Forbes – *Granard*, E.
Fox-Strangways – *Ilchester*, E.
Frankland – *Zouche*
Fraser – *F. of Carmyllie*[*]
Fraser – *F. of Kilmorack*[*]
Fraser – *Lovat*
Fraser – *Saltoun*
Fraser – *Strathalmond*
Freeman-Grenville – *Kinloss*
Fremantle – *Cottesloe*
French – *De Freyne*
Galbraith – *Strathclyde*
Ganzoni – *Belstead*
Gardner – *G. of Parkes*[*]
Gathorne-Hardy – *Cranbrook*, E.
Gibbs – *Aldenham*
Gibbs – *Wraxall*
Gibson – *Ashbourne*

Giffard – *Halsbury*, E.
Gilbey – *Vaux of Harrowden*
Gillmore – *G. of Thamesfield*[*]
Gilmour – *G. of Craigmillar*[*]
Gladwin – *G. of Clee*[*]
Glyn – *Wolverton*
Godley – *Kilbracken*
Goff – *G. of Chieveley*[*]
Gordon – *Aberdeen*, M.
Gordon – *Huntly*, M.
Gordon Lennox – *Richmond*, D.
Gore – *Arran*, E.
Gough-Calthorpe – *Calthorpe*
Gould – *G. of Potternewton*[*]
Graham – *G. of Edmonton*[*]
Graham – *Montrose*, D.
Graham-Toler – *Norbury*, E.
Grant of Grant – *Strathspey*
Grant-Ferris – *Harvington*[*]
Granville – *G. of Eye*[*]
Gray – *G. of Contin*[*]
Greaves – *Dysart*, C.
Greenall – *Daresbury*
Greene – *G. of Harrow Weald*[*]
Greenhill – *G. of Harrow*[*]
Greville – *Warwick*, E.
Grey – *G. of Naunton*[*]
Griffiths – *G. of Fforestfach*[*]
Grigg – *Altrincham*
Grimston – *G. of Westbury*
Grimston – *Verulam*, E.
Grosvenor – *Ebury*
Grosvenor – *Westminster*, D.
Gueterbock – *Berkeley*
Guest – *Wimborne*, V.
Guinness – *Iveagh*, E.
Guinness – *Moyne*
Gully – *Selby*, V.
Gurdon – *Cranworth*
Gwynne Jones – *Chalfont*[*]
Hamilton – *Abercorn*, D.
Hamilton – *Belhaven and Stenton*
Hamilton – *Dudley*
Hamilton – *H. of Dalzell*
Hamilton – *Holm Patrick*
Hamilton-Russell – *Boyne*, V.
Hamilton-Smith – *Colwyn*
Hanbury-Tracy – *Sudeley*
Handcock – *Castlemaine*
Harbord-Hamond – *Suffield*
Harding – *H. of Petherton*
Hardinge – *H. of Penshurst*
Hare – *Blakenham*, V.
Hare – *Listowel*, E.
Harmsworth – *Rothermere*, V.
Harris – *H. of Greenwich*[*]
Harris – *H. of High Cross*[*]
Harris – *Malmesbury*, E.
Harvey – *H. of Tasburgh*

Hastings Bass – *Huntingdon*, E.
Hay – *Erroll*, E.
Hay – *Kinnoull*, E.
Hay – *Tweeddale*, M.
Heathcote-Drummond-Willoughby – *Willoughby de Eresby*
Hely-Hutchinson – *Donoughmore*, E.
Henderson – *Faringdon*
Henderson – *H. of Brompton*[*]
Hennessy – *Windlesham*
Henniker-Major – *Henniker*
Hepburne-Scott – *Polwarth*
Herbert – *Carnarvon*, E.
Herbert – *Hemingford*
Herbert – *Pembroke*, E.
Herbert – *Powis*, E.
Hermon-Hodge – *Wyfold*
Hervey – *Bristol*, M.
Hewitt – *Lifford*, V.
Hicks Beach – *St Aldwyn*, E.
Hill – *Downshire*, M.
Hill – *Sandys*
Hill-Trevor – *Trevor*
Hilton – *H. of Eggardon*[*]
Hobart-Hampden – *Buckinghamshire*, E.
Hogg – *Hailsham of St Marylebone*[*]
Holland-Hibbert – *Knutsford*, V.
Hollis – *H. of Heigham*[*]
Holme – *H. of Cheltenham*[*]
Holmes à Court – *Heytesbury*
Hood – *Bridport*, V.
Hope – *Glendevon*
Hope – *H. of Craighead*[*]
Hope – *Linlithgow*, M.
Hope – *Rankeillour*
Hope Johnstone – *Annandale and Hartfell*, E.
Hope-Morley – *Hollenden*
Hopkinson – *Colyton*
Hore Ruthven – *Gowrie*, E.
Houghton – *H. of Sowerby*[*]
Hovell-Thurlow-Cumming-Bruce – *Thurlow*
Howard – *Carlisle*, E.
Howard – *Effingham*, E.
Howard – *H. of Penrith*
Howard – *Strathcona*
Howard – *Suffolk and Berkshire*, E.
Howe – *H. of Aberavon*[*]
Howells – *Geraint*[*]
Howie – *H. of Troon*[*]
Hubbard – *Addington*
Huggins – *Malvern*, V.
Hughes – *Cledwyn of Penrhos*[*]
Hughes-Young – *St Helens*
Hunt – *H. of Tanworth*[*]
Hutchinson – *H. of Lullington*[*]

Ponsonby – *Sysonby*
Porter – *P. of Luddenham**
Powys – *Lilford*
Pratt – *Camden, M.*
Preston – *Gormanston, V.*
Primrose – *Rosebery, E.*
Prittie – *Dunalley*
Prout – *Kingsland**
Ramsay – *Dalhousie, E.*
Ramsbotham – *Soulbury, V.*
Rawlinson – *R. of Ewell**
Rees-Williams – *Ogmore*
Renfrew – *R. of Kaimsthorn**
Rhys – *Dynevor*
Richards – *Milverton*
Richardson – *R. of Duntisbourne**
Rippon – *R. of Hexham**
Ritchie – *R. of Dundee*
Robens – *R. of Woldingham**
Roberts – *Clwyd*
Robertson – *R. of Oakridge*
Robertson – *Wharton*
Robinson – *Martonmere*
Robson – *R. of Kiddington**
Roche – *Fermoy*
Rodd – *Rennell*
Rodger – *R. of Earlsferry**
Rodgers – *R. of Quarry Bank**
Roll – *R. of Ipsden**
Roper-Curzon – *Teynham*
Rospigliosi – *Newburgh, E.*
Rous – *Stradbroke, E.*
Rowley-Conwy – *Langford*
Royle – *Fanshawe of Richmond**
Runciman – *R. of Doxford, V.*
Russell – *Ampthill*
Russell – *Bedford, D.*
Russell – *de Clifford*
Russell – *R. of Liverpool*
Ryder – *Harrowby, E.*
Ryder – *R. of Eaton Hastings**
Ryder – *R. of Warsaw**
Sackville – *De La Warr, E.*
Sackville-West – *Sackville*
Sainsbury – *S. of Preston Candover**
St Aubyn – *St Levan*
St Clair – *Sinclair*
St Clair-Erskine – *Rosslyn, E.*
St John – *Bolingbroke and St John, V.*
St John – *St John of Blesto*
St John-Stevas – *St John of Fawsley**
St Leger – *Doneraile, V.*
Samuel – *Bearsted, V.*
Sanderson – *S. of Ayot*
Sanderson – *S. of Bowden**
Sandilands – *Torphichen*
Saumarez – *De Saumarez*
Savile – *Mexborough, E.*
Scarlett – *Abinger*
Schreiber – *Marlesford**
Sclater-Booth – *Basing*
Scott – *Eldon, E.*

Scott-Ellis – *Howard de Walden*
Scrymgeour – *Dundee, E.*
Seager – *Leighton of St Mellons*
Seely – *Mottistone*
Sefton – *S. of Garston**
Seymour – *Hertford, M.*
Seymour – *Somerset, D.*
Shaw – *Craigmyle*
Shaw – *S. of Northstead**
Sheppard – *S. of Didgemere**
Shirley – *Ferrers, E.*
Short – *Glenamara**
Siddeley – *Kenilworth*
Sidney – *De L'Isle, V.*
Sieff – *S. of Brimpton**
Simon – *S. of Glaisdale**
Simon – *S. of Wythenshawe*
Sinclair – *Caithness, E.*
Sinclair – *S. of Cleeve*
Sinclair – *Thurso, V.*
Skeffington – *Massereene, V.*
Slynn – *S. of Hadley**
Smith – *Bicester*
Smith – *Hambleden, V.*
Smith – *Kirkhill**
Smith – *S. of Gilmorehill**
Somerset – *Beaufort, D.*
Somerset – *Raglan*
Souter – *Audley*
Spencer – *Churchill, V.*
Spencer-Churchill – *Marlborough, D.*
Spring Rice – *Monteagle of Brandon*
Stanhope – *Harrington, E.*
Stanley – *Derby, E.*
Stanley – *Stanley of Alderley & Sheffield*
Stapleton-Cotton – *Combermere, V.*
Sterling – *S. of Plaistow**
Stevens – *S. of Ludgate**
Stewart – *Galloway, E.*
Stewart – *Stewartby**
Stodart – *S. of Leaston**
Stoddart – *S. of Swindon**
Stonor – *Camoys*
Stopford – *Courtown, E.*
Stourton – *Mowbray*
Strachey – *O'Hagan*
Strutt – *Belper*
Strutt – *Rayleigh*
Stuart – *Castle Stewart, E.*
Stuart – *Moray, E.*
Stuart – *S. of Findhorn, V.*
Suenson-Taylor – *Grantchester*
Taylor – *Ingrow**
Taylor – *T. of Blackburn**
Taylor – *T. of Gosforth**
Taylor – *T. of Gryfe**
Taylour – *Headfort, M.*
Temple-Gore-Langton – *Temple of Stowe, E.*
Tennant – *Glenconner*
Thellusson – *Rendlesham*
Thesiger – *Chelmsford, V.*

Thomas – *T. of Gwydir**
Thomas – *T. of Swynnerton**
Thomas – *T. of Walliswood**
Thomas – *Tonypandy, V.*
Thomson – *T. of Fleet*
Thomson – *T. of Monifieth**
Thynn – *Bath, M.*
Thynne – *Bath, M.*
Tottenham – *Ely, M.*
Trefusis – *Clinton*
Trench – *Ashtown*
Trevor-Roper – *Dacre of Glanton**
Tufton – *Hothfield*
Turner – *Netherthorpe*
Turner – *T. of Camden**
Turnour – *Winterton, E.*
Tyrell-Kenyon – *Kenyon*
Vanden-Bempde-Johnstone – *Derwent*
Vane – *Barnard*
Vane – *Inglewood*
Vane-Tempest-Stewart – *Londonderry, M.*
Vanneck – *Huntingfield*
Vaughan – *Lisburne, E.*
Vereker – *Gort, V.*
Verney – *Willoughby de Broke*
Vernon – *Lyveden*
Vesey – *De Vesci, V.*
Villiers – *Clarendon, E.*
Vivian – *Swansea*
Wade – *W. of Chorlton**
Walker – *W. of Worcester**
Wallace – *W. of Campsie**
Wallace – *W. of Coslany**
Wallace – *W. of Saltaire**
Wallop – *Portsmouth, E.*
Walton – *W. of Detchant**
Ward – *Bangor, V.*
Ward – *Dudley, E.*
Warrender – *Bruntisfield*
Watson – *Manton*
Wedderburn – *W. of Charlton**
Weir – *Inverforth*
Weld-Forester – *Forester*
Wellesley – *Cowley, E.*
Wellesley – *Wellington, D.*
Westenra – *Rossmore*
White – *Annaly*
White – *James of Holland Park**
Whiteley – *Marchamley*
Whitfield – *Kenswood*
Williams – *W. of Crosby**
Williams – *W. of Elvel**
Williams – *W. of Mostyn**
Williamson – *Forres*
Willoughby – *Middleton*
Wills – *Dulverton*
Wilson – *Moran*
Wilson – *Nunburnholme*
Wilson – *W. of Langside**
Wilson – *W. of Tillyorn**
Windsor – *Gloucester, D.*
Windsor – *Kent, D.*
Windsor-Clive – *Plymouth, E.*

Wingfield – *Powerscourt, V.*
Winn – *St Oswald*
Wodehouse – *Kimberley, E.*
Wolfson – *W. of Sunningdale**
Wood – *Halifax, E.*
Wood – *Holderness**
Woodhouse – *Terrington*
Wright – *W. of Richmond**
Wyatt – *W. of Weeford**
Wyndham – *Egremont & Leconfield*
Wyndham-Quin – *Dunraven, E.*
Wynn – *Newborough*
Yarde-Buller – *Churston*
Yerburgh – *Alvingham*
Yorke – *Hardwicke, E.*
Young – *Kennet*
Young – *Y. of Dartington**
Young – *Y. of Graffham**
Younger – *Y. of Leckie, V.*
Younger – *Y. of Prestwick**

Orders of Chivalry

THE MOST NOBLE ORDER OF THE GARTER (1348)

KG

Ribbon, Blue
Motto, Honi soit qui mal y pense
(*Shame on him who thinks evil of it*)
The number of Knights Companions is limited to 24

SOVEREIGN OF THE ORDER
The Queen

LADIES OF THE ORDER
HM Queen Elizabeth the Queen
  Mother, 1936
HRH The Princess Royal, 1994

ROYAL KNIGHTS
HRH The Prince Philip, Duke of
  Edinburgh, 1947
HRH The Prince of Wales, 1958
HRH The Duke of Kent, 1985

EXTRA KNIGHTS COMPANIONS AND LADIES
HRH Princess Juliana of the
  Netherlands, 1958
HRH The Grand Duke of
  Luxembourg, 1972
HM The Queen of Denmark, 1979
HM The King of Sweden, 1983
HM The King of Spain, 1988
HM The Queen of the Netherlands,
  1989

KNIGHTS AND LADY COMPANIONS
The Earl of Longford, 1971
The Marquess of Abergavenny, 1974
The Duke of Grafton, 1976
The Lord Hunt, 1979
The Duke of Norfolk, 1983
The Lord Lewin, 1983
The Lord Richardson of
  Duntisbourne, 1983
The Lord Carrington, 1985
The Lord Callaghan of Cardiff, 1987
The Viscount Leverhulme, 1988
The Lord Hailsham of St
  Marylebone, 1988
The Duke of Wellington, 1990
Field Marshal the Lord Bramall,
  1990
Sir Edward Heath, 1992
The Viscount Ridley, 1992
The Lord Sainsbury of Preston
  Candover, 1992
The Lord Ashburton, 1994
The Lord Kingsdown, 1994

Sir Ninian Stephen, 1994
The Baroness Thatcher, 1995
Sir Edmund Hillary, 1995
The Duke of Devonshire, 1996
Sir Timothy Coleman, 1996

Prelate, The Bishop of Winchester
Chancellor, The Lord Carrington, KG,
  GCMG, CH, MC
Register, The Dean of Windsor
Garter King of Arms, P. Gwynn-Jones,
  LVO
Gentleman Usher of the Black Rod, Gen.
  Sir Edward Jones, KCB, CBE
Secretary, D. H. B. Chesshyre, LVO

THE MOST ANCIENT AND MOST NOBLE ORDER OF THE THISTLE (REVIVED 1687)

KT

Ribbon, Green
Motto, Nemo me impune lacessit (*No
  one provokes me with impunity*)
The number of Knights is limited to 16

SOVEREIGN OF THE ORDER
The Queen

LADY OF THE THISTLE
HM Queen Elizabeth the Queen
  Mother, 1937

ROYAL KNIGHTS
HRH The Prince Philip, Duke of
  Edinburgh, 1952
HRH The Prince of Wales, Duke of
  Rothesay, 1977

KNIGHTS
The Earl of Wemyss and March, 1966
The Earl of Dalhousie, 1971
The Lord Clydesmuir, 1972
Sir Donald Cameron of Lochiel, 1973
The Duke of Buccleuch and
  Queensberry, 1978
The Earl of Elgin and Kincardine,
  1981
The Lord Thomson of Monifieth,
  1981
The Lord MacLehose of Beoch, 1983
The Earl of Airlie, 1985
Capt. Sir Iain Tennant, 1986
The Viscount Whitelaw, 1990
The Lord Younger of Prestwick, 1995

Chancellor, The Duke of Buccleuch
  and Queensberry, KT, VRD
Dean, The Very Revd G. I. Macmillan

Secretary and Lord Lyon King of Arms, Sir
  Malcolm Innes of Edingight, KCVO,
  WS
Usher of the Green Rod, Rear-Adm. D.A.
  Dunbar-Nasmith, CB, DSC

THE MOST HONOURABLE ORDER OF THE BATH (1725)

GCB *Military*   GCB *Civil*

GCB   Knight (or Dame) Grand
        Cross
KCB   Knight Commander
DCB   Dame Commander
CB   Companion
Ribbon, Crimson
Motto, Tria juncta in uno (*Three joined
  in one*)

Remodelled 1815, and enlarged many
times since. The Order is divided into
civil and military divisions. Women
became eligible for the Order from 1
January 1971

THE SOVEREIGN

GREAT MASTER AND FIRST OR
PRINCIPAL KNIGHT GRAND
CROSS
HRH The Prince of Wales, KG, KT,
  GCB

Dean of the Order, The Dean of
  Westminster
Bath King of Arms, Air Chief Marshal
  Sir David Evans, GCB, CBE
Registrar and Secretary, Rear-Adm.
  D. E. Macey, CB
Genealogist, P. Gwynn-Jones, LVO
Gentleman Usher of the Scarlet Rod, Air
  Vice-Marshal Sir Richard Peirse,
  KCVO, CB
Deputy Secretary, The Secretary of the
  Central Chancery of the Orders of
  Knighthood
Chancery, Central Chancery of the
  Orders of Knighthood, St James's
  Palace, London SW1A 1BH

THE ORDER OF MERIT
(1902)

OM *Military*   OM *Civil*

OM

Ribbon, Blue and crimson

This Order is designed as a special distinction for eminent men and women without conferring a knighthood upon them. The Order is limited in numbers to 24, with the addition of foreign honorary members. Membership is of two kinds, military and civil, the badge of the former having crossed swords, and the latter oak leaves

THE SOVEREIGN

HRH The Prince Philip, Duke of Edinburgh, 1968
Dame Veronica Wedgwood, 1969
Sir Isaiah Berlin, 1971
Sir George Edwards, 1971
Sir Alan Hodgkin, 1973
The Lord Todd, 1977
Revd Prof. Owen Chadwick, KBE, 1983
Sir Andrew Huxley, 1983
Sir Michael Tippett, 1983
Frederick Sanger, 1986
The Lord Menuhin, 1987
Prof. Sir Ernst Gombrich, 1988
Dr Max Perutz, 1988
Dame Cicely Saunders, 1989
The Lord Porter of Luddenham, 1989
The Baroness Thatcher, 1990
Dame Joan Sutherland, 1991
Prof. Francis Crick, 1991
Dame Ninette de Valois, 1992
Sir Michael Atiyah, 1992
Lucian Freud, 1993
The Lord Jenkins of Hillhead, 1993
Sir Aaron Klug, 1995
Honorary Members, Mother Teresa, 1983; Nelson Mandela, 1995

Secretary and Registrar, Sir Edward Ford, KCB, KCVO, ERD
Chancery, Central Chancery of the Orders of Knighthood, St James's Palace, London SW1A 1BH

THE MOST EXALTED
ORDER OF THE STAR OF
INDIA (1861)

GCSI   Knight Grand Commander
KCSI   Knight Commander
CSI   Companion
Ribbon, Light blue, with white edges
Motto, Heaven's Light our Guide

THE SOVEREIGN
Registrar, The Secretary of the Central Chancery of the Orders of Knighthood
No conferments have been made since 1947

THE MOST
DISTINGUISHED ORDER
OF ST MICHAEL AND ST
GEORGE (1818)

GCMG   KCMG

GCMG   Knight (or Dame) Grand Cross
KCMG   Knight Commander
DCMG   Dame Commander
CMG   Companion

Ribbon, Saxon blue, with scarlet centre
Motto, Auspicium melioris aevi (*Token of a better age*)

THE SOVEREIGN

GRAND MASTER
HRH The Duke of Kent, KG, GCMG, GCVO, ADC

Prelate, The Rt. Revd the Bishop of Coventry
Chancellor, Sir Antony Acland, GCMG, GCVO
Secretary, Sir John Coles, KCMG
Registrar, Sir John Graham, Bt., GCMG
King of Arms, Sir Ewen Fergusson, GCMG, GCVO
Gentleman Usher of the Blue Rod, Sir John Margetson, KCMG
Dean, The Dean of St Paul's
Deputy Secretary, The Secretary of the Central Chancery of the Orders of Knighthood
Chancery, Central Chancery of the Orders of Knighthood, St James's Palace, London SW1A 1BH

THE MOST EMINENT
ORDER OF THE INDIAN
EMPIRE (1868)

GCIE   Knight Grand Commander
KCIE   Knight Commander
CIE   Companion
Ribbon, Imperial purple
Motto, Imperatricis auspiciis (*Under the auspices of the Empress*)

THE SOVEREIGN
Registrar, The Secretary of the Central Chancery of the Orders of Knighthood

THE SOVEREIGN
Registrar, The Secretary of the Central Chancery of the Orders of Knighthood
No conferments have been made since 1947

THE IMPERIAL ORDER OF
THE CROWN OF INDIA
(1877) FOR LADIES

CI
Badge, the royal cipher in jewels within an oval, surmounted by an heraldic crown and attached to a bow of light blue watered ribbon, edged white
The honour does not confer any rank or title upon the recipient
No conferments have been made since 1947

HM The Queen, 1947
HM Queen Elizabeth the Queen Mother, 1931
HRH The Princess Margaret, Countess of Snowdon, 1947
HRH Princess Alice, Duchess of Gloucester, 1937

THE ROYAL VICTORIAN
ORDER (1896)

GCVO   KCVO

GCVO   Knight or Dame Grand Cross
KCVO   Knight Commander
DCVO   Dame Commander
CVO   Commander
LVO   Lieutenant
MVO   Member
Ribbon, Blue, with red and white edges
Motto, Victoria

THE SOVEREIGN
GRAND MASTER
HM Queen Elizabeth the Queen Mother

Chancellor, The Lord Chamberlain
Secretary, The Keeper of the Privy Purse
Registrar, The Secretary of the Central Chancery of the Orders of Knighthood
Chaplain, The Revd J. Robson
Hon. Genealogist, D. H. B. Chesshyre, LVO

THE MOST EXCELLENT ORDER OF THE BRITISH EMPIRE (1917)

GBE   KBE

The Order was divided into military and civil divisions in December 1918

GBE Knight or Dame Grand Cross
KBE Knight Commander
DBE Dame Commander
CBE Commander
OBE Officer
MBE Member

Ribbon, Rose pink edged with pearl grey with vertical pearl stripe in centre (military division); without vertical pearl stripe (civil division)
Motto, For God and the Empire

THE SOVEREIGN

GRAND MASTER
HRH The Prince Philip, Duke of Edinburgh, KG, KT, OM, GBE, PC, FRS

Prelate, The Bishop of London
King of Arms, Adm. Sir Anthony Morton, GBE, KCB
Registrar, The Secretary of the Central Chancery of the Orders of Knighthood
Secretary, Sir Robin Butler, GCB, CVO
Dean, The Dean of St Paul's
Gentleman Usher of the Purple Rod, Sir Robin Gillett, Bt., GBE, RD
Chancery, Central Chancery of the Orders of Knighthood, St James's Palace, London SW1A 1BH

ORDER OF THE COMPANIONS OF HONOUR (1917)

CH

Ribbon, Carmine, with gold edges
This Order consists of one class only and carries with it no title. The number of awards is limited to 65 (excluding honorary members).

Anthony, Rt. Hon. John, 1981
Ashley of Stoke, The Lord, 1975
Astor, Hon. David, 1993
Attenborough, Sir David, 1995
Baker, Dame Janet, 1993
Baker, Rt. Hon. Kenneth, 1992
Brenner, Sydney, 1986
Brooke, Rt. Hon. Peter, 1992

Carrington, The Lord, 1983
Casson, Sir Hugh, 1984
Cledwyn of Penrhos, The Lord, 1976
de Valois, Dame Ninette, 1981
Doll, Sir Richard, 1995
Eccles, The Viscount, 1984
Fraser, Rt. Hon. Malcolm, 1977
Freud, Lucian, 1983
Gielgud, Sir John, 1977
Glenamara, The Lord, 1976
Gorton, Rt. Hon. Sir John, 1971
Guinness, Sir Alec, 1994
Hailsham of St Marylebone, The Lord, 1974
Hawking, Prof. Stephen, 1989
Healey, The Lord, 1979
Howe of Aberavon, The Lord, 1996
Hurd, Rt. Hon. Douglas, 1995
Jones, James, 1977
Jones, Prof. Reginald, 1994
King, Rt. Hon. Tom, 1992
Lange, Rt. Hon. David, 1989
Lasdun, Sir Denys, 1995
Milstein, César, 1994
Owen, The Lord, 1994
Pasmore, Victor, 1980
Perutz, Prof. Max, 1975
Powell, Anthony, 1987
Powell, Sir Philip, 1984
Pritchett, Sir Victor, 1992
Runciman, Hon. Sir Steven, 1984
Rylands, George, 1987
Sanger, Frederick, 1981
Sisson, Charles, 1993
Smith, Sir John, 1993
Somare, Rt. Hon. Sir Michael, 1978
Talboys, Rt. Hon. Sir Brian, 1981
Tebbit, The Lord, 1987
Tippett, Sir Michael, 1979
Trudeau, Rt. Hon. Pierre, 1984
Weight, Prof. Carel, 1994
Whitelaw, The Viscount, 1974
Widdowson, Dr Elsie, 1993
Worlock, Most Revd Derek, 1995
Honorary Members, Lee Kuan Yew, 1970; Dr Joseph Luns, 1971

Secretary and Registrar, The Secretary of the Central Chancery of the Orders of Knighthood

THE DISTINGUISHED SERVICE ORDER (1886)

DSO

Ribbon, Red, with blue edges
Bestowed in recognition of especial services in action of commissioned officers in the Navy, Army and Royal Air Force and (since 1942) Mercantile Marine. The members are Companions only. A Bar may be awarded for any additional act of service

THE IMPERIAL SERVICE ORDER (1902)

ISO

Ribbon, Crimson, with blue centre

Appointment as Companion of this Order is open to members of the Civil Services whose eligibility is determined by the grade they hold. The Order consists of The Sovereign and Companions to a number not exceeding 1,900, of whom 1,300 may belong to the Home Civil Services and 600 to Overseas Civil Services. The Prime Minister announced in March 1993 that he would make no further recommendations for appointments to the Order.

Secretary, Sir Robin Butler, GCB, CVO
Registrar, The Secretary of the Central Chancery of the Orders of Knighthood, St James's Palace, London SW1A 1BH

THE ROYAL VICTORIAN CHAIN (1902)

It confers no precedence on its holders

HM THE QUEEN
HM Queen Elizabeth the Queen Mother, 1937
HRH Princess Juliana of the Netherlands, 1950
HM The King of Thailand, 1960
HIH The Crown Prince of Ethiopia, 1965
HM The King of Jordan, 1966
HM King Zahir Shah of Afghanistan, 1971
HM The Queen of Denmark, 1974
HM The King of Nepal, 1975
HM The King of Sweden, 1975
The Lord Coggan, 1980
HM The Queen of the Netherlands, 1982
Gen. Antonio Eanes, 1985
HM The King of Spain, 1986
HM The King of Saudi Arabia, 1987
HRH The Princess Margaret, Countess of Snowdon, 1990
The Lord Runcie, 1991
The Lord Charteris of Amisfield, 1992
HE Richard von Weizsäcker, 1992
HM The King of Norway, 1994

Baronetage and Knightage

BARONETS

Style, 'Sir' before forename and surname, followed by 'Bt.'
Wife's style, 'Lady' followed by surname
For forms of address, *see* page 136

There are five different creations of baronetcies: Baronets of England (creations dating from 1611); Baronets of Ireland (creations dating from 1619); Baronets of Scotland or Nova Scotia (creations dating from 1625); Baronets of Great Britain (creations after the Act of Union 1707 which combined the kingdoms of England and Scotland); and Baronets of the United Kingdom (creations after the union of Great Britain and Ireland in 1801).

Badge of Baronets of the United Kingdom   *Badge of Baronets of Nova Scotia*

Badge of Ulster

The patent of creation limits the destination of a baronetcy, usually to male descendants of the first baronet, although special remainders allow the baronetcy to pass, if the male issue of sons fail, to the male issue of daughters of the first baronet. In the case of baronetcies of Scotland or Nova Scotia, a special remainder of 'heirs male and of tailzie' allows the baronetcy to descend to heirs general, including women. There are four existing Scottish baronets with such a remainder, one of whom, the holder of the Dunbar of Hempriggs creation, is a Baronetess.

The Official Roll of Baronets is kept at the Home Office by the Registrar of the Baronetage. Anyone who considers that he is entitled to be entered on the Roll may petition the Crown through the Home Secretary. Every person succeeding to a baronetcy must exhibit proofs of succession to the Home Secretary. A person whose name is not entered on the Official Roll will not be addressed or mentioned by the title of baronet in any official document, nor will he be accorded precedence as a baronet.

BARONETCIES EXTINCT SINCE THE LAST EDITION
Corbet (*cr.* 1808); Kitson (*cr.* 1886), by the death of Lord Airedale; Levy (*cr.* 1913); Neville (*cr.* 1927); Vaughan-Morgan (*cr.* 1960), by the death of Lord Reigate.

Registrar of the Baronetage, Miss C. E. C. Sinclair
Assistant Registrar, Mrs F. G. Bright
Office, Home Office, 50 Queen Anne's Gate, London SW1H 9AT. Tel: 0171-273 3498

KNIGHTS

Style, 'Sir' before forename and surname, followed by appropriate post-nominal initials if a Knight Grand Cross, Knight Grand Commander or Knight Commander
Wife's style, 'Lady' followed by surname
For forms of address, *see* page 136

The prefix 'Sir' is not used by knights who are clerics of the Church of England, who do not receive the accolade. Their wives are entitled to precedence as the wife of a knight but not to the style of 'Lady'.

ORDERS OF KNIGHTHOOD

Knight Grand Cross, Knight Grand Commander, and Knight Commander are the higher classes of the Orders of Chivalry (*see* pages 170–2). Honorary knighthoods of these Orders may be conferred on men who are citizens of countries of which The Queen is not head of state. As a rule, the prefix 'Sir' is not used by honorary knights.

KNIGHTS BACHELOR

The Knights Bachelor do not constitute a Royal Order, but comprise the surviving representation of the ancient State Orders of Knighthood. The Register of Knights Bachelor, instituted by James I in the 17th century, lapsed, and in 1908 a voluntary association under the title of The Society of Knights (now The Imperial Society of Knights Bachelor by Royal Command) was formed with the primary objects of continuing the various registers dating from 1257 and obtaining the uniform registration of every created Knight Bachelor. In 1926 a design for a badge to be worn by Knights Bachelor was approved and adopted; in 1974 a neck badge and miniature were added.

Knight Principal, Sir Conrad Swan, KCVO
Chairman of Council, The Lord Lane of Horsell
Prelate, Rt. Revd and Rt. Hon. The Bishop of London
Hon. Registrar, Sir Kenneth Newman, GBE, QPM
Hon. Treasurer, Sir Douglas Morpeth, TD
Clerk to the Council, R. M. Esden
Office, 21 Old Buildings, Lincoln's Inn, London WC2A 3UJ

LIST OF BARONETS AND KNIGHTS
Revised to 31 August 1996

Peers are not included in this list

†   Not registered on the Official Roll of the Baronetage at the time of going to press
()   The date of creation of the baronetcy is given in parenthesis
I   Baronet of Ireland
NS   Baronet of Nova Scotia
S   Baronet of Scotland

If a baronet or knight has a double barrelled or hyphenated surname, he is listed under the final element of the name
A full entry in italic type indicates that the recipient of a knighthood died during the year in which the honour was conferred. The name is included for purposes of record

Abal, Sir Tei, Kt., CBE
Abbott, Sir Albert Francis, Kt., CBE
Abbott, *Vice-Adm.* Sir Peter Charles, KCB
Abdy, Sir Valentine Robert Duff, Bt. (1850)
Abel, Sir Seselo (Cecil) Charles Geoffrey, Kt., OBE
Aheles, Sir (Emil Herbert) Peter, Kt.
Abercromby, Sir Ian George, Bt. (s. 1636)
Abraham, Sir Edward Penley, Kt., CBE, FRS
Acheson, *Prof.* Sir (Ernest) Donald, KBE
Ackers, Sir James George, Kt.
†Ackroyd, Sir Timothy Robert Whyte, Bt. (1956)
Acland, Sir Antony Arthur, GCMG, GCVO
Acland, *Lt.-Col.* Sir (Christopher) Guy (Dyke), Bt., MVO (1890)
Acland, Sir John Dyke, Bt. (1644)
Acland, *Maj.-Gen.* Sir John Hugh Bevil, KCB, CBE
Adam, Sir Christopher Eric Forbes, Bt. (1917)
Adams, Sir Philip George Doyne, KCMG
Adams, Sir William James, KCMG
Adamson, Sir (William Owen) Campbell, Kt.
Adrien, *Hon.* Sir Maurice Latour-, Kt.
Adye, Sir John Anthony, KCMG
Agnew, Sir Crispin Hamlyn, Bt. (s. 1629)
Agnew, Sir John Keith, Bt. (1895)
Aiken, *Air Chief Marshal* Sir John Alexander Carlisle, KCB
Ainsworth, Sir (Thomas) David, Bt. (1916)
Aird, *Capt.* Sir Alastair Sturgis, KCVO
Aird, Sir (George) John, Bt. (1901)
Airey, Sir Lawrence, KCB
Airy, *Maj.-Gen.* Sir Christopher John, KCVO, CBE
Aitchison, Sir Charles Walter de Lancey, Bt. (1938)
Aitken, Sir Robert Stevenson, Kt., MD, D.phil.
Akehurst, *Gen.* Sir John Bryan, KCB, CBE
Albert, Sir Alexis François, Kt., CMG, VRD
Albu, Sir George, Bt. (1912)
Alcock, *Air Chief Marshal* Sir (Robert James) Michael, GCB, KBE
Aldous, *Rt. Hon.* Sir William, Kt.
Alexander, Sir Charles Gundry, Bt. (1945)
Alexander, Sir Claud Hagart-, Bt. (1886)
Alexander, Sir Douglas, Bt. (1921)
Alexander, Sir (John) Lindsay, Kt.
Alexander, *Prof.* Sir Kenneth John Wilson, Kt.
Alexander, Sir Michael O'Donal Bjarne, GCMG

Alexander, Sir Norman Stanley, Kt., CBE
†Alexander, Sir Patrick Desmond William Cable-, Bt. (1809)
Allan, Sir Anthony James Allan Havelock-, Bt. (1858)
Allen, *Prof.* Sir Geoffrey, Kt., PH.D., FRS
Allen, Sir John Derek, Kt., CBE
Allen, *Hon.* Sir Peter Austin Philip Jermyn, Kt.
Allen, Sir William Guilford, Kt.
Allen, Sir (William) Kenneth (Gwynne), Kt.
Alleyne, Sir George Allanmoore Ogarren, Kt.
Alleyne, *Revd* Sir John Olpherts Campbell, Bt. (1769)
Alliance, Sir David, Kt., CBE
Allinson, Sir (Walter) Leonard, KCVO, CMG
Alliott, *Hon.* Sir John Downes, Kt.
Allison, *Air Chief Marshal* Sir John Shakespeare, KCB, CBE
Alment, Sir (Edward) Anthony John, Kt.
Althaus, Sir Nigel Frederick, Kt.
Ambo, *Rt. Revd* George, KBE
Amet, *Hon.* Sir Arnold Karibone, Kt.
Amies, Sir (Edwin) Hardy, KCVO
Amory, Sir Ian Heathcoat, Bt. (1874)
Anderson, Sir John Anthony, KBE
Anderson, *Maj.-Gen.* Sir John Evelyn, KBE
Anderson, Sir John Muir, Kt., CMG
Anderson, *Hon.* Sir Kevin Victor, Kt.
Anderson, *Vice-Adm.* Sir Neil Dudley, KBE, CB
Anderson, *Prof.* Sir (William) Ferguson, Kt., OBE
Anderton, Sir (Cyril) James, Kt., CBE, QPM
Andrew, Sir Robert John, KCB
Andrews, Sir Derek Henry, KCB, CBE
Andrews, *Hon.* Sir Dormer George, Kt.
Angus, Sir Michael Richardson, Kt.
Annesley, Sir Hugh Norman, Kt., QPM
Anson, *Vice-Adm.* Sir Edward Rosebery, KCB
Anson, Sir John, KCB
Anson, *Rear-Adm.* Sir Peter, Bt., CB (1831)
Anstey, *Brig.* Sir John, Kt., CBE, TD
Anstruther, *Maj.* Sir Ralph Hugo, Bt., GCVO, MC (s. 1694)
Antico, Sir Tristan Venus, Kt.
†Antrobus, Sir Edward Philip, Bt. (1815)
Appleyard, Sir Leonard Vincent, KCMG
Appleyard, Sir Raymond Kenelm, KBE
Arbuthnot, Sir Keith Robert Charles, Bt. (1823)
Arbuthnot, Sir William Reierson, Bt. (1964)
Archdale, *Capt.* Sir Edward Folmer, Bt., DSC, RN (1928)

Archer, *Gen.* Sir (Arthur) John, KCB, OBE
Arculus, Sir Ronald, KCMG, KCVO
Armitage, *Air Chief Marshal* Sir Michael John, KCB, CBE
Armour, *Prof.* Sir James, Kt., CBE
Armstrong, Sir Andrew Clarence Francis, Bt., CMG (1841)
Armytage, Sir John Martin, Bt. (1738)
Arnold, *Rt. Hon.* Sir John Lewis, Kt.
Arnold, Sir Malcolm Henry, Kt., CBE
Arnold, Sir Thomas Richard, Kt., MP
Arnott, Sir Alexander John Maxwell, Bt. (1896)
Arnott, *Prof.* Sir (William) Melville, Kt., TD, MD
Arrindell, Sir Clement Athelston, GCMG, GCVO, QC
Arthur, *Lt.-Gen.* Sir (John) Norman Stewart, KCB
Arthur, Sir Stephen John, Bt. (1841)
Ash, *Prof.* Sir Eric Albert, Kt., CBE, FRS, FEng.
Ashburnham, Sir Denny Reginald, Bt. (1661)
Ashe, Sir Derick Rosslyn, KCMG
Ashley, Sir Bernard Albert, Kt.
Ashmore, *Admiral of the Fleet* Sir Edward Beckwith, GCB, DSC
Ashmore, *Vice-Adm.* Sir Peter William Beckwith, KCB, KCVO, DSC
Ashworth, Sir Herbert, Kt.
Aske, *Revd* Sir Conan, Bt. (1922)
Askew, Sir Bryan, Kt.
Asscher, *Prof.* (Adolf) William, Kt., MD, FRCP
Astill, *Hon.* Sir Michael John, Kt.
Aston, Sir Harold George, Kt., CBE
Aston, *Hon.* Sir William John, KCMG
Astor, *Hon.* Sir John Jacob, Kt., MBE
Astwood, *Hon.* Sir James Rufus, KBE
Astwood, *Lt.-Col.* Sir Jeffrey Carlton, Kt., CBE, ED
Atcherley, Sir Harold Winter, Kt.
Atiyah, Sir Michael Francis, Kt., OM, PH.D., FRS
Atkinson, *Air Marshal* Sir David William, KBE
Atkinson, Sir Frederick John, KCB
Atkinson, Sir John Alexander, KCB, DFC
Atkinson, Sir Robert, Kt., DSC, FEng.
Attenborough, Sir David Frederick, Kt., CH, CVO, CBE, FRS
Atwell, Sir John William, Kt., CBE, FRSE, FEng.
Atwill, Sir (Milton) John (Napier), Kt.
Audland, Sir Christopher John, KCMG
Audley, Sir George Bernard, Kt.
Augier, *Prof.* Sir Fitz-Roy Richard, Kt.
Auld, *Rt. Hon.* Sir Robin Ernest, Kt.
†Austin, Sir Anthony Leonard, Bt. (1894)
Austin, *Vice-Adm.* Sir Peter Murray, KCB

Austin, *Air Marshal* Sir Roger Mark, KCB, AFC

Axford, Sir William Ian, Kt.

Aykroyd, Sir James Alexander Frederic, Bt. (1929)

Aykroyd, Sir William Miles, Bt., MC (1920)

Aylmer, Sir Richard John, Bt. (I. 1622)

Bacha, Sir Bhinod, Kt., CMG

Backhouse, Sir Jonathan Roger, Bt. (1901)

Bacon, Sir Nicholas Hickman Ponsonby, Bt. *Premier Baronet of England* (1611 and 1627)

Bacon, Sir Sidney Charles, Kt., CB, FEng.

Baddeley, Sir John Wolsey Beresford, Bt. (1922)

Baddiley, *Prof.* Sir James, Kt., PH.D., D.SC., FRS, FRSE

Badger, Sir Geoffrey Malcolm, Kt.

Bagge, Sir (John) Jeremy Picton, Bt. (1867)

Bagnall, *Field Marshal* Sir Nigel Thomas, GCB, CVO, MC

Bailey, Sir Alan Marshall, KCB

Bailey, Sir Brian Harry, Kt., OBE

Bailey, Sir Derrick Thomas Louis, Bt., DFC (1919)

Bailey, Sir John Bilsland, KCB

Bailey, Sir Richard John, Kt., CBE

Bailey, Sir Stanley Ernest, Kt., CBE, QPM

Bailhache, Sir Philip Martin, Kt.

Baillie, Sir Gawaine George Hope, Bt. (1823)

Baines, *Prof.* Sir George Grenfell-, Kt., OBE

Baird, Sir David Charles, Bt. (1809)

Baird, *Lt.-Gen.* Sir James Parlane, KBE, MD

Baird, Sir James Richard Gardiner, Bt., MC (s. 1695)

Baird, *Vice-Adm.* Sir Thomas Henry Eustace, KCB

Bairsto, *Air Marshal* Sir Peter Edward, KBE, CB

Baker, Sir Robert George Humphrey Sherston-, Bt. (1796)

Baker, *Hon.* Sir (Thomas) Scott (Gillespie), Kt.

Balchin, Sir Robert George Alexander, Kt.

Balcombe, *Rt. Hon.* Sir (Alfred) John, Kt.

Balderstone, Sir James Schofield, Kt.

Baldwin, Sir Peter Robert, KCB

Ball, *Air Marshal* Sir Alfred Henry Wynne, KCB, DSO, DFC

Ball, Sir Charles Irwin, Bt. (1911)

Ball, Sir Christopher John Elinger, Kt.

Ball, *Prof.* Sir Robert James, Kt., PH.D.

Bamford, Sir Anthony Paul, Kt.

Banham, Sir John Michael Middlecott, Kt.

Bannerman, Sir David Gordon, Bt., OBE (s. 1682)

Bannister, Sir Roger Gilbert, Kt., CBE, DM, FRCP

Barber, Sir (Thomas) David, Bt., (1960)

Barbour, *Very Revd* Sir Robert Alexander Stewart, KCVO, MC

Barclay, Sir Colville Herbert Sanford, Bt. (s. 1668)

Barclay, Sir Peter Maurice, Kt., CBE

Barclay, Sir Roderick Edward, GCVO, KCMG

Barder, Sir Brian Leon, KCMG

Barker, Sir Alwyn Bowman, Kt., CMG

Barker, Sir Colin, Kt.

Barker, *Hon.* Sir (Richard) Ian, Kt.

Barlow, Sir Christopher Hilaro, Bt. (1803)

Barlow, Sir (George) William, Kt., FEng.

Barlow, Sir John Kemp, Bt. (1907)

Barlow, Sir Thomas Erasmus, Bt., DSC (1902)

Barnard, Sir Joseph Brian, Kt.

Barnes, Sir (James) David (Francis), Kt., CBE

Barnes, Sir James George, Kt., MBE

Barnes, Sir Kenneth, KCB

Barnewall, Sir Reginald Robert, Bt. (I. 1623)

Baron, Sir Thomas, Kt., CBE

Barraclough, *Air Chief Marshal* Sir John, KCB, CBE, DFC, AFC

Barraclough, Sir Kenneth James Priestley, Kt., CBE, TD

Barran, Sir David Haven, Kt.

Barran, Sir John Napoleon Ruthven, Bt. (1895)

Barratt, Sir Lawrence Arthur, Kt.

Barratt, Sir Richard Stanley, Kt., CBE, QPM

Barrett, *Lt.-Gen.* Sir David William Scott-, KBE, MC

Barrett, *Lt.-Col.* Sir Dennis Charles Titchener, Kt., TD

Barrett, Sir Stephen Jeremy, KCMG

Barrington, Sir Alexander (Fitzwilliam Croker), Bt. (1831)

Barrington, Sir Nicholas John, KCMG, CVO

Barron, Sir Donald James, Kt.

Barrow, *Capt.* Sir Richard John Uniacke, Bt. (1835)

Barrowclough, Sir Anthony Richard, Kt., QC

Barry, Sir (Lawrence) Edward (Anthony Tress), Bt. (1899)

Bartlett, Sir John Hardington, Bt. (1913)

Barton, *Prof.* Sir Derek Harold Richard, Kt., FRS, FRSE

Barttelot, *Col.* Sir Brian Walter de Stopham, Bt., OBE (1875)

Barwick, *Rt. Hon.* Sir Garfield Edward John, GCMG

Batchelor, Sir Ivor Ralph Campbell, Kt., CBE

Bate, Sir David Lindsay, KBE

Bate, Sir (Walter) Edwin, Kt., OBE

Bateman, Sir Cecil Joseph, KBE

Bateman, Sir Geoffrey Hirst, Kt., FRCS

Bates, Sir Geoffrey Voltelin, Bt., MC (1880)

Bates, Sir (John) Dawson, Bt., MC (1937)

Batho, Sir Peter Ghislain, Bt. (1928)

Bathurst, *Admiral of the Fleet* Sir (David) Benjamin, GCB

Bathurst, Sir Frederick John Charles Gordon Hervey-, Bt. (1818)

Bathurst, Sir Maurice Edward, Kt., CMG, CBE, QC

Batten, Sir John Charles, KCVO

Battersby, *Prof.* Sir Alan Rushton, Kt., FRS

Battishill, Sir Anthony Michael William, KCB

Batty, Sir William Bradshaw, Kt., TD

Baxendell, Sir Peter Brian, Kt., CBE, FEng.

Bayliss, *Prof.* Sir Noel Stanley, Kt., CBE

Bayliss, Sir Richard Ian Samuel, KCVO, MD, FRCP

Bayly, *Vice-Adm.* Sir Patrick Uniacke, KBE, CB, DSC

Bayne, Sir Nicholas Peter, KCMG

Baynes, Sir John Christopher Malcolm, Bt. (1801)

Bazley, Sir Thomas Stafford, Bt. (1869)

Beach, *Gen.* Sir (William Gerald) Hugh, GBE, KCB, MC

Beale, *Lt.-Gen.* Sir Peter John, KBE, FRCP

Beament, Sir James William Longman, Kt., SC.D., FRS

Beattie, *Hon.* Sir Alexander Craig, Kt.

Beattie, *Hon.* Sir David Stuart, GCMG, GCVO

Beauchamp, Sir Christopher Radstock Proctor-, Bt. (1745)

Beaumont, *Capt.* the Hon. Sir (Edward) Nicholas (Canning), KCVO

Beaumont, Sir George (Howland Francis), Bt. (1661)

Beaumont, Sir Richard Ashton, KCMG, OBE

Beavis, *Air Chief Marshal* Sir Michael Gordon, KCB, CBE, AFC

Becher, Sir William Fane Wrixon, Bt., MC (1831)

Beck, Sir Edgar Charles, Kt., CBE, FEng.

Beck, Sir Edgar Philip, Kt.

Beckett, *Capt.* Sir (Martyn) Gervase, Bt., MC (1921)

Beckett, Sir Terence Norman, KBE, FEng.

Bedingfeld, *Capt.* Sir Edmund George Felix Paston-, Bt. (1661)

Beecham, Sir Jeremy Hugh, Kt.

Beecham, Sir John Stratford Roland, Bt. (1914)

Beeley, Sir Harold, KCMG, CBE

Beetham, *Marshal of the Royal Air Force* Sir Michael James, GCB, CBE, DFC, AFC

Beevor, Sir Thomas Agnew, Bt. (1784)
Begg, Sir Neil Colquhoun, KBE
Beith, Sir John Greville Stanley, KCMG
Belch, Sir Alexander Ross, Kt., CBE, FRSE
Beldam, Rt. Hon. Sir (Alexander) Roy (Asplan), Kt.
Belich, Sir James, Kt.
Bell, Sir Brian Ernest, KBE
Bell, Sir (George) Raymond, KCMG, CB
Bell, Sir John Lowthian, Bt. (1885)
Bell, Hon. Sir Rodger, Kt.
Bell, Sir Timothy John Leigh, Kt.
Bell, Sir (William) Ewart, KCB
Bell, Sir William Hollin Dayrell Morrison-, Bt. (1905)
Bellew, Sir Henry Charles Gratton-, Bt. (1838)
Bellinger, Sir Robert Ian, GBE
Bellingham, Sir Noel Peter Roger, Bt. (1796)
Bengough, Col. Sir Piers, KCVO, OBE
Benn, Sir (James) Jonathan, Bt. (1914)
Bennett, Sir Charles Moihi Te Arawaka, Kt., DSO
Bennett, Air Vice-Marshal Sir Erik Peter, KBE, CB
Bennett, Rt. Hon. Sir Frederic Mackarness, Kt.
Bennett, Sir Hubert, Kt.
Bennett, Hon. Sir Hugh Peter Derwyn, Kt.
Bennett, Sir John Mokonuiarangi, Kt.
Bennett, Gen. Sir Phillip Harvey, KBE, DSO
Bennett, Sir Reginald Frederick Brittain, Kt., VRD
Bennett, Sir Ronald Wilfrid Murdoch, Bt. (1929)
Benson, Sir Christopher John, Kt.
Bentley, Sir William, KCMG
Benyon, Sir William Richard, Kt.
Beresford, Sir (Alexander) Paul, Kt., MP
Berger, Vice-Adm. Sir Peter Egerton Capel, KCB, LVO, DSC
Berghuser, Hon. Sir Eric, Kt., MBE
Berlin, Sir Isaiah, Kt., OM, CBE
Berman, Sir Franklin Delow, KCMG
Bernard, Sir Dallas Edmund, Bt. (1954)
Berney, Sir Julian Reedham Stuart, Bt. (1620)
Berrill, Sir Kenneth Ernest, GBE, KCB
Berriman, Sir David, Kt.
Berry, Prof. Sir Colin Leonard, Kt., FRCpath.
Berry, Prof. Sir Michael Victor, Kt., FRS
Berthon, Vice-Adm. Sir Stephen Ferrier, Kt.
Berthoud, Sir Martin Seymour, KCVO, CMG
Best, Sir Richard Radford, KCVO, CBE

Bethune, Sir Alexander Maitland Sharp, Bt. (s. 1683)
Bethune, Hon. Sir (Walter) Angus, Kt.
Bett, Sir Michael, Kt., CBE
Bevan, Sir Martyn Evan Evans, Bt. (1958)
Bevan, Sir Timothy Hugh, Kt.
Beveridge, Sir Gordon Smith Grieve, Kt., FRSE, FEng., FRSA
Beverley, Lt.-Gen. Sir Henry York La Roche, KCB, OBE, RM
Bibby, Sir Derek James, Bt., MC (1959)
Bick, Hon. Sir Martin James Moore-, Kt.
Bickersteth, Rt. Revd John Monier, KCVO
Biddulph, Sir Ian D'Olier, Bt. (1664)
Bide, Sir Austin Ernest, Kt.
Bidwell, Sir Hugh Charles Philip, GBE
Biggam, Sir Robin Adair, Kt.
Biggs, Vice-Adm. Sir Geoffrey William Roger, KCB
Biggs, Sir Norman Paris, Kt.
Bilas, Sir Angmai Simon, Kt., OBE
Billière, Gen. Sir Peter Edgar de la Cour de la, KCB, KBE, DSO, MC
Bing, Sir Rudolf Franz Josef, KBE
Bingham, Hon. Sir Eardley Max, Kt., QC
Bingham, Rt. Hon. Sir Thomas Henry, Kt.
Birch, Sir John Allan, KCVO, CMG
Birch, Sir Roger, Kt., CBE, QPM
Bird, Sir Richard Geoffrey Chapman, Bt. (1922)
Birkin, Sir John Christian William, Bt. (1905)
Birkin, Sir (John) Derek, Kt., TD
Birkmyre, Sir Archibald, Bt. (1921)
Birley, Sir Derek Sydney, Kt.
Birrell, Sir James Drake, Kt.
Birtwistle, Sir Harrison, Kt.
Bishop, Sir Frederick Arthur, Kt., CB, CVO
Bishop, Sir George Sidney, Kt., CB, OBE
Bishop, Sir Michael David, Kt., CBE
Bisson, Rt Hon. Sir Gordon Ellis, Kt.
Black, Prof. Sir Douglas Andrew Kilgour, Kt., MD, FRCP
Black, Sir James Whyte, Kt., FRCP, FRS
Black, Adm. Sir (John) Jeremy, GBE, KCB, DSO
Black, Sir Robert Brown, GCMG, OBE
Black, Sir Robert David, Bt. (1922)
Blackburne, Hon. Sir William Anthony, Kt.
Blacker, Gen. Sir (Anthony Stephen) Jeremy, KCB, CBE
Blacker, Gen. Sir Cecil Hugh, GCB, OBE, MC
Blackett, Sir Hugh Francis, Bt. (1673)
Blacklock, Surgeon Capt. Prof. Sir Norman James, KCVO, OBE
Blackman, Sir Frank Milton, KCVO, OBE

Blackwell, Sir Basil Davenport, Kt., FEng.
Blackwood, Sir John Francis, Bt. (1814)
Blair, Sir Alastair Campbell, KCVO, TD, WS
Blair, Lt.-Gen. Sir Chandos, KCVO, OBE, MC
Blair, Sir Edward Thomas Hunter, Bt. (1786)
Blake, Sir Alfred Lapthorn, KCVO, MC
Blake, Sir Francis Michael, Bt. (1907)
Blake, Sir Peter James, KBE
Blake, Sir (Thomas) Richard (Valentine), Bt. (I. 1622)
Blaker, Sir John, Bt. (1919)
Blakiston, Sir Ferguson Arthur James, Bt. (1763)
Bland, Sir (Francis) Christopher (Buchan), Kt.
Bland, Sir Henry Armand, Kt., CBE
Bland, Lt.-Col. Sir Simon Claud Michael, KCVO
Blelloch, Sir John Nial Henderson, KCB
Blennerhassett, Sir (Marmaduke) Adrian Francis William, Bt. (1809)
Blewitt, Maj. Sir Shane Gabriel Basil, GCVO
Blofeld, Hon. Sir John Christopher Calthorpe, Kt.
Blois, Sir Charles Nicholas Gervase, Bt. (1686)
Blomefield, Sir Thomas Charles Peregrine, Bt. (1807)
Bloomfield, Sir Kenneth Percy, KCB
Blosse, Capt. Sir Richard Hely Lynch-, Bt. (1622)
Blount, Sir Walter Edward Alpin, Bt., DSC (1642)
Blunden, Sir George, Kt.
†Blunden, Sir Philip Overington, Bt. (I. 1766)
Blunt, Sir David Richard Reginald Harvey, Bt. (1720)
Boardman, Prof. Sir John, Kt., FSA, FBA
Bodilly, Hon. Sir Jocelyn, Kt., VRD
Bodmer, Sir Walter Fred, Kt., PH.D., FRS
Body, Sir Richard Bernard Frank Stewart, Kt., MP
Boevey, Sir Thomas Michael Blake Crawley-, Bt. (1784)
Bogarde, Sir Dirk (Derek Niven van den Bogaerde), Kt.
Boileau, Sir Guy (Francis), Bt. (1838)
Boles, Sir Jeremy John Fortescue, Bt. (1922)
Boles, Sir John Dennis, Kt., MBE
Bolland, Sir Edwin, KCMG
Bollers, Hon. Sir Harold Brodie Smith, Kt.
Bolton, Sir Frederic Bernard, Kt., MC
Bona, Sir Kina, KBE
Bond, Sir Kenneth Raymond Boyden, Kt.
Bond, Prof. Sir Michael Richard, Kt., FRCPsych., FRCPGlas., FRCSE
Bondi, Prof. Sir Hermann, KCB, FRS

Bonfield, Sir Peter Leahy, Kt., CBE, FEng.

Bonham, *Maj.* Sir Antony Lionel Thomas, Bt. (1852)

Bonington, Sir Christian John Storey, Kt., CBE

Bonsall, Sir Arthur Wilfred, KCMG, CBE

Bonsor, Sir Nicholas Cosmo, Bt., MP (1925)

Boolell, Sir Satcam, Kt.

Boon, Sir Peter Coleman, Kt.

Boord, Sir Nicolas John Charles, Bt. (1896)

Boorman, *Lt.-Gen.* Sir Derek, KCB

Booth, Sir Christopher Charles, Kt., MD, FRCP

Booth, Sir Douglas Allen, Bt. (1916)

Booth, Sir Gordon, KCMG, CVO

†Booth, Sir Josslyn Henry Robert Gore-, Bt. (I. 1760)

Booth, Sir Michael Addison John Wheeler-, KCB

Booth, Sir Robert Camm, Kt., CBE, TD

Boothby, Sir Brooke Charles, Bt. (1660)

Boreel, Sir Francis David, Bt. (1645)

Boreham, *Hon.* Sir Leslie Kenneth Edward, Kt.

Bornu, The Waziri of, KCMG, CBE

Borthwick, Sir John Thomas, Bt., MBE (1908)

Bossom, *Hon.* Sir Clive, Bt. (1953)

Boswall, Sir (Thomas) Alford Houstoun-, Bt. (1836)

Boswell, *Lt.-Gen.* Sir Alexander Crawford Simpson, KCB, CBE

Bosworth, Sir Neville Bruce Alfred, Kt., CBE

Bottomley, Sir James Reginald Alfred, KCMG

Boughey, Sir John George Fletcher, Bt. (1798)

Boulton, Sir Clifford John, GCB

Boulton, Sir (Harold Hugh) Christian, Bt. (1905)

Boulton, Sir William Whytehead, Bt., CBE, TD (1944)

Bourn, Sir John Bryant, KCB

Bourne, Sir (John) Wilfrid, KCB

Bovell, *Hon.* Sir (William) Stewart, Kt.

Bowater, Sir Euan David Vansittart, Bt. (1939)

Bowater, Sir (John) Vansittart, Bt. (1914)

Bowden, Sir Andrew, Kt., MBE, MP

Bowden, Sir Frank, Bt. (1915)

Bowen, Sir Geoffrey Fraser, Kt.

Bowen, Sir Mark Edward Mortimer, Bt. (1921)

†Bowlby, Sir Richard Peregrine Longstaff, Bt. (1923)

Bowman, Sir Jeffery Haverstock, Kt.

Bowman, Sir Paul Humphrey Armytage, Bt. (1884)

Bowmar, Sir Charles Erskine, Kt.

Bowness, Sir Alan, Kt., CBE

Boxer, *Air Vice-Marshal* Sir Alan Hunter Cachemaille, KCVO, CB, DSO, DFC

Boyce, *Vice-Adm.* Sir Michael Cecil, KCB, OBE

Boyce, Sir Robert Charles Leslie, Bt. (1952)

Boyd, Sir Alexander Walter, Bt. (1916)

Boyd, Sir John Dixon Iklé, KCMG

Boyd, The Hon. Sir Mark Alexander Lennox-, Kt., MP

Boyd, *Prof.* Sir Robert Lewis Fullarton, Kt., CBE, D.SC., FRS

Boyes, Sir Brian Gerald Barratt-, KBE

Boyle, Sir Stephen Gurney, Bt. (1904)

Boyne, Sir Henry Brian, Kt., CBE

Boynton, Sir John Keyworth, Kt., MC

Boys, *Rt. Hon.* Sir Michael Hardie, GCMG

Boyson, *Rt. Hon.* Sir Rhodes, Kt., MP

Brabham, Sir John Arthur, Kt., OBE

Bradbeer, Sir John Derek Richardson, Kt., OBE, TD

Bradbury, *Surgeon Vice-Adm.* Sir Eric Blackburn, KBE, CB

Bradford, Sir Edward Alexander Slade, Bt. (1902)

Bradley, Sir Burton Gyrth Burton-, Kt., OBE

Bradman, Sir Donald George, Kt.

Bradshaw, Sir Kenneth Anthony, KCB

Bradshaw, *Lt.-Gen.* Sir Richard Phillip, KBE

Brain, Sir (Henry) Norman, KBE, CMG

Braithwaite, Sir (Joseph) Franklin Madders, Kt.

Braithwaite, *Rt. Hon.* Sir Nicholas Alexander, Kt., OBE

Braithwaite, Sir Rodric Quentin, GCMG

Bramall, Sir (Ernest) Ashley, Kt.

Bramley, *Prof.* Sir Paul Anthony, Kt.

Branigan, Sir Patrick Francis, Kt., QC

Bray, Sir Theodor Charles, Kt., CBE

Brennan, *Hon.* Sir (Francis) Gerard, KBE

Brett, Sir Charles Edward Bainbridge, Kt., CBE

Brickwood, Sir Basil Greame, Bt. (1927)

Bridges, *Hon.* Sir Phillip Rodney, Kt., CMG

Brierley, Sir Ronald Alfred, Kt.

Bright, Sir Graham Frank James, Kt., MP

Bright, Sir Keith, Kt.

Brinckman, Sir Theodore George Roderick, Bt. (1831)

Brisco, Sir Donald Gilfrid, Bt. (1782)

Briscoe, Sir John Geoffrey James, Bt. (1910)

Brise, Sir John Archibald Ruggles-, Bt., CB, OBE, TD (1935)

Bristow, *Hon.* Sir Peter Henry Rowley, Kt.

Brittan, *Rt. Hon.* Sir Leon, Kt., QC

Brittan, Sir Samuel, Kt.

Britton, Sir Edward Louis, Kt., CBE

Broackes, Sir Nigel, Kt.

†Broadbent, Sir Andrew George, Bt. (1893)

Brocklebank, Sir Aubrey Thomas, Bt. (1885)

Brockman, *Vice-Adm.* Sir Ronald Vernon, KCB, CSI, CIE, CVO, CBE

Brodie, Sir Benjamin David Ross, Bt. (1834)

Bromhead, Sir John Desmond Gonville, Bt. (1806)

Bromley, Sir Rupert Charles, Bt. (1757)

Bromley, Sir Thomas Eardley, KCMG

Brook, Sir Robin, Kt., CMG, OBE

†Brooke, Sir Alistair Weston, Bt. (1919)

Brooke, Sir Francis George Windham, Bt. (1903)

Brooke, *Rt. Hon.* Sir Henry, Kt.

Brooke, Sir Richard Neville, Bt. (1662)

Brookes, Sir Wilfred Deakin, Kt., CBE, DSO

Brooksbank, Sir (Edward) Nicholas, Bt. (1919)

Broom, *Air Marshal* Sir Ivor Gordon, KCB, CBE, DSO, DFC, AFC

Broomfield, Sir Nigel Hugh Robert Allen, KCMG

Broughton, *Air Marshal* Sir Charles, KBE, CB

†Broughton, Sir David Delves, Bt. (1661)

Broun, Sir William Windsor, Bt. (s. 1686)

Brown, Sir Allen Stanley, Kt., CBE

Brown, Sir (Arthur James) Stephen, KBE

Brown, Sir (Austen) Patrick, KCB

Brown, *Adm.* Sir Brian Thomas, KCB, CBE

Brown, *Lt.-Col.* Sir Charles Frederick Richmond, Bt. (1863)

Brown, Sir (Cyril) Maxwell Palmer, KCB, CMG

Brown, *Vice-Adm.* Sir David Worthington, KCB

Brown, Sir Derrick Holden-, Kt.

Brown, Sir Douglas Denison, Kt.

Brown, *Hon.* Sir Douglas Dunlop, Kt.

Brown, Sir (Frederick Herbert) Stanley, Kt., CBE, FEng.

Brown, *Prof.* Sir (George) Malcolm, Kt., FRS

Brown, Sir George Noel, Kt.

Brown, Sir John Douglas Keith, Kt.

Brown, Sir John Gilbert Newton, Kt., CBE

Brown, Sir Mervyn, KCMG, OBE

Brown, *Hon.* Sir Ralph Kilner, Kt., OBE, TD

Brown, Sir Robert Crichton-, KCMG, CBE, TD

Brown, *Rt. Hon.* Sir Simon Denis, Kt.

Brown, *Rt. Hon.* Sir Stephen, Kt.

Brown, Sir Thomas, Kt.

Brown, Sir William, Kt., CBE

Brown, Sir William Brian Piggott-, Bt. (1903)

Browne, *Rt. Hon.* Sir Patrick Reginald Evelyn, Kt., OBE, TD

Brownrigg, Sir Nicholas (Gawen), Bt. (1816)

Browse, *Prof.* Sir Norman Leslie, Kt., MD, FRCS

Bruce, Sir (Francis) Michael Ian, Bt. (s. 1628)

Bruce, Sir Hervey James Hugh, Bt. (1804)

Bruce, *Rt. Hon.* Sir (James) Roualeyn Hovell-Thurlow-Cumming-, Kt.

Brunner, Sir John Henry Kilian, Bt. (1895)

Brunton, Sir (Edward Francis) Lauder, Bt. (1908)

Brunton, Sir Gordon Charles, Kt.

Bryan, Sir Arthur, Kt.

Bryan, Sir Paul Elmore Oliver, Kt., DSO, MC

Bryce, *Hon.* Sir (William) Gordon, Kt., CBE

Bryson, *Adm.* Sir Lindsay Sutherland, KCB, FEng.

Buchan, Sir John, Kt., CMG

Buchanan, Sir Andrew George, Bt. (1878)

Buchanan, Sir Charles Alexander James Leith-, Bt. (1775)

Buchanan, *Prof.* Sir Colin Douglas, Kt., CBE

Buchanan, *Vice-Adm.* Sir Peter William, KBE

Buchanan, Sir Robert Wilson (Robin), Kt.

Buchanan, Sir (Ranald) Dennis, Kt., MBE

Buck, Sir (Philip) Antony (Fyson), Kt., QC

Buckley, *Rt. Hon.* Sir Denys Burton, Kt., MBE

Buckley, Sir John William, Kt.

Buckley, *Lt.-Cdr.* Sir (Peter) Richard, KCVO

Buckley, *Hon.* Sir Roger John, Kt.

Bulkeley, Sir Richard Thomas Williams-, Bt. (1661)

Bull, Sir Simeon George, Bt. (1922)

Bullard, Sir Julian Leonard, GCMG

Bullus, Sir Eric Edward, Kt.

Bulmer, Sir William Peter, Kt.

Bultin, Sir Bato, Kt., MBE

Bunbury, Sir Michael William, Bt. (1681)

Bunbury, Sir (Richard David) Michael Richardson-, Bt. (I. 1787)

Bunch, Sir Austin Wyeth, Kt., CBE

Bunyard, Sir Robert Sidney, Kt., CBE, QPM

Burbidge, Sir Herbert Dudley, Bt. (1916)

Burbury, *Hon.* Sir Stanley Charles, KCMG, KCVO, KBE

Burdett, Sir Savile Aylmer, Bt. (1665)

Burgen, Sir Arnold Stanley Vincent, Kt., FRS

Burgess, *Gen.* Sir Edward Arthur, KCB, OBE

Burgess, Sir (Joseph) Stuart, Kt., CBE, ph.D., FRSC

Burgh, Sir John Charles, KCMG, CB

Burke, Sir James Stanley Gilbert, Bt. (I. 1797)

Burke, Sir (Thomas) Kerry, Kt.

Burley, Sir Victor George, Kt., CBE

Burman, Sir (John) Charles, Kt.

Burnet, Sir James William Alexander (Sir Alastair Burnet), Kt.

Burnett, *Air Chief Marshal* Sir Brian Kenyon, GCB, DFC, AFC

Burnett, Sir David Humphery, Bt., MBE, TD (1913)

Burnett, Sir John Harrison, Kt.

Burnett, Sir Walter John, Kt.

Burney, Sir Cecil Denniston, Bt. (1921)

Burns, Sir Terence, GCB

Burns, *Maj.-Gen.* Sir (Walter Arthur) George, GCVO, CB, DSO, OBE, MC

Burrell, Sir John Raymond, Bt. (1774)

Burrenchobay, Sir Dayendranath, KBE, CMG, CVO

Burrows, Sir Bernard Alexander Brocas, GCMG

Burston, Sir Samuel Gerald Wood, Kt., OBE

Burt, *Hon.* Sir Francis Theodore Page, KCMG

Burton, Sir Carlisle Archibald, Kt., OBE

Burton, Sir George Vernon Kennedy, Kt., CBE

Burton, Sir Michael St Edmund, KCVO, CMG

Bush, *Adm.* Sir John Fitzroy Duyland, GCB, DSC

Butler, *Rt. Hon.* Sir Adam Courtauld, Kt.

Butler, *Hon.* Sir Arlington Griffith, KCMG

Butler, Sir Clifford Charles, Kt., ph.D., FRS

Butler, Sir (Frederick) (Edward) Robin, GCB, CVO

Butler, Sir Michael Dacres, GCMG

Butler, Sir (Reginald) Michael (Thomas), Bt. (1922)

Butler, *Hon.* Sir Richard Clive, Kt.

†Butler, Sir Richard Pierce, Bt. (1628)

Butt, Sir (Alfred) Kenneth Dudley, Bt. (1929)

Butter, *Maj.* Sir David Henry, KCVO, MC

Butterfield, *Hon.* Sir Alexander Neil Logie, Kt.

Buxton, *Hon.* Sir Richard Joseph, Kt.

Buxton, Sir Thomas Fowell Victor, Bt. (1840)

Buzzard, Sir Anthony Farquhar, Bt. (1929)

Byatt, Sir Hugh Campbell, KCVO, CMG

Byers, Sir Maurice Hearne, Kt., CBE, QC

Byford, Sir Lawrence, Kt., CBE, QPM

Cable, Sir James Eric, KCVO, CMG

Cadbury, Sir (George) Adrian (Hayhurst), Kt.

Cadell, *Vice-Adm.* Sir John Frederick, KBE

Cadogan, *Prof.* Sir John Ivan George, Kt., CBE, FRS, FRSE

Cahn, Sir Albert Jonas, Bt. (1934)

Cain, Sir Edward Thomas, Kt., CBE

Cain, Sir Henry Edney Conrad, Kt.

Caine, Sir Michael Harris, Kt.

Caines, Sir John, KCB

Cairncross, Sir Alexander Kirkland, KCMG

Calcutt, Sir David Charles, Kt., QC

Calderwood, Sir Robert, Kt.

Caldwell, *Surgeon Vice-Adm.* Sir (Eric) Dick, KBE, CB

Callard, Sir Eric John, Kt., FEng.

Callaway, *Prof.* Sir Frank Adams, Kt., CMG, OBE

Calley, Sir Henry Algernon, Kt., DSO, DFC

Calman, *Prof.* Sir Kenneth Charles, KCB, MD, FRCP, FRCS, FRSE

Calne, *Prof.* Sir Roy Yorke, Kt., FRS

Calthorpe, Sir Euan Hamilton Anstruther-Gough-, Bt. (1929)

Cameron of Lochiel, Sir Donald Hamish, KT, CVO, TD

Cameron, Sir (Eustace) John, Kt., CBE

Cameron, Sir John Watson, Kt., OBE

Campbell, Sir Alan Hugh, GCMG

Campbell, Sir Colin Moffat, Bt., MC (s. 1668)

Campbell, *Prof.* Sir Colin Murray, Kt.

Campbell, *Prof.* Sir Donald, Kt., CBE, FRCS, FRCPGlas.

Campbell, Sir Ian Tofts, Kt., CBE, VRD

Campbell, Sir Ilay Mark, Bt. (1808)

Campbell, Sir Lachlan Philip Kemeys, Bt. (1815)

Campbell, Sir Matthew, KBE, CB, FRSE

Campbell, Sir Niall Alexander Hamilton, Bt. (1831)

Campbell, Sir Robin Auchinbreck, Bt. (s. 1628)

Campbell, Sir Thomas Cockburn-, Bt. (1821)

Campbell, *Hon.* Sir Walter Benjamin, Kt.

Campbell, *Hon.* Sir William Anthony, Kt.

†Carden, Sir Christopher Robert, Bt. (1887)

Carden, Sir John Craven, Bt. (I. 1787)

Carew, Sir Rivers Verain, Bt. (1661)

Carey, Sir Peter Willoughby, GCB

Carlisle, Sir James Beethoven, GCMG

Carlisle, Sir John Michael, Kt.

Carlisle, Sir Kenneth Melville, Kt., MP

Carmichael, Sir David Peter William Gibson-Craig-, Bt. (s. 1702 and 1831)

Carnac, *Revd Canon* Sir (Thomas) Nicholas Rivett-, Bt. (1836)

Carnegie, *Lt.-Gen.* Sir Robin Macdonald, KCB, OBE

Carnegie, Sir Roderick Howard, Kt.

Carnwath, Sir Robert John
Anderson, Kt., CVO
Caro, Sir Anthony Alfred, Kt., CBE
Carpenter, *Very Revd* Edward
Frederick, KCVO
Carpenter, *Lt.-Gen.* the Hon. Sir
Thomas Patrick John Boyd-, KBE
Carr, Sir (Albert) Raymond
(Maillard), Kt.
Carr, *Air Marshal* Sir John Darcy
Baker-, KBE, CB, AFC
Carrick, *Hon.* Sir John Leslie, KCMG
Carrick, Sir Roger John, KCMG, LVO
Carsberg, *Prof.* Sir Bryan Victor, Kt.
Carswell, *Rt. Hon.* Sir Robert
Douglas, Kt.
Carter, Sir Charles Frederick, Kt.,
FBA
Carter, *Prof.* Sir David Craig, Kt.,
FRCSE, FRCSGlas., FRCPE
Carter, Sir Derrick Hunton, Kt., TD
Carter, Sir John, Kt., QC
Carter, Sir John Alexander, Kt.
Carter, Sir Philip David, Kt., CBE
Carter, Sir Richard Henry Alwyn,
Kt.
Carter, Sir William Oscar, Kt.
Cartland, Sir George Barrington, Kt.,
CMG
Cartledge, Sir Bryan George, KCMG
Cary, Sir Roger Hugh, Bt. (1955)
Casey, *Rt. Hon.* Sir Maurice Eugene,
Kt.
Cash, Sir Gerald Christopher, GCMG,
GCVO, OBE
Cass, Sir Geoffrey Arthur, Kt.
Cass, Sir John Patrick, Kt., OBE
Cassel, Sir Harold Felix, Bt., TD, QC
(1920)
Cassels, *Field Marshal* Sir (Archibald)
James Halkett, GCB, KBE, DSO
Cassels, Sir John Seton, Kt., CB
Cassels, *Adm.* Sir Simon Alastair
Cassillis, KCB, CBE
Cassidi, *Adm.* Sir (Arthur) Desmond,
GCB
Casson, Sir Hugh Maxwell, CH,
KCVO, PPRA, FRIBA
Cater, Sir Jack, KBE
Cater, Sir John Robert, Kt.
Catford, Sir (John) Robin, KCVO, CBE
Catherwood, Sir (Henry) Frederick
(Ross), Kt., MEP
Catling, Sir Richard Charles, Kt.,
CMG, OBE
Cato, *Hon.* Sir Arnott Samuel, KCMG
Cave, Sir Charles Edward Coleridge,
Bt. (1896)
Cave, Sir (Charles) Philip Haddon-,
KBE, CMG
Cave, Sir Robert Cave-Browne-, Bt.
(1641)
Cawley, Sir Charles Mills, Kt., CBE,
ph.D.
Cayley, Sir Digby William David,
Bt. (1661)
Cayzer, Sir James Arthur, Bt. (1904)
Cazalet, *Hon.* Sir Edward Stephen,
Kt.
Cazalet, Sir Peter Grenville, Kt.

Cecil, *Rear-Adm.* Sir (Oswald) Nigel
Amherst, KBE, CB
Chacksfield, *Air Vice-Marshal* Sir
Bernard Albert, KBE, CB
Chadwick, *Revd Prof.* Henry, KBE
Chadwick, *Hon.* Sir John Murray, Kt.,
ED
Chadwick, Sir Joshua Kenneth
Burton, Bt. (1935)
Chadwick, *Revd Prof.* (William)
Owen, OM, KBE, FBA
Chalstrey, Sir (Leonard) John, Kt.,
MD, FRCS
Chan, *Rt. Hon.* Sir Julius, GCMG, KBE
Chance, Sir (George) Jeremy
ffolliott, Bt. (1900)
Chandler, Sir Colin Michael, Kt.
Chandler, Sir Geoffrey, Kt., CBE
Chaney, *Hon.* Sir Frederick Charles,
KBE, AFC
Chantler, *Prof.* Sir Cyril, Kt., MD, FRCP
Chaplin, Sir Malcolm Hilbery, Kt.,
CBE
Chapman, Sir David Robert
Macgowan, Bt. (1958)
Chapman, Sir George Alan, Kt.
Chapman, Sir Sidney Brookes, Kt.,
MP
Chapple, *Field Marshal* Sir John
Lyon, GCB, CBE
Charlton, Sir Robert (Bobby), Kt.,
CBE
Charnley, Sir (William) John, Kt., CB,
FEng.
Chataway, *Rt. Hon.* Sir Christopher,
Kt.
Chatfield, Sir John Freeman, Kt., CBE
Chaytor, Sir George Reginald, Bt.
(1831)
Checketts, *Sqn. Ldr.* Sir David John,
KCVO
Checkland, Sir Michael, Kt.
Cheetham, Sir Nicolas John
Alexander, KCMG
Cheshire, *Air Marshal* Sir John
Anthony, KBE, CB
Chessells, Sir Arthur David (Tim),
Kt.
Chesterman, Sir (Dudley) Ross, Kt.,
ph.D.
Chesterton, Sir Oliver Sidney, Kt.,
MC
Chetwood, Sir Clifford Jack, Kt.
Chetwynd, Sir Arthur Ralph Talbot,
Bt. (1795)
Cheung, Sir Oswald Victor, Kt., CBE
Cheyne, Sir Joseph Lister Watson,
Bt., OBE (1908)
Chichester, Sir (Edward) John, Bt.
(1641)
Chilcot, Sir John Anthony, KCB
Child, Sir (Coles John) Jeremy, Bt.
(1919)
Chilton, *Brig.* Sir Frederick Oliver,
Kt., CBE, DSO
Chilwell, *Hon.* Sir Muir Fitzherbert,
Kt.
Chinn, Sir Trevor Edwin, Kt., CVO
Chipperfield, Sir Geoffrey Howes,
KCB

Chitty, Sir Thomas Willes, Bt. (1924)
Cholmeley, Sir Montague John, Bt.
(1806)
Christie, Sir George William
Langham, Kt.
Christie, Sir William, Kt., MBE
Christopherson, Sir Derman Guy,
Kt., OBE, D.Phil., FRS, FEng.
Chung, Sir Sze-yuen, GBE, FEng.
Clapham, Sir Michael John Sinclair,
KBE
Clark, Sir Francis Drake, Bt. (1886)
Clark, Sir John Allen, Kt.
Clark, Sir John Stewart-, Bt., MEP
(1918)
†Clark, Sir Jonathan George, Bt.
(1917)
Clark, Sir Robert Anthony, Kt., DSC
Clark, Sir Robin Chichester-, Kt.
Clark, Sir Terence Joseph, KBE, CMG,
CVO
Clark, Sir Thomas Edwin, Kt.
Clarke, *Hon.* Sir Anthony Peter, Kt.
Clarke, Sir (Charles Mansfield)
Tobias, Bt. (1831)
Clarke, *Prof.* Sir Cyril Astley, KBE,
MD, SC.D., FRS, FRCP
Clarke, Sir Ellis Emmanuel
Innocent, GCMG
Clarke, Sir Jonathan Dennis, Kt.
Clarke, *Maj.* Sir Peter Cecil, KCVO
Clarke, Sir Robert Cyril, Kt.
Clarke, Sir Rupert William John, Bt.,
MBE (1882)
Clay, Sir Richard Henry, Bt. (1841)
Clayton, Sir David Robert, Bt. (1732)
Clayton, Sir Robert James, Kt., CBE,
FEng.
Cleaver, Sir Anthony Brian, Kt.
Cleminson, Sir James Arnold Stacey,
KBE, MC
Clerk, Sir John Dutton, Bt., CBE, VRD
(s. 1679)
Clerke, Sir John Edward
Longueville, Bt. (1660)
Clifford, Sir Roger Joseph, Bt. (1887)
Clothier, Sir Cecil Montacute, KCB,
QC
Clucas, Sir Kenneth Henry, KCB
Clutterbuck, *Vice-Adm.* Sir David
Granville, KBE, CB
Coates, Sir David Frederick
Charlton, Bt. (1921)
Coats, Sir Alastair Francis Stuart, Bt.
(1905)
Coats, Sir William David, Kt.
Cobban, Sir James Macdonald, Kt.,
CBE, TD
Cobham, Sir Michael John, Kt., CBE
Cochrane, Sir (Henry) Marc
(Sursock), Bt. (1903)
Cockburn, Sir John Elliot, Bt.
(s. 1671)
Cockcroft, Sir Wilfred Halliday, Kt.,
D.Phil.
Cockerell, Sir Christopher Sydney,
Kt., CBE, FRS
Cockram, Sir John, Kt.
Cockshaw, Sir Alan, Kt., FEng.

Codrington, Sir Simon Francis
Bethell, Bt. (1876)
Codrington, Sir William Alexander,
Bt. (1721)
Coghill, Sir Egerton James Nevill
Tobias, Bt. (1778)
Cohen, Sir Edward, Kt.
Cohen, Sir Ivor Harold, Kt., CBE, TD
Cohen, Sir Stephen Harry Waley-,
Bt. (1961)
Coldstream, Sir George Phillips,
KCB, KCVO, QC
Cole, Sir (Alexander) Colin, KCB,
KCVO, TD
Cole, Sir David Lee, KCMG, MC
Cole, Sir (Robert) William, Kt.
Coleman, Sir Timothy, KG
Coles, Sir (Arthur) John, KCMG
Colfox, Sir (William) John, Bt.
(1939)
Collett, Sir Christopher, GBE
Collett, Sir Ian Seymour, Bt. (1934)
Collins, Hon. Sir Andrew David, Kt.
Collins, Sir Arthur James Robert,
KCVO
Collins, Sir John Alexander, Kt.
Collyear, Sir John Gowen, Kt., FEng.
Colman, Hon. Sir Anthony David, Kt.
Colman, Sir Michael Jeremiah, Bt.
(1907)
Colquhoun of Luss, Sir Ivar Iain, Bt.
(1786)
Colt, Sir Edward William Dutton Bt.
(1694)
Colthurst, Sir Richard La Touche,
Bt. (1744)
Colvin, Sir Howard Montagu, Kt.,
CVO, CBE, FBA
Compston, Vice-Adm. Sir Peter
Maxwell, KCB
Comyn, Hon. Sir James, Kt.
Conant, Sir John Ernest Michael, Bt.
(1954)
Condon, Sir Paul Leslie, Kt., QPM
Connell, Hon. Sir Michael Bryan, Kt.
Conran, Sir Terence Orby, Kt.
Cons, Hon. Sir Derek, Kt.
Constable, Sir Frederic Strickland-,
Bt. (1641)
Cook, Prof. Sir Alan Hugh, Kt.
Cook, Sir Christopher Wymondham
Rayner Herbert, Bt. (1886)
Cooke, Sir Charles Fletcher-, Kt., QC
Cooke, Lt.-Col. Sir David William
Perceval, Bt. (1661)
Cooke, Sir Howard Felix Hanlan,
ON, GCMG, GCVO, CD
Cooksey, Sir David James Scott, Kt.
Cooley, Sir Alan Sydenham, Kt., CBE
Cooper, Rt. Hon. Sir Frank, GCB, CMG
Cooper, Sir (Frederick Howard)
Michael Craig-, Kt., CBE, TD
Cooper, Gen. Sir George Leslie
Conroy, GCB, MC
Cooper, Sir Louis Jacques Blom-,
Kt., QC
Cooper, Sir Patrick Graham Astley,
Bt. (1821)
Cooper, Sir Richard Powell, Bt.
(1905)

Cooper, Maj.-Gen. Sir Simon
Christie, KCVO
Cooper, Sir William Daniel Charles,
Bt. (1863)
Coote, Sir Christopher John, Bt.,
Premier Baronet of Ireland (I. 1621)
Copas, Most Revd Virgil, KBE, DD
Cope, Rt. Hon. Sir John Ambrose, Kt.,
MP
Copisarow, Sir Alcon Charles, Kt.
Corbett, Maj.-Gen. Sir Robert John
Swan, KCVO, CB
Corby, Sir (Frederick) Brian, Kt.
Corfield, Rt. Hon. Sir Frederick
Vernon, Kt., QC
Corfield, Sir Kenneth George, Kt.,
FEng.
Corley, Sir Kenneth Sholl Ferrand,
Kt.
Cormack, Sir Magnus Cameron, KBE
Cormack, Sir Patrick Thomas, Kt.,
MP
Corness, Sir Colin Ross, Kt.
Cornford, Sir (Edward) Clifford, KCB,
FEng.
Cornforth, Sir John Warcup, Kt., CBE,
D.Phil., FRS
Corry, Sir William James, Bt. (1885)
Cortazzi, Sir (Henry Arthur) Hugh,
GCMG
Cory, Sir (Clinton Charles) Donald,
Bt. (1919)
Cossons, Sir Neil, Kt., OBE
Cotter, Lt.-Col. Sir Delaval James
Alfred, Bt., DSO (I. 1763)
Cotterell, Sir John Henry Geers, Bt.
(1805)
Cotton, Sir John Richard, KCMG, OBE
Cotton, Hon. Sir Robert Carrington,
KCMG
Cottrell, Sir Alan Howard, Kt., ph.D.,
FRS, FEng.
†Cotts, Sir Richard Crichton
Mitchell, Bt. (1921)
Coulson, Sir John Eltringham, KCMG
Couper, Sir (Robert) Nicholas
(Oliver), Bt. (1841)
Court, Hon. Sir Charles Walter
Michael, KCMG, OBE
Cousins, Air Marshal Sir David, KCB,
AFC
Coutts, Sir David Burdett Money-,
KCVO
Couzens, Sir Kenneth Edward, KCB
Covacevich, Sir (Anthony) Thomas,
Kt., DFC
Coward, Vice-Adm. Sir John Francis,
KCB, DSO
Cowdrey, Sir (Michael) Colin, Kt.,
CBE
Cowen, Rt. Hon. Prof. Sir Zelman,
GCMG, GCVO, QC
Cowie, Sir Thomas (Tom), Kt., OBE
Cowperthwaite, Sir John James, KBE,
CMG
Cox, Sir Alan George, Kt., CBE
Cox, Prof. Sir David Roxbee, Kt., FRS
Cox, Sir Geoffrey Sandford, Kt., CBE
Cox, Vice-Adm. Sir John Michael
Holland, KCB

Cradock, Rt. Hon. Sir Percy, GCMG
Craig, Sir (Albert) James
(Macqueen), GCMG
Craufurd, Sir Robert James, Bt.
(1781)
Craven, Sir John Anthony, Kt.
Craven, Air Marshal Sir Robert
Edward, KBE, CB, DFC
Crawford, Prof. Sir Frederick
William, Kt., FEng.
Crawford, Sir (Robert) Stewart,
GCMG, CVO
Crawford, Vice-Adm. Sir William
Godfrey, KBE, CB, DSC
Crawshay, Col. Sir William Robert,
Kt., DSO, ERD, TD
Creagh, Maj.-Gen. Sir (Kilner)
Rupert Brazier-, KBE, CB, DSO
Cresswell, Hon. Sir Peter John, Kt.
Crill, Sir Peter Leslie, KBE
Cripps, Sir Cyril Humphrey, Kt.
Crisp, Sir (John) Peter, Bt. (1913)
Critchett, Sir Ian (George Lorraine),
Bt. (1908)
Critchley, Sir Julian Michael
Gordon, Kt., MP
Croft, Sir Owen Glendower, Bt.
(1671)
Croft, Sir Thomas Stephen Hutton,
Bt. (1818)
†Crofton, Sir Hugh Denis, Bt. (1801)
Crofton, Prof. Sir John Wenman, Kt.
Crofton, Sir Malby Sturges, Bt.
(1838)
Croker, Sir Walter Russell, KBE
Crookenden, Lt.-Gen. Sir Napier,
KCB, DSO, OBE
Cross, Air Chief Marshal Sir Kenneth
Brian Boyd, KCB, CBE, DSO, DFC
Crossland, Prof. Sir Bernard, Kt., CBE,
FEng.
Crossland, Sir Leonard, Kt.
Crossley, Sir Nicholas John, Bt.
(1909)
Crouch, Sir David Lance, Kt.
Cruthers, Sir James Winter, Kt.
Cubbon, Sir Brian Crossland, GCB
Cubitt, Sir Hugh Guy, Kt., CBE
Cullen, Sir (Edward) John, Kt., F.ENG.
Cumming, Sir William Gordon
Gordon-, Bt. (1804)
Cuninghame, Sir John Christopher
Foggo Montgomery-, Bt. (NS
1672)
†Cuninghame, Sir William Henry
Fairlie-, Bt. (s. 1630)
Cunliffe, Sir David Ellis, Bt. (1759)
Cunningham, Sir Charles Craik, GCB,
KBE, CVO
Cunningham, Lt.-Gen. Sir Hugh
Patrick, KBE
Cunynghame, Sir Andrew David
Francis, Bt. (s. 1702)
Curle, Sir John Noel Ormiston,
KCVO, CMG
Curran, Sir Samuel Crowe, Kt., D.SC.,
ph.D., FRS, FRSE, FEng.
†Currie, Sir Donald Scott, Bt. (1847)
Currie, Sir Neil Smith, Kt., CBE
Curtis, Sir Barry John, Kt.

Dowson, Sir Philip Manning, Kt.,
CBE, ARA
Doyle, Sir Reginald Derek Henry,
Kt., CBE
D'Oyly, Sir Nigel Hadley Miller, Bt.
(1663)
Drake, Sir (Arthur) Eric (Courtney),
Kt., CBE
Drake, Hon. Sir (Frederick) Maurice,
Kt., DFC
Dreyer, Adm. Sir Desmond Parry,
GCB, CBE, DSC
Drinkwater, Sir John Muir, Kt., QC
Driver, Sir Antony Victor, Kt.
Driver, Sir Eric William, Kt.
Drummond, Sir John Richard Gray,
Kt., CBE
Drury, Sir (Victor William) Michael,
Kt., OBE
Dryden, Sir John Stephen Gyles, Bt.
(1733 and 1795)
du Cann, Rt. Hon. Sir Edward Dillon
Lott, KBE
Duckworth, Maj. Sir Richard Dyce,
Bt. (1909)
du Cros, Sir Claude Philip Arthur
Mallet, Bt. (1916)
Duff, Rt. Hon. Sir (Arthur) Antony,
GCMG, CVO, DSO, DSC
Duffell, Lt.-Gen. Sir Peter Royson,
KCB, CBE, MC
Duffus, Hon. Sir William Algernon
Holwell, Kt.
Duffy, Sir (Albert) (Edward) Patrick,
Kt., ph.D.
Dugdale, Sir William Stratford, Bt.,
MC (1936)
Dunbar, Sir Archibald Ranulph, Bt.
(s. 1700)
Dunbar, Sir David Hope-, Bt. (s.
1664)
Dunbar, Sir Drummond Cospatrick
Ninian, Bt., MC (s. 1698)
Dunbar, Sir James Michael, Bt. (s.
1694)
Dunbar of Hempriggs, Dame
Maureen Daisy Helen (Lady
Dunbar of Hempriggs), Btss. (s.
1706)
Duncan, Sir James Blair, Kt.
Duncombe, Sir Philip Digby
Pauncefort-, Bt. (1859)
Dunham, Sir Kingsley Charles, Kt.,
ph.D., FRS, FRSE, FEng.
Dunlop, Sir Thomas, Bt. (1916)
Dunlop, Sir William Norman
Gough, Kt.
Dunn, Air Marshal Sir Eric Clive,
KBE, CB, BEM
Dunn, Air Marshal Sir Patrick
Hunter, KBE, CB, DFC
Dunn, Rt. Hon. Sir Robin Horace
Walford, Kt., MC
Dunne, Sir Thomas Raymond, KCVO
Dunnett, Sir Alastair MacTavish, Kt.
Dunnett, Sir (Ludovic) James, GCB,
CMG
Dunning, Sir Simon William Patrick,
Bt. (1930)

Dunphie, Maj.-Gen. Sir Charles
Anderson Lane, Kt., CB, CBE, DSO
Dunstan, Lt.-Gen. Sir Donald
Beaumont, KBE, CB
†Duntze, Sir Daniel Evans, Bt. (1774)
Dupre, Sir Tumun, Kt., MBE
Dupree, Sir Peter, Bt. (1921)
Durand, Sir Edward Alan
Christopher David Percy, Bt.
(1892)
Durant, Sir (Robert) Anthony
(Bevis), Kt., MP
Durham, Sir Kenneth, Kt.
Durie, Sir Alexander Charles, Kt.,
CBE
Durkin, Air Marshal Sir Herbert, KBE,
CB
Durrant, Sir William Alexander
Estridge, Bt. (1784)
Duthie, Prof. Sir Herbert Livingston,
Kt.
Duthie, Sir Robert Grieve (Robin),
Kt., CBE
Duxbury, Air Marshal Sir (John)
Barry, KCB, CBE
Dyer, Prof. Sir (Henry) Peter
(Francis) Swinnerton-, Bt., KBE, FRS
(1678)
Dyke, Sir David William Hart, Bt.
(1677)
Dyson, Hon. Sir John Anthony, Kt.
Earle, Sir (Hardman) George
(Algernon), Bt. (1869)
East, Sir (Lewis) Ronald, Kt., CBE
Easton, Sir Robert William Simpson,
Kt., CBE
Eaton, Adm. Sir Kenneth John, GBE,
KCB
Eberle, Adm. Sir James Henry Fuller,
GCB
Ebrahim, Sir (Mahomed)
Currimbhoy, Bt. (1910)
Eccles, Sir John Carew, Kt., D.phil.,
FRS
Echlin, Sir Norman David Fenton,
Bt. (I. 1721)
Eckersley, Sir Donald Payze, Kt., OBE
Edge, Capt. Sir (Philip) Malcolm,
KCVO
†Edge, Sir William, Bt. (1937)
Edmonstone, Sir Archibald Bruce
Charles, Bt. (1774)
Edwardes, Sir Michael Owen, Kt.
Edwards, Sir Christopher John
Churchill, Bt. (1866)
Edwards, Sir George Robert, Kt., OM,
CBE, FRS, FEng.
Edwards, Sir (John) Clive
(Leighton), Bt. (1921)
Edwards, Sir Llewellyn Roy, Kt.
Edwards, Prof. Sir Samuel Frederick,
Kt., FRS
Egan, Sir John Leopold, Kt.
Egerton, Sir John Alfred Roy, Kt.
Egerton, Sir (Philip) John (Caledon)
Grey-, Bt. (1617)
Egerton, Sir Seymour John Louis,
GCVO
Egerton, Sir Stephen Loftus, KCMG

Eggleston, Hon. Sir Richard Moulton,
Kt.
Eichelbaum, Rt. Hon. Sir Thomas,
GBE
Eliott of Stobs, Sir Charles Joseph
Alexander, Bt. (s. 1666)
Ellerton, Sir Geoffrey James, Kt.,
CMG, MBE
Elliot, Sir Gerald Henry, Kt.
Elliott, Sir Clive Christopher Hugh,
Bt. (1917)
Elliott, Sir David Murray, KCMG, CB
Elliott, Prof. Sir John Huxtable, Kt.,
FBA
Elliott, Sir Randal Forbes, KBE
Elliott, Prof. Sir Roger James, Kt., FRS
Elliott, Sir Ronald Stuart, Kt.
Ellis, Sir John Rogers, Kt., MBE, MD,
FRCP
Ellis, Sir Ronald, Kt., FEng.
Ellison, Col. Sir Ralph Harry Carr-,
Kt., TD
Elphinstone, Sir John, Bt. (s. 1701)
Elphinstone, Sir (Maurice) Douglas
(Warburton), Bt., TD (1816)
Elton, Sir Arnold, Kt., CBE
Elton, Sir Charles Abraham
Grierson, Bt. (1717)
Elwes, Sir Jeremy Vernon, Kt., CBE
Elwood, Sir Brian George Conway,
Kt., CBE
Elworthy, Sir Peter Herbert, Kt.
Elyan, Sir (Isadore) Victor, Kt.
Emery, Rt. Hon. Sir Peter Frank
Hannibal, Kt., MP
Empson, Adm. Sir (Leslie) Derek,
GBE, KCB
Engineer, Sir Noshirwan Phirozshah,
Kt.
Engle, Sir George Lawrence Jose,
KCB, QC
English, Sir Cyril Rupert, Kt.
English, Sir David, Kt.
English, Sir Terence Alexander
Hawthorne, KBE, FRCS
Epstein, Prof. Sir (Michael) Anthony,
Kt., CBE, FRS
Ereaut, Sir (Herbert) Frank Cobbold,
Kt.
Errington, Col. Sir Geoffrey
Frederick, Bt. (1963)
Errington, Sir Lancelot, KCB
Erskine, Sir (Thomas) David, Bt.
(1821)
Esmonde, Sir Thomas Francis
Grattan, Bt. (I. 1629)
Espie, Sir Frank Fletcher, Kt., OBE
Esplen, Sir John Graham, Bt. (1921)
Eustace, Sir Joseph Lambert, GCMG,
GCVO
Evans, Sir Anthony Adney, Bt. (1920)
Evans, Rt. Hon. Sir Anthony Howell
Meurig, Kt., RD
Evans, Air Chief Marshal Sir David
George, GCB, CBE
Evans, Air Chief Marshal Sir David
Parry-, GCB, CBE
Evans, Hon. Sir Haydn Tudor, Kt.
Evans, Sir Richard Harry, Kt., CBE

Evans, Sir Richard Mark, KCMG, KCVO

Evans, Sir Robert, Kt., CBE, FEng.

Evans, *Very Revd (Thomas) Eric*, KCVO

Evans, Sir (William) Vincent (John), GCMG, MBE, QC

Eveleigh, *Rt. Hon.* Sir Edward Walter, Kt., ERD

Everard, Sir Robin Charles, Bt. (1911)

Everson, Sir Frederick Charles, KCMG

Every, Sir Henry John Michael, Bt. (1641)

Ewans, Sir Martin Kenneth, KCMG

†Ewart, Sir William Michael, Bt. (1887)

Ewbank, *Hon.* Sir Anthony Bruce, Kt.

Ewin, Sir (David) Ernest Thomas Floyd, Kt., OBE, LVO

Ewing, *Vice-Adm.* Sir (Robert) Alastair, KBE, CB, DSC

Ewing, Sir Ronald Archibald Orr-, Bt. (1886)

Eyre, Sir Graham Newman, Kt., QC

Eyre, *Maj.-Gen.* Sir James Ainsworth Campden Gabriel, KCVO, CBE

Eyre, Sir Reginald Edwin, Kt.

Faber, Sir Richard Stanley, KCVO, CMG

Fadahunsi, Sir Joseph Odeleye, KCMG

Fagge, Sir John William Frederick, Bt. (1660)

Fairbairn, *Hon.* Sir David Eric, KBE, DFC

Fairbairn, Sir (James) Brooke, Bt. (1869)

Fairclough, Sir John Whitaker, Kt., FEng.

Fairgrieve, Sir (Thomas) Russell, Kt., CBE, TD

Fairhall, *Hon.* Sir Allen, KBE

Fairweather, Sir Patrick Stanislaus, KCMG

Falconer, *Hon.* Sir Douglas William, Kt., MBE

Falk, Sir Roger Salis, Kt., OBE

Falkiner, Sir Edmond Charles, Bt. (I. 1778)

Fall, Sir Brian James Proetel, GCVO, KCMG

Falle, Sir Samuel, KCMG, KCVO, DSC

Fareed, Sir Djamil Sheik, Kt.

Farmer, Sir (Lovedin) George Thomas, Kt.

Farndale, *Gen.* Sir Martin Baker, KCB

Farquhar, Sir Michael Fitzroy Henry, Bt. (1796)

Farquharson, *Rt. Hon.* Sir Donald Henry, Kt.

Farquharson, Sir James Robbie, KBE

Farr, Sir John Arnold, Kt.

Farrer, Sir (Charles) Matthew, GCVO

Farrington, Sir Henry Francis Colden, Bt. (1818)

Fat, Sir (Maxime) Edouard (Lim Man) Lim, Kt.

Faulkner, Sir (James) Dennis (Compton), Kt., CBE, VRD

Fawcus, Sir (Robert) Peter, KBE, CMG

Fawkes, Sir Randol Francis, Kt.

Fay, Sir (Humphrey) Michael Gerard, Kt.

Fayrer, Sir John Lang Macpherson, Bt. (1896)

Fearn, Sir (Patrick) Robin, KCMG

Feilden, Sir Bernard Melchior, Kt., CBE

Feilden, Sir Henry Wemyss, Bt., (1846)

Fell, Sir Anthony, Kt.

Fell, Sir David, KCB

Fellowes, *Rt. Hon.* Sir Robert, GCVO, KCB

Fenn, Sir Nicholas Maxted, GCMG

Fennell, *Hon.* Sir (John) Desmond Augustine, Kt., OBE

Fennessy, Sir Edward, Kt., CBE

Ferguson, Sir Ian Edward Johnson-, Bt. (1906)

Fergusson of Kilkerran, Sir Charles, Bt. (s. 1703)

Fergusson, Sir Ewan Alastair John, GCMG, GCVO

Fergusson, Sir James Herbert Hamilton Colyer-, Bt. (1866)

Feroze, Sir Rustam Moolan, Kt., FRCS

Ferris, *Hon.* Sir Francis Mursell, Kt., TD

ffolkes, Sir Robert Francis Alexander, Bt, OBE (1774)

Field, Sir Malcolm David, Kt.

Fielding, Sir Colin Cunningham, Kt., CB

Fielding, Sir Leslie, KCMG

Fiennes, Sir Ranulph Twisleton-Wykeham-, Bt., OBE (1916)

Figg, Sir Leonard Clifford William, KCMG

Figgess, Sir John George, KBE, CMG

Figgis, Sir Anthony St John Howard, KCVO, CMG

Figures, Sir Colin Frederick, KCMG, OBE

Fingland, Sir Stanley James Gunn, KCMG

Finlay, Sir David Ronald James Bell, Bt. (1964)

Firth, *Prof.* Sir Raymond William, Kt., PH.D., FBA

Fish, Sir Hugh, Kt., CBE

Fisher, Sir George Read, Kt., CMG

Fisher, *Hon.* Sir Henry Arthur Pears, Kt.

Fisher, Sir Nigel Thomas Loveridge, Kt., MC

Fison, Sir (Richard) Guy, Bt., DSC (1905)

†Fitzgerald, *Revd* (Sir) Daniel Patrick, Bt. (1903)

FitzGerald, Sir George Peter Maurice, Bt., MC (*The Knight of Kerry*) (1880)

FitzHerbert, Sir Richard Ranulph, Bt. (1784)

Fitzpatrick, *Gen.* Sir (Geoffrey Richard) Desmond, GCB, DSO, MBE, MC

Fitzpatrick, *Air Marshal* Sir John Bernard, KBE, CB

Flanagan, Sir James Bernard, Kt., CBE

Fletcher, Sir Henry Egerton Aubrey-, Bt. (1782)

Fletcher, Sir James Muir Cameron, Kt.

Fletcher, Sir Leslie, Kt., DSC

Fletcher, *Air Chief Marshal* Sir Peter Carteret, KCB, OBE, DFC, AFC

Floissac, *Hon.* Sir Vincent Frederick, Kt., CMG, OBE, QC

Floyd, Sir Giles Henry Charles, Bt. (1816)

Foley, *Lt.-Gen.* Sir John Paul, KCB, OBE, MC

Foley, Sir (Thomas John) Noel, Kt., CBE

Follett, *Prof.* Sir Brian Keith, Kt., FRS

Foot, Sir Geoffrey James, Kt.

Foots, Sir James William, Kt.

Forbes, *Hon.* Sir Alastair Granville, Kt.

Forbes, *Maj.* Sir Hamish Stewart, Bt., MBE, MC (1823)

Forbes of Craigievar, Sir John Alexander Cumnock, Bt. (s. 1630)

Forbes, *Vice-Adm.* Sir John Morrison, KCB

Forbes, *Hon.* Sir Thayne John, Kt.

†Forbes of Pitsligo, Sir William Daniel Stuart-, Bt. (s. 1626)

Ford, Sir Andrew Russell, Bt. (1929)

Ford, Sir David Robert, KBE, LVO, OBE

Ford, *Maj.* Sir Edward William Spencer, KCB, KCVO

Ford, *Air Marshal* Sir Geoffrey Harold, KBE, CB, FEng.

Ford, *Prof.* Sir Hugh, Kt., FRS, FEng.

Ford, Sir James Anson St Clair-, Bt. (1793)

Ford, Sir John Archibald, KCMG, MC

Ford, Sir Richard Brinsley, Kt., CBE

Ford, *Gen.* Sir Robert Cyril, GCB, CBE

Foreman, Sir Philip Frank, Kt., CBE, FEng.

Forman, Sir John Denis, Kt., OBE

Forrest, *Prof.* Sir (Andrew) Patrick (McEwen), Kt.

Forrest, *Rear-Adm.* Sir Ronald Stephen, KCVO

Forster, Sir Archibald William, Kt., FEng.

Forster, Sir Oliver Grantham, KCMG, LVO

Forte, Hon. Sir Rocco John Vincent, Kt.

Forwood, Sir Dudley Richard, Bt. (1895)

Foster, *Prof.* Sir Christopher David, Kt.

Foster, Sir John Gregory, Bt. (1930)

Foster, Sir Norman Robert, Kt.

Foster, Sir Robert Sidney, GCMG, KCVO

Foulis, Sir Ian Primrose Liston-, Bt. (s. 1634)

Foulkes, Sir Nigel Gordon, Kt.

Fountain, *Hon.* Sir Cyril Stanley Smith, Kt.

Fowden, Sir Leslie, Kt., FRS
Fowke, Sir David Frederick
Gustavus, Bt. (1814)
Fowler, Sir (Edward) Michael
Coulson, Kt.
Fowler, Rt. Hon. Sir (Peter) Norman,
Kt., MP
Fox, Sir (Henry) Murray, GBE
Fox, Rt. Hon. Sir (John) Marcus, Kt.,
MBE, MP
Fox, Rt. Hon. Sir Michael John, Kt.
Fox, Sir Paul Leonard, Kt., CBE
France, Sir Arnold William, GCB
France, Sir Christopher Walter, GCB
France, Sir Joseph Nathaniel, KCMG,
CBE
Francis, Sir Horace William
Alexander, Kt., CBE, FEng.
Frank, Sir Douglas George Horace,
Kt., QC
Frank, Sir (Frederick) Charles, Kt.,
OBE, FRS
Frank, Sir Robert Andrew, Bt. (1920)
Frankel, Sir Otto Herzberg, Kt., D.SC.,
FRS
Franklin, Sir Michael David Milroy,
KCB, CMG
Franks, Sir Arthur Temple, KCMG
Fraser, Sir Angus McKay, KCB, TD
Fraser, Sir Charles Annand, KCVO
Fraser, Gen. Sir David William, GCB,
OBE
Fraser, Air Marshal Revd Sir (Henry)
Paterson, KBE, CB, AFC
Fraser, Sir Ian, Kt., DSO, OBE
Fraser, Sir Ian James, Kt., CBE, MC
Fraser, Sir (James) Campbell, Kt.
Fraser, Prof. Sir James David, Bt.
(1943)
Fraser, Sir William Kerr, GCB
Frederick, Sir Charles Boscawen, Bt.
(1723)
Freeland, Sir John Redvers, KCMG
Freeman, Sir James Robin, Bt. (1945)
Freeman, Sir Ralph, Kt., CVO, CBE,
FEng.
Freer, Air Chief Marshal Sir Robert
William George, GBE, KCB
Freeth, Hon. Sir Gordon, KBE
French, Hon. Sir Christopher James
Saunders, Kt.
Frere, Vice-Adm. Sir Richard Tobias,
KCB
Fretwell, Sir (Major) John (Emsley),
GCMG
Freud, Sir Clement Raphael, Kt.
Froggatt, Sir Leslie Trevor, Kt.
Froggatt, Sir Peter, Kt.
Frossard, Sir Charles Keith, KBE
Frost, Sir David Paradine, Kt., OBE
Frost, Hon. Sir (Thomas) Sydney, Kt.
Fry, Sir Peter Derek, Kt., MP
Fry, Hon. Sir William Gordon, Kt.
Fryberg, Sir Abraham, Kt., MBE
Fuchs, Sir Vivian Ernest, Kt., PH.D.
Fuller, Hon. Sir John Bryan Munro,
Kt.
Fuller, Sir John William Fleetwood,
Bt. (1910)

Fung, Hon. Sir Kenneth Ping-Fan,
Kt., CBE
Furness, Sir Stephen Roberts, Bt.
(1913)
Gadsden, Sir Peter Drury
Haggerston, GBE, FEng.
Gage, Hon. Sir William Marcus, Kt.
Gainsford, Sir Ian Derek, Kt., DDS
Gairy, Rt. Hon. Sir Eric Matthew, Kt.
Gaius, Rt. Revd Saimon, KBE
Gallwey, Sir Philip Frankland
Payne-, Bt. (1812)
Gam, Rt. Revd Sir Getake, KBE
Gamble, Sir David Hugh Norman,
Bt. (1897)
Garden, Air Marshal Sir Timothy,
KCB
Gardiner, Sir George Arthur, Kt., MP
Gardner, Sir Douglas Bruce Bruce-,
Bt. (1945)
Gardner, Sir Edward Lucas, Kt., QC
Garland, Hon. Sir Patrick Neville, Kt.
Garland, Hon. Sir Ransley Victor, KBE
Garlick, Sir John, KCB
Garner, Sir Anthony Stuart, Kt.
Garnier, Rear-Adm. Sir John, KCVO,
CBE
Garrick, Sir Ronald, Kt., CBE, FEng.
Garrioch, Sir (William) Henry, Kt.
Garrod, Lt.-Gen. Sir (John) Martin
Carruthers, KCB, OBE
Garthwaite, Sir (William) Mark
(Charles), Bt. (1919)
Gaskell, Sir Richard Kennedy
Harvey, Kt.
Gatehouse, Hon. Sir Robert
Alexander, Kt.
Geddes, Sir (Anthony) Reay
(Mackay), KBE
George, Sir Arthur Thomas, Kt.
George, Sir Richard William, Kt.
Gerken, Vice-Adm. Sir Robert
William Frank, KCB, CBE
Gery, Sir Robert Lucian Wade-,
KCMG, KCVO
Gethin, Sir Richard Joseph St
Lawrence, Bt. (I. 1665)
Ghurburrun, Sir Rabindrah, Kt.
Gibb, Sir Francis Ross (Frank), Kt.,
CBE, FEng.
Gibbings, Sir Peter Walter, Kt.
Gibbon, Gen. Sir John Houghton,
GCB, OBE
Gibbons, Sir (John) David, KBE
Gibbons, Sir William Edward Doran,
Bt. (1752)
Gibbs, Hon. Sir Eustace Hubert
Beilby, KCVO, CMG
Gibbs, Rt. Hon. Sir Harry Talbot,
GCMG, KBE
Gibbs, Sir Roger Geoffrey, Kt.
Gibbs, Field Marshal Sir Roland
Christopher, GCB, CBE, DSO, MC
†Gibson, Revd Sir Christopher
Herbert, Bt. (1931)
Gibson, Revd Sir David, Bt. (1926)
Gibson, Vice-Adm. Sir Donald
Cameron Ernest Forbes, KCB, DSC
Gibson, Rt. Hon. Sir Peter Leslie, Kt.
Gibson, Rt. Hon. Sir Ralph Brian, Kt.

Giddings, Air Marshal Sir (Kenneth
Charles) Michael, KCB, OBE, DFC,
AFC
Gielgud, Sir (Arthur) John, Kt., CH
Giffard, Sir (Charles) Sydney
(Rycroft), KCMG
Gilbert, Air Chief Marshal Sir Joseph
Alfred, KCB, CBE
Gilbert, Sir Martin John, Kt., CBE
†Gilbey, Sir Walter Gavin, Bt. (1893)
Giles, Rear-Adm. Sir Morgan Charles
Morgan-, Kt., DSO, OBE, GM
Gill, Sir Anthony Keith, Kt., FEng.
Gillett, Sir Robin Danvers Penrose,
Bt., GBE, RD (1959)
Gilmour, Col. Sir Allan Macdonald,
KCVO, OBE, MC
Gilmour, Sir John Edward, Bt., DSO,
TD (1897)
Gina, Sir Lloyd Maepeza, KBE
Gingell, Air Chief Marshal Sir John,
GBE, KCB, KCVO
Girolami, Sir Paul, Kt.
Girvan, Hon. Sir (Frederick) Paul, Kt.
Gladstone, Sir (Erskine) William, Bt.
(1846)
Glasspole, Sir Florizel Augustus,
GCMG, GCVO
Glen, Sir Alexander Richard, KBE,
DSC
Glenn, Sir (Joseph Robert)
Archibald, Kt., OBE
Glidewell, Rt. Hon. Sir Iain Derek
Laing, Kt.
Glock, Sir William Frederick, Kt.,
CBE
Glover, Gen. Sir James Malcolm,
KCB, MBE
Glover, Sir Victor Joseph Patrick, Kt.
Glyn, Sir Alan, Kt., ERD
Glyn, Sir Anthony Geoffrey Leo
Simon, Bt. (1927)
Glyn, Sir Richard Lindsay, Bt. (1759
and 1800)
Goad, Sir (Edward) Colin (Viner),
KCMG
Godber, Sir George Edward, GCB, DM
Goff, Sir Robert (William) Davis-,
Bt. (1905)
Gold, Sir Arthur Abraham, Kt., CBE
Gold, Sir Joseph, Kt.
Goldberg, Prof. Sir Abraham, Kt., MD,
D.SC., FRCP
Goldberg, Prof. Sir David Paul
Brandes, Kt.
Goldman, Sir Samuel, KCB
Goldsmith, Sir James Michael, Kt.
Gombrich, Prof. Sir Ernst Hans Josef,
Kt., OM, CBE, PH.D., FBA, FSA
Gooch, Sir (Richard) John Sherlock,
Bt. (1746)
Gooch, Sir Trevor Sherlock (Sir
Peter), Bt. (1866)
Goodall, Sir (Arthur) David
Saunders, GCMG
Goodenough, Sir Richard Edmund,
Bt. (1943)
Goodhart, Sir Philip Carter, Kt.
Goodhart, Sir Robert Anthony
Gordon, Bt. (1911)

Goodhart, Sir William Howard, Kt., QC
Goodhew, Sir Victor Henry, Kt.
Goodison, Sir Alan Clowes, KCMG
Goodison, Sir Nicholas Proctor, Kt.
Goodman, Sir Patrick Ledger, Kt., CBE
Goodson, Sir Mark Weston Lassam, Bt. (1922)
Goodwin, Sir Matthew Dean, Kt., CBE
Goold, Sir George Leonard, Bt. (1801)
Gordon, Sir Alexander John, Kt., CBE
Gordon, Sir Andrew Cosmo Lewis Duff-, Bt. (1813)
Gordon, Sir Charles Addison Somerville Snowden, KCB
Gordon, Sir Keith Lyndell, Kt., CMG
Gordon, Sir (Lionel) Eldred (Peter) Smith-, Bt. (1838)
Gordon, Sir Robert James, Bt. (s. 1706)
Gordon, Sir Sidney Samuel, Kt., CBE
Gordon Lennox, Lord Nicholas Charles, KCMG, KCVO
†Gore, Sir Nigel Hugh St George, Bt. (I. 1622)
Gorham, Sir Richard Masters, Kt., CBE, DFC
Goring, Sir William Burton Nigel, Bt. (1627)
Gorst, Sir John Michael, Kt., MP
Gorton, Rt. Hon. Sir John Grey, GCMG, CH
Goschen, Sir Edward Christian, Bt., DSO (1916)
Gosling, Sir (Frederick) Donald, Kt.
Goswell, Sir Brian Lawrence, Kt.
Goulden, Sir (Peter) John, KCMG
Goulding, Sir (Ernest) Irvine, Kt.
Goulding, Sir (William) Lingard Walter, Bt. (1904)
Gourlay, Gen. Sir (Basil) Ian (Spencer), KCB, OBE, MC, RM
Gourlay, Sir Simon Alexander, Kt.
Govan, Sir Lawrence Herbert, Kt.
Gow, Gen. Sir (James) Michael, GCB
Gowans, Sir James Learmonth, Kt., CBE, FRCP, FRS
Graaff, Sir de Villiers, Bt., MBE (1911)
Grabham, Sir Anthony Henry, Kt.
Graham, Sir Alexander Michael, GBE
Graham, Sir Charles Spencer Richard, Bt. (1783)
Graham, Sir James Bellingham, Bt. (1662)
Graham, Sir James Thompson, Kt., CMG
Graham, Sir John Alexander Noble, Bt., GCMG (1906)
Graham, Sir John Moodie, Bt. (1964)
Graham, Sir Norman William, Kt., CB
Graham, Sir Peter, KCB, QC
Graham, Sir Peter Alfred, Kt., OBE
Graham, Lt.-Gen. Sir Peter Walter, KCB, CBE
†Graham, Sir Ralph Stuart, Bt. (1629)

Graham, Hon. Sir Samuel Horatio, Kt., CMG, OBE
Grandy, Marshal of the Royal Air Force Sir John, GCB, GCVO, KBE, DSO
Grant, Sir Archibald, Bt. (s. 1705)
Grant, Sir Clifford, Kt.
Grant, Sir (John) Anthony, Kt., MP
Grant, Sir (Matthew) Alistair, Kt.
Grant, Sir Patrick Alexander Benedict, Bt. (s. 1688)
Gray, Sir John Archibald Browne, Kt., SC.D., FRS
Gray, Vice-Adm. Sir John Michael Dudgeon, KBE, CB
Gray, Sir John Walton David, KBE, CMG
Gray, Lt.-Gen. Sir Michael Stuart, KCB, OBE
Gray, Sir Robert McDowall (Robin), Kt.
Gray, Sir William Hume, Bt. (1917)
Gray, Sir William Stevenson, Kt.
Graydon, Air Chief Marshal Sir Michael James, GCB, CBE
Grayson, Sir Jeremy Brian Vincent Harrington, Bt. (1922)
Green, Sir Allan David, KCB, QC
Green, Hon. Sir Guy Stephen Montague, KBE
Green, Sir Kenneth, Kt.
Green, Sir Owen Whitley, Kt.
†Green, Sir Stephen Lycett, Bt., TD (1886)
Greenaway, Sir John Michael Burdick, Bt. (1933)
Greenborough, Sir John, KBE
Greenbury, Sir Richard, Kt.
Greene, Sir (John) Brian Massy-, Kt.
Greengross, Sir Alan David, Kt.
Greening, Rear-Adm. Sir Paul Woollven, GCVO
Greenwell, Sir Edward Bernard, Bt. (1906)
Gregson, Sir Peter Lewis, GCB
Greig, Sir (Henry Louis) Carron, KCVO, CBE
Grenside, Sir John Peter, Kt., CBE
Grey, Sir Anthony Dysart, Bt. (1814)
Grierson, Sir Michael John Bewes, Bt. (s. 1685)
Grierson, Sir Ronald Hugh, Kt.
Griffin, Adm. Sir Anthony Templer Frederick Griffith, GCB
Griffin, Maj. Sir (Arthur) John (Stewart), KCVO
Griffin, Sir (Charles) David, Kt., CBE
Griffiths, Sir Eldon Wylie, Kt.
Griffiths, Sir John Norton-, Bt. (1922)
Grimwade, Sir Andrew Sheppard, Kt., KBE
Grindrod, Most Revd John Basil Rowland, KBE
Grinstead, Sir Stanley Gordon, Kt.
Grose, Vice-Adm. Sir Alan, KBE
Grotrian, Sir Philip Christian Brent, Bt. (1934)
Grove, Sir Charles Gerald, Bt. (1874)
Grove, Sir Edmund Frank, KCVO
Grugeon, Sir John Drury, Kt.

Grylls, Sir (William) Michael (John), Kt., MP
Guinness, Sir Alec, Kt., CH, CBE
Guinness, Sir Howard Christian Sheldon, Kt., VRD
Guinness, Sir Kenelm Ernest Lee, Bt. (1867)
Guise, Sir John Grant, Bt. (1783)
Gujadhur, Sir Radhamohun, Kt., CMG
Gull, Sir Rupert William Cameron, Bt. (1872)
Gumbs, Sir Emile Rudolph, Kt.
Gunn, Prof. Sir John Currie, Kt., CBE
Gunn, Sir Robert Norman, Kt.
Gunn, Sir William Archer, KBE, CMG
†Gunning, Sir Charles Theodore, Bt. (1778)
Gunston, Sir John Wellesley, Bt. (1938)
Gurdon, Prof. Sir John Bertrand, Kt., D.phil., FRS
Guthrie, Gen. Sir Charles Ronald Llewelyn, GCB, LVO, OBE
Guthrie, Sir Malcolm Connop, Bt., (1936)
Guy, Gen. Sir Roland Kelvin, GCB, CBE, DSO
Habakkuk, Sir John Hrothgar, Kt., FBA
Hackett, Gen. Sir John Winthrop, GCB, CBE, DSO, MC
Hadfield, Sir Ronald, Kt., QPM
Hadlee, Sir Richard John, Kt., MBE
Hadley, Sir Leonard Albert, Kt.
Hague, Prof. Sir Douglas Chalmers, Kt., CBE
Halberg, Sir Murray Gordon, Kt., MBE
Hale, Prof. Sir John Rigby, Kt.
Hall, Sir Arnold Alexander, Kt., FRS, FEng.
Hall, Sir Basil Brodribb, KCB, MC, TD
Hall, Air Marshal Sir Donald Percy, KCB, CBE, AFC
Hall, Sir Douglas Basil, Bt., KCMG (s. 1687)
Hall, Sir Ernest, Kt., OBE
Hall, Sir (Frederick) John (Frank), Bt. (1923)
Hall, Sir John, Kt.
Hall, Sir John Bernard, Bt. (1919)
Hall, Sir Peter Edward, KBE, CMG
Hall, Sir Peter Reginald Frederick, Kt., CBE
Hall, Sir Robert de Zouche, KCMG
Hall, Brig. Sir William Henry, KBE, DSO, ED
Halliday, Vice-Adm. Sir Roy William, KBE, DSC
Hallinan, Sir (Adrian) Lincoln, Kt.
Halpern, Sir Ralph Mark, Kt.
Halsey, Revd Sir John Walter Brooke, Bt. (1920)
Halstead, Sir Ronald, Kt., CBE
Ham, Sir David Kenneth Rowe-, GBE
Hambling, Sir (Herbert) Hugh, Bt. (1924)
Hamburger, Sir Sidney Cyril, Kt., CBE

Hamer, *Hon.* Sir Rupert James,
KCMG, ED
Hamill, Sir Patrick, Kt., QPM
Hamilton, *Rt. Hon.* Sir Archibald
Gavin, Kt., MP
Hamilton, Sir Edward Sydney, Bt.
(1776 and 1819)
Hamilton, Sir James Arnot, KCB, MBE,
FEng.
Hamilton, Sir Malcolm William
Bruce Stirling-, Bt. (s. 1673)
Hamilton, Sir Michael Aubrey, Kt.
Hamilton, Sir (Robert Charles)
Richard Caradoc, Bt. (s. 1646)
Hammett, *Hon.* Sir Clifford James,
Kt.
Hammick, Sir Stephen George, Bt.
(1834)
Hampel, Sir Ronald Claus, Kt.
Hampshire, Sir Stuart Newton, Kt.,
FBA
Hancock, Sir David John Stowell,
KCB
Hancock, *Air Marshal* Sir Valston
Eldridge, KBE, CB, DFC
Hand, *Most Revd* Geoffrey David,
KBE
Handley, Sir David John Davenport-,
Kt., OBE
Hanham, Sir Michael William, Bt.,
DFC (1667)
Hanley, Sir Michael Bowen, KCB
Hanmer, Sir John Wyndham
Edward, Bt. (1774)
Hann, Sir James, Kt., CBE
Hannam, Sir John Gordon, Kt., MP
Hannay, Sir David Hugh Alexander,
GCMG
Hanson, Sir Anthony Leslie Oswald,
Bt. (1887)
†Hanson, Sir Charles Rupert Patrick,
Bt. (1918)
Hanson, Sir John Gilbert, KCMG, CBE
Hardcastle, Sir Alan John, Kt.
Harders, Sir Clarence Waldemar, Kt.,
OBE
Hardie, Sir Charles Edgar Mathewes,
Kt., CBE
Hardie, Sir Douglas Fleming, Kt.,
CBE
Harding, Sir Christopher George
Francis, Kt.
Harding, Sir George William, KCMG,
CVO
Harding, *Marshal of the Royal Air Force*
Sir Peter Robin, GCB
Harding, Sir Roy Pollard, Kt., CBE
Hardman, Sir Henry, KCB
Hardy, Sir David William, Kt.
Hardy, Sir James Gilbert, Kt., OBE
Hardy, Sir Rupert John, Bt. (1876)
Hare, Sir Philip Leigh, Bt. (1818)
Harford, Sir (John) Timothy, Bt.
(1934)
Hargroves, *Brig.* Sir Robert Louis,
Kt., CBE
Harington, *Gen.* Sir Charles Henry
Pepys, GCB, CBE, DSO, MC
Harington, Sir Nicholas John, Bt.
(1611)

Harland, *Air Marshal* Sir Reginald
Edward Wynyard, KBE, CB
Harley, *Lt.-Gen.* Sir Alexander
George Hamilton, KBE, CB
Harman, *Gen.* Sir Jack Wentworth,
GCB, OBE, MC
Harman, *Hon.* Sir Jeremiah LeRoy,
Kt.
Harmsworth, Sir Hildebrand Harold,
Bt. (1922)
Harpham, Sir William, KBE, CMG
Harris, *Prof.* Sir Alan James, Kt., CBE,
FEng.
Harris, Sir Anthony Kyrle Travers,
Bt. (1953)
Harris, *Prof.* Sir Henry, Kt., FRCP,
FRCPath., FRS
Harris, *Lt.-Gen.* Sir Ian Cecil, KBE, CB,
DSO
Harris, Sir Jack Wolfred Ashford, Bt.
(1932)
Harris, *Air Marshal* Sir John Hulme,
KCB, CBE
Harris, Sir William Gordon, KBE, CB,
FEng.
Harrison, *Prof.* Sir Donald Frederick
Norris, Kt., FRCS
Harrison, Sir Ernest Thomas, Kt.,
OBE
Harrison, Sir Francis Alexander
Lyle, Kt., MBE, QC
Harrison, *Surgeon Vice-Adm.* Sir John
Albert Bews, KBE
Harrison, *Hon.* Sir (John) Richard,
Kt., ED
Harrison, *Hon.* Sir Michael Guy
Vicat, Kt.
Harrison, Sir Michael James
Harwood, Bt. (1961)
Harrison, *Prof.* Sir Richard John, Kt.,
FRS
Harrison, Sir (Robert) Colin, Bt.
(1922)
Harrison, Sir Terence, Kt., FEng.
Harrop, Sir Peter John, KCB
Hart, Sir Graham Allan, KCB
Hartley, *Air Marshal* Sir Christopher
Harold, KCB, CBE, DFC, AFC
Hartley, Sir Frank, Kt., CBE, Ph.D.
†Hartopp, *Lt. Cdr* Sir Kenneth Alston
Cradock-, Bt., MBE, DSC (1796)
Hartwell, Sir (Francis) Anthony
Charles Peter, Bt. (1805)
Harvey, Sir Charles Richard
Musgrave, Bt. (1933)
Haselhurst, Sir Alan Gordon
Barraclough, Kt., MP
Haskard, Sir Cosmo Dugal Patrick
Thomas, KCMG, MBE
Haslam, *Hon.* Sir Alec Leslie, Kt.
Haslam, *Rear-Adm.* Sir David
William, KBE, CB
Hassan, Sir Joshua Abraham, GBE,
KCMG, LVO, QC
Hassett, *Gen.* Sir Francis George, KBE,
CB, DSO, LVO
Hastings, Sir Stephen Lewis
Edmonstone, Kt., MC
Hatty, *Hon.* Sir Cyril James, Kt.
Haughton, Sir James, Kt., CBE, QPM

Havelock, Sir Wilfrid Bowen, Kt.
Hawkins, Sir Arthur Ernest, Kt.
†Hawkins, Sir Howard Caesar, Bt.
(1778)
Hawkins, Sir Paul Lancelot, Kt., TD
Hawley, Sir Donald Frederick,
KCMG, MBE
†Hawley, Sir Henry Nicholas, Bt.
(1795)
Haworth, Sir Philip, Bt. (1911)
Hawthorne, *Prof.* Sir William Rede,
Kt., CBE, SC.D., FRS, FEng.
Hay, Sir David Osborne, Kt., CBE, DSO
Hay, Sir David Russell, Kt., CBE,
FRCP, MD
Hay, Sir Hamish Grenfell, Kt.
Hay, Sir James Brian Dalrymple-, Bt.
(1798)
†Hay, Sir John Erroll Audley, Bt. (s.
1663)
†Hay, Sir Ronald Frederick
Hamilton, Bt. (s. 1703)
Haydon, Sir Walter Robert, KCMG
Hayes, Sir Brian David, GCB
Hayes, Sir Claude James, KCMG
Hayes, *Vice-Adm.* Sir John Osier
Chattock, KCB, OBE
Hayr, *Air Marshal* Sir Kenneth
William, KCB, KBE, AFC
Hayward, Sir Anthony William
Byrd, Kt.
Hayward, Sir Jack Arnold, Kt., OBE
Haywood, Sir Harold, KCVO, OBE
Head, Sir Francis David Somerville,
Bt. (1838)
Healey, Sir Charles Edward
Chadwyck-, Bt. (1919)
Heap, Sir Desmond, Kt.
Heap, Sir Peter William, KCMG
Heath, *Rt. Hon.* Sir Edward Richard
George, KG, MBE, MP
Heath, Sir Mark Evelyn, KCVO, CMG
Heath, *Air Marshal* Sir Maurice
Lionel, KBE, CB, CVO
Heathcote, *Brig.* Sir Gilbert Simon,
Bt., CBE (1733)
Heathcote, Sir Michael Perryman,
Bt. (1733)
Heatley, Sir Peter, Kt., CBE
Heaton, Sir Yvo Robert Henniker-,
Bt. (1912)
Heiser, Sir Terence Michael, GCB
Hellaby, Sir (Frederick Reed) Alan,
Kt.
Henderson, Sir Denys Hartley, Kt.
Henderson, Sir (John) Nicholas,
GCMG, KCVO
Henderson, Sir William MacGregor,
Kt., D.SC., FRS
Henley, Sir Douglas Owen, KCB
Henley, *Rear-Adm.* Sir Joseph
Charles Cameron, KCVO, CB
Hennessy, Sir James Patrick Ivan,
KBE, CMG
†Henniker, Sir Adrian Chandos, Bt.
(1813)
Henry, Sir Denis Aynsley, Kt., OBE,
QC
Henry, *Rt. Hon.* Sir Denis Robert
Maurice, Kt.

Henry, *Hon.* Sir Geoffrey Arama, KBE
Henry, Sir James Holmes, Bt., CMG, MC, TD, QC (1923)
Henry, *Hon.* Sir Trevor Ernest, Kt.
Hepburn, Sir John Alastair Trant Kidd Buchan-, Bt. (1815)
Herbecq, Sir John Edward, KCB
Herbert, *Adm.* Sir Peter Geoffrey Marshall, KCB, OBE
Hermon, Sir John Charles, Kt., OBE, QPM
Heron, Sir Conrad Frederick, KCB, OBE
Heron, Sir Michael Gilbert, Kt.
Hervey, Sir Roger Blaise Ramsay, KCVO, CMG
Heseltine, *Rt. Hon.* Sir William Frederick Payne, GCB, GCVO
Hetherington, Sir Arthur Ford, Kt., DSC, FEng.
Hetherington, Sir Thomas Chalmers, KCB, CBE, TD, QC
Hewetson, Sir Christopher Raynor, Kt., TD
Hewett, Sir Peter John Smithson, Bt., MM (1813)
Hewitt, Sir (Cyrus) Lenox (Simson), Kt., OBE
Hewitt, Sir Nicholas Charles Joseph, Bt. (1921)
Heygate, Sir Richard John Gage, Bt. (1831)
Heyman, Sir Horace William, Kt.
Heywood, Sir Peter, Bt. (1838)
Hezlet, *Vice-Adm.* Sir Arthur Richard, KBE, CB, DSO, DSC
Hibbert, Sir Jack, KCB
Hibbert, Sir Reginald Alfred, GCMG
Hickey, Sir Justin, Kt.
Hickman, Sir (Richard) Glenn, Bt. (1903)
Hicks, Sir Robert, Kt., MP
Hidden, *Hon.* Sir Anthony Brian, Kt.
Hielscher, Sir Leo Arthur, Kt.
Higgins, Sir Christopher Thomas, Kt.
Higgins, *Hon.* Sir Malachy Joseph, Kt.
Higgins, *Rt. Hon.* Sir Terence Langley, KBE, MP
Higginson, Sir Gordon Robert, Kt., Ph.D., FEng.
Highgate, Sir James Brown, Kt., CBE
Hildyard, Sir David Henry Thoroton, KCMG, DFC
Hill, Sir Alexander Rodger Erskine-, Bt. (1945)
Hill, Sir Arthur Alfred, Kt., CBE
Hill, Sir Brian John, Kt.
Hill, Sir James Frederick, Bt. (1917)
Hill, Sir John McGregor, Kt., Ph.D., FEng.
Hill, Sir John Maxwell, Kt., CBE, DFC
†Hill, Sir John Rowley, Bt. (I. 1779)
Hill, *Vice-Adm.* Sir Robert Charles Finch, KBE, FEng.
Hill, Sir (Stanley) James (Allen), Kt., MP
Hillary, Sir Edmund, KG, KBE
Hillhouse, Sir (Robert) Russell, KCB

Hills, Sir Graham John, Kt.
Hine, *Air Chief Marshal* Sir Patrick Bardon, GCB, GBE
Hines, Sir Colin Joseph, Kt., OBE
Hinsley, *Prof.* Sir Francis Harry, Kt., OBE, FBA
Hirsch, *Prof.* Sir Peter Bernhard, Kt., Ph.D., FRS
Hirst, *Rt. Hon.* Sir David Cozens-Hardy, Kt.
Hirst, Sir Michael William, Kt.
Hoare, Sir Peter Richard David, Bt. (1786)
Hoare, Sir Timothy Edward Charles, Bt., OBE (I. 1784)
Hobart, Sir John Vere, Bt. (1914)
Hobday, Sir Gordon Ivan, Kt.
Hobhouse, Sir Charles John Spinney, Bt. (1812)
Hobhouse, *Rt. Hon.* Sir John Stewart, Kt.
Hockaday, Sir Arthur Patrick, KCB, CMG
Hockley, *Gen.* Sir Anthony Heritage Farrar-, GBE, KCB, DSO, MC
†Hodge, Sir Andrew Rowland, Bt. (1921)
Hodge, Sir Julian Stephen Alfred, Kt.
Hodges, *Air Chief Marshal* Sir Lewis MacDonald, KCB, CBE, DSO, DFC
Hodgkin, *Prof.* Sir Alan Lloyd, OM, KBE, FRS, Sc.D.
Hodgkin, Sir Gordon Howard Eliot, Kt., CBE
Hodgkinson, *Air Chief Marshal* Sir (William) Derek, KCB, CBE, DFC, AFC
Hodgson, Sir Maurice Arthur Eric, Kt., FEng.
Hodgson, *Hon.* Sir (Walter) Derek (Thornley), Kt.
Hodson, Sir Michael Robin Adderley, Bt. (I. 1789)
Hoffenberg, *Prof.* Sir Raymond, KBE
Hogg, Sir Christopher Anthony, Kt.
Hogg, Sir Edward William Lindsay-, Bt. (1905)
Hogg, *Vice-Adm.* Sir Ian Leslie Trower, KCB, DSC
Hogg, Sir John Nicholson, Kt., TD
†Hogg, Sir Michael David, Bt. (1846)
Holcroft, Sir Peter George Culcheth, Bt. (1921)
Holden, Sir David Charles Beresford, KBE, CB, ERD
Holden, Sir Edward, Bt. (1893)
Holden, Sir John David, Bt. (1919)
Holder, Sir John Henry, Bt. (1898)
Holder, *Air Marshal* Sir Paul Davie, KBE, CB, DSO, DFC, Ph.D.
Holderness, Sir Richard William, Bt. (1920)
Holdgate, Sir Martin Wyatt, Kt., CB, Ph.D.
Holdsworth, Sir (George) Trevor, Kt.
Holland, *Hon.* Sir Alan Douglas, Kt.
Holland, *Hon.* Sir Christopher John, Kt.

Holland, Sir Clifton Vaughan, Kt.
Holland, Sir Geoffrey, KCB
Holland, Sir Guy (Hope), Bt. (1917)
Holland, Sir Kenneth Lawrence, Kt., CBE, QFSM
Holland, Sir Philip Welsby, Kt.
Holliday, *Prof.* Sir Frederick George Thomas, Kt., CBE, FRSE
Hollings, *Hon.* Sir (Alfred) Kenneth, Kt., MC
Hollis, *Hon.* Sir Anthony Barnard, Kt.
Hollom, Sir Jasper Quintus, KBE
Holloway, *Hon.* Sir Barry Blyth, KBE
Holm, Sir Carl Henry, Kt., OBE
Holman, *Hon.* Sir (Edward) James, Kt.
Holmes, *Prof.* Sir Frank Wakefield, Kt.
Holmes, Sir Maurice Andrew, Kt.
Holmes, Sir Peter Fenwick, Kt., MC
Holroyd, *Air Marshal* Sir Frank Martyn, KBE, CB, FEng.
Holt, *Prof.* Sir James Clarke, Kt.
Holt, Sir Michael, Kt., CBE
Home, Sir William Dundas, Bt. (s. 1671)
Honeycombe, *Prof.* Sir Robert William Kerr, Kt., FRS, FEng.
Honywood, Sir Filmer Courtenay William, Bt. (1660)
Hood, Sir Harold Joseph, Bt., TD (1922)
Hookway, Sir Harry Thurston, Kt.
Hoole, Sir Arthur Hugh, Kt.
Hooper, *Hon.* Sir Anthony, Kt.
Hope, Sir (Charles) Peter, KCMG, TD
Hope, Sir Colin Frederick Newton, Kt.
Hope, *Rt. Revd and Rt. Hon.* David Michael, KCVO
Hope, Sir John Carl Alexander, Bt. (s. 1628)
Hopkin, Sir David Armand, Kt.
Hopkin, Sir (William Aylsham) Bryan, Kt., CBE
Hopkins, Sir Anthony Philip, Kt., CBE
Hopkins, Sir Michael John, Kt., CBE, RA, RIBA
Hopwood, *Prof.* Sir David Alan, Kt., FRS
Hordern, *Rt. Hon.* Sir Peter Maudslay, Kt., MP
Horlick, *Vice-Adm.* Sir Edwin John, KBE, FEng.
Horlick, Sir James Cunliffe William, Bt. (1914)
Horlock, *Prof.* Sir John Harold, Kt., FRS, FEng.
Hornby, Sir Derek Peter, Kt.
Hornby, Sir Simon Michael, Kt.
Horne, Sir Alan Gray Antony, Bt. (1929)
Horsfall, Sir John Musgrave, Bt., MC, TD (1909)
Horsley, *Air Marshal* Sir (Beresford) Peter (Torrington), KCB, CBE, LVO, AFC
†Hort, Sir Andrew Edwin Fenton, Bt. (1767)
Hosker, Sir Gerald Albery, KCB, QC

Hoskyns, Sir Benedict Leigh, Bt. (1676)
Hoskyns, Sir John Austin Hungerford Leigh, Kt.
Hotung, Sir Joseph Edward, Kt.
Houghton, Sir John Theodore, Kt., CBE, FRS
†Houldsworth, Sir Richard Thomas Reginald, Br. (1887)
Hounsfield, Sir Godfrey Newbold, Kt., CBE
House, *Lt.-Gen.* Sir David George, GCB, KCVO, CBE, MC
Houssemayne du Boulay, Sir Roger William, KCVO, CMG
Howard, Sir (Hamilton) Edward de Coucey, Bt., GBE (1955)
Howard, *Prof.* Sir Michael Eliot, Kt., CBE, MC
Howard, *Maj.-Gen.* Lord Michael Fitzalan-, GCVO, CB, CBE, MC
Howard, Sir Walter Stewart, Kt., MBE
Howell, Sir Ralph Frederic, Kt., MP
Howells, Sir Eric Waldo Benjamin, Kt., CBE
Howlett, *Gen.* Sir Geoffrey Hugh Whitby, KBE, MC
Hoyle, *Prof.* Sir Fred, Kt., FRS
Hoyos, *Hon.* Sir Fabriciano Alexander, Kt.
Huddie, Sir David Patrick, Kt., FEng.
Hudson, Sir Havelock Henry Trevor, Kt.
Hudson, *Lt.-Gen.* Sir Peter, KCB, CBE
Huggins, *Hon.* Sir Alan Armstrong, Kt.
Hughes, Sir David Collingwood, Bt. (1773)
Hughes, *Prof.* Sir Edward Stuart Reginald, Kt., CBE
Hughes, Sir Jack William, Kt.
Hughes, *Air Marshal* Sir (Sidney Weetman) Rochford, KCB, CBE, AFC
Hughes, Sir Trevor Denby Lloyd-, Kt.
Hughes, Sir Trevor Poulton, KCB
Hugo, *Lt.-Col.* Sir John Mandeville, KCVO, OBE
Hull, *Prof.* Sir David, Kt.
†Hulse, Sir Edward Jeremy Westrow, Bt. (1739)
Hume, Sir Alan Blyth, Kt., CB
Humphreys, Sir Olliver William, Kt., CBE
Humphreys, Sir (Raymond Evelyn) Myles, Kt.
Hunn, Sir Jack Kent, Kt., CMG
Hunt, Sir David Wathen Stather, KCMG, OBE
Hunt, Sir John Leonard, Kt., MP
Hunt, *Adm.* Sir Nicholas John Streynsham, GCB, LVO
Hunt, Sir Peter John, Kt., FRICS
Hunt, Sir Rex Masterman, Kt., CMG
Hunt, Sir Robert Frederick, Kt., CBE, FEng.
Hunter, *Hon.* Sir Alexander Albert, KBE
Hunter, Sir Alistair John, KCMG
Hunter, Sir Ian Bruce Hope, Kt., MBE

Hunter, *Prof.* Sir Laurence Colvin, Kt., CBE, FRSE
Hurn, Sir (Francis) Roger, Kt.
Hurrell, Sir Anthony Gerald, KCVO, CMG
Husbands, Sir Clifford Straugh, GCMG
Hutchinson, *Hon.* Sir Ross, Kt., DFC
Hutchison, *Lt.-Cdr.* Sir (George) Ian Clark, Kt., RN
Hutchison, *Rt. Hon.* Sir Michael, Kt.
Hutchison, Sir Peter, Bt., CBE (1939)
Hutchison, Sir Peter Craft, Bt. (1956)
Hutton, *Rt. Hon.* Sir (James) Brian Edward, Kt.
Huxley, *Prof.* Sir Andrew Fielding, Kt., OM, FRS
Huxtable, *Gen.* Sir Charles Richard, KCB, CBE
Hyatali, *Hon.* Sir Isaac Emanuel, Kt.
Hyslop, Sir Robert John (Robin) Maxwell-, Kt.
Ibbs, Sir (John) Robin, KBE
Imbert, Sir Peter Michael, Kt., QPM
Imray, Sir Colin Henry, KBE, CMG
Inge, *Field Marshal* Sir Peter Anthony, GCB
Ingham, Sir Bernard, Kt.
Ingilby, Sir Thomas Colvin William, Bt. (1866)
Inglis, Sir Brian Scott, Kt.
Inglis of Glencorse, Sir Roderick John, Bt. (s. 1703)
Ingram, Sir James Herbert Charles, Bt. (1893)
Ingram, Sir John Henderson, Kt., CBE
Inkin, Sir Geoffrey David, Kt., OBE
†Innes, Sir David Charles Kenneth Gordon, Bt. (NS 1686)
Innes of Edingight, Sir Malcolm Rognvald, KCVO
Innes, Sir Peter Alexander Berowald, Bt. (s. 1628)
Inniss, *Hon.* Sir Clifford de Lisle, Kt.
Irvine, Sir Donald Hamilton, Kt., CBE, MD, FRCGP
Irvine, *Dr* Sir Robin Orlando Hamilton, Kt.
Irving, *Prof.* Sir Miles Horsfall, Kt., MD, FRCS, FRCSE
Isaacs, Sir Jeremy Israel, Kt.
Isham, Sir Ian Vere Gyles, Bt. (1627)
Jack, *Hon.* Sir Alieu Sulayman, Kt.
Jack, Sir David, Kt., CBE, FRS, FRSE
Jack, Sir David Emmanuel, GCMG, MBE
Jackson, *Air Chief Marshal* Sir Brendan James, GCB
Jackson, Sir (John) Edward, KCMG
Jackson, Sir Michael Roland, Bt. (1902)
Jackson, Sir Nicholas Fane St George, Bt. (1913)
Jackson, Sir Robert, Bt. (1815)
Jackson, *Gen.* Sir William Godfrey Fothergill, GBE, KCB, MC
Jackson, Sir William Thomas, Bt. (1869)
Jacob, Sir Isaac Hai, Kt., QC

Jacob, *Hon.* Sir Robert Raphael Hayim (Robin), Kt.
Jacobi, Sir Derek George, Kt., CBE
Jacobi, *Dr* Sir James Edward, Kt., OBE
Jacobs, Sir David Anthony, Kt.
Jacobs, *Hon.* Sir Kenneth Sydney, KBE
Jacobs, Sir Piers, KBE
Jacobs, Sir Wilfred Ebenezer, GCMG, GCVO, OBE, QC
Jacomb, Sir Martin Wakefield, Kt.
Jaffray, Sir William Otho, Bt. (1892)
James, Sir Cynlais Morgan, KCMG
James, Sir Gerard Bowes Kingston, Bt. (1823)
James, Sir Robert Vidal Rhodes, Kt.
James, Sir Stanislaus Anthony, GCMG, OBE
Jamieson, *Air Marshal* Sir David Ewan, KBE, CB
Jansen, Sir Ross Malcolm, KBE
Jardine, Sir Andrew Colin Douglas, Bt. (1916)
Jardine, *Maj.* Sir (Andrew) Rupert (John) Buchanan-, Bt., MC (1885)
Jardine of Applegirth, Sir Alexander Maule, Bt. (s. 1672)
Jarratt, Sir Alexander Anthony, Kt., CB
Jawara, *Hon.* Sir Dawda Kairaba, Kt.
Jay, Sir Antony Rupert, Kt., CVO
Jeewoolall, Sir Ramesh, Kt.
Jefferson, Sir George Rowland, Kt., CBE, FEng.
Jefferson, Sir Mervyn Stewart Dunnington-, Bt. (1958)
Jeffreys, *Prof.* Sir Alec John, Kt., FRS
Jeffries, *Hon.* Sir John Francis, Kt.
Jehangir, Sir Hirji, Bt. (1908)
Jejeebhoy, Sir Rustom, Bt. (1857)
Jenkins, Sir Brian Garton, GBE
Jenkins, Sir Elgar Spencer, Kt., OBE
Jenkins, Sir Michael Romilly Heald, KCMG
Jenkinson, Sir John Banks, Bt. (1661)
†Jenks, Sir Maurice Arthur Brian, Bt. (1932)
Jennings, *Prof.* Sir Robert Yewdall, Kt., QC
Jephcott, Sir (John) Anthony, Kt. (1962)
Jessel, Sir Charles John, Bt. (1883)
Jewkes, Sir Gordon Wesley, KCMG
Joel, *Hon.* Sir Asher Alexander, KBE
John, Sir Rupert Godfrey, Kt.
Johns, *Air Chief Marshal* Sir Richard Edward, KBE, CBE, LVO
Johnson, *Rt. Hon.* Sir David Powell Croom-, Kt., DSC, VRD
Johnson, *Gen.* Sir Garry Dene, KCB, OBE, MC
Johnson, Sir John Rodney, KCMG
†Johnson, Sir Patrick Eliot, Bt. (1818)
Johnson, Sir Peter Colpoys Paley, Bt. (1755)
Johnson, *Hon.* Sir Robert Lionel, Kt.
Johnson, Sir Ronald Ernest Charles, Kt., CB
Johnson, Sir Vassel Godfrey, Kt., CBE
Johnston, Sir (David) Russell, Kt., MP

Johnston, Sir John Baines, GCMG, KCVO

Johnston, Lt.-Col. Sir John Frederick Dame, GCVO, MC

Johnston, Lt.-Gen. Sir Maurice Robert, KCB, OBE

Johnston, Sir Thomas Alexander, Bt. (s. 1626)

Johnston, Sir William Robert Patrick Knox- (Sir Robin), Kt., CBE, RD

Johnstone, Sir (George) Richard Douglas, Bt. (s. 1700)

Johnstone, Sir (John) Raymond, Kt., CBE

Jolliffe, Sir Anthony Stuart, GBE

Jones, Gen. Sir (Charles) Edward Webb, KCB, CBE

Jones, Sir Christopher Lawrence-, Bt. (1831)

Jones, Sir David Akers-, KBE, CMG

Jones, Air Marshal Sir Edward Gordon, KCB, CBE, DSO, DFC

Jones, Sir (Edward) Martin Furnival, Kt., CBE

Jones, Sir Ewart Ray Herbert, Kt., D.SC., Ph.D., FRS

Jones, Sir Francis Avery, Kt., CBE, FRCP

Jones, Sir Gordon Pearce, Kt.

Jones, Sir Harry Ernest, Kt., CBE

Jones, Sir (John) Derek Alun-, Kt.

Jones, Sir John Henry Harvey-, Kt., MBE

Jones, Sir John Lewis, KCB, CMG

Jones, Sir John Prichard-, Bt. (1910)

Jones, Sir Keith Stephen, Kt.

Jones, Hon. Sir Kenneth George Illtyd, Kt.

Jones, Sir (Owen) Trevor, Kt.

Jones, Sir (Peter) Hugh (Jefferd) Lloyd-, Kt.

Jones, Sir Richard Anthony Lloyd, KCB

Jones, Sir Robert Edward, Kt.

Jones, Sir Simon Warley Frederick Benton, Bt. (1919)

Jones, Sir (Thomas) Philip, Kt., CB

Jones, Sir (William) Emrys, Kt.

Jones, Hon. Sir William Lloyd Mars-, Kt., MBE

Jones, Sir Wynn Normington Hugh-, Kt., LVO

†Joseph, Hon. Sir James Samuel, Bt. (1943)

Jowitt, Hon. Sir Edwin Frank, Kt.

Joyce, Lt.-Gen. Sir Robert John Hayman-, KCB, CBE

Judge, Rt. Hon. Sir Igor, Kt.

Judge, Sir Paul Rupert, Kt.

Jugnauth, Rt. Hon. Sir Anerood, KCMG, QC

Jungius, Vice-Adm. Sir James George, KBE

Junor, Sir John Donald Brown, Kt.

Jupp, Hon. Sir Kenneth Graham, Kt., MC

Kaberry, Hon. Sir Christopher Donald, Bt. (1960)

Kalms, Sir (Harold) Stanley, Kt.

Kalo, Sir Kwamala, Kt., MBE

Kan Yuet-Keung, Sir, GBE

Kapi, Hon. Sir Mari, Kt., CBE

Kaputin, Sir John Rumet, KBE, CMG

Katsina, The Emir of, KBE, CMG

Katz, Sir Bernard, Kt., FRS

Kausimae, Sir David Nanau, KBE

Kavali, Sir Thomas, Kt., OBE

Kawharu, Prof. Sir Ian Hugh, Kt.

Kay, Prof. Sir Andrew Watt, Kt.

Kay, Hon. Sir John William, Kt.

Kay, Hon. Sir Maurice Ralph, Kt.

Kaye, Sir David Alexander Gordon, Bt. (1923)

Kaye, Sir Emmanuel, Kt., CBE

Kaye, Sir John Phillip Lister Lister-, Bt. (1812)

Keane, Sir Richard Michael, Bt. (1801)

Keatinge, Sir Edgar Mayne, Kt., CBE

Keeble, Sir (Herbert Ben) Curtis, GCMG

Keene, Hon. Sir David Wolfe, Kt.

Keith, Prof. Sir James, KBE

Kellett, Sir Stanley Charles, Bt. (1801)

Kelly, Sir David Robert Corbett, Kt., CBE

Kelly, Rt. Hon. Sir (John William) Basil, Kt.

Kelly, Sir William Theodore, Kt., OBE

Kemball, Air Marshal Sir (Richard) John, KCB, CBE

Kemp, Sir (Edward) Peter, KCB

Kendrew, Sir John Cowdery, Kt., CBE, SC.D., FRS

Kenilorea, Rt. Hon. Sir Peter, KBE

Kennard, Lt.-Col. Sir George Arnold Ford, Bt. (1891)

Kennaway, Sir John Lawrence, Bt. (1791)

Kennedy, Sir Clyde David Allen, Kt.

Kennedy, Sir Francis, KCMG, CBE

Kennedy, Hon. Sir Ian Alexander, Kt.

Kennedy, Sir Ludovic Henry Coverley, Kt.

†Kennedy, Sir Michael Edward, Bt., (1836)

Kennedy, Rt. Hon. Sir Paul Joseph Morrow, Kt.

Kennedy, Air Chief Marshal Sir Thomas Lawrie, GCB, AFC

Kennedy-Good, Sir John, KBE

Kenny, Sir Anthony John Patrick, Kt., D.Phil., D.Litt., FBA

Kenny, Gen. Sir Brian Leslie Graham, GCB, CBE

Kent, Sir Harold Simcox, GCB, QC

Kenyon, Sir George Henry, Kt.

Kermode, Sir (John) Frank, Kt., FBA

Kermode, Sir Ronald Graham Quale, KBE

Kerr, Hon. Sir Brian Francis, Kt.

Kerr, Adm. Sir John Beverley, GCB

Kerr, Sir John Olav, KCMG

Kerr, Rt. Hon. Sir Michael Robert Emanuel, Kt.

Kerruish, Sir (Henry) Charles, Kt., OBE

Kerry, Sir Michael James, KCB, QC

Kershaw, Sir (John) Anthony, Kt., MC

Keswick, Sir John Chippendale Lindley, Kt.

Kidd, Sir Robert Hill, KBE, CB

Kikau, Ratu Sir Jone Latianara, KBE

Killen, Hon. Denis James, KCMG

Killick, Sir John Edward, GCMG

Kimber, Sir Charles Dixon, Bt. (1904)

Kinahan, Sir Robert George Caldwell, Kt., ERD

King, Sir Albert, Kt., OBE

King, Gen. Sir Frank Douglas, GCB, MBE

King, Sir John Christopher, Bt. (1888)

King, Vice-Adm. Sir Norman Ross Dutton, KBE

King, Sir Richard Brian Meredith, KCB, MC

King, Sir Wayne Alexander, Bt. (1815)

Kingman, Prof. Sir John Frank Charles, Kt., FRS

Kingsland, Sir Richard, Kt., CBE, DFC

Kingsley, Sir Patrick Graham Toler, KCVO

Kinloch, Sir David, Bt. (s. 1686)

Kinloch, Sir David Oliphant, Bt. (1873)

Kipalan, Sir Albert, Kt.

Kirby, Hon. Sir Richard Clarence, Kt.

Kirkham, Sir Graham, Kt.

Kirkpatrick, Sir Ivone Elliott, Bt. (s. 1685)

Kirkwood, Hon. Sir Andrew Tristram Hammett, Kt.

Kirwan, Sir (Archibald) Laurence Patrick, KCMG, TD

Kitcatt, Sir Peter Julian, Kt., CB

Kitson, Gen. Sir Frank Edward, GBE, KCB, MC

Kitson, Sir Timothy Peter Geoffrey, Kt.

Kleinwort, Sir Richard Drake, Bt. (1909)

Klug, Sir Aaron, Kt., OM

Kneller, Sir Alister Arthur, Kt.

Knight, Sir Allan Walton, Kt., CMG

Knight, Sir Arthur William, Kt.

Knight, Sir Harold Murray, KBE, DSC

Knight, Air Chief Marshal Sir Michael William Patrick, KCB, AFC

Knill, Sir John Kenelm Stuart, Bt. (1893)

Knill, Prof. Sir John Lawrence, Kt., FEng.

Knott, Sir John Laurence, Kt., CBE

Knowles, Sir Charles Francis, Bt. (1765)

Knowles, Sir Durward Randolph, Kt., OBE

Knowles, Sir Leonard Joseph, Kt., CBE

Knowles, Sir Richard Marchant, Kt.

Knox, Sir Bryce Muir, KCVO, MC, TD

Knox, Sir David Laidlaw, Kt., MP

Knox, Hon. Sir John Leonard, Kt.

Knox, Hon. Sir William Edward, Kt.

Koraea, Sir Thomas, Kt.

Lewthwaite, *Brig.* Sir Rainald Gilfrid, Bt., CVO, OBE, MC (1927)

Ley, Sir Ian Francis, Bt. (1905)

Leyland, Sir Philip Vyvyan Naylor-, Bt. (1895)

Lickiss, Sir Michael Gillam, Kt.

Lickley, Sir Robert Lang, Kt., CBE, FEng.

Lidderdale, Sir David William Shuckburgh, KCB

Liggins, *Prof.* Sir Graham Collingwood, Kt., CBE, FRS

Lighthill, Sir (Michael) James, Kt., FRS

Lightman, *Hon.* Sir Gavin Anthony, Kt.

Lighton, Sir Thomas Hamilton, Bt. (I. 1791)

Lim, Sir Han-Hoe, Kt., CBE

Linacre, Sir (John) Gordon (Seymour), Kt., CBE, AFC, DFM

Lindop, Sir Norman, Kt.

Lindsay, Sir James Harvey Kincaid Stewart, Kt.

Lindsay, *Hon.* Sir John Edmund Frederic, Kt.

Lindsay, Sir Ronald Alexander, Bt., (1962)

Lipworth, Sir (Maurice) Sydney, Kt.

Lithgow, Sir William James, Bt. (1925)

Little, *Most Revd* Thomas Francis, KBE

Littler, Sir (James) Geoffrey, KCB

Livesay, *Adm.* Sir Michael Howard, KCB

Llewellyn, Sir Henry Morton, Bt., CBE (1922)

Llewelyn, Sir John Michael Dillwyn-Venables-, Bt. (1890)

Lloyd, Sir Ian Stewart, Kt.

Lloyd, Sir (John) Peter (Daniel), Kt.

Lloyd, Sir Nicholas Markley, Kt.

Lloyd, *Rt. Hon.* Sir Peter Robert Cable, Kt., MP

Lloyd, Sir Richard Ernest Butler, Bt. (1960)

Loader, Sir Leslie Thomas, Kt., CBE

Loane, *Most Revd* Marcus Lawrence, KBE

Lobo, Sir Rogerio Hyndman, Kt., CBE

Lock, *Cdr.* Sir (John) Duncan, Kt.

Lockhart, Sir Simon John Edward Francis Sinclair-, Bt. (s. 1636)

Loder, Sir Giles Rolls, Bt. (1887)

Lodge, Sir Thomas, Kt.

Lofthouse, Sir Geoffrey, Kt., MP

Logan, Sir Donald Arthur, KCMG

Logan, Sir Raymond Douglas, Kt.

Lokoloko, Sir Tore, GCMG, GCVO, OBE

Lombe, *Hon.* Sir Edward Christopher Evans-, Kt.

Longden, Sir Gilbert James Morley, Kt., MBE

Longmore, *Hon.* Sir Andrew Centlivres, Kt.

Loram, *Vice-Adm.* Sir David Anning, KCB, CVO

Lorimer, Sir (Thomas) Desmond, Kt.

Los, *Hon.* Sir Kubulan, Kt., CBE

Lovell, Sir (Alfred Charles) Bernard, Kt., OBE, FRS

Lovelock, Sir Douglas Arthur, KCB

Loveridge, Sir John Warren, Kt.

Lovill, Sir John Roger, Kt., CBE

Low, Sir Alan Roberts, Kt.

Low, Sir James Richard Morrison-, Bt. (1908)

Lowe, *Air Chief Marshal* Sir Douglas Charles, GCB, DFC, AFC

Lowe, Sir Thomas William Gordon, Bt. (1918)

Lowry, Sir John Patrick, Kt., CBE

Lowson, Sir Ian Patrick, Bt. (1951)

Lowther, *Maj.* Sir Charles Douglas, Bt. (1824)

Loyd, Sir Francis Alfred, KCMG, OBE

Loyd, Sir Julian St John, KCVO

Lu, Sir Tseng Chi, Kt.

Lucas, Sir Cyril Edward, Kt., CMG, FRS

Lucas, Sir Thomas Edward, Bt. (1887)

Luce, *Rt Hon.* Sir Richard Napier, Kt.

Luckhoo, Sir Lionel Alfred, KCMG, CBE, QC

Lucy, Sir Edmund John William Hugh Cameron-Ramsay-Fairfax, Bt. (1836)

Luddington, Sir Donald Collin Cumyn, KBE, CMG, CVO

Lumsden, Sir David James, Kt.

Lus, *Hon.* Sir Pita, Kt., OBE

Lush, *Hon.* Sir George Hermann, Kt.

Lushington, Sir John Richard Castleman, Bt. (1791)

Luttrell, *Col.* Sir Geoffrey Walter Fownes, KCVO, MC

Lyell, *Rt. Hon.* Sir Nicholas Walter, Kt., QC, MP

Lygo, *Adm.* Sir Raymond Derek, KCB

Lyle, Sir Gavin Archibald, Bt. (1929)

Lyons, Sir Edward Houghton, Kt.

Lyons, Sir James Reginald, Kt.

Lyons, Sir John, Kt.

McAdam, Sir Ian William James, Kt., OBE

Macadam, Sir Peter, Kt.

McAlpine, Sir William Hepburn, Bt. (1918)

†Macara, Sir Hugh Kenneth, Bt. (1911)

Macartney, Sir John Barrington, Bt. (I. 1799)

McAvoy, Sir (Francis) Joseph, Kt., CBE

McCaffrey, Sir Thomas Daniel, Kt.

McCall, Sir (Charles) Patrick Home, Kt., MBE, TD

McCallum, Sir Donald Murdo, Kt., CBE, FEng.

McCamley, Sir Graham Edward, Kt., MBE

McCarthy, *Rt. Hon.* Sir Thaddeus Pearcey, KBE

McClellan, *Col.* Sir Herbert Gerard Thomas, Kt., CBE, TD

McClintock, Sir Eric Paul, Kt.

McColl, Sir Colin Hugh Verel, KCMG

McCollum, *Hon.* Sir William, Kt.

McConnell, Sir Robert Shean, Bt. (1900)

McCorkell, *Col.* Sir Michael William, KCVO, OBE, TD

McCowan, *Rt. Hon.* Sir Anthony James Denys, Kt.

McCowan, Sir Hew Cargill, Bt. (1934)

McCrea, *Prof.* Sir William Hunter, Kt., FRS

McCrindle, Sir Robert Arthur, Kt.

McCullough, *Hon.* Sir (Iain) Charles (Robert), Kt.

McCusker, Sir James Alexander, Kt.

MacDermott, *Rt. Hon.* Sir John Clarke, Kt.

McDermott, Sir (Lawrence) Emmet, KBE

MacDonald, *Gen.* Sir Arthur Leslie, KBE, CB

McDonald, Sir Duncan, Kt., CBE, FEng.

Macdonald of Sleat, Sir Ian Godfrey Bosville, Bt. (s. 1625)

Macdonald, Sir Kenneth Carmichael, KCB

Macdonald, *Vice-Adm.* Sir Roderick Douglas, KBE

McDonald, Sir Tom, Kt., OBE

McDonald, *Hon.* Sir William John Farquhar, Kt.

MacDougall, Sir (George) Donald (Alastair), Kt., CBE, FBA

McDowell, Sir Eric Wallalce, Kt., CBE

McDowell, Sir Henry McLorinan, KBE

Mace, *Lt.-Gen.* Sir John Airth, KBE, CB

McEwen, Sir John Roderick Hugh, Bt. (1953)

McFarland, Sir John Talbot, Bt. (1914)

Macfarlane, Sir (David) Neil, Kt.

Macfarlane, Sir George Gray, Kt., CB, FEng.

McFarlane, Sir Ian, Kt.

McGeoch, *Vice-Adm.* Sir Ian Lachlan Mackay, KCB, DSO, DSC

McGrath, Sir Brian Henry, KCVO

Macgregor, Sir Edwin Robert, Bt. (1828)

MacGregor of MacGregor, Sir Gregor, Bt. (1795)

McGregor, Sir Ian Alexander, Kt., CBE, FRS

MacGregor, Sir Ian Kinloch, Kt.

McGrigor, *Capt.* Sir Charles Edward, Bt. (1831)

McIntosh, *Vice-Adm.* Sir Ian Stewart, KBE, CB, DSO, DSC

McIntosh, Sir Malcolm Kenneth, Kt., ph.D.

McIntosh, Sir Ronald Robert Duncan, KCB

McIntyre, Sir Donald Conroy, Kt., CBE

McIntyre, Sir Meredith Alister, Kt.

MacKay, *Prof.* Sir Donald Iain, Kt., FRSE

Mackay, Sir (George Patrick) Gordon, Kt., CBE

McKay, Sir John Andrew, Kt., CBE
Mackechnie, Sir Alistair John, Kt.
McKee, *Maj.* Sir (William) Cecil, Kt.,
ERD
McKellen, Sir Ian Murray, Kt., CBE
McKenzie, Sir Alexander, KBE
Mackenzie, Sir Alexander Alwyne
Henry Charles Brinton Muir-, Bt.
(1805)
Mackenzie, *Vice-Adm.* Sir Hugh
Stirling, KCB, DSO, DSC
†Mackenzie, Sir (James William)
Guy, Bt. (1890)
Mackenzie, *Gen.* Sir Jeremy John
George, KCB, OBE
†Mackenzie, Sir Peter Douglas, Bt.
(s. 1673)
†Mackenzie, Sir Roderick McQuhae,
Bt. (s. 1703)
McKenzie, Sir Roy Allan, KBE
Mackeson, Sir Rupert Henry, Bt.
(1954)
MacKinlay, Sir Bruce, Kt., CBE
McKinnon, Sir James, Kt.
McKinnon, *Hon.* Sir Stuart Neil, Kt.
Mackintosh, Sir Cameron Anthony,
Kt.
Macklin, Sir Bruce Roy, Kt., OBE
Mackworth, *Cdr.* Sir David Arthur
Geoffrey, Bt. (1776)
McLaren, Sir Robin John Taylor,
KCMG
MacLaurin, Sir Ian Charter, Kt.
Maclean, Sir Donald Og Grant, Kt.
†Maclean of Dunconnell, Sir Charles
Edward, Bt. (1957)
McLean, Sir Francis Charles, Kt., CBE
MacLean, *Vice-Adm.* Sir Hector
Charles Donald, KBE, CB, DSC
Maclean, Sir Lachlan Hector
Charles, Bt. (NS 1631)
Maclean, Sir Robert Alexander, KBE
McLennan, Sir Ian Munro, KCMG,
KBE
McLeod, Sir Charles Henry, Bt.
(1925)
McLeod, Sir Ian George, Kt.
MacLeod, Sir (John) Maxwell
Norman, Bt. (1924)
Macleod, Sir (Nathaniel William)
Hamish, KBE
McLintock, Sir Michael William, Bt.
(1934)
Maclure, Sir John Robert Spencer,
Bt. (1898)
McMahon, Sir Brian Patrick, Bt.
(1817)
McMahon, Sir Christopher William,
Kt.
Macmillan, Sir (Alexander
McGregor) Graham, Kt.
MacMillan, *Lt.-Gen.* Sir John
Richard Alexander, KCB, CBE
McMullin, *Rt. Hon.* Sir Duncan
Wallace, Kt.
Macnaghten, Sir Patrick Alexander,
Bt. (1836)
McNamara, *Air Chief Marshal* Sir
Neville Patrick, KBE

Macnaughton, *Prof.* Sir Malcolm
Campbell, Kt.
McNee, Sir David Blackstock, Kt.,
QPM
McNeice, Sir (Thomas) Percy
(Fergus), Kt., CMG, OBE
MacPhail, Sir Bruce Dugald, Kt.
Macpherson, Sir Ronald Thomas
Steward (Tommy), CBE, MC, TD
Macpherson of Cluny, *Hon.* Sir
William Alan, Kt., TD
McQuarrie, Sir Albert, Kt.
MacRae, Sir (Alastair) Christopher
(Donald Summerhayes), KCMG
Macrae, *Col.* Sir Robert Andrew
Scarth, KCVO, MBE
Macready, Sir Nevil John Wilfrid,
Bt. (1923)
Mactaggart, Sir John Auld, Bt. (1938)
Macwhinnie, Sir Gordon Menzies,
Kt., CBE
McWilliam, Sir Michael Douglas,
KCMG
McWilliams, Sir Francis, GBE, FEng.
Madden, *Adm.* Sir Charles Edward,
Bt., GCB (1919)
Maddocks, Sir Kenneth Phipson,
KCMG, KCVO
Maddox, Sir John Royden, Kt.
Madel, Sir (William) David, Kt., MP
Madigan, Sir Russel Tullie, Kt., OBE
Magnus, Sir Laurence Henry Philip,
Bt. (1917)
Maguire, *Air Marshal* Sir Harold
John, KCB, DSO, OBE
Mahon, Sir (John) Denis, Kt., CBE
Mahon, Sir William Walter, Bt.
(1819)
Maiden, Sir Colin James, Kt., D.phil.
Main, Sir Peter Tester, Kt., ERD
Maini, Sir Amar Nath, Kt., CBE
Maino, Sir Charles, KBE
†Maitland, Sir Charles Alexander,
Bt. (1818)
Maitland, Sir Donald James Dundas,
GCMG, OBE
Makins, Sir Paul Vivian, Bt. (1903)
Malcolm, Sir James William
Thomas Alexander, Bt. (s. 1665)
Malet, Sir Harry Douglas St Lo, Bt.
(1791)
Mallaby, Sir Christopher Leslie
George, GCMG, GCVO
†Mallinson, Sir William James, Bt.
(1935)
Malone, *Hon.* Sir Denis Eustace
Gilbert, Kt.
Mamo, Sir Anthony Joseph, Kt., OBE
Mance, *Hon.* Sir Jonathan Hugh, Kt.
Manchester, Sir William Maxwell,
KBE
Mander, Sir Charles Marcus, Bt.
(1911)
Manduell, Sir John, Kt., CBE
Mann, *Rt. Hon.* Sir Michael, Kt.
Mann, *Rt. Revd* Michael Ashley, KCVO
Mann, Sir Rupert Edward, Bt. (1905)
Mansel, Sir Philip, Bt. (1622)
Mansfield, *Vice-Adm.* Sir (Edward)
Gerard (Napier), KBE, CVO

Mansfield, *Prof.* Sir Peter, Kt., FRS
Mansfield, Sir Philip (Robert Aked),
KCMG
Mantell, *Hon.* Sir Charles Barrie
Knight, Kt.
Manton, Sir Edwin Alfred Grenville,
Kt.
Manuella, Sir Tulaga, GCMG, MBE
Manzie, Sir (Andrew) Gordon, KCB
Mara, *Rt. Hon. Ratu* Sir Kamisese
Kapaiwai Tuimacilai, GCMG, KBE
Margetson, Sir John William Denys,
KCMG
Marjoribanks, Sir James Alexander
Milne, KCMG
Mark, Sir Robert, GBE
Markham, Sir Charles John, Bt.
(1911)
Marking, Sir Henry Ernest, KCVO,
CBE, MC
Marling, Sir Charles William
Somerset, Bt. (1882)
Marr, Sir Leslie Lynn, Bt. (1919)
Marriner, Sir Neville, Kt., CBE
Marriott, Sir Hugh Cavendish
Smith-, Bt. (1774)
Marriott, Sir John Brook, KCVO
Marsden, Sir Nigel John Denton, Bt.
(1924)
Marshall, Sir Arthur Gregory
George, Kt., OBE
Marshall, Sir Colin Marsh, Kt.
Marshall, Sir Denis Alfred, Kt.
Marshall, *Prof.* Sir (Oshley) Roy, Kt.,
CBE
Marshall, Sir Peter Harold Reginald,
KCMG
Marshall, Sir Robert Braithwaite,
KCB, MBE
Marshall, Sir (Robert) Michael, Kt.,
MP
Martell, *Vice-Adm.* Sir Hugh Colenso,
KBE, CB
Martin, Sir George Henry, Kt., CBE
Martin, *Vice-Adm.* Sir John Edward
Ludgate, KCB, DSC
Martin, *Prof.* Sir (John) Leslie, Kt.,
ph.D.
Martin, *Prof.* Sir Laurence
Woodward, Kt.
Martin, Sir (Robert) Bruce, Kt., QC
Marychurch, Sir Peter Harvey, KCMG
Masefield, Sir Peter Gordon, Kt.
Masire, Sir Ketumile, GCMG
Mason, *Hon.* Sir Anthony Frank, KBE
Mason, Sir (Basil) John, Kt., CB, D.SC.,
FRS
Mason, *Prof.* Sir David Kean, Kt., CBE
Mason, Sir Frederick Cecil, KCVO,
CMG
Mason, Sir Gordon Charles, Kt., OBE
Mason, Sir John Charles Moir, KCMG
Mason, Sir John Peter, Kt., CBE
Mason, *Prof.* Sir Ronald, KCB, FRS
Matane, Sir Paulias Nguna, Kt., CMG,
OBE
Mather, Sir (David) Carol
(Macdonell), Kt., MC
Mather, Sir William Loris, Kt., CVO,
OBE, MC, TD

Mathers, Sir Robert William, Kt.
Matheson, Sir (James Adam) Louis, KBE, CMG, FEng.
Matheson of Matheson, Sir Fergus John, Bt. (1882)
Matthews, Sir Peter Alec, Kt.
Matthews, Sir Peter Jack, Kt., CVO, OBE, QPM
Matthews, Sir Stanley, Kt., CBE
Maud, The Hon. Sir Humphrey John Hamilton, KCMG
†Maxwell, Sir Michael Eustace George, Bt. (s. 1681)
Maxwell, Sir Nigel Mellor Heron-, Bt. (s. 1683)
May, *Hon.* Sir Anthony Tristram Kenneth, Kt.
May, *Rt. Hon.* Sir John Douglas, Kt.
May, Sir Kenneth Spencer, Kt., CBE
May, *Prof.* Sir Robert McCredie, Kt., FRS
Mayhew, *Rt. Hon.* Sir Patrick Barnabas Burke, Kt., QC, MP
Maynard, *Hon.* Sir Clement Travelyan, Kt.
Maynard, *Air Chief Marshal* Sir Nigel Martin, KCB, CBE, DFC, AFC
Medlycott, Sir Mervyn Tregonwell, Bt. (1808)
Megarry, *Rt. Hon.* Sir Robert Edgar, Kt., FBA
Megaw, *Rt. Hon.* Sir John, Kt., CBE, TD
Meinertzhagen, Sir Peter, Kt., CMG
Melhuish, Sir Michael Ramsay, KBE, CMG
Mellon, Sir James, KCMG
Melville, Sir Harry Work, KCB, ph.D., D.SC., FRS
Melville, Sir Leslie Galfreid, KBE
Melville, Sir Ronald Henry, KCB
Mensforth, Sir Eric, Kt., CBE, F.Eng.
Menter, Sir James Woodham, Kt., ph.D., SC.D., FRS
Menteth, Sir James Wallace Stuart-, Bt. (1838)
Menzies, Sir Peter Thomson, Kt.
Meyer, Sir Anthony John Charles, Bt. (1910)
Meyjes, Sir Richard Anthony, Kt.
Meyrick, Sir David John Charlton, Bt. (1880)
Meyrick, Sir George Christopher Cadafael Tapps-Gervis-, Bt. (1791)
Miakwe, *Hon.* Sir Akepa, KBE
Michael, Sir Peter Colin, Kt., CBE
Middleton, Sir George Humphrey, KCMG
Middleton, Sir Lawrence Monck, Bt. (1662)
Middleton, Sir Peter Edward, GCB
Miers, Sir (Henry) David Alastair Capel, KBE, CMG
Milbank, Sir Anthony Frederick, Bt. (1882)
Milburn, Sir Anthony Rupert, Bt. (1905)
Miles, Sir Peter Tremayne, KCVO
Miles, Sir William Napier Maurice, Bt. (1859)

Millais, Sir Geoffrey Richard Everett, Bt. (1885)
Millar, Sir Oliver Nicholas, GCVO, FBA
Millar, Sir Ronald Graeme, Kt.
Millard, Sir Guy Elwin, KCMG, CVO
Miller, Sir Donald John, Kt., FRSE, FEng.
Miller, Sir Hilary Duppa (Hal), Kt.
Miller, Sir (Ian) Douglas, Kt.
Miller, Sir John Holmes, Bt. (1705)
Miller, *Lt.-Col.* Sir John Mansel, GCVO, DSO, MC
Miller, Sir (Oswald) Bernard, Kt.
Miller, Sir Peter North, Kt.
Miller, Sir Ronald Andrew Baird, Kt., CBE
Miller of Glenlee, Sir Stephen William Macdonald, Bt. (1788)
Millett, *Rt. Hon.* Sir Peter Julian, Kt.
Millichip, Sir Frederick Albert (Bert), Kt.
Milling, *Air Marshal* Sir Denis Crowley-, KCB, CBE, DSO, DFC
Mills, *Vice-Adm.* Sir Charles Piercy, KCB, CBE, DSC
Mills, Sir Frank, KCVO, CMG
Mills, Sir John Lewis Ernest Watts, Kt., CBE
Mills, Sir Peter Frederick Leighton, Bt. (1921)
Milman, *Lt.-Col.* Sir Derek, Bt. (1800)
Milne, Sir John Drummond, Kt.
†Milner, Sir Timothy William Lycett, Bt. (1717)
Milnes Coates, Sir Anthony Robert, Bt. (1911)
Mitchell, *Air Cdre* Sir (Arthur) Dennis, KBE, CVO, DFC, AFC
Mitchell, Sir David Bower, Kt., MP
Mitchell, Sir Derek Jack, KCB, CVO
Mitchell, *Prof.* Sir (Edgar) William John, Kt., CBE, FRS
Mitchell, *Rt. Hon.* Sir James FitzAllen, KCMG
Mitchell, *Hon.* Sir Stephen George, Kt.
Moate, Sir Roger Denis, Kt., MP
Mobbs, Sir (Gerald) Nigel, Kt.
Moberly, Sir John Campbell, KBE, CMG
Moberly, Sir Patrick Hamilton, KCMG
Moffat, Sir Brian Scott, Kt., OBE
Moffat, *Lt.-Gen.* Sir (William) Cameron, KBE
Mogg, *Gen.* Sir (Herbert) John, GCB, CBE, DSO
Moir, Sir Ernest Ian Royds, Bt. (1916)
Moller, *Hon.* Sir Lester Francis, Kt.
†Molony, Sir Thomas Desmond, Bt. (1925)
Molyneaux, *Rt. Hon.* Sir James Henry, KBE, MP
Monck, Sir Nicholas Jeremy, KCB
Monro, Sir Hector Seymour Peter, Kt., MP
Montgomery, Sir (Basil Henry) David, Bt. (1801)

Montgomery, Sir (William) Fergus, Kt., MP
Mookerjee, Sir Birendra Nath, Kt.
Moollan, Sir Abdool Hamid Adam, Kt.
Moollan, *Hon.* Sir Cassam (Ismael), Kt.
Moon, Sir Peter Wilfred Giles Graham-, Bt. (1855)
†Moon, Sir Roger, Bt. (1887)
Moore, *Most Revd* Desmond Charles, KBE
Moore, Sir Francis Thomas, Kt.
Moore, Sir Henry Roderick, Kt., CBE
Moore, *Hon.* Sir John Cochrane, Kt.
Moore, *Maj.-Gen.* Sir (John) Jeremy, KCB, OBE, MC
Moore, Sir John Michael, KCVO, CB, DSC
Moore, *Prof.* Sir Norman Winfrid, Bt. (1919)
Moore, Sir Patrick William Eisdell, Kt., OBE
Moore, Sir William Roger Clotworthy, Bt., TD (1932)
Morauta, Sir Mekere, Kt.
Mordaunt, Sir Richard Nigel Charles, Bt. (1611)
Moreton, Sir John Oscar, KCMG, KCVO, MC
Morgan, *Vice-Adm.* Sir Charles Christopher, KBE
Morgan, *Maj.-Gen.* Sir David John Hughes-, Bt., CB, CBE (1925)
Morgan, Sir John Albert Leigh, KCMG
Morison, *Hon.* Sir Thomas Richard Atkin, Kt.
Morland, *Hon.* Sir Michael, Kt.
Morland, Sir Robert Kenelm, Kt.
Morpeth, Sir Douglas Spottiswoode, Kt., TD
Morris, *Air Marshal* Sir Arnold Alec, KBE, CB, FEng.
Morris, Sir (James) Richard (Samuel), Kt., CBE, FEng.
Morris, Sir Keith Elliot Hedley, KBE, CMG
Morris, *Prof.* Sir Peter John, Kt., FRS
Morris, Sir Robert Byng, Bt. (1806)
Morris, Sir Trefor Alfred, Kt., CBE, QPM
Morris, *Very Revd* Sir William James, KCVO, ph.D.
Morrison, *Hon.* Sir Charles Andrew, Kt.
Morrison, Sir Howard Leslie, Kt., OBE
Morritt, *Hon.* Sir (Robert) Andrew, Kt., CVO
Morrow, Sir Ian Thomas, Kt.
Morse, Sir Christopher Jeremy, KCMG
Morton, *Adm.* Sir Anthony Storrs, GBE, KCB
Morton, Sir (Robert) Alastair (Newton), Kt.
Moseley, Sir George Walker, KCB
Moser, *Prof.* Sir Claus Adolf, KCB, CBE, FBA

†Moss, Sir David John Edwards-, Bt.
(1868)
Mostyn, *Gen.* Sir (Joseph) David
Frederick, KCB, CBE
†Mostyn, Sir William Basil John, Bt.
(1670)
Mott, Sir John Harmer, Bt. (1930)
†Mount, Sir (William Robert)
Ferdinand, Bt. (1921)
Mountain, Sir Denis Mortimer, Bt.
(1922)
Mowbray, Sir John, Kt.
Mowbray, Sir John Robert, Bt.
(1880)
Muir, Sir Laurence Macdonald, Kt.
†Muir, Sir Richard James Kay, Bt.
(1892)
Muirhead, Sir David Francis, KCMG,
CVO
Mulcahy, Sir Geoffrey John, Kt.
Mullens, *Lt.-Gen.* Sir Anthony
Richard Guy, KCB, OBE
Mummery, *Hon.* Sir John Frank, Kt.
Munn, Sir James, Kt., OBE
Munro, Sir Alan Gordon, KCMG
Munro, Sir Alasdair Thomas Ian, Bt.
(1825)
Munro, Sir Ian Talbot, Bt. (s. 1634)
Munro, Sir Sydney Douglas Gun-,
GCMG, MBE
Muria, *Hon.* Sir Gilbert John Baptist,
Kt.
Murley, Sir Reginald Sydney, KBE,
TD, FRCS
Murphy, Sir Leslie Frederick, Kt.
Murray, *Rt. Hon.* Sir Donald Bruce,
Kt.
Murray, Sir Donald Frederick, KCVO,
CMG
Murray, Sir James, KCMG
Murray, Sir John Antony
Jerningham, Kt., CBE
Murray, *Prof.* Sir Kenneth, Kt.,
FRCPath., FRS, FRSE
Murray, Sir Nigel Andrew Digby, Bt.
(s. 1628)
Murray, Sir Patrick Ian Keith, Bt.
(s. 1673)
†Murray, Sir Rowland William
Patrick, Bt. (s. 1630)
Mursell, Sir Peter, Kt., MBE
Musgrave, Sir Christopher Patrick
Charles, Bt. (1611)
Musgrave, Sir Richard James, Bt.
(I. 1782)
Musson, *Gen.* Sir Geoffrey Randolph
Dixon, GCB, CBE, DSO
Myers, Sir Kenneth Ben, Kt., MBE
Myers, Sir Philip Alan, Kt., OBE, QPM
Myers, *Prof.* Sir Rupert Horace, KBE
Mynors, Sir Richard Baskerville, Bt.
(1964)
Nabarro, Sir John David Nunes, Kt.,
MD, FRCP
Naipaul, Sir Vidiadhar Surajprasad,
Kt.
Nairn, Sir Michael, Bt. (1904)
Nairn, Sir Robert Arnold Spencer-,
Bt. (1933)

Nairne, *Rt. Hon.* Sir Patrick
Dalmahoy, GCB, MC
Naish, Sir (Charles) David, Kt.
Nall, Sir Michael Joseph, Bt., RN
(1954)
Namaliu, *Rt. Hon.* Sir Rabbie
Langanai, Kt., CMG
†Napier, Sir Charles Joseph, Bt.
(1867)
Napier, Sir John Archibald Lennox,
Bt. (s. 1627)
Napier, Sir Oliver John, Kt.
Nasmith, *Prof.* Sir James Duncan
Dunbar-, Kt., CBE, RIBA, FRSE
Neal, Sir Eric James, Kt., CVO
Neal, Sir Leonard Francis, Kt., CBE
Neale, Sir Gerrard Anthony, Kt.
Neave, Sir Paul Arundell, Bt. (1795)
Nedd, *Hon.* Sir Robert Archibald, Kt.
Neill, *Rt. Hon.* Sir Brian Thomas, Kt.
Neill, Sir Francis Patrick, Kt., QC
Neill, *Rt. Hon.* Sir Ivan, Kt., PC (NI)
Neill, Sir (James) Hugh, KCVO, CBE,
TD
†Nelson, Sir Jamie Charles Vernon
Hope, Bt. (1912)
Nelson, *Hon.* Sir Robert Franklyn, Kt.
Nelson, *Air Marshal* Sir (Sidney)
Richard (Carlyle), KCB, OBE, MD
Nepean, *Lt.-Col.* Sir Evan Yorke, Bt.
(1802)
Neubert, Sir Michael John, Kt., MP
Nevile, *Capt.* Sir Henry Nicholas,
KCVO
Neville, Sir Roger Albert Gartside,
Kt., VRD
New, *Maj.-Gen.* Sir Laurence
Anthony Wallis, Kt., CB, CBE
Newall, Sir Paul Henry, Kt., TD
Newington, Sir Michael John, KCMG
Newman, Sir Francis Hugh Cecil, Bt.
(1912)
Newman, Sir Geoffrey Robert, Bt.
(1836)
Newman, *Hon.* Sir George Michael,
Kt.
Newman, Sir Jack, Kt., CBE
Newman, Sir Kenneth Leslie, GBE,
QPM
Newman, *Vice-Adm.* Sir Roy
Thomas, KCB
Newman, *Col.* Sir Stuart Richard, Kt.,
CBE, TD
Newns, Sir (Alfred) Foley (Francis
Polden), KCMG, CVO
Newsam, Sir Peter Anthony, Kt.
Newton, Sir (Charles) Wilfred, Kt.,
CBE
Newton, Sir (Harry) Michael (Rex),
Bt. (1900)
Newton, Sir Kenneth Garnar, Bt.,
OBE, TD (1924)
Newton, Sir (Leslie) Gordon, Kt.
Ngata, Sir Henare Kohere, KBE
Nichol, Sir Duncan Kirkbride, Kt.,
CBE
Nicholas, Sir David, Kt., CBE
Nicholas, Sir Herbert Richard, Kt.,
OBE

Nicholas, Sir John William, KCVO,
CMG
Nicholls, *Air Marshal* Sir John
Moreton, KCB, CBE, DFC, AFC
Nicholson, Sir Bryan Hubert, Kt.
†Nicholson, Sir Charles Christian,
Bt. (1912)
Nicholson, *Hon.* Sir David Eric, Kt.
Nicholson, *Rt. Hon.* Sir Michael, Kt.
Nicholson, Sir Paul Douglas, Kt.
Nicholson, Sir Robin Buchanan, Kt.,
ph.D., FRS, FEng.
Nicoll, Sir William, KCMG
Nield, Sir Basil Edward, Kt., CBE, QC
Nightingale, Sir Charles Manners
Gamaliel, Bt. (1628)
Nightingale, Sir John Cyprian, Kt.,
CBE, BEM, QPM
Nimmo, *Hon.* Sir John Angus, Kt.,
CBE
Nixon, Sir Edwin Ronald, Kt., CBE
Nixon, *Revd* Sir Kenneth Michael
John Basil, Bt. (1906)
Noble, Sir David Brunel, Bt. (1902)
Noble, Sir Iain Andrew, Bt., OBE
(1923)
Noble, Sir (Thomas Alexander)
Fraser, Kt., MBE
Nombri, Sir Joseph Karl, Kt., ISO, BEM
Norman, Sir Arthur Gordon, KBE,
DFC
Norman, Sir Mark Annesley, Bt.
(1915)
Norman, Sir Robert Henry, Kt., OBE
Norman, Sir Robert Wentworth, Kt.
Norman, Sir Ronald, Kt., OBE
Normanton, Sir Tom, Kt., TD
Norris, *Air Chief Marshal* Sir
Christopher Neil Foxley-, GCB,
DSO, OBE
Norris, Sir Eric George, KCMG
North, Sir Thomas Lindsay, Kt.
North, Sir (William) Jonathan
(Frederick), Bt. (1920)
Norton, *Vice-Adm.* *Hon.* Sir Nicholas
John Hill-, KCB
Norwood, Sir Walter Neville, Kt.
Nossal, Sir Gustav Joseph Victor,
Kt., CBE
Nott, *Rt. Hon.* Sir John William
Frederic, KCB
Nourse, *Rt. Hon.* Sir Martin Charles,
Kt.
Nugent, Sir John Edwin Lavallin, Bt.
(I. 1795)
Nugent, *Maj.* Sir Peter Walter James,
Bt. (1831)
Nugent, Sir Robin George Colborne,
Bt. (1806)
Nursaw, Sir James, KCB, QC
Nuttall, Sir Nicholas Keith
Lillington, Bt. (1922)
Nutting, *Rt. Hon.* Sir (Harold)
Anthony, Bt. (1903)
Oakeley, Sir John Digby Atholl, Bt.
(1790)
Oakes, Sir Christopher, Bt. (1939)
Oakshott, *Hon.* Sir Anthony
Hendrie, Bt. (1959)
Oates, Sir Thomas, Kt., CMG, OBE

Obolensky, *Prof.* Sir Dimitri, Kt.
O'Brien, Sir Frederick William
Fitzgerald, Kt.
O'Brien, Sir Richard, Kt., DSO, MC
O'Brien, Sir Timothy John, Bt.
(1849)
O'Brien, *Adm.* Sir William Donough,
KCB, DSC
O'Connell, Sir Maurice James
Donagh MacCarthy, Bt. (1869)
O'Connor, *Rt. Hon.* Sir Patrick
McCarthy, Kt.
O'Dea, Sir Patrick Jerad, KCVO
Odell, Sir Stanley John, Kt.
Ogden, Sir (Edward) Michael, Kt., QC
Ogilvie, Sir Alec Drummond, Kt.
Ogilvy, *Hon.* Sir Angus James Bruce,
KCVO
Ogilvy, Sir Francis Gilbert Arthur,
Bt. (s. 1626)
Ognall, *Hon.* Sir Harry Henry, Kt.
Ohlson, Sir Brian Eric Christopher,
Bt. (1920)
Okeover, *Capt.* Sir Peter Ralph
Leopold Walker-, Bt. (1886)
Olewale, *Hon.* Sir Niwia Ebia, Kt.
Oliphant, Sir Mark (Marcus
Laurence Elwin), KBE, FRS
O'Loghlen, Sir Colman Michael, Bt.
(1838)
Olver, Sir Stephen John Linley, KBE,
CMG
O'Neil, *Hon.* Sir Desmond Henry, Kt.
Ongley, *Hon.* Sir Joseph Augustine,
Kt.
Onslow, *Rt. Hon.* Sir Cranley Gordon
Douglas, KCMG, MP
Onslow, Sir John Roger Wilmot, Bt.
(1797)
Oppenheim, Sir Alexander, Kt., OBE,
D.SC., FRSE
Oppenheim, Sir Duncan Morris, Kt.
Oppenheimer, Sir Michael Bernard
Grenville, Bt. (1921)
Orde, Sir John Alexander Campbell-,
Bt. (1790)
O'Regan, *Hon.* Sir John Barry, Kt.
O'Regan, *Dr* Sir Stephen Gerard
(Tipene), Kt.
Orlebar, Sir Michael Keith Orlebar
Simpson-, KCMG
Ormond, Sir John Davies Wilder,
Kt., BEM
Orr, Sir David Alexander, Kt., MC
Osborn, Sir John Holbrook, Kt.
Osborn, Sir Richard Henry Danvers,
Bt. (1662)
Osborne, Sir Peter George, Bt.
(I. 1629)
Osifelo, Sir Frederick Aubarua, Kt.,
MBE
Osman, Sir (Abdool) Raman
Mahomed, GCMG, CBE
Osmond, Sir Douglas, Kt., CBE
Osmond, Sir (Stanley) Paul, Kt., CB
Oswald, *Admiral of the Fleet* Sir (John)
Julian Robertson, GCB
Otton, Sir Geoffrey John, KCB
Otton, *Rt. Hon.* Sir Philip Howard, Kt.

Oulton, Sir Antony Derek Maxwell,
GCB, QC
Outram, Sir Alan James, Bt. (1858)
Overall, Sir John Wallace, Kt., CBE,
MC
Owen, Sir Geoffrey, Kt.
Owen, Sir Hugh Bernard Pilkington,
Bt. (1813)
Owen, Sir Hugo Dudley Cunliffe-,
Bt. (1920)
Owen, *Hon.* Sir John Arthur Dalziel,
Kt.
Owo, The Olowo of, Kt.
Oxburgh, *Prof.* Sir Ernest Ronald,
KBE, PH.D., FRS
Oxford, Sir Kenneth Gordon, Kt.,
CBE, QPM
Packard, *Lt.-Gen.* Sir (Charles)
Douglas, KBE, CB, DSO
Page, Sir (Arthur) John, Kt.
Page, Sir Frederick William, Kt., CBE,
FENG.
Page, Sir John Joseph Joffre, Kt., OBE
Paget, Sir Julian Tolver, Bt., CVO
(1871)
Paget, Sir Richard Herbert, Bt.
(1886)
Pain, *Lt.-Gen.* Sir (Horace) Rollo
(Squarey), KCB, MC
Pain, *Hon.* Sir Peter Richard, Kt.
Paine, Sir Christopher Hammon, Kt.,
FRCP, FRCR
Palin, *Air Chief Marshal* Sir Roger
Hewlett, KCB, OBE
Palliser, *Rt. Hon.* Sir (Arthur)
Michael, GCMG
Palmar, Sir Derek James, Kt.
Palmer, Sir (Charles) Mark, Bt.
(1886)
Palmer, *Gen.* Sir (Charles) Patrick
(Ralph), KBE
Palmer, Sir Geoffrey Christopher
John, Bt. (1660)
Palmer, *Rt. Hon.* Sir Geoffrey
Winston Russell, KCMG
Palmer, Sir John Chance, Kt.
Palmer, Sir John Edward Somerset,
Bt. (1791)
Palmer, *Maj.-Gen.* Sir (Joseph)
Michael, KCVO
Palmer, Sir Reginald Oswald, GCMG,
MBE
Pantlin, Sir Dick Hurst, Kt., CBE
Paolozzi, Sir Eduardo Luigi, Kt., CBE,
RA
Parbo, Sir Arvi Hillar, Kt.
Parish, Sir David Elmer Woodbine,
Kt., CBE
Park, *Hon.* Sir Hugh Eames, Kt.
Parker, Sir (Arthur) Douglas Dodds-,
Kt.
Parker, Sir Eric Wilson, Kt.
Parker, *Hon.* Sir Jonathan Frederic,
Kt.
Parker, Sir Peter, KBE, LVO
Parker, Sir Richard (William) Hyde,
Bt. (1681)
Parker, *Rt. Hon.* Sir Roger Jocelyn,
Kt.

Parker, *Vice-Adm.* Sir (Wilfred) John,
KBE, CB, DSC
Parker, Sir William Peter Brian, Bt.
(1844)
Parkes, Sir Edward Walter, Kt., FENG
Parkinson, Sir Nicholas Fancourt, Kt.
Parsons, Sir (John) Michael, Kt.
Parsons, Sir Richard Edmund
(Clement Fownes), KCMG
Partridge, Sir Michael John
Anthony, KCB
Pascoe, *Gen.* Sir Robert Alan, KCB,
MBE
Pasley, Sir John Malcolm Sabine, Bt.
(1794)
Paterson, Sir Dennis Craig, Kt.
Paterson, Sir John Valentine Jardine,
Kt.
Patnick, Sir (Cyril) Irvine, Kt., OBE,
MP
Paton, Sir (Thomas) Angus (Lyall),
Kt., CMG, FRS, FENG.
Pattie, *Rt. Hon.* Sir Geoffrey Edwin,
Kt., MP
Pattinson, Sir (William) Derek, Kt.
Pattullo, Sir (David) Bruce, Kt., CBE
Paul, Sir John Warburton, GCMG,
OBE, MC
Paul, *Air Marshal* Sir Ronald Ian
Stuart-, KBE
Payne, Sir Norman John, Kt., CBE,
FENG.
Peach, Sir Leonard Harry, Kt.
Peacock, *Prof.* Sir Alan Turner, Kt.,
DSC
Pearce, Sir Austin William, Kt., CBE,
PH.D., FENG.
Pearce, Sir (Daniel Norton) Idris, Kt.,
CBE, TD
Pearce, Sir Eric Herbert, Kt., OBE
Pearse, Sir Brian Gerald, Kt.
Pearson, Sir Francis Nicholas Fraser,
Bt. (1964)
Pearson, *Gen.* Sir Thomas Cecil
Hook, KCB, CBE, DSO
Peart, *Prof.* Sir William Stanley, Kt.,
MD, FRS
Pease, Sir (Alfred) Vincent, Bt.
(1882)
Pease, Sir Richard Thorn, Bt. (1920)
Peat, Sir Gerrard Charles, KCVO
Peat, Sir Henry, KCVO, DFC
Peck, Sir Edward Heywood, GCMG
Peckham, *Prof.* Sir Michael John, Kt.,
FRCP, FRCPGlas., FRCR, FRCPath.
Pedder, *Air Marshal* Sir Ian Maurice,
KCB, OBE, DFC
†Peek, Sir William Grenville, Bt.
(1874)
Peek, *Vice-Adm.* Sir Richard Innes,
KBE, CB, DSC
Peel, Sir John Harold, KCVO
Peel, Sir (William) John, Kt.
Peirse, Sir Henry Grant de la Poer
Beresford-, Bt. (1814)
Peirse, *Air Vice-Marshal* Sir Richard
Charles Fairfax, KCVO, CB
Pelgen, Sir Harry Friedrich, Kt., MBE
Pelly, Sir Richard John, Bt. (1840)

Pemberton, Sir Francis Wingate William, Kt., CBE

Penrose, *Prof.* Sir Roger, Kt., FRS

Percival, *Rt. Hon.* Sir (Walter) Ian, Kt., QC

Pereira, Sir (Herbert) Charles, Kt., D.SC., FRS

Perring, Sir Ralph Edgar, Bt. (1963)

Perris, Sir David (Arthur), Kt., MBE

Perry, Sir David Howard, KCB

Perry, Sir (David) Norman, Kt., MBE

Perry, Sir Michael Sydney, Kt., CBE

Pestell, Sir John Richard, KCVO

Peterkin, Sir Neville, Kt.

Peters, *Prof.* Sir David Keith, Kt., FRCP

Petersen, Sir Jeffrey Charles, KCMG

Petersen, Sir Johannes Bjelke-, KCMG

Peterson, Sir Christopher Matthew, Kt., CBE, TD

Petit, Sir Dinshaw Manockjee, Bt. (1890)

Peto, Sir Henry George Morton, Bt. (1855)

Peto, Sir Michael Henry Basil, Bt. (1927)

Petrie, Sir Peter Charles, Bt., CMG (1918)

Pettigrew, Sir Russell Hilton, Kt.

Pettit, Sir Daniel Eric Arthur, Kt.

Philips, *Prof.* Sir Cyril Henry, Kt.

Phillips, Sir Fred Albert, Kt., CVO

Phillips, Sir Henry Ellis Isidore, Kt., CMG, MBE

Phillips, Sir Horace, KCMG

Phillips, *Hon.* Sir Nicholas Addison, Kt.

Phillips, Sir Peter John, Kt., OBE

Phillips, Sir Robin Francis, Bt. (1912)

Pickering, Sir Edward Davies, Kt.

†Pickthorn, Sir James Francis Mann, Bt. (1959)

Pidgeon, Sir John Allan Stewart, Kt.

†Piers, Sir James Desmond, Bt. (I. 1661)

Pigot, Sir George Hugh, Bt. (1764)

Pigott, Sir Berkeley Henry Sebastian, Bt. (1808)

Pike, Sir Michael Edmund, KCVO, CMG

Pike, Sir Philip Ernest Housden, Kt., QC

Pilditch, Sir Richard Edward, Bt. (1929)

Pile, Sir Frederick Devereux, Bt., MC (1900)

Pile, Sir William Dennis, GCB, MBE

Pilkington, Sir Antony Richard, Kt.

Pilkington, Sir Thomas Henry Milborne-Swinnerton-, Bt. (s. 1635)

Pill, *Rt. Hon.* Sir Malcolm Thomas, Kt.

Pillar, *Adm.* Sir William Thomas, GBE, KCB

Pindling, *Rt. Hon.* Sir Lynden Oscar, KCMG

Pinker, Sir George Douglas, KCVO

Pinsent, Sir Christopher Roy, Bt. (1938)

Pippard, *Prof.* Sir (Alfred) Brian, Kt., FRS

Pirie, *Gp Capt* Sir Gordon Hamish, Kt., CVO, CBE

Pitakaka, Sir Moses Puibangara, GCMG

Pitblado, Sir David Bruce, KCB, CVO

Pitcher, Sir Desmond Henry, Kt.

Pitman, Sir Brian Ivor, Kt.

Pitoi, Sir Sere, Kt., CBE

Pitt, Sir Harry Raymond, Kt., PH.D., FRS

Pitts, Sir Cyril Alfred, Kt.

Plastow, Sir David Arnold Stuart, Kt.

†Platt, Sir (Frank) Lindsey, Bt. (1958)

Platt, Sir Harold Grant, Kt.

Platt, *Prof.* Hon. Sir Peter, Bt. (1959)

Playfair, Sir Edward Wilder, KCB

Pliatzky, Sir Leo, KCB

Plowman, *Hon.* Sir John Robin, Kt., CBE

Plumb, *Prof.* Sir John Harold, Kt.

Pohai, Sir Timothy, Kt., MBE

Pole, Sir (John) Richard (Walter Reginald) Carew, Bt. (1628)

Pole, Sir Peter Van Notten, Bt. (1791)

Pollen, Sir John Michael Hungerford, Bt. (1795)

Pollock, Sir George Frederick, Bt. (1866)

Pollock, Sir Giles Hampden Montagu-, Bt. (1872)

Pollock, *Admiral of the Fleet* Sir Michael Patrick, GCB, LVO, DSC

Ponsonby, Sir Ashley Charles Gibbs, Bt., KCVO, MC (1956)

Pontin, Sir Frederick William, Kt.

Poole, *Hon.* Sir David Anthony, Kt.

Poore, Sir Herbert Edward, Bt. (1795)

Pope, *Vice-Adm.* Sir (John) Ernle, KCB

Pope, Sir Joseph Albert, Kt., D.SC., PH.D.

Popplewell, *Hon.* Sir Oliver Bury, Kt.

†Porritt, Sir Jonathon Espie, Bt. (1963)

Portal, Sir Jonathan Francis, Bt. (1901)

Porter, Sir John Simon Horsbrugh-, Bt. (1902)

Porter, Sir Leslie, Kt.

Porter, *Air Marshal* Sir (Melvin) Kenneth (Drowley), KCB, CBE

Porter, *Rt. Hon.* Sir Robert Wilson, Kt., PC (NI), QC

Posnett, Sir Richard Neil, KBE, CMG

Potter, *Rt. Hon.* Sir Mark Howard, Kt.

Potter, *Maj.-Gen.* Sir (Wilfrid) John, KBE, CB

Potts, *Hon.* Sir Francis Humphrey, Kt.

Pound, Sir John David, Bt. (1905)

Pountain, Sir Eric John, Kt.

Powell, Sir (Arnold Joseph) Philip, Kt., CH, OBE, RA, FRIBA

Powell, Sir Charles David, KCMG

Powell, Sir Nicholas Folliott Douglas, Bt. (1897)

Powell, Sir Raymond, Kt., MP

Powell, Sir Richard Royle, GCB, KBE, CMG

Power, Sir Alastair John Cecil, Bt. (1924)

Prance, *Prof.* Sir Ghillean Tolmie, Kt., FRS

Prendergast, Sir (Walter) Kieran, KCVO, CMG

Prentice, *Hon.* Sir William Thomas, Kt., MBE

Prescott, Sir Mark, Bt. (1938)

Preston, Sir Ronald Douglas Hildebrand, Bt. (1815)

Prevost, Sir Christopher Gerald, Bt. (1805)

Price, Sir Charles Keith Napier Rugge-, Bt. (1804)

Price, Sir David Ernest Campbell, Kt.

Price, Sir Francis Caradoc Rose, Bt. (1815)

Price, Sir Frank Leslie, Kt.

Price, Sir (James) Robert, KBE

Price, Sir Leslie Victor, Kt., OBE

Price, Sir Norman Charles, KCB

Price, Sir Robert John Green-, Bt. (1874)

Prickett, *Air Chief Marshal* Sir Thomas Other, KCB, DSO, DFC

Prideaux, Sir Humphrey Povah Treverbian, Kt., OBE

†Primrose, Sir John Ure, Bt. (1903)

Pringle, *Air Marshal* Sir Charles Norman Seton, KBE, FENG.

Pringle, *Hon.* Sir John Kenneth, Kt.

Pringle, *Lt.-Gen.* Sir Steuart (Robert), Bt., KCB, RM (S. 1683)

Pritchard, Sir Neil, KCMG

Pritchett, Sir Victor Sawdon, Kt., CH, CBE

Proby, Sir Peter, Bt. (1952)

Prosser, Sir Ian Maurice Gray, Kt.

Proud, Sir John Seymour, Kt.

Pryke, Sir David Dudley, Bt. (1926)

Pugh, Sir Idwal Vaughan, KCB

Pugsley, *Prof.* Sir Alfred Grenvile, Kt., OBE, D.SC., FRS, FENG.

Pullen, Sir William Reginald James, KCVO

Pullinger, Sir (Francis) Alan, Kt., CBE

Pumphrey, Sir (John) Laurence, KCMG

Purchas, *Rt. Hon.* Sir Francis Brooks, Kt.

Purves, Sir William, Kt., CBE, DSO

Purvis, *Vice-Adm.* Sir Neville, KCB

Puttnam, Sir David Terrance, Kt., CBE

Quicke, Sir John Godolphin, Kt., CBE

Quigley, Sir (William) George (Henry), Kt., CB, PH.D.

Quilliam, *Hon.* Sir (James) Peter, Kt.

Quilter, Sir Anthony Raymond Leopold Cuthbert, Bt. (1897)

Quinlan, Sir Michael Edward, GCB

Quinton, Sir James Grand, Kt.

Radcliffe, Sir Sebastian Everard, Bt. (1813)

Radzinowicz, *Prof.* Sir Leon, Kt., LLD

Rae, *Hon.* Sir Wallace Alexander Ramsay, Kt.
Raeburn, Sir Michael Edward Norman, Bt. (1923)
Raeburn, *Maj.-Gen.* Sir (William) Digby (Manifold), KCVO, CB, DSO, MBE
Raffray, Sir Piat Joseph Raymond Andre, Kt.
Raikes, *Vice-Adm.* Sir Iwan Geoffrey, KCB, CBE, DSC
Raison, *Rt. Hon.* Sir Timothy Hugh Francis, Kt.
Ralli, Sir Godfrey Victor, Bt., TD (1912)
Ramdanee, Sir Mookteswar Baboolall Kailash, Kt.
Ramphal, Sir Shridath Surendranath, GCMG
Ramphul, Sir Baalkhristna, Kt.
Ramphul, Sir Indurduth, Kt.
Ramsay, Sir Alexander William Burnett, Bt. (1806)
Ramsay, Sir Allan John (Hepple), KBE, CMG
Ramsbotham, *Gen.* Sir David John, GCB, CBE
Ramsbotham, *Hon.* Sir Peter Edward, GCMG, GCVO
Ramsden, Sir John Charles Josslyn, Bt. (1689)
Ramsey, Sir Alfred Ernest, Kt.
Randle, *Prof.* Sir Philip John, Kt.
Ranger, Sir Douglas, Kt., FRCS
Rank, Sir Benjamin Keith, Kt., CMG
Rankin, Sir Alick Michael, Kt., CBE
Rankin, Sir Ian Niall, Bt. (1898)
Rasch, *Maj.* Sir Richard Guy Carne, Bt. (1903)
Rashleigh, Sir Richard Harry, Bt. (1831)
Ratford, Sir David John Edward, KCMG, CVO
Rattee, *Hon.* Sir Donald Keith, Kt.
Rattle, Sir Simon Dennis, Kt., CBE
Rault, Sir Louis Joseph Maurice, Kt.
Rawlins, *Surgeon Vice-Adm.* Sir John Stuart Pepys, KBE
Rawlinson, Sir Anthony Henry John, Bt. (1891)
Read, *Air Marshal* Sir Charles Frederick, KBE, CB, DFC, AFC
Read, Sir (John) Antony (Jervis), GCB, CBE, DSO, MC
Read, Sir John Emms, Kt.
†Reade, Sir Kenneth Ray, Bt. (1661)
Reay, *Lt.-Gen.* Sir (Hubert) Alan John, KBE
Redgrave, *Maj.-Gen.* Sir Roy Michael Frederick, KBE, MC
Redmayne, Sir Nicholas, Bt. (1964)
Redmond, Sir James, Kt., FEng.
Redwood, Sir Peter Boverton, Bt. (1911)
Reece, Sir Charles Hugh, Kt.
Reece, Sir James Gordon, Kt.
Reed, *Hon.* Sir Nigel Vernon, Kt., CBE
Rees, Sir (Charles William) Stanley, Kt., TD

Rees, Sir David Allan, Kt., PH.D., D.SC., FRS
Rees, *Prof.* Sir Martin John, Kt., FRS
Reeve, Sir Anthony, KCMG, KCVO
Reeves, *Most Revd* Paul Alfred, GCMG, GCVO
Reffell, *Adm.* Sir Derek Roy, KCB
Refshauge, *Maj-Gen.* Sir William Dudley, Kt., CBE
Reid, Sir Alexander James, Bt. (1897)
Reid, Sir (Harold) Martin (Smith), KBE, CMG
Reid, Sir Hugh, Bt. (1922)
Reid, Sir Norman Robert, Kt.
Reid, Sir Robert Paul, Kt.
Reid, Sir William Kennedy, KCB
Reiher, Sir Frederick Bernard Carl, KBE, CMG
Reilly, Sir (D'Arcy) Patrick, GCMG, OBE
Reilly, *Lt.-Gen.* Sir Jeremy Calcott, KCB, DSO
Renals, Sir Stanley, Bt. (1895)
Rennie, Sir John Shaw, GCMG, OBE
Renouf, Sir Clement William Bailey, Kt.
Renouf, Sir Francis Henry, Kt.
Renshaw, Sir (Charles) Maurice Bine, Bt. (1903)
Renwick, Sir Richard Eustace, Bt. (1921)
Renwick, Sir Robin William, KCMG
Reporter, Sir Shapoor Ardeshirji, KBE
Reynolds, Sir David James, Bt. (1923)
Reynolds, Sir Peter William John, Kt., CBE
Rhodes, Sir Basil Edward, Kt., CBE, TD
Rhodes, Sir John Christopher Douglas, Bt. (1919)
Rhodes, Sir Peregrine Alexander, KCMG
Rice, *Maj.-Gen.* Sir Desmond Hind Garrett, KCVO, CBE
Rice, Sir Timothy Miles Bindon, Kt.
Richard, Sir Cliff, Kt., OBE
Richards, Sir (Francis) Brooks, KCMG, D.SC.
Richards, *Lt.-Gen.* Sir John Charles Chisholm, KCB, KCVO, RM
Richards, Sir Rex Edward, Kt., D.SC., FRS
Richardson, Sir Anthony Lewis, Bt. (1924)
Richardson, *Rt. Hon.* Sir Ivor Lloyd Morgan, Kt.
Richardson, Sir (John) Eric, Kt., CBE
Richardson, Sir Michael John de Rougemont, Kt.
Richardson, *Lt.-Gen.* Sir Robert Francis, KCB, CVO, CBE
Richardson, Sir Simon Alaisdair Stewart-, Bt. (s. 1630)
Riches, Sir Derek Martin Hurry, KCMG
Riches, *Gen.* Sir Ian Hurry, KCB, DSO
Richmond, Sir Alan James, Kt.
Richmond, *Rt. Hon.* Sir Clifford Parris, KBE

Richmond, Sir John Frederick, Bt. (1929)
Richmond, *Prof.* Sir Mark Henry, Kt., FRS
Rickett, Sir Denis Hubert Fletcher, KCMG, CB
Ricketts, Sir Robert Cornwallis Gerald St Leger, Bt. (1828)
Riddell, Sir John Charles Buchanan, Bt., CVO (s. 1628)
Ridley, Sir Adam (Nicholas), Kt.
Ridsdale, Sir Julian Errington, Kt., CBE
Rigby, *Lt.-Col.* Sir (Hugh) John (Macbeth), Bt. (1929)
Riley, Sir Ralph, Kt., FRS
Rimer, *Hon.* Sir Colin Percy Farquharson, Kt.
Ring, Sir Lindsay Roberts, GBE
Ringadoo, *Hon.* Sir Veerasamy, GCMG
Ripley, Sir Hugh, Bt. (1880)
Risk, Sir Thomas Neilson, Kt.
Rix, *Hon.* Sir Bernard Anthony, Kt.
Rix, Sir John, Kt., MBE, FEng.
Roberts, Sir Bryan Clieve, KCMG, QC
Roberts, *Hon.* Sir Denys Tudor Emil, KBE, QC
Roberts, Sir Derek Harry, Kt., CBE, FRS, FEng.
Roberts, Sir (Edward Fergus) Sidney, Kt., CBE
Roberts, Sir Frank Kenyon, GCMG, GCVO
Roberts, *Brig.* Sir Geoffrey Paul Hardy-, KCVO, CB, CBE
Roberts, Sir Gilbert Howland Rookehurst, Bt. (1809)
Roberts, Sir Gordon James, Kt., CBE
Roberts, *Rt. Hon.* Sir (Ieuan) Wyn Pritchard, Kt., MP
Roberts, Sir Samuel, Bt. (1919)
Roberts, Sir Stephen James Leake, Kt.
Roberts, Sir William James Denby, Bt. (1909)
Robertson, Sir John Fraser, KCMG, CBE
Robertson, Sir Lewis, Kt., CBE, FRSE
Robertson, *Prof.* Sir Rutherford Ness, Kt., CMG
Robins, Sir Ralph Harry, Kt., FEng.
Robinson, Sir Albert Edward Phineas, Kt.
†Robinson, Sir Christopher Philipse, Bt. (1854)
Robinson, Sir John James Michael Laud, Bt. (1660)
†Robinson, Sir Dominick Christopher Lynch-, Bt. (1920)
Robinson, Sir Wilfred Henry Frederick, Bt. (1908)
Robotham, *Hon.* Sir Lascelles Lister, Kt.
Robson, *Prof.* Sir James Gordon, Kt., CBE
Robson, Sir John Adam, KCMG
Roch, *Rt. Hon.* Sir John Ormond, Kt.
Roche, Sir David O'Grady, Bt. (1838)
Rodgers, Sir (John Fairlie) Tobias, Bt. (1964)

Rodrigues, Sir Alberto Maria, Kt., CBE, ED
Roe, *Air Chief Marshal* Sir Rex David, GCB, AFC
Rogers, Sir Frank Jarvis, Kt.
Rogers, *Air Chief Marshal* Sir John Robson, KCB, CBE
Rogers, Sir Richard George, Kt., RA
Roll, *Revd* Sir James William Cecil, Bt. (1921)
Rooke, Sir Denis Eric, Kt., CBE, FRS, FEng.
Ropner, Sir John Bruce Woollacott, Bt. (1952)
Ropner, Sir Robert Douglas, Bt. (1904)
Roscoe, Sir Robert Bell, KBE
Rose, *Rt. Hon.* Sir Christopher Dudley Roger, Kt.
Rose, Sir Clive Martin, GCMG
Rose, Sir David Lancaster, Bt. (1874)
Rose, *Gen.* Sir (Hugh) Michael, KCB, CBE, DSO, QGM
Rose, Sir Julian Day, Bt. (1872 and 1909)
Rosier, *Air Chief Marshal* Sir Frederick Ernest, GCB, CBE, DSO
Ross, Sir (James) Keith, Bt., RD, FRCS (1960)
Ross, *Lt.-Gen.* Sir Robert Jeremy, KCB, OBE
Rosser, Sir Melvyn Wynne, Kt.
Rossi, Sir Hugh Alexis Louis, Kt.
Roth, *Prof.* Sir Martin, Kt., MD, FRCP
Rothnie, Sir Alan Keir, KCVO, CMG
Rothschild, Sir Evelyn Robert Adrian de, Kt.
Rougier, *Hon.* Sir Richard George, Kt.
Rous, *Lt.-Gen.* Hon. Sir William Edward, KCB, OBE
Rowe, Sir Jeremy, Kt., CBE
Rowell, Sir John Joseph, Kt., CBE
Rowland, *Air Marshal* Sir James Anthony, KBE, DFC, AFC
Rowlands, *Air Marshal* Sir John Samuel, GC, KBE
Rowley, Sir Charles Robert, Bt. (1836)
Rowley, Sir Joshua Francis, Bt. (1786)
Roxburgh, *Vice-Adm.* Sir John Charles Young, KCB, CBE, DSO, DSC
Royden, Sir Christopher John, Bt. (1905)
Rudd, Sir (Anthony) Nigel (Russell), Kt.
Rumbold, Sir Henry John Sebastian, Bt. (1779)
Rumbold, Sir Jack Seddon, Kt.
Runchorelal, Sir (Udayan) Chinubhai Madhowlal, Bt. (1913)
Runciman, *Hon.* Sir James Cochran Stevenson (Sir Steven Runciman), Kt., CH Rusby, *Vice-Adm.* Sir Cameron, KCB, LVO
Russell, Sir Charles Ian, Bt. (1916)
Russell, *Hon.* Sir David Sturrock West-, Kt.
Russell, Sir George, Kt., CBE

Russell, Sir George Michael, Bt. (1812)
Russell, *Prof.* Sir Peter Edward Lionel, Kt., D.Litt., FBA
Russell, Sir (Robert) Mark, KCMG
Russell, Sir Spencer Thomas, Kt.
Russell, *Rt. Hon.* Sir (Thomas) Patrick, Kt.
Rutter, Sir Frank William Eden, KBE
Rutter, *Prof.* Sir Michael Llewellyn, Kt., CBE, MD, FRS
Ryan, Sir Derek Gerald, Bt. (1919)
Rycroft, Sir Richard Newton, Bt. (1784)
Ryrie, Sir William Sinclair, KCB
Sabola, *Hon.* Sir Joaquim Claudino Gonsalves-, Kt.
Sachs, *Hon.* Sir Michael Alexander Geddes, Kt.
Sainsbury, Sir Robert James, Kt.
Sainsbury, *Rt. Hon.* Sir Timothy Alan Davan, Kt., MP
St Aubyn, Sir (John) Arscott Molesworth-, Bt. (1689)
St George, Sir George Bligh, Bt. (1. 1766)
St Johnston, Sir Kerry, Kt.
Sainty, Sir John Christopher, KCB
Sakzewski, Sir Albert, Kt.
Salt, Sir Patrick MacDonnell, Bt. (1869)
Salt, Sir (Thomas) Michael John, Bt. (1899)
Sampson, Sir Colin, Kt., CBE, QPM
Samuel, Sir Jon Michael Glen, Bt. (1898)
Samuelson, Sir (Bernard) Michael (Francis), Bt. (1884)
Samuelson, Sir Sydney Wylie, Kt., CBE
Sandberg, Sir Michael Graham Ruddock, Kt., CBE
Sanders, Sir John Reynolds Mayhew-, Kt.
Sanders, Sir Robert Tait, KBE, CMG
Sanderson, Sir Frank Linton, Bt. (1920)
Sarei, Sir Alexis Holyweek, Kt., CBE
Sarell, Sir Roderick Francis Gisbert, KCMG, KCVO
Sargant, Sir (Henry) Edmund, Kt.
Saunders, *Hon.* Sir John Anthony Holt, Kt., CBE, DSO, MC
Saunders, Sir Peter, Kt.
Sauzier, Sir (André) Guy, Kt., CBE, ED
Savage, Sir Ernest Walter, Kt.
Savile, Sir James Wilson Vincent, Kt., OBE
Saville, *Rt. Hon.* Sir Mark Oliver, Kt.
Say, *Rt. Revd* Richard David, KCVO
Schiemann, *Rt. Hon.* Sir Konrad Hermann Theodor, Kt.
Schneider, *Rt. Hon.* Sir Lancelot Raymond Adams-, KCMG
Scholey, Sir David Gerald, Kt., CBE
Scholey, Sir Robert, Kt., CBE, FEng.
Scholtens, Sir James Henry, KCVO
Schubert, Sir Sydney, Kt.
Schuster, Sir (Felix) James Moncrieff, Bt., OBE (1906)

Scipio, Sir Hudson Rupert, Kt.
Scoon, Sir Paul, GCMG, GCVO, OBE
Scopes, Sir Leonard Arthur, KCVO, CMG, OBE
Scott, Sir Anthony Percy, Bt. (1913)
Scott, Sir (Charles) Peter, KBE, CMG
Scott, Sir David Aubrey, GCMG
Scott, Sir Dominic James Maxwell-, Bt. (1642)
Scott, Sir Ian Dixon, KCMG, KCVO, CIE
Scott, Sir James Jervoise, Bt. (1962)
Scott, Sir Kenneth Bertram Adam, KCVO, CMG
Scott, Sir Michael, KCVO, CMG
Scott, *Rt. Hon.* Sir Nicholas Paul, KBE, MP
Scott, Sir Oliver Christopher Anderson, Bt. (1909)
Scott, *Prof.* Sir Philip John, KBE
Scott, *Rt. Hon.* Sir Richard Rashleigh Folliott, Kt.
Scott, Sir Robert David Hillyer, Kt.
Scott, Sir Walter John, Bt. (1907)
Scott, *Rear-Adm.* Sir (William) David (Stewart), KBE, CB
Scowen, Sir Eric Frank, Kt., MD, D.SC., LLD, FRCP, FRCS
Scrivenor, Sir Thomas Vaisey, Kt., CMG
Seale, Sir John Henry, Bt. (1838)
Seaman, Sir Keith Douglas, KCVO, OBE
Sebastian, Sir Cuthbert Montraville, GCMG, OBE
†Sebright, Sir Peter Giles Vivian, Bt. (1626)
Seccombe, Sir (William) Vernon Stephen, Kt.
Secombe, Sir Harry Donald, Kt., CBE
Seconde, Sir Reginald Louis, KCMG, CVO
Sedley, *Hon.* Sir Stephen John, Kt.
Seely, Sir Nigel Edward, Bt. (1896)
Seeto, Sir Ling James, Kt., MBE
Seeyave, Sir Rene Sow Choung, Kt., CBE
Seligman, Sir Peter Wendel, Kt., CBE
Sergeant, Sir Patrick, Kt.
Series, Sir (Joseph Michel) Emile, Kt., CBE
Serpell, Sir David Radford, KCB, CMG, OBE
Seton, Sir Iain Bruce, Bt. (s. 1663)
†Seton, Sir James Christall, Bt. (s. 1683)
Severne, *Air Vice-Marshal* Sir John de Milt, KCVO, OBE, AFC
Seymour, *Cdr.* Sir Michael Culme-, Bt., RN (1809)
Shakerley, Sir Geoffrey Adam, Bt. (1838)
†Shakespeare, Sir Thomas William, Bt. (1942)
Shapland, Sir William Arthur, Kt.
Sharp, Sir Adrian, Bt. (1922)
Sharp, Sir George, Kt., OBE
Sharp, Sir Kenneth Johnston, Kt., TD
Sharp, Sir Leslie, Kt., QPM
Sharp, Sir Milton Reginald, Bt. (1920)

Sharp, Sir Richard Lyall, KCVO, CB
Sharpe, *Hon.* Sir John Henry, Kt., CBE
Sharples, Sir James, Kt., QPM
Shattock, Sir Gordon, Kt.
Shaw, Sir Brian Piers, Kt.
Shaw, Sir (Charles) Barry, Kt., CB, QC
Shaw, Sir (George) Neville Bowan-, Kt.
Shaw, *Prof.* Sir John Calman, Kt., CBE, FRSE
Shaw, Sir (John) Giles (Dunkerley), Kt., MP
Shaw, Sir John Michael Robert Best-, Bt. (1665)
Shaw, Sir Neil McGowan, Kt.
Shaw, Sir Robert, Bt. (1821)
Shaw, Sir Roy, Kt.
Shaw, Sir Run Run, Kt., CBE
Sheehy, Sir Patrick, Kt.
Sheen, *Hon.* Sir Barry Cross, Kt.
Sheffield, Sir Reginald Adrian Berkeley, Bt. (1755)
Shehadie, Sir Nicholas Michael, Kt., OBE
Sheil, *Hon.* Sir John, Kt.
Sheldon, *Hon.* Sir (John) Gervase (Kensington), Kt.
Shelley, Sir John Richard, Bt. (1611)
Shelton, Sir William Jeremy Masefield, Kt.
Shepheard, Sir Peter Faulkner, Kt., CBE
Shepherd, Sir Colin Ryley, Kt., MP
Shepperd, Sir Alfred Joseph, Kt.
Sherlock, Sir Philip Manderson, KBE
Sherman, Sir Alfred, Kt.
Sherman, Sir Louis, Kt., OBE
Shersby, Sir (Julian) Michael, Kt., MP
Shields, Sir Neil Stanley, Kt., MC
Shields, *Prof.* Sir Robert, Kt., MD
Shiffner, Sir Henry David, Bt. (1818)
Shillington, Sir (Robert Edward) Graham, Kt., CBE
Shinwell, Sir Maurice Adrian, Kt.
Shock, Sir Maurice, Kt.
Short, *Brig.* Sir Noel Edward Vivian, Kt., MBE, MC
Shuckburgh, Sir Rupert Charles Gerald, Bt. (1660)
Siaguru, Sir Anthony Michael, KBE
Siddall, Sir Norman, Kt., CBE, FEng.
Sidey, *Air Marshal* Sir Ernest Shaw, KBE, CB, AFC
Sie, Sir Banja Tejan-, GCMG
Simeon, Sir John Edmund Barrington, Bt. (1815)
Simmons, *Air Marshal* Sir Michael George, KCB, AFC
Simmons, Sir Stanley Clifford, Kt., FRCS, FRCOG
Simon, Sir David Alec Gwyn, Kt., CBE
Simonet, Sir Louis Marcel Pierre, Kt., CBE
Simpson, *Hon.* Sir Alfred Henry, Kt.
Simpson, Sir William James, Kt.
Sims, Sir Roger Edward, Kt., MP
Sinclair, Sir Clive Marles, Kt.
Sinclair, Sir George Evelyn, Kt., CMG, OBE

Sinclair, Sir Ian McTaggart, KCMG, QC
Sinclair, *Air Vice-Marshal* Sir Laurence Frank, GC, KCB, CBE, DSO
Sinclair, Sir Patrick Robert Richard, Bt. (s. 1704)
Sinclair, Sir Ronald Ormiston, KBE
Singer, *Prof.* Sir Hans Wolfgang, Kt.
Singer, *Hon.* Sir Jan Peter, Kt.
Singh, *Hon.* Sir Vijay Raghubir, Kt.
Singhania, Sir Padampat, Kt.
Sitwell, Sir (Sacheverell) Reresby, Bt. (1808)
Skeet, Sir Trevor Herbert Harry, Kt., MP
Skeggs, Sir Clifford George, Kt.
Skehel, Sir John James, Kt., FRS
Skingsley, *Air Chief Marshal* Sir Anthony Gerald, GBE, KCB
Skinner, Sir (Thomas) Keith (Hewitt), Bt. (1912)
Skipwith, Sir Patrick Alexander d'Estoteville, Bt. (1622)
Skyrme, Sir (William) Thomas (Charles), KCVO, CB, CBE, TD
Slack, Sir William Willatt, KCVO, FRCS
Slade, Sir Benjamin Julian Alfred, Bt. (1831)
Slade, *Rt. Hon.* Sir Christopher John, Kt.
Slaney, *Prof.* Sir Geoffrey, KBE
Slater, *Adm.* Sir John (Jock) Cunningham Kirkwood, GCB, LVO
Sleight, Sir Richard, Bt. (1920)
Sloan, Sir Andrew Kirkpatrick, Kt., QPM
Sloman, Sir Albert Edward, Kt., CBE
Smallwood, *Air Chief Marshal* Sir Denis Graham, GBE, KCB, DSO, DFC
Smart, *Prof.* Sir George Algernon, Kt., MD, FRCP
Smart, Sir Jack, Kt., CBE
Smedley, *Hon.* Sir (Frank) Brian, Kt.
Smedley, Sir Harold, KCMG, MBE
Smiley, *Lt.-Col.* Sir John Philip, Bt. (1903)
Smith, Sir Alan, Kt., CBE, DFC
Smith, Sir Alexander Mair, Kt., PH.D.
Smith, Sir Andrew Colin Hugh-, Kt.
Smith, *Lt.-Gen.* Sir Anthony Arthur Denison-, KBE
Smith, Sir Charles Bracewell-, Bt. (1947)
Smith, Sir Christopher Sydney Winwood, Bt. (1809)
Smith, *Prof.* Sir Colin Stansfield, Kt., CBE
Smith, Sir Cyril, Kt., MBE
Smith, *Prof.* Sir David Cecil, Kt., FRS
Smith, *Air Chief Marshal* Sir David Harcourt-, GBE, KCB, DFC
Smith, Sir David Iser, KCVO
Smith, Sir Douglas Boucher, KCB
Smith, Sir Dudley (Gordon), Kt., MP
Smith, *Maj.-Gen.* Sir (Francis) Brian Wyldbore-, Kt., CB, DSO, OBE
Smith, *Prof.* Sir Francis Graham-, Kt., FRS
Smith, Sir Geoffrey Johnson, Kt., MP

Smith, Sir John Alfred, Kt., QPM
Smith, *Prof.* Sir John Cyril, Kt., CBE, QC, FBA
Smith, Sir John Hamilton-Spencer-, Bt. (1804)
Smith, Sir John Jonah Walker-, Bt. (1960)
Smith, Sir John Kenneth Newson-, Bt. (1944)
Smith, Sir John Lindsay Eric., Kt., CH, CBE
†Smith, Sir John Rathbone Vassar-, Bt. (1917)
Smith, Sir Joseph William Grenville, Kt., MD, FRCP
Smith, Sir Leslie Edward George, Kt.
Smith, Sir Michael John Llewellyn, KCVO, CMG
Smith, *Rt. Hon.* Sir Murray Stuart-, Kt.
Smith, Sir Raymond Horace, KBE
Smith, Sir Robert Courtney, Kt., CBE
Smith, Sir Robert Hill, Bt. (1945)
Smith, *Prof.* Sir Roland, Kt.
Smith, *Air Marshal* Sir Roy David Austen-, KBE, CB, CVO, DFC
Smith, *Lt.-Gen.* Sir Rupert Anthony, KCB, DSO, OBE, QGM
Smith, Sir (Thomas) Gilbert, Bt. (1897)
Smith, *Prof.* Sir Trevor Arthur, Kt.
Smith, *Adm.* Sir Victor Alfred Trumper, KBE, CB, DSC
Smith, Sir (William) Antony (John) Reardon-, Bt. (1920)
Smith, Sir (William) Richard Prince-, Bt. (1911)
Smithers, Sir Peter Henry Berry Otway, Kt., VRD, D.phil.
Smyth, Sir Thomas Weyland Bowyer-, Bt. (1661)
Smyth, Sir Timothy John, Bt. (1955)
Soakimori, Sir Frederick Pa-Nukuanca, KBE, CPM
Soame, Sir Charles John Buckworth-Herne-, Bt. (1697)
Sobers, Sir Garfield St Auburn, Kt.
Solomon, Sir David Arnold, Kt., MBE
Solomon, Sir Harry, Kt.
Solti, Sir Georg, KBE
Somare, *Rt. Hon.* Sir Michael Thomas, GCMG, CH
Somers, *Rt. Hon.* Sir Edward Jonathan, Kt.
Somerset, Sir Henry Beaufort, Kt., CBE
Somerville, *Brig.* Sir John Nicholas, Kt., CBE
Somerville, Sir Quentin Charles Somerville Agnew-, Bt. (1957)
Sopwith, Sir Charles Ronald, Kt.
Soutar, *Air Marshal* Sir Charles John Williamson, KBE
South, Sir Arthur, Kt.
Southby, Sir John Richard Bilbe, Bt. (1937)
Southern, Sir Richard William, Kt., FBA
Southern, Sir Robert, Kt., CBE
Southey, Sir Robert John, Kt., CMG

Southgate, Sir Colin Grieve, Kt.
Southgate, Sir William David, Kt.
Southward, Sir Leonard Bingley, Kt.,
OBE
Southward, Sir Ralph, KCVO, FRCP
Southwood, *Prof.* Sir (Thomas)
Richard (Edmund), Kt., FRS
Southworth, Sir Frederick, Kt., QC
Souyave, *Hon.* Sir (Louis) Georges,
Kt.
Sowrey, *Air Marshal* Sir Frederick
Beresford, KCB, CBE, AFC
Sparkes, Sir Robert Lyndley, Kt.
Sparrow, Sir John, Kt.
Spearman, Sir Alexander Young
Richard Mainwaring, Bt. (1840)
Spedding, *Prof.* Sir Colin Raymond
William, Kt., CBE
Spedding, Sir David Rolland, KCMG,
CVO, OBE
Speed, Sir (Herbert) Keith, Kt., RD,
MP
Speed, Sir Robert William Arney,
Kt., CB, QC
Speelman, Sir Cornelis Jacob, Bt.
(1686)
Speight, *Hon.* Sir Graham Davies, Kt.
Speir, Sir Rupert Malise, Kt.
Spencer, Sir Derek Harold, Kt., QC,
MP
Spicer, Sir James Wilton, Kt., MP
Spicer, Sir Nicholas Adrian Albert,
Bt., MB (1906)
Spicer, Sir William Michael Hardy,
Kt., MP
Spiers, Sir Donald Maurice, Kt., CB,
TD
Spooner, Sir James Douglas, Kt.
Spotswood, *Marshal of the Royal Air
Force* Sir Denis Frank, GCB, CBE,
DSO, DFC
Spratt, *Col.* Sir Greville Douglas, GBE,
TD
Spring, Sir Dryden Thomas, Kt.
Spry, *Hon.* Sir John Farley, Kt.
Stabb, *Hon.* Sir William Walter, Kt.,
QC
Stainton, Sir (John) Ross, Kt., CBE
Stakis, Sir Reo Argiros, Kt.
Stamer, Sir (Lovelace) Anthony, Bt.
(1809)
Stanbridge, *Air Vice-Marshal* Sir
Brian Gerald Tivy, KCVO, CBE, AFC
Stanier, Sir Beville Douglas, Bt.
(1917)
Stanier, *Field Marshal* Sir John
Wilfred, GCB, MBE
Stanley, *Rt. Hon.* Sir John Paul, Kt.,
MP
†Staples, Sir Thomas, Bt. (I. 1628)
Stark, Sir Andrew Alexander Steel,
KCMG, CVO
Starke, *Hon.* Sir John Erskine, Kt.
Starkey, Sir John Philip, Bt. (1935)
Starrit, Sir James, KCVO
Statham, Sir Norman, KCMG, CVO
Staughton, *Rt. Hon.* Sir Christopher
Stephen Thomas Jonathan
Thayer, Kt.
Staveley, Sir John Malfroy, KBE, MC

Staveley, *Admiral of the Fleet* Sir
William Doveton Minet, GCB
Stear, *Air Chief Marshal* Sir Michael
James Douglas, KCB, CBE
Steel, Sir David Edward Charles, Kt.,
DSO, MC, TD
Steel, *Rt. Hon.* Sir David Martin Scott,
KBE, MP
Steel, *Maj.* Sir (Fiennes) Michael
Strang, Bt. (1938)
Steele, Sir (Philip John) Rupert, Kt.
Steere, Sir Ernest Henry Lee-, KBE
Stenhouse, Sir Nicol, Kt.
Stening, *Col.* Sir George Grafton
Lees, Kt., ED
Stephen, *Rt. Hon.* Sir Ninian Martin,
KG, GCMG, GCVO, KBE
Stephenson, Sir Henry Upton, Bt.
(1936)
Stephenson, *Rt. Hon.* Sir John
Frederick Eustace, Kt.
Sternberg, Sir Sigmund, Kt.
Stevens, Sir Jocelyn Edward
Greville, Kt., CVO
Stevens, Sir Laurence Houghton, Kt.,
CBE
Stevenson, *Vice-Adm.* Sir (Hugh)
David, KBE
Stevenson, Sir Simpson, Kt.
Stewart, Sir Alan, KBE
Stewart, Sir Alan d'Arcy, Bt. (I. 1623)
Stewart, Sir David James
Henderson-, Bt. (1957)
Stewart, Sir David John Christopher,
Bt. (1803)
Stewart, Sir Edward Jackson, Kt.
Stewart, *Prof.* Sir Frederick Henry,
Kt., Ph.D., FRS, FRSE
Stewart, Sir Houston Mark Shaw-,
Bt., MC, TD (S. 1667)
Stewart, Sir James Douglas, Kt.
Stewart, Sir James Moray, KCB
Stewart, Sir (John) Simon (Watson),
Bt. (1920)
Stewart, Sir Robertson Huntly, Kt.,
CBE
Stewart, Sir Robin Alastair, Bt. (1960)
Stewart, Sir Ronald Compton, Bt.
(1937)
Stewart, *Prof.* Sir William Duncan
Paterson, Kt., FRS, FRSE
Stibbon, *Gen.* Sir John James, KCB,
OBE
Stirling, Sir Alexander John
Dickson, KBE, CMG
Stirling, Sir Angus Duncan Aeneas,
Kt.
Stockdale, Sir Arthur Noel, Kt.
Stockdale, Sir Thomas Minshull, Bt.
(1960)
Stocker, *Rt. Hon.* Sir John Dexter, Kt.,
MC, TD
Stoddart, *Wg Cdr.* Sir Kenneth
Maxwell, KCVO, AE
Stoker, *Prof.* Sir Michael George
Parke, Kt., CBE, FRCP, FRS, FRSE
Stokes, Sir John Heydon Romaine,
Kt.
Stone, Sir Alexander, Kt., OBE

Stones, Sir William Frederick, Kt.,
OBE
Stonhouse, Sir Philip Allan, Bt.
(1628)
Stonor, *Air Marshal* Sir Thomas
Henry, KCB
Storey, *Hon.* Sir Richard, Bt., CBE
(1960)
Stormonth Darling, Sir James
Carlisle, Kt., CBE, MC, TD
Stott, Sir Adrian George Ellingham,
Bt. (1920)
Stow, Sir Christopher Philipson-, Bt.,
DFC (1907)
Stow, Sir John Montague, GCMG,
KCVO
Stowe, Sir Kenneth Ronald, GCB, CVO
Stracey, Sir John Simon, Bt. (1818)
Strachan, Sir Curtis Victor, Kt., CVO
Strachey, Sir Charles, Bt. (1801)
Straker, Sir Michael Ian Bowstead,
Kt., CBE
Strawson, *Prof.* Sir Peter Frederick,
Kt., FBA
Street, *Hon.* Sir Laurence Whistler,
KCMG
Streeton, Sir Terence George, KBE,
CMG
Stringer, Sir Donald Edgar, Kt., CBE
Strong, Sir Roy Colin, Kt., Ph.D., FSA
Stronge, Sir James Anselan Maxwell,
Bt. (1803)
Stroud, *Prof.* Sir (Charles) Eric, Kt.,
FRCP
Strutt, Sir Nigel Edward, Kt., TD
Stuart, Sir James Keith, Kt.
Stuart, Sir Kenneth Lamonte, Kt.
†Stuart, Sir Phillip Luttrell, Bt.
(1660)
Stubblefield, Sir (Cyril) James, Kt.,
D.SC., FRS
Stubbs, Sir James Wilfrid, KCVO, TD
Stubbs, Sir William Hamilton, Kt.,
Ph.D.
Stucley, *Lt.* Sir Hugh George
Coplestone Bampfylde, Bt. (1859)
Studd, Sir Edward Fairfax, Bt. (1929)
Studd, Sir Peter Malden, GBE, KCVO
Studholme, Sir Henry William, Bt.
(1956)
Stuttaford, Sir William Royden, Kt.,
CBE
Style, *Lt.-Cdr.* Sir Godfrey William,
Kt., CBE, DSC, RN
†Style, Sir William Frederick, Bt.
(1627)
Suffield, Sir (Henry John) Lester, Kt.
Sugden, Sir Arthur, Kt.
Sullivan, Sir Desmond John, Kt.
Sullivan, Sir Richard Arthur, Bt.
(1804)
Summerfield, *Hon.* Sir John
Crampton, Kt., CBE
Sutherland, Sir John Brewer, Bt.
(1921)
Sutherland, Sir Maurice, Kt.
Sutherland, *Prof.* Sir Stewart Ross,
Kt., FBA
Sutherland, Sir William George
MacKenzie, Kt.

Suttie, Sir (George) Philip Grant-,
Bt. (s. 1702)
Sutton, Sir Frederick Walter, Kt., OBE
Sutton, *Air Marshal* Sir John
Matthias Dobson, KCB
Sutton, Sir Richard Lexington, Bt.
(1772)
Swaffield, Sir James Chesebrough,
Kt., CBE, RD
Swaine, Sir John Joseph, Kt., CBE
Swallow, Sir William, Kt.
Swan, Sir Conrad Marshall John
Fisher, KCVO, PH.D.
Swan, Sir John William David, KBE
Swann, Sir Michael Christopher, Bt.,
TD (1906)
Swanwick, Sir Graham Russell, Kt.,
MBE
Swartz, *Hon.* Sir Reginald William
Colin, KBE, ED
Sweetnam, Sir (David) Rodney,
KCVO, CBE, FRCS
Swinburn, *Lt.-Gen.* Sir Richard Hull,
KCB
Swinson, Sir John Henry Alan, Kt.,
OBE
Swinton, *Maj.-Gen.* Sir John, KCVO,
OBE
Swire, Sir Adrian Christopher, Kt.
Swire, Sir John Anthony, Kt., CBE
Swynnerton, Sir Roger John Massy,
Kt., CMG, OBE, MC
Sykes, Sir Francis John Badcock, Bt.
(1781)
Sykes, Sir John Charles Anthony le
Gallais, Bt. (1921)
Sykes, *Prof.* Sir (Malcolm) Keith, Kt.
Sykes, Sir Richard, Kt.
Sykes, Sir Tatton Christopher Mark,
Bt. (1783)
Symington, *Prof.* Sir Thomas, Kt.,
MD, FRSE
Symons, *Vice-Adm.* Sir Patrick
Jeremy, KBE
Synge, Sir Robert Carson, Bt. (1801)
Tait, *Adm.* Sir (Allan) Gordon, KCB,
DSC
Tait, Sir James Sharp, Kt., D.SC., LLD.,
PH.D.
Tait, Sir Peter, KBE
Talbot, *Vice-Adm.* Sir (Arthur
Allison) FitzRoy, KBE, CB, DSO
Talbot, *Hon.* Sir Hilary Gwynne, Kt.
Talboys, *Rt. Hon.* Sir Brian Edward,
CH, KCB
Tancred, Sir Henry Lawson-, Bt.
(1662)
Tangaroa, *Hon.* Sir Tangoroa, Kt.,
MBE
Tange, Sir Arthur Harold, Kt., CBE
Tapsell, Sir Peter Hannay Bailey,
Kt., MP
Tate, Sir (Henry) Saxon, Bt. (1898)
Tavare, Sir John, Kt., CBE
Taylor, *Lt.-Gen.* Sir Allan Macnab,
KBE, MC
Taylor, Sir (Arthur) Godfrey, Kt.
Taylor, Sir Cyril Julian Hebden, Kt.

Taylor, Sir Edward Macmillan
(Teddy), Kt., MP
Taylor, Sir John Lang, KCMG
Taylor, Sir Nicholas Richard Stuart,
Bt. (1917)
Taylor, *Prof.* Sir William, Kt., CBE
Teagle, *Vice-Adm.* Sir Somerford
Francis, KBE
Tebbit, Sir Donald Claude, GCMG
Te Heuheu, Sir Hepi Hoani, KBE
Telford, Sir Robert, Kt., CBE, FEng.
Temple, Sir Ernest Sanderson, Kt.,
MBE, QC
Temple, Sir Rawden John Afamado,
Kt., CBE, QC
Temple, *Maj.* Sir Richard Anthony
Purbeck, Bt., MC (1876)
Templeton, Sir John Marks, Kt.
Tenison, Sir Richard Hanbury-,
KCVO
Tennant, *Capt.* Sir Iain Mark, KT
Tennant, Sir Anthony John, Kt.
Tennant, Sir Peter Frank Dalrymple,
Kt., CMG, OBE
Teo, Sir Fiatau Penitala, GCMG,
GCVO, ISO, MBE
Terry, Sir Michael Edward Stanley
Imbert-, Bt. (1917)
Terry, *Air Chief Marshal* Sir Peter
David George, GCB, AFC
Tetley, Sir Herbert, KBE, CB
Tett, Sir Hugh Charles, Kt.
Thatcher, Sir Denis, Bt., MBE, TD
(1990)
Thesiger, Sir Wilfred Patrick, KBE,
DSO
Thomas, Sir Derek Morison David,
KCMG
Thomas, Sir Frederick William, Kt.
Thomas, Sir (Godfrey) Michael
(David), Bt. (1694)
Thomas, Sir Jeremy Cashel, KCMG
Thomas, Sir (John) Alan, Kt.
Thomas, Sir John Maldwyn, Kt.
Thomas, *Prof.* Sir John Meurig, Kt.,
FRS
Thomas, Sir Keith Vivian, Kt.
Thomas, Sir Robert Evan, Kt.
Thomas, *Hon.* Sir Roger John
Laugharne, Kt.
Thomas, *Hon.* Sir Swinton Barclay,
Kt.
Thomas, Sir William James Cooper,
Bt., TD (1919)
Thomas, Sir (William) Michael
(Marsh), Bt. (1918)
Thomas, *Adm.* Sir (William) Richard
Scott, KCB, KCVO, OBE
Thompson, Sir Christopher Peile,
Bt. (1890)
Thompson, Sir Clive Malcolm, Kt.
Thompson, Sir Donald, Kt., MP
Thompson, Sir Gilbert Williamson,
Kt., OBE
Thompson, *Surgeon Vice-Adm.* Sir
Godfrey James Milton-, KBE
Thompson, *Vice-Adm.* Sir Hugh
Leslie Owen, KBE, FEng.
Thompson, Sir (Humphrey) Simon
Meysey-, Bt. (1874)

Thompson, *Prof.* Sir Michael
Warwick, Kt., D.SC
Thompson, Sir Paul Anthony, Bt.
(1963)
Thompson, Sir Peter Anthony, Kt.
Thompson, Sir Richard Hilton
Marler, Bt. (1963)
Thompson, Sir (Thomas) Lionel
Tennyson, Bt. (1806)
Thomson, Sir Adam, Kt., CBE
Thomson, Sir (Frederick Douglas)
David, Bt. (1929)
Thomson, Sir John, KBE, TD
Thomson, Sir John Adam, GCMG
Thomson, Sir John (Ian) Sutherland,
KBE, CMG
Thomson, Sir Mark Wilfrid Home,
Bt. (1925)
Thomson, Sir Thomas James, Kt.,
CBE, FRCP
Thorn, Sir John Samuel, Kt., OBE
Thorne, *Maj.-Gen.* Sir David
Calthrop, KBE, CVO
Thorne, Sir Neil Gordon, Kt., OBE,
TD
Thorne, Sir Peter Francis, KCVO, CBE
Thornton, Sir (George) Malcolm,
Kt., MP
Thornton, *Lt.-Gen.* Sir Leonard
Whitmore, KCB, CBE
Thornton, Sir Peter Eustace, KCB
Thorold, Sir Anthony Henry, Bt.,
OBE, DSC (1642)
Thorpe, *Hon.* Sir Mathew Alexander,
Kt.
Thouron, Sir John Rupert Hunt, KBE
Thwaites, Sir Bryan, Kt., PH.D.
Thwin, Sir U, Kt.
Tibbits, *Capt.* Sir David Stanley, Kt.,
DSC
Tickell, Sir Crispin Charles
Cervantes, GCMG, KCVO
Tidbury, Sir Charles Henderson, Kt.
Tikaram, Sir Moti, KBE
Tims, Sir Michael David, KCVO
Tindle, Sir Ray Stanley, Kt., CBE
Tippet, *Vice-Adm.* Sir Anthony
Sanders, KCB
Tippett, Sir Michael Kemp, Kt., OM,
CH, CBE
†Tipping, Sir David Gwynne Evans-,
Bt. (1913)
Tirvengadum, Sir Harry Krishnan,
Kt.
Titman, Sir John Edward Powis,
KCVO
Tod, *Air Marshal* Sir John Hunter
Hunter-, KBE, CB
Tod, *Vice-Adm.* Sir Jonathan James
Richard, KCB, CBE
Todd, *Prof.* Sir David, Kt., CBE
Todd, Sir Ian Pelham, KBE, FRCS
Todd, *Hon.* Sir (Reginald Stephen)
Garfield, Kt.
Tollemache, Sir Lyonel Humphry
John, Bt. (1793)
Tololo, Sir Alkan, KBE
Tomkins, Sir Alfred George, Kt., CBE
Tomkins, Sir Edward Emile, GCMG,
CVO

Tomkys, Sir (William) Roger, KCMG
Tomlinson, *Prof.* Sir Bernard Evans, Kt., CBE
Tooley, Sir John, Kt.
Tooth, Sir (Hugh) John Lucas-, Bt. (1920)
ToRobert, Sir Henry Thomas, KBE
Tory, Sir Geofroy William, KCMG
Touche, Sir Anthony George, Bt. (1920)
Touche, Sir Rodney Gordon, Bt. (1962)
Toulson, *Hon.* Sir Roger Grenfell, Kt.
Tovey, Sir Brian John Maynard, KCMG
ToVue, Sir Ronald, Kt., OBE
Towneley, Sir Simon Peter Edmund Cosmo William, KCVO
Townsend, *Rear-Adm.* Sir Leslie William, KCVO, CBE
Townsing, Sir Kenneth Joseph, Kt., CMG
Traill, Sir Alan Towers, GBE
Trant, *Gen.* Sir Richard Brooking, KCB
Travers, Sir Thomas à'Beckett, Kt.
Treacher, *Adm.* Sir John Devereux, KCB
Trehane, Sir (Walter) Richard, Kt.
Trelawny, Sir John Barry Salusbury-, Bt. (1628)
Trench, Sir Peter Edward, Kt., CBE, TD
Trescowthick, Sir Donald Henry, KBE
Trevelyan, Sir Geoffrey Washington, Bt. (1874)
Trevelyan, Sir Norman Irving, Bt. (1662)
Trewby, *Vice-Adm.* Sir (George Francis) Allan, KCB, FEng.
Trezise, Sir Kenneth Bruce, Kt., OBE
Trippier, Sir David Austin, Kt., RD
Tritton, Sir Anthony John Ernest, Bt. (1905)
†Trollope, Sir Anthony Simon, Bt. (1642)
Trotter, Sir Ronald Ramsay, Kt.
Troubridge, Sir Thomas Richard, Bt. (1799)
Troup, *Vice-Adm.* Sir (John) Anthony (Rose), KCB, DSC
Trowbridge, *Rear-Adm.* Sir Richard John, KCVO
Truscott, Sir George James Irving, Bt. (1909)
Tuck, Sir Bruce Adolph Reginald, Bt. (1910)
Tucker, *Hon.* Sir Richard Howard, Kt.
Tuckey, *Hon.* Sir Simon Lane, Kt.
Tuita, Sir Mariano Kelesimalefo, Kt., OBE
Tuite, Sir Christopher Hugh, Bt., Ph.D. (1622)
Tuivaga, Sir Timoci Uluiburotu, Kt.
Tuke, Sir Anthony Favill, Kt.
Tumim, *His Hon.* Sir Stephen, Kt.
Tupper, Sir Charles Hibbert, Bt. (1888)

Turbott, Sir Ian Graham, Kt., CMG, CVO
Turing, Sir John Dermot, Bt. (s. 1638)
Turnberg, *Prof.* Sir Leslie Arnold, Kt., MD, FRCP
Turnbull, Sir Richard Gordon, GCMG
Turner, Sir Colin William Carstairs, Kt., CBE, DFC
Turner, *Hon.* Sir Michael John, Kt.
Turnquest, Sir Orville Alton, GCMG, QC
Tuti, *Revd* Dudley, KBE
Tuzo, *Gen.* Sir Harry Craufurd, GCB, OBE, MC
Tweedie, *Prof.* Sir David Philip, Kt.
Tyree, Sir (Alfred) William, Kt., OBE
Tyrwhitt, Sir Reginald Thomas Newman, Bt. (1919)
Udoma, *Hon.* Sir (Egbert) Udo, Kt.
Unsworth, *Hon.* Sir Edgar Ignatius Godfrey, Kt., CMG
Unwin, Sir (James) Brian, KCB
Ure, Sir John Burns, KCMG, LVO
Urquhart, Sir Brian Edward, KCMG, MBE
Urwick, Sir Alan Bedford, KCVO, CMG
Usher, Sir Leonard Gray, Kt.
Usher, Sir (William) John Tevenar, Bt. (1899)
Ustinov, Sir Peter Alexander, Kt., CBE
Utting, Sir William Benjamin, Kt., CB
Vai, Sir Mea, Kt., CBE, ISO
Vallance, Sir Iain David Thomas, Kt.
Vallat, Sir Francis Aimé, GBE, KCMG, QC
Vallings, *Vice-Adm.* Sir George Montague Francis, KCB
Vanderfelt, Sir Robin Victor, KBE
van der Post, Sir Laurens Jan, Kt., CBE
Vane, Sir John Robert, Kt., D.Phil., D.SC., FRS
Vanneck, *Air Cdre* Hon. Sir Peter Beckford Rutgers, GBE, CB, AFC
van Straubenzee, Sir William Radcliffe, Kt., MBE
Vasquez, Sir Alfred Joseph, Kt., CBE, QC
Vaughan, Sir Gerard Folliott, Kt., MP, FRCP
Vavasour, *Cdr.* Sir Geoffrey William, Bt., DSC, RN (1828)
Veale, Sir Alan John Ralph, Kt., FEng.
Verco, Sir Walter John George, KCVO
†Verney, Sir John Sebastian, Bt. (1946)
Verney, *Hon.* Sir Lawrence John, Kt., TD
Verney, Sir Ralph Bruce, Bt., KBE (1818)
Vernon, Sir James, Kt., CBE
Vernon, Sir Nigel John Douglas, Bt. (1914)
Vernon, Sir (William) Michael, Kt.
Vesey, Sir (Nathaniel) Henry (Peniston), Kt., CBE
Vestey, Sir (John) Derek, Bt. (1921)
Vial, Sir Kenneth Harold, Kt., CBE

Vick, Sir (Francis) Arthur, Kt., OBE, Ph.D.
Vickers, *Lt.-Gen.* Sir Richard Maurice Hilton, KCB, LVO, OBE
Victoria, Sir (Joseph Aloysius) Donatus, Kt., CBE
Vincent, *Field Marshal* Sir Richard Frederick, GBE, KCB, DSO
Vincent, Sir William Percy Maxwell, Bt. (1936)
Vinelott, *Hon.* Sir John Evelyn, Kt.
Vines, Sir William Joshua, Kt., CMG
†Vyvyan, Sir Ralph Ferrers Alexander, Bt. (1645)
Waddell, Sir Alexander Nicol Anton, KCMG, DSC
Waddell, Sir James Henderson, Kt., CB
Wade, *Prof.* Sir Henry William Rawson, Kt., QC, FBA
Wade, *Air Chief Marshal* Sir Ruthven Lowry, KCB, DFC
Waite, *Rt. Hon.* Sir John Douglas, Kt.
Wake, Sir Hereward, Bt., MC (1621)
Wakefield, Sir (Edward) Humphry (Tyrell), Bt. (1962)
Wakefield, Sir Norman Edward, Kt.
Wakefield, Sir Peter George Arthur, KBE, CMG
Wakeford, *Air Marshal* Sir Richard Gordon, KCB, OBE, LVO, AFC
Wakeley, Sir John Cecil Nicholson, Bt., FRCS (1952)
†Wakeman, Sir Edward Offley Bertram, Bt. (1828)
Walford, Sir Christopher Rupert, Kt.
Walker, *Revd* Alan Edgar, Kt., OBE
Walker, *Gen.* Sir Antony Kenneth Frederick, KCB
Walker, Sir Baldwin Patrick, Bt. (1856)
Walker, Sir (Charles) Michael, GCMG
Walker, Sir Colin John Shedlock, Kt., OBE
Walker, Sir David Alan, Kt.
Walker, Sir Gervas George, Kt.
Walker, *Rt. Hon.* Sir Harold, Kt., MP
Walker, Sir Harold Berners, KCMG
Walker, *Maj.* Sir Hugh Ronald, Bt. (1906)
Walker, Sir James Graham, Kt., MBE
Walker, Sir James Heron, Bt. (1868)
Walker, *Air Marshal* Sir John Robert, KCB, CBE, AFC
Walker, *Lt.-Gen.* Sir Michael John Dawson, KCB, CBE
Walker, Sir Michael Leolin Forestier-, Bt. (1835)
Walker, Sir Patrick Jeremy, KCB
Walker, *Hon.* Sir Robert, Kt.
Walker, Sir Rodney Myerscough, Kt.
Walker, *Gen.* Sir Walter Colyear, KCB, CBE, DSO
Wall, Sir (John) Stephen, KCMG, LVO
Wall, *Hon.* Sir Nicholas Peter Rathbone, Kt.
Wall, Sir Patrick Henry Bligh, Kt., MC, VRD
Wall, Sir Robert William, Kt., OBE
Wallace, Sir Ian James, Kt., CBE

Waller, *Hon.* Sir (George) Mark, Kt.
Waller, *Rt. Hon.* Sir George Stanley, Kt., OBE
Waller, Sir Robert William, Bt. (I. 1780)
Walley, Sir John, KBE, CB
Wallis, Sir Peter Gordon, KCVO
Wallis, Sir Timothy William, Kt.
Walmsley, *Vice-Adm.* Sir Robert, KCB
Walsh, Sir Alan, Kt., D.SC., FRS
Walsh, *Prof.* Sir John Patrick, KBE
†Walsham, Sir Timothy John, Bt. (1831)
Walter, Sir Harold Edward, Kt.
Walters, *Prof.* Sir Alan Arthur, Kt.
Walters, Sir Dennis Murray, Kt., MBE
Walters, Sir Frederick Donald, Kt.
Walters, Sir Peter Ingram, Kt.
Walters, Sir Roger Talbot, KBE, FRIBA
Walton, Sir John Robert, Kt.
Wan, Sir Wamp, Kt., MBE
Wanstall, *Hon.* Sir Charles Gray, Kt.
Ward, *Rt. Hon.* Sir Alan Hylton, Kt.
Ward, Sir Joseph James Laffey, Bt. (1911)
Ward, *Maj.-Gen.* Sir Philip John Newling, KCVO, CBE
Ward, Sir Timothy James, Kt.
Wardale, Sir Geoffrey Charles, KCB
Wardlaw, Sir Henry (John), Bt. (s. 1631)
Wardle, Sir Thomas Edward Jewell, Kt.
Waring, Sir (Alfred) Holburt, Bt. (1935)
Warmington, Sir Marshall Denham Malcolm, Bt. (1908)
Warner, Sir (Edward Courtenay) Henry, Bt. (1910)
Warner, Sir Edward Redston, KCMG, OBE
Warner, *Prof.* Sir Frederick Edward, Kt., FRS, FEng.
Warner, Sir Gerald Chierici, KCMG
Warner, *Hon.* Sir Jean-Pierre Frank Eugene, Kt.
†Warren, Sir Michael Blackley, Bt. (1784)
Warren, Sir (Frederick) Miles, KBE
Warren, Sir Kenneth Robin, Kt.
Wass, Sir Douglas William Gretton, GCB
Waterhouse, *Hon.* Sir Ronald Gough, Kt.
Waterlow, Sir Christopher Rupert, Bt. (1873)
Waterlow, Sir (James) Gerard, Bt. (1930)
Waters, *Gen.* Sir (Charles) John, GCB, CBE
Waters, Sir Thomas Neil Morris, Kt.
Wates, Sir Christopher Stephen, Kt.
Watkins, *Rt. Hon.* Sir Tasker, VC, GBE
Watson, Sir Bruce Dunstan, Kt.
Watson, Sir Duncan Amos, Kt., CBE
Watson, Sir (James) Andrew, Bt. (1866)
Watson, Sir John Forbes Inglefield-, Bt. (1895)

Watson, Sir Michael Milne-, Bt., CBE (1937)
Watson, Sir (Noel) Duncan, KCMG
Watson, *Vice-Adm.* Sir Philip Alexander, KBE, LVO
Watt, *Surgeon Vice-Adm.* Sir James, KBE, FRCS
Watt, Sir James Harvie-, Bt. (1945)
Watts, Sir Arthur Desmond, KCMG
Watts, *Lt.-Gen.* Sir John Peter Barry Condliffe, KBE, CB, MC
Wauchope, Sir Roger (Hamilton) Don-, Bt. (s. 1667)
Way, Sir Richard George Kitchener, KCB, CBE
Weatherall, *Prof.* Sir David John, Kt., FRS
Weatherall, *Vice-Adm.* Sir James Lamb, KBE
Weatherstone, Sir Dennis, KBE
Weaver, Sir Tobias Rushton, Kt., CB
Webb, Sir Thomas Langley, Kt.
Webber, Sir Andrew Lloyd, Kt.
Webster, *Very Revd* Alan Brunskill, KCVO
Webster, *Vice-Adm.* Sir John Morrison, KCB
Webster, *Hon.* Sir Peter Edlin, Kt.
Wedderburn, Sir Andrew John Alexander Ogilvy-, Bt. (1803)
Wedgwood, Sir (Hugo) Martin, Bt. (1942)
Weekes, Sir Everton DeCourcey, KCMG, OBE
Weinberg, Sir Mark Aubrey, Kt.
Weir, Sir Michael Scott, KCMG
Weir, Sir Roderick Bignell, Kt.
Welby, Sir (Richard) Bruno Gregory, Bt. (1801)
Welch, Sir John Reader, Bt. (1957)
Weldon, Sir Anthony William, Bt. (I. 1723)
Wellings, Sir Jack Alfred, Kt., CBE
†Wells, Sir Christopher Charles, Bt. (1944)
Wells, Sir John Julius, Kt.
Westbrook, Sir Neil Gowanloch, Kt., CBE
Westerman, Sir (Wilfred) Alan, Kt., CBE
Weston, Sir Michael Charles Swift, KCMG, CVO
Weston, Sir (Philip) John, KCMG
Whalen, Sir Geoffrey Henry, Kt., CBE
Wheeler, Sir Frederick Henry, Kt., CBE
Wheeler, Sir Harry Anthony, Kt., OBE
Wheeler, *Air Chief Marshal* Sir (Henry) Neil (George), GCB, CBE, DSO, DFC, AFC
Wheeler, *Rt. Hon.* Sir John Daniel, Kt., MP
Wheeler, Sir John Hieron, Bt. (1920)
Wheeler, *Hon.* Sir Kenneth Henry, Kt.
Wheeler, *Lt.-Gen.* Sir Roger Neil, KCB, CBE
Wheler, Sir Edward Woodford, Bt. (1660)

Whent, Sir Gerald Arthur, Kt., CBE
Whishaw, Sir Charles Percival Law, Kt.
Whitaker, *Maj.* Sir James Herbert Ingham, Bt., OBE (1936)
White, Sir Christopher Robert Meadows, Bt. (1937)
White, *Hon.* Sir Christopher Stuart Stuart-, Kt.
White, Sir David Harry, Kt.
White, Sir George Stanley James, Bt. (1904)
White, *Wg Cdr.* Sir Henry Arthur Dalrymple-, Bt., DFC (1926)
White, *Adm.* Sir Hugo Moresby, GCB, CBE
White, *Hon.* Sir John Charles, Kt., MBE
White, Sir John Woolmer, Bt. (1922)
White, Sir Lynton Stuart, Kt., MBE, TD
White, *Adm.* Sir Peter, GBE
White, Sir Thomas Astley Woollaston, Bt. (1802)
Whitehead, Sir John Stainton, GCMG, CVO
Whitehead, Sir Rowland John Rathbone, Bt. (1889)
Whiteley, Sir Hugo Baldwin Huntington-, Bt. (1918)
Whiteley, *Gen.* Sir Peter John Frederick, GCB, OBE, RM
Whitfield, Sir William, Kt., CBE
Whitford, *Hon.* Sir John Norman Keates, Kt.
Whitley, *Air Marshal* Sir John René, KBE, CB, DSO, AFC
Whitmore, Sir Clive Anthony, GCB, CVO
Whitmore, Sir John Henry Douglas, Bt. (1954)
Whittome, Sir (Leslie) Alan, Kt.
Wickerson, Sir John Michael, Kt.
Wicks, Sir James Albert, Kt.
Wicks, Sir Nigel Leonard, KCB, CVO, CBE
†Wigan, Sir Michael Iain, Bt. (1898)
Wiggin, Sir Alfred William (Jerry), Kt., TD, MP
†Wiggin, Sir Charles Rupert John, Bt. (1892)
Wigram, *Revd Canon* Sir Clifford Woolmore, Bt. (1805)
Wilbraham, Sir Richard Baker, Bt. (1776)
Wilford, Sir (Kenneth) Michael, GCMG
Wilkes, *Gen.* Sir Michael John, KCB, CBE
Wilkins, Sir Graham John, Kt.
Wilkinson, Sir (David) Graham (Brook) Bt. (1941)
Wilkinson, *Prof.* Sir Denys Haigh, Kt., FRS
Wilkinson, *Prof.* Sir Geoffrey, Kt., FRS
Wilkinson, Sir Peter Allix, KCMG, DSO, OBE
Wilkinson, Sir Philip William, Kt.
Willatt, Sir (Robert) Hugh, Kt.

Willcocks, Sir David Valentine, Kt., CBE, MC
Williams, Sir Alastair Edgcumbe James Dudley-, Bt. (1964)
Williams, Sir Alwyn, Kt., Ph.D., FRS
Williams, Sir Arthur Dennis Pitt, Kt.
Williams, Sir (Arthur) Gareth Ludovic Emrys Rhys, Bt. (1918)
Williams, Prof. Sir Bruce Rodda, KBE
Williams, Adm. Sir David, GCB
Williams, Prof. Sir David Glyndwr Tudor, Kt.
Williams, Sir David Innes, Kt.
Williams, Hon. Sir Denys Ambrose, KCMG
Williams, Sir Donald Mark, Bt. (1866)
Williams, Prof. Sir (Edward) Dillwyn, Kt., FRCP
Williams, Hon. Sir Edward Stratten, KCMG, KBE
Williams, Prof. Sir Glanmor, Kt., CBE, FBA
Williams, Sir Henry Sydney, Kt., OBE
Williams, Sir John Robert, KCMG
Williams, Sir (Lawrence) Hugh, Bt. (1798)
Williams, Sir Leonard, KBE, CB
Williams, Sir Osmond, Bt., MC (1909)
Williams, Prof. Sir Robert Evan Owen, Kt., MD, FRCP
Williams, Sir (Robert) Philip Nathaniel, Bt. (1915)
Williams, Sir Robin Philip, Bt. (1953)
Williams, Sir (William) Maxwell (Harries), Kt.
Williamson, Marshal of the Royal Air Force Sir Keith Alec, GCB, AFC
Williamson, Sir (Nicholas Frederick) Hedworth, Bt. (1642)
Willink, Sir Charles William, Bt. (1957)
Willis, Hon. Sir Eric Archibald, KBE, CMG
Willis, Vice-Adm. Sir (Guido) James, KBE
Willis, Air Chief Marshal Sir John Frederick, KCB, CBE
Willison, Lt.-Gen. Sir David John, KCB, OBE, MC
Willison, Sir John Alexander, Kt., OBE
Wills, Sir David Seton, Bt. (1904)
Wills, Sir (Hugh) David Hamilton, Kt., CBE, TD
Wills, Sir John Vernon, Bt., TD (1923)
Wilmot, Sir Henry Robert, Bt. (1759)
†Wilmot, Sir Michael John Assheton Eardley-, Bt. (1821)
Wilsey, Gen. Sir John Finlay Willasey, GCB, CBE
Wilson, Lt.-Gen. Sir (Alexander) James, KBE, MC
Wilson, Sir Anthony, Kt.
Wilson, Vice-Adm. Sir Barry Nigel, KCB
Wilson, Lt.-Col. Sir Blair Aubyn Stewart-, KCVO
Wilson, Sir Charles Haynes, Kt.

Wilson, Sir David, Bt. (1920)
Wilson, Sir David Mackenzie, Kt.
Wilson, Sir Geoffrey Masterman, KCB, CMG
Wilson, Sir James William Douglas, Bt. (1906)
Wilson, Sir John Foster, Kt., CBE
Wilson, Brig. Sir Mathew John Anthony, Bt., OBE, MC (1874)
Wilson, Hon. Sir Nicholas Allan Roy, Kt.
Wilson, Sir Patrick Michael Ernest David McNair-, Kt., MP
Wilson, Sir Reginald Holmes, Kt.
Wilson, Sir Robert, Kt., CBE
Wilson, Sir Robert Donald, KBE
Wilson, Rt. Revd Roger Plumpton, KCVO, DD
Wilson, Sir Roland, KBE
Wilson, Air Chief Marshal Sir (Ronald) Andrew (Fellowes), KCB, AFC
Wilson, Hon. Sir Ronald Darling, KBE, CMG
Wilton, Sir (Arthur) John, KCMG, KCVO, MC
Wiltshire, Sir Frederick Munro, Kt., CBE
Wingate, Capt. Sir Miles Buckley, KCVO
Winnington, Sir Francis Salwey William, Bt. (1755)
Winskill, Air Cdre Sir Archibald Little, KCVO, CBE, DFC
Winterbottom, Sir Walter, Kt., CBE
Wiseman, Sir John William, Bt. (1628)
Wolfendale, Prof. Sir Arnold Whittaker, Kt., FRS
Wolfson, Sir Brian Gordon, Kt.
Wolseley, Sir Charles Garnet Richard Mark, Bt. (1628)
†Wolseley, Sir James Douglas, Bt. (I. 1745)
Wolstenholme, Sir Gordon Ethelbert Ward, Kt., OBE
Wombwell, Sir George Philip Frederick, Bt. (1778)
Womersley, Sir Peter John Walter, Bt. (1945)
Woo, Sir Leo Joseph, Kt.
Wood, Sir Alan Marshall Muir, Kt., FRS, FEng.
Wood, Sir Andrew Marley, KCMG
Wood, Sir Anthony John Page, Bt. (1837)
Wood, Sir David Basil Hill-, Bt. (1921)
Wood, Sir Frederick Ambrose Stuart, Kt.
Wood, Sir Ian Clark, Kt., CBE
Wood, Prof. Sir John Crossley, Kt., CBE
Wood, Hon. Sir John Kember, Kt., MC
Wood, Sir Martin Francis, Kt., OBE
Wood, Sir Russell Dillon, KCVO, VRD
Wood, Sir William Alan, KCVO, CB
Woodard, Rear Adm. Sir Robert Nathaniel, KCVO
Woodcock, Sir John, Kt., CBE, QPM

Woodfield, Sir Philip John, KCB, CBE
Woodhead, Vice-Adm. Sir (Anthony) Peter, KCB
Woodhouse, Rt. Hon. Sir (Arthur) Owen, KBE, DSC
Wooding, Sir Norman Samuel, Kt., CBE
Woodroffe, Most Revd George Cuthbert Manning, KBE
Woodroofe, Sir Ernest George, Kt., Ph.D.
Woodruff, Prof. Sir Michael Francis Addison, Kt., D.SC., FRS, FRCS
Woods, Sir Colin Philip Joseph, KCVO, CBE
Woods, Rt. Revd Robert Wilmer, KCMG, KCVO
Woodward, Hon. Sir (Albert) Edward, Kt., OBE
Woodward, Adm. Sir John Forster, GBE, KCB
Woolf, Sir John, Kt.
Woollaston, Sir (Mountford) Tosswill, Kt.
Wordie, Sir John Stewart, Kt., CBE, VRD
Worsley, Gen. Sir Richard Edward, GCB, OBE
Worsley, Sir (William) Marcus (John), Bt. (1838)
Worsthorne, Sir Peregrine Gerard, Kt.
Wraight, Sir John Richard, KBE, CMG
Wratten, Air Chief Marshal Sir William John, KBE, CB, AFC
Wraxall, Sir Charles Frederick Lascelles, Bt. (1813)
Wrey, Sir George Richard Bourchier, Bt. (1628)
Wrigglesworth, Sir Ian William, Kt.
Wright, Sir Allan Frederick, KBE
Wright, Sir David John, KCMG, LVO
Wright, Sir Denis Arthur Hepworth, GCMG
Wright, Sir Edward Maitland, Kt., D.Phil., LLD, D.SC., FRSE
Wright, Hon. Sir (John) Michael, Kt.
Wright, Sir (John) Oliver, GCMG, GCVO, DSC
Wright, Sir Paul Hervé Giraud, KCMG, OBE
Wright, Sir Peter Robert, Kt., CBE
Wright, Sir Richard Michael Cory-, Bt. (1903)
Wrightson, Sir Charles Mark Garmondsway, Bt. (1900)
Wrigley, Prof. Sir Edward Anthony (Sir Tony), Kt., Ph.D., FBA
Wynn, Sir David Watkin Williams-, Bt. (1688)
Yacoub, Prof. Sir Magdi Habib, Kt., FRCS
Yang, Hon. Sir Ti Liang, Kt.
Yapp, Sir Stanley Graham, Kt.
Yardley, Sir David Charles Miller, Kt., LLD
Yarranton, Sir Peter George, Kt.
Yarrow, Sir Eric Grant, Bt., MBE (1916)
Yellowlees, Sir Henry, KCB

Yocklunn, Sir John (Soong Chung), KCVO
Yoo Foo, Sir (François) Henri, Kt.
Youens, Sir Peter William, Kt., CMG, OBE
Young, Sir Brian Walter Mark, Kt.
Young, Sir Colville Norbert, GCMG, MBE
Young, Lt.-Gen. Sir David Tod, KBE, CB, DFC
Young, Rt. Hon. Sir George Samuel Knatchbull, Bt., MP (1813)

Young, Hon. Sir Harold William, KCMG
Young, Sir John Kenyon Roe, Bt. (1821)
Young, Hon. Sir John McIntosh, KCMG
Young, Sir Leslie Clarence, Kt., CBE
Young, Sir Norman Smith, Kt.
Young, Sir Richard Dilworth, Kt.
Young, Sir Robert Christopher Mackworth-, GCVO
Young, Sir Roger William, Kt.

Young, Sir Stephen Stewart Templeton, Bt. (1945)
Young, Sir William Neil, Bt. (1769)
Younger, Maj.-Gen. Sir John William, Bt., CBE (1911)
Zeeman, Prof. Sir (Erik) Christopher, Kt., FRS
Zeidler, Sir David Ronald, Kt., CBE
Zissman, Sir Bernard Philip, Kt.
Zoleveke, Sir Gideon Pitabose, KBE
Zunz, Sir Gerhard Jacob (Jack), Kt., FEng.
Zurenuoc, Sir Zibang, KBE

The Military Knights of Windsor

The Military Knights of Windsor take part in all ceremonies of the Noble Order of the Garter and attend Sunday morning service in St George's Chapel, Windsor Castle, as representatives of the Knights of the Garter. The Knights receive a small stipend in addition to their army pensions and quarters in Windsor Castle.

The Knights of Windsor were originally founded in 1348 after the wars in France to assist English knights, who, having been prisoners in the hands of the French, had become impoverished by the payments of heavy ransoms. When Edward III founded the Order of the Garter later the same year, he incorporated the Knights of Windsor and the College of St George into its foundation and raised the number of Knights to 26 to correspond with the number of the Knights of the Garter. Known later as the Alms Knights or Poor Knights of Windsor, their establishment was

reduced under the will of King Henry VIII to 13 and Statutes were drawn up by Queen Elizabeth I.

In 1833 King William IV changed their designation to The Military Knights and granted them their present uniform which consists of a scarlet tail-coat with white cross sword-belt, crimson sash and cocked hat with plume. The badges are the Shield of St George and the Star of the Order of the Garter.

Governor, Maj.-Gen. Peter Downward, CB, DSO, DFC

Military Knights, Brig. A. L. Atkinson, OBE; Brig. J. F. Lindner, OBE, MC; Maj. W. L. Thompson, MVO, MBE, DCM; Maj. L. W. Dickerson; Maj. J. C. Cowley, OBE, DCM; Maj. G. R. Mitchell, MBE, BEM; Lt.-Col. R. L. C. Tamplin; Maj. P. H. Bolton, MBE; Brig. T. W. Hackworth, OBE; Maj. R. J. Moore; Lt.-Col. R. R. Giles

Supernumerary, Brig. A. C. Tyler, CBE, MC

Dames Grand Cross and Dames Commanders

Style, 'Dame' before forename and surname, followed by appropriate post-nominal initials. Where such an award is made to a lady already in enjoyment of a higher title, the appropriate initials follow her name
Husband, Untitled
For forms of address, *see* page 136

Dame Grand Cross and Dame Commander are the higher classes for women of the Order of the Bath, the Order of St Michael and St George, the Royal Victorian Order, and the Order of the British Empire. Dames Grand Cross rank after the wives of Baronets and before the wives of Knights Grand Cross. Dames Commanders rank after the wives of Knights Grand Cross and before the wives of Knights Commanders

Honorary Dames Commanders may be conferred on women who are citizens of countries of which The Queen is not head of state

---

LIST OF DAMES *Revised to 31 August 1996*

Women peers in their own right and life peers are not included in this list. Female members of the royal family are not included in this list; details of the orders they hold are given on pages 117–8

If a dame has a double barrelled or hyphenated surname, she is listed under the final element of the name

Abaijah, Dame Josephine, DBE
Abel Smith, Lady, DCVO
Abergavenny, The Marchioness of, DCVO
Airlie, The Countess of, DCVO
Albemarle, The Countess of, DBE
Anderson, *Brig*. Hon. Dame Mary Mackenzie (Mrs Pihl), DBE
Anelay, Dame Joyce Anne, DBE
Anglesey, The Marchioness of, DBE
Anson, Lady (Elizabeth Audrey), DBE
Anstee, Dame Margaret Joan, DCMG
Arden, *Hon*. Dame Mary Howarth (Mrs Mance), DBE
Baker, Dame Janet Abbott (Mrs Shelley), CH, DBE
Ballin, Dame Reubina Ann, DBE
Barnes, Dame (Alice) Josephine (Mary Taylor), DBE, FRCP, FRCS
Barrow, Dame Jocelyn Anita (Mrs Downer), DBE
Barstow, Dame Josephine Clare (Mrs Anderson), DBE
Basset, Lady Elizabeth, DCVO
Bean, Dame Majorie Louise, DBE
Beaurepaire, Dame Beryl Edith, DBE
Bergquist, *Prof.* Dame Patricia Rose, DBE
Berry, Dame Alice Miriam, DBE
Blaize, Dame Venetia Ursula, DBE
Blaxland, Dame Helen Frances, DBE
Booth, *Hon*. Dame Margaret Myfanwy Wood, DBE
Bottomley, Dame Bessie Ellen, DBE
Bowman, Dame (Mary) Elaine Kellett-, DBE, MP
Boyd, Dame Vivienne Myra, DBE
Bracewell, *Hon*. Dame Joyanne Winifred (Mrs Copeland), DBE
Brain, Dame Margaret Anne (Mrs Wheeler), DBE
Brazill, Dame Josephine (Sister Mary Philippa), DBE

Bridges, Dame Mary Patricia, DBE
Brown, Dame Beryl Paston, DBE
Brown, Dame Gillian Gerda, DCVO, CMG
Browne, Lady Moyra Blanche Madeleine, DBE
Bryans, Dame Anne Margaret, DBE
Bryce, Dame Isabel Graham, DBE
Buttfield, Dame Nancy Eileen, DBE
Byford, Dame Hazel, DBE
Bynoe, Dame Hilda Louisa, DBE
Caldicott, Dame Fiona, DBE, FRCP, FRCPsych.
Cartland, Dame Barbara Hamilton, DBE
Cartwright, Dame Mary Lucy, DBE, SC.D., D.Phil., FRS
Cartwright, Dame Silvia Rose, DBE
Casey, Dame Stella Katherine, DBE
Cayford, Dame Florence Evelyn, DBE
Charles, Dame (Mary) Eugenia, DBE
Chesterton, Dame Elizabeth Ursula, DBE
Clark, *Prof.* Dame (Margaret) June, DBE, ph.D.
Clay, Dame Marie Mildred, DBE
Clayton, Dame Barbara Evelyn (Mrs Klyne), DBE
Cleland, Dame Rachel, DBE
Coll, Dame Elizabeth Anne Loosemore Esteve-, DBE
Cookson, Dame Catherine Ann, DBE
Corsar, The Hon. Dame Mary Drummond, DBE
Coulshed, Dame (Mary) Frances, DBE, TD
Crowe, Dame Sylvia, DBE
Daws, Dame Joyce Margaretta, DBE
Dell, Dame Miriam Patricia, DBE
Dench, Dame Judith Olivia (Mrs Williams), DBE
de Valois, Dame Ninette, OM, CH, DBE
Digby, Lady, DBE
Donaldson, Dame (Dorothy) Mary (Lady Donaldson of Lymington), GBE
Doyle, *Air Comdt*. Dame Jean Lena Annette Conan (Lady Bromet), DBE
Drake, *Brig*. Dame Jean Elizabeth Rivett-, DBE
Drew, Dame Jane Beverley (Mrs Fry), DBE, FRIBA

Dugdale, Kathryn, Lady, DCVO
Dumont, Dame Ivy Leona, DCMG
Ebsworth, *Hon*. Dame Ann Marian, DBE
Emerton, Dame Audrey Caroline, DBE
Engel, Dame Pauline Frances (Sister Pauline Engel), DBE
Evison, Dame Helen June Patricia, DBE
Fenner, Dame Peggy Edith, DBE, MP
Fitton, Dame Doris Alice (Mrs Mason), DBE
Fookes, Dame Janet Evelyn, DBE, MP
Fraser, Dame Dorothy Rita, DBE
Friend, Dame Phyllis Muriel, DBE
Fritchie, Dame Irene Tordoff (Dame Rennie Fritchie), DBE
Frost, Dame Phyllis Irene, DBE
Fry, Dame Margaret Louise, DBE
Gallagher, Dame Monica Josephine, DBE
Gardiner, Dame Helen Louisa, DBE, MVO
Gibbs, Dame Molly Peel, DBE
Giles, *Air Comdt*. Dame Pauline (Mrs Parsons), DBE, RRC
Golding, Dame (Cecilie) Monica, DBE
Goodman, Dame Barbara, DBE
Gordon, Dame Minita Elmira, GCMG, GCVO
Gow, Dame Jane Elizabeth (Mrs Whiteley), DBE
Grafton, The Duchess of, GCVO
Green, Dame Mary Georgina, DBE
Grey, Dame Beryl Elizabeth (Mrs Svenson), DBE
Grimthorpe, The Lady, DCVO
Guilfoyle, Dame Margaret Georgina Constance, DBE
Guthardt, *Revd Dr* Dame Phyllis Myra, DBE
Haig, Dame Mary Alison Glen-, DBE
Hale, *Hon*. Dame Brenda Marjorie (Mrs Farrand), DBE
Hammond, Dame Joan Hood, DBE
Harper, Dame Elizabeth Margaret Way, DBE
Harris, Dame (Muriel) Diana Reader-, DBE
Heilbron, *Hon*. Dame Rose, DBE

Decorations and Medals

PRINCIPAL DECORATIONS AND MEDALS
In order of precedence

VICTORIA CROSS (VC), 1856 (*see* page 209)
GEORGE CROSS (GC), 1940 (*see* page 210)

British Orders of Knighthood, etc.
BARONET'S BADGE
KNIGHT BACHELOR'S BADGE

Decorations
CONSPICUOUS GALLANTRY CROSS (CGC), 1995
ROYAL RED CROSS Class I (RRC), 1883
DISTINGUISHED SERVICE CROSS (DSC), 1914. For all ranks for actions at sea
MILITARY CROSS (MC), December 1914. For all ranks for actions on land
DISTINGUISHED FLYING CROSS (DFC), 1918. For all ranks for acts of gallantry when flying in active operations against the enemy
AIR FORCE CROSS (AFC), 1918. For all ranks for acts of courage when flying, although not in active operations against the enemy
ROYAL RED CROSS Class II (ARRC)
ORDER OF BRITISH INDIA
KAISAR-I-HIND MEDAL
ORDER OF ST JOHN

Medals for Gallantry and Distinguished Conduct
UNION OF SOUTH AFRICA QUEEN'S MEDAL FOR BRAVERY, in Gold
DISTINGUISHED CONDUCT MEDAL (DCM), 1854
CONSPICUOUS GALLANTRY MEDAL (CGM), 1874
CONSPICUOUS GALLANTRY MEDAL (FLYING)
GEORGE MEDAL (GM), 1940
QUEEN'S POLICE MEDAL FOR GALLANTRY
QUEEN'S FIRE SERVICE MEDAL FOR GALLANTRY
ROYAL WEST AFRICAN FRONTIER FORCE DISTINGUISHED CONDUCT MEDAL
KING'S AFRICAN RIFLES DISTINGUISHED CONDUCT MEDAL
INDIAN DISTINGUISHED SERVICE MEDAL
UNION OF SOUTH AFRICA QUEEN'S MEDAL FOR BRAVERY, in Silver
DISTINGUISHED SERVICE MEDAL (DSM), 1914
MILITARY MEDAL (MM), 1916
DISTINGUISHED FLYING MEDAL (DFM), 1918
AIR FORCE MEDAL (AFM)
CONSTABULARY MEDAL (IRELAND)
MEDAL FOR SAVING LIFE AT SEA
SEA GALLANTRY MEDAL
INDIAN ORDER OF MERIT (Civil)
INDIAN POLICE MEDAL FOR GALLANTRY
CEYLON POLICE MEDAL FOR GALLANTRY
SIERRA LEONE POLICE MEDAL FOR GALLANTRY
SIERRA LEONE FIRE BRIGADES MEDAL FOR GALLANTRY
COLONIAL POLICE MEDAL FOR GALLANTRY (CPM)
QUEEN'S GALLANTRY MEDAL, 1974
ROYAL VICTORIAN MEDAL (RVM), Gold, Silver and Bronze

BRITISH EMPIRE MEDAL (BEM), (formerly the Medal of the Order of the British Empire, for Meritorious Service; also includes the Medal of the Order awarded before 29 December 1922)
CANADA MEDAL
QUEEN'S POLICE (QPM) AND QUEEN'S FIRE SERVICE MEDALS (QFSM) FOR DISTINGUISHED SERVICE
QUEEN'S MEDAL FOR CHIEFS

War Medals and Stars (in order of date)

Polar Medals (in order of date)

IMPERIAL SERVICE MEDAL

Police Medals for Valuable Service
BADGE OF HONOUR

Jubilee, Coronation and Durbar Medals
KING GEORGE V, KING GEORGE VI AND QUEEN ELIZABETH II LONG AND FAITHFUL SERVICE MEDALS

Efficiency and Long Service Decorations and Medals
MEDAL FOR MERITORIOUS SERVICE
ACCUMULATED CAMPAIGN SERVICE MEDAL
THE MEDAL FOR LONG SERVICE AND GOOD CONDUCT (Military)
NAVAL LONG SERVICE AND GOOD CONDUCT MEDAL
ROYAL MARINES MERITORIOUS SERVICE MEDAL
ROYAL AIR FORCE MERITORIOUS SERVICE MEDAL
ROYAL AIR FORCE LONG SERVICE AND GOOD CONDUCT MEDAL
MEDAL FOR LONG SERVICE AND GOOD CONDUCT (ULSTER DEFENCE REGIMENT)
POLICE LONG SERVICE AND GOOD CONDUCT MEDAL
FIRE BRIGADE LONG SERVICE AND GOOD CONDUCT MEDAL
COLONIAL POLICE AND FIRE BRIGADES LONG SERVICE MEDALS
COLONIAL PRISON SERVICE MEDAL
HONG KONG DISCIPLINED SERVICES MEDAL
ARMY EMERGENCY RESERVE DECORATION (ERD), 1952
VOLUNTEER OFFICERS' DECORATION (VD)
VOLUNTEER LONG SERVICE MEDAL
VOLUNTEER OFFICERS' DECORATION for India and the Colonies
VOLUNTEER LONG SERVICE MEDAL for India and the Colonies
COLONIAL AUXILIARY FORCES OFFICERS' DECORATION
COLONIAL AUXILIARY FORCES LONG SERVICE MEDAL
MEDAL FOR GOOD SHOOTING (Naval)
MILITIA LONG SERVICE MEDAL
IMPERIAL YEOMANRY LONG SERVICE MEDAL
TERRITORIAL DECORATION (TD), 1908
EFFICIENCY DECORATION (ED)
TERRITORIAL EFFICIENCY MEDAL
EFFICIENCY MEDAL
SPECIAL RESERVE LONG SERVICE AND GOOD CONDUCT MEDAL
DECORATION FOR OFFICERS, ROYAL NAVY RESERVE (RD), 1910
DECORATION FOR OFFICERS, —RNVR (VRD)
ROYAL NAVAL RESERVE LONG SERVICE AND GOOD CONDUCT MEDAL
RNVR LONG SERVICE AND GOOD CONDUCT MEDAL
ROYAL NAVAL AUXILIARY SICK BERTH RESERVE LONG SERVICE AND GOOD CONDUCT MEDAL

ROYAL FLEET RESERVE LONG SERVICE AND GOOD
CONDUCT MEDAL
ROYAL NAVAL WIRELESS AUXILIARY RESERVE LONG
SERVICE AND GOOD CONDUCT MEDAL
AIR EFFICIENCY AWARD (AE), 1942
ULSTER DEFENCE REGIMENT MEDAL
THE QUEEN'S MEDAL. For champion shots in the RN, RM,
RNZN, Army, RAF
CADET FORCES MEDAL, 1950
COASTGUARD AUXILIARY SERVICE LONG SERVICE
MEDAL (formerly Coast Life Saving Corps Long
Service Medal)
SPECIAL CONSTABULARY LONG SERVICE MEDAL
ROYAL OBSERVER CORPS MEDAL
CIVIL DEFENCE LONG SERVICE MEDAL
AMBULANCE SERVICE (EMERGENCY DUTIES) LONG
SERVICE AND GOOD CONDUCT MEDAL
RHODESIA MEDAL
ROYAL ULSTER CONSTABULARY SERVICE MEDAL
SERVICE MEDAL OF THE ORDER OF ST JOHN
BADGE OF THE ORDER OF THE LEAGUE OF MERCY
VOLUNTARY MEDICAL SERVICE MEDAL, 1932
WOMEN'S VOLUNTARY SERVICE MEDAL
COLONIAL SPECIAL CONSTABULARY MEDAL

Foreign Orders, Decorations and Medals (in order of date)

THE VICTORIA CROSS (1856)
FOR CONSPICUOUS BRAVERY

VC

Ribbon, Crimson, for all Services (until 1918 it was blue for
the Royal Navy)

Instituted on 29 January 1856, the Victoria Cross was
awarded retrospectively to 1854, the first being held by Lt.
C. D. Lucas, RN, for bravery in the Baltic Sea on 21 June
1854 (gazetted 24 February 1857). The first 62 Crosses
were presented by Queen Victoria in Hyde Park, London,
on 26 June 1857.

The Victoria Cross is worn before all other decorations,
on the left breast, and consists of a cross-pattée of bronze,
one and a half inches in diameter, with the Royal Crown
surmounted by a lion in the centre, and beneath there is
the inscription *For Valour.* Holders of the VC receive a tax-
free annuity of £1,300, irrespective of need or other
conditions. In 1911, the right to receive the Cross was
extended to Indian soldiers, and in 1920 to Matrons,
Sisters and Nurses, and the staff of the Nursing Services
and other services pertaining to hospitals and nursing, and
to civilians of either sex regularly or temporarily under
the orders, direction or supervision of the Naval, Military,
or Air Forces of the Crown.

SURVIVING RECIPIENTS OF THE VICTORIA CROSS
as at 31 August 1996

Agansing Rai, *Havildar,* MM (Gurkha Rifles)
1944 *World War*
Ali Haidar, *Jemadar* (Frontier Force Rifles)
1945 *World War*
Annand, *Capt.* R. W. (Durham Light Infantry)
1940 *World War*

Bhan Bhagta Gurung, *Capt.* (2nd Gurkha Rifles)
1945 *World War*
Bhandari Ram, *Capt.* (Baluch R.)
1944 *World War*
Chapman, *Sgt.* E. T., BEM (Monmouthshire R.)
1945 *World War*
Cruickshank, *Flt. Lt.* J. A. (RAFVR)
1944 *World War*
Cutler, Sir Roden, AK, KCMG, KCVO, CBE (Australia)
1941 *World War*
Fraser, *Lt.-Cdr.* I. E., DSC (RNR)
1945 *World War*
Gaje Ghale, *Subedar* (Gurkha Rifles)
1943 *World War*
Ganju Lama, *Jemadar,* MM (Gurkha Rifles)
1944 *World War*
Gardner, *Capt.* P. J., MC (RTR)
1941 *World War*
Gian Singh, *Jemadar* (Punjab R.)
1945 *World War*
Gould, *Lt.* T. W. (RN)
1942 *World War*
Hinton, *Sgt.* J. D. (NZMF)
1941 *World War*
Jamieson, *Maj.* D. A., CVO (R. Norfolk R.)
1944 *World War*
Kenna, *Pte.* E. (Australian M. F.)
1945 *World War*
Kenneally, *C-Q-M-S* J. P. (Irish Guards)
1943 *World War*
Lachiman Gurung, *Rifleman* (Gurkha Rifles)
1945 *World War*
Merritt, *Lt.-Col.* C. C. I., CD (S. Saskatchewan R.)
1942 *World War*
Norton, *Capt.* G. R., MM (SAMF)
1944 *World War*
Payne, *WO* K. (Australian Army)
1969 *Vietnam*
Porteous, *Col.* P. A. (RA)
1942 *World War*
Rambahadur Limbu, *Lt.,* MVO (Gurkha Rifles)
1965 *Sarawak*
Reid, *Flt. Lt.* W. (RAFVR)
1943 *World War*
Smith, *Sgt.* E. A., CD (Seaforth Highlanders of Canada)
1944 *World War*
Smythe, *Capt.* Q. G. M. (SAMF)
1942 *World War*
Speakman-Pitt, *Sgt.* W. (Black Watch)
1951 *Korea*
Tulbahadur Pun, *WOI* (Gurkha Rifles)
1944 *World War*
Umrao Singh, *Sub-Major* (IA)
1944 *World War*
Watkins, *Maj. Rt. Hon.* Sir Tasker, GBE (Welch R.)
1944 *World War*
Wilson, *Lt.-Col.* E. C. T. (E. Surrey R.)
1940 *World War*

THE GEORGE CROSS (1940)
FOR GALLANTRY

GC

Ribbon, Dark blue, threaded through a bar adorned with laurel leaves

Instituted 24 September 1940 (with amendments, 3 November 1942).

The George Cross is worn before all other decorations (except the VC) on the left breast (when worn by a woman it may be worn on the left shoulder from a ribbon of the same width and colour fashioned into a bow). It consists of a plain silver cross with four equal limbs, the cross having in the centre a circular medallion bearing a design showing St George and the Dragon. The inscription *For Gallantry* appears round the medallion and in the angle of each limb of the cross is the Royal cypher 'G VI' forming a circle concentric with the medallion. The reverse is plain and bears the name of the recipient and the date of the award. The cross is suspended by a ring from a bar adorned with laurel leaves on dark blue ribbon one and a half inches wide.

The cross is intended primarily for civilians; awards to the fighting services are confined to actions for which purely military honours are not normally granted. It is awarded only for acts of the greatest heroism or of the most conspicuous courage in circumstances of extreme danger. From 1 April 1965, holders of the Cross have received a tax-free annuity of £1,300.

The royal warrant which ordained that the grant of the Empire Gallantry Medal should cease authorized holders of that medal to return it to the Central Chancery of the Orders of Knighthood and to receive in exchange the George Cross. A similar provision applied to posthumous awards of the Empire Gallantry Medal made after the outbreak of war in 1939. In October 1971 all surviving holders of the Albert Medal and the Edward Medal exchanged those decorations for the George Cross.

SURVIVING RECIPIENTS OF THE GEORGE CROSS
as at 31 August 1996

If the recipient originally received the Empire Gallantry Medal (EGM), the Albert Medal (AM) or the Edward Medal (EM), this is indicated by the initials in parenthesis.

Archer, *Col.* B. S. T., GC, OBE, ERD, 1941
Atkinson, T., GC (EGM), 1939
Baker, J. T., GC (EM), 1929
Bamford, J., GC, 1952
Beaton, J., GC, CVO, 1974
Biggs, *Maj.* K. A., GC, 1946
Bridge, *Cdr.* J., GC, GM, 1944
Butson, *Col.* A. R. C., GC, CD, MD (AM), 1948
Bywater, R. A. S., GC, GM, 1944
Errington, H., GC, 1941
Fairfax, F. W., GC, 1953
Farrow, K., GC (AM), 1948
Flintoff, H. H., GC (EM), 1944
Gledhill, A. J., GC, 1967
Gregson, J. S., GC (AM), 1943
Hawkins, E., GC (AM), 1943
Hodge, *Capt.* A. M., GC, VRD (EGM), 1940
Johnson, *WO1* (*SSM*) B., GC, 1990

Kinne, D. G., GC, 1954
Lowe, A. R., GC (AM), 1949
Lynch, J., GC, BEM (AM), 1948
Malta, GC, 1942
Manwaring, T. G., GC (EM), 1949
Moore, R. V., GC, 1940
Moss, B., GC, 1940
Naughton, F., GC (EGM), 1937
Pearson, Miss J. D. M., GC (EGM), 1940
Pratt, M. K., GC, 1978
Purves, Mrs M., GC (AM), 1949
Raweng, Awang anak, GC, 1951
Riley, G., GC (AM), 1944
Rowlands, *Air Marshal* Sir John, GC, KBE, 1943
Sinclair, *Air Vice-Marshal* Sir Laurence, GC, KCB, CBE, DSO, 1941
Stevens, H. W., GC, 1958
Stronach, *Capt.* G. P., GC, 1943
Styles, *Lt.-Col.* S. G., GC, 1972
Taylor, *Lt.-Cdr.* W. H., GC, MBE, 1941
Walker, C., GC, 1972
Walker, C. H., GC (AM), 1942
Walton, E. W. K., GC (AM), 1948
Wilcox, C., GC (EM), 1949
Wiltshire, S. N., GC (EGM), 1930
Yates, P. W., GC (EM), 1932

Chiefs of Clans and Names in Scotland

Only chiefs of whole Names or Clans are included, except certain special instances (marked *) who, though not chiefs of a whole name, were or are for some reason (e.g. the Macdonald forfeiture) independent. Under decision (*Campbell-Gray*, 1950) that a bearer of a 'double or triple-barrelled' surname cannot be held chief of a part of such, several others cannot be included in the list at present.

THE ROYAL HOUSE: HM The Queen

AGNEW: Sir Crispin Agnew of Lochnaw, Bt., QC, 6 Palmerston Road, Edinburgh EH9 1TN

ANSTRUTHER: Sir Ralph Anstruther of that Ilk, Bt., GCVO, MC, Balcaskie, Pittenweem, Fife KY10 2RD

ARBUTHNOTT: The Viscount of Arbuthnott, CBE, DSC, Arbuthnott House, Laurencekirk, Kincardineshire AB30 1PA

BARCLAY: Peter C. Barclay of Towie Barclay and of that Ilk, 28A Gordon Place, London W8 4JE

BORTHWICK: The Lord Borthwick, TD, Crookston, Heriot, Midlothian EH38 5YS

BOYD: The Lord Kilmarnock, 194 Regent's Park Road, London NW1 8XP

BOYLE: The Earl of Glasgow, Kelburn, Fairlie, Ayrshire KA29 0BE

BRODIE: Ninian Brodie of Brodie, Brodie Castle, Forres, Morayshire IV36 0TE

BRUCE: The Earl of Elgin and Kincardine, KT, Broomhall, Dunfermline, Fife KY11 3DU

BUCHAN: David S. Buchan of Auchmacoy, Auchmacoy House, Ellon, Aberdeenshire

BURNETT: J. C. A. Burnett of Leys, Crathes Castle, Banchory, Kincardineshire

CAMERON: Sir Donald Cameron of Lochiel, KT, CVO, TD, Achnacarry, Spean Bridge, Inverness-shire

CAMPBELL: The Duke of Argyll, Inveraray, Argyll PA32 8XF

CARMICHAEL: Richard J. Carmichael of Carmichael, Carmichael, Thankerton, Biggar, Lanarkshire

CARNEGIE: The Duke of Fife, Elsick House, Stonehaven, Kincardineshire AB3 2NT

CATHCART: Maj.-Gen. The Earl Cathcart, CB, DSO, MC, Moor Hatches, West Amesbury, Salisbury SP4 7BH

CHARTERIS: The Earl of Wemyss and March, KT, Gosford House, Longniddry, East Lothian EH32 0PX

CLAN CHATTAN: M. K. Mackintosh of Clan Chattan, Maxwell Park, Gwelo, Zimbabwe

CHISHOLM: Alastair Chisholm of Chisholm (*The Chisholm*), Silver Willows, Beck Row, Bury St Edmunds

COCHRANE: The Earl of Dundonald, Lochnell Castle, Ledaig, Argyllshire

COLQUHOUN: Sir Ivar Colquhoun of Luss, Bt., Camstraddan, Luss, Dunbartonshire G83 8NX

CRANSTOUN: David A. S. Cranstoun of that Ilk, Corehouse, Lanark

CRICHTON: vacant

DARROCH: Capt. Duncan Darroch of Gourock, The Red House, Branksome Park Road, Camberley, Surrey

DAVIDSON: Duncan Davidson of Davidston, Durham Drive, Havelock North, New Zealand

DEWAR: Kenneth Dewar of that Ilk and Vogrie, The Dower House, Grayshott, Nr. Hindhead, Surrey

DRUMMOND: The Earl of Perth, PC, Stobhall, Perth PH2 6DR

DUNBAR: Sir James Dunbar of Mochrum, Bt., Bld 848 C.2, 66877 Flugplatz, Ramstein, Germany

DUNDAS: David D. Dundas of Dundas, 8 Derna Road, Kenwyn 7700, South Africa

DURIE: Raymond V. D. Durie of Durie, Court House, Pewsey, Wilts

ELIOTT: Mrs Margaret Eliott of Redheugh, Redheugh, Newcastleton, Roxburghshire

ERSKINE: The Earl of Mar and Kellie, Erskine House, Kirk Wynd, Clackmannan FK10 4JF

FARQUHARSON: Capt. A. Farquharson of Invercauld, MC, Invercauld, Braemar, Aberdeenshire AB35 5TT

FERGUSSON: Sir Charles Fergusson of Kilkerran, Bt., Kilkerran, Maybole, Ayrshire

FORBES: The Lord Forbes, KBE, Balforbes, Alford, Aberdeenshire AB33 8DR

FORSYTH: Alistair Forsyth of that Ilk, Ethie Castle, by Arbroath, Angus DD11 5SP

FRASER: The Lady Saltoun, Cairnbulg Castle, Fraserburgh, Aberdeenshire AB43 5TN

*FRASER (OF LOVAT): The Lord Lovat, Beaufort Lodge, Beauly, Inverness-shire IV4 7AZ

GAYRE: R. Gayre of Gayre and Nigg, Minard Castle, Minard, Inverary, Argyll PA32 8YB

GORDON: The Marquess of Huntly, Aboyne Castle, Aberdeenshire AB34 5JP

GRAHAM: The Duke of Montrose, Buchanan Auld House, Drymen, Stirlingshire

GRANT: The Lord Strathspey, The House of Lords, London SW1A 0PW

GRIERSON: Sir Michael Grierson of Lag, Bt., 40c Palace Road, London SW2 3NJ

HAIG: The Earl Haig, OBE, Bemersyde, Melrose, Roxburghshire TD6 9DP

HALDANE: Martin Haldane of Gleneagles, Gleneagles, Auchterarder, Perthshire

HANNAY: Ramsey Hannay of Kirkdale and of that Ilk, Cardoness House, Gatehouse-of-Fleet, Kirkcudbrightshire

HAY: The Earl of Erroll, Woodbury Hall, Sandy, Beds

HENDERSON: John Henderson of Fordell, 7 Owen Street, Toowoomba, Queensland, Australia

HUNTER: Pauline Hunter of Hunterston, Plovers Ridge, Lon Cecrist, Treaddur Bay, Holyhead, Gwynedd

IRVINE OF DRUM: David C. Irvine of Drum, 20 Enville Road, Bowden, Altrincham, Cheshire WA14 2PQ

JARDINE: Sir Alexander Jardine of Applegirth, Bt., Ash House, Thwaites, Millom, Cumbria LA18 5HY

JOHNSTONE: The Earl of Annandale and Hartfell, Raehills, Lockerbie, Dumfriesshire

KEITH: The Earl of Kintore, The Stables, Keith Hall, Inverurie, Aberdeenshire AB51 0LD

KENNEDY: The Marquess of Ailsa, Cassillis House, Maybole, Ayrshire

KERR: The Marquess of Lothian, KCVO, Ferniehurst Castle, Jedburgh, Roxburghshire TN8 6NX

KINCAID: Mrs Heather V. Kincaid of Kincaid, 4 Watling Street, Leintwardine, Craven Arms, Shropshire

LAMONT: Peter N. Lamont of that Ilk, St Patrick's College, Manly, NSW 2095, Australia

LEASK: Madam Leask of Leask, 1 Vincent Road, Sheringham, Norfolk

LENNOX: Edward J. H. Lennox of that Ilk, Pools Farm, Downton on the Rock, Ludlow, Shropshire

LESLIE: The Earl of Rothes, Tanglewood, West Tytherley, Salisbury, Wilts SP5 1LX

LINDSAY: The Earl of Crawford and Balcarres, PC, Balcarres, Colinsburgh, Fife

LOCKHART: Angus H. Lockhart of the Lee, Newholme, Dunsyre, Lanark

LUMSDEN: Gillem Lumsden of that Ilk and Blanerne, Kinderslegh, Bois Avenue, Chesham Bois, Amersham

MACALESTER: William St J. S. McAlester of Loup and Kennox, 2 Avon Road East, Christchurch, Dorset

McBAIN: J. H. McBain of McBain, 7025, North Finger Rock Place, Tucson, Arizona, USA

MALCOLM (MACCALLUM): Robin N. L. Malcolm of Poltalloch, Duntrune Castle, Lochgilphead, Argyll

MACDONALD: The Lord Macdonald (*The Macdonald of Macdonald*), Kinloch Lodge, Sleat, Isle of Skye

*MACDONALD OF CLANRANALD: Ranald A. Macdonald of Clanranald, Grooms Bell, The Haining, Selkirk TD7 5LR

*MACDONALD OF SLEAT (CLAN HUSTEAIN): Sir Ian Bosville Macdonald of Sleat, Bt., Thorpe Hall, Rudston, Driffield, N. Humberside YO25 0JE

*MACDONELL OF GLENGARRY: Air Cdre Aeneas R. MacDonell of Glengarry, CB, DFC, Elonbank, Castle Street, Fortrose, Ross-shire IV10 8TH

MACDOUGALL: vacant

MACDOWALL: Fergus D. H. Macdowall of Garthland, 16 Tower Road, Nepean, Ontario, Canada

MACGREGOR: Sir Gregor MacGregor of MacGregor, Bt., Bannatyne, Newtyle, Blairgowrie, Perthshire PH12 8TR

MACINTYRE: James W. MacIntyre of Glenoe, 15301 Pine Orchard Drive, Apartment 3H, Silver Spring, Maryland, USA

MACKAY: The Lord Reay, House of Lords, London SW1

MACKENZIE: The Earl of Cromartie, Castle Leod, Strathpeffer, Ross-shire IV14 9AA

MACKINNON: Madam Anne Mackinnon of Mackinnon, 16 Purleigh Road, Bridgwater, Somerset

MACKINTOSH: *The Mackintosh of Mackintosh*, Moy Hall, Inverness IV13 7YQ

MACLACHLAN: Madam Marjorie MacLachlan of MacLachlan, Castle Lachlan, Argyll

MACLAREN: Donald MacLaren of MacLaren and Achleskine, Achleskine, Kirkton, Balquidder, Lochearnhead

MACLEAN: The Hon. Sir Lachlan Maclean of Duart, Bt., Arngask House, Glenfarg, Perthshire PH2 9QA

MACLENNAN: vacant

MACLEOD: John MacLeod of MacLeod, Dunvegan Castle, Isle of Skye

MACMILLAN: George MacMillan of MacMillan, Finlaystone, Langbank, Renfrewshire

MACNAB: J. C. Macnab of Macnab (*The Macnab*), Leuchars Castle Farmhouse, Leuchars, Fife KY16 0EY

MACNAGHTEN: Sir Patrick Macnaghten of Macnaghten and Dundarave, Bt., Dundarave, Bushmills, Co. Antrim

MACNEACAIL: Iain Macneacail of Macneacail and Scorrybreac, 12 Fox Street, Ballina, NSW, Australia

MACNEIL OF BARRA: Ian R. Macneil of Barra (*The Macneil of Barra*), Kisimul Castle, Barra

MACPHERSON: The Hon. Sir William Macpherson of Cluny, TD, Newtown Castle, Blairgowrie, Perthshire

MACTHOMAS: Andrew P. C. MacThomas of Finegand, c/o The Clan MacThomas Society, 19 Warriston Avenue, Edinburgh

MAITLAND: The Earl of Lauderdale, 12 St Vincent Street, Edinburgh

MAKGILL: The Viscount of Oxfuird, Hill House, St Mary Bourne, Andover, Hants SP11 6BG

MAR: The Countess of Mar, St Michael's Farm, Great Witley, Worcs WR6 6JB

MARJORIBANKS: Andrew Marjoribanks of that Ilk

MATHESON: Maj. Sir Fergus Matheson of Matheson, Bt., Old Rectory, Hedenham, Bungay, Suffolk NR35 2LD

MENZIES: David R. Menzies of Menzies, 20 Nardina Crescent, Dalkeith, Western Australia

MOFFAT: Madam Moffat of that Ilk, St Jasual, Bullocks Farm Lane, Wheeler End Common, High Wycombe

MONCREIFFE: vacant

MONTGOMERIE: The Earl of Eglinton and Winton, The Dutch House, West Green, Hartley Wintney, Hants

MORRISON: Dr Iain M. Morrison of Ruchdi, Magnolia Cottage, The Street, Walberton, Sussex

MUNRO: Hector W. Munro of Foulis, TD, Foulis Castle, Evanton, Ross-shire IV16 9UX

MURRAY: The Duke of Atholl, Blair Castle, Blair Atholl, Perthshire

NESBITT (or NISBET): Robert Nesbitt of that Ilk, Upper Roundhurst Farm, Roundhurst, Haslemere, Surrey

NICOLSON: The Lord Carnock, 90 Whitehall Court, London SW1A 2EL

OGILVY: The Earl of Airlie, KT, GCVO, PC, Cortachy Castle, Kirriemuir, Angus

RAMSAY: The Earl of Dalhousie, KT, GCVO, GBE, MC, Brechin Castle, Brechin, Angus DD7 6SH

RATTRAY: James S. Rattray of Rattray, Craighall, Rattray, Perthshire

ROBERTSON: Alexander G. H. Robertson of Struan (*Struan-Robertson*), The Breach Farm, Goudhurst Road, Cranbrook, Kent

ROLLO: The Lord Rollo, Pitcairns, Dunning, Perthshire

ROSE: Miss Elizabeth Rose of Kilravock, Kilravock Castle, Croy, Inverness

ROSS: David C. Ross of that Ilk, The Old Schoolhouse, Fettercairn, Kincardineshire

RUTHVEN: The Earl of Gowrie, PC, Castlemartin, Kilcullen, Co. Kildare, Republic of Ireland

SCOTT: The Duke of Buccleuch and Queensberry, KT, VRD, Bowhill, Selkirk

SCRYMGEOUR: The Earl of Dundee, Birkhill, Cupar, Fife

SEMPILL: The Lord Sempill, East Lodge, Druminnor, Rhynie, Aberdeenshire AB5 4LT

SHAW: John Shaw of Tordarroch, Newhall, Balblair, By Conon Bridge, Ross-shire

SINCLAIR: The Earl of Caithness, Churchill, Chipping Norton, Oxford OX7 5UX

SKENE: Danus Skene of Skene, Nether Pitleur, Strathmiglo, Fife

STIRLING: Fraser J. Stirling of Cader, 17 Park Row, Farnham, Surrey

STRANGE: Maj. Timothy Strange of Balcaskie, Little Holme, Porton Road, Amesbury, Wilts

SUTHERLAND: The Countess of Sutherland, House of Tongue, Brora, Sutherland

SWINTON: John Swinton of that Ilk, 123 Superior Avenue SW, Calgary, Alberta, Canada

TROTTER: Alexander Trotter of Mortonhall, Charterhall, Duns, Berwickshire

URQUHART: Kenneth T. Urquhart of Urquhart, 507 Jefferson Park Avenue, Jefferson, New Orleans, Louisiana 70121, USA

WALLACE: Ian F. Wallace of that Ilk, 5 Lennox Street, Edinburgh EH4 1QB

WEDDERBURN OF THAT ILK: The Master of Dundee, Birkhill, Cupar, Fife

WEMYSS: David Wemyss of that Ilk, Invermay, Forteviot, Perthshire

The Privy Council

The Sovereign in Council, or Privy Council, was the chief source of executive power until the system of Cabinet government developed in the 18th century. Now the Privy Council's main functions are to advise the Sovereign and to exercise its own statutory responsibilities independent of the Sovereign in Council (*see also* page 216).

Membership of the Privy Council is automatic upon appointment to certain government and judicial positions in the United Kingdom, e.g. Cabinet ministers must be Privy Counsellors and are sworn in on first assuming office. Membership is also accorded by The Queen to eminent people in the UK and independent countries of the Commonwealth of which Her Majesty is Queen, on the recommendation of the British Prime Minister. Membership of the Council is retained for life, except for very occasional removals.

The administrative functions of the Privy Council are carried out by the Privy Council Office (*see* page 334) under the direction of the Lord President of the Council, who is always a member of the Cabinet.

Lord President of the Council, The Rt. Hon. Antony Newton, OBE, MP
Clerk of the Council, N. H. Nicholls, CBE

MEMBERS *as at 31 August 1996*

HRH The Duke of Edinburgh, 1951
HRH The Prince of Wales, 1977

Aberdare, Lord, 1974
Ackner, Lord, 1980
Airlie, Earl of, 1984
Aitken, Jonathan, 1994
Aldington, Lord, 1954
Aldous, Sir William, 1995
Alebua, Ezekiel, 1988
Alison, Michael, 1981
Alport, Lord, 1960
Amery of Lustleigh, Lord, 1960
Ampthill, Lord, 1995
Ancram, Michael, 1996
Anthony, Douglas, 1971
Archer of Sandwell, Lord, 1977
Arnold, Sir John, 1979
Arthur, Hon. Owen, 1995
Ashdown, Paddy, 1989
Ashley of Stoke, Lord, 1979
Atkins, Robert, 1995
Auld, Sir Robin, 1995
Baker, Kenneth, 1984
Balcombe, Sir John, 1985
Barber, Lord, 1963

Barnett, Lord, 1975
Barwick, Sir Garfield, 1964
Beckett, Margaret, 1993
Beith, Alan, 1992
Beldam, Sir Roy, 1989
Belstead, Lord, 1983
Benn, Anthony, 1964
Bennett, Sir Frederic, 1985
Bevins, John, 1959
Biffen, John, 1979
Bingham of Cornhill, Lord, 1986
Birch, William, 1992
Bird, Vere, 1982
Bisson, Sir Gordon, 1987
Blair, Anthony, 1994
Blaker, Lord, 1983
Blatch, Baroness, 1993
Bolger, James, 1991
Booth, Albert, 1976
Boothroyd, Betty, 1992
Boscawen, Hon. Robert, 1992
Bottomley, Virginia, 1992
Boyd-Carpenter, Lord, 1954
Boyson, Sir Rhodes, 1987
Braine, Lord, 1985
Brandon of Oakbrook, Lord, 1978
Brathwaite, Sir Nicholas, 1991
Bridge of Harwich, Lord, 1975
Brightman, Lord, 1979
Brittan, Sir Leon, 1981
Brooke, Sir Henry, 1996
Brooke, Peter, 1988
Brown, Gordon, 1996
Brown, Sir Simon, 1992
Brown, Sir Stephen, 1983
Browne, Sir Patrick, 1974
Browne-Wilkinson, Lord, 1983
Buckley, Sir Denys, 1970
Butler, Sir Adam, 1984
Butler-Sloss, Dame Elizabeth, 1988
Caithness, Earl of, 1990
Callaghan of Cardiff, Lord, 1964
Cameron of Lochbroom, Lord, 1984
Campbell of Croy, Lord, 1970
Canterbury, The Archbishop of, 1991
Carlisle of Bucklow, Lord, 1979
Carr of Hadley, Lord, 1963
Carrington, Lord, 1959
Carswell, Sir Robert, 1993
Casey, Sir Maurice, 1986
Castle of Blackburn, Baroness, 1964
Cato, Robert, 1981
Chalfont, Lord, 1964
Chalker of Wallasey, Baroness, 1987
Chan, Sir Julius, 1981
Channon, Paul, 1980
Charteris of Amisfield, Lord, 1972
Chataway, Sir Christopher, 1970
Clark, Alan, 1991
Clark, Helen, 1990
Clark of Kempston, Lord, 1990
Clarke, Kenneth, 1984
Cledwyn of Penrhos, Lord, 1966
Cockfield, Lord, 1982

Cocks of Hartcliffe, Lord, 1976
Coggan, Lord, 1961
Colman, Fraser, 1986
Colnbrook, Lord, 1973
Compton, John, 1983
Concannon, John, 1978
Cook, Robin, 1996
Cooke of Thorndon, Lord, 1977
Cooper, Sir Frank, 1983
Cope, Sir John, 1988
Corfield, Sir Frederick, 1970
Cowen, Sir Zelman, 1981
Cradock, Sir Percy, 1993
Cranborne, Viscount, 1994
Crawford and Balcarres, Earl of, 1972
Crickhowell, Lord, 1979
Croom-Johnson, Sir David, 1984
Cumming-Bruce, Sir Roualeyn, 1977
Cunningham, Jack, 1993
Curry, David, 1996
Davies, Denzil, 1978
Davison, Sir Ronald, 1978
Dean of Harptree, Lord, 1991
Deedes, Lord, 1962
Dell, Edmund, 1970
Denham, Lord, 1981
Denning, Lord, 1948
Devonshire, Duke of, 1964
Dewar, Donald, 1996
Diamond, Lord, 1965
Dillon, Sir Brian, 1982
Dixon, Donald, 1996
Donaldson of Lymington, Lord, 1979
Dorrell, Stephen, 1994
Douglas, Sir William, 1977
Douglas-Hamilton, Lord James, 1996
du Cann, Sir Edward, 1964
Duff, Sir Antony, 1980
Dunn, Sir Robin, 1980
Eccles, Viscount, 1951
Eden of Winton, Lord, 1972
Eggar, Timothy, 1995
Eichelbaum, Sir Thomas, 1989
Emery, Sir Peter, 1993
Emslie, Lord, 1972
Erroll of Hale, Lord, 1960
Esquivel, Manuel, 1986
Evans, Sir Anthony, 1992
Eveleigh, Sir Edward, 1977
Farquharson, Sir Donald, 1989
Fellowes, Sir Robert, 1990
Ferrers, Earl, 1982
Floissac, Sir Vincent, 1992
Foot, Michael, 1974
Forsyth, Michael, 1995
Foster, Derek, 1993
Fowler, Sir Norman, 1979
Fox, Sir Marcus, 1995
Fox, Sir Michael, 1981
Fraser, Malcolm, 1976
Fraser of Carmyllie, Lord, 1989
Freeman, John, 1966
Freeman, Roger, 1993

Freeson, Reginald, 1976
Gairy, Sir Eric, 1977
Garel-Jones, Tristan, 1992
Gault, Thomas, 1992
Georges, Telford, 1986
Gibbs, Sir Harry, 1972
Gibson, Sir Peter, 1993
Gibson, Sir Ralph, 1985
Gibson-Watt, Lord, 1974
Gilbert, John, 1978
Gilmour of Craigmillar, Lord, 1973
Glenamara, Lord, 1964
Glidewell, Sir Iain, 1985
Goff of Chieveley, Lord, 1982
Goodlad, Alastair, 1992
Gorton, Sir John, 1968
Gowrie, Earl of, 1984
Gray of Contin, Lord, 1982
Griffiths, Lord, 1980
Gummer, John, 1985
Habgood, Rt Revd Lord, 1983
Hague, William, 1995
Hailsham of St Marylebone, Lord,
  1956
Hamilton, Sir Archie, 1991
Hanley, Jeremy, 1994
Hardie Boys, Sir Michael, 1989
Harrison, Walter, 1977
Harvington, Lord, 1971
Hattersley, Roy, 1975
Hayhoe, Lord, 1985
Healey, Lord, 1964
Heath, Sir Edward, 1955
Heathcoat-Amory, David, 1996
Henry, Sir Denis, 1993
Herbison, Margaret, 1964
Heseltine, Michael, 1979
Heseltine, Sir William, 1986
Hesketh, Lord, 1991
Higgins, Sir Terence, 1979
Hirst, Sir David, 1992
Hobhouse, Sir John, 1993
Hoffmann, Lord, 1992
Hogg, Hon. Douglas, 1992
Holderness, Lord, 1959
Hope of Craighead, Lord, 1989
Hordern, Sir Peter, 1993
Howard, Michael, 1990
Howe of Aberavon, Lord, 1972
Howell, David, 1979
Howell, Lord, 1976
Hughes, Lord, 1970
Hunt, David, 1990
Hunt, Jonathan, 1989
Hurd, Douglas, 1982
Hutchison, Sir Michael, 1995
Hutton, Sir Brian, 1988
Ingraham, Hubert, 1993
Jauncey of Tullichettle, Lord, 1988
Jellicoe, Earl, 1963
Jenkin of Roding, Lord, 1973
Jenkins of Hillhead, Lord, 1964
Jones, Aubrey, 1955
Jopling, Michael, 1979
Judge, Sir Igor, 1996
Jugnauth, Sir Anerood, 1987
Kaufman, Gerald, 1978
Keith of Kinkel, Lord, 1976
Kelly, Sir Basil, 1984
Kenilorea, Sir Peter, 1979

Kennedy, Sir Paul, 1992
Kerr, Sir Michael, 1981
King, Thomas, 1979
Kingsdown, Lord, 1987
Kingsland, Lord, 1994
Kinnock, Neil, 1983
Knight, Gregory, 1995
Lamont, Norman, 1986
Lane, Lord, 1975
Lang, Ian, 1990
Lange, David, 1984
Lansdowne, Marquess of, 1964
Latasi, Kamuta, 1996
Latey, Sir John, 1986
Lauti, Sir Toaripi, 1979
Lawson of Blaby, Lord, 1981
Lawton, Sir Frederick, 1972
Leggatt, Sir Andrew, 1990
Leonard, Rt. Revd Graham, 1981
Lilley, Peter, 1990
Listowel, Earl of, 1946
Llewelyn-Davies of Hastoe,
  Baroness, 1975
Lloyd of Berwick, Lord, 1984
Lloyd, Sir Peter, 1994
London, The Bishop of, 1995
Longford, Earl of, 1948
Louisy, Allan, 1981
Lowry, Lord, 1974
Luce, Sir Richard, 1986
Lyell, Sir Nicholas, 1990
Mabon, Dickson, 1977
McCarthy, Sir Thaddeus, 1968
McCowan, Sir Anthony, 1989
MacDermott, Sir John, 1987
MacGregor, John, 1985
MacIntyre, Duncan, 1980
McKay, Ian, 1992
Mackay of Ardbrecknish, Lord, 1996
Mackay of Clashfern, Lord, 1979
Mackay of Drumadoon, Lord, 1996
McKinnon, Donald, 1992
Maclean, David, 1995
McMullin, Sir Duncan, 1980
Major, John, 1987
Manley, Michael, 1989
Mann, Sir Michael, 1988
Mara, Ratu Sir Kamisese, 1973
Marsh, Lord, 1966
Mason of Barnsley, Lord, 1968
Maude, Hon. Francis, 1992
Mawhinney, Brian, 1994
May, Sir John, 1982
Mayhew, Sir Patrick, 1986
Megarry, Sir Robert, 1978
Megaw, Sir John, 1969
Mellish, Lord, 1967
Mellor, David, 1990
Merlyn-Rees, Lord, 1974
Millan, Bruce, 1975
Millett, Sir Peter, 1994
Mitchell, Sir James, 1985
Molyneaux, Sir James, 1983
Monro, Sir Hector, 1995
Moore of Lower Marsh, Lord, 1986
Moore, Michael, 1990
Moore of Wolvercote, Lord, 1977
Morris, Alfred, 1979
Morris, Charles, 1978
Morris, John, 1970

Morris, Michael, 1994
Morritt, Sir Robert, 1994
Moyle, Roland, 1978
Murray, Hon. Lord, 1974
Murray, Sir Donald, 1989
Murray of Epping Forest, Lord, 1976
Murton of Lindisfarne, Lord, 1976
Mustill, Lord, 1985
Nairne, Sir Patrick, 1982
Namaliu, Sir Rabbie, 1989
Needham, Richard, 1994
Neill, Sir Brian, 1985
Newton, Antony, 1988
Nicholls of Birkenhead, Lord, 1995
Nicholson, Sir Michael, 1995
Nolan, Lord, 1991
Nott, Sir John, 1979
Nourse, Sir Martin, 1985
Nutting, Sir Anthony, 1954
Oakes, Gordon, 1979
O'Connor, Sir Patrick, 1980
O'Donnell, Turlough, 1979
O'Flynn, Francis, 1987
Oliver of Aylmerton, Lord, 1980
Onslow, Sir Cranley, 1988
Oppenheim-Barnes, Baroness, 1979
Orme, Stanley, 1974
Otton, Sir Philip, 1995
Owen, Lord, 1976
Paeniu, Bikenibeu, 1991
Palliser, Sir Michael, 1983
Palmer, Sir Geoffrey, 1986
Parker, Sir Roger, 1983
Parkinson, Lord, 1981
Patten, Christopher, 1989
Patten, John, 1990
Patterson, Percival, 1993
Pattie, Sir Geoffrey, 1987
Percival, Sir Ian, 1983
Perth, Earl of, 1957
Peyton of Yeovil, Lord, 1970
Phillips, Sir Nicholas, 1995
Pill, Sir Malcolm, 1995
Pindling, Sir Lynden, 1976
Portillo, Michael, 1992
Potter, Sir Mark, 1996
Powell, Enoch, 1960
Prentice, Lord, 1966
Prescott, John, 1994
Price, George, 1982
Prior, Lord, 1970
Puapua, Tomasi, 1982
Purchas, Sir Francis, 1982
Pym, Lord, 1970
Raison, Sir Timothy, 1982
Ramsden, James, 1963
Rawlinson of Ewell, Lord, 1964
Redwood, John, 1993
Rees, Lord, 1983
Renton, Lord, 1962
Renton, Timothy, 1989
Richard, Lord, 1993
Richardson, Sir Ivor, 1978
Richardson of Duntisbourne, Lord,
  1976
Richmond, Sir Clifford, 1973
Rifkind, Malcolm, 1986
Rippon of Hexham, Lord, 1962
Robens of Woldingham, Lord, 1951
Roberts, Sir Wyn, 1991

Roch, Sir John, 1993
Rodger of Earlsferry, Lord, 1992
Rodgers of Quarry Bank, Lord, 1975
Rose, Sir Christopher, 1992
Roskill, Lord, 1971
Ross, *Hon.* Lord, 1985
Rumbold, Dame Angela, 1991
Runcie, Lord, 1980
Russell, Sir Patrick, 1987
Ryder, Richard, 1990
Sainsbury, Sir Timothy, 1992
St John of Fawsley, Lord, 1979
Sandiford, Erskine, 1989
Saville, Sir Mark, 1994
Scarman, Lord, 1973
Schiemann, Sir Konrad, 1995
Scott, Sir Nicholas, 1989
Scott, Sir Richard, 1991
Seaga, Edward, 1981
Seear, Baroness, 1985
Shawcross, Lord, 1946
Shearer, Hugh, 1969
Sheldon, Robert, 1977
Shephard, Gillian, 1992
Shepherd, Lord, 1965
Shore, Peter, 1967
Simmonds, Kennedy, 1984
Simon of Glaisdale, Lord, 1961
Sinclair, Ian, 1977
Slade, Sir Christopher, 1982
Slynn of Hadley, Lord, 1992

Smith, Sir Geoffrey Johnson, 1996
Somare, Sir Michael, 1977
Somers, Sir Edward, 1981
Stanley, Sir John, 1984
Staughton, Sir Christopher, 1988
Steel, Sir David, 1977
Stephen, Sir Ninian, 1979
Stephenson, Sir John, 1971
Stewartby, Lord, 1989
Steyn, Lord, 1992
Stocker, Sir John, 1986
Stodart of Leaston, Lord, 1974
Stott, Lord, 1964
Strathclyde, Lord, 1995
Stuart-Smith, Sir Murray, 1988
Talboys, Sir Brian, 1977
Taylor of Gosforth, Lord, 1988
Tebbit, Lord, 1981
Templeman, Lord, 1978
Thatcher, Baroness, 1970
Thomas of Gwydir, Lord, 1964
Thomas, Sir Swinton, 1994
Thomson, David, 1981
Thomson of Monifieth, Lord, 1966
Thorpe, Jeremy, 1967
Thorpe, Sir Matthew, 1995
Tizard, Robert, 1986
Tonypandy, Viscount, 1968
Trefgarne, Lord, 1989
Trumpington, Baroness, 1992
Ullswater, Viscount, 1994

Varley, Lord, 1974
Waddington, Lord, 1987
Waite, Sir John, 1993
Wakeham, Lord, 1983
Waldegrave, William, 1990
Walker, Sir Harold, 1979
Walker of Worcester, Lord, 1970
Waller, Sir George, 1976
Ward, Sir Alan, 1995
Watkins, Sir Tasker, 1980
Weatherill, Lord, 1980
Wheeler, Sir John, 1993
Whitelaw, Viscount, 1967
Wilberforce, Lord, 1964
Williams, Alan, 1977
Williams of Crosby, Baroness, 1974
Wilson of Langside, Lord, 1967
Windlesham, Lord, 1973
Wingti, Paias, 1987
Withers, Reginald, 1977
Woodhouse, Sir Owen, 1974
Woolf, Lord, 1986
Wylie, *Hon.* Lord, 1970
York, The Archbishop of, 1991
Young, Baroness, 1981
Young, Sir George, 1993
Young of Graffham, Lord, 1984
Younger of Prestwick, Lord, 1979
Zacca, Edward, 1992

The Privy Council of Northern Ireland

The Privy Council of Northern Ireland had responsibilities in Northern Ireland similar to those of the Privy Council in Great Britain until the Northern Ireland Act 1974 instituted direct rule and a UK Cabinet minister became responsible for the functions previously exercised by the Northern Ireland government.

Membership of the Privy Council of Northern Ireland is retained for life. The postnominal initials PC (NI)

are used to differentiate its members from those of the Privy Council.

MEMBERS   *as at 31 August 1996*

Bailie, Robin, 1971
Bleakley, David, 1971
Bradford, Roy, 1969
Craig, William, 1963
Dobson, John, 1969
Kelly, Sir Basil, 1969

Kirk, Herbert, 1962
Long, William, 1966
Lowry, The Lord, 1971
McConnell, The Lord, 1964
McIvor, Basil, 1971
Morgan, William, 1961
Moyola, The Lord, 1966
Neill, Sir Ivan, 1950
Porter, Sir Robert, 1969
Simpson, Robert, 1969
Taylor, John, MP, 1970
West, Henry, 1960

Parliament

The United Kingdom constitution is not contained in any single document but has evolved in the course of time, formed partly by statute, partly by common law and partly by convention. A constitutional monarchy, the United Kingdom is governed by Ministers of the Crown in the name of the Sovereign, who is head both of the state and of the government.

The organs of government are the legislature (Parliament), the executive and the judiciary. The executive consists of HM Government (Cabinet and other Ministers) (*see* pages 275–6), government departments (*see* pages 277–356), local authorities (*see* Local Government), and public corporations operating nationalized industries or social or cultural services (*see* pages 277–356). The judiciary (*see* Law Courts and Offices) pronounces on the law, both written and unwritten, interprets statutes and is responsible for the enforcement of the law; the judiciary is independent of both the legislature and the executive.

THE MONARCHY

The Sovereign personifies the state and is, in law, an integral part of the legislature, head of the executive, head of the judiciary, the commander-in-chief of all armed forces of the Crown and the 'Supreme Governor' of the Church of England. The seat of the monarchy is in the United Kingdom. In the Channel Islands and the Isle of Man, which are Crown dependencies, the Sovereign is represented by a Lieutenant-Governor. In the member states of the Commonwealth of which the Sovereign is head of state, her representative is a Governor-General; in United Kingdom dependencies the Sovereign is usually represented by a Governor, who is responsible to the British Government.

Although the powers of the monarchy are now very limited, restricted mainly to the advisory and ceremonial, there are important acts of government which require the participation of the Sovereign. These include summoning, proroguing and dissolving Parliament, giving royal assent to bills passed by Parliament, appointing important office-holders, e.g. government ministers, judges, bishops and governors, conferring peerages, knighthoods and other honours, and granting pardon to a person wrongly convicted of a crime. An important function is appointing a Prime Minister, by convention the leader of the political party which enjoys, or can secure, a majority of votes in the House of Commons. In international affairs the Sovereign as head of state has the power to declare war and make peace, to recognize foreign states and governments, to conclude treaties and to annex or cede territory. However, as the Sovereign entrusts executive power to Ministers of the Crown and acts on the advice of her Ministers, which she cannot ignore, in practice royal prerogative powers are exercised by Ministers, who are responsible to Parliament.

Ministerial responsibility does not diminish the Sovereign's importance to the smooth working of government. She holds meetings of the Privy Council, gives audiences to her Ministers and other officials at home and overseas, receives accounts of Cabinet decisions, reads dispatches and signs state papers; she must be informed and consulted on every aspect of national life; and she must show complete impartiality.

COUNSELLORS OF STATE
In the event of the Sovereign's absence abroad, it is necessary to appoint Counsellors of State under letters patent to carry out the chief functions of the Monarch, including the holding of Privy Councils and giving royal assent to acts passed by Parliament. The normal procedure is to appoint as Counsellors three or four members of the royal family among those remaining in the United Kingdom.

In the event of the Sovereign on accession being under the age of eighteen years, or at any time unavailable or incapacitated by infirmity of mind or body for the performance of the royal functions, provision is made for a regency.

THE PRIVY COUNCIL

The Sovereign in Council, or Privy Council, was the chief source of executive power until the system of Cabinet government developed. Now its main function is to advise the Sovereign to approve Orders in Council and to advise on the issue of royal proclamations. The Council's own statutory responsibilities (independent of the powers of the Sovereign in Council) include powers of supervision over the registering bodies for the medical and allied professions. A full Council is summoned only on the death of the Sovereign or when the Sovereign announces his or her intention to marry. (For full list of Counsellors, *see* pages 213–5)

There are a number of advisory Privy Council committees, whose meetings the Sovereign does not attend. Some are prerogative committees, such as those dealing with legislative matters submitted by the legislatures of the Channel Islands and the Isle of Man or with applications for charters of incorporation; and some are provided for by statute, e.g. those for the universities of Oxford and Cambridge and the Scottish universities.

The Judicial Committee of the Privy Council is the final court of appeal from courts of the United Kingdom dependencies, courts of independent Commonwealth countries which have retained the right of appeal, courts of the Channel Islands and the Isle of Man, some professional and disciplinary committees, and church sources. The Committee is composed of Privy Counsellors who hold, or have held, high judicial office, although usually only three or five hear each case.

Administrative work is carried out by the Privy Council Office under the direction of the Lord President of the Council, a Cabinet Minister.

PARLIAMENT

Parliament is the supreme law-making authority and can legislate for the United Kingdom as a whole or for any parts of it separately (the Channel Islands and the Isle of Man are Crown dependencies and not part of the United Kingdom).

The main functions of Parliament are to pass laws, to provide (by voting taxation) the means of carrying on the work of government and to scrutinize government policy and administration, particularly proposals for expenditure. International treaties and agreements are by custom presented to Parliament before ratification.

Parliament emerged during the late 13th and early 14th centuries. The officers of the King's household and the King's judges were the nucleus of early Parliaments, joined by such ecclesiastical and lay magnates as the King might summon to form a prototype 'House of Lords', and occasionally by the knights of the shires, burgesses and proctors of the lower clergy. By the end of Edward III's reign a 'House of Commons' was beginning to appear; the first known Speaker was elected in 1377.

Parliamentary procedure is based on custom and precedent, partly formulated in the Standing Orders of both Houses (*see* Standing Orders, page 222), and each House has the right to control its own internal proceedings and to commit for contempt. The system of debate in the two Houses is similar; when a motion has been moved, the Speaker proposes the question as the subject of a debate. Members speak from wherever they have been sitting. Questions are decided by a vote on a simple majority. Draft legislation is introduced, in either House, as a bill. Bills can be introduced by a Government Minister or a private Member, but in practice the majority of bills which become law are introduced by the Government. To become law, a bill must be passed by each House (for parliamentary stages, *see* Bill, page 220) and then sent to the Sovereign for the royal assent, after which it becomes an Act of Parliament.

Proceedings of both Houses are public, except on extremely rare occasions. The minutes (called Votes and Proceedings in the Commons, and Minutes of Proceedings in the Lords) and the speeches (The Official Report of Parliamentary Debates, *Hansard*) are published daily. Proceedings are also recorded for transmission on radio and television and stored in the Parliamentary Recording Unit before transfer to the National Sound Archive. Television cameras have been allowed into the House of Lords since January 1985 and into the House of Commons since November 1989; committee meetings may also be televised.

By the Parliament Act of 1911, the maximum duration of a Parliament is five years (if not previously dissolved), the term being reckoned from the date given on the writs for the new Parliament. The maximum life has been prolonged by legislation in such rare circumstances as the two world wars (31 January 1911 to 25 November 1918; 26 November 1935 to 15 June 1945). Dissolution and writs for a general election are ordered by the Sovereign on the advice of the Prime Minister. The life of a Parliament is divided into sessions, usually of one year in length, beginning and ending most often in October or November.

THE HOUSE OF LORDS
London SW1A 0PW
Tel 0171-219 3000

The House of Lords consists of the Lords Spiritual and Temporal. The Lords Spiritual are the Archbishops of Canterbury and York, the Bishops of London, Durham and Winchester, and the 21 senior diocesan bishops of the Church of England. The Lords Temporal consist of all hereditary peers of England, Scotland, Great Britain and the United Kingdom who have not disclaimed their peerages, life peers created under the Life Peerages Act 1958, and those Lords of Appeal in Ordinary created life peers under the Appellate Jurisdiction Act 1876, as

amended (law lords). Disclaimants of a hereditary peerage lose their right to sit in the House of Lords but gain the right to vote at parliamentary elections and to offer themselves for election to the House of Commons (*see also* page 137). Those peers disqualified from sitting in the House include:
– aliens, i.e. any peer who is not a British citizen, a Commonwealth citizen (under the British Nationality Act 1981) or a citizen of the Republic of Ireland
– peers under the age of 21
– undischarged bankrupts or, in Scotland, those whose estate is sequestered
– peers convicted of treason

Peers who do not wish to attend sittings of the House of Lords may apply for leave of absence for the duration of a Parliament.

Until the beginning of this century the House of Lords had considerable power, being able to veto any bill submitted to it by the House of Commons, but those powers were greatly reduced by the Parliament Acts of 1911 and 1949 (*see* page 221).

Combined with its legislative role, the House of Lords has judicial powers as the ultimate Court of Appeal for courts in Great Britain and Northern Ireland, except for criminal cases in Scotland. These powers are exercised by the Lord Chancellor and the law lords.

Members of the House of Lords are unpaid. However, they are entitled to reimbursement of travelling expenses on parliamentary business within the UK and certain other expenses incurred for the purpose of attendance at sittings of the House, within a maximum for each day of £74.00 for overnight subsistence, £33.00 for day subsistence and incidental travel, and £32.00 for secretarial costs, postage and certain additional expenses.

COMPOSITION *as at 17 July 1996*
Archbishops and Bishops, 26
Peers by succession, 756 (16 women)
Hereditary Peers of first creation (including the Prince of Wales), 11
Life Peers under the Appellate Jurisdiction Act 1876, 24
Life Peers under the Life Peerages Act 1958, 378 (65 women)
Total 1,195
Of whom:
Peers without Writs of Summons, 84 (3 minors)
Peers on leave of absence from the House, 67

STATE OF PARTIES *as at 17 July 1996*
About half of the members of the House of Lords take the whip of one of the political parties. The other members sit on the cross-benches as independents or have no party affiliation.

Conservative, 468
Labour, 110
Liberal Democrats, 56
Cross-bench, 298
Other (including Bishops), 260 (of whom 151 are ineligible to attend)

OFFICERS

The House is presided over by the Lord Chancellor, who is *ex officio* Speaker of the House. A panel of deputy Speakers is appointed by Royal Commission. The first deputy Speaker is the Chairman of Committees, appointed at the beginning of each session, a salaried officer of the House who takes the chair in committee of the whole House and in some select committees. He is assisted by a panel of deputy chairmen, headed by the salaried Principal Deputy

Chairman of Committees, who is also chairman of the European Communities Committee of the House.

The permanent officers include the Clerk of the Parliaments, who is in charge of the administrative staff collectively known as the Parliament Office; the Gentleman Usher of the Black Rod, who is also Serjeant-at-Arms in attendance upon the Lord Chancellor and is responsible for security and for accommodation and services in the House of Lords; and the Yeoman Usher, who is Deputy Serjeant-at-Arms and assists Black Rod in his duties.

Speaker (£18,607), The Lord Mackay of Clashfern, PC
    Private Secretary, P. Kennedy
Chairman of Committees (£51,652), The Lord Boston of
    Faversham, QC
Principal Deputy Chairman of Committees (£47,673), The Lord
    Tordoff
Clerk of the Parliaments (£103,425), Sir Michael Wheeler-
    Booth, KCB
Clerk Assistant and Principal Finance Officer (£67,500 –
    £98,000), J. M. Davies
Reading Clerk and Clerk of Public Bills (£57,000 –£84,500),
    P. D. G. Hayter, LVO
Counsel to Chairman of Committees (£57,000 –£84,500),
    D. Rippengal, CB, QC; Sir James Nursaw, KCB, QC; Dr C. S.
    Kerse
Principal Clerks (£51,103 –£84,500), J. A. Vallance White
    (*Judicial Office and Fourth Clerk at the Table*); M. G.
    Pownall (*Clerk of the Journals*); B. P. Keith (*Private Bills*);
    D. R. Beamish (*Committees*); R. H. Walters, D.Phil.
Chief Clerks (£41,978 –£61,493), Dr F. P. Tudor; T. V.
    Mohan; E. C. Ollard
Senior Clerks (£29,107 –£44,101), Mrs M. E. Ollard (*seconded
    as Secretary to the Leader of the House and Chief Whip*); A.
    Makower; E. J. J. Wells; S. P. Burton; J. L. Goddard; Mrs
    M. B. Bloor; T. E. Radice
Clerks (£15,172 –£26,365), D. J. Batt; Dr C. Andrew Mylne;
    Miss L. J. Mouland; J. A. Vaughan
Clerk of the Records (£41,978 –£61,493), D. J. Johnson, FSA
Deputy Clerk of the Records (£32,962 –£53,481), S. K. Ellison
Establishment Officer, R. H. Walters, D.Phil.
Deputy Establishment Officer (£29,107 –£44,101), G.
    Embleton
Accountant (£29,107 –£53,481), C. Preece
Assistant Accountant (£22,410 –£28,932), Miss J. M.
    Lansdown
Computer Executive (£29,107 –£44,101), Ms S. C. White
Internal Auditor (£29,107 –£44,101), C. H. Rogers
Staff Adviser (£29,107 –£44,101), D. A. W. Dunn, ISO
Judicial Taxing Clerk (£22,410 –£28,932), C. G. Osborne
Librarian (£41,978 –£61,493), D. L. Jones
Deputy Librarian (£32,962 –£53,481), P. G. Davis, PH.D.
Senior Library Clerk (£29,107 –£44,101), Miss I. L. Victory,
    PH.D.
Examiners of Petitions for Private Bills, B. P. Keith; R. J.
    Willoughby
Gentleman Usher of the Black Rod and Serjeant-at-Arms
    (£57,000 –£84,500), Gen. Sir Edward Jones, KCB, CBE
Yeoman Usher of the Black Rod and Deputy Serjeant-at-Arms
    (£29,107 –£44,101), Air Vice-Marshal D. R. Hawkins,
    CB, MBE
Administration Officer (£29,107 –£44,101), Brig. A. J. M.
    Clark
Staff Superintendent, Maj. A. M. Charlesworth
Shorthand Writer (fees), Mrs P. J. Woolgar
Editor, Official Report (*Hansard*), (£39,566 –£57,910), Mrs
    M. E. Villiers
Deputy Editor, Official Report (£29,843 –£48,311), G. R.
    Goodbarne

THE HOUSE OF COMMONS
London SW1A 0AA
Tel 0171-219 3000

The members of the House of Commons are elected by universal adult suffrage. For electoral purposes, the United Kingdom is divided into constituencies, each of which returns one member to the House of Commons, the member being the candidate who obtains the largest number of votes cast in the constituency. To ensure equitable representation the four Boundary Commissions keep constituency boundaries under review and recommend any redistribution of seats which may seem necessary because of population movements, etc. The number of seats was raised to 640 in 1945, then reduced to 625 in 1948, and subsequently rose to 630 in 1955, 635 in 1970, 650 in 1983 and 651 in 1992. Of the present 651 seats, there are 524 for England, 38 for Wales, 72 for Scotland and 17 for Northern Ireland.

At the next general election the number of constituencies will increase to 659; 529 seats in England, 40 seats in Wales, 72 seats in Scotland, and 18 seats in Northern Ireland.

ELECTIONS

Elections are by secret ballot, each elector casting one vote; voting is not compulsory. When a seat becomes vacant between general elections, a by-election is held.

British subjects and citizens of the Irish Republic can stand for election as Members of Parliament (MPs) provided they are 21 or over and not subject to disqualification. Those disqualified from sitting in the House include:

– undischarged bankrupts
– people sentenced to more than one year's imprisonment
– clergy of the Church of England, Church of Scotland, Church of Ireland and Roman Catholic Church
– members of the House of Lords
– holders of certain offices listed in the House of Commons Disqualification Act 1975, e.g. members of the judiciary, Civil Service, regular armed forces, police forces, some local government officers and some members of public corporations and government commissions

For entitlement to vote in parliamentary elections, *see* Legal Notes section.

A candidate does not require any party backing but his or her nomination for election must be supported by the signatures of ten people registered in the constituency. A candidate must also deposit with the returning officer £500, which is forfeit if the candidate does not receive more than 5 per cent of the votes cast. All election expenses at a general election, except the candidate's personal expenses, are subject to a statutory limit of £4,330, plus 3.7 pence for each elector in a borough constituency or 4.9 pence for each elector in a county constituency.

See pages 226 –32 for an alphabetical list of MPs, pages 237 –67 for the results of the last General Election, and pages 234 –5 for the results of recent by-elections.

STATE OF PARTIES *as at 13 July 1996*
Conservative, 324 (17 women)
Elected as Conservative but has resigned the whip, 1
Labour, 272 (38 women)
Liberal Democrats, 25 (4 women)
Plaid Cymru, 4
Scottish Nationalist, 4 (2 women)
Democratic Unionist, 3
Social Democratic and Labour, 4
Ulster Unionist, 9
United Kingdom Unionist, 1

The Speaker and three Deputy Speakers, 4 (2 women) Total, 651 (63 women)

BUSINESS

The week's business of the House is outlined each Thursday by the Leader of the House, after consultation between the Chief Government Whip and the Chief Opposition Whip. A quarter to a third of the time will be taken up by the Government's legislative programme, and the rest by other business, e.g. question time. As a rule, bills likely to raise political controversy are introduced in the Commons before going on to the Lords, and the Commons claims exclusive control in respect of national taxation and expenditure. Bills such as the Finance Bill, which imposes taxation, and the Consolidated Fund Bills, which authorize expenditure, must begin in the Commons. A bill of which the financial provisions are subsidiary may begin in the Lords; and the Commons may waive its rights in regard to Lords' amendments affecting finance.

The Commons has a public register of MPs' financial and certain other interests; this is published annually as a House of Commons paper. Members must also disclose any relevant financial interest or benefit in a matter before the House when taking part in a debate, in certain other proceedings of the House, or in consultations with other MPs, with Ministers or civil servants.

MEMBERS' PAY AND ALLOWANCES

Since 1911 members of the House of Commons have received salary payments; facilities for free travel were introduced in 1924. Members are entitled to claim income tax relief on expenses incurred in the course of their parliamentary duties. Salary rates since 1911 are as follows:

1911	£400 p.a.	1981 June	£13,950 p.a.
1931	360	1982 June	14,510
1934	380	1983 June	15,308
1935	400	1984 Jan	16,106
1937	600	1985 Jan	16,904
1946	1,000	1986 Jan	17,702
1954	1,250	1987 Jan	18,500
1957	1,750	1988 Jan	22,548
1964	3,250	1989 Jan	24,107
1972 Jan	4,500	1990 Jan	26,701
1975 June	5,750	1991 Jan	28,970
1976 June	6,062	1992 Jan	30,854
1977 July	6,270	1994 Jan	31,687
1978 June	6,897	1995 Jan	33,189
1979 June	9,450	1996 Jan	34,085
1980 June	11,750	1996 July	43,000

In 1969 MPs were granted an allowance for secretarial and research expenses. In 1987 this became known as the Office Costs Allowance. From April 1996 the allowance is £43,098 a year.

Since 1972 MPs can claim reimbursement for the additional cost of staying overnight away from their main residence while on parliamentary business. From April 1996 this has been £11,976 a year and since 1984 has been non-taxable.

From 1980 provision was made enabling each MP in receipt of Office Costs Allowance to contribute sums to an approved pension scheme for the provision of a pension, or other benefits, for or in respect of persons whose salary is met by him/her from the Office Costs Allowance.

MEMBERS' PENSIONS

Pension arrangements for MPs were first introduced in 1964. The arrangements currently provide a pension of one-fiftieth of salary for each year of pensionable service with a maximum of two-thirds of salary at age 65. Pension is payable normally at age 65, for men and women, or on later retirement. Pensions may be paid earlier, e.g. on ill-health retirement. The widow/widower of a former MP receives a pension of five-eighths of the late MP's pension. Pensions are index-linked. Members currently contribute 6 per cent of salary to the pension fund; there is an Exchequer contribution, currently slightly more than the amount contributed by MPs.

The House of Commons Members' Fund provides for annual or lump sum grants to ex-MPs, their widows or widowers, and children whose income are below certain limits. Alternatively, payments of £2,116 a year to ex-MPs with at least ten years' service and who left the House of Commons before October 1964, and £1,323 a year to their widows or widowers are made as of right. Members contribute £24 a year and the Exchequer £215,000 a year to the fund.

OFFICERS AND OFFICIALS

The House of Commons is presided over by the Speaker, who has considerable powers to maintain order in the House. A deputy, the Chairman of Ways and Means, and two Deputy Chairmen may preside over sittings of the House of Commons; they are elected by the House, and, like the Speaker, neither speak nor vote other than in their official capacity.

The staff of the House are employed by a Commission chaired by the Speaker. The heads of the six House of Commons departments are permanent officers of the House, not MPs. The Clerk of the House is the principal adviser to the Speaker on the privileges and procedures of the House, the conduct of the business of the House, and committees. The Serjeant-at-Arms is responsible for security, ceremonial, and for accommodation in the Commons part of the Palace of Westminster.

Speaker (£69,651), The Rt. Hon. Betty Boothroyd, MP (West Bromwich West)

Chairman of Ways and Means (£56,785), The Rt. Hon. Michael Morris, MP (Northampton South)

First Deputy Chairman of Ways and Means (£53,015), Sir Geoffrey Lofthouse, MP (Pontefract and Castleford)

Second Deputy Chairman of Ways and Means (£53,015), Dame Janet Fookes, DBE, MP (Plymouth Drake)

OFFICES OF THE SPEAKER AND CHAIRMAN OF WAYS AND MEANS

Speaker's Secretary (£42,180–£61,595), N. Bevan, CB

Chaplain to the Speaker, The Revd Canon D. Gray, TD

Secretary to the Chairman of Ways and Means, (£28,954–£43,802), Ms L. M. Gardner

DEPARTMENT OF THE CLERK OF THE HOUSE

Clerk of the House of Commons (£101,827), D. W. Limon, CB

Clerk Assistant (£67,500–£83,450), W. R. McKay, CB

Clerk of Committees (£67,500–£83,450), C. B. Winnifrith

Principal Clerks (£55,000–£67,650)

Public Bills, R. B. Sands

Table Office, G. Cubie

Journals, A. J. Hastings

Private Bills, R. J. Willoughby

Select Committees, D. G. Millar

Domestic Committees, M. R. Jack, PH.D.

Overseas Office, R. W. G. Wilson

Standing Committees, W. A. Proctor

Second Clerk, Select Committees, Ms H. E. Irwin

Financial Committees, Mrs J. Sharpe

Deputy Principal Clerks (£42,180–£61,595), S. A. L. Panton; Ms A. Milner-Barry; F. A. Cranmer; R. J. Rogers; C. R. M. Ward, ph.D.; D. W. N. Doig; D. L. Natzler; E. P. Silk; A. R. Kennon; L. C. Laurence Smyth; S. J. Patrick; D. J. Gerhold; C. J. Poyser; D. F. Harrison; S. J. Priestley; A. H. Doherty; P. A. Evans; R. I. S. Phillips; R. G. James, ph.D.; Ms P. A. Helme; D. R. Lloyd; B. M. Hutton; J. S. Benger, D.phil.; Ms E. C. Samson; N. P. Walker; M. D. Hamlyn

Senior Clerks (£28,954–£43,802), Mrs E. J. Flood; P. C. Seaward, D.phil.; C. G. Lee; C. D. Stanton; A. Y. A. Azad; C. A. Shaw; Ms L. M. Gardner; K. J. Brown; F. J. Reid; M. Hennessy; G. R. Devine; Mrs E. A. J. Attridge (*acting*); A. M. Kidner (*acting*); Ms J. Eldred (*acting*)

Clerks of Domestic Committees (£28,954–£43,802), P. G. Moon; M. Clark

Examiners of Petitions for Private Bills, R. J. Willoughby; B. P. Keith

Registrar of Members' Interests, R. J. Willoughby

Taxing Officer, R. J. Willoughby

Vote Office

Deliverer of the Vote (£42,180–£61,595), H. C. Foster

Deputy Deliverers of the Vote (£28,954–£43,802), J. F. Collins (*Distribution*); F. W. Hallett (*Production*)

Speaker's Counsel

Speaker's Counsel (£55,000–£67,650), J. S. Mason, cb

Speaker's Counsel (European legislation) (£55,000–£67,650), T. J. G. Pratt, cb

Speaker's Assistant Counsel (£42,180–£61,595), A. Akbar; J. R. Mallinson

Department of the Serjeant-at-Arms

Serjeant-at-Arms (£55,000–£67,650), P. N. W. Jennings

Deputy Serjeant-at-Arms (£42,180–£61,595), M. J. A. Cummins

Assistant Serjeant-at-Arms (£32,791–£53,108), P. A. J. Wright

Deputy Assistant Serjeant-at-Arms (£28,954–£43,802), J. M. Robertson; M. C. D. Harvey

Parliamentary Works Directorate

Director of Works (£55,060–£61,595), H. P. Webber

Deputy Director of Works (£32,791–£53,108), L. Brantingham

Communications Directorate

Director of Communications (£42,180–£61,595), C. G. Gilbert

Department of the Library

Librarian (£55,000–£67,650), Miss J. B. Tanfield

Deputy Librarian (£51,135–£61,595), Miss P. J. Baines

Service Directors (£42,180–£61,595), S. Z. Young; K. G. Cuningham; Mrs J. M. Wainwright

Heads of Section (£32,791–£53,108), C. C. Pond, ph.D.; Mrs C. B. Andrews; R. C. Clements; Mrs J. M. Lourie; R. J. Ware, D.phil.; C. R. Barclay; Mrs J. M. Fiddick; Mrs C. M. Gillie; R. J. Twigger; Mrs G. L. Allen

Senior Library Clerks (£28,954–£43,802), Ms F. Poole; T. N. Edmonds; R. J. Cracknell; Miss O. M. Gay; Miss E. M. McInnes; Dr D. J. Gore; B. K. Winetrobe; Miss M. Baber; Ms A. Walker; Mrs H. V. Holden; Mrs P. L. Carling; Miss J. Seaton; A. J. L. Crompton; Miss P. J. Strickland; Miss V. A. Miller; Ms H. M. Jeffs; M. P. Hillyard; Ms J. Roll; Ms W. T. Wilson; S. A. Wise; E. H. Wood; P. Bowers; T. E. Dodd; A. C. Seely; Ms J. K. Dyson; K. N. H. Parry (*acting*)

Department of Finance and Administration

Director of Finance and Administration (£55,000–£67,650), J. Rodda

Accountant (£51,135–£61,595), A. R. Marskell

Deputy Accountant (£32,791–£53,108), M. Fletcher

Head of Establishments Office (£51,135–£61,595), B. A. Wilson

Deputy Head of Establishments Office (£32,791–£53,108), J. A. Robb

Head of Finance Office (£42,180–£61,595), M. J. Barram

Staff Inspector (£32,791–£53,108), R. C. Collins

Department of the Official Report

Editor (£51,135–£61,595), I. D. Church

Deputy Editor (£42,180–£61,595), P. Walker

Principal Assistant Editors (£32,791–£53,108), J. Gourley; W. G. Garland; Miss H. Hales; Miss L. Sutherland

Assistant Editors (£32,791–£49,325), Miss V. Grainger; Miss V. A. A. Clarke; S. M. Hutchinson; Miss C. Fogarty; Miss V. A. Widgery; Ms K. Stewart; P. R. Hadlow

Refreshment Department

Director of Catering Services (£42,180–£61,595), Mrs S. J. Harrison

Financial Controller (£28,954–£43,802), Mrs J. A. Rissen

Operations Manager (£28,954–£43,802), N. M. Hutson

PARLIAMENTARY INFORMATION

The following is a short glossary of aspects of the work of Parliament. Unless otherwise stated, references are to House of Commons procedures.

BILL – Proposed legislation is termed a bill. The stages of a public bill (for private bills, *see* page 221) in the House of Commons are as follows:

First Reading: There is no debate at this stage, which merely constitutes an order to have the bill printed

Second Reading: The debate on the principles of the bill

Committee Stage: The detailed examination of a bill, clause by clause. In most cases this takes place in a standing committee, or the whole House may act as a committee. A special standing committee may take evidence before embarking on detailed scrutiny of the bill. Very rarely, a bill may be examined by a select committee (*see* page 222)

Report Stage: Detailed review of a bill as amended in committee

Third Reading: Final debate on a bill

Public bills go through the same stages in the House of Lords, except that in almost all cases the committee stage is taken in committee of the whole House.

A bill may start in either House, and has to pass through both Houses to become law. Both Houses have to agree the same text of a bill, so that the amendments made by the second House are then considered in the originating House, and if not agreed, sent back or themselves amended, until agreement is reached.

CHILTERN HUNDREDS – A legal fiction, a nominal office of profit under the Crown, the acceptance of which requires an MP to vacate his seat. The Manor of Northstead is similar. These are the only means by which an MP may resign.

CLOSURE AND GUILLOTINE – To prevent deliberate waste of time of either House, a motion may be made that the question be now put. In the House of Commons, if the Speaker decides that the rights of a minority are not being prejudiced and 100 members support the closure motion in a division, if carried, the original motion is put to the House without further debate.

The guillotine represents a more rigorous and systematic application of the closure. Under this system, a bill proceeds in accordance with a rigid timetable and discussion is limited to the time allotted to each group of clauses. The closure is hardly ever used in the Lords, and there is no procedure for a guillotine. The completion of business in the Lords is ensured by agreement from all sides of the House.

CONSOLIDATED FUND BILL – A bill to authorize issue of money to maintain Government services. The bill is dealt with without debate.

DISSOLUTION – Parliament comes to an end either by dissolution by the Sovereign, on the advice of the Prime Minister, or on the expiration of the term of five years for which the House of Commons was elected. Dissolution is normally effected by a royal proclamation.

EARLY DAY MOTION – A motion put on the notice paper by an MP without in general the real prospect of its being debated. Such motions are expressions of back-bench opinion.

EMERGENCY DEBATE – In the Commons a method of obtaining prompt discussion of a matter of urgency is by moving the adjournment under Standing Order No. 20 for the purpose of discussing a specific and important matter that should have urgent consideration. A member may ask leave to make this motion by giving written notice to the Speaker, usually before 12 noon, and if the Speaker considers the matter of sufficient importance and the House agrees, it is discussed usually at 7 p.m. on the following day.

FATHER OF THE HOUSE – The Member whose continuous service in the House of Commons is the longest. The present Father of the House is the Rt. Hon. Sir Edward Heath, KG, MBE, MP, elected first in 1950.

HANSARD – The official report of debates in both Houses (and in standing committees) published by HMSO, normally on the day after the sitting concerned.

HOURS OF MEETING – The House of Commons meets on Monday, Tuesday and Thursday at 2.30 p.m., on Wednesday at 10 a.m. and on Friday at 9.30 a.m.; there are ten Fridays without sittings in each session. The House of Lords normally meets at 2.30 p.m. Monday to Wednesday and at 3 p.m. on Thursday. In the latter part of the session, the House of Lords sometimes sits on Fridays at 11 a.m.

HYBRIDITY – A public bill which is considered to affect specific private or local interests, as distinct from all such interests of a single category, is called a hybrid bill and is subject to a special form of scrutiny to enable people affected to object. In the House of Lords, affirmative instruments may also be treated as hybrid.

LEADER OF THE OPPOSITION – In 1937 the office of Leader of the Opposition was recognized and a salary was assigned to the post. Since July 1996 the salary has been £83,332 (including parliamentary salary of £43,000). The present Leader of the Opposition is the Rt. Hon. Tony Blair, MP.

THE LORD CHANCELLOR – The Lord High Chancellor of Great Britain is (*ex officio*) the Speaker of the House of Lords. Unlike the Speaker of the House of Commons, he is a member of the Government, takes part in debates and votes in divisions. He has none of the powers to maintain order that the Speaker in the Commons has, these powers being exercised in the Lords by the House as a whole. The Lord Chancellor sits in the Lords on one of the Woolsacks, couches covered with red cloth and stuffed with wool. If he wishes to address the House in any way except formally as Speaker, he leaves the Woolsack.

NAMING – When a member has been named by the Speaker for a breach of order, i.e. contrary to the practice of the House, called by surname and not addressed as the 'Hon. Member for … (her/his constituency)', the Leader of the House moves that the offender 'be suspended from the service of the House' for (in the case of a first offence) a period of five sitting days. Should the member offend again, the period of suspension is increased.

OPPOSITION DAY – A day on which the topic for debate is chosen by the Opposition. There are twenty such days in a normal session. On seventeen days, subjects are chosen by the Leader of the Opposition; on the remaining three days by the leader of the next largest opposition party.

PARLIAMENT ACTS 1911 AND 1949 – Under these Acts, bills may become law without the consent of the Lords.
Since at least the 18th century the Commons has had the privilege of having bills concerned with supply (i.e. taxation and money matters) passed without amendment by the Lords, though until 1911 the Lords retained the right to reject such bills outright.
By the Parliament Act 1911, a bill which has been endorsed by the Speaker of the House of Commons as a money bill, and has been passed by the Commons and sent up to the Lords at least one month before the end of a session, can become law without the consent of the Lords if it is not passed by them without amendment within a month.
Under the Parliament Acts 1911 and 1949, if the Lords reject any other public bill (except one to prolong the life of a Parliament) which has been passed by the Commons in two successive sessions, then that bill shall (unless the Commons direct to the contrary) become law without the consent of the Lords. The Lords have power, therefore, to delay a public bill for thirteen months from its first second reading in the House of Commons.

PRIME MINISTER'S QUESTIONS – The Prime Minister answers questions from 3.15 to 3.30 p.m. on Tuesdays and Thursdays. Nowadays the 'open question' predominates. Members tend to ask the Prime Minister what are his or her official engagements for the day; a supplementary question on virtually any topic can then be put.

PRIVATE BILL – A bill promoted by a body or an individual to give powers additional to, or in conflict with, the general law, and to which a special procedure applies to enable people affected to object.

PRIVATE MEMBERS' BILL – A public bill promoted by a Member who is not a member of the Government.

PRIVATE NOTICE QUESTION – A question adjudged of urgent importance on submission to the Speaker (in the Lords, the Leader of the House), answered at the end of oral questions, usually at 3.30 p.m.

PRIVILEGE – The following are covered by the privilege of Parliament:
(i)   freedom from interference in going to, attending at, and going from, Parliament
(ii) freedom of speech in parliamentary proceedings
(iii) the printing and publishing of anything relating to the proceedings of the two Houses is subject to privilege
(iv) each House is the guardian of its dignity and may punish any insult to the House as a whole

PROROGATION – The bringing to an end, by the Sovereign on the advice of the Government, of a session of Parliament. Public bills which have not completed all their stages lapse on prorogation.

QUEEN'S SPEECH – The speech delivered by The Queen at the State Opening of Parliament, in which the Government's programme for the session is set forth. The speech is drafted by civil servants and approved by the Cabinet.

QUESTION TIME – Oral questions are answered by Ministers in the Commons from 2.30 to 3.30 p.m. every day except Friday. They are also taken at the start of the Lords sittings, with a daily limit of four oral questions.

ROYAL ASSENT – The royal assent is signified by letters patent to such bills and measures as have passed both Houses of Parliament (or bills which have been passed under the Parliament Acts 1911 and 1949). The Sovereign has not given royal assent in person since 1854. On occasion, for instance in the prorogation of Parliament, royal assent may be pronounced to the two Houses by Lords Commissioners. More usually royal assent is notified to each House sitting separately in accordance with the Royal Assent Act 1967. The old French formulae for royal assent are then endorsed on the acts by the Clerk of the Parliaments.

The power to withhold assent resides with the Sovereign but has not been exercised in the United Kingdom since 1707, in the reign of Queen Anne.

SCOTTISH GRAND COMMITTEE – Established in its present form in 1957, the committee consists of all 72 MPs representing Scottish constituencies, with a quorum of ten. The functions of the committee are to consider the principle of all public bills relating exclusively to Scotland (constituting in effect the bill's second reading); to consider the Scottish estimates on not less than six days a session; and to consider matters relating exclusively to Scotland on not more than six days a session. From the beginning of the 1994-5 session, the committee's powers were enhanced to allow oral questions, short debates, ministerial statements, and consideration of appropriate statutory instruments. The committee can meet on appointed days at specified places in Scotland.

The Scottish Affairs select committee is empowered to examine the expenditure, administration and policy of the Scottish Office, and the expenditure and administration of the Lord Advocate's Office.

SELECT COMMITTEES – Consisting usually of ten to 15 members of all parties, select committees are a means used by both Houses in order to investigate certain matters.

Most select committees in the House of Commons are now tied to departments; each committee investigates subjects within a government department's remit. There are other House of Commons select committees dealing with public accounts (i.e. the spending by the Government of money voted by Parliament) and European legislation, and also domestic committees dealing, for example, with privilege and procedure. Major select committees usually take evidence in public; their evidence and reports are published by HMSO.

The principal select committee in the House of Lords is that on the European Communities, which has, at present, six sub-committees dealing with all areas of Community policy. The House of Lords also has a select committee on science and technology, which appoints sub-committees to deal with specific subjects. In addition, *ad hoc* select committees have been set up from time to time to investigate specific subjects, e.g. overseas trade, murder and life imprisonment. There are also some joint committees of the two Houses, e.g. the Joint Committee on Statutory Instruments.

The following are the more important select committees:

DEPARTMENTAL COMMITTEES
Agriculture – Chair, Sir Jerry Wiggin, MP; Clerk, Mr Walker
Defence – Chair, Michael Colvin, MP; Clerks, Mr Kennon; Mr Shaw
Education and Employment – Chair, Sir Malcolm Thornton, MP; Clerk, Mr Hamlyn
Environment – Chair, Andrew Bennett, MP; Clerks, Mr Priestley; Ms Payne
Foreign Affairs – Chair, Rt. Hon. David Howell, MP; Clerks, Dr Ward; Mrs Davies
Health – Chair, Marion Roe, MP; Clerks, Dr James; Mr Healey
Home Affairs – Chair, Sir Ivan Lawrence, MP; Clerks, Mr Poyser; Mr Fox
National Heritage – Chair, Rt. Hon. Gerald Kaufman, MP; Clerk, Mr Patrick
Northern Ireland – Chair, Clive Soley, MP, Clerk, Mr Phillips
Science and Technology – Chair, Sir Giles Shaw, MP; Clerk, Ms Samson
Scottish Affairs – Chair, William McKelvey, MP; Clerks, Mr Doherty; Mr McGlashan
Social Security – Chair, Frank Field, MP; Clerk, Mr Laurence Smyth
Trade and Industry – Chair, Martin O'Neill, MP; Clerks, Mr Gerhold; Mrs Mulley
Transport – Chair, Rt. Hon. Paul Channon, MP; Clerks, Ms Long; Mr Stanton
Treasury – Chair, Sir Thomas Arnold, MP; Clerk, Mrs Sharpe
Welsh Affairs – Chair, Gareth Wardell, MP; Clerk, Ms Helme

NON-DEPARTMENTAL COMMITTEES
Deregulation – Chair, Barry Field, MP; Clerks, Mr Rogers; Mrs Flood
European Legislation – Chair, James Hood, MP; Clerks, Mr Rogers; Mr Lloyd
Parliamentary Commissioner – Chair, James Pawsey, MP; Clerk, Mr Azad
Procedure – Chair, Rt. Hon. Sir Peter Emery, MP; Clerks, Mr Natzler; Mr Rhys
Public Accounts – Chair, Rt. Hon. Robert Sheldon, MP; Clerk, Mr Brown
Public Service – Chair, Giles Radice, MP; Clerk, Dr Seaward
Standards and Privileges – Chair, Rt. Hon. Antony Newton, MP; Clerks, Mr Hastings; Mr Reid

THE SPEAKER – The Speaker of the House of Commons is the spokesman and president of the Chamber. He or she is elected by the House at the beginning of each Parliament or when the previous Speaker retires or dies. The Speaker neither speaks in debates nor votes in divisions except when the voting is equal.

STANDING ORDERS – Rules which have from time to time been agreed by each House of Parliament to regulate the conduct of its business. These orders may be amended or repealed, and are from time to time suspended or dispensed with.

STATE OPENING – This marks the start of each new session of Parliament. Parliament is normally opened, in the presence of both Houses, by The Queen in person, who makes the speech from the throne which outlines the Government's policies for the coming session (*see* Queen's Speech). In the absence of The Queen, Parliament is opened by Royal Commission, and The Queen's Speech is read by one of the Lords Commissioners specially appointed by letters patent for the occasion.

STRANGERS – Anyone who is not a Member or Officer of the House is a stranger. Visitors are generally admitted to debates of both Houses but may be excluded if the House so decides; in practice this happens only in time of war.

However, the cry of 'I spy strangers' causes the public gallery to be cleared, and occurs often.

VACANT SEATS – When a vacancy occurs in the House of Commons during a session of Parliament, the writ for the by-election is moved by a Whip of the party to which the member whose seat has been vacated belonged. If the House is in recess, the Speaker can issue a warrant for a writ, should two members certify to him that a seat is vacant.

WELSH GRAND COMMITTEE – First appointed in the 1959-60 session, the committee consists of all 38 MPs representing Welsh constituencies plus five other members nominated by the selection committee. The functions of the committee are to consider the principle of all public bills referred to it (constituting in effect the second reading of such a bill); and to consider matters relating exclusively to Wales.

The Welsh Affairs select committee is empowered to examine the expenditure, administration and policy of the Welsh Office.

WHIPS – In order to secure the attendance of Members of a particular party in Parliament on all occasions, and particularly on the occasion of an important vote, Whips (originally known as 'Whippers-in') are appointed. The written appeal or circular letter issued by them is also known as a 'whip', its urgency being denoted by the number of times it is underlined. Failure to respond to a three-line whip, headed 'Most important', is tantamount in the Commons to secession (at any rate temporarily) from the party. Whips are officially recognized by Parliament and are provided with office accommodation in both Houses. In both Houses, Government and some Opposition Whips receive salaries from public funds.

PUBLIC INFORMATION SERVICES

HOUSE OF COMMONS – Public Information Office, House of Commons, London SW1A 0AA. Tel: 0171-219 4272
HOUSE OF LORDS – The Journal and Information Office, House of Lords, London SW1A 0PW. Tel: 0171–219 3107

GOVERNMENT OFFICE

The Government is the body of Ministers responsible for the administration of national affairs, determining policy and introducing into Parliament any legislation necessary to give effect to government policy. The majority of Ministers are members of the House of Commons but members of the House of Lords or of neither House may also hold ministerial responsibility. The Lord Chancellor is always a member of the House of Lords. The Prime Minister is, by current convention, always a member of the House of Commons.

THE PRIME MINISTER

The office of Prime Minister, which had been in existence for nearly 200 years, was officially recognized in 1905 and its holder was granted a place in the table of precedence. The Prime Minister, by tradition also First Lord of the Treasury and Minister for the Civil Service, is appointed by the Sovereign and is usually the leader of the party which enjoys, or can secure, a majority in the House of Commons. Other Ministers are appointed by the Sovereign on the recommendation of the Prime Minister, who also allocates functions amongst Ministers and has the power to obtain their resignation or dismissal individually.

The Prime Minister informs the Sovereign of state and political matters, advises on the dissolution of Parliament, and makes recommendations for important Crown appointments, the award of honours, etc.

As the chairman of Cabinet meetings and leader of a political party, the Prime Minister is responsible for translating party policy into government activity. As leader of the Government, the Prime Minister is responsible to Parliament and to the electorate for the policies and their implementation.

The Prime Minister also represents the nation in international affairs, e.g. summit conferences.

THE CABINET

The Cabinet developed during the 18th century as an inner committee of the Privy Council, which was the chief source of executive power until that time. The Cabinet is composed of about twenty Ministers chosen by the Prime Minister, usually the heads of government departments (generally known as Secretaries of State unless they have a special title, e.g. Chancellor of the Exchequer), the leaders of the two Houses of Parliament, and the holders of various traditional offices.

The Cabinet's functions are the final determination of policy, control of government and co-ordination of government departments. The exercise of its functions is dependent upon enjoying majority support in the House of Commons. Cabinet meetings are held in private, taking place once or twice a week during parliamentary sittings and less often during a recess. Proceedings are confidential, the members being bound by their oath as Privy Counsellors not to disclose information about the proceedings.

The convention of collective responsibility means that the Cabinet acts unanimously even when Cabinet Ministers do not all agree on a subject. The policies of departmental Ministers must be consistent with the policies of the Government as a whole, and once the Government's policy has been decided, each Minister is expected to support it or resign.

The convention of ministerial responsibility holds a Minister, as the political head of his or her department, accountable to Parliament for the department's work. Departmental Ministers usually decide all matters within their responsibility, although on matters of political importance they normally consult their colleagues collectively. A decision by a departmental Minister is binding on the Government as a whole.

POLITICAL PARTIES

Before the reign of William and Mary the principal officers of state were chosen by and were responsible to the Sovereign alone and not to Parliament or the nation at large. Such officers acted sometimes in concert with one another but more often independently, and the fall of one did not, of necessity, involve that of others, although all were liable to be dismissed at any moment.

In 1693 the Earl of Sunderland recommended to William III the advisability of selecting a ministry from the political party which enjoyed a majority in the House of Commons and the first united ministry was drawn in 1696 from the Whigs, to which party the King owed his throne. This group became known as the Junto and was regarded with suspicion as a novelty in the political life of the nation, being a small section meeting in secret apart from the main body of Ministers. It may be regarded as the forerunner of the Cabinet and in course of time it led to the establishment of the principle of joint responsibility of Ministers, so that internal disagreement caused a change of personnel or resignation of the whole body of Ministers.

The accession of George I, who was unfamiliar with the English language, led to a disinclination on the part of the Sovereign to preside at meetings of his Ministers and caused the appearance of a Prime Minister, a position first acquired by Robert Walpole in 1721 and retained without interruption for 20 years and 326 days.

DEVELOPMENT OF PARTIES

In 1828 the Whigs became known as Liberals, a name originally given to it by its opponents to imply laxity of principles, but gradually accepted by the party to indicate its claim to be pioneers and champions of political reform and progressive legislation. In 1861 a Liberal Registration Association was founded and Liberal Associations became widespread. In 1877 a National Liberal Federation was formed, with headquarters in London. The Liberal Party was in power for long periods during the second half of the 19th century and for several years during the first quarter of the 20th century, but after a split in the party the numbers elected were small from 1931. In 1988, a majority of the Liberals agreed on a merger with the Social Democratic Party under the title Social and Liberal Democrats; since 1989 they have been known as the Liberal Democrats. A minority continue separately as the Liberal Party.

Soon after the change from Whig to Liberal the Tory Party became known as Conservative, a name believed to have been invented by John Wilson Croker in 1830 and to have been generally adopted about the time of the passing of the Reform Act of 1832 to indicate that the preservation of national institutions was the leading principle of the party. After the Home Rule crisis of 1886 the dissentient Liberals entered into a compact with the Conservatives, under which the latter undertook not to contest their seats, but a separate Liberal Unionist organization was maintained until 1912, when it was united with the Conservatives.

Labour candidates for Parliament made their first appearance at the general election of 1892, when there were 27 standing as Labour or Liberal-Labour. In 1900 the Labour Representation Committee was set up in order to establish a distinct Labour group in Parliament, with its own whips, its own policy, and a readiness to co-operate with any party which might be engaged in promoting legislation in the direct interest of labour. In 1906 the LRC became known as the Labour Party.

The Council for Social Democracy was announced by four former Labour Cabinet Ministers in January 1981 and on 26 March 1981 the Social Democratic Party was launched. Later that year the SDP and the Liberal Party formed an electoral alliance. In 1988 a majority of the SDP agreed on a merger with the Liberal Party (*see* above) but a minority continued as a separate party under the SDP title. In 1990 it was decided to wind up the party organization and its three sitting MPs were known as independent social democrats. None were returned at the 1992 general election.

Plaid Cymru was founded in 1926 to provide an independent political voice for Wales and to campaign for self-government in Wales.

The Scottish National Party was founded in 1934 to campaign for independence for Scotland.

The Social Democratic and Labour Party was founded in 1970, emerging from the civil rights movement of the 1960s, with the aim of promoting reform, reconciliation and partnership across the sectarian divide in Northern Ireland and of opposing violence from any quarter.

The Ulster Democratic Unionist Party was founded in 1971 to resist moves by the Official Unionist Party which were considered a threat to the Union. Its aims are to maintain Northern Ireland as an integral part of the United Kingdom; and to express unionist opinion and defend the interests of Ulster unionism.

The Ulster Unionist Council first met formally in 1905. Its objectives are to maintain Northern Ireland as an integral part of the United Kingdom; to express unionist opinion and defend the interests of Ulster unionism; and to promote the aims of the Ulster Unionist Party.

GOVERNMENT AND OPPOSITION

The government of the day is formed by the party which wins the largest number of seats in the House of Commons at a general election, or which has the support of a majority of members in the House of Commons. By tradition, the leader of the majority party is asked by the Sovereign to form a government, while the largest minority party becomes the official Opposition with its own leader and 'Shadow' Cabinet. Leaders of the Government and Opposition sit on the front benches of the Commons with their supporters (the back-benchers) sitting behind them.

FINANCIAL SUPPORT

Financial support to Opposition parties was introduced in 1975 and is commonly known as Short Money, after Edward Short, the Leader of the House at that time, who introduced the scheme. For 1996–7 financial assistance is:

Labour	£1,530,190.51
Liberal Democrats	316,480.54
Plaid Cymru	22,040.36
SNP	36,782.68
SDLP	23,134.12
Democratic Unionists	15,954.37
Ulster Unionists	46,357.18

PARTIES

The parties included here are those with MPs sitting in the House of Commons in the present Parliament. Addresses of other political parties may be found in the Societies and Institutions section.

CONSERVATIVE AND UNIONIST PARTY
Central Office, 32 Smith Square, London SW1P 3HH
Tel 0171-222 9000
Chairman, The Rt. Hon. Brian Mawhinney, MP
Deputy Chairman, Hon. Michael Trend, MP
Senior Treasurer, The Lord Hambro

SCOTTISH CONSERVATIVE AND UNIONIST CENTRAL OFFICE
Suite 1/1, 14 Links Place, Leith, Edinburgh EH6 7EZ
Tel 0131-555 2900
Chairman, Sir Michael Hirst
Deputy Chairman, Miss A. Goldie
Hon. Treasurer, W. Y. Hughes, CBE
Director of the Party in Scotland, R. Pratt, CBE

LABOUR PARTY
John Smith House, 150 Walworth Road, London SE17 1JT
Tel 0171-701 1234
Parliamentary Party Leader, The Rt. Hon. Tony Blair, MP
Deputy Party Leader, The Rt. Hon. John Prescott, MP
Leader in the Lords, The Lord Richard, PC, QC
Chair, Ms D. Jeuda
Vice-Chair, Ms C. Short, MP
Treasurer, T. Burlison
General Secretary, T. Sawyer

Shadow Cabinet as at end July 1996
Leader of the Opposition, The Rt. Hon. Tony Blair, MP
Deputy Leader, The Rt. Hon. John Prescott, MP
Defence, David Clark, MP
Disabled People's Rights, Tom Clarke, MP
Education and Employment, David Blunkett, MP
Environment and London, Frank Dobson, MP
Environment Protection, Michael Meacher, MP
Food, Agriculture and Rural Affairs, Gavin Strang, MP
Foreign and Commonwealth Affairs, The Rt. Hon. Robin Cook, MP
Health, Chris Smith, MP
Home Affairs, Jack Straw, MP
Leader of the House, Ann Taylor, MP
Northern Ireland, Marjorie Mowlam, MP
Overseas Development, Claire Short, MP
Scotland, George Robertson, MP
Social Security, Harriet Harman, MP
Trade and Industry, The Rt. Hon. Margaret Beckett, MP
Transport, Andrew Smith, MP
Treasury and Economic Affairs, The Rt. Hon. Gordon Brown, MP
Wales, Ron Davies, MP

National Heritage, The Rt. Hon. Jack Cunningham, MP
Chancellor of the Duchy of Lancaster, The Rt. Hon. Derek Foster, MP
Chief Secretary to the Treasury, Alistair Darling, MP

LABOUR CHIEF WHIPS
House of Lords, The Lord Graham of Edmonton
House of Commons, The Rt. Hon. Donald Dewar, MP

LIBERAL DEMOCRATS
4 Cowley Street, London SW1P 3NB
Tel 0171-222 7999
President, Robert Maclennan, MP
Hon. Treasurer, T. Razzall, CBE
General Secretary, G. Elson
Parliamentary Party Leader, The Rt. Hon. Paddy Ashdown, MP
Leader in the Lords, The Rt. Hon. the Lord Jenkins of Hillhead

LIBERAL DEMOCRAT SPOKESMEN *as at end May 1996*
Deputy Leader and Home Affairs, Alan Beith, MP
Agriculture and Rural Affairs, Paul Tyler, MP
Central/East Europe, Sir Russell Johnston, MP
Community Care, Archy Kirkwood, MP
Education, Employment and Training, Don Foster, MP
Energy, Fisheries, Jim Wallace, MP
Environment, Matthew Taylor, MP
EU Affairs, Charles Kennedy, MP
Foreign Affairs, Defence and Sport, Menzies Campbell, MP
Health and Welfare, Urban Policy, Simon Hughes, MP
Home Affairs, and Justice, Alex Carlile, QC, MP
Housing, Family and Women's Issues, Diana Maddock, MP
Local Government, David Rendel, MP
National Heritage, Constitution, Arts, Robert Maclennan, MP
Northern Ireland, The Lord Holme of Cheltenham
Overseas Development, Emma Nicholson, MP
Science and Technology, Nigel Jones, MP
Scottish Affairs, Ray Michie, MP
Social Security and Disability, Liz Lynne, MP
Trade and Industry, Nick Harvey, MP
Transport, David Chidgey, MP
Treasury, Malcolm Bruce, MP

LIBERAL DEMOCRAT WHIPS
House of Lords, The Lord Harris of Greenwich
House of Commons, Archy Kirkwood, MP (*Chief Whip*); Simon Hughes, MP (*Deputy Whip*)

WELSH LIBERAL DEMOCRATS
57 St Mary Street, Cardiff CF1 1FE
Tel 01222-382210
Party President, M. Thomas, OBE, QC
Party Leader, Alex Carlile, QC, MP
Chairman, P. Black
Treasurer, N. Howells
Secretary, J. Burree
Party Manager, Ms J. Lewis, MBE

SCOTTISH LIBERAL DEMOCRATS
4 Clifton Terrace, Edinburgh EH12 5DR
Tel 0131-337 2314
Party President, R. Thomson
Party Leader, Jim Wallace, MP
Convenor, Ms M. MacLaren
Hon. Treasurer, D. R. Sullivan
Chief Executive, A. Myles

PLAID CYMRU
51 Cathedral Road, Cardiff CF1 9HD
Tel 01222-231944
Party President, Dafydd Wigley, MP
Chairman, J. Evans
Treasurer, S. Morgan
Chief Executive/General Secretary, K. Davies

SCOTTISH NATIONAL PARTY
6 North Charlotte Street, Edinburgh EH2 4JH
Tel 0131-226 3661
Parliamentary Party Leader, Margaret Ewing, MP
Chief Whip, Andrew Welsh, MP
National Convener, Alex Salmond, MP
Senior Vice-Convener, Dr A. Macartney, MEP
National Treasurer, K. MacAskill
National Secretary, A. Morgan

NORTHERN IRELAND

SOCIAL DEMOCRATIC AND LABOUR PARTY
Cranmore House, 611 Lisburn Road, Belfast BT9 7GT
Tel 01232-668100
Parliamentary Party Leader, John Hume, MP, MEP
Deputy Leader, Seamus Mallon, MP
Chief Whip, Eddie McGrady, MP
Chairman, I. Stephenson
Hon. Treasurer, P. O'Hagan
Party Administrator, Mrs G. Cosgrove

ULSTER DEMOCRATIC UNIONIST PARTY
91 Dundela Avenue, Belfast BT4 3BU
Tel 01232-471155
Parliamentary Party Leader, Ian Paisley, MP, MEP
Deputy Leader, Peter Robinson, MP
Chairman, W. J. McClure
Hon. Treasurer, G. Campbell
General Secretary, N. Dodds

ULSTER UNIONIST PARTY
3 Glengall Street, Belfast BT12 5AE
Tel 01232-324601
Party Leader, David Trimble, MP
Chief Whip, Revd Martin Smyth, MP
Ulster Unionist Council
President, J. Cunningham
Chairman, D. Rogan
Hon. Treasurer, J. Allen, OBE
Party Secretary, J. Wilson

MEMBERS OF PARLIAMENT AS AT 31 JULY 1996

For abbreviations, *see* page 237
* Denotes membership of the last Parliament
†Elected at a by-election since the 1992 general election

*Abbott, Ms Diane J. (*b.* 1953) *Lab., Hackney North and Stoke Newington*, maj. 10,727
*Adams, Mrs Irene (*b.* 1948) *Lab., Paisley North*, maj. 9,329
Ainger, Nicholas R. (*b.* 1949) *Lab., Pembroke*, maj. 755
Ainsworth, Peter M. (*b.* 1956) *C., Surrey East*, maj. 17,656
Ainsworth, Robert W. (*b.* 1952) *Lab., Coventry North East*, maj. 11,676
*Aitken, Jonathan W. P. (*b.* 1942) *C., Thanet South*, maj. 11,513
*Alexander, Richard T. (*b.* 1934) *C., Newark*, maj. 8,229
*Alison, Rt. Hon. Michael J. H. (*b.* 1926) *C., Selby*, maj. 9,508
*Allason, Rupert W. S. (*b.* 1951) *C., Torbay*, maj. 5,787
*Allen, Graham W. (*b.* 1953) *Lab., Nottingham North*, maj. 10,743
*Alton, David P. (*b.* 1951) *LD, Liverpool, Mossley Hill*, maj. 2,606
*Amess, David A. A. (*b.* 1952) *C., Basildon*, maj. 1,480
Ancram, Rt. Hon. Michael A. F. J. K. (Earl of Ancram) (*b.* 1945) *C., Devizes*, maj. 19,712
*Anderson, Donald (*b.* 1939) *Lab., Swansea East*, maj. 23,482
Anderson, Mrs Janet (*b.* 1949) *Lab., Rossendale and Darwen*, maj. 120
*Arbuthnot, James N. (*b.* 1952) *C., Wanstead and Woodford*, maj. 16,885
*Armstrong, Miss Hilary J. (*b.* 1945) *Lab., Durham North West*, maj. 13,987
*Arnold, Jacques A. (*b.* 1947) *C., Gravesham*, maj. 5,493
*Arnold, Sir Thomas (*b.* 1947) *C., Hazel Grove*, maj. 929
*Ashby, David G. (*b.* 1940) *C., Leicestershire North West*, maj. 979
*Ashdown, Rt. Hon. J. J. D. (Paddy) (*b.* 1941) *LD, Yeovil*, maj. 8,833
*Ashton, Joseph W. (*b.* 1933) *Lab., Bassetlaw*, maj. 9,997
*Aspinwall, Jack H. (*b.* 1933) *C., Wansdyke*, maj. 13,341
*Atkins, Rt. Hon. Robert J. (*b.* 1946) *C., South Ribble*, maj. 5,973
*Atkinson, David A. (*b.* 1940) *C., Bournemouth East*, maj. 14,823
Atkinson, Peter (*b.* 1943) *C., Hexham*, maj. 13,438
Austin-Walker, John E. (*b.* 1944) *Lab., Woolwich*, maj. 2,225
*Baker, Rt. Hon. Kenneth W., CH (*b.* 1934) *C., Mole Valley*, maj. 15,950
*Baker, Nicholas B. (*b.* 1938) *C., Dorset North*, maj. 10,080
*Baldry, Antony B. (*b.* 1950) *C., Banbury*, maj. 16,720
Banks, Matthew (*b.* 1961) *C., Southport*, maj. 3,063
*Banks, Robert G., MBE (*b.* 1937) *C., Harrogate*, maj. 12,589
*Banks, Tony L. (*b.* 1943) *Lab., Newham North West*, maj. 9,171
*Barnes, Harold (*b.* 1936) *Lab., Derbyshire North East*, maj. 6,270
*Barron, Kevin J. (*b.* 1946) *Lab., Rother Valley*, maj. 17,222
Bates, Michael W. (*b.* 1961) *C., Langbaurgh*, maj. 1,564
†Batiste, Spencer L. (*b.* 1945) *C., Elmet*, maj. 3,261
*Battle, John D. (*b.* 1951) *Lab., Leeds West*, maj. 13,828
Bayley, Hugh (*b.* 1952) *Lab., York*, maj. 6,342
*Beckett, Rt. Hon. Margaret M. (*b.* 1953) *Lab., Derby South*, maj. 6,936
*Beggs, Roy (*b.* 1936) *UUP, Antrim East*, maj. 7,422
*Beith, Rt. Hon. Alan J. (*b.* 1943) *LD, Berwick-upon-Tweed*, maj. 5,043
*Bell, Stuart (*b.* 1938) *Lab., Middlesbrough*, maj. 15,784
*Bellingham, Henry C. (*b.* 1955) *C., Norfolk North West*, maj. 11,564

*Bendall, Vivian W. H. (*b.* 1938) *C., Ilford North*, maj. 9,071
*Benn, Rt. Hon. Anthony N. W. (*b.* 1925) *Lab., Chesterfield*, maj. 6,414
*Bennett, Andrew F. (*b.* 1939) *Lab., Denton and Reddish*, maj. 12,084
*Benton, Joseph E. (*b.* 1933) *Lab., Bootle*, maj. 29,442
Beresford, Sir Paul (*b.* 1946) *C., Croydon Central*, maj. 9,650
*Bermingham, Gerald E. (*b.* 1940) *Lab., St Helens South*, maj. 18,209
Berry, Roger L., D.Phil (*b.* 1948) *Lab., Kingswood*, maj. 2,370
Betts, Clive J. C. (*b.* 1950) *Lab., Sheffield, Attercliffe*, maj. 15,480
*Biffen, Rt. Hon. John W. (*b.* 1930) *C., Shropshire North*, maj. 16,211
*Blair, Rt. Hon. Anthony C. L. (*b.* 1953) *Lab., Sedgefield*, maj. 14,859
*Blunkett, David (*b.* 1947) *Lab., Sheffield, Brightside*, maj. 22,681
*Boateng, Paul Y. (*b.* 1951) *Lab., Brent South*, maj. 9,705
*Body, Sir Richard (*b.* 1927) *C., Holland with Boston*, maj. 13,831
*Bonsor, Sir Nicholas, Bt. (*b.* 1942) *C., Upminster*, maj. 13,821
Booth, Hartley, Ph.D. (*b.* 1946) *C., Finchley*, maj. 6,388
*Boothroyd, Rt. Hon. Betty (*b.* 1929) *The Speaker, West Bromwich West*, maj. 7,830
*Boswell, Timothy E. (*b.* 1942) *C., Daventry*, maj. 20,274
*Bottomley, Peter J. (*b.* 1944) *C., Eltham*, maj. 1,666
*Bottomley, Rt. Hon. Virginia H. B. M. (*b.* 1948) *C., Surrey South West*, maj. 14,975
*Bowden, Sir Andrew, MBE (*b.* 1930) *C., Brighton, Kemptown*, maj. 3,056
*Bowis, John C., OBE (*b.* 1945) *C., Battersea*, maj. 4,840
*Boyes, Roland (*b.* 1937) *Lab., Houghton and Washington*, maj. 20,808
*Boyson, Rt. Hon. Sir Rhodes (*b.* 1925) *C., Brent North*, maj. 10,131
*Bradley, Keith J. C. (*b.* 1950) *Lab., Manchester, Withington*, maj. 9,735
Brandreth, Gyles D. (*b.* 1948) *C., City of Chester*, maj. 1,101
*Bray, Jeremy W., Ph.D. (*b.* 1930) *Lab., Motherwell South*, maj. 14,013
*Brazier, Julian W. H. (*b.* 1953) *C., Canterbury*, maj. 10,805
*Bright, Sir Graham (*b.* 1942) *C., Luton South*, maj. 799
*Brooke, Rt. Hon. Peter L., CH (*b.* 1934) *C., City of London and Westminster South*, maj. 13,369
*Brown, Rt. Hon. J. Gordon, Ph.D. (*b.* 1951) *Lab., Dunfermline East*, maj. 17,444
*Brown, Michael R. (*b.* 1951) *C., Brigg and Cleethorpes*, maj. 9,269
*Brown, Nicholas H. (*b.* 1950) *Lab., Newcastle upon Tyne East*, maj. 13,877
Browning, Mrs Angela F. (*b.* 1946) *C., Tiverton*, maj. 11,089
*Bruce, Ian C. (*b.* 1947) *C., Dorset South*, maj. 13,508
*Bruce, Malcolm G. (*b.* 1944) *LD, Gordon*, maj. 274
*Budgen, Nicholas W. (*b.* 1937) *C., Wolverhampton South West*, maj. 4,966
Burden, Richard (*b.* 1954) *Lab., Birmingham, Northfield*, maj. 630
*Burns, Simon H. M. (*b.* 1952) *C., Chelmsford*, maj. 18,260
*Burt, Alistair J. H. (*b.* 1955) *C., Bury North*, maj. 4,764
*Butcher, John P. (*b.* 1946) *C., Coventry South West*, maj. 1,436
Butler, Peter (*b.* 1951) *C., Milton Keynes North East*, maj. 14,176
*Butterfill, John V. (*b.* 1941) *C., Bournemouth West*, maj. 12,703
Byers, Stephen J. (*b.* 1953) *Lab., Wallsend*, maj. 19,470

*Caborn, Richard G. (*b.* 1943) *Lab., Sheffield Central,* maj. 17,294

*Callaghan, James (*b.* 1927) *Lab., Heywood and Middleton,* maj. 8,074

Campbell, Mrs Anne (*b.* 1940) *Lab., Cambridge,* maj. 580

*Campbell, Ronald (*b.* 1943) *Lab., Blyth Valley,* maj. 8,044

*Campbell, W. Menzies, CBE, QC (*b.* 1941) *LD, Fife North East,* maj. 3,308

*Campbell-Savours, Dale N. (*b.* 1943) *Lab., Workington,* maj. 10,449

*Canavan, Dennis A. (*b.* 1942) *Lab., Falkirk West,* maj. 9,812

Cann, James (*b.* 1946) *Lab., Ipswich,* maj. 265

*Carlile, Alexander C., QC (*b.* 1948) *LD, Montgomery,* maj. 5,209

*Carlisle, John R. (*b.* 1942) *C., Luton North,* maj. 13,094

*Carlisle, Sir Kenneth (*b.* 1941) *C., Lincoln,* maj. 2,049

*Carrington, Matthew H. M. (*b.* 1947) *C., Fulham,* maj. 6,579

*Carttiss, Michael R. H. (*b.* 1938) *C., Great Yarmouth,* maj. 5,309

*Cash, William N. P. (*b.* 1940) *C., Stafford,* maj. 10,900

*Channon, Rt. Hon. H. Paul G. (*b.* 1935) *C., Southend West,* maj. 11,902

*Chapman, Sir Sydney (*b.* 1935) *C., Chipping Barnet,* maj. 13,951

†Chidgey, David W. G. (*b.* 1942) *LD, Eastleigh,* maj. 9,239

Chisholm, Malcolm (*b.* 1949) *Lab., Edinburgh, Leith,* maj. 4,985

†Church, Ms Judith A. (*b.* 1953), *Lab., Dagenham,* maj. 13,344

*Churchill, Winston S. (*b.* 1940) *C., Davyhulme,* maj. 4,426

Clapham, Michael (*b.* 1943) *Lab., Barnsley West and Penistone,* maj. 14,504

Clappison, W. James (*b.* 1956) *C., Hertsmere,* maj. 18,735

*Clark, David G., PH.D. (*b.* 1939) *Lab., South Shields,* maj. 13,477

Clarke, Eric L. (*b.* 1933) *Lab., Midlothian,* maj. 10,334

*Clarke, Rt. Hon. Kenneth H., QC (*b.* 1940) *C., Rushcliffe,* maj. 19,766

*Clarke, Thomas, CBE (*b.* 1941) *Lab., Monklands West,* maj. 17,065

*Clelland, David G. (*b.* 1943) *Lab., Tyne Bridge,* maj. 15,210

Clifton-Brown, Geoffrey R. (*b.* 1953) *C., Cirencester and Tewkesbury,* maj. 16,058

*Clwyd, Ms Ann (*b.* 1937) *Lab., Cynon Valley,* maj. 21,364

Coe, Sebastian N., OBE (*b.* 1956) *C., Falmouth and Camborne,* maj. 3,267

Coffey, Ms M. Ann (*b.* 1946) *Lab., Stockport,* maj. 1,422

*Cohen, Harry (*b.* 1949) *Lab., Leyton,* maj. 11,484

*Colvin, Michael K. B. (*b.* 1932) *C., Romsey and Waterside,* maj. 15,304

Congdon, David L. (*b.* 1949) *C., Croydon North East,* maj. 7,473

Connarty, Michael (*b.* 1949) *Lab., Falkirk East,* maj. 7,969

*Conway, Derek L. (*b.* 1953) *C., Shrewsbury and Atcham,* maj. 10,965

*Cook, Francis (*b.* 1935) *Lab., Stockton North,* maj. 10,474

*Cook, Rt. Hon. R. F. (Robin) (*b.* 1946) *Lab., Livingston,* maj. 8,105

*Coombs, Anthony M. V. (*b.* 1952) *C., Wyre Forest,* maj. 10,341

*Coombs, Simon C. (*b.* 1947) *C., Swindon,* maj. 2,826

*Cope, Rt. Hon. Sir John (*b.* 1937) *C., Northavon,* maj. 11,861

*Corbett, Robin (*b.* 1933) *Lab., Birmingham, Erdington,* maj. 4,735

*Corbyn, Jeremy B. (*b.* 1949) *Lab., Islington North,* maj. 12,784

*Cormack, Sir Patrick (*b.* 1939) *C., Staffordshire South,* maj. 22,633

Corston, Ms Jean (*b.* 1942) *Lab., Bristol East,* maj. 2,692

*Couchman, James R. (*b.* 1942) *C., Gillingham,* maj. 16,638

*Cousins, James M. (*b.* 1944) *Lab., Newcastle upon Tyne Central,* maj. 5,288

*Cox, Thomas M. (*b.* 1930) *Lab., Tooting,* maj. 4,107

*Cran, James D. (*b.* 1944) *C., Beverley,* maj. 16,517

*Critchley, Sir Julian (*b.* 1930) *C., Aldershot,* maj. 19,188

*Cummings, John S. (*b.* 1943) *Lab., Easington,* maj. 26,390

*Cunliffe, Lawrence F. (*b.* 1929) *Lab., Leigh,* maj. 18,827

Cunningham, James (*b.* 1941) *Lab., Coventry South East,* maj. 1,311

*Cunningham, Rt. Hon. Dr John A. (Jack) (*b.* 1939) *Lab., Copeland,* maj. 2,439

†Cunningham, Ms Roseanna (*b.* 1951), *SNP, Perth and Kinross,* maj. 7,311

*Currie, Mrs Edwina (*b.* 1946) *C., Derbyshire South,* maj. 4,658

*Curry, Rt. Hon. David M. (*b.* 1944) *C., Skipton and Ripon,* maj. 19,330

Dafis, Cynog G. (*b.* 1938) *PC, Ceredigion and Pembroke North,* maj. 3,193

*Dalyell, Tam (Sir Thomas Dalyell of the Binns, Bt.) (*b.* 1932) *Lab., Linlithgow,* maj. 7,026

*Darling, Alistair M. (*b.* 1953) *Lab., Edinburgh Central,* maj. 2,126

Davidson, Ian (*b.* 1950) *Lab., Glasgow, Govan,* maj. 4,125

Davies, Bryan (*b.* 1939) *Lab., Oldham Central and Royton,* maj. 8,606

†Davies, Christopher (Chris) (*b.* 1954), *LD, Littleborough and Saddleworth,* maj. 1,993

*Davies, Rt. Hon. D. J. Denzil (*b.* 1938) *Lab., Llanelli,* maj. 19,270

*Davies, J. Quentin (*b.* 1944) *C., Stamford and Spalding,* maj. 22,869

*Davies, Ronald (*b.* 1946) *Lab., Caerphilly,* maj. 22,672

*Davis, David M. (*b.* 1948) *C., Boothferry,* maj. 17,535

*Davis, Terence A. G. (*b.* 1938) *Lab., Birmingham, Hodge Hill,* maj. 7,068

*Day, Stephen R. (*b.* 1948) *C., Cheadle,* maj. 15,778

Denham, John V. (*b.* 1953) *Lab., Southampton, Itchen,* maj. 551

Deva, Niranjan J. A. (*b.* 1948) *C., Brentford and Isleworth,* maj. 2,086

*Devlin, Timothy R. (*b.* 1959) *C., Stockton South,* maj. 3,369

*Dewar, Rt. Hon. Donald C. (*b.* 1937) *Lab., Glasgow, Garscadden,* maj. 13,340

*Dicks, Terence P. (*b.* 1937) *C., Hayes and Harlington,* maj. 53

*Dixon, Rt. Hon. Donald (*b.* 1929) *Lab., Jarrow,* maj. 17,907

*Dobson, Frank G. (*b.* 1940) *Lab., Holborn and St Pancras,* maj. 10,824

Donohoe, Brian H. (*b.* 1948) *Lab., Cunninghame South,* maj. 10,680

*Dorrell, Rt. Hon. Stephen J. (*b.* 1952) *C., Loughborough,* maj. 10,883

*Douglas-Hamilton, Rt. Hon. Lord James (*b.* 1942) *C., Edinburgh West,* maj. 879

*Dover, Densmore (*b.* 1938) *C., Chorley,* maj. 4,246

*Dowd, James P. (*b.* 1951) *Lab., Lewisham West,* maj. 1,809

Duncan, Alan J. C. (*b.* 1957) *C., Rutland and Melton,* maj. 25,535

Duncan-Smith, G. Iain (*b.* 1954) *C., Chingford,* maj. 14,938

*Dunn, Robert J. (*b.* 1946) *C., Dartford,* maj. 10,314

*Dunnachie, James F. (*b.* 1930) *Lab., Glasgow, Pollok,* maj. 7,883

*Dunwoody, Hon. Mrs Gwyneth P. (*b.* 1930) *Lab., Crewe and Nantwich,* maj. 2,695

*Durant, Sir Anthony (*b.* 1928) *C., Reading West,* maj. 13,298

*Dykes, Hugh J. (*b.* 1939) *C., Harrow East,* maj. 11,098

Eagle, Ms Angela (*b.* 1961) *Lab., Wallasey,* maj. 3,809

Eastham, Kenneth (*b.* 1927) *Lab., Manchester, Blackley,* maj. 12,389

*Eggar, Rt. Hon. Timothy J. C. (*b.* 1951) *C., Enfield North,* maj. 9,430

Elletson, Harold D. H. (*b.* 1960) *C., Blackpool North,* maj. 3,040

*Higgins, Rt. Hon. Sir Terence, KBE (*b.* 1928) *C., Worthing,* maj. 16,533

*Hill, Sir James (*b.* 1926) *C., Southampton, Test,* maj. 585

Hill, T. Keith (*b.* 1943) *Lab., Streatham,* maj. 2,317

*Hinchliffe, David M. (*b.* 1948) *Lab., Wakefield,* maj. 6,590

†Hodge, Ms Margaret E. (*b.* 1944) *Lab., Barking,* maj. 11,414

*Hoey, Ms Catharine (Kate) L. (*b.* 1946) *Lab., Vauxhall,* maj. 10,488

*Hogg, Rt. Hon. Douglas M., QC (*b.* 1945) *C., Grantham,* maj. 19,588

*Hogg, Norman (*b.* 1938) *Lab., Cumbernauld and Kilsyth,* maj. 9,215

*Home Robertson, John D. (*b.* 1948) *Lab., East Lothian,* maj. 10,036

*Hood, James (*b.* 1948) *Lab., Clydesdale,* maj. 10,187

Hoon, Geoffrey W. (*b.* 1953) *Lab., Ashfield,* maj. 12,987

Horam, John R. (*b.* 1939) *C., Orpington,* maj. 12,935

*Hordern, Rt. Hon. Sir Peter (*b.* 1929) *C., Horsham,* maj. 25,072

*Howard, Rt. Hon. Michael, QC (*b.* 1941) *C., Folkestone and Hythe,* maj. 8,910

*Howarth, Alan T., CBE (*b.* 1944) *Lab., Stratford-upon-Avon,* maj. 22,892

*Howarth, George E. (*b.* 1949) *Lab., Knowsley North,* maj. 22,403

*Howell, Rt. Hon. David A. R. (*b.* 1936) *C., Guildford,* maj. 13,404

*Howell, Sir Ralph (*b.* 1923) *C., Norfolk North,* maj. 12,545

*Howells, Kim S., PH.D. (*b.* 1946) *Lab., Pontypridd,* maj. 19,797

*Hoyle, E. Douglas H. (*b.* 1930) *Lab., Warrington North,* maj. 12,622

Hughes, Kevin M. (*b.* 1952) *Lab., Doncaster North,* maj. 19,813

*Hughes, Robert (*b.* 1932) *Lab., Aberdeen North,* maj. 9,237

*Hughes, Robert G. (*b.* 1951) *C., Harrow West,* maj. 17,897

*Hughes, Royston J. (*b.* 1925) *Lab., Newport East,* maj. 9,899

*Hughes, Simon H. W. (*b.* 1951) *LD, Southwark and Bermondsey,* maj. 9,845

*Hume, John, MEP (*b.* 1937) *SDLP, Foyle,* maj. 13,005

*Hunt, Rt. Hon. David J. F., MBE (*b.* 1942) *C., Wirral West,* maj. 11,064

*Hunt, Sir John (*b.* 1929) *C., Ravensbourne,* maj. 19,714

*Hunter, Andrew R. F. (*b.* 1943) *C., Basingstoke,* maj. 21,198

*Hurd, Rt. Hon. Douglas R., CH, CBE (*b.* 1930) *C., Witney,* maj. 22,568

Hutton, John M. P. (*b.* 1955) *Lab., Barrow and Furness,* maj. 3,578

*Illsley, Eric E. (*b.* 1955) *Lab., Barnsley Central,* maj. 19,361

*Ingram, Adam P. (*b.* 1947) *Lab., East Kilbride,* maj. 11,992

*Jack, J. Michael (*b.* 1946) *C., Fylde,* maj. 20,991

Jackson, Ms Glenda, CBE (*b.* 1936) *Lab., Hampstead and Highgate,* maj. 1,440

Jackson, Mrs Helen (*b.* 1939) *Lab., Sheffield, Hillsborough,* maj. 7,068

*Jackson, Robert V. (*b.* 1946) *C., Wantage,* maj. 16,473

Jamieson, David C. (*b.* 1947) *Lab., Plymouth, Devonport,* maj. 7,412

*Janner, Hon. Greville E., QC (*b.* 1928) *Lab., Leicester West,* maj. 3,978

Jenkin, Hon. Bernard (*b.* 1959) *C., Colchester North,* maj. 16,492

†Jenkins, Brian D. (*b.* 1942) *Lab., Staffordshire South East,* maj. 13,762

*Jessel, Toby F. H. (*b.* 1934) *C., Twickenham,* maj. 5,711

*Johnson Smith, Rt. Hon. Sir Geoffrey (*b.* 1924) *C., Wealden,* maj. 20,931

*Johnston, Sir Russell (*b.* 1932) *LD, Inverness, Nairn and Lochaber,* maj. 458

*Jones, Gwilym H. (*b.* 1947) *C., Cardiff North,* maj. 2,969

*Jones, Ieuan W. (*b.* 1949) *PC, Ynys Môn,* maj. 1,106

Jones, Jon O. (*b.* 1954) *Lab., Cardiff Central,* maj. 3,465

Jones, Ms Lynne M., PH.D. (*b.* 1951) *Lab., Birmingham, Selly Oak,* maj. 2,060

*Jones, Martyn D. (*b.* 1947) *Lab., Clwyd South West,* maj. 4,941

Jones, Nigel D. (*b.* 1948) *LD, Cheltenham,* maj. 1,668

*Jones, Robert B. (*b.* 1950) *C., Hertfordshire West,* maj. 13,940

*Jones, S. Barry (*b.* 1938) *Lab., Alyn and Deeside,* maj. 7,851

*Jopling, Rt. Hon. T. Michael (*b.* 1930) *C., Westmorland and Lonsdale,* maj. 16,436

Jowell, Ms Tessa (*b.* 1947) *Lab., Dulwich,* maj. 2,056

*Kaufman, Rt. Hon. Gerald B. (*b.* 1930) *Lab., Manchester, Gorton,* maj. 16,279

Keen, Alan (*b.* 1937) *Lab., Feltham and Heston,* maj. 1,995

*Kellett-Bowman, Dame Elaine, DBE (*b.* 1924) *C., Lancaster,* maj. 2,953

*Kennedy, Charles P. (*b.* 1959) *LD, Ross, Cromarty and Skye,* maj. 7,630

Kennedy, Mrs Jane (*b.* 1958) *Lab., Liverpool, Broadgreen,* maj. 7,027

*Key, S. Robert (*b.* 1945) *C., Salisbury,* maj. 8,973

Khabra, Piara C. (*b.* 1924) *Lab., Ealing, Southall,* maj. 6,866

*Kilfoyle, Peter (*b.* 1946) *Lab., Liverpool, Walton,* maj. 28,299

*King, Rt. Hon. Thomas J., CH (*b.* 1933) *C., Bridgwater,* maj. 9,716

*Kirkhope, Timothy J. R. (*b.* 1945) *C., Leeds North East,* maj. 4,244

*Kirkwood, Archibald J. (*b.* 1946) *LD, Roxburgh and Berwickshire,* maj. 4,257

*Knapman, Roger M. (*b.* 1944) *C., Stroud,* maj. 13,405

*Knight, Mrs Angela A. (*b.* 1950) *C., Erewash,* maj. 5,703

*Knight, Rt. Hon. Gregory (*b.* 1949) *C., Derby North,* maj. 4,453

*Knight, Dame Jill, DBE (*b.* 1923) *C., Birmingham, Edgbaston,* maj. 4,307

*Knox, Sir David (*b.* 1933) *C., Staffordshire Moorlands,* maj. 7,410

Kynoch, George A. B. (*b.* 1946) *C., Kincardine and Deeside,* maj. 4,495

Lait, Ms Jacqui (*b.* 1947) *C., Hastings and Rye,* maj. 6,634

*Lamont, Rt. Hon. Norman S. H. (*b.* 1942) *C., Kingston upon Thames,* maj. 10,153

*Lang, Rt. Hon. Ian B. (*b.* 1940) *C., Galloway and Upper Nithsdale,* maj. 2,468

*Lawrence, Sir Ivan, QC (*b.* 1936) *C., Burton,* maj. 5,996

Legg, Barry (*b.* 1949) *C., Milton Keynes South West,* maj. 4,687

*Leigh, Edward J. E. (*b.* 1950) *C., Gainsborough and Horncastle,* maj. 16,245

*Lennox-Boyd, Hon. Sir Mark (*b.* 1943) *C., Morecambe and Lunesdale,* maj. 11,509

*Lester, Sir James (*b.* 1932) *C., Broxtowe,* maj. 9,891

*Lestor, Miss Joan (*b.* 1931) *Lab., Eccles,* maj. 13,226

*Lewis, Terence (*b.* 1935) *Lab., Worsley,* maj. 10,012

†Liddell, Mrs Helen (*b.* 1950) *Lab., Monklands East,* maj. 1,640

Lidington, David R., PH.D. (*b.* 1956) *C., Aylesbury,* maj. 18,860

*Lilley, Rt. Hon. Peter B. (*b.* 1943) *C., St Albans,* maj. 16,404

*Litherland, Robert K. (*b.* 1930) *Lab., Manchester Central,* maj. 18,037

*Livingstone, Ken (*b.* 1945) *Lab., Brent East,* maj. 5,971

*Lloyd, Anthony J. (*b.* 1950) *Lab., Stretford,* maj. 11,137

*Lloyd, Rt. Hon. Sir Peter (*b.* 1937) *C., Fareham,* maj. 24,141

Llwyd, Elfyn (*b.* 1951) *PC, Meirionnydd Nant Conwy,* maj. 4,613

*Lofthouse, Sir Geoffrey (*b.* 1925) *Lab., Pontefract and Castleford,* maj. 23,495

*Lord, Michael N. (*b.* 1938) *C., Suffolk Central,* maj. 16,031

*Loyden, Edward (*b.* 1923) *Lab., Liverpool, Garston,* maj. 12,279

Luff, Peter J. (*b.* 1955) *C., Worcester,* maj. 6,152

*Lyell, Rt. Hon. Sir Nicholas, QC (*b.* 1938) *C., Bedfordshire Mid,* maj. 25,138

*Paice, James E. T. (*b.* 1949) *C., Cambridgeshire South East,* maj. 23,810

*Paisley, Revd Ian R. K., MEP (*b.* 1926) *DUP, Antrim North,* maj. 14,936

*Parry, Robert (*b.* 1933) *Lab., Liverpool, Riverside,* maj. 17,437

*Patchett, Terry (*b.* 1940) *Lab., Barnsley East,* maj. 24,777

*Patnick, Sir Irvine, OBE (*b.* 1929) *C., Sheffield, Hallam,* maj. 6,741

*Patten, Rt. Hon. John H. C. (*b.* 1945) *C., Oxford West and Abingdon,* maj. 3,539

*Pattie, Rt. Hon. Sir Geoffrey (*b.* 1936) *C., Chertsey and Walton,* maj. 22,819

*Pawsey, James F. (*b.* 1933) *C., Rugby and Kenilworth,* maj. 13,247

*Peacock, Mrs Elizabeth J. (*b.* 1937) *C., Batley and Spen,* maj. 1,408

†Pearson, Ian P. (*b.* 1949) *Lab., Dudley West,* maj. 20,694

*Pendry, Thomas (*b.* 1934) *Lab., Stalybridge and Hyde,* maj. 8,831

Pickles, Eric J. (*b.* 1952) *C., Brentwood and Ongar,* maj. 15,145

Pickthall, Colin (*b.* 1944) *Lab., Lancashire West,* maj. 2,077

*Pike, Peter L. (*b.* 1937) *Lab., Burnley,* maj. 11,491

Pope, Gregory J. (*b.* 1960) *Lab., Hyndburn,* maj. 1,960

*Porter, David J. (*b.* 1948) *C., Waveney,* maj. 6,702

*Porter, G. B. (Barry) (*b.* 1939) *C., Wirral South,* maj. 8,183

*Portillo, Rt. Hon. Michael D. X. (*b.* 1953) *C., Enfield, Southgate,* maj. 15,563

*Powell, Sir Raymond (*b.* 1928) *Lab., Ogmore,* maj. 23,827

*Powell, William R. (*b.* 1948) *C., Corby,* maj. 342

Prentice, Mrs Bridget (*b.* 1952) *Lab., Lewisham East,* maj. 1,095

Prentice, Gordon (*b.* 1951) *Lab., Pendle,* maj. 2,113

*Prescott, Rt. Hon. John L. (*b.* 1938) *Lab., Hull East,* maj. 18,719

*Primarolo, Ms Dawn (*b.* 1954) *Lab., Bristol South,* maj. 8,919

Purchase, Kenneth (*b.* 1939) *Lab., Wolverhampton North East,* maj. 3,939

*Quin, Miss Joyce G. (*b.* 1944) *Lab., Gateshead East,* maj. 18,530

*Radice, Giles H. (*b.* 1936) *Lab., Durham North,* maj. 19,637

*Randall, Stuart J. (*b.* 1938) *Lab., Hull West,* maj. 10,585

*Rathbone, J. R. (Tim) (*b.* 1933) *C., Lewes,* maj. 12,175

Raynsford, W. R. N. (Nick) (*b.* 1945) *Lab., Greenwich,* maj. 1,357

*Redmond, Martin (*b.* 1937) *Lab., Don Valley,* maj. 13,534

*Redwood, Rt. Hon. John A. (*b.* 1951) *C., Wokingham,* maj. 25,709

*Reid, Dr John (*b.* 1947) *Lab., Motherwell North,* maj. 18,910

†Rendel, David D. (*b.* 1949) *LD, Newbury,* maj. 22,055

*Renton, Rt. Hon. R. Timothy (*b.* 1932) *C., Sussex Mid,* maj. 20,528

Richards, Roderick (*b.* 1947) *C., Clwyd North West,* maj. 6,050

*Riddick, Graham E. G. (*b.* 1955) *C., Colne Valley,* maj. 7,225

*Rifkind, Rt. Hon. Malcolm L., QC (*b.* 1946) *C., Edinburgh, Pentlands,* maj. 4,290

Robathan, Andrew R. G. (*b.* 1951) *C., Blaby,* maj. 25,347

*Roberts, Rt. Hon. Sir Wyn (*b.* 1930) *C., Conwy,* maj. 995

*Robertson, George I. M. (*b.* 1946) *Lab., Hamilton,* maj. 16,603

Robertson, Raymond S. (*b.* 1959) *C., Aberdeen South,* maj. 1,517

*Robinson, Geoffrey (*b.* 1938) *Lab., Coventry North West,* maj. 6,432

Robinson, Mark N. F. (*b.* 1946) *C., Somerton and Frome,* maj. 4,341

*Robinson, Peter D. (*b.* 1948) *DUP, Belfast East,* maj. 7,787

Roche, Mrs Barbara M. R. (*b.* 1954) *Lab., Hornsey and Wood Green,* maj. 5,177

*Roe, Mrs Marion A. (*b.* 1936) *C., Broxbourne,* maj. 23,970

*Rogers, Allan R. (*b.* 1932) *Lab., Rhondda,* maj. 28,816

*Rooker, Jeffrey W. (*b.* 1941) *Lab., Birmingham, Perry Barr,* maj. 8,590

*Rooney, Terence H. (*b.* 1950) *Lab., Bradford North,* maj. 7,664

*Ross, Ernest (*b.* 1942) *Lab., Dundee West,* maj. 10,604

*Ross, William (*b.* 1936) *UUP, Londonderry East,* maj. 18,527

*Rowe, Andrew (*b.* 1935) *C., Kent Mid,* maj. 19,649

*Rowlands, Edward (*b.* 1940) *Lab., Merthyr Tydfil and Rhymney,* maj. 26,713

*Ruddock, Mrs Joan M. (*b.* 1943) *Lab., Lewisham, Deptford,* maj. 12,238

*Rumbold, Rt. Hon. Dame Angela, DBE (*b.* 1932) *C., Mitcham and Morden,* maj. 1,734

*Ryder, Rt. Hon. Richard A., OBE (*b.* 1949) *C., Norfolk Mid,* maj. 18,948

*Sackville, Hon. Thomas G. (*b.* 1950) *C., Bolton West,* maj. 1,079

*Sainsbury, Rt. Hon. Sir Timothy (*b.* 1932) *C., Hove,* maj. 12,268

*Salmond, Alexander E. A. (*b.* 1954) *SNP, Banff and Buchan,* maj. 4,108

*Scott, Rt. Hon. Sir Nicholas, KBE (*b.* 1933) *C., Chelsea,* maj. 12,789

*Sedgemore, Brian C. J. (*b.* 1937) *Lab., Hackney South and Shoreditch,* maj. 9,016

*Shaw, David L. (*b.* 1950) *C., Dover,* maj. 833

*Shaw, Sir Giles (*b.* 1931) *C., Pudsey,* maj. 8,972

*Sheerman, Barry J. (*b.* 1940) *Lab., Huddersfield,* maj. 7,258

*Sheldon, Rt. Hon. Robert E. (*b.* 1923) *Lab., Ashton-under-Lyne,* maj. 10,935

*Shephard, Rt. Hon. Gillian P. (*b.* 1940) *C., Norfolk South West,* maj. 16,931

*Shepherd, Sir Colin (*b.* 1938) *C., Hereford,* maj. 3,413

*Shepherd, Richard C. S. (*b.* 1942) *C., Aldridge-Brownhills,* maj. 11,024

*Shersby, Sir Michael (*b.* 1933) *C., Uxbridge,* maj. 13,179

*Shore, Rt. Hon. Peter D. (*b.* 1924) *Lab., Bethnal Green and Stepney,* maj. 12,230

*Short, Ms Clare (*b.* 1946) *Lab., Birmingham, Ladywood,* maj. 15,283

Simpson, Alan (*b.* 1948) *Lab., Nottingham South,* maj. 3,181

*Sims, Sir Roger (*b.* 1930) *C., Chislehurst,* maj. 15,276

*Skeet, Sir Trevor (*b.* 1918) *C., Bedfordshire North,* maj. 11,618

*Skinner, Dennis E. (*b.* 1932) *Lab., Bolsover,* maj. 20,660

*Smith, Andrew D. (*b.* 1951) *Lab., Oxford East,* maj. 7,538

*Smith, Christopher R., ph.D. (*b.* 1951) *Lab., Islington South and Finsbury,* maj. 10,652

*Smith, Sir Dudley (*b.* 1926) *C., Warwick and Leamington,* maj. 8,935

Smith, Llewellyn T. (*b.* 1944) *Lab., Blaenau Gwent,* maj. 30,067

*Smith, Timothy J. (*b.* 1947) *C., Beaconsfield,* maj. 23,597

*Smyth, Revd W. Martin (*b.* 1931) *UUP, Belfast South,* maj. 10,070

*Snape, Peter C. (*b.* 1942) *Lab., West Bromwich East,* maj. 2,813

*Soames, Hon. A. Nicholas W. (*b.* 1948) *C., Crawley,* maj. 7,765

*Soley, Clive S. (*b.* 1939) *Lab., Hammersmith,* maj. 4,754

*Spearing, Nigel J. (*b.* 1930) *Lab., Newham South,* maj. 2,502

*Speed, Sir Keith, RD (*b.* 1934) *C., Ashford,* maj. 17,359

*Spellar, John F. (*b.* 1947) *Lab., Warley West,* maj. 5,472

Spencer, Sir Derek, QC (*b.* 1936) *C., Brighton, Pavilion,* maj. 3,675

*Spicer, Sir James (*b.* 1925) *C., Dorset West,* maj. 8,010

*Spicer, Sir Michael (*b.* 1943) *C., Worcestershire South,* maj. 16,151

Spink, Dr Robert M. (*b.* 1948) *C., Castle Point,* maj. 16,830

Spring, Richard J. G. (*b.* 1946) *C., Bury St Edmunds,* maj. 18,787

Sproat, Iain M. (*b.* 1938) *C., Harwich,* maj. 17,159
Squire, Ms Rachel (*b.* 1954) *Lab., Dunfermline West,* maj. 7,484
*Squire, Robin C. (*b.* 1944) *C., Hornchurch,* maj. 9,165
*Stanley, Rt. Hon. Sir John (*b.* 1942) *C., Tonbridge and Malling,* maj. 21,558
*Steel, Rt. Hon. Sir David, KBE (*b.* 1938) *LD, Tweeddale, Ettrick and Lauderdale,* maj. 2,520
*Steen, Anthony D. (*b.* 1939) *C., South Hams,* maj. 13,711
*Steinberg, Gerald N. (*b.* 1945) *Lab., City of Durham,* maj. 15,058
Stephen, B. Michael L. (*b.* 1942) *C., Shoreham,* maj. 14,286
*Stern, Michael C. (*b.* 1942) *C., Bristol North West,* maj. 45
Stevenson, George W. (*b.* 1938) *Lab., Stoke-on-Trent South,* maj. 6,909
*Stewart, J. Allan (*b.* 1942) *C., Eastwood,* maj. 11,688
*Stott, Roger, CBE (*b.* 1943) *Lab., Wigan,* maj. 21,842
*Strang, Gavin S., PH.D. (*b.* 1943) *Lab., Edinburgh East,* maj. 7,211
*Straw, J. W. (Jack) (*b.* 1946) *Lab., Blackburn,* maj. 6,027
Streeter, Gary (*b.* 1955) *C., Plymouth, Sutton,* maj. 11,950
*Sumberg, David A. G. (*b.* 1941) *C., Bury South,* maj. 788
†Sutcliffe, Gerard (*b.* 1953) *Lab., Bradford South,* maj. 9,664
Sweeney, Walter E. (*b.* 1949) *C., Vale of Glamorgan,* maj. 19
Sykes, John D. (*b.* 1956) *C., Scarborough,* maj. 11,734
*Tapsell, Sir Peter (*b.* 1930) *C., Lindsey East,* maj. 11,846
*Taylor, Sir Edward (Teddy) (*b.* 1937) *C., Southend East,* maj. 13,111
*Taylor, Ian C., MBE (*b.* 1945) *C., Esher,* maj. 20,371
*Taylor, Rt. Hon. John D. (*b.* 1937) *UUP, Strangford,* maj. 8,911
*Taylor, John M. (*b.* 1941) *C., Solihull,* maj. 25,146
*Taylor, Matthew O. J. (*b.* 1963) *LD, Truro,* maj. 7,570
*Taylor, Mrs W. Ann (*b.* 1947) *Lab., Dewsbury,* maj. 634
*Temple-Morris, Peter (*b.* 1938) *C., Leominster,* maj. 16,680
Thomason, K. Roy, OBE (*b.* 1944) *C., Bromsgrove,* maj. 13,702
*Thompson, Sir Donald (*b.* 1931) *C., Calder Valley,* maj. 4,878
*Thompson, H. Patrick (*b.* 1935) *C., Norwich North,* maj. 266
*Thompson, John (*b.* 1928) *Lab., Wansbeck,* maj. 18,174
*Thornton, Sir Malcolm (*b.* 1939) *C., Crosby,* maj. 14,806
*Thurnham, Peter G. (*b.* 1938) *Ind. C., Bolton North East,* maj. 185
†Timms, Stephen C. (*b.* 1955) *Lab., Newham North East,* maj. 11,818
Tipping, S. Paddy (*b.* 1949) *Lab., Sherwood,* maj. 2,910
†Touhig, J. Donnelly (Don) (*b.* 1959) *Lab., Islwyn,* maj. 13,097
*Townend, John E. (*b.* 1934) *C., Bridlington,* maj. 16,358
*Townsend, Cyril D. (*b.* 1937) *C., Bexleyheath,* maj. 14,086
*Tracey, Richard P. (*b.* 1943) *C., Surbiton,* maj. 9,639
*Tredinnick, David A. S. (*b.* 1950) *C., Bosworth,* maj. 19,094
Trend, Hon. Michael St J. (*b.* 1952) *C., Windsor and Maidenhead,* maj. 12,928
†Trickett, Jon H. (*b.* 1950) *Lab., Hemsworth,* maj. 13,875
*Trimble, W. David (*b.* 1944) *UUP, Upper Bann,* maj. 16,163
*Trotter, Neville G. (*b.* 1932) *C., Tynemouth,* maj. 597
*Turner, Dennis (*b.* 1942) *Lab., Wolverhampton South East,* maj. 10,240
*Twinn, Dr Ian D. (*b.* 1950) *C., Edmonton,* maj. 593
Tyler, Paul A., CBE (*b.* 1941) *LD, Cornwall North,* maj. 1,921
*Vaughan, Sir Gerard (*b.* 1923) *C., Reading East,* maj. 14,555
*Vaz, N. Keith A. S. (*b.* 1956) *Lab., Leicester East,* maj. 11,316
*Viggers, Peter J. (*b.* 1938) *C., Gosport,* maj. 16,318
*Waldegrave, Rt. Hon. William A. (*b.* 1946) *C., Bristol West,* maj. 6,071
*Walden, George G. H., CMG (*b.* 1939) *C., Buckingham,* maj. 19,791
*Walker, A. Cecil (*b.* 1924) *UUP, Belfast North,* maj. 9,625
*Walker, Rt. Hon. Sir Harold (*b.* 1927) *Lab., Doncaster Central,* maj. 10,682

*Walker, William C. (*b.* 1929) *C., Tayside North,* maj. 3,995
*Wallace, James R. (*b.* 1954) *LD, Orkney and Shetland,* maj. 5,033
*Waller, Gary P. A. (*b.* 1945) *C., Keighley,* maj. 3,596
*Walley, Ms Joan L. (*b.* 1949) *Lab., Stoke-on-Trent North,* maj. 14,777
*Ward, John D., CBE (*b.* 1925) *C., Poole,* maj. 12,831
*Wardell, Gareth L. (*b.* 1944) *Lab., Gower,* maj. 7,018
*Wardle, Charles F. (*b.* 1939) *C., Bexhill and Battle,* maj. 16,307
*Wareing, Robert N. (*b.* 1930) *Lab., Liverpool, West Derby,* maj. 20,425
Waterson, Nigel C. (*b.* 1950) *C., Eastbourne,* maj. 5,481
*Watson, Michael G. (*b.* 1949) *Lab., Glasgow Central,* maj. 11,019
*Watts, John A. (*b.* 1947) *C., Slough,* maj. 514
*Wells, Bowen (*b.* 1935) *C., Hertford and Stortford,* maj. 20,210
*Welsh, Andrew P. (*b.* 1944) *SNP, Angus East,* maj. 954
*Wheeler, Rt. Hon. Sir John (*b.* 1940) *C., Westminster North,* maj. 3,733
*Whitney, Raymond W., OBE (*b.* 1930) *C., Wycombe,* maj. 17,076
Whittingdale, John F. L., OBE (*b.* 1959) *C., Colchester South and Maldon,* maj. 21,821
Wicks, Malcolm H. (*b.* 1947) *Lab., Croydon North West,* maj. 1,526
*Widdecombe, Miss Ann N. (*b.* 1947) *C., Maidstone,* maj. 16,286
*Wiggin, Sir Jerry, TD (*b.* 1937) *C., Weston-super-Mare,* maj. 5,342
*Wigley, Dafydd (*b.* 1943) *PC, Caernarfon,* maj. 14,476
*Wilkinson, John A. D. (*b.* 1940) *C., Ruislip-Northwood,* maj. 19,791
Willetts, David L. (*b.* 1956) *C., Havant,* maj. 17,584
*Williams, Rt. Hon. Alan J. (*b.* 1930) *Lab., Swansea West,* maj. 9,478
*Williams, Dr Alan W. (*b.* 1945) *Lab., Carmarthen,* maj. 2,922
*Wilshire, David (*b.* 1943) *C., Spelthorne,* maj. 19,843
*Wilson, Brian D. H. (*b.* 1948) *Lab., Cunninghame North,* maj. 2,939
*Winnick, David J. (*b.* 1933) *Lab., Walsall North,* maj. 3,824
*Winterton, Mrs J. Ann (*b.* 1941) *C., Congleton,* maj. 11,120
*Winterton, Nicholas R. (*b.* 1938) *C., Macclesfield,* maj. 22,767
*Wise, Mrs Audrey (*b.* 1935) *Lab., Preston,* maj. 12,175
*Wolfson, G. Mark (*b.* 1934) *C., Sevenoaks,* maj. 19,154
*Wood, Timothy J. R. (*b.* 1940) *C., Stevenage,* maj. 4,888
*Worthington, Anthony (*b.* 1941) *Lab., Clydebank and Milngavie,* maj. 12,430
*Wray, James (*b.* 1938) *Lab., Glasgow, Provan,* maj. 10,703
Wright, Anthony W., D.PHIL. (*b.* 1948) *Lab., Cannock and Burntwood,* maj. 1,506
*Yeo, Timothy S. K. (*b.* 1945) *C., Suffolk South,* maj. 17,289
*Young, David W. (*b.* 1930) *Lab., Bolton South East,* maj. 12,691
*Young, Rt. Hon. Sir George, Bt. (*b.* 1941) *C., Ealing, Acton,* maj. 7,007

RETIRING MPs

The following MPs have announced that they will not be standing at the next general election:

Michael Alison, C., Selby
David Alton, LD, Liverpool Mossley Hill
Kenneth Baker, C., Mole Valley
Robert Banks, C., Harrogate and Knaresborough
John Biffen, C., Shropshire North
Jeremy Bray, Lab., Motherwell South
John Butcher, C., Coventry South West
Alex Carlile, LD, Montgomery
Sir Kenneth Carlisle, C., Lincoln
Paul Channon, C., Southend West
Sir Julian Critchley, C., Aldershot
Edwina Currie, C., Derbyshire South
Terry Dicks, C., Hayes and Harlington
Sir Anthony Durant, C., Reading West
Tim Eggar, C., Enfield North
Andrew Faulds, Lab., Warley East
Dudley Fishburn, C., Kensington
Sir Anthony Grant, C., Cambridgeshire South West
Sir Michael Grylls, C., Surrey North West
Sir John Hannam, C., Exeter
Peter Hardy, Lab., Wentworth
Roy Hattersley, Lab., Birmingham Sparkbrook
Sir Robert Hicks, C., Cornwall South East
Sir Peter Hordern, C., Horsham
David Howell, C.,Guildford
Sir John Hunt, C., Ravensbourne
Douglas Hurd, C., Witney
Greville Janner, Lab., Leicester West
Sir Russell Johnston, LD, Inverness, Nairn and Lochaber
Dame Jill Knight, C., Birmingham Edgbaston
Sir Patrick McNair-Wilson, C., New Forest
Sir Patrick Mayhew, C., Tunbridge Wells
Sir David Mitchell, C., Hampshire North West
Sir Hector Monro, C., Dumfries
Sir Fergus Montgomery, C., Altrincham and Sale
Alf Morris, Lab., Manchester Wythenshawe
Steven Norris, C., Epping Forest
Sir Cranley Onslow, C., Woking
Stan Orme, Lab., Salford East
Bob Parry, Lab., Liverpool Riverside
Terry Patchett, Lab., Barnsley
John Patten, C., Oxford West and Abingdon
Sir Geoffrey Pattie, C., Chertsey and Walton
Tim Renton, C., Sussex Mid
Sir Wyn Roberts, C., Conwy
Richard Ryder, C., Mid Norfolk
Sir Giles Shaw, C., Pudsey
Peter Shore, Lab., Bethnal Green and Stepney
Sir Keith Speed, C., Ashford
Sir James Spicer, C., Dorset West
Sir David Steel, LD, Tweeddale, Ettrick and Lauderdale
Patrick Thompson, C., Norwich North
Peter Thurnham, Ind. C., Bolton North East
Neville Trotter, C., Tynemouth
George Walden, C., Buckingham
John Ward, C., Poole
Sir Jerry Wiggin, C., Weston-super-Mare
Mark Wolfson, C., Sevenoaks

The following MPs have been deselected by their constituency parties:
David Ashby, C., Leicestershire North West
David Young, Lab., Bolton South East

MEMBERS WITH SMALL MAJORITIES

The following MPs were returned in April 1992 with majorities of fewer than 1,000 votes

*Denotes membership of last Parliament

	Maj.
Walter Sweeney, C., Vale of Glamorgan	19
*Michael Stern, C., Bristol North West	45
*Terry Dicks, C., Hayes and Harlington	53
Phil Gallie, C., Ayr	85
Janet Anderson, Lab., Rossendale and Darwen	120
Jonathan Evans, C., Brecon and Radnor	130
Estelle Morris, Lab., Birmingham Yardley	162
*Peter Thurnham, C., Bolton North East	185
Mike Hall, Lab., Warrington South	191
*David Martin, C., Portsmouth South	242
Jamie Cann, Lab., Ipswich	265
*Patrick Thompson, C., Norwich North	266
*Malcolm Bruce, LD, Gordon	274
*William Powell, C., Corby	342
Mike Gapes, Lab., Ilford South	402
*Sir Russell Johnston, LD, Inverness, Nairn and Lochaber	458
*Alice Mahon, Lab., Halifax	478
*John Watts, C., Slough	514
John Denham, Lab., Southampton Itchen	551
Anne Campbell, Lab., Cambridge	580
*James Hill, C., Southampton Test	585
Dr Joe Hendron, SDLP, Belfast West	589
*Dr Ian Twinn, C., Edmonton	593
Neville Trotter, C., Tynemouth	597
Richard Burden, Lab., Birmingham Northfield	630
*Ann Taylor, Lab., Dewsbury	634
*Michael Forsyth, C., Stirling	703
*Phillip Oppenheim, C., Amber Valley	712
Nick Ainger, Lab., Pembroke	755
*David Sumberg, C., Bury South	788
Nick Harvey, LD, Devon North	794
*Graham Bright, C., Luton South	799
*David Shaw, C., Dover	833
*Lord James Douglas-Hamilton, C., Edinburgh West	879
*Sir Tom Arnold, C., Hazel Grove	929
*Andrew Welsh, SNP, Angus East	954
*David Ashby, C., Leicestershire North West	979
*Sir Wyn Roberts, C., Conwy	995

BY-ELECTIONS SINCE THE 1992 GENERAL ELECTION

NEWBURY
(6 May 1993)
E.81,081   T.71.25%

D. Rendel, *LD*	37,590
J. Davidson, *C.*	15,535
S. Billcliffe, *Lab.*	1,151
A. Sked, *Anti-Maastricht Anti Fed.*	601
A. Bannon, *C. Candidate*	561
S. Martin, *Commoners Party Movement*	435
'Lord' D. Sutch, *Loony*	432
J. Wallis, *Green*	341
R. Marlar, *Referendum*	338
J. Browne, *C. Rebel*	267
Ms L. St Clair, *Corrective*	170
W. Board, *Maastricht Referendum for Britain*	84
M. Grenville, *NLP*	60
J. Day, *People and Pensioners*	49
C. Palmer, *21st Century*	40
M. Grbin, *Defence of Children's Humanity Bosnia*	33
A. Page, *SDP*	33
Ms A. Murphy, *Comm. GB*	32
M. Stone, *Give Royal Billions to Schools*	21
LD majority	22,055

CHRISTCHURCH
(29 July 1993)
E.71,868   T.74.2%

Mrs D. Maddock, *LD*	33,164
R. Hayward, *C.*	16,737
N. Lickley, *Lab.*	1,453
A. Sked, *Anti-Maastricht Anti Fed.*	878
'Lord' D. Sutch, *Loony Rock-Roll*	404
A. Bannon, *C. Candidate*	357
P. Newman, *Sack Graham Taylor*	80
Ms T. B. Jackson, *Buy Daily Sport*	67
P. Hollyman, *Save NHS*	60
J. Crockard, *Highlander IV Wednesday Promotion Night*	48
M. Griffiths, *NLP*	45
M. Belcher, *Ian for King*	23
K. Fitzhugh, *Alfred Chicken*	18
J. Walley, *Rainbow Alliance Coalition*	16
LD majority	16,427

ROTHERHAM
(5 May 1994)
E.60,937   T.44.14%

D. MacShane, *Lab.*	14,912
D. Wildgoose, *LD*	7,958
N. Gibb, *C.*	2,649
'Lord' D. Sutch, *Loony*	1,114
K. Laycock, *NLP*	173
Lab. majority	6,954

BARKING
(9 June 1994)
E.50,454   T.38.6%

Ms M. Hodge, *Lab.*	13,704
G. White, *LD*	2,290
Ms T. May, *C.*	1,976
G. Needs, *NF*	551
G. Batten, *UK Ind.*	406
Ms H. Butensky, *NLP*	90
Lab. majority	11,414

BRADFORD SOUTH
(9 June 1994)
E.69,914   T.44.0%

G. Sutcliffe, *Lab.*	17,014
Ms H. Wright, *LD*	7,350
R. Farley, *C.*	5,475
'Lord' D. Sutch, *Loony*	727
K. Laycock, *NLP*	187
Lab. majority	9,664

DAGENHAM
(9 June 1994)
E.59,645   T.37.2%

Ms J. Church, *Lab.*	15,474
J. Fairrie, *C.*	2,130
P. Dunphy, *LD*	1,804
J. Tyndall, *BNP*	1,511
P. Compobassi, *UK Ind.*	457
M. Leighton, *NLP*	116
Lab. majority	13,344

EASTLEIGH
(9 June 1994)
E.91,736   T.58.9%

D. Chidgey, *LD*	24,473
Ms M. Birks, *Lab.*	15,234
S. Reid, *C.*	13,675
N. Farage, *UK Ind.*	952
'Lord' D. Sutch, *Loony*	783
P. Warburton, *NLP*	145
LD majority	9,239

NEWHAM NORTH EAST
(9 June 1994)
E.59,555   T.34.5%

S. Timms, *Lab.*	14,668
P. Hammond, *C.*	2,850
A. Kellaway, *LD*	821
A. Scholefield, *UK Ind.*	509
J. Homeless, *House Homeless People*	342
R. Archer, *NLP*	228
Ms V. Garman, *Buy the Daily Sport*	155
Lab. majority	11,818

MONKLANDS EAST
(30 June 1994)
E.48,391   T.70.17%

Mrs H. Liddell, *Lab.*	16,960
Ms K. Ullrich, *SNP*	15,320
S. Gallagher, *LD*	878
Ms S. Bell, *C.*	799
A. Bremner, *Network Against Criminal Justice Bill*	69
D. Paterson, *NLP*	58
Lab. majority	1,640

DUDLEY WEST
(15 December 1994)
E.87,633   T.46.95%

I. Pearson, *Lab.*	28,400
G. Postles, *C.*	7,706
M. Hadley, *LD*	3,154
M. S. Hyde, *Lib.*	548
M. R. Floyd, *UK Ind.*	590
A. Carmichael, *NF*	561
M. H. Nattrass, *New Britain*	146
Ms M. Nicholson, *FOREST*	77
J. D. Oldbury, *NLP*	70
C. R. Palmer, *21st Century*	55
Lab. majority	20,694

ISLWYN
(16 February 1995)
E.50,737   T.45.6%

D. Touhig, *Lab.*	16,030
J. Davies, *PC*	2,933
J. Bushell, *LD*	2,448
R. Buckland, *C.*	913
'Lord' D. Sutch, *Loony*	506
H. Hughes, *UK Ind.*	289
T. Rees, *NLP*	47
Lab. majority	13,097

PERTH AND KINROSS
(25 May 1995)
E.65,410   T.62.0%

Ms R. Cunningham, *SNP*	16,931
D. Alexander, *Lab.*	9,620
J. Godfrey, *C.*	8,990
Ms V. Linklater, *LD*	4,952
'Lord' D. Sutch, *Loony*	586
V. Linacre, *UK Ind.*	504
R. Harper, *Green*	223
M. Halford, *Scots Conservatory*	88
G. Black, *NLP*	54
SNP majority	7,311

DOWN NORTH
(15 June 1995)
E.68,662   T.38.7%

R. McCartney, *UK Unionist*	10,124
A. McFarland, *UUP*	7,232
Sir Oliver Napier, *All.*	6,970
A. Chambers, *Ind. Unionist*	2,170
S. Sexton, *C.*	583
M. Brooks, *Free Para Lee Clegg Now*	108
C. Carter, *Ulster's Ind. Voice*	101
J. Anderson, *NLP*	100
UK Unionist majority	2,892

LITTLEBOROUGH AND
SADDLEWORTH
(27 July 1995)
*E.*65,576   *T.*63.6%
C. Davies, *LD*	16,231
P. Woolas, *Lab.*	14,238
J. Hudson, *C.*	9,934
'Lord' D. Sutch, *Loony*	782
J. Whittaker, *UK Ind.*	549
P. Douglas, *C. Party*	193
Mr Blobby, *House Party*	105
A. Pitts, *Soc.*	46
L. D. McLaren, *Old Lab.*	33
C. R. Palmer, *21st Century*	25
LD majority	1,993

HEMSWORTH
(1 February 1996)
*E.*55,679   *T.*39.5%
J. Trickett, *Lab.*	15,817
N. Hazell, *C.*	1,942
D. Ridgway, *LD*	1,516
Ms B. Nixon, *Soc. Lab.*	1,193
'Lord' D. Sutch, *Loony*	652
P. Davies, *UK Ind.*	455
Ms P. Alexander, *Green*	157
M. Thomas, *Mark Thomas Friday Nights Channel 4*	122
M. Cooper, *National Democrat*	111
Ms D. Leighton, *NLP*	28
Lab. majority	13,875

STAFFORDSHIRE SOUTH EAST
(11 April 1996)
*E.*70,199   *T.*60.3%
B. Jenkins, *Lab.*	26,155
J. James, *C.*	12,393
Ms J. Davey, *LD*	2.042
A. Smith, *UK Independence*	1,272
'Lord' D. Sutch, *Loony*	506
Ms S. Edwards, *National Democrats*	358
S. Mountford, *Lib.*	332
L.Taylor, *Churchill C.*	123
News Bunny, *Official Bunny News Party*	85
N. Samuelson, *Daily Loonylugs Earring-up the World*	80
D. Lucas, *NLP*	53
F. Sandy, *Action Against Crime Life Means Life*	53
A. Wood, *Restoration of Death Penalty*	45
Lab. majority	13,762

Prime Ministers since 1782

Over the centuries there has been some variation in the determination of the dates of appointment of Prime Ministers. Where possible, the date given is that on which a new Prime Minister kissed the Sovereign's hands and accepted the commission to form a ministry. However, until the middle of the 19th century the dating of a commission or transfer of seals could be the date of taking office. Where the composition of the Government changed, e.g. became a coalition, but the Prime Minister remained the same, the date of the change of government is given.

The Marquess of Rockingham, *Whig*, 27 March 1782
The Earl of Shelburne, *Whig*, 4 July 1782
The Duke of Portland, *Coalition*, 2 April 1783
William Pitt, *Tory*, 19 December 1783
Henry Addington, *Tory*, 17 March 1801
William Pitt, *Tory*, 10 May 1804
The Lord Grenville, *Whig*, 11 February 1806
The Duke of Portland, *Tory*, 31 March 1807
Spencer Perceval, *Tory*, 4 October 1809
The Earl of Liverpool, *Tory*, 8 June 1812
George Canning, *Tory*, 10 April 1827
Viscount Goderich, *Tory*, 31 August 1827
The Duke of Wellington, *Tory*, 22 January 1828
The Earl Grey, *Whig*, 22 November 1830
The Viscount Melbourne, *Whig*, 16 July 1834
The Duke of Wellington, *Tory*, 17 November 1834
Sir Robert Peel, *Tory*, 10 December 1834
The Viscount Melbourne, *Whig*, 18 April 1835
Sir Robert Peel, *Tory*, 30 August 1841
Lord John Russell (subsequently the Earl Russell), *Whig*, 30 June 1846
The Earl of Derby, *Tory*, 23 February 1852
The Earl of Aberdeen, *Peelite*, 19 December 1852
The Viscount Palmerston, *Liberal*, 6 February 1855
The Earl of Derby, *Conservative*, 20 February 1858
The Viscount Palmerston, *Liberal*, 12 June 1859
The Earl Russell, *Liberal*, 29 October 1865

The Earl of Derby, *Conservative*, 28 June 1866
Benjamin Disraeli, *Conservative*, 27 February 1868
William Gladstone, *Liberal*, 3 December 1868
Benjamin Disraeli, *Conservative*, 20 February 1874
William Gladstone, *Liberal*, 23 April 1880
The Marquess of Salisbury, *Conservative*, 23 June 1885
William Gladstone, *Liberal*, 1 February 1886
The Marquess of Salisbury, *Conservative*, 25 July 1886
William Gladstone, *Liberal*, 15 August 1892
The Earl of Rosebery, *Liberal*, 5 March 1894
The Marquess of Salisbury, *Conservative*, 25 June 1895
Arthur Balfour, *Conservative*, 12 July 1902
Sir Henry Campbell-Bannerman, *Liberal*, 5 December 1905
Herbert Asquith, *Liberal*, 7 April 1908
Herbert Asquith, *Coalition*, 25 May 1915
David Lloyd-George, *Coalition*, 7 December 1916
Andrew Bonar Law, *Conservative*, 23 October 1922
Stanley Baldwin, *Conservative*, 22 May 1923
Ramsay MacDonald, *Labour*, 22 January 1924
Stanley Baldwin, *Conservative*, 4 November 1924
Ramsay MacDonald, *Labour*, 5 June 1929
Ramsay MacDonald, *Coalition*, 24 August 1931
Stanley Baldwin, *Coalition*, 7 June 1935
Neville Chamberlain, *Coalition*, 28 May 1937
Winston Churchill, *Coalition*, 10 May 1940
Winston Churchill, *Conservative*, 23 May 1945
Clement Attlee, *Labour*, 26 July 1945
Sir Winston Churchill, *Conservative*, 26 October 1951
Sir Anthony Eden, *Conservative*, 6 April 1955
Harold Macmillan, *Conservative*, 10 January 1957
Sir Alec Douglas-Home, *Conservative*, 19 October 1963
Harold Wilson, *Labour*, 16 October 1964
Edward Heath, *Conservative*, 19 June 1970
Harold Wilson, *Labour*, 4 March 1974
James Callaghan, *Labour*, 5 April 1976
Margaret Thatcher, *Conservative*, 4 May 1979
John Major, *Conservative*, 28 November 1990

General Election statistics

PRINCIPAL PARTIES IN PARLIAMENT since 1970

	1970	1974 Feb.	1974 Oct.	1979	1983	1987	1992
Conservative	330*	296	276	339	397	375	336
Labour	287	301	319	268	209	229	270
Liberal/LD	6	14	13	11	17	17	20
Social Democrat	—	1	—	—	6	5	—
Independent	5†	1	1	2	—	—	—
Plaid Cymru	—	2	3	2	2	3	4
Scottish Nationalist	1	7	11	2	2	3	3
Democratic Unionist	—	—	—	3	3	3	3
SDLP	—	1	1	1	1	3	4
Sinn Fein	—	—	—	—	1	1	—
Ulster Popular Unionist	—	—	—	—	1	1	1
Ulster Unionist‡	*	11	10	6	10	9	9
The Speaker	1	1	1	1	1	1	1
Total	630	635	635	635	650	650	651

* Including 8 Ulster Unionists
† Comprising: Independent Labour 1, Independent Unity 1, Protestant Unity 1, Republican Labour 1, Unity 1
‡ Comprises:
1974 (February) United Ulster Unionist Council 11
1974 (October) United Ulster Unionist 10
1979 Ulster Unionist 5, United Ulster Unionist 1
1983 Official Unionist 10

PARLIAMENTS since 1970

Assembled	Dissolved	Duration yr	m.	d.
29 June 1970	8 February 1974	3	7	10
6 March 1974	20 September 1974	0	6	14
22 October 1974	7 April 1979	4	5	16
9 May 1979	13 May 1983	4	0	4
15 June 1983	18 May 1987	3	11	3
17 June 1987	16 March 1992	4	8	28
27 April 1992				

MAJORITIES IN THE COMMONS since 1970

Year	Party	Maj.
1970	Conservative	31
1974 Feb.	No majority	
1974 Oct.	Labour	5
1979	Conservative	43
1983	Conservative	144
1987	Conservative	102
1992	Conservative	21

VOTES CAST 1987 and 1992*

GENERAL ELECTION 1987

Conservative	13,760,525
Labour	10,029,944
Liberal/SDP Alliance	7,341,152
Scottish Nationalist	416,873
Plaid Cymru	123,589
†Green	89,753
Others	37,576

GENERAL ELECTION 1992

Conservative	14,048,283
Labour	11,559,735
Liberal Democrats	5,999,384
Scottish Nationalist	629,552
Plaid Cymru	154,439
Others	436,207

*Excluding Northern Ireland seats
†Excluding Ecology candidate in Northern Ireland

SIZE OF ELECTORATE 1992

	No. of electors	Average no. of electors per seat
England and Wales	38,648,000	68,800
Scotland	3,929,000	54,600
Northern Ireland	1,141,000	67,100
Total	43,719,000	67,200

PARLIAMENTARY CONSTITUENCIES as at 9 April 1992

The results of voting in each parliamentary division at the general election of 9 April 1992 are given below. The majority in the 1987 general election, and any by-elections between 1987 and 1992, is given below the 1992 result.

Symbols

E.	Total number of electors in the constituency at the 1992 general election
T.	Turnout of electors at the 1992 general election
*	Member of the last Parliament

Abbreviations

All.	Alliance Party (NI)
C.	Conservative
DUP	Democratic Unionist Party
Green	Green Party
Ind.	Independent
Lab.	Labour
L./All.	Liberal Alliance
LD	Liberal Democrat
Lib.	Liberal
PC	Plaid Cymru
SD	Social Democrat
SDLP	Social Democratic and Labour Party
SDP	Social Democrat Party
SF	Sinn Fein
SNP	Scottish National Party
UPUP	Ulster Popular Unionist Party
UUP	Ulster Unionist Party
ADS	After Dinner Speaker
AFE	Anti-Federal Europe
Alt.	Alternative
Anti Fed.	Anti Federalist League
Anti H.	Anti-Heseltine Independent
APAKBI	Anti-Paddy Ashdown Keep Britain Independent

AS	Anglo Saxon
Bastion	Bastion Party
BNP	British National Party
Brewer	Jolly Small Brewers Party
Brit. Ind.	British Independence Party
CD	Christian Democrat
Century	21st Century Party
Choice	People's Choice
CL	Communist League
Comm. GB	Communist Party of Great Britain
CRA	Chauvinist Raving Alliance
CSP	Common Sense Party
C. Thatch.	Conservative Thatcherite
DLC	Democrat Liberal Conservative
DOS	Doctor of Stockwell
EFRA	Epping Forest Residents Association
ERIP	Equal Representation in Parliament
EUVJJ	End Unemployment Vote Justice for the Jobless
FDP	Fancy Dress Party
Fellowship	Fellowship Party
FP	Feudal Party
FTA	Fair Trials Abroad
FTM	Forward to Mars Party
Fun	Funstermentalist
Gremloids	Gremloids
Hardcore	The Altern-8-ive (Hardcore) Party
Homeland	Independent British Homeland Defence
Hove C.	Official Conservative Hove Party
IFM	Irish Freedom Movement
ILP	Independent Labour Party
Ind. U.	Independent Unionist
Int. Comm.	International Communist Party
Islamic	Islamic Party
ISS	Illegal Sunday Shopping
JBR	Justice from British Rail

Loony	Official Monster Raving Loony Party
Loony G.	Loony Green
LP	Lodestar Party
LTU	Labour and Trade Union
MBI	Morecambe Bay Independent
NA	Noise Abatement
Nat.	Nationalist
NF	National Front
NLP	Natural Law Party
Pensioners	Pensioners' Party
PP	People's Party
PPP	Peoples' Peace Party
PR	Proportional Representation
Prog. Soc.	Independent Progressive Socialist
Prot. Ref.	Protestant Reformation
QFL	Quality for Life Party
RAVA	Rainbow Ark Voters Association
RCC	Revolutionary Christian Communist
Real Bean	Real Bean
Rev. Comm.	Revolutionary Communist
Rizz	Rizz Party – Rainbow
Scallywagg	Scallywagg
SML	Scottish Militant Labour
SOADDA	Struck Off and Die Doctor's Alliance
Soc.	Socialist
Soc. Lab.	Socialist Labour
True Lab.	True Labour
UTCHAP	Up The Creek Have A Party
WAR	Workers Against Racism
Wessex	Save Wessex
Whiplash	Whiplash Corrective
WP	Workers' Party
WRP	Workers' Revolutionary Party
WUWC	Wake Up Wokingham Campaign
YSOR	Young Socialist – Occupy Ravenscraig

ENGLAND

Aldershot (Hants)
E.81,754   T.78.71%

*J. Critchley, C.	36,974
A. Collett, LD	17,786
J. Anthony Smith, Lab.	8,552
D. Robinson, Lib.	1,038
C. majority	19,188
(June 1987, C. maj. 17,784)	

Aldridge-Brownhills (W. Midlands)
E.63,404   T.82.55%

*R. Shepherd, C.	28,431
N. Fawcett, Lab.	17,407
S. Reynolds, LD	6,503
C. majority	11,024
(June 1987, C. maj. 12,396)	

Altrincham and Sale (Greater Manchester)
E.65,897   T.80.66%

*Sir F. Montgomery, C.	29,066
Ms M. Atherton, Lab.	12,275
J. Mulholland, LD	11,601
J. Renwick, NLP	212

C. majority	16,791
(June 1987, C. maj. 14,228)	

Amber Valley (Derbys)
E.70,155   T.84.69%

*Hon. P. Oppenheim, C.	27,418
J. Cooper, Lab.	26,706
G. Brocklebank, LD	5,294
C. majority	712
(June 1987, C. maj. 9,500)	

Arundel (W. Sussex)
E.79,241   T.77.06%

*Sir M. Marshall, C.	35,405
Dr J. Walsh, LD	15,542
R. Nash, Lab.	8,321
Mrs D. Renson, Lib.	1,103
R. Corbin, Green	693
C. majority	19,863
(June 1987, C. maj. 18,880)	

Ashfield (Notts)
E.75,075   T.77.70%

G. Hoon, Lab.	32,018
L. Robertson, C.	19,031

J. Turton, LD	7,291
Lab. majority	12,987
(June 1987, Lab. maj. 4,400)	

Ashford (Kent)
E.71,767   T.79.20%

*K. Speed, C.	31,031
Ms C. Headley, LD	13,672
Ms D. Cameron, Lab.	11,365
Dr A. Porter, Green	773
C. majority	17,359
(June 1987, C. maj. 15,488)	

Ashton-under-Lyne (Greater Manchester)
E.58,701   T.73.87%

*Rt. Hon. R. Sheldon, Lab.	24,550
J. Pinniger, C.	13,615
C. Turner, LD	4,005
C. Hall, Lib.	907
J. Brannigan, NLP	289
Lab. majority	10,935
(June 1987, Lab. maj. 9,286)	

AYLESBURY (Bucks)
E.79,208   T.80.29%

D. Lidington, *C.*	36,500
Ms S. Bowles, *LD*	17,640
R. Priest, *Lab.*	8,517
N. Foster, *Green*	702
B. D'Arcy, *NLP*	239
C. majority	18,860

(June 1987, C. maj. 16,558)

BANBURY (Oxon)
E.71,840   T.81.51%

*A. Baldry, *C.*	32,215
Ms A. Billingham, *Lab.*	15,495
G. Fisher, *LD*	10,602
Dr R. Ticiiati, *NLP*	250
C. majority	16,720

(June 1987, C. maj. 17,330)

BARKING (Greater London)
E.50,454   T.69.99%

*Ms J. Richardson, *Lab.*	18,224
J. Kennedy, *C.*	11,956
S. Churchman, *LD*	5,133
Lab. majority	6,268

(June 1987, Lab. maj. 3,409)
See also page 234

BARNSLEY CENTRAL (S. Yorks)
E.55,373   T.70.53%

*E. Illsley, *Lab.*	27,048
D. Senior, *C.*	7,687
S. Cowton, *LD*	4,321
Lab. majority	19,361

(June 1987, Lab. maj. 19,051)

BARNSLEY EAST (S. Yorks)
E.54,051   T.72.73%

*T. Patchett, *Lab.*	30,346
J. Procter, *C.*	5,569
Ms S. Anginotti, *LD*	3,399
Lab. majority	24,777

(June 1987, Lab. maj. 23,511)

BARNSLEY WEST AND PENISTONE (S. Yorks)
E.63,374   T.75.75%

M. Clapham, *Lab.*	27,965
G. Sawyer, *C.*	13,461
I. Nicolson, *LD*	5,610
D. Jones, *Green*	970
Lab. majority	14,504

(June 1987, Lab. maj. 14,191)

BARROW AND FURNESS (Cumbria)
E.67,764   T.82.11%

J. Hutton, *Lab.*	26,568
*C. Franks, *C.*	22,990
C. Crane, *LD*	6,089
Lab. majority	3,578

(June 1987, C. maj. 3,928)

BASILDON (Essex)
E.67,585   T.79.61%

*D. Amess, *C.*	24,159
J. Potter, *Lab.*	22,679
G. Williams, *LD*	6,967
C. majority	1,480

(June 1987, C. maj. 2,649)

BASINGSTOKE (Hants)
E.82,952   T.82.79%

*A. Hunter, *C.*	37,521
D. Bull, *Lab.*	16,323

C. Curtis, *LD*	14,119
Ms V. Oldaker, *Green*	714
C. majority	21,198

(June 1987, C. maj. 17,893)

BASSETLAW (Notts)
E.58,583   T.92.97%

*J. Ashton, *Lab.*	29,061
Mrs C. Spelman, *C.*	19,064
M. Reynolds, *LD*	6,340
Lab. majority	9,997

(June 1987, Lab. maj. 5,613)

BATH (Avon)
E.63,689   T.82.54%

D. Foster, *LD*	25,718
*Rt. Hon. C. Patten, *C.*	21,950
Ms P. Richards, *Lab.*	4,102
D. McCanlis, *Green*	433
Ms M. Barker, *Lib.*	172
Dr A. Sked, *Anti Fed.*	117
J. Rumming, *Ind.*	79
LD majority	3,768

(June 1987, C. maj. 1,412)

BATLEY AND SPEN (W. Yorks)
E.76,417   T.79.63%

*Mrs E. Peacock, *C.*	27,629
Mrs E. Durkin, *Lab.*	26,221
G. Beever, *LD*	6,380
C. Lord, *Green*	628
C. majority	1,408

(June 1987, C. maj. 1,362)

BATTERSEA (Greater London)
E.68,218   T.76.63%

*J. Bowis, *C.*	26,390
A. Dubs, *Lab.*	21,550
R. O'Brien, *LD*	3,659
I. Wingrove, *Green*	584
W. Stevens, *NLP*	98
C. majority	4,840

(June 1987, C. maj. 857)

BEACONSFIELD (Bucks)
E.64,268   T.82.27%

*T. Smith, *C.*	33,817
Ms A. Purse, *LD*	10,220
G. Smith, *Lab.*	7,163
W. Foulds, *Ind. C.*	1,317
A. Foss, *NLP*	196
Ms J. Martin, *ERIP*	166
C. majority	23,597

(June 1987, C. maj. 21,339)

BECKENHAM (Greater London)
E.59,440   T.77.86%

P. Merchant, *C.*	26,323
K. Ritchie, *Lab.*	11,038
Ms M. Williams, *LD*	8,038
G. Williams, *Lib.*	643
P. Shaw, *NLP*	243
C. majority	15,285

(June 1987, C. maj. 13,464)

BEDFORDSHIRE MID
E.81,864   T.84.45%

*Rt. Hon. Sir N. Lyell, *C.*	40,230
R. Clayton, *Lab.*	15,092
N. Hills, *LD*	11,957
P. Cottier, *Lib.*	1,582
M. Lorys, *NLP*	279

C. majority	25,138

(June 1987, C. maj. 22,851)

BEDFORDSHIRE NORTH
E.73,789   T.80.03%

*Sir T. Skeet, *C.*	29,920
P. Hall, *Lab.*	18,302
M. Smithson, *LD*	10,014
Ms L. Smith, *Green*	643
B. Bench, *NLP*	178
C. majority	11,618

(June 1987, C. maj. 16,505)

BEDFORDSHIRE SOUTH WEST
E.79,662   T.82.39%

*W. D. Madel, *C.*	37,498
B. Elliott, *Lab.*	16,225
M. Freeman, *LD*	10,988
P. Rollings, *Green*	689
D. Gilmour, *NLP*	239
C. majority	21,273

(June 1987, C. maj. 22,305)

BERKSHIRE EAST
E.90,365   T.81.41%

*A. Mackay, *C.*	43,898
Ms L. Murray, *LD*	15,218
K. Dibble, *Lab.*	14,458
C. majority	28,680

(June 1987, C. maj. 22,626)

BERWICK-UPON-TWEED (Northumberland)
E.54,919   T.79.12%

*A. Beith, *LD*	19,283
Dr A. Henfrey, *C.*	14,240
Dr G. Adam, *Lab.*	9,933
LD majority	5,043

(June 1987, L./All. maj. 13,945)

BETHNAL GREEN AND STEPNEY (Greater London)
E.55,675   T.65.45%

*Rt. Hon. P. Shore, *Lab.*	20,350
J. Shaw, *LD*	8,120
Miss J. Emmerson, *C.*	6,507
R. Edmonds, *BNP*	1,310
S. Kelsey, *Comm. GB*	156
Lab. majority	12,230

(June 1987, Lab. maj. 5,284)

BEVERLEY (Humberside)
E.81,198   T.79.69%

*J. Cran, *C.*	34,503
A. Collinge, *LD*	17,986
C. Challen, *Lab.*	12,026
D. Hetherington, *NLP*	199
C. majority	16,517

(June 1987, C. maj. 12,595)

BEXHILL AND BATTLE (E. Sussex)
E.65,850   T.78.99%

*C. Wardle, *C.*	31,330
Ms S. Prochak, *LD*	15,023
F. Taylor, *Lab.*	4,883
J. Prus, *Green*	594
Mrs M. Smith, *CSP*	190
C. majority	16,307

(June 1987, C. maj. 20,519)

BEXLEYHEATH (Greater London)
E.57,684   T.82.17%

*C. Townsend, *C.*	25,606
J. Browning, *Lab.*	11,520

Ms W. Chaplin, *LD* 10,107
R. Cundy, *Ind.* 170
C. majority 14,086
(June 1987, C. maj. 11,687)

BILLERICAY (Essex)
E.80,388 T.82.34%
*Mrs T. Gorman, *C.* 37,406
F. Bellard, *LD* 14,912
Ms A. Miller, *Lab.* 13,880
C. majority 22,494
(June 1987, C. maj. 18,016)

BIRKENHEAD (Merseyside)
E.62,682 T.72.96%
*F. Field, *Lab.* 29,098
R. Hughes, *C.* 11,485
P. Williams, *LD* 4,417
Ms T. Fox, *Green* 543
Ms B. Griffiths, *NLP* 190
Lab. majority 17,613
(June 1987, Lab. maj. 15,372)

BIRMINGHAM EDGBASTON
(W. Midlands)
E.53,041 T.71.29%
*Dame J. Knight, *C.* 18,529
J. Wilton, *Lab.* 14,222
I. Robertson-Steel, *LD* 4,419
P. Simpson, *Green* 643
C. majority 4,307
(June 1987, C. maj. 8,581)

BIRMINGHAM ERDINGTON
(W. Midlands)
E.52,398 T.70.15%
*R. Corbett, *Lab.* 18,549
S. Hope, *C.* 13,814
Dr J. Campbell, *LD* 4,398
Lab. majority 4,735
(June 1987, Lab. maj. 2,467)

BIRMINGHAM HALL GREEN
(W. Midlands)
E.60,091 T.78.17%
*A. Hargreaves, *C.* 21,649
Ms J. Slowey, *Lab.* 17,984
D. McGrath, *LD* 7,342
C. majority 3,665
(June 1987, C. maj. 7,621)

BIRMINGHAM HODGE HILL
(W. Midlands)
E.57,651 T.70.82%
*T. Davis, *Lab.* 21,895
Miss E. Gibson, *C.* 14,827
S. Hagan, *LD* 3,740
E. Whicker, *NF* 370
Lab. majority 7,068
(June 1987, Lab. maj. 4,789)

BIRMINGHAM LADYWOOD
(W. Midlands)
E.56,970 T.65.92%
*Ms C. Short, *Lab.* 24,887
Mrs B. Ashford, *C.* 9,604
B. Worth, *LD* 3,068
Lab. majority 15,283
(June 1987, Lab. maj. 10,028)

BIRMINGHAM NORTHFIELD
(W. Midlands)
E.70,533 T.76.08%
R. Burden, *Lab.* 24,433
*R. King, *C.* 23,803
D. Cropp, *LD* 5,431
Lab. majority 630
(June 1987, C. maj. 3,135)

BIRMINGHAM PERRY BARR
(W. Midlands)
E.72,161 T.71.62%
*J. Rooker, *Lab.* 27,507
G. Green, *C.* 18,917
T. Philpott, *LD* 5,261
Lab. majority 8,590
(June 1987, Lab. maj. 6,933)

BIRMINGHAM SELLY OAK
(W. Midlands)
E.72,150 T.76.61%
Ms L. Jones, *Lab.* 25,430
*A. Beaumont-Dark, *C.* 23,370
D. Osborne, *LD* 5,679
P. Slatter, *Green* 535
C. Barwood, *NLP* 178
K. Malik, *Rev Comm* 84
Lab. majority 2,060
(June 1987, C. maj. 2,584)

BIRMINGHAM SMALL HEATH
(W. Midlands)
E.55,213 T.62.95%
R. Godsiff, *Lab.* 22,675
A. Qayyum Chaudhary, *C.* 8,686
H. Thomas, *LD* 2,575
Ms H. Clawley, *Green* 824
Lab. majority 13,989
(June 1987, Lab. maj. 15,521)

BIRMINGHAM SPARKBROOK
(W. Midlands)
E.51,677 T.66.80%
*Rt. Hon. R. Hattersley, *Lab.* 22,116
M. Khamisa, *C.* 8,544
D. Parry, *LD* 3,028
C. Alldrick, *Green* 833
Lab. majority 13,572
(June 1987, Lab. maj. 11,859)

BIRMINGHAM YARDLEY
(W. Midlands)
E.54,749 T.77.98%
Ms E. Morris, *Lab.* 14,884
*A. D. G. Bevan, *C.* 14,722
J. Hemming, *LD* 12,899
Miss P. Read, *NF* 192
Lab. majority 162
(June 1987, C. maj. 2,522)

BISHOP AUCKLAND (Durham)
E.72,572 T.76.52%
*D. Foster, *Lab.* 27,763
D. Williamson, *C.* 17,676
W. Wade, *LD* 10,099
Lab. majority 10,087
(June 1987, Lab. maj. 7,035)

BLABY (Leics)
E.81,790 T.83.39%
A. Robathan, *C.* 39,498
Ms E. Ranson, *Lab.* 14,151
Ms M. Lewin, *LD* 13,780

J. Peacock, *BNP* 521
Ms S. Lincoln, *NLP* 260
C. majority 25,347
(June 1987, C. maj. 22,176)

BLACKBURN (Lancs)
E.73,251 T.75.05%
*J. Straw, *Lab.* 26,633
R. Coates, *C.* 20,606
D. Mann, *LD* 6,332
R. Field, *Green* 878
Mrs M. Carmichael-Grimshaw, *LP* 334
W. Ayliffe, *NLP* 195
Lab. majority 6,027
(June 1987, Lab. maj. 5,497)

BLACKPOOL NORTH (Lancs)
E.58,087 T.77.55%
H. Elletson, *C.* 21,501
E. Kirton, *Lab.* 18,461
A. Lahiff, *LD* 4,786
Sir G. Francis, *Loony* 178
H. Walker, *NLP* 125
C. majority 3,040
(June 1987, C. maj. 7,321)

BLACKPOOL SOUTH (Lancs)
E.56,801 T.77.35%
N. Hawkins, *C.* 19,880
G. Marsden, *Lab.* 18,213
R. Wynne, *LD* 5,675
D. Henning, *NLP* 173
C. majority 1,667
(June 1987, C. maj. 6,744)

BLAYDON (Tyne & Wear)
E.66,044 T.77.69%
*J. McWilliam, *Lab.* 27,028
P. Pescod, *C.* 13,685
P. Nunn, *LD* 10,602
Lab. majority 13,343
(June 1987, Lab. maj. 12,488)

BLYTH VALLEY (Northumberland)
E.60,913 T.80.77%
*R. Campbell, *Lab.* 24,542
P. Tracey, *LD* 16,498
M. Revell, *C.* 7,691
S. Tyley, *Green* 470
Lab. majority 8,044
(June 1987, Lab. maj. 853)

BOLSOVER (Derbys)
E.66,693 T.78.94%
*D. Skinner, *Lab.* 33,973
T. James, *C.* 13,313
Ms S. Barber, *LD* 5,363
Lab. majority 20,660
(June 1987, Lab. maj. 14,120)

BOLTON NORTH EAST (Greater
Manchester)
E.58,659 T.82.26%
*P. Thurnham, *C.* 21,644
D. Crausby, *Lab.* 21,459
B. Dunning, *LD* 4,971
P. Tong, *NLP* 181
C. majority 185
(June 1987, C. maj. 813)

BOLTON SOUTH EAST (Greater Manchester)
E.65,600   T.75.53%
*D. Young, *Lab.* — 26,906
N. Wood-Dow, *C.* — 14,215
D. Lee, *LD* — 5,243
W. Hardman, *Ind. Lab.* — 2,894
L. Walch, *NLP* — 290
Lab. majority — 12,691
(June 1987, Lab. maj. 11,381)

BOLTON WEST (Greater Manchester)
E.71,344   T.83.53%
*Hon. T. Sackville, *C.* — 26,452
C. Morris, *Lab.* — 25,373
Ms B. Ronson, *LD* — 7,529
Ms J. Phillips, *NLP* — 240
C. majority — 1,079
(June 1987, C. maj. 4,593)

BOOTHFERRY (Humberside)
E.80,747   T.79.73%
*D. Davis, *C.* — 35,266
Ms L. Coubrough, *Lab.* — 17,731
J. Goss, *LD* — 11,388
C. majority — 17,535
(June 1987, C. maj. 18,970)

BOOTLE (Merseyside)
E.69,308   T.72.46%
*J. Benton, *Lab.* — 37,464
C. Varley, *C.* — 8,022
J. Cunningham, *LD* — 3,301
Ms M. Hall, *Lib.* — 1,174
T. Haynes, *NLP* — 264
Lab. majority — 29,442
(June 1987, Lab. maj. 24,477)
(May 1990, Lab. maj. 23,517)
(November 1990, Lab. maj. 19,465)

BOSWORTH (Leics)
E.80,234   T.84.13%
*D. Tredinnick, *C.* — 36,618
D. Everitt, *Lab.* — 17,524
G. Drozdz, *LD* — 12,643
B. Fewster, *Green* — 716
C. majority — 19,094
(June 1987, C. maj. 17,016)

BOURNEMOUTH EAST (Dorset)
E.75,089   T.72.82%
*D. Atkinson, *C.* — 30,820
N. Russell, *LD* — 15,997
P. Brushett, *Lab.* — 7,541
Ms S. Holmes, *NLP* — 329
C. majority — 14,823
(June 1987, C. maj. 14,683)

BOURNEMOUTH WEST (Dorset)
E.74,738   T.75.72%
*J. Butterfill, *C.* — 29,820
Ms J. Dover, *LD* — 17,178
B. Grower, *Lab.* — 9,423
A. Springham, *NLP* — 232
C. majority — 12,642
(June 1987, C. maj. 12,651)

BOW AND POPLAR (Greater London)
E.56,685   T.65.84%
*Mrs M. Gordon, *Lab.* — 18,487
P. Hughes, *LD* — 10,083
S. Pearce, *C.* — 6,876

J. Tyndall, *BNP* — 1,107
S. Petter, *Green* — 612
W. Hite, *NLP* — 158
Lab. majority — 8,404
(June 1987, Lab. maj. 4,631)

BRADFORD NORTH (W. Yorks)
E.66,719   T.73.38%
*T. Rooney, *Lab.* — 23,420
M. Riaz, *C.* — 15,756
D. Ward, *LD* — 9,133
W. Beckett, *Loony* — 350
M. Nasr, *Islamic* — 304
Lab. majority — 7,664
(June 1987, Lab. maj. 1,663)
(November 1990, Lab. maj. 9,514)

BRADFORD SOUTH (W. Yorks)
E.69,914   T.75.61%
*G. R. Cryer, *Lab.* — 25,185
A. Popat, *C.* — 20,283
B. Boulton, *LD* — 7,243
M. Naseem, *Islamic* — 156
Lab. majority — 4,902
(June 1987, Lab. maj. 309)
See also page 234

BRADFORD WEST (W. Yorks)
E.70,016   T.69.90%
*M. Madden, *Lab.* — 26,046
Dr A. Ashworth, *C.* — 16,544
Dr. A. Griffiths, *LD* — 5,150
P. Braham, *Green* — 735
D. Pidcock, *Islamic* — 471
Lab. majority — 9,502
(June 1987, Lab. maj. 7,551)

BRAINTREE (Essex)
E.78,880   T.83.41%
*Rt. Hon. A. Newton, *C.* — 34,415
I. Willmore, *Lab.* — 16,921
Ms D. Wallis, *LD* — 13,603
J. Abbott, *Green* — 855
C. majority — 17,494
(June 1987, C. maj. 16,857)

BRENT EAST (Greater London)
E.53,319   T.68.82%
*K. Livingstone, *Lab.* — 19,387
D. Green, *C.* — 13,416
M. Cummins, *LD* — 3,249
Ms T. Dean, *Green* — 548
Ms A. Murphy, *Comm. GB* — 96
Lab. majority — 5,971
(June 1987, Lab. maj. 1,653)

BRENT NORTH (Greater London)
E.58,917   T.70.57%
*Rt. Hon. Sir R. Boyson, *C.* — 23,445
J. Moher, *Lab.* — 13,314
P. Lorber, *LD* — 4,149
T. Vipul, *Ind.* — 356
T. Davids, *NLP* — 318
C. majority — 10,131
(June 1987, C. maj. 15,720)

BRENT SOUTH (Greater London)
E.56,034   T.64.10%
*P. Boateng, *Lab.* — 20,662
R. Blackman, *C.* — 10,957
M. Harskin, *LD* — 3,658
D. Johnson, *Green* — 479
C. Jani, *NLP* — 166

Lab. majority — 9,705
(June 1987, Lab. maj. 7,931)

BRENTFORD AND ISLEWORTH (Greater London)
E.70,880   T.76.22%
N. Deva, *C.* — 24,752
Ms A. Keen, *Lab.* — 22,666
Ms J. Salmon, *LD* — 5,683
J. Bradley, *Green* — 927
C. majority — 2,086
(June 1987, C. maj. 7,953)

BRENTWOOD AND ONGAR (Greater London)
E.65,830   T.84.70%
E. Pickles, *C.* — 32,145
Ms E. Bottomley, *LD* — 17,000
F. Keohane, *Lab.* — 6,080
Ms C. Bartley, *Green* — 535
C. majority — 15,145
(June 1987, C. maj. 18,921)

BRIDGWATER (Somerset)
E.71,567   T.79.51%
*Rt. Hon. T. King, *C.* — 26,610
W. Revans, *LD* — 16,894
P. James, *Lab.* — 12,365
G. Dummett, *Green* — 746
A. Body, *Ind.* — 183
Ms G. Sanson, *NLP* — 112
C. majority — 9,716
(June 1987, C. maj. 11,195)

BRIDLINGTON (Humberside)
E.84,829   T.77.93%
*J. Townend, *C.* — 33,604
J. Leeman, *LD* — 17,246
S. Hatfield, *Lab.* — 15,263
C. majority — 16,358
(June 1987, C. maj. 17,321)

BRIGG AND CLEETHORPES (Humberside)
E.82,377   T.77.98%
*M. Brown, *C.* — 31,673
I. Cawsey, *Lab.* — 22,404
Ms M. Cockbill, *LD* — 9,374
N. Jacques, *Green* — 790
C. majority — 9,269
(June 1987, C. maj. 12,250)

BRIGHTON KEMPTOWN (E. Sussex)
E.57,646   T.76.14%
*A. Bowden, *C.* — 21,129
Ms G. Haynes, *Lab.* — 18,073
P. Scott, *LD* — 4,461
Ms E. Overall, *NLP* — 230
C. majority — 3,056
(June 1987, C. maj. 9,260)

BRIGHTON PAVILION (E. Sussex)
E.57,616   T.76.81%
D. Spencer, *C.* — 20,630
D. Lepper, *Lab.* — 16,955
T. Pearce, *LD* — 5,606
I. Brodie, *Green* — 963
Ms E. Turner, *NLP* — 103
C. majority — 3,675
(June 1987, C. maj. 9,142)

BRISTOL EAST (Avon)
E.62,577   T.80.40%
Ms J. Corston, *Lab.* — 22,418
*J. Sayeed, *C.* — 19,726
J. Kiely, *LD* — 7,903
I. Anderson, *NF* — 270
Lab. majority — 2,692
(June 1987, C. maj. 4,123)

BRISTOL NORTH WEST (Avon)
E.72,726   T.82.35%
*M. Stern, *C.* — 25,354
D. Naysmith, *Lab.* — 25,309
J. Taylor, *LD* — 8,498
H. Long, *SD* — 729
C. majority — 45
(June 1987, C. maj. 6,952)

BRISTOL SOUTH (Avon)
E.64,309   T.78.04%
*Ms D. Primarolo, *Lab.* — 25,164
J. Bercow, *C.* — 16,245
P. Crossley, *LD* — 7,892
J. Boxall, *Green* — 756
N. Phillips, *NLP* — 136
Lab. majority — 8,919
(June 1987, Lab. maj. 1,404)

BRISTOL WEST (Avon)
E.70,579   T.74.37%
*Rt. Hon. W. Waldegrave, *C.* — 22,169
C. Boney, *LD* — 16,098
H. Bashforth, *Lab.* — 12,992
A. Sawday, *Green* — 906
D. Cross, *NLP* — 104
B. Brent, *Rev. Comm.* — 92
P. Hammond, *SOADDA* — 87
T. Hedges, *Anti Fed.* — 42
C. majority — 6,071
(June 1987, C. maj. 7,703)

BROMSGROVE (H & W)
E.71,111   T.82.49%
K. R. Thomason, *C.* — 31,709
Ms C. Mole, *Lab.* — 18,007
Ms A. Cassin, *LD* — 8,090
J. Churchman, *Green* — 856
C. majority — 13,702
(June 1987, C. maj. 16,685)

BROXBOURNE (Herts)
E.72,116   T.79.95%
*Mrs M. Roe, *C.* — 36,094
M. Hudson, *Lab.* — 12,124
Mrs J. Davies, *LD* — 9,244
G. Woolhouse, *NLP* — 198
C. majority — 23,970
(June 1987, C. maj. 22,995)

BROXTOWE (Notts)
E.73,123   T.83.40%
*J. Lester, *C.* — 31,096
J. Walker, *Lab.* — 21,205
J. Ross, *LD* — 8,395
D. Lukehurst, *NLP* — 293
C. majority — 9,891
(June 1987, C. maj. 16,651)

BUCKINGHAM
E.56,063   T.84.21%
*G. Walden, *C.* — 29,496
T. Jones, *LD* — 9,705
K. White, *Lab.* — 7,662

L. Sheaff, *NLP* — 353
C. majority — 19,791
(June 1987, C. maj. 18,526)

BURNLEY (Lancs)
E.68,952   T.74.38%
*P. Pike, *Lab.* — 27,184
Mrs B. Binge, *C.* — 15,693
G. Birtwistle, *LD* — 8,414
Lab. majority — 11,491
(June 1987, Lab. maj. 7,557)

BURTON (Staffs)
E.75,292   T.82.43%
*I. Lawrence, *C.* — 30,845
Ms P. Muddyman, *Lab.* — 24,849
R. Renold, *LD* — 6,375
C. majority — 5,996
(June 1987, C. maj. 9,830)

BURY NORTH (Greater Manchester)
E.69,529   T.84.77%
*A. Burt, *C.* — 29,266
J. Dobbin, *Lab.* — 24,502
C. McGrath, *LD* — 5,010
M. Sullivan, *NLP* — 163
C. majority — 4,764
(June 1987, C. maj. 6,929)

BURY SOUTH (Greater Manchester)
E.65,793   T.82.10%
*D. Sumberg, *C.* — 24,873
Ms H. Blears, *Lab.* — 24,085
A. Cruden, *LD* — 4,832
Mrs N. Sullivan, *NLP* — 228
C. majority — 788
(June 1987, C. maj. 2,679)

BURY ST EDMUNDS (Suffolk)
E.79,967   T.78.38%
R. Spring, *C.* — 33,554
T. Sheppard, *Lab.* — 14,767
J. Williams, *LD* — 13,814
Ms J. Lillis, *NLP* — 550
C. majority — 18,787
(June 1987, C. maj. 21,458)

CALDER VALLEY (W. Yorks)
E.74,417   T.82.09%
*Sir D. Thompson, *C.* — 27,753
D. Chaytor, *Lab.* — 22,875
S. Pearson, *LD* — 9,842
Ms V. Smith, *Green* — 622
C. majority — 4,878
(June 1987, C. maj. 6,045)

CAMBRIDGE
E.69,022   T.73.18%
Mrs A. Campbell, *Lab.* — 20,039
M. Bishop, *C.* — 19,459
D. Howarth, *LD* — 10,037
T. Cooper, *Green* — 720
D. Brettell-Winnington, *Loony* — 175
R. Chalmers, *NLP* — 83
Lab. majority — 580
(June 1987, C. maj. 5,060)

CAMBRIDGESHIRE NORTH EAST
E.79,935   T.79.38%
*M. Moss, *C.* — 34,288
M. Leeke, *LD* — 19,195
R. Harris, *Lab.* — 8,746
C. Ash, *Lib.* — 998
Mrs M. Chalmers, *NLP* — 227

C. majority — 15,093
(June 1987, C. maj. 1,428)

CAMBRIDGESHIRE SOUTH EAST
E.78,600   T.80.57%
*J. Paice, *C.* — 36,693
R. Wotherspoon, *LD* — 12,883
M. Jones, *Lab.* — 12,688
J. Marsh, *Green* — 836
Ms B. Langridge, *NLP* — 231
C. majority — 23,810
(June 1987, C. maj. 17,502)

CAMBRIDGESHIRE SOUTH WEST
E.84,418   T.81.10%
*Sir A. Grant, *C.* — 38,902
Ms S. Sutton, *LD* — 19,265
K. Price, *Lab.* — 9,378
Ms L. Whitebread, *Green* — 699
F. Chalmers, *NLP* — 225
C. majority — 19,637
(June 1987, C. maj. 18,251)

CANNOCK AND BURNTWOOD
(Staffs)
E.72,600   T.84.21%
A. Wright, *Lab.* — 28,139
*G. Howarth, *C.* — 26,633
P. Treasaden, *LD* — 5,899
M. Hartshorne, *Loony* — 469
Lab. majority — 1,506
(June 1987, C. maj. 2,689)

CANTERBURY (Kent)
E.75,181   T.78.12%
*J. Brazier, *C.* — 29,827
M. Vye, *LD* — 19,022
M. Whitemore, *Lab.* — 8,936
Ms W. Arnall, *Green* — 747
Ms S. Curphey, *NLP* — 203
C. majority — 10,805
(June 1987, C. maj. 14,891)

CARLISLE (Cumbria)
E.55,140   T.79.39%
*E. Martlew, *Lab.* — 20,479
C. Condie, *C.* — 17,371
R. Aldersey, *LD* — 5,740
Ms N. Robinson, *NLP* — 190
Lab. majority — 3,108
(June 1987, Lab. maj. 916)

CARSHALTON AND WALLINGTON
(Surrey)
E.65,179   T.80.94%
*F. N. Forman, *C.* — 26,243
T. Brake, *LD* — 16,300
Ms M. Moran, *Lab.* — 9,333
R. Steel, *Green* — 614
D. Bamford, *Loony G.* — 266
C. majority — 9,943
(June 1987, C. maj. 14,409)

CASTLE POINT (Essex)
E.66,229   T.80.50%
Dr R. Spink, *C.* — 29,629
D. Flack, *Lab.* — 12,799
A. Petchey, *LD* — 10,208
Ms I. Willis, *Green* — 683
C. majority — 16,830
(June 1987, C. maj. 19,248)

CHEADLE (Greater Manchester)
E.66,131   T.84.43%
*S. Day, C.   32,504
Ms P. Calton, LD   16,726
Ms S. Broadhurst, Lab.   6,442
Ms P. Whittle, NLP   168
C. majority   15,778
(June 1987, C. maj. 10,631)

CHELMSFORD (Essex)
E.83,441   T.84.61%
*S. Burns, C.   39,043
H. Nicholson, LD   20,783
Dr R. Chad, Lab.   10,010
Ms E. Burgess, Green   769
C. majority   18,260
(June 1987, C. maj. 7,761)

CHELSEA (Greater London)
E.42,371   T.63.31%
*Rt. Hon. N. Scott, C.   17,471
Ms R. Horton, Lab.   4,682
Ms S. Broidy, LD   4,101
Ms N. Kortvelyessy, Green   485
D. Armstrong, Anti Fed.   88
C. majority   12,789
(June 1987, C. maj. 13,319)

CHELTENHAM (Glos)
E.79,808   T.80.32%
N. Jones, LD   30,351
J. Taylor, C.   28,683
Ms P. Tatlow, Lab.   4,077
M. Rendall, AFE   665
H. Brighouse, NLP   169
M. Bruce-Smith, Ind.   162
LD majority   1,668
(June 1987, C. maj. 4,896)

CHERTSEY AND WALTON (Surrey)
E.70,465   T.80.52%
*Rt. Hon. Sir G. Pattie, C.   34,163
A. Kremer, LD   11,344
Ms I. Hamilton, Lab.   10,791
Ms S. Bennell, NLP   444
C. majority   22,819
(June 1987, C. maj. 17,469)

CHESHAM AND AMERSHAM (Bucks)
E.69,895   T.81.93%
Ms C. Gillan, C.   36,273
A. Ketteringham, LD   14,053
Ms C. Atherton, Lab.   5,931
Ms C. Strickland, Green   753
T. Griffith-Jones, NLP   255
C. majority   22,220
(June 1987, C. maj. 19,440)

CHESTER, CITY OF
E.63,370   T.83.84%
G. Brandreth, C.   23,411
D. Robinson, Lab.   22,310
G. Smith, LD   6,867
T. Barker, Green   448
S. Cross, NLP   98
C. majority   1,101
(June 1987, C. maj. 4,855)

CHESTERFIELD (Derbys)
E.71,783   T.77.98%
*A. Benn, Lab.   26,461
A. Rogers, LD   20,047
P. Lewis, C.   9,473

Lab. majority   6,414
(June 1987, Lab. maj. 8,577)

CHICHESTER (W. Sussex)
E.82,124   T.77.77%
*R. A. Nelson, C.   37,906
P. Gardiner, LD   17,019
Ms D. Andrewes, Lab.   7,192
E. Paine, Green   876
Ms J. Weights, Lib.   643
Ms J. Jackson, NLP   238
C. majority   20,887
(June 1987, C. maj. 20,177)

CHINGFORD (Greater London)
E.55,401   T.78.41%
G. I. Duncan-Smith, C.   25,730
P. Dawe, Lab.   10,792
S. Banks, LD   5,705
D. Green, Lib.   602
J. Baguley, Green   575
Revd C. John, Ind.   41
C. majority   14,938
(June 1987, C. maj. 17,955)

CHIPPING BARNET (Greater London)
E.57,153   T.78.57%
*S. Chapman, C.   25,589
A. Williams, Lab.   11,638
D. Smith, LD   7,247
Ms D. Derksen, NLP   222
C. Johnson, Fun.   213
C. majority   13,951
(June 1987, C. maj. 14,871)

CHISLEHURST (Greater London)
E.53,782   T.78.89%
*R. Sims, C.   24,761
I. Wingfield, Lab.   9,485
W. Hawthorne, LD   6,683
I. Richmond, Lib.   849
Dr F. Speed, Green   652
C. majority   15,276
(June 1987, C. maj. 14,507)

CHORLEY (Lancs)
E.78,531   T.82.81%
*D. Dover, C.   30,715
R. McManus, Lab.   26,469
Ms J. Ross-Mills, LD   7,452
P. Leadbetter, NLP   402
C. majority   4,246
(June 1987, C. maj. 8,057)

CHRISTCHURCH (Dorset)
E.71,438   T.80.70%
*R. Adley, C.   36,627
Revd D. Bussey, LD   13,612
A. Lloyd, Lab.   6,997
J. Barratt, NLP   243
A. Wareham, CRA   175
C. majority   23,015
(June 1987, C. maj. 22,374)
See also page 234

CIRENCESTER AND TEWKESBURY (Glos)
E.88,299   T.82.05%
G. Clifton-Brown, C.   40,258
E. Weston, LD   24,200
T. Page, Lab.   7,262
R. Clayton, NLP   449

P. Trice-Rolph, Ind.   287
C. majority   16,058
(June 1987, C. maj. 12,662)

CITY OF LONDON AND WESTMINSTER SOUTH
E.55,021   T.63.08%
*Rt. Hon. P. Brooke, C.   20,938
C. Smith, Lab.   7,569
Ms J. Smithard, LD   5,392
G. Herbert, Green   458
P. Stockton, Loony   147
A. Farrell, IFM   107
R. Johnson, NLP   101
C. majority   13,369
(June 1987, C. maj. 12,034)

COLCHESTER NORTH (Essex)
E.86,479   T.79.11%
Hon. B. Jenkin, C.   35,213
Dr J. Raven, LD   18,721
D. Lee, Lab.   13,870
M. Tariq Shabbeer, Green   372
M. Mears, NLP   238
C. majority   16,492
(June 1987, C. maj. 13,623)

COLCHESTER SOUTH AND MALDON (Essex)
E.86,410   T.79.22%
J. Whittingdale, C.   37,548
I. Thorn, LD   15,727
C. Pearson, Lab.   14,158
M. Patterson, Green   1,028
C. majority   21,821
(June 1987, C. maj. 15,483)

COLNE VALLEY (W. Yorks)
E.72,043   T.81.97%
*G. Riddick, C.   24,804
J. Harman, Lab.   17,579
N. Priestley, LD   15,953
R. Stewart, Green   443
Mrs M. Staniforth, Loony   160
J. Hasty, Ind.   73
J. Tattersall, NLP   44
C. majority   7,225
(June 1987, C. maj. 1,677)

CONGLETON (Cheshire)
E.70,477   T.84.47%
*Mrs J. A. Winterton, C.   29,163
I. Brodie-Browne, LD   18,043
M. Finnegan, Lab.   11,927
P. Brown, NLP   399
C. majority   11,120
(June 1987, C. maj. 7,969)

COPELAND (Cumbria)
E.54,911   T.83.54%
*Dr J. Cunningham, Lab.   22,328
P. Davies, C.   19,889
R. Putnam, LD   3,508
J. Sinton, NLP   148
Lab. majority   2,439
(June 1987, Lab. maj. 1,894)

CORBY (Northants)
E.68,333   T.82.88%
*W. Powell, C.   25,203
A. Feather, Lab.   24,861
M. Roffe, LD   5,792
Ms J. Wood, Lib.   784

C. majority 342
(June 1987, C. maj. 1,805)

CORNWALL NORTH
E.76,844   T.81.51%
*P. Tyler, LD 29,696
*Sir G. Neale, C. 27,775
F. Jordan, Lab. 4,103
P. Andrews, Lib. 678
G. Rowe, Ind. 276
Mrs H. Treadwell, NLP 112
LD majority 1,921
(June 1987, C. maj. 5,682)

CORNWALL SOUTH EAST
E.73,027   T.82.14%
*R. Hicks, C. 30,565
R. Teverson, LD 22,861
Mrs L. Gilroy, Lab. 5,536
Miss M. Cook, Lib. 644
A. Quick, Anti Fed. 227
Miss R. Allen, NLP 155
C. majority 7,704
(June 1987, C. maj. 6,607)

COVENTRY NORTH EAST
(W. Midlands)
E.64,787   T.73.20%
R. Ainsworth, Lab. 24,896
K. Perrin, C. 13,220
V. McKee, LD 5,306
*J. Hughes, Ind. Lab. 4,008
Lab. majority 11,676
(June 1987, Lab. maj. 11,867)

COVENTRY NORTH WEST
(W. Midlands)
E.50,670   T.77.63%
*G. Robinson, Lab. 20,349
Mrs A. Hill, C. 13,917
Ms A. Simpson, LD 5,070
Lab. majority 6,432
(June 1987, Lab. maj. 5,663)

COVENTRY SOUTH EAST
(W. Midlands)
E.48,796   T.74.87%
J. Cunningham, Lab. 11,902
Mrs M. Hyams, C. 10,591
*D. Nellist, Ind. Lab. 10,551
A. Armstrong, LD 3,318
N. Tompkinson, NF 173
Lab. majority 1,311
(June 1987, Lab. maj. 6,653)

COVENTRY SOUTH WEST
(W. Midlands)
E.63,474   T.80.14%
*J. Butcher, C. 23,225
R. Slater, Lab. 21,789
G. Sewards, LD 4,666
R. Wheway, Lib. 989
D. Morris, NLP 204
C. majority 1,436
(June 1987, C. maj. 3,210)

CRAWLEY (W. Sussex)
E.78,277   T.79.16%
*Hon. A. N. Soames, C. 30,204
Ms L. Moffatt, Lab. 22,439
G. Seekings, LD 8,558
M. Wilson, Green 766

C. majority 7,765
(June 1987, C. maj. 12,138)

CREWE AND NANTWICH (Cheshire)
E.74,993   T.81.87%
*Hon. Mrs G. Dunwoody, Lab. 65
B. Silvester, C. 25,370
G. Griffiths, LD 7,315
Ms N. Wilkinson, Green 651
Lab. majority 2,695
(June 1987, Lab. maj. 1,092)

CROSBY (Merseyside)
E.82,537   T.82.45%
*M. Thornton, C. 32,267
Ms M. Eagle, Lab. 17,461
Ms F. Clucas, LD 16,562
J. Marks, Lib. 1,052
S. Brady, Green 559
N. Paterson, NLP 152
C. majority 14,806
(June 1987, C. maj. 6,853)

CROYDON CENTRAL (Greater
London)
E.55,798   T.71.73%
Sir P. Beresford, C. 22,168
G. Davies, Lab. 12,518
Ms D. Richardson, LD 5,342
C. majority 9,650
(June 1987, C. maj. 12,617)

CROYDON NORTH EAST (Greater
London)
E.64,405   T.72.01%
D. Congdon, C. 23,835
Ms M. Walker, Lab. 16,362
J. Fraser, LD 6,186
C. majority 7,473
(June 1987, C. maj. 12,519)

CROYDON NORTH WEST (Greater
London)
E.57,241   T.70.76%
M. Wicks, Lab. 19,152
*H. Malins, C. 17,626
Ms L. Hawkins, LD 3,728
Lab. majority 1,526
(June 1987, C. maj. 3,988)

CROYDON SOUTH (Greater London)
E.64,768   T.77.57%
R. Ottaway, C. 31,993
P. Billenness, LD 11,568
Miss H. Salmon, Lab. 6,444
M. Samuel, Choice 239
C. majority 20,425
(June 1987, C. maj. 19,063)

DAGENHAM (Greater London)
E.59,645   T.70.65%
*B. Gould, Lab. 22,027
D. Rossiter, C. 15,294
C. Marquand, LD 4,824
Lab. majority 6,733
(June 1987, Lab. maj. 2,469)
See also page 234

DARLINGTON (Durham)
E.66,094   T.83.60%
A. Milburn, Lab. 26,556
*M. Fallon, C. 23,758
P. Bergg, LD 4,586

Dr D. Clarke, BNP 355
Lab. majority 2,798
(June 1987, C. maj. 2,661)

DARTFORD (Kent)
E.72,366   T.83.14%
*B. Dunn, C. 31,194
Dr H. Stoate, Lab. 20,880
Dr P. Bryden, LD 7,584
A. Munro, FDP 262
Ms A. Holland, NLP 247
C. majority 10,314
(June 1987, C. maj. 14,929)

DAVENTRY (Northants)
E.71,824   T.82.75%
*T. Boswell, C. 34,734
Ms L. Koumi, Lab. 14,460
A. Rounthwaite, LD 9,820
R. France, NLP 422
C. majority 20,274
(June 1987, C. maj. 19,690)

DAVYHULME (Greater Manchester)
E.61,679   T.81.82%
*W. Churchill, C. 24,216
B. Brotherton, Lab. 19,790
Ms J. Pearcey, LD 5,797
T. Brotheridge, NLP 665
C. majority 4,426
(June 1987, C. maj. 8,199)

DENTON AND REDDISH (Greater
Manchester)
E.68,463   T.76.77%
*A. Bennett, Lab. 29,021
J. Horswell, C. 16,937
Dr F. Ridley, LD 4,953
M. Powell, Lib. 1,296
J. Fuller, NLP 354
Lab. majority 12,084
(June 1987, Lab. maj. 8,250)

DERBY NORTH
E.73,176   T.80.65%
*G. Knight, C. 28,574
R. Laxton, Lab. 24,121
R. Charlesworth, LD 5,638
E. Wall, Green 383
P. Hart, NF 245
N. Onley, NLP 58
C. majority 4,453
(June 1987, C. maj. 6,280)

DERBY SOUTH
E.66,328   T.75.52%
*Mrs M. Beckett, Lab. 25,917
N. Brown, C. 18,981
S. Hartropp, LD 5,198
Lab. majority 6,936
(June 1987, Lab. maj. 1,516)

DERBYSHIRE NORTH EAST
E.70,707   T.83.61%
*H. Barnes, Lab. 28,860
J. Hayes, C. 22,590
D. Stone, LD 7,675
Lab. majority 6,270
(June 1987, Lab. maj. 3,720)

DERBYSHIRE SOUTH
E.82,342   T.85.49%
*Mrs E. Currie, C. 34,266
M. Todd, Lab. 29,608

Ms D. Brass, *LD* — 6,236
T. Mercer, *NLP* — 291
C. majority — 4,658
(June 1987, C. maj. 10,311)

DERBYSHIRE WEST
*E.*71,201   *T.*84.99%
*P. McLoughlin, *C.* — 32,879
R. Fearn, *LD* — 14,110
S. Clamp, *Lab.* — 13,528
C. majority — 18,769
(June 1987, C. maj. 10,527)

DEVIZES (Wilts)
*E.*89,745   *T.*81.67%
M. Ancram, *C.* — 39,090
Ms J. Mactaggart, *LD* — 19,378
Ms R. Berry, *Lab.* — 13,060
S. Coles, *Lib.* — 962
D. Ripley, *Green* — 808
C. majority — 19,712
(June 1987, C. maj. 17,830)

DEVON NORTH
*E.*68,998   *T.*84.36%
N. Harvey, *LD* — 27,414
*A. Speller, *C.* — 26,620
P. Donner, *Lab.* — 3,410
Ms C. Simmons, *Green* — 658
G. Treadwell, *NLP* — 107
LD majority — 794
(June 1987, C. maj. 4,469)

DEVON WEST AND TORRIDGE
*E.*76,933   *T.*81.46%
*Miss E. Nicholson, *C.* — 29,627
D. McBride, *LD* — 26,013
D. Brenton, *Lab.* — 5,997
Dr F. Williamson, *Green* — 898
D. Collins, *NLP* — 141
C. majority — 3,614
(June 1987, C. maj. 6,468)

DEWSBURY (W. Yorks)
*E.*72,839   *T.*80.18%
*Mrs W. A. Taylor, *Lab.* — 25,596
J. Whitfield, *C.* — 24,962
R. Meadowcroft, *LD* — 6,570
Lady J. Birdwood, *BNP* — 660
N. Denby, *Green* — 471
Mrs J. Marsden, *NLP* — 146
Lab. majority — 634
(June 1987, Lab. maj. 445)

DONCASTER CENTRAL (S. Yorks)
*E.*68,890   *T.*74.24%
*Rt. Hon. H. Walker, *Lab.* — 27,795
W. Glossop, *C.* — 17,113
C. Hampson, *LD* — 6,057
M. Driver, *WRP* — 184
Lab. majority — 10,682
(June 1987, Lab. maj. 8,196)

DONCASTER NORTH (S. Yorks)
*E.*74,732   *T.*73.92%
K. Hughes, *Lab.* — 34,135
R. Light, *C.* — 14,322
S. Whiting, *LD* — 6,787
Lab. majority — 19,813
(June 1987, Lab. maj. 19,938)

DON VALLEY (S. Yorks)
*E.*76,327   *T.*76.25%
*M. Redmond, *Lab.* — 32,008

N. Paget-Brown, *C.* — 18,474
M. Jevons, *LD* — 6,920
S. Platt, *Green* — 803
Lab. majority — 13,534
(June 1987, Lab. maj. 11,467)

DORSET NORTH
*E.*76,718   *T.*81.79%
*N. Baker, *C.* — 34,234
Ms L. Siegle, *LD* — 24,154
J. Fitzmaurice, *Lab.* — 4,360
C. majority — 10,080
(June 1987, C. maj. 11,907)

DORSET SOUTH
*E.*75,788   *T.*76.91%
*I. Bruce, *C.* — 29,319
B. Ellis, *LD* — 15,811
Dr A. Chedzoy, *Lab.* — 12,298
Mrs J. Nager, *Ind.* — 673
M. Griffiths, *NLP* — 191
C. majority — 13,508
(June 1987, C. maj. 15,067)

DORSET WEST
*E.*67,256   *T.*81.18%
*Sir J. Spicer, *C.* — 27,766
R. Legg, *LD* — 19,756
J. Mann, *Lab.* — 7,082
C. majority — 8,010
(June 1987, C. maj. 12,364)

DOVER (Kent)
*E.*68,962   *T.*83.50%
*D. Shaw, *C.* — 25,395
G. Prosser, *Lab.* — 24,562
M. Sole, *LD* — 6,212
A. Sullivan, *Green* — 637
P. Sherred, *Ind.* — 407
B. Philp, *Ind. C.* — 250
C. Percy, *NLP* — 127
C. majority — 833
(June 1987, C. maj. 6,541)

DUDLEY EAST (W. Midlands)
*E.*75,355   *T.*74.96%
*Dr J. Gilbert, *Lab.* — 29,806
J. Holland, *C.* — 20,606
I. Jenkins, *LD* — 5,400
G. Cartwright, *NF* — 675
Lab. majority — 9,200
(June 1987, Lab. maj. 3,473)

DUDLEY WEST (W. Midlands)
*E.*86,632   *T.*82.08%
*J. Blackburn, *C.* — 34,729
K. Lomax, *Lab.* — 28,940
G. Lewis, *LD* — 7,446
C. majority — 5,789
(June 1987, C. maj. 10,244)
See also page 234

DULWICH (Greater London)
*E.*55,141   *T.*67.91%
Ms T. Jowell, *Lab.* — 17,714
*G. Bowden, *C.* — 15,658
Dr A. Goldie, *LD* — 4,078
Lab. majority — 2,056
(June 1987, C. maj. 180)

DURHAM, CITY OF
*E.*68,165   *T.*74.61%
*G. Steinberg, *Lab.* — 27,095
M. Woodroofe, *C.* — 12,037

N. Martin, *LD* — 10,915
Ms S. J. Banks, *Green* — 812
Lab. majority — 15,058
(June 1987, Lab. maj. 6,125)

DURHAM NORTH
*E.*73,694   *T.*76.08%
*G. Radice, *Lab.* — 33,567
Ms E. Sibley, *C.* — 13,930
P. Appleby, *LD* — 8,572
Lab. majority — 19,637
(June 1987, Lab. maj. 18,433)

DURHAM NORTH WEST
*E.*61,139   *T.*75.58%
*Miss H. Armstrong, *Lab.* — 26,734
Mrs T. May, *C.* — 12,747
T. Farron, *LD* — 6,728
Lab. majority — 13,987
(June 1987, Lab. maj. 10,162)

EALING ACTON (Greater London)
*E.*58,687   *T.*76.03%
*Sir G. Young, *C.* — 22,579
Ms Y. Johnson, *Lab.* — 15,572
L. Rowe, *LD* — 5,487
Ms A. Seibe, *Green* — 554
T. Pitt-Aikens, *Ind. C.* — 432
C. majority — 7,007
(June 1987, C. maj. 12,233)

EALING NORTH (Greater London)
*E.*63,528   *T.*78.84%
*H. Greenway, *C.* — 24,898
M. Stears, *Lab.* — 18,932
P. Hankinson, *LD* — 5,247
D. Earl, *Green* — 554
C. Hill, *NF* — 277
R. Davis, *CD* — 180
C. majority — 5,966
(June 1987, C. maj. 15,153)

EALING SOUTHALL (Greater London)
*E.*65,574   *T.*75.49%
P. Khabra, *Lab.* — 23,476
P. Treleaven, *C.* — 16,610
*S. Bidwell, *True Lab.* — 4,665
Ms P. Nandhra, *LD* — 3,790
N. Goodwin, *Green* — 964
Lab. majority — 6,866
(June 1987, Lab. maj. 7,977)

EASINGTON (Durham)
*E.*65,061   *T.*72.46%
*J. Cummings, *Lab.* — 34,269
W. Perry, *C.* — 7,879
P. Freitag, *LD* — 5,001
Lab. majority — 26,390
(June 1987, Lab. maj. 24,639)

EASTBOURNE (E. Sussex)
*E.*76,103   *T.*80.97%
N. Waterson, *C.* — 31,792
*D. Bellotti, *LD* — 26,311
I. Gibbons, *Lab.* — 2,834
D. Aherne, *Green* — 391
Ms T. Williamson, *Lib.* — 296
C. majority — 5,481
(June 1987, C. maj 16,923)
(October 1990, LD maj. 4,550)

EASTLEIGH (Hants)
E.91,736   T.82.91%
S. Milligan, *C.*	38,998
D. Chidgey, *LD*	21,296
Ms J. Sugrue, *Lab.*	15,768
C. majority	17,702

(June 1987, C. maj. 13,355)
See also page 234

ECCLES (Greater Manchester)
E.64,910   T.74.12%
*Miss J. Lestor, *Lab.*	27,357
G. Ling, *C.*	14,131
G. Reid, *LD*	5,835
R. Duriez, *Green*	521
Miss J. Garner, *NLP*	270
Lab. majority	13,226

(June 1987, Lab. maj. 9,699)

EDDISBURY (Cheshire)
E.75,089   T.82.55%
*A. Goodlad, *C.*	31,625
Ms N. Edwards, *Lab.*	18,928
D. Lyon, *LD*	10,543
A. Basden, *Green*	783
N. Pollard, *NLP*	107
C. majority	12,697

(June 1987, C. maj. 15,835)

EDMONTON (Greater London)
E.63,052   T.75.66%
*Dr I. Twinn, *C.*	22,076
A. Love, *Lab.*	21,483
E. Jones, *LD*	3,940
Ms E. Solley, *NLP*	207
C. majority	593

(June 1987, C. maj. 7,286)

ELLESMERE PORT AND NESTON
(Cheshire)
E.71,572   T.84.12%
A. Miller, *Lab.*	27,782
A. Pearce, *C.*	25,793
Ms E. Jewkes, *LD*	5,944
Dr M. Money, *Green*	589
Dr A. Rae, *NLP*	105
Lab. majority	1,989

(June 1987, Lab. maj. 1,853)

ELMET (W. Yorks)
E.70,558   T.82.53%
*S. Batiste, *C.*	27,677
C. Burgon, *Lab.*	24,416
Mrs A. Beck, *LD*	6,144
C. majority	3,261

(June 1987, C. maj. 5,356)

ELTHAM (Greater London)
E.51,989   T.78.72%
*P. Bottomley, *C.*	18,813
C. Efford, *Lab.*	17,147
C. McGinty, *LD*	4,804
A. Graham, *Ind. C.*	165
C. majority	1,666

(June 1987, C. maj. 6,460)

ENFIELD NORTH (Greater London)
E.67,421   T.77.91%
*T. Eggar, *C.*	27,789
M. Upham, *Lab.*	18,359
Ms S. Tustin, *LD*	5,817
J. Markham, *NLP*	565

C. majority   9,430
(June 1987, C. maj. 14,015)

ENFIELD SOUTHGATE (Greater
London)
E.64,311   T.76.28%
*M. Portillo, *C.*	28,422
Ms K. Livney, *Lab.*	12,859
K. Keane, *LD*	7,080
Ms M. Hollands, *Green*	696
C. majority	15,563

(June 1987, C. maj. 18,345)

EPPING FOREST (Essex)
E.67,585   T.80.55%
*S. Norris, *C.*	32,407
S. Murray, *Lab.*	12,219
Mrs B. Austen, *LD*	9,265
A. O'Brien, *EFRA*	552
C. majority	20,188

(June 1987, C. maj. 21,513)
(December 1988, C. maj. 4,504)

EPSOM AND EWELL (Surrey)
E.68,138   T.80.14%
*Rt. Hon. A. Hamilton, *C.*	32,861
M. Emerson, *LD*	12,840
R. Warren, *Lab.*	8,577
G. Hatchard, *NLP*	334
C. majority	20,021

(June 1987, C. maj. 20,761)

EREWASH (Derbys)
E.75,627   T.83.78%
Mrs A. Knight, *C.*	29,907
S. Stafford, *Lab.*	24,204
P. Tuck, *LD*	8,606
L. Johnson, *BNP*	645
C. majority	5,703

(June 1987, C. maj. 9,754)

ERITH AND CRAYFORD (Kent)
E.59,213   T.79.66%
*D. Evennett, *C.*	21,926
N. Beard, *Lab.*	19,587
Ms F. Jamieson, *LD*	5,657
C. majority	2,339

(June 1987, C. maj. 6,994)

ESHER (Surrey)
E.58,840   T.80.80%
*I. Taylor, *C.*	31,115
J. Richling, *LD*	10,744
Ms J. Reay, *Lab.*	5,685
C. majority	20,371

(June 1987, C. maj. 19,068)

EXETER (Devon)
E.76,723   T.82.21%
*Sir J. Hannam, *C.*	26,543
J. Lloyd, *Lab.*	22,498
G. Oakes, *LD*	12,059
Ms A. Micklem, *Lib.*	1,119
T. Brenan, *Green*	764
M. Turnbull, *NLP*	98
C. majority	4,045

(June 1987, C. maj. 7,656)

FALMOUTH AND CAMBORNE
(Cornwall)
E.70,702   T.81.10%
S. Coe, *C.*	21,150
Ms T. Jones, *LD*	17,883
J. Cosgrove, *Lab.*	16,732

P. Holmes, *Lib.*	730
K. Saunders, *Green*	466
F. Zapp, *Loony*	327
A. Pringle, *NLP*	56
C. majority	3,267

(June 1987, C. maj. 5,039)

FAREHAM (Hants)
E.81,124   T.81.85%
*P. Lloyd, *C.*	40,482
J. Thompson, *LD*	16,341
Ms E. Weston, *Lab.*	8,766
M. Brimecome, *Green*	818
C. majority	24,141

(June 1987, C. maj. 18,795)

FAVERSHAM (Kent)
E.81,977   T.79.71%
*R. Moate, *C.*	32,755
Ms H. Brinton, *Lab.*	16,404
R. Truelove, *LD*	15,896
R. Bradshaw, *NLP*	294
C. majority	16,351

(June 1987, C. maj. 13,978)

FELTHAM AND HESTON (Greater
London)
E.81,221   T.73.90%
A. Keen, *Lab.*	27,660
*P. Ground, *C.*	25,665
M. Hoban, *LD*	6,700
Lab. majority	1,995

(June 1987, C. maj. 5,430)

FINCHLEY (Greater London)
E.52,907   T.77.64%
H. Booth, *C.*	21,039
Ms A. Marjoram, *Lab.*	14,651
Ms H. Leighter, *LD*	4,568
A. Gunstock, *Green*	564
Ms S. Johnson, *Loony*	130
J. Macrae, *NLP*	129
C. majority	6,388

(June 1987, C. maj. 8,913)

FOLKESTONE AND HYTHE (Kent)
E.65,856   T.79.61%
*Rt. Hon. M. Howard, *C.*	27,437
Mrs L. Cufley, *LD*	18,527
P. Doherty, *Lab.*	6,347
A. Hobbs, *NLP*	123
C. majority	8,910

(June 1987, C. maj. 9,126)

FULHAM (Greater London)
E.52,740   T.76.16%
*M. Carrington, *C.*	21,438
N. Moore, *Lab.*	14,859
P. Crystal, *LD*	3,339
Ms E. Streeter, *Green*	443
J. Darby, *NLP*	91
C. majority	6,579

(June 1987, C. maj. 6,322)

FYLDE (Lancs)
E.63,573   T.78.50%
*M. Jack, *C.*	30,639
N. Cryer, *LD*	9,648
Ms C. Hughes, *Lab.*	9,382
P. Leadbetter, *NLP*	239
C. majority	20,991

(June 1987, C. maj. 17,772)

GAINSBOROUGH AND HORNCASTLE
(Lincs)
E.72,038   T.80.87%
*E. Leigh, *C.*   31,444
N. Taylor, *LD*   15,199
Ms F. Jones, *Lab.*   11,619
C. majority   16,245
(June 1987, C. maj. 9,723)

GATESHEAD EAST (Tyne & Wear)
E.64,355   T.73.63%
*Miss J. Quin, *Lab.*   30,100
M. Callanan, *C.*   11,570
R. Beadle, *LD*   5,720
Lab. majority   18,530
(June 1987, Lab. maj. 17,228)

GEDLING (Notts)
E.68,953   T.82.34%
*A. J. B. Mitchell, *C.*   30,191
V. Coaker, *Lab.*   19,554
D. George, *LD*   6,863
Ms A. Miszeweka, *NLP*   168
C. majority   10,637
(June 1987, C. maj. 16,539)

GILLINGHAM (Kent)
E.71,851   T.80.32%
*J. Couchman, *C.*   30,201
P. Clark, *Lab.*   13,563
M. Wallbank, *LD*   13,509
C. MacKinlay, *Ind.*   248
D. Jolicoeur, *NLP*   190
C. majority   16,638
(June 1987, C. maj. 12,549)

GLANFORD AND SCUNTHORPE
(Humberside)
E.73,479   T.78.91%
*E. Morley, *Lab.*   30,623
Dr A. Saywood, *C.*   22,211
W. Paxton, *LD*   4,172
C. Nottingham, *SD*   982
Lab. majority   8,412
(June 1987, Lab. maj. 512)

GLOUCESTER
E.80,578   T.80.24%
*D. French, *C.*   29,870
K. Stephens, *Lab.*   23,812
J. Sewell, *LD*   10,978
C. majority   6,058
(June 1987, C. maj. 12,035)

GLOUCESTERSHIRE WEST
E.80,007   T.83.89%
*P. Marland, *C.*   29,232
Ms D. Organ, *Lab.*   24,274
L. Boait, *LD*   13,366
A. Reeve, *Brit. Ind.*   172
C. Palmer, *Century*   75
C. majority   4,958
(June 1987, C. maj. 11,679)

GOSPORT (Hants)
E.69,638   T.76.79%
*P. Viggers, *C.*   31,094
M. Russell, *LD*   14,776
Ms M. Angus, *Lab.*   7,275
P. Ettie, *Pensioners*   332
C. majority   16,318
(June 1987, C. maj. 13,723)

GRANTHAM (Lincs)
E.83,463   T.79.29%
*Hon. D. Hogg, *C.*   37,194
S. Taggart, *Lab.*   17,606
J. Heppell, *LD*   9,882
J. Hiley, *Lib.*   1,500
C. majority   19,588
(June 1987, C. maj. 21,303)

GRAVESHAM (Kent)
E.70,740   T.83.48%
*J. Arnold, *C.*   29,322
G. Green, *Lab.*   23,829
D. Deedman, *LD*   5,269
A. Bunstone, *Ind.*   273
R. Khilkoff-Boulding, *ILP*   187
B. Buxton, *Soc.*   174
C. majority   5,493
(June 1987, C. maj. 8,792)

GREAT GRIMSBY (Humberside)
E.67,427   T.75.28%
*A. V. Mitchell, *Lab.*   25,895
P. Jackson, *C.*   18,391
Ms P. Frankish, *LD*   6,475
Lab. majority   7,504
(June 1987, Lab. maj. 8,784)

GREAT YARMOUTH (Norfolk)
E.68,263   T.77.94%
*M. Carttiss, *C.*   25,505
Ms B. Baughan, *Lab.*   20,196
M. Scott, *LD*   7,225
Ms P. Larkin, *NLP*   284
C. majority   5,309
(June 1987, C. maj. 10,083)

GREENWICH (Greater London)
E.47,789   T.74.63%
W. R. N. Raynsford, *Lab.*   14,630
*Mrs R. Barnes, *SD*   13,273
Mrs A. McNair, *C.*   6,960
R. McCracken, *Green*   483
R. Mallone, *Fellowship*   147
M. Hardee, *UTCHAP*   103
J. Small, *NLP*   70
Lab. majority   1,357
(June 1987, SDP/All. maj. 2,141)

GUILDFORD (Surrey)
E.77,265   T.78.48%
*Rt. Hon. D. Howell, *C.*   33,516
Mrs M. Sharp, *LD*   20,112
H. Mann, *Lab.*   6,781
A. Law, *NLP*   234
C. majority   13,404
(June 1987, C. maj. 12,607)

HACKNEY NORTH AND STOKE
NEWINGTON (Greater London)
E.54,655   T.63.53%
*Ms D. Abbott, *Lab.*   20,083
C. Manson, *C.*   9,356
K. Fitchett, *LD*   3,996
Ms H. Hunt, *Green*   1,111
J. Windsor, *NLP*   178
Lab. majority   10,727
(June 1987, Lab. maj. 7,678)

HACKNEY SOUTH AND SHOREDITCH
(Greater London)
E.57,935   T.63.82%
*B. Sedgemore, *Lab.*   19,730
A. Turner, *C.*   10,714
G. Wintle, *LD*   5,533
L. Lucas, *Green*   772
Ms G. Norman, *NLP*   226
Lab. majority   9,016
(June 1987, Lab. maj. 7,522)

HALESOWEN AND STOURBRIDGE (W.
Midlands)
E.77,644   T.82.28%
P. W. Hawksley, *C.*   32,312
A. Hankon, *Lab.*   22,730
V. Sharma, *LD*   7,941
T. Weller, *Green*   908
C. majority   9,582
(June 1987, C. maj. 13,808)

HALIFAX (W. Yorks)
E.73,401   T.78.69%
*Ms A. Mahon, *Lab.*   25,115
T. Martin, *C.*   24,637
I. Howell, *LD*   7,364
R. Pearson, *Nat.*   649
Lab. majority   478
(June 1987, Lab. maj. 1,212)

HALTON (Cheshire)
E.74,906   T.78.34%
*Rt. Hon. G. Oakes, *Lab.*   35,025
G. Mercer, *C.*   16,821
D. Reaper, *LD*   6,104
S. Herley, *Loony*   398
N. Collins, *NLP*   338
Lab. majority   18,204
(June 1987, Lab. maj. 14,578)

HAMMERSMITH (Greater London)
E.47,229   T.71.90%
*C. Soley, *Lab.*   17,329
A. Hennessy, *C.*   12,575
J. Bates, *LD*   3,380
R. Crosskey, *Green*   546
K. Turner, *NLP*   89
Ms H. Szamuely, *Anti Fed.*   41
Lab. majority   4,754
(June 1987, Lab. maj. 2,415)

HAMPSHIRE EAST
E.92,139   T.80.35%
*M. Mates, *C.*   47,541
Ms S. Baring, *LD*   18,376
J. Phillips, *Lab.*   6,840
I. Foster, *Green*   1,113
S. Hale, *RCC*   165
C. majority   29,165
(June 1987, C. maj. 23,786)

HAMPSHIRE NORTH WEST
E.73,101   T.80.75%
*Sir D. Mitchell, *C.*   34,310
M. Simpson, *LD*   16,462
M. Stockwell, *Lab.*   7,433
Ms D. Ashley, *Green*   825
C. majority   17,848
(June 1987, C. maj. 13,437)

HAMPSTEAD AND HIGHGATE
(Greater London)
E.58,203　T.73.04%
Ms G. Jackson, *Lab.*　19,193
O. Letwin, *C.*　17,753
D. Wrede, *LD*　4,765
S. Games, *Green*　594
Dr R. Prosser, *NLP*　86
Ms A. Hall, *RAVA*　44
C. Scallywag Wilson, *Scallywag*　44
Captain Rizz, *Rizz*　33
Lab. majority　1,440
(June 1987, C. maj. 2,221)

HARBOROUGH (Leics)
E.76,514　T.82.11%
E. Garnier, *C.*　34,280
M. Cox, *LD*　20,737
Ms C. Mackay, *Lab.*　7,483
A. Irwin, *NLP*　328
C. majority　13,543
(June 1987, C. maj. 18,810)

HARLOW (Essex)
E.68,615　T.82.56%
*J. Hayes, *C.*　26,608
W. Rammell, *Lab.*　23,668
Ms L. Spenceley, *LD*　6,375
C. majority　2,940
(June 1987, C. maj. 5,877)

HARROGATE (N. Yorks)
E.76,250　T.77.98%
*R. Banks, *C.*　32,023
T. Hurren, *LD*　19,434
A. Wright, *Lab.*　7,230
A. Warneken, *Green*　780
C. majority　12,589
(June 1987, C. maj. 11,902)

HARROW EAST (Greater London)
E.74,733　T.77.83%
*H. Dykes, *C.*　30,752
A. McNulty, *Lab.*　19,654
Ms V. Chamberlain, *LD*　6,360
P. Burrows, *Lib.*　1,142
Mrs S. Hamza, *NLP*　212
J. Lester, *Anti Fed.*　49
C. majority　11,098
(June 1987, C. maj. 18,273)

HARROW WEST (Greater London)
E.69,616　T.78.69%
*R. G. Hughes, *C.*　30,240
C. Moraes, *Lab.*　12,343
C. Noyce, *LD*　11,050
G. Aitman, *Lib.*　845
Mrs J. Argyle, *NLP*　306
C. majority　17,897
(June 1987, C. maj. 15,444)

HARTLEPOOL (Cleveland)
E.67,968　T.76.07%
P. Mandelson, *Lab.*　26,816
G. Robb, *C.*　18,034
I. Cameron, *LD*　6,860
Lab. majority　8,782
(June 1987, Lab. maj. 7,289)

HARWICH (Essex)
E.80,260　T.77.70%
I. Sproat, *C.*　32,369
Mrs P. Bevan, *LD*　15,210

R. Knight, *Lab.*　14,511
Mrs E. McGrath, *NLP*　279
C. majority　17,159
(June 1987, C. maj. 12,082)

HASTINGS AND RYE (E. Sussex)
E.71,838　T.74.86%
Ms J. Lait, *C.*　25,573
M. Palmer, *LD*　18,939
R. Stevens, *Lab.*　8,458
Ms S. Phillips, *Green*　640
T. Howell, *Loony*　168
C. majority　6,634
(June 1987, C. maj. 7,347)

HAVANT (Hants)
E.74,217　T.79.01%
D. Willetts, *C.*　32,233
S. van Hagen, *LD*　14,649
G. Morris, *Lab.*　10,968
T. Mitchell, *Green*　793
C. majority　17,584
(June 1987, C. maj. 16,510)

HAYES AND HARLINGTON (Greater London)
E.54,449　T.79.70%
*T. Dicks, *C.*　19,489
J. McDonnell, *Lab.*　19,436
T. Little, *LD*　4,472
C. majority　53
(June 1987, C. maj. 5,965)

HAZEL GROVE (Greater Manchester)
E.64,302　T.84.94%
*Sir T. Arnold, *C.*　24,479
A. Stunell, *LD*　23,550
C. McAllister, *Lab.*　6,390
M. Penn, *NLP*　204
C. majority　929
(June 1987, C. maj. 1,840)

HEMSWORTH (W. Yorks)
E.55,679　T.75.91%
*D. Enright, *Lab.*　29,942
G. Harrison, *C.*　7,867
Ms V. Megson, *LD*　4,459
Lab. majority　22,075
(June 1987, Lab. maj. 20,700)
(November 1991, Lab. maj. 11,087)
See also page 235

HENDON NORTH (Greater London)
E.51,513　T.75.08%
*J. Gorst, *C.*　20,569
D. Hill, *Lab.*　13,447
P. Kemp, *LD*　4,136
Ms P. Duncan, *Green*　430
Ms P. Orr, *NLP*　95
C. majority　7,122
(June 1987, C. maj. 10,932)

HENDON SOUTH (Greater London)
E.48,401　T.72.38%
*J. Marshall, *C.*　20,593
Ms L. Lloyd, *Lab.*　8,546
J. Cohen, *LD*　5,609
J. Leslie, *NLP*　289
C. majority　12,047
(June 1987, C. maj. 11,124)

HENLEY (Oxon)
E.64,702　T.79.84%
*Rt. Hon. M. Heseltine, *C.*　30,835
D. Turner, *LD*　12,443
I. Russell-Swinnerton, *Lab.*　7,676
A. Plane, *Anti H.*　431
Ms S. Banerji, *NLP*　274
C. majority　18,392
(June 1987, C. maj. 17,082)

HEREFORD
E.69,676　T.81.29%
*C. Shepherd, *C.*　26,727
G. Jones, *LD*　23,314
Ms J. Kelly, *Lab.*　6,005
C. Mattingly, *Green*　596
C. majority　3,413
(June 1987, C. maj. 1,413)

HERTFORD AND STORTFORD
E.76,654　T.81.05%
*B. Wells, *C.*　35,716
C. White, *LD*　15,506
A. Bovaird, *Lab.*　10,125
J. Goth, *Green*　780
C. majority　20,210
(June 1987, C. maj. 17,140)

HERTFORDSHIRE NORTH
E.80,066　T.84.44%
O. Heald, *C.*　33,679
R. Liddle, *LD*　17,148
Ms S. Bissett Johnson, *Lab.*　16,449
B. Irving, *NLP*　339
C. majority　16,531
(June 1987, C. maj. 11,442)

HERTFORDSHIRE SOUTH WEST
E.70,836　T.83.76%
*R. Page, *C.*　33,825
Ms A. Shaw, *LD*　13,718
A. Gale, *Lab.*　11,512
C. Adamson, *NLP*　281
C. majority　20,107
(June 1987, C. maj. 15,784)

HERTFORDSHIRE WEST
E.78,573　T.82.36%
*R. Jones, *C.*　33,340
Mrs E. McNally, *Lab.*　19,400
M. Trevett, *LD*　10,464
J. Hannaway, *Green*　674
J. McAuley, *NF*　665
G. Harvey, *NLP*　175
C. majority　13,940
(June 1987, C. maj. 14,924)

HERTSMERE (Herts)
E.69,951　T.80.89%
W. J. Clappison, *C.*　32,133
Dr D. Souter, *Lab.*　13,398
Mrs Z. Gifford, *LD*　10,681
Ms D. Harding, *NLP*　373
C. majority　18,735
(June 1987, C. maj. 18,106)

HEXHAM (Northumberland)
E.57,812　T.82.37%
P. Atkinson, *C.*　24,967
I. Swithenbank, *Lab.*　11,529
J. Wallace, *LD*　10,344
J. Hartshorne, *Green*　781

C. majority 13,438
(June 1987, C. maj. 8,066)

HEYWOOD AND MIDDLETON
(Greater Manchester)
*E.*57,176   *T.*74.92%
*J. Callaghan, *Lab.* 22,380
E. Ollerenshaw, *C.* 14,306
Dr M. Taylor, *LD* 5,262
P. Burke, *Lib.* 757
Ms A. Scott, *NLP* 134
Lab. majority 8,074
(June 1987, Lab. maj. 6,848)

HIGH PEAK (Derbys)
*E.*70,793   *T.*84.62%
C. Hendry, *C.* 27,538
T. Levitt, *Lab.* 22,719
S. Molloy, *LD* 8,861
R. Floyd, *Green* 794
C. majority 4,819
(June 1987, C. maj. 9,516)

HOLBORN AND ST PANCRAS
(Greater London)
*E.*64,480   *T.*62.99%
*F. Dobson, *Lab.* 22,243
A. McHallam, *C.* 11,419
Ms J. Horne-Roberts, *LD* 5,476
P. Wolf-Light, *Green* 959
M. Hersey, *NLP* 212
R. Headicar, *Soc.* 175
N. Lewis, *WAR* 133
Lab. majority 10,824
(June 1987, Lab. maj. 8,853)

HOLLAND WITH BOSTON (Lincs)
*E.*67,900   *T.*77.93%
*Sir R. Body, *C.* 29,159
J. Hough, *Lab.* 15,328
N. Ley, *LD* 8,434
C. majority 13,831
(June 1987, C. maj. 17,595)

HONITON (Devon)
*E.*79,223   *T.*80.74%
*Sir P. Emery, *C.* 33,533
Ms J. Sharratt, *LD* 17,022
R. Davison, *Lab.* 8,142
D. Owen, *Ind. C.* 2,175
S. Hughes, *Loony G.* 1,442
G. Halliwell, *Lib.* 1,005
A. Tootill, *Green* 650
C. majority 16,511
(June 1987, C. maj. 16,562)

HORNCHURCH (Greater London)
*E.*60,522   *T.*79.78%
*R. Squire, *C.* 25,817
Ms L. Cooper, *Lab.* 16,652
B. Oddy, *LD* 5,366
T. Matthews, *SD* 453
C. majority 9,165
(June 1987, C. maj. 10,694)

HORNSEY AND WOOD GREEN
(Greater London)
*E.*73,491   *T.*75.85%
Mrs B. Roche, *Lab.* 27,020
A. Boff, *C.* 21,843
P. Dunphy, *LD* 5,547
Ms L. Crosbie, *Green* 1,051
P. Davies, *NLP* 197

W. Massey, *Rev. Comm.* 89
Lab. majority 5,177
(June 1987, C. maj. 1,779)

HORSHAM (W. Sussex)
*E.*84,158   *T.*81.27%
*Sir P. Hordern, *C.* 42,210
Ms J. Stainton, *LD* 17,138
S. Uwins, *Lab.* 6,745
Ms J. Elliott, *Lib.* 1,281
T. King, *Green* 692
J. Duggan, *PPP* 332
C. majority 25,072
(June 1987, C. maj. 23,907)

HOUGHTON AND WASHINGTON
(Tyne & Wear)
*E.*79,325   *T.*70.60%
*R. Boyes, *Lab.* 34,733
A. Tyrie, *C.* 13,925
O. Dumpleton, *LD* 7,346
Lab. majority 20,808
(June 1987, Lab. maj. 20,193)

HOVE (E. Sussex)
*E.*67,450   *T.*74.26%
*Hon. T. Sainsbury, *C.* 24,525
D. Turner, *Lab.* 12,257
A. Jones, *LD* 9,709
N. Furness, *Hove C.* 2,658
G. Sinclair, *Green* 814
J. Morilly, *NLP* 126
C. majority 12,268
(June 1987, C. maj. 18,218)

HUDDERSFIELD (W. Yorks)
*E.*67,604   *T.*72.32%
*B. Sheerman, *Lab.* 23,832
Ms J. Kenyon, *C.* 16,574
Ms A. Denham, *LD* 7,777
N. Harvey, *Green* 576
M. Cran, *NLP* 135
Lab. majority 7,258
(June 1987, Lab. maj. 7,278)

HULL EAST
*E.*69,036   *T.*69.29%
*J. Prescott, *Lab.* 30,092
J. Fareham, *C.* 11,373
J. Wastling, *LD* 6,050
C. Kinzell, *NLP* 323
Lab. majority 18,719
(June 1987, Lab. maj. 14,689)

HULL NORTH
*E.*71,363   *T.*66.71%
*J. K. McNamara, *Lab.* 26,619
B. Coleman, *C.* 11,235
A. Meadowcroft, *LD* 9,504
G. Richardson, *NLP* 253
Lab. majority 15,384
(June 1987, Lab. maj. 12,169)

HULL WEST
*E.*56,111   *T.*65.70%
*S. Randall, *Lab.* 21,139
D. Stewart, *C.* 10,554
R. Tress, *LD* 4,867
B. Franklin, *NLP* 308
Lab. majority 10,585
(June 1987, Lab. maj. 8,130)

HUNTINGDON (Cambs)
*E.*92,913   *T.*79.16%
*Rt. Hon. J. Major, *C.* 48,662
H. Seckleman, *Lab.* 12,432
A. Duff, *LD* 9,386
P. Wiggin, *Lib.* 1,045
Miss D. Birkhead, *Green* 846
Lord D. Sutch, *Loony* 728
M. Flanagan, *C. Thatch.* 231
Lord Buckethead, *Gremloids* 107
C. Cockell, *FTM* 91
D. Shepheard, *NLP* 26
C. majority 36,230
(June 1987, C. maj. 27,044)

HYNDBURN (Lancs)
*E.*58,539   *T.*83.97%
G. Pope, *Lab.* 23,042
*K. Hargreaves, *C.* 21,082
Ms Y. Stars, *LD* 4,886
S. Whittle, *NLP* 150
Lab. majority 1,960
(June 1987, C. maj. 2,220)

ILFORD NORTH (Greater London)
*E.*58,670   *T.*77.98%
*V. Bendall, *C.* 24,698
Ms L. Hilton, *Lab.* 15,627
R. Scott, *LD* 5,430
C. majority 9,071
(June 1987, C. maj. 12,090)

ILFORD SOUTH (Greater London)
*E.*55,741   *T.*76.83%
M. Gapes, *Lab.* 19,418
*N. Thorne, *C.* 19,016
G. Hogarth, *LD* 4,126
N. Bramachari, *NLP* 269
Lab. majority 402
(June 1987, C. maj. 4,572)

IPSWICH (Suffolk)
*E.*67,261   *T.*80.32%
J. Cann, *Lab.* 23,680
*M. Irvine, *C.* 23,415
J. White, *LD* 6,159
Ms J. Scott, *Green* 591
E. Kaplan, *NLP* 181
Lab. majority 265
(June 1987, C. maj. 874)

ISLE OF WIGHT
*E.*99,838   *T.*79.76%
*B. Field, *C.* 38,163
Dr P. Brand, *LD* 36,336
K. Pearson, *Lab.* 4,784
C. Daly, *NLP* 350
C. majority 1,827
(June 1987, C. maj. 6,442)

ISLINGTON NORTH (Greater
London)
*E.*56,270   *T.*67.26%
*J. Corbyn, *Lab.* 21,742
Mrs L. Champagnie, *C.* 8,958
Ms S. Ludford, *LD* 5,732
C. Ashby, *Green* 1,420
Lab. majority 12,784
(June 1987, Lab. maj. 9,657)

ISLINGTON SOUTH AND FINSBURY
(Greater London)
E.55,541   T.72.52%
*C. Smith, Lab.	20,586
M. Jones, C.	9,934
C. Pryce, LD	9,387
Ms R. Hersey, JBR	149
Ms M. Avino, Loony	142
M. Spinks, NLP	83
Lab. majority	10,652
(June 1987, Lab. maj. 805)

JARROW (Tyne & Wear)
E.62,611   T.74.44%
*D. Dixon, Lab.	28,956
T. Ward, C.	11,049
K. Orrell, LD	6,608
Lab. majority	17,907
(June 1987, Lab. maj. 18,795)

KEIGHLEY (W. Yorks)
E.66,358   T.82.58%
*G. Waller, C.	25,983
T. Flanagan, Lab.	22,387
I. Simpson, LD	5,793
M. Crowson, Green	642
C. majority	3,596
(June 1987, C. maj. 5,606)

KENSINGTON (Greater London)
E.42,129   T.73.29%
*J. D. Fishburn, C.	15,540
Ms A. Holmes, Lab.	11,992
C. Shirley, LD	2,770
Ms A. Burlingham-Johnson, Green	
	415
A. Hardy, NLP	90
Ms A. Bulloch, Anti Fed.	71
C. majority	3,548
(June 1987, C. maj. 4,447)
(July 1988, C. maj. 815)

KENT MID
E.74,459   T.79.66%
*A. Rowe, C.	33,633
T. Robson, Lab.	13,984
G. Colley, LD	11,476
G. Valente, NLP	224
C. majority	19,649
(June 1987, C. maj. 14,768)

KETTERING (Northants)
E.67,853   T.82.58%
*R. Freeman, C.	29,115
P. Hope, Lab.	17,961
R. Denton-White, LD	8,962
C. majority	11,154
(June 1987, C. maj. 11,327)

KINGSTON UPON THAMES (Greater
London)
E.51,077   T.78.41%
*Rt. Hon. N. Lamont, C.	20,675
D. Osbourne, LD	10,522
R. Markless, Lab.	7,748
A. Amer, Lib.	771
D. Beaupre, Loony	212
G. Woollcoombe, NLP	81
A. Scholefield, Anti Fed.	42
C. majority	10,153
(June 1987, C. maj. 11,186)

KINGSWOOD (Avon)
E.71,727   T.83.85%
R. Berry, Lab.	26,774
*R. Hayward, C.	24,404
Ms J. Pinkerton, LD	8,960
Lab. majority	2,370
(June 1987, C. maj. 4,393)

KNOWSLEY NORTH (Merseyside)
E.48,761   T.72.81%
*G. Howarth, Lab.	27,517
S. Mabey, C.	5,114
J. Murray, LD	1,515
Mrs K. Lappin, Lib.	1,180
V. Ruben, NLP	179
Lab. majority	22,403
(June 1987, Lab. maj. 21,098)

KNOWSLEY SOUTH (Merseyside)
E.62,260   T.74.77%
*E. O'Hara, Lab.	31,933
L. Byrom, C.	9,922
I. Smith, LD	4,480
M. Raiano, NLP	217
Lab. majority	22,011
(June 1987, Lab. maj. 20,846)
(September 1990, Lab. maj. 11,367)

LANCASHIRE WEST
E.77,462   T.82.55%
C. Pickthall, Lab.	30,128
*K. Hind, C.	28,051
P. Reilly, LD	4,884
P. Pawley, Green	546
B. Morris, NLP	336
Lab. majority	2,077
(June 1987, C. maj. 1,353)

LANCASTER (Lancs)
E.58,714   T.78.78%
*Dame E. Kellett-Bowman, C.	21,084
Ms R. Henig, Lab.	18,131
J. Humberstone, LD	6,524
Ms G. Dowding, Green	433
R. Barcis, NLP	83
C. majority	2,953
(June 1987, C. maj. 6,453)

LANGBAURGH (Cleveland)
E.79,566   T.83.05%
M. Bates, C.	30,018
*A. Kumar, Lab.	28,454
P. Allen, LD	7,615
C. majority	1,564
(June 1987, C. maj. 2,088)
(November 1991, C. maj. 1,975)

LEEDS CENTRAL (W. Yorks)
E.62,058   T.61.29%
*D. Fatchett, Lab.	23,673
Mrs T. Holdroyd, C.	8,653
D. Pratt, LD	5,713
Lab. majority	15,020
(June 1987, Lab. maj. 11,505)

LEEDS EAST (W. Yorks)
E.61,695   T.70.02%
G. Mudie, Lab.	24,929
N. Carmichael, C.	12,232
P. Wrigley, LD	6,040
Lab. majority	12,697
(June 1987, Lab. maj. 9,526)

LEEDS NORTH EAST (W. Yorks)
E.64,372   T.76.89%
*T. Kirkhope, C.	22,462
F. Hamilton, Lab.	18,218
C. Walmsley, LD	8,274
J. Noble, Green	546
C. majority	4,244
(June 1987, C. maj. 8,419)

LEEDS NORTH WEST (W. Yorks)
E.69,406   T.72.84%
*Dr K. Hampson, C.	21,750
Ms B. Pearce, LD	14,079
Ms S. Egan, Lab.	13,782
D. Webb, Green	519
N. Nowosielski, Lib.	427
C. majority	7,671
(June 1987, C. maj. 5,201)

LEEDS SOUTH AND MORLEY
(W. Yorks)
E.63,107   T.72.58%
W. J. Gunnell, Lab.	23,896
R. Booth, C.	16,524
Ms J. Walmsley, LD	5,062
R. Thurston, NLP	327
Lab. majority	7,372
(June 1987, Lab. maj. 6,711)

LEEDS WEST (W. Yorks)
E.67,084   T.71.14%
*J. Battle, Lab.	26,310
P. Bartlett, C.	12,482
G. Howard, LD	4,252
M. Meadowcroft, Lib.	3,980
Ms A. Mander, Green	569
R. Tenny, NF	132
Lab. majority	13,828
(June 1987, Lab. maj. 4,692)

LEICESTER EAST
E.63,434   T.78.40%
*N. K. A. S. Vaz, Lab.	28,123
J. Stevens, C.	16,807
Ms S. Mitchell, LD	4,043
M. Frankland, Green	453
D. Taylor, Homeland	308
Lab. majority	11,316
(June 1987, Lab. maj. 1,924)

LEICESTER SOUTH
E.71,120   T.75.09%
*J. Marshall, Lab.	27,934
Dr M. Dutt, C.	18,494
Ms A. Crumbie, LD	6,271
J. McWhirter, Green	554
Ms P. Saunders, NLP	154
Lab. majority	9,440
(June 1987, Lab. maj. 1,877)

LEICESTER WEST
E.65,510   T.73.66%
*Hon. G. Janner, Lab.	22,574
J. Guthrie, C.	18,596
G. Walker, LD	6,402
Ms C. Wintram, Green	517
Ms J. Rosta, NLP	171
Lab. majority	3,978
(June 1987, Lab. maj. 1,201)

LEICESTERSHIRE NORTH WEST
E.72,414   T.86.11%

*D. Ashby, C.	28,379
D. Taylor, Lab.	27,400
J. Beckett, LD	6,353
J. Fawcett, NLP	229
C. majority	979

(June 1987, C. maj. 7,828)

LEIGH (Greater Manchester)
E.70,064   T.75.02%

*L. Cunliffe, Lab.	32,225
J. Egerton, C.	13,398
R. Bleakley, LD	6,621
A. Tayler, NLP	320
Lab. majority	18,827

(June 1987, Lab. maj. 16,606)

LEOMINSTER (H & W)
E.70,873   T.81.69%

*P. Temple-Morris, C.	32,783
D. Short, LD	16,103
C. Chappell, Lab.	6,874
Ms F. Norman, Green	1,503
Capt. E. Carlise, Anti Fed.	640
C. majority	16,680

(June 1987, C. maj. 14,075)

LEWES (E. Sussex)
E.73,918   T.81.81%

*J. R. Rathbone, C.	33,042
N. Baker, LD	20,867
Ms A. Chapman, Lab.	5,758
A. Beaumont, Green	719
N. Clinch, NLP	87
C. majority	12,175

(June 1987, C. maj. 13,620)

LEWISHAM DEPTFORD (Greater London)
E.57,014   T.65.05%

*Mrs J. Ruddock, Lab.	22,574
Miss T. O'Neill, C.	10,336
Ms J. Brightwell, LD	4,181
Lab. majority	12,238

(June 1987, Lab. maj. 6,771)

LEWISHAM EAST (Greater London)
E.57,674   T.74.78%

Mrs B. Prentice, Lab.	19,576
*Hon. C. Moynihan, C.	18,481
J. Hawkins, LD	4,877
Ms G. Mansour, NLP	196
Lab. majority	1,095

(June 1987, Lab. maj. 4,814)

LEWISHAM WEST (Greater London)
E.59,317   T.73.11%

J. Dowd, Lab.	20,378
*J. Maples, C.	18,569
Ms E. Neale, LD	4,295
P. Coulam, Anti Fed.	125
Lab. majority	1,809

(June 1987, C. maj. 3,772)

LEYTON (Greater London)
E.57,271   T.67.38%

*H. Cohen, Lab.	20,334
Miss C. Smith, C.	8,850
J. Fryer, LD	8,180
L. de Pinna, Lib.	561
K. Pervez, Green	412
R. Archer, NLP	256

Lab. majority	11,484

(June 1987, Lab. maj. 4,641)

LINCOLN
E.78,905   T.79.15%

*K. Carlisle, C.	28,792
N. Butler, Lab.	26,743
D. Harding-Price, LD	6,316
Ms S. Wiggin, Lib.	603
C. majority	2,049

(June 1987, C. maj. 7,483)

LINDSEY EAST (Lincs)
E.80,026   T.78.07%

*Sir P. Tapsell, C.	31,916
J. Dodsworth, LD	20,070
D. Shepherd, Lab.	9,477
Ms R. Robinson, Green	1,018
C. majority	11,846

(June 1987, C. maj. 8,616)

LITTLEBOROUGH AND SADDLEWORTH (Greater Manchester)
E.65,576   T.81.61%

*G. Dickens, C.	23,682
C. Davies, LD	19,188
A. Brett, Lab.	10,649
C. majority	4,494

(June 1987, C. maj. 6,202)
See also page 235

LIVERPOOL BROADGREEN
E.60,080   T.69.59%

Mrs J. Kennedy, Lab.	18,062
Ms R. Cooper, LD	11,035
*T. Fields, Soc. Lab.	5,952
Mrs H. Roche, C.	5,405
S. Radford, Lib.	1,211
Mrs A. Brennan, NLP	149
Lab. majority	7,027

(June 1987, Lab. maj. 6,047)

LIVERPOOL GARSTON
E.57,538   T.70.60%

*E. Loyden, Lab.	23,212
J. Backhouse, C.	10,933
W. Roberts, LD	5,398
A. Conrad, Lib.	894
P. Chandler, NLP	187
Lab. majority	12,279

(June 1987, Lab. maj. 13,777)

LIVERPOOL MOSSLEY HILL
E.60,409   T.68.52%

*D. Alton, LD	19,809
N. Bann, Lab.	17,203
S. Syder, C.	4,269
B. Rigby, NLP	114
LD majority	2,606

(June 1987, L./All. maj. 2,226)

LIVERPOOL RIVERSIDE
E.49,595   T.54.57%

*R. Parry, Lab.	20,550
Dr A. Zsigmond, C.	3,113
M. Akbar Ali, LD	2,498
L. Brown, Green	738
J. Collins, NLP	169
Lab. majority	17,437

(June 1987, Lab. maj. 20,689)

LIVERPOOL WALTON
E.70,102   T.67.40%

*P. Kilfoyle, Lab.	34,214
B. Greenwood, C.	5,915
J. Lang, LD	5,672
T. Newall, Lib.	963
D. Carson, Prot. Ref.	393
Ms D. Raiano, NLP	98
Lab. majority	28,299

(June 1987, Lab. maj. 23,253)
(July 1991, Lab. maj. 6,860)

LIVERPOOL WEST DERBY
E.56,718   T.69.84%

*R. Wareing, Lab.	27,014
S. Fitzsimmons, C.	6,589
Ms G. Bundred, LD	4,838
D. Curtis, Lib.	1,021
C. Higgins, NLP	154
Lab. majority	20,425

(June 1987, Lab. maj. 20,496)

LOUGHBOROUGH (Leics)
E.75,450   T.78.52%

*S. Dorrell, C.	30,064
A. Reed, Lab.	19,181
A. Stott, LD	8,953
I. Sinclair, Green	817
P. Reynolds, NLP	233
C. majority	10,883

(June 1987, C. maj. 17,648)

LUDLOW (Salop)
E.68,935   T.80.87%

*C. Gill, C.	28,719
D. Phillips, LD	14,567
Ms B. Mason, Lab.	11,709
N. Appleton-Fox, Green	758
C. majority	14,152

(June 1987, C. maj. 11,699)

LUTON NORTH (Beds)
E.76,857   T.81.91%

*J. Carlisle, C.	33,777
A. McWalter, Lab.	20,683
Ms J. Jackson, LD	7,570
R. Jones, Green	633
K. Buscombe, NLP	292
C. majority	13,094

(June 1987, C. maj. 15,573)

LUTON SOUTH (Beds)
E.73,016   T.79.10%

*G. Bright, C.	25,900
W. McKenzie, Lab.	25,101
D. Rogers, LD	6,020
Ms L. Bliss, Green	550
D. Cooke, NLP	191
C. majority	799

(June 1987, C. maj. 5,115)

MACCLESFIELD (Cheshire)
E.76,548   T.82.29%

*N. Winterton, C.	36,447
Mrs M. Longworth, Lab.	13,680
Dr P. Beatty, LD	12,600
Mrs C. Penn, NLP	268
C. majority	22,767

(June 1987, C. maj. 19,092)

MAIDSTONE (Kent)
E.72,834   T.80.08%
*Miss A. Widdecombe, C.	31,611
Ms P. Yates, LD	15,325
Ms A. Logan, Lab.	10,517
Ms P. Kemp, Green	707
F. Ingram, NLP	172
C. majority	16,286
(June 1987, C. maj. 10,364)

MAKERFIELD (Greater Manchester)
E.71,425   T.76.09%
*I. McCartney, Lab.	32,832
Mrs D. Dickson, C.	14,714
S. Jeffers, LD	5,097
Ms S. Cairns, Lib.	1,309
C. Davies, NLP	397
Lab. majority	18,118
(June 1987, Lab. maj. 15,558)

MANCHESTER BLACKLEY
E.55,234   T.69.31%
*K. Eastham, Lab.	23,031
W. Hobhouse, C.	10,642
S. Wheale, LD	4,324
M. Kennedy, NLP	288
Lab. majority	12,389
(June 1987, Lab. maj. 10,122)

MANCHESTER CENTRAL
E.56,446   T.56.90%
*R. Litherland, Lab.	23,336
P. Davies, C.	5,299
M. Clayton, LD	3,151
A. Buchanan, CL	167
Ms V. Mitchell, NLP	167
Lab. majority	18,037
(June 1987, Lab. maj. 19,867)

MANCHESTER GORTON
E.62,410   T.60.84%
*Rt. Hon. G. Kaufman, Lab.	23,671
J. Bullock, C.	7,392
P. Harris, LD	5,327
T. Henderson, Lib.	767
M. Daw, Green	595
Ms P. Lawrence, Rev. Comm.	108
P. Mitchell, NLP	84
Ms C. Smith, Int. Comm.	30
Lab. majority	16,279
(June 1987, Lab. maj. 14,065)

MANCHESTER WITHINGTON
E.63,838   T.71.27%
*K. Bradley, Lab.	23,962
E. Farthing, C.	14,227
G. Hennell, LD	6,457
B. Candeland, Green	725
C. Menhinick, NLP	128
Lab. majority	9,735
(June 1987, Lab. maj. 3,391)

MANCHESTER WYTHENSHAWE
E.53,548   T.69.68%
*Rt. Hon. A. Morris, Lab.	22,591
K. McKenna, C.	10,595
S. Fenn, LD	3,633
G. Otten, Green	362
Ms E. Martin, NLP	133
Lab. majority	11,996
(June 1987, Lab. maj. 11,855)

MANSFIELD (Notts)
E.66,964   T.82.23%
*J. A. Meale, Lab.	29,932
G. Mond, C.	18,208
S. Thompstone, LD	6,925
Lab. majority	11,724
(June 1987, Lab. maj. 56)

MEDWAY (Kent)
E.61,736   T.80.22%
*Dame P. Fenner, C.	25,924
R. Marshall-Andrews, Lab.	17,138
C. Trice, LD	4,751
M. Austin, Lib.	1,480
P. Kember, NLP	234
C. majority	8,786
(June 1987, C. maj. 9,929)

MERIDEN (W. Midlands)
E.76,994   T.78.85%
*I. Mills, C.	33,462
N. Stephens, Lab.	18,763
Ms J. Morris, LD	8,489
C. majority	14,699
(June 1987, C. maj. 16,820)

MIDDLESBROUGH (Cleveland)
E.58,844   T.69.85%
*S. Bell, Lab.	26,343
P. Rayner, C.	10,559
Ms R. Jordan, LD	4,201
Lab. majority	15,784
(June 1987, Lab. maj. 14,958)

MILTON KEYNES NORTH EAST
(Bucks)
E.62,748   T.80.95%
P. Butler, C.	26,212
Ms M. Cosin, Lab.	12,036
P. Gaskell, LD	11,693
A. Francis, Green	529
Mrs M. Kavanagh-Dowsett, Ind. C.	249
M. Simson, NLP	79
C. majority	14,176
(New constituency)

MILTON KEYNES SOUTH WEST
(Bucks)
E.66,422   T.77
B. Legg, C.	23,840
K. Wilson, Lab.	19,153
C. Pym, LD	7,429
Dr C. Field, Green	525
H. Kelly, NLP	202
C. majority	4,687
(New constituency)

MITCHAM AND MORDEN (Greater London)
E.63,723   T.80.32%
*Rt. Hon. A. Rumbold, C.	23,789
Ms S. McDonagh, Lab.	22,055
J. Field, LD	4,687
T. Walsh, Green	655
C. majority	1,734
(June 1987, C. maj. 6,183)

MOLE VALLEY (Surrey)
E.66,949   T.81.97%
*Rt. Hon. K. Baker, C.	32,549
M. Watson, LD	16,599
Dr T. Walsh, Lab.	5,291

| Ms J. Thomas, NLP | 442 |
| C. majority | 15,950 |
(June 1987, C. maj. 16,076)

MORECAMBE AND LUNESDALE
(Lancs)
E.56,426   T.78.35%
*Hon. M. Lennox-Boyd, C.	22,507
Ms J. Yates, Lab.	10,998
A. Saville, LD	9,584
M. Turner, MBI	916
R. Marriott, NLP	205
C. majority	11,509
(June 1987, C. maj. 11,785)

NEWARK (Notts)
E.68,801   T.82.17%
*R. Alexander, C.	28,494
D. Barton, Lab.	20,265
P. Harris, LD	7,342
Ms P. Wood, Green	435
C. majority	8,229
(June 1987, C. maj. 13,543)

NEWBURY (Berks)
E.80,252   T.82.75%
Mrs J. Chaplin, C.	37,135
D. Rendel, LD	24,778
R. Hall, Lab.	3,962
J. Wallis, Green	539
C. majority	12,357
(June 1987, C. maj. 16,658)
See also page 234

NEWCASTLE UNDER LYME (Staffs)
E.66,595   T.80.34%
*Mrs L. Golding, Lab.	25,652
A. Brierley, C.	15,813
A. Thomas, LD	11,727
R. Lines, NLP	314
Lab. majority	9,839
(June 1987, Lab. maj. 5,132)

NEWCASTLE UPON TYNE CENTRAL
E.59,973   T.71.32%
*J. Cousins, Lab.	21,123
M. Summersby, C.	15,835
L. Opik, LD	5,816
Lab. majority	5,288
(June 1987, Lab. maj. 2,483)

NEWCASTLE UPON TYNE EAST
E.57,165   T.70.73%
*N. Brown, Lab.	24,342
J. Lucas, C.	10,465
A. Thompson, LD	4,883
G. Edwards, Green	744
Lab. majority	13,877
(June 1987, Lab. maj. 12,500)

NEWCASTLE UPON TYNE NORTH
E.66,187   T.76.80%
*D. Henderson, Lab.	25,121
I. Gordon, C.	16,175
P. Maughan, LD	9,542
Lab. majority	8,946
(June 1987, Lab. maj. 5,243)

NEW FOREST (Hants)
E.75,413   T.80.76%
*Sir P. McNair-Wilson, C.	37,986
Ms J. Vernon-Jackson, LD	17,581
M. Shutler, Lab.	4,989
Ms F. Carter, NLP	350

C. majority 20,405
(June 1987, C. maj. 21,732)

NEWHAM NORTH EAST (Greater London)
*E.*59,555 *T.*60.34%
*R. Leighton, *Lab.* 20,952
J. Galbraith, *C.* 10,966
J. Aves, *LD* 4,020
Lab. majority 9,986
(June 1987, Lab. maj. 8,236)
See also page 234

NEWHAM NORTH WEST (Greater London)
*E.*46,471 *T.*56.02%
*T. Banks, *Lab.* 15,911
M. Prisk, *C.* 6,740
A. Sawdon, *LD* 2,445
Ms A. Standford, *Green* 587
T. Jug, *Loony G.* 252
D. O'Sullivan, *Int. Comm.* 100
Lab. majority 9,171
(June 1987, Lab. maj. 8,496)

NEWHAM SOUTH (Greater London)
*E.*51,143 *T.*60.19%
*N. Spearing, *Lab.* 14,358
Ms J. Foster, *C.* 11,856
A. Kellaway, *LD* 4,572
Lab. majority 2,502
(June 1987, Lab. maj. 2,766)

NORFOLK MID
*E.*80,336 *T.*81.64%
*Rt. Hon. R. Ryder, *C.* 35,620
M. Castle, *Lab.* 16,672
J. Gleed, *LD* 13,072
Ms C. Waite, *NLP* 226
C. majority 18,948
(June 1987, C. maj. 18,008)

NORFOLK NORTH
*E.*73,780 *T.*80.84%
*R. Howell, *C.* 28,810
N. Lamb, *LD* 16,265
M. Cullingham, *Lab.* 13,850
Ms A. Zelter, *Green* 559
Ms S. Jackson, *NLP* 167
C. majority 12,545
(June 1987, C. maj. 15,310)

NORFOLK NORTH WEST
*E.*77,438 *T.*80.67%
*H. Bellingham, *C.* 32,554
Dr G. Turner, *Lab.* 20,990
A. Waterman, *LD* 8,599
S. Pink, *NLP* 330
C. majority 11,564
(June 1987, C. maj. 10,825)

NORFOLK SOUTH
*E.*81,647 *T.*83.99%
*Rt. Hon. J. MacGregor, *C.* 36,081
C. Brocklebank-Fowler, *LD* 18,516
C. Needle, *Lab.* 12,422
Ms S. Ross-Wagenknecht, *Green* 702
N. Clark, *NLP* 320
R. Peacock, *Ind.* 304
R. Watkins, *Ind. C.* 232
C. majority 17,565
(June 1987, C. maj. 12,418)

NORFOLK SOUTH WEST
*E.*77,652 *T.*79.30%
*Mrs G. Shephard, *C.* 33,637
Ms M. Page, *Lab.* 16,706
J. Marsh, *LD* 11,237
C. majority 16,931
(June 1987, C. maj. 20,436)

NORMANTON (W. Yorks)
*E.*65,562 *T.*76.35%
*W. O'Brien, *Lab.* 25,936
R. Sturdy, *C.* 16,986
M. Galdas, *LD* 7,137
Lab. majority 8,950
(June 1987, Lab. maj. 7,287)

NORTHAMPTON NORTH
*E.*69,139 *T.*78.52%
*A. Marlow, *C.* 24,865
Ms J. Thomas, *Lab.* 20,957
R. Church, *LD* 8,236
B. Spivack, *NLP* 232
C. majority 3,908
(June 1987, C. maj. 9,256)

NORTHAMPTON SOUTH
*E.*83,477 *T.*79.90%
*M. Morris, *C.* 36,882
J. Dickie, *Lab.* 19,909
G. Mabbutt, *LD* 9,912
C. majority 16,973
(June 1987, C. maj. 17,803)

NORTHAVON (Avon)
*E.*83,496 *T.*84.16%
*Rt. Hon. Sir J. Cope, *C.* 35,338
Ms H. Larkins, *LD* 23,477
Ms J. Norris, *Lab.* 10,290
Ms J. Greene, *Green* 789
P. Marx, *Lib.* 380
C. majority 11,861
(June 1987, C. maj. 14,270)

NORWICH NORTH (Norfolk)
*E.*63,308 *T.*81.82%
*H. P. Thompson, *C.* 22,419
I. Gibson, *Lab.* 22,153
D. Harrison, *LD* 6,706
L. Betts, *Green* 433
R. Arnold, *NLP* 93
C. majority 266
(June 1987, C. maj. 7,776)

NORWICH SOUTH (Norfolk)
*E.*63,603 *T.*80.60%
*J. Garrett, *Lab.* 24,965
D. Baxter, *C.* 18,784
C. Thomas, *LD* 6,609
A. Holmes, *Green* 803
B. Parsons, *NLP* 104
Lab. majority 6,181
(June 1987, Lab. maj. 336)

NORWOOD (Greater London)
*E.*52,496 *T.*65.87%
*J. Fraser, *Lab.* 18,391
J. Samways, *C.* 11,175
Ms S. Lawman, *LD* 4,087
S. Collins, *Green* 790
M. Leighton, *NLP* 138
Lab. majority 7,216
(June 1987, Lab. maj. 4,723)

NOTTINGHAM EAST
*E.*67,939 *T.*70.08%
J. Heppell, *Lab.* 25,026
*M. Knowles, *C.* 17,346
T. Ball, *LD* 3,695
A. Jones, *Green* 667
C. Roylance, *Lib.* 598
J. Ashforth, *NLP* 283
Lab. majority 7,680
(June 1987, C. maj. 456)

NOTTINGHAM NORTH
*E.*69,494 *T.*74.98%
*G. Allen, *Lab.* 29,052
I. Bridge, *C.* 18,309
A. Skelton, *LD* 4,477
A. Cadman, *NLP* 274
Lab. majority 10,743
(June 1987, Lab. maj. 1,665)

NOTTINGHAM SOUTH
*E.*72,796 *T.*74.22%
A. Simpson, *Lab.* 25,771
*M. Brandon-Bravo, *C.* 22,590
G. D. Long, *LD* 5,408
Ms J. Christou, *NLP* 263
Lab. majority 3,181
(June 1987, C. maj. 2,234)

NUNEATON (Warwicks)
*E.*70,906 *T.*83.70%
W. Olner, *Lab.* 27,157
*L. Stevens, *C.* 25,526
Ms R. Merritt, *LD* 6,671
Lab. majority 1,631
(June 1987, C. maj. 5,655)

OLD BEXLEY AND SIDCUP (Greater London)
*E.*49,449 *T.*81.94%
*Rt. Hon. E. Heath, *C.* 24,450
Ms D. Brierly, *Lab.* 8,751
D. Nicolle, *LD* 6,438
B. Rose, *Alt. C.* 733
R. Stephens, *NLP* 148
C. majority 15,699
(June 1987, C. maj. 16,274)

OLDHAM CENTRAL AND ROYTON (Greater Manchester)
*E.*61,333 *T.*74.20%
B. Davies, *Lab.* 23,246
Mrs T. Morris, *C.* 14,640
Ms A. Dunn, *LD* 7,224
I. Dalling, *NLP* 403
Lab. majority 8,606
(June 1987, Lab. maj. 6,279)

OLDHAM WEST (Greater Manchester)
*E.*54,063 *T.*75.65%
*M. Meacher, *Lab.* 21,580
J. Gillen, *C.* 13,247
J. Smith, *LD* 5,525
Ms S. Dalling, *NLP* 551
Lab. majority 8,333
(June 1987, Lab. maj. 5,967)

ORPINGTON (Greater London)
*E.*57,318 *T.*83.67%
J. Horam, *C.* 27,421
C. Maines, *LD* 14,486
S. Cowan, *Lab.* 5,512

R. Almond, *Lib.* 539
C. majority 12,935
(June 1987, C. maj. 12,732)

OXFORD EAST
*E.*63,075 *T.*74.59%
*A. Smith, *Lab.* 23,702
Dr M. Mayall, *C.* 16,164
M. Horwood, *LD* 6,105
Mrs C. Lucas, *Green* 933
Miss A. Wilson, *NLP* 101
K. Thompson, *Rev. Comm.* 48
Lab. majority 7,538
(June 1987, Lab. maj. 1,288)

OXFORD WEST AND ABINGDON
*E.*72,328 *T.*76.68%
*Rt. Hon. J. Patten, *C.* 25,163
Sir W. Goodhart, *LD* 21,624
B. Kent, *Lab.* 7,652
M. Woodin, *Green* 660
R. Jenking, *Lib.* 194
Miss S. Nelson, *Anti Fed.* 98
G. Wells, *NLP* 75
C. majority 3,539
(June 1987, C. maj. 4,878)

PECKHAM (Greater London)
*E.*58,269 *T.*53.87%
*Ms H. Harman, *Lab.* 19,391
C. Frazer, *C.* 7,386
Mrs R. Colley, *LD* 4,331
G. Dacres, *WRP* 146
V. Emmanuel, *Whiplash* 140
Lab. majority 12,005
(June 1987, Lab. maj. 9,489)

PENDLE (Lancs)
*E.*64,063 *T.*82.91%
G. Prentice, *Lab.* 23,497
*J. Lee, *C.* 21,384
A. Davies, *LD* 7,976
Mrs V. Thorne, *Anti Fed.* 263
Lab. majority 2,113
(June 1987, C. maj. 2,639)

PENRITH AND THE BORDER
(Cumbria)
*E.*73,769 *T.*79.67%
*D. Maclean, *C.* 33,808
G. Walker, *LD* 15,359
J. Metcalfe, *Lab.* 8,871
R. Gibson, *Green* 610
I. Docker, *NLP* 129
C. majority 18,449
(June 1987, C. maj. 17,366)

PETERBOROUGH (Cambs)
*E.*87,638 *T.*75.12%
*B. Mawhinney, *C.* 31,827
Ms J. Owens, *Lab.* 26,451
Ms A. Taylor, *LD* 5,208
E. Murat, *Lib.* 1,557
R. Heaton, *BNP* 311
P. Beasley, *PP* 271
C. Brettell, *NLP* 215
C. majority 5,376
(June 1987, C. maj. 9,784)

PLYMOUTH DEVONPORT (Devon)
*E.*65,799 *T.*77.83%
D. Jamieson, *Lab.* 24,953
K. Simpson, *C.* 17,541

M. Mactaggart, *LD* 6,315
H. Luscombe, *SD* 2,152
F. Lyons, *NLP* 255
Lab. majority 7,412
(June 1987, SDP/All. maj. 6,470)

PLYMOUTH DRAKE (Devon)
*E.*51,667 *T.*75.56%
*Dame J. Fookes, *C.* 17,075
P. Telford, *Lab.* 15,062
Ms V. Cox, *LD* 5,893
D. Stanbury, *SD* 476
Ms A. Harrison, *Green* 441
T. Pringle, *NLP* 95
C. majority 2,013
(June 1987, C. maj. 3,125)

PLYMOUTH SUTTON (Devon)
*E.*67,430 *T.*81.17%
G. Streeter, *C.* 27,070
A. Pawley, *Lab.* 15,120
J. Brett-Freeman, *LD* 12,291
J. Bowler, *NLP* 256
C. majority 11,950
(June 1987, C. maj. 4,013)

PONTEFRACT AND CASTLEFORD
(W. Yorks)
*E.*64,648 *T.*74.25%
*G. Lofthouse, *Lab.* 33,546
A. Rockall, *C.* 10,051
D. Ryan, *LD* 4,410
Lab. majority 23,495
(June 1987, Lab. maj. 21,626)

POOLE (Dorset)
*E.*79,221 *T.*79.39%
*J. Ward, *C.* 33,445
B. Clements, *LD* 20,614
H. White, *Lab.* 6,912
M. Steen, *Ind. C.* 1,620
A. Bailey, *NLP* 303
C. majority 12,831
(June 1987, C. maj. 14,808)

PORTSMOUTH NORTH (Hants)
*E.*79,592 *T.*77.05%
*P. Griffiths, *C.* 32,240
A. Burnett, *Lab.* 18,359
A. Bentley, *LD* 10,101
Ms H. Palmer, *Green* 628
C. majority 13,881
(June 1987, C. maj. 18,401)

PORTSMOUTH SOUTH (Hants)
*E.*77,645 *T.*69.09%
*D. Martin, *C.* 22,798
M. Hancock, *LD* 22,556
S. Rapson, *Lab.* 7,857
A. Zivkovic, *Green* 349
W. Trend, *NLP* 91
C. majority 242
(June 1987, C. maj. 205)

PRESTON (Lancs)
*E.*64,158 *T.*71.74%
*Mrs A. Wise, *Lab.* 24,983
S. O'Toole, *C.* 12,808
W. Chadwick, *LD* 7,897
Ms J. Ayliffe, *NLP* 341
Lab. majority 12,175
(June 1987, Lab. maj. 10,645)

PUDSEY (W. Yorks)
*E.*70,847 *T.*80.14%
*Sir G. Shaw, *C.* 25,067
A. Giles, *Lab.* 16,095
D. Shutt, *LD* 15,153
Ms J. Wynne, *Green* 466
C. majority 8,972
(June 1987, C. maj. 6,436)

PUTNEY (Greater London)
*E.*61,914 *T.*77.91%
*Rt. Hon. D. Mellor, *C.* 25,188
Ms J. Chegwidden, *Lab.* 17,662
J. Martyn, *LD* 4,636
K. Hagenbach, *Green* 618
P. Levy, *NLP* 139
C. majority 7,526
(June 1987, C. maj. 6,907)

RAVENSBOURNE (Greater London)
*E.*57,259 *T.*81.24%
*Sir J. Hunt, *C.* 29,506
P. Booth, *LD* 9,792
E. Dyer, *Lab.* 6,182
I. Mouland, *Green* 617
P. White, *Lib.* 318
J. Shepheard, *NLP* 105
C. majority 19,714
(June 1987, C. maj. 16,919)

READING EAST (Berks)
*E.*72,151 *T.*75.02%
*Sir G. Vaughan, *C.* 29,148
Ms G. Parker, *Lab.* 14,593
D. Thair, *LD* 9,528
Ms A. McCubbin, *Green* 861
C. majority 14,555
(June 1987, C. maj. 16,217)

READING WEST (Berks)
*E.*67,937 *T.*77.98%
*Sir A. Durant, *C.* 28,048
P. Ruhemann, *Lab.* 14,750
K. Lock, *LD* 9,572
P. Unsworth, *Green* 613
C. majority 13,298
(June 1987, C. maj. 16,753)

REDCAR (Cleveland)
*E.*62,494 *T.*77.73%
*Dr M. Mowlam, *Lab.* 27,184
R. Goodwill, *C.* 15,607
C. Abbott, *LD* 5,789
Lab. majority 11,577
(June 1987, Lab. maj. 7,735)

REIGATE (Surrey)
*E.*71,853 *T.*78.54%
*Sir G. Gardiner, *C.* 32,220
B. Newsome, *LD* 14,556
Ms H. Young, *Lab.* 9,150
M. Dilcliff, *SD* 513
C. majority 17,664
(June 1987, C. maj. 18,173)

RIBBLE VALLEY (Lancs)
*E.*64,996 *T.*85.73%
N. Evans, *C.* 29,178
*M. Carr, *LD* 22,636
R. Pickup, *Lab.* 3,649
D. Beesley, *Loony G.* 152
Ms N. Holmes, *NLP* 112

C. majority 6,542
(June 1987, C. maj. 19,528)
(March 1991, LD maj. 4,641)

RICHMOND AND BARNES (Greater London)
E.53,081   T.85.01%
*J. Hanley, *C.* 22,894
Dr J. Tonge, *LD* 19,025
D. Touhig, *Lab.* 2,632
Ms J. Maciejowska, *Green* 376
C. Cunningham, *NLP* 89
R. Meacock, *QFL* 62
Ms A. Ellis-Jones, *Anti Fed.* 47
C. majority 3,869
(June 1987, C. maj. 1,766)

RICHMOND (N. Yorks)
E.82,879   T.78.41%
*W. Hague, *C.* 40,202
G. Irwin, *LD* 16,698
R. Cranston, *Lab.* 7,523
M. Barr, *Ind.* 570
C. majority 23,504
(June 1987, C. maj. 19,576)
(Feb 1989, C. maj. 2,634)

ROCHDALE (Greater Manchester)
E.69,522   T.76.47%
Ms E. Lynne, *LD* 22,776
D. Williams, *Lab.* 20,937
D. Goldie-Scott, *C.* 8,626
K. Henderson, *BNP* 620
V. Lucker, *NLP* 211
LD majority 1,839
(June 1987, L./All. maj. 2,779)

ROCHFORD (Essex)
E.76,869   T.82.99%
*Dr M. Clark, *C.* 38,967
N. Harris, *LD* 12,931
D. Quinn, *Lab.* 10,537
Ms L. Farmer, *Lib.* 1,362
C. majority 26,036
(June 1987, C. maj. 19,694)

ROMFORD (Greater London)
E.54,001   T.78%
*Sir M. Neubert, *C.* 23,834
Ms E. Gordon, *Lab.* 12,414
Ms P. Atherton, *LD* 5,329
F. Gibson, *Green* 546
C. majority 11,420
(June 1987, C. maj. 13,471)

ROMSEY AND WATERSIDE (Hants)
E.82,628   T.83.15%
*M. Colvin, *C.* 37,375
G. Dawson, *LD* 22,071
Mrs A. Mawle, *Lab.* 8,688
J. Spottiswood, *Green* 577
C. majority 15,304
(June 1987, C. maj. 15,272)

ROSSENDALE AND DARWEN (Lancs)
E.76,909   T.83.06%
Mrs J. Anderson, *Lab.* 28,028
*D. Trippier, *C.* 27,908
K. Connor, *LD* 7,226
J. Gaffney, *Green* 596
P. Gorrod, *NLP* 125
Lab. majority 120
(June 1987, C. maj. 4,982)

ROTHERHAM (S. Yorks)
E.60,937   T.71.68%
J. Boyce, *Lab.* 27,933
S. Yorke, *C.* 10,372
D. Wildgoose, *LD* 5,375
Lab. majority 17,561
(June 1987, Lab. maj. 16,012)
See also page 234

ROTHER VALLEY (S. Yorks)
E.68,303   T.74.98%
*K. Barron, *Lab.* 30,977
T. Horton, *C.* 13,755
K. Smith, *LD* 6,483
Lab. majority 17,222
(June 1987, Lab. maj. 15,790)

RUGBY AND KENILWORTH (Warwicks)
E.77,766   T.83.72%
*J. Pawsey, *C.* 34,110
J. Airey, *Lab.* 20,863
J. Roodhouse, *LD* 9,934
S. Withers, *NLP* 202
C. majority 13,247
(June 1987, C. maj. 16,264)

RUISLIP-NORTHWOOD (Greater London)
E.54,151   T.81.91%
*J. Wilkinson, *C.* 28,097
Ms R. Brooks, *Lab.* 8,306
H. Davies, *LD* 7,739
M. Sheehan, *NLP* 214
C. majority 19,791
(June 1987, C. maj. 16,971)

RUSHCLIFFE (Notts)
E.76,253   T.83.04%
*Rt. Hon. K. Clarke, *C.* 34,448
A. Chewings, *Lab.* 14,682
Dr A. Wood, *LD* 12,660
S. Anthony, *Green* 775
M. Maelor-Jones, *Ind. C.* 611
D. Richards, *NLP* 150
C. majority 19,766
(June 1987, C. maj. 20,839)

RUTLAND AND MELTON (Leics)
E.80,976   T.80.82%
A. Duncan, *C.* 38,603
Ms J. Taylor, *Lab.* 13,068
R. Lustig, *LD* 12,682
J. Berreen, *Green* 861
R. Grey, *NLP* 237
C. majority 25,535
(June 1987, C. maj. 23,022)

RYEDALE (N. Yorks)
E.87,048   T.81.73%
*J. Greenway, *C.* 39,888
Mrs E. Shields, *LD* 21,449
J. Healey, *Lab.* 9,812
C. majority 18,439
(June 1987, C. maj. 9,740)

SAFFRON WALDEN (Essex)
E.74,878   T.83.21%
*A. Haselhurst, *C.* 35,272
M. Hayes, *LD* 17,848
J. Kotz, *Lab.* 8,933
M. Miller, *NLP* 260

C. majority 17,424
(June 1987, C. maj. 16,602)

ST ALBANS (Herts)
E.74,188   T.83.47%
*Rt. Hon. P. Lilley, *C.* 32,709
Ms M. Howes, *LD* 16,305
K. Pollard, *Lab.* 12,016
C. Simmons, *Green* 734
D. Lucas, *NLP* 161
C. majority 16,404
(June 1987, C. maj. 10,881)

ST HELENS NORTH (Merseyside)
E.71,261   T.77.35%
*J. Evans, *Lab.* 31,930
B. Anderson, *C.* 15,686
J. Beirne, *LD* 7,224
Ms A. Lynch, *NLP* 287
Lab. majority 16,244
(June 1987, Lab. maj. 14,260)

ST HELENS SOUTH (Merseyside)
E.67,507   T.73.77%
*G. Bermingham, *Lab.* 30,391
Mrs P. Buzzard, *C.* 12,182
B. Spencer, *LD* 6,933
Dr H. Jump, *NLP* 295
Lab. majority 18,209
(June 1987, Lab. maj. 13,801)

ST IVES (Cornwall)
E.71,152   T.80.29%
*D. Harris, *C.* 24,528
A. George, *LD* 22,883
S. Warran, *Lab.* 9,144
Dr G. Stephens, *Lib.* 577
C. majority 1,645
(June 1987, C. maj. 7,555)

SALFORD EAST (Greater Manchester)
E.52,616   T.64.36%
*Rt. Hon. S. Orme, *Lab.* 20,327
D. Berens, *C.* 9,092
N. Owen, *LD* 3,836
M. Stanley, *Green* 463
C. Craig, *NLP* 150
Lab. majority 11,235
(June 1987, Lab. maj. 12,056)

SALISBURY (Wilts)
E.75,916   T.79.89%
*S. R. Key, *C.* 31,546
P. Sample, *LD* 22,573
S. Fear, *Lab.* 5,483
Dr S. Elcock, *Green* 609
S. Fletcher, *Ind.* 233
T. Abbott, *Wessex* 117
Ms A. Martell, *NLP* 93
C. majority 8,973
(June 1987, C. maj. 11,443)

SCARBOROUGH (N. Yorks)
E.76,364   T.77.18%
J. Sykes, *C.* 29,334
D. Billing, *Lab.* 17,600
B. Davenport, *LD* 11,133
Dr D. Richardson, *Green* 876
C. majority 11,734
(June 1987, C. maj. 13,626)

SEDGEFIELD (Durham)
E.61,024   T.77.06%

*A. Blair, *Lab.*	28,453
N. Jopling, *C.*	13,594
G. Huntington, *LD*	4,982
Lab. majority	14,859
(June 1987, Lab. maj. 13,058)	

SELBY (N. Yorks)
E.77,178   T.80.16%

*Rt. Hon. M. Alison, *C.*	31,067
J. Grogan, *Lab.*	21,559
E. Batty, *LD*	9,244
C. majority	9,508
(June 1987, C. maj. 13,779)	

SEVENOAKS (Kent)
E.71,050   T.81.35%

*G. M. Wolfson, *C.*	33,245
R. Walshe, *LD*	14,091
Ms J. Evans, *Lab.*	9,470
Ms M. Lawrence, *Green*	786
P. Wakeling, *NLP*	210
C. majority	19,154
(June 1987, C. maj. 17,345)	

SHEFFIELD ATTERCLIFFE (S. Yorks)
E.69,177   T.71.81%

C. Betts, *Lab.*	28,563
G. Millward, *C.*	13,083
Ms H. Woolley, *LD*	7,283
G. Ferguson, *Green*	751
Lab. majority	15,480
(June 1987, Lab. maj. 17,191)	

SHEFFIELD BRIGHTSIDE (S. Yorks)
E.63,810   T.66.26%

*D. Blunkett, *Lab.*	29,771
T. Loughton, *C.*	7,090
R. Franklin, *LD*	5,273
D. Hyland, *Int. Comm.*	150
Lab. majority	22,681
(June 1987, Lab. maj. 24,191)	

SHEFFIELD CENTRAL (S. Yorks)
E.59,059   T.56.12%

*R. Caborn, *Lab.*	22,764
V. Davies, *C.*	5,470
A. Sangar, *LD*	3,856
G. Wroe, *Green*	750
M. Clarke, *EUVJJ*	212
Ms J. O'Brien, *CL*	92
Lab. majority	17,294
(June 1987, Lab. maj. 19,342)	

SHEFFIELD HALLAM (S. Yorks)
E.76,584   T.70.83%

*C. I. Patnick, *C.*	24,693
Dr P. Gold, *LD*	17,952
Ms V. Hardstaff, *Lab.*	10,930
M. Baker, *Green*	473
R. Hurford, *NLP*	101
Ms T. Clifford, *Rev. Comm.*	99
C. majority	6,741
(June 1987, C. maj. 7,637)	

SHEFFIELD HEELEY (S. Yorks)
E.70,953   T.70.89%

*W. Michie, *Lab.*	28,005
D. Beck, *C.*	13,051
P. Moore, *LD*	9,247
Lab. majority	14,954
(June 1987, Lab. maj. 14,440)	

SHEFFIELD HILLSBOROUGH
(S. Yorks)
E.77,343   T.77.19%

Mrs H. Jackson, *Lab.*	27,568
D. Chadwick, *LD*	20,500
S. Cordle, *C.*	11,640
Lab. majority	7,068
(June 1987, Lab. maj. 3,286)	

SHERWOOD (Notts)
E.73,354   T.85.48%

S. P. Tipping, *Lab.*	29,788
*A. Stewart, *C.*	26,878
J. Howard, *LD*	6,039
Lab. majority	2,910
(June 1987, C. maj. 4,495)	

SHIPLEY (W. Yorks)
E.68,816   T.82.12%

*Sir M. Fox, *C.*	28,463
Ms A. Lockwood, *Lab.*	16,081
J. Cole, *LD*	11,288
C. Harris, *Green*	680
C. majority	12,382
(June 1987, C. maj. 12,630)	

SHOREHAM (W. Sussex)
E.71,252   T.81.17%

B. M. L. Stephen, *C.*	32,670
M. King, *LD*	18,384
P. Godwin, *Lab.*	6,123
W. Weights, *Lib.*	459
J. Dreben, *NLP*	200
C. majority	14,286
(June 1987, C. maj. 17,070)	

SHREWSBURY AND ATCHAM (Salop)
E.70,620   T.82.45%

*D. Conway, *C.*	26,681
K. Hemsley, *LD*	15,716
Ms E. Owen, *Lab.*	15,157
G. Hardy, *Green*	677
C. majority	10,965
(June 1987, C. maj. 9,064)	

SHROPSHIRE NORTH
E.82,675   T.77.68%

*Rt. Hon. J. Biffen, *C.*	32,443
J. Stevens, *LD*	16,232
R. Hawkins, *Lab.*	15,550
C. majority	16,211
(June 1987, C. maj. 14,415)	

SKIPTON AND RIPON (N. Yorks)
E.75,628   T.81.34%

*D. Curry, *C.*	35,937
R. Hall, *LD*	16,607
Ms K. Allott, *Lab.*	8,978
C. majority	19,330
(June 1987, C. maj. 17,174)	

SLOUGH (Berks)
E.73,889   T.78.24%

*J. Watts, *C.*	25,793
E. Lopez, *Lab.*	25,279
P. Mapp, *LD*	4,041
J. Clark, *Lib.*	1,426
D. Alford, *Ind. Lab.*	699
A. Carmichael, *NF*	290
M. Creese, *NLP*	153
Ms E. Smith, *ERIP*	134
C. majority	514
(June 1987, C. maj. 4,090)	

SOLIHULL (W. Midlands)
E.77,303   T.81.61%

*J. Taylor, *C.*	38,385
M. Southcombe, *LD*	13,239
Ms N. Kutapan, *Lab.*	10,544
C. Hards, *Green*	925
C. majority	25,146
(June 1987, C. maj. 21,786)	

SOMERTON AND FROME (Somerset)
E.71,354   T.82.75%

M. Robinson, *C.*	28,052
D. Heath, *LD*	23,711
R. Ashford, *Lab.*	6,154
Ms L. Graham, *Green*	742
Ms J. Pollock, *Lib.*	388
C. majority	4,341
(June 1987, C. maj. 9,538)	

SOUTHAMPTON ITCHEN (Hants)
E.72,104   T.76.93%

J. Denham, *Lab.*	24,402
*C. Chope, *C.*	23,851
J. Hodgson, *LD*	7,221
Lab. majority	551
(June 1987, C. maj. 6,716)	

SOUTHAMPTON TEST (Hants)
E.72,932   T.77.40%

*S. J. A. Hill, *C.*	24,504
A. Whitehead, *Lab.*	23,919
Ms D. Maddock, *LD*	7,391
J. Michaelis, *Green*	535
D. Plummer, *NLP*	101
C. majority	585
(June 1987, C. maj. 6,954)	

SOUTHEND EAST (Essex)
E.56,708   T.73.80%

*Sir E. Taylor, *C.*	24,591
G. Bramley, *Lab.*	11,480
Ms J. Horne, *LD*	5,107
B. Lynch, *Lib.*	673
C. majority	13,111
(June 1987, C. maj. 13,847)	

SOUTHEND WEST (Essex)
E.64,198   T.77.80%

*Rt. Hon. P. Channon, *C.*	27,319
Ms N. Stimson, *LD*	15,417
G. Viney, *Lab.*	6,139
A. Farmer, *Lib.*	495
C. Keene, *Green*	451
P. Warburton, *NLP*	127
C. majority	11,902
(June 1987, C. maj. 8,400)	

SOUTH HAMS (Devon)
E.83,061   T.81.09%

*A. Steen, *C.*	35,951
V. Evans, *LD*	22,240
Ms E. Cohen, *Lab.*	8,091
C. Titmuss, *Green*	846
Mrs L. Summerville, *NLP*	227
C. majority	13,711
(June 1987, C. maj. 13,146)	

SOUTHPORT (Merseyside)
E.71,443   T.77.60%

M. Banks, *C.*	26,081
*R. Fearn, *LD*	23,018
J. King, *Lab.*	5,637
J. Walker, *Green*	545

G. Clements, *NLP* 159
C. majority 3,063
(June 1987, L./All. maj. 1,849)

SOUTH RIBBLE (Lancs)
*E.*78,173   *T.*82.99%
*R. Atkins, *C.* 30,828
Dr G. Smith, *Lab.* 24,855
S. Jones, *LD* 8,928
Dr R. Decter, *NLP* 269
C. majority 5,973
(June 1987, C. maj. 8,430)

SOUTH SHIELDS (Tyne & Wear)
*E.*59,392   *T.*70.07%
*D. Clark, *Lab.* 24,876
J. Howard, *C.* 11,399
A. Preece, *LD* 5,344
Lab. majority 13,477
(June 1987, Lab. maj. 13,851)

SOUTHWARK AND BERMONDSEY
(Greater London)
*E.*60,251   *T.*62.62%
*S. Hughes, *LD* 21,459
R. Balfe, *Lab.* 11,614
A. Raca, *C.* 3,794
S. Tyler, *BNP* 530
T. Blackham, *NF* 168
Dr G. Barnett, *NLP* 113
J. Grogan, *CL* 56
LD majority 9,845
June 1987, L./All. maj. 2,779

SPELTHORNE (Surrey)
*E.*69,343   *T.*80.36%
*D. Wilshire, *C.* 32,627
Ms A. Leedham, *Lab.* 12,784
R. Roberts, *LD* 9,202
Ms J. Wassell, *Green* 580
D. Rea, *Loony* 338
D. Ellis, *NLP* 195
C. majority 19,843
(June 1987, C. maj. 20,050)

STAFFORD
*E.*74,663   *T.*82.91%
*W. Cash, *C.* 30,876
D. Kidney, *Lab.* 19,976
Mrs J. Calder, *LD* 10,702
C. Peat, *Hardcore* 178
P. Lines, *NLP* 176
C. majority 10,900
(June 1987, C. maj. 13,707)

STAFFORDSHIRE MID
*E.*73,414   *T.*85.66%
M. Fabricant, *C.* 31,227
*Mrs S. Heal, *Lab.* 24,991
B. Stamp, *LD* 6,432
Ms D. Grice, *NLP* 239
C. majority 6,236
(June 1987, C. maj. 14,654)
(March 1990, Lab. maj. 9,449)

STAFFORDSHIRE MOORLANDS
*E.*75,036   *T.*83.66%
*D. Knox, *C.* 29,240
J. Siddelley, *Lab.* 21,830
Ms C. Jebb, *LD* 9,326
M. Howson, *Anti Fed.* 2,121
P. Davies, *NLP* 261

C. majority 7,410
(June 1987, C. maj. 14,427)

STAFFORDSHIRE SOUTH
*E.*82,758   *T.*81.54%
*P. Cormack, *C.* 40,266
B. Wylie, *Lab.* 17,633
I. Sadler, *LD* 9,584
C. majority 22,633
(June 1987, C. maj. 25,268)

STAFFORDSHIRE SOUTH EAST
*E.*70,199   *T.*82.05%
*D. Lightbown, *C.* 29,180
B. Jenkins, *Lab.* 21,988
Dr G. Penlington, *LD* 5,540
Miss J. Taylor, *SD* 895
C. majority 7,192
(June 1987, C. maj. 10,885)
See also page 235

STALYBRIDGE AND HYDE (Greater
Manchester)
*E.*68,189   *T.*73.46%
*T. Pendry, *Lab.* 26,207
S. Mort, *C.* 17,376
I. Kirk, *LD* 4,740
R. Powell, *Lib.* 1,199
D. Poyzer, *Loony* 337
E. Blomfield, *NLP* 238
Lab. majority 8,831
(June 1987, Lab. maj. 5,663)

STAMFORD AND SPALDING (Lincs)
*E.*75,153   *T.*81.16%
*J. Q. Davies, *C.* 35,965
C. Burke, *Lab.* 13,096
B. Lee, *LD* 11,939
C. majority 22,869
(June 1987, C. maj. 14,007)

STEVENAGE (Herts)
*E.*70,233   *T.*83.03%
*T. Wood, *C.* 26,652
Ms J. Church, *Lab.* 21,764
A. Reilly, *LD* 9,668
A. Calcraft, *NLP* 233
C. majority 4,888
(June 1987, C. maj. 5,340)

STOCKPORT (Greater Manchester)
*E.*58,095   *T.*82.27%
Ms M. A. Coffey, *Lab.* 21,096
*A. Favell, *C.* 19,674
Ms A. Corris, *LD* 6,539
Ms J. Filmore, *Green* 436
D. Saunders, *NLP* 50
Lab. majority 1,422
(June 1987, C. maj. 2,853)

STOCKTON NORTH (Cleveland)
*E.*69,451   *T.*76.83%
*F. Cook, *Lab.* 27,918
S. Brocklebank-Fowler, *C.* 17,444
Ms S. Fletcher, *LD* 7,454
K. McGarvey, *Ind. Lab.* 550
Lab. majority 10,474
(June 1987, Lab. maj. 8,801)

STOCKTON SOUTH (Cleveland)
*E.*75,959   *T.*82.77%
*T. Devlin, *C.* 28,418
J. Scott, *Lab.* 25,049
Ms K. Kirkham, *LD* 9,410

C. majority 3,369
(June 1987, C. maj. 774)

STOKE-ON-TRENT CENTRAL
(Staffs)
*E.*65,527   *T.*68.12%
*M. Fisher, *Lab.* 25,897
N. Gibb, *C.* 12,477
M. Dent, *LD* 6,073
N. Pullen, *NLP* 196
Lab. majority 13,420
(June 1987, Lab. maj. 9,770)

STOKE-ON-TRENT NORTH (Staffs)
*E.*73,141   *T.*73.42%
*Ms J. Walley, *Lab.* 30,464
L. Harris, *C.* 15,687
J. Redfern, *LD* 7,167
A. Morrison, *NLP* 387
Lab. majority 14,777
(June 1987, Lab. maj. 8,513)

STOKE-ON-TRENT SOUTH (Staffs)
*E.*71,316   *T.*74.33%
G. Stevenson, *Lab.* 26,380
R. Ibbs, *C.* 19,471
F. Jones, *LD* 6,870
Mrs E. Lines, *NLP* 291
Lab. majority 6,909
(June 1987, Lab. maj. 5,053)

STRATFORD-UPON-AVON
(Warwicks)
*E.*82,824   *T.*82.07%
*A. Howarth, *C.* 40,251
N. Fogg, *LD* 17,359
Ms S. Brookes, *Lab.* 8,932
R. Roughan, *Green* 729
A. Saunders, *Ind. C.* 573
M. Twite, *NLP* 130
C. majority 22,892
(June 1987, C. maj. 21,165)

STREATHAM (Greater London)
*E.*56,825   *T.*69.03%
K. Hill, *Lab.* 18,925
*Sir W. Shelton, *C.* 16,608
J. Pindar, *LD* 3,858
R. Baker, *Green* 443
A. Hankin, *Islamic* 154
Mrs C. Payne, *ADS* 145
J. Parsons, *NLP* 97
Lab. majority 2,317
(June 1987, C. maj. 2,407)

STRETFORD (Greater Manchester)
*E.*54,467   *T.*68.76%
*A. Lloyd, *Lab.* 22,300
C. Rae, *C.* 11,163
F. Beswick, *LD* 3,722
A. Boyton, *NLP* 268
Lab. majority 11,137
(June 1987, Lab. maj. 9,402)

STROUD (Glos)
*E.*82,553   *T.*84.49%
*R. Knapman, *C.* 32,201
D. Drew, *Lab.* 18,796
M. Robinson, *LD* 16,751
Ms S. Atkinson, *Green* 2,005
C. majority 13,405
(June 1987, C. maj. 12,375)

SUFFOLK CENTRAL
E.82,735   T.80.26%
*M. Lord, C.   32,917
Ms L. Henniker-Major, LD   16,886
J. Harris, Lab.   15,615
J. Matthissen, Green   800
Ms J. Wilmot, NLP   190
C. majority   16,031
(June 1987, C. maj. 16,290)

SUFFOLK COASTAL
E.79,333   T.81.62%
*Rt. Hon. J. Gummer, C.   34,680
P. Monk, LD   15,395
T. Hodgson, Lab.   13,508
A. Slade, Green   943
Ms F. Kaplan, NLP   232
C. majority   19,285
(June 1987, C. maj. 15,280)

SUFFOLK SOUTH
E.84,833   T.81.73%
*T. Yeo, C.   34,793
Ms K. Pollard, LD   17,504
S. Hesford, Lab.   16,623
T. Aisbitt, NLP   420
C. majority   17,289
(June 1987, C. maj. 16,243)

SUNDERLAND NORTH (Tyne &
Wear)
E.72,874   T.68.86%
W. Etherington, Lab.   30,481
Miss J. Barnes, C.   13,477
V. Halom, LD   5,389
Ms W. Lundgren, Lib.   841
Lab. majority   17,004
(June 1987, Lab. maj. 14,672)

SUNDERLAND SOUTH (Tyne &
Wear)
E.72,607   T.69.87%
*C. Mullin, Lab.   29,399
G. Howe, C.   14,898
J. Lennox, LD   5,844
T. Scouler, Green   596
Lab. majority   14,501
(June 1987, Lab. maj. 12,613)

SURBITON (Greater London)
E.42,421   T.82.44%
*R. Tracey, C.   19,033
Ms B. Janke, LD   9,394
R. Hutchinson, Lab.   6,384
W. Parker, NLP   161
C. majority   9,639
(June 1987, C. maj. 9,741)

SURREY EAST
E.57,878   T.82.53%
P. Ainsworth, C.   29,767
R. Tomlin, LD   12,111
Mrs G. Roles, Lab.   5,075
I. Kilpatrick, Green   819
C. majority   17,656
(June 1987, C. maj. 18,126)

SURREY NORTH WEST
E.83,648   T.78.27%
*Sir M. Grylls, C.   41,772
Mrs C. Clark, LD   13,378
M. Hayhurst, Lab.   8,886
Ms Y. Hockey, Green   1,441

C. majority   28,394
(June 1987, C. maj. 23,575)

SURREY SOUTH WEST
E.72,288   T.82.77%
*Mrs V. Bottomley, C.   35,008
N. Sherlock, LD   20,033
P. Kelly, Lab.   3,840
N. Bedrock, Green   710
K. Campbell, NLP   147
D. Newman, AS   98
C. majority   14,975
(June 1987, C. maj. 14,343)

SUSSEX MID
E.80,827   T.82.85%
*Rt. Hon. T. Renton, C.   39,524
Ms M. Collins, LD   18,996
Ms L. Gregory, Lab.   6,951
H. Stevens, Green   772
P. Berry, Loony   392
P. Hodkin, PR   246
Dr A. Hankey, NLP   89
C. majority   20,528
(June 1987, C. maj. 18,292)

SUTTON AND CHEAM (Greater
London)
E.60,949   T.82.39%
Lady O. Maitland, C.   27,710
P. Burstow, LD   16,954
G. Martin, Lab.   4,980
J. Duffy, Green   444
Ms A. Hatchard, NLP   133
C. majority   10,756
(June 1987, C. maj. 15,718)

SUTTON COLDFIELD (W. Midlands)
E.71,410   T.79.51%
*Rt. Hon. Sir N. Fowler, C.   37,001
J. Whorwood, LD   10,965
Ms J. Bott-Obi, Lab.   8,490
H. Meads, NLP   324
C. majority   26,036
(June 1987, C. maj. 21,183)

SWINDON (Wilts)
E.90,067   T.81.46%
*S. Coombs, C.   31,749
J. D'Avila, Lab.   28,923
S. Cordon, LD   11,737
W. Hughes, Green   647
R. Gillard, Loony G.   236
V. Farrar, Ind.   78
C. majority   2,826
(June 1987, C. maj. 4,857)

TATTON (Cheshire)
E.71,085   T.80.83%
*M. N. Hamilton, C.   31,658
J. Kelly, Lab.   15,798
Ms C. Hancox, LD   9,597
M. Gibson, FP   410
C. majority   15,860
(June 1987, C. maj. 17,094)

TAUNTON (Somerset)
E.78,036   T.82.32%
*D. Nicholson, C.   29,576
Ms J. Ballard, LD   26,240
Ms J. Hole, Lab.   8,151
P. Leavey, NLP   279

C. majority   3,336
(June 1987, C. maj. 10,380)

TEIGNBRIDGE (Devon)
E.74,892   T.83.43%
*P. Nicholls, C.   31,272
R. Younger-Ross, LD   22,416
R. Kennedy, Lab.   8,128
A. Hope, Loony   437
N. Hayes, NLP   234
C. majority   8,856
(June 1987, C. maj. 10,425)

THANET NORTH (Kent)
E.70,978   T.76.02%
*R. Gale, C.   30,867
A. Bretman, Lab.   12,657
Ms J. Phillips, LD   9,563
Ms H. Dawe, Green   873
C. majority   18,210
(June 1987, C. maj. 17,480)

THANET SOUTH (Kent)
E.62,441   T.78.17%
*J. Aitken, C.   25,253
M. James, Lab.   13,740
W. Pitt, LD   8,948
Ms S. Peckham, Green   871
C. majority   11,513
(June 1987, C. maj. 13,683)

THURROCK (Essex)
E.69,171   T.78.15%
A. MacKinlay, Lab.   24,791
*T. Janman, C.   23,619
A. Banton, LD   5,145
C. Rogers, Pensioners   391
P. Compobassi, Anti Fed.   117
Lab. majority   1,172
(June 1987, C. maj. 690)

TIVERTON (Devon)
E.71,024   T.82.98%
Mrs A. Browning, C.   30,376
D. Cox, LD   19,287
Ms S. Gibb, Lab.   5,950
D. Morrish, Lib.   2,225
P. Foggitt, Green   1,007
B. Rhodes, NLP   96
C. majority   11,089
(June 1987, C. maj. 9,212)

TONBRIDGE AND MALLING (Kent)
E.77,292   T.82.66%
*Rt. Hon. Sir J. Stanley, C.   36,542
P. Roberts, LD   14,984
Ms M. O'Neill, Lab.   11,533
J. Tidy, Green   612
Mrs J. Hovarth, NLP   221
C. majority   21,558
(June 1987, C. maj. 16,429)

TOOTING (Greater London)
E.68,306   T.74.79%
*T. Cox, Lab.   24,601
M. Winters, C.   20,494
B. Bunce, LD   3,776
Ms C. Martin, Lib.   1,340
P. Owens, Green   694
F. Anklesalria, NLP   119
M. Whitelaw, CD   64
Lab. majority   4,107
(June 1987, Lab. maj. 1,441)

TORBAY (Devon)
E.71,171   T.80.63%
*R. Allason, *C.*	28,624
A. Sanders, *LD*	22,837
P. Truscott, *Lab.*	5,503
R. Jones, *NF*	268
Ms A. Thomas, *NLP*	157
C. majority	5,787
(June 1987, C. maj. 8,820)	

TOTTENHAM (Greater London)
E.68,319   T.65.60%
*B. Grant, *Lab.*	25,309
A. Charalambous, *C.*	13,341
A. L'Estrange, *LD*	5,120
P. Budge, *Green*	903
Ms M. Obomanu, *NLP*	150
Lab. majority	11,968
(June 1987, Lab. maj. 4,141)	

TRURO (Cornwall)
E.75,101   T.82.35%
*M. Taylor, *LD*	31,230
N. St Aubyn, *C.*	23,660
J. Geach, *Lab.*	6,078
L. Keating, *Green*	569
C. Tankard, *Lib.*	208
Ms M. Hartley, *NLP*	108
LD majority	7,570
(June 1987, L./All. maj. 4,753)	

TUNBRIDGE WELLS (Kent)
E.76,808   T.78.11%
*Rt. Hon. Sir P. Mayhew, *C.*	34,162
A. Clayton, *LD*	17,030
E. Goodman, *Lab.*	8,300
E. Fenna, *NLP*	267
R. Edey, *ISS*	236
C. majority	17,132
(June 1987, C. maj. 16,122)	

TWICKENHAM (Greater London)
E.63,072   T.84.27%
*T. Jessel, *C.*	26,804
Dr V. Cable, *LD*	21,093
M. Gold, *Lab.*	4,919
G. Gill, *NLP*	152
D. Griffith, *DLC*	103
A. Miners, *Lib.*	85
C. majority	5,711
(June 1987, C. maj. 7,127)	

TYNE BRIDGE (Tyne & Wear)
E.53,079   T.62.64%
*D. Clelland, *Lab.*	22,328
C. Liddell-Grainger, *C.*	7,118
J. Burt, *LD*	3,804
Lab. majority	15,210
(June 1987, Lab. maj. 15,573)	

TYNEMOUTH (Tyne & Wear)
E.74,955   T.80.39%
*N. Trotter, *C.*	27,731
P. Cosgrove, *Lab.*	27,134
P. Selby, *LD*	4,855
A. Buchanan-Smith, *Green*	543
C. majority	597
(June 1987, C. maj. 2,583)	

UPMINSTER (Greater London)
E.64,138   T.80.46%
*Sir N. Bonsor, *C.*	28,791
T. Ward, *Lab.*	14,970

T. Hurlstone, *LD*   7,848
C. majority   13,821
(June 1987, C. maj. 16,857)

UXBRIDGE (Greater London)
E.61,744   T.78.87%
*J. M. Shersby, *C.*	27,487
R. Evans, *Lab.*	14,308
S. Carey, *LD*	5,900
I. Flindall, *Green*	538
M. O'Rourke, *BNP*	350
A. Deans, *NLP*	120
C. majority	13,179
(June 1987, C. maj. 15,970)	

VAUXHALL (Greater London)
E.62,473   T.62.35%
*Ms C. Hoey, *Lab.*	21,328
B. Gentry, *C.*	10,840
M. Tuffrey, *LD*	5,678
Ms P. Shepherd, *Green*	803
A. Khan, *DOS*	156
Ms S. Hill, *Rev. Comm.*	152
Lab. majority	10,488
(June 1987, Lab. maj. 9,019)	
(June 1989, Lab. maj. 9,766)	

WAKEFIELD (W. Yorks)
E.69,794   T.76.27%
*D. Hinchliffe, *Lab.*	26,964
D. Fanthorpe, *C.*	20,374
T. Wright, *LD*	5,900
Lab. majority	6,590
(June 1987, Lab. maj. 2,789)	

WALLASEY (Merseyside)
E.65,676   T.82.50%
Ms A. Eagle, *Lab.*	26,531
*Rt. Hon. L. Chalker, *C.*	22,722
N. Thomas, *LD*	4,177
Ms S. Davis, *Green*	650
G. Gay, *NLP*	105
Lab. majority	3,809
(June 1987, C. maj. 279)	

WALLSEND (Tyne & Wear)
E.77,941   T.74.12%
S. Byers, *Lab.*	33,439
Miss M. Gibbon, *C.*	13,969
M. Huscroft, *LD*	10,369
Lab. majority	19,470
(June 1987, Lab. maj. 19,384)	

WALSALL NORTH (W. Midlands)
E.69,604   T.74.98%
*D. Winnick, *Lab.*	24,387
R. Syms, *C.*	20,563
A. Powis, *LD*	6,629
K. Reynolds, *NF*	614
Lab. majority	3,824
(June 1987, Lab. maj. 1,790)	

WALSALL SOUTH (W. Midlands)
E.65,642   T.76.26%
*B. George, *Lab.*	24,133
L. Jones, *C.*	20,955
G. Williams, *LD*	4,132
R. Clarke, *Green*	673
J. Oldbury, *NLP*	167
Lab. majority	3,178
(June 1987, Lab. maj. 1,116)	

WALTHAMSTOW (Greater London)
E.49,140   T.72.35%
N. Gerrard, *Lab.*	16,251
*H. Summerson, *C.*	13,229
P. Leighton, *LD*	5,142
Ms J. Lambert, *Green*	594
V. Wilkinson, *Lib.*	241
A. Planton, *NLP*	94
Lab. majority	3,022
(June 1987, C. maj. 1,512)	

WANSBECK (Northumberland)
E.63,457   T.79.29%
*J. Thompson, *Lab.*	30,046
G. Sanderson, *C.*	11,872
B. Priestley, *LD*	7,691
N. Best, *Green*	710
Lab. majority	18,174
(June 1987, Lab. maj. 16,789)	

WANSDYKE (Avon)
E.77,156   T.84.33%
*J. Aspinwall, *C.*	31,389
D. Norris, *Lab.*	18,048
Ms D. Darby, *LD*	14,834
F. Hayden, *Green*	800
C. majority	13,341
(June 1987, C. maj. 16,144)	

WANSTEAD AND WOODFORD
(Greater London)
E.55,821   T.78.28%
*J. Arbuthnot, *C.*	26,204
Ms L. Brown, *Lab.*	9,319
G. Staight, *LD*	7,362
F. Roads, *Green*	637
A. Brickell, *NLP*	178
C. majority	16,885
(June 1987, C. maj. 16,412)	

WANTAGE (Oxon)
E.68,328   T.82.68%
*R. Jackson, *C.*	30,575
R. Morgan, *LD*	14,102
V. Woodell, *Lab.*	10,955
R. Ely, *Green*	867
C. majority	16,473
(June 1987, C. maj. 12,156)	

WARLEY EAST (W. Midlands)
E.51,717   T.71.72%
*A. Faulds, *Lab.*	19,891
G. Marshall, *C.*	12,097
A. Harrod, *LD*	4,547
A. Groucott, *NLP*	561
Lab. majority	7,794
(June 1987, Lab. maj. 5,585)	

WARLEY WEST (W. Midlands)
E.57,164   T.73.90%
J. Spellar, *Lab.*	21,386
Mrs S. Whitehouse, *C.*	15,914
Ms E. Todd, *LD*	4,945
Lab. majority	5,472
(June 1987, Lab. maj. 5,393)	

WARRINGTON NORTH (Cheshire)
E.78,548   T.77.38%
*E. D. H. Hoyle, *Lab.*	33,019
C. Daniels, *C.*	20,397
I. Greenhalgh, *LD*	6,965
B. Davies, *NLP*	400

Lab. majority	12,622
(June 1987, Lab. maj. 8,013)	

WARRINGTON SOUTH (Cheshire)
E.77,694   T.82.04%

M. Hall, Lab.	27,819
*C. Butler, C.	27,628
P. Walker, LD	7,978
S. Benson, NLP	321
Lab. majority	191
(June 1987, C. maj. 3,609)	

WARWICK AND LEAMINGTON
E.71,259   T.81.54%

*Sir D. Smith, C.	28,093
M. Taylor, Lab.	19,158
Ms S. Boad, LD	9,645
Ms J. Alty, Green	803
R. Newby, Ind.	251
J. Brewster, NLP	156
C. majority	8,935
(June 1987, C. maj. 13,982)	

WARWICKSHIRE NORTH
E.71,473   T.83.82%

M. O'Brien, Lab.	27,599
*Hon. F. Maude, C.	26,145
N. Mitchell, LD	6,167
Lab. majority	1,454
(June 1987, C. maj. 2,829)	

WATFORD (Herts)
E.72,291   T.82.34%

*W. A. T. T. Garel-Jones, C.	29,072
M. Jackson, Lab.	19,482
M. Oaten, LD	10,231
J. Hywel-Davies, Green	566
L. Davis, NLP	176
C. majority	9,590
(June 1987, C. maj. 11,736)	

WAVENEY (Suffolk)
E.84,181   T.81.81%

*D. Porter, C.	33,174
E. Leverett, Lab.	26,472
A. Rogers, LD	8,925
D. Hook, NLP	302
C. majority	6,702
(June 1987, C. maj. 11,783)	

WEALDEN (E. Sussex)
E.74,665   T.80.83%

*Sir G. Johnson Smith, C.	37,263
M. Skinner, LD	16,332
S. Billcliffe, Lab.	5,579
I. Guy-Moore, Green	1,002
Dr R. Graham, NLP	182
C. majority	20,931
(June 1987, C. maj. 20,110)	

WELLINGBOROUGH (Northants)
E.73,875   T.81.89%

*P. Fry, C.	32,302
P. Sawford, Lab.	20,486
Ms J. Trevor, LD	7,714
C. majority	11,816
(June 1987, C. maj. 14,070)	

WELLS (Somerset)
E.69,833   T.82.71%

*D. Heathcoat-Amory, C.	28,620
H. Temperley, LD	21,971
J. Pilgrim, Lab.	6,126
M. Fenner, Green	1,042

C. majority	6,649
(June 1987, C. maj. 8,541)	

WELWYN HATFIELD (Herts)
E.72,146   T.84.39%

*D. Evans, C.	29,447
R. Little, Lab.	20,982
R. Parker, LD	10,196
Ms E. Lucas, NLP	264
C. majority	8,465
(June 1987, C. maj. 10,903)	

WENTWORTH (S. Yorks)
E.64,914   T.74.03%

*P. Hardy, Lab.	32,939
M. Brennan, C.	10,490
Ms C. Roderick, LD	4,629
Lab. majority	22,449
(June 1987, Lab. maj. 20,092)	

WEST BROMWICH EAST
(W. Midlands)
E.56,940   T.75.25%

*P. Snape, Lab.	19,913
C. Blunt, C.	17,100
M. Smith, LD	5,360
J. Lord, NF	477
Lab. majority	2,813
(June 1987, Lab. maj. 983)	

WEST BROMWICH WEST
(W. Midlands)
E.57,655   T.70.41%

*Miss B. Boothroyd, Lab.	22,251
D. Swayne, C.	14,421
Miss S. Broadbent, LD	3,925
Lab. majority	7,830
(June 1987, Lab. maj. 5,253)	

WESTBURY (Wilts)
E.87,356   T.82.99%

D. Faber, C.	36,568
Ms V. Rayner, LD	23,962
W. Stallard, Lab.	9,642
P. Macdonald, Lib.	1,440
P. French, Green	888
C. majority	12,606
(June 1987, C. maj. 10,097)	

WESTMINSTER NORTH (Greater
London)
E.58,847   T.75.75%

*Sir J. Wheeler, C.	21,828
Ms J. Edwards, Lab.	18,095
J. Wigoder, LD	3,341
Ms A. Burke, Green	1,017
J. Hinde, NLP	159
M. Kelly, Anti Fed.	137
C. majority	3,733
(June 1987, C. maj. 3,310)	

WESTMORLAND AND LONSDALE
(Cumbria)
E.71,865   T.77.76%

*Rt. Hon. M. Jopling, C.	31,798
S. Collins, LD	15,362
D. Abbott, Lab.	8,436
R. Johnstone, NLP	287
C. majority	16,436
(June 1987, C. maj. 14,920)	

WESTON-SUPER-MARE (Avon)
E.78,839   T.79.75%

*A. W. Wiggin, C.	30,022
B. Cotter, LD	24,680
D. Murray, Lab.	6,913
Dr R. Lawson, Green	1,262
C. majority	5,342
(June 1987, C. maj. 7,998)	

WIGAN (Greater Manchester)
E.72,739   T.76.16%

*R. Stott, Lab.	34,910
E. Hess, C.	13,068
G. Davies, LD	6,111
K. White, Lib.	1,116
Ms A. Taylor, NLP	197
Lab. majority	21,842
(June 1987, Lab. maj. 20,462)	

WILTSHIRE NORTH
E.85,851   T.81.71%

*R. Needham, C.	39,028
Ms C. Napier, LD	22,640
Ms C. Reid, Lab.	6,945
Ms L. Howitt, Green	850
G. Hawkins, Lib.	622
S. Martienssen, Bastion	66
C. majority	16,388
(June 1987, C. maj. 10,939)	

WIMBLEDON (Greater London)
E.61,917   T.80.23%

*Dr C. Goodson-Wickes, C.	26,331
K. Abrams, Lab.	11,570
Ms A. Willott, LD	10,569
V. Flood, Green	860
H. Godfrey, NLP	181
G. Hadley, Ind.	170
C. majority	14,761
(June 1987, C. maj. 11,301)	

WINCHESTER (Hants)
E.79,218   T.83.46%

P. G. Malone, C.	33,113
A. Barron, LD	24,992
P. Jenks, Lab.	4,917
*J. Browne, Ind. C.	3,095
C. majority	8,121
(June 1987, C. maj. 7,479)	

WINDSOR AND MAIDENHEAD
(Berks)
E.77,327   T.81.68%

Hon. M. Trend, C.	35,075
J. Hyde, LD	22,147
Ms C. Attlee, Lab.	4,975
R. Williams, Green	510
D. Askwith, Loony	236
Miss E. Bigg, Ind.	110
M. Grenville, NLP	108
C. majority	12,928
(June 1987, C. maj. 17,836)	

WIRRAL SOUTH (Merseyside)
E.61,116   T.82.37%

*G. B. Porter, C.	25,590
Ms H. Southworth, Lab.	17,407
E. Cunniffe, LD	6,581
N. Birchenough, Green	584
G. Griffiths, NLP	182
C. majority	8,183
(June 1987, C. maj. 10,963)	

WIRRAL WEST (Merseyside)
E.62,453   T.81.57%

*Rt. Hon. D. Hunt, C.	26,852
Ms H. Stephenson, Lab.	15,788
J. Thornton, LD	7,420
Ms G. Bowler, Green	700
N. Broome, NLP	188
C. majority	11,064
(June 1987, C. maj. 12,723)	

WITNEY (Oxon)
E.78,521   T.81.89%

*Rt. Hon. D. Hurd, C.	36,256
J. Plaskitt, Lab.	13,688
I. Blair, LD	13,393
Ms C. Beckford, Green	716
Ms S. Catling, NLP	134
Miss M. Brown, FTA	119
C. majority	22,568
(June 1987, C. maj. 18,464)	

WOKING (Surrey)
E.80,842   T.79.20%

*Rt. Hon. C. Onslow, C.	37,744
Mrs D. Buckrell, LD	17,902
J. Dalgleish, Lab.	8,080
Mrs T. Macintyre, NLP	302
C. majority	19,842
(June 1987, C. maj. 16,544)	

WOKINGHAM (Berks)
E.85,914   T.82.41%

*J. Redwood, C.	43,497
P. Simon, LD	17,788
N. Bland, Lab.	8,846
P. Owen, Loony	531
P. Harriss, WUWC	148
C. majority	25,709
(June 1987, C. maj. 20,387)	

WOLVERHAMPTON NORTH EAST
(W. Midlands)
E.62,695   T.78%

K. Purchase, Lab.	24,106
*Mrs M. Hicks, C.	20,167
M. Gwinnett, LD	3,546
K. Bullman, Lib.	1,087
Lab. majority	3,939
(June 1987, C. maj. 204)	

WOLVERHAMPTON SOUTH EAST
(W. Midlands)
E.56,158   T.72.86%

*D. Turner, Lab.	23,215
P. Bradbourn, C.	12,975
R. Whitehouse, LD	3,881
Ms C. Twelvetrees, Lib.	850
Lab. majority	10,240
(June 1987, Lab. maj. 6,398)	

WOLVERHAMPTON SOUTH WEST
(W. Midlands)
E.67,288   T.78.28%

*N. Budgen, C.	25,969
S. Murphy, Lab.	21,003
M. Wiggin, LD	4,470
C. Hallmark, Lib.	1,237
C. majority	4,966
(June 1987, C. maj. 10,318)	

WOODSPRING (Avon)
E.77,534   T.83.21%

Dr L. Fox, C.	35,175
Ms N. Kirsen, LD	17,666
R. Stone, Lab.	9,942
N. Brown, Lib.	836
Ms R. Knifton, Green	801
B. Lee, NLP	100
C. majority	17,509
(June 1987, C. maj. 17,852)	

WOOLWICH (Greater London)
E.55,977   T.70.91%

J. Austin-Walker, Lab.	17,551
*J. Cartwright, SD	15,326
K. Walmsley, C.	6,598
Ms S. Hayward, NLP	220
Lab. majority	2,225
(June 1987, SDP/All. maj. 1,937)	

WORCESTER
E.74,211   T.80.99%

P. Luff, C.	27,883
R. Berry, Lab.	21,731
J. Caiger, LD	9,561
M. Foster, Green	592
M. Soden, Brewer	343
C. majority	6,152
(June 1987, C. maj. 10,453)	

WORCESTERSHIRE MID
E.84,269   T.81.07%

*E. Forth, C.	33,964
Ms J. Smith, Lab.	24,094
D. Barwick, LD	9,745
P. Davis, NLP	520
C. majority	9,870
(June 1987, C. maj. 14,911)	

WORCESTERSHIRE SOUTH
E.80,423   T.79.99%

*W. M. H. Spicer, C.	34,792
P. Chandler, LD	18,641
N. Knowles, Lab.	9,727
G. Woodford, Green	1,178
C. majority	16,151
(June 1987, C. maj. 13,645)	

WORKINGTON (Cumbria)
E.57,597   T.81.52%

*D. Campbell-Savours, Lab.	26,719
S. Sexton, C.	16,270
Ms C. Neale, LD	3,028
D. Langstaff, Loony	755
Ms N. Escott, NLP	183
Lab. majority	10,449
(June 1987, Lab. maj. 7,019)	

WORSLEY (Greater Manchester)
E.72,244   T.77.74%

*T. Lewis, Lab.	29,418
N. Cameron, C.	19,406
R. Boyd, LD	6,490
P. Connolly, Green	677
G. Phillips, NLP	176
Lab. majority	10,012
(June 1987, Lab. maj. 7,337)	

WORTHING (W. Sussex)
E.77,540   T.77.41%

*Rt. Hon. T. Higgins, C.	34,198
Mrs S. Bucknall, LD	17,665
J. Deen, Lab.	6,679

Mrs P. Beever, Green	806
N. Goble, Lib.	679
C. majority	16,533
(June 1987, C. maj. 18,501)	

THE WREKIN (Salop)
E.90,892   T.77.14%

*B. Grocott, Lab.	33,865
Mrs E. Holt, C.	27,217
A. West, LD	8,032
R. Saunders, Green	1,008
Lab. majority	6,648
(June 1987, Lab. maj. 1,456)	

WYCOMBE (Bucks)
E.72,564   T.78.01%

*R. Whitney, C.	30,081
T. Andrews, LD	13,005
J. Huddart, Lab.	12,222
J. Laker, Green	686
A. Page, SD	449
T. Anton, NLP	168
C. majority	17,076
(June 1987, C. maj. 13,819)	

WYRE (Lancs)
E.67,778   T.79.54%

*K. Mans, C.	29,449
D. Borrow, Lab.	17,785
J. Ault, LD	6,420
R. Perry, NLP	260
C. majority	11,664
(June 1987, C. maj. 14,661)	

WYRE FOREST (H & W)
E.73,550   T.82.36%

*A. Coombs, C.	28,983
R. Maden, Lab.	18,642
M. Jones, LD	12,958
C. majority	10,341
(June 1987, C. maj. 7,224)	

YEOVIL (Somerset)
E.73,057   T.81.98%

*Rt. Hon. J. J. D. Ashdown, LD	58
J. Davidson, C.	22,125
Ms V. Nelson, Lab.	5,765
J. Risbridger, Green	639
D. Sutch, Loony	338
R. Simmerson, APAKBI	70
LD majority	8,833
(June 1987, L./All. maj. 5,700)	

YORK (N. Yorks)
E.79,242   T.80.97%

H. Bayley, Lab.	31,525
*C. Gregory, C.	25,183
Ms K. Anderson, LD	6,811
S. Kenwright, Green	594
Ms P. Orr, NLP	54
Lab. majority	6,342
(June 1987, C. maj. 147)	

WALES

ABERAVON (W. Glamorgan)
E.51,650 T.77.57%

*Rt. Hon. J. Morris, *Lab.*	26,877
H. Williams, *C.*	5,567
Mrs M. Harris, *LD*	4,999
D. Saunders, *PC*	1,919
Capt. Beany, *Real Bean*	707
Lab. majority	21,310

(June 1987, Lab. maj. 20,609)

ALYN AND DEESIDE (Clwyd)
E.60,477 T.80.08%

*S. B. Jones, *Lab.*	25,206
J. Riley, *C.*	17,355
R. Britton, *LD*	4,687
J. Rogers, *PC*	551
V. Button, *Green*	433
J. Cooksey, *Ind.*	200
Lab. majority	7,851

(June 1987, Lab. maj. 6,383)

BLAENAU GWENT
E.55,638 T.78.13%

L. Smith, *Lab.*	34,333
D. Melding, *C.*	4,266
A. Burns, *LD*	2,774
A. Davies, *PC*	2,099
Lab. majority	30,067

(June 1987, Lab. maj. 27,861)

BRECON AND RADNOR (Powys)
E.51,509 T.85.94%

J. P. Evans, *C.*	15,977
*R. Livsey, *LD*	15,847
C. Mann, *Lab.*	11,634
Ms S. Meredudd, *PC*	418
H. Richards, *Green*	393
C. majority	130

(June 1987, L./All. maj. 56)

BRIDGEND (Mid Glamorgan)
E.58,531 T.80.44%

*W. Griffiths, *Lab.*	24,143
D. Unwin, *C.*	16,817
D. Mills, *LD*	4,827
A. Lloyd Jones, *PC*	1,301
Lab. majority	7,326

(June 1987, Lab. maj. 4,380)

CAERNARFON (Gwynedd)
E.46,468 T.78.15%

*D. Wigley, *PC*	21,439
P. Fowler, *C.*	6,963
Ms S. Mainwaring, *Lab.*	5,641
R. Arwel Williams, *LD*	2,101
G. Evans, *NLP*	173
PC majority	14,476

(June 1987, PC maj. 12,812)

CAERPHILLY (Mid Glamorgan)
E.64,529 T.77.20%

*R. Davies, *Lab.*	31,713
H. Philpott, *C.*	9,041
L. Whittle, *PC*	4,821
S. Wilson, *LD*	4,247
Lab. majority	22,672

(June 1987, Lab. maj. 19,167)

CARDIFF CENTRAL (S. Glamorgan)
E.57,716 T.74.35%

J. O. Jones, *Lab.*	18,014
*I. Grist, *C.*	14,549

Ms J. Randerson, *LD*	9,170
H. Marshall, *PC*	748
C. von Ruhland, *Green*	330
B. Francis, *NLP*	105
Lab. majority	3,465

(June 1987, C. maj. 1,986)

CARDIFF NORTH (S. Glamorgan)
E.56,721 T.84.15%

*G. H. Jones, *C.*	21,547
Ms J. Morgan, *Lab.*	18,578
Ms E. Warlow, *LD*	6,487
Ms E. Bush, *PC*	916
J. Morse, *BNP*	121
D. Palmer, *NLP*	86
C. majority	2,969

(June 1987, C. maj. 8,234)

CARDIFF SOUTH AND PENARTH
(S. Glamorgan)
E.61,484 T.77.25%

*A. Michael, *Lab.*	26,383
T. Hunter Jarvie, *C.*	15,958
P. Verma, *LD*	3,707
Ms B. Anglezarke, *PC*	776
L. Davey, *Green*	676
Lab. majority	10,425

(June 1987, Lab. maj. 4,574)

CARDIFF WEST (S. Glamorgan)
E.58,898 T.77.56%

*H. R. Morgan, *Lab.*	24,306
M. Prior, *C.*	15,015
Ms J. Gasson, *LD*	5,002
Ms P. Bestic, *PC*	1,177
A. Harding, *NLP*	184
Lab. majority	9,291

(June 1987, Lab. maj. 4,045)

CARMARTHEN (Dyfed)
E.68,887 T. 82.70%

*Dr A. W. Williams, *Lab.*	20,879
R. Thomas, *PC*	17,957
S. Cavenagh, *C.*	12,782
Mrs J. Hughes, *LD*	5,353
Lab. majority	2,922

(June 1987, Lab. maj. 4,317)

CEREDIGION AND PEMBROKE
NORTH (Dyfed)
E.66,180 T.77.36%

C. Dafis, *PC*	16,020
*G. Howells, *LD*	12,827
J. Williams, *C.*	12,718
J. Davies, *Lab.*	9,637
PC majority	3,193

(June 1987, L./All. maj. 4,700)

CLWYD NORTH WEST
E.67,351 T.78.64%

R. Richards, *C.*	24,488
C. Ruane, *Lab.*	18,438
R. Ingham, *LD*	7,999
T. Neil, *PC*	1,888
Ms M. Swift, *NLP*	158
C. majority	6,050

(June 1987, C. maj. 11,781)

CLWYD SOUTH WEST
E.60,607 T.81.52%

*M. Jones, *Lab.*	21,490
G. Owen, *C.*	16,549

G. Williams, *LD*	6,027
E. Lloyd Jones, *PC*	4,835
N. Worth, *Green*	351
Mrs J. Leadbetter, *NLP*	155
Lab. majority	4,941

(June 1987, Lab. maj. 1,028)

CONWY (Gwynedd)
E.53,576 T.78.85%

*Rt. Hon. Sir W. Roberts, *C.*	14,250
Revd R. Roberts, *LD*	13,255
Ms E. Williams, *Lab.*	10,883
R. Davies, *PC*	3,108
O. Wainwright, *Ind. C.*	637
Ms D. Hughes, *NLP*	114
C. majority	995

(June 1987, C. maj. 3,024)

CYNON VALLEY (Mid Glamorgan)
E.49,695 T.76.46%

*Ms A. Clwyd, *Lab.*	26,254
A. Smith, *C.*	4,890
T. Benney, *PC*	4,186
M. Verma, *LD*	2,667
Lab. majority	21,364

(June 1987, Lab. maj. 21,571)

DELYN (Clwyd)
E.66,591 T.83.40%

D. Hanson, *Lab.*	24,979
M. Whitby, *C.*	22,940
R. Dodd, *LD*	6,208
A. Drake, *PC*	1,414
Lab. majority	2,039

(June 1987, C. maj. 1,224)

GOWER (W. Glamorgan)
E.57,231 T.81.84%

*G. Wardell, *Lab.*	23,455
A. Donnelly, *C.*	16,437
C. Davies, *LD*	4,655
A. Price, *PC*	1,658
B. Kingzett, *Green*	448
G. Egan, *Loony G.*	114
M. Beresford, *NLP*	74
Lab. majority	7,018

(June 1987, Lab. maj. 5,764)

ISLWYN (Gwent)
E.51,079 T.81.48%

*Rt. Hon. N. Kinnock, *Lab.*	30,908
P. Bone, *C.*	6,180
M. Symonds, *LD*	2,352
Ms H. Jones, *PC*	1,636
Lord Sutch, *Loony*	547
Lab. majority	24,728

(June 1987, Lab. maj. 22,947)
See also page 234

LLANELLI (Dyfed)
E.65,058 T.77.80%

*Rt. Hon. D. Davies, *Lab.*	27,802
G. Down, *C.*	8,532
M. Phillips, *PC*	7,878
K. Evans, *LD*	6,404
Lab. majority	19,270

(June 1987, Lab. maj. 20,935)

MEIRIONNYDD NANT CONWY
(Gwynedd)
E.32,413   T.81.47%

E. Llwyd, *PC*	11,608
G. Lewis, *C.*	6,995
R. Williams, *Lab.*	4,978
Mrs R. Parry, *LD*	2,358
W. Pritchard, *Green*	471
PC. majority	4,613
(June 1987, PC maj. 3,026)	

MERTHYR TYDFIL AND RHYMNEY
(Mid Glamorgan)
E.58,430   T.75.84%

*E. Rowlands, *Lab.*	31,710
R. Rowland, *LD*	4,997
M. Hughes, *C.*	4,904
A. Cox, *PC*	2,704
Lab. majority	26,713
(June 1987, Lab. maj. 28,207)	

MONMOUTH (Gwent)
E.59,147   T.86.06%

R. Evans, *C.*	24,059
*H. Edwards, *Lab.*	20,855
Mrs F. David, *LD*	5,562
M. Witherden, *Green/PC*	431
C. majority	3,204
(June 1987, C. maj. 9,350)	
(May 1991, Lab. maj. 2,406)	

MONTGOMERY (Powys)
E.41,386   T.79.87%

*A. Carlile, *LD*	16,031
Mrs J. France-Hayhurst, *C.*	10,822
S. Wood, *Lab.*	4,115
H. Parsons, *PC*	1,581
P. Adams, *Green*	508
LD majority	5,209
(June 1987, L./All. maj. 2,558)	

NEATH (W. Glamorgan)
E.56,392   T.80.58%

*P. Hain, *Lab.*	30,903
D. Adams, *C.*	6,928
Dr D. Evans, *PC*	5,145
M. Phillips, *LD*	2,467
Lab. majority	23,975
(June 1987, Lab. maj. 20,578)	
(April 1991, Lab. maj. 9,830)	

NEWPORT EAST (Gwent)
E.51,603   T.81.21%

*R. J. Hughes, *Lab.*	23,050
Mrs A. Emmett, *C.*	13,151
W. Oliver, *LD*	4,991
S. Ainley, *Green/PC*	716
Lab. majority	9,899
(June 1987, Lab. maj. 7,064)	

NEWPORT WEST (Gwent)
E.54,871   T.82.82%

*P. Flynn, *Lab.*	24,139
A. Taylor, *C.*	16,360
A. Toye, *LD*	4,296
P. Keelan, *PC*	653
Lab. majority	7,779
(June 1987, Lab. maj. 2,708)	

OGMORE (Mid Glamorgan)
E.52,195   T.80.62%

*R. Powell, *Lab.*	30,186
D. Edwards, *C.*	6,359
J. Warman, *LD*	2,868
Ms L. McAllister, *PC*	2,667
Lab. majority	23,827
(June 1987, Lab. maj. 22,292)	

PEMBROKE (Dyfed)
E.73,187   T.82.86%

N. Ainger, *Lab.*	26,253
*N. Bennett, *C.*	25,498
P. Berry, *LD*	6,625
C. Bryant, *PC*	1,627
R. Coghill, *Green*	484
M. Stoddart, *Anti Fed.*	158
Lab. majority	755
(June 1987, C. maj. 5,700)	

PONTYPRIDD (Mid Glamorgan)
E.61,685   T.79.25%

*K. Howells, *Lab.*	29,722
Dr P. Donnelly, *C.*	9,925
Dr D. Bowen, *PC*	4,448
S. Belzak, *LD*	4,180
Ms E. Jackson, *Green*	615
Lab. majority	19,797
(June 1987, Lab. maj. 17,277)	
(Feb. 1989, Lab. maj. 10,794)	

RHONDDA (Mid Glamorgan)
E.59,955   T.76.61%

*A. Rogers, *Lab.*	34,243
G. Davies, *PC*	5,427
J. Richards, *C.*	3,588
P. Nicholls-Jones, *LD*	2,431
M. Fisher, *Comm. GB*	245
Lab. majority	28,816
(June 1987, Lab. maj. 30,596)	

SWANSEA EAST (W. Glamorgan)
E.59,196   T.75.56%

*D. Anderson, *Lab.*	31,179
H. Davies, *C.*	7,697
R. Barton, *LD*	4,248
Ms E. Bonner-Evans, *PC*	1,607
Lab. majority	23,482
(June 1987, Lab. maj. 19,338)	

SWANSEA WEST (W. Glamorgan)
E.59,785   T.73.34%

*Rt. Hon. A. Williams, *Lab.*	23,238
R. Perry, *C.*	13,760
M. Shrewsbury, *LD*	4,620
Dr D. Lloyd, *PC*	1,668
B. Oubridge, *Green*	564
Lab. majority	9,478
(June 1987, Lab. maj. 7,062)	

TORFAEN (Gwent)
E.61,104   T.77.47%

*P. Murphy, *Lab.*	30,352
M. Watkins, *C.*	9,598
M. Hewson, *LD*	6,178
Dr J. Cox, *Green/PC*	1,210
Lab. majority	20,754
(June 1987, Lab. maj. 17,550)	

VALE OF GLAMORGAN
(S. Glamorgan)
E.66,672   T.81.93%

W. Sweeney, *C.*	24,220
*J. Smith, *Lab.*	24,201
K. Davies, *LD*	5,045
D. Haswell, *PC*	1,160
C. majority	19
(June 1987, C. maj 6,251)	
(May 1989, Lab. maj. 6,028)	

WREXHAM (Clwyd)
E.63,720   T.80.71%

*J. Marek, *Lab.*	24,830
O. Paterson, *C.*	18,114
A. Thomas, *LD*	7,074
G. Wheatley, *PC*	1,415
Lab. majority	6,716
(June 1987, Lab. maj. 4,152)	

YNYS MÔN (Gwynedd)
E.53,412   T.80.62%

*I. W. Jones, *PC*	15,984
G. Price Rowlands, *C.*	14,878
Dr R. Jones, *Lab.*	10,126
Ms P. Badger, *LD*	1,891
Mrs S. Parry, *NLP*	182
PC majority	1,106
(June 1987, PC maj. 4,298)	

SCOTLAND

ABERDEEN NORTH (Grampian)
E.60,217   T.66.52%

*R. Hughes, *Lab.*	18,845
J. McGugan, *SNP*	9,608
P. Cook, *C.*	6,836
Dr M. Ford, *LD*	4,772
Lab. majority	9,237
(June 1987, Lab. maj. 16,278)	

ABERDEEN SOUTH (Grampian)
E.58,881   T.69.78%

R. Robertson, *C.*	15,808
*F. Doran, *Lab.*	14,291
J. Davidson, *SNP*	6,223
Ms I. Keith, *LD*	4,767
C. majority	1,517
(June 1987, Lab. maj. 1,198)	

ANGUS EAST (Tayside)
E.63,170   T.75.03%

*A. Welsh, *SNP*	19,006
Dr R. Harris, *C.*	18,052
G. Taylor, *Lab.*	5,994
C. McLeod, *LD*	3,897
D. McCabe, *Green*	449
SNP majority	954
(June 1987, SNP maj. 1,544)	

ARGYLL AND BUTE (Strathclyde)
E.47,894   T.76.19%
*Mrs J. R. Michie, *LD*	12,739
J. Corrie, *C.*	10,117
Prof. N. MacCormick, *SNP*	8,689
D. Browne, *Lab.*	4,946
LD majority	2,622
(June 1987, L./All. maj. 1,394)

AYR (Strathclyde)
E.65,481   T.83.08%
P. Gallie, *C.*	22,172
A. Osborne, *Lab.*	22,087
Mrs B. Mullin, *SNP*	5,949
J. Boss, *LD*	4,067
R. Scott, *NLP*	132
C. majority	85
(June 1987, C. maj. 182)

BANFF AND BUCHAN (Grampian)
E.64,873   T.71.20%
*A. Salmond, *SNP*	21,954
S. Manson, *C.*	17,846
B. Balcombe, *Lab.*	3,803
Mrs R. Kemp, *LD*	2,588
SNP majority	4,108
(June 1987, SNP maj. 2,441)

CAITHNESS AND SUTHERLAND
(Highland)
E.30,905   T.71.93%
*R. Maclennan, *LD*	10,032
G. Bruce, *C.*	4,667
K. MacGregor, *SNP*	4,049
M. Coyne, *Lab.*	3,483
LD majority	5,365
(June 1987, SDP/All. maj. 8,494)

CARRICK, CUMNOCK AND DOON
VALLEY (Strathclyde)
E.55,330   T.76.94%
*G. Foulkes, *Lab.*	25,142
J. Boswell, *C.*	8,516
C. Douglas, *SNP*	6,910
Ms M. Paris, *LD*	2,005
Lab. majority	16,626
(June 1987, Lab. maj. 16,802)

CLACKMANNAN (Central)
E.48,963   T.78.34%
*M. O'Neill, *Lab.*	18,829
A. Brophy, *SNP*	10,326
J. Mackie, *C.*	6,638
Ms A. Watters, *LD*	2,567
Lab. majority	8,503
(June 1987, Lab. maj. 12,401)

CLYDEBANK AND MILNGAVIE
(Strathclyde)
E.47,337   T.77.79%
*A. Worthington, *Lab.*	19,637
G. Hughes, *SNP*	7,207
W. Harvey, *C.*	6,654
A. Tough, *LD*	3,216
Ms J. Barrie, *NLP*	112
Lab. majority	12,430
(June 1987, Lab. maj. 16,304)

CLYDESDALE (Strathclyde)
E.61,878   T.77.62%
*J. Hood, *Lab.*	21,418
Ms C. Goodwin, *C.*	11,231
I. Gray, *SNP*	11,084

Ms E. Buchanan, *LD*	3,957
S. Cartwright, *BNP*	342
Lab. majority	10,187
(June 1987, Lab. maj. 10,502)

CUMBERNAULD AND KILSYTH
(Strathclyde)
E.46,489   T.79.06%
*N. Hogg, *Lab.*	19,855
T. Johnston, *SNP*	10,640
I. Mitchell, *C.*	4,143
Ms J. Haddow, *LD*	2,118
Lab. majority	9,215
(June 1987, Lab. maj. 14,403)

CUNNINGHAME NORTH
(Strathclyde)
E.54,803   T.78.21%
*B. Wilson, *Lab.*	17,564
Ms E. Clarkson, *C.*	14,625
D. Crossan, *SNP*	7,813
D. Herbison, *LD*	2,864
Lab. majority	2,939
(June 1987, Lab. maj. 4,422)

CUNNINGHAME SOUTH
(Strathclyde)
E.49,010   T.75.88%
B. Donohoe, *Lab.*	19,687
R. Bell, *SNP*	9,007
S. Leslie, *C.*	6,070
B. Ashley, *LD*	2,299
W. Jackson, *NLP*	128
Lab. majority	10,680
(June 1987, Lab. maj. 16,633)

DUMBARTON (Strathclyde)
E.57,222   T.77.11%
*J. McFall, *Lab.*	19,255
T. Begg, *C.*	13,126
W. McKechnie, *SNP*	8,127
J. Morrison, *LD*	3,425
Ms D. Krass, *NLP*	192
Lab. majority	6,129
(June 1987, Lab. maj. 5,222)

DUMFRIES (D & G)
E.61,145   T.79.97%
*Sir H. Monro, *C.*	21,089
P. Rennie, *Lab.*	14,674
A. Morgan, *SNP*	6,971
N. Wallace, *LD*	5,749
G. McLeod, *Ind. Green*	312
T. Barlow, *NLP*	107
C. majority	6,415
(June 1987, C. maj. 7,493)

DUNDEE EAST (Tayside)
E.58,959   T.72.10%
*J. McAllion, *Lab.*	18,761
D. Coutts, *SNP*	14,197
S. Blackwood, *C.*	7,549
I. Yuill, *LD*	1,725
Ms S. Baird, *Green*	205
R. Baxter, *NLP*	77
Lab. majority	4,564
(June 1987, Lab. maj. 1,015)

DUNDEE WEST (Tayside)
E.59,953   T.69.82%
*E. Ross, *Lab.*	20,498
K. Brown, *SNP*	9,894
A. Spearman, *C.*	7,746

Ms E. Dick, *LD*	3,132
Ms E. Hood, *Green*	432
D. Arnold, *NLP*	159
Lab. majority	10,604
(June 1987, Lab. maj. 16,526)

DUNFERMLINE EAST (Fife)
E.50,179   T.75.62%
*J. G. Brown, *Lab.*	23,692
M. Tennant, *C.*	6,248
J. Lloyd, *SNP*	5,746
Ms T. Little, *LD*	2,262
Lab. majority	17,444
(June 1987, Lab. maj. 19,589)

DUNFERMLINE WEST (Fife)
E.50,948   T.76.44%
Ms R. Squire, *Lab.*	16,374
M. Scott-Hayward, *C.*	8,890
J. Smith, *SNP*	7,563
Ms E. Harris, *LD*	6,122
Lab. majority	7,484
(June 1987, Lab. maj. 9,402)

EAST KILBRIDE (Strathclyde)
E.64,080   T.80.01%
*A. Ingram, *Lab.*	24,055
Ms K. McAlorum, *SNP*	12,063
G. Lind, *C.*	9,781
Ms S. Grieve, *LD*	5,377
Lab. majority	11,992
(June 1987, Lab. maj. 12,624)

EAST LOTHIAN
E.66,699   T.82.37%
*J. Home Robertson, *Lab.*	25,537
J. Hepburne Scott, *C.*	15,501
G. Thomson, *SNP*	7,776
T. McKay, *LD*	6,126
Lab. majority	10,036
(June 1987, Lab. maj. 10,105)

EASTWOOD (Strathclyde)
E.63,685   T.80.97%
*J. A. Stewart, *C.*	24,124
P. Grant-Hutchison, *Lab.*	12,436
Miss M. Craig, *LD*	8,493
P. Scott, *SNP*	6,372
Dr L. Fergusson, *NLP*	146
C. majority	11,688
(June 1987, C. maj. 6,014)

EDINBURGH CENTRAL (Lothian)
E.56,527   T.69.26%
*A. Darling, *Lab.*	15,189
P. Martin, *C.*	13,063
Ms L. Devine, *SNP*	5,539
A. Myles, *LD*	4,500
R. Harper, *Green*	630
D. Wilson, *Lib.*	235
Lab. majority	2,126
(June 1987, Lab. maj. 2,262)

EDINBURGH EAST (Lothian)
E.45,687   T.73.89%
*G. Strang, *Lab.*	15,446
K. Ward, *C.*	8,235
D. McKinney, *SNP*	6,225
D. Scobie, *LD*	3,432
G. Farmer, *Green*	424
Lab. majority	7,211
(June 1987, Lab. maj. 9,295)

EDINBURGH LEITH (Lothian)
E.56,520   T.71.30%
M. Chisholm, *Lab.*		13,790
Ms F. Hyslop, *SNP*		8,805
M. Bin Ashiq Rizvi, *C.*		8,496
Mrs H. Campbell, *LD*		4,975
*R. Brown, *Ind. Lab.*		4,142
A. Swan, *NLP*		96
Lab. majority		4,985
(June 1987, Lab. maj. 11,327)

EDINBURGH PENTLANDS (Lothian)
E.55,567   T.80.18%
*Rt. Hon. M. Rifkind, *C.*		18,128
M. Lazarowicz, *Lab.*		13,838
Ms K. Caskie, *SNP*		6,882
K. Smith, *LD*		5,597
D. Rae, *NLP*		111
C. majority		4,290
(June 1987, C. maj. 3,745)

EDINBURGH SOUTH (Lothian)
E.61,355   T.72.67%
*N. Griffiths, *Lab.*		18,485
S. Stevenson, *C.*		14,309
B. McCreadie, *LD*		5,961
R. Knox, *SNP*		5,727
G. Manclark, *NLP*		108
Lab. majority		4,176
(June 1987, Lab. maj. 1,859)

EDINBURGH WEST (Lothian)
E.58,998   T.82.67%
*Lord J. Douglas-Hamilton, *C.*		18,071
D. Gorrie, *LD*		17,192
Ms I. Kitson, *Lab.*		8,759
G. Sutherland, *SNP*		4,117
A. Fleming, *Lib.*		272
Ms L. Hendry, *Green*		234
D. Bruce, *BNP*		133
C. majority		879
(June 1987, C. maj. 1,234)

FALKIRK EAST (Central)
E.51,918   T.76.91%
M. Connarty, *Lab.*		18,423
R. Halliday, *SNP*		10,454
K. Harding, *C.*		8,279
Miss D. Storr, *LD*		2,775
Lab. majority		7,969
(June 1987, Lab. maj. 14,023)

FALKIRK WEST (Central)
E.50,126   T.76.77%
*D. Canavan, *Lab.*		19,162
W. Houston, *SNP*		9,350
M. Macdonald, *C.*		7,558
M. Reilly, *LD*		2,414
Lab. majority		9,812
(June 1987, Lab. maj. 13,552)

FIFE CENTRAL
E.56,152   T.74.33%
*H. McLeish, *Lab.*		21,036
Mrs T. Marwick, *SNP*		10,458
Ms C. Cender, *C.*		7,353
C. Harrow, *LD*		2,892
Lab. majority		10,578
(June 1987, Lab. maj. 15,709)

FIFE NORTH EAST
E.53,747   T.77.84%
*W. M. Campbell, *LD*		19,430
Mrs M. Scanlon, *C.*		16,122
D. Roche, *SNP*		3,589
Miss L. Clark, *Lab.*		2,319
T. Flynn, *Green*		294
D. Senior, *Lib.*		85
LD majority		3,308
(June 1987, L./All. maj. 1,447)

GALLOWAY AND UPPER NITHSDALE (D & G)
E.54,474   T.81.66%
*Rt. Hon. I. Lang, *C.*		18,681
M. Brown, *SNP*		16,213
J. Dowson, *Lab.*		5,766
J. McKerchar, *LD*		3,826
C. majority		2,468
(June 1987, C. maj. 3,673)

GLASGOW CATHCART (Strathclyde)
E.44,689   T.75.38%
*J. Maxton, *Lab.*		16,265
J. Young, *C.*		8,264
W. Steven, *SNP*		6,107
G. Dick, *LD*		2,614
Ms K. Allan, *Green*		441
Lab. majority		8,001
(June 1987, Lab. maj. 11,203)

GLASGOW CENTRAL (Strathclyde)
E.48,107   T.63.05%
*M. Watson, *Lab.*		17,341
B. O'Hara, *SNP*		6,322
E. Stewart, *C.*		4,208
Dr A. Rennie, *LD*		1,921
Ms I. Brandt, *Green*		435
T. Burn, *Comm. GB*		106
Lab. majority		11,019
(June 1987, Lab. maj. 17,253)
(June 1989, Lab. maj. 6,462)

GLASGOW GARSCADDEN (Strathclyde)
E.41,289   T.71.13%
*D. Dewar, *Lab.*		18,920
R. Douglas, *SNP*		5,580
J. Scott, *C.*		3,385
C. Brodie, *LD*		1,425
W. Orr, *NLP*		61
Lab. majority		13,340
(June 1987, Lab. maj. 18,977)

GLASGOW GOVAN (Strathclyde)
E.45,822   T.76.03%
I. Davidson, *Lab.*		17,051
*J. Sillars, *SNP*		12,926
J. Donnelly, *C.*		3,458
R. Stewart, *LD*		1,227
D. Spaven, *Green*		181
Lab. majority		4,125
(June 1987, Lab. maj. 19,509)
(Nov. 1988, SNP maj. 3,554)

GLASGOW HILLHEAD (Strathclyde)
E.57,223   T.68.80%
*G. Galloway, *Lab.*		15,148
C. Mason, *LD*		10,322
Ms A. Bates, *C.*		6,728
Miss S. White, *SNP*		6,484
Ms L. Collie, *Green*		558
Ms H. Gold, *Rev. Comm.*		73

D. Patterson, *NLP*   60
Lab. majority		4,826
(June 1987, Lab. maj. 3,251)

GLASGOW MARYHILL (Strathclyde)
E.48,426   T.65.16%
*Mrs M. Fyfe, *Lab.*		19,452
C. Williamson, *SNP*		6,033
J. Godfrey, *C.*		3,248
J. Alexander, *LD*		2,215
P. O'Brien, *Green*		530
M. Henderson, *NLP*		78
Lab. majority		13,419
(June 1987, Lab. maj. 19,364)

GLASGOW POLLOK (Strathclyde)
E.46,139   T.70.74%
*J. Dunnachie, *Lab.*		14,170
T. Sheridan, *SML*		6,287
R. Gray, *C.*		5,147
G. Leslie, *SNP*		5,107
D. Jago, *LD*		1,932
Lab. majority		7,883
(June 1987, Lab. maj. 17,983)

GLASGOW PROVAN (Strathclyde)
E.36,560   T.65.31%
*J. Wray, *Lab.*		15,885
Ms A. MacRae, *SNP*		5,182
A. Rosindell, *C.*		1,865
C. Bell, *LD*		948
Lab. majority		10,703
(June 1987, Lab. maj. 18,372)

GLASGOW RUTHERGLEN (Strathclyde)
E.52,709   T.75.23%
*T. McAvoy, *Lab.*		21,962
B. Cooklin, *C.*		6,692
J. Higgins, *SNP*		6,470
D. Baillie, *LD*		4,470
Ms B. Slaughter, *Int. Comm.*		62
Lab. majority		15,270
(June 1987, Lab. maj. 13,995)

GLASGOW SHETTLESTON (Strathclyde)
E.51,910   T.68.91%
*D. Marshall, *Lab.*		21,665
Ms N. Sturgeon, *SNP*		6,831
N. Mortimer, *C.*		5,396
Ms J. Orskov, *LD*		1,881
Lab. majority		14,834
(June 1987, Lab. maj. 18,981)

GLASGOW SPRINGBURN (Strathclyde)
E.45,842   T.65.65%
*M. Martin, *Lab.*		20,369
S. Miller, *SNP*		5,863
A. Barnett, *C.*		2,625
R. Ackland, *LD*		1,242
Lab. majority		14,506
(June 1987, Lab. maj. 22,063)

GORDON (Grampian)
E.80,103   T.73.86%
*M. Bruce, *LD*		22,158
J. Porter, *C.*		21,884
B. Adam, *SNP*		8,445
P. Morrell, *Lab.*		6,682
LD majority		274
(June 1987, L./All. maj. 9,519)

GREENOCK AND PORT GLASGOW
(Strathclyde)
E.52,053   *T*.73.72%
*N. Godman, *Lab.*   22,258
I. Black, *SNP*   7,279
Dr J. McCullough, *C.*   4,479
C. Lambert, *LD*   4,359
Lab. majority   14,979
(June 1987, Lab. maj. 20,055)

HAMILTON (Strathclyde)
E.61,531   *T*.76.15%
*G. Robertson, *Lab.*   25,849
W. Morrison, *SNP*   9,246
Ms M. Mitchell, *C.*   8,250
J. Oswald, *LD*   3,515
Lab. majority   16,603
(June 1987, Lab. maj. 21,662)

INVERNESS NAIRN AND LOCHABER
(Highland)
E.69,468   *T*.73.27%
*Sir R. Johnston, *LD*   13,258
D. Stewart, *Lab.*   12,800
F. Ewing, *SNP*   12,562
J. Scott, *C.*   11,517
J. Martin, *Green*   766
LD majority   458
(June 1987, L./All maj. 5,431)

KILMARNOCK AND LOUDOUN
(Strathclyde)
E.62,002   *T*.79.99%
*W. McKelvey, *Lab.*   22,210
A. Neil, *SNP*   15,231
R. Wilkinson, *C.*   9,438
Mrs K. Philbrick, *LD*   2,722
Lab. majority   6,979
(June 1987, Lab. maj. 14,127)

KINCARDINE AND DEESIDE
(Grampian)
E.66,617   *T*.78.74%
G. Kynoch, *C.*   22,924
*N. Stephen, *LD*   18,429
Dr A. Macartney, *SNP*   5,927
M. Savidge, *Lab.*   4,795
S. Campbell, *Green*   381
C. majority   4,495
(June 1987, C. maj. 2,063)
(Nov. 1991, LD maj. 7,824)

KIRKCALDY (Fife)
E.51,762   *T*.75.06%
*Dr L. Moonie, *Lab.*   17,887
S. Hosie, *SNP*   8,761
S. Wosley, *C.*   8,476
Ms S. Leslie, *LD*   3,729
Lab. majority   9,126
(June 1987, Lab. maj. 11,570)

LINLITHGOW (Lothian)
E.61,082   *T*.78.66%
*T. Dalyell, *Lab.*   21,603
K. MacAskill, *SNP*   14,577
Ms E. Forbes, *C.*   8,424
M. Falchikov, *LD*   3,446
Lab. majority   7,026
(June 1987, Lab. maj. 10,373)

LIVINGSTON (Lothian)
E.61,092   *T*.74.62%
*R. Cook, *Lab.*   20,245
P. Johnston, *SNP*   12,140
H. Gordon, *C.*   8,824
F. Mackintosh, *LD*   3,911
A. Ross-Smith, *Green*   469
Lab. majority   8,105
(June 1987, Lab. maj. 11,105)

MIDLOTHIAN
E.60,255   *T*.77.87%
E. Clarke, *Lab.*   20,588
A. Lumsden, *SNP*   10,254
J. Stoddart, *C.*   9,443
P. Sewell, *LD*   6,164
I. Morrice, *Green*   476
Lab. majority   10,334
(June 1987, Lab. maj. 12,253)

MONKLANDS EAST (Strathclyde)
E.48,391   *T*.75.07%
*Rt. Hon. J. Smith, *Lab.*   22,266
J. Wright, *SNP*   6,554
S. Walters, *C.*   5,830
P. Ross, *LD*   1,679
Lab. majority   15,712
(June 1987, Lab. maj. 16,389)
See also page 234

MONKLANDS WEST (Strathclyde)
E.49,269   *T*.77.45%
*T. Clarke, *Lab.*   23,384
K. Bovey, *SNP*   6,319
A. Lownie, *C.*   6,074
Ms S. Hamilton, *LD*   2,382
Lab. majority   17,065
(June 1987, Lab. maj. 18,333)

MORAY (Grampian)
E.63,255   *T*.72.46%
*Mrs M. Ewing, *SNP*   20,299
Ms R. Hossack, *C.*   17,455
C. Smith, *Lab.*   5,448
B. Sheridan, *LD*   2,634
SNP majority   2,844
(June 1987, SNP maj. 3,685)

MOTHERWELL NORTH
(Strathclyde)
E.57,290   *T*.76.71%
*Dr J. Reid, *Lab.*   27,852
D. Clark, *SNP*   8,942
R. Hargrave, *C.*   5,011
Miss H. Smith, *LD*   2,145
Lab. majority   18,910
(June 1987, Lab. maj. 23,595)

MOTHERWELL SOUTH
(Strathclyde)
E.50,042   *T*.76.17%
*J. Bray, *Lab.*   21,771
Mrs K. Ullrich, *SNP*   7,758
G. McIntosh, *C.*   6,097
A. Mackie, *LD*   2,349
D. Lettice, *YSOR*   146
Lab. majority   14,013
(June 1987, Lab. maj. 16,930)

ORKNEY AND SHETLAND
E.31,472   *T*.65.53%
*J. Wallace, *LD*   9,575
Dr P. McCormick, *C.*   4,542

J. Aberdein, *Lab.*   4,093
Mrs F. McKie, *SNP*   2,301
Ms C. Wharton, *NLP*   115
LD majority   5,033
(June 1987, L./All. maj. 3,922)

PAISLEY NORTH (Strathclyde)
E.46,403   *T*.73.39%
*Mrs I. Adams, *Lab.*   17,269
R. Mullin, *SNP*   7,940
D. Sharpe, *C.*   5,576
Miss E. McCartin, *LD*   2,779
D. Mellor, *Green*   412
N. Brennan, *NLP*   81
Lab. majority   9,329
(June 1987, Lab. maj. 14,442)
(Nov. 1990, Lab. maj. 3,770)

PAISLEY SOUTH (Strathclyde)
E.47,889   *T*.75.01%
*G. McMaster, *Lab.*   18,202
I. Lawson, *SNP*   8,653
Ms S. Laidlaw, *C.*   5,703
A. Reid, *LD*   3,271
S. Porter, *NLP*   93
Lab. majority   9,549
(June 1987, Lab. maj. 15,785)
(Nov. 1990, Lab. maj. 5,030)

PERTH AND KINROSS (Tayside)
E.65,410   *T*.76.86%
*Sir N. Fairbairn, *C.*   20,195
Ms R. Cunningham, *SNP*   18,101
M. Rolfe, *Lab.*   6,267
M. Black, *LD*   5,714
C. majority   2,094
(June 1987, C. maj. 5,676)
See also page 234

RENFREW WEST AND INVERCLYDE
(Strathclyde)
E.58,122   *T*.80.32%
*T. Graham, *Lab.*   17,085
Ms A. Goldie, *C.*   15,341
C. Campbell, *SNP*   9,444
S. Nimmo, *LD*   4,668
D. Maltman, *NLP*   149
Lab. majority   1,744
(June 1987, Lab. maj. 4,063)

ROSS, CROMARTY AND SKYE
(Highland)
E.55,524   *T*.73.90%
*C. Kennedy, *LD*   17,066
J. Gray, *C.*   9,436
R. Gibson, *SNP*   7,618
J. MacDonald, *Lab.*   6,275
D. Jardine, *Green*   642
LD majority   7,630
(June 1987, SDP/All. maj. 11,319)

ROXBURGH AND BERWICKSHIRE
(Borders)
E.43,485   *T*.77.71%
*A. Kirkwood, *LD*   15,852
S. Finlay-Maxwell, *C.*   11,595
M. Douglas, *SNP*   3,437
S. Lambert, *Lab.*   2,909
LD majority   4,257
(June 1987, L./All maj. 4,008)

STIRLING (Central)
E.58,266 T.82.29%
*M. Forsyth, C. — 19,174
Ms K. Phillips, Lab. — 18,471
G. Fisher, SNP — 6,558
W. Robertson, LD — 3,337
W. Thomson, Green — 342
R. Sharp, Loony — 68
C. majority — 703
(June 1987, C. maj. 548)

STRATHKELVIN AND BEARSDEN (Strathclyde)
E.61,116 T.82.33%
*S. Galbraith, Lab. — 21,267
M. Hirst, C. — 18,105
T. Chalmers, SNP — 6,275

Ms B. Waterfield, LD — 4,585
D. Whitley, NLP — 90
Lab. majority — 3,162
(June 1987, Lab. maj. 2,452)

TAYSIDE NORTH
E.55,969 T.77.64%
*W. Walker, C. — 20,283
J. Swinney, SNP — 16,288
S. Horner, LD — 3,791
S. Maclennan, Lab. — 3,094
C. majority — 3,995
(June 1987, C. maj. 5,016)

TWEEDDALE, ETTRICK AND LAUDERDALE (Borders)
E.39,493 T.78.04%
*Rt. Hon. Sir D. Steel, LD — 12,296

L. Beat, C. — 9,776
Mrs C. Creech, SNP — 5,244
A. Dunton, Lab. — 3,328
J. Hein, Lib. — 177
LD majority — 2,520
(June 1987, L./All. maj. 5,942)

WESTERN ISLES
E.22,784 T.70.35%
*C. MacDonald, Lab. — 7,664
Ms F. MacFarlane, SNP — 5,961
R. Heany, C. — 1,362
N. Mitchison, LD — 552
A. Price, Ind. — 491
Lab. majority — 1,703
(June 1987, Lab. maj. 2,340)

NORTHERN IRELAND

ANTRIM EAST
E.62,839 T.62.46%
*R. Beggs, UUP — 16,966
N. Dodds, DUP — 9,544
S. Neeson, All. — 9,132
Miss M. Boal, C. — 3,359
Ms A. Palmer, NLP — 250
UUP majority — 7,422
(June 1987, UUP maj. 15,360)

ANTRIM NORTH
E.69,124 T.65.82%
*Revd I. Paisley, DUP — 23,152
J. Gaston, UUP — 8,216
S. Farren, SDLP — 6,512
G. Williams, All. — 3,442
R. Sowler, C. — 2,263
J. McGarry, SF — 1,916
DUP majority — 14,936
(June 1987, DUP maj. 23,234)

ANTRIM SOUTH
E.68,013 T.62.10%
*C. Forsythe, UUP — 29,956
D. McClelland, SDLP — 5,397
J. Blair, All. — 5,224
H. Cushinan, SF — 1,220
D. Martin, Loony G. — 442
UUP majority — 24,559
(June 1987, UUP maj. 19,587)

BELFAST EAST
E.52,833 T.67.74%
*P. Robinson, DUP — 18,437
Dr J. Alderdice, All. — 10,650
D. Greene, C. — 3,314
Ms D. Dunlop, Ind. U. — 2,256
J. O'Donnell, SF — 679
J. Bell, WP — 327
G. Redden, NLP — 128
DUP majority — 7,787
(June 1987, DUP maj. 9,798)

BELFAST NORTH
E.55,062 T.65.22%
*A. C. Walker, UUP — 17,240
A. Maginness, SDLP — 7,615
P. McManus, SF — 4,693
T. Campbell, All. — 2,246
Ms M. Redpath, C. — 2,107

S. Lynch, NA — 1,386
Ms M. Smith, WP — 419
D. O'Leary, NLP — 208
UUP majority — 9,625
(June 1987, UUP maj. 8,560)

BELFAST SOUTH
E.52,032 T.64.54%
*Revd W. M. Smyth, UUP — 16,336
Dr A. McDonnell, SDLP — 6,266
J. Montgomery, All. — 5,054
L. Fee, C. — 3,356
S. Hayes, SF — 1,123
P. Hadden, LTU — 875
P. Lynn, WP — 362
Ms T. Mullan, NLP — 212
UUP majority — 10,070
(June 1987, UUP maj. 11,954)

BELFAST WEST
E.54,609 T.73.19%
Dr J. Hendron, SDLP — 17,415
*G. Adams, SF — 16,826
F. Cobain, UUP — 4,766
J. Lowry, WP — 750
M. Kennedy, NLP — 213
SDLP majority — 589
(June 1987, SF maj. 2,221)

DOWN NORTH
E.68,662 T.65.47%
*J. Kilfedder, UPUP — 19,305
Dr L. Kennedy, C. — 14,371
Ms A. Morrow, All. — 6,611
D. Vitty, DUP — 4,414
A. Wilmot, NLP — 255
UPUP majority — 4,934
(June 1987, UPUP maj. 3,953)
See also page 234

DOWN SOUTH
E.76,093 T.80.92%
*E. McGrady, SDLP — 31,523
D. Nelson, UUP — 25,181
S. Fitzpatrick, SF — 1,843
M. Healey, All. — 1,542
Mrs S. McKenzie-Hill, C. — 1,488
SDLP majority — 6,342
(June 1987, SDLP maj. 731)

FERMANAGH AND SOUTH TYRONE
E.70,192 T.78.53%
*K. Maginnis, UUP — 26,923
T. Gallagher, SDLP — 12,810
F. Molloy, SF — 12,604
D. Kettyles, Prog. Soc. — 1,094
E. Bullick, All. — 950
G. Cullen, NA — 747
UUP majority — 14,113
(June 1987, UUP maj. 12,823)

FOYLE
E.74,585 T.69.57%
*J. Hume, SDLP — 26,710
G. Campbell, DUP — 13,705
M. McGuinness, SF — 9,149
Ms L. McIlroy, All. — 1,390
G. McKenzie, WP — 514
J. Burns, NLP — 422
SDLP majority — 13,005
(June 1987, SDLP maj. 9,860)

LAGAN VALLEY
E.72,645 T.67.39%
*Rt. Hon. J. H. Molyneaux, UUP — 29,772
S. Close, All. — 6,207
H. Lewsley, SDLP — 4,626
T. Coleridge, C. — 4,423
P. Rice, SF — 3,346
Ms A.-M. Lowry, WP — 582
UUP majority — 23,565
(June 1987, UUP maj. 23,373)

LONDONDERRY EAST
E.75,559 T.69.79%
*W. Ross, UUP — 30,370
A. Doherty, SDLP — 11,843
Ms P. Davey-Kennedy, SF — 5,320
P. McGowan, All. — 3,613
A. Elder, C. — 1,589
UUP majority — 18,527
(June 1987, UUP maj. 20,157)

NEWRY AND ARMAGH
E.67,508 T.77.87%
*S. Mallon, SDLP — 26,073
J. Speers, UUP — 18,982
B. Curran, SF — 6,547
Mrs E. Bell, All. — 972

SDLP majority	7,091	ULSTER MID		UPPER BANN		
(June 1987, SDLP maj. 5,325)		*E.*69,071 *T.*79.28%		*E.*67,446 *T.*67.43%		
STRANGFORD		*Revd Dr R. T. W. McCrea, *DUP*		*W. D. Trimble, *UUP*	26,824
*E.*68,870 *T.*65.02%			23,181	Mrs B. Rodgers, *SDLP*	10,661
*Rt. Hon. J. Taylor, *UUP*	19,517	D. Haughey, *SDLP*	16,994	B. Curran, *SF*	2,777
S. Wilson, *DUP*	10,606	B. McElduff, *SF*	10,248	Dr W. Ramsey, *All.*	2,541
K. McCarthy, *All.*	7,585	J. McLoughlin, *Ind.*	1,996	Mrs C. Jones, *C.*	1,556
S. Eyre, *C.*	6,782	Ms A. Gormley, *All.*	1,506	T. French, *WP*	1,120
D. Shaw, *NLP*	295	H. Hutchinson, *LTU*	389	*UUP majority*	16,163
UUP majority	8,911	T. Owens, *WP*	285	(June 1987, OUP maj. 17,361)
(June 1987, UUP maj. 20,646)		J. Anderson, *NLP*	164	(May 1990, OUP maj. 13,849)
		DUP majority	6,187		
		(June 1987, DUP maj. 9,360)			

COMMONWEALTH PARLIAMENTARY ASSOCIATION (1911)

The Commonwealth Parliamentary Association consists of 135 branches in the national, state, provincial or territorial parliaments in the countries of the Commonwealth. Conferences and general assemblies are held every year in different countries of the Commonwealth.

President (1995–6), Y. B. Tan Sri Dato' Zahir Haji Ismail, MP, Speaker of the House of Representatives, Malaysia

Vice-President, (1995–6), Hon. Sir Ramesh Jeewoolall, MP, Speaker of the National Assembly, Mauritius

Chairman of the Executive Committee (1993–), Colin Shepherd, MP (United Kingdom)

Secretary-General, A. R. Donahoe, QC, Suite 700, Westminster House, 7 Millbank, London SW1P 3JA

UNITED KINGDOM BRANCH

Hon. Presidents, The Lord Chancellor; Madam Speaker
Chairman of Branch, The Rt. Hon. John Major, MP

Chairman of Executive Committee, Sir Ivan Lawrence, QC, MP
Secretary, P. Cobb, OBE, Westminster Hall, Houses of Parliament, London, SW1A 0AA

THE INTER-PARLIAMENTARY UNION (1889)

To facilitate personal contact between members of all Parliaments in the promotion of representative institutions, peace and international co-operation.

Secretary-General, P. Cornillon, Place du Petit-Saconnex. BP 99, 1211 Geneva 19, Switzerland

BRITISH GROUP

Palace of Westminster, London SW1A 0AA

Hon. Presidents, The Lord Chancellor; Madam Speaker
President, The Rt. Hon. John Major, MP
Chairman, Dame Jill Knight, DBE, MP
Secretary, D. Ramsay

European Parliament

European Parliament elections take place at five-yearly intervals. In mainland Britain MEPs are elected in all constituencies on a first-past-the-post basis; in Northern Ireland three MEPs are elected by proportional representation. From 1979 to 1994 the number of seats held by the UK in the European Parliament was 81. At the June 1994 election the number of seats increased to 87 (England 71, Wales 5, Scotland 8, Northern Ireland 3).

Since 1994, nationals of member states of the European Union have the right to vote in elections to the European Parliament in the UK. British subjects and citizens of the Irish Republic can stand in the UK for election to the European Parliament provided they are 21 or over and not subject to disqualification.

MEPs receive a salary from the parliaments or governments of their respective member states, set at the level of the national parliamentary salary and subject to national taxation rules (for salary of British MPs, *see* page 219).

UK MEMBERS AS AT END JULY 1996

*Denotes membership of the last European Parliament

*Adam, Gordon J., PH.D. (*b.* 1934), *Lab., Northumbria*, maj. 66,158

*Balfe, Richard A. (*b.* 1944), *Lab., London South Inner*, maj. 59,220

*Barton, Roger (*b.* 1945), *Lab., Sheffield*, maj. 50,288

Billingham, Mrs Angela T. (*b.* 1939), *Lab., Northamptonshire and Blaby*, maj. 26,085

*Bowe, David R. (*b.* 1955), *Lab., Cleveland and Richmond*, maj. 57,568

*Cassidy, Bryan M. D. (*b.* 1934), *C., Dorset and Devon East*, maj. 2,264

Chichester, Giles B. (*b.* 1946), *C., Devon and Plymouth East*, maj. 700

*Coates, Kenneth S. (*b.* 1930), *Lab., Nottinghamshire North and Chesterfield*, maj. 76,260

*Collins, Kenneth D. (*b.* 1939), *Lab., Strathclyde East*, maj. 52,340

Corrie, John A. (*b.* 1935), *C., Worcestershire and Warwickshire South*, maj. 1,204

*Crampton, Peter D. (*b.* 1932), *Lab., Humberside*, maj. 40,618

*Crawley, Mrs Christine M. (*b.* 1950), *Lab., Birmingham East*, maj. 55,120

Cunningham, Thomas A. (Tony) (*b.* 1952), *Lab., Cumbria and Lancashire North*, maj. 22,988

*David, Wayne (*b.* 1957), *Lab., South Wales Central*, maj. 86,082

*Donnelly, Alan J. (*b.* 1957), *Lab., Tyne and Wear*, maj. 88,380

Donnelly, Brendan P. (*b.* 1950), *C., Sussex South and Crawley*, maj. 1,746

*Elles, James E. M. (*b.* 1949), *C., Buckinghamshire and Oxfordshire East*, maj. 30,665

*Elliott, Michael N. (*b.* 1932), *Lab., London West*, maj. 42,275

Evans, Robert J. E. (*b.* 1956), *Lab., London North West*, maj. 17,442

*Ewing, Mrs Winifred M. (*b.* 1929), *SNP, Highlands and Islands*, maj. 54,916

*Falconer, Alexander (*b.* 1940), *Lab., Scotland Mid and Fife*, maj. 31,413

*Ford, J. Glyn (*b.* 1950), *Lab., Greater Manchester East*, maj. 55,986

*Green, Mrs Pauline (*b.* 1948), *Lab., London North*, maj. 48,348

Hallam, David J. A. (*b.* 1948), *Lab., Herefordshire and Shropshire*, maj. 1,850

Hardstaff, Mrs Veronica M. (*b.* 1941), *Lab., Lincolnshire and Humberside South*, maj. 13,745

*Harrison, Lyndon H. A. (*b.* 1947), *Lab., Cheshire West and Wirral*, maj. 47,176

Hendrick, Mark P. (*b.* 1958), *Lab., Lancashire Central*, maj. 12,191

*Hindley, Michael J. (*b.* 1947), *Lab., Lancashire South*, maj. 41,404

Howitt, Richard (*b.* 1961), *Lab., Essex South*, maj. 21,367

*Hughes, Stephen S. (*b.* 1952), *Lab., Durham*, maj. 111,638

*Hume, John, MP (*b.* 1937), *SDLP, Northern Ireland*, polled 161,992 votes

*Jackson, Mrs Caroline F., D.PHIL. (*b.* 1946), *C., Wiltshire North and Bath*, maj. 8,787

*Kellett-Bowman, Edward T. (*b.* 1931), *C., Itchen, Test and Avon*, maj. 6,903

Kerr, Hugh (*b.* 1944), *Lab., Essex West and Hertfordshire East*, maj. 3,067

Kinnock, Mrs Glenys E. (*b.* 1944), *Lab., South Wales East*, maj. 120,247

*Lomas, Alfred (*b.* 1928), *Lab., London North East*, maj. 57,085

Macartney, W. J. Allan, PH.D. (*b.* 1941), *SNP, Scotland North East*, maj. 31,227

McCarthy, Ms Arlene (*b.* 1960), *Lab., Peak District*, maj. 49,307

*McGowan, Michael (*b.* 1940), *Lab., Leeds*, maj. 53,082

*McIntosh, Ms Anne C. B. (*b.* 1954), *C., Essex North and Suffolk South*, maj. 3,633

*McMahon, Hugh R. (*b.* 1938), *Lab., Strathclyde West*, maj. 25,023

*McMillan-Scott, Edward H. C. (*b.* 1949), *C., Yorkshire North*, maj. 7,072

McNally, Mrs Eryl M. (*b.* 1942), *Lab., Bedfordshire and Milton Keynes*, maj. 33,209

*Martin, David W. (*b.* 1954), *Lab., Lothians*, maj 37,207

Mather, Graham C. S. (*b.* 1954), *C., Hampshire North and Oxford*, maj. 9,194

*Megahy, Thomas (*b.* 1929), *Lab., Yorkshire South West*, maj. 59,562

Miller, Bill (*b.* 1954), *Lab., Glasgow*, maj. 43,158

*Moorhouse, C. James O. (*b.* 1924), *C., London South and Surrey East*, maj. 8,739

Morgan, Ms Eluned (*b.* 1967), *Lab., Wales Mid and West*, maj. 29,234

*Morris, Revd David R. (*b.* 1930), *Lab., South Wales West*, maj. 84,970

Murphy, Simon F., PH.D. (*b.* 1962), *Lab., Midlands West*, maj. 54,823

Needle, Clive (*b.* 1956), *Lab., Norfolk*, maj. 26,287

*Newens, A. Stanley (*b.* 1930), *Lab., London Central*, maj. 25,059

*Newman, Edward (*b.* 1953), *Lab., Greater Manchester Central*, maj. 42,445

*Nicholson, James F. (*b.* 1945), *UUUP, Northern Ireland*, polled 133,459 votes

*Oddy, Ms Christine M. (*b.* 1955), *Lab., Coventry and Warwickshire North*, maj. 43,901

*Paisley, Revd Ian R. K., MP (*b.* 1926), *DUP, Northern Ireland*, polled 163,246 votes

Perry, Roy J. (*b.* 1943), *C., Wight and Hampshire South*, maj. 5,101

*Plumb, The Lord (*b.* 1925), *C., Cotswolds,* maj. 4,268
*Pollack, Ms Anita J. (*b.* 1946), *Lab., London South West,* maj. 30,975
Provan, James L. C. (*b.* 1936), *C., South Downs West,* maj. 21,067
*Read, Ms I. M. (Mel) (*b.* 1939), *Lab., Nottingham and Leicestershire North West,* maj. 39,668
*Seal, Barry H., PH.D. (*b.* 1937), *Lab., Yorkshire West,* maj. 48,197
*Simpson, Brian (*b.* 1953), *Lab., Cheshire East,* maj. 39,279
Skinner, Peter W. (*b.* 1959), *Lab., Kent West,* maj. 16,777
*Smith, Alexander (*b.* 1943), *Lab., Scotland South,* maj. 45,155
*Spencer, Thomas N. B. (*b.* 1948), *C., Surrey,* maj. 27,018
Spiers, Shaun M. (*b.* 1962), *Lab., London South East,* maj. 8,022
*Stevens, John C. C. (*b.* 1955), *C., Thames Valley,* maj. 758
*Stewart, Kenneth A. (*b.* 1925), *Lab., Merseyside West,* maj. 51,811 (*see* Stop-press)
*Stewart-Clark, Sir John, Bt. (*b.* 1929), *C., Sussex East and Kent South,* maj. 6,212
Sturdy, Robert W. (*b.* 1944), *C., Cambridgeshire,* maj. 3,942
Tappin, Michael (*b.* 1946), *Lab., Staffordshire West and Congleton,* maj. 40,277

Teverson, Robin (*b.* 1952), *LD, Cornwall and Plymouth West,* maj. 29,498
Thomas, David E. (*b.* 1955), *Lab., Suffolk and Norfolk South West,* maj. 12,535
*Titley, Gary (*b.* 1950), *Lab., Greater Manchester West,* maj. 58,635
*Tomlinson, John E. (*b.* 1939), *Lab., Birmingham West,* maj. 39,350
*Tongue, Ms Carole (*b.* 1955), *Lab., London East,* maj. 57,389
Truscott, Peter, PH.D. (*b.* 1959), *Lab., Hertfordshire,* maj. 10,304
Waddington, Mrs Susan A. (*b.* 1944), *Lab., Leicester,* maj. 20,284
Watson, Graham R. (*b.* 1956), *LD, Somerset and Devon North,* maj. 22,509
Watts, Mark F. (*b.* 1964), *Lab., Kent East,* maj. 635
*West, Norman, (*b.* 1935), *Lab., Yorkshire South,* maj. 88,309
*White, Ian (*b.* 1947), *Lab., Bristol,* maj. 29,955
Whitehead, Phillip (*b.* 1937), *Lab., Staffordshire East and Derby,* maj. 72,196
*Wilson, A. Joseph (*b.* 1937), *Lab., Wales North,* maj. 15,242
*Wynn, Terence (*b.* 1946), *Lab., Merseyside East and Wigan,* maj. 74,087

UK CONSTITUENCIES AS AT 9 JUNE 1994

Abbreviations	
Anti Fed.	UK Independence Anti-Federal
Anti Fed. C.	Official Anti-Federalist Conservative
Beanus	Eurobean from Planet Beanus
C. Non Fed.	Conservative Non-Federal Party
Capital P.	Restoration of Capital Punishment
Comm.	Communist
Comm. YBG	Communist Y Blaid Gomiwyddol
Const. NI	Constitutional Independence for N. Ireland
Corr.	Corrective Party
CPP	Christian People's Party
ICP	International Communist Party
ICP4	International Communist Party (4th International)
Ind. AES	Independent Anti-European Superstate
Ind. Out	Independent Out of Europe
Judo	European People's Party Judo Christian Alliance
Loony C	Raving Loony Commonsense
Loony CP	Monster Raving Loony Christian Party
Loony X	Monster Raving Loony Project X Party
MCCARTHY	Make Criminals Concerned About Our Response To Hostility and Yobbishness
MK	Mebyon Kernow
NCSA	Network Against Child Support Agency
Neeps	North East Ethnic Party, The Neeps
Rainbow	Rainbow Connection – Oui-Say-Non-Party
Sportsman	Sportsman Anti-Common Market Bureaucracy
UUUP	United Ulster Unionist Party

For other abbreviations, *see* page 237

ENGLAND

BEDFORDSHIRE AND MILTON KEYNES
E. 525,524   *T.* 38.74%

E. McNally, *Lab.*	94,837
Mrs E. Currie, *C.*	61,628
Ms M. Howes, *LD*	27,994
A. Sked, *UK Independence*	7,485
A. Francis, *Green*	6,804
A. Howes, *New Britain*	3,878
L. Sheaff, *NLP*	939
Lab. majority	33,209

(Boundary change since June 1989)

BIRMINGHAM EAST
E. 520,782   *T.* 29.77%

Mrs C. Crawley, Lab.	90,291
A. Turner, *C.*	35,171
Ms C. Cane, *LD*	19,455
P. Simpson, *Green*	6,268
R. Cook, *Soc.*	1,969
M. Brierley, *NLP*	1,885
Lab. majority	55,120

(June 1989, Lab. maj. 46,948)

BIRMINGHAM WEST
E. 509,948   *T.* 28.49%

J. Tomlinson, Lab.	77,957
D. Harman, *C.*	38,607
N. McGeorge, *LD*	14,603
Dr B. Juby, *Anti Fed.*	5,237
M. Abbott, *Green*	4,367
A. Carmichael, *NF*	3,727
H. Meads, *NLP*	789
Lab. majority	39,350

(June 1989, Lab. maj. 30,860)

BRISTOL
E. 503,218   *T.* 40.91%

I. White, Lab.	90,790
The Earl of Stockton, *C.*	60,835
J. Barnard, *LD*	40,394

J. Boxall, *Green*	7,163
T. Whittingham, *UK Independence*	5,798
T. Dyball, *NLP*	876
Lab. majority	29,955

(Boundary change since June 1989)

BUCKINGHAMSHIRE AND OXFORDSHIRE EAST
E. 487,692   *T.* 37.31%

J. Elles, C.	77,037
D. Enright, *Lab.*	46,372
Ms S. Bowles, *LD*	42,836
L. Roach, *Green*	8,433
Ms A. Micklem, *Lib.*	5,111
Dr G. Clements, *NLP*	2,156
C. majority	30,665

(Boundary change since June 1989)

CAMBRIDGESHIRE
E. 495,383   *T.* 35.91%

R. Sturdy, *C.*	66,921
Ms M. Johnson, *Lab.*	62,979
A. Duff, *LD*	36,114
Ms M. Wright, *Green*	5,756
P. Wiggin, *Lib.*	4,051
F. Chalmers, *NLP*	2,077
C. majority	3,942

(Boundary change since June 1989)

CHESHIRE EAST
E. 502,726   *T.* 32.46%

B. Simpson, Lab.	87,586
P. Slater, *C.*	48,307
P. Harris, *LD*	20,552
D. Wild, *Green*	3,671
P. Dixon, *Loony CP*	1,600
P. Leadbetter, *NLP*	1,488
Lab. majority	39,279

(Boundary change since June 1989)

CHESHIRE WEST AND WIRRAL
E. 538,571   T. 36.78%

*L. Harrison, *Lab.*	106,160
D. Senior, *C.*	58,984
I. Mottershaw, *LD*	20,746
D. Carson, *British Home Rule*	6,167
M. Money, *Green*	5,096
A. Wilmot, *NLP*	929
Lab. majority	47,176

(Boundary change since June 1989)

CLEVELAND AND RICHMOND
E. 499,580   T. 35.26%

*D. Bowe, *Lab.*	103,355
R. Goodwill, *C.*	45,787
B. Moore, *LD*	21,574
G. Parr, *Green*	4,375
R. Scott, *NLP*	1,068
Lab. majority	57,568

(Boundary change since June 1989)

CORNWALL AND PLYMOUTH WEST
E. 484,697   T. 44.92%

R. Teverson, *LD*	91,113
*C. Beazley, *C.*	61,615
Mrs D. Kirk, *Lab.*	42,907
Mrs P. Garnier, *UK Independence*	
	6,466
P. Holmes, *Lib.*	6,414
Ms K. Westbrook, *Green*	4,372
Dr L. Jenkin, *MK*	3,315
F. Lyons, *NLP*	921
M. Fitzgerald, *Subsidiarity*	606
LD majority	29,498

(Boundary change since June 1989)

COTSWOLDS
E. 497,588   T. 39.27%

*The Lord Plumb, *C.*	67,484
Ms T. Kingham, *Lab.*	63,216
J. Thomson, *LD*	44,269
M. Rendell, *New Britain*	11,044
D. McCanlis, *Green*	8,254
H. Brighouse, *NLP*	1,151
C. majority	4,268

(Boundary change since June 1989)

COVENTRY AND WARWICKSHIRE NORTH
E. 523,448   T. 32.54%

*Ms C. Oddy, *Lab.*	89,500
Ms J. Crabb, *C.*	45,599
G. Sewards, *LD*	17,453
R. Meacham, *Free Trade*	9,432
P. Baptie, *Green*	4,360
R. Wheway, *Lib.*	2,885
R. France, *NLP*	1,098
Lab. majority	43,901

(Boundary change since June 1989)

CUMBRIA AND LANCASHIRE NORTH
E. 498,557   T. 40.78%

A. Cunningham, *Lab.*	97,599
*The Lord Inglewood, *C.*	74,611
R. Putnam, *LD*	24,233
R. Frost, *Green*	5,344
I. Docker, *NLP*	1,500
Lab. majority	22,988

(Boundary change since June 1989)

DEVON AND PLYMOUTH EAST
E. 524,320   T. 45.07%

G. Chichester, *C.*	74,953
A. Sanders, *LD*	74,253
Ms L. Gilroy, *Lab.*	47,596
D. Morrish, *Lib.*	14,621
P. Edwards, *Green*	11,172
R. Huggett, *Literal Democrat*	10,203
J. Everard, *Ind.*	2,629
A. Pringle, *NLP*	908
C. majority	700

(Boundary change since June 1989)

DORSET AND DEVON EAST
E. 531,842   T. 41.21%

*B. Cassidy, *C.*	81,551
P. Goldenberg, *LD*	79,287
A. Gardner, *Lab.*	34,856
M. Floyd, *UK Independence*	10,548
Mrs K. Bradbury, *Green*	8,642
I. Mortimer, *C. Non-Fed.*	3,229
M. Griffiths, *NLP*	1,048
C. majority	2,264

(Boundary change since June 1989)

DURHAM
E. 532,051   T. 35.62%

*S. Hughes, *Lab.*	136,671
P. Bradbourn, *C.*	25,033
Dr N. Martin, *LD*	20,935
S. Hope, *Green*	5,670
C. Adamson, *NLP*	1,198
Lab. majority	111,638

(June 1989, Lab. maj. 86,848)

ESSEX NORTH AND SUFFOLK SOUTH
E. 497,098   T. 41.33%

*Ms A. McIntosh, *C.*	68,311
C. Pearson, *Lab.*	64,678
S. Mole, *LD*	52,536
S. de Chair, *Ind. AES*	12,409
J. Abbott, *Green*	6,641
N. Pullen, *NLP*	884
C. majority	3,633

(Boundary change since June 1989)

ESSEX SOUTH
E. 487,221   T. 33.08%

R. Howitt, *Lab.*	71,883
L. Stanbrook, *C.*	50,516
G. Williams, *LD*	26,132
B. Lynch, *Lib.*	6,780
G. Rumens, *Green*	4,691
M. Heath, *NLP*	1,177
Lab. majority	21,367

(Boundary change since June 1989)

ESSEX WEST AND HERTFORDSHIRE EAST
E. 504,095   T. 36.39%

H. Kerr, *Lab.*	66,379
*Ms P. Rawlings, *C.*	63,312
Ms G. James, *LD*	35,695
B. Smalley, *Britain*	10,277
Ms F. Mawson, *Green*	5,632
P. Carter, *Sportsman*	1,127
L. Davis, *NLP*	1,026
Lab. majority	3,067

(Boundary change since June 1989)

GREATER MANCHESTER CENTRAL
E. 481,779   T. 29.11%

*E. Newman, *Lab.*	74,935
Mrs S. Mason, *C.*	32,490
J. Begg, *LD*	22,988
B. Candeland, *Green*	4,952
P. Burke, *Lib.*	3,862
P. Stanley, *NLP*	1,017
Lab. majority	42,445

(Boundary change since June 1989)

GREATER MANCHESTER EAST
E. 501,125   T. 27.17%

*G. Ford, *Lab.*	82,289
J. Pinniger, *C.*	26,303
A. Riley, *LD*	20,545
T. Clarke, *Green*	5,823
W. Stevens, *NLP*	1,183
Lab. majority	55,986

(Boundary change since June 1989)

GREATER MANCHESTER WEST
E. 512,618   T. 29.70%

*G. Titley, *Lab.*	94,129
D. Newns, *C.*	35,494
F. Harasiwka, *LD*	13,650
R. Jackson, *Green*	3,950
G. Harrison, *MCCARTHY*	3,693
T. Brotheridge, *NLP*	1,316
Lab. majority	58,635

(Boundary change since June 1989)

HAMPSHIRE NORTH AND OXFORD
E. 525,982   T. 38.31%

G. Mather, *C.*	72,209
Ms J. Hawkins, *LD*	63,015
J. Tanner, *Lab.*	48,525
D. Wilkinson, *UK Independence*	8,377
Dr M. Woodin, *Green*	7,310
H. Godfrey, *NLP*	1,027
R. Boston, *Boston Tea Party*	1,018
C. majority	9,194

(Boundary change since June 1989)

HEREFORDSHIRE AND SHROPSHIRE
E. 536,470   T. 38.69%

D. Hallam, *Lab.*	76,120
*Sir C. Prout, *C.*	74,270
J. Gallagher, *LD*	44,130
Ms F. Norman, *Green*	11,578
T. Mercer, *NLP*	1,480
Lab. majority	1,850

(Boundary change since June 1989)

HERTFORDSHIRE
E. 522,338   T. 40.11%

Dr P. Truscott, *Lab.*	81,821
P. Jenkinson, *C.*	71,517
D. Griffiths, *LD*	38,995
Ms L. Howitt, *Green*	7,741
M. Biggs, *New Britain*	6,555
J. McAuley, *NF*	1,755
D. Lucas, *NLP*	734
J. Laine, *Century*	369
Lab. majority	10,304

(Boundary change since June 1989)

HUMBERSIDE
E. 519,013   T. 32.38%

*P. Crampton, *Lab.*	87,296
D. Stewart, *C.*	46,678
Ms D. Wallis, *LD*	28,818
Ms S. Mummery, *Green*	4,170

Ms A. Miszewska, *NLP* — 1,100
Lab. majority — 40,618
(Boundary change since June 1989)

ITCHEN, TEST AND AVON
E. 550,406   T. 41.83%
*E. Kellett-Bowman, *C.* — 81,456
A. Barron, *LD* — 74,553
E. Read, *Lab.* — 52,416
N. Farage, *UK Independence* — 12,423
Ms F. Hulbert, *Green* — 7,998
A. Miller-Smith, *NLP* — 1,368
C. majority — 6,903
(Boundary change since June 1989)

KENT EAST
E. 499,662   T. 40.34%
M. Watts, *Lab.* — 69,641
*C. Jackson, *C.* — 69,006
J. Macdonald, *LD* — 44,549
C. Bullen, *UK Independence* — 9,414
S. Dawe, *Green* — 7,196
C. Beckley, *NLP* — 1,746
Lab. majority — 635
(Boundary change since June 1989)

KENT WEST
E. 505,658   T. 37.33%
P. Skinner, *Lab.* — 77,346
*B. Patterson, *C.* — 60,569
J. Daly, *LD* — 33,869
C. Mackinlay, *UK Independence* — 9,750
Ms P. Kemp, *Green* — 5,651
J. Bowler, *NLP* — 1,598
Lab. majority — 16,777
(Boundary change since June 1989)

LANCASHIRE CENTRAL
E. 505,224   T. 33.23%
M. Hendrick, *Lab.* — 73,420
*M. Welsh, *C.* — 61,229
Ms J. Ross-Mills, *LD* — 20,578
D. Hill, *Home Rule* — 6,751
C. Maile, *Green* — 4,169
Ms J. Ayliffe, *NLP* — 1,727
Lab. majority — 12,191
(Boundary change since June 1989)

LANCASHIRE SOUTH
E. 514,840   T. 33.14%
*M. Hindley, *Lab.* — 92,598
R. Topham, *C.* — 51,194
J. Ault, *LD* — 17,008
J. Gaffney, *Green* — 4,774
Mrs E. Rokas, *Ind.* — 3,439
J. Renwick, *NLP* — 1,605
Lab. majority — 41,404
(Boundary change since June 1989)

LEEDS
E. 521,989   T. 30.03%
*M. McGowan, *Lab.* — 89,160
N. Carmichael, *C.* — 36,078
Ms J. Harvey, *LD* — 17,575
M. Meadowcroft, *Lib.* — 6,617
Ms C. Nash, *Green* — 6,283
Ms S. Hayward, *NLP* — 1,018
Lab. majority — 53,082
(June 1989, Lab. maj. 42,518)

LEICESTER
E. 515,343   T. 37.63%
Ms S. Waddington, *Lab.* — 87,048
A. Marshall, *C.* — 66,764
M. Jones, *LD* — 28,890
G. Forse, *Green* — 8,941
Ms P. Saunders, *NLP* — 2,283
Lab. majority — 20,284
(Boundary change since June 1989)

LINCOLNSHIRE AND HUMBERSIDE SOUTH
E. 539,981   T. 36.34%
Mrs V. Hardstaff, *Lab.* — 83,172
*W. Newton Dunn, *C.* — 69,427
K. Melton, *LD* — 27,241
Ms R. Robinson, *Green* — 8,563
E. Wheeler, *Lib.* — 3,434
I. Selby, *NCSA* — 2,973
H. Kelly, *NLP* — 1,429
Lab. majority — 13,745
(Boundary change since June 1989)

LONDON CENTRAL
E. 494,610   T. 32.57%
*S. Newens, *Lab.* — 75,711
A. Elliott, *C.* — 50,652
Ms S. Ludford, *LD* — 20,176
Ms N. Kortvelyessy, *Green* — 7,043
H. Le Fanu, *UK Independence* — 4,157
C. Slapper, *Soc.* — 1,593
Ms S. Hamza, *NLP* — 1,215
G. Weiss, *Rainbow* — 547
Lab. majority — 25,059
(June 1989, Lab. maj. 11,542)

LONDON EAST
E. 511,523   T. 33.38%
*Ms C. Tongue, *Lab.* — 98,759
Ms V. Taylor, *C.* — 41,370
K. Montgomery, *LD* — 15,566
G. Batten, *UK Independence* — 5,974
J. Baguley, *Green* — 4,337
O. Tillett, *Third Way Independence* — 3,484
N. Kahn, *NLP* — 1,272
Lab. majority — 57,389
(June 1989, Lab. maj. 27,385)

LONDON NORTH
E. 541,269   T. 34.00%
*Mrs P. Green, *Lab.* — 102,059
M. Keegan, *C.* — 53,711
I. Mann, *LD* — 15,739
Ms H. Jago, *Green* — 5,666
I. Booth, *UK Independence* — 5,099
G. Sabrizi, *Judo* — 880
J. Hinde, *NLP* — 856
Lab. majority — 48,348
(June 1989, Lab. maj. 5,837)

LONDON NORTH EAST
E. 486,016   T. 26.60%
*A. Lomas, *Lab.* — 80,256
S. Gordon, *C.* — 23,171
K. Appiah, *LD* — 10,242
Ms J. Lambert, *Green* — 8,386
E. Murat, *Lib.* — 2,573
P. Compobassi, *UK Independence* — 2,015
R. Archer, *NLP* — 1,111
M. Fischer, *Comm. GB* — 869
A. Hyland, *ICP4* — 679

Lab. majority — 57,085
(June 1989, Lab. maj. 47,767)

LONDON NORTH WEST
E. 481,272   T. 35.13%
R. Evans, *Lab.* — 80,192
*The Lord Bethell, *C.* — 62,750
Ms H. Leighter, *LD* — 18,998
D. Johnson, *Green* — 4,743
Ms A. Murphy, *Comm. GB* — 858
Ms T. Sullivan, *NLP* — 807
C. Palmer, *Century* — 740
Lab. majority — 17,442
(June 1989, C. maj. 7,400)

LONDON SOUTH AND SURREY EAST
E. 486,358   T. 34.38%
*J. Moorhouse, *C.* — 64,813
Ms G. Rolles, *Lab.* — 56,074
M. Reinisch, *LD* — 32,059
J. Cornford, *Green* — 7,046
J. Major, *Loony X* — 3,339
A. Reeve, *Capital P.* — 2,983
P. Levy, *NLP* — 887
C. majority — 8,739
(Boundary change since June 1989)

LONDON SOUTH EAST
E. 493,178   T. 35.38%
S. Spiers, *Lab.* — 71,505
*P. Price, *C.* — 63,483
J. Fryer, *LD* — 25,271
I. Mouland, *Green* — 6,399
R. Almond, *Lib.* — 3,881
K. Lowne, *NF* — 2,926
J. Small, *NLP* — 1,025
Lab. majority — 8,022
(Boundary change since June 1989)

LONDON SOUTH INNER
E. 510,609   T. 27.30%
*R. Balfe, *Lab.* — 85,079
A. Boff, *C.* — 25,859
A. Graves, *LD* — 20,708
S. Collins, *Green* — 6,570
M. Leighton, *NLP* — 1,179
Lab. majority — 59,220
(Boundary change since June 1989)

LONDON SOUTH WEST
E. 479,246   T. 34.35%
*Ms A. Pollack, *Lab.* — 81,850
Prof. P. Treleaven, *C.* — 50,875
G. Blanchard, *LD* — 18,697
T. Walsh, *Green* — 5,460
A. Scholefield, *UK Independence* — 4,912
C. Hopewell, *Capital P.* — 1,840
M. Simson, *NLP* — 625
J. Quanjer, *Spirit of Europe* — 377
Lab. majority — 30,975
(Boundary change since June 1989)

LONDON WEST
E. 505,791   T. 36.02%
*M. Elliott, *Lab.* — 94,562
R. Guy, *C.* — 52,287
W. Mallinson, *LD* — 21,561
J. Bradley, *Green* — 6,134
G. Roberts, *UK Independence* — 4,583
W. Binding, *NF* — 1,963
R. Johnson, *NLP* — 1,105
Lab. majority — 42,275
(June 1989, Lab. maj. 14,808)

MERSEYSIDE EAST AND WIGAN
E. 518,196　T. 24.66%

*T. Wynn,	*Lab.*	91,986
C. Manson,	*C.*	17,899
Ms F. Clucas,	*LD*	8,874
J. Melia,	*Lib.*	4,765
L. Brown,	*Green*	3,280
G. Hutchard,	*NLP*	1,009
Lab. majority		74,087
(June 1989, Lab. maj. 76,867)		

MERSEYSIDE WEST
E. 515,909　T. 26.18%

*K. Stewart,	*Lab.*	78,819
C. Varley,	*C.*	27,008
D. Bamber,	*LD*	19,097
S. Radford,	*Lib.*	4,714
Ms L. Lever,	*Green*	4,573
J. Collins,	*NLP*	852
Lab. majority		51,811
(June 1989, Lab. maj. 49,817)		

MIDLANDS WEST
E. 533,742　T. 31.28%

S. Murphy,	*Lab.*	99,242
M. Simpson,	*C.*	44,419
G. Baldauf-Good,	*LD*	12,195
M. Hyde,	*Lib.*	5,050
C. Mattingly,	*Green*	4,390
J. Oldbury,	*NLP*	1,641
Lab. majority		54,823
(June 1989, Lab. maj. 42,364)		

NORFOLK
E. 513,553　T. 44.25%

C. Needle,	*Lab.*	102,711
*P. Howell,	*C.*	76,424
P. Burall,	*LD*	39,107
A. Holmes,	*Green*	7,938
B. Parsons,	*NLP*	1,075
Lab. majority		26,287
(Boundary change since June 1989)		

NORTHAMPTONSHIRE AND BLABY
E. 524,916　T. 39.37%

Mrs A. Billingham,	*Lab.*	95,317
*A. Simpson,	*C.*	69,232
K. Scudder,	*LD*	27,616
Ms A. Bryant,	*Green*	9,121
I. Whitaker,	*Ind.*	4,397
B. Spivack,	*NLP*	972
Lab. majority		26,085
(Boundary change since June 1989)		

NORTHUMBRIA
E. 516,680　T. 33.65%

*G. Adam,	*Lab.*	103,087
J. Flack,	*C.*	36,929
L. Opik,	*LD*	20,195
D. Lott,	*UK Independence*	7,210
J. Hartshorne,	*Green*	5,714
L. Walch,	*NLP*	740
Lab. majority		66,158
(June 1989, Lab. maj. 60,040)		

NOTTINGHAM AND LEICESTERSHIRE NORTH WEST
E. 507,915　T. 37.68%

*Ms M. Read,	*Lab.*	95,344
M. Brandon-Bravo,	*C.*	55,676
A. Wood,	*LD*	23,836
Ms S. Blount,	*Green*	7,035
J. Downes,	*UK Independence*	5,849

P. Walton,	*Ind. Out*	2,710
Mrs J. Christou,	*NLP*	927
Lab. majority		39,668
(Boundary change since June 1989)		

NOTTINGHAMSHIRE NORTH AND CHESTERFIELD
E. 490,330　T. 36.95%

*K. Coates,	*Lab.*	114,353
D. Hazell,	*C.*	38,093
Ms S. Pearce,	*LD*	21,936
G. Jones,	*Green*	5,159
Ms S. Lincoln,	*NLP*	1,632
Lab. majority		76,260
(Boundary change since June 1989)		

PEAK DISTRICT
E. 511,357　T. 39.02%

Ms A. McCarthy,	*Lab.*	105,853
R. Fletcher,	*C.*	56,546
Ms S. Barber,	*LD*	29,979
M. Shipley,	*Green*	5,598
D. Collins,	*NLP*	1,533
Lab. majority		49,307
(Boundary change since June 1989)		

SHEFFIELD
E. 476,530　T. 27.50%

*R. Barton,	*Lab.*	76,397
Ms S. Anginotti,	*LD*	26,109
Ms K. Twitchen,	*C.*	22,374
B. New,	*Green*	4,742
M. England,	*Comm.*	834
R. Hurford,	*NLP*	577
Lab. majority		50,288
(Boundary change since June 1989)		

SOMERSET AND DEVON NORTH
E. 517,349　T. 47.09%

G. Watson,	*LD*	106,187
*Mrs M. Daly,	*C.*	83,678
J. Pilgrim,	*Lab.*	34,540
D. Taylor,	*Green*	10,870
G. Livings,	*New Britain*	7,165
M. Lucas,	*NLP*	1,200
LD majority		22,509
(Boundary change since June 1989)		

SOUTH DOWNS WEST
E. 486,793　T. 39.45%

J. Provan,	*C.*	83,813
Dr J. Walsh,	*LD*	62,746
Ms L. Armstrong,	*Lab.*	32,344
E. Paine,	*Green*	7,703
W. Weights,	*Lib.*	3,630
P. Kember,	*NLP*	1,794
C. majority		21,067
(Boundary change since June 1989)		

STAFFORDSHIRE EAST AND DERBY
E. 519,553　T. 35.46%

P. Whitehead,	*Lab.*	102,393
Ms J. Evans,	*C.*	50,197
Ms D. Brass,	*LD*	17,469
I. Crompton,	*UK Independence*	6,993
R. Clarke,	*Green*	4,272
R. Jones,	*NF*	2,098
Ms D. Grice,	*NLP*	793
Lab. majority		72,196
(Boundary change since June 1989)		

STAFFORDSHIRE WEST AND CONGLETON
E. 502,395　T. 31.60%

M. Tappin,	*Lab.*	84,337
A. Brown,	*C.*	44,060
J. Stevens,	*LD*	24,430
D. Hoppe,	*Green*	4,533
D. Lines,	*NLP*	1,403
Lab. majority		40,277
(Boundary change since June 1989)		

SUFFOLK AND NORFOLK SOUTH WEST
E. 477,668　T. 38.38%

D. Thomas,	*Lab.*	74,304
*A. Turner,	*C.*	61,769
R. Atkins,	*LD*	37,975
A. Slade,	*Green*	7,760
E. Kaplan,	*NLP*	1,530
Lab. majority		12,535
(Boundary change since June 1989)		

SURREY
E. 514,130　T. 37.51%

*T. Spencer,	*C.*	83,405
Mrs S. Thomas,	*LD*	56,387
Ms F. Wolf,	*Lab.*	30,894
Mrs S. Porter,	*UK Independence*	7,717
H. Charlton,	*Green*	7,198
J. Walker,	*Ind. Britain in Europe*	4,627
Mrs J. Thomas,	*NLP*	2,638
C. majority		27,018
(Boundary change since June 1989)		

SUSSEX EAST AND KENT SOUTH
E. 513,550　T. 41.90%

*Sir J. Stewart-Clark,	*C.*	83,141
D. Bellotti,	*LD*	76,929
N. Palmer,	*Lab.*	35,273
A. Burgess,	*UK Independence*	9,058
Ms R. Addison,	*Green*	7,439
Ms T. Williamson,	*Lib.*	2,558
P. Cragg,	*NLP*	765
C. majority		6,212
(Boundary change since June 1989)		

SUSSEX SOUTH AND CRAWLEY
E. 492,413　T. 37.64%

B. Donnelly,	*C.*	62,860
Ms J. Edmond Smith,	*Lab.*	61,114
J. Williams,	*LD*	41,410
Ms P. Beever,	*Green*	9,348
D. Horner,	*Ind. Euro-Sceptic*	7,106
N. Furness,	*Anti-Fed. C.*	2,618
A. Hankey,	*NLP*	901
C. majority		1,746
(Boundary change since June 1989)		

THAMES VALLEY
E. 543,685　T. 34.80%

*J. Stevens,	*C.*	70,485
J. Howarth,	*Lab.*	69,727
N. Bathurst,	*LD*	33,187
P. Unsworth,	*Green*	6,120
J. Clark,	*Lib.*	5,381
P. Owen,	*Loony C*	2,859
M. Grenville,	*NLP*	1,453
C. majority		758
(June 1989, C. maj. 26,491)		

TYNE AND WEAR
E. 516,436   T. 28.02%

*A. Donnelly, *Lab.*	107,604
I. Liddell-Grainger, *C.*	19,224
P. Maughan, *LD*	8,706
G. Edwards, *Green*	4,375
Ms W. Lundgren, *Lib.*	4,164
A. Fisken, *NLP*	650
Lab. majority	88,380
(June 1989, Lab. maj. 95,780)	

WIGHT AND HAMPSHIRE SOUTH
E. 488,398   T. 37.16%

R. Perry, *C.*	63,306
M. Hancock, *LD*	58,205
Ms S. Fry, *Lab.*	40,442
J. Browne, *Ind.*	12,140
P. Fuller, *Green*	6,697
W. Treend, *NLP*	722
C. majority	5,101
(Boundary change since June 1989)	

WILTSHIRE NORTH AND BATH
E. 496,591   T. 41.46%

*Mrs C. Jackson, *C.*	71,872
Ms J. Matthew, *LD*	63,085
Ms J. Norris, *Lab.*	50,489
P. Cullen, *Lib.*	6,760
M. Davidson, *Green*	5,974
T. Hedges, *UK Independence*	5,842
D. Cooke, *NLP*	1,148
Dr J. Day, *CPP*	725
C. majority	8,787
(Boundary change since June 1989)	

WORCESTERSHIRE AND
WARWICKSHIRE SOUTH
E. 551,162   T. 37.98%

J. Corrie, *C.*	73,573
Ms G. Gschaider, *Lab.*	72,369
P. Larner, *LD*	44,168
Ms J. Alty, *Green*	9,273
C. Hards, *National Independence*	8,447
J. Brewster, *NLP*	1,510
C. majority	1,204
(Boundary change since June 1989)	

YORKSHIRE NORTH
E. 475,686   T. 38.70%

*E. McMillan-Scott, *C.*	70,036
B. Regan, *Lab.*	62,964
M. Pitts, *LD*	43,171
Dr R. Richardson, *Green*	7,036
S. Withers, *NLP*	891
C. majority	7,072
(Boundary change since June 1989)	

YORKSHIRE SOUTH
E. 523,401   T. 28.64%

*N. West, *Lab.*	109,004
J. Howard, *C.*	20,695
Ms C. Roderick, *LD*	11,798
P. Davies, *UK Independence*	3,948
J. Waters, *Green*	3,775
N. Broome, *NLP*	681
Lab. majority	88,309
(June 1989, Lab. maj. 91,784)	

YORKSHIRE SOUTH WEST
E. 547,469   T. 29.03%

*T. Megahy, *Lab.*	94,025
Mrs C. Adamson, *C.*	34,463
D. Ridgway, *LD*	21,595

A. Cooper, *Green*	7,163
G. Mead, *NLP*	1,674
Lab. majority	59,562
(Boundary change since June 1989)	

YORKSHIRE WEST
E. 490,078   T. 34.61%

*B. Seal, *Lab.*	90,652
R. Booth, *C.*	42,455
C. Bidwell, *LD*	20,452
R. Pearson, *New Britain*	8,027
C. Harris, *Green*	7,154
D. Whitley, *NLP*	894
Lab. majority	48,197
(Boundary change since June 1989)	

WALES

SOUTH WALES CENTRAL
E. 477,182   T. 39.40%

*W. David, *Lab.*	115,396
Ms L. Verity, *C.*	29,314
G. Llywelyn, *PC*	18,857
J. Dixon, *LD*	18,471
C. von Ruhland, *Green*	4,002
R. Griffiths, *Comm. YBG*	1,073
G. Duguay, *NLP*	889
Lab. majority	86,082
(Boundary change since June 1989)	

SOUTH WALES EAST
E. 454,794   T. 43.07%

Mrs G. Kinnock, *Lab.*	144,907
Mrs R. Blomfield-Smith, *C.*	24,660
C. Woolgrove, *LD*	9,963
C. Mann, *PC*	9,550
R. Coghill, *Green*	4,509
Ms S. Williams, *Welsh Soc.*	1,270
Dr R. Brussatis, *NLP*	1,027
Lab. majority	120,247
(Boundary change since June 1989)	

SOUTH WALES WEST
E. 395,131   T. 39.92%

*Revd D. Morris, *Lab.*	104,263
R. Buckland, *C.*	19,293
J. Bushell, *LD*	15,499
Ms C. Adams, *PC*	12,364
Ms J. Evans, *Green*	4,114
Ms H. Evans, *NLP*	1,112
Capt. Beany, *Beanus*	1,106
Lab. majority	84,970
(Boundary change since June 1989)	

WALES MID AND WEST
E. 401,529   T. 48.00%

Ms E. Morgan, *Lab.*	78,092
M. Phillips, *PC*	48,858
P. Bone, *C.*	31,606
Ms J. Hughes, *LD*	23,719
D. Rowlands, *UK Independence*	5,536
Dr C. Busby, *Green*	3,938
T. Griffith-Jones, *NLP*	988
Lab. majority	29,234
(Boundary change since June 1989)	

WALES NORTH
E. 475,829   T. 45.34%

*J. Wilson, *Lab.*	88,091
D. Wigley, *PC*	72,849
G. Mon Hughes, *C.*	33,450

Ms R. Parry, *LD*	14,828
P. Adams, *Green*	2,850
D. Hughes, *NLP*	2,065
M. Cooksey, *Ind.*	1,623
Lab. majority	15,242
(Boundary change since June 1989)	

SCOTLAND

GLASGOW
E. 463,364   T. 34.46%

W. Miller, *Lab.*	83,953
T. Chalmers, *SNP*	40,795
T. Sheridan, *SML*	12,113
R. Wilkinson, *C.*	10,888
J. Money, *LD*	7,291
P. O'Brien, *Green*	2,252
J. Fleming, *Soc.*	1,125
M. Wilkinson, *NLP*	868
C. Marsden, *ICP*	381
Lab. majority	43,158
(June 1989, Lab. maj. 59,232)	

HIGHLANDS AND ISLANDS
E. 328,104   T. 39.09%

*Mrs W. Ewing, *SNP*	74,872
M. Macmillan, *Lab.*	19,956
M. Tennant, *C.*	15,767
H. Morrison, *LD*	12,919
Dr E. Scott, *Green*	3,140
M. Carr, *UK Independence*	1,096
Ms M. Gilmour, *NLP*	522
SNP majority	54,916
(June 1989, SNP maj. 44,695)	

LOTHIANS
E. 520,943   T. 38.69%

*D. Martin, *Lab.*	90,531
K. Brown, *SNP*	53,324
Dr P. McNally, *C.*	33,526
Ms H. Campbell, *LD*	17,883
R. Harper, *Green*	5,149
J. McGregor, *Soc.*	637
M. Siebert, *NLP*	500
Lab. majority	37,207
(June 1989, Lab. maj. 38,826)	

SCOTLAND MID AND FIFE
E. 546,060   T. 38.25%

*A. Falconer, *Lab.*	95,667
R. Douglas, *SNP*	64,254
P. Page, *C.*	28,192
Ms H. Lyall, *LD*	17,192
M. Johnston, *Green*	3,015
T. Pringle, *NLP*	532
Lab. majority	31,413
(June 1989, Lab. maj. 52,157)	

SCOTLAND NORTH EAST
E. 575,748   T. 37.72%

A. Macartney, *SNP*	92,892
*H. McCubbin, *Lab.*	61,665
Dr R. Harris, *C.*	40,372
S. Horner, *LD*	18,008
K. Farnsworth, *Green*	2,569
Ms M. Ward, *Comm. GB*	689
L. Mair, *Neeps*	584
D. Paterson, *NLP*	371
SNP majority	31,227
(June 1989, Lab. maj. 2,613)	

SCOTLAND SOUTH	
E. 500,643 *T*. 40.14%	
*A. Smith, *Lab*.	90,750
A. Hutton, *C*.	45,595
Mrs C. Creech, *SNP*	45,032
D. Millar, *LD*	13,363
J. Hein, *Lib.*	3,249
Ms L. Hendry, *Green*	2,429
G. Gay, *NLP*	539
Lab. majority	45,155
(June 1989, Lab. maj. 15,693)	

STRATHCLYDE EAST	
E. 492,618 *T*. 37.26%	
*K. Collins, *Lab*.	106,476
I. Hamilton, *SNP*	54,136
B. Cooklin, *C*.	13,915
R. Stewart, *LD*	6,383
A. Whitelaw, *Green*	1,874
D. Gilmour, *NLP*	787
Lab. majority	52,340
(June 1989, Lab. maj. 60,317)	

STRATHCLYDE WEST	
E. 489,129 *T*. 40.05%	
*H. McMahon, *Lab*.	86,957
C. Campbell, *SNP*	61,934
J. Godfrey, *C*.	28,414
D. Herbison, *LD*	14,772
Ms K. Allan, *Green*	2,886
Ms S. Gilmour, *NLP*	918
Lab. majority	25,023
(June 1989, Lab. maj. 39,591)	

NORTHERN IRELAND

Northern Ireland forms a three-member seat with a single transferable vote system

E. 1,150,304 *T*. 48.67%	
*Revd I. Paisley, *DUP*	163,246
*J. Hume, *SDLP*	161,992
*J. Nicholson, *UUUP*	133,459
Mrs M. Clark-Glass, *All.*	23,157
T. Hartley, *SF*	21,273
Ms D. McGuinness, *SF*	17,195
F. Molloy, *SF*	16,747
Revd H. Ross, *Ulster Independence*	7,858
Miss M. Boal, *C*.	5,583
J. Lowry, *WP*	2,543
N. Cusack, *Ind. Lab.*	2,464
J. Anderson, *NLP*	1,418
Mrs J. Campion, *Peace Coalition*	1,088
D. Kerr, *Independence for Ulster*	571
Ms S. Thompson, *NLP*	454
M. Kennedy, *NLP*	419
R. Mooney, *Const. NI*	400

Speakers of the Commons since 1708

The date of appointment given is the day on which the Speaker was first elected by the House of Commons. The appointment requires royal approbation before it is confirmed and this is usually given within a few days. The present Speaker is the 155th.

PARLIAMENT OF GREAT BRITAIN

Sir Richard Onslow (*Lord Onslow*), 16 November 1708
William Bromley, 25 November 1710
Sir Thomas Hanmer, 16 February 1714
Spencer Compton (*Earl of Wilmington*), 17 March 1715
Arthur Onslow, 23 January 1728
Sir John Cust, 3 November 1761
Sir Fletcher Norton (*Lord Grantley*), 22 January 1770
Charles Cornwall, 31 October 1780
Hon. William Grenville (*Lord Grenville*), 5 January 1789
Henry Addington (*Viscount Sidmouth*), 8 June 1789

PARLIAMENT OF THE UNITED KINGDOM

Sir John Mitford (*Lord Redesdale*), 11 February 1801

Charles Abbot (*Lord Colchester*), 10 February 1802
Charles Manners-Sutton (*Viscount Canterbury*), 2 June 1817
James Abercromby (*Lord Dunfermline*), 19 February 1835
Charles Shaw-Lefevre (*Viscount Eversley*), 27 May 1839
J. Evelyn Denison (*Viscount Ossington*), 30 April 1857
Sir Henry Brand (*Viscount Hampden*), 9 February 1872
Arthur Wellesley Peel (*Viscount Peel*), 26 February 1884
William Gully (*Viscount Selby*), 10 April 1895
James Lowther (*Viscount Ullswater*), 8 June 1905
John Whitley, 27 April 1921
Hon. Edward Fitzroy, 20 June 1928
Douglas Clifton-Brown (*Viscount Ruffside*), 9 March 1943
William Morrison (*Viscount Dunrossil*), 31 October 1951
Sir Harry Hylton-Foster, 20 October 1959
Horace King (*Lord Maybray-King*), 26 October 1965
Selwyn Lloyd (*Lord Selwyn-Lloyd*), 12 January 1971
George Thomas (*Viscount Tonypandy*), 2 February 1976
Bernard Weatherill (*Lord Weatherill*), 15 June 1983
Betty Boothroyd, 27 April 1992

The Government

THE CABINET AS AT 31 JULY 1996

Prime Minister, First Lord of the Treasury and Minister for the Civil Service
The Rt. Hon. John Major, MP, since November 1990
First Secretary of State and Deputy Prime Minister
The Rt. Hon. Michael Heseltine, MP, since July 1995
Lord High Chancellor
The Lord Mackay of Clashfern, PC, since October 1987
Chancellor of the Exchequer
The Rt. Hon. Kenneth Clarke, QC, MP, since May 1993
Secretary of State for the Home Department
The Rt. Hon. Michael Howard, QC, MP, since May 1993
Secretary of State for Foreign and Commonwealth Affairs
The Rt. Hon. Malcolm Rifkind, QC, MP, since July 1995
Lord President of the Council and Leader of the House of Commons
The Rt. Hon. Antony Newton, OBE, MP, since April 1992
Secretary of State for the Environment
The Rt. Hon. John Gummer, MP, since May 1993
Secretary of State for Social Security
The Rt. Hon. Peter Lilley, MP, since April 1992
Chief Secretary to the Treasury
The Rt. Hon. William Waldegrave, MP, since July 1995
Secretary of State for Trade and Industry and President of the Board of Trade
The Rt. Hon. Ian Lang, MP, since July 1995
Secretary of State for Northern Ireland
The Rt. Hon. Sir Patrick Mayhew, QC, MP, since April 1992
Secretary of State for National Heritage
The Rt. Hon. Virginia Bottomley, MP, since July 1995
Secretary of State for Education and Employment
The Rt. Hon. Gillian Shephard, MP, since July 1994
(Education)/July 1995 (Employment)
Secretary of State for Defence
The Rt. Hon. Michael Portillo, MP, since July 1995
Minister without Portfolio (Party chairman)
The Rt. Hon. Brian Mawhinney, MP, since July 1995
Secretary of State for Health
The Rt. Hon. Stephen Dorrell, MP, since July 1995
Lord Privy Seal and Leader of the House of Lords
Viscount Cranborne, PC, since July 1994
Secretary of State for Transport
The Rt. Hon. Sir George Young, Bt., MP, since July 1995
Minister of Agriculture, Fisheries and Food
The Rt. Hon. Douglas Hogg, QC, MP, since July 1995
Secretary of State for Scotland
The Rt. Hon. Michael Forsyth, MP, since July 1995
Chancellor of the Duchy of Lancaster and Minister for Public Service
The Rt. Hon. Roger Freeman, MP, since July 1995
Secretary of State for Wales
The Rt. Hon. William Hague, MP, since July 1995

LAW OFFICERS

Attorney-General
The Rt. Hon. Sir Nicholas Lyell, QC, MP, since April 1992

Lord Advocate
The Lord Mackay of Drumadoon, PC, QC, since May 1995
Solicitor-General
Sir Derek Spencer, QC, MP, since April 1992
Solicitor-General for Scotland
Paul Cullen, QC

MINISTERS OF STATE

Agriculture, Fisheries and Food
Anthony Baldry, MP
Office of Public Service
David Willetts, MP (*Paymaster-General*)
Defence
The Hon. Nicholas Soames, MP (*Armed Forces*)
James Arbuthnot, MP (*Defence Procurement*)
Education and Employment
Eric Forth, MP
The Lord Henley
Environment
The Rt. Hon. David Curry, MP (*Minister for Local Government*)
The Earl Ferrars, PC (*Minister for Environment and Countryside*)
Robert Jones, MP (*Minister for Construction, Planning and Energy Efficiency*)
Foreign and Commonwealth Affairs
The Baroness Chalker of Wallasey, PC (*Minister for Overseas Development*)
David Davis, MP (*Minister for Europe*)
The Rt. Hon. Jeremy Hanley, MP
Sir Nicholas Bonsor, MP
Health
Gerald Malone, MP
Home Office
The Rt. Hon. David Maclean, MP
The Baroness Blatch, PC
Ann Widdecombe, MP
National Heritage
Iain Sproat, MP (*Minister for Sport*)
Northern Ireland Office
The Rt. Hon. Sir John Wheeler, MP
The Rt. Hon. Michael Ancram, MP
Scottish Office
The Rt. Hon. Lord James Douglas-Hamilton, MP (*Home Affairs and Health*)
Social Security
The Lord Mackay of Ardbrecknish, PC
Alistair Burt, MP (*Social Security and Disabled People*)
Trade and Industry
The Lord Fraser of Carmyllie, PC, QC
Anthony Nelson, MP (*Minister for Trade*)
Gregory Knight, MP (*Minister of Industry and Energy*)
Transport
John Watts, MP
Treasury
Michael Jack, MP (*Financial Secretary*)
Angela Knight, MP (*Economic Secretary*)

UNDER-SECRETARIES OF STATE

Agriculture, Fisheries and Food
  Angela Browning, MP
  Timothy Boswell, MP
Defence
  The Earl Howe
Education and Employment
  Robin Squire, MP
  James Paice, MP
  Cheryl Gillan, MP
Environment
  Sir Paul Beresford, MP
  James Clappison, MP
Foreign Office
  Liam Fox, MP
Health
  The Baroness Cumberlege, CBE
  John Horam, MP
  Simon Burns, MP
Home Office
  Timothy Kirkhope, MP
  The Hon. Thomas Sackville, MP
Lord Chancellor's Department
  Gary Streeter, MP
National Heritage
  The Lord Inglewood
Northern Ireland
  The Baroness Denton of Wakefield, CBE
  Malcolm Moss, MP
Scottish Office
  George Kynoch, MP (*Industry and Local Government*)
  Raymond Robertson, MP (*Education, Housing and Fisheries*)
  The Earl of Lindsay (*Agriculture, Forestry and the Environment*)
Social Security
  Roger Evans, MP
  Oliver Heald, MP
  Andrew Mitchell, MP
Trade and Industry
  Ian Taylor, MBE, MP (*Science and Technology*)
  Richard Page, MP (*Small Business, Industry and Energy*)
  John Taylor, MP (*Competition and Consumer Affairs*)
Transport
  The Viscount Goschen
  John Bowis, OBE, MP
Treasury
  Phillip Oppenheim, MP (*Exchequer Secretary*)
  The Lords Commissioners, *see* Government whips
Welsh Office
  Gwilym Jones, MP
  Jonathan Evans, MP

GOVERNMENT WHIPS

HOUSE OF LORDS

Captain of the Honourable Corps of Gentlemen-at-Arms (Chief Whip)
  The Lord Strathclyde, PC
Captain of The Queen's Bodyguard of the Yeoman of the Guard (Deputy Chief Whip)
  The Lord Chesham
Lords-in-Waiting
  The Viscount Long; The Lord Lucas of Crudwell; The Earl of Courtown

Baronesses-in-Waiting
  The Baroness Trumpington, PC; The Baroness Miller of Hendon

HOUSE OF COMMONS

Parliamentary Secretary to the Treasury (Chief Whip)
  The Rt. Hon. Alastair Goodlad, MP
Treasurer of HM Household (Deputy Chief Whip)
  Andrew Mackay, MP
Comptroller of HM Household
  Timothy Wood, MP
Vice-Chamberlain of HM Household
  Derek Conway, MP
Lords Commissioners
  Bowen Wells, MP; Michael Bates, MP;
  Patrick McLoughlin, MP; Roger Knapman, MP;
  Richard Ottaway, MP
Assistant Whips
  Gyles Brandeth, MP; Sebastian Coe, MP;
  Anthony Coombs, MP; Jacqui Lait, MP;
  Peter Ainsworth, MP

Government Departments and Public Offices

This section covers central government departments, executive agencies, regulatory bodies, other statutory independent organizations, and bodies which are government-financed or whose head is appointed by a government minister.

THE CIVIL SERVICE

Changes are currently being introduced into the civil service with the aim of reducing its functions to a central core and privatizing or contracting out the rest of its work. Many semi-autonomous executive agencies have already been established under the 'Next Steps' programme. Executive agencies operate within a framework set by the responsible minister which specifies policies, objectives and available resources. They are usually headed by a chief executive, who is responsible for the day-to-day operations of the agency and who is accountable to the minister for the use of resources and for the performance of the agency. Nearly 52 per cent of civil servants now work in executive agencies. Customs and Excise and the Inland Revenue, which employ a further 15 per cent of civil servants, also operate on 'Next Steps' lines. In April 1996 there were 494,300 permanent civil servants.

Most of the Home Civil Service's senior grades were formerly absorbed into an Open pay and grading structure. The Senior Civil Service came into being on 1 April 1996 and comprises civil servants formerly at Grade 5 level and above and all agency chief executives. All government departments and executive agencies are now responsible for their own pay and grading systems for civil servants outside the Senior Civil Service. In practice the grades of the former Open structure ar still currently being used in many organizations. The Open structure represented the following:

Grade	Title
1	Permanent Secretary
1A	Second Permanent Secretary
2	Deputy Secretary
3	Under-Secretary
4	Chief Scientific Officer B, Professional and Technology Directing A
5	Assistant Secretary, Deputy Chief Scientific Officer, Professional and Technology Directing B
6	Senior Principal, Senior Principal Scientific Officer, Professional and Technology Superintending Grade
7	Principal, Principal Scientific Officer, Principal Professional and Technology Officer

SALARIES

MINISTERIAL SALARIES 1996–7

Ministers who are Members of the House of Commons receive a parliamentary salary (£43,000) in addition to their ministerial salary. The salaries in the right-hand column will come into effect on the day after the general election.

	From July 1996	After general election
Prime Minister	£58,557	£100,000
Secretary of State (Commons)	£43,991	£60,000
Secretary of State (Lords)	£58,876	£77,963
Minister of State (Commons)	£31,125	£31,125
Minister of State (Lords)	£51,838	£51,838
Parliamentary Under-Secretary (Commons)	£23,623	£23,623
Parliamentary Under-Secretary (Lords)	£43,632	£43,632

CIVIL SERVICE SALARIES 1996–7

Senior Civil Service (SCS)

Secretary of the Cabinet and Head of the Home Civil Service	£90,000–£154,500
Permanent Secretary to the Treasury	£90,000–£154,500
Head of the Diplomatic Service	£90,000–£154,500
Permanent Secretary	£90,000–£154,500
Band 9	£80,000–£113,300
Band 8	£73,200–£106,900
Band 7	£67,000–£100,900
Band 6	£61,200–£95,300
Band 5	£55,900–£90,000
Band 4	£51,000–£85,000
Band 3	£46,200–£75,600
Band 2	£41,900–£67,200
Band 1	£38,000–£59,700

Staff are placed in pay bands according to their level of responsibility and taking account of other factors such as experience and marketability. Movement within and between bands is based on performance. A recruitment and retention allowance of up to £3,000 may be paid at each department's discretion in addition to the salary ranges shown for bands 1 to 9.

Other Civil Servants

Following the delegation of responsibility for pay and grading to government departments and agencies from 1 April 1996, it is now not possible to show the pay rates for staff outside the Senior Civil Service. Individual departments and agencies have introduced or will be introducing their own pay systems.

ADJUDICATOR'S OFFICE
Haymarket House, 28 Haymarket, London SW1Y 4SP
Tel 0171-930 2292

The Adjudicator's Office opened in 1993 and investigates complaints made about the way the Inland Revenue, Customs and Excise or the Contributions Agency have handled an individual's affairs.
The Adjudicator, Ms E. Filkin
Head of Office, D. I. Richardson

ADVISORY, CONCILIATION AND ARBITRATION SERVICE

Brandon House, 180 Borough High Street, London
SEI ILW
Tel 0171-210 3613

The Advisory, Conciliation and Arbitration Service (ACAS) is an independent organization set up under the Employment Protection Act 1975 (the provisions now being found in the Trade Union and Labour Relations (Consolidation) Act 1992). ACAS is directed by a Council consisting of a full-time chairman and part-time employer, trade union and independent members, all appointed by the Secretary of State for Trade and Industry. The functions of the Service are to promote the improvement of industrial relations in general, to provide facilities for conciliation, mediation and arbitration as means of avoiding and resolving industrial disputes, and to provide advisory and information services on industrial relations matters to employers, employees and their representatives.

ACAS also has regional offices in Birmingham, Bristol, Cardiff, Fleet, Glasgow, Leeds, Liverpool, London, Manchester, Newcastle upon Tyne and Nottingham.

Chairman, J. Hougham, CBE
Chief Conciliation Officer (*G4*), D. Evans

MINISTRY OF AGRICULTURE, FISHERIES AND FOOD

Whitehall Place, London SWIA 2HH
Tel 0171-238 6000; *enquiries* 0645-335577

The Ministry of Agriculture, Fisheries and Food is responsible for administering government policies on agriculture, horticulture and fisheries in England and policies relating to the safety and quality of food in the UK as a whole. In association with the Agriculture Departments of the Scottish, Welsh and Northern Ireland Offices and with the Intervention Board (*see* page 315), the Ministry is responsible for the negotiation and administration of the EU common agricultural and fisheries policies, for matters relating to the single European market, and for international agricultural and food trade policy. It commissions research to assist in the formulation and assessment of policy.

The Ministry administers policies on the control and eradication of animal, plant and fish diseases, and on assistance to capital investment in farm and horticultural businesses; it also has responsibilities relating to the protection and enhancement of the countryside and the marine environment as well as to flood defence and other rural issues.

The Ministry is responsible for ensuring public health standards in the manufacture, preparation and distribution of basic foods, and for planning to safeguard essential food supplies in times of emergency. It is responsible for government relations with the UK food and drink manufacturing industries and the food and drink importing, distributive and catering trades.

The Food Safety Directorate is responsible for many aspects of food safety and quality. These include pesticide safety approval, biotechnology, meat hygiene, animal health and welfare, and related public health issues.

Minister, The Rt. Hon. Douglas Hogg, QC, MP
　Principal Private Secretary (*G7*), W. F. G. Strang
　Private Secretary, M. H. Nisbet
　Parliamentary Private Secretary, G. Clifton-Brown, MP

Minister of State, Tony Baldry, QC, MP (*Farming and Fisheries*)
　Private Secretary, Miss R. J. Gower
　Parliamentary Private Secretary, N. Evans, MP
Parliamentary Secretary, Timothy Boswell, MP (*Countryside*)
　Private Secretary, P. Green
Parliamentary Secretary, Angela Browning, MP (*Food*)
　Private Secretary, Mrs E. C. Ratcliffe
Parliamentary Clerk, Miss A. Evans
Permanent Secretary (*G1*), R. J. Packer
　Private Secretary, R. Campbell

ESTABLISHMENT DEPARTMENT
Director of Establishments (*G3*), J. W. Hepburn

†ESTABLISHMENTS (GENERAL) AND OFFICE SERVICES DIVISION
Head of Division (*G6*), Dr J. A. Bailey

WELFARE BRANCH
Whitehall Place (West Block), London SWIA 2HH
Tel 0171-238 6000
Chief Welfare Officer (*SEO*), D. J. Jones

†PERSONNEL MANAGEMENT AND DEVELOPMENT DIVISION
Head of Division (*G5*), T. J. Osmond

DEPARTMENTAL HEALTH AND SAFETY UNIT
Government Buildings, Hook Rise South, Tolworth, Surbiton, Surrey KT6 7NF
Tel 0181-330 4411
Head of Unit (*G7*), C. R. Bradburn

†TRAINING AND DEVELOPMENT BRANCH
Principal (*G7*), J. M. Cowley

BUILDING AND ESTATE MANAGEMENT
Eastbury House, 30–34 Albert Embankment, London SEI 7TL
Tel 0171-238 6000
Head of Division (*G5*), J. A. S. Nickson

INFORMATION TECHNOLOGY DIRECTORATE
Government Buildings, Epsom Road, Guildford, Surrey GUI 2LD
Tel 01483-68121
Director (*G5*), A. G. Matthews
Head of Strategies (*G6*), R. J. Long
Head of Applications (*G6*), D. D. Brown
Head of Infrastructure (*G6*), S. V. Soper

INFORMATION DIVISION
Whitehall Place (West Block), London SWIA 2HH
Tel 0171-238 6000
Chief Information Officer (*G5*), G. Blakeway
Chief Press Officer (*G7*), M. Smith
Chief Publicity Officer (*G7*), N. Wagstaffe
Principal Librarian (*G7*), P. McShane

FINANCE DEPARTMENT
19–29 Woburn Place, London WCIH OLU
Tel 0171-270 8080
Principal Finance Officer (*G3*), P. Elliott

FINANCIAL POLICY DIVISION
Head of Division (*G5*), P. P. Nash

FINANCIAL MANAGEMENT DIVISION
Head of Division (*G5*), J. M. Lowi

†At Nobel/Ergon House, 17 Smith Square, London SWIP 3JR. Tel: 0171-238 6000

PROCUREMENT AND CONTRACTS DIVISION
Director of Audit (G5), D. V. Fisher

CAP SCHEMES MANAGEMENT
Head of Division (G5), Miss V. A. Smith

MARKET TESTING AND PROCUREMENT ADVICE
Director (G5), D. B. Rabey

RESOURCE MANAGEMENT STRATEGY UNIT
Head of Division (G5), Mrs J. Flint

LEGAL DEPARTMENT
55 Whitehall, London SWIA 2EY
Tel 0171-238 6000
Legal Adviser and Solicitor (G2), R. Woolman
Principal Assistant Solicitors (G3), D. J. Pearson; Ms C. A.
  Crisham

LEGAL DIVISIONS
Assistant Solicitor, Division A1 (G5), Dr M. R. Parke
Assistant Solicitor, Division A2 (G5), P. Kent
Assistant Solicitor, Division A3 (G5), T. J. Middleton
Assistant Solicitor, Division A4 (G5), P. D. Davis
Assistant Solicitor, Division B1 (G5), Mrs C. A. Davis
Assistant Solicitor, Division B2 (G4), Ms S. B. Spence
Assistant Solicitor, Division B3 (G5), A. I. Corbett
Assistant Solicitor, Division B4 (G5), Mrs F. C. Nash

INVESTIGATION UNIT
Chief Investigation Officer, Miss J. Panting

AGRICULTURAL COMMODITIES, TRADE AND FOOD PRODUCTION
Deputy Secretary (G2), Ms V. K. Timms

EUROPEAN UNION AND LIVESTOCK GROUP
Under-Secretary (G3), D. P. Hunter

DIVISIONS
Head, European Union I (G5), A. J. Lebrecht
Head, European Union II (G6), L. G. Mitchell
Head, Beef and Sheep (G5), J. R. Cowan
Head, Milk, Pigs, Eggs and Poultry (G5), B. J. Harding
Head, Livestock Quota Unit (G6), Ms L. Cornish

ARABLE CROPS AND HORTICULTURE
Under-Secretary (G3), D. H. Griffiths

DIVISIONS
Head, Cereals and Set-Aside (G4), G. M. Trevelyan
Head, Sugar, Tobacco, Oilseeds and Protein (G5), Mrs
  A. M. Blackburn
†*Head, Horticulture and Potatoes (G5)*, R. A. Saunderson

PLANT VARIETY RIGHTS OFFICE AND SEEDS DIVISION
White House Lane, Huntingdon Road, Cambridge
CB3 0LF
Tel 01223-277151
Head of Office (G5), D. A. Boreham

FOOD, DRINK AND MARKETING POLICY
Under-Secretary (G3), N. Thornton

DIVISIONS
Head, Food and Drinks Industry (G5), R. E. Melville
Head, International Relations and Export Promotion (G5),
  D. V. Orchard
Head, Trade Policy and Tropical Foods (G5), Miss S. E. Brown
†*Head, Market Task Force (G5)*, H. B. Brown

REGIONAL SERVICES AND DEFENCE GROUP
Under-Secretary (G3), R. A. Saunderson
Head, Deregulation, Agricultural Training and Resources (G5),
  A. R. Burne
*Head, Plant Health and Plant Health and Seeds Inspectorate
  (G5)*, A. J. Perrins
Head, Flood and Coastal Protection (G5), Dr. J. Park

REGIONAL ORGANIZATION
Head, Regional Support Unit (G7), D. Putley

Regional Service Centres

ANGLIA REGION, Block B, Government Buildings,
  Brooklands Avenue, Cambridge CB2 2DR. Tel: 01223-
  462727. *Regional Director (G5)*, Miss C. J. Rabagliati
EAST MIDLANDS REGION, Government Buildings, Block
  7, Chalfont Drive, Nottingham NG8 3SN. Tel: 0115-929
  1191. *Regional Director (G6)*, G. Norbury
NORTH-EAST REGION, Government Buildings, Crosby
  Road, Northallerton, N. Yorks DL6 1AD. Tel: 01609-
  773751. *Regional Director (G6)*, P. Watson
NORTHERN REGION, Eden Bridge House, Lowther
  Street, Carlisle, Cumbria CA3 8DX. Tel: 01228-
  23400. *Regional Director (G5)*, J. P. Bradbury
NORTH MERCIA REGION, Berkeley Towers, Nantwich
  Road, Crewe, Cheshire CW2 6PT. Tel: 01270-
  69211. *Regional Director (G6)*, R. Bettley-Smith
SOUTH-EAST REGION, Block A, Government Buildings,
  Coley Park, Reading, Berks RG1 6DT. Tel: 01734-
  581222. *Regional Director (G6)*, Mrs V. Silvester
SOUTH MERCIA REGION, Block C, Government
  Buildings, Whittington Road, Worcester WR5 2LQ. Tel:
  01905-763355. *Regional Director (G6)*, B. Davies
SOUTH-WEST REGION, Government Buildings,
  Alphington Road, Exeter EX2 8NQ. Tel: 01392-77951.
  Regional Director (G6), M. R. W. Highman
WESSEX REGION, Block 3, Government Buildings,
  Burghill Road, Westbury-on-Trym, Bristol
  BS10 6NJ. Tel: 01272-591000. *Regional Director (G6)*, Mrs
  A. J. L. Ould

FOOD SAFETY AND ENVIRONMENT GROUP
Deputy Secretary (G2), R. J. D. Carden

ENVIRONMENT GROUP
Under-Secretary (G3), D. J. Coates
Head, Conservation and Woodlands Policy (G5), Ms J. Allfrey
Head, Conservation Management Division (G5), P. M. Boyling
Head, Land Use and Rural Economy (G5), R. C. McIvor
Head, Land Use Planning Unit (G5), D. G. Sisson
Head, Environmental Protection (G5), D. E. Jones

†FOOD SAFETY AND SCIENCE GROUP
Under-Secretary (G3), G. Podger

DIVISIONS
Head, Food Hygiene (G5), Ms S. Nason
Head, Additives and Novel Foods (G5), Dr J. R. Bell
Head, Food Labelling and Standards (G5), G. Meekings
Head, Food Contaminants (G5), Dr R. Burt
Head, Consumers and Nutrition (G5), Miss E. J. Wordley
Head, Radiological Safety (G5), Dr M. G. Segal

†CHIEF SCIENTIST'S GROUP
Chief Scientist (G3), Dr D. W. F. Shannon

DIVISIONS
Head, Agriculture and Food Technology (G5), Dr J. C. Sherlock

Head, Food and Veterinary Science Division (*G5*),
Dr K. J. MacOwan
Head, Environment, Fisheries and International Science (*G5*),
Dr M. Parker
Head, Research Policy Co-ordination (*G5*), J. C. Suich

ANIMAL HEALTH AND VETERINARY GROUP
Government Buildings, Hook Rise South, Tolworth,
Surbiton, Surrey KT6 7NF
Tel 0181-330 4411

Under-Secretary (*G3*), B. H. B. Dickinson
Chief Veterinary Officer (*G3*), K. C. Meldrum, CB

DIVISIONS
Head, Animal Health (Disease Control) (*G5*), T. E. D. Eddy
Head, Animal Health (International Trade) (*G5*), R. A. Bell
Head, Meat Hygiene (*G5*), C. J. Lawson
Head, Services (*G6*), R. Gurd
Head, Animal Welfare (*G5*), C. J. Ryder

STATE VETERINARY SERVICE
Government Buildings, Hook Rise South, Tolworth,
Surbiton, Surrey KT15 3NB
Tel 0181-330 4411
Director of Veterinary Field Services (*G3*), I. Crawford

LASSWADE VETERINARY LABORATORY
East of Scotland College of Agriculture, The Bush Estate,
Penicuik, Midlothian EH26 0SA
Tel 0131-445 5371
Head of Laboratory (*G6*), Miss G. Mackenzie

†FISHERIES DEPARTMENT
Fisheries Secretary (*G3*), S. Wentworth

DIVISIONS
Head, Fisheries I (*G5*), A. Kuyk
Head, Fisheries II (*G5*), C. I. Llewellyn
Head, Fisheries III (*G5*), J. E. Robbs
Head, Fisheries IV (*G6*), B. S. Edwards
Chief Inspector, Sea Fisheries Inspectorate (*G6*), S. G. Elson

FISHERIES RESEARCH
Pakefield Road, Lowestoft, Suffolk NR33 0HT
Tel 01502-562244
Director of Fisheries Research and Development for Great Britain
(*G4*), P. W. Greig-Smith
Deputy Directors of Fisheries Research (*G5*), J. W. Horwood;
J. E. Portmann

FISHERIES LABORATORY
Pakefield Road, Lowestoft, Suffolk NR33 0HT
Tel 01502-562244

FISHERIES LABORATORY
Remembrance Avenue, Burnham-on-Crouch, Essex
CM0 8HA
Tel 01621-782658

FISHERIES EXPERIMENT STATION
Benarth Road, Conwy LL32 8UB
Tel 01492-593883

FISH DISEASES LABORATORY
33–33A Albany Road, Granby Industrial Estate,
Weymouth, Dorset DT4 9TU
Tel 01305-772137
Officer-in-Charge (*Principal Scientific Officer*) (*G6*), B. J. Hill,
PH.D.

ECONOMICS AND STATISTICS
Under-Secretary (*G3*), Dr J. M. Slater

DIVISIONS
Senior Economic Adviser, Economics and Statistics (Farm Business) (*G5*), J. P. Muriel
Senior Economic Adviser, Economics (International and Food) (*G5*), vacant
Senior Economic Adviser, Economics (Resource Use) (*G5*),
R. W. Irving

STATISTICS DIVISION
Foss House, 1–2 Peasholme Green, King's Pool, York
YO1 2PX
Tel 01904-455328

Chief Statistician (Commodities and Food) (*G4*), Dr P. J. Lund
Chief Statistician (Census and Surveys) (*G5*), P. F. Helm

EXECUTIVE AGENCIES

ADAS (AGRICULTURAL DEVELOPMENT AND ADVISORY SERVICE)
ADAS Headquarters, Oxford Spires Business Park, The
Boulevard, Kidlington, Oxon OX5 1NZ
Tel 01865-842742

ADAS provides a range of consultancy services to the land-based industries. It is a joint executive agency of MAFF and the Welsh Office and carries out research, performs certain statutory functions and provides advice on policy for both departments. The Government has announced its intention of privatizing the commercial parts of ADAS.
Chief Executive, P. Needham
Director of Operations and Director for Wales, W. I. C. Davies
Research Director, Dr A. D. Hughes
Marketing Director, D. J. Hall
Finance Director, Dr C. Herring
Personnel Director, C. Ouseley

CENTRAL SCIENCE LABORATORY
The Innovation Centre, York Science Park, University
Road, Heslington, York YO1 5DG
Tel 01904-435120

The Central Science Laboratory was enlarged in 1994 by merging with the Food Science Laboratory, Norwich and the Torry Research Station, Aberdeen. The agency provides MAFF with technical support and policy advice on the protection and quality of the food supply and on related environmental issues.
Chief Executive (*G3*), Prof. P. I. Stanley
Research Director (*G5*), Prof. A. R. Hardy
Head of Food Science Laboratory (*G5*), Dr J. Gilbert, Norwich
Research Park, Colney Lane, Norwich NR4 7UQ. Tel:
01603-259350
Director, Torry Research Station (*G5*), Dr L. Cox, PO Box 31,
135 Abbey Road, Aberdeen AB9 8DG. Tel: 01224-877071

INTERVENTION BOARD
— *see* page 315

MEAT HYGIENE SERVICE
Foss House, 1–2 Peasholme Green, King's Pool, York
YO1 2PX
Tel 01904-455500

The Agency was launched in April 1995 and is responsible for the fresh meat hygiene enforcement arrangements formerly carried out by local authorities.
Chief Executive (*G4*), J. McNeill

---

†At Nobel/Ergon House, 17 Smith Square, London SW1P 3JR. Tel: 0171-238 6000

PESTICIDES SAFETY DIRECTORATE
Mallard House, King's Pool, 3 Peasholme Green, York
YO1 2PX
Tel 01904-640500
The Pesticides Safety Directorate is responsible for the
evaluation and approval of pesticides and the development
of policies relating to them, in order to protect consumers,
users and the environment.
Chief Executive (G4), G. K. Bruce
Director (Policy) (G5), J. A. Bainton
Director (Approvals) (G5), Dr A. D. Martin

VETERINARY LABORATORIES AGENCY
Woodham Lane, New Haw, Addlestone, Surrey KT15 3NB
Tel 01932-341111
The Veterinary Laboratories Agency provides scientific
and technical expertise in animal and public health.
Director and Chief Executive (G3), Dr T. W. A. Little
Director of Research (G4), Dr J. A. Morris
Director of Operations (G5), J. W. Harkness
Director of Veterinary Investigation Centres (G5),
W. A. Edwards

VETERINARY MEDICINES DIRECTORATE
Woodham Lane, New Haw, Addlestone, Surrey KT15 3NB
Tel 01932-336911
The Veterinary Medicines Directorate is responsible for
all aspects of licensing and control of animal medicines,
including the protection of the consumer from hazardous
or unacceptable residues.
Chief Executive and Director of Veterinary Medicines (G4),
Dr J. M. Rutter
Director (Policy) (G5), R. Anderson
Director (Licensing) (G5), Dr K. N. Woodward
Secretary and Head of Business Unit (G6), J. FitzGerald
Licensing Manager, Pharmaceuticals and Feed Additives (G6),
J. P. O'Brien
*Licensing Manager, Immunologicals and Suspected Adverse
Reactions (SARS) (G6)*, vacant

COLLEGE OF ARMS OR HERALDS
COLLEGE
Queen Victoria Street, London EC4V 4BT
Tel 0171-248 2762

The Sovereign's Officers of Arms (Kings, Heralds and
Pursuivants of Arms) were first incorporated by Richard
III. The powers vested by the Crown in the Earl Marshal
(the Duke of Norfolk) with regard to state ceremonial are
largely exercised through the College. The College is also
the official repository of the arms and pedigrees of English,
Northern Irish and Commonwealth (except Canadian)
families and their descendants, and its records include
official copies of the records of Ulster King of Arms, the
originals of which remain in Dublin. The 13 officers of the
College specialize in genealogical and heraldic work for
their respective clients.
    Arms have been and still are granted by letters patent
from the Kings of Arms. A right to arms can only be
established by the registration in the official records of the
College of Arms of a pedigree showing direct male line
descent from an ancestor already appearing therein as
being entitled to arms, or by making application through
the College of Arms for a grant of arms. Grants are made to
corporations as well as to individuals.
    The College of Arms is open Monday–Friday 10–4.
Earl Marshal, His Grace the Duke of Norfolk, KG, GCVO,
CB, CBE, MC

KINGS OF ARMS
Garter, P. L. Gwynn-Jones, LVO
Clarenceux, J. P. B. Brooke-Little, CVO, FSA
Norroy and Ulster (and Registrar), D. H. B. Chesshyre, LVO,
FSA

HERALDS
Windsor, T. D. Mathew
Somerset, T. Woodcock, LVO, FSA
Richmond (and Earl Marshal's Secretary), P. L. Dickinson
York, H. E. Paston-Bedingfeld
Chester, T. H. S. Duke
Lancaster, vacant

PURSUIVANTS
Bluemantle, R. J. B. Noel
Portcullis, W. G. Hunt, TD
Rouge Croix, D. V. White
Rouge Dragon, vacant

COURT OF THE LORD LYON
HM New Register House, Edinburgh EH1 3YT
Tel 0131-556 7255

The Court of the Lord Lyon is the Scottish Court of
Chivalry (including the genealogical jurisdiction of the *Ri-
Sennachie* of Scotland's Celtic Kings). The Lord Lyon King
of Arms has jurisdiction, subject to appeal to the Court of
Session and the House of Lords, in questions of heraldry
and the right to bear arms. The Court also administers the
Scottish Public Register of All Arms and Bearings and the
Public Register of All Genealogies. Pedigrees are established by decrees of Lyon Court and by letters patent. As
Royal Commissioner in Armory, the Lord Lyon grants
patents of arms (which constitute the grantee and heirs
noble in the Noblesse of Scotland) to 'virtuous and well-
deserving' Scotsmen and to petitioners (personal or
corporate) in Her Majesty's overseas realms of Scottish
connection, and issues birthbrieves.
Lord Lyon King of Arms, Sir Malcolm Innes of Edingight,
KCVO, WS

HERALDS
Albany, J. A. Spens, RD, WS
Rothesay, Sir Crispin Agnew of Lochnaw, Bt., QC
Ross, C. J. Burnett, FSA Scot

PURSUIVANTS
Kintyre, J. C. G. George, FSA Scot
Unicorn, Alastair Campbell of Airds, FSA Scot
Carrick, Mrs C. G. W. Roads, MVO, FSA Scot

Lyon Clerk and Keeper of Records, Mrs C. G. W. Roads, MVO,
FSA Scot
Procurator-Fiscal, D. F. Murby, WS
Herald Painter, Mrs J. Phillips
Macer, A. M. Clark

ARTS COUNCILS

The Arts Council of Great Britain was established as an
independent body in 1946 to be the principal channel for
the Government's support of the arts. In 1994 the Scottish
and Welsh Arts Councils became autonomous and the Arts
Council of Great Britain became the Arts Council of
England.
    The Arts Councils are responsible for the distribution of
one-fifth of the proceeds of the National Lottery allocated

to 'good causes'. They had made awards to the value of £402.760 million by the end of April 1996.

ARTS COUNCIL OF ENGLAND
14 Great Peter Street, London SW1P 3NQ
Tel 0171-333 0100

The Arts Council of England funds the major arts organizations in England and the ten Regional Arts Boards. It is funded by the Department of National Heritage and works closely with the Scottish Arts Council and the Arts Council of Wales.

The Council also provides advice, information and help to artists and arts organizations. Its objectives are to develop and improve the understanding and practice of the arts and to increase their accessibility to the public.

The Council distributes an annual grant from the Department of National Heritage; the grant for 1996–7 is £186.133 million.

Chairman, The Lord Gowrie, PC
Vice-Chairman, Sir Richard Rogers, RA
Members, R. Cork; Prof. R. Cowell; Prof. B. Cox, CBE; C. Denton; Prof. C. Frayling; Ms M. Guillebaud; Sir Ernest Hall, OBE; Dr D. Harrison, CBE; G. Henderson; Ms T. Holt, CBE; Prof. A. Motion; S. Phillips; Ms U. Prashar, CBE; C. Priestley, CB; R. Reed; D. Reid; Ms S. Robinson; Ms P. Skene; R. Southgate; two vacancies
Secretary-General, Ms M. Allen

REGIONAL ARTS BOARDS

EASTERN ARTS BOARD, Cherry Hinton Hall, Cherry Hinton Road, Cambridge CB1 4DW. Tel: 01223-215355. *Chair*, Dr D. Harrison
EAST MIDLANDS ARTS BOARD, Mountfields House, Forest Road, Loughborough, Leics LE11 3HU. Tel: 01509-218292. *Chair*, Prof. R. Cowell
LONDON ARTS BOARD, Elme House, 133 Long Acre, London WC2E 9AF. Tel: 0171-240 1313. *Chair*, C. Priestley
NORTHERN ARTS BOARD, 9–10 Osborne Terrace, Newcastle upon Tyne NE2 1NZ. Tel: 0191-281 6334. *Chair*, Mrs S. Robinson
NORTH-WEST ARTS BOARD, Manchester House, 22 Bridge Street, Manchester M3 3AB. Tel: 0161-834 9131. *Chair*, Prof. B. Cox
SOUTH-EAST ARTS BOARD, 10 Mount Ephraim, Tunbridge Wells, Kent TN4 8AS. Tel: 01892-515210. *Chair*, R. Reed
SOUTHERN ARTS BOARD, 13 St Clement Street, Winchester SO23 9DQ. Tel: 01962-855099. *Chair*, D. Reid
SOUTH-WEST ARTS BOARD, Bradninch Place, Gandy Street, Exeter EX4 3LS. Tel: 01392-218188. *Chair*, Ms M. Guillebaud
WEST MIDLANDS ARTS BOARD, 82 Granville Street, Birmingham B1 2LH. Tel: 0121-631 3121. *Chair*, R. Southgate
YORKSHIRE AND HUMBERSIDE ARTS BOARD, 21 Bond Street, Dewsbury, W. Yorks WF13 1AX. Tel: 01924-455555. *Chair*, Sir Ernest Hall

SCOTTISH ARTS COUNCIL
12 Manor Place, Edinburgh EH3 7DD
Tel 0131-226 6051

The Scottish Arts Council funds arts organizations in Scotland and is funded directly by the Scottish Office. The grant for 1996–7 is £24.47 million.
Chairman, M. Linklater
Vice-Chairman, Ms F. Walker

Members, Dr Sheila Brock; D. Connell; J. Denholm; K. Geddes; G. Hallewell; P. Hamilton; R. Love; Dr Rita McAllister; Dr I. McGowan; Ms M. MacLean; Ms J. Richardson; Prof. E. Spiller; Ms L. Thomson
Director, Ms S. Reid
Lottery Director, D. Bonnar

ARTS COUNCIL OF WALES
Museum Place, Cardiff CF1 3NX
Tel 01222-394 711

The Arts Council of Wales funds arts organizations in Wales and is funded directly by the Welsh Office. The grant for 1996–7 is £14 million.
Chairman, Sir Richard Lloyd Jones, KCB
Members, Ms J. Davidson; M. Edwards; F. Evans; K. Evans; Ms K. Gass; P. Griffiths; G. S. Jones; R. G. Jones; M. Pepper; D. Richards; A. Roberts; E. Thomas; Prof. G. Thomas; Ms M. Vincentelill
Chief Executive, E. Jenkins

ARTS COUNCIL OF NORTHERN IRELAND
185 Stranmillis Road, Belfast BT9 5DU
Tel 01232-381591

The Arts Council of Northern Ireland disburses government funds in support of the arts in Northern Ireland. It is funded by the Department of Education for Northern Ireland, and the grant for 1996–7 is £6.85 million.
Chairman, D. Deeny, QC
Vice-Chairman, Sir Charles Brett
Members, J. Aiken; S. Burnside; F. Cobain; P. Donnelly; Ms R. Duffy; Dr Tess Hurson; Ms K. Ingram; Prof. Edna Longley; W. O'Connell; R. Pierce; Ms C. Poulter; Ms I. Sandford; Prof. R. Welch
Chief Executive, B. Ferran

ART GALLERIES, ETC

ROYAL FINE ART COMMISSION
7 St James's Square, London SW1Y 4JU
Tel 0171-839 6537

Established in 1924, the Commission is an autonomous authority on the aesthetic implications of any project or development, primarily but not exclusively architectural, which affects the visual environment.
Chairman, The Lord St John of Fawsley, PC, FRSL
Commissioners, Miss S. Andreae; Prof. R. D. Carter, CBE; E. Cullinan, CBE, RA; Sir Philip Dowson, CBE, PRA; D. H. Fraser, RA; E. Hollinghurst; Sir Michael Hopkins, CBE, RA; S. A. Lipton; Prof. Margaret MacKeith, PH.D.; H. T. Moggridge, OBE; Mrs J. Nutting; T. Osborne, FRICS; I. Ritchie; Prof. J. R. Steer, FSA; Miss W. Taylor, CBE; Q Terry, FRIBA; Dr G. Worsley
Secretary, F. Golding

ROYAL FINE ART COMMISSION FOR SCOTLAND
9 Atholl Crescent, Edinburgh EH3 8HA
Tel 0131-229 1109

The Commission was established in 1927 and advises ministers and local authorities on the visual impact and quality of design of construction projects. It is an independent body and gives its opinions impartially.
Chairman, The Lord Cameron of Lochbroom, PC, FRSE
Commissioners, Prof. G. Benson; W. A. Cadell; Mrs K. Dalyell; A. S. Matheson, FRIBA; R. G. Maund; D. Page; Miss B. Rae; Prof. T. Ridley, FRSE; M. Turnbull; Prof. R. Webster; R. Wedgwood
Secretary, C. Prosser

NATIONAL GALLERY

Trafalgar Square, London WC2N 5DN
Tel 0171-839 3321

The National Gallery, which houses a permanent collection of western painting since the 13th century, was founded in 1824, following a parliamentary grant of £60,000 for the purchase and exhibition of the Angerstein collection of pictures. The present site was first occupied in 1838; a substantial extension to the north of the building with a public entrance in Orange Street was opened in 1975, and the Sainsbury wing was opened in 1991. Total government grant-in-aid for 1996–7 is £18.724 million.

BOARD OF TRUSTEES
Chairman, P. Hughes, CBE
Trustees, P. Troughton; Sir Derek Oulton, GCB, QC;
 E. Uglow; Sir Keith Thomas, FBA; The Hon. Simon
 Sainsbury; Lady Bingham; Sir Mark Richmond, SC.D.,
 FRS; A. Bennett; Lady Monck; Mrs P. Ridley; Sir Ewen
 Fergusson, GCMG, GCVO; R. Gavron, CBE; C. Le Brun;
 The Hon. R. G. H. Seitz

OFFICERS
Director, R. N. MacGregor
Chief Curator, Dr C. P. H. Brown
Senior Curators, Dr N. Penny; Dr S. Foister; Dr D. Gordon;
 J. Leighton
Chief Restorer, M. H. Wyld
Head of Exhibitions, M. J. Wilson
Scientific Adviser, Dr A. Roy
Director of Administration, J. MacAuslan
Head of Press and Public Relations, Miss J. Liddiard

NATIONAL PORTRAIT GALLERY

St Martin's Place, London WC2H 0HE
Tel 0171-306 0055

A grant was made in 1856 to form a gallery of the portraits of the most eminent persons in British history. The present building was opened in 1896 and an extension in 1933. There are four outstations displaying portraits in appropriate settings: Montacute House, Gawthorpe Hall, Beningbrough Hall and Bodelwyddan Castle. Total government grant-in-aid for 1996–7 is £4.914 million.

BOARD OF TRUSTEES
Chairman, H. Keswick
Trustees, The Lord President of the Council (*ex officio*);
 The President of the Royal Academy of Arts (*ex officio*);
 J. Roberts, CBE, D.Phil.; The Lord Morris of Castle
 Morris, D.Phil.; Prof. N. Lynton; Sir Eduardo Paolozzi;
 J. Tusa; Sir Antony Acland, GCMG, GCVO; Mrs
 J. E. Benson, LVO, OBE; Mrs W. Tumim, OBE; Sir David
 Scholey, CBE; Mrs C. Tomalin; Baroness Willoughby de
 Eresby; M. Hastings; Prof. The Earl Russell, FBA
Director (G3), C. Saumarez-Smith, PH.D.

TATE GALLERY

Millbank, London SW1P 4RG
Tel 0171-887 8000

The Tate Gallery comprises the national collections of British painting and 20th-century painting and sculpture. The Gallery was opened in 1897, the cost of erection (£80,000) being defrayed by Sir Henry Tate, who also contributed the nucleus of the present collection. The Turner wing was opened in 1910, galleries to contain the collection of modern foreign painting in 1926, and a new sculpture hall in 1937. In 1979 a further extension was built, and the Clore Gallery, for the Turner collection, was opened in 1987. The Tate Gallery Liverpool opened in 1988 and the Tate Gallery St Ives in 1993. Total government grant-in-aid for 1996–7 is £18.775 million.

BOARD OF TRUSTEES
Chairman, D. Stevenson, CBE
Trustees, Prof. Dawn Ades; The Lord Attenborough, CBE;
 The Hon. Mrs J. de Botton; Sir Richard Carew Pole;
 M. Craig-Martin; P. Doig; B. Gascoigne, FRSL;
 D. Gordon; Mrs P. Ridley; D. Verey; W. Woodrow

OFFICERS
Director (G3), N. Serota
Director of Public and Regional Services (G5), S. Nairne
Keeper of the British Collection (G5), A. Wilton
Keeper of the Modern Collection (G5), R. Morphet
Curator, Tate Gallery Liverpool (G6), L. Biggs
Curator, Tate Gallery St Ives (G6), M. Tooby

WALLACE COLLECTION

Hertford House, Manchester Square, London W1M 6BN
Tel 0171-935 0687

The Wallace Collection was bequeathed to the nation by the widow of Sir Richard Wallace, Bt. in 1897, and Hertford House was subsequently acquired by the Government. Total government grant-in-aid for 1996–7 is £1.9 million.
Director, Miss R. J. Savill
Head of Administration, A. W. Houldershaw

NATIONAL GALLERIES OF SCOTLAND

The Mound, Edinburgh EH2 2EL
Tel 0131-556 8921

The National Galleries of Scotland comprise the National Gallery of Scotland, the Scottish National Portrait Gallery and the Scottish National Gallery of Modern Art. There are also outstations at Paxton House, Berwickshire, and Duff House, Banffshire. Total government grant-in-aid for 1996–7 is £8.268 million.

TRUSTEES
Chairman of the Trustees, A. M. Grossart, CBE
Trustees, Mrs L. W. Gibbs; Lord Macfarlane of Bearsden;
 Dr T. Johnston; Prof. A. A. Tait; E. Hagman;
 Prof. E. Fernie; M. Shea; The Countess of Airlie, CVO;
 Mrs A. McCurley; Prof. J. R. Harper, CBE; Prof.
 Christina Lodder

OFFICERS
Director (G4), T. Clifford
Keeper of Conservation (G6), J. P. Dick, OBE
Head of Press and Information (G7), Mrs A. M. Wagener
Keeper of Education (G7), M. Cassin
Registrar (G7), Miss A. Buddle
Secretary (G6), Ms S. Edwards
Buildings (G7), R. Galbraith
Keeper, National Gallery of Scotland (G6), M. Clarke
Keeper, Scottish National Portrait Gallery (G6), D. Thomson,
 PH.D.
 Curator of Photography, Miss S. F. Stevenson
Keeper, Scottish National Gallery of Modern Art (G6),
 R. Calvocoressi

ASSEMBLY OMBUDSMAN FOR NORTHERN IRELAND AND NORTHERN IRELAND COMMISSIONER FOR COMPLAINTS

Progressive House, 33 Wellington Place, Belfast BT1 6HN
Tel 01232-233821

The Ombudsman is appointed under legislation with powers to investigate complaints by people claiming to have sustained injustice in consequence of maladministration arising from action taken by a Northern Ireland government department, or any other public body within

his remit. Staff are presently seconded from the Northern Ireland Civil Service.
Commissioner, G. Burns, MBE
Deputy Commissioner, G. R. Dawson
Directors, C. O'Hare; R. Doherty

UK ATOMIC ENERGY AUTHORITY
Harwell, Didcot, Oxon OX11 ORA
Tel 01235-820220

The UKAEA was established by the Atomic Energy Authority Act 1954 and took over responsibility for the research and development of the civil nuclear power programme. The Authority increasingly evolved its operations, selling its products and services to the nuclear and non-nuclear sectors under the marketing title of AEA Technology while also continuing with the development of nuclear research and development.

The commercial arm, AEA Technology PLC, is now a science engineering services business which is legally separate from UKAEA and is due to be privatized by the end of 1996. UKAEA itself is responsible for the safe management and decommissioning of its radioactive plant and facilities used for the development of the UK's nuclear power programme. It is also responsible for maximizing the income from its still-operating active facilities, buildings and land on its six sites. UKAEA also undertakes special nuclear tasks for the Government, including the UK's contribution to the international fusion programme.
Chairman, UKAEA, Adm. Sir Kenneth Eaton
Chairman, AEA Technology PLC, Sir Anthony Cleaver
Chief Executive, UKAEA, Dr D. Pooley, CBE
Chief Executive, AEA Technology PLC, Dr P. Watson

AUDIT COMMISSIONS

AUDIT COMMISSION FOR LOCAL AUTHORITIES AND THE NATIONAL HEALTH SERVICE IN ENGLAND AND WALES
1 Vincent Square, London SW1P 2PN
Tel 0171-828 1212

The Audit Commission was set up in 1983 with responsibility for the external audit of local authorities. This remit was extended from 1990 to include the audit of the National Health Service bodies in England and Wales. The Commission appoints the auditors, who may be from the District Audit Service or from a private firm of accountants. The Commission is also responsible for promoting value for money in the services provided by local authorities and health bodies.

The Commission has 15–17 members appointed by the Secretary of State for the Environment in consultation with the Secretaries of State for Wales and for Health. Though appointed by the Secretary of State, the Commissioners are responsible to Parliament.
Chairman, R. Brooke
Deputy Chairman, C. Thompson
Controller of Audit, A. Foster
Chief Executive of District Audit Service, D. Prince

ACCOUNTS COMMISSION FOR SCOTLAND
18 George Street, Edinburgh EH2 2QU
Tel 0131-477 1234

The Commission was set up in 1975. It is responsible for securing the audit of the accounts of Scottish local authorities and certain joint boards and joint committees. On 1 April 1995 it assumed responsibility for securing the audit of National Health Service bodies in Scotland. Amongst its duties the Commission is required to deal with reports made by the Controller of Audit on items of account contrary to law; on incorrect accounting; and on losses due to misconduct, negligence and failure to carry out statutory duties. Since 1988 the Commission has had responsibility for value-for-money audits of authorities.

Members are appointed by the Secretary of State for Scotland.
Chairman, Prof. J. P. Percy
Controller of Audit, R. W. Black
Secretary, W. F. Magee

THE BANK OF ENGLAND
Threadneedle Street, London EC2R 8AH
Tel 0171-601 4444

The Bank of England was incorporated in 1694 under royal charter. It is the banker of the Government, on whose behalf it executes monetary policy and manages the note issue and the national debt. It is also responsible for promoting the efficiency and competitiveness of financial services. As the central reserve bank of the country, the Bank keeps the accounts of British banks, who maintain with it a proportion of their cash resources, and of most overseas central banks. The Bank is divided into two divisions, Monetary Stability and Financial Stability. (*See* also pages 604–5.)
Governor, E. A. J. George
Deputy Governor, H. J. Davies
Directors, Sir David Cooksey; M. D. K. W. Foot; Sir John Hall; Mrs F. A. Heaton; P. H. Kent; Sir John Keswick; M. A. King; Sir David Lees; Ms S. V. Masters; Sir Christopher Morse, KCMG; J. Neill, CBE, Ph.D.; I. Plenderleith; Sir David Scholey, CBE, FRSA; N. I. Simms; D. A. G. Simon; Sir Colin Southgate
Advisers to the Governor, Sir Peter Petrie; L. Berkowitz; I. G. Watt
Chief Cashier and Deputy Director, Banking and Market Services, G. E. A. Kentfield
Chief Registrar, P. W. F. Ironmonger
General Manager, Printing Works, A. W. Jarvis
Secretary, J. R. E. Footman
The Auditor, M. J. W. Phillips

BOUNDARY COMMISSIONS

The Commissions are constituted under the Parliamentary Constituencies Act 1986. The Speaker of the House of Commons is ex-officio chairman of all four commissions in the UK. Each of the four commissions is required by law to keep the parliamentary constituencies in their part of the UK under review. The latest review was completed in April 1995; the final proposals have been approved by Parliament and take effect at the next general election. Each of the three commissions in Great Britain is required by law to keep the European parliamentary constituencies in their part of Great Britain under review.

ENGLAND
St Catherine's House, 10 Kingsway, London WC2B 6JP
Tel 0171-396 2105
Deputy Chairman, vacant
Joint Secretaries, R. McLeod; S. Limpkin

WALES
St Catherine's House, 10 Kingsway, London WC2B 6JP
Tel 0171-396 2105
Deputy Chairman, The Hon. Mr Justice Kay
Joint Secretaries, R. McLeod; S. Limpkin

SCOTLAND
St Andrew's House, Edinburgh EH1 3DG
Tel 0131-244 2196/2027
Deputy Chairman, The Hon. Lord Davidson
Secretary, D. K. C. Jeffrey

NORTHERN IRELAND
Room 1/77, Old Admiralty Building, Whitehall, London
SW1A 2AZ
Tel 0171-210 6569
Deputy Chairman, The Hon. Mr Justice Pringle
Secretary, Ms C. Marson

BRITISH BROADCASTING CORPORATION
Broadcasting House, Portland Place, London W1A 1AA
Tel 0171-580 4468
Television Centre, Wood Lane, London W12 7RJ
Tel 0181-743 8000

The BBC was incorporated under royal charter as successor to the British Broadcasting Company Ltd, whose licence expired in 1926. Its current charter came into force in 1981 and a new charter will come into force on 1 January 1997. The chairman, vice-chairman and other governors are appointed by The Queen-in-Council. The BBC is financed by revenue from receiving licences for the home services and by grant-in-aid from Parliament for the World Service (radio). In June 1996 the BBC announced a restructuring of the corporation into six divisions: Production, Broadcast, News, Worldwide, Resources, and Corporate Centre.
For services, *see* Broadcasting section.

BOARD OF GOVERNORS

Chairman (£63,670), Sir Christopher Bland
Vice-Chairman (£16,340), The Lord Cocks of Hartcliffe, PC
National Governors (*each* £16,340), Sir Kenneth Bloomfield, KCB (*N. Ireland*); Dr G. Jones (*Wales*); N. Drummond (*Scotland*)
Governors (*each* £8,170), W. B. Jordan, CBE; Lord Nicholas Gordon Lennox, KCMG, KCVO; Mrs M. Spurr, OBE; Mrs J. Cohen; Sir David Scholey, CBE; R. Eyre, CBE; A. White, CBE

BOARD OF MANAGEMENT

EXECUTIVE COMMITTEE
Director-General, J. Birt
Deputy Director-General and Chief Executive, BBC Worldwide, R. Phillis
Chief Executives, R. Neil (*BBC Production*); W. Wyatt (*BBC Broadcast*); T. Hall (*BBC News*); R. Lynch (*BBC Resources*)
Directors, Ms M. Salmon (*Personnel*); Ms P. Hodgson (*Policy and Planning*); R. Baker-Bates (*Finance and IT*); C. Browne (*Corporate Affairs*)

WIDER BOARD OF MANAGEMENT
Managing Director, World Service, S. Younger

Directors, A. Yentob (*Programmes*); M. Jackson (*Television*); M. Bannister (*Radio*); Ms J. Drabble (*Education*); M. Byford (*Regional Broadcasting*)

OTHER SENIOR STAFF

The Secretary, M. Stevenson
Head of Continuous News, Ms J. Abramsky
Controller, BBC1, M. Jackson
Controller, BBC2, M. Thompson
Controller, Radio 1, M. Bannister
Controller, Radio 2, J. Moir
Controller, Radio 3, N. Kenyon
Controller, Radio 4, J. Boyle
Controller, Radio 5 Live, vacant
Controller, BBC Scotland, J. McCormick
Controller, BBC Wales, G. Talfan Davies
Controller, BBC N. Ireland, P. Loughrey
Head of Broadcasting, BBC South, J. Shearer
Head of Broadcasting, BBC North, C. Adams
Head of Broadcasting, BBC Midlands and East, N. Chapman
Controller, Editorial Policy, R. Ayre
Legal Adviser, G. Roscoe

BRITISH COAL CORPORATION
Charles House, 5–11 Lower Regent Street, London
SW1Y 4LR
Tel 0171-201 4141

The British Coal Corporation (formerly the National Coal Board) was constituted in 1946 and took over the mines on 1 January 1947. The Coal Industry Act 1994 established the statutory framework for the privatization of British Coal's mining operations. British Coal's ownership of coal reserves and responsibility for licensing other coal producers were transferred to the Coal Authority, a non-departmental public body (*see* page 291). The sale of regional coal companies, into which British Coal's operational mining assets had been transferred, was concluded in December 1994. The Act also charged British Coal with the disposal of its non-mining activities. This process is continuing, and the bulk of the assets are expected to have been disposed of by early 1997. The British Coal Corporation will be wound up when the process is completed.
Chairman, J. N. Clarke
Executive Member, P. L. Hutchinson (*Secretary/Legal Adviser*)
Non-Executive Members, A. P. Hichens; Sir Robert Davidson, FEng.; D. B. Vaughan

THE BRITISH COUNCIL
10 Spring Gardens, London SW1A 2BN
Tel 0171-930 8466
Medlock Street, Manchester M15
Tel 0161-957 7000

The British Council was established in 1934, incorporated by royal charter in 1940 and granted a supplemental charter in 1993. It is an independent, non-political organization which promotes Britain abroad. It is the UK's international network for education, culture and development services. The Council is represented in 228 towns and cities in 109 countries and runs 185 libraries, 95 teaching centres and 29 resource centres around the world.
Total funding in 1995–6, including Foreign and Commonwealth Office grants and contracted money, was £423.5 million.

Chairman, Sir Martin Jacomb
Deputy Chairman, The Lord Chorley
Director-General, Sir John Hanson, KCMG, CBE

BRITISH FILM COMMISSION
70 Baker Street, London W1M 1DJ
Tel 0171-224 5000

The British Film Commission was set up in 1991 and is funded by the Department of National Heritage. The Commission promotes the UK as an international production centre, encourages the use of locations, facilities, services and personnel, and provides, at no charge to the enquirer, comprehensive advice and information relating to the practical aspects of filming in the UK.
Commissioner, Sir Sydney Samuelson, CBE
Chief Executive, A. Patrick

BRITISH FILM INSTITUTE
21 Stephen Street, London W1P 2LN
Tel 0171-255 1444

The British Film Institute was established in 1933 under royal charter. Its aims are to encourage the development of the art of film and its use as a record of contemporary life in Great Britain, and to foster the study, appreciation and use of films for television. It includes the National Film and Television Archive, the National Film Theatre and the Museum of the Moving Image, and it supports a network of 38 regional film theatres. The BFI Library contains the world's largest collection of material relating to film and television. Total government funding for 1996–7 is £16.5 million.
Chairman, J. Thomas
Director, W. Stevenson

BRITISH PHARMACOPOEIA COMMISSION
Market Towers, 1 Nine Elms Lane, London SW8 5NQ
Tel 0171-273 0561

The British Pharmacopoeia Commission sets standards for medicinal products used in human and veterinary medicines and is responsible for publication of the British Pharmacopoeia (a publicly-available statement of the standard that a product must meet throughout its shelf-life), the British Pharmacopoeia (Veterinary) and the selection of British Approved Names. It also participates in the work of the European Pharmacopoeia on behalf of the UK. It has 13 members who are appointed by the Secretary of State for Health, the Minister for Agriculture, Fisheries and Food, the Secretaries of State for Scotland and Wales, and the relevant Northern Ireland departments.
Chairman, Prof. D. Ganderton, OBE
Vice-Chairman, Dr D. H. Calam
Secretary and Scientific Director, Dr R. C. Hutton

BRITISH RAILWAYS BOARD
Euston House, 24 Eversholt Street, PO Box 100, London NW1 1DZ
Tel 0171-928 5151

The British Railways Board came into being in 1963 under the terms of the Transport Act 1962. Under the Railways Act 1993, the activities of the Board have been restructured and are gradually being transferred to the private sector. For details of privatization and railway operations, *see* Transport section.
Chairman and Chief Executive (£180,000), J. K. Welsby, CBE
Finance and Planning, J. J. Jerram, CBE
Personnel, A. P. Watkinson
Engineering, Services and Safety, A. D. Roche
Part-time executive member, C. J. Campbell, CBE
Part-time non-executive members, P. Allen, CBE; J. Butler;
    K. H. M. Dixon; Sir William Francis, CBE; Miss
    K. T. Kantor; W. Wilson
Secretary, P. Trewin

BRITISH STANDARDS INSTITUTION (BSI)
389 Chiswick High Road, London W4 4AL
Tel 0181-996 9000

The British Standards Institution is the recognized authority in the UK for the preparation and publication of national standards for industrial and consumer products. In consultation with the interests concerned, BSI prepares standards relating to nearly every sector of the nation's industry and trade. It also represents the UK at European and international standards meetings. About 90 per cent of its standards work is now internationally linked. British Standards are issued for voluntary adoption, though in a number of cases compliance with a British Standard is required by legislation. Industrial and consumer products certified as complying with the relevant British Standard may carry the Institution's certification trade mark, known as the 'Kitemark'.
Chairman, V. E. Thomas, OBE
Chief Executive, B. Davis

BRITISH TOURIST AUTHORITY
Thames Tower, Black's Road, London W6 9EL
Tel 0181-846 9000

Established under the Development of Tourism Act 1969, the British Tourist Authority has specific responsibility for promoting tourism to Great Britain from overseas. It also has a general responsibility for the promotion and development of tourism and tourist facilities within Great Britain as a whole, and for advising the Secretary of State for National Heritage on tourism matters.
Chairman (*part-time*), D. Quarmby
Chief Executive, A. Sell

BRITISH WATERWAYS
Willow Grange, Church Road, Watford, Herts WD1 3QA
Tel 01923-226422

British Waterways is the navigation authority for over 2,000 miles of canals and river navigations in England,

Scotland and Wales. Some 380 miles are maintained and are being developed as commercial waterways for use by freight-carrying vessels. Another 1,200 miles, the cruising waterways, are being developed for boating, fishing and other leisure activities. The remaining 500 miles, the remainder waterways, are maintained with due regard to safety, public health and the preservation of amenities.

Chairman (part-time), B. Henderson, CBE
Vice-Chairman (part-time), Sir Peter Hutchison, Bt.
Members (all part-time), J. Gordon; D. H. R. Yorke;
  M. Cairns; Sir Neil Cossons; Ms J. Elvey; Ms J. Lewis-Jones
Chief Executive, D. Fletcher
Director of Corporate Services, R. J. Duffy

BROADCASTING STANDARDS COUNCIL
7 The Sanctuary, London SW1P 3JS
Tel 0171-233 0544

The Council was set up in 1988 but received its statutory powers under the Broadcasting Act 1990. Its role is advisory, not regulatory. It monitors the portrayal of violence, sex and matters of taste and decency in all broadcast programmes and advertisements on television, radio, cable and satellite services. The Council publishes a code of practice, considers complaints and conducts research into audience attitudes. Members of the Council are appointed by the Secretary of State for National Heritage. The appointments are part-time.
  The Broadcasting Act 1996 provides for the merger of the BSC with the Broadcasting Complaints Commission to form the Broadcasting Standards Commission from 1 April 1997.

Chair (£42,700), The Lady Howe of Aberavon
Deputy Chairman (£32,250), The Lord Dubs
Members (each £12,845), Ms R. Bevan; Dame Fiona
  Caldicott, DBE; R. Kernohan, OBE; the Very
  Revd J. Lang; M. Parris; Ms S. O'Sullivan
Director, S. Whittle

THE BROADS AUTHORITY
Thomas Harvey House, 18 Colegate, Norwich NR3 1BQ
Tel 01603-610734

The Broads Authority is a special statutory authority set up under the Norfolk and Suffolk Broads Act 1988, with powers and responsibilities similar to those of National Park Authorities. The functions of the Authority are to conserve and enhance the natural beauty of the Broads; to promote the enjoyment of the Broads by the public; and to protect the interests of navigation. The Authority comprises 35 members, appointed by the local authorities in the area covered, environmental conservation bodies, the Environment Agency, and the Great Yarmouth Port Authority.

Chairman, J. S. Peel, CBE, MC
Chief Executive, M. A. Clark

THE CABINET OFFICE

The Cabinet Office comprises the Secretariat, who support Ministers collectively in the conduct of Cabinet business; and the Office of Public Service (OPS) which is responsible for the competitiveness agenda, the progress and develop-

ment of deregulation, the Citizen's Charter initiative, the Next Steps programme, policy on open government, senior Civil Service and public appointments, market testing and efficiency in the Civil Service, and Civil Service recruitment.
  The OPS supports the Prime Minister in his capacity as Minister for the Civil Service, with responsibility for day-to-day supervision delegated to the Chancellor of the Duchy of Lancaster.

Prime Minister and Minister for the Civil Service,
  The Rt. Hon. John Major, MP

PRIME MINISTER'S OFFICE
10 Downing Street, London SW1A 2AA
Tel 0171-270 3000

Principal Private Secretary (G3), A. Allan
Private Secretaries (G5), J. E. Holmes (*Overseas Affairs*);
  M. Wallace (*Economic Affairs*); M. Adams (*Parliamentary
  Affairs*); (*G7*), Ms R. Reynolds (*Home Affairs*)
Assistant Private Secretaries, K. Waldock; Miss
  J. L. Wilkinson
Diary Secretary, Ms A. Warburton
Political Secretary, H. James
Policy Unit, N. Blackwell; Mrs K. Ramsey; D. Morris;
  J. Rees; D. Soskin; S. Williams; Ms C. Fairbairn;
  S. Walker
Parliamentary Private Secretary, J. Ward, MP
Chief Press Secretary (G2), J. Haslam
Deputy Chief Press Secretary (G5), vacant
*Secretary for Appointments, and Ecclesiastical Secretary to the
  Lord Chancellor (G2),* J. Holroyd, CB
Parliamentary Clerk, R. Stone
Secretary of the Cabinet and Head of Home Civil Service,
  Sir Robin Butler, GCB, CVO
Private Secretary, Ms J. A. Polley

SECRETARIAT
70 Whitehall, London SW1A 2AS
Tel 0171-270 3000

Economic and Domestic Secretariat, K. Mackenzie, CB;
  W. A. Jeffrey
Defence and Overseas Affairs Secretariat, C. R. Budd, CMG;
  A. J. D. Pawson
Joint Intelligence Organization, J. Alpass; W. R. Fittall
European Secretariat, B. Bender; A. T. Cahn
Telecommunications Secretariat, R. Hope

OFFICE OF PUBLIC SERVICE (OPS)
*Horse Guards Road, London SW1P 3AL
Tel 0171-270 1234
70 Whitehall, London SW1A 2AS
Tel 0171-270 3000

First Secretary of State and Deputy Prime Minister,
  The Rt. Hon. Michael Heseltine, MP
  Principal Private Secretary, M. Gibson
  Private Secretary, R. Huxter
  Special Advisers, Eileen, Lady Strathnaver; Dr A. Kemp
Chancellor of the Duchy of Lancaster, The Rt. Hon. Roger
  Freeman, MP
  Principal Private Secretary, Ms J. Lemprière
  Private Secretary, Mrs H. R. M. Paxman
Paymaster-General, David Willetts, MP
  Private Secretary, J. B. McLaren
Second Permanent Secretary, R. Mountfield, CB
  Private Secretary, M. S. Langdale

---

*Unless otherwise stated, this is the address and telephone number for
divisions of the OPS

Parliamentary Clerk, Miss D. Smailes
Press Secretary (G5), B. Sutlieff

CITIZEN'S CHARTER UNIT
Government Offices, Great George Street, London
SWIP 3AL
Tel 0171-270 1826

Director, Miss E. C. Turton, CB
Deputy Directors, Mrs G. Craig; Dr C. Sanger

CENTRAL IT UNIT
1st Floor, Hampton House, 20 Albert Embankment,
London SEI 7TJ
Tel 0171-238 2015

Head of Unit, G. H. B. Jordan

EFFICIENCY AND EFFECTIVENESS GROUP
70 Whitehall, London SWIA 2AS
Tel 0171-270 0273

Prime Minister's Adviser on Efficiency and Effectiveness,
    Sir Peter Levene, KBE
Head of Unit (G3), J. R. C. Oughton
Head of Next Steps Project Team, M. J. Cowper

AGENCIES GROUP
Ashley House, Monck Street, London SWIP 2BQ
Tel 0171-270 1234
Ministers' Adviser on Agencies, C. M. Brendish
Head of Agencies Group A, J. P. Henry
Head of Agencies Group B, Mrs M. J. Bloom

CIVIL SERVICE EMPLOYER GROUP
Head of Group, H. H. Taylor
Training and Development White Paper, Mrs J. I. Britton
Development and Equal Opportunities Division, Dr R. Price
Fast Stream and European Staffing Division, Dr J. G. Fuller
International Public Service Unit, C. J. Parry
Personnel Management and Conditions of Service Division,
    J. Strachan
Top Management Programme, Ms H. Dudley (*Course Director*)
Civil Service Pensions Division, D. G. Pain

OFFICE OF THE COMMISSIONER FOR PUBLIC
APPOINTMENTS (OCPA)
Horse Guards Road, London SWIP 3AL
Tel 0171-270 5792
The role of the Commissioner for Public Appointments
(CPA) is to monitor, regulate and approve departmental
appointment procedures for ministerial appointments to
executive non-departmental public bodies and NHS
bodies. The Commissioner is appointed by Order in
Council.
Commissioner, Sir Leonard Peach
Head of the Office, Miss E. M. Goodison

OFFICE OF THE CIVIL SERVICE COMMISSIONERS
(OCSC)
Horse Guards Road, London SWIP 3AL
Tel 0171-270 5081

First Commissioner, Sir Michael Bett, CBE
Commissioners (part-time), D. J. Burr; M. D. Geddes; Ms J.
    A. Hunt; H. J. F. McLean, CBE; Sir Leonard Peach;
    K. Singh
Secretary to the Commissioners and Head of the Office, Miss
    E. M. Goodison

INFORMATION OFFICER MANAGEMENT UNIT
Ashley House, 2 Monck Street, London SWIP 2BQ
Tel 0171-270 1234

Director, T. J. Perks

COMPETITIVENESS DIVISION
Head of Division, Dr R. C. Dobbie, CB

DEREGULATION UNIT
Director, Miss L. J. Neville-Rolfe

SENIOR CIVIL SERVICE GROUP
Director, B. M. Fox
Head of Senior Staff and Interchange Division, D. Laughrin
Head of Senior Pay and Contracts Division, J. A. Barker

MACHINERY OF GOVERNMENT AND STANDARDS
GROUP
70 Whitehall, London SWIA 2AS
Tel 0171-270 1234

Head of Group, D. A. Wilkinson
Head of Security Division, J. K. Barron

CEREMONIAL BRANCH
53 Parliament Street, London SWIA 2NG
Tel 0171-210 5056
Honours Nomination Unit: Tel 0171-210 5071

Ceremonial Officer, A. J. Merifield, CB

ESTABLISHMENT OFFICER'S GROUP
Queen Anne's Chambers, 28 Broadway, London SWIH 9JS
Tel 0171-270 3000

Principal Establishment and Finance Officer, R. W. D. Venning
Deputy Establishment Officer, K. Bastin
Senior Finance Officer, K. Tolladay

HISTORICAL AND RECORDS SECTION
Hepburn House, Marsham Street, London SWIP 4HW
Tel 0171-217 6032

Head of Section, Miss P. M. Andrews, OBE

EXECUTIVE AGENCIES

THE BUYING AGENCY
Royal Liver Building, Pier Head, Liverpool L3 1PE
Tel 0151-227 4262

The Agency provides a professional purchasing service to
government departments and other public bodies.
Chief Executive (G5), S. P. Sage

CCTA (THE GOVERNMENT CENTRE FOR
INFORMATION SYSTEMS)
Hampton House, 20 Albert Embankment, London SEI 7TJ
Tel 0171-238 2250
Rosebery Court, St Andrew's Business Park, Norwich
NR7 0HS
Tel 01603-704807

CCTA offers a range of specialist services in the field of
information technology and telecommunications. It became an executive agency in April 1996.
Chief Executive, R. Assirati

CENTRAL OFFICE OF INFORMATION
— see page 289

CIVIL SERVICE COLLEGE
Sunningdale Park, Ascot, Berks SL5 0QE
Tel 01344-634000
11 Belgrave Road, London SWIV 1RB
Tel 0171-834 6644

The College provides training in management and pro-
fessional skills for the public and private sectors.
Chief Executive (G3), Dr S. H. F. Hickey
Business Executives (G5/G6), C. W. H. Aitken; M. N. Barnes;
    Mrs M. B. Chapman; Ms E. Chennells; G. W. Llewellyn;
    M. Timmis; Miss M. A. Wood; Dr A. Wyatt

HMSO
— see page 346

PROPERTY ADVISERS TO THE CIVIL ESTATE
St Christopher House, Southwark Street, London SEI OTE
Tel 0171-921 1000

The Agency co-ordinates government activity on the civil estate, and provides general property guidance and support to government departments without in-house facilities. It was established in April 1996.
Chief Executive, N. Borrett

SECURITY FACILITIES EXECUTIVE
St Christopher House, Southwark Street, London SEI OTE
Tel 0171-921 4813

The Agency provides a range of security support services, products and systems for central government, the wider public sector and other approved customers.
Chief Executive (G5), J. C. King

CENTRAL ADJUDICATION SERVICES
Quarry House, Quarry Hill, Leeds LS2 7UB
Tel 0113-232 4000
New Court, 48 Carey Street, London WC2A 2LS
Tel 0171-412 1504

The Chief Adjudication Officer and Chief Child Support Officer are independent statutory authorities under the Social Security Act 1975 (as amended) and the Child Support Act 1991. They are appointed by the Secretary of State for Social Security to give advice to adjudication officers and child support officers, to keep under review the operation of the systems of adjudication, and to report annually to the Secretary of State on adjudication standards.

Adjudication officers make decisions of first instance on all claims for social security cash benefits, and child support officers make decisions of first instance on applications for child maintenance made to the Child Support Agency. Officers of the Chief Adjudication Officer also enter written observations on all appeals made to the Social Security Commissioners, and officers of the Chief Child Support Officer make written observations on appeals to the Child Support Commissioners.
Chief Adjudication Officer and Chief Child Support Officer,
E. W. Hazlewood

CENTRAL OFFICE OF INFORMATION
Hercules Road, London SEI 7DU
Tel 0171-928 2345

The Central Office of Information (COI) is an executive agency which offers consultancy, procurement and project management services to central government for publicity, and provides specialist services in certain areas. Though the majority of COI's work is for government departments in the UK, it also procures a range of publicity materials for overseas consumption. Administrative responsibility for the COI rests with the Minister of Public Service within the Cabinet Office.
Chief Executive and Head of the Government Information Service
(G3), G. M. Devereau
Senior Personal Secretary, Mrs J. Rodrigues

MANAGEMENT BOARD
Members, G. M. Devereau; K. Williamson; R. Windsor;
R. Smith
Secretary, Miss K. Gilding

DIRECTORS
Director, Client Services and Marketing (G6), vacant

Director, Advertising (G6), P. Buchanan
Director, Research (G6), M. Rigg
Director, Direct Marketing (G6), C. Noble
Director, Events (G6), A. Chard
Director, Press and Pictures (G6), V. Rowlands
Director, Publications (G6), J. Murray
Director, Publishing and Translations (G6), D. Beynon
Director, Films and Radio (G6), I. Hamilton
Principal Finance Officer (G5), K. Williamson
Director, Regional Network (G6), R. Haslam

NETWORK OFFICES

EASTERN, Three Crowns House, 72–80 Hills Road,
Cambridge CB2 ILL. *Network Director (G7)*, Mrs
V. Burdon
MIDLANDS EAST, 1st Floor, Severns House, 20 Middle
Pavement, Nottingham NGI 7DW. *Network Director (G7)*,
P. Smith
MIDLANDS WEST, Five Ways House, Islington Row
Middleway, Edgbaston, Birmingham B15 ISH. *Network
Director (G6)*, B. Garner
NORTH-EAST, Wellbar House, Gallowgate, Newcastle
upon Tyne NEI 4TB. *Network Director (G7)*, H. Cozens
NORTH-WEST, Sunley Tower, Piccadilly Plaza,
Manchester MI 4BD. *Network Director (G7)*, Mrs E. Jones
SOUTH-EAST, Hercules Road, London SEI 7DU. *Network
Director (G6)*, D. Smith
SOUTH-WEST, The Pithay, Bristol BSI 2NF. *Network
Director (G7)*, P. Whitbread
YORKSHIRE AND HUMBERSIDE, City House, New Station
Street, Leeds LSI 4JG. *Network Director (G7)*, vacant

CERTIFICATION OFFICE FOR TRADE
UNIONS AND EMPLOYERS' ASSOCIATIONS
180 Borough High Street, London SEI ILW
Tel 0171-210 3734/5

The Certification Office is an independent statutory authority. The Certification Officer is appointed by the Secretary of State for Trade and Industry and is responsible for receiving and scrutinizing annual returns from trade unions and employers' associations; for investigating allegations of financial irregularities in the affairs of a trade union or employers' association; for dealing with complaints concerning trade union elections; for ensuring observance of statutory requirements governing political funds and trade union mergers; and for certifying the independence of trade unions.
Certification Officer, E. G. Whybrew
Assistant Certification Officer, G. S. Osborne

SCOTLAND
58 Frederick Street, Edinburgh EH2 ILN
Tel 0131-226 3224
Assistant Certification Officer for Scotland, J. L. J. Craig

CHARITY COMMISSION
St Alban's House, 57–60 Haymarket, London SW1Y 4QX
Tel 0171-210 4556
2nd Floor, 20 King's Parade, Queen's Dock, Liverpool
L3 4DQ
Tel 0151-703 1500
Woodfield House, Tangier, Taunton, Somerset TA1 4BL
Tel 01823-345000

The Charity Commission is established under the Charities Act 1993 with the general function of promoting the effective use of charitable resources in England and

Wales. The Commission gives information and advice to charity trustees to make the administration of their charity more effective; investigates misconduct and the abuse of charitable assets, and takes or recommends remedial action; and maintains a public register of charities. The Commission does not have at its disposal any funds with which to make grants to organizations or individuals.

At the end of 1995 the total number of registered charities was 181,467.

Chief Commissioner (G3), R. Fries
Commissioner (G3), R. M. C. Venables
Commissioners (part-time) (G4), J. Bonds; Mrs T. Baring; Ms J. Warburton
Heads of Legal Sections (G5), J. A. Dutton; G. S. Goodchild; K. M. Dibble; S. Slack
Executive Director (G4), Mrs E. A. Shaw
Head of Policy Division (G5), Ms J. Munday
Establishment Officer (G5), Ms C. Stewart
Information Systems Controller (G5), Ms G. Cruickshank

The offices responsible for charities in Scotland and Northern Ireland are:
SCOTLAND – Scottish Charities Office, Crown Office, 25 Chambers Street, Edinburgh EH1 1LA. Tel: 0131-226 2626
NORTHERN IRELAND – Department of Health and Social Services, Charities Branch, Annexe 3, Castle Buildings, Stormont Estate, Belfast BT4 3RA. Tel: 01232-522 780

CHIEF ADJUDICATION OFFICER AND CHIEF CHILD SUPPORT OFFICER
— *see* Central Adjudication Services

CHILD SUPPORT AGENCY
— *see* page 345

CHURCH COMMISSIONERS
1 Millbank, London SW1P 3JZ
Tel 0171-222 7010

The Church Commissioners were established in 1948 by the amalgamation of Queen Anne's Bounty (established 1704) and the Ecclesiastical Commissioners (established 1836).

The Commissioners are responsible for the management of most of the Church of England's assets, the income from which is predominantly used to pay, house and pension the clergy. The Commissioners own nearly 137,000 acres of agricultural land, a number of residential estates in central London, and commercial property in Great Britain and the USA. They also carry out administrative duties in connection with pastoral reorganization and redundant churches, and have been designated by the General Synod as the central stipends authority of the Church of England.

The Commissioners are: the Archbishops of Canterbury and of York; the 41 diocesan bishops; five deans or provosts, ten other clergy and ten lay persons appointed by the General Synod; four lay persons nominated by The Queen; four persons nominated by the Archbishop of Canterbury; the Lord Chancellor; the Lord President of the Council; the First Lord of the Treasury; the Chancellor of the Exchequer; the Secretary of State for the Home Department; the Speaker of the House of Commons; the Lord Chief Justice; the Master of the Rolls; the Attorney-General; the Solicitor-General; the Lord Mayor and two Aldermen of the City of London; the Lord Mayor of York;

and one representative from each of the Universities of Oxford and Cambridge.

INCOME AND EXPENDITURE
for year ended 31 December 1995

	£ million
Total income	154.2
Net income	137.2
Investments	74.4
Property	63.5
Interest from loans, etc.	16.3
Total expenditure	143.0
Clergy stipends	41.7
Clergy and widows' pensions	76.9
Clergy houses	0.3
Episcopal and cathedral housing	2.3
Financial provision for resigning clergy	3.3
Commissioners' administration of central church functions	5.3
Episcopal administration and payments to Chapters	10.1
Church buildings	0.9
Administration costs of other bodies	2.2
Deficit for year	(5.6)

CHURCH ESTATES COMMISSIONERS
First, Sir Michael Colman, Bt.
Second, The Rt. Hon. Michael Alison, MP
Third, Mrs M. H. Laird

OFFICERS
Secretary, P. Locke
Deputy Secretary (Policy and Planning), R. S. Hopgood
Deputy Secretary (Finance and Investment), C. W. Daws
Assistant Secretaries:
  The Accountant, G. C. Baines
  Management Accountant, B. J. Hardy
  Chief Surveyor, A. C. Brown
  Computer Manager, J. W. Ferguson
  Estates, P. H. P. Shaw, LVO
  Investments Manager, A. S. Hardy
  Pastoral, Houses and Redundant Churches, M. D. Elengorn
  Stipends and Allocations, M. G. S. Farrell
  Senior Architect, J. A. Taylor
Official Solicitor, J. P. Guy

CIVIL AVIATION AUTHORITY
CAA House, 45–59 Kingsway, London WC2B 6TE
Tel 0171-379 7311

The CAA is responsible for the economic regulation of UK airlines by licensing air routes and air travel organizers and by approving fares for journeys outside the European Union; for the safety regulation of UK civil aviation by the certification of airlines and aircraft and by licensing aerodromes, flight crew and aircraft engineers; and, through a subsidiary company, National Air Traffic Services Ltd, for the provision of air traffic control and telecommunications services.

The CAA also advises the Government on aviation issues, represents consumer interests, conducts economic and scientific research, produces statistical data and provides specialist services and other training, and consultancy services to clients world-wide.
Chairman (part-time), Sir Malcolm Field
Secretary, R. J. Britton

THE COAL AUTHORITY
200 Lichfield Lane, Mansfield, Notts NG18 4RG
Tel 01623-427162

The Coal Authority was established under the Coal Industry Act 1994 to manage certain functions previously undertaken by British Coal, including ownership of unworked coal. It is responsible for licensing coal mining operations and for providing information on coal reserves and past and future coal mining. It settles subsidence claims not falling on coal mining operators. It is also responsible for the management and disposal of property, and for dealing with surface hazards such as abandoned coal mine shafts.

Chairman, Sir David White
Chief Executive, N. Washington, OBE

COMMONWEALTH DEVELOPMENT CORPORATION
1 Bessborough Gardens, London SW1V 2JQ
Tel 0171-828 4488

The Commonwealth Development Corporation (CDC) assists overseas countries in the development of their economies. Its sponsoring department is the Overseas Development Administration. Its main activity is providing long-term finance, as loans and risk capital, for financially viable and developmentally sound business enterprises. CDC's area of operations includes British dependent territories and, with ministerial approval, Commonwealth or other developing countries. At present, CDC is authorized to operate in more than 60 countries and territories. Its investments at the end of 1995 were £1,487 million.

Chairman (part-time), The Earl Cairns, CBE
Deputy Chairman (part-time), Sir William Ryrie, KCB
Chief Executive, Dr R. Reynolds

COMMONWEALTH SECRETARIAT
— *see* Index

COMMONWEALTH WAR GRAVES COMMISSION
2 Marlow Road, Maidenhead, Berks SL6 7DX
Tel 01628-34221

The Commonwealth War Graves Commission (formerly Imperial War Graves Commission) was founded by royal charter in 1917. It is responsible for the commemoration of 1,695,190 members of the forces of the Commonwealth who fell in the two world wars. More than one million graves are maintained in 23,198 burial grounds throughout the world. Over three-quarters of a million men and women who have no known grave or who were cremated are commemorated by name on memorials built by the Commission.

The funds of the Commission are derived from the six participating governments, i.e. the UK, Australia, Canada, India, New Zealand and South Africa.

President, HRH The Duke of Kent, KG, GCMG, GCVO, ADC
Chairman, The Secretary of State for Defence in the UK
Vice-Chairman, Air Chief Marshal Sir Joseph Gilbert, KCB, CBE

Members, The Secretary of State for the Environment in the UK; The High Commissioners in London for Australia, Canada, India, New Zealand and South Africa; Dame Janet Fookes, DBE, MP; Sir Nigel Mobbs; The Viscount Ridley, KG, GCVO, TD; Prof. R. J. O'Neill, AO; Mrs L. Golding, MP; Sir Harold Walker, KCMG; Gen. Sir John Akehurst, KCB, CBE; Adm. Sir John Kerr, GCB
Director-General and Secretary to the Commission, D. Kennedy
Deputy Director-General, R. J. Dalley
Directors, P. Noakes (*Finance*); A. Coombe (*Works*); D. C. Parker (*Horticulture*); D. R. Parker (*Personnel*); J. P. D. Gee, OBE (*Information and Secretariat*)
Legal Adviser and Solicitor, G. C. Reddie

IMPERIAL WAR GRAVES ENDOWMENT FUND
Trustees, The Lord Remnant, CVO (*Chairman*); Air Chief Marshal Sir Joseph Gilbert, KCB, CBE; A. C. Barker
Secretary to the Trustees, P. Noakes

COUNTRYSIDE COMMISSION
John Dower House, Crescent Place, Cheltenham, Glos GL50 3RA
Tel 01242-521381

The Countryside Commission was set up in 1968 and is an independent agency which promotes the conservation and enhancement of landscape beauty in England. It encourages the provision and improvement of facilities in the countryside, and works to secure access for open air recreation. Since 1982 the Commission has been funded by an annual grant from the Department of the Environment. Members of the Commission are appointed by the Secretary of State for the Environment.

In April 1996 the Commission's Countryside Stewardship initiative was transferred to the Ministry of Agriculture, Fisheries and Food.

Chairman, R. Simmonds
Commissioners, D. Barker, MBE; the Rt Revd A. Chesters; the Lord Denham, KBE; Dr Susan Owens; Prof. A. Patmore, CBE; W. Rogers-Coltman, OBE; R. Swarbrick, CBE; Mrs R. Thomas; Mrs S. Ward; D. Woodhall, CBE
Chief Executive (G3), R. G. Wakeford
Directors (G5), R. Clarke (*Policy*); M. J. Kirby (*Operations*); M. Taylor (*Resources*)
National Heritage Adviser, P. Walshe
Head of Corporate Planning (G7), N. Holliday
Head of Land Use Branch (G7), Ms P. Jones
Head of Recreation and Access Branch (G7), T. Robinson
Head of Public Affairs (G7), R. Roberts
Head of Finance and Establishments (G7), V. Ellis
Head of National Parks and Planning Branch (G7), R. Lloyd
Head of Environmental Protection Branch (G7), J. Worth
Regional Officers (G7), K. Buchanan (*Newcastle*); M. Carroll (*Cambridge*); Dr S. A. Buchanan (*Leeds*); E. Holdaway (*Bristol*); Dr Liz Newton (*Manchester*); D. E. Coleman (*London*); T. Allen (*Birmingham*)
Special Initiatives, Dr M. Rawson (*Community Forests*)

COUNTRYSIDE COUNCIL FOR WALES/ CYNGOR CEFN GWLAD CYMRU
Plas Penrhos, Fford Penrhos, Bangor LL57 2LQ
Tel 01248-385500

The Countryside Council for Wales is the Government's statutory adviser on wildlife, countryside and maritime conservation matters in Wales, and it is the executive

authority for the conservation of habitats and wildlife. It promotes the protection of the Welsh landscape and encourages opportunities for public access and enjoyment of the countryside. It provides grant aid to local authorities, voluntary organizations and individuals to pursue countryside management. It is funded by the Welsh Office and accountable to the Secretary of State for Wales, who appoints its members.
Chairman, E. M. W. Griffith, CBE
Chief Executive, P. E. Loveluck, CBE
Director, Policy and Science, Dr M. E. Smith
Director, Conservation, I. R. Bonner

COVENT GARDEN MARKET AUTHORITY
Covent House, New Covent Garden Market, London SW8 5NX
Tel 0171-720 2211

The Covent Garden Market Authority is constituted under the Covent Garden Market Acts 1961 to 1977, the members being appointed by the Minister of Agriculture, Fisheries and Food. The Authority owns and operates the 56-acre New Covent Garden Markets (fruit, vegetables, flowers) which have been trading since 1974.
Chairman (part-time), W. P. Bowman, CBE
General Manager, Dr P. M. Liggins
Secretary, C. Farey

CRIMINAL INJURIES COMPENSATION AUTHORITY AND BOARD
Morley House, 26–30 Holborn Viaduct, London ECIA 2JQ
Tel 0171-842 6800
Tay House, 300 Bath Street, Glasgow G2 4JR
Tel 0141-331 2726

All applications for compensation for personal injury arising from crimes of violence in England, Scotland and Wales are dealt with at the above locations. (Separate arrangements apply in Northern Ireland.) Applications received up to 31 March 1996 were assessed on the basis of common law damages under the 1990 compensation scheme by the Criminal Injuries Compensation Board (CICB), which also hears appeals. Applications received on or after 1 April 1996 are assessed under a tariff-based scheme, made under the Criminal Injuries Compensation Act 1995, by the Criminal Injuries Compensation Authority (CICA); there is a separate avenue of appeal to the Criminal Injuries Compensation Appeals Panel (CICAP).
The Board was founded in 1964 by the Home Secretary and Secretary of State for Scotland under the prerogative powers of the Crown. The Authority and the Panel are established by the tariff-based scheme made under the Criminal Injuries Compensation Act 1995.
Chairman of the Criminal Injuries Compensation Board (part-time) (£35,306), The Lord Carlisle of Bucklow, PC, QC
Chief Executive of the Board and of the Criminal Injuries Compensation Authority, P. G. Spurgeon
Head of Legal Services, Mrs A. M. Johnstone
Operations Manager, E. McKeown
Chairman of the Criminal Injuries Compensation Appeals Panel, M. Lewer, QC
Secretary to the Board, Miss V. Jenson

CROFTERS COMMISSION
4–6 Castle Wynd, Inverness IV2 3EQ
Tel 01463-663450

The Crofters Commission is a statutory body established in 1955. It advises the Secretary of State for Scotland on all matters relating to crofting. It controls the letting, sub-letting and, in certain cases, the assignation or enlargement of crofts; the removal of land from crofting tenure; and the regulation of common grazings. It also administers schemes of agricultural assistance to crofters.
Chairman, I. MacAskill
Secretary (G6), M. Grantham

CROWN AGENTS FOR OVERSEA GOVERNMENTS AND ADMINISTRATIONS
St Nicholas House, St Nicholas Road, Sutton, Surrey SM1 1EL
Tel 0181-643 3311

Incorporated under the Crown Agents Act 1979, the Crown Agents are commercial, financial and professional agents for governments and public authorities in over 120 countries, and for international bodies and other organizations, primarily in the public sector. The Government has announced its intention to transfer the Crown Agents to an independent foundation and the necessary legislation was passed in 1995.
Chairman, D. H. Probert, CBE
Managing Director, P. F. Berry

CROWN ESTATE
16 Carlton House Terrace, London SW1Y 5AH
Tel 0171-210 4377

The land revenues of the Crown in England and Wales have been collected on the public account since 1760, when George III surrendered them to Parliament and received a fixed annual payment or Civil List. At the time of the surrender the gross revenues amounted to about £89,000 and the net return to about £11,000.
The land revenues in Ireland have been carried to the Consolidated Fund since 1820; from 1923, as regards the Republic of Ireland, they have been collected and administered by the Irish Government.
The land revenues in Scotland were transferred to the predecessors of the Crown Estate Commissioners in 1833.
In the year ended 31 March 1996, the gross income from the Crown Estate totalled £143 million. The sum of £94.6 million was paid to the Exchequer in 1995–6 as surplus revenue.
First Commissioner and Chairman (part-time), Sir Denys Henderson
Second Commissioner and Chief Executive, C. K. Howes, CB
Commissioners (part-time), R. B. Caws, CBE, FRICS; J. N. C. James, CBE; I. Grant; J. H. M. Norris, CBE; The Lord De Ramsey
Commissioner and Deputy Chief Executive, D. E. G. Griffiths
Deputy Chief Executive, D. E. Murray
Legal Adviser, M. L. Davies
Crown Estate Surveyor, C. F. Hynes
Urban Estates Managers, M. W. Dillon; A. Bickmore; R. Wyatt
Agricultural Estates Manager, R. J. Mulholland

Marine Estates Manager, F. G. Parrish
Information Systems Manager, D. Kingston-Smith
Valuation and Investment Analysis Manager, P. Shearmur
Internal Audit Manager, J. E. Ford
Finance Manager, J. G. Lelliott
Corporate Services Manager, M. E. Beckwith
Personnel Manager, R. J. Blake
Public Relations and Press Officer, Mrs G. Coates

SCOTLAND
10 Charlotte Square, Edinburgh EH2 4BR
Tel 0131-226 7241
Crown Estate Receiver for Scotland, M. J. Gravestock

WINDSOR ESTATE
The Great Park, Windsor, Berks SL4 2HT
Tel 01753-860222
Deputy Ranger and Surveyor, M. J. O'Lone

CROWN PROSECUTION SERVICE
— *see* pages 366–7

BOARD OF CUSTOMS AND EXCISE
*New King's Beam House, 22 Upper Ground, London
SE1 9PJ
Tel 0171-620 1313

Commissioners of Customs were first appointed in 1671 and housed by the King in London. The Excise Department was formerly under the Inland Revenue Department and was amalgamated with the Customs Department in 1909.

HM Customs and Excise is responsible for collecting and administering customs and excise duties and VAT, and advises the Chancellor of the Exchequer on any matters connected with them. The Department is also responsible for preventing and detecting the evasion of revenue laws and for enforcing a range of prohibitions and restrictions on the importation of certain classes of goods. In addition, the Department undertakes certain agency work on behalf of other departments, including the compilation of UK overseas trade statistics from customs import and export documents.

THE BOARD
Chairman (G1), Mrs V. P. M. Strachan, CB
  Private Secretaries, Ms C. Davis; A. Jones
Deputy Chairman, A. W. Russell, CB
Commissioners (G3), D. F. O. Battle; A. C. Sawyer; Mrs
  E. A. Woods; M. J. Eland; D. R. Howard; A. Paynter;
  M. Brown; R. McAfee
Head of Board's Secretariat, J. Bone

PUBLIC RELATIONS OFFICE
Tel 0171-865 5665
Head of Public Relations, Ms L. J. Sinclair

INFORMATION SYSTEMS DIRECTORATE
Alexander House, Victoria Avenue, Southend-on-Sea
SS99 1AU
Tel 01702-348944
Director, A. Paynter

CUSTOMS POLICY DIRECTORATE
Director, M. Eland

---

*Unless otherwise stated, this is the address and telephone number of directorates of the Board

EXCISE AND CENTRAL POLICY DIRECTORATE
Director, D. Howard

VAT POLICY DIRECTORATE
Director, M. Brown

PERSONNEL AND FINANCE DIRECTORATE
Director, D. Battle

CENTRAL OPERATIONS DIRECTORATE
Director, R. McAfee

Tariff and Statistical Office
Alexander House, Victoria Avenue, Southend-on-Sea
SS99 1AU
Tel 01702-348944
Controller, A. Cowley

Accounting Services Division
Alexander House, Victoria Avenue, Southend-on-Sea
SS99 1AU
Tel 01702-348944
Accountant and Comptroller-General, D. Robinson

COMPLIANCE DIRECTORATE
Director, Mrs E. A. Woods

PREVENTION DIRECTORATE
Director, A. Sawyer

National Investigation Service
Custom House, Lower Thames Street, London EC3R 6EE
Tel 0171-283 5353
Chief Investigation Officer, R. Kellaway

SOLICITOR'S OFFICE
Solicitor, D. Pickup
Deputy Solicitor, G. Fotherby

COLLECTORS OF HM CUSTOMS AND EXCISE (G5)
Anglia, R. C. Shepherd
Central England, A. Bowen
Eastern England, M. D. Patten
London Airports, M. Peach
London Central, J. Maclean
Northern England, H. Peden
Northern Ireland, T. W. Logan
North-west England, A. Allen
Scotland, C. Arnott
South-east England, W. I. Stuttle
South London and Thames, J. Priestly
Southern England, C. J. Packman
Thames Valley, J. Barnard
Wales, the West and Borders, H. Burnard

OFFICE OF THE DATA PROTECTION
REGISTRAR
Wycliffe House, Water Lane, Wilmslow, Cheshire
SK9 5AF
Tel 01625-545700

The Office of the Data Protection Registrar was created by the Data Protection Act 1984. It is the Registrar's duty to compile and maintain the Register of data users and computer bureaux and to provide facilities for members of the public to examine the Register; to promote observance of data protection principles; to consider complaints made by data subjects; to disseminate information about the Act; to encourage the production of codes of practice by trade associations and other bodies; to guide data users in complying with data protection principles; to co-operate

with other parties to the Council of Europe Convention and act as UK authority for the purposes of Article 13 of the Convention; and to report annually to Parliament on the performance of her functions.
Registrar, Mrs E. France

DEER COMMISSION FOR SCOTLAND
Knowsley, 82 Fairfield Road, Inverness IV3 5LH
Tel 01463-231751

The Deer Commission for Scotland has the general functions of furthering the conservation and control of deer in Scotland. It has the statutory duty, with powers, to prevent damage to agriculture, forestry and the habitat by deer. The Commission also has the power to advise in the interest of conservation any owner of land on questions relating to the carrying of stocks of deer on that land, and to carry out research into matters of scientific importance relating to deer. It is funded by the Scottish Office.
Chairman (part-time), P. Gordon-Duff-Pennington, OBE
Chief Executive and Secretary, A. Rinning
Technical Director, R. W. Youngson

MINISTRY OF DEFENCE
— *see* pages 381–4

DESIGN COUNCIL
1 Oxendon Street, London SW1Y 4EE
Tel 0171-208 2121

The Design Council is incorporated by royal charter and is a registered charity. It aims to inspire the best use of design by the UK in order to improve prosperity and well-being. It works with government, industry and academia to generate information and practical tools for uptake in industry and education which demonstrate the contribution, value and effectiveness of design. Its sponsoring department is the Department of Trade and Industry.
Chairman, J. Sorrell, CBE
Chief Executive, A. Summers

THE DUCHY OF CORNWALL
10 Buckingham Gate, London SW1E 6LA
Tel 0171-834 7346

The Duchy of Cornwall was created by Edward III in 1337 for the support of his eldest son Edward, later known as the Black Prince. It is the oldest of the English duchies. The precursor of the duchy was the earldom of Cornwall, granted to Richard, younger brother of Henry III on his marriage four years after he had been granted the title of earl in 1227. The duchy is acquired by inheritance by the sovereign's eldest son either at birth or on the accession of his parent to the throne, whichever is the later. The primary purpose of the estate remains to provide an income for the Prince of Wales. The estate is mainly agricultural, consisting of 129,000 acres in 24 counties mainly in the south-west of England. The duchy also has some residential property, a number of shops and offices, and a Stock Exchange portfolio. Prince Charles is the 24th Duke of Cornwall.
THE PRINCE'S COUNCIL
Chairman, HRH The Prince of Wales, KG, KT, GCB

Lord Warden of the Stannaries, The Earl Peel
Receiver-General, The Earl Cairns, CBE
Attorney-General to the Prince of Wales, J. M. Sullivan, QC
Secretary and Keeper of the Records, J. N. C. James, CBE
Other members, Earl of Shelburne; Cdr. R. J. Aylard, CVO, RN; J. E. Pugsley; A. M. J. Galsworthy; C. Howes, CB; W. N. Hood, CBE; W. R. A. Ross

OTHER OFFICERS
Auditors, I. Brindle; H. Hughes
Sheriff (1996–7), Mrs J. Trench Morison

THE DUCHY OF LANCASTER
Lancaster Place, Strand, London WC2E 7ED
Tel 0171-836 8277

The estates and jurisdiction known as the Duchy of Lancaster have belonged to the reigning monarch since 1399 when John of Gaunt's son came to the throne as Henry IV. As the Lancaster Inheritance it goes back as far as 1265 when Henry III granted his youngest son Edmund lands and possessions following the Baron's war. In 1267 Henry gave Edmund the County, Honor and Castle of Lancaster and created him the first Earl of Lancaster. In 1351 Edward III created Lancaster a County Palatine.

The Chancellor of the Duchy of Lancaster is responsible for the administration of the Duchy, the appointment of justices of the peace in Lancashire, Greater Manchester and Merseyside and ecclesiastical patronage in the Duchy gift. The Chancellor is also a member of the Cabinet.
Chancellor of the Duchy of Lancaster, The Rt. Hon. Roger Freeman, MP
Attorney-General, T. A. W. Lloyd, QC
Receiver-General, M. C. G. Peat, CVO
Clerk of the Council, M. K. Ridley, CVO
Chief Clerk, Col. F. N. J. Davies

DEPARTMENT FOR EDUCATION AND EMPLOYMENT
Sanctuary Buildings, Great Smith Street, London SW1P 3BT
Tel 0171-925 5000
Caxton House, Tothill Street, London SW1H 9NF
Tel 0171-273 3000
Moorfoot, Sheffield S1 4PQ
Tel 0114-275 3275
Mowden Hall, Staindrop Road, Darlington DL3 9BG
Tel 01325-460155

The Department for Education and Employment was formed in July 1995, bringing together the functions of the former Department of Education with the training and labour market functions of the former Employment Department Group. It includes an executive agency, the Employment Service. The new Department aims to support economic growth and improve the nation's competitiveness and quality of life by raising standards of educational achievement and skill and by promoting an efficient and flexible labour market.
Secretary of State for Education and Employment, The Rt. Hon. Gillian Shephard, MP
Principal Private Secretary, A. T. Evans
Special Advisers, Dr. E. Cottrell; N. Heslop
Ministers of State, Eric Forth, MP; The Lord Henley
Private Secretaries, Ms C. Maye; Ms P. Clarke

Parliamentary Under-Secretaries of State, Robin Squire, MP;
James Paice, MP; Cheryl Gillan, MP
  Private Secretaries, D. McGrath; J. Kittmer;
  Ms S. Battarbee
Permanent Secretary, M. Bichard
  Private Secretary, Ms J. Ruff

EMPLOYMENT AND LIFETIME LEARNING DIRECTORATE

Director-General, N. Stuart
Heads of Divisions, M. Nicholas (Employer Training Policy);
  Ms F. Everiss (Individual Commitment)

EMPLOYMENT AND ADULT TRAINING
Director, P. Makeham
Heads of Divisions, I. Berry (Employment Policy and
  Programmes); A. Cranston (Employment and Benefits);
  E. Galvin (Training Programmes)

JSA PROJECT
Director, I. Stewart
JSA Project Manager, M. Allen

EQUAL OPPORTUNITIES, TECHNOLOGY AND OVERSEAS LABOUR
Director, B. Niven
Heads of Divisions, Mrs J. Anderson, Ms S. Weber (Sex and
  Race Equality); Miss D. Fordham (Disability Policy);
  R. Ritzema (Education and Training Technology);
  N. Atkinson (Overseas Labour Service)

FINANCE DIRECTORATE

Director, L. Lewis
Heads of Divisions, D. Sandeman (Expenditure); Mrs I. Wilde
  (Finance Policy); D. Russell (Programme Performance and
  Evaluation); K. Beeton (Efficiency); P. Connor (Accounting
  and Systems); N. Thirtle (Internal Audit); P. Slade (Private
  Finance Initiative).

FURTHER AND HIGHER EDUCATION AND YOUTH TRAINING DIRECTORATE

Director-General, R. Dawe
Head of Division, M. Waring (Education Business Links)

FURTHER EDUCATION AND YOUTH TRAINING
Director, D. Forrester
Heads of Divisions, S. Kershaw (16–19 Policy); Mrs L.
  Ammon (Choice and Careers); J. Stanyer (Further Education
  Support Unit); Miss J. Benham (Further Education);
  R. Wye (Training for Young People)

HIGHER EDUCATION
Director, T. Clark
Heads of Divisions, Miss K. Fleay (Higher Education Funding);
  Miss C. Macready (Higher Education Quality); J. Moore
  (Student Support); T. Fellowes (Higher Education and
  Employment)

QUALIFICATIONS
Director, M. Richardson
Heads of Divisions, Miss C. Bienkowska (School and College
  Based Qualifications); J. West (Qualifications for Work);
  C. Barnham (Qualifications Framework and GNVQ)

INFORMATION DIRECTORATE

Director, J. Coe
Heads of Divisions, M. Paterson (Media Relations); J. Ross
  (Publicity)

LEGAL ADVISER'S OFFICE

Legal Adviser, R. Ricks
Heads of Divisions, F. Clarke; S. Harker; C. House; Ms R.
  Jeffreys; A. Preston

OPERATIONS DIRECTORATE

Director, J. Hedger
Heads of Divisions, P. Houten (TECs and Careers Service
  Policy); P. Lauener (Resources and Budget Management);
  Mrs P. Jones (Financial Control, Operations); P. Thomas
  (Quality and Performance Improvement); H. Sharp
  (Government Office Policy and Management); J. Fuller
  (Sector Skills Partnership)

PERSONNEL AND SUPPORT SERVICES DIRECTORATE

Director, D. Normington
Heads of Divisions, Ms C. Tyler (Senior Staff Appointments
  and Development); R. Hinchcliffe (Information Systems); Ms
  C. Johnson (Personnel); K. Jordan (Procurement and
  Contracting); J. Gordon (Training and Development);
  L. Webb (Estates and Office Services); T. Jeffery (Human
  Resource Policy)

SCHOOLS DIRECTORATE

Director-General, P. Owen
Head of Division, M. Richardson (Curriculum and Assessment)

SCHOOL PLACES, BUILDINGS AND GOVERNANCE GROUP
Director, P. Shaw
Heads of Divisions, S. Marston (Grant-Maintained Schools
  Policy); A. Shaw (Supply of School Places); Ms A. Jackson
  (Specialist Schools and School Governance); J. Whitaker
  (Schools Capital); M. Hipkins (Under-Fives); C. Wells
  (Nursery Vouchers Implementation)

SCHOOL FUNDING, EFFECTIVENESS AND TEACHERS GROUP
Director, N. Saunders
Heads of Divisions, A. Clarke (School Recurrent Funding);
  J. Street (LEA Finance); A. Wye (School Teachers' Pay and
  Pensions); Ms S. Scales (Teacher Supply, Training and
  Qualifications); M. Stark (School Effectiveness)

PUPILS, PARENTS AND YOUTH GROUP
Director, R. Smith
Heads of Divisions, A. Sargent (Parental Choice); R. Green
  (Special Educational Needs Policy); P. Thorpe (Discipline
  and Attendance); G. Holley (Youth Service and Preparation
  for Adulthood); M. Phipps (Pupil Welfare)

STRATEGY, INTERNATIONAL AND ANALYTICAL SERVICES DIRECTORATE

Director-General, G. Reid
Heads of Divisions, J. Dewsbury (Briefing); R. Harrison
  (Strategy and Board Secretariat)

ANALYTICAL SERVICES
Director, D. Allnutt
Heads of Divisions, J. Gardner (Qualifications); J. Elliott
  (Youth and Further Education); M. Chaplin (Skills and
  Training Analysis); D. Thompson (Higher Education); Ms
  J. Walton (Schools, Teachers and General); B. Butcher
  (TECs and Lifetime Learning); B. Wells (Labour Market
  Analysis); R. Bartholomew (Social Analysis and Research);
  Ms A. Brown (School Resources and Modelling)

INTERNATIONAL
Director, C. Tucker, CB

Heads of Divisions, Miss E. Hodkinson (*EC Education and Training*); Ms W. Harris (*European Union*); Ms E. Trewartha (*European Social Fund*); D. Brown (*International Relations*)
Assistant Director, Exports, Assistance and European Schools, R. Morgan

EXECUTIVE AGENCY

THE EMPLOYMENT SERVICE
St Vincent House, 30 Orange Street, London WC2H 7HT
Tel 0171-839 5600
The Employment Service is responsible for providing services and administering programmes to help unemployed people get back to work as quickly as possible and to make payments to those entitled to benefit.
Chief Executive (G3+), M. E. G. Fogden, CB
Senior Director of Operations (G3), D. Grover
Director of Finance and Resources (G3), D. Horne
Director of Policy and Process Design (G3), R. Phillips
Director of Human Resources (G4), K. White
Regional Directors (G4), R. Foster (*London and South-east*); (*G5*), Mrs A. Le Sage (*East Midlands*); P. Robson (*Northern*); J. Roberts (*North-west*); K. Pascoe (*South-west*); Miss R Thew (*West Midlands*); R. Lasko (*Yorkshire and Humberside*)
Director for Scotland (G5), A. R. Brown
Director for Wales (G5), Mrs S. Keyse

OFFICE OF ELECTRICITY REGULATION

Hagley House, Hagley Road, Birmingham B16 8QG
Tel 0121-456 2100
SCOTLAND: Regent Court, 70 West Regent Street, Glasgow G2 2QZ
Tel 0141-331 2678

The Office of Electricity Regulation (OFFER) is the regulatory body for the electricity supply industry in England, Scotland and Wales. Its functions are to promote competition in the generation and supply of electricity; to ensure that all reasonable demands for electricity are satisfied; to protect customers' interests in relation to prices, security of supply and quality of services; and to promote the efficient use of electricity. Headed by the Director-General of Electricity Supply, OFFER was set up under the Electricity Act 1989 but is independent of ministerial control.
Director-General of Electricity Supply, Prof. S. C. Littlechild
Deputy Director-General, C. P. Carter
Deputy Director-General for Scotland, G. L. Sims
Directors of Regulation and Business Affairs, T. M. Davis; J. Saunders
Director of Supply Competition, A. J. Boorman
Director of Consumer Affairs, Dr D. P. Hauser
Technical Director, Dr B. Wharmby
Director of Public Affairs, Miss J. D. Luke
Director of Administration, H. P. Jones
Legal Adviser, D. R. B. Bevan
Chief Examiner, J. D. Cooper

OFFICE OF ELECTRICITY REGULATION NORTHERN IRELAND

Brookmount Buildings, 42 Fountain Street, Belfast BT1 5EE
Tel 01232-311575

OFFER NI is the regulatory body for the electricity supply industry in Northern Ireland.

Director-General of Electricity Supply for Northern Ireland, D. McIldoon
Deputy Director-General, C. H. Coulthard

ENGLISH HERITAGE
— *see* Historic Buildings and Monuments Commission for England

ENGLISH NATURE

Northminster House, Peterborough PE1 1UA
Tel 01733-340345

English Nature (the Nature Conservancy Council for England) was established in 1991 and is responsible for advising the Secretary of State for the Environment on nature conservation in England. It promotes, directly and through others, the conservation of England's wildlife and natural features. It selects, establishes and manages National Nature Reserves and identifies and notifies Sites of Special Scientific Interest. It provides advice and information about nature conservation, and supports and conducts research relevant to these functions. Through the Joint Nature Conservation Committee (*see* page 329), it works with its sister organizations in Scotland and Wales on UK and international nature conservation issues.
Chairman, The Earl of Cranbrook
Chief Executive, Dr D. R. Langslow
Directors, Dr K. L. Duff; E. T. Idle; Miss C. E. M. Wood; Ms S. Collins

ENGLISH PARTNERSHIPS

16–18 Old Queen Street, London SW1H 9HP
Tel 0171-976 7070

English Partnerships, in statute the Urban Regeneration Agency, came into full operation in April 1994. Its primary aim is to secure the reclamation and reuse of vacant and derelict land throughout England for employment, green space, housing or any other use that will help to regenerate the area. It works in partnership with the public, private and voluntary sectors. Its sponsoring department is the Department of the Environment.
Chairman, The Lord Walker of Worcester, MBE, PC
Deputy Chairman, Sir Idris Pearce, CBE
Chief Executive, D. Taylor

DEPARTMENT OF THE ENVIRONMENT

Eland House, Bressenden Place, London SW1E 5DU
Tel 0171-890 3000
Ashdown House, 123 Victoria Street, London SW1E 6DE
Tel 0171-890 3000

The Department of the Environment is responsible for planning and land use; local government; housing and construction; inner city areas; new towns; environmental protection; conservation areas and countryside affairs; health and safety at work and energy efficiency.
Secretary of State for the Environment, The Rt. Hon. John Gummer, MP
  Private Secretary, A. Davis
  Special Advisers, T. Burke; K. Adams; L. O'Connor; G. Barwell
  Parliamentary Private Secretary, D. French, MP

Minister for Local Government, The Rt. Hon. David Curry,
MP
  Private Secretary, B. Hackland
Minister for Planning, Construction and Energy Efficiency,
Robert Jones, MP
  Private Secretary, Mrs T. Vokes
  Parliamentary Private Secretary to Mr Curry and Mr Jones,
M. Banks, MP
Minister for Environment and Countryside, The Earl Ferrers,
PC
  Private Secretary, C. T. Wood
Parliamentary Under-Secretaries of State, Sir Paul Beresford,
MP; James Clappison, MP
  Private Secretaries, D. Gleave; J. Humphreys
Lord-in-Waiting, The Lord Lucas
  Private Secretary, Miss A. Hemming
Parliamentary Clerk, T. Teehan
Permanent Secretary (G1), A. Turnbull, CB, CVO
  Private Secretary, Mrs P. Allars

ORGANIZATION AND ESTABLISHMENTS
Principal Establishments Officer (G3), R. S. Dudding
Principal Finance Officer (G3), W. F. S. Rickett

PERSONNEL
Grade 5, K. G. Arnold; L. B. Hicks; Mrs M. Winckler
Chief Welfare Officer (G7), Miss E. T. Haines

FINANCE CENTRAL
Heads of Divisions (G5), M. J. Bailey; A. C. Allberry;
  P. D. Walton; M. R. Haselip; I. C. McBrayne
Grade 6, M. J. Burt; A. Brooks

ADMINISTRATION RESOURCES
Grade 5, J. J. O'Callaghan; Mrs H. Parker-Brown

DIRECTORATE OF COMMUNICATION
Director (G4), S. Dugdale
Grade 5, K. Kerslake

GOVERNMENT OFFICES CENTRAL UNIT
Under-Secretary (G3), A. G. Watson
Grade 5, T. Abraham; B. Hopson

HOUSING CONSTRUCTION, PLANNING AND COUNTRYSIDE GROUP
Deputy Secretary (G2), Mrs M. McDonald

SECRETARIAT
Grade 7, P. G. Tobia

HOUSING POLICY AND PRIVATE SECTOR
Under-Secretary (G3), Dr C. P. Evans
Grade 5, J. E. Roberts; Mrs H. Chipping; C. L. L. Braun

HOUSING AND URBAN MONITORING AND ANALYSIS
Under-Secretary (G3), Dr C. P. Evans
Grade 5, J. E. Turner; Mrs J. Littlewood; M. Hughes;
  S. Aldridge

HOUSING, SOCIAL POLICY AND RESOURCES
Under-Secretary (G3), Mrs D. S. Phillips
Grade 5, A. Wells; C. H. Bowden; R. S. Horsman;
  L. G. Packer

CONSTRUCTION SPONSORSHIP
Director (G3), P. Ward
Grade 5, J. P. Channing; J. N. Lithgow; Dr
  R. P. Thorogood
Grade 6, R. Wood

WILDLIFE AND COUNTRYSIDE DIRECTORATE
Under-Secretary (G3), J. P. Plowman
Grade 5, R. M. Pritchard; R. W. Bunce; R. Hepworth

PROPERTY AND BUILDINGS
Director (G4), D. O. McCreadie
Grade 5, J. M. Leigh-Pollitt; P. F. Everall
Grade 6, W. J. Marsh

PLANNING DIRECTORATE
Under-Secretary (G3), J. F. Ballard
Heads of Divisions (G5), D. N. Donaldson; R. Jones;
  W. E. Chapman; M. R. Ash; J. Zetter; R. C. Mabey;
  A. M. Oliver

CHIEF ECONOMIST DIRECTORATE
Chief Economist (G3), C. Riley
Economist (G6), R. Davies

LOCAL DEVELOPMENT GROUP
Deputy Secretary (G2), C. J. S. Brearley, CB

SECRETARIAT
HEO, E. A. Carter

LOCAL GOVERNMENT FINANCE POLICY DIRECTORATE
Director, Local Government Finance Policy (G3), N. Kinghan
Heads of Divisions (G5), Miss L. F. Bell; R. J. Gibson;
  M. J. C. Faulkner; Mrs P. Peneck; Dr C. Myerscough

LOCAL GOVERNMENT DIRECTORATE
Director (G3), Mrs L. A. Heath
Heads of Divisions (G5), M. H. Coulshed; P. Rowsell;
  J. R. Footit

REGENERATION DIRECTORATE
Director (G3), M. B. Gahagan
Heads of Divisions (G5), J. Jacobs; G. Lanfer; D. Liston-
  Jones; (G6), I. Nicol

PRIVATE FINANCE UNIT
Head of Unit (G5), J. McCarthy

LEGAL
Solicitor and Legal Adviser (G2), Mrs M. A. Morgan, CB
Deputy Solicitors (G3), A. D. Roberts; Ms S. D. Unerman;
  P. J. Szell
Assistant Solicitors (G5), J. L. Comber; I. D. Day; Mrs
  S. Headley; Mrs P. J. Conlon; Mrs G. Hedley-Dent;
  D. W. Jordan; Miss D. C. S. Phillips; Ms A. Brett-Holt;
  D. J. Noble

OFFICE OF THE CHIEF SCIENTIST
Chief Scientist (G3), Dr D. J. Fisk
Head of Division (G5), Dr A. J. Apling

ENVIRONMENT PROTECTION
Senior Director (G2), Miss D. A. Nichols

ENVIRONMENT AND INTERNATIONAL DIRECTORATE
Under-Secretary (G3), Dr D. J. Fisk
Heads of Divisions (G5), R. Mills; C. Whaley; Dr P.
  Hinchcliffe; Dr S. Brown; P. F. Unwin

ENVIRONMENT PROTECTION STATEGY AND WASTES DIRECTORATE
Under-Secretary (G3), P. J. Britton
Heads of Divisions (G5), Mrs L. A. C. Simcock; Mrs H. C.
  Hillier; B. Glicksman; J. Stevens; R. Wilson; J. Adams

WATER AND LAND DIRECTORATE
Director (G3), N. W. Summerton
Heads of Divisions (G5), A. J. C. Simcock; Dr N. R.
  Williams; P. Bristow

Drinking Water Inspectorate
Grade 5, M. J. Rouse

ENVIRONMENTAL AND ENERGY MANAGEMENT
DIRECTORATE
Under-Secretary (G3), J. Hobson
Heads of Divisions (G5), A. K. Galloway; Mrs G. Hackman;
H. Cleary
Grade 6, Dr A. Vincent

REGIONAL OFFICES
— *see* pages 302–3

EXECUTIVE AGENCIES

BUILDING RESEARCH ESTABLISHMENT
Garston, Watford, Herts WD2 7JR
Tel 01923-894040

The BRE carries out research and provides advice on the
design, construction and performance of buildings, and
supports government departments in their related respon-
sibilities. The BRE is due to be privatized by February
1997.
Chief Executive (G3), R. G. Courtney
Deputy Chief Executive and Group Director (G4),
N. O. Milbank
Directors of Groups (G5), Dr V. H. C. Crisp; Dr A. B. Birtles;
R. Driscoll; M. Shaw
Director and Privatization Co-ordinator (G4), Dr W. D.
Woolley
Finance Director (G5), J. Horan
Personnel Director (G6), Mrs A. Elkeles

ORDNANCE SURVEY
— *see* page 331

PLANNING INSPECTORATE
Tollgate House, Houlton Street, Bristol BS2 9DJ
Tel 0117-987 8927

The Inspectorate is responsible for casework involving
planning, housing, roads, environmental and related legis-
lation. It is a joint executive agency of the Department of
the Environment and the Welsh Office.
Chief Executive and Chief Planning Inspector (G3), C. Shepley
Deputy Chief Planning Inspector (G4), J. Greenfield
Assistant Chief Planning Inspectors (G5), R. E. Wilson; Mrs
S. Bruton; J. T. Graham; D. E. John
Director of Planning Appeals (G5), Ms S. Carter
Director of Finance and Management Services (G5), M. Brasher

QUEEN ELIZABETH II CONFERENCE CENTRE
Broad Sanctuary, London SW1P 3EE
Tel 0171-798 4010

The Centre provides conference and banqueting facilities
for both private sector and government use.
Chief Executive (G5), M. C. Buck

THE ENVIRONMENT AGENCY
Hampton House, 20 Albert Embankment, London SE1 7TJ
Tel 0171-820 5012
Rio House, Waterside Drive, Aztec West, Almondsbury,
Bristol BS12 4UD
Tel 01454-624400

The Environment Agency came into being on 1 April 1996
under the Environment Act 1995. It brings together the
work formerly undertaken by the National Rivers Authority, HM Inspectorate of Pollution, the waste regulation
authorities and some technical units of the Department of
the Environment. The Agency is responsible for pollution
prevention and control in England and Wales, and for the
management and use of water resources, including flood

defences, fisheries and navigation. It has head offices in
London and Bristol and eight regional offices which are
mainly concerned with operational activities.

THE BOARD
Chairman, The Lord de Ramsey
Members, P. Burnham; Prof. R. Edwards; I. Farookhi;
E. Gallagher; Sir Richard George; N. Haigh, OBE;
C. Hampson, CBE; J. Harman; Mrs K. Morgan; J. Norris;
D. Osborn, Dr A. Powell, T. Rodgers, Mrs J. Wykes

THE EXECUTIVE
Chief Executive, E. Gallagher
Director of Finance, N. Reader
Director of Personnel, G. Duncan
Director of Pollution Prevention and Control, D. Slater
Director of Water Management, G. Mance
Director of Operations, A. Robertson
Director of Public Affairs, M. Wilson
Director of Legal Services, R. Navarro
Chief Scientist, J. Pentreath

ROYAL COMMISSION ON
ENVIRONMENTAL POLLUTION
Church House, Great Smith Street, London SW1P 3BZ
Tel 0171-276 2080

The Commission was set up in 1970 to advise on matters,
both national and international, concerning the pollution
of the environment; on the adequacy of research in this
field; and the future possibilities of danger to the environ-
ment.
Chairman, Sir John Houghton, CBE, FRS
Members, Sir Geoffrey Allen, FRS; Revd Prof. M. C. Banner;
Prof. G.S. Boulton, FRS, FRSE; Prof. C. E. D. Chilvers;
Prof. R. Clift, OBE, FENG.; Dr P. Doyle, CBE, FRSE;
J. Flemming; Sir Martin Holdgate, CB; Prof. R. Macrory;
Prof. M. G. Marmot, PH.D.; Prof. J. G. Morris, CBE, FRS;
Dr Penelope A. Rowlatt; The Earl of Selborne, KBE, FRS
Secretary, D. R. Lewis

EQUAL OPPORTUNITIES COMMISSION
Overseas House, Quay Street, Manchester M3 3HN
Tel 0161-833 9244

Press Office, 36 Broadway, London SW1H 0XH. Tel: 0171-
222 1110
Other Offices, Stock Exchange House, 7 Nelson Mandela
Place, Glasgow G2 1QW. Tel: 0141-248 5833; Caerwys
House, Windsor Place, Cardiff. Tel: 01222-343552

The Commission was set up by Parliament in 1975 as a
result of the passing of the Sex Discrimination Act. It works
towards the elimination of discrimination on the grounds
of sex or marital status and to promote equality of
opportunity between men and women generally. It is
responsible to the Department for Education and Employ-
ment.
Chairwoman (£45,320), Ms K. Bahl
Deputy Chairwomen, Lady (Diana) Brittan, CBE; Mrs E.
Hodder
Members, Ms A. Gibson; Ms C. Wells, OBE; P. Smith;
Ms M. Berg; R. K.Fleeman; R. Grayson; Dr J. Stringer;
Ms E. Symons; Prof. T. Rees; Ms G. James
Chief Executive, P. Naish

EQUAL OPPORTUNITIES COMMISSION FOR NORTHERN IRELAND
Chamber of Commerce House, 22 Great Victoria Street, Belfast BT2 7BA
Tel 01232-242752
Chair and Chief Executive, Mrs J. Smyth

EXCHEQUER AND AUDIT DEPARTMENT
— *see* National Audit Office

ECGD (EXPORT CREDITS GUARANTEE DEPARTMENT)
PO Box 2200, 2 Exchange Tower, Harbour Exchange Square, London E14 9GS
Tel 0171-512 7000

ECGD (Export Credits Guarantee Department), the official export credit insurer, is a separate government department responsible to the President of the Board of Trade and functions under the Export and Investment Guarantees Act 1991. This enables ECGD to facilitate UK exports by making available export credit insurance to British firms engaged in selling overseas and to guarantee repayment to banks in Britain providing finance for export credit for goods sold on credit terms of two years or more. The Act also empowers ECGD to insure British private investment overseas against political risks such as war, expropriation and restrictions on remittances.
Chief Executive, W. B. Willott, CB
Group Directors (*G3*), V. P. Lunn-Rockliffe (*Asset Management*); J. R. Weiss (*Underwriting*); T. M. Jaffray (*Resource Management*)

DIVISIONS
Head, Finance (*G5*), J. C. W. Croall
Head, Central Services (*G5*), P. J. Callaghan
Head, Underwriting Divisions (*G5*), M. Lemmon (*Division 1*); M. D. Pentecost (*Division 3*); Mrs M. E. Maddox (*Division 4*); S. R. Dodgson (*Division 5*); C. J. Leeds (*Division 6*)
Head, Office of the General Counsel (*G5*), R. G. Elden
Head, International Debt (*G5*), A. Steele
Head, Claims (*G5*), R. F. Lethbridge
Head, Treasury Management (*G5*), J. S. Snowdon
Head, Risk Management (*G5*), P. J. Radford
Head, Chief Executive's Division (*G5*), R. Gotts
Head, IT Services (*G6*), E. J. Walsby
Head, Internal Audit (*G6*), G. Cassell
Head, Operational Research (*G6*), Ms R. Kaufman

EXPORT GUARANTEES ADVISORY COUNCIL
Chairman, R. T. Fox, CBE
Other Members, B. P. Dewe Mathews, CBE, TD; T. M. Evans, CBE; Sir Frank Lampl; G. W. Lynch; J. W. Melbourn, CBE; D. B. Newlands; Sir Derek Thomas, KCMG; The Viscount Weir

OFFICE OF FAIR TRADING
Field House, Bream's Buildings, London EC4A 1PR
Tel 0171-242 2858

The Office of Fair Trading is a non-ministerial government department headed by the Director-General of Fair Trading. It keeps commercial activities in the UK under review and seeks to protect consumers against unfair trading practices. The Director-General's consumer protection duties under the Fair Trading Act 1973, together with his responsibilities under the Consumer Credit Act 1974, the Estate Agents Act 1979, the Control of Misleading Advertisements Regulations 1988, and the Unfair Terms in Consumer Contracts Regulations 1994, are administered by the Office's Consumer Affairs Division. The Competition Policy Division is concerned with monopolies and mergers (under the Fair Trading Act 1973), and the Director-General's other responsibilities for competition matters, including those under the Restrictive Trade Practices Act 1976, the Resale Prices Act 1976, the Competition Act 1980, the Financial Services Act 1986 and the Broadcasting Act 1990. The Office is the UK competent authority on the application of the European Commission's competition rules, and also liaises with the Commission on consumer protection initiatives.
Director-General, J. Bridgeman
Deputy Director-General, J. W. Preston, CB

CONSUMER AFFAIRS DIVISION
Director (*G3*), G. Horton
Assistant Directors (*G5*), P. Casey; R. Watson; M. Graham

COMPETITION POLICY DIVISION
Director (*G3*), Dr M. Howe, CB
Assistant Directors (*G5*), A. J. White; H. L. Emden; E. L. Whitehorn; S. Wood; M. Parr

LEGAL DIVISION
Director (*G3*), Miss P. Edwards
Assistant Directors (*G5*), M. A. Khan; P. T. Rostron
Establishment and Finance Officer (*G5*), Miss C. Banks
Chief Information Officer (*G6*), D. Hill

FOREIGN AND COMMONWEALTH OFFICE
Downing Street, London SW1A 2AL
Tel 0171-270 3000

The Foreign and Commonwealth Office provides, mainly through diplomatic missions, the means of communication between the British Government and other governments and international governmental organizations for the discussion and negotiation of all matters falling within the field of international relations. It is responsible for alerting the British Government to the implications of developments overseas; for protecting British interests overseas; for protecting British citizens abroad; for explaining British policies to, and cultivating friendly relations with, governments overseas; and for the discharge of British responsibilities to the dependent territories.

Secretary of State, The Rt. Hon. Malcolm Rifkind, QC, MP
  Principal Private Secretary, W. G. Ehrman
  Private Secretaries, D. J. Chilcott; S. J. Sharpe
  Special Advisers, C. Blunt; G. Carter
Minister of State (*Minister for Overseas Development*), The Baroness Chalker of Wallasey, PC
  Private Secretary, R. Calvert
  Parliamentary Private Secretary, A. Hargreaves, MP
Ministers of State, David Davis, MP (*Minister for Europe*); The Rt. Hon. Jeremy Hanley, MP; Sir Nicholas Bonsor, Bt, MP
  Private Secretaries, M. Tatham; J. Slater; T. Barrow
Parliamentary Under-Secretary of State, Dr Liam Fox, MP
Parliamentary Relations Unit, E. Jenkinson (*Head*); A. Mehmet, MVO (*Deputy Head and Parliamentary Clerk*)
Permanent Under-Secretary of State and Head of the Diplomatic Service, Sir John Coles, KCMG
  Private Secretary, J. King

Deputy Under-Secretaries, J. R. Young, CMG (*Chief Clerk*);
P. Lever, CMG (*Economic Director*); J. Q. Greenstock, CMG
(*Political Director*); A. Galsworthy; A. Burns, CMG;
J. Rollo
Legal Adviser, Sir Franklin Berman, KCMG, QC
*Deputy Political Director and UK Perm. Rep. on the Council of
WEU*, E. Jones Parry
Director of Information Systems, R. Dibble
Principal Finance Officer and Chief Inspector, K. R. Tebbit
Assistant Under-Secretaries, S. J. L. Wright; J. R. de
Fonblanque; D. J. M. Dain; C. Battiscombe, CMG;
W. Marsden, CMG; P. J. Torry; F. F. Mingay, CMG;
R. H. Smith; F. N. Richards, CVO, CMG; R. Dales; G. Fry;
A. Hunt, CMG; J. A. Shepherd, CMG
HM Vice-Marshal of the Diplomatic Corps, P. S. Astley, LVO

HEADS OF DEPARTMENTS (DS4)

*Aid Policy Department, S. Chakrabarti
Aviation and Maritime Department, R. A. Kealy
British Diplomatic Spouses Association, Mrs C. Young
Central European Department, H. Pearce
Commonwealth Co-ordination Department, D. A. Broad
Commonwealth Foreign and Security Policy Unit, Ms A. Pringle
Conference Unit, M. Dalton
Consular Division, S. F. Howarth
Cultural Relations Department, A. D. Sprake
Counter Terrorism Policy Department, T. Fean
Eastern Adriatic Unit, N. K. Darroch
Eastern Department, R. D. Wilkinson
*Economic Advisers Department, J. Rollo
*Economic Relations Department, N. Westcott
Engineering Services, I. Whitehead
Environment, Science and Energy Department, D. E. Lyscom
Equatorial Africa Department, Ms A. Grant
European Community Department (External), R. Stagg
European Community Department (Internal), A. J. Cary
Far Eastern and Pacific Department, D. Coates
Financial Compliance Unit, M. Mayhew
Fundamental Expenditure Review Unit, R. Brinkley
Home Estate Department, D. C. Brown, CMG
Hong Kong Department, S. L. Cowper Coles
Honours Unit, R. M. Sands
Human Rights Policy Unit, R. P. Nash
Information Department, P. J. Dun
Information Systems Department, P. McDermott
Internal Audit, R. Elias
Joint Assistance Unit (Central Europe), S. Laing
Joint Assistance Unit (Eastern Europe), M. McCulloch
†*Joint Export Promotion Directorate*, A. Hunt
Latin America Department, H. Hogger
Library and Records Department, S. I. Soutar
*Management Consultancy and Inspection Department,
S. R. H. Pease
Medical and Welfare Unit, Miss D. M. Symes, OBE
Middle East Department, N. W. Browne
Migration and Visa Department, M. E. Frost
National Audit Office, R. Burwood
Near East and North Africa Department, P. W. Ford
News Department, N. E. Sheinwald
Non-Proliferation Department, B. Cleghorn
North America Department, P. J. Priestley
OSCE and Council of Europe, C. A. Munro
Overseas Estate Department, M. H. R. Bertram, CBE
Overseas Inspectorate, K. R. Tebbit (*Chief Inspector and
Principal Finance Officer*)

Overseas Police Adviser, L. Grundy (*Senior Police Adviser*)
Permanent Under-Secretary's Department, P. January
Personnel Management Department, P. R. Sizeland
Personnel Policy Unit, Ms P. Major
Personnel Services Department, G. G. Wetherell
Policy Planning Staff, Miss A. M. Leslie
PROSPER, C. J. Edgerton, OBE
Protocol Department, R. S. Gorham (*First Assistant Marshal of
the Diplomatic Corps*)
Purchasing Directorate, M. Gower
Republic of Ireland Department, D. A. Lamont
Research and Analysis Department, S. Jack
Resource and Finance Department, J. W. Thorp
Royal Matters Unit, B. Money
Security Department, T. Duggin
Security Policy Department, R. H. Gozney
Services, Planning and Resources Department, Mrs J. Link, LVO
South Asian Department, C. Elmes
South Atlantic and Antarctic Department, A. J. Longrigg
South-East Asian Department, N. J. Cox
Southern Africa Department, B. H. Dinwiddy
Southern European Department, H. B. Warren-Gash
Support Services Department, M. Carr
Training Department, I. W. Mackley
United Nations Department, Miss M. G. D. Evans, CMG
Western European Department, A. Layden
West Indian and Atlantic Department, C. Drace-Francis
Whitley Council, W. Evans

EXECUTIVE AGENCY

WILTON PARK CONFERENCE CENTRE
Wiston House, Steyning, W. Sussex BN44 3DZ
Tel 01903-815020

The Centre organizes international affairs conferences and
is hired out to government departments and commercial
users.
Chief Executive, R. Langhorne

THE SECRET INTELLIGENCE SERVICE
(MI6)
Vauxhall Cross, PO Box 1300, London SE1 1BD

The Secret Intelligence Service produces secret intelligence in support of the Government's security, defence,
foreign and economic policies. It was placed on a statutory
footing by the Intelligence Services Act 1994. The Act also
established an Intelligence Services Tribunal, which hears
complaints made against the Service.
Director-General, Sir David Spedding, KCMG, CVO, OBE

GOVERNMENT COMMUNICATIONS
HEADQUARTERS (GCHQ)
Priors Road, Cheltenham, Glos GL52 5AJ
Tel 01242-221491

GCHQ produces signal intelligence in support of the
Government's security, defence, foreign and economic
policies. It also provides advice and assistance to government departments and the armed forces on the security of
their communications and information technology systems. It was placed on a statutory footing by the Intelligence Services Act 1994. The Act also established an
Intelligence Services Tribunal, which hears complaints
made against GCHQ.
Director, D. B. Omand

*Joint Foreign and Commonwealth Office/Overseas Development
Administration department

†Joint Foreign and Commonwealth Office/Department of Trade and
Industry directorate

CORPS OF QUEEN'S MESSENGERS
Support Services Department, Foreign and
Commonwealth Office, London SW1A 2AH
Tel 0171-270 2779

Superintendent of the Corps of Queen's Messengers,
Maj. I. G. M. Bamber
Queen's Messengers, Maj. J. E. A. Andre;
Cdr. D. H. Barraclough; Maj. A. N. D. Bols;
Lt.-Cdr. K. E. Brown; Lt.-Col. W. P. A. Bush;
Lt.-Col. M. B. de S. Clayton; Capt. G. Courtauld;
Maj. P. C. H. Dening-Smitherman;
Sqn. Ldr. J. S. Frizzell; Capt. N. C. E. Gardner;
Cdr. P. G. Gregson; Maj. D. A. Griffiths;
Wg Cdr. J. O. Jewiss; Lt.-Col. J. M. C. Kimmins;
Lt.-Col. R. C. Letchworth; Maj. D. R. Nevile;
Maj. K. J. Rowbottom; Maj. M. R. Senior;
Cdr. K. M. C. Simmons, AFC; Maj. P. M. O. Springfield;
Maj. J. S. Steele; Col. D. W. F. Taylor

FOREIGN COMPENSATION COMMISSION
Room 013, 4 Central Buildings, Matthew Parker Street,
London SW1H 9NL
Tel 0171-210 0400/5

The Commission was set up by the Foreign Compensation Act 1950 primarily to distribute, under Orders in
Council, funds received from other governments in
accordance with agreements to pay compensation for
expropriated British property and other losses sustained
by British nationals.

The Commission also has the duty of registering claims
for British-owned property in contemplation of agreements with other countries, and it has done so in seven
instances since 1950.

Chairman, A. W. E. Wheeler, CBE
Secretary, A. N. Grant

FORESTRY COMMISSION
231 Corstorphine Road, Edinburgh EH12 7AT
Tel 0131-334 0303

The Forestry Commission is the government department
responsible for forestry policy in Great Britain. It reports
directly to forestry ministers (i.e. the Secretary of State for
Scotland, who takes the lead role, the Minister of Agriculture, Fisheries and Food and the Secretary of State for
Wales), to whom it is responsible for advice on forestry
policy and for the implementation of that policy. There is a
statutorily-appointed Chairman and Board of Commissioners (four executive and seven non-executive) with
prescribed duties and powers.

The Commission's principal objectives are to protect
Britain's forests and woodlands; expand Britain's forest
area; enhance the economic value of the forest resources;
conserve and improve the biodiversity, landscape and
cultural heritage of forests and woodlands; develop opportunities for woodland recreation; and increase public
understanding of and community participation in forestry.
Forest Enterprise, a trading body operating as an executive
agency of the Commission, manages its forestry estate on a
multi-use basis.

Chairman (part-time) (£36,965), Sir Peter Hutchison, Bt.,
   CBE
Director-General and Deputy Chairman (G2), D. J. Bills
Commissioner, Administration and Finance (G3), D. S. Grundy

Head of the Forestry Authority (G3), D. L. Foot
Secretary to the Commissioners (G5), T. J. D. Rollinson

FOREST ENTERPRISE, 231 Corstorphine Road, Edinburgh
   EH12 7AT. Tel: 0131-334 0303. *Chief Executive (acting),*
   G. M. Cowie

REGISTRY OF FRIENDLY SOCIETIES
15 Great Marlborough Street, London W1V 2LL
Tel 0171-437 9992

The Registry of Friendly Societies is a government
department serving three statutory bodies, the Building
Societies Commission, the Friendly Societies Commis-
sion, and the Central Office of the Registry of Friendly
Societies (together with the Assistant Registrar of Friendly
Societies for Scotland).

The Building Societies Commission was established by
the Building Societies Act 1986. The Commission is
responsible for the supervision of building societies and
administers the system of regulation. It also advises the
Treasury and other government departments on matters
relating to building societies.

The Friendly Societies Commission was established by
the Friendly Societies Act 1992. Its responsibilities for the
supervision of friendly societies parallel those of the
Building Societies Commission for building societies.

The Central Office of the Registry of Friendly Societies
provides a public registry for mutual organizations registered under the Building Societies Act 1986, Friendly
Societies Acts 1974 and 1992, and the Industrial and
Provident Societies Act 1965. It is responsible for the
supervision of friendly societies and credit unions, and
advises the Government on issues affecting those societies.

BUILDING SOCIETIES COMMISSION
Chairman, G. E. Fitchew
Deputy Chairman, M. Owen
Commissioners, J. M. Palmer; *T. F. Mathews, CBE;
   *F. E. Worsley; *F. G. Sunderland; *N. Fox Bassett; *Sir
   James Birrell
* part-time

FRIENDLY SOCIETIES COMMISSION
Chairman, D. W. Lee
Commissioners, F. da Rocha; *A. Wilson; *J. A. Geddes;
   *P. E. Couse; *Dr J. Dine
* part-time

CENTRAL OFFICE
Chief Registrar, G. E. Fitchew
Assistant Registrars, A. J. Perrett; Ms S. Eden; D. A. W.
   Stevens

THE REGISTRY
First Commissioner and Chief Registrar (G2), G. E. Fitchew

BUILDING SOCIETIES COMMISSION STAFF
Grade 3, M. Owen
Grade 4, J. M. Palmer
Grade 5, D. A. W. Stevens; W. Champion; M. Coombs;
   E. Engstrom
Grade 6, N. F. Digance

FRIENDLY SOCIETIES COMMISSION STAFF
Grade 4, D. W. Lee
Grade 6, F. da Rocha

CENTRAL SERVICES STAFF
Legal Adviser (G4), A. J. Perrett
Establishment and Finance Officer (G5), J. Stevens

Legal Staff (G5), C. Gregory; *(G6)*, P. G. Ashcroft;
C. Stallard

REGISTRY OF FRIENDLY SOCIETIES, SCOTLAND
58 Frederick Street, Edinburgh EH2 1NB
Tel 0131-226 3224
Assistant Registrar (G5), J. L. J. Craig, WS

GAMING BOARD FOR GREAT BRITAIN
Berkshire House, 168–173 High Holborn, London
WC1V 7AA
Tel 0171-306 6200

The Board was established in 1968 and is responsible to the
Home Secretary. It is the regulatory body for casinos, bingo
clubs, gaming machines and the larger society and all local
authority lotteries in Great Britain. Its functions are to
ensure that those involved in organizing gaming and
lotteries are fit and proper to do so and to keep gaming free
from criminal infiltration; to ensure that gaming and
lotteries are run fairly and in accordance with the law; and
to advise the Home Secretary on developments in gaming
and lotteries so that the law can respond to change.
Chairman (part-time) (£33,995), Lady Littler
Secretary, T. Kavanagh

OFFICE OF GAS SUPPLY
Stockley House, 130 Wilton Road, London SW1V 1LQ
Tel 0171-828 0898

The Office of Gas Supply (Ofgas) is a regulatory body set
up under the Gas Act 1986. It is headed by the Director-
General of Gas Supply, who is independent of ministerial
control.
  The principal functions of Ofgas are to control British
Gas prices and levels of service; to protect the interests of
the gas consumer; and to facilitate the development of
competition in the gas market. Other functions are to grant
licences to gas suppliers and to investigate complaints.
Director-General, Ms C. Spottiswoode
Chief Economic Adviser, Dr Eileen Marshall
Legal Adviser, D. R. M. Long
Director, Public Affairs, C. Webb
Director, Consumer Affairs and Licensing, J. Golay
Director, Administration, R. Field

OFFICE OF GAS REGULATION NORTHERN
IRELAND
Brookmount Buildings, 42 Fountain Street, Belfast BT1 5EE
Tel 01232-311575

OFGAS NI is the regulatory body for the gas industry in
Northern Ireland.
Director-General of Gas for Northern Ireland, D. McIldoon

GOVERNMENT ACTUARY'S DEPARTMENT
22 Kingsway, London WC2B 6LE
Tel 0171-211 2600

The Government Actuary provides a consulting service to
government departments, the public sector, and overseas
governments. The actuaries advise on social security
schemes and superannuation arrangements in the public
sector at home and abroad, on population and other
statistical studies, and on government supervision of
insurance companies and friendly societies.
Government Actuary, C. D. Daykin, CB
Directing Actuaries, D. G. Ballantine; D. H. Loades, CB; A. G.
Young
Chief Actuaries, E. I. Battersby; Ms W. M. Beaver; A. J.
Chamberlain; T. W. Hewitson; A. I. Johnston; D. Lewis;
J. C. A. Rathbone

GOVERNMENT HOSPITALITY FUND
8 Cleveland Row, London SW1A 1DH
Tel 0171-210 3000

The Government Hospitality Fund was instituted in 1908
for the purpose of organizing official hospitality on a
regular basis with a view to the promotion of international
goodwill. It is responsible to the Foreign and Commonwealth Office.
Minister in Charge, Sir Nicholas Bonsor, Bt., MP
Secretary, Col. T. Earl

GOVERNMENT OFFICES FOR THE
REGIONS

The Government Offices for the Regions were established
in April 1994. They combine the former regional offices of
the Departments of the Environment, Trade and Industry,
Education and Employment, and Transport. The regional
directors are accountable to the Secretaries of State of all
four Departments. The offices' role is to promote a
coherent approach to competitiveness, sustainable economic development and regeneration using public and
private resources.
Central Unit, Room C10/19A, 2 Marsham Street, London
SW1P 3EB
Tel 0171-276 4629
Head of Central Unit (G3), G. Watson
Resources, Planning and Administration (G5), T. Abraham
Personnel Policy (G5), B. Hopson

EASTERN
Secretariat: Enterprise House, Vision Park, Histon,
Cambridge CB4 4DZ
Tel 01223-202065

Regional Director (G3), J. Turner
Directors (G5), C. Dunabin (*Housing, Environment and
Regeneration*); T. Bird (*Planning, Transport and Europe*);
M. Oldham (*Trade and Industry*); Mrs C. Hunter
(*Employment and Training*)

EAST MIDLANDS
Secretariat: The Belgrave Centre, Stanley Place, Talbot
Street, Nottingham NG1 5GG
Tel 0115-971 9971

Regional Director (G3), M. Lanyon
Directors (G4), D. Morrison (*Environment and Transport*);
(*G5*), M. Briggs (*Trade and Industry*); A. Davies
(*Employment and Training*)

LONDON
Secretariat: 10th Floor, Riverwalk House, 157–161
Millbank, London SW1P 4RR
Tel 0171-217 3456

Regional Director (G2), R. Young

Directors (*G3*), J. A. Owen (*Regeneration*); M. Lambirth
(*Planning and Transport*); B. Glickman (*Skills Enterprise
and Education*); (*G5*), Mrs J. Bridges (*Planning*); G. Emes
(*Transport Assessment*); Mrs L. Meek (*Strategy and Co-
ordination Unit*); (*G6*), A. Weeden (*Transport*)

MERSEYSIDE
Secretariat: Room 403, Graeme House, Derby Square,
Liverpool L2 7SU
Tel 0151-224 6300

Regional Director (*G3*), J. Stoker
Directors (*G5*), I. Urqhart (*Skills and Enterprise*); S. Dunmore
(*Regeneration, Transport and Planning*); Ms P. Jackson
(*Competitiveness and Europe*)

NORTH-EAST
Secretariat: Room 404, Stangate House, 2 Groat Market,
Newcastle upon Tyne NE1 1YN
Tel 0191-201 3300

Regional Director (*G3*), Ms P. Denham
Directors (*G5*), J. Darlington (*Planning, Environment and
Transport*); Miss D. Caudle (*Regeneration and Housing*);
A. Dell (*Competitiveness, Industry and Europe*); S. Geary
(*Education Skills and Business Development*); (*G6*), Mrs D.
Pearce (*Strategy and Resources*)

NORTH-WEST
Secretariat: 20th Floor, Sunley Tower, Piccadilly Plaza,
Manchester M1 4BE
Tel 0161-952 4000

Regional Director (*G3*), Miss M. Neville-Rolfe
Directors, (*G5*), B. Isherwood (*Regeneration*); D. Higham
(*Competitiveness*); P. Styche (*Infrastructure and Planning*);
P. Keen (*Skills and Enterprise*); (*G6*), D. Duff (*TEC
Operations and Finance*); D. Stewart (*Europe*)

SOUTH-EAST
Secretariat: 2nd Floor, Bridge House, 1 Walnut Tree Close,
Guildford, Surrey GU1 4GA
Tel 01483-882481

Regional Director (*G3*), Mrs G. Ashmore
Directors (*G5*), G. B. Wilson (*Hants/IOW*); N. Wilson
(*Berks/Oxon/Bucks*); J. Vaughan (*Kent*); E. Beston
(*Surrey/E. and W. Sussex*); Mrs E. A. Baker (*Regional
Strategy Team*)

SOUTH-WEST
Secretariat: 4th Floor, The Pithay, Bristol BS1 2PB
Tel 0117-900 1708

Regional Director (*G3*), B. H. Leonard
Directors (*G5*), S. McQuillin (*Devon and Cornwall*);
M. Quinn (*Environment and Transport*); T. Shearer
(*Education, Trade and Industry*); (*G6*), D. Way (*Strategy
and Resources*)

WEST MIDLANDS
Secretariat: 6th Floor, 77 Paradise Circus, Queensway,
Birmingham B1 2DT
Tel 0121-212 5000

Regional Director (*G3*), D. Ritchie
Directors (*G4*), Dr H. M. Sutton (*Trade, Industrial
Development and Europe*); (*G5*), Mrs P. Holland (*Housing
and Regeneration*); P. Langley (*Planning, Transport and
Environment*); H. Tollyfield (*Education, Skills and
Enterprise*); Mrs L. Eastwood (*Resource Management*)

YORKSHIRE AND HUMBERSIDE
Secretariat: PO Box 213, City House, New Station Street,
Leeds LS1 4US
Tel 0113-280 0600

Regional Director (*G3*), J. Walker
Directors (*G4*), Ms S. Seymour (*Strategy and Europe*); (*G5*),
I. Crowther (*Environment, Planning and Transport*);
I. Kerry (*Regeneration*); G. Dyche (*Business, Enterprise and
Skills*); (*G6*), N. Best (*Personnel and Resources*)

DEPARTMENT OF HEALTH
Richmond House, 79 Whitehall, London SW1A 2NS
Tel 0171-210 3000

The Department of Health is responsible for the provision
of the National Health Service in England and for social
care, including oversight of personal social services run by
local authorities in England for children, the elderly, the
infirm, the handicapped and other persons in need. It is
responsible for health promotion and has functions relating
to public and environmental health, food safety and nutrition. The Department is also responsible for the ambulance
and emergency first aid services, under the Civil Defence
Act 1948. The Department represents the UK at the
European Union and other international organizations
including the World Health Organization. It also supports
UK-based healthcare and pharmaceutical industries.
Secretary of State for Health, The Rt. Hon. Stephen Dorrell, MP
    Principal Private Secretary, Ms C. Moriarty
    Private Secretaries, J. Holden; S. Gallagher
    Special Advisers, T. Hockley; T. Rycroft
    Parliamentary Private Secretary, D. Faber, MP
Minister of State, Gerald Malone, MP
    Private Secretary, Ms K. Fraser
    Parliamentary Private Secretary, N. Waterson, MP
Parliamentary Under-Secretaries of State, The Baroness
    Cumberlege, CBE; John Horam, MP; Simon Burns, MP
    Private Secretaries, Ms E. Woodeson;
    Mrs M. Weatherseed; A. Lapsley
Parliamentary Clerk, G. Wakeman
Permanent Secretary (*G1*), Sir Graham Hart, KCB
    Private Secretary, Dr M. Gray
Chief Medical Officer (*G1A*), Dr Sir Kenneth Calman, KCB
Chief Executive, NHS Executive (*G1A*), A. Langlands
Deputy Chief Medical Officer (*G2*), Dr J. S. Metters, CB

NATIONAL HEALTH SERVICE POLICY BOARD
Chairman, The Secretary of State for Health
Members, Gerald Malone, MP (*Minister of State*); The
    Baroness Cumberlege, CBE; J. Horam, MP; J. Bowis, OBE,
    MP (*Parliamentary Under-Secretaries*); Dr Sir Kenneth
    Calman, KCB (*Chief Medical Officer*); A. Langlands (*Chief
    Executive, NHS Executive*); Sir Graham Hart, KCB
    (*Permanent Secretary*); Mrs Y. Moores; B. Baker; Dr Sir
    Stuart Burgess, CBE; K. Ackroyd; Miss J. Trotter, OBE;
    J. Greetham, CBE; I. Mills; W. Wells; Prof. A.
    Breckenridge

PUBLIC HEALTH POLICY GROUP

HEALTH ASPECTS OF ENVIRONMENT AND FOOD
DIVISION
Under-Secretary (*G3*), Dr E. Rubery
Head of Branches, Dr R. Skinner; Dr E. Smales; Mrs M. Fry;
    C. P. Kendall

SOCIAL CARE GROUP
Chief Social Services Inspector, Sir Herbert Laming, CBE
Head of Social Care Policy, T. R. H. Luce, CB
Deputy Chief Inspectors, D. Gilroy; Ms A. Nottage
Assistant Secretaries (*G5*), R. M. Orton; N. F. Duncan;
    D. P. Walden; Mrs E. Hunter-Johnston; R. Tyrrell

Assistant Chief Inspectors (HQ), J. Kennedy; F. Tolan; Mrs
W. Rose
Assistant Chief Inspectors (Regions), S. Allard; J. Cypher;
B. Riddell; A. Jones; D. G. Lambert; Mrs P. K. Hall;
C. P. Brearley; J. Fraser; Mrs L. Hoare; Ms J. Owen

HEALTH PROMOTION DIVISION
Under-Secretary (G3), G. J. F. Podger
Principal Medical Officer (G4), Dr D. McInnes
Assistant Secretaries (G5), J. F. Sharpe, CBE; Miss A. Mithani;
Ms L. Lockyer; K. J. Guinness

NURSING GROUP
Chief Nursing Officer/Director of Nursing (G3), Mrs
Y. Moores
Assistant Chief Nursing Officers (G4), Mrs P. Cantrill; Mrs G.
Stevens; (G5), Dr G. Chapman; C. Butler

NHS EXECUTIVE
Quarry House, Quarry Hill, Leeds LS2 7UE
Tel 0113-254 5000
Chief Executive, A. Langlands
Director of Human and Corporate Resources, K. Jarrold
Director of Finance and Corporate Information, C. Reeves
Medical Director, Dr G. Winyard
Chief Nursing Officer, Mrs Y. Moores
Director of Research and Development, Prof. J. D. Swales
Director of Planning and Performance Management,
A. D. M. Liddell

PERSONNEL DIRECTORATE
Director of Human and Corporate Resources (G2), K. Jarrold

PERSONNEL DIVISION
Deputy Director (G3), M. Deegan
Under-Secretary (G3), R. M. Drury
Assistant Secretaries (G5), B. A. J. Bennett; Miss G. Newton;
Miss A. Simkins; Mrs E. Alkalifa

RESEARCH AND DEVELOPMENT DIVISION
Director of Research and Development, Prof. J. D. Swales
Deputy Director of Research Management (G4), Dr C.
Henshall
Assistant Secretaries (G5), Mrs J. Griffin; Dr P. Greenaway;
J. Ennis; Dr D. Gardiner
Senior Medical Officers (G5), Dr J. Toy; Dr S. Bannerjee; Dr
C. Law
Senior Principal Research Officers (G6), Ms A. Kauder;
Dr C. Davies
Nursing Officer (G6), Dr E. Meerabeau

HEALTH CARE DIRECTORATE
Deputy Chief Medical Officer (G2), Dr G. Winyard

PUBLIC HEALTH DIVISION
Grade 4, Dr T. Mann
Assistant Secretary (G5), P. Spellman
Senior Medical Officers (G5), Dr M. Charny; Dr I. Bowns;
Dr A. Lakhani; Dr J. Carpenter; Dr A. Burnett

MEDICAL EDUCATION, TRAINING AND STAFFING
DIVISION
Senior Principal Medical Officer (G3), J. R. W. Hangartner
Senior Medical Officers (G5), Dr R. Cairncross; Dr
C. Marvin; Dr S. Horsley
Assistant Secretaries (G5), S. D. Catling; T. Ashe;
R. Naysmith

PRIMARY CARE AND DENTAL SERVICES
Deputy Secretary (G2), A. D. M. Liddell

PRIMARY CARE DIVISION 2
Grade 4, J. A. Thompson
Senior Dental Officers, C. Audrey; K. A. Eaton; I. Cooper

DENTAL SERVICES BRANCH
Grade 4, J. A. Thompson
Head of Pharmaceutical and Optical Services (G5), G. Denham

OFFICE OF THE CHIEF DENTAL OFFICER
Chief Dental Officer, R. B. Mouatt
Dental Officer, A. J. Hawkes

OFFICE OF THE CHIEF PHARMACIST
Chief Pharmaceutical Officer (G4), B. H. Hartley

FINANCE AND PERFORMANCE DIRECTORATE
Director (G2), C. L. Reeves

FINANCE BRANCH
Under-Secretary (Health) (G3), A. B. Barton
Assistant Secretaries (G5), J. M. Brownlee; A. McNeil; R. J.
Tredgett; J. Stopes-Roe

FINANCE AND PERFORMANCE DIRECTORATE A
Deputy Director (G3), P. Garland
Heads of Branches (G5), H. Gwynn; A. Angilley; M. Sturges;
G. Hetherington; B. Derry; S. Bell

FINANCE AND PERFORMANCE DIVISION B
Deputy Director (G3), R. Douglas
Heads of Branches (G5), J. Tomlinson; S. Saunders;
M. Harris; D. J. Havelock

REGIONAL OFFICES
ANGLIA AND OXFORD, 6–12 Capital Drive, Linford
Wood, Milton Keynes MK14 6QP. *Chairman*, Sir Stuart
Burgess, CBE, PH.D., FRSC; *Regional Director*, Ms
B. Stocking
NORTHERN AND YORKSHIRE, John Snow House, Durham
University Science Park, Durham DH1 3YE. *Chairman*,
J. Greetham, CBE; *Regional Director*, Prof. L. Donaldson
NORTH THAMES, 40 Eastbourne Terrace, London W2 3QR.
Chairman, I. Mills; *Regional Director*, R. Kerr
NORTH WEST, 930–932 Birchwood Boulevard,
Millennium Park, Birchwood, Warrington WA3 7QN.
Chairman, Prof. A. Breckenridge; *Regional Director*,
R. Tinston
SOUTH AND WEST, Westward House, Lime Kiln Close,
Stoke Gifford, Bristol BS12 6SR. *Chairman*, Miss J.
Trotter, OBE; *Regional Director*, A. Laurance
SOUTH THAMES, 40 Eastbourne Terrace, London W2 3QR.
Chairman, W. Wells; *Regional Director*, C. Spry
TRENT, Fulwood House, Old Fulwood Road, Sheffield
S10 3TH. *Chairman*, K. Ackroyd, CBE; *Regional Director*,
N. McKay
WEST MIDLANDS, Arthur Thompson House, 146 Hagley
Road, Birmingham B16 9PA. *Chairman*, B. W. Baker;
Regional Director, B. Edwards, CBE

COMMISSIONING BOARD FOR HIGH SECURITY
PSYCHIATRIC SERVICES
NHS Executive North Thames Regional Office, 40
Eastbourne Terrace, London W2 3QR
Tel 0171-725 5662
Chairman, Mrs A.-M. Nelson
Director, R. Rowden

DEPARTMENTAL RESOURCES AND SERVICES GROUP
Deputy Secretary (G2), J. Pilling, CB

STATISTICS DIVISION
Director of Statistics (G3), Mrs R. J. Butler
Chief Statisticians (G5), R. K. Willmer; G. J. O. Phillpotts

DEPARTMENTAL MANAGEMENT
Principal Establishment Officer (G3), D. J. Clark
Assistant Secretaries (G5), Miss A. Stephenson; P. Allen;
J. E. Knight; Ms P. A. Stewart

INFORMATION SERVICES DIVISION
Head of Division (G4), Dr A. A. Holt
Heads of Branches (G5), J. Bilsby; Mrs L. Wishart; *(G6)*,
Miss S. Blackburn; C. Horsey; Mrs R. Chinn; M.
Rainsford; *(G7)*, Mrs J. Dainty

ECONOMICS AND OPERATIONAL RESEARCH DIVISION
(HEALTH)
Chief Economic Adviser (G3), C. H. Smee
Senior Economic Advisers (G5), Dr S. Harding; J. W. Hurst

INFORMATION DIVISION
Director of Information, Miss R. Christopherson
Deputy Directors, C. P. Wilson (*news*); Mrs A. Rea (*publicity*)

SOLICITOR'S OFFICE
Solicitor (G2), P. K. J. Thompson
Principal Assistant Solicitor (G3), Mrs G. S. Kerrigan

ADVISORY COMMITTEES

ADVISORY COMMITTEE ON THE MICROBIOLOGICAL
SAFETY OF FOOD, Room 601A, Skipton House, 80
London Road, London SEI 6LW. Tel: 0171-972 5049.
Chairman, Prof. D. Georgala
CLINICAL STANDARDS ADVISORY GROUP, Wellington
House, 133–155 Waterloo Road, London SEI 8UG. Tel:
0171-972 4926. *Chairman*, Prof. M. Harris
COMMITTEE ON THE SAFETY OF MEDICINES, Market
Towers, 1 Nine Elms Lane, London SW8 5NQ. Tel:
0171-273 0451. *Chairman*, Prof. M. D. Rawlins
MEDICINES COMMISSION, Market Towers, 1 Nine Elms
Lane, London SW8 5NQ. Tel: 0171-273 0365. *Chairman*,
Prof. D. Lawson, CBE, MD, FRCPEd., FRCP(Glas.)

EXECUTIVE AGENCIES

MEDICINES CONTROL AGENCY
Market Towers, 1 Nine Elms Lane, London SW8 5NQ
Tel 0171-273 0000
The Agency controls medicines through licensing,
monitoring and inspection, and enforces safety standards.
Chief Executive, Dr K. H. Jones

MEDICAL DEVICES AGENCY
Hannibal House, Elephant and Castle, London SEI 6TE
Tel 0171-972 2000
The Agency safeguards the performance, quality and
safety of medical devices.
Director (G4), A. Kent

NHS ESTATES
1 Trevelyan Square, Boar Lane, Leeds LSI 6AE
Tel 0113-254 7000
The agency provides advice and support in the area of
healthcare estate functions to the NHS and the healthcare
industry.
Chief Executive (G3), J. C. Locke

NHS PENSIONS
Hesketh House, 200–220 Broadway, Fleetwood, Lancs
FY7 8LG
Tel 01253-774774
The agency administers the NHS occupational pension
scheme.
Chief Executive (G5), A. F. Cowan

SPECIAL HEALTH AUTHORITIES

ASHWORTH HOSPITAL, Parkbourn, Maghull, Merseyside
L31 IHW. Tel: 0151-473 0303. *Chief Nursing Officer*, Mrs J.
Miles
BROADMOOR HOSPITAL, Crowthorne, Berks RG45 7EG.
Tel: 01344-773111. *Chief Executive*, A. Franey
CENTRE FOR APPLIED MICROBIOLOGY AND RESEARCH,
Porton Down, Salisbury, Wilts SP4 0JG. Tel: 01980-
612100. *Director*, vacant
HEALTH EDUCATION AUTHORITY, Hamilton House,
Mabledon Place, London WCIH 9TX. Tel: 0171-383
3833. *Chairman*, A. Close; *Chief Executive*, S. Fortescue
NATIONAL BLOOD AUTHORITY, Oak House, Reeds
Crescent, Watford, Herts WDI 1QH. Tel: 01923-212121.
Chairman, Sir Colin Walker, OBE; *Chief Executive*, J. Adey
NHS LITIGATION AUTHORITY, 22–23 Blayds Yard,
Leeds LSI 4AD. Tel: 0113-244 6077. *Chairman*, Sir Bruce
Martin, QC
NHS SUPPLIES AUTHORITY, Apex Plaza, Forbury Road,
Reading, Berks RGI IAX. Tel: 01734-595085. *Chairman*,
N. Ward; *National Director of Supplies*, T. Hunt, CBE
RAMPTON HOSPITAL, Retford, Notts DN22 0PD. Tel:
01777-248321. *Manager*, Mrs S. Foley

HEALTH AND SAFETY COMMISSION
Rose Court, 2 Southwark Bridge, London SEI 9HS
Tel 0171-717 6000

The Health and Safety Commission was created under the
Health and Safety at Work etc. Act 1974, with duties to
reform health and safety law, to propose new regulations,
and generally to promote the protection of people at work
and of the public from hazards arising from industrial and
commercial activity, including major industrial accidents
and the transportation of hazardous materials.

The Commission members are appointed by the
Secretary of State for the Environment, although the
Commission assists a number of Secretaries of State
concerned with aspects of its functions. It is made up of
representatives of employers, trades unions and local
authorities, and has a full-time chairman.

The Commission can appoint agents, and it works in
conjunction with local authorities who enforce the Act in
such premises as offices and warehouses.
Chairman, F. J. Davies, CBE
Members, R. Symons, CBE; E. Carrick; C. Chope, OBE; Dr
G. M. Schofield; A. Grant; Ms A. Scully, OBE; Ms C.
Atwell; Ms A. Gibson; Dr M. McKiernan
Secretary, T. A. Gates

HEALTH AND SAFETY EXECUTIVE
Rose Court, 2 Southwark Bridge, London SEI 9HS
Tel 0171-717 6000

The Health and Safety Executive is the Health and Safety
Commission's major instrument. Through its inspectorates it enforces health and safety law in the majority of

industrial premises, to protect people at work and the public. The Executive advises the Commission in its major task of laying down safety standards through regulations and practical guidance for many industrial processes, liaising as necessary with government departments and other institutions. The Executive is also the licensing authority for nuclear installations and the reporting officer on the severity of nuclear incidents in Britain. In carrying out its functions the Executive acts independently of the Government, guided only by the Commission as to general health and safety policy.

Director-General (G2), Miss J. H. Bacon, CB (*at G1A*)
Deputy Director-General (G2), D. C. T. Eves, CB (*HM Chief Inspector of Factories*)
Director, Field Operations Division (G3), Dr A. Ellis
Director, Nuclear Safety (G3), Dr S. A. Harbison
Director, Science and Technology (G3), Dr J. McQuaid
Director, Safety and Major Hazards Policy (G3), M. E. Addison
Director, Health Division (G3), Dr P. J. Graham
Director, Resources and Planning (G3), R. Hillier
Director, Offshore Safety (G3), R. S. Allison, CB

HIGHLANDS AND ISLANDS ENTERPRISE
Bridge House, 20 Bridge Street, Inverness IV1 1QR
Tel 01463-234171

Highlands and Islands Enterprise (HIE) was set up under the Enterprise and New Towns (Scotland) Act 1991. Its role is to design, direct and deliver enterprise development, training, environmental and social projects and services. HIE is made up of a strategic core body and ten Local Enterprise Companies (LECs) to which many of its individual functions are delegated. The LECs design and develop initiatives at local level covering a wide range of economic and community development, training and environmental improvements.

Chairman, F. Morrison, CBE
Chief Executive, I. A. Robertson, CBE

HISTORIC BUILDINGS AND MONUMENTS COMMISSION FOR ENGLAND (ENGLISH HERITAGE)
23 Savile Row, London W1X 1AB
Tel 0171-973 3000

Under the National Heritage Act 1983, the duties of the Commission are to secure the preservation of ancient monuments and historic buildings; to promote the preservation and enhancement of conservation areas; and to promote the public's enjoyment of, and advance their knowledge of, ancient monuments and historic buildings and their preservation. The Commission has advisory committees on historic buildings and areas, ancient monuments, cathedrals and churches, parks and gardens, and London. It is funded by the Department of National Heritage.

Chairman, Sir Jocelyn Stevens, CVO
Commissioners, HRH The Duke of Gloucester; The Lord Cavendish of Furness; Ms B. Cherry; Sir David Wilson; Mrs C. Lycett-Green; J. Seymour; G. Wilson; A. Fane; Lady Gass; Prof. E. Fernie, CBE; R. MacCormac; Ms K. McLeod; R. Morris, FSA
Chief Executive (acting), Ms J. Sharman

HISTORIC BUILDINGS COUNCIL FOR WALES
Brunel House, 2 Fitzalan Road, Cardiff CF2 1UY
Tel 01222-500200

The Council's function is to advise the Secretary of State for Wales on the built heritage through Cadw: Welsh Historic Monuments (*see* page 356), which is an executive agency within the Welsh Office.

Chairman, T. Lloyd, FSA
Members, W. Lindsay Evans; R. Haslam; Dr P. Morgan; Mrs S. Furse; Dr S. Unwin; Dr E. Wiliam
Secretary, R. W. Hughes

HISTORIC BUILDINGS COUNCIL FOR SCOTLAND
Longmore House, Salisbury Place, Edinburgh EH9 1SH
Tel 0131-668 8787

The Historic Buildings Council for Scotland is the advisory body to the Secretary of State for Scotland on matters related to buildings of special architectural or historical interest and in particular to proposals for awards by him of grants for the repair of buildings of outstanding architectural or historical interest or lying within outstanding conservation areas.

Chairman, Sir Raymond Johnstone, CBE
Members, R. Cairns; Sir Ilay Campbell, Bt.; M. Ellington; Dr J. Frew; Lady Jane Grosvenor; J. Hunter Blair; I. Hutchison, OBE; K. Martin; Miss G. Nayler; Revd C. Robertson; Mrs F. Walker
Secretary, Ms S. Adams

ROYAL COMMISSION ON THE HISTORICAL MONUMENTS OF ENGLAND
National Monuments Record Centre, Kemble Drive, Swindon SN2 2GZ
Tel 01793-414700
London Search Room: 55 Blandford Street, London W1H 3AF.
Tel: 0171-208 8200

The Royal Commission on the Historical Monuments of England was established in 1908. It is the national body of architectural and archaeological survey and record and manages England's public archive of heritage information the National Monuments Record. It is funded by the Department of National Heritage.

Chairman, The Lord Faringdon
Commissioners, Prof. R. Bradley, FSA; D. J. Keene, Ph.D.; Prof. G. I. Meirion-Jones, Ph.D., FSA; Prof. A. C. Thomas, CBE, D.Litt., FSA; R. D. H. Gem, Ph.D., FSA; T. R. M. Longman; R. A. Yorke; Miss A. Riches, FSA; Dr M. Airs, FSA; Prof. M. Fulford, Ph.D., FSA; Dr M. Palmer, FSA; Miss A. Arrowsmith
Secretary, T. G. Hassall, FSA

ROYAL COMMISSION ON THE ANCIENT AND HISTORICAL MONUMENTS OF WALES

Crown Building, Plas Crug, Aberystwyth SY23 1NJ
Tel 01970-621233

The Royal Commission was established in 1908 to make an inventory of the ancient and historical monuments of Wales and Monmouthshire. It is currently empowered by a royal warrant of 1992 to survey, record, publish and maintain a database of ancient and historical and maritime sites and structures, and landscapes in Wales. The Commission is funded by the Welsh Office and is also responsible for the National Monuments Record of Wales, which is open daily for public reference, for the supply of archaeological information to the Ordnance Survey, for the co-ordination of archaeological aerial photography in Wales, and for sponsorship of the regional Sites and Monuments Records.

Chairman, Prof. J. B. Smith
Commissioners, Prof. R. W. Brunskill, OBE, Ph.D., FSA (*Vice-Chairman*); Prof. R. A. Griffiths, Ph.D., D.Litt.; D. Gruffyd Jones; R. M. Haslam, FSA; Prof. G. B. D. Jones, D.Phil., FSA; Mrs A. Nicol; S. B. Smith; Prof. G. J. Wainwright, MBE, Ph.D., FSA; E. Wiliam, Ph.D., FSA
Secretary, P. R. White, FSA

ROYAL COMMISSION ON THE ANCIENT AND HISTORICAL MONUMENTS OF SCOTLAND

John Sinclair House, 16 Bernard Terrace, Edinburgh EH8 9NX
Tel 0131-662 1446

The Royal Commission was established in 1908 and is appointed to provide for the survey and recording of ancient and historical monuments connected with the culture, civilization and conditions of life of the people in Scotland from the earliest times. It is funded by the Scottish Office. The Commission compiles and maintains the National Monuments Record of Scotland as the national record of the archaeological and historical environment. The National Monuments Record is open for reference Monday–Thursday 9.30–4.30, Friday 9.30–4.

Chairman, Sir William Fraser, GCB, FRSE
Commissioners, Prof. J. M. Coles, Ph.D., FBA; Prof. J. D. Dunbar-Nasmith, CBE, FRIBA; Prof. Rosemary Cramp, CBE, FSA; Prof. T. C. Smout, CBE, FRSE, FBA; The Hon. Lord Cullen; Dr Deborah Howard, FSA; Prof. R. A. Paxton, FRSE; Dr Barbara Crawford, FSA, FSA SCOT.; Miss A. Riches
Secretary, R. J. Mercer, FSA, FRSE

ANCIENT MONUMENTS BOARD FOR WALES

Brunel House, 2 Fitzalan Road, Cardiff CF2 1UY
Tel 01222-500200

The Ancient Monuments Board for Wales advises the Secretary of State for Wales on his statutory functions in respect of ancient monuments.
Chairman, Prof. R. R. Davies, CBE, D.Phil., FBA

Members, R. G. Keen; Mrs F. M. Lynch Llewellyn, FSA; Prof. W. H. Manning, Ph.D., FSA; Prof. J. B. Smith; Prof. W. E. Davies, Ph.D., FBA; M. J. Garner
Secretary, S. Morris

ANCIENT MONUMENTS BOARD FOR SCOTLAND

Longmore House, Salisbury Place, Edinburgh EH9 1SH
Tel 0131-668 8764

The Ancient Monuments Board for Scotland advises the Secretary of State for Scotland on the exercise of his functions, under the Ancient Monuments and Archaeological Areas Act 1979, of providing protection for monuments of national importance. Protection may be provided by including a monument in a statutory list of protected monuments, by acquisition, or by guardianship in which the Secretary of State assumes responsibility for maintenance.

Chairman, Prof. M. Lynch, Ph.D., FRSE
Members, A. Wright; Mrs E. V. W. Proudfoot, FSA, FSA SCOT.; Mrs K. Dalyell, FSA SCOT.; J. H. A. Gerrard, FRSA, FSA SCOT.; P. Clarke; L. J. Masters, FSA; Dr Anna Ritchie, FSA, FSA SCOT.; R. D. Kernohan, OBE; Dr Janet Morgan, FSA SCOT.; Prof. C. D. Morris, FSA, FSA SCOT.; R. J. Mercer, FRSE, FSA, FSA SCOT.; W. D. H. Sellar, FSA SCOT.; B. Mackie; Miss L. M. Thoms, FSA SCOT.
Secretary, R. A. J. Dalziel
Assessor, D. J. Breeze, Ph.D., FRSE, FSA SCOT.

HOME-GROWN CEREALS AUTHORITY

Hamlyn House, Highgate Hill, London N19 5PR
Tel 0171-263 3391

Set up under the Cereals Marketing Act 1965, the Authority consists of seven members representing UK cereal growers, seven representing dealers in, or processors of, grain and two independent members. The Authority's functions are to improve the production and marketing of UK-grown cereals and oilseeds through a research and development programme, to provide a market information service, to promote UK cereals in export markets and to support work at Food from Britain. The Authority also undertakes agency work for the Intervention Board in connection with the application in the UK of the Common Agricultural Policy for cereals.

Chairman, G. B. Nelson, CBE
Chief Executive, A. J. Williams

HOME OFFICE

50 Queen Anne's Gate, London SW1H 9AT
Tel 0171-273 4000

The Home Office deals with those internal affairs in England and Wales which have not been assigned to other government departments. The Home Secretary is particularly concerned with the administration of justice; criminal law; the treatment of offenders, including probation and the prison service; the police; immigration and nationality; passport policy matters; community relations; certain public safety matters; and fire and civil emergencies services. The Home Secretary personally is the link between The Queen and the public, and exercises certain powers on her behalf, including that of the Royal Pardon.

Other subjects dealt with include electoral arrangements; addresses and petitions to The Queen; ceremonial and formal business connected with honours; requests for extradition of criminals; scrutiny of local authority bye-laws; granting of licences for scientific procedures involving animals; cremations, burials and exhumations; firearms; dangerous drugs and poisons; general policy on laws relating to shops, liquor licensing, gaming and lotteries, and marriage; theatre and cinema licensing; and race relations policy.

The Home Secretary is also the link between the UK government and the governments of the Channel Islands and the Isle of Man.

Secretary of State for the Home Department, The Rt. Hon. Michael Howard, QC, MP
  Principal Private Secretary (SCS), K. D. Sutton
  Private Secretaries, Mrs M. K. Bramwell; C. Harnett; D. Redhouse
  Special Adviser, P. Rock
  Parliamentary Private Secretary, D. Lidington, MP
Ministers of State, The Rt. Hon. David Maclean, MP; Ann Widdecombe, MP; The Baroness Blatch, CBE, PC
  Private Secretaries, Miss S. Gooch; A. E. Jones; J. Sedgwick
  Special Adviser, Miss R. Whetstone
  Parliamentary Private Secretary to Baroness Blatch and Mr Maclean, D. Evennett, MP
Parliamentary Under-Secretary of State, Timothy Kirkhope, MP
  Private Secretary, G. Park
Parliamentary Under-Secretary of State, The Hon. Tom Sackville, MP
  Private Secretary, Miss C. McCombie
Parliamentary Clerk, Mrs R. Robinson
Permanent Under-Secretary of State (G1), R. T. J. Wilson, CB
  Private Secretary, Ms J. L. Hutcheon
Chief Medical Officer (at Department of Health), Dr Sir Kenneth Calman, KCB

CENTRAL SECRETARIAT

Head of Secretariat (acting) (SCS), Mrs M. Wooldridge

COMMUNICATION DIRECTORATE

Director, Communication (SCS), M. Granatt
Deputy Head of Communication (Head of News) (SCS), B. Butler
Head of Publicity and Corporate Services (G6), C. Skinner
Assistant Director, Co-ordination (G7), A. Underwood
Chief Press Officer (G7), B. McBride
Head of Information and Library Services (G7), P. Griffiths

CONSTITUTIONAL AND COMMUNITY POLICY DIRECTORATE

Director (SCS), Miss C. Sinclair
Heads of Units (SCS), Mrs G. Catto; R. Evans; M. Gillespie; S. B. Hickson

ANIMALS (SCIENTIFIC PROCEDURES) INSPECTORATE
Chief Inspector (SCS), Dr R. Watt
Superintendent Inspector (SCS), Dr J. Anderson
Inspectors (G6), Dr R. Curtis; Dr V. Navaratnam; D. Rutty; Dr R. South; Dr C. Wilkins

GAMING BOARD FOR GREAT BRITAIN
— *see* page 302

CORPORATE RESOURCES DIRECTORATE
Grenadier House, 99–105 Horseferry House, London SW1P 2DD
Tel 0171-273 4000
Clive House, Petty France, London SW1H 9HD
Tel 0171-273 4000

Director (SCS), Miss P. Drew
Heads of Units (SCS), Dr M. Allnutt; B. Caffarey; A. R. Edwards; S. Wharton
Senior Principals (G6), T. Cobley; J. Daly; D. Houghton; J. G. Jones; R. Jones; T. Lewis; D. Meakin

CRIMINAL POLICY DIRECTORATE

Director (SCS), J. Halliday, CB
Deputy Director (SCS), J. Lyon
Heads of Units (SCS), M. Boyle; R. Childs; I. Chisholm; Mrs F. Clarkson; E. Grant; A. Harding; P. Honour; Ms H. Jackson; N. Varney
Senior Principals (G6), Ms A. Fletcher; H. Marriage; A. Macfarlane

CENTRAL DRUGS PREVENTION UNIT
Horseferry House, Dean Ryle Street, London SW1P 2AW
Tel 0171-273 4000
Head of Unit (G6), A. Norbury

HOME OFFICE CRIME PREVENTION COLLEGE
The Hawkhills, Easingwold, York YO6 3EG
Tel 01347-825060
Director, J. Acton

HM INSPECTORATE OF PROBATION
Chief Inspector (SCS), G. W. Smith, CBE
Assistant Chief Inspector (G6), G. Childs

CRIMINAL INJURIES COMPENSATION AUTHORITY
— *see* page 292

FIRE AND EMERGENCY PLANNING DIRECTORATE
Horseferry House, Dean Ryle Street, London SW1P 2AW
Tel 0171-273 4000
50 Queen Anne's Gate, London SW1H 9AT
Tel 0171-273 4000

Director (SCS), Mrs S. Street
Heads of Units (SCS), E. Guy; Mrs V. Harris; Miss S. Paul; Dr D. Peace
Civil Emergencies Adviser, D. Bawtree, CB

HM FIRE SERVICE INSPECTORATE
HM Chief Inspector, B. T. A. Collins, OBE
HM Territorial Inspectors, D. McCallum, OBE; P. Morphew, QFSM; N. Musselwhite, CBE; G. P. Reid, QFSM; A. Rule, QFSM
Lay Inspector, P. Cummings
HM Inspectors, W. Ambalino; D. Berry; G. P. Bowles; S. D. Christian; M. T. Franklin; D. Kent; E. G. Pearn, QFSM; K. Phillips; R. M. Simpson, OBE; A. C. Wells, QFSM; D. Wright
Principal (G7), K. O'Sullivan

EMERGENCY PLANNING COLLEGE
The Hawkhills, Easingwold, Yorks YO6 3EG
Tel 01347-821406
Senior Principal (G6), A. R. Blackley
College Secretary (G7), A. Richmond

IMMIGRATION AND NATIONALITY DIRECTORATE, AND EU AND INTERNATIONAL UNIT

Lunar House, 40 Wellesley Road, Croydon, Surrey CR9 2BY
Tel 0181-686 0688
Apollo House, 36 Wellesley Road, Croydon, Surrey CR9 3RR
Tel 0181-686 0333
50 Queen Anne's Gate, London SW1H 9AT
Tel 0171-273 4000
India Buildings, 3rd Floor, Water Street, Liverpool L2 0QN
Tel 0151-227 3939

Director-General (*SCS*), T. Walker
Deputy Directors-General (*SCS*), A. R. Rawsthorne (*Policy*); T. Flesher (*Operations*)
Heads of Directorates (*SCS*), J. Acton; Miss V. M. Dews; E. B. Nicholls; Mrs E. C. L. Pallett; J. Potts; A. Walmsley; R. M. Whalley; R. G. Yates
Senior Principals (*G6*), P. Dawson; B. Downie; C. Saunders; G. Stadlen

IMMIGRATION SERVICE
Director (*Ports*) (*SCS*), T. Farrage
Deputy Directors (*G6*), G. Boiling, MBE; V. Hogg
Director (*Enforcement*) (*SCS*), D. Cooke
Deputy Director (*G6*), D. McDonough

EU AND INTERNATIONAL UNIT
Head of Unit (*SCS*), P. Edwards

LEGAL ADVISER'S BRANCH

Legal Adviser (*SCS*), D. E. J. Nissen
Deputy Legal Advisers (*SCS*), Mrs S. A. Evans; D. Seymour
Assistant Legal Advisers (*SCS*), R. J. Clayton; J. R. O'Meara; C. M. L. Osborne; S. A. Parker

ORGANIZED AND INTERNATIONAL CRIME DIRECTORATE

Director (*SCS*), J. Warne
Heads of Units (*SCS*), J. Duke-Evans; P. Wrench
Senior Principal (*G6*), J. Nicholson

NATIONAL CRIMINAL INTELLIGENCE SERVICE
— *see* page 376

INQUIRY INTO LEGISLATION AGAINST TERRORISM
Reviewer, The Lord Lloyd
SCS, A. Cory

PLANNING AND FINANCE DIRECTORATE

50 Queen Anne's Gate, London SW1H 9AT
Tel 0171-273 4000
Horseferry House, Dean Ryle Street, London SW1P 2AW
Tel 0171-273 4000

Director (*SCS*), S. Norris, CB
Heads of Units (*SCS*), R. Eagle; L. Haugh
Senior Principals (*G6*), P. Davies; B. Elliott; I. Gaskell; A. K. Holman; R. McBurney; Ms E. Sparrow

POLICE POLICY DIRECTORATE

Director (*SCS*), S. Boys Smith
Heads of Units (*SCS*), N. Benger; R. Fulton; Miss D. Loudon; C. Pelham; N. Sanderson
Senior Principals (*G6*), N. Burham; R. Ginman; Dr G. Laycock

NATIONAL DIRECTORATE OF POLICE TRAINING
National Director of Police Training, P. Ryan, QPM

Central Administration Unit
Senior Principal (*G6*), P. Curwen

POLICE STAFF COLLEGE
Bramshill House, Bramshill, Hook, Hants RG27 0JW
Tel 0125-126 2931
Head of Higher Training, Mrs S. Davies, QPM

POLICE INFORMATION TECHNOLOGY ORGANIZATION
Horseferry House, Dean Ryle Street, London SW1P 2AW
Tel 0171-273 4000

Chief Executive (*SCS*), Miss J. MacNaughton
Senior Managers (*SCS*), B. Buck; M. Goulding
Senior Principals (*G6*), M. Hart; J. Hamer; D. Rowe; Dr G. Turnbull

HENDON DATA CENTRE
Aerodrome Road, Colindale, London NW9 5LN
Tel 0181-200 2424

Head of Unit (*G6*), J. Ladley

POLICE SCIENTIFIC DEVELOPMENT BRANCH
Woodcock Hill, Sandridge, St Albans, Herts AL4 9HQ
Tel 01727-865051
Director (*SCS*), B. R. Coleman, OBE
Research Director (*G6*), Dr P. Young

Langhurst House, Langhurstwood Road, Nr Horsham, W. Sussex RH12 4WX
Tel 01403-255451
Head of Unit Langhurst (*G6*), Dr G. Thomas

HM INSPECTORATE OF CONSTABULARY

HM Chief Inspector of Constabulary (*SCS*), D. J. O'Dowd, CBE, QPM
HM Inspectors (*SCS*), D. Crompton, CBE, QPM; G. J. Dear, QPM; C. Smith, CBE, CVO, QPM; P. J. Winship, QPM; J. Stevens, QPM
Lay Inspectors, P. T. G. Hobbs; Dr A. Williams
Senior Principal (*G6*), L. Davidoff

METROPOLITAN POLICE COMMITTEE AND SECRETARIAT
Clive House, Petty France, London SW1H 9HD
Tel 0171-273 4000

Head of Secretariat (*SCS*), Mrs C. Crawford

RESEARCH AND STATISTICS DIRECTORATE

Director (*SCS*), C. Nuttall
Heads of Units (*SCS*), C. Lewis; D. Moxon; P. Wood
Senior Principals (*G6*), G. Barclay; Dr B. Butcher; Dr S. Field; P. Jordan; Mrs C. Lehman; Mrs P. Mayhew; R. Taylor; Ms J. Vennard; Mrs M. Wilkinson

PRISON SERVICE MONITORING UNIT

Head of Unit (*SCS*), R. Weatherill

HM INSPECTORATE OF PRISONS

HM Chief Inspector (*SCS*), Gen. Sir David Ramsbotham, GCB, CBE
HM Deputy Chief Inspector (*SCS*), C. Allen
HM Inspectors (*Governor 1*), R. Jacques; T. Wood

PRISONS OMBUDSMAN
— *see* page 334

PAROLE BOARD FOR ENGLAND AND WALES
— *see* pages 332–3

THE SECURITY SERVICE (MI5)

Thames House, PO Box 3255, London SWIP IAE

The Security Service was placed on a statutory footing by the Security Service Act 1989 and is headed by a director-general who is directly accountable to the Home Secretary. The function of the Service is the protection of national security, in particular against threats from espionage, terrorism and sabotage, from the activities of agents of foreign powers, and from actions intended to overthrow or undermine parliamentary democracy by political, industrial or violent means. It is also the Service's function to safeguard the economic well-being of the UK against threats posed by the actions or intentions of persons outside the British Islands. Under the Security Service Act 1996 the Service's role has been extended to support the police and customs in the prevention and detection of serious crime. Under the Intelligence Services Act 1994, the Intelligence and Security Committee of Parliamentarians was established to oversee the work of all three intelligence services. The Security Service Tribunal and Commissioner (*see* page 344) investigate complaints about the Service from the public.

Director-General, S. Lander

HM PRISON SERVICE

Cleland House, Page Street, London SWIP 4LN
Tel 0171-217 6000

An executive agency of the Home Office.

SALARIES 1996–7

Governor 1	£46,467–£48,025
Governor 2	£41,959–£43,206
Governor 3	£36,236–£36,566
Governor 4	£29,817–£31,974
Governor 5	£26,320–£28,639

THE PRISONS BOARD
Director-General (*SCS*), R. R. Tilt
Director of Personnel (*SCS*), D. Scott
Director of Finance (*SCS*), B. Landers
Director of Security and Programmes (*SCS*), A. J. Pearson
Directors of Operations (*SCS*), A. Papps (*North*); A. Walker (*South*); P. Wheatley (*Dispersals*)
Director of Services (*SCS*), H. Taylor
Director of Health Care (*SCS*), Dr M. Longfield
Non-Executive Members, F. W. Bentley; Sir Duncan Nichol, CBE

PRISON SERVICE HEADQUARTERS
Heads of Groups (*SCS*), R. Smith (*Custody*); W. J. Abbott (*Security*); I. Boon (*Pay and Industrial Relations*); K. Heal (*Programmes Policy*); Miss S. Paul (*Health Care Policy*); Mrs E. J. Grimsey (*Personnel Planning*); T. Wilson (*Contracts and Competitions*); J. Le Vay (*Planning*); P. Sleightholme (*Systems Strategy*); (*G6*), Mrs H. Bayne (*Lifer*); Mrs A. Nelson (*Prison Service Communications*); K. Lockyer (*Secretariat*)
Strategic Development Adviser (*SMO*), Dr L. Joyce
Heads of Services (*Gov. 1*), C. Davidson (*Training*); (*Gov. 3*), Mrs U. McCullom-Gordon (*Staff Care and Welfare*); (*SCS*), R. Haines (*Construction*); Miss L. Gill (*Prisoner Services*); (*G6*), vacant (*Office Services*); Mrs Y. Wilmott (*Nursing*); Dr C. McDougall (*Personnel*); J. Gunderson (*Prisoner Escorts and Custody*); S. Jenner (*Internal Audit*); J. Powls (*IT Services*); A. Pay (*Accounting*); (*G7*), T. Kelly (*Personnel Finance*); (*PMO*), Dr D. Howells (*Healthcare Professional Development*)
Chaplain-General and Archdeacon of the Prison Service, Ven. D. Fleming
Chief Education Adviser (*G6*), I. G. Benson
Chief Physical Education Adviser (*G6*), M. W. Denton

PRISON ENTERPRISE AND ACTIVITY SERVICES
Block A, Whitgift Centre, Wellesley Road, Croydon, Surrey CR9 3LY
Tel 0181-686 8710
Director (*SCS*), P. R. A. Fulton

SUPPLY AND TRANSPORT SERVICES
Crown House, 52 Elizabeth Street, Corby, Northants
Tel 01536-202101
Director (*SCS*), D. J. C. Kent

AREA MANAGERS
Directorate of Operations (*North*)
East Midlands (*SCS*), J. Blakey
Mercia (*SCS*), D. Curtis
Mersey and Manchester (*SCS*), R. Halward
North-East (*SCS*), R. Mitchell
North-West (*SCS*), D. I. Lockwood
Yorkshire (*SCS*), T. Bone

Directorate of Operations (*South*)
Central (*SCS*), J. Dring
Kent (*SCS*), T. Murtagh, OBE
London North and East Anglia (*SCS*), A. de Frisching
London South (*SCS*), P. J. Kitteridge
South Coast (*SCS*), J. Perriss
Wales and the West (*SCS*), J. May

PRISONS
ACKLINGTON, Morpeth, Northumberland NE65 9XF. *Governor*, I. Woods
ALBANY, Newport, Isle of Wight PO30 5RS. *Governor*, S. O'Neill
ALDINGTON, Ashford, Kent TN25 7BQ. *Governor*, D. A. Bratton
ASHWELL, Oakham, Leics LE15 7LS. *Governor*, C. Bushell
*ASKHAM GRANGE, Askham Richard, York YO2 3PT. *Governor*, H. E. Crew
BEDFORD, St Loyes Street, Bedford MK40 1HG. *Governor*, E. Willets
BELMARSH, Western Way, Thamesmead, London SE28 0EB. *Governor*, W. S. Duff
BIRMINGHAM, Winson Green Road, Birmingham B18 4AS. *Governor*, G. Gregory-Smith
BLAKENHURST (private prison), Hewell Lane, Redditch, Worcs B97 6QS. *Monitor*, P. J. Hanglin
BLANTYRE HOUSE, Goudhurst, Cranbrook, Kent TN17 2NH. *Governor*, B. Pollett
BLUNDESTON, Lowestoft, Suffolk NR32 5BG. *Governor*, S. Robinson
BRISTOL, Cambridge Road, Bristol BS7 8PS. *Governor*, R. D. Dixon
BRIXTON, PO Box 369, Jebb Avenue, London SW2 5XF. *Governor*, Dr A. Coyle
BROCKHILL, Redditch, Worcs B97 6RD. *Governor*, K. Naisbitt
BUCKLEY HALL (private prison), Buckley Road, Rochdale, Lancs OL12 9DP. *Monitor*, Miss V. Bird
BULLINGDON, Padrick Haugh Road, Arncott, Bicester, Oxon OX6 0PZ. *Governor*, Mrs S. E. Payne
*BULLWOOD HALL, High Road, Hockley, Essex SS5 4TE. *Governor*, Mrs E. Butler
CAMP HILL, Newport, Isle of Wight PO30 5PB. *Governor*, S. Moore
CANTERBURY, Longport, Canterbury, Kent CT1 1PJ. *Governor*, G. Davies
CARDIFF, Knox Road, Cardiff CF2 1UG. *Governor*, N. D. Clifford
CHANNINGS WOOD, Denbury, Newton Abbott, Devon TQ12 6DW. *Governor*, J. K. Petherick
CHELMSFORD, Springfield Road, Chelmsford, Essex CM2 6LQ. *Governor*, vacant

COLDINGLEY, Bisley, Woking, Surrey GU24 9EX. *Governor*, J. Smith

*COOKHAM WOOD, Cookham Wood, Rochester, Kent MEI 3LU. *Governor*, I. Smout

DARTMOOR, Princetown, Yelverton, Devon PL20 6RR. *Governor*, J. Lawrence

DONCASTER (private prison), Off North Bridge, Marshgate, Doncaster DN5 8UX. *Director*, K. Rogers

DORCHESTER, North Square, Dorchester, Dorset DT1 1JD. *Governor*, R. Walker

DOWNVIEW, Sutton Lane, Sutton, Surrey SM2 5PD. *Governor*, D. M. Lancaster

*DRAKE HALL, Eccleshall, Staffs ST21 6LQ. *Governor*, G. Hughes

*DURHAM, Old Elvet, Durham DHI 3HU. *Governor*, R. Mitchell

*EAST SUTTON PARK, Sutton Valence, Maidstone, Kent MEI7 3DF. *Governor*, Mrs C. J. Galbally

*ELMLEY, Church Road, Eastchurch, Sheerness, Kent MEI2 4DZ. *Governor*, A. Smith

ERLESTOKE HOUSE, Devizes, Wilts SNI0 5TU. *Governor*, vacant

EVERTHORPE, Brough, North Humberside HUI5 IRB. *Governor*, R. Smith

EXETER, New North Road, Exeter, Devon EX4 4EX. *Governor*, T. C. H. Newth

FEATHERSTONE, New Road, Featherstone, Wolverhampton WVI0 7PU. *Governor*, C. Scott

FORD, Arundel, W. Sussex BNI8 0BX. *Governor*, D. A. Godfrey

FRANKLAND, Frankland, Brasside, Durham, DHI 5YD. *Governor*, P. J. Leonard

FULL SUTTON, Full Sutton, York YO4 IPS. *Governor*, J. W. Staples

GARTH, Ulnes Walton Lane, Leyland, Preston, Lancs PR5 3NE. *Governor*, W. Rose-Quirie

GARTREE, Leicester Road, Market Harborough, Leics LEI6 7RP. *Governor*, R. J. Perry

GLOUCESTER, Barrack Square, Gloucester GLI 2JN. *Governor*, R. Dempsey

GRENDON, Grendon Underwood, Aylesbury, Bucks HPI8 0TL. *Governor*, T. C. Newell

HASLAR, Dolphin Way, Gosport, Hants POI2 2AW. *Governor*, I. Truffet

HAVERIGG, Haverigg Camp, Millom, Cumbria LAI8 4NA. *Governor*, B. Wilson

HEWELL GRANGE, Redditch, Worcs B97 6QQ. *Governor*, D. W. Bamber

HIGHDOWN, Sutton Lane, Sutton, Surrey SM2 5PJ. *Governor*, S. Pryor

HIGHPOINT, Stradishall, Newmarket, Suffolk CB8 9YG. *Governor*, C. D. Sherwood

HINDLEY, Gibson Street, Bickershaw, Hindley, Wigan, Lancs WN2 5TH. *Governor*, L. Lavender

HOLLESLEY BAY COLONY, Hollesley, Woodbridge, Suffolk IPI2 3JS. *Governor*, M. F. Clarke

*HOLLOWAY, Parkhurst Road, London N7 0NU. *Governor*, M. Sheldrick

HOLME HOUSE, Holme House Road, Stockton-on-Tees, Cleveland TSI8 2QU. *Governor*, D. Roberts

HULL, Hedon Road, Hull, N. Humberside HU9 5LS. *Governor*, M. Newell

KINGSTON, Milton Road, Portsmouth PO3 6AS. *Governor*, J. R. Dovell

KIRKHAM, Preston, Lancs PR4 2RA. *Governor*, A. F. Jennings

KIRKLEVINGTON GRANGE, Yarm, Cleveland TSI5 9PA. *Governor*, Mrs P. Midgley

LANCASTER, The Castle, Lancaster LAI IYL. *Governor*, D. G. McNaughton

LATCHMERE HOUSE, Church Road, Ham Common, Richmond, Surrey TWI0 5HH. *Governor*, E. Butt

LEEDS, Armley, Leeds LSI2 2TJ. *Governor*, A. J. Fitzpatrick

LEICESTER, Welford Road, Leicester LE2 7AJ. *Governor*, M. Egan

LEWES, Brighton Road, Lewes, E. Sussex BN7 IEA. *Governor*, J. F. Dixon

LEYHILL, Wotton-under-Edge, Glos GLI2 8HL. *Governor*, D. T. Williams

LINCOLN, Greetwell Road, Lincoln LN2 4BD. *Governor*, D. Shaw

LINDHOLME, Bawtry Road, Hatfield, Woodhouse, Doncaster DN7 6EE. *Governor*, M. Shann

LITTLEHEY, Perry, Huntingdon, Cambs PEI8 0SR. *Governor*, M. L. Knight

LIVERPOOL, 68 Hornby Road, Liverpool L9 3DF. *Governor*, B. Duncan

LONG LARTIN, South Littleton, Evesham, Worcs WRII 5TZ. *Governor*, J. Mullen

MAIDSTONE, County Road, Maidstone MEI4 IUZ. *Governor*, H. Bagshaw

MANCHESTER, Southall Street, Manchester M60 9AH. *Governor*, P. Earnshaw

MOORLAND, Hatfield Woodhouse, Doncaster DN7 6BW. *Governor*, C. R. Griffiths

MORTON HALL, Swinderby, Lincoln LN6 9PS. *Governor*, S. G. Wagstaffe

THE MOUNT, Molyneaux Avenue, Bovingdon, Hemel Hempstead HP3 0NZ. *Governor*, Mrs M. Donnelly

*NEW HALL, Dial Wood, Flockton, Wakefield, W. Yorks WF4 4AX. *Governor*, D. England

NORTH SEA CAMP, Freiston, Boston, Lincs PE22 0QX. *Governor*, M. A. Lewis

NORWICH, Mousehold, Norwich NRI 4LU. *Governor*, N. Wall

NOTTINGHAM, Perry Road, Sherwood, Nottingham NG5 3AG. *Governor*, P. J. Bennett

OXFORD, New Road, Oxford OXI ILZ. *Governor*, Mrs S. E. Payne

PARKHURST, Newport, Isle of Wight PO30 5NX. *Governor*, D. M. Morrison

PENTONVILLE, Caledonian Road, London N7 8TT. *Governor*, K. Brewer

PRESTON, 2 Ribbleton Lane, Preston, Lancs ORI 5AB. *Governor*, R. J. Crouch

RANBY, Ranby, Retford, Notts DN22 8EU. *Governor*, T. J. Williams

*RISLEY, Warrington Road, Risley, Warrington WA3 6BP. *Governor*, vacant

ROCHESTER, Rochester, Kent MEI 3QS. *Governor*, R. A. Chapman

RUDGATE, Wetherby, W. Yorks LS23 7AZ. *Governor*, H. Jones

SEND, Ripley Road, Send, Woking, Surrey GU23 7LJ. *Governor*, S. Guy-Gibbons

SHEPTON MALLET, Cornhill, Shepton Mallet, Somerset BA4 5LU. *Governor*, P. O'Sullivan

SHREWSBURY, The Dana, Shrewsbury, Salop SYI 2HR. *Governor*, K. Beaumont

STAFFORD, 54 Gaol Road, Stafford STI6 3AW. *Governor*, R. Feeney

STANDFORD HILL, Church Road, Eastchurch, Sheerness, Kent MEI2 4AA. *Governor*, D. M. Twiner

STOCKEN, Stocken Hall Road, Stretton, Nr Oakham, Leics LEI5 7RD. *Governor*, D. Hall

STOKE HEATH, Market Drayton, Shropshire TF9 2JL. *Governor*, J. Aldridge

*Women's establishments/establishments with units for women

*STYAL, Wilmslow, Cheshire SK9 4HR. *Governor,*
M. Goodwin
SUDBURY, Sudbury, Derbys DE6 5HW. *Governor,* P. E. Salter
SWALESIDE, Eastchurch, Isle of Sheppey, Kent ME12 4AX.
Governor, R. Tasker
SWANSEA, Oystermouth Road, Swansea SA1 2SR. *Governor,*
J. Heyes
USK, 29 Maryport Street, Usk, Gwent NP5 1XP. *Governor,*
N. J. Evans
THE VERNE, Portland, Dorset DT5 1EQ. *Governor,*
T. M. Turner
WAKEFIELD, Love Lane, Wakefield WF2 9AG. *Governor,*
R. Doughty
WANDSWORTH, PO Box 757, Heathfield Road, London
SW18 3HS. *Governor,* C. G. Clark, OBE
WAYLAND, Wayland, Griston, Thetford, Norfolk IP25 6RL.
Governor, M. Spurr
WEALSTUN, Wetherby, W. Yorks LS23 7AY. *Governor,*
G. Barnard
WELLINGBOROUGH, Millers Park, Doddington Road,
Wellingborough, Northants NN8 2NH. *Governor,*
J. Whetton
WHATTON, Whatton, Notts NG13 9FQ. *Governor,*
B. McCourt
WHITEMOOR, Longhill Road, March, Cambs PE15 0PR.
Governor, R. B. Clarke
WINCHESTER, Romsey Road, Winchester, Hants
SO22 5DF. *Governor,* M. K. Pascoe
WOODHILL, Tattenhoe Street, Milton Keynes MK4 4DA.
Governor, Ms M. Gorman
WORMWOOD SCRUBBS, PO Box 757, Du Cane Road,
London W12 0AE. *Governor,* J. F. Perris
WYMOTT, Moss Lane, Ulnes Walton, Leyland, Preston,
Lancs PR5 3LW. *Governor,* G. Brunskill

YOUNG OFFENDER INSTITUTIONS

AYLESBURY, Bierton Road, Aylesbury, Bucks HP20 1EH.
Governor, N. Pascoe
BRINSFORD, New Road, Featherstone, Wolverhampton
WV10 7PY. *Governor,* B. Payling
*BULLWOOD HALL, High Road, Hockley, Essex SS5 4TE.
Governor, Mrs E. Butler
CASTINGTON, Morpeth, Northumberland NE65 9XF.
Governor, C. Harder
DEERBOLT, Bowes Road, Barnard Castle, Co. Durham
DL12 9BG. *Governor,* P. Atkinson
DOVER, The Citadel, Western Heights, Dover, Kent
CT17 9DR. *Governor,* B. W. Sutton
*DRAKE HALL, Eccleshall, Staffs ST21 6LQ. *Governor,*
G. Hughes
*EAST SUTTON PARK, Sutton Valence, Maidstone, Kent
ME17 3DF. *Governor,* Mrs C. J. Galbally
EASTWOOD PARK, Falfield, Wotton-under-Edge, Glos
GL12 8DB. *Governor,* P. Winkley
FELTHAM, Bedfont Road, Feltham, Middx TW13 4ND.
Governor, I. Ward
GLEN PARVA, Tigers Road, Wigston, Leics LE8 2TN.
Governor, C. Williams
GUYS MARSH, Shaftesbury, Dorset SP7 0AH. *Governor,*
R. Gaines
HATFIELD, Hatfield, Doncaster DN7 6EL. *Governor,*
H. Jones
HOLLESLEY BAY COLONY, Hollesley, Woodbridge,
Suffolk IP12 3JS. *Governor,* M. F. Clarke
HUNTERCOMBE, Huntercombe Place, Nuffield, Henley-
on-Thames RG9 5SB. *Governor,* D. Strong
LANCASTER FARMS, Stone Row Head, off Quernmore
Road, Lancaster LA1 3QZ. *Governor,* D. J. Waplington

*Women's establishments/establishments with units for women

*NEW HALL, Dial Wood, Flockton, Wakefield WF4 4AX.
Governor, D. England
NORTHALLERTON, East Road, Northallerton, N. Yorks
DL6 1NW. *Governor,* D. P. G. Appleton
ONLEY, Willoughby, Rugby, Warks CV23 8AP. *Governor,*
J. N. Brooke
PORTLAND, Easton, Portland, Dorset DT5 1DL. *Governor,*
D. Brisco
PRESCOED, 29 Maryport Street, Usk NP4 0TD. *Governor,*
N. J. Evans
STOKE HEATH, Market Drayton, Salop TF9 2JL. *Governor,*
J. Aldridge
*STYAL, Wilmslow, Cheshire, SK9 4HR. *Governor,*
M. Goodwin
SWINFEN HALL, Lichfield, Staffs WS14 9QS. *Governor,* J. P.
Francis
THORN CROSS, Arley Road, Appleton Thorn,
Warrington WA4 4RL. *Governor,* I. Windebank
WERRINGTON, Stoke-on-Trent ST9 0DX. *Governor,*
B. Stanhope
WETHERBY, York Road, Wetherby, W. Yorks LS22 5ED.
Governor, P. J. Atkinson

REMAND CENTRES

BRINSFORD, New Road, Featherstone, Wolverhampton
WV10 7PY. *Governor,* B. Payling
CARDIFF, Knox Road, Cardiff CF2 1UG. *Governor,*
N. D. Clifford
EXETER, New North Road, Exeter, Devon EX4 4EX.
Governor, T. C. H. Newth
FELTHAM, Bedfont Road, Feltham, Middx TW13 4ND.
Governor, I. Ward
GLEN PARVA, Tigers Road, Wigston, Leics LE8 2TN.
Governor, C. Williams
LANCASTER FARMS, Stone Rowe Head, Off Quernmore
Road, Lancaster LA1 3QZ. *Governor,* D. J. Waplington
LOW NEWTON, Brasside, Durham DH1 5SD. *Governor,*
vacant
NORWICH, Mousehold, Norwich, Norfolk NR1 4LU.
Governor, N. Wall
READING, Forbury Road, Reading, Berks RG1 3HY.
Governor, W. Payne
THE WOLDS (private remand prison), Everthorpe,
Brough, N. Humberside HU15 2JZ. *Director,* J. McDonnell

FIRE SERVICE COLLEGE
Moreton-in-Marsh, Glos GL56 0RH
Tel 01608-650831

An executive agency of the Home Office.
Chief Executive, N. K. Finlayson
Commandant, T. Glossop, QFSM
Dean, Dr R. Willis-Lee
Director of Development and Services (G7), Dr T. Jeans

FORENSIC SCIENCE SERVICE
HEADQUARTERS
Metropolitan Police Forensic Science Laboratory, 109
Lambeth Road, London SE1 7LP
Tel 0171-230 1212
Priory House, Gooch Street North, Birmingham B5 6QQ
Tel 0121-607 6800

An executive agency of the Home Office.
Director-General (SCS), Dr J. Thompson
Director of Business Development (SCS), T. Howitt
Director of Finance (SCS), R. Anthony
Chief Scientist (G6), Dr. B. Bramley
Corporate Service Manager (G6), Dr W. D. Wilson
Director of Operations and Head of Personnel (G6),
M. Loveland
Director of Service (G6), Dr D. Werrett

UK PASSPORT AGENCY
Clive House, Petty France, London SW1H 9HD
Tel 0171-799 2728
An executive agency of the Home Office.
Chief Executive (SCS), D. Gatenby
Deputy Chief Executive and Director of Operations (G6),
 T. Lonsdale
Director of Resources (G6), K. J. Sheehan
Director of Systems (G6), R. G. Le Marechal

HORSERACE TOTALISATOR BOARD
74 Upper Richmond Road, London SW15 2SU
Tel 0181-874 6411

The Horserace Totalisator Board was established by the
Betting, Gaming and Lotteries Act 1963, as successor to the
Racecourse Betting Control Board. Its function is to
operate totalisators on approved racecourses in Great
Britain, and it also provides on- and off-course cash and
credit offices. Under the Horserace Totalisator and Betting
Levy Board Act 1972, it is further empowered to offer bets
at starting price (or other bets at fixed odds) on any sporting
event. The chairman and members of the Board are
appointed by the Home Secretary.
Chairman (£95,000), The Lord Wyatt of Weeford (*until
April 1997*)
Chief Executive, B. McDonnell

HOUSING CORPORATION
149 Tottenham Court Road, London W1P 0BN
Tel 0171-393 2000

Established by Parliament in 1964, the Housing Corporation registers, promotes, funds and supervises housing
associations. The Corporation's duties were extended
under the provisions of the Housing Act 1988 to cover the
payment of capital and revenue grants to housing associations, advice for tenants interested in Tenants' Choice,
and the approval and revocation of potential new landlords
under this policy. The Corporation is funded by the
Department of the Environment.
  There are over 2,200 registered associations in England
providing more than 600,000 homes for people in need of
housing. Housing associations are non-profit making
bodies run by voluntary committees.
Chairman, Sir Brian Pearse
Chief Executive, A. Mayer

HUMAN FERTILIZATION AND EMBRYOLOGY AUTHORITY
Paxton House, 30 Artillery Lane, London E1 7LS
Tel 0171-377 5077

The Authority was established under the Human Fertili-
zation and Embryology Act 1990. Its function is to license
persons carrying out any of the following activities: the
creation or use of embryos outside the body in the
provision of infertility treatment services; the use of
donated gametes in infertility treatment; the storage of
gametes or embryos; and research on human embryos. The
Authority also keeps under review information about
embryos and, when requested to do so, gives advice to the
Secretary of State for Health.
Chairman, Mrs R. Deech

Deputy Chairman, Lady (Diana) Brittan
Members, Prof. R. J. Berry; Mrs J. Denton; Ms E. Forgan;
 D. Greggains; Mrs J. Harbison; Prof. S. Hillier; The
 Most Revd R. Holloway; Prof. M. Johnson; R. Jones;
 Miss P. Keith; Dr B. Lieberman; Mrs A. Mays; Dr
 A. McLaren; Dr J. Naish; Prof. A. Nichol; Prof.
 A. Templeton; Prof. Revd A. Thiselton; Ms
 J. Tugendhat; J. Williams
Chief Executive, Mrs S. McCarthy

INDEPENDENT COMMISSION FOR POLICE COMPLAINTS FOR NORTHERN IRELAND
Chamber of Commerce House, 22 Great Victoria Street,
Belfast BT2 7LP
Tel 01232-244821

The Independent Commission for Police Complaints was
established under the Police (Northern Ireland) Order
1987. It has powers to supervise the investigation of certain
categories of serious complaints, can direct that disciplinary charges be brought, and has oversight of the
informal resolution procedure for less serious complaints.
Chairman, J. Grew
Chief Executive, B. McClelland

INDEPENDENT REVIEW SERVICE FOR THE SOCIAL FUND
4th Floor, Centre City Podium, 5 Hill Street,
Birmingham B5 4UB
Tel 0121-606 2100

The Social Fund Commissioner is appointed by the
Secretary of State for Social Security. The Commissioner
appoints Social Fund Inspectors, who provide an independent review of decisions made by Social Fund Officers in
the Benefits Agency of the Department of Social Security.
Social Fund Commissioner, J. Scampion

INDEPENDENT TELEVISION COMMISSION
33 Foley Street, London W1P 7LB
Tel 0171-255 3000

The Independent Television Commission replaced the
Independent Broadcasting Authority in 1991. The Com-
mission is responsible for licensing and regulating all
commercially funded television services broadcast from
the UK. Members are appointed by the Secretary of State
for National Heritage.
Chairman (£63,670), Sir George Russell, CBE
Deputy Chairman, Earl of Dalkeith
Members, R. Goddard; Mrs E. Wynne Jones; Dr J. Beynon,
 FEng.; Ms J. Goffe; Dr Maria Moloney; J. Ranelagh; Dr
 M. Shea
Chief Executive, P. Rogers
Secretary, M. Redley

INDUSTRIAL INJURIES ADVISORY COUNCIL
6th Floor, The Adelphi, 1–11 John Adam Street, London WC2N 6HT
Tel 0171-962 8066

The Industrial Injuries Advisory Council is a statutory body under the Social Security Act 1975 which considers and advises the Secretary of State for Social Security on regulations and other questions relating to industrial injuries benefits or their administration.
Chairman, Prof. A. J. Newman Taylor, OBE, FRCP
Secretary, R. Wakely

BOARD OF INLAND REVENUE
Somerset House, London WC2R 1LB
Tel 0171-438 6420

The Board of Inland Revenue was constituted under the Inland Revenue Board Act 1849, by the consolidation of the Board of Excise and the Board of Stamps and Taxes. In 1909 the administration of excise duties was transferred to the Board of Customs. The Board of Inland Revenue administers and collects direct taxes – income tax, corporation tax, capital gains tax, inheritance tax, stamp duty, and petroleum revenue tax – and advises the Chancellor of the Exchequer on policy questions involving them.
   The Department is organized into a series of accountable management units. The day-to-day operations in assessing and collecting tax and in providing internal support services are carried out by Executive Offices. The Department's Valuation Office is an executive agency responsible for providing valuation services for rating, council tax, Inland Revenue and other public sector purposes. In 1995–6 the Inland Revenue collected £97,000 million in tax.

THE BOARD
Chairman (G1), Sir Anthony Battishill, KCB
   Private Secretary, Miss S. Woollard
Deputy Chairmen (G2), S. C. T. Matheson, CB; C. W. Corlett, CB
Director-General (G2), G. H. Bush

DIVISIONS
Director, Personnel Division (G3), J. Gant
Director, Business and Management Services Division (G3), J. Yard
Director, Change Management Division and Self-Assessment Programme, D. A. Smith
Principal Finance Officer (G3), R. R. Martin
Director, Policy Co-ordination Unit, P. Lewis
Director, Business Operations Division (G3), M. A. Johns
Director, Quality Development Division (G3), K. V. Deacon
Director, Company Tax Division and Financial Institutions Division (G3), M. F. Cayley
Director, International Division (G3), I. Spence
Director, Business Profits Division (G3), E. J. Gribbon
Director, Personal Tax Division (G3), E. McGivern
Director, Capital and Valuation Division, and Savings and Investment Division (G3), B. A. Mace

EXECUTIVE OFFICES

ACCOUNTS OFFICE (CUMBERNAULD), Cumbernauld, Glasgow G70 5TR. *Controller*, A. Geddes, OBE

ACCOUNTS OFFICE (SHIPLEY), Shipley, Bradford, W. Yorks BD98 8AA. *Controller*, P. Clark, OBE

CAPITAL TAXES OFFICE
Ferrers House, PO Box 38, Castle Meadow Road, Nottingham NG2 1BB
Controller, B. D. Kent

CAPITAL TAXES OFFICE (SCOTLAND)
Mulberry House, 16 Picardy Place, Edinburgh EH1 3NB
Registrar, I. Fraser

CORPORATE COMMUNICATIONS OFFICE
North-West Wing, Bush House, Aldwych, London WC2B 4PP
Controller, R. N. Hooper

ENFORCEMENT OFFICE
Durrington Bridge House, Barrington Road, Worthing, W. Sussex BN12 4SE
Controller, Mrs S. F. Walsh

FINANCIAL ACCOUNTING OFFICE
South Block, Barrington Road, Worthing, W. Sussex BN12 4XH
Controller, J. D. Easey

FINANCIAL INTERMEDIARIES AND CLAIMS OFFICE
St John's House, Merton Road, Bootle L26 9BB
Controller, D. A. Hartnett

INTERNAL AUDIT OFFICE
North-West Wing, Bush House, Aldwych, London WC2B 4PP
Controller, N. R. Buckley

LARGE GROUP OFFICE
New Court, Carey Street, London WC2A 2JE
Controller, R. A. J. Jones

OIL TAXATION OFFICE
Melbourne House, Aldwych, London WC2B 4LL
Controller, R. C. Mountain

PENSION SCHEMES OFFICE
Yorke House, PO Box 62, Castle Meadow Road, Nottingham NG2 1BG
Controller, S. J. McManus

SOLICITOR'S OFFICE
East Wing, Somerset House, London WC2R 1LB
Solicitor (G2), B. E. Cleave, CB

SOLICITOR'S OFFICE (SCOTLAND)
80 Lauriston Place, Edinburgh EH3 9SL
Solicitor, I. K. Laing

SPECIAL COMPLIANCE OFFICE
Angel Court, 199 Borough High Street, London SE1 1HZ
Controller, F. J. Brannigan

STAMP OFFICE
South-West Wing, Bush House, Strand, London WC2B 4QN
Controller, K. S. Hodgson

STATISTICS AND ECONOMICS OFFICE
West Wing, Somerset House, Strand, London WC2R 1LB
Director, R. Ward

TRAINING OFFICE
Lawres Hall, Riseholme Park, Lincoln LN2 2BJ
Controller, T. Kuczys

REGIONAL EXECUTIVE OFFICES

INLAND REVENUE EAST, Midgate House, Peterborough PE1 1TD. *Controller*, M. J. Hodgson

INLAND REVENUE LONDON, New Court, Carey Street, London WC2A 2JE. *Controller*, J. F. Carling
INLAND REVENUE NORTH, 100 Russell Street, Middlesbrough, Cleveland TS1 2RZ. *Controller*, R. I. Ford
INLAND REVENUE NORTH-WEST, The Triad, Stanley Road, Bootle, Merseyside L20 3PD. *Controller*, I. S. Gerrie
INLAND REVENUE SOUTH-EAST, Dukes Court, Dukes Street, Woking GU21 5XR. *Controller*, D. L. S. Bean
INLAND REVENUE SOUTH-WEST, Longbrook House, New North Road, Exeter EX4 4QU. *Controller*, Mrs M. E. Williams
INLAND REVENUE SOUTH YORKSHIRE, Concept House, 5 Young Street, Sheffield S1 4LF. *Controller*, A. C. Sleeman
INLAND REVENUE WALES AND MIDLANDS, 1st Floor, Phase 11 Building, Ty Glas Avenue, Llanishen, Cardiff CF4 5TS. *Controller*, M. W. Kirk
INLAND REVENUE SCOTLAND, 80 Lauriston Place, Edinburgh EH3 9SL. *Controller*, O. J. Clarke
INLAND REVENUE NORTHERN IRELAND, Dorchester House, 52–58 Great Victoria Street, Belfast BT2 7QE. *Controller*, R. S. T. Ewing

VALUATION OFFICE AGENCY
New Court, 48 Carey Street, London WC2A 2JE
Tel 0171-324 1183/1057
Meldrum House, 15 Drumsheugh Gardens, Edinburgh EH3 7UN
Tel 0131-225 4938

Chief Executive, Ms V. Lowe
Chief Valuer, Scotland, A. MacLaren

ADJUDICATOR'S OFFICE
— *see* page 277

INTERCEPTION COMMISSIONER
c/o The Home Office, 50 Queen Anne's Gate, London SW1H 9AT

The Commissioner is appointed by the Prime Minister. He keeps under review the issue by the Home Secretary, the Foreign Secretary, and the Secretaries of State for Scotland and for Northern Ireland, of warrants under the Interception of Communications Act 1985 and safeguards made in respect of intercepted material obtained through the use of such warrants. He is also required to give all such assistance as the Interception of Communications Tribunal may require to enable it to carry out its functions, and to submit an annual report to the Prime Minister with respect to the carrying out of his functions.
Commissioner, The Lord Nolan, PC

INTERCEPTION OF COMMUNICATIONS TRIBUNAL
PO Box 44, London SE1 0TX
Tel 0171-273 4096

Under the Interception of Communications Act 1985, the Tribunal is required to investigate applications from any person who believes that communications sent to or by them have been intercepted in the course of their transmission by post or by means of a public telecommunications system. The Tribunal comprises senior members of the legal profession, who are appointed by The Queen.
President, The Hon. Mr Justice Macpherson of Cluny
Vice-President, Sir David Calcutt, QC
Members, P. Scott, QC; W. Carmichael; R. Seabrook, QC

INTERVENTION BOARD
PO Box 69, Reading RG1 3YD
Tel 0118-958 3626

The Intervention Board was established as a government department in 1972 and became operational in 1973; it became an executive agency in 1990. The Board is responsible for the implementation of European Union regulations covering the market support arrangements of the Common Agricultural Policy. Members are appointed by and are responsible to the Minister of Agriculture, Fisheries and Food and the Secretaries of State for Scotland, Wales and Northern Ireland.
Chairman, A. Marshall
Chief Executive (G3), G. Trevelyan

HEADS OF DIVISIONS
External Trade Division (G5), G. N. Dixon
Internal Market Division (G5), H. MacKinnon
Corporate Services Division (G5), J. W. M. Peffers
Finance Division (G5), G. R. R. Jenkins
Legal Division (G5), J. F. McCleary
Chief Accountant (G6), R. Bryant
Procurement and Supply (G6), P. J. Offer
Information Systems (G7), T. G. Lamberstock
Internal Market Operations (G6), J. A. Sutton

LAND AUTHORITY FOR WALES
The Custom House, Customhouse Street, Cardiff CF1 5AP
Tel 01222-223444

The Authority, established under the Local Government Planning and Land Act 1980, is responsible for identifying and acquiring land suitable for development in Wales and making it available for development by others.
Chairman (part-time) (£33,305), Sir Geoffrey Inkin, OBE
Chief Executive, B. Ryan, FRICS

LAND REGISTRIES

HM LAND REGISTRY
Lincoln's Inn Fields, London WC2A 3PH
Tel 0171-917 8888

The registration of title to land was first introduced in England and Wales by the Land Registry Act 1862; HM Land Registry operates today under the Land Registration Acts 1925 to 1988. The object of registering title to land is to create and maintain a register of landowners whose title is guaranteed by the state and so to simplify the transfer, mortgage and other dealings with real property. Registration on sale is now compulsory throughout England and Wales. The register has been open to inspection by the public since 1990.

HM Land Registry is an executive agency administered under the Lord Chancellor by the Chief Land Registrar. The work is decentralized to a number of regional offices. The Chief Land Registrar is also responsible for the Land Charges Department and the Agricultural Credits Department.

HEADQUARTERS OFFICE
Chief Land Registrar and Chief Executive, Dr S. J. Hill
Solicitor to Land Registry, C. J. West
Director of Corporate Services, E. G. Beardsall
Senior Land Registrar, Mrs J. G. Totty
Director of Operations, G. N. French

Director of Information Technology, P. J. Smith
Director of Management Services, P. R. Laker
Land Registrar, M. L. Wood
Deputy Establishment Officer, J. Hodder
Controller of Operations Development, A. W. Howarth

COMPUTER SERVICES DIVISION
Burrington Way, Plymouth PL5 3LP
Tel 01752-779831
Head of Services Division, P. A. Maycock
Head of Development Division, R. J. Smith

LAND CHARGES AND AGRICULTURAL CREDITS
DEPARTMENT
Burrington Way, Plymouth PL5 3LP
Tel 01752-635600
Superintendent of Land Charges (G7), J. Hughes

DISTRICT LAND REGISTRIES
BIRKENHEAD – Old Market House, Hamilton Street,
Birkenhead L41 5FL. Tel: 0151-473 1110. *District Land
Registrar*, M. G. Garwood
COVENTRY – Leigh Court, Torrington Avenue, Coventry
CV4 9XZ. Tel: 01203-860860. *District Land Registrar*,
S. P. Kelway
CROYDON – Sunley House, Bedford Park, Croydon
CR9 3LE. Tel: 0181-781 9100. *District Land Registrar*,
D. M. J. Moss
DURHAM – Southfield House, Southfield Way, Durham
DH1 5TR. Tel: 0191-301 3500. *District Land Registrar*,
C. W. Martin
GLOUCESTER – Twyver House, Bruton Way, Gloucester
GL1 1DQ. Tel: 01452-511111. *District Land Registrar*,
W. W. Budden
HARROW – Lyon House, Lyon Road, Harrow, Middx
HA1 2EU. Tel: 0181-427 8811. *District Land Registrar*,
J. V. Timothy
KINGSTON UPON HULL – Earle House, Portland Street,
Hull HU2 8JN. Tel: 01482-223244. *District Land Registrar*,
S. R. Coveney
LEICESTER – Thames Tower, 99 Burleys Way, Leicester
LE1 3UB. Tel: 0116-265 4000. *District Land Registrar*, Mrs
J. A. Goodfellow
LYTHAM – Birkenhead House, Lytham St Annes, Lancs
FY8 5AB. Tel: 01253-849849. *District Land Registrar*,
J. G. Cooper
NOTTINGHAM – Chalfont Drive, Nottingham NG8 3RN.
Tel: 0115-935 1166. *District Land Registrar*,
P. J. Timothy
PETERBOROUGH – Touthill Close, City Road,
Peterborough PE1 1XN. Tel: 01733-288288. *District Land
Registrar*, L. M. Pope
PLYMOUTH – Plumer House, Tailyour Road, Crownhill,
Plymouth PL6 5HY. Tel: 01752-636000. *District Land
Registrar*, A. J. Pain
PORTSMOUTH – St Andrews Court, St Michael's Road,
Portsmouth PO1 2JH. Tel: 01705-768888. *District Land
Registrar*, S. R. Sehrawat
STEVENAGE – Brickdale House, Swingate, Stevenage,
Herts SG1 1XG. Tel: 01438-788888. *District Land Registrar*,
C. Tate
SWANSEA – Tybryn Glas, High Street, Swansea SA1 1PW.
Tel: 01792-458877. *District Land Registrar*,
G. A. Hughes.
TELFORD – Parkside Court, Hall Park Way, Telford TF3
4LR. Tel: 01952-290355. *District Land Registrar*,
M. A. Roche
TUNBRIDGE WELLS – Curtis House, Hawkenbury,
Tunbridge Wells, Kent TN2 5AQ. Tel: 01892-510015.
District Land Registrar, G. R. Tooke

WEYMOUTH – 1 Cumberland Drive, Weymouth, Dorset
DT4 9TT. Tel: 01305-776161. *District Land Registrar*, Mrs
P. M. Reeson
YORK – James House, James Street, York YO1 3YZ. Tel:
01904-450000. *District Land Registrar*, Mrs R. F. Lovel

REGISTERS OF SCOTLAND (EXECUTIVE
AGENCY)
Meadowbank House, 153 London Road, Edinburgh
EH8 7AU
Tel 0131-659 6111

The Registers of Scotland is an executive agency of the
Scottish Office. The Registers consist of: General Register
of Sasines and Land Register of Scotland; Register of
Deeds in the Books of Council and Session; Register of
Protests; Register of Judgments; Register of Service of
Heirs; Register of the Great Seal; Register of the Quarter
Seal; Register of the Prince's Seal; Register of Crown
Grants; Register of Sheriffs' Commissions; Register of the
Cachet Seal; Register of Inhibitions and Adjudications;
Register of Entails; Register of Hornings.

The General Register of Sasines and the Land Register
of Scotland form the chief security in Scotland of the rights
of land and other heritable (or real) property.
Chief Executive and Keeper of the Registers of Scotland (G4),
A. W. Ramage
Deputy Chief Executive (G5), J. K. Mason
Deputy Keeper (G5), A. G. Rennie
Senior Directors (G6), B. J. Corr; A. M. Falconer
Directors (G7), R. Glen (*Human resources*); Miss
M. M. D. Archer (*Land Register*); D. McCallum (*Land
Register*); L. J. Mitchell (*Sasines*); A. M. Gardiner (*Land
Register*); I. M. Nicol (*Finance*); Ms A. Rooney
(*Communications*); T. Wilson (*Commercial*)

LAW COMMISSION
Conquest House, 37–38 John Street, London WC1N 2BQ
Tel 0171-453 1220

The Law Commission was set up in 1965, under the Law
Commissions Act 1965, to make proposals to the Government for the examination of the law in England and Wales
and for its revision where it is unsuited for modern
requirements, obscure, or otherwise unsatisfactory. It
recommends to the Lord Chancellor programmes for the
examination of different branches of the law and suggests
whether the examination should be carried out by the
Commission itself or by some other body. The Commission is also responsible for the preparation of Consolidation
and Statute Law (Repeals) Bills.
Chairman, The Hon. Mrs Justice Arden
Commissioners, C. Harpum; A. S. Burrows; Miss D. Faber;
S. Silber, QC
Secretary, M. W. Sayers

SCOTTISH LAW COMMISSION
140 Causewayside, Edinburgh EH9 1PR
Tel 0131-668 2131

The Commission keeps the law in Scotland under review
and makes proposals for its development and reform. It is
responsible to the Scottish Courts Administration (*see* page
368).
Chairman, The Hon. Lord Davidson

Commissioners (full-time), Dr E. M. Clive; N. R. Whitty;
(*part-time*) Prof. K. G. C. Reid; W. Nimmo Smith, QC
Secretary, J. G. S. MacLean

LAW OFFICERS' DEPARTMENTS
Legal Secretariat to the Law Officers, Attorney-General's
Chambers, 9 Buckingham Gate, London SW1E 6JP
Tel 0171-828 7155
Attorney-General's Chambers, Royal Courts of Justice,
Belfast BT1 3JY
Tel 01232-235111

The Law Officers of the Crown for England and Wales are
the Attorney-General and the Solicitor-General. The
Attorney-General, assisted by the Solicitor-General, is
the chief legal adviser to the Government and is also
ultimately responsible for all Crown litigation. He has
overall responsibility for the work of the Law Officers'
Departments (the Treasury Solicitor's Department, the
Crown Prosecution Service, the Serious Fraud Office and
the Legal Secretariat to the Law Officers). He has a specific
statutory duty to superintend the discharge of their duties
by the Director of Public Prosecutions (who heads the
Crown Prosecution Service) and the Director of the
Serious Fraud Office. The Director of Public Prosecutions
for Northern Ireland is also responsible to the Attorney-
General for the performance of his functions. The
Attorney-General has additional responsibilities in rela-
tion to aspects of the civil and criminal law.
Attorney-General (*£46,745), The Rt. Hon. Sir Nicholas
Lyell, QC, MP
  Private Secretary, S. M. Whatton
Solicitor-General (*£38,329), Sir Derek Spencer, QC, MP
  Private Secretary, S. M. Whatton
  Parliamentary Private Secretary, E. Garnier, QC, MP
Legal Secretary (*G2*), Miss J. L. Wheldon, CB
Deputy Legal Secretary (*G3*), S. J. Wooler
* In addition to a parliamentary salary of £43,000

LEGAL AID BOARD
85 Gray's Inn Road, London WC1X 8AA
Tel 0171-813 1000

The Legal Aid Board has the general function of ensuring
that advice, assistance and representation are available in
accordance with the Legal Aid Act 1988. In 1989 it took
over from the Law Society responsibility for administering
legal aid. The Board is a non-departmental government
body whose members are appointed by the Lord Chancellor.
Chairman, Sir Tim Chessells
Deputy Chairman, H. Hodge
Members, S. Orchard (*Chief Executive*); J. Crosby; Ms
  J. Dunkley; C. George; B. Harvey; Ms K. Markus; Ms
  D. Payne; Ms P. Pearce; G. Pulman, QC; D. Sinker;
  K. Winberg

SCOTTISH LEGAL AID BOARD
44 Drumsheugh Gardens, Edinburgh EH3 7SW
Tel 0131-226 7061

The Scottish Legal Aid Board was set up under the Legal
Aid (Scotland) Act 1986. It is responsible for ensuring that
advice, assistance and representation are available in

accordance with the Act. The Board is a non-departmental
government body whose members are appointed by the
Secretary of State for Scotland.
Chairman, Ms C. A. M. Davis
Members, Mrs K. Blair; Mrs P. M. M. Bowman; Mrs
  S. Campbell; Mrs J. Couper; Prof. P. H. Grinyer; Sheriff
  A. Jessop; N. Kuensberg; R. J. Livingstone;
  C. N. McEachran, QC; Ms Y. Osman; R. Scott;
  A. F. Wylie, QC
Chief Executive, R. Scott

OFFICE OF THE LEGAL SERVICES OMBUDSMAN
22 Oxford Court, Oxford Street, Manchester M2 3WQ
Tel 0161-236 9532

The Legal Services Ombudsman is appointed by the Lord
Chancellor under the Courts and Legal Services Act 1990
to oversee the handling of complaints against solicitors,
barristers and licensed conveyancers by their professional
bodies. A complainant must first complain to the relevant
professional body before raising the matter with the
Ombudsman. The Ombudsman is independent of the legal
profession and his services are free of charge.
Legal Services Ombudsman, M. Barnes
Secretary, S. Murray

OFFICE OF THE SCOTTISH LEGAL SERVICES
OMBUDSMAN
2 Greenside Lane, Edinburgh EH1 3AH
Tel 0131-556 5574
Scottish Legal Services Ombudsman, G. S. Watson

LIBRARIES

LIBRARY AND INFORMATION COMMISSION
2 Sheraton Street, London W1V 4BH
Tel 0171-411 0056

The Commission is an independent body set up by the
Secretary of State for National Heritage in 1995 to advise
the Government and others on library and information
matters, notably in the areas of research strategy and
international links. It also aims to promote co-operation
and co-ordination between different types of information
services.
Chairman, M. Evans
Commissioners, D. Adams; E. Arram; Sir Charles
  Chadwyck-Healey; Dr G. Chambers; Prof. M. Collier;
  Prof. Judith Elkin; Dr B. Lang; D. Law; Dr R. McKee;
  Rabbi Julia Neuberger; Sir Peter Swinnerton-Dyer; Dr
  Sandra Ward; M. Wood
Executive Secretary, vacant

THE BRITISH LIBRARY
96 Euston Road, London NW1 2DB
Tel 0171-412 7000

The British Library was established in 1973. It is the UK's
national library and occupies the central position in the
library and information network. The Library aims to serve
scholarship, research, industry, commerce and all other
major users of information. Its services are based on
collections which include over 18 million volumes, 1
million discs, and 55,000 hours of tape recordings, at 18
buildings in London and one complex in West Yorkshire.
The British Library's new purpose-built accommodation

at St Pancras, London NW1 is scheduled to open to the public in a phased programme starting in late 1997. Government grant-in-aid to the British Library in 1996–7 is £85.1 million; the British Library St Pancras Project receives £21.5 million. The Library's sponsoring department is the Department of National Heritage.

Access to the Humanities and Social Sciences reading rooms is limited to holders of a British Library Reader's Pass; information about eligibility is available from the Reader Admissions Office. The reading rooms of the Science Reference and Information Service are open to the general public without charge or formality.

Opening hours of services vary; most services are closed for one week each year. Specific information should be checked by telephone.

BRITISH LIBRARY BOARD
96 Euston Road, London NW1 2DB
Tel 0171-412 7262

Chairman, Dr J. Ashworth
Chief Executive and Deputy Chairman (*G2*), Dr B. Lang
Deputy Chief Executive (*G4*), D. Russon
Director-General, Collections and Services (*G4*), D. Bradbury
Part-time Members, T. J. Rix; D. Peake; The Hon.
    E. Adeane, CVO; Sir Matthew Farrer, GCVO; Mrs
    P. M. Lively, OBE; Prof. M. Anderson, FBA, FRSE;
    A. Bloom; B. Naylor; J. Ritblat

BRITISH LIBRARY, BOSTON SPA
Boston Spa, Wetherby, W. Yorks LS23 7BQ
Tel 01937-546000

DOCUMENT SUPPLY CENTRE, *Director (acting)* (G5), M.
    Smith
NATIONAL BIBLIOGRAPHIC SERVICE. Tel: 01937-546585.
    Director (*G6*), R. Smith
London Unit, 2 Sheraton Street, London WIV 4BH. Tel:
    0171-412 7077
ACQUISITIONS PROCESSING AND CATALOGUING, *Director*
    (*G5*), S. Ede
COMPUTING AND TELECOMMUNICATIONS. Tel: 01937-
    546879. *Director* (*G5*), J. R. Mahoney

BRITISH LIBRARY, LONDON
Great Russell Street, London WCIB 3DG
Tel 0171-412 7000

St Pancras Project Director (*G4*), D. Lyman
Director of Project Services St Pancras Planning (*G6*), Dr
    R. Coman

ADMINISTRATION, 2 Sheraton Street, London WIV 4BH.
    Tel: 0171-412 7132. *Director* (*G5*), D. Gesua
PRESS AND PUBLIC RELATIONS, 96 Euston Road, London
    NW1 2DB. Tel: 0171-412 7111. *Head* (*G7*), M. Jackson
PUBLIC SERVICES. Tel: 0171-412 7626. *Director* (*G5*), Ms
    J. Carr
Exhibitions and Education Service. Tel: 0171-412 7595
Reader Admissions. Tel: 0171-412 7677

HUMANITIES AND SOCIAL SCIENCES. Tel: 0171-412 7676.
    Director (*G5*), A. Phillips
*West European Collections, Slavonic and East European
    Collections, English Language Collections.* Tel: 0171-412
    7676
Social Policy Information Service. Tel: 0171-412 7536
Information Sciences Service (BLISS), Ridgmount Street,
    London WCIE 7AE. Tel: 0171-412 7688
Newspaper Library, Colindale Avenue, London NW9 5HE.
    Tel: 0171-412 7353
National Sound Archive, 29 Exhibition Road, London SW7
    2AS. Tel: 0171-412 7440

COLLECTIONS AND PRESERVATION. Tel: 0171-412 7676.
    Director (*G5*), Dr M. Foot
Preservation Service (National Preservation Office). Tel: 0171-
    412 7612

SPECIAL COLLECTIONS. Tel: 0171-412 7513. *Director*
    (*G5*), Dr A. Prochaska
Oriental and India Office Collections, 197 Blackfriars Road,
    London SE1 8NG. Tel: 0171-412 7873
Western Manuscripts. Tel: 0171-412 7513
Map Library. Tel: 0171-412 7700
Music Library. Tel: 0171-412 7528
Philatelic Collections. Tel: 0171-412 7729

SCIENCE REFERENCE AND INFORMATION SERVICE,
    25 Southampton Buildings, London WC2A 1AW. Tel:
    0171-412 7494; 9 Kean Street, London WC2B 4AT. Tel:
    0171-412 7288. *Director* (*G5*), A. Gomersall

RESEARCH AND INNOVATION CENTRE, 2 Sheraton
    Street, London WIV 4BH. Tel: 0171-412 7055. *Director*
    (*G6*), N. Macartney

NATIONAL LIBRARY OF SCOTLAND
George IV Bridge, Edinburgh EHI 1EW
Tel 0131-226 4531

The Library, which was founded as the Advocates' Library in 1682, became the National Library of Scotland in 1925. It is funded by the Scottish Office. It contains about six million books and pamphlets, 18,000 current periodicals, 230 newspaper titles and 100,000 manuscripts. It has an unrivalled Scottish collection.

The Reading Room for reference and research which cannot conveniently be pursued elsewhere. Admission is by ticket issued to an approved applicant. Opening hours: Reading Room, weekdays, 9.30–8.30 (Wednesday, 10–8.30); Saturday 9.30–1. Map Library, weekdays, 9.30–5 (Wednesday, 10–5); Saturday 9.30–1. Exhibition, weekdays, 10–5; Saturday 10–5; Sunday 2–5. Scottish Science Library, weekdays, 9.30–5 (Wednesday, 10–8.30).

Chairman of the Trustees, The Earl of Crawford and
    Balcarres, PC
Librarian and Secretary to the Trustees (*G4*), I. D. McGowan
Secretary of the Library (*G6*), M. C. Graham
Keeper of Printed Books (*G6*), Ms A. Matheson, PH.D.
Keeper of Manuscripts (*G6*), I. C. Cunningham
Director of Public Services (*G6*), A. M. Marchbank, PH.D.
Director of Electronic Information (*G6*), B. Gallivan

NATIONAL LIBRARY OF WALES/
LLYFRGELL GENEDLAETHOL CYMRU
Aberystwyth SY23 3BU
Tel 01970-623816

The National Library of Wales was founded by Royal Charter in 1907, and is maintained by annual grant from the Welsh Office. It contains about four million printed books, 40,000 manuscripts, four million deeds and documents, numerous maps, prints and drawings, and a sound and moving image collection. It specializes in manuscripts and books relating to Wales and the Celtic peoples. It is the repository for pre-1858 Welsh probate records, manorial records and tithe documents, and certain legal records. Readers' room open weekdays, 9.30–6 (Saturday 9.30–5); closed first week of October. Admission by Reader's Ticket.

President, Prof. Emeritus J. Gwynn Williams
Librarian (*G4*), Dr J. L. Madden
Heads of Departments (*G6*), M. W. Mainwaring
    (*Administration and Technical Services*); G. Jenkins
    (*Manuscripts and Records*); Dr W. R. M. Griffiths (*Printed
    Books*); Dr D. H. Owen (*Pictures and Maps*)

LIGHTHOUSE AUTHORITIES

CORPORATION OF TRINITY HOUSE
Trinity House, Tower Hill, London EC3N 4DH
Tel 0171-480 6601

Trinity House, the first general lighthouse and pilotage authority in the kingdom, was granted its first charter by Henry VIII in 1514. The Corporation is the general lighthouse authority for England, Wales and the Channel Islands and maintains 67 lighthouses (of which 11 are manned), 14 major floating aids to navigation (e.g. light vessels) and more than 400 buoys. It also has certain statutory jurisdiction over aids to navigation maintained by local harbour authorities and is responsible for dealing with wrecks dangerous to navigation, except those occurring within port limits or wrecks of HM ships.

The Trinity House Lighthouse Service is maintained out of the General Lighthouse Fund which is provided from light dues levied on ships calling at ports of the UK and the Republic of Ireland. The Corporation is also a deep-sea pilotage authority and a charitable organization.

The affairs of the Corporation are controlled by a board of Elder Brethren and the Secretary. A separate board, which comprises Elder Brethren, senior staff and outside representatives, currently controls the Lighthouse Service. The Elder Brethren also act as nautical assessors in marine cases in the Admiralty Division of the High Court of Justice.

ELDER BRETHREN
Master, HRH The Duke of Edinburgh, KG, KT
Deputy Master, Rear-Adm. P. B. Rowe, CBE, LVO
Elder Brethren, Capt. D. J. Orr; Capt. N. M. Turner, RD;
   Capt. Sir Malcolm Edge, KCVO; HRH The Prince of
   Wales, KG, KT; HRH The Duke of York, CVO, ADC; Capt.
   R. N. Mayo, CBE; Capt. Sir David Tibbits, DSC, RN; Capt.
   D. A. G. Dickens; Capt. J. E. Bury; Capt. J. A. N. Bezant,
   DSC, RD, RNR (retd.); Capt. D. J. Cloke; Capt. Sir Miles
   Wingate, KCVO; The Rt. Hon. Sir Edward Heath, KG,
   MBE, MP; Capt. I. R. C. Saunders; Capt. P. F. Mason, CBE;
   Capt. T. Woodfield, OBE; Sir Eric Drake, CBE; The Lord
   Simon of Glaisdale, PC; Admiral of the Fleet the Lord
   Lewin, KG, GCB, LVO, DSC; Capt. D. T. Smith, RN; Cdr. Sir
   Robin Gillett, Bt., GBE, RD, RNR; The Lord Cuckney;
   The Lord Carrington, KG, GCMG, CH, MC, PC; Sir Brian
   Shaw; The Lord Mackay of Clashfern, PC; Sir Adrian
   Swire; Capt. P. H. King; The Lord Sterling of Plaistow,
   CBE, RNR; Cdr. M. J. Rivett-Carnac, RN; Capt. C. M. C.
   Stewart; Adm. Sir Jock Slater, GCB, LVO

OFFICERS
Secretary, R. F. Dobb
Director of Finance, K. W. Clark
Director of Engineering, M. G. B. Wannell
Director of Administration, D. I. Brewer
General Manager Operations, Capt. J. M. Barnes
Human Resources and Communications Manager,
   N. J. Cutmore
Operations Administration Manager, S. J. W. Dunning
Legal and Insurance Manager, J. D. Price
Navigation Manager, Mrs K. Hossain
Deputy Director of Engineering, P. N. Hyde
Senior Inspector of Shipping, J. R. Dunnett
Media and Communication Officer, H. L. Cooper

COMMISSIONERS OF NORTHERN LIGHTHOUSES
84 George Street, Edinburgh EH2 3DA
Tel 0131-226 7051

The Commissioners of Northern Lighthouses are the general lighthouse authority for Scotland and the Isle of Man. The present board owes its origin to an Act of Parliament passed in 1786. At present the Commissioners operate under the Merchant Shipping Act 1894 and are 19 in number.

The Commissioners control 8 major manned lighthouses, 76 major automatic lighthouses, 112 minor lights and many lighted and unlighted buoys. They have a fleet of two motor vessels.

COMMISSIONERS
The Lord Advocate; the Solicitor-General for Scotland; the Lord Provosts of Edinburgh, Glasgow and Aberdeen; the Provost of Inverness; the Convener of Argyll and Bute Council; the Sheriffs-Principal of North Strathclyde, Tayside, Central and Fife, Grampian, Highlands and Islands, South Strathclyde, Dumfries and Galloway, Lothians and Borders, and Glasgow and Strathkelvin; A. J. Struthers; W. F. Hay, CBE; Capt. D. M. Cowell; Adm. Sir Michael Livesay, KCB; The Lord Maclay

OFFICERS
Chief Executive, Capt. J. B. Taylor, RN
Director of Finance, D. Gorman
Director of Engineering, W. Paterson
Director of Operations and Navigational Requirements,
   P. J. Christmas

LOCAL COMMISSIONERS

COMMISSION FOR LOCAL ADMINISTRATION IN ENGLAND
21 Queen Anne's Gate, London SW1H 9BU
Tel 0171-915 3210

Local Commissioners (local government ombudsmen) are responsible for investigating complaints from members of the public against local authorities (but not town and parish councils); police authorities; the Commission for New Towns (housing functions); urban development corporations (town and country planning functions) and certain other authorities. The Commissioners are appointed by the Crown on the recommendation of the Secretary of State for the Environment.

Certain types of action are excluded from investigation, including personnel matters and commercial transactions unless they relate to the purchase or sale of land. Complaints can be sent direct to the Local Government Ombudsman or through a councillor, although the Local Government Ombudsman will not consider a complaint unless the council has had an opportunity to investigate and reply to a complainant.

A free booklet *Complaint about the council? How to complain to the Local Government Ombudsman* is available from the Commission's office.

Chairman of the Commission and Local Commissioner
   (£95,051), E. B. C. Osmotherly, CB
Vice-Chairman and Local Commissioner (£77,875), Mrs
   P. A. Thomas
Local Commissioner (£76,875), J. R. White
Member (ex officio), The Parliamentary Commissioner for
   Administration
Secretary (£48,135), G. D. Adams

COMMISSION FOR LOCAL ADMINISTRATION IN WALES
Derwen House, Court Road, Bridgend CF31 1BN
Tel 01656-661325

The Local Commissioner for Wales has similar powers to the Local Commissioners in England. The Commissioner is appointed by the Crown on the recommendation of the Secretary of State for Wales. A free leaflet *Your Local Ombudsman in Wales* is available from the Commission's office.
Local Commissioner, E. R. Moseley
Secretary, D. Bowen
Member (ex officio), The Parliamentary Commissioner for Administration

COMMISSIONER FOR LOCAL ADMINISTRATION IN SCOTLAND
23 Walker Street, Edinburgh EH3 7HX
Tel 0131-225 5300

The Local Commissioner for Scotland has similar powers to the Local Commissioners in England, and is appointed by the Crown on the recommendation of the Secretary of State for Scotland.
Local Commissioner, F. C. Marks, OBE
Deputy and Secretary, Ms J. H. Renton

LONDON REGIONAL TRANSPORT
55 Broadway, London SW1H 0BD
Tel 0171-222 5600

Subject to the financial objectives and principles approved by the Secretary of State for Transport, London Regional Transport has a general duty to provide or secure the provision of public transport services for Greater London.
Chairman (£154,500), P. Ford
Member, and Managing Director of London Transport Board (£68,967), C. Hodson, CBE
Member for Finance (£92,784), A. J. Sheppeck
Member, and Managing Director of London Underground Ltd (£108,635), D. Tunnicliffe

LORD ADVOCATE'S DEPARTMENT
2 Carlton Gardens, London SW1Y 5AA
Tel 0171-210 1010

The Law Officers for Scotland are the Lord Advocate and the Solicitor-General for Scotland. The Lord Advocate's Department is responsible for drafting Scottish legislation, for providing legal advice to other departments on Scottish questions and for assistance to the Law Officers for Scotland in certain of their legal duties.
Lord Advocate (£57,241), The Lord Mackay of Drumadoon, PC, QC
Private Secretary, A. G. Maxwell
Solicitor-General for Scotland (£48,985), Paul Cullen, QC
Private Secretary, A. G. Maxwell
Legal Secretary and First Scottish Parliamentary Counsel (G2), J. C. McCluskie, QC
Assistant Legal Secretaries and Scottish Parliamentary Counsel (G3), G. M. Clark; G. Kowalski; P. J. Layden, TD; C. A. M. Wilson
Assistant Legal Secretary and Depute Scottish Parliamentary Counsel (G5), J. D. Harkness

LORD CHANCELLOR'S DEPARTMENT
Selborne House, 54–60 Victoria Street, London SW1E 6QB
Tel 0171-210 8500

The Lord Chancellor is the principal legal adviser of the Crown, Speaker of the House of Lords, President of the House of Lords as an Appellate Court, of the Court of Appeal, and of the Chancery Division of the High Court of Justice, and acting President of the Judicial Committee of the Privy Council. The Lord Chancellor appoints Justices of the Peace (except in Lancashire) and advises the Crown on the appointment of most members of the higher judiciary. He is responsible for promoting general reforms in the civil law, for the procedure of the civil courts and for legal aid schemes. He is a member of the Cabinet. He also has ministerial responsibility for magistrates' courts, which are administered locally. Administration of the Supreme Court and county courts in England and Wales was taken over by the Court Service, an executive agency of the department, in April 1995.

The Lord Chancellor is also responsible for ensuring that letters patent and other formal documents are passed in the proper form under the Great Seal of the Realm, of which he is the custodian. The work in connection with this is carried out under his direction in the Office of the Clerk of the Crown in Chancery.
Lord Chancellor (£132,178), The Lord Mackay of Clashfern, PC
Private Secretary, P. Kennedy
Parliamentary Private Secretary, P. Luff, MP
Parliamentary Secretary, Gary Streeter, MP
Private Secretary, A. Clegg
Permanent Secretary (G1), Sir Thomas Legg, KCB, QC
Private Secretary, Ms M. Cale

CROWN OFFICE
House of Lords, London SW1A 0PW
Clerk of the Crown in Chancery (G1), Sir Thomas Legg, KCB, QC
Deputy Clerk of the Crown in Chancery (G2), M. Huebner, CB
Clerk of the Chamber, C. I. P. Denyer

JUDICIAL APPOINTMENTS GROUP
Tel 0171-210 8926

Head of Group (G3), R. E. K. Holmes
Grade 5, D. E. Staff (*Policy and Conditions of Service*); Mrs M. Pigott (*Circuit Bench*); Miss J. Killick (*Circuit Bench*); E. Adams (*District Bench and Tribunals*); R. Venne (*Magistrates' Appointments*)

Judicial Studies Board
14 Little St James's Street, London SW1A 1DP
Tel 0171-925 0185
Grade 5, P. G. Taylor

POLICY GROUP
Tel 0171-210 8719

Head of Group (G2), I. M. Burns, CB
Heads of Divisions (G5), S. Smith (*Legal Aid*); Ms J. Rowe (*Criminal Policy*); D. Gladwell (*Civil Justice*); R. Sams (*Law Reform and Tribunals*); W. Arnold (*Family Policy*); P. G. Harris (*Legal Aid Reform*); A. J. Finlay (*Woolf Inquiry*)
Head of Secretariat and Agency Monitoring Unit (G7), Ms A. Jones

LEGAL ADVISER'S GROUP
Tel 0171-210 0711

Legal Adviser (G3), R. H. H. White

Grade 4, M. H. Collon (*Legal Advice and Litigation*)
Grade 5, J. Watherston (*International*); M. Kron (*Rules of Court and Regulations*)

CORPORATE SERVICES GROUP
Tel 0171-210 5503

Director of Corporate Services and Principal Establishment and Finance Officer (G3), Mrs N. A. Oppenheimer
Grade 5, Ms H. Tuffs (*Personnel Management*); A. Cogbill (*Finance*); A. Maultby (*Planning and Communications*)
Grade 6, K. Cregeen (*Accommodation and Magistrates' Courts Building*); A. Rummins (*Internal Audit*); K. Garrett (*Statutory Publications Office*)

MAGISTRATES' COURTS GROUP
Tel 0171-210 8809

Head of Group (G3), L. C. Oates
Grade 5, M. E. Ormerod
Grade 6, P. Duffin

ECCLESIASTICAL PATRONAGE
10 Downing Street, London SW1A 2AA
Tel 0171-930 4433

Secretary for Ecclesiastical Patronage, J. H. Holroyd, CB
Assistant Secretary for Ecclesiastical Patronage, N. C. Wheeler

MAGISTRATES' COURTS' SERVICE INSPECTORATE
Southside, 105 Victoria Street, London SW1E 6QJ
Tel 0171-210 1655

Chief Inspector (G5), Mrs R. L. Melling
Senior Inspectors (G6), Ms J. Eeles; D. Gear; C. Monson; Ms S. Steel

LORD CHANCELLOR'S ADVISORY COMMITTEE ON STATUTE LAW
6 Spring Gardens, London SW1A 2BP
Tel 0171-389 3244

The Advisory Committee advises the Lord Chancellor on all matters relating to the revision, modernization and publication of the statute book.

Chairman, The Lord Chancellor
Deputy Chairman, Sir Thomas Legg, KCB, QC
Members, Sir Michael Wheeler-Booth, KCB; Sir Clifford Boulton, KCB; The Hon. Mr Justice Brooke; The Hon. Lord Davidson; C. Jenkins, CB, QC; J. C. McCluskie, QC; G. Hosker, CB, QC; R. Brodie, CB; R. H. H White; J. Gibson; Dr P. Freeman; (*ex officio*) First Legislative Counsel, Northern Ireland
Secretary, C. Carey

EXECUTIVE AGENCIES

THE COURT SERVICE
Southside, 105 Victoria Street, London SW1E 6QT
Tel 0171-210 1775

The Court Service provides administrative support to the Supreme Court of England and Wales, county courts and a number of tribunals.

Chief Executive (G2), M. Huebner
Grade 5, P. Handcock (*operational support*)

Finance and Administration Group
Director (G3), C. W. V. Everett
Grade 5, K. Pogson (*resources*); Miss B. Kenny (*personnel and training*); P. Jacobs (*project manager, LOCCS*); A. Shaw (*accommodation, procurement, libraries and records*); P. White (*information technology (ISD)*)

Royal Courts of Justice
Strand, London WC2A 2LL
Tel 0171-936 6000
Administrator, G. E. Calvett

For Supreme Court departments and offices and circuit administrators, *see* Law Courts and Offices section

HM LAND REGISTRY
— *see* pages 315–16

PUBLIC RECORD OFFICE
— *see* pages 336–7

PUBLIC TRUST OFFICE
— *see* page 335

LORD GREAT CHAMBERLAIN'S OFFICE
House of Lords, London SW1A 0PW
Tel 0171-219 3100

The Lord Great Chamberlain is a Great Officer of State, the office being hereditary since the grant of Henry I to the family of De Vere, Earls of Oxford. The Lord Great Chamberlain is responsible for the Royal Apartments of the Palace of Westminster, i.e. The Queen's Robing Room, the Royal Gallery and, in conjunction with the Lord Chancellor and Madam Speaker, Westminster Hall. The Lord Great Chamberlain has particular responsibility for the internal administrative arrangements within the House of Lords for State Openings of Parliament.

Lord Great Chamberlain, The Marquess of Cholmondeley
Secretary to the Lord Great Chamberlain, Gen. Sir Edward Jones, KCB, CBE
Clerks to the Lord Great Chamberlain, Mrs S. E. Douglas; Miss R. M. Wilkinson

LORD PRIVY SEAL'S OFFICE
Privy Council Office, 68 Whitehall, London SW1A 2AT
Tel 0171-270 3000

The Lord Privy Seal is a member of the Cabinet and Leader of the House of Lords. He has no departmental portfolio, but is a member of a number of domestic and economic Cabinet committees. He is responsible to the Prime Minister for the organization of government business in the House and has a responsibility to the House itself to advise it on procedural matters and other difficulties which arise.

Lord Privy Seal, and Leader of the House of Lords, Viscount Cranborne, PC
Principal Private Secretary, Mrs J. Hope
Private Secretary (House of Lords), Mrs M. Ollard
Special Adviser, Ms S. McEwen
Parliamentary Private Secretary, J. Sykes, MP

LOTTERY, OFFICE OF THE NATIONAL
— *see* page 328

OFFICE OF MANPOWER ECONOMICS
Oxford House, 76 Oxford Street, London W1N 9FD
Tel 0171-467 7244

The Office of Manpower Economics was set up in 1971. It is an independent non-statutory organization which is responsible for servicing independent review bodies which advise on the pay of various public service groups (*see* Review Bodies, page 337), the Pharmacists Review Panel and the Police Negotiating Board. The Office is also responsible for servicing *ad hoc* bodies of inquiry and for undertaking research into pay and associated matters as requested by the Government.

OME Director, M. J. Horsman
Director, Statistics and Office Services, G. S. Charles
Director, Armed Forces Secretariat, A. Hughes
Director, Health Secretariat, and OME Deputy Director, Miss S. M. Haird
Director, Teachers' and Police Secretariats, P. J. H. Edwards
Director, Senior Salaries Secretariat, Mrs C. Haworth
Press Liaison Officer, M. C. Cahill

MENTAL HEALTH ACT COMMISSION
Maid Marian House, 56 Hounds Gate, Nottingham
NGI 6BG
Tel 0115-950 4040

The Mental Health Act Commission was established in 1983. Its functions are to keep under review the operation of the Mental Health Act 1983; to visit and meet patients detained under the Act; to investigate complaints falling within the Commission's remit; to operate the consent to treatment safeguards in the Mental Health Act; to publish a biennial report on its activities; to monitor the implementation of the Code of Practice; and to advise ministers. Commissioners are appointed by the Secretary of State for Health.

Chairman, The Viscountess Runciman of Doxford, OBE
Vice-Chairman, N. Pleming
Chief Executive (G6), W. Bingley

MILLENNIUM COMMISSION
2 Little Smith Street, London SWIP 3DH
Tel 0171-340 2001

The Millennium Commission was established in February 1994 and is funded by the Department of National Heritage. It is an independent body which distributes 20 per cent of the money allocated to 'good causes' from National Lottery proceeds to projects to mark the millennium. The Commission had made awards totalling £494 million by April 1996.

Chairman, The Rt. Hon. Virginia Bottomley, MP
Members, Prof. Heather Couper, FRAS; Earl of Dalkeith; The Lord Glentoran, CBE; Sir John Hall; The Rt. Hon. M. Heseltine, MP; S. Jenkins; M. Montague, CBE; Miss P. Scotland, QC
Chief Executive, Miss J. A. Page, CBE

MONOPOLIES AND MERGERS COMMISSION
New Court, 48 Carey Street, London WC2A 2JT
Tel 0171-324 1407

The Commission was established in 1949 as the Monopolies and Restrictive Practices Commission and became the Monopolies and Mergers Commission under the Fair Trading Act 1973. Its role is to investigate and report on matters which are referred to it by the Secretary of State for Trade and Industry or the Director-General of Fair Trading or, in the case of privatized industries, by the appropriate regulator. Its decisions are determined by the criteria set out in the legislation covering the different types of reference. The main types of reference which can be made are: monopolies; mergers; newspaper mergers; general, involving general practices in an industry; restrictive labour practices; competition, involving anti-competitive practices of individual firms; public sector audits; privatized industries; and Channel 3 (ITV) networking arrangements between holders of regional Channel 3 licences. References may be made under the Fair Trading Act 1973, the Competition Act 1980, the Broadcasting Act or other relevant statutes.

The Commission consists of about 35 members, including a full-time chairman and three part-time deputy chairmen, all appointed by the Secretary of State for Trade and Industry. Each inquiry is conducted on behalf of the Commission by a group of four to six members who are appointed by the chairman.

Chairman (£97,440), G. D. W. Odgers
Deputy Chairmen (£40–£60,000), D. Morris, PH.D.; P. H. Dean, CBE; D. G. Goyder, CBE
Members (£13,765/*£9,175 each), Prof. J. Beatson; Prof. M. Cave; R. H. F. Croft, CB; *R. Davies; Prof. S. Eilon; *J. Evans; *N. H. Finney, OBE; *Sir Archibald Forster; *Sir Ronald Halstead, CBE; D. B. Hammond; *Ms P. A. Hodgson; D. J. Jenkins, MBE; H. H. Liesner, CB; R. Lyons; P. Mackay; *N. F. Matthews; Prof. J. S. Metcalfe, CBE; *Mrs K. Mortimer; *R. Munson; Prof. D. Newbery; Dr Gill Owen; *Prof. J. F. Pickering; *L. Priestley; R. Prosser; Prof. Judith Rees; Dr Ann Robinson; *J. K. Roe; *Dr Lynda Rouse; *G. H. Stacy, CBE; Mrs C. Tritton, QC; Prof. G. Whittington
Secretary, Miss P. Boys
* Reserve members

MUSEUMS

MUSEUMS AND GALLERIES COMMISSION
16 Queen Anne's Gate, London SWIH 9AA
Tel 0171-233 4200

Established in 1931 as the Standing Commission on Museums and Galleries, the Commission was renamed and took up new functions in 1981. Its sponsor department is the Department of National Heritage. The Commission advises the Government, including the Department of Education for Northern Ireland, the Scottish Education Department and the Welsh Office, on museum affairs. Commissioners are appointed by the Prime Minister.

The Commission's executive functions include providing the services of the Museums Security Adviser; allocating grants to the seven Area Museum Councils in England; funding and monitoring the work of the Museum Documentation Association; and administering grant schemes for non-national museums. The Commission administers the arrangements for government indemnities and the acceptance of works of art in lieu of inheritance tax, and its Conservation Unit advises on conservation and environmental standards. A registration scheme for museums in the UK is operated by the Commission.

Chairman, J. Joll
Members, The Marchioness of Anglesey, DBE; J. Baer; Prof. P. Bateson, FRS; The Baroness Brigstocke; Prof. R. Buchanan;The Viscountess Cobham; R. Foster; L. Grossman; Adm. Sir John Kerr, GCB; J. Last, CBE; Prof. D. Michie; The Lord Rees, PC, QC; R. H. Smith; A. Warhurst, CBE; Mrs C. Wilson
Director and Secretary, T. Mason

THE BRITISH MUSEUM
Great Russell Street, London WC1B 3DG
Tel 0171-636 1555

The British Museum houses the national collection of antiquities, coins and paper money, medals, and prints and drawings. The ethnographical collections are displayed at the Museum of Mankind. The British Museum may be said to date from 1753, when Parliament approved the holding of a public lottery to raise funds for the purchase of the collections of Sir Hans Sloane and the Harleian manuscripts, and for their proper housing and maintenance. The building (Montagu House) was opened in 1759. The present buildings were erected between 1823 and the present day, and the original collection has increased to its present dimensions by gifts and purchases. Total government grant-in-aid for 1996–7 is £33.196 million.

BOARD OF TRUSTEES
Appointed by the Sovereign, HRH The Duke of Gloucester, GCVO
Appointed by the Prime Minister, N. Barber; Prof. Gillian Beer, FBA; Sir John Boyd; J. Browne, FEng.; Sir Matthew Farrer, GCVO; Sir Peter Harrop, KCB; Sir Michael Hopkins, CBE, RA, RIBA; Sir Joseph Hotung; S. Keswick; Hon. Mrs M. Marten, OBE; Sir John Morgan, KCMG; The Rt. Hon. Sir Timothy Raison; Prof. G. H. Treitel, DCL, FBA, QC
Nominated by the Learned Societies, Prof. Jean Thomas, CBE (*Royal Society*); A. Jones, RA (*Royal Academy*); Sir Claus Moser, KCB, CBE, FBA (*British Academy*); The Lord Renfrew of Kaimsthorn, FBA, FSA (*Society of Antiquaries*)
Appointed by the Trustees of the British Museum, G. C. Greene, CBE (*Chairman*); Sir David Attenborough, CH, CVO, CBE, FRS; Prof. Rosemary Cramp, CBE, FSA; The Lord Egremont; Dr Jennifer Montagu, FBA

OFFICERS
Director (*G2*), Dr R. G. W. Anderson, FRSC, FSA
Deputy Director (*G4*), Miss J. M. Rankine
Secretary (*G6*), Mrs C. Nihoul Parker
Head of Public Services (*G6*), G. A. L. House
Head of Press and Public Relations (*SIO*), A. E. Hamilton
Head of Design (*G6*), Miss M. Hall, OBE
Head of Education (*G7*), J. F. Reeve
Head of Administration (*G5*), C. E. I. Jones
Head of Building Development and Planning (*G5*), K. T. Stannard
Head of Building Management (*G6*), T. R. A. Giles
Head of Finance (*G7*), Miss S. E. Davies
Head of Personnel and Office Services (*G7*), Miss B. A. Hughes

KEEPERS
Keeper of Prints and Drawings (*G5*), A. V. Griffiths
Keeper of Coins and Medals (*G5*), Dr A. M. Burnett
Keeper of Egyptian Antiquities (*G5*), W. V. Davies
Keeper of Western Asiatic Antiquities (*G5*), Dr J. E. Curtis
Keeper of Greek and Roman Antiquities (*G5*), Dr D. J. R. Williams
Keeper of Medieval and Later Antiquities (*G5*), N. M. Stratford
Keeper of Prehistoric and Romano-British Antiquities (*G5*), Dr T. M. Potter
Keeper of Japanese Antiquities (*G5*), L. R. H. Smith
Keeper of Oriental Antiquities (*G5*), R. J. Knox
Keeper of Ethnography (*G5*), B. J. Mack
Keeper of Scientific Research (*G5*), Dr S. G. E. Bowman
Keeper of Conservation (*G5*), W. A. Oddy

NATURAL HISTORY MUSEUM
Cromwell Road, London SW7 5BD
Tel 0171-938 9123

The Natural History Museum originates from the natural history departments of the British Museum, which grew extensively during the 19th century and in 1860 the natural history collection was moved from Bloomsbury to a new location. Part of the site of the 1862 International Exhibition in South Kensington was acquired for the new museum, and the Museum opened to the public in 1881. In 1963 the Natural History Museum became completely independent with its own body of trustees. The Walter Rothschild Zoological Museum, Tring, bequeathed by the second Lord Rothschild, has formed part of the Museum since 1938. The Geological Museum merged with the Natural History Museum in 1985. Total government grant-in-aid for 1996–7 is £27.445 million.

BOARD OF TRUSTEES
Appointed by the Prime Minister: Sir Robert May, FRS (*Chairman*); The Baroness Blackstone, PH.D.; Mrs J. M. d'Abo; Sir Denys Henderson; Sir Crispin Tickell, GCMG, KCVO; Dame Anne McLaren, DBE, FRS; Prof. Sir Ronald Oxburgh, FRS; Sir Richard Sykes
Nominated by the Royal Society, Prof. J. L. Harper, CBE, FRS
Appointed by the Trustees of the Natural History Museum, Prof. Sir Brian Follett, FRS; Prof. K. O'Nions, FRS; The Lord Palumbo

SENIOR STAFF
Director, N. R. Chalmers, PH.D.
Director of Science, Prof. P. Henderson, D.phil.
Science Policy Co-ordinator, Ms N. Donlon
Secretary and Head of Corporate Services, C. J. E. Legg
Head of Development and Marketing, Mrs T. Burman
Keeper of Zoology, C. R. Curds, D.SC
Director, Tring Zoological Museum, I. R. Bishop, OBE
Keeper of Entomology, Dr R. P. Lane
Keeper of Botany, S. Blackmore, PH.D.
Keeper of Palaeontology, L. R. M. Cocks, D.SC
Keeper of Mineralogy, Dr A. Fleet
Head of Finance, J. Card
Head of Personnel, Mrs P. H. I. Orchard
Head of Library and Information Services, vacant
Head of Education and Exhibitions (*G5*), Dr G. Clarke
Head of Visitor Services, Mrs W. B. Gullick
Head of Estates, G. Pellow

THE SCIENCE MUSEUM
South Kensington, London SW7 2DD
Tel 0171-938 8000

The Science Museum, part of the National Museum of Science and Industry, houses the national collections of science, technology, industry and medicine. The Museum began as the science collection of the South Kensington Museum and first opened in 1857. In 1883 it acquired the collections of the Patent Museum and in 1909 the science collections were transferred to the new Science Museum, leaving the art collections with the Victoria and Albert Museum.

Some of the Museum's commercial aircraft, agricultural machinery, and road and rail transport collections are at Wroughton, Wilts. The Museum is also responsible for the National Railway Museum, York; the National Museum of Photography, Film and Television, Bradford; and the Concorde Exhibition at the Fleet Air Arm Museum, Yeovilton.

Total government grant-in-aid for 1996–7 is £20.63 million.

BOARD OF TRUSTEES
Chairman, Dr P. Williams, CBE
Members, HRH The Duke of Kent, KG, GCMG, GCVO, ADC;
Dr Mary Archer; The Viscount Downe; G. Dyke;
Miss M. S. Goldring, OBE; Dr Anne Grocock; Mrs
A. Higham, OBE; Mrs J. Kennedy, OBE; Dr Bridget
Ogilvie; Sir David Puttnam; Sir Michael Quinlan, GCB;
L. de Rothschild, CBE; Sir Christopher Wates

OFFICERS
Director, Sir Neil Cossons, OBE, FSA
*Assistant Director and Head of Resource Management
Division,* J. J. Defries
Head of Personnel and Training, C. Gosling
Head of Finance, Ms A. Caine
Assistant Director and Head of Collections Division, Dr T.
Wright
Head of Physical Sciences and Engineering Group,
Dr D. A. Robinson
Head of Life and Communications Technologies Group,
Dr R. F. Bud
Head of Collections Management Group, Dr S. Keene
Assistant Director and Head of Public Affairs Division,
C. M. Pemberton
Assistant Director and Head of Science Communication Division,
Prof. J. R. Durant
Head of Education and Programmes, Dr R. Jackson
Head of Exhibitions, Dr G. Farmelo
Assistant Director and Head of Project Development Division,
Mrs G. M. Thomas
Head of Design, T. Molloy
Head of National Railway Museum, A. Scott
Head of National Museum of Photography, Film and Television,
Ms A. Nevill

VICTORIA AND ALBERT MUSEUM
South Kensington, London SW7 2RL
Tel 0171-938 8500

The national museum of all branches of fine and applied art
and design, the Victoria and Albert Museum descends
directly from the Museum of Manufactures, which opened
in Marlborough House in 1852 after the Great Exhibition
of 1851. The Museum was moved in 1857 to become part of
the South Kensington Museum. It was renamed the
Victoria and Albert Museum in 1899. It also houses the
National Art Library and Print Room.

The branch museum at Bethnal Green, which houses
the Museum of Childhood, was opened in 1872 and the
building is the most important surviving example of the
type of glass and iron construction used by Paxton for the
Great Exhibition. The Museum is also responsible for the
Wellington Museum (Apsley House), and the Theatre
Museum. Total government grant-in-aid for 1996–7 is
£30.6 million.

BOARD OF TRUSTEES
Chairman, The Lord Armstrong of Ilminster, GCB, CVO
Deputy Chairman, Sir Michael Butler, GCMG
Members, The Lord Barnett, PC; Miss N. Campbell; Sir
Clifford Chetwood; The Viscountess Cobham;
E. Dawe; R. Fitch, CBE; Prof. C. Frayling, PH.D.;
R. Gorlin; Pamela, Lady Harlech; Sir Terence Heiser,
GCB; A. Irby III; Sir Nevil Macready, Bt., CBE;
Miss A. Plowden; Prof. M. Podro, PH.D., FBA; M. Saatchi;
J. Scott, FSA; A. Snow; Prof. J. Steer, FSA; A. Wheatley
Secretary to the Board of Trustees (G7), P. A. Wilson

OFFICERS
Director (G3), A. C. N. Borg, CBE, PH.D.
Assistant Directors (G5), T. Stevens (*Collections*); J. W. Close
(*Administration*)

Head of Buildings and Estate (G5), J. G. Charlesworth
Head of Collections (G5), Mrs G. F. Miles
Head of Conservation Department (G5), Dr J. Ashley-Smith
Head of Finance and Central Services (G5), Miss R. M. Sykes
Development Director, D. Charlton
Head of Education (G6), D. Anderson
Curator, Ceramics Collection (G6), Dr O. Watson
Curator, Far Eastern Collection (G6), Miss R. Kerr
Curator, Furniture and Woodwork Collection (G6), C. Wilk
Curator, Indian and South-East Asian Collection (G6),
Dr D. Swallow
Curator, Metalwork Collection (G6), Mrs P. Glanville
Head of Personnel (G6), Mrs G. Henchley
Curator, Prints, Drawings and Paintings Collection (G6),
Miss S. B. Lambert
Head of Public Affairs (G5), R. Cole-Hamilton
Head of Research (G5), P. Greenhalgh
Curator, Sculpture Collection (G6), P. E. D. Williamson
Curator, Textiles and Dress Collection (G6), Mrs V. D. Mendes
Managing Director, V. and A. Enterprises Ltd, M. Cass
Curator and Chief Librarian, National Art Library (G5),
J. F. van den Wateren
Head of Bethnal Green Museum of Childhood (G6), A. P. Burton
Head of Theatre Museum (G6), Ms M. Benton
Curator of Wellington Museum (*Apsley House*), J. R. S. Voak

MUSEUM OF LONDON
London Wall, London EC2Y 5HN
Tel 0171-600 3699

The Museum of London illustrates the history of London
from prehistoric times to the present day. It opened in 1976
and is based on the amalgamation of the former Guildhall
Museum and London Museum. The Museum is controlled by a Board of Governors, appointed (nine each) by
the Government and the Corporation of London. The
Museum is funded jointly by the Department of National
Heritage and the Corporation of London, each contributing £4.313 million in 1996–7.
Chairman of Board of Governors, P. Revell-Smith, CBE
Director, M. G. Hebditch, CBE, FSA

COMMONWEALTH INSTITUTE
Kensington High Street, London W8 6NQ
Tel 0171-603 4535

The Commonwealth Institute is the UK centre responsible
for promoting the Commonwealth in Britain through
exhibitions, educational programmes, publications, resources and information. The Institute houses an Education Centre, a Commonwealth Resource Centre and
Literature Library, and a Conference and Events Centre.
Its galleries are currently closed for refurbishment and will
reopen with new exhibitions in spring 1997.

The Institute is an independent statutory body, partially
funded by the British government with contributions from
other Commonwealth governments. It is controlled by a
Board of Governors which includes the High Commis-
sioners of all Commonwealth countries represented in
London. Total government grant-in-aid for 1996–7 is
£1 million.
Director-General, S. Cox
Administrative and Commercial Director, P. Kennedy
Projects Director, Dr J. Stevenson

IMPERIAL WAR MUSEUM
Lambeth Road, London SE1 6HZ
Tel 0171-416 5000

The Museum, founded in 1917, illustrates and records all
aspects of the two world wars and other military operations

involving Britain and the Commonwealth since 1914. It was opened in its present home, formerly Bethlem Hospital or Bedlam, in 1936. The Museum also administers HMS *Belfast* in the Pool of London, Duxford Airfield near Cambridge and the Cabinet War Rooms in Westminster.

Total government grant-in-aid for 1996–7 is £10.678 million.

Director-General, R. W. K. Crawford
Secretary, J. J. Chadwick
Assistant Directors, D. A. Needham (*Administration*); Miss K. J. Carmichael (*Collections*); G. Marsh (*Planning and Development*)
Head of Personnel Services, Miss L. Court
Head of Finance, Mrs P. A. Whitfield
Head of Information Systems, J. C. Barrett
Head of Support Systems, G. P. McCartney
Director of Duxford Airfield, E. O. Inman
Director of HMS Belfast, E. J. Wenzel

KEEPERS
Department of Museum Services, C. Dowling, D.Phil.
Department of Documents, R. W. A. Suddaby
Department of Exhibits and Firearms, D. J. Penn
Department of Printed Books, G. M. Bayliss, PH.D.
Department of Art, Miss A. H. Weight
Department of Film, R. B. N. Smither
Department of Photographs, Miss K. J. Carmichael
Department of Sound Records, Mrs M. A. Brooks
Department of Marketing and Trading, Miss A. Godwin
Curator of the Cabinet War Rooms, P. Reed

NATIONAL MARITIME MUSEUM
Greenwich, London SE10 9NF
Tel 0181-858 4422

Established by Act of Parliament in 1934, the National Maritime Museum illustrates the maritime history of Great Britain in the widest sense, underlining the importance of the sea and its influence on the nation's power, wealth, culture, technology and institutions. The Museum is in three groups of buildings in Greenwich Park – the main building, the Queen's House (built by Inigo Jones, 1616–35) and the Old Royal Observatory (including Wren's Flamsteed House). Total government grant-in-aid for 1996–7 is £10.5 million.
Director, R. L. Ormond

NATIONAL ARMY MUSEUM
Royal Hospital Road, London SW3 4HT
Tel 0171-730 0717

The National Army Museum covers the history of five centuries of the British Army. It was established by royal charter in 1960. Total government grant-in-aid for 1996–7 is £3.293 million.
Director, I. G. Robertson
Assistant Directors, D. K. Smurthwaite; A. J. Guy; Maj. P. R. Bateman

ROYAL AIR FORCE MUSEUM
Grahame Park Way, London NW9 5LL
Tel 0181-205 2266

Situated on the former airfield at RAF Hendon, the Museum illustrates the development of aviation from before the Wright brothers to the present-day RAF. Total government grant-in-aid for 1996–7 is £3.14 million.
Director, Dr M. A. Fopp
Deputy Director, J. D. Freeborn
Keepers, P. Elliott; D. F. Lawrence

NATIONAL MUSEUMS AND GALLERIES ON MERSEYSIDE
William Brown Street, Liverpool L3 8EN
Tel 0151-207 0001

The Board of Trustees of the National Museums and Galleries on Merseyside was established in 1986 to take over responsibility for the museums and galleries previously administered by Merseyside County Council. The Board is responsible for the Liverpool Museum, the Merseyside Maritime Museum (incorporating HM Customs and Excise National Museum), the Museum of Liverpool Life, the Lady Lever Art Gallery, the Walker Art Gallery and Sudley House, and a centre for museum conservation which opened in autumn 1996. Total government grant-in-aid for 1996–7 is £13.1 million.
Chairman of the Board of Trustees, D. McDonnell
Director, R. Foster
Head of Central Services, P. Sudbury, PH.D.
Keeper of Art Galleries, J. Treuherz
Keeper of Conservation, A. Durham
Keeper, Liverpool Museum, E. Greenwood
Keeper, Merseyside Maritime Museum and Museum of Liverpool Life, M. Stammers

NATIONAL MUSEUMS AND GALLERIES OF WALES/AMGUEDDFEYDD AC ORIELAU CENEDLAETHOL CYMRU
Cathays Park, Cardiff CF1 3NP
Tel 01222-397951

The National Museums and Galleries of Wales comprise the National Museum and Gallery, the Museum of Welsh Life, the Roman Legionary Museum, Turner House Art Gallery, the Welsh Slate Museum, the Segontium Roman Museum, the Museum of the Welsh Woollen Industry and the Welsh Industrial and Maritime Museum. Total funding from the Welsh Office for 1996–7 is £11.552 million.
President, C. R. T. Edwards
Vice-President, M. C. T. Pritchard, CBE

OFFICERS
Director, C. Ford, CBE
Assistant Directors, T. Arnold (*Resource Management*); C. Thomas (*Public Services*); A. Southall (*Museums Development*); I. Fell (*Education and Interpretation*); Dr E. Williams (*Collections and Research*)
Keeper of Geology, M. G. Bassett, PH.D.
Keeper of Botany, B. A. Thomas, PH.D.
Keeper of Zoology, P. M. Morgan
Keeper of Archaeology (*acting*), R. Brewer
Curator, Museum of Welsh Life, vacant
Keepers, E. Scourfield, PH.D.; J. Williams-Davies
Officer in Charge, Roman Legionary Museum, P. Guest, PH.D.
Keeper in Charge, Turner House Art Gallery, D. Alston
Keeper in Charge, Welsh Slate Museum, D. Roberts, PH.D.
Officer in Charge, Segontium Roman Museum, R. J. Brewer
Officer in Charge, Museum of the Welsh Woollen Industry, E. Scourfield, PH.D.
Keeper, Welsh Industrial and Maritime Museum, E. S. Owen-Jones, PH.D.

NATIONAL MUSEUMS OF SCOTLAND
Chambers Street, Edinburgh EH1 1JF
Tel 0131-225 7534

The National Museums of Scotland comprise the Royal Museum of Scotland, the Scottish United Services Museum, the Scottish Agricultural Museum, the Museum of Flight, the Biggar Gasworks Museum and Shambellie House Museum of Costume. Total funding from the Scottish Office for 1996–7 is £19.685 million.

BOARD OF TRUSTEES
Chairman, R. Smith, FSA scot.
Members, Prof. L. Bown, OBE; R. D. Cramond, CBE, FSA scot.;
Countess of Dalkeith; Prof. T. Devine; Dr Lesley
Glasser, FRSE; S. G. Gordon, CBE; Sir Alistair Grant;
Prof. P. H. Jones; A. Massie; Dr Anna Ritchie; The
Countess of Rosebery; Sir John Thomson; Dr Veronica
Van Heyingen

OFFICERS
Director (G3), M. Jones, FSA, FSA scot., FRSA
*Depute Director (Resources) and Project Director, Museum of
Scotland (G5)*, I. Hooper, FSA scot.
*Depute Director (Collections) and Keeper of History and Applied
Art (G5)*, Miss D. Idiens, FRSA, FSA scot.
Keeper of Archaeology, D. V. Clarke, PH.D., FSA, FSA scot.
Keeper of Geology (G5), vacant
Keeper of Natural History (G5), M. Shaw, D.PHIL.
Keeper of Science, Technology and Working Life (G5),
D. J. Bryden, PH.D., FSA
Head of Public Affairs (G6), Ms M. Bryden
Head of Museum Services (G6), S. R. Elson, FSA scot.
Head of Administration (G6), A. G. Young
Campaign Director, Museum of Scotland, S. Brock, PH.D., FRSA
Keeper, Scottish United Services Museum, S. C. Wood
Curator, Scottish Agricultural Museum, G. Sprott
Curator, Museum of Flight, Sqn. Ldr. R. Major
Curator, Biggar Gasworks Museum, J. Crompton
Keeper, Shambellie House Museum of Costume, Miss N. Tarrant

NATIONAL AUDIT OFFICE
157–197 Buckingham Palace Road, London SW1W 9SP
Tel 0171–798 7000
Audit House, 23–24 Park Place, Cardiff CF1 3BA
Tel 01222-378661
22 Melville Street, Edinburgh EH3 7NS
Tel 0131-244 2736

The National Audit Office came into existence under the
National Audit Act 1983 to replace and continue the work
of the former Exchequer and Audit Department. The Act
reinforced the Office's total financial and operational
independence from the Government and brought its head,
the Comptroller and Auditor-General, into a closer
relationship with Parliament as an officer of the House of
Commons.

The National Audit Office provides independent information, advice and assurance to Parliament and the
public about all aspects of the financial operations of
government departments and many other bodies receiving
public funds. It does this by examining and certifying the
accounts of these organizations and by regularly publishing reports to Parliament on the results of its value for
money investigations of the economy, efficiency and
effectiveness with which public resources have been used.
The National Audit Office is also the auditor by agreement
of the accounts of certain international and other organizations. In addition, the Office authorizes the issue of
public funds to government departments.
Comptroller and Auditor-General, Sir John Bourn, KCB
Private Secretary, F. Grogan
Deputy Comptroller and Auditor-General, R. N. Le Marechal,
CB
Assistant Auditors-General, T. Burr; J. A. Higgins;
L. H. Hughes, CB; J. Marshall; M. C. Pfleger; Miss C.
Mawhood

Directors, C. K. Beauchamp; B. Hogg; J. Parsons;
J. M. Pearce; A. G. Roberts; R. A. Skeen; A. Fiander;
M. Daynes; R. J. Eales; J. Colman; B. Payne; N. Sloan;
D. Woodward; Ms W. Kenway-Smith; R. Frith;
J. Cavanagh; R. Maggs; M. Sinclair; J. Robertson;
M. Whitehouse

NATIONAL CONSUMER COUNCIL
20 Grosvenor Gardens, London SW1W 0DH
Tel 0171-730 3469

The National Consumer Council was set up by the
Government in 1975 to give an independent voice to
consumers in the UK. Its job is to advocate the consumer
interest to decision-makers in national and local government, industry and regulatory bodies, business and the
professions. It does this through a combination of research
and campaigning. It is funded by a grant-in-aid from the
Department of Trade and Industry.
Chairman, D. Hatch, CBE
Vice-Chairman, Mrs A. Scully, OBE
Director, R. Evans

NATIONAL DEBT OFFICE
— *see* National Investment and Loans Office

DEPARTMENT OF NATIONAL HERITAGE
2–4 Cockspur Street, London SW1Y 5DH
Tel 0171-211 6000

The Department of National Heritage was established in
1992 and is responsible for government policy relating to
the arts, broadcasting, the press, museums and galleries,
libraries, sport and recreation, heritage and tourism. It
funds the Arts Councils and other arts bodies, including the
National Heritage Memorial Fund. It also funds the
Museums and Galleries Commission, the national
museums and galleries in England, the British Library, the
Sports Council, the British Tourist Authority and the
English Tourist Board, and the British Film Institute. It is
responsible for the issue of export licences on works of art,
antiques and collector's items; the Government Art Collection; the built heritage, including the Royal Parks and
Historic Royal Palaces executive agencies; and statistical
services including the International Passenger Survey and
broadcasting statistics. The Department is also responsible
for policy and implementation of the National Lottery. On
1 May 1996 the Department assumed responsibility from
the Home Office for the voluntary sector and charities.
Secretary of State for National Heritage, The Rt. Hon. Virginia
Bottomley, MP
Private Secretary, D. Fawcett
Special Adviser, A. Pepper
Parliamentary Private Secretary, N. Hawkins, MP
Minister of State, Iain Sproat, MP
Private Secretary, Ms D. Wells
Parliamentary Private Secretary, A. Robathan, MP
Parliamentary Under-Secretary, The Lord Inglewood
Lady-in-Waiting, The Baroness Trumpington
Parliamentary Clerk, C. Hutson
Permanent Secretary (G1), G. H. Phillips, CB
Private Secretary, Ms C. Pillmen

LIBRARIES, GALLERIES AND MUSEUMS GROUP
Head of Group (G3), Miss S. Booth, CBE
Head of Libraries and Information Services Division (G5),
D. Wilson
Head of Museums and Galleries Division (G5), P. Gregory

Director, Government Art Collection (G6), Dr Wendy Baron, OBE
Head of Cultural Property Unit (G7), M. Helston

ARTS, SPORTS AND LOTTERY GROUP
Head of Group (G3), A. Ramsay
Head of Arts Division (G5), Ms M. Leech
Head of National Lottery Division (G5), S. MacDonald
Head of Sport and Recreation Division (G5), S. Broadley

BROADCASTING AND MEDIA GROUP
Head of Group (G3), P. Wright
Head of Broadcasting Policy Division (G5), N. Kroll
Head of Media Division (G5), Dr K. Gray

HERITAGE AND TOURISM GROUP
Head of Group (G3), D. Chesterton
Head of Heritage Division (G5), A. Corner
Head of Tourism Division (G5), Ms J. Evans

VOLUNTARY AND COMMUNITY DIVISION
Head of Division (G5), H. Webber

RESOURCES AND SERVICES GROUP
Director (G4), N. Pittman
Director of Finance and Corporate Planning (G5), Ms A. Stewart
Director of Implementation and Review (G5), R. MacLachlan
Director of Personnel (G5), G. Jones

INFORMATION
Head of Information (G5), A. Marre

EXECUTIVE AGENCIES

HISTORIC ROYAL PALACES
Hampton Court Palace, East Molesey, Surrey KT8 9AU
Tel 0181-781 9750

The Historic Royal Palaces agency manages the Tower of London, Hampton Court Palace, Kensington Palace State Apartments and the Royal Ceremonial Dress Collection, Kew Palace with Queen Charlotte's Cottage, and the Banqueting House, Whitehall.
Chief Executive, D. C. Beeton
Director of Finance and Resources, A. Cornwell
Surveyor of the Fabric, S. Bond
Director of Public Affairs, P. D. Hammond
Curator, Historic Royal Palaces, Dr S. J. Thurley
Commercial Director, C. MacDonald
Director, Hampton Court Palace, R. Evans, FRICS
Resident Governor, HM Tower of London, Maj.-Gen. M. G. Field
Administrator, Kensington Palace, N. J. Arch

ROYAL PARKS AGENCY
The Old Police House, Hyde Park, London W2 2UH
Tel 0171-298 2000

The agency is responsible for maintaining and developing the royal parks.
Chief Executive (G5), D. Welch

NATIONAL HERITAGE MEMORIAL FUND
20 King Street, London SW1Y 6QY
Tel 0171-930 0963

The National Heritage Memorial Fund is an independent body established in 1980 as a memorial to those who have died for the UK. The Fund is empowered by the National Heritage Act 1980 to give financial assistance towards the cost of acquiring, maintaining or preserving land, buildings, works of art and other objects of outstanding interest which are also of importance to the national heritage. The Fund is administered by 13 trustees who are appointed by the Prime Minister.

The National Lottery Act 1993 designated the Fund as distributor of the heritage share of proceeds from the National Lottery (one fifth of the proceeds to the 'good causes'). In effect, this positioned the Fund as an umbrella organization operating two funds: the Heritage Memorial Fund and the Heritage Lottery Fund. The Heritage Memorial Fund receives an annual grant from the Department of National Heritage (£8 million in 1996–7). The Heritage Lottery Fund had made awards to the value of £256.6 million by July 1996.
Chairman, The Lord Rothschild
Trustees, Dr E. Anderson; Sir Richard Carew Pole, Bt.; W. L. Evans; Sir Nicholas Goodison; Sir Martin Holdgate; Mrs C. Hubbard; Sir Martin Jacomb; J. Keegan; The Lord Macfarlane of Bearsden; Prof. P. J. Newbould; Mrs J. Nutting; Mrs C. Porteous; Dame Sue Tinson, DBE
Director, Ms A. Case

NATIONAL INSURANCE JOINT AUTHORITY
The Adelphi, 1–11 John Adam Street, London WC2N 6HT
Tel 0171-962 8523

The Authority's function is to co-ordinate the operation of social security legislation in Great Britain and Northern Ireland, including the necessary financial adjustments between the two National Insurance Funds.
Members, The Secretary of State for Social Security; the Head of the Department of Health and Social Services for Northern Ireland.
Secretary, M. Driver

NATIONAL INVESTMENT AND LOANS OFFICE
1 King Charles Street, London SW1A 2AP
Tel 0171-270 3861

The National Investment and Loans Office was set up in 1980 by the merger of the National Debt Office and the Public Works Loan Board. The Office provides staff and services for the National Debt Commissioners and the Public Works Loan Commissioners. The National Debt Office is responsible for the investment and management of statutory funds relating to the surplus monies of certain government bodies; the management of some residual operations relating to the national debt; and the facilitation of raising funds by central government following Article 104 of the Maastricht Treaty, in pursuance of section 211 of the Finance Act 1993. The function of the Public Works Loan Board is to make loans for capital purposes from central government funds to local authorities and to collect repayments.
Director, I. H. Peattie
Establishment Officer, A. G. Ladd

NATIONAL DEBT OFFICE
Comptroller-General, I. H. Peattie

PUBLIC WORKS LOAN BOARD
Chairman, Sir Robin Dent, KCVO
Deputy Chairman, A. D. Loehnis, CMG

Other Commissioners, Miss V. J. Di Palma, OBE;
R. A. Chapman; A. Morton; G. G. Williams;
L. B. Woodhall; Ms S. V. Masters; Mrs R. V. Hale;
R. Burton; J. A. Parkes; J. Andrews
Secretary, I. H. Peattie
Assistant Secretary, Miss L. M. Ashcroft

OFFICE OF THE NATIONAL LOTTERY
2 Monck Street, London SW1P 2BQ
Tel 0345-125596

The Office of the National Lottery (OFLOT) was
established as a non-ministerial government department
under the National Lottery Act 1993. It regulates the
National Lottery operations and licenses games promoted
as part of the Lottery.

About 28 per cent of national lottery proceeds is
currently allocated equally to five 'good causes': the arts,
charities, heritage, sport and the Millennium Fund. More
than £1,400 million had been allocated to the good causes
by 31 March 1996.

Director-General (G2), P. Davis
Deputy Director-General (G5), Ms D. Kahn
Head of Compliance Regulation (G5), K. Dunn

NATIONAL LOTTERY CHARITIES BOARD
St Vincent House, 30 Orange Street, London WC2H 7HH
Tel 0171-747 5300

The Board is the independent body set up under the
National Lottery Act 1993 to distribute funds from the
Lottery to support charitable, benevolent and philan-
thropic organizations (one-fifth of the 28 per cent allocated
to 'good causes'). There are 22 Board members including
the chairman. Members are appointed by the Secretary of
State for National Heritage. The Board's main aim is to
help meet the needs of those at greatest disadvantage in
society and to improve the quality of life in the community
through themed grants programmes in the UK and an
international grants programme for UK-based charities
working abroad. The Board is also piloting a small grants
scheme in Wales. By June 1996 the Board had awarded
4,689 grants totalling £319 million.

Chairman, The Hon. D. Sieff
Chief Executive, T. Hornsby
Members, Mrs T. Baring; A. Bhatia; G. Bowie; Mrs
J. Churchman; I. Clarke; Ms S. Clarke; Ms P. de Lima;
A. Higgins; T. Jones; Ms A. Jordan; Ms J. Kaufmann;
W. Kirkpatrick; Ms A. McGinley; Ms M. McWilliams;
W. G. Morrison; A. Phillips; Ms L. Quinn; Sir Adam
Ridley; J. Simpson, OBE; N. Stewart; Prof. Sir Eric
Stroud, FRCP; C. Woodcock

NATIONAL PHYSICAL LABORATORY
Queen's Road, Teddington, Middx TW11 0LW
Tel 0181-977 3222

The Laboratory is government-owned but contractor-
operated. It develops and disseminates national measurement standards.
Managing Director, Dr J. Rae

NATIONAL RADIOLOGICAL
PROTECTION BOARD
Chilton, Didcot, Oxon OX11 0RQ
Tel 01235-831600

The National Radiological Protection Board is an independent statutory body created by the Radiological
Protection Act 1970. It is the national point of authoritative
reference on radiological protection for both ionizing and
non-ionizing radiations, and has issued recommendations
on limiting human exposure to electromagnetic fields and
radiation from a range of sources, including X-rays, the Sun
and power generators. Its sponsoring department is the
Department of Health.
Chairman, Prof. Sir Keith Peters
Director, Prof. R. H. Clarke

DEPARTMENT FOR NATIONAL SAVINGS
Charles House, 375 Kensington High Street, London
W14 8SD
Tel 0171-605 9300

The Department for National Savings was established as a
government department in 1969. It became an executive
agency of the Treasury in July 1996. The Department is
responsible for the administration of a wide range of
schemes for personal savers.
Chief Executive, P. Bareau
Deputy Director (G3), K. Chivers
Director, Operations (G5), D. H. Monaghan
Director, Information Systems (G5), A. S. McGill
Director, Personnel (G5), D. S. Speedie
Director, Finance (G5), M. A. Nicholls
Director, Marketing (G5), Miss A. Nash
Director, Policy and Product Development (G5),
P. N. S. Hickman-Robertson

For details of schemes, *see* National Savings section

OFFICE FOR NATIONAL STATISTICS
Great George Street, London SW1P 3AQ
Tel 0171-270 3000

The Office for National Statistics was created in April 1996
by the merger of the Central Statistical Office and the
Office of Population, Censuses and Surveys. It is an
executive agency of the Treasury and is responsible for
the full range of functions previously carried out by those
offices. This includes responsibility for preparing and
interpreting key economic statistics for government
policy; collecting and publishing business statistics; publishing annual and monthly statistical digests; providing
researchers, analysts and other customers with a statistical
service; administration of the marriage laws and local
registration of births, marriages and deaths in England and
Wales; provision of population estimates and projections
and statistics on health and other demographic matters in
England and Wales; population censuses in England and
Wales; surveys for government departments and public
bodies; and promoting these functions within the UK, the
European Union and internationally to provide a statistical
service to meet European Union and international requirements.

The office for National Statistics is also responsible for
establishing and maintaining a central database of key

economic and social statistics produced to common classifications, definitions and standards.
Chief Executive, Prof. T. Holt
Directors (G3), J. Calder; J. Fox; J. Kidgell; L. Mayhew; M. Pepper; D. Roberts
Principal Establishment Officer (G5), E. Williams
Principal Finance Officer (G5), B. Smith
Head of Information (G6), I. Scott
Parliamentary Clerk, L. Land

JOINT NATURE CONSERVATION COMMITTEE
Monkstone House, City Road, Peterborough PE1 1JY
Tel 01733-62626

The Committee was established under the Environmental Protection Act 1990. It advises the Government and others on UK and international nature conservation issues and disseminates knowledge on these subjects. It establishes common standards for the monitoring of nature conservation and research, and analyses the resulting information. It commissions research relevant to these roles, and provides guidance to English Nature, Scottish Natural Heritage, the Countryside Council for Wales and the Department of the Environment for Northern Ireland.
Chairman, The Earl of Selborne, KBE, FRS
Chief Officer, Dr A. E. Brown
Director, Dr M. A. Vincent

NOLAN COMMITTEE
— *see* page 346

NORTHERN IRELAND AUDIT OFFICE
106 University Street, Belfast BT7 1EU
Tel 01232-251000

The primary aim of the Northern Ireland Audit Office is to provide independent assurance, information and advice to Parliament on the proper accounting for Northern Ireland departmental and certain other public expenditure, revenue, assets and liabilities, on regularity and propriety; and on the economy, efficiency and effectiveness of the use of resources.
Comptroller and Auditor-General for Northern Ireland, J. M. Dowdall

NORTHERN IRELAND OFFICE
Whitehall, London SW1A 2AZ
Tel 0171-210 3000
Stormont Castle, Belfast BT4 3ST
Tel 01232-520700

The Northern Ireland Office was established in 1972, when the Northern Ireland (Temporary Provisions) Act transferred the legislative and executive powers of the Northern Ireland Parliament and Government to the UK Parliament and a Secretary of State.
The Northern Ireland Office is responsible primarily for security issues, law and order and prisons, and for matters relating to the political and constitutional future of the province. It also deals with international issues as they affect Northern Ireland, including the Anglo-Irish Agreement. The Northern Ireland departments are responsible

for the administration of social, industrial and economic policies.
The names of most civil servants are not listed for security reasons.
Secretary of State for Northern Ireland, The Rt. Hon. Sir Patrick Mayhew, QC, MP
Special Adviser, D. Campbell-Bannerman
Parliamentary Private Secretary, J. Cran, MP
Ministers of State, The Rt. Hon. Michael Ancram, MP; The Rt. Hon. Sir John Wheeler, MP
Parliamentary Private Secretary to Michael Ancram, H. Elletson, MP
Parliamentary Under-Secretaries of State, The Baroness Denton of Wakefield, CBE; Malcolm Moss, MP
Permanent Under-Secretary of State (G1), Sir John Chilcot, KCB
Second Permanent Under-Secretary of State, Head of the Northern Ireland Civil Service, Sir David Fell, KCB

LONDON
Deputy Secretary (Political Director)
Under-Secretaries (G3), (Associate Political Director); (Security and International; Constitutional and Political; Economic and Social); (Establishment and Finance)
SCS, (Information Services)

BELFAST
Deputy Secretary (Political Director)
Under-Secretaries (Associate Political Director); (Security); (Criminal Justice); (Political); (Establishment and Finance)

EXECUTIVE AGENCIES
COMPENSATION AGENCY, Royston House, Upper Queen Street, Belfast BT1 6FD. Tel: 01232-2499444
PRISON SERVICE AGENCY, Dundonald House, Upper Newtownards Road, Belfast B4 3SU. Tel: 01232-520700

DEPARTMENT OF AGRICULTURE FOR NORTHERN IRELAND
Dundonald House, Upper Newtownards Road, Belfast BT4 3SB
Tel 01232-520100

Parliamentary Under-Secretary of State, The Baroness Denton of Wakefield, CBE
Permanent Secretary (G2)
Under-Secretaries (G3), (Central Services and Rural Development); (Food and Farm Policy); (Agri-Environment Policy, Forestry and Fisheries); (Veterinary); (Science); (Agri-Food Development)

EXECUTIVE AGENCY
INTERVENTION BOARD
— *see* page 315

DEPARTMENT OF ECONOMIC DEVELOPMENT NORTHERN IRELAND
Netherleigh, Massey Avenue, Belfast BT4 2JP
Tel 01232-529900

Parliamentary Under-Secretary of State, The Baroness Denton of Wakefield, CBE
Permanent Secretary (G2)
Under-Secretaries (G3), (Resources Group); (Regulatory Services Group)
INDUSTRIAL DEVELOPMENT BOARD, IDB House, 64 Chichester Street, Belfast BT1 4JX. Tel: 01232-233233

EXECUTIVE AGENCIES

INDUSTRIAL RESEARCH AND TECHNOLOGY UNIT,
Netherleigh, Massey Avenue, Belfast BT4 2JP. Tel:
01232-529900
TRAINING AND EMPLOYMENT AGENCY (NORTHERN
IRELAND), Clarendon House, 39–49 Adelaide Street,
Belfast BT2 8FD. Tel: 01232-541541

DEPARTMENT OF EDUCATION FOR NORTHERN IRELAND
Rathgael House, Balloo Road, Bangor, Co. Down BT19 7PR
Tel 01247-279279

Minister of State, The Rt. Hon. Michael Ancram, MP
Permanent Secretary (G2)
Under-Secretaries (G3), (Schools); (Finance and Corporate
Services); (Education and Training Inspectorate)

DEPARTMENT OF THE ENVIRONMENT FOR NORTHERN IRELAND
Clarence Court, 10–18 Adelaide Street, Belfast BT2 8GB
Tel 01232-540540

Parliamentary Under-Secretary of State, Malcolm Moss, MP
Permanent Secretary (G2)
Under-Secretaries (G3), (Personnel, Finance, Housing and
Local Government); (Rural and Urban Affairs); (Roads,
Water and Transport); (Planning, Works and
Environment)

EXECUTIVE AGENCIES

CONSTRUCTION SERVICE, Churchill House, Victoria
Square, Belfast BT1 4QW. Tel: 01232-250284
DRIVER AND VEHICLE LICENSING AGENCY (NORTHERN
IRELAND), County Hall, Castlerock Road, Coleraine,
Co. Londonderry BT51 3HS. Tel: 01265-41200
DRIVER AND VEHICLE TESTING AGENCY (NORTHERN
IRELAND), Balmoral Road, Belfast BT12 6QL. Tel: 01232-
681831
ENVIRONMENT AND HERITAGE SERVICE,
Commonwealth House, Castle Street, Belfast BT1 1GU.
Tel: 01232-251477
LAND REGISTERS OF NORTHERN IRELAND, Lincoln
Building, 27–45 Great Victoria Street, Belfast BT2 7SL.
Tel: 01232-251515
ORDNANCE SURVEY OF NORTHERN IRELAND, Colby
House, Stranmillis Court, Belfast BT9 5BJ. Tel: 01232-
255755
PLANNING SERVICE, Clarence Court, 10–18 Adelaide
Street, Belfast BT2 8GB. Tel: 01232-540540
PUBLIC RECORD OFFICE (NORTHERN IRELAND) – *see*
page 337
RATE COLLECTION AGENCY (NORTHERN IRELAND),
Oxford House, 49–55 Chichester Street, Belfast
BT1 4HH. Tel: 01232-252252
ROADS SERVICE, Clarence Court, 10–18 Adelaide Street,
Belfast BT2 8GB. Tel: 01232-540540
WATER SERVICE, Northland House, 3 Frederick Street,
Belfast BT1 2NR. Tel: 01232-244711

ADVISORY BODIES

HISTORIC BUILDINGS COUNCIL FOR NORTHERN
IRELAND, c/o Environment and Heritage Service,
Historic Monuments and Buildings, Commonwealth
House, Castle Street, Belfast BT1 1GU. Tel: 01232-
251477
COUNCIL FOR NATURE CONSERVATION AND THE
COUNTRYSIDE, c/o Environment and Heritage Service,
Commonwealth House, Castle Street, Belfast BT1 1GU.
Tel: 01232-251477

DEPARTMENT OF FINANCE AND PERSONNEL
Rosepark, Belfast BT4 3SW
Tel 01232-520400

Minister of State, The Rt. Hon. Sir John Wheeler, MP
Permanent Secretary (G2)
Under-Secretaries (G3), (Supply Group); (Resources
Control and Professional Services Group); (Central
Personnel Group); (Government Purchasing Service)

NORTHERN IRELAND CIVIL SERVICE (NICS)
Stormont Castle, Belfast BT4 3TT
Tel 01232-520700

Head of Civil Service (G1A), Sir David Fell, KCB
Under-Secretaries (G3), (Central Secretariat); (Legal
Services); (Office of the Legislative Council)

GENERAL REGISTER OFFICE (NORTHERN IRELAND)
Oxford House, 49–65 Chichester Street, Belfast BT1 4HL
Tel 01232-252000

Registrar-General (G6)

EXECUTIVE AGENCY

VALUATION AND LANDS AGENCY, Queen's Court, 56–66
Upper Queen Street, Belfast BT4 6FD. Tel: 01232-
439303

DEPARTMENT OF HEALTH AND SOCIAL SERVICES NORTHERN IRELAND
Dundonald House, Upper Newtownards Road, Belfast
BT4 3SF
Tel 01232-520500

Parliamentary Under-Secretary of State, Malcolm Moss, MP
Permanent Secretary (G2)
Chief Medical Officer (G2A)
Under-Secretaries (G3), (Health and Social Services
Group); (Health and Social Policy); (Medical and
Allied Services); (Central Management and Social
Security Policy Group)

EXECUTIVE AGENCIES

NORTHERN IRELAND CHILD SUPPORT AGENCY, Great
Northern Tower, 17 Great Victoria Street, Belfast
BT2 7AD. Tel: 01232-339000
NORTHERN IRELAND HEALTH AND SOCIAL SERVICES
ESTATES AGENCY, Stoney Road, Dundonald, Belfast
BT16 0US. Tel: 01232-520025
NORTHERN IRELAND SOCIAL SECURITY AGENCY, Castle
Buildings, Stormont, Belfast BT4 3SJ. Tel: 01232-520520

OCCUPATIONAL PENSIONS BOARD
PO Box 2EE, Newcastle upon Tyne NE99 2EE
Tel 0191-225 6414

The Occupational Pensions Board (OPB) is an independent statutory body set up under the Social Security Act
1973 to administer the contracting-out of occupational
pensions from the State Earnings Related Pension Scheme
(SERPS), and to advise the Secretary of State. Its functions
have been extended by subsequent legislation and it is now
also responsible for administering equal access, preservation and modification requirements and appropriate
personal pension schemes. Following the Social Security
Act 1990, the OPB was appointed as Registrar of Occupational and Personal Pension Schemes and granted powers
to make grants to approved bodies in the field. The OPB

now funds the operation of the Occupational Pensions Advisory Service (OPAS).

The OPB is to be dissolved on 5 April 1997 under the Pension Act 1995. It will be replaced by the Occupational Pensions Regulatory Authority (OPRA).
Chairman, P. D. Carr, CBE
Deputy Chairman, Miss C. H. Dawes, OBE
Secretary to the Board and General Manager of Executive Office (*G6*), M. McLean
Chief Executive, OPRA, Ms C. Johnston

OMBUDSMEN

— *see* Local Commissioners *and* Parliamentary Commissioner. For non-statutory Ombudsmen, *see* Index

ORDNANCE SURVEY

Romsey Road, Maybush, Southampton SO16 4GU
Tel 01703-792000

Ordnance Survey is the national mapping agency for Britain. It became an executive agency in 1990 and reports to the Secretary of State for the Environment.

Ordnance Survey maintains a large-scale database (which replaces the large-scale plans previously available) from which site-centred plans can be plotted at a variety of scales. It also produces a wide range of small-scale maps, co-publishes several series of atlases and guidebooks, and is becoming increasingly involved in the supply of mapping as data.
Director-General and Chief Executive, Prof. D. Rhind

OVERSEAS DEVELOPMENT ADMINISTRATION

94 Victoria Street, London SW1E 5JL
Tel 0171-917 7000
Abercrombie House, Eaglesham Road, East Kilbride, Glasgow G75 8EA
Tel 01355-844000

The Overseas Development Administration of the Foreign and Commonwealth Office deals with British development assistance to overseas countries. This includes both capital aid on concessional terms and technical assistance (mainly in the form of specialist staff abroad and training facilities in the UK), whether provided directly to developing countries or through the various multilateral aid organizations, including the United Nations and its specialized agencies.
Minister for Overseas Development, The Baroness Chalker of Wallasey, PC
Private Secretary (*G7*), R. Calvert
Parliamentary Private Secretary, A. Hargreaves, MP
Permanent Secretary (*SCS*), J. M. M. Vereker
Private Secretary, B. Mellor

PROGRAMMES

Director-General (*SCS*), B. R. Ireton
Head of Emergency Aid Department (*SCS*), P. A. Bearpark

AFRICA
Director (*SCS*), P. D. M. Freeman
Heads of Departments (*SCS*), Mrs B. M. Kelly, CBE (*Africa, Greater Horn and Co-ordination*); S. Ray (*West and North Africa*); M. A. Wickstead (*British Development Division in East Africa*); A. G. Coverdale (*British Development Division in Central Africa*); J. H. S. Chard (*British Development Division in South Africa*)

ASIA
Director (*SCS*), J. V. Kerby
Heads of Departments (*SCS*), A. D. Davis (*East Asia and Pacific*); Ms S. E. Unsworth (*British Development Co-operation Office*); Ms M. H. Vowles (*Western Asia*); A. K. C. Wood (*South-East Asia Development Division*); K. L. Sparkhall (*Aid Management Office*)

EASTERN EUROPE AND WESTERN HEMISPHERE
Director (*SCS*), J. A. L. Faint
Heads of Departments (*SCS*), M. C. McCulloch (*Joint Assistance Department (Eastern)*); J. S. Laing (*Joint Assistance Department (Central Europe)*); B. P. Thomson (*British Development Division in the Caribbean*); (*G6*), D. R. Curran (*Latin America, Caribbean and Atlantic*); (*G7*), J. D. Moye (*EBRD Unit*)

ECONOMICS AND GOVERNANCE
Director, and Chief Economic Adviser (*SCS*), J. B. W. Wilmshurst
Chief Statistician (*SCS*), A. B. Williams
Head of Asia, Latin America and Oceans Economics (*G6*), P. J. Ackroyd
Head of African Economics Department (*SCS*), M. G. Foster
Head of International Economics Department (*SCS*), P. D. Grant
Senior Small-Scale Enterprise Adviser (*G6*), D. L. Wright
Senior Economic Advisers (*G6*), Ms R. L. Turner; P. L. Owen; P. J. Dearden; P. J. Landymore; E. Hawthorn; F. C. Clift; J. L. Hoy
Head of Government Institutions Advisory Department (*SCS*), R. J. Wilson
Senior Government and Institutions Advisers (*G6*), Dr G. W. Glentworth; D. W. Baker; Mrs A. Newsum; S. Sharples; J. G. Clarke
Senior Police Adviser (*G6*), L. H. Grundy

HUMAN RESOURCE DEVELOPMENT
Director, and Chief Health and Population Adviser (*SCS*), Dr D. N. Nabarro
Senior Health and Population Advisers (*G6*), Dr P. J. Key; J. N. Lambert; Ms J. M. Isard; S. Tyson; R. N. Grose; Ms C. M. Sergeant
Chief Social Development Adviser (*G6*), Dr R. Eyben
Senior Social Development Advisers (*G6*), Ms P. M. Holden; Dr A. M. Coles
Chief Education Adviser (*SCS*), Ms M. A. Harrison
Senior Education Advisers (*G6*), Dr C. Treffgarne; M. E. Seath; M. D. Francis; R. T. Allsop; Dr D. B. Pennycuick; S. E. Packer; Dr K. M. Lillis; Dr G. R. H. Jones
Senior Technical Education Adviser (*G6*), C. Lewis

PRODUCTIVE CAPACITY AND ENVIRONMENT
Director, and Chief Natural Resources Adviser (*SCS*), A. J. Bennett
Head of Environment Policy Department (*SCS*), D. P. Turner
Head of Natural Resources Policy and Advisory Department, and Deputy Chief Natural Resources Adviser (*SCS*), J. M. Scott
Head of Natural Resources Research Department (*SCS*), Dr I. H. Haines
Senior Natural Resources Advisers (*G6*), Ms F. Proctor; R. C. Fox; M. J. Wilson; A. J. Tainsh; J. R. F. Hansell; Dr B. E. Grimwood; J. A. Harvey; A. Hall
Natural Resources Systems Programme Manager (*G6*), J. C. Barrett
Senior Environment and Research Adviser (*G6*), Ms L. C. Brown
Senior Fisheries Advisers (*G6*), R. W. Beales; Dr J. Tarbit
Senior Forestry Advisers (*G6*), J. M. Hudson; I. A. Napier
Senior Animal Health Advisers (*G6*), G. G. Freeland; Ms L. M. Bell
Chief Engineering Adviser (*SCS*), J. W. Hodges

Senior Engineering Advisers (G6), B. Dolton; C. I. Ellis; P. J. Davies; D. F. Gillett; P. W. D. H. Roberts; M. F. Sergeant; R. J. Cadwallader; C. J. Hunt
Senior Water Resources Adviser (G6), A. Wray
Senior Architectural and Physical Planning Adviser (G6), M. W. Parkes
Senior Electrical and Mechanical Adviser (G6), R. P. Jones
Senior Renewable Energy and Research Adviser (G6), A. Gilchrist
Industrial Training Adviser (G7), D. G. Marr

RESOURCES

Director-General (SCS), R. G. Manning
Heads of Departments (SCS), J. R. Drummond (*Personnel*); D. S. Fish (*Procurement, Appointments and NGO*); P. Aylett (*Information*); G. M. Stegmann (*Aid Policy and Resources*); B. W. Hammond (*Information Systems*); R. A. Elias (*Internal Audit Unit*); C. P. Raleigh (*Evaluation*); (*G6*), R. Plumb (*Overseas Pensions*); K. D. Grimshaw (*Sponsored Organizations Unit*)
Assistant Establishment Officer (G6), J. A. Anning

INTERNATIONAL DEVELOPMENT AFFAIRS
Director (SCS), N. B. Hudson, CB
Heads of Departments (SCS), D. J. Batt (*European Union*); J. C. Machin (*United Nations and Commonwealth*); M. E. Cund (*International Financial Institutions*)

OFFICE OF THE PARLIAMENTARY COMMISSIONER FOR ADMINISTRATION AND HEALTH SERVICE COMMISSIONER
Church House, Great Smith Street, London SW1P 3BW
Tel 0171-276 2130 (*Parliamentary Commissioner*); 0171-217 4051 (*Health Service Commissioner*)

The Parliamentary Commissioner for Administration (the Parliamentary Ombudsman) is independent of Government and is an officer of Parliament. He is responsible for investigating complaints referred to him by MPs from members of the public who claim to have sustained injustice in consequence of maladministration by or on behalf of government departments and certain non-departmental public bodies. Certain types of action by government departments or bodies are excluded from investigation. The Parliamentary Commissioner is also responsible for investigating complaints, referred by MPs, alleging that access to official information has been wrongly refused under the Code of Practice on Access to Government Information 1994.

The Health Service Commissioners (the Health Service Ombudsmen) for England, for Scotland and for Wales are responsible for investigating complaints against National Health Service authorities and trusts that are not dealt with by those authorities to the satisfaction of the complainant. Complaints can be referred direct by the member of the public who claims to have sustained injustice or hardship in consequence of the failure in a service provided by a relevant body, failure of that body to provide a service or in consequence of any other action by that body. (The Ombudsmens' jurisdiction now covers complaints about family doctors, dentists, pharmacists and opticians, and complaints about actions resulting from clinical judgment.) The Health Service Ombudsmen are also responsible for investigating complaints that information has been wrongly refused under the Code of Practice on Openness in the National Health Service 1995. The three offices are presently held by the Parliamentary Commissioner.
Parliamentary Commissioner and Health Service Commissioner (G1), Sir William Reid, KCB (*until end 1996*)

Deputy Parliamentary Commissioners (G3), J. E. Avery; J. Tate
Deputy Health Service Commissioners (G3), C. I I. Wilson; Miss M. I. Nisbet
Directors, Parliamentary Commissioner (G5), Mrs A. H. P. Bates; D. J. Coffey; Mrs S. P. Maunsell; J. L. Railton; A. Watson
Directors, Health Service Commissioners (G5), Miss H. Bainbridge; D. P. Flaherty; N. J. Jordan; R. H. Keynes; D. R. G. Pinchin; P. Pugh
Finance and Establishment Officer (G6), T. G. Hull

PARLIAMENTARY COMMISSIONER FOR STANDARDS
House of Commons, London SW1A 0AA
Tel 0171-219 0320

Following recommendations of the Committee on Standards in Public Life (the Nolan Committee) the House of Commons agreed to the appointment of an independent Parliamentary Commissioner for Standards. The Commissioner was appointed with effect from November 1995 and has responsibility for maintaining and monitoring the operation of the Register of Members' Interests; advising Members of Parliament and the new select committee on standards and privileges on the interpretation of the rules on disclosure and advocacy and on other questions of propriety; and receiving and, if he thinks fit, investigating complaints about the conduct of MPs.
Parliamentary Commissioner for Standards, Sir Gordon Downey, KCB

PARLIAMENTARY COUNSEL
36 Whitehall, London SW1A 2AY
Tel 0171-210 6633

Parliamentary Counsel draft all government bills (i.e. primary legislation) except those relating exclusively to Scotland, the latter being drafted by the Lord Advocate's Department. They also advise on all aspects of parliamentary procedure in connection with such bills and draft government amendments to them as well as any motions (including financial resolutions) necessary to secure their introduction to, and passage through, Parliament.
First Counsel (SCS), J. C. Jenkins, CB, QC
Counsel (SCS), D. W. Saunders, CB; E. G. Caldwell, CB; E. G. Bowman, CB; G. B. Sellers, CB; E. R. Sutherland, CB; P. F. A. Knowles, CB; S. C. Laws, CB; R. S. Parker; Miss C. E. Johnston; P. J. Davies

---

PAROLE BOARD FOR ENGLAND AND WALES
Abell House, John Islip Street, London SW1P 4LH
Tel 0171-217 5314

The Board was constituted under the Criminal Justice Act 1967 and continued under the Criminal Justice Act 1991. Its duty is to advise the Home Secretary with respect to matters referred to it by him which are connected with the early release or recall of prisoners. Its functions include giving directions concerning the release on licence of prisoners serving discretionary life sentences and of certain prisoners serving long-term determinate sentences; and making recommendations to the Home Secretary concerning the early release on licence of other prisoners, the conditions of parole and licences and the variation and

cancellation of such conditions, and the recall of long-term and life prisoners while on licence.
Chairman, The Lord Belstead, PC
Vice-Chairman, The Hon. Mr Justice Alliott
Chief Executive, M. S. Todd

PAROLE BOARD FOR SCOTLAND
Calton House, 5 Redheughs Rigg, Edinburgh EH12 9HW
Tel 0131-244 8755

The Board directs and advises the Secretary of State for Scotland on the release of prisoners on licence, and related matters.
Chairman, I. McNee
Vice-Chairman, Sheriff G. Shiach
Secretary, H. P. Boyle

PATENT OFFICE
Cardiff Road, Newport NP9 1RH
Tel 0645-500505

The Patent Office is an executive agency of the Department of Trade and Industry. The duties of the Patent Office are to administer the Patent Acts, the Registered Designs Act and the Trade Marks Act, and to deal with questions relating to the Copyright, Designs and Patents Act 1988. The Search and Advisory Service carries out commercial searches through patent information. In 1994–5 the Office granted 9,530 patents and registered 7,806 designs and 28,828 trade and service marks.
Comptroller-General (G3), P. R. S. Hartnack
Assistant Comptroller, Intellectual Property Policy Directorate (Supt. Examiner), G. Jenkins
Assistant Comptroller, Patents and Designs (G4), R. J. Marchant
Assistant Registrar, Trade Marks (G4), Miss A. Brimelow
Head of Administration and Resources (G5), C. Octon
Head of ADP Unit (G6), G. Bennett

PAYMASTER
The Office of HM Paymaster-General
Sutherland House, Russell Way, Crawley, W. Sussex
RH10 1UH
Tel 01293-560999
Alencon Link, Basingstoke, Hants RG21 7JB
Tel 01256-846488

PAYMASTER, the Office of HM Paymaster-General, was formed by the consolidation in 1835 of various separate pay departments. Its function is that of paying agent for government departments other than the revenue departments. Most of its payments are made through banks, to whose accounts the necessary transfers are made at the Bank of England. The calculation and payment of over 1.5 million public service pensions is an important feature of its work. The Office became an executive agency of the Treasury in 1993 but is to be privatized in 1997.
Paymaster-General, David Willetts, MP
Assistant Paymaster-General/Chief Executive (G5), K. Sullens

OFFICE OF THE PENSIONS OMBUDSMAN
11 Belgrave Road, London SW1V 1RB
Tel 0171-834 9144

The Pensions Ombudsman is appointed by the Secretary of State for Social Security under the Pension Schemes Act 1993 to deal with complaints against, and disputes with, occupational and personal pension schemes. He is completely independent.
Pensions Ombudsman, Dr J. T. Farrand

POLICE COMPLAINTS AUTHORITY
10 Great George Street, London SW1P 3AE
Tel 0171-273 6450

The Police Complaints Authority was established under the Police and Criminal Evidence Act 1984 to provide an independent system for dealing with serious complaints by members of the public against police officers in England and Wales. It is funded by the Home Office. The authority has powers to supervise the investigation of certain categories of serious complaints and certain statutory functions in relation to the disciplinary aspects of complaints. It does not deal with police operational matters; these are usually dealt with by the Chief Constable of the relevant force.
Chairman (acting), P. Moorhouse
Deputy Chairman (Investigations), J. Cartwright
Deputy Chairman (Discipline), P. W. Moorhouse
Members, Mrs L. Cawsey; N. Dholakia, OBE; J. Elliott; Miss L. Haye; A. Kelly; Mrs M. Meacher; Mrs C. Mitchell; E. Wignall; A. Williams

INDEPENDENT COMMISSION FOR POLICE COMPLAINTS FOR NORTHERN IRELAND
— see page 313

POLITICAL HONOURS SCRUTINY COMMITTEE
Cabinet Office, 53 Parliament Street, London SW1A 2NG
Tel 0171-210 5058

The function of the Political Honours Scrutiny Committee (a committee of Privy Councillors) was set out in an Order of Council in 1991 and amended by Orders in Council in 1992 and 1994. The Prime Minister submits certain particulars to the Committee about persons proposed to be recommended for honour for their political services. The Committee, after such enquiry as they think fit, report to the Prime Minister whether, so far as they believe, the persons whose names are submitted to them are fit and proper persons to be recommended.
Chairman, The Lord Pym, MC, PC
Members, The Lord Cledwyn of Penrhos, CH, PC; The Lord Thomson of Monifieth, KT, PC
Secretary, A. J. Merifield, CB

PORT OF LONDON AUTHORITY
Devon House, 58–60 St Katharine's Way, London E1 9LB
Tel 0171-265 2656

The Port of London Authority is a public trust constituted under the Port of London Act 1908 and subsequent legislation. It is the governing body for the Port of London, covering the tidal portion of the River Thames from Teddington to the seaward limit. The Board comprises a chairman and up to seven but not less than four non-executive members appointed by the Secretary of State for Transport, and up to four but not less than one executive members appointed by the Board.

Chairman, Sir Brian Shaw
Vice-Chairman, J. H. Kelly, CBE
Chief Executive, D. Jeffery
Secretary, G. E. Ennals

THE POST OFFICE
148 Old Street, London EC1V 9HQ
Tel 0171-490 2888

Crown services for the carriage of government dispatches were set up in about 1516. The conveyance of public correspondence began in 1635 and the mail service was made a parliamentary responsibility with the setting up of a Post Office in 1657. Telegraphs came under Post Office control in 1870 and the Post Office Telephone Service began in 1880. The National Girobank service of the Post Office began in 1968. The Post Office ceased to be a government department in 1969 when responsibility for the running of the postal, telecommunications, giro and remittance services was transferred to a public authority called the Post Office. The 1981 British Telecommunications Act separated the functions of the Post Office, making it solely responsible for postal services and Girobank. Girobank was privatized in 1990.

The chairman, chief executive and members of the Post Office Board are appointed by the Secretary of State for Trade and Industry but responsibility for the running of the Post Office as a whole rests with the Board in its corporate capacity.

FINANCIAL RESULTS £m	1994–5	1995–6
Post Office Group		
Turnover	5,878	6,210
Profit before tax	472	422
Royal Mail		
Turnover	4,540	4,804
Profit before tax	430	354
Parcelforce		
Turnover	481	471
Profit (loss) before tax	(30)	1
Post Office Counters		
Turnover	1,118	1,195
Profit before tax	30	35

POST OFFICE BOARD
Chairman, Sir Michael Heron
Chief Executive, J. Roberts, CBE
Members, R. Close (*Managing Director, Finance*); J. Cope (*Managing Director, Strategy and Personnel*)
Secretary, R. Osmond
For postal services, *see* pages 510–12

PRIME MINISTER'S OFFICE
— *see* page 287

PRISONS OMBUDSMAN FOR ENGLAND AND WALES
St Vincent House, 30 Orange Street, London WC2H 7HH
Tel 0171-389 1527

The post of Prisons Ombudsman was instituted in 1994. The Ombudsman is appointed by the Home Secretary and is an independent point of appeal for prisoners' grievances about their lives in prison, including disciplinary issues. The Ombudsman cannot investigate grievances relating to issues which are the subject of litigation or criminal proceedings, decisions taken by ministers, or actions of bodies outside the prison service.
Prisons Ombudsman, Sir Peter Woodhead, KCB

For Scotland, *see* Scottish Prisons Complaints Commission

PRIVY COUNCIL OFFICE
Whitehall, London SW1A 2AT
Tel 0171-270 3000

The Office is responsible for the arrangements leading to the making of all royal proclamations and Orders in Council; for certain formalities connected with ministerial changes; for considering applications for the granting (or amendment) of royal charters; for the scrutiny and approval of by-laws and statutes of chartered bodies; and for the appointment of High Sheriffs and many Crown and Privy Council appointments to governing bodies.
Lord President of the Council (and Leader of the House of Commons), The Rt. Hon. Antony Newton, OBE, MP
Private Secretary, P. Cohen
Special Adviser, P. Moman
Parliamentary Private Secretary, J. Couchman, MP
Clerk of the Council (G3), N. H. Nicholls, CBE
Deputy Clerk of the Council (G5), Miss K. P. Makin, OBE
Senior Clerk, Miss M. A. McCullagh

PROCURATOR FISCAL SERVICE
— *see* pages 369–70

PUBLIC HEALTH LABORATORY SERVICE
61 Colindale Avenue, London NW9 5DF
Tel 0181-200 1295

The Public Health Laboratory Service comprises nine groups of laboratories, the Central Public Health Laboratory and the Communicable Disease Surveillance Centre. The PHLS provides diagnostic microbiological services to hospitals, and has reference facilities that are available nationally. It collates information on the incidence of infection, and when necessary it institutes special inquiries into outbreaks and the epidemiology of infectious disease. It also undertakes bacteriological surveillance of the quality of food and water for local authorities and others.
Chairman, Dr M. P. W. Godfrey, CBE, FRCP
Deputy Chairman, A. Graham-Dixon, QC
Director, Dr Diana Walford, FRCP, FRCPath.
Deputy Directors, Prof. B. I. Duerden, MD, FRCPath.
(*Programmes*); K. M. Saunders (*Corporate Planning and Resources*)
Board Secretary, K. M. Saunders

CENTRAL PUBLIC HEALTH LABORATORY
Colindale Avenue, London NW9 5HT
Director, Prof. S. P. Borriello

COMMUNICABLE DISEASES SURVEILLANCE CENTRE
Colindale Avenue, NW9 5EQ
Director, Dr C. L. R. Bartlett

OTHER SPECIAL LABORATORIES AND UNITS

ANAEROBE REFERENCE UNIT, Public Health Laboratory,
Cardiff. *Director*, Prof. B. I. Duerden, MD, FRCpath.
CRYPTOSPROIDIUM REFERENCE UNIT, Public Health
Laboratory, Rhyl. *Director*, D. N. Looker
GONOCOCCUS REFERENCE UNIT, Public Health
Laboratory, Bristol. *Director*, A. E. Jephcott, MD
LEPTOSPIRA REFERENCE LABORATORY, Public Health
Laboratory, Hereford. *Director*, Dr T. J. Coleman
MALARIA REFERENCE LABORATORY, London School of
Hygiene and Tropical Medicine, London WC1. *Directors*,
Prof. D. J. Bradley, DM; D. C. Warhurst, PH.D., FRCpath.
MENINGOCOCCAL REFERENCE LABORATORY, Public
Health Laboratory, Manchester. *Director*, Dr
B. A. Oppenheim
MYCOBACTERIUM REFERENCE UNIT, Public Health
Laboratory, Dulwich, London. *Director*,
Dr F. Drobniewski
MYCOLOGY REFERENCE LABORATORY, Public Health
Laboratory, Bristol. *Director*, Dr D. Warnock; Public
Health Laboratory, Leeds. *Director*, Prof. E. G. V. Evans
PARASITOLOGY REFERENCE LABORATORY, Hospital for
Tropical Diseases, London. *Director*, Dr P. L. Chiodini
TOXOPLASMA REFERENCE LABORATORIES, Public Health
Laboratory, Swansea. *Director*, D. H. M. Joynson; Public
Health Laboratory, Tooting, London. *Director*, Prof.
A. R. M. Coates

PHLS GROUPS OF LABORATORIES AND GROUP
DIRECTORS

East, Dr Philippa M. B. White
Midlands, Dr R. E. Warren
North, Dr N. F. Lightfoot
North-West, Dr P. Morgan-Capner
South Thames, Prof. R. Y. Cartwright
South-West, Dr K. A. V. Cartwright
Trent, Dr P. J. Wilkinson
Wessex, Dr S. A. Rousseau
Wales, Dr A. J. Howard

REGISTRAR OF PUBLIC LENDING RIGHT
Bayheath House, Prince Regent Street,
Stockton-on-Tees TS18 1DF
Tel 01642-604699

Under the Public Lending Right system, in operation since
1983, payment is made from public funds to authors whose
books are lent out from public libraries. Payment is made
once a year and the amount each author receives is
proportionate to the number of times (established from a
sample) that each registered book has been lent out during
the previous year. The Registrar of PLR, who is appointed
by the Secretary of State for National Heritage, compiles
the register of authors and books. Only living authors
resident in the UK or Germany are eligible to apply. (The
term 'author' covers writers, illustrators, translators, and
some editors/compilers.)

A payment of two pence was made in 1995–6 for each
estimated loan of a registered book, up to a top limit of
£6,000 for the books of any one registered author; the
money for loans above this level is used to augment the
remaining PLR payments. In February 1996, the sum of

£4.330 million was made available for distribution to
20,127 registered authors and assignees as the annual
payment of PLR.

The PLR Advisory Committee advises the Secretary of
State for National Heritage and the Registrar of Public
Lending Right. Its members are appointed by the Secretary
of State.

Chairman of Advisory Committee, P. S. Ziegler, CVO
Registrar, Dr J. G. Parker

PUBLIC RECORD OFFICE
— *see* page 336

PUBLIC TRUST OFFICE
Stewart House, 24 Kingsway, London WC2B 6JX
Tel 0171-269 7000

COURT FUNDS OFFICE, 22 Kingsway, London WC2B 6LE
Tel 0171-936 6000

The Public Trust Office became an executive agency of
the Lord Chancellor's Department in 1994. The chief
executive of the agency holds the statutory titles of Public
Trustee and Accountant-General of the Supreme Court.

The Public Trustee is a trust corporation created to
undertake the business of executorship and trusteeship; she
can act as executor or administrator of the estate of a
deceased person, or as trustee of a will or settlement. The
Public Trustee is also responsible for the performance of
all the administrative, but not the judicial, tasks required of
the Court of Protection under Part VII of the Mental
Health Act 1983, relating to the management and administration of the property and affairs of persons suffering
from mental disorder. The Public Trustee also acts as
Receiver when so directed by the Court, usually where
there is no other person willing or able so to act.

The Accountant-General of the Supreme Court,
through the Court Funds Office, is responsible for the
investment and accounting of funds in court for persons
under a disability, monies in court subject to litigation and
statutory deposits.

Chief Executive (Public Trustee and Accountant-General), Ms
J. C. Lomas
Assistant Public Trustee, Mrs S. Hutcheson
Investment Manager, H. Stevenson
Chief Property Adviser, A. Nightingale

MENTAL HEALTH SECTOR
Head, Mrs H. M. Bratton
Receivership Activity, D. Adams
Protection Activity, P. L. Hales

TRUSTS AND FUNDS SECTOR
Head, F. J. Eddy
Court Funds Activity, R. Anns
Trust Activity, M. Munt

ESTABLISHMENTS AND FINANCE SECTOR
Head, E. A. Bloomfield
Finance, M. Guntrip
Planning, Mrs N. M. Hunt

PUBLIC WORKS LOAN BOARD
— *see* National Investment and Loans Office

COMMISSION FOR RACIAL EQUALITY
Elliot House, 10–12 Allington Street, London SW1E 5EH
Tel 0171-828 7022

The Commission was established in 1977, under the Race Relations Act 1976, to work towards the elimination of discrimination and promote equality of opportunity and good relations between different racial groups. It is funded by the Home Office.
Chairman, H. Ouseley
Deputy Chairs, Mrs Z. Manzoor; H. Harris
Members, R. Purkiss; Dr D. Neil; Ms M. Cunningham; Dr R. Chandran; Dr Z. Khan; M. Hastings; M. Jogee; Dr J. Singh; Ms J. Mellor
Executive Director, D. Sharma

THE RADIO AUTHORITY
Holbrook House, 14 Great Queen Street, London WC2B 5DG
Tel 0171-430 2724

The Radio Authority was established in 1991 under the Broadcasting Act 1990. It is the regulator and licensing authority for all independent radio services. Members of the Authority are appointed by the Secretary of State for National Heritage; senior executive staff are appointed by the Authority.
Chairman, Sir Peter Gibbings
Deputy Chairman, M. Moriarty, CB
Members, Ms J. Francis; M. Reupke; Lady Sheil; A. Reid; Mrs H. Tennant
Chief Executive, A. Stoller
Deputy Chief Executive, D. Vick
Secretary to the Authority, J. Norrington

OFFICE OF THE RAIL REGULATOR
1 Waterhouse Square, 138–142 Holborn, London EC1N 2ST
Tel 0171-282 2000

The Office of the Rail Regulator was set up under the Railways Act 1993. It is headed by the Rail Regulator, who is independent of ministerial control. The Regulator's main functions are the licensing of operators of railway assets; the approval of agreements for access by those operators to track, stations and light maintenance depots; the enforcement of domestic competition law; and consumer protection. The Regulator also sponsors a network of rail users' consultative committees, which represent the interests of passengers.
Rail Regulator, J. A. Swift, QC
Director, Personnel, Finance and Administration, P. D. Murphy
Director, Economic Regulation Group, C. W. Bolt
Director, Railway Network Group, C. J. F. Brown
Director, Passenger Services Group, J. A. Rhodes
Chief Legal Adviser, M. R. Brocklehurst

RECORD OFFICES

ADVISORY COUNCIL ON PUBLIC RECORDS
Secretariat: Public Record Office, Ruskin Avenue, Kew, Richmond, Surrey TW9 4DU
Tel 0181-876 3444

Council members are appointed by the Lord Chancellor, under the Public Records Act 1958, to advise him on matters concerning public records in general and, in particular, on those aspects of the work of the Public Record Office which affect members of the public who make use of it. The Council meets quarterly and produces an annual report which is published alongside the Report of the Keeper of Public Records as a House of Commons sessional paper.
Chairman, The Master of the Rolls
Secretary, T. R. Padfield

THE PUBLIC RECORD OFFICE
Ruskin Avenue, Kew, Richmond, Surrey TW9 4DU
Tel 0181-876 3444

The Public Record Office, originally established in 1838 under the Master of the Rolls, was placed under the direction of the Lord Chancellor in 1958. It became an executive agency in 1992. The Lord Chancellor appoints a Keeper of Public Records, whose duties are to co-ordinate and supervise the selection of records of government departments and the law courts for permanent preservation, to safeguard the records and to make them available to the public. There is a separate record office for Scotland (*see* page 337).

The Office holds records of central government dating from the Domesday Book (1086) to the present. Under the Public Records Act 1967 they are normally open to inspection when 30 years old, and are then available, without charge, in the reading rooms, Monday–Friday, 9.30–5.
Keeper of Public Records (G3), Mrs S. Tyacke
Director, Public Services Division (G5), Dr E. Hallam Smith
Director, Archival Services Division (G5), Dr N. G. Cox
Director, Corporate Services Division (G5), Dr D. Simpson

HOUSE OF LORDS RECORD OFFICE
House of Lords, London SW1A 0PW
Tel 0171-219 3074

Since 1497, the records of Parliament have been kept within the Palace of Westminster. They are in the custody of the Clerk of the Parliaments. In 1946 a record department was established to supervise their preservation and their availability to the public. The search room of the office is open to the public Monday–Friday, 9.30–5 (Tuesday to 8, by appointment).

Some three million documents are preserved, including Acts of Parliament from 1497, journals of the House of Lords from 1510, minutes and committee proceedings from 1610, and papers laid before Parliament from 1531. Amongst the records are the Petition of Right, the Death Warrant of Charles I, the Declaration of Breda, and the Bill of Rights. The House of Lords Record Office also has charge of the journals of the House of Commons (from 1547), and other surviving records of the Commons (from 1572), including documents relating to private bill legislation from 1818. Among other documents are the records of the Lord Great Chamberlain, the political papers of certain members of the two Houses, and documents relating to

Parliament acquired on behalf of the nation. A permanent exhibition was established in the Royal Gallery in 1979.

Clerk of the Records (£40,807–£59,754), D. J. Johnson, FSA
Deputy Clerk of the Records (£32,054–£51,975), S. K. Ellison
Assistant Clerk of the Records (£18,611–£32,731), D. L. Prior

ROYAL COMMISSION ON HISTORICAL MANUSCRIPTS

Quality House, Quality Court, Chancery Lane, London WC2A 1HP
Tel 0171-242 1198

The Commission was set up by royal warrant in 1869 to enquire and report on collections of papers of value for the study of history which were in private hands. In 1959 a new warrant enlarged these terms of reference to include all historical records, wherever situated, outside the Public Records and gave it added responsibilities as a central co-ordinating body to promote, assist and advise on their proper preservation and storage. The Commission, which is responsible to the Department of National Heritage, has published over 200 volumes of reports.

It also maintains the National Register of Archives (NRA), which contains over 39,000 unpublished lists and catalogues of manuscript collections describing the holdings of local record offices, national and university libraries, specialist repositories and others in the UK and overseas. The NRA can be searched using computerized indices which are available in the Commission's search room.

The Commission also administers the Manorial and Tithe Documents Rules on behalf of the Master of the Rolls.

Chairman, The Rt. Hon. Sir Thomas Bingham
Commissioners, The Lord Blake, FBA; Prof. S. F. C. Milsom, FBA; P. T. Cormack, FSA, MP; D. G. Vaisey, FSA; The Lord Egremont and Leconfield; Sir Matthew Farrer, GCVO; Miss B. Harvey, FBA, FSA; Sir John Sainty, KCB, FSA; Prof. R. H. Campbell, OBE, PH.D.; Very Revd H. E. C. Stapleton, FSA; Sir Keith Thomas, PBA; Mrs C. M. Short; The Earl of Scarbrough; Mrs A. Dundas-Bekker; G. E. Aylmer, D.Phil, FBA; Mrs S. J. Davies, PH.D.
Secretary, C. J. Kitching, PH.D., FSA

SCOTTISH RECORDS ADVISORY COUNCIL

HM General Register House, Edinburgh EH1 3YY
Tel 0131-556 6585

The Council was established under the Public Records (Scotland) Act 1937. Its members are appointed by the Secretary of State for Scotland and it may submit proposals or make representations to the Secretary of State, the Lord Justice General or the Lord President of the Court of Session on questions relating to the public records of Scotland.

Chairman, Prof. M. Anne Crowther
Secretary, D. M. Abbott

SCOTTISH RECORD OFFICE

HM General Register House, Edinburgh EH1 3YY
Tel 0131-535 1314

The history of the national archives of Scotland can be traced back to the 13th century. The Scottish Record Office keeps the administrative records of pre-Union Scotland, the registers of central and local courts of law, the public registers of property rights and legal documents, and many collections of local and church records and private archives. Certain groups of records, mainly the modern records of government departments in Scotland, the Scottish railway records, the plans collection, and

private archives of an industrial or commercial nature, are preserved in the branch repository at the West Register House in Charlotte Square. The search rooms in both buildings are open Monday–Friday, 9–4.45. A permanent exhibition at the West Register House and changing exhibitions at the General Register House are open to the public on weekdays, 10–4. The National Register of Archives (Scotland), which is a branch of the Scottish Record Office, is based in the West Register House.

The Scottish Record Office became an executive agency of the Scottish Office in 1993.

Keeper of the Records of Scotland, P. M. Cadell
Deputy Keeper, Dr P. D. Anderson

PUBLIC RECORD OFFICE (NORTHERN IRELAND)

66 Balmoral Avenue, Belfast BT9 6NY
Tel 01232-251318

The Public Record Office (Northern Ireland) is responsible for identifying and preserving Northern Ireland's archival heritage and making it available to the public. It is an executive agency of the Department of the Environment for Northern Ireland. The search room is open on weekdays, 9.15–4.15 (Thursday, 9.15–8.45).

Chief Executive (G5), Dr A. P. Malcomson

CORPORATION OF LONDON RECORDS OFFICE

Guildhall, London EC2P 2EJ
Tel 0171-332 1251

The Corporation of London Records Office contains the municipal archives of the City of London which are regarded as the most complete collection of ancient municipal records in existence. The collection includes charters of William the Conqueror, Henry II, and later kings and queens to 1957; ancient custumals: Liber Horn, Dunthorne, Custumarum, Ordinacionum, Memorandorum and Albus, Liber de Antiquis Legibus, and collections of Statutes; continuous series of judicial rolls and books from 1252 and Council minutes from 1275; records of the Old Bailey and Guildhall Sessions from 1603; financial records from the 16th century; the records of London Bridge from the 12th century; and numerous subsidiary series and miscellanea of historical interest. Readers' Room open Monday–Friday, 9.30–4.45.

Keeper of the City Records, The City Secretary
City Archivist, J. R. Sewell
Deputy City Archivist, Mrs J. M. Bankes

RESEARCH COUNCILS

— see pages 701–6

REVIEW BODIES

The secretariat for these bodies is provided by the Office of Manpower Economics (*see* page 321)

ARMED FORCES PAY

The Review Body on Armed Forces Pay was appointed in 1971 to advise the Prime Minister on the pay and allowances of members of naval, military and air forces of the Crown and of any women's service administered by the Defence Council.

Chairman, G. M. Hourston

Members, C. M. Bolton; Mrs K. Coleman, OBE; J. C. L. Cox, CBE; J. Crosby; Sir Gavin Laird; G. Neely; Air Chief Marshal Sir Roger Palin, KCB, OBE; Mrs D. Venables

DOCTORS' AND DENTISTS' REMUNERATION

The Review Body on Doctors' and Dentists' Remuneration was set up in 1971 to advise the Prime Minister on the remuneration of doctors and dentists taking any part in the National Health Service.
Chairman, C. B. Gough
Members, Mrs B. Brewer; Mrs C. Hui; M. Innes; R. Jackson; C. King, CBE; Dr E. Nelson; D. Penton

NURSING STAFF, MIDWIVES, HEALTH VISITORS AND PROFESSIONS ALLIED TO MEDICINE

The Review Body for nursing staff, midwives, health visitors and professions allied to medicine was set up in 1983 to advise the Prime Minister on the remuneration of nursing staff, midwives and health visitors employed in the National Health Service; and also of physiotherapists, radiographers, remedial gymnasts, occupational therapists, orthoptists, chiropodists, dietitians and related grades employed in the National Health Service.
Chairman, B. Rigby
Members, Mrs A. Dean; Mrs S. Gleig; L. Haddon; Ms R. Lea; Miss A. Mackie, OBE; K. Miles; Prof. Gillian Raab

SCHOOL TEACHERS

The School Teachers' Review Body (STRB) is a statutory body, set up under the School Teachers' Pay and Conditions Act 1991. It is required to examine and report on such matters relating to the statutory conditions of employment of school teachers in England and Wales as may be referred to it by the Secretary of State for Education and Employment. The STRB's reports are submitted to the Prime Minister and the Secretary of State and the latter is required to publish them.
Chairman, A. R. Vineall
Members, Mrs B. Amey; Mrs J. Cuthbertson; P. Gedling; M. Harding; Miss J. Langdon

SENIOR SALARIES

A Top Salaries Review Body was set up in 1971 to advise the Prime Minister on the remuneration of the higher judiciary and other judicial appointments, senior civil servants, and senior officers of the armed forces. In 1993 its name was changed to the Senior Salaries Review Body, and its remit was officially extended to cover the pay, pensions and allowances of MPs, ministers and others whose pay is determined by a Ministerial and Other Salaries Order, and the allowances of peers.
Chairman, Sir Michael Perry, CBE
Members, M. Beloff, QC; Mrs R. Day; G. M. Hourston; Sir Sydney Lipworth, QC; Miss P. Mann; Mrs Y. Newbold; M. Sheldon; Sir Anthony Wilson

ROYAL BOTANIC GARDEN EDINBURGH
Inverleith Row, Edinburgh EH3 5LR
Tel 0131-552 7171

The Royal Botanic Garden Edinburgh (RBGE) originated as the Physic Garden, established in 1670 beside the Palace of Holyroodhouse. Since 1986, RBGE has been administered by a Board of Trustees established under the National Heritage (Scotland) Act 1985. It receives an annual grant from the Scottish Office.

RBG Edinburgh is an international centre for scientific research on plant diversity, maintaining collections of living plants and reference resources, including a herbarium of some two million specimens of preserved plants. Other statutory functions of RBGE include the provision of education and information on botany and horticulture, and the provision of public access to the living plant collections.

The Garden moved to its present site at Inverleith, Edinburgh in 1821. There are also three specialist gardens: Younger Botanic Garden Benmore, near Dunoon, Argyllshire; Logan Botanic Garden, near Stranraer, Wigtownshire; and Dawyck Botanic Garden, near Stobo, Peeblesshire. Public opening hours: RBGE, daily (except Christmas Day and New Year's Day) November–February 10–4; March–April and September–October 10–6; May–August 10–8; specialist gardens, 15 March–October 10–6. Admission free to RBGE; small admission charge to specialist gardens.
Chairman of the Board of Trustees, Prof. M. Wilkins, FRSE
Regius Keeper, Prof. D. S. Ingram, SC.D., FRSE
Deputy Keeper, Dr D. J. Mann

ROYAL BOTANIC GARDENS KEW
Richmond, Surrey TW9 3AB
Tel 0181-940 1171
Wakehurst Place, Ardingly, nr Haywards Heath, W. Sussex RH17 6TN
Tel 01444-892701

The Royal Botanic Gardens (RBG) Kew were originally laid out as a private garden for Kew House for George III's mother, HRH Princess Augusta, in 1759. They were much enlarged in the 19th century, notably by the inclusion of the grounds of the former Richmond Lodge. In 1965 the garden at Wakehurst Place was acquired; it is owned by the National Trust and managed by RBG Kew. Under the National Heritage Act 1983 a Board of Trustees was set up to administer the Gardens which in 1984 became an independent body supported by a grant-in-aid from the Ministry of Agriculture, Fisheries and Food.

The functions of RBG Kew are to carry out research into plant sciences, to disseminate knowledge about plants and to provide the public with the opportunity to gain knowledge and enjoyment from the Gardens' collections. There are extensive national reference collections of living and preserved plants and a comprehensive library and archive. The main emphasis is on plant conservation and biodiversity.

Open daily (except Christmas Day and New Year's Day) from 9.30 a.m. The closing hour varies from 4 p.m. in midwinter to 6 p.m. on weekdays and 7.30 p.m. on Sundays and Bank Holidays in mid-summer. Admission (1996, £4.50. Concessionary schemes available. Glasshouses, 9.30–4.30 (winter); 9.30–5.30 (summer). No dogs except guide-dogs for the blind.

BOARD OF TRUSTEES
Chairman, R. A. E. Herbert, CBE

Members, R. P. Bauman; The Viscount Blakenham; Sir Jeffery Bowman; C. D. Brickell, CBE; Prof. W. G. Chaloner, FRS; Prof. H. Dickinson; Miss A. Ford; S. de Grey; Lady Lennox-Boyd; The Lady Renfrew of Kaimsthorn, PH.D.; The Earl of Selbourne, KBE, FRS (*Queen's Trustee*)
Director, Prof. Sir Ghillean Prance, FRS

ROYAL COMMISSION FOR THE EXHIBITION OF 1851
Sherfield Building, Imperial College of Science, Technology and Medicine, London SW7 2AZ
Tel 0171-594 8790

The Royal Commission was incorporated by supplemental charter as a permanent Commission after winding up the affairs of the Great Exhibition of 1851. Its object is to promote scientific and artistic education by means of funds derived from its Kensington estate, purchased with the surplus left over from the Great Exhibition.
President, HRH The Duke of Edinburgh, KG, KT, PC
Chairman, Board of Management, Sir Denis Rooke, CBE, FRS, FENG.
Secretary to Commissioners, J. P. W. Middleton, CB

THE ROYAL MINT
Llantrisant, Pontyclun, Mid Glamorgan CF72 8YT
Tel 01443-222111

The prime responsibility of the Royal Mint is the provision of United Kingdom coinage, but it actively competes in world markets for a share of the available circulating coin business and, based on the last ten years, two-thirds of the 15,000 tonnes of coins produced annually is exported to more than 100 countries. The Mint also manufactures special proof and uncirculated quality coins in gold, silver and other metals; military and civil decorations and medals; commemorative and prize medals; and royal and official seals.
The Royal Mint became an executive agency of the Treasury in 1990.
Master of the Mint, The Chancellor of the Exchequer (*ex officio*)
Deputy Master and Comptroller, R. de L. Holmes

ROYAL NATIONAL THEATRE BOARD
South Bank, London, SE1 9PX
Tel 0171-928 2033

The chairman and members of the Board of the Royal National Theatre are appointed by the Secretary of State for National Heritage.
Chairman, Sir Christopher Hogg
Members, The Hon. P. Benson; The Hon. Lady Cazalet; M. Codron, CBE; Lady Greenbury; Ms S. Hall; Ms K. Jones; S. Lipton; D. Nandy; M. Oliver; The Rt. Hon. Sir Michael Palliser, GCMG; T. Stoppard, CBE; P. Wiegand; S. Yassukovich, CBE
Company Secretary and Head of Finance, A. Blackstock
Board and Committee Secretary, M. McGregor

RURAL DEVELOPMENT COMMISSION
141 Castle Street, Salisbury, Wilts. SP1 3TP
Tel 01722-336255

The Rural Development Commission is the government agency for economic and social development in rural England. The Commission gives advice to the Government and undertakes activities aimed at stimulating job creation and the provision of essential services in the countryside. Its sponsoring department is the Department of the Environment.
Chairman, The Lord Shuttleworth
Deputy Chairman, R. Thompson
Chief Executive, R. Butt

SCOTTISH COURTS ADMINISTRATION
— see page 368

SCOTTISH ENTERPRISE
120 Bothwell Street, Glasgow G2 7JP
Tel 0141-248 2700

In 1991 Scottish Enterprise took over the economic development and environmental improvement functions of the Scottish Development Agency and the training functions of the Training Agency in lowland Scotland. It is funded by the Scottish Office and its remit is to further the development of Scotland's economy, to enhance the skills of the Scottish workforce, to promote Scotland's international competitiveness and to improve the environment. Many of its functions are contracted out to a network of local enterprise companies. Through Locate in Scotland (*see* page 342), Scottish Enterprise is also concerned with attracting firms to Scotland.
Chairman, Sir Donald MacKay
Chief Executive, C. Beveridge, CBE

SCOTTISH ENVIRONMENT PROTECTION AGENCY
Erskine Court, The Castle Business Park, Stirling FK9 4TR
Tel 01786-457700

The Scottish Environment Protection Agency came into being on 1 April 1996 under the Environment Act 1995. It brings together the work formerly undertaken by HM Industrial Pollution Inspectorate, the river purification authorities, and district and islands councils in respect of waste regulation and some air pollution controls. It has regional offices in East Kilbride, Riccarton and Dingwall, and 17 local offices throughout Scotland. It receives funding from the Scottish Office.

THE BOARD
Chairman, Prof. W. Turmeau, CBE
Members, B. Baird; A. Buchan; B. Fitzgerald; G. Gordon, OBE; D. Hughes Hallett, FRICS; Prof. C. Johnston; C. McChord; C. McLatchie; Ms A. Magee; Ms J. Shaw

THE EXECUTIVE
Chief Executive, A. Paton
Director of Corporate Services, Dr G. King
Director of Environmental Strategy, Ms P. Henton
Director, North Region, Prof. D. Mackay
Director, East Region, W. Halcrow
Director, West Region, J. Beveridge

SCOTTISH HOMES
Thistle House, 91 Haymarket Terrace, Edinburgh
EH12 5HE
Tel 0131-313 0044

Scottish Homes, the national housing agency for Scotland, aims to improve the quality and variety of housing available in Scotland by working in partnership with the public and private sectors. The agency is a major funder of new and improved housing provided by housing associations and private developers. It is currently transferring its own 34,000 rented houses to alternative landlords. It is also involved in housing research and in piloting innovative housing solutions. Board members are appointed by the Secretary of State for Scotland.
Chairman, J. Ward, CBE
Chief Executive, P. McKinlay

SCOTTISH NATURAL HERITAGE
12 Hope Terrace, Edinburgh EH9 2AS
Tel 0131-447 4784

Scottish Natural Heritage came into existence in 1992 under the Natural Heritage (Scotland) Act 1991. It provides advice on nature conservation to all those whose activities affect wildlife, landforms and features of geological interest in Scotland, and seeks to develop and improve facilities for the enjoyment of the Scottish countryside. It is funded by the Scottish Office.
Chairman, M. Magnusson, KBE
Chief Executive, R. Crofts
Chief Scientific Adviser, M. B. Usher
Director of Policy, J. Thomson
Director of Resources, L. Montgomery

SCOTTISH OFFICE

The Secretary of State for Scotland is responsible in Scotland for a wide range of statutory functions which in England and Wales are the responsibility of a number of departmental ministers. He also works closely with ministers in charge of Great Britain departments on topics of special significance to Scotland within their fields of responsibility. His statutory functions are administered by five main departments collectively known as the Scottish Office. The departments are: the Scottish Office Agriculture, Environment and Fisheries Department; the Scottish Office Development Department; the Scottish Office Education and Industry Department; the Scottish Office Department of Health; and the Scottish Office Home Department.
In addition there are a number of other Scottish departments for which the Secretary of State has some degree of responsibility; these include the Scottish Courts Administration, the General Register Office, the Scottish Record Office and the Department of the Registers of Scotland. The Secretary of State also bears ministerial responsibility for the activities in Scotland of several statutory bodies, such as the Forestry Commission, whose functions extend throughout Great Britain.

Dover House, Whitehall, London, SW1A 2AU
Tel 0171-270 3000

Secretary of State for Scotland, The Rt. Hon. Michael Forsyth, MP
Private Secretary (G5), C. M. A. Lugton
Special Advisers, G. Warner; Mrs J. Low
Parliamentary Private Secretary, B. Jenkin, MP
Minister of State, The Rt. Hon. Lord James Douglas-Hamilton, MP (*Home Affairs and Health*)
Private Secretary, A. T. F. Johnston
Parliamentary Private Secretary, N. Deva, MP
Parliamentary Under-Secretaries of State, Raymond Robertson, MP (*Education, Housing and Fisheries*); George Kynoch, MP (*Industry and Local Government*); The Earl of Lindsay (*Agriculture, Forestry and the Environment*)
Private Secretaries, S. Farrell; D. McLaren; J. M. Pryce
Parliamentary Clerk, Mrs L. J. Stirling
Permanent Under-Secretary of State (G1), Sir Russell Hillhouse, KCB
Private Secretary, Miss L. M. Harper

LIAISON DIVISION
Assistant Secretary (G5), E. W. Ferguson

MANAGEMENT GROUP SUPPORT STAFF
Principal (G7), M. Grant

St Andrew's House, Edinburgh EH1 3DG
Tel 0131-556 8400

PERSONNEL GROUP
16 Waterloo Place, Edinburgh EH1 3DN
Tel 0131-556 8400
Principal Establishment Officer (G3), C. C. MacDonald
Assistant Secretary (G5), G. D. Calder

FINANCE DIVISION
Victoria Quay, Edinburgh EH6 6QQ
Tel 0131-556 8400
Principal Finance Officer (G3), J. S. G. Graham
Assistant Secretaries (G5), Dr P. S. Collings; D. Crawley; D. G. N. Reid; W. T. Tait
Head of Accountancy Services Unit (G6), I. M. Smith
Assistant Director of Finance Strategy (G6), I. A. McLeod

SOLICITOR'S OFFICE
For the Scottish departments and certain UK services, including HM Treasury, in Scotland
Solicitor (G2), R. Brodie, CB
Deputy Solicitor (G3), R. M. Henderson
Divisional Solicitors (G4), J. L. Jamieson; (*G5*), R. Bland (*seconded to Scottish Law Commission*); G. C. Duke; I. H. Harvie; H. F. Macdiarmid; J. G. S. Maclean; N. Raven; Mrs L. A. Wallace

SCOTTISH OFFICE INFORMATION DIRECTORATE
For the Scottish departments and certain UK services
Director (G5), Ms E. S. B. Drummond
Deputy Director (G6), W. A. McNeill

SCOTTISH OFFICE AGRICULTURE, ENVIRONMENT AND FISHERIES DEPARTMENT
Pentland House, 47 Robb's Loan, Edinburgh EH14 1TY
Tel 0131-556 8400
Secretary (G2), A. M. Russell
Under-Secretaries (G3), T. A. Cameron (*Agriculture*); S. F. Hampson (*Environment*)
Fisheries Secretary (G3), I. W. Gordon
Assistant Secretaries (G5), D. A. Brew; D. R. Dickson; J. Duffy; M. B. Foulis; R. A. Grant; C. K. McIntosh; A. J. Matheson; A. J. Rushworth; I. M. Whitelaw
Chief Agricultural Officer (G4), W. A. Macgregor
Deputy Chief Agricultural Officer (G5), J. I. Woodrow

Assistant Chief Agricultural Officers (G6), J. A. Hardie;
A. Robb; A. J. Robertson
Chief Agricultural Economist (G6), J. R. Wildgoose, D.Phil.
Chief Food and Dairy Officer (G7), S. D. Rooke
Principal Surveyor (G6), I. W. Anderson, FRICS
Scientific Adviser (G5), T. W. Hegarty, Ph.D.
Senior Principal Scientific Officers (G6), Mrs L. A. D. Turl;
Dr Rosi Waterhouse

FISHERIES RESEARCH SERVICES
Marine Laboratory, PO Box 101, Victoria Road, Torry,
Aberdeen AB9 8DB
Tel 01224-876544

Director of Fisheries Research for Scotland (G4),
Prof. A. D. Hawkins, Ph.D., FRSE
Deputy Director (G5), J. Davies

Freshwater Fisheries Laboratory
Faskally, Pitlochry, Perthshire PH6 5LB
Tel 01796-472060

Senior Principal Scientific Officers (G6), Dr R. M. Cook; Dr
J. M. Davies; Dr A. E. Ellis; Dr A. L. S. Munro;
R. G. J. Shelton; Dr P. A. Stewart; Dr C. S. Wardle
Inspector of Salmon and Freshwater Fisheries for Scotland (G7),
D. A. Dunkley

ENVIRONMENTAL AFFAIRS GROUP
Under-Secretary (G3), S. F. Hampson
Assistant Secretaries (G5), J. W. L. Lonie; T. D. MacDonald;
J. A. Rennie
Chief Water Engineer, D. MacDonald
Ecological Adviser (G6), Dr J. Miles

DIRECTORATE OF ADMINISTRATIVE SERVICES
Victoria Quay, Edinburgh EH6 6QQ
Tel 0131-556 8400

Director of Administrative Services (G3), R. S. B. Gordon
Director of Efficiency Unit (G5), Ms I. M. Low
Chief Estates Officer (G6), J. A. Andrew

Saughton House, Broomhouse Drive, Edinburgh EH11 3DX
Head of Information Technology (G5), A. M. Brown
Head of IT Services (G6), I. W. Goodwin
Director of Telecommunications (G6), K. Henderson, OBE

James Craig Walk, Edinburgh EH1 3BA
Head of Purchasing and Supplies (G5), D. Ramsay

EXECUTIVE AGENCIES

INTERVENTION BOARD
— see page 315

SCOTTISH AGRICULTURAL SCIENCE AGENCY
East Craig, Edinburgh EH12 8NJ
The Agency provides scientific information and advice on
agricultural and horticultural crops and the environment,
and has various statutory and regulatory functions.
Director (G5), Dr R. K. M. Hay
Deputy Director (G6), S. R. Cooper
Senior Principal Scientific Officers (G6), A. D. Ruthven;
W. J. Rennie

SCOTTISH FISHERIES PROTECTION AGENCY
Pentland House, 47 Robb's Loan, Edinburgh EH14 1TY
Tel 0131-556 8400
The Agency enforces fisheries law and regulations in
Scottish waters and ports.
Chief Executive (G5), Capt. P. Du Vivier, RN
Director of Corporate Strategy and Resources (G6), J. B. Roddin
Director of Operational Enforcement (G6), R. J. Walker
Marine Superintendent, Capt. R. M. Mill-Irving

SCOTTISH OFFICE DEVELOPMENT
DEPARTMENT
Victoria Quay, Edinburgh EH6 6QQ
Tel 0131-556 8400

Secretary (G2), H. H. Mills, CB
Under-Secretaries (G3), D. J. Belfall; J. W. Elvidge
Assistant Secretaries (G5), M. T. Affolter; J. A. Ewing;
D. Hart; D. Henderson; J. D. Gallacher; W. Howat;
K. W. McKay; J. R. McQueen; D. A. Middleton; R. Tait;
G. M. D. Thomson
Senior Economic Adviser (G5), C. L. Wood

PROFESSIONAL STAFF
*Director of Construction and Building Control Group and Chief
Architect (G3)*, J. E. Gibbons, Ph.D., FSA SCOT.
*Deputy Director of Construction and Building Control Group and
Deputy Chief Architect (G5)*, G. Gray
*Deputy Director of Construction and Building Control Group and
Chief Quantity Surveyor (G5)*, A. J. Wyllie
Chief Planner (G4), A. Mackenzie
Chief Statistician (G5), Dr J. Cuthbert

INQUIRY REPORTERS
Robert Stevenson House, 2 Greenside Lane, Edinburgh
EH1 3AG
Tel 0131-244 5680
Chief Reporter (G3), Miss G. Pain
Deputy Chief Reporter (G5), R. M. Hickman

NATIONAL ROADS DIRECTORATE
Victoria Quay, Edinburgh EH6 6QQ
Tel 0131-556 8400

Director of Roads (G3), J. Innes
Deputy Chief Engineers (G5), J. A. Howison (*Roads*),
N. B. MacKenzie (*Bridges*)

EXECUTIVE AGENCY

HISTORIC SCOTLAND
Longmore House, Salisbury Place, Edinburgh EH9 1SH
Tel 0131-668 8600
The agency's role is to protect Scotland's historic monu-
ments, buildings and lands, and to promote public under-
standing and enjoyment of them.
Chief Executive (G3), G. N. Munro
Directors (G5), F. J. Lawrie; I. Maxwell; B. Naylor; (*G6*),
S. Rosie
Chief Inspector of Ancient Monuments, Dr D. J. Breeze
Chief Inspector, Building Division, J. R. Hume

SCOTTISH OFFICE EDUCATION AND
INDUSTRY DEPARTMENT
Victoria Quay, Edinburgh EH6 6QQ
Tel 0131-556 8400

Secretary (G2), G. R. Wilson, CB
Under-Secretaries (G3), J. S. B. Martin; E. J. Weeple
Assistant Secretaries (G5), A. W. Fraser; I. G. F. Gray;
R. Irvine; R. D. Jackson; G. McHugh; Miss M. Maclean;
A. K. MacLeod; Mrs R. Menlowe; Mrs V. Macniven
Chief Statistician (G5), C. R. Macleans

HM INSPECTORS OF SCHOOLS
Senior Chief Inspector (G3), D. A. Osler
Depute Senior Chief Inspector (G4), Dr G. H. C. Donaldson
Chief Inspectors (G5), J. Boyes; J. T. Donaldson; Miss
K. M. Fairweather; D. E. Kelso; J. J. McDonald;
A. S. McGlynn; M. Roebuck; H. M. Stalker;
R. M. S. Tuck
There are 79 Grade 6 Inspectors

INDUSTRIAL EXPANSION
Meridian Court, 5 Cadogan Street, Glasgow G2 6AT
Tel 0141-248 2855

Under-Secretary (G3), G. Robson
Industrial Adviser, D. Blair
Scientific Adviser, Prof. D. J. Tedford
Assistant Secretaries (G5), M. T. S. Batho; W. Malone; Ms J. Morgan; Dr J. Rigg

LOCATE IN SCOTLAND
120 Bothwell Street, Glasgow G2 7JP
Tel 0141-248 2700

Director (G4), M. Togneri

SCOTTISH TRADE INTERNATIONAL
120 Bothwell Street, Glasgow G2 7JP
Tel 0141-248 2700

Director, D. Taylor

EXECUTIVE AGENCIES

STUDENT AWARDS AGENCY FOR SCOTLAND
Gyleview House, 3 Redheughs Rigg, Edinburgh EH12 9HH
Tel 0131-244 5867

Chief Executive, K. MacRae

SCOTTISH OFFICE PENSIONS AGENCY
St Margaret's House, 151 London Road, Edinburgh
EH8 7TG
Tel 0131-556 8400

The Agency is responsible for the pension arrangements of some 300,000 people, mainly NHS and teaching services employees and pensioners.
Chief Executive, N. MacLeod
Directors (G7), G. Mowat (*Policy*); A. M. Small (*Operations*); M. J. McDermott (*Resources and Customer Services*)

SCOTTISH OFFICE DEPARTMENT OF HEALTH
St Andrew's House, Edinburgh EH1 3DG
Tel 0131-556 8400

NATIONAL HEALTH SERVICE IN SCOTLAND
MANAGEMENT EXECUTIVE
Chief Executive (G3), G. R. Scaife
Director of Purchasing (G4), Dr K. J. Woods
Director of Primary Care (G5), Mrs A. Robson
Director of Finance (G5), S. Featherstone
Director of Human Resources (G5), M. Sibbald
Director of Nursing, Miss A. Jarvie
Medical Director (G3), Dr A. B. Young, FRCPE
Director of Trusts (G4), P. Wilson
Director of Information Services, NHS, C. B. Knox
Director of Estates, H. R. McCallum
Chief Pharmacist (G5), W. Scott
Chief Scientist, Prof. I. A. D. Bouchier, CBE, FRCP
Chief Dental Officer, J. R. Wild

PUBLIC HEALTH POLICY UNIT
Head of Unit and Chief Medical Officer (G2), Dr R. E. Kendell, CBE
Deputy Chief Medical Officer (G3), Dr A. B. Young, FRCPE
Under-Secretary (G3), Mrs N. Munro
Assistant Secretary (G5), J. T. Brown
Principal Medical Officers, Dr J. V. Basson; Dr Rosalind Skinner; Dr Elizabeth Sowler
Senior Medical Officers, Dr Angela Anderson; P. W. Brooks; Dr J. Cumming; Dr D. J. Ewing; Dr A. Findlay; Dr D. Jolliffe; Dr A. Keel; Dr Patricia Madden; Dr R. Simmons

NATIONAL HEALTH SERVICE, SCOTLAND

HEALTH BOARDS
ARGYLL AND CLYDE, Ross House, Hawkhead Road, Paisley PA2 7BN. *Chairman*, M. D. Jones; *General Manager*, I. C. Smith
AYRSHIRE AND ARRAN, PO Box 13, Seafield House, Doonfoot Road, Ayr KA7 4DW. *Chairman*, J. W. G. Donaldson, CBE; *General Manager*, J. M. Eckford, OBE
BORDERS, Huntlyburn, Melrose, Roxburghshire TD6 9DB. *Chairman*, D. A. C. Kilshaw; *General Manager*, D. A. Peters, OBE
DUMFRIES AND GALLOWAY, Nithbank, Dumfries DG1 2SD. *Chairman*, Mrs J. D. Tulloch; *General Manager*, D. Banks
FIFE, Springfield House, Cupar KY7 5PR. *Chairman*, R. Baker, OBE; *General Manager*, Miss P. Frost
FORTH VALLEY, 33 Spittal Street, Stirling FK8 1DX. *Chairman (acting)*, E. Bell-Scott; *General Manager*, D. Hird
GRAMPIAN, Summerfield House, 2 Eday Road, Aberdeen AB9 1RE. *Chairman*, C. MacLeod, CBE; *General Manager*, F. E. L. Hartnett, OBE
GREATER GLASGOW, 112 Ingram Street, Glasgow G1 1ET. *Chairman*, Sir Robert Calderwood; *General Manager (acting)*, T. A. Divers
HIGHLAND, Reay House, 17 Old Edinburgh Road, Inverness IV2 3HG. *Chairman*, J. D. M. Robertson, CBE; *General Manager*, Dr G. V. Stone
LANARKSHIRE, 14 Beckford Street, Hamilton, Lanarkshire ML3 0TA. *Chairman*, I. Livingstone, OBE; *General Manager*, Prof. F. Clark, CBE
LOTHIAN, 148 The Pleasance, Edinburgh EH8 9RS. *Chairman*, Dr J. W. Baynham, CBE; *General Manager*, J. Lusby
ORKNEY, Balfour Hospital, New Scapa Road, Kirkwall, Orkney KW15 1BQ. *Chairman*, J. Leslie; *General Manager*, E. Jackson
SHETLAND, Brevik House, South Road, Lerwick ZW1 0RB. *Chairman*, Mrs F. Grains, OBE; *General Manager*, B. J. Atherton
TAYSIDE, PO Box 75, Vernonholme, Riverside Drive, Dundee DD1 9NL. *Chairman*, J. C. MacFarlane, CBE; *General Manager*, Miss L. Barrie
WESTERN ISLES, 37 South Beach Street, Stornoway, Isle of Lewis PA87 2BN. *Chairman*, A. Matheson; *General Manager*, R. Mullan

HEALTH EDUCATION BOARD FOR SCOTLAND
Woodburn House, Canaan Lane, Edinburgh EH10 4SG
Tel 0131-447 8044

Chairman, D. Campbell
General Manager, Dr A. Tannahill

STATE HOSPITAL
Carstairs Junction, Lanark ML11 8RP
Tel 01555-840293

Chairman, P. Hamilton-Grierson
General Manager, R. Manson

COMMON SERVICES AGENCY
Trinity Park House, South Trinity Road, Edinburgh
EH5 3SE
Tel 0131-552 6255

Chairman, G. Scaife
General Manager (acting), Dr F. Gibb

SCOTTISH OFFICE HOME DEPARTMENT
St Andrew's House, Edinburgh EH1 3DG
Tel 0131-556 8400

Secretary (G2), J. Hamill

Under-Secretaries (G3), N. G. Campbell; D. J. Essery; Mrs G. M. Stewart
Assistant Secretaries (G5), C. Baxter; Mrs M. H. Brannan; Mrs M. B. Gunn; R. S. T. MacEwen; D. Macniven, TD
Chief Research Officer, Dr C. P. A. Levein
Senior Principal Research Officer (G6), Dr Jacqueline Tombs

SOCIAL WORK SERVICES GROUP
James Craig Walk, Edinburgh EH1 3BA
Tel 0131-556 8400

Under-Secretary (G3), N. G. Campbell
Assistant Secretaries (G5), G. A. Anderson; Ms L. J. Clare; J. W. Sinclair
Chief Inspector of Social Work Services, A. Skinner
Assistant Chief Inspectors, Ms M. L. Hunt; F. A. O'Leary; Mrs G. Ottley; D. Pia; I. C. Robertson; A. Sabine

OTHER APPOINTMENTS
HM Chief Inspector of Constabulary, J. Boyd, CBE, QPM
HM Chief Inspector of Prisons, C. Fairweather, OBE
Commandant, Scottish Police College, H. I. Watson, QPM
HM Chief Inspector of Fire Services, N. Morrison
Commandant, Scottish Fire Service Training School, D. Grant, QFSM

MENTAL WELFARE COMMISSION FOR SCOTLAND
25 Drumsheugh Gardens, Edinburgh EH3 7NS
Tel 0131-225 7034

Chairman, Hon. Lady Cosgrove
Commissioners, Mrs N. Bennie; P. H. Brodie; Mrs F. Cotter; Mrs M. Jeffcoat; Dr M. Livingston; Dr D. McCall-Smith; Dr M. McCreadie; D. J. Macdonald; Ms L. M. Noble; I. Ross; Dr E. M. Thomas; W. Gent; Ms M. Whoriskey; A. Robb

COUNSEL TO THE SECRETARY OF STATE FOR SCOTLAND UNDER THE PRIVATE LEGISLATION PROCEDURE (SCOTLAND) ACT 1936
50 Frederick Street, Edinburgh EH2 1EN
Tel 0131-226 6499

Senior Counsel, G. S. Douglas, QC
Junior Counsel, N. M. P. Morrison

EXECUTIVE AGENCIES

REGISTERS OF SCOTLAND
— see page 316

SCOTTISH COURT SERVICE
— see page 368

SCOTTISH PRISON SERVICE
Calton House, 5 Redheughs Rigg, Edinburgh EH12 9HW
Tel 0131-556 8400

Chief Executive of Scottish Prison Service (G3), E. W. Frizzell
Director of Custody (G4), P. Withers
Director, Human Resources (G5), F. Coyle
Director, Finance and Information Systems (G5), W. Pretswell
Director, Strategy and Corporate Affairs (G5), D. A. Stewart
Deputy Director, Regime Services and Supplies (G6), vacant
Deputy Director, Estates and Buildings (G6), B. Paterson
Area Director, South and West (G5), J. Pearce
Area Director, North and East (G5), P. Russell
Governor, Scottish Prison Service College, J. Matthews

PRISONS

ABERDEEN, Craiginches, Aberdeen AB9 2HN. *Governor*, J. Bywalec

BARLINNIE, Barlinnie, Glasgow G33 2QX. *Governor*, R. L. Houchain
CASTLE HUNTLY YOUNG OFFENDERS INSTITUTION, Castle Huntly, Longforgan, nr Dundee DD2 5HL. *Governor*, K. Rennie
CORNTON VALE, Cornton Road, Stirling FK9 5NY. *Governor*, vacant
DUMFRIES YOUNG OFFENDERS INSTITUTION, Terregles Street, Dumfries DG2 9AX. *Governor*, G. Taylor
DUNGAVEL, Dungavel House, Strathaven, Lanarkshire ML10 6RF. *Governor*, Ms M. Wood
EDINBURGH, 33 Stenhouse Road, Edinburgh EH11 3LN. *Governor*, J. Durno
FRIARTON, Friarton, Perth PH2 8DW. *Governor*, E. A. Gordon
GLENOCHIL PRISON AND YOUNG OFFENDERS INSTITUTION, King O'Muir Road, Tullibody, Clackmannanshire FK10 3AD. *Governor*, L. McBain
GREENOCK, Gateside, Greenock PA16 9AH. *Governor*, R. MacCowan
LONGRIGGEND REMAND INSTITUTION, Longriggend, nr Airdrie, Lanarkshire ML6 7TL. *Governor*, A. MacDonald
LOW MOSS, Low Moss, Bishopbriggs, Glasgow G64 2QB. *Governor*, W. Middleton
NORANSIDE, Noranside, Fern, by Forfar, Angus DD8 3QY. *Governor*, E. Brownsmith
PENNINGHAME, Penninghame, Newton Stewart DG8 6RG. *Governor*, H. Ross
PERTH, 3 Edinburgh Road, Perth PH2 8AT. *Governor*, M. Duffy
PETERHEAD, Salthouse Head, Peterhead, Aberdeenshire AB4 6YY. *Governor*, W. Rattray
POLMONT YOUNG OFFENDERS INSTITUTION, Brightons, Falkirk, Stirlingshire FK2 0AB. *Governor*, D. Gunn
PORTERFIELD, Porterfield, Inverness IV2 3HH. *Governor*, W. M. Weir
SHOTTS, Shotts ML7 4LF. *Governor*, W. McKinlay
SHOTTS UNIT, Shotts ML7 4LF. *Governor*, A. McVicar
SHOTTS NATIONAL INDUCTION UNIT, Shotts ML7 4LE. *Governor*, Ms S. Brookes

SCOTTISH RECORD OFFICE
— see page 337

GENERAL REGISTER OFFICE
New Register House, Edinburgh EH1 3YT
Tel 0131-334 0380

The General Register Office for Scotland is an associated department of the Scottish Office. It is the office of the Registrar-General for Scotland, who has responsibility for civil registration and the taking of censuses in Scotland and has in his custody the following records: the statutory registers of births, deaths, still births, adoptions, marriages and divorces; the old parish registers (recording births, deaths and marriages, etc., before civil registration began in 1855); and records of censuses of the population in Scotland. Hours of public access: Monday–Friday 9–4.30.
Registrar-General, J. Meldrum
Deputy Registrar-General, B. V. Philp
Senior Principal (G6), D. A. Orr
Principals (G7), D. B. L. Brownlee; R. C. Lawson; F. D. Garvie
Statisticians (G7), J. Arrundale; G. W. L. Jackson; F. G. Thomas

SCOTTISH PRISONS COMPLAINTS COMMISSION

Government Buildings, Broomhouse Drive, Edinburgh EH11 3XD
Tel 0131-244 8423

The Commission was established in 1994. It is an independent body to which prisoners in Scottish prisons can make application in relation to any matter where they have failed to obtain satisfaction from the Prison Service's internal grievance procedures. Clinical judgments made by medical officers, matters which are the subject of legal proceedings and matters relating to sentence, conviction and parole decision-making are excluded from the Commission's jurisdiction. The Commissioner is appointed by the Secretary of State for Scotland.
Commissioner, Dr J. McManus

SEA FISH INDUSTRY AUTHORITY

18 Logie Mill, Logie Green Road, Edinburgh EH7 4HG
Tel 0131-558 3331

Established under the Fisheries Act 1981, the Authority is required to promote the efficiency of the sea fish industry. It carries out research relating to the industry and gives advice on related matters. It provides training, promotes the marketing, consumption and export of sea fish and sea fish products, and may provide financial assistance for the improvement of fishing vessels in respect of essential safety equipment. It is responsible to the Ministry of Agriculture, Fisheries and Food.
Chairman, E. Davey
Chief Executive, P. D. Chaplin

THE SECURITY SERVICE COMMISSIONER

c/o PO Box 18, London SEI OTZ

The Commissioner is appointed by the Prime Minister. He keeps under review the issue of warrants by the Home Secretary under the Intelligence Services Act 1994, and is required to help the Security Service Tribunal by investigating complaints which allege interference with property and by offering all such assistance in discharging its functions as it may require. He is also required to submit an annual report on the discharge of his functions to the Prime Minister.
Commissioner, The Rt. Hon. Lord Justice Stuart-Smith

SECURITY SERVICE TRIBUNAL

PO Box 18, London SEI OTZ
Tel 0171-273 4095

The Security Service Act 1989 established a tribunal of three to five senior members of the legal profession, independent of the Government and appointed by The Queen, to investigate complaints from any person about anything which they believe the Security Service has done to them or to their property.
President, The Rt. Hon. Lord Justice Simon Brown
Vice-President, Sheriff J. McInnes, QC
Member, Sir Richard Gaskell

SERIOUS FRAUD OFFICE

Elm House, 10–16 Elm Street, London WCIX OBJ
Tel 0171-239 7272

The Serious Fraud Office is an autonomous department under the superintendence of the Attorney-General. Its remit is to investigate and prosecute serious and complex fraud. (Other fraud cases are currently handled by the fraud investigation unit of the Crown Prosecution Service.) The scope of its powers covers England, Wales and Northern Ireland. The staff includes lawyers, accountants and other support staff; investigating teams work closely with the police.
Director, G. Staple, CB

DEPARTMENT OF SOCIAL SECURITY

Richmond House, 79 Whitehall, London SWIA 2NS
Tel 0171-238 0800

The Department of Social Security is responsible for the payment of benefits and the collection of contributions under the National Insurance and Industrial Injuries schemes, and for the payment of child benefit, one-parent benefit, Income Support and Family Credit. It administers the Social Fund, and is responsible for assessing the means of applicants for legal aid. It is also responsible for the payment of war pensions and the operation of the child maintenance system.
Secretary of State for Social Security, The Rt. Hon. Peter Lilley, MP
    Private Secretary, S. Czerniawski
    Special Adviser, P. Barnes
    Parliamentary Private Secretary, P. Merchant, MP
Minister of State, Alistair Burt, MP (*Social Security and Disabled People*)
    Private Secretary, G. Tempest-Hay
Minister of State, The Lord Mackay of Ardbrecknish, PC
    Private Secretary, Ms C. Payne
Parliamentary Under-Secretaries of State, Roger Evans, MP; Andrew Mitchell, MP; Oliver Heald, MP
    Private Secretaries, M. Baldock; J. Vincent; C. Lewis
    Parliamentary Private Secretary, D. Congdon, MP
Permanent Secretary (G1), Mrs A. E. Bowtell, CB
    Private Secretary, B. Hearn

CORPORATE MANAGEMENT GROUP
Director (G2), J. Tross

PERSONNEL AND HQ SUPPORT SERVICES DIRECTORATE
Director, S. Hewitt
Section Heads (G5), T. Perl; (G7), R. Yeats; B. Glew; J. Elliott

*ANALYTICAL SERVICES DIVISION
Director (G3), D. Stanton
Chief Statisticians (G5), N. Dyson; M. McDowall
Senior Economic Advisers (G5), J. Ball; G. Harris
Deputy Chief Scientific Officer (G5), D. Barnbrook
Chief Research Officer (G5), Ms S. Duncan

FINANCE DIVISION
Grade 3, S. Lord

---

*At the Adelphi, 1–11 John Adam Street, London WC2N 6HT. Tel: 0171-962 8000

SOCIAL SECURITY POLICY GROUP
Head of Policy Group (G2), C. Kelly
Policy Directors (G3), R. Allen; M. Whippman; Miss
  M. Peirson, CB; D. Brereton
Policy Managers (G5), Mrs A. Lingwood; D. Jackson; Ms
  S. Graham; B. O'Gorman; Miss J. Moore; M. Street;
  J. Groombridge; Mrs C. Rookes; B. Calderwood; Miss
  J. Leibling; D. Allsop; C. Evans; J. Hughes; P. Cleasby;
  G. Bowen; Ms K. Limm; P. Morgan; Mrs L. Richards;
  Ms J. Shersby; (G6), B. Layton; I. Williams

INFORMATION DIRECTORATE
Head of Information (G5), S. Reardon
Deputy Head of Information (G6), T. Grace
Principal Information Officer (G7), J. Bretherton
Chief Publicity Officer (G7), Ms H. Midlane

SOLICITOR'S OFFICE
Solicitor (G2), P. K. J. Thompson

SOLICITOR'S DIVISION A
New Court, 48 Carey Street, London WC2A 2LS
Tel 0171-412 1465

Principal Assistant Solicitor (G3), J. A. Catlin
Assistant Solicitors (G5), R. Powell; J. M. Swainson; Mrs
  G. Massiah; K. K. Baublys; Mrs F. A. Logan;
  S. M. Cooper

SOLICITOR'S DIVISION B
New Court, 48 Carey Street, London WC2A 2LS
Tel 0171-412 1404

Solicitor (G2), P. K. J. Thompson
Assistant Solicitors (G5), R. G. S. Aitken; W. H. Connell; Ms
  S. Edwards

SOLICITOR'S DIVISION C
New Court, 48 Carey Street, London WC2A 2LS
Tel 0171-412 1341

Principal Assistant Solicitor (G3), Mrs G. S. Kerrigan
Assistant Solicitors (G5), P. Milledge; R. J. Dormer; Miss
  M. E. Trefgarne; Mrs S. Walker; Miss G. E. Parker

MAXWELL PENSIONS UNIT
7 St James's Square, London SW1Y 4JU
Tel 0171-839 3599

Director (G5), R. P. Cleasby

EXECUTIVE AGENCIES

BENEFITS AGENCY
Quarry House, Quarry Hill, Leeds LS2 7UA
Tel 0113-232 4000

The Agency administers claims for and payments of social
security benefits.
Chief Executive, P. Mathison
  Private Secretary, Ms E. Clayton
Directors, D. Riggs (*Finance*); P. Murphy (*Personnel and
  Communications*); Ms U. Brennan (*Change Management*);
  A. Cleveland (*Project Director*); G. McCorkell (*Project
  Director*); J. Lutton (*North*); T. Edge (*South*)

Benefits Agency Medical Services
Principal Medical Officers, Dr M. Aylward; Dr P. Dewis; Dr
  C. Hudson; Dr P. Doughty

CHILD SUPPORT AGENCY
Quay House, The Waterfront, Brierley Hill, W. Midlands
DY1 1XZ
Tel 01384-488488

The Agency was set up in April 1993. It is responsible for
the administration of the Child Support Act and for the

assessment, collection and enforcement of maintenance
payments for all new cases.
Chief Executive, Miss A. Chant
Directors, S. Heminsley; C. Francis; M. Davison; C. Peters;
  M. Isaacs

CONTRIBUTIONS AGENCY
DSS Longbenton, Benton Park Road, Newcastle upon
Tyne NE98 1YX
Tel 0191-213 5000

The Agency collects and records National Insurance
contributions, maintains individual records, and provides
an advisory service on National Insurance matters.
Chief Executive (G3), Mrs F. Boardman
Deputy Chief Executive (G5), G. Bertram
Management Board, K. Wilson; T. Lord; D. Slater; K. Elliott
Non-Executive Members, J. Wilson; B. Glassberg

INFORMATION TECHNOLOGY SERVICES AGENCY
4th Floor, Verulam Point, Station Way, St Albans, Herts
AL1 5HE
Tel 01727-815838

The Agency maintains and oversees policies on infor-
mation technology strategy, procurement, technical stan-
dards and security.
Chief Executive, I. Magee
Directors, J. Thomas; N. Haighton; G. Hextall; J. Brewood;
  G. Kemp; P. Sharkey; C. Brown; T. Edkins
Non-Executive Director, T. Drury

WAR PENSIONS AGENCY
Norcross, Blackpool, Lancs FY5 3WP
Tel 01253-858858

The Agency administers the payment of war disablement
and war widows' pensions and provides welfare services
and support to war disablement pensioners, war widows
and their dependants and carers. It became an executive
agency in 1994.
Chief Executive, K. Caldwell

Central Advisory Committee on War Pensions
Room 1138, The Adelphi, 1–11 John Adam Street,
London WC2N 6HT
Tel 0171-962 8028
Secretary, S. Adams

ADVISORY BODIES

NATIONAL DISABILITY COUNCIL, 6th Floor, The
  Adelphi, 1–11 John Adam Street, London WC2N 6HT.
  Tel: 0171-712 2099. *Chairman*, D. Grayson; *Secretary*,
  Ms K. Archer
SOCIAL SECURITY ADVISORY COMMITTEE, New Court,
  Carey Street, London WC2A 2LS. Tel 0171-412 1507.
  Chairman, Sir Thomas Boyd-Carpenter, KBE; *Secretary*,
  L. C. Smith

SPORTS COUNCIL
16 Upper Woburn Place, London WC1H 0QP
Tel 0171-388 1277

The Sports Council is an independent body established in
1972 by royal charter. It promotes the development of sport
and fosters the provision of facilities for sport and recreation in Great Britain. Government funding for 1996–7 is
£47 million.
  The Council is also responsible, with the other Sports
Councils, for administering the Lottery Sports Fund,

which distributes the funds allocated to sport from the proceeds of the National Lottery. The Council had made awards to the value of £248 million by July 1996.

In the autumn of 1996 the Council will be replaced by a United Kingdom Sports Council and an English Sports Council.

Chairman, Sir Rodney Walker
Chief Executive, D. Casey

For Sports Councils for Scotland, Wales and N. Ireland, *see* page 707.

OFFICE FOR STANDARDS IN EDUCATION (OFSTED)
Alexandra House, 33 Kingsway, London WC2B 6SE
Tel 0171-421 6800

A non-ministerial government department established in 1992 to keep the Secretary of State and the public informed about the standards and management of schools in England, and to establish and monitor an independent inspection system for maintained schools in England. *See also* page 432.

HM Chief Inspector, C. Woodhead
Director of Administration, Mrs H. Douglas
Directors of Inspection, A. J. Rose, CBE; M. J. Tomlinson

TEAM MANAGERS

Planning and Resource, Miss J. Phillips
Personnel Management, C. Payne
Contracts, C. Bramley
Communications, Media and Public Relations, J. Lawson
Information Systems, M. Childs
Administrative Support and Estates Management, K. Francis
Competition and Compliance, Ms E. Slater
Training and Assessment of Independent Inspectors, Miss E. Pagliacci
Inspection Quality, Monitoring and Development, P. Matthews
LEA Reviews, Reorganization Proposals and Independent Schools, D. Singleton
School Improvement, Ms E. Passmore
Additional Inspector Project, Ms S. O'Sullivan
Nursery and Primary, K. Lloyd
Secondary, C. Gould
Post-Compulsory, D. West
Special Educational Needs, C. Marshall
Research, Analysis and International, Ms C. Agambar
Teacher Education and Training, D. Taylor
Nursery Education Scheme, D. Bradley
Specialist Advisers, J. Stannard; N. Bufton; B. Ponchaud; A. Dobson; M. Ive; G. Goldstein; J. Hamer; P. Smith; Ms J. Mills; G. Clay; P. Jones; I. Wragg
There are about 200 HM Inspectors

COMMITTEE ON STANDARDS IN PUBLIC LIFE
Horse Guards Road, London SW1P 3AL
Tel 0171-270 5875

The Committee on Standards in Public Life (the Nolan Committee) was set up in October 1994. It is a standing body whose chairman and members are appointed by the Prime Minister. Its remit is to examine concerns about standards of conduct of all holders of public office, including arrangements relating to financial and commercial activities, and to make recommendations as to any

changes in current arrangements which might be required to ensure the highest standards of propriety in public life. The committee does not investigate individual allegations of misconduct.

Chairman, The Lord Nolan, PC
Members, Sir Clifford Boulton, GCB; Sir Martin Jacomb; Prof. A. King; The Rt. Hon. T. King, CH, MP; The Rt. Hon. P. Shore, MP; The Lord Thomson of Monifieth, PC; Sir William Utting, CB; Dame Anne Warburton, DCVO, CMG; Ms D. Warwick
Secretary (SCS), A. Riddell

HMSO (HER MAJESTY'S STATIONERY OFFICE)
St Crispins, Duke Street, Norwich NR3 1PD
Tel 01603-622211

HMSO (Her Majesty's Stationery Office) was established in 1786. It provides printing, binding and business supplies to government departments and publicly funded organizations. It was an executive agency accountable to the Chancellor of the Duchy of Lancaster (the Minister of Public Service) within the Cabinet Office but was privatized in September 1996. HMSO is also the Government's publisher, and has bookshops for the sale of government publications in seven cities as well as appointed agents in other UK cities and throughout the world. HMSO obtains most of its supplies and printing from commercial sources, but about 20 per cent of its printing requirement, such as Hansard and Bills and Acts of Parliament, is produced in its own printing works.

Controller and Chief Executive (acting), M. D. Lynn
Board Directors, C. J. Penn; C. N. Southgate; P. J. Macdonald, CBE

DIRECTORS

Client Publishing, A. Cole
Parliamentary and Statutory Publishing, E. Hendry
Book Sales and Service, B. Minett
Office Supplies, V. G. Bell
Business Systems, D. C. Kerry
Copiers, P. Barnard
Print, A. A. Smith (*Norwich*); G. Aldus (*London*); M. McNeill (*Manchester and Logistics*); C. Mills (*Security*)
Furniture, G. A. H. Turner
HMSO Wales, A. McCabe
HMSO Scotland, G. Heaford
HMSO N. Ireland, S. Barker

BIRMINGHAM – *Bookshop*, 68–69 Bull Street, Birmingham B4 6AB
BRISTOL, Distribution Park, Hawkley Drive, Woodlands Lane, Bradley Stoke, Bristol BS12 0BF. *Bookshop*, 33 Wine Street, Bristol BS1 2BH
LONDON – *Publications Centre*, 51 Nine Elms Lane, London SW8 5DR. *Bookshop*, 49 High Holborn, London WC1V 6HB
MANCHESTER, Broadway, Chadderton, Oldham, Lancs OL9 9QH. *Bookshop*, 9–21 Princess Street, Manchester M60 8AS
SCOTLAND, South Gyle Crescent, Edinburgh EH12 9EB. *Bookshop*, 71 Lothian Road, Edinburgh EH3 9AZ
WALES – *Bookshop*, The Friary, Cardiff CF1 4AA
NORTHERN IRELAND, IDB House, Chichester Street, Belfast BT1 4PS. *Bookshop*, 16 Arthur Street, Belfast BT1 4GD

OFFICE OF TELECOMMUNICATIONS
50 Ludgate Hill, London EC4M 7JJ
Tel 0171-634 8700

The Office of Telecommunications (Oftel) is a non-ministerial government department which is responsible for supervising telecommunications activities in the UK. Its principal functions are to ensure that holders of telecommunications licences comply with their licence conditions; to maintain and promote effective competition in telecommunications; and to promote the interests of purchasers and other users of telecommunication services and apparatus in respect of prices, quality and variety.

The Director-General has powers to deal with anti-competitive practices and monopoly situations. He also has a duty to consider all reasonable complaints and representations about telecommunication apparatus and services.

Director-General, D. G. Cruickshank
Deputy Director-General, Mrs A. Walker
Director of Network Competition, Mrs A. Taylor
Director of Consumer Affairs, Ms C. Farnish
Director of Licensing, Ms S. Chambers
Director of Licence Enforcement and Fair Trading, C. J. C. Wright
Technical Director, P. Walker
Economic Director, A. Bell
Legal Director, D. H. M. Ingham
Director of Information, D. Redding
Director of Service Competition and International Affairs, Ms C. Varley

TOURIST BOARDS
(For British Tourist Authority, *see* page 286)

The English Tourist Board, the Scottish Tourist Board, the Wales Tourist Board and the Northern Ireland Tourist Board are responsible for developing and marketing the tourist industry in their respective countries. The Boards' main objectives are to promote holidays and to encourage the provision and improvement of tourist amenities.

ENGLISH TOURIST BOARD, Thames Tower, Black's Road, London W6 9EL. Tel: 0181-846 9000. *Chief Executive*, T. Bartlett
SCOTTISH TOURIST BOARD, 23 Ravelston Terrace, Edinburgh EH4 3EU. Tel: 0131-332 2433. *Chief Executive*, D. D. Reid
WALES TOURIST BOARD, Brunel House, 2 Fitzalan Road, Cardiff CF2 1UY. Tel: 01222-499909. *Chief Executive*, J. French
NORTHERN IRELAND TOURIST BOARD, St Anne's Court, 59 North Street, Belfast BT1 1NB. Tel: 01232-231221. *Chief Executive*, I. Henderson

DEPARTMENT OF TRADE AND INDUSTRY
1 Victoria Street, London SW1H 0ET
Tel 0171-215 5000

Business Link: Tel 0800-500200
Business in Europe: Tel 0117-944 4888
Innovation Enquiry Line: Tel 0171-215 1217

The Department is responsible for international trade policy, including the promotion of UK trade interests in the European Union, GATT, OECD, UNCTAD and other international organizations; the promotion of UK exports and assistance to exporters; policy in relation to industry and commerce, including industrial relations policy; policy towards small firms; regional industrial assistance; legislation and policy in relation to the Post Office; competition policy and consumer protection; the development of national policies in relation to all forms of energy and the development of new sources of energy, including international aspects of energy policy; policy on science and technology research and development; space policy; standards, quality and design; company legislation; and the regulation of insurance industries.

President of the Board of Trade and Secretary of State for Trade and Industry, The Rt. Hon. Ian Lang, MP
Principal Private Secretary, J. Alty
Private Secretaries, R. Jenkinson; A. Phillipson
Parliamentary Private Secretary, S. Coombe, MP
Minister for Industry and Energy, The Rt. Hon. Gregory Knight, MP
Private Secretary, M. Hilton
Parliamentary Private Secretary, R. Spring, MP
Minister for Trade, Anthony Nelson, MP
Private Secretary, U. Marthaler
Minister of State, The Rt. Hon. The Lord Fraser of Carmyllie, QC
Private Secretary, C. Pook
Parliamentary Under-Secretary of State for Science and Technology, Ian Taylor, MBE, MP
Private Secretary, Ms H. Stanley
Parliamentary Under-Secretary of State for Small Business, Industry and Energy, Richard Page, MP
Private Secretary, I. McKenzie
Parliamentary Under-Secretary of State for Competition and Consumer Affairs, John Taylor, MP
Private Secretary, P. Hadley
British Overseas Trade Board Chairman, M. Laing, CBE
Private Secretary, Ms S. Brown
Parliamentary Clerk, T. Williams
Permanent Secretary, M. Scholar, CB
Private Secretary, C. Hannant
Second Permanent Secretary, Chief Scientific Adviser and Head of Office of Science and Technology, Sir Robert May, FRS
Private Secretary, R. Clay
Directors-General, Sir John Cadogan, CBE, FRS (*Director-General of the Research Councils*); C. W. Roberts, CB (*Trade Policy and Export Promotion*); D. Durie, CMG (*Regional and Small- and Medium-Sized Enterprises*); B. Hilton, CB (*Corporate and Consumer Affairs*); A. Hammond, CB (*The Solicitor*); C. Henderson, CB (*Energy*); A. C. Hutton (*Resources and Services*); A. Macdonald, CB (*Industry*)

DIVISIONAL ORGANIZATION

‡AEROSPACE AND DEFENCE INDUSTRIES DIRECTORATE
Director of Aerospace and Defence Industries, R. Foster
Directors, M. Coolican; S. I. Charik

BRITISH NATIONAL SPACE CENTRE
Bridge Place, 88–89 Eccleston Square, London SW1V 1PT
Director-General, D. R. Davis
Deputy Director-General, D. Leadbeater
Directors, H. Evans; Dr P. Murdin; Dr D. Lumley

BUSINESS LINK DIRECTORATE
Director of Business Link, V. Brown
Directors, J. Reid; P. Bentley; P. Waller

CENTRAL POLICY UNIT
Director, Dr C. Bell

‡At 151 Buckingham Palace Road, London SW1W 9SS

‡CHEMICALS AND BIOTECHNOLOGY DIRECTORATE
Director of Chemicals and Biotechnology, M. Baker
Directors, Ms G. Alliston; Dr E. A. M. Baker

COAL DIRECTORATE
Director, A. Berry

‡COMMUNICATIONS AND INFORMATION INDUSTRIES
DIRECTORATE
Director of Communications and Information Industries,
    W. MacIntyre
Directors, J. Neilson; N. McMillan; D. Hendon;
    N. Worman; D. Hopkins; S. Pride

COMPANY LAW DIRECTORATE
Director of Company Law, Mrs S. Brown
Directors, N. D. Peace; D. E. Love

CONSUMER AFFAIRS AND COMPETITION POLICY
DIRECTORATE
Director of Consumer Affairs and Competiton Policy, P. Salvidge
Directors, A. Cooper; M. Higson; P. Masson; Miss D. Gane;
    Dr A. Eggington; G. Boon

ECONOMICS AND STATISTICS DIRECTORATE
Chief Economic Adviser, D. R. Coates
Directors, Dr D. S. Higham; S. Penneck; M. S. Bradley

ELECTRICITY DIRECTORATE
Director of Electricity, J. Green

ENERGY POLICY AND ANALYSIS UNIT
Director of Energy Policy and Analysis, M. Keay
Directors, E. Evans; G. C. White

ENERGY TECHNOLOGIES DIRECTORATE
Director, G. Bevan

‡ENGINEERING, AUTOMOTIVE AND METALS
DIRECTORATE
Director of Engineering, Automotive and Metals, M. O'Shea
Directors, H. Brown; J. Grewe; R. Poole; A. Vinall; A. Wilks

ENGINEERING INSPECTORATE
Director of Engineering Inspectorate, Dr P. Fenwick

‡ENVIRONMENT DIRECTORATE
Director of Environment, Dr C. Hicks

‡ESTATES AND FACILITIES MANAGEMENT
DIRECTORATE
Director, M. Coolican

EUROPEAN COHESION DIRECTORATE
Director, D. Miner

EUROPE DIRECTORATE
Kingsgate House, 66–74 Victoria Street, London
SW1E 6SW
Director, B. Stow

EXPORT CONTROL AND NON-PROLIFERATION
DIRECTORATE
Kingsgate House, 66–74 Victoria Street, London
SW1E 6SW
Director of Export Control and Non-Proliferation,
    R. J. Meadway
Directors, A. J. Mantle, P. H. Agrell

EXPORT PROMOTION DIRECTORATE
Kingsgate House, 66–74 Victoria Street, London
SW1E 6SW
Directors, M. Mowlam (*The Americas*); M. Cohen (*Asia
    Pacific*); K. Levinson (*Central and Eastern Europe*); S. Lyle
    Smythe (*Business in Europe*); N. Armour (*Middle East,
    Near East and North Africa*); N. McInnes (*Sub-Saharan
    Africa and South Asia*)

EXPORT SERVICES DIRECTORATE
Kingsgate House, 66–74 Victoria Street, London
SW1E 6SW
Director, A. Reynolds

FINANCE AND RESOURCE MANAGEMENT DIRECTORATE
Director of Finance and Resource Management, M. Roberts
Directors, Dr S. Sklaroff; K. Hills; N. Nandra; J. P. Clayton

IMPORT POLICY DIRECTORATE
Kingsgate House, 66–74 Victoria Street, London
SW1E 6SW
Director, S. Bowen

INDUSTRIAL RELATIONS DIRECTORATE
Director of Industrial Relations, Ms H. Leiser
Directors, K. Masson; R. Niblett; A. Wright; Mrs
    Z. Hornstein; P. Parker

‡INDUSTRY ECONOMICS AND STATISTICS
DIRECTORATE
Director, Dr N. Owen

INFORMATION DIRECTORATE
Director of Information, Ms J. M. Caines
Director of News, M. Ricketts
Director of Publicity, Miss P. R. A. Freedman

‡INFORMATION MANAGEMENT AND TECHNOLOGY
DIRECTORATE
Director, R. Wheeler

‡INNOVATION UNIT
Director, Dr A. Keddie

INSURANCE DIRECTORATE
Director of Insurance, J. Spencer
Directors, R. Allen; R. Hobbs; K. Long; J. Whitlock

INTERNAL AUDIT
Bridge Place, 88–89 Eccleston Square, London SW1V 1PT
Director of Internal Audit, A. C. Elkington

INTERNATIONAL ECONOMICS DIRECTORATE
Kingsgate House, 66–74 Victoria Street, London
SW1E 6SW
Director, C. Moir

INVEST IN BRITAIN BUREAU
Chief Executive, A. Fraser

INVESTIGATIONS AND ENFORCEMENT DIRECTORATE
10 Victoria Street, London SW1H 0NN
Director of Investigations and Enforcement, J. Phillips
Directors, G. Horne; J. Sibley; R. Burns; T. Dunstan;
    S. Clements

JOINT EXPORT PROMOTION DIRECTORATE
(FCO/DTI)
Kingsgate House, 66–74 Victoria Street, London
SW1E 6SW
Director-General of Export Promotion, F. R. Mingay, CMG
Directors, D. Saunders; (*DS4*), M. Dougal

LEGAL RESOURCE MANAGEMENT AND BUSINESS LAW
UNIT
10 Victoria Street, London SW1H 0NN
The Solicitor and Director-General, A. Hammond, CB
Director, J. Burnett

LEGAL SERVICES DIRECTORATE A
10 Victoria Street, London SW1H 0NN
Director of Legal A, J. Stanley

---

‡At 151 Buckingham Palace Road, London SW1W 9SS

Legal Directors, I. Mathers; J. Roberts; Miss N. O'Flynn;
  S. Hyett; Miss G. Richmond

LEGAL SERVICES DIRECTORATE B
10 Victoria Street, London SWIH ONN

Director of Legal B, P. Bovey
Legal Directors, R. Baker; Ms R. Jeffreys; T. Susman;
  B. Welch; A. Woods

LEGAL SERVICES DIRECTORATE C
10 Victoria Street, London SWIH ONN

Director of Legal C, Miss K. Morton
Legal Directors, S. Milligan; R. Perkins; R. Green;
  M. Bucknill; C. Raikes

MANAGEMENT BEST PRACTICE
Director of Management Best Practice, Dr K. Poulter
Directors, Dr I. Harrison; J. Sutton

NEW ISSUES AND DEVELOPING COUNTRIES
Kingsgate House, 66–74 Victoria Street, London
SWIE 6SW

Director, C. Bridge

NUCLEAR INDUSTRIES DIRECTORATE
Director of Nuclear Industries, N. Hirst
Directors, Mrs H. Haddon; S. D. Spivey; Dr M. Draper;
  J. Rhodes

NUCLEAR POWER PRIVATIZATION TEAM
Director, C. Wilcock

OFFICE OF SCIENCE AND TECHNOLOGY: SCIENCE AND
ENGINEERING BASE DIRECTORATE
Albany House, 84–86 Petty France, London SWIH 9ST

Director, Science and Engineering Base, A. Quigley
Directors, A. Carter; K. Root

OFFICE OF SCIENCE AND TECHNOLOGY:
TRANSDEPARTMENTAL SCIENCE AND TECHNOLOGY
DIRECTORATE
Albany House, 84–86 Petty France, London SWIH 9ST

Director, Transdepartmental Science and Technology, Ms H.
  Williams
Directors, R. Wright; C. De Grouchy

OIL AND GAS DIRECTORATE
Director of Oil and Gas, M. J. Michell
Directors, J. R. V. Brook; S. Price; A. Wilson
Director of Oil and Gas Royalties Office, A. Cran

Oil and Gas Office (Aberdeen)
Atholl House, 86–88 Guild Street, Aberdeen AB9 IDR
Tel 01224-213557

Director, A. S. Wilson

OIL AND GAS PROJECTS AND SUPPLIES OFFICE
Tay House, 300 Bath Street, Glasgow G2 4DX
Tel 0141-228 3646
Kingsgate House, 66–74 Victoria Street, London
SWIH 6SW
Tel 0171-215 5000

Chief Executive, Oil Supplies Office, M. Stanley
Directors, P. Dunn; K. Forrest; B. Gallagher; K. Mayo

‡POST OFFICE RETAILING AND TEXTILES
DIRECTORATE
Director of Post Office Retailing and Textiles, I. M. Jones
Director, C. Jackson

PROJECTS EXPORT PROMOTION DIRECTORATE
Director of Projects Export Promotion, D. J. Hall
Directors, A. G. Atkinson; D. Marsh

REGIONAL ASSISTANCE DIRECTORATE
Director, D. Miner

REGIONAL POLICY DIRECTORATE
Director, D. Smith

SENIOR STAFF MANAGEMENT
Director, R. Rogers

SMALL- AND MEDIUM-SIZED ENTERPRISES (SME)
POLICY DIRECTORATE
St Mary's House, Level 2, c/o Moorfoot, Sheffield SI 4PQ
Director, R. Anderson

SMALL- AND MEDIUM-SIZED ENTERPRISES (SME)
TECHNOLOGY DIRECTORATE
Director, R. Allpress

STAFF PAY AND CONDITIONS
Director of Personnel, vacant
Director, C. Johnston

STAFF PERSONNEL OPERATIONS
Director, I. Cameron

‡TECHNOLOGY AND STANDARDS DIRECTORATE
Director of Technology and Standards, Dr D. Evans
Directors, R. T. King; I. C. Downing; J. M. Barber;
  G. C. Riggs

TRADE POLICY DIRECTORATE
Kingsgate House, 66–74 Victoria Street, London
SWIE 6SW

Director, J. Hunt

BRITISH OVERSEAS TRADE BOARD
Kingsgate House, 66–74 Victoria Street, London SWIE
6SW
Tel 0171-215 5000

President, The President of the Board of Trade
Chairman, M. Laing, CBE
Vice-Chairman, HRH The Duke of Kent, KG, GCMG, GCVO
Members, Dr D. Baldwin, CBE; A. Buxton; I. L. Dale, OBE;
  A. Turner; P. Goodwin, CBE; D. Lanigan, CBE;
  R. Mingay, CMG; R. Burman, CBE; The Rt. Hon. Sir
  Michael Palliser, GCMG; Sir Brian Pearse;
  C. W. Roberts, CB; B. D. Taylor, CBE; B. Willott;
  A. Burns, CMG; D. Peake; A. Hunt, CMG
Secretary, Dr D. Walker

REGIONAL OFFICES
— *see* pages 302–3

EXECUTIVE AGENCIES

COMPANIES HOUSE
Companies House, Crown Way, Cardiff CF4 3UZ
Tel 01222-388588
London Search Room, 55–71 City Road, London ECIY IBB
Tel 0171-253 9393
37 Castle Terrace, Edinburgh EHI 2EB
Tel 0131-535 5800
Companies House incorporates companies, registers company documents and provides company information.
Registrar of Companies for England and Wales, J.Holden
Registrar for Scotland, J. Henderson

THE INSOLVENCY SERVICE
PO Box 203, 21 Bloomsbury Street, London WCIB 3QW
Tel 0171-637 1110
The Service administers and investigates the affairs of bankrupts and companies in compulsory liquidation; deals with the disqualification of directors in all corporate

failures; regulates insolvency practitioners and their professional bodies; provides banking and investment services for bankruptcy and liquidation estates; and advises ministers on insolvency policy issues.

Inspector-General and Chief Executive, P. R. Joyce
Deputy Inspectors-General, D. J. Flynn; M. C. A. Osborne

NATIONAL WEIGHTS AND MEASURES LABORATORY
Stanton Avenue, Teddington, Middx TW11 0JZ
Tel 0181-943 7272

The Laboratory administers weights and measures legislation, carries out type examination, calibration and testing, and runs courses on metrological topics.
Chief Executive (*G5*), Dr S. Bennett

PATENT OFFICE
— *see* page 333

RADIOCOMMUNICATIONS AGENCY
New King's Beam House, 22 Upper Ground, London
SE1 9SA
Tel 0171-211 0211

The Agency is responsible for most civil radio matters other than telecommunications broadcasting policy and the radio equipment market.
Chief Executive (*G3*), J. Norton

DEPARTMENT OF TRANSPORT
Great Minster House, 76 Marsham Street, London
SW1P 4DR
Tel 0171-271 5000

The Department of Transport is responsible for land, sea and air transport, including sponsorship of the rail and bus industries; airports; domestic and international civil aviation; shipping and the ports industry; navigational lights, pilotage, HM Coastguard and marine pollution; motorways and other trunk roads; oversight of road transport including vehicle standards, registration and licensing, driver testing and licensing, bus and road freight licensing, regulation of taxis and private hire cars and road safety; and oversight of local authorities' transport planning, including payment of Transport Supplementary Grant.

Secretary of State for Transport, The Rt. Hon. Sir George Young, Bt., MP
  Private Secretary, Miss B. Hill
  Parliamentary Private Secretary, Dr C. Goodson-Wickes, MP
Minister of State, John Watts, MP (*Railways, Roads and Local Transport*)
  Private Secretary, S. M. Ghagan
  Parliamentary Private Secretary, T. Dicks, MP
Parliamentary Under-Secretaries, The Viscount Goschen (*Aviation and Shipping*); John Bowis, OBE, MP (*Transport in London and Road Safety*)
  Private Secretaries, S. Heard; L. Sambrook
Parliamentary Clerk, Miss P. Gaunt
Permanent Under-Secretary of State, Sir Patrick Brown, KCB
  Private Secretary, Miss V. H. Dickinson

INFORMATION
Head of Information, D. McMillan

RESOURCES
Director of Resources, D. J. Rowlands, CB

PERSONNEL
Director of Personnel and Change Management, R. Bird
SCS, R. D. Bayly; G. Kemp

Grade 6, B. Meakins
Grade 7, J. Gibson
Chief Welfare Officer (*G7*), Miss E. T. Haines

FINANCE
SCS, B. Wadsworth
Accounting Adviser, A. R. Allum
Heads of Divisions, R. Bennett; M. Reece; P. A. Sanders

EXECUTIVE AGENCIES DIRECTORATE
SCS, A. C. Melville

INTERNAL AUDIT
Ashdown House, Sedlescombe Road North, Hastings, E. Sussex TN37 7GA
Tel 01424-458306

Head of Branch, M. J. Reece

CENTRAL SERVICES
Ashdown House, Sedlescombe Road North, Hastings, E. Sussex TN37 7GA
Tel 01424-458306

Director, M. R. Newey
Heads of Divisions, I. R. Heawood (*Management Support Services*); G. L. Jones (*Departmental Procurement Unit*)
Grade 6, I. Harris (*Accommodation and Office Services*); P. Waller (*IT Management Unit*)

STATISTICAL SERVICES
Romney House, 43 Marsham Street, London SW1P 3PY
Tel 0171-276 8513

SCS, Miss B. J. Wood; Dr R. L. Butchart; P. J. Capell; R. P. Donachie

CHIEF SCIENTIST
Chief Scientist, Dr D. H. Metz

TRANSPORT SECURITY
Portland House, Stag Place, London SW1E 5BH
Tel 0171-460 3016

Director and Co-ordinator, R. D. Lord
SCS, Mrs A. M. Moss

MOBILITY UNIT
Head of Unit, Miss E. A. Frye

RAILWAYS
Director of Railways, N. L. J. Montagu, CB

RAILWAY INFRASTRUCTURE
Director of Railways (*General*), R. J. Griffins
Heads of Divisions, Dr J. H. Denning (*Railways 1A*); Miss P. M. Williams (*International Railways*); M. Fuhr (*Rail Link Bill*); P. Cox (*Railways Economics*); A. P. Moss (*Channel Tunnel*)

RAILWAY PRIVATIZATION
Director of Railway Privatization, Mrs J. M. Williams
Heads of Divisions, P. H. McCarthy; R. Linnard; R. S. Peal; D. Priestley

CHANNEL TUNNEL SAFETY AUTHORITY
SCS, E. A. Ryder, CB

ROADS, LOCAL TRANSPORT AND TRANSPORT POLICY
Director of Roads and Local Transport, P. Wood

NATIONAL ROADS POLICY DIRECTORATE
Director of National Roads Policy, H. Wenban-Smith
Heads of Divisions, T. Worsley (*Highways Economic and Traffic Appraisal*); Dr C. M. Woodman (*Highways Policy and Programmes*); Mrs C. M. Dixon (*Tolling and Private Finance*)

URBAN AND LOCAL TRANSPORT
Director of Urban and Local Transport, R. A. Allan
Heads of Divisions, A. B. Murray (*Buses and London Transport*); E. C. Neve (*Taxis and London Projects*); M. R. Pitwood (*Local Transport Policy*); M. A. Walsh (*Economics, Local Transport and General*); A. S. D. Whybrow (*Traffic Policy*); M. F. Talbot (*Driver Information and Traffic Management*)

ROAD AND VEHICLE SAFETY
Director of Road and Vehicle Safety, Miss S. J. Lambert
Heads of Divisions, I. R. Jordan (*Vehicle Standards and Engineering*); Dr R. M. Kimber (*Road Safety*); J. L. Gansler (*Licensing and Roadworthiness Policy*); J. R. Fells (*Road Haulage*); (*G6*), J. Winder (*Traffic Area Network Unit*)

TRANSPORT POLICY UNIT
Head of Unit, D. R. Instone

DEPARTMENTAL MEDICAL ADVISER
SCS, Dr P. A. M. Diamond, OBE

AVIATION GROUP
Director of General Civil Aviation, A. J. Goldman, CB
SCS, Ms A. Munro (*Airport Policy*); Ms M. J. Clare (*CAA and Safety Policy*); M. C. Mann (*Economics Aviation Maritime International*); Ms E. A. Duthie (*Noise and Pollution*)

INTERNATIONAL AVIATION NEGOTIATIONS
Director of International Aviation Negotiations, A. T. Baker
SCS, N. J. Starling; Dr P. H. Martin

AIR ACCIDENTS INVESTIGATION BRANCH
Royal Aerospace Establishment, Farnborough, Hants GU14 6TD
Tel 01252-510300
Chief Inspector of Air Accidents, K. P. R. Smart, CBE
Deputy Chief Inspector of Air Accidents, R. C. McKinlay

SHIPPING DIRECTORATE
Director of Shipping, R. E. Clarke
Heads of Divisions, J. F. Wall; R. T. Bishop; G. D. Rowe

MARINE ACCIDENTS INVESTIGATION BRANCH
5–7 Brunswick Place, Southampton SO1 2AN
Tel 01703-232424
Chief Inspector of Marine Accidents, Capt. P. B. Marriott

REGIONAL OFFICES
— see pages 302–3

EXECUTIVE AGENCIES

COASTGUARD AGENCY
Spring Place, 105 Commercial Road, Southampton SO15 1EG
Tel 01703-329100
The Agency's role is to minimize loss of life among seafarers and coastal users, and to minimize pollution from ships to sea and coastline.
Chief Executive, C. J. Harris
Chief Coastguard, J. Astbury

DRIVER AND VEHICLE LICENSING AGENCY
Longview Road, Morriston, Swansea SA6 7JL
Tel 01792-772151
The Agency issues driving licences, registers and licenses vehicles, and collects excise duty.
Chief Executive, Dr S. J. Ford
Heads of Divisions, R. J. Verge; T. J. Horton; J. C. Betts

DRIVING STANDARDS AGENCY
Stanley House, Talbot Street, Nottingham NG1 5GU
Tel 0115-947 4222
The Agency's role is to carry out driving tests and approve driving instructors.
Chief Executive, B. L. Herdan

HIGHWAYS AGENCY
St Christopher House, Southwark Street, London SE1 0TE
Tel 0171-928 3666
The Agency is responsible for the management and maintenance of the motorway and trunk road network and for road construction and improvement.
Chief Executive, L. J. Haynes

Finance Directorate
Director, J. Seddon
Heads of Divisions, P. A. Houston (*Finance and Procurement*); J. Bradley (*Lands, Claims and Graphics*); D. Kershaw (*Computing*)

Private Finance Directorate
Director, P. G. Collis

Human Resources Directorate
Director, K. A. Wyatt

Engineering and Environmental Policy Directorate
Director, T. A. Rochester
Deputy Director, J. A. Kerman
Head of Divisions, Mrs V. A. Bodnar (*Agency Environmental Policy*); N. S. Organ (*Road Engineering and Environmental*); A. J. Pickett (*Bridges Engineering*)

Road Programme Directorate
Director, J. W. Fellows
Deputy Director, D. York
Heads of Divisions, D. A. Holland (*Technical Services*); K. McKenzie (*Administrative Services*); D. E. Oddy (*Motorways Operations*); R. R. Bineham (*Northern Operations*); D. Ward (*Southern Operations*); J. P. Boud (*Construction Operations*); D. E. Oddy (*Administrative Operations*)

Network Management and Maintenance Directorate
Director, B. J. Billington
Deputy Director, P. E. Nutt
Heads of Divisions, R. Eastman (*Network Policy Division*); M. G. Quinn (*Network Control Division*); K. A. Lasbury (*Northern Network Management*); W. S. C. Wadrup (*Midland Network Management*); A. D. Rowland (*Southern Network Management*); R. T. Thorndike (*London Network Management*)

MARINE SAFETY AGENCY
Spring Place, 105 Commercial Road, Southampton SO15 1EG
Tel 01703-329100
The Agency's role is to develop, promote and enforce high standards of marine safety and to minimize the risk of pollution of the marine environment from ships.
Chief Executive, R. M. Bradley
Directors, W. A. Graham (*Ship Construction and Navigation*); A. Cubbin (*Marine Safety Operations and Seafarers Standards*); (*G6*), R. Padgett (*Finance, Personnel and Corporate Services*)

VEHICLE CERTIFICATION AGENCY
1 Eastgate Office Centre, Eastgate Road, Bristol BS5 6XX
Tel 0117-951 5151
The Agency tests and certificates vehicles to UK and international standards.
Chief Executive, D. W. Harvey

VEHICLE INSPECTORATE
Berkeley House, Croydon Street, Bristol BS5 0DA
Tel 0117-954 3274

The Agency carries out annual testing and inspection of heavy goods and other vehicles and administers the MOT testing scheme.
Chief Executive, R. J. Oliver
Deputy Chief Executive, J. A. T. David

TRAFFIC DIRECTOR FOR LONDON
College House, Great Peter Street, London SW1P 3LN
Tel 0171-222 4545

The Traffic Director for London is a non-departmental public body which is independent from the Department of Transport but responsible to the Secretary of State for Transport and to Parliament. Its role is to co-ordinate the introduction of the Priority (Red) Route Network in London and monitor its operation.
Traffic Director for London, D. Turner

TRAFFIC AREA OFFICES

LICENSING AUTHORITIES AND TRAFFIC COMMISSIONERS
EASTERN (Nottingham and Cambridge), Brig. C. M. Boyd
NORTH-EASTERN (Newcastle upon Tyne and Leeds), K. R. Waterworth
NORTH-WESTERN (Manchester), K. R. Waterworth
SCOTTISH (Edinburgh), Brig. M. W. Betts
SOUTH-EASTERN AND METROPOLITAN (Eastbourne), Brig. M. H. Turner
SOUTH WALES (Cardiff), J. Mervyn
WESTERN (Bristol), J. Mervyn
WEST MIDLANDS (Birmingham), J. Mervyn

THE TREASURY
Parliament Street, London SW1P 3AG
Tel 0171-270 3000

The Office of the Lord High Treasurer has been continuously in commission for well over 200 years. The Lord High Commissioners of HM Treasury are the First Lord of the Treasury (who is also the Prime Minister), the Chancellor of the Exchequer and five junior Lords (who are government whips in the House of Commons). This Board of Commissioners is assisted at present by the Chief Secretary, a Parliamentary Secretary who is also the government Chief Whip, a Financial Secretary, an Economic Secretary, the Paymaster-General, and the Permanent Secretary.

The Prime Minister is not primarily concerned in the day-to-day aspects of Treasury business; the management of the Treasury devolves upon the Chancellor of the Exchequer and the other Treasury ministers.

The Chief Secretary is responsible for the planning and control of public expenditure; public sector pay, excluding the Civil Service; value for money in the public services (including the 'Next Steps' programme); and export credit.

The Financial Secretary has responsibility for parliamentary financial business; the legislative programme; oversight of the Inland Revenue; Inland Revenue taxes (excluding stamp duties); and privatization, competition and deregulation policy.

The Economic Secretary has responsibility for monetary policy; the financial system (including financial institutions); international finance issues and institutions; Economic and Monetary Union; stamp duties; wider share-ownership; Treasury interest in small firms' policy; procurement policy; economic briefing; the Valuation Office Agency; the Royal Mint; the Department for National Savings; the Registry of Friendly Societies; the National Investment and Loans Office; the Office for National Statistics; and the Government Actuary's Department.

The Exchequer Secretary to the Treasury is responsible for general oversight of Customs and Excise; Customs and Excise duties and taxes; assisting the Chief Secretary on public expenditure planning and control; Treasury interest in women's issues; charities; the environment (including energy efficiency); the EC budget; general accounting issues; PAYMASTER (*see* page 333) and ministerial correspondence.

All Treasury ministers are concerned in tax matters.
Prime Minister and First Lord of the Treasury, The Rt. Hon. John Major, MP
Chancellor of the Exchequer, The Rt. Hon. Kenneth Clarke, QC, MP
  Principal Private Secretary, N. I. MacPherson
  Private Secretary, A. Gibbs
  Special Adviser, A. Teasdale
Chief Secretary to the Treasury, The Rt. Hon. William Waldegrave, MP
  Private Secretary, P. Raynes
  Special Adviser, P. Gardner
Financial Secretary to the Treasury, Michael Jack, MP
  Private Secretary, D. Finch
  Parliamentary Private Secretary, M. Fabricant, MP
Economic Secretary, Angela Knight, MP
  Private Secretary, Ms S. Tebbutt
Exchequer Secretary to the Treasury, The Rt. Hon. Phillip Oppenheim, MP
  Private Secretary, Ms P. Murray
  Special Adviser to the Treasury Ministers, E. Troup
Parliamentary Secretary to the Treasury and Government Chief Whip (*£36,613), The Rt. Hon. Alastair Goodlad, MP
  Private Secretary, M. Maclean
  Special Adviser, Miss S. C. Hole, OBE
Treasurer of HM Household and Deputy Chief Whip (*£31,125), Andrew Mackay, MP
Comptroller of HM Household (*£20,029), Timothy Wood, MP
Vice-Chamberlain of HM Household (*20,029), Derek Conway, MP
Lord Commissioners of the Treasury (*£20,029), M. Bates, MP; B. Wells, MP; P. McLoughlin, MP; R. Knapman, MP; R. Ottaway, MP
Assistant Whips (*£20,029), G. Brandreth, MP; S. Coe, MP; A. Coombs, MP; Mrs J. Lait, MP; P. Ainsworth, MP
Parliamentary Clerk, D. S. Martin
Panel of Independent Forecasters to the Treasury, G. Davies; T. Congdon; Prof. P. Minford, CBE; Ms K. Barker; Ms B. Rosewell; M. Weale
Permanent Secretary to the Treasury (*G1*), Sir Terence Burns, GCB
  Private Secretary, C. Guest
Head of Government Accountancy Service and Chief Accountancy Adviser to the Treasury, A. Likierman

DIRECTORATES

Leader, Ministerial Support Team, N. Macpherson
Leader, Communications Team, Ms J. Rutter
Leader, Strategy Team, N. Holgate

---

*In addition to a parliamentary salary of £43,000

MACROECONOMIC POLICY AND PROSPECTS
Director, Prof. A. Budd
Deputy Directors, J. Grice; A. O'Donnell, CB (*until end 1996*)
Team Leaders, M. Bradbury; J. S. Cunliffe; C. M. Kelly;
A. Kilpatrick; S. W. Matthews; S. Pickford; D. Savage

INTERNATIONAL FINANCE
Director, Sir Nigel Wicks, KCB, CVO, CBE
Deputy Directors, P. McIntyre; D. L. C. Peretz, CB
Team Leaders, S. Brooks; R. Fellgett; N. J. Ilett;
Ms S. Owen; D. Roe

BUDGET AND PUBLIC FINANCES
Director, P. R. C. Gray
Deputy Directors, S. W. Boys-Smith; †E. J. W. Gieve; C. J.
Mowl
Team Leaders, B. Byers; D. Deaton; Ms R. Kosmin;
N. M. Hansford; S. N. Matthews; M. Parkinson;
A. W. Ritchie; P. Short; S. N. Wood; P. Wynn Owen

SPENDING
Director, R. P. Culpin, CB, CVO
Deputy Directors, †N. Glass; Miss G. M. Noble;
Ms A. Perkins; P. N. Sedgwick
Team Leaders, P. Brook; S. Chakrabarti; D. Griffiths;
J. Halligan; A. Hudson; M. Neale; T. J. Sutton;
I. V. W. Taylor; Ms R. Thompson; Ms S. Walker

FINANCIAL MANAGEMENT, REPORTING AND AUDIT
Director (Chief Accountancy Adviser), A. Likierman
Deputy Director, †J. E. Mortimer
Team Leaders, K. Bradley; C. Butler; Mrs R. M. Dunn;
P. Holden; N. Holgate; Ms A. M. Jones

FINANCE, REGULATION AND INDUSTRY
Director, S. Robson
Deputy Directors, A. Whiting; M. L. Williams
Team Leaders, H. J. Bush; J. Colling; Mrs P. C. Diggle;
C. Farthing; J. J. Heywood; J. May; C. R. Pickering;
A. Sharples; Ms J. Simpson; P. Wanless

PERSONNEL AND SUPPORT
Director, Ms M. O'Mara
Team Leaders, I. Cooper; S. Judge; D. Rayson

EXECUTIVE AGENCIES

DEPARTMENT FOR NATIONAL SAVINGS
— *see* page 328

PAYMASTER
— *see* page 333

ROYAL MINT
— *see* page 339

OFFICE FOR NATIONAL STATISTICS
— *see* page 328

THE TREASURY SOLICITOR
DEPARTMENT OF HM PROCURATOR-GENERAL AND
TREASURY SOLICITOR
Queen Anne's Chambers, 28 Broadway, London
SW1H 9JS
Tel 0171-210 3000

The Treasury Solicitor's Department provides legal services for many government departments. Those without their own lawyers are provided with legal advice, and both they and other departments are provided with litigation services. The Treasury Solicitor is also the Queen's

---

† Combined Deputy Director and Head of Team

Proctor, and is responsible for collecting Bona Vacantia on behalf of the Crown. The Department became an executive agency in April 1996.

HM Procurator-General and Treasury Solicitor (SCS), M. L.
Saunders, CB, QC
Deputy Treasury Solicitor (SCS), D. A. Hogg

CENTRAL ADVISORY DIVISION
SCS, Mrs I. G. Letwin

LITIGATION DIVISION
SCS, D. Brummell; F. L. Croft; Mrs D. Babar;
A. D. Lawton; A. Leithead; P. R. Messer; Mrs
J. B. C. Oliver; D. Palmer; R. J. Phillips; A. J. Sandal;
P. F. O. Whitehurst
Grade 6, Miss P. J. Carroll

QUEEN'S PROCTOR DIVISION
Queen's Proctor (SCS), M. L. Saunders, CB, QC
Assistant Queen's Proctor (SCS), Mrs D. Babar

RESOURCES AND SERVICES DIVISION
Principal Establishment and Finance Officer and Security Officer
(SCS), A. J. E. Hollis
Deputy Establishment Officer (G7), Ms H. Donnelly
Finance Officer (G7), C. A. Woolley
Information Systems Manager (G7), G. N. Younger
Business Support Manager (G7), J. Hoadly

BONA VACANTIA DIVISION
SCS, R. A. D. Jackson

EUROPEAN DIVISION
SCS, J. E. G. Vaux; J. E. Collins; D. Macrae

NATIONAL HERITAGE DIVISION
SCS, P. C. Jenkins

OFFICE OF PUBLIC SERVICE DIVISION
SCS, M. C. L. Carpenter

MINISTRY OF DEFENCE ADVISORY DIVISION
Metropole Building, Northumberland Avenue, London
WC2N 5BL
Tel 0171-218 4691
SCS, A. M. C. Inglese; Mrs P. A. Dayer; C. P. J.
Muttukumaru

DEPARTMENT FOR EDUCATION AND EMPLOYMENT
ADVISORY DIVISION
Caxton House, Tothill Street, London SW1H 9NF
Tel 0171-273 3000
SCS, R. N. Ricks; C. House; Miss R. Jeffreys;
N. A. D. Lambert; F. D. W. Clarke; A. D. Preston;
S. T. Harker

DEPARTMENT OF TRANSPORT ADVISORY DIVISION
Great Minster House, 76 Marsham Street, London
SW1P 4DR
Tel 0171-271 5000
SCS, M. C. P. Thomas; D. J. Aries; P. D. Coopman;
C. W. M. Ingram; A. G. Jones; R. Lines; N. C. Thomas

HM TREASURY ADVISORY DIVISION
Treasury Chambers, Parliament Street, London SW1P 3AG
Tel 0171-270 3000
SCS, M. A. Blythe; M. J. Hemming; Mrs V. Collett; Miss
J. V. Stokes; J. R. J. Braggins

GOVERNMENT PROPERTY LAWYERS
Riverside Chambers, Castle Street, Taunton, Somerset
TA1 4AP
Tel 01823-345200
An executive agency of the Treasury Solicitor's Department.
Chief Executive (G3), P. Horner

Group Directors (G5), M. Denmayor, I. P. Parker;
M. F. Rawlins; A. M. Scarfe
Director of Lands Advisory (G5), R. C. Paddock

COUNCIL ON TRIBUNALS
7th Floor, 22 Kingsway, London WC2B 6LE
Tel 0171-936 7045

The Council on Tribunals is an independent statutory body. It keeps under review the constitution and working of the various tribunals which have been placed under its general supervision, and considers and reports on administrative procedures relating to statutory inquiries. It is consulted by government departments on proposals for legislation affecting tribunals and inquiries, and on proposals where the need for an appeals procedure may arise. It also offers advice on draft primary legislation. Some 70 tribunals are currently under the Council's supervision.

The Scottish Committee of the Council generally considers Scottish tribunals and matters relating only to Scotland.

Members of the Council are appointed by the Lord Chancellor and the Lord Advocate. The Scottish Committee is composed partly of members of the Council designated by the Lord Advocate and partly of others appointed by him. The Parliamentary Commissioner for Administration is *ex officio* a member of both the Council and the Scottish Committee.

Chairman, The Lord Archer of Sandwell, PC, QC
Members, The Parliamentary Commissioner for Administration; Mrs A. Anderson; T. N. Biggart, CBE, WS (*Chairman of the Scottish Committee*); Mrs S. Friend, MBE; C. Heaps; Prof. M. J. Hill; R. H. Jones, CVO; Dr C. A. Kaplan; I. D. Penman, CB; Prof. M. Partington; S. M. D. Brown; S. R. Davie, CB
Secretary, J. D. Saunders

SCOTTISH COMMITTEE OF THE COUNCIL ON
TRIBUNALS
44 Palmerston Place, Edinburgh EH12 5BJ
Tel 0131-220 1236

Chairman, T. N. Biggart, CBE, WS
Members, The Parliamentary Commissioner for Administration; Mrs H. Sheerin, OBE; Ms M. Burns; Mrs A. Middleton; I. D. Penman, CB; Mrs P. Y. Berry, MBE
Secretary, Mrs E. M. MacRae

TRIBUNALS
— *see* pages 372–5

UNRELATED LIVE TRANSPLANT REGULATORY AUTHORITY
Department of Health, Room 520, Eileen House, 80–94 Newington Causeway, London SE1 6EF
Tel 0171-972 2739

The Unrelated Live Transplant Regulatory Authority (ULTRA) is a statutory body established in 1990. In every case where the transplant of an organ within the definition of the Human Organ Transplants Act 1989 is proposed between a living donor and a recipient who are not genetically related, the proposal must be referred to ULTRA. Applications must be made by registered medical practitioners.

The Authority comprises a chairman and ten members appointed by the Secretary of State for Health. The secretariat is provided by Department of Health officials.
Chairman, Prof. M. Bobrow, CBE
Members, Revd Prof. G. R. Dunstan, CBE; Dr J. F. Douglas; Dr P. A. Dyer; Mrs D. Eccles; A. Hooker; S. G. Macpherson; Prof. N. P. Mallick; Prof. J. R. Salaman; Miss S. M. Taber; J. Wellbeloved
Administrative Secretary, J. R. Walden
Medical Secretary, Dr P. Doyle

WALES YOUTH AGENCY
Leslie Court, Lon-y-Llyn, Caerphilly CF83 1BQ
Tel 01222-880088

The Wales Youth Agency is a non-departmental public body funded by the Welsh Office. Its functions include the encouragement and development of the partnership between statutory and voluntary agencies relating to young people; the promotion of staff development and training; and the extension of marketing and information services in the relevant fields. The board of directors is appointed by the Secretary of State for Wales; directors do not receive a salary.
Chairman of the Board of Directors, G. Davies
Vice-Chairman of the Board of Directors, Dr H. Williamson
Executive Director, B. Williams

OFFICE OF WATER SERVICES
Centre City Tower, 7 Hill Street, Birmingham B5 4UA
Tel 0121-625 1300

The Office of Water Services (Ofwat) was set up under the Water Act 1989 and is the independent economic regulator of the water and sewerage companies in England and Wales. Ofwat's main duties are to ensure that the companies can finance and carry out the functions specified in the Water Industry Act 1991 and to protect the interests of water customers. Ofwat is a non-ministerial government department headed by the Director-General of Water Services. The Director-General has established ten regional customer service committees which are concerned solely with the interests of water customers. They are fully independent of the water industry with their own statutory identity and duty to investigate customer complaints and represent the interest of water customers. Representation of customer interests at national level is the responsibility of the Ofwat National Customer Council (ONCC), whose membership comprises the ten regional chairmen and the Director-General.

The Director-General is independent of ministerial control and directly accountable to Parliament.
Director-General of Water Services, I. C. R. Byatt

WELSH DEVELOPMENT AGENCY
Principality House, The Friary, Cardiff CF1 4AE
Tel 0345-775577/66

The Agency was established under the Welsh Development Agency Act 1975. Its remit is to help further the regeneration of the economy and improve the environment in Wales. The Agency's main activities include site assembly, provision of premises, encouraging investment by the private sector in property development, grant-aiding land reclamation, stimulating quality urban and rural development, promoting Wales as a location for inward investment, helping to boost the growth, profitability and competitiveness of indigenous Welsh companies, and providing investment capital for industry. Its sponsoring department is the Welsh Office.

Chairman, D. Rowe-Beddoe
Deputy Chairman, R. Lewis
Chief Executive, B. Hartop

WELSH OFFICE

The Welsh Office has responsibility in Wales for ministerial functions relating to health and personal social services; education, except for terms and conditions of service and student awards; training; the Welsh language, arts and culture; the implementation of the Citizen's Charter in Wales; local government; housing; water and sewerage; environmental protection; sport; agriculture and fisheries; forestry; land use, including town and country planning and countryside and nature conservation; new towns; non-departmental public bodies and appointments in Wales; ancient monuments and historic buildings and the Welsh Arts Council; roads; tourism; financial assistance to industry; the Strategic Development Scheme in Wales and the Programme for the Valleys; the operation of the European Regional Development Fund in Wales and other European Community matters; civil emergencies; and all financial aspects of these matters, including Welsh rate support grant.

Gwydyr House, Whitehall, London SW1A 2ER
Tel 0171-270 3000

Secretary of State for Wales, The Rt. Hon. William Hague, MP
  Private Secretary, Dr J. Milligan
Parliamentary Under-Secretaries, Gwilym Jones, MP;
  Jonathan Evans, MP
  Private Secretaries, V. R. Watkin; W. S. Gear
  Special Adviser, B. Towns
Parliamentary Clerk, A. Green
Permanent Secretary (G1), Mrs R. Lomax
  Private Secretary, Ms J. M. Brown

Cathays Park, Cardiff CF1 3NQ
Tel 01222-825111

LEGAL GROUP
Legal Adviser (G3), D. G. Lambert
Deputy Legal Adviser (G5), J. H. Turnbull

INFORMATION DIVISION
Director of News (G7), R. Lehnert
Principal Publicity Officer (G7), W. J. Edwards

ESTABLISHMENT GROUP
Principal Establishment Officer (G3), C. D. Stevens
Heads of Divisions (G5), R. M. Abel; G. A. Thomas;
  Ms H. Angus
Chief Statistician (G5), W. R. L. Alldritt
Head of Health Statistics and Analysis Unit (G6), P. J.
  Fullerton
Head of Training and Education Intelligence Unit (G6), Mrs C.
  Fullerton

FINANCE GROUP
Principal Finance Officer (G3), R. A. Wallace
Heads of Divisions (G5), D. T. Richards; L. A. Pavelin
Senior Economic Adviser (G5), M. G. Phelps

Grade 6, M. G. Horlock
Head of Internal Audit (G6), D. Howarth

AGRICULTURE, ECONOMIC DEVELOPMENT, AND INDUSTRY AND TRAINING
Deputy Secretary (G2), J. F. Craig, CB

AGRICULTURE DEPARTMENT
Head of Department (G3), L. K. Walford
Heads of Divisions (G5), D. R. Thomas; Mrs A. M. Jackson
Divisional Executive Officers (G7), W. K. Griffiths
  (*Carmarthen*); E. Hughes (*Caernarfon*); J. C. Alexander
  (*Llandrindod Wells*)

ECONOMIC DEVELOPMENT GROUP
Head of Group (G3), M. J. Cochlin
Heads of Divisions (G5), B. J. Mitchell; A. D. Lansdown;
  M. L. Evans

INDUSTRY AND TRAINING DEPARTMENT
Director (G3), D. W. Jones
Industrial Director (G4), J. Cameron
Heads of Divisions (G5), G. T. Evans; H. Brodie;
  N. E. Thomas; (G6), Dr R. J. Loveland

EDUCATION, HOUSING, HEALTH AND SOCIAL SERVICES, TRANSPORT, LOCAL GOVERNMENT, PLANNING AND ENVIRONMENT
Deputy Secretary (G2), J. W. Lloyd, CB

EDUCATION DEPARTMENT
Head of Department (G3), S. H. Martin
Heads of Divisions (G5)°, W. G. Davies; H. Evans;
  R. J. Davies; Dr H. F. Rawlings

OFFICE OF HM CHIEF INSPECTOR FOR SCHOOLS IN WALES
Chief Inspector (G4)°, R. L. James
Staff Inspectors (G5)°, S. J. Adams; J. R. N. Evans;
  T. E. Parry; G. Thomas; P. Thomas
There are 45 Grade 6 Inspectors.
Head of Administration (G7), J. Roberts

LOCAL GOVERNMENT GROUP
Head of Group (G3), J. D. Shortridge
Heads of Divisions (G5), A. C. Wood; M. J. Clancy;
  Mrs B. J. M. Wilson; Mrs E. A. Taylor
Chief Inspector, Social Services Inspectorate (*Wales*) (G5),
  D. G. Evans
Deputy Chief Inspectors, J. F. Mooney; R. C. Woodward
Social Services Inspectors (G7), D, Barker; D. A. Brushett;
  G. H. Davies; Miss R. E. Evans; I. Forster;
  Mrs J. Jenkins; C. D. Vyvyan; Mrs P. White

HEALTH DEPARTMENT
Director (G3), P. R. Gregory
Heads of Divisions (G5), D. H. Jones; D. A. Pritchard; M. D.
  Chown; B. Wilcox; R. C. Williams; A. G. Thornton

HEALTH PROFESSIONAL GROUP
Chief Medical Officer (G3), Dr D. J. Hine
Principal Medical Officers (G4), Dr B. Fuge; Dr J. K.
  Richmond
Senior Medical Officers (G5), Dr J. Ludlow; Dr H. N.
  Williams; Dr D. Salter; Dr P. Lyne
Medical Adviser (*part-time*), Dr J. Andrew
Chief Dental Officer (G5), D. M. Heap
Senior Dental Officer (G5), P. Langmaid
Chief Scientific Adviser (G5), Dr J. A. V. Pritchard
Deputy Scientific Adviser (G6), Dr E. O. Crawley
Chief Pharmaceutical Adviser (G5), Miss C. W. Howells

°Based at Ty Glas Road, Llanishen, Cardiff CF4 5LE. Tel: 01222-761456

Chief Environmental Health Adviser (G5), R. Alexander
Deputy Environmental Health Adviser (G6), D. Worthington

NURSING DIVISION
Chief Nursing Officer, Miss M. Bull
Deputy Chief Nursing Officer, Mrs B. Melvin
Nursing Officers, Mrs S. M. Drayton; P. Johnson; Mrs
J. Sait; M. F. Tonkin

TRANSPORT, PLANNING AND ENVIRONMENT GROUP
Head of Group (G3), G. C. G. Craig
Director of Highways (G4), K. J. Thomas°
Deputy Director of Highways (G5), J. G. Evans*
Head of Division (G5), D. I. Westlake°
Chief Planning Adviser (G5), W. P. Roderick
Superintending Engineers (G6), J. R. Rees*; B. H. Hawker,
OBE*
Chief Estates Adviser (G6), G. K. Hoad
Senior Principal (G6), P. R. Marsden
Scientific Adviser (G6), Dr H. Prosser
Principal Planning Officers (G7), L. Owen; J. V. Spear
Principal Research Officers (G7), A. S. Dredge;
Ms L. J. Roberts
Principal Estates Officer (G7), R. W. Wilson
*Principal Professional and Technology Officers, Highways
Directorate° (G7)*, M. J. Gilbert*; I. A. Grindulis;
A. P. Howcroft; A. L. Perry; R. H. Powell; S. C. Shouler;
J. Collins; K. J. Alexander; R. H. Hooper*; R. K. Cone;
J. Dawkins; T. Dorken; R. Shaw; M. J. A. Parker;
V. S. Pownall*

LOCAL GOVERNMENT REORGANIZATION GROUP
Head of Group (G3), J. D. Shortridge

HEALTH AUTHORITIES

BRO TAF, Churchill House, Churchill Way, Cardiff CF1
4TW. *Chair*, Mrs K. Thomas; *Chief Executive*, Mrs G.
Todd
DYFED POWYS, St David's Hospital, Carmarthen SA31 3HB.
Chair, Mrs V. Bourne; *Chief Executive*, Mrs P. Stansbie
GWENT, Mamhilad House, Mamhilad, Pontypool NP4
0YP. *Chair*, Hon. Mrs L. Price; *Chief Executive*, J. Hallett
MORGANNWG, The Oldway Centre, 36 Orchard Street,
Swansea SA1 5AQ. *Chair*, H. Thomas; *Chief Executive*,
Mrs J. Williams
NORTH WALES, Preswylfa, Hendy Road, Mold CH7 1PZ.
Chair, Dr A. Kenrick; *Chief Executive*, B. Jones

EXECUTIVE AGENCIES

AGRICULTURAL DEVELOPMENT AND ADVISORY
SERVICE (ADAS)
— *see* page 280

CADW: WELSH HISTORIC MONUMENTS
Brunel House, Fitzalan Road, Cardiff CF2 1UY
Tel 01222-500200
Cadw supports the preservation, conservation, apprecia-
tion and enjoyment of the built heritage in Wales.
Chief Executive, T. Cassidy
Director of Policy and Administration, R. W. Hughes
Conservation Architect (G6), J. D. Hogg
*Principal Inspector of Ancient Monuments and Historic
Buildings*, J. R. Avent

Based at:
°Ty Glas Road, Llanishen, Cardiff CF4 5LE. Tel: 01222-761456
*Government Buildings, Dinerth Road, Rhos-on-Sea, Colwyn Bay
LL28 4UL. Tel: 01492-44261

Inspectors of Ancient Monuments and Historic Buildings,
J. K. Knight; A. D. McLees; Dr S. E. Rees; R. C. Turner;
M. J. Yates

INTERVENTION BOARD
— *see* page 315

PLANNING INSPECTORATE
Cathays Park, Cardiff CF1 3NQ
Tel 01222-823892
A joint executive agency of the Department of the
Environment and the Welsh Office (*see* page 298).
Chief Executive and Chief Inspector of Planning (G3),
C. Shepley
Assistant Chief Planning Inspector (G5), Mrs S. Bruton

WOMEN'S NATIONAL COMMISSION
Level 4, Caxton House, Tothill Street, London SW1H 9NF
Tel 0171-273 5486

The Women's National Commission is an independent
advisory committee to the Government. Its remit is to
ensure that the informed opinions of women are given their
due weight in the deliberations of the Government. The
Commission's 50 members are all women who are elected
or appointed by national organizations with a large and
active membership of women. The organizations include
the women's sections of the major political parties, trade
unions and religious groups, professional women's organizations and other bodies broadly representative of women.
The Commission's sponsoring department is the Department for Education and Employment.
Government Co-Chairman, Mrs A. Browning, MP
Elected Co-Chairman, Mrs E. Bavidge
Joint Secretaries, Ms J. Bailey; Ms W. Brown

CIVIL SERVICE STAFF

BY PRINCIPAL DEPARTMENTS *As at 1 April 1995*

	Total	Of whom in agencies
Agriculture, Fisheries and Food	10,567	4,164
Cabinet Office	2,405	887
Customs and Excise	24,132	—
Defence	116,139	32,403
Education	2,507	391
Employment Department Group	49,553	39,852
Environment	7,054	2,541
Foreign Office	5,978	30
Health	4,496	1,058
Home Office	50,889	41,323
Inland Revenue	59,093	4,531
Lord Chancellor's Department	11,605	10,383
Scottish Departments	13,158	7,571
Social Security	89,248	86,455
Trade and Industry	10,247	5,103
Transport	12,792	10,491
Treasury	1,127	—
Welsh Office	2,224	227
Other departments	43,679	19,238
TOTAL	516,893	266,648

Law Courts and Offices

THE JUDICIAL COMMITTEE OF THE PRIVY COUNCIL

The Judicial Committee of the Privy Council is primarily the final court of appeal for the United Kingdom dependent territories and those independent Commonwealth countries which have retained the avenue of appeal upon achieving independence (Antigua and Barbuda, The Bahamas, Barbados, Belize, Brunei, Dominica, The Gambia, Jamaica, Kiribati, Mauritius, New Zealand, St Christopher and Nevis, St Lucia, St Vincent and the Grenadines, Trinidad and Tobago, and Tuvalu). The Committee also hears appeals from the Channel Islands and the Isle of Man and the disciplinary and health committees of the medical and allied professions. It has a limited jurisdiction to hear appeals under the Pastoral Measure 1983. In 1995 the Judicial Committee heard 69 appeals and 69 petitions for special leave to appeal.

The members of the Judicial Committee include the Lord Chancellor, the Lords of Appeal in Ordinary (*see* page 358), other Privy Councillors who hold or have held high judicial office and certain judges from the Commonwealth.

PRIVY COUNCIL OFFICE (JUDICIAL COMMITTEE), Downing Street, London SWIA 2AJ. Tel: 0171-270 0483. *Registrar of the Privy Council*, D. H. O. Owen; *Chief Clerk*, F. G. Hart

The Judicature of England and Wales

The legal system of England and Wales is separate from those of Scotland and Northern Ireland and differs from them in law, judicial procedure and court structure, although there is a common distinction between civil law (disputes between individuals) and criminal law (acts harmful to the community).

The supreme judicial authority for England and Wales is the House of Lords, which is the ultimate Court of Appeal from all courts in Great Britain and Northern Ireland (except criminal courts in Scotland) for all cases except those concerning the interpretation and application of European Community law, including preliminary rulings requested by British courts and tribunals, which are decided by the European Court of Justice (*see* page 773). As a Court of Appeal the House of Lords consists of the Lord Chancellor and the Lords of Appeal in Ordinary (law lords).

The Supreme Court of Judicature comprises the Court of Appeal, the High Court of Justice and the Crown Court. The High Court of Justice is the superior civil court and is divided into three divisions. The Chancery Division is concerned mainly with equity, bankruptcy and contentious probate business. The Queen's Bench Division deals with commercial and maritime law, serious personal injury and medical negligence cases, cases involving a breach of contract and professional negligence actions. The Family Division deals with matters relating to family law. Sittings are held at the Royal Courts of Justice in London or at 126 District Registries outside the capital. High Court judges sit alone to hear cases at first instance. Appeals from lower courts are heard by two or three judges, or by single judges of the appropriate division. The Restrictive Practices Court, set up under the Restrictive Trade Practices Act 1956, and the Official Referees' Courts, which deal almost exclusively with cases concerning the construction industry, are also part of the High Court. Appeals from the High Court are heard in the Court of Appeal (Civil Division), presided over by the Master of the Rolls, and may go on to the House of Lords.

In criminal matters the decision to prosecute in the majority of cases rests with the Crown Prosecution Service, the independent prosecuting body in England and Wales (*see* page 366–7). At the head of the service is the Director of Public Prosecutions, who discharges her duties under the superintendence of the Attorney-General. Certain categories of offence continue to require the Attorney-General's consent for prosecution.

The Crown Court sits in about 90 centres, divided into six circuits, and is presided over by High Court judges, full-time circuit judges, and part-time recorders and assistant recorders, sitting with a jury in all trials which are contested. There were 332 assistant recorders at 30 June 1996. The Crown Court deals with trials of the more serious criminal offences, the sentencing of offenders committed for sentence by magistrates' courts (when the magistrates consider their own power of sentence inadequate), and appeals from magistrates' courts. Magistrates usually sit with a circuit judge or recorder to deal with appeals and committals for sentence. Appeals from the Crown Court, either against sentence or conviction, are made to the Court of Appeal (Criminal Division), presided over by the Lord Chief Justice. A further appeal from the Court of Appeal to the House of Lords can be brought if a point of law of general public importance is considered to be involved.

Minor criminal offences (summary offences) are dealt with in magistrates' courts, which usually consist of three unpaid lay magistrates (justices of the peace) sitting without a jury, who are advised on points of law and procedure by a legally-qualified clerk to the justices. There were 30,326 justices of the peace at 1 January 1996. In busier courts a full-time, salaried and legally-qualified stipendiary magistrate presides alone. Cases involving people under 18 are heard in youth courts, specially constituted magistrates' courts which sit apart from other courts. Preliminary proceedings in a serious case to decide whether there is evidence to justify committal for trial in the Crown Court are also dealt with in the magistrates' courts. Appeals from magistrates' courts against sentence or conviction are made to the Crown Court. Appeals upon a point of law are made to the High Court, and may go on to the House of Lords.

Most minor civil cases are dealt with by the county courts, of which there are about 270 (details may be found in the local telephone directory). Cases are heard by circuit judges or district judges. There were 331 district judges at 31 May 1996. For cases involving small claims there are special simplified procedures. Where there are financial limits on county court jurisdiction, claims which exceed those limits may be tried in the county courts with the consent of the parties, or in certain circumstances on transfer from the High Court. Outside London, bankruptcy proceedings can be heard in designated county courts. Magistrates' courts can deal with certain classes of civil case and committees of magistrates license public houses, clubs and betting shops. For the implementation of the Children Act 1989, a new structure of hearing centres was set up in 1991 for family proceedings cases, involving magistrates' courts (family proceedings courts), divorce county courts, family hearing centres and care centres. Appeals in family matters heard in the family proceedings courts go to the Family Division of the High Court; affiliation appeals and appeals from decisions of the licensing committees of magistrates go to the Crown Court. Appeals from county courts are heard in the Court of Appeal (Civil Division), and may go on to the House of Lords.

On 26 July 1996 the Master of the Rolls (Lord Woolf) published proposals for a radical reform of the civil justice system in England and Wales aimed at making procedures simpler, quicker and cheaper.

Coroners' courts investigate violent and unnatural deaths or sudden deaths where the cause is unknown. Cases may be brought before a local coroner (a senior lawyer or doctor) by doctors, the police, various public authorities or members of the public. Where a death is sudden and the cause is unknown, the coroner may order a post-mortem examination to determine the cause of death rather than hold an inquest in court.

Judicial appointments are made by The Queen; the most senior appointments are made on the advice of the Prime Minister and other appointments on the advice of the Lord Chancellor.

Under the provisions of the Criminal Appeal Act 1995, a Commission is being set up to direct and supervise investigations into possible miscarriages of justice and to refer cases to the courts on the grounds of conviction and sentence; these functions were formerly the responsibility of the Home Secretary. The Commission will be based in Birmingham and is expected to start work by the end of 1996.

THE HOUSE OF LORDS
AS FINAL COURT OF APPEAL

The Lord High Chancellor
The Rt. Hon. the Lord Mackay of Clashfern, *born* 1927, *apptd* 1987

LORDS OF APPEAL IN ORDINARY (each £122,231)
Style, The Rt. Hon. Lord —

Rt. Hon. Lord Goff of Chieveley, *born* 1926, *apptd* 1986
Rt. Hon. Lord Browne-Wilkinson, *born* 1930, *apptd* 1991
Rt. Hon. Lord Mustill, *born* 1931, *apptd* 1992
Rt. Hon. Lord Slynn of Hadley, *born* 1930, *apptd* 1992
Rt. Hon. Lord Lloyd of Berwick, *born* 1929, *apptd* 1993
Rt. Hon. Lord Nolan, *born* 1928, *apptd* 1994
Rt. Hon. Lord Nicholls of Birkenhead, *born* 1933, *apptd* 1994
Rt. Hon. Lord Steyn, *born* 1932, *apptd* 1995
Rt. Hon. Lord Hoffman, *born* 1934, *apptd* 1995
Rt. Hon. Lord Hope of Craighead, *born* 1938, *apptd* 1996
Rt. Hon. Lord Clyde, *born* 1932, *apptd* 1996

Registrar, The Clerk of the Parliaments (*see* page 218)

SUPREME COURT OF JUDICATURE

COURT OF APPEAL

The Master of the Rolls (£122,231), The Rt. Hon. Lord Woolf, *born* 1933, *apptd* 1996
Secretary, Miss V. Seymour
Clerk, D. G. Grimmett

LORDS JUSTICES OF APPEAL (each £117,190)
Style, The Rt. Hon. Lord/Lady Justice [surname]

Rt. Hon. Sir Martin Nourse, *born* 1932, *apptd* 1985
Rt. Hon. Dame Elizabeth Butler-Sloss, DBE, *born* 1933, *apptd* 1988
Rt. Hon. Sir Murray Stuart-Smith, *born* 1927, *apptd* 1988
Rt. Hon. Sir Christopher Staughton, *born* 1933, *apptd* 1988
Rt. Hon. Sir Anthony McCowan, *born* 1928, *apptd* 1989
Rt. Hon. Sir Roy Beldam, *born* 1925, *apptd* 1989
Rt. Hon. Sir Andrew Leggatt, *born* 1930, *apptd* 1990
Rt. Hon. Sir Paul Kennedy, *born* 1935, *apptd* 1992
Rt. Hon. Sir David Hirst, *born* 1925, *apptd* 1992
Rt. Hon. Sir Simon Brown, *born* 1937, *apptd* 1992
Rt. Hon. Sir Anthony Evans, *born* 1934, *apptd* 1992
Rt. Hon. Sir Christopher Rose, *born* 1937, *apptd* 1992
Rt. Hon. Sir John Waite, *born* 1932, *apptd* 1993
Rt. Hon. Sir John Roch, *born* 1934, *apptd* 1993
Rt. Hon. Sir Peter Gibson, *born* 1934, *apptd* 1993
Rt. Hon. Sir John Hobhouse, *born* 1932, *apptd* 1993
Rt. Hon. Sir Denis Henry, *born* 1931, *apptd* 1993
Rt. Hon. Sir Mark Saville, *born* 1936, *apptd* 1994
Rt. Hon. Sir Peter Millett, *born* 1932, *apptd* 1994
Rt. Hon. Sir Swinton Thomas, *born* 1931, *apptd* 1994
Rt. Hon. Sir Andrew Morritt, CVO, *born* 1938, *apptd* 1994
Rt. Hon. Sir Philip Otton, *born* 1933, *apptd* 1995
Rt. Hon. Sir Robin Auld, *born* 1937, *apptd* 1995
Rt. Hon. Sir Malcolm Pill, *born* 1938, *apptd* 1995
Rt. Hon. Sir William Aldous, *born* 1936, *apptd* 1995
Rt. Hon. Sir Alan Ward, *born* 1938, *apptd* 1995
Rt. Hon. Sir Michael Hutchison, *born* 1933, *apptd* 1995
Rt. Hon. Sir Konrad Schiemann, *born* 1937, *apptd* 1995
Rt. Hon. Sir Nicholas Phillips, *born* 1938, *apptd* 1995
Rt. Hon. Sir Mathew Thorpe, *born* 1938, *apptd* 1995
Rt. Hon. Sir Mark Potter, *born* 1937, *apptd* 1996
Rt. Hon. Sir Henry Brooke, *born* 1936, *apptd* 1996
Rt. Hon. Sir Igor Judge, *born* 1941, *apptd* 1996
Rt. Hon. Sir Mark Waller, *born* 1940, *apptd* 1996
Rt. Hon. Sir John Mummery, *born* 1938, *apptd* 1996

Ex officio Judges, The Lord High Chancellor; the Lord Chief Justice of England; the Master of the Rolls; the President of the Family Division; and the Vice-Chancellor

COURT OF APPEAL (CRIMINAL DIVISION)

Judges, The Lord Chief Justice of England; the Master of the Rolls; Lords Justices of Appeal; and Judges of the High Court of Justice

COURTS-MARTIAL APPEAL COURT

Judges, The Lord Chief Justice of England; the Master of the Rolls; Lords Justices of Appeal; and Judges of the High Court of Justice

HIGH COURT OF JUSTICE
CHANCERY DIVISION

President, The Lord High Chancellor
The Vice-Chancellor (£117,190), The Rt. Hon. Sir Richard Scott, *born* 1934, *apptd* 1994
Clerk, W. Northfield, BEM

JUDGES (each £104,431)
Style, The Hon. Mr/Mrs Justice [surname]

Hon. Sir Jeremiah Harman, *born* 1930, *apptd* 1982
Hon. Sir John Knox, *born* 1925, *apptd* 1985
Hon. Sir Donald Rattee, *born* 1937, *apptd* 1989
Hon. Sir Francis Ferris, TD, *born* 1932, *apptd* 1990
Hon. Sir John Chadwick, ED, *born* 1941, *apptd* 1991
Hon. Sir Jonathan Parker, *born* 1937, *apptd* 1991
Hon. Sir John Lindsay, *born* 1935, *apptd* 1992
Hon. Dame Mary Arden, DBE, *born* 1947, *apptd* 1993
Hon. Sir Edward Evans-Lombe, *born* 1937, *apptd* 1993
Hon. Sir Robin Jacob, *born* 1941, *apptd* 1993
Hon. Sir William Blackburne, *born* 1944, *apptd* 1993
Hon. Sir Gavin Lightman, *born* 1939, *apptd* 1994
Hon. Sir Robert Walker, *born* 1938, *apptd* 1994
Hon. Sir Robert Carnwath, *born* 1945, *apptd* 1994
Hon. Sir Colin Rimer, *born* 1944, *apptd* 1994
Hon. Sir Hugh Laddie, *born* 1946, *apptd* 1995

HIGH COURT OF JUSTICE IN BANKRUPTCY

Judges, The Vice-Chancellor and judges of the Chancery
Division of the High Court

COMPANIES COURT

Judges, The Vice Chancellor and judges of the Chancery
Division of the High Court

PATENT COURT (APPELLATE SECTION)

Judge, The Hon. Mr Justice Jacob

QUEEN'S BENCH DIVISION

The Lord Chief Justice of England (£132,178) The Rt. Hon.
the Lord Bingham of Cornhill, *born* 1933, *apptd* 1996
Private Secretary, E. Adams
Clerk, J. Bond

JUDGES (each £104,431)
Style, The Hon. Mr/Mrs Justice [surname]

Hon. Sir Christopher French, *born* 1925, *apptd* 1979
Hon. Sir Charles McCullough, *born* 1931, *apptd* 1981
Hon. Sir Oliver Popplewell, *born* 1927, *apptd* 1983
Hon. Sir Richard Tucker, *born* 1930, *apptd* 1985
Hon. Sir Patrick Garland, *born* 1929, *apptd* 1985
Hon. Sir Michael Turner, *born* 1931, *apptd* 1985
Hon. Sir John Alliott, *born* 1932, *apptd* 1986
Hon. Sir Harry Ognall, *born* 1934, *apptd* 1986
Hon. Sir John Owen, *born* 1925, *apptd* 1986
Hon. Sir Humphrey Potts, *born* 1931, *apptd* 1986
Hon. Sir Richard Rougier, *born* 1932, *apptd* 1986
Hon. Sir Ian Kennedy, *born* 1930, *apptd* 1986
Hon. Sir Stuart McKinnon, *born* 1938, *apptd* 1988
Hon. Sir Scott Baker, *born* 1937, *apptd* 1988
Hon. Sir Edwin Jowitt, *born* 1929, *apptd* 1988
Hon. Sir Douglas Brown, *born* 1931, *apptd* 1996
Hon. Sir Michael Morland, *born* 1929, *apptd* 1989
Hon. Sir Roger Buckley, *born* 1939, *apptd* 1989
Hon. Sir Anthony Hidden, *born* 1936, *apptd* 1989
Hon. Sir Michael Wright, *born* 1932, *apptd* 1990
Hon. Sir Charles Mantell, *born* 1937, *apptd* 1990
Hon. Sir John Blofeld, *born* 1932, *apptd* 1990
Hon. Sir Peter Cresswell, *born* 1944, *apptd* 1991
Hon. Sir Anthony May, *born* 1940, *apptd* 1991
Hon. Sir John Laws, *born* 1945, *apptd* 1992
Hon. Dame Ann Ebsworth, DBE, *born* 1937, *apptd* 1992
Hon. Sir Simon Tuckey, *born* 1941, *apptd* 1992
Hon. Sir David Latham, *born* 1942, *apptd* 1992
Hon. Sir Christopher Holland, *born* 1937, *apptd* 1992
Hon. Sir John Kay, *born* 1943, *apptd* 1992
Hon. Sir Richard Curtis, *born* 1933, *apptd* 1992

Hon. Sir Stephen Sedley, *born* 1939, *apptd* 1992
Hon. Dame Janet Smith, DBE, *born* 1940, *apptd* 1992
Hon. Sir Anthony Colman, *born* 1938, *apptd* 1992
Hon. Sir Anthony Clarke, *born* 1943, *apptd* 1993
Hon. Sir John Dyson, *born* 1943, *apptd* 1993
Hon. Sir Thayne Forbes, *born* 1938, *apptd* 1993
Hon. Sir Michael Sachs, *born* 1932, *apptd* 1993
Hon. Sir Stephen Mitchell, *born* 1941, *apptd* 1993
Hon. Sir Rodger Bell, *born* 1939, *apptd* 1993
Hon. Sir Michael Harrison, *born* 1939, *apptd* 1993
Hon. Sir Bernard Rix, *born* 1944, *apptd* 1993
Hon. Dame Heather Steel, DBE, *born* 1940, *apptd* 1993
Hon. Sir William Gage, *born* 1938, *apptd* 1993
Hon. Sir Jonathan Mance, *born* 1943, *apptd* 1993
Hon. Sir Andrew Longmore, *born* 1944, *apptd* 1993
Hon. Sir Thomas Morison, *born* 1939, *apptd* 1993
Hon. Sir Richard Buxton, *born* 1938, *apptd* 1993
Hon. Sir David Keene, *born* 1941, *apptd* 1994
Hon. Sir Andrew Collins, *born* 1942, *apptd* 1994
Hon. Sir Maurice Kay, *born* 1942, *apptd* 1995
Hon. Sir Brian Smedley, *born* 1934, *apptd* 1995
Hon. Sir Anthony Hooper, *born* 1937, *apptd* 1995
Hon. Sir Alexander Butterfield, *born* 1942, *apptd* 1995
Hon. Sir George Newman, *born* 1941, *apptd* 1995
Hon. Sir David Poole, *born* 1938, *apptd* 1995
Hon. Sir Martin Moore-Bick, *born* 1946, *apptd* 1995
Hon. Sir Gordon Langley, *born* 1943, *apptd* 1995
Hon. Sir Roger Thomas, *born* 1947, *apptd* 1996
Hon. Sir Robert Nelson, *born* 1942, *apptd* 1996
Hon. Sir Roger Toulson, *born* 1946, *apptd* 1996
Hon. Sir Michael Astill, *born* 1938, *apptd* 1996
Hon. Sir Alan Moses, *born* 1945, *apptd* 1996

FAMILY DIVISION

President (£117,190) Rt. Hon. Sir Stephen Brown, *born*
1929, *apptd* 1988
Secretary, Mrs S. Leung
Clerk, Mrs S. Bell

JUDGES (each £104,431)
Style, The Hon. Mr/Mrs Justice [surname]

Hon. Sir Anthony Hollis, *born* 1927, *apptd* 1982
Hon. Sir Edward Cazalet, *born* 1936, *apptd* 1988
Hon. Sir Robert Johnson, *born* 1933, *apptd* 1989
Hon. Dame Joyanne Bracewell, DBE, *born* 1934, *apptd* 1990
Hon. Sir Michael Connell, *born* 1939, *apptd* 1991
Hon. Sir Peter Singer, *born* 1944, *apptd* 1993
Hon. Sir Nicholas Wilson, *born* 1945, *apptd* 1993
Hon. Sir Nicholas Wall, *born* 1945, *apptd* 1993
Hon. Sir Andrew Kirkwood, *born* 1944, *apptd* 1993
Hon. Sir Christopher Stuart-White, *born* 1933, *apptd* 1993
Hon. Dame Brenda Hale, DBE, *born* 1945, *apptd* 1994
Hon. Sir Hugh Bennett, *born* 1943, *apptd* 1995
Hon. Sir Edward Holman, *born* 1947, *apptd* 1995
Hon. Dame Mary Hogg, *born* 1947, *apptd* 1995
Hon. Sir Christopher Sumner, *born* 1939, *apptd* 1996

RESTRICTIVE PRACTICES COURT

Room 410, Thomas More Building, Royal Courts of
Justice, Strand, London WC2A 2LL
Tel 0171-936 6727

President, The Hon. Mr Justice Buckley
Judges, The Hon. Mr Justice Ferris; The Hon. Mr Justice
Buxton
Lay Members, B. M. Currie; Sir Lewis Robertson, CBE;
R. Garrick, CBE; S. J. Ahearne; J. A. Graham; Mrs D. H.
Hatfield; S. McDowall; J. A. Scott; B. D. Colgate;
J. A. C. King
Clerk of the Court, M. Buckley

OFFICIAL REFEREES' COURTS
St Dunstan's House, 133–137 Fetter Lane, London
EC4A 1HD
Tel 0171-936 7427

JUDGES (each £89,123)
His Hon. Judge Lewis, QC (*Senior Official Referee*)
His Hon. Judge Bowsher, QC
His Hon. Judge Loyd, QC
His Hon. Judge Hicks, QC
His Hon. Judge Havery, QC
His Hon. Judge Lloyd, QC
His Hon. Judge Newman, QC
His Hon. Judge Thornton, QC
His Hon. Judge Wilcox

Chief Clerk, Miss B. Joy

LORD CHANCELLOR'S DEPARTMENT
— *see* Government Departments and Public Offices

SUPREME COURT DEPARTMENTS AND OFFICES
Royal Courts of Justice, London WC2A 2LL
Tel 0171-936 6000

DIRECTOR'S OFFICE
Director, G. E. Calvett
Deputy Director, J. Selch
Group Manager, Family Proceedings and Probate Service, R. P. Knight
Finance and Court Business Officer, K. T. Fairweather

ADMIRALTY AND COMMERCIAL REGISTRY AND MARSHAL'S OFFICE
Registrar (£62,621), P. Miller
Marshal and Chief Clerk (G7), A. Ferrigno

BANKRUPTCY DEPARTMENT
Chief Registrar (£76,716), G. L. Pimm
Bankruptcy Registrars (£62,621), W. S. James;
  J. A. Simmonds; D. G. Scott; P. J. S. Rawson
Chief Clerk (SEO), M. Brown

CENTRAL OFFICE OF THE SUPREME COURT
Senior Master of the Supreme Court (*QBD*), *and Queen's Remembrancer* (£76,716), R. L. Turner
Masters of the Supreme Court (*QBD*) (£62,621),
  P. B. Creightmore; D. L. Prebble; G. H. Hodgson;
  J. Trench; M. Tennant; P. Miller; N. O. G. Murray;
  I. H. Foster; G. H. Rose; P. G. A. Eyre
Chief Clerk (G7), P. Emery

CHANCERY DIVISION
Chief Clerk (G7), P. Emery

CHANCERY CHAMBERS
Chief Master of the Supreme Court (£76,716), J. M. Dyson
Masters of the Supreme Court (£62,621), G. A. Barratt; J. I. Winegarten; J. A. Moncaster, R. A. Bowman
Chief Clerk (SEO), G. Robinson
Conveyancing Counsel of the Supreme Court, W. D. Ainger;
  H. M. Harrod; A. C. Taussig

COMPANIES COURT
Registrar (£62,621), M. Buckley
Chief Clerk (SEO), M. Brown

COURT OF APPEAL CIVIL DIVISION
Registrar (£76,716), J. D. R. Adams
Chief Clerk (SEO), Miss H. M. Goddard

COURT OF APPEAL CRIMINAL DIVISION
Registrar (£76,716), M. McKenzie, QC
Deputy Registrar (G5), Mrs L. G. Knapman
Chief Clerk (G7), M. Bishop

COURTS-MARTIAL APPEALS OFFICE
Registrar (£76,716), M. McKenzie, QC
Chief Clerk (G7), M. Bishop

CROWN OFFICE OF THE SUPREME COURT
Master of the Crown Office, and Queen's Coroner and Attorney
  (£76,716), M. McKenzie, QC
Head of Crown Office (G5), Mrs L. Knapman
Chief Clerk (G7), M. Bishop

EXAMINERS OF THE COURT
Empowered to take examination of witnesses in all Divisions of the High Court
R. G. Wood; Mrs G. M. Kenne; R. M. Planterose; Miss V. E. I. Selvaratnam

RESTRICTIVE PRACTICES COURT
Clerk of the Court, M. Buckley
Chief Clerk (SEO), M. Brown

SUPREME COURT TAXING OFFICE
Chief Master (£76,716), P. T. Hurst
Masters of the Supreme Court (£62,621), M. Ellis; T. H. Seager Berry; C. C. Wright; P. A. Rogers; G. N. Pollard; J. E. O'Hare
Court Manager, Mrs H. Oakey
Chief Taxing Officer (G7), T. J. Ryan

COURT OF PROTECTION
Stewart House, 24 Kingsway, London WC2B 6HD
Tel 0171-269 7000
Master (£76,716), D. A. Lush

ELECTION PETITIONS OFFICE
Room E218, Royal Courts of Justice, Strand, London WC2A 2LL
Tel 0171-936 6131
The office accepts petitions and deals with all matters relating to the questioning of parliamentary, European Parliament and local government elections, and with applications for relief under the Representation of the People legislation.
Prescribed Officer, R. L. Turner
Chief Clerk, Miss J. L. Waine

OFFICE OF THE LORD CHANCELLOR'S VISITORS
Stewart House, 24 Kingsway, London WC2B 6HD
Tel 0171-269 7317
Legal Visitor, A. R. Tyrrell
Medical Visitors, K. Khan; W. B. Sprey; E. Mateu; S. E. Malapatra; A. Bailey; A. Kaeser

OFFICIAL RECEIVERS' DEPARTMENT
21 Bloomsbury Street, London WC1B 3SS
Tel 0171-323 3090
Senior Official Receiver, M. C. A. Osborne
Official Receivers, M. J. Pugh; L. T. Cramp; J. Norris

OFFICIAL SOLICITOR'S DEPARTMENT
81 Chancery Lane, London WC2B 6HD
Tel 0171-911 7105
Official Solicitor to the Supreme Court, P. M. Harris

Deputy Official Solicitor, H. J. Baker
Chief Clerk (G7), R. Lancaster

PRINCIPAL REGISTRY (FAMILY DIVISION)
Somerset House, London WC2R ILP
Tel 0171-936 6000

Senior District Judge (£76,716), G. B. N. A. Angel
District Judges (£62,621), R. B. Rowe; B. P. F. Kenworthy-
Browne; Mrs K. T. Moorhouse; M. J. Segal; R. Conn;
Miss I. M. Plumstead; G. J. Maple; Miss H. C. Bradley;
K. J. White; A. R. S. Bassett-Cross; N. A. Grove;
M. C. Berry; Miss S. M. Bowman; C. Million; P. Waller;
Miss P. Cushing; R. Harper; G. C. Brasse
Group Manager, Family Proceedings and Probate Service (G6),
R. P. Knight

District Probate Registrars

Birmingham and Stoke-on-Trent, C. Marsh
Brighton and Maidstone, M. N. Emery
Bristol, Exeter and Bodmin, R. H. P. Joyce
Ipswich, Norwich and Peterborough, D. N. Mee
Leeds, Lincoln and Sheffield, A. P. Dawson
Liverpool, Lancaster and Chester, B. J. Thomas
Llandaff, Bangor, Carmarthen and Gloucester, R. F. Yeldam
Manchester and Nottingham, M. A. Moran
Newcastle, Carlisle, York and Middlesbrough, P. Sanderson
Oxford, R. R. Da Costa
Winchester, A. K. Biggs

OFFICE OF THE JUDGE ADVOCATE OF
THE FLEET
The Law Courts, Barker Road, Maidstone ME16 8EQ
Tel 01622-754966

Judge Advocate of the Fleet (£76,716), His Hon. Judge
Sessions

OFFICE OF THE JUDGE ADVOCATE-
GENERAL OF THE FORCES
(*Joint Service for the Army and the Royal Air Force*)
22 Kingsway, London WC2B 6LE
Tel 0171-305 7910

Judge Advocate-General (£89,123), His Hon. Judge J. W.
Rant, CB, QC
Vice-Judge Advocate-General (£76,716), E. G. Moelwyn-
Hughes
Assistant Judge Advocates-General (£49,400–£57,000), D. M.
Berkson; M. A. Hunter; J. P. Camp; Miss S. E. Woollam;
R. C. C. Seymour; I. H. Pearson; R. G. Chapple; J. F. T.
Bayliss

HIGH COURT AND CROWN COURT
CENTRES

First-tier centres deal with both civil and criminal cases
and are served by High Court and circuit judges. Second-
tier centres deal with criminal cases only and are served
by High Court and circuit judges. Third-tier centres deal
with criminal cases only and are served only by circuit
judges.
  A management structure review of the Court Service is
currently in progress and is likely to result in changes in
the groups within circuits, which would take effect by 1
April 1997.

MIDLAND AND OXFORD CIRCUIT
First-tier – Birmingham, Lincoln, Nottingham, Oxford,
Stafford, Warwick
Second-tier – Leicester, Northampton, Shrewsbury,
Worcester
Third-tier – Coventry, Derby, Grimsby, Hereford,
Peterborough, Stoke-on-Trent, Wolverhampton
Circuit Administrator, R. Stoate, The Priory Courts, 6th
Floor, 33 Bull Street, Birmingham B4 6DW. Tel: 0121-
681 3000
Courts Administrators: Birmingham Group, P. Barton;
Nottingham Group, Mrs E. A. Folman; *Stafford Group*, A. F.
Parker

NORTH-EASTERN CIRCUIT
First-tier – Leeds, Newcastle upon Tyne, Sheffield,
Teesside
Second-tier – Bradford, York
Third-tier – Doncaster, Durham, Kingston-upon-Hull
Circuit Administrator, P. J. Farmer, 17th Floor, West Riding
House, Albion Street, Leeds LS1 5AA. Tel: 0113-251
1200
Courts Administrators: Leeds Group, P. Delany, OBE; *Newcastle
upon Tyne Group*, K. Budgen; *Sheffield Group*, G. Bingham

NORTHERN CIRCUIT
First-tier – Carlisle, Liverpool, Manchester, Preston
Third-tier – Barrow-in-Furness, Bolton, Burnley,
Lancaster
Circuit Administrator, R. A. Vincent, 15 Quay Street,
Manchester M60 9FD. Tel: 0161-833 1005
Courts Administrators: Manchester Group, Mrs A. Prior;
Liverpool Group, D. A. Beaumont; *Preston Group*,
Mrs C. A. Mayer

SOUTH-EASTERN CIRCUIT
First-tier – Chelmsford, Lewes, Norwich
Second-tier – Ipswich, London (Central Criminal Court),
Luton, Maidstone, Reading, St Albans
Third-tier – Aylesbury, Basildon, Brighton, Bury St
Edmunds, Cambridge, Canterbury, Chichester,
Guildford, King's Lynn, London (Croydon, Harrow,
Inner London Sessions House, Isleworth, Kingston
upon Thames, Knightsbridge, Middlesex Guildhall,
Snaresbrook, Southwark, Wood Green, Woolwich),
Southend
Circuit Administrator, J. Brindley, New Cavendish House,
18 Maltravers Street, London WC2R 3EU. Tel: 0171-936
7235
Deputy Circuit Administrator, P. Stockton
Courts Administrators: Chelmsford Group, M. Littlewood;
Maidstone Group, Mrs H. Hartwell; *Kingston Group*,
J. L. Powell; *London Group (Civil)*, D. Marsh; *London
Group (Crime)*, G. F. Addicott

The High Court in Greater London sits at the Royal
Courts of Justice.

WALES AND CHESTER CIRCUIT
First-tier – Caernarfon, Cardiff, Chester, Mold, Swansea
Second-tier – Carmarthen, Merthyr Tydfil, Newport,
Welshpool
Third-tier – Dolgellau, Haverfordwest, Knutsford,
Warrington
Circuit Administrator, V. Grove, Churchill House,
Churchill Way, Cardiff CF1 4HH. Tel: 01222-396925

Courts Administrators: Cardiff Group, A. M. Eshelby; *Chester Group*, T. D. Beckett

WESTERN CIRCUIT

First-tier – Bristol, Exeter, Truro, Winchester
Second-tier – Dorchester, Gloucester, Plymouth, Weymouth
Third-tier – Barnstaple, Bournemouth, Newport (IOW), Portsmouth, Salisbury, Southampton, Swindon, Taunton
Circuit Administrator, R. J. Clark, Bridge House, Clifton Down, Bristol BS8 4BN. Tel: 0117-974 3763
Courts Administrators: Bristol Group, A. C. Butler; *Exeter Group*, J. Ardern; *Winchester Group*, D. Ryan

CIRCUIT JUDGES

*Senior Circuit Judges, each £89,123
Circuit Judges, each £76,716
Style, His/Her Hon. Judge [surname]
Senior Presiding Judge, The Rt. Hon. Lord Justice Auld

MIDLAND AND OXFORD CIRCUIT

Presiding Judges, Hon. Mr Justice Jowitt; Hon. Mr Justice Latham

W. A. L. Allardice; F. A. Allen; Miss C. Alton;
B. J. Appleby, QC; D. P. Bennett; R. S. A. Benson;
I. J. Black, QC; J. G. Boggis, QC; R. W. A. Bray;
D. W. Brunning; J. J. Cavell; F. A. Chapman;
P. N. R. Clark; R. R. B. Cole; T. G. E. Corrie; P. F. Crane;
*P. J. Crawford, QC (*Recorder of Birmingham*);
I. T. R. Davidson, QC; P. N. de Mille; T. M. Dillon, QC;
C. H. Durman; B. A. Farrer, QC; Miss E. N. Fisher;
J. E. Fletcher; A. C. Geddes; R. J. H. Gibbs, QC; V. E. Hall;
J. Hall; D. R. D. Hamilton; S. T. Hammond;
G. C. W. Harris, QC; M. K. Harrison-Hall; M. J. Heath;
C. R. Hodson; J. R. Hopkin; R. H. Hutchinson;
R. P. V. Jenkins; A. W. P. King; M. K. Lee, QC;
D. L. McCarthy; A. W. McCreath; D. D. McEvoy, QC;
M. H. Mander; K. Matthewman, QC; W. D. Matthews;
R. G. May; H. R. Mayor, QC; N. J. Mitchell; P. R. Morrell;
J. I. Morris; A. J. H. Morrison; M. D. Mott; A. J. D. Nicholl;
R. T. N. Orme; R. C. C. O'Rorke; J. F. F. Orrell;
D. S. Perrett, QC; C. J. Pitchers; R. F. D. Pollard;
F. M. Potter; D. P. Pugsley; J. R. Pyke; R. J. Rubery;
J. A. O. Shand; J. R. S. Smyth; D. P. Stanley; P. J. Stretton;
G. C. Styler; H. C. Tayler, QC; A. B. Taylor; M. B. Ward;
D. J. R. Wilcox; H. Wilson; J. W. Wilson;
K. S. W. Wilson Mellor, QC; C. G. Young

NORTH-EASTERN CIRCUIT

Presiding Judges, Hon. Mr Justice Hooper; Hon. Mrs Justice Smith

J. R. S. Adams; J. Altman; T. G. F. Atkinson; T. W. Barber;
J. E. Barry; G. N. Barr Young; R. Bartfield;
D. R. Bentley, QC; P. H. Bowers; A. N. J. Briggs;
D. M. A. Bryant; J. W. M. Bullimore; B. Bush; M. C. Carr;
M. L. Cartlidge; P. J. Charlesworth; P. J. Cockroft;
G. J. K. Coles, QC; J. Crabtree; M. T. Cracknell;
W. H. R. Crawford, QC; Mrs J. Davies; I. J. Dobkin;
E. J. Faulks; P. J. Fox, QC; A. N. Fricker, QC; M. S. Garner;
A. R. Goldsack, QC; R. A. Grant; S. P. Grenfell;
G. F. R. Harkins; P. M. L. Hoffman; R. Hunt;
A. E. Hutchinson, QC; N. H. Jones, QC; G. H. Kamil;
T. D. Kent-Jones, TD; G. M. Lightfoot; R. P. Lowden;
A. G. McCallum; A. C. Macdonald; M. K. Mettyear;
R. J. Moore; A. L. Myerson, QC; D. A. Orde;
Miss H. E. Paling; P. E. Robertshaw; R. M. Scott;
A. Simpson; L. Spittle; J. Stephenson; *R. A. R. Stroyan, QC

(*Recorder of Newcastle upon Tyne*); Mrs L. Sutcliffe;
J. A. Swanson; M. J. Taylor; R. C. Taylor; J. D. G. Walford;
M. Walker; P. H. C. Walker; *B. Walsh, QC;
J. S. Wolstenholme; D. R. Wood

NORTHERN CIRCUIT

Presiding Judge, Hon. Mr Justice Forbes

M. P. Allweis; H. H. Andrew, QC; J. F. Appleton; A. W. Bell;
R. C. W. Bennett; Miss I. Bernstein; M. S. Blackburn;
R. Brown; J. K. Burke, QC; I. B. Campbell; F. B. Carter, QC;
B. I. Caulfield; D. Clark; D. C. Clarke, QC; G. M. Clifton;
I. W. Crompton; *R. E. Davies, QC (*Recorder of Manchester*);
M. Dean, QC; Miss A. E. Downey; B. R. Duckworth;
S. B. Duncan; Miss D. B. Eaglestone; T. K. Earnshaw;
G. A. Ensor; D. M. Evans, QC; S. J. D. Fawcus; P. S. Fish;
J. R. B. Geake; D. S. Gee; W. George; J. A. D. Gilliland, QC;
R. G. Hamilton; J. A. Hammond; F. D. Hart, QC;
M. Hedley; T. B. Hegarty, QC; T. D. T. Hodson;
F. R. B. Holloway; R. C. Holman; N. J. G. Howarth;
G. W. Humphries; C. E. F. James; P. M. Kershaw, QC
(*Commercial Circuit Judge*); H. L. Lachs; P. M. Lakin;
J. M. Lever, QC; R. J. D. Livesey, QC; R. Lockett; D. Lynch;
D. I. Mackay; J. B. Macmillan; D. G. Maddison;
B. C. Maddocks; C. J. Mahon; J. A. Morgan; W. P. Morris;
T. J. Mort; F. D. Owen, TD; R. E. I. Pickering; J. C. Phipps;
D. A. Pirie; A. J. Proctor; J. H. Roberts; Miss G. D. Ruaux;
H. S. Singer; E. Slinger; W. P. Smith; Miss E. M. Steel;
C. B. Tetlow; J. P. Townend; I. J. C. Trigger;
P. W. G. Urquhart; W. R. Wickham (*Recorder of Liverpool*);
K. H. P. Wilkinson; B. Woodward

SOUTH-EASTERN CIRCUIT

Presiding Judges, Hon. Mr Justice Gage; Hon. Mr Justice Wright

M. F. Addison; F. J. Aglionby; A. R. L. Ansell;
S. A. Anwyl, QC; J. A. Baker; J. B. Baker, QC;
M. F. Baker, QC; M. J. D. Baker; A. F. Balston;
G. S. Barham; C. J. A. Barnett, QC; W. E. Barnett, QC;
K. Bassingthwaighte; G. A. Bathurst Norman;
P. J. L. Beaumont, QC; N. E. Beddard; M. G. Binning;
G. J. Binns; J. E. Bishop; B. M. B. Black; H. O. Blacksell,
QC; J. G. Boal, QC; A. V. Bradbury; P. N. Brandt;
L. J. Bromley, QC; A. E. Brooks; R. G. Brown;
J. M. Bull, QC; G. N. Butler, QC; *N. M. Butter, QC;
H. J. Byrt, QC; C. V. Callman; J. Q. Campbell;
B. E. Capstick, QC; M. J. Carroll; B. E. F. Catlin;
B. L. Charles, QC; P. C. L. Clark; P. C. Clegg; S. H. Colgan;
P. H. Collins; C. C. Colston, QC; S. S. Coltart; Viscount
Colville of Culross, QC; J. S. Colyer, QC; C. D. Compston;
T. A. C. Coningsby, QC; J. G. Conner; R. D. Connor;
M. J. Cook; R. A. Cooke; G. H. Coombe; M. R. Coombe;
A. Cooray; P. E. Copley; Dr E. Cotran; P. R. Cowell;
R. C. Cox; J. F. Crocker; D. L. Croft, QC; H. M. Crush;
D. M. Cryan; P. Curl; G. L. Davies; I. H. Davies, TD;
W. L. M. Davies, QC; W. N. Denison, QC (*Common Serjeant*);
J. E. Devaux; M. N. Devonshire, TD; A. E. J. Diamond, QC;
P. H. Downes; W. H. Dunn, QC; A. H. Durrant;
C. M. Edwards; Q. T. Edwards, QC; D. F. Elfer; QC;
D. R. Ellis; C. Elwen; P. F. L. Evans; S. J. Evans;
J. D. Farnworth; P. Fingret; J. J. Finney; P. Ford;
J. J. Fordham; G. C. F. Forrester; Ms D. A. Freedman;
R. Gee; L. Gerber; C. A. H. Gibson;
Miss A. F. Goddard, QC; S. A. Goldstein; P. W. Goldstone;
M. B. Goodman; C. G. M. Gordon; J. B. Gosschalk;
J. H. Gower, QC; M. Graham, QC; B. S. Green, QC;
P. B. Greenwood; D. J. Griffiths; G. D. Grigson;
R. B. Groves, TD, VRD; N. T. Hague, QC;
A. B. R. Hallgarten, QC; Miss G. Hallon; P. J. Halnan;
J. Hamilton; C. R. H. Hardy; B. Hargrove, OBE, QC;

M. F. Harris; R. G. Hawkins, QC; R. J. Haworth; R. M. Hayward; A. H. Head; A. N. Hitching; D. Holden; A. C. W. Hordern, QC; K. A. D. Hornby; R. W. Howe; M. Hucker; Sir David Hughes-Morgan, Bt., CB, CBE; J. G. Hull, QC; M. J. Hyam; D. A. Inman; A. B. Issard-Davies; Dr P. J. E. Jackson; C. P. James; T. J. C. Joseph; S. S. Katkhuda; M. Kennedy, QC; A. M. Kenny; T. R. King; L. G. Krikler; L. H. C. Lait; P. St J. H. Langan, QC; Capt. J. B. R. Langdon, RN; G. F. B. Laughland, QC; R. Laurie; T. Lawrence; D. M. Levy, QC; S. H. Lloyd; F. R. Lockhart; D. B. D. Lowe; Capt. S. Lyons; K. M. McHale; K. A. Machin, QC; K. C. Macrae; T. Maher; B. A. Marder, QC; F. J. M. Marr-Johnson; L. A. Marshall; D. N. N. Martineau; N. A. Medawar, QC; D. B. Meier; D. J. Mellor; G. D. Mercer; D. Q. Miller; F. I. Mitchell; H. M. Morgan; D. Morton Jack; R. T. Moss; Miss M. J. S. Mowat; J. I. Murchie; T. M. E. Nash; Mrs N. F. Negus; M. H. D. Neligan; Mrs M. F. Norrie; Brig. A. P. Norris, OBE; P. W. O'Brien; M. A. Oppenheimer; D. A. Paiba; D. J. Parry; Mrs N. Pearce; Prof. D. S. Pearl; Miss V. A. Pearlman; B. P. Pearson; J. R. Peppitt, QC; F. H. L. Petre; N. A. J. Philpot; D. C. Pitman; J. R. Platt; P. B. Pollock; T. G. Pontius; W. D. C. Poulton; H. C. Pownall, QC; S. Pratt; R. J. C. V. Prendergast; J. E. Prévité, QC; B. H. Pryor, QC; J. E. Pullinger; D. W. Radford; J. W. Rant, QC; E. V. P. Reece; M. P. Reynolds; G. K. Rice; M. S. Rich, QC; N. P. Riddell; G. Rivlin, QC; S. D. Robbins; D. A. H. Rodwell, QC; J. W. Rogers, QC; G. H. Rooke, TD, QC; P. C. R. Rountree; J. H. Rucker; T. R. G. Ryland; R. B. Sanders; A. R. G. Scott-Gall; J. S. Sennitt; J. L. Sessions; J. D. Sheerin; D. R. A. Sich; A. G. Simmons; K. T. Simpson; P. R. Simpson; M. Singh, QC; J. K. E. Slack, TD; S. P. Sleeman; P. M. J. Slot; C. M. Smith, QC; S. A. R. Smith; R. J. Southan; S. B. Spence; W. F. C. Thomas; A. G. Y. Thorpe; A. H. Tibber; C. H. Tilling; J. T. Turner; C. J. M. Tyrer; Mrs A. P. Uziell-Hamilton; J. E. van der Werff; Sir Lawrence Verney, TD (*Recorder of London*); A. O. R. Vick, QC; T. L. Viljoen; Miss M. S. Viner, CBE, QC; R. Wakefield; R. Walker; S. P. Waller; D. B. Watling, QC; V. B. Watts; *F. J. White; S. R. Wilkinson; R. J. Winstanley; E. G. Wintmore; K. H. Zucker, QC

WALES AND CHESTER CIRCUIT

Presiding Judges, Hon. Mr Justice Curtis; Hon. Mr Justice Kay

K. E. Barnett; M. R. Burr; S. P. Clarke; T. R. Crowther, QC; J. T. Curran; Miss J. M. P. Daley; G. H. M. Daniel; Sir Robin David, QC; D. T. A. Davies; J. B. S. Diehl, QC; D. E. H. Edwards; G. O. Edwards; Lord Elystan-Morgan; D. R. Evans, QC; T. M. Evans, QC; J. W. Gaskell; *M. Gibbon, QC; D. R. Halbert; D. J. Hale; D. M. Hughes; G. J. Jones; H. D. H. Jones; G. E. Kilfoil; T. E. I. Lewis-Bowen; C. G. Masterman; D. G. Morgan; D. G. Morris; D. C. Morton; T. H. Moseley; C. P. J. Price, QC; E. J. Prosser, QC; H. E. P. Roberts; S. M. Stephens; H. V. Williams, QC

WESTERN CIRCUIT

Presiding Judges, Hon. Mr Justice Butterfield; Hon. Mr Justice Tuckey

P. T. S. Batterbury; J. F. Beashel; Miss J. A. M. Bonvin; C. L. Boothman; M. J. L. Brodrick; J. M. J. Burford, QC; R. D. H. Bursell; J. R. Chalkley; M. G. Cotterill; G. W. A. Cottle; S. C. Darwall Smith; Mrs S. P. Darwall Smith; Mrs L. H. Davies; *M. Dyer; J. D. Foley; D. L. Griffiths; J. D. Griggs; Mrs C. M. A. Hagen; P. J. C. R. Hooton; G. B. Hutton; R. E. Jack, QC; A. G. H. Jones; T. N. Mackean; Miss S. M. D. McKinney;

I. S. McKintosh; I. G. McLean; J. G. McNaught; T. J. Milligan; J. Neligan; E. G. Neville; S. K. O'Malley; S. K. Overend; R. Price; R. C. Pryor, QC; J. N. P. Rudd; A. Rutherford; Miss A. O. H. Sander; D. H. D. Selwood; R. M. Shawcross; D. A. Smith, QC; W. E. M. Taylor; P. M. Thomas; A. A. R. Thompson, QC; H. J. M. Tucker, QC; D. M. Webster, QC; J. H. Weeks, QC; J. R. Whitley; J. S. Wiggs; J. A. J. Wigmore; J. C. Willis; J. H. Wroath

RECORDERS (each £366 per day)

F. A. Abbott; R. D. I. Adam; J. D. R. Adams; P. C. Ader; R. J. P. Aikens, QC; J. F. Akast; D. J. Ake; R. Akenhead, QC; I. D. G. Alexander, QC; C. D. Allan, QC; C. J. Alldis; J. H. Allen, QC; D. M. Altaras; A. J. Anderson, QC; W. P. Andreae-Jones, QC; P. J. Andrews, QC; R. A. Anelay, QC; M. G. Anthony; Miss L. E. Appleby, QC; J. F. A. Archer, QC; Lord Archer of Sandwell, PC, QC; A. J. Arlidge, QC; E. K. Armitage, QC; P. J. B. Armstrong; G. K. Arran; R. Ashton; J. M. Aspinall, QC; E. G. Aspley; N. J. Atkinson, QC; D. S. Aubrey; M. G. Austin-Smith, QC; M. J. S. Axtell; W. S. Aylen, QC; P. D. Babb; J. F. Badenoch, QC; Miss P. H. Badley; A. B. Baillie; N. R. J. Baker, QC; S. W. Baker; C. G. Ball, QC; P. R. Barclay; A. Barker, QC; B. J. Barker, QC; D. Barker, QC; G. E. Barling, QC; D. N. Barnard; D. M. W. Barnes, QC; H. J. Barnes; T. P. Barnes, QC; A. J. Barnett; R. A. Barratt, QC; R. Bartfield; D. A. Bartlett; G. R. Bartlett, QC; J. C. T. Barton, QC; D. C. Bate, QC; S. D. Batten, QC; P. D. Batty, QC; J. J. Baughan, QC; R. A. Bayliss; D. M. Bean; J. Beatson; C. H. Beaumont; R. V. M. E. Behar; C. O. J. Behrens; R. W. Belben; P. Bennett, QC; P. C. Benson; R. A. Benson, QC; H. L. Bentham, QC; D. M. Berkson; C. R. Berry; M. Bethel, QC; J. P. V. Bevan; C. Beveridge, QC; Mrs C. V. Bevington; N. Bidder; I. G. Bing; P. V. Birkett, QC; M. I. Birnbaum; W. J. Birtles; P. W. Birts, QC; B. G. D. Blair, QC; J. A. Blair-Gould; A. N. H. Blake; P. E. Bleasdale; C. Bloom, QC; D. J. Blunt, QC; O. S. P. Blunt, QC; D. R. L. Bodey, QC; R. H. Bond; G. T. K. Boney, QC; J. J. Boothby; D. J. Boulton; S. N. Bourne-Arton, QC; S. C. Boyd, QC; J. J. Boyle; D. L. Bradshaw; W. T. S. Braithwaite, QC; N. D. Bratza, QC; G. B. Breen; D. J. Brennan; M. L. Brent, QC; G. J. B. G. Brice, QC; J. N. W. Bridges-Adams; A. J. Brigden; P. J. Briggs; D. R. Bright; R. P. Brittain; R. A. Britton; J. Bromley-Davenport; S. C. Brown, QC; D. J. M. Browne, QC; N. Browne; A. J. N. Brunner, QC; R. V. Bryan; A. Bueno, QC; P. E. Bullock; J. P. Burgess; J. P. Burke, QC; H. W. Burnett, QC; R. H. Burns; S. J. Burnton, QC; G. Burrell, QC; M. J. Burton, QC; K. Bush; A. J. Butcher, QC; Miss J. Butler; C. W. Byers; M. D. Byrne; Mrs B. A. Calvert, QC; D. Calvert-Smith; R. Camden Pratt, QC; Miss S. M. C. Cameron, QC; A. N. Campbell, QC; J. M. Caplan, QC; G. M. C. Carey, QC; A. C. Carlile, QC, MP; The Lord Carlisle of Bucklow, PC, QC; H. B. H. Carlisle, QC; J. J. Carter-Manning, QC; R. Carus, QC; Mrs J. R. Case; P. D. Cattan; Miss M. T. Catterson; J. A. Chadwin, QC; N. M. Chambers, QC; Miss D. C. Champion; V. R. Chapman; J. M. Cherry, QC; J. R. Cherryman, QC; C. F. Chruszcz, QC; C. H. Clark, QC; C. S. C. S. Clarke, QC; P. W. Clarke; P. R. J. Clarkson, QC; T. Clayson; A. S. L. Cleary; W. Clegg, QC; T. A. Clover; M. F. Coates; Miss S. Coates; W. P. Coates; D. J. Cocks, QC; J. J. Coffey, QC; T. A. Coghlan, QC; W. J. Coker, QC; J. R. Cole; A. J. S. Coleman; N. J. Coleman; P. J. D. Coleridge, QC; N. B. C. Coles, QC;

A. R. Collender, QC; P. N. Collier, QC; J. M. Collins;
I. Collis; Ms M. Colton; Mrs J. R. Comyns; G. D. Conlin;
C. S. Cook; K. B. Coonan, QC; A. E. M. Cooper;
Miss B. P. Cooper, QC; P. J. Cooper, QC;
Miss S. M. Corkhill; C. J. Cornwall; P. J. Cosgrove, QC;
Miss D. R. Cotton, QC; J. S. Coward, QC;
Mrs L. M. Cox, QC; P. Crampin, QC; N. Crichton;
D. I. Crigman, QC; M. L. S. Cripps; C. A. Critchlow;
D. R. Crome; Mrs J. Crowley; J. D. Crowley, QC;
W. R. H. Crowther, QC; T. S. Culver;
Miss E. A. M. Curnow, QC; P. D. Curran;
J. W. O. Curtis, QC; M. J. Curwen; K. C. Cutler;
A. J. G. Dalziel; Mrs P. M. T. Dangor; P. M. Darlow;
A. M. Darroch; G. W. Davey; C. P. M. Davidson;
A. R. M. Davies; J. T. L. Davies; R. L. Davies, QC;
W. E. Davis; A. W. Dawson; D. H. Day, QC; J. J. Deave;
J. B. Deby, QC; P. G. Dedman; Mrs P. A. Deeley;
C. F. Dehn, QC; P. A. de la Piquerie; M. A. de Navarro, QC;
R. L. Denyer, QC; S. C. Desch, QC; H. A. D. de Silva;
P. N. Digney; C. E. Dines; A. D. Dinkin, QC; D. R. Dobbin;
P. Dodgson; R. A. M. Doggett; Ms B. Dohmann, QC;
D. T. Donaldson, QC; A. M. Donne, QC; A. F. S. Donovan;
A. K. Dooley; J. Dowse; S. M. Duffield; P. R. Dunkels, QC;
J. D. Durham Hall, QC; R. T. Dutton; J. M. Dyson;
D. Eady, QC; H. W. P. Eccles, QC; C. N. Edelman, QC;
A. H. Edwards; Miss S. M. Edwards, QC; G. Elias, QC;
E. A. Elliott; R. C. Elly; J. A. Elvidge; R. M. Englehart, QC;
T. M. English; D. A. Evans, QC; D. H. Evans, QC;
F. W. H. Evans; G. W. R. Evans, QC; M. Evans, QC;
M. J. Evans; M. A. Everall, QC; Sir Graham Eyre, QC;
T. M. Faber; W. D. Fairclough; R. B. Farley, QC;
P. M. Farmer, QC; D. J. Farrer, QC; P. E. Feinberg, QC;
R. Fernyhough, QC; M. C. Field; J. E. Finestein;
J. E. P. Finnigan; D. T. Fish; D. P. Fisher, QC;
G. D. Flather, CBE, QC; P. E. J. Focke, QC;
R. A. Fordham, QC; A. J. Forrest; M. D. P. Fortune;
D. R. Foskett, QC; J. R. Foster, QC; Miss R. M. Foster;
J. H. Fryer-Spedding, OBE; M. Furness; M. Gale, QC;
C. J. E. Gardner, QC; C. R. Garside, QC; R. C. Gaskell;
S. A. G. L. Gault; A. H. Gee, QC; I. W. Geering, QC;
D. S. Geey; D. C. Gerrey; J. S. Gibbons, QC;
A. J. Gilbart; F. H. S. Gilbert, QC; N. J. Gilchrist;
K. Gillance; N. B. D. Gilmour, QC; L. Giovene;
A. T. Glass, QC; H. B. Globe, QC; Miss E. Gloster, QC;
H. K. Goddard, QC; H. A. Godfrey, QC;
Ms L. S. Godfrey, QC; J. J. Goldberg, QC;
J. B. Goldring, QC; P. H. Goldsmith, QC;
L. C. Goldstone, QC; I. F. Goldsworthy, QC;
A. J. J. Gompertz, QC; A. A. Gordon; J. R. W. Goss;
T. J. C. Goudie, QC; A. A. Goymer; G. Gozem;
A. S. Grabiner, QC; C. A. St J. Gray, QC; G. Gray, QC;
H. Green, QC; Miss J. E. G. Greenberg, QC;
A. E. Greenwood; J. C. Greenwood; J. G. Grenfell, QC;
R. D. Grey, QC; R. H. Griffith-Jones; J. P. G. Griffiths, QC;
M. G. Grills; M. S. E. Grime, QC; P. Grobel;
P. H. Gross, QC; M. A. W. Grundy; S. J. Gullick;
A. S. Hacking, QC; M. F. Haigh; J. W. Haines; N. J. Hall;
S. J. Hall; J. P. N. Hallam; D. T. Hallchurch;
Miss H. C. Hallett, QC; G. M. Hamilton, TD, QC;
I. M. Hamilton; Miss S. Hamilton, QC; P. L. Hamlin;
J. Hampton; J. L. Hand, QC; Miss R. S. A. Hare, QC;
R. D. Harman, QC; G. T. Harrap; P. J. Harrington, QC;
D. M. Harris, QC; R. D. Harrison; R. M. Harrison, QC;
H. M. Harrod; J. M. Harrow; C. P. Hart-Leverton, QC;
B. Harvey; C. S. Harvey, MBE, TD; J. G. Harvey;
M. L. T. Harvey, QC; D. W. Hatton, QC;
T. S. A. Hawkesworth, QC; W. G. Hawkesworth;
J. M. Haworth; R. W. P. Hay; Prof. D. J. Hayton;
Miss J. E. Hayward; R. Hayward-Smith, QC;
A. T. Hedworth, QC; G. E. Heggs; R. A. Henderson, QC;

R. H. Q. Henriques, QC; M. J. Henshell;
P. J. M. Heppel, QC; R. C. Herman; M. S. Heslop QC;
T. Hewitt; B. J. Higgs, QC; E. M. Hill, QC; J. W. Hillyer;
A. J. H. Hilton, QC; Ms E. J. Hindley, QC; W. T. J. Hirst;
J. D. Hitchen; S. A. Hockman, QC; A. J. C. Hoggett, QC;
D. A. Hollis, VRD, QC; C. J. Holmes; J. F. Holt; R. M. Hone;
A. T. Hoolahan, QC; A. D. Hope; S. Hopkins;
M. A. P. Hopmeier; M. Horowitz, QC; Miss R. Horwood-Smart;
C. P. Hotten, QC; B. F. Houlder, QC;
M. N. Howard, QC; C. I. Howells; M. J. Hubbard, QC;
A. P. G. Hughes, QC; Mrs H. M. Hughes; Miss
J. C. A. Hughes, QC; P. T. Hughes, QC; R. P. Hughes;
T. M. Hughes; J. Hugill, QC; L. D. Hull;
W. G. B. Hungerford; D. P. Hunt; D. R. N. Hunt, QC;
P. J. Hunt, QC; I. G. A. Hunter, QC; M. Hussain, QC;
J. G. K. Hyland; B. A. Hytner, QC; R. A. G. Inglis;
P. R. Isaacs; S. Jack; D. G. A. Jackson; M. R. Jackson;
R. M. Jackson, QC; I. E. Jacob; P. J. Jacobs;
N. F. B. Jarman, QC; J. M. Jarvis, QC; J. R. Jarvis;
A. H. Jeffreys; D. A. Jeffreys, QC; J. Jeffs, QC;
J. D. Jenkins; D. B. Johnson, QC; D. A. F. Jones;
D. L. Jones; N. G. Jones; R. A. Jones; S. E. Jones, QC;
T. G. Jones; W. H. Joss; H. M. Joy; P. S. L. Joyce, QC;
R. W. S. Juckes; M. D. L. Kalisher, QC; M. L. Kallipetis, QC;
I. G. F. Karsten, QC; R. G. Kaye, QC; C. B. Kealy;
M. L. Keane; K. R. Keen, QC; B. R. Keith, QC; C. L. Kelly;
C. J. B. Kemp; D. Kennett Brown; D. M. Kerr;
L. D. Kershen, QC; M. I. Khan; G. M. Khayat, QC;
R. I. Kidwell, QC; T. R. A. King, QC; W. M. Kingston, QC;
R. C. Klevan, QC; B. J. Knight, QC; M. S. Knott;
Miss P. E. Knowles; C. Knox; Miss J. C. M. Korner, QC;
S. E. Kramer, QC; Miss L. J. Kushner, QC; P. E. Kyte, QC;
L. P. Laity; C. A. Lamb; N. R. W. Lambert; D. A. Landau;
D. G. Lane, QC; T. J. Langdale, QC; B. F. J. Langstaff, QC;
D. H. Latham; R. B. Latham, QC; S. W. Lawler, QC;
Sir Ivan Lawrence, QC, MP; M. H. Lawson, QC;
G. S. Lawson-Rogers, QC; P. L. O. Leaver, QC;
D. Lederman, QC; B. W. T. Leech; I. Leeming, QC;
C. H. de V. Leigh, QC; Sir Godfrey Le Quesne, QC;
H. B. G. Lett; B. L. Lever; B. H. Leveson, QC; S. Levine;
A. E. Levy, QC; M. E. Lewer, QC; A. K. Lewis, QC;
B. W. Lewis; M. ap G. Lewis, QC; R. S. Lewis;
C. C. D. Lindsay, QC; S. J. Linehan, QC; J. S. Lipton;
B. J. E. Livesey, QC; C. G. Llewellyn-Jones, QC;
C. J. Lockhart-Mummery, QC; A. J. C. Lodge, QC;
T. Longbotham; D. C. Lovell-Pank, QC; G. W. Lowe;
N. H. Lowe; J. A. M. Lowen; G. W. Lowther; F. D. L. Loy;
Mrs C. M. Ludlow; E. Lyons, QC; R. G. B. McCombe, QC;
A. G. McDowall; A. G. MacDuff, QC; K. M. P. Macgill;
C. I. McGonigal; R. J. McGregor-Johnson;
R. D. Machell, QC; J. V. Machin; B. M. McIntyre;
C. C. Mackay, QC; D. L. Mackie; R. G. McKinnon;
W. N. McKinnon; N. A. McKittrick; I. A. B. McLaren, QC;
I. McLeod; N. R. B. Macleod; N. J. C. McLusky;
A. G. Mainds; A. H. R. Maitland; A. R. Malcolm;
H. J. Malins; M. E. Mann, QC; The Hon. G. R. J. Mansfield;
A. C. B. Markham-David; R. L. Marks; A. S. Marron, QC;
P. Marsh; R. G. Marshall-Andrews; G. C. Marson;
H. R. A. Martineau; C. P. Mather; D. Matheson, QC;
P. R. Matthews; Mrs S. P. Matthews, QC;
P. B. Mauleverer, QC; R. B. Mawrey, QC; J. F. M. Maxwell;
R. Maxwell, QC; Mrs P. R. May; M. Meggeson;
N. F. Merriman, QC; C. S. J. Metcalf; J. T. Milford, QC;
K. S. H. Miller; R. A. Miller; S. M. Miller, QC;
J. B. M. Milmo, QC; D. C. Milne, QC; Miss C. M. Miskin;
Miss A. E. Mitchell; A. P. Mitchell; C. R. Mitchell;
D. C. Mitchell; J. R. Mitchell; J. E. Mitting, QC; F. R. Moat;
E. G. Moelwyn-Hughes; C. R. D. Moger, QC;
D. R. P. Mole, QC; H. J. Montlake; M. G. C. Moorhouse;
D. W. Morgan; G. E. Moriarty, QC; A. P. Morris, QC; The

Rt. Hon. J. Morris, QC, MP; C. Morris-Coole;
C. J. Moss, QC; P. C. Mott, QC; R. W. Moxon-Browne, QC;
J. H. Muir; F. J. Muller, QC; G. S. Murdoch, QC;
I. P. Murphy, QC; M. J. A. Murphy, QC; N. O. G. Murray;
N. J. Mylne, QC; H. G. Narayan; D. E. Neuberger, QC;
R. E. Newbold; A. R. H. Newman, QC; G. Nice, QC;
C. A. A. Nicholls, QC; C. V. Nicholls, QC; A. S. T. E. Nicol;
A. E. R. Noble; B. Nolan, QC; M. C. Norman; J. M. Norris;
P. H. Norris; J. G. Nutting, QC; D. P. O'Brien, QC;
E. M. Ogden, QC; Mrs F. M. Oldham, QC; S. Oliver-
Jones, QC; R. W. Onions; C. P. L. Openshaw, QC;
M. N. O'Sullivan; D. B. W. Ouseley, QC; R. M. Owen, QC;
T. W. Owen; N. D. Padfield, QC; S. R. Page;
D. C. J. Paget, QC; A. O. Palmer, QC; A. W. Palmer, QC;
D. P. Pannick, QC; A. D. W. Pardoe, QC; S. A. B. Parish;
G. C. Parkins, QC; G. E. Parkinson; M. P. Parroy, QC;
D. J. Parry; E. O. Parry; M. A. Parry Evans;
N. S. K. Pascoe, QC; A. Patience, QC; J. G. Paulusz;
W. E. Pawlak; R. J. Pearse Wheatley; J. V. Pegden;
D. H. Penry-Davey, QC; J. Perry, QC; M. Pert, QC;
B. J. Phelvin; J. A. Phillips; W. B. Phillips;
M. A. Pickering, QC; T. O. Pillay; C. J. Pitchford, QC;
The Hon. B. M. D. Pitt; Miss E. F. Platt, QC; R. Platts;
J. R. Playford, QC; A. G. S. Pollock, QC; A. R. Porten, QC;
L. R. Portnoy; Mrs M. Poulet, QC; T. W. Preston, QC;
D. Price; G. A. L. Price, QC; J. A. Price, QC; J. C. Price;
N. P. L. Price, QC; H. W. Prosser; A. C. Pugh, QC;
G. V. Pugh, QC; G. F. Pulman, QC; C. P. B. Purchas, QC;
R. M. Purchas, QC; N. R. Purnell, QC; P. O. Purnell, QC;
Q. C. W. Querelle; D. A. Radcliffe; Mrs N. P. Radford, QC;
Ms A. J. Rafferty, QC; T. W. H. Raggatt, QC; A. Rankin, QC;
A. D. Rawley, QC; P. R. Raynor, QC; L. F. Read, QC;
J. H. Reddihough; A. R. F. Redgrave; J. Reeder, QC;
P. Rees; C. E. Reese, QC; J. R. Reid, QC; P. C. Reid;
P. C. Rhodes; R. E. Rhodes, QC; D. G. Rice; D. W. Richards;
S. P. Richards; H. A. Richardson; S. V. Riordan, QC;
G. Risius; Miss J. H. Ritchie, QC; M. W. Roach;
J. A. Roberts, QC; J. M. Roberts; J. M. G. Roberts, QC;
A. J. Robertson; V. Robinson, QC; D. E. H. Robson, QC;
G. W. Roddick, QC; Miss D. J. Rodgers;
J. M. T. Rogers, QC; P. F. G. Rook, QC; W. M. Rose;
J. G. Ross; J. G. Ross Martyn; P. C. Rouch; J. J. Rowe, QC;
R. J. Royce, QC; M. W. Rudland; A. A. Rumbelow, QC;
N. J. Rumfitt, QC; R. J. Rundell; R. R. Russell;
G. C. Ryan, QC; J. R. T. Rylance; C. R. A. Sallon, QC;
C. N. Salmon; D. A. Salter; J. E. A. Samuels, QC;
A. T. Sander; G. R. Sankey, QC; N. L. Sarony;
J. H. B. Saunders, QC; M. P. Sayers, QC; R. J. Scholes, QC;
Miss P. Scriven, QC; R. J. Seabrook, QC; C. Seagroatt, QC;
M. R. Selfe; W. P. L. Sellick; O. M. Sells, QC; D. Serota, QC;
R. W. Seymour; A. J. Seys-Llewellyn; A. R. F. Sharp;
P. P. Shears; S. J. Sher, QC; Miss J. Shipley;
J. M. Shorrock, QC; S. R. Silber, QC; P. R. Singer, QC;
J. C. N. Slater, QC; A. C. Smith; A. C. Smith, QC;
A. T. Smith, QC; R. D. H. Smith, QC; R. S. Smith, QC;
Ms Z. P. Smith; C. J. Smyth; S. M. Solley, QC; R. F. Solman;
E. Somerset Jones, QC; R. C. Southwell, QC,
R. C. E. Southwell; M. H. Spence, QC; J. Spencer, QC;
M. G. Spencer; S. M. Spencer, QC;
R. V. Spencer Bernard; D. P. Spens; R. W. Spon-Smith;
D. W. Steel, QC; D. Steer, QC; M. T. Steiger, QC;
D. H. Stembridge, QC; Mrs L. J. Stern, QC;
A. W. Stevenson, TD; J. S. H. Stewart, QC;
R. M. Stewart, QC; W. R. Stewart Smith; A. C. Steynor;
G. J. C. Still; D. A. Stockdale, QC; D. M. A. Stokes, QC;
M. G. T. Stokes, QC; E. D. R. Stone, QC; J. B. Storey, QC;
P. L. Storr; T. M. F. Stow, QC; D. M. A. Strachan, QC;
M. Stuart-Moore, QC; F. R. C. Such; A. B. Suckling, QC;
J. M. Sullivan, QC; Ms L. E. Sullivan, QC; D. M. Sumner;
J. P. C. Sumption, QC; M. A. Supperstone, QC; P. J. Susman;

R. P. Sutton, QC; C. J. Sutton-Mattocks;
Miss C. J. Swift, QC; D. R. Swift; L. Swift, QC;
M. R. Swift, QC; Miss H. H. Swindells, QC;
C. J. M. Symons, QC; J. P. Tabor, QC; J. A. Tackaberry, QC;
R. K. K. Talbot; R. B. Tansey, QC; G. F. Tattersall, QC;
E. Taylor; J. J. Teare; R. H. Tedd, QC; A. D. Temple, QC;
V. B. A. Temple, QC; M. H. Tennant;
D. M. Thomas, OBE, QC; D. O. Thomas, QC; P. A. Thomas;
R. L. Thomas, QC; R. M. Thomas; R. U. Thomas, QC;
P. J. Thompson; D. K. Ticehurst, QC; A. C. Tickle;
J. Tiley; M. B. Tillett, QC; J. W. Tinnion;
R. N. Titheridge, QC; S. M. Tomlinson, QC;
R. S. W. Tonking; J. K. Toulmin, CMG, QC;
J. B. S. Townend, QC; C. M. Treacy, QC; H. B. Trethowan;
A. D. H. Trollope, QC; M. G. Tugendhat, QC;
H. W. Turcan; D. A. Turner, QC; P. A. Twigg, QC;
A. R. Tyrrell, QC; N. E. Underhill, QC; J. G. G. Ungley;
N. P. Valios, QC; N. C. van der Bijl; A. R. Vandermeer, QC;
D. A. J. Vaughan, QC; M. J. D. Vere-Hodge, QC;
J. P. Wadsworth, QC; S. P. Waine; J. J. Wait; Miss
A. P. Wakefield; R. M. Wakerley, QC; W. H. Waldron, QC;
Mrs E. A. Walker; R. A. Walker, QC; R. J. Walker, QC;
T. E. Walker, QC; Sir Jonah Walker-Smith, Bt.;
T. M. Walsh; C. T. Walton; J. J. Wardlow; J. C. Warner;
J. Warren, QC; N. J. Warren; D. E. B. Waters; Sir James
Watson, Bt.; B. J. Waylen; A. R. Webb; R. S. Webb, QC;
A. S. Webster, QC; M. Weisman; P. Weitzman, QC;
C. S. Welchman; C. P. C. Whelon; G. Whitburn, QC;
C. H. Whitby; G. B. N. White; W. J. M. White;
D. R. B. Whitehouse, QC; R. P. Whitehurst;
P. G. Whiteman, QC; P. J. M. Whiteman, TD;
A. Whitfield, QC; D. G. Widdicombe, QC; C. T. Wide, QC;
R. Wigglesworth; A. D. F. Wilcken; A. F. Wilkie, QC;
N. V. M. Wilkinson; Miss E. Willers;
G. H. G. Williams, QC; The Lord Williams of Mostyn, QC;
Miss J. A. Williams, QC; J. G. Williams, QC; J. L. Williams, QC;
M. J. Williams; W. L. Williams, QC;
Miss H. E. Williamson, QC; S. W. Williamson, QC;
A. J. D. Wilson, QC; A. M. Wilson, QC; C. Wilson-
Smith, QC; G. W. Wingate-Saul, QC; M. E. Wolff;
H. Wolton, QC; D. A. Wood, QC; N. A. Wood; W. R. Wood;
L. G. Woodley, QC; Miss S. Woodley; J. T. Woods;
W. C. Woodward, QC; N. G. Wootton; T. H. Workman;
Miss A. M. Worrall, QC; D. Worsley; P. F. Worsley, QC;
J. J. Wright; M. P. Yelton; D. E. M. Young, QC

STIPENDIARY MAGISTRATES

PROVINCIAL (each £62,621)

Cheshire, P. K. Dodd, OBE, *apptd* 1991
Devon, P. H. Wassall, *apptd* 1994
East and West Sussex, P. C. Tain, *apptd* 1992
Essex, K. A. Gray, *apptd* 1995
Greater Manchester, W. D. Fairclough, *apptd* 1982;
    Miss J. E. Hayward, *apptd* 1991; A. Berg, *apptd* 1994;
    C. R. Darnton, *apptd* 1994
Hampshire, T. G. Cowling, *apptd* 1989
Humberside, N. H. White, *apptd* 1985
Lancashire/Merseyside, J. Finestein, *apptd* 1992
Leicestershire, D. M. Meredith, *apptd* 1995
Merseyside, D. R. G. Tapp, *apptd* 1992; P. S. Ward, *apptd*
    1994; P. J. Firth, *apptd* 1994
Middlesex, N. A. McKittrick, *apptd* 1989; S. N. Day, *apptd*
    1991
Mid Glamorgan, Miss P. J. Watkins, *apptd* 1995
Norfolk, N. P. Heley, *apptd* 1994
North-East London, G. E. Cawdron, *apptd* 1993

Nottinghamshire, P. F. Nuttall, *apptd* 1991; M. L. R. Harris, *apptd* 1991
Shropshire, P. H. R. Browning, *apptd* 1994
South Glamorgan, G. R. Watkins, *apptd* 1993
South Yorkshire, J. A. Browne, *apptd* 1992; W. D. Thomas, *apptd* 1989; M. A. Rosenberg, *apptd* 1993; P. H. F. Jones, *apptd* 1995; Mrs S. E. Driver, *apptd* 1995
Staffordshire, P. G. G. Richards, *apptd* 1991
West Midlands, W. M. Probert, *apptd* 1983; B. Morgan, *apptd* 1989; I. Gillespie, *apptd* 1991; M. F. James, *apptd* 1991; C. M. McColl, *apptd* 1994
West Yorkshire, F. D. L. Loy, *apptd* 1972; Mrs P. A. Hewitt, *apptd* 1990; G. A. K. Hodgson, *apptd* 1993

METROPOLITAN

Chief Metropolitan Stipendiary Magistrate and Chairman of Magistrates' Courts Committee for Inner London Area (£76,716), P. G. N. Badge, *apptd* 1992 (*Bow Street*)

Magistrates (each £62,621)

Bow Street, The Chief Magistrate; R. D. Bartle, *apptd* 1972; H. N. Evans, *apptd* 1990; P. A. M. Clark, *apptd* 1996
Camberwell Green, C. P. M. Davidson, *apptd* 1984; H. Gott, *apptd* 1992; Miss E. Roscoe, *apptd* 1994; R. House, *apptd* 1995; Miss C. S. R. Tubbs, *apptd* 1996
Clerkenwell, M. L. R. Romer, *apptd* 1972; C. J. Bourke, *apptd* 1972; B. Loosley, *apptd* 1989
Family Proceedings and Youth Courts, London NW1, G. Wicks, *apptd* 1987; N. Crichton, *apptd* 1987
Greenwich and Woolwich, D. A. Cooper, *apptd* 1991; P. S. Wallis, *apptd* 1993; H. Riddle, *apptd* 1995
Highbury Corner, Miss D. Quick, *apptd* 1986; A. T. Evans, *apptd* 1990; D. Simpson, *apptd* 1993
Horseferry Road, G. Parkinson, *apptd* 1982; A. R. Davies, *apptd* 1985; G. Breen, *apptd* 1986; Mrs K. R. Keating, *apptd* 1987
Marlborough Street, T. H. Workman, *apptd* 1986; Miss D. Wickham, *apptd* 1989
Marylebone, D. Kennett-Brown, *apptd* 1982; K. Maitland-Davies, *apptd* 1984; A. C. Baldwin, *apptd* 1990; C. Pratt, *apptd* 1990
Old Street, M. A. Johnstone, *apptd* 1980; Mrs L. Morgan, *apptd* 1995
South-Western, S. G. Clixby, *apptd* 1981; C. D. Voelcker, *apptd* 1982; A. Ormerod, *apptd* 1988
Thames, I. Bing, *apptd* 1989; W. A. Kennedy, *apptd* 1991; M. J. Read, *apptd* 1993; S. Dawson, *apptd* 1994
Tower Bridge, Mrs J. R. Comyns, *apptd* 1982; R. D. Philips, *apptd* 1989; M. Kelly, *apptd* 1992
Wells Street, Miss A. M. Jennings, *apptd* 1972; Ms G. Babington-Browne, *apptd* 1991
West London, T. English, *apptd* 1986; D. Thomas, *apptd* 1990
Unattached Magistrates, C. S. F. Black, *apptd* 1993; I. M. Baker, *apptd* 1990; Mrs E. Rees, *apptd* 1994; S. Somjee, *apptd* 1995; J. B. Coleman, *apptd* 1995; Miss D. Lachhar, *apptd* 1996

MAGISTRATES' COURTS COMMITTEE FOR THE INNER LONDON AREA
65 Romney Street, London SW1P 3RD
Tel 0171-799 3332
Justices' Chief Executive and Clerk to the Committee (*£80,000), Miss C. Glenn
Justices' Clerk (Training) (£*48,971), Miss A. F. Damazer

* 1995–6 figure

CROWN PROSECUTION SERVICE
50 Ludgate Hill, London EC4M 7EX
Tel 0171-273 8000

The Crown Prosecution Service (CPS) is responsible for the independent review and conduct of criminal proceedings instituted by police forces in England and Wales, with the exception of cases conducted by the Serious Fraud Office (*see* page 344) and certain minor offences.

The Director of Public Prosecutions is the head of the Service and discharges her statutory functions under the superintendence of the Attorney-General.

The Service comprises a headquarters office and 14 Areas covering England and Wales. Each of the CPS Areas is supervised by a Chief Crown Prosecutor.

For salary information, *see* page 277

Director of Public Prosecutions (G1), Mrs B. Mills, QC
Director of Corporate Services (G3), D. Nooney
Director of Casework Evaluation (G3), C. Newell
Director of Casework Services (G3), G. Duff

CPS AREAS

CPS ANGLIA, Queen's House, 58 Victoria Street, St Albans AL1 3HZ. Tel: 01727-818100. *Chief Crown Prosecutor (G4)*, R. J. Chronnell
CPS CENTRAL CASEWORK, 50 Ludgate Hill, London EC4M 7EX. Tel: 0171-273 8000. *Chief Crown Prosecutor (G4)*, D. Kyle
CPS EAST MIDLANDS, 2 King Edward Court, King Edward Street, Nottingham NG1 1EL. Tel: 0115-948 0480 *Chief Crown Prosecutor (G4)*, B. T. McArdle
CPS HUMBER, Greenfield House, Scotland Street, Sheffield S3 7DQ. Tel: 0114-291 2164. *Chief Crown Prosecutor (G4)*, D. Adams, CBE
CPS LONDON, Portland House, Stag Place, London SW1E 5BH. Tel: 0171-915 5700. *Chief Crown Prosecutor (G3)*, G. D. Etherington
CPS MERSEY/LANCASHIRE, 7th Floor (South), Royal Liver Building, Pier Head, Liverpool L3 1HN. Tel: 0151-236 7575. *Chief Crown Prosecutor (G4)*, G. Brown
CPS MIDLANDS, 14th Floor, Colmore Gate, 2 Colmore Row, Birmingham B3 2QA. Tel: 0121-629 7202. *Chief Crown Prosecutor (G4)*, D. Blundell
CPS NORTH, Wellbar House, Gallowgate, Newcastle upon Tyne NE1 4TX. Tel: 0191-261 1858. *Chief Crown Prosecutor (G4)*, M. Graham
CPS NORTH-WEST, PO Box 377, 8th Floor, Sunlight House, Quay Street, Manchester M60 3LU. Tel: 0161-83 7402. *Chief Crown Prosecutor (G4)*, A. R. Taylor
CPS SEVERN/THAMES, Artillery House, Heritage Way, Droitwich, Worcester WR9 8YB. Tel: 01905-793763. *Chief Crown Prosecutor (G4)*, N. Franklin
CPS SOUTH-EAST, 1 Onslow Street, Guildford, Surrey GU1 4YA. Tel: 01483-882600. *Chief Crown Prosecutor (G4)*, C. Nicholls
CPS SOUTH-WEST, 8 Kew Court, Pynes Hill, Rydon Lane, Exeter EX2 5SS. Tel: 01392-445422. *Chief Crown Prosecutor (G4)*, P. Boeuf
CPS WALES, Tudor House, 16 Cathedral Road, Cardiff CF1 9LJ. Tel: 01222-783000. *Chief Crown Prosecutor (G4)*, R. A. Prickett
CPS YORKSHIRE, 6th Floor, Ryedale Building, 60 Piccadilly, York YO1 1NS. Tel: 01904-610726. *Chief Crown Prosecutor (G4)*, D. V. Dickenson

The Scottish Judicature

Scotland has a legal system separate from and differing greatly from the English legal system in enacted law, judicial procedure and the structure of courts.

In Scotland the system of public prosecution is headed by the Lord Advocate and is independent of the police, who have no say in the decision to prosecute. The Lord Advocate, discharging his functions through the Crown Office in Edinburgh, is responsible for prosecutions in the High Court, sheriff courts and district courts. Prosecutions in the High Court are prepared by the Crown Office and conducted in court by one of the law officers, by an advocate-depute, or by a solicitor advocate. In the inferior courts the decision to prosecute is made and prosecution is preferred by procurators fiscal, who are lawyers and full-time civil servants subject to the directions of the Crown Office. A permanent legally-qualified civil servant known as the Crown Agent is responsible for the running of the Crown Office and the organization of the Procurator Fiscal Service, of which he is the head.

Scotland is divided into six sheriffdoms, each with a full-time Sheriff Principal. The sheriffdoms are further divided into sheriff court districts, each of which has a legally-qualified, resident sheriff or sheriffs, who are the judges of the court.

In criminal cases sheriffs principal and sheriffs have the same powers; sitting with a jury of 15 members, they may try more serious cases on indictment, or, sitting alone, may try lesser cases under summary procedure. Minor summary offences are dealt with in district courts which are administered by the district and the islands local government authorities and presided over by lay justices of the peace (of whom there are about 4,200) and, in Glasgow only, by stipendiary magistrates. Juvenile offenders (children under 16) may be brought before an informal children's hearing comprising three local lay people. The superior criminal court is the High Court of Justiciary which is both a trial and an appeal court. Cases on indictment are tried by a High Court judge, sitting with a jury of 15, in Edinburgh and on circuit in other towns. Appeals from the lower courts against conviction or sentence are heard also by the High Court, which sits as an appeal court only in Edinburgh. There is no further appeal to the House of Lords in criminal cases.

In civil cases the jurisdiction of the sheriff court extends to most kinds of action. Appeal against decisions of the sheriff may be made to the Sheriff Principal and thence to the Court of Session, or direct to the Court of Session, which sits only in Edinburgh. The Court of Session is divided into the Inner and the Outer House. The Outer House is a court of first instance in which cases are heard by judges sitting singly, sometimes with a jury of 12. The Inner House, itself subdivided into two divisions of equal status, is mainly an appeal court. Appeals may be made to the Inner House from the Outer House as well as from the sheriff court. An appeal may be made from the Inner House to the House of Lords.

The judges of the Court of Session are the same as those of the High Court of Justiciary, the Lord President of the Court of Session also holding the office of Lord Justice General in the High Court. Senators of the College of Justice are Lords Commissioners of Justiciary as well as judges of the Court of Session. On appointment, a Senator takes a judicial title, which is retained for life. Although styled 'The Hon./Rt. Hon. Lord —', the Senator is not a peer.

The office of coroner does not exist in Scotland. The local procurator fiscal inquires privately into sudden or suspicious deaths and may report findings to the Crown Agent. In some cases a fatal accident inquiry may be held before the sheriff.

COURT OF SESSION AND HIGH COURT OF JUSTICIARY

The Lord President and Lord Justice General (£122,231)
The Rt. Hon. the Lord Rodger of Earlsferry, *born* 1944, *apptd* 1996
Secretary, Mrs M. Small

INNER HOUSE

Lords of Session (each £117,190)

FIRST DIVISION
The Lord President
Hon. Lord Sutherland (Ranald Sutherland), *born* 1932, *apptd* 1985
Hon. Lord Cullen (William Cullen), *born* 1935, *apptd* 1986

SECOND DIVISION
Lord Justice Clerk (£121,190), The Rt. Hon. Lord Ross (Donald Ross), *born* 1927, *apptd* 1985
Rt. Hon. The Lord McCluskey, *born* 1929, *apptd* 1984
Hon. Lord Morison (Alastair Morison), *born* 1931, *apptd* 1985
Hon. Lord Weir (Bruce Weir), *born* 1931, *apptd* 1985

OUTER HOUSE

Lords of Session (each £104,431)

Hon. Lord Prosser (William Prosser), *born* 1934, *apptd* 1986
Hon. Lord Kirkwood (Ian Kirkwood), *born* 1932, *apptd* 1987
Hon. Lord Coulsfield (John Cameron), *born* 1934, *apptd* 1987
Hon. Lord Milligan (James Milligan), *born* 1934, *apptd* 1988
Hon. Lord Caplan (Philip Caplan), *born* 1929, *apptd* 1989
Rt. Hon. The Lord Cameron of Lochbroom, *born* 1931, *apptd* 1989
Hon. Lord Marnoch (Michael Bruce), *born* 1938, *apptd* 1990
Hon. Lord MacLean (Ranald MacLean), *born* 1938, *apptd* 1990
Hon. Lord Penrose (George Penrose), *born* 1938, *apptd* 1990
Hon. Lord Osborne (Kenneth Osborne), *born* 1937, *apptd* 1990
Hon. Lord Abernethy (Alistair Cameron), *born* 1938, *apptd* 1992
Hon. Lord Johnston (Alan Johnston), *born* 1942, *apptd* 1994
Hon. Lord Gill (Brian Gill), *born* 1942, *apptd* 1994
Hon. Lord Hamilton (Arthur Hamilton), *born* 1942, *apptd* 1995
Hon. Lord Dawson (Thomas Dawson), *born* 1948, *apptd* 1995
Hon. Lord Macfadyen (Donald Macfadyen), *born* 1945, *apptd* 1995
Hon. Lady Cosgrove (Hazel Aronson), *born* 1946, *apptd* 1996

COURT OF SESSION AND HIGH COURT OF JUSTICIARY

Parliament House, Parliament Square, Edinburgh EH1 1RQ
Tel 0131-225 2595

Principal Clerk of Session and Justiciary (£36,739–£54,815), H. S. Foley
Deputy Principal Clerk of Justiciary and Administration (£24,724–£38,290), T. Fyffe
Deputy Principal Clerk of Session and Principal Extractor (£24,724–£38,290), G. McKeand
Deputy Principal Clerk (Keeper of the Rolls) (£24,724–£38,290), T. M. Thomson
Depute Clerks of Session and Justiciary (£19,215–£25,289), N. J. Dowie; I. Smith; T. Higgins; T. B. Cruickshank; Q. Oliver; F. Shannly; A. S. Moffat; D. J. Shand; G. Ellis; D. G. Lynn; R. Cockburn; W. Dunn; A. Finlayson; C. Armstrong; S. Hindes; P. Crow; R. McMillan; G. Prentice; S. Walker; R. Jenkins; J. O. McLean; M. Weir

SCOTTISH COURTS ADMINISTRATION

Hayweight House, 23 Lauriston Street, Edinburgh EH3 9DQ
Tel 0131-229 9200

The Scottish Courts Administration is responsible to the Secretary of State for Scotland for the performance of the Scottish Court Service and central administration pertaining to the judiciary in the Supreme and Sheriff Courts; and to the Lord Advocate for certain aspects of court procedures, jurisdiction and legislation, law reform and other matters.
Director (*G2*), J. Hamill
Deputy Director (*Legal Policy*) (*Assistant Solicitor*) (*G5*), P. M. Beaton
Deputy Director (*Resources and Liaison*) (*G6*), D. Stewart

SCOTTISH COURT SERVICE

Hayweight House, 23 Lauriston Street, Edinburgh EH3 9DQ
Tel 0131-229 9200

The Scottish Court Service became an executive agency within the Scottish Courts Administration in 1995. It is responsible to the Secretary of State for Scotland for the provision of staff, court houses and associated services for the Supreme and Sheriff Courts.
Chief Executive, M. Ewart

SHERIFF COURT OF CHANCERY

27 Chambers Street, Edinburgh EH1 1LB
Tel 0131-225 2525

The Court deals with service of heirs and completion of title in relation to heritable property.
Sheriff of Chancery, C. G. B. Nicholson, QC

HM COMMISSARY OFFICE

27 Chambers Street, Edinburgh EH1 1LB
Tel 0131-225 2525

The Office is responsible for issuing confirmation, a legal document entitling a person to execute a deceased person's will, and other related matters.
Commissary Clerk, J. L. Anderson

SCOTTISH LAND COURT

1 Grosvenor Crescent, Edinburgh EH12 5ER
Tel 0131-225 3595

The court deals with disputes relating to agricultural and crofting land in Scotland.

Chairman (£89,123), The Hon. Lord Philip (Alexander Philip), QC
Members, D. D. McDiarmid; D. M. Macdonald; J. Kinloch (*part-time*)
Principal Clerk, K. H. R. Graham, WS

SHERIFFDOMS

SALARIES

Sheriff Principal	£89,123
Sheriff	£76,716
Regional Sheriff Clerk	£28,975–£56,295
Sheriff Clerk	£11,208–£39,324

*Floating Sheriff

GRAMPIAN, HIGHLANDS AND ISLANDS

Sheriff Principal, D. J. Risk
Regional Sheriff Clerk, J. Robertson

SHERIFFS AND SHERIFF CLERKS

Aberdeen and Stonehaven, D. W. Bogie; G. C. Warner; D. Kelbie; L. A. S. Jessop; A. Pollock; *Sheriff Clerks*, Mrs E. Laing (*Aberdeen*); I. Smith (*Stonehaven*)
Peterhead and Banff, K. A. McLernan; *Sheriff Clerk*, A. Hempseed (*Peterhead*); *Sheriff Clerk Depute*, Mrs F. L. MacPherson (*Banff*)
Elgin, N. McPartlin; *Sheriff Clerk*, M. McBey
Inverness, Lochmaddy, Portree, Stornoway, Dingwall, Tain, Wick and Dornoch, W. J. Fulton; D. Booker-Milburn; J. O. A. Fraser; I. A. Cameron; *Sheriff Clerks*, J. Robertson (*Inverness*); W. Cochrane (*Dingwall*); *Sheriff Clerks Depute*, Miss M. Campbell (*Lochmaddy and Portree*); Mrs M. Macdonald (*Stornoway*); L. MacLachlan (*Tain*); Mrs J. McEwan (*Wick*); Miss R. MacSween (*Dornoch*)
Kirkwall and Lerwick, C. S. Mackenzie; *Sheriff Clerks Depute*, R. Cantwell (*Kirkwall*); A. C. Norris (*Lerwick*)
Fort William, C. G. McKay (also *Oban*); *Sheriff Clerk Depute*, D. Hood

TAYSIDE, CENTRAL AND FIFE

Sheriff Principal, J. J. Maguire, QC
Regional Sheriff Clerk, J. S. Doig

SHERIFFS AND SHERIFF CLERKS

Arbroath and Forfar, K. A. Veal; *C. N. R. Stein; *Sheriff Clerks*, M. Herbertson (*Arbroath*); S. Munro (*Forfar*)
Dundee, R. A. Davidson; A. L. Stewart, QC; *J. N. Young; C. Smith (also *Cupar*); *Sheriff Clerk*, J. S. Doig
Perth, J. F. Wheatley; J. C. McInnes, QC; *Sheriff Clerk*, W. Jones
Falkirk, A. V. Sheehan; A. J. Murphy; *Sheriff Clerk*, D. Forrester
Stirling, The Hon. R. E. G. Younger; *Mrs A. M. Cowan; *Sheriff Clerk*, J. Clark
Alloa, W. M. Reid; *Sheriff Clerk*, G. McKeand
Cupar, C. Smith (also *Dundee*); *Sheriff Clerk*, R. Hughes
Dunfermline, J. S. Forbes; C. W. Palmer; *Sheriff Clerk*, W. McCulloch
Kirkcaldy, W. J. Christie; Mrs L. G. Patrick; *Sheriff Clerk*, I. Hay

LOTHIAN AND BORDERS

Sheriff Principal, C. G. B. Nicholson, QC
Regional Sheriff Clerk, J. Anderson

SHERIFFS AND SHERIFF CLERKS

Edinburgh, vacant (also *Peebles*); R. G. Craik, QC;
G. I. W. Shiach; Miss I. A. Poole; R. J. D. Scott;
A. M. Bell; J. M. S. Horsburgh, QC; G. W. S. Presslie (also
Haddington); J. A. Farrell; *A. Lothian; *F. J. Keane;
I. D. Macphail, QC; C. N. Stoddart; A. B. Wilkinson, QC;
Mrs D. J. B. Robertson; N. M. P. Morrison, QC; *Sheriff
Clerk*, J. Anderson
Peebles, vacant (also *Edinburgh*); *Sheriff Clerk Depute*,
R. McArthur
Linlithgow, H. R. MacLean; G. R. Fleming; *Sheriff Clerk*,
R. Sinclair
Haddington, G. W. S. Presslie (also *Edinburgh*); *Sheriff Clerk*,
J. O'Donnell
Jedburgh and Duns, J. V. Paterson; *Sheriff Clerk*,
J. W. Williamson
Selkirk, J. V. Paterson; *Sheriff Clerk Depute*, L. McFarlane

NORTH STRATHCLYDE

Sheriff Principal, R. C. Hay, CBE
Regional Sheriff Clerk, A. A. Brown

SHERIFFS AND SHERIFF CLERKS

Oban, C. G. McKay (also *Fort William*); *Sheriff Clerk Depute*,
G. Whitelaw
Dumbarton, J. T. Fitzsimons; T. Scott; S. W. H. Fraser;
Sheriff Clerk, P. Corcoran
Paisley, R. G. Smith; J. Spy; C. K. Higgins; N. Douglas;
*D. J. Pender; *W. Dunlop (also *Campbeltown*); *Sheriff
Clerk*, A. A. Brown
Greenock, J. Herald (also *Rothesay*); Sir Stephen Young;
Sheriff Clerk, J. Tannahill
Kilmarnock, T. M. Croan; D. B. Smith; T. F. Russell; *Sheriff
Clerk*, N. R. Weir
Dunoon, A. W. Noble; *Sheriff Clerk Depute*, Mrs C. Carson
Campbeltown, *W. Dunlop (also *Paisley*); *Sheriff Clerk Depute*,
P. G. Hay
Rothesay, J. Herald (also *Greenock*); *Sheriff Clerk Depute*, Mrs
S. Gracie

GLASGOW AND STRATHKELVIN

Sheriff Principal, N. D. MacLeod, QC
Regional Sheriff Clerk, I. Scott

SHERIFFS AND SHERIFF CLERKS

Glasgow, A. C. Horsfall, QC (*seconded to Scottish Lands
Tribunal*); B. Kearney; G. H. Gordon, CBE, PH.D., QC;
B. A. Lockhart; I. G. Pirie; Mrs A. L. A. Duncan;
G. J. Evans; E. H. Galt; A. C. Henry; J. K. Mitchell;
A. G. Johnston; J. P. Murphy; M. Sischy; Miss
S. A. O. Raeburn, QC; D. Convery; J. McGowan;
B. A. Kerr, QC; Mrs C. M. A. F. Gimblett;
I. A. S. Peebles, QC; C. W. McFarlane, QC; K. M. Maciver;
Sheriff Clerk, I. Scott

SOUTH STRATHCLYDE, DUMFRIES AND GALLOWAY

Sheriff Principal, G. L. Cox, QC
Regional Sheriff Clerk, M. Bonar

HERIFFS AND SHERIFF CLERKS

Hamilton, L. Cameron; A. C. MacPherson; W. F. Lunny;
D. C. Russell; V. J. Canavan (also *Airdrie*); W. E. Gibson;
H. Stirling; J. H. Stewart; *Sheriff Clerk*, P. Feeney
Lanark, J. D. Allan; *H. S. Neilson; *Sheriff Clerk*, J. Lynn
Ayr, N. Gow, QC; R. G. McEwan, QC; *C. B. Miller; *Sheriff
Clerk*, G. W. Waddell

Stranraer and Kirkcudbright, J. R. Smith (also *Dumfries*);
Sheriff Clerks, W. McIntosh (*Stranraer*); B. Lindsay
(*Kirkcudbright*)
Dumfries, K. G. Barr; M. J. Fletcher; J. R. Smith (also
Stranraer and Kirkcudbright); *Sheriff Clerk*, P. McGonigle
Airdrie, V. J. Canavan (also *Hamilton*); R. H. Dickson;
I. C. Simpson; *Sheriff Clerk*, M. Bonar

STIPENDIARY MAGISTRATES

GLASGOW

R. Hamilton, *apptd* 1984; J. B. C. Nisbet, *apptd* 1984;
R. B. Christie, *apptd* 1985; Mrs J. A. M. MacLean, *apptd*
1990

PROCURATOR FISCAL SERVICE

CROWN OFFICE
25 Chambers Street, Edinburgh EH1 1LA
Tel 0131-226 2626
Crown Agent (*£65,990–£79,396), J. D. Lowe, CB
Deputy Crown Agent (*£45,278–£54,815), N. McFadyen

PROCURATORS FISCAL

*SALARIES

Regional Procurator Fiscal–grade 3	£52,704–£62,817
Regional Procurator Fiscal–grade 4	£45,278–£54,815
Procurator Fiscal–upper level	£36,739–£54,815
Procurator Fiscal–lower level	£26,418–£45,078

*1994–5 figures; grades and salaries were under review at the time
of going to press

GRAMPIAN, HIGHLANDS AND ISLANDS REGION

Regional Procurator Fiscal, A. D. Vannett (*Aberdeen*)
Procurators Fiscal, E. K. Barbour (*Stonehaven*);
A. J. M. Colley (*Banff*); Mrs D. Wilson (*Peterhead*);
J. F. MacKay (*Elgin*); A. N. MacDonald (*Wick*);
J. Bamber (*Portree, Lochmaddy*); F. Redman (*Stornoway*);
G. K. Buchanan (*Inverness*); D. K. Adam (*Kirkwall,
Lerwick*); Mrs A. Neizer (*Fort William*); D. R. Hingston
(*Dingwall, Dornoch, Tain*)

TAYSIDE, CENTRAL AND FIFE REGION

Regional Procurator Fiscal, B. K. Heywood (*Dundee*)
Procurators Fiscal, I. C. Walker (*Forfar*); I. A. McLeod
(*Perth*); J. J. Miller (*Falkirk*); C. Ritchie (*Stirling*);
I. D. Douglas (*Alloa*); E. B. Russell (*Cupar*);
R. T. Hamilton (*Dunfermline*); Miss E. C. Munro
(*Kirkcaldy*)

LOTHIAN AND BORDERS REGION

Regional Procurator Fiscal, R. F. Lees (*Edinburgh*)
Procurators Fiscal, D. McNeill (*Peebles*); Miss L. M. Ruxton
(*Linlithgow*); A. J. P. Reith (*Haddington*); A. R. G. Fraser
(*Duns, Jedburgh*); D. McNeill (*Selkirk*)

NORTH STRATHCLYDE REGION

Regional Procurator Fiscal, J. D. Friel (*Paisley*)
Procurators Fiscal, I. Henderson (*Campbeltown*);
C. C. Donnelly (*Dumbarton*); W. S. Carnegie (*Greenock,
Rothesay*); D. L. Webster (*Dunoon*); J. G. MacGlennan
(*Kilmarnock*); B. R. Maguire (*Oban*)

GLASGOW AND STRATHKELVIN REGION
Regional Procurator Fiscal, A. C. Normand (*Glasgow*)

SOUTH STRATHCLYDE, DUMFRIES AND GALLOWAY
REGION
Regional Procurator Fiscal, F. R. Crowe (*Hamilton*)
Procurators Fiscal, S. R. Houston (*Lanark*); D. A. Brown
(*Ayr*); F. Walkingshaw (*Stranraer*); D. J. Howdle
(*Dumfries, Stranraer, Kirkcudbright*); D. Spiers (*Airdrie*)

Northern Ireland Judicature

In Northern Ireland the legal system and the structure of
courts closely resemble those of England and Wales; there
are, however, often differences in enacted law.

The Supreme Court of Judicature of Northern Ireland
comprises the Court of Appeal, the High Court of Justice
and the Crown Court. The practice and procedure of
these courts is similar to that in England. The superior
civil court is the High Court of Justice, from which an
appeal lies to the Northern Ireland Court of Appeal; the
House of Lords is the final civil appeal court.

The Crown Court, served by High Court and county
court judges, deals with criminal trials on indictment.
Cases are heard before a judge and, except those involving
offences specified under emergency legislation, a jury.
Appeals from the Crown Court against conviction or
sentence are heard by the Northern Ireland Court of
Appeal; the House of Lords is the final court of appeal.

The decision to prosecute in cases tried on indictment
and in summary cases of a serious nature rests in Northern
Ireland with the Director of Public Prosecutions, who is
responsible to the Attorney-General. Minor summary
offences are prosecuted by the police.

Minor criminal offences are dealt with in magistrates'
courts by a legally qualified resident magistrate and,
where an offender is under 17, by juvenile courts each
consisting of a resident magistrate and two lay members
specially qualified to deal with juveniles (at least one of
whom must be a woman). In June 1996 there were 942
justices of the peace in Northern Ireland. Appeals from
magistrates' courts are heard by the county court, or by
the Court of Appeal on a point of law or an issue as to
jurisdiction.

Magistrates' courts in Northern Ireland can deal with
certain classes of civil case but most minor civil cases are
dealt with in county courts. Judgments of all civil courts
are enforceable through a centralized procedure administered by the Enforcement of Judgments Office.

SUPREME COURT OF JUDICATURE
The Royal Courts of Justice, Belfast BT1 3JF
Tel 01232-235111

Lord Chief Justice of Northern Ireland (£122,231)
    The Rt. Hon. Sir Brian Hutton, *born* 1931, *apptd* 1988
Principal Secretary, G. W. Johnston

LORDS JUSTICES OF APPEAL (each £117,190)
Style, The Rt. Hon. Lord Justice [surname]

Rt. Hon. Sir John MacDermott, *born* 1927, *apptd* 1987
Rt. Hon. Sir Robert Carswell, *born* 1934, *apptd* 1993
Rt. Hon. Sir Michael Nicholson, *born* 1933, *apptd* 1995

PUISNE JUDGES (each £104,431)
Style, The Hon. Mr Justice [surname]
Hon. Sir William McCollum, *born* 1933, *apptd* 1987
Hon. Sir Anthony Campbell, *born* 1936, *apptd* 1988
Hon. Sir John Sheil, *born* 1938, *apptd* 1989
Hon. Sir Brian Kerr, *born* 1948, *apptd* 1993
Hon. Sir John Pringle, *born* 1929, *apptd* 1993
Hon. Sir Malachy Higgins, *born* 1944, *apptd* 1993
Hon. Sir Paul Girvan, *born* 1948, *apptd* 1995

MASTERS OF THE SUPREME COURT (each £62,621)
Master, Queen's Bench and Appeals and Clerk of the Crown,
    J. W. Wilson, QC
Master, High Court, Mrs D. M. Kennedy
Master, Office of Care and Protection, F. B. Hall
Master, Chancery Office, R. A. Ellison
Master, Bankruptcy and Companies Office, J. B. C. Glass
Master, Probate and Matrimonial Office, R. T. Millar
Master, Taxing Office, J. C. Napier

OFFICIAL SOLICITOR
Official Solicitor to the Supreme Court of Northern Ireland,
    C. W. G. Redpath

COUNTY COURTS

JUDGES (each £89,123)
Style, His Hon. Judge [surname]

Judge Curran, QC; Judge McKee, QC; Judge Gibson, QC;
Judge Hart, QC; Judge Petrie, QC; Judge Smyth, QC; Judge
Markey, QC; Judge McKay, QC; Judge Chambers, QC
(*Chief Social Security and Child Support Commissioner*); Judge
Martin, QC; Judge Brady, QC

RECORDERS (each £89,123)
Belfast, Judge Russell, QC
Londonderry, Judge Burgess

MAGISTRATES' COURTS

RESIDENT MAGISTRATES (each £62,621)
There are 17 resident magistrates in Northern Ireland.

CROWN SOLICITOR'S OFFICE
PO Box 410, Royal Courts of Justice, Belfast BT1 3JY
Tel 01232-542555

Crown Solicitor, N. P. Roberts

DEPARTMENT OF THE DIRECTOR OF
PUBLIC PROSECUTIONS
Royal Courts of Justice, Belfast BT1 3NX
Tel 01232-542444

Director of Public Prosecutions, A. Fraser, CB, QC
Deputy Director of Public Prosecutions, D. Magill

NORTHERN IRELAND COURT SERVICE
Windsor House, Bedford Street, Belfast BT2 7LT
Tel 01232-328594

Director (G3)

Ecclesiastical Courts

Original jurisdiction is exercised by the consistory court of each diocese in England, presided over by the Chancellor of that diocese. Appellate jurisdiction is exercised by the provincial courts detailed below, by the Court for Ecclesiastical Causes Reserved, and by commissions of review (the membership of these being newly constituted for each case).

COURT OF ARCHES (PROVINCE OF CANTERBURY)
Registry, 16 Beaumont Street, Oxford OXI 2LZ
Tel 01865-241974

Dean of the Arches, The Rt. Worshipful Sir John Owen

COURT OF THE VICAR-GENERAL OF THE PROVINCE OF CANTERBURY
Registry, 16 Beaumont Street, Oxford OXI 2LZ
Tel 01865-241974

Vicar-General, The Rt. Worshipful Miss S. Cameron, QC

CHANCERY COURT OF YORK
Registry, 1 Peckitt Street, York YOI ISG
Tel 01904-623487

Auditor, The Rt. Worshipful Sir John Owen

THE VICAR-GENERAL OF THE PROVINCE OF YORK
Registry, 1 Peckitt Street, York YOI ISG
Tel 01904-623487

Vicar-General, His Honour the Worshipful Judge T. A. C. Coningsby, QC

COURT OF FACULTIES
Registry, 1 The Sanctuary, London SWIP 3JT
Tel 0171-222 5381

Office for the issue of special and common marriage licences, appointment of notaries public, etc. Office hours, Monday–Friday, 10–4.

Master of the Faculties, The Rt. Worshipful Sir John Owen

The Probation Service

ENGLAND AND WALES

The Probation Service is employed in each area (55 in total) by an independent committee of justices and it provides a professional social work agency in the courts, with responsibility for a wide range of duties which include:

(a) a pre-sentence report service for the criminal courts
(b) provision of a range of non-custodial measures involving the supervision of offenders in the community
(c) supervisory aftercare for offenders released from custody, together with social work in penal establishments and help for the families of those serving sentences
(d) an enquiry, conciliation and supervision service in the divorce and domestic courts
(e) support for and promotion of preventive and containment measures in the community designed to reduce the level of crime and domestic breakdown

It is a direct grant service funded 80 per cent from the Home Office and 20 per cent from the relevant local authority.

Its national representative bodies are:

THE CENTRAL PROBATION COUNCIL, 38 Belgrave Square, London SWIX 8NT. Tel: 0171-245 9364. *Director*, I. Miles

THE ASSOCIATION OF CHIEF OFFICERS OF PROBATION, 20–30 Lawefield Lane, Wakefield WF2 8SP. Tel: 01924-361156. *General Secretary*, Ms M. Honeyball

THE NATIONAL ASSOCIATION OF PROBATION OFFICERS, 3 Chivalry Road, London SWII IHT. Tel: 0171-223 4887. *General Secretary*, Ms J. McKnight

SCOTLAND

The probation service in Scotland is a statutory duty of local authorities under section 27 of the Social Work (Scotland) Act 1968. Social workers supervise and provide advice, guidance and assistance to those persons living in their area who are subject to a court's supervision order. This is done by social workers as part of their normal duties and not by a separate probation staff.

NORTHERN IRELAND

The Probation Board for Northern Ireland provides a probation service throughout Northern Ireland. Its function and range of duties is similar to that of the Probation Service in England and Wales (*see* above), except that in Northern Ireland work in divorce and domestic courts is the responsibility of the social services and not the Probation Board. The Probation Board is a statutory body whose 14 members are appointed by the Secretary of State for Northern Ireland and it receives its funding from the Northern Ireland Office.

Tribunals

AGRICULTURAL LAND TRIBUNALS
c/o Land Use and Rural Economy Division, Ministry of Agriculture, Fisheries and Food, Nobel House, 17 Smith Square, London SW1P 3JR
Tel 0171-238 6991

Agricultural Land Tribunals were set up under the Agriculture Act 1947 and settle disputes and other issues between agricultural landlords and tenants. They also settle drainage disputes between neighbours.

There are seven tribunals covering England and one covering Wales. For each tribunal the Lord Chancellor appoints a chairman and one or more deputies, who must be barristers or solicitors of at least seven years standing. The Lord Chancellor also appoints lay members to three statutory panels of members: the 'landowners' panel, the 'farmers' panel and the 'drainage' panel.

Each of the eight tribunals is an independent statutory body with jurisdiction only within its own area. A separate tribunal is constituted for each case, and consists of a chairman (who may be the chairman or one of the deputy chairmen) and two lay members nominated by the chairman.
Chairmen (England) (£233 a day), W. D. Greenwood; K. J. Fisher; P. A. de la Piquerie; C. H. Beaumont; M. K. Lee; G. L. Newsom; His Hon. Judge Robert Taylor
Chairman (Wales) (£233 a day), W. J. Owen

COMMONS COMMISSIONERS
4th Floor, 35 Old Queen Street, London SW1H 9JA
Tel 0171-222 0038

The Commons Commissioners are responsible for deciding disputes arising under the Commons Registration Act 1965 and the Common Land (Rectification of Registers) Act 1989. They also enquire into the ownership of unclaimed common land. Commissioners are appointed by the Lord Chancellor.
Chief Commons Commissioner (part-time) (£40,358), D. M. Burton
Commissioner, I. L. R. Romer
Clerk, Miss F. A. A. Buchan

COPYRIGHT TRIBUNAL
25 Southampton Buildings, London WC2A 1AY
Tel 0171-438 4776

The Copyright Tribunal is the successor to the Performing Right Tribunal which was established by the Copyright Act 1956 to resolve various classes of copyright dispute, principally in the field of collective licensing. Its jurisdiction was extended by the Copyright, Designs and Patents Act 1988 and the Broadcasting Act 1990.

The chairman and two deputy chairmen are appointed by the Lord Chancellor. Up to eight ordinary members are appointed by the Secretary of State for Trade and Industry.
Chairman (£316 a day), J. M. Bowers
Secretary, Miss J. E. M. Durdin

DATA PROTECTION TRIBUNAL
c/o The Home Office, Queen Anne's Gate, London SW1H 9AT
Tel 0171-273 3386

The Data Protection Tribunal was established under the Data Protection Act 1984 to determine appeals against decisions of the Data Protection Registrar (*see* page 293). The chairman and two deputy chairmen are appointed by the Lord Chancellor and must be legally qualified. Lay members are appointed by the Home Secretary to represent the interests of data users or data subjects.

A tribunal consists of a legally-qualified chairman sitting with equal numbers of the lay members appointed to represent the interests of data users and data subjects.
Chairman (£359 a day), J. A. C. Spokes, QC
Secretary, D. Anderson

EMPLOYMENT APPEAL TRIBUNAL
Central Office, Audit House, 58 Victoria Embankment, London EC4Y 0DS
Tel 0171-273 1041
Divisional Office, 52 Melville Street, Edinburgh EH3 7HF
Tel 0131-225 3963

The Employment Appeal Tribunal was established as a superior court of record under the provisions of the Employment Protection Act 1975, hearing appeals on a question of law arising from any decision of an industrial tribunal.

A tribunal consists of a legally-qualified chairman and two lay members, one from each side of industry. They are appointed by The Queen on the recommendation of the Lord Chancellor and the Secretary of State for Trade and Industry.
President, The Hon. Mr Justice Morison
Scottish Chairman, The Hon. Lord Johnston
Registrar, Miss V. J. Selio

IMMIGRATION APPELLATE AUTHORITIES
Thanet House, 231 Strand, London WC2R 1DA
Tel 0171-353 8060

The Immigration Appeal Adjudicators hear appeals from immigration decisions concerning the need for, and refusal of, leave to enter or remain in the UK, refusals to grant asylum, decisions to make deportation orders and directions to remove persons subject to immigration control from the UK. The Immigration Appeal Tribunal hears appeals direct from decisions to make deportation orders in matters concerning conduct contrary to the public good and refusals to grant asylum. Its principal jurisdiction is however, the hearing of appeals from adjudicators by the party (Home Office or individual) who is aggrieved by the decision. Appeals are subject to leave being granted by the tribunal.

An adjudicator sits alone. The tribunal sits in divisions of three, normally a legally qualified member and two lay members. Members of the tribunal and adjudicators are appointed by the Lord Chancellor.

IMMIGRATION APPEAL TRIBUNAL
President (£80,176), G. W. Farmer
Vice-Presidents, Prof. D. C. Jackson; Mrs J. Chatwani

IMMIGRATION APPEAL ADJUDICATORS
Chief Adjudicator, His Hon. Judge Pearl
Deputy Chief Adjudicator, vacant

INDEPENDENT TRIBUNAL SERVICE
City Gate House, 39–45 Finsbury Square, London
EC2A 1PX
Tel 0171-814 6500

The service is the judicial authority which exercises judicial and administrative control over the independent social security and child support appeal tribunals, medical and disability appeal tribunals, and vaccine damage tribunals.
President, His Hon. Judge Bassingthwaighte
Chief Executive, S. Williams

INDUSTRIAL TRIBUNALS

CENTRAL OFFICE (ENGLAND AND WALES)
19–29 Woburn Place, London WC1H 0LU
Tel 0171-273 8659

Industrial Tribunals for England and Wales sit in 11 regions. The tribunals deal with matters of employment law, redundancy, dismissal, contract disputes, sexual, racial and disability discrimination, and related areas of dispute which may arise in the workplace. A central registration unit records all applications and maintains a public register at Southgate Street, Bury St Edmunds, Suffolk IP33 2AQ. The tribunals are funded by the Department of Trade and Industry. In April 1997 the tribunals will be renamed the Employment Tribunal Service.

Chairmen, who may be full-time or part-time, are legally qualified. They are appointed by the Lord Chancellor. Tribunal members are nominated by specified employer and employee groups and appointed by the Secretary of State for Trade and Industry.
President, His Hon. Judge Lawrence

CENTRAL OFFICE (SCOTLAND)
Eagle Building, 215 Bothwell Street, Glasgow G2 7TS
Tel 0141-204 0730

Tribunals in Scotland have the same remit as those in England and Wales. Chairmen are appointed by the Lord President of the Court of Session and lay members by the Secretary of State for Trade and Industry.
President (£89,123), Mrs D. Littlejohn

INDUSTRIAL TRIBUNALS AND THE FAIR EMPLOYMENT TRIBUNAL (NORTHERN IRELAND)
Long Bridge House, 20–24 Waring Street, Belfast BT1 2EB
Tel 01232-327666

The industrial tribunal system in Northern Ireland was set up in 1965 and is similar to the system operating in the rest of the UK. The main legislation in Northern Ireland giving jurisdiction to industrial tribunals to hear complaints relating to employment matters corresponds to legislation enacted in Great Britain, except that there is no equivalent legislation to the Race Relations Act.

Since 1990 there has been a separate Fair Employment Tribunal in Northern Ireland. The Fair Employment Tribunal hears and determines individual cases of alleged religious or political discrimination in employment. Employers can also appeal to the Fair Employment Tribunal if they consider the directions of the Fair Employment Commission to be unreasonable, inappropriate or unnecessary, and the Fair Employment Commission can make application to the Tribunal for the enforcement of undertakings or directions with which an employer has not complied.

The president, vice-president and part-time chairmen of the Fair Employment Tribunal are appointed by the Lord Chancellor. The full-time chairman and the part-time chairmen of the industrial tribunals and the panel members to both the industrial tribunals and the Fair Employment Tribunal are appointed by the Department of Economic Development Northern Ireland.
President of the Industrial Tribunals and the Fair Employment Tribunal (£89,123), J. Maguire, CBE
Vice-President of the Industrial Tribunals and the Fair Employment Tribunal, Mrs M. P. Price
Secretary, J. Murphy

LANDS TRIBUNAL
48–49 Chancery Lane, London WC2A 1JR
Tel 0171-936 7200

The Lands Tribunal is an independent judicial body constituted by the Lands Tribunal Act 1949 for the purpose of determining a wide range of questions relating to the valuation of land, rating appeals from valuation tribunals and the discharge or modification of restrictive covenants. The Act also empowers the tribunal to accept the function of arbitration under references by consent. The tribunal consists of a president and a number of other members, who are appointed by the Lord Chancellor.
President, His Hon. Judge Marder, QC
Members (£76,716), Dr T. Hoyes, FRICS; M. St J. Hopper, FRICS; P. H. Clarke, FRICS
Member (part-time), His Hon. Judge Rich, QC
Members (part-time) (£349 a day), J. C. Hill, TD; A. P. Musto, FRICS
Registrar, C. A. McMullan

LANDS TRIBUNAL FOR SCOTLAND
1 Grosvenor Crescent, Edinburgh EH12 5ER
Tel 0131-225 7996

The Lands Tribunal for Scotland was constituted by the Lands Tribunal Act 1949. Its remit is the same as the tribunal for England and Wales but also covers questions relating to tenants' rights. The president is appointed by the Lord President of the Court of Session.
President, The Hon. Lord Philip, QC
Members (£76,716), Sheriff A. C. Horsfall, QC; A. R. MacLeary; J. Devine
Member (part-time) (£349 a day), R. A. Edwards, CBE, WS
Clerk, N. Tainsh

MENTAL HEALTH REVIEW TRIBUNALS

The Mental Health Review Tribunals are independent judicial bodies established under the Mental Health Act 1959 and which now operate under the Mental Health Act 1983. They are responsible for reviewing the cases of patients compulsorily detained under the Act's provisions. They have the power to discharge the patient, to recommend leave of absence, delayed discharge, transfer to another hospital or that a guardianship order be made, and to reclassify both restricted and unrestricted patients. There are eight tribunals in England, each headed by a regional chairman who is appointed by the Lord Chancellor's Department on a part-time basis. Each tribunal is made up of at least three members, and must include a lawyer, who acts as president (£239 a day), a medical member (£226 a day) and a lay member (£97 a day).

The Mental Health Review Tribunals' secretariat is based in five regional offices:

LIVERPOOL, 3rd Floor, Cressington House, 249 St Mary's Road, Garston, Liverpool L19 0NF. Tel: 0151-494 0095. *Clerk*, Mrs B. Foot

LONDON (NORTH), Spur 3, Block 1, Government Buildings, Honeypot Lane, Stanmore, Middx HA7 1AY. Tel: 0171-972 3734. *Clerk*, P. Barnett

LONDON (SOUTH), Block 3, Crown Offices, Kingston Bypass Road, Surbiton, Surrey KT6 5QN. Tel: 0181-268 4520. *Clerk*, C. Lilly

NOTTINGHAM, Spur A, Block 5, Government Buildings, Chalfont Drive, Western Boulevard, Nottingham NG8 3RZ. Tel: 0115-929 4222. *Clerk*, M. Chapman

WALES, 4th Floor, Crown Buildings, Cathays Park, Cardiff CF1 3NQ. Tel: 01222-825328. *Clerk*, Mrs C. Thomas

NATIONAL HEALTH SERVICE TRIBUNAL

The NHS Tribunal was set up under the National Health Service Act 1977. It inquires into representations that the continued inclusion of a family practitioner (doctor, dentist, pharmacist or optician) on a Family Practitioner Committee's list would be prejudicial to the efficiency of the services concerned. The tribunal sits when required, about eight times a year, and usually in London. The chairman is appointed by the Lord Chancellor and members are appointed by the Secretary of State for Health.
Chairman (£295 a day), A. Whitfield, QC
Deputy Chairmen, Miss E. Platt, QC; Dr R. N. Ough
Clerk, I. D. Keith, East Hookers, Twineham, nr Haywards Heath, W. Sussex RH17 5NN. Tel: 01444-881345

NATIONAL HEALTH SERVICE TRIBUNAL (SCOTLAND)
Erskine House, 68 Queen Street, Edinburgh EH2 4NN
Tel 0131-226 6541

The tribunal was set up under the National Health Service (Scotland) Act 1978, and exists to consider representations that the continued inclusion of a registered doctor, dentist, optometrist or pharmacist on a health board's list would be prejudicial to the continuing efficiency of the service in question.

The tribunal meets when required and is composed of a chairman, one lay member, and one practitioner member drawn from a representative professional panel. The chairman is appointed by the Lord President of the Court of Session, and the lay member and the members of the professional panel are appointed by the Secretary of State for Scotland.
Chairman (£295 a day), W. C. Galbraith, QC
Lay member, J. D. M. Robertson
Clerk to the Tribunal, D. G. Brash, WS

PENSIONS APPEAL TRIBUNALS

CENTRAL OFFICE (ENGLAND AND WALES)
48–49 Chancery Lane, London WC2A 1JR
Tel 0171-936 7034

The Pensions Appeal Tribunals are responsible for hearing appeals from ex-servicemen or women and widows who have had their claims for a war pension rejected by the Secretary of State for Social Security. The Entitlement Appeal Tribunals hear appeals in cases where the Secretary of State has refused to grant a war pension. The Assessment Appeal Tribunals hear appeals against the Secretary of State's assessment of the degree of disablement caused by an accepted condition.

The tribunal members are appointed by the Lord Chancellor.
President (£62,621), J. R. T. Holt
Secretary, W. Thomas

PENSIONS APPEAL TRIBUNALS FOR SCOTLAND
20 Walker Street, Edinburgh EH3 7HS
Tel 0131-220 1404
President (£282 a day), C. N. McEachran, QC

OFFICE OF THE SOCIAL SECURITY AND CHILD SUPPORT COMMISSIONERS
Harp House, 83–86 Farringdon Street, London EC4A 4DH
Tel 0171-353 5145
23 Melville Street, Edinburgh EH3 7PW
Tel 0131-225 2201

The Social Security Commissioners are the final statutory authority to decide appeals relating to entitlement to social security benefits. The Child Support Commissioners are the final statutory authority to decide appeals relating to child support. Appeals may be made in relation to both matters only on a point of law. The Commissioners' jurisdiction covers England, Wales and Scotland. There are 17 commissioners; they are all qualified lawyers.
Chief Social Security Commissioner and Chief Child Support Commissioner, His Hon. Judge Machin, QC
Secretary, S. Hill (*London*); E. Barschtschyk (*Edinburgh*)

OFFICE OF THE SOCIAL SECURITY AND CHILD SUPPORT COMMISSIONERS FOR NORTHERN IRELAND
Lancashire House, 5 Linenhall Street, Belfast BT2 8AA
Tel 01232-332344

The role of Northern Ireland Social Security and Child Support Commissioners is similar to that of the Commissioners in Great Britain. There are two commissioners for Northern Ireland.
Chief Commissioner, His Hon. Judge Chambers, QC
Registrar of Appeals, W. D. Pollock

THE SOLICITORS' DISCIPLINARY TRIBUNAL

227–228 Strand, London WC2A IBA
Tel 0171-242 0219

The Solicitors' Disciplinary Tribunal was constituted under the provisions of the Solicitors Act 1974. It is an independent statutory body whose members are appointed by the Master of the Rolls. The tribunal considers applications made to it alleging either professional misconduct and/or a breach of the statutory rules by which solicitors are bound against an individually named solicitor, former solicitor, or registered foreign lawyer. The tribunal's jurisdiction extends to solicitor's clerks, in respect of whom they may make an order restricting that clerk's employment by solicitors. The president and solicitor members do not receive remuneration.
President, G. B. Marsh
Clerk, Mrs S. C. Elson

SPECIAL COMMISSIONERS OF INCOME TAX

15–19 Bedford Avenue, London WC1B 3AS
Tel 0171-631 4242

The Special Commissioners are an independent body appointed by the Lord Chancellor to hear complex appeals against decisions of the Board of Inland Revenue and its officials. In addition to the Presiding Special Commissioner there are two full-time and 12 deputy special commissioners; all are legally qualified.
Presiding Special Commissioner, His Hon. Stephen Oliver, QC
Special Commissioners (£62,621), T. H. K. Everett;
   D. A. Shirley
Clerk, R. P. Lester

TRAFFIC COMMISSIONERS

c/o Scottish Traffic Area, Argyle House, 3 Lady Lawson Street, Edinburgh EH3 9SE
Tel 0131-529 8500

The Traffic Commissioners are responsible for the licensing of operators of heavy goods and public service vehicles. They also have responsibility for appeals relating to the licensing of operators and for disciplinary cases involving the conduct of drivers of these vehicles. There are seven Commissioners in the eight traffic areas covering Great Britain. Each Traffic Commissioner constitutes a tribunal for the purposes of the Tribunals and Inquiries Act 1971. For Traffic Area Offices and Commissioners, *see* page 352.
Senior Traffic Commissioner (£54,029), M. Betts

TRANSPORT TRIBUNAL

48–49 Chancery Lane, London WC2A IJR
Tel 0171-936 7493

The Transport Tribunal was set up in 1947 and hears appeals against decisions made by Traffic Commissioners at public inquiries. The tribunal consists of a legally-qualified president, two legal members who may sit as chairmen, and five lay members. The president and legal members are appointed by the Lord Chancellor and the lay members are appointed by the Secretary of State for Transport.
President (part-time), His Hon. Judge Main, QC
Legal members (£257 a day), His Hon. Judge Brodrick (*part-time*); R. Owen, QC
Lay members (£206 a day), T. W. Hall; J. W. Whitworth;
   G. Simms; Miss E. B. Haran; P. Rogers
Secretary, W. Thomas

VALUATION TRIBUNALS

c/o Warwickshire Valuation Tribunal, 2nd Floor, Walton House, 11 Parade, Leamington Spa, Warks CV32 4DG
Tel 01926-421875

The Valuation Tribunals hear appeals concerning the council tax, non-domestic rating and land drainage rates in England and Wales. They also have residual jurisdiction to hear appeals concerning the community charge, the pre-1990 rating list, disabled rating and mixed hereditaments. There are 56 tribunals in England, and eight in Wales. Each tribunal is a separate independent body; those in England are funded by the Department of the Environment and those in Wales by the Welsh Office. A separate tribunal is constituted for each hearing, and normally consists of a chairman and two other members. Members are appointed by the local authority/authorities, and serve on a voluntary basis. A National Committee of Valuation Tribunals considers all matters affecting valuations tribunals in England, and the President of the Council of Wales Valuation Tribunals performs the same function in Wales.
President, National Committee of Valuation Tribunals,
   A. H. W. Kennard
Secretary, National Committee of Valuation Tribunals,
   B. P. Massen
National President, Council of Wales Valuation Tribunal,
   P. J. Law

VAT AND DUTIES TRIBUNALS

15–19 Bedford Avenue, London WC1B 3AS
Tel 0171-631 4242

VAT and Duties Tribunals are administered by the Lord Chancellor's Department in England and Wales, and by the Secretary of State in Scotland. They are independent, and decide disputes between taxpayers and the Commissioners of Customs and Excise. In England and Wales, the president and chairmen are appointed by the Lord Chancellor and members are appointed by the Treasury. Chairmen in Scotland are appointed by the Lord President of the Court of Session.
President, His Hon. Stephen Oliver, QC
Vice-President, England and Wales (£66,621), A. W. Simpson
Vice-President, Scotland (£66,621), R. A. Bennett, CBE, QC
Vice-President, Northern Ireland (£66,621), D. C. Morgan, QC
Registrar, R. P. Lester

TRIBUNAL CENTRES

EDINBURGH, 44 Palmerston Place, Edinburgh EH12 5BJ.
   Tel: 0131-226 3551
LONDON (including Belfast), 15–19 Bedford Avenue,
   London WC1B 3AS. Tel: 0171-631 4242
MANCHESTER, Warwickgate House, Warwick Road, Old
   Trafford, Manchester M16 0GP. Tel: 0161-872 6471

The Police Service

There are 52 police forces in the United Kingdom, each responsible for policing in its area. Most forces' area is conterminous with one or more local authority areas. Policing in London is carried out by the Metropolitan Police and the City of London Police; in Northern Ireland by the Royal Ulster Constabulary; and by the Isle of Man, States of Jersey, and Guernsey forces in their respective islands and bailiwicks. National services include the National Criminal Intelligence Service and the National Missing Persons Bureau (*see* below).

Each police force is maintained by a police authority. The authorities of English and Welsh forces comprise local councillors, magistrates and independent members. In Scotland, there are eight joint police boards made up of local councillors. In London the authority for the Metropolitan Police is the Home Secretary, advised by the Metropolitan Police Committee; for the City of London Police the authority is a committee of the Corporation of London and includes councillors and magistrates. In Northern Ireland the Secretary of State appoints the police authority.

Police authorities are financed by central and local government grants and a precept on the council tax. Subject to the approval of the Home Secretary and to regulations, they appoint the chief constable. In England and Wales they are responsible for publishing annual policing plans and annual reports, setting local objectives and a budget, and levying the precept. The police authorities in Scotland are responsible for setting a budget, providing the resources necessary to police the area adequately, appointing officers of the rank of Assistant Chief Constable and above, and determining the number of officers and civilian staff in the force. The structure and responsibilities of the police authority in Northern Ireland are under review.

The Home Secretary and the Secretaries of State for Scotland and Northern Ireland are responsible for the organization, administration and operation of the police service. They make regulations covering matters such as police ranks, discipline, hours of duty, and pay and allowances. All police forces are subject to inspection by HM Inspectors of Constabulary, who report to the respective Secretary of State.

COMPLAINTS

The investigation and resolution of a serious complaint against a police officer in England and Wales is subject to the scrutiny of the Police Complaints Authority. An officer who is disciplined by his chief constable, whether as a result of a complaint or not, may appeal to the Home Secretary. In Scotland, chief constables are obliged to investigate a complaint against one of their officers; if there is a suggestion of criminal activity, the complaint is investigated by an independent public prosecutor. In Northern Ireland complaints are investigated by the Independent Commission for Police Complaints.

BASIC RATES OF PAY *from 1 September 1996**

Chief Constable	
No fixed term	£59,742–£85,431
Fixed term appointment	£62,730–£89,598
Assistant Chief Constable-designate	80% of their Chief Constable's pay

Assistant Chief Constable	
No fixed term	£50,769–£58,278
Fixed term appointment	£53,310–£61,191
Superintendent	£38,724–£46,362
Chief Inspector	£32,937–£35,589*
Inspector	£29,466–£32,067*
Sergeant	£22,785–£26,574*
Constable	£14,916–£23,607*

Metropolitan Police

Metropolitan Commissioner	£90,148
Deputy Commissioner	£83,712–£94,593
Assistant Commissioner	£75,699–£83,343
Commander	£50,769–£61,191

The rank of Chief Superintendent was abolished in April 1995. Existing appointments continue and receive the higher ranges of the pay scale for Superintendents
*These pay scales apply from 1 September 1996. Other pay scales apply from 1 September 1995; pay negotiations still in progress at time of going to press

THE SPECIAL CONSTABULARY

Each police force has its own special constabulary, made up of volunteers who work in their spare time. Special Constables have full police powers within their force and adjoining force areas, and assist regular officers with routine policing duties.

NATIONAL CRIMINAL INTELLIGENCE SERVICE

The function of the National Criminal Intelligence Service (NCIS) is to gather, collate and disseminate information and intelligence on serious crime of a regional national and international nature. It is independent of any other police organization.

Headquarters: Spring Gardens, 2 Citadel Place, London SEII 5EF. Tel: 0171-238 8000
Strength, 570
Director-General, A. H. Pacey, CBE, QPM
Deputy Director-General (Director (Intelligence)), J. P. Hamilton, QPM
Director, International Division, P. J. Byrne, MBE
Director, UK Division, P. L. Clay
Director, Resources Division, R. Creedon

NATIONAL MISSING PERSONS BUREAU

The Police National Missing Persons Bureau (PNMPB acts as a central clearing house of information, receiving reports about vulnerable missing persons that are still outstanding after 28 days and details of unidentified persons or remains within 48 hours of being found from all forces in England and Wales. Reports are also received from Scottish police forces, the RUC, and foreign police forces via Interpol.

Headquarters: New Scotland Yard, Broadway, London SWIH 0BG. Tel: 0171-230 1212
Director, C. J. Coombes

FORENSIC SCIENCE SERVICE

A new national Forensic Science Service was created in April 1996 by the merger of the Forensic Science Service and the Metropolitan Police Forensic Science Laboratory. It provides support and advice for the investigation of scenes of crime, scientific analysis of material, and inter

pretation of scientific results. Services are concentrated at sites in London, Birmingham, Chorley and Wetherby.
Headquarters: Priory House, Gooch Street North, Birmingham B5 6QQ. Tel: 0121-666 6606
Chief Executive, Dr J. Thompson

POLICE AUTHORITIES

Strength: actual strength of force as at mid 1996
Chair: chairman/convener of the police authority/police committee/joint police board

ENGLAND

AVON AND SOMERSET CONSTABULARY, *HQ,* PO Box 37, Valley Road, Portishead, Bristol BS20 8QJ. Tel: 01275-818181. *Strength,* 2,978; *Chief Constable,* D. J. Shattock, CBE, QPM; *Chair,* I. Hoddell

BEDFORDSHIRE POLICE, *HQ,* Woburn Road, Kempston, Bedford MK43 9AX. Tel: 01234-841212. *Strength,* 1,130; *Chief Constable,* M. O'Byrne, QPM; *Chair,* A. P. Hendry, CBE

CAMBRIDGESHIRE CONSTABULARY, *HQ,* Hinchingbrooke Park, Huntingdon, Cambs PE18 8NP. Tel: 01480-456111. *Strength,* 1,270; *Chief Constable,* D. G. Gunn, QPM; *Chair,* J. Reynolds

CHESHIRE CONSTABULARY, *HQ,* Nuns Road, Chester CH1 2PP. Tel: 01244-350000. *Strength,* 2,003; *Chief Constable,* J. M. Jones, QPM; *Chair,* R. Tilling

CLEVELAND CONSTABULARY, *HQ,* PO Box 70, Ladgate Lane, Middlesbrough TS8 9EH. Tel: 01642-326326. *Strength,* 1,428; *Chief Constable,* B. D. D. Shaw, QPM; *Chair,* A. Gwenlan

CUMBRIA CONSTABULARY, *HQ,* Carleton Hall, Penrith, Cumbria CA10 2AU. Tel: 01768-891999. *Strength,* 1,118; *Chief Constable,* A. G. Elliott, QPM; *Chair,* R. Watson

DERBYSHIRE POLICE, *HQ,* Butterley Hall, Ripley, Derbyshire DE5 3RS. Tel: 01773-570100. *Strength,* 1,765; *Chief Constable,* J. F. Newing, QPM; *Chair,* K. Wilkinson

DEVON AND CORNWALL CONSTABULARY, *HQ,* Middlemoor, Exeter EX2 7HQ. Tel: 0990-777444. *Strength,* 2,944; *Chief Constable,* J. S. Evans, QPM; *Chair,* B. Homer, OBE

DORSET POLICE FORCE, *HQ,* Winfrith, Dorchester, Dorset DT2 8DZ. Tel: 01929-462727. *Strength,* 1,269; *Chief Constable,* D. W. Aldous, QPM; *Chair,* Sir Stephen Hammick, Bt.

DURHAM CONSTABULARY, *HQ,* Aykley Heads, Durham DH1 5TT. Tel: 0191-386 4929. *Strength,* 1,404; *Chief Constable,* F. W. Taylor, QPM; *Chair,* J. Knox

ESSEX POLICE, *HQ,* PO Box 2, Springfield, Chelmsford CM2 6DA. Tel: 01245-491491. *Strength,* 2,915; *Chief Constable,* J. H. Burrow, CBE; *Chair,* E. Peel

GLOUCESTERSHIRE CONSTABULARY, *HQ,* Holland House, Lansdown Road, Cheltenham, Glos GL51 6QH. Tel: 01242-521321. *Strength,* 1,160; *Chief Constable,* A. J. P. Butler, QPM; *Chair,* R. Somers, PH.D.

GREATER MANCHESTER POLICE, *HQ,* PO Box 22 (S. West PDO), Chester House, Boyer Street, Manchester M16 0RE. Tel: 0161-872 5050. *Strength,* 7,186; *Chief Constable,* D. Wilmot, QPM; *Chair,* S. Murphy

HAMPSHIRE POLICE, *HQ,* West Hill, Winchester, Hants SO22 5DB. Tel: 01962-868133. *Strength,* 3,351; *Chief Constable,* J. C. Hoddinott, CBE, QPM; *Chair,* M. J. Clark

HERTFORDSHIRE CONSTABULARY, *HQ,* Stanborough Road, Welwyn Garden City, Herts AL8 6XF. Tel: 01707-354200. *Strength,* 1,716; *Chief Constable,* P. Sharpe, QPM; *Chair,* R. Gordon

HUMBERSIDE POLICE, *HQ,* Queens Gardens, Kingston upon Hull HU1 3DJ. Tel: 01482-326111. *Strength,* 2,036; *Chief Constable,* D. A. Leonard, QPM; *Chair,* I. A. Cawsey

KENT CONSTABULARY, *HQ,* Sutton Road, Maidstone, Kent ME15 9BZ. Tel: 01622-690690. *Strength,* 3,156; *Chief Constable,* J. D. Phillips, QPM; *Chair,* Sir John Grugeon

LANCASHIRE CONSTABULARY, *HQ,* PO Box 77, Hutton, Preston, Lancs PR4 5SB. Tel: 01772-614444. *Strength,* 3,202; *Chief Constable,* Mrs P. A. Clare, QPM; *Chair,* Mrs R. B. Henig

LEICESTERSHIRE CONSTABULARY, *HQ,* PO Box 999, Leicester LE99 1AZ. Tel: 0116-253 0066. *Strength,* 1,919; *Chief Constable,* K. Povey, QPM; *Chair,* R. A. Wann

LINCOLNSHIRE POLICE, *HQ,* PO Box 999, Lincoln LN5 7PH. Tel: 01522-532222. *Strength,* 1,176; *Chief Constable,* J. P. Bensley, QPM; *Chair,* R. Staples

MERSEYSIDE POLICE, *HQ,* PO Box 59, Canning Place, Liverpool L69 1JD. Tel: 0151-709 6010. *Strength,* 4,446; *Chief Constable,* Sir James Sharples, QPM; *Chair,* Ms C. Gustafson

NORFOLK CONSTABULARY, *HQ,* Martineau Lane, Norwich NR1 2DJ. Tel: 01603-768769. *Strength,* 1,392; *Chief Constable,* K. R. Williams, QPM; *Chair,* B. J. Landale

NORTHAMPTONSHIRE POLICE, *HQ,* Wootton Hall, Northampton NN4 0JQ. Tel: 01604-700700. *Strength,* 1,200; *Chief Constable,* new appointment awaited; *Chair,* Dr M. Dickie

NORTHUMBRIA POLICE, *HQ,* Ponteland, Newcastle upon Tyne NE20 0BL. Tel: 01661-872555. *Strength,* 3,736; *Chief Constable,* J. A. Stevens, QPM; *Chair,* G. Gill

NORTH YORKSHIRE POLICE, *HQ,* Newby Wiske Hall, Newby Wiske, Northallerton, N. Yorks DL7 9HA. Tel: 01609-783131. *Strength,* 1,331; *Chief Constable,* D. M. Burke, QPM; *Chair,* Mrs A. F. Harris

NOTTINGHAMSHIRE CONSTABULARY, *HQ,* Sherwood Lodge, Arnold, Nottingham NG5 8PP. Tel: 0115-967 0999. *Strength,* 2,367; *Chief Constable,* C. F. Bailey, QPM; *Chair,* C. P. Winterton

SOUTH YORKSHIRE POLICE, *HQ,* Snig Hill, Sheffield S3 8LY. Tel: 0114-276 8522. *Strength,* 4,825; *Chief Constable,* R. Wells, QPM; *Chair,* C. Swindells

STAFFORDSHIRE POLICE, *HQ,* Cannock Road, Stafford ST17 0QG. Tel: 01785-257717. *Strength,* 2,215; *Chief Constable,* J. W. Giffard; *Chair,* J. T. Meir

SUFFOLK CONSTABULARY, *HQ,* Martlesham Heath, Ipswich IP5 7QS. Tel: 01473-613500. *Strength,* 1,127; *Chief Constable,* A. T. Coe, QPM; *Chair,* M. N. Smith

SURREY POLICE, *HQ,* Mount Browne, Sandy Lane, Guildford, Surrey GU3 1HG. Tel: 01483-571212. *Strength,* 1,676; *Chief Constable,* D. J. Williams, QPM; *Chair,* A. C. Tisdall

SUSSEX POLICE, *HQ,* Malling House, Church Lane, Lewes, E. Sussex BN7 2DZ. Tel: 01273-475432. *Strength,* 3,099; *Chief Constable,* P. Whitehouse, QPM; *Chair,* Dr J. M. M. Walsh, RD

THAMES VALLEY POLICE, *HQ,* Oxford Road, Kidlington, Oxon OX5 2NX. Tel: 01865-846000. *Strength,* 3,724; *Chief Constable,* C. Pollard, QPM; *Chair,* Mrs D. J. Priestley

WARWICKSHIRE CONSTABULARY, *HQ,* PO Box 4, Leek Wootton, Warwick CV35 7QB. Tel: 01926-415000. *Strength,* 977; *Chief Constable,* P. D. Joslin, QPM; *Chair,* F. Pithie

WEST MERCIA CONSTABULARY, *HQ,* PO Box 55, Hindlip Hall, Hindlip, Worcester WR3 8SP. Tel: 01905-723000. *Strength,* 2,061; *Chief Constable,* D. C. Blakey, QPM; *Chair,* G. Raxster

WEST MIDLANDS POLICE, *HQ,* PO Box 52, Lloyd House, Colmore Circus, Queensway, Birmingham B4 6NQ. Tel: 0121-626 5000. *Strength,* 7,280; *Chief Constable,* E. Crew, QPM; *Chair,* R. Jones

WEST YORKSHIRE POLICE, *HQ,* PO Box 9, Laburnum
Road, Wakefield, W. Yorks WF1 3QP. Tel: 01924-375222.
Strength, 5,118; *Chief Constable,* K. Hellawell, QPM; *Chair,*
T. Brennan
WILTSHIRE CONSTABULARY, *HQ,* London Road, Devizes,
Wilts SN10 2DN. Tel: 01380-722341. *Strength,* 1,120; *Chief
Constable,* W. R. Girven, QPM; *Chair,* H. A. Woolnough

WALES

DYFED–POWYS POLICE, *HQ,* PO Box 99, Llangunnor,
Carmarthen, Dyfed SA31 2PF. Tel: 01267-222020.
Strength, 1,002; *Chief Constable,* R. White, CBE, QPM; *Chair,*
W. J. W. Evans
GWENT CONSTABULARY, *HQ,* Croesyceiliog, Cwmbran
NP44 2XJ. Tel: 01633-838111. *Strength,* 1,210; *Chief
Constable,* new appointment awaited; *Chair,* D. Turnbull
NORTH WALES POLICE, *HQ,* Glan-y-don, Colwyn Bay,
Clwyd LL29 8AW. Tel: 01492-517171. *Strength,* 1,381;
Chief Constable, M. J. Argent, QPM; *Chair,* G. Bartley
SOUTH WALES CONSTABULARY, *HQ,* Cowbridge Road,
Bridgend CF31 3SU. Tel: 01656-655555. *Strength,* 2,994;
Chief Constable, A. T. Burden, QPM; *Chair,* B. P. Murray

SCOTLAND

CENTRAL SCOTLAND POLICE, *HQ,* Randolphfield, Stirling
FK8 2HD. Tel: 01786-456000. *Strength,* 657; *Chief Constable,*
W. J. M. Wilson, QPM; *Convener,* Mrs J. Burness
DUMFRIES AND GALLOWAY CONSTABULARY, *HQ,*
Cornwall Mount, Dumfries DG1 1PZ. Tel: 01387-252112.
Strength, 383; *Chief Constable,* W. Rae; *Chair,* K. Cameron
FIFE CONSTABULARY, *HQ,* Detroit Road, Glenrothes, Fife
KY6 2RJ. Tel: 01592-418888. *Strength,* 797; *Chief Constable,*
J. P. Hamilton, QPM; *Chair,* A. Keddie
GRAMPIAN POLICE, *HQ,* Queen Street, Aberdeen AB10 1ZA.
Tel: 01224-639111. *Strength,* 1,166; *Chief Constable,*
I. T. Oliver, QPM, PH.D.; *Chair,* Prof. J. Thomaneck
LOTHIAN AND BORDERS POLICE, *HQ,* Fettes Avenue,
Edinburgh EH4 1RB. Tel: 0131-311 3131. *Strength,* 2,519;
Chief Constable, R. Cameron, QPM; *Chair,* E. Drummond
NORTHERN CONSTABULARY, *HQ,* Perth Road, Inverness
IV2 3SY. Tel: 01463-715555. *Strength,* 643; *Chief Constable,*
W. A. Robertson, QPM; *Chair,* N. Graham
STRATHCLYDE POLICE, *HQ,* 173 Pitt Street, Glasgow
G2 4JS. Tel: 0141-532 2000. *Strength,* 7,216; *Chief
Constable,* J. Orr, OBE; *Chair,* W. Timoney
TAYSIDE POLICE, *HQ,* PO Box 59, West Bell Street,
Dundee DD1 9JU. Tel: 01382-223200. *Strength,* 1,090;
Chief Constable, W. A. Spence, QPM; *Chair,* A. Shand

NORTHERN IRELAND

ROYAL ULSTER CONSTABULARY, *HQ,* Brooklyn, Knock
Road, Belfast BT5 6LE. Tel: 01232-650222. *Strength,* 8,429;
Chief Constable, R. Flanagan; *Chair,* P. Armstrong

ISLANDS

ISLAND POLICE FORCE, *HQ,* Hospital Lane, St Peter Port,
Guernsey GY1 2QN. Tel: 01481-725111. *Strength,* 146;
Chief Officer (acting), Supt. G. W. Denning; *President, States
Committee for Home Affairs,* M. Torode
STATES OF JERSEY POLICE, *HQ,* Rouge Bouillon, PO Box
789, St Helier, Jersey JE2 3ZA. Tel: 01534-612612.
Strength, 243; *Chief Officer,* R. H. Le Breton; *Chair,*
M. Wavell
ISLE OF MAN CONSTABULARY, *HQ,* Glencrutchery Road,
Douglas, Isle of Man IM2 4RG. Tel: 01624-631212.
Strength, 213; *Chief Constable,* R. E. N. Oake; *Chairman,
Police Committee,* Hon. R. K. Corkill

METROPOLITAN POLICE SERVICE
New Scotland Yard, Broadway, London SW1H 0BG
Tel 0171-230 1212

Establishment, 27,994
Commissioner, Sir Paul Condon, QPM
Deputy Commissioner, B. Hayes, CBE, QPM
Receiver, P. Fletcher

OPERATIONAL AREAS
Assistant Commissioners, A. J. Speed, QPM (*Central*);
B. H. Skitt, BEM, QPM (*North-West*); A. Dunn, QPM (*North
East*); W. I. R. Johnston, QPM (*South-East*); P. Manning,
QPM (*South-West*)
Deputy Assistant Commissioners, D. Flanders, QPM;
M. J. Sullivan, OBE, QPM
Commanders, D. M. T. Kendrick, QPM; J. F. Purnell, GM, QP
T. D. Laidlaw, QPM; C. R. Pearman; A. L. Rowe, QPM;
M. Briggs; M. R. Campbell; W. I. Griffiths, BEM; S. C.
Pilkington; D. A. Ray, QPM; R. Gaspar; D. Gilbertson;
Mrs J. Stichbury; J. Townsend

SPECIALIST OPERATIONS DEPARTMENT
Assistant Commissioner, D. C. Veness, QPM
Deputy Assistant Commissioners, J. A. Howley, QPM;
A. G. Fry, QPM
Commanders, R. C. Marsh, QPM; B. G. Moss, QPM;
J. G. D. Grieve; R. A. C. Ramm

COMPLAINTS INVESTIGATION BUREAU
Commander, I. G. Quinn

INSPECTORATE
Commander, B. J. Luckhurst

OTHER DEPARTMENTS
Director, Strategic Co-ordination, Mrs B. Reeves
Director, Personnel, Mrs H. Maslen
Director, Consultancy and Information Services, Mrs
S. Merchant
Director, Public Affairs, Mrs S. Cullum
Solicitor, D. Hamilton
Director, Technology, N. Boothman
Director, Property Services, T. G. Lawrence

CITY OF LONDON POLICE
26 Old Jewry, London EC2R 8DJ
Tel 0171-601 2222

Strength (January 1996), 937

The City of London Police is responsible for policing t
City of London. Though small, the area includes one of t
most important financial centres in the world and the for
has particular expertise in areas such as fraud investigati
as well as the areas required of any police force.

The force has a wholly elected police authority, t
police committee of the Corporation of London, whi
appoints the Commissioner.
Commissioner (£91,764), W. Taylor, QPM
Assistant Commissioner (£71,577), P. Nove
Commander (£61,191), J. Davison
Chairman of Police Committee, Maj.-Gen. P. Maclellan, CB,
CVO, MBE

BRITISH TRANSPORT POLICE
15 Tavistock Place, London WC1H 9SJ
Tel 0171-388 7541

Strength (March 1996), 2,165

British Transport Police is the national police force for the railways in England, Wales and Scotland, including the London Underground system and the Docklands Light Railway. The Chief Constable reports to the British Transport Police Committee. The members of the Committee are appointed by the British Railways Board, Railtrack and London Underground Ltd.
Chief Constable, D. O'Brien, OBE, QPM
Deputy Chief Constable, A. Parker, QPM

MINISTRY OF DEFENCE POLICE
MDP Wethersfield, Braintree, Essex CM7 4AZ
Tel 01371-854000

Strength (April 1996), 4,019

The Ministry of Defence Police is an agency of the Ministry of Defence. It is a national civilian police force whose officers are appointed by the Secretary of State for Defence. It is responsible for the policing of all military land, stations and establishments in the United Kingdom. The agency also has certain responsibilities for the civilian Ministry of Defence Guard Service.
Chief Constable, W. E. E. Boreham, OBE
Deputy Chief Constable, A. V. Comben
Head of Secretariat, J. A. Smallwood

ROYAL PARKS CONSTABULARY
The Old Police House, Hyde Park, London W2 2UH
Tel 0171-298 2000

Strength (May 1996), 177

The Royal Parks Constabulary is maintained by the Royal Parks Agency, an executive agency of the Department of National Heritage, and is responsible for the policing of eight royal parks in and around London. These comprise an area in excess of 6,300 acres. Officers of the force are appointed under the Parks Regulations Act 1872 as amended.
Chief Officer, W. Ross
Deputy Chief Officer, A. McLean

UK ATOMIC ENERGY AUTHORITY CONSTABULARY
Building E6, Culham Laboratory, Abingdon,
Oxon OX14 3DB
Tel 01235-463760

Strength (July 1996), 479

The Constabulary is responsible for policing UK Atomic Energy Authority and British Nuclear Fuels PLC establishments and for escorting nuclear material between establishments. The Chief Constable is responsible, through the Atomic Energy Authority Police Committee, to the President of the Board of Trade.
Chief Constable, A. J. Pointer, QPM
Assistant Chief Constable, W. H. Pryke

STAFF ASSOCIATIONS

ASSOCIATION OF CHIEF POLICE OFFICERS OF ENGLAND, WALES AND NORTHERN IRELAND, Room 311, Wellington House, 67–73 Buckingham Gate, London SW1E 6BE. Tel: 0171-230 7184. Represents Chief Constables, Deputy and Assistant Chief Constables in England, Wales and Northern Ireland, and officers of the rank of Commander and above in the Metropolitan and City of London Police. *General Secretary*, Miss M. C. E. Barton

THE POLICE SUPERINTENDENTS' ASSOCIATION OF ENGLAND AND WALES, 67A Reading Road, Pangbourne, Reading RG8 7JD. Tel: 01189-844005. Represents officers of the rank of Superintendent. *Secretary*, Chief Supt. D. A. Clark

THE POLICE FEDERATION OF ENGLAND AND WALES, 15–17 Langley Road, Surbiton, Surrey KT6 6LP. Tel: 0181-399 2224. Represents officers up to and including the rank of Chief Inspector. *General Secretary*, L. Williams

ASSOCIATION OF CHIEF POLICE OFFICERS IN SCOTLAND, Police Headquarters, Fettes Avenue, Edinburgh EH4 1RB. Tel: 0131-311 3051. Represents the Chief Constables, Deputy and Assistant Chief Constables of the Scottish police forces. *Hon. Secretary*, H. R. Cameron, QPM

THE ASSOCIATION OF SCOTTISH POLICE SUPERINTENDENTS, Secretariat, 173 Pitt Street, Glasgow G2 4JS. Tel: 0141-221 5796. Represents officers of the rank of Superintendent. *Hon. Secretary*, Chief Supt. A. Forrest

THE SCOTTISH POLICE FEDERATION, 5 Woodside Place, Glasgow G3 7QF. Tel: 0141-332 5234. Represents officers up to and including the rank of Chief Inspector. *General Secretary*, D. J. Keil, QPM

THE SUPERINTENDENTS' ASSOCIATION OF NORTHERN IRELAND, MSU RUC Station, Musgrave Street, Belfast BT1 3HX. Tel: 01232-700507. Represents Superintendents and Chief Superintendents in the RUC. *Hon. Secretary*, Supt. W. T. Brown

THE POLICE FEDERATION FOR NORTHERN IRELAND, Royal Ulster Constabulary, Garnerville, Garnerville Road, Belfast BT4 2NX. Tel: 01232-760831. Represents officers up to and including the rank of Chief Inspector. *Secretary*, D. A. McClurg

Crime Statistics

ENGLAND AND WALES

CRIMINAL JUSTICE STATISTICS 1994

Number of arrests	1,753,000,000
Notifiable offences recorded	5,036,000
Notifiable offences cleared up	1,320,000
Clear-up rate	26%
*Number of offenders cautioned	308,000
Defendants proceeded against at magistrates' courts	1,947,000
Defendants found guilty at magistrates' courts	1,340,000
Defendants tried at Crown Courts	86,000
Defendants found guilty at Crown Courts	68,000
Defendants sentenced at Crown Courts after summary conviction	3,000
Total offenders found guilty at both courts	1,408,000
*Total offenders found guilty or cautioned	1,716,000

*Excludes motoring offences

AVERAGE LENGTH OF SENTENCE 1994 *in months*

	Males aged 21 and over	Females aged 21 and over
Magistrates' courts	3.1	2.5–2.6
Crown court	21.6	18.6

OFFENDERS SENTENCED BY TYPE OF SENTENCE OR ORDER 1994

Absolute discharge	25,900
Conditional discharge	108,900
Fine	1,055,200
Probation order	50,500
Supervision order	9,200
Community service order	49,500
Attendance sentence order	7,300
Combination order	12,400
Young offender institution	16,800
Imprisonment:	
Suspended	3,200
Unsuspended	52,400
Otherwise dealt with	19,100
All sentences or orders: total	1,407,100
Of which:	
Immediate custody	69,200
Community sentences	128,900

Source: HMSO – *Criminal Statistics England and Wales 1994*

SCOTLAND

CRIMINAL JUSTICE STATISTICS 1994

Total crimes and offences recorded	990,981
Number of persons proceeded against	178,292
Persons with charge proved	158,119

PERSONS WITH CHARGE PROVED *by main penalty* 1994

Absolute discharge	430
Remit to children's hearing	122
Admonition or caution	15,967
Compensation order	1,659
Fine	112,428
Probation	6,011
Community service order	5,430
Insanity, hospital or guardianship order	118
Detention of child	28
Young offender institution	4,426
Prison	11,500
All penalties: total	158,119

Source: Scottish Office – *Annual Abstract of Statistics 1995*

POLICE STRENGTHS 1996

	Male	Female	Total
ENGLAND AND WALES			
Total officers	108,615	18,262	126,877
Ethnic minority officers	1,793	484	2,277
Special constables	12,803	6,925	19,728
Civilians	20,821	32,112	52,933
SCOTLAND			
Officers	12,627	1,885	14,512
Special constables	1,523	454	1,977
Civilians	1,539	2,518	4,057
NORTHERN IRELAND			
Officers	7,536	893	8,429
Special constables	977	545	1,522
Civilians	732	2,032	2,764

Sources: Home Office; Scottish Office; RUC

Defence

The armed forces of the United Kingdom comprise the Royal Navy, the Army and the Royal Air Force. The Queen is commander-in-chief of all the armed forces. The Ministry of Defence, headed by a Secretary of State, provides the support structure for the armed forces. Within the Ministry of Defence, the Defence Council has overall responsibility for running the armed forces. The Chief of Staff of each service reports through the Chief of the Defence Staff to the Secretary of State on matters relating to the running of his service. The Chief of Staff also chairs the executive committee of the appropriate service board, which manages the service in accordance with centrally-determined objectives and budgets. The military-civilian Central Staffs, headed by the Vice-Chief of the Defence Staff and the Second Permanent Under-Secretary of State, are responsible for policy, operational requirements, commitments, financial management, resource planning and civilian personnel management. The Procurement Executive is responsible for purchasing equipment. The Defence Intelligence Staff and the Defence Scientific Staff also form part of the Ministry of Defence.

As a result of the 1994 'Front Line First' defence costs study, the Ministry of Defence has been restructured and a permanent Joint Headquarters for the conduct of joint operations was set up at Northwood in April 1996. The Joint Headquarters connects the policy and strategic functions of the MoD Head Office with the conduct of operations and strengthens the policy/executive division.

ARMED FORCES STRENGTHS *as at 1 April 1996*

All Services	222,417
Men	206,660
Women	15,757
Royal Naval Services	48,307
Men	44,676
Women	3,631
Army	109,387
Men	102,858
Women	6,529
Royal Air Force	64,723
Men	59,126
Women	5,597

DEPLOYMENT; *as at April 1996*

Outside Great Britain, army units were stationed in the South Atlantic, Belize, Brunei, Cyprus, the Falkland Islands, Germany, Gibraltar, the Gulf, Hong Kong (the Brigade of Gurkhas), Northern Ireland and Turkey. Royal Air Force units were stationed in the central Atlantic, the eastern Atlantic and North Sea, the Channel, Cyprus, the Falkland Islands, Germany, Gibraltar, the Gulf, Hong Kong, Italy, Northern Ireland, Turkey and the former Yugoslavia.

Members of the British armed forces were also deployed with the United Nations Force in Cyprus (UNFICYP), the United Nations Iraq-Kuwait Observer Mission (UNIKOM), the Implementation Force in the former Yugoslavia (IFOR) and as military observers with the United Nations Mission in Georgia/Organization for Security and Co-operation in Europe (UNOMIG/OSCE).

DEFENCE CUTS

*DEFENCE CASH PROVISION IN REAL TERMS

	£ million
1994–5 outturn	22,562
1995–6 estimated outturn	20,653
1996–7 plans	20,293
1997–8 plans	20,258

*At 1994–5 prices, based on GDP assumptions in the 1996–7 Financial Statement and Budget Report

SERVICE PERSONNEL

	Royal Navy	Army	RAF
1990 strength	63,200	152,800	89,700
1991 target for 1995	55,000	116,000	75,000
July 1994 target for 2000	49,100	117,800	62,500
May 1995 plans for 1996	48,000	117,000	66,500
May 1996 plans for 1 April 1997	46,000	111,000	57,000

MoD CIVILIAN PERSONNEL

1990–1 level	170,642
February 1994 level	144,010
April 1994 target for 1996	128,700
1 April 1996 level	127,700
July 1994 target for 2000	121,600
May 1996 target for 2002	115,800

MINISTRY OF DEFENCE

Main Building, Whitehall, London SW1A 2HB
Tel 0171-218 6645

For ministerial and civil service salaries, *see* page 277
For Services salaries, *see* pages 390–2

Secretary of State for Defence, The Rt. Hon. Michael Portillo, MP
 Private Secretary, Ms M. Aldred
 Special Adviser, Ms A. Broom
 Parliamentary Private Secretary, D. Ames, MP
Minister of State for the Armed Forces, The Hon. Nicholas Soames, MP
 Private Secretary, D. King
Minister of State for Defence Procurement, The Rt. Hon. James Arbuthnot, MP
 Private Secretary, J. Wright
Parliamentary Private Secretary to Mr Soames and Mr Arbuthnot, N. Hawkins, MP
Parliamentary Under-Secretary of State, The Earl Howe
 Private Secretary, G. Dean
Permanent Under-Secretary of State (G1), R. C. Mottram
 Private Secretary, D. Stephens
Chief of the Defence Staff, Field Marshal Sir Peter Inge, GCB
 (*until early 1997*)

THE DEFENCE COUNCIL

The Defence Council is responsible for running the Armed Forces. It is chaired by the Secretary of State for Defence and consists of: the Ministers of State; the Parliamentary Under-Secretary of State; the Permanent Under-Secretary of State; the Chief of the Defence Staff; the Chief of the

Naval Staff; the Chief of the General Staff; the Chief of the Air Staff; the Vice-Chief of the Defence Staff; the Chief Scientific Adviser; the Chief of Defence Procurement; and the Second Permanent Under-Secretary of State.

CHIEFS OF STAFF

CHIEF OF THE NAVAL STAFF
Chief of the Naval Staff and First Sea Lord, Adm. Sir Jock Slater, GCB, LVO, ADC
Asst Chief of the Naval Staff, Rear-Adm. J. J. Blackham

CHIEF OF THE GENERAL STAFF
Chief of the General Staff, Gen. Sir Charles Guthrie, GCB, LVO, OBE, ADC (*Gen.*)
Asst Chief of the General Staff, Maj.-Gen. M. A. Willcocks
Director-General, Development and Doctrine, Lt.-Gen. M. D. Jackson, CBE

CHIEF OF THE AIR STAFF
Chief of the Air Staff, Air Chief Marshal Sir Michael Graydon, GCB, CBE, ADC
Asst Chief of the Air Staff, Air Vice-Marshal T. I. Jenner, CB
British-American Community Relations, Air Marshal Sir John Kemball (retd)
Chief Executive, National Air Traffic Services (G2), D. J. McLauchlan

CENTRAL STAFFS

Vice-Chief of the Defence Staff, Air Chief Marshal Sir John Willis, KCB, CBE
Second Permanent Under-Secretary of State (G1A), Sir Moray Stewart, KCB
Defence Services Secretary, Air Vice-Marshal P. J. Harding, CB, CBE, AFC
Deputy CDS (Commitments), Lt.-Gen. Sir Alexander Harley, KBE, CB
Asst Under-Secretary (Home and Overseas) (G3), B. R. Hawtin
Asst CDS (Operations), Air Vice-Marshal A. J. Harrison
Asst CDS (Logistics), Maj.-Gen. G. A. Ewer
Deputy CDS (Systems), Vice-Adm. J. H. Dunt
Asst CDS, Operational Requirements (Sea Systems), Rear-Adm. R. T. R. Phillips
Asst CDS, Operational Requirements (Land Systems), Maj.-Gen. E. F. G. Burton, OBE
Asst CDS, Operational Requirements (Air Systems), Air Vice-Marshal C. C. C. Coville, CB
Director-General, Information and Communications Services, Maj.-Gen. W. J. P. Robins, OBE
Deputy CDS (Programmes and Personnel), Air Marshal P. T. Squire, DFC, AFC
Asst CDS (Programmes), Rear-Admiral N. R. Essenhigh
Surgeon-General, Surgeon Vice-Adm. A. L. Revell, QHS
Chief Executive, Defence Dental Agency, Air Vice-Marshal J. Mackey, QHDS
Director, Defence Nursing Services, Air Cdre V. M. Hand
Director-General, Defence Medical Training, Maj.-Gen. C. G. Callow
Deputy Under-Secretary (Policy) (G2), R. P. Hatfield, CBE
Asst Under-Secretary (Policy) (G3), G. W. Hopkinson
Asst CDS (Policy), Air Vice-Marshal J. C. French

DEFENCE INFORMATION STAFF
Press Secretary and Chief of Information (G4), Ms G. Samuel
Deputy Press Secretary and Director of Information (Policy and Procurement) (G5), I. Lee
Director, Public Relations (Navy), Capt. C. Beagley, RN
Director, Public Relations (Army), Brig. P. C. C. Trousdell
Director, Public Relations (RAF), Air Cdre G. L. McRobbie

MANAGEMENT AND FINANCE
Deputy Under-Secretaries (G2), J. F. Howe, CB, OBE (*Civilian Management*); R. T. Jackling, CB, CBE (*Resources, Finance and Programmes*)
Defence Housing Executive (G3), C. J. I. James
Asst Under-Secretaries (G3), D. C. R. Heyhoe (*General Finance*); I. D. Fauset (*Civilian Personnel Management*); B. A. E. Taylor (*Civilian Policy Management*); C. V. Balmer (*Financial Management*); Miss A. Walker (*Service Personnel*); vacant (*Director-General of Management and Organization*); D. J. Seammen (*Programmes*); D. Fisher (*Systems*); A. Inglese (*Legal Adviser*)
Defence Estate Organization (G4), J. Mustow (*Works*); A. Boardman (*Land*)
Chief Statistical Adviser and Chief Executive of Defence Analytical Services Agency, P. Altobell
Chief Executive, Defence Bills Agency, T. R. Thurgate

DEFENCE INTELLIGENCE STAFF
Chief of Defence Intelligence
Director-General, Intelligence (Assessments)
Director-General, Scientific and Technical Intelligence
Director-General, Management and Support of Intelligence
Director-General, Intelligence Geographic Resources
Director, Defence Intelligence (Secretariat) (G5)

DEFENCE SCIENTIFIC STAFF
Chief Scientific Adviser (G1A), Prof. Sir David Davies, KBE
Chief Scientist (G2), P. D. Ewins, CB
Nuclear Weapon Safety Adviser (G2), Dr A. Ferguson
Deputy Chief Scientists (G3), P. M. Sutcliffe (*Research and Technology*); M. Earwicker (*Scrutiny and Analysis*)
Asst Chief Scientific Adviser (Nuclear) (G4), P. W. Roper
Chief Executive, Defence Evaluation and Research Agency (G2), J. A. R. Chisholm

SECOND SEA LORD/COMMANDER-IN-CHIEF NAVAL HOME COMMAND
Second Sea Lord and C.-in-C. Naval Home Command, Adm. Sir Michael Boyce, KCB, OBE
Director-General, Naval Personnel (Strategy and Plans) and Chief of Staff to Second Sea Lord, Rear-Adm. R. B. Lees
Asst Under-Secretary (Naval Personnel) (G3), J. M. Moss, CB
Flag Officer Training and Recruiting, Rear-Adm. J. H. S. McAnally, LVO
Naval Secretary and Director-General, Naval Manning, Rear-Adm. F. M. Malbon
Director-General, Naval Medical Services, Surgeon Rear-Adm. A. Craig, QHP
Director-General, Naval Chaplaincy Services, Ven. M. W. Bucks, QHC

NAVAL SUPPORT COMMAND
Chief of Fleet Support, Vice-Adm. Sir Toby Frere, KCB
Asst Under-Secretary (Fleet Support) (G3), D. J. Gould
Director-General, Fleet Support (Ships) (G3), R. V. Babbington
Director-General, Naval Bases and Supply (N), Rear-Adm. J. A. Trewby
Director-General, Naval Bases and Supply and Chief Inspector of Explosives (G4), D. J. Stevens
Director-General, Fleet Support (Operations and Plans), Rear-Adm. P. Spencer
Director-General, Aircraft (Navy), Rear-Adm. D. J. Wood
Flag Officer Scotland, N. England and N. Ireland, Rear-Adm. J. G. Tolhurst, CB

Hydrographer of the Royal Navy and Chief Executive, Hydrographic Office, Rear-Adm. J. P. Clarke, CB, LVO, MBE

COMMANDER-IN-CHIEF FLEET

C.-in-C. Fleet, Adm. Sir Peter Abbott, KCB
Deputy Commander Fleet and Chief of Staff, Vice-Adm. Sir Jonathan Tod, KCB, CBE
Chief of Staff (Operations) and Flag Officer Submarines, Rear-Adm. J. F. Perowne
Flag Officer Surface Flotilla, Vice-Adm. J. R. Brigstocke
Flag Officer Sea Training, Rear-Adm. P. M. Franklyn
Flag Officer Naval Aviation, Rear-Adm. T. W. Loughran
Commandant-General, Royal Marines, Maj.-Gen. D. A. S. Pennefather, CB, OBE

QUARTERMASTER-GENERAL'S DEPARTMENT

Quartermaster-General, Lt.-Gen. S. Cowan, CBE
Chief of Staff, Maj.-Gen. K. O'Donoghue, CBE
Asst Under-Secretary (Quartermaster) (G3), N. H. R. Evans
Director-General, Logistic Support (Army), Maj.-Gen. M. S. White, CBE
Director-General, Equipment (Army), Maj.-Gen. P. J. G. Corp, CB
Chief Executive, Logistics Information Systems Agency, Brig. A. W. Pollard
Chief Executive, Defence Postal and Courier Service, Brig. T. M. Brown, OBE
Chief Executive, Defence Transport and Movements Executive, Brig. M. G. R. Hodson, CBE
Chief Executive, Defence Clothing and Textiles Agency, Brig. M. J. Roycroft

ADJUTANT-GENERAL'S DEPARTMENT

Adjutant-General, Gen. Sir Michael Rose, KCB, CBE, DSO, QGM
Chief of Staff to the Adjutant-General, Maj.-Gen. R. A. Oliver, OBE
Director-General, Army Manning and Recruiting, Maj.-Gen. D. L. Burden, CB, CBE
Chaplain-General, Revd Dr V. Dobbins
Director, Army Legal Services, Maj.-Gen. A. P. V. Rogers, OBE
Head, Command Secretariat (G4), W. A. Perry
Military Secretary, Maj.-Gen. M. I. E. Scott, CBE, DSO
Director-General, Army Medical Services, Maj.-Gen. W. R. Short
Director-General, Individual Training, and Chief Executive, Army Individual Training Organization, Maj.-Gen. C. L. Elliott, MBE
Commandant, Royal Military Academy, Sandhurst, Maj.-Gen. J. F. Deverell, OBE
Commandant, Royal Military College of Science, Maj.-Gen. D. J. M. Jenkins, CBE

COMMANDER-IN-CHIEF LAND COMMAND

Commander-in-Chief, Land Command, Gen. Sir Roger Wheeler, KCB, CBE
Deputy Commander-in-Chief, Land Command, and Inspector-General, Territorial Army, Lt.-Gen. H. W. R. Pike, DSO, MBE
Chief of Staff, HQ Land Command, Maj.-Gen. C. G. C. Vyvyan, CBE
Deputy Chief of Staff, HQ Land Command, Maj.-Gen. R. A. Cordy-Simpson
Command Secretariat (G3), J. S. Pitt-Brooke

HQ STRIKE COMMAND

Air Officer Commanding-in-Chief, Air Chief Marshal Sir William Wratten, KBE, CB, AFC
Chief of Staff and Deputy Commander-in-Chief, Air Marshal G. A. Robertson, CBE
Senior Air Staff Officer, Air Vice-Marshal D. A. Hurrell
Air Officer Administration, Air Vice-Marshal T. B. Sherrington, OBE
Air Officer Commanding, No. 1 Group, Air Vice-Marshal J. R. Day
Air Officer Engineering and Supply, Air Vice-Marshal D. J. Saunders, CBE
Air Officer Commanding, No. 11/18 Group, Air Vice-Marshal C. R. Spink
Head, Command Secretariat (G5), J. P. Thatcher

HQ LOGISTIC COMMAND

Air Officer Commanding-in-Chief and Air Member for Logistics, Air Chief Marshal Sir John Allison, KCB, CBE
Chief of Staff, Land Command, Air Vice-Marshal C. G. Terry, CB, OBE
Air Officer Communications Information Systems and Air Officer Commanding Signals Units, Air Vice-Marshal B. C. McCandless
Director-General, Support Management (RAF), Air Vice-Marshal P. D. Markey
Command Secretary (G3), H. Griffiths
Chief Executive, RAF Maintenance Group Agency, Air Vice-Marshal R. H. Kyle, MBE

HQ PERSONNEL AND TRAINING COMMAND

Air Member for Personnel and Air Officer Commanding-in-Chief, Air Marshal Sir David Cousins, KCB, AFC
Chief of Staff and Director-General, Strategic Policy and Plans, Air Vice-Marshal M. D. Smart
Air Officer Training, Air Vice-Marshal J. A. G. May, CB, CBE
Air Secretary, Air Vice-Marshal R. P. O'Brien, OBE
Commandant, RAF Staff College, Bracknell, Air Vice-Marshal M. Van der Veen
Commandant, RAF Staff College, Cranwell, Air Vice-Marshal A. J. Stables
Director-General, Medical Services (RAF), Air Vice-Marshal J. A. Baird, QHP
Director, Legal Services (RAF), Air Vice-Marshal G. W. Carleton
Chaplain-in-Chief (RAF), Ven. P. R. Turner, QHC

PROCUREMENT EXECUTIVE

EXECUTIVE

Chief of Defence Procurement, Vice-Adm. Sir Robert Walmsley, KCB
Director-General, Land Systems and Master-General of the Ordnance, Lt.-Gen. Sir Robert Hayman-Joyce, KCB, CBE
Deputy Chief of Defence Procurement (Operations), Air Marshal Sir Roger Austin, KCB, AFC
Deputy Chief of Defence Procurement (Support) (G3), M. J. V. Bell

BUSINESS UNITS

Director-General (Business Strategy) (G3), J. A. Gulvin, CB
Director-General (Finance) (G3), B. Miller
President of the Ordnance Board, Air Vice-Marshal P. J. O'Reilly
Director-General, Commercial Directorate (G3), A. T. Phipps
Principal Director, Pricing and Quality Services (G4), N. J. Bennett

Director-General, Submarines (*G3*), C. V. Betts
Director-General, Surface Ships and Acting Controller of the Navy, Rear-Adm. F. P. Scourse, MBE
Director-General, Surface Weapons (*Naval*) (*G4*), A. M. Stagg
Chief, Strategic Systems Executive, Rear-Adm. P. A. M. Thomas
Director-General (*Nuclear*) (*G4*), Dr D. R. Glue
Director, Nuclear Projects (*G4*), R. A. Russell
Director-General, Command Information Systems (*G3*), J. D. Maines
Director-General, Air Systems 1, Air Vice-Marshal P. C. Norriss, CB, AFC
Director-General, Air Systems 2 (*G3*), G. E. Roe
Director-General, Weapons and Electronic Systems (*G3*), G. N. Beaven
Head of Defence Export Services (*G2*), C. B. G. Masefield
Military Deputy to Head of DES, Rear-Adm. J. F. T. G. Salt (retd)
Director-General, Marketing (*G3*), D. J. Bowen
Asst Under-Secretary (*Export Policy and Finance*) (*G4*), Dr A. M. Fox
Director-General, Saudi Armed Forces Project, Air Marshal I. D. Macfadyen, CB, OBE
Principal Directors of Contracts (*G4*), P. A. Gerard (*Navy*); A. V. Carey (*Ordnance*); S. L. Porter (*Air*)

DEFENCE AGENCIES

ARMY BASE REPAIR ORGANIZATION, Monxton Road, Andover, Hants SP11 8HT. Tel: 01264-383295. *Chief Executive*, J. R. Drew, CBE
ARMY BASE STORAGE AND DISTRIBUTION AGENCY, Monxton Road, Andover, Hants SP11 8HT. Tel: 01264-383334. *Chief Executive*, Brig. K. J. W. Goad, ADC
ARMY INDIVIDUAL TRAINING ORGANIZATION, Trenchard Lines, Upavon, Pewsey, Wilts SN9 6BE. Tel: 01980-615024. *Chief Executive*, Maj.-Gen. C. L. Elliott, MBE
ARMY TECHNICAL SUPPORT AGENCY, Room 23/11, Portway, Monxton Road, Andover, Hants SP11 8HT. Tel: 01264-383161. *Chief Executive*, J. R. Prince
DEFENCE ANALYTICAL SERVICES AGENCY, Northumberland House, Northumberland Avenue, London WC2N 5BP. Tel: 0171-218 0729. *Chief Executive*, P. Altobell
DEFENCE ANIMAL CENTRE, Welby Lane, Melton Mowbray, Leics LE13 0SL. Tel: 01664-410694. *Chief Executive*, Col. A. H. Roache
DEFENCE BILLS AGENCY, Room 410, Mersey House, Drury Lane, Liverpool L2 7PX. Tel: 0151-242 2234. *Chief Executive*, T. R. Thurgate
DEFENCE CLOTHING AND TEXTILES AGENCY, Monxton Road, Andover, Hants SP11 8HT. Tel: 01264-382216. *Chief Executive*, Brig. M. J. Roycroft
DEFENCE DENTAL AGENCY, Room 102, Lacon House, Theobalds Road, London WC1X 8RY. Tel: 0171-305 5733. *Chief Executive*, Air Vice-Marshal J. Mackey, QHDS
DEFENCE EVALUATION AND RESEARCH AGENCY, Farnborough, Hants GU14 6TD. Tel: 01252-392000. *Chief Executive*, J. A. R. Chisholm
DEFENCE MEDICAL SUPPLIES AGENCY, Defence Medical Equipment Depot, Drummond Barracks, Ludgershall, Andover, Hants SP11 9RU. Tel: 01264-798606. *Chief Executive*, B. Nimick
DEFENCE POSTAL AND COURIER SERVICE, Inglis Barracks, Mill Hill, London NW7 1PX. Tel: 0181-818 6300. *Director and Chief Executive*, Brig. T. M. Brown, OBE
DEFENCE SECONDARY CARE AGENCY, Room 1216, Empress State Building, Lillie Road, London SW6 1TR. Tel: 0171-305 6190. *Chief Executive*, R. Smith

DEFENCE TRANSPORT AND MOVEMENTS EXECUTIVE, Monxton Road, Andover, Hants SP11 8HT. Tel: 01264-382139. *Chief Executive*, Brig. M. G. R. Hodson, CBE
DISPOSAL SALES AGENCY, 7th Floor, 6 Hercules Road, London SE1. Tel: 0171-261 8853. *Chief Executive*, M. Westgate
HYDROGRAPHIC OFFICE, ADMIRALTY WAY, Taunton, Somerset TA1 2DN. Tel: 01823-337900. *Chief Executive, and Hydrographer of the Royal Navy*, Rear-Adm. J. P. Clarke, CB, LVO, MBE
JOINT AIR RECONNAISSANCE INTELLIGENCE CENTRE, RAF Brampton, Huntingdon, Cambs PE18 8QL. Tel: 01480-52151. *Chief Executive*, Gp Capt N. J. Pearson
LOGISTIC INFORMATION SYSTEMS AGENCY, Monxton Road, Andover, Hants SP11 8HT. Tel: 01264-382815. *Chief Executive*, Brig. A. W. Pollard
METEOROLOGICAL OFFICE, London Road, Bracknell, Berks RG12 2SZ. Tel: 01344-420242. *Chief Executive*, Prof. J. C. R. Hunt, FRS
MILITARY SURVEY, Elmwood Avenue, Feltham, Middx TW13 7AH. Tel: 0181-818 2193. *Chief Executive*, Brig. P. R. Wildman, OBE
MINSTRY OF DEFENCE POLICE, Wethersfield, Braintree, Essex CM7 4AZ. Tel: 01371-854000. *Chief Executive*, Chief Constable W. E. E. Boreham, OBE
NAVAL AIRCRAFT REPAIR ORGANIZATION, Royal Naval Yard, Fleetlands, Gosport, Hants PO13 0AW. Tel: 01705-544910. *Chief Executive*, Capt. W. S. Graham, RN
NAVAL RECRUITING AND TRAINING AGENCY, Victory Building, HM Naval Base, Portsmouth, Hants PO1 3LS. Tel: 01705-727602. *Chief Executive*, Rear-Adm. J. H. S. McAnally, LVO
PAY AND PERSONNEL AGENCY, Warminster Road, Bath BA1 5AA. Tel: 01225-828105. *Chief Executive*, M. A. Rowe
RAF MAINTENANCE GROUP AGENCY, RAF Brampton, Huntingdon, Cambs PE18 8QL. Tel: 01480-52151 ext. 6300. *Chief Executive*, Air Vice-Marshal R. H. Kyle, MBE
RAF SIGNALS ENGINEERING ESTABLISHMENT, RAF Henlow, Beds SG16 6DN. Tel: 01462-851515 ext. 7625. *Chief Executive*, Air Cdre P. C. Ayee
RAF TRAINING GROUP AGENCY, RAF Innsworth, Gloucester GL3 1EZ. Tel: 01452-712612 ext. 5302. *Chief Executive*, Air Vice-Marshal J. A. G. May, CB, CBE
SERVICE CHILDREN'S EDUCATION, BFPO 140. Tel: 00-49 2161 473296. *Chief Executive*, I. S. Mitchelson

The Royal Navy

LORD HIGH ADMIRAL OF THE UNITED KINGDOM
HM The Queen

ADMIRALS OF THE FLEET
HRH The Prince Philip, Duke of Edinburgh, KG, KT, OM, GBE, AC, QSO, PC, *apptd* 1953
The Lord Hill-Norton, GCB, *apptd* 1971
Sir Michael Pollock, GCB, LVO, DSC, *apptd* 1974
Sir Edward Ashmore, GCB, DSC, *apptd* 1977
The Lord Lewin, KG, GCB, LVO, DSC, *apptd* 1979
Sir Henry Leach, GCB, *apptd* 1982
Sir William Staveley, GCB, *apptd* 1989
Sir Julian Oswald, GCB, *apptd* 1993
Sir Benjamin Bathurst, GCB, *apptd* 1995

ADMIRALS
Slater, Sir Jock, GCB, LVO, ADC (*Chief of the Naval Staff and First Sea Lord*)
White, Sir Hugo, GCB, CBE (*Governor and C.-in-C. Gibraltar*)

Boyce, Sir Michael, KCB, OBE, ADC (*C.-in-C. Naval Home Command and Second Sea Lord*)

Abbott, Sir Peter, KCB (*C.-in-C. Fleet*)

VICE-ADMIRALS

Frere, Sir Toby, KCB (*Chief of Fleet Support*)

Moore, M. A. C., LVO (*Chief of Staff to Commander, Allied Naval Forces Southern Europe*)

Walmsley, Sir Robert, KCB (*Chief of Defence Procurement*)

Revell, A. L., QHS (*Surgeon-General*)

Tod, Sir Jonathan, KCB, CBE (*Deputy Comd. Fleet and Chief of Staff*)

Gretton, M. P. (*Supreme Allied Commander Atlantic's Representative in Europe*)

Dunt, J. H. (*Deputy CDS (Systems)*)

Brigstocke, J. R. (*Flag Officer Surface Flotilla*)

Garnett, I. D. G. (*Military Assistant, Supreme Allied Commander Atlantic*)

REAR-ADMIRALS

Wilkinson, N. J., CB (*Commandant, Joint Services Defence College*)

Tolhurst, J. G., CB (*Flag Officer Scotland, N. England and N. Ireland*)

Blackham, J. J. (*Asst Chief of Naval Staff*)

Essenhigh, N. R. (*Asst CDS (Programmes)*)

Craig, A., QHP (*Director-General, Naval Medical Services*)

Haddacks, P. K. (*Asst CDS (Policy and Requirements*) to *Supreme Allied Commander Europe*)

West, A. W. J., DSC (*Commander, UK Task Group*)

Trewby, J. A. (*Director-General Naval Bases and Supply*)

Clarke, J. P., CB, LVO, MBE (*Hydrographer of the Navy and Chief Executive, Hydrographic Office Defence Support Agency*)

Blackburn, D. A. J. (*Head of British Defence Staff Washington*)

Scourse, F. P., MBE (*Director-General, Surface Ships and Acting Controller of the Navy*)

Franklyn, P. M. (*Flag Officer Sea Training*)

Perowne, J. F. (*Chief of Staff (Operations), Flag Officer Submarines, COMSUBEASTLANT and COMSUBNORTHWEST*)

Wood, D. J. (*Director-General, Aircraft (Navy)*)

Lees, R. B. (*Director-General, Naval Personnel (Strategy and Plans) and Chief of Staff to Second Sea Lord*)

Spencer, P. (*Director-General, Fleet Support (Operations and Plans)*)

Loughran, T. W. (*Flag Officer Naval Aviation*)

Thomas, P. A. M. (*Chief, Strategic Systems Executive*)

Malbon, F. M. (*Naval Secretary and Director-General, Naval Manning*)

Armstrong, J. H. A. J. (*Senior Naval Member, Royal College of Defence Studies*)

McAnally, J. H. S., LVO (*Flag Officer Training and Recruiting*)

Phillips, R. T. R. (*Asst CDS Operational Requirements (Sea Systems)*)

Ross, A. B. (*Asst Director Operations Divn International Military Staff*)

HM FLEET AS AT 1 APRIL 1996

SUBMARINES

TRIDENT
Operational: Vanguard, Victorious*

POLARIS
Operational: Repulse

FLEET
Operational: Sceptre, Spartan, Splendid, Talent, Trafalgar, Trenchant, Triumph
Refitting/standby: Sovereign, Superb, Tireless, Torbay, Turbulent

ANTI-SUBMARINE WARFARE (ASW) CARRIERS

Operational: Illustrious, Invincible
Refitting/standby: Ark Royal

ASSAULT SHIPS

Operational: Fearless
Refitting/standby: Intrepid

DESTROYERS

TYPE 42
Operational: Birmingham, Edinburgh, Exeter, Glasgow, Gloucester, Liverpool, Manchester, Nottingham, Southampton, York
Refitting/standby: Cardiff, Newcastle

FRIGATES

TYPE 23
Operational: Argyll, Iron Duke, Lancaster, Marlborough, Monmouth, Montrose, Northumberland, Richmond*, Somerset*, Westminster
Refitting/standby: Norfolk

TYPE 22
Operational: Battleaxe, Beaver, Boxer, Brave, Brazen, Brilliant, Campbeltown, Chatham, Cornwall, Cumberland, London, Sheffield
Refitting/standby: Coventry

OFFSHORE PATROL

CASTLE CLASS
Operational: Dumbarton Castle, Leeds Castle

ISLAND CLASS
Operational: Alderney, Anglesey, Guernsey, Lindisfarne, Orkney, Shetland

MINEHUNTERS

HUNT CLASS
Operational: Atherstone, Berkeley, Bicester, Brecon, Chiddingfold, Cottesmore, Dulverton, Hurworth, Ledbury, Middleton, Quorn
Refitting/standby: Brocklesby, Cattistock

SANDOWN CLASS
Operational: Bridport, Cromer, Inverness, Sandown, Walney

PATROL CRAFT

PEACOCK CLASS
Operational: Peacock, Plover, Starling

RIVER CLASS
Operational: Arun, Blackwater, Itchen, Orwell, Spey

COASTAL TRAINING CRAFT †
Operational: Archer, Biter, Blazer, Charger, Dasher, Example, Exploit, Explorer, Express, Loyal Chancellor, Loyal Watcher, Puncher, Pursuer, Smiter

---

* Engaged in trials or training
† Operated by the University Royal Naval Units

GIBRALTAR SEARCH AND RESCUE CRAFT
Operational: Ranger, Trumpeter

ROYAL YACHT

Operational: Britannia

ICE PATROL SHIP

Operational: Endurance

SURVEY SHIPS

Operational: Bulldog, Gleaner, Hecla, Herald
Refitting/standby: Beagle, Roebuck

SOLD/DECOMMISSIONED 1995–6

Renown

OTHER PARTS OF THE NAVAL SERVICE

ROYAL MARINES

The Royal Marines were formed in 1664 and are part of the Naval Service. Their primary purpose is to conduct amphibious and land warfare. The principal operational units are 3 Commando Brigade Royal Marines, an amphibious all-arms brigade trained to operate in arduous environments, which is a core element of the UK's Joint Rapid Reaction Force; Comacchio Group Royal Marines, which is responsible for the security of nuclear weapon facilities; and Special Boat Service Royal Marines, the maritime special forces. The Royal Marines also provide detachments for warships and land-based naval parties as required. The Royal Marines Band Service provides military musical support for the Naval Service. The headquarters of the Royal Marines is at Portsmouth, along with the Royal Marines School of Music, and principal bases are at Plymouth, Arbroath, Poole, Taunton and Chivenor. The Corps of Royal Marines is about 6,500 strong.
Commandant-General, Royal Marines, Maj.-Gen. D. A. S. Pennefather, CB, OBE

ROYAL MARINES RESERVE (RMR)

The Royal Marines Reserve is a commando-trained volunteer force with the principal role, when mobilized, of supporting the Royal Marines. There are RMR centres in London, Glasgow, Bristol, Liverpool and Newcastle. The current strength of the RMR is about 1,000.
Director, RMR, Col. J. Q. Davis

ROYAL FLEET AUXILIARY (RFA)

The Royal Fleet Auxiliary supplies ships of the fleet with fuel, food, water, spares and ammunition while at sea. Its ships are manned by merchant seamen. In April 1996 there were 21 ships in the RFA.

FLEET AIR ARM

The Fleet Air Arm was established in 1937 and operates aircraft (including helicopters) for the Royal Navy. In April 1996 there were 218 aircraft in the Fleet Air Arm.

ROYAL NAVAL RESERVE (RNR)

The Royal Naval Reserve is a totally integrated part of the Royal Navy. It comprises about 3,500 men and women nationwide who volunteer to train in their spare time for a variety of sea and shore tasks which they would carry out in time of crisis or war.
Director, Naval Reserves, Capt N. R. Hodgson, RN

QUEEN ALEXANDRA'S ROYAL NAVAL NURSING SERVICE

The first nursing sisters were appointed to naval hospitals in 1884 and the Queen Alexandra's Royal Naval Nursing Service (QARNNS) gained its current title in 1902. Nursing ratings were introduced in 1960 and men were integrated into the Service in 1982; both men and women serve as officers and ratings. Female medical assistants were introduced in 1987. Qualified staff and learners are mainly based at the UK Royal Naval Hospitals, and continue their responsibility for the health and fitness of naval personnel. The strength is about 600.
Patron, HRH Princess Alexandra, the Hon. Lady Ogilvy
Matron-in-Chief, Capt. C. M. Taylor

The Army

THE QUEEN

FIELD MARSHALS

HRH The Prince Philip, Duke of Edinburgh, KG, KT, OM, GBE, AC, QSO, PC, *apptd* 1953
Sir James Cassels, GCB, KBE, DSO, *apptd* 1968
The Lord Carver, GCB, CBE, DSO, MC, *apptd* 1973
Sir Roland Gibbs, GCB, CBE, DSO, MC, *apptd* 1979
The Lord Bramall, KG, GCB, OBE, MC, *apptd* 1982
Sir John Stanier, GCB, MBE, *apptd* 1985
Sir Nigel Bagnall, GCB, CVO, MC, *apptd* 1988
The Lord Vincent of Coleshill, GBE, KCB, DSO, Col. Cmdt. RA, *apptd* 1991
Sir John Chapple, GCB, CBE, *apptd* 1992
HRH The Duke of Kent, KG, GCMG, GCVO, ADC, *apptd* 1993
Sir Peter Inge, GCB, Col. Green Howards, Col. Cmdt. APTC (*Chief of the Defence Staff, until early* 1997), *apptd* 1994

GENERALS

Guthrie, Sir Charles, GCB, LVO, OBE, ADC (*Gen.*), (*Chief of the General Staff*)
Mackenzie, Sir Jeremy, KCB, OBE, Col. Cmdt. AG Corps, Col. The Highlanders (*D. SACEUR*)
Rose, Sir Michael, KCB, CBE, DSO, QGM, ADC (*Adjutant-General*)
Wheeler, Sir Roger, KCB, CBE, Col. Cmdt. Int. Corps, Col. RIR (*C.-in-C., Land*)

LIEUTENANT-GENERALS

Foley, Sir John, KCB, OBE, MC, Col. Cmdt. The Light Division
Walker, Sir Michael, KCB, CBE, Col. Cmdt. The Queen's Division, Col. Cmdt. AAC (*Commandant NATO Rapid Reaction Corps*)
Harley, Sir Alexander, KBE, CB, Col. Cmdt. RRA (*Deputy CDS (Commitments)*)
Smith, Sir Rupert, KCB, DSO, OBE, QGM, Col. Cmdt. Parachute Regiment, Col. Cmdt. Corps of REME (*GOC Northern Ireland*)
Cowan, S., CBE, Col. QGS (*Quartermaster-General*)
Hayman-Joyce, Sir Robert, KCB, CBE, Col. Cmdt. RAC (*Director-General, Land Systems and Master-General of the Ordnance*)

Pike, H. W. R., DSO, MBE, Col. Cmdt. SASC (*Deputy C.-in-C., Land, and Inspector-General, Territorial Army*)

Grant, S. C., CB, Col. QLR (*Commandant, Royal College of Defence Studies*)

Jackson, M. D., CBE (*Director-General, Development and Doctrine*)

Wallace, C. B. Q., OBE, Col. Cmdt. 2 RGJ (*Comd. Permanent Joint HQ*)

MAJOR-GENERALS

Courage, W. J., CB, MBE (*Director-General, TA*)

Burton, E. F. G., OBE (*Asst CDS, Operational Requirements (Land Systems)*)

Freer, I. L., CB, CBE, Col. Staffords

Dutton, B. H., CBE, Col. Cmdt. POW Division (*Comd. British Forces Hong Kong*)

Robins, W. J. P., OBE (*Director-General, Information and Communications Services*)

Kennedy, A. I. G., CB, CBE (*Senior Army Member, Royal College of Defence Studies*)

Mackay-Dick, I. C., MBE (*GOC London District*)

Scott, M. I. E., CBE, DSO (*Military Secretary*)

Burden, D. L., CB, CBE, Col. Cmdt. Royal Logistics Corps (*Director-General, Army Manning and Recruiting*)

Cordingley, P. A. J., DSO (*GOC 2 Divn*)

Willcocks, M. A. (*Asst Chief of the General Staff*)

Cordy-Simpson, R. A. (*Deputy Chief of Staff, HQ Land Command*)

Deverell, J. F., OBE (*Commandant RMAS*)

Pigott, A. D., CBE, Col. Cmdt. The Queen's Gurkha Engineers (*Comdt. Staff College*)

Hall, J. M. F. C., OBE, Col. Cmdt. The Scottish Division, Col. Cmdt. RAVC (*GOC Scotland*)

McAfee, R. W. M., Col. Cmdt. RTR (*Comd. Multinational Divn Central (Airmobile)*)

Richards, N. W. F., OBE (*GOC HQ 4 Divn*)

Vyvyan, C. G. C., Col. Cmdt. 1 RGJ (*Chief of Staff, HQ Land*)

White, M. S., CBE (*Director-General, Logistic Support (Army)*)

Jenkins, D. J. M., CBE (*Commandant RMCS*)

Rogers, A. P. V., OBE (*Director, Army Legal Services*)

Granville-Chapman, T. J., CBE (*Commandant Joint Services Command and Staff College*)

Drewienkiewicz, K. J. (*Director of Support LANDCENT*)

Oliver, R. A., OBE (*Chief of Staff, Adjutant-General's Dept.*)

Sulivan, T. J., CBE (*Chief of Staff HQ ACE Rapid Reaction Corps*)

Corp, P. J. G., CB, Col. Cmdt. REME (*Director-General, Equipment (Army)*)

Pack, S. J. (*Comd. British Forces Gibraltar*)

Pennefather, D. A. S., CB, OBE (*Commandant-General, Royal Marines*)

Elliott, C. L., MBE (*Chief Executive, Army Individual Training Organization*)

Drewry, C. F., CBE (*GOC UK Support Command (Germany)*)

Ewer, G. A. (*Asst CDS (Logistics)*)

Short, W. R., QHP (*Director-General, Army Medical Services*)

Callow, C. G., OBE (*Director-General, Defence Medical Training*)

O'Donoghue, K., CBE (*Chief of Staff, HQ Quartermaster-General*)

Kiszely, J. P., MC (*GOC 1 (UK) Armd Division*)

Searby, R. V. (*GOC 5 Divn*)

CONSTITUTION OF THE ARMY

The regular forces include the following arms, branches and corps. They are listed in accordance with the order of precedence within the British Army. Soldiers' record offices are shown at the end of each group; all the record offices are due to move to Kentigern House, Glasgow, by July 1997. Records of officers are maintained at the Ministry of Defence.

THE ARMS

HOUSEHOLD CAVALRY – The Household Cavalry Regiment (The Life Guards and The Blues and Royals). *Records*, Queen's Park, Chester

ROYAL ARMOURED CORPS – Cavalry Regiments: 1st The Queen's Dragoon Guards; The Royal Scots Dragoon Guards (Carabiniers and Greys); The Royal Dragoon Guards; The Queen's Royal Hussars (The Queen's Own and Royal Irish); 9th/12th Royal Lancers (Prince of Wales's); The King's Royal Hussars; The Light Dragoons; The Queen's Royal Lancers; Royal Tank Regiment, comprising two regular regiments. *Records*, Queen's Park, Chester

ARTILLERY – Royal Regiment of Artillery. *Records*, Imphal Barracks, Fulford Road, York

ENGINEERS – Corps of Royal Engineers. *Records*, Kentigern House, Brown Street, Glasgow

SIGNALS – Royal Corps of Signals. *Records*, Kentigern House, Brown Street, Glasgow

THE INFANTRY

The Foot Guards and regiments of Infantry of the Line are grouped in divisions as follows:

GUARDS DIVISION – Grenadier, Coldstream, Scots, Irish and Welsh Guards. *Divisional Office*, HQ Infantry, Imber Road, Warminster, Wilts. *Training Centre*, Infantry Training Centre, Vimy Barracks, Catterick, N. Yorks. *Records*, Imphal Barracks, Fulford Road, York

SCOTTISH DIVISION – The Royal Scots (The Royal Regiment); The Royal Highland Fusiliers (Princess Margaret's Own Glasgow and Ayrshire Regiment); The King's Own Scottish Borderers; The Black Watch (Royal Highland Regiment); The Highlanders (Seaforth, Gordons and Camerons); The Argyll and Sutherland Highlanders (Princess Louise's). *Divisional Office*, HQ Infantry, Imber Road, Warminster, Wilts. *Training Centre*, Infantry Training Centre, Vimy Barracks, Catterick, N. Yorks. *Records*, Imphal Barracks, Fulford Road, York.

QUEEN'S DIVISION – The Princess of Wales's Royal Regiment (Queen's and Royal Hampshire's); The Royal Regiment of Fusiliers; The Royal Anglian Regiment. *Divisional Office*, HQ Infantry, Imber Road, Warminster, Wilts. *Training Centre*, Infantry Training Centre, Vimy Barracks, Catterick, N. Yorks. *Records*, Higher Barracks, Exeter

KING'S DIVISION – The King's Own Royal Border Regiment; The King's Regiment; The Prince of Wales's Own Regiment of Yorkshire; The Green Howards (Alexandra, Princess of Wales's Own Yorkshire Regiment); The Queen's Lancashire Regiment; The Duke of Wellington's Regiment (West Riding). *Divisional Office*, HQ Infantry, Imber Road, Warminster, Wilts. *Training Centre*, Infantry Training Centre, Vimy Barracks, Catterick, N. Yorks. *Records*, Imphal Barracks, Fulford Road, York

THE ROYAL IRISH REGIMENT (one general service and six home service battalions) – 27th (Inniskilling), 83rd, 87th and the Ulster Defence Regiment. *Regimental HQ* and *Training Centre*, St Patrick's Barracks, BFPO 808. *Records*, Imphal Barracks, Fulford Road, York

PRINCE OF WALES'S DIVISION – The Devonshire and Dorset Regiment; The Cheshire Regiment; The Royal Welch Fusiliers; The Royal Regiment of Wales (24th/41st Foot); The Royal Gloucestershire, Berkshire and Wiltshire Regiment; The Worcestershire and Sherwood Foresters Regiment (29th/45th Foot); The Staffordshire Regiment (The Prince of Wales's). *Divisional Office*, HQ Infantry, Imber Road, Warminster, Wilts. *Training Centre*, Infantry Training Centre, Vimy Barracks, Catterick, N. Yorks. *Records*, Imphal Barracks, Fulford, York

LIGHT DIVISION – The Light Infantry; The Royal Green Jackets. *Divisional Office*, HQ Infantry, Imber Road, Warminster, Wilts. *Training Centre*, Infantry Training Centre, Vimy Barracks, Catterick, N. Yorks. *Records*, Higher Barracks, Exeter

BRIGADE OF GURKHAS – The Royal Gurkha Rifles; The Queen's Gurkha Engineers; Queen's Gurkha Signals; The Queen's Own Gurkha Transport Regiment. *Regimental HQ, Training Centre* and *Records*, Queen Elizabeth Barracks, Church Crookham, Fleet, Aldershot, Hants

THE PARACHUTE REGIMENT (three regular battalions) – *Regimental HQ*, Browning Barracks, Aldershot, Hants. *Training Centre*, Infantry Training Centre, Vimy Barracks, Catterick, N. Yorks. *Records*, Higher Barracks, Exeter

SPECIAL AIR SERVICE REGIMENT – *Regimental HQ and Training Centre*, Stirling Lines, Hereford. *Records*, Higher Barracks, Exeter

ARMY AIR CORPS – *Regimental HQ* and *Training Centre*, Middle Wallop, Stockbridge, Hants. *Records*, Higher Barracks, Exeter

SERVICES/ARMS*

Royal Army Chaplains' Department – *Regimental HQ* and *Training Centre*, Netheravon House, Netheravon, Wilts SP4 9NF

The Royal Logistic Corps – *Regimental HQ,* Blackdown Barracks, Deepcut, Camberley, Surrey. *Training Centre*, Princess Royal Barracks, Deepcut, Camberley, Surrey. *Records*, Kentigern House, Brown Street, Glasgow; South Wigston, Leicester; Higher Barracks, Exeter

Royal Army Medical Corps – *Regimental HQ* and *Training Centre*, Keogh Barracks, Ashvale, Aldershot, Hants. *Records*, Queen's Park, Chester

Corps of Royal Electrical and Mechanical Engineers – *Regimental HQ* and *Training Centre*, Hazebrouck Barracks, Isaac Newton Road, Arborfield, Reading, Berks. *Records*, Glen Parva Barracks, Saffron Road, Wigston, Leicester

Adjutant-General's Corps – *Corps HQ* and *Training Centre*, Worthy Down, Winchester, Hants. *Records*, Queen's Park, Chester

Royal Army Veterinary Corps – *Corps HQ,* Galloway Road, Aldershot, Hants. *Regimental HQ* and *Training Centre*, Welby Lane Camp, Elmhurst Avenue, Melton Mowbray, Leics. *Records*, Higher Barracks, Exeter

Small Arms School Corps – *Corps HQ* and *Training Centre*, School of Infantry, Imber Road, Warminster, Wilts. *Records*, Higher Barracks, Exeter

Royal Army Dental Corps – *Regimental HQ,* Evelyn Woods Road, Aldershot, Hants. *Training Centre*, Keogh Barracks, Ashvale, Aldershot, Hants. *Records*, Queen's Park, Chester

*Intelligence Corps – *Corps HQ* and *Training Centre*, Templer Barracks, Ashford, Kent. *Records*, Higher Barracks, Exeter

Army Physical Training Corps – *Regimental HQ* and *Training Centre*, Queen's Avenue, Aldershot, Hants. *Records*, Higher Barracks, Exeter

General Service Corps – *Records*, Imphal Barracks, Fulford Road, York

Queen Alexander's Royal Army Nursing Corps – *Regimental HQ* and *Training Centre*, Keogh Barracks, Ashvale, Aldershot, Hants. *Records*, Queen's Park, Chester

Corps of Army Music – *Corps HQ* and *Training Centre,* Army School of Music, Netherhall, Kneller Road, Twickenham, Middx. *Records*, Higher Barracks, Exeter

ARMY EQUIPMENT HOLDINGS

The Army is equipped (as at November 1995) with 662 tanks, 3,470 armoured combat vehicles or ACV lookalikes, 511 artillery pieces, 48 landing craft and 236 helicopters.

THE TERRITORIAL ARMY (TA)

The Territorial Army is designed to be a General Reserve to the Army. It exists to reinforce the regular Army as and when required, with individuals, sub-units or units either in the UK or overseas, and to provide the framework and basis for regeneration and reconstitution in times of national emergency. The TA also provides an essential link between the military and civilian communities. Its structure has recently been reviewed. Its peacetime establishment is 59,000.

Inspector-General, Lt.-Gen. H. W. R. Pike, DSO, MBE

QUEEN ALEXANDRA'S ROYAL ARMY NURSING CORPS

The Queen Alexandra's Royal Army Nursing Corps (QARANC) was founded in 1902 as Queen Alexandra's Imperial Military Nursing Service (QAIMNS) and gained its present title in 1949. The QARANC has trained nurses for the register since 1950 and has many other nursing employments. Since 1992 men have been eligible to join the QARANC. The Corps provides service in military hospitals in the UK (including Northern Ireland), Germany, Hong Kong, Cyprus, Falkland Islands, Belize and wherever they may be needed world-wide.

Colonel-in-Chief, HRH The Princess Margaret, Countess of Snowdon, GCVO, CI

Matron-in-Chief (Army) and Director, Army Nursing Services, Col. J. Arigho

---

The Royal Air Force

THE QUEEN

MARSHALS OF THE ROYAL AIR FORCE

HRH The Prince Philip, Duke of Edinburgh, KG, KT, OM, GBE, AC, QSO, PC, *apptd* 1953

Sir John Grandy, GCB, GCVO, KBE, DSO, *apptd* 1971

Sir Denis Spotswood, GCB, CBE, DSO, DFC, *apptd* 1974

Sir Michael Beetham, GCB, CBE, DFC, AFC, *apptd* 1982

Sir Keith Williamson, GCB, AFC, *apptd* 1985

The Lord Craig of Radley, GCB, OBE, *apptd* 1988

AIR CHIEF MARSHALS

Graydon, Sir Michael, GCB, CBE, ADC (*Chief of the Air Staff*)

Stear, Sir Michael, KCB, CBE (*Deputy C.-in-C. Allied Forces Central Europe*)

Johns, Sir Richard, KCB, CBE, LVO (*C.-in-C. Allied Forces North-Western Europe*)

Wratten, Sir William, KBE, CB, AFC, ADC (*AOC.-in-C. Strike Command and Comd. Allied Air Forces North-Western Europe*)

Willis, Sir John, KCB, CBE (*Vice-Chief of the Defence Staff*)

Allison, Sir John, KCB, CBE (*Air Officer Commanding-in-Chief and Air Member for Logistics*)

AIR MARSHALS

Austin, Sir Roger, KCB, AFC (*Deputy Chief of Defence Procurement (Operations)*)

Macfadyen, I. D., CB, OBE (*Director-General, Saudi Armed Forces Project*)

Cheshire, Sir John, KBE, CB (*UK Military Representative to NATO Military Committee, Brussels*)

Cousins, Sir David, KCB, AFC (*Air Member for Personnel and Air Officer Commanding-in-Chief*)

Squire, P. T., DFC, AFC (*Deputy CDS (Programmes and Personnel)*)

Robertson, G. A., CBE (*Chief of Staff and Deputy C.-in-C. Strike Command*)

Bagnall, A. J. C., CB, OBE (*Deputy C.-in-C. Allied Air Forces Central Europe*)

AIR VICE-MARSHALS

Harding, P. J., CB, CBE, AFC (*Defence Services Secretary*)

Baird, J. A., QHP (*Director-General, Medical Services (RAF)*)

Saunders, D. J., CBE (*Air Officer Engineering and Supply*)

Chapple, R., QHP (*Principal Medical Officer, RAF Support Command*)

Norriss, P. C., CB, AFC (*Director-General, Air Systems 1*)

Kyle, R. H., MBE (*Chief Executive, RAF Maintenance Group Agency*)

Mackey, J., QHDS (*Chief Executive, Defence Dental Agency*)

Sherrington, T. B., OBE (*Air Officer Admin., Strike Command*)

Carleton, G. W. (*Director, Legal Services (RAF)*)

Coville, C. C. C., CB (*Asst CDS Operational Requirements (Air Systems)*)

O'Brien, R. P., OBE (*Air Secretary*)

May, J. A. G., CB (*Air Officer Training*)

Terry, C. G., CB, OBE (*Chief of Staff, Logistic Command, and Chief Engineer (RAF)*)

Feesey, J. D. L. (*Director-General, Policy and Plans*)

Goddard, P. J., AFC (*Senior Directing Staff (Air), Royal College of Defence Studies*)

Goodall, R. H., CBE, AFC (*Chief of Staff, Permanent Joint HQ*)

Jenner, T. I., CB (*Asst Chief of the Air Staff*)

Day, J. R. (*AOC No. 1 Group*)

Harrison, A. J. (*Asst CDS (Operations)*)

Millar, P. (*Comd. British Forces Cyprus*)

Stables, A. J. (*Commandant RAF Staff College, Cranwell*)

Hull, D. H., QHS (*Dean of Air Force Music*)

Hurrell, D. A. (*Senior Air Staff Officer*)

Markey, P. D. (*Director-General, Support Management (RAF)*)

McCandless, B. C. (*Air Officer Communications Information Systems and Air Officer Commanding Signals Units*)

French, J. C. (*Asst CDS (Policy)*)

Van der Veen, M. (*Cmdt., RAF Staff College Bracknell*)

Smart, M. D. (*Chief of Staff, Personnel and Training Command, and Director-General, Strategic Policy and Plans*)

O'Reilly, P. J. (*President of the Ordnance Board*)

Spink, C. R. (*AOC No. 11/18 Group*)

Elder, R. D.

Jackson, M. R.

Thompson, J. H.

CONSTITUTION OF THE ROYAL AIR FORCE

The RAF consists of three commands: Strike Command, Personnel and Training Command and Logistics Command. Strike Command is responsible for all the RAF's front-line forces. Its roles include strike/attack, air defence, reconnaissance, maritime patrol, strategic air transport, air-to-air refuelling, search and rescue, and aero-medical facilities. Personnel and Training Command is responsible for personnel administration and training in the RAF. Logistics Command is responsible for all logistics, engineering and materiel support.

RAF EQUIPMENT *as at 1 July 1996*

Aircraft – 249 Tornado, 70 Harrier, 54 Jaguar, 9 Canberra, 29 Nimrod, 26 VC10, 9 Tristar, 55 Hercules, 11 BAe, 7 Sentry, 4 Andover, 100 Hawk, 116 Bulldog, 10 Domenie, 2 Islander, 10 Jetstream, 73 Tucano

Helicopters – 37 Puma, 50 Wessex, 19 Sea King, 34 Chinook, 21 Gazelle

Rapier missiles

ROYAL AUXILIARY AIR FORCE (RAUXAF)

Formed in 1924, the Auxiliary Air Force received the prefix 'Royal' in 1947 in recognition of its war record. The RAUXAF supports the RAF in maritime air operations, air and ground defence of airfields, air movements and aero-medical evacuation. The RAUXAF and the RAFVR are due to be merged in 1997.

Air Commodore-in-Chief, HM The Queen

Director of Personnel Management (Airmen) and Controller of Reserve Forces (RAF), Air Cdre M. L. Jackson, OBE

ROYAL AIR FORCE VOLUNTEER RESERVE (RAFVR)

The Royal Air Force Volunteer Reserve was created in 1936 to train the increased number of aircrew who were seen as necessary for the forthcoming conflict. The RAFVR was reconstituted in 1947 following war service. It provides specialist personnel who fill specific wartime intelligence support, photo interpretation and public relations appointments. A small number of RAFVR aircrew augment regular crews on Nimrod (Maritime Reconnaissance) aircraft in wartime. The RAFVR and the RAUXAF are due to be merged in 1997.

Director of Personnel Management (Airmen) and Controller of Reserve Forces (RAF), Air Cdre M. L. Jackson, OBE

PRINCESS MARY'S ROYAL AIR FORCE NURSING SERVICE

The Princess Mary's Royal Air Force Nursing Service (PMRAFNS) offers commissions to Registered General Nurses (RGN) with a minimum of two years experience after obtaining RGN and normally with a second qualification. RGNs with no additional experience or qualification are recruited as non-commissioned officers in the grade of Staff Nurse.

Air Chief Commandant, HRH Princess Alexandra, the Hon. Lady Ogilvy, GCVO

Matron-in-Chief, Gp Capt R. H. Williams

SERVICE SALARIES

The following rates of pay apply from 1 December 1996. The increasing integration of women in the armed services is reflected in equal pay for equal work and the X factor addition is now the same for men and women (12 per cent).

Annual salaries are derived from daily rates in whole pence and rounded to the nearest £.

The pay rates shown are for Army personnel. The rates apply also to personnel of equivalent rank and pay band in the other services.

OFFICERS' SALARIES

MAIN SCALE

Rank	Daily	Annual	Rank	Daily	Annual
Second Lieutenant	£38.53	£14,063	Special List Lieutenant-Colonel	£113.72	£41,508
Lieutenant			Lieutenant-Colonel		
On appointment	50.93	18,589	On appointment with less than 19 years service	115.84	42,282
After 1 year in the rank	52.27	19,079			
After 2 years in the rank	53.61	19,568	After 2 years in the rank or with 19 years service	118.89	43,395
After 3 years in the rank	54.95	20,057			
After 4 years in the rank	56.29	20,546	After 4 years in the rank or with 21 years service	121.94	44,508
Captain			After 6 years in the rank or with 23 years service	124.99	45,621
On appointment	64.90	23,689			
After 1 year in the rank	66.65	24,327	After 8 years in the rank or with 25 years service	128.04	46,735
After 2 years in the rank	68.40	24,966	Colonel		
After 3 years in the rank	70.15	25,605	On appointment	134.65	49,147
After 4 years in the rank	71.90	26,244	After 2 years in the rank	138.19	50,439
After 5 years in the rank	73.65	26,882	After 4 years in the rank	141.73	51,731
After 6 years in the rank	75.40	27,521	After 6 years in the rank	145.27	53,024
Major			After 8 years in the rank	148.81	54,316
On appointment	82.34	30,054	Brigadier	165.09	60,258
After 1 year in the rank	84.38	30,799			
After 2 years in the rank	86.42	31,543	Major-General	181.62	66,291
After 3 years in the rank	88.46	32,288			
After 4 years in the rank	90.50	33,033	Lieutenant-General	205.58	75,000
After 5 years in the rank	92.54	33,777			
After 6 years in the rank	94.58	34,522	General	277.35	101,233
After 7 years in the rank	96.62	35,266			
After 8 years in the rank	98.66	36,011	Field Marshal	344.80	125,852

SALARIES OF OFFICERS COMMISSIONED FROM THE RANKS (LIEUTENANTS AND CAPTAINS ONLY)

YEARS OF COMMISSIONED SERVICE	YEARS OF NON-COMMISSIONED SERVICE FROM AGE 18					
	Less than 12 years		12 years but less than 15 years		15 years or more	
	Daily	Annual	Daily	Annual	Daily	Annual
On commissioning	£71.67	£26,160	£75.36	£27,506	£79.05	£28,853
After 1 year service	73.52	26,835	77.21	28,182	80.26	29,295
After 2 years service	75.36	27,506	79.05	28,853	81.45	29,729
After 3 years service	77.21	28,182	80.26	29,295	82.64	30,164
After 4 years service	79.05	28,853	81.45	29,729	83.83	30,598
After 5 years service	80.26	29,295	82.64	30,164	85.02	31,032
After 6 years service	81.45	29,729	83.83	30,598	86.21	31,467
After 8 years service	82.64	30,164	85.02	31,032	87.40	31,901
After 10 years service	83.83	30,598	86.21	31,467	87.40	31,901
After 12 years service	85.02	31,032	87.40	31,901	87.40	31,901
After 14 years service	86.21	31,467	87.40	31,901	87.40	31,901
After 16 years service	87.40	31,901	87.40	31,901	87.40	31,901

SOLDIERS' SALARIES

The pay structure below officer level is divided into pay bands. Jobs at each rank are allocated to bands according to their score in the job evaluation system. Length of service is from age 18.

Scale A: committed to serve/have completed less than 6 years

Scale B: committed to serve/have completed 6 years but less than 9 years

Scale C: committed to serve/have completed more than 9 years

Daily rates of pay effective from 1 December 1996 are:

RANK — SCALE A

	Band 1	Band 2	Band 3
Private			
Class 4	£24.14	£ —	£ —
Class 3	27.04	31.39	36.22
Class 2	30.23	34.62	39.45
Class 1	32.88	37.26	42.08
Lance-Corporal			
Class 3	32.88	37.26	42.08
Class 2	35.12	39.51	44.73
Class 1	37.78	42.17	47.39
Corporal			
Class 2	40.41	44.78	50.00
Class 1	43.38	47.74	52.96

	Band 4	Band 5	Band 6	Band 7
Sergeant	£47.80	£52.56	£57.75	£ —
Staff Sergeant	50.55	55.29	60.51	66.78
Warrant Officer				
Class 2	54.05	58.81	65.21	71.62
Class 1	57.64	62.38	68.88	75.27

SCALE B

	Band 1	Band 2	Band 3
Private			
Class 4	£24.44	£ —	£ —
Class 3	27.34	31.69	36.52
Class 2	30.53	34.92	39.75
Class 1	33.18	37.56	42.38

RANK — SCALE B (CONTD)

	Band 1	Band 2	Band 3
Lance-Corporal			
Class 3	33.18	37.56	42.38
Class 2	35.42	39.81	45.03
Class 1	38.08	42.47	47.69
Corporal			
Class 2	40.71	45.08	50.30
Class 1	43.68	48.04	53.26

	Band 4	Band 5	Band 6	Band 7
Sergeant	£48.10	£52.86	£58.05	£ —
Staff Sergeant	50.85	55.59	60.81	66.08
Warrant Officer				
Class 2	54.35	59.11	65.51	71.92
Class 1	57.94	62.68	69.18	75.57

SCALE C

	Band 1	Band 2	Band 3
Private			
Class 4	£24.89	£ —	£ —
Class 3	27.79	32.14	36.97
Class 2	30.98	35.37	40.20
Class 1	33.63	38.01	42.83
Lance-Corporal			
Class 3	33.63	38.01	42.83
Class 2	35.87	40.26	45.48
Class 1	38.53	42.92	48.14
Corporal			
Class 2	41.16	45.53	50.75
Class 1	44.13	48.49	53.71

	Band 4	Band 5	Band 6	Band 7
Sergeant	£48.55	£53.31	£58.50	£ —
Staff Sergeant	51.30	56.04	61.26	67.53
Warrant Officer				
Class 2	54.80	59.56	65.96	72.37
Class 1	58.39	63.13	69.63	76.02

RELATIVE RANK – ARMED FORCES

	Royal Navy		Army		Royal Air Force
1	Admiral of the Fleet	1	Field Marshal	1	Marshal of the RAF
2	Admiral (Adm.)	2	General (Gen.)	2	Air Chief Marshal
3	Vice-Admiral (Vice-Adm.)	3	Lieutenant-General (Lt.-Gen.)	3	Air Marshal
4	Rear-Admiral (Rear-Adm.)	4	Major-General (Maj.-Gen.)	4	Air Vice-Marshal
5	Commodore (1st & 2nd class) (Cdre)	5	Brigadier (Brig.)	5	Air Commodore (Air Cdre)
6	Captain (Capt.)	6	Colonel (Col.)	6	Group Captain (Gp Capt)
7	Commander (Cdr.)	7	Lieutenant-Colonel (Lt.-Col.)	7	Wing Commander (Wg Cdr.)
8	Lieutenant-Commander (Lt.-Cdr.)	8	Major (Maj.)	8	Squadron Leader (Sqn. Ldr.)
9	Lieutenant (Lt.)	9	Captain (Capt.)	9	Flight Lieutenant (Flt. Lt.)
10	Sub-Lieutenant (Sub-Lt.)	10	Lieutenant (Lt.)	10	Flying Officer (FO)
11	Acting Sub-Lieutenant (Acting Sub-Lt.)	11	Second Lieutenant (2nd Lt.)	11	Pilot Officer (PO)

SERVICE RETIRED PAY ON COMPULSORY RETIREMENT

Those who leave the services having served at least five years, but not long enough to qualify for the appropriate immediate pension, now qualify for a preserved pension and terminal grant, both of which are payable at age 60. The tax-free resettlement grants shown below are payable on release to those who qualify for a preserved pension and who have completed nine years service from age 21 (officers) or 12 years from age 18 (other ranks).

The annual rates for army personnel are given. The rates apply also to personnel of equivalent rank in the other services, including the nursing services.

OFFICERS

Applicable to officers who give full pay service on the active list on or after 30 November 1996

No. of years reckonable service over age 21	Capt. and below	Major	Lt.-Col.	Colonel	Brigadier	Major-General	Lieutenant-General	General
16	£ 7,843	£ 9,414	£12,368	£ —	£ —	£ —	£ —	£ —
17	8,208	9,861	12,940	—	—	—	—	—
18	8,573	10,309	13,512	15,705	—	—	—	—
19	8,937	10,756	14,084	16,370	—	—	—	—
20	9,302	11,203	14,656	17,035	—	—	—	—
21	9,667	11,650	15,229	17,699	—	—	—	—
22	10,032	12,098	15,801	18,364	21,190	—	—	—
23	10,397	12,545	16,373	19,029	21,860	—	—	—
24	10,762	12,992	16,945	19,694	22,529	24,785	—	—
25	11,126	13,440	17,517	20,359	23,199	25,552	—	—
26	11,491	13,887	18,089	21,024	23,869	26,258	—	—
27	11,856	14,334	18,661	21,689	24,538	26,995	30,542	—
28	12,221	14,781	19,233	22,354	25,208	27,731	31,375	—
29	12,586	15,229	19,805	23,019	25,877	28,468	32,209	—
30	12,951	15,676	20,378	23,683	26,547	29,205	33,042	44,598
31	13,315	16,123	20,950	24,348	27,216	29,941	33,875	45,723
32	13,680	16,570	21,522	25,013	27,886	30,678	34,708	46,848
33	14,045	17,018	22,094	25,678	28,555	31,414	35,542	47,972
34	14,410	17,465	22,666	26,343	29,225	32,151	36,375	49,097

Field Marshal – active list retired pay at the rate of £61,037 a year

WARRANT OFFICERS, NCOS AND PRIVATES

Applicable to soldiers who give full pay service on or after 30 November 1996

No. of years reckonable service	Below Corporal	Corporal	Sergeant	Staff Sergeant	Warrant Officer Class II	Warrant Officer Class I
22	£4,551	£5,798	£6,433	£ 7,323	£ 7,570	£ 8,368
23	4,710	6,000	6,658	7,579	7,838	8,669
24	4,869	6,203	6,882	7,834	8,106	8,970
25	5,028	6,405	7,107	8,090	8,375	9,270
26	5,186	6,608	7,331	8,346	8,643	9,571
27	5,345	6,810	7,556	8,601	8,911	9,872
28	5,504	7,012	7,781	8,857	9,179	10,173
29	5,663	7,215	8,005	9,113	9,447	10,474
30	5,822	7,417	8,230	9,368	9,716	10,774
31	5,981	7,620	8,454	9,624	9,984	11,075
32	6,140	7,822	8,679	9,880	10,252	11,376
33	6,299	8,024	8,904	10,135	10,520	11,677
34	6,457	8,227	9,128	10,391	10,788	11,978
35	6,616	8,429	9,353	10,647	11,057	12,278
36	6,775	8,632	9,577	10,902	11,325	12,579
37	6,934	8,834	9,802	11,158	11,593	12,880

RESETTLEMENT GRANTS

Terminal grants are in each case three times the rate of retired pay or pension. There are special rates of retired pay for certain other ranks not shown above. Lower rates are payable in cases of voluntary retirement.

A gratuity of £2,665 is payable for officers with short service commissions for each year completed. Resettlement grants are: officers £9,174; non-commissioned ranks £6,041.

Archbishops of Canterbury since 1414

Henry Chichele (1362–1443), translated 1414
John Stafford (?–1452), translated 1443
John Kemp (c.1380–1454), translated 1452
Thomas Bourchier (c.1410–86), translated 1454
John Morton (c.1420–1500), translated 1486
Henry Deane (?–1503), translated 1501
William Warham (1450–1532), translated 1503
Thomas Cranmer (1489–1556), translated 1533
Reginald Pole (1500–58), translated 1556
Matthew Parker (1504–75), translated 1559
Edmund Grindal (c.1519–83), translated 1576
John Whitgift (c.1530–1604), translated 1583
Richard Bancroft (1544–1610), translated 1604
George Abbot (1562–1633), translated 1611
William Laud (1573–1645), translated 1633
William Juxon (1582–1663), translated 1660
Gilbert Sheldon (1598–1677), translated 1663
William Sancroft (1617–93), translated 1678
John Tillotson (1630–94), translated 1691
Thomas Tenison (1636–1715), translated 1695
William Wake (1657–1737), translated 1716

John Potter (c.1674–1747), translated 1737
Thomas Herring (1693–1757), translated 1747
Matthew Hutton (1693–1758), translated 1757
Thomas Secker (1693–1768), translated 1758
Hon. Frederick Cornwallis (1713–83), translated 1768
John Moore (1730–1805), translated 1783
Charles Manners-Sutton (1755–1828), translated 1805
William Howley (1766–1848), translated 1828
John Bird Sumner (1780–1862), translated 1848
Charles Longley (1794–1868), translated 1862
Archibald Campbell Tait (1811–82), translated 1868
Edward White Benson (1829–96), translated 1883
Frederick Temple (1821–1902), translated 1896
Randall Davidson (1848–1930), translated 1903
Cosmo Lang (1864–1945), translated 1928
William Temple (1881–1944), translated 1942
Geoffrey Fisher (1887–1972), translated 1945
Michael Ramsey (1904–88), translated 1961
Donald Coggan (1909–), translated 1974
Robert Runcie (1921–), translated 1980
George Carey (1935–), translated 1991

Archbishops of York since 1606

Tobias Matthew (1546–1628), translated 1606
George Montaigne (1569–1628), translated 1628
Samuel Harsnett (1561–1631), translated 1629
Richard Neile (1562–1640), translated 1632
John Williams (1582–1650), translated 1641
Accepted Frewen (1588–1664), translated 1660
Richard Sterne (1596–1683), translated 1664
John Dolben (1625–86), translated 1683
Thomas Lamplugh (1615–91), translated 1688
John Sharp (1645–1714), translated 1691
William Dawes (1671–1724), translated 1714
Launcelot Blackburn (1658–1743), translated 1724
Thomas Herring (1693–1757), translated 1743
Matthew Hutton (1693–1758), translated 1747
John Gilbert (1693–1761), translated 1757
Robert Hay Drummond (1711–76), translated 1761

William Markham (1719–1807), translated 1777
Edward Vernon Harcourt (1757–1847), translated 1808
Thomas Musgrave (1788–1860), translated 1847
Charles Longley (1794–1868), translated 1860
William Thomson (1819–90), translated 1862
William Connor Magee (1821–91), translated 1891
William Maclagan (1826–1910), translated 1891
Cosmo Lang (1864–1945), translated 1909
William Temple (1881–1944), translated 1929
Cyril Garbett (1875–1955), translated 1942
Michael Ramsey (1904–88), translated 1956
Donald Coggan (1909–), translated 1961
Stuart Blanch (1918–94), translated 1975
John Habgood (1927–), translated 1983
David Hope (1940–), translated 1995

Popes since 1800

The family name is in italics

Pius VII, *Chiaramonti*, elected 1800
Leo XII, *della Genga*, elected 1823
Pius VIII, *Castiglioni*, elected 1829
Gregory XVI, *Cappellari*, elected 1831
Pius IX, *Mastai-Ferretti*, elected 1846
Leo XIII, *Pecci*, elected 1878
Pius X, *Sarto*, elected 1903
Benedict XV, *della Chiesa*, elected 1914

Pius XI, *Ratti*, elected 1922
Pius XII, *Pacelli*, elected 1939
John XXIII, *Roncalli*, elected 1958
Paul VI, *Montini*, elected 1963
John Paul I, *Luciani*, elected 1978
John Paul II, *Wojtyla*, elected 1978

Adrian IV is the only Englishman to be elected pope. He was born Nicholas Breakspear at Langley, near St Albans, and was elected Pope in 1154 on the death of Anastasius IV. He died in 1159.

The Christian Churches

The Church of England

The Church of England is the established (i.e. state) church in England and the mother church of the Anglican Communion. A Church of England already existed when Pope Gregory sent Augustine to evangelise the English in AD 596. During the Middle Ages conflicts between Church and State culminated in the Act of Supremacy in 1534. This repudiated papal supremacy and declared Henry VIII to be the supreme head of the Church in England. Since 1559 the English monarch has been termed the Supreme Governor of the Church of England. The Thirty-Nine Articles, a set of doctrinal statements which, together with the Book of Common Prayer of 1662 and the Ordinal, define the position of the Church of England, were adopted in their final form in 1571 and include the emphasis on personal faith and the authority of the scriptures common to the Protestant Reformation throughout Europe.

The Church of England is divided into the two provinces of Canterbury and York, each under an archbishop. The two provinces are subdivided into 44 dioceses. Decisions on matters concerning the Church of England are made by the General Synod, established in 1970. It also discusses and expresses opinion on any other matter of religious or public interest. The General Synod has 574 members in total, divided between three houses: the House of Bishops, the House of Clergy and the House of Laity. It is presided over jointly by the Archbishops of Canterbury and York and normally meets twice a year. The Synod has the power, delegated by Parliament, to frame statute law (known as a Measure) on any matter concerning the Church of England. A Measure must be laid before both Houses of Parliament, who may accept or reject it but cannot amend it. Once accepted the Measure is submitted for royal assent and then has the full force of law. The Synod appoints a number of committees, boards and councils which deal with, or advise on, a wide range of matters. In addition to the General Synod, there are synods of clergy and laity at diocesan level.

A report of a commission headed by the Bishop of Durham recommending changes to the national structures of the Church of England was accepted by the General Synod in November 1995; a draft Measure will be brought before the Synod in November 1996 and the changes, which include the creation of an Archbishops' Council, are likely to be implemented in 1998.

In 1994 the Church of England had an electoral roll membership of 1.5 million, of whom about 1.1 million regularly attended Sunday services. There are (1995 figures) two archbishops, 106 diocesan, suffragan and (stipendiary) assistant bishops, 9,333 other male and 820 female full-time stipendiary clergy, and over 16,000 churches and places of worship. (The Diocese in Europe is not included in these figures.)

The Ordination of Women

On 11 November 1992, the General Synod of the Church of England voted to permit the ordination of women as priests by majorities of 75 per cent in the House of Bishops, 70.4 per cent in the House of Clergy, and 67.3 per cent in the House of Laity. After receiving parliamentary approval and royal assent, the canon was promulged in the General Synod in February 1994 and the first 32 women priests were ordained on 12 March 1994 by the Bishop of Bristol.

The Priests (Ordination of Women) Measure 1993 contains provisions safeguarding the position of bishops and parishes who are opposed to the priestly ministry of women. In November 1993 the General Synod agreed to the appointment of up to three 'provincial visitors' to work with those who are unable to accept the ministry of bishops ordaining women priests. The provincial visitors, who are suffragan bishops in the newly created sees of Ebbsfleet (Province of Canterbury), Beverley (Province of York) and Richborough (Province of Canterbury), are allowed to carry out confirmations and ordinations in parishes opposed to women priests, as long as they have the permission of the diocesan bishop. Clergy who feel compelled to leave the ministry are entitled to financial assistance.

Porvoo Common Statement

The Porvoo Common Statement was drawn up by the British and Irish Anglican churches and the Nordic and Baltic Lutheran churches and was approved by the General Synod of the Church of England in July 1995. In the House of Bishops the motion was approved by 34 votes to 0, in the House of Clergy by 176 votes to 8, and in the House of Laity by 169 votes to 15.

Churches that agree the statement regard baptized members of each other's churches as members of their own, and allow free interchange of episcopally ordained ministers within the rules of each church.

GENERAL SYNOD OF THE CHURCH OF ENGLAND, Church House, Dean's Yard, London SWIP 3NZ. Tel: 0171-222 9011. *Secretary-General*, P. Mawer

HOUSE OF BISHOPS: *Chairman*, The Archbishop of Canterbury; *Vice-Chairman*, The Archbishop of York

HOUSE OF CLERGY: *Joint Chairmen*, Revd Dr J. Sentamu; Canon J. Stanley

HOUSE OF LAITY: *Chairman*, Dr Christina Baxter; *Vice-Chairman*, Dr P. Giddings

Stipends 1996–7

Archbishop of Canterbury	£47,070
Archbishop of York	£41,420
Bishop of London	£38,440
Other diocesan bishops	£25,520
Suffragan bishops	£20,980
Deans and provosts	£20,980
Residentiary canons	£17,160
Incumbents and clergy of similar status	£13,450*

*national average

Stipendiary Clergy *as at 31 December 1995*

	Male	Female
Bath and Wells	234	20
Birmingham	192	25
Blackburn	261	5
Bradford	123	8
Bristol	143	19
Canterbury	179	15
Carlisle	159	13
Chelmsford	406	31

	Male	Female
Chester	284	14
Chichester	348	8
Coventry	153	17
Derby	184	10
Durham	229	28
Ely	154	20
Exeter	279	9
Gloucester	168	14
Guildford	187	23
Hereford	121	12
Leicester	162	14
Lichfield	348	37
Lincoln	204	28
Liverpool	256	32
London	514	45
Manchester	304	22
Newcastle	160	9
Norwich	203	16
Oxford	404	46
Peterborough	147	9
Portsmouth	116	9
Ripon	147	24
Rochester	226	19
St Albans	270	29
St Edmundsbury and Ipswich	175	15
Salisbury	234	14
Sheffield	195	18
Sodor and Man	22	0
Southwark	350	49
Southwell	187	23
Truro	125	3
Wakefield	184	17
Winchester	250	12
Worcester	153	16
York	300	23
TOTAL	9,440	820

Province of Canterbury

CANTERBURY

103RD ARCHBISHOP AND PRIMATE OF ALL ENGLAND
Most Revd and Rt. Hon. George L. Carey, PH.D., *cons.* 1987, *trans.* 1991, *apptd* 1991; Lambeth Palace, London SE1 7JU. *Signs* George Cantuar:

BISHOPS SUFFRAGAN
Dover, Rt. Revd J. Richard A. Llewellin, *cons.* 1985, *apptd* 1992; Upway, St Martin's Hill, Canterbury, CT1 1PR
Maidstone, Rt. Revd Gavin H. Reid, *cons.* 1992, *apptd* 1992; Bishop's House, Pett Lane, Charing, Ashford TN27 0DL
Ebbsfleet, Rt. Revd John Richards, *cons.* 1994, *apptd* 1994 (provincial episcopal visitor); The Rectory, Church Leigh, Stoke-on-Trent, Staffs ST10 4PT
Richborough, Rt. Revd Edwin Barnes, *cons.* 1995, *apptd* 1995 (provincial episcopal visitor); St Stephen's House, Marston Street, Oxford OX4 1JX

DEAN
Very Revd John Arthur Simpson, *apptd* 1986

CANONS RESIDENTIARY
P. Brett, *apptd* 1983; R. H. C. Symon, *apptd* 1994; Dr M. Chandler, *apptd* 1995; Ven. J. Pritchard, *apptd* 1996
Organist, D. Flood, FRCO, *apptd* 1988

ARCHDEACONS
Canterbury, Ven. J. Pritchard, *apptd* 1996
Maidstone, Ven. P. Evans, *apptd* 1989

Vicar-General of Province and Diocese, Chancellor S. Cameron, QC
Commissary-General, His Hon. Judge Richard Walker
Joint Registrars of the Province, F. E. Robson, OBE; B. J. T. Hanson, CBE
Diocesan Registrar and Legal Adviser, R. H. B. Sturt
Diocesan Secretary, D. Kemp, Diocesan House, Lady Wootton's Green, Canterbury CT1 1NQ. Tel: 01227-459401

LONDON

132ND BISHOP
Rt. Revd Richard C. Chartres; The Old Deanery, Dean's Court, London EC4V 5AA. *Signs* Richard Londin:

AREA BISHOPS
Edmonton, Rt. Revd Brian J. Masters, *cons.* 1982, *apptd* 1984; 1 Regent's Park Terrace, London NW1 7EE
Kensington, Rt. Revd Michael Colclough, *cons.* 1996, *apptd* 1996; 19 Campden Hill Square, London W8 7JY
Stepney, Rt. Revd Dr John M. Sentamu, *cons.* 1996, *apptd* 1996; 63 Coborn Road, London E3 2DB
Willesden, Rt. Revd Graham G. Dow, *cons.* 1992, *apptd* 1992; 173 Willesden Lane, London NW6 7YN

BISHOP SUFFRAGAN
Fulham, Rt. Revd John Broadhurst, *cons.* 1996, *apptd* 1996; c/o The Old Deanery, Dean's Court, London EC4V 5AA

DEAN OF ST PAUL'S
Very Revd John H. Moses, PH.D., *apptd* 1996

CANONS RESIDENTIARY
Ven. G. Cassidy, *apptd* 1987; R. J. Halliburton, *apptd* 1990; M. J. Saward, *apptd* 1991
Registrar and Receiver of St Paul's, Brig. R. W. Acworth, CBE
Organist, J. Scott, FRCO, *apptd* 1990

ARCHDEACONS
Charing Cross, Ven. W. Jacob, *apptd* 1996
Hackney, Ven. C. Young, *apptd* 1992
Hampstead, Ven. P. Wheatley, *apptd* 1995
London, Ven. G. Cassidy, *apptd* 1987
Middlesex, Ven. M. Colmer, *apptd* 1996
Northolt, Ven. P. Broadbent, *apptd* 1995

Chancellor, Miss S. Cameron, QC, *apptd* 1992
Registrar and Legal Secretary, D. W. Faull, OBE
Diocesan Secretary, C. J. A. Smith, 36 Causton Street, London SW1P 4AU. Tel: 0171-932 1100

WINCHESTER

96TH BISHOP
Rt. Revd Michael C. Scott-Joynt, *cons.* 1987, *trans.* 1995, *apptd* 1995; Wolvesey, Winchester SO23 9ND. *Signs* Michael Winton:

BISHOPS SUFFRAGAN
Basingstoke, Rt. Revd D. Geoffrey Rowell, *cons.* 1994, *apptd* 1994; Little Acorns, Boynes Wood Road, Medstead GU34 5EA
Southampton, vacant; Ham House, The Crescent, Romsey SO51 7NG

DEAN
Very Revd Michael Till, *apptd* 1996

Dean of Jersey (A Peculiar), Very Revd John Seaford, *apptd* 1993
Dean of Guernsey (A Peculiar), Very Revd Marc Trickey, *apptd* 1995

CANONS RESIDENTIARY
A. K. Walker, *apptd* 1987; Ven. A. F. Knight, *apptd* 1991; P. B. Morgan, *apptd* 1994
Organist, D. Hill, FRCO, *apptd* 1988

ARCHDEACONS
Basingstoke, Ven. A. F. Knight, *apptd* 1990
Winchester, Ven. A. G. Clarkson, *apptd* 1984

Chancellor, C. Clark, *apptd* 1993
Registrar and Legal Secretary, P. M. White
Diocesan Secretary, R. Anderton, Church House, 9 The Close, Winchester, Hants SO23 9LS. Tel: 01962-844644

BATH AND WELLS

76TH BISHOP
Rt. Revd James L. Thompson, *cons.* 1978, *apptd* 1991; The Palace, Wells BA5 2PD. *Signs* James Bath & Wells

BISHOP SUFFRAGAN
Taunton, Rt. Revd J. H. Richard Lewis, *cons.* 1992, *apptd* 1992; Sherford Farm House, Sherford, Taunton TA1 3RF

DEAN
Very Revd Richard Lewis, *apptd* 1990

CANONS RESIDENTIARY
P. de N. Lucas, *apptd* 1988; G. O. Farran, *apptd* 1985; R. Acworth, *apptd* 1993; P. G. Walker, *apptd* 1994
Organist, M. Archer, *apptd* 1996

ARCHDEACONS
Bath, Ven. R. J. S. Evens, *apptd* 1996
Taunton, Ven. R. M. C. Frith, *apptd* 1992
Wells, Ven. R. Acworth, *apptd* 1993

Chancellor, T. Briden, *apptd* 1993
Registrar and Legal Secretary, T. Berry
Diocesan Secretary, N. Denison, The Old Deanery, Wells, Somerset BA5 2UG. Tel: 01749-670777

BIRMINGHAM

7TH BISHOP
Rt. Revd Mark Santer, *cons.* 1981, *apptd* 1987; Bishop's Croft, Harborne, Birmingham B17 0BG. *Signs* Mark Birmingham

BISHOP SUFFRAGAN
Aston, Rt. Revd John Austin, *cons.* 1992, *apptd* 1992; Strensham House, 8 Strensham Hill, Moseley, Birmingham B13 8AG

PROVOST
Very Revd Peter A. Berry, *apptd* 1986

CANONS RESIDENTIARY
Ven. C. J. G. Barton, *apptd* 1990; Revd D. Lee, *apptd* 1996
Organist, M. Huxley, FRCO, *apptd* 1986

ARCHDEACONS
Aston, Ven. C. J. G. Barton, *apptd* 1990
Birmingham, Ven. J. F. Duncan, *apptd* 1985

Chancellor, His Honour Judge Aglionby, *apptd* 1970
Registrar and Legal Secretary, H. Carslake
Diocesan Secretary, J. Drennan, 175 Harborne Park Road, Harborne, Birmingham B17 0BH. Tel: 0121-427 5141

BRISTOL

54TH BISHOP
Rt. Revd Barry Rogerson, *cons.* 1979, *apptd* 1985; Bishop's House, Clifton Hill, Bristol BS8 1BW. *Signs* Barry Bristol

BISHOP SUFFRAGAN
Swindon, Rt. Revd Michael Doe, *cons.* 1994, *apptd* 1994; Mark House, Field Rise, Old Town, Swindon SN1 4HP

DEAN
vacant

CANONS RESIDENTIARY
A. L. J. Redfern, *apptd* 1987; J. L. Simpson, *apptd* 1989; P. F. Johnson, *apptd* 1990
Organist, C. Brayne, *apptd* 1990

ARCHDEACONS
Bristol, Ven. D. J. Banfield, *apptd* 1990
Swindon, Ven. M. Middleton, *apptd* 1992

Chancellor, Sir David Calcutt, QC, *apptd* 1971
Registrar and Legal Secretary, D. Ratcliffe
Diocesan Secretary, Mrs L. Farrall, Diocesan Church House, 23 Great George Street, Bristol, Avon BS1 5QZ. Tel: 0117-921 4411

CHELMSFORD

8TH BISHOP
Rt. Revd John F. Perry, *cons.* 1989, *apptd* 1996; Bishopscourt, Margaretting, Ingatestone CM4 0HD. *Signs* John Chelmsford

BISHOPS SUFFRAGAN
Barking, Rt. Revd Roger F. Sainsbury, *cons.* 1991, *apptd* 1991; 110 Capel Road, Forest Gate, London E7 0JS
Bradwell, Rt. Revd Laurence Green, *cons.* 1993, *apptd* 1993; The Vicarage, Orsett Road, Horndon-on-the-Hill, Stanford-le-Hope, Essex SS17 8NS
Colchester, Rt. Revd Edward Holland, *cons.* 1986, *apptd* 1995; 1 Fitzwalter Road, Lexden, Colchester CO3 3SS

PROVOST
vacant

CANONS RESIDENTIARY
T. Thompson, *apptd* 1988; B. P. Thompson, *apptd* 1988; D. Knight, *apptd* 1991
Organist, Dr G. Elliott, PH.D., FRCO, *apptd* 1981

ARCHDEACONS
Colchester, Ven. E. C. F. Stroud, *apptd* 1983
Harlow, Ven. P. F. Taylor, *apptd* 1996
Southend, Ven. D. Jennings, *apptd* 1992
West Ham, Ven. M. J. Fox, *apptd* 1996

Chancellor, Miss S. M. Cameron, QC, *apptd* 1970
Registrar and Legal Secretary, B. Hood
Diocesan Secretary, D. Phillips, 53 New Street, Chelmsford, Essex CM1 1AT. Tel: 01245-266731

CHICHESTER

102ND BISHOP
Rt. Revd Eric W. Kemp, DD, *cons.* 1974, *apptd* 1974; The
Palace, Chichester PO19 1PY. *Signs* Eric Cicestr:

BISHOPS SUFFRAGAN
Horsham, Rt. Revd Lindsay G. Urwin, *cons.* 1993, *apptd* 1993;
Bishop's House, 21 Guildford Road, Horsham,
W. Sussex RH12 1LU
Lewes, vacant; Beacon House, Berwick, Polegate BN26 6ST

DEAN
Very Revd John D. Treadgold, LVO, *apptd* 1989

CANONS RESIDENTIARY
R. T. Greenacre, *apptd* 1975; F. J. Hawkins, *apptd* 1981
Organist, A. J. Thurlow, FRCO, *apptd* 1980

ARCHDEACONS
Chichester, Ven. M. Brotherton, *apptd* 1991
Horsham, Ven. W. C. L. Filby, *apptd* 1983
Lewes and Hastings, Ven. H. Glaisyer, *apptd* 1991

Chancellor, His Honour Judge Q. T. Edwards, QC, *apptd* 1978
Registrar and Legal Secretary, C. L. Hodgetts
Diocesan Secretary, J. Prichard, Diocesan Church House,
211 New Church Road, Hove, E. Sussex BN3 4ED. Tel:
01273-421021

COVENTRY

7TH BISHOP
Rt. Revd Simon Barrington-Ward, *cons.* 1985, *apptd* 1985;
The Bishop's House, 23 Davenport Road, Coventry
CV5 6PW. *Signs* Simon Coventry

BISHOP SUFFRAGAN
Warwick, Rt. Revd Anthony M. Priddis, *cons.* 1996, *apptd*
1996; 139 Kenilworth Road, Coventry CV4 7AF

PROVOST
Very Revd John F. Petty, *apptd* 1987

CANONS RESIDENTIARY
P. Oestreicher, *apptd* 1986; V. Faull, *apptd* 1994; J. C. Burch,
apptd 1995
Organist, A. P. Leddington Wright, *apptd* 1984

ARCHDEACONS
Coventry, Ven. H. I. L. Russell, *apptd* 1989
Warwick, Ven. M. J. J. Paget-Wilkes, *apptd* 1990

Chancellor, Sir William Gage, *apptd* 1980
Registrar and Legal Secretary, D. J. Dumbleton
Diocesan Secretary, Mrs I. Chapman, Church House,
Palmerston Road, Coventry CV5 6FJ. Tel: 01203-674328

DERBY

6TH BISHOP
Rt. Revd Jonathan S. Bailey, *cons.* 1992, *apptd* 1995; Derby
Church House, Full Street, Derby DE1 3DR. *Signs*
Jonathan Derby

BISHOP SUFFRAGAN
Repton, Rt. Revd F. Henry A. Richmond, *cons.* 1986, *apptd*
1986; Repton House, Lea, Matlock DE4 5JP

PROVOST
Very Revd Benjamin H. Lewers, *apptd* 1981

CANONS RESIDENTIARY
G. A. Chesterman, *apptd* 1989; Ven. I. Gatford, *apptd* 1992;
G. O. Marshall, *apptd* 1992; R. M. Parsons, *apptd* 1993
Organist, P. Gould, *apptd* 1982

ARCHDEACONS
Chesterfield, Ven. D. C. Garnett, *apptd* 1996
Derby, Ven. I. Gatford, *apptd* 1992

Chancellor, J. W. M. Bullimore, *apptd* 1981
Registrar and Legal Secretary, J. S. Battie
Diocesan Secretary, R. J. Carey, Derby Church House, Full
Street, Derby DE1 3DR. Tel: 01332-382233

ELY

67TH BISHOP
Rt. Revd Stephen W. Sykes, *cons.* 1990, *apptd* 1990; The
Bishop's House, Ely, Cambs CB7 4DW. *Signs* Stephen Ely

BISHOP SUFFRAGAN
Huntingdon, vacant; 14 Lynn Road, Ely, Cambs CB6 1DA

DEAN
Very Revd Michael Higgins, *apptd* 1991

CANONS RESIDENTIARY
D. J. Green, *apptd* 1980; J. Inge, *apptd* 1996
Organist, P. Trepte, FRCO, *apptd* 1991

ARCHDEACONS
Ely, Ven. J. Watson, *apptd* 1993
Huntingdon, vacant
Wisbech, Ven. J. Rone, *apptd* 1995

Chancellor, W. Gage, QC
Joint Registrars, W. H. Godfrey; P. F. B. Beesley (*Legal
Secretary*)
Diocesan Secretary, Dr M. Lavis, Bishop Woodford House,
Barton Road, Ely, Cambs CB7 4DX. Tel: 01353-663579

EXETER

69TH BISHOP
Rt. Revd G. Hewlett Thompson, *cons.* 1974, *apptd* 1985;
The Palace, Exeter EX1 1HY. *Signs* Hewlett Exon:

BISHOPS SUFFRAGAN
Crediton, Rt. Revd Richard S. Hawkins, *cons.* 1988, *apptd*
1996; 10 The Close, Exeter EX1 1EZ
Plymouth, Rt. Revd John H. Garton, *cons.* 1996, *apptd* 1996;
31 Riverside Walk, Tamerton Foliot, Plymouth PL5 4AQ

DEAN
Very Revd Keith B. Jones, *apptd* 1996

CANONS RESIDENTIARY
A. C. Mawson, *apptd* 1979; K. C. Parry, *apptd* 1991
Organist, L. A. Nethsingha, FRCO, *apptd* 1973

ARCHDEACONS
Barnstaple, Ven. T. Lloyd, *apptd* 1989
Exeter, Ven. A. F. Tremlett, *apptd* 1994
Plymouth, Ven. R. G. Ellis, *apptd* 1982
Totnes, Preb. R. T. Gilpin, *apptd* 1996

Chancellor, Sir David Calcutt, QC, *apptd* 1971
Registrar and Legal Secretary, R. K. Wheeler

Diocesan Secretary, Revd R. Huddleson, Diocesan House, Palace Gate, Exeter, Devon EX1 1HX. Tel: 01392-72686

GIBRALTAR IN EUROPE

BISHOP
Rt. Revd John Hind, *cons.* 1991, *apptd* 1993; 14 Tufton Street, London SW1P 3QZ. *Signs* John Gibraltar

BISHOP SUFFRAGAN
In Europe Rt. Revd Henry Scriven, *cons.* 1995, *apptd* 1994; 14 Tufton Street, London SW1P 3QZ

Vicar-General, Canon W. G. Reid
Dean, Cathedral Church of the Holy Trinity, Gibraltar, Very Revd B. W. Horlock, OBE
Chancellor, Pro-Cathedral of St Paul, Valletta, Malta, Canon A. Woods
Chancellor, Pro-Cathedral of the Holy Trinity, Brussels, Belgium, Canon N. Walker

ARCHDEACONS
Aegean, Ven. S. J. B. Peake
North-West Europe, Ven. G. G. Allen
France, Ven. M. Draper
Gibraltar, Ven. K. Robinson
Italy, Rt. Revd E. Devenport
Scandinavia and Germany, Ven. D. Ratcliff
Switzerland, Ven. P. J. Hawker, OBE

Chancellor, Sir David Calcutt, QC
Registrar and Legal Secretary, J. G. Underwood
Diocesan Secretary, Canon W. G. Reid, 14 Tufton Street, London SW1P 3QZ. Tel: 0171-976 8001

GLOUCESTER

39TH BISHOP
Rt. Revd David Bentley, *cons.* 1986, *apptd* 1993; Bishopscourt, Gloucester GL1 2BQ. *Signs* David Gloucestr

BISHOP SUFFRAGAN
Tewkesbury, Rt. Revd John S. Went, *cons.* 1995, *apptd* 1995; Green Acre, Hempsted, Gloucester GL2 6LG

DEAN
Very Revd Nicholas A. S. Bury, *apptd* 1996

CANONS RESIDENTIARY
R. D. M. Grey, *apptd* 1982; N. Chatfield, *apptd* 1992; N. Heavisides, *apptd* 1993; C. H. Morgan, *apptd* 1996

Organist, D. Briggs, FRCO, *apptd* 1994

ARCHDEACONS
Cheltenham, Ven. J. A. Lewis, *apptd* 1988
Gloucester, Ven. C. J. H. Wagstaff, *apptd* 1982

Chancellor and Vicar-General, Ms D. J. Rogers, *apptd* 1990
Registrar and Legal Secretary, C. G. Peak
Diocesan Secretary, M. Williams, Church House, College Green, Gloucester GL1 2LY. Tel: 01452-410022

GUILDFORD

8TH BISHOP
Rt. Revd John W. Gladwin, *cons.* 1994, *apptd* 1994; Willow Grange, Woking Road, Guildford GU4 7QS. *Signs* John Guildford

BISHOP SUFFRAGAN
Dorking, Rt. Revd Ian Brackley, *cons.* 1996, *apptd* 1995; 13 Pilgrims Way, Guildford GU4 8AD

DEAN
Very Revd Alexander G. Wedderspoon, *apptd* 1987

CANONS RESIDENTIARY
R. D. Fenwick, *apptd* 1990; J. Schofield, *apptd* 1995; Revd Dr Maureen Palmer

Organist, A. Millington, FRCO, *apptd* 1982

ARCHDEACONS
Dorking, Ven. M. Wilson, *apptd* 1995
Surrey, Ven. R. Reiss, *apptd* 1995

Chancellor, His Hon. Judge Goodman
Registrar and Legal Secretary, P. F. B. Beesley
Diocesan Secretary, Mrs K. Ingate, Diocesan House, Quarry Street, Guildford GU1 3XG. Tel: 01483-571826

HEREFORD

103RD BISHOP
Rt. Revd John Oliver, *cons.* 1990, *apptd* 1990; The Palace, Hereford HR4 9BN. *Signs* John Hereford

BISHOP SUFFRAGAN
Ludlow, Rt. Revd Dr John Saxbee, *cons.* 1994, *apptd* 1994; Bishop's House, Halford, Craven Arms, Shropshire SY7 9BT

DEAN
Very Revd Robert A. Willis, *apptd* 1992

CANONS RESIDENTIARY
P. Iles, *apptd* 1983; J. Tiller, *apptd* 1984; J. Butterworth, *apptd* 1994

Organist, Dr R. Massey, FRCO, *apptd* 1974

ARCHDEACONS
Hereford, Ven. L. G. Moss, *apptd* 1992
Ludlow, Rt. Revd J. C. Saxbee, *apptd* 1992

Chancellor, J. M. Henty
Joint Registrars and Legal Secretaries, V. T. Jordan; P. F. B. Beesley
Diocesan Secretary, Miss S. Green, The Palace, Hereford HR4 9BL. Tel: 01432-353863

LEICESTER

5TH BISHOP
Rt. Revd Thomas F. Butler, PH.D., LL D, *cons.* 1985, *apptd* 1991; Bishop's Lodge, 10 Springfield Road, Leicester LE2 3BD. *Signs* Thomas Leicester

STIPENDIARY ASSISTANT BISHOP
Rt. Revd William Down, *cons.* 1990, *apptd* 1995

PROVOST
Very Revd Derek Hole, *apptd* 1992

CANONS RESIDENTIARY
M. T. H. Banks, *apptd* 1988; M. Wilson, *apptd* 1988
Organist, J. T. Gregory, *apptd* 1994

ARCHDEACONS
Leicester, Ven. M. Edson, *apptd* 1994
Loughborough, Ven. I. Stanes, *apptd* 1992

Chancellor, N. Seed, *apptd* 1989
Registrars and Legal Secretaries, P. C. E. Morris; R. H. Bloor

Diocesan Secretary, J. Cryer, Church House, 3–5 St Martin's East, Leicester LEI 5FX. Tel: 0116-262 7445

LICHFIELD

97TH BISHOP
Rt. Revd Keith N. Sutton, *cons.* 1978, *apptd* 1984; Bishop's House, The Close, Lichfield WS13 7LG. *Signs* Keith Lichfield

BISHOPS SUFFRAGAN
Shrewsbury, Rt. Revd David M. Hallatt, *cons.* 1994, *apptd* 1994; 68 London Road, Shrewsbury SY2 6PG
Stafford, Rt. Revd Christopher J. Hill, *cons.* 1996, *apptd* 1996; Ash Garth, Broughton Crescent, Barlaston, Staffs ST12 9DD
Wolverhampton, Rt. Revd Michael G. Bourke, *cons.* 1993, *apptd* 1993; 61 Richmond Road, Wolverhampton WV3 9JH

DEAN
Very Revd Tom Wright, *apptd* 1993

CANONS RESIDENTIARY
Ven. R. B. Ninis, *apptd* 1974; A. N. Barnard, *apptd* 1977; J. Howe, *apptd* 1988; C. W. Taylor, *apptd* 1995

Organist, A. Lumsden, *apptd* 1992

ARCHDEACONS
Lichfield, Ven. R. B. Ninis, *apptd* 1974
Salop, Ven. G. Frost, *apptd* 1987
Stoke-on-Trent, Ven. D. Ede, *apptd* 1989

Chancellor, His Honour Judge Shand
Registrar and Legal Secretary, J. P. Thorneycroft
Diocesan Secretary, D. R. Taylor, St Mary's House, The Close, Lichfield, Staffs WS13 7LD. Tel: 01543-414551

LINCOLN

70TH BISHOP
Rt. Revd Robert M. Hardy, *cons.* 1980, *apptd* 1987; Bishop's House, Eastgate, Lincoln LN2 1QQ. *Signs* Robert Lincoln

BISHOPS SUFFRAGAN
Grantham, Rt. Revd William Ind, *cons.* 1987, *apptd* 1987; Fairacre, Barrowby High Road, Grantham NG31 8NP
Grimsby, Rt. Revd David Tustin, *cons.* 1979, *apptd* 1979; Bishop's House, Church Lane, Irby-upon-Humber, Grimsby DN37 7JR

DEAN
Very Revd Brandon D. Jackson, *apptd* 1989

CANONS RESIDENTIARY
B. R. Davis, *apptd* 1977; A. J. Stokes, *apptd* 1992; V. White, *apptd* 1994

Organist, C. S. Walsh, FRCO, *apptd* 1988

ARCHDEACONS
Lincoln, Ven. A. Hawes, *apptd* 1995
Lindsey, vacant
Stow, Ven. R. J. Wells, *apptd* 1989

Chancellor, His Honour Judge Goodman, *apptd* 1971
Registrar and Legal Secretary, D. M. Wellman
Diocesan Secretary, P. Hamlyn Williams, The Old Palace, Lincoln LN2 1PU. Tel: 01522-529241

NORWICH

70TH BISHOP
Rt. Revd Peter J. Nott, *cons.* 1977, *apptd* 1985; Bishop's House, Norwich NR3 1SB. *Signs* Peter Norvic:

BISHOPS SUFFRAGAN
Lynn, Rt. Revd David Conner, *cons.* 1994, *apptd* 1994; The Old Vicarage, Castle Acre, King's Lynn PE32 2AA
Thetford, Rt. Revd Hugo F. de Waal, *cons.* 1992, *apptd* 1992; Rectory Meadow, Bramerton, Norwich NR14 7DW

DEAN
Very Revd Stephen Platten, *apptd* 1995

CANONS RESIDENTIARY
M. F. Perham, *apptd* 1992; Ven. C. J. Offer, *apptd* 1994; R. J. Hanmer, *apptd* 1994

Organist, D. Dunnett, *apptd* 1996

ARCHDEACONS
Lynn, Ven. A. C. Foottit, *apptd* 1987
Norfolk, Ven. A. M. Handley, *apptd* 1993
Norwich, Ven. C. J. Offer, *apptd* 1994

Chancellor, His Honour J. H. Ellison, VRD, *apptd* 1955
Registrar and Legal Secretary, J. W. F. Herring
Diocesan Secretary, D. Adeney, Diocesan House, 109 Dereham Road, Easton, Norwich, Norfolk NR9 5ES. Tel: 01603-880853

OXFORD

41ST BISHOP
Rt. Revd Richard D. Harries, *cons.* 1987, *apptd* 1987; Diocesan Church House, North Hinksey, Oxford OX2 0NB. *Signs* Richard Oxon:

AREA BISHOPS
Buckingham, Rt. Revd Colin J. Bennetts, *cons.* 1994, *apptd* 1994; Sheridan, Grimms Hill, Great Missenden HP16 9BD
Dorchester, Rt. Revd Anthony J. Russell, *cons.* 1988, *apptd* 1988; Holmby House, Sibford Ferris, Banbury, Oxon OX15 5RG
Reading, vacant; Greenbanks, Old Bath Road, Sonning, Reading RG4 0SY

DEAN OF CHRIST CHURCH
Very Revd John H. Drury, *apptd* 1991

CANONS RESIDENTIARY
Ven. F. V. Weston, *apptd* 1982; O. M. T. O'Donovan, D.phil., *apptd* 1982; J. M. Pierce, *apptd* 1987; J. S. K. Ward, *apptd* 1991; R. Jeffery, *apptd* 1996; Prof. J. Webster, *apptd* 1996

Organist, S. Darlington, FRCO, *apptd* 1985

ARCHDEACONS
Berkshire, Ven. M. A. Hill, *apptd* 1992
Buckingham, Ven. J. A. Morrison, *apptd* 1989
Oxford, Ven. F. V. Weston, *apptd* 1982

Chancellor, P. T. S. Boydell, QC, *apptd* 1958
Registrar and Legal Secretary, Dr F. E. Robson
Secretary to the Diocesan Board of Finance, T. Landsbert, Diocesan Church House, North Hinksey, Oxford OX2 0NB. Tel: 01865-244566

PETERBOROUGH

37TH BISHOP
Rt. Revd Ian P. M. Cundy, *cons.* 1992, *apptd* 1996; The Palace, Peterborough PE1 1YA. *Signs* Ian Petriburg:

BISHOP SUFFRAGAN
Brixworth, Rt. Revd Paul E. Barber, *cons.* 1989, *apptd* 1989; 4 The Avenue, Dallington, Northampton NN1 4RZ

DEAN
Very Revd Michael Bunker, *apptd* 1992

CANONS RESIDENTIARY
T. R. Christie, *apptd* 1980; J. Higham, *apptd* 1983; T. Willmott, *apptd* 1989
Organist, C. S. Gower, FRCO, *apptd* 1977

ARCHDEACONS
Northampton, Ven. M. R. Chapman, *apptd* 1991
Oakham, Ven. B. Fernyhough, *apptd* 1977

Chancellor, T. A. C. Coningsby, QC, *apptd* 1989
Registrar and Legal Secretary, R. Hemingray
Diocesan Secretary, K. H. Hope-Jones, The Palace, Peterborough, Cambs PE1 1YB. Tel: 01733-64448

PORTSMOUTH

8TH BISHOP
Rt. Revd Dr Kenneth W. Stevenson, *cons.* 1995, *apptd* 1995; Bishopswood, 23 The Avenue, Fareham, Hants PO14 1NT. *Signs* Kenneth Portsmouth

PROVOST
Very Revd Michael Yorke, *apptd* 1994

CANONS RESIDENTIARY
C. J. Bradley, *apptd* 1990; D. T. Isaac, *apptd* 1990; Jane Hedges, *apptd* 1993
Organist, D. Price, *apptd* 1996

ARCHDEACONS
Isle of Wight, Ven. K. M. L. H. Banting, *apptd* 1996
Portsmouth, Ven. G. P. Knowles, *apptd* 1993

Chancellor, His Honour Judge Aglionby, *apptd* 1978
Registrar and Legal Secretary, Miss H. A. G. Tyler
Diocesan Secretary, M. F. Jordan, Cathedral House, St Thomas's Street, Portsmouth, Hants PO1 2HA. Tel: 01705-825731

ROCHESTER

106TH BISHOP
Rt. Revd Dr Michael Nazir-Ali, *cons.* 1984, *apptd* 1994; Bishopscourt, Rochester ME1 1TS. *Signs* Michael Roffen:

BISHOP SUFFRAGAN
Tonbridge, Rt. Revd Brian A. Smith, *cons.* 1993, *apptd* 1993; Bishop's Lodge, St Botolph's Road, Sevenoaks TN13 3AG

DEAN
Very Revd Edward F. Shotter, *apptd* 1990

CANONS RESIDENTIARY
E. R. Turner, *apptd* 1981; R. J. R. Lea, *apptd* 1988; J. Armson, *apptd* 1989; N. Warren, *apptd* 1989
Organist, R. Sayer, FRCO, *apptd* 1995

ARCHDEACONS
Bromley, Ven. G. Norman, *apptd* 1994
Rochester, Ven. N. L. Warren, *apptd* 1989
Tonbridge, Ven. Judith Rose

Chancellor, His Honour Judge M. B. Goodman, *apptd* 1971
Registrar, O. R. Woodfield
Legal Secretary, D. W. Faull, OBE
Diocesan Secretary, P. Law, St Nicholas Church, Boley Hill, Rochester ME1 1SL. Tel: 01634-830333

ST ALBANS

9TH BISHOP
Rt. Revd Christopher W. Herbert, *cons.* 1995, *apptd* 1995; Abbey Gate House, St Albans AL3 4HD. *Signs* Christopher St Albans

BISHOPS SUFFRAGAN
Bedford, Rt. Revd John H. Richardson, *cons.* 1994, *apptd* 1994; 168 Kimbolton Road, Bedford MK41 8DN
Hertford, Rt. Revd Robin J. N. Smith, *cons.* 1990, *apptd* 1990; Hertford House, Abbey Mill Lane, St Albans AL3 4HE

DEAN
Very Revd Christopher Lewis, *apptd* 1993

CANONS RESIDENTIARY
C. Garner, *apptd* 1984; G. R. S. Ritson, *apptd* 1987; M. Sansom, *apptd* 1988; C. R. J. Foster, *apptd* 1994
Organist, Dr B. Rose, *apptd* 1988

ARCHDEACONS
Bedford, Ven. M. L. Lesiter, *apptd* 1993
St Albans, Ven. P. B. Davies, *apptd* 1987

Chancellor, His Honour Judge Bursell, QC, *apptd* 1992
Registrar and Legal Secretary, D. N. Cheetham
Diocesan Secretary, L. Nicholls, Holywell Lodge, 41 Holywell Hill, St Albans AL1 1HE. Tel: 01727-854532

ST EDMUNDSBURY AND IPSWICH

BISHOP
vacant; Bishop's House, 4 Park Road, Ipswich IP1 3ST. *Signs –* St Edmundsbury and Ipswich

BISHOP SUFFRAGAN
Dunwich, Rt. Revd Timothy J. Stevens, *cons.* 1995, *apptd* 1995; The Old Vicarage, Stowupland, Stowmarket IP14 4BQ

PROVOST
Very Revd J. Atwell, *apptd* 1995

CANONS RESIDENTIARY
A. M. Shaw, *apptd* 1989; M. E. Mingins, *apptd* 1993
Organist, M. Cousins, *apptd* 1993

ARCHDEACONS
Ipswich, Ven. T. A. Gibson, *apptd* 1987
Sudbury, Ven. J. Cox, *apptd* 1995
Suffolk, Ven. G. Arrand, *apptd* 1994

Chancellor, His Honour Sir John Blofeld, QC, *apptd* 1974
Registrar and Legal Secretary, Revd J. D. Mitson
Diocesan Secretary, I. Dodd, 13–15 Tower Street, Ipswich IP1 3BG. Tel: 01473-211028

SALISBURY

77TH BISHOP
Rt. Revd David S. Stancliffe, *cons.* 1993, *apptd* 1993; South
Canonry, The Close, Salisbury SP1 2ER. *Signs* David
Sarum

BISHOPS SUFFRAGAN
Ramsbury, Rt. Revd Peter St G. Vaughan, *cons.* 1989, *apptd*
1989; Bishop's House, Urchfont, Devizes, Wilts SN10
4QH
Sherborne, Rt. Revd John D. G. Kirkham, *cons.* 1976, *apptd*
1976; Little Bailie, Sturminster Marshall, Wimborne
BH21 4AD

DEAN
Very Revd Derek Watson, *apptd* 1996

CANONS RESIDENTIARY
D. J. C. Davies, *apptd* 1985; D. M. K. Durston, *apptd* 1992;
June Osborne, *apptd* 1995
Organist, R. G. Seal, FRCO, *apptd* 1968

ARCHDEACONS
Dorset, Ven. G. E. Walton, *apptd* 1982
Sarum, Ven. B. J. Hopkinson, *apptd* 1986
Sherborne, Ven. P. C. Wheatley, *apptd* 1991
Wilts, Ven. B. J. Smith, *apptd* 1980

Chancellor, His Honour J. H. Ellison, VRD, *apptd* 1955
Registrar and Legal Secretary, F. M. Broadbent
Diocesan Secretary, Revd Karen Curnock, Church House,
Crane Street, Salisbury SP1 2QB. Tel: 01722-411922

SOUTHWARK

8TH BISHOP
Rt. Revd Robert K. Williamson, *cons.* 1984, *trans.* 1991,
apptd 1991; Bishop's House, 38 Tooting Bec Gardens,
London SW16 1QZ. *Signs* Robert Southwark

AREA BISHOPS
Croydon, Rt. Revd Dr Wilfred D. Wood, DD, *cons.* 1985, *apptd*
1985; St Matthew's House, George Street, Croydon CR0
1PE
Kingston upon Thames, Rt Revd Martin Wharton, *cons.* 1992,
apptd 1992; *Kingston Episcopal Area Office*, Whitelands
College, West Hill, London SW15 3SN
Woolwich, Rt. Revd Colin O. Buchanan, *cons.* 1985, *apptd*
1996; c/o Trinity House, 4 Chapel Court, Borough High
Street, London SE1 1HW

PROVOST
Very Revd Colin B. Slee, *apptd* 1994

CANONS RESIDENTIARY
Dr M. Kitchen, *apptd* 1988; D. Painter, *apptd* 1991; Helen
Cunliffe, *apptd* 1995
Organist, P. Wright, FRCO, *apptd* 1989

ARCHDEACONS
Croydon, Ven. V. A. Davies, *apptd* 1994
Lambeth, Ven. C. R. B. Bird, *apptd* 1988
Lewisham, Ven. D. J. Atkinson, *apptd* 1996
Reigate, Ven. M. Baddeley, *apptd* 1996
Southwark, Ven. D. L. Bartles-Smith, *apptd* 1985
Wandsworth, Ven. D. Gerrard, *apptd* 1989

Chancellor, vacant
Registrar and Legal Secretary, P. Morris

Diocesan Secretary, M. Cawte, Trinity House, 4 Chapel
Court, Borough High Street, London SE1 1HW. Tel: 0171-
403 8686

TRURO

13TH BISHOP
Rt. Revd Michael T. Ball, *cons.* 1980, *apptd* 1990; Lis Escop,
Truro TR3 6QQ. *Signs* Michael Truro

BISHOP SUFFRAGAN
St Germans, Rt. Revd Graham R. James, *cons.* 1993, *apptd*
1993; 32 Falmouth Road, Truro TR1 2HX

DEAN
Very Revd David J. Shearlock, *apptd* 1982

CANONS RESIDENTIARY
P. R. Gay, *apptd* 1994; K. P. Mellor, *apptd* 1994; P. D.
Goodridge, *apptd* 1996
Organist, A. Nethsingha, FRCO, *apptd* 1994

ARCHDEACONS
Cornwall, Ven. J. T. McCabe, *apptd* 1996
Bodmin, Ven. R. D. C. Whiteman, *apptd* 1989

Chancellor, P. T. S. Boydell, QC, *apptd* 1957
Registrar and Legal Secretary, M. J. Follett
Diocesan Secretary, C. B. Gorton, Diocesan House, Kenwyn,
Truro TR1 3DU. Tel: 01872-74351

WORCESTER

BISHOP
vacant; The Bishop's House, Hartlebury Castle,
Kidderminster DY11 7XX. *Signs* – Worcester

BISHOP SUFFRAGAN
Dudley, Rt. Revd Dr Rupert Hoare, *cons.* 1993, *apptd* 1993;
The Bishop's House, Brooklands, Halesowen Road,
Cradley Heath B64 7JF

DEAN
vacant

CANONS RESIDENTIARY
Ven. F. Bentley, *apptd* 1984; D. G. Thomas, *apptd* 1987;
I. M. MacKenzie, *apptd* 1989
Organist, A. Lucas, *apptd* 1996

ARCHDEACONS
Dudley, Ven. J. Gathercole, *apptd* 1987
Worcester, Ven. F. Bentley, *apptd* 1984

Chancellor, P. T. S. Boydell, QC, *apptd* 1959
Registrar and Legal Secretary, M. Huskinson
Diocesan Secretary, J. Stanbury, The Old Palace, Deansway,
Worcester WR1 2JE. Tel: 01905-20537

ROYAL PECULIARS

WESTMINSTER
The Collegiate Church of St Peter

Dean, vacant
Sub Dean and Archdeacon, A. E. Harvey, *apptd* 1987
Canons of Westminster, A. E. Harvey, *apptd* 1982; D. C. Gray,
apptd 1987; C. D. Semper, *apptd* 1987; D. H. Hutt, *apptd*
1995

Chapter Clerk and Receiver-General, Rear-Adm. K. A. Snow,
CB, *apptd* 1987
Organist, M. Neary, FRCO, *apptd* 1988
Registrar, S. J. Holmes, MVO, 20 Dean's Yard, London
SWIP 3PA
Legal Secretary, C. L. Hodgetts

WINDSOR

The Queen's Free Chapel of St George within Her Castle of Windsor
Dean, Very Revd Patrick R. Mitchell, FSA, *apptd* 1989
Canons Residentiary, J. A. White, *apptd* 1982; D. M. Stanesby,
PH.D., *apptd* 1985; M. A. Moxon, *apptd* 1990; L. F. P.
Gunner, *apptd* 1996
Chapter Clerk, Lt.-Col. N. J. Newman, *apptd* 1990, Chapter
Office, The Cloisters, Windsor Castle, Windsor, Berks
SL4 INJ
Organist, J. Rees-Williams, FRCO, *apptd* 1991

Province of York

YORK

96TH ARCHBISHOP AND PRIMATE OF ENGLAND
Most Revd and Rt. Hon. David M. Hope, KCVO, D.Phil., LL D,
cons. 1985, *trans.* 1995, *apptd* 1995; Bishopthorpe, York
YO2 1QE. *Signs* David Ebor:

BISHOPS SUFFRAGAN
Hull, Rt. Revd James S. Jones, *cons.* 1994, *apptd* 1994; Hullen
House, Woodfield Lane, Hessle, Hull HU13 0ES
Selby, Rt. Revd Humphrey V. Taylor, *cons.* 1991, *apptd* 1991;
10 Precentor's Court, York YO1 2ES
Whitby, Rt. Revd Gordon Bates, *cons.* 1983, *apptd* 1983;
60 West Green, Stokesley, Middlesbrough TS9 5BD
Beverley, Rt. Revd John Gaisford, *cons.* 1994, *apptd* 1994
(provincial episcopal visitor); 3 North Lane, Roundhay,
Leeds LS8 2QJ

DEAN
Very Revd Raymond Furnell, *apptd* 1994

CANONS RESIDENTIARY
J. Toy, PH.D., *apptd* 1983; R. Metcalfe, *apptd* 1988;
P. J. Ferguson, *apptd* 1995; E. R. Norman, PH.D., DD, *apptd* 1995
Organist, P. Moore, FRCO, *apptd* 1983

ARCHDEACONS
Cleveland, Ven. C. J. Hawthorn, *apptd* 1991
East Riding, Ven. H. F. Buckingham, *apptd* 1988
York, Ven. G. B. Austin, *apptd* 1988

Official Principal and Auditor of the Chancery Court,
J. A. D. Owen, QC
Chancellor of the Diocese, His Honour Judge Coningsby, QC,
apptd 1977
Vicar-General of the Province and Official Principal of the
Consistory Court, His Honour Judge Coningsby, QC
Registrar and Legal Secretary, L. P. M. Lennox
Diocesan Secretary, K. W. Dodgson, Church House,
Ogleforth, York YO1 2JE. Tel: 01904-611696

DURHAM

92ND BISHOP
Rt. Revd A. Michael A. Turnbull, *cons.* 1988, *apptd* 1994;
Auckland Castle, Bishop Auckland DL14 7NR. *Signs*
Michael Dunelm:

BISHOP SUFFRAGAN
Jarrow, Rt. Revd Alan Smithson, *cons.* 1990, *apptd* 1990; The
Old Vicarage, Hallgarth, Pittington, Durham DH6 1AB

DEAN
Very Revd John R. Arnold, *apptd* 1989

CANONS RESIDENTIARY
M. C. Perry, *apptd* 1970; R. L. Coppin, *apptd* 1974; Ven. J. D.
Hodgson, *apptd* 1983; D. W. Brown, *apptd* 1990; G. S. Pedley,
apptd 1993
Organist, J. B. Lancelot, FRCO, *apptd* 1985

ARCHDEACONS
Auckland, Ven. G. G. Gibson, *apptd* 1993
Durham, Ven. J. D. Hodgson, *apptd* 1993

Chancellor, His Honour Judge Bursell, QC, *apptd* 1989
Registrar and Legal Secretary, D. M. Robertson
Diocesan Secretary, W. Hurworth, Auckland Castle, Bishop
Auckland, Co. Durham DL14 7QJ. Tel: 01388-604515

BLACKBURN

7TH BISHOP
Rt. Revd Alan D. Chesters, *cons.* 1989, *apptd* 1989; Bishop's
House, Ribchester Road, Blackburn BB1 9EF. *Signs* Alan
Blackburn

BISHOPS SUFFRAGAN
Burnley, Rt. Revd Martyn W. Jarrett, *cons.* 1994, *apptd* 1994;
Dean House, 449 Padiham Road, Burnley BB12 6TE
Lancaster, Rt. Revd John Nicholls, *cons.* 1990, *apptd* 1990;
Wheatfields, 7 Dallas Road, Lancaster LA1 1TN

PROVOST
Very Revd David Frayne, *apptd* 1992

CANONS RESIDENTIARY
K. J. Parfitt, *apptd* 1994; J. R. Hall, *apptd* 1994; D. M. Galilee,
apptd 1995; A. D. Hindley, *apptd* 1996
Organist, G. Stewart, *apptd* 1995

ARCHDEACONS
Blackburn, Ven. F. J. Marsh, *apptd* 1996
Lancaster, Ven. K. H. Gibbons, *apptd* 1981

Chancellor, J. W. M. Bullimore, *apptd* 1990
Registrar and Legal Secretary, T. A. Hoyle
Diocesan Secretary, Revd M. J. Wedgeworth, Diocesan
Office, Cathedral Close, Blackburn BB1 5AA. Tel: 01254-
54421

BRADFORD

8TH BISHOP
Rt. Revd David J. Smith, *cons.* 1987, *apptd* 1992;
Bishopscroft, Ashwell Road, Heaton, Bradford BD9 4AU.
Signs David Bradford

PROVOST
Very Revd John S. Richardson, *apptd* 1990

CANONS RESIDENTIARY
C. G. Lewis, *apptd* 1993; G. Smith, *apptd* 1996
Organist, A. Horsey, FRCO, *apptd* 1986

ARCHDEACONS
Bradford, Ven. D. H. Shreeve, *apptd* 1984
Craven, Ven. M. L. Grundy, *apptd* 1994

Chancellor, D. M. Savill, QC, *apptd* 1976
Registrar and Legal Secretary, J. G. H. Mackrell
Diocesan Secretary, M. Halliday, Cathedral Hall, Stott Hill,
    Bradford BDI 4ET. Tel: 01274-725958

CARLISLE

65TH BISHOP
Rt. Revd Ian Harland, *cons.* 1985, *apptd* 1989; Rose Castle,
    Dalston, Carlisle CA5 7BZ. *Signs* Ian Carliol:

BISHOP SUFFRAGAN
Penrith, Rt. Revd Richard Garrard, *cons.* 1994, *apptd* 1994;
    Holm Croft, Castle Road, Kendal, Cumbria LA9 7AU

DEAN
Very Revd Henry E. C. Stapleton, *apptd* 1988

CANONS RESIDENTIARY
R. A. Chapman, *apptd* 1978; Ven. D. C. Turnbull, *apptd* 1993;
D. W. V. Weston, *apptd* 1994; C. Hill, *apptd* 1996
Organist, J. Suter, FRCO, *apptd* 1991

ARCHDEACONS
Carlisle, Ven. D. C. Turnbull, *apptd* 1993
West Cumberland, vacant
Westmorland and Furness, Ven. D. T. I. Jenkins, *apptd* 1995

Chancellor, His Honour Judge Aglionby, *apptd* 1991
Registrar and Legal Secretary, Mrs S. Holmes
Diocesan Secretary, Canon C. Hill, Church House, West
    Walls, Carlisle CA3 8UE. Tel: 01228-22573

CHESTER

40TH BISHOP
Rt. Revd Peter R. Forster, PH.D., *cons.* 1996, *apptd* 1996;
    Bishop's House, Chester CHI 2JD. *Signs* Peter Cestr:

BISHOPS SUFFRAGAN
Birkenhead, Rt. Revd Michael L. Langrish, *cons.* 1993, *apptd*
    1993; 67 Bidston Road, Oxton, Birkenhead L43 6TR
Stockport, Rt. Revd Geoffrey M. Turner, *cons.* 1994, *apptd*
    1994; Bishop's Lodge, Back Lane, Dunham Town,
    Altrincham, Cheshire WA14 4SG

DEAN
Very Revd Dr Stephen S. Smalley, *apptd* 1986

CANONS RESIDENTIARY
R. M. Rees, *apptd* 1990; O. A. Conway, *apptd* 1991; Dr
T. J. Dennis, *apptd* 1994; J. W. S. Newcome, *apptd* 1994
Organist, R. Fisher, FRCO, *apptd* 1968

ARCHDEACONS
Chester, Ven. C. Hewetson, *apptd* 1994
Macclesfield, Ven. R. J. Gillings, *apptd* 1994

Chancellor, H. H. Lomas, *apptd* 1977
Registrar and Legal Secretary, A. K. McAllester
Diocesan Secretary, P. J. Mills, Diocesan House, Raymond
    Street, Chester CHI 4PN. Tel: 01244-379222

LIVERPOOL

6TH BISHOP
Rt. Revd David S. Sheppard, *cons.* 1969, *apptd* 1975; Bishop's
    Lodge, Woolton Park, Liverpool L25 6DT. *Signs* David
    Liverpool

BISHOP SUFFRAGAN
Warrington, Rt. Revd John Packer, *cons.* 1996, *apptd* 1996;
    c/o Martinsfield, Elm Avenue, Great Crosby, Liverpool
    L23 2SX

DEAN
Very Revd Rhys D. C. Walters, OBE, *apptd* 1983

CANONS RESIDENTIARY
D. J. Hutton, *apptd* 1983; M. C. Boyling, *apptd* 1994; N. T.
    Vincent, *apptd* 1995
Organist, Prof. I. Tracey, *apptd* 1980

ARCHDEACONS
Liverpool, Ven. R. L. Metcalf, *apptd* 1994
Warrington, Ven. C. D. S. Woodhouse, *apptd* 1981

Chancellor, R. G. Hamilton
Registrar and Legal Secretary, R. H. Arden
Diocesan Secretary, K. Cawdron, Church House, 1 Hanover
    Street, Liverpool LI 3DW. Tel: 0151-709 9722

MANCHESTER

10TH BISHOP
Rt. Revd Christopher J. Mayfield, *cons.* 1985, *apptd* 1993;
    Bishopscourt, Bury New Road, Manchester M7 4LE.
    Signs Christopher Manchester

BISHOPS SUFFRAGAN
Bolton, Rt. Revd David Bonser, *cons.* 1991, *apptd* 1991;
    4 Sandfield Drive, Lostock, Bolton BL6 4DU
Hulme, Rt. Revd Colin J. F. Scott, *cons.* 1984, *apptd* 1984;
    1 Raynham Avenue, Didsbury, Manchester M20 0BW
Middleton, Rt. Revd Stephen Venner, *cons.* 1994, *apptd* 1994;
    The Hollies, Manchester Road, Rochdale OLII 3QY

DEAN
Very Revd Kenneth Riley, *apptd* 1993

CANONS RESIDENTIARY
Ven. R. B. Harris, *apptd* 1980; J. R. Atherton, PH.D., *apptd* 1984;
A. E. Radcliffe, *apptd* 1991; P. Denby, *apptd* 1995
Organist, C. Stokes, *apptd* 1992

ARCHDEACONS
Bolton, Ven. L. M. Davies, *apptd* 1992
Manchester, Ven. R. B. Harris, *apptd* 1980
Rochdale, Ven. J. M. M. Dalby, *apptd* 1991

Chancellor, G. C. H. Spafford, *apptd* 1976
Registrar and Legal Secretary, M. Darlington
Diocesan Secretary, Mrs J. Park, Diocesan Church House,
    90 Deansgate, Manchester M3 2GH. Tel: 0161-833 9521

NEWCASTLE

10TH BISHOP
Rt. Revd Andrew A. K. Graham, *cons.* 1977, *apptd* 1981;
    Bishop's House, 29 Moor Road South, Gosforth,
    Newcastle upon Tyne NE3 IPA. *Signs* A. Newcastle

Stipendiary Assistant Bishop
Rt. Revd Kenneth Gill, *cons.* 1972, *apptd* 1980

Provost
Very Revd Nicholas G. Coulton, *apptd* 1990

Canons Residentiary
R. Langley, *apptd* 1985; P. R. Strange, *apptd* 1986;
I. F. Bennett, *apptd* 1988; Ven. P. Elliott, *apptd* 1993

Organist, T. G. Hone, FRCO, *apptd* 1987

Archdeacons
Lindisfarne, Ven. M. E. Bowering, *apptd* 1987
Northumberland, Ven. P. Elliott, *apptd* 1993

Chancellor, His Honour A. J. Blackett-Ord, CVO, *apptd* 1971
Registrar and Legal Secretary, Mrs B. J. Lowdon
Diocesan Secretary, J. M. Craster, Church House, Grainger
Park Road, Newcastle upon Tyne NE4 8SX. Tel: 0191-
226 0622

RIPON

11TH BISHOP
Rt. Revd David N. de L. Young, *cons.* 1977, *apptd* 1977;
Bishop Mount, Ripon HG4 5DP. *Signs* David Ripon

Bishop Suffragan
Knaresborough, Rt. Revd Malcolm J. Menin, *cons.* 1986, *apptd*
1986; 16 Shaftesbury Avenue, Roundhay, Leeds LS8 1DT

Dean
Very Revd John Methuen, *apptd* 1995

Canons Residentiary
P. J. Marshall, *apptd* 1985; M. R. Glanville-Smith, *apptd* 1990;
Revd K. Punshon, *apptd* 1996

Organist, K. Beaumont, FRCO, *apptd* 1994

Archdeacons
Leeds, Ven. J. M. Oliver, *apptd* 1992
Richmond, Ven. K. Good, *apptd* 1993

Chancellor, His Honour Judge Grenfell, *apptd* 1992
Registrar and Legal Secretary, J. R. Balmforth
Diocesan Secretary, G. M. Royal, Diocesan Office, St Mary's
Street, Leeds LS9 7DP. Tel: 0113-248 7487

SHEFFIELD

5TH BISHOP
Rt. Revd David R. Lunn, *cons.* 1980, *apptd* 1980;
Bishopscroft, Snaithing Lane, Sheffield S10 3LG. *Signs*
David Sheffield

Bishop Suffragan
Doncaster, Rt. Revd. Michael F. Gear, *cons.* 1993, *apptd* 1993;
Bishops Lodge, Hooton Roberts, Rotherham S65 4PF

Provost
Very Revd Michael Sadgrove, *apptd* 1995

Canons Residentiary
T. M. Page, *apptd* 1982; Ven. S. R. Lowe, *apptd* 1988;
C. M. Smith, *apptd* 1991; Jane E. M. Sinclair, *apptd* 1993

Organist, S. Lole, *apptd* 1994

Archdeacons
Doncaster, Ven. B. L. Holdridge, *apptd* 1994
Sheffield, Ven. S. R. Lowe, *apptd* 1988

Chancellor, Prof. J. D. McClean, *apptd* 1992

Registrar and Legal Secretary, C. P. Rothwell
Diocesan Secretary, C. A. Beck, FCIS, Diocesan Church
House, 95–99 Effingham Street, Rotherham S65 1BL. Tel:
0114-283 7547

SODOR AND MAN

79TH BISHOP
Rt. Revd Noel D. Jones, CB, *cons.* 1989, *apptd* 1989; The
Bishop's House, Quarterbridge Road, Douglas, Isle of
Man IM2 3RF. *Signs* Noel Sodor and Man

Canons
B. H. Kelly, *apptd* 1980; J. Sheen, *apptd* 1991; F. H. Bird, *apptd*
1993; D. Whitworth, *apptd* 1996

Archdeacon
Isle of Man, Ven. B. H. Partington, *apptd* 1996

Vicar-General and Chancellor, Ms C. Faulds
Registrar and Legal Secretary, C. J. Callow
Diocesan Secretary, The Hon. C. Murphy, c/o Cooil
Voorath, The Cronk, Ballaugh, Isle of Man IM7 5AX. Tel:
01624-897880

SOUTHWELL

9TH BISHOP
Rt. Revd Patrick B. Harris, *cons.* 1973, *apptd* 1988; Bishop's
Manor, Southwell NG25 0JR. *Signs* Patrick Southwell

Bishop Suffragan
Sherwood, Rt. Revd Alan W. Morgan, *cons.* 1989, *apptd* 1989;
Sherwood House, High Oakham Road, Mansfield
NG18 5AJ

Provost
Very Revd David Leaning, *apptd* 1991

Canons Residentiary
D. P. Keene, *apptd* 1981; I. G. Collins, *apptd* 1985;
M. R. Austin, *apptd* 1988

Organist, P. Hale, *apptd* 1989

Archdeacons
Newark, Ven. D. C. Hawtin, *apptd* 1992
Nottingham, Ven. G. Ogilvie, *apptd* 1996

Chancellor, J. Shand, *apptd* 1981
Registrar and Legal Secretary, C. C. Hodson
Diocesan Secretary, B. Noake, Dunham House, Westgate,
Southwell, Notts NG25 0JL. Tel: 01636-814331

WAKEFIELD

11TH BISHOP
Rt. Revd Nigel S. McCulloch, *cons.* 1986, *apptd* 1992;
Bishop's Lodge, Woodthorpe Lane, Wakefield WF2 6JL.
Signs Nigel Wakefield

Bishop Suffragan
Pontefract, Rt. Revd John Finney, *cons.* 1993, *apptd* 1993;
Pontefract House, 181A Manygates Lane, Wakefield
WF2 7DR

Provost
Very Revd John E. Allen, *apptd* 1982

CANONS RESIDENTIARY
R. D. Baxter, *apptd* 1986; I. C. Knox, *apptd* 1989; G. Nairn-Briggs, *apptd* 1992
Organist, J. Bielby, FRCO, *apptd* 1972

ARCHDEACONS
Halifax, Ven. R. Inwood, *apptd* 1995
Pontefract, Ven. J. Flack, *apptd* 1992

Chancellor, P. Collier, QC, *apptd* 1992
Registrar and Legal Secretary, L. Box
Diocesan Secretary, J. Clark, Church House, 1 South Parade, Wakefield WF1 ILP. Tel: 01924-371802

The Anglican Communion

The Anglican Communion consists of 37 independent provincial or national Christian churches throughout the world, many of which are in Commonwealth countries and originated from missionary activity by the Church of England. There is no single world authority linking the Communion, but all recognize the leadership of the Archbishop of Canterbury and have strong ecclesiastical and historical links with the Church of England. Every ten years all the bishops in the Communion meet at the Lambeth Conference, convened by the Archbishop of Canterbury. The Conference has no policy-making authority but is an important forum for the discussion of issues of common concern. The Anglican Consultative Council was set up in 1968 to function between conferences and the meeting of the Primates every two years.

There are about 70 million Anglicans and 800 archbishops and bishops world-wide.

THE CHURCH IN WALES

The Anglican Church was the established church in Wales from the 16th century until 1920, when the estrangement of the majority of Welsh people from Anglicanism resulted in disestablishment. Since then the Church in Wales has been an autonomous province consisting of six sees, with one of the diocesan bishops being elected Archbishop of Wales by an electoral college comprising elected lay and clerical members.

The legislative body of the Church in Wales is the Governing Body, which has 356 members in total, divided between the three orders of bishops, clergy and laity. It is presided over by the Archbishop of Wales and meets twice annually. Its decisions are binding upon all members of the Church. There are about 100,000 members of the Church in Wales, with six bishops, about 700 stipendiary clergy and 1,142 parishes.

THE GOVERNING BODY OF THE CHURCH IN WALES, 39 Cathedral Road, Cardiff CF1 9XF. Tel: 01222–231638. *Secretary-General*, J. W. D. McIntyre

10TH ARCHBISHOP OF WALES, Most Revd Alwyn R. Jones (Bishop of St Asaph), *elected* 1991

THE RT. REVD BISHOPS
Bangor (79*th*), Rt. Revd Dr Barry C. Morgan, *b.* 1947, *cons.* 1993, *elected* 1992; Tŷ'r Esgob, Bangor LL57 2SS. *Signs* Barry Bangor. *Stipendiary clergy*, 69
Llandaff (101*st*), Rt. Revd Roy T. Davies, *b.* 1934, *cons.* 1985, *elected* 1985; Llys Esgob, The Cathedral Green, Llandaff, Cardiff CF5 2YE. *Signs* Roy Landav. *Stipendiary clergy*, 158

Monmouth (8*th*), Rt. Revd Rowan D. Williams, *b.* 1950, *cons.* 1992, *elected* 1992; Bishopstow, Stow Hill, Newport NP9 4EA. *Signs* Rowan Monmouth. *Stipendiary clergy*, 120
St Asaph (74*th*), Most Revd Alwyn R. Jones, *b.* 1934, *cons.* 1982, *elected* 1982; Esgobty, St Asaph, Clwyd LL17 0TW. *Signs* Alwyn Cambrensis. *Stipendiary clergy*, 112
St David's (126*th*), Rt. Revd D. Huw Jones, *b.* 1934, *cons.* 1993, *elected* 1995; Llys Esgob, Abergwili, Carmarthen SA31 2JG. *Signs* Huw St Davids. *Stipendiary clergy*, 132
Swansea and Brecon (7*th*), Rt. Revd Dewi M. Bridges, *b.* 1933, *cons.* 1988, *elected* 1988; Ely Tower, Brecon, Powys LD3 9DE. *Signs* Dewi Swansea & Brecon. *Stipendiary clergy*, 100

The stipend of a diocesan bishop of the Church in Wales is £24,901 a year from 1996

THE SCOTTISH EPISCOPAL CHURCH

The Scottish Episcopal Church was founded after the Act of Settlement (1690) established the presbyterian nature of the Church of Scotland. The Scottish Episcopal Church is in full communion with the Church of England but is autonomous. The governing authority is the General Synod, an elected body of 180 members which meets once a year. The diocesan bishop who convenes and presides at meetings of the General Synod is called the Primus and is elected by his fellow bishops.

There are 54,382 members of the Scottish Episcopal Church, of whom 33,795 are communicants. There are seven bishops, 210 stipendiary clergy, and 320 churches and places of worship.

THE GENERAL SYNOD OF THE SCOTTISH EPISCOPAL CHURCH, 21 Grosvenor Crescent, Edinburgh EH12 5EE. Tel: 0131-225 6357. *Secretary-General*, J. F. Stuart

PRIMUS OF THE SCOTTISH EPISCOPAL CHURCH, Most Revd Richard F. Holloway (Bishop of Edinburgh), *elected* 1992

THE RT. REVD BISHOPS
Aberdeen and Orkney, A. Bruce Cameron, *b.* 1941, *cons.* 1992, *apptd* 1992. *Clergy*, 19
Argyll and the Isles, Douglas M. Cameron, *b.* 1935, *cons.* 1993, *apptd* 1992. *Clergy*, 9
Brechin, Robert T. Halliday, *b.* 1932, *cons.* 1990, *apptd* 1990. *Clergy*, 19
Edinburgh, Richard F. Holloway, *b.* 1933, *cons.* 1986, *apptd* 1986. *Clergy*, 53
Glasgow and Galloway, John M. Taylor, *b.* 1932, *cons.* 1991, *apptd* 1991. *Clergy*, 48
Moray, Ross and Caithness, Gregor Macgregor, *b.* 1933, *cons.* 1994, *apptd* 1994. *Clergy*, 13
St Andrews, Dunkeld and Dunblane, Michael H. G. Henley, *b.* 1938, *cons.* 1995, *apptd* 1995. *Clergy*, 30

The minimum stipend of a diocesan bishop of the Scottish Episcopal Church was £19,278 in 1996

THE CHURCH OF IRELAND

The Anglican Church was the established church in Ireland from the 16th century but never secured the allegiance of a majority of the Irish and was disestablished in 1871. The Church in Ireland is divided into the provinces of Armagh and Dublin, each under an archbishop. The provinces are subdivided into 12 dioceses.

The legislative body is the General Synod, which has 660 members in total, divided between the House of Bishops and the House of Representatives. The Archbishop of Armagh is elected by the House of Bishops; other episcopal elections are made by an electoral college.

There are about 375,000 members of the Church of Ireland, with two archbishops, ten bishops, about 600 clergy and about 1,000 churches and places of worship.

CENTRAL OFFICE, Church of Ireland House, Church Avenue, Rathmines, Dublin 6. Tel: 00-353-1-4978422. *Chief Officer and Secretary of the Representative Church Body*, R. H. Sherwood; *Assistant Secretary of the General Synod*, D. G. Meredith

PROVINCE OF ARMAGH

ARCHBISHOP OF ARMAGH AND PRIMATE OF ALL IRELAND, Most Revd Robert H. A. Eames, PH.D., *b.* 1937, *cons.* 1975, *trans.* 1986. *Clergy*, 50

THE RT. REVD BISHOPS
Clogher, Brian D. A. Hannon, *b.* 1936, *cons.* 1986, *apptd* 1986. *Clergy*, 34
Connor, James E. Moore, *b.* 1933, *cons.* 1995, *apptd.* 1995. *Clergy*, 104
Derry and Raphoe, James Mehaffey, PH.D., *b.* 1931, *cons.* 1980, *apptd* 1980. *Clergy*, 55
Down and Dromore, Gordon McMullan, PH.D., TH.D., *b.* 1934, *cons.* 1980, *trans.* 1986. *Clergy*, 107
Kilmore, Elphin and Ardagh, Michael H. G. Mayes, *b.* 1941, *cons.* 1993, *apptd* 1993. *Clergy*, 28
Tuam, Killala and Achonry, John R. W. Neill, *b.* 1945, *cons.* 1986, *apptd* 1986. *Clergy*, 12

PROVINCE OF DUBLIN

ARCHBISHOP OF DUBLIN, BISHOP OF GLENDALOUGH, AND PRIMATE OF IRELAND, Most Revd Walton N. F. Empey, *b.* 1934, *cons.* 1981, *trans.* 1985, 1996. *Clergy*, 88

THE RT. REVD BISHOPS
Cashel and Ossory, Noel V. Willoughby, *b.* 1926, *cons.* 1980, *apptd* 1980. *Clergy*, 34
Cork, Cloyne and Ross, Robert A. Warke, *b.* 1930, *cons.* 1988, *apptd* 1988. *Clergy*, 29
Limerick and Killaloe, Edward F. Darling, *b.* 1933, *cons.* 1985, *apptd* 1985. *Clergy*, 24
Meath and Kildare, Most Revd Robert L. Clarke, *b.* 1949, *cons.* 1996, *trans.* 1996. *Clergy*, 23

Anglican Communion Overseas

ANGLICAN CHURCH OF AOTEAROA, NEW ZEALAND AND POLYNESIA

PRIMATE AND ARCHBISHOP OF AOTEAROA, NEW ZEALAND AND POLYNESIA, The Most Revd Brian N. Davis (Bishop of Wellington), *cons.* 1980, *apptd* 1986

THE RT. REVD BISHOPS
Aotearoa, Whakahuhui Vercoe, *cons.* 1981, *apptd* 1981
Auckland, John Paterson, *cons.* 1995, *apptd* 1995
Christchurch, David Coles, *cons.* 1990, *apptd* 1990
Dunedin, Penelope Jamieson, *cons.* 1990, *apptd* 1990
Nelson, Derek Eaton, *cons.* 1990, *apptd* 1990
Polynesia, Jabez Bryce, *cons.* 1975, *apptd* 1975
Waiapu, Murray Mills, *cons.* 1991, *apptd* 1991

Waikato, David Moxon, *cons.* 1993, *apptd* 1993
Wellington, *see* above

ANGLICAN CHURCH OF AUSTRALIA

PRIMATE OF AUSTRALIA, The Most Revd Keith Rayner (Archbishop of Melbourne), *cons.* 1969, *apptd* 1991

PROVINCE OF NEW SOUTH WALES

METROPOLITAN
Archbishop of Sydney, The Most Revd R. Harry Goodhew, *cons.* 1982, *apptd* 1993

THE RT. REVD BISHOPS
Armidale, Peter Chiswell, *cons.* 1976, *apptd* 1976
Bathurst, Bruce W. Wilson, *cons.* 1984, *apptd* 1989
Canberra and Goulburn, George V. Browning, *cons.* 1985, *apptd* 1993
Grafton, Bruce A. Schultz, *cons.* 1983, *apptd* 1985
Newcastle, Roger A. Herft, *cons.* 1986, *apptd* 1993
Riverina, Bruce Q. Clark, *cons.* 1993, *apptd* 1993

PROVINCE OF QUEENSLAND

METROPOLITAN
Archbishop of Brisbane, The Most Revd Peter Hollingworth, *cons.* 1985, *apptd* 1990

THE RT. REVD BISHOPS
North Queensland, Clyde M. Wood, *cons.* 1983, *apptd* 1996
Northern Territory, Richard F. Appleby, *cons.* 1992, *apptd* 1992
Rockhampton, Ronald F. Stone, *cons.* 1992, *apptd* 1996

PROVINCE OF SOUTH AUSTRALIA

METROPOLITAN
Archbishop of Adelaide, The Most Revd Ian G. C. George, *cons.* 1989, *apptd* 1991

THE RT. REVD BISHOPS
The Murray, Graham H. Walden, *cons.* 1981, *apptd* 1989
Willochra, W. David H. McCall, *cons.* 1987, *apptd* 1987

PROVINCE OF VICTORIA

METROPOLITAN
Archbishop of Melbourne, The Most Revd Keith Rayner, *cons.* 1969, *apptd* 1990 (*see* above)

THE RT. REVD BISHOPS
Ballarat, R. David Silk, *cons.* 1994, *apptd* 1994
Bindigo, R. David Bowden, *cons.* 1995, *apptd* 1995
Gippsland, Arthur L. V. Jones, *cons.* 1994, *apptd* 1994
Wangaratta, Paul Richardson, *cons.* 1987, *apptd* 1995

PROVINCE OF WESTERN AUSTRALIA

METROPOLITAN
Archbishop of Perth, The Most Revd Peter F. Carnley, PH.D., *cons.* 1981, *apptd* 1981

THE RT. REVD BISHOPS
Bunbury, Hamish J. U. Jamieson, *cons.* 1974, *apptd* 1984
North-West Australia, Anthony Nicholls, *cons.* 1992, *apptd* 1992

EXTRA-PROVINCIAL DIOCESE

Bishop of Tasmania, Rt. Revd Phillip K. Newell, AO, *cons.* 1982, *apptd* 1982

EPISCOPAL ANGLICAN CHURCH OF BRAZIL
Igreja Episcopal Anglicana Do Brasil

PRIMATE, The Most Revd Glauco Soares de Lima (Bishop of São Paulo), *cons.* 1989, *apptd* 1994

THE RT. REVD BISHOPS
Brasilia, Almir dos Santos, *cons.* 1989, *apptd* 1989
Central Brazil, Sydney A. Ruiz, *cons.* 1985, *apptd* 1985
Northern Brazil, Clovis E. Rodrigues, *cons.* 1985, *apptd* 1986
Pelotas, Luiz O. P. Prado, *cons.* 1987, *apptd* 1989
São Paulo, see above, *apptd* 1989
Southern Brazil, Claudio V. S. Gastal, *cons.* 1984, *apptd* 1984
South-Western Brazil, Jubal P. Neves, *cons.* 1993, *apptd* 1993

CHURCH OF THE PROVINCE OF BURUNDI

ARCHBISHOP OF PROVINCE, The Most Revd Samuel Sindamuka (Bishop of Matana), *cons.* 1975, *apptd* 1989

THE RT. REVD BISHOPS
Bujumbura, Pie Ntukamazina, *cons.* 1990, *apptd* 1990
Buye, Samuel Ndayisenga, *apptd* 1979
Gitega, Jean Nduwayo, *apptd* 1985
Matana, see above

ANGLICAN CHURCH OF CANADA

ARCHBISHOP AND PRIMATE, The Most Revd Michael G. Peers, *cons.* 1977, *elected* 1986

PROVINCE OF BRITISH COLUMBIA
METROPOLITAN
Archbishop of Kootenay, The Most Revd David Crawley, *cons.* 1990, *elected* 1994

THE RT. REVD BISHOPS
British Columbia, Barry Jenks, *cons.* 1992, *elected* 1992
Caledonia, John Hannen, *cons.* 1981, *elected* 1981
Cariboo, James Cruickshank, *cons.* 1992, *elected* 1992
Kootenay, see above, *elected* 1990
New Westminster, Michael Ingham, *cons.* 1994, *elected* 1993
Yukon, Terrence O. Buckle, *cons.* 1993, *elected* 1995

PROVINCE OF CANADA
METROPOLITAN
Archbishop of Western Newfoundland, The Most Revd Stewart S. Payne, *cons.* 1978, *elected* 1990

THE RT. REVD BISHOPS
Central Newfoundland, Edward Marsh, *cons.* 1990, *elected* 1990
Eastern Newfoundland and Labrador, Donald Harvey, *cons.* 1993, *elected* 1992
Fredericton, George Lemon, *cons.* 1989, *elected* 1989
Montreal, Andrew Hutchison, *cons.* 1990, *elected* 1990
Nova Scotia, Arthur Peters, *cons.* 1982, *elected* 1982
Quebec, Bruce Stavert, *cons.* 1991, *elected* 1991
Western Newfoundland, see above

PROVINCE OF ONTARIO
METROPOLITAN
Archbishop of Huron, The Most Revd Percival O'Driscoll, *cons.* 1987, *elected* 1993

THE RT. REVD BISHOPS
Algoma, Ronald Ferris, *cons.* 1981, *elected* 1995
Huron, see above
Moosonee, Caleb Lawrence, *cons.* 1980, *elected* 1980
Niagara, Walter Asbil, *cons.* 1990, *elected* 1990
Ontario, Peter Mason, *cons.* 1992, *elected* 1992
Ottawa, John Baycroft, *cons.* 1985, *elected* 1993
Toronto, Terence Finlay, *cons.* 1986, *elected* 1990

PROVINCE OF RUPERT'S LAND
METROPOLITAN
Archbishop of Calgary, The Most Revd Barry Curtis, *cons.* 1983, *elected* 1994

THE RT. REVD BISHOPS
Arctic, J. Christopher Williams, *cons.* 1987, *elected* 1991
Athabasca, John Clarke, *cons.* 1992, *elected* 1992
Brandon, Malcolm Harding, *cons.* 1992, *elected* 1992
Calgary, see above, *elected* 1983
Edmonton, Kenneth Genge, *cons.* 1988, *elected* 1988
Keewatin, vacant
Qu' Appelle, Eric Bays, *cons.* 1986, *elected* 1986
Rupert's Land, Patrick Lee, *cons.* 1994, *elected* 1994
Saskatchewan, Anthony Burton, *cons.* 1993, *elected* 1993
Saskatoon, Thomas Morgan, *cons.* 1985, *elected* 1993

CHURCH OF THE PROVINCE OF CENTRAL AFRICA

ARCHBISHOP OF PROVINCE, The Most Revd Walter P. K. Makhulu (Bishop of Botswana), *cons.* 1979, *apptd* 1980

THE RT. REVD BISHOPS
Botswana, see above
Central Zambia, Titus Zhenje
Eastern Zambia, John R. Osmers
Harare, Jonathan Siyachitema, *cons.* 1981
Lake Malawi, Peter Nyanja, *cons.* 1978, *apptd* 1978
The Lundi, vacant
Lusaka, Stephen Mumba, *cons.* 1981, *apptd* 1981
Manicaland, Elijah Masuko, *cons.* 1981, *apptd* 1981
Matabeleland, Theophilus Naledi, *cons.* 1987, *apptd* 1987
Northern Malawi, Jackson C. Biggers
Northern Zambia, Bernard Malango, *cons.* 1988, *apptd* 1988
Southern Malawi, Nathaniel Aipa, *cons.* 1987, *apptd* 1987

CHURCH OF THE PROVINCE OF THE INDIAN OCEAN

ARCHBISHOP OF PROVINCE, The Most Revd Remi Rabenirina (Bishop of Atananarivo), *cons.* 1984, *apptd* 1995

THE RT. REVD BISHOPS
Antananarivo, see above, *apptd* 1984
Antsiranana, Keith Benzies, OBE, *cons.* 1982, *apptd* 1982
Mahajanga, vacant
Mauritius, Rex Donat, *cons.* 1984, *apptd* 1984
Seychelles, French Chang-Him, *cons.* 1979, *apptd* 1979
Toamasina, Donald Smith, *cons.* 1990, *apptd* 1990

HOLY CATHOLIC CHURCH IN JAPAN
Nippon Sei Ko Kai

PRIMATE, The Most Revd James T. Yashiro (Bishop of Kita Kanto), *cons.* 1985, *apptd* 1994

THE RT. REVD BISHOPS
Chubu, Samuel W. Hoyo, *cons.* 1987, *apptd* 1987
Hokkaido, Augustine H. Amagi, *cons.* 1987, *apptd* 1987
Kita Kanto, see above, *apptd* 1985
Kobe, John J. Furumoto, *cons.* 1992, *apptd* 1992
Kyoto, Barnabas M. Muto, *cons.* 1995, *apptd* 1995
Kyushu, Joseph N. Iida, *cons.* 1982, *apptd* 1982
Okinawa, Paul S. Nakamura, *cons.* 1972, *apptd* 1972
Osaka, Augustine K. Takano, *cons.* 1995, *apptd* 1995
Tohoku, John T. Sato, *cons.* 1996, *apptd* 1996
Tokyo, John M. Takeda, *cons.* 1988, *apptd* 1988
Yokohama, Raphael S. Kajiwara, *cons.* 1984, *apptd* 1984

EPISCOPAL CHURCH IN JERUSALEM AND THE MIDDLE EAST

PRESIDENT-BISHOP, Rt. Revd Samir Kafity, *apptd* 1986

THE RT. REVD BISHOPS
Jerusalem, Samir Kafity, *cons.* 1984, *apptd* 1986
Iran, Iraj Mottahedeh, *cons.* 1990, *apptd* 1990
Egypt, Ghais A. Malik, *cons.* 1984, *apptd* 1984
Cyprus and the Gulf, Clive Handford, *cons.* 1990, *apptd* 1996

CHURCH OF THE PROVINCE OF KENYA

ARCHBISHOP OF PROVINCE (*acting*), Rt Revd David Gitari (Bishop of Kirinyaga), *cons.* 1975, *apptd* 1994

THE RT. REVD BISHOPS
Butere, Horace Etemesi, *cons.* 1993, *apptd* 1993
Eldoret, Stephen Kewasis, *cons.* 1992, *apptd* 1992
Embu, Moses Njue, *cons.* 1990, *apptd* 1990
Kajiado, vacant
Katakwa, Eliud Okiring, *cons.* 1991, *apptd* 1991
Kirinyaga, see above, *apptd* 1975
Kitui, Benjamin Nzimbi, *cons.* 1985, *apptd* 1995
Machakos, vacant
Maseno North, vacant
Maseno South, Francis Mwayi-Abiero, *cons.* 1994, *apptd* 1994
Maseno West, Joseph Wasonga, *cons.* 1991, *apptd* 1991
Mombasa, Julius Kalu, *cons.* 1994, *apptd* 1994
Mount Kenya Central, Julius G. Gachuche, *cons.* 1993, *apptd* 1993
Mount Kenya South, vacant
Mount Kenya West, Alfred Chipman, *cons.* 1993, *apptd* 1993
Mumias, William Wesa
Nairobi, vacant
Nakuru, Stephen M. Njihia, *cons.* 1990, *apptd* 1990
Nambale, Josiah M. Were, *cons.* 1993, *apptd* 1993
Southern Nyanza, Haggai Nyang', *cons.* 1990, *apptd* 1993
Taita/Taveta, Samson M. Mwaluda, *cons.* 1993, *apptd* 1993

CHURCH OF THE PROVINCE OF KOREA

ARCHBISHOP OF PROVINCE, The Most Revd Bundo C. H. Kim (Bishop of Pusan), *cons.* 1988, *apptd* 1995

THE RT. REVD BISHOPS
Daejon, Paul Hwan Yoon, *cons.* 1987, *apptd* 1988
Pusan, see above
Seoul, Matthew C. B. Chung, *cons.* 1995, *apptd* 1995

CHURCH OF THE PROVINCE OF MELANESIA

ARCHBISHOP OF PROVINCE, The Most Revd Ellison L. Pogo (Bishop of Central Melanesia), *cons.* 1981, *apptd* 1994

THE RT. REVD BISHOPS
Banks and Torres, Walter Ling, *cons.* 1996, *apptd* 1996
Central Melanesia, see above
Hanuato'o, James Mason, *cons.* 1991, *apptd* 1991
Malaita, Terry M. Brown, *cons.* 1996, *apptd* 1996
Temotu, Lazarus Munamua, *cons.* 1987, *apptd* 1987
Vanuatu, Michael Tavoa, *cons.* 1990, *apptd* 1990
Ysabel, Walter Siba, *cons.* 1990, *apptd* 1994

EPISCOPAL CHURCH OF MEXICO

ARCHBISHOP OF PROVINCE, The Most Revd José G. Saucedo (Bishop of Cuernavaca), *cons.* 1958, *elected* 1995

THE RT. REVD BISHOPS
Cuernavaca, see above, *apptd* 1989
Mexico, Sergio Carrauza-Gomez, *cons.* 1989, *apptd* 1989
Northern Mexico, German Martinez-Marquez, *cons.* 1987, *apptd* 1987
South-East Mexico, Claro Huerta-Rames, *cons.* 1980, *apptd* 1989
Western Mexico, Samuel Espinoza-Venegas, *cons.* 1981, *apptd* 1983

CHURCH OF THE PROVINCE OF MYANMAR

ARCHBISHOP OF PROVINCE, The Most Revd Andrew Mya Han (Bishop of Yangon), *cons.* 1988, *apptd* 1988

THE RT. REVD BISHOPS
Hpa'an, Daniel Hoi Kyin, *cons.* 1992, *apptd* 1992
Mandalay, Andrew Hla Aung, *cons.* 1988, *apptd* 1988
Myitkyina, John Shan Lum, *cons.* 1994, *apptd* 1994
Sittwe, Barnabas Theaung Hawi, *cons.* 1978, *apptd* 1980
Toungoo, John Wilme, *cons.* 1994, *apptd* 1994
Yangon (Rangoon), see above

CHURCH OF THE PROVINCE OF NIGERIA

ARCHBISHOP OF PROVINCE, The Most Revd Joseph Adetiloye (Bishop of Lagos), *apptd* 1991

THE RT. REVD BISHOPS
Aba, A. O. Iwuagwu, *apptd* 1985
Abuja, Peter Akinola, *apptd* 1989
Akoko, J. O. K. Olowokure, *apptd* 1986
Akure, Emmanuel B. Gbonigi, *apptd* 1983
Asaba, Roland N. C. Nwosu, *apptd* 1977
Awka, Maxwell S. C. Anikwenwa, *apptd* 1987
Bauchi, Emmanuel O. Chukwuma, *apptd* 1990
Benin, Peter Onekpe

Calabar, W. G. Ekprikpo
Egba-Abeokuta, Matthew O. Owadayo
Egbado, Timothy I. O. Bolaji
Ekiti, C. A. Akinbola, *apptd* 1986
Enugu, Gideon N. Otubelu, *apptd* 1969
Ibadan, Gideon I. Olajide, *apptd* 1988
Ife, Gabriel B. Oloniyo
Ijebu, Abraham O. Olowoyo, *apptd* 1990
Ijebu Remo, E. O. I. Ogundana, *apptd* 1984
Ikale-Ilaje, J. Akin Omoyajowo
Ilesha, E. A. Ademowo, *apptd* 1989
Jos, B. A. Kwashi
Kaduna, Titus Ogbonyomi, *apptd* 1975
Kafanchan, William Diya, *apptd* 1990
Kano, B. O. Omosebi, *apptd* 1990
Katsina, J. S. Kwasu, *apptd* 1990
Kwara, Jeremiah O. A. Fabuluje
Lagos, see above, *apptd* 1985
Lokoja, George Bako
Maiduguri, E. K. Mani, *apptd* 1990
Makurdi, Nathan Nyom
Mbaise, Cyril Chukwka Anyanwu
Minna, Nathaniel Yisa, *apptd* 1990
The Niger, Jonathan A. Onyemelukwe, *apptd* 1975
Niger Delta, Samuel O. Elenwo, *apptd* 1981
Nsukka, Jonah Ilonuba
Oke-Osun, Abraham O. Awoson
Okigwe North, Alfred Nwaizuzu
Okigwe South, Bennett Okoro
Orlu, Samuel C. N. Ebo, *apptd* 1984
Ondo, Samuel O. Aderin, *apptd* 1981
Osun, Seth O. Fagbemi, *apptd* 1987
Owerri, Benjamin C. Nwankiti, *apptd* 1968
Owo, Peter A. Adebiyi
Sabongida Ora, Albert A. Agbaje
Sokoto, J. A. Idowu-Fearon, *apptd* 1990
Ukwa, Uju Obinya
Umuahia, Ngochukwe U. Ezuoke
Uyo, Ebenezar E. Nglass
Warri, Nathaniel Enuku
Yola, Chris O. Efobi, *apptd* 1990

ANGLICAN CHURCH OF PAPUA NEW GUINEA

ARCHBISHOP OF PROVINCE, The Most Revd James Ayong (Bishop of Aipo Rongo), *cons.* 1995, *elected* 1996

THE RT. REVD BISHOPS
Aipo Rongo, see above, *elected* 1995
Dogura, Tevita Talanoa, *cons.* 1992, *elected* 1992
New Guinea Islands, Michael Hough, *cons.* 1996, *elected* 1996
Popondota, Reuben Tariambari, *cons.* 1995, *elected* 1994
Port Moresby, Isaac Gadebo, *cons.* 1983, *elected* 1983

EPISCOPAL CHURCH IN THE PHILIPPINES

PRIME BISHOP, The Most Revd Narciso V. Ticobay, *cons.* 1986, *apptd* 1993

THE RT. REVD BISHOPS
Central Philippines, Manuel C. Lumpias, *cons.* 1977, *apptd* 1978
North Central Philippines, Joel A. Pachao, *cons.* 1993, *apptd* 1993
Northern Luzon, Ignacio C. Soliba, *cons.* 1990, *apptd* 1990
Northern Philippines, Robert L. Longid, *cons.* 1983, *apptd* 1986

Southern Philippines, James B. Manguramas, *cons.* 1993, *apptd* 1993

CHURCH OF THE PROVINCE OF RWANDA

ARCHBISHOP OF PROVINCE, The Most Revd Augustin Nshamihigo (Bishop of Shyira), *apptd* 1992 (currently in exile)

THE RT. REVD BISHOPS
Butare, Venuste Mutiganda
Byumba, Onesphore Rwaje
Cyangugu, Daniel Nduhura (currently in exile)
Kibungo, Augustin Mvunabandi (currently in exile)
Kigali, Jonathan Ruhumuliza
Kigeme, Norman Kayumba
Shyira, see above, *apptd* 1984
Shyogwe, Samuel Musubyimana (currently in exile)

CHURCH OF THE PROVINCE OF SOUTHERN AFRICA

Metropolitan
Archbishop of Cape Town, The Most Revd Winston H. N. Ndungane, *cons.* 1991, *trans.* 1996

THE RT. REVD BISHOPS
Bloemfontein, Thomas Stanage, *cons.* 1978, *trans.* 1982
Christ the King, Peter Lee, *cons.* 1990, *elected* 1990
George, Derek Damant, *cons.* 1985, *elected* 1985
Grahamstown, David Russell, *cons.* 1986, *trans.* 1987
Johannesburg, Duncan Buchanan, *cons.* 1986, *elected* 1986
Kimberley and Kuruman, vacant
Klerksdorp, David Nkwe, *cons.* 1990, *elected* 1990
Lebombo, Dinis Sengulane, *cons.* 1976, *elected* 1976
Lesotho, Philip Mokuku, *cons.* 1978, *elected* 1978
Namibia, James Kauluma, *cons.* 1978, *elected* 1981
Natal, Michael Nuttall, *cons.* 1975, *trans.* 1982
Niassa, Paulino Manhique, *cons.* 1986, *elected* 1986
Port Elizabeth, Eric Pike, *cons.* 1989, *trans.* 1993
Pretoria, Richard Kraft, *cons.* 1982, *elected* 1982
St Helena, John Ruston, *cons.* 1985, *trans.* 1991
St John's, Jacob Dlamini, *cons.* 1980, *elected* 1985
St Mark the Evangelist, Rollo Le Feuvre, *cons.* 1987, *elected* 1987
South-Eastern Transvaal, David Beetge, *cons.* 1990, *elected* 1990
Swaziland, Lawrence Zulu, *cons.* 1975, *trans.* 1993
Umzimvubu, Geoffrey Davies, *cons.* 1987, *elected* 1991
Zululand, Peter Harker, *cons.* 1993, *elected* 1993

Order of Ethiopia, Sigqibo Dwane, *cons.* 1983, *apptd* 1983

ANGLICAN CHURCH OF THE SOUTHERN CONE OF AMERICA

PRESIDING BISHOP, Rt. Revd Maurice Sinclair (Bishop of Northern Argentina), *cons.* 1990

THE RT. REVD BISHOPS
Argentina, David Leake, *cons.* 1969, *apptd* 1990
Bolivia, Gregory Venables, *cons.* 1993
Chile, Colin Bazley, *cons.* 1969, *apptd* 1977
Northern Argentina, see above, *apptd* 1990
Paraguay, John Ellison, *cons.* 1988, *apptd* 1988

Peru and Bolivia, vacant
Uruguay, Harold Godfrey, *cons.* 1986, *apptd* 1986

PROVINCE OF THE EPISCOPAL CHURCH OF THE SUDAN

ARCHBISHOP OF PROVINCE, The Most Revd Benjamin W. Yugusuk (Bishop of Juba)

THE RT. REVD BISHOPS
Bor, Nathaniel Garang
Cueibet, Ruben M. Makoi
El Obeil, Kurkeil M. Khamis
Juba, see above
Kaduguli, Peter El Birish
Kajo-keji, Manaseh B. Dawidi
Khartoum, Bulus Idris Tia
Lainya, Eliaba L. Menasona
Lui, Ephraim Natana
Malakal, Kedekia Mabior
Maridi, Joseph Marona
Mundri, Dr Eluzai G. Munda
Port Sudan, vacant
Rajaf, Michael S. Lugor
Renk, Daniel Deng
Rokon, Francis Loyo
Rumbek, Gabriel R. Jur
Torit, Wilson A. Ogwok
Wau, Henery Riak
Yambio, Daniel Zindo, *cons.* 1984, *apptd* 1984
Yei, Seme L. Solomone
Yirol, Benjamin Mangar

CHURCH OF THE PROVINCE OF TANZANIA

ARCHBISHOP OF PROVINCE, The Most Revd John A. Ramadhani (Bishop of Zanzibar and Tanga), *cons.* 1980, *apptd* 1984

THE RT. REVD BISHOPS
Central Tanganyika, Godfrey Mhogolo, *cons.* 1989, *apptd* 1989
Dar es Salaam, Basil Sambano, *cons.* 1992, *apptd* 1992
Kagera, Edwin Nyamubi, *cons.* 1993, *apptd* 1993
Mara, vacant
Masasi, Christopher Sadiki, *cons.* 1992, *apptd* 1992
Morogoro, Dudley Mageni, *cons.* 1987, *apptd* 1987
Mount Kilimanjaro, Simon Makundi, *cons.* 1991, *apptd* 1991
Mpwapwa, Simon Chiwanga, *cons.* 1991, *apptd* 1991
Rift Valley, Alpha Mohamed, *cons.* 1982, *apptd* 1991
Ruaha, Donald Mtetemela, *cons.* 1982, *apptd* 1990
Ruvuma, Stanford Shauri, *cons.* 1989, *apptd* 1989
South-West Tanganyika, Charles Mwaigoga, *cons.* 1983, *apptd* 1983
Tabora, Francis Ntiruka, *cons.* 1989, *apptd* 1989
Victoria Nyanza, John Changae, *cons.* 1993, *apptd* 1993
Western Tanganyika, Gerard Mpango, *cons.* 1983, *apptd* 1983
Zanzibar and Tanga, see above

CHURCH OF THE PROVINCE OF UGANDA

ARCHBISHOP OF PROVINCE, The Most Revd Livingstone Mpalanyi-Nkoyoyo (Bishop of Kampala)

THE RT. REVD BISHOPS
Bukedi, Nicodemus Okille, *apptd* 1984
Bunyoro-Kitara, Wilson N. Turumanya
Busoga, Cyprian Bamwoze, *apptd* 1972
Central Buganda, George Sinabulya
East Ankole, Elisha Kyamugambi, *cons.* 1992, *apptd* 1992
Kampala, see above
Karamoja, Peter Lomongin, *apptd* 1987
Kigezi, William Rukirande
Kinkizi, John Ntegyereize
Kitgum, Macleord B. Ochola II
Lango, Melchizedek Otim, *apptd* 1976
Luwero, Mesusera Bugimbi, *cons.* 1990, *apptd* 1990
Madi and West Nile, Enoch Drati
Mbale, Israel Koboyi, *cons.* 1992, *apptd* 1992
Mityana, Wilson Mutebi, *apptd* 1977
Muhabura, Ernest M. Shalita, *cons.* 1990, *apptd* 1990
Mukono, Michael Ssenyimba
Namirembe, Samuel B. Ssekkadde
Nebbi, Henry L. Orombi, *cons.* 1993, *apptd* 1993
North Kigezi, John Kahijwa
North Mbale, Peter Mudonyi, *cons.* 1992, *apptd* 1992
Northern Uganda, Gideon Oboma
Ruwenzori, Eustace Kamanyire, *apptd* 1981
Soroti, Geresom Ilukor, *apptd* 1976
South Ruwenzori, Zebidee Masereka
West Ankole, Yorumu Bamunoba, *apptd* 1977
West Buganda, Christopher Senyonjo, *apptd* 1974

EPISCOPAL CHURCH IN THE USA

PRESIDING BISHOP AND PRIMATE, Most Revd Edmond Lee Browning, DD, *cons.* 1968, *apptd* 1986

RT. REVD BISHOPS
Province I
Connecticut, Clarence Coleridge, *cons.* 1981, *apptd* 1994
Maine, vacant
Massachusetts, M. Thomas Shaw, *cons.* 1994, *apptd* 1995
New Hampshire, Douglas E. Theuner, *cons.* 1986, *apptd* 1986
Rhode Island, Geralyn Wolfe, *cons.* 1996, *apptd* 1996
Vermont, Mary A. Mcleod, *cons.* 1993, *apptd* 1993
Western Massachusetts, vacant

Province II
Albany, David S. Ball, *cons.* 1984, *apptd* 1984
Central New York, David B. Joslin, *cons.* 1991, *apptd* 1992
Europe, Convocation of American Churches in, Jeffery Rowthorn, *cons.* 1987
*Haiti, Zaché Duracin, *cons.* 1993, *apptd* 1994
Long Island, Orris Walker, *cons.* 1988, *apptd* 1991
New Jersey, Joe M. Doss, *cons.* 1993, *apptd* 1993
New York, Richard Grein, *cons.* 1981, *apptd* 1989
Newark, John S. Spong, *cons.* 1976, *apptd* 1979
Rochester, William G. Burrill, *cons.* 1984, *apptd* 1984
*Virgin Islands, Telésforo Isaac (*Bishop-in-charge*), *cons.* 1972
Western New York, David C. Bowman, *cons.* 1986, *apptd* 1987

Province III
Bethlehem, Paul Marshall, *cons.* 1996, *apptd* 1996
Central Pennsylvania, Michael W. Creighton, *cons.* 1995
Delaware, C. Cabell Tennis, *cons.* 1986, *apptd* 1986
Easton, Martin G. Townsend, *cons.* 1992, *apptd* 1993
Maryland, Robert Ihloff, *cons.* 1995

---

*missionary diocese

North-Western Pennsylvania, Robert D. Rowley jun., *cons.*
  1989, *apptd* 1991
Pennsylvania, Allen L. Bartlett, *cons.* 1986, *apptd* 1987
Pittsburgh, Alden M. Hathaway, *cons.* 1981, *apptd* 1983
Southern Virginia, Frank Vest, *cons.* 1985, *apptd* 1991
South-Western Virginia, A. Heath Light, *cons.* 1979, *apptd*
  1979
Virginia, Peter J. Lee, *cons.* 1984, *apptd* 1985
Washington, Ronald Haines, *cons.* 1986, *apptd* 1990
West Virginia, John H. Smith, *cons.* 1989, *apptd* 1989

Province IV

Alabama, Robert O. Miller, *cons.* 1988, *apptd* 1988
Atlanta, Frank K. Allan, *cons.* 1988, *apptd* 1989
Central Florida, John Howe, *cons.* 1989, *apptd* 1990
Central Gulf Coast, Charles F. Duvall, *cons.* 1981, *apptd* 1981
East Carolina, Sidney Saunders, *cons.* 1979, *apptd* 1983
East Tennessee, Robert G. Tharp, *cons.* 1991, *apptd* 1992
Florida, Stephen Jecko, *cons.* 1994, *apptd* 1994
Georgia, Henry Louttit, *cons.* 1994, *apptd* 1994
Kentucky, Ted Gulick, *cons.* 1964
Lexington, Don A. Wimberley, *cons.* 1984, *apptd* 1985
Louisiana, James B. Brown, *cons.* 1976, *apptd* 1976
Mississippi, Alfred C. Marble jun., *cons.* 1991, *apptd* 1993
North Carolina, Robert Johnson, *cons.* 1994, *apptd* 1994
South Carolina, Edward Salmon jun., *cons.* 1990, *apptd* 1990
South-East Florida, Calvin O. Schofield jun. *cons.* 1979, *apptd*
  1980
South-West Florida, Rogers Harris, *cons.* 1989, *apptd* 1989
Tennessee, Bertram N. Herlong, *cons.* 1993, *apptd* 1993
Upper South Carolina, Dorsey F. Henderson, *cons.* 1995
West Tennessee, James Coleman, *cons.* 1993
Western North Carolina, Robert Johnson, *cons* 1989, *apptd*
  1990

Province V

Chicago, Frank T. Griswold III, *cons.* 1985, *apptd* 1987
Eastern Michigan, Edwin M. Leidel jun., *cons.* 1996, *apptd*
  1996
Eau Claire, William C. Wantland, *cons.* 1980, *apptd* 1980
Fond Du Lac, Russell Jacobus, *cons.* 1994, *apptd* 1994
Indianapolis, Edward W. Jones, *cons.* 1977, *apptd* 1977
Michigan, R. Stewart Wood, *cons.* 1990, *apptd* 1990
Milwaukee, Roger J. White, *cons.* 1984, *apptd* 1985
Missouri, Hays Rockwell, *cons.* 1991, *apptd* 1993
Northern Indiana, Francis C. Gray, *cons.* 1986, *apptd* 1987
Northern Michigan, Thomas K. Ray, *cons.* 1982, *apptd* 1982
Ohio, J. Clark Grew, *cons.* 1994, *apptd* 1994
Quincy, Keith L. Ackerman, *cons.* 1994, *apptd* 1994
Southern Ohio, Herbert Thompson jun., *cons.* 1988, *apptd*
  1992
Springfield, Peter H. Beckwith, *cons.* 1991
Western Michigan, Edward L. Lee jun., *cons.* 1989, *apptd* 1989

Province VI

Colorado, William Winterrowd, *cons.* 1991, *apptd* 1991
Iowa, C. Christopher Epting, *cons.* 1988, *apptd* 1988
Minnesota, James Jelinek, *cons.* 1993, *apptd* 1993
Montana, Charles I. Jones, *cons.* 1986, *apptd* 1986
Nebraska, James E. Krotz, *cons.* 1989, *apptd* 1989
North Dakota, Andrew H. Fairfield, *cons.* 1990, *apptd* 1990
South Dakota, Creighton Robertson, *cons.* 1994, *apptd* 1994
Wyoming, Bob G. Jones, *cons.* 1977, *apptd* 1977

Province VII

Arkansas, Larry Maze, *cons.* 1994, *apptd* 1994
Dallas, James Stanton, *cons.* 1993, *apptd* 1993
Fort Worth, Jack Iker, *cons.* 1993, *apptd* 1994
Kansas, William E. Smalley, *cons.* 1989, *apptd* 1989
North-West Texas, Sam B. Hulsey, *cons.* 1980, *apptd* 1980

Oklahoma, Robert M. Moodey, *cons.* 1988, *apptd* 1989
Rio Grande, Terence Kelshaw, *cons.* 1989, *apptd* 1989
Texas, Claude Payne, *cons.* 1994
West Missouri, John C. Buchanan, *cons.* 1989, *apptd* 1989
West Texas, James E. Folts, *cons.* 1996, *apptd* 1996
Western Kansas, Vernon Strickland, *cons.* 1995
Western Louisiana, Robert Hargrove, *cons.* 1989, *apptd* 1990

Province VIII

Alaska, vacant
Arizona, Robert R. Shahan, *cons.* 1992, *apptd* 1993
California, William E. Swing, *cons.* 1979, *apptd* 1980
El Camino Real, Richard L. Skimpfky, *cons.* 1990, *apptd* 1990
Eastern Oregon, Rustin R. Kimsey, *cons.* 1980, *apptd* 1980
Hawaii, Richard Chang, *cons.* 1997, *apptd* 1996
Idaho, John Thornton, *cons.* 1990, *apptd* 1990
Los Angeles, Frederick L. Borsch, *cons.* 1988, *apptd* 1988
*Navajoland Area Mission, Steven T. Plummer, *cons.* 1989,
  apptd 1989
Nevada, Stewart C. Zabriskie, *cons.* 1986, *apptd* 1986
Northern California, Jerry A. Lamb, *cons.* 1991, *apptd* 1992
Olympia, Vincent W. Warner, *cons.* 1989, *apptd* 1990
Oregon, Robert L. Ladehoff, *cons.* 1985, *apptd* 1986
San Diego, Gethin B. Hughes, *cons.* 1992, *apptd* 1992
San Joaquin, John-David Schofield, *cons.* 1988, *apptd* 1989
Spokane, Frank Terry, *cons.* 1990, *apptd* 1991
*Taiwan, John C. T. Chien, *cons.* 1988, *apptd* 1988
Utah, George E. Bates, *cons.* 1986, *apptd* 1986

Province IX

*Central Ecuador, Neptali L. Moreno, *cons.* 1990, *apptd* 1990
*Colombia, Bernardo Merino-Botero, *cons.* 1979, *apptd* 1979
*Dominican Republic, Julio C. Holguin, *apptd* 1991
*Guatemala, Armando Guerra, *cons.* 1982, *apptd* 1982
*Honduras, Leopold Frade, *cons.* 1984, *apptd* 1984
*Nicaragua, Sturdie W. Downs, *cons.* 1985, *apptd* 1985
*Panama, Clarence W. Hayes, *cons.* 1995
*El Salvador, Martin Barahona, *cons.* 1992, *apptd* 1992

Extra-Provincial

Costa Rica, Cornelius J. Wilson, *cons.* 1978, *apptd* 1978
Puerto Rico, David Alvarez, *cons.* 1987, *apptd* 1987
Venezuela, Orlando Guerrero, *cons.* 1995

CHURCH OF THE PROVINCE OF WEST AFRICA

Archbishop of Province, The Most Revd Robert Okine
  (Bishop of Koforidua), *cons.* 1981, *apptd* 1993

The Rt. Revd Bishops
Accra, Francis W. B. Thompson, *cons.* 1983, *apptd* 1983
Bo, Samuel S. Gbonda, *cons.* 1994, *apptd* 1994
Cape Coast, Kobina Quashie, *apptd* 1992
Freetown, vacant
Gambia, Solomon T. Johnson, *cons.* 1990, *apptd* 1990
Guinea, vacant
Koforidua, *see* above, *apptd* 1981
Kumasi, Edmund Yeboah, *cons.* 1985, *apptd* 1985
Liberia, vacant
Sekondi, Theophilus Annobil, *cons.* 1981, *apptd* 1981
Sunyani/Tamale, Joseph Dadson, *cons.* 1981, *apptd* 1981

The Anglican Church of Cameroon is a missionary area of
the Province

CHURCH IN THE PROVINCE OF THE WEST INDIES

ARCHBISHOP OF PROVINCE, The Most Revd Orland Lindsay (Bishop of North-Eastern Caribbean and Aruba), *cons.* 1970, *apptd* 1986

THE RT. REVD BISHOPS
Barbados, Rufus Broome
Belize, Sylvestre D. Romero-Palma
Guyana, Randolph George, *cons.* 1976, *apptd* 1980
Jamaica, Neville de Souza, *cons.* 1973, *apptd* 1979
Nassau and the Bahamas, Michael Eldon, CMG, *cons.* 1971, *apptd* 1972
North-Eastern Caribbean and Aruba, see above
Trinidad and Tobago, Rawle Douglin
Windward Islands, Sehon Goodridge

CHURCH OF THE PROVINCE OF ZAÏRE

ARCHBISHOP OF PROVINCE, The Most Revd Byankya Njojo (Bishop of Boga-Zaïre), *cons.* 1980, *apptd* 1992

THE RT. REVD BISHOPS
Boga-Zaïre, see above, *apptd* 1980
Bukavu, Balafuga Dirokpa, *cons.* 1982, *apptd* 1982
Kisangani, Sylvestre Tibafa, *cons.* 1980, *apptd* 1980
Maniema, vacant
Nord-Kivu, Methusela Munzenda, *cons.* 1992, *apptd* 1992
Shaba, Emmanuel Kolini, *cons.* 1980, *apptd* 1980

OTHER CHURCHES AND EXTRA-PROVINCIAL DIOCESES

ANGLICAN CHURCH OF BERMUDA, The Rt. Revd Ewen Ratteray, *apptd* 1996
EPISCOPAL CHURCH OF CUBA, The Rt. Revd Jorge Perera Hurtado, *apptd* 1995
HONG KONG AND MACAO, The Rt. Revd Peter Kwong
KUCHING, The Rt. Revd Datuk John Leong Chee Yun
LUSITANIAN CHURCH (*Portuguese Episcopal Church*), The Rt. Revd Fernando da Luz Soares, *apptd* 1971
SPANISH REFORMED EPISCOPAL CHURCH, The Rt. Revd Carlos Lozano Lopez, *apptd* 1995

The Church of Scotland

The Church of Scotland is the established (i.e. state) church of Scotland. The Church is Reformed and evangelical in doctrine, and presbyterian in constitution. In 1560 the jurisdiction of the Roman Catholic Church in Scotland was abolished and the first assembly of the Church of Scotland ratified the Confession of Faith, drawn up by a committee including John Knox. In 1592 Parliament passed an Act guaranteeing the liberties of the Church and its presbyterian government. James VI (James I of England) and later Stuart monarchs attempted to restore episcopacy, but a presbyterian church was finally restored in 1690 and secured by the Act of Settlement (1690) and the Act of Union (1707). The Free Church of Scotland was formed in 1843 in a dispute over patronage and state interference; in 1900 most of its ministers joined with the United Presbyterian Church (formed in 1847) to form the United

Free Church of Scotland. In 1929 most of this body rejoined the Church of Scotland to form the united Church of Scotland.

The Church of Scotland is presbyterian in its organization, i.e. based on a hierarchy of councils of ministers and elders and, since 1990, of members of a diaconate. At local level the kirk session consists of the parish minister and ruling elders. At district level the presbyteries, of which there are 47, consist of all the ministers in the district, one ruling elder from each congregation, and those members of the diaconate who qualify for membership. The General Assembly is the supreme authority, and is presided over by a Moderator chosen annually by the Assembly. The Sovereign, if not present in person, is represented by a Lord High Commissioner who is appointed each year by the Crown.

The Church of Scotland has about 700,000 members, 1,200 ministers and 1,600 churches. There are about 100 ministers and other personnel working overseas.

Lord High Commissioner (1996), HRH The Princess Royal KG, GCVO
Moderator of the General Assembly (1996), The Rt. Revd J. H. McIndoe
Principal Clerk, The Very Revd J. L. Weatherhead, DD
Depute Clerk, Revd F. A. J. MacDonald
Procurator, A. Dunlop, QC
Law Agent and Solicitor of the Church, Mrs J. S. Wilson
Parliamentary Agent, I. McCulloch (*London*)
General Treasurer, D. F. Ross
CHURCH OFFICE, 121 George Street, Edinburgh EH2 4YN. Tel: 0131-225 5722

PRESBYTERIES AND CLERKS

Edinburgh, Revd W. P. Graham
West Lothian, Revd D. Shaw
Lothian, J. D. McCulloch

Melrose and Peebles, Revd J. H. Brown
Duns, Revd A. C. D. Cartwright
Jedburgh, Revd A. D. Reid

Annandale and Eskdale, Revd C. B. Haston
Dumfries and Kirkcudbright, Revd G. M. A. Savage
Wigtown and Stranraer, Revd D. Dutton

Ayr, Revd J. Crichton
Irvine and Kilmarnock, Revd C. G. F. Brockie
Ardrossan, Revd D. Broster

Lanark, Revd I. D. Cunningham
Paisley, Revd J. P. Cubie
Greenock, Revd D. Mill
Glasgow, Revd A. Cunningham
Hamilton, Revd J. H. Wilson
Dumbarton, Revd D. P. Munro

South Argyll, Revd R. H. McNidder
Dunoon, Revd R. Samuel
Lorn and Mull, Revd W. Hogg

Falkirk, Revd D. E. McClements
Stirling, Revd B. W. Dunsmore

Dunfermline, Revd W. E. Farquhar
Kirkcaldy, Revd B. L. Tomlinson
St Andrews, Revd J. W. Patterson

Dunkeld and Meigle, Revd A. F. Chisholm
Perth, Revd D. Main
Dundee, Revd J. A. Roy
Angus, Revd R. J. Ramsay

Aberdeen, Revd A. Douglas
Kincardine and Deeside, Revd J. W. S. Brown
Gordon, Revd I. U. Thomson
Buchan, Revd R. Neilson
Moray, Revd D. J. Ferguson

Abernethy, Revd J. A. I. MacEwan
Inverness, Revd A. S. Younger
Lochaber, Revd A. Ramsay

Ross, Revd R. M. MacKinnon
Sutherland, Revd J. L. Goskirk
Caithness, Revd M. G. Mappin
Lochcarron/Skye, Revd A. I. Macarthur
Uist, Revd A. P. J. Varwell
Lewis, Revd T. S. Sinclair

Orkney (Finstown), Revd T. Hunt
Shetland (Lerwick), Revd N. R. Whyte
England (London), Revd W. A. Cairns

Europe (Portugal), Revd J. W. McLeod

The minimum stipend of a minister in the Church of Scotland in 1996 was £15,348

The Roman Catholic Church

The Roman Catholic Church is one world-wide Christian Church acknowledging as its head the Bishop of Rome, known as the Pope (Father). The Pope is held to be the successor of St Peter and thus invested with the power which was entrusted to St Peter by Jesus Christ. A direct line of succession is therefore claimed from the earliest Christian communities. Papal authority over the doctrine and jurisdiction of the Church in western Europe developed early and was unrivalled after the split with the Eastern Orthodox Church until the Protestant Reformation in the 16th century. With the fall of the Roman Empire the Pope also became an important political leader. His temporal power is now limited to the 107 acres of the Vatican City State.

The Pope exercises spiritual authority over the Church with the advice and assistance of the Sacred College of Cardinals, the supreme council of the Church. He is also advised about the concerns of the Church locally by his ambassadors, who liaise with the Bishops' Conference in each country.

In addition to advising the Pope, those members of the Sacred College of Cardinals who are under the age of 80 also elect a successor following the death of a Pope. The assembly of the Cardinals at the Vatican for the election of a new Pope is known as the Conclave in which, in complete seclusion, the Cardinals elect by a secret ballot; a two-thirds majority is necessary before the vote can be accepted as final. When a Cardinal receives the necessary votes, the Dean of the Sacred College formally asks him if he will accept election and the name by which he wishes to be known. On his acceptance of the office the Conclave is dissolved and the First Cardinal Deacon announces the election to the assembled crowd in St Peter's Square. On the first Sunday or Holyday following the election, the new Pope assumes the pontificate at High Mass in St Peter's Square. A new pontificate is dated from the assumption of the pontificate.

The number of cardinals was fixed at 70 by Pope Sixtus V in 1586, but has been steadily increased since the pontificate of John XXIII and now stands at 160 (as at end June 1996).

The Roman Catholic Church universally and the Vatican City State are run by the Curia, which is made up of the Secretariat of State, the Sacred Council for the Public Affairs of the Church, and various congregations, secretariats and tribunals assisted by commissions and offices. The congregations are permanent commissions for conducting the affairs of the Church and are made up of cardinals, one of whom occupies the office of prefect. Below the Secretariat of State and the congregations are the secretariats and tribunals, all of which are headed by cardinals. (The Curial cardinals are analagous to ministers in charge of government departments.)

The Vatican State has its own diplomatic service, with representatives known as nuncios. Papal nuncios with full diplomatic recognition are given precedence over all other ambassadors to the country to which they are appointed; where precedence is not recognized the Papal representative is known as a pro-nuncio. Where the representation is only to the local churches and not to the government of a country, the Papal representative is known as an apostolic delegate. The Roman Catholic Church has an estimated 890.9 million adherents world-wide.

SOVEREIGN PONTIFF

His Holiness Pope John Paul II (Karol Wojtyla), *born* Wadowice, Poland, 18 May 1920; *ordained priest* 1946; *appointed Archbishop* of Krakow 1964; *created Cardinal* 1967; *assumed pontificate* 16 October 1978

SECRETARIAT OF STATE
Secretary of State, HE Cardinal Angelo Sodano
First Section (General Affairs), Mgr G. Re (Archbishop of Vescovio)
Second Section (Relations with other states), Mgr J. L. Tauran (Archbishop of Telepte)

BISHOPS' CONFERENCE

The Roman Catholic Church in England and Wales is governed by the Bishops' Conference, membership of which includes the Diocesan Bishops, the Apostolic Exarch of the Ukrainians, the Bishop of the Forces and the Auxiliary Bishops. The Conference is headed by the President (Cardinal Basil Hume, Archbishop of Westminster) and Vice-President. There are five departments, each with an episcopal chairman: the Department for Christian Life and Worship (the Archbishop of Southwark), the Department for Mission and Unity (the Bishop of Arundel and Brighton), the Department for Catholic Education and Formation (the Bishop of Leeds), the Department for Christian Responsibility and Citizenship (the Bishop of Plymouth), and the Department for International Affairs.

The Bishops' Standing Committee, made up of all the Archbishops and the chairman of each of the above departments, has general responsibility for continuity and policy between the plenary sessions of the Conference. It prepares the Conference agenda and implements its decisions. It is serviced by a General Secretariat. There are also agencies and consultative bodies affiliated to the Conference.

The Bishops' Conference of Scotland has as its president Archbishop Winning of Glasgow and is the permanently constituted assembly of the Bishops of Scotland. To promote its work, the Conference establishes various agencies which have an advisory function in relation to the Conference. The more important of these agencies are called Commissions and each one has a Bishop President who, with the other members of the Commissions, are appointed by the Conference.

The Irish Episcopal Conference has as its acting president Archbishop Connell of Dublin. Its membership comprises all the Archbishops and Bishops of Ireland and it appoints various Commissions to assist it in its work. There are three types of Commissions: (a) those made up of lay and clerical members chosen for their skills and experience, and staffed by full-time expert secretariats; (b) Commissions whose members are selected from existing institutions and whose services are supplied on a part-time basis; and (c) Commissions of Bishops only.

The Roman Catholic Church in Britain and Ireland has an estimated 8,992,000 members, 11 archbishops, 67 bishops, 11,260 priests, and 8,588 churches and chapels open to the public.

Bishops' Conferences secretariats:

ENGLAND AND WALES, 39 Eccleston Square, London SWIV IPD. Tel: 0171-630 8220. *General Secretary*, The Rt. Revd Philip Carroll

SCOTLAND, Candida Casa, 8 Corsehill Road, Ayr, Scotland KA7 2ST. Tel: 01292-256750. *General Secretary*, The Rt. Revd Maurice Taylor, Bishop of Galloway

IRELAND, Iona, 65 Newry Road, Dundalk, Co. Louth. *Executive Secretary*, Revd Hugh G. Connelly

GREAT BRITAIN

APOSTOLIC NUNCIO TO THE UNITED KINGDOM OF GREAT BRITAIN AND NORTHERN IRELAND
The Most Revd Luigi Barbarito, 54 Parkside, London SWI9 5NE. Tel: 0181-946 1410

ENGLAND AND WALES

THE MOST REVD ARCHBISHOPS
Westminster, HE Cardinal Basil Hume, *cons*. 1976
   Auxiliaries, Victor Guazzelli, *cons*. 1970; Vincent Nichols, *cons*. 1992; James J. O'Brien, *cons*. 1977; Patrick O'Donoghue, *cons*. 1993
   Clergy, 789
   Archbishop's Residence, Archbishop's House, Ambrosden Avenue, London SWIP IQJ. Tel: 0171-834 4717
Birmingham, Maurice Couve de Murville, *cons*. 1982, *apptd* 1982
   Auxiliaries, Terence Brain, *cons*. 1991; Philip Pargeter, *cons*. 1989
   Clergy, 524
   Diocesan Curia, Cathedral House, St Chad's Queensway, Birmingham B4 6EX. Tel: 0121-236 5535
Cardiff, John A. Ward, *cons*. 1981, *apptd* 1983
   Clergy, 146
   Diocesan Curia, Archbishop's House, 41–43 Cathedral Road, Cardiff CFI 9HD. Tel: 01222-220411
Liverpool, Patrick Kelly, *cons*. 1984, *apptd* 1996
   Auxiliaries, John Rawsthorne, *cons*. 1981; Vincent Malone, *cons*. 1989
   Clergy, 602
   Diocesan Curia, 152 Brownlow Hill, Liverpool L3 5RQ. Tel: 0151-709 4801
Southwark, Michael Bowen, *cons*. 1970, *apptd* 1977
   Auxiliaries, Charles Henderson, *cons*. 1972; Howard Tripp, *cons*. 1980; John Jukes, *cons*. 1980
   Clergy, 504
   Diocesan Curia, Archbishop's House, 150 St George's Road, London SEI 6HX. Tel: 0171-928 5592

THE RT. REVD BISHOPS
Arundel and Brighton, Cormac Murphy-O'Connor, *cons*. 1977. *Clergy*, 286. *Diocesan Curia*, Bishop's House, The Upper Drive, Hove, E. Sussex BN3 6NE. Tel: 01273-506387
Brentwood, Thomas McMahon, *cons*. 1980, *apptd* 1980. *Clergy*, 167. *Bishop's Office*, Cathedral House, Ingrave Road, Brentwood, Essex CMI5 8AT. Tel: 01277-232266
Clifton, Mervyn Alexander, *cons*. 1972, *apptd* 1975. *Clergy*, 235. *Diocesan Curia*, Egerton Road, Bishopston, Bristol BS7 8HU. Tel: 0117-924 1378

East Anglia, Peter Smith, *cons*. 1995, *apptd* 1995. *Clergy*, 133. *Diocesan Curia*, The White House, 21 Upgate, Poringland, Norwich NRI4 7SH. Tel: 01508-492202
Hallam, Gerald Moverley, *cons*. 1968, *apptd* 1980 (has retired, but continuing until successor appointed). *Clergy*, 98. *Bishop's Residence*, 'Quarters', Carsick Hill Way, Sheffield SIO 3LT. Tel: 0114-230 9101
Hexham and Newcastle, Michael Ambrose Griffiths, *cons*. 1992. *Clergy*, 281. *Diocesan Curia*, Bishop's House, East Denton Hall, 800 West Road, Newcastle upon Tyne NE5 2BJ. Tel: 0191-228 0003
Lancaster, John Brewer, *cons*. 1971, *apptd* 1985. *Clergy*, 255. *Bishop's Residence*, Bishop's House, Cannon Hill, Lancaster LAI 5NG. Tel: 01524-32231
Leeds, David Konstant, *cons*. 1977, *apptd* 1985. *Clergy*, 235. *Diocesan Curia*, 7 St Marks Avenue, Leeds LS2 9BN. Tel: 0113-244 4788
Menevia (Wales), Daniel Mullins, *cons*. 1970, *apptd* 1987. *Clergy*, 63. *Diocesan Curia*, 115 Walter Road, Swansea SAI 5RE. Tel: 01792-644017
Middlesbrough, John Crowley, *cons*. 1986, *apptd* 1992. *Clergy*, 182. *Diocesan Curia*, 50A The Avenue, Linthorpe, Middlesbrough, Cleveland TS5 6QT. Tel: 01642-850505
   Auxiliary, Thomas O'Brien, *cons*. 1981
Northampton, Patrick Leo McCartie, *cons*. 1977, *apptd* 1990. *Clergy*, 163. *Diocesan Curia*, Bishop's House, Marriott Street, Northampton NN2 6AW. Tel: 01604-715635
Nottingham, James McGuinness, *cons*. 1972, *apptd* 1975. *Clergy*, 204. *Diocesan Curia*, Willson House, Derby Road, Nottingham NGI 5AW. Tel: 0115-953 9800
Plymouth, Christopher Budd, *cons*. 1986. *Clergy*, 156. *Diocesan Curia*, Vescourt, Hartley Road, Plymouth PL3 5LR. Tel: 01752-772950
Portsmouth, F. Crispian Hollis, *cons*. 1987, *apptd* 1989. *Clergy*, 264. *Bishop's Residence*, Bishop's House, Edinburgh Road, Portsmouth, Hants POI 3HG. Tel: 01705-820894
Salford, vacant. *Clergy*, 391. *Diocesan Curia*, Cathedral House, 250 Chapel Street, Salford M3 5LL. Tel: 0161-834 9052
Shrewsbury, Brian Noble, *cons*. 1995, *apptd* 1995. *Clergy*, 202. *Diocesan Curia*, 2 Park Road South, Birkenhead, Merseyside L43 4UX. Tel: 0151-652 9855
Wrexham (Wales), Edwin Regan, *apptd* 1994. *Clergy*, 91. *Diocesan Curia*, Bishop's House, Sontley Road, Wrexham, Clwyd LLI3 7EW. Tel: 01978-262726

SCOTLAND

THE MOST REVD ARCHBISHOPS
St Andrews and Edinburgh, Keith Patrick O'Brian, *cons*. 1985
   Auxiliary, Kevin Rafferty, *cons*. 1990
   Clergy, 201
   Diocesan Curia, 106 Whitehouse Loan, Edinburgh EH9 IBD. Tel: 0131-452 8244
Glasgow, HE Cardinal Thomas Winning, *cons*. 1971, *apptd* 1974
   Clergy, 303
   Diocesan Curia, 196 Clyde Street, Glasgow GI 4JY. Tel: 0141-226 5898

THE RT. REVD BISHOPS
Aberdeen, Mario Conti, *cons*. 1977. *Clergy*, 58. *Bishop's Residence*, 156 King's Gate, Aberdeen AB2 6BR. Tel: 01224-319154
Argyll and the Isles, Roderick Wright, *cons*. 1990. *Clergy*, 32. *Diocesan Curia*, St Mary's, Belford Road, Fort William, Inverness-shire PH33 6BT. Tel: 01397-706046
Dunkeld, Vincent Logan, *cons*. 1981. *Clergy*, 55. *Diocesan Curia*, 26 Roseangle, Dundee DDI 4LR. Tel: 01382-25453
Galloway, Maurice Taylor, *cons*. 1981. *Clergy*, 66. *Diocesan Curia*, 8 Corsehill Road, Ayr KA7 2ST. Tel: 01292-266750

Motherwell, Joseph Devine, *cons.* 1977, *apptd* 1983. *Clergy*, 180. Diocesan Curia, Coursington Road, Motherwell MLI IPW. Tel: 01698-269114
Paisley, John A. Mone, *cons.* 1984, *apptd* 1988. *Clergy*, 95. Diocesan Curia, Cathedral House, 8 East Buchanan Street, Paisley, Renfrewshire PAI IHS. Tel: 0141-889 3601

IRELAND

There is one hierarchy for the whole of Ireland. Several of the dioceses have territory partly in the Republic of Ireland and partly in Northern Ireland.

APOSTOLIC NUNCIO TO IRELAND
The Most Revd Emanuele Gerada (titular Archbishop of Nomenta), 183 Navan Road, Dublin 7. Tel: 00 353 1-380577

THE MOST REVD ARCHBISHOPS
Armagh, HE Cardinal Cahal B. Daly, *cons.* 1990
Coadjutor, Sean Brady
Auxiliary, Gerard Clifford, *cons.* 1991
Clergy, 183
Diocesan Curia, Ara Coeli, Armagh BT61 7QY. Tel: 01861-522045
Cashel, Dermot Clifford, *cons.* 1986
Clergy, 136
Archbishop's Residence, Archbishop's House, Thurles, Co. Tipperary. Tel: 00 353 504-21512
Dublin, Desmond Connell, *cons.* 1988, *apptd* 1988
Auxiliaries, Donal Murray, *cons.* 1982; Dermot O'Mahony, *cons.* 1975; James Moriarty, *cons.* 1992; Eamonn Walsh, *cons.* 1990; Desmond Williams, *cons.* 1985; Fiachra O'Ceallaigh, *cons* 1994; James Kavanagh, *cons.* 1996
Clergy, 994
Archbishop's Residence, Archbishop's House, Drumcondra, Dublin 9. Tel: 00 353 1-8373732
Tuam, Michael Neary, *cons.* 1992
Clergy, 180
Archbishop's Residence, Archbishop's House, Tuam, Co. Galway. Tel: 00 353 93-24166

THE MOST REVD BISHOPS
Achonry, Thomas Flynn, *cons.* 1975. *Clergy*, 62. *Bishop's Residence*, Bishop's House, Ballaghaderreen, Co. Roscommon. Tel: 00 353 907-60021
Ardagh and Clonmacnois, Colm O'Reilly, *cons.* 1983. *Clergy*, 100. Diocesan Office, Bishop's House, St Michael's, Longford, Co. Longford. Tel: 00 353 43-46432
Clogher, Joseph Duffy, *cons.* 1979. *Clergy*, 108. *Bishop's Residence*, Bishop's House, Monaghan. Tel: 00 353 47-81019
Clonfert, Joseph Kirby, *cons.* 1988. *Clergy*, 71. *Bishop's Residence*, St Brendan's, Coorheen, Loughrea, Co. Galway. Tel: 00 353 91-41560
Cloyne, John Magee, *cons.* 1987. *Clergy*, 158. Diocesan Centre, Cobh, Co. Cork. Tel: 00 353 21-811430
Cork and Ross, Michael Murphy, *cons.* 1976. *Clergy*, 338. Diocesan Office, Bishop's House, Redemption Road, Cork. Tel: 00 353 21-301717
Auxiliary, John Buckley, *cons.* 1984
Derry, Seamus Hegarty, *cons.* 1984, *apptd* 1994. *Clergy*, 157. *Bishop's Residence*, Bishop's House, St Eugene's Cathedral, Derry BT48 9AP. Tel: 01504-262302
Auxiliary, Francis Lagan, *cons.* 1988

Down and Connor, Patrick J. Walsh, *cons.* 1991. *Clergy*, 248. *Bishop's Residence*, Lisbreen, 73 Somerton Road, Belfast, Co. Antrim DT15 4DE. Tel: 01232-776185
Auxiliaries, Anthony Farquhar, *cons.* 1983; William Philbin, *cons.* 1991; Michael Dallat, *cons.* 1994
Dromore, Francis Brooks, *cons.* 1976. *Clergy*, 78. *Bishop's Residence*, Bishop's House, Violet Hill, Newry, Co. Down BT35 6PN. Tel: 01693-62444
Elphin, Christopher Jones, *cons.* 1994. *Clergy*, 101. *Bishop's Residence*, St Mary's, Sligo. Tel: 00 353 71-62670
Ferns, Brendon Comiskey, *cons.* 1980. *Clergy*, 161. *Bishop's Office*, Bishop's House, Summerhill, Wexford. Tel: 00 353 53-22177
Galway and Kilmacduagh, James McLoughlin, *cons.* 1993. *Clergy*, 90. Diocesan Office, The Cathedral, Galway. Tel: 00 353 91-63566
Kerry, William Murphy, *cons.* 1995. *Clergy*, 149. *Bishop's Residence*, Bishop's House, Killarney, Co. Kerry. Tel: 00 353 64-31168
Kildare and Leighlin, Laurence Ryan, *cons.* 1984. *Clergy*, 136. *Bishop's Residence*, Bishop's House, Carlow. Tel: 00 353 503-31102
Killala, Thomas Finnegan, *cons.* 1970. *Clergy*, 62. *Bishop's Residence*, Bishop's House, Ballina, Co. Mayo. Tel: 00 353 96-21518
Killaloe, William Walsh, *cons.* 1994. *Clergy*, 149. *Bishop's Residence*, Westbourne, Ennis, Co. Clare. Tel: 00 353 65-28638
Kilmore, Francis McKiernan, *cons.* 1972. *Clergy*, 115. *Bishop's Residence*, Bishop's House, Cullies, Co. Cavan. Tel: 00 353 49-31496
Limerick, Donal Murray, *cons.* 1996. *Clergy*, 152. Diocesan Offices, 66 O'Connell Street, Limerick. Tel: 00 353 61-315856
Meath, Michael Smith, *cons.* 1984, *apptd* 1990. *Clergy*, 141. *Bishop's Residence*, Bishop's House, Dublin Road, Mullingar, Co. Westmeath. Tel: 00 353 44-48841
Ossory, Laurence Forristal, *cons.* 1980. *Clergy*, 111. *Bishop's Residence*, Sion House, Kilkenny. Tel: 00 353 56-62448
Raphoe, Philip Boyce, *cons.* 1994. *Clergy*, 96. *Bishop's Residence*, Ard Adhamhnáin, Letterkenny, Co. Donegal. Tel: 00 353 74-21208
Waterford and Lismore, William Lee, *cons.* 1993. *Clergy*, 130. *Bishop's Residence*, Woodleigh, Summerville Avenue, Waterford. Tel: 00 353 51-71432

RESIDENTIAL ARCHBISHOPRICS THROUGHOUT THE WORLD

ALBANIA
Durrës-Tirana, Brok K. Mirdita
Shkodër, Frano Illia

ALGERIA
Algiers, Henri Teissier

ANGOLA
Huambo, Francisco Viti
Luanda, HE Cardinal Alexandre do Nascimento
Lubango, Manuel Franklin da Costa
Coadjutor, Zacarias Kamwenho

ARGENTINA
Bahia Blanca, Romulo Garcia
Buenos Aires, HE Cardinal Antonio Quarracino
Córdoba, HE Cardinal Raúl Francisco Primatesta
Corrientes, Domingo S. Castagna
La Plata, Carlos Galán
Mendoza, Jose M. Arancibia

Paraná, Estanislao Esteban Karlic
Resistencia, Carmelo J. Giaquinta
Rosario, Eduardo Vicente Miras
Salta, Moises J. Blanchoud
San Juan de Cuyo, Italo Severino Di Stefano
Santa Fe, Edgardo Gabriel Storni
Tucumán, Arsenio R. Casado

AUSTRALIA
Adelaide, Leonard Anthony Faulkner
Brisbane, John A. Bathersby
Canberra, Francis P. Carroll
Hobart, Joseph E. D'Arcy
Melbourne, Thomas Francis Little
Perth, Barry J. Hickey
Sydney, HE Cardinal Edward B. Clancy

AUSTRIA
Salzburg, Georg Eder
Vienna, Christoph Schoenborn

BANGLADESH
Dhaka, Michael Rozario

BELARUS
Minsk-Mobilev Archdiocese, HE Cardinal Kazimierz Swiatek

BELGIUM
Malines-Bruxelles, HE Cardinal Godfried Danneels

BENIN
Cotonou, Isidore de Souzá

BOLIVIA
Cochabamba, Rene Fernandez Apaza
La Paz, Luis Sainz Hinojosa
Santa Cruz de la Sierra, Julio T. Sandoval
Sucre, Jesus G. Pérez Rodriguez

BOSNIA HERCEGOVINA
Vrhbosna, Sarajevo, HE Cardinal Vinko Puljić

BRAZIL
Aparacida, HE Cardinal Aloisio Lorscheider
Aracaju, Luciano José Cabral Duarte
Bélem do Pará, Vicente Joaquim Zico
Belo Horizonte, Serafim Fernandes de Araújo
Botucatu, Antonio M. Mucciolo
Brasilia, HE Cardinal Jose Freire Falcao
Campinas, Gilberto Pereira Lopes
Campo Grande, Vitorio Pavanello
Cascavel, Lucio I. Baumgaertner
Cuiaba, Bonifacio Piccinini
Curitiba, Pedro Antonio Fedalto
Diamantina, Geraldo Majelo Reis
Florianópolis, Eusebio Oscar Scheid
Fortaleza, vacant
Goiania, Antonio Ribeiro de Oliveira
Juiz de Fora, Clovis Frainer
Londrina, Albano Bortoletto Cavallin
Maceió, Edvaldo G. Amaral
Manaus, Luiz S. Vieira
Mariana, Luciano Mendes de Almeida
Maringá, Jaime Luis Coelho
Natal, Heitor de Araujo Sales
Niteroi, Carlos A. Navarro
Olinda and Recife, José Cardoso Sobrinho
Palmas, Alberto T. Corrèa
Paraiba, Marcello Pinto Carvalheira
Porto Alegre, Altamiro Rossato
Porto Velho, José Martins da Silva
Pouso Alegre, vacant
Ribeirão Preto, Arnaldo Ribeiro
São Luis do Maranhão, Paulo Eduardo de Andrade Ponte

São Paulo, HE Cardinal Paulo Evaristo Arns
São Salvador da Bahia, HE Cardinal Lucas Moreira Neves
São Sebastião do Rio de Janeiro, HE Cardinal Eugenio de Araújo Sales
Sorocaba, José Lambert
Teresina, Miguel F. Camara Filho
Uberaba, Aloisio R. Oppermann
Vitória, Silvestre L. Scandian

BURKINA
Ouagadougou, Jean-Marie Untaani Compaore

BURUNDI
Gitega, Joachim Ruhuna

CAMEROON
Bamenda, Paul Verdzekov
Douala, HE Cardinal Christian W. Tumi
Garoua, Antoine Ntalou
Yaoundé, Jean Zoa

CANADA
Edmonton, Joseph N. MacNeil
Gatineau-Hull, Roger Ebacher
Grouard-McLennon, Henri Légaré
Halifax, Austin-Emile Burke
Keewatin-Le Pas, Peter Alfred Sutton
Kingston, Francis John Spence
Moncton, vacant
Montreal, HE Cardinal Jean-Claude Turcotte
Ottawa, Marcel A. Gervais
Quebec, Maurice Couture
Regina, Peter Mallon
Rimouski, Bertrand Blanchet
St Boniface, Antoine Hacault
St Johns, Newfoundland, James H. MacDonald
Sherbrooke, Jean Marie Fortier
    Coadjutor, Andre Gaumond
Toronto, Aloysius Matthew Ambrosic
Vancouver, Adam J. Exner
Winnipeg, Leonard J. Wall; (Ukrainian rite), Michael Bzdel

CAUCASIA
Caucasia Apostolic Administrator, Jean-Paul Gobel

CENTRAL AFRICAN REPUBLIC
Bangui, Joachim N'Dayen

CHAD
Ndjamena, Charles Vandame

CHILE
Antofagasta, Patricio Infante Alfonso
Concepción, Antonio M. Casamitjana
La Serena, Francisco J. Cox Huneeus
Puerto Montt, Savino B. Cazzaro Bertollo
Santiago de Chile, HE Cardinal Carlos Oviedo Cavada

CHINA
Anking, Huai-Ning, vacant
Canton, vacant
Changsha, vacant
Chungking, vacant
Foochow, Min-Hou, vacant
Hangchow, vacant
Hankow, vacant
Kaifeng, vacant
Kunming, vacant
Kweyang, vacant
Lanchow, vacant
Mukden, vacant
Nanchang, vacant
Nanking, vacant
Nanning, vacant

Peking (Beijing), vacant
Sian, vacant
Suiyūan, Francis Wang Hsueh-Ming
Taiyuan, vacant
Tsinan, vacant

COLOMBIA
Barranquilla, Felix Maria Torres Parra
Bogotá, Pedro Rubiano Sáenz
Bucaramanga, Dario Castrillon Hoyos
Cali, Isaias Duarte Cancino
Cartagena, Carlos José Ruiseco Vieira
Ibague, Juan S. Jaramillo
Manizales, José de Jesús Pimiento Rodriguez
Medellin, Hector Rueda Hernández
Nueva Pamplona, Victor M. Lopez Forero
Popayán, Alberto G. Jaramillo
Santa Fe de Antioquia, Ignacio Gomez Aŕistizabal
Tunja, Augusto Trujillo Arango

CONGO
Brazzaville, Barthélémy Batantu

COSTA RICA
San José, Román Arrieta Villalobos

CÔTE D'IVOIRE
Abidjan, Bernard Agre
Bouake, Vital Komenan Yao
Gagnoa, Noel Kokora-Tekry
Korhogo, Auguste Nobou

CROATIA
Rijeka-Senj, Anton Tamarut
Split-Makarska, Ante Juric
Zadar, Marijan Oblak
Zagreb, HE Cardinal Franjo Kuharić

CUBA
San Cristóbal de la Habana, HE Cardinal Jaime Lucas Ortega
  y Alamino
Santiago de Cuba, Pedro Meurice Estiu

CYPRUS
Cyprus (Maronite seat at Nicosia), Boutros Gemayel

CZECH REPUBLIC
Olomouc, Jan Graubner
Prague, HE Cardinal Miloslav Vlk

DOMINICAN REPUBLIC
Santiago de los Caballeros, Juan A. F. Santana
Santo Domingo, HE Cardinal Nicolás de Jesús López
  Rodriguez

ECUADOR
Cuenca, Alberto Luna Tobar
Guayaquil, Ignacio Larrea Holguin
Quito, Antonio J. González Zumárraga

EQUATORIAL GUINEA
Malabo, Idlefonso Obama Obono

ETHIOPIA
Addis Ababa, HE Cardinal Paul Tzadua

FRANCE
Aix, Louis-Marie Bille
Albi, Roger Meindre
Auch, vacant
Avignon, Raymond Bouchex
Besançon, Lucien Daloz
Bordeaux, HE Cardinal Pierre Eyt
Bourges, Pierre Plateau
Cambrai, Jacques Delaporte
Chambéry, Claude Feidt

Lyon, Jean Balland
Marseilles, Bernard Panafieu
Paris, HE Cardinal J. M. Lustiger
Reims, Gerard Defois
Rennes, Jacques Jullien
Rouen, Joseph Duval
Sens, vacant
Strasbourg, Charles Amarin Brand
Toulouse, André Collini
Tours, Jean Honoré

FRENCH POLYNESIA
Papeete, Michel Coppenrath

GABON
Libreville, André Fernand Anguilé

GERMANY
Bamberg, Karl Braun
Berlin, HE Cardinal George M. Sterzinsky
Cologne, HE Cardinal Joachim Meisner
Freiburg im Breisgau, Oskar Saier
Munich and Freising, HE Cardinal Friedrich Wetter
Paderborn, Johannes Joachim Degenhardt

GHANA
Accra, Dominic K. Andoh
Cape Coast, Peter Kodwo A. Turkson
Tamale, Gregory E. Kpiebaya

GREECE
Athens, Nicholaos Foscolos
Corfu, Antonio Varthalitis
Naxos, Nicolaos Printesis
Rhodes, vacant (Apostolic Administrator, Nicholaos
  Foscolos)

GUATEMALA
Guatemala, Prospero Penados del Barrio

GUINEA
Conakry, Robert Sarah

HAITI
Cap-Haitien, François Gayot
Port au Prince, François-Wolff Ligondé

HONDURAS
Tegucigalpa, Oscar A. Maradiaga

HONG KONG
Hong Kong, HE Cardinal J. B. Wu Cheng Chung

HUNGARY
Eger, Istvan Seregely
Esztergom, HE Cardinal Laslo Paskai
Kalocsa, Laszlo Danko

INDIA
Agra, Cecil de Sa
Bangalore, Alphonsus Mathias
Bhopal, Paschal Topno
Bombay, HE Cardinal I. Pimenta
Calcutta, Henry Sebastian D'Souza
Changanacherry, Joseph Powathil
Cuttack-Bhubaneswar, Raphael Cheenath
Delhi, Alan de Lastic
Ernakulam, HE Cardinal Anthony Padiyara
Goa and Daman, Raul Nicolau Gonsalves
Hyderabad, Saminini Arulappa
Madras and Mylapore, James M. Arul Das
Madurai, Marianus Arokiasamy
Nagpur, Leobard D'Souza
Pondicherry and Cuddalore, Michael Augustine
Ranchi, Telesphore P. Toppo
Shillong-Gauhati, Tarcisius Resto Phanrang

Trivandrum (Syrian Melekite rite), Cyril Baselios
  Malancharuvil
Verapoly, Cornelius Elanjikal

INDONESIA
Ende, Donatus Djagom
Jakarta, vacant
Kupang, Gregorius Manteiro
Medan, Alfred Gonti Pius Datubara
Merauke, Jacobus Duivenvoorde
Pontianak, Hieronymus Herculanus Bumbun
Semarang, HE Cardinal Julius R. Darmaatmadja
Ujung Pandang, Johannes Liku Ada'

IRAN
Ahváz, Hanna Zora
Tehran, Youhannan Semaan Issayi
Urmyā, Thomas Meram

IRAQ
Arbil, Hanna Markho
Baghdad (Latin rite), Paul Dahdah; (Syrian rite), Athanase
  M. S. Matoka; (Armenian rite), Paul Coussa; (Chaldean
  rite), Raphaël Bidawid
Basra, vacant
Kirkuk, André Sana
Mosul (Chaldean rite), Georges Garmo; (Syrian rite),
  Cyrille E. Benni

ISRAEL (*see also* Patriarchs, page 421)
Akka (Greek Melekite Catholic rite), Maximos Salloum

ITALY
Acerenza, Michele Scandiffio
Amalfi, Beniamino De Palma
Ancona, Franco Festorazzi
Bari, Mariano Magrassi
Benevento, Serafino Sprovieri
Bologna, HE Cardinal Giacomo Biffi
Brindisi, Settimio Todisco
Cagliari, Otterino Pietro Alberti
Camerino, Piergiorgio Nesti
Campobasso-Boiano, Ettore Di Filippo
Capua, Luigi Diligenza
Catania, Luigi Bommarito
Catanzaro, Antonio Cantisani
Chieti, Edoardo Menichelli
Conza, Mario Milano
Cosenza, Dino Trabalzini
Crotone-Santa Severina, Giuseppe Agostino
Fermo, Cleto Bellucci
Ferrara, Carlo Caffarra
Florence, HE Cardinal Silvano Piovanelli
Foggia, Giuseppe Casale
Gaeta, Vincenzo Farano
Genoa, Dionigi Tettamanzi
Gorizia and Gradisca, Antonio Vitale Bommarco
Lanciano, Enzio d'Antonio
L'Aquila, Mario Peressin
Lecce, Cosmo F. Ruppi
Lucca, Bruno Tommasi
Manfredonia, Vincenzo D'Addario
Matera, Antonio Ciliberti
Messina, Ignazio Cannavó
Milan, HE Cardinal Carlo Maria Martini
Modena, Santo B. Quadri
Monreale, Salvatore Cassisa
Naples, HE Cardinal Michele Giordano
Oristano, Pier Luigi Tiddia
Otranto, Francesco Cacucci
Palermo, Salvatore De Giorgi
Perugia, Giuseppe Chiaretti

Pescara-Penne, Francesco Cuccarese
Pisa, Alessandro Plotti
Potenza, Ennio Appignanesi
Ravenna, Luigi Amaducci
Reggio Calabria, Vittorio L. Mondello
Rossano-Cariati, Andrea Cassone
Salerno, Gerardo Pierro
Sassari, Salvatore Isgrò
Siena, Gaetano Bonicelli
Siracusa, Giuseppe Costanzo
Sorrento, Felice Cece
Spoleto, Riccardo Fontana
Taranto, Luigi Papa
Trani and Barletta, Carmelo Cassati
Trento, Giovanni Sartori
Turin, HE Cardinal Giovanni Saldarini
Udine, Alfredo Battisti
Urbino, Donato U. Bianchi
Vercelli, Enrico Masseroni

JAMAICA
Kingston, Edgerton R. Clarke

JAPAN
Nagasaki, Francis Xavier Shimamoto
Osaka, Paul Hisao Yasuda
Tokyo, HE Cardinal Peter Seiichi Shirayanagi

JORDAN
Petra and Filadelfia (Greek Melekite Catholic rite), George
  El-Murr

KAZAKHSTAN
Karaganda Apostolic Administration (Latin rite), Apostolic
  Administrator, Mgr Jan Lenga (titular Bishop of Arba)

KENYA
Kisumu, Zacchaeus Okoth
Mombasa, John Njenga
Nairobi, HE Cardinal Maurice Otunga
Nyeri, Nicodemus Kirima

KOREA
Kwang Ju, Victorinus Kong-Hi Youn
Seoul, HE Cardinal Stephen Sou Hwan Kim
Tae Gu, Paul Moun-Hi Ri

LATVIA
Riga, Jānis Pujats

LEBANON
Antelias (Maronite rite), Joseph Mohsen Bechara
Baalbek, Eliopoli (Greek Melekite Catholic rite), Salim
  Bustros
Baniyas (Greek Melekite Catholic rite), Antoine Hayek
Beirut (Greek Melekite Catholic rite), Habib Bacha;
  (Maronite rite), Khalil Abinader; (Armenian rite), Jean
  P. Kasparian
Saïda (Greek Melekite Catholic rite), Georges Kwaiter
Tripoli (Maronite rite), Gabriel Toubia; (Greek Melekite
  Catholic rite), George Riashi
Tyre (Greek Melekite Catholic rite), Jean A. Haddad;
  (Maronite rite), Maroun Sader
Zahle and Furzol (Greek Melekite Catholic rite), Andre
  Haddad

LESOTHO
Maseru, Bernard Mohlalisi

LIBERIA
Monrovia, Michael Kpakala Francis

LITHUANIA
Kaunas, Sigitas Tamkevicius
Vilnius, Audris J. Bačkis

LUXEMBOURG
Luxembourg, Fernand Franck

MADAGASCAR
Antananarive, HE Cardinal Armand G. Razafindratandra
Antsiranana, Albert Joseph Tsiahoana
Fianarantsoa, Philibert Randriambololona

MALAWI
Blantyre, James Chiona

MALAYSIA
Kuala Lumpur, Anthony S. Fernandez
Kuching, Peter Chung Hoan Ting

MALI
Bamako, Luc Auguste Sangaré

MALTA
Malta, Joseph Mercieca

MARTINIQUE
Fort de France, Maurice Marie-Sainte

MEXICO
Acapulco, Rafael Bello Ruiz
Antequera, Hector G. Martinez
Chihuahua, José Fernández Arteaga
Durango, José M. Perez
Guadalajara, HE Cardinal Juan Sandoval Iniguez
Hermosillo, Carlos Quintero Arce
Jalapa, Sergio Obeso Rivera
Mexico City, Norberto R. Carrera
Monterrey, HE Cardinal Adolfo Suarez Rivera
Morelia, Alberto S. Inda
Puebla de los Angeles, Rosendo Huesca Pacheco
San Luis Potosi, Arturo A. Szymanski Ramirez
Tlalnepantla, Manuel P. Gil Gonzalez
Yucatán, Emilio C. B. Belaunzaran

MONACO
Monaco, Joseph-Marie Sardou

MOROCCO
Rabat, Hubert Michon
Tangier, Antonio J. Peteiro Freire

MOZAMBIQUE
Beira, Jaime P. Goncalves
Maputo, HE Cardinal Alexandre José Maria dos Santos
Nampula, Manuel Vieira Pinto

MYANMAR (BURMA)
Mandalay, Alphonse U. Than Aung
Yangon (Rangoon), Gabriel Thohey Mahn Gaby

NAMIBIA
Windhoek, Bonifatius Haushiku

NETHERLANDS
Utrecht, HE Cardinal Adrianus J. Simonis

NEW ZEALAND
Wellington, HE Cardinal Thomas Stafford Williams

NICARAGUA
Managua, HE Cardinal Miguel Obando Bravo

NIGERIA
Jos, Gabriel G. Ganaka
Kaduna, Peter Yariyok Jatau
Lagos, Anthony Okogie
Onitsha, Albert K. Obiefuna

OCEANIA
Agaña, Anthony Sablan Apuron
Honiara, Adrian Thomas Smith
Nouméa, Michel-Marie-Bernard Calvet

Papeete, Michel-Gaspard Copenrath
Samoa, Apia and Tokelau, HE Cardinal Pio Taofino'u
Suva, Petero Mataca

PAKISTAN
Karachi, Simeon Pereira

PANAMA
Panama, Jose Dimas C. Delgado

PAPUA NEW GUINEA
Madang, Benedict To Varpin
Mount Hagen, Michael Meier
Port Moresby, Peter Kurongku
Rabaul, Karl Hesse

PARAGUAY
Asuncion, Felipe Santiago B. Avalos

PERU
Arequipa, Luis Sanchez-Moreno Lira
Ayacucho o Huamanga, Juan L. C. Thorne
Cuzco, Alcides Mendoza Castro
Huancayo, Jose P. Rios Reynoso
Lima, HE Cardinal Augusto Vargas Alzamora
Piura, Oscar Rolando Cantuarias Pastor
Trujillo, Manuel Prado Pérez-Rosas

PHILIPPINES
Caceres, Leonardo Legazpi
Cagayan de Oro, Jesus B. Tuquib
Capiz, Onesimo C. Gordoncillo
Cebu, HE Cardinal Ricardo Vidal
Cotabato, Philip Francis Smith
Davao, Antonio Mabutas
Jaro, Alberto J. Piamonte
Lingayen-Dagupan, Oscar V. Cruz
Lipa, Gaudencio B. Rosales
Manila, HE Cardinal Jaime L. Sin
Nueva Segovia, Orlando Quevedo
Ozamiz, Jesus Dosado
Palo, Pedro R. Dean
San Fernando, Paciano Aniceto
Tuguegarao, Diosdado A. Talamayan
Zamboanga, Carmelo D. F. Morelos

POLAND
Bialystok, Stanislaw Szymecki
Czestochowa, Stanislaw Nowak
Gdańsk, Tadeusz Goclowski
Gniezno, Henryk Muszyński
Katowice, Damian Zimoń
Kraków, HE Cardinal Franciszek Macharski
Lodz, Wladyslaw Ziolek
Lublin, Boleslaw Pylak
Poznań, Jerzy Stroba
Przemyśl of the Latins, Jozef Michalik
Szczecin-Kamień, Marian Przykucki
Warmia, Edmund Piszcz
Warsaw, HE Cardinal Józef Glemp
Wroclaw, HE Cardinal Henryk Roman Gulbinowicz

PORTUGAL
Braga, Eurico Dias Nogueira
Evora, Maurilio Jorge Quintal de Gouveia

PUERTO RICO
San Juan, HE Cardinal Luis Aponte Martinez

ROMANIA
Alba Julia (Latin rite), Gyorgy-Miklos Jakubinyi
Bucureşti, Ioan Robu
Fagaras and Alba Julia (Romanian Byzantine rite), Lucian Muresan

RUSSIA
Moscow Apostolic Administration (covering European Russia), Apostolic Administrator, Archbishop Tadeusz Kondrusiewicz
Novosibirsk Apostolic Administration (covering Siberia), Apostolic Administrator, Mgr Joseph Werth, SJ (titular Bishop of Bulna)

RWANDA
Kigali, Thaddée Ntihinyurwa

ST LUCIA
Castries, Kelvin E. Felix, OBE

EL SALVADOR
San Salvador, Fernando S. Lacalle

SENEGAL
Dakar, HE Cardinal Hyacinthe Thiandoum

SIERRA LEONE
Freetown and Bo, Joseph Ganda

SINGAPORE
Singapore, Gregory Yong Sooi Ngean

SLOVAK REPUBLIC
Trnava, Jan Sokol

SLOVENIA
Ljubljana, Alojzij Suštar

SOUTH AFRICA
Bloemfontein, Peter John Butelezi
Cape Town, Lawrence Patrick Henry
Durban, Wilfrid Fox Napier
Pretoria, George Francis Daniel

SPAIN
Barcelona, HE Cardinal Ricardo Maria Carles Gordó
Burgos, Santiago Martinez Acebes
Granada, José Méndez Asensio
Madrid, Antonio M. Rouco Varela
Oviedo, Gabino Diaz Merchán
Pamplona, Fernando S. Aquilar
Santiago de Compostela, vacant
Sevilla, Carlos Amigo Vallejo
Tarragona, Ramon Torrella Cascante
Toledo, Francisco A. Martinez
Valencia, Agustin Garcia-Gasco Vicente
Valladolid, José Delicado Baeza
Zaragoza, Elíaz Yanez Alvarez

SRI LANKA
Colombo, Nicholas Marcus Fernando

SUDAN
Juba, Paulino Lukudu Loro
Khartoum, Gabriel Zubeir Wako

SYRIA
Alep, Beroea, Halab (Greek Melekite Catholic rite), Jean-Clement Jeanbart; (Syrian rite), Raboula A. Beylouni; (Maronite rite), Pierre Callaos; (Armenian rite), Boutros Marayati
Baniyas (Greek Melekite Catholic rite), Antoine Hayek
Bosra, Bostra, Boulos Nassif Borkhoche
Damascus (Greek Melekite Catholic rite), S. B. Maximos V. Hakim; (Syrian rite), Eustache J. Mounayer; (Maronite rite), Hamid A. Mourany
Hassaké-Nisibi, Georges Habib Hafouri
Homs, Emesa (Greek Melekite Catholic rite), Abraham Nehmé; (Syrian Catholic rite), Basile Daoud
Laodicea (Greek Melekite Catholic rite), Fares Maakaroun

TAIWAN
Taipei, Joseph Ti-Kang

TANZANIA
Dar es Salaam, Polycarp Pengo
Mwanza, Antony Mayala
Songea, Norbert W. Mtega
Tabora, Mario E. A. Mgulunde

THAILAND
Bangkok, HE Cardinal Michael Michai Kitbunchu
Tharé and Nonseng, Lawrence Khai Saen-Phon-On

TOGO
Lomé, Philippe F. K. Kpodzro

TRINIDAD
Port of Spain, Gordon Anthony Pantin

TURKEY
Diarbekir, Paul Karatas
Istanbul (Constantinople), Jean Tcholakian
Izmir, Giuseppe G. Bernardini

UGANDA
Kampala, HE Cardinal Emmanuel Wamala

UKRAINE
Lvov (Latin rite), Marian Jaworski (Archbishop of Lvov of the Latins); (Ukrainian rite), HE Cardinal Myroslav I. Lubachivsky (Major Archbishop of Lvov of the Ukrainians)

URUGUAY
Montevideo, José Gottardi Cristelli

USA
Anchorage, Francis Thomas Hurley
Atlanta, John F. Donoghue
Baltimore, HE Cardinal William Henry Keeler
Boston, HE Cardinal Bernard F. Law
Chicago, HE Cardinal Joseph L. Bernardin
Cincinnati, Daniel E. Pilarczyk
Denver, James Francis Stafford
Detroit, HE Cardinal Adam J. Maida
Dubuque, Jerome G. Hanus
Hartford, Daniel A. Cronin
Indianapolis, Daniel Mark Buechlein
Kansas City, James P. Keleher
Los Angeles, HE Cardinal Roger M. Mahony
Louisville, Thomas C. Kelly
Miami, John C. Favalora
Milwaukee, Rembert G. Weakland
Mobile, Oscar H. Lipscomb
Newark, Theodore E. McCarrick
New Orleans, Francis B. Schulte
New York, HE Cardinal John J. O'Connor
Oklahoma City, Eusebius Joseph Beltran
Omaha, Elden Curtiss
Philadelphia, HE Cardinal Anthony J. Bevilacqua; (Ukrainian rite), Stephen Sulyk
Pittsburgh (Byzantine rite), Judson M. Procyk
Portland (Oregon), vacant
St Louis (Missouri), Justin F. Rigali
St Paul and Minneapolis, Harry J. Flynn
San Antonio, Patrick F. Flores
San Francisco, William J. Levada
Santa Fe, Michael Sheehan
Seattle, Thomas J. Murphy
Washington, HE Cardinal James A. Hickey

VENEZUELA
Barquisimeto, Julio Manuel Chirivella Varela
Calabozo, Helimenas de J. R. Paredes
Caracas, Ignacio A. V. Garcia
Ciudad Bolivar, Medardo Luzardo Romero
Cumana, Alfredo J. R. Figueroa

Maracaibo, Ramon O. Perez Morales
Mérida, Baltazar P. Cardozo
Valencia, Jorge Liberato Urosa Savino

VIETNAM
Hanoi, HE Cardinal Paul Joseph Pham Dinh Tung
Hue, Apostolic Administrator, Etienne N. N. Thê
Thanh-Phô Hôchiminh, Apostolic Administrator, Mgr Nicolas
    Huynh Van Nghi

YUGOSLAV FEDERAL REPUBLIC
Bar, Petar Perkolić
Belgrade, Franc Perko

ZAÏRE
Bukavu, Christophe Munzihirwa Mwene Ngabo
Kananga, Bakole wa Ilunga
Kinshasa, HE Cardinal Frederick Etsou-Nzabi-
    Bamungwabi
Kisangani, Laurent Monsengwo Pasinya
Lubumbashi, Kabanga Songasonga
Mbandaka-Bikoro, Joseph Kumuondala Mbimba

ZAMBIA
Kasama, James Spaita
Lusaka, Adrian Mungandu

ZIMBABWE
Harare, Patrick Chakaipa

PATRIARCHS IN COMMUNION WITH THE ROMAN CATHOLIC CHURCH

Alexandria, HB Stephanos II Ghattas (Patriarch for Catholic
    Copts); HB Parthenios III (Greek Orthodox Patriarch of
    Alexandria and All Africa)
Antioch, HB Ignace Antoine II Hayek (Patriarch for Syrian
    rite Catholics); HB Maximos V. Hakim (Patriarch for
    Greek Melekite rite Catholics); HE Cardinal Nasrallah
    Pierre Sfeir (Patriarch for Maronite rite Catholics)
Jerusalem, HB Michel Sabbah (Patriarch for Latin rite
    Catholics); HB Maximos V. Hakim (Patriarch for Greek
    Melekite rite Catholics)
Babilonia of the Chaldeans, HB Raphael I Bidawid
Cilicia of the Armenians, HB Jean Pierre XVIII Kasparian
    (Patriarch for Armenian rite Catholics)
Oriental India, Archbishop Raul Nicolau Gonsalves
Lisbon, HE Cardinal Antonio Ribeiro
Venice, HE Cardinal Marco Ce

Other Churches in the UK

AFRICAN AND AFRO-CARIBBEAN CHURCHES

There are more than 160 Christian churches or groups of
African or Afro-Caribbean origin in the UK. These include
the Apostolic Faith Church, the Cherubim and Seraphim
Church, the New Testament Church Assembly, the New
Testament Church of God, the Wesleyan Holiness Church
and the Aladura Churches.

The Afro-West Indian United Council of Churches and
the Council of African and Afro-Caribbean Churches UK
(which was initiated as the Council of African and Allied
Churches in 1979 to give one voice to the various Christian
churches of African origin in the UK) are the media
through which the member churches can work jointly to
provide services they cannot easily provide individually.

There are about 70,000 adherents of African and Afro-
Caribbean churches in the UK, and about 1,000 congregations. The Afro-West Indian United Council of
Churches has about 30,000 individual members, 135
ministers and 65 places of worship. The Council of African
and Afro-Caribbean Churches UK has about 17,000
members, 250 ministers and 75 congregations.

AFRO-WEST INDIAN UNITED COUNCIL OF CHURCHES,
    c/o New Testament Church of God, Arcadian Gardens,
    High Road, London N22 5AA. Tel: 0181-888 9427.
    Chairman, Revd E. Brown
COUNCIL OF AFRICAN AND AFRO-CARIBBEAN CHURCHES
    UK, 31 Norton House, Sidney Road, London SW9 0UJ.
    Tel: 0171-274 5589. *Chairman,* His Grace The Most
    Revd Father Olu A. Abiola

ASSOCIATED PRESBYTERIAN CHURCHES OF SCOTLAND

The Associated Presbyterian Churches came into being in
1989 as a result of a division within the Free Presbyterian
Church of Scotland. Following two controversial disciplinary cases, the culmination of deepening differences
within the Church, a presbytery was formed calling itself
the Associated Presbyterian Churches (APC). The Associated Presbyterian Churches has about 1,000 members, 15
ministers and 20 churches.
Clerk of the Scottish Presbytery, Revd Dr M. MacInnes,
    Drumalin, 16 Drummond Road, Inverness IV2 4NB. Tel:
    01463-223983

THE BAPTIST CHURCH

Baptists trace their origins to John Smyth, who in 1609 in
Amsterdam reinstituted the baptism of conscious believers
as the basis of the fellowship of a gathered church.
Members of Smyth's church established the first Baptist
church in England in 1612. They came to be known as
'General' Baptists and their theology was Arminian,
whereas a later group of Calvinists who adopted the
baptism of believers came to be known as 'Particular'
Baptists. The two sections of the Baptists were united into
one body, the Baptist Union of Great Britain and Ireland, in
1891. In 1988 the title was changed to the Baptist Union of
Great Britain.

Baptists emphasize the complete autonomy of the local
church, although individual churches are linked in various
kinds of associations. There are international bodies (such
as the Baptist World Alliance) and national bodies, but
some Baptist churches belong to neither. However, in
Great Britain the majority of churches and associations
belong to the Baptist Union of Great Britain. There are also
Baptist Unions in Wales, Scotland and Ireland which are
much smaller than the Baptist Union of Great Britain, and
there is some overlap of membership.

There are over 38 million Baptist church members
world-wide; in the Baptist Union of Great Britain there are
157,000 members, 1,864 pastors and 2,130 churches. In the
Baptist Union of Scotland there are 14,328 members, 140
pastors and 171 churches. In the Baptist Union of Wales
there are 24,178 members, 118 pastors and 537 churches. In
the Baptist Union of Ireland there are 8,454 members, 83
pastors and 109 churches.
President of the Baptist Union of Great Britain (1996–7), Revd
    John C. James

General Secretary, Revd D. R. Coffey, Baptist House, PO Box 44, 129 Broadway, Didcot, Oxon OXII 8RT. Tel: 01235-512077

THE CHURCH OF CHRIST, SCIENTIST

The Church of Christ, Scientist was founded by Mary Baker Eddy in the USA in 1879 to 'reinstate primitive Christianity and its lost element of healing'. Christian Science teaches the need for spiritual regeneration and salvation from sin, but is best known for its reliance on prayer alone in the healing of sickness. Adherents believe that such healing is a law, or Science, and is in direct line with that practised by Jesus Christ (revered, not as God, but as the Son of God) and by the early Christian Church.

The denomination consists of The First Church of Christ, Scientist, in Boston, Massachusetts, USA (the Mother Church) and its branch churches in over 60 countries world-wide. Branch churches are democratically governed by their members, while a five-member Board of Directors, based in Boston, is authorized to transact the business of the Mother Church. The Bible and Mary Baker Eddy's book, *Science and Health with Key to the Scriptures*, are used at services; there are no clergy. Those engaged in full-time healing are called practitioners, of whom there are 3,500 world-wide.

No membership figures are available, since Mary Baker Eddy felt that numbers are no measure of spiritual vitality and ruled that such statistics should not be published. There are over 2,400 branch churches world-wide, including nearly 200 in the UK.

CHRISTIAN SCIENCE COMMITTEE ON PUBLICATION, 2 Elysium Gate, 126 New Kings Road, London SW6 4LZ. Tel: 0171-371 0600. *District Manager for Great Britain and Ireland*, A. Grayson

THE CHURCH OF JESUS CHRIST OF LATTER-DAY SAINTS

The Church (often referred to as 'the Mormons') was founded in New York State, USA, in 1830, and came to Britain in 1837. The oldest continuous branch in the world is to be found in Preston, Lancs. Mormons are Christians who claim to belong to the 'Restored Church' of Jesus Christ. They believe that true Christianity died when the last original apostle died, but that it was given back to the world by God and Christ through Joseph Smith, the Church's founder and first president. They accept and use the Bible as scripture, but believe in continuing revelation from God and use additional scriptures, including *The Book of Mormon: Another Testament of Jesus Christ*. The importance of the family is central to the Church's beliefs and practices. Church members set aside Monday evenings as Family Home Evenings when Christian family values are taught. Polygamy was formally discontinued in 1890.

The Church has no paid ministry; local congregations are headed by a leader chosen from amongst their number. The world governing body, based in Utah, USA, is the three-man First Presidency, assisted by the Quorum of the Twelve Apostles.

There are about 9 million members world-wide, with about 170,000 adherents in Britain in over 350 congregations.

President of the Europe North Area (including Britain), Elder C. O. Samuelson, jun.

BRITISH HEADQUARTERS, Church Offices, 751 Warwick Road, Solihull, W. Midlands B91 3DQ. Tel: 0121-711 2244

THE CONGREGATIONAL FEDERATION

The Congregational Federation was founded by members of Congregational churches in England and Wales who did not join the United Reformed Church (q.v.) in 1972. There are also churches in Scotland and Australia affiliated to the Federation. The Federation exists to encourage congregations of believers to worship in free assembly, but it has no authority over them and emphasizes their right to independence and self-government.

The Federation has 11,923 members, 71 recognized ministers and 313 churches in England, Wales and Scotland.

President of the Federation (1996–7), F. Wroe

General Secretary, G. M. Adams, The Congregational Centre, 4 Castle Gate, Nottingham NGI 7AS. Tel: 0115-941 3801

THE FREE CHURCH OF ENGLAND

The Free Church of England is a union of two bodies in the Anglican tradition, the Free Church of England, founded in 1844 as a protest against the Oxford Movement in the established Church, and the Reformed Episcopal Church, founded in America in 1873 but which also had congregations in England. As both Churches sought to maintain the historic faith, tradition and practice of the Anglican Church since the Reformation, they decided to unite as one body in England in 1927. The historic episcopate was conferred on the English Church in 1876 through the line of the American bishops, who had pioneered an open table Communion policy towards members of other denominations.

The Free Church of England has 1,550 members, 38 ministers and 26 churches in England. It also has three house churches and three ministers in New Zealand, and one church and one minister in St Petersburg, Russia.

General Secretary, Revd W. J. Lawler, 45 Broughton Road, Wallasey, Merseyside L44 4DT. Tel: 0151-638 2564

THE FREE CHURCH OF SCOTLAND

The Free Church of Scotland was formed in 1843 when over 400 ministers withdrew from the Church of Scotland as a result of interference in the internal affairs of the church by the civil authorities. In 1900, all but 26 ministers joined with others to form the United Free Church (most of which rejoined the Church of Scotland in 1929). In 1904 the remaining 26 ministers were recognized by the House of Lords as continuing the Free Church of Scotland.

The Church maintains strict adherence to the Westminster Confession of Faith (1648) and accepts the Bible as the sole rule of faith and conduct. Its General Assembly meets annually. It also has links with Reformed Churches overseas. The Free Church of Scotland has 6,000 members 110 ministers and 140 churches.

General Treasurer, I. D. Gill, The Mound, Edinburgh EHI 2LS. Tel: 0131-226 5286

THE FREE PRESBYTERIAN CHURCH OF SCOTLAND

The Free Presbyterian Church of Scotland was formed in 1893 by two ministers of the Free Church of Scotland who refused to accept a Declaratory Act passed by the Free Church General Assembly in 1892. The Free Presbyterian Church of Scotland is Calvinistic in doctrine and emphasizes observance of the Sabbath. It adheres strictly to the Westminster Confession of Faith of 1648.

The Church has about 3,000 members in Scotland and about 7,000 in overseas congregations. It has 26 ministers and 50 churches.

Moderator, Revd J. R. Tallach, Free Presbyterian Manse, Raasay, by Kyle IV40 8PB. Tel: 01478-660216
Clerk of Synod, Revd J. MacLeod, 16 Matheson Road, Stornoway, Isle of Lewis HSI 2LA. Tel: 01851-702755

THE INDEPENDENT METHODIST CHURCHES

The Independent Methodist Churches seceded from the Wesleyan Methodist Church in 1805 and remained independent when the Methodist Church in Great Britain was formed in 1932. They are mainly concentrated in the industrial areas of the north of England.

The churches are Methodist in doctrine but their organization is congregational. All the churches are members of the Independent Methodist Connexion of Churches. The controlling body of the Connexion is the Annual Meeting, to which churches send delegates. The Connexional President is elected annually. Between annual meetings the affairs of the Connexion are handled by departmental committees. Ministers are appointed by the churches and trained through the Connexion. The ministry is open to both men and women and is unpaid.

There are 3,400 members, 106 ministers and 101 churches in Great Britain.

Connexional President (1996–7), H. G. Gleave
General Secretary, J. M. Day, The Old Police House, Croxton, Stafford ST21 6PE. Tel: 0163-062 0671

JEHOVAH'S WITNESSES

The movement now known as Jehovah's Witnesses grew from a Bible study group formed by Charles Taze Russell in 1872 in Pennsylvania, USA. In 1896 it adopted the name of the Watch Tower Bible and Tract Society, and in 1931 its members became known as Jehovah's Witnesses. Jehovah's (God's) Witnesses believe in the Bible as the word of God, and consider it to be inspired and historically accurate. They take the scriptures literally, except where there are obvious indications that they are figurative or symbolic, and reject the doctrine of the Trinity. Witnesses believe that the earth will remain for ever and that all those approved of by Jehovah will have eternal life on a cleansed and beautified earth; only 144,000 will go to heaven to rule with Christ. They believe that the second coming of Christ and his thousand-year reign on earth have been imminent since 1914, and that Armageddon (a final battle in which evil will be defeated) will precede Christ's rule of peace. They refuse to take part in military service, and do not accept stimulants or blood transfusions. They publish a magazine, *The Watchtower.*

The 12-member world governing body is based in New York, USA. Witnesses world-wide are divided into branches, countries or areas, districts, circuits and congregations. There are overseers at each level, and two assemblies are held annually for each circuit. There is no paid ministry, but each congregation has elders assigned to look after various duties and every Witness is assigned homes to visit in their congregation.

There are over 5 million Jehovah's Witnesses world-wide, with 130,000 Witnesses in the UK organized into over 1,400 congregations.

BRITISH ISLES HEADQUARTERS, Watch Tower House, The Ridgeway, London NW7 IRN. Tel: 0181-906 2211

THE LUTHERAN CHURCH

Lutheranism is based on the teachings of Martin Luther, the German leader of the Protestant Reformation. The authority of the scriptures is held to be supreme over Church tradition and creeds, and the key doctrine is that of justification by faith alone.

Lutheranism is one of the largest Protestant denominations and it is particularly strong in northern Europe and the USA. Some Lutheran churches are episcopal, while others have a synodal form of organization; unity is based on doctrine rather than structure. Most Lutheran churches are members of the Lutheran World Federation, based in Geneva.

Lutheran services in Great Britain are held in many languages to serve members of different nationalities. English-language congregations are members either of the Lutheran Church in Great Britain–United Synod, or of the Evangelical Lutheran Church of England. The United Synod and most of the various national congregations are members of the Lutheran Council of Great Britain.

There are over 70 million Lutherans world-wide; in Great Britain there are 27,000 members, 45 ministers and 100 churches.

Chairman of the Lutheran Council of Great Britain, Very Revd R. J. Patkai, 8 Collingham Gardens, London SW5 OHW. Tel: 0171-373 1141

THE METHODIST CHURCH

The Methodist movement started in England in 1729 when the Revd John Wesley, an Anglican priest, and his brother Charles met with others in Oxford and resolved to conduct their lives and study by 'rule and method'. In 1739 the Wesleys began evangelistic preaching and the first Methodist chapel was founded in Bristol in the same year. In 1744 the first annual conference was held, at which the Articles of Religion were drawn up. Doctrinal emphases included repentance, faith, the assurance of salvation, social concern and the priesthood of all believers. After John Wesley's death in 1791 the Methodists withdrew from the established Church to form the Methodist Church. Methodists gradually drifted into many groups, but in 1932 the Wesleyan Methodist Church, the United Methodist Church and the Primitive Methodist Church united to form the Methodist Church in Great Britain as it now exists.

The governing body and supreme authority of the Methodist Church is the Conference, but there are also 33 district synods, consisting of all the ministers and selected lay people in each district, and circuit meetings of the ministers and lay people of each circuit.

424   The Christian Churches

There are over 60 million Methodists world-wide; in Great Britain (1995 figures) there are 380,269 members, 3,660 ministers, 12,611 lay preachers and 6,678 churches.
President of the Conference in Great Britain (1996–7), Revd N. T. Collinson
Vice-President of the Conference (1996–7), Ms J. S. Pickard
Secretary of the Conference, Revd B. E. Beck, Methodist Church, Conference Office, 25 Marylebone Road, London NW1 5JR. Tel: 0171-486 5502

THE METHODIST CHURCH IN IRELAND

The Methodist Church in Ireland is closely linked to British Methodism but is autonomous. It has 17,964 members, 199 ministers, 289 lay preachers and 233 churches.
President of the Conference in Ireland (1996–7), Revd K. Best, 11 Clearwater, Clooney Road, Londonderry BT47 1BE. Tel: 01504-42644
Secretary of the Conference in Ireland, Revd E. T. I. Mawhinney, 1 Fountainville Avenue, Belfast BT9 6AN. Tel: 01232-324554

THE ORTHODOX CHURCH

The Orthodox Church (or Eastern Orthodox Church) is a communion of self-governing Christian churches recognizing the honorary primacy of the Oecumenical Patriarch of Constantinople.

In the first millennium of the Christian era the faith was slowly formulated. Between AD 325 and 787 there were seven Oecumenical Councils at which bishops from the entire Christian world assembled to resolve various doctrinal disputes which had arisen. The estrangement between East and West began after Constantine moved the centre of the Roman Empire from Rome to Constantinople, and it gained momentum after the temporal administration was divided. Linguistic and cultural differences between Greek East and Latin West served to encourage separate ecclesiastical developments which became pronounced in the tenth and early 11th centuries.

The administration of the church was divided between five ancient patriarchates: Rome and all the West, Constantinople (the imperial city – the 'New Rome'), Jerusalem and all Palestine, Antioch and all the East, and Alexandria and all Africa. Of these, only Rome was in the Latin West and after the Great Schism in 1054, Rome developed a structure of authority centralized on one source, the Papacy, while the Orthodox East maintained the style of localized administration.

To the older patriarchates were later added the Patriarchates of Russia, Georgia, Serbia, Bulgaria and Romania. The Orthodox Church also includes autocephalous (self-governing) national churches in Greece, Cyprus, Poland, Albania, Czechoslovakia and Sinai, and autonomous national churches in Finland and Japan. The Estonian and Latvian Orthodox Churches are in practice part of the Moscow Patriarchate. The Belorussians and Ukrainians have recently been given greater autonomy by Moscow, but some Ukrainians have broken away to establish an independent Ukrainian Patriarchate. In Macedonia the local hierarchy has declared itself independent of the Serbian Patriarchate. The Russian dioceses in the diaspora fall into four groups: those under the direct control of the Moscow Patriarchate; the Russian Orthodox Church Outside Russia, sometimes known as the Synod in Exile; the Russian Archdiocese centred at the cathedral in rue Daru, Paris, which is part of the Patriarchate in Constantinople;

and the Orthodox Church in America, which was granted autocephalous status in 1970.

The position of Orthodox Christians is that the faith was fully defined during the period of the Oecumenical Councils. In doctrine it is strongly trinitarian, and stresses the mystery and importance of the sacraments. It is episcopal in government. The structure of the Orthodox Christian year differs from that of western Churches (*see* page 82).

Orthodox Christians throughout the world are estimated to number about 150 million.

PATRIARCHS

Archbishop of Constantinople, New Rome and Oecumenical Patriarch, Bartholomew, *elected* 1991
Pope and Patriarch of Alexandria and All Africa, Parthenios III, *elected* 1987
Patriarch of Antioch and All the East, Ignatios IV, *elected* 1979
Patriarch of Jerusalem and All Palestine, Diodoros, *elected* 1981
Patriarch of Moscow and All Russia, Alexei II, *elected* 1990
Archbishop of Tbilisi and Mtskheta, Catholicos-Patriarch of All Georgia, Ilia II, *elected* 1977
Archbishop of Pec, Metropolitan of Belgrade and Karlovci, Patriarch of Serbia, Paul, *elected* 1990
Archbishop of Bucharest and Patriarch of Romania, Teoctist, *elected* 1986
Metropolitan of Sofia and Patriarch of Bulgaria, Maxim, *elected* 1971
Patriarch of Kiev and All Ukraine, Philaret, *elected* 1995 (not recognized by any other Patriarchate)

ORTHODOX CHURCHES IN THE UK

THE PATRIARCHATE OF ANTIOCH

Until 1995 the Patriarchate of Antioch was represented in Britain by one Arabic language parish with one priest. A group of ex-Anglicans (the 'Pilgrimage to Orthodoxy') was received into the Patriarchate of Antioch in 1995. There are now eight parishes served by eight priests. In Britain the Patriarchate is represented by the Revd Fr Samir Gholam, 1A Redhill Street, London NW1 4BG. Tel: 0171-383 0403

THE GREEK ORTHODOX CHURCH (PATRIARCHATE OF CONSTANTINOPLE)

The presence of Greek Orthodox Christians in Britain dates back to 1677 when Archbishop Joseph Geogirenes of Samos fled from Turkish persecution and came to London, where a church was built for him in Soho. The present Greek cathedral in Moscow Road, Bayswater, was opened for public worship in 1879 and the Diocese of Thyateira and Great Britain was established in 1922. There are now 114 parishes and other communities (including monasteries) in Great Britain, served by five bishops and 91 churches.

In Great Britain the Patriarchate of Constantinople is represented by Archbishop Gregorios of Thyateira and Great Britain, 5 Craven Hill, London W2 3EN. Tel: 0171-723 4787.

THE RUSSIAN ORTHODOX CHURCH (PATRIARCHATE OF MOSCOW) AND THE RUSSIAN ORTHODOX CHURCH OUTSIDE RUSSIA

The earliest records of Russian Orthodox Church activities in Britain date from the visit to England of Tsar Peter I at the beginning of the 18th century. Clergy were sent from Russia to serve the chapel established to minister to the staff of the Imperial Russian Embassy in London.

After 1917 the Church of Russia was persecuted. The Patriarch of Moscow, St Tikhon the New Martyr, anathematized both the atheistic persecutors of the Church and all who collaborated with them. Because of the civil war normal administrative contact with Russian Orthodox Christians outside the country was impossible, and he therefore authorized the establishment of a higher church administration, i.e. a synod in exile, by Russian bishops who were then outside Russia. This is the origin of the Russian Orthodox Church Outside Russia. The attitude of the Church of Russia to the former Soviet regime was always a source of contention between the two hierarchies; tensions are now lessening but remain unresolved.

In Britain the Patriarchate of Moscow is represented by Metropolitan Anthony of Sourozh, 67 Ennismore Gardens, London SW7 1NH. Tel: 0171-584 0096. He is assisted by one archbishop, one vicar bishop and 13 priests. There are 27 parishes and smaller communities.

The Russian Orthodox Church Outside Russia is represented by Archbishop Mark of Richmond and Great Britain (also Archbishop of Berlin and Germany), 14 St Dunstan's Road, London W6 8RB. Tel: 0181-748 4232. There are eight communities, including two monasteries, served by four priests.

THE SERBIAN ORTHODOX CHURCH (PATRIARCHATE OF SERBIA)

There was a small congregation of Orthodox Christian Serbs in London before the Second World War, but most Serbian parishes in Britain have been established since 1945. There is no resident bishop as the parishes are part of the Serbian Orthodox Diocese of Western Europe, which has its centre in Germany. There are 33 parishes and smaller communities in Britain served by 13 priests.

In Britain the Patriarchate of Serbia is represented by the Episcopal Vicar, the Very Revd Milun Kostic, 89 Lancaster Road, London W11 1QQ. Tel: 0171-727 8367.

OTHER NATIONALITIES

Most of the Ukrainian parishes in Britain have now joined the Patriarchate of Constantinople, leaving just one Ukrainian parish in Britain under the care of the Patriarch of Kiev. The Latvian, Polish and some Belorussian parishes are also under the care of the Patriarchate of Constantinople. The Patriarchate of Romania has one parish served by two priests. The Patriarchate of Bulgaria has one parish served by one priest. The Belorussian Autocephalous Orthodox Church has five parishes served by two priests.

ORTHODOX CHURCH PUBLIC RELATIONS OFFICE, St George Orthodox Information Service, 64 Prebend Gardens, London W6 0XU. Tel: 0181-741 9624. *Secretary,* A. Bond

PENTECOSTAL CHURCHES

Pentecostalism is inspired by the descent of the Holy Spirit upon the apostles at Pentecost. The movement began in Los Angeles, USA, in 1906 and is characterized by baptism with the Holy Spirit, divine healing, speaking in tongues (glossolalia), and a literal interpretation of the scriptures. The Pentecostal movement in Britain dates from 1907. Initially, groups of Pentecostalists were led by laymen and did not organize formally. However, in 1915 the Elim Foursquare Gospel Alliance (more usually called the Elim Pentecostal Church) was founded in Ireland by George Jeffreys and in 1924 about 70 independent assemblies formed a fellowship, the Assemblies of God in Great Britain and Ireland. The Apostolic Church grew out of the 1904–5 revivals in South Wales and was established in 1916, and the New Testament Church of God was

established in England in 1953. In recent years many aspects of Pentecostalism have been adopted by the growing charismatic movement within the Roman Catholic, Protestant and Eastern Orthodox churches.

There are about 22 million Pentecostalists world-wide, with about 130,000 adult adherents in Great Britain and Ireland.

THE APOSTOLIC CHURCH, International Administration Offices, PO Box 389, 24–27 St Helens Road, Swansea SA1 1ZH. Tel: 01792-473992. *President,* Pastor P. Cawthorne; *Administrator,* Pastor M. Davies. The Apostolic Church has about 130 churches, 5,500 adherents and 83 ministers

THE ASSEMBLIES OF GOD IN GREAT BRITAIN AND IRELAND, General Offices, 106–114 Talbot Street, Nottingham NG1 5GH. Tel: 0115-947 4525. *General Superintendent,* W. Shenton; *General Administrator,* B. D. Varnam. The Assemblies of God has 645 churches, about 75,000 adherents (including children) and 678 accredited ministers

THE ELIM PENTECOSTAL CHURCH, PO Box 38, Cheltenham, Glos GL50 3HN. Tel: 01242-519904. *General Superintendent,* Pastor I. W. Lewis; *Administrator,* Pastor B. Hunter. The Elim Pentecostal Church has about 470 churches, 50,000 adherents and 475 accredited ministers

THE NEW TESTAMENT CHURCH OF GOD, Main House, Overstone Park, Overstone, Northampton NN6 0AD. Tel: 01604-645944. *National Overseer,* Revd Dr R. O. Brown. The New Testament Church of God has 110 organized congregations, 7,500 baptized members, about 20,000 adherents and 242 accredited ministers

---

THE PRESBYTERIAN CHURCH IN IRELAND

The Presbyterian Church in Ireland is Calvinistic in doctrine and presbyterian in constitution. Presbyterianism was established in Ireland as a result of the Ulster plantation in the early 17th century, when English and Scottish Protestants settled in the north of Ireland.

There are 21 presbyteries and five regional synods under the chief court known as the General Assembly. The General Assembly meets annually and is presided over by a Moderator who is elected for one year. The ongoing work of the Church is undertaken by 18 boards under which there are a number of specialist committees.

There are about 304,000 Presbyterians in Ireland, mainly in the north, in 562 congregations and with 400 ministers.

Moderator (1996–7), Rt. Revd Dr D. H. Allen
Clerk of Assembly and General Secretary, Revd S. Hutchinson, Church House, Belfast BT1 6DW. Tel: 01232-322284

THE PRESBYTERIAN CHURCH OF WALES

The Presbyterian Church of Wales or Calvinistic Methodist Church of Wales is Calvinistic in doctrine and presbyterian in constitution. It was formed in 1811 when Welsh Calvinists severed the relationship with the established church by ordaining their own ministers. It secured its own confession of faith in 1823 and a Constitutional Deed in 1826, and since 1864 the General Assembly has met annually, presided over by a Moderator elected for a year. The doctrine and constitutional structure of the Presbyterian Church of Wales was confirmed by Act of Parliament in 1931–2.

The Church has 51,720 members, 136 ministers and 939 churches.

Moderator (1996–7), Revd A. Wynne Edwards

General Secretary, Revd D. H. Owen, 53 Richmond Road, Cardiff CF2 3UP. Tel: 01222-494913

THE RELIGIOUS SOCIETY OF FRIENDS (QUAKERS)

Quakerism is a movement, not a church, which was founded in the 17th century by George Fox and others in an attempt to revive what they saw as 'primitive Christianity'. The movement was based originally in the Midlands, Yorkshire and north-west England, but there are now Quakers in 36 countries around the world. The colony of Pennsylvania, founded by William Penn, was originally Quaker.

Emphasis is placed on the experience of God in daily life rather than on sacraments or religious occasions. There is no church calendar. Worship is largely silent and there are no appointed ministers; the responsibility for conducting a meeting is shared equally among those present. Social reform and religious tolerance have always been important to Quakers, together with a commitment to non-violence in resolving disputes.

There are 213,800 Quakers world-wide, with over 19,000 in Great Britain and Ireland. There are about 490 meeting houses in Great Britain.

CENTRAL OFFICES: (GREAT BRITAIN) Friends House, Euston Road, London NW1 2BJ. Tel: 0171-387 3601; (IRELAND) Swanbrook House, Morehampton Road, Dublin 4. Tel: 00 353 1-683684

THE SALVATION ARMY

The Salvation Army was founded by a Methodist minister, William Booth, in the east end of London in 1865, and has since become established in 101 countries world-wide. It was first known as the Christian Mission, and took its present name in 1878 when it adopted a quasi-military command structure intended to inspire and regulate its endeavours and to reflect its view that the Church was engaged in spiritual warfare. Salvationists emphasize evangelism, social work and the relief of poverty.

The world leader, known as the General, is elected by a High Council composed of the Chief of the Staff and senior ranking officers known as commissioners.

There are 1,341,841 members, 17,276 active officers (full-time ordained ministers) and 14,558 worship centres and outposts world-wide. In Great Britain and Ireland there are 66,183 members, 1,763 active officers and 993 worship centres.

General, P. A. Rader

UK Territorial Commander, Commissioner D. Pender

TERRITORIAL HEADQUARTERS, PO Box 249, 101 Queen Victoria Street, London EC4P 4EP. Tel: 0171-236 5222

THE SEVENTH-DAY ADVENTIST CHURCH

The Seventh-day Adventist Church was founded in 1863 in the USA. Its members look forward to the second coming of Christ and observe the Sabbath (the seventh day) as a day of rest, worship and ministry. The Church bases its faith and practice wholly on the Bible and has developed 27 fundamental beliefs.

The World Church is divided into 12 divisions, each made up of unions of churches. The Seventh-day Adventist Church in the British Isles is known as the British Union of Seventh-day Adventists and is a member of the Trans-European Division. In the British Isles the administrative organization of the church is arranged in three tiers: the local churches; the regional conferences for south England, north England, Wales, Scotland and Ireland; and the national 'union' conference.

There are about 9 million Adventists and 38,816 churches in 208 countries world-wide. In the UK and Ireland there are 18,734 members, 162 ministers and 247 churches.

President of the British Union Conference, Pastor C. R. Perry

BRITISH ISLES HEADQUARTERS, Stanborough Park, Watford WD2 6JP. Tel: 01923-672251

UNDEB YR ANNIBYNWYR CYMRAEG
The Union of Welsh Independents

The Union of Welsh Independents was formed in 1872 and is a voluntary association of Welsh Congregational Churches and personal members. It is entirely Welsh-speaking. Congregationalism in Wales dates back to 1639 when the first Welsh Congregational Church was opened in Gwent. Member Churches are Calvinistic in doctrine and congregationalist in organization. Each church has complete independence in the government and administration of its affairs.

The Union has 42,442 members, 150 ministers and 555 member churches.

President of the Union (1996–7), Revd F. M. Jones

General Secretary, Revd D. Morris Jones, Tŷ John Penry, 11 Heol Sant Helen, Swansea SA1 4AL. Tel: 01792-652542

UNITARIAN AND FREE CHRISTIAN CHURCHES

Unitarianism has its historical roots in the Judaeo-Christian tradition but questions the deity of Christ and the doctrine of the trinity. It allows the individual to embrace insights from all the world's faiths and philosophies, as there is no formal creed. It is accepted that beliefs may evolve in the light of personal experience.

Unitarian communities first became established in Poland and Transylvania in the 16th century. The first avowedly Unitarian place of worship in the British Isles opened in London in 1774. The General Assembly of Unitarian and Free Christian Churches came into existence in 1928 as the result of the amalgamation of two earlier organizations.

There are about 10,000 Unitarians in Great Britain and Ireland, and 150 Unitarian ministers. About 250 self-governing congregations and fellowship groups, including a small number overseas, are members of the General Assembly.

GENERAL ASSEMBLY OF UNITARIAN AND FREE CHRISTIAN CHURCHES, Essex Hall, 1–6 Essex Street, Strand, London WC2R 3HY. Tel: 0171-240 2384. *General Secretary*, J. J. Teagle

THE UNITED REFORMED CHURCH

The United Reformed Church was formed by the union of most of the Congregational churches in England and Wales with the Presbyterian Church of England in 1972.

Congregationalism dates from the mid 16th century. It is Calvinistic in doctrine, and its followers form independent self-governing congregations bound under God by covenant, a principle laid down in the writings of Robert Browne (1550–1633). From the late 16th century the movement was driven underground by persecution, but the cause was defended at the Westminster Assembly in 1643 and the Savoy Declaration of 1658 laid down its principles. Congregational churches formed county associations for mutual support and in 1832 these associations merged to form the Congregational Union of England and Wales.

The Presbyterian Church in England also dates from the mid 16th century, and was Calvinistic and evangelical in its doctrine. It was governed by a hierarchy of courts.

In the 1960s there was close co-operation locally and nationally between Congregational and Presbyterian Churches. This led to union negotiations and a Scheme of Union, supported by Act of Parliament in 1972. In 1981 a further unification took place, with the Reformed Association of Churches of Christ becoming part of the URC. In its basis the United Reformed Church reflects local church initiative and responsibility with a conciliar pattern of oversight. The General Assembly is the central body, and is made up of equal numbers of ministers and lay members.

The United Reformed Church is divided into 12 Provinces, each with a Provincial Moderator who chairs the Synod, and 75 Districts. There are 102,582 members, 774 full-time stipendiary ministers, 219 non-stipendiary ministers and 1,768 local churches.

General Secretary, Revd A. G. Burnham, 86 Tavistock Place, London WC1H 9RT. Tel: 0171-916 2020

THE WESLEYAN REFORM UNION

The Wesleyan Reform Union was founded by Methodists who left or were expelled from Wesleyan Methodism in 1849 following a period of internal conflict. Its doctrine is conservative evangelical and its organization is congregational, each church having complete independence in the government and administration of its affairs. The main concentration of churches is in Yorkshire.

The Union has 2,516 members, 20 ministers, 143 lay preachers and 122 churches.

President (1996–7), S. Bown

General Secretary, Revd E. W. Downing, Wesleyan Reform Church House, 123 Queen Street, Sheffield S1 2DU. Tel: 0114-272 1938

Non-Christian Faiths

BUDDHISM

Buddhism originated in northern India, in the teachings of Siddharta Gautama, who was born near Kapilavastu about 560 BC. After a long spiritual quest he experienced enlightenment beneath a tree at the place now known as Bodhgaya, and began missionary work.

Fundamental to Buddhism is the concept that there is no such thing as a permanent soul or self; when someone dies, consciousness is the only one of the elements of which they were composed which is lost. All the other elements regroup in a new body and carry with them the consequences of the conduct of the earlier life (known as the law of *karma*). This cycle of death and rebirth is broken only when the state of *nirvana* has been reached. Buddhism steers a middle path between belief in personal immortality and belief in death as the final end.

The Four Noble Truths of Buddhism (*dukkha*, suffering; *tanha*, a thirst or desire for continued existence which causes dukkha; *nirvana*, the final liberation from desire and ignorance; and *ariya*, the path to nirvana) are all held to be universal and to sum up the *dhamma* or true nature of life. Necessary qualities to promote spiritual development are *sila* (morality), *samadhi* (meditation) and *panna* (wisdom).

There are two main schools of Buddhism: *Theravada* Buddhism, the earliest extant school, which is more traditional, and *Mahayana* Buddhism, which began to develop about 100 years after the Buddha's death and is more liberal; it teaches that all people may attain Buddahood. Important schools which have developed within Mahayana Buddhism are *Zen* Buddhism, *Nichiren* Buddhism and Pure Land Buddhism or *Amidism*. There are also distinctive Tibetan forms of Buddhism. Buddhism began to establish itself in the West at the beginning of the 20th century.

The scripture of Theravada Buddhism is the *Pali Canon*, which dates from the first century BC. Mahayana Buddhism uses a Sanskrit version of the Pali Canon but also has many other works of scripture.

There is no set time for Buddhist worship, which may take place in a temple or in the home. Worship centres around *paritta* (chanting), acts of devotion centring on the image of the Buddha, and, where possible, offerings to a relic of the Buddha. Buddhist festivals vary according to local traditions and within Theravada and Mahayana Buddhism. For religious purposes Buddhists use solar and lunar calendars, the New Year being celebrated in April. Other festivals mark events in the life of the Buddha.

There is no supreme governing authority in Buddhism. In the United Kingdom communities representing all schools of Buddhism have developed and operate independently. The Buddhist Society was established in 1924; it runs courses and lectures, and publishes books about Buddhism. It represents no one school of Buddhism.

There are estimated to be at least 300 million Buddhists world-wide, and about 275 organizations and groups, an estimated 25,000 adherents and 15 temples or monasteries in the United Kingdom.

THE BUDDHIST SOCIETY, 58 Eccleston Square, London SW1V 1PH. Tel: 0171-834 5858. *General Secretary*, R. C. Maddox

HINDUISM

Hinduism has no historical founder but is known to have been highly developed in India by about 1200 BC. Its adherents originally called themselves Aryans; Muslim invaders first called the Aryans 'Hindus' (derived from the word 'Sindhu', the name of the river Indus) in the eighth century.

Hinduism's evolution has been complex and it embraces many different religious beliefs, mythologies and practices. Most Hindus hold that *satya* (truthfulness), *ahimsa* (non-violence), honesty, physical labour and tolerance of other faiths are essential for good living. They believe in one supreme spirit (*Brahman*), and in the transmigration of *atman* (the soul). Most Hindus accept the doctrine of *karma* (consequences of actions), the concept of *samsara* (successive lives) and the possibility of all atmans achieving *moksha* (liberation from samsara) through *jnana* (knowledge), *yoga* (meditation), *karma* (work or action) and *bhakti* (devotion).

Most Hindus offer worship to *murtis* (images or statues) representing different aspects of Brahman, and follow their *dharma* (religious and social duty) according to the traditions of their *varna* (social class), *ashrama* (stage in life), *jati* (caste) and *kula* (family).

Hinduism's sacred texts are divided into *shruti* ('heard' or divinely inspired), including the *Vedas*, or *smriti* ('remembered' tradition), including the *Ramayana*, the *Mahabharata*, the *Puranas* (ancient myths), and the sacred law books. Most Hindus recognize the authority of the *Vedas*, the oldest holy books, and accept the philosophical teachings of the *Upanishads*, the *Vedanta Sutras* and the *Bhagavad-Gita*.

Brahman is formless, limitless and all-pervading, and is represented in worship by murtis which may be male or female and in the form of a human, animal or bird. Brahma, Vishnu and Shiva are the most important gods worshipped by Hindus; their respective consorts are Saraswati, Lakshmi and Durga or Parvati, also known as Shakti. There are held to have been ten *avatars* (incarnations) of Vishnu, of whom the most important are Rama and Krishna. Other popular gods are Ganesha, Hanuman and Subrahmanyam. All gods are seen as aspects of the supreme God, not as competing deities.

Orthodox Hindus revere all gods and goddesses equally, but there are many sects, including the Hare-Krishna movement (ISKCon), the Arya Samaj, the Swami Narayan Hindu mission and the Satya Sai-Baba movement. Worship in the sects is concentrated on one deity to the exclusion of others. In some sects a human *guru* (spiritual teacher), usually the head of the organization, is revered more than the deity, while in other sects the guru is seen as the source of spiritual guidance.

Hinduism does not have a centrally-trained and ordained priesthood. The pronouncements of the *shankaracharyas* (heads of monasteries) of Shringeri, Puri, Dwarka and Badrinath are heeded by the orthodox but may be ignored by the various sects.

The commonest form of worship is a *puja*, in which offerings of red and yellow powders, rice grains, water, flowers, food, fruit, incense and light are made to the image of a deity. Puja may be done either in a home shrine or a *mandir* (temple). Many British Hindus celebrate life-cycle rituals with Sanskrit mantras for naming a baby, the sacred thread (an initiation ceremony), marriage and cremation. For details of the Hindu calendar, main festivals etc, *see* pages 84–5.

The largest communities of Hindus in Britain are in Leicester, London, Birmingham and Bradford, and developed as a result of immigration from India, east Africa and Sri Lanka. Many Hindus now are British by birth, with English as their first language; the main ethnic languages are Gujarati, Hindi, Punjabi, Tamil, Bengali and Marathi.

There are an estimated 800 million Hindus world-wide; there are about 360,000 adherents and over 150 temples in the UK.

ARYA PRATINIDHI SABHA (UK) AND ARYA SAMAJ LONDON, 69A Argyle Road, London W13 0LY. Tel: 0181-991 1732. *Director,* Prof. S. N. Bharadwaj

BHARATIYA VIDYA BHAVAN, Old Church Building, 4A Castletown Road, London W14 9HQ. Tel: 0171-381 3086. *Executive Director,* Dr M. Nandakumara

INTERNATIONAL SOCIETY FOR KRISHNA CONSCIOUSNESS (ISKCon), Bhaktivedanta Manor, Letchmore Heath, nr Watford, Herts WD2 8EP. Tel: 01923-857244. *Governing Body Commissioner,* H. H. Sivarama Swami

NATIONAL COUNCIL OF HINDU TEMPLES (UK), c/o Shree Sanatan Mandir, Weymouth Street, off Catherine Street, Leicester LE4 6FP. Tel: 0116-266 1402. *Secretary,* V. Aery

SWAMINARAYAN HINDU MISSION, 105-119 Brentfield Road, London NW10 8JB. Tel: 0181-965 2651. *Head of Mission,* Admaswarup Swami

VISHWA HINDU PARISHAD (UK), 48 Wharfedale Gardens, Thornton Heath, Surrey CR7 6LB. Tel: 0181-684 9716. *General Secretary,* K. Ruparelia

ISLAM

Islam (which means 'peace arising from submission to the will of Allah' in Arabic) is a monotheistic religion which originated in Arabia through the Prophet Muhammad, who was born in Mecca (Makkah) in AD 570. Islam spread to Egypt, North Africa, Spain and the borders of China in the century following the prophet's death, and is now the predominant religion in Indonesia, the Near and Middle East, North and parts of West Africa, Pakistan, Bangladesh, Malaysia and some of the republics of the former Soviet Union. There are also large Muslim communities in many other countries.

For Muslims (adherents of Islam), God (*Allah*) is one and holds absolute power. His commands were revealed to mankind through the prophets, who include Abraham, Moses and Jesus, but his message was gradually corrupted until revealed finally and in perfect form to Muhammad through the angel *Jibril* (Gabriel) over a period of 23 years. This last, incorruptible message has been recorded in the *Qur'an* (Koran), which contains 114 divisions called *surahs,* each made up of *ayahs,* and is held to be the essence of all previous scriptures. The *Ahadith* are the records of the Prophet Muhammad's deeds and sayings (the *Sunnah*) as recounted by his immediate followers. A culture and a system of law and theology gradually developed to form a distinctive Islamic civilization. Islam makes no distinction between sacred and worldly affairs and provides rules for every aspect of human life. The *Shari'ah* is the sacred law of Islam based upon prescriptions derived from the Qur'an and the Sunnah of the Prophet.

The 'five pillars of Islam' are *shahadah* (a declaration of faith in the oneness and supremacy of Allah and the messengership of Muhammad); *salat* (formal prayer, to be performed five times a day facing the *Ka'bah* (sacred house) in the holy city of Mecca); *zakat* (welfare due); *saum* (fasting during the month of Ramadan); and *hajj* (pilgrimage to Mecca); some Muslims would add *jihad* (striving for the cause of good and resistance to evil).

Two main groups developed among Muslims. *Sunni* Muslims accept the legitimacy of Muhammad's first four *caliphs* (successors as head of the Muslim community) and of the authority of the Muslim community as a whole. About 90 per cent of Muslims are *Sunni* Muslims. *Shi'ites* recognize only Muhammad's son-in-law Ali as his rightful successor and the *Imams* (descendants of Ali, not to be confused with *imams* (prayer leaders or religious teachers)) as the principal legitimate religious authority. The largest group within *Shi'ism* is *Twelver Shi'ism,* which has been the official school of law and theology in Iran since the 16th century; other subsects include the *Ismailis* and the *Druze,* the latter being an offshoot of the Ismailis and differing considerably from the main body of Muslims.

There is no organized priesthood, but learned men such as *ulama, imams* and *ayatollahs* are accorded great respect. The *Sufis* are the mystics of Islam. Mosques are centres for worship and teaching and also for social and welfare activities. For details of the Muslim calendar and festivals, *see* page 86.

Islam was first known in western Europe in the eighth century AD when 800 years of Muslim rule began in Spain. Later, Islam spread to eastern Europe. More recently, Muslims came to Europe from Africa, the Middle East and Asia in the late 19th century. Both the Sunni and Shi'ah traditions are represented in Britain, but the majority of Muslims in Britain adhere to Sunni Islam.

The largest communities are in London, Liverpool, Manchester, Birmingham, Bradford, Cardiff, Edinburgh and Glasgow. There is no central organization, but the Islamic Cultural Centre, which is the London Central Mosque, and the Imams and Mosques Council are influential bodies; there are many other Muslim organizations in Britain.

There are about 1,000 million Muslims world-wide, with more than one million adherents and about 900 mosques in Britain.

IMAMS AND MOSQUES COUNCIL, 20–22 Creffield Road, London W5 3RP. Tel: 0181-992 6636. *Director of the Council and Principal of the Muslim College,* Dr M. A. Z. Badawi

ISLAMIC CULTURAL CENTRE, 146 Park Road, London NW8 7RG. Tel: 0171-724 3363. *Director (acting),* H. Al-Majed

MUSLIM WORLD LEAGUE, 46 Goodge Street, London W1P 1FJ. Tel: 0171-636 7568. *Director,* B. A. Alim

UNION OF MUSLIM ORGANIZATIONS OF THE UK AND EIRE, 109 Campden Hill Road, London W8 7TL. Tel: 0171-229 0538. *Geneal Secretary,* Dr S. A. Pasha

JUDAISM

Judaism is the oldest monotheistic faith. The primary authority of Judaism is the Hebrew Bible or *Tanakh,* which records how the descendants of Abraham were led by Moses out of their slavery in Egypt to Mount Sinai where God's law (*Torah*) was revealed to them as the chosen people. The *Talmud,* which consists of commentaries on the *Mishnah* (the first text of rabbinical Judaism), is also held to be authoritative, and may be divided into two main categories: the *halakah* (dealing with legal and ritual matters) and the *Aggadah* (dealing with theological and ethical matters not directly concerned with the regulation of conduct). The *Midrash* comprises rabbinic writings containing biblical interpretations in the spirit of the *Aggadah*. The *halakah* has become a source of division; Orthodox Jews regard Jewish law as derived from God and therefore unalterable; Reform and Liberal Jews seek to interpret it in the light of contemporary considerations; and Conservative Jews aim to maintain most of the traditional rituals but to allow changes in accordance with that tradition. Reconstructionist Judaism, a 20th-century movement, regards Judaism as a culture rather than a theological system and therefore accepts all forms of Jewish practice.

The family is the basic unit of Jewish ritual, with the synagogue playing an important role as the centre for public worship and religious study. A synagogue is led by a group of laymen who are elected to office. The Rabbi is primarily a teacher and spiritual guide. The Sabbath is the central religious observance. For details of the Jewish calendar, fasts and festivals, *see* page 85. Most British Jews are descendants of either the *Ashkenazim* of central and eastern Europe or the *Sephardim* of Spain and Portugal.

The Chief Rabbi of the United Hebrew Congregations of the Commonwealth is appointed by a Chief Rabbinate Conference, and is the rabbinical authority of the Orthodox sector of the Ashkenazi Jewish community. His authority is not recognized by the Reform Synagogues of Great Britain (the largest progressive group), the Union of Liberal and Progressive Synagogues, the Union of Orthodox Hebrew Congregations, the Federation of Synagogues, the Sephardi community, or the Assembly of Masorti Synagogues. He is, however, generally recognized both outside the Jewish community and within it as the public religious representative of the totality of British Jewry.

The *Beth Din* (Court of Judgment) is the rabbinic court. The *Dayanim* (Assessors) adjudicate in disputes or on matters of Jewish law and tradition; they also oversee dietary law administration. The Chief Rabbi is President of the *Beth Din* of the United Synagogue.

The Board of Deputies of British Jews was established in 1760 and is the representative body of British Jewry. The basis of representation is mainly synagogal, but communal organizations are also represented. It watches over the interests of British Jewry and seeks to counter anti-Jewish discrimination.

There are over 12.5 million Jews world-wide; in Great Britain and Ireland there are an estimated 300,000 adherents and about 350 synagogues. Of these, 185 congregations and about 150 rabbis and ministers are under the jurisdiction of the Chief Rabbi; 99 orthodox congregations have a more independent status; and 72 congregations do not recognize the authority of the Chief Rabbi.

CHIEF RABBINATE, 735 High Road, London N12 0US. Tel: 0181-343 6301. *Chief Rabbi*, Dr Jonathan Sacks; *Executive Director*, J. Kestenbaum

BETH DIN (COURT OF THE CHIEF RABBI), 735 High Road, London N12 0US. Tel: 0181-343 6280. *Registrar*, J. Phillips; *Dayanim*, Rabbi C. Ehrentreu; Rabbi I. Binstock; Rabbi C. D. Kaplin; Rabbi M. Gelley

BOARD OF DEPUTIES OF BRITISH JEWS, Commonwealth House, 1–19 New Oxford Street, London WC1A 1NF. Tel: 0171-543 5400. *President*, E. Tabachnik, QC; *Chief Executive*, N. A. Nagler

ASSEMBLY OF MASORTI SYNAGOGUES, 766 Finchley Road, London NW11 7TH. Tel: 0181-201 8772. *Development Director*, H. Freedman

FEDERATION OF SYNAGOGUES, 65 Watford Way, London NW4 3AQ. Tel: 0181-202 2263. *Administrator*, G. Kushner

REFORM SYNAGOGUES OF GREAT BRITAIN, The Sternberg Centre for Judaism, Manor House, 80 East

End Road, London N3 2SY. Tel: 0181-349 4731. *Chief Executive*, Rabbi T. Bayfield

SPANISH AND PORTUGUESE JEWS' CONGREGATION, 2 Ashworth Road, London W9 1JY. Tel: 0171-289 2573. *Chief Executive*, Mrs J. Velleman

UNION OF LIBERAL AND PROGRESSIVE SYNAGOGUES, The Montagu Centre, 21 Maple Street, London W1P 6DS. Tel: 0171-580 1663. *Director*, Mrs R. Rosenberg

UNION OF ORTHODOX HEBREW CONGREGATIONS, 140 Stamford Hill, London N16 6QT. Tel: 0181-802 6226. *Executive Director*, Rabbi A. Klein

UNITED SYNAGOGUE HEAD OFFICE, 735 High Road, London N12 0US. Tel: 0181-343 8989. *Chief Executive*, J. M. Lew

SIKHISM

The Sikh religion dates from the birth of Guru Nanak in the Punjab in 1469. 'Guru' means teacher but in Sikh tradition has come to represent the divine presence of God giving inner spiritual guidance. Nanak's role as the human vessel of the divine guru was passed on to nine successors, the last of whom (Guru Gobind Singh) died in 1708. The immortal guru is now held to reside in the sacred scripture, *Guru Granth Sahib*, and so to be present in all Sikh gatherings.

Guru Nanak taught that there is one God and that different religions are like different roads leading to the same destination. He condemned religious conflict, ritualism and caste prejudices. The fifth Guru, Guru Arjan, largely compiled the Sikh Holy Book, a collection of hymns (*gurbani*) known as the *Adi Granth*. It includes the writings of the first five Gurus and the ninth Guru, and selected writings of Hindu and Muslim saints whose views are in accord with the Gurus' teachings. Guru Arjan also built the Golden Temple at Amritsar, the centre of Sikhism. The tenth Guru, Guru Gobind Singh, passed on the guruship to the sacred scripture, Guru Granth Sahib. He also founded the *Khalsa*, an order intended to fight against tyranny and injustice. Male initiates to the order added 'Singh' to their given names and women added 'Kaur'. Guru Gobind Singh also made five symbols obligatory: *kaccha* (a special undergarment), *kara* (a steel bangle), *kirpan* (a small sword), *kesh* (long unshorn hair, and consequently the wearing of a turban), and *kangha* (a comb). These practices are still compulsory for those Sikhs who are initiated into the *Khalsa* (the *Amritdharis*). Those who do not seek initiation are known as *Sahajdharis*.

There are no professional priests in Sikhism; anyone with a reasonable proficiency in the Punjabi language can conduct a service. Worship can be offered individually or communally, and in a private house or a *gurdwara* (temple). Sikhs are forbidden to eat meat prepared by ritual slaughter; they are also asked to abstain from smoking alcohol and other intoxicants. For details of the Sikh calendar and main celebrations, *see* page 86.

There are about 20 million Sikhs world-wide and about 400,000 adherents and more than 250 gurdwaras in Great Britain. The largest communities are in London, Bradford, Leeds, Huddersfield, Birmingham, Nottingham, Coventry and Wolverhampton. Every gurdwara manages its own affairs and there is no central body in the UK. The Sikh Missionary Society provides an information service.

SIKH CULTURAL SOCIETY OF GREAT BRITAIN, 88 Mollison Way, Edgware, Middx HA8 5QW. Tel: 0181-95 1215. *General Secretary*, A. S. Chhatwal

SIKH MISSIONARY SOCIETY UK, 10 Featherstone Road, Southall, Middx UB2 5AA. Tel: 0181-574 1902. *Hon. Secretary*, T. S. Manget

Education

For addresses of national education departments, *see* Government Departments and Public Offices. For other addresses, *see* Education Directory

Responsibility for education in the United Kingdom is largely decentralized. Overall responsibility for all aspects of education in England lies with the Secretary of State for Education and Employment; in Wales with the Secretary of State for Wales; in Scotland with the Secretary of State for Scotland acting through the Scottish Office Education and Industry Department; and in Northern Ireland with the Secretary of State for Northern Ireland.

The main concerns of the education departments (the Department for Education and Employment (DFEE), the Welsh Office, the Scottish Office Education and Industry Department (SOEID), and the Department of Education for Northern Ireland (DENI)) are the formulation of national policies for education and the maintenance of consistency in educational standards. They are responsible for the broad allocation of resources for education, for the rate and distribution of educational building and for the supply, training and superannuation of teachers.

EXPENDITURE

In the UK in 1993–4, provisional expenditure on education was (£ million):

Schools	19,676.2
Further and higher education	8,965.3
Other education and related expenditure	3,336.5

Most of this expenditure is incurred by local authorities, which make their own expenditure decisions according to their local situations and needs. Expenditure on education by central government departments, in real terms, was (£ million):

	1995–6 estimated outturn	1996–7 planned
DFEE	10,753	10,766
Welsh Office	520.6	529.4
SOEID	1,281	1,326
DENI	1,323	1,370

The bulk of direct expenditure by the DFEE, the Welsh Office and SOEID is directed towards supporting higher education in universities and colleges through the Higher Education Funding Councils (HEFCs) and further education and sixth form colleges through the Further Education Funding Councils (FEFCs) in England and Wales and directly from central government in Scotland. In addition, the DFEE funds grant-maintained schools (through the Funding Agency for Schools), the City Technology Colleges (CTCs) and the City College for the Technology of the Arts, and pays grants to Technology Colleges.

The Welsh Office also funds grants for higher and further education, grant-maintained schools, educational services and research, and supports bilingual education and the Welsh language.

In Scotland the main elements of central government expenditure, in addition to those outlined above, are grant-aided special schools, self-governing schools, student awards and bursaries, curriculum development, special educational needs and community education.

The Department of Education for Northern Ireland directly funds higher education, teacher education, teacher salaries and superannuation, student awards, further education, grant-maintained integrated schools, and voluntary grammar schools.

Current net expenditure on education by local education authorities in England, Wales, and Scotland, and education and library boards in Northern Ireland is (£ million):

	1995–6 estimated outturn	1996–7 planned
England	19,990	18,000
Wales	1,235.5	1,241.5
Scotland	2,515.5	2,503.1
Northern Ireland	953	936

LOCAL EDUCATION ADMINISTRATION

The education service at present is a national service in which the provision of most school education is locally administered; its administration is still largely decentralized.

In England and Wales the education service is administered by local education authorities (LEAs), which carry the day-to-day responsibility for providing most state primary and secondary education in their areas, although the planning and supply of school places is to be shared with the Funding Agency for Schools as the number of grant-maintained schools grows. They also share with the FEFCs the duty to provide adult education to meet the needs of their areas.

The LEAs own and maintain schools and colleges, build new ones and provide equipment. Most of the public money spent on education is disbursed by the local authorities. LEAs are financed largely from the council tax and aggregate external finance (AEF) from the Department of the Environment in England and the Welsh Office in Wales.

The powers of local education authorities as regards the control of schools have been modified in recent years and schools can choose to opt out of local authority control. These grant-maintained (GM) schools are funded by the Funding Agency for Schools in England. Those in Wales are funded by the Welsh Office at present but the Schools Funding Council for Wales will take over when the number of grant-maintained schools is sufficient to warrant the change. Primary schools can apply for grant-maintained status as a group as well as individually. An Education Association can be set up to take over the management of failing schools where both the LEA and the governing body have not brought about improvements identified as necessary by inspection.

The duty of providing education locally in Scotland rests with the education authorities. They are responsible for the construction of buildings, the employment of teachers and other staff, and the provision of equipment and materials. Devolved School Management (DSM) was introduced for all primary and secondary schools by April 1996, although the deadline has been extended to April 1998 in primary schools with headteachers who teach full-time and to April 1997 in all special schools.

The powers of local authorities over educational institutions under their control have been reduced also in Scotland. Education authorities are required to establish school boards consisting of parents and teachers as well as co-opted members, responsible among other things for the appointment of staff. Schools can choose to withdraw from local authority control and become self-governing; the institution of Technology Academies directly funded by central government has been provided for; at least half the members of further education college councils must be drawn from employers, and substantial functions have been delegated to these new councils.

Education is administered locally in Northern Ireland by five education and library boards, whose costs are met in full by DENI. A review of educational administration has taken place and as a result the boards are to be reduced in number from five to three. All grant-aided schools include elected parents and teachers on their boards of governors. Provision has been made for schools wishing to provide integrated education to have grant-maintained integrated status from the outset. All schools and colleges of further education have full responsibility for their own budgets, including staffing costs. The Council for Catholic Maintained Schools forms an upper tier of management for Catholic schools and provides advice on matters relating to management and administration.

THE INSPECTORATE

The Office for Standards in Education (OFSTED) is a non-ministerial government department in England headed by HM Chief Inspector of Schools (HMCI). OFSTED's remit is regularly to inspect all maintained schools and report on and thereby improve standards of achievement. All state schools are inspected by teams of independent inspectors on contract to OFSTED, including educationalists and lay people and headed by registered inspectors. There are also additional inspectors (AIs), who are mostly headteachers and deputy heads on secondment to OFSTED for the inspection of primary schools. HM Inspectors (HMI) within OFSTED report on good practice in schools and other educational issues based on inspection evidence. From 1997 for secondary and from 1998 for primary, schools will be inspected once every six years or more frequently if there is cause. A summary of the inspection report must be sent to parents of each pupil by the school, followed by a copy of the governors' action plan thereon. OFSTED's counterpart in Wales is the Office of HM Chief Inspector of Schools in Wales (OHMCI Wales), where inspection of maintained schools is carried out on a five-year cycle. The inspection of further and higher education in England and Wales is the responsibility of inspectors appointed to the respective funding councils.

HM Inspectorate in Scotland carries out the inspection of schools and further education institutions in Scotland, using teams which include lay people, and in addition requires schools to produce a document setting out their educational targets for two years ahead and a report on progress over the previous two years. The inspection of higher education is the responsibility of inspectors appointed to the Higher Education Funding Council for Scotland.

Inspection is carried out in Northern Ireland by the Department of Education's Education and Training Inspectorate, using teams which include lay people. The Inspectorate also performs an advisory function to the Secretary of State for Northern Ireland. From September 1992 a five-year cycle of inspection was introduced.

There were, in 1996–7, 200 HMIs who act as special advisers to OFSTED, 1,500 registered inspectors, 6,400 team inspectors in England, 40 HMIs and about 888 registered inspectors and team members in Wales, 93 HMIs in Scotland and 60 members of the Inspectorate in Northern Ireland.

SCHOOLS AND PUPILS

Schooling is compulsory in Great Britain for all children between five and 16 years and between four and 16 years in Northern Ireland. Some provision is made for children under five and many pupils remain at school after the minimum leaving age. No fees are charged in any publicly maintained school in England, Wales and Scotland. In Northern Ireland, fees are paid by pupils in preparatory departments of grammar schools, but pupils admitted to the secondary departments of grammar schools do not pay fees.

In the UK, parents have a right to express a preference for a particular school and have a right to appeal if dissatisfied. The policy, known as more open enrolment, requires schools to admit children up to the limit of their capacity if there is a demand for places, and to publish their criteria for selection if they are over-subscribed, in which case parents have a right of appeal.

The 'Parents' Charter', available free from education departments, is a booklet which tells parents about the education system. Schools are now required to make available information about themselves, their public examination results, truancy rates, and destination of leavers. Corporal punishment is no longer legal in publicly maintained schools in the UK.

FALL AND RISE IN NUMBERS

In primary education, and increasingly in secondary education, pupil numbers in the UK declined through the 1980s. In nursery and primary schools pupil numbers reached their lowest figure of 4.6 million in 1986. They stood at 5.1 million in 1995 and are expected to increase gradually year by year until by 2000 they reach about 5.6 million. In secondary schools pupil numbers peaked at 4.6 million in 1981. They stood at 3.65 million in 1995 and are projected to rise to about 4.1 million in 2005.

ENGLAND AND WALES

There are two main categories of school in England and Wales: publicly maintained schools, which charge no fees and independent schools, which charge fees (*see* pages 435–6). Publicly maintained schools are maintained by local education authorities except for grant-maintained schools and City Technology Colleges.

The number of schools by category in 1995 was:

Maintained schools	24,116
County	15,876
Voluntary	7,175
controlled	2,991
aided	4,134
special agreement*	50
Grant-maintained	1,032
Wales	17
CTCs and CCTAs	16
Independent schools	2,325
TOTAL	26,441

* There are no special agreement schools in Wales

County schools are owned by LEAs and wholly funded by them. They are non-denominational and provide primary and secondary education. Voluntary schools also provide primary and secondary education. Although the buildings are in many cases provided by the voluntary bodies (mainly religious denominations), they are financially maintained by an LEA. In controlled schools the LEA bears all costs. In aided schools the building is usually provided by the voluntary body. The managers or governors are responsible for repairs to the school building and for improvements and alterations to it, though the DFEE may reimburse part of approved capital expenditure, while the LEA pays for internal maintenance and other running costs. Special agreement schools are those where the LEA may, by special agreement, pay between one-half and three-quarters of the cost of building a new, or extending an existing, voluntary school, almost always a secondary school

Under the Local Management of Schools (LMS) initiative, LEAs are required to delegate at least 85 per cent of school budgets, including staffing costs, directly to schools. LEAs continue to retain responsibility for various services, including transport and school meals.

Governing bodies – All publicly maintained schools have a governing body, usually made up of a number of parent representatives, governors appointed by the LEA if the school is LEA maintained, the headteacher (unless he or she chooses otherwise), and serving teachers. Schools can appoint up to four sponsor governors from business who will be expected to provide financial and managerial assistance. Governors are responsible for the overall policies of schools and their academic aims and objectives; they also control matters of school discipline and the appointment and dismissal of staff. Governing bodies select inspectors for their schools, are responsible for action as a result of inspection reports and are required to make those reports and their action plans thereon available to parents.

Technology Colleges and Language Colleges – The Specialist Schools programme is open to all state secondary schools wishing to specialize in the teaching of technology, mathematics and science (Technology Colleges) and modern foreign languages (Language Colleges). In addition to the normal funding arrangements, the colleges receive business sponsorship (up to four sponsor governors may sit on governing bodies) and complementary capital grants up to £100,000 from central government, together with extra annual funding of £100 a pupil to assist the delivery of an enhanced curriculum. By September 1996, there were 151 technology colleges and 30 language colleges. In Wales the Technology Schools Initiative provides grants to enhance technology teaching to those schools successful in attracting funding through open competition.

Grant-maintained (GM) schools – All secondary and primary schools, whether maintained or independent, are eligible to apply for grant-maintained status, subject to a ballot of parents. GM schools are maintained directly by the Secretary of State and the Welsh Office, not the LEA, and are wholly run by their own governing body. They also have the freedom to borrow commercially to fund capital projects. The Funding Agency for Schools pays grants to GM schools in England. The Schools Funding Council for Wales will be instituted when the number of GM schools justifies the change in funding arrangements. As of September 1996 about 60 per cent of grant-maintained schools were secondary schools.

City Technology Colleges (CTCs) and *City Colleges for the Technology of the Arts (CCTAs)* are state-aided but independent of LEAs. Their aim is to widen the choice of secondary education in disadvantaged urban areas and to teach a broad curriculum with an emphasis on science, technology, business understanding and arts technologies. Capital costs are shared by government and sponsors from industry and commerce, and running costs are covered by a per capita grant from the DFEE in line with comparable

costs in an LEA maintained school. The first city technology college opened in 1988 in Solihull. The first CCTA, known as Britschool, opened in Croydon in 1991.

SCOTLAND

The number of schools by category in 1995 was:

Publicly maintained schools:

Education authority	3,843
Grant-aided	10
Self-governing	3
Independent schools	116
TOTAL	3,972

Education authority schools (known as public schools) are financed jointly by the authorities and central government. Grant-aided schools are conducted by voluntary managers who receive grants direct from the SOEID. Independent schools receive no direct grant and charge fees, but are subject to inspection and registration. An additional category is that of self-governing schools opting to be managed entirely by a board of management consisting of the headteacher, parent and staff representatives and co-opted members. The change of status requires a ballot of parents and the publication of proposals by the board, and the achievement of self-government is subject to a final decision by the Secretary of State. These schools remain in the public sector and are funded by direct government grant set to match the resources the school would have received under education authority management. Three have so far been established.

Education authorities are required to establish school boards to participate in the administration and management of schools. These boards consist of elected parents and staff members as well as co-opted members.

Technology Academies (TAs) – The Self-Governing Schools etc. (Scotland) Act 1989 provides for setting up technology academies in areas of urban deprivation. These secondary schools are intended to be so placed as to draw on a wide catchment, and to offer a broad curriculum with an emphasis on science and technology. They are to be founded and managed in partnership with industrial sponsors, with central government meeting the running costs by grant-aid thereafter. None has yet been set up.

NORTHERN IRELAND

The number of schools by category in 1995 was:

Grant-aided schools:

Controlled	683
Voluntary maintained	555
Voluntary grammar	53
Integrated schools	32
Independent schools	20
TOTAL	1,343

Controlled schools are controlled by the education and library boards with all costs paid from public funds. Voluntary maintained schools, mainly under Roman Catholic management, receive grants towards capital costs and running costs in whole or in part. Voluntary grammar schools may be under Roman Catholic or non-denominational management and receive grants from the DENI. All grant-aided schools include elected parents and teachers on their boards of governors, whose responsibilities also include financial management under the Local Management of Schools (LMS) initiative. About 85 per cent of the potential funds available to schools are now delegated to them. Voluntary maintained and voluntary grammar schools can apply for designation as a new category of voluntary school, which is eligible for a 100 per cent as opposed to 85 per cent grant. Such schools are managed by a board of governors on which no single interest group has a majority of nominees.

The majority of children in Northern Ireland are educated in schools which in practice are segregated on religious lines. Integrated schools exist to educate Protestant and Roman Catholic children together. There are two types: grant-maintained integrated schools which are funded by DENI; and controlled integrated schools funded by the education and library boards. Procedures are in place for balloting parents in existing segregated schools to determine whether they want instead to have integrated schools. By September 1996, 32 integrated schools had been established, 11 of them secondary.

THE STATE SYSTEM

NURSERY EDUCATION – Nursery education is for children from two to five years and is not compulsory. It takes place in nursery schools or nursery classes in primary schools. The number of children receiving nursery education in the UK in 1994-5 was:

In maintained nursery schools	85,100
In primary schools	976,100
In non-maintained nursery schools	63,900
TOTAL	1,125,100
% of total three- and four-year-old population	57%

Many children also attend pre-school playgroups organized by parents and voluntary bodies such as the Pre-School Learning Alliance. In order to increase participation in nursery education, every parent of a four-year-old is to be given a voucher worth £1,100 exchangeable for up to three terms of pre-school education. The scheme was piloted in 1996 and will be fully operational in England and Wales by April 1997 and in Northern Ireland by September 1997. In Scotland the pilot began in August 1996, prior to the introduction of the scheme in August 1997.

PRIMARY EDUCATION – Primary education begins at five years in Great Britain and four years in Northern Ireland, and is almost always co-educational. In England, Wales and Northern Ireland the transfer to secondary school is generally made at 11 years. In Scotland, the primary school course lasts for seven years and pupils transfer to secondary courses at about the age of 12.

Primary schools consist mainly of infants' schools for children aged five to seven, junior schools for those aged seven to 11, and combined junior and infant schools for both age groups. First schools in some parts of England cater for ages five to ten as the first stage of a three-tier system: first, middle and secondary. Many primary schools provide nursery classes for children under five (see above).

Primary schools (UK) 1994-5	
No. of primary schools	23,938
No. of pupils	5,250,600
Pupils under five years	976,100

Pupil-teacher ratios in maintained primary schools were:

	1992–3	1993–4
England	22.2	22.5
Wales	22.1	22.3
Scotland	19.3	19.5
Northern Ireland	22.3	21.7
UK	21.9	21.5

The average size of classes 'as taught' was 25.8 in 1994 but fell to 25.5 in 1995.

MIDDLE SCHOOLS – Middle schools (which take children from first schools), mostly in England, cover varying age ranges between eight and 14 and usually lead on to comprehensive upper schools.

SECONDARY EDUCATION – Secondary schools are for children aged 11 to 16 and for those who choose to stay on to 18. At 16, many students prefer to move on to tertiary or sixth form colleges (see page 439). Most secondary schools in England, Wales and Scotland are co-educational. The largest secondary schools have over 1,500 pupils but only 27 per cent of the schools take over 1,000 pupils.

Secondary schools 1995

	England and Wales	Scotland	N. Ireland
No. of pupils	3,128,401	314,904	150,036
% over 16 years	9.9%	11.3%	13.6%
Average class size	21	19.4	n/a
Pupil-teacher ratio	16.1	12.9	15.2

In England and Wales the main types of secondary schools are: comprehensive schools (86.2 per cent of pupils in England, 100 in Wales), whose admission arrangements are without reference to ability or aptitude; middle deemed secondary schools for children aged variously between eight and 14 years who then move on to senior comprehensive schools at 12, 13 or 14 (5.5 per cent of pupils in England); secondary modern schools (3.1 per cent of pupils in England) providing a general education with a practical bias; secondary grammar schools (4.0 per cent of pupils in England) with selective intake providing an academic course from 11 to 16–18 years; and technical schools (0.1 per cent in England), providing an integrated academic and technical education.

In Scotland all pupils in education authority secondary schools attend schools with a comprehensive intake. Most of these schools provide a full range of courses appropriate to all levels of ability from first to sixth year.

In most areas of Northern Ireland there is a selective system of secondary education with pupils transferring either to grammar schools (40 per cent of pupils in 1995) or secondary schools (59.7 per cent of pupils in 1995) at 11–12 years of age. Parents can choose the school they would like their children to attend and all those who apply must be admitted if they meet the criteria. If a school is oversubscribed beyond its statutory admissions number, selection is on the basis of published criteria, which, for most grammar schools, place emphasis on performance in the transfer procedure tests which are set and administered by the Northern Ireland Council for the Curriculum, Examinations and Assessment. When parents consider that a school has not applied its criteria fairly they have access to independent appeals tribunals. Grammar schools provide an academic type of secondary education with A-levels at the end of the seventh year, while secondary non-grammar schools follow a curriculum suited to a wider range of aptitudes and abilities.

SPECIAL EDUCATION – Special education is provided for children with special educational needs, usually because they have a disability which either prevents or hinders them from making use of educational facilities of a kind generally provided for children of their age in schools within the area of the local authority concerned. Wherever possible, such children are educated in ordinary schools taking the parents' wishes into account, and schools are required to publish their policy for pupils with special educational needs. LEAs in England and Wales are required to identify and secure provision for the needs of children with learning difficulties, to involve the parents in any decision and draw up a formal statement of the child's special educational needs and how they intend to meet them, all within statutory time limits. Parents have a right to appeal to a Special Educational Needs (SEN) Tribunal if they disagree with the statement. A code of practice similar to that in England and Wales is to be introduced in

Northern Ireland. A SEN Tribunal will operate there from September 1997.

Maintained special schools are run by education authorities which pay all the costs of maintenance, but under the terms of Local Management of Schools (LMS), those able and wishing to manage their own budgets may choose to do so. These schools are also able to apply to become grant-maintained. Non-maintained special schools are run by voluntary bodies; they may receive some grant from central government for capital expenditure and for equipment but their current expenditure is met primarily from the fees charged to education authorities for pupils placed in the schools. Some independent schools provide education wholly or mainly for children with special educational needs and are required to meet similar standards to those for maintained and non-maintained special schools. It is intended that pupils with special education needs should have access to as much of the national curriculum as possible, but there is provision for them to be exempt from it or for it to be modified to suit their capabilities.

The number of full-time pupils with special needs in January 1995 was:

Special schools: total	112,300
England	95,300
Wales	3,300
Scotland	9,100
N. Ireland	4,600
Hospital schools: total	200
Public sector primary and secondary	
schools: total	134,300
England	112,800
Wales	10,900
Scotland	5,700
N. Ireland	3,200

In Scotland, school placing is a matter of agreement between education authorities and parents. Parents have the right to say which school they want their child to attend, and a right of appeal where their wishes are not being met. Whenever possible, children with special needs are integrated into ordinary schools. However, for those who require a different environment or specialized facilities, there are special schools, both grant-aided by central government and independent, and special classes within ordinary schools. Education authorities are required to respond to reasonable requests for independent special schools and to send children with special needs to schools outside Scotland if appropriate provision is not available within the country.

Alternative Provision

There is no legal obligation on parents in the UK to educate their children at school provided that the local education authority is satisfied that the child is receiving full-time education suited to its age, abilities and aptitudes. The education authority need not be informed that a child is being educated at home unless the child is already registered at a state school. In this case the parents must arrange for the child's name to be removed from the school's register (by writing to the headteacher) before education at home can begin. Failure to do so leaves the parents liable to prosecution for condoning non-attendance.

In most cases an initial visit is made by an education adviser or education welfare officer, and sometimes subsequent inspections are made, but practice varies according to the individual education authority. There is no requirement for parents educating their children at home to be in possession of a teaching qualification.

Information and support on all aspects of home education can be obtained from Education Otherwise (*see* page 449).

INDEPENDENT SCHOOLS

Independent schools receive no grants from public funds, but they can apply to the Secretaries of State for grant-maintained status within the public sector. They charge fees, and are owned and managed under special trusts, with profits being used for the benefit of the schools concerned. There is a wide variety of provision, from kindergartens to large day and boarding schools, and from experimental schools to traditional institutions. A number of independent schools have been instituted by religious and ethnic minorities.

All independent schools in the UK are open to inspection by approved inspectors (*see* page 432) and must register with the appropriate government education department. The education departments lay down certain minimum standards and can make schools remedy any unacceptable features of their building or instruction and exclude any unsuitable teacher or proprietor. Most independent schools offer a similar range of courses to state schools and enter pupils for the same public examinations. Introduction of the national curriculum and the associated education targets and assessment procedures is not obligatory in the independent sector.

The term public schools is often applied to those independent schools in membership of the Headmasters' and Headmistresses' Conference, the Governing Bodies Association or the Governing Bodies of Girls' Schools Association. Most public schools are single-sex but there are some mixed schools and an increasing number of schools have mixed sixth forms.

Preparatory schools are so-called because they prepare pupils for the common entrance examination to senior independent schools. Most cater for pupils from about seven to 13 years. The common entrance examination is set by the Common Entrance Examination Board, but marked by the independent school to which the pupil intends to go. It is taken at 13 by boys, and from 11 to 13 by girls.

The number of schools and pupils in 1994-5 was:

	No. of schools	No. of pupils	Pupil-teacher ratio
England	2,259	556,572	10.3
Wales	62	10,297	10.1
Scotland	116	32,600	10.2
N. Ireland	21	941	10.8

Most independent schools in Scotland follow the English examination system, i.e. GCSE followed by A-levels, although some take the Scottish Education Certificate at Standard grade followed by Highers or Advanced Highers.

Assisted Places Scheme

The Assisted Places Scheme enables children to attend independent secondary schools which their parents could not otherwise afford. The scheme provides help with tuition fees and other expenses, except boarding costs, on a sliding scale depending on the family's income. The proportion of pupils receiving full fee remission is about 46 per cent. In the 1996–7 academic year, 35,830 places were offered at the 372 participating schools in England and Wales. The 55 participating schools in Scotland admitted about 3,000 pupils on the scheme in 1995–6, which, unlike that in England and Wales, is cash-limited.

The proportion of pupils receiving full fee remission was about 47 per cent.

The scheme is administered and funded in England by the DFEE, in Wales by the Welsh Office, and in Scotland by the SOEID. The scheme does not operate in Northern Ireland as the independent sector admits non-fee-paying pupils. There is, however, a similar scheme known as the Talented Children's Scheme to help pupils gifted in music and dance.

Further information can be obtained from the Independent Schools Information Service (*see* page 449).

THE CURRICULUM

ENGLAND AND WALES

The national curriculum was introduced in primary and secondary schools between autumn 1989 and autumn 1996, for the period of compulsory schooling from five to 16. It is mandatory in all maintained schools. As originally proposed, it was widely criticized for being too prescriptive and time-consuming. Following revision in 1994 its requirements were substantially reduced; the revisions were implemented in August 1995 for key stages 1 to 3 and from August 1996 for key stage 4.

The statutory subjects at key stages 1 and 2 (5–11 year olds) are:

Core subjects	Foundation subjects
English	Design and technology
Welsh, for Welsh-speaking schools in Wales	Information technology
Mathematics	History
Science	Geography
	Welsh, in Wales
	Art
	Music
	PE

At key stage 3 (11- to 14-year olds) all pupils must study a modern foreign language. At key stage 4 (14- to 16-year olds) pupils are required to take GCSEs in the core subjects and at least a GCSE short course in a modern foreign language and design and technology (optional subjects in Wales); they must also continue to study, although they are not required to take examinations in, information technology and PE. Other foundation subjects are optional. Religious education must be taught across all key stages, following a locally agreed syllabus; parents have the right to remove their children if they wish.

National tests and tasks in English and mathematics at key stage 1, with the addition of science at key stages 2 and 3, are in place. Teachers make their own assessments of their pupils' progress to set alongside the test results. At key stage 4 the GCSE and vocational equivalents will be the main form of assessment.

For several years the DFEE and the Welsh Office have published tables showing pupils' performance in A-level, AS-level, GCSE and GNVQ examinations school by school. Similar tables showing the results of the 1996 tests and teacher assessments for 11-year-olds will be published for the first time in 1997. Approximately 700,000 pupils in each of the age groups take the tests each year in England and Wales.

In Wales in 1994–5 the Welsh language was in use as the main or secondary medium of instruction or taught as a second language in 98.4 per cent of primary schools. In secondary schools Welsh was taught as a first or second language in 96.6 per cent of schools. It constitutes a core subject of the national curriculum in schools in which Welsh is taught as a first language and a foundation subject in the others, although there is provision for exemptions to

be made; by September 1999 all pupils will be taught Welsh throughout the period of compulsory schooling. A two-year review of assessment arrangements for the national curriculum is taking place.

In England the School Curriculum and Assessment Authority (SCAA), an independent government agency funded by the DFEE, is responsible for advising the Secretary of State on the school curriculum and school tests and examinations. In Wales its functions are performed by the Curriculum and Assessment Authority for Wales (ACAC), funded by the Welsh Office.

SCOTLAND

The content and management of the curriculum in Scotland are not prescribed by statute but are the responsibility of education authorities and individual headteachers. Advice and guidance is provided by the SOEID and the Scottish Consultative Council on the Curriculum. SOEID has produced guidelines on the structure and balance of the curriculum for the 5–14 age group as well as for each of the curriculum areas. There are also guidelines on assessment across the whole curriculum, on reporting to parents, and on standardized national tests for English language and mathematics at five levels for this age group. A major programme to extend modern language teaching to primary schools is in progress. The curriculum for 14- to 16-year-olds includes study within each of eight modes: language and communication, mathematical studies, science, technology, social studies, creative activities, physical education, and religious and moral education. There is a recommended percentage of class time to be devoted to each area over the two years. Provision is made for teaching in Gaelic in Gaelic-speaking areas.

For 16- to 18-year-olds, there is available a modular system of vocational courses, certificated by the Scottish Vocational Education Council, in addition to academic courses and a new unified framework of courses and awards is to be introduced in 1998–9.

The Scottish Consultative Council on the Curriculum has responsibility for development and advisory work on the curriculum in Scottish schools.

NORTHERN IRELAND

A curriculum common to all grant-aided schools exists. Pupils are required to study religious education and, depending on which key stage they have reached, certain subjects from six broad areas of study: English, mathematics, science and technology; the environment and society; creative and expressive studies and, in key stages 3 and 4, language studies. The statutory curriculum requirements at key stages 1 to 3 have been revised and new programmes of study were introduced in September 1996. Six cross-curricular educational themes, which include information technology and education for mutual understanding, are woven through the main subjects of the curriculum. Irish is a foundation subject in schools that use it as a medium of instruction.

The assessment of pupils for all compulsory subjects, broadly in line with practice in England and Wales, will take place at the ages of eight, 11, 14 and 16. Statutory assessment will be introduced in 1996–7. The GCSE will be used to assess 16-year-olds.

The Northern Ireland Council for the Curriculum, Examinations and Assessment (NICCEA) monitors and advises the department and teachers on all matters relating to the curriculum, assessment arrangements and examinations in grant-aided schools in Northern Ireland. It conducts GCSE, A- and AS-level examinations, pupil assessment at key stages and administers the transfer procedure tests.

RECORDS OF ACHIEVEMENT

The National Record of Achievement (NRA) is being reviewed and will be relaunched in September 1997. It sets down the range of a school-leaver's achievements and activities both inside and outside the classroom, including those not tested by examination. It is issued to all those leaving school in England, Wales and Northern Ireland and its use is to be extended within further and higher education, training and employment. It is not compulsory in Scotland but is available to all education authorities for issue to school leavers. Parents in England and Wales must receive a written yearly progress report on all aspects of their child's achievements. There is a similar commitment for Northern Ireland. In Scotland the school report card gives parents information on their child's progress.

THE PUBLIC EXAMINATION SYSTEM

ENGLAND, WALES AND NORTHERN IRELAND

Until the end of 1987, secondary school pupils at the end of compulsory schooling around the age of 16, and others, took the General Certificate of Education (GCE) Ordinary-level or the Certificate of Secondary Education (CSE). From 1988 these were replaced by a single system of examinations, the General Certificate of Secondary Education (GCSE), which is usually taken after five years of secondary education. The GCSE is the main method of assessing the performance of pupils at age 16 in all national curriculum subjects required to be assessed at the end of compulsory schooling. The structure of the exam is being adapted in accordance with national curriculum requirements; new subject criteria were published in 1995 to govern GCSE syllabuses introduced in 1996 for first examination in 1998. From September 1996 GCSE short course qualifications in a wide range of subjects were introduced. As a rule the syllabus will take half the time of a GCSE course.

The GCSE differs from its predecessors in that there are syllabuses based on national criteria covering course objectives, content and assessment methods; differentiated assessment (i.e. different papers or questions for different ranges of ability); and grade-related criteria (i.e. grades awarded on absolute rather than relative performance). The GCSE certificates are awarded on a seven-point scale, A to G. From 1994 there has been an additional 'starred' A grade (A*), to recognize the achievement of the highest attainers at GCSE. Grades A to C are the equivalent of the corresponding O-level grades A to C or CSE grade 1. Grades D, E, F and G record achievement at least as high as that represented by CSE grades 2 to 5. All GCSE syllabuses, assessments and grading procedures are monitored by the School Curriculum and Assessment Authority (see page 436) to ensure that they conform to the national criteria

In the UK in 1993–4, 84 per cent of all 15-year-olds achieved one or more higher grade GCSE, SCE Standard grade, or equivalent results, 1.4 per cent fewer than in 1992-3.

In Wales the Certificate of Education is intended for 16-year-olds for whom no suitable examination exists. In 1995, 17,107 candidates took the examination, of whom 92.8 per cent obtained pass or better.

From 1991, many maintained schools have offered BTEC Firsts (see page 439) and an increasing number offer BTEC Nationals. National Vocational Qualifications in the form of General NVQs have been available to students in schools from 1992 (see page 440). The Part 1 GNVQ has been piloted from 1995. It is a two-year course available at foundation and intermediate levels, broadly equivalent to two GCSEs.

The General Diploma was introduced in 1995 for 16- to 18-year-olds achieving GCSE at grades A* to C in English, mathematics and science, plus two other GCSEs at the same grades or their vocational equivalent.

Advanced (A-level) examinations are taken by those who choose to continue their education after GCSE. A-level courses last two years and have traditionally provided the foundation for entry to higher education. A-levels are marked on a seven-point scale, from A to E, N (narrow failure) and U (unclassified), which latter grade will not be certificated.

Advanced Supplementary level (AS-level) examinations were introduced in 1987 as an alternative to, and to complement, A-level examinations. AS-levels are for full-time A-level students but are also open to other students. An AS-level syllabus covers not less than half the amount of ground covered by the corresponding A-level syllabus and, where possible, is related to it. An AS-level course lasts two years and requires not less than half the teaching time of the corresponding A-level course, and two AS-levels are equivalent to one A-level. AS-level passes are graded A to E, with grade standards related to the A-level grades.

In the UK in 1993–4, 190,000 school pupils (47 per cent boys, 53 per cent girls) achieved one or more passes at A-level or SCE H-grade, an increase of 1.6 per cent on the previous year. Of those in Great Britain who entered for at least one A-level, or at least two SCE H-grades, 44 per cent studied sciences (58 per cent boys, 42 per cent girls) and 56 per cent studied arts/social studies (41 per cent of boys, 59 per cent of girls).

Most examining boards allow the option of an additional paper of greater difficulty to be taken by A-level candidates to obtain what is known as a Special-level or Scholarship-level qualification. S-level papers are available in most of the traditional academic subjects and are marked on a three-point scale.

The City & Guilds Foundation Programmes at pre-16 and Diploma of Vocational Education at post-16 replaced the Certificate of Pre-Vocational Education (CPVE) at post-16 in schools and colleges from 1992. It is intended for a wide ability range, including pupils who might not go on to A-levels but would like to continue their education on completion of compulsory secondary schooling.

The Diploma of Vocational Education provides recognition of achievement at two levels: foundation and intermediate; the latter broadly corresponding to the GNVQ (see page 440) at intermediate and advanced levels. The intermediate level is being phased out in favour of the corresponding GNVQs. Within guidelines schools and colleges design their own courses, which stress activity-based learning, core skills which include application of number, communication and information technology, and work experience. The Diploma of Vocational Education is mainly for those who want to find out what aptitudes they may have and to prepare themselves for work, but who are not yet committed to a particular occupation. According to level, it can be taken alongside other courses such as GCSEs, A- or AS-levels. At foundation level it can provide a context for the introduction of GNVQ units into the key stage 4 curriculum.

SCOTLAND

Scotland has its own system of public examinations. At the end of the fourth year of secondary education, at about the age of 16, pupils take the Standard grade (which has replaced the Ordinary grade) of the Scottish Certificate of Education. Standard grade courses and examinations have been designed to suit every level of ability, with assessment against nationally determined standards of performance.

For most courses there are three separate examination papers at the end of the two-year Standard grade course. They are set at Credit (leading to awards at grade 1 or 2), General (leading to awards at grade 3 or 4) and Foundation (leading to awards at grade 5 or 6) levels. Grade 7 is available to those who, although they have completed the course, have shown no significant level of attainment. Normally pupils will take examinations covering two pairs of grades, either grades 1–4 or grades 3–6. Most candidates take seven or eight Standard grade examinations.

The Higher grade of the Scottish Certificate of Education is normally taken one year after Standard grade, at the age of 17 or thereabouts. It is common for pupils to be presented for four or more Higher grades at a single diet of the examination.

The Certificate of Sixth Year Studies (CSYS) is designed to give direction and purpose to sixth-year work by encouraging pupils who have completed their main subjects at Higher grade to study a maximum of three of these subjects in depth. Pupils may also use the sixth year to gain improved or additional Higher grades or Standard grades. A major programme of reform, 'Higher Still', is afoot which will draw all upper secondary qualifications into a single framework by 1998–9. There will be five levels of attainment, the first three corresponding to Standard grade levels, plus Higher and Advanced Higher (which will replace CSYS). Students will study individual units (of 40 or 80 hours) which will be internally assessed, and may combine these into courses (with external assessment) or group awards.

The examining body for the Scottish Certificate of Education and the Certificate of Sixth Year Studies is the Scottish Examination Board (SEB).

National Certificates provide an alternative to, and complement Highers and CSYS. They are awarded to pupils normally over the age of 16 who have successfully completed a programme of vocational courses based on modular study units, and the assessment system is based on national criteria. National Certificates are awarded by the Scottish Vocational Education Council (SCOTVEC) (*see also* page 440).

The Scottish Qualifications Authority (SQA) will take over the existing functions of SEB and SCOTVEC and will administer the new 'Higher Still' qualifications from April 1997.

THE INTERNATIONAL BACCALAUREATE

The International Baccalaureate is an internationally recognized two-year pre-university course and examination designed to facilitate the mobility of students and to promote international understanding. Candidates must offer one subject from each of six subject groups, at least three at higher level and the remainder at subsidiary level. Single subjects can be offered, for which a certificate is received. There are 34 schools and colleges in the UK which offer the International Baccalaureate diploma.

TEACHERS

ENGLAND AND WALES

Teachers are appointed by local education authorities, school governing bodies, or school managers. Those in publicly maintained schools must be approved as qualified by the Secretary of State. To become a qualified teacher it is necessary to have successfully completed a course of initial teacher training, usually either a Bachelor of Education (B.Ed.) degree or the Postgraduate Certificate of Education (PGCE) at an accredited institution, but a one-year course is being considered which will qualify certain non-graduates to teach at nursery and infant level.

With certain exceptions the profession at present has an all-graduate entry. Teachers in further education are not required to have qualified teacher status, though roughly half have a teaching qualification and most have industrial, commercial or professional experience. The new National Qualification for Headship (NQH) is to be piloted until July 1997 and will be introduced in September of that year.

Teacher training was formerly largely integrated with the rest of higher education, with training places concentrated in universities and institutes or colleges of education, but it has now become largely school-based, with student teachers on secondary PGCE courses spending two-thirds of their training in the classroom. Changes have also been made to primary phase teacher training to make it more school-based and to give schools a role in course design and delivery. Individual schools or consortia of schools and CTCs can bid for funds from the DFEE to carry out their own teacher training, including recruitment of students, subject to approval of their proposed training programme by the Teacher Training Agency (TTA) and monitoring and evaluation by the Office for Standards in Education (OFSTED). Funds are given to schools to meet the costs of designing and delivering the courses, and students receive flat-rate bursaries.

The Teacher Training Agency began operations in September 1994. The TTA accredits institutions in England providing initial teacher training for school teachers which meet both criteria published by the Secretary of State and appropriate quality standards. The TTA funds all types of teacher training in England, whether run by universities, colleges or schools, and some educational research. It has responsibility for the Licensed Teacher Scheme, which is designed to attract into the teaching profession entrants over 24 years of age without formal teaching qualifications but with relevant training and experience; licensees undertake a two-year training programme devised by the school which appoints them.

The Higher Funding Council for Wales exercises similar functions in respect of Wales. The TTA also acts as a central source of information and advice for both England and Wales about entry to teaching, and has responsibilities relating to the continuing professional development of teachers.

The Specialist Teacher Assistant (STA) scheme was introduced in September 1994 to provide trained support to qualified teachers in the teaching of reading, writing and arithmetic to young pupils.

SCOTLAND

All teachers in maintained schools must be registered with the General Teaching Council for Scotland. They are registered provisionally for a two-year probationary period which can be extended if necessary. Only graduates are accepted as entrants to the profession; primary school teachers undertake either a four-year vocational degree course or a one-year postgraduate course, while teachers of academic subjects in secondary school undertake the latter. As a result of a review of initial teacher training instituted in 1992 a greater proportion of training is now classroom-based. The colleges of education provide both in-service and pre-service training for teachers and are funded by the Scottish Higher Education Funding Council.

NORTHERN IRELAND

Teacher training in Northern Ireland is provided by the two universities and two colleges of education. The colleges are concerned with teacher education mainly for the primary school sector. They also provide B.Ed. courses for intending secondary school teachers of religious education, commercial studies, and craft, design and technology. With these exceptions, the training of teachers for secondary schools is provided in the education departments of the universities. A professional qualification is not mandatory to teach in secondary schools. A review of primary and secondary teacher training has taken place as a result of which from 1996–7 all student teachers will spend more time in the classroom. The current probationary year is to be replaced by a two-year induction period by 1996–7.

ACCREDITATION OF TRAINING INSTITUTIONS

Advice to central government on the accreditation, content and quality of initial teacher training courses is given in England by the TTA, in Wales by the HEFCW and in Northern Ireland by validating bodies. These bodies also monitor and disseminate good practice, assisted in Northern Ireland by the Teacher Education Committee.

In Scotland all training courses in colleges of education must be approved by the SOEID and a validating body.

NEWLY-TRAINED TEACHERS

Of teachers who in 1994 had successfully completed initial training courses in the UK, 17,400 had completed a postgraduate course and 10,000 a course for non-graduates.

Because of a shortage of teachers in certain secondary subjects, from 1996-7 providers of initial teacher training will be able to apply for funds from the TTA to provide enhanced courses, and scholarships and bursaries to attract trainee teachers onto one- or two-year full-time courses in priority subjects. The subjects are: science; mathematics; modern languages (including Welsh in Wales); design and technology; information technology, and religious education.

SERVING TEACHERS 1993-4 *(full-time and full-time equivalent)*

Public sector schools	452,000
Primary	212,000
Secondary	223,000
Special	17,000
FE and HE establishments	145,380
Universities	32,000
TOTAL	629,380

SALARIES

Qualified teachers in England, Wales and Northern Ireland, other than heads and deputy heads, are paid on an 18-point scale. Entry points and placement depend on qualifications, experience, responsibilities, excellence, and recruitment and retention factors as calculated by the relevant body, i.e. the governing body or the LEA. There is a statutory superannuation scheme in maintained schools.

Teachers in Scotland are paid on a ten-point scale. The entry point depends on type of qualification, and additional allowances are payable under certain circumstances.

Salaries from 1 April 1996

	England, Wales and N. Ireland	Scotland
Head	£25,371–£55,566	£26,376–£48,858
Deputy head	£24,564–£40,407	£26,376–£36,558
Teacher	£12,462–£33,375	£12,510–£20,796

FURTHER EDUCATION

The Education Reform Act 1988 defines further education as all provision outside schools to people aged over 16 of education up to and including A-level and its equivalent. The Further Education Funding Councils for England and Wales, the Scottish Office Education and Industry Department and the Education and Library Boards in Northern Ireland have a duty to secure provision of adequate facilities for further education in their areas.

ENGLAND AND WALES

Further education and sixth form colleges are funded directly by central government through the Further Education Funding Council for England (FEFCE) and the Further Education Funding Council for Wales (FEFCW). These councils are also responsible for the assessment of quality, in which the Councils' inspectorates play a key role. The colleges are controlled by autonomous further education corporations, which include substantial representation from industry and commerce, and which own their own assets and employ their own staff. Their funding is determined in part by the number of students enrolled.

In England and Wales further education courses are taught at a variety of institutions. These include universities which were formerly polytechnics, colleges of higher education, colleges of further education (some of which also offer higher education courses), and tertiary colleges and sixth form colleges, which concentrate on the provision of normal sixth form school courses as well as a range of vocational courses. A number of institutions specific to a particular form of training, e.g. the Royal College of Music, are also involved.

Teaching staff in further education establishments are not necessarily required to have teaching qualifications although many do so, but they are subject to regular appraisal of teaching performance.

Further education tends to be broadly vocational in purpose and employers are often involved in designing courses. It ranges from lower-level technical and commercial courses through courses for those aiming at higher-level posts in industry, commerce and administration, to professional courses. Facilities for GCSE courses, the Diploma of Vocational Education, AS-levels and A-level courses are also provided (*see* pages 437–8). These courses can form the foundation for progress to higher education qualifications.

The main courses and examinations in the vocational field, all of which link with the National Vocational Qualification (NVQ) framework (*see* below), are offered by the following bodies, but there are also many others:

The Business and Technology Education Council (BTEC) and London Examinations have merged to form the Edexcel Foundation. Edexcel courses and qualifications will continue to be known by their original names. They provide programmes of study across a wide range of subject areas. The main qualifications are the BTEC First Certificate and the BTEC First Diploma; the BTEC National Certificate and the BTEC National Diploma; the BTEC Higher National Diploma; BTEC NVQs; and BTEC foundation, intermediate and advanced GNVQs in some vocational areas. BTEC First and National diplomas will be phased out gradually as GNVQs are introduced.

City & Guilds specializes in developing qualifications and assessments for work-related, general education and leisure qualifications. It awards nationally recognized certificates in over 500 subjects, many of which are NVQs, SVQs and GNVQs. Its progressive structure of awards spans seven levels, from foundation to the highest level of professional competence.

RSA Examinations Board schemes cover a wide range of vocational qualifications, including accounting, business administration, customer service, management, language schemes, information technology and teaching qualifications. A wide range of NVQs and GNVQs are offered and a policy operates of credit accumulation, so that candidates can take a single unit or complete qualifications.

There are 589 further education establishments and sixth form colleges in England and Wales and 4,390 adult education centres. In 1994–5 there were 702,200 full-time and sandwich-course students and 1,369,384 part-time students on further education courses.

SCOTLAND

Further education comprises non-advanced courses up to SCE Highers grade, GCE A-level and SCOTVEC vocational courses. Further education colleges are currently funded by central government but a further education funding council is proposed at a later stage. Courses are taught mainly at colleges of further education, including technical colleges, and in some schools.

Further education colleges are incorporated bodies, with boards of management which run them and employ staff. The boards include the principal and staff and student representatives among their ten to 16 members, and at least half the members must have experience of commerce, industry or the practice of a profession.

The Scottish Vocational Education Council (SCOTVEC) awards qualifications for most occupations. It awards at non-advanced level the National Certificate which is available in over 3,000 individual modules and covers the whole range of non-advanced further education provision in Scotland. Students may study for the National Certificate on a full-time, part-time, open learning or work-based learning basis. National Certificate modules can be taken in further education colleges, secondary schools and other centres, normally from the age of 16 onwards. SCOTVEC also offers modular advanced-level HNC/HND qualifications and a few post-graduate or post-experience qualifications which are available in further education colleges and higher education institutions. SCOTVEC accredits and awards Scottish Vocational Qualifications (SVQs) which are analogous with the system of NVQs which operates in the rest of the UK. SVQs are essentially work-based but are also available in further education colleges and other centres.

The Record of Education and Training (RET) has been introduced to provide a single certificate recording SCOTVEC achievements; an updated version is provided as and when necessary. SCOTVEC also administers the National Record of Achievement in Scotland on behalf of the Scottish Office.

In 1993–4 there were 40,654 full-time and sandwich-course students and 80,051 part-time students on non-advanced vocational courses of further education in the 43 further education colleges and five colleges of education.

NORTHERN IRELAND

The Education and Library Boards currently plan the further education provision to be made by colleges under their management subject to approval by the Department of Education for Northern Ireland. From August 1997 all colleges will become free-standing corporate bodies and the planning will transfer to DENI, which will also fund the colleges directly.

Financial powers and responsibilities are delegated to the boards of governors of the colleges. The boards must include at least 50 per cent membership from the professions, local business or industry, or other fields of employment relevant to the activities of the college.

On reaching school-leaving age, pupils may attend colleges of further education to pursue the same type of vocational courses as are provided in colleges in England and Wales, administered by the same examining bodies.

In 1995–6 Northern Ireland had 17 institutions of further education, and there were 21,096 full-time students and 51,885 part-time students on non-advanced vocational courses of further education.

COURSE INFORMATION

Applications for further education courses are generally made directly to the colleges concerned. Information on further education courses in the UK and addresses of colleges can be found in the *Directory of Further Education* published annually by the Careers Research and Advisory Centre.

NATIONAL VOCATIONAL QUALIFICATIONS

The National Council for Vocational Qualifications (NCVQ) was set up by the Government in 1986 to achieve a coherent national framework for vocational qualifications in England, Wales and Northern Ireland. The Council does not award qualifications but accredits National Vocational Qualifications (NVQs), General National Vocational Qualifications (GNVQs) and core skills. Candidates are assessed through awarding bodies who bestow the qualifications where candidates reach the required standards. SCOTVEC (*see* above) performs similar functions in Scotland, but its role includes the awarding of qualifications.

From September 1992 General National Vocational Qualifications (GNVQs) were introduced into colleges and schools as a vocational alternative to academic qualifications. They cover broad categories in the NVQ framework and are aimed at those wishing to familiarize themselves with a range of opportunities. Advanced GNVQ or the vocational A-level is designed to be equivalent to two A-levels; intermediate is equivalent to four or five good GCSEs. Foundation GNVQs became available in September 1994.

HIGHER EDUCATION

The term higher education is used to describe education above A-level, Advanced Higher grade and their equivalent, which is provided in universities and colleges of higher education and in some further education colleges.

The Further and Higher Education Act 1992 and parallel legislation in Scotland removed the distinction between higher education provided by the universities, which were funded by the Universities Funding Council (UFC), and that provided in England and Wales by the former polytechnics and colleges of higher education, funded by the Polytechnics and Colleges Funding Council (PCFC), and in Scotland by the former central institutions and other institutions funded by central government. All are now funded by the Higher Education Funding Councils for England, Wales and Scotland. Other provisions brought the non-university sector in line with the universities, allowing all polytechnics, and other higher education institutions which satisfy the necessary criteria, to award their own taught course and research degrees and to adopt the title of university. All the polytechnics and other colleges have since adopted the title of university. The change of name does not affect the legal constitution of the institutions.

The number of students in higher eduction in the UK in 1994-5 was:

	Universities	Other	Total
Full-time, sandwich	814,000	206,000	1,420,000
% female	48%	51%	
Part-time	525,000	162,000	687,000
% female	24%	49%	
Overseas	114,400	9,700	124,100
TOTAL	1,453,400	377,700	1,831,100

The proportion of 16- to 20-year-olds entering full-time higher education in Great Britain rose from 12.2 per cent in 1985–6 to 25.6 per cent in 1994–5. The number of mature entrants (those aged 21 and over when starting an undergraduate course and 25 and over when starting a postgraduate course) to higher education in Great Britain in 1995 (excluding those at the Open University) was 459,000. The number of full-time and part-time students on science courses in 1994–5 was 365,600, of whom 21.5 per cent were female.

UNIVERSITIES AND COLLEGES

The universities are self-governing institutions established by royal charter or Act of Parliament. They have academic freedom and are responsible for their own academic appointments, curricula and student admissions and award their own degrees.

Responsibility for universities in England rests with the Secretary of State for Education and Employment, and in their territories with the Secretaries of State for Scotland, Wales and Northern Ireland. Advice to the Government on matters relating to the universities is provided by the Higher Education Funding Councils for England, Wales and Scotland, and by the Northern Ireland Higher Education Council. The HEFCs receive a block grant from central government which they allocate to the universities and colleges. The grant is allocated directly by central government in Northern Ireland.

There are now 88 universities in the UK, where only 47 existed prior to the Further and Higher Education Acts 1992. Of the 88, 71 are in England (including one federal university), two (one a federal institution) in Wales, 13 in Scotland and two in Northern Ireland.

The pre-1992 universities each have their own system of internal government but broad similarities exist. Most are run by two main bodies: the senate, which deals primarily with academic issues and consists of members elected from within the university; and the council, which is the supreme body and is responsible for all appointments and promotions, and bidding for and allocation of financial resources. At least half the members of the council are drawn from outside the university. Joint committees of senate and council are becoming increasingly common.

Those universities which were formerly polytechnics (38) or other higher education institutions (3) and the colleges of higher education (47) are run by higher education corporations (HECs), which are controlled by boards of governors whose members were initially appointed by the Secretaries of State but which will subsequently make their own appointments. At least half the members of each board must be drawn from industry, business, commerce and the professions.

In 1994-5 full-time student enrolments in England and Wales were:

	Universities	Other
England		
Undergraduates	660,200	146,800
% overseas	10%	4%
Postgraduates	95,800	9,600
% overseas	34%	14.5%
Wales		
Undergraduates	39,500	16,600
% overseas	11.4%	6%
Postgraduates	5,900	700
% overseas	30.5%	0%

Higher education courses funded by the respective HEFCs are also taught in some further education colleges in England and Wales. In England in 1994-5 there were over 36,000 students (8 per cent of total higher education student numbers) on such courses and 564 (0.72 per cent of higher education student numbers) in Wales.

The non-residential Open University provides courses nationally leading to degrees. Teaching is through a combination of television and radio programmes, correspondence, tutorials, short residential courses and local audio-visual centres. No qualifications are needed for entry. The Open University offers a modular programme of undergraduate courses by credit accumulation and post-experience and postgraduate courses, including a programme of higher degrees which comprises B.Phil., M.Phil. and Ph.D. through research, and MA, MBA and M.Sc. through taught courses. The Open University throughout the UK is funded by the Higher Education Funding Council for England. Its recurrent grant for 1994-5 was £110.8 million. In 1996, about 97,000 undergraduates were registered at the Open University, of whom about 50 per cent were women. Estimated cost (1996) of a six-credit degree was around £3,200 including course fees of £1,800.

The independent University of Buckingham provides a two-year course leading to a bachelor's degree and its tuition fees were £9,460 for 1996. It receives no capital or recurrent income from the Government but its students are eligible for mandatory awards from local education authorities. Its academic year consists of four terms of ten weeks each.

ACADEMIC STAFF

Each university and college appoints its own academic staff on its own conditions. However, there is a common salary structure and, except for Oxford and Cambridge, a common career structure in those universities formerly funded by the UFC and a common salary structure for the former PCFC sector. The Universities and Colleges Employers Association (UCEA) acts as a pay agency for universities and colleges.

Teaching staff in higher education require no formal teaching qualification, but teacher trainers are required to spend a certain amount of time in schools to ensure that they have sufficient recent practical experience.

In 1994–5, there were 70,439 full-time and part-time teaching and research staff in institutions of higher education in the UK.

Salary scales for staff in the former UFC sector differ from those in the former polytechnics and colleges; it is hoped eventually to amalgamate them. The 1995–6 salary scales for non-clinical academic staff in universities formerly funded by the UFC are:

Professor from	£31,999
Senior lecturer	£27,747–£31,357
Lecturer grade B	£20,677–£26,430
Lecturer grade A	£15,154–£19,848

The salaries of clinical academic staff are kept broadly comparable to those of doctors and dentists in the National Health Service.

Salary scales for lecturers in the former polytechnics, now universities, and colleges of higher education in England, Wales and Northern Ireland are (September 1995):

Head of Department	from £26,304
Principal lecturer	£25,474–£32,030
Senior lecturer	£20,381–£26,931
Lecturer	£13,100–£21,838

The salary scales for staff in Scotland are (April 1995):

Head of department/professor	from £32,058
Senior lecturer	£24,044–£31,081
Lecturer	£14,607–£26,216

FINANCE

Although universities and colleges are expected to look to a wider range of funding sources than before, and to generate additional revenue in collaboration with industry, they are still largely financed, directly or indirectly, from government resources.

In 1994–5 the total income of institutions of higher education in the UK was £10 million (£9.4 million in 1993–4). Grants from the funding councils amounted to £4.4 million (£3.5 million in 1993–4), forming 43.6 per cent of total income (37 per cent in 1993-4). Income from research grants and contracts was £1.4 million, an increase of 0.1 per cent on the previous year.

In the academic year 1994–5 the HEFCs' recurrent grant to institutions outside their sector and to LEAs for the provision of higher education courses was £79.4 million.

COURSES

In the UK all universities, including the Open University, and some colleges award their own degrees and other qualifications and can act as awarding and validating bodies for neighbouring colleges which are not yet accredited. The Higher Education Quality Council (HEQC), funded by institutional contributions, advises the Secretaries of State on applications for degree-awarding powers.

Higher education courses last full-time for at least four weeks or, if part-time, involve more than 60 hours of instruction. Facilities exist for full-time and part-time study, day release, sandwich or block release. Credit accumulation and transfer (CATS) is a system of study which is becoming widely available. It allows a student to achieve a final qualification by accumulating credits for courses of study successfully achieved, or even professional experience, over a period. Credit transfer information and values are carried on an electronic database called ECCTIS 2000, which is available in most careers offices and many schools and colleges.

Higher education courses include: first degree and postgraduate (including research); Diploma in Higher Education (Dip.HE); Higher National Diploma (HND) and Higher National Certificate (HNC); and preparation for professional examinations. The in-service training of teachers is also included, but from September 1994 has been funded in England by the TTA (*see* page 438), not the HEFC.

The Diploma of Higher Education (Dip.HE) is a two-year diploma usually intended to serve as a stepping-stone to a degree course or other further study. The Dip.HE is awarded by the institution itself if it is accredited; by an accredited institution of its choice if not. The BTEC Higher National Certificate (HNC) is awarded after two years part-time study. The BTEC Higher National Diploma (HND) is awarded after two years full-time, or three years sandwich-course or part-time study.

With the exception of certain Scottish universities where master is sometimes used for a first degree in arts subjects, undergraduate courses lead to the title of Bachelor, Bachelor of Arts (BA) and Bachelor of Science (B.Sc.) being the most common. For a higher degree the titles are: Master of Arts (MA), Master of Science (M.Sc.) (usually taught courses) and the research degrees of Master of Philosophy (M Phil) and Doctor of Philosophy (Ph.D. or, at a few universities, D.Phil.).

Most undergraduate courses at British universities and colleges of higher education run for three years, except in Scotland and at the University of Keele where they may take four years. Professional courses in subjects such as medicine, dentistry and veterinary science take longer. Details of courses on offer and of predicted entry requirements for the following year's intake are provided in *University and College Entrance: Official Guide*, published annually by the Universities and Colleges Admissions Service (UCAS), which includes degree, Dip.HE and HND courses at all universities (excluding the Open University) and most colleges of HE (for address, *see* page 451.

Postgraduate studies vary in length. Taught courses which lead to certificates, diplomas or master's degrees usually take one year full-time or two years part-time. Research degrees take from two to three years full-time and much longer if completed on a part-time basis. Details of taught courses and research degree opportunities can be found in *Graduate Studies*, published annually for the Careers Research and Advisory Centre (CRAC) by Hobsons Publishing plc (for address, *see* page 451).

Post-experience short courses are forming an increasing part of higher education provision, reflecting the need to update professional and technical training. Most of these courses fund themselves.

ADMISSIONS

The target number of students entering higher education has been set at 30 per cent of the 18- to 19-year-old age group. Apart from quotas for medical, dental and veterinary students, there are no limits set for other subjects and the individual university or college decides which students to accept. The formal entry requirements to most degree courses are two A-levels at grade E or above (or equivalent), and to HND courses one A-level (or equivalent). In practice, most offers of places require qualifications in excess of this, higher requirements usually reflecting the popularity of a course. These requirements do not, however, exclude applications from students with a variety of non-GCSE qualifications or unquantified experience and skills.

For admission to a degree, Dip.HE or HND, potential students apply through a central clearing house. All universities and most colleges providing higher education courses in the UK are members of the Universities and Colleges Admission Service (UCAS). Applicants are supplied with an application form and a *UCAS Handbook*, available from schools, colleges and careers offices or direct from UCAS, and may apply to a maximum of eight institutions/courses on the UCAS form. The only exception among universities is the Open University, which conducts its own admissions.

Applications for undergraduate teacher training courses are made through UCAS. Details of initial teacher training courses in Scotland can be obtained from colleges of education and those universities offering such courses, and from the Committee of Scottish Higher Education Principals (COSHEP).

For admission as a postgraduate student, universities and colleges normally require a good first degree in a subject related to the proposed course of study or research, but other experience and qualifications will be considered on merit. Most applications are made to individual institutions but there are two clearing houses of relevance. Postgraduate teacher training courses in England and Wales utilize the Graduate Teacher Training Registry (*see* page 451). Applications to postgraduate teacher training courses in Scotland are made through the Teacher Education Admissions Clearing House (TEACH) (*see* page 451). Applications for PGCE courses at institutions in Northern Ireland are made to the Department of Education for Northern Ireland. For social work the Social Work Admissions System operates (*see* page 451).

SCOTLAND

The Scottish Higher Education Funding Council (SHEFC) funds 21 institutions of higher education, including 13 universities. The universities are broadly managed as described above and each institution of higher education is managed by an independent governing body which includes representatives of industrial, commercial, professional and educational interests. Most of the courses outside the universities have a vocational orientation and a substantial number are sandwich courses.

Full-time higher education student enrolments in 1994–5 were:

	Universities	Other
Undergraduates	91,100	36,200
% overseas	8.2%	2.2%
Postgraduates	12,300	1,900
% overseas	48.2%	10.5%

There were 29,098 students on higher education courses in further education colleges, 21 per cent of total higher education students.

NORTHERN IRELAND

In Northern Ireland advanced courses are provided by 17 institutions of further education and by the two universities. As well as offering first and postgraduate degrees, the University of Ulster offers courses leading to the BTEC Higher National Diploma and professional qualifications. Applications to undertake courses of higher education other than degree courses are made to the institutions direct. Full-time higher education student enrolments in 1994–5 were:

	Universities	Other
Undergraduates	21,000	3,600
% overseas	16.6%	9%
Postgraduates	2,700	600
% overseas	7.4%	0%

There were 6,832 students enrolled on advanced courses of higher education in the institutions of further education, 25 per cent of higher education student numbers.

FEES

The tuition fees for students with mandatory awards (*see* below) are paid by the grant-awarding body. Students from member states of the European Union pay fees at home student rates. Since 1980–1 students from outside the EU have paid fees that are meant to cover the cost of their education, but financial help is available under a number of schemes. Information about these schemes is available from British Council offices world-wide.

Universities and colleges are free to set their own charges for students from non-EU countries. Undergraduate fees for the academic year 1996–7 for home and EU students are £750 for arts courses (band 1), £1,600 for laboratory or workshop based courses, mainly science (band 2), and £2,800 for clinical courses (band 3).

For postgraduate students, the maximum tuition fee that will be reimbursed through the awards system is £2,490 in 1996–7.

GRANTS FOR STUDENTS

Students in the UK who plan to take a full-time or sandwich course of further study after leaving school may be eligible for a grant. A parental contribution is deductible on a sliding scale dependent on income. For married students this may be deducted from their spouse's income instead. However, parental contribution is not deducted from the grant to students over 25 years of age who have been self-supporting for at least three years. The main rates of mandatory grant have been frozen since 1991–2 as it is envisaged that students will increasingly support themselves by loans. Tuition fees are paid in full for all students in receipt of a grant, regardless of parental income, and they are usually paid direct to the university or college by the education authority.

Grants are paid by local education authorities in England, Wales and Northern Ireland, of which 100 per cent of the cost is reimbursed by central government, and by the SOEID in Scotland through the Students Award Agency. Applications are made to the authority in the area in which the student normally lives. Applications should not, however, be made earlier than the January preceding the start of the course.

TYPES OF GRANT

Grants are of two kinds: mandatory and discretionary. Mandatory grants are those which awarding authorities must pay to students who are attending designated courses and who can satisfy certain other conditions. Such a grant is awarded normally to enable the student to attend only one designated course and there is no general entitlement to an award for any particular number of years. Discretionary grants are those for which each awarding authority has discretion to decide its own policy.

Designated courses are those full-time or sandwich courses leading to: a degree; the Diploma of Higher Education; the BTEC Higher National Diploma; initial teacher-training courses, including those for the postgraduate certificate of education and the art teachers' certificate or diploma; a university certificate or diploma course lasting at least three years; other qualifications which are specifically designated as being comparable to first degree courses; and the SCOTVEC Higher National Diploma. The local education authority should be consulted for advice about eligibility for a grant.

A means-tested maintenance grant, usually paid once a term, covers periods of attendance during term as well as the Christmas and Easter vacations, but not the summer vacation. The basic grant rates for 1996–7 are:

Living in	Grant	Grant to Scottish students
College/lodgings in London area	2,105	2,035
College/lodgings outside London area	1,710	1,645
Parental home	1,400	1,260

Additional allowances are available if, for example, the course requires a period of study abroad.

LEA and SOEID expenditure on student fees and maintenance in 1994–5 was £2,926.8 million; 923,465 mandatory awards were made.

STUDENT LOANS

The Education (Student Loans) Act 1990 legislated for interest-free but indexed top-up loans of up to £2,035 in 1996–7 to be made available to eligible students in the UK. The Government expects that at least £766.7 million will be taken up in loans in 1996–7.

Students apply direct to the Student Loans Company Ltd (see page 451), which will require a certificate of eligibility from their place of study. Loans are available to students on designated courses within the scope of mandatory awards and the same residency conditions apply. Repayment is normally over five to seven years, although it can be deferred if income is at or below 85 per cent of national average earnings (about £14,500 a year). From the 1997-8 academic year private financial institutions will receive subsidies to allow them to offer loans on the same terms as the Student Loans Company.

ACCESS FUNDS

Access funds are allocated by education departments to the appropriate funding councils in England, Wales and Scotland and administered by further and higher education institutions. In Northern Ireland they are allocated by central government to the institutions direct. They are available to students whose access to higher education might otherwise be inhibited by financial considerations or where real financial difficulties are faced. For the academic year 1996–7, provision in the UK will be £28.9 million.

POSTGRADUATE AWARDS

Unlike funding for undergraduates, which is mandatory for most degree and equivalent level courses, grants for postgraduate study are usually discretionary. Grants are also often dependent on the class of first degree, especially for research degrees.

An increasing number of scholarships are available from research charities, endowments, and particular industries or companies. For residents in England and Wales, several schemes of postgraduate bursaries or studentships are funded by the DFEE, the government research councils, the Ministry of Agriculture, Fisheries and Food, and the British Academy, which awards grants for study in the humanities.

In Scotland postgraduate funding is provided by the SOEID, the Scottish Office Agriculture and Fisheries Department, and the research councils as in England and Wales.

Awards in Northern Ireland are made by the DENI, the Department of Agriculture for Northern Ireland, and the Medical Research Council.

In the UK in 1993–4, 21,400 awards were made. The national rates in 1996–7 are:

Living in	12-month scholarship	30-week bursary
College/lodgings in London area	5,845	3,460
College/lodgings outside London area	4,645	2,735
Parental home	3,420	2,065

ADULT AND CONTINUING EDUCATION

The term adult education covers a broad spectrum of educational activities ranging from non-vocational courses of general interest, through the acquiring of special vocational skills needed in industry or commerce, to study for a degree at the Open University.

The responsibility for securing adult and continuing education in England and Wales is statutory and shared between the Further Education Funding Councils, which are responsible for and fund those courses which take place in their sector and lead to academic and vocational qualifications, prepare students to undertake further or higher education courses, or confer basic skills; the Higher Education Funding Councils, which fund advanced courses of continuing education; and LEAs, which are responsible for those courses which do not fall within the remit of the funding councils. Funding in Northern Ireland is through the education and library boards and in Scotland by the Scottish Office Education and Industry Department.

PROVIDERS

Courses specifically for adults are provided by many bodies. They include, in the statutory sector: local education authorities in England and Wales; in Scotland the education authorities and the SOEID; education and library boards in Northern Ireland; further education colleges; higher education colleges; universities, especially the Open University and Birkbeck College of the University of London; residential colleges; the BBC, independent television and local radio stations. There are also a number of voluntary bodies.

The LEAs in England and Wales operate through 'area' adult education centres (4,390 in 1995), institutes or colleges, and the adult studies departments of colleges of further education. The SOEID funds adult education, including that provided by the universities and the Workers' Educational Association, at vocational further education colleges (47 in 1995) and evening centres (162 in 1995). In addition, SOEID provides grants to a number of voluntary organizations. Provision in the statutory sector in Northern Ireland is the responsibility of the universities and the education and library boards, which operate 17 further education colleges and a number of community schools.

The involvement of universities in adult education and continuing education has diversified considerably and is supported by a variety of administrative structures ranging from dedicated departments to a devolved approach. Birkbeck College in the University of London caters solely for part-time students. Those institutions and colleges formerly in the PCFC sector in England and Wales, because of their range of courses and flexible patterns of student attendance, provide opportunities in the field of adult and continuing education. The Forum for the Advancement of Continuing Education (FACE) promotes collaboration between institutions of higher education active in this area. The Open University, in partnership with the BBC, provides distance teaching leading to first degrees, and also offers post-experience and higher degree courses (*see* page 459).

Of the voluntary bodies, the biggest is the Workers' Educational Association (WEA) which operates throughout the UK, reaching about 150,000 adult students annually. The FEFC for England, the SOEID, and LEAs make grants towards provision.

The National Institute of Adult Continuing Education (England and Wales) (NIACE) provides information and advice to organizations and providers on all aspects of adult continuing education. NIACE conducts research, project and development work, and is funded by the DFEE, the LEAs and other funding bodies. The Welsh committee, NIACE Cymru, receives financial support from the Welsh Office, support in kind from the Welsh Joint Education Committee, and advises government, voluntary bodies and education providers on adult continuing education and training matters in Wales. In Scotland advice on adult and community education, and promotion thereof, is provided by the Scottish Community Education Council. The Northern Ireland Council for Adult Education has an advisory role. Its membership includes representatives of the education and library boards and of most organizations involved in the field, together with an assessor appointed by DENI.

Membership of the Universities Association for Continuing Education is open to any university or university college in the UK. It promotes university continuing education, facilitates the interchange of information, and supports research and development work in continuing education.

Courses

Although lengths vary, most courses are part-time. Long-term residential colleges in England and Wales are grant-aided by the FEFCs and provide full-time courses lasting one or two years. Some colleges and centres offer short-term residential courses, lasting from a few days to a few weeks, in a wide range of subjects. Local education authorities directly sponsor many of the colleges, while others are sponsored by universities or voluntary organizations. A directory of learning holidays, *Time to Learn*, is published by NIACE.

Grants

Although full-time courses at degree level attract mandatory awards, for courses below that level all students over the age of 19 must pay a fee. However, discretionary grants may be available. Adult education bursaries for students at the long-term residential colleges of adult education are the responsibility of the colleges themselves. The awards are administered for the colleges by the Awards Officer of the Residential Colleges Committee for students resident in England and are funded by the FEFC for England in English colleges; for colleges in Wales they are funded and administered by the FEFC for Wales; and for colleges in Scotland and Northern Ireland they are funded by central government and administered by the education authorities. A booklet, *Adult Education Bursaries,* can be obtained from the Awards Officer, Adult Education Bursaries, c/o Ruskin College (*see* page 461).

Numbers

There are no comprehensive statistics covering all aspects of adult education. However, enrolments on evening courses in the UK numbered 1,480,000 in 1994–5 (65.8 per cent women). This number included 722,000 students at adult education centres.

Education Directory

LOCAL EDUCATION AUTHORITIES

ENGLAND

County Councils

BEDFORDSHIRE, County Hall, Cauldwell Street, Bedford MK42 9AP. Tel: 01234-363222. *Director*, D. G. Wadsworth

BERKSHIRE, PO Box 902, Shire Hall, Shinfield Park, Reading RG2 9XE. Tel: 0118-923 3652. *Chief Education Officer*, S. R. Goodchild

BUCKINGHAMSHIRE, County Hall, Aylesbury HP20 1UA. Tel: 01296-382641. *Director*, D. McGahey

CAMBRIDGESHIRE, Castle Court, Shire Hall, Cambridge CB3 0AP. Tel: 01223-317990. *Director*, A. Baxter

CHESHIRE, County Hall, Chester CHI 1SQ. Tel: 01244-602306. *Director*, D. Cracknell

CORNWALL, County Hall, Truro TRI 3AY. Tel: 01872-322000. *Secretary for Education*, J. Harris

CUMBRIA, 5 Portland Square, Carlisle CAI IPU. Tel: 01228-606060. *Director*, J. Nellist

DERBYSHIRE, County Hall, Matlock DE4 3AG. Tel: 01629-580000. *Chief Education Officer*, Ms V. Hannon

DEVON, County Hall, Topsham Road, Exeter EX2 4QG. Tel: 01392-382039. *Chief Education Officer*, S. W. Jenkin

DORSET, County Hall, Colliton Park, Dorchester DTI IXJ. Tel: 01305-224166. *Director*, R. H. Ely

DURHAM, County Hall, Durham DHI 5UJ. Tel: 0191-386 4411. *Director*, K. Mitchell

EAST SUSSEX, PO Box 4, County Hall, St Anne's Crescent, Lewes BN7 1SG. Tel: 01273-481000. *Director*, D. Mallen

ESSEX, PO Box 47, A Block, County Hall, Victoria Road South, Chelmsford CMI ILD. Tel: 01245-492211. *Director*, P. A. Lincoln

GLOUCESTERSHIRE, Shire Hall, Gloucester GLI 2TP. Tel: 01452-425302. *Chief Education Officer*, K. D. Anderson, CBE

HAMPSHIRE, The Castle, Winchester SO23 8UG. Tel: 01962-841841. *Director*, P. J. Coles

HEREFORD AND WORCESTER, County Hall, Spetchley Road, Worcester WR5 2NP. Tel: 01905-766347. *County Education Officer*, D. A. J. Stanley

HERTFORDSHIRE, County Hall, Hertford SGI3 8DF. Tel: 01992-555701. *Director*, M. Instone

ISLE OF WIGHT, County Hall, Newport PO30 IUD. Tel: 01983-823400. *Director*, A. Kaye

KENT, Springfield, Maidstone MEI4 2LJ. Tel: 01622-671411. *Director*, R. Pryke

LANCASHIRE, PO Box 61, County Hall, Preston PRI 8RJ. Tel: 01772-254868. *Chief Education Officer*, C. J. Trinick

LEICESTERSHIRE, County Hall, Glenfield, Leicester LE3 8RF. Tel: 0116-265 6300. *Director*, Mrs J. A. M. Strong

LINCOLNSHIRE, County Offices, Newland, Lincoln LNI IYQ. Tel: 01522-552222. *Director*, N. J. Riches

NORFOLK, County Hall, Martineau Lane, Norwich NRI 2DH. Tel: 01603-222222. *Director*, M. H. Edwards

NORTHAMPTONSHIRE, PO Box 149, County Hall, Northampton NNI IAU. Tel: 01604-236252. *Director*, J. R. Atkinson

NORTHUMBERLAND, County Hall, Morpeth NE61 2EF. Tel: 01670-533000. *Director*, C. C. Tipple

NORTH YORKSHIRE, County Hall, Northallerton DL7 8AD. Tel: 01609-780780. *Director*, Miss C. Welbourn

NOTTINGHAMSHIRE, County Hall, West Bridgford, Nottingham NG2 7QP. Tel: 0115-982 3823. *Director*, R. Valentine

OXFORDSHIRE, Macclesfield House, New Road, Oxford OXI INA. Tel: 01865-815449. *Director*, G. Badman

SHROPSHIRE, The Shirehall, Abbey Foregate, Shrewsbury SY2 6ND. Tel: 01743-254302. *Director*, Ms C. Adams

SOMERSET, County Hall, Taunton TAI 4DY. Tel: 01823-333451. *Chief Education Officer*, N. Henwood

STAFFORDSHIRE, Wedgwood Building, Tipping Street, Stafford STI6 2DH. Tel: 01785-223121. *Chief Education Officer*, P. J. Hunter, PH.D.

SUFFOLK, St Andrew House, County Hall, Ipswich IP4 ILJ. Tel: 01473-264627. *County Education Officer*, D. J. Peachey

SURREY, County Hall, Penrhyn Road, Kingston upon Thames KTI 2DN. Tel: 0181-541 9501. *County Education Officer*, Dr P. Gray

WARWICKSHIRE, PO Box 24, 22 Northgate Street, Warwick CV34 4SR. Tel: 01926-410410. *Director*, E. Wood

WEST SUSSEX, County Hall, West Street, Chichester POI9 IRF. Tel: 01243-777100. *Director*, R. D. C. Bunker

WILTSHIRE, County Hall, Trowbridge BAI4 8JH. Tel: 01225-713000. *Chief Education Officer*, Dr L. Davies

Unitary Councils

BARNSLEY, Berneslai Close, Barnsley S70 2HS. Tel: 01226-770770. *Director*, D. Dalton

BATH AND NORTH-EAST SOMERSET, Northgate House, Upper Borough Walls, Bath BAI 2JD. Tel: 01225-460628. *Director*, R. Jones

BIRMINGHAM, Council House, Margaret Street, Birmingham B3 3BU. Tel: 0121-235 2550. *Chief Education Officer*, T. Brighouse

BOLTON, Paderborn House, Civic Centre, Bolton BLI IJW. Tel: 01204-522311. *Director*, Mrs M. Blenkinsop

BRADFORD, Flockton House, Flockton Road, Bradford BD4 7RY. Tel: 01274-751840. *Director*, Ms D. Cavanagh

BRISTOL, Council House, College Green, Bristol BSI 5TR. Tel: 0117-922 2000. *Director*, R. Riddell

BURY, Athenaeum House, Market Street, Bury BL9 0BN. Tel: 0161-253 5652. *Chief Education Officer (acting)*, G. Talbot

CALDERDALE, Northgate House, Northgate, Halifax HXI IUN. Tel: 01422-357257. *Director*, I. Jennings

COVENTRY, Council House, Earl Street, Coventry CVI 5RR. Tel: 01203-833333. *Chief Education Officer*, Ms. C. Goodwin

DONCASTER, PO Box 266, The Council House, College Road, Doncaster DNI 3AD. Tel: 01302-734444. *Director*, A. M. Taylor

DUDLEY, Westox House, 1 Trinity Road, Dudley DYI IJB. Tel: 01384-452200. *Chief Education Officer*, R. Colligan

EAST RIDING OF YORKSHIRE, County Hall, Beverley HUI7 9BA. Tel: 01482-887700. *Director*, J. Ginnever

GATESHEAD, Civic Centre, Regent Street, Gateshead NE8 IHH. Tel: 0191-477 1011. *Director*, J. D. Arbon

HARTLEPOOL, Civic Centre, Victoria Road, Hartlepool TS24 8AY. Tel: 01429-266522. *Director*, J. J. Fitt

KINGSTON UPON HULL, Essex House, Alfred Gelder Street, Kingston upon Hull HUI IYD. Tel: 01482-610610. *Director*, Ms J. E. Taylor

KIRKLEES, Oldgate House, 2 Oldgate, Huddersfield HD1 6QW. Tel: 01484-422133. *Chief Education Officer,* R. Vincent

KNOWSLEY, Huyton Hey Road, Huyton, Merseyside L36 5YH. Tel: 0151-443 3232. *Director of Education,* P. Wylie

LEEDS, Merrion House, Leeds LS2 8DT. Tel: 0113-247 5575. *Chief Education Officer,* J. Rawlinson

LIVERPOOL, 14 Sir Thomas Street, Liverpool L1 6BJ. Tel: 0151-227 3911. *Director,* M. F. Cogley

MANCHESTER, Cumberland House, Crown Square, Manchester M60 3BB. Tel: 0161-234 7125. *Chief Education Officer,* R. Jobson

MIDDLESBROUGH, Civic Centre, Middlesbrough TS1 2QQ. Tel: 01642-262001. *Director,* M. Shorney

NEWCASTLE UPON TYNE, Civic Centre, Newcastle upon Tyne NE1 8PU. Tel: 0191-232 8520. *Education Officer,* D. Bell

NORTH EAST LINCOLNSHIRE, Eleanor Street, Grimsby DN31 1HU. Tel: 01472-323025. *Head of Education,* G. Hill

NORTH LINCOLNSHIRE, Pittwood House, Ashby Road, Scunthorpe DN16 1AB. Tel: 01724-296296. *Director,* T. Thomas

NORTH SOMERSET, Town Hall, Weston-Super-Mare BS23 1UJ. Tel: 01934-888888. *Director,* Ms J. Wreford

NORTH TYNESIDE, Stephenson House, Stephenson Street, North Shields NE30 1QA. Tel: 0191-200 5151. *Director,* L. Walton

OLDHAM, Town Hall, Middleton Road, Chadderton, Oldham OL9 6PP. Tel: 0161-911 4203. *Director,* Mrs H. Holmes

REDCAR AND CLEVELAND, Council Offices, Kirkleatham Street, Redcar TS10 1RT. Tel: 01642-444000. *Chief Education Officer,* K. Bruton

ROCHDALE, PO Box 70, Municipal Offices, Smith Street, Rochdale OL16 1YD. Tel: 01706-47474. *Director,* B. Atkinson

ROTHERHAM, Norfolk House, Walker Place, Rotherham S60 1QT. Tel: 01709-822500. *Education Officer,* H. C. Bower

ST HELENS, Rivington Centre, Rivington Road, St Helens WA10 4ND. Tel: 01744-456000. *Director,* B. M. Mainwaring

SALFORD, Chapel Street, Salford M3 5LT. Tel: 0161-832 9751. *Chief Education Officer,* D. Johnston

SANDWELL, PO Box 41, Shaftesbury House, 402 High Street, West Bromwich B70 9LT. Tel: 0121-525 7366. *Director,* S. Gallacher

SEFTON, Town Hall, Oriel Road, Bootle, Merseyside L20 7AE. Tel: 0151-922 4040. *Education Officer,* J. A. Marsden

SHEFFIELD, Leopold Street, Sheffield S1 1RJ. Tel: 0114-272 6341. *Director,* vacant

SOLIHULL, PO Box 20, Council House, Solihull B91 3QU. Tel: 0121-704 6000. *Director,* D. Nixon

SOUTH GLOUCESTERSHIRE, Bowling Hill, Chipping Sodbury BS17 6JX. Tel: 01454-863253. *Director,* Ms T. Gillespie

SOUTH TYNESIDE, Town Hall and Civic Offices, Westoe Road, South Shields NE32 2RL. Tel: 0191-427 1717. *Director,* I. L. Reid

STOCKPORT, Stopford House, Piccadilly, Stockport SK1 3XE. Tel: 0161-474 3808. *Director,* M. K. J. Hunt

STOCKTON-ON-TEES, Municipal Buildings, Church Road, Stockton-on-Tees TS18 1XE. Tel: 01642-670067. *Head of Education,* S. Bradford

SUNDERLAND, PO Box 101, Civic Centre, Burdon Road, Sunderland SR2 7DN. Tel: 0191-553 1000. *Director,* J. Williams

TAMESIDE, Council Offices, Wellington Road, Ashton-under-Lyne OL6 6DL. Tel: 0161-342 8355. *Director,* A. M. Webster

TRAFFORD, PO Box 19, Sale Town Hall, Tatton Road, Sale M33 1YR. Tel: 0161-912 1212. *Director,* A. Lee

WAKEFIELD, County Hall, Bond Street, Wakefield WF1 2QL. Tel: 01924-306090. *Education Officer,* J. McLeod

WALSALL, Civic Centre, Darwall Street, Walsall WS1 1DQ. Tel: 01922-650000. *Director,* T. Howard

WIGAN, Gateway House, Standishgate, Wigan WN1 1AE. Tel: 01942-244991. *Education Officer,* R. Clark

WIRRAL, Hamilton Building, Conway Street, Birkenhead L41 4FD. Tel: 0151-666 2121. *Director,* D. Rigby

WOLVERHAMPTON, Civic Centre, St Peter's Square, Wolverhampton WV1 1RR. Tel: 01902-27811. *Director,* R. Lockwood

YORK, 10–12 George Hudson Street, York YO1 1ZG. Tel: 01904-615191. *Director,* M. Peters

LONDON

*Inner London borough

BARKING AND DAGENHAM, Town Hall, Barking, Essex IG11 7LU. Tel: 0181-592 4500. *Education Officer,* A. Larbalestier

BARNET, Old Town Hall, Friern Barnet Lane, London N11 3DL. Tel: 0181-359 2000. *Director,* M. Daubney

BEXLEY, Hill View, Hill View Drive, Welling, Kent DA16 3RY. Tel: 0181-303 7777. *Director,* P. McGee

BRENT, Chesterfield House, 9 Park Lane, Wembley, Middx HA9 7RW. Tel: 0181-937 3020. *Chief Education Officer (acting),* P. Doherty

BROMLEY, Civic Centre, Stockwell Close, Bromley BR1 3UH. Tel: 0181-464 3333. *Director,* vacant

*CAMDEN, Crowndale Centre, 218–220 Eversholt Street, London NW1 1BD. Tel: 0171-911 1525. *Education Officer,* R. Litchfield

*CITY OF LONDON, Education Department, Corporation of London, PO Box 270, Guildhall, London EC2P 2EJ. Tel: 0171-332 1750. *City Education Officer,* D. Smith

*CITY OF WESTMINSTER, PO Box 240, City Hall, 64 Victoria Street, London SW1E 6QP. Tel: 0171-798 2771. *Director,* Mrs D. McGrath

CROYDON, Taberner House, Park Lane, Croydon CR9 1TP. Tel: 0181-686 4433. *Director,* P. Benians

EALING, Perceval House, 14–16 Uxbridge Road, London W5 2HL. Tel: 0181-758 5484. *Director,* vacant

ENFIELD, PO Box 56, Civic Centre, Silver Street, Enfield EN1 3XQ. Tel: 0181-967 9423. *Director,* Ms L. Graham

*GREENWICH, Riverside House, Woolwich High Street, London, SE18 6DN. Tel: 0181-854 8888. *Director,* J. Kramer

*HACKNEY, Edith Cavell Building, Enfield Road, London N1 5AZ. Tel: 0171-214 8400. *Director (acting),* S. Roberts

*HAMMERSMITH AND FULHAM, Cambridge House, Cambridge Grove, London W6 4LE. Tel: 0181-576 5477. *Director,* Ms C. Whatford

HARINGEY, 48 Station Road, Wood Green, London N22 4TY. Tel: 0181-975 9700. *Director,* Miss J. Tonge

HARROW, PO Box 22, Civic Centre, Harrow HA1 2UW. Tel: 0181-424 1304. *Director,* Mrs C. Gilbert

HAVERING, Broxhill Centre, Broxhill Road, Harold Hill, Romford RM4 1XN. Tel: 01708-772222. *Director,* C. Hardy

HILLINGDON, Civic Centre, High Street, Uxbridge, Middx UB8 1UW. Tel: 01895-250111. *Director,* Mrs G. Andrews

HOUNSLOW, Civic Centre, Lampton Road, Hounslow, Middx TW3 4DN. Tel: 0181-862 5301. *Director,* J. D. Trickett

*ISLINGTON, Laycock Street, London N1 ITH. Tel: 0171-457 5753. *Education Officer,* Dr H. Nicole

*KENSINGTON AND CHELSEA, Town Hall, Hornton Street, London W8 7NX. Tel: 0171-937 5464. *Director,* R. Wood

KINGSTON UPON THAMES, Guildhall, High Street, Kingston upon Thames KT1 IEU. Tel: 0181-547 5220. *Director,* J. Braithwaite

*LAMBETH, Blue Star House, 234–244 Stockwell Road, London SW9 9SP. Tel: 0171-926 2248. *Director,* Ms H. DuQuesnay, CBE

*LEWISHAM, Laurence House, 1 Catford Road, London SE6 4SW. Tel: 0181-695 6000. *Director,* Ms A. Efunshile

MERTON, Civic Centre, London Road, Morden, Surrey SM4 5DX. Tel: 0181-554 3251. *Director,* Ms J. Cairns

NEWHAM, Broadway House, 322 High Street, London E15 IAJ. Tel: 0181-555 5552. *Director,* I. Harrison

REDBRIDGE, Lynton House, 255–259 High Road, Ilford IG1 INN. Tel: 0181-478 3020. *Director,* D. E. Capper

RICHMOND UPON THAMES, Regal House, London Road, Twickenham TW1 3QS. Tel: 0181-891 7500. *Director,* G. Alexander

*SOUTHWARK, 1 Bradenham Close, London SE17 2BA. Tel: 0171-525 5000. *Director,* G. Mott

SUTTON, The Grove, Carshalton, Surrey SM5 3AL. Tel: 0181-770 6568. *Director,* Dr I. Birnbaum

*TOWER HAMLETS, Mulberry Place, 5 Clove Crescent, London E14 2BG. Tel: 0171-364 5000. *Education Officer,* Mrs A. Sofer

WALTHAM FOREST, Municipal Offices, High Road, Leyton, London E10 5QJ. Tel: 0181-527 5544. *Chief Education Officer,* A. Lockhart

*WANDSWORTH, Town Hall, Wandsworth High Street, London SW18 2PU. Tel: 0181-871 6000. *Director,* P. Robinson

WALES

ANGLESEY, Glanhwfa Road, Llangefni LL77 7EY. Tel: 01248-752900. *Director,* R. P. Jones

BLAENAU GWENT, Civic Centre, Ebbw Vale NP3 6XB. Tel: 01495-355434. *Director,* B. Mawby

BRIDGEND, Sunnyside Offices, Bridgend CF31 4AR. Tel: 01656-766211. *Director,* D. Matthews

CAERNARFONSHIRE AND MERIONETHSHIRE, Swyddfa'r Cyngor, Caernarfon LL55 ISH. Tel: 01286-679012. *Director,* D. Whittall

CAERPHILLY, Caerphilly Road, Ystrad Mynach, Hengoed CF82 7EP. Tel: 01443-816016. *Director,* N. Harries

CARDIFF, County Hall, Atlantic Wharf, Cardiff CF1 5UW. Tel: 01222-872000. *Director,* T. Davies

CARMARTHENSHIRE, Pibwrlwyd, Carmarthen SA31 2NH. Tel: 01267-234567. *Director,* K. P. Davies

CEREDIGION, Swyddfa'r Sir, Aberystwyth SY23 2DE. Tel: 01970-633600. *Director,* R. Williams

CONWY, Government Buildings, Dinerth Road, Colwyn Bay LL28 5AX. Tel: 01492-544261. *Director,* R. E. Williams

DENBIGHSHIRE, Phase IV, Shire Hall, Mold CH7·6GR. Tel: 01824-706700. *Director,* E. Lewis

FLINTSHIRE, County Hall, Mold CH7 6ND. Tel: 01352-704010. *Director,* K. McDonogh

MERTHYR TYDFIL, Civic Centre, Castle Street, Merthyr Tydfil CF47 8AN. Tel: 01685-724614. *Director,* D. Jones

MONMOUTHSHIRE, County Hall, Cwmbran NP44 2XH. Tel: 01633-838838. *Director,* D. Young

NEATH AND PORT TALBOT, Civic Centre, Port Talbot SA13 IPJ. Tel: 01639-763333. *Director,* V. Thomas

NEWPORT, Civic Centre, Newport NP9 4UR. Tel: 01633-232000. *Director,* G. Bingham

PEMBROKESHIRE, Cambria House, Haverfordwest SA61 ITP. Tel: 01437-764551. *Director,* G. Davies

POWYS, County Hall, Llandrindod Wells LD1 5LG. Tel: 01597-826433. *Director,* M. Barker

RHONDDA, CYNON, TAFF, Grawen Street, Porth CF39 0BU. Tel: 01433-687666. *Director,* K. Ryley

SWANSEA, Room 1.1.10, County Hall, Oystermouth Road, Swansea SA1 3SN. Tel: 01792-636351. *Director,* M. Brunt

TORFAEN, County Hall, Cwmbran NP44 2WH. Tel: 01633-832403. *Director,* M. de Val

VALE OF GLAMORGAN, Civic Offices, Holton Road, Barry CF63 4RU. Tel: 01466-709100. *Director,* A. Davies

WREXHAM, Roxburgh House, Hill Street, Wrexham LL11 ISN. Tel: 01978-297400. *Director,* T. Garner

SCOTLAND

ABERDEEN CITY, Summerhill Education Centre, Stronsay Drive, Aberdeen AB15 6JA. Tel: 01224-208626. *Director,* J. Stodter

ABERDEENSHIRE, Woodhill House, Westburn Road, Aberdeen AB16 5GB. Tel: 01224-665420. *Director,* M. White

ANGUS, County Buildings, Market Street, Forfar DD8 3LG. Tel: 01307-461460. *Director,* J. Anderson

ARGYLL AND BUTE, Argyll House, Alexandra Parade, Dunoon PA23 8HI. Tel: 01369-704000. *Director,* A. C. Morton

CITY OF EDINBURGH, Council Headquarters, George IV Bridge, Edinburgh EH1 IUQ. Tel: 0131-200 2000. *Director,* Ms E. Reid

CLACKMANNANSHIRE, Lime Tree House, Alloa FK10 IEX. Tel: 01259-452435. *Director,* K. Bloomer

DUMFRIES AND GALLOWAY, Education Headquarters, 30 Edinburgh Road, Dumfries DG1 IJQ. Tel: 01387-260000. *Director,* K. MacLeod

DUNDEE CITY, Floor 8, Tayside House, 28 Crichton Street, Dundee DD1 3RJ. Tel: 01382-223281. *Director,* Ms A. Wilson

EAST AYRSHIRE, Council Headquarters, London Road, Kilmarnock KA3 7BU. Tel: 01563-576017. *Director,* J. Mulgrew

EAST DUMBARTONSHIRE, Bocleirla House, 100 Milngavie Road, Bearsden, Glasgow G61 2TQ. Tel: 0141-942 9000. *Director,* I. Mills

EAST LOTHIAN, Council Buildings, Haddington EH41 3HA. Tel: 01620-827827. *Director,* A. Blackie

EAST RENFREWSHIRE, Council Offices, Eastwood Park, Rouken Glen Road, Giffnock, Glasgow G46 6UG. Tel: 0141-621 3430. *Director,* Ms E. J. Currie

FALKIRK, McLaren House, Marchmont Avenue, Polmont, Falkirk FK2 0NZ. Tel: 01324-506600. *Director,* G. Young

FIFE, Rothesay House, North Street, Glenrothes KY7 5PN. Tel: 01592-413656. *Director,* A. Mackay

GLASGOW CITY, Education Offices, 129 Bath Street, Glasgow G2 2SY. Tel: 0141-287 6898. *Director,* K. Corsar

HIGHLAND, Glenurquhart Road, Inverness IV3 5NX. Tel: 01463-702801. *Director,* A. C. Gilchrist

INVERCLYDE, 105 Dalrymple Street, Greenock PA15 IHT. Tel: 01475-724400. *Director,* B. McLeary

MIDLOTHIAN, Education Division, Greenhall Centre, Gowkshill, Gorebridge EH23 4PE. Tel: 01875-823699. *Director,* D. MacKay

MORAY, Academy Street, Elgin IV30 ILL. Tel. 01343-541144. *Director,* K. Gavin

NORTH AYRSHIRE, Cunninghame House, Irvine KA12 8EE. Tel: 01294-324100. *Director,* J. Travers

NORTH LANARKSHIRE, Municipal Buildings, Kildonan Street, Coatbridge ML5 3LF. Tel: 01236-812222. *Director,* M. O'Neil

ORKNEY ISLANDS, Council Offices, School Place, Kirkwall, Orkney KW15 1WY. Tel: 01856-873535. *Director,* J. J. Anderson

PERTH AND KINROSS, 6–8 South Methven Street, Perth PH1 5PF. Tel: 01783-476200. *Director,* R. McKay

RENFREWSHIRE, South Building, Cotton Street, Paisley PA1 1BU. Tel: 0141-842 5601. *Director,* Mrs S. Rae

SCOTTISH BORDERS, Council Headquarters, Newtown St Boswells, Melrose TD6 0SA. Tel: 01835-824000. *Director,* J. Christie

SHETLAND ISLANDS, Schlumberger, Gremista Industrial Estate, Lerwick ZE1 0PX. Tel: 01595-744300. *Director,* J. Halcrow

SOUTH AYRSHIRE, County Buildings, Wellington Square, Ayr KA7 1DR. Tel: 01292-612000. *Director,* M. McCabe

SOUTH LANARKSHIRE, Council Offices, Almada Street, Hamilton ML3 0AA. Tel: 01698-454444. *Director,* Ms M. Allan

STIRLING, Council Headquarters, Viewforth, Stirling FK8 2ET. Tel: 01786-442680. *Director,* G. Jeyes

WEST DUMBARTONSHIRE, Garshake Road, Dumbarton G82 3PU. Tel: 01389-737000. *Director,* I. McMurdo

WEST LOTHIAN, Lindsay House, South Bridge Street, Bathgate EH48 1TS. Tel: 01506-776000. *Director,* R. Stewart

WESTERN ISLES ISLANDS, Council Offices, Sandwick Road, Stornoway HS1 2BW. Tel: 01851-703773. *Director,* N. Galbraith

NORTHERN IRELAND

EDUCATION AND LIBRARY BOARDS

BELFAST, 40 Academy Street, Belfast BT1 2NQ. Tel: 01232-564000. *Chief Executive,* T. G. J. Moag

NORTH EASTERN, County Hall, 182 Galgorm Road, Ballymena, Co. Antrim BT43 1HN. Tel: 01266-653333. *Chief Executive,* G. Topping

SOUTH EASTERN, 18 Windsor Avenue, Belfast BT9 6EF. Tel: 01232-381188. *Chief Executive,* T. Nolan, OBE

SOUTHERN, 3 Charlemont Place, The Mall, Armagh BT61 9AX. Tel: 01861-512200. *Chief Executive,* J. G. Kelly

WESTERN, 1 Hospital Road, Omagh, Co. Tyrone BT79 0AW. Tel: 01662-240240. *Chief Executive,* J. Martin

ISLANDS

GUERNSEY, Grange Road, St Peter Port GY1 1RQ. Tel: 01481-710821. *Director,* D. T. Neale

JERSEY, PO Box 142, JE4 8QJ. Tel: 01534-509500. *Director,* B. Grady

ISLE OF MAN, Department of Education, Murray House, 5–11 Mount Havelock, Douglas IM1 2SG. Tel: 01624-685685. *Director,* G. A. Baker

ISLES OF SCILLY, Town Hall, St Mary's TR21 0LW. Tel: 01720-422537. *Secretary for Education,* P. S. Hygate

ADVISORY BODIES

SCHOOLS

EDUCATION OTHERWISE, PO Box 7420, London N9 9SG. *Helpline,* tel: 0891-518303

INTERNATIONAL BACCALAUREATE, Peterson House, Fortran Road, St Mellons, Cardiff CF3 0LT. Tel: 01222-774000. *Director of Examinations,* C. Carthew

NATIONAL ADVISORY COUNCIL FOR EDUCATION TRAINING AND TARGETS, 7th Floor, 222 Grays Inn Road, London WC1X 8HL. Tel: 0171-211 4529. *Chairman,* P. Davis; *Director,* P. Chorley

NATIONAL COUNCIL FOR EDUCATIONAL TECHNOLOGY, Milburn Hill Road, Science Park, Coventry CV4 7JJ. Tel: 01203-416994. *Chief Executive,* Mrs M. Bell

SPECIAL EDUCATIONAL NEEDS TRIBUNAL, 71 Victoria Street, London SW1H 0HW. Tel: 0171-925 6925. *President,* T. Aldridge; *Secretary,* Ms J. Saraga

INDEPENDENT SCHOOLS

GOVERNING BODIES ASSOCIATION, The Coach House, Pickforde Lane, Ticehurst, E. Sussex TN5 7BJ. Tel: 01580-200855. *Secretary,* D. G. Banwell

GOVERNING BODIES OF GIRLS' SCHOOLS ASSOCIATION, The Coach House, Pickforde Lane, Ticehurst, E. Sussex TN5 7BJ. Tel: 01580-200855. *Secretary,* D. G. Banwell

INDEPENDENT SCHOOLS EXAMINATIONS BOARD, Jordan House, Christchurch Road, New Milton, Hants BH25 6QJ. Tel: 01425-621111. *Administrator,* Mrs J. Williams

INDEPENDENT SCHOOLS INFORMATION SERVICE, 56 Buckingham Gate, London SW1E 6AG. Tel: 0171-630 8793. *National Director,* D. J. Woodhead

THE ISJC ASSISTED PLACES COMMITTEE, 26 Queen Anne's Gate, London SW1H 9AN. Tel: 0171-222 9595. *Secretary,* P. F. V. Waters

FURTHER EDUCATION

FURTHER EDUCATION DEVELOPMENT AGENCY, Dumbarton House, 68 Oxford Street, London W1N 0DA. Tel: 0171-436 0020. *Chief Executive,* S. Crowne

NATIONAL COUNCIL FOR VOCATIONAL QUALIFICATIONS, 222 Euston Road, London NW1 2BZ. Tel: 0171-387 9898. *Chief Executive,* J. Hillier

Regional Advisory Councils

ASSOCIATION OF COLLEGES IN THE EASTERN REGION , Merlin Place, Milton Road, Cambridge CB4 4DP. Tel: 01223–424022. *Chief Executive,* J. Graystone

CENTRA (EDUCATION AND TRAINING SERVICES) LTD, Duxbury Park, Duxbury Hall Road, Chorley, Lancs PR7 4AT. Tel: 01257-241428. *Chief Executive,* N. Bailey

EMFEC (EAST MIDLAND FURTHER EDUCATION COUNCIL), Robins Wood House, Robins Wood Road, Aspley, Nottingham NG8 3NH. Tel: 0115-929 3291. *Chief Executive,* R. Ainscough

NCFE (NORTHERN COUNCIL FOR FURTHER EDUCATION), 5 Grosvenor Villas, Grosvenor Road, Newcastle upon Tyne NE2 2RU. Tel: 0191-281 3242. *Chief Executive,* J. F. Pearce

SOUTHERN REGIONAL COUNCIL FOR FURTHER EDUCATION AND TRAINING, The Mezzanine Suite, PO Box 2055, Civic Centre, Reading RG1 7ET. Tel: 01734-390592. *Chief Executive,* B. J. Knowles

SOUTH WEST ASSOCIATION FOR FURTHER EDUCATION AND TRAINING, Bishops Hull House, Bishops Hull, Taunton, Somerset TA1 5RA. Tel: 01823-335491. *Chief Executive,* S. Fisher

WELSH JOINT EDUCATION COMMITTEE, 245 Western Avenue, Cardiff CF5 2YX. Tel: 01222-265000. *Secretary,* C. Heycock

YORKSHIRE AND HUMBERSIDE ASSOCIATION FOR FURTHER AND HIGHER EDUCATION, 13 Wellington Road East, Dewsbury, W. Yorks WF13 1XG. Tel: 01924-450900. *Chief Executive*, Prof. N. Woodhead

HIGHER EDUCATION

ASSOCIATION OF COMMONWEALTH UNIVERSITIES, John Foster House, 36 Gordon Square, London WC1H 0PF. Tel: 0171–387 8572. *Secretary-General*, Prof. M. G. Gibbons

COMMITTEE OF VICE-CHANCELLORS AND PRINCIPALS OF THE UNIVERSITIES OF THE UNITED KINGDOM, 29 Tavistock Square, London WC1H 9EZ. Tel: 0171-387 9231. *Chairman*, Prof. G. Roberts, FRS; *Chief Executive* Ms D. Warwick

HIGHER EDUCATION QUALITY COUNCIL, 344–354 Gray's Inn Road, London WC1X 8BP. Tel: 0171-837 2223. *Company Secretary*, G. L. Middleton

NORTHERN IRELAND HIGHER EDUCATION COUNCIL, Rathgael House, Balloo Road, Bangor BT19 7PR. Tel: 01247–279333. *Chairman*, Sir Kenneth Bloomfield, KCB; *Secretary*, J. Coote

CURRICULUM COUNCILS

AWDURDOD CWRICWLWM ACASESU CYMRU/ CURRICULUM AND ASSESSMENT AUTHORITY FOR WALES, Castle Buildings, Womanby Street, Cardiff CF1 9SX. Tel: 01222-344946. *Chief Executive*, J. V. Williams

NORTHERN IRELAND COUNCIL FOR THE CURRICULUM, EXAMINATIONS AND ASSESSMENT, 29 Clarendon Road, Belfast BT1 3BG. Tel: 01232-261200. *Chief Executive*, Mrs C. Coxhead

SCHOOL CURRICULUM AND ASSESSMENT AUTHORITY, Newcombe House, 45 Notting Hill Gate, London W11 3JB. Tel: 0171– 229 1234. *Chairman*, Sir Ron Dearing, CB; *Chief Executive*, N. Tate, PH.D.

SCOTTISH CONSULTATIVE COUNCIL ON THE CURRICULUM, Gardyne Road, Broughty Ferry, Dundee DD5 1NY. Tel: 01382-455053. *Chief Executive*, C. E. Harrison

EXAMINING BODIES

GCSE

LONDON EXAMINATIONS AND ASSESSMENT COUNCIL, Stewart House, 32 Russell Square, London WC1B 5DN. Tel: 0171-331 4000. *Chief Executive*, Ms C. Townsend, PH.D.

MIDLAND EXAMINING GROUP, 1 Hills Road, Cambridge CB1 2EU. Tel: 01223-553311. *Chief Executive*, R. R. McLone, PH.D. (Part of UCLES)

NORTHERN EXAMINATIONS AND ASSESSMENT BOARD, Devas Street, Manchester M15 6EX. Tel: 0161-953 1180. *Chief Executive*, Mrs K. Tattersall

NORTHERN IRELAND COUNCIL FOR THE CURRICULUM, EXAMINATIONS AND ASSESSMENT, Beechill House, 42 Beechill Road, Belfast BT8 4RS. Tel: 01232-704666. *Chief Executive*, Mrs C. Coxhead

SEG (SOUTHERN EXAMINING GROUP), Stag Hill House, Guildford, Surrey GU2 5XJ. Tel: 01483-506506. *Secretary-General*, J. A. Day

WELSH JOINT EDUCATION COMMITTEE, 245 Western Avenue, Cardiff CF5 2YX. Tel: 01222-265000. *Chief Executive*, C. Heycock

A-LEVEL

ASSOCIATED EXAMINING BOARD, Stag Hill House, Guildford, Surrey GU2 5XJ. Tel: 01483-506506. *Secretary-General*, J. A. Day

LONDON EXAMINATIONS AND ASSESSMENT COUNCIL, Stewart House, 32 Russell Square, London WC1B 5DN. Tel: 0171-331 4000. *Chief Executive*, Ms C. Townsend, PH.D.

NORTHERN EXAMINATIONS AND ASSESSMENT BOARD, Devas Street, Manchester M15 6EX. Tel: 0161-953 1180. *Chief Executive*, Mrs K. Tattersall

NORTHERN IRELAND COUNCIL FOR THE CURRICULUM, EXAMINATIONS AND ASSESSMENT, Beechill House, 42 Beechill Road, Belfast BT8 4RS. Tel: 01232-704666. *Chief Executive*, Mrs C. Coxhead

OXFORD AND CAMBRIDGE EXAMINATIONS AND ASSESSMENT COUNCIL (OCEAC), Syndicate Buildings, 1 Hills Road, Cambridge CB1 2EU. Tel: 01223-553311; Ewert House, Ewert Place, Oxford OX2 7BZ. Tel: 01865-54291 (OCEAC is part of UCLES)

OXFORD AND CAMBRIDGE SCHOOLS EXAMINATION BOARD, *see* OCEAC

UNIVERSITY OF CAMBRIDGE LOCAL EXAMINATIONS SYNDICATE (UCLES), *see* OCEAC

UNIVERSITY OF OXFORD DELEGACY OF LOCAL EXAMINATIONS, *see* OCEAC

WELSH JOINT EDUCATION COMMITTEE, 245 Western Avenue, Cardiff CF5 2YX. Tel: 01222-265000. *Chief Executive*, C. Heycock

SCOTLAND

SCOTTISH EXAMINATION BOARD, Ironmills Road, Dalkeith, Midlothian EH22 1LE. Tel: 0131-663 6601. *Chief Executive*, H. A. Long, PH.D.

SCOTTISH QUALIFICATIONS AUTHORITY, Hanover House, 24 Douglas Street, Glasgow G2 7NQ. Tel: 0141-248 7900

SCOTTISH VOCATIONAL EDUCATION COUNCIL (SCOTVEC), Hanover House, 24 Douglas Street, Glasgow G2 7NQ. Tel: 0141-248 7900. *Chief Executive*, T. J. McCool, CBE

FURTHER EDUCATION

CITY & GUILDS, 1 Giltspur Street, London EC1A 9DD. Tel: 0171-294 2468. *Director-General*, N. Carey, PH.D.

THE EDEXCEL FOUNDATION (BTEC and London Examinations and Assessment Council), Stewart House, 32 Russell Square, London WC1B 5DN. Tel: 0171-331 4000. *Chief Executive*, Ms C. Townsend, PH.D.

RSA EXAMINATIONS BOARD, Westwood Way, Coventry CV4 8HS. Tel: 01203-470033. *Chief Executive*, M. F. Cross

FUNDING COUNCILS

SCHOOLS

FUNDING AGENCY FOR SCHOOLS, Albion Wharf, 25 Skeldergate, York YO1 2XL. Tel: 01904-661661. *Chairman*, Sir Christopher Benson; *Chief Executive*, M. Collier

FURTHER EDUCATION

FURTHER EDUCATION FUNDING COUNCIL FOR ENGLAND, Cheylesmore House, Quinton Road, Coventry CV1 2WT. Tel: 01203-863000. *Chief Executive*, Prof. D. Melville

FURTHER EDUCATION FUNDING COUNCIL FOR WALES, Lambourne House, Cardiff Business Park, Llanishen, Cardiff CF4 5GL. Tel: 01222-761861. *Chief Executive*, Prof. J. A. Andrews

SCOTTISH FURTHER EDUCATION FUNDING UNIT, Scottish Office Education and Industry Department, First Floor West, Victoria Quay, Edinburgh EH6 6QQ. Tel: 0131-244 0278. *Director*, R. D. Jackson

HIGHER EDUCATION

HIGHER EDUCATION FUNDING COUNCIL FOR ENGLAND, Northavon House, Coldharbour Lane, Bristol BS16 1QD. Tel: 0117-931 7317. *Chief Executive*, Prof. B. Fender

HIGHER EDUCATION FUNDING COUNCIL FOR WALES, Lambourne House, Cardiff Business Park, Llanishen, Cardiff CF4 5GL. Tel: 01222-761861. *Chief Executive*, Prof. J. A. Andrews

SCOTTISH HIGHER EDUCATION FUNDING COUNCIL, Donaldson House, 97 Haymarket Terrace, Edinburgh EH12 5HD. Tel: 0131-313 6500. *Chief Executive*, Prof. J. Sizer, CBE

STUDENT LOANS COMPANY LTD, 100 Bothwell Street, Glasgow G2 7JD. Tel: 0141-306 2000. *Chief Executive*, C. Ward

TEACHER TRAINING AGENCY, Portland House, Stag Place, London SW1E 5TT. Tel: 0171-925 3700. *Chairman*, G. Parker, CBE; *Chief Executive*, Ms A. Millett

---

ADMISSIONS AND COURSE INFORMATION

CAREERS RESEARCH AND ADVISORY CENTRE (CRAC), Sheraton House, Castle Park, Cambridge CB3 0AX. Tel: 01223-460277. *Director*, D. McGregor. *Publishers*, Hobsons Publishing PLC, Bateman Street, Cambridge CB2 1LZ

COMMITTEE OF SCOTTISH HIGHER EDUCATION PRINCIPALS (COSHEP), St Andrew House, 141 West Nile Street, Glasgow G1 2RN. Tel: 0141-353 1880. *Secretary*, Dr R. L. Crawford

GRADUATE TEACHER TRAINING REGISTRY, Fulton House, Jessop Avenue, Cheltenham, Glos GL50 3SH. Tel: 01242-225868. *Registrar*, Mrs M. Griffiths

SOCIAL WORK ADMISSIONS SYSTEM, Fulton House, Jessop Avenue, Cheltenham, Glos GL50 3SH. Tel: 01242-225977. *Admissions Officer*, Mrs M. Griffiths

TEACHER EDUCATION ADMISSIONS CLEARING HOUSE (TEACH) (Scottish postgraduate only), PO Box 165, Holyrood Road, Edinburgh EH8 8AT. *Registrar*, Miss R. C. Williamson

UNIVERSITIES AND COLLEGES ADMISSIONS SERVICE, Fulton House, Jessop Avenue, Cheltenham, Glos GL50 3SH. Tel: 01242-222444. *Chief Executive*, M. A. Higgins, PH.D.

UNIVERSITIES

THE UNIVERSITY OF ABERDEEN (1495)
Regent Walk, Aberdeen AB9 1FX
Tel 01224-272014
Full-time students (1995–6), 10,843
Chancellor, Sir Kenneth Alexander, FRSE (1987)
Vice-Chancellor, Prof. C. D. Rice
Registrar, Dr P. J. Murray

Secretary, N. R. D. Begg
Rector, I. Hamilton, QC (1993–6)

THE UNIVERSITY OF ABERTAY DUNDEE (1994)
Bell Street, Dundee DD1 1HG
Tel: 01382-308000
Full-time students (1995–6), 4,000
Chancellor, The Earl of Airlie, KT, GCVO, PC
Vice-Chancellor, Prof. B. King
Registrar, Prof. J. McGoldrick
Secretary, D. Hogarth

ANGLIA POLYTECHNIC UNIVERSITY (1992)
Bishop Hall Lane, Chelmsford, Essex CM1 1SQ
Tel 01245-493131
Full-time students (1995–6), 10,545
Chancellor, The Lord Prior, PC (1992)
Vice-Chancellor, M. Malone-Lee, CB
Head of Student Administration, D. Davies
Secretary, S. G. Bennett

ASTON UNIVERSITY (1966)
Aston Triangle, Birmingham B4 7ET
Tel 0121-359 3611
Full-time students (1995–6), 4,500
Chancellor, Sir Adrian Cadbury (1979)
Vice-Chancellor, Prof. M. Wright
Registrar and Secretary, R. D. A. Packhan

THE UNIVERSITY OF BATH (1966)
Claverton Down, Bath BA2 7AY
Tel 01225-826826
Full-time students (1995–6), 5,610
Chancellor, Sir Denys Henderson (1993)
Vice-Chancellor, Prof. V. D. Vandelinde
Registrar, J. A. Bursey

THE UNIVERSITY OF BIRMINGHAM (1900)
Edgbaston, Birmingham B15 2TT
Tel 0121-414 3344
Full-time students (1995–6), 17,000
Chancellor, Sir Alexander Jarratt, CB (1983)
Vice-Chancellor, Prof. M. Irvine, PH.D.
Registrar and Secretary, D. R. Holmes

BOURNEMOUTH UNIVERSITY (1992)
Poole House, Talbot Campus, Fern Barrow, Dorset BH12 5BB
Tel 01202-524111
Full-time students (1994–5), 8,200
Chancellor, The Baroness Cox (1992)
Vice-Chancellor, Prof. G. Slater
Registrar, N. Richardson
Secretary, R. Allen

THE UNIVERSITY OF BRADFORD (1966)
Bradford BD7 1DP
Tel 01274-733466
Full-time students (1995–6), 6,769
Chancellor, Sir Trevor Holdsworth (1992)
Vice-Chancellor, Prof. D. J. Johns, PH.D., D.SC. (1989)
Registrar and Secretary, N. J. Andrew

THE UNIVERSITY OF BRIGHTON (1992)
Mithras House, Lewes Road, Brighton BN2 4AT
Tel 01273-600900
Full-time students (1995–6), 10,800
Chairman of the Board, M. J. Aldrich

Director, Prof. D. J. Watson
Deputy Director, D. E. House

THE UNIVERSITY OF BRISTOL (1909)
Senate House, Tyndall Avenue, Bristol BS8 1TH
Tel 0117-928 9000
Full-time students (1995–6), 10,833
Chancellor, Sir Jeremy Morse, KCMG (1989)
Vice-Chancellor, Sir John Kingman, FRS
Registrar, J. H. M. Parry
Secretary, Ms K. McKenzie, D.phil.

BRUNEL UNIVERSITY (1966)
Uxbridge, Middx UB8 3PH
Tel 01895-274000
Full-time students (1995–6), 12,441
Chancellor, The Earl of Halsbury, FRS (1966)
Vice-Chancellor, Prof. M. J. H. Sterling
Secretary-General and Registrar, D. Neave

THE UNIVERSITY OF BUCKINGHAM (1983)
(Founded 1976 as University College at Buckingham)
Buckingham MK18 1EG
Tel 01280-814080
Full-time students (1995–6), 976
Chancellor, The Baroness Thatcher, KG, OM, PC, FRS (1992)
Vice-Chancellor, Prof. R. H. Taylor (from Jan. 1997)
Director of Administration, J. Elder

THE UNIVERSITY OF CAMBRIDGE
University Offices, The Old Schools, Cambridge CB2 1TN
Tel 01223-337733
Undergraduates in residence (1995–6), 11,115

UNIVERSITY OFFICERS, ETC.
Chancellor, HRH The Duke of Edinburgh, KG, KT, OM, GBE,
  PC (1977)
Vice-Chancellor, Prof. A. N. Broers, ph.D., FRS (1996)
High Steward, The Lord Runcie, PC, DD (1991)
Deputy High Steward, The Lord Richardson of
  Duntisbourne, PC, MBE, TD (1983)
Commissary, The Lord Oliver of Aylmerton, PC (*Trinity
  Hall*) (1989)
Proctors, D. J. H. Garling, SC.D. (*St John's*); O. Rackham, ph.D.
  (*Corpus Christi*) (1996)
Orator, A. J. Bowen (*Jesus*) (1993)
Registrary, S. G. Fleet, ph.D. (*Downing*) (1983)
Deputy Registrary, N. J. B. A. Branson, ph.D. (*Darwin*) (1993)
Librarian, P. K. Fox (*Selwyn*) (1994)
Treasurer, Ms J. Womack (*Trinity*) (1993)
Secretary-General of the Faculties, D. A. Livesey,
  ph.D. (*Emmanuel*) (1992)
Director of the Fitzwilliam Museum, D. D. Robinson (*Clare*)
  (1995)

COLLEGES AND HALLS, ETC.
with dates of foundation

CHRIST'S (1505), *Master,* A. J. Munro, ph.D. (1995)
CHURCHILL (1960), *Master,* Sir John Boyd, KCMG (1996)
CLARE (1326), *Master,* Prof. B. A. Hepple, LL D (1993)
CLARE HALL (1966), *President,* Prof. G. P. K. Beer, Litt.D.,
  FBA (1994)
CORPUS CHRISTI (1352), *Master,* Prof. Sir Tony Wrigley,
  ph.D. (1994)
DARWIN (1964), *Master,* Prof. G. E. R. Lloyd, ph.D., FBA
  (1989)
DOWNING (1800), *Master,* Prof. D. A. King, FRS (1995)
EMMANUEL (1584), *Master,* Prof. J. E. Ffowcs-Williams,
  SC.D. (1996)

FITZWILLIAM (1966), *Master,* Prof. A. W. Cuthbert, ph.D.,
  FRS (1991)
GIRTON (1869), *Mistress,* Mrs J. J. d'A. Campbell, CMG
  (1992)
GONVILLE AND CAIUS (1348), *Master,* N. MacKendrick
  (1996)
HOMERTON (1824) (for B.Ed. students), *Principal,*
  Mrs K. B. Pretty, ph.D. (1991)
HUGHES HALL (1885) (for post-graduate students),
  President, J. T. Dingle, D.SC. (1993)
JESUS (1496), *Master,* Prof. the Lord Renfrew of
  Kaimsthorn, SC.D. (1986)
KING'S (1441), *Provost,* Prof. P. P. G. Bateson, SC.D., FRS
  (1987)
*LUCY CAVENDISH COLLEGE (1965) (for women research
  students and mature and affiliated undergraduates),
  President, The Baroness Perry of Southwark (1994)
MAGDALENE (1542), *Master,* Prof. Sir John Gurdon,
  D.phil., FRS (1995)
*NEW HALL (1954), *President,* Mrs A. Lonsdale (1996)
*NEWNHAM (1871), *Principal,* Ms O. S. O'Neill, CBE
  (1992)
PEMBROKE (1347), *Master,* Sir Roger Tomkys, KCMG
  (1992)
PETERHOUSE (1284), *Master,* Prof. Sir John Meurig
  Thomas, FRS (1993)
QUEENS' (1448), *President,* Lord Eatwell (from Jan. 1997)
ROBINSON (1977), *Warden,* Prof. the Lord Lewis of
  Newnham, SC.D., FRS (1977)
ST CATHARINE'S (1473), *Master,* Prof. Sir Terence
  English (1993)
ST EDMUND'S (1896), *Master,* Prof. R. B. Heap, SC.D. (1996)
ST JOHN'S (1511), *Master,* Prof. P. Goddard, ph.D., FRS
  (1994)
SELWYN (1882), *Master,* D. Harrison, CBE, SC.D., F.eng.
  (1993)
SIDNEY SUSSEX (1596), *Master,* Prof. G. Horn, SC.D., FRS
  (1992)
TRINITY (1546), *Master,* Sir Michael Atiyah, ph.D., FRS,
  FRSE (1990)
TRINITY HALL (1350), *Master,* Sir John Lyons, ph.D.
  (1984)
WOLFSON (1965), *President,* G. Johnson ph.D. (1994)
*College for women only

THE UNIVERSITY OF CENTRAL ENGLAND IN BIRMINGHAM (1992)
Perry Barr, Birmingham B42 2SU
Tel 0121-331 5000
Full-time students (1995–6), 11,000
Chancellor, The Lord Mayor of Birmingham
Vice-Chancellor, Dr P. C. Knight, CBE
Secretary and Registrar, Ms M. Penlington

THE UNIVERSITY OF CENTRAL LANCASHIRE (1992)
Preston PR1 2HE
Tel 01772-201201
Full-time students (1995–6), 13,856
Chancellor, Sir Francis Kennedy, KCMG, CBE
Vice-Chancellor, B. G. Booth
Academic Registrar, L. Munro
Secretary, Ms P. M. Ackroyd

THE CITY UNIVERSITY (1966)
Northampton Square, London EC1V 0HB
Tel 0171-477 8000
Full-time students (1995–6), 6,837
Chancellor, The Rt. Hon. the Lord Mayor of London

Vice-Chancellor, Prof. R. N. Franklin, CBE, D.Phil., D.SC.
Academic Registrar, A. H. Seville, Ph.D.
Secretary, M. M. O'Hara

COVENTRY UNIVERSITY (1992)
Priory Street, Coventry CV1 5FB
Tel 01203-631313
Full-time students (1995–6), 13,035
Chancellor, The Lord Plumb, MEP
Vice-Chancellor, M. Goldstein, Ph.D., D.SC.
Academic Registrar, J. Gledhill, Ph.D.
Secretary, Ms L. Arlidge

CRANFIELD UNIVERSITY (1969)
(Founded as Cranfield Institute of Technology)
Cranfield, Beds MK43 0AL
Tel 01234-750111
Full-time students (1995–6), 2,355
Chancellor, The Lord Kings Norton, Ph.D., FEng. (1969)
Vice-Chancellor, Prof. F. R. Hartley, D.SC.
Secretary and Registrar, J. K. Pettifer

DE MONTFORT UNIVERSITY (1992)
The Gateway, Leicester LE1 9BH
Tel 0116-255 1551
Full-time students (1995–6), 26,000
Chancellor, Sir Clive Whitmore, GCB, CVO
Vice-Chancellor, Prof. K. Barker, CBE
Academic Registrar, V. E. Critchlow

THE UNIVERSITY OF DERBY (1993)
(formerly Derbyshire College of Higher Education)
Kedleston Road, Derby DE22 1GB
Tel 01332-622222
Full-time students (1995–6), 9,500
Chancellor, Sir Christopher Ball
Vice-Chancellor, Prof. R. Waterhouse
Registrar, Mrs J. Fry
Secretary, R. Gillis

THE UNIVERSITY OF DUNDEE (1967)
Dundee DD1 4HN
Tel 01382-223181
Full-time students (1995–6), 8,170
Chancellor, Sir James Black, FRCP, FRS (1992)
Vice-Chancellor, Dr I. J. Graham-Bryce
Academic Secretary, Dr I. Francis
Secretary, R. Seaton
Rector, S. Fry (1995–8)

THE UNIVERSITY OF DURHAM
(Founded 1832; re-organized 1908, 1937 and 1963)
Old Shire Hall, Durham DH1 3HP
Tel 0191-374 2000
Full-time students (1995–6), 8,804
Chancellor, Sir Peter Ustinov, CBE, FRSL
Vice-Chancellor, Prof. E. A. V. Ebsworth, CBE, Ph.D., SC.D.,
   FRSE
Registrar and Secretary, J. C. F. Hayward

COLLEGES
COLLINGWOOD, *Principal*, Prof. G. H. Blake, Ph.D.
GRADUATE SOCIETY, *Principal*, M. Richardson, Ph.D.
GREY, *Master*, V. E. Watts
HATFIELD, *Master*, Prof. T. P. Burt, Ph.D.
ST AIDAN'S, *Principal*, R. J. Williams
ST CHAD'S, *Principal*, Revd D. W. H. Arnold, Ph.D.
ST CUTHBERT'S SOCIETY, *Principal*, S. G. C. Stoker
ST HILD AND ST BEDE, *Principal*, J. V. Armitage, Ph.D.
ST JOHN'S, *Principal*, D. V. Day

ST MARY'S, *Principal*, Miss J. M. Kenworthy
TREVELYAN, *Principal*, Prof. M. Todd
UNIVERSITY (DURHAM), *Master*, E. C. Salthouse, Ph.D.
UNIVERSITY (STOCKTON), *Principal*, J. C. F. Hayward
USHAW, *President*, Rt. Revd Mgr R. Atherton, OBE
VAN MILDERT, *Principal*, Ms J. Turner, Ph.D.

THE UNIVERSITY OF EAST ANGLIA (1963)
Norwich NR4 7TJ
Tel 01603-456161
Full-time students (1995–6), 7,500
Chancellor, Sir Geoffrey Allen, FEng, FRS (1994)
Vice-Chancellor, Dame Elizabeth Esteve-Coll, DBE
Registrar and Secretary, M. G. E. Paulson-Ellis, OBE

THE UNIVERSITY OF EAST LONDON (1992)
Longbridge Road, Dagenham, Essex RM8 2AS
Tel 0181-590 7000
Full-time students (1995–6), 10,080
Chancellor, vacant
Vice-Chancellor, Prof. F. Gould
Secretary and Registrar, A. Ingle

THE UNIVERSITY OF EDINBURGH (1583)
7–11 Nicolson Street, Edinburgh EH8 9BE
Tel 0131-650 1000
Full-time students (1995–6), 15,358
Chancellor, HRH The Prince Philip, Duke of Edinburgh,
   KG, KT, OM, GBE, PC, FRS (1952)
Vice-Chancellor, Prof. Sir Stewart Sutherland, FBA, FRSE
Secretary, M. J. B. Lowe, Ph.D.
Rector, Dr. M. Macleod (1994–7)

THE UNIVERSITY OF ESSEX (1964)
Wivenhoe Park, Colchester CO4 3SQ
Tel 01206-873333
Full-time students (1995–6), 5,645
Chancellor, The Rt. Hon. Sir Patrick Nairne, GCB, MC, LL D
   (1983)
Vice-Chancellor, I. Crewe
Registrar and Secretary, A. F. Woodburn

THE UNIVERSITY OF EXETER (1955)
Northcote House, The Queen's Drive, Exeter EX4 4QJ
Tel 01392-263263
Full-time students (1995–6), 8,000
Chancellor, Sir Rex Richards, D.SC., FRS (1981)
Vice-Chancellor, Sir Geoffrey Holland, KCB
Academic Registrar and Secretary, I. H. C. Powell

GLAMORGAN UNIVERSITY (1992)
Treforest, Pontypridd CF37 1DL
Tel 01443-480480
Full-time students (1995–6), 11,598
Chancellor, The Lord Rees, PC, QC
Vice-Chancellor, Prof. A. L. Webb
Academic Registrar, J. O'Shea
Secretary, J. L. Bracegirdle

THE UNIVERSITY OF GLASGOW (1451)
Glasgow G12 8QQ
Tel 0141-339 8855
Full-time students (1995–6), 15,302
Chancellor, Sir William Kerr Fraser
Vice-Chancellor, Prof. G. Davies, Ph.D., FEng.
Secretary, D. Mackie
Rector, R. Wilson (1996–9)

GLASGOW CALEDONIAN UNIVERSITY
(1993)
Cowcaddens Road, Glasgow G4 0BA
Tel 0141-331 3000
Full-time students (1995–6), 9,700
Chancellor, The Lord Nickson, KBE
Vice-Chancellor, Prof. J. S. Mason, PH.D.
Secretary, B. M. Murphy

THE UNIVERSITY OF GREENWICH (1992)
Bexley Road, Eltham, London SE9 2PQ
Tel 0181-331 8000
Full-time students (1995–6), 15,130
Chancellor, The Baroness Young
Vice-Chancellor, Dr D. E. Fussey
Academic Registrar, A. I. Mayfield
Secretary, J. M. Charles

HERIOT-WATT UNIVERSITY (1966)
Riccarton, Edinburgh EH14 4AS
Tel 0131-449 5111
Full-time students (1995–6), 9,219
Chancellor, The Lord Mackay of Clashfern, PC, QC, FRSE
(1979)
Vice-Chancellor, Prof. A. G. J. MacFarlane, CBE, PH.D., FRS,
FRSE, FEng. (1989)
Secretary, P. L. Wilson

THE UNIVERSITY OF HERTFORDSHIRE
(1992)
College Lane, Hatfield, Herts AL10 9AB
Tel 01707-284000
Full-time students (1995–6), 13,504
Chancellor, Sir Ian MacLaurin
Vice-Chancellor, Prof. N. K. Buxton
Registrar and Secretary, P. G. Jeffreys

THE UNIVERSITY OF HUDDERSFIELD
(1992)
Queensgate, Huddersfield HD1 3DH
Tel 01484-422288
Full-time students (1995–6), 10,524
Chancellor, vacant
Vice-Chancellor, Prof. J. R. Tarrant, PH.D.
Academic Registrar, M. E. Bond
Secretary, G. W. Downs

THE UNIVERSITY OF HULL (1954)
Cottingham Road, Hull HU6 7RX
Tel 01482-346311
Full-time students (1995–6), 12,200
Chancellor, The Lord Armstrong of Ilminster, GCB, CVO
Vice-Chancellor, Prof. D. Dilks, FRSL
Registrar and Secretary, D. J. Lock

KEELE UNIVERSITY (1962)
Keele, Newcastle under Lyme, Staffs ST5 5BG
Tel 01782-621111
Full-time students (1995–6), 5,700
Chancellor, Sir Claus Moser, KCB, CBE, FBA (1986)
Vice-Chancellor, Prof. J. V. Finch
Registrar, D. Cohen, PH.D.
Director of Academic Affairs, Dr E. F. Slade

THE UNIVERSITY OF KENT AT
CANTERBURY (1965)
Canterbury CT2 7NZ
Tel 01227-764000
Full-time students (1995–6), 8,441
Chancellor, Sir Crispin Tickell, GCMG, KCVO

Vice-Chancellor, Prof. R. Sibson, PH.D.
Secretary and Registrar, T. Mead, PH.D.

KINGSTON UNIVERSITY (1992)
Penrhyn Road, Kingston upon Thames,
Surrey KT1 2EE
Tel 0181-547 2000
Full-time students (1995–6), 13,678
Chancellor, Sir Frank Lampl
Vice-Chancellor, R. C. Smith, CBE, PH.D.
Secretary, R. Abdulla

THE UNIVERSITY OF LANCASTER (1964)
Bailrigg, Lancaster LA1 4YW
Tel 01524-65201
Full-time students (1995–6), 9,926
Chancellor, HRH Princess Alexandra, the Hon. Lady
Ogilvy, GCVO (1964)
Vice-Chancellor, Prof. W. Ritchie, OBE
Secretary, S. A. C. Lamley

THE UNIVERSITY OF LEEDS (1904)
Leeds LS2 9JT
Tel 0113-243 1751
Full-time students (1995–6), 19,419
Chancellor, HRH The Duchess of Kent, GCVO (1966)
Vice-Chancellor, Prof. A. G. Wilson
Secretary and Registrar, D. Robinson, PH.D.

LEEDS METROPOLITAN UNIVERSITY (1992)
Calverley Street, Leeds LS1 3HE
Tel 0113-283 2600
Full-time students (1995–6), 10,825
Chairman of the Board of Governors, L. Silver
Vice-Chancellor, Prof. L. Wagner
Head of Registry Services, M. Christie
Secretary, M. Wilkinson

THE UNIVERSITY OF LEICESTER (1957)
University Road, Leicester LE1 7RH
Tel 0116-252 2522
Full-time students (1995–6), 8,516
Chancellor, Sir Michael Atiyah, OM, PH.D., D.SC. (1995)
Vice-Chancellor, K. J. R. Edwards, PH.D.
Registrar and Secretary, K. J. Julian

THE UNIVERSITY OF LINCOLNSHIRE AND
HUMBERSIDE
(University of Humberside founded 1992; re-organized
1996)
Humberside Campus: Cottingham Road, Hull HU6 7RT
Tel 01482-440550
Lincoln Campus: Lincoln LN2 4YF
Tel 01522-882000
Full-time students (1995–6), 11,410
Chancellor, Dr J. H. Hooper, CBE
Vice-Chancellor, Prof. R. P. King
Registrar, F. S. Marks
Secretary, Ms M. Harries-Jenkins

THE UNIVERSITY OF LIVERPOOL (1903)
Senate House, Abercromby Square, Liverpool L69 3BX
Tel 0151-794 2010
Full-time students (1995–6), 12,993
Chancellor, The Lord Owen, CH, PC
Vice-Chancellor, Prof. P. N. Love, CBE
Registrar and Secretary, M. D. Carr

LIVERPOOL JOHN MOORES UNIVERSITY (1992)

Rodney House, 70 Mount Pleasant, Liverpool L3 5UX
Tel 0151-231 2121
Full-time students (1995–6), 14,825
Chancellor, J. Moores, CBE
Vice-Chancellor, Prof. P. Toyne
Registrar and Secretary, Ms A. Wild

THE UNIVERSITY OF LONDON (1836)

Senate House, Malet Street, London WC1E 7HU
Tel 0171-636 8000
Internal students (1995–6), 79,230, External students, 22,116
Visitor, HM The Queen in Council
Chancellor, HRH The Princess Royal, KG, GCVO, FRS (1981)
Vice-Chancellor, Prof. A. Rutherford, CBE
Chairman of the Council, The Lord Woolf, PC
Chairman of Convocation, Prof. Sir William Taylor, CBE

COLLEGES OF THE UNIVERSITY
BIRKBECK COLLEGE, Malet Street, London
   WC1E 7HX. *Master*, The Baroness Blackstone, PH.D.
CHARING CROSS AND WESTMINSTER MEDICAL SCHOOL,
   The Reynolds Building, St Dunstan's Road, London
   W6 8RP. *Dean*, Prof. R. M. Greenhalgh, FRCS
GOLDSMITHS COLLEGE, Lewisham Way, New Cross,
   London SE14 6NW. *Warden*, Prof. K. J. Gregory, PH.D.
HEYTHROP COLLEGE, Kensington Square, London
   W8 5HQ. *Principal*, C. J. Moss, D.phil.
IMPERIAL COLLEGE OF SCIENCE, TECHNOLOGY AND
   MEDICINE (includes St Mary's Hospital Medical
   School), South Kensington, London SW7 2AZ. *Rector*,
   Prof. Sir Ronald Oxburgh, KBE, FRS
INSTITUTE OF CANCER RESEARCH, Royal Cancer
   Hospital, Chester Beatty Laboratories, 17A Onslow
   Gardens, London SW7 3AL. *Chief Executive*, Prof.
   P. B. Garland, PH.D., FRSE
INSTITUTE OF EDUCATION, 20 Bedford Way, London
   WC1H 0AL. *Director*, Prof. P. Mortimore
KING'S COLLEGE LONDON (includes King's College
   School of Medicine and Dentistry), Strand, London
   WC2R 2LS. *Principal*, Prof. A. Lucas, PH.D.
   Associated Institute:
   Institute of Psychiatry, De Crespigny Park, Denmark Hill,
   London SE5 8AF. *Dean*, Prof. S. Checkley
LONDON BUSINESS SCHOOL, Sussex Place, Regent's Park,
   London NW1 4SA. *Principal*, Prof. G. S. Bain, D.phil.
THE LONDON HOSPITAL MEDICAL COLLEGE, Turner
   Street, London E1 2AD. *Dean*, Prof. Sir Colin Berry,
   FRCPath.
LONDON SCHOOL OF ECONOMICS AND POLITICAL
   SCIENCE, Houghton Street, London WC2A 2AE. *Director*,
   J. M. Ashworth, PH.D., D.SC.
LONDON SCHOOL OF HYGIENE AND TROPICAL
   MEDICINE, Keppel Street, London WC1E 7HT. *Dean*,
   Prof. H. Spencer
QUEEN MARY AND WESTFIELD COLLEGE (incorporating
   St Bartholomew's and the Royal London School of
   Medicine and Dentistry), Mile End Road, London
   E1 4NS. *Principal*, Prof. G. Zellick, PH.D.
ROYAL FREE HOSPITAL SCHOOL OF MEDICINE, Rowland
   Hill Street, London NW3 2PF. *Dean*, Prof. A. J.
   Zuckerman, MD, FRCP
ROYAL HOLLOWAY, Egham Hill, Egham, Surrey TW20
   0EX. *Principal*, Prof. N. Gowar, M.phil.
ROYAL POSTGRADUATE MEDICAL SCHOOL,
   Hammersmith Hospital, Du Cane Road, London
   W12 7HT. *Dean*, Prof. Sir Colin Dollery, FRCP

ROYAL VETERINARY COLLEGE, Royal College Street,
   London NW1 0TU. *Principal and Dean*, Prof. L. E. Lanyon,
   PH.D.
ST BARTHOLOMEW'S AND THE ROYAL LONDON SCHOOL
   OF MEDICINE AND DENTISTRY, *see* Queen Mary and
   Westfield College
ST GEORGE'S HOSPITAL MEDICAL SCHOOL, Cranmer
   Terrace, London SW17 0RE. *Dean*, Prof. R. Boyd
SCHOOL OF ORIENTAL AND AFRICAN STUDIES,
   Thornhaugh Street, Russell Square, London
   WC1H 0XG. *Director*, Sir Tim Lankester, KCB
SCHOOL OF PHARMACY, 29–39 Brunswick Square,
   London WC1N 1AX. *Dean*, Prof. A. T. Florence, PH.D.,
   FRSE
SCHOOL OF SLAVONIC AND EAST EUROPEAN STUDIES,
   Senate House, Malet Street, London WC1E 7HU. *Director*,
   Prof. M. A. Branch, PH.D.
UNITED MEDICAL AND DENTAL SCHOOLS OF GUY'S AND
   ST THOMAS' HOSPITALS, Guy's, London Bridge,
   London SE1 9RT; St Thomas', Lambeth Palace Road,
   London SE1 7EH. *Principal*, Prof. C. Chantler, FRCP
UNIVERSITY COLLEGE LONDON (including UCL
   Medical School), Gower Street, London
   WC1E 6BT. *Provost*, Sir Derek Roberts, CBE, FRS
WYE COLLEGE, Wye, Near Ashford, Kent
   TN25 5AH. *Principal*, Prof. J. H. D. Prescott, PH.D.

SCHOOL OF ADVANCED STUDY
Senate House, Malet Street, London WC1E 7HU. *Dean*, Prof.
   T. C. Daintith
Comprises:
INSTITUTE OF ADVANCED LEGAL STUDIES, Charles
   Clore House, 17 Russell Square, London
   WC1B 5DR. *Director*, Prof. B. A. K. Rider
INSTITUTE OF CLASSICAL STUDIES, 31–34 Gordon
   Square, London WC1H 0PY. *Director*, Prof.
   R. R. K. Sorabji, FBA
INSTITUTE OF COMMONWEALTH STUDIES, 27–28 Russell
   Square, London WC1B 5DS. *Director*, Prof. J. Manor
INSTITUTE OF GERMANIC STUDIES, 29 Russell Square,
   London WC1B 5DP. *Hon. Director*, E. M. Batley
INSTITUTE OF HISTORICAL RESEARCH, Senate House,
   Malet Street, London WC1E 7HU. *Director*, Prof.
   P. K. O'Brien, D.phil.
INSTITUTE OF LATIN AMERICAN STUDIES, 31 Tavistock
   Square, London WC1H 9HA. *Director*, Prof. V. G. Bulmer-
   Thomas, D.phil.
INSTITUTE OF ROMANCE STUDIES, Senate House, Malet
   Street, London WC1E 7HU. *Hon. Director*, Prof. A. Lavers,
   PH.D.
INSTITUTE OF UNITED STATES STUDIES, Senate House,
   Malet Street, London WC1E 7HU. *Director*, Prof.
   G. L. McDowell, PH.D.
WARBURG INSTITUTE, Woburn Square, London
   WC1H 0AB. *Director*, Prof. C. N. J. Mann, PH.D.

INSTITUTES AND ASSOCIATE INSTITUTIONS
BRITISH INSTITUTE IN PARIS, 9–11 rue de Constantine,
   75340 Paris, Cedex 07, France. *Director*, Prof.
   C. L. Campos, PH.D. *London office:* Senate House, Malet
   Street, London WC1E 7HU
CENTRE FOR DEFENCE STUDIES, King's College London,
   Strand, London WC2R 2LS. *Director*, Prof. L. Freedman
CENTRE FOR ENGLISH STUDIES, Senate House, Malet
   Street, London WC1E 7HU. *Director*, Dr W. L. Chernaik
COURTAULD INSTITUTE OF ART, North Block, Somerset
   House, Strand, London WC2R 0RN. *Director*, Prof. E. C.
   Fernie
INSTITUTE OF ZOOLOGY, Royal Zoological Society,
   Regent's Park, London NW1 4RY. *Director*, Prof. M.
   Gosling.

JEWS' COLLEGE, 44A Albert Road, London NW4 2SJ.
Principal, Rabbi Dr D. Sinclair
ROYAL ACADEMY OF MUSIC, Marylebone Road, London
NW1 5HT. *Principal,* Prof. C. Price
ROYAL COLLEGE OF MUSIC, Prince Consort Road,
London SW7 2BS. *Director,* Ms J. Ritterman, PH.D.
TRINITY COLLEGE OF MUSIC, 11–13 Mandeville Place,
London WIM 6AQ. *Principal,* G. Henderson
UNIVERSITY MARINE BIOLOGICAL STATION MILLPORT,
Isle of Cumbrae, Scotland KA28 0EG. *Director,* Prof.
J. Davenport, PH.D., D.SC., FRSE

LONDON GUILDHALL UNIVERSITY (1993)
133 Whitechapel High Street, London E1 7QA
Tel 0171-320 1000
Full-time students (1995–6), 13,000
Patron, HRH The Prince Philip, Duke of Edinburgh, KG,
KT, OM, GBE, PC, FRS
Provost, Prof. R. Floud, D.Phil.
Academic Registrar, Ms J. Grinstead
Secretary, N. Maude

**LOUGHBOROUGH UNIVERSITY OF
TECHNOLOGY** (1966)
Loughborough, Leics LE11 3TU
Tel 01509-263171
Full-time students (1994–5), 9,963
Chancellor, Sir Denis Rooke, CBE, FRS, FEng (1989)
Vice-Chancellor, Prof. D.Wallace, PH.D., FRS, FRSE
Registrar, D. E. Fletcher, PH.D.
Academic Secretary, N. A. McHard

THE UNIVERSITY OF LUTON (1993)
(formerly Luton College of Higher Education)
Park Square, Luton LU1 3JU
Tel 01582-34111
Full-time students (1995–6), 9,000
Chancellor, Sir David Plastow
Vice-Chancellor, Dr A. Wood
Head of Admissions, S. Kendall

THE UNIVERSITY OF MANCHESTER
(Founded 1851; re-organized 1880 and 1903)
Oxford Road, Manchester M13 9PL
Tel: 0161-275 2000
Full-time students (1995–6), 16,569
Chancellor, The Lord Flowers, FRS
Vice-Chancellor, Prof. M. B. Harris, CBE, PH.D.
Registrar and Secretary, E. Newcomb
Academic Secretary, D. A. Richardson

**UNIVERSITY OF MANCHESTER
INSTITUTE OF SCIENCE AND
TECHNOLOGY** (1824)
PO Box 88, Manchester M60 1QD
Tel 0161-236 3311
Full-time students (1995–6), 6,000
Chancellor, Prof. Sir Roland Smith, PH.D. (1995)
Vice-Chancellor, Prof. R. F. Boucher, FEng.
Registrar and Secretary, P. C. C. Stephenson

**MANCHESTER METROPOLITAN
UNIVERSITY** (1992)
All Saints, Manchester M15 6BH
Tel 0161-247 2000
Full-time students (1995–6), 22,000
Chancellor, The Duke of Westminster, OBE, TD
Vice-Chancellor, Sir Kenneth Green
Academic Registrar, J. Karczewski-Slowikowski
Secretary, T. A. Hendley

MIDDLESEX UNIVERSITY (1992)
White Hart Lane, London N17 8HR
Tel 0181-362 5000
Full-time students (1994–5), 16,084
Chancellor, The Baroness Platt of Writtle
Vice-Chancellor, vacant
Registrar and Secretary, G. Jones

NAPIER UNIVERSITY (1992)
219 Colinton Road, Edinburgh EH14 1DJ
Tel 0131-444 2266
Full-time students (1995–6), 7,753
Chancellor, The Lord Younger of Prestwick, KCVO, TD, PC,
FRSE
Vice-Chancellor, Prof. J. Mavor
Secretary and Registrar, I. J. Miller

**THE UNIVERSITY OF NEWCASTLE UPON
TYNE**
(Founded 1852; re-organized 1908, 1937 and 1963)
6 Kensington Terrace, Newcastle upon Tyne NE1 7RU
Tel 0191-222 6000
Full-time students (1995–6), 12,703
Chancellor, The Viscount Ridley, KG, GCVO, TD (1989)
Vice-Chancellor, J. R. G. Wright
Registrar, D. E. T. Nicholson

THE UNIVERSITY OF NORTH LONDON
(1992)
166–220 Holloway Road, London N7 8DB
Tel 0171-607 2789
Full-time students (1995–6), 10,710
Vice-Chancellor, B. Roper
Academic Registrar, Dr M. Storey
Secretary, J. McParland

**THE UNIVERSITY OF NORTHUMBRIA AT
NEWCASTLE** (1992)
Ellison Place, Newcastle upon Tyne NE1 8ST
Tel 0191-232 6002
Full-time students (1995–6), 16,656
Chancellor, The Lord Glenamara, CH, PC (1984)
Vice-Chancellor, Prof. G. Smith
Registrar, Mrs C. Penna
Secretary, R. A. Bott

THE UNIVERSITY OF NOTTINGHAM (1948)
University Park, Nottingham NG7 2RD
Tel 0115-951 5151
Full-time students (1995–6), 13,425
Chancellor, Sir Ron Dearing, CB, FEng. (1993)
Vice-Chancellor, Prof. Sir Colin Campbell
Registrar, D. J. Allen

NOTTINGHAM TRENT UNIVERSITY (1992)
Burton Street, Nottingham NG1 4BU
Tel 0115-941 8418
Full-time students (1995–6), 18,213
Vice-Chancellor, Prof. R. Cowell, PH.D.
Academic Registrar, D. W. Samson
Secretary, S. Smith

THE UNIVERSITY OF OXFORD
University Offices, Wellington Square, Oxford OX1 2JD
Tel 01865-270001
Students in residence (1995–6), 15,300

UNIVERSITY OFFICERS, ETC.
Chancellor, The Lord Jenkins of Hillhead, OM, PC (*Balliol*),
elected 1987

High Steward, The Lord Goff of Chieveley, PC (*Lincoln* and
New College), *elected* 1990
Vice-Chancellor, Dr P. M. North, CBE, QC, FBA (*Jesus*), *elected*
1993
Proctors, Dr J. R. T. Garfitt (*Magdalen*); Dr J. C. N. Horder
(*Worcester*), *elected* 1996
Assessor, Dr N. G. Bowles (*St Anne's*), *elected* 1996
Public Orator, J. Griffin (*Balliol*), *elected* 1992
Bodley's Librarian, D. G. Vaisey (*Exeter*), *elected* 1986
Keeper of Archives, D. G. Vaisey (*Exeter*), *elected* 1995
Director of the Ashmolean Museum, Prof. C. J. White, CVO
(*Worcester*), *elected* 1985
Registrar of the University, A. J. Dorey, D.phil. (*Linacre*), *elected*
1979
Surveyor to the University, P. M. R. Hill, *elected* 1993
Secretary of Faculties, A. P. Weale (*Worcester*), *elected* 1984
Secretary of the Chest, J. R. Clements, *elected* 1995
Deputy Registrar (*Administration*), P. W. Jones (*Green*), *elected*
1991

OXFORD COLLEGES AND HALLS
with dates of foundation

ALL SOULS (1438), *Warden*, Prof. J. Davis (1994)
BALLIOL (1263), *Master*, C. R. Lucas, D.phil. (1994)
BRASENOSE (1509), *Principal*, The Lord Windlesham, CVO,
PC (1989)
CHRIST CHURCH (1546), *Dean*, Very Revd J. H. Drury
(1991)
CORPUS CHRISTI (1517), *President*, Prof. Sir Keith
Thomas, FBA (1986)
EXETER (1314), *Rector*, Prof. M. Butler (1994)
GREEN (1979), *Warden*, Sir Crispin Tickell, GCMG, KCVO
(1990)
HERTFORD (1874), *Principal*, Sir Walter Bodmer, FRS
(1996)
JESUS (1571), *Principal*, Dr P. M. North, CBE, FBA (1984)
KEBLE (1868), *Warden*, A. Cameron, FBA, FSA (1994)
KELLOG (1990), *President*, G. P. Thomas, Ph.D. (1990)
LADY MARGARET HALL (1878), *Principal*, Sir Brian Fall,
KCMG (1995)
LINACRE (1962), *Principal*, Dr P. A. Slack (1996)
LINCOLN (1427), *Rector*, E. K. Anderson, FRSE (1994)
MAGDALEN (1458), *President*, A. D. Smith, CBE (1988)
MANSFIELD (1886), *Principal*, D. I. Marquand (1996)
MERTON (1264), *Warden*, Dr. J Rawson, FBA (1994)
NEW COLLEGE (1379), *Warden*, Prof. A. J. Ryan (1996)
NUFFIELD (1937), *Warden*, Prof. A. Atkinson, FBA (1994)
ORIEL (1326), *Provost*, E. W. Nicholson, DD, FBA (1990)
PEMBROKE (1624), *Master*, Prof. R. Stevens, DCL (1993)
QUEEN'S (1340), *Provost*, G. Marshall (1993)
ST ANNE'S (1952) (originally Society of Oxford Home-
Students (1879)), *Principal*, Mrs R. L. Deech (1991)
ST ANTONY'S (1950), *Warden*, The Lord Dahrendorf, KBE,
ph.D., FBA (1987)
ST CATHERINE'S (1962), *Master*, The Lord Plant of
Highfield (1994)
ST CROSS (1965), *Master*, R. C. Repp, D.phil. (1987)
ST EDMUND HALL (*c*.1278), *Principal*, His Hon. Stephen
Tumin (1996)
*ST HILDA'S (1893), *Principal*, Miss E. Llewellyn-Smith,
CB (1990)
ST HUGH'S (1886), *Principal*, D. Wood, QC (1991)
ST JOHN'S (1555), *President*, W. Hayes, D.phil. (1987)
ST PETER'S (1929), *Master*, J. P. Barron, D.phil. (1991)
SOMERVILLE (1879), *Principal*, Dr F. Caldicott (1996)
TEMPLETON (1965), *President*, Dr M. van Clemm (1996)

_____

* College for women only

TRINITY (1554), *President*, The Hon. Michael J. Beloff, QC
(1996)
UNIVERSITY (1249), *Master*, W. J. Albery, D.phil., FRS
(1989)
WADHAM (1612), *Warden*, J. S. Flemming (1993)
WOLFSON (1966), *President*, Sir David Smith, D.phil. (1994)
WORCESTER (1714), *Provost*, R. G. Smethurst (1991)

BLACKFRIARS (1921), *Regent*, Revd B. E. A. Davies (1994)
CAMPION HALL (1896), *Master*, Revd J. A. Munitiz (1989)
GREYFRIARS (1910), *Warden*, Revd M. W. Sheehan,
D.phil. (1990)
MANCHESTER (1786), *Principal*, Revd R. Waller, Ph.D.
(1990)
REGENT'S PARK (1810), *Principal*, Revd P. S. Fiddes,
D.phil. (1989)
ST BENET'S HALL (1897), *Master*, Revd H. Wansbrough,
OSB (1991)

OXFORD BROOKES UNIVERSITY (1993)
Headington, Oxford OX3 0BP
Tel 01865-741111
Full-time students (1995–6), 8,000
Chancellor, Ms H. Kennedy, QC
Vice-Chancellor, Dr C. Booth
Deputy Vice-Chancellor, Corporate Services, B. Summers
Academic Secretary, Ms L. Winders

THE UNIVERSITY OF PAISLEY (1992)
(formerly Paisley College of Technology)
High Street, Paisley PA1 2BE
Tel 0141-848 3000
Full-time students (1993–4), 6,162
Chancellor, Sir Robert Easton, CBE
Vice-Chancellor, Prof. R. W. Shaw
Registrar, D. Rigg
Secretary, J. Fraser

THE UNIVERSITY OF PLYMOUTH (1992)
Drake Circus, Plymouth PL4 8AA
Tel 01752-600600
Full-time students (1995–6), 18,305
Vice-Chancellor, Prof. J. Bull
Registrar, Dr C. J. Sparrow

THE UNIVERSITY OF PORTSMOUTH (1992)
University House, Winston Churchill Avenue,
Portsmouth PO1 2UP
Tel 01705-876543
Full-time students (1995–6), 14,612
Chancellor, The Lord Palumbo
Vice-Chancellor (*acting*), Dr M. Bateman
Academic Registrar, A. Rees
Secretary, R. Moore

THE QUEEN'S UNIVERSITY OF BELFAST
(1908)
Belfast BT7 1NN
Tel 01232-245133
Full-time students (1994–5), 11,000
Chancellor, Sir David Orr
Vice-Chancellor, Sir Gordon Beveridge, Ph.D., FRSE
Academic Secretary, Dr G. Baird
Administrative Secretary, D. Wilson

THE UNIVERSITY OF READING (1926)
Whiteknights, PO Box 217, Reading RG6 2AH
Tel 0118-987 5123
Full-time students (1995–6), 11,000

Chancellor, The Lord Carrington, KG, GCMG, CH, MC, PC (1992)
Vice-Chancellor, Prof. R. Williams
Registrar, D. C. R. Frampton

THE ROBERT GORDON UNIVERSITY (1992)
Schoolhill, Aberdeen AB10 1FR
Tel 01224-262210
Full-time students (1995–6), 6,500
Chancellor, Sir Bob Reid (1993)
Vice-Chancellor, Dr D. A. Kennedy
Secretary, D. Caldwell

THE UNIVERSITY OF ST ANDREWS (1411)
College Gate, St Andrews KY16 9AJ
Tel 01334-476161
Full-time students (1995–6), 5,930
Chancellor, Sir Kenneth Dover, D.Litt., FRSE, FBA (1981)
Vice-Chancellor, Prof. S. Arnott, CBE, SC.D., FRS, FRSE
Secretary of Court, D. J. Corner
Rector, D. Findlay, QC (1994–7)

THE UNIVERSITY OF SALFORD (1967)
Salford M5 4WT
Tel 0161-745 5000
Full-time students (1995–6), 13,000
Chancellor, Sir Walter Bodmer, Ph.D., FRS
Vice-Chancellor, Prof. T. M. Husband, Ph.D., FEng.
Registrar, M. D. Winton, Ph.D.

THE UNIVERSITY OF SHEFFIELD (1905)
8 Palmerston Road, Sheffield S10 2TE
Tel 0114-276 8555
Full-time students (1995–6), 18,400
Chancellor, The Lord Dainton, Ph.D., SC.D., FRS (1979)
Vice-Chancellor, Prof. G. G. Roberts, Ph.D., D.SC., FRS
Registrar and Secretary, J. S. Padley, Ph.D.

SHEFFIELD HALLAM UNIVERSITY (1992)
Pond Street, Sheffield S1 1WB
Tel 0114-272 0911
Full-time students (1995–6), 20,000
Chancellor, Sir Bryan Nicholson
Vice-Chancellor, J. Stoddart, CBE
Registrar, Ms J. Tory
Secretary, Ms S. Neocosmos

THE UNIVERSITY OF SOUTHAMPTON (1952)
Highfield, Southampton SO17 1BJ
Tel 01703-595000
Full-time students (1995–6), 12,500
Chancellor, The Earl of Selbourne, KBE, FRS
Vice-Chancellor, Prof. H. Newby, CBE, Ph.D.
Secretary and Registrar, J. F. D. Lauwerys
Academic Registrar, R. Knight

SOUTH BANK UNIVERSITY (1992)
103 Borough Road, London SE1 0AA
Tel 0171-898 8989
Full-time students (1994–5), 15,000
Chancellor, C. McLaren
Vice-Chancellor, Prof. G. Bernbaum
Registrar, R. Phillips
Secretary, Mrs L. Gander

STAFFORDSHIRE UNIVERSITY (1992)
College Road, Stoke-on-Trent ST4 2DE
Tel 01782-294000
Full-time students (1995–6), 13,223

Chancellor, The Lord Ashley of Stoke, CH, PC
Vice-Chancellor, Prof. C. E. King, Ph.D.
Academic Registrar, Miss F. Francis
Secretary, K. Sproston

THE UNIVERSITY OF STIRLING (1967)
Stirling FK9 4LA
Tel 01786-467055
Full-time students (1995–6), 5,300
Chancellor, The Lord Balfour of Burleigh, FRSE (1988)
Vice-Chancellor, Prof. A. Miller, Ph.D., FRSE
Academic Registrar, D. Wood
Secretary, K. J. Clarke

THE UNIVERSITY OF STRATHCLYDE (1964)
McCance Building, John Anderson Campus, Glasgow G1 1XQ
Tel 0141-552 4400
Full-time students (1995–6), 14,100
Chancellor, The Lord Tombs, LL D, D.SC., FEng. (1990)
Vice-Chancellor, Prof. J. P. Arbuthnott, SC.D., FRSE
Secretary, P. W. A. West

THE UNIVERSITY OF SUNDERLAND (1992)
Langham Tower, Ryhope Road, Sunderland SR2 7EE
Tel 0191-515 2000
Full-time students (1994–5), 12,588
Vice-Chancellor, Ms A. Wright, Ph.D.
Academic Registrar, S. Porteous
Secretary, J. D. Pacey

THE UNIVERSITY OF SURREY (1966)
Guildford, Surrey GU2 5XH
Tel 01483-300800
Full-time students (1995–6), 7,500
Chancellor, HRH The Duke of Kent, KG, GCMG, GCVO (1977)
Vice-Chancellor, Prof. R. J. Dowling, Ph.D., FEng.
Secretary and Registrar, H. W. B. Davies

THE UNIVERSITY OF SUSSEX (1961)
Falmer, Brighton BN1 9RH
Tel 01273-606755
Full-time students (1995–6), 8,731
Chancellor, The Duke of Richmond and Gordon (1985)
Vice-Chancellor, Prof. G. Conway, Ph.D.
Registrar and Secretary, B. Gooch

THE UNIVERSITY OF TEESSIDE (1992)
Middlesbrough TS1 3BA
Tel 01642-218121
Full-time students (1994–5), 9,700
Chancellor, Sir Leon Brittan
Vice-Chancellor, Prof. D. Fraser
University Secretary, J. M. McClintock

THAMES VALLEY UNIVERSITY (1992)
St Mary's Road, Ealing, London W5 5RF
Tel 0181-579 5000
Full-time students (1995–6), 11,500
Chancellor, P. Hamlyn, CBE
Vice-Chancellor, M. Fitzgerald, Ph.D.
Head of Registry, P. Head
Secretary, Ms M. Joyce

THE UNIVERSITY OF ULSTER (1984)
(Amalgamation of New University of Ulster and Ulster Polytechnic)
Cromore Road, Coleraine BT52 1SA
Tel 01265-44141
Full-time students (1995–6), 13,548

Chancellor, Rabbi J. Neuberger
Vice-Chancellor, Prof. Sir Trevor Smith
Academic Registrar, K. Miller, ᴘʜ.ᴅ.

THE UNIVERSITY OF WALES (1893)
King Edward VII Avenue, Cathays Park, Cardiff ᴄꜰ1 3ɴs
Tel 01222-382656
Full-time students (1995–6), 45,000
Chancellor, HRH The Prince of Wales, ᴋɢ, ᴋᴛ, ɢᴄʙ, ᴘᴄ (1976)
Senior Vice-Chancellor, Prof. K. Robbins, ᴅ.ʟitt., ᴅ.ᴘʜil., ꜰʀsᴇ
Secretary-General, J. D. Pritchard

Cᴏʟʟᴇɢᴇs ᴀɴᴅ Iɴsᴛɪᴛᴜᴛɪᴏɴs

Uɴɪᴠᴇʀsɪᴛʏ Cᴏʟʟᴇɢᴇ ᴏꜰ Nᴏʀᴛʜ Wᴀʟᴇs, Bangor
ʟʟ57 2ᴅɢ. Tel: 01248-351151. *Vice-Chancellor*, Prof. H. R.
Evans, ᴘʜ.ᴅ., ꜰᴇng. (1995)
Uɴɪᴠᴇʀsɪᴛʏ Cᴏʟʟᴇɢᴇ ᴏꜰ Wᴀʟᴇs, Aʙᴇʀʏsᴛᴡʏᴛʜ, Old
College, King Street, Aberystwyth sʏ23 2ᴀx. Tel:
01970-623111. *Vice-Chancellor*, Prof. D. Llwyd Morgan,
ᴅ.ᴘʜil. (1995)
Uɴɪᴠᴇʀsɪᴛʏ ᴏꜰ Wᴀʟᴇs, Cᴀʀᴅɪꜰꜰ, PO Box 920, Cardiff
ᴄꜰ1 3xᴘ. Tel: 01222-874000. *Vice-Chancellor*, Prof.
E. B. Smith, ᴘʜ.ᴅ., ᴅ.sᴄ. (1993)
Uɴɪᴠᴇʀsɪᴛʏ ᴏꜰ Wᴀʟᴇs Cᴏʟʟᴇɢᴇ, Nᴇᴡᴘᴏʀᴛ, College
Crescent, Caerleon ɴᴘ6 1ʏɢ. Tel: 01633-432020.
Principal, Prof. K. J. Overshott, ᴘʜ.ᴅ.
Uɴɪᴠᴇʀsɪᴛʏ ᴏꜰ Wᴀʟᴇs Cᴏʟʟᴇɢᴇ ᴏꜰ Mᴇᴅɪᴄɪɴᴇ, Heath
Park, Cardiff ᴄꜰ4 4xɴ. Tel: 01222-747747. *Vice-Chancellor*, Prof. I. R. Cameron, ꜰʀᴄᴘ (1994)
Uɴɪᴠᴇʀsɪᴛʏ ᴏꜰ Wᴀʟᴇs Iɴsᴛɪᴛᴜᴛᴇ, Cᴀʀᴅɪꜰꜰ, Llandaff
Centre, Western Avenue, Cardiff ᴄꜰ5 2sɢ. Tel: 01222-551111. *Principal*, J. D. Winslow
Uɴɪᴠᴇʀsɪᴛʏ ᴏꜰ Wᴀʟᴇs, Lᴀᴍᴘᴇᴛᴇʀ, Lampeter sᴀ48 7ᴇᴅ.
Tel: 01570-422351. *Principal*, Prof. K. Robbins, ᴅ.ʟitt.,
ᴅ.ᴘʜil., ꜰʀsᴇ (1992)
Uɴɪᴠᴇʀsɪᴛʏ ᴏꜰ Wᴀʟᴇs, Sᴡᴀɴsᴇᴀ, Singleton Park,
Swansea sᴀ2 8ᴘᴘ. Tel: 01792-205678. *Vice-Chancellor*,
Prof. R. H. Williams, ᴘʜ.ᴅ., ꜰʀs (1994)

THE UNIVERSITY OF WARWICK (1965)
Coventry ᴄᴠ4 7ᴀʟ
Tel 01203-523523
Full-time students (1995–6), 13,300
Chancellor, Sir Shridath Surendranath Ramphal, ɢᴄᴍɢ, ǫᴄ
(1989)
Vice-Chancellor, Prof. Sir Brian Follett, ꜰʀs, ᴅ.sᴄ.
Registrar, M. L. Shattock, ᴏʙᴇ

THE UNIVERSITY OF WESTMINSTER (1992)
309 Regent Street, London ᴡ1ʀ 8ᴀʟ
Tel 0171-911 5000
Full-time students (1995–6), 9,000
Rector, Dr G. M. Copland
Deputy-Rector, A. Dart
Registrar, Ms J. Hopkinson

THE UNIVERSITY OF THE WEST OF ENGLAND, BRISTOL (BRISTOL UWE) (1992)
Coldharbour Lane, Bristol ʙs16 1ǫʏ
Tel 0117-965 6261
Full-time students (1995–6), 13,622
Chancellor, Dame Elizabeth Butler-Sloss, ᴅʙᴇ
Vice-Chancellor, A. C. Morris
Academic Registrar, Ms M. J. Carter
Secretary, W. Evans

THE UNIVERSITY OF WOLVERHAMPTON (1992)
Wulfruna Street, Wolverhampton ᴡᴠ1 1sʙ
Tel 01902-321000
Full-time students (1995–6), 17,296
Chancellor, The Earl of Shrewsbury and Talbot
Vice-Chancellor, Prof. M. J. Harrison

THE UNIVERSITY OF YORK (1963)
Heslington, York ʏᴏ1 5ᴅᴅ
Tel 01904-430000
Full-time students (1995–6), 5,600
Chancellor, Dame Janet Baker, ᴄʜ, ᴅʙᴇ
Vice-Chancellor, Prof. R. U. Cooke, ᴘʜ.ᴅ.
Registrar, D. J. Foster

THE OPEN UNIVERSITY (1969)
Walton Hall, Milton Keynes ᴍᴋ7 6ᴀᴀ
Tel 01908-274066
Students and clients (1996), c.200,000
Tuition by correspondence linked with special radio and
television programmes, video and audio cassettes, computing, residential schools and a locally-based tutorial and
counselling service. The University awards degrees of
ʙᴀ, ʙ.sᴄ., ʙ.ᴘʜil., ᴍᴀ, ᴍʙᴀ, ᴍʙᴀ (Technology), ᴍ.ᴇng., ᴍ.sᴄ.,
ᴍ.ᴘʜil., ᴘʜ.ᴅ., ᴅ.ᴇᴅ., ᴅ.sᴄ. and ᴅ.ʟitt. There are faculties and
schools of arts; education; health and social welfare;
management; mathematics and computing; modern
languages; science; social sciences; technology; and a wide
range of qualification courses and study packs.
Chancellor, The Rt. Hon. Betty Boothroyd, ᴍᴘ
Vice-Chancellor, Sir John Daniel
Secretary, D. J. Clinch

THE ROYAL COLLEGE OF ART (1837)
Kensington Gore, London sᴡ7 2ᴇᴜ
Tel 0171-584 5020
Under royal charter (1967) the Royal College of Art grants
the degrees of Doctor, Doctor of Philosophy, Master of
Philosophy and Master of Arts.
Students (1995–6), 770 (all postgraduate)
Provost, The Earl of Snowdon, ɢᴄᴠᴏ
Rector and Vice-Provost, Prof. C. Frayling
Registrar, A. Selby

COLLEGES

It is not possible to name here all the colleges offering
courses of higher or further education. The list does not
include colleges forming part of a polytechnic or a university. The English colleges that follow are confined to those
in the Higher Education Funding Council for England
sector; there are many more colleges in England providing
higher education courses, some with HEFCFE funding.
The list of colleges in Wales, Scotland and Northern
Ireland includes institutions providing at least one full-time course leading to a first degree granted by an
accredited validating body.

ENGLAND

Bᴀᴛʜ Cᴏʟʟᴇɢᴇ ᴏꜰ Hɪɢʜᴇʀ Eᴅᴜᴄᴀᴛɪᴏɴ, Newton Park,
Newton St Loe, Bath ʙᴀ2 9ʙɴ. Tel: 01225-873701.
Director, F. Morgan
Bɪsʜᴏᴘ Gʀᴏssᴇᴛᴇsᴛᴇ Cᴏʟʟᴇɢᴇ, Lincoln ʟɴ1 3ᴅʏ. Tel:
01522-527347. *Principal*, Ms E. Baker

BOLTON INSTITUTE OF HIGHER EDUCATION, Deane Road, Bolton BL3 5AB. Tel: 01204-528851. *Principal,* R. Oxtoby, PH.D.

BRETTON HALL, West Bretton, Wakefield, W. Yorks WF4 4LG. Tel: 01924-830261. *Principal,* Prof. G. H. Bell

BUCKINGHAMSHIRE COLLEGE, Queen Alexandra Road, High Wycombe, Bucks HP11 2JZ. Tel: 01494-522141. *Director,* Prof. P. B. Mogford

CANTERBURY CHRIST CHURCH COLLEGE, North Holmes Road, Canterbury, Kent CT1 1QU. Tel: 01227-767700. *Principal,* M. H. A. Berry, TD

THE CENTRAL SCHOOL OF SPEECH AND DRAMA, Embassy Theatre, Eton Avenue, London NW3 3HY. Tel: 0171-722 8183. *Principal,* Prof. R. S. Fowler, FRSA

CHELTENHAM AND GLOUCESTER COLLEGE OF HIGHER EDUCATION, PO Box 220, The Park, Cheltenham, Glos GL50 2QF. Tel: 01242-532700. *Director,* Miss J. O. Trotter, OBE

CHICHESTER INSTITUTE OF HIGHER EDUCATION, College Lane, Chichester, West Sussex PO19 4PE. Tel: 01243-816000. *Director,* P. E. D. Robinson

COLLEGE OF ST MARK AND ST JOHN, Derriford Road, Plymouth PL6 8BH. Tel: 01752-777188. *Principal,* Dr W. J. Rea

DARTINGTON COLLEGE OF ARTS, Totnes, Devon TQ9 6EJ. Tel: 01803-862224. *Principal,* Prof. K. Thompson

EDGE HILL UNIVERSITY COLLEGE, St Helens Road, Ormskirk, Lancs L39 4QP. Tel: 01695-575171. *Director,* Dr. J. Cater

FALMOUTH COLLEGE OF ARTS, Woodlane, Falmouth, Cornwall TR11 4RA. Tel: 01326-211077. *Principal,* Prof. A. G. Livingston

HARPER ADAMS AGRICULTURAL COLLEGE, Newport, Shropshire TF10 8NB. Tel: 01952-820280. *Principal,* G. R. McConnell

HOMERTON COLLEGE, Cambridge CB2 2PH. Tel: 01223-507111. *Principal,* Mrs K. Pretty, PH.D.

INSTITUTE OF ADVANCED NURSING EDUCATION, Royal College of Nursing, 20 Cavendish Square, London W1M 0AB. Tel: 0171-409 3333. *Director,* Prof. A. Kitson

KENT INSTITUTE OF ART AND DESIGN, Oakwood Park, Maidstone ME16 8AG (*also* New Dover Road, Canterbury CT1 3AN; and Fort Pitt, Rochester ME1 1DZ). Tel: 01622-691471/757286. *Director,* Prof. V. Grylls

KING ALFRED'S COLLEGE OF HIGHER EDUCATION, Winchester SO22 4NR. Tel: 01962-841515. *Principal,* Prof. J. P. Dickinson

LIVERPOOL HOPE UNIVERSITY COLLEGE, Hope Park, Liverpool L16 9JD. Tel: 0151-737 3477. *Rector,* Prof. S. Lee

THE LONDON INSTITUTE, 65 Davies Street, London W1Y 2DA. Tel: 0171-514 6000. *Rector,* Sir William Stubbs Comprising:
Camberwell College of Arts, Peckham Road, London SE5 8UF
Central St Martins College of Art and Design, Southampton Row, London WC1B 4AP
Chelsea College of Art and Design, Manresa Road, London SW3 6LS
London College of Fashion, 20 John Prince's Street, London W1M 0BJ
London College of Printing and Distributive Trades, Elephant and Castle, London SE1 6SB

LOUGHBOROUGH COLLEGE OF ART AND DESIGN, Epinal Way, Loughborough, Leics LE11 3GE. Tel: 01509-261515. *Principal,* T. Kavanagh

LSU COLLEGE OF HIGHER EDUCATION, The Avenue, Southampton SO17 1BG. Tel: 01703-228761. *Principal,* Dr A. C. Chitnis

NENE COLLEGE, Park Campus, Boughton Green Road, Northampton NN2 7AL. Tel: 01604-735500. *Director,* S. M. Gaskell, PH.D.

NEWMAN COLLEGE, Genners Lane, Bartley Green, Birmingham B32 3NT. Tel: 0121-476 1181. *Principal,* Prof. B. Ray

ROEHAMPTON INSTITUTE LONDON, Senate House, Roehampton Lane, London SW15 5PU. Comprises Digby Stuart College, Froebel Institute College, Southlands College and Whitelands College. Tel: 0181-392 3000. *Rector,* Prof. S. C. Holt, PH.D.

ROSE BRUFORD COLLEGE, Lamorbey Park, Sidcup, Kent DA15 9DF. Tel: 0181-300 3024. *Principal,* R. Ely

ROYAL NORTHERN COLLEGE OF MUSIC, 124 Oxford Road, Manchester M13 9RD. Tel: 0161-273 6283. *Principal,* Prof. E. Gregson

SOUTHAMPTON INSTITUTE, East Park Terrace, Southampton SO14 0YN. Tel: 01703-319000. *Director,* Prof. D. G. Leyland

SURREY INSTITUTE OF ART AND DESIGN, Falkner Road, The Hart, Farnham, Surrey GU9 7DS. Tel: 01252-722441. *Director,* N. J. Taylor

TRINITY AND ALL SAINTS' COLLEGE, Brownberrie Lane, Horsforth, Leeds LS18 5HD. Tel: 0113-283 7100. *Principal,* Dr G. L. Turnbull

UNIVERSITY COLLEGE CHESTER, Cheyney Road, Chester CH1 4BJ. Tel: 01244-375444. *Principal,* Canon E. V. Binks

UNIVERSITY COLLEGE OF RIPON AND YORK ST JOHN, Lord Mayor's Walk, York YO3 7EX. Tel: 01904-656771. *Principal,* Prof. R. A. Butlin

UNIVERSITY COLLEGE OF S. MARTIN, Lancaster LA1 3JD. Tel: 01524-63446. *Principal,* D. Edynbry, PH.D.

UNIVERSITY COLLEGE SCARBOROUGH, Filey Road, Scarborough YO11 3AZ. Tel: 01723-362392. *Principal,* R. A. Withers, PH.D.

WESTHILL COLLEGE, Weoley Park Road, Selly Oak, Birmingham B29 6LL. Tel: 0121-472 7245. *Principal,* Dr J. G. Priestley

WESTMINSTER COLLEGE, Oxford OX2 9AT. Tel: 01865-247644. *Principal,* Revd Dr R. Ralph

WINCHESTER SCHOOL OF ART, Park Avenue, Winchester, Hants SO23 8DL. Tel: 01962-842500. *Head of School,* Prof. K. Crouan

WORCESTER COLLEGE OF HIGHER EDUCATION, Henwick Grove, Worcester WR2 6AJ. Tel: 01905-855000. *Principal,* Ms D. Urwin

WALES

THE NORTH-EAST WALES INSTITUTE OF HIGHER EDUCATION, Plas Coch, Mold Road, Wrexham LL11 2AW. Tel: 01978-290666. *Principal,* Prof. J. O. Williams, PH.D, D.SC.

SWANSEA INSTITUTE OF HIGHER EDUCATION, Townhill Road, Swansea SA2 0UT. Tel: 01792-481000. *Principal,* G. Stockdale, PH.D.

TRINITY COLLEGE, Carmarthen SA31 3EP. Tel: 01267-237971. *Principal,* D. C. Jones-Davies, OBE

WELSH COLLEGE OF MUSIC AND DRAMA, Castle Grounds, Cathays Park, Cardiff CF1 3ER. Tel: 01222-342854. *Principal,* E. Fivet

SCOTLAND

BELL COLLEGE OF TECHNOLOGY, Almada Street, Hamilton ML3 0JB. Tel: 01698-283100. *Principal,* J. Reid

DUMFRIES AND GALLOWAY COLLEGE, Heathhall, Dumfries DG1 3QZ. Tel: 01387-261261. *Principal,* J. W. M. Neil

FIFE COLLEGE OF FURTHER AND HIGHER EDUCATION, St Brycedale Avenue, Kirkcaldy, Fife KY1 1EX. Tel: 01592-268591. *Principal*, D. A. Huckle

GLASGOW SCHOOL OF ART, 167 Renfrew Street, Glasgow G3 6RQ. Tel: 0141-353 4500. *Director*, Prof. D. Cameron

NORTHERN COLLEGE OF EDUCATION, Hilton Place, Aberdeen AB24 4FA. Tel: 01224-283500; Gardyne Road, Dundee DD5 1NY. Tel: 01382-464000. *Principal*, D. A. Adams

QUEEN MARGARET COLLEGE, Clerwood Terrace, Edinburgh EH12 8TS. Tel: 0131-317 3000; Duke Street, Edinburgh EH6 8HF. Tel: 0131-317 3355. *Principal*, Dr J. Stringer

ROYAL SCOTTISH ACADEMY OF MUSIC AND DRAMA, 100 Renfrew Street, Glasgow G2 3DB. Tel: 0141-332 4101. *Principal*, Dr P. Ledger, CBE, FRSE

SAC (SCOTTISH AGRICULTURAL COLLEGE), Central Office, West Mains Road, Edinburgh EH9 3JG. Tel: 0131-535 4000. Campuses at Aberdeen, Auchincruive, Ayr, and Edinburgh. *Principal*, Prof. P. C. Thomas

ST ANDREW'S COLLEGE OF EDUCATION, Duntocher Road, Bearsden, Glasgow G61 4QA. Tel: 0141-943 1424. *Principal*, Prof. B. J. McGettrick, OBE

NORTHERN IRELAND

EAST DOWN INSTITUTE OF FURTHER AND HIGHER EDUCATION, Market Street, Downpatrick, Co. Down BT30 6ND. Tel: 01396-615815. *Principal*, T. L. Place

ST MARY'S COLLEGE, 191 Falls Road, Belfast BT12 6FE. Tel: 01232-327678. *Principal*, Revd M. O'Callaghan

STRANMILLIS COLLEGE, Stranmillis Road, Belfast BT9 5DY. Tel: 01232-381271. *Principal*, Dr J. R. McMinn

ADULT AND CONTINUING EDUCATION

FORUM FOR THE ADVANCEMENT OF CONTINUING EDUCATION (FACE), Department of Continuing Education, University of Plymouth, Plymouth PL4 8AA. Tel: 01752-232374. *Chair*, C. Bell

NATIONAL INSTITUTE OF ADULT CONTINUING EDUCATION, 21 De Montfort Street, Leicester LE1 7GE. Tel: 0116-255 1451. *Director*, A. Tuckett

NIACE CYMRU, 245 Western Avenue, Cardiff CF5 2YX. Tel: 01222-265001. *Associate Director*, Ms A. Poole

NORTHERN IRELAND COUNCIL FOR ADULT EDUCATION, c/o Western Education and Library Board, 1 Hospital Road, Omagh, Co. Tyrone BT79 0AW. Tel: 01662-240240. *Chairman*, J. Martin; *Education Officer*, Ms T. Devine

THE RESIDENTIAL COLLEGES COMMITTEE, c/o Ruskin College, Oxford OX1 2HE. Tel: 01865-556360. *Awards Officer*, Mrs F. A. Bagchi

SCOTTISH COMMUNITY EDUCATION COUNCIL, Rosebery House, 9 Haymarket Terrace, Edinburgh EH12 5EZ. Tel: 0131-313 2488. *Chief Executive*, C. McConnell

THE UNIVERSITIES ASSOCIATION FOR CONTINUING EDUCATION, Department of Adult Continuing Education, University of Leeds, Leeds LS2 9JT. Tel: 0113-233 3184. *Secretary*, Prof. R. Taylor

THE WORKERS' EDUCATIONAL ASSOCIATION, Temple House, 17 Victoria Park Square, London E2 9PB. Tel: 0181-983 1515. *General Secretary*, R. Lochrie

LONG-TERM RESIDENTIAL COLLEGES FOR ADULT EDUCATION

COLEG HARLECH, Harlech, Gwynedd LL46 2PU. Tel: 01766-780363. *Warden*, J. W. England

CO-OPERATIVE COLLEGE, Stanford Hall, Loughborough, Leics LE12 5QR. Tel: 01509-852333. *Chief Executive*, R. Wildgusp

FIRCROFT COLLEGE, 1018 Bristol Road, Selly Oak, Birmingham B29 6LH. Tel: 0121-472 0116. *Principal*, K. Jackson

HILLCROFT COLLEGE, South Bank, Surbiton, Surrey KT6 6DF. Tel: 0181-399 2688. For women only. *Principal*, Ms J. Ireton

NEWBATTLE ABBEY COLLEGE, Dalkeith, Midlothian EH22 3LL. Tel: 0131-663 1921. *Principal*, W. M. Conboy

NORTHERN COLLEGE, Wentworth Castle, Stainborough, Barnsley, S. Yorks S75 3ET. Tel: 01226-776000. *Principal*, Prof. R. H. Fryer

PLATER COLLEGE, Pullens Lane, Oxford OX3 0DT. Tel: 01865-741676. *Principal*, M. Blades

RUSKIN COLLEGE, Walton Street, Oxford OX1 2HE. Tel: 01865-54331. *Principal*, S. Yeo, D.Phil.

PROFESSIONAL EDUCATION

Excluding postgraduate study

The organizations listed below are those which, by providing specialist training or conducting examinations, control entry into a profession, or organizations responsible for maintaining a register of those with professional qualifications in their sector.

Many professions now have a largely graduate entry, and possession of a first degree can exempt entrants from certain of the professional examinations. Enquiries about obtaining professional qualifications should be made to the relevant professional organization(s). Details of higher education providers of first degrees may be found in *University and College Entrance: Official Guide* (available from UCAS, *see* page 451).

ACCOUNTANCY

The main bodies granting membership on examination after a period of practical work are:

INSTITUTE OF CHARTERED ACCOUNTANTS IN ENGLAND AND WALES, Chartered Accountants' Hall, PO Box 433, Moorgate Place, London EC2P 2BJ. Tel: 0171-920 8100. *Secretary and Chief Executive*, A. J. Colquhoun

INSTITUTE OF CHARTERED ACCOUNTANTS OF SCOTLAND, 27 Queen Street, Edinburgh EH2 1LA. Tel: 0131-225 5673. *Chief Executive*, P. W. Johnston

CHARTERED ASSOCIATION OF CERTIFIED ACCOUNTANTS, 29 Lincoln's Inn Fields, London WC2A 3EE. Tel: 0171-242 6855. *Chief Executive*, Mrs A. L. Rose

CHARTERED INSTITUTE OF MANAGEMENT ACCOUNTANTS, 63 Portland Place, London W1N 4AB. Tel: 0171-637 2311. *Secretary*, J. S. Chester, OBE

CHARTERED INSTITUTE OF PUBLIC FINANCE AND ACCOUNTANCY, 3 Robert Street, London WC2N 6BH. Tel: 0171-543 5600. *Director*, N. P. Hepworth, OBE

ACTUARIAL SCIENCE

Two professional organizations grant qualifications after examination:

INSTITUTE OF ACTUARIES, Staple Inn Hall, High Holborn, London WC1V 7QJ. Tel: 0171-242 0106. *Secretary-General*, A. G. Tait. Enquiries to Actuarial Education Service, Napier House, 4 Worcester Street, Oxford OX1 2AW. Tel: 01865-794144

FACULTY OF ACTUARIES IN SCOTLAND, 40–44 Thistle Street, Edinburgh EH2 1EN. Tel: 0131-220 4555. *Secretary*, W. W. Mair

ARCHITECTURE

The Education and Professional Development Committee of the Royal Institute of British Architects sets standards and guides the whole system of architectural education throughout the UK. The RIBA recognizes courses at 38 schools of architecture in the UK for exemption from their own examinations.

THE ROYAL INSTITUTE OF BRITISH ARCHITECTS, 66 Portland Place, London W1N 4AD. Tel: 0171-580 5533. *President*, O. Luder; *Director-General*, A. Reid, PH.D.

Schools of architecture outside the universities include:

THE ARCHITECTURAL ASSOCIATION, 34–36 Bedford Square, London WC1B 3ES. *Secretary*, E. A. Le Maistre

PRINCE OF WALES'S INSTITUTE OF ARCHITECTURE, 14–15 Gloucester Gate, London NW1 4HG. Tel: 0171-916 7380. *Director*, Dr R. John

BANKING

Professional organizations granting qualifications after examination are:

CHARTERED INSTITUTE OF BANKERS, 90 Bishopsgate, London EC2N 4AS. Tel: 0171-444 7111. *Chief Executive*, G. Shreeve

CHARTERED INSTITUTE OF BANKERS IN SCOTLAND, 19 Rutland Square, Edinburgh EH1 2DE. Tel: 0131-229 9869. *Chief Executive*, Dr C. W. Munn

BIOLOGY, CHEMISTRY, PHYSICS

Professional qualifications are awarded by:

INSTITUTE OF BIOLOGY, 20–22 Queensberry Place, London SW7 2DZ. Tel: 0171-581 8333. *President*, Prof. R. B. Heap; *General Secretary*, Dr R. H. Priestley

INSTITUTE OF PHYSICS, 76–78 Portland Place, London W1N 4AA. Tel: 0171-470 4800. *Chief Executive*, Dr A. D. W. Jones

ROYAL SOCIETY OF CHEMISTRY, Burlington House, Piccadilly, London W1V 0BN. Tel: 0171-437 8656. *President*, E. Able; *Secretary-General*, T. D. Inch, PH.D.

BUILDING

Examinations are conducted by:

CHARTERED INSTITUTE OF BUILDING, Englemere, King's Ride, Ascot, Berks SL5 8TB. Tel: 01344-23355. *Chief Executive*, K. Banbury

INSTITUTE OF BUILDING CONTROL, 21 High Street, Ewell, Epsom, Surrey KT17 1SB. Tel: 0181-393 6860. *Chief Executive*, Ms R. Raywood

INSTITUTE OF CLERKS OF WORKS OF GREAT BRITAIN, 41 The Mall, London W5 3TJ. Tel: 0181-579 2917/8. *Secretary*, A. P. Macnamara

BUSINESS, MANAGEMENT AND ADMINISTRATION

Professional bodies conducting training and/or examinations in business, administration, management or commerce include:

AMETS (ASSOCIATION FOR MANAGEMENT EDUCATION AND TRAINING IN SCOTLAND), c/o University of Stirling, Stirling FK9 4LA. Tel: 01786-450906. *Vice-Chairman*, M. Makower

THE ASSOCIATION OF MBAS, 15 Duncan Terrace, London N1 8BZ. Tel: 0171-837 3375. Publishes a directory giving details of MBA courses provided at UK institutions. *Director*, R. McCormick

CAM FOUNDATION (COMMUNICATIONS, ADVERTISING AND MARKETING EDUCATION FOUNDATION), Abford House, 15 Wilton Road, London SW1V 1NJ. Tel: 0171-828 7506. *General Secretary*, J. Knight

CHARTERED INSTITUTE OF HOUSING, Octavia House, Westwood Business Park, Westwood Way, Coventry CV4 8JP. Tel: 01203-694433. *Chief Executive*, Ms C. Laird

CHARTERED INSTITUTE OF MARKETING, Moor Hall, Cookham, Maidenhead, Berks SL6 9QH. Tel: 01628-427500. *Director-General*, S. Cuthbert

CHARTERED INSTITUTE OF PURCHASING AND SUPPLY, Easton House, Easton on the Hill, Stamford, Lincs PE9 3NZ. Tel: 01780-56777. *Director-General*, P. Thomson

CHARTERED INSTITUTE OF TRANSPORT, 80 Portland Place, London W1N 4DP. Tel: 0171-636 9952. *Director*, Mrs S. Gross

FACULTY OF SECRETARIES AND ADMINISTRATORS, Brightstowe, Catteshall Lane, Godalming, Surrey GU7 1LJ. Tel: 01483-454213. *Secretary*, Mrs D. M. Rummery

HENLEY MANAGEMENT COLLEGE, Greenlands, Henley-on-Thames, Oxon RG9 3AU. Tel: 01491-571454. *Principal*, Prof. R. Wild, PH.D., D.SC.

INSTITUTE OF ADMINISTRATIVE MANAGEMENT, 40 Chatsworth Parade, Petts Wood, Orpington, Kent BR5 1RW. Tel: 01689-875555. *Chief Executive*, Prof. G. Robinson

INSTITUTE OF CHARTERED SECRETARIES AND ADMINISTRATORS, 16 Park Crescent, London W1N 4AH. Tel: 0171-580 4741. *Chief Executive*, M. J. Ainsworth

INSTITUTE OF CHARTERED SHIPBROKERS, 3 St Helen's Place, London EC3A 6EJ. Tel: 0171-628 5559. *Director*, Mrs B. Fletcher

INSTITUTE OF EXPORT, Export House, 64 Clifton Street, London EC2A 4HB. Tel: 0171-247 9812. *Director-General*, I. J. Campbell

INSTITUTE OF HEALTH SERVICES MANAGEMENT, 39 Chalton Street, London NW1 1JD. Tel: 0171-388 2626. *Director*, Ms K. Caines

INSTITUTE OF MANAGEMENT, Management House, Cottingham Road, Corby, Northants NN17 1TT. Tel: 01536-204222. *Director-General*, R. Young

INSTITUTE OF PERSONNEL AND DEVELOPMENT, IPD House, Camp Road, London SW19 4UX. Tel: 0181-971 9000. *Director-General*, G. Armstrong

INSTITUTE OF PRACTITIONERS IN ADVERTISING, 44 Belgrave Square, London SW1X 8QS. Tel: 0171-235 7020. *Secretary*, J. Raad

LONDON CHAMBER OF COMMERCE AND INDUSTRY EXAMINATIONS BOARD, Marlowe House, Station Road, Sidcup, Kent DA15 7BJ. Tel: 0181-302 0261. *Chief Executive*, W. J. Swords

DANCE

IMPERIAL SOCIETY OF TEACHERS OF DANCING, Imperial House, 22–26 Paul Street, London EC2A 4QE. Tel: 0171-377 1577. *Chief Executive*, M. J. Browne

ROYAL ACADEMY OF DANCING, 36 Battersea Square, London SW11 3RA. Tel: 0171-223 0091. *Chief Executive*, D. Watchman; *Artistic Director*, Miss L. Wallis

ROYAL BALLET SCHOOL, 155 Talgarth Road, London
W14 9DE. Tel: 0181-748 6335. Also at White Lodge,
Richmond Park, Surrey TW10 5HR. Tel: 0181-876 5547.
Director, Dame Merle Park, DBE

DEFENCE

ROYAL COLLEGE OF DEFENCE STUDIES, Seaford House,
37 Belgrave Square, London SW1X 8NS. Tel: 0171-915
4800. Prepares selected senior officers and officials for
responsibilities in the direction and management of
defence and security. *Commandant*, Lt.-Gen. S. C. Grant,
CB

ROYAL NAVAL COLLEGES

BRITANNIA ROYAL NAVAL COLLEGE, Dartmouth, Devon
TQ6 0HJ. Tel: 01803-832141. Provides general and
academic officer training. *Captain*, Capt. A. P.
Masterton-Smith
ROYAL NAVAL COLLEGE, Greenwich, London SE10 9NN.
Tel: 0181-858 2154. *Admiral President*, Rear-Adm.
J. B. Blackham; *Dean of the College*, Prof. G. Till, PH.D.

MILITARY COLLEGES

DIRECTORATE OF EDUCATIONAL AND TRAINING
SERVICES, Director-General Adjutant General's Corp,
Worthy Down, Winchester, Hants SO21 2RG. Tel:
01962-887665. *Director*, Brig. A. D. Thompson
ROYAL MILITARY ACADEMY SANDHURST, Camberley,
Surrey GU15 4PQ. Tel: 01276-63344. *Commandant*, Maj.-
Gen. J. F. Deverell, OBE
ROYAL MILITARY COLLEGE OF SCIENCE, Shrivenham,
Swindon, Wilts SN6 8LA. Tel: 01793-785435. Students
from UK and overseas study from degree to
postgraduate levels in management, science and
technology. The College is a faculty of Cranfield
University. *Commandant*, Maj.-Gen. D. J. M. Jenkins,
CBE; *Principal*, Prof. P. Hutchinson
STAFF COLLEGE, Camberley, Surrey GU15 4NP. Tel:
01276-412632. *Commandant*, Maj.-Gen. A. D. Piggott,
CBE

ROYAL AIR FORCE COLLEGES

ROYAL AIR FORCE COLLEGE, Cranwell, Sleaford, Lincs.
NG34 8HB. Selects all officer and aircrew entrants to the
RAF and provides initial training for all officer entrants
to the RAF. Also provides specialist training for junior
officers of some ground branches and supervision of
elementary flying training, general service training for
University Air Squadrons, and supervision of the Air
Cadet Organization. *Air Officer Commanding and
Commandant*, Air Vice-Marshal A. J. Stables, CBE
ROYAL AIR FORCE STAFF COLLEGE, Bracknell,
Berks RG12 9DD. Prepares selected senior officers for
high-grade command and staff appointments. Two-
thirds of the students are RAF officers; the others are
officers from the other UK Services and overseas air
forces. *Air Officer Commanding and Commandant*, Air
Vice-Marshal M. van der Veen
ROYAL AIR FORCE TRAINING, DEVELOPMENT AND
SUPPORT UNIT, RAF Halton, Aylesbury, Bucks HP22
5PG. Tel: 01296-623535. *Commanding Officer*,
Gp Capt K. L. Sherit

DENTISTRY

To be entitled to be registered in the Dentists Register, a
person must hold the degree or diploma in dental surgery
of a university in the UK or the diploma of any of the
licensing authorities (the Royal Colleges of Surgeons of
England and of Edinburgh, and the Royal College of

Physicians and Surgeons of Glasgow). Nationals of an EU
member state holding an appropriate European diploma,
and holders of certain overseas diplomas, may also be
registered. The Dentists Register is maintained by:
THE GENERAL DENTAL COUNCIL, 37 Wimpole Street,
London W1M 8DQ. Tel: 0171-486 2171. *Chief Executive*,
Mrs R. M. J. Hepplewhite

DIETETICS
See also FOOD AND NUTRITION SCIENCE

The professional association is the British Dietetic
Association. Full membership is open to dietitians holding
a recognized qualification, who may also become State
Registered Dietitians through the Council for Professions
Supplementary to Medicine (*see* Medicine)
THE BRITISH DIETETIC ASSOCIATION, 7th Floor,
Elizabeth House, 22 Suffolk Street, Queensway,
Birmingham B1 1LS. Tel: 0121-643 5483. *Administrator*,
J. Grigg

DRAMA

The national validating body for courses providing train-
ing in drama for the professional theatre is the National
Council for Drama Training. It currently has accredited
courses at the following: Academy of Live and Recorded
Arts; Arts Educational Schools; Birmingham School of
Speech Training and Dramatic Art; Bristol Old Vic
Theatre School; Central School of Speech and Drama;
Drama Centre, London; Drama Studio, London; Guild-
ford School of Acting; Guildhall School of Music and
Drama, London; London Academy of Music and Dramatic
Art; Manchester Metropolitan University School of
Theatre; Mountview Theatre School; Oxford School of
Drama, Woodstock; Queen Margaret College, Edinburgh;
Rose Bruford College, Sidcup; Royal Academy of
Dramatic Art, London; Royal Scottish Academy of Music
and Drama; Webber Douglas Academy of Dramatic Art;
Welsh College of Music and Drama.
  The accreditation of a course in a school does not
necessarily imply that other courses of different type or
duration in the same school are also accredited.
THE NATIONAL COUNCIL FOR DRAMA TRAINING, 5
Tavistock Place, London WC1H 9SN. *Executive Secretary*,
Ms A. Bailey

ENGINEERING

The Engineering Council supervises the engineering
profession through the 39 nominated engineering institutions who are represented on its Board for Engineers'
Regulation. Working with and through the institutions, the
Council sets the standards for the registration of individuals, and also the accreditation for academic courses in
universities and colleges and the practical training in
industry.
THE ENGINEERING COUNCIL, 10 Maltravers Street,
London WC2R 3ER. Tel: 0171-240 7891. *Director-General*,
M. Heath

The principal qualifying bodies are:
BRITISH COMPUTER SOCIETY, 1 Sanford Street, Swindon
SN1 1HJ. Tel: 01793-417417. *Chief Executive*, Ms J. Scott
CHARTERED INSTITUTION OF BUILDING SERVICES
ENGINEERS, 222 Balham High Road, London SW12 9BS.
Tel: 0181-675 5211. *Secretary*, A. V. Ramsay
INSTITUTION OF CHEMICAL ENGINEERS, Davis Building,
165–189 Railway Terrace, Rugby, Warks CV21 3HQ. Tel:
01788-578214. *Chief Executive*, Dr T. J. Evans

INSTITUTION OF CIVIL ENGINEERS, 1 Great George
Street, London SWIP 3AA. Tel: 0171-222 7722. *Director-General*, R. S. Dobson, OBE, FENG.

INSTITUTION OF ELECTRICAL ENGINEERS, Savoy Place,
London WC2R OBL. Tel: 0171-240 1871. *Secretary*, Dr
J. C. Williams, FENG.

INSTITUTE OF ENERGY, 18 Devonshire Street, London
WIN 2AU. Tel: 0171-580 7124. *Secretary*, J. E. H. Leach

INSTITUTION OF GAS ENGINEERS, 21 Portland Place,
London WIN 3AF. Tel: 0171-636 6603. *Secretary*, Mrs
S. M. Raine

INSTITUTE OF MARINE ENGINEERS, The Memorial
Building, 76 Mark Lane, London EC3R 7JN. Tel: 0171-
481 8493. *Secretary*, J. E. Sloggett, OBE

INSTITUTE OF MATERIALS, 1 Carlton House Terrace,
London SWIY 5DB. Tel: 0171-839 4071. *Secretary*, Dr
J. A. Catterall

INSTITUTE OF MEASUREMENT AND CONTROL, 87 Gower
Street, London WCIE 6AA. Tel: 0171-387 4949. *Secretary*,
M. J. Yates

INSTITUTION OF MECHANICAL ENGINEERS, 1 Birdcage
Walk, London SWIH 9JJ. Tel: 0171-222 7899. *Director-General*, Dr R. Pike

INSTITUTION OF MINING AND METALLURGY, 44
Portland Place, London WIN 4BR. Tel: 0171-580 3802.
Secretary, M. J. Jones

INSTITUTION OF MINING ENGINEERS, Danum House, 6A
South Parade, Doncaster DNI 2DY. Tel: 01302-320486.
Secretary, Dr G. J. M. Woodrow

INSTITUTE OF PHYSICS, 76–78 Portland Place, London
WIN 4AA. Tel: 0171-470 4800. *Chief Executive*, Dr A.
Jones

INSTITUTION OF STRUCTURAL ENGINEERS, 11 Upper
Belgrave Street, London SWIX 8BH. Tel: 0171-235 4535.
Chief Executive, Dr J. W. Dougill

ROYAL AERONAUTICAL SOCIETY, 4 Hamilton Place,
London OBQ. Tel: 0171-499 3515. *Director*,
R. J. Kennett

ROYAL INSTITUTION OF NAVAL ARCHITECTS, 10 Upper
Belgrave Street, London SWIX 8BQ. Tel: 0171-235 4622.
Secretary, J. Rosewarn

FILM AND TELEVISION

Training for graduates intending to make a career in film
and television production is provided by the National Film
and Television School, which provides courses in production, direction, animation, camera work and other
specialisms. Short post-experience courses to enable
professionals to update or expand their skills are also
provided.

NATIONAL FILM AND TELEVISION SCHOOL, Station
Road, Beaconsfield, Bucks HP9 ILJ. Tel: 01494-671234.
Director, H. Camre

FOOD AND NUTRITION SCIENCE
See also DIETETICS

Scientific and professional bodies include:

INSTITUTE OF FOOD SCIENCE & TECHNOLOGY, 5
Cambridge Court, 210 Shepherd's Bush Road, London
W6 7NJ. Tel: 0171-603 6316. *Chief Executive*, Ms H. G.
Wild

NUTRITION SOCIETY, 10 Cambridge Court, 210
Shepherds Bush Road, London W6 7NJ. Tel: 0171-602
0228. *Hon. Secretary*, Prof. J. Mathers

FORESTRY AND TIMBER STUDIES

Professional organizations include:

COMMONWEALTH FORESTRY ASSOCIATION, c/o Oxford
Forestry Institute, South Parks Road, Oxford OXI 3RB.
Tel: 01865-275072. *Chairman*, P. J. Wood

INSTITUTE OF CHARTERED FORESTERS, 7A St Colme
Street, Edinburgh EH3 6AA. Tel: 0131-225 2705.
Secretary, Mrs M. W. Dick

ROYAL FORESTRY SOCIETY OF ENGLAND, WALES AND
NORTHERN IRELAND, 102 High Street, Tring, Herts
HP23 4AF. Tel: 01442-822028. *Director*, J. E. Jackson,
PH.D.

ROYAL SCOTTISH FORESTRY SOCIETY, The Stables,
Dalkeith Country Park, Dalkeith, Midlothian EH22 2NA.
Tel: 0131-660 9480. *Director*, M. Osborne

FUEL AND ENERGY SCIENCE

The principal professional bodies are:

INSTITUTE OF ENERGY, 18 Devonshire Street, London
WIN 2AU. Tel: 0171-580 7124. *Secretary*, J. Leach

INSTITUTION OF GAS ENGINEERS, 21 Portland Place,
London WIN 3AF. Tel: 0171-636 6603. *Secretary*, Mrs
S. M. Raine

INSTITUTE OF PETROLEUM, 61 New Cavendish Street,
London WIM 8AR. Tel: 0171-467 7100. *Director-General*,
I. Ward

HOTELKEEPING, CATERING AND INSTITUTIONAL MANAGEMENT
See also DIETETICS, and FOOD AND NUTRITION SCIENCE

The qualifying professional body in these areas is:

HOTEL AND CATERING INTERNATIONAL MANAGEMENT
ASSOCIATION, 191 Trinity Road, London SW17 7HN.
Tel: 0181-672 4251. *Chief Executive*, D. Wood

INDUSTRIAL AND VOCATIONAL TRAINING

There are 120 industry training organizations, employer-
led independent organizations whose role includes setting
the standards of National and Scottish Vocational Qualifications.

NATIONAL COUNCIL OF INDUSTRY TRAINING
ORGANIZATIONS, 10 Meadowcourt, Amos Road,
Sheffield S9 IBX. Tel: 0114-261 9926. *Chair*, Ms L.
Millington; *Administrator*, Miss J. Maisari

INSURANCE

Organizations conducting examinations and awarding
diplomas are:

ASSOCIATION OF AVERAGE ADJUSTERS, 200 Aldersgate
Street, London ECIA 4JJ. Tel: 0171-956 0099. *Hon.
Secretary*, D. W. Taylor

CHARTERED INSTITUTE OF LOSS ADJUSTERS, Manfield
House, 1 Southampton Street, London WC2R OLR. Tel:
0171-240 1496. *Director*, A. F. Clack

CHARTERED INSURANCE INSTITUTE, 20 Aldermanbury,
London EC2V 7HY. Tel: 0171-606 3835. *Director-General*,
Prof. D. E. Bland

JOURNALISM

Courses for trainee newspaper journalists are available at
20 centres. One-year full-time courses are available for
selected students and 18-week courses for graduates.
Particulars of all these courses are available from the
National Council for the Training of Journalists. Short
courses for mid-career development can be arranged, as
can various distance learning courses. The NCTJ also

offers Assessor, Internal Verifier (IV) and Accreditation of Prior Achievement (APA) training, and NVQs.

For periodical journalists, there are eight centres running courses approved by the Periodicals Training Council.

THE NATIONAL COUNCIL FOR TRAINING OF JOURNALISTS, Latton Bush Centre, Southern Way, Harlow, Essex CM18 7BL. Tel: 01279-430009. *Chief Executive*, R. Selwood

THE PERIODICALS TRAINING COUNCIL, Queen's House, 55–56 Lincoln's Inn Field, London WC2A 3LJ. Tel: 0171-404 4168. *Executive Director*, Ms J. Butcher

LAW

THE BAR

Admission to the Bar of England and Wales is controlled by the Inns of Court, admission to the Bar of Northern Ireland by the Honorable Society of the Inn of Court of Northern Ireland and admission as an Advocate of the Scottish Bar is controlled by the Faculty of Advocates. The governing body of the barristers' branch of the legal profession in England and Wales is the General Council of the Bar. The governing body in Northern Ireland is the Honorable Society of the Inn of Court of Northern Ireland, and the Faculty of Advocates is the governing body of the Scottish Bar. The education and examination of students training for the Bar of England and Wales is regulated by the General Council of the Bar. The Inns of Court School of Law is currently the sole provider of the Bar's vocational course but from September 1997 there will be other institutions validated to provide the course. Those who intend to practise at the Bar of England and Wales must pass the Bar's vocational course.

THE GENERAL COUNCIL OF THE BAR, 3 Bedford Row, London WC1R 4DB. Tel: 0171-242 0082. *Chairman*, D. Peury-Davey, QC; *Chief Executive*, N. Morison

FACULTY OF ADVOCATES, Advocates Library, Parliament House, Edinburgh EH1 1RF. Tel: 0131-226 5071. *Dean*, A. R. Hardie, QC; *Clerk*, I. G. Armstrong

THE HONORABLE SOCIETY OF THE INN OF COURT OF NORTHERN IRELAND, Royal Courts of Justice, Belfast BT1 3JF. Tel: 01232-235111. *Treasurer* (1996), F. C. Elliott, QC; *Under-Treasurer*, J. A. L. McLean, QC

The Inns of Court

THE INNER TEMPLE, London EC4Y 7HL. Tel: 0171-797 8250. *Treasurer*, The Rt. Hon. Lord Justice Staughton; *Sub-Treasurer*, Brig. P. A. Little, CBE

THE MIDDLE TEMPLE, London EC4Y 9AT. Tel: 0171-427 4800. *Treasurer*, The Lord Nicholls, QC; *Deputy Treasurer*, Sir David Calcutt, QC

GRAY'S INN, 8 South Square, London WC1R 5EU. Tel: 0171-405 8164. *Treasurer*, His Hon. Judge Lewis, QC; *Under-Treasurer*, D. Machin

LINCOLN'S INN, London WC2A 3TL. Tel: 0171-405 1393. *Treasurer*, Sir Maurice Drake, DFC; *Under-Treasurer*, Capt. P. M. Carver, RN

INNS OF COURT SCHOOL OF LAW, 39 Eagle Street, London WC1R 4AJ. Tel: 0171-404 5787. *Chairman*, The Hon. Mr Justice Hooper; *Dean*, Mrs M. A. Phillips

SOLICITORS

Qualifications for solicitor are obtainable only from one of the Law Societies, which control the education and examination of trainee solicitors and the admission of solicitors.

LAW SOCIETY OF ENGLAND AND WALES, 113 Chancery Lane, London WC2A 1PL. Tel: 0171-242 1222. *President* (1996–7), J. A. Girling; *Vice-President* (1996–7), P. Sycamore; *Secretary-General*, Ms J. M. Betts

THE COLLEGE OF LAW provides courses for the Common Professional Examination and Legal Practice Course at Braboeuf Manor, St Catherines, Guildford, Surrey GU3 1HA; 14 Store Street, London WC1E 7DE; Christleton Hall, Chester CH3 7AB; Bishopthorpe Road, York YO2 1QA

OFFICE FOR THE SUPERVISION OF SOLICITORS, Victoria Court, 8 Dormer Place, Leamington Spa, Warks CV32 5AE. Tel: 01926-820082. The Office is an establishment of the Law Society set up to handle complaints about solicitors

LAW SOCIETY OF SCOTLAND, Law Society's Hall, 26 Drumsheugh Gardens, Edinburgh EH3 7YR. Tel: 0131-226 7411. *President* (1996–7), A. G. McCulloch; *Secretary*, K. W. Pritchard, OBE

LAW SOCIETY OF NORTHERN IRELAND, Law Society House, 98 Victoria Street, Belfast BT1 3JZ. Tel: 01232-231614. *Secretary*, M. C. Davey

LIBRARIANSHIP AND INFORMATION SCIENCE/MANAGEMENT

The Library Association accredits degree and post-graduate courses in library and information science which are offered by 18 universities in the UK. A full list of accredited degree and postgraduate courses is available from its Information Service. The Association also maintains a professional register of Chartered Members open to graduate ordinary members of the Association.

THE LIBRARY ASSOCIATION, 7 Ridgmount Street, London WC1E 7AE. Tel: 0171-636 7543. *Chief Executive*, R. Shimmon

MATERIALS STUDIES

The qualifying body is:

INSTITUTE OF MATERIALS, 1 Carlton House Terrace, London SW1Y 5DB. Tel: 0171-839 4071. *Secretary*, Dr J. A. Catterall

MEDICINE

EXAMINING BODY FOR DIPLOMAS

UNITED EXAMINING BOARD, Apothecaries Hall, Black Friars Lane, London EC4V 6EJ. Tel: 0171-236 1180. *Chairman*, P. Edmond, CBE; *Registrar*, A. M. Wallington-Smith

COLLEGES/SOCIETIES HOLDING POSTGRADUATE MEMBERSHIP AND DIPLOMA EXAMINATIONS

ROYAL COLLEGE OF ANAESTHETISTS, 48–49 Russell Square, London WC1B 4JY. Tel: 0171-813 1900. *President*, Prof. C. Prys-Roberts; *Chief Executive*, Sir Geoffrey de Deney, KCVO

ROYAL COLLEGE OF GENERAL PRACTITIONERS, 14 Princes Gate, London SW7 1PU. Tel: 0171-581 3232. *Hon. President*, Dr L. Newman, OBE; *Hon. Secretary*, Dr W. Reith

ROYAL COLLEGE OF OBSTETRICIANS AND GYNAECOLOGISTS, 27 Sussex Place, London NW1 4RG. Tel: 0171-262 5425. *President*, Dr N. Patel; *Secretary*, P. A. Barnett

ROYAL COLLEGE OF PATHOLOGISTS, 2 Carlton House Terrace, London SW1Y 5AF. Tel: 0171-930 5861. *President*, Prof. A. J. Bellingham, FRCP, FRCPath.; *Secretary*, K. Lockyer

ROYAL COLLEGE OF PHYSICIANS, 11 St Andrews Place, London NW1 4LE. Tel: 0171-935 1174. *President*, Prof. Sir Leslie Turnberg; *Secretary*, D. B. Lloyd

ROYAL COLLEGE OF PHYSICIANS AND SURGEONS OF GLASGOW, 232–242 St Vincent Street, Glasgow G2 5RJ. Tel: 0141-221 6072. *President,* Prof. N. McKay; *Hon. Secretary,* Dr S. Slater

ROYAL COLLEGE OF PHYSICIANS OF EDINBURGH, 9 Queen Street, Edinburgh EH2 1JQ. Tel: 0131-225 7324. *President,* Dr J. D. Cash; *Secretary,* Dr J. Thomas

ROYAL COLLEGE OF PSYCHIATRISTS, 17 Belgrave Square, London SW1X 8PG. Tel: 0171-235 2351. *President,* Dr R. Kendell; *Secretary,* Mrs V. Cameron

ROYAL COLLEGE OF RADIOLOGISTS, 38 Portland Place, London W1N 4QJ. Tel: 0171-636 4432. *President,* Dr M. J. Brindle; *Secretary,* A. J. Cowles

ROYAL COLLEGE OF SURGEONS OF EDINBURGH, Nicolson Street, Edinburgh EH8 9DW. Tel: 0131-527 1600. *President,* Prof. Sir Robert Shields; *Secretary,* Ms A. Campbell

ROYAL COLLEGE OF SURGEONS OF ENGLAND, 35–43 Lincoln's Inn Fields, London WC2A 3PN. Tel: 0171-405 3474. *President,* Sir Rodney Sweetnam, KCVO, CBE; *Secretary,* R. H. E. Duffett

SOCIETY OF APOTHECARIES OF LONDON, 14 Black Friars Lane, London EC4V 6EJ. Tel: 0171-236 1189. *Clerk,* R. J. Stringer

PROFESSIONS SUPPLEMENTARY TO MEDICINE

The standard of professional education in biomedical sciences, chiropody, dietetics, occupational therapy, orthoptics, physiotherapy and radiography is the responsibility of seven professional boards, which also publish an annual register of qualified practitioners. The work of the boards is co-ordinated by the Council for Professions Supplementary to Medicine.

THE COUNCIL FOR PROFESSIONS SUPPLEMENTARY TO MEDICINE, Park House, 184 Kennington Park Road, London SE11 4BU. Tel: 0171-582 0866. *Registrar,* M. D. Hall

BIOMEDICAL SCIENCES

Qualifications from higher or further education establishments and training in medical laboratories are required for progress to the professional examinations and qualifications of the Institute of Biomedical Science.

INSTITUTE OF BIOMEDICAL SCIENCE, 12 Coldbath Square, London EC1R 5HL. Tel: 0171-636 8192. *Chief Executive,* A. Potter

CHIROPODY

Professional recognition is granted by the Society of Chiropodists and Podiatrists to students who are awarded B.Sc. degrees in Podiatry or Podiatric Medicine after attending a course of full-time training for three or four years at one of the 14 recognized schools in the UK (11 in England and Wales, two in Scotland and one in Northern Ireland). Qualifications granted and degrees recognized by the Society are approved by the Chiropodists Board for the purpose of State Registration, which is a condition of employment within the National Health Service.

THE SOCIETY OF CHIROPODISTS AND PODIATRISTS, 53 Welbeck Street, London W1M 7HE. Tel: 0171-486 3381. *General Secretary,* J. G. C. Trouncer

See also DIETETICS

OCCUPATIONAL THERAPY

Professional qualifications are awarded by the College of Occupational Therapists upon completion of one of the 29 training courses approved by the College. The courses are normally degree-level courses based in higher education institutions.

COLLEGE OF OCCUPATIONAL THERAPISTS, 6–8 Marshalsea Road, London SE1 1HL. Tel: 0171-357 6480. *Secretary,* J. Thompson

See also OPHTHALMIC AND DISPENSING OPTICS

ORTHOPTICS

Orthoptists undertake the diagnosis and treatment of all types of squint and other anomalies of binocular vision, working in close collaboration with ophthalmologists. The training and maintenance of professional standards are the responsibility of the Orthoptists Board of the Council for the Professions Supplementary to Medicine. The professional body is the British Orthoptic Society. Training is at degree level.

THE BRITISH ORTHOPTIC SOCIETY, Tavistock House North, Tavistock Square, London WC1H 9HX. *Hon. Secretary,* Mrs A. Charnock

OSTEOPATHY

Osteopathy is accorded statutory regulation by the Osteopaths Act 1993. There are currently four bodies that accredit courses leading to a qualification in Osteopathy but these are due to be replaced by a General Osteopathic Council when it opens a new register, expected to be in 1997. Osteopathy is becoming an all-graduate profession. Courses vary in length from three to five years, granting various qualifications from diploma to honours degree. Shorter courses are available for qualified doctors. Details of accrediting institutions and courses can be obtained from the Osteopathic Information Service.

OSTEOPATHIC INFORMATION SERVICE, PO Box 2074, Reading, Berks RG1 4YR. Tel: 01734-512051. *Public Relations Manager,* B. Daniels

PHYSIOTHERAPY

Full-time three- or four-year degree courses are available at 31 recognized schools in the UK. Information about courses leading to eligibility for Membership of the Chartered Society of Physiotherapy and to State Registration is available from the Chartered Society of Physiotherapy.

THE CHARTERED SOCIETY OF PHYSIOTHERAPY, 14 Bedford Row, London WC1R 4ED. Tel: 0171-306 6666. *Secretary,* vacant

RADIOGRAPHY AND RADIOTHERAPY

In order to practise both diagnostic and therapeutic radiography in the UK, it is necessary to have successfully completed a course of education and training recognized by the Privy Council. Such courses are offered by universities throughout the UK and lead to the award of a degree in radiography. Further information is available from the college.

THE COLLEGE OF RADIOGRAPHERS, 2 Carriage Row, 183 Eversholt Street, London NW1 1BU. Tel: 0171-391 4500. *Chief Executive,* S. Evans

COMPLEMENTARY MEDICINE

Professional courses are validated by:

INSTITUTE FOR COMPLEMENTARY MEDICINE, PO Box 194, London SE16 1QZ. Tel: 0171-237 5165. *Director,* A. Baird

MERCHANT NAVY TRAINING SCHOOLS

OFFICERS

WARSASH MARITIME CENTRE, Southampton Institute, Newtown Road, Warsash, Southampton SO31 9ZL. Tel: 01489-576161. *Dean*, Capt. G. B. Angas

SEAFARERS

INDEFATIGABLE SCHOOL, Plas Llanfair, Llanfairpwll, Anglesey LL61 6NT. Tel: 01248-714338. *Headmaster*, Capt. P. White

NATIONAL SEA TRAINING CENTRE, North West Kent College, Dering Way, Gravesend, Kent DA12 2JJ. Tel: 01474-363656. *Head of Faculty*, R. MacDonald

MUSIC

ASSOCIATED BOARD OF THE ROYAL SCHOOLS OF MUSIC, 14 Bedford Square, London WC1B 3JG. Tel: 0171-636 5400. The Board conducts graded music examinations in over 80 countries and provides other services to music education through its professional development department and publishing company. *Chief Executive*, R. Morris

GUILDHALL SCHOOL OF MUSIC AND DRAMA, Silk Street, London EC2Y 8DT. Tel: 0171-628 2571. *Principal*, I. Horsbrugh

LONDON COLLEGE OF MUSIC, Thames Valley University, St Mary's Road, London W5 5RF. Tel: 0181-231 2304. *Director*, A. Creamer

ROYAL ACADEMY OF MUSIC, Marylebone Road, London NW1 5HT. Tel: 0171-873 7373. *Principal*, Prof. C. Price

ROYAL COLLEGE OF MUSIC, Prince Consort Road, London SW7 2BS. Tel: 0171-589 3643. *Director*, Ms J. Ritterman, PH.D.

ROYAL COLLEGE OF ORGANISTS, 7 St Andrew Street, London EC4A 3LQ. Tel: 0171-936 3606. *Chief Executive*, Dr M. Nicholas

ROYAL NORTHERN COLLEGE OF MUSIC, 124 Oxford Road, Manchester M13 9RD. Tel: 0161-273 6283. *Principal*, Prof. E. Gregson

ROYAL SCOTTISH ACADEMY OF MUSIC AND DRAMA, 100 Renfrew Street, Glasgow G2 3DB. Tel: 0141-332 4101. *Principal*, Dr P. Ledger, CBE, FRSE

TRINITY COLLEGE OF MUSIC, 11–13 Mandeville Place, London W1M 6AQ. Tel: 0171-935 5773. *Principal*, G. Henderson

NURSING

All nurses must be registered with the UK Central Council for Nursing, Midwifery and Health Visiting. Courses leading to registration as a nurse are at least three years in length. There are also some programmes which are combined with degrees. Students study in colleges of nursing or in institutions of higher education. Courses offer a combination of theoretical and practical experience in a variety of settings. Different courses lead to different types of registration, including: Registered General Nurse (RGN) or Registered Nurse (RN), Registered Mental Nurse (RMN), Registered Mental Handicap Nurse (RMHN), Registered Sick Children Nurse (RSCN), Registered Midwife (RM) and Registered Health Visitor (RHV). The various national boards, listed below, are responsible for validating courses in nursing.

The Royal College of Nurses is the professional union representing nurses and provides higher education through its Institute.

UK CENTRAL COUNCIL FOR NURSING, MIDWIFERY AND HEALTH VISITING, 23 Portland Place, London W1N 4JT. Tel: 0171-637 7181. *Chief Executive and Registrar*, Ms S. Norman

ENGLISH NATIONAL BOARD FOR NURSING, MIDWIFERY AND HEALTH VISITING, Victory House, 170 Tottenham Court Road, London OHA. Tel: 0171-388 3131. *Chief Executive*, A. P. Smith

NATIONAL BOARD FOR NURSING, MIDWIFERY AND HEALTH VISITING FOR NORTHERN IRELAND, Centre House, 79 Chichester Street, Belfast BT1 4JE. Tel: 01232-238152. *Chief Executive*, Dr O. D'A. Slevin

NATIONAL BOARD FOR NURSING, MIDWIFERY AND HEALTH VISITING FOR SCOTLAND, 22 Queen Street, Edinburgh EH2 1NT. Tel: 0131-226 7371. *Chief Executive*, Mrs L. Mitchell

WELSH NATIONAL BOARD FOR NURSING, MIDWIFERY AND HEALTH VISITING, Floor 13, Pearl Assurance House, Greyfriars Road, Cardiff CF1 3AG. Tel: 01222-395535. *Chief Executive*, D. A. Ravey

THE ROYAL COLLEGE OF NURSING OF THE UNITED KINGDOM, 20 Cavendish Square, London W1M 0AB. Tel: 0171-409 3333. *General Secretary*, Miss C. Hancock; *Principal of the RCN Institute*, Prof. A. Kitson

OPHTHALMIC AND DISPENSING OPTICS

Professional bodies are:

THE ASSOCIATION OF BRITISH DISPENSING OPTICIANS, 6 Hurlingham Business Park, Sulivan Road, London SW6 3DU. Tel: 0171-736 0088. Grants qualifications as a dispensing optician. *Registrar*, D. G. Baker

THE COLLEGE OF OPTOMETRISTS, 10 Knaresborough Place, London SW5 0TG. Tel: 0171-373 7765. Grants qualifications as an optometrist. *General Secretary*, P. D. Leigh

PHARMACY

Information may be obtained from the Secretary and Registrar of the Royal Pharmaceutical Society of Great Britain.

ROYAL PHARMACEUTICAL SOCIETY OF GREAT BRITAIN, 1 Lambeth High Street, London SE1 7JN. Tel: 0171-735 9141. *Secretary and Registrar*, J. Ferguson, OBE

PHOTOGRAPHY

The professional body is:

BRITISH INSTITUTE OF PROFESSIONAL PHOTOGRAPHY, Fox Talbot House, Amwell End, Ware, Herts SG12 9HN. Tel: 01920-464011. *Chief Executive*, A. Mair

PRINTING

Details of training courses in printing can be obtained from the Institute of Printing and the British Printing Industries Federation. In addition to these examining and organizing bodies, examinations are held by various independent regional examining boards in further education.

BRITISH PRINTING INDUSTRIES FEDERATION, 11 Bedford Row, London WC1R 4DX. Tel: 0171-242 6904. *Director-General*, T. P. E. Machin

INSTITUTE OF PRINTING, 8A Lonsdale Gardens, Tunbridge Wells, Kent TN1 1NU. Tel: 01892-538118. *Secretary-General*, D. Freeland

SOCIAL WORK

The Central Council for Education and Training in Social Work promotes education and training for social work and social care in the UK. It approves education and training programmes, including those leading to its qualifying award, the Diploma in Social Work.

THE CENTRAL COUNCIL FOR EDUCATION AND TRAINING IN SOCIAL WORK, Derbyshire House, St Chad's Street, London WC1H 8AD. Tel: 0171-278 2455. *Chairman,* J. Greenwood; *Director,* T. Hall

SPEECH AND LANGUAGE THERAPY

The Royal College of Speech and Language Therapists provides details of courses leading to qualification as a speech and language therapist. Other professionals may become Associates of the College. A directory of registered members is published annually.

THE ROYAL COLLEGE OF SPEECH AND LANGUAGE THERAPISTS, 7 Bath Place, Rivington Street, London EC2A 3DR. Tel: 0171-613 3855. *Director,* Mrs P. Evans

SURVEYING

The qualifying professional bodies include:

ARCHITECTS AND SURVEYORS INSTITUTE, St Mary House, 15 St Mary Street, Chippenham, Wilts SN15 3WD. Tel: 01249-444505. *Chief Executive,* C. G. A. Nash, OBE

ASSOCIATION OF BUILDING ENGINEERS, Jubilee House, Billing Brook Road, Weston Favell, Northampton NN3 8NW. Tel: 01604-404121. *Chief Executive,* B. D. Hughes

INCORPORATED SOCIETY OF VALUERS AND AUCTIONEERS (1968), 3 Cadogan Gate, London SW1X 0AS. Tel: 0171-235 2282. *Chief Executive,* H. Whitty

INSTITUTE OF REVENUES, RATING AND VALUATION, 41 Doughty Street, London WC1N 2LF. Tel: 0171-831 3505. *Director,* C. Farrington

ROYAL INSTITUTION OF CHARTERED SURVEYORS (incorporating The Institute of Quantity Surveyors), 12 Great George Street, London SW1P 3AD. Tel: 0171-222 7000. *Chief Executive,* Ms C. Makin

TEACHING

Teachers in publicly maintained schools must be approved as qualified by the Secretary of State in England and the General Teaching Council in Scotland, usually after a course at an accredited institution. Non-graduates usually qualify by way of a three- or four-year course leading to a Bachelor of Education (B.Ed.) honours degree, or a first degree course (BA, B.Sc.) taken concurrently with a certificate of education. Graduates take a one-year postgraduate certificate of education (PGCE). Teacher training courses may now also be developed and delivered by schools in England, subject to approval of their proposed training programme by the Teacher Training Agency and monitoring and evaluation by OFSTED (*see also* pages 438–9).

Details of courses in England and Wales are contained in the *Handbook of Degree and Advanced Courses* published annually by the National Association of Teachers in Further and Higher Education. Details of courses in Scotland can be obtained from colleges of education, universities, from COSHEP, and from TEACH (*see* page 451). Details of courses in Northern Ireland can be obtained from the Department of Education for Northern Ireland. Applications for teacher training courses in Northern Ireland are made to the institutions direct. For applications, *see* pages 442–3.

TEXTILES

THE TEXTILE INSTITUTE, International Headquarters, 10 Blackfriars Street, Manchester M3 5DR. Tel: 0161-834 8457. *Chief Executive (acting),* Dr J. McPhee

THEOLOGICAL COLLEGES

The number of students training for the ministry in the academic year 1995–6 is shown in parenthesis. Those marked * show figures for 1994–5.

ANGLICAN

COLLEGE OF THE RESURRECTION, Mirfield, W. Yorks WF14 0BW. Tel: 01924-490441. (20). *Principal,* Revd Dr D. J. Lane

CRANMER HALL, St John's College, Durham DH1 3RJ. Tel: 0191-374 3579. (59). *Principal,* D. V. Day

OAK HILL COLLEGE, Chase Side, London N14 4PS. Tel: 0181-449 0467. (45). *Principal,* Revd Dr D. Peterson

RIDLEY HALL, Cambridge CB3 9HG. Tel: 01223-353040. (50). *Principal,* Revd G. A. Cray

RIPON COLLEGE, Cuddesdon, Oxford OX44 9EX. Tel: 01865-874404. (75). *Principal (acting),* Revd Dr B. Castle

ST JOHN'S COLLEGE, Chilwell Lane, Bramcote, Nottingham NG9 3DS. Tel: 0115-925 1114. (75). *Principal,* Revd Dr J. Goldingay

ST MICHAEL'S THEOLOGICAL COLLEGE, Llandaff, Cardiff CF5 2YJ. Tel: 01222-563379/116. (30). *Principal,* Revd Canon J. H. L. Rowlands

ST STEPHEN'S HOUSE, 16 Marston Street, Oxford OX4 1JX. Tel: 01865-247874. (50). *Principal,* Revd J. Sheehy

THEOLOGICAL INSTITUTE OF THE SCOTTISH EPISCOPAL CHURCH, 21 Inverleith Terrace, Edinburgh EH3 5NS. Tel: 0131-343 2038. (27). *Principal,* Revd R. A. Nixon

TRINITY COLLEGE, Stoke Hill, Bristol BS9 1JP. Tel: 0117-968 2803. (120). *Principal,* Revd Canon D. Gillett

WESTCOTT HOUSE, Jesus Lane, Cambridge CB5 8BP. Tel: 01223-350074. (57). *Principal,* Revd M. G. V. Roberts

WYCLIFFE HALL, 54 Banbury Road, Oxford OX2 6PW. Tel: 01865-274200. (67). *Principal,* Revd Dr A. McGrath

BAPTIST

BRISTOL BAPTIST COLLEGE, Woodland Road, Bristol BS8 1UN. Tel: 0117-926 0248. (25). *Principal,* Revd Dr B. Haymes

NORTHERN BAPTIST COLLEGE, Luther King House, Brighton Grove, Rusholme, Manchester M14 5JP. Tel: 0161-224 2214. (21). *Principal,* Revd Dr R. L. Kidd

NORTH WALES BAPTIST COLLEGE, Ffordd Ffriddoedd, Bangor LL57 2EH. Tel: 01248-362608. (2). *Warden,* Revd Dr D. D. Morgan

REGENT'S PARK COLLEGE, Oxford OX1 2LB. Tel: 01865-288120. (24). *Principal,* Revd Dr P. S. Fiddes

THE SCOTTISH BAPTIST COLLEGE, 12 Aytoun Road, Glasgow G41 5RN. Tel: 0141-424 0747. (13). *Principal,* Revd K. B. E. Roxburgh

SOUTH WALES BAPTIST COLLEGE, 54 Richmond Road, Cardiff CF2 3UR. Tel: 01222-496060. (24). *Principal,* Revd D. H. Matthews

SPURGEON'S COLLEGE, South Norwood Hill, London SE25 6DJ. Tel: 0181-653 0850. (80). *Principal,* Revd M. Quicke

CHURCH OF SCOTLAND

CHRIST'S COLLEGE, 25 High Street, Old Aberdeen AB2 3EE. Tel: 01224-272138. (30). *Master,* Revd Prof. A. Main, TD, ph.D.

NEW COLLEGE, Mound Place, Edinburgh EH1 2LU. Tel: 0131-650 8900. (33). *Principal,* Revd Dr R. Page

TRINITY COLLEGE, 4 The Square, University of
Glasgow, Glasgow G12 8QQ. Tel: 0141-339 8855. (70).
Principal, Revd Prof. G. M. Newlands

CONGREGATIONAL

COLLEGE OF THE WELSH INDEPENDENTS, 38 Pier Street,
Aberystwyth. *Principal*, Revd Dr E. S. John
SCOTTISH CONGREGATIONAL COLLEGE, St Colm's, 20
Inverleith Terrace, Edinburgh EH3 5NS. Tel: 0131-315
3595. (1). *Principal*, Revd Dr J. W. S. Clark

ECUMENICAL

QUEEN'S COLLEGE, Somerset Road, Edgbaston,
Birmingham B15 2QH. Tel: 0121-454 1527. (70).
Principal, Revd P. Fisher

METHODIST

EDGHILL THEOLOGICAL COLLEGE, 9 Lennoxvale, Belfast
BT9 5BY. Tel: 01232-665870. (19). *Principal*, Revd D. D.
Cooke, PH.D.
HARTLEY VICTORIA COLLEGE, Northern Federation for
Training in Ministry, Luther King House, Brighton
Grove, Manchester M14 5JP. Tel: 0161-224 2215. (22).
Principal, Revd G. Slater
WESLEY COLLEGE, College Park Drive, Henbury Road,
Bristol BS10 7QD. Tel: 0117-959 1200. (63). *Principal*,
Revd Dr N. Richardson
WESLEY HOUSE, Jesus Lane, Cambridge CB5 8BJ. Tel:
01223-350609. (30). *Principal*, Revd Dr I. H. Jones
WESLEY STUDY CENTRE, 55 The Avenue, Durham
DH1 4EB. Tel: 0191-386 1833. (24). *Director*, Revd
P. Luscombe, PH.D.

NON-DENOMINATIONAL

ST MARY'S COLLEGE, The University, St Andrews, Fife
KY16 9JU. Tel: 01334-462851. (180). *Principal*, Dr
R. A. Piper

PRESBYTERIAN

UNION THEOLOGICAL COLLEGE, Belfast BT7 1JT. Tel:
01232-325374. (*41). *Principal*, Revd Prof. T. S. Reid

PRESBYTERIAN CHURCH OF WALES

UNITED THEOLOGICAL COLLEGE, Aberystwyth SY23 2LT.
Tel: 01970-624574. (20). *Principal*, Revd Prof. E. N.
Roberts

ROMAN CATHOLIC

ALLEN HALL, 28 Beaufort Street, London SW3 5AA. Tel:
0171-351 1296. (*35). *Principal*, Revd K. Barltrop, STL
CAMPION HOUSE COLLEGE, 112 Thornbury Road,
Isleworth, Middx TW7 4NN. Tel: 0181-560 1924. (23).
Principal, Revd C. C. Dykehoff, SJ
OSCOTT COLLEGE, Chester Road, Sutton Coldfield,
W. Midlands B73 5AA. Tel: 0121-354 7117. (50). *Rector*,
Rt. Revd P. McKinney, STL
ST JOHN'S SEMINARY, Wonersh, Guildford, Surrey
GU5 0QX. Tel: 01483-892217. (70). *Rector*, Fr
K. Haggerty, STL
SCOTUS COLLEGE, 2 Chesters Road, Bearsden, Glasgow
G61 4AG. Tel: 0141-942 8384. (50). *Rector*, Rt Revd M. J.
Conway
USHAW COLLEGE, Durham DH7 9RH. Tel: 0191-373 1366.
(64). *President*, Revd J. O'Keefe

UNITARIAN

UNITARIAN COLLEGE, Northern Federation for Training
in Ministry, Luther King House, Brighton Grove,
Rusholme, Manchester M14 5JP. Tel: 0161-224 2849. (5).
Principal, Revd L. Smith, PH.D.

UNITED REFORMED

BALA-BANGOR INDEPENDENT COLLEGE, Bangor
LL57 2EH. (*15). *Principal*, R. T. Jones, D.PHIL., DD
MANSFIELD COLLEGE, Mansfield Road, Oxford OX1 3TF.
Tel: 01865-270999. (25). *Principal*, Prof. D. Marquand
NORTHERN COLLEGE, Northern Federation for Training
in Ministry, Luther King House, Brighton Grove,
Rusholme, Manchester M14 5JP. Tel: 0161-224 4381.
(24). *Principal*, Revd Dr D. R. Peel
WESTMINSTER COLLEGE, Madingley Road, Cambridge
CB3 0AA. Tel: 01223-353997. (28). *Principal*, Revd D. G.
Cornick, PH.D.

JEWISH

JEWS' COLLEGE, Albert Road, London NW4 2SJ. Tel: 0181-
203 6427. (10). *Principal*, Rabbi Dr D. Sinclair
LEO BAECK COLLEGE, Sternberg Centre for Judaism, 80
East End Road, London N3 2SY. Tel: 0181-349 4525.
(17). *Principal*, Rabbi Prof. J. Magonet

TOWN AND COUNTRY PLANNING

Degree and diploma courses in town planning are accred-
ited by the Royal Town Planning Institute.
THE ROYAL TOWN PLANNING INSTITUTE, 26 Portland
Place, London W1N 4BE. Tel: 0171-636 9107. *Secretary-
General*, R. Upton

TRANSPORT

Qualifying examinations in transport management and
logistics leading to chartered professional status are
conducted by the Chartered Institute of Transport.
THE CHARTERED INSTITUTE OF TRANSPORT, 80
Portland Place, London W1N 4DP. Tel: 0171-636 9952.
Director, Mrs S. Gross

Independent Schools

The following pages list those independent schools whose Head is a member of the Headmasters' and Headmistress' Conference, the Society of Headmasters and Headmistresses of Independent Schools or the Girls' Schools Association

---

THE HEADMASTERS' AND HEADMISTRESS' CONFERENCE

Chairman (1997), M. B. Mavor (Rugby School)
Secretary, V. S. Anthony, 130 Regent Road, Leicester
LEI 7PG. Tel: 0116-285 4810
Membership Secretary, D. E. Prince, 1 Russell House, Bepton Road, Midhurst, W. Sussex GU29 9NB. Tel: 01730-815635. The annual meeting is, as a rule, held at the end of September or early in October

* Woodard Corporation School, 1 The Sanctuary, London SWIP 3JT. Tel: 0171-222 5381
† Girls in VI form
‡ Co-educational
° 1995 figures

Name of School	Foun-ded	No. of pupils	Annual fees £		Head (with date of appointment)
ENGLAND AND WALES			Boarding	Day	
Abbotsholme School, Staffs	1889	240‡	11,850	7,920	D. J. Farrant (1984)
Abingdon School, Oxon	1256	780	10,332	5,571	M. St J. Parker (1975)
Ackworth School, W. Yorks	1779	375‡	9,705	5,529	M. J. Dickinson (1995)
Aldenham School, Herts	1597	377†	11,919	8,175	S. R. Borthwick (1994)
Alleyn's School, London SE22	1619	925‡	—	5,895	Dr C. H. R. Niven (1992)
Ampleforth College (*RC*), Yorks	1802	540	12,555	6,480	Revd G. F. L. Chamberlain, OSB (1993)
*Ardingly College, W. Sussex	1858	450‡	12,225	9,465	J. W. Flecker (1980)
Arnold School, Blackpool	1896	823‡	—	3,900	W. T. Gillen (1993)
Ashville College, Harrogate	1877	574‡	9,237	4,938	M. H. Crosby (1987)
Bablake School, Coventry	1560	876‡	—	3,975	Dr S. Nuttall (1991)
Bancroft's School, Essex	1727	749‡	—	6,051	Dr P. R. Scott (1996)
Barnard Castle School, Co. Durham	1883	516‡	8,940	5,292	F. S. McNamara (1980)
Batley Grammar School, W. Yorks	1612	547‡	—	3,882	W. M. Duggan (1995)
Bedales School, Hants	1893	400‡	13,647	10,236	Mrs A. A. Willcocks (1995)
Bedford Modern School	1566	930	9,179	4,839	S. Smith (1996)
Bedford School	1552	708	11,670	7,350	Dr I. P. Evans (1990)
Berkhamsted School, Herts	1541	500†	11,664	9,821	Dr P. Chadwick (1996)
Birkenhead School, Merseyside	1860	690	—	3,897	S. J. Haggett (1991)
°Bishop's Stortford College, Herts	1868	337†	10,320	7,440	J. Trotman (1996)
*Bloxham School, Oxon	1860	356†	12,655	9,915	D. K. Exham (1991)
Blundell's School, Devon	1604	420‡	12,135	7,410	J. Leigh (1992)
Bolton School	1524	850	—	4,626	A. W. Wright (1983)
Bootham School, York	1823	346‡	10,161	6,594	I. M. Small (1988)
Bradfield College, Berks	1850	620†	12,825	9,621	P. B. Smith (1985)
Bradford Grammar School	1662	920†	—	4,428	S. R. Davidson (1996)
Brentwood School, Essex	1557	1,048‡	10,620	6,075	J. A. B. Kelsall (1993)
Brighton College, E. Sussex	1845	488‡	12,450	8,190	J. D. Leach (1987)
Bristol Grammar School	1532	1,040‡	—	4,089	C. E. Martin (1986)
Bromsgrove School, Worcs	1553	640‡	10,605	6,750	T. M. Taylor (1986)
Bryanston School, Dorset	1928	630‡	13,230	8,820	T. D. Wheare (1983)
Bury Grammar School, Lancs	1634	700	—	3,876	K. Richards (1990)
Canford School, Dorset	1923	540‡	13,000	9,750	J. D. Lever (1992)
Caterham School, Surrey	1811	750‡	11,730	6,090	R. A. E. Davey (1995)
Charterhouse, Surrey	1611	720†	13,341	11,022	Revd J. S. Witheridge (1996)
Cheadle Hulme School, Cheshire	1855	980‡	—	4,296	D. J. Wilkinson (1990)
Cheltenham College, Glos	1841	580†	12,690	9,585	P. D. V. Wilkes (1990)
Chetham's School of Music, Manchester	1653	258‡	15,975	12,366	Revd Canon P. F. Hullah (1992)
Chigwell School, Essex	1629	370†	9,993	6,573	D. F. Gibbs (1996)
Christ College, Brecon	1541	340‡	9,972	7,728	D. P. Jones (1996)
Christ's Hospital, W. Sussex	1553	820‡	varies	—	Dr P. C. D. Southern (1996)
Churcher's College, Hants	1722	575‡	9,810	5,250	G. W. Buttle (1988)

Name of School	Founded	No. of pupils	Annual fees £ Boarding	Day	Head (with date of appointment)
City of London Freemen's School, Surrey	1854	530‡	9,988	6,291	D. C. Haywood (1987)
City of London, London EC4	1442	870	—	6,120	R. Dancey (1995)
Clifton College, Bristol	1862	630‡	12,500	8,900	H. Monro (1991)
Colfe's School, London SE12	1652	720†	—	5,730	Dr D. Richardson (1990)
Colston's Collegiate School, Bristol	1710	450‡	10,590	5,745	D. G. Crawford (1995)
Cranleigh School, Surrey	1863	490†	12,990	9,615	T. A. A. Hart (1984)
Culford School, Suffolk	1881	400‡	10,920	7,107	J. S. Richardson (1992)
Dame Allan's School, Newcastle upon Tyne	1705	418†	—	3,570	D. W. Welsh (*Principal*) (1996)
Dauntsey's School, Wilts	1543	640‡	11,070	6,816	C. R. Evans (1985)
Dean Close School, Cheltenham	1884	445‡	12,840	8,955	C. J. Bacon (1979)
Denstone College, Staffs	1873	300‡	11,328	8,052	D. Derbyshire (from January 1997)
Douai School (*RC*), Berks	1903	205‡	10,545	6,780	Dr E. Power, OSB (1993)
Dover College, Kent	1871	250‡	11,820	6,450	M. P. G. Wright (1991)
Downside School (*RC*), Somerset	1607	301	11,685	6,180	Revd Dom. A. Sutch (*Master*) (1995)
Dulwich College, London SE21	1619	1,390	12,636	6,318	G. G. Able (*Master*) (from January 1997)
Durham School	1414	299†	11,748	7,644	M. A. Lang (1982)
Eastbourne College, E Sussex	1867	477‡	12,084	8,936	C. M. P. Bush (1993)
Ellesmere College, Shropshire	1884	300‡	11,100	7,350	B. J. Wignall (1996)
Eltham College, London SE9	1842	590†	12,081	5,724	D. M. Green (1990)
Emanuel School, London SE11	1594	760‡	—	4,950	T. Jones-Parry (1994)
Epsom College, Surrey	1855	652‡	12,204	9,066	A. H. Beadles (1993)
Eton College, Berks	1440	1,270	13,410	—	J. E. Lewis (1994)
Exeter School	1633	700†	8,475	4,470	N. W. Gamble (1992)
Felsted School, Essex	1564	350‡	12,978	10,239	S. C. Roberts (1993)
Forest School, London E17	1834	825†	9,087	5,790	A. G. Boggis (*Warden*) (1992)
Framlingham College, Suffolk	1864	450‡	10,170	6,528	Mrs. G. M. Randall (1994)
Frensham Heights, Surrey	1925	295‡	11,985	7,770	P. de Voil (1993)
Giggleswick School, N. Yorks	1512	320‡	12,120	8,040	A. P. Millard (1993)
The Grange School, Cheshire	1978	575‡	—	3,675	E. S. Marshall (1977)
Gresham's School, Norfolk	1555	520‡	12,435	8,700	J. H. Arkell (1991)
Haberdashers' Aske's School, Herts	1690	1,100	—	6,021	J. W. R. Goulding (1996)
Haileybury, Herts	1862	586†	13,338	9,672	S. A. Westley (*Master*) (1996)
Hampton School, Middx	1557	945	—	5,280	B. R. Martin (from April 1997)
Harrow School, Middx	1571	785	13,830	—	N. R. Bomford (1991)
Hereford Cathedral School	1384	622‡	8,235	4,755	Dr H. C. Tomlinson (1987)
Highgate School, London N6	1565	615	—	7,515	R. P. Kennedy (1989)
Hulme Grammar School, Oldham	1611	684	—	3,726	T. J. Turvey (1995)
Hurstpierpoint College, W. Sussex	1849	350‡	11,940	9,330	S. Meek (1995)
Hymers College, Hull	1889	743‡	—	3,735	J. C. Morris (1990)
Ipswich School, Suffolk	1390	595‡	9,111	5,331	I. G. Galbraith (1993)
John Lyon School, Middx	1876	520	—	5,790	Revd T. J. Wright (1986)
Kelly College, Devon	1877	300‡	11,670	7,335	M. Turner (1995)
Kent College, Canterbury	1885	500‡	10,770	6,048	E. B. Halse (1995)
Kimbolton School, Cambs	1600	560‡	9,450	5,520	R. V. Peel (1987)
King Edward VI School, Southampton	1553	950‡	—	5,016	P. B. Hamilton (1996)
King Edward VII School, Lytham	1908	495	—	3,875	P. J. Wilde (1993)
King Edward's School, Bath	1552	665†	—	4,548	P. J. Winter (1993)
King Edward's School, Birmingham	1552	890	—	4,725	H. R. Wright (*Chief Master*) (1991)
King Edward's School, Witley, Surrey	1553	421‡	9,450	6,540	R. J. Fox (1988)
King Henry VIII School, Coventry	1545	810‡	—	3,975	T. J. Vardon (1994)
King's College, Taunton	1880	450‡	12,030	7,920	R. S. Funnell (1988)
King's College School, London SW19	1829	720	—	6,840	R. M. Reeve (1980)
King's School, Bruton, Somerset	1519	334†	11,355	8,055	R. I. Smyth (1993)
King's School, Canterbury	600	740‡	13,440	9,285	Revd K. H. Wilkinson (1996)
King's School, Chester	1541	510	—	4,230	A. R. D. Wickson (1981)
King's School, Ely, Cambs	970	400‡	12,030	8,055	R. H. Youdale (1992)
King's School, Gloucester	1541	350‡	10,650	6,300	P. Lacey (1992)
King's School, Macclesfield	1502	1,120‡	—	4,350	A. G. Silcock (1987)
King's School, Rochester, Kent	604	320‡	12,375	7,110	Dr I. R. Walker (1986)
King's School, Tynemouth	1860	670‡	—	3,924	Dr D. Younger (1993)

Name of School	Founded	No. of pupils	Annual fees £		Head (with date of appointment)
			Boarding	Day	
King's School, Worcester	1541	802‡	9,099	5,250	Dr J. M. Moore (1983)
Kingston Grammar School, Surrey	1561	600‡	—	5,715	C. D. Baxter (1991)
Kingswood School, Bath	1748	450‡	11,829	7,350	G. M. Best (1987)
*Lancing College, W. Sussex	1848	515†	12,630	9,495	C. J. Saunders (1993)
Latymer Upper School, London w6	1624	955†	—	6,180	C. Diggory (1991)
Leeds Grammar School	1552	917	—	4,845	B. W. Collins (1986)
Leicester Grammar School	1981	606‡	—	4,320	J. B. Sugden (1989)
Leighton Park School, Reading	1890	370‡	11,754	8,820	J. Dunston (1996)
The Leys School, Cambridge	1875	420‡	12,300	8,790	Revd J. C. A. Barrett (1990)
Liverpool College	1840	620‡	—	4,290	B. R. Martin (*Principal*) (1992)
Llandovery College, Carmarthenshire	1848	235‡	9,987	6,516	Dr C. E. Evans (*Warden*) (1988)
Lord Wandsworth College, Hants	1912	475‡	9,972	7,752	G. de W. Waller (1993)
Loughborough Grammar School	1495	940	8,586	4,662	D. N. Ireland (1984)
Magdalen College School, Oxford	1480	516	—	5,094	P. M. Tinniswood (*Master*) (1991)
Malvern College, Worcs	1865	648‡	12,750	9,270	H. C. K. Carson (from January 1997)
Manchester Grammar School	1515	1,411	—	4,344	G. M. Stephen, ph.d (*High Master*) (1994)
Marlborough College, Wilts	1843	800‡	13,425	9,465	E. J. H. Gould (*Master*) (1993)
Merchant Taylors' School, Liverpool	1620	730	—	3,933	S. J. R. Dawkins (1985)
Merchant Taylors' School, Middx	1561	750	11,520	6,920	J. R. Gabitass (1991)
Millfield, Street, Somerset	1935	1,220‡	13,785	8,820	C. S. Martin (1990)
Mill Hill School, London NW7	1807	530†	12,045	7,815	W. R. Winfield (1996)
Monkton Combe School, Bath	1868	326‡	12,195	8,400	M. J. Cuthbertson (1990)
Monmouth School, Gwent	1614	570	8,664	5,202	T. H. P. Haynes (1995)
Mount St Mary's College (*RC*), Sheffield	1842	290‡	9,420	6,150	P. B. Fisher (1991)
Newcastle under Lyme School	1874	1,150‡	—	3,755	Dr R. M. Reynolds (*Principal*) (1990)
Norwich School	1250	630†	—	4,800	C. D. Brown (1984)
Nottingham High School	1513	826	—	4,923	C. S. Parker (1995)
Oakham School, Rutland	1584	1,000‡	12,240	6,840	A. R. M. Little (1996)
The Oratory School (*RC*), Berks	1859	380	12,300	8,595	S. W. Barrow (1992)
Oundle School, Northants	1556	835‡	13,380	—	D. B. McMurray (1984)
Pangbourne College, Berks	1917	329‡	11,880	8,310	A. B. E. Hudson (1988)
Perse School, Cambridge	1615	525†	—	4,839	N. P. V. Richardson (1994)
Plymouth College	1877	587‡	9,580	4,995	A. J. Morsley (1992)
Pocklington School, York	1514	620‡	8,904	5,109	J. N. D. Gray (1992)
Portsmouth Grammar School	1732	820‡	—	4,755	A. C. V. Evans (1983)
Prior Park College (*RC*), Bath	1830	500‡	10,758	5,949	R. G. G. Mercer, d.phil (1996)
Queen Elizabeth GS, Wakefield	1591	751	—	4,368	R. P. Mardling (1985)
Queen Elizabeth's GS, Blackburn	1567	950†	—	4,140	Dr D. S. Hempsall (1995)
Queen Elizabeth's Hospital, Bristol	1590	500	7,431	4,131	Dr R. Gliddon (1986)
Queen's College, Taunton	1843	480‡	9,693	6,354	C. T. Bradnock (1991)
Radley College, Oxon	1847	614	12,900	—	R. M. Morgan (*Warden*) (1991)
Ratcliffe College (*RC*), Leicester	1844	490‡	9,459	6,309	T. A. Kilbride (1996)
Reading Blue Coat School	1646	550‡	10,050	5,514	Revd A. C. E. Sanders (1974)
Reed's School, Surrey	1813	350†	10,767	8,142	D. E. Prince (1983)
Reigate Grammar School, Surrey	1675	820‡	—	5,160	P. V. Dixon (1996)
Rendcomb College, Glos	1920	241‡	10,800	8,550	J. Tolputt (1987)
Repton School, Derby	1557	560‡	12,120	9,120	G. E. Jones (1987)
RNIB New College, Worcester	1987	122‡	22,636	15,090	Mrs H. Williams (*Principal*) (1995)
Rossall School, Lancs	1844	400‡	11,628	4,368	R. D. W. Rhodes (1988)
Royal Grammar School, Guildford	1552	840	—	5,980	T. M. S. Young (1992)
Royal Grammar School, Newcastle upon Tyne	1545	935	—	3,885	J. F. X. Miller (1994)
Royal Grammar School, Worcester	1291	773	—	4,590	W. A. Jones (1993)
Rugby School, Warwicks	1567	740‡	13,290	10,440	M. B. Mavor, cvo (1990)
Rydal Penrhos School, Conwy	1880	380‡	10,242	7,389	N. W. Thorne (1991)
Ryde School (with Upper Chine), Isle of Wight	1921	460‡	8,870	4,350	M. D. Featherstone (1990)
St. Albans School, Herts	1570	654†	—	5,865	A. R. Grant (1993)
St Ambrose College, Cheshire	1946	700	—	3,624	G. E. Hester (1991)
St. Bede's College (*RC*), Manchester	1876	1,000‡	—	3,990	J. Byrne (1983)
St Bees School, Cumbria	1583	285‡	11,016	7,578	P. A. Chamberlain (1988)

Name of School	Foun-ded	No. of pupils	Annual fees £		Head (with date of appointment)
			Boarding	Day	
St Benedict's School (RC), London w5	1902	591†	—	5,220	Dr A. J. Dachs (1987)
St Dunstan's College, London se6	1888	643‡	—	5,745	J. D. Moore (1993)
St Edmund's College (RC), Herts	1568	450‡	10,320	6,480	D. J. J. McEwen (1984)
St Edmund's School, Canterbury	1749	300‡	12,570	8,220	A. N. Ridley (1994)
St Edward's College (RC), Liverpool	1853	750‡	—	3,798	J. E. Waszek (1992)
St Edward's School, Oxford	1863	560†	12,855	9,465	D. Christie (Warden) (1988)
St George's College (RC), Surrey	1869	530†	—	6,795	J. A. Peake (1995)
St John's School, Surrey	1851	400†	11,100	7,650	C. H. Tongue (1993)
St Lawrence College in Thanet, Kent	1879	370‡	11,835	7,905	M. Slater (1996)
St Mary's College (RC), Merseyside	1919	630‡	—	3,894	W. Hammond (1991)
St Paul's School, London sw13	1509	780	12,765	8,490	R. S. Baldock (High Master) (1992)
St Peter's School, York	627	479‡	10,419	6,066	A. F. Trotman (1995)
Sedbergh School, Cumbria	1525	315	12,150	8,505	C. H. Hirst (1995)
Sevenoaks School, Kent	1418	939‡	12,087	7,362	T. R. Cookson (1996)
Sherborne School, Dorset	1550	600	13,125	10,005	P. H. Lapping (1988)
Shrewsbury School	1552	690	12,990	9,150	F. E. Maidment (1988)
Silcoates School, W. Yorks	1820	422‡	—	5,562	A. P. Spillane (1991)
Solihull School, W. Midlands	1560	810†	—	4,530	P. S. J. Derham (1996)
Stamford School, Lincs	1532	570	8,600	4,300	G. J. Timm (1978)
Stockport Grammar School	1487	985‡	—	4,086	I. Mellor (1996)
Stonyhurst College (RC), Lancs	1593	400†	12,045	7,500	A. J. F. Aylward (1996)
Stowe School, Bucks	1923	550†	4,263	2,935	J. G. L. Nichols (1988)
Sutton Valence School, Kent	1576	380‡	11,700	7,485	N. A. Sampson (1994)
Taunton School	1847	483‡	11,355	7,260	B. B. Sutton (1987)
Tettenhall College, Wolverhampton	1863	220‡	9,147	5,640	Dr P. C. Bodkin (1994)
Tonbridge School, Kent	1553	680	13,620	9,612	J. M. Hammond (1990)
Trent College, Nottingham	1868	700‡	10,899	6,690	J. S. Lee (1988)
Trinity School, Surrey	1596	850	—	5,622	B. J. Lenon (1995)
Truro School	1879	810‡	8,958	4,812	G. A. G. Dodd (1993)
University College School, London nw3	1830	700	—	7,200	K. J. Durham (1996)
Uppingham School, Leics	1584	630†	13,320	7,995	Dr S. C. Winkley (1991)
Warwick School	914	806	10,419	4,854	Dr P. J. Cheshire (1988)
Wellingborough School, Northants	1595	510‡	9,780	5,595	F. R. Ullmann (1993)
Wellington College, Berks	1856	795†	12,750	9,300	C. J. Driver (Master) (1989)
Wellington School, Somerset	1837	547‡	8,394	4,596	A. J. Rogers (1990)
Wells Cathedral School, Somerset	1180	598‡	9,651	5,667	J. S. Baxter (1986)
West Buckland School, Devon	1858	455‡	9,450	5,130	M. Downward (1979)
Westminster School, London sw1	1560	675†	13,530	10,125	D. M. Summerscale (1986)
Whitgift School, Surrey	1596	1,105	—	5,826	C. A. Barnett, D.phil (1991)
William Hulme's GS, Manchester	1887	761‡	—	4,449	P. D. Briggs (1987)
Winchester College, Hants	1382	680	13,944	10,458	J. P. Sabben-Clare (1985)
Wisbech Grammar School, Cambs	1379	640‡	—	4,890	R. S. Repper (1988)
Wolverhampton Grammar School	1512	770‡	—	5,100	B. Trafford (1990)
Woodbridge School, Suffolk	1662	540‡	9,279	5,646	S. H. Cole (1994)
Woodhouse Grove School, Bradford	1812	560‡	9,450	5,565	D. Humphreys (1996)
Worksop College, Notts	1895	350‡	11,325	7,800	R. A. Collard (1994)
Worth School (RC), W. Sussex	1959	315	11,952	8,109	Fr C. Jamison (1994)
Wrekin College, Shropshire	1880	270‡	11,910	6,540	P. M. Johnson (1991)
Wycliffe College, Glos	1882	364‡	12,750	9,000	D. C. M. Prichard (1994)
Yarm School, N. Yorks	1978	520†	—	4,750	R. N. Tate (1978)

SCOTLAND

Name of School	Foun-ded	No. of pupils	Boarding	Day	Head
Daniel Stewart's and Melville College, Edinburgh	1832	780	8,640	4,320	P. J. F. Tobin (Principal) (1989)
Dollar Academy, Clackmannanshire	1818	767‡	9,612	4,338	J. S. Roberston (Rector) (1994)
The Edinburgh Academy	1824	580†	11,265	5,283	J. V. Light (Rector) (1995)
Fettes College, Edinburgh	1870	495‡	12,810	8,655	M. T. Thyne, frse (1988)
George Heriot's School, Edinburgh	1659	980‡	—	3,936	K. P. Pearson (1983)
George Watson's College, Edinburgh	1741	1,278‡	8,646	4,299	F. E. Gerstenberg (Principal) (1985)
Glasgow Academy	1845	585‡	—	4,485	D. Comins (Rector) (1994)
Glenalmond College, Perth	1841	325‡	12,480	8,325	I. G. Templeton (Warden) (1992)
Gordonstoun School, Moray	1934	420‡	12,480	8,055	M. C. S.-R. Pyper (1990)

Name of School	Founded	No. of pupils	Annual fees £ Boarding	Annual fees £ Day	Head (with date of appointment)
High School of Dundee	1239	750‡	—	4,170	R. Nimmo, OBE (*Rector*) (1977)
High School of Glasgow	1124	635‡	—	4,518	R. G. Easton (1983)
Hutcheson's Grammar School, Glasgow	1641	1,213‡	—	3,986	D. R. Ward (*Rector*) (1987)
Kelvinside Academy, Glasgow	1878	425	—	4,720	J. H. Duff (*Rector*) (1980)
Loretto School, Midlothian	1827	317‡	12,195	8,130	K. J. Budge (1995)
Merchiston Castle School, Edinburgh	1833	330	11,985	7,965	D. M. Spawforth (1980)
Morrison's Academy, Crieff	1860	449‡	11,121	3,828	G. H. Edwards (*Rector*) (1996)
Robert Gordon's College, Aberdeen	1729	958‡	—	4,185	B. R. W. Lockhart (1996)
St Aloysius' College, Glasgow	1859	820‡	—	3,300	Revd A. Porter, SJ (1995)
Strathallan School, Perth	1913	495‡	11,775	8,211	A. W. McPhail (1993)

NORTHERN IRELAND

Name of School	Founded	No. of pupils	Boarding	Day	Head
°Bangor Grammar School, Co. Down	1856	920	—	400	T. W. Patton (1979)
Belfast Royal Academy	1785	1,364‡	—	80	W. M. Sillery (1980)
Campbell College, Belfast	1894	705	5,556	1,041	Dr R. J. I. Pollock (1987)
Coleraine Academical Institution	1856	850	6,600	2,910	R. S. Forsythe (1984)
Methodist College, Belfast	1868	1,853‡	5,792	230	T. W. Mulryne (*Principal*) (1988)
Portora Royal School, Enniskillen	1618	100	—	42	R. L. Bennett (1983)
Royal Belfast Academical Institution	1810	1,050	—	420	R. M. Ridley (*Principal*) (1990)

CHANNEL ISLANDS AND ISLE OF MAN

Name of School	Founded	No. of pupils	Boarding	Day	Head
Elizabeth College, Guernsey	1563	555†	6,660	2,610	J. H. F. Doulton (1988)
King William's College, Isle of Man	1668	320‡	11,580	8,250	P. K. Fulton-Peebles (*Principal*) (1996)
Victoria College, Jersey	1852	620	—	1,776	J. Hydes (1992)

EUROPE

Name of School	Founded	No. of pupils	Boarding	Day	Head
Aiglon College, Switzerland	1949	280‡	Fr.45,340	Fr.31,170	R. McDonald (1994)
British School in the Netherlands	1935	490‡	—	Gld.20,490	M. J. Cooper (*Principal*) (1990)
British School of Brussels	1970	502‡	—	Fr.648,000	Ms J. M. Bray (*Principal*) (1992)
British School of Paris	1954	320‡	Fr.105,000	Fr.75,000	M. Honour (*Principal*) (1991)
°The English School, Nicosia, Cyprus	1900	834‡	—	C£1,700	A. M. Hudspeth (1988)
The International School of Geneva	1924	1,000‡	Fr.42,720	Fr.19,040	G. Walker, OBE (*Director-General*) (1991)
The International School of Paris	1964	220‡	—	Fr.82,000	N. M. Prentki (1988)
King's College, Madrid		n/a‡	—	n/a	Dr G. Percy
St Columba's College, Dublin	1843	265‡	Ir£6,135	Ir£3,540	T. E. Macey (*Warden*) (1988)
St Edward's College, Malta	1929	600†	—	LM.765	G. Briscoe (1989)
St George's English School, Rome	1958	350‡	—	L.19.4m	B. Gardner (1994)
°Sir James Henderson British School, Milan	1969	170‡	—	L.15m	C. T. G. Leech (*Principal*) (1986)

OTHER OVERSEAS MEMBERS

AFRICA

DIOCESAN COLLEGE, Rondebosch, SA. *Head*, C. N. Watson

FALCON COLLEGE, PO Esigodini, Zimbabwe. *Head*, P. N. Todd

HILTON COLLEGE, Kwazulu-Natal, SA. *Head*, M. J. Nicholson

MICHAELHOUSE, Balgowan, SA. *Head*, J. H. Pluke

PETERHOUSE, Marondera, Zimbabwe. *Head*, M. A. Bawden

ST GEORGE'S COLLEGE, Harare, Zimbabwe. *Head*, K. F. Brennan

ST JOHN'S COLLEGE, Johannesburg, SA. *Head*, R. J. D. Clarence

ST STITHIAN'S COLLEGE, Randburg, SA. *Head*, D. B. Wylde

AUSTRALIA

ANGLICAN CHURCH GRAMMAR SCHOOL, Brisbane, Queensland. *Head*, C. V. Ellis

BRIGHTON GRAMMAR SCHOOL, Brighton, Victoria. *Head*, R. L. Rofe

BRISBANE BOYS' COLLEGE, Toowong, Queensland. *Head*, G. M. Cujes

CAMBERWELL GRAMMAR SCHOOL, Balwyn, Victoria. *Head*, C. F. Black

CANBERRA GRAMMAR SCHOOL, Redhill, ACT. *Head*, T. C. Murray

CAULFIELD GRAMMAR SCHOOL, Elsternwick, Victoria. *Head*, S. H. Newton

CHRIST CHURCH GRAMMAR SCHOOL, Claremont, W. Australia. *Head*, J. J. S. Madin

CRANBROOK SCHOOL, Sydney, NSW. *Head*, Dr B. N. Carter

THE GEELONG COLLEGE, Geelong, Victoria. *Head*, Ms P. Turner

GEELONG GRAMMAR SCHOOL, Corio, Victoria. *Head*, L. Hannah

GUILDFORD GRAMMAR SCHOOL, Guildford, W. Australia. *Head*, J. M. Moody

HAILEYBURY COLLEGE, Keysborough, Victoria. *Head*, A. H. M. Aikman

THE HALE SCHOOL, Wembley Downs, W. Australia. *Head*, R. J. Inverarity

THE ILLAWARRA GRAMMAR SCHOOL, Wollongong, NSW. *Head*, Revd P. J. R. Smart

THE KING'S SCHOOL, Parramatta, NSW. *Head*, J. A. Wickham

KINROSS WOLAROI SCHOOL, Orange, NSW. *Head*, A. E. S. Anderson

KNOX GRAMMAR SCHOOL, Wahroonga, NSW. *Head*, Dr I. Paterson

MELBOURNE GRAMMAR SCHOOL, South Yarra, Victoria. *Head*, A. P. Sheahan

MENTONE GRAMMAR SCHOOL, Mentone, Victoria. *Head*, N. Clark

NEWINGTON COLLEGE, Stanmore, NSW. *Head*, M. E. Smee

ST PETER'S COLLEGE, St Peter's, S. Australia. *Head*, R. L. Burchnall

SCOTCH COLLEGE, Adelaide, S. Australia. *Head*, K. Webb

SCOTCH COLLEGE, Melbourne, Victoria. *Head*, Dr F. G. Donaldson

SCOTCH COLLEGE, Claremont, W. Australia. *Head*, W. R. Dickinson

THE SCOTS COLLEGE, Sydney, NSW. *Head*, Dr R. L. Iles

THE SCOTS SCHOOL, Bathurst, NSW. *Head*, R. D. Fraser

THE SOUTHPORT SCHOOL, Southport, Queensland. *Head*, B. A. Cook

SYDNEY CHURCH OF ENGLAND GRAMMAR SCHOOL, Sydney, NSW. *Head*, R. A. I. Grant

SYDNEY GRAMMAR SCHOOL, Darlinghurst, NSW. *Head*, Dr R. D. Townsend

WESLEY COLLEGE, Melbourne, Victoria. *Head*, D. G. McArthur

WESTBOURNE AND WILLIAMSTOWN GRAMMAR SCHOOLS, Hoppers Crossing, Victoria. *Head*, G. G. Ryan

CANADA

BRENTWOOD COLLEGE SCHOOL, Mill Bay, BC. *Head*, W. T. Ross

GLENLYON-NORFOLK SCHOOL, Victoria, BC. *Head*, D. Brooks

HILLFIELD-STRATHALLAN COLLEGE, Hamilton, Ontario. *Head*, W. S. Boyer

PICKERING COLLEGE, Newmarket, Ontario. *Head*, vacant

ST ANDREW'S COLLEGE, Aurora, Ontario. *Head*, R. P. Bedard

TRINITY COLLEGE SCHOOL, Port Hope, Ontario. *Head*, R. C. N. Wright

UPPER CANADA COLLEGE, Toronto, Ontario. *Head*, J. D. Blakey

HONG KONG

ISLAND SCHOOL, Borrett Road. *Head*, D. J. James

KING GEORGE V SCHOOL, Kowloon. *Head*, M. J. Behennah

INDIA

BISHOP COTTON SCHOOL, Shimla. *Head*, K. Mustafi

THE CATHEDRAL AND JOHN CONNON SCHOOL, Bombay. *Head*, D. E. W. Shaw

THE LAWRENCE SCHOOL, Sanawar. *Head*, Dr H. S. Dhillon

THE SCINDIA SCHOOL, Gwalior. *Head*, A. N. Dar

MALAYSIA

KOLEJ TUANKU JA'AFAR, Negeri Sembilan. *Head*, S. Morris

NEW ZEALAND

CHRIST'S COLLEGE, Christchurch. *Head*, Dr M. J. Rosser

KING'S COLLEGE, Auckland. *Head*, J. S. Taylor

ST ANDREW'S COLLEGE, Christchurch. *Head*, B. Maister

THE COLLEGIATE SCHOOL, Wanganui. *Head*, T. S. McKinley

WAITAKI BOYS' HIGH SCHOOL, Oamaru. *Head*, B. R. Gollop

PAKISTAN

AITCHISON COLLEGE, Lahore. *Head*, S. Khan

SOUTH AMERICA

ACADEMIA BRITANICA CUSCATLECA, Santa Tecla, El Salvador. *Head*, R. Braund

THE BRITISH SCHOOLS, Montevideo, Uruguay. *Head*, C. D. T. Smith

MARKHAM COLLEGE, Lima, Peru. *Head*, W. J. Baker

ST ANDREW'S SCOTS SCHOOL, Buenos Aires, Argentina. *Head*, A. G. F. Fisher

ST GEORGE'S COLLEGE, Buenos Aires, Argentina. *Head*, N. P. O. Green

ST PAULS' SCHOOL, São Paulo, Brazil. *Head*, M. T. M. C. McCann

USA

ST MARK'S COLLEGE, Southborough, Massachusetts. *Head*, A. J. de V. Hill

ADDITIONAL MEMBERS

The headteachers of some maintained schools are by invitation Additional Members of the HMC. They include the following:

BISHOP WORDSWORTH'S SCHOOL, Salisbury. *Head*, C. D. Barnett

DURHAM JOHNSTON COMPREHENSIVE SCHOOL, Durham. *Head*, J. Dunford

EGGBUCKLAND COMMUNITY COLLEGE, Plymouth. *Head*, H. E. Green

HAYWARDS HEATH SIXTH FORM COLLEGE, W. Sussex. *Head*, B. W. Derbyshire

HINCHINGBROOKE SCHOOL, Huntington, Cambs. *Head*, P. J. Downes

THE JUDD SCHOOL, Tonbridge, Kent. *Head*, K. A. Starling

LISKEARD SCHOOL AND COMMUNITY COLLEGE, Liskeard, Cornwall. *Head*, A. D. Wood

THE LONDON ORATORY SCHOOL, London sw6. *Head*, J. C. McIntosh

PRESCOT SCHOOL, Prescot, Merseyside. *Head*, P. A. Barlow

PRINCE HENRY'S GRAMMAR SCHOOL, Otley, W Yorks. *Head*, M. Franklin

PRINCE WILLIAM SCHOOL, Oundle, Cambs. *Head*, C. J. Lowe

THE ROYAL GRAMMAR SCHOOL, Lancaster. *Head*, P. J. Mawby

ST ANSELM'S COLLEGE, Birkenhead, Merseyside. *Head*, C. J. Cleugh

ST JOHN'S SCHOOL, Marlborough, Wilts. *Head*, J. T. Price

SOCIETY OF HEADMASTERS AND HEADMISTRESSES OF INDEPENDENT SCHOOLS

The Society was founded in 1961 and, in general, represents smaller boarding schools.

Secretary, I. D. Cleland, Celedston, Rhosesmore Road, Halkyn, Holywell CH8 8DL. Tel: 01352-781102

Headmasters of the following schools are members of both HMC and SHMIS; details of these schools appear in the HMC list: Abbotsholme School, Bedales School, Churcher's College, City of London Freemen's School, Colston's Collegiate School, King's School, Gloucester, King's School, Tynemouth, Lord Wandsworth College, Pang-

bourne College, Reading Blue Coat School, Reed's School, Rendcomb College, Ryde School, St George's College, Silcoates School, Tettenhall College, Wisbech Grammar School, Woodbridge School, Yarm School

* Woodard Corporation School
† Girls in VI form
‡ Co-educational
° 1995 figures
§ Entry into SHMIS subject to confirmation

Name of School	Foun-ded	No. of pupils	Annual fees £ Boarding	Day	Head (with date of appointment)
Abbey Gate College, Saighton, Chester	1977	300‡	—	4,221	E. W. Mitchell (1991)
Austin Friars School (*RC*), Carlisle	1951	304‡	7,956	4,734	M. G. Taylor (1994)
Bearwood College, Berks	1827	220‡	10,500	5,850	Dr R. J. Belcher (1993)
Bedstone College, Shropshire	1948	200‡	10,500	6,006	M. S. Symonds (1991)
°Bembridge School, Isle of Wight	1919	200‡	9,270	4,620	J. High (1986)
Bentham School, N. Yorks	1726	220‡	9,450	4,710	T. Halliwell (1995)
Bethany School, Kent	1866	275‡	9,819	6,282	W. M. Harvey (1988)
Birkdale School, Sheffield	1904	500†	—	4,599	Revd M. D. A. Hepworth (1983)
Box Hill School, Surrey	1959	260‡	10,530	6,300	Dr R. A. S. Atwood (1987)
Carmel College (*Jewish*), Oxon	1948	143‡	13,000	7,500	P. D. Skelker (1984)
Claremont Fan Court School, Surrey	1932	306‡	9,435	5,970	Mrs. P. B. Farrar (*Principal*) (1994)
Clayesmore School, Dorset	1896	290‡	11,640	8,145	D. J. Beeby (1986)
Cokethorpe School, Oxon	1957	225‡	12,420	8,010	P. J. S. Cantwell (1995)
Duke of York's Royal Military School, Dover	1803	500‡	795	—	Col. G. H. Wilson (1992)
Elmhurst Ballet School, Surrey	1903	72‡	9,570	7,020	J. McNamara (*Principal*) (1995)
Embley Park School, Romsey, Hants	1946	250‡	9,945	6,060	D. F. Chapman (1987)
Ewell Castle School, Surrey	1926	320†	—	4,635	R. A. Fewtrell (1983)
Friends' School, Essex	1702	230‡	10,614	6,369	Ms J. Laing (1996)
°Fulneck School (Boys), W. Yorks	1753	425‡	8,655	4,620	Mrs B. A. Heppell (1994)
*Grenville College, Devon	1954	300‡	10,551	5,175	Dr M. C. V. Cane (1992)
Halliford School, Middx	1956	281†	—	4,680	J. R. Crook (1984)
Hipperholme Grammar School, Halifax	1648	322‡	—	3,750	C. C. Robinson (1988)
Keil School, Dumbarton	1915	220‡	9,300	5,100	J. A. Cummings (1993)
Kingham Hill School, Oxon	1886	210‡	9,945	5,970	M. H. Payne (*Warden*) (1990)
Kirkham Grammar School, Lancs	1549	545‡	7,500	3,870	B. Stacey (1991)
Langley School, Norfolk	1910	247‡	10,500	5,460	S. J. W. McArthur (1989)
Lord Mayor Treloar College, Hants	1908	114‡	40,452	30,339	N. Clark (1989)
Milton Abbey School, Dorset	1954	83	12,090	8,070	W. J. Hughes-D'Aeth (1995)
Oswestry School, Shropshire	1407	245‡	9,591	5,556	P. K. Smith (1995)
The Purcell School (music), Middx	1962	144‡	17,343	11,283	K. J. Bain (1983)
Rannoch School, Perth	1959	230‡	10,764	5,655	M. Barratt (1982)
Rishworth School, W. Yorks	1724	400‡	9,900	4,818	M. J. Elford (1992)
°Rougemont School, Torfaen	1919	170‡	—	4,602	I. Brown (1995)
Royal Hospital School, Ipswich	1712	650‡	7,875	4,050	N. K. D. Ward (1995)
Royal Russell School, Surrey	1853	450‡	10,035	5,550	Dr J. R. Jennings (1996)
°Royal School, Dungannon, N. Ireland	1614	700‡	5,726	85	P. D. Hewitt (1984)
Royal Wolverhampton School	1850	310‡	10,545	5,385	Mrs B. A. Evans (1995)
Ruthin School, Denbighshire	1574	171‡	10,350	6,510	J. S. Rowlands (1993)
St Bede's School, E. Sussex	1979	450‡	11,925	7,200	R. A. Perrin (1978)
St Christopher School, Letchworth	1915	330‡	11,454	6,489	C. Reid (1980)
St David's College, Conwy	1965	210	10,178	6,619	W. Seymour (1991)
Scarborough College, N. Yorks	1898	360‡	9,843	5,337	T. L. Kirkup (1996)
Seaford College, W. Sussex	1884	290‡	10,250	6,450	R. C. Hannaford (1990)
Shebbear College, Devon	1841	240‡	9,816	5,268	R. J. Buley (1983)
Shiplake College, Oxon	1959	295	11,730	7,890	N. V. Bevan (1988)
Sibford School, Oxon	1842	250‡	10,035	5,310	Ms S. Freestone (from January 1997)
Sidcot School, North Somerset	1808	405‡	9,930	5,925	C. J. Greenfield (1986)

Name of School	Foun-ded	No. of pupils	Annual fees £ Boarding	Day	Head (with date of appointment)
Stafford Grammar School, Staffs	1982	300‡	—	4,080	M. S. James (1992)
Stanbridge Earls School, Hants	1952	180‡	12,120	3,690	H. Moxon (1984)
Sunderland High School	1887	246‡	—	3,915	Ms C. Rendle-Short (1993)
Warminster School, Wilts	1707	290‡	9,690	5,610	T. D. Holgate (1990)
Yehudi Menuhin School (music), Surrey	1963	50‡	varies	varies	N. Chisholm (1988)

GIRLS' SCHOOLS ASSOCIATION

THE GIRLS' SCHOOLS ASSOCIATION, 130 Regent Road, Leicester LEI 7PG. Tel: 0116-254 1619
President (from Jan. 1997), Mrs J. Lang
Secretary, Ms S. Cooper

CSC Church Schools Company, Church Schools House, Chapel Street, Titchmarsh, Kettering, Northants NNI4 3DA. Tel: 01832-735105
§ Girls Public Day School Trust, 26 Queen Anne's Gate, London SWIH 9AN. Tel: 0171-222 9595
* Woodard Corporation School
† Boys in VI form
‡ Co-educational
° 1995 figures

Name of School	Foun-ded	No. of pupils	Annual fees £ Boarding	Day	Head (with date of appointment)
ENGLAND AND WALES					
Abbey School, Reading	1887	710	—	4,350	Miss B. C. L. Sheldon (1991)
Abbot's Hill, Herts	1912	160	10,710	6,330	Mrs K. Lewis (from January 1997)
Adcote School for Girls, Shropshire	1907	94	9,540	5,295	Mrs S. B. Cecchet (1979)
Alice Ottley School, Worcester	1883	573	—	5,052	Miss C. Sibbit (1986)
Amberfield School, Ipswich	1952	170	—	3,990	Mrs L. A. Lewis (1992)
Ashford School, Kent	1910	366	11,319	6,513	Mrs P. Metham (1992)
Atherley School, Southampton (*CSC*)	1926	246	—	4,482	Mrs C. Madina (1994)
Badminton School, Bristol	1858	300	11,850	6,600	C. J. T. Gould (1981)
Bath High School	1875	450	—	4,140	Miss M. A. Winfield (1985)
Bedford High School	1882	740	9,453	4,995	Mrs B. E. Stanley (1995)
Bedgebury School, Kent	1860	224	11,301	6,996	Mrs L. J. Griffin (1995)
Beechwood Sacred Heart (*RC*), Kent	1915	160	11,190	6,675	T. S. Hodkinson (1993)
Belvedere School, Liverpool	1880	482	—	4,140	Mrs C. H. Evans (1992)
Benenden School, Kent	1923	430	13,260	—	Mrs G. duCharme (1985)
Berkhamsted School, Herts	1888	400†	10,113	5,973	Dr P. Chadwick (1996)
Birkenhead High School	1901	682	—	4,140	Mrs K. R. Irving (1986)
Blackheath High School, London SE3	1880	358	—	4,920	Miss R. K. Musgrave (1989)
Bolton School, Lancs	1877	804	—	4,626	Miss E. J. Panton (1994)
Bradford Girls' Grammar School	1875	650	—	4,200	Mrs L. J. Warrington (1987)
Brighton and Hove High School	1876	506	—	4,140	Miss R. A. Woodbridge (1989)
Brigidine School, Windsor	1948	210	—	4,680	Mrs M. B. Cairns (1986)
Bromley High School, Kent	1883	543	—	4,920	Mrs E. J. Hancock (1989)
Bruton School, Somerset	1900	501	7,761	4,011	Mrs J. M. Wade (1987)
Burgess Hill School, W. Sussex	1906	360	9,675	5,730	Mrs R. F. Lewis (1992)
Bury Grammar School, Lancs	1884	800	—	3,876	Miss J. M. Lawley (1987)
Casterton School, Carnforth, Lancs	1823	350	9,618	6,030	A. F. Thomas (1990)
Central Newcastle High School	1895	612	—	4,140	Mrs A. M. Chapman (1985)
Channing School, London N6	1885	322	—	5,880	Mrs I. R. Raphael (1984)
Cheltenham Ladies' College, Glos	1853	844	12,900	8,190	Mrs A. V. Tuck (*Principal*) (1996)
City of London School for Girls, London EC2	1894	548	—	5,427	Mrs Y. A. Burne, PH.D. (1995)
Clifton High School, Bristol	1877	412	8,535	4,470	Mrs Y. G. Graham (1996)
Cobham Hall, Kent	1962	180	13,500	8,250	Mrs R. J. McCarthy (1989)
Colston's Girls' School, Bristol	1891	490	—	3,840	Mrs J. P. Franklin (1989)
Combe Bank School, Kent	1868	210	—	6,030	Miss N. Spurr (1993)
Commonweal Lodge School, Surrey	1916	100	—	4,680	Mrs S. Law (1995)
Cranford House School, Oxon	1931	80	—	4,920	Mrs A. B. Gray (1992)
Croft House School, Dorset	1941	100	10,215	7,215	M. P. Hawkins (1993)

Name of School	Foun-ded	No. of pupils	Annual fees £ Boarding	Day	Head (with date of appointment)
Croham Hurst School, Surrey	1899	320	—	4,890	Miss S. C. Budgen (1994)
§Croydon High School, Surrey	1874	714	—	4,920	Mrs P. E. Davies (1990)
°Dame Allan's Girls' School, Newcastle upon Tyne	1705	388†	—	3,570	T. A. Willcocks (*Principal*) (1988)
Derby High School	1892	320	—	4,500	G. H. Goddard, PH.D. (1983)
Downe House, Berks	1907	640	12,915	9,360	Mrs A. G Watkin (*acting*) (1996)
Dunottar School, Surrey	1926	290	—	4,875	Ms M. Skinner (from January 1997)
Durham High School for Girls	1884	273	—	4,593	Miss M. L. Walters (1992)
°Edgbaston Church of England College	1886	350	—	4,275	Mrs A. Varley-Tipton (1992)
Edgbaston High School for Girls	1876	495	—	4,425	Mrs S. J. Horsman (1987)
Edgehill College, Devon	1884	350‡	10,050	5,490	Mrs E. M. Burton (1987)
Elmslie Girls' School, Lancs	1918	170	—	4,425	Miss E. M. Smithies (1978)
Farlington School, W. Sussex	1896	250	9,870	6,090	Mrs P. M. Mawer (1992)
Farnborough Hill, Hants	1889	530	—	4,782	Miss R. McGeoch (1996)
Farringtons and Stratford House, Kent	1911	260	10,278	5,205	Mrs B. J. Stock (1987)
Francis Holland School, London NW1	1878	366	—	5,640	Mrs P. H. Parsonson (1988)
Francis Holland School, London SW1	1881	190	—	6,330	Mrs J. A. Anderson (1982)
Gateways School, Leeds	1941	180	—	3,750	Mrs J. E. Stephen (1994)
°Godolphin School, Wilts	1726	387	10,779	6,456	Miss J. Horsburgh (1996)
Godolphin and Latymer School, London W6	1905	716	—	6,285	Miss M. Rudland (1986)
Greenacre School, Surrey	1933	218	—	5,250	Mrs P. M. Wood (1990)
Guildford High School (*CSC*)	1888	519	—	5,385	Mrs S. H. Singer (1991)
Haberdashers' Aske's School for Girls, Herts	1873	825	—	4,410	Mrs P. Penney (1991)
Haberdashers' Monmouth School	1891	646	8,592	4,521	Mrs. D. L. Newman (1992)
Harrogate Ladies' College	1893	300	9,495	6,324	Dr M. J. Hustler (1996)
Headington School, Oxford	1915	541	9,600	4,830	Mrs H. A. Fender (1996)
Heathfield School, Ascot, Berks	1900	210	13,125	—	Mrs J. M. Benammar (1992)
§Heathfield School, Pinner, Middx	1900	293	—	4,920	Mrs J. Merritt (1988)
Hethersett Old Hall School, Norwich	1928	215	9,225	4,650	Mrs V. M. Redington (1983)
Highclare School, W. Midlands	1932	173†	—	4,380	Mrs C. A. Hanson (1974)
Hollygirt School, Nottingham	1877	220	—	3,795	Mrs M. R. Banks (1985)
Holy Child School, Birmingham	1933	148	—	4,725	Mrs J. M. C. Hill (1993)
Holy Trinity College, Bromley	1886	270	—	4,347	Mrs D. A. Bradshaw (1994)
Holy Trinity School, Kidderminster	1903	200	—	3,885	Mrs S. M. Bell (1990)
Howell's School, Denbigh	1859	206	10,485	6,840	Mrs M. Steel (1991)
§Howell's School, Llandaff, Cardiff	1860	552	—	4,140	Mrs C. J. Fitz (1991)
Hull High School (*CSC*)	1890	146	—	4,125	Mrs M. A. Benson (1994)
Hulme Grammar School, Oldham	1895	530	—	3,726	Miss M. S. Smolenski (1992)
Ilford Ursuline High School, Essex	1903	350	—	4,575	Miss J. Reddington (1990)
§Ipswich High School	1878	463	—	4,140	Miss V. C. MacCuish (1993)
James Allen's Girls' School, London SE22	1741	740	—	6,150	Mrs M. Gibbs (1994)
Kent College	1885	240	11,700	6,960	Miss B. J. Crompton (1990)
King Edward VI High School for Girls, Birmingham	1883	550	—	4,500	Ms S. H. Evans (1996)
King's HS for Girls, Warwick	1879	560	—	4,350	Mrs J. M. Anderson (1987)
Kingsley School, Warks	1884	600	—	4,485	Mrs M. A. Webster (1988)
Lady Eleanor Holles School, Middx	1711	692	—	5,520	Miss E. M. Candy (1981)
La Retraite School, Wilts	1953	120	—	4,845	Mrs R. A. Simmons (1994)
Lavant House Rosemead School, W. Sussex	1919	134	10,425	5,850	Mrs S. E. Watkins (1996)
Leeds Girls' High School	1876	600	—	4,617	Miss P. A. Randall (1977)
Leicester High School	1906	300	—	4,500	Mrs P. A. Watson (1992)
Lincoln Minster School	1905	200‡	8,000	4,500	Mrs M. Bradley (1996)
Loughborough High School	1850	529	—	4,194	Miss J. E. L. Harvatt (1978)
Luckley-Oakfield School, Berks	1895	240	8,349	5,175	R. C. Blake (1984)
Malvern Girls' College, Worcs	1893	160	12,285	8,190	Revd P. D. Newton (*acting*) (1996)
Manchester High School	1874	700‡	—	4,185	Miss E. M. Diggory (1994)
Manor House School, Little Bookham, Surrey	1927	140	8,190	5,640	Mrs L. Mendes (1989)
Maynard School, Exeter	1877	484	—	4,440	Miss F. Murdin (1980)
Merchant Taylors' School, Liverpool	1888	660	—	3,933	Mrs J. I. Mills (1994)
Moira House School, E. Sussex	1875	215	11,340	7,320	A. R. Underwood (1975)
More House School, London SW1	1953	200	—	5,700	Miss M. Connell (1991)
Moreton Hall, Shropshire	1913	280	11,700	8,100	J. Forster (1992)

Name of School	Founded	No. of pupils	Annual fees £ Boarding	Day	Head (with date of appointment)
Mount School, York	1831	251	10,170	6,255	Miss B. J. Windle (1986)
Newcastle upon Tyne Church HS	1885	365	—	3,960	Mrs L. G. Smith (1996)
New Hall School, Chelmsford, Essex	1642	410	10,830	6,930	Sr Anne-Marie (1996)
Northampton High School	1878	587	—	4,275	Mrs L. A. Mayne (1988)
North Foreland Lodge, Hants	1909	150	11,550	7,050	Miss S. Cameron (1996)
North London Collegiate School	1850	745	—	5,124	Mrs J. L. Clanchy (1986)
Northwood College, Middx	1878	418	—	5,172	Mrs J. A. Mayou (1991)
Norwich High School	1875	645	—	4,140	Mrs V. C. Bidwell (1985)
Nottingham High School	1875	820	—	4,140	Mrs A. C. Rees (1996)
Notting Hill and Ealing High School	1873	564	—	4,920	Mrs S. M. Whitfield (1991)
Ockbrook School, Derby	1799	470	7,392	3,978	Miss D. P. Bolland (1995)
Old Palace School, Surrey	1887	599	—	4,293	Miss K. L. Hilton (1974)
Oxford High School	1875	551	—	4,140	Miss F. Lusk (from January 1997)
Palmers Green High School, London N21	1905	140	—	4,650	Mrs S. Grant (1989)
Parsons Mead, Surrey	1897	250	9,270	5,280	Miss E. B. Plant (1990)
Perse School for Girls, Cambridge	1881	540	—	4,935	Miss H. S. Smith (1989)
Peterborough High School	1939	170	8,838	4,401	Mrs A. J. V. Storey (1977)
Pipers Corner School, Bucks	1930	300	9,702	5,808	Mrs V. M. Staltensfield (1996)
Polam Hall School, Co. Durham	1848	320	9,159	4,479	Mrs H. C. Hamilton (1986)
Portsmouth High School	1882	511	—	4,140	Mrs J. M. Dawtrey (1984)
Princess Helena College, Herts	1820	150	10,410	7,245	J. Jarvis (1995)
Prior's Field, Surrey	1902	230	10,287	6,867	Mrs J. M. McCallum (1987)
Putney High School, London SW15	1893	573	—	4,920	Mrs E. Merchant (1991)
Queen Anne's School, Berks	1698	175	11,820	7,740	Mrs D. Forbes (1993)
Queen Ethelburga's College, York	1912	200	11,397	7,497	Mrs G. L. Richardson (Principal) (1993)
Queen Margaret's School, York	1901	360	10,626	6,732	Dr G. A. H. Chapman (1992)
Queen Mary School, Lytham, Lancs	1930	460	—	3,870	Miss M. C. Ritchie (1981)
Queen's College, London W1	1848	368	—	6,105	Lady Goodhart (1991)
Queen's Gate School, London SW7	1891	240	—	5,325	Mrs A. M. Holyoak (Principal) (1988)
Queen's School, Chester	1878	468	—	4,545	Miss D. M. Skilbeck (1989)
Queenswood, Herts	1894	400	11,958	7,374	Ms C. Farr (Principal) (1996)
Redland High School for Girls, Bristol	1882	352	—	4,200	Mrs C. Lear (1989)
Red Maids' School, Bristol	1634	503	7,776	3,888	Miss S. Hampton (1987)
Rickmansworth Masonic School, Herts	1788	540	8,811	5,361	Mrs I. M. Andrews (1992)
Roedean School, Brighton	1885	400	13,635	7,740	Mrs A. R. Longley (1984)
The Royal School, Bath	1864	210	11,001	5,886	Mrs E. McKendrick (1994)
The Royal School, Surrey	1840	320	10,017	6,363	C. Brooks (1985)
Rydal Penrhos School (Girls), Colwyn Bay	1880	216	9,720	6,660	C. M. J. Allen (1993)
Rye St Antony School (RC), Oxford	1930	350	8,880	5,280	Miss A. M. Jones (1990)
St Albans High School, Herts	1889	532	—	5,040	Mrs C. Y. Daly (1994)
St Andrew's School, Bedford	1897	140	—	3,912	Mrs J. M. Mark (1995)
St Anne's School, Windermere, Cumbria	1863	250	9,540	6,330	R. D. Hunter (1994)
St Antony's-Leweston School (RC), Dorset	1891	290	10,935	7,140	Miss B. A. King (1996)
St Catherine's School, Surrey	1885	471	9,630	5,880	Mrs C. M. Oulton (1994)
St David's School, Middx	1716	230	9,585	5,394	Mrs J. G. Osborne (1985)
St Dunstan's Abbey School, Devon	1850	180	8,652	4,860	R. A. Bye (1990)
St Elphin's School, Derbys	1844	160	10,197	5,940	Mrs V. E. Fisher (1994)
St Felix School, Suffolk	1897	195	11,100	7,200	Mrs S. R. Campion (1991)
St Francis' College (RC), Herts	1933	196	9,810	5,025	Miss M. Hegarty (1993)
St Gabriel's School, Berks	1929	158	—	5,034	D. Cobb (1990)
St George's School, Ascot, Berks	1923	290	12,150	7,350	Mrs A. M. Griggs (1989)
School of S. Helen and S. Katharine, Oxon	1903	522	—	4,704	Mrs C. L. Hall (1993)
St Helen's School, Middx	1899	609	9,576	5,082	Mrs D. M. Jefkins (1995)
S. Hilary's School, Cheshire	1880	120	—	4,230	Ms G. M. Case (1995)
St James's and the Abbey, Worcs	1896	177	11,565	7,308	Mrs E. M. Mullenger (1986)
St Joseph's Convent School (RC), Berks	1909	378	—	4,065	Mrs V. Brookes (1990)
St Leonards-Mayfield School, E. Sussex	1850	525	10,740	7,160	Sr J. Sinclair (1980)
St Margaret's School, Bushey, Herts	1749	335	9,210	5,625	Miss M. de Villiers (1992)
St Margaret's School, Exeter	1904	350	7,104	4,323	Mrs M. D'Albertanson (1993)
St Martin's School, Solihull	1941	212	—	4,590	Mrs S. J. Williams (1988)
School of S. Mary and S. Anne, Abbots Bromley, Staffs	1874	227	11,205	7,485	A. J. Grigg (1989)

Name of School	Foun-ded	No. of pupils	Annual fees £		Head (with date of appointment)
			Boarding	Day	
St Mary's Convent School, Worcester	1934	220	—	3,780	Miss G. Morrissey (1995)
St Mary's Hall, Brighton	1836	263	9,315	6,180	Mrs P. J. James (1991)
St Mary's School (*RC*), Ascot, Berks	1885	338	12,246	7,705	Sr M. F. Orchard (1982)
°St Mary's School, Calne, Wilts	1872	307	11,550	6,825	Mrs C. Shaw (1996)
St Mary's School, Cambridge	1898	555	7,410	4,140	Ms M. Conway (1989)
St Mary's School, Colchester	1908	210	—	3,960	Mrs G. M. G. Mouser (1981)
°St Mary's School, Gerrards Cross	1872	190	—	4,995	Mrs F. Balcombe (1995)
St Mary's School (*RC*), Shaftesbury	1945	310	9,990	6,420	Sr M. Campion Livesey (1985)
St Mary's School, Wantage, Oxon	1873	220	11,550	7,698	Mrs S. Bodinham (1994)
St Maur's Senior School, Weybridge	1898	390	—	4,530	Mrs M. E. Dodds (1991)
St Paul's Girls' School, London w6	1904	620	—	6,627	Miss J. Gough (*High Mistress*) (1992)
St Swithun's School, Winchester	1884	455	11,580	6,990	Ms H. Harvey, ph.d. (1995)
St Teresa's School, Dorking	1928	330	10,785	5,325	L. Allan (1987)
Selwyn School, Glos		130	8,430	4,800	Miss L. M. Brown (1994)
§Sheffield High School	1878	545	—	4,140	Mrs M. A. Houston (1989)
Sherborne School for Girls, Dorset	1899	430	12,240	8,550	Miss J. M. Taylor (1985)
§Shrewsbury High School	1885	406	—	4,140	Miss S. Gardner (1990)
Sir William Perkins's School, Surrey	1725	590	—	4,170	Miss S. Ross (1994)
§South Hampstead High School, London nw3	1876	630	—	4,920	Mrs J. G. Scott (1993)
Stamford High School, Lincs	1876	713	8,616	4,308	Miss G. K. Bland (1978)
Stonar School, Wilts	1921	402	9,915	5,490	Mrs S. Hopkinson (1985)
Stover School, Devon	1932	188	8,580	4,559	P. E. Bujak (1994)
§Streatham Hill and Clapham High School, London sw2	1887	419	—	4,920	Miss G. M. Ellis (1979)
Surbiton High School, Surrey (*CSC*)	1884	597	—	5,130	Miss M. G. Perry (1993)
§Sutton High School, Surrey	1884	494	—	4,920	Mrs A. J. Coutts (1995)
§Sydenham High School, London se26	1887	458	—	4,920	Mrs G. Baker (1988)
Talbot Heath, Dorset	1886	418	9,150	5,250	Mrs C. Dipple (1991)
Teesside High School, Stockton-on-Tees	1970	400	—	3,936	Miss J. F. Hamilton (1995)
Tormead School, Surrey	1905	502	—	5,370	Mrs H. E. M. Alleyne (1992)
Truro High School	1880	350	8,364	4,551	J. Graham-Brown (1992)
Tudor Hall School, Oxon	1850	262	10,545	6,570	Miss N. Godfrey (1984)
Ursuline College, Kent	1904	360‡	10,600	5,400	Sr A. Montgomery (1995)
Wakefield Girls' High School	1878	741	—	4,368	Mrs P. A. Langham (1987)
Walthamstow Hall, Kent	1838	315	12,360	6,660	Mrs J. S. Lang (1984)
Wentworth College, Dorset	1871	241	9,330	5,850	Miss S. D. Coe (1990)
Westfield School, Newcastle upon Tyne	1962	220	—	4,392	Mrs M. Farndale (1990)
West Heath, Kent	1867	110	12,030	8,070	Mrs A. Williamson (*Principal*) (1994)
Westholme School, Lancs	1923	625	—	3,690	Mrs L. Croston (*Principal*) (1988)
Westonbirt School, Glos	1928	220	11,340	7,380	Mrs G. Hylson-Smith (1986)
§Wimbledon High School, London sw19	1880	569	—	4,920	Dr J. L. Clough (1995)
Wispers School, Surrey	1946	120	9,507	6,117	L. H. Beltran (1980)
Withington Girls' School, Manchester	1890	525	—	3,930	Mrs M. Kenyon (1986)
Woldingham School, Surrey	1842	530	12,009	7,263	P. Dineen, ph.d. (1985)
°Wychwood School, Oxford	1897	160	6,885	4,350	Mrs M. L. Duffill (1981)
Wycombe Abbey School, Bucks	1896	500	12,780	9,585	Mrs J. M. Goodland (1989)
Wykeham House School, Fareham, Hants	1913	300	—	4,059	Mrs R. M. Kamaryc (1995)

Scotland

Kilgraston School, Perthshire	1930	180	10,335	5,955	Mrs J. L. Austin (1993)
Laurel Park School, Glasgow	1903	550	—	3,969	Mrs E. Surber (1996)
Mary Erskine School, Edinburgh	1694	652	8,640	4,320	P. F. J. Tobin (*Principal*) (1989)
St Denis and Cranley School, Edinburgh	1858	130	9,975	5,085	Mrs S. Duncanson (1996)
St George's School, Edinburgh	1888	568	9,075	4,575	J. McClure, d.phil. (1994)
St Leonards School, St Andrews	1877	280	12,366	6,540	Mrs M. James (1988)
St Margaret's School, Aberdeen	1846	219	—	3,924	Miss L. M. Ogilvie (1989)
St Margaret's School, Edinburgh	1890	363	8,685	4,305	Miss A. Mitchell (1994)

Channel Islands

The Ladies' College, Guernsey	1872	359	—	2,250	Miss M. E. Macdonald (*Principal*) (1992)

Social Welfare

National Health Service
and Local Authority Personal Social Services

The National Health Service came into being on 5 July 1948 as a result of the National Health Service Act 1946, covering England and Wales, and separate legislation for Scotland and Northern Ireland. The Acts placed a duty on the relevant Secretaries of State to promote the establishment of a comprehensive health service designed to secure improvement in the mental and physical health of the people and the prevention, diagnosis and treatment of illness. The National Health Service is administered in England by the Secretary of State for Health, and in Wales, Scotland and Northern Ireland by the Secretaries of State for Wales, Scotland and Northern Ireland.

The National Health Service covers a comprehensive range of hospital, specialist, family practitioner (medical, dental, ophthalmic and pharmaceutical), artificial limb and appliance, ambulance, and community health services. Everyone normally resident in the UK is entitled to use any of these services without charge, except where charges are specifically provided for by statute, e.g. prescriptions.

In addition, the Secretary of State for Health is responsible under the Local Authority Social Services Act 1970 for the provision by local authorities of social services for the elderly, the disabled, those with mental disorders and for families and children.

The NHS is financed mainly from taxation and the cost met from moneys voted by Parliament. The estimated level of expenditure in 1996–7 is £42,600 million.

STRUCTURE

The National Health Service and Community Care Act 1990 reformed management and patient care. The Act provided for more streamlined Regional and District Health Authorities and Family Health Services Authorities, and for the establishment of NHS Trusts, which operate as self-governing health care providers. One result of the Act is that health care is provided through NHS contracts, where one body (the purchaser) is responsible for obtaining the appropriate health care for its population from another body (the provider). From 1 April 1993, the Community Care Reforms introduced changes in the way care is administered for the elderly, the mentally ill, the physically handicapped and people with learning disabilities.

On 31 March 1996 the eight Regional Health Authorities (RHAs) in England were replaced by eight NHS Executive regional offices which have taken on the functions of the RHAs. They are responsible for regional planning, the allocation of resources to Health Authorities (HAs) and general practitioner fundholders, and the promotion of national policies and priorities, and are directly accountable to the Secretary of State for Health.

From April 1996, 100 new Health Authorities (HAs) replaced the District Health Authorities and Family Health Service Authorities and have taken on the combined duties and responsibilities of both. They are responsible for developing strategies, in liaison with general practitioners, the public, local authorities and other public bodies, to improve health and secure a comprehensive range of health and health-care services for their local populations within national guidelines. HAs'

resources are allocated by the NHS Executive headquarters, to which they are also accountable for their performance.

HEALTH SERVICES

FAMILY DOCTOR SERVICE

In England and Wales the Family Doctor Service (or General Medical Services) was managed by 98 Family Health Services Authorities (FHSAs) which also organized the general dental, pharmaceutical and ophthalmic services for their areas. These functions are now the responsibility of the Health Authorities (HAs). In England the chairman is appointed by the Secretary of State and the non-executive members by the regional offices of the NHS Executive. In Wales the chairman and non-executive members are appointed by the Secretary of State.

Any doctor may take part in the Family Doctor Service (provided the area in which he/she wishes to practise has not already an adequate number of doctors) and about 28,000 general practitioners in England and Wales do so. They may at the same time have private fee-paying patients. Family doctors are paid for their NHS work in accordance with a scheme of remuneration which includes a basic practice allowance, capitation fees, reimbursement of certain practice expenses and payments for out-of-hours work.

The National Health Service and Community Care Act 1990 enables general practitioner practices to apply for fundholding status. This makes the practice responsible for its own NHS budget for a specified range of goods and services. Since 1 April 1996 there have been two types of general practitioner fundholding: Standard fundholders, for practices with at least 5,000 patients, who purchase a full range of in- and out-patient services; and Community fundholders, for smaller practices of at least 3,000 patients, who purchase only community nursing services and diagnostic tests. There are currently 3,000 fundholding units, comprising 3,735 practices. Fundholding practices are monitored by the HAs on behalf of the NHS Executive regional offices.

Everyone aged 16 or over can choose their doctor (parents or guardians choose for children under 16) and the doctor is also free to accept a person or not as he or she chooses. A person may change their doctor if they wish, by going to the surgery of a general practioner of their choice who is willing to accept them, and either handing in their medical card to register or filling in a form. When people are away from home they can still use the Family Doctor Service if they ask to be treated as temporary residents, and in an emergency, if a person's own doctor is not available, any doctor in the service will give treatment and advice.

Patients are treated either in the doctor's surgery or, when necessary, at home. Doctors may prescribe for their patients all drugs and medicines which are medically necessary for their treatment and also a certain number of surgical appliances (the more elaborate being provided through hospitals).

DENTAL SERVICE

Dentists, like doctors, may take part in the NHS and also have private patients. About 16,000 of the dentists available for general practice in England provide NHS general dental services. They are responsible to the HAs in whose areas they provide services.

Patients are free to go to any dentist who is taking part in the NHS and willing to accept them. Dentists are paid a capitation fee and payment for certain treatments for patients registered with them who are under 18 years of age. They receive payment for items of treatment for individual adult patients and, in addition, a continuing care payment for those registered with them.

Patients are asked to pay 80 per cent of the cost of NHS dental treatment. The maximum charge for a course of treatment is £325. There is no charge for arrest of bleeding, repairs to dentures, home visits by the dentist or re-opening a surgery in an emergency (in these two cases, payment will be for treatment given in the normal way). The following are exempt from dental charges/have charges remitted:

(i)   young people under 18
(ii) full-time students under 19
(iii) women who were pregnant when accepted for treatment
(iv) women who have had a child in the previous 12 months
(v)   people or the partners of people who receive income support, family credit, disability working allowance or income-based jobseeker's allowance

Leaflet HC11 available from post offices and local social security offices explains how other people on a low income can, depending on their financial circumstances, get free treatment or help with charges.

PHARMACEUTICAL SERVICE

Patients may obtain medicines, appliances and oral contraceptives prescribed under the NHS from any pharmacy whose owner has entered into arrangements with the HA to provide this service. Almost all pharmacy owners have done so and display notices that they dispense under the NHS; the number of these pharmacies in England and Wales in March 1996 was about 10,500. There are also some appliance suppliers who only provide special appliances. In rural areas where access to a pharmacy may be difficult, patients may be able to obtain medicines, etc., from their doctor.

Except for contraceptives (for which there is no charge), a charge of £5.50 is payable for each item supplied unless the patient is exempt and the declaration on the back of the prescription form is completed. Exemptions cover:

(i)   children under 16
(ii)   full-time students under 19
(iii) men and women aged 60 and over
(iv)   pregnant women
(v)   women who have had a baby within the last 12 months
(vi)   people suffering from certain medical conditions
(vii) people who receive income support or family credit and their dependants
(viii) people who receive disability working allowance and their partners
(ix)   people who receive income-based jobseeker's allowance, and their partners
(x)   people who hold an AG2 certificate issued by the Health Benefits Division, and their dependants
(xi)   war pensioners (for their accepted disablements)

Prepayment certificates (£28.50 valid for four months, £78.40 valid for a year) may be purchased by those patients not entitled to exemption who require frequent pre-scriptions. Further information about the exemption and prepayment arrangements is given in leaflet HC11.

GENERAL OPHTHALMIC SERVICES

General Ophthalmic Services, which are administered by HAs, form part of the ophthalmic services available under the NHS. The NHS sight test is available free to:

(i)   children under 16
(ii)   full-time students under the age of 19
(iii) people in receipt of income support, income-based jobseeker's allowance or family credit, and their partners
(iv)   people in receipt of disability working allowance and their partners
(v)   people prescribed complex lenses
(vi)   the registered blind and partially sighted
(vii) diagnosed diabetic and glaucoma patients
(viii) close relatives aged 40 or over of diagnosed glaucoma patients

Those on a low income may qualify for help with the cost.

Certain groups are automatically entitled to help with the purchase of glasses under an NHS voucher scheme:

(i)   children under 16
(ii)   full-time students under 19
(iii) people in receipt of income support, income-based jobseeker's allowance or family credit, and their partners
(iv)   people in receipt of disability working allowance and their partners
(v)   people wearing certain complex lenses
(vi)   people whose spectacles are lost or damaged as a result of their disability, injury or illness

The value of the voucher depends on the lenses required. Vouchers may be used to help pay for the glasses or contact lenses of the patient's choice. People with a low income may claim help on form AG1. Glasses or contact lenses should not be purchased until the result of a claim is known as no refunds can be given. Booklet G11 gives further details.

Diagnosis and specialist treatment of eye conditions is available through the Hospital Eye Service as well as the provision of glasses of a special type.

Testing of sight may be carried out by any ophthalmic medical practitioner or ophthalmic optician. The optician must give the prescription, and a voucher if eligible, to the patient who can take this to any supplier of glasses of his/her choice to have dispensed. However, only registered opticians can supply glasses to children and to people registered as blind or partially sighted.

PRIMARY HEALTH CARE SERVICES

Primary health care services include the general medical, dental, ophthalmic and pharmaceutical services. They also include community services run by HAs, health centres and clinics, family planning outside the hospital service, and preventive activities in the community including vaccination, immunization and fluoridation.

The district nursing and health visiting services include community psychiatric nursing for mentally ill people living outside hospital, and school nursing for the health surveillance of schoolchildren of all ages. Ante- and post-natal care and chiropody are also an integral part of the primary health care service.

COMMUNITY CHILD HEALTH SERVICES

Pre-school services at GP surgeries or child health clinics provide regular surveillance of children's physical, mental and emotional health and development, and advice to parents on their children's health and welfare.

The School Health Service provides for the medical and dental examination of schoolchildren, and advises the local education authority, the school, the parents and the pupil of any health factors which may require special consideration during the pupil's school life. GPs are increasingly undertaking child health surveillance to improve the preventive health care of children.

HOSPITALS AND OTHER SERVICES

The Secretary of State for Health has a duty to provide, to such extent as he/she considers necessary to meet all reasonable requirements, hospital and other accommodation; medical, dental, nursing and ambulance services; other facilities for the care of expectant and nursing mothers and young children; facilities for the prevention of illness and the care and after-care of persons suffering from illness; and such other services as are required for the diagnosis and treatment of illness. Rehabilitation services (occupational therapy, physiotherapy and speech therapy) may also be provided for those who need it and surgical and medical appliances are supplied in appropriate cases. NHS services and equipment should be free of charge unless current legislation on prescriptions states otherwise.

Specialists and consultants who work in the NHS can engage in private practice, including the treatment of their private patients in NHS hospitals. Any private work a consultant does is additional to NHS duties.

Trusts

The National Health Service and Community Care Act 1990 enables hospitals and other providers of health care to become independent of health authority control as self-governing NHS Trusts run by boards of directors. The Trusts derive their income principally from contracts to provide health services to health authorities and fund-holding general practitioners. As at April 1995 there were 433 trusts, representing the majority of hospitals in England.

Charges

In a number of hospitals, accommodation is available for the treatment of private in-patients who undertake to pay the full costs of hospital accommodation and services and (usually) separate medical fees to a specialist as well. The amount of the medical fees is a matter for agreement between doctor and patient. Hospital charges for private in-patients are set locally at a commercial rate.

Certain hospitals have accommodation in single rooms or small wards which, if not required for patients who need privacy for medical reasons, may be made available to patients who desire it as an amenity for a small charge. These patients are still NHS patients and are treated as such.

There is no charge for drugs supplied to NHS hospital in-patients but out-patients pay £5.50 an item unless they are exempt.

With certain exceptions, hospital out-patients have to pay fixed charges for dentures, contact lenses and certain appliances. Glasses may be obtained either from the hospital or an optician and the charge will be related to the type of lens prescribed and the choice of frame.

PERSONAL SOCIAL SERVICES

Local authorities are responsible for personal social services within their area. Each authority has a Director of

Social Services and a Social Services Committee responsible for the social services functions placed upon them by the Local Authority Social Services Act 1970.

FINANCE

ENGLAND

COST OF NATIONAL HEALTH AND PERSONAL SOCIAL SERVICES 1994

	£ million
All services	38,466
Central government services: total	31,275
Central administration	227
Health Authorities, current	22,656
Health Authorities, capital	618
Family Health Services Authorities:	
Administration and related services	78
General medical	1,840
Pharmaceutical	3,051
General dental	1,223
General ophthalmic	192
Other	1,391
Personal social services	7,191

Source: HMSO – *Health and Personal Social Services Statistics for England 1995*

WALES

GROSS CENTRAL GOVERNMENT SUPPORT FOR HEALTH AND PERSONAL SOCIAL SERVICES 1993–4*

	£ thousand
Total	2,095,990
District Health Authorities	1,308,658
NHS Trusts	47,743
General medical	110,195
Pharmaceutical	224,038
General dental	67,963
General ophthalmic	13,532
Welfare foods	13,470
Other	310,391

* Excludes local authority expenditure on personal social services funded through general grants
Source: Welsh Office – *Digest of Welsh Statistics 1995*

SCOTLAND

NET COSTS OF THE NATIONAL HEALTH SERVICE 1994–5

	£ thousand
Total cost	4,335,737
Central administration	8,966
Total NHS cost	4,326,771
NHS contributions	423,293
Net costs to Exchequer	3,903,478
Health Board administration	93,844
Hospital and community health services	3,087,729
Family practitioner services	855,141
Centre health services	198,478
State hospital	19,824
Training	27,165
Research	10,062
Disabled services	2,230
Welfare foods	13,910
Miscellaneous health services	18,388

Source: Scottish Office – *Annual Abstract of Statistics 1995*

EMPLOYEES

NUMBER OF BEDS AND PATIENT ACTIVITY

HEALTH AND PERSONAL SOCIAL SERVICES WORKFORCE (*Great Britain*)

Health Service staff and practitioners: total	979,081
Dental Practice Board staff	722
Statutory authorities staff	4,380
Family Health Services practitioners: total	60,965
Of whom:	
General medical practitioners	34,421
General dental practitioners	18,630
Ophthalmic medical practitioners	735
Ophthalmic opticians	7,179
Directly employed staff: total	913,014
Of whom:	
Medical staff	56,736
Dental staff	2,947
Nursing and midwifery staff	429,160
Professionals allied to medical staff	48,338
Scientific and professional staff	17,043
Professional and technical staff	43,458
Administrative and clerical staff	182,390
Works and maintenance staff	19,249
Ambulance staff	21,379
Ancillary staff	91,064
Others	1,250
*Personal social services staff	237,752
Total	1,216,833

*England only

Source: HMSO – *Annual Abstract of Statistics 1996*

ENGLAND AND WALES 1993

	England	Wales
In-patients:		
Average daily available beds	219,000	17,500
Average daily occupation of beds	n/a	13,500
Persons waiting for admission at 31 March	995,000	61,000
Day-case admissions	2,106,000	201,400
Ordinary admissions	7,988,000	n/a
Out-patient attendances:		
New patients	9,685,000	1,254,100*
Total attendances	38,233,000	3,494,800
Accident and emergency:		
New patients	11,365,000	n/a
Total attendances	13,289,000	n/a
Family Health Services:		
Number of patients per doctor	1,902	1,739
Prescriptions dispensed	413,300,000	34,300,000
NHS sight tests conducted	5,935,000	397,000
Pairs of glasses dispensed/ vouchers paid for	3,485,000	254,000
Number of adult courses of dental treatment	24,848,000	1,399,000

n/a not available
* 1992 figure

SCOTLAND 1993

In-patients:	
Average available staffed beds	46,700
Average occupied beds	38,100
Out-patient attendances:	
New patients	2,457,000
Total attendances	6,086,000
Primary Care Services:	
Average number of patients per principal doctor	1,542
Prescriptions dispensed	48,180,000
NHS sight tests conducted	568,000
Pairs of glasses supplied	440,000
Number of courses of dental treatment completed	2,647,000

Source: HMSO – *Annual Abstract of Statistics 1996*

National Insurance and Related Cash Benefits

The state insurance and assistance schemes, comprising schemes of national insurance and industrial injuries insurance, national assistance, and non-contributory old age pensions came into force from 5 July 1948. The Ministry of Social Security Act 1966 replaced national assistance and non-contributory old age pensions with a scheme of non-contributory benefits. These and subsequent measures relating to social security provision in Great Britain were consolidated by the Social Security Act 1975; the Social Security (Consequential Provisions) Act 1975; and the Industrial Injuries and Diseases (Old Cases) Act 1975. Corresponding measures were passed for Northern Ireland. The Social Security Pensions Act 1975 introduced a new state pensions scheme in 1978, and the graduated pension scheme 1961 to 1975 has been wound up, existing rights being preserved. Under the Pensions Act 1995 the age of retirement is to be 65 for both men and women, this being phased in between 2010 and 6 April 2020. The Pensioners' Payments and Social Security Act 1979 provided for a £10 Christmas bonus for pensioners in 1979 and for the payment of a bonus in succeeding years at levels then to be determined. The Child Benefit Act 1975 replaced family allowances (introduced 1946) with child benefit and one parent benefit. Some of this legislation has been superseded by the provisions of the Social Security Acts 1968 to 1992.

NATIONAL INSURANCE SCHEME

The National Insurance (NI) scheme operates under the Social Security Contributions and Benefits Act 1992 and the Social Security Administration Act 1992, and orders and regulations made thereunder. The scheme is financed by contributions payable by earners, employers and others (such as non-employed persons paying voluntary contributions). It provides the funds required for paying the benefits payable under the Social Security Acts out of the National Insurance Fund and not out of other public money, and for the making of payments towards the cost of the National Health Service. In 1991 the Redundancy Fund was absorbed into the National Insurance Fund. The yearly Treasury supplement to the National Insurance Fund was abolished in 1989. A Treasury grant was introduced from 1993.

CONTRIBUTIONS

National Insurance contributions are of four classes:

CLASS 1 CONTRIBUTIONS

These are earnings-related, based on a percentage of the employee's earnings.

Primary Class 1 contributions are payable by employed earners and office-holders over age 16 with gross earnings at or above the lower earnings limit of £61.00 per week. Employees earning less than the lower earnings limit do not pay any contributions. For those with gross earnings at or above this level, contributions are payable on all earnings up to an upper limit of £455.00 per week. 'Gross earnings' include overtime pay, commission, bonus, etc., without deduction of any superannuation contributions. Contributions are paid at 2 per cent of earnings up to the lower earnings limit, plus contributions at a higher percentage on earnings between the lower earning limit and the employees' upper earnings limit. Employees contributing at the reduced rate continue to pay at that rate on earnings up to and including the employees' upper earnings limit.

Secondary Class 1 contributions are payable by employers of employed earners, and by the appropriate authorities in the case of office-holders. In 1985 the upper earnings limit for employers' contributions was abolished and secondary contributions are payable on all the employee's earnings if they reach or exceed £61.00 per week.

Women who marry for the first time no longer have a right to elect not to pay the full contribution rate. Married women and widows who before 12 May 1977 elected not to pay contributions at the full rate retain the right to pay a reduced rate over the same earnings range, which includes a contribution to the National Health Service. They lose this right if, after 5 April 1978, there are two consecutive tax years in which they receive no earnings on which primary Class 1 contributions are payable and in which they have not been at any time self-employed earners. No primary contributions are due on earnings paid for a period on or after the employee's pension age, even when retirement is deferred.

Primary contributions are deducted from earnings by the employer and are paid, together with the employer's contributions, to the Inland Revenue along with income tax collected under the PAYE system.

For the period 6 April 1996 to 5 April 1997 the earnings brackets determining Class 1 contributions are:

Earnings bracket	Weekly earnings
1	£61.00–109.99
2	110.00–154.99
3	155.00–209.99
4	210.00–455.00
5	over 455.00

CLASS 2 CONTRIBUTIONS

These are flat-rate, paid weekly by self-employed earners over age 16. Those with earnings below £3,430 a year for the tax year 1996–7 can apply for exemption from liability to pay Class 2 contributions. People who while self-employed are exempted from liability to pay contributions on the grounds of small earnings may pay either Class 2 or Class 3 contributions voluntarily. Self-employed earners (whether or not they pay Class 2 contributions) may also be liable to pay Class 4 contributions based on profits or gains within certain limits. There are special rules for those who are concurrently employed and self-employed.

Married women and widows can no longer choose not to pay Class 2 contributions. Those who elected not to pay Class 2 contributions before 12 May 1977 retain the right until there is a period of two consecutive tax years after 5 April 1978 in which they were not at any time either self-employed earners or had earnings on which primary Class 1 contributions were payable.

CLASS 3 CONTRIBUTIONS

These are voluntary flat-rate contributions payable by persons over age 16 who would otherwise be unable to qualify for retirement pension and certain other benefits because they have an insufficient record of Class 1 or Class 2 contributions. Married women and widows who on or before 11 May 1977 elected not to pay Class 1 (full rate) or Class 2 contributions cannot pay Class 3 contributions while they retain this right.

CLASS 4 CONTRIBUTIONS

These are payable by self-employed earners, whether or not they pay Class 2 contributions, on annual profits or gains from a trade, profession or vocation chargeable to income tax under Schedule D, where these fall between £6,860 and £23,660 a year. The maximum Class 4 contribution, payable on profits or gains of £23,660 or more, is £1,008.

Class 4 contributions are generally assessed and collected by the Inland Revenue along with Schedule D income tax. Self-employed persons under 16 or who at the beginning of a tax year are over pension age even where retirement is deferred, are not liable to pay Class 4 contributions. There are special rules for people who have more than one job or who pay Class 1 contributions on earnings which are chargeable to income tax under Schedule D.

Regulations state the cases in which earners may be exempted from liability to pay contributions, and the conditions upon which contributions are credited to persons who are exempted. Leaflet NI 208 is obtainable from local social security offices.

CONTRIBUTION RATES
FROM 6 APRIL 1996 TO 5 APRIL 1997

CLASS 1 CONTRIBUTIONS – EMPLOYEE'S RATES
Not Contracted Out

	Percentage of reckonable income			
Earnings bracket	On first £61.00		On earnings from £61.00–£455.00	
	standard	reduced	standard	reduced
1	2	3.85	10	3.85
2	2	3.85	10	3.85
3	2	3.85	10	3.85
4	2	3.85	10	3.85
5	*2	*3.85	*10	*3.85

CLASS 1 CONTRIBUTIONS – EMPLOYEE'S RATES
Contracted Out (see also page 487)

Earnings bracket	On first £61.00		On earnings from £61.00–£455.00	
	standard	reduced	standard	reduced
1	2	3.85	8.2	3.85
2	2	3.85	8.2	3.85
3, 4	2	3.85	8.2	3.85
5	*2	*3.85	*8.2	*3.85

*To a maximum of £455.00 per week

CLASS 1 CONTRIBUTIONS – EMPLOYER'S RATES

Earnings bracket	On first £61.00	On earnings from £61.00– £455.00	On any earnings over £455.00
1	3.0	0.0	0
2	5.0	2.0	0
3	7.0	4.0	0
4	10.2	7.2	0
5	10.2	7.2	10.2

CLASS 2 CONTRIBUTIONS, £6.05 weekly flat rate

CLASS 3 CONTRIBUTIONS, £5.95

CLASS 4 CONTRIBUTIONS, 8% of profits or gains

The Social Security (Contributions) Act 1991 added a new class of contributions: 1A, payable in respect of car fuel by persons liable to pay secondary Class 1 contributions. It was effective from the 1991–2 tax year.

THE STATE EARNINGS RELATED PENSION SCHEME (SERPS)

The Social Security Pensions Act 1975 which came into force in 1978 aimed to reduce reliance upon means-tested benefit in old age, in widowhood and in chronic ill-health by providing better pensions; to ensure that occupational pension schemes which are contracted out of part of the state scheme fulfil the conditions of a good scheme; that pensions are adequately protected against inflation; and that in both the state and occupational schemes men and women are treated equally. Modifications to the schemes have been made since 1978 and further changes come into effect in April 1997 (see below).

Under the state earnings-related pension scheme, retirement, invalidity and widow's pensions for employees are related to the earnings on which NI contributions have been paid. For employees of either sex with a complete insurance record, the scheme provides a category A retirement pension in two parts, a basic and an additional pension. The basic pension corresponds to the old personal flat-rate national insurance pension. The additional pension is 1.25 per cent of average earnings between the lower weekly earnings limit for Class 1 contribution liability and the upper earnings limit for each year of such earnings under the scheme, and will thus build up to 25 per cent in twenty years. Retirement, widow's and invalidity pensions under the new scheme started to be paid in 1979. Since 1979 the basic retirement pension has been augmented for employed earners by the additional pension related to earnings, but it will be 20 years before these additional pensions become payable at the full rate.

The additional pension will be calculated in a different way for individuals who reach pension age after 6 April 1999. The changes are to be phased in over ten years. From 2010 a lifetime's earnings will be included in the calculation and for years from 1988–9 onwards the accrual rate on these surplus earnings will be 20 per cent. The accrual rate on surplus earnings for the years from 1978–9 to 1987–8 will remain at 25 per cent.

Actual earnings are to be revalued in terms of the earnings level current in the last complete tax year before pension age (or death or incapacity). Both components of pensions in payment are to be uprated annually in line with the movement of prices. Graduated retirement pensions in payment, and rights to such pensions earned by people who are still working, will be brought into the annual review of benefits.

Self-employed persons pay contributions towards the basic pension. Employees with earnings below the lower limit and people not in employment may contribute voluntarily for basic pension. Although no primary Class 1 contributions or Class 2 or Class 4 contributions are payable by persons who work beyond pension age (65 for men, 60 for women), the employer's liability for secondary Class 1 contributions continues if earnings are at or above the lower earnings limit. Class 4 contributions are still payable up to the end of the tax year during which pension age is reached.

Widows will get the whole of any additional pensions earned by their husbands with their widowed mother's allowances or widow's pensions; and can add to the retirement pensions earned by their own contributions any additional pensions earned by their husbands up to the maximum payable on one person's contributions. Men whose wives die when they are both over pension age can add together their own and their wives' pension rights in the same way.

The scheme permits years of home responsibilities to reduce the number of qualifying years (since 1978) needed by women for retirement pension. The range of short-term social security benefits and industrial injury benefits under the Social Security Act 1975 continues with only minor changes.

CONTRACTED-OUT AND PERSONAL PENSION SCHEMES

Members of occupational pension schemes which meet the standards laid down in the Pension Schemes Act 1993 can be contracted-out of the state earnings-related pension scheme (SERPS).

Until 1988 occupational pension schemes could contract out only if they promised a pension that was related to earnings (a contracted-out salary-related scheme). They must provide a pension that is not less than the guaranteed minimum pension (GMP), which is broadly equivalent to the state earnings-related pension. Since 6 April 1988 occupational pension schemes which promise a minimum level of contributions (a contracted-out money purchase scheme) have also been able to contract out. They provide a pension based on how much has been paid in and invested and how much these investments have grown.

Since 1988 employees have been able to start their own personal pension instead of staying in SERPS. This choice is open to all employees even if their employer has a pension scheme. A personal pension, like a contracted-out money purchase scheme, provides a pension based on the fund built up in the scheme over the years plus the results of the way they have been invested.

The decision on whether or not an occupational pension scheme may become contracted-out lies with the Occupational Pension Board, an independent statutory body which has a general responsibility for supervising contracting-out. They also consider and approve personal pension schemes which can be used instead of state additional pension.

The state earnings-related pension payable to a member of a contracted-out salary-related scheme, or his widow, will be reduced by the amount of GMP payable (which in the case of a widow must be at least half of the late husband's GMP entitlement). Members of contracted-out money purchase schemes and personal pension schemes, or their widows, have no GMP entitlement as such. But the state earnings-related pension payable will be reduced by an amount equivalent to a GMP (or widow's GMP).

Since 1988 contracted-out salary-related schemes must also provide a widower's GMP which must be at least half of the late wife's GMP entitlement built up from 6 April 1988. (A scheme need not provide entitlement to a GMP for widowers of earners dying before April 1989.) Contracted-out money purchase schemes and personal pension schemes must provide half-rate widower's benefit.

In contracted-out occupational pension schemes, both the employee and the employer pay the lower (rebated) rate of National Insurance contributions on earnings between the lower and upper earnings limits in recognition that full SERPS will not be paid. The amount of the rebate is determined by the Secretary of State after receiving advice from the Government Actuary and is normally reviewed every five years (see also page 486).

An employee who chooses a personal pension in place of SERPS or their employer's pension scheme must pay NI contributions at the full ordinary rate (the employer's share must also be paid at the same rate). The DSS pays the difference between the lower contracted-out rate and the full ordinary rate directly into the personal pension scheme.

The Pensions Act 1995 introduces a number of changes to the present system of contracting-out. From April 1997, the links between SERPS and contracting-out will be broken, and thereafter people will no longer accrue entitlement to SERPS for periods of contracted-out service, but will still be entitled to pension rights earned before April 1997. Contracted-out salary-related schemes will no longer have to provide a GMP. Instead, they will have to satisfy a new scheme-based test as one of the requirements for the issue of a contracting-out certificate. GMPs accrued before April 1997 will still form part of the occupational pension and will broadly continue to be subject to the rules currently in force. All occupational pension schemes will be required to provide inflation-proofing of up to 5 per cent on the whole pension accrued after April 1997. There will also be age-related National Insurance contribution rebates, from April 1997, for people who leave SERPS and join a contracted-out money purchase or personal pension scheme. The rebate will be lower for younger people and higher for older people. This should mean that most people will be able to stay in their contracted-out money purchase or personal pension scheme until they retire.

The Occupational Pensions Board will be abolished from April 1997, and the Contributions Agency, an executive agency of the Department of Social Security, will process elections to contract-out.

NATIONAL INSURANCE FUND

The National Insurance Fund receives all social security contributions (less only the National Health Service) and it bears the cost of all contributory benefits provided by the Social Security Acts and the cost of administration.

Approximate receipts and payments of the National Insurance Fund for the year ended 31 March 1995, were:

Receipts	£'000
Balance, 1 April 1994	4,548,652
Contributions under the Social Security Acts (net of SSP/SMP)	37,863,479
Treasury Grant	6,280,000
Compensation from Consolidated Fund for SSP/SMP recoveries	541,000
Income from investments	363,950
Other receipts	82,003
	49,679,084

Payments	£'000	£'000
Unemployment benefit	1,299,483	
Sickness benefit	341,840	
Invalidity benefit	7,705,134	
Maternity allowance	27,000	
Widow's benefit	1,022,000	
Guardian's allowance and child's special allowance	1,000	
Retirement pension	28,744,810	
Pensioners' lump sum payments	123,305	39,264,572
Personal pensions		1,956,618
Transfers to Northern Ireland		145,000
Administration		1,279,888
Other payments		8,879
Redundancy payments		196,528
Balance, 31 March 1995		6,827,599
		49,679,084

BENEFITS

The benefits payable under the Social Security Acts are as follows:

CONTRIBUTORY BENEFITS
Incapacity benefit
Maternity allowance
Widow's benefit, comprising widow's payment, widowed mother's allowance and widow's pension
Retirement pensions, categories A and B

NON-CONTRIBUTORY BENEFITS
Child benefit
One parent benefit
Guardian's allowance
Invalid care allowance
Mobility allowance
Severe disablement allowance
Attendance allowance
Disability living allowance
Disability working allowance
Retirement pensions, categories C and D
Income support
Family credit
Social fund

BENEFITS FOR INDUSTRIAL INJURIES, DISABLEMENT AND DEATH

OTHER
Statutory sick pay
Statutory maternity pay
Jobseeker's allowance

Leaflets relating to the various benefits and payments are obtainable from local social security offices.

CONTRIBUTORY BENEFITS

Entitlement to contributory benefits depends on contribution conditions being satisfied either by the claimant or by some other person (depending on the kind of benefit). The class or classes of contribution which for this purpose are relevant to each benefit are:

Jobseeker's allowance (contribution-based)	Class 1
Incapacity benefit	Class 1 or 2
Maternity allowance	Class 1 or 2
Widow's benefits	Class 1, 2 or 3
Retirement pensions categories A and B	Class 1, 2 or 3

The system of contribution conditions relates to yearly levels of earnings on which contributions have been paid. The contribution conditions for different benefits are set out in leaflets available at local social security offices.

JOBSEEKER'S ALLOWANCE

Jobseeker's allowance replaced unemployment benefit and income support for unemployed people under pension age from 7 October 1996. There are two routes of entitlement: a contribution-based route, paid as a personal rate to individuals for up to six months, and an income-based route, based on savings and income and payable for a claimant and their dependants for as long as they satisfy the rules. Rates of jobseeker's allowance correspond to income support rates.

A person wishing to claim jobseeker's allowance must be unemployed, capable of work and available for any work which they can reasonably be expected to do, usually for at least 40 hours a week. They must actively seek work. They must agree and sign a 'Jobseeker's Agreement', which will set out each claimant's plans to find work.

A person will be disqualified from jobseeker's allowance if they have left a job voluntarily or through misconduct, if they refuse to take up an offer of employment or if they fail to attend a training scheme or employment programme. Hardship payments may not be available except where a person may be vulnerable, e.g. if sick or pregnant, or for those with children or caring responsibilities.

INCAPACITY BENEFIT

Incapacity benefit replaced state sickness benefit and invalidity benefit on 13 April 1995. Short-term incapacity benefit consists of a lower rate payable for the first 28 weeks of sickness, and a higher rate payable after 28 weeks. Long-term benefit is payable after 52 weeks and is not payable after pension age. The terminally ill and those entitled to the highest rate care component of disability living allowance are able to get the long-term rate after 28 weeks rather than 52 weeks. Incapacity benefit is taxable after 28 weeks of incapacity. Former sickness and invalidity benefit claimants were transferred to incapacity benefit on equivalent rates and special transitional arrangements apply.

Two rates of age addition are paid with long-term benefit based on the claimant's age when incapacity started. The higher rate is payable where incapacity for work commenced before the age of 35; and the lower rate where incapacity commenced before the age of 45. Increases for dependents are also payable with short and long-term incapacity benefit.

A new medical test of incapacity, the 'all work test', was introduced for incapacity benefit as well as other benefits paid on the basis of incapacity for work. The medical test normally applies after 28 weeks of incapacity for work and assesses ability to perform a range of work-related activities rather than the ability to perform a specific job. The new test applies to most former sickness and invalidity benefit claimants.

MATERNITY BENEFIT

Statutory maternity pay (SMP) is administered by employers (see page 493). The state maternity allowance scheme covers women who are self-employed or otherwise do not qualify for SMP. The Maternity (Compulsory Leave) Regulations 1994 apply to both schemes and effectively prohibit women from working for two weeks after the date of childbirth.

A woman may qualify for maternity allowance (MA) if she has been working and paying contributions at the full rate for at least 26 weeks in the 66-week period which ends one week before the week the baby is due. She also has an element of choice in deciding when to stop work and receive MA, which is not payable for any period she works. Women employed at the 15th week before the baby is due will receive £54.55 per week for up to 18 weeks, and self-employed and unemployed women will receive £47.35 for up to 18 weeks.

WIDOW'S BENEFITS

Only the late husband's contributions of any class count for widow's benefit in any of its three forms:

Widow's payment – may be received by a woman who at her husband's death is under 60, or whose husband was not entitled to a Category A retirement pension when he died

Widowed mother's allowance – payable to a widow if she is entitled or treated as entitled to child benefit, or if she is expecting her husband's baby

Widow's pension – a widow may receive this pension if aged 45 or over at the time of her husband's death (40 or over if widowed before 11 April 1988) or when her widowed mother's allowance ends. If aged 55 or over (50 or over if widowed before 11 April 1988) she will receive the full widow's pension rate

Widow's benefit of any form ceases upon remarriage or during a period in which she lives with a man as his wife.

RETIREMENT PENSION: CATEGORIES A AND B

A Category A pension is payable for life to men or women on their own contributions if they are over pension age (65 for a man and 60 for a woman).

Where a person defers making a claim at 65 (60 for a woman) or later opts to be treated as if he/she had not made a claim, and does not draw a Category A pension, the weekly rate of pension is increased when he or she finally makes a claim or reaches the age of 70 (65 for a woman), in respect of weeks when pension is forgone during the five years after reaching minimum pension age. Details of the increase in the rate of pension due to deferred retirement are given in leaflet NP46, available at social security offices. If a married man defers his own Category A pension, his wife has to defer receiving her Category B pension based on his contribution record. During this time she earns increments to the Category B pension, provided she does not claim retirement pension or graduated retirement benefit in her own right; increments are payable to her (and not her husband) when they both claim their pensions.

A Category B pension is normally payable for life to a woman on her husband's contributions when he has claimed, or is over 70, and has qualified for his own Category A pension, and she has reached 60. It is also payable on widowhood after 60 whether or not the late husband had retired and qualified for his own pension. The pension is payable at the rate of the increase for a wife while the husband is alive, and at the single person's rate on widowhood after 60. Where a woman is widowed before she reaches 60, a Category B pension is paid to her on reaching 60 at the same rate as her widow's pension if she claims. If a woman qualifies for a pension of each category she receives whichever pension is the larger.

The earnings rule, which stated that anyone who had qualified for a pension would have it reduced if he or she earned more than a certain amount, was abolished in 1989. Where an adult dependant is living with the claimant, an adult dependants increase (£36.60) will only be payable if the dependant's earnings do not exceed the rate of jobseeker's allowance for a single person (*see* below). For the purpose of the dependency rule only, earnings will include payments by way of occupational or personal pension. The earnings of a separated spouse affect the increase of retirement pension if they exceed £36.60 a week.

Income support is payable to men between 65 and 70 and women between 60 and 65 who have not claimed their retirement pension and who would have been entitled to a retirement pension if they had claimed at pension age. This applies in the case of incapacity benefit if incapacity for work is the result of an industrial accident or prescribed disease. These rates of benefit for people over pension age are shown in leaflet NI 196. A retirement pension will be increased by the amount of any invalidity allowance the pensioner was getting within the period of eight weeks and one day before reaching minimum pension age but this will be offset against any additional pension or GMP. An age addition of 25p per week is payable if a retirement pensioner is aged 80 or over.

GRADUATED RETIREMENT BENEFIT

Graduated NI contributions were first payable from 1961 and were calculated as a percentage of earnings between certain bands. They were discontinued in 1975. Any graduated pension which an employed person over 18 and under 70 (65 for a woman) had earned by paying graduated contributions will be paid when the contributor claims retirement pension or at 70 (65 for a woman), in addition to any retirement pension for which he or she qualifies.

Graduated retirement benefit is at the rate of 7.90p a week (April 1996) for each 'unit' of graduated contributions paid by the employee (half a unit or more counts as a whole unit). A unit of contributions is £7.50 for men and £9.00 for women of graduated contributions paid.

A wife can get a graduated pension in return for her own graduated contributions, but not for her husband's. A widow, or a widower whose wife died after 5 April 1979 when they were both over pensionable age, gets a graduated addition to his/her retirement pension equal to half of any graduated additions earned by his/her late spouse, plus any additions earned by his/her own graduated contributions. If a person defers making a claim beyond 65 (60 for a woman), entitlement may be increased by one seventh of a penny per £1 of its weekly rate for each complete week of deferred retirement, as long as the retirement is deferred for a minimum of seven weeks.

WEEKLY RATES OF BENEFIT
from April 1996

Jobseeker's allowance (contribution-based)

Person under 18	£28.85
Person aged 18–24	37.90
Person over 25	47.90
Couple	75.20

Short-term incapacity benefit

Person under pension age – lower rate	46.15
*Person under pension age – higher rate	54.55
Increase for adult dependant	28.55
*Person over pension age	58.65
Increase for adult dependant	33.15

*Long-term incapacity benefit

Person (under or over pension age)	61.15
Increase for adult dependant	36.60
Age addition – lower rate	6.45
Age addition – higher rate	12.90

Invalidity allowance: maximum amount payable

Higher rate	12.90
Middle rate	8.10
Lower rate	4.05

Maternity allowance

Employed	54.55
Self-employed or unemployed	47.35

Widow's benefits

Widow's payment (lump sum)	1,000.00
*Widowed mother's allowance	61.15
*Widow's pension	61.15

*Retirement pension: categories A and B

Single person	61.15
Increase for wife/other adult dependant	36.60

*These benefits attract an increase for each dependent child (in addition to child benefit) of £9.90 for the first or only child and £11.15 for each subsequent child

NON-CONTRIBUTORY BENEFITS

CHILD BENEFIT

Child benefit is payable for virtually all children aged under 16, and for those aged 16 to 18 who are studying full-time up to and including A-level or equivalent standard. It is also payable for a short period if the child has left school recently and is registered for work or youth training at a careers office.

ONE-PARENT BENEFIT

This benefit may be paid to a person in receipt of child benefit who is responsible for bringing up one or more children on his/her own. It is a flat rate non-means tested, non-contributory benefit payable for the eldest child.

GUARDIAN'S ALLOWANCE

Where the parents of a child are dead, the person who has the child in his/her family may claim a guardian's allowance in addition to child benefit. The allowance, in exceptional circumstances, is payable on the death of only one parent.

INVALID CARE ALLOWANCE

Invalid care allowance is payable to persons of working age who are not gainfully employed because they are regularly and substantially engaged in caring for a severely disabled person who is receiving attendance allowance, the middle or highest rate of disability living allowance care component or constant attendance allowance, paid at not less than the normal maximum rate, under the industrial injuries or war pensions schemes.

SEVERE DISABLEMENT ALLOWANCE

Persons who have been incapable of work for a continuous period of at least 28 weeks but who do not qualify for contributory incapacity benefit may be entitled to severe disablement allowance. People who first become incapable of work after their 20th birthday must also be at least 80 per cent disabled or have been disabled for a continuous period of at least 28 weeks.

ATTENDANCE ALLOWANCE

This is payable to disabled people over 65 who need a lot of care or supervision because of physical or mental disability for a period of at least six months. People not expected to live for six months because of an illness do not have to wait six months. The allowance has two rates: the lower rate is for day or night care, and the higher rate is for day and night care.

DISABILITY LIVING ALLOWANCE

This is payable to disabled people under 65 who have personal care and mobility needs because of an illness or disability for a period of at least three months and are likely to have those needs for a further six months or more. People not expected to live for six months because of an illness do not have to wait three months. The allowance has two components: the care component, which has three rates, and the mobility component, which has two rates. The rates depend on the care and mobility needs of the claimant. The mobility component is payable only to those aged five or over.

DISABILITY WORKING ALLOWANCE

This is a tax-free, income-related benefit for people who are working 16 hours a week or more but have an illness or disability which puts them at a disadvantage in getting a job. To qualify a person must be aged 16 or over and must, at the date of the claim, have one of the 'qualifying benefits',

such as disability living allowance. The amount payable depends on the size of the family and weekly income. The allowance is not payable if any savings exceed £16,000.

RETIREMENT PENSION: CATEGORIES C AND D

A Category C pension is provided, subject to a residence test, for persons who were over pensionable age on 5 July 1948, and for women whose husbands are so entitled if they are over pension age, with increases for adult and child dependants. A Category D pension is provided for others when they reach 80 if they are not already getting a retirement pension of any category or if they are getting that pension at less than these rates. An age addition of 25p per week is payable if persons entitled to retirement pension are aged 80 or over.

WEEKLY RATES OF BENEFIT
from April 1996

Child benefit (first child)	£10.80
Each subsequent child	8.80
One-parent benefit	
First or only child of certain lone parents	6.30
Guardian's allowance (eldest child)	9.85
Each subsequent child	11.05
*Severe disablement allowance	
†Basic rate	35.55
Under 40	12.40
40–49	7.80
50–59	3.90
Increase for wife/other adult dependant	21.15
*Invalid care allowance	36.60
Increase for wife/other adult dependant	21.90
Attendance allowance	
Higher rate	46.70
Lower rate	31.20
Disability living allowance	
Care component	
Higher rate	46.70
Middle rate	31.20
Lower rate	12.40
Mobility component	
Higher rate	32.65
Lower rate	12.40
Disability working allowance	
Single person	48.25
Couple or single parent	75.60
Child aged under 11	11.75
aged 11–15	19.45
aged 16–17	24.15
aged 18	33.80
Disabled child allowance	20.40
Thirty hours allowance	10.30
‡Applicable amount (income threshold)	
Single person	54.75
Couple or single parent	73.00
Retirement pension: categories *C and D	
Single person	36.60
Increase for wife/other adult dependant	21.90
(not payable with Category D pension)	

*These benefits attract an increase for each dependent child (in addition to child benefit) of £9.90 for the first or only child and £11.15 for each subsequent child
†The age addition applies to the age when incapacity began
‡70 pence is deducted from the maximum DWA payable (this is obtained by adding up the appropriate allowance for each person in the family) for every £ coming in each week over the appropriate applicable amount. Where weekly income is below the applicable amount, maximum DWA is payable

INCOME SUPPORT

Income support is a benefit for those aged 18 and over (although certain vulnerable 16- and 17-year-olds may be eligible) whose income falls below set levels. Others who may be eligible include people who are over 60, bringing up children alone, unable to work through sickness or disability, or caring for a disabled person. Except in special cases income support is not available to those who work for more than 24 hours per week or who have a partner who works for more than 16 hours per week. Income support for unemployed people was replaced by jobseeker's allowance from 7 October 1996.

Income support is not payable if the claimant, or claimant and partner, have capital or savings in excess of £8,000. For capital or savings in excess of £3,000 a deduction of £1 is made for every £250, or part of £250, held.

Sums payable depend on fixed allowances laid down by law for people in different circumstances. If both partners are entitled to income support, either may claim it for the couple. People receiving income support may be able to receive housing benefit, help with mortgage or home loan interest and help with health care. They may also be eligible for help with exceptional expenses from the Social Fund. Leaflet IS20 gives a detailed explanation of income support.

Special rates may apply to some people living in residential care or nursing homes. Details are available from local social security offices.

INCOME SUPPORT PREMIUMS

Income support premiums are additional weekly payments for those with special needs. People qualifying for more than one premium will normally only receive the highest single premium for which they qualify. However, family premium, disabled child's premium, severe disability premium and carer premium are payable in addition to other premiums.

People with children qualify for a family premium if they have at least one child; a disabled child's premium if they have a child who receives disability living allowance or is registered blind; or a lone parent premium if they are bringing up one or more children alone. If someone receives invalid care allowance, they qualify for the carer premium.

Long-term sick or disabled people qualify for a disability premium if they or their partner are receiving certain benefits because they are disabled or cannot work; are registered blind; or if the claimant, but not their partner, is incapable of work or receiving statutory sick pay for at least 364 days (not broken by any period longer than 56 days), or 196 days if terminally ill. If someone is living alone and they are in receipt of attendance allowance, or disability living allowance at the middle or higher rate, without anyone receiving invalid care allowance for looking after them, they may qualify for a severe disability premium in addition to a disability premium.

People qualify for a pensioner premium if they or their partner are aged between 60 and 74, an enhanced pensioner premium if they or their partner are aged between 75 and 79, and a higher pensioner premium if they or their partner are aged 80 or over. A higher pensioner premium is also payable to people aged between 60 and 79 who receive attendance allowance, disability living allowance, long-term incapacity benefit or severe disablement allowance, or who are registered blind.

WEEKLY RATES OF BENEFIT
from April 1996

Income support

Single people	
aged 16–17	£28.85
aged 16–17 (certain circumstances)	37.90
aged 18–24	37.90
aged 25 and over	47.90
aged 18 and over and a single parent	47.90

Couples*	
both under 18	57.20
one or both aged 18 or over	75.20

For each child in a family	
under 11	16.45
aged 11–15	24.10
†aged 16–17	28.85
†aged 18 and over	37.90

Premiums

Family premium	10.55
Disabled child's premium	20.40
Carer's premium	13.00
Lone parent premium	5.20
Disability premium	
Single	20.40
Couple	29.15
Severe disability premium	
Single	36.40
Couple (one person qualified)	36.40
Couple (both qualified)	72.80
Pensioner premium	
Single	19.15
Couple	28.90
Higher pensioner premium	
Single	25.90
Couple	37.05
Enhanced pensioner premium	
Single	21.30
Couple	31.90

*Where one or both partners are aged under 18, their personal allowance will depend on their situation
†If in full-time education up to A-level or equivalent standard

FAMILY CREDIT

Family credit is a tax-free benefit for working families with children. To qualify, a family must include at least one child under 16 (under 19 if in full-time education up to A-level or equivalent standard) and the claimant, or partner if there is one, must be working for at least 16 hours per week. It does not matter which partner is working and they may be employed or self-employed. The right to family credit does not depend on NI contributions and the same rates of benefit are paid to one- and two-parent families. Family credit is not payable if the claimant, or claimant and partner, have capital or savings in excess of £8,000. The rate of benefit is affected if capital or savings in excess of £3,000 are held. The rate of benefit payable depends upon the claimant's (and partner's) net income (excluding child benefit, one-parent benefit and the first £15.00 of any maintenance in payment), number of children and children's ages, and the number of hours worked. Family credit is paid for 26 weeks and the amount payable will usually remain the same throughout this period, regardless of change of circumstances. In certain cases where there are formal childcare arrangements for children under 11, costs of up to £60 per week will be taken into account. Up to £10.30 a week extra is paid to parents working 30 hours or more a week. Payment is made weekly via post offices or every four weeks directly into a bank or building society account. Family credit is claimed by post. A claim pack FC1 which includes a claim form can be obtained at a post office or social security office or call the Family Credit Helpline on 01253-500050. In two-parent families the woman should claim.

WEEKLY RATES OF BENEFIT
from week commencing 9 April 1996

The maximum amount will be payable where net income is no more than £73.00 a week. Where net income exceeds that amount, the maximum credit is reduced by 70 per cent of the excess and the result is the family credit payable. The maximum rate consists of:

Adult credit (for one or two parents)	£46.45
plus for each child	
aged under 11	11.75
aged 11–15	19.45
aged 16–17	24.15
aged 18	33.80

CLAIMS AND QUESTIONS

With a few exceptions, claims and questions relating to social security benefits are decided by statutory authorities who act independently of the Department of Social Security and Department for Education and Employment.

The first of the statutory authorities, the Adjudication Officer, determines entitlement to benefit. A client who is dissatisfied with that decision has the right of appeal to an independent social security appeal tribunal. There is a further right of appeal to a Social Security Commissioner against the tribunal's decision but leave to appeal must first be obtained. Appeals to the Commissioner must be on a point of law. Provision is also made for the determination of certain questions by the Secretary of State for Social Security.

Disablement questions are decided by adjudicating medical authorities or medical appeal tribunals. Appeal to the Commissioner against a tribunal's decision is with leave and on a point of law only.

Leaflet NI246, which is available from social security offices, explains how to appeal, and leaflet NI260 is a guide to reviews and appeals.

THE SOCIAL FUND

The Social Fund helps people with expenses which are difficult to meet from regular income. Regulated maternity, funeral and cold weather payments are decided by Adjudication Officers and are not cash-limited. Discretionary community care grants, and budgeting and crisis loans are decided by Social Fund Officers and come out of a yearly budget which is allocated to each district (1996–7, grants £97 million; loans £321.5 million; £1 million set aside as a contingency reserve).

REGULATED PAYMENTS
Maternity Payments

A payment of up to £100 for each baby expected, born or adopted. It is payable to people on income support, disability working allowance and family credit and is non-repayable.

Funeral Payments

Payable for specified funeral director's charges, plus the necessary cost of all burial or cremation expenses reasonably incurred by people receiving income support, disability working allowance, family credit, council tax benefit or housing benefit. It is recoverable from the estate of the deceased.

Cold Weather Payments

£8.50 for any consecutive seven days when the average temperature is 0°C or below in their area. These are paid to people on income support who are pensioners, disabled or parents with a child under the age of five. They are non-repayable.

DISCRETIONARY PAYMENTS
Community Care Grants

They are intended to help people on income support to move into the community or avoid institutional or residential care; ease exceptional pressures on families; care for a prisoner on release on temporary licence; and/or meet certain essential travelling expenses. They are non-repayable.

Budgeting Loans

These are interest-free loans to people who have been receiving income support for at least six months, for intermittent expenses that may be difficult to budget for.

Crisis Loans

These are interest-free loans to anyone, whether receiving benefit or not, who is without resources in an emergency, where there is no other means of preventing serious risk or damage to their health or safety.

Loans are normally repaid over a period of up to 78 weeks at 15, 10 or 5 per cent of income support (less housing costs), depending on other commitments.

SAVINGS

Savings over £500 (£1,000 for people aged 60 or over) are taken into account for maternity and funeral payments, community care grants and budgeting loans. All savings are taken into account for crisis loans. Savings are not taken into account for cold weather payments.

APPEALS AND REVIEWS

For regulated payments there is a right of appeal (except in the case of cold weather payments, which do not carry the right of appeal although a question may be raised by a claimant if they believe they should have received a payment) to an independent Social Security Appeal Tribunal and thereafter to a Social Security Commissioner. For discretionary payments there is a review system where persons can ask for a review at the local office with a further right of review to an independent Social Fund Inspector.

INDUSTRIAL INJURIES, DISABLEMENT AND DEATH BENEFITS

The industrial injuries scheme, administered under the Social Security Contributions and Benefits Act 1992, provides a range of benefits designed to compensate for disablement resulting from an industrial accident (i.e. an accident arising out of and in the course of an employed earner's employment) or from a prescribed disease due to the nature of a person's employment. Rates of benefit are increased annually.

BENEFITS

Disablement benefit is normally payable 15 weeks (90 days) after the date of accident or onset of disease if the employed earner suffers from loss of physical or mental faculty such that the resulting disablement is assessed at not less than 14 per cent. The amount of disablement benefit payable varies according to the degree of disablement (in the form of a percentage) assessed by an adjudicating medical authority or medical appeal tribunal.

Disablement assessed at less than 14 per cent does not normally attract basic benefit except for certain chest diseases. A weekly pension is payable where the assessment of disablement is between 14 and 100 per cent (assessments of 14 to 19 per cent are payable at the 20 per cent rate). Payment can be made for a limited period or for life. The basic rates are applicable to adults and to juveniles entitled to an increase for a child or adult dependant; other juveniles receive lower rates.

Basic rates of pension are not related to the pensioner's loss of earning power, and are payable whether he/she is in work or not. There is provision for increases of pension if the pensioner requires constant attendance or if his/her disablement is exceptionally severe. A pensioner may draw statutory sick pay or incapacity benefit as appropriate, in addition to disablement pension, during spells of incapacity for work.

Regulations impose certain obligations on claimants and beneficiaries and on employers, including, in the case of claimants for disablement benefit, that of submitting themselves for medical examination.

SUPPLEMENTARY ALLOWANCES

Special schemes under the Industrial Injuries and Diseases (Old Cases) Act 1975 provide supplementary allowances to those entitled to receive weekly payments of workmen's compensation for loss of earnings due to injury at work, or disease contracted during employment before 5 July 1948 when the industrial injuries scheme was introduced. Other schemes under the Act provide allowances to those who contracted slowly-developing diseases during employment before July 1948 where neither workmen's compensation nor industrial injuries benefits are payable. A lump sum death benefit of up to £300 may also be payable to a dependant of such a person. Leaflet NI196 provides details relating to these allowances.

WEEKLY RATES OF BENEFIT
from April 1996

*Disablement benefit/pension
Degree of disablement

100 per cent	£99.00
90	89.10
80	79.20
70	69.30
60	59.40
50	49.50
40	39.60
30	29.70
20	19.80
†Unemployability supplement	61.15
Addition for adult dependant (subject to earnings rule)	36.60
Reduced earnings allowance (maximum)	£39.60
Constant attendance allowance (normal maximum rate)	39.70
Exceptionally severe disablement allowance	39.70

*There is a weekly benefit for those under 18 with no dependants which is set at a lower rate
†This benefit attracts an increase for each dependent child (in addition to child benefit) of £9.90 for the first child and £11.15 for each subsequent child

CLAIMS AND QUESTIONS

Provision is made for the determination of certain questions by the Secretary of State for Social Security, and of 'disablement questions' by a medical board (or a single doctor) or, on appeal, by a medical appeal tribunal. An appeal on a point of law against a medical appeal tribunal decision is determined by the Social Security Commissioner.

Claims for benefit and certain questions arising in connection with a claim for or award of benefit (e.g. whether the accident arose out of and in the course of the employment) are determined by an adjudication officer appointed by the Secretary of State, or a social security appeal tribunal, or in certain circumstances, on further appeal, by the Commissioners.

OTHER BENEFITS

STATUTORY SICK PAY

Employers usually pay statutory sick pay (SSP) to their employees for up to 28 weeks of sickness in any period of incapacity for work. SSP is paid at £54.55 a week and is subject to PAYE tax and NI deductions. Employees who cannot get SSP may be able to claim incapacity benefit. Employers can recover some SSP costs under the percentage threshold scheme where a large part of the workforce is off sick at the same time. Where SSP payments exceed 13 per cent of the employer's total NI liability for any tax month the employer can recover excess SSP paid above the 13 per cent threshold. Leaflet NI 244 is obtainable from local Social Security offices.

STATUTORY MATERNITY PAY

In general, employers pay statutory maternity pay to pregnant women who have been employed by them full or part-time for at least 26 weeks before the end of the 'qualifying week', which is 15 weeks before the week the baby is due, and whose earnings are on average at least at the lower earnings limit for the payment of NI contributions. All women who meet these conditions receive payment of 90 per cent of their average earnings for six weeks, followed by a maximum of 12 weeks at £54.55. Women have some choice in deciding when to begin maternity leave but SMP is not payable for any week in which work is done. Employers are reimbursed for 92 per cent of the SMP they pay (105.5 per cent for those whose annual NI liability is £20,000 or less).

War Pensions

The War Pensions Agency, an executive agency of the Department of Social Security (DSS), awards war pensions under The Naval, Military and Air Forces, Etc. (Disablement and Death) Service Pensions Order 1983 to members of the armed forces in respect of the periods 4 August 1914 to 30 September 1921 and subsequent to 3 September 1939 (including present members of the armed forces). War pensions for the period 1 October 1921 to 2 September 1939 were dealt with by the Ministry of Defence until July 1996 when the DSS became responsible for the provision of war pensions for this period. There is also a scheme for civilians and civil defence workers in respect of the 1939–45 war, and other schemes for groups such as merchant seamen and Polish armed forces who served under British command.

Pensions

War disablement pension is awarded for the disabling effects of any injury, wound or disease which is attributable to, or has been aggravated by, conditions of service in the armed forces. It cannot be paid until the serviceman or woman has left the armed forces.

Disablement is assessed by comparison of the disabled person's health with that of a normal, healthy person of the same age and sex, without taking into account the disabled person's earning capacity or occupation, and is expressed on a percentage scale up to 100 per cent. Disablement of 20 per cent and above, for which a pension is awarded, is assessed in steps of 10 per cent. Maximum assessment does not necessarily imply total incapacity. For assessment of less than 20 per cent a lump sum is usually payable. No award is made where disablement in respect of noise-induced sensorineural hearing loss is assessed at less than 20 per cent.

The dependency allowance in respect of a wife or child was abolished in 1992 and an equivalent amount incorporated into the basic war disablement pension.

War widow's pension is awarded where death occurs as a result of service or where a war disablement pensioner was receiving constant attendance allowance at the time of his death, or would have been receiving it if he were not in hospital, in which case his widow has automatic entitlement to a war widow's pension, regardless of the cause of death. Additional allowances are payable for dependent children, in addition to child benefit. From July 1995 a war widow's pension, which is withdrawn on remarriage, can be restored on subsequent widowhood or divorce.

A lower weekly rate is payable to war widows of men below the rank of Lieutenant-Colonel who are under the age of 40, without children and capable of maintaining themselves. This is increased to the standard rate at age 40.

Rank additions to both disablement gratuities and widow's pensions may be paid where the rank held was above that of private (or equivalent).

Supplementary Allowances

A number of supplementary allowances may be awarded to a war pensioner which are intended to meet various needs, such as mobility, unemployability, constant nursing care, which may result from disablement or death and take account of its particular effect on the pensioner or spouse.

The principal supplementary allowances are:
Unemployability supplement – paid to a war pensioner whose pensioned disablement is so serious as to make him unemployable. An invalidity allowance may also be payable if the incapacity for work began more than five years before normal retirement age.
Allowance for lowered standard of occupation – awarded to a partially disabled pensioner whose pensioned disablement permanently prevents him from following his regular occupation. The allowance, together with the basic war disablement pension, must not exceed pension at the 100 per cent rate.

Constant attendance allowance – awarded if the pensioner is receiving a pension at the 80 per cent rate or more and needs care and attendance because of the disability. It is paid at one of four rates depending on how much care is needed.
Widow's child's allowance – paid in addition to child benefit.

Other supplementary allowances include exceptionally severe disablement allowance, severe disablement occupational allowance, treatment allowance, mobility supplement, comforts allowance, clothing allowance, age allowance and widow's age allowance. There is a rent allowance available on a war widow's pension.

Decisions on supplementary allowances are made on a discretionary basis and there is no provision for a statutory right of appeal against them. However, war pensioners may discuss any aspect of their pension position with their local war pensions committee, which may be able to arrange help or make representations to the DSS.

War Pensioners Abroad

The DSS is responsible for the payment of war pensions, and, where necessary, meeting the cost of treatment for accepted disablement, to pensioners who reside overseas. They receive the same pension rates and annual upratings as war pensioners in this country.

Social Security Benefits

Most social security benefits are paid in addition to the basic war disablement pension or war widow's pension. Any retirement pension for which a war widow qualifies on her own contributions, and any graduated retirement benefit or additional earnings-related pension inherited from her husband, can be paid in addition to her war widow's pension.

A war pensioner or war widow who claims income support, family credit or disability working allowance has the first £10 of pension disregarded. A similar provision operates for housing benefit and council tax benefit; but the local authority may, at its discretion, disregard any or all of the balance.

Claims and Questions

Where a claim in respect of death or disablement is made no later than seven years after the termination of service, the claimant does not have to prove that the disablement or death on which the claim is based is related to service and receives the benefit of any reasonable doubt. Where a claim in respect of death or disablement is made more than seven years after the termination of service the claimant has to show that disablement or death is related to service. However, the claim succeeds if reliable evidence is produced which raises a reasonable doubt whether or not disablement or death is related to service. There is no time limit for making a claim for war pension.

Independent pensions appeal tribunals hear appeals against the decisions of the DSS on entitlement and assessment of disablement in respect of the 1939–45 war and subsequent service cases. There are no time limits within which an entitlement appeal must be made but there are time limits within which an assessment appeal should be made. However, there are now no rights of appeal in the 1914–21 war disablement cases, the great majority of which were given final assessment in the 1920s with a 12 months' right of appeal at the time. An appeal by a 1914 war widow must be made within twelve months of the date on which the rejection of the claim is notified.

War Pensioners Welfare Service

The DSS operates a war pensioners welfare service to advise and assist war pensioners and their widows on any matters affecting their welfare. Welfare officers are attached to war pensioners' welfare offices located in the major towns, and the service is available to any war pensioner or war widow who needs it.

The current rates of all war pensions and allowances are listed in WPA leaflet 9, *Rates of War Pensions and Allowances*, obtainable from war pensioners welfare offices, HMSO, Broadway, Chadderton, Oldham OL9 9QH, or by phoning the War Pension Helpline on 01253-858858.

WEEKLY RATES OF PENSIONS AND ALLOWANCES
from week commencing 8 April 1996

War disablement pension
Degree of disablement:

100 per cent	£105.00
90 per cent	94.50
80 per cent	84.00
70 per cent	73.50
60 per cent	63.00
50 per cent	52.50
40 per cent	42.00
30 per cent	31.50
20 per cent	21.00

Unemployability supplement

Personal allowance	64.90
Increase for wife/other adult dependant	36.50
Increase for first child	9.90
Increase for other children	11.15

Allowance for lowered standard of occupation

(maximum)	39.60

Widow's pension
(widow of Private or equivalent rank)

Standard rate	79.35
Increase for first child	14.10
Increase for other children	15.35
Childless widow under 40	18.35

Widow's age allowance

aged 65–69	9.05
aged 70–79	17.40
aged 80 and over	25.90

The Water Industry

ENGLAND AND WALES

In England and Wales the Secretaries of State for the Environment and for Wales have overall responsibility for water policy and set the environmental and health and safety standards for the water industry. The Director-General of Water Services, as the independent economic regulator, is responsible for ensuring that the private water companies are able to fulfil their statutory obligation to provide water supply and sewerage services, and for protecting the interests of consumers.

The Minister of Agriculture, Fisheries and Food and the Secretary of State for Wales are responsible for policy relating to land drainage, flood protection, sea defences and the protection and development of fisheries.

The Environment Agency is responsible for water quality and the control of pollution, the management of water resources and nature conservation. The Drinking Water Inspectorate and local authorities are responsible for the quality of drinking water.

THE WATER COMPANIES

Until 1989 nine regional water authorities in England and the Welsh Water Authority in Wales were responsible for water supply and the development of water resources, sewerage and sewage disposal, pollution control, fresh-water fisheries, flood protection, water recreation, and environmental conservation. The Water Act 1989 provided for the creation of a privatized water industry under public regulation, and the functions of the regional water authorities were taken over by ten holding companies and the regulatory bodies.

Of the 99 per cent of the population of England and Wales who are connected to a public water supply, 75 per cent are supplied by the water companies (through their principal operating subsidiaries, the water service companies). The remaining 25 per cent are supplied by statutory water companies which were already in the private sector. Most of these have public limited company (PLC) status and many are now French-owned. They are represented by the Water Companies Association. The ten water service companies are also responsible for sewerage and sewage disposal in England and Wales. The Water Services Association is the trade association for all the water service companies except Wessex Water Services.

Water Service Companies

ANGLIAN WATER SERVICES LTD, Anglian House, Ambury Road, Huntingdon, Cambs PE18 6NZ

DWR CYMRU (WELSH WATER), Cambrian Way, Brecon, Powys LD3 7HP

NORTHUMBRIAN WATER LTD, Abbey Road, Pity Me, Durham DHI 5FJ

NORTH WEST WATER LTD, Dawson House, Liverpool Road, Great Sankey, Warrington WA5 3LW

SEVERN TRENT WATER LTD, 2297 Coventry Road, Sheldon, Birmingham B26 3PU

SOUTHERN WATER SERVICES LTD, Southern House, Yeoman Road, Worthing, W. Sussex BNI3 3NX

SOUTH WEST WATER SERVICES LTD, Peninsula House, Rydon Lane, Exeter EX2 7HR

THAMES WATER UTILITIES LTD, Nugent House, Vastern Road, Reading RGI 8DB

WESSEX WATER SERVICES LTD, Wessex House, Passage Street, Bristol BS2 OJQ

YORKSHIRE WATER SERVICES LTD, West Riding House, 67 Albion Street, Leeds LSI 5AA

WATER COMPANIES ASSOCIATION, 1 Queen Anne's Gate, London SWIH 9BT. Tel: 0171-222 0644. *Chief Executive*, Ms P. Taylor

WATER SERVICES ASSOCIATION, 1 Queen Anne's Gate, London SWIH 9BT. Tel: 0171-957 4567. *Chief Executive*, Miss J. Langdon

REGULATORY BODIES

The Office of Water Services (Ofwat) (*see* page 354) was set up under the Water Act 1989 and is the independent economic regulator of the water and sewerage companies in England and Wales. Ofwat's main duty is to ensure that the companies can finance and carry out their statutory functions and to protect the interests of water customers. Ofwat is a non-ministerial government department headed by the Director-General of Water Services, who is appointed by the Secretaries of State for the Environment and for Wales.

An independent national body, the National Rivers Authority, took over the regulatory and river management functions of the regional water authorities. It had statutory duties and powers in relation to water resources, pollution control, flood defence, fisheries, recreation, conservation and navigation in England and Wales. On 1 April 1996 the statutory duties, powers and functions of the National Rivers Authority were transferred to the new Environment Agency (*see* page 298).

The Drinking Water Inspectorate (*see* page 297) is responsible for assessing the quality of the drinking water supplied by the water companies, inspecting the companies themselves and investigating any accidents affecting drinking water quality. The Chief Inspector presents an annual report to the Secretaries of State for the Environment and for Wales.

METHODS OF CHARGING

In England and Wales, most householders still pay for domestic water supply and sewerage services through charges based on the assessed value of their property under the old domestic rating system. Industrial and most commercial users are charged according to consumption, which is recorded by meter.

The Water Industry Act 1991 gives the water companies until 2000 to decide on and introduce a suitable method of charging. The main options under consideration are a flat-rate licence fee, property banding, and metering. The Government believes metering to be the best basis for payment. However, extension of the use of meters to all households will take considerable time to achieve. The Government has therefore decided to allow water companies to continue to use the old domestic rating system as a basis for their unmeasured charges after 2000.

SCOTLAND

Overall responsibility for national water policy in Scotland rests with the Secretary of State for Scotland. Most aspects of water policy are administered through the Scottish Office Agriculture, Environment and Fisheries Department.

Water supply and sewerage services were formerly local authority responsibilities and the Central Scotland Water Development Board had the function of developing new sources of water supply for the purpose of providing water in bulk to water authorities whose limits of supply were within the board's area. The Local Government etc. (Scotland) Act 1994 provided for three new public water authorities, covering the north, east and west of Scotland respectively, to be established to take over the provision of water and sewerage services from 1 April 1996. From that date the Central Scotland Water Development Board was abolished. The new authorities are accountable to Parliament through the Secretary of State for Scotland. The Act also provided for a Scottish Water and Sewerage Customers Council to be established to represent consumer interests. It will monitor the performance of the authorities; approve charges schemes; investigate complaints; and keep the Secretary of State advised on standards of service and customer relations.

The new Scottish Environment Protection Agency (SEPA) (*see* page 339) is responsible for promoting the cleanliness of Scotland's rivers, lochs and coastal waters. SEPA is also responsible for controlling pollution.

East of Scotland Water Authority, Pentland Gait, 597 Calder Road, Edinburgh EH11 4HJ. Tel: 0131-453 7500. *Chief Executive*, R. Rennet

North of Scotland Water Authority, Caledonia House, 63 Academy Street, Inverness IV1 1LU. Tel: 01463-245400. *Chief Executive*, A. Findlay

Scottish Water and Sewerage Customers Council, Suite 4, Ochil House, Springkerse Business Park, Stirling FK7 7XE. Tel: 01786-430200. *Director*, Dr V. Nash

West of Scotland Water Authority, 419 Balmore Road, Glasgow G22 6NU. Tel: 0141-355 3555. *Chief Executive*, E. Chambers

Methods of Charging

The water authorities set charges for domestic and non-domestic water and sewerage provision through charges schemes which have to be approved by the Scottish Water and Sewerage Customers Council. The authorities must publish a summary of their charges schemes.

NORTHERN IRELAND

In Northern Ireland ministerial responsibility for water services lies with the Secretary of State for Northern Ireland. The Water Service, which is an executive agency of the Department of the Environment for Northern Ireland, is responsible for policy and co-ordination with regard to supply, distribution and cleanliness of water, and the provision and maintenance of sewerage services.

The Water Service (*see* page 330) is divided into four regions, the Eastern, Northern, Western and Southern Divisions. These are based in Belfast, Ballymena, Londonderry and Craigavon respectively.

On major issues the Department of the Environment for Northern Ireland seeks the views of the Northern Ireland Water Council, a body appointed to advise the Department on the exercise of its water and sewerage functions. The Council includes representatives from agriculture, angling, industry, commerce, tourism, trade unions and local government.

Methods of Charging

Usually householders do not pay separately for water and sewerage services; the costs of these services are allowed for in the Northern Ireland regional rate. Water consumed by industry, commerce and agriculture in excess of 100 cubic metres (22,000 gallons) per half year is charged through meters. Traders operating from industrially rated premises are required to pay for the treatment and disposal of the trade effluent which they discharge into the public sewerage system.

Energy

THE COAL INDUSTRY

Coal has been mined in Britain for centuries and the availability of coal was crucial to the industrial revolution of the 18th and 19th centuries. Mines were in private ownership until 1947 when they were nationalized and came under the management of the National Coal Board (later the British Coal Corporation). In addition to producing coal at its own deep-mine and opencast sites, British Coal was responsible for licensing private operators.

PRIVATIZATION

Under the Coal Industry Act 1994, a new body, the Coal Authority (*see* page 291), was established to take over ownership of coal reserves and to issue licences to private mining companies as part of the privatization of British Coal. The Coal Authority also deals with the physical legacy of mining, e.g. subsidence damage claims, and is responsible for holding and making available all existing records.

The Government offered the mines for sale in five businesses based in the separate regions of Scotland, Wales and the North-East and two based on the central areas of the Midlands and Yorkshire. All five businesses were sold, the three businesses in England being sold to a single purchaser as one company. Coal production in the UK is now undertaken entirely in the private sector.

SUPPLY AND DEMAND

The main domestic customer for coal is the electricity supply industry, but the latter's demand for coal has declined as it turns increasingly to alternative fuels. National Power has announced that it expects to close ten of its 18 coal-fired power stations by 2000.

Supply 1994	million tonnes
Production of deep-mined coal	31.1
Production of opencast coal	16.6
Recovered slurry, fines, etc.	0.3
Imports	15.0
Change in colliery stocks	−4.2
Change in stocks at opencast sites	−0.5
Total supply	67.7

Home consumption 1994	
Electricity supply industry	62.4
Coke ovens	8.6
Low temperature carbonization plants	0.5
Manufactured fuel plants	0.7
Railways	—
Collieries	—
Industry	4.9
Domestic	3.9
Public services	0.5
Miscellaneous	0.2
Total home consumption	81.7
Overseas shipments and bunkers	1.0
Total consumption and shipments	82.7
*Change in distributed stocks	−14.6
†Balance	0.4

*Stock change excludes industrial and domestic stocks
†This is the balance between supply and consumption, shipments and changes in known distributed stocks
Source: HMSO – *Annual Abstract of Statistics 1996*

THE GAS INDUSTRY

The gas industry in the United Kingdom was nationalized in 1949 under the Gas Act 1948, and operated as the Gas Council. The Gas Act 1972 replaced the Gas Council with the British Gas Corporation and led to greater centralization of the industry. The British Gas Corporation was privatized in 1986 as British Gas PLC and is currently the main supplier of gas in Great Britain. The Office of Gas Supply (*see* page 302) is the regulatory body for the gas industry.

In 1993 the Monopolies and Mergers Commission found that British Gas's integrated business in Great Britain as a gas trader and the owner of the gas transportation system could be expected to operate against the public interest, and it recommended that the company divest itself of its gas trading activities in Great Britain. The President of the Board of Trade subsequently announced that competition would be introduced into the domestic gas supply market, and that British Gas should separate fully its supply and transportation operations; it would not, however, be required to divest itself of its supply business. Competition is now being introduced into the domestic gas market. The first tranche took place in April 1996 when a pilot project involving 500,000 customers in Cornwall, Devon and Wales was implemented. The second tranche will commence in April 1997, when competition will be extended to cover two million customers in the south of England. In April 1998 competition will be extended to cover all customers in Great Britain.

FUEL INPUT AND GAS OUTPUT: GAS SALES 1994

Fuel input to gas industry	GWh
Petroleum (*million tonnes*)	—
*Petroleum gases	52
Natural gas	—
Coke oven gas	—
Total to gas works	—
Natural gas for direct supply	729,374
Total fuel input	729,426

Gas output and sales	
Gas output:	
Town gas	30
Natural gas supplied direct	729,374
Gross total available	729,404
Own use	−2,743
†Statistical difference	−20,444
Total sales	706,217

*Butane, propane, ethane and refinery tail gases
†Supply greater than recorded demand (−). Includes losses in distribution
Source: HMSO – *Annual Abstract of Statistics 1996*

NATURAL GAS CONSUMPTION 1995p

	GWh
Domestic	326,010
Electricity generators	145,455
Iron and steel industry	20,581
Other industries	152,896
Other	109,585
Total	754,527

p provisional
Source: Department of Trade and Industry

BRITISH GAS

The principal business of British Gas PLC is the purchase, transmission and sale of natural gas to domestic, industrial and commercial customers in Great Britain. It is increasingly seeking to exploit overseas markets. British Gas has hydrocarbon exploration and production operations offshore and onshore, both in Great Britain and overseas, and it has an interest in gas-related activities world-wide.

British Gas is divided into three parts: the UK Gas Business, Exploration and Production, and International Downstream. In 1994 it restructured its UK operations to separate its gas supply business from its gas transportation business. Its regional structure was abolished and has been replaced by four business units: TransCo, which provides transportation and storage services to shippers; British Gas Trading, which sells gas to domestic, industrial and commercial customers; Retail, which markets gas and other appliances through a national chain of shops; and Service, which handles the servicing and installation of gas central heating and other equipment. British Gas has announced plans to demerge; final proposals will be tabled in 1997.

BRITISH GAS PLC, The Adelphi, 1–11 John Adam Street, London WC2N 6HT. Tel: 0171-321 2880. *Chairman and Chief Executive*, R. V. Giordano

BRITISH GAS FINANCE
£ million

	1994	1995
Turnover		
TransCo	3,103	3,126
Trading	8,238	7,604
Exploration and production	1,161	1,268
Other activities	480	821
†Overseas gas supply	669	—
Less: intra-group sales	(3,953)	(4,218)
Total	9,698	8,601
Operating costs include:		
Raw materials and consumables	3,397	2,955
Employee costs	1,691	1,492
Exceptional costs	195	394
Current cost depreciation	1,365	1,275
Total	8,711	8,018
Current cost profit on ordinary activities	1,020	590
Gearing adjustment	67	92
Net interest payable	(184)	(92)
Current cost profit before tax	918	607
Current cost profit after tax	414	136
Minority shareholders' interest	(4)	(6)
Current cost profit attributable to British Gas shareholders	410	130
Dividends	(631)	(637)
Transfer from reserves	(221)	(507)

1994 restated on an estimated basis
†Discontinued June 1994

SUPPLY AND TRANSMISSION

British Gas obtains natural gas from fields on mainland Britain, in coastal waters and in the North Sea. It also imports gas from other countries. In 1994 total production of gas by British Gas from UK continental shelf fields was 450 billion cubic feet; in 1995 total production was 429 billion cubic feet.

The mainland national transmission system is operated by British Gas, with other gas suppliers entering contracts to use the system. British Gas operates six reception terminals. The length of mains in use in 1995 was 269,600

km: 251,700 km of distribution mains and 17,900 km of transmission mains.

THE ELECTRICITY INDUSTRY

Under the Electricity Act 1989 twelve regional public electricity supply companies were formed from the twelve area electricity boards in England and Wales; the companies were floated on the stock market in 1990. Four companies were formed from the Central Electricity Generating Board: three generating companies (National Power PLC, Nuclear Electric PLC and PowerGen PLC) and the National Grid Company PLC. National Power PLC and PowerGen PLC were floated on the stock market in 1991, the Government retaining a 40 per cent holding in both companies. In 1995 a second flotation took place when the Government sold its remaining 40 per cent holding in the two companies. Shares in the National Grid Company PLC were demerged from the regional electricity companies and floated on the stock market in December 1995.

In Scotland, three new companies were formed: Scottish Power PLC, Scottish Hydro-Electric PLC and Scottish Nuclear Ltd. Flotation of Scottish Power PLC and Scottish Hydro-Electric PLC on the stock market took place in 1991.

Two new companies, British Energy PLC and Magnox Electric PLC, were formed from the combined assets of Scottish Nuclear Ltd and Nuclear Electric PLC in April 1996. British Energy PLC is due to be floated on the stock market in the summer of 1996; Magnox Electric is to remain in public ownership.

In Northern Ireland, Northern Ireland Electricity PLC was set up in 1993 under a 1991 Order in Council. It has been floated on the stock market.

A trade and representational organization, the Electricity Association, was created by the newly formed electricity companies; its principal subsidiaries were Electricity Association Services Ltd (for representational and professional services) and Electricity Association Technology Ltd (for distribution and utilization research, development and technology transfer). Electricity Association Technology Ltd (now renamed EA Technology Ltd) left the Electricity Association group of companies in 1993.

The Offices of Electricity Regulation (*see* page 296) are the regulatory bodies for the industry.

Competition is to be introduced into the domestic electricity market on 1 April 1998.

ELECTRICITY ASSOCIATION SERVICES LTD, 30 Millbank, London SW1P 4RD. Tel: 0171-963 5700. *Chief Executive*, P. E. G. Daubeney

EA TECHNOLOGY LTD, Capenhurst, Chester CH1 6ES. Tel: 0151-339 4181. *Managing Director*, Dr S. F. Exell

SUPPLY COMPANIES

BRITISH ENERGY PLC, 10 Lochside Place, Edinburgh EH12 9DF. Tel: 0131-527 2000. *Chief Executive*, Dr R. Hawley

MAGNOX ELECTRIC PLC, Berkeley Centre, Berkeley, Glos GL13 9PB. Tel: 01453-810451. *Chief Executive*, R. Hall

THE NATIONAL GRID COMPANY PLC, National Grid House, Kirby Corner Road, Coventry CV4 8JY. Tel: 01203-537777. *Chief Executive*, D. Jones

NATIONAL POWER PLC, Windmill Hill Business Park, Whitehill Way, Swindon, Wilts SN5 9NX. Tel: 01793-877777. *Chief Executive*, E. Wallis

POWERGEN PLC, 53 New Broad Street, London EC2M 1JJ. Tel: 0171-638 5742. *Chief Executive*, E. Wallis

REGIONAL ELECTRICITY COMPANIES

EASTERN ELECTRICITY PLC, PO Box 40, Wherstead, Ipswich IP2 9AQ

EAST MIDLANDS ELECTRICITY PLC, PO Box 444, Wollaton, Nottingham NG8 IEZ

LONDON ELECTRICITY PLC, Templar House, 81–87 High Holborn, London WCIV 6NU

MANWEB PLC, Sealand Road, Chester CHI 4LR

MIDLANDS ELECTRICITY PLC, Mucklow Hill, Halesowen, W. Midlands B62 8BP

NORTHERN ELECTRIC PLC, Carliol House, Newcastle upon Tyne NE99 ISE

NORWEB PLC, Talbot Road, Manchester MI6 OMQ

SEEBOARD PLC, Forest Gate, Brighton Road, Crawley, W. Sussex RHII 9BH

SOUTHERN ELECTRIC PLC, Littlewick Green, Maidenhead, Berks SL6 3QB

SWALEC PLC, St Mellons, Cardiff CF3 9XW

SOUTH WESTERN ELECTRICITY PLC, 800 Park Avenue, Aztec West, Almondsbury, Avon BS12 4SE

YORKSHIRE ELECTRICITY GROUP PLC, Scarcroft, Leeds LS14 3HS

SCOTTISH COMPANIES

SCOTTISH HYDRO-ELECTRIC PLC, 16 Rothesay Terrace, Edinburgh EH3 7SE. Tel: 0131-225 1361. *Chief Executive*, R. Young

SCOTTISH POWER PLC, 1 Atlantic Quay, Glasgow G2 8SP. Tel: 0141-248 8200. *Chief Executive*, I. Robinson

NORTHERN IRELAND

NORTHERN IRELAND ELECTRICITY PLC, PO Box 2, Danesfort, 120 Malone Road, Belfast BT9 5HT. Tel: 01232-661100. *Chief Executive*, Dr P. Haren

GENERATION, SUPPLY AND CONSUMPTION
gigawatt-hours

	1993	1994
Electricity generated		
Major power producers: total	300,514	302,807
Conventional steam stations	187,786	175,362
Nuclear stations	84,433	83,944
Gas turbines and oil engines	359	244
Combined cycle gas turbine stations	22,811	36,971
Hydro-electric stations:		
Natural flow	3,522	4,317
Pumped storage	1,437	1,463
Renewables other than hydro	165	506
Electricity used on works: total	19,287	17,504
Major generating companies	17,391	15,921
Other generators	1,896	1,583
Electricity supplied (gross)		
Major power producers: total	283,123	286,886
Conventional steam stations	178,312	167,289
Nuclear stations	76,839	76,412
Gas turbines and oil engines	324	233
Combined cycle gas turbine stations	22,611	36,815
Hydro-electric stations:		
Natural flow	3,513	4,265
Pumped storage	1,388	1,417
Renewables other than hydro	136	455
Electricity used in pumping		
Major power producers	1,948	2,051

Electricity supplied (net): total	301,845	305,828
Major power producers	281,175	284,835
Other generators	20,670	20,993
Net imports	16,721	16,887
Electricity available	318,561	322,715
Losses in transmission, etc	22,815	26,520
Electricity consumption: total	295,746	296,195
Fuel industries	9,615	7,669
Final users: total	286,130	288,527
Industrial sector	96,842	97,855
Domestic sector	100,456	100,644
Other sectors	88,833	90,028

Source: HMSO – *Annual Abstract of Statistics 1996*

Transport

GOODS TRANSPORT 1994

TOTAL TONNE KILOMETRES (*millions*)	220,800
Road	143,700
Rail (British Rail only)	13,300
Water: coastwise oil products*	28,700
Water: other*	23,500
Pipelines (except gases)	11,600
TOTAL (*million tonnes*)	2,051
Road	1,689
Rail (British Rail only)	97
Water: coastwise oil products*	43
Water: other*	97
Pipelines (except gases)	125

*'Coastwise' includes all sea traffic within the UK, Isle of Man and Channel Islands. 'Other' means other coastwise plus inland water-way traffic and one-port traffic
Source: HMSO – *Annual Abstract of Statistics 1996*

PASSENGER TRANSPORT 1994p
Million passenger kilometres (estimated)

TOTAL	689,000
Air	5,000
Rail*	35,000
Road: Public service vehicles	43,000
Cars, vans and taxis	596,000
Motorcycles	4,000
Pedal cycles	5,000

p provisional
* Including London Regional Transport and Passenger Transport Executive railway systems
Source: HMSO – *Annual Abstract of Statistics 1996*

AIR PASSENGERS 1995*

ALL UK AIRPORTS: TOTAL	131,100,157
LONDON AREA AIRPORTS: TOTAL	83,330,537
Battersea Heliport	4,022
Gatwick	22,550,131
Heathrow	54,469,173
London City	553,989
Luton	1,829,205
Southend	4,210
Stansted	3,919,827
OTHER UK AIRPORTS: TOTAL	47,769,600
Aberdeen	2,255,557
Barra	7,665
Barrow-in-Furness	344
Belfast City	1,283,500
Belfast International	2,374,506
Benbecula	38,942
Biggin Hill	5,259
Birmingham	5,328,469
Blackpool	75,961
Bournemouth	103,388
Bristol	1,468,123
Cambridge	33,004
Cardiff	1,068,582
Carlisle	1,514
Coventry	3,523
Dundee	16,397
East Midlands	1,891,215
Edinburgh	3,384,432
Exeter	191,101
Glasgow	5,528,771
Gloucestershire	2,763
Hawarden	46
Humberside	289,348
Inverness	285,221
Islay	20,400
Isle of Man	561,235
Isles of Scilly–St Mary's	119,110
–Tresco	24,094
Kent International	2,621
Kirkwall	104,994
Leeds/Bradford	931,697
Lerwick (Tingwall)	4,411
Liverpool	505,786
Londonderry	64,897
Lydd	258
Manchester	14,750,949
Newcastle	2,527,503
Norwich	258,470
Penzance Heliport	90,462
Plymouth	106,182
Prestwick	330,691
Scatsta	14,623
Shoreham	2,398
Southampton	519,841
Stornoway	95,733
Sumburgh	505,407
Teesside	462,127
Tiree	5,602
Unst	74,505
Wick	47,973
CHANNEL IS. AIRPORTS: TOTAL	2,569,589
Alderney	85,472
Guernsey	833,464
Jersey	1,650,653

*Total terminal, transit, scheduled and charter passengers
Source: Civil Aviation Authority

AERODROMES/AIRPORTS

The following aerodromes in the UK, the Isle of Man and the Channel Islands are either state owned or licensed for use by civil aircraft. A number of unlicensed aerodromes not included in this list are also available for private use by special permission. Aerodromes designated as Customs airports are printed in small capitals. Customs facilities are available at certain other aerodromes by special arrangement.

BAA   Owned by BAA PLC
H   Licensed for helicopters
HIAL Operated by Highland and
        Islands Airports Ltd
L   Owned by municipal
        authority
M   Military aerodromes – civil
        availability by prior
        permission
P   Private ownership
S   Government owned and
        operated

ENGLAND AND WALES
Aberporth, Dyfed   M
Andrewsfield, Essex
Barrow (Walney Island), Cumbria
Bembridge, IOW
Benson, Oxon   M
Beverley/Linley Hill,
   N. Humberside
BIGGIN HILL, Kent   P
BIRMINGHAM   P
Blackbushe, Hants
BLACKPOOL, Lancs   P
Bodmin, Cornwall
Boscombe Down, Wilts   M
Bourn, Cambridge
BOURNEMOUTH, Dorset   P
BRISTOL   P
Brize Norton, Oxford   M
Brough, N. Humberside
Caernarfon, Gwynedd
CAMBRIDGE   P
CARDIFF   P
Carlisle, Cumbria   L
Chichester (Goodwood), Sussex
Chivenor, Devon   M
Church Fenton, N. Yorks   M
Clacton, Essex
Compton Abbas, Dorset
Cosford, Wolverhampton   M
COVENTRY, W. Midlands   L
Cranfield, Beds
Cranwell, Lincs   M
Crowfield, Suffolk
Culdrose, Cornwall   M
Denham, Bucks
Derby
Dishforth, N. Yorks   M
Dunkeswell, Devon
Dunsfold, Surrey   L
Duxford, Cambs   L
Eaglescott, Devon
Earls Colne, Halstead

EAST MIDLANDS, Derbys   P
Elstree, Herts
EXETER, Devon
Fairoaks, Surrey
Farnborough, Hants   S
Fenland, Lincs
Filton, Bristol
Finningley, S. Yorks   M
Fowlmere, Cambs
Full Sutton, N. Yorks
Gloucestershire (Staverton)   P
Great Yarmouth (North Denes),
   Norfolk   H
Halfpenny Green, Staffs
Halton, Bucks   M
Haverfordwest, Dyfed   L
Hawarden, Clywd
Hucknall, Notts
HUMBERSIDE   P
Ipswich, Suffolk
Isle of Wight/Sandown
Land's End (St Just), Cornwall
Lashenden, Headcorn, Kent
LEEDS/BRADFORD   P
Lee-on-Solent, Hants   M
Leicester
Linton-on-Ouse, Yorks   M
Little Gransden, Beds
LIVERPOOL   P
Llanbedr, Gwynedd   M
LONDON/CITY
LONDON/GATWICK   BAA
LONDON/HEATHROW   BAA
LONDON/LUTON   P
LONDON/STANSTED   BAA
London/Westland Heliport   H
LYDD, Kent
Lyneham, Wilts   M
MANCHESTER   P
Manchester (Barton)
MANSTON/KENT
   INTERNATIONAL   M
Mona, Gwynedd   M
Netherthorpe, S. Yorks
NEWCASTLE UPON TYNE   P
Newton, Notts   M
Northampton (Sywell)
Northolt, Middx   M
NORWICH, Norfolk   L
Nottingham
Old Sarum, Wilts
Oxford (Kidlington)
Penzance, Cornwall   H
Perranporth, Cornwall
Peterborough (Conington)
Peterborough (Sibson)
PLYMOUTH (ROBOROUGH), Devon
Portland Naval, Dorset   MH
Redhill, Surrey
Retford/Gamston, Notts
Rochester, Kent
St Mawgan, Cornwall   M
Sandtoft, Humberside
Scilly Isles (St Mary's)   L
Seething, Norfolk
Shawbury, Shropshire   M
Sherburn-in-Elmet, N. Yorks
Shipdham, Norfolk
Shobdon, Herefordshire
SHOREHAM, W. Sussex   P
Silverstone, Northants

Sleap, Shropshire
SOUTHAMPTON   P
SOUTHEND, Essex   P
Stapleford, Essex
Sturgate, Lincs
Swansea   L
TEESSIDE   P
Thruxton, Hants
Tresco, Isles of Scilly   H
Turweston, Northants
Valley, Gwynedd   M
Warton, Lancs
Wattisham, Suffolk   M
Wellesbourne Mountford, Warwick
Welshpool, Powys
Weston, Avon   H
White Waltham, Berks
Wickenby, Lincs
Woodford, Gtr Manchester
Woodvale, Merseyside   M
Wycombe Air Park (Booker), Bucks
Yeovil, Somerset
Yeovilton, Somerset   M

SCOTLAND
ABERDEEN (DYCE)   BAA
Barra, Hebrides
Benbecula, Hebrides   HIAL
Campbeltown   HIAL
Cumbernauld, Strathclyde
Dundee   L
Eday, Orkneys   L
EDINBURGH   BAA
Fair Isle, Shetlands
Fife   L
Flotta, Orkneys
GLASGOW   BAA
Inverness (Dalcross)   HIAL
Islay (Port Ellen), Hebrides   HIAL
Kirkwall, Orkneys   HIAL
Lerwick (Tingwall), Shetlands   L
Leuchars, Fife   M
North Ronaldsay, Orkneys   L
Papa Westray, Orkneys   L
Perth (Scone)
PRESTWICK, Ayrshire   BAA
Sanday, Orkneys   L
Scatsta, Shetlands
Stornoway, Hebrides   HIAL
Stronsay, Orkneys   L
SUMBURGH, Shetlands   HIAL
Tiree, Hebrides   HIAL
Unst, Shetlands   L
West Freugh, Dumfries   S
Westray, Orkneys   L
Whalsay, Shetlands
Wick, Caithness   HIAL

NORTHERN IRELAND
BELFAST (ALDERGROVE)
Belfast (City)
Enniskillen (St Angelo), Co.
   Fermanagh   P
Londonderry (Eglinton)   L
Newtownards, Co. Down

ISLANDS
ALDERNEY, CI   S
GUERNSEY, CI   S
ISLE OF MAN   S
JERSEY, CI   S

RAILWAYS

Britain pioneered railways and a railway network was developed across Britain by private companies in the course of the 19th century. In 1948 the main railway companies were nationalized and were run by a public authority, the British Transport Commission. The Commission was replaced by the British Railways Board in 1963. On 1 April 1994 the British Railways Board ceased to be responsible for the provision of rail services in Britain but continues as operator (under the operating name British Rail) of all train services until they are sold or franchised to the private sector.

Prior to privatization, management of the railways had been organized into the business sectors of InterCity, Network SouthEast, Regional Railways, Trainload Freight and Railfreight Distribution. These businesses have ceased to exist corporately but the names will continue to be used for trading purposes in the short term. European Passenger Services Ltd was set up to manage international passenger rail services through the Channel Tunnel and ownership was transferred to the Government in May 1994.

PRIVATIZATION

Since 1 April 1994, ownership of track and land has been vested in a new company, Railtrack, which was floated on the Stock Exchange in May 1996. Railtrack manages the track and charges for access to it and is responsible for signalling and timetabling. It does not operate train services. It owns the freehold of stations, but station management is being privatized under management contract or lease arrangements. Initially, Railtrack's infrastructure support functions were provided by 20 British Rail service companies; these companies have now been sold into the private sector. Railtrack will invest in infrastructure principally using finance raised by track charges, and will take investment decisions in consultation with rail operators.

Passenger services have been divided into 25 train-operating units, which are gradually being franchised to private sector operators. The private sector will eventually also be able to run completely new services with a right of open access to the track. The Government will continue to subsidize loss-making but socially necessary rail services. The franchising director is responsible for awarding franchises by competitive tendering, monitoring the performance of the franchisees, and allocating and administering government subsidy payments.

British Rail's passenger rolling stock has been divided between three subsidiary companies which will lease rolling stock to franchisees. The three companies were transferred to government ownership in July 1995 and were sold to the private sector in February 1996. The bulk freight haulage companies and Rail Express Systems, which carries Royal Mail traffic, have been sold to English, Welsh and Scottish Railways. The European business of Railfreight Distribution will be privatized when the Channel Tunnel freight services have been developed. The domestic and deep-sea container business (Freightliner) was sold in May 1996. British Rail's technical support and specialist function businesses are also being sold.

The independent Rail Regulator is responsible for the licensing of new railway operators, approving access agreements, promoting the use and development of the network, and protecting the interests of rail users.

BRITISH RAILWAYS BOARD, see page 286

RAILTRACK, 40 Bernard Street, London WC1N 1BY. Tel: 0171-344 7100. *Chairman*, R. Horton. *Chief Executive*, J. Edmonds, CBE
OFFICE OF PASSENGER RAIL FRANCHISING (OPRAF), Golding's House, 2 Hay's Lane, London SE1 2HB. Tel: 0171-940 4200. *Franchising Director*, J. O'Brien
OFFICE OF THE RAIL REGULATOR (ORR), 1 Waterhouse Square, Holborn Bars, 138–142 Holborn, London EC1N 2SU. Tel: 0171-282 2000. *Rail Regulator*, J. Swift

RAIL OPERATIONS

At 31 March 1996, Railtrack had about 20,000 miles of standard gauge lines and sidings in use, representing over 10,000 miles of route of which about 3,000 miles were electrified. Standard rail on main line has a weight of 110 lb per yard.

Loaded train miles run in passenger service totalled 231.3 million. Passenger journeys made during the year totalled 718.7 million, including 325.6 million made by holders of season tickets. The average distance of each passenger journey on ordinary fare was 34.1 miles; and on season ticket, 14.5 miles. Passenger stations in use in 1996 numbered 2,514. Train miles run in freight service totalled 24.5 million.

On 31 March 1996 British Rail employed 63,982 staff (94,344 at 31 March 1995). Including subsidiaries, the group total at 31 March 1996 was 64,259 (100,264 at 31 March 1995).

FINANCIAL RESULTS

Railtrack

In 1994–5 Railtrack showed an operating profit of £305 million and a pre-tax profit of £189 million.

	£ million
Income	
Passenger	1,955
Freight	191
Property rental	82
Other	47
Total	2,275
Costs	
Production and management	501
Infrastructure maintenance	696
Asset maintenance plan charge	483
Joint industry costs	197
Depreciation	93
Total	1,970

British Rail

British Rail's profit and loss account for 1995–6 showed a profit of £58 million after interest and extraordinary items, compared with a profit of £362 million in 1994–5. The railway operating surplus was £13.7 million (including a write-off of £500 million against Channel Tunnel freight services) compared with a surplus of £571 million for the previous year.

	£ million
*Income	
Passenger	4,394
Freight and Parcels	444
Railfreight Distribution	47
Others	164
Infrastructure services	1,019
Group Services	317
Total	6,385

Operating expenditure

Staff costs	1,919
Railtrack access charges	2,155
Rolling stock leasing	487
Materials, supplies and services	1,162
Depreciation	102
Amortization of deferred grant	(27)
Own work capitalized	(1)
Total	5,797

Operating profit	588
Profit on disposals	176
Restructuring costs	(51)
Exceptional items	(575)
Profit before interest	138
Interest	(80)
Group profit	58

*Income includes government grants totalling £2,010 million

ACCIDENTS ON RAILWAYS

	1993–4	1994–5
Train accidents: total	977	907
Persons killed: total	6	12
Passengers	0	3
Railway staff	0	5
Others	6	4
Persons injured: total	246	296
Passengers	134	190
Railway staff	95	83
Others	17	23
Other accidents through movement of railway vehicles		
Persons killed	26	27
Persons injured	2,373	2,417
Other accidents on railway premises		
Persons killed	9	3
Persons injured	8,244	7,933
Trespassers and suicides		
Persons killed	253	254
Persons injured	97	85

THE CHANNEL TUNNEL

The earliest recorded scheme for a submarine transport connection between Britain and France was in 1802. Tunnelling has begun simultaneously on both sides of the Channel three times: in 1881, in the early 1970s, and on 1 December 1987, when construction workers began to bore the first of the three tunnels which form the current project. They 'holed through' the first tunnel (the service tunnel) on 1 December 1990 and tunnelling was completed in June 1991. The tunnel was officially inaugurated by The Queen and President Mitterrand of France on 6 May 1994.

In January 1986 the concession for construction and operation of the tunnel and its services was awarded to a paired Anglo-French private-sector company, CTG-FM, wholly owned by Eurotunnel. Eurotunnel's costs from establishment in 1986 to the first commercial service in 1994 were about £8,700 million. The funds available to Eurotunnel amount to £10,535 million, raised through equity and loans. Eurotunnel expect to achieve cash-flow break-even in 1998. On 14 September 1995 Eurotunnel suspended interest payments on its 'junior' debt (i.e. all money raised before a rights issue in 1994) in line with its credit agreement. This gives Eurotunnel up to March 1997 to discuss a restructuring of its finances with interested parties.

Passenger services (Eurostar) run from Waterloo station in London to Paris and Brussels. Connecting services from Edinburgh and Manchester via London began in 1995 and through services from these cities, not stopping in London, are scheduled to begin in September 1996. Vehicle shuttle services (Le Shuttle) operate between Folkestone and Calais.

The submarine link comprises three tunnels. There are two rail tunnels, each carrying trains in one direction, which measure 24.93 ft (7.6 m) in diameter. Between them lies a smaller service tunnel, measuring 15.75 ft (4.8 m) in diameter. The service tunnel is linked to the rail tunnels by 130 cross-passages for maintenance and safety purposes. The tunnels are 31 miles (50 km) long, 24 miles (38 km) of which is under the sea-bed at an average depth of 132 ft (40 m). The rail terminals are situated at Folkestone and Calais, and the tunnels go underground at Shakespeare Cliff, Dover, and Sangatte, west of Calais.

RAIL LINKS

The route for the British Channel Tunnel rail link was confirmed by the Government in 1994. The rail link will run from Folkestone to a proposed new terminal at St Pancras station, London, but at present services run into a terminal at Waterloo station, London.

Construction of the rail link will be financed by the private sector with a substantial government contribution. A private sector consortium, London and Continental Railways Ltd, will be responsible for the design, construction and ownership of the rail link, and has taken over Union Railways and European Passenger Services Ltd who will operate international services from London through the Channel tunnel. Construction is expected to be completed in 2003.

Infrastructure developments in France have been completed and high-speed trains run from Calais to Paris linking the Channel tunnel with the high-speed European network.

ROADS

Highway Authorities

The powers and responsibilities of highway authorities in England and Wales are set out in the Highways Acts 1980; for Scotland there is separate legislation.

Responsibility for trunk road motorways and other trunk roads in Great Britain rests in England with the Secretary of State for Transport, in Scotland with the Secretary of State for Scotland, and in Wales with the Secretary of State for Wales. The costs of construction, improvement and maintenance are paid for by central government. The highway authority for non-trunk roads in England, Wales and Scotland is, in general, the unitary authority, county council or London borough council in whose area the roads lie. In Northern Ireland the Department of the Environment for Northern Ireland is the statutory road authority responsible for public roads and their maintenance and construction; the Roads Service executive agency (*see* page 330) carries out these functions on behalf of the Department.

Finance

The Government contributes towards capital expenditure through Transport Supplementary Grant (TSG) in England and Transport Grant (TG) in Wales. Grant rates are determined by the respective Secretaries of State; at present, grant is paid at 50 per cent of expenditure accepted for grant in England and Wales.

In England TSG is paid towards capital spending on highways and the regulation of traffic; current expenditure is funded by revenue support grant (i.e. central government grants to local authorities for non-specific services). TSG is also paid towards capital spending on bridge assessment and strengthening; towards structural maintenance on the primary route network; and towards all principal 'A' roads. In Wales TG is paid towards capital expenditure only; current expenditure is funded by revenue support grant.

For the financial year 1996–7 local authorities in England will receive £236 million in TSG. Total estimated expenditure on building and maintaining motorways and trunk roads in England in 1995–6 was £1,785 million; estimated outturn for 1996–7 is £1,569 million.

For the financial year 1996–7 local authorities in Wales will receive up to £39 million in TG. Total expenditure on roads in Wales in 1994–5 was £298.4 million.

The Scottish Office receives a block vote from Parliament and the Secretary of State for Scotland determines how much is allocated towards roads. Total expenditure on building and maintaining trunk roads in Scotland was estimated at £234 million in 1995–6.

In Northern Ireland expenditure on roads in 1995–6 was estimated at £150 million, and estimated expenditure for 1996–7 is £153 million.

Private Finance

The Government is seeking to encourage greater involvement by the private sector in the design, finance, construction and operation of roads. A research programme is under way to assess the technology necessary for the introduction of electronic motorway tolls.

Road Building Programme

In 1995 the Government conducted a review of its programme of improving the motorway and trunk road network, resulting in the withdrawal in November 1995 of 77 schemes deemed to be unnecessary or environmentally unacceptable and the suspension of preparation work on 104 other schemes. In winter 1995, 35 schemes were under construction, 37 schemes were being taken forward as Design, Build, Finance and Operate (DBFO), i.e. privately-financed, schemes and a further 112 were being progressed under conventional funding arrangements.

Road Lengths (in miles) as at April 1995

	Total roads	Trunk roads (including motorways)	Motorways*
England	174,207	6,448	1,678
Wales	21,001	1,057	78
Scotland	32,698	1,950	179
N. Ireland	15,018	1,460†	69
UK	242,925	10,916	2,004

*There were in addition 27.3 miles of local authority motorway in England and 16.7 miles in Scotland
†'A' roads; there are no designated trunk roads in N. Ireland

Motorways

England and Wales:

M1	London to Yorkshire
M2	London to Faversham
M3	London to Southampton
M4	London to South Wales
M5	Birmingham to Exeter
M6	Catthorpe to Carlisle
M10	St Albans spur
M11	London to Cambridge
M18	Rotherham to Goole
M20	London to Folkestone
M23	London to Gatwick
M25	London orbital
M26	M20 to M25 spur
M27	Southampton bypass
M32	M4 to Bristol spur
M40	London to Birmingham
M41	London to West Cross
M42	South-west of Birmingham to Measham
M45	Dunchurch spur
M50	Ross spur
M53	Chester to Birkenhead
M54	M6 to Telford
M55	Preston to Blackpool
M56	Manchester to Chester
M57	Liverpool outer ring
M58	Liverpool to Wigan
M61	Manchester to Preston
M62	Liverpool to Hull
M63	Manchester southern ring road
M65	Calder Valley
M66	Manchester eastern ring road to Rochdale
M67	Manchester Hyde to Denton
M69	Coventry to Leicester
M180	South Humberside

Scotland:

M8	Edinburgh-Newhouse, Baillieston-West Ferry Interchange
M9	Edinburgh to Stirling
M73	Maryville to Mollisburn
M74	Glasgow-Paddy's Ridde Bridge, Cleughbrae-Gretna
M77	Ayr Road Route
M80	Stirling to Haggs/Glasgow (M8) to Stepps
M90	Inverkeithing to Perth
M876	Dennyloanhead (M80) to Kincardine Bridge

Northern Ireland:

M1	Belfast to Dungannon
M2	Belfast to Antrim
M3	Belfast Cross Harbour Bridge
M5	M2 to Greencastle
M12	M1 to Craigavon
M22	Antrim to Randalstown

ROAD USE

Estimated Traffic on all Roads (Great Britain) 1995

Million vehicle kilometres

All motor vehicles	430,900
Cars and taxis	353,200
Two-wheeled motor vehicles	4,100
Buses and coaches	4,700
Light vans	39,100
Other goods vehicles	29,800
Total goods vehicles	68,900
Pedal cycles	4,500

Source: Department of Transport

Buses and Coaches (Great Britain) 1994–5

Number of vehicles (31 March 1995)	75,300
Vehicle kilometres (millions)	4,106
Local bus passenger journeys (millions)	4,420
Passenger receipts (£ million)	3,335

Road Goods Transport (Great Britain) 1995

Analysis by mode of working and by gross weight of vehicle

Estimated tonne kilometres (thousand million)	143.7
Own account	37.2
Public haulage	106.5
By gross weight of vehicle (billion tonne kilometres)	
Not over 25 tonnes	24.7
Over 25 tonnes	119.0
Estimated tonnes carried (millions)	1,609.0
Own account	622.0
Public haulage	987.0
By gross weight of vehicle (million tonnes)	
Not over 25 tonnes	467.0
Over 25 tonnes	1,142.0

Source: Department of Transport

Road Accidents 1995

Road accidents	230,376
Vehicles involved:	
Pedal cycles	25,462
Motor vehicles	388,603
Total casualties	310,506
Pedestrians	47,029
Vehicle users	263,477
Killed*	3,621
Pedestrians	1,038
Pedal cycles	213
All two-wheeled motor vehicles	445
Cars and taxis	1,749
Others	176

*Died within 30 days of accident

	Killed	Injured
1965	7,952	389,986
1970	7,499	355,869
1975	6,366	318,584
1980	6,010	323,000
1985	5,165	312,359
1990	5,217	335,924
1993	3,814	302,206
1994	3,650	311,539
1995	3,621	306,885

DRIVING LICENCES

It is necessary to hold a valid full licence in order to drive on public roads in the UK. Learner drivers obtain a provisional driving licence before starting to learn to drive and must then pass a test to obtain a full driving licence. There are separate tests for driving motor cycles, cars, passenger-carrying vehicles (PCVs) and large goods vehicles (LGVs). Drivers must hold full car entitlement before they can apply for PCV or LGV entitlements. In 1996, 36.4 million people in the UK held a valid driving licence (full or provisional). The minimum age for driving motor cars, light goods vehicles up to 3.5 tonnes and motor cycles is 17 (moped, 16).

The Driver and Vehicle Licensing Agency is responsible for issuing driving licences, registering and licensing vehicles, and collecting excise duty in Great Britain. In Northern Ireland the Driver and Vehicle Licensing Agency (Northern Ireland) has similar responsibilities.

Driving Licence Fees *since October 1994*

First provisional licence	£21.00
Changing a provisional to a full licence after passing a driving test	free
Renewal of licence	£6.00
Renewal of licence including PCV or LGV entitlements	£21
Medical renewal	free
Medical renewal (over 70)	£6.00
Duplicate Licence	£6.00
Exchange Licence	£6.00
Removing endorsements	£6.00
New licence after a period of disqualification	£12.00
New licence after disqualification for some drinking and driving offences	£20

Driving Tests

The Driving Standards Agency is responsible for carrying out driving tests and approving driving instructors in Great Britain. In Northern Ireland the Driver and Vehicle Testing Agency (Northern Ireland) is responsible for testing drivers and vehicles.

About 1.6 million car driving tests were conducted in Great Britain in 1995–6 of which 45.7 per cent resulted in a pass. In addition over 80,000 lorry and bus tests were undertaken, of which 48 per cent were successful. Over 108,000 motorcycle tests were undertaken, of which 70.1 per cent were successful.

*Driving Test Fees (weekday rate/evening and Saturday rate)

For cars	£28.50/£38.50
†For motor cycles	£36/£47.50
For lorries, buses	£62/£80
For invalid carriages	free

*Since 1 July 1996 most candidates for car and motor cycle tests have also been required to take a written driving theory test, for which there is a separate fee of £15. Theory tests for lorry and bus drivers will be introduced on 1 January 1997

†Almost all motor cyclists are required to have completed Compulsory Basic Training, organized by DSA-approved training bodies. Prices vary. The exemption from CBT for full car licence holders will end on 1 January 1997

An extended driving test was introduced in 1992 for those convicted of dangerous driving. The fee is £57/£77.50 (car) or £72/£92 (motorcycle)

MOTOR VEHICLES

Vehicles must be licensed before they can be driven on public roads. They must also be approved as roadworthy by the Vehicle Certification Agency. The Vehicle Inspectorate carries out annual testing and inspection of goods vehicles, buses and coaches.

The number of vehicles with current licences in 1995 was:

	Britain	N. Ireland
Private and light goods	23,000,000	523,000
Motor cycles, scooters, mopeds	603,000	9,000
Public transport vehicles	82,000	2,000
Heavy goods vehicles	410,000	16,000
Agricultural tractors	317,000	2,000
Others	45,000	11,000
Total	25,679,000	612,000

These totals include 1,094,000 vehicles exempt from licensing.

Vehicle Licences

Since 1974 registration and first licensing of vehicles has been through local offices (known as Vehicle Registration Offices) of the Department of Transport's Driver and Vehicle Licensing Centre in Swansea. The records of existing vehicles are held at Swansea. Local facilities for relicensing are available as follows:

(i) with a licence reminder (form V11) in person at any post office which deals with vehicle licensing, or post it to the post office shown on the form

(ii) with a vehicle licence renewal (form V10). Applicants may normally apply in person at any licensing post office. They will need to take their vehicle registration document; if this is not available the applicant must complete form V62 which is held at post offices. Postal applications can be made to the post offices shown on form V100, available at any post office. This form also provides guidance on registering and licensing vehicles.

Details of the present duties chargeable on motor vehicles are available at post offices and Vehicle Registration Offices. The Vehicle Excise and Registration Act 1994 provides *inter alia* that any vehicle kept on a public road but not used on roads is chargeable to excise duty as if it were in use. All non-commercial vehicles over 25 years old are exempt from vehicle excise duty.

Vehicle Excise Duty Rates *since 1 July 1995*

	12 months £	6 months £
Motor Cars		
Light vans, cars, taxis, etc.	140.00	77.00
Motor Cycles		
With or without sidecar, not over 150 cc	15.00	—
With or without sidecar, 150–250 cc	35.00	—
Electric motorcycles (including tricycles)	15.00	—
Others	55.00	30.25
Tricycles *(not over 450 kg)*		
Not over 150 cc	15.00	—
Others	55.00	30.25
Buses		
Seating 9–16 persons	150.00	82.50
Seating 17–35 persons	200.00	110.00
Seating 36–60 persons	300.00	165.00
Seating over 60 persons	450.00	247.50

MoT Testing

Cars, motor cycles, motor caravans, light goods and dual-purpose vehicles more than three years old must be covered by a current MoT test certificate. The certificate must be renewed annually. Copies of the legislation governing MoT testing can be obtained from any bookshop which stocks HMSO publications. The legislation comprises the Road Traffic Act 1988 (Sections 45 and 46), the Motor Vehicles (Test) Regulations 1981, and subsequent amendments. The MoT testing scheme is administered by the Vehicle Inspectorate.

A fee is payable to MoT testing stations, which must be authorized to carry out tests. The maximum fees, which are prescribed by regulations, are:

For cars and light vans	£28.66
For solo motor cycles	£11.90
For motor cycle combinations	£20.00
For three-wheeled vehicles	£23.40
For non-public service vehicle buses	£35.12
For light goods vehicles	£28.66
For goods vehicles	£30.68

SHIPPING

PRINCIPAL MERCHANT FLEETS 1995

Flag	No	Gross tonnage
Panama	5,777	71,921,698
Liberia	1,666	59,800,742
Greece	1,863	29,434,695
Cyprus	1,674	24,652,547
Bahamas	1,176	23,602,812
Japan	9,438	19,913,211
Norway (NIS)	700	18,902,880
Malta	1,164	17,678,303
China	2,948	16,943,220
Russia	5,160	15,202,349
Singapore	1,344	13,610,818
*United States of America	5,292	12,760,810
Hong Kong	399	8,794,766
Philippines	1,524	8,743,769
India	916	7,126,850
Korea (South)	2,246	6,972,148
Italy	1,397	6,699,484
Turkey	1,075	6,267,629
Saint Vincent	1,029	6,164,878
Taiwan	683	6,104,294
Germany	1,146	5,626,178
Denmark (DIS)	450	5,119,877
Brazil	551	5,076,695
Ukraine	1,142	4,613,003
United Kingdom	1,454	4,412,683
Netherlands	1,059	3,409,241
Malaysia	685	3,282,878
Marshall Islands	95	3,098,574
Bermuda	86	3,047,535
Sweden	621	2,955,425
Iran	424	2,902,431
Australia	627	2,853,061
Indonesia	2,196	2,770,513
Norway	1,515	2,648,030
Romania	421	2,536,421
Canada	886	2,401,047
Poland	516	2,358,043
Isle of Man	146	2,300,402
French Antarctic Territory	77	2,266,040
Kuwait	213	2,057,044
WORLD TOTAL	82,890	490,662,091

NIS   Norwegian International Ship Register – offshore registry
*Excluding ships of United States Reserve Fleet
DIS   Danish International Register of Shipping – offshore registry

Source: Lloyd's Register of Shipping

MERCHANT SHIPS COMPLETED 1995

Country of Build	No.	Gross tonnage
Japan	592	9,262,882
Korea (South)	158	6,264,282
Germany	91	1,120,991
Denmark	25	1,003,032
*China	64	783,688
Poland	39	523,650
Taiwan	16	488,083
Italy	19	395,360
Finland	8	316,606
France	13	253,991
Spain	41	250,743
Romania	18	229,321
Netherlands	76	205,181
*Ukraine	16	184,637
Croatia	7	178,626
Brazil	7	172,245
Norway	35	146,785
United Kingdom	22	125,775
Singapore	51	98,933
Bulgaria	7	91,598
*Russia	19	82,846
India	13	40,840
Turkey	12	30,506
Slovakia	13	29,856
Sweden	2	28,916
Other countries	169	157,528

For Registration in		
Panama	256	7,186,380
Liberia	71	3,804,849
Hong Kong	39	1,260,039
Philippines	31	819,842
Japan	296	796,653
Germany	61	742,393
China	49	679,636
Greece	20	641,015
Cyprus	33	537,732
Marshall Islands	9	481,513
Singapore	95	469,173
Malaysia	27	436,376
Denmark (DIS)	12	412,601
Bahamas	16	369,536
Taiwan	14	357,355
Norway (NIS)	15	351,101
Italy	16	310,739
United Kingdom	20	307,695
India	17	266,996
Norway	15	194,948
Malta	13	187,482
Netherlands	45	178,159
Antigua and Barbuda	29	169,684
French Antarctic Territory	6	155,132
Isle of Man	4	147,144
Other countries	324	1,202,728
WORLD TOTAL	1,533	22,466,901

*Information incomplete
DIS   Danish International Register of Shipping – offshore registry
NIS   Norwegian International Ship Register – offshore registry

Source: Lloyd's Register of Shipping

BRITISH-REGISTERED* TRADING VESSELS
of 500 Gross Tons and Over *as at end 1994*

Type of vessel	No.	Gross tonnage
Tankers[1]	113	2,481,000
Bulk carriers[2]	14	294,000
Specialized carriers[3]	13	110,000
Container (fully cellular)	34	1,236,000
Ro-Ro[4]	84	874,000
Other general cargo	93	212,000
Passenger[5]	9	281,000
Total	360	5,488,000

* Registered in the UK and British Crown dependencies
1 Includes oil, gas, chemical and other specialized tankers
2 Includes combination bulk carriers: ore/oil and ore bulk/oil carriers
3 Includes livestock, car and chemical carriers
4 Roll-on, roll-off passenger and cargo vessels
5 Cruise liner and other passenger vessels

Source: HMSO – *Annual Abstract of Statistics 1996*

SEAPORT TRAFFIC OF GREAT BRITAIN 1994
By Mode of Appearance

	Million gross tonnes
Foreign Traffic: *Imports*	184.9
Bulk fuel traffic	71.2
Other bulk traffic	46.2
Container and roll-on traffic	49.6
Semi-bulk traffic	16.6
Conventional traffic	1.4
Foreign Traffic: *Exports*	178.6
Bulk fuel traffic	112.1
Other bulk traffic	21.3
Container and roll-on traffic	38.8
Semi-bulk traffic	5.3
Conventional traffic	1.1
Domestic Traffic*	154.6
Bulk fuel traffic	105.1
Other bulk traffic	33.9
Container and roll-on traffic	10.5
Semi-bulk traffic	0.4
Conventional traffic	0.5
Non-oil traffic with UK offshore installations	4.1
Total Foreign and Domestic Traffic	518.1

Domestic traffic refers to traffic through the ports of Great Britain only, to all parts of the UK, Isle of Man and the Channel Islands. Traffic to and from offshore installations, landing of sea-dredged aggregates and material shipped for dumping at sea included

Source: HMSO – *Annual Abstract of Statistics 1996*

SEABORNE TRADE OF THE UK 1994p
Exports (Including Re-exports) Plus Imports by Sea

	Million tonnes	% *carried by* UK-registered vessels*
By weight		
All cargo	352.9	12
Dry bulk cargo	84.9	9
Other dry cargo	110.8	15
Tanker cargo	157.2	12
	£ *million*	
By value		
All cargo	2,178,800	25
Dry bulk cargo	74,800	9
Other dry cargo	1,970,800	28
Tanker cargo	133,200	12

p provisional
* Relates to trade with countries outside the EU
Source: HMSO – *Annual Abstract of Statistics 1996*

PASSENGER MOVEMENT BY SEA 1994

Arrivals plus departures at UK seaports by place of embarkation or landing

All passenger movements	37,038,000
Irish Republic	3,478,000
Belgium	2,878,000
France†	27,224,000
Netherlands	1,987,000
Other EU countries	896,000
Other European and Mediterranean countries‡	305,000
USA	31,100
Rest of the world	3,100
Pleasure cruises beginning and/or ending at UK seaports	236,000

* Passengers are included at both departure and arrival if their journeys begin and end at a UK seaport
† Includes hovercraft passengers
‡ Includes North Africa and Middle East Mediterranean countries

Source: HMSO – *Annual Abstract of Statistics 1996*

Communications

Postal Services

Responsibility for running postal services rests in the UK with a public authority, the Post Office (*see* page 334). The Secretary of State for Trade and Industry has powers to suspend the monopoly of the Post Office in certain areas and to issue licences to other bodies to provide an alternative service. Non-Post Office bodies are permitted to transfer mail between document exchanges and to deliver letters, provided that a minimum fee of £1 per letter is charged. Charitable organizations are allowed to carry and deliver Christmas and New Year cards.

INLAND POSTAL SERVICES AND REGULATIONS

INLAND LETTER POST RATES*

Not over	1st class†	2nd class†
60 g	26p	20p
100 g	39p	31p
150 g	49p	38p
200 g	60p	45p
250 g	70p	55p
300 g	80p	64p
350 g	92p	73p
400 g	£1.04	83p
450 g	£1.17	93p
500 g	£1.30	£1.05
600 g	£1.60	£1.25
700 g	£2.00	£1.45
750 g	£2.15	£1.55 (not
800 g	£2.30	admissible
900 g	£2.55	over 750 g)
1,000 g	£2.50	
Each extra 250 g or part thereof	70p	

UK PARCEL RATES

Not over		Not over	
1 kg	£2.70	8 kg	£6.10
2 kg	£3.30	10 kg	£7.10
4 kg	£4.70	30 kg	£8.40
6 kg	£5.25		

*Postcards travel at the same rates as letter post
†There is a two-tier postal delivery system in the UK with first class letters normally being delivered the following day and second class post within three days

STAMPS

Postage stamps are sold in values of 1p, 2p, 4p, 5p, 6p, 10p, 19p, 20p, 25p, 26p, 29p, 30p, 31p, 35p, 36p, 37p, 38p, 39p, 41p, 43p, 50p, 63p, £1, £1.50, £2.00, £5.00, and £10.00. Books or rolls of first and second class stamps are also available. Stamps are sold at Post Offices and some other outlets, including stationers and newsagents.

PREPAID STATIONERY

Aerogrammes to all destinations are 36p. Forces Aerogrammes are free to certain destinations.

OVERSEAS POSTAL SERVICES AND REGULATIONS

OVERSEAS SURFACE MAIL RATES

Letters

Not over		Not over	
20 g	31p	450 g	£2.88
60 g	52p	500 g	£3.18
100 g	75p	750 g	£4.70
150 g	£1.06	1,000 g	£6.21
200 g	£1.36	1,250 g	£7.71
250 g	£1.66	1,500 g	£9.21
300 g	£1.97	1,750 g	£10.71
350 g	£2.27	2,000 g	£12.21
400 g	£2.57		

AIRMAIL LETTER RATES

Europe: Letters

Not over		Not over	
20 g	26p	260 g	£1.82
20 g non EC	31p	280 g	£1.95
40 g	44p	300 g	£2.07
60 g	56p	320 g	£2.20
80 g	69p	340 g	£2.32
100 g	82p	360 g	£2.45
120 g	94p	380 g	£2.57
140 g	£1.07	400 g	£2.70
160 g	£1.19	420 g	£2.82
180 g	£1.32	440 g	£2.95
200 g	£1.44	460 g	£3.08
220 g	£1.57	480 g	£3.20
240 g	£1.69	*500 g	£3.33

* Max. 2 kg

Outside Europe: Letters

	Not over 10 g	Not over 20 g	Over 20 g
Zone 1	43p	63p	varies
Zone 2	43p	63p	varies

For airmail letter zones outside Europe, *see* pages 515–6

Prepaid envelopes:
Standard services (DL size)

	1st class	2nd class
single	31p	25p
packet of 10	£2.85	£2.25

Guaranteed services	Special Delivery	Registered	Registered Plu
C4, 500g	£4.00	£4.30	£4.9
C5, 250g	3.30	3.60	4.2(

Printed postage stamps cut from envelopes, postcards newspaper wrappers, etc., may be used as stamps i payment of postage, provided that they are not imperfec or defaced.

POSTAL ORDERS

Postal orders (British pattern) are issued and paid at nearly all post offices in the UK and in many other countries.

Postal orders are printed with a counterfoil for denominations of 50p and £1, followed by £1 steps to £10, £15 and £20. Postage stamps may be affixed in the space provided to increase the value of the postal order by up to 49p. Charges (in addition to the value of the postal order): Up to £1, 25p; £2–£4, 42p; £5–£7, 58p; £8–£10, 66p; £15, 80p; £20, 85p.

The name of the payee must be inserted on the postal order. If not presented within six months of the last day of the month of issue, orders must be sent to the local customer services manager of Post Office Counters Ltd (listed in the telephone directory) to ascertain whether the order may still be paid. If the counterfoil has been retained postal orders not more than four years out of date may be paid when presented with the counterfoil at a post office.

RESTRICTIONS

Articles which may not be sent in the post include offensive or dangerous articles, packets likely to impede Post Office sorters, and certain kinds of advertisement.

Under Department of Trade and Industry regulations the exportation of some goods by post is prohibited except under Department of Trade licence. Enquiries should be addressed to the Export Data Branch, Overseas Trade Divisions, Department of Trade and Industry, 1 Victoria Street, London SW1H 0ET. Tel: 0171-215 5000.

SPECIAL DELIVERY SERVICES

DATAPOST

A guaranteed service for the delivery of documents and packages: (i) Datapost Sameday offers same working day collection and delivery in many areas; (ii) Datapost 10 (for delivery before 10 a.m.) and Datapost 12 (for delivery before noon) offer next working day delivery nationwide and are available only to certain destinations. Items may be collected or handed in at post offices. There are also Datapost links with a number of overseas countries. Parcelforce 24 (next working day delivery) and 48 (delivery in two working days) offer a similar guaranteed service.

ROYAL MAIL SPECIAL DELIVERY

A guaranteed next-day delivery service by 12.30 p.m. to most UK destinations for first class letters and packets. Fee of £2.70 plus first class postage is refunded if next working day delivery is not achieved, provided that items are posted before latest recommended posting times.

SWIFTAIR

Express delivery of airmail letters and packets up to 2 kg anywhere in the world. Items normally arrive at least one day in advance of normal air mail. Charge (in addition to postage), £2.70.

OTHER SERVICES

ADVICE OF DELIVERY

Written confirmation of delivery from the post office at the stated destination. Charge: 33p (inland); 40p (international); plus postage.

CASH ON DELIVERY (INLAND AND INTERNATIONAL)

Inland: an amount up to £500 can, under certain conditions, be collected and remitted to the sender of a parcel containing an invoice. Invoice values of over £100 are only collectable at Post Office premises. Charge per parcel (exclusive of postage and registration): customers under contract, £1.70; other customers, £2.00; COD enquiry, £1.70.

Overseas: this service is only available with Parcelforce International Standard or Economy service. The following fee is added to postage charges, based on the value of the item to be delivered:

Value	Fee
Up to £200	£5.20
£200–£400	£9.85
£400–£600	£15.00
£600–£1,000	£19.15
£1,000–£1,500	£23.30

CERTIFICATE OF POSTING

Issued free on request at time of posting.

COMPENSATION (INLAND AND INTERNATIONAL)

Inland: compensation up to a maximum of £26 may be paid where it can be shown that a letter was damaged or lost in the post due to the fault of the Post Office, its employees or agents. The Post Office does not accept responsibility for loss or damage arising from faulty packing. Charges: Parcelforce – compensation up to £20 per parcel for loss or damage if a certificate of posting has been obtained. Compensation Fee Certificate of Posting – 70p, up to £150 compensation; £1.25, up to £500 compensation.

International: if a certificate of posting is produced, compensation up to a maximum of £26 may be given for loss or damage in the UK to uninsured parcels to or from most overseas countries. No compensation will be paid for any loss or damage due to the action of the Queen's Enemies.

INTERNATIONAL REPLY COUPONS

Coupons used to prepay replies to letters, exchangeable abroad for stamps representing the minimum surface mail letter rate from the country concerned to the UK. Charge: 60p each.

NEWSPAPER POST

Copies of newspapers registered at the Post Office may be posted only by the publisher or their agents in open-ended wrappers or unsealed envelopes approved by the Post Office, or tied with string removable without cutting. Wrappers and envelopes must be prominently marked 'newspaper post' in the top left-hand corner. The only additional writing or printing permitted is 'with compliments', the name and address of sender, request for return if undeliverable, and a page reference. Items receive first class letter service.

POSTE RESTANTE

Poste Restante is solely for travellers and is for three months in any one town. A packet may be addressed to any post office, except town sub-offices, and should state 'Poste Restante' or 'to be called for' in the address. Redirection from a Poste Restante is undertaken for up to three months. Letters for an expected ship at a port are kept for two months, otherwise letters are kept for two weeks, or one month if from abroad. At the end of this period mail is treated as undeliverable or is returned.

RECORDED DELIVERY (INLAND)

Provides a record of posting and delivery of letters and ensures a signature on delivery. This service is recommended for items of little or no monetary value. Charge: 60p plus postage.

By agent of addressee: mail other than parcels, business reply and freepost items may be reposted free not later than the day after delivery (not counting Sundays and public holidays) if unopened and if original addressee's name is unobscured. Parcels may be redirected free within the same time limits only if the original and substituted address are in the same local parcel delivery area (or the London postal area). Registred packets must be taken to a post office and are re-registered free up to the day after delivery.

By the Post Office: a printed form obtainable from the Post Office must be signed by the person to whom the letters are to be addressed. A fee is payable for each different surname on the application form. Charges: up to 1 calendar month, £6.00 (abroad, £12.00); up to 3 calendar months, £13.00 (£26.00); up to 12 calendar months, £30.00 (£60.00).

REGISTERED MAIL (INLAND AND INTERNATIONAL)

Inland: all packets must be handed to the post office and a certificate of posting obtained. Charges (plus postage): up to £500 compensation, £3.00; Registered Plus for compensation between £500 and £1,500, £3.30; up to £2,200 compensation, £3.60. Consequential Loss Insurance provides cover up to £10,000:

Compensation up to	Standard fee in addition to registered fee and postage
£1,000	45p
£2,500	60p
£5,000	85p
£7,500	£1.10
£10,000	£1.35

Compensation in respect of currency or other forms of monetary worth is given only if money is sent by registered letter post. Compensation cannot be paid in the case of any packet containing prohibited articles (*see* Restrictions). Compensation is only paid for well-packed fragile articles and not for exceptionally fragile or perishable articles.

International: packets containing valuable papers, documents or articles can be insured as letters, or as parcels if the country of destination does not accept dutiable goods in the letter post. For HM ships abroad and members of the Army

and RAF overseas using BFPO numbers, parcels only are insurable up to £140 at a fee of £1.20. Charges (plus airmail postage): compensation up to £500, £3.00; up to £1,000, £4.00.

SMALL PACKETS POST (INTERNATIONAL)

Permits the transmission of goods up to 2 kg to all countries, in the same mails as printed papers (NB: to Myanmar (Burma) and Papua New Guinea there is a limit of 500 g). Packets can be sealed and can contain personal correspondence relating to the contents. Registration is allowed as insurance as long as the item is packed in a way complying with any insurance regulations. A customs declaration is required and the packet must be marked with 'small packet' and a return address. Instructions for the disposal of undelivered packets must be given at the time of posting. An undeliverable packet will be returned to the sender at his/her expense.

Surface Mail: World-wide

Not over		Not over	
100 g	50p	450 g	£1.67
150 g	67p	500 g	£1.84
200 g	84p	750 g	£2.68
250 g	£1.00	1,000 g	£3.51
300 g	£1.17	1,500 g	£5.21
350 g	£1.34	2,000 g	£6.91
400 g	£1.51		

SPECIAL DELIVERY
See above

UNDELIVERED AND UNPAID MAIL

Undelivered mail is returned to the sender provided the return address is indicated either on the outside of the envelope or inside. If the sender's address is not available items not containing property are destroyed. If the packet contains something of value it is retained for up to three months. Undeliverable second class mail containing newspapers, magazines or commercial advertising is destroyed.

All unpaid or underpaid letters are treated as second class mail. The recipient is charged the amount of underpayment plus 15p per item. Parcels over 750 g are charged at first class rates plus 15p.

Public Telecommunications Services

Under the British Telecommunications Act 1981 British Telecom (now BT) was created to provide a national public telecommunications service. The Telecommunications Act 1984 removed BT's monopoly on running the public telecommunications system and BT was privatized in 1984.

The Telecommunications Act 1984 also established the Office of Telecommunications (Oftel) as the independent regulatory body for the telecommunications industry (*see also* Government Departments and Public Offices).

PUBLIC TELECOMMUNICATIONS OPERATORS

Until 1991 the three licensed fixed-link public telecommunications operators (PTOs) in the UK were BT, Mercury Communications Ltd, and Kingston Communications (Hull) PLC. In March 1991 the Government announced that it was opening up the existing duopoly of the two major fixed-link operators and would be en-

couraging applications for telecommunications licences Since then the Department of Trade and Industry has received over 200 applications for new licences. Around 25 PTO licences have been granted.

BT's obligations under its operating licence continue to include the provision of a universal telecommunication service; a service in rural areas; and essential services, such as public call boxes and emergency services.

Mercury Communications is licensed to provide national and international public telecommunication services for residential and business customers. These services utilize the digital network created by Mercury. Mercury can also provide the following services: public and private telephone services; national and international switched voice and data services; electronic messaging (private circuits and networks (national and international) integrated voice and data); data network services; customer equipment; and mobile communications services.

In June 1996 the Government announced that it was liberalizing international facilities licensing in the UK. The end of the BT/Mercury duopoly means that other operators are now able to apply for licences to own and operate their own international telecommunications networks.

PRIVATE TELEPHONE SERVICES

There are over 260 private telephone companies which offer information on a variety of subjects such as the weather, stock market analysis, horoscopes, etc., on the BT network. Other services are available on the Mercury and Racal Vodaphone networks.

The lines and equipment are provided by BT under condition that services adhere to the codes of practice of the Independent Committee for the Supervision of Standards of Telephone Information Services. All services are charged at 48p per minute (peak and standard rate) or 36p per minute (cheap rate).

MOBILE TELEPHONE SYSTEMS

Cellular telephone network systems allow calls to be made to and from mobile telephones. The four companies licensed by the Department of Trade and Industry to provide competing cellular telephone systems are Cellnet, jointly owned by BT and Securicor; One-2-One, jointly owned by Cable and Wireless and US West; Orange, owned by Hutchison Telecom UK Ltd; and Racal Vodafone Ltd, owned by the Racal Electronics Group.

INLAND TELEPHONES

An individual customer can install an extension telephone socket or apparatus in their own home without the need to buy the items from any of the licensed public telecommunications operators. However, it is necessary to possess a special style of master-socket which must be supplied by the public network operator. Although an individual need not buy or rent an apparatus from a PTO, a telephone bought from a retail outlet must be of an approved standard compatible with the public network (indicated by a green disc on the label).

BT EXCHANGE LINE RENTALS (*including VAT*)

	Per quarter
Residential, exclusive	£25.69
Light user scheme	£25.69
Business, exclusive	£41.13

BT TELEPHONE APPARATUS RENTAL

Residential	from £4.47
Business	from £4.70
Private payphone	from £35.00

EXCHANGE LINE CONNECTION AND TAKE-OVER CHARGES (*including VAT*)
BT

New line	£116.33
Removing customer	£0.00
Take-over of existing lines:	
Simultaneous (same day)	£0.00
Non-simultaneous	£9.99

Mercury

Initial and annual administration charge	£23.00

RATES

BT and Mercury local and dialled national calls are charged by the second. Calls made from payphones are charged in 10p units. There is a 5p minimum charge on all BT calls and a 3p minimum charge on Mercury calls. All charges are subject to VAT, except those from payphones which are VAT inclusive. VAT charges on ordinary lines are calculated as a percentage of the total quarterly (BT)/monthly (Mercury) bill.

The charge per second depends on the time of day and the distance of the call:

BT	Mercury	
Daytime	Standard	Monday to Friday 8 a.m. to 6 p.m.
Cheap	Economy	Monday to Friday 6 p.m. to 8 a.m.*
Weekend	Weekend	Midnight Friday to midnight Sunday

*also Christmas Day, Boxing Day and New Year's Day

Local rate
Regional rate – up to 35 miles (56 km)
National rate – over 35 miles (56 km) (including Channel Islands and Isle of Man)
'm' rate – dialled calls to mobile phones

DIALLED CALL TIME pence per minute charges (*including VAT*)

	BT	Mercury
Local		
Daytime	4.00	*
Cheap	1.70	*
Weekend	1.00	*
Regional rate		
Daytime/Standard	8.30	7.52
Cheap/Economy	4.00	2.82
Weekend	3.30	2.82
National rate		
Daytime/Standard	8.80	7.52
Cheap/Economy	4.65	2.82
Weekend	3.30	2.82
'm' rate		
Daytime/Standard	41.05	32.90†
Cheap/Economy	28.32	23.03†
Weekend	12.05	23.03†

*Mercury advises customers to use BT or cable for local calls
†Calls to One-2-One and Orange mobile phones are charged at the following pence per minute rates:

Standard	12.69
Economy/Weekend	7.99

OPERATOR-CONNECTED CALLS

Operator-connected calls from ordinary lines are generally subject to a three-minute minimum charge (and thereafter by the minute) which varies with distance and time of day. Operator-connected calls from payphones are charged in three-minute periods at the payphone tariff. For calls that have to be placed through the operator because a dialled call has failed, the charge is equivalent to the dialled rate, subject normally to the three-minute minimum.

Higher charges apply to other operator-connected calls, including special services calls and those to mobile phones, the Irish Republic and the Channel Islands.

PHONECARDS

BT phonecards to the value of £2, £5, £10 and £20 are available from post offices and other outlets for use in specially designated public telephone boxes. Each phonecard unit is equivalent to a 10p coin in a payphone. Special public payphones at major railway stations and airports also accept commercial credit cards.

INTERNATIONAL TELEPHONES

All UK customers have access to International Direct Dialling (IDD) and can dial direct to numbers on most exchanges in over 200 countries world-wide. Details about how to make calls are given in dialling code information and in the International Telephone Guide.

For countries without IDD, calls have to be made through the International Operator. All operator-connected calls are subject to a three-minute minimum charge. Thereafter the call is charged by the minute.

Countries which can be called on IDD fall into one of 13 international charge bands depending on location. Charges in each band also vary according to the time of day; cheap rate dialled calls are available to all countries at certain times, but there is no reduced rate for operator-connected calls. Details of current international telephone charges can be obtained from the International Operator.

For International Dialling Codes, *see* pages 515–6

OTHER TELECOMMUNICATIONS SERVICES

TELEX SERVICE

There are now 208 countries that can be reached by the BT telex service from the UK, over 200 of them by direct dialling. For most customers, direct dialled calls to international destinations are charged by the second. Calls via the BT operator are charged in one-minute steps with a three-minute minimum, plus a surcharge of £1.30 a call. Operator-connected calls are charged at between 39p and £1.60 a minute depending upon the country called.

Calls made via BT's Telex Plus store and forward facility attract normal telex charges and a handling charge of 13p for inland delivered messages and 30p for international delivered messages.

TELEMESSAGE

Telemessages can be sent by telephone or telex within the UK for 'hard copy' delivery the next working day, including Saturdays. To achieve this, a telemessage must be telephoned/telexed before 10 p.m. Monday to Saturday (7 p.m. Sundays and Bank Holidays). Dial 100 (190 in London, Birmingham and Glasgow) and ask for the Telemessage Service or see the telex directory for codes.

A telemessage costs £5 for the first 50 words and £2.75 for each subsequent group of 50 words – the name and address are free. A sender's copy costs 85p. A selection of cards is available for special occasions at 80p per card. All prices are subject to VAT.

INTERNATIONAL TELEMESSAGE

Telemessage is also available to the USA. For next working day delivery a telemessage must be filed by 10 p.m. UK time Monday to Saturday (7 p.m. Sundays and Bank Holidays). US addresses must include the ZIP code. Charges are £7.25 for the first 50 words and £3.60 for each subsequent group of 50 words. The name and address are free but all charges are subject to VAT.

BT SERVICES

OPERATOR SERVICES – 100
  For difficulties
  For the following call services: alarm calls (booking charge £2.70); advice of duration and charge (charge £1.80); charge card calls (charge £1.50); freephone calls; international personal calls (charge £2.15–£4.30); transferred charge calls (charge £1.80); subscriber controlled transfer (All charges exclude VAT)
INTERNATIONAL OPERATOR – 155
DIRECTORY ENQUIRIES – 192 (25p charge per call)
INTERNATIONAL DIRECTORY ENQUIRIES – 153
EMERGENCY SERVICES – 999
  Services include fire service; police service; ambulance service; coastguard; lifeboat; cave rescue; mountain rescue
FAULTS – 151
TELEMESSAGE – 100 (190 in London, Birmingham and Glasgow)
INTERNATIONAL TELEMESSAGE – 100 (190 in London, Birmingham and Glasgow). The service is only available to the USA
INTERNATIONAL TELEGRAMS – 100 (190 in London, Birmingham and Glasgow). The service is available world-wide
MARITIME SERVICES – 100
  Includes Ship's Telegram Service and Ship's Telephone Service
BT INMARSAT SATELLITE SERVICE – 155
ALL OTHER CALL ENQUIRIES – 191

Airmail and IDD Codes

AIRMAIL ZONES (AZ)
The table includes airmail letter zones for countries outside Europe, and destinations to which European and European Union airmail letter rates apply (*see also* page 510).
(*Source: Post Office*)

1   airmail zone 1
2   airmail zone 2
e   Europe
eu   European Union

INTERNATIONAL DIRECT DIALLING (IDD)
International dialling codes are composed of four elements which are dialled in sequence:

(i)   the international code
(ii)   the country code (*see* below)
(iii)   the area code
(iv)   the customer's telephone number

Calls to some countries must be made via the international operator. (*Source: BT*)

†   Calls must be made via the international operator
p   A pause in dialling is necessary whilst waiting for a second tone
*   Varies in some areas

Country	AZ	IDD from UK	IDD to UK
Afghanistan	1	00 93	†
Albania	*e*	00 355	†
Algeria	1	00 213	00*p*44
Andorra	*eu*	00 376	00 44
Angola	1	00 244	†
Anguilla	1	00 1 809	001 44
Antigua and Barbuda	1	00 1 268	011 44
Argentina	1	00 54	00 44
Armenia	*e*	00 374	810 44
Aruba	1	00 297	†
Ascension Island	1	00 247	01 44
Australia	2	00 61	00 11 44
Austria	*eu*	00 43	00 44
Azerbaijan	*e*	00 994	810 44
Azores	*eu*	00 351	00 44
Bahamas	1	00 1 809	011 44
Bahrain	1	00 973	0 44
Bangladesh	1	00 880	00 44
Barbados	1	00 1 246	011 44
Belarus	*e*	00 375	810 44
Belgium	*eu*	00 32	00 44
Belize	1	00 501	†
Benin	1	00 229	00*p*44
Bermuda	1	00 1 441	1 44
Bhutan	1	00 975	00 44
Bolivia	1	00 591	00 44
Bosnia-Hercegovina	*e*	00 387	99 44
Botswana	1	00 267	00 44
Brazil	1	00 55	00 44
British Virgin Islands	1	00 1 809 49	011 44
Brunei	1	00 673	00 44
Bulgaria	*e*	00 359	00 44
Burkina Faso	1	00 226	00 44
Burundi	1	00 257	90 44
Cambodia	1	00 855	†
Cameroon	1	00 237	00 44
Canada	1	00 1	011 44
Canary Islands	*eu*	00 34	07*p*44
Cape Verde	1	00 238	00 44
Cayman Islands	1	00 1 345	0 44
Central African Republic	1	00 236	00*p*44
Chad	1	00 235	†
Chile	1	00 56	00 44
China	2	00 86	00 44
Colombia	1	00 57	90 44
Comoros	1	00 269	†
Congo	1	00 242	00 44
Cook Islands	2	00 682	00 44
Costa Rica	1	00 506	00 44
Côte d'Ivoire	1	00 225	00 44
Croatia	*e*	00 385	99 44
Cuba	1	00 53	†
Cyprus	*e*	00 357	00 44
Czech Republic	*e*	00 42	00 44
Denmark	*eu*	00 45	009 44
Djibouti	1	00 253	00 44
Dominica	1	00 1 809	011 44
Dominican Republic	1	00 1 809	†
Ecuador	1	00 593	00 44
Egypt	1	00 20	00 44
Equatorial Guinea	1	00 240	19 44
Eritrea	1	00 291	†
Estonia	*e*	00 372	810 44
Ethiopia	1	00 251	00 44
Falkland Islands	1	00 500	01 44
Faroe Islands	*e*	00 298	009 44
Fiji	2	00 679	05 44
Finland	*eu*	00 358	00 44
France	*eu*	00 33	00 44
French Guiana	1	00 594	†
French Polynesia	2	00 689	00 44
Gabon	1	00 241	00 44
The Gambia	1	00 220	00 44
Georgia	*e*	00 7	810 44
Germany	*eu*	00 49	00 44
Ghana	1	00 233	00 44
Gibraltar	*eu*	00 350	00 44
Greece	*eu*	00 30	00 44
Greenland	*e*	00 299	009 44
Grenada	1	00 1 809	011 44
Guadeloupe	1	00 590	00 44
Guam	2	00 671	00 44
Guatemala	1	00 502	00 44
Guinea	1	00 224	†
Guinea-Bissau	1	00 245	†
Guyana	1	00 592	011 44
Haiti	1	00 509	†
Honduras	1	00 504	00 44
Hong Kong	1	00 852	001 44
Hungary	*e*	00 36	00 44
Iceland	*e*	00 354	00 44
India	1	00 91	00 44
Indonesia	1	00 62	00 44
Iran	1	00 98	00 44
Iraq	1	00 964	00 44
Ireland, Republic of	*eu*	00 353	00 44
Israel	1	00 972	00 44
Italy	*eu*	00 39	00 44
Jamaica	1	00 1 809	†
Japan	2	00 81	001 44
Jordan	1	00 962	00 44*
Kazakhstan	*e*	00 7	810 44
Kenya	1	00 254	00 44
Kiribati	2	00 686	09 44

Country	AZ	IDD from UK	IDD to UK
Korea, North	2	00 850	010 44
Korea, South	2	00 82	001 44
Kuwait	1	00 965	00 44
Kyrgystan	e	00 7	810 44
Laos	1	00 856	†
Latvia	e	00 371	810 44
Lebanon	1	00 961	00 44
Lesotho	1	00 266	00 44
Liberia	1	00 231	00 44
Libya	1	00 218	00 44
Liechtenstein	e	00 41 75	00 44
Lithuania	e	00 370	810 44
Luxembourg	eu	00 352	00 44
Macao	1	00 853	00 44
Macedonia	e	00 389	99 44
Madagascar	1	00 261	16p44
Madeira	eu	00 351 91	00 44*
Malawi	1	00 265	101 44
Malaysia	1	00 60	00 44
Maldives	1	00 960	00 44
Mali	1	00 223	00 44
Malta	e	00 356	00 44
Mariana Islands, Northern	2	00 670	010 44
Marshall Islands	2	00 692	012 44
Martinique	1	00 596	19p44
Mauritania	1	00 222	00 44
Mauritius	1	00 230	00 44
Mayotte	1	00 269	19p44
Mexico	1	00 52	98 44
Micronesia, Federated States of	2	00 691	†
Moldova	e	00 373	810 44
Monaco	eu	00 377 93	19p44
Mongolia	2	00 976	†
Montenegro	e	00 381	99 44
Montserrat	1	00 1 664	†
Morocco	1	00 212	00p44
Mozambique	1	00 258	00 44
Myanmar	1	00 95	0 44
Namibia	1	00 264	09 44
Nauru	2	00 674	00 44
Nepal	1	00 977	00 44
Netherlands	eu	00 31	00 44
Netherlands Antilles	1	00 599	00 44
New Caledonia	2	00 687	00 44
New Zealand	2	00 64	00 44
Nicaragua	1	00 505	00 44
Niger	1	00 227	00 44
Nigeria	1	00 234	009 44
Niue	2	00 683	†
Norfolk Island	2	00 672	00 44
Norway	e	00 47	095 44
Oman	1	00 968	00 44
Pakistan	1	00 92	00 44
Palau	2	00 680	†
Panama	1	00 507	00 44
Papua New Guinea	2	00 675	05 44
Paraguay	1	00 595	002 44 / 003 44
Peru	1	00 51	00 44
Philippines	1	00 63	00 44
Poland	e	00 48	0p044
Portugal	eu	00 351	00 44
Puerto Rico	1	00 1 787	135 44
Qatar	1	00 974	044
Réunion	1	00 262	19p44
Romania	e	00 40	00 44

Country	AZ	IDD from UK	IDD to UK
Russia	e	00 7	810 44
Rwanda	1	00 250	00 44
St Helena	1	00 290	01 44
St Kitts and Nevis	1	00 1 809	†
St Lucia	1	00 1 758	0 44
St Pierre and Miquelon	1	00 508	19p44
St Vincent and the Grenadines	1	00 1 809	00 44
El Salvador	1	00 503	00 44
Samoa, American	1	00 684	144
San Marino	eu	00 378	00 44
São Tomé and Príncipe	1	00 239	00 44
Saudi Arabia	1	00 966	00 44
Senegal	1	00 221	00p44
Serbia	e	00 381	99 44
Seychelles	1	00 248	0 44
Sierra Leone	1	00 232	00 44
Singapore	1	00 65	005 44
Slovak Republic	e	00 42	00 44
Slovenia	e	00 386	99 44
Solomon Islands	1	00 677	00 44
Somalia	1	00 252	†
South Africa	1	00 27	09 44
Spain	eu	00 34	07p44
Sri Lanka	1	00 94	00 44
Sudan	1	00 249	†
Suriname	1	00 597	00 44
Swaziland	1	00 268	00 44
Sweden	eu	00 46	009 44p
Switzerland	e	00 41	00 44
Syria	2	00 963	00 44
Taiwan	1	00 886	002 44
Tajikistan	e	00 7	810 44
Tanzania	1	00 255	00 44
Thailand	1	00 66	001 44
Tibet	2	00 86	00 44
Togo	1	00 228	00 44
Tonga	2	00 676	00 44
Trinidad and Tobago	1	00 1 809	01 44
Tristan da Cunha	1	†	†
Tunisia	2	00 216	00 44
Turkey	1	00 90	00 44
Turkmenistan	e	00 993	810 44
Turks and Caicos Islands	1	00 1 809	0 44
Tuvalu	1	00 688	00 44
Uganda	1	00 256	00 44
Ukraine	e	00 380	810 44
United Arab Emirates	1	00 971	00 44
Uruguay	2	00 598	00 44
USA	1	00 1	011 44
Alaska		00 1 907	011 44
Hawaii		00 1 808	011 44
Uzbekistan	e	00 7	810 44
Vanuatu	1	00 678	00 44
Vatican City State	eu	00 39 66982	00 44
Venezuela	1	00 58	00 44
Vietnam	1	00 84	00 44
Virgin Islands (US)	2	00 1 809	011 44
Western Samoa	1	00 685	†
Yemen	1	00 967	00 44
Yugoslav Fed. Rep.	e	00 381	99 44
Zaïre	1	00 243	00 44
Zambia	1	00 260	00 44
Zimbabwe	1	00 263	00 44

Development Corporations

NEW TOWNS

COMMISSION FOR THE NEW TOWNS
Glen House, Stag Place, London SW1E 5AJ
Tel 0171-828 7722

The Commission was established under the New Towns Act 1959. Its remit is to hold, manage and turn to account the property of development corporations transferred to the Commission; and to dispose of property so transferred and any other property held by it, as soon as it considers it expedient to do so. In carrying out its remit the Commission must have due regard to the convenience and welfare of persons residing, working or carrying on business there and, until disposal, the maintenance and enhancement of the value of the land held and return obtained from it.

The Commission has such responsibilities in Basildon, Bracknell, Central Lancashire, Corby, Crawley, Harlow, Hatfield, Hemel Hempstead, Milton Keynes, Northampton, Peterborough, Redditch, Skelmersdale, Stevenage, Telford, Warrington and Runcorn, Washington, and Welwyn Garden City. The Commission has minimal responsibilities (principally financial and litigation) in Aycliffe and Peterlee, and Cwmbran following the wind-up of their development corporations in 1988.

In May 1996 the Government proposed that the Commission should take on responsibility for any assets and liabilities remaining when urban development corporations and housing action trusts are wound up. Legislation relating to the extension of the Commission's role was before Parliament at the time of going to press.
Chairman, Dr J. R. G. Bradfield, CBE
Members, R. B. Caws, CBE; F. C. Graves, OBE; Sir Brian Jenkins, GBE; M. H. Mallinson; Lady Marsh; J. Trustram Eve
Chief Executive, N. J. Walker

REGIONAL OFFICES

NORTH (Central Lancashire, Skelmersdale, Warrington and Runcorn, Washington, Aycliffe and Peterlee), New Town House, Buttermarket Street, Warrington WA1 2LF. Tel: 01925-651144. *Director*, C. Mackrell
CENTRAL (Milton Keynes, Corby, Northampton), Saxon Court, 502 Avebury Boulevard, Central Milton Keynes MK9 3HS. Tel: 01908-692692. *Director*, J. Napleton
WEST MIDLANDS (Redditch, Telford), Jordan House West, Hall Court, Hall Park Way, Telford TF3 4NN. Tel: 01952-293131. *Director*, C. Mackrell
SOUTH (Basildon, Bracknell, Crawley, Harlow, Hatfield, Hemel Hempstead, Peterborough, Stevenage, Welwyn Garden City), Glen House, Stag Place, London SW1E 5AJ. Tel: 0171-828 7722. *Director*, G. D. Johnston

DEVELOPMENT CORPORATIONS

WALES

DEVELOPMENT BOARD FOR RURAL WALES (1977), Ladywell House, Newtown, Powys SY16 1JB. Tel: 01686-626965. *Chairman*, D. Rowe-Beddoe; *Chief Executive*, J. Taylor

SCOTLAND

CUMBERNAULD (1956), Cumbernauld House, Cumbernauld G67 3JH. *Chairman*, D. W. Mitchell, CBE. *General Manager*, D. R. Lind. Area, 7,788 acres. Population, 52,200. To be wound up December 1996
EAST KILBRIDE (1947), wound up 31 December 1995
GLENROTHES (1948), wound up 31 December 1995
IRVINE (1966), Perceton House, Irvine, Ayrshire KA11 2AL. *Chairman*, M. Crichton, CBE. *Managing Director*, J. Murdoch. Area, 16,000 acres. Population, 56,300. To be wound up March 1997
LIVINGSTON (1962), 1 Bell Square, Brucefield Industrial Park, Livingston, West Lothian EH54 9BY. *Chairman*, R. S. Watt, CBE. *Chief Executive*, J. A. Pollock. Area, 6,868 acres. Population, 44,000. To be wound up December 1996

URBAN DEVELOPMENT CORPORATIONS

Urban development corporations were established under the Local Government, Planning and Land Act 1980. Their remit is to bring land and buildings in selected areas back into effective use by developing infrastructure, housing, employment and the environment. The corporations encourage business, especially from overseas, to invest in the area and can provide grants to assist commercial and industrial development.

ENGLAND

BIRMINGHAM HEARTLANDS (1992), Waterlinks House, Richard Street, Birmingham, B7 4AA. Tel: 0121-333 3060. *Chairman*, Sir Reginald Eyre; *Chief Executive*, J. Beeston. Area, 1,000 hectares. To be wound up March 1998
BLACK COUNTRY (1987), Black Country House, Rounds Green Road, Oldbury B69 2RD. Tel: 0121-511 2000. *Chairman*, G. Carter, CBE; *Chief Executive*, D. Morgan. Area, 2,600 hectares. To be wound up March 1998
BRISTOL, wound up 31 December 1995
CENTRAL MANCHESTER, wound up 31 March 1996
LEEDS, wound up 31 March 1995
LONDON DOCKLANDS (1981), Thames Quay, 191 Marsh Wall, London E14 9TJ. Tel: 0171-512 3000. *Chairman*, M. Pickard; *Chief Executive*, E. Sorensen. Area, 2,226 hectares. To be wound up March 1998
MERSEYSIDE (1981), Royal Liver Buildings, Pier Head, Liverpool L3 1JH. Tel: 0151-236 6090. *Chairman*, Sir Desmond Pitcher; *Chief Executive*, C. Farrow. Area, 960 hectares. To be wound up March 1998
PLYMOUTH (1993), Royal William Yard, Plymouth PL1 3RP. Tel: 01752-256132. *Chairman*, Lord Chilver, FRS; *Chief Executive*, G. Tinbrell. Area, 67 hectares. To be wound up March 1998
SHEFFIELD (1988), Don Valley House, Saville Street East, Sheffield S4 7UQ. Tel: 0114-272 0100. *Chairman*, H. Sykes; *Chief Executive*, G. Kendall. Area, 800 hectares. To be wound up March 1997
TEESSIDE (1987), Dunedin House, Riverside Quay, Stockton-on-Tees TS17 6BJ. Tel: 01642-677123. *Chairman*, Sir Ronald Norman, OBE; *Chief Executive*, D. Hall. Area, 4,600 hectares. To be wound up March 1998

TRAFFORD PARK (1987), Waterside, Trafford Wharf Road, Trafford Park, Manchester M17 1EX. Tel: 0161-848 8000. *Chairman*, W. Morgan; *Chief Executive*, M. Shields. Area, 1,270 hectares. To be wound up March 1998

TYNE AND WEAR (1987), Scotswood House, Newcastle Business Park, Newcastle upon Tyne NE4 7YL. Tel: 0191-226 1234. *Chairman*, Sir Paul Nicholson; *Chief Executive*, A. Balls, CB. Area, 2,400 hectares. To be wound up March 1998

WALES

CARDIFF BAY (1987), Baltic House, Mount Stuart Square, Cardiff CF1 6DH. Tel: 01222-823958. *Chairman*, Sir Geoffrey Inkin, OBE; *Chief Executive*, M. Boyce. Area, 1,094 hectares

NORTHERN IRELAND

LAGANSIDE (1989), Clarendon Building, 15 Clarendon Road, Belfast BT1 3BG. Tel: 01232-328507. *Chairman*, The Duke of Abercorn; *Chief Executive*, G. Mackey. Area, 122 hectares

---

HM Coastguard

Founded in 1822, originally to guard the coasts against smuggling, HM Coastguard's role today is the very different one of guarding and saving life at sea. The Service is responsible for co-ordinating all civil maritime search and rescue operations around the 10,500 mile coastline of Great Britain and Northern Ireland and 1,000 miles into the Atlantic. In addition, it co-operates with search and rescue organizations of neighbouring countries in western Europe and around the Atlantic seaboard. The Service maintains a 24-hour radar watch on the Dover Strait, providing a Channel navigation information service for all shipping in one of the busiest sea lanes in the world. It also liaises very closely with the off-shore oil and gas industry and with merchant shipping companies.

Since 1978 HM Coastguard has been organized into six regions, each with a Regional Controller. Each region is subdivided into districts under District Controllers, operating from Maritime Rescue Co-ordination Centres or Sub-Centres. In all there are 21 of these centres. They are on 24-hour watch and are fitted with a comprehensive range of communications equipment. They are supported by some 357 smaller stations staffed by part-time Auxiliary Coastguards under the direction of Regulars, each of which keeps its parent centre fully informed of day-to-day casualty risk, particularly on the more remote danger spots around the coast.

Between 1 January and 31 December 1995, the 450 Regular and 3,500 Auxiliary Coastguards co-ordinated 12,220 incidents requiring search and rescue facilities, resulting in assistance being given to 19,384 persons. All distress telephone and radio calls are centralized on the 21 centres, which are on the alert for people or vessels in distress, shipping hazards and pollution incidents. Using telecommunications equipment, including satellite, they can alert and co-ordinate the most appropriate rescue facilities; RNLI lifeboats, Royal Navy, RAF or Coastguard helicopters, fixed-wing aircraft, vessels in the vicinity, or Coastguard shore and cliff rescue teams.

For those who regularly sail in local waters or make longer passages, the Coastguard Yacht and Boat Safety Scheme provides a valuable free service. Its aim is to give the Coastguard a record of the details of craft, their equipment fit and normal operating areas. Yacht and Boat Safety Scheme cards are available from all Coastguard stations, harbourmasters' offices, and most yacht clubs and marinas as well as Coastguard Headquarters.

Members of the public who see an accident or a potentially dangerous incident on or around the coast should dial 999 and ask for the Coastguard.

On 1 April 1994 HM Coastguard and the Marine Pollution Control Unit together formed the Coastguard Agency, an executive agency of the Department of Transport.

Coastguard Headquarters and Office of the Chief Coastguard,
Spring Place, 105 Commercial Road, Southampton SO15 1EG. Tel: 01703-329100

Local Government

The Local Government Acts of 1972, 1985 and 1992, the Local Government (Wales) Act 1994, the Local Government (Scotland) Act 1973 and the London Government Act 1963 are the main six Acts which have brought about the present structure of local government in Great Britain. This structure has been in effect in England and Wales since 1974, with alterations in 1986, 1995 and 1996; and in Scotland since 1975.

The structure in England is based on two tiers of local authorities (county councils and district councils) in the non-metropolitan areas; and a single tier of metropolitan and London borough councils in the six metropolitan areas of England and in London respectively.

Following recent reviews of the structure of local government in England by the Local Government Commission, 46 unitary (all-purpose) authorities have been or are being created to cover certain areas in the non-metropolitan counties. The remaining county areas will continue to have two tiers of local authorities. The county and district councils in the Isle of Wight were replaced by a single unitary authority on 1 April 1995; the former counties of Avon, Cleveland and Humberside were abolished on 1 April 1996 and replaced by unitary authorities; York became a unitary authority at the same date. Changes in other areas will take effect in April 1997 and April 1998.

Legislation passed in 1994 abolishes the two-tier structure in Wales and Scotland with effect from 1 April 1996 and replaces it with a single tier of unitary authorities.

Local authorities are empowered or required by various Acts of Parliament to carry out functions in their areas. The legislation concerned comprises public general Acts and 'local' Acts which local authorities have promoted as private bills.

ELECTIONS

Local elections are normally held on the first Thursday in May. Generally, all British subjects or citizens of the Republic of Ireland of 18 years or over who are resident on the qualifying date in the area for which the election is being held, are entitled to vote at local government elections. A register of electors is prepared and published annually by local electoral registration officers.

A returning officer has the overall responsibility for an election. Voting takes place at polling stations, arranged by the local authority and under the supervision of a presiding officer specially appointed for the purpose. Candidates, who are subject to various statutory qualifications and disqualifications designed to ensure that they are suitable persons to hold office, must be nominated by electors for the electoral area concerned.

In England, the Local Government Commission is responsible for carrying out periodic reviews of electoral arrangements and making proposals to the Secretary of State for changes found necessary. In Wales and Scotland these matters are the responsibility of the Local Boundary Commission for Wales and the Local Boundary Commission for Scotland respectively.

LOCAL GOVERNMENT COMMISSION FOR ENGLAND, Dolphyn Court, 10–11 Great Turnstile, Lincoln's Inn Fields, London WC1V 7JU. Tel: 0171-430 8400

INTERNAL ORGANIZATION

The council as a whole is the final decision-making body within any authority. Councils are free to a great extent to make their own internal organizational arrangements.

Normally, questions of policy are settled by the full council, while the administration of the various services is the responsibility of committees of councillors. Day-to-day decisions are delegated to the council's officers, who act within the policies laid down by the councillors.

FINANCE

Local government in England, Wales and Scotland is financed from four sources: the council tax, non-domestic rates, government grants, and income from fees and charges for services. (For arrangements in Northern Ireland, see page 522.)

COUNCIL TAX

Under the Local Government Finance Act 1992, from 1 April 1993 the council tax replaced the community charge (which had been introduced in April 1989 in Scotland and April 1990 in England and Wales in place of domestic rates).

The council tax is a local tax levied by each local council. Liability for the council tax bill usually falls on the owner-occupier or tenant of a dwelling which is their sole or main residence. Council tax bills may be reduced because of the personal circumstances of people resident in a property, and there are discounts in the case of dwellings occupied by fewer than two adults.

In England, each county council, each district council and, from 1 April 1996, each police authority sets its own council tax rate. The district councils collect the combined council tax, and the county councils and police authorities claim their share from the district councils' collection funds. In Wales, each county and county borough council and each police authority sets its own council tax rate. The county and county borough councils collect the combined council tax and the police authorities claim their share from the collection funds. In Scotland each island council and unitary authority sets its own rate of council tax.

The tax relates to the value of the dwelling. Each dwelling is placed in one of eight valuation bands, ranging from A to H, based on the property's estimated market value as at 1 April 1991.

The valuation bands and ranges of values in England, Wales and Scotland are:

England

A	Up to £40,000	E	£88,001–£120,000
B	£40,001–£52,000	F	£120,001–£160,000
C	£52,001–£68,000	G	£160,001–£320,000
D	£68,001–£88,000	H	Over £320,000

Wales

A	Up to £30,000	E	£66,001–£90,000
B	£30,001–£39,000	F	£90,001–£120,000
C	£39,001–£51,000	G	£120,001–£240,000
D	£51,001–£66,000	H	Over £240,000

Scotland

A	Up to £27,000	E	£58,001–£80,000
B	£27,001–£35,000	F	£80,001–£106,000
C	£35,001–£45,000	G	£106,001–£212,000
D	£45,001–£58,000	H	Over £212,000

The council tax within a local area varies between the different bands according to proportions laid down by law. The charge attributable to each band as a proportion of the Band D charge set by the council is approximately:

A	67%	E	122%
B	78%	F	144%
C	89%	G	167%
D	100%	H	200%

The band D rate is given in the tables on pages 540–45 (England), 552 (London), 555 (Wales), and 560 (Scotland). There may be variations from the given figure within each district council area because of different parish or community precepts being levied.

NON-DOMESTIC RATES

Non-domestic (business) rates are collected by billing authorities; these are the district councils in those areas of England with two tiers of local government and unitary authorities in other parts of England, the county and county borough councils in Wales (since April 1996), and the councils and islands councils in Scotland. In respect of England and Wales, the Local Government Finance Act 1988 provides for liability for rates to be assessed on the basis of a poundage (multiplier) tax on the rateable value of property (hereditaments). Separate multipliers are set by the appropriate Secretaries of State in England, Wales and Scotland, and rates are collected by the billing authority for the area where a property is located. Rate income collected by billing authorities is paid into a national non-domestic rating (NNDR) pool and redistributed to individual authorities on the basis of the adult population figure as prescribed by the appropriate Secretary of State. The rates pools are maintained separately in England, Wales and Scotland. For the years 1995–6 to 2000–1 actual payment of rates in certain cases are subject to transitional arrangements, to phase in the larger increases and reductions in rates resulting from the effects of the 1995 revaluation.

Rates are levied in Scotland in accordance with the Local Government (Scotland) Act 1975. For 1995–6, the Secretary of State for Scotland prescribed a single non-domestic rates poundage to apply throughout the country at the same level as the uniform business rate (UBR) in England. Rate income is pooled and redistributed to local authorities on a per capita basis. For the year 1995–6 payment of rates was subject to transitional arrangements to phase in the effect of the 1995 revaluation.

Rateable values for the rating lists came into force on 1 April 1995. They are derived from the rental value of property as at 1 April 1993 and determined on certain statutory assumptions by valuation officers of the Valuation Office Agency in England and Wales, and by Regional Assessors in Scotland. New property which is added to the list, and significant changes to existing property, necessitate amendments to the rateable value on the same basis. Rating lists (valuation rolls in Scotland) remain in force until the next general revaluation. Such revaluations take place every five years, the next being in 2000.

Certain types of property are exempt from rates, e.g. agricultural land and buildings, and places of public religious worship. Charities and other non-profit-making organizations may receive full or partial relief. Empty property is liable to pay rates at 50 per cent, except for certain specified classes which are exempt entirely.

GOVERNMENT GRANTS

In addition to specific grants in support of revenue expenditure on particular services, central government pays revenue support grant to local authorities. This grant is paid to each local authority so that if each authority spends at a level sufficient to provide a standard level of service, all authorities in the same class can set broadly the same council tax.

COMPLAINTS

Commissioners for Local Administration in England, Wales and Scotland (*see* pages 319–20) are responsible for investigating complaints from members of the public who claim to have suffered injustice as a consequence of maladministration in local government or in certain local bodies.

The Northern Ireland Commissioner for Complaints fulfils a similar function in Northern Ireland, investigating complaints about local authorities and certain public bodies.

THE QUEEN'S REPRESENTATIVES

The Lord Lieutenant of a county is the permanent local representative of the Crown in that county. The appointment of Lord Lieutenants is now regulated by the Reserve Forces Act 1980. They are appointed by the Sovereign on the recommendation of the Prime Minister. The retirement age is 75. The office of Lord Lieutenant dates from 1557, and its holder was originally responsible for the maintenance of order and for local defence in the county. The duties of the post include attending on royalty during official visits to the county, performing certain duties in connection with armed forces of the Crown (and in particular the reserve forces), and making presentations of honours and awards on behalf of the Crown. In England, Wales and Northern Ireland, the Lord Lieutenant usually also holds the office of *Custos Rotulorum*. As such, he or she acts as head of the county's commission of the peace (which recommends the appointment of magistrates).

The office of Sheriff (from the Old English shire-reeve) of a county was created in the tenth century. The Sheriff was the special nominee of the Sovereign, and the office reached the peak of its influence under the Norman kings. The Provisions of Oxford (1258) laid down a yearly tenure of office. Since the mid-16th century the office has been purely civil, with military duties taken over by the Lord Lieutenant of the county. The Sheriff (commonly known as 'High Sheriff') attends on royalty during official visits to the county, acts as the returning officer during parliamentary elections in county constituencies, attends the opening ceremony when a High Court judge goes on circuit, executes High Court writs, and appoints under-sheriffs to act as deputies. The appointments and duties of the High Sheriffs in England and Wales are laid down by the Sheriffs Act 1887.

The serving High Sheriff submits a list of names of possible future sheriffs to a tribunal which chooses three names to put to the Sovereign. The tribunal nominates the High Sheriff annually on 12 November and the Sovereign pricks the name of the Sheriff to succeed in the following year. The term of office runs from 25 March to the following 24 March (the civil and legal year before 1752). No person may be chosen twice in three years if there is any other suitable person in the county.

CIVIC DIGNITIES

District councils in England may petition for a royal charter granting borough or 'city' status to the district. County councils in Wales may petition for a royal charter granting county borough or 'city' status to the council.

In England and Wales the chairman of a borough or county borough council may be called a mayor, and the chairman of a city council a Lord Mayor. Parish councils in England and Wales may call themselves 'town councils', in which case their chairman is the town mayor.

In Scotland the chairman of a district council may be known as a convener; a provost is the equivalent of a mayor. The chairmen of the councils for the cities of Aberdeen, Dundee, Edinburgh and Glasgow are Lord Provosts.

ENGLAND
(For London, *see* below)

There are currently 36 non-metropolitan counties; all (apart from the Isle of Wight) are divided into non-metropolitan districts. In addition, there are 13 unitary authorities created in April 1996, and a further 36 unitary authorities will come into being in April 1997 and April 1998. At present there are 286 non-metropolitan districts; by 1998 there will be 282. The populations of most of the new unitary authorities are in the range of 100,000 to 300,000. The non-metropolitan districts have populations broadly in the range of 60,000 to 100,000; some, however, have larger populations, because of the need to avoid dividing large towns, and some in mainly rural areas have smaller populations.

Six metropolitan counties cover the main conurbations outside Greater London: Tyne and Wear, West Midlands, Merseyside, Greater Manchester, West Yorkshire and South Yorkshire. They are divided into 36 metropolitan districts, most of which have a population of over 200,000.

There are also about 10,000 parishes, in 219 of the non-metropolitan and 18 of the metropolitan districts.

ELECTIONS

For districts, non-metropolitan counties and for about 8,000 parishes, there are elected councils, consisting of directly elected councillors. The councillors elect annually one of their number as chairman.

Generally, councillors serve four years and there are no elections of district and parish councillors in county election years. In metropolitan districts, one-third of the councillors for each ward are elected each year except in the year when county elections take place elsewhere. Non-metropolitan districts can choose whether to have elections by thirds or whole council elections. In the former case, one-third of the council, as nearly as may be, is elected in each year of metropolitan district elections. If whole council elections are chosen, these are held in the year midway between county elections.

FUNCTIONS

In non-metropolitan areas, functions are divided between the districts and counties, those requiring the larger area or population for their efficient performance going to the county. The metropolitan district councils, with the larger population in their areas, already had wider functions than non-metropolitan councils, and following abolition of the metropolitan county councils were given most of those functions also. A few functions continue to be exercised over the larger area by joint bodies, made up of councillors from each district.

The allocation of functions is as follows:

County councils: education; strategic planning; traffic, transport and highways; fire service; consumer protection; refuse disposal; smallholdings; social services; libraries

Non-metropolitan district councils: local planning; housing; highways (maintenance of certain urban roads and off-street car parks); building regulations; environmental health; refuse collection; cemeteries and crematoria

Non-metropolitan unitary councils: their functions are all those listed above, except that the fire service is exercised by a joint body

Concurrently by county and district councils: recreation (parks, playing fields, swimming pools); museums; encouragement of the arts, tourism and industry

The Police and Magistrates Court Act 1994 set up police authorities in England and Wales separate from the local authorities.

PARISH COUNCILS

Parishes with 200 or more electors must generally have parish councils, which means that over three-quarters of the parishes have councils. A parish council comprises at least five members, the number being fixed by the district council. Elections are held every four years, at the time of the election of the district councillor for the ward including the parish. All parishes have parish meetings, comprising the electors of the parish. Where there is no council, the meeting must be held at least twice a year.

Parish council functions include: allotments; encouragement of arts and crafts; community halls, recreational facilities (e.g. open spaces, swimming pools), cemeteries and crematoria; and many minor functions. They must also be given an opportunity to comment on planning applications. They may, like county and district councils, spend limited sums for the general benefit of the parish. They levy a precept on the district councils for their funds.

FINANCE

Aggregate external finance for 1996–7 was originally determined at £35,652 million. Of this, specific and special grants were estimated at £4,892 million. £18,024 million was in respect of revenue support grant and £12,736 million was support from the national non-domestic rate pool. Total standard spending by local authorities considered for grant purposes was £44,927 million.

The average council taxes, expressed in terms of Band C, two-adult properties for 1996–7, were: inner London boroughs and the City of London £633; outer London boroughs £606; metropolitan districts £725; shire areas £632. The average for England was £647.

National non-domestic rate (or uniform business rate) for 1996–7 is 44.9p. The provisional amount estimated to be raised from central, local and Crown lists is £12.5 billion. Total rateable value held on draft local authority lists at 31 December 1995 was £29.7 billion. The amount to be redistributed to authorities from the pool in 1996–7 is £12.7 billion.

Under the Local Government and Housing Act 1989, local authorities have four main ways of paying for capital expenditure: borrowing and other forms of extended credit; capital grants from central government towards some types of capital expenditure; 'usable' capital receipts from the sale of land, houses and other assets; and revenue.

The amount of capital expenditure which a local authority can finance by borrowing (or other forms of credit) is effectively limited by the credit approvals issued to it by central government. Most credit approvals can be used for any local authority service; these are known as basic credit approvals. Others are for particular projects or services; these are known as supplementary credit approvals.

Generally, the 'usable' part of a local authority's capital receipts consists of 25 per cent of receipts from the sale of council houses and 50 per cent of most other receipts. The balance has to be set aside as provision for repaying debt and meeting other credit liabilities.

EXPENDITURE

Local authority budgeted net revenue expenditure for 1996–7 was (1996–7 cash prices):

Service	£m
Education	19,062
Personal social services	7,903
Police	6,296
Highway maintenance	1,730
Fire	1,285
Civil defence and other Home Office services	542
Magistrates courts	306
Public transport and parking	646
Housing benefit administration	5,406
Non-housing revenue account housing	354
Libraries, museums and art galleries	755
Swimming pools and recreation	497
Local environmental services	5,247
Other services	365
Net current expenditure	50,394
Capital charges	2,307
Capital charged to revenue	800
Other non-current expenditure	3,645
Interest receipts	−699
Gross revenue expenditure	56,447
Specific and special grants outside AEF	−9,032
Other income	−73
Revenue expenditure	47,342
Specific and special grants inside AEF	−1,549
Net revenue expenditure	45,793
AEF = aggregate external finance	

LONDON

Since the abolition of the Greater London Council in 1986, the Greater London area has not had a single local government body. The area is divided into 32 borough councils, which have a status similar to the metropolitan district councils in the rest of England, and the Corporation of the City of London.

LONDON BOROUGH COUNCILS

The London boroughs have whole council elections every four years, in the year immediately following the county council election year. The next elections will be held in 1998.

The borough councils have responsibility for the following functions: building regulations; cemeteries and crematoria; consumer protection; education; youth employment; environmental health; electoral registration; food; drugs; housing; leisure services; libraries; local planning; local roads; museums; parking; recreation (parks, playing fields, swimming pools); refuse collection and street cleansing; social services; town planning; and traffic management.

THE CORPORATION OF LONDON
(*see also* pages 547–9)

The Corporation of London is the local authority for the City of London. Its legal definition is 'The Mayor and Commonalty and Citizens of the City of London'. It is governed by the Court of Common Council, which consists of the Lord Mayor, 24 other aldermen, and 130 common councilmen. The Lord Mayor and two sheriffs are nominated annually by the City guilds (the livery companies) and elected by the Court of Aldermen. Aldermen and councilmen are elected by businesses in the 25 wards into which the City is divided; councilmen must stand for re-election annually. The Council is a legislative assembly, and there are no political parties.

The Corporation has the same functions as the London borough councils. In addition, it runs the City of London Police; is the health authority for the Port of London; has health control of animal imports throughout Greater London, including at Heathrow airport; owns and manages public open spaces throughout Greater London; runs the Central Criminal Court; and runs Billingsgate, Smithfield and Spitalfields markets.

THE CITY GUILDS (LIVERY COMPANIES)

The livery companies of the City of London grew out of early medieval religious fraternities and began to emerge as trade and craft guilds, retaining their religious aspect, in the 12th century. From the early 14th century, only members of the trade and craft guilds could call themselves citizens of the City of London. The guilds began to be called livery companies, because of the distinctive livery worn by the most prosperous guild members on ceremonial occasions, in the late 15th century.

By the early 19th century the power of the companies within their trades had begun to wane, but those wearing the livery of a company continued to play an important role in the government of the City of London. Liverymen still have the right to nominate the Lord Mayor and sheriffs, and most members of the Court of Common Council are liverymen (*see also* page 549).

GREATER LONDON SERVICES

After the abolition of the Greater London Council (GLC) in 1986, the London boroughs took over most of its functions. Successor bodies have also been set up for certain functions.

The London Residuary Body (LRB) was set up in 1986 to deal with residual matters of the GLC which could not easily be transferred elsewhere and in 1990 became responsible for residual matters relating to the Inner London Education Authority. The LRB completed its work and was wound up in 1995, having transferred most residual Greater London matters to the London Borough of Bromley and inner London matters to the Royal Borough of Kensington and Chelsea.

WALES

The Local Government (Wales) Act 1994 abolished the two-tier structure of eight county and 37 district councils which had existed since 1974, and replaced it, from 1 April 1996, with 22 unitary authorities. The new authorities were elected in May 1995. Each unitary authority has inherited all the functions of the previous county and district councils, except fire services (which are provided by three combined fire authorities, composed of representatives of the unitary authorities) and National Parks (which are the responsibility of three independent National Park authorities).

The Police and Magistrates Courts Act 1994 set up four police authorities with effect from 1 April 1995: Dyfed-Powys, Gwent, North Wales, and South Wales.

COMMUNITY COUNCILS

In Wales parishes have been replaced by communities. Unlike England, where many areas are not in any parish, communities have been established for the whole of Wales, approximately 865 communities in all. Community meetings may be convened as and when desired.

Community councils exist in 734 communities and further councils may be established at the request of a community meeting. Community councils have broadly the same range of powers as English parish councils. Community councillors are elected en bloc at the same time as a unitary authority election and for a term of four years.

FINANCE

Aggregate external finance for 1996–7 is £2,517.9 million. This comprises revenue support grant of £1,821.1 million, specific grants of £237.8 million, and support from the national non-domestic rate pool of £459.0 million. Total standard spending by local authorities considered for grant purposes is £2,867.6 million.

The average council tax levied in Wales for 1996–7 is £462, comprising unitary authorities £416 and police authorities £46.

National non-domestic rates (or uniform business rate) in Wales for 1996–7 is 40.5p. The amount estimated to be raised is £459 million. Total rateable value held on local authority lists at 31 December 1995 was £1,324 million.

SCOTLAND

The Local Government etc. (Scotland) Act abolished the two-tier structure of nine regional and 53 district councils which had existed since 1975 and replaced it, from 1 April 1996, with 29 unitary authorities on the mainland; the three islands councils remain. The new authorities were elected in April 1995. Each unitary authority has inherited all the functions of the regional and district councils, except water and sewerage (which are provided by three public bodies whose members will be appointed by the Secretary of State for Scotland) and reporters panels (which have become a national agency).

ELECTIONS

The unitary authorities consist of directly elected councillors. Elections take place every three years; the next elections are in 1999. In 1996 the register showed 3,971,203 electors in Scotland.

FUNCTIONS

The functions of the councils and islands councils are: education; social work; strategic planning; the provision of infrastructure such as roads; consumer protection; flood prevention; coast protection; valuation and rating; the police and fire services; civil defence; electoral registration; public transport; registration of births, deaths and marriages; housing; leisure and recreation; development control and building control; environmental health; licensing; allotments; public conveniences; the administration of district courts

COMMUNITY COUNCILS

Unlike the parish councils and community councils in England and Wales, Scottish community councils are not local authorities. Their purpose as defined in statute is to ascertain and express the views of the communities which they represent, and to take in the interests of their communities such action as appears to be expedient or practicable. Over 1,000 community councils have been established under schemes drawn up by district and islands councils in Scotland.

Since April 1996 community councils have had an enhanced role, becoming statutory consultees on local planning issues and on the decentralization schemes which the new councils have to draw up for delivery of services.

FINANCE

Figures for 1995–6 show total receipts from non-domestic rates of £1,244.4 million and £759.6 million from the council tax. The unified business rate for 1995–6 was 43p and the average Band D council tax payable was £624. The average Band D council water charge payable was £84.

NORTHERN IRELAND

For the purpose of local government Northern Ireland has a system of 26 single-tier district councils.

ELECTIONS

There are 582 members of the councils, elected for periods of four years at a time on the principle of proportional representation.

FUNCTIONS

The district councils have three main roles. These are:

Executive: responsibility for a wide range of local services including building regulations; community services; consumer protection; cultural facilities; environmental health; miscellaneous licensing and registration provisions, including dog control; litter prevention; recreational and social facilities; refuse collection and disposal; street cleansing; and tourist development

Representative: nominating representatives to sit as members of the various statutory bodies responsible for the administration of regional services such as drainage, education, fire, health and personal social services, housing, and libraries

Consultative: acting as the medium through which the views of local people are expressed on the operation in their area of other regional services, notably conservation (including water supply and sewerage services), planning, and roads, provided by those departments of central government which have an obligation, statutory or otherwise, to consult the district councils about proposals affecting their areas

FINANCE

Local government in Northern Ireland is funded by a system of rates (a local property tax calculated by using the rateable value of a property multiplied by an amount per pound of rateable value). Rates are collected by the Department of the Environment for Northern Ireland and consist of a regional rate made by the Department of Finance and Personnel and a district rate made by individual district councils.

In 1995–6 approximately £430 million was raised in rates in Northern Ireland and the total rateable value was £237.3 million. The average domestic poundage levied was 167.27p and the average non-domestic rate poundage was 241.27p.

Political Composition of Local Councils

AS AT END MAY 1996

Abbreviations:

C.	Conservative
Com.	Communist
Dem.	Democrat
Green	Green
Ind.	Independent
Lab.	Labour
Lib.	Liberal
LD	Liberal Democrat
MK	Mebyon Kernow
NP	Non-political/Non-party
PC	Plaid Cymru
RA	Ratepayers'/Residents' Associations
SD	Social Democrat
SNP	Scottish National Party

ENGLAND

COUNTY COUNCILS

*Unitary council

Bedfordshire	*Lab.* 31, *C.* 27, *LD* 14, *Ind.* 1
Berkshire	*LD* 34, *Lab.* 25, *C.* 14, *Ind.* 2, *Lib.* 1
Buckinghamshire	*C.* 37, *LD* 16, *Lab.* 13, *Ind.* 4, *Ind. C.* 1
Cambridgeshire	*C.* 33, *Lab.* 21, *LD* 21, *Ind.* 1, *Lib.* 1
Cheshire	*Lab.* 34, *C.* 22, *LD* 14
Cornwall	*LD* 40, *Ind.* 25, *Lab.* 7, *C.* 6, *MK* 1
Cumbria	*Lab.* 39, *C.* 28, *Ind.* 2, *LD* 14
Derbyshire	*Lab.* 51, *C.* 21, *LD* 8, *Ind.* 1, *vacant* 3
Devon	*LD* 39, *Lab.* 21, *C.* 17, *Ind.* 4, *Lib.* 3, *Ind. C.* 1
Dorset	*LD* 39, *C.* 27, *Lab.* 6, *Ind.* 5
Durham	*Lab.* 56, *C.* 6, *LD* 6, *Ind.* 4
East Sussex	*LD* 30, *C.* 22, *Lab.* 18
Essex	*Lab.* 35, *LD* 32, *C.* 30, *Ind.* 1
Gloucestershire	*LD* 30, *Lab.* 19, *Ind. C.* 12
Hampshire	*LD* 48, *C.* 28, *Lab.* 23, *Ind.* 3
Hereford and Worcester	*C.* 25, *Lab.* 24, *LD* 20, *Ind.* 6, *vacant* 1
Hertfordshire	*Lab.* 31, *C.* 24, *LD* 19, *Ind.* 2, *vacant* 1
*Isle of Wight	*LD* 34, *C.* 5, *Ind.* 5, *Lab* 3, *others* 1
Kent	*C.* 41, *Lab.* 31, *LD* 27
Lancashire	*Lab.* 53, *C.* 34, *LD* 11, *vacant* 1
Leicestershire	*Lab.* 37, *C.* 30, *LD* 17, *Ind. C.* 1
Lincolnshire	*C.* 31, *Lab.* 24, *LD* 16, *Ind.* 5
Norfolk	*C.* 33, *Lab.* 32, *LD* 17, *Ind.* 2
Northamptonshire	*Lab.* 35, *C.* 26, *LD* 5, *Ind.* 2
Northumberland	*Lab.* 39, *C.* 13, *LD* 13, *Ind.* 1
North Yorkshire	*LD* 29, *C.* 26, *Lab.* 11, *Ind.* 7, *vacant* 1
Nottinghamshire	*Lab.* 58, *C.* 24, *LD* 6
Oxfordshire	*Lab.* 24, *C.* 23, *LD* 20, *Green* 2, *Ind. C.* 1

Shropshire	*C.* 24, *Lab.* 24, *LD* 15, *Ind.* 2, *Ind. Lab.* 1
Somerset	*LD* 40, *C.* 13, *Lab.* 3, *Ind.* 1
Staffordshire	*Lab.* 52, *C.* 20, *LD* 5, *Ind.* 2, *RA* 2, *vacant* 1
Suffolk	*Lab.* 32, *C.* 25, *LD* 19, *Ind.* 4
Surrey	*C.* 33, *LD* 28, *Lab.* 10, *RA* 3, *Ind.* 2
Warwickshire	*Lab.* 30, *C.* 19, *LD* 10, *Ind.* 3
West Sussex	*LD* 34, *C.* 26, *Lab.* 9, *vacant* 1
Wiltshire	*LD* 34, *C.* 17, *Lab.* 17

UNITARY COUNCILS

Barnsley	*Lab.* 63, *Ind.* 2, *C.* 1
Bath and North-East Somerset	*LD* 27, *Lab.* 21, *C.* 16, *vacant* 1
Birmingham	*Lab.* 87, *LD* 17, *C.* 13
Bolton	*Lab.* 48, *C.* 6, *LD* 6
Bradford	*Lab.* 71, *C.* 13, *LD* 6
Bristol	*Lab.* 52, *C.* 6, *LD* 10
Bury	*Lab.* 41, *C.* 4, *LD* 3
Calderdale	*Lab.* 29, *C.* 7, *LD* 7, *Ind.* 1
Coventry	*Lab.* 50, *C.* 4
Doncaster	*Lab.* 58, *C.* 3, *LD* 2
Dudley	*Lab.* 60, *C.* 8, *LD* 4
East Riding of Yorkshire	*Lab.* 23, *C.* 19, *LD* 18, *Ind.* 7
Gateshead	*Lab.* 51, *LD* 14, *Lib.* 1
Hartlepool	*Lab.* 40, *LD* 4, *C.* 2, *Ind. C.* 1
Kingston upon Hull	*Lab.* 59, *LD* 1
Kirklees	*Lab.* 45, *LD* 18, *C.* 6, *Green* 1, *Ind.* 1, *vacant* 1
Knowsley	*Lab.* 65, *LD* 1
Leeds	*Lab.* 82, *LD* 9, *C.* 8
Liverpool	*Lab.* 51, *LD* 42, *Ind. Lab.* 3, *Lib.* 2, *C.* 1
Manchester	*Lab.* 84, *LD* 15
Middlesbrough	*Lab.* 45, *LD* 4, *C.* 2, *Ind.* 1, *Ind. Lab.* 1
Newcastle upon Tyne	*Lab.* 65, *LD* 13
North East Lincolnshire	*Lab.* 32, *LD* 7, *C.* 2, *Ind.* 1
North Lincolnshire	*Lab.* 35, *C.* 7
North Somerset	*LD* 30, *C.* 17, *Lab.* 6, *Ind.* 4, *Green* 1, *Lib.* 1
North Tyneside	*Lab.* 45, *C.* 8, *LD* 6, *Ind.* 1
Oldham	*Lab.* 36, *LD* 24
Redcar and Cleveland	*Lab.* 49, *LD* 7, *Ind.* 2, *C.* 1
Rochdale	*Lab.* 36, *LD* 17, *C.* 6, *vacant* 1
Rotherham	*Lab.* 65, *C.* 1
St Helens	*Lab.* 44, *LD* 9, *C.* 1
Salford	*Lab.* 57, *LD* 3
Sandwell	*Lab.* 60, *LD* 9, *C.* 2, *Ind. Lab.* 1
Sefton	*Lab.* 32, *LD* 24, *C.* 13
Sheffield	*Lab.* 55, *LD* 31, *C.* 1
Solihull	*C.* 16, *Lab.* 16, *LD* 12, *Ind.* 6, *vacant* 1
South Gloucestershire	*Lab.* 31, *LD* 30, *C.* 8, *Ind. Lab.* 1
South Tyneside	*Lab.* 52, *LD* 6, *others* 2
Stockport	*LD* 31, *Lab.* 27, *Ind.* 3, *C.* 2
Stockton-on-Tees	*Lab.* 44, *C.* 7, *LD* 4
Sunderland	*Lab.* 67, *C.* 4, *LD* 3, *Ind.* 1
Tameside	*Lab.* 54, *LD* 1, *others* 2
Trafford	*Lab.* 35, *C.* 23, *LD* 5
Wakefield	*Lab.* 61, *C.* 2
Walsall	*Lab.* 25, *C.* 13, *LD* 5, *Ind. C.* 1, *Ind.* 1, *others* 15
Wigan	*Lab.* 69, *LD* 2, *Ind.* 1
Wirral	*Lab.* 41, *C.* 16, *LD* 9
Wolverhampton	*Lab.* 46, *C.* 12, *LD* 2
York	*Lab.* 30, *LD* 17, *C.* 3, *Ind.* 2, *vacant* 1

NON-METROPOLITAN DISTRICT
COUNCILS

*Denotes councils where one-third of councillors retire
each year except in the year of county council elections

*Adur   LD 29, Lab. 6, C. 2, Ind. 2
Allerdale   Lab. 37, C. 7, Ind. 7, LD 4
Alnwick   LD 11, Lab. 7, Ind. 3, C. 2,
                               others 6
Amber Valley   Lab. 39, C. 4
Arun   C. 29, LD 14, Lab. 10, Ind. 3
Ashfield   Lab. 33
Ashford   C. 19, LD 14, Lab. 11, Ind. C. 1,
                               Ind. 1, others 3
Aylesbury Vale   LD 33, C. 12, Ind. 6, Lab. 5,
                               others 2
Babergh   Ind. 12, Lab. 12, C. 9, LD 7,
                               others 2
*Barrow-in-Furness   Lab. 29, C. 4, others 5
*Basildon   Lab. 24, LD 17, C. 1
*Basingstoke and Deane   C. 23, LD 17, Lab. 14, Ind. 3
*Bassetlaw   Lab. 35, C. 6, LD 3, Ind. 2,
                               others 4
*Bedford   Lab. 22, LD 14, C. 10, Ind. 7
Berwick upon Tweed   LD 12, Ind. 10, C. 2, Lab. 2, Ind.
                               Lib. 1, others 1
Blaby   Lab. 16, C. 11, LD 9, Ind. 2,
                               Ind. C. 1
*Blackburn   Lab. 45, C. 12, LD 3
Blackpool   Lab. 38, LD 3, C. 2, vacant 1
Blyth Valley   Lab. 39, LD 7, Ind. Lab. 1
Bolsover   Lab. 35, Ind. 1, RA 1
Boston   Lab. 10, Ind. 7, LD 7, C. 5,
                               others 5
Bournemouth   LD 28, C. 19, Ind. 4, Lab. 6
Bracknell Forest   Lab. 22, C. 12, LD 6
Braintree   Lab. 37, C. 10, Ind. 7, LD 6
Breckland   Lab. 24, C. 18, Ind. 8, LD 2,
                               Green 1
*Brentwood   Lib. 25, C. 12, Lab. 2
Bridgnorth   Ind. 9, Lab. 6, Ind. C. 5, LD 4,
                               C. 3, Ind. Lab. 1, NP 1,
                               others 4
*Brighton   Lab. 29, C. 16, Ind. C. 3
Broadland   Lab. 20, C. 12, LD 12, Ind. 5
Bromsgrove   Lab. 24, C. 12, LD 1, others 2
*Broxbourne   C. 25, Lab. 15, LD 2
Broxtowe   Lab. 36, C. 7, LD 5, Ind. 1
*Burnley   Lab. 38, LD 8, C. 1, Ind. 1
*Cambridge   Lab. 23, LD 18, C. 1
*Cannock Chase   Lab. 40, LD 2
Canterbury   LD 24, Lab. 15, C. 10
Caradon   Ind. 18, LD 18, Lab. 2, RA 2,
                               C. 1
*Carlisle   Lab. 33, C. 14, LD 3, Ind. 1
Carrick   LD 19, Ind. 8, Lab. 8, C. 7,
                               MK 1, others 2
Castle Morpeth   Lab. 12, Ind. 10, C. 6, LD 6
Castle Point   Lab. 34, C. 5
Charnwood   Lab. 30, C. 15, LD 5, Ind. 2
Chelmsford   LD 32, C. 13, Lab. 7, Ind. 4
*Cheltenham   LD 34, C. 3, Ind. 3, Lab. 1
*Cherwell   Lab. 28, C. 16, LD 8
*Chester   Lab. 27, LD 18, C. 13, Ind. 2
Chesterfield   Lab. 37, LD 10
Chester-le-Street   Lab. 30, C. 1, Ind. 1, LD 1
Chichester   LD 25, C. 21, Ind. 4, Lab. 1
Chiltern   LD 24, C. 22, RA 2, Ind. 1,
                               Lab. 1
*Chorley   Lab. 35, LD 7, C. 5, Ind. 1

Christchurch   LD 11, C. 8, Ind. 6
*Colchester   LD 33, Lab. 15, C. 11, RA 1
*Congleton   LD 28, Lab. 11, C. 5, Ind. LD 1
Copeland   Lab. 37, C. 12, Ind. 2
Corby   Lab. 24, LD 2, C. 1
Cotswold   Ind. 16, LD 9, Ind. C. 5, Lab. 4,
                               C. 3, others 8
*Craven   LD 18, C. 6, Lab. 6, Ind. 4
*Crawley   Lab. 28, C. 2, LD 2
*Crewe and Nantwich   Lab. 38, C. 15, LD 3, Ind. 1
Dacorum   Lab. 33, C. 19, LD 4, Ind. 2
Darlington   Lab. 36, C. 13, LD 2, Ind. 1
Dartford   Lab. 35, C. 10, RA 1, Ind. Lab. 1
*Daventry   C. 15, Lab. 15, Ind. 3, LD 2
*Derby   Lab. 39, C. 3, LD 2
Derbyshire Dales   LD 16, Ind. C. 15, Lab. 8
Derwentside   Lab. 50, Ind. 5
Dover   Lab. 39, C. 13, LD 4
Durham   Lab. 38, LD 7, Ind. 4
Easington   Lab. 44, Lib. 3, Ind. 2,
                               Ind. Lab. 2
*Eastbourne   LD 21, C. 8, vacant 1
East Cambridgeshire   Ind. 14, LD 13, NP 6, Lab. 3,
                               Ind. C. 1
East Devon   C. 31, LD 19, Ind. 10
East Dorset   LD 23, C. 12, Ind. 1
East Hampshire   LD 26, C. 12, Ind. 4
East Hertfordshire   C. 23, LD 16, Lab. 8, Ind. 2,
                               RA 1
*Eastleigh   LD 31, C. 7, Lab. 6
East Lindsey   NP 34, Lab. 14, LD 7, Green 3,
                               others 2
East Northamptonshire   Lab. 25, C. 9, LD 2
East Staffordshire   Lab. 36, C. 4, Ind. C. 3, LD 3
Eden   Ind. 31, LD 4, Lab. 2
*Ellesmere Port and
   Neston   Lab. 36, C. 5
*Elmbridge   C. 21, RA 21, LD 9, Lab. 8,
                               Ind. 1
*Epping Forest   Lab. 18, LD 16, C. 13, RA 9,
                               Ind. 3
Epsom and Ewell   RA 33, Lab. 3, LD 3
Erewash   Lab. 39, C. 10, Ind. 2, LD 1
*Exeter   Lab. 24, LD 7, Lib. 3, C. 2
*Fareham   LD 21, C. 8, Lab. 8, others 5
Fenland   Lab. 19, C. 14, Ind. 4, LD 2,
                               vacant 1
Forest Heath   C. 10, LD 6, Ind. 5, Lab. 4
Forest of Dean   Lab. 28, Ind. 8, LD 5, NP 5,
                               C. 1, others 1, vacant 1
Fylde   C. 17, Ind. 12, Lab. 6, LD 4,
                               others 10
Gedling   Lab. 29, C. 20, LD 7, Ind. 1
*Gillingham   LD 29, Lab. 10, C. 2, Ind. 1
*Gloucester   Lab. 25, LD 8, C. 2
*Gosport   LD 18, Lab. 7, C. 5
Gravesham   Lab. 33, C. 10, Ind. 1
*Great Yarmouth   Lab. 38, C. 9, LD 1
Guildford   LD 23, C. 13, Lab. 6, Ind. 3
*Halton   Lab. 46, LD 7
Hambleton   C. 25, Ind. 15, Lab. 4, LD 3
Harborough   LD 16, C. 11, Lab. 8, Ind. 2
*Harlow   Lab. 39, LD 3
*Harrogate   LD 44, C. 10, Lab. 4, Ind. 1
*Hart   LD 15, C. 12, Lab. 8
*Hastings   LD 17, Lab. 15
*Havant   LD 20, Lab. 11, C. 8, Ind. 3
*Hereford   LD 22, Lab. 5
*Hertsmere   Lab. 22, C. 8, LD 8, Ind. 1
High Peak   Lab. 30, C. 5, LD 5, Ind. 4

Hinckley and Bosworth   *LD* 16, *Lab.* 13, *C.* 5
Horsham   *LD* 22, *C.* 18, *Ind.* 3
Hove   *Lab.* 16, *C.* 11, *LD* 3
*Huntingdonshire   *C.* 33, *LD* 13, *Lab.* 5, *Ind.* 2
*Hyndburn   *Lab.* 44, *C.* 3
*Ipswich   *Lab.* 41, *C.* 6, *LD* 1
Kennet   *Ind.* 14, *Lab.* 9, *C.* 9, *LD* 8
Kerrier   *Lab.* 15, *LD* 13, *Ind.* 12, *others* 4
Kettering   *Lab.* 32, *C.* 6, *Ind.* 3, *LD* 3, *vacant* 1
Kings Lynn and West Norfolk   *Lab.* 37, *Ind. C.* 16, *LD* 6, *Ind.* 1
Lancaster   *Lab.* 33, *C.* 11, *Ind.* 9, *LD* 5, *Ind. C.* 1, *others* 1
Leicester   *Lab.* 40, *LD* 8, *C.* 7, *vacant* 1
*Leominster   *Ind.* 16, *LD* 7, *Lab.* 6, *C.* 3, *Ind. C.* 3, *Green* 1
Lewes   *LD* 28, *C.* 16, *Lab.* 2, *Ind.* 1, *RA* 1
Lichfield   *Lab.* 33, *C.* 19, *LD* 2, *Ind.* 1, *Ind. Lab.* 1
*Lincoln   *Lab.* 33
Luton   *Lab.* 36, *LD* 9, *C.* 3
*Macclesfield   *C.* 33, *Lab.* 12, *LD* 11, *RA* 3, *vacant* 1
*Maidstone   *LD* 22, *Lab.* 18, *C.* 10, *Ind.* 5
Maldon   *C.* 16, *Lab.* 7, *Ind.* 6, *LD* 1
Malvern Hills   *LD* 18, *Ind.* 11, *NP* 7, *C.* 6, *Green* 3, *Lab.* 3, *Ind. C.* 2, *vacant* 1
Mansfield   *Lab.* 45, *C.* 1
Melton   *LD* 9, *C.* 8, *Lab.* 5, *Ind.* 4
Mendip   *LD* 21, *Lab.* 9, *C.* 8, *Ind.* 3, *RA* 2
Mid Bedfordshire   *C.* 22, *Lab.* 20, *Ind.* 6, *LD* 5
Mid Devon   *LD* 21, *Ind.* 17, *Lab.* 1, *Lib.* 1
Mid Suffolk   *Lab.* 17, *LD* 11, *C.* 6, *Ind.* 5, *others* 1
*Mid Sussex   *LD* 28, *C* 18, *Ind.* 4, *Lab.* 4
Milton Keynes   *Lab.* 30, *LD* 18, *C.* 2, *Ind.* 1
*Mole Valley   *LD* 18, *C.* 11, *Ind.* 9, *Lab.* 2, *vacant* 1
Newark and Sherwood   *Lab.* 37, *C.* 10, *LD* 5, *Ind.* 2
Newbury   *LD* 37, *C.* 6, *Ind.* 2
*Newcastle-under-Lyme   *Lab.* 42, *LD* 10, *C.* 4
New Forest   *LD* 32, *C.* 23, *Ind.* 3
Northampton   *Lab.* 34, *LD* 8, *C.* 1
North Cornwall   *Ind.* 25, *LD* 12, *C.* 1
North Devon   *LD* 31, *Ind.* 11, *C.* 1, *others* 1
North Dorset   *LD* 19, *Ind.* 12, *C.* 1, *Lab.* 1,
North East Derbyshire   *Lab.* 42, *C.* 4, *LD* 3, *Ind. Lab.* 2, *Ind.* 1, *vacant* 1
*North Hertfordshire   *Lab.* 26, *C.* 16, *LD* 7, *Ind.* 1
North Kesteven   *Lab.* 15, *LD* 8, *Ind.* 6, *C.* 4, *others* 6
North Norfolk   *Lab.* 19, *Ind.* 12, *LD* 12, *C.* 3
North Shropshire   *Ind.* 7, *Lab.* 6, *C.* 2, *LD* 1, *others* 24
North Warwickshire   *Lab.* 29, *C.* 4, *Ind.* 1
North West Leicestershire   *Lab.* 35, *C.* 3, *Ind. C.* 2
North Wiltshire   *LD* 30, *C.* 12, *Lab.* 6, *Ind.* 4
*Norwich   *Lab.* 37, *LD* 11
Nottingham   *Lab.* 51, *LD* 2, *C.* 1, *Green* 1
*Nuneaton and Bedworth   *Lab.* 42, *C.* 3
*Oadby and Wigston   *LD* 25, *C.* 1
Oswestry   *Lab.* 10, *C.* 5, *LD* 5, *others* 9
*Oxford   *Lab.* 39, *LD* 9, *Green* 3
*Pendle   *LD* 29, *Lab.* 19, *C.* 3

*Penwith   *LD* 11, *Lab.* 9, *Ind.* 8, *C.* 4, *MK* 2
*Peterborough   *Lab.* 29, *C.* 13, *Lib.* 3, *LD* 2, *Ind.* 1
Plymouth   *Lab.* 55, *C.* 5
Poole   *LD* 23, *C.* 13, *Lab.* 3
*Portsmouth   *Lab.* 21, *LD* 12, *C.* 6
*Preston   *Lab.* 32, *C.* 13, *SD* 12
*Purbeck   *LD* 11, *Ind.* 5, *C.* 3, *Lab.* 3
*Reading   *Iab.* 35, *LD* 6, *C.* 4
*Redditch   *Lab.* 25, *C.* 3, *LD* 1
*Reigate and Banstead   *C.* 15, *Lab.* 14, *LD* 14, *RA* 4, *Ind.* 2
Restormel   *LD* 30, *NP* 9, *Lab.* 4, *C.* 1
Ribble Valley   *LD* 19, *C.* 18, *Ind. C.* 1, *Lab.* 1
Richmondshire   *Ind.* 22, *LD* 9, *C.* 2, *SD* 1
Rochester-upon-Medway   *Lab.* 44, *LD* 5, *C.* 1
*Rochford   *LD* 23, *Lab.* 11, *RA* 3, *C.* 2
*Rossendale   *Lab.* 31, *C.* 5
Rother   *LD* 21, *C.* 14, *Ind.* 5, *Lab.* 5
*Rugby   *Lab.* 22, *C.* 11, *LD* 5, *others* 10
*Runneymede   *C.* 21, *Lab.* 14, *Ind.* 6, *LD* 1
Rushcliffe   *C.* 26, *Lab.* 17, *LD* 10, *Ind.* 1
*Rushmoor   *LD* 18, *Lab.* 14, *C.* 13
Rutland   *Ind.* 11, *LD* 5, *C.* 2, *Lab.* 2
Ryedale   *Ind.* 9, *LD* 9, *C.* 4, *Lab.* 1
*St Albans   *LD* 39, *Lab.* 11, *C.* 6, *vacant* 1
St Edmundsbury   *Lab.* 22, *C.* 15, *LD* 5, *Ind.* 2
Salisbury   *LD* 30, *Lab.* 11, *C.* 9, *Ind.* 8
Scarborough   *Lab.* 24, *C.* 13, *Ind.* 8, *LD* 4
Sedgefield   *Lab.* 47, *Ind.* 2
Sedgemoor   *C.* 21, *Lab.* 13, *LD* 12, *Ind.* 3
Selby   *Lab.* 26, *C.* 9, *Ind.* 5, *LD* 1
Sevenoaks   *LD* 20, *C.* 17, *Lab.* 11, *Ind.* 5
Shepway   *LD* 20, *C.* 19, *Lab.* 14, *Ind.* 3
*Shrewsbury and Atcham   *Lab.* 22, *LD* 13, *C.* 8, *Ind.* 5
*Slough   *Lab.* 36, *Lib.* 3, *Ind.* 1
*Southampton   *Lab.* 29, *LD* 13, *C.* 3
*South Bedfordshire   *Lab.* 24, *LD* 15, *C.* 11, *Ind.* 3
South Bucks   *C.* 19, *Ind.* 17, *LD* 4
*South Cambridgeshire   *Ind.* 21, *C.* 13, *LD* 11, *Lab.* 10
South Derbyshire   *Lab.* 27, *C.* 6, *others* 1
*Southend-on-Sea   *LD* 18, *Lab.* 11, *C.* 10
South Hams   *C.* 16, *Ind.* 16, *LD* 10, *Lab.* 2
*South Herefordshire   *Ind.* 23, *LD* 13, *others* 2, *vacant* 1
South Holland   *Ind.* 17, *Lab.* 10, *C.* 7, *others* 4
South Kesteven   *Lab.* 18, *C.* 13, *Ind.* 11, *LD* 7, *Ind. Lab.* 3, *Lib.* 2, *others* 3
*South Lakeland   *LD* 25, *Ind.* 11, *C.* 10, *Lab.* 6
South Norfolk   *LD* 30, *C.* 12, *Lab.* 3, *Ind.* 2
South Northamptonshire   *C.* 15, *Lab.* 10, *Ind.* 8, *LD* 7
South Oxfordshire   *LD* 21, *Lab.* 13, *C.* 9, *Ind.* 5, *others* 2
South Ribble   *Lab.* 29, *C.* 16, *LD* 9
South Shropshire   *NP* 9, *Lab.* 8, *Ind.* 7, *Green* 2, *Lab.* 1, *others* 13
South Somerset   *LD* 45, *C.* 8, *Ind.* 6, *Lab.* 1
South Staffordshire   *C.* 26, *Lab.* 15, *Lib.* 4, *RA* 3, *Ind. C.* 1, *Ind.* 1
Spelthorne   *C.* 21, *Lab.* 16, *LD* 3
Stafford   *Lab.* 33, *C.* 16, *LD* 10, *Ind.* 1
*Staffordshire Moorlands   *Lab.* 27, *C.* 11, *LD* 7, *Ind.* 3, *others* 8
*Stevenage   *Lab.* 38, *LD* 1
*Stoke-on-Trent   *Lab.* 60
*Stratford-upon-Avon   *LD* 24, *C.* 17, *Ind.* 9, *Lab.* 3
*Stroud   *Lab.* 27, *LD* 11, *C.* 7, *Ind.* 5, *Green* 4, *vacant* 1

Suffolk Coastal	*C.* 19, *LD* 16, *Lab.* 15, *Ind.* 5
Surrey Heath	*C.* 24, *LD* 8, *Lab.* 4
*Swale	*LD* 23, *Lab.* 19, *C.* 6, *Ind.* 1,
*Tamworth	*Lab.* 27, *Ind.* 3
*Tandridge	*LD* 19, *C.* 16, *Lab.* 7
Taunton Deane	*LD* 29, *C.* 14, *Lab.* 7, *Ind.* 3
Teesdale	*Lab.* 12, *Ind.* 11, *NP* 6, *C.* 2
Teignbridge	*LD* 25, *Ind.* 21, *Lab.* 7, *C.* 5
Tendring	*Lab.* 37, *Ind.* 9, *C.* 8, *LD* 6
Test Valley	*C.* 22, *LD* 22
Tewkesbury	*Ind.* 22, *LD* 8, *Lab.* 5, *others* 1
*Thamesdown	*Lab.* 41, *LD* 9, *C.* 3, *Ind.* 1
Thanet	*Lab.* 44, *LD* 4, *C.* 4, *Ind.* 2
*Three Rivers	*LD* 23, *C.* 17, *Lab.* 8
*Thurrock	*Lab.* 37, *C.* 2
*Tonbridge and Malling	*C.* 23, *LD* 21, *Lab.* 11
*Torbay	*LD* 25, *C.* 5, *Lab.* 5, *Ind. LD* 1
Torridge	*LD* 13, *Ind.* 9, *NP* 6, *Lab.* 5, *C.* 2, *Green* 1
*Tunbridge Wells	*LD* 27, *C.* 14, *Lab.* 6, *Ind.* 1
Tynedale	*Lab.* 19, *LD* 13, *C.* 11, *Ind.* 4
Uttlesford	*LD* 19, *C.* 12, *Ind.* 7, *Lab.* 4
Vale of White Horse	*LD* 34, *C.* 11, *Lab.* 5, *Ind.* 1
Vale Royal	*Lab.* 42, *C.* 15, *LD* 3
Wansbeck	*Lab.* 46
Warrington	*Lab.* 48, *LD* 11, *C.* 1
Warwick	*Lab.* 17, *C.* 13, *LD* 11, *Ind.* 4
*Watford	*Lab.* 21, *LD* 9, *C.* 6
*Waveney	*Lab.* 44, *C.* 2, *LD* 2
Waverley	*LD* 37, *C.* 17, *Lab.* 2, *Ind.* 1
Wealden	*C.* 29, *LD* 24, *Ind.* 5
Wear Valley	*Lab.* 35, *Ind.* 3, *LD* 2
Wellingborough	*Lab.* 16, *C.* 15, *Ind.* 3
*Welwyn Hatfield	*Lab.* 32, *C.* 15
West Devon	*LD* 15, *Ind.* 14, *Lab.* 1
West Dorset	*C.* 18, *Lab.* 17, *LD* 14, *Lab.* 5, *SD* 1
*West Lancashire	*Lab.* 35, *C.* 20
*West Lindsey	*LD* 19, *Ind.* 10, *Lab.* 3, *C.* 2, *others* 3
*West Oxfordshire	*Ind.* 15, *LD* 14, *Lab.* 11, *C.* 9
West Somerset	*C.* 11, *Ind.* 10, *Lab.* 8, *LD* 3
West Wiltshire	*LD* 28, *C.* 8, *Lab.* 4, *Ind.* 3
*Weymouth and Portland	*Lab.* 15, *LD* 14, *RA* 4, *Ind.* 2
*Winchester	*LD* 36, *C.* 9, *Lab.* 6, *Ind.* 4
Windsor and Maidenhead	*LD* 32, *C.* 17, *Ind.* 7, *Lab.* 2
*Woking	*LD* 18, *C.* 10, *Lab.* 7
*Wokingham	*LD* 29, *C.* 24, *Ind.* 1
*Worcester	*Lab.* 23, *C.* 9, *LD* 3, *Ind.* 1
*Worthing	*LD* 25, *C.* 11
Wrekin	*Lab.* 38, *C.* 3, *Ind. Lab.* 2, *LD* 2, *Ind.* 1
Wychavon	*C.* 18, *LD* 15, *Lab.* 9, *Ind.* 5, *vacant* 2
Wycombe	*C.* 24, *LD* 19, *Lab.* 15, *Ind.* 2
Wyre	*Lab.* 30, *C.* 18, *LD* 4, *RA* 2, *Ind. C.* 1, *vacant* 1
*Wyre Forest	*Lab.* 26, *LD* 8, *C.* 3, *Lab.* 3, *Ind.* 2

GREATER LONDON BOROUGHS

Barking and Dagenham	*Lab.* 47, *RA* 3, *LD* 1
Barnet	*C.* 29, *Lab.* 25, *LD* 6
Bexley	*C.* 24, *Lab.* 24, *LD* 14
Brent	*C.* 33, *Lab.* 28, *LD* 5
Bromley	*C.* 32, *LD* 21, *Lab.* 7
Camden	*Lab.* 48, *C.* 7, *LD* 4
City of Westminster	*C.* 45, *Lab.* 15
Croydon	*Lab.* 40, *C.* 30

Ealing	*Lab.* 49, *C.* 19, *LD* 3
Enfield	*Lab.* 41, *C.* 24, *Ind. C.* 1
Greenwich	*Lab.* 46, *C.* 8, *SD* 4, *LD* 3, *Ind. Lab.* 1
Hackney	*Lab.* 33, *C* 13, *LD* 2, *vacant* 2
Hammersmith and Fulham	*Lab.* 33, *C.* 13, *LD* 2, *vacant* 2
Haringey	*Lab.* 57, *C.* 2
Harrow	*LD* 29, *C.* 16, *Lab.* 14, *Ind.* 1, *others* 3
Havering	*Lab.* 28, *RA* 17, *C.* 12, *LD* 2, *others* 4
Hillingdon	*Lab.* 41, *C.* 25, *others* 3
Hounslow	*Lab.* 50, *C.* 6, *LD* 4
Islington	*Lab.* 37, *LD* 13, *C.* 1, *Ind.* 1
Kensington and Chelsea	*C.* 39, *Lab.* 15
Kingston upon Thames	*LD* 27, *C.* 17, *Lab.* 6
Lambeth	*LD* 25, *Lab.* 24, *C.* 14, *Ind.* 1
Lewisham	*Lab.* 63, *LD* 2, *C.* 1, *others* 1
Merton	*Lab.* 39, *C.* 10, *Ind.* 5, *LD* 3
Newham	*Lab.* 60
Redbridge	*Lab.* 28, *C.* 24, *Lib.* 9, *vacant* 1
Richmond upon Thames	*LD* 43, *C.* 7, *Lab.* 2
Southwark	*Lab.* 35, *LD* 24, *C.* 3, *Ind. Lib.* 1, *others* 1
Sutton	*LD* 47, *Lab.* 5, *C.* 4
Tower Hamlets	*Lab.* 43, *LD* 7
Waltham Forest	*Lab.* 26, *C.* 16, *LD* 14, *Ind. Lab.* 1
Wandsworth	*C.* 45, *Lab.* 16

WALES SINCE 1 APRIL 1996

Anglesey	*Ind.* 26, *PC* 7, *Lab.* 6, *C.* 1
Blaenau Gwent	*Lab.* 33, *Ind.* 5, *C.* 1, *Ind. Lab.* 1, *Lib.* 1, *PC* 1
Bridgend	*Lab.* 45, *Ind.* 2, *Ind. Lab.* 1
Caernarfonshire and Merionethshire	*PC* 45, *Ind.* 20, *Lab.* 11, *LD* 4, *others* 2
Caerphilly	*Lab.* 56, *PC* 9, *Ind.* 3
Cardiff	*Lab.* 56, *LD* 9, *C.* 1, *PC* 1
Carmarthenshire	*Lab.* 37, *Ind.* 29, *PC* 8, *LD* 3, *Ind. Lab.* 2, *others* 1, *vacant* 1
Ceredigion	*Ind.* 24, *LD* 11, *PC* 8, *Lab.* 1
Conwy	*LD* 18, *Ind.* 10, *C.* 9, *PC* 4
Denbighshire	*Lab.* 20, *Ind.* 19, *PC* 7, *LD* 3
Flintshire	*Lab.* 45, *LD* 6, *C.* 3, *others* 18
Merthyr Tydfil	*Lab.* 30, *Ind.* 3
Monmouthshire	*Lab.* 26, *C.* 11, *Ind.* 4, *LD* 1
Neath and Port Talbot	*Lab.* 50, *PC* 3, *RA* 3, *Ind.* 2, *LD* 2, *SD* 1, *others* 2, *vacant* 1
Newport	*Lab.* 46, *C.* 1
Pembrokeshire	*Ind.* 39, *Lab.* 14, *LD* 3, *PC* 3, *others* 1
Powys	*Ind.* 61, *Lab.* 9, *LD* 9, *C.* 3, *PC* 1
Rhondda, Cynon, Taff	*Lab.* 58, *PC* 12, *Ind.* 3, *vacant* 1
Swansea	*Lab.* 56, *Ind.* 9, *LD* 7, *C.* 1
Torfaen	*Lab.* 41, *C.* 1, *Ind.* 1, *LD* 1
Vale of Glamorgan	*Lab.* 36, *C.* 5, *PC* 5, *Ind. C.* 1
Wrexham	*Lab.* 33, *Ind. C.* 7 , *Ind. Lab.* 2, *NP* 1, *others* 8

SCOTLAND SINCE 1 APRIL 1996

Aberdeen City	*Lab.* 30, *LD* 10, *C.* 9, *SNP* 1
Aberdeenshire	*LD* 15, *SNP* 15, *Ind.* 13, *C.* 4
Angus	*SNP* 21, *C.* 2, *LD* 2, *Ind.* 1
Argyll and Bute	*Ind.* 21, *SNP* 4, *C.* 3, *LD* 3, *Lab.* 2
City of Edinburgh	*Lab.* 34, *C.* 14, *LD* 10
Clackmannanshire	*Lab.* 8, *SNP* 3, *C.* 1
Dumfries and Galloway	*Ind.* 28, *Lab.* 20, *LD* 10, *SNP* 9, *C.* 2, *others* 1
Dundee City	*Lab.* 28, *C.* 4, *SNP* 3, *Ind. Lab.* 1
East Ayrshire	*Lab.* 22, *SNP* 8
East Dumbartonshire	*Lab.* 15, *LD* 9, *C.* 2
East Lothian	*Lab.* 15, *C.* 3
East Renfrewshire	*C.* 9, *Lab.* 8, *LD* 2, *RA* 1
Falkirk	*Lab.* 23, *SNP* 8, *Ind.* 3, *C.* 2
Fife	*Lab.* 54, *LD* 25, *SNP* 9, *Ind.* 2, *others* 2
Glasgow City	*Lab.* 77, *C.* 3, *LD* 1, *SNP* 1, *others* 1
Highland	*Ind.* 48, *SNP* 9, *Lab.* 7, *LD* 6, *C.* 1, *vacant* 1
Inverclyde	*Lab.* 14, *LD* 5, *C.* 1
Midlothian	*Lab.* 13, *SNP* 2
Moray	*SNP* 13, *Lab.* 3, *Ind.* 2
North Ayrshire	*Lab.* 27, *C.* 1, *Ind.* 1, *SNP* 1
North Lanarkshire	*Lab.* 60, *SNP* 7, *Ind.* 2
Orkney Islands	*Ind.* 28
Perth and Kinross	*SNP* 18, *Lab.* 6, *LD* 5, *C.* 2, *Ind.* 1
Renfrewshire	*Lab.* 20, *SNP* 13, *LD* 3, *C.* 2, *others* 2
Scottish Borders	*Ind.* 22, *LD* 17, *SNP* 8, *NP* 6, *C.* 3, *Lab.* 2,
Shetland Islands	*NP* 11, *Ind.* 8, *LD* 2, *Lab.* 1, *Ind. Lab.* 1, *others* 3
South Ayrshire	*Lab.* 21, *C.* 4
South Lanarkshire	*Lab.* 54, *SNP* 8, *C.* 2, *LD* 2, *others* 8
Stirling	*Lab.* 13, *C.* 7, *SNP* 2
West Dumbartonshire	*Lab.* 14, *SNP* 7, *Ind.* 1
Western Isles	*Ind.* 25, *Lab.* 5
West Lothian	*Lab.* 15, *SNP* 11, *C.* 1

Patron Saints

ST GEORGE
Patron Saint of England

St George is believed to have been born in Cappadocia, of Christian parents, in the latter part of the third century and to have served with distinction as a soldier under the Emperor Diocletian, including a visit to England on a military mission. When the persecution of Christians was ordered, St George sought a personal interview to remonstrate with the Emperor and after a profession of faith resigned his military commission. Arrest and torture followed and he was martyred at Nicomedia on 23 April 303, a day ordered to be kept in remembrance as a national festival by the Council of Oxford in 1222, although it was not until the reign of Edward III that he was made patron saint of England.

St George's connection with a dragon seems to date from the close of the sixth century and to be due to the transfer of his remains from Nicomedia to Lydda, close to the scene of the legendary exploit of Perseus in rescuing Andromeda and slaying the sea monster, credit for which became attached to the Christian martyr.

ST DAVID
Patron Saint of Wales

St David is believed to have been born towards the beginning and to have died towards the end of the sixth century. St David was an eloquent preacher, who founded the monastery at Menevia, now St David's. He became the patron of Wales, but there is no record of any papal canonization before 1181. His annual festival is observed on 1 March.

ST ANDREW
Patron Saint of Scotland

St Andrew, one of the apostles and brother of Simon Peter, was born at Bethsaida on the Sea of Galilee and lived at Capernaum. He preached the Gospel in Asia Minor and in Scythia along the shores of the Black Sea and became the patron saint of Russia. It is believed that he suffered crucifixion at Patras in Achaea, on a *crux decussata* (now known as St Andrew's Cross) and that his relics were removed from Patras to Constantinople and thence to St Andrews, probably in the eighth century, since which time he has been the patron saint of Scotland. The festival of St Andrew is held on 30 November.

ST PATRICK
Patron Saint of Ireland

St Patrick was born, probably in England, about 389 and was carried off to Ireland as a slave about 16 years later, escaping to Gaul at the age of 22. He was ordained deacon at Auxerre and having been consecrated Bishop in 432 was dispatched to Wicklow to reorganize the Christian communities in Ireland. He founded the see of Armagh and introduced Latin into Ireland as the language of the Church. He died *c.*461 and his festival is celebrated on 17 March.

England

The Kingdom of England lies between 55° 46′ and 49° 57′ 30″ N. latitude (from a few miles north of the mouth of the Tweed to the Lizard), and between 1° 46′ E. and 5° 43′ W. (from Lowestoft to Land's End). England is bounded on the north by the Cheviot Hills; on the south by the English Channel; on the east by the Straits of Dover (Pas de Calais) and the North Sea; and on the west by the Atlantic Ocean, Wales and the Irish Sea. It has a total area of 50,351 sq. miles (130,410 sq. km): land 50,058 sq. miles (129,652 sq. km); inland water 293 sq. miles (758 sq. km).

POPULATION

The population at the 1991 census was 46,382,050 (males 22,469,707; females 23,912,343). The average density of the population in 1991 was 3.6 persons per hectare.

FLAG

The flag of England is the cross of St George, a red cross on a white field (cross gules in a field argent). The cross of St George, the patron saint of England, has been used since the 13th century.

RELIEF

There is a marked division between the upland and lowland areas of England. In the extreme north the Cheviot Hills (highest point, The Cheviot, 2,674 ft) form a natural boundary with Scotland. Running south from the Cheviots, though divided from them by the Tyne Gap, is the Pennine range (highest point, Cross Fell, 2,930 ft), the main orological feature of the country. The Pennines culminate in the Peak District of Derbyshire (Kinder Scout, 2,088 ft). West of the Pennines are the Cumbrian mountains, which include Scafell Pike (3,210 ft), the highest peak in England, and to the east are the Yorkshire Moors, their highest point being Urra Moor (1,490 ft).

In the west, the foothills of the Welsh mountains extend into the bordering English counties of Shropshire (the Wrekin, 1,334 ft; Long Mynd, 1,694 ft) and Hereford and Worcester (the Malvern Hills – Worcestershire Beacon, 1,394 ft). Extensive areas of high land and moorland are also to be found in the south-western peninsula formed by Somerset, Devon and Cornwall: principally Exmoor (Dunkery Beacon, 1,704 ft), Dartmoor (High Willhays, 2,038 ft) and Bodmin Moor (Brown Willy, 1,377 ft). Ranges of low, undulating hills run across the south of the country, including the Cotswolds in the Midlands and south-west, the Chilterns to the north of London, and the North (Kent) and South (Sussex) Downs of the south-east coastal areas.

The lowlands of England lie in the Vale of York, East Anglia and the area around the Wash. The lowest-lying are the Cambridgeshire Fens in the valleys of the Great Ouse and the River Nene, which are below sea-level in places. Since the 17th century extensive drainage has brought much of the Fens under cultivation. The North Sea coast between the Thames and the Humber, low-lying and formed of sand and shingle for the most part, is subject to erosion and defences against further incursion have been built along many stretches.

HYDROGRAPHY

The Severn is the longest river in Great Britain, rising in the north-eastern slopes of Plynlimon (Wales) and entering England in Shropshire with a total length of 220 miles (354 km) from its source into its outflow into the Bristol Channel, where it receives on the east the Bristol Avon, and on the west the Wye, its other tributaries being the

Vyrnwy, Tern, Stour, Teme and Upper (or Warwickshire) Avon. The Severn is tidal below Gloucester, and a high bore or tidal wave sometimes reverses the flow as high as Tewkesbury (13½ miles above Gloucester). The scenery of the greater part of the river is very picturesque and beautiful, and the Severn is a noted salmon river, some of its tributaries being famous for trout. Navigation is assisted by the Gloucester and Berkeley Ship Canal (16¾ miles), which admits vessels of 350 tons to Gloucester. The Severn Tunnel was begun in 1873 and completed in 1886 at a cost of £2 million and after many difficulties from flooding. It is 4 miles 628 yards in length (of which 2¼ miles are under the river). The Severn road bridge between Haysgate, Gwent, and Almondsbury, Glos, with a centre span of 3,240 ft, was opened in 1966.

The longest river wholly in England is the Thames, with a total length of 215 miles (346 km) from its source in the Cotswold hills to the Nore, and is navigable by ocean-going ships to London Bridge. The Thames is tidal to Teddington (69 miles from its mouth) and forms county boundaries almost throughout its course; on its banks are situated London, Windsor Castle, the oldest royal residence still in regular use, Eton College and Oxford, the oldest university in the kingdom.

Of the remaining English rivers, those flowing into the North Sea are the Tyne, Wear, Tees, Ouse and Trent from the Pennine Range, the Great Ouse (160 miles), which rises in Northamptonshire, and the Orwell and Stour from the hills of East Anglia. Flowing into the English Channel are the Sussex Ouse from the Weald, the Itchen from the Hampshire Hills, and the Axe, Teign, Dart, Tamar and Exe from the Devonian hills. Flowing into the Irish Sea are the Mersey, Ribble and Eden from the western slopes of the Pennines and the Derwent from the Cumbrian mountains.

The English Lakes, noteworthy for their picturesque scenery and poetic associations, lie in Cumbria, the largest being Windermere (10 miles long), Ullswater and Derwent Water.

ISLANDS

The Isle of Wight is separated from Hampshire by the Solent. The capital, Newport, stands at the head of the estuary of the Medina, Cowes (at the mouth) being the chief port. Other centres are Ryde, Sandown, Shanklin, Ventnor, Freshwater, Yarmouth, Totland Bay, Seaview and Bembridge.

Lundy (the name means Puffin Island), 11 miles north-west of Hartland Point, Devon, is about two miles long and about half a mile wide on average, with a total area of about 1,116 acres, and a population of about 20. It became the property of the National Trust in 1969 and is now principally a bird sanctuary.

The Isles of Scilly consist of about 140 islands and skerries (total area, 6 sq. miles/10 sq. km) situated 28 miles south-west of Land's End. Only five are inhabited: St Mary's, St Agnes, Bryher, Tresco and St Martin's. The population is 1,978. The entire group has been designated a Conservation Area, a Heritage Coast, and an Area of Outstanding Natural Beauty, and has been given National Nature Reserve status by the Nature Conservancy Council because of its unique flora and fauna. Tourism and the winter/spring flower trade for the home market form the basis of the economy of the Isles. The island group is a recognized rural development area.

EARLY HISTORY

Archaeological evidence suggests that England has been inhabited since at least the Palaeolithic period, though the extent of the various Palaeolithic cultures was dependent upon the degree of glaciation. The succeeding Neolithic and Bronze Age cultures have left abundant remains throughout the country, the best-known of these being the henges and stone circles of Stonehenge (ten miles north of Salisbury, Wilts) and Avebury (Wilts), both of which are believed to have been of religious significance. In the latter part of the Bronze Age the Goidels, a people of Celtic race, and in the Iron Age other Celtic races of Brythons and Belgae, invaded the country and brought with them Celtic civilization and dialects, place names in England bearing witness to the spread of the invasion over the whole kingdom.

THE ROMAN CONQUEST

The Roman conquest of Gaul (57–50 BC) brought Britain into close contact with Roman civilization, but although Julius Caesar raided the south of Britain in 55 BC and 54 BC, conquest was not undertaken until nearly 100 years later. In AD 43 the Emperor Claudius dispatched Aulus Plautius, with a well-equipped force of 40,000, and himself followed with reinforcements in the same year. Success was delayed by the resistance of Caratacus (Caractacus), the British leader from AD 48–51, who was finally captured and sent to Rome, and by a great revolt in AD 61 led by Boudicca (Boadicea), Queen of the Iceni; but the south of Britain was secured by AD 70, and Wales and the area north to the Tyne by about AD 80.

In AD 122, the Emperor Hadrian visited Britain and built a continuous rampart, since known as Hadrian's Wall, from Wallsend to Bowness (Tyne to Solway). The work was entrusted by the Emperor Hadrian to Aulus Platorius Nepos, legate of Britain from AD 122 to 126, and it was intended to form the northern frontier of the Roman Empire.

The Romans administered Britain as a province under a Governor, with a well-defined system of local government, each Roman municipality ruling itself and its surrounding territory, while London was the centre of the road system and the seat of the financial officials of the Province of Britain. Colchester, Lincoln, York, Gloucester and St Albans stand on the sites of five Roman municipalities, and Wroxeter, Caerleon, Chester, Lincoln and York were at various times the sites of legionary fortresses. Well-preserved Roman towns have been uncovered at or near Silchester (*Calleva Atrebatum*), ten miles south of Reading, Wroxeter (*Viroconium Cornoviorum*), near Shrewsbury, and St Albans (*Verulamium*) in Hertfordshire.

Four main groups of roads radiated from London, and a fifth (the Fosse) ran obliquely from Lincoln through Leicester, Cirencester and Bath to Exeter. Of the four groups radiating from London, one ran south-east to Canterbury and the coast of Kent, a second to Silchester and thence to parts of western Britain and south Wales, a third (later known as Watling Street) ran through Verulamium to Chester, with various branches, and the fourth reached Colchester, Lincoln, York and the eastern counties.

In the fourth century Britain was subject to raids along the east coast by Saxon pirates, which led to the establishment of a system of coast defence from the Wash to Southampton Water, with forts at Brancaster, Burgh Castle (Yarmouth), Walton (Felixstowe), Bradwell, Reculver, Richborough, Dover, Lympne, Pevensey and Porchester (Portsmouth). The Irish (Scoti) and Picts in the north were also becoming more aggressive; from about AD 350

incursions became more frequent and more formidable. As the Roman Empire came under attack increasingly towards the end of the fourth century, many troops were removed from Britain for service in other parts of the empire. The island was eventually cut off from Rome by the Teutonic conquest of Gaul, and with the withdrawal of the last Roman garrison early in the fifth century, the Romano-British were left to themselves.

SAXON SETTLEMENT

According to legend, the British King Vortigern called in the Saxons to defend him against the Picts, the Saxon chieftains being Hengist and Horsa, who landed at Ebbsfleet, Kent, and established themselves in the Isle of Thanet; but the events during the one and a half centuries between the final break with Rome and the re-establishment of Christianity are unclear. However, it would appear that in the course of this period the raids turned into large-scale settlement by invaders traditionally known as Angles (England north of the Wash and East Anglia), Saxons (Essex and southern England) and Jutes (Kent and the Weald), which pushed the Romano-British into the mountainous areas of the north and west, Celtic culture outside Wales and Cornwall surviving only in topographical names. Various kingdoms were established at this time which attempted to claim overlordship of the whole country, hegemony finally being achieved by Wessex (capital, Winchester) in the ninth century. This century also saw the beginning of raids by the Vikings (Danes), which were resisted by Alfred the Great (871–899), who fixed a limit to the advance of Danish settlement by the Treaty of Wedmore (878), giving them the area north and east of Watling Street, on condition that they adopt Christianity.

In the tenth century the kings of Wessex recovered the whole of England from the Danes, but subsequent rulers were unable to resist a second wave of invaders. England paid tribute (*Danegeld*) for many years, and was invaded in 1013 by the Danes and ruled by Danish kings from 1016 until 1042, when Edward the Confessor was recalled from exile in Normandy. On Edward's death in 1066 Harold Godwinson (brother-in-law of Edward and son of Earl Godwin of Wessex) was chosen King of England. After defeating (at Stamford Bridge, Yorkshire, 25 September) an invading army under Harald Hadraada, King of Norway (aided by the outlawed Earl Tostig of Northumbria, Harold's brother), Harold was himself defeated at the Battle of Hastings on 14 October 1066, and the Norman conquest secured the throne of England for Duke William of Normandy, a cousin of Edward the Confessor.

CHRISTIANITY

Christianity reached the Roman province of Britain from Gaul in the third century (or possibly earlier); Alban, traditionally Britain's first martyr, was put to death as a Christian during the persecution of Diocletian (22 June 303), at his native town Verulamium; and the Bishops of Londinium, Eboracum (York), and Lindum (Lincoln) attended the Council of Arles in 314. However, the Anglo-Saxon invasions submerged the Christian religion in England until the sixth century when conversion was undertaken in the north from 563 by Celtic missionaries from Ireland led by St Columba, and in the south by a mission sent from Rome in 597 which was led by St Augustine, who became the first archbishop of Canterbury. England appears to have been converted again by the end of the seventh century and followed, after the Council of Whitby in 663, the practices of the Roman Church, which brought the kingdom into the mainstream of European thought and culture.

PRINCIPAL CITIES

BIRMINGHAM

Birmingham (West Midlands) is Britain's second city. It is a focal point in national communications networks with a rapidly expanding International Airport. The generally accepted derivation of 'Birmingham' is the *ham* (dwelling-place) of the *ing* (family) of *Beorma*, presumed to have been Saxon. During the Industrial Revolution the town grew into a major manufacturing centre. In 1889 Birmingham was granted city status.

Despite the decline in manufacturing, Birmingham is still a major hardware trade and motor component industry centre. As well as the National Exhibition Centre and the Aston Science Park, recent developments include the International Convention Centre and the National Indoor Arena.

The principal buildings are the Town Hall (1834–50); the Council House (1879); Victoria Law Courts (1891); Birmingham University (1906–9); the 13th-century Church of St Martin-in-the-Bull-Ring (rebuilt 1873); the Cathedral (formerly St Philip's Church) (1711) and the Roman Catholic Cathedral of St Chad (1839–41).

BRADFORD

Bradford (West Yorkshire) lies on the southern edge of the Yorkshire Dales National Park, including within its boundaries the village of Haworth, home of the Brontë sisters, and Ilkley Moor.

Originally a Saxon township, Bradford received a market charter in 1251 but developed only slowly until the industrialization of the textile industry brought rapid growth during the 19th century; it was granted its city charter in 1897. The prosperity of that period is reflected in much of the city's architecture, particularly the public buildings: City Hall (1873), Wool Exchange (1867), St George's Hall (Concert Hall, 1853), Cartwright Hall (Art Gallery, 1904) and the Technical College (1882). Other chief buildings are the Cathedral (15th century) and Bolling Hall (14th century).

Textiles still play an important part in the city's economy but industry is now more broadly based, including engineering, micro-electronics, printing and chemicals. The city has a strong financial services sector, and a growing tourism industry.

BRISTOL

Bristol was a Royal Borough before the Norman Conquest. The earliest form of the name is *Bricgstow*. In 1373 it received from Edward III a charter granting it county status.

The chief buildings include the 12th-century Cathedral (with later additions), with Norman chapter house and gateway, the 14th-century Church of St Mary Redcliffe, Wesley's Chapel, Broadmead, the Merchant Venturers' Almshouses, the Council House (1956), Guildhall, Exchange (erected from the designs of John Wood in 1743), Cabot Tower, the University and Clifton College. The Roman Catholic Cathedral at Clifton was opened in 1973.

The Clifton Suspension Bridge, with a span of 702 feet over the Avon, was projected by Brunel in 1836 but was not completed until 1864. Brunel's SS *Great Britain*, the first ocean-going propeller-driven ship, is now being restored in the City Docks from where she was launched in 1843.

The docks themselves have been extensively restored and redeveloped.

CAMBRIDGE

Cambridge, a settlement far older than its ancient University, lies on the River Cam or Granta. The city is a county town and regional headquarters. Its industries include electronics, high technology research and development, and biotechnology. Among its open spaces are Jesus Green, Sheep's Green, Coe Fen, Parker's Piece, Christ's Pieces, the University Botanic Garden, and the Backs, or lawns and gardens through which the Cam winds behind the principal line of college buildings. East of the Cam, King's Parade, upon which stand Great St Mary's Church, Gibbs' Senate House and King's College Chapel with Wilkins' screen, joins Trumpington Street to form one of the most beautiful throughfares in Europe.

University and college buildings provide the outstanding features of Cambridge architecture but several churches (especially St Benet's, the oldest building in the city, and St Sepulchre's, the Round Church) are also notable. The Guildhall (1939) stands on a site of which at least part has held municipal buildings since 1224.

CANTERBURY

Canterbury, the Metropolitan City of the Anglican Communion, has a history going back to prehistoric times. It was the Roman *Durovernum Cantiacorum* and the Saxon *Cant-wara-byrig* (stronghold of the men of Kent). Here in 597 St Augustine began the conversion of the English to Christianity, when Ethelbert, King of Kent, was baptized.

Of the Benedictine St Augustine's Abbey, burial place of the Jutish Kings of Kent (whose capital Canterbury was), only ruins remain. St Martin's Church, on the eastern outskirts of the city, is stated by Bede to have been the place of worship of Queen Bertha, the Christian wife of King Ethelbert, before the advent of St Augustine.

In 1170 the rivalry of Church and State culminated in the murder in Canterbury Cathedral, by Henry II's knights, of Archbishop Thomas Becket, whose shrine became a great centre of pilgrimage, as described by Chaucer in his *Canterbury Tales*. After the Reformation pilgrimages ceased, but the prosperity of the city was strengthened by an influx of Huguenot refugees, who introduced weaving. The poet and playwright Christopher Marlowe was born and reared in Canterbury, and there are also literary associations with Defoe, Dickens, Joseph Conrad and Somerset Maugham.

The Cathedral, with architecture ranging from the 11th to the 15th centuries, is world famous. Modern pilgrims are attracted particularly to the Martyrdom, the Black Prince's Tomb, the Warriors' Chapel and the many examples of medieval stained glass.

The medieval city walls are built on Roman foundations and the 14th-century West Gate is one of the finest buildings of its kind in the country.

The 1,000 seat Marlowe Theatre is a centre for the Canterbury Arts Festival each autumn.

CARLISLE

Carlisle is situated at the confluence of the River Eden and River Caldew, 309 miles north-west of London and about ten miles from the Scottish border. It was granted a charter in 1158.

The city stands at the western end of Hadrian's Wall and dates from the original Roman settlement of *Luguvalium*. Granted to Scotland in the tenth century, Carlisle is not included in the Domesday Book. William Rufus reclaimed the area in 1092 and the castle and city walls were built to guard Carlisle and the western border; the citadel is a Tudor addition to protect the south of the city. Border disputes were common until the problem of the Debateable Lands was settled in 1552. During the Civil War the city remained Royalist; in 1745 Carlisle was besieged for the last time by the Young Pretender.

The Cathedral, originally a 12th-century Augustinian priory, was enlarged in the 13th and 14th centuries after the diocese was created in 1133. To the south is a restored Tithe Barn and nearby the 18th-century church of St Cuthbert, the third to stand on a site dating from the seventh century.

Carlisle is the major shopping, commercial and agricultural centre for the area, and industries include the manufacture of metal goods, biscuits and textiles. However, the largest employer is the services sector, notably in central and local government, retailing and transport. The city has an important communications position at the centre of a network of major roads, as an important stage on the main west coast rail services, and with its own airport at Crosby-on-Eden.

CHESTER

Chester is situated on the River Dee, and was granted borough and city status in 1974. Its recorded history dates from the first century when the Romans founded the fortress of *Deva*. The city's name is derived from the Latin *castra* (a camp or encampment). During the Middle Ages, Chester was the principal port of north-west England but declined with the silting of the Dee estuary and competition from Liverpool. The city was also an important military centre, notably during Edward I's Welsh campaigns and the Elizabethan Irish campaigns. During the Civil War, Chester supported the King and was besieged from 1643 to 1646. Chester's first charter was granted *c.*1175 and the city was incorporated in 1506. The office of Sheriff is the earliest created in the country (*c.*1120s), and in 1992 the Mayor was granted the title of Lord Mayor. He/she also enjoys the title 'Admiral of the Dee'.

The city's architectural features include the city walls (an almost complete two-mile circuit), the unique 13th-century Rows (covered galleries above the street-level shops), the Victorian Gothic Town Hall (1869), the Castle (rebuilt 1788 and 1822) and numerous half-timbered buildings. The Cathedral was a Benedictine abbey until the Dissolution. Remaining monastic buildings include the chapter house, refectory and cloisters and there is a modern free-standing bell tower. The Norman church of St John the Baptist was a cathedral church in the early Middle Ages.

Chester is a thriving retail, business and tourist centre.

COVENTRY

Coventry (West Midlands) is an important industrial centre, producing vehicles, machine tools, agricultural machinery, man-made fibres, aerospace components and telecommunications equipment. New investment has come from financial services, power transmission, professional services and education.

The city owes its beginning to Leofric, Earl of Mercia, and his wife Godiva who, in 1043, founded a Benedictine monastery. The guildhall of St Mary dates from the 14th century, three of the city's churches date from the 14th and 15th centuries, and 16th-century almshouses may still be seen. Coventry's first cathedral was destroyed at the Reformation, its second in the 1940 blitz (the walls and spire remain) and the new cathedral designed by Sir Basil Spence, consecrated in 1962, now draws innumerable visitors.

Coventry is the home of the University of Warwick and its Science Park, Coventry University, the Westwood Business Park, the Cable and Wireless College, and the Museum of British Road Transport.

DERBY

Derby stands on the banks of the River Derwent, and its name dates back to 880 when the Danes settled in the locality and changed the original Saxon name of *Northworthy* to *Deoraby*.

Derby has a wide range of industries: its products include aero engines, pipework, specialized mechanical engineering equipment, textiles, chemicals, plastics and the Royal Crown Derby porcelain. The city is an established railway centre, the site of British Rail's Technical Centre with its research laboratories.

Buildings of interest include St Peter's Church and the Old Abbey Building (14th century), the Cathedral (1525), St Mary's Roman Catholic Church (1839) and the Industrial Museum, formerly the Old Silk Mill (1721). The traditional city centre is complemented by the Eagle Centre and 'out-of-centre' retail developments. In addition to the Derby Playhouse, the Assembly Rooms are a multi-purpose venue.

The first charter granting a Mayor and Aldermen was that of Charles I in 1637. Previous charters date back to 1154. It was granted city status in 1977.

DURHAM

The city of Durham is a district in the county of Durham and a major tourist attraction because of its prominent Norman Cathedral and Castle set high on a wooded peninsula overlooking the River Wear. The Cathedral was founded as a shrine for the body of St Cuthbert in 995. The present building dates from 1093 and among its many treasures is the tomb of the Venerable Bede (673–735). Durham's Prince Bishops had unique powers up to 1836, being lay rulers as well as religious leaders. As a palatinate Durham could have its own army, nobility, coinage and courts. The Castle was the main seat of the Prince Bishops for nearly 800 years; it is now used as a college by the University. The University, founded on the initiative of Bishop William Van Mildert, is England's third oldest.

Among other buildings of interest is the Guildhall in the Market Place which dates originally from the 14th century. Much work has been carried out to conserve this area, forming part of the city's major contribution to the Council of Europe's Urban Renaissance Campaign. Annual events include Durham's Regatta in June (claimed to be the oldest rowing event in Britain) and the Annual Gala (formerly Durham Miners' Gala) in July.

The economy of Durham has undergone a significant change with the replacement of mining as the dominant industry by 'white collar' employment. Although still a predominantly rural area, the industrial and commercial sector is growing and a wide range of manufacturing and service industries are based on industrial estates in and around the city.

EXETER

Exeter lies on the River Exe ten miles from the sea. It was granted a charter by Henry II. The Romans founded *Isca Dumnoniorum* in the first century AD, and in the third century a stone wall (much of which remains) was built, providing protection against Saxon, and then Danish invasions. After the Conquest, the city led resistance to William in the west until reduced by siege. The Normans built the ringwork castle of Rougemont, the gatehouse and one tower of which remain, although the rest was pulled down in 1784. The first bridge across the Exe was built in the early 13th century. The city's main port was situated downstream at Topsham until the construction in the 1560s of the first true canal in England, the redevelopment of which in 1700 brought seaborne trade direct to the city. Exeter was the Royalist headquarters in the west during the Civil War.

The diocese of Exeter was established by Edward the Confessor in 1050, although a minster existed near the Cathedral site from the late seventh century. A new cathedral was built in the 12th century but the present building was begun c.1275, although incorporating the Norman towers, and completed about a century later. The Guildhall dates from the 12th century and there are many other medieval buildings in the city, as well as architecture in the Georgian and Regency styles, and the Custom House (1680). Damage suffered by bombing in 1942 led to the redevelopment of the city centre.

Exeter's prosperity from medieval times was based on trade in wool and woollen cloth (commemorated by Tuckers Hall), which remained at its height until the late 18th century when export trade was hit by the French wars. Subsequently Exeter has developed as an administrative and commercial centre, notably in the distributive trades, light manufacturing industries and tourism.

KINGSTON UPON HULL

Hull (officially Kingston upon Hull) lies at the junction of the River Hull with the Humber, 22 miles from the North Sea. It is one of the major seaports of the United Kingdom. It has docks covering a water area of 172 acres, equipped to handle cargoes by unit-load techniques, and is a departure point for car ferry services to continental Europe. There is a variety of industry and service industries, as well as increasing tourism and conference business.

The city, restored after heavy air raid damage during the Second World War, has good office and administrative buildings, its municipal centre being the Guildhall, its educational centres the University of Hull and Humberside University and its religious centre the Parish Church of the Holy Trinity. The old town area is being renovated and includes a marina and shopping complex. Just west of the city is the Humber Bridge, the world's longest single-span suspension bridge.

Kingston upon Hull was so named by Edward I. City status was accorded in 1897 and the office of Mayor raised to the dignity of Lord Mayor in 1914.

LEEDS

Leeds (West Yorkshire), situated in the lower Aire Valley, is a junction for road, rail, canal and air services and an important manufacturing and commercial centre. Seventy-three per cent of employment is in services, notably the distributive trades, public administration, medical services and business services. The main manufacturing industries are mechanical engineering, printing and publishing, metal goods and furniture.

The principal buildings are the Civic Hall (1933), the Town Hall (1858), the Municipal Buildings and Art Gallery (1884) with the Henry Moore Gallery (1982), the Corn Exchange (1863) and the University. The Parish Church (St Peter's) was rebuilt in 1841; the 17th-century St John's Church has a fine interior with a famous English Renaissance screen; the last remaining 18th-century church in the city is Holy Trinity in Boar Lane (1727). Kirkstall Abbey (about three miles from the centre of the city), founded by Henry de Lacy in 1152, is one of the most

complete examples of Cistercian houses now remaining. Temple Newsam, birthplace of Lord Darnley, was acquired by the Council in 1922. The present house was largely rebuilt by Sir Arthur Ingram in about 1620. Adel Church, about five miles from the centre of the city, is a fine Norman structure. The new Royal Armouries Museum houses the collection of antique arms and armour formerly held at the Tower of London.

Leeds was first incorporated by Charles I in 1626. The earliest forms of the name are *Loidis* or *Ledes*, the origins of which are obscure.

LEICESTER

Leicester is situated geographically in the centre of England. It dates back to pre-Roman times and was one of the five Danish *Burghs*. In 1589 Queen Elizabeth I granted a charter to the city and the ancient title was confirmed by letters patent in 1919.

The principal industries are hosiery, knitwear, footwear manufacturing and engineering. The growth of Leicester as a hosiery centre increased rapidly from the introduction there of the first stocking frame in 1670 and today it has some of the largest hosiery factories in the world.

The principal buildings are the Town Hall, the New Walk Centre, the University of Leicester, De Montfort University, De Montfort Hall, one of the finest concert halls in the provinces seating over 2,750 people, and the Granby Halls, an indoor sports facility. The ancient churches of St Martin (now Leicester Cathedral), St Nicholas, St Margaret, All Saints, St Mary de Castro, and buildings such as the Guildhall, the 14th-century Newarke Gate, the Castle and the Jewry Wall Roman site still exist. The Haymarket Theatre was opened in 1973 and The Shires shopping centre in 1992.

LINCOLN

Situated 40 miles inland on the River Witham, Lincoln derives its name from a contraction of *Lindum Colonia*, the settlement founded in AD 48 by the Romans to command the crossing of Ermine Street and Fosse Way. Sections of the third-century Roman city wall can be seen, including an extant gateway (Newport Arch), and excavations have discovered traces of a sewerage system unique in Britain. The Romans also drained the surrounding fenland and created a canal system, laying the foundations of Lincoln's agricultural prosperity and also of the city's importance in the medieval wool trade as a port and Staple town.

As one of the Five Boroughs of the Danelaw, Lincoln was an important trading centre in the ninth and tenth centuries and medieval prosperity from the wool trade lasted until the 14th century, enabling local merchants to build parish churches (of which three survive), and attracting in the 12th century a Jewish community (Jew's House and Court, Aaron's House). However, the removal of the Staple to Boston in 1369 heralded a decline from which the city only recovered fully in the 19th century when improved fen drainage made Lincoln agriculturally important and improved canal and rail links led to industrial development, mainly in the manufacture of machinery, components and engineering products.

The castle was built shortly after the Conquest and is unusual in having two mounds; on one motte stands a Keep (Lucy's Tower) added in the 12th century. It currently houses one of the four surviving copies of the Magna Carta. The Cathedral was begun c.1073 when the first Norman bishop moved the see of Lindsey to Lincoln, but was mostly destroyed by fire and earthquake in the 12th century. Rebuilding was begun by St Hugh and completed over a century later. Other notable architectural features are the 12th-century High Bridge, the oldest in Britain still to carry buildings, and the Guildhall situated above the 15th–16th-century Stonebow gateway.

LIVERPOOL

Liverpool (Merseyside) on the right bank of the River Mersey, three miles from the Irish Sea, is the United Kingdom's foremost port for the Atlantic trade. Tunnels link Liverpool with Birkenhead and Wallasey.

There are 2,100 acres of dockland on both sides of the river and the Gladstone and Royal Seaforth Docks can accommodate the largest vessels afloat. Annual tonnage of cargo handled is approximately 27.8 million tonnes. The main imports are crude oil, grain, ores, edible oils, timber, containers and break-bulk cargo. Liverpool Free Port, Britain's largest, was opened in 1984.

Liverpool was created a free borough in 1207 and a city in 1880. From the early 18th century it expanded rapidly with the growth of industrialization and the Atlantic trade. Surviving buildings from this date include the Bluecoat Chambers (1717, formerly the Bluecoat School), the Town Hall (1754, rebuilt to the original design 1795), and buildings in Rodney Street, Canning Street and the suburbs. Notable from the 19th and 20th centuries are the Anglican Cathedral, built from the designs of Sir Giles Gilbert Scott (the foundation stone was laid in 1904, the building was completed only in 1980), the Catholic Metropolitan Cathedral (designed by Sir Frederick Gibberd, consecrated 1967) and St George's Hall (1838–54), regarded as one of the finest modern examples of classical architecture. The refurbished Albert Dock (designed by Jesse Hartley) contains the Merseyside Maritime Museum and Tate Gallery, Liverpool.

In 1852 an Act was obtained for establishing a public library, museum and art gallery; as a result Liverpool had one of the first public libraries in the country. The Brown, Picton and Hornby libraries now form one of the country's major libraries. The Victoria Building of Liverpool University, the Royal Liver, Cunard and Mersey Docks & Harbour Company buildings at the Pier Head, the Municipal Buildings and the Philharmonic Hall are other examples of the city's fine buildings.

MANCHESTER

Manchester (the *Mamucium* of the Romans, who occupied it in AD 79) is a commercial and industrial centre with a population engaged in the engineering, chemical, clothing, food processing and textile industries and in education. Banking, insurance and a growing leisure industry are among the prime commercial activities. The city is connected with the sea by the Manchester Ship Canal, opened in 1894, 35½ miles long, and accommodating ships up to 15,000 tons. Manchester Airport handles 15 million passengers yearly.

The principal buildings are the Town Hall, erected in 1877 from the designs of Alfred Waterhouse, together with a large extension of 1938; the Royal Exchange (1869, enlarged 1921); the Central Library (1934); Heaton Hall; the 17th-century Chetham Library; the Rylands Library (1900), which includes the Althorp collection; the University precinct; the 15th-century Cathedral (formerly the parish church); G-MEX exhibition centre and the Free Trade Hall. Recent developments include the Manchester Arena, the largest indoor arena in Europe. Manchester is the home of the Hallé Orchestra, the Royal Northern College of Music, the Royal Exchange Theatre and seven public art galleries. Metrolink, the new light rail system, opened in 1992.

The town received its first charter of incorporation in 1838 and was created a city in 1853. The title of City was retained under local government reorganization.

NEWCASTLE UPON TYNE

Newcastle upon Tyne (Tyne and Wear), on the north bank of the River Tyne, is eight miles from the North Sea. A cathedral and university city, it is the administrative, commercial and cultural centre for north-east England and the principal port. It is an important manufacturing centre with a wide variety of industries.

The principal buildings include the Castle Keep (12th century), Black Gate (13th century), Blackfriars (13th century), West Walls (13th century), St Nicholas's Cathedral (15th century, fine lantern tower), St Andrew's Church (12th–14th century), St John's (14th–15th century), All Saints (1786 by Stephenson), St Mary's Roman Catholic Cathedral (1844), Trinity House (17th century), Sandhill (16th-century houses), Guildhall (Georgian), Grey Street (1834–9), Central Station (1846–50), Laing Art Gallery (1904), University of Newcastle Physics Building (1962) and Medical Building (1985), Civic Centre (1963), Central Library (1969) and Eldon Square Shopping Development (1976). Open spaces include the Town Moor (927 acres) and Jesmond Dene. Nine bridges span the Tyne at Newcastle.

The city derives its name from the 'new castle' (1080) erected as a defence against the Scots. In 1400 it was made a county, and in 1882 a city.

NORWICH

Norwich (Norfolk) grew from an early Anglo-Saxon settlement near the confluence of the Rivers Yare and Wensum, and now serves as provincial capital for the predominantly agricultural region of East Anglia. The name is thought to relate to the most northerly of a group of Anglo-Saxon villages or *wics*. The city's first known charter was granted in 1158 by Henry II.

Norwich serves its surrounding area as a market town and commercial centre, banking and insurance being prominent among the city's businesses. From the 14th century until the Industrial Revolution, Norwich was the regional centre of the woollen industry, but now the biggest single industry is financial services and principal trades are engineering, printing, shoemaking, double glazing, and the production of chemicals, clothing and food processing. Norwich is accessible to seagoing vessels by means of the River Yare, entered at Great Yarmouth, 20 miles to the east.

Among many historic buildings are the Cathedral (completed in the 12th century and surmounted by a 15th-century spire 315 feet in height), the keep of the Norman castle (now a museum and art gallery), the 15th-century flint-walled Guildhall (now a tourist information centre), some thirty medieval parish churches, St Andrew's and Blackfriars' Halls, the Tudor houses preserved in Elm Hill and the Georgian Assembly House. The University of East Anglia is located on a site at Earlham on the city's western boundary.

NOTTINGHAM

Nottingham stands on the River Trent and is connected by canal with the Atlantic Ocean and the North Sea. *Snotinga-ham* or *Notingeham*, literally the homestead of the people of Snot, is the Anglo-Saxon name for the Celtic settlement of *Tigguocobauc*, or the house of caves. In 878, Nottingham became one of the Five Boroughs of the Danelaw. William the Conqueror ordered the construction of Nottingham

Castle, while the town itself developed rapidly under Norman rule. Its laws and rights were later formally recognized by Henry II's charter in 1155. The Castle became a favoured residence of King John. In 1642 King Charles I raised his personal standard at Nottingham Castle at the start of the Civil War.

Nottingham is a major sporting centre, home to Nottingham Forest FC, Notts County FC (the world's oldest Football league side), Nottingham Racecourse and the National Watersports Centre. The principal industries include textiles, pharmaceuticals, food manufacturing, engineering and telecommunications. There are two universities within the city boundaries.

Architecturally, Nottingham has a wealth of notable buildings, particularly those designed in the Victorian era by T. C. Hine and Watson Fothergill. The City Council owns the Castle, of Norman origin but restored in 1878, Wollaton Hall (1580–8), Newstead Abbey (home of Lord Byron), the Guildhall (1888) and Council House (1929). St Mary's, St Peter's and St Nicholas's Churches are of interest, as is the Roman Catholic Cathedral (Pugin, 1842–4).

Nottingham was granted city status in 1897.

OXFORD

Oxford is a university city, an important industrial centre, and a market town. Industry played a minor part in Oxford until the motor industry was established in 1912.

It is for its architecture that Oxford is of most interest to the visitor, its oldest specimens being the reputedly Saxon tower of St Michael's church, the remains of the Norman castle and city walls, and the Norman church at Iffley. It is chiefly famous, however, for its Gothic buildings, such as the Divinity Schools, the Old Library at Merton College, William of Wykeham's New College, Magdalen College and Christ Church and many other college buildings. Later centuries are represented by the Laudian quadrangle at St John's College, the Renaissance Sheldonian Theatre by Wren, Trinity College Chapel, and All Saints Church; Hawksmoor's mock-Gothic at All Souls College, and the 18th-century Queen's College. In addition to individual buildings, High Street and Radcliffe Square, just off it, both form architectural compositions of great beauty. Most of the Colleges have gardens, those of Magdalen, New College, St John's and Worcester being the largest.

PLYMOUTH

Plymouth is situated on the borders of Devon and Cornwall at the confluence of the Rivers Tamar and Plym. The city has a long maritime history; it was the home port of Sir Francis Drake and the starting point for his circumnavigation of the world, as well as the last port of call for the *Mayflower* when the Pilgrim Fathers sailed for the New World in 1620. Today Plymouth is host to many international yacht races. The Barbican harbour area has many Elizabethan buildings and on Plymouth Hoe stands Smeaton's lighthouse, the third to be built on the Eddystone Rocks 13 miles offshore.

The city centre was rebuilt following extensive war damage, and comprises a large shopping centre, municipal offices, law courts and public buildings. The main employment is provided at the naval base, though many industrial firms and service industries have become established in the post-war period and the city is a growing tourism centre. In 1982 the Theatre Royal was opened. In conjunction with the Cornwall County Council, the Tamar Bridge was constructed linking the city by road with Cornwall.

PORTSMOUTH

Portsmouth occupies Portsea Island, Hampshire, with boundaries extending to the mainland. It is a centre of industry and commerce, including many high technology and manufacturing industries. It is the British headquarters of several major international companies. The Royal Navy base still has a substantial work-force, although this has decreased in recent years. The commercial port and continental ferry port is owned and run by the City Council, and carries passengers and vehicles to France and northern Spain.

A major port since the 16th century, Portsmouth is also a thriving seaside resort catering for thousands of visitors annually. Among many historic attractions are Lord Nelson's flagship, HMS *Victory*, the Tudor warship *Mary Rose*, Britain's first 'ironclad' warship, HMS *Warrior*, the D-Day Museum, Charles Dickens' birthplace at 393 Old Commercial Road, the Royal Naval and Royal Marine museums, Southsea Castle (built by Henry VIII), the Round Tower and Point Battery, which for hundreds of years have guarded the entrance to Portsmouth Harbour, Fort Nelson on Portsdown Hill and the Sealife Centre.

ST ALBANS

The origins of St Albans, situated on the River Ver, stem from the Roman town of *Verulamium*. Named after the first Christian martyr in Britain, who was executed here, St Albans has developed around the Norman Abbey and Cathedral Church (consecrated 1115), built partly of materials from the old Roman city. The museums house Iron Age and Roman artefacts and the Roman Theatre, unique in Britain, has a stage as opposed to an amphitheatre. Archaeological excavations in the city centre have revealed evidence of pre-Roman, Saxon and medieval occupation.

The town's significance grew to the extent that it was a signatory and venue for the drafting of the Magna Carta. It was also the scene of riots during the Peasants' Revolt, the French King John was imprisoned there after the Battle of Poitiers, and heavy fighting took place there during the Wars of the Roses.

Previously controlled by the Abbot, the town achieved a charter in 1553 and city status in 1877. The street market, first established in 1553, is still an important feature of the city, as are many hotels and inns which survive from the days when St Albans was an important coach stop. Tourist attractions include historic churches and houses, and a 15th-century clock tower.

The city now contains a wide range of firms, with special emphasis on micro-technology and electronics, particularly in the medical field. In addition, it is the home of the Royal National Rose Society, and of Rothamsted Park, the agricultural research centre.

SHEFFIELD

Sheffield (South Yorkshire), the centre of the special steel and cutlery trades, is situated at the junction of the Sheaf, Porter, Rivelin and Loxley valleys with the River Don. Though its cutlery, silverware and plate have long been famous, Sheffield has other and now more important industries: special and alloy steels, engineering, toolmaking and medical equipment. Sheffield has two universities and is an important research centre.

The parish church of St Peter and St Paul, founded in the 12th century, became the Cathedral Church of the Diocese of Sheffield in 1914. The Roman Catholic Cathedral Church of St Marie (founded 1847) was created Cathedral for the new diocese of Hallam in 1980. Parts of the present building date from *c*.1435. The principal buildings are the Town Hall (1897), the Cutlers' Hall (1832), City Hall (1932), Graves Art Gallery (1934), Mappin Art Gallery, the Crucible Theatre and the restored 19th-century Lyceum theatre, which dates from 1897 and was reopened in 1990. Three major sports venues were opened in 1990 to 1991.

Sheffield was created a city in 1893 and in 1974 retained its city status.

Master Cutler of the Company of Cutlers in Hallamshire 1995– 6,
D. R. Stone

SOUTHAMPTON

Southampton is the leading British deep-sea port on the Channel and is situated on one of the finest natural harbours in the world. The first charter was granted by Henry II and Southampton was created a county of itself in 1447. In 1964 it was granted city status.

There were Roman and Saxon settlements on the site of the city, which has been an important port since the time of the Conquest due to its natural deep-water harbour. The oldest church is St Michael's (1070) which has an unusually tall spire built in the 18th century as a landmark for navigators of Southampton Water. Other buildings and monuments within the city walls are the Tudor House Museum, God's House Tower, the Bargate museum, the Tudor Merchants Hall, the Weigh-house, West Gate, King John's House, Long House, Wool House, the ruins of Holy Rood Church, St Julien's Church and the Mayflower Memorial. The medieval town walls, built for artillery, are among the most complete in Europe. Public open spaces total over 1,000 acres and comprise 9 per cent of the city's area. The Common covers an area of 328 acres in the central district of the city and is mostly natural parkland. Two recent additions to work in marine technology in Southampton are Europe's leading oceanographic research centre (part of the University) and the marine science and technology business park.

STOKE-ON-TRENT

Stoke-on-Trent (Staffordshire), standing on the River Trent and familiarly known as The Potteries, is the main centre of employment for the population of North Staffordshire. The city is the largest clayware producer in the world (china, earthenware, sanitary goods, refractories, bricks and tiles) and also has a wide range of other manufacturing industry, including steel, chemicals, engineering and tyres. Extensive reconstruction has been carried out in recent years.

The city was formed by the federation of the separate municipal authorities of Tunstall, Burslem, Hanley, Stoke, Fenton, and Longton in 1910 and received its city status in 1925.

WINCHESTER

Winchester, the ancient capital of England, is situated on the River Itchen. The city is rich in architecture of all types but the Cathedral takes pride of place. The longest Gothic cathedral in the world, it was built in 1079–93 and exhibits examples of Norman, Early English and Perpendicular styles. Winchester College, founded in 1382, is one of the most famous public schools, the original building (1393) remaining largely unaltered. St Cross Hospital, another great medieval foundation, lies one mile south of the city. The almshouses were founded in 1136 by Bishop Henry de Blois, and Cardinal Henry Beaufort added a new almshouse of 'Noble Poverty' in 1446. The chapel and dwellings are of great architectural interest, and visitors may still receive the 'Wayfarer's Dole' of bread and ale.

Excavations have done much to clarify the origins and development of Winchester. Part of the forum and several of the streets of the Roman town have been discovered; excavations in the Cathedral Close have uncovered the entire site of the Anglo-Saxon cathedral (known as the Old Minster) and parts of the New Minster which was built by Alfred's son Edward the Elder and is the burial place of the Alfredian dynasty. The original burial place of St Swithun, before his remains were translated to a site in the present cathedral, was also uncovered.

Excavations in other parts of the city have thrown much light on Norman Winchester, notably on the site of the Royal Castle (adjacent to which the new Law Courts have been built) and in the grounds of Wolvesey Castle, where the great house built by Bishops Giffard and Henry de Blois in the 12th century has been uncovered. The Great Hall, built by Henry III between 1222 and 1236 survives and houses the Arthurian Round Table.

YORK

The city of York is an archiepiscopal seat. Its recorded history dates from AD 71, when the Roman Ninth Legion established a base under Petilius Cerealis which later became the fortress of *Eburacum*. In Anglo-Saxon times the city was the royal and ecclesiastical centre of Northumbria, and after capture by a Viking army in AD 866 it became the capital of the Viking kingdom of Jorvik. By the 14th century the city had become a great mercantile centre, mainly because of its control of the wool trade, and was used as the chief base against the Scots. Under the Tudors its fortunes declined, though Henry VIII made it the headquarters of the Council of the North. Excavations on many sites, including Coppergate, have greatly expanded knowledge of Roman, Viking and medieval urban life.

With its development as a railway centre in the 19th century the commercial life of York expanded. The principal industries are the manufacture of chocolate, scientific instruments and sugar. It is the location of several government departments.

The city is rich in examples of architecture of all periods. The earliest church was built in AD 627 and, in the 12th to 15th centuries, the present Minster was built in a succession of styles. Other examples within the city are the medieval city walls and gateways, churches and guildhalls. Domestic architecture includes the Georgian mansions of The Mount, Micklegate and Bootham.

English Counties and Shires

LORD LIEUTENANTS AND HIGH SHERIFFS

County/Shire	Lord Lieutenant	High Sheriff, 1996–7
Bedfordshire	S. C. Whitbread	J. J. M. Glasse
Berkshire	P. L. Wroughton	C. Spence
Bristol	J. Tidmarsh, MBE	G. Ferguson
Buckinghamshire	Sir Nigel Mobbs (from Jan. 1997)	R. E. Morris-Adams
Cambridgeshire	J. G. P. Crowden	N. H. M. Chancellor
Cheshire	W. Bromley Davenport	Sir Anthony Pilkington
Cornwall	Lady Holborow	Mrs D. Morrison
Cumbria	J. A. Cropper	H. C. F. Bowring
Derbyshire	J. K. Bather	Brig. C. E. Wilkinson, CBE, TD
Devon	The Earl of Morley	Mrs Y. M. V. Tremlett
Dorset	The Lord Digby	W. J. Weld
Durham	D. J. Grant, CBE	J. A. Marr
East Riding of Yorkshire	R. Marriott, TD	T. Martin
East Sussex	Adm. Sir Lindsay Bryson, KCB, FEng.	J. Fooks
Essex	The Lord Braybrooke	P. T. Thistlethwayte
Gloucestershire	H. W. G. Elwes	J. G. Peel
Greater London	Field Marshal the Lord Bramall, KG, GCB, OBE, MC	Sir Cyril Taylor
Greater Manchester	Col. J. B. Timmins, OBE, TD	Mrs M. F. MacKinnon Firth, OBE
Hampshire	Mrs F. M. Fagan	M. Radcliffe
Hereford and Worcester	Sir Thomas Dunne, KCVO	Mrs R. S. Clive
Hertfordshire	S. A. Bowes Lyon	R. Dimsdale
Isle of Wight	*C. D. J. Bland	Mrs J. A. Griffin
Kent	The Lord Kingsdown, KG, PC	P. Smallwood
Lancashire	Sir Simon Towneley, KCVO	T. R. H. Kimber
Leicestershire	T. G. M. Brooks	G. N. Corah
Lincolnshire	Mrs B. K. Cracroft-Eley	J. Milligan-Manby
Merseyside	A. W. Waterworth	Mrs J. A. Grundy
Norfolk	Sir Timothy Colman, KG	I. D. R. MacNicol, FRICS
Northamptonshire	J. L. Lowther, CBE	M. F. Collcutt
Northumberland	The Viscount Ridley, KG, GCVO, TD	J. F. C. Festing
North Yorkshire	Sir Marcus Worsley, Bt.	J. L. C. Pratt
Nottinghamshire	Sir Andrew Buchanan, Bt.	T. Parr
Oxfordshire	H. L. J. Brunner	M. Cochrane
Shropshire	A. E. H. Heber-Percy	T. W. E. Corbett
Somerset	Sir John Vernon Wills, Bt., TD	C. Thomas-Everard, FRICS
South Yorkshire	The Earl of Scarbrough	W. G. A. Warde-Norbury
Staffordshire	J. A. Hawley, TD	S. E. Mitchell
Suffolk	The Lord Belstead, PC	J. Kerr, MBE
Surrey	R. E. Thornton, OBE	A. Sanders
Tyne and Wear	Sir Ralph Carr-Ellison, TD	Dr M. L. Fisher
Warwickshire	The Viscount Daventry	Maj. J. W. Oakes
West Midlands	R. R. Taylor, OBE	J. D. Saville
West Sussex	Maj.-Gen. Sir Philip Ward, KCVO, CBE	J. Knight
West Yorkshire	J. Lyles	J. S. Behrens
Wiltshire	Lt.-Gen. Sir Maurice Johnston, KCB, OBE	A. W. M. Christie-Miller

* Lord Lieutenant and Governor

COUNTY COUNCILS: Area, Population, Finance

Council	Administrative headquarters	Area (hectares)	Population 1994	Total demand upon collection fund 1996–7
Bedfordshire	County Hall, Bedford	123,468	543,100	£89,379,000
Berkshire	Shire Hall, Shinfield Park, Reading	125,901	769,200	137,660,000
Buckinghamshire	County Hall, Aylesbury	188,279	658,400	118,700,000
Cambridgeshire	Shire Hall, Cambridge	340,181	686,900	107,400,000
Cheshire	County Hall, Chester	233,325	975,600	178,581,418
Cornwall	County Hall, Truro	356,442†	479,600†	76,054,000
Cumbria	The Courts, Carlisle	682,451	490,200	86,787,000
Derbyshire	County Offices, Matlock	263,098	954,100	152,900,000
Devon	County Hall, Exeter	671,096	1,053,400	164,585,000
Dorset	County Hall, Dorchester	265,433	673,000	117,656,209
Durham	County Hall, Durham	243,369	607,800	81,899,510
East Sussex	Pelham House, St Andrew's Lane, Lewes	179,530	726,500	129,431,000
Essex	County Hall, Chelmsford	367,167	1,569,900	259,656,000
Gloucestershire	Shire Hall, Gloucester	264,270	549,500	88,913,412
Hampshire	The Castle, Winchester	378,022	1,605,700	255,214,000
Hereford and Worcester	County Hall, Worcester	392,650	699,900	109,882,000
Hertfordshire	County Hall, Hertford	163,601	1,005,400	179,025,000
§Isle of Wight	County Hall, Newport, IOW	38,063	124,600	27,783,500
Kent	County Hall, Maidstone	373,063	1,546,300	25,500,000
Lancashire	County Hall, Preston	306,957	1,424,000	237,191,000
Leicestershire	County Hall, Glenfield, Leicester	255,297	916,900	133,221,000
Lincolnshire	County Offices, Newland, Lincoln	591,791	605,600	91,135,000
Norfolk	County Hall, Norwich	537,482	768,500	118,458,000
Northamptonshire	County Hall, Northampton	236,721	594,800	90,465,384
Northumberland	County Hall, Morpeth	503,165	307,700	51,222,531
North Yorkshire	County Hall, Northallerton	803,741	726,100	91,048,594
Nottinghamshire	County Hall, Nottingham	216,090	1,030,900	172,615,513
Oxfordshire	County Hall, Oxford	260,798	590,200	109,594,000
Shropshire	The Shirehall, Shrewsbury	349,013	416,500	63,709,000
Somerset	County Hall, Taunton	345,233	477,900	82,000,000
Staffordshire	County Buildings, Stafford	271,616	1,054,400	145,145,432
Suffolk	County Hall, Ipswich	379,664	649,500	101,722,000
Surrey	County Hall, Kingston upon Thames	167,924	1,041,200	211,700,000
Warwickshire	Shire Hall, Warwick	198,052	496,300	90,714,000
West Sussex	County Hall, Chichester	198,935	722,100	134,600,000
Wiltshire	County Hall, Trowbridge	347,883	586,300	95,323,000

Source for population figures: OPCS Monitor PP1 96/1, 29 February 1996
† Including Isles of Scilly
§ Unitary authority since April 1995

COUNTY COUNCILS: Officers and Chairman

Council	Chief Executive	County Treasurer	Chairman of County Council
Bedfordshire	D. Cleggett	*B. Phelps	B. K. W. Gibbons
Berkshire	°G. B. Scotford, OBE	†I. Thompson	M. L. Tomkinson
Buckinghamshire	I. Crookall	**J. Beckerlegg	K. I. Ross
Cambridgeshire	A. G. Lister	*D. Earle	J. L. Gluza
Cheshire	M. E. Pitt	‡‡J. E. H. Whiteoak	W. E. Leathwood
Cornwall	J. Mills	F. Twyning	A. R. J. Horn
Cumbria	J. E. Burnet	§R. F. Mather	C. L. Tuley, MBE
Derbyshire	J. S. Raine	P. Swaby	H. Lowe
Devon	P. Jenkinson	J. Glasby	E. J. Kingston
Dorset	P. K. Harvey	A. P. Peel	Mrs P. A. Hymers
Durham	K. W. Smith	J. Kirkby	J. Walker
East Sussex	††Mrs C. Miller	J. Davies	D. Norcross
Essex	K. W. S. Ashurst	K. D. Neale	W. Archibald
Gloucestershire	M. Honey	**J. R. Cockroft	F. R. Thompson
Hampshire	P. C. B. Robertson	J. E. Scotford, CBE	N. A. Best, CBE
Hereford and Worcester	J. W. Turnbull	P. Middleborough	J. W. Wardle, MBE
Hertfordshire	B. Ogley	*C. Sweeney	Mrs I. Tarry, CBE
Isle of Wight	†F. Hetherington	J. Pulsford	Mrs M. O'Neill Stolworthy
Kent	P. R. Sabin	*P. Martin	P. Morgan
Lancashire	G. A. Johnson	B. G. Aldred	D. Yates
Leicestershire	J. B. Sinnott	R. Hale	J. M. Roberts
Lincolnshire	J. Barrow	P. Brittain	Mrs E. Davies
Norfolk	T. J. Byles	R. D. Summers	R. D. Phelan
Northamptonshire	J. V. Picking	*R. Paver	J. J. Gardner
Northumberland	°°K. Morris	*K. Morris	T. Wallace
North Yorkshire	J. A. Ransford	J. S. Moore	T. K. Hull
Nottinghamshire	P. Housden	R. Latham	B. Grocock
Oxfordshire	J. Harwood	C. Gray	D. Buckle
Shropshire	A. J. Barnish	N. T. Pursey	G. Raxster
Somerset	B. M. Tanner	C. N. Bilsland	R. B. Clark
Staffordshire	B. A. Price	R. G. Tettenborn, OBE	W. F. Austin
Suffolk	P. F. Bye	P. B. Atkinson	K. J. Doran
Surrey	P. Coen	‡‡P. Derrick	Baroness Thomas of Walliswood, OBE
Warwickshire	I. G. Caulfield	S. R. Freer	B. Kirton
West Sussex	D. P. Rigg	Mrs H. Kilpatrick	C. Robinson
Wiltshire	Dr K. Robinson	D. Chalker	Mrs J. M. Wood

* Director of Finance
° County Manager
† County Finance Officer
** Director of Corporate Services
°° Managing Director
†† Head of Paid Service
‡‡ Director of Resources
§ Director of Corporate Finance
‡ Clerk to the Council

Unitary Councils

Small capitals denote City status
§ Denotes Metropolitan council

Council	Population 1994	Band D charge 1996*	Chief Executive	Mayor (a) Lord Mayor (b) Chairman 1996–7
§Barnsley	226,500	£554.08	J. Edwards	C. Rowe
Bath and North-East Somerset	†158,692	675.00	T. du Sautoy	Ms M. Feeny
§Birmingham	1,008,400	681.02	M. Lyons	(a) Ms M. Arnott-Job
§Bolton	265,200	732.90	B. Collinge	E. Johnson
§Bradford	481,700	646.94	R. Penn	(a) G. Mitchell
Bristol	†374,300	871.46	Ms L. de Groot	Ms J. McLaren
§Bury	182,200	651.71	D. J. Burton	T. Holt
§Calderdale	193,600	740.80	M. Ellison	Ms D. Neal
§Coventry	302,500	808.68	I. Roxburgh	(a) S. Hodson
§Doncaster	292,500	592.52	J. D. Hale	Mrs D. M. Layton
§Dudley	312,200	637.29	A. V. Astling	W. P. Cody
East Riding of Yorkshire	†310,000	729.87	D. Stephenson	(b) P. Rounding
§Gateshead	202,400	778.50	L. N. Elton	W. Maddison
Hartlepool	†90,409	836.69	B. J. Dinsdale	H. J. Bishop
Kingston upon Hull	†265,000	655.29	I. Crookham	(a) J. S. Mulgrove, MBE
§Kirklees	386,900	759.00	R. V. Hughes	Ms A. Harrison
§Knowsley	154,000	774.04	D. Henshaw	J. Gallagher
§Leeds	724,400	635.29	‡P. Smith	(a) M. J. Bedford
§Liverpool	474,000	1006.46	P. Bounds	(a) F. Doran
§Manchester	431,100	838.36	A. Sandford	(a) D. Shaw
Middlesbrough	†146,000	639.45	D. W. Ashton	R. Regan
§Newcastle upon Tyne	283,600	770.82	G. N. Cook	(a) L. A. Russell
North East Lincolnshire	†164,000	735.48	R. Bennett	(b) L. T. Taylor
North Lincolnshire	†153,000	886.82	Dr M. Garnett	Ms J. Metcalfe
North Somerset	†177,000	615.93	P. May	(b) D. Walker
§North Tyneside	194,100	743.17	Executive Directorate	R. W. Schofield
§Oldham	220,400	768.00	C. Smith	(a) A. Griffiths
Redcar and Cleveland	†144,000	858.00	A. W. Kilburn	(b) Ms F. Christie
§Rochdale	207,100	726.68	J. F. D. Pierce	S. Emmott
§Rotherham	256,300	676.89	J. Bell	J. P. Wardle
§St Helens	181,000	777.87	Mrs C. Hudson	A. Worth
§Salford	230,700	813.75	J. C. Willis	J. Gaffney
§Sandwell	293,700	679.23	N. Summers	R. S. Badham
§Sefton	292,400	749.82	G. J. Haywood	T. J. Francis
§Sheffield	530,100	725.17	Mrs P. J. Gordon	(a) P. Price
§Solihull	202,000	616.73	Dr N. H. Perry	L. W. P. Kyles
South Gloucestershire	†220,000	640.00	**M. Robinson	(b) L. Bishop
§South Tyneside	156,700	708.66	‡‡P. J. Haigh	W. E. Brady
§Stockport	291,400	803.48	J. Schultz	Ms A. Graham
Stockton-on-Tees	†176,600	746.03	G. Garlick	R. Gibson
§Sunderland	297,200	652.24	Dr C. W. Sinclair	(a) I. Galbraith
§Tameside	221,800	756.00	M. J. Greenwood	M. P. Ballagher
§Trafford	218,100	591.66	W. Allan Lewis	L. T. Murkin
§Wakefield	317,300	580.53	R. Mather	(a) K. Bolland
§Walsall	263,900	718.49	D. C. Winchurch	R. Worrall
§Wigan	310,000	699.60	S. M. Jones	A. B. Coyle, OBE
§Wirral	333,100	773.70	A. White	Mrs N. M. Lea
§Wolverhampton	245,100	725.04	D. Anderson	G. F. Howells
York	†104,100	574.24	D. Clark	(a) K. King

Source of 1994 population figures: OPCS Monitor PP1 96/1, 29 February 1996
† 1996 figures given for new unitary authorities
* For explanation of council tax, *see* pages 519–20
‡ The Chief Officer
** Head of Paid Service
‡‡ Director of Corporate Services

Non-Metropolitan Councils

SMALL CAPITALS denote CITY status
§ Denotes Borough status
Source of population figures: OPCS Monitor PP1 96/1, 29 February 1996
For explanation of council tax, *see* pages 519–20

Council	Population 1994	Band D charge 1996	Chief Executive	Chairman 1996–7 (a) Mayor (b) Lord Mayor
Adur, West Sussex	57,900	£654.00	F. M. G. Staden	D. Hancock
§Allerdale, Cumbria	96,100	699.39	C. J. Hart	(a) Mrs J. Tweddle
Alnwick, Northumberland	30,600	680.00	L. St Ruth	J. Hinson
§Amber Valley, Derbyshire	114,500	679.14	P. M. Carney	(a) E. J. Chapman
Arun, West Sussex	134,300	628.03	I. Sumnall	Mrs J. Goad
Ashfield, Nottinghamshire	109,900	690.72	†N. Bernasconi	Mrs G. Thierry
§Ashford, Kent	94,800	585.35	D. Lambert	(a) S. J. G. Koowaree
Aylesbury Vale, Bucks	152,000	570.00	B. Hurley	Mrs A. Davies
Babergh, Suffolk	78,800	598.44	D. C. Bishop	Mrs J. Law
§Barrow-in-Furness, Cumbria	72,100	733.33	T. O. Campbell	(a) S. Derbyshire
Basildon, Essex	162,100	651.96	J. Robb	Ms A. Bruce
§Basingstoke and Deane, Hants	147,200	569.64	Ms K. Sporle	(a) L. T. Garland
Bassetlaw, Notts	105,500	716.93	M. S. Havenhand	B. Macaulay
§Bedford	137,000	635.51	L. W. Gould	(a) A. Bagchi
§Berwick-upon-Tweed, Northumberland	26,500	683.46	E. O. Cawthorn	(a) J. D. Lockie
Blaby, Leics	85,300	528.52	‡E. Hemsley	J. T. Roper
§Blackburn, Lancs	140,100	781.31	G. L. Davies	(a) Ms M. Leaver
§Blackpool, Lancs	154,600	665.93	G. E. Essex-Crosby	(a) L. Kersh
§Blyth Valley, Northumberland	80,600	663.50	D. Crawford	(a) R. Allan
Bolsover, Derbyshire	70,800	721.25	J. R. Fotherby	C. R. Moseby
§Boston, Lincs	54,200	628.92	I. Ward	(a) C. A. Tebbs
§Bournemouth, Dorset	160,000	579.96	D. Newell	(a) Mrs J. Moore
§Bracknell Forest, Berks	104,600	551.08	A. J. Targett	(a) T. Wheaton
Braintree, Essex	123,600	588.33	Ms A. Ralph	E. Bishop
Breckland, Norfolk	112,200	577.00	R. Garnett	A. Stasiak
Brentwood, Essex	71,800	583.38	C. P. Sivell	(a) C. Myers
Bridgnorth, Shropshire	50,400	611.30	Mrs T. M. Elliott	R. Lane
§Brighton, East Sussex	154,900	579.94	G. Jones	(a) I. Duncan
Broadland, Norfolk	110,100	574.72	J. H. Bryant	D. Dewgrade
Bromsgrove, Hereford and Worcs	94,000	566.41	R. P. Bradshaw	R. Clayton
§Broxbourne, Herts	82,400	558.73	M. J. Walker	(a) Mrs J. E. E. Ball
§Broxtowe, Notts	112,200	716.29	M. Brown	(a) J. White
§Burnley, Lancs	90,500	747.19	R. Ellis	(a) P. A. White
CAMBRIDGE	113,000	629.65	R. Hammond	(a) J. Durrant
Cannock Chase, Staffs	90,800	633.45	M. G. Kemp	T. F. Smith
CANTERBURY, Kent	133,900	607.95	Dr C. Gay	(b) C. Wake
Caradon, Cornwall	78,900	611.00	J. Neal	E. G. Lewis
CARLISLE, Cumbria	103,300	727.97	R. S. Brackley	(a) C. Johnston
Carrick, Cornwall	84,400	628.98	P. M. Kidwell-Talbot	P. C. Tregunna
§Castle Morpeth, Northumberland	50,200	680.05	P. Wilson	(a) Mrs K. Morris
§Castle Point, Essex	85,900	636.84	B. Rollinson	(a) D. Williams
§Charnwood, Leics	153,100	616.89	S. M. Peatfield	(a) K. Brailsford
§Chelmsford, Essex	155,800	597.28	M. Easteal	(a) F. Mountain
§Cheltenham, Glos	106,800	596.52	C. Nye	(a) Mrs P. Thomas
Cherwell, Oxon	127,500	621.00	G. J. Handley	R. E. Groves, MBE
CHESTER, Cheshire	120,600	666.00	P. F. Durham	(b) Ms L. Price
§Chesterfield, Derbyshire	101,600	676.08	D. R. Shaw	(a) G. Waddours
Chester-le-Street, Co. Durham	54,200	623.34	J. A. Greensmith	D. Meek
Chichester, West Sussex	103,100	584.45	C. E. Evans	A. J. French
Chiltern, Bucks	91,400	613.35	A. Goodrum	Miss P. A. Appleby, MBE
§Chorley, Lancs	96,900	687.35	J. W. Davies	(a) M. Coombes
§Christchurch, Dorset	42,700	568.67	M. A. Turvey	(a) E. W. Wood
§Colchester, Essex	149,600	607.61	J. Cobley	(a) W. Sanford

†Managing Director
‡ Finance and General Manager

Council	Population 1994	Band D charge 1996	Chief Executive	Chairman 1996–7 (a) Mayor (b) Lord Mayor
§Congleton, Cheshire	85,500	£656.22	†P. Cooper	(a) Mrs K. A. Thomas
§Copeland, Cumbria	71,000	681.85	Dr J. Stanforth	(a) Ms J. Pickering
Corby, Northants	52,800	616.30	T. Simmons	(a) J. Cowling
Cotswold, Glos	80,800	585.00	N. Howells	Mrs S. M. H. Herdman
Craven, North Yorkshire	51,100	581.00	Ms G. Taylor, PH.D	R. Walker
§Crawley, W. Sussex	90,000	614.79	M. D. Sander	(a) J. G. Smith
§Crewe and Nantwich, Cheshire	111,400	674.68	A. Wenham	(a) L. Cooper
§Dacorum, Herts	134,200	569.85	K. Hunt	(a) M. Young
§Darlington, Co. Durham	100,600	659.71	B. Keel	(a) G. Plummer
§Dartford, Kent	83,400	597.67	C. R. Shepherd	(a) H. Phillips
Daventry, Northants	64,100	744.69	R. J. Symons, RD	J. S. H. Russell
DERBY	230,500	664.79	R. H. Cowlishaw	(a) A. Mullarkey
Derbyshire Dales	68,600	656.92	D. Wheatcroft	C. P. Brindley
Derwentside, Co. Durham	87,000	706.16	N. F. Johnson	H. S. Guildford
Dover, Kent	106,900	598.68	J. P. Moir, TD	P. T. Wilson
DURHAM	89,100	642.39	C. G. Firmin	(a) J. S. Anderson
Easington, Co. Durham	98,000	744.00	*P. Innes	D. Myers
§Eastbourne, East Sussex	88,200	639.07	S. E. Conway	(a) R. G. Kirtley
East Cambridgeshire	63,300	447.03	R. C. Carr	H. J. L. Fitch
East Devon	122,800	572.09	F. J. Vallender	B. Willoughby
East Dorset	80,700	586.40	A. Breakwell	N. P. Evans
East Hampshire	108,200	593.73	B. P. Roynon	H. Cunliffe
East Hertfordshire	121,600	550.97	R. J. Bailey	J. O. Ranger
§Eastleigh, Hants	110,800	589.57	C. Tapp	(a) D. Horne
East Lindsey, Lincs	121,400	611.69	P. Haigh	Lt.-Gen. J. L. M. Dymoke, MBE
East Northamptonshire	70,000	606.47	R. K. Heath	Dr P. Wix
East Staffordshire	99,000	601.98	F. W. Saunders	(a) Mrs J. Dean
Eden, Cumbria	47,300	704.42	I. W. Bruce	J. B. Thornborrow
§Ellesmere Port and Neston, Cheshire	81,400	689.86	S. Ewbank	(a) Ms J. Walker
§Elmbridge, Surrey	119,700	616.95	D. W. L. Jenkins	(a) H. Ashton
Epping Forest, Essex	118,900	597.67	J. Burgess	R. Barnes
§Epsom and Ewell, Surrey	69,000	582.16	D. J. Smith	(a) Mrs H. Dodd
§Erewash, Derbyshire	107,100	664.74	G. A. Pook	(a) P. A. Jeffery
EXETER, Devon	104,500	562.37	W. H. Bassett	(a) I. Mitchell
§Fareham, Hants	101,800	526.98	A. A. Davies	(a) D. J. Murray
Fenland, Cambs	78,500	499.00	N. R. Topliss	B. E. A. Diggle
Forest Heath, Suffolk	64,000	566.07	S. W. Catchpole	Mrs S. D. Crickmere
Forest of Dean, Glos	75,400	619.89	‡R. A. Willis	B. W. Hobman
§Fylde, Lancs	74,000	692.12	J. R. Wilkinson	(a) A. W. Jealous
§Gedling, Notts	111,700	705.54	D. Kennedy	(a) R. B. Marshall
§Gillingham, Kent	96,200	583.80	J. A. McBride	(a) Mrs D. Smith
GLOUCESTER	104,700	572.93	G. Garbutt	(a) T. Haines
§Gosport, Hants	74,700	609.52	M. Crocker	(a) K. H. Brown
§Gravesham, Kent	92,900	558.63	E. V. J. Seager	(a) A. Cunningham, MBE
§Great Yarmouth, Norfolk	88,700	577.94	R. Packham	P. W. Dye
§Guildford, Surrey	126,200	586.11	D. T. Watts	(a) J. D. Woodhatch
§Halton, Cheshire	123,700	646.05	M. Cuff	(a) F. Nyland
Hambleton, North Yorkshire	82,900	497.52	P. C. O'Brien (acting)	D. J. Dennis
Harborough, Leics	70,900	619.32	M. C. Wilson	B. Summers
Harlow, Essex	73,100	704.55	*D. Byrne	Ms D. Pennick
§Harrogate, North Yorkshire	148,400	626.30	P. M. Walsh	(a) P. Broadbank
Hart, Hants	83,300	588.41	G. R. Jelbart	H. Eastwood
§Hastings, East Sussex	82,600	643.35	R. A. Carrier	(a) G. White
§Havant, Hants	119,400	613.78	R. Smith	(a) Mrs V. Steel
HEREFORD	50,500	577.68	C. E. S. Willis	(a) L. M. H. Andrews
§Hertsmere, Hertfordshire	94,200	582.44	P. H. Copland	(a) J. Nolan
§High Peak, Derbyshire	87,300	696.53	R. P. H. Brady	(a) D. Lomax
§Hinckley and Bosworth, Leics	97,700	586.85	°I. G. Davis	(a) D. J. Wood
Horsham, West Sussex	114,300	587.34	M. J. Pearson	A. Chisholm
§Hove, East Sussex	91,300	604.28	J. P. Teasdale	(a) L. E. Hamilton

† Managing Director
* General Manager
‡ Head of Paid Service
° Head of Technical Services

Council	Population 1994	Band D charge 1996	Chief Executive	Chairman 1996–7 (a) Mayor (b) Lord Mayor
Huntingdonshire, Cambs	149,900	£537.91	D. Monks	J. G. Rignall
§Hyndburn, Lancs	79,600	751.49	M. Chambers	(a) M. M. Yousaf
§Ipswich, Suffolk	114,100	671.13	J. D. Herir	(a) P. Smart
Kennet, Wilts	73,800	578.60	P. L. Owens	D. Parker
Kerrier, Cornwall	88,900	613.87	G. G. Cox	T. J. Bray
§Kettering, Northants	79,200	626.49	P. Walker	(a) B. Morgan
§King's Lynn and West Norfolk	131,000	587.47	A. E. Pask	(a) A. M. Evans
Lancaster, Lancs	135,000	689.64	J. Burrows	(a) Mrs J. Horner
Leicester	293,400	686.41	R. Green	(b) C. S. Batty
Leominster, Hereford and Worcs	40,900	558.96	†Mrs M. Holborow	M. J. Kimberly
Lewes, East Sussex	88,400	633.13	J. N. Crawford	J. E. Lewry
Lichfield, Staffs	93,600	533.40	J. T. Thompson	W. J. Wilson
Lincoln	84,600	625.17	A. Sparke	(a) A. Morgan
§Luton, Beds	180,800	650.64	Mrs K. Jones	(a) M. D. Hand
§Macclesfield, Cheshire	151,300	669.95	B. W. Longden	(a) H. R. Harrison
§Maidstone, Kent	138,500	627.95	J. D. Makepeace	(a) M. Robertson
Maldon, Essex	53,500	581.46	E. A. P. Plumridge	R. G. Boyce
Malvern Hills, Hereford and Worcs	90,700	595.50	M. J. Jones	J. Tretheway
Mansfield, Notts	102,100	692.93	R. P. Goad	M. Hall
§Melton, Leics	46,600	616.25	P. M. Murphy	(a) R. Hyslop
Mendip, Somerset	98,000	639.45	G. Jeffs	C. F. Lockey
Mid Bedfordshire	114,900	616.58	C. A. Tucker	D. Harrowell
Mid Devon	66,400	585.37	M. I. R. Bull	D. J. Allen
Mid Suffolk	79,100	608.17	G. Chilton	M. Shave
Mid Sussex	125,100	604.00	W. J. H. Hatton	Ms A. Jones
§Milton Keynes, Bucks	188,400	657.13	H. Miller	(a) D. L. Lewis
Mole Valley, Surrey	79,000	567.22	H. Kerswell	Mrs J. Marsh
Newark and Sherwood, Notts	104,100	766.34	†R. G. Dix	B. L. D'Arcy
Newbury, Berks	141,600	595.94	P. E. McMahon	J. I. Morgan
§Newcastle under Lyme, Staffs	123,100	589.06	J. Dunn	(a) G. O'Kane Cairns
New Forest, Hants	166,400	609.00	†I. B. Mackintosh	Miss S. A. Cooke
§Northampton	187,600	670.05	R. J. B. Morris	(a) J. S. Bains
North Cornwall	76,900	616.73	D. Brown	A. Hirst
North Devon	86,200	567.15	D. T. Cunliffe	Mrs F. E. Webber
North Dorset	55,300	575.92	Ms E. Peters	M. F. Lane
North East Derbyshire	99,200	704.60	‡Mrs C. A. Gilbey	Ms M. Simpson
North Hertfordshire	114,300	585.42	J. S. Philp	Mrs A. E. Carss
North Kesteven, Lincs	82,000	600.71	S. Lamb	G. W. Chambers
North Norfolk	94,300	588.13	B. A. Barrell	A. L. Dennis
North Shropshire	54,400	636.72	D. Pearce	A. Boughey
§North Warwickshire	61,400	665.00	J. Hutchinson	(a) Mrs A. Forwood
North West Leicestershire	83,100	619.79	M. J. Diaper	W. J. Wildgoose
North Wiltshire	118,900	622.21	R. Marshall	A. S. R. Jackson
Norwich, Norfolk	127,800	641.38	J. R. Packer	(b) R. Quinn
Nottingham	282,400	769.23	E. F. Cantle	(a) B. Parker
§Nuneaton and Bedworth, Warwickshire	119,100	705.79	‡‡J. Walton	(a) J. Glass
§Oadby and Wigston, Leics	53,100	627.06	Mrs R. E. Hyde	(a) J. Kaufman
§Oswestry, Shropshire	34,300	621.14	D. A. Towers	(a) Mrs A. H. Bickerton
Oxford	132,800	688.40	R. S. Block	(b) Ms B. Keen
§Pendle, Lancs	85,700	751.49	S. Barnes	(a) F. Clifford
Penwith, Cornwall	59,600	613.60	‡F. H. Murton	P. Badrock
Peterborough, Cambs	158,700	588.10	W. E. Samuel	(a) M. A. Choudhary
Plymouth, Devon	255,800	649.78	Mrs A. Stone	(b) Mrs S. Y. Bellamy
§Poole, Dorset	138,100	587.70	J. W. Brooks	(a) B. A. Greenwood
Portsmouth, Hants	189,300	572.13	N. Gurney	(b) M. Hancock
§Preston, Lancs	133,100	748.48	J. Carr	(a) R. Marshall
Purbeck, Dorset	44,500	500.00	P. B. Croft	D. A. Budd
Reading, Berks	138,500	696.26	D. Bligh	(a) R. J. Day
§Redditch, Hereford and Worcs	78,400	619.60	**Ms S. Manzie	(a) R. T. Vickers
§Reigate and Banstead, Surrey	118,300	591.21	M. Bacon	(a) J. A. Chiles

† Managing Director
‡ Head of Paid Service
‡‡ Borough Manager
** Borough Director

Council	Population 1994	Band D charge 1996	Chief Executive	Chairman 1996–7 (a) Mayor (b) Lord Mayor
§Restormel, Cornwall	89,000	£600.15	Mrs P. Crowson	(a) Mrs S. Blaylock
§Ribble Valley, Lancs	51,800	697.33	O. Hopkins	(a) Ms E. Lowe
Richmondshire, N. Yorkshire	45,100	579.07	H. Tabiner	R. Alderson
ROCHESTER UPON MEDWAY, Kent	145,500	512.82	R. I. Gregory	(a) H. Housby
Rochford, Essex	75,800	604.00	R. Lovell	P. Beckers
§Rossendale, Lancs	65,600	761.69	J. S. Hartley	(a) L. Forshaw
Rother, East Sussex	86,000	619.20	D. F. Powell	M. J. Jones
§Rugby, Warwickshire	86,600	676.06	Miss D. M. Colley	(a) S. G. Humphries
§Runnymede, Surrey	75,100	528.15	T. N. Williams	(a) Mrs M. H. Taylor
§Rushcliffe, Notts	103,000	681.04	J. Saxton	(a) A. H. Cooper
§Rushmoor, Hants	85,800	580.79	R. Upton	(a) M. Banner
Rutland, Leics	33,600	631.70	F. Allen Dobson	B. Montgomery
Ryedale, North Yorkshire	93,900	618.01	M. Walker	A. C. Farnaby
ST ALBANS, Herts	128,700	587.58	E. A. Hackford	(a) Revd R. Donald
§St Edmundsbury, Suffolk	92,800	597.13	G. R. Toft	(a) W. Cownley
Salisbury, Wilts	110,000	598.54	D. R. J. Rawlinson	I. West
§Scarborough, N. Yorkshire	108,700	578.97	J. M. Trebble	(a) J. E. Agar
Sedgefield, Co. Durham	91,400	728.07	A. J. Roberts	K. Noble
Sedgemoor, Somerset	101,400	605.24	A. G. Lovell	G. A. Buchanan
Selby, North Yorkshire	92,000	559.68	M. Connor	J. A. Heppenstal
Sevenoaks, Kent	109,900	618.74	B. C. Cova, MBE	D. Coates
Shepway, Kent	96,500	631.67	R. J. Thompson	K. D. Hudson
§Shrewsbury and Atcham	94,600	610.55	D. Bradbury	(a) K. Brennand
§Slough, Berks	104,900	534.28	Mrs C. Coppell	(a) Mrs M. Atkinson
SOUTHAMPTON, Hants	211,700	592.48	J. Cairns	(a) Ms D. Altwood
South Bedfordshire	110,400	670.72	T. D. Rix	E. Snoxell
South Buckinghamshire	63,900	560.00	C. R. Furness	Mrs P. Burry
South Cambridgeshire	123,600	517.02	J. S. Ballantyne	Mrs S. Saunders
South Derbyshire	75,100	667.96	D. J. Dugdale	Mrs J. Mead
§Southend-on-Sea, Essex	169,900	581.73	°D. Moulson	(a) H. P. Gibeon
South Hams, Devon	79,100	585.89	M. S. Carpenter	Mrs J. I. Roskruge
South Herefordshire	54,100	580.73	A. Hughes	Mrs R. F. Lincoln
South Holland, Lincs	70,400	636.77	C. J. Simpkins	J. R. Pearl
South Kesteven, Lincs	115,200	605.38	K. R. Cann	K. Joynson
South Lakeland, Cumbria	100,300	700.96	A. F. Winstanley	M. C. Bentley
South Norfolk	104,500	562.59	A. G. T. Kellett	Viscountess Knollys
South Northamptonshire	73,000	655.33	K. Whitehead	P. Henson
South Oxfordshire	121,800	514.45	R. Watson	Mrs S. M. Cooper
§South Ribble, Lancs	103,600	688.56	P. Halsall	(a) Mrs B. R. Greenland
South Shropshire	39,300	601.82	G. C. Biggs, MBE	R. D. Phillips
South Somerset	148,300	640.52	M. Usher	Mrs Gail Coleshill
South Staffordshire	104,400	529.24	L. Barnfield	J. L. Evans
§Spelthorne, Surrey	91,400	591.78	M. B. Taylor	(a) G. G. Blampied
§Stafford	122,500	577.86	J. K. M. Krawiec	(a) J. T. Holland
Staffordshire Moorlands	95,100	594.16	B. J. Preedy	G. S. Eyre
§Stevenage, Herts	75,900	626.05	H. L. Miller	(a) B. G. Dunnell
STOKE-ON-TRENT, Staffs	245,200	644.64	B. Smith	(b) J. P. Birkin
Stratford-on-Avon, Warwicks	109,500	632.62	I. B. Prosser	S. B. Ribbans
Stroud, Glos	106,300	647.68	R. M. Ollin	Mrs M. E. A. Nolder
Suffolk Coastal	113,200	608.38	T. K. Griffin	R. Burgon
§Surrey Heath	81,900	587.52	N. M. Pughe	(a) C. Gimblett
§Swale, Kent	117,200	558.87	J. C. Edwards	(a) E. Madgwick
§Tamworth, Staffs	71,800	571.52	C. Moore	(a) R. R. Dermid
Tandridge, Surrey	76,700	601.00	P. J. D. Thomas	R. B. Clements
§Taunton Deane, Somerset	98,200	596.17	†Mrs S. Douglas	(a) J. G. Dunkley, OBE
Teesdale, Co. Durham	24,200	644.93	C. M. Anderson	O. Hedley
Teignbridge, Devon	114,100	573.48	B. T. Jones	R. Astbury
Tendring, Essex	130,900	596.80	D. Mitchell-Gears	B. Mixter
§Test Valley, Hants	105,300	573.61	A. Jones	(a) B. I. Palmer
§Tewkesbury, Glos	75,400	503.59	H. Davis	(a) H. Chamberlayne
§Thamesdown, Wilts	173,500	619.73	‡R. Clegg	(a) M. K. Caton
Thanet, Kent	125,300	434.00	D. Ralls, CBE, DFC	Mrs M. Davies

° Town Clerk
‡ General Manager
‡ Head of Paid Service

Council	Population 1994	Band D charge 1996	Chief Executive	Chairman 1996–7 (a) Mayor (b) Lord Mayor
Three Rivers, Herts	83,100	£606.60	A. Robertson	Ms N. Spellman
§Thurrock, Essex	131,400	605.34	K. Barnes	(a) S. Josling
§Tonbridge and Malling, Kent	102,800	591.09	T. Thompson	(a) Ms J. Cresswell
§Torbay, Devon	123,000	567.86	A. J. Hodgkiss (acting)	(a) Mrs C. Milward
Torridge, Devon	54,700	546.26	R. K. Brasington	W. J. Brook
§Tunbridge Wells, Kent	102,900	580.34	R. J. Stone	(a) R. Baker
Tynedale, Northumberland	57,700	659.85	A. Baty	Mrs M. J. Howard
Uttlesford, Essex	67,500	591.81	K. Ivory	E. C. Abrahams
Vale of White Horse, Oxon	113,200	612.63	D. J. Heavens	R. T. Johnston
§Vale Royal, Cheshire	114,700	670.00	W. R. T. Woods	(a) E. G. Redford
Wansbeck, Northumberland	62,200	690.90	A. G. White	J. A. Graham
§Warrington, Cheshire	186,700	680.12	M. I. M. Sanders	(a) Mrs M. Roblin
Warwick	119,800	654.21	Ms J. Barrett	Mrs J. Evans
§Watford, Herts	76,200	666.47	Ms C. Hassan	(a) P. Harrison
Waveney, Suffolk	107,600	590.41	M. Berridge	T. Carter
§Waverley, Surrey	114,800	575.30	Miss C. L. Pointer	(a) Mrs G. Beel
Wealden, East Sussex	134,900	613.14	D. R. Holness	Mrs V. Chidson
Wear Valley, Co. Durham	63,300	714.09	°Mrs C. Hughes	S. Dent
§Wellingborough, Northants	68,100	499.50	J. E. Thewlass	(a) S. Dholakia
Welwyn Hatfield, Herts	94,700	610.69	D. Riddle	A. Appleby
§West Devon	46,700	603.18	J. S. Ligo	(a) J. Darch
West Dorset	88,600	561.53	R. C. Rennison	T. Frost
West Lancashire	110,200	717.32	B. A. Knight	R. A. Pendleton
West Lindsey, Lincs	77,700	623.67	R. W. Nelsey	J. Turner
West Oxfordshire	95,000	557.41	N. J. B. Robson	E. J. Cooper
West Somerset	32,000	636.19	C. Rockall	S. Pugsley
West Wiltshire	110,000	585.33	R. S. While	T. Chivers
§Weymouth and Portland, Dorset	62,900	582.49	M. N. Ashby	(a) B. Ellis
WINCHESTER, Hants	101,800	599.83	D. H. Cowan	(a) B. V. Blunt
§Windsor and Maidenhead, Berks	137,800	590.94	D. Lunn	(a) Mrs A. Sheldon
§Woking, Surrey	89,000	575.30	P. Russell	(a) J. G. B. Coombe
Wokingham, Berks	141,700	623.75	Mrs G. C. Norton	Ms D. Carpenter
WORCESTER	89,500	582.15	††D. Wareing	(a) L. Thomas
§Worthing, West Sussex	97,400	610.11	M. J. Ball	(a) P. Green
Wrekin, Shropshire	143,900	660.00	D. G. Hutchison	S. Bradley
Wychavon, Hereford and Worcs	104,600	578.80	W. S. Nott	R. Mason
Wycombe, Bucks	162,600	603.52	R. J. Cummins	(a) Mrs E. M. Barratt
§Wyre, Lancs	103,900	694.29	M. Brown	(a) R. V. Allen
Wyre Forest, Hereford and Worcs	97,200	601.00	W. S. Baldwin	N. Knowles

° Executive Director
†† Principal Director

Roman Names of English Towns and Cities

Bath	*Aquae Sulis*	Leicester	*Ratae Corieltauvorum*
Canterbury	*Durovernum Cantiacorum*	Lincoln	*Lindum*
Carlisle	*Luguvalium*	London	*Londinium*
Chelmsford	*Caesaromagus*	Manchester	*Mamucium*
Chester	*Deva*	Newcastle upon Tyne	*Pons Aelius*
Chichester	*Noviomagus Regnensium*	Pevensey	*Anderetium*
Cirencester	*Corinium Dobunnorum*	Rochester	*Durobrivae*
Colchester	*Camulodunum*	St Albans	*Verulamium*
Doncaster	*Danum*	Salisbury (Old Sarum)	*Sorviodunum*
Dorchester	*Durnovaria*	Silchester	*Calleva Atrebatum*
Dover	*Dubris*	Winchester	*Venta Belgarum*
Exeter	*Isca Dumnoniorum*	Wroxeter	*Viroconium Cornoviorum*
Gloucester	*Glevum*	York	*Eburacum*

LOCAL GOVERNMENT CHANGES IN ENGLAND

CHANGES FROM 1 APRIL 1997

UA Unitary Authority

Present county (no. of DCs at present)

Bedfordshire (4)	UA in Luton; rest remain two-tier
Buckinghamshire (5)	UA in Milton Keynes; rest remain two-tier
Derbyshire (9)	UA in Derby; rest remain two-tier
Dorset (8)	UAs in Bournemouth, Poole; rest remain two-tier
Durham (8)	UA in Darlington; rest remain two-tier
East Sussex	UA in Brighton and Hove; rest remain two-tier
Hampshire (13)	UAs in Portsmouth, Southampton; rest remain two-tier
Leicestershire (9)	UAs in Leicester, Rutland; rest remain two-tier
Staffordshire (9)	UA in Stoke-on-Trent; rest remain two-tier
Wiltshire (5)	UA in Thamesdown; rest remain two-tier

CHANGES PROPOSED FROM 1 APRIL 1998

Present county (no. of DC's at present)

Berkshire (6)	UAs in Bracknell Forest, Newbury, Reading, Slough, Windsor and Maidenhead, Wokingham
Cambridgeshire (6)	UA in Peterborough; rest remain two-tier
Cheshire (8)	UAs in Halton, Warrington; rest remain two-tier
Devon (10)	UAs in Plymouth, Torbay; rest remain two-tier
Essex (14)	UAs in Southend, Thurrock; rest remain two-tier
Hereford and Worcester (9)	UA in Herefordshire (pre-1974 boundary); Worcestershire retains two tiers
Kent (14)	UA in Rochester and Gillingham; rest remain two-tier
Lancashire (14)	UAs in Blackburn, Blackpool; rest remain two-tier
Nottinghamshire (8)	UA in Nottingham; rest remain two-tier
Shropshire (6)	UA in The Wrekin; rest remain two-tier

No changes are proposed in the following:
Cornwall; Cumbria; Gloucestershire; Hertfordshire; Lincolnshire; Norfolk; Northamptonshire; Northumberland; Oxfordshire; Somerset; Suffolk; Surrey; Warwickshire; West Sussex

The Cinque Ports

As their name implies, the Cinque Ports were originally five in number: Hastings, New Romney, Hythe, Dover and Sandwich. They were formed during the 11th century to defend the Channel coast and, after the Norman Conquest, were recognized as a Confederation by a charter of 1278. The 'antient towns' of Winchelsea and Rye were added at some time after the Conquest. The other members of the Confederation, known as Limbs, are Lydd, Faversham, Folkestone, Deal, Tenterden, Margate and Ramsgate.

Until 1855 the duty of the Cinque Ports was to provide ships and men for the defence of the state in return for considerable privileges, such as tax exemptions and the framing of by-laws. Of these privileges only jurisdiction in Admiralty remains.

The Barons of the Cinque Ports have the ancient privilege of attending the Coronation ceremony and are allotted special places in Westminster Abbey.

Lord Warden of the Cinque Ports, HM Queen Elizabeth the Queen Mother
Judge, Court of Admiralty, G. Darling, RD, QC
Registrar, I. G. Gill, LVO, 3 Waterloo Crescent, Dover, Kent CT16 1LA. Tel: 01304-225225

LORD WARDENS OF THE CINQUE PORTS *since* 1904

The Marquess Curzon	1904
The Prince of Wales	1905
The Earl Brassey	1908
The Earl Beauchamp	1913
The Marquess of Reading	1934
The Marquess of Willingdon	1936
Winston Churchill	1941
Sir Robert Menzies	1965
HM Queen Elizabeth the Queen Mother	1978

London

THE CORPORATION OF LONDON
(*see also* page 522)

THE CORPORATION OF LONDON
(*see also* page 522)

The City of London is the historic centre at the heart of London known as 'the square mile' around which the vast metropolis has grown over the centuries. The City's residential population is 5,500. The civic government is carried on by the Corporation of London through the Court of Common Council.

The City is the financial and business centre of London and includes the head offices of the principal banks, insurance companies and mercantile houses, in addition to buildings ranging from the historic interest of the Roman Wall and the 15th-century Guildhall, to the massive splendour of St Paul's Cathedral and the architectural beauty of Wren's spires.

The City of London was described by Tacitus in AD 62 as 'a busy emporium for trade and traders'. Under the Romans it became an important administration centre and hub of the road system. Little is known of London in Saxon times, when it formed part of the kingdom of the East Saxons. In 886 Alfred recovered London from the Danes and reconstituted it a burgh under his son-in-law. In 1066 the citizens submitted to William the Conqueror who in 1067 granted them a charter, which is still preserved, establishing them in the rights and privileges they had hitherto enjoyed.

THE MAYORALTY

The Mayoralty was probably established about 1189, the first Mayor being Henry Fitz Ailwyn who filled the office for 23 years and was succeeded by Fitz Alan (1212–14). A new charter was granted by King John in 1215, directing the Mayor to be chosen annually, which has ever since been done, though in early times the same individual often held the office more than once. A familiar instance is that of 'Whittington, thrice Lord Mayor of London' (in reality four times, 1397, 1398, 1406, 1419); and many modern cases have occurred. The earliest instance of the phrase 'Lord Mayor' in English is in 1414. It was used more generally in the latter part of the 15th century and became invariable from 1535 onwards. At Michaelmas the liverymen in Common Hall choose two Aldermen who have served the office of Sheriff for presentation to the Court of Aldermen, and one is chosen to be Lord Mayor for the following mayoral year.

LORD MAYOR'S DAY

The Lord Mayor of London was previously elected on the feast of St Simon and St Jude (28 October), and from the time of Edward I, at least, was presented to the King or to the Barons of the Exchequer on the following day, unless that day was a Sunday. The day of election was altered to 16 October in 1346, and after some further changes was fixed for Michaelmas Day in 1546, but the ceremonies of admittance and swearing-in of the Lord Mayor continued to take place on 28 and 29 October respectively until 1751. In 1752, at the reform of the calendar, the Lord Mayor was continued in office until 8 November, the 'New Style' equivalent of 28 October. The Lord Mayor is now presented to the Lord Chief Justice at the Royal Courts of Justice on the second Saturday in November to make the final declaration of office, having been sworn in at Guildhall on the preceding day. The procession to the Royal Courts of Justice is popularly known as the Lord Mayor's Show.

REPRESENTATIVES

Aldermen are mentioned in the 11th century and their office is of Saxon origin. They were elected annually between 1377 and 1394, when an Act of Parliament of Richard II directed them to be chosen for life.

The Common Council, elected annually on the first Friday in December, was, at an early date, substituted for a popular assembly called the *Folkmote*. At first only two representatives were sent from each ward, but the number has since been greatly increased.

OFFICERS

Sheriffs were Saxon officers; their predecessors were the *wic-reeves* and *portreeves* of London and Middlesex. At first they were officers of the Crown, and were named by the Barons of the Exchequer; but Henry I (in 1132) gave the citizens permission to choose their own Sheriffs, and the annual election of Sheriffs became fully operative under King John's charter of 1199. The citizens lost this privilege, as far as the election of the Sheriff of Middlesex was concerned, by the Local Government Act 1888; but the liverymen continue to choose two Sheriffs of the City of London, who are appointed on Midsummer Day and take office at Michaelmas.

The office of Chamberlain is an ancient one, the first contemporary record of which is 1237. The Town Clerk (or Common Clerk) is mentioned in 1274.

ACTIVITIES

The work of the Corporation is assigned to a number of committees which present reports to the Court of Common Council. These Committees are: City Lands and Bridge House Estates, Policy and Resources, Finance, Planning and Transportation, Central Markets, Billingsgate and Leadenhall Markets, Spitalfields Market, Police, Port and City of London Health and Social Services, Libraries, Art Galleries and Records, Boards of Governors of Schools, Music and Drama (Guildhall School of Music and Drama), Establishment, Housing, Gresham (City side), Hampstead Heath Management, Epping Forest and Open Spaces, West Ham Park, Privileges, Barbican Residential and Barbican Centre (Barbican Arts and Conference Centre).

The City's estate, in the possession of which the Corporation of London differs from other municipalities, is managed by the City Lands and Bridge House Estates Committee, the chairmanship of which carries with it the title of Chief Commoner.

The Honourable the Irish Society, which manages the Corporation's estates in Ulster, consists of a Governor and five other Aldermen, the Recorder, and 19 Common Councilmen, of whom one is elected Deputy Governor.

THE LORD MAYOR 1995–6*

The Rt. Hon. the Lord Mayor, Sir Leonard Chalstrey
  Secretary, Air Vice-Marshal M. Dicken, CB

THE SHERIFFS 1996–7

Sir Peter Levene, KBE (*Alderman, Portsoken*) and K. E. Ayers; *elected*, 26 June 1995; *assumed office*, 28 September 1995

---

*The Lord Mayor for 1996–7 was elected on Michaelmas Day. *See* Stop-press

OFFICERS, ETC

Town Clerk and Chamberlain, B. P. Harty
Chief Commoner (1996), P. J. Willoughby
Clerk, The Honourable the Irish Society, S. Waley, The Irish Chamber, St Dunstan's House, 2–4 Carey Lane, London EC2V 8AA

THE ALDERMEN

Name and Ward	CC	Ald.	Shff.	Lord Mayor
Sir Peter Gadsden, GBE,				
Farringdon Wt.	1969	1971	1970	1979
Sir Christopher Leaver, GBE,				
Dowgate	1973	1974	1979	1981
Sir Alan Traill, GBE,				
Langbourn	1970	1975	1982	1984
Sir David Rowe-Ham, GBE,				
Bridge	—	1976	1984	1986
Sir Christopher Collett, GBE,				
Broad Street	1973	1979	1985	1988
Sir Hugh Bidwell, GBE,				
Billingsgate	—	1979	1986	1989
Sir Alexander Graham, GBE,				
Queenhithe	1978	1979	1986	1990
Sir Brian Jenkins, GBE,				
Cordwainer	—	1980	1987	1991
Sir Paul Newall, TD, Walbrook	1980	1981	1989	1993
Sir Christopher Walford,				
Farringdon Wn.	—	1982	1990	1994
Sir Leonard Chalstrey, Vintry	1981	1984	1993	1995

All the above have passed the Civic Chair

Roger Cork, *Tower*	1978	1983	1992
Richard Nichols, *Candlewick*	1983	1984	1994
Sir Peter Levene, KBE,			
Portsoken	1983	1984	
Clive Martin, OBE, TD, *Aldgate*	—	1985	
Bryan Toye, *Lime Street*	—	1983	
Peter Bull, *Cheap*	1968	1984	
David Howard, *Cornhill*	1972	1986	
James Oliver, *Bishopsgate*	1980	1987	
Gavyn Arthur, *Cripplegate*	1988	1991	
Robert Finch, *Coleman Street*	—	1992	
Richard Agutter, *Castle Baynard*	—	1995	
Michael Savory, *Bread Street*	1980	1996	
David Brewer, *Bassishaw*	1992	1996	
Nicholas Anstee, *Aldersgate*	1987	1996	

THE COMMON COUNCIL

Deputy: Each Common Councilman so described serves as deputy to the Alderman of her/his ward

Absalom, J. D. (1994)	Farringdon Wt.
Angell, E. H. (1991)	Cripplegate Wt.
Archibald, *Deputy* W. W. (1986)	Cornhill
Bailey, J. (1993)	Cripplegate Wt.
Ballard, K. A., MC (1969)	Castle Baynard
Balls, H. D. (1970)	Castle Baynard
Barker, *Deputy* J. A. (1981)	Cripplegate Wt.
Barnes-Yallowley, H. M. F. (1986)	Coleman Street
Beale, *Deputy* M. J. (1979)	Lime Street
Bird, J. L. (1977)	Bridge
Biroum-Smith, P. L. (1988)	Dowgate
Block, S. A. A. (1983)	Cheap
Bowman, J. C. R. (1995)	Aldgate
Bradshaw, D. J. (1991)	Cripplegate Wn.
Bramwell, F. M. (1983)	Langbourn
Brewster, J. W., OBE (1994)	Bassishaw
Brighton, R. L. (1984)	Portsoken
Brooks, W. I. B. (1988)	Billingsgate
Brown, *Deputy* D. T. (1971)	Walbrook
Caspi, D. (1994)	Bridge
Cassidy, *Deputy* M. J. (1989)	Coleman Street
Catt, B. F. (1982)	Farringdon Wn.
Chadwick, R. A. H. (1994)	Tower
Challis, G. H., CBE (1978)	Langbourn
Cohen, Mrs C. M. (1986)	Lime Street
Cole, Lt.-Col. Sir Colin, KCB, KCVO, TD (1964)	Castle Baynard
Collinson, Miss A. H. (1991)	Farringdon Wt.
Cotgrove, D. (1991)	Lime Street
Coven, *Deputy* Mrs E. O., CBE (1972)	Dowgate
Currie, Miss S. E. M. (1985)	Cripplegate Wt.
Daily-Hunt, R. B. (1989)	Cripplegate Wt.
Darwin, G. E. (1995)	Farringdon Wt.
Davis, C. B. (1991)	Bread Street
Delderfield, D. W. (1995)	Farringdon Wt.
Dove, W. H., MBE (1993)	Bishopsgate
Dunitz, A. A. (1984)	Portsoken
Edwards, *Deputy* R. D. K. (1978)	Bassishaw
Eskenzi, A. N. (1970)	Farringdon Wn.
Evans, *Deputy* Mrs J. (1975)	Farringdon Wt.
Eve, R. A. (1980)	Cheap
Everett, K. M. (1984)	Candlewick
Farthing, R. B. C. (1981)	Aldgate
Fell, J. A. (1982)	Queenhithe
FitzGerald, *Deputy* R. C. A. (1981)	Bread Street
Forbes, G. B. (1993)	Bishopsgate
Fraser, S. J. (1993)	Coleman Street
Fraser, W. B. (1981)	Vintry
Galloway, A. D. (1981)	Broad Street
Gillon, G. M. F. (1995)	Cordwainer
Ginsburg, S. (1990)	Bishopsgate
Gowman, Miss A. (1991)	Dowgate
Graves, A. C. (1985)	Bishopsgate
Green, C. (1994)	Aldersgate
Hall, B. R. H. (1995)	Farringdon Wn.
Halliday, Mrs P. (1992)	Walbrook
Hardwick, Dr P. B. (1987)	Aldgate
Harries, R. E. (1995)	Cripplegate Wt.
Harris, B. N. (1996)	Broad Street
Hart, *Deputy* M. G. (1970)	Bridge
Haynes, J. E. H. (1986)	Cornhill
Henderson, *Deputy* J. S., OBE (1975)	Langbourn
Henderson-Begg, M. (1977)	Coleman Street
Hilliard, N. R. M. (1994)	Farringdon Wt.
Holland, *Deputy* J., CBE (1972)	Aldgate
Holliday, Mrs E. H. L. (1987)	Vintry
Horlock, *Deputy* H. W. S. (1969)	Farringdon Wn.
Hughesdon, J. S. (1991)	Broad Street
Jackson, L. St J. T. (1978)	Bread Street
Keep, Mrs B. (1987)	Cripplegate Wn.
Kellett, Mrs M. W. F. (1986)	Tower
Kemp, D. L. (1984)	Coleman Street
Knowles, S. K. (1984)	Candlewick
Lawrence, G. A. (1994)	Farringdon Wt.
Lawson, G. C. H. (1971)	Portsoken
Littlestone, N. (1993)	Aldersgate
MacLellan, A. P. W. (1989)	Walbrook
McNeil, I. D. (1977)	Lime Street
Malins, J. H., QC (1981)	Farringdon Wt.
Martin, R. C. (1986)	Queenhithe
Martinelli, P. J. (1994)	Bassishaw
Mayhew, Miss J. (1986)	Queenhithe
Mitchell, *Deputy* C. R. (1971)	Castle Baynard
Mizen, *Deputy* D. H. (1979)	Broad Street
Mobsby, *Deputy* D. J. L. (1985)	Billingsgate

Morgan, *Deputy* B. L., CBE (1963)	*Bishopsgate*
Moss, A. D. (1989)	*Tower*
Nash, *Deputy* Mrs J. C. (1983)	*Aldersgate*
Neary, J. E. (1982)	*Aldgate*
Newman, Mrs P. B. (1989)	*Aldersgate*
Northall-Laurie, P. D. (1975)	*Walbrook*
Owen, Mrs J. (1975)	*Langbourn*
Owen-Ward, J. R. (1983)	*Bridge*
Parmley, A. C. (1992)	*Vintry*
Pembroke, *Deputy* Mrs A. M. F. (1978)	*Cheap*
Platts-Mills, J. F. F., QC	*Farringdon Wt.*
Ponsonby of Shulbrede, *Deputy* Lady (1981)	*Farringdon Wt.*
Pulman, *Deputy* G. A. G. (1983)	*Tower*
Punter, C. (1993)	*Cripplegate Wn.*
Reed, *Deputy* J. L., MBE (1967)	*Farringdon Wn.*
Revell-Smith, *Deputy* P. A., CBE (1959)	*Vintry*
Rigby, P. P., CBE (1972)	*Farringdon Wn.*
Robinson, Mrs D. C. (1989)	*Bishopsgate*
Roney, *Deputy* E. P. T., CBE (1974)	*Bishopsgate*
Samuel, *Deputy* Mrs I., MBE (1971)	*Portsoken*
Sargant, K. A. (1991)	*Cornhill*
Saunders, *Deputy* R. (1975)	*Candlewick*
Scriven, R. G. (1984)	*Candlewick*
Sellon, S. A., OBE, TD (1990)	*Cordwainer*
Shalit, D. M. (1972)	*Farringdon Wn.*
Sharp, *Deputy* Mrs I. M. (1974)	*Queenhithe*
Sherlock, M. R. C. (1992)	*Dowgate*
Simpson, A. S. J. (1987)	*Aldersgate*
Smith, Miss A. M. (1995)	*Farringdon Wt.*
Snyder, *Deputy* M. J. (1986)	*Cordwainer*
Spanner, J. H., TD (1984)	*Broad Street*
Stevenson, F. P. (1994)	*Cripplegate Wn.*
Stone, H. V. (1993)	*Billingsgate*
Taylor, J. A. F., TD (1991)	*Bread Street*
Trotter, J. (1993)	*Billingsgate*
Walsh, S. (1989)	*Farringdon Wt.*
Warner, D. W. (1994)	*Cripplegate Wn.*
White, Dr J. W. (1986)	*Cornhill*
Willoughby, P. J. (1985)	*Bishopsgate*
Wilmot, R. T. D. (1973)	*Cordwainer*
Wilson, A. B., CBE (1984)	*Cheap*
Wixley, G. R. A., CBE, TD (1964)	*Coleman Street*
Woodward, *Deputy* C. D., CBE (1971)	*Cripplegate Wn.*
Wooldridge, F. D. (1988)	*Farringdon Wn.*

The City Guilds (Livery Companies)

The constitution of the livery companies has been unchanged for centuries. There are three ranks of membership: freemen, liverymen and assistants. A person can become a freeman by patrimony (through a parent having been a freeman); by servitude (through having served an apprenticeship to a freeman); or by redemption (by purchase).

Election to the livery is the prerogative of the company, who can elect any of its freemen as liverymen. Assistants are usually elected from the livery and form a Court of Assistants which is the governing body of the company. The Master (in some companies called the Prime Warden) is elected annually from the assistants.

As at June 1996, 23,750 liverymen of the guilds were entitled to vote at elections at Common Hall.

The order of precedence, omitting extinct companies, is given in parenthesis after the name of each company in the list below. In certain companies the election of Master or Prime Warden for the year does not take place till the autumn. In such cases the Master or Prime Warden for 1995–6 is given.

THE TWELVE GREAT COMPANIES
In order of civic precedence

MERCERS (*1*). *Hall,* Ironmonger Lane, London EC2V 8HE. *Livery,* 226. *Clerk,* G. M. M. Wakeford, OBE. *Master,* J. Hedges

GROCERS (*2*). *Hall,* Princes Street, London EC2R 8AD. *Livery,* 312. *Clerk,* C. G. Mattingley, CBE. *Master,* C. D. Stewart-Smith, CBE

DRAPERS (*3*). *Hall,* Throgmorton Avenue, London EC2N 2DQ. *Livery,* 243. *Clerk,* A. L. Lang, MBE. *Master,* Vice-Adm. Sir Geoffrey Dalton, KCB

FISHMONGERS (*4*). *Hall,* London Bridge, London EC4R 9EL. *Livery,* 366. *Clerk,* K. S. Waters. *Prime Warden,* M. Drummond, OBE

GOLDSMITHS (*5*). *Hall,* Foster Lane, London EC2V 6BN. *Livery,* 275. *Clerk,* R. D. Buchanan-Dunlop, CBE. *Prime Warden,* S. L. Devlin, CMG

MERCHANT TAYLORS (*6/7*). *Hall,* 30 Threadneedle Street, London EC2R 8AY. *Livery* 312. *Clerk,* D. A. Peck. *Master,* P. H. Ryan, CBE

SKINNERS (*6/7*). *Hall,* 8 Dowgate Hill, London EC4R 2SP. *Livery,* 370. *Clerk,* Capt. D. Hart-Dyke, CBE, LVO, RN. *Master,* A. Crawshaw

HABERDASHERS (*8*). *Hall,* Staining Lane, London EC2V 7DD. *Livery,* 320. *Clerk,* Capt. R. J. Fisher, RN. *Master,* D. G. C. Inglefield

SALTERS (*9*). *Hall,* 4 Fore Street, London EC2Y 5DE. *Livery,* 165. *Clerk,* Col. M. P. Barneby. *Master,* A. Dawson Paul

IRONMONGERS (*10*). *Hall,* Shaftesbury Place, Barbican, London EC2Y 8AA. *Livery,* 224. *Clerk,* J. A. Oliver. *Master,* R. H. Hunting

VINTNERS (*11*). *Hall,* Upper Thames Street, London EC4V 3BJ. *Livery,* 308. *Clerk,* Brig. G. Read, CBE. *Master* T. J. Hood

CLOTHWORKERS (*12*). *Hall,* Dunster Court, Mincing Lane, London EC3R 7AH. *Livery,* 200. *Clerk,* M. G. T. Harris. *Master,* R. L. L. Davis

OTHER CITY GUILDS
In alphabetical order

ACTUARIES (*91*). *Livery*, 190. *Clerk*, P. D. Esslemont, 16A Cadogan Square, London SW1X 0JU. *Master*, M. H. Field, CBE

AIR PILOTS AND AIR NAVIGATORS, GUILD OF (*81*). *Livery*, 415. *Grand Master*, HRH The Prince Philip, Duke of Edinburgh, KG, KT. *Clerk*, Gp Capt. W. M. Watkins, Cobham House, 291 Gray's Inn Road, London WC1X 8QF. *Master*, Dr I. C. Perry

APOTHECARIES, SOCIETY OF (*58*). *Hall*, 14 Black Friars Lane, London EC4V 6EJ. *Livery*, 1,286. *Clerk*, Lt.-Col. R. J. Stringer. *Master*, Dr F. B. Gibberd

ARBITRATORS (*93*). *Livery*, 234. *Clerk*, Lt.-Col. I. R. P. Green, 2 Bolts Hill, Castle Camps, Cambs CB1 6TL. *Master*, C. J. Evans

ARMOURERS AND BRASIERS (*22*). *Hall*, 81 Coleman Street, London EC2R 5BJ. *Livery*, 125. *Clerk*, Cdr. T. J. K. Sloane, OBE. *Master*, M. J. Paton

BAKERS (*19*). *Hall*, Harp Lane, London EC3R 6DP. *Livery*, 389. *Clerk (acting)*, J. W. Tompkins. *Master*, J. Moon

BARBERS (*17*). *Hall*, Monkwell Square, Wood Street, London EC2Y 5BL. *Livery*, 235. *Clerk*, Brig. A. F. Eastburn. *Master*, R. R. C. Bloomfield, CBE

BASKETMAKERS (*52*). *Livery*, 341. *Clerk*, Maj. G. J. Flint-Shipman, TD, 48 Seymour Walk, London SW10 9NF. *Prime Warden*, J. Heffernan

BLACKSMITHS (*40*). *Livery*, 239. *Clerk*, R. C. Jorden, 27 Cheyne Walk, Grange Park, London N21 1DB. *Prime Warden*, R. Lyons

BOWYERS (*38*). *Livery*, 105. *Clerk*, J. R. Owen-Ward, 261 Green Lanes, London N13 4XE. *Master*, P. J. Begent

BREWERS (*14*). *Hall*, Aldermanbury Square, London EC2V 7HR. *Livery*, 115. *Clerk*, C. W. Dallmeyer. *Master*, M. R. M. Foster

BRODERERS (*48*). *Livery*, 158. *Clerk*, P. J. C. Crouch, 11 Bridge Road, East Molesey, Surrey KT8 9EU. *Master*, B. E. Toye

BUILDERS MERCHANTS (*88*). *Livery*, 183. *Clerk*, Miss S. M. Robinson, TD, 14 Charterhouse Square, London EC1M 6AX. *Master*, D. Bedford

BUTCHERS (*24*). *Hall*, 87 Bartholomew Close, London EC1A 7EB. *Livery*, 650. *Clerk*, J. C. M. Chapman. *Master*, Mrs S. Reid

CARMEN (*77*). *Livery*, 430. *Clerk*, Cdr. R. M. H. Bawtree, OBE, 35–37 Ludgate Hill, London EC4M 7JN. *Master*, J. M. B. Gotch

CARPENTERS (*26*). *Hall*, 1 Throgmorton Avenue, London EC2N 2JJ. *Livery*, 150. *Clerk*, Maj.-Gen. P. T. Stevenson, OBE. *Master*, F. D. Hornsby

CHARTERED ACCOUNTANTS (*86*). *Livery*, 345. *Clerk*, C. Bygrave, The Rustlings, Valley Close, Studham, Dunstable, Beds LU6 2QN. *Master*, W. S. C. Richards

CHARTERED ARCHITECTS (*98*). *Livery*, 150. *Clerk*, J. Griffiths, 28 Palace Road, East Molesey, Surrey KT8 9DL. *Master*, Mrs S. Reid

CHARTERED SECRETARIES AND ADMINISTRATORS (*87*). *Livery*, 225. *Hon. Clerk*, W. C. Hammond, MBE, St Dunstan's House, Carey Lane, London EC2V 8AA. *Master*, G. S. Finn

CHARTERED SURVEYORS (*85*). *Livery*, 350. *Clerk*, Mrs A. L. Jackson, 16 St Mary-at-Hill, London EC3R 8EE. *Master*, D. H. Pepper

CLOCKMAKERS (*61*). *Livery*, 220. *Clerk*, Gp Capt P. H. Gibson, MBE, Room 66–67 Albert Buildings, 49 Queen Victoria Street, London EC4N 4SE. *Master*, Air Vice-Marshal P. H. Latham, CB, AFC

COACHMAKERS AND COACH-HARNESS MAKERS (*72*). *Livery*, 420. *Clerk*, Maj. W. H. Wharfe, 149 Banstead Road, Ewell, Epsom, Surrey KT17 3HL. *Master*, J. Smillie

CONSTRUCTORS (*99*). *Livery*, 119. *Clerk*, L. L. Brace, 181 Fentiman Road, London SW8 1JY. *Master*, P. A. Everett

COOKS (*35*). *Livery*, 75. *Clerk*, M. C. Thatcher, 35 Great Peter Street, London SW1P 3LR. *Master*, Revd J. K. L. Powell

COOPERS (*36*). *Hall*, 13 Devonshire Square, London EC2M 4TH. *Livery*, 260. *Clerk*, J. A. Newton. *Master*, J. B. Holden

CORDWAINERS (*27*). *Livery* 152. *Clerk*, Lt.-Col. J. R. Blundell, RM, Eldon Chambers, 30 Fleet Street, London EC4Y 1AA. *Master*, T. C. Weber-Brown

CURRIERS (*29*). *Livery*, 96. *Clerk*, Gp Capt F. J. Hamilton, Kestrel Cottage, East Knoyle, Salisbury SP3 6AD. *Master*, R. G. Blaber

CUTLERS (*18*). *Hall*, Warwick Lane, London EC4M 7BR. *Livery*, 115. *Clerk*, K. S. G. Hinde, TD. *Master*, J. A. L. Evans, CBE

DISTILLERS (*69*). *Livery*, 260. *Clerk*, C. V. Hughes, 71 Lincoln's Inn Fields, London WC2A 3JF. *Master*, A. W. C. Edwards

DYERS (*13*). *Hall*, 10 Dowgate Hill, London EC4R 2ST. *Livery*, 121. *Clerk*, J. R. Chambers. *Prime Warden*, R. S. Brooks

ENGINEERS (*94*). *Livery*, 281. *Clerk*, Cdr. B. D. Gibson, Kiln Bank, Bodle Street Green, Hailsham, E. Sussex BN27 4UA. *Master*, Prof. Sir Frederick Crawford, FENG.

ENVIRONMENTAL CLEANERS (*97*). *Livery*, 185. *Clerk*, S. J. Holt, Whitethorns, Rannoch Road, Crowborough, E. Sussex TN6 1RA. *Master*, A. W. E. Ellison

FAN MAKERS (*76*). *Livery*, 205. *Clerk*, Lt.-Col. I. R. P. Green, 2 Bolts Hill, Castle Camps, Cambs CB1 6TL. *Master*, A. S. Collins, TD

FARMERS (*80*). *Hall*, 3 Cloth Street, London EC1A 7LD. *Livery*, 300. *Clerk*, Miss M. L. Winter. *Master*, W. M. Cornish

FARRIERS (*55*). *Livery*, 360. *Clerk*, H. W. H. Ellis, 37 The Uplands, Loughton, Essex IG10 1NQ. *Master*, T. L. Baker

FELTMAKERS (*63*). *Livery*, 170. *Clerk*, Lt.-Col. C. J. Holroyd, Providence Cottage, Chute Cadley, Andover, Hants SP11 9EB. *Master*, Capt. P. Cobb, OBE, RN

FLETCHERS (*39*). *Hall*, 3 Cloth Street, London EC1A 7LD. *Livery*, 110. *Clerk*, J. R. Owen-Ward. *Master*, L. S. Johnson

FOUNDERS (*33*). *Hall*, 1 Cloth Fair, London EC1A 7HT. *Livery*, 175. *Clerk*, A. J. Gillett. *Master*, R. G. Lightfoot

FRAMEWORK KNITTERS (*64*). *Livery*, 210. *Clerk*, H. W. H. Ellis, Whitegarth Chambers, 37 The Uplands, Loughton, Essex IG10 1NQ. *Master*, T. M. Fraser

FRUITERERS (*45*). *Livery*, 270. *Clerk*, Lt.-Col. L. G. French, Chapelstones, 84 High Street, Codford St Mary, Warminster, Wilts BA12 0ND. *Master*, M. J. Tanguy

FUELLERS (*95*). *Livery*, 65. *Clerk*, S. J. Lee, Fords, 134 Ockford Road, Godalming, Surrey GU7 1RG. *Master*, Brig. C. E. Wilkinson

FURNITURE MAKERS (*83*). *Livery*, 257. *Clerk*, Mrs J. A. Wright, 9 Little Trinity Lane, London EC4V 2AD. *Master*, H. P. Joscelyne

GARDENERS (*66*). *Livery*, 248. *Clerk*, Col. N. G. S. Gray, 25 Luke Street, London EC2A 4AR. *Master*, I. B. Flanagan

GIRDLERS (*23*). *Hall*, Basinghall Avenue, London EC2V 5DD. *Livery*, 80. *Clerk*, Lt.-Col. R. Sullivan. *Master*, Sir Gordon Pirie, CVO, CBE

GLASS-SELLERS (*71*). *Livery*, 165. *Hon. Clerk*, B. J. Rawles, 43 Aragon Avenue, Thames Ditton, Surrey KT7 0PY. *Master*, J. G. Thorpe

GLAZIERS AND PAINTERS OF GLASS (*53*). *Hall*, 9 Montague Close, London SE1 9DD. *Livery*, 270. *Clerk*, P. R. Batchelor. *Master*, M. C. Tosh

GLOVERS (*62*). *Livery*, 280. *Clerk*, Mrs M. Hood, 71 Ifield Road, London SW10 9AU. *Master*, A. S. Fishman

GOLD AND SILVER WYRE DRAWERS (74). *Livery*, 325. *Clerk*, J. R. Williams, 50 Cheyne Avenue, London E18 2DR. *Master*, N. S. Nichols

GUNMAKERS (73). *Livery*, 280. *Clerk*, J. M. Riches, The Proof House, 48–50 Commercial Road, London E1 1LP. *Master*, R. W. Whittaker

HORNERS (54). *Livery*, 260. *Clerk*, S. J. Holt, Whitethorns, Rannoch Road, Crowborough, E. Sussex TN6 1RA. *Master*, D. J. Rogers

INFORMATION TECHNOLOGISTS (100). *Livery*, 255. *Clerk*, Mrs G. Davies, 30 Aylesbury Street, London EC1R 0ER. *Master*, K. Arnold, OBE

INNHOLDERS (32). *Hall*, College Street, London EC4R 2RH. *Livery*, 130. *Clerk*, J. R. Edwardes Jones. *Master*, A. House

INSURERS (92). *Hall*, 20 Aldermanbury, London EC2V 7HY. *Livery*, 373. *Clerk*, V. D. Webb. *Master*, B. V. Day

JOINERS AND CEILERS (41). *Livery*, 130. *Clerk*, Mrs A. L. Jackson, 75 Meadway Drive, Horsell, Woking, Surrey GU21 4TF. *Master*, S. K. Riddick

LAUNDERERS (89). *Hall*, 9 Montague Close, London SE1 9DD. *Livery*, 230. *Clerk*, vacant. *Master*, D. R. Browne

LEATHERSELLERS (15). *Hall*, 15 St Helen's Place, London EC3A 6DQ. *Livery*, 150. *Clerk*, Capt. J. G. F. Cooke, OBE, RN. *Master*, D. W. Dove

LIGHTMONGERS (96). *Livery*, 132. *Clerk*, D. B. Wheatley, 53 Leithcote Gardens, London SW16 2UX. *Master*, D. J. Collins

LORINERS (57). *Livery*, 350. *Clerk*, J. R. Williams, 50 Cheyne Avenue, London E18 2DR. *Master*, A. Bischoff

MAKERS OF PLAYING CARDS (75). *Livery*, 149. *Clerk*, M. J. Smyth, 6 The Priory, Godstone, Surrey RH9 8NL. *Master*, M. H. Goodall

MARKETORS (90). *Livery*, 243. *Clerk*, Mrs G. Dutty, 14 Charterhouse Square, London EC1M 6AX. *Master*, D. Thomas

MASONS (30). *Livery*, 125. *Clerk*, T. F. Ackland, 261 Green Lanes, London N13 4XE. *Master*, B. Woodman

MASTER MARINERS, HONOURABLE COMPANY OF (78). HQS *Wellington*, Temple Stairs, Victoria Embankment, London WC2R 2PN. *Livery*, 250. *Clerk*, J. A. V. Maddock. *Admiral*, HRH The Duke of Edinburgh, KG, KT. *Master*, Capt. G. T. Davies

MUSICIANS (50). *Livery*, 320. *Clerk*, S. F. N. Waley, St Dunstan's House, 2–4 Carey Lane, London EC2V 8AA. *Master*, A. M. Burnett-Brown

NEEDLEMAKERS (65). *Livery*, 240. *Clerk*, M. G. Cook, 5 Staple Inn, London WC1V 7QH. *Master*, B. G. Amery

PAINTER-STAINERS (28). *Hall*, 9 Little Trinity Lane, London EC4V 2AD. *Livery*, 308. *Clerk*, Col. W. J. Chesshyre. *Master*, G. F. Jacobs

PATTENMAKERS (70). *Livery*, 179. *Clerk*, C. L. K. Ledger, 17 Orchard Close, The Rutts, Bushey Heath, Herts WD2 1LW. *Master*, J. A. V. Townsend

PAVIORS (56). *Livery*, 250. *Clerk*, R. F. Coe, 154 Dukes Avenue, New Malden, Surrey KT3 4HR. *Master*, J. Luff

PEWTERERS (16). *Hall*, Oat Lane, London EC2V 7DE. *Livery*, 113. *Clerk*, Cdr. A. Steiner, OBE. *Master*, J. P. Hull

PLAISTERERS (46). *Hall*, 1 London Wall, London EC4Y 5JU. *Livery*, 208. *Clerk*, R. Vickers. *Master*, B. Lincoln

PLUMBERS (31). *Livery*, 349. *Clerk*, Lt.-Col. R. J. A. Paterson-Fox, 49 Queen Victoria Street, London EC4N 4SA. *Master*, C. D. Smith

POULTERS (34). *Livery*, 173. *Clerk*, A. W. Scott, 23 Orchard Drive, Chorleywood, Herts WD3 5QN. *Master*, M. B. Savory

SADDLERS (25). *Hall*, 40 Gutter Lane, London EC2V 6BR. *Livery*, 70. *Clerk*, Gp Capt W. S. Brereton Martin, CBE. *Master*, W. Price

SCIENTIFIC INSTRUMENT MAKERS (84). *Hall*, 9 Montague Close, London SE1 9DD. *Livery*, 232. *Clerk*, F. G. Everard. *Master*, W. Lyons

SCRIVENERS (44). *Livery*, 215. *Clerk*, P. C. Stevens, HQS *Wellington*, Temple Stairs, Victoria Embankment, London WC2R 2PN. *Master*, H. J. W. Harman

SHIPWRIGHTS (59). *Livery*, 420. *Clerk*, Capt. R. F. Channon, RN, Ironmongers' Hall, Barbican, London EC2Y 8AA. *Permanent Master*, HRH The Duke of Edinburgh, KG, KT. *Prime Warden*, J. G. M. Hart

SOLICITORS (79). *Livery*, 265. *Clerk*, Miss S. M. Robinson, TD, 14 Charterhouse Square, London EC1M 6AX. *Master*, W. King

SPECTACLE MAKERS (60). *Livery*, 370. *Clerk*, C. J. Eldridge, Apothecaries' Hall, Black Friars Lane, London EC4V 6EL. *Master*, C. Stone

STATIONERS AND NEWSPAPER MAKERS (47). *Hall*, Ave Maria Lane, London EC4M 7DD. *Livery*, 439. *Clerk*, Brig. D. G. Sharp. *Master*, R. Fullick

TALLOW CHANDLERS (21). *Hall*, 4 Dowgate Hill, London EC4R 2SH. *Livery*, 180. *Clerk*, Brig. W. K. L. Prosser, CBE, MC. *Master*, C. A. Holborow, OBE, TD, MD, FRCS

TIN PLATE WORKERS alias Wire Workers (67). *Livery*, 174. *Clerk*, S. J. Holt, Whitethorns, Rannoch Road, Crowborough, E. Sussex TN6 1RA. *Master*, Dr R. S. A. White

TOBACCO PIPE MAKERS AND TOBACCO BLENDERS (82). *Livery*, 161. *Clerk*, N. J. Hallings-Pott, Hackhurst Farm, Lower Dicker, Hailsham, E. Sussex BN27 4BP. *Master*, R. L. H. Merton

TURNERS (51). *Livery*, 180. *Clerk*, Maj.-Gen. D. Shaw, CB, CBE, c/o Apothecaries' Hall, Black Friars Lane, London EC4V 6EL. *Master*, J. N. Ciclitira

TYLERS AND BRICKLAYERS (37). *Livery*, 130. *Clerk*, J. Griffiths, 28 Palace Road, East Molesey, Surrey KT8 9DL. *Master*, B. G. Holliday, MC.

UPHOLDERS (49). *Livery*, 200. *Clerk*, G. J. K. Darby, Kirstone, Beckenham Place Park, Beckenham, Kent BR3 2BN. *Master*, D. S. Austin

WAX CHANDLERS (20). *Hall*, Gresham Street, London EC2V 7AD. *Livery*, 88. *Clerk*, Cdr J. Stevens. *Master*, D. La Riece

WEAVERS (42). *Livery*, 125. *Clerk*, Mrs F. Newcombe, Saddlers' House, Gutter Lane, London EC2V 6BR. *Upper Bailiff*, S. A. A. Block

WHEELWRIGHTS (68). *Livery*, 250. *Clerk*, M. G. Cook, 9 Staple Inn, London WC1V 7QH. *Master*, B. P. Boreham

WOOLMEN (43). *Livery*, 135. *Clerk*, F. Allen, Hollands, Hedsor Road, Bourne End, Bucks SL8 5EC. *Master*, M. D. Abrahams, CBE

FIREFIGHTERS (*No livery*), Freemen, 110. *Clerk*, T. Morris, 20 Aldermanbury, London EC2V 7GF. *Master*, K. Barnes

PARISH CLERKS (*No livery*). *Members*, 90. *Clerk*, Lt.-Col. B. J. N. Coombes, 1 Dean Trench Street, London SW1P 3HB. *Master*, Revd G. L. Blacktop

WATER CONSERVATORS (*No livery*). Freemen, 162. *Clerk*, H. B. Berridge, MBE, 20 Aldermanbury, London EC2V 7GF. *Master*, E. W. Flaxman.

WATERMEN AND LIGHTERMEN (*No livery*). *Craft Owning Freemen*, 300. *Hall*, 18 St Mary-at-Hill, London EC3R 8EE. *Clerk*, R. G. Crouch. *Master*, Capt. Sir Malcolm Edge, KCVO

WORLD TRADERS (*No livery*). Freemen, 83. *Clerk*, J. T. Norman, 13 Pinewood Road, Branksome Park, Poole, Dorset BH13 6JP. *Master*, J. Davis, CBE

LONDON BOROUGH COUNCILS

Council	Municipal offices	Population 1994	Band D charge 1996	Chief Executive (*Managing Director)	Mayor (a) Lord Mayor 1996−7
Barking and Dagenham	°Dagenham, RM10 7BN	155,000	£576.00	W. C. Smith	J. Thomas
Barnet	†The Burroughs, Hendon, NW4 4BG	308,200	636.85	M. M. Caller	Ms P. Coleman
Bexley	‡Bexleyheath, Kent DA6 7LB	220,400	583.92	C. Duffield	R. Brierly
Brent	†Forty Lane, Wembley, HA9 9EZ	244,500	455.50	G. Benham	Ms L. Patel
Bromley	°Bromley, BR1 3UH	293,000	540.00	M. Blanch	P. Woods
§Camden	†Judd Street, WC1H 9JE	182,500	778.60	S. Bundred	Ms G. Lazenby
§CITY OF WESTMINSTER	City Hall, Victoria Street, SW1E 6QP	190,100	295.00	*W. C. Roots	(a) R. Davis
Croydon	Taberner House, Park Lane, Croydon CR9 3JS	326,800	593.00	D. Wechsler	P. Spalding
Ealing	†Uxbridge Road, W5 2HL	289,800	532.00	Ms G. Guy	M. Patil
Enfield	°Enfield, EN1 3XA	259,800	616.88	D. Plank	P. Cunneen
§Greenwich	†Wellington Street, SE18 6PW	212,200	763.29	C. Roberts	Ms J. Gillman
§Hackney	†Mare Street, E8 1EA	192,500	855.13	A. Elliston	Ms L. Hibberd
§Hammersmith and Fulham	†King Street, W6 9JU	156,600	725.00	*N. Newton	I. Coleman
Haringey	°Wood Green, N22 4LE	212,300	780.00	G. Singh	R. Blanchard
Harrow	°Harrow, HA1 2UH	210,300	579.69	A. G. Redmond	A. Hamlin
Havering	†Romford, RM1 3BD	231,700	595.00	H. W. Tinworth	I. Cameron
Hillingdon	°Uxbridge, UB8 1UW	243,000	593.32	C. Rippingale	Ms J. Blundell
Hounslow	°Lampton Road, Hounslow, TW3 4DN	202,700	661.68	R. Kerslake	Ms M. Brister
§Islington	†Upper Street, N1 2UD	175,200	853.39	Ms L. Fullick	Ms S. Marks
§Kensington and Chelsea (RB)	†Hornton Street, W8 7NX	151,500	503.94	R. A. Taylor	J. Corbet-Singleton
Kingston upon Thames (RB)	Guildhall, Kingston upon Thames KT1 1EU	138,500	569.48	B. Quoroll	I. Reid
§Lambeth	†Brixton Hill, SW2 1RW	260,700	665.00	Ms H. Rabbatts	A. Bays
§Lewisham	†Catford, SE6 4RU	242,400	629.45	B. Quirk	Ms F. Hayee
Merton	°London Road, Morden, SM4 5DX	177,200	644.67	Ms S. Charteris	S. Flegg
Newham	†East Ham, E6 2RP	226,800	594.00	Ms W. Thomson	Ms S. Ahmad
Redbridge	†Ilford, IG1 1DD	225,100	581.00	M. J. Frater	R. Hoskins
Richmond upon Thames	°York Street, Twickenham, TW1 3AA	172,000	683.00	R. L. Harbord	M. Rolands
§Southwark	†Peckham Road, SE5 8UB	228,800	730.91	W. Coomber	Ms J. Khachik
Sutton	‡St Nicholas Way, Sutton, SM1 1EA	173,400	579.06	Mrs P. Hughes	S. Theed
§Tower Hamlets	107 Commercial Street, E1 6BG	170,500	645.91	Ms S. Pierce	A. Jacob
Waltham Forest	†Forest Road, Walthamstow, E17 4JF	221,800	737.83	A. Tobias	R. J. Wheatley
§Wandsworth	†Wandsworth, SW18 2PU	266,600	431.26	G. K. Jones	Miss D. Whittingham

§   Inner London Borough
RB Royal Borough
°   Civic Centre
†   Town Hall
‡   Civic Offices
Source of population statistics: OPCS Monitor PP1 95/1, 17 August 1995
For explanation of council tax, *see* pages 519−20

Wales

The Principality of Wales (Cymru) occupies the extreme west of the central southern portion of the island of Great Britain, with a total area of 8,015 sq. miles (20,758 sq. km): land 7,965 sq. miles (20,628 sq. km); inland water 50 sq. miles (130 sq. km). It is bounded on the north by the Irish Sea, on the south by the Bristol Channel, on the east by the English counties of Cheshire, Shropshire, Hereford and Worcester, and Gloucestershire, and on the west by St George's Channel.

Across the Menai Straits is the island of Ynys Môn (Anglesey) (276 sq. miles), communication with which is facilitated by the Menai Suspension Bridge (1,000 ft long) built by Telford in 1826, and by the tubular railway bridge (1,100 ft long) built by Stephenson in 1850. Holyhead harbour, on Holy Isle (north-west of Anglesey), provides accommodation for ferry services to Dublin (70 miles).

POPULATION

The population at the 1991 Census was 2,811,865 (males 1,356,886; females 1,454,979). The average density of population in 1991 was 1.36 persons per hectare.

RELIEF

Wales is a country of extensive tracts of high plateau and shorter stretches of mountain ranges deeply dissected by river valleys. Lower-lying ground is largely confined to the coastal belt and the lower parts of the valleys. The highest mountains are those of Snowdonia in the north-west (Snowdon, 3,559 ft), Berwyn (Aran Fawddwy, 2,971 ft), Cader Idris (Pen y Gadair, 2,928 ft), Dyfed (Plynlimon, 2,467 ft), and the Black Mountain, Brecon Beacons and Black Forest ranges in the south-east (Carmarthen Van, 2,630 ft, Pen y Fan, 2,906 ft, Waun Fâch, 2,660 ft).

HYDROGRAPHY

The principal river rising in Wales is the Severn (*see* page 529), which flows from the slopes of Plynlimon to the English border. The Wye (130 miles) also rises in the slopes of Plynlimon. The Usk (56 miles) flows to the Bristol Channel, through Gwent. The Dee (70 miles) rises in Bala Lake and flows through the Vale of Llangollen, where an aqueduct (built by Telford in 1805) carries the Pontcysyllte branch of the Shropshire Union Canal across the valley. The estuary of the Dee is the navigable portion, 14 miles in length and about five miles in breadth, and the tide rushes in with dangerous speed over the 'Sands of Dee'. The Towy (68 miles), Teifi (50 miles), Taff (40 miles), Dovey (30 miles), Taf (25 miles) and Conway (24 miles), the last named broad and navigable, are wholly Welsh rivers.

The largest natural lake is Bala (Llyn Tegid) in Gwynedd, nearly four miles long and about one mile wide. Lake Vyrnwy is an artificial reservoir, about the size of Bala, and forms the water supply of Liverpool; Birmingham is supplied from reservoirs in the Elan and Claerwen valleys.

WELSH LANGUAGE

According to the 1991 Census results, the percentage of persons of three years and over able to speak Welsh was:

Clwyd	18.2	Powys	20.2
Dyfed	43.7	S. Glamorgan	6.5
Gwent	2.4	W. Glamorgan	15.0
Gwynedd	61.0		
Mid Glamorgan	8.5	Wales	18.7

The 1991 figure represents a slight decline from 18.9 per cent in 1981 (1971, 20.8 per cent; 1961, 26 per cent).

FLAG

The flag of Wales, the Red Dragon (Y Ddraig Goch), is a red dragon on a field divided white over green (per fess argent and vert a dragon passant gules). The flag was augmented in 1953 by a royal badge on a shield encircled with a riband bearing the words *Ddraig Goch Ddyry Cychwyn* and imperially crowned, but this augmented flag is rarely used.

EARLY HISTORY

The earliest inhabitants of whom there is any record appear to have been subdued or exterminated by the Goidels (a people of Celtic race) in the Bronze Age. A further invasion of Celtic Brythons and Belgae followed in the ensuing Iron Age. The Roman conquest of southern Britain and Wales was for some time successfully opposed by Caratacus (Caractacus or Caradog), chieftain of the Catuvellauni and son of Cunobelinus (Cymbeline). South-east Wales was subjugated and the legionary fortress at Caerleon-on-Usk established by about AD 75–77; the conquest of Wales was completed by Agricola about AD 78. Communications were opened up by the construction of military roads from Chester to Caerleon-on-Usk and Caerwent, and from Chester to Conwy (and thence to Carmarthen and Neath). Christianity was introduced during the Roman occupation, in the fourth century.

ANGLO-SAXON ATTACKS

The Anglo-Saxon invaders of southern Britain drove the Celts into the mountain stronghold of Wales, and into Strathclyde (Cumberland and south-west Scotland) and Cornwall, giving them the name of *Waelisc* (Welsh), meaning 'foreign'. The West Saxons' victory of Deorham (AD 577) isolated Wales from Cornwall and the battle of Chester (AD 613) cut off communication with Strathclyde and northern Britain. In the eighth century the boundaries of the Welsh were further restricted by the annexations of Offa, King of Mercia, and counter-attacks were largely prevented by the construction of an artificial boundary from the Dee to the Wye (Offa's Dyke).

In the ninth century Rhodri Mawr (844–878) united the country and successfully resisted further incursions of the Saxons by land and raids of Norse and Danish pirates by sea, but at his death his three provinces of Gwynedd (north), Powys (mid) and Deheubarth (south) were divided among his three sons, Anarawd, Mervyn and Cadell. Cadell's son Hywel Dda ruled a large part of Wales and codified its laws but the provinces were not united again until the rule of Llewelyn ap Seisyllt (husband of the heiress of Gwynedd) from 1018 to 1023.

THE NORMAN CONQUEST

After the Norman conquest of England, William I created palatine counties along the Welsh frontier, and the Norman barons began to make encroachments into Welsh territory. The Welsh princes recovered many of their losses during the civil wars of Stephen's reign and in the early 13th century Owen Gruffydd, prince of Gwynedd, was the dominant figure in Wales. Under Llywelyn ap Iorwerth (1194–1240) the Welsh united in powerful resistance to English incursions and Llwelyn's privileges and *de facto* independence were recognized in Magna Carta. His grandson, Llywelyn ap Gruffydd, was the last native prince; he was killed in 1282 during hostilities between the Welsh and English, allowing Edward I of England to establish his authority over the country. On 7 February 1301, Edward of Caernarvon, son of Edward I, was created Prince of Wales, a title which has subsequently been borne by the eldest son of the sovereign.

Strong Welsh national feeling continued, expressed in the early 15th century in the rising led by Owain Glyndŵr, but the situation was altered by the accession to the English throne in 1485 of Henry VII of the Welsh House of Tudor. Wales was politically assimilated to England under the Act of Union of 1535, which extended English laws to the Principality and gave it parliamentary representation for the first time.

EISTEDDFOD

The Welsh are a distinct nation, with a language and literature of their own, and the national bardic festival (Eisteddfod), instituted by Prince Rhys ap Griffith in 1176, is still held annually (for date, *see* page 12). These *Eisteddfodau* (sessions) form part of the *Gorsedd* (assembly), which is believed to date from the time of Prydian, a ruling prince in an age many centuries before the Christian era.

PRINCIPAL CITIES

CARDIFF

Cardiff, at the mouth of the Rivers Taff, Rhymney and Ely, is the capital city of Wales and a major administrative, commercial and business centre. It has many industries, including steel and cigars, and its flourishing port is within the Cardiff Bay area, subject of a major redevelopment until the year 2000.

The many fine buildings include the City Hall, the National Museum of Wales, University Buildings, Law Courts, Welsh Office, County Hall, Police Headquarters, the Temple of Peace and Health, Llandaff Cathedral, the Welsh National Folk Museum at St Fagans, Cardiff Castle, the New Theatre, the Sherman Theatre and the Welsh College of Music and Drama. More recent buildings include St David's Hall, Cardiff International Arena and World Trade Centre, and the Welsh National Ice Rink. The Millenium Stadium is to be completed for the 1999 rugby World Cup.

SWANSEA

Swansea (*Abertawe*) is a city and a seaport. The Gower peninsula was brought within the city boundary under local government reform in 1974. The trade of the port includes coal, steel products, containerized goods and the import and export of petroleum products and petrochemicals.

The principal buildings are the Norman Castle (rebuilt *c.*1330), the Royal Institution of South Wales, founded in 1835 (including Library), the University College at Singleton, and the Guildhall, containing the Brangwyn panels. More recent buildings include the Industrial and Maritime Museum, the new Maritime Quarter and Marina and the leisure centre.

Swansea was chartered by the Earl of Warwick, *c.*1158–84, and further charters were granted by King John, Henry III, Edward II, Edward III and James II, Cromwell (two) and the Marcher Lord William de Breos.

LOCAL COUNCILS

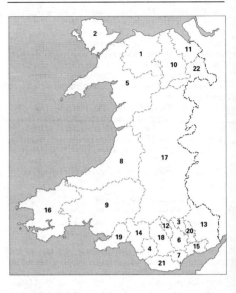

Key	County
1	Conwy
2	Anglesey
3	Blaenau Gwent
4	Bridgend
5	Caernarfonshire and Merionethshire
6	Caerphilly
7	Cardiff
8	Ceredigion
9	Carmarthenshire
10	Denbighshire
11	Flintshire
12	Merthyr Tydfil
13	Monmouthshire
14	Neath and Port Talbot
15	Newport
16	Pembrokeshire
17	Powys
18	Rhondda, Cynon, Taff
19	Swansea
20	Torfaen
21	The Vale of Glamorgan
22	Wrexham

LORD LIEUTENANTS AND HIGH SHERIFFS

County	Lord Lieutenant	High Sheriff, 1996–7
Clwyd	Sir William Gladstone, Bt.	R. H. W. Graham-Palmer
Dyfed	Sir David Mansel Lewis, KCVO	D. C. Jones-Davies, OBE
Gwent	Sir Richard Hanbury-Tenison, KCVO	I. F. Donald
Gwynedd	R. E. Meuric Rees, CBE	Maj. D. O. Carpenter
Mid Glamorgan	M. A. McLaggan	D. Clayton-Jones, TD
Powys	M. L. Bourdillon	W. A. D. Windham
South Glamorgan	Capt. N. Lloyd-Edwards	R. P. V. Rees, OBE
West Glamorgan	R. C. Hastie, CBE	R. Lewis

LOCAL COUNCILS

SMALL CAPITALS denote CITY status
§ Denotes Borough status

Council	Administrative headquarters	Population (latest estimate)	Band D charge 1996	Chief Executive	Chairman 1996–7 (a) Mayor (b) Lord Mayor
Anglesey	Llangefni	70,000	£416.81	L. Gibson	G. W. Roberts
§Blaenau Gwent	Ebbw Vale	73,300	430.00	R. Leadbetter, OBE	(a) M. B. Dally
§Bridgend	Bridgend	130,874	542.04	I. K. Lewis	(a) Mrs M. Butcher
Caernarfonshire and Merionethshire	Caernarfon	117,000	469.00	G. Jones	D. Orwig
§Caerphilly	Hengoed	170,000	462.69	M. Davies	(a) L. Lewis
CARDIFF	Cardiff	306,500	375.83	B. Davies	(b) J. Phillips
Carmarthenshire	Carmarthen	169,000	520.00	R. Morgan	D. T. Davies, OBE, MM
Ceredigion	Aberaeron	69,700	446.53	O. Watkin	G. Ellis
§Conwy	Conwy	110,700	401.26	C. D. Barker	W. Jones
Denbighshire	Ruthin	91,000	491.22	H. V. Thomas	R. Webb
Flintshire	Mold	144,000	500.48	P. McGreevy	Mrs I. Fellows, MBE
§Merthyr Tydfil	Merthyr Tydfil	60,000	495.46	R. V. Morris	(a) W. Smith
Monmouthshire	Cwmbran	81,000	409.06	J. Redfearn	V. G. Thomas
§Neath and Port Talbot	Port Talbot	140,000	561.76	K. Sawyers	(a) R. Jones
§Newport	Newport	130,000	389.00	R. D. Blair	(a) L. R. Turnball
Pembrokeshire	Haverfordwest	117,000	373.22	B. Parry-Jones	D. J. Thomas
Powys	Llandrindod Wells	123,600	433.86	N. Pringle	D. M. Jones
§Rhondda Cynon Taff	Tonypandy	232,581	493.00	G. R. Thomas	(a) R. Roberts
SWANSEA	Swansea	231,000	402.69	Ms V. Sugar	(b) D. Thomas
§Torfaen	Pontypool	90,700	438.35	Dr C. L. Grace	(a) S. P. Smith
§Vale of Glamorgan	Barry	119,200	424.92	D. Foster	N. Brown
§Wrexham	Wrexham	123,500	489.13	D. A. Griffin	(a) Mrs B. Greenaway

For explanation of council tax, *see* pages 519–20

Scotland

The Kingdom of Scotland occupies the northern portion of the main island of Great Britain and includes the Inner and Outer Hebrides, and the Orkney, Shetland, and many other islands. It lies between 60° 51′ 30″ and 54° 38′ N. latitude and between 1° 45′ 32″ and 6° 14′ W. longitude, with England to the south, the Atlantic Ocean on the north and west, and the North Sea on the east.

The greatest length of the mainland (Cape Wrath to the Mull of Galloway) is 274 miles, and the greatest breadth (Buchan Ness to Applecross) is 154 miles. The customary measurement of the island of Great Britain is from the site of John o' Groats house, near Duncansby Head, Caithness, to Land's End, Cornwall, a total distance of 603 miles in a straight line and approximately 900 miles by road.

The total area of Scotland is 30,420 sq. miles (78,789 sq. km); land 29,767 sq. miles (77,097 sq. km), inland water 653 sq. miles (1,692 sq. km).

POPULATION

The population at the 1991 Census was 4,998,567 (males 2,391,961; females 2,606,606). The average density of the population in 1991 was 0.65 persons per hectare.

RELIEF

There are three natural orographic divisions of Scotland. The southern uplands have their highest points in Merrick (2,766 ft), Rhinns of Kells (2,669 ft), and Cairnsmuir of Carsphairn (2,614 ft), in the west; and the Tweedsmuir Hills in the east (Hartfell 2,651 ft, Dollar Law 2,682 ft, Broad Law 2,756 ft).

The central lowlands, formed by the valleys of the Clyde, Forth and Tay, divide the southern uplands from the northern Highlands, which extend almost from the extreme north of the mainland to the central lowlands, and are divided into a northern and a southern system by the Great Glen.

The Grampian Mountains, which entirely cover the southern Highland area, include in the west Ben Nevis (4,406 ft), the highest point in the British Isles, and in the east the Cairngorm Mountains (Cairn Gorm 4,084 ft, Braeriach 4,248 ft, Ben Macdui 4,296 ft). The north-western Highland area contains the mountains of Wester and Easter Ross (Carn Eige 3,880 ft, Sgurr na Lapaich 3,775 ft).

Created, like the central lowlands, by a major geological fault, the Great Glen (60 miles long) runs between Inverness and Fort William, and contains Loch Ness, Loch Oich and Loch Lochy. These are linked to each other and to the north-east and south-west coasts of Scotland by the Caledonian Canal, providing a navigable passage between the Moray Firth and the Inner Hebrides.

HYDROGRAPHY

The western coast is fragmented by peninsulas and islands, and indented by fjords (sea-lochs), the longest of which is Loch Fyne (42 miles long) in Argyll. Although the east coast tends to be less fractured and lower, there are several great drowned inlets (firths), e.g. Firth of Forth, Firth of Tay, Moray Firth, as well as the Firth of Clyde in the west.

The lochs are the principal hydrographic feature. The largest in Scotland and in Britain is Loch Lomond (27 sq. miles), in the Grampian valleys; the longest and deepest is Loch Ness (24 miles long and 800 feet deep), in the Great Glen; and Loch Shin (20 miles long) and Loch Maree in the Highlands.

The longest river is the Tay (117 miles), noted for its salmon. It flows into the North Sea, with Dundee on the estuary, which is spanned by the Tay Bridge (10,289 ft) opened in 1887 and the Tay Road Bridge (7,365 ft) opened in 1966. Other noted salmon rivers are the Dee (90 miles) which flows into the North Sea at Aberdeen, and the Spey (110 miles), the swiftest flowing river in the British Isles, which flows into Moray Firth. The Tweed, which gave its name to the woollen cloth produced along its banks, marks in the lower stretches of its 96-mile course the border between Scotland and England.

The most important river commercially is the Clyde (106 miles), formed by the junction of the Daer and Portrail water, which flows through the city of Glasgow to the Firth of Clyde. During its course it passes over the picturesque Falls of Clyde, Bonnington Linn (30 ft), Corra Linn (84 ft), Dundaff Linn (10 ft) and Stonebyres Linn (80 ft), above and below Lanark. The Forth (66 miles), upon which stands Edinburgh, the capital, is spanned by the Forth (Railway) Bridge (1890), which is 5,330 feet long, and the Forth (Road) Bridge (1964), which has a total length of 6,156 feet (over water) and a single span of 3,000 feet.

The highest waterfall in Scotland, and the British Isles, is Eas a'Chùal Aluinn with a total height of 658 feet (200 m), which falls from Glas Bheinn in Sutherland. The Falls of Glomach, on a head-stream of the Elchaig in Wester Ross, have a drop of 370 feet.

GAELIC LANGUAGE

According to the 1991 Census, 1.4 per cent of the population of Scotland, mainly in the Highlands and western coastal regions, were able to speak the Scottish form of Gaelic.

FLAG

The flag of Scotland is known as the Saltire. It is a white diagonal cross on a blue field (saltire argent in a field azure) and represents St Andrew, the patron saint of Scotland.

THE SCOTTISH ISLANDS

The Hebrides did not become part of the Kingdom of Scotland until 1266, when they were ceded to Alexander III by Magnus of Norway. Orkney and Shetland fell to the Scottish Crown as a pledge for the unpaid dowry of Margaret of Denmark, wife of James III, in 1468, the Danish claims to suzerainty being relinquished in 1590 when James VI married Anne of Denmark.

ORKNEY

The Orkney Islands (total area 375½ sq. miles) lie about six miles north of the mainland, separated from it by the Pentland Firth. Of the 90 islands and islets (holms and skerries) in the group, about one-third are inhabited.

The total population at the 1991 Census was 19,612; the 1991 populations of the islands shown here include those of smaller islands forming part of the same civil parish.

Mainland, 15,128	Rousay, 291
Burray, 363	Sanday, 533
Eday, 166	Shapinsay, 322
Flotta and Fara, 126	South Ronaldsay, 943
Graemsay and Hoy, 477	Stronsay, 382
North Ronaldsay, 92	Westray, 704
Papa Westray, 85	

The islands are rich in Pictish and Scandinavian remains, the most notable being the Stone Age village of Skara Brae, the burial chamber of Maeshowe, the many brochs (Pictish towers) and St Magnus Cathedral. Scapa Flow, between the

Mainland and Hoy, was the war station of the British Grand Fleet from 1914 to 1919 and the scene of the scuttling of the surrendered German High Seas Fleet (21 June, 1919).

Most of the islands are low-lying and fertile, and farming (principally beef cattle) is the main industry. Flotta, to the south of Scapa Flow, is now the site of the oil terminal for the Piper, Claymore and Tartan fields in the North Sea.

The capital is Kirkwall (population 6,881) on Mainland.

SHETLAND

The Shetland Islands have a total area of 551 sq. miles and a population at the 1991 Census of 22,522. They lie about 50 miles north of the Orkneys, with Fair Isle about half-way between the two groups. Out Stack, off Muckle Flugga, one mile north of Unst, is the most northerly part of the British Isles (60° 51′ 30″ N. lat.).

There are over 100 islands, of which 16 are inhabited. Populations at the 1991 census were:

Mainland, 17,596	Muckle Roe, 115
Bressay, 352	Trondra, 117
East Burra, 72	Unst, 1,055
Fair Isle, 67	West Burra, 857
Fetlar, 90	Whalsay, 1,041
Housay, 85	Yell, 1,075

Shetland's many archaeological sites include Jarlshof, Mousa and Clickhimin, and its long connection with Scandinavia has resulted in a strong Norse influence on its place-names and dialect.

Industries include fishing, knitwear and farming. In addition to the fishing fleet there are fish processing factories, while the traditional handknitting of Fair Isle and Unst is supplemented now with machine-knitted garments. Farming is mainly crofting, with sheep being raised on the moorland and hills of the islands. Latterly the islands have become an important centre of the North Sea oil industry, with pipelines from the Brent and Ninian fields running to the terminal at Sullom Voe, the largest of its kind in Europe. Lerwick is the main centre for supply services for offshore oil exploration and development.

The capital is Lerwick (population 7,901) on Mainland.

THE HEBRIDES

Until the closing years of the 13th century the Hebrides included other Scottish islands in the Firth of Clyde, the peninsula of Kintyre (Argyllshire), the Isle of Man, and the (Irish) Isle of Rathlin. The origin of the name is stated to be the Greek *Eboudai*, latinized as *Hebudes* by Pliny, and corrupted to its present form. The Norwegian name *Sudreyjar* (Southern Islands) was latinized as *Sodorenses*, a name that survives in the Anglican bishopric of Sodor and Man.

There are over 500 islands and islets, of which about 100 are inhabited, though mountainous terrain and extensive peat bogs mean that only a fraction of the total area is under cultivation. Stone, Bronze and Iron Age settlement has left many remains, including those at Callanish on Lewis, and Norse colonization has influenced language, customs and place-names. Occupations include farming (mostly crofting and stock-raising), fishing and the manufacture of tweeds and other woollens. Tourism is also an important factor in the economy.

The Inner Hebrides lie off the west coast of Scotland and relatively close to the mainland. The largest and best-known is Skye (area 643 sq. miles; pop. 8,868; chief town, Portree), which contains the Cuillin Hills (Sgurr Alasdair 3,257 ft), the Red Hills (Beinn na Caillich 2,403 ft), Bla Bheinn (3,046 ft) and The Storr (2,358 ft). Skye is also

famous as the refuge of the Young Pretender in 1746. Other islands in the Highland Region include Raasay (pop. 163), Rum, Eigg and Muck.

Islands in the Strathclyde Region include Arran (pop. 4,474) containing Goat Fell (2,868 ft); Coll and Tiree (pop. 940); Colonsay and Oronsay (pop. 106); Islay (area 235 sq. miles; pop. 3,538); Jura (area 160 sq. miles; pop. 196) with a range of hills culminating in the Paps of Jura (Beinn-an-Oir, 2,576 ft, and Beinn Chaolais, 2,477 ft); and Mull (area 367 sq. miles; pop. 2,708; chief town Tobermory) containing Ben More (3,171 ft).

The Outer Hebrides, separated from the mainland by the Minch, now form the Western Isles Islands Council area (area 1,119 sq. miles; population at the 1991 Census 29,600). The main islands are Lewis with Harris (area 770 sq. miles, pop. 21,737), whose chief town, Stornoway, is the administrative headquarters; North Uist (pop. 1,404); South Uist (pop. 2,106); Baleshare (55); Benbecula (pop. 1,803) and Barra (pop. 1,244). Other inhabited islands include Bernera (262), Berneray (141), Eriskay (179), Grimsay (215), Scalpay (382) and Vatersay (72).

EARLY HISTORY

The Picts, believed to be of non-Aryan origin, seem to have inhabited the whole of northern Britain and to have spread over the north of Ireland. Remains are most frequent in Caithness and Sutherland and the Orkney Islands.

Celts arrived from Belgic Gaul during the latter part of the Bronze Age and in the early Iron Age and, except in the extreme north of the mainland and in the islands, the civilization and speech of the people were definitely Celtic at the time of the Roman invasion of Britain.

THE ROMAN INVASION

In AD 79–80 Julius Agricola extended the Roman conquests in Britain by advancing into Caledonia and building a line of fortifications across the isthmus between the Forth and Clyde, but after a victory at Mons Graupius he was recalled. Hadrian's Wall, mostly complete by AD 130, marked the frontier until about AD 143 when the frontier moved north to the Forth–Clyde isthmus and was secured by the Antonine Wall. From about AD 155 the Antonine Wall was damaged by frequent attacks and by the end of the second century the northern limit of Roman Britain had receded to Hadrian's Wall.

THE SCOTS

After the withdrawal or absorption of the Roman garrison of Britain there were many years of tribal warfare between the Picts and Scots (the Gaelic tribe then dominant in Ireland), the Brythonic Waelisc (Welsh) of Strathclyde (south-west Scotland and Cumberland), and the Anglo-Saxons of Lothian. The Waelisc were isolated from their kinsmen in Wales by the victory of the West Saxons at Chester (613), and towards the close of the ninth century the Scots under Kenneth Mac Alpin became the dominant power in Caledonia. In the reign of Malcolm I (943–954) Strathclyde was brought into subjection, the English lowland kingdom (Lothian) being conquered by Malcolm II (1005–1034).

From the late 11th century until the mid 16th century there were constant wars between Scotland and England, the outstanding figures in the struggle being William Wallace, who defeated the English at Stirling Bridge (1297) and Robert Bruce, who won the battle of Bannockburn (1314). James IV and many of his nobles fell at the disastrous battle of Flodden (1513).

THE JACOBITE REVOLTS

In 1603 James VI of Scotland succeeded Elizabeth I on the throne of England (his mother, Mary Queen of Scots, was the great-granddaughter of Henry VII), his successors reigning as sovereigns of Great Britain, although political union of the two countries did not occur until 1707. After the abdication (by flight) in 1688 of James VII and II, the crown devolved upon William III (grandson of Charles I) and Mary (elder daughter of James VII and II). In 1689 Graham of Claverhouse roused the Highlands on behalf of James VII and II, but died after a military success at Killiecrankie.

After the death of Anne (younger daughter of James VII and II), the throne devolved upon George I (great-grandson of James VI and I). In 1715, armed risings on behalf of James Stuart (the Old Pretender) led to the indecisive battle of Sheriffmuir, and the Jacobite movement died down until 1745, when Charles Stuart (the Young Pretender) defeated the Royalist troops at Prestonpans and advanced to Derby (1746). From Derby, the adherents of 'James VIII and III' (the title claimed for his father by Charles Stuart) fell back on the defensive, and the movement was finally crushed at Culloden (16 April 1746).

PRINCIPAL CITIES

ABERDEEN

Aberdeen, 130 miles north-east of Edinburgh, received its charter as a Royal Burgh in 1179. Scotland's third largest city, Aberdeen is the second largest Scottish fishing port and the main centre for offshore oil exploration and production. It is also an ancient university town and distinguished research centre. Other industries include engineering, food processing, textiles, paper manufacturing and chemicals.

Places of interest include King's College, St Machar's Cathedral, Brig o' Balgownie, Duthie Park and Winter Gardens, Hazlehead Park, the Kirk of St Nicholas, Mercat Cross, Marischal College and Marischal Museum, Provost Skene's House, Art Gallery, James Dun's House, Satrosphere Hands-On Discovery Centre, and Aberdeen Maritime Museum in Provost Ross's House.

DUNDEE

Dundee, a Royal Burgh, is situated on the north bank of the Tay estuary. The city's port and dock installations are important to the offshore oil industry and the airport also provides servicing facilities. Principal industries include textiles, computers and other electronic industries, lasers, printing, tyre manufacture, food processing, carpets, engineering, clothing manufacture and tourism.

The unique City Churches – three churches under one roof, together with the 15th-century St Mary's Tower – are the most prominent architectural feature. Dundee has two historic ships: the Dundee-built RRS *Discovery* which took Capt. Scott to the Antarctic lies alongside Discovery Quay, and the frigate *Unicorn*, the only British-built wooden warship still afloat, is moored in Victoria Dock. Places of interest include Mills Public Observatory, the Tay road and rail bridges, McManus Galleries, Barrack Street Museum, Claypotts Castle, Broughty Castle and Verdant Works (Textile Heritage Centre).

EDINBURGH

Edinburgh is the capital of and seat of government in Scotland. The city is built on a group of hills and contains in Princes Street one of the most beautiful thoroughfares in the world.

The principal buildings are the Castle, which includes St Margaret's Chapel, the oldest building in Edinburgh, and near it, the Scottish National War Memorial; the Palace of Holyroodhouse; Parliament House, the present seat of the judicature; three universities (Edinburgh, Heriot-Watt, Napier); St Giles' Cathedral (restored 1879–83); St Mary's (Scottish Episcopal) Cathedral (Sir Gilbert Scott); the General Register House (Robert Adam); the National and the Signet Libraries; the National Gallery; the Royal Scottish Academy; the National Portrait Gallery; and the Edinburgh International Conference Centre, opened in 1995.

GLASGOW

Glasgow, a Royal Burgh, is the principal commercial and industrial centre in Scotland. The city occupies the north and south banks of the Clyde, formerly one of the chief commercial estuaries in the world. The principal industries include engineering, electronics, finance, chemicals and printing. The city has also developed recently as a tourism and conference centre.

The chief buildings are the 13th-century Gothic Cathedral, the University (Sir Gilbert Scott), the City Chambers, the Royal Concert Hall, St Mungo Museum of Religious Life and Art, Pollok House, the School of Art (Mackintosh), Kelvingrove Art Galleries, the Gallery of Modern Art, the Burrell Collection museum and the Mitchell Library. The city is home to the Scottish National Orchestra, Scottish Opera and Scottish Ballet.

LORD LIEUTENANTS

Title	Name
Aberdeenshire	Capt. C. A. Farquharson
Angus	The Earl of Airlie, KT, GCVO, PC
Argyll and Bute	The Duke of Argyll
Ayrshire and Arran	Maj. R. Y. Henderson, TD
Banffshire	J. A. S. McPherson, CBE
Berwickshire	Maj.-Gen. Sir John Swinton, KCVO, OBE
Caithness	Maj. G. T. Dunnett, TD
Clackmannan	Lt.-Col. R. C. Stewart, CBE, TD
Dumfries	Capt. R. C. Cunningham-Jardine
Dumbartonshire	Brig. D. D. G. Hardie, TD
East Lothian	Sir Hew Hamilton-Dalrymple, Bt., KCVO
Fife	The Earl of Elgin and Kincardine, KT
Inverness	The Lord Gray of Contin, PC
Kincardineshire	The Viscount of Arbuthnott, CBE, DSC, FRSE
Lanarkshire	H. B. Sneddon, CBE
Midlothian	Capt. G. W. Burnet, LVO
Moray	Air Vice-Marshal G. A. Chesworth, CB, OBE, DFC
Nairn	The Earl of Leven and Melville
Orkney	Brig. M. G. Dennison
Perth and Kinross	Sir David Montgomery, Bt.
Renfrewshire	The Lord Goold
Ross and Cromarty	Capt. R. W. K. Stirling of Fairburn, TD

Roxburgh, Ettrick and Lauderdale	The Duke of Buccleugh and Queensberry, KT, VRD	Tweeddale	Capt. J. D. B. Younger
Shetland	J. H. Scott	West Lothian	The Earl of Morton
Stirling and Falkirk	Lt.-Col. J. Stirling of Garden, CBE, TD, FRICS	Western Isles	The Viscount Dunrossil, CMG
		Wigtown	Maj. E. S. Orr-Ewing
Sutherland	Maj.-Gen. D. Houston, CBE		
The Stewartry of Kirkcudbright	Lt.-Gen. Sir Norman Arthur, KCB		

The Lord Provosts of the four city districts of Aberdeen, Dundee, Edinburgh and Glasgow are Lord Lieutenants for those districts *ex officio*

LOCAL COUNCILS

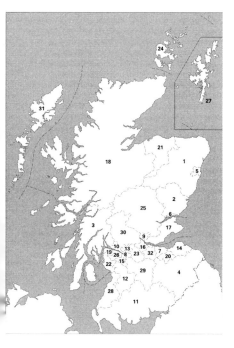

Key	Council
1	Aberdeenshire
2	Angus
3	Argyll and Bute
4	Scottish Borders
5	Aberdeen City
6	Dundee City
7	City of Edinburgh
8	Glasgow City
9	Clackmannanshire
10	West Dumbartonshire
11	Dumfries and Galloway
12	East Ayrshire
13	East Dumbartonshire
14	East Lothian
15	East Renfrewshire
16	Falkirk
17	Fife
18	Highland
19	Inverclyde
20	Midlothian
21	Moray
22	North Ayrshire
23	North Lanarkshire
24	Orkney Islands Council
25	Perth and Kinross
26	Renfrewshire
27	Shetland Islands Council
28	South Ayrshire
29	South Lanarkshire
30	Stirling
31	Western Isles Islands Council
32	West Lothian

LOCAL COUNCILS

Council	Administrative headquarters	Population (latest estimate)	Band D charge 1996	Chief Executive	Chairman (a) Convener (b) Provost (c) Lord Provost
Aberdeen City	Aberdeen	219,120	£909.51	D. Paterson	(c) Ms M. Farquhar
Aberdeenshire	Aberdeen	226,530	591.00	A. Campbell	(a) Dr C. S. Millar
Angus	Forfar	111,750	659.00	A. B. Watson	(b) Mrs F. M. Duncan
Argyll and Bute	Lochgilphead	90,000	652.00	J. McLellan	(a) J. Wilson
City of Edinburgh	Edinburgh	447,550	812.00	T. Aitchson	(c) E. Milligan
Clackmannanshire	Alloa	47,679	744.50	R. Allan	(b) R. Elder
Dundee City	Dundee	151,010	882.50	A. Stephen	(c) M. J. Rolfe
Dumfries and Galloway	Dumfries	147,900	833.33	I. F. Smith	(a) A. T. Baldwick
East Ayrshire	Kilmarnock	124,000	793.50	D. Montgomery	(b) R. Stirling
East Dumbartonshire	Glasgow	110,000	668.00	C. Mallon	(b) J. Dempsey
East Lothian	Haddington	86,800	670.00	J. Linsay	(a) P. O'Brien
East Renfrewshire	Glasgow	86,780	621.00	P. Daniels	O. Taylor
Falkirk	Falkirk	142,800	624.00	W. Weir	(b) A. Fowler
Fife	Glenrothes	351,600	694.00	Dr J. A. Markland	(a) J. W. MacDougall
Glasgow City	Glasgow	618,430	897.00	J. F. Anderson	(c) P. Lally
Highland	Inverness	207,500	620.00	A. McCourt	(a) P. J. Peacock
Inverclyde	Greenock	89,380	762.00	G. H. Bettison	(b) Ms C. Allen
Midlothian	Dalkeith	79,880	718.00	T. Muir	(b) D. Molloy
Moray	Elgin	87,150	607.50	A. Connell	(a) G. McDonald
North Ayrshire	Irvine	139,000	660.00	B. Devine	(a) G. Steven
North Lanarkshire	Motherwell	326,750	758.00	A. Cowe	(b) V. Matheison
Orkney Islands	Kirkwall	19,700	480.00	R. H. Gilbert	(a) H. Halcro-Johnston
Perth and Kinross	Perth	130,740	696.50	H. Robertson	(b) J. Culliven
Renfrewshire	Paisley	176,970	830.00	T. Scholes	(b) Ms N. Allison
Scottish Borders	Melrose	105,300	558.00	A. M. Croall	(a) A. L. Tulley
Shetland Islands	Lerwick	23,090	443.21	M. E. Green	(a) Canon L. S. Smith
South Ayrshire	Ayr	114,000	731.00	G. W. F. Thorley	(b) R. Campbell
South Lanarkshire	Hamilton	307,510	717.75	A. MacNish	(b) S. Casserly
Stirling	Stirling	81,630	730.50	K. Yates	(b) J. Paterson
West Dumbartonshire	Dumbarton	97,790	812.00	M. J. Watters	(b) P. O'Neill
West Lothian	Livingston	148,190	678.00	A. M. Linkston	(a) J. Thomas
West Isles Islands	Stornoway	29,393	550.00	B. W. Stewart	(a) D. Mackay

For explanation of council tax, *see* pages 519–20

Northern Ireland

Northern Ireland has a total area of 5,461 sq. miles (14,144 sq. km): land, 5,215 sq. miles (13,506 sq. km); inland water and tideways, 246 sq. miles (638 sq. km).

The population of Northern Ireland at the 1991 Census was 1,577,836 (males, 769,071; females, 808,765). The average density of population in 1991 was 1.11 persons per hectare.

In 1991 the number of persons in the various religious denominations (expressed as percentages of the total population) were: Roman Catholic, 38.4; Presbyterian, 21.4; Church of Ireland, 17.7; Methodist, 3.8; others 7.7; none, 3.7; not stated, 7.3.

PRINCIPAL CITIES

BELFAST

Belfast, the administrative centre of Northern Ireland, is situated at the mouth of the River Lagan at its entrance to Belfast Lough. The city grew, owing to its easy access by sea to Scottish coal and iron, to be a great industrial centre.

The principal buildings are of a relatively recent date and include the Parliament Buildings at Stormont, the City Hall, the Law Courts, the Public Library and the Museum and Art Gallery.

Belfast received its first charter of incorporation in 1613 and was created a city in 1888; the title of Lord Mayor was conferred in 1892.

LONDONDERRY

Londonderry (originally Derry) is situated on the River Foyle, and has important associations with the City of London. The Irish Society was created by the City of London in 1610, and under its royal charter of 1613 it fortified the city and was for long closely associated with its administration. Because of this connection the city was incorporated in 1613 under the new name of Londonderry.

The city is famous for the great siege of 1688–9, when for 105 days the town held out against the forces of James II until relieved by sea. The city walls are still intact and form a circuit of almost a mile around the old city.

Interesting buildings are the Protestant Cathedral of St Columb's (1633) and the Guildhall, reconstructed in 1912 and containing a number of beautiful stained glass windows, many of which were presented by the livery companies of London.

CONSTITUTION AND GOVERNMENT

As part of the United Kingdom, Northern Ireland is subject to the same fundamental constitutional provisions which apply to the rest of the United Kingdom. It had its own parliament and government from 1921 to 1972, but after increasing civil unrest the Northern Ireland (Temporary Provisions) Act 1972 transferred the legislative and executive powers of the Northern Ireland parliament and government to the UK Parliament and a Secretary of State. The Northern Ireland Constitution Act 1973 provided for devolution in Northern Ireland through an assembly and executive, and in January 1974 a power-sharing executive was formed by the Northern Ireland political parties. This arrangement collapsed in May 1974 and since then Northern Ireland has been governed by direct rule under the provisions of the Northern Ireland Act 1974. This allows Parliament to approve all laws for Northern Ireland and places the Northern Ireland department under the direction and control of the Secretary of State for Northern Ireland.

Attempts have been made by successive governments to find a means of restoring a widely acceptable form of devolved government to Northern Ireland. A 78-member Assembly was elected by proportional representation in 1982. However, it was dissolved four years later after it failed to discharge its responsibilities of making proposals for the resumption of devolved government and of monitoring the work of the Northern Ireland departments.

In 1985 the governments of the United Kingdom and the Republic of Ireland signed the Anglo-Irish Agreement, establishing an intergovernmental conference in which the Irish government may put forward views and proposals on certain aspects of Northern Ireland affairs.

Discussions between the British and Irish governments and the main Northern Ireland parties began in 1991. It was agreed that any political settlement would need to address three key relationships: those within Northern Ireland; those within the island of Ireland (north/south); and those between the British and Irish governments (east/west). Although round table talks ended in 1992 the process continued from September 1993 as separate bilateral discussions with three of the Northern Ireland parties (the DUP declined to participate).

On 15 December 1993 the British and Irish governments published the Joint Declaration complementing the political talks, and making clear that any settlement would need to be founded on principles of democracy and consent. The declaration also stated that all democratically mandated parties could be involved in political talks as long as they permanently renounced paramilitary violence.

The provisional IRA and loyalist paramilitary groups announced cease-fires on 31 August and 13 October 1994 respectively. The Government initiated a series of separate exploratory meetings with Sinn Fein and loyalist representatives in December 1994. The purposes of these were: to explore the basis upon which Sinn Fein and the loyalist representatives would come to be admitted to an inclusive political talks process; to exchange views on how they would be able to play the same role as the current constitutional parties in the public life of Northern Ireland; and to examine the practical consequences of the ending of violence.

In February 1995 the Prime Minister launched *A Framework for Accountable Government in Northern Ireland* and, with the Irish Prime Minister, *A New Framework for Agreement*. These outlined what a comprehensive political settlement might look like. The ideas were intended to facilitate multilateral dialogue involving the Northern Ireland parties and the British government. To this end the Secretary of State for Northern Ireland (Sir Patrick Mayhew) initiated separate bilateral meetings with the leaders of the main parties. The Government had previously given an undertaking to submit the final outcome of political talks to the electorate of Northern Ireland for approval in a referendum.

In the autumn of 1995 the Prime Minister said that Sinn Fein would not be invited to all-party talks until the IRA had decommissioned its arms; the IRA ruled out any decommissioning of weapons in advance of a political settlement. In November 1995 the Prime Minister and the

Irish Prime Minister agreed to set up a three-member international body chaired by a former US senator, George Mitchell, to advise both governments on suitable methods of decommissioning arms. The international body reported in January 1996 that no weapons would be decommissioned before the start of all-party talks and that a compromise agreement was necessary under which weapons would be decommissioned during negotiations. The Prime Minister accepted the report and proposed that elections should be held to provide a pool of representatives to conduct all-party talks. On 9 February 1996 the IRA called off its cease-fire. On 30 May 1996 elections were held to a peace forum. On 10 June all-party talks opened at Stormont Castle; Sinn Fein delegates were turned away because the IRA had failed to reinstate its cease-fire. The peace forum met for the first time on 14 June 1996; it was boycotted by Sinn Fein members. On 29 June 1996 the all-party talks were suspended for six weeks after disagreements over the issue of decommissioning arms.

FLAG

The official national flag of Northern Ireland is now the Union Flag. The flag formerly in use (a white, six-pointed star in the centre of a red cross on a white field, enclosing a red hand and surmounted by a crown) has not been used since the imposition of direct rule.

ECONOMY

FINANCE

Taxation in Northern Ireland is largely imposed and collected by the United Kingdom government. After deducting the cost of collection and of Northern Ireland's contributions to the European Community the balance, known as the Attributed Share of Taxation, is paid over to the Northern Ireland Consolidated Fund. Northern Ireland's revenue is insufficient to meet its expenditure and is supplemented by a grant-in-aid.

	1995–6*	1996–7**
Public income	£6,579,018,105	£7,027,800,000
Public expenditure	6,510,447,437	7,027,800,000

* Outturn
** Estimate

PRODUCTION

The products of the engineering and allied industries, which employed 25,400 persons in 1993, were valued at £1,723 million. The textiles industry, employing about 11,200 persons, produced products valued at approximately £536 million. The food products, beverages and tobacco industry, employing about 22,700 persons, produced goods valued at £3,962 million.

In 1995 1,375 persons were employed in mining and quarrying operations in Northern Ireland and the minerals raised (22,119,008 tonnes) were valued at £55,982,254.

COMMUNICATIONS

The total tonnage handled by Northern Ireland ports in 1995 was 20 million. Regular ferry, freight and container services operate to ports in Great Britain and Europe from 18 ports, including Belfast, Coleraine, Larne, Londonderry and Warrenpoint.

The Northern Ireland Transport Holding Company is largely responsible for the supervision of the subsidiary companies, Ulsterbus and Citybus (which operate the public road passenger services) and Northern Ireland Railways. Road freight services are also provided by a large number of hauliers operating competitively under licence.

Belfast International Airport was privatized in July 1994. It has substantial passenger and freight handling facilities and provides scheduled and chartered services on domestic and international routes.

Scheduled services also operate from Belfast City Airport (BCA) to 21 UK destinations and from City of Derry Airport (Londonderry) to Glasgow, Manchester and to Belfast, providing links to many of the locations serviced by BCA.

Northern Ireland Counties

County	Area* (sq. miles)	Lord Lieutenant	High Sheriff, 1996
Antrim	1,093	The Lord O'Neill, TD	D. de Burgh Kinahan
‡Belfast City	25	Col. J. E. Wilson, OBE	S. Bride
Armagh	484	The Earl of Caledon	Dr M. Patton
Down	945	W. J. Hall	W. S. Brown
Fermanagh	647	The Earl of Erne	G. Burns
†Londonderry	798	Sir Michael McCorkell, KCVO, OBE, TD	T. C. Boyd
‡Londonderry City	3.4	J. T. Eaton, CBE, TD	D. Chatis
Tyrone	1,211	The Duke of Abercorn	J. R. H. Ellis

* Excluding inland waters and tideways
‡ Denotes County Borough
† Excluding the City of Londonderry

District Councils

SMALL CAPITALS denotes CITY status
§ Denotes Borough Council

Council	Population (30 June 1994)	Net Annual Value	Council Clerk	Chairman †Mayor 1996
§Antrim, Co. Antrim	46,039	£7,445,831	S. J. Magee	†F. R. H. Marks
§Ards, Co. Down	66,533	8,447,579	D. J. Fallows	†R. Gibson
				†R. Ferguson
ARMAGH, Co. Armagh	52,053	5,548,105	D. R. D. Mitchall	†J. A. Speers
§Ballymena, Co. Antrim	57,132	8,903,765	M. G. Rankin	†J. Currie
§Ballymoney, Co. Antrim	24,478	2,770,364	J. C. Alderdice	†J. A. Gaston
Banbridge, Co. Down	37,083	4,384,059	R. Gilmore	W. McCracken
Belfast, Co. Antrim and Co. Down	295,649	57,800,052	B. Hanna	S. I. G. Adamson (Lord Mayor)
§Carrickfergus, Co. Antrim	34,747	4,798,829	R. Boyd	†S. McCambey
§Castlereagh, Co. Down	63,206	8,734,158	J. White	†Mrs I. Robinson
§Coleraine, Co. Londonderry	53,866	8,193,577	W. E. Andrews	†Mrs P. E. A. Armitage
Cookstown, Co. Tyrone	31,096	3,345,957	M. McGuckin	S. A. Glasgow
§Craigavon, Co. Armagh	77,359	11,363,669	M. Graham (acting)	†M. Casey
Derry, Co. Londonderry	100,614	13,540,468	T. J. Keanie	†R. Dallas
Down, Co. Down	59,695	6,627,612	O. O'Connor	W. J. F. Biggerstaff
Dungannon, Co. Tyrone	45,847	5,159,683	W. J. Beattie	V. Currie N. R. D. Mulligan
Fermanagh, Co. Fermanagh	54,446	6,384,167	Mrs A. McGinley	S. Foster
§Larne, Co. Antrim	29,904	4,157,956	G. McKinley	†S. C. McAllister
§Limavady, Co. Londonderry	29,845	3,101,729	J. K. Stevenson	†M. Gault
§Lisburn, Co. Antrim and Co. Down	102,882	14,813,451	M. S. Fielding	†G. Morrison
Magherafelt, Co. Londonderry	36,643	3,859,691	J. A. McLaughlin	P. H. McErlain
Moyle, Co. Antrim	14,751	1,632,504	R. G. Lewis	A. G. Kane
Newry and Mourne, Co. Down and Co. Armagh	82,671	8,865,124	K. O'Neill	J. E. B. Hanna
§Newtownabbey, Co. Antrim	78,145	11,882,556	N. Dunn (acting)	†W. G. Snoddy
§North Down, Co. Down	72,914	10,437,089	A. McDowell	†Mrs R. L. Cree
Omagh, Co. Tyrone	45,915	5,014,191	J. P. McKinney	S. Shields
Strabane, Co. Tyrone	35,886	3,446,404	Dr V. R. Eakin	E. Turner

The Isle of Man

Ellan Vannin

The Isle of Man is an island situated in the Irish Sea, in latitude 54° 3'–54° 25' N. and longitude 4° 18'–4° 47' W., nearly equidistant from England, Scotland and Ireland. Although the early inhabitants were of Celtic origin, the Isle of Man was part of the Norwegian Kingdom of the Hebrides until 1266, when this was ceded to Scotland. Subsequently granted to the Stanleys (Earls of Derby) in the 15th century and later to the Dukes of Atholl, it was brought under the administration of the Crown in 1765. The island forms the bishopric of Sodor and Man.

The total land area is 221 sq. miles (572 sq. km). The report on the 1991 Census showed a resident population of 69,788 (males, 33,693; females, 36,095). The main language in use is English. There are no remaining native speakers of Manx Gaelic but 643 people are able to speak the language.

CAPITAL – ΨDouglas; population (1991), 22,214. ΨCastletown (3,152) is the ancient capital; the other towns are ΨPeel (3,829) and ΨRamsey (6,496)

FLAG – A red flag charged with three conjoined armoured legs in white and gold

TYNWALD DAY – 5 July.

GOVERNMENT

The Isle of Man is a self-governing Crown dependency, having its own parliamentary, legal and administrative system. The British Government is responsible for international relations and defence. Under the UK Act of Accession, Protocol 3, the island's relationship with the European Community is limited to trade alone and does not extend to financial aid. The Lieutenant-Governor is The Queen's personal representative in the island.

The legislature, Tynwald, is the oldest parliament in the world in continuous existence. It has two branches: the Legislative Council and the House of Keys. The Council consists of the President of Tynwald, the Bishop of Sodor and Man, the Attorney-General (who does not have a vote) and eight members elected by the House of Keys. The House of Keys has 24 members, elected by universal adult suffrage. The branches sit separately to consider legislation and sit together, as Tynwald Court, for most other parliamentary purposes.

The presiding officer in Tynwald Court is the President of Tynwald, elected by the members, who also presides over sittings of the Legislative Council. The presiding officer of the House of Keys is Mr Speaker, who is elected by members of the House.

The principal members of the Manx Government are the Chief Minister and nine departmental ministers, who comprise the Council of Ministers.

Lieutenant-Governor, His Excellency Sir Timothy Daunt, KCMG
    ADC to the Lieutenant-Governor, M. M. Wood
President of Tynwald, The Hon. Sir Charles Kerruish, OBE
Speaker, House of Keys, The Hon. J. C. Cain
The First Deemster and Clerk of the Rolls, His Honour J. W. Corrin, CBE
Clerk of Tynwald, Secretary to the House of Keys and Counsel to the Speaker, Prof. T. St J. N. Bates
Clerk of Legislative Council and Clerk Assistant of Tynwald, T. A. Bawden
Attorney-General, J. M. Kerruish, QC
Chief Minister, The Hon. M. R. Walker, CBE
Chief Secretary, J. F. Kissack
Chief Financial Officer, J. A. Cashen

ECONOMY

Most of the income generated in the island is earned in the services sector with financial and business services being considerably larger than the traditional industry of tourism. Manufacturing industry is also a major generator of income whilst the island's other traditional industries of agriculture and fishing now play a smaller role in the economy.

Under the terms of Protocol 3, the island has free access to EU markets for its products.

The island's unemployment rate is approximately 4 per cent and price inflation is around 3 per cent per annum.

FINANCE

The budget for 1996–7 provided for net expenditure of £226 million. The principal sources of government revenue are taxes on income and expenditure. Income tax is payable at a rate of 15 per cent on the first £9,000 of taxable income for single resident individuals and 20 per cent on the balance, after personal allowances; these bands are doubled for married couples. The rate of income tax is 20 per cent on the whole taxable income of non-residents and companies. By agreement with the British Government, the island keeps most of its rates of indirect taxation (VAT and duties) the same as those in the United Kingdom, but this agreement may be terminated by either party. However, VAT on tourist accommodation is charged at 5 per cent. A reciprocal agreement on national insurance benefits and pensions exists between the Governments of the Isle of Man and the United Kingdom. Taxes are also charged on property (rates), but these are comparatively low.

The major government expenditure items are health, social security and education, which account for 60 per cent of the government budget. The island makes a voluntary annual contribution to the United Kingdom for defence and other external services.

Although the island has a limited relationship with the European Union, it neither contributes money to nor receives funds from the EU budget.

The Channel Islands

The Channel Islands, situated off the north-west coast of France (at distances of from ten to 30 miles), are the only portions of the Dukedom of Normandy still belonging to the Crown, to which they have been attached since the Conquest. They were the only British territory to come under German occupation during the Second World War, following invasion on 30 June to 1 July 1940. The islands were relieved by British forces on 9 May 1945, and 9 May (Liberation Day) is now observed as a bank and public holiday.

The islands consist of Jersey (28,717 acres/11,630 ha), Guernsey (15,654 acres/6,340 ha), and the dependencies of Guernsey: Alderney (1,962 acres/795 ha), Brechou (74/30), Great Sark (1,035/419), Little Sark (239/97), Herm (320/130), Jethou (44/18) and Lihou (38/15) – a total of 48,083 acres/19,474 ha, or 75 sq. miles/194 sq. km. In 1991 the population of Jersey was 84,082; and of Guernsey, 58,867; Alderney, 2,297 and Sark, 575. The official languages are English and French but French is being supplanted by English, which is the language in daily use. In country districts of Jersey and Guernsey and throughout Sark a Norman-French *patois* is also in use, though to a declining extent.

GOVERNMENT

The islands are Crown dependencies with their own legislative assemblies (the States in Jersey, Guernsey and Alderney, and the Court of Chief Pleas in Sark), and systems of local administration and of law, and their own courts. Acts passed by the States require the sanction of The Queen-in-Council. The British Government is responsible for defence and international relations. The Channel Islands have trading rights alone within the European Union; these rights do not include financial aid.

In both Bailiwicks the Lieutenant-Governor and Commander-in-Chief, who is appointed by the Crown, is the personal representative of The Queen and the channel of communication between the Crown (via the Privy Council) and the island's government.

The government of each Bailiwick is conducted by committees appointed by the States. Justice is administered by the Royal Courts of Jersey and Guernsey, each consisting of the Bailiff and 12 elected Jurats. The Bailiffs of Jersey and Guernsey, appointed by the Crown, are President of the States and of the Royal Courts of their respective islands.

Each Bailiwick constitutes a deanery under the jurisdiction of the Bishop of Winchester (*see* Index).

ECONOMY

A mild climate and good soil have led to the development of intensive systems of agriculture and horticulture, which form a significant part of the economy. Equally important are invisible earnings, principally from tourism and banking and finance, the low rate of income tax (20p in the £ in Jersey and Guernsey; no tax of any kind in Sark) and the absence of super-tax and death duties making the islands a popular tax-haven.

Principal exports are agricultural produce and flowers; imports are chiefly machinery, manufactured goods, food, fuel and chemicals. Trade with the UK is regarded as internal.

British currency is legal tender in the Channel Islands but each Bailiwick issues its own coins and notes (*see* page 603). They also issue their own postage stamps; UK stamps are not valid.

JERSEY

Lieutenant-Governor and Commander-in-Chief of Jersey, His Excellency Gen. Sir Michael Wilkes, KCB, CBE, *apptd* 1995
    Secretary and ADC, Col. A. J. C. Woodrow, OBE
Bailiff of Jersey, Sir Philip Bailhache, Kt.
Deputy Bailiff, F. C. Hamon
Attorney-General, M. C. St J. Burt, QC
Receiver-General, Gp Capt R. Green, OBE
Solicitor-General, Miss S. C. Nicolle, QC
Greffier of the States, G. H. C. Coppock
States Treasurer, G. M. Baird

FINANCE

Year to 31 Dec.	1994	1995
Revenue income	£393,418,443	£417,271,388
Revenue expenditure	356,827,170	376,752,850
Capital expenditure	74,762,593	67,886,094
Public debt	0	0

CHIEF TOWN – ΨSt Helier, on the south coast of Jersey
FLAG – A white field charged with a red saltire cross, and the arms of Jersey in the upper centre

GUERNSEY AND DEPENDENCIES

Lieutenant-Governor and Commander-in-Chief of the Bailiwick of Guernsey and its Dependencies, His Excellency Vice-Adm. Sir John Coward, KCB, DSO, *apptd* 1994
    Secretary and ADC, Capt. D. P. L. Hodgetts
Bailiff of Guernsey, Sir Graham Dorey
Deputy Bailiff, de V. G. Carey
HM Procureur and Receiver-General, A. C. K. Day, QC
HM Comptroller, G. R. Rowland, QC
States Supervisor, M. J. Brown

FINANCE

Year to 31 Dec.	1994	1995
Revenue	£164,719,000	£171,506,000
Expenditure	143,957,000	152,222,000

CHIEF TOWNS – ΨSt Peter Port, on the east coast of Guernsey; St Anne on Alderney
FLAG – White, bearing a red cross of St George, with a gold cross overall in the centre

ALDERNEY

President of the States, G. W. Baron
Clerk of the States, D. V. Jenkins
Clerk of the Court, A. Johnson

SARK

Seigneur of Sark, J. M. Beaumont
The Seneschal, L. P. de Carteret
The Greffier, J. P. Hamon

OTHER DEPENDENCIES

Brechou, Lihou and Jethou are leased by the Crown. Herm is leased by the States of Guernsey.

Conservation and Heritage

Countryside Conservation

see page 567

NATIONAL PARKS

ENGLAND AND WALES

The ten National Parks of England and Wales were set up under the provisions of the National Parks and Access to the Countryside Act 1949 to conserve and protect scenic landscapes from inappropriate development and to provide access to the land for public enjoyment.

The Countryside Commission is the statutory body which has the power to designate National Parks in England, and the Countryside Council for Wales is responsible for National Parks in Wales. Designations in England are confirmed by the Secretary of State for the Environment, and those in Wales by the Secretary of State for Wales. The designation of a National Park does not affect the ownership of the land or remove the rights of the local community. Although the parks are administered through local government, the majority of the land is owned by private landowners (74 per cent) or by bodies such as the National Trust (7 per cent) and the Forestry Commission (7 per cent). The National Park Authorities own only 2.3 per cent of the land in the National Parks.

The Environment Act 1995 will replace the existing National Park committees and boards with free-standing National Park Authorities (NPAs) and will also widen the duties of the NPAs to include fostering the economic and social well-being of local communities within the National Parks. NPAs are the authorities responsible for park administration. They also influence land use and development, and deal with planning applications. The NPAs appoint the National Park Officer for the National Park they administer.

In Wales, the three National Parks have had free-standing NPAs since 1 April 1996. Two-thirds of the members are local authority representatives and one-third are appointed by the Secretary of State for Wales with advice from the Countryside Council for Wales.

In England, two free-standing NPAs already exist: the Peak Park Joint Planning Board and the Lake District Special Planning Board. These are autonomous authorities which are financially independent. These two Boards and the five other NPAs in England will be replaced on 1 April 1997 by free-standing NPAs. Membership will be split between local authority representatives and members appointed by the Secretary of State for the Environment, with the local authority representatives in a majority of one.

Central government provides 75 per cent of the funding for the parks through the National Park Supplementary Grant (the National Park Grant in Wales). The remaining 25 per cent is supplied by the local authorities concerned. Approved net expenditure for all National Parks in England and Wales in 1996–7 was £28,372,602.

The Countryside Commission has stated that other areas are regarded as being worthy of National Parks status. Two areas considered as having equivalent status are the Broads and the New Forest (*see* page 567).

The National Parks (with date designation confirmed) are:

BRECON BEACONS (1957), 1,351 sq. km/522 sq. miles – The park lies in Powys (66 per cent), Carmarthenshire, Rhondda, Cynon and Taff, Merthyr Tydfil, Blaenau Gwent and Monmouthshire. The park is centred on the Beacons, Pen y Fan, Corn Du and Cribyn, but also includes the valley of the Usk, the Black Mountains to the east and the Black Mountain to the west. There are information centres at Brecon, Craig-y-nos Country Park, Abergavenny and Llandovery, a study centre at Danywenallt and a day visitor centre near Libanus. *Information Office*, 7 Glamorgan Street, Brecon, Powys LD3 7DP. Tel: 01874-624437. *National Park Officer*, M. Fitton

DARTMOOR (1951 and 1994), 954 sq. km/368 sq. miles – The park lies wholly in Devon. It consists of moorland and rocky granite tors, and is rich in prehistoric remains. There are information centres at Newbridge, Tavistock, Bovey Tracey, Steps Bridge, Princetown and Postbridge. *Information Office*, Parke, Haytor Road, Bovey Tracey, Devon TQ13 9JQ. Tel: 01626-832093. *National Park Officer*, N. Atkinson

EXMOOR (1954), 693 sq. km/268 sq. miles – The park lies in Somerset (71 per cent) and Devon. Exmoor is a moorland plateau inhabited by wild ponies and red deer. There are many ancient remains and burial mounds. There are information centres at Lynmouth, County Gate, Dulverton and Combe Martin. *Information Office*, Exmoor House, Dulverton, Somerset TA22 9HL. Tel: 01398-23665. *National Park Officer*, K. Bungay

LAKE DISTRICT (1951), 2,292 sq. km/885 sq. miles – The park lies wholly in Cumbria. The Lake District includes England's highest mountains (Scafell Pike, Helvellyn and Skiddaw) but it is most famous for its glaciated lakes. There are information centres at Keswick, Waterhead, Hawkshead, Seatoller, Bowness, Grasmere, Coniston, Glenridding and Pooley Bridge, an information van at Gosforth and a park centre at Brockhole, Windermere. *Information Office*, Brockhole, Windermere, Cumbria LA23 1LJ. Tel: 01539-446601. *National Park Officer*, J. Toothill

NORTHUMBERLAND (1956), 1,049 sq. km/405 sq. miles – The park lies wholly in Northumberland. It is an area of hill country stretching from Hadrian's Wall to the Scottish Border. There are information centres at Ingram, Once Brewed, Rothbury, Housesteads, Harbottle and Kielder, and an information caravan at Cawfields. *Information Office*, Eastburn, South Park, Hexham, Northumberland NE46 1BS. Tel: 01434-605555. *National Park Officer*, G. Taylor

NORTH YORK MOORS (1952), 1,436 sq. km/554 sq. miles – The park lies in North Yorkshire (96 per cent) and Redcar and Cleveland. It consists of woodland and moorland, and includes the Hambleton Hills and the Cleveland Way. There are information centres at Danby, Pickering, Sutton Bank, Ravenscar, Helmsley and Hutton-le-Hole, and a day study centre at Danby.

Information Office, The Old Vicarage, Bondgate, Helmsley, York Y06 5BP. Tel: 01439-70657. *National Park Officer*, D. Arnold-Forster

PEAK DISTRICT (1951), 1,438 sq. km/555 sq. miles – The park lies in Derbyshire (64 per cent), Staffordshire, South Yorkshire, Cheshire, West Yorkshire and Greater Manchester. The Peak District includes the gritstone moors of the 'Dark Peak' and the limestone dales of the 'White Peak'. There are information centres at Bakewell, Edale, Fairholmes and Castleton, and information points at Torside (in the Longdendale Valley) and at Hartington (former station). *Information Office*, Aldern House, Baslow Road, Bakewell, Derbyshire DE45 1AE. Tel: 01629-814321. *National Park Officer*, C. Harrison

PEMBROKESHIRE COAST (1952 and 1995), 584 sq. km/225 sq. miles – The park lies wholly in Pembrokeshire. It includes cliffs, moorland and Skomer Island. There are information centres at Tenby, St David's, Pembroke, Newport, Kilgetty, Haverfordwest and Broad Haven. *Information Office*, Winch Lane, Haverfordwest, Pembrokeshire SA61 1PY. Tel: 01437-764636. *National Park Officer*, N. Wheeler

SNOWDONIA (1951), 2,142 sq. km/827 sq. miles – Snowdonia lies in Gwynedd and Conwy. It is an area of deep valleys and rugged mountains. There are information centres at Aberdovey, Bala, Betws y Coed, Blaenau Ffestiniog, Conwy, Harlech, Dolgellau and Llanberis. *Information Office*, Penrhyndeudraeth, Gwynedd LL48 6LF. Tel: 01766-770274. *National Park Officer*, I. Huws.

YORKSHIRE DALES (1954), 1,769 sq. km/683 sq. miles – The park lies in North Yorkshire (88 per cent) and Cumbria. The Yorkshire Dales are composed primarily of limestone overlaid in places by millstone grit. The three peaks of Ingleborough, Whernside and Pen-y-Ghent are within the park. There are information centres at Clapham, Grassington, Hawes, Aysgarth Falls, Malham and Sedbergh. *Information Office*, Yorebridge House, Bainbridge, Leyburn, N. Yorks DL8 3BP. Tel: 01969-50456. *National Park Officer*, R. Harvey

Two other areas considered to have equivalent status to national parks are the Broads and the New Forest. The Broads Authority, a special statutory authority, was established in 1989 to develop, conserve and manage the Norfolk and Suffolk Broads (*see also* Government Departments and Public Offices). The Government declared in 1992 its intention of giving the New Forest a status equivalent to that of a National Park by declaring it an 'area of national significance'.

THE BROADS (1989), 303 sq. km/117 sq. miles – The Broads are located between Norwich and Great Yarmouth on the flood plains of five rivers flowing through the area to the sea. The area is one of fens, winding waterways, woodland and marsh. The 40 or so broads are man-made, and are connected to the rivers by dykes, providing over 200 km of navigable waterways. There are information centres at Beccles, Hoveton, North-west Tower (Yarmouth), Ranworth and Toad Hole. *Broads Authority*, Thomas Harvey House, 18 Colegate, Norwich NR3 1BQ. Tel: 01603-610734. *Chief Executive*, A. Clark

THE NEW FOREST, 376 sq. km/145 sq. miles – The forest has been protected since 1079 when it was declared a royal hunting forest. The area consists of forest, ancient woodland and heathland. Much of the Forest is managed by the Forestry Commission, which provides several camp-sites. The main villages are Brockenhurst, Burley and Lyndhurst, which has a visitor centre.
The Forestry Commission, Office of the Deputy Surveyor of the New Forest and the New Forest Committee, The Queen's House, Lyndhurst, Hants SO43 7NH. Tel: 01703-284149

SCOTLAND AND NORTHERN IRELAND

The National Parks and Access to the Countryside Act 1949 dealt only with England and Wales and made no provision for Scotland or Northern Ireland. Although there are no national parks in these two countries, there is power to designate them in Northern Ireland under the Amenity Lands Act 1965 and the Nature Conservation and Amenity Lands Order (Northern Ireland) 1985. In 1989 the Scottish Office asked Scottish Natural Heritage to report on whether national parks should be designated in Scotland.

AREAS OF OUTSTANDING NATURAL BEAUTY

ENGLAND AND WALES

Under the National Parks and Access to the Countryside Act 1949, provision was made for the designation of Areas of Outstanding Natural Beauty (AONBs) by the Countryside Commission. The Countryside Act 1968 further defines the role of AONBs, suggesting that they should show due regard for the interests of other land users, such as agriculture and forestry groups. The Countryside Commission continues to be responsible for AONBs in England but since April 1991 the Countryside Council for Wales has been responsible for the Welsh AONBs. Designations in England are confirmed by the Secretary of State for the Environment and those in Wales by the Secretary of State for Wales.

Although less emphasis is placed upon the provision of open-air enjoyment for the public than in the national parks, AONBs are areas which are no less beautiful and require the same degree of protection to conserve and enhance the natural beauty of the countryside. This includes protecting flora and fauna, geological and other landscape features. In AONBs planning and management responsibilities are split between county and district councils. There are 19 which cross local authority boundaries. Finance for the AONBs is provided by grant-aid.

The 41 Areas of Outstanding Natural Beauty (with date designation confirmed) are:

ANGLESEY (1967), Anglesey, 215 sq. km/83 sq. miles

ARNSIDE AND SILVERDALE (1972), Cumbria/Lancashire, 75 sq. km/29 sq. miles

BLACKDOWN HILLS (1991), Devon/Somerset, 370 sq. km/143 sq. miles.

CANNOCK CHASE (1958), Staffordshire, 68 sq. km/26 sq. miles

CHICHESTER HARBOUR (1964), Hampshire/West Sussex, 74 sq. km/29 sq. miles

CHILTERNS (1965; extended 1990), Bedfordshire/Hertfordshire/Buckinghamshire/Oxfordshire, 833 sq. km/322 sq. miles

CLWYDIAN RANGE (1985), Denbighshire/Flintshire, 156 sq. km/60 sq. miles

CORNWALL (1959; Camel estuary 1983), 958 sq. km/370 sq. miles

COTSWOLDS (1966; extended 1990), Gloucestershire/Wiltshire/Warwickshire/Hereford and Worcester/Somerset, 2,038 sq. km/787 sq. miles

CRANBORNE CHASE AND WEST WILTSHIRE DOWNS
(1983), Dorset/Hampshire/Somerset/Wiltshire, 983
sq. km/379 sq. miles
DEDHAM VALE (1970; extended 1978, 1991), Essex/
Suffolk, 90 sq. km/35 sq. miles
EAST DEVON (1963), 268 sq. km/103 sq. miles
NORTH DEVON (1960), 171 sq. km/66 sq. miles
SOUTH DEVON (1960), 337 sq. km/130 sq. miles
DORSET (1959), 1,129 sq. km/436 sq. miles
FOREST OF BOWLAND (1964), Lancashire/North
Yorkshire, 802 sq. km/310 sq. miles
GOWER (1956), Swansea, 189 sq. km/73 sq. miles
EAST HAMPSHIRE (1962), 383 sq. km/148 sq. miles
SOUTH HAMPSHIRE COAST (1967), 77 sq. km/30 sq.
miles
HIGH WEALD (1983), Kent/Surrey/East Sussex/West
Sussex, 1,460 sq. km/564 sq. miles
HOWARDIAN HILLS (1987), North Yorkshire, 204 sq. km/
79 sq. miles
KENT DOWNS (1968), 878 sq. km/339 sq. miles
LINCOLNSHIRE WOLDS (1973), 558 sq. km/215 sq. miles
LLEYN (1957), Gwynedd, 155 sq. km/60 sq. miles
MALVERN HILLS (1959), Hereford and Worcester/
Gloucestershire, 105 sq. km/40 sq. miles
MENDIP HILLS (1972; extended 1989), Somerset, 198 sq.
km/76 sq. miles
NIDDERDALE (1994), North Yorkshire, 603 sq. km/233 sq.
miles
NORFOLK COAST (1968), 451 sq. km/174 sq. miles
NORTH PENNINES (1988), Cumbria/Durham/
Northumberland, 1,983 sq. km/766 sq. miles
NORTHUMBERLAND COAST (1958), 135 sq. km/52 sq.
miles
QUANTOCK HILLS (1957), Somerset, 99 sq. km/38 sq.
miles
ISLES OF SCILLY (1976), 16 sq. km/6 sq. miles
SHROPSHIRE HILLS (1959), 804 sq. km/310 sq. miles
SOLWAY COAST (1964), Cumbria, 115 sq. km/44 sq. miles
SUFFOLK COAST AND HEATHS (1970), 403 sq. km/156 sq.
miles
SURREY HILLS (1958), 419 sq. km/162 sq. miles
SUSSEX DOWNS (1966), 983 sq. km/379 sq. miles
TAMAR VALLEY (1995), Cornwall/Devon, 195 sq. km/115
sq. miles
NORTH WESSEX DOWNS (1972), Berkshire/Hampshire/
Oxfordshire/Wiltshire, 1,730 sq. km/668 sq. miles
ISLE OF WIGHT (1963), 189 sq. km/73 sq. miles
WYE VALLEY (1971), Monmouthshire/Gloucestershire/
Hereford and Worcester, 326 sq. km/126 sq. miles

NORTHERN IRELAND

The Department of the Environment for Northern Ireland, with advice from the Council for Nature Conservation and the Countryside, designates Areas of Outstanding
Natural Beauty in Northern Ireland. At present there are
nine and these cover a total area of approximately 284,948
hectares (704,121 acres).

ANTRIM COAST AND GLENS, Co. Antrim, 70,600 ha/
174,452 acres
CAUSEWAY COAST, Co. Antrim, 4,200 ha/10,378 acres
LAGAN VALLEY, Co. Down, 2,072 ha/5,119 acres
LECALE COAST, Co. Down, 3,108 ha/7,679 acres
MOURNE, Co. Down, 57,012 ha/140,876 acres
NORTH DERRY, Co. Londonderry, 12,950 ha/31,999 acres
RING OF GULLION, Co. Armagh, 15,353 ha/37,938 acres
SPERRIN, Co. Tyrone/Co. Londonderry, 101,006 ha/
249,585 acres
STRANGFORD LOUGH, Co. Down, 18,647 ha/46,077 acres

NATIONAL SCENIC AREAS

No Areas of Outstanding Natural Beauty are designated in
Scotland. However, National Scenic Areas have a broadly
equivalent status. Scottish Natural Heritage recognizes
areas of national scenic significance. At mid 1996 there
were 40, covering a total area of 1,001,800 hectares
(2,475,448 acres).

Development within National Scenic Areas is dealt with
by the local planning authority, who are required to consult
Scottish Natural Heritage concerning certain categories of
development. Land management uses can also be modified
in the interest of scenic conservation. The Secretary of
State for Scotland has limited powers of intervention
should a planning authority and Scottish Natural Heritage
disagree.

ASSYNT-COIGACH, Highland, 90,200 ha/222,884 acres
BEN NEVIS AND GLEN COE, Highland/Argyll and Bute/
Perthshire and Kinross, 101,600 ha/251,053 acres
CAIRNGORM MOUNTAINS, Highland/Aberdeenshire/
Moray, 67,200 ha/166,051 acres
CUILLIN HILLS, Highland, 21,900 ha/54,115 acres
DEESIDE AND LOCHNAGAR, Aberdeenshire/Angus,
40,000 ha/98,840 acres
DORNOCH FIRTH, Highland, 7,500 ha/18,532 acres
EAST STEWARTRY COAST, Dumfries and Galloway, 4,500
ha/11,119 acres
EILDON AND LEADERFOOT, Borders, 3,600 ha/8,896 acres
FLEET VALLEY, Dumfries and Galloway, 5,300 ha/13,096
acres
GLEN AFFRIC, Highland, 19,300 ha/47,690 acres
GLEN STRATHFARRAR, Highland, 3,800 ha/9,390 acres
HOY AND WEST MAINLAND, Orkney Islands, 14,800 ha/
36,571 acres
JURA, Argyll and Bute, 21,800 ha/53,868 acres
KINTAIL, Highland, 15,500 ha/38,300 acres
KNAPDALE, Argyll and Bute, 19,800 ha/48,926 acres
KNOYDART, Highland, 39,500 ha/97,604 acres
KYLE OF TONGUE, Highland, 18,500 ha/45,713 acres
KYLES OF BUTE, Argyll and Bute, 4,400 ha/10,872 acres
LOCHNA KEAL, MULL, Argyll and Bute, 12,700 ha/31,382
acres
LOCH LOMOND, Argyll and Bute/Stirling/West
Dumbartonshire, 27,400 ha/67,705 acres
LOCH RANNOCH AND GLEN LYON, Perthshire and
Kinross/Stirling, 48,400 ha/119,596 acres
LOCH SHIEL, Highland, 13,400 ha/33,111 acres
LOCH TUMMEL, Perthshire and Kinross, 9,200 ha/22,733
acres
LYNN OF LORN, Argyll and Bute, 4,800 ha/11,861 acres
MORAR, MOIDART AND ARDNAMURCHAN, Highland,
13,500 ha/33,358 acres
NORTH-WEST SUTHERLAND, Highland, 20,500 ha/50,655
acres
NITH ESTUARY, Dumfries and Galloway, 9,300 ha/
22,980 acres
NORTH ARRAN, North Ayrshire, 23,800 ha/58,810 acres
RIVER EARN, Perthshire and Kinross, 3,000 ha/7,413
acres
RIVER TAY, Perthshire and Kinross, 5,600 ha/13,838
acres
ST KILDA, Western Isles, 900 ha/2,224 acres
SCARBA, LUNGA AND THE GARVELLACHS, Argyll and
Bute, 1,900 ha/4,695 acres
SHETLAND, Shetland Islands, 11,600 ha/28,664 acres
SMALL ISLES, Highland, 15,500 ha/38,300 acres

SOUTH LEWIS, HARRIS AND NORTH UIST, Western Isles, 109,600 ha/270,822 acres

SOUTH UIST MACHAIR, Western Isles, 6,100 ha/15,073 acres

THE TROSSACHS, Stirling, 4,600 ha/11,367 acres

TROTTERNISH, Highland, 5,000 ha/12,355 acres

UPPER TWEEDDALE, Borders, 10,500 ha/25,945 acres

WESTER ROSS, Highland, 145,300 ha/359,036 acres

THE NATIONAL FOREST

The National Forest will be planted in about 200 square miles of Derbyshire, Leicestershire and Staffordshire. About 30 million trees, of mixed species but mainly broadleaved, will be planted over the next 20 years and beyond, and will eventually cover about one-third of the designated area. The project is funded by the Department of the Environment. It was developed in 1992–5 by the Countryside Commission and is now run by the National Forest Company. Competitive bids for woodland creation projects are submitted to the National Forest Company by anybody who wishes to undertake a project, and are considered under the National Forest tender scheme. Sixteen tenders were approved in the first round of the scheme in 1995. The second round of the scheme closed for bids on 31 March 1996; approval of these tenders will be given in autumn 1996. The third round opens for bids on 1 January 1997.

NATIONAL FOREST COMPANY, Enterprise Glade, Bath Lane, Moira, Swadlincote, Derbys DE12 6BD. Tel: 01283-551211. *Chief Executive*, Ms S. Bell

Nature Conservation Areas

SITES OF SPECIAL SCIENTIFIC INTEREST

Site of Special Scientific Interest (SSSI) is a legal notification applied to land in England, Scotland or Wales which English Nature (EN), Scottish Natural Heritage (SNH), or the Countryside Council for Wales (CCW) identifies as being of special interest because of its flora, fauna, geological or physiographical features. In some cases, SSSI are managed as nature reserves.

EN, SNH and CCW must notify the designation of a SSSI to the local planning authority, every owner/occupier of the land, and the relevant Secretary of State. Forestry and agricultural departments and a number of other bodies are also informed of this notification.

Objections to the notification of a SSSI can be made and ultimately considered at a full meeting of the Council of EN or the Statutory Protection Committee of CCW. In Scotland an objection will be dealt with by the appropriate regional board or the main board of SNH, depending on the nature of the objection. Unresolved objections on scientific grounds must be referred to the Advisory Committee for SSSI.

The protection of these sites depends on the co-operation of individual landowners and occupiers. Owner/occupiers must consult EN, SNH or CCW and gain written consent before they can undertake certain listed activities on the site. Funds are available through management agreements and grants to assist owners and occupiers in conserving sites' interests. As a last resort a site can be purchased.

The number and area of SSSIs in Britain as at 31 March 1996 was:

	no.	hectares	acres
England	3,874	920,696	2,274,119
Scotland	1,398	895,227	2,211,211
Wales	909	208,076	514,156

NORTHERN IRELAND

In Northern Ireland 93 Areas of Special Scientific Interest (ASSIs) have been established by the Department of the Environment for Northern Ireland. These cover a total area of 76,061.5 hectares (704,121 acres).

NATIONAL NATURE RESERVES

National Nature Reserves are defined in the National Parks and Access to the Countryside Act 1949 as land designated for the study and preservation of flora and fauna, or of geological or physiographical features.

English Nature (EN), Scottish Natural Heritage (SNH) or the Countryside Council for Wales (CCW) can designate as a National Nature Reserve land which is being managed as a nature reserve under an agreement with one of the statutory nature conservation agencies; land held and managed by EN, SNH or CCW; or land held and managed as a nature reserve by another approved body. EN, SNH or CCW can make by-laws to protect reserves from undesirable activities; these are subject to confirmation by the relevant Secretary of State.

The number and area of National Nature Reserves in Britain as at 31 March 1996 was:

	no.	hectares	acres
England	173	68,222	168,577
Scotland	70	113,238	279,698
Wales	55	17,719	43,784

NORTHERN IRELAND

National Nature Reserves are established and managed by the Department of the Environment for Northern Ireland, with advice from the Council for Nature Conservation and the Countryside. There are 45 National Nature Reserves covering 4,574 hectares (11,297 acres).

LOCAL NATURE RESERVES

Local Nature Reserves are defined in the National Parks and Access to the Countryside Act 1949 as land designated for the study and preservation of flora and fauna, or of geological or physiographical features. The Act gives local authorities in England, Scotland and Wales the power to acquire, declare and manage local nature reserves in consultation with English Nature, Scottish Natural Heritage and the Countryside Council for Wales. Conservation trusts can also own and manage non-statutory local nature reserves.

The number and area of designated Local Nature Reserves in Britain as at 31 March 1996 was:

	no.	hectares	acres
England	519	18,431	45,543
Scotland	23	7,456	18,416
Wales	31	5,006	12,370

An additional 33 km of linear trails are designated as Local Nature Reserves.

FOREST NATURE RESERVES

Forest Enterprise (an executive agency of the Forestry Commission) is responsible for the management of the Commission's forests. It has created 46 Forest Nature Reserves with the aim of protecting and conserving special forms of natural habitat, flora and fauna. There are about 300 SSSI on the estates, some of which are also Nature Reserves.

Forest Nature Reserves extend in size from under 50 hectares (124 acres) to over 500 hectares (1,236 acres). The largest include the Black Wood of Rannoch, by Loch Rannoch; Cannop Valley Oakwoods, Forest of Dean; Culbin Forest, near Forres; Glen Affric, near Fort Augustus; Kylerhea, Skye; Pembrey, Carmarthen Bay; Starr Forest, in Galloway Forest Park; and Wyre Forest, near Kidderminster.

NORTHERN IRELAND
There are 36 Forest Nature Reserves in Northern Ireland, covering 1,759 hectares (4,346 acres). They are designated and administered by the Forest Service, a division of the Department of Agriculture for Northern Ireland. There are also 15 National Nature Reserves on Forest Service-owned property.

MARINE NATURE RESERVES

The Wildlife and Countryside Act 1981 gives the Secretary of State for the Environment (and the Secretaries of State for Wales and for Scotland where appropriate) power to designate Marine Nature Reserves, and English Nature, Scottish Natural Heritage and the Countryside Council for Wales powers to select and manage these reserves.

Marine Nature Reserves provide protection for marine flora and fauna, and geological and physiographical features on land covered by tidal waters or parts of the sea in or adjacent to Great Britain. Reserves also provide opportunities for study and research.

The three statutory Marine Nature Reserves are:

LUNDY (1986), Bristol Channel
SKOMER (1990), Dyfed
STRANGFORD LOUGH (1995), Northern Ireland

Two other areas proposed for designation as reserves are: the Menai Strait, and Bardsey Island and part of the Lleyn peninsula, both in Wales.

A number of non-statutory marine reserves have been set up by conservation groups.

Wildlife Conservation

PROTECTED SPECIES

The Wildlife and Countryside Act 1981 gives legal protection to a wide range of wild animals and plants. Subject to parliamentary approval, the Secretary of State for the Environment may vary the animals and plants given legal protection. The most recent variation of Schedules 5 and 8 came into effect in October 1992.

ANIMALS, ETC.

Under Section 9 and Schedule 5 of the Act it is illegal without a licence to kill, injure, take, possess or sell any of the animals mentioned below (whether alive or dead) and to disturb its place of shelter and protection or to destroy that place.

‡Adder (*Vipera berus*)
§Allis shad (*alosa alosa*)
Anemone, Ivell's Sea (*Edwardsia ivelli*)
Anemone, Startlet Sea (*Nematosella vectensis*)
Apus (*Triops cancriformis*)
Bat, Horseshoe (*Rhinolophidae*, all species)
Bat, Typical (*Vespertilionidae*, all species)
Beetle (*Hypebaeus flavipes*)
Beetle, Lesser Silver Water (*Hydrochara caraboides*)
§Beetle, Mire Pill (*Curimopsis nigrita*)
Beetle, Rainbow Leaf (*Chrysolina cerealis*)
Beetle, Violet Click (*Limoniscus violaceus*)
Beetle, Water (*Graphoderus zonatus*)
Beetle, Water (*Paracymus aeneus*)
Burbot (*Lota lota*)
*Butterfly, Adonis Blue (*Lysandra bellargus*)
*Butterfly, Black Hairstreak (*Strymonidia pruni*)
*Butterfly, Brown Hairstreak (*Thecla betulae*)
*Butterfly, Chalkhill Blue (*Lysandra coridon*)
*Butterfly, Chequered Skipper (*Carterocephalus palaemon*)
*Butterfly, Duke of Burgundy Fritillary (*Hamearis lucina*)
*Butterfly, Glanville Fritillary (*Melitaea cinxia*)
Butterfly, Heath Fritillary (*Mellicta athalia* (or *Melitaea athalia*))
Butterfly, High Brown Fritillary (*Argynnis adippe*)
Butterfly, Large Blue (*Maculinea arion*)
*Butterfly, Large Copper (*Lycaena dispar*)
*Butterfly, Large Heath (*Coenonympha tullia*)
*Butterfly, Large Tortoiseshell (*Nymphalis polychloros*)
Butterfly, Lulworth Skipper (*Thymelicus acteon*)
Butterfly, Marsh Fritillary (*Eurodryas aurinia*)
Butterfly, Mountain Ringlet (*Erebia epiphron*)
Butterfly, Northern Brown Argus (*Aricia artaxerxes*)
Butterfly, Pearl-bordered Fritillary (*Boloria euphrosyne*)
Butterfly, Purple Emperor (*Apatura iris*)
Butterfly, Silver Spotted Skipper (*Hesperia comma*)
*Butterfly, Silver-studded Blue (*Plebejus argus*)
Butterfly, Small Blue (*Cupido minimus*)
Butterfly, Swallowtail (*Papilio machaon*)

*Butterfly, White Letter Hairstreak (*Stymonida w-album*)
*Butterfly, Wood White (*Leptidea sinapis*)
Cat, Wild (*Felis silvestris*)
Cicada, New Forest (*Cicadetta montana*)
**Crayfish, Atlantic Stream (*Austropotamobius pallipes*)
Cricket, Field (*Gryllus campestris*)
Cricket, Mole (*Gryllotalpa gryllotalpa*)
Dolphin (*Cetacea*)
Dormouse (*Muscardinus avellanarius*)
Dragonfly, Norfolk Aeshna (*Aeshna isosceles*)
*Frog, Common (*Rana temporaria*)
Grasshopper, Wart-biter (*Decticus verrucivorus*)
Hatchet Shell, Northern (*Thyasira gouldi*)
Lagoon Snail (*Paludinella littorina*)
Lagoon Snail, De Folin's (*Caecum armoricum*)
Lagoon Worm, Tentacled (*Alkmaria romijni*)
Leech, Medicinal (*Hirudo medicinalis*)
Lizard, Sand (*Lacerta agilis*)
‡Lizard, Viviparous (*Lacerta vivipara*)
Marten, Pine (*Martes martes*)
Moth, Barberry Carpet (*Pareulype berberata*)
Moth, Black-veined (*Siona lineata* (or *Idaea lineata*))
Moth, Essex Emerald (*Thetidia smaragdaria*)
Moth, New Forest Burnet (*Zygaena viciae*)
Moth, Reddish Buff (*Acosmetia caliginosa*)
Moth, Sussex Emerald (*Thalera fimbrialis*)
Moth, Viper's Bugloss (*Hadena irregularis*)
†Mussel, Freshwater Pearl (*Margaritifera margaritifera*)
Newt, Great Crested (or Warty) (*Triturus cristatus*)
*Newt, Palmate (*Triturus helveticus*)
*Newt, Smooth (*Triturus vulgaris*)
Otter, Common (*Lutra lutra*)
Porpoise (*Cetacea*)
Sandworm, Lagoon (*Armandia cirrhosa*)
††Sea Fan, Pink (*Eunicella verrucosa*)
Sea-Mat, Trembling (*Victorella pavida*)
Sea Slug, Lagoon (*Tenellia adspersa*)
Shrimp, Fairy (*Chirocephalus diaphanus*)
Shrimp, Lagoon Sand (*Gammarus insensibilis*)
‡Slow-worm (*Anguis fragilis*)
Snail, Glutinous (*Myxas glutinosa*)
Snail, Sandbowl (*Catinella arenaria*)
‡Snake, Grass (*Natrix natrix* (*Natrix helvetica*))
Snake, Smooth (*Coronella austriaca*)
Spider, Fen Raft (*Dolomedes plantarius*)
Spider, Ladybird (*Eresus niger*)
Squirrel, Red (*Sciurus vulgaris*)
Sturgeon (*Acipenser sturio*)
*Toad, Common (*Bufo bufo*)
Toad, Natterjack (*Bufo calamita*)
Turtle, Marine (*Dermochelyidae* and *Cheloniidae*, all species)
Vendace (*Coregonus albula*)
Walrus (*Odobenus rosmarus*)
Whale (*Cetacea*)
Whitefish (*Coregonus lavaretus*)

PLANTS

Under Section 13 and Schedule 8 of the Wildlife and Countryside Act 1981, it is illegal without a licence to pick, uproot, sell or destroy any of the plants mentioned below and, unless authorized, to uproot any wild plant.

Adder's tongue, Least (*Ophioglossum lusitanicum*)
Alison, Small (*Alyssum alyssoides*)
Blackwort (*Southbya nigrella*)
Broomrape, Bedstraw (*Orobanche caryophyllacea*)

* the offence relates to 'sale' only
** the offence relates to 'taking' and 'sale' only
† the offence relates to 'killing and injuring' only
‡ the offence relates to 'killing, injuring and take'
§ the offence relates to 'killing, injuring and taking'
§§ the offence relates only to damaging, destroying or obstructing access to a shelter or protection
†† the offence relates to killing, injuring, taking, possession and sale

Broomrape, Oxtongue (*Orobanche loricata*)
Broomrape, Thistle (*Orobanche reticulata*)
Cabbage, Lundy (*Rhynchosinapis wrightii*)
Calamint, Wood (*Calamintha sylvatica*)
Caloplaca, Snow (*Caloplaca nivalis*)
Catapyrenium, Tree (*Catapyrenium psoromoides*)
Catchfly, Alpine (*Lychnis alpina*)
Catillaria, Laurer's (*Catellaria laureri*)
Centaury, Slender (*Centaurium tenuiflorum*)
Cinquefoil, Rock (*Potentilla rupestris*)
Cladonia, Upright Mountain (*Cladonia stricta*)
Clary, Meadow (*Salvia pratensis*)
Club-rush, Triangular (*Scirpus triquetrus*)
Colt's-foot, Purple (*Homogyne alpina*)
Cotoneaster, Wild (*Cotoneaster integerrimus*)
Cottongrass, Slender (*Eriophorum gracile*)
Cow-wheat, Field (*Melampyrum arvense*)
Crocus, Sand (*Romulea columnae*)
Crystalwort, Lizard (*Riccia bifurca*)
Cudweed, Broad-leaved (*Filago pyramidata*)
Cudweed, Jersey (*Gnaphalium luteoalbum*)
Cudweed, Red-tipped (*Filago lutescens*)
Diapensia (*Diapensia lapponica*)
Dock, Shore (*Rumex rupestris*)
Earwort, Marsh (*Jamesoniella undulifolia*)
Eryngo, Field (*Eryngium campestre*)
Fern, Dickie's bladder (*Cystopteris dickieana*)
Fern, Killarney (*Trichomanes speciosum*)
Flapwort, Norfolk (*Leiocolea rutheana*)
Fleabane, Alpine (*Erigeron borealis*)
Fleabane, Small (*Pulicaria vulgaris*)
Frostwort, Pointed (*Gymnomitrion apiculatum*)
Galingale, Brown (*Cyperus fuscus*)
Gentian, Alpine (*Gentiana nivalis*)
Gentian, Dune (*Gentianella uliginosa*)
Gentian, Early (*Gentianella anglica*)
Gentian, Fringed (*Gentianella ciliata*)
Gentian, Spring (*Gentiana verna*)
Germander, Cut-leaved (*Teucrium botrys*)
Germander, Water (*Teucrium scordium*)
Gladiolus, Wild (*Gladiolus illyricus*)
Goosefoot, Stinking (*Chenopodium vulvaria*)
Grass-poly (*Lythrum hyssopifolia*)
Grimmia, Blunt-leaved (*Grimmia unicolor*)
Gyalecta, Elm (*Gyalecta ulmi*)
Hare's-ear, Sickle-leaved (*Bupleurum falcatum*)
Hare's-ear, Small (*Bupleurum baldense*)
Hawk's-beard, Stinking (*Crepis foetida*)
Hawkweed, Northroe (*Hieracium northroense*)
Hawkweed, Shetland (*Hieracium zetlandicum*)
Hawkweed, Weak-leaved (*Hieracium attenuatifolium*)
Heath, Blue (*Phyllodoce caerulea*)
Helleborine, Red (*Cephalanthera rubra*)
Helleborine, Young's (*Epipactis youngiana*)
Horsetail, Branched (*Equisetum ramosissimum*)
Hound's-tongue, Green (*Cynoglossum germanicum*)
Knawel, Perennial (*Scleranthus perennis*)
Knotgrass, Sea (*Polygonum maritimum*)
Lady's-slipper (*Cypripedium calceolus*)
Lecanactis, Churchyard (*Lecanactis hemisphaerica*)
Lecanora, Tarn (*Lecanora archariana*)
Lecidea, Copper (*Lecidea inops*)
Leek, Round-headed (*Allium sphaerocephalon*)
Lettuce, Least (*Lactuca saligna*)
Lichen, Arctic Kidney (*Nephroma arcticum*)
Lichen, Ciliate Strap (*Heterodermia leucomelos*)
Lichen, Coralloid Rosette (*Heterodermia propagulifera*)
Lichen, Ear-lobed Dog (*Peltigera lepidophora*)
Lichen, Forked Hair (*Bryoria furcellata*)
Lichen, Golden Hair (*Teloschistes flavicans*)

Lichen, Orange Fruited Elm (*Caloplaca luteoalba*)
Lichen, River Jelly (*Collema dichotomum*)
Lichen, Scaly Breck (*Squamarina lentigera*)
Lichen, Stary Breck (*Buellia asterella*)
Lily, Snowdon (*Lloydia serotina*)
Liverwort (*Petallophyllum ralfsi*)
Liverwort, Lindenberg's Leafy (*Adelanthus lindenbergianus*)
Marsh-mallow, Rough (*Althaea hirsuta*)
Marshwort, Creeping (*Apium repens*)
Milk-parsley, Cambridge (*Selinum carvifolia*)
Moss (*Drepanocladius vernicosus*)
Moss, Alpine Copper (*Mielichoferia mielichoferi*)
Moss, Baltic Bog (*Sphagnum balticum*)
Moss, Blue Dew (*Saelania glaucescens*)
Moss, Blunt-leaved Bristle (*Orthotrichum obtusifolium*)
Moss, Bright Green Cave (*Cyclodictyon laetevirens*)
Moss, Cordate Beard (*Barbula cordata*)
Moss, Cornish Path (*Ditrichum cornubicum*)
Moss, Derbyshire Feather (*Thamnobryum angustifolium*)
Moss, Dune Thread (*Bryum mamillatum*)
Moss, Glaucous Beard (*Barbula glauca*)
Moss, Green Shield (*Buxbaumia viridis*)
Moss, Hair Silk (*Plagiothecium piliferum*)
Moss, Knothole (*Zygodon forsteri*)
Moss, Large Yellow Feather (*Scorpidium turgescens*)
Moss, Millimetre (*Micromitrium tenerum*)
Moss, Multifruited River (*Cryphaea lamyana*)
Moss, Nowell's Limestone (*Zygodon gracilis*)
Moss, Rigid Apple (*Bartramia stricta*)
Moss, Round-leaved Feather (*Rhyncostegium rotundifolium*)
Moss, Schleicher's Thread (*Bryum schleicheri*)
Moss, Triangular Pygmy (*Acaulon triquetrum*)
Moss, Vaucher's Feather (*Hypnum vaucheri*)
Mudwort, Welsh (*Limosella australis*)
Naiad, Holly-leaved (*Najas marina*)
Naiad, Slender (*Najas flexilis*)
Orache, Stalked (*Halimione pedunculata*)
Orchid, Early Spider (*Ophrys sphegodes*)
Orchid, Fen (*Liparis loeselii*)
Orchid, Ghost (*Epipogium aphyllum*)
Orchid, Lapland Marsh (*Dactylorhiza lapponica*)
Orchid, Late Spider (*Ophrys fuciflora*)
Orchid, Lizard (*Himantoglossum hircinum*)
Orchid, Military (*Orchis militaris*)
Orchid, Monkey (*Orchis simia*)
Pannaria, Caledonia (*Pannaria ignobilis*)
Parmelia, New Forest (*Parmelia minarum*)
Parmentaria, Oil Stain (*Parmentaria chilensis*)
Pear, Plymouth (*Pyrus cordata*)
Penny-cress, Perfoliate (*Thlaspi perfoliatum*)
Pennyroyal (*Mentha pulegium*)
Pertusaria, Alpine Moss (*Pertusaria bryontha*)
Physcia, Southern Grey (*Physcia tribacioides*)
Pigmyweed (*Crassula aquatica*)
Pine, Ground (*Ajuga chamaepitys*)
Pink, Cheddar (*Dianthus gratianopolitanus*)
Pink, Childling (*Petroraghia nanteuilii*)
Plantain, Floating Water (*Luronium natans*)
Pseudocyphellaria, Ragged (*Pseudocyphellaria lacerata*)
Psora, Rusty Alpine (*Psora rubiformis*)
Ragwort, Fen (*Senecio paludosus*)
Ramping-fumitory, Martin's (*Fumaria martinii*)
Rampion, Spiked (*Phyteuma spicatum*)
Restharrow, Small (*Ononis reclinata*)
Rock-cress, Alpine (*Arabis alpina*)
Rock-cress, Bristol (*Arabis stricta*)
Rustworth, Western (*Marsupella profunda*)
Sandwort, Norwegian (*Arenaria norvegica*)
Sandwort, Teesdale (*Minuartia stricta*)
Saxifrage, Drooping (*Saxifraga cernua*)

Saxifrage, Marsh (*Saxifrage hirulus*)
Saxifrage, Tufted (*Saxifraga cespitosa*)
Solenopsora, Serpentine (*Solenopsora liparina*)
Solomon's-seal, Whorled (*Polygonatum verticillatum*)
Sow-thistle, Alpine (*Cicerbita alpina*)
Spearwort, Adder's-tongue (*Ranunculus ophioglossifolius*)
Speedwell, Fingered (*Veronica triphyllos*)
Speedwell, Spiked (*Veronica spicata*)
Star-of-Bethlehem, Early (*Gagea bohemica*)
Starfruit (*Damasonium alisma*)
Stonewort, Bearded (*Chara canescens*)
Stonewort, Foxtail (*Lamprothamnium papulosum*)
Strapwort (*Corrigiola litoralis*)
Turpswort (*Geocalyx graveolens*)
Violet, Fen (*Viola persicifolia*)
Viper's-grass (*Scorzonera humilis*)
Water-plantain, Ribbon-leaved (*Alisma gramineum*)
Wood-sedge, Starved (*Carex depauperata*)
Woodsia, Alpine (*Woodsia alpina*)
Woodsia, Oblong (*Woodsia ilvensis*)
Wormwood, Field (*Artemisia campestris*)
Woundwort, Downy (*Stachys germanica*)
Woundwort, Limestone (*Stachys alpina*)
Yellow-rattle, Greater (*Rhinanthus serotinus*)

Wild Birds

The Wildlife and Countryside Act 1981 lays down a close season for wild birds (other than game birds) from 1 February to 31 August inclusive, each year. Exceptions to these dates are made for:

Capercaillie and (except Scotland) *Woodcock* – 1 February to 30 September
Snipe – 1 February to 11 August
Wild Duck and *Wild Goose* (below high water mark) – 21 February to 31 August

Birds which may be killed or taken outside the close season (except on Sundays and on Christmas Day in Scotland, and on Sundays in prescribed areas of England and Wales) are the above-named, plus coot, certain wild duck (gadwall, goldeneye, mallard, pintail, pochard, shoveler, teal, tufted duck, wigeon), certain wild geese (Canada, greylag, pink-footed, white-fronted (in England and Wales only)), moorhen, golden plover and woodcock.

Certain wild birds may be killed or taken subject to the conditions of a general licence at any time by authorized persons: crow, collared dove, gull (great and lesser black-backed or herring), jackdaw, jay, magpie, pigeon (feral or wood), rook, sparrow (house), and starling. Conditions usually apply where the birds pose a threat to agriculture, public health, air safety, other bird species, and to prevent the spread of disease.

All other British birds are fully protected by law throughout the year.

CLOSE SEASONS AND TIMES

Game Birds

In each case the dates are inclusive:

Black game – 11 December to 19 August (31 August in Somerset, Devon and New Forest)
Grouse – 11 December to 11 August
Partridge – 2 February to 31 August
Pheasant – 2 February to 30 September
Ptarmigan – (Scotland only) 11 December to 11 August

It is also unlawful in England and Wales to kill this game on a Sunday or Christmas Day

Hunting and Ground Game

There is no statutory close time for fox-hunting or rabbit-shooting, nor for hares. However, by an Act passed in 1892 the sale of hares or leverets in Great Britain is prohibited from 1 March to 31 July inclusive. The recognized date for the opening of the fox-hunting season is 1 November, and it continues till the following April.

Deer

The statutory close seasons for deer (all dates inclusive) are:

	England and Wales	Scotland
Fallow deer		
Male	1 May–31 July	1 May–31 July
Female	1 Mar.–31 Oct.	16 Feb.–20 Oct.
Red deer		
Male	1 May–31 July	21 Oct.–30 June
Female	1 Mar.–31 Oct.	16 Feb.–20 Oct.
Roe deer		
Male	1 Nov.–31 Mar.	21 Oct.–31 Mar.
Female	1 Mar.–31 Oct.	1 April–20 Oct.
Sika deer		
Male	1 May–31 July	21 Oct.–30 June
Female	1 Mar.–31 Oct.	16 Feb.–20 Oct.
Red/Sika hybrids		
Male	—	21 Oct.–30 June
Female	—	16 Feb.–20 Oct.

Angling

Game Fishing

Where local by-laws neither specify nor dispense with an annual close season, the statutory close times for game fishing are: Trout, 1 October to end February; Salmon, 1 November to 31 January.

Coarse Fishing

Responsibility for the fisheries function of the National Rivers Authority, including licensing and regulation, passed to the Environment Agency on 1 April 1996. The statutory close season for coarse fish in England and Wales runs from 15 March to 15 June on all rivers, streams and drains. Close season arrangements for canals vary from region to region. The close season on all lakes, ponds and reservoirs is at the discretion of the fishery owner, except on the Norfolk Broads and certain Sites of Special Scientific Interest where the statutory close season still applies. It is necessary in all cases to check with the Environment Agency regional office concerning the area (details can be found in the local telephone directory).

Licences

Purchase of a national rod fishing licence is legally required of anglers wishing to fish with rod and line in all waters within the area of the Environment Agency.

	Salmon and sea trout	Non-migratory trout and coarse fish
Full	£55.00	£15.00
Concessionary	27.50	7.50
Eight-day	13.50	4.50
One-day	4.50	1.50

Concessionary licences are available for juniors (12–16 years), for senior citizens (65 years and over), and disabled who are in receipt of invalidity benefit or severe disability allowance. Those in receipt of a war pension which includes unemployability supplements are also eligible.

Historic Buildings and Monuments

LISTING

Under the Planning (Listed Buildings and Conservation Areas) Act 1990, the Secretary of State for National Heritage has a statutory duty to compile lists of buildings or groups of buildings in England which are of special architectural or historic interest. Under the Ancient Monuments and Archaeological Areas Act 1979 as amended by the National Heritage Act 1983, the Secretary of State is also responsible for compiling a schedule of ancient monuments. Decisions are taken on the advice of English Heritage (see page 306).

Listed buildings are classified into Grade I, Grade II* and Grade II. There are currently about 500,000 individual listed buildings in England, of which about 95 per cent are Grade II listed. Almost all pre-1700 buildings are listed, and most buildings of 1700 to 1840. English Heritage is carrying out thematic surveys of particular types of buildings with a view to making recommendations for listing, and members of the public may propose a building for consideration. The main purpose of listing is to ensure that care is taken in deciding the future of a building. No changes which affect the architectural or historic character of a listed building can be made without listed building consent (in addition to planning permission where relevant). Applications for listed building consent are normally dealt with by the local planning authority, although English Heritage is always consulted about proposals affecting Grade I and Grade II* properties. It is a criminal offence to demolish a listed building, or alter it in such a way as to affect its character, without consent.

There are currently about 16,000 scheduled monuments in England. English Heritage is carrying out a Monuments Protection Programme assessing archaeological sites with a view to making recommendations for scheduling, and members of the public may propose a monument for consideration. All monuments proposed for scheduling are considered to be of national importance. Where buildings are both scheduled and listed, ancient monuments legislation takes precedence. The main purpose of scheduling a monument is to preserve it for the future and to protect it from damage, destruction or any unnecessary interference. Once a monument has been scheduled, scheduled monument consent is required before any works are carried out which would damage or alter the monument in any way. The scope of the control is more extensive and more detailed than that applied to listed buildings, but certain minor works, as detailed in the Ancient Monuments Class Consents Order 1994, may be carried out without consent. It is a criminal offence to carry out unauthorized work to scheduled monuments.

Under the Planning (Listed Buildings and Conservation Areas) Act 1990 and the Ancient Monuments and Archaeological Areas Act 1979, the Secretary of State for Wales is responsible for listing buildings and scheduling monuments in Wales on the advice of Cadw (see page 356), the Historic Buildings Council for Wales (see page 306) and the Ancient Monuments Board for Wales (see page 307). The criteria for evaluating buildings are similar to those in England and the same listing system is used. There are about 18,000 listed buildings and about 2,800 scheduled monuments in Wales.

Under the Town and County Planning (Scotland) Act 1972 and the Ancient Monuments and Archaeological Areas Act 1979, the Secretary of State for Scotland is responsible for listing buildings and scheduling monuments in Scotland on the advice of Historic Scotland (see page 341), the Historic Buildings Council for Scotland (see page 306) and the Ancient Monuments Board for Scotland (see page 307). The criteria for evaluating buildings are similar to those in England but an A, B, C grading system is used. There are about 42,000 listed buildings and about 6,000 scheduled monuments in Scotland.

Under the Planning (Northern Ireland) Order 1991 and the Historic Monuments and Archaeological Objects (Northern Ireland) Order 1995, the Department of the Environment for Northern Ireland (see page 330) is responsible for listing buildings and scheduling monuments in Northern Ireland on the advice of the Historic Buildings Council for Northern Ireland and the Historic Monuments Council for Northern Ireland. The criteria for evaluating buildings are similar to those in England but no official grading system is used. There are about 8,565 listed buildings and 1,120 scheduled monuments in Northern Ireland.

The Government proposes to reform the system for protecting the built heritage in Great Britain. In March 1995 public consultation was introduced on listing recommendations arising from English Heritage's thematic surveys of particular building types, and a Green Paper was published in May 1996.

OPENING TO THE PUBLIC

The following is a selection of the many historic buildings and monuments open to the public. The admission charges given are the standard charges for 1996–7; many properties have concessionary rates for children, etc. Opening hours vary. Many properties are closed in winter and some are also closed in the mornings. Most properties are closed on Christmas Eve, Christmas Day, Boxing Day and New Year's Day, and many are closed on Good Friday. During the winter season, most English Heritage monuments are closed on Mondays and Tuesdays and monuments in the care of Cadw are closed on Sunday mornings. Information about a specific property should be checked by telephone.

*Closed in winter (usually November-March)
†Closed in winter, and in mornings in summer

ENGLAND

EH English Heritage property
NT National Trust property

*A LA RONDE (NT), Exmouth, Devon. Tel: 01395-265514. Closed Sat. morning and Fri. Adm. £3.10. Unique 16-sided house built in 1796

*ALNWICK CASTLE, Northumberland. Tel: 01665-510777. Closed Fri. Adm. £4.70; grounds only £4.20. Seat of the Dukes of Northumberland since 1309; Italian Renaissance-style interior

ALTHORP, Northants. Tel: 01604-770107. Opening times and prices subject to change. House originally built in early 16th century. Fine art collection

†ANGLESEY ABBEY (NT), Cambs. Tel: 01223-811200. Closed Mon. (except Bank Holidays) and Tues. Gardens open daily July to Sept. Adm. £5.50 (£6.50 Sun. and Bank Holidays); gardens only, £3.20. House built c.1600; bought by Lord Fairhaven in early 20th century. Outstanding grounds with unique statuary

APSLEY HOUSE, London W1. Tel: 0171-499 5676. Closed Mon. Adm £3.00. Built by Robert Adam 1771-8, home of the Dukes of Wellington since 1817 and known as 'No. 1 London'. Collection of fine and decorative arts

†ARUNDEL CASTLE, W. Sussex. Tel: 01903-883136. Closed Sat. and Good Fri. Adm. charge. Castle dating from the Norman Conquest. Seat of the Dukes of Norfolk

AVEBURY (NT), Wilts. Adm. free. Remains of stone circles constructed 4,000 years ago surrounding the later village of Avebury. Also *Alexander Keiller Museum*. Tel: 01672-539250. Adm. £1.50

BANQUETING HOUSE, Whitehall, London SW1. Tel: 0171-839 8919. Closed Sun. and Bank Holidays. Adm. £3.00. Designed by Inigo Jones; ceiling paintings by Rubens. Site of the execution of Charles I

†BASILDON PARK (NT), Berks. Tel: 01734-843040. Closed Mon. (except Bank Holidays) and Tues. Adm. £3.70; grounds only, £1.50. Palladian house built in 1776; unusual octagonal room

BATTLE ABBEY (EH), E. Sussex. Tel: 01424-773792. Adm. £3.50. Remains of the abbey founded by William the Conqueror on the site of the Battle of Hastings

BEAULIEU, Hants. Tel: 01590-612345. Adm. charge. House and gardens, Beaulieu Abbey and exhibition of monastic life, National Motor Museum (*see also* page 581)

BEESTON CASTLE (EH), Cheshire. Tel: 01829-260464. Adm. £2.20. Thirteenth-century inner ward with gatehouse and towers, and remains of large outer ward

*BELTON HOUSE (NT), Grantham, Lincs. Tel: 01476-566116. Closed Mon. (except Bank Holidays) and Tues. Adm. £4.50. Fine 17th-century house in landscaped park

BELVOIR CASTLE, nr Grantham, Lincs. Tel: 01476-870262. Closed Mon. and Fri. except Bank Holidays. Adm. £4.25. Seat of the Dukes of Rutland; 19th-century Gothic-style castle

BERKELEY CASTLE, Glos. Tel: 01453-810332. Opening times vary. Adm. £4.50. Completed 1153; site of the murder of Edward II (1327). Elizabethan terraced gardens

BLENHEIM PALACE, Woodstock, Oxon. Tel: 01993-811325. Adm. charge. Seat of the Dukes of Marlborough and Winston Churchill's birthplace; designed by Vanbrugh

BLICKLING HALL (NT), Norfolk. Tel: 01263-733084. Closed Mon. (except Bank Holidays) and Thurs. Adm. £5.50 (£6.50 Sun. and Bank Holidays); garden only tickets available. Jacobean house with state rooms, Long Gallery, formal gardens, temple and 18th-century orangery

BODIAM CASTLE (NT), E. Sussex. Tel: 01580-830436. Closed Mon. in winter. Adm. £2.70. Well-preserved medieval moated castle

BOLSOVER CASTLE (EH), Derbys. Tel: 01246-823349. Closed Mon. and Tues. in winter. Adm. £2.60. Notable for its 17th-century buildings

BOSCOBEL HOUSE (EH), Shropshire. Tel: 01902-850244. Closed Mon. and Tues. in winter. Adm. £3.50. Timber-framed 17th-century hunting lodge, refuge of fugitive Charles II

BOUGHTON HOUSE, Northants. Tel: 01536-515731. House open Aug. only; grounds May to Sept. except Fri. State rooms by prior booking. Adm. £4.00; grounds £1.50. A 17th-century house with French-style additions

BOWOOD HOUSE, Wilts. Tel: 01249-812102. Adm. £4.80. An 18th-century house in Capability Brown park, with lake, temple and arboretum

BROADLANDS, Hants. Tel: 01794-516878. Open July-Sept. Adm. £5.00. Palladian mansion in Capability Brown parkland. Mountbatten exhibition

BRONTË PARSONAGE, Haworth, W. Yorks. Tel: 01535-642323. Closed Jan.- Feb. Adm. £3.80. Home of the Brontë sisters; museum and memorabilia

BUCKFAST ABBEY, Devon. Tel: 01364-642519. Adm. free. Medieval monastery rebuilt 1907-1938

*BUCKINGHAM PALACE, London SW1. Tel: 0171-839 1377. Open daily for eight weeks from early Aug. each year. Adm. £8.50. Purchased by George III in 1762, it has been the Sovereign's official London residence since 1837. Eighteen state rooms, including the Throne Room; also the Picture Gallery

BUCKLAND ABBEY (NT), Devon. Tel: 01822-853607. Closed Thurs. In winter open only weekend afternoons. Adm. £4.20. A 13th-century Cistercian monastery. Home of Sir Francis Drake

*BURGHLEY HOUSE, Stamford, Lincs. Tel: 01780-52451. Adm. £5.50. Late Elizabethan house; vast state apartments

†CALKE ABBEY (NT), Derbys. Tel: 01332-863822. Closed Thurs. and Fri. Adm. £4.70, by timed ticket. Baroque 18th-century mansion

CARISBROOKE CASTLE (EH), Isle of Wight. Tel: 01983-522107. Adm. £3.80. Norman castle; prison of Charles I 1647-8

CARLISLE CASTLE (EH), Cumbria. Tel: 01228-591922. Adm. £2.50. Medieval castle, prison of Mary Queen of Scots

*CARLYLE'S HOUSE (NT), Cheyne Row, London SW3. Tel: 0171-352 7087. Home of Thomas Carlyle

CASTLE ACRE PRIORY (EH), Norfolk. Tel: 01760-755394. Closed Mon. and Tues. in winter. Adm. £2.50. Remains include 12th-century church and prior's lodgings

*CASTLE DROGO (NT), Devon. Tel: 01647-433306. Castle closed Fri. Adm. £4.80; grounds only, £2.20. Granite castle designed by Lutyens

*CASTLE HOWARD, N. Yorks. Tel: 01653-684333. Adm. £6.50; grounds only, £4.00. Designed by Vanbrugh 1699-1726; mausoleum designed by Hawksmoor

CASTLE RISING CASTLE (EH), Norfolk. Tel: 01553-631330. Closed Mon. and Tues. in winter. Adm. £2.00. A 12th-century keep in a massive earthwork with gatehouse and bridge

†CHARTWELL (NT), Kent. Tel: 01732-866368. Closed Fri. and Mon. (except Bank Holidays). Adm. £4.50; grounds only, £2.00. Home of Sir Winston Churchill

*CHATSWORTH, Derbys. Tel: 01246-582204. Adm. £5.75. Tudor mansion with later additions in magnificent parkland

CHESTERS ROMAN FORT (EH), Northumberland. Tel: 01434-681379. Adm. £2.50. Fine example of a Roman cavalry fort

*CHYSAUSTER ANCIENT VILLAGE (EH), Cornwall. Tel: 01326-212044. Adm. £1.50. Romano-Cornish village, 2nd and 3rd century AD, on a probably late Iron Age site

CLIFFORD'S TOWER (EH), York. Tel: 01904-646940. Adm. £1.60. A 13th-century tower built on a mound

†CLIVEDEN (NT), Berks. Tel: 01628-605069. House open Thurs. and Sun. only, gardens daily. Adm. £4.00, £1.00 extra for house. Former home of the Astors, now an hotel set in garden and woodland

CORBRIDGE ROMAN SITE (EH), Northumberland. Tel: 01434-632349. Closed Mon. and Tues. in winter. Adm. £2.50. Excavated central area of a Roman town and successive military bases

CORFE CASTLE (NT), Dorset. Tel: 01929-481294. Nov.-Jan. open weekend afternoons only. Adm. £3.00. Ruined former royal castle dating from 11th century

†CROFT CASTLE (NT), Herefordshire. Tel: 01568-780246. Closed Mon. (except Bank Holidays) and Tues.; April and Oct. open weekends only. Adm. £3.20. Pre-Conquest border castle with Georgian-Gothic interior

DEAL CASTLE (EH), Kent. Tel: 01304-372762. Closed Mon. and Tues. in winter. Adm. £2.80. Largest and most complete of the coastal defence forts built by Henry VIII

DICKENS HOUSE, Doughty Street, London WC1. Tel: 0171-405 2127. Closed Sun. Adm. £3.50. House occupied by Dickens 1837-9; manuscripts, furniture and portraits

DR JOHNSON'S HOUSE, 17 Gough Square, London EC4. Tel: 0171-353 3745. Closed Sun. and Bank Holidays. Adm. £3.00. Home of Samuel Johnson

DOVE COTTAGE, Grasmere, Cumbria. Tel: 015394-35544. Closed Jan. and early Feb. Adm. £4.10. Wordsworth's home 1799-1808; museum and memorabilia

DOVER CASTLE (EH), Kent. Tel: 01304-201628. Adm. £6.00. Castle with Roman, Saxon and Norman features; wartime operations rooms

DUNSTANBURGH CASTLE (EH), Northumberland. Tel: 01665-576231. Closed Mon. and Tues. in winter. Adm. £1.50. A 14th-century castle on a cliff, with a substantial gatehouse-keep

FARLEIGH HUNGERFORD CASTLE (EH), Somerset. Tel: 01225-754026. Adm. £1.50. Late 14th-century castle with two courts and chapel with tomb of Sir Thomas Hungerford

*FARNHAM CASTLE KEEP (EH), Surrey. Tel: 01252-713393. Adm. £2.00. Large 12th-century shell-keep on motte

FOUNTAINS ABBEY (NT), nr Ripon, N. Yorks. Tel: 01765-608888. Closed Fri. Nov.-Jan. Adm. £4.00. Ruined Cistercian monastery; 18th-century landscaped gardens of Studley Royal estate

FRAMLINGHAM CASTLE (EH), Suffolk. Tel: 01728-724189. Adm. £2.50. Castle (c.1200) with high curtain walls enclosing an almshouse (1639)

FURNESS ABBEY (EH), Cumbria. Tel: 01229-823420. Adm. £2.30. Remains of church and conventual buildings founded in 1123

GLASTONBURY ABBEY, Somerset. Tel: 01458-832267. Adm. £2.50. Ruins of a 12th-century abbey rebuilt after fire. Site of an early Christian settlement

GOODRICH CASTLE (EH), Herefordshire. Tel: 01600-890538. Adm. £2.20. Remains of 13th- and 14th-century castle with 12th-century keep

GREENWICH, London SE10. *Royal Observatory*. Closed Sun. mornings. Adm. charge. Former Royal Observatory (founded 1675) where the time ball and zero meridian of longitude can be seen. *The Queen's House*. Tel: 0181-858 4422. Closed Sun. mornings. Adm. charge. Designed for Queen Anne, wife of James I, by Inigo Jones. *Painted Hall and Chapel* (Royal Naval College). Closed mornings. Visitors are admitted to Sunday service in the chapel at 11 a.m. except during college vacations

GRIMES GRAVES (EH), Norfolk. Tel: 01842-810656. Closed Mon. and Tues. in winter. Adm. £1.50. Neolithic flint mines. One shaft can be descended

*GUILDHALL, London EC2. Tel: 0171-332 1460. Closed Sat. Adm. free. Centre of civic government of the City. Built c.1440; facade built 1788-9

*HADDON HALL, Derbys. Tel: 01629-812855. Closed Sun. in July and Aug. except Bank Holiday weekend. Adm. £4.50. Well-preserved 12th-century manor house

HAILES ABBEY, Glos. Tel: 01242-602398. Closed Mon. and Tues. in winter. Adm. £2.20. Ruins of a 13th-century Cistercian monastery

†HAM HOUSE (NT), Richmond, Surrey. Tel: 0181-940 1950. Closed Thurs. and Fri. Adm. £4.00. Garden open all year except Fri. Adm. free. Stuart house with fine interiors

HAMPTON COURT PALACE, East Molesey, Surrey. Tel: 0181-781 9500. Adm. £7.50. A 16th-century palace with additions by Wren. Gardens with maze; Tudor tennis court (summer only)

†HARDWICK HALL (NT), Derbys. Tel: 01246-850430. Closed Mon. (except Bank Holidays), Tues. and Fri.: grounds open daily, all year. Adm £5.50; grounds only £2.50. Built 1591-7 by Bess of Hardwick; notable furnishings

*HARDY'S COTTAGE (NT), Higher Bockhampton, Dorset. Tel: 01305-262366. Interior open only by appointment. Adm. £2.50. Garden open daily, adm. free. Birthplace of Thomas Hardy

*HAREWOOD HOUSE, W. Yorks. Tel: 0113-288 6331. Adm. charge. An 18th-century house designed by John Carr and Robert Adam; park by Capability Brown

†HATFIELD HOUSE, Herts. Tel: 01707-262823. Closed Mon. (except Bank Holidays). Adm. charge. Jacobean house built by Robert Cecil, and family home of the Cecils. Surviving wing of royal Palace of Hatfield (1497)

HELMSLEY CASTLE (EH), N. Yorks. Tel: 01439-770442. Closed Mon. and Tues. in winter. Adm. £2.00. A 12th-century keep and curtain wall with 16th-century buildings. Spectacular earthwork defences

†HEVER CASTLE, Kent. Tel: 01732-865224. Adm. charge. A 13th-century double-moated castle, childhood home of Anne Boleyn

*HOLKER HALL, Cumbria. Tel: 015395-58328. Closed Sat. Adm. charge. Former home of the Dukes of Devonshire; award-winning gardens

†HOLKHAM HALL, Norfolk. Tel: 01328-710227. Closed Fri. and Sat. Adm. £3.00. Fine Palladian mansion

HOUSESTEADS ROMAN FORT (EH), Northumberland. Tel: 01434-344363. Adm. £2.50. Excavated infantry fort on Hadrian's Wall with extra-mural civilian settlement

†HUGHENDEN MANOR (NT), High Wycombe. Tel: 01494-532580. Closed Mon. (except Bank Holidays) and Tues.; open weekends only in March. Adm. £3.60. Home of Disraeli; small formal garden

JANE AUSTEN'S HOUSE, Chawton, Hants. Tel: 01420-83262. Closed Mon.-Fri. in Jan. and Feb. Adm. £2.00. Jane Austen's home 1809-17

KEATS HOUSE, Keats Grove, London NW3. Tel: 0171-435 2062. Closed Sun. mornings in summer, mornings except Sat. in winter. Adm. free. Home of John Keats 1818-20

*KELMSCOTT MANOR, nr Lechlade, Glos. Tel: 01367-252486. Open Wed. and third Sat. in every month. Adm. £6.00. Summer home of William Morris, with products of Morris and Co.

KENILWORTH CASTLE (EH), Warks. Tel: 01926-852078. Adm. £2.50. Castle showing many styles of building from 1155 to 1649

*KENSINGTON PALACE, London W8. Tel: 0171-937 9561. Adm. £5.50. Built in 1605 and enlarged by Wren; bought by William and Mary in 1689. Birthplace of Queen Victoria

KENWOOD (EH), Hampstead Lane, London NW3. Tel: 0181-348 1286. Adm. free. Adam villa housing the Iveagh bequest of paintings and furniture. Open-air concerts in summer

*KEW PALACE, Surrey. Tel: 0181-332 5189. Adm. £1.00 (plus £4.50 adm. to Kew Gardens). Built in 1631 as the Dutch House; residence of George III.

†KINGSTON LACY HOUSE (NT), Dorset. Tel: 01202-883402. Closed Thurs. and Fri. Adm. £5.50; grounds only, £2.20. A 17th-century house with 19th-century alterations; important collection of paintings

†KNEBWORTH HOUSE, Herts. Tel: 01438-812661. Closed Mon. (except Bank Holidays), and Mon.-Fri. April, May and Sept. Adm. £4.50; grounds only, £3.50. Tudor manor house concealed by 19th-century Gothic decoration; Lutyens gardens

*Knole (NT), Kent. Tel: 01732-450608. Closed Mon. (except Bank Holidays), Tues. and Thurs. morning. Adm. £4.50; park free to pedestrians. House dating from 1456 set in parkland; fine art treasures

Lambeth Palace, London SE1. Tel: 0171-928 8282. Visits by written application. Official residence of the Archbishop of Canterbury. A 19th-century house with parts dating from the 12th century

*Lanercost Priory (EH), Cumbria. Tel: 016977-3030. Adm. £1.00. The nave of the Augustinian priory church, c.1166, is still used; remains of other claustral buildings

*Lanhydrock (NT), Cornwall. Tel: 01208-73320. Closed Mon. (except Bank Holidays). Garden open daily including in winter. Adm. £5.90; gardens only, £3.00. House dating from the 17th century; 45 rooms, including kitchen and nursery

Leeds Castle, Kent. Tel: 01622-765400. Adm. £8.00; park only, £6.00. Castle dating from the 9th century, on two islands in a lake

*Levens Hall, Cumbria. Tel: 015395-60321. Closed Fri. and Sat. Adm. charge. Elizabethan house with unique topiary garden (1694). Steam engine collection

Lincoln Castle. Tel: 01522-511068. Adm. £2.00. Built by William the Conqueror in 1068

Lindisfarne Priory (EH), Northumberland. Tel: 01289-389200. Open all year, subject to tide times. Adm. £2.50. Bishopric of the Northumbrian kingdom destroyed by the Danes; re-established in the 11th century as a Benedictine priory, now ruined

Little Moreton Hall (NT), Cheshire. Tel: 01260-272018. Closed Mon. (except Bank Holidays) and Tues. Adm. £3.60. Timber-framed moated manor house with knot garden

Longleat House, Warminster. Tel: 01985-844400. Open daily; safari park closed winter. Adm. charge. Elizabethan house in Italian Renaissance style

Lullingstone Roman Villa (EH), Kent. Tel: 01322-863467. Adm. £2.00. Large villa occupied for much of the Roman period; fine mosaics

Luton Hoo, Beds. Tel: 01582-22955. Open Fri.-Sun. and Bank Holiday Mon. Adm. £5.50. Houses the Wernher collection of china, glass, pictures and other *objets d'art*

Mansion House, London EC4. Tel: 0171-626 2500. Group visits only, by prior arrangement. Adm. free. The official residence of the Lord Mayor of London

Marble Hill House (EH), Twickenham, Middx. Tel: 0181-892 5115. Closed Mon. and Tues. in winter. Adm. £2.50. English Palladian villa with Georgian paintings and furniture

Michelham Priory, E. Sussex. Tel: 01323-844224. Adm. £3.80. Tudor house built onto an Augustinian priory

Middleham Castle (EH), N. Yorks. Tel: 01969-623899. Closed Mon. and Tues. in winter. Adm. £1.60. A 12th-century keep within later fortifications. Childhood home of Richard III

Montacute House (NT), Somerset. Tel: 01935-823289. Closed Tues; grounds open all year. Adm. £5.00; grounds only, £2.80. Elizabethan house with National Portrait Gallery portraits from period

Mount Grace Priory (EH), N. Yorks. Tel: 01609-883494. Closed Mon. and Tues. in winter. Adm. £2.40. Carthusian monastery, with remains of monastic buildings

Netley Abbey (EH), Hants. Tel: 01705-527667. Adm. free. Remains of Cistercian abbey, used as house in Tudor period

Old Sarum (EH), Wilts. Tel: 01722-335398. Adm. £1.70. Earthworks enclosing remains of the castle and the 11th-century cathedral

Orford Castle (EH), Suffolk. Tel: 013944-50472. Adm. £2.00. Circular keep of c.1170 and remains of coastal defence castle built by Henry II

*Osborne House (EH), Isle of Wight. Tel: 01983-200022. Adm. £6.00. Queen Victoria's seaside residence

†Osterley Park House (NT), Isleworth, Middx. Tel: 0181-560 3918. Closed Mon. (except Bank Holidays) and Tues; grounds open all year. Adm. £3.70; grounds free. Elizabethan mansion set in parkland

Pendennis Castle (EH), Cornwall. Tel: 01326-316594. Adm. £2.50. Well-preserved coastal defence castle built by Henry VIII

†Penshurst Place, Kent. Tel: 01892-870307. Adm. £5.50; grounds only, £4.00. House with medieval Baron's Hall and 14th-century gardens

†Petworth (NT), W. Sussex. Tel: 01798-342207. Closed Mon. (except Bank Holidays) and Fri. Adm. £4.20; grounds free. Late 17th-century house set in deer park

Pevensey Castle (EH), E. Sussex. Tel: 01323-762604. Closed Mon. and Tues. in winter. Adm. £2.00. Walls of a 4th-century Roman fort enclosing remains of an 11th-century castle

Peveril Castle (EH), Derbys. Tel: 01433-620613. Adm. £1.50. A 12th-century castle defended on two sides by precipitous rocks

†Polesden Lacy (NT), Surrey. Tel: 01372-458203. Closed Mon. (except Bank Holidays) and Tues.; open weekends only in March. Grounds open daily all year. Adm. £6.00; grounds only £3.00. Regency villa remodelled in the Edwardian era. Fine paintings and furnishings

Portchester Castle (EH), Hants. Tel: 01705-378291. Adm. £2.50. Walls of a late Roman fort enclosing a Norman keep and an Augustinian priory church

*Powderham Castle, Devon. Tel: 01626-890243. Closed Sat. Adm. £4.40. Medieval castle with 18th- and 19th-century alterations

†Raby Castle, Co. Durham. Tel: 01833-660202. Closed Sat. (except Bank Holiday weekends). Limited opening in May and June. Adm. £3.50; grounds only, £1.00. A 14th-century castle with walled gardens

*Ragley Hall, Warks. Tel: 01789-762090. Closed Mon. (except Bank Holidays) and Fri.; grounds open daily. Adm. £4.50. A 17th-century house with gardens, park and lake

Richborough Castle (EH), Kent. Tel: 01304-612013. Adm. £2.00. Landing-site of the Claudian invasion in AD 43, with 3rd-century stone walls

Richmond Castle (EH), N. Yorks. Tel: 01748-822493. Adm. £1.80. A 12th-century keep with 11th-century curtain wall and domestic buildings

Rievaulx Abbey (EH), N. Yorks. Tel: 01439-798228. Adm. £2.50. Remains of a Cistercian abbey founded c.1131

Rochester Castle (EH), Kent. Tel: 01634-402276. Adm. £2.50. An 11th-century castle partly on the Roman city wall, with a square keep of c.1130

†Rockingham Castle, Northants. Tel: 01536-770240. Open Sun. and Thurs. only (and Bank Holiday Mon. and Tues., and Tues. in Aug.). Adm. £3.80; gardens only, £2.40. Built by William the Conqueror

Royal Pavilion, Brighton. Tel: 01273-603005. Adm. charge. Palace of George IV, in Chinese style with Indian exterior and Regency gardens

†Rufford Old Hall (NT), Lancs. Tel: 01704-821254. Closed Thurs. and Fri. Adm. £3.00; garden only, £1.60. A 16th-century hall with unique screen

St Augustine's Abbey (EH), Canterbury, Kent. Tel: 01227-767345. Adm. £1.50. Remains of Benedictine monastery, with Norman church, on site of abbey founded AD 598 by St Augustine

St Mawes Castle (EH), Cornwall. Tel: 01326-270526. Closed Mon. and Tues. in winter. Adm. £2.00. Coastal defence castle built by Henry VIII comprising central tower and three bastions

St Michael's Mount (NT), Cornwall. Tel: 01736-710507. Closed Sat. and Sun. No regular ferry service in winter; castle open as tide, weather, etc., permit. Adm. £3.70. A 14th-century castle with later additions and alterations, off the coast at Marazion

*Sandringham, Norfolk. Tel: 01553-772675. Closed for three weeks in summer and when the Royal Family is in residence. Adm. £4.00; grounds only, £3.00. The Queen's private residence; a neo-Jacobean house built in 1870

Scarborough Castle (EH), N. Yorks. Tel: 01723-372451. Closed Mon. and Tues. in winter. Adm. £1.80. Remains of 12th-century keep and curtain walls

†Sherborne Castle, Dorset. Tel: 01935-813182. Open Thurs., Sat., Sun. and Bank Holiday Mon. Adm. charge. Early 12th-century castle owned by Sir Walter Raleigh

*Shugborough (NT), Staffs. Tel: 01889-881388. Adm. house, servants' quarters and farm, £8.00; each site alone, £3.50. House set in 18th-century park with monuments, temples and pavilions in the Greek Revival style

Skipton Castle, N. Yorks. Tel: 01756-792442. Closed Sun. mornings. Adm. £3.40. D-shaped castle with six round towers and beautiful inner courtyard

†Smallhythe Place (NT), Kent. Tel: 01580-762334. Closed Thurs.-Fri. (open Good Friday). Adm. £2.50. Half-timbered 16th-century house; home of Ellen Terry 1899-1928

†Stanford Hall, Leics. Tel: 01788-860250. Open Sat.-Sun.; also Bank Holiday Mon. and Tues. Adm. £3.50; grounds only, £1.90. William and Mary house with Stuart portraits. Motorcycle museum

Stonehenge (EH), Wilts. Tel: 01980-624715. Adm. £3.50. Prehistoric monument consisting of a series of concentric stone circles surrounded by a ditch and bank

Stoneleigh Abbey, Warks. Tel: 01285-659771. Open by appointment only; closed weekends. Early 18th-century Georgian mansion on the site of a Cistercian abbey

†Stonor Park, Oxon. Tel: 01491-638587. Opening days vary. Adm. £4.00. Medieval house with Georgian facade. Centre of Roman Catholicism after the Reformation

†Stourhead (NT), Wilts. Tel: 01985-844785. Closed Thurs.-Fri. Gardens open daily all year. Adm. £4.20; gardens, £4.20. English Palladian mansion with famous gardens

*Stratfield Saye House, Hants. Tel: 01256-882882. Closed Fri. Adm. charge. House built 1630-40; home of the Dukes of Wellington since 1817

Stratford-upon-Avon, Warks. Shakespeare's Birthplace with Shakespeare Centre; Anne Hathaway's Cottage, home of Shakespeare's wife; Mary Arden's House, home of Shakespeare's mother; New Place, where Shakespeare died; and Hall's Croft, home of Shakespeare's daughter. Tel: 01789-204016. Adm. charges. Also Grammar School attended by Shakespeare, Holy Trinity Church, where Shakespeare is buried, Royal Shakespeare Theatre (burnt down 1926, rebuilt 1932) and Swan Theatre (opened 1986)

*Sudeley Castle, Glos. Tel: 01242-602308. Adm. £5.40; grounds only, £4.00. Castle built in 1442; restored in the 19th century

*Syon House, Brentford, Middx. Tel: 0181-560 0881. Opening times vary. Adm. £5.50; grounds only, £2.50. Built on the site of a former monastery; Adam interior

Tilbury Fort (EH), Essex. Tel: 01375-858489. Closed Mon. and Tues. in winter. Adm. £2.00. A 17th-century coastal fort

Tintagel Castle (EH), Cornwall. Tel: 01840-770328. Adm. £2.50. A 12th-century cliff-top castle and Dark Age settlement site

Tower of London, London EC3. Tel: 0171-709 0765. Adm. charge. Royal palace and fortress begun by William the Conqueror in 1078. Houses the Crown Jewels

*Trerice (NT), Cornwall. Tel: 01637-875404. Closed Tues. Adm. £3.80. Elizabethan manor house

Tynemouth Priory and Castle (EH), Tyne and Wear. Tel: 0191-257 1090. Closed Mon. and Tues. in winter. Adm. £1.50. Remains of a Benedictine priory, founded 1090, on Saxon monastic site. First World War gun battery open Sat., Sun. and Bank Holidays

†Uppark (NT), W. Sussex. Tel: 01730-825415. Closed Fri. and Sat. Adm. £5.00 by timed ticket. Late 17th-century house, completely restored after fire. Fetherstonhaugh art collection.

Walmer Castle (EH), Kent. Tel: 01304-364288. Closed Mon. and Tues. in winter; closed Jan.-Feb. and when the Lord Warden is in residence. Adm. £3.80. One of Henry VIII's coastal defence castles, now the residence of the Lord Warden of the Cinque Ports

Waltham Abbey (EH), Essex. Adm. free. Ruined abbey including the nave of the abbey church, 'Harold's Bridge' and late 14th-century gatehouse. Traditionally the burial place of Harold II (1066)

Warkworth Castle (EH), Northumberland. Tel: 01665-711423. Adm. £2.00. A 15th-century keep amidst earlier ruins, with 14th-century hermitage (open Wed. and Sun. in summer only) upstream

Warwick Castle. Tel: 01926-408000. Adm. £8.75. Medieval castle with Madam Tussaud's waxworks, in Capability Brown parkland

Whitby Abbey (EH), N. Yorks. Tel: 01947-603568. Adm. £1.60. Remains of Norman church on the site of a monastery founded in AD 657

*Wilton House, Wilts. Tel: 01722-743115. Adm. £6.00; grounds only, £3.50. A 17th-century house on the site of a Tudor house and Saxon abbey. Notable art collection

Windsor Castle, Berks. Tel: 01753-831118 for recorded information on opening times. Adm. £9.50, including the Castle precincts. Official residence of The Queen; oldest royal residence still in regular use. Includes state apartments and Queen Mary's Dolls' House. Restoration work in progress on fire-damaged state rooms (which may still be viewed). Also St George's Chapel

Woburn Abbey, Beds. Tel: 01525-290666. Closed Nov. and Dec.; also Mon.-Fri. in Jan. and Feb. Adm. £6.80. Built on the site of a Cistercian abbey; seat of the Dukes of Bedford. Important art collection; antiques centre

Wroxeter Roman City (EH), Shropshire. Tel: 01743-761330. Closed Mon. and Tues. in winter. Adm. £2.50. Second-century public baths and part of the forum of the Roman town of Viroconium

WALES

c   Property of Cadw: Welsh Historic Monuments
nt National Trust property

Beaumaris Castle (c), Anglesey. Tel: 01248-810361. Adm. £2.20. Fine concentrically-planned castle, still almost intact

CAERLEON ROMAN BATHS AND AMPHITHEATRE (C), nr Newport. Tel: 01633-422518. Closed Sun. morning in winter. Adm. £1.70, joint ticket with Legionary Museum £2.85. Rare example of a legionary bath-house and late 1st-century arena surrounded by bank for spectators

CAERNARFON CASTLE (C). Tel: 01286-677617. Adm. £3.80. Important Edwardian castle built, with the town wall, between 1283 and 1330

CAERPHILLY CASTLE (C). Tel: 01222-883143. Adm. £2.20. Concentrically-planned castle (c.1270) notable for its scale and use of water defences

CARDIFF CASTLE. Tel: 01222-878100. Adm. charge. Castle built on the site of a Roman fort; spectacular towers and rich interior

CASTELL COCH (C), nr Cardiff. Tel: 01222-810101. Adm. £2.20. Rebuilt 1875-90 on medieval foundations

CHEPSTOW CASTLE (C). Tel: 01291-624065. Adm. £3.00. Rectangular keep amid extensive fortifications

CONWY CASTLE (C). Tel: 01492-592358. Adm. £3.00. Built by Edward I, 1283-7

*CRICCIETH CASTLE (C). Tel: 01766-522227. Adm. £2.20. Native Welsh 13th-century castle, altered by Edward I

DENBIGH CASTLE (C). Tel: 01745-813979. Adm. free. Remains of the castle (begun 1282), including triple-towered gatehouse

HARLECH CASTLE (C). Tel: 01766-780552. Adm. £3.00. Well-preserved Edwardian castle, constructed 1283-90, on an outcrop above the former shore-line

PEMBROKE CASTLE. Tel: 01646-681510. Adm. £2.95. Castle founded in 1093, with a Great Tower 75 feet tall; birthplace of King Henry VII

†PENRHYN CASTLE (NT), Bangor. Tel: 01248-353084. Closed Tues. Adm. £4.50; grounds only, £3.00. Neo-Norman castle built in the 19th century. Industrial railway museum

PORTMEIRION, Penrhyndeudraeth. Tel: 01766-770228. Adm. £3.20 (April-Oct.); reduced rate in winter. Village in Italianate style

†POWIS CASTLE (NT), nr Welshpool. Tel: 01938-554336. Closed Mon. (except Bank Holidays) and Tues. (except July and Aug.). Adm. £6.00; garden only, £4.00. Medieval castle with interior in variety of styles; 17th-century gardens and Clive of India museum

RAGLAN CASTLE (C). Tel: 01291-690228. Adm. £2.20. Remains of 15th-century castle with moated hexagonal keep

ST DAVIDS BISHOP'S PALACE (C), St Davids. Tel: 01437-720517. Closed Sun. mornings in winter. Adm. £1.70. Remains of residence of Bishops of St Davids built 1328-47

TINTERN ABBEY (C), nr Chepstow. Tel: 01291-689251. Adm. £2.20. Remains of 13th-century church and conventual buildings of a Cistercian monastery

TRETOWER COURT AND CASTLE (C), nr Crickhowell. Tel: 01874-730279. Adm. £2.20. Medieval house with remains of 12th-century castle nearby

SCOTLAND

HS Historic Scotland property
NTS National Trust for Scotland property

ANTONINE WALL (HS), between the Clyde and the Forth. Adm. free. Built about AD 142, consists of ditch, turf rampart and road, with forts every two miles

BALMORAL CASTLE, Aberdeenshire. Tel: 013397-42334. Open May-July. Closed Sun. Adm. £3.00. Mid 19th-century Baronial-style castle built for Victoria and Albert. The Queen's private residence

BLACK HOUSE, ARNOL (HS), Lewis, Western Isles. Tel: 01851-710395. Closed Sun.; also Fri. in winter. Adm. £1.50. Traditional Lewis thatched house

*BLAIR CASTLE, Blair Atholl. Tel: 01796-481207. Adm. £5.00. Mid 18th-century mansion with 13th-century tower; seat of the Dukes of Atholl

*BONAWE IRON FURNACE (HS), Argyll and Bute. Tel: 01866-822432. Closed Sun. mornings. Adm. £2.00. Charcoal-fuelled ironworks founded in 1753

†BOWHILL, Selkirk. Tel: 01750-22204. House open July only; grounds early May to late summer except Fri. Adm. £4.00; grounds only, £1.00. Seat of the Dukes of Buccleuch and Queensberry. Fine collection of paintings, including portrait miniatures

BROUGH OF BIRSAY (HS), Orkney. Adm. free. Remains of Norse church and village on the tidal island of Birsay

CAERLAVEROCK CASTLE (HS), nr Dumfries. Tel: 01387-770244. Closed Sun. mornings. Adm. £2.00. Fine early classical Renaissance building

CALLANISH STANDING STONES (HS), Lewis, Western Isles. Adm. free. Standing stones in a cross-shaped setting, dating from 3000 BC

CATHER TUNS (BROWN AND WHITE) (HS), Aberdeenshire. Adm. free. Two large Iron Age hill forts

*CAWDOR CASTLE, Inverness. Tel: 01667-404615. Adm. £4.70; grounds only, £2.50. A 14th-century keep with 15th- and 17th-century additions

CLAVA CAIRNS (HS), Highland. Adm. free. Late Neolithic or early Bronze Age cairns

*CRATHES CASTLE (NTS), nr Banchory. Tel: 01330-844525. Garden and grounds open all year. Adm. £4.10; garden and grounds only, £1.60; castle only, £1.60. A 16th-century baronial castle in woodland, fields and gardens

*CULZEAN CASTLE (NTS), S. Ayrshire. Tel: 01655-760274. Country park open all year. Adm. £5.50; country park only, £3.00; castle only, £3.50. An 18th-century Adam castle with oval staircase and circular saloon

*DRUMLANRIG CASTLE, nr Dumfries. Tel: 01848-331682. Closed Thurs. Adm. charge. Castle with baroque decorative features and notable art and furniture collections

DRYBURGH ABBEY (HS), Borders. Tel: 01835-822381. Closed Sun. mornings. Adm. £2.00. A 12th-century abbey containing tomb of Sir Walter Scott

*DUNVEGAN CASTLE, Skye. Tel: 01470-521206. Closed Sun. mornings. Adm. £4.00; gardens only, £2.50. A 13th-century castle with later additions; the home of the chiefs of the Clan MacLeod. Boat trips to seal colony

EDINBURGH CASTLE (HS). Tel: 0131-225 9846. Adm. £5.50; war memorial free. Includes the Scottish National War Memorial, Scottish United Services Museum and historic apartments

EDZELL CASTLE (HS), Aberdeenshire. Tel: 01356-648631. Closed Sun. mornings; also Thurs. afternoons and Fri. in winter. Adm. £2.00. Medieval tower house; unique walled garden

*EILEAN DONAN CASTLE, Wester Ross. Tel: 01599-555202. Adm. £2.50. A 13th-century castle with Jacobite relics

ELGIN CATHEDRAL (HS), Moray. Tel: 01343-547171. Closed Sun. mornings; also Thurs. afternoons and Fri. in winter. Adm. £1.50. A 13th-century cathedral with fine chapterhouse

*FLOORS CASTLE, Kelso. Tel: 01573-223333. In Oct. open Sun. and Wed. only. Adm. £3.80. Largest inhabited castle in Scotland; seat of the Dukes of Roxburghe

FORT GEORGE (HS), Highland. Tel: 01667-462777. Closed Sun. mornings. Adm. £2.50. An 18th-century fort

*GLAMIS CASTLE, Angus. Tel: 01307-840242. Adm. £4.70; grounds only, £2.20. Seat of the Lyon family (later Earls of Strathmore and Kinghorne) since 1372

GLASGOW CATHEDRAL (HS). Tel: 0141-552 6891. Closed Sun. mornings. Adm. free. Medieval cathedral with elaborately vaulted crypt

GLENELG BROCH (HS), Highland. Adm. free. Two broch towers with well-preserved structural features

*HOPETOUN HOUSE, nr Edinburgh. Tel: 0131-331 2451. Adm. £3.80; grounds only, £2.00. House designed by Sir William Bruce, enlarged by William Adam

HUNTLY CASTLE (HS). Tel: 01466-793191. Closed Sun. mornings; also Thurs. afternoons and Fri. in winter. Adm. £2.00. Ruin of a 16th- and 17th-century house

*INVERARAY CASTLE, Argyll. Tel: 01499-302203. Closed Fri. (except July-Aug.) and Sun. morning. Woods open all year. Adm. £4.00. Gothic-style 18th-century castle; seat of the Dukes of Argyll

IONA ABBEY, Inner Hebrides. Tel: 01681-700404. Adm. £2.00. Monastery founded by St Columba in AD 563

*JARLSHOF (HS), Shetland. Tel: 01950-460112. Closed Sun. mornings. Adm. £2.00. Remains from Stone Age

JEDBURGH ABBEY (HS), Borders. Tel: 01835-863925. Closed Sun. mornings. Adm. £2.50. Romanesque and early Gothic church founded about 1138

KELSO ABBEY (HS), Borders. Closed Sun. mornings. Adm. free. Remains of great abbey church founded 1128

LINLITHGOW PALACE (HS). Tel: 01506-842896. Closed Sun. mornings. Adm. £2.00. Ruin of royal palace in park setting. Birthplace of Mary, Queen of Scots

MAES HOWE CHAMBERED CAIRN (HS), Orkney. Tel: 01856-761606. Closed Sun. Mornings; also Thurs. mornings and Wed. in winter. Adm. £2.00. Neolithic tomb plundered by Vikings

*MEIGLE SCULPTURED STONE (HS), Angus. Tel: 011828-64612. Closed Sun. mornings. Adm. £1.20. Celtic Christian stones

MELROSE ABBEY (HS), Borders. Tel: 01896-822562. Closed Sun. mornings. Adm. £2.50. Ruin of Cistercian abbey founded c.1136

MOUSA BROCH (HS), Shetland. Adm. free. Finest surviving Iron Age broch tower

NETHER LARGIE CAIRNS (HS), Argyll and Bute. Adm. free. Bronze Age and Neolithic cairns

NEW ABBEY CORN MILL (HS), nr Dumfries. Tel: 01387-850260. Closed Sun. mornings; also Thurs. afternoons and Fri. in winter. Adm. £2.00. Water-powered mill

PALACE OF HOLYROODHOUSE, Edinburgh. Tel: 0131-556 7371. Closed when The Queen is in residence. Adm. £5.00. The Queen's official Scottish residence. Main part of the palace built 1671-9

RING OF BROGAR (HS), Orkney. Adm. free. Neolithic circle of upright stones with an enclosing ditch

RUTHWELL CROSS (HS), Dumfries and Galloway. Adm. free. Seventh-century Anglian cross

ST ANDREWS CASTLE AND CATHEDRAL (HS), Fife. Tel: 01334-477196 (castle); 01334-472563 (cathedral). Adm. £2.00 (castle); £1.50 (cathedral). Closed Sun. mornings. Ruins of 13th-century castle and remains of the largest cathedral in Scotland

*SCONE PALACE, Perth. Tel: 01738-552300. Adm. £4.70; grounds only, £2.35. House built 1802-13 on the site of a medieval palace

SKARA BRAE (HS), Orkney. Tel: 01856-841815. Closed Sun. mornings. Adm. £2.50. Stone-Age village

*SMAILHOLM TOWER (HS), Borders. Closed Sun. mornings. Adm. £1.50. Well-preserved tower-house

STIRLING CASTLE (HS). Tel: 01786-450000. Adm. £3.50. Great Hall and gatehouse of James IV, palace of James V, Chapel Royal remodelled by James VI

TANTALLON CASTLE (HS), E. Lothian. Tel: 01620-892727. Closed Sun. mornings; also Thurs. afternoons and Fri. in winter. Adm. £2.00. Fortification with earthwork defences and a 14th-century curtain wall with towers

*THREAVE CASTLE (HS), Dumfries and Galloway. Tel: 08314-168512. Closed Sun. mornings. Adm. £1.50, including ferry trip. Late 14th-century tower on an island; reached by boat, long walk to castle

URQUHART CASTLE (HS), Loch Ness. Tel: 01456-450551. Adm. £3.00. Closed Sun. morning in winter. Castle remains with well-preserved tower on shore of loch

---

NORTHERN IRELAND

DE Property in the care of the Northern Ireland Department of the Environment

NT National Trust property

CARRICKFERGUS CASTLE (DE), Co. Antrim. Tel: 01960-351273. Closed Sun. mornings. Adm. £2.70. Castle begun in 1180 and garrisoned until 1928

†CASTLE COOLE (NT), Enniskillen. Tel: 01365-322690. Closed Thurs. May-Aug. and Mon.-Fri. in April and Sept. Adm. house, £2.60; estate, £1.50 per car. An 18th-century mansion by James Wyatt in parkland

†CASTLE WARD (NT), Co. Down. Tel: 01396-881204. Closed Thurs. May-Aug. and Mon.-Fri. in April, Sept. and Oct; grounds open all year. Adm. house, £2.60; estate, £3.50 per car. An 18th-century house with Classical west and Gothic east fronts

*DEVENISH ISLAND (DE), Co. Fermanagh. Closed Sun. mornings and Mon. Adm. £2.25. Island monastery founded in the 6th century by St Molaise

DOWNHILL CASTLE (NT), Co. Londonderry. Tel: 01265-848728. Adm. free. Ruins of palatial house in landscaped estate including Mussenden Temple. Temple closed in winter and Mon.-Fri. (except Bank Holidays) in April-June and Sept.

DUNLUCE CASTLE (DE), Co. Antrim. Tel: 012657-31938. Closed Sun. morning (except July and Aug.) Adm. £1.50. Ruins of 16th-century stronghold of the MacDonnells

†FLORENCE COURT (NT), Co. Fermanagh. Tel: 01365-348249. Closed Tues., and Mon.-Fri. (except Bank Holidays) in April and Sept.; grounds open all year. Adm. £2.60; estate £1.50 per car. Mid 18th-century house with rococo plasterwork

*GREY ABBEY (DE), Co. Down. Tel: 01247-788585. Closed Sun. morning and Mon. Adm £1.00. Substantial remains of a Cistercian abbey founded in 1193

HILLSBOROUGH FORT (DE), Co. Down. Closed Sun. mornings and Mon. Adm. free. Built in 1650

†MOUNT STEWART (NT), Co. Down. Tel: 012477-88387. Closed Tues., and Mon.-Fri. in April and Oct. Adm. £3.00. An 18th-century house, childhood home of Lord Castlereagh

NENDRUM MONASTERY (DE), Mahee Island, Co. Down. Closed Sun. mornings and Mon., also Mon.-Fri. in winter. Adm 75p. Founded in the 5th century by St Machaoi

*TULLY CASTLE (DE), Co. Fermanagh. Closed Sun. mornings and Mon. Adm. £1.00. Fortified house and bawn built in 1613

*WHITE ISLAND (DE), Co. Fermanagh. Closed Sun. mornings and Mon. Adm. £2.25. Tenth-century monastery and 12th-century church. Access by ferry

Museums and Galleries

There are more than 2,000 museums and galleries in the United Kingdom. About 1,600 are registered with the Museums and Galleries Commission (*see* page 322), which indicates that they have an appropriate constitution, are soundly financed, have adequate collection management standards and public services, and have access to professional curatorial advice. Museums must achieve full or provisional registration status in order to be eligible for grants from the Museums and Galleries Commission and from Area Museums Councils. Over 700 of the registered museums are run by a local authority.

The national museums and galleries (i.e. the British Museum, the Imperial War Museum, the National Army Museum, the National Galleries of Scotland, the National Gallery, the National Maritime Museum, the National Museums and Galleries on Merseyside, the National Museum of Wales, the National Museums of Scotland, the National Portrait Gallery, the Natural History Museum, the RAF Museum, the Royal Armouries, the Science Museum, the Tate Gallery, the Ulster Folk and Transport Museum, the Ulster Museum, the Victoria and Albert Museum, and the Wallace Collection) receive direct government grant-in-aid. Local authority museums are funded by the local authority and may also receive grants from the Museums and Galleries Commission. Independent museums and galleries mainly rely on their own resources but are also eligible for grants from the Museums and Galleries Commission.

Ten Area Museum Councils in the United Kingdom, which are independent charities that receive an annual grant from the Museums and Galleries Commission, give advice and support to the museums in their area and may offer improvement grants. They also circulate exhibitions and assist with training and marketing.

Opening to the Public

The following is a selection of the museums and art galleries in the United Kingdom. The admission charges given are the standard charges for 1996-7, where a charge is made; many museums have concessionary rates for children, etc. Opening hours vary. Most museums are closed on Christmas Eve, Christmas Day, Boxing Day and New Year's Day; many are closed on Good Friday, and some are closed on May Day Bank Holiday. Some smaller museums close at lunchtimes. Information about a specific museum or gallery should be checked by telephone.

* Local authority museum/gallery

ENGLAND

BARNARD CASTLE, Co. Durham – *The Bowes Museum*, Westwick Road. Tel: 01833-690606. Closed Sun. mornings. Adm. £3.00. European art from the late medieval period to the 19th century; music and costume galleries; English period rooms from Elizabeth I to Victoria; local archaeology

BATH – *American Museum in Britain*, Claverton Manor. Tel: 01225-460503. Closed mornings and Mon. (except Bank Holidays); also closed in winter (except on application). Adm. £5.00 (including house); grounds and galleries only, £2.00. American decorative arts from the 17th to 19th centuries

**Museum of Costume*, Bennett Street. Tel: 01225-477752. Adm. £3.50. Fashion from the 16th century to the present day

**Roman Baths Museum*, Abbey Church Yard. Tel: 01225-477774. Adm. (including 18th-century Pump Room) £5.60. Museum adjoins the remains of a Roman baths and temple complex

**Victoria Art Gallery*, Bridge Street. Tel: 01225-477772. Closed Sun. and Bank Holidays. Adm. free. European Old Masters and British art since the 18th century

BEAMISH, Co. Durham – *Beamish, The North of England Open Air Museum*. Tel: 01207-231811. Closed Mon. and Fri. in winter. Adm. charge. Recreated northern town c.1900, with rebuilt and furnished local buildings, colliery village, farm, railway station, tramway, Pockerley Manor and horse-yard (set c.1800)

BEAULIEU, Hants – *National Motor Museum*. Tel: 01590-612345. Adm. charge. Displays of over 250 vehicles dating from 1895 to the present day

BEVERLEY, N. Humberside – *Museum of Army Transport*, Flemingate. Tel: 01482-860445. Adm. charge. Field workshop, amphibious assault landing, railway section and aircraft

BIRMINGHAM – *Aston Hall*, Albert Road. Tel: 0121-327 0062. Closed mornings and in winter. Adm. free. Jacobean house containing paintings, furniture and tapestries from 17th to 19th centuries

**Birmingham Nature Centre*, Edgbaston. Tel: 0121-472 7775. Closed Mon.-Sat. in winter. Adm. £1.50. Indoor and outdoor enclosures displaying British wildlife

**City Museum and Art Gallery*, Chamberlain Square. Tel: 0121-235 2834. Closed Sun. mornings. Adm. free (except Gas Hall). Includes notable collection of Pre-Raphaelites

**Museum of Science and Industry*, Newhall Street. Tel: 0121-235 1661. Closed Sun. mornings. Adm. free. Vehicles and industrial machinery from the Industrial Revolution to the present; interactive science centre and mechanical musical instrument collection

BRADFORD – *Cartwright Hall Art Gallery*, Lister Park. Tel: 01274-493313. Closed Mon. (except Bank Holidays). Adm. free. British 19th- and 20th-century fine art

**Industrial Museum and Horses at Work*, Moorside Road. Tel: 01274-631756. Closed Mon. (except Bank Holidays). Adm. charge. Engineering, textiles, transport and social history exhibits, including recreated back-to-back cottages, shire horses and horse tram-rides

National Museum of Photography, Film and Television, Pictureville. Tel: 01274-727488. Closed Mon. Adm. free. Photography, film and television equipment and materials, including the only IMAX cinema in the UK and the only public Cinerama theatre in the world

BRIGHTON – *Brighton Museum and Art Gallery*, Church Street. Tel: 01273-603005. Closed Sun. mornings and Wed. Adm. free. Includes fine art, design, fashion, archaeology, Brighton history

BRISTOL – *Arnolfini Gallery*, Narrow Quay. Tel: 0117-929 9191. Adm. free; charge for cinema and events. Contemporary visual arts, dance, theatre, film and music

**Blaise Castle House Museum*, Henbury. Tel: 0117-950 6789. Closed Mon. Adm. free. Agricultural and social history collections in an 18th-century mansion

**Bristol Industrial Museum*, Prince Street. Tel: 0117-925 1470. Closed Mon. Adm. charge. Industrial, maritime and transport collections

*City Museum and Art Gallery, Queen's Road. Tel: 0117-922 3571. Adm. charge. Includes fine and decorative art, oriental art, and Bristol ceramics and paintings

CAMBRIDGE – Duxford Airfield, Duxford. Tel: 01223-835000. Adm. £5.95. Displays of military and civil aircraft, tanks, guns and naval exhibits

Fitzwilliam Museum, Trumpington Street. Tel: 01223-332900. Closed Mon. (except some Bank Holidays) and Sun. mornings. Adm. free. Antiquities, fine and applied arts, clocks, ceramics, manuscripts, furniture, sculpture, coins and medals, temporary exhibitions

CARLISLE – * Tullie House Museum and Art Gallery, Castle Street. Tel: 01228-34781. Closed Sun. mornings. Adm. charge to Border galleries only; ground floor, Old Tullie House and Jacobean galleries, adm. free. Prehistoric archaeology, Hadrian's Wall, Viking and medieval Cumbria, and the social history of Carlisle; also British 19th- and 20th-century art and English porcelain

CHESTER – * Grosvenor Museum, Grosvenor Street. Tel: 01244-321616. Closed Sun. mornings. Adm. free. Roman collections, natural history, art, Chester silver, local history and costume

CHICHESTER – Weald and Downland Open Air Museum, Singleton. Tel: 01243-811348. Closed Mon.,Tues., Thurs., Fri. in winter. Adm. £4.20. Rebuilt vernacular buildings from south-east England; includes medieval houses, agricultural and rural craft buildings and a working watermill

COLCHESTER – * Colchester Castle Museum, Castle Park. Tel: 01206-282939. Closed Sun. mornings. Adm. £3.00. Local archaeological antiquities and displays on Roman Colchester; tours of the Roman vaults, castle walls and chapel with medieval and prison displays

COVENTRY – * Herbert Art Gallery and Museum, Jordan Well. Tel: 01203-832381. Closed Sun. mornings. Local history, archaeology and industry, natural history, oriental ceramics, and fine and decorative art

*Museum of British Road Transport, Hales Street. Tel: 01203-832425. Adm. £3.30. Hundreds of motor vehicles and bicycles

CRICH, nr Matlock, Derbys – National Tramway Museum. Tel: 01773-852565. Closed in winter. Open weekends and Bank Holidays, Mon.-Thurs. April-Sept., and some Fridays. Adm. £5.40. Open-air working museum with tram rides

DERBY – * Derby Museum and Art Gallery, The Strand. Tel: 01332-255586. Closed Sun. mornings and Bank Holiday mornings. Adm. free. Includes paintings by Joseph Wright of Derby and Derby porcelain

*Industrial Museum, off Full Street. Tel: 01332-255308. Closed Sun. mornings and Bank Holiday mornings. Adm. free. Rolls-Royce aero engine collection and a railway engineering gallery

DORCHESTER – Dorset County Museum, High West Street. Tel: 01305-262735. Closed Sun. (except July and Aug.) Adm. £2.35. Includes a collection of Thomas Hardy's manuscripts, books, notebooks and drawings

EXETER – Exeter Maritime Museum, The Haven. Tel: 01392-58075. Adm. £4.25. Collection of working boats from around the world

*Royal Albert Memorial Museum, Queen Street. Tel: 01392-265858. Closed Sun. Adm. free. Natural history, archaeology, ethnography, and fine and decorative art including Exeter silver

GAYDON, Warwick – British Motor Industry Heritage Trust, Banbury Road. Tel: 019626-641188. Adm. charge. History of British motor industry from 1890 to present; classic vehicles; engineering gallery; Corgi and Lucas collections

GLOUCESTER, – National Waterways Museum, The Docks. Tel: 01452-318054. Adm. £4.50. History of Britain's canals and inland waterways

GOSPORT, Hants. – Royal Navy Submarine Museum, Haslar Jetty Road. Tel: 01705-529217. Adm. £3.50. Underwater warfare, including the submarine Alliance; historical and nuclear galleries; and first Royal Navy submarine

HALIFAX – Eureka! The Museum for Children, Discovery Road. Tel: 01426-983191. Adm. £4.75 (over age 12), £3.75 (ages 3-12), free (under age 3). Saver ticket £14.75. Museum designed for children up to age 12

HULL – * Ferens Art Gallery, Queen Victoria Square. Tel: 01482-613902. Closed Sun. mornings. Adm.: non-residents £1.00; residents free. European art, especially Dutch 17th-century paintings, British portraits from 17th to 20th centuries, and marine paintings

*Town Docks Museum, Queen Victoria Square. Tel: 01482-613902. Closed Sun. mornings. Adm.: non-residents £1.00; residents free. Whaling, fishing and navigation exhibits

HUNTINGDON – * Cromwell Museum, Grammar School Walk. Tel: 01480-425830. Closed Mon., and mornings (except Sat. and Sun.) in winter. Adm. free. Portraits and memorabilia relating to Oliver Cromwell

IPSWICH – * Christchurch Mansion and Wolsey Art Gallery, Christchurch Park. Tel: 01473-253246. Closed Sun. mornings and Mon. Adm. free. Tudor house with paintings by Gainsborough, Constable and other Suffolk artists; furniture and 18th-century ceramics. Art gallery for temporary exhibitions

LEEDS – * Abbey House Museum, Kirkstall. Tel: 0113-275 5821. Closed Sun. mornings and Mon. Adm. charge. Toys, games, dolls, and three full-sized period streets

*City Art Gallery, The Headrow. Tel: 0113-247 8248. Closed Sun. mornings. Adm. free. British and European paintings including English watercolours, modern sculpture, Henry Moore gallery, print room

*City Museum, Calverley Street. Tel: 0113-247 8275. Closed Sun. and Mon. Adm. free. Natural history, archaeology, ethnography and coin collections

*Royal Armouries Museum, Armouries Drive. Tel: 0113-220 1900. Adm. £6.95. Antique arms and armour formerly held by Tower of London; five galleries including tournament, war, oriental arms, etc., jousting and simulated fights

LEICESTER – * Jewry Wall Museum, St Nicholas Circle. Tel: 0116-247 3021. Closed Sun. mornings. Adm. free. Archaeology, Roman Jewry Wall and baths, and mosaics

*Leicestershire Museum and Art Gallery, New Walk. Tel: 0116-255 4100. Closed Sun. mornings. Adm. free. Natural history, geology, ancient Egypt gallery, European art and decorative arts

*Snibston Discovery Park, Coalville. Tel: 01530-510851. Adm. charge. Open-air science and industry museum on site of a coal mine; country park with nature trail

LINCOLN – * Museum of Lincolnshire Life, Burton Road. Tel: 01522-528448. Closed Sun. mornings in winter. Adm. charge. Social history and agricultural collection

*Usher Gallery, Lindum Road. Tel: 01522-527980. Closed Sun. mornings. Adm. £1.00. Watches, miniatures, porcelain, silver; collection of Peter de Wint works; Lincolnshire topography; Tennyson memorabilia

LIVERPOOL – Lady Lever Art Gallery, Wirral. Tel: 0151-645 3623. Closed Sun. mornings. Adm. free. Paintings, furniture and porcelain

Liverpool Museum, William Brown Street. Tel: 0151-207 0001. Closed Sun. mornings. Adm. free (except to the Planetarium). Includes Egyptian mummies, weapons and classical sculpture; planetarium, aquarium, vivarium and natural history centre

Merseyside Maritime Museum, Albert Dock. Tel: 0151-207 0001. Joint adm. charge with the Museum of Liverpool Life. Floating exhibits, working displays and craft demonstrations; incorporates *HM Customs and Excise National Museum*

Museum of Liverpool Life, Mann Island. Tel: 0151-207 0001. Joint adm. charge with the Merseyside Maritime Museum. The history of Liverpool

Sudley House, Mossley Hill Road. Tel: 0151-724 3245. Closed Sun. mornings. Adm. free. Late 18th- and 19th-century British paintings in former shipowner's home

Tate Gallery Liverpool, Albert Dock. Tel: 0151-709 3223. Closed Mon. (except Bank Holidays). Adm. free. Twentieth-century painting and sculpture

Walker Art Gallery, William Brown Street. Tel: 0151-207 0001. Closed Sun. mornings. Adm. free. Paintings from the 14th to 20th centuries

LONDON: GALLERIES – *Barbican Art Gallery*, Barbican Centre, EC2. Tel: 0171-382 7105. Temporary exhibitions

Courtauld Institute Galleries, Somerset House, Strand, WC2. Tel: 0171-873 2526. Closed Sun. mornings. Adm. £3.00. The University of London galleries

Dulwich Picture Gallery, College Road, SE21. Tel: 0181-693 5254. Closed Sun. mornings and Mon. Adm. £2.00 (free on Fri.). Built by Sir John Soane to house 17th- and 18th-century paintings

Hayward Gallery, South Bank Centre, SE1. Tel: 0171-928 3144. Adm. £5.00. Temporary exhibitions

National Gallery, Trafalgar Square, WC2. Tel: 0171-839 3321. Closed Sun. mornings. Adm. free. Western painting from the 13th to 20th centuries; early Renaissance collection in the Sainsbury wing

National Portrait Gallery, St Martin's Place, WC2. Tel: 0171-306 0055. Closed Sun. mornings and some Bank Holidays. Adm. free. Portraits of eminent people in British history

Percival David Foundation of Chinese Art, Gordon Square, WC1. Tel: 0171-387 3909. Closed weekends and Bank Holidays. Adm free. Chinese ceramics; charge for use of reference library

Photographers Gallery, Great Newport Street, WC2. Tel: 0171-831 1772. Closed Sun. Adm. free. Temporary exhibitions

The Queen's Gallery, Buckingham Palace, SW1. Tel: 0171-839 1377. Adm. £3.50. Art from the Royal Collection

Royal Academy of Arts, Piccadilly, W1. Tel: 0171-439 7438. Adm. charge. British art since 1750 and temporary exhibitions; annual Summer Exhibition

Serpentine Gallery, Kensington Gardens, W2. Tel: 0171-723 9072. Adm. free. Temporary exhibitions

Tate Gallery, Millbank, SW1. Tel: 0171-887 8000. Closed Sun. mornings. Adm. free (charge for special exhibitions). British painting and 20th-century painting and sculpture

Wallace Collection, Manchester Square, W1. Tel: 0171-935 0687. Closed Sun. mornings. Adm. free. Paintings and drawings, French 18th-century furniture, armour, porcelain and clocks

Whitechapel Art Gallery, Whitechapel High Street, E1. Tel: 0171-522 7878. Closed Mon. Adm. free to most exhibitions. Temporary exhibitions of modern art

LONDON: MUSEUMS – *Bank of England Museum*, Threadneedle Street, EC2. Tel: 0171-601 5545. Closed weekends and Bank Holidays. Adm. free. History of the Bank since 1694

Bethnal Green Museum of Childhood, Cambridge Heath Road, E2. Tel: 0181-980 3204. Closed Sun. mornings and Fri. Adm. free but donations invited. Toys, games and exhibits relating to the social history of childhood

British Museum, Great Russell Street, WC1. Tel: 0171-636 1555. Closed Sun. mornings. Adm. free. Antiquities, coins, medals, prints and drawings, European history galleries

Cabinet War Rooms, King Charles Street, SW1. Tel: 0171-930 6961. Adm. £4.20. Underground rooms used by Churchill and the Government during the Second World War

Commonwealth Institute, Kensington High Street, W8. Tel: 0171-603 4535. Closed for redevelopment until spring 1997. Exhibitions on Commonwealth nations, visual arts and crafts

Cutty Sark, Greenwich, SE10. Tel: 0181-858 3445. Adm. £3.25. Restored and rerigged tea clipper with exhibits on board. Sir Francis Chichester's round-the-world yacht, *Gipsy Moth IV*, can also be seen (separate adm. charge)

Design Museum, Shad Thames, SE1. Tel: 0171-378 6055. Adm. £4.75. The development of design and the mass-production of consumer objects

Geffrye Museum, Kingsland Road, E2. Tel: 0171-739 9893. Closed Mon.; also Sun. and Bank Holiday mornings. Adm. free. English urban domestic interiors from 1600–1950s; also paintings, furniture, decorative arts, walled herb garden and knot garden

HMS Belfast, Morgans Lane, Tooley Street, SE1. Tel: 0171-407 6434. Adm £4.40. Life on a warship, illustrated on World War II warship

Horniman Museum and Gardens, London Road, SE23. Tel: 0181-699 1872. Closed Sun. mornings. Adm. free. Museum of ethnography, musical instruments, natural history and aquarium. Reference library (by appointment)

Imperial War Museum, Lambeth Road, SE1. Tel: 0171-416 5000. Reference departments closed Sat. (except by appointment) and Sun. Adm. £4.50 (free after 4.30 p.m. daily). All aspects of the two world wars and other military operations involving Britain and the Commonwealth since 1914

Jewish Museum, Albert Street, NW1. Tel: 0171-284 1997. Closed Fri., Sat., public and Jewish holidays. Adm. £3.00. Jewish life, history and religion

London Transport Museum, Covent Garden, WC2. Tel: 0171-379 6344. Adm. charge. Vehicles, photographs and graphic art relating to the history of transport in London

MCC Museum, Lord's, NW8. Tel: 0171-289 1611. Open match days (closed Sun. mornings); also conducted tours by appointment with Tours Manager. Adm. charge. Cricket museum

Museum of Garden History, Lambeth Palace Road SE1. Tel: 0171-401 8865. Open daily except Sat. Closed Dec.-Feb. Adm free. Exhibition of aspects of garden history and re-created 17th-century garden

Museum of London, London Wall, EC2. Tel: 0171-600 3699. Closed Sun. mornings and Mon. Adm. £3.50 (free after 4.30 p.m. daily). History of London from prehistoric times to present day

Museum of Mankind, Burlington Gardens, W1. Tel: 0171-437 2224. Closed Sun. mornings. Adm. free. The ethnographical collections of the British Museum

Museum of the Moving Image, South Bank, SE1. Tel: 0171-401 2636. Adm. £5.95. History of the moving image in cinema and television

National Army Museum, Royal Hospital Road, SW3. Tel: 0171-730 0717. Adm. free. History of the British soldier; the Indian Army room at the Royal Military Academy, Sandhurst, may be viewed by appointment

National Maritime Museum, Greenwich, SE10. Tel: 0181-858 4422. Reference library closed Sat. (except by appointment) and Sun. Comprises the main building,

the Old Royal Observatory and the Queen's House (*see* page 576). Adm. charge. Maritime history of Britain
Natural History Museum, Cromwell Road, sw7. Tel: 0171-938 9123. Adm. £5.50. Natural history collections
Royal Air Force Museum, Colindale, nw9. Tel: 0181-205 2266. Adm. £5.20. Aviation from before the Wright brothers to the present-day RAF; historic aircraft
Royal Mews, Buckingham Palace, sw1. Tel: 0171-839 1377. Open Tues.-Thurs. afternoons in summer, Wed. only in winter. Adm. £3.50. Carriages, coaches, stables and horses
Science Museum, Exhibition Road, sw7. Tel: 0171-938 8000. Adm. charge. Science, technology, industry and medicine collections
Shakespeare Globe Exhibition, Bankside, se1. Tel: 0171-928 6406. Adm. £4.00. Recreation of Elizabethan theatre using 16th-century techniques
Sherlock Holmes Museum, Baker Street, nw1. Tel: 0171-935 8866. Adm. £5.00. Recreated rooms of the fictional detective
Sir John Soane's Museum, Lincoln's Inn Fields, wc2. Tel: 0171-430 0175. Closed Sun. and Mon. Adm. free. Art and antiques, temporary exhibitions
Theatre Museum, Russell Street, wc2. Tel: 0171-836 7891. Closed Mon. Adm. £3.00. History of the performing arts
Tower Bridge Experience, se1. Tel: 0171-378 1928. Adm. £5.50. History of the bridge and display of Victorian steam machinery; panoramic views from walkways
Victoria and Albert Museum, Cromwell Road, sw7. Tel: 0171-938 8500. Closed Mon. mornings. Adm. £5.00. Includes National Art Library and Print Room (closed Sun. and Mon.) Adm. free but donations invited. Fine and applied art and design, including furniture, glass, textiles, dress collections
Wellington Museum, Apsley House, w1 (*see* page 574)
Wimbledon Lawn Tennis Museum, Church Road, sw19. Tel; 0181-946 6131. Closed Sun. mornings and Mon. Adm. £2.50. Tennis trophies, fashion and memorabilia
Manchester – *City Art Galleries*, Mosley Street and Princess Street. Tel: 0161-236 5244. Closed Sun. mornings. Adm. free. Includes Old Masters, Turner, Gainsborough, Stubbs, the Pre-Raphaelites and 20th century art
Gallery of English Costume, Rusholme. Tel: 0161-224 5217. Closed Sun., Mon. Adm. free. Exhibits from the 16th to 20th centuries
Manchester Museum, Oxford Road. Tel: 0161-275 2634. Closed Sun. Adm. free. Archaeology, archery, botany, Egyptology, entomology, ethnography, geology, natural history, numismatics, oriental and zoology collections
Museum of Science and Industry, Castlefield. Tel: 0161-832 1830. Adm. £4.00. On site of world's oldest passenger railway station; galleries relating to space, energy, power, transport, aviation and social history; interactive science centre
Whitworth Art Gallery, Oxford Road. Tel: 0161-275 7450. Closed Sun. mornings. Adm. free. Watercolours, drawings, prints, textiles, wallpapers and 20th-century British art
Newcastle upon Tyne – *Laing Art Gallery*, Higham Place. Tel: 0191-232 7734. Closed Sun. mornings. Adm. free. British and European art, ceramics, glass, silver, textiles and costume; local arts and crafts
Newcastle Discovery Museum, West Blandford Square. Tel: 0191-232 6789. Closed Sun. Adm. free. Local history, fashion, power, and Tyneside's maritime history; hands-on science centre

Newmarket – *National Horseracing Museum*, High Street. Tel: 01638-667333. Closed Mon. (except Bank Holidays, July and Aug.), Sun. mornings and Jan.-March. Adm. £3.30. Paintings, trophies and exhibits relating to horseracing
Norwich – *Castle Museum*. Tel: 01603-223624. Closed Sun. mornings. in winter. Adm. charge. Art (including Norwich school), archaeology, natural history, teapot collection; guided tours of battlements and dungeons
Nottingham – *Brewhouse Yard Museum*, Castle Boulevard. Tel: 0115-948 3504. Adm. free (except weekends and Bank Holidays). Daily life from the 17th to 20th centuries
Castle Museum. Tel: 0115-948 3504. Adm. free (except weekends and Bank Holidays). Paintings, ceramics, silver and glass; history of Nottingham
Industrial Museum, Wollaton Park. Tel: 0115-928 4602. Closed Sun. mornings, and Mon.-Wed. in winter. Adm. free (except weekends and Bank Holidays). Lacemaking machinery, steam engines and transport exhibits
Museum of Costume and Textiles, Castle Gate. Tel: 0115-948 3504. Adm. free. Costume displays from 1790 to the mid 20th-century in period rooms
Natural History Museum, Wollaton Park. Tel: 0115-928 1333. Closed Sun. mornings. Adm. free (except weekends and Bank Holidays) Local natural history and wildlife dioramas
Oxford – *Ashmolean Museum*, Beaumont Street. Tel: 01865-278000. Closed Mon. (except Bank Holidays) and Sun. mornings. Adm. free. European and Oriental fine and applied arts, archaeology, Egyptology and numismatics
Museum of Modern Art, Pembroke Street. Tel: 01865-722733. Closed Mon. Adm. £2.50. Temporary exhibitions
Oxford University Museum, Parks Road. Tel: 01865-272950. Closed mornings (except for school parties by appointment) and Sun. Adm. free. Entomology, geology, mineralogy and zoology
Plymouth – *City Museum and Art Gallery*, Drake Circus. Tel: 01752-264878. Closed Mon. (except Bank Holidays) and Sun. Adm. free. Local and natural history, ceramics, silver, Old Masters, temporary exhibitions
The Dome, The Hoe. Tel: 01752-603300. Adm. charge. Maritime history museum
Portsmouth – *Charles Dickens Birthplace Museum*, Old Commercial Road. Tel: 01705-827261. Closed in winter. Adm. charge. Dickens memorabilia
D-Day Museum, Clarence Esplanade. Tel: 01705-827261. Adm. charge. Includes the Overlord Embroidery
Naval Heritage Area, HM Naval Base. Story of the Royal Navy using HMS *Victory* (tel: 01705-819604), HMS *Warrior* (tel: 01705-291379), and the *Mary Rose* (tel: 01705-750521). Separate adm. charge to each, combined tickets available
Royal Naval Museum, HM Naval Base. Tel: 01705-733060. Adm. charge. History of the Royal Navy
Preston – *Harris Museum and Art Gallery*, Market Square. Tel: 01772-258248. Closed Sun. and Bank Holidays. Adm. free. British art since the 18th century, ceramics, glass, costume and local history; also contemporary exhibitions
St Albans – *Verulamium Museum*, St Michael's. Tel: 01727-819339. Closed Sun. mornings. Adm. £2.60. Iron Age and Roman Verulamium, including wall plasters, jewellery, mosaics and room reconstructions
St Ives, Cornwall – *Tate Gallery St Ives*, Porthmeor Beach. Tel: 01736-796226. Closed Mon. Oct.-March. Adm. £3.00. Painting and sculpture by artists associated with St Ives

SHEFFIELD – *City Museum and Mappin Art Gallery*, Weston Park. Tel: 0114-276 8588. Closed Mon. Adm. free. Includes applied arts, natural history, archaeology and ethnography, 19th- and 20th-century art
Graves Art Gallery, Surrey Street. Tel: 0114-273 5858. Closed Sun. Adm. free. British art from the 16th to 20th centuries. Old Masters and non-European art
Kelham Island Industrial Museum, off Alma Street. Tel: 0114-272 2106. Closed Fri. and Sat. Adm. charge. Local industrial and social history
Shepherd Wheel, off Hangingwater Road. Tel: 0114-236 7731. Closed Mon. and Tues. Adm. free. Water-powered cutlery-grinding wheel and workshops
STOKE-ON-TRENT – *City Museum and Art Gallery*, Hanley. Tel: 01782-202173. Closed Sun. mornings. Adm. free. Pottery, china and porcelain collections
Etruria Industrial Museum, Etruria. Tel: 01782-287557. Closed Mon. and Tues. Adm. free. Britain's sole surviving steam-powered potter's mill
Gladstone Pottery Museum, Longton. Tel: 01782-319232. Adm. charge. A working Victorian pottery. Pottery factory tours are available by arrangement Mon.–Fri., except during factory holidays, at the following: *Royal Doulton*, Burslem; *Spode*, Stoke; *John Beswick*, Longton; *Wedgwood*, Barlaston; *W. Moorcroft*, Cobridge; *H & R Johnson Tiles*, Tunstall; *Moorland Pottery*, Burslem; *Peggy Davies Ceramics*, Stoke; *Staffordshire Enamels*, Longton; *St George's Fine Bone China*, Hanley
STYAL, Cheshire – *Quarry Bank Mill*. Tel: 01625-527468. Closed Mon. in winter. Adm. charge. Working mill illustrating history of cotton industry; costumed display at restored Apprentice House
TELFORD – *Ironbridge Gorge Museum*. Tel: 01952-433522. Smaller sites closed in winter. Adm. charge for each site; £8.95 for all sites (ticket valid until all sites have been visited). First iron bridge; early 20th-century working town; Museum of the River; Museum of Iron; Jackfield Tile Museum; Coalport China Museum
TRING, Herts – *Tring Zoological Museum*, Akeman Street. Tel: 01442-824181. Closed Sun. mornings. Adm. £2.20. Display of more than 4,000 animal species
WAKEFIELD – *Yorkshire Sculpture Park*, West Bretton. Tel: 01924-830302. Adm. free. Open-air sculpture gallery including works by Moore, Hepworth, Frink and others
WORCESTER – *City Museum and Art Gallery*, Foregate Street. Tel: 01905-25371. Closed Thurs. and Sun. Adm. free. Includes a military museum, 19th-century chemist's shop and changing art exhibitions
Museum of Worcester Porcelain and Royal Worcester Factory, Severn Street. Tel: 01905-23221. Closed Sun. Adm. £1.50. Worcester porcelain collection; factory tours on weekdays
WROUGHTON, nr Swindon, Wilts – *Science Museum*, Wroughton Airfield. Tel: 01793-814466. Open selected summer weekends only. Adm. charge. Air displays and some of the Science Museum's transport and agricultural collection
YEOVIL, Somerset – *Fleet Air Arm Museum*, Royal Naval Air Station, Yeovilton. Tel: 01935-840565. Adm. charge. History of naval aviation; historic aircraft, including Concorde 002
Montacute House, Montacute. Tel: 01935-823289. Closed mornings and Tues.; also closed in winter. Adm. £4.80. Elizabethan and Jacobean portraits from the National Portrait Gallery
YORK – *Beningbrough Hall*, Shipton-by-Beningbrough. Tel: 01904-470666. Closed Thurs. and Fri. (except Good Friday and July-Aug.); also closed in winter. Adm. £4.50. Portraits from the National Portrait Gallery

Castle Museum. Tel: 01904-653611. Adm. £4.20. Reconstructed streets; costume and military collections
City Art Gallery, Exhibition Square. Tel: 01904-623839. Closed Sun. mornings. Adm. free. European and British painting spanning seven centuries; modern pottery
Jorvik Viking Centre, Coppergate. Tel: 01904-643211. Adm. £4.95. Reconstruction of Viking York
National Railway Museum, Leeman Road. Tel: 01904-621261. Adm. £4.50. Includes locomotives, rolling stock and carriages
Yorkshire Museum, Museum Gardens. Tel: 01904-629745. Closed Sun. mornings in winter. Adm. £3.00. Yorkshire life from Roman to medieval times; geology gallery

WALES

BODELWYDDAN, Denbighshire – *Bodelwyddan Castle*. Tel: 01745-584060. Opening times vary. Adm. charge. Portraits from the National Portrait Gallery, furniture from the Victoria and Albert Museum and sculptures from the Royal Academy
CAERLEON – *Roman Legionary Museum*. Tel: 01633-423134. Closed Sun. mornings. Adm. charge. Material from the site of the Roman fortress of Isca and its suburbs
CARDIFF – *National Museum of Wales*, Cathays Park. Tel: 01222-397951. Closed Sun. mornings and Mon. (except Bank Holidays). Adm. charge. Includes natural sciences, archaeology and Impressionist paintings
Museum of Welsh Life, St Fagans. Tel: 01222-569441. Adm. charge. Open-air museum with re-erected buildings, agricultural equipment and costume
Welsh Industrial and Maritime Museum, Bute Street. Tel: 01222-481919. Closed Sun. mornings and Mon. (except Bank Holidays). Adm. charge. Power, railways, locomotives and shipping exhibitions; miniature railway
DRE-FACH FELINDRE, nr Llandysul – *Museum of the Welsh Woollen Industry*. Tel: 01559-370929. Closed Sun., and Sat. in winter. Adm. charge. Exhibitions, a working woollen mill and craft workshops
LLANBERIS, nr Caernarfon – *Welsh Slate Museum*. Tel: 01286-870630. Closed in winter (except by appointment). Adm. charge. Former slate quarry with original machinery and plant; slate crafts demonstrations
SWANSEA – *Glyn Vivian Art Gallery and Museum*, Alexandra Road. Tel: 01792-655006. Closed Mon. (except Bank Holidays). Adm. free. Paintings, ceramics, Swansea pottery and porcelain, clocks, glass and Welsh art
Swansea Maritime and Industrial Museum, Museum Square. Tel: 01792-650351. Closed Mon. (except Bank Holidays). Adm. free. Includes a working woollen mill and historic boats

SCOTLAND

ABERDEEN – *Aberdeen Art Gallery*, Schoolhill. Tel: 01224-646333. Closed Sun. mornings. Adm. free. Art from the 18th to 20th centuries
Aberdeen Maritime Museum, Shiprow. Tel: 01224-585788. Closed Sun. Adm. free. Maritime history, including shipbuilding and North Sea oil
EDINBURGH – *City Art Centre*, Market Street. Tel: 0131-529 3993. Closed Sun. Adm. free. Late 19th- and 20th-century art and temporary exhibitions

Huntly House Museum, Canongate. Tel: 0131-529 4143.
Closed Sun. Adm. free. Local history, silver, glass and
Scottish pottery
Museum of Childhood, High Street. Tel: 0131-529 4142.
Closed Sun. Adm. free. Toys, games, clothes and
exhibits relating to the social history of childhood
Museum of Flight, East Fortune Airfield, nr North
Berwick. Tel: 01620-880308. Closed in winter. Adm.
charge. Display of more than 30 aircraft
National Gallery of Scotland, The Mound. Tel: 0131-556
8921. Closed Sun. mornings. Adm. free. Paintings,
drawings and prints from the 16th to 20th centuries, and
the national collection of Scottish art
The People's Story, Canongate. Tel: 0131-529 4057.
Closed Sun. Adm. free. Edinburgh life since the 18th
century
Royal Museum of Scotland, Chambers Street. Tel: 0131-
225 7534. Closed Sun. mornings. Adm. free. Scottish and
international collections from prehistoric times to the
present
Scottish Agricultural Museum, Ingliston. Tel: 0131-225
7534. Closed in winter and on Sun.; also on Sat. in May
and Sept. Adm. free. History of agriculture in Scotland
Scottish National Portrait Gallery, Queen Street. Tel:
0131-556 8921. Closed Sun. mornings. Adm. free.
Portraits of eminent people in Scottish history, and the
national collection of photography
Scottish National Gallery of Modern Art, Belford Road. Tel:
0131-556 8921. Closed Sun. mornings. Adm. free.
Twentieth-century painting, sculpture and graphic art
Scottish United Services Museum, Edinburgh Castle. Tel:
0131-225 7534. Closed Sun. mornings in winter. Adm.
free. History of the armed forces of Scotland
The Writer's Museum, Lawnmarket. Tel: 0131-529 4901.
Closed Sun. Adm. free. Robert Louis Stevenson, Walter
Scott and Robert Burns exhibits
FORT WILLIAM – *West Highland Museum*, Cameron Square.
Tel: 01397-702169. Closed until May 1997. Includes
tartan collections and exhibits relating to 1745 uprising
GLASGOW – *Burrell Collection*, Pollokshaws Road. Tel:
0141-649 7151. Adm. free. Nineteenth-century
paintings, textiles, furniture, ceramics, stained glass and
silver
Gallery of Modern Art, Queen Street. Tel: 0141-229 1996.
Adm. free. Collection of contemporary Scottish and
world art
Glasgow Art Gallery and Museum, Kelvingrove. Tel: 0141-
287 2000. Adm. free. Includes Old Masters, 19th-
century French paintings and armour collection
Hunterian Art Gallery, Hillhead Street. Tel: 0141-330
5431. Closed Sun. Adm. free. Rennie Mackintosh and
Whistler collections; also Old Masters and modern
prints
McLellan Galleries, Sauchiehall Street. Tel: 0141-331
1854. Adm. charge. Temporary exhibitions
Museum of Transport, Bunhouse Road. Tel: 0141-287
2000. Adm. free. Includes a reproduction of a 1938
Glasgow street, cars since the 1930s, trams and a
Glasgow subway station
People's Palace Museum, Glasgow Green. Tel: 0141-554
0223. Adm. free. History of Glasgow since 1175
Pollok House, Pollokshaws Road. Tel: 0141-649 7547.
Adm. free. Spanish paintings, furniture, silver and
ceramics
St Mungo Museum of Religious Life and Art, Castle Street.
Tel: 0141-553 2557. Adm. free. Explores universal
themes through objects of all the main world religions

NORTHERN IRELAND

BELFAST – *Ulster Museum*, Botanic Gardens. Tel: 01232-
383000. Closed weekend mornings. Adm. free. Irish
antiquities, natural and local history, fine and applied
arts
HOLYWOOD, Co. Down – *Ulster Folk and Transport Museum*,
Cultra. Tel. 01232-428428. Closed Sun. mornings, also
Sat. mornings in winter. Adm. £3.30. Indoor galleries
and reconstructed buildings in the open air, Irish
National Railway and Titanic exhibitions
LONDONDERRY – *The Tower Museum*, Union Hall Place.
Tel: 01504-372411. Closed Sun. morning July-Aug.;
Sun. and Mon. (except Bank Holidays) Sep.-June. Adm.
£3.00. Tells the story of Ireland through the history of
Londonderry
OMAGH, Co. Tyrone – *Ulster American Folk Park*,
Castletown. Tel: 01662-243292. Closed weekends in
winter. Adm. £3.50. Open-air museum telling the story
of Ulster's emigrants to America; restored or recreated
dwellings and workshops; ship and dockside gallery

Cost of Living and Inflation Rates

The first cost of living index to be calculated took July 1914 as 100 and was based on the pattern of expenditure of working-class families in 1914. The cost of living index was superseded in 1947 by the general index of retail prices (RPI), although the older term is still popularly applied to it.

GENERAL INDEX OF RETAIL PRICES

The general index of retail prices measures the changes month by month in the average level of prices of goods and services purchased by most households in the United Kingdom. The spending pattern on which the index is based is revised each year, mainly using information from the Family Expenditure Survey. The expenditure of certain higher income households and of households mainly dependent on state pensions is excluded.

The index is compiled using a selection of over 600 goods and services and the prices charged for these items are collected at regular intervals in about 180 locations throughout the country. For the index, the price changes are weighted in accordance with the pattern of consumption of the average family.

INFLATION RATE

The twelve-monthly percentage change in the 'all items' index of the RPI is usually referred to as the rate of inflation. The percentage change in prices between any two months/years can be obtained using the following formula:

$$\frac{\text{Later date RPI} - \text{Earlier date RPI}}{\text{Earlier date RPI}} \times 100$$

e.g. to find the rate of inflation for 1988, using the annual averages for 1987 and 1988:

$$\frac{106.9 - 101.9}{101.9} \times 100 = 4.9\%$$

PURCHASING POWER OF THE POUND

Changes in the internal purchasing power of the pound may be defined as the 'inverse' of changes in the level of prices; when prices go up, the amount which can be purchased with a given sum of money goes down. To find the purchasing power of the pound in one month or year, given that it was 100p in a previous month or year, the calculation would be:

$$100p \times \frac{\text{Earlier month/year RPI}}{\text{Later month/year RPI}}$$

Thus, if the purchasing power of the pound is taken to be 100p in 1975, the comparable purchasing power in 1995 would be:

$$100p \times \frac{34.2}{149.1} = 22.94p$$

For longer term comparisons, it has been the practice to use an index which has been constructed by linking together the RPI for the period 1962 to date; an index derived from the consumers expenditure deflator for the period from 1938 to 1962; and the prewar 'Cost of Living' index for the period 1914 to 1938. This long-term index enables the internal purchasing power of the pound to be calculated for any year from 1914 onwards. It should be noted that these figures can only be approximate.

	Long-term index of consumer goods and services (Jan. 1987 = 100)	Comparable purchasing power of £1 in 1995	Rate of inflation (annual average)
1914	2.8	53.25	
1915	3.5	42.60	
1920	7.0	21.30	
1925	5.0	29.82	
1930	4.5	33.13	
1935	4.0	37.28	
1938	4.4	33.89	
There are no official figures for 1939–45			
1946	7.4	20.15	
1950	9.0	16.57	
1955	11.2	13.31	
1960	12.6	11.83	
1965	14.8	10.07	
1970	18.5	8.06	
1975	34.2	4.36	
1980	66.8	2.23	18.0
1981	74.8	1.99	11.9
1982	81.2	1.84	8.6
1983	84.9	1.76	4.6
1984	89.2	1.67	5.0
1985	94.6	1.58	6.1
1986	97.8	1.52	3.4
1987	101.9	1.46	4.2
1988	106.9	1.39	4.9
1989	115.2	1.29	7.8
1990	126.1	1.18	9.5
1991	133.5	1.12	5.9
1992	138.5	1.08	3.7
1993	140.7	1.06	1.6
1994	144.1	1.03	2.4
1995	149.1	1.00	3.5

Gaming and Lotteries

Gaming and lotteries in the UK are officially regulated and may only be run by licensed operators or in licensed premises. Responsibility for policy and the laws on gaming and lotteries rests with the Home Secretary. Supervision of gaming and lottery operations is mostly the responsibility of the Gaming Board of Great Britain, although the National Lottery (*see* below) is regulated by the Director-General of the National Lottery through the Office of the National Lottery.

Most betting is on horseracing and greyhound racing, and may take place at racecourses and greyhound tracks, or at off-course betting offices. The amount spent on on-course betting cannot be calculated precisely since no duty is payable on it and therefore no returns are made; however, it is estimated to be about 10 per cent of the figures for off-course betting.

Off-Course Betting (UK)

	£ million
1993–4	6,385
1994–5	6,562
1995–6	6,257p

p provisional
Source: Horserace Totalisator Board

Other forms of gaming and lotteries include the following (for National Lottery, *see* below):

Number of casinos operating	119
Drop	£2,461m
Bingo clubs licensed	972
Amount staked (£ million)	£811m
Gaming machines licensed	271,272*
Society lottery schemes registered	377
Local authority lottery schemes registered	25
Number of lotteries held under registered schemes	1,144
Total ticket sales (£ million)	£38.74m

* 1993–4 figure
Source: Annual Report of the Gaming Board of Great Britain 1994–5

THE NATIONAL LOTTERY

The National Lottery is run by a private company, Camelot. The Office of the National Lottery regulates the National Lottery operations and licenses games promoted as part of the Lottery.

The first National Lottery tickets draw was made on 19 November 1994 and scratchcards were introduced on 25 March 1995. Tickets and scratchcards cost £1. The average number of tickets sold each week in the first year of the Lottery was about 63,893,000, and the average number of scratchcards sold each week was about 32,813,000. An estimated two-thirds of the adult population buy lottery tickets each week and spend an average of £2.60. About 15–20 per cent of the adult population purchases scratchcards; accurate data is difficult to obtain but it is estimated that most players buy about three scratchcards a week. From November 1994 to February 1996 more than £5,900 million was raised by the National Lottery.

Fifty per cent of the proceeds are used in prize money; the Government receives 12 per cent in tax; the retailer receives 5 per cent; Camelot receives 5 per cent; and the remaining 28 per cent is divided equally between the five 'good causes' (*see* below). If the jackpot prize is not won, it is 'rolled over' to the following week; the first multi-million jackpot prize of £17,880,000 was won by one individual on 10 December 1994 as the result of a roll-over. The highest individual win to date was £22,590,000 on 10 June 1995.

LOTTERY AWARDS

Seventy-seven per cent of awards made by the 11 disbursing bodies were for less than £100,000; 2.4 per cent were for more than £1 million. Most awards are conditional on partnership funding being obtained from other sources.

Awards Made *to February 1996*

Awards, Total - 5,121 to the total value of £1,225,957,787

Arts Awards, Total - 842 awards to the total value of £319,533,744

Arts Council of England - 466 awards to the total value of £280,876,872. Twelve awards were for more than £3 million, including £55 million to the Royal Opera House, Covent Garden, £41.1 million to the Lowry Centre and £30 million to Sadler's Wells Theatre

Arts Council of Wales - 159 awards to the total value of £10,263,012. Three awards were for more than £1 million, including £2 million to the Cardiff Old Library Trust

Scottish Arts Council - 142 awards to the total value of £22,986,792. Six awards were for more than £1 million, including £3 million to the Edinburgh Festival Society

Arts Council of Northern Ireland - 75 awards to the total value of £5,407,067. Three awards were for more than £300,000, including £3 million to Armagh City and District Council for a new theatre/arts centre

Millennium Commission - 310 awards to the total value of £443,448,385. Thirteen awards were for more than £10 million, including £50 million to the new Tate Gallery of Modern Art, £50 million to the Earth Centre, Conisbrough, £46 million to South Glamorgan County Council and the Welsh Rugby Union for the Millennium Stadium, £42.5 million to Sustrans National Cycle Network, £40 million to the Renaissance of Portsmouth Harbour and £21.5 million to the Millennium Seed Bank at the Royal Botanic Gardens, Kew

National Heritage Memorial Fund - 221 awards to the total value of £117,001,647. Seven awards were for more than £5 million, including £13.25 million to the Sir Winston Churchill Archive Trust, £10.277 million to the National Trust for Scotland for the Mar Lodge Estate, £8 million to the National Gallery for Seurat's *The Channel of Gravelines* and £7.65 million to the Lowry Centre

National Lottery Charities Board - 2,460 awards to the total value of £159,081,946. Twelve awards were for more than £500,000, including £682,000 to St Chad's Community Project, Tyne and Wear, £666,177 to Strathclyde Poverty Alliance, £647,725 to Wirral Mind and £600,000 to Barnado's

Sport Awards, Total - 1,288 awards to the total value of £186,892,065

THE SPORTS COUNCIL - 911 awards to the total value of £152,066,880. Nine awards were for more than £3 million, including £5.756 to North Tyneside Council for the regeneration of Smith Park, £4.895 million to the London Borough of Hackney for the Clissold Leisure Centre and £4.417 million to the Jubilee Sailing Trust, Hants

SPORTS COUNCIL FOR WALES - 111 awards to the total value of £9,763,218. Two awards were for more than £500,000, including £1.418 million to Wrexham Maelor Borough Council for its swimming baths

SCOTTISH SPORTS COUNCIL - 166 awards to the total value of £18,474,658. Four awards were for more than £700,000, including £1.5 million to Tayside Regional Council for the Maryfield Regional Sports Complex

SPORTS COUNCIL FOR NORTHERN IRELAND - 100 awards to the value of £6,587,309. Three awards were for more than £400,000, including £500,000 to Lisburn Racquets Club

REGIONAL BREAKDOWN OF AWARDS BY VALUE
To February 1996

	% of total UK population	% of value of total awards made
England	83.3	71.86
London		22.67
North-West		10.04
North-East		3.95
Yorks and Humberside		7.15
Eastern		5.50
East Midlands		2.25
West Midlands		4.52
South-West		4.34
South-East		9.65
Merseyside		1.28
England-wide		0.52
Scotland	8.9	10.10
Wales	5.0	10.33
N. Ireland	2.8	2.27
UK-wide projects		5.45

Sources: Department of National Heritage; Office of the National Lottery

Duty and Tax-free Allowances

Travellers are entitled to the allowances in either of the columns below (but not both) for any category of goods (*see* Notes on Allowances). Passengers under 17 are not, however, entitled to tobacco and drinks allowances.

COLUMN 1

Goods obtained duty and tax-free in the European Union (e.g. in duty-free shops), or duty and tax-free on a ship or aircraft, or goods obtained outside the European Union

COLUMN 2

Suggested guidelines for goods obtained duty and tax paid in the European Union

COLUMN 1	COLUMN 2
Tobacco goods	*Tobacco goods*
200 cigarettes	800 cigarettes
or	*plus*
100 cigarillos	400 cigarillos
or	*plus*
50 cigars	200 cigars
or	*plus*
250 grammes of tobacco	1 kg of tobacco
Alcoholic drinks	*Alcoholic drinks*
2 litres of still table wine	90 litres of still table wine (not more than 60 litres should
plus	be sparkling wine)
1 litre over 22% vol. (e.g. spirits and strong liqueurs)	*plus*
	10 litres over 22% vol. (e.g. spirits and strong liqueurs)
or	*plus*
2 litres not over 22% vol. (e.g. low strength liqueurs, fortified wine or sparkling wine)	20 litres not over 22% vol. (e.g. low strength liqueurs, fortified wine)
or	*plus*
A further 2 litres of still table wine	110 litres of beer
Perfume	*Perfume*
50 grammes (60 cc or 2 fl oz)	No limit
Toilet water	*Toilet water*
250 cc (9 fl oz)	No limit
Other goods	*Other goods*
£75 worth	No limit

NB: A maximum of 50 litres of beer may be imported duty-free, subject to the limitations of the 'Other goods' monetary allowance.

Anyone visiting the United Kingdom for less than six months is also entitled to bring in, free of duty and tax, all personal effects (except tobacco goods, alcoholic drinks and perfume) which they intend to take with them when they leave.

NOTES ON ALLOWANCES

1 The countries of the European Union are Austria, Belgium, Denmark, Finland, France, Germany, Greece, the Irish Republic, Italy, Luxembourg, the Netherlands, Portugal, Spain (but not the Canary Islands), Sweden, and the United Kingdom (but not the Channel Islands)

2 The allowances apply only to goods carried and cleared by travellers at the time of their arrival

3 The allowances do not apply to goods brought in for sale or for other commercial purposes

4 Reduced allowances apply to certain persons crossing the Irish land boundary and to seamen and aircrew members

5 Whisky, gin, rum, brandy, vodka and most liqueurs normally exceed 22% vol. (38.8° proof) but advocaat, cassis, fraise, suze and aperitifs may be less. Fortified wines include port, sherry, vermouth and madeira. Sparkling wines include champagne, perelada, spumante and semi-sparkling wines. Still table wines include claret, Sauterne, Graves and Chianti. Burgundy, Chablis, hock and Moselle may be either sparkling or still, depending on manufacture

6 Goods obtained duty and tax-free or outside the European Union may not be mixed with goods of the same category obtained duty and tax paid in the European Union to obtain the higher allowance, e.g. the higher allowance for tobacco goods will not apply if any of the items in that category were obtained duty and tax-free or outside the European Union

7 Where there are alternative quantities within a category of goods they may be apportioned. For example, 100 cigarettes (half allowance) plus 50 cigarillos (half allowance)

8 One litre is approximately $1\frac{3}{4}$ pints or 35 fl oz

9 A cigarillo is a cigar with a maximum weight of 3 grammes

PROHIBITED AND RESTRICTED GOODS

Customs officers are able to provide full information. This is a list of more frequently met items:

Controlled drugs (such as opium, heroin, morphine, cocaine, cannabis, amphetamines, lysergide (LSD) and barbiturates)

Firearms (including gas pistols, electric shock batons and similar weapons), ammunition and explosives (including fireworks)

Offensive weapons (including certain types of knife, swordsticks, knuckle-dusters and other martial arts equipment)

Counterfeit currency and other counterfeit goods, such as fake watches and sports shirts; goods bearing a false indication of their place of manufacture or in breach of UK copyright

Obscene books, magazines, films, videotapes, laser discs, computer discs and other material, horror comics

Radio transmitters (walkie-talkies, Citizen's Band radios, cordless telephones, etc.) not approved for use in the UK

Meat and poultry, and most of their products, including ham, bacon, sausage, paté, eggs, milk and cream. (Exception: 1 kg per passenger of fully cooked meat or poultrymeat products in cans or other hermetically-sealed containers of glass or foil)

Plants, parts thereof and plant produce, including trees and shrubs, soil, potatoes and certain other vegetables, fruit, bulbs and seeds

Anglers' lead weights

Most animals and birds, whether alive or dead (e.g. stuffed), certain fish and fish eggs, whether live or dead, or bees

Certain articles derived from rare species including fur skins, ivory, reptile leather and goods made from them

NB: Cats, dogs and other mammals, including mice, rats, guinea-pigs and gerbils, must not be landed unless a British import licence (rabies) has previously been issued.

EXPORT CONTROL

The following are some of the goods subject to export control and should be declared to the customs officer. There are formalities to be completed in respect of these goods prior to arrival at the port of exportation and further information is available through any local office of Customs and Excise (address in the telephone directory).

Controlled drugs

Firearms and ammunition

Photographic material over 50 years old and valued at £6,000 or more

Portraits (including sculptures) of British historical personages which are over 50 years old and valued at £6,000 or more

Antiques, collectors' items, etc. (including paintings and other works of art) over 50 years old and valued at £39,600 or more

Certain archaeological material

Most live animals and birds, and items made from animals occurring wild in the UK

Nobel Prizes

For prize winners for the years 1901–92, *see* earlier editions of *Whitaker's Almanack*.

The Nobel Prizes are awarded each year from the income of a trust fund established by the Swedish scientist Alfred Nobel, the inventor of dynamite, who died on 10 December 1896 leaving a fortune of £1,750,000. The prizes are awarded to those who have contributed most to the common good in the domain of:

Physics – awarded by the Royal Swedish Academy of Sciences

Chemistry – awarded by the Royal Swedish Academy of Sciences

Physiology or Medicine – awarded by the Karolinska Institute

Literature – awarded by the Swedish Academy of Arts

Peace – awarded by a five-person committee elected by the Norwegian Storting

Economic Sciences (instituted 1969) – awarded by the Royal Swedish Academy of Sciences

The first awards were made in 1901 on the fifth anniversary of Nobel's death. The prizes are awarded every year on 10 December, the anniversary of Nobel's death.

The Trust is administered by the board of directors of the Nobel Foundation, Stockholm, consisting of five members and three deputy members. The Swedish Government appoints a chairman and a deputy chairman, the remaining members being appointed by the awarding authorities.

The awards have been distributed as follows:

Physics
American 60, British 20, German 19 (1948–90, West German 8), French 11, Soviet 7, Dutch 6, Swedish 4, Austrian 3, Danish 3, Italian 3, Japanese 3, Canadian 2, Chinese 2, Swiss 2, Indian 1, Irish 1, Pakistani 1

Chemistry
American 40, German 27 (1948–90, West German 10), British 23, French 7, Swiss 5, Swedish 4, Canadian 3, Dutch 3, Argentinian 1, Austrian 1, Belgian 1, Czech 1, Finnish 1, Hungarian 1, Italian 1, Japanese 1, Mexican 1, Norwegian 1, Soviet 1

Physiology or Medicine
American 74, British 23, German 15 (1948–90, West German 4), French 7, Swedish 7, Danish 5, Swiss 5, Austrian 4, Belgian 4, Italian 3, Australian 2, Canadian 2, Dutch 2, Hungarian 2, Russian 2, Argentinian 1, Japanese 1, Portuguese 1, South African 1, Spanish 1

Literature
French 12, American 10, British 8, Swedish 7, German 6 (1948–90, West German 1), Italian 5, Spanish 5, Danish 3, Irish 3, Norwegian 3, Soviet 3, Chilean 2, Greek 2, Japanese 2, Polish 2, Swiss 2, Australian 1, Belgian 1, Colombian 1, Czech 1, Egyptian 1, Finnish 1, Guatemalan 1, Icelandic 1, Indian 1, Israeli 1, Mexican 1, Nigerian 1, South African 1, Trinidadian 1, Yugoslav 1, Stateless 1

Peace
American 17, Institutions 17, British 10, French 9, Swedish 5, German 4 (1948–90, West German 1), South African 4, Belgian 3, Israeli 3, Swiss 3, Argentinian 2, Austrian 2, Norwegian 2, Soviet 2, Burmese 1, Canadian 1, Costa Rican 1, Danish 1, Dutch 1, Egyptian 1, Guatemalan 1, Irish 1, Italian 1, Japanese 1, Mexican 1, Palestinian 1, Polish 1, Tibetan 1, Vietnamese 1, Yugoslav 1

Economics
American 24, British 6, Norwegian 2, Swedish 2, Dutch 1, French 1, German 1, Soviet 1

Prize	1993	1994	1995
Physics	Dr R. Hulse (American) Dr J. Taylor (American)	Prof. B. Brockhouse (Canadian) Prof. C. Shull (American)	Dr M. Perl (American) Dr F. Reines (American)
Chemistry	Prof. M. Smith (Canadian) Dr K. Mullis (American)	Prof. G. Olah (American)	P. Crutzen (Dutch) Dr M. Molina (Mexican) Dr S. Rowland (American)
Physiology or Medicine	R. Roberts (British) Prof. P. Sharp (American)	Dr A. Gilman (American) Dr M. Rodbell (American)	Dr E. Lewis (American) Dr C. Nuesslein-Volhard (German) Dr E. Wieschaus (American)
Literature	Ms T. Morrison (American)	K. Oe (Japanese)	S. Heaney (Irish)
Peace	N. Mandela (South African) Pres. F. W. de Klerk (South African)	Y. Rabin (Israeli) Y. Arafat (Palestinian) S. Peres (Israeli)	Prof. J. Rotblat (British) The Pugwash Conference on Science and World Affairs
Economics	Prof. R. Fogel (American) Prof. D. North (American)	J. Harsanyi (American) J. Nash (American) R. Selten (German)	R. Lucas (American)

Countries of the World

WORLD AREA AND POPULATION

The total population of the world in mid-1990 was estimated at 5,292 million, compared with 3,019 million in 1960 and 2,070 million in 1930.

Continent, etc.	Area sq. miles '000	sq. km '000	Estimated population mid-1990
Africa	11,704	30,313	642,000,000
North America[1]	8,311	21,525	276,000,000
Latin America[2]	7,933	20,547	448,000,000
Asia[3]	10,637	27,549	3,113,000,000
Europe[4]	1,915	4,961	498,000,000
Former USSR	8,649	22,402	289,000,000
Oceania[5]	3,286	8,510	26,500,000
TOTAL	52,435	135,807	5,292,000,000

[1] Includes Greenland and Hawaii
[2] Mexico and the remainder of the Americas south of the USA
[3] Includes European Turkey, excludes former USSR
[4] Excludes European Turkey and former USSR
[5] Includes Australia, New Zealand and the islands inhabited by Micronesian, Melanesian and Polynesian peoples
Source: UN Demographic Yearbook 1990 (pub. 1992)

A United Nations report *The Sex and Age Distribution of the World Populations* (revised 1994) puts the world's population in the late 20th and 21st centuries at the following levels (medium variant data):

1995	5,716.4m	2030	8,670.6m
2000	6,158.0m	2040	9,318.2m
2010	7,032.3m	2050	9,833.2m
2020	7,887.8m		

The population forecast for the years 2000 and 2050 is:

Continent, etc.	Estimated population (million) 2000	2050
Africa	831.596	2,140.844
North America[1]	306.280	388.997
Latin America[2]	523.875	838.527
Asia	3,753.846	5,741.005
Europe	729.803	677.764
Oceania	30.651	46.070
TOTAL	6,158.051	9,833.207

[1] Includes Bermuda, Greenland, and St Pierre and Miquelon
[2] Mexico and the remainder of the Americas south of the USA

AREA AND POPULATION BY CONTINENT

No complete survey of many countries has yet been achieved and consequently accurate area figures are not always available. Similarly, many countries have not recently, or have never, taken a census. The areas of countries given below are derived from estimated figures published by the United Nations. The conversion factors used are:
(i) to convert square miles to square km, multiply by 2.589988
(ii) to convert square km to square miles, multiply by 0.3861022
Population figures for countries are derived from the most recent estimates available. Accurate and up-to-date data for the populations of capital cities are scarce, and definitions of cities' extent differ. The figures given below are the latest estimates available, and where it is known that the figure applies to an urban agglomeration this is indicated.
*   latest census figure
Ψ   seaport
u.a.   urban agglomeration

AFRICA

COUNTRY/TERRITORY	AREA sq. miles	sq. km	POPULATION	CAPITAL	POPULATION OF CAPITAL
Algeria	919,595	2,381,741	26,722,000	Ψ Algiers	3,250,000
Angola	481,354	1,246,700	10,276,000	Ψ Luanda	3,000,000
Benin	43,484	112,622	5,215,000	Ψ Porto Novo	208,258
Botswana	224,607	581,730	1,326,796*	Gaborone	133,458*
Burkina Faso	105,869	274,200	9,682,000	Ouagadougou	441,514
Burundi	10,747	27,834	5,958,000	Bujumbura	235,440
Cameroon	183,569	475,442	12,600,000	Yaoundé	653,670
Cape Verde	1,557	4,033	370,000	Ψ Praia	57,748
Central African Republic	240,535	622,984	3,173,000	Bangui	473,817
Chad Republic	495,755	1,284,000	5,961,000	Ndjaména	402,000
The Comoros	838	2,171	585,000	Moroni	17,267
Congo	132,047	342,000	2,443,000	Brazzaville	600,000
Côte d'Ivoire	124,503	322,463	13,316,000	Yamoussoukro	106,786
Djibouti	8,494	22,000	520,000*	Ψ Djibouti	340,700
Egypt	386,662	1,001,449	58,978,000	Cairo	13,000,000
Equatorial Guinea	10,830	28,051	379,000	Ψ Malabo	30,418
Eritrea	36,170	93,679	3,500,000	Asmara	275,000
Ethiopia	471,778	1,221,900	51,859,000	Addis Ababa	3,500,000
Gabon	103,347	267,667	1,035,000	Ψ Libreville	251,000
Gambia	4,361	11,295	1,081,000	Ψ Banjul (*u.a.*)	44,536

Country/Territory	Area sq. miles	sq. km	Population	Capital	Population of Capital
Ghana	92,100	238,537	16,944,000	Ψ Accra (u.a.)	1,781,100
Guinea	94,926	245,857	6,501,000	Ψ Conakry	763,000
Guinea-Bissau	13,948	36,125	1,050,000	Ψ Bissau	109,486*
Kenya	224,961	582,646	26,017,000	Nairobi	1,400,000
Lesotho	11,720	30,355	1,943,000	Maseru	288,951*
Liberia	43,000	111,369	2,640,000	Ψ Monrovia	425,000
Libya	679,362	1,759,540	5,222,000	Ψ Tripoli	1,000,000
Madagascar	226,669	587,041	13,101,000	Antananarivo	1,250,000
Malawi	45,747	118,484	10,843,000	Lilongwe	223,973
Mali	478,791	1,240,000	9,524,000	Bamako	658,275*
Mauritania	397,955	1,030,700	2,217,000	Nouakchott	850,000
Mauritius	790	2,045	1,082,998	Ψ Port Louis	144,250
Mayotte (Fr.)	144	372	94,410*	Mamoundzou	12,000
Morocco	172,414	446,550	26,448,000	Ψ Rabat	1,494,000
Western Sahara	102,703	266,000	183,000	Laayoune	96,784*
Mozambique	309,495	801,590	16,500,000	Ψ Maputo	1,150,000
Namibia	318,261	824,292	1,500,000	Windhoek	110,000
Niger	489,191	1,267,080	8,846,000	Niamey	410,000
Nigeria	356,669	923,768	107,900,000	Abuja	378,671
Réunion (Fr.)	969	2,510	643,000	St Denis	122,000
Rwanda	10,169	26,338	7,750,000	Kigali	156,000
St Helena (UK)	47	122	5,644	Ψ Jamestown	1,332
Ascension Island	34	88	1,160	Ψ Georgetown	—
Tristan da Cunha	38	98	292	Ψ Edinburgh of the Seven Seas	—
São Tomé and Príncipe	372	964	125,000	Ψ São Tomé	25,000
Senegal	75,750	196,192	8,102,000	Ψ Dakar	1,000,000
Seychelles	108	280	73,000	Ψ Victoria	24,324
Sierra Leone	27,699	71,740	4,587,000	Ψ Freetown	470,000*
Somalia	246,201	637,657	9,077,000	Ψ Mogadishu	1,000,000
South Africa	471,445	1,221,031	40,049,000	Pretoria (u.a.) / Ψ Cape Town (u.a.)	822,925 / 1,911,521
Sudan	967,500	2,505,813	27,361,000	Khartoum (u.a.)	3,000,000
Swaziland	6,704	17,363	906,000	Mbabane	38,290
Tanzania	364,900	945,087	28,846,000	Dodoma	88,474
Togo	21,925	56,785	4,010,000	Ψ Lomé	366,476
Tunisia	63,170	163,610	8,815,000	Ψ Tunis	1,394,749
Uganda	91,259	236,036	18,592,000	Kampala (u.a.)	750,000
Zaïre	905,567	2,345,409	42,552,000	Kinshasa	2,778,281
Zambia	290,586	752,614	9,196,000	Lusaka (u.a.)	1,000,000
Zimbabwe	150,804	390,580	11,200,000	Harare	1,184,000

AMERICA

North America

Country/Territory	Area sq. miles	sq. km	Population	Capital	Population of Capital
Canada	3,849,670	9,970,599	29,606,100	Ottawa (u.a.)	313,987*
Greenland (Den.)	840,004	2,175,600	55,700	Ψ Godthåb	—
Mexico	761,605	1,972,547	91,858,000	Mexico City (u.a.)	14,987,051*
St Pierre and Miquelon (Fr.)	93	242	6,300	Ψ St Pierre	—
United States	3,787,318	9,809,108	259,681,000	Washington DC	585,221

Central America and the West Indies

Country/Territory	Area sq. miles	sq. km	Population	Capital	Population of Capital
Anguilla (UK)	35	91	8,960*	The Valley	1,400
Antigua and Barbuda	170	440	65,962*	Ψ St John's	30,000
Aruba (Neth.)	75	193	71,000	Ψ Oranjestad	25,000
Bahamas	5,380	13,935	269,000	Ψ Nassau	171,000*
Barbados	166	431	264,000	Ψ Bridgetown	108,000
Belize	8,867	22,965	205,000*	Belmopan	3,739*
Bermuda (UK)	20	53	60,075	Ψ Hamilton	2,277
Cayman Islands (UK)	100	259	33,600	Ψ George Town	17,500
Costa Rica	19,575	50,700	3,232,526	San José (u.a.)	86,178
Cuba	42,804	110,861	10,905,000	Ψ Havana	2,143,406
Dominica	290	751	71,000	Ψ Roseau	15,850
Dominican Republic	18,816	48,734	7,684,000	Ψ Santo Domingo (u.a.)	1,313,172*
Grenada	133	344	95,000	Ψ St George's	10,000
Guadeloupe (Fr.)	687	1,779	420,000	Ψ Basse Terre	14,000

Country/Territory	Area sq. miles	sq. km	Population	Capital	Population of Capital
Guatemala	42,042	108,889	10,332,000	Guatemala City	1,675,589
Haiti	10,714	27,750	7,035,000	Ψ Port-au-Prince	1,000,000
Honduras	43,277	112,088	5,493,900	Tegucigalpa	670,100
Jamaica	4,244	10,991	2,960,000	Ψ Kingston (u.a.)	696,300
Martinique (Fr.)	425	1,102	375,000	Ψ Fort de France	101,540
Montserrat (UK)	38	98	9,000	Ψ Plymouth	2,500
Netherlands Antilles (Neth.)	371	961	197,000	Ψ Willemstad	50,000
Nicaragua	50,193	130,000	4,275,000	Managua	615,000
Panama	29,762	77,082	2,631,013	Ψ Panama City	1,064,221
Puerto Rico (USA)	3,435	8,897	3,600,000	Ψ San Juan (u.a.)	437,745
St Christopher and Nevis	101	261	41,000	Ψ Basseterre	15,000
St Lucia	238	616	143,000	Ψ Castries	56,000
St Vincent and the Grenadines	150	388	110,000	Ψ Kingstown	33,694
El Salvador	8,124	21,041	5,641,000	San Salvador	497,644
Trinidad and Tobago	1,981	5,130	1,239,908	Ψ Port of Spain	50,878
Turks and Caicos Is. (UK)	166	430	19,000	Ψ Grand Turk	4,000
Virgin Islands:					
British (UK)	59	153	16,108*	Ψ Road Town	3,983
US (USA)	132	342	101,809	Ψ Charlotte Amalie	11,756

South America

Argentina	1,073,512	2,780,400	32,370,298	Ψ Buenos Aires	2,960,976
Bolivia	424,165	1,098,581	6,440,000*	La Paz	1,115,000
Brazil	3,286,488	8,511,965	156,275,000	Brasilia	1,596,274*
Chile	292,258	756,945	13,813,000	Santiago	5,443,000
Colombia	439,737	1,138,914	36,000,000	Bogotá	8,000,000
Ecuador	109,484	283,561	10,980,972	Quito	1,387,887
Falkland Islands (UK)	4,700	12,173	2,121	Ψ Stanley	1,643
French Guiana (Fr.)	35,135	91,000	140,000	Ψ Cayenne	41,000
Guyana	83,000	214,969	825,000	Ψ Georgetown	185,000
Paraguay	157,048	406,752	4,830,000	Asunción (u.a.)	729,307*
Peru	496,225	1,285,216	22,331,000	Lima (u.a.)	6,483,901*
South Georgia (UK)	1,580	4,092	—		—
Suriname	63,037	163,265	418,000	Ψ Paramaribo (u.a.)	110,000
Uruguay	68,037	176,215	3,116,802	Ψ Montevideo	1,383,660
Venezuela	353,857	916,490	21,378,000	Caracas (u.a.)	2,784,000

ASIA

Afghanistan	251,772	652,090	17,691,000	Kabul	1,424,400*
Bahrain	240	622	539,000	Ψ Manama	108,684*
Bangladesh	55,598	143,998	108,000,000*	Dhaka	6,537,308*
Bhutan	18,147	47,000	650,000	Thimphu	15,000
Brunei	2,226	5,765	276,300	Bandar Seri Begawan	56,300
Cambodia	69,898	181,035	9,308,000	Ψ Phnom Penh	920,000
China[1]	3,705,408	9,596,961	1,200,000,000	Beijing (Peking)	6,560,000
Hong Kong (UK)	416	1,074	6,307,900		—
India	1,269,346	3,287,590	846,302,688*	Delhi	8,375,188
Indonesia	735,358	1,904,569	189,907,000	Ψ Jakarta	7,885,519
Iran	636,296	1,648,000	66,000,000	Tehran	6,042,584
Iraq	167,925	434,924	19,951,000	Baghdad	3,841,286
Israel[2]	8,019	20,770	5,090,000	Tel Aviv	1,781,500
West Bank and Gaza Strip	2,406	6,231	1,635,000	Gaza City	120,000
Japan	145,834	377,700	124,764,215	Tokyo (u.a.)	11,935,700
Jordan	37,738	97,740	4,095,579	Amman	1,270,000
Kazakhstan	1,049,155	2,716,626	16,963,600	Alma-Ata	1,500,000
Korea, D.P.R. (North)	46,540	120,538	23,472,000	Pyongyang	2,000,000
Korea, Rep. of (South)	38,025	98,484	44,563,000	Seoul	10,229,000
Kuwait	6,969	18,049	1,575,983*	Ψ Kuwait (city)	400,000
Kyrgyzstan	76,642	198,501	4,500,000	Bishkek	616,000
Laos	91,429	231,800	4,605,300*	Vientiane	120,000
Lebanon	4,015	10,400	2,806,000	Ψ Beirut	1,500,000
Macao (Port.)	6	16	395,000	Ψ Macao	—
Malaysia	127,317	329,749	20,103,000	Kuala Lumpur	1,231,500
Maldives	115	298	246,000	Ψ Malé	46,334
Mongolia	604,250	1,565,000	2,363,000	Ulan Bator	600,500

Country/Territory	Area sq. miles	sq. km	Population	Capital	Population of Capital
Myanmar (Burma)	261,218	676,552	45,555,000	Ψ Yangon (Rangoon) (u.a.)	3,973,872
Nepal	54,342	140,747	21,360,000	Kathmandu	300,000
Oman	82,030	212,457	2,000,000*	Ψ Muscat	400,000
Pakistan	341,026	883,254	126,284,000	Islamabad (u.a.)	350,000
Philippines	115,831	300,000	66,188,000	Ψ Manila	1,876,195
Qatar	4,247	11,000	537,000	Ψ Doha	220,000
Saudi Arabia	830,000	2,149,640	16,929,294*	Riyadh	2,000,000
Singapore	247	639	2,930,200	—	—
Sri Lanka	25,332	65,610	17,619,000	Ψ Colombo	2,026,000
Syria	71,498	185,180	14,171,000	Damascus	1,451,000
Taiwan	13,800	35,742	20,944,066	Taipei	2,719,659
Tajikistan	55,251	143,100	5,513,400	Dushanbe	595,000
Thailand	198,457	514,000	58,336,072	Ψ Bangkok	5,572,712
Turkey[3]	301,382	780,576	60,771,000	Ankara	3,236,626
Turkmenistan	188,456	488,100	4,483,000*	Ashkhabad	407,000
United Arab Emirates	32,278	83,600	2,310,000	Abu Dhabi	450,000
Uzbekistan	172,742	447,229	21,206,800	Tashkent	2,073,000
Vietnam	127,242	329,556	72,500,000	Hanoi	2,150,000
Yemen	203,850	527,696	15,800,000*	Sana'a	972,000

[1] Including Tibet
[2] Including East Jerusalem, the Golan Heights and Israeli citizens on the West Bank
[3] Including Turkey in Europe

EUROPE

Country/Territory	Area sq. miles	sq. km	Population	Capital	Population of Capital
Albania	11,099	28,748	3,500,000	Tirana	244,153
Andorra	180	468	64,311	Andorra la Vella	22,821
Armenia	11,306	29,271	3,754,000	Yerevan	1,254,000
Austria	32,375	83,853	8,015,000	Vienna	1,539,848*
Azerbaijan	33,436	86,565	7,553,000	Baku	1,149,000
Belarus	80,300	207,897	10,265,000	Minsk	1,589,000
Belgium	11,781	30,513	10,100,631	Brussels (u.a.)	949,070
Bosnia-Hercegovina	19,735	51,129	2,900,000	Sarajevo	453,324
Bulgaria	42,823	110,912	8,472,000	Sofia	1,114,925
Croatia	21,823	56,538	4,784,265	Zagreb	867,865
Cyprus	3,572	9,251	740,000	Nicosia	185,000
Czech Republic	30,372	78,664	10,302,000*	Prague	1,215,076
Denmark	16,630	43,063	5,215,718	Ψ Copenhagen (u.a.)	1,339,395
Faroe Islands	540	1,399	43,700	Ψ Tórshavn	—
Estonia	17,413	45,082	1,491,583	Talinn	434,763
Finland	130,500	338,000	5,098,754	Ψ Helsinki	515,765
France	211,208	547,026	57,218,000	Paris (u.a.)	9,318,800
Georgia	26,911	69,673	5,401,000	Tbilisi	1,260,000
Germany	137,738	365,755	81,075,000	Berlin	3,454,200
Gibraltar (UK)	2	6	28,051	Ψ Gibraltar	—
Greece	50,944	131,944	10,256,464	Athens (u.a.)	3,096,775*
Hungary	35,919	93,030	10,278,000	Budapest	2,004,000
Iceland	39,768	103,000	266,786	Ψ Reykjavik (u.a.)	103,036
Ireland, Republic of	27,136	70,283	3,621,035	Ψ Dublin	480,996*
Italy	116,304	301,225	57,154,000	Rome (u.a.)	2,693,383*
Latvia	24,695	63,935	2,529,600	Riga	840,000
Liechtenstein	61	157	31,000	Vaduz	5,072
Lithuania	26,173	67,761	3,724,000	Vilnius	579,000
Luxembourg	998	2,586	406,600	Luxembourg	75,800
Macedonia	9,925	25,713	1,936,877*	Skopje	448,229*
Malta	122	316	76,335*	Ψ Valletta	7,184*
Moldova	13,912	36,018	4,335,000	Kishinev	665,000*
Monaco	0.4	1	29,972	Monaco-Ville	1,151
Netherlands	15,770	40,844	15,391,000	Ψ Amsterdam (u.a.)	1,031,000
Norway[1]	125,181	324,219	4,348,410	Ψ Oslo	483,401
Poland	120,725	312,677	38,600,000	Warsaw	1,641,900
Portugal[2]	35,553	92,082	9,862,700*	Ψ Lisbon	2,128,000
Romania	91,699	237,500	22,760,449*	Bucharest	2,064,474*
Russia[3]	6,593,391	17,070,289	148,100,000	Moscow	8,700,000
San Marino	23	61	25,058	San Marino	—

Country/Territory	Area sq. miles	sq. km	Population	Capital	Population of Capital
Slovakia	18,932	49,035	5,336,455	Bratislava	448,785
Slovenia	7,816	20,251	1,989,477	Ljubljana	269,972
Spain[4]	194,897	504,782	38,872,268*	Madrid (u.a.)	4,947,555
Sweden	173,732	449,964	8,745,109*	Ψ Stockholm (u.a.)	1,532,803
Switzerland	15,943	41,293	7,127,000	Berne	135,600*
Ukraine	233,090	603,700	51,471,000*	Kiev	2,577,000
United Kingdom[5]	94,248	244,101	58,395,000	Ψ London (u.a.)	6,961,900
England	50,351	130,410	48,708,000	—	—
Wales	8,015	20,758	2,913,000	Ψ Cardiff	300,000
Scotland	30,420	78,789	5,132,000	Ψ Edinburgh	444,000
Northern Ireland	5,461	14,144	1,642,000	Ψ Belfast (u.a.)	297,000
Vatican City State	0.2	0.44	1,000	Vatican City	—
Yugoslavia, Fed. Rep. of	39,506	102,350	10,410,000	Belgrade	1,455,000

[1] Excludes Svalbard and Jan Mayen Islands (approx. 24,101 sq. miles (62,422 sq. km) and 3,000 population)
[2] Includes Madeira (314 sq. miles) and the Azores (922 sq. miles)
[3] Includes Russia in Asia
[4] Includes Balearic Islands, Canary Islands, Ceuta and Melilla
[5] Excludes Isle of Man (221 sq. miles (572 sq. km), 69,788* population), and Channel Islands (75 sq. miles (194 sq. km), 142,949* population)

OCEANIA

Country/Territory	Area sq. miles	sq. km	Population	Capital	Population of Capital
American Samoa (USA)	76	197	46,773	Ψ Pago Pago	—
Australia	2,967,909	7,686,848	18,114,000	Canberra	328,000
Norfolk Island	14	36	1,912	Ψ Kingston	—
Fiji	7,055	18,274	758,000	Ψ Suva	69,665
French Polynesia (Fr.)	1,544	4,000	215,000	Ψ Papeete	24,200
Guam (USA)	212	549	133,152	Agaña	—
Kiribati	281	728	77,000	Tarawa	17,921
Marshall Islands	70	181	52,000	Majuro	20,000
Micronesia, Fed. States of	271	701	107,000	Palikir	—
Nauru	8	21	10,000	Ψ Nauru	—
New Caledonia (Fr.)	7,358	19,058	178,000	Ψ Noumea	65,000
New Zealand	103,736	268,676	3,494,300	Ψ Wellington (u.a.)	329,000
Cook Islands	91	236	18,300	Avarua	—
Niue	100	259	2,239	Alofi	—
Ross Dependency[1]	286,696	750,310	—	—	—
Tokelau	5	12.9	1,700	—	—
Northern Mariana Islands (USA)	184	476	43,345	Saipan	39,090
Palau (USA)	192	497	15,122*	Koror	10,493
Papua New Guinea	178,260	461,691	4,205,000	Ψ Port Moresby	173,500
Pitcairn Islands (UK)	1.9	5	54	—	—
Solomon Islands	10,983	28,446	328,723*	Ψ Honiara	40,000
Tonga	270	699	98,000	Ψ Nuku'alofa	30,000
Tuvalu	10	25	12,000	Ψ Funafuti	2,856
Vanuatu	4,706	12,190	159,800	Ψ Port Vila	26,100
Wallis and Futuna Islands (Fr.)	106	274	13,705	Ψ Mata-Utu	—
Western Samoa	1,097	2,842	158,000	Ψ Apia	36,000*

[1] Includes permanent shelf ice

Currencies of the World
AND EXCHANGE RATES AGAINST £ STERLING

Franc CFA = Franc de la Communauté financière africaine
Franc CFP = Franc des Comptoirs français du Pacifique

COUNTRY/TERRITORY	MONETARY UNIT	AVERAGE RATE TO £ 1 September 1995	AVERAGE RATE TO £ 30 August 1996
Afghanistan	Afghani (Af) of 100 puls	Af 6896.21	Af 7424.25
Albania	Lek (Lk) of 100 qindarka	Lk 177.063	Lk 170.523
Algeria	Algerian dinar (DA) of 100 centimes	DA 80.6524	DA 81.9872
American Samoa	Currency is that of USA	US$ 1.5525	US$ 1.5630
Andorra	French and Spanish currencies in use	—	—
Angola	Readjusted kwanza (Kzrl) of 100 lwei, replaced new kwanza (Nkz)	Nkz 5005.26	Kzrl 49678.4
Anguilla	East Caribbean dollar (EC$) of 100 cents	EC$ 4.1918	EC$ 4.2201
Antigua and Barbuda	East Caribbean dollar (EC$) of 100 cents	EC$ 4.1918	EC$ 4.2201
Argentina	Peso of 10,000 australes	Pesos 1.5517	Pesos 1.5609
Armenia	Dram of 100 couma	Dram 635.097	Dram 654.585
Aruba	Aruban florin	Florins 2.7790	Florins 2.7978
Australia	Australian dollar ($A) of 100 cents	$A 2.0714	$A 1.9754
Austria	Schilling of 100 Groschen	Schilling 15.9756	Schilling 16.2535
Azerbaijan	Manat of 100 gopik	Manat 6823.24	Manat 6727.15
Bahamas	Bahamian dollar (B$) of 100 cents	B$ 1.5525	B$ 1.5630
Bahrain	Bahrain dinar (BD) of 1,000 fils	BD 0.5853	BD 0.5893
Bangladesh	Taka (Tk) of 100 poisha	Tk 61.7895	Tk 65.4898
Barbados	Barbados dollar (BD$) of 100 cents	BD$ 3.1226	BD$ 3.1437
Belarus	Rouble of 100 kopeks	Roubles 17853.8	Roubles 26852.4
Belgium	Belgian franc (or frank) of 100 centimes (centiemen)	Francs 46.7225	Francs 47.5621
Belize	Belize dollar (BZ$) of 100 cents	BZ$ 3.1050	BZ$ 3.1260
Benin	Franc CFA	Francs 784.440	Francs 790.270
Bermuda	Bermuda dollar of 100 cents	$ 1.5525	$ 1.5630
Bhutan	Ngultrum of 100 chetrum (Indian currency is also legal tender)	Ngultrum 49.5403	Ngultrum 55.7523
Bolivia	Boliviano ($b) of 100 centavos	$b 7.5141	$b 8.0182
Bosnia-Hercegovina	Dinar of 100 paras	—	—
Botswana	Pula (P) of 100 thebe	P 4.3551	P 5.4508
Brazil	Real of 100 centavos	Real 1.4740	Real 1.5888
British Virgin Islands	US dollar (US$) (£ sterling and EC$ also circulate)	US$ 1.5525	US$ 1.5630
Brunei	Brunei dollar of 100 sen (fully interchangeable with Singapore currency)	$ 2.2061	$ 2.1995
Bulgaria	Lev of 100 stotinki	Leva 105.469	Leva 329.012
Burkina Faso	Franc CFA	Francs 784.440	Francs 790.270
Burundi	Burundi franc of 100 centimes	Francs 393.171	Francs 338.437
Cambodia	Riel of 100 sen	Riel 3570.75	Riel 3594.90
Cameroon	Franc CFA	Francs 784.440	Francs 790.270
Canada	Canadian dollar (C$) of 100 cents	C$ 2.0858	C$ 2.1386
Cape Verde	Escudo Caboverdiano of 100 centavos	Esc 128.811	Esc 129.682
Cayman Islands	Cayman Islands dollar (CI$) of 100 cents	CI$ 1.2858	CI$ 1.3303
Central African Republic	Franc CFA	Francs 784.440	Francs 790.270
Chad	Franc CFA	Francs 784.440	Francs 790.270
Chile	Chilean peso of 100 centavos	Pesos 610.676	Pesos 641.846
China	Renminbi Yuan of 10 jiao or 100 fen	Yuan 12.9156	Yuan 12.9828
Christmas Island	Currency is that of Australia	$A 2.0714	$A 1.9754
Cocos (Keeling) Islands	Currency is that of Australia	$A 2.0714	$A 1.9754
Colombia	Colombian peso of 100 centavos	Pesos 1474.56	Pesos 1628.65
Comoros	Franc CFA/Franc	Francs 588.476	Francs 593.921
Congo	Franc CFA	Francs 784.440	Francs 790.270
Cook Islands	Currency is that of New Zealand	NZ$ 2.3755	NZ$ 2.2644
Costa Rica	Costa Rican colón (₡) of 100 céntimos	₡ 286.343	₡ 329.715
Côte d'Ivoire	Franc CFA	Francs 784.440	Francs 790.270
Croatia	Kuna of 100 lipas	Kuna 8.3241	Kuna 8.1782

Country/Territory	Monetary Unit	Average Rate to £ 1 September 1995	Average Rate to £ 30 August 1996
Cuba	Cuban peso of 100 centavos	Pesos 1.5525	Pesos 1.5630
Cyprus	Cyprus pound (C£) of 100 cents	C£ 0.7114	C£ 0.7164
Czech Republic	Koruna (Kčs) of 100 haléřu	Kčs 41.8570	Kčs 40.5380
Denmark	Danish krone of 100 øre	Kroner 8.8252	Kroner 8.9275
Djibouti	Djibouti franc of 100 centimes	Francs 275.911	Francs 250.080
Dominica	East Caribbean dollar (EC$) of 100 cents	EC$ 4.1918	EC$ 4.2201
Dominican Republic	Dominican Republic peso (RD$) of 100 centavos	RD$ 21.4245	RD$ 21.7023
Ecuador	Sucre of 100 centavos	Sucres 3890.57	Sucres 5125.86
Egypt	Egyptian pound (£E) of 100 piastres or 1,000 millièmes	£E 5.2770	£E 5.3123
Equatorial Guinea	Franc CFA	Francs 784.440	Francs 790.270
Eritrea	Ethiopian currency is in use	EB 9.0045	EB 9.0654
Estonia	Kroon of 100 sents	Kroons 18.2251	Kroons 18.5316
Ethiopia	Ethiopian birr (EB) of 100 cents	EB 9.0045	EB 9.0654
Falkland Islands	Falkland pound of 100 pence	*at parity with £ sterling*	
Faroe Islands	Currency is that of Denmark	Kroner 8.8252	Kroner 8.9275
Fiji	Fiji dollar (F$) of 100 cents	F$ 2.1971	F$ 2.1799
Finland	Markka (Mk) of 100 penniä	Mk 6.8109	Mk 6.9845
France	Franc of 100 centimes	Francs 7.8444	Francs 7.9027
French Guiana	Currency is that of France	Francs 7.8444	Francs 7.9027
French Polynesia	Franc CFP	Francs 142.661	Francs 143.981
Gabon	Franc CFA	Francs 784.440	Francs 790.270
Gambia	Dalasi (D) of 100 butut	D 14.9040	D 15.3643
Georgia	Georgian Coupon	—	—
Germany	Deutsche Mark (DM) of 100 Pfennig	DM 2.2717	DM 2.3098
Ghana	Cedi of 100 pesewas	Cedi 1870.76	Cedi 2633.66
Gibraltar	Gibraltar pound of 100 pence	*at parity with £ sterling*	
Greece	Drachma of 100 leptae	Drachmae 365.723	Drachmae 369.415
Greenland	Currency is that of Denmark	Kroner 8.8252	Kroner 8.9275
Grenada	East Caribbean dollar (EC$) of 100 cents	EC$ 4.1918	EC$ 4.2201
Guadeloupe	Currency is that of France	Francs 7.8444	Francs 7.9027
Guam	Currency is that of USA	US$ 1.5525	US$ 1.5630
Guatemala	Quetzal (Q) of 100 centavos	Q 9.0919	Q 9.5038
Guinea	Guinea franc of 100 centimes	Francs 1536.04	Francs 1558.31
Guinea-Bissau	Guinea-Bissau peso of 100 centavos	Pesos 26001.3	Pesos 28190.3
Guyana	Guyana dollar (G$) of 100 cents	G$ 223.250	G$ 217.101
Haiti	Gourde of 100 centimes	Gourdes 29.4975	Gourdes 23.2178
Honduras	Lempira of 100 centavos	Lempiras 14.6867	Lempiras 18.8654
Hong Kong	Hong Kong dollar (HK$) of 100 cents	HK$ 12.0176	HK$ 12.0863
Hungary	Forint of 100 fillér	Forints 201.771	Forints 235.958
Iceland	Icelandic króna (Kr) of 100 aurar	Kr 101.906	Kr 103.471
India	Indian rupee (Rs) of 100 paisa	Rs 49.5403	Rs 55.7523
Indonesia	Rupiah (Rp) of 100 sen	Rp 3519.91	Rp 3660.55
Iran	Rial	Rials 4657.50	Rials 4689.00
Iraq	Iraqi dinar (ID) of 1,000 fils	ID 0.9315	ID 0.4860
Ireland, Republic of	Punt (IR£) of 100 pence	IR£ 0.9774	IR£ 0.9630
Israel	Shekel of 100 agora	Shekels 4.7219	Shekels 4.9060
Italy	Lira of 100 centesimi	Lire 2523.90	Lire 2358.53
Jamaica	Jamaican dollar (J$) of 100 cents	J$ 51.2325	J$ 53.5328
Japan	Yen of 100 sen	Yen 151.237	Yen 169.742
Jordan	Jordanian dinar (JD) of 1,000 fils	JD 1.1054	JD 1.1094
Kazakhstan	Tenge	—	Tenge 106.597
Kenya	Kenya shilling (Ksh) of 100 cents	Ksh 85.8533	Ksh 88.9348
Kiribati	Australian dollar ($A) of 100 cents	$A 2.0714	$A 1.9754
Korea, North	Won of 100 jun	Won 3.3379	Won 3.3605
Korea, South	Won of 100 jeon	Won 1200.32	Won 1280.49
Kuwait	Kuwaiti dinar (KD) of 1,000 fils	KD 0.4697	KD 0.4678
Kyrgyzstan	Som	—	—
Laos	Kip (K) of 100 at	K 1428.30	K 1437.96
Latvia	Lats of 100 santimes	Lats 0.8339	Lats 0.8502
Lebanon	Lebanese pound (L£) of 100 piastres	L£ 2504.96	L£ 2441.41
Lesotho	Loti (M) of 100 lisente	M 5.6802	M 7.0140
Liberia	Liberian dollar (L$) of 100 cents	L$ 1.5525	L$ 1.5630
Libya	Libyan dinar (LD) of 1,000 dirhams	LD 0.5519	LD 0.5557

Country/Territory	Monetary Unit	Average Rate to £ 1 September 1995	Average Rate to £ 30 August 1996
Liechtenstein	Swiss franc of 100 rappen (or centimes)	Francs 1.8588	Francs 1.8718
Lithuania	Litas	Litas 6.2100	Litas 6.2520
Luxembourg	Luxembourg franc (LF) of 100 centimes (Belgian currency is also legal tender)	LF 46.7225	LF 47.5621
Macao	Pataca of 100 avos	Pataca 12.3984	Pataca 12.4867
Macedonia, Former Yugoslav Rep.	Dinar of 100 paras	Dinars 61.0139	Dinars 63.2940
Madagascar	Franc malgache (FMG) of 100 centimes	FMG 6908.63	FMG 6017.55
Malawi	Kwacha (K) of 100 tambala	K 23.6878	K 23.9139
Malaysia	Malaysian dollar (ringgit) (M$) of 100 sen	M$ 3.8743	M$ 3.8978
Maldives	Rufiyaa of 100 laaris	Rufiyaa 18.2730	Rufiyaa 18.3965
Mali	Franc CFA	Francs 784.440	Francs 790.270
Malta	Maltese lira (LM) of 100 cents or 1,000 mils	LM 0.5559	LM 0.5594
Marshall Islands	Currency is that of USA	US$ 1.5525	US$ 1.5630
Martinique	Currency is that of France	Francs 7.8444	Francs 7.9027
Mauritania	Ouguiya (UM) of 5 khoums	UM 200.257	UM 214.233
Mauritius	Mauritius rupee of 100 cents	Rs 28.2788	Rs 31.6430
Mayotte	Currency is that of France	Francs 7.8444	Francs 7.9027
Mexico	Peso of 100 centavos	Pesos 9.7187	Pesos 11.8585
Moldova	Leu	Leu 7.0383	Leu 7.2445
Monaco	French franc of 100 centimes	Francs 7.8444	Francs 7.9027
Mongolia	Tugrik of 100 möngö	Tugriks 697.228	Tugriks 729.406
Montserrat	East Caribbean dollar (EC$) of 100 cents	EC$ 4.1918	EC$ 4.2201
Morocco	Dirham (DH) of 100 centimes	DH 13.3586	DH 13.4903
Mozambique	Metical (MT) of 100 centavos	MT 14908.7	MT 17412.6
Myanmar (Burma)	Kyat (K) of 100 pyas	K 8.8421	K 9.1519
Namibia	Namibian dollar of 100 cents	*at parity with SA Rand*	
Nauru	Australian dollar ($A) of 100 cents	$A 2.0714	$A 1.9754
Nepal	Nepalese rupee of 100 paisa	Rs 78.2305	Rs 87.5671
Netherlands	Gulden (guilder) or florin of 100 cents	Guilders 2.5461	Guilders 2.5893
Netherlands Antilles	Netherlands Antilles guilder of 100 cents	Guilders 2.7790	Guilders 2.7978
New Caledonia	Franc CFP	Francs 142.661	Francs 143.981
New Zealand	New Zealand dollar (NZ$) of 100 cents	NZ$ 2.3755	NZ$ 2.2644
Nicaragua	Córdoba (C$) of 100 centavos	C$ 11.9061	C$ 13.3918
Niger	Franc CFA	Francs 784.440	Francs 790.270
Nigeria	Naira (N) of 100 kobo	N 34.1519	N 34.3860
Niue	Currency is that of New Zealand	NZ$ 2.3755	NZ$ 2.2644
Norfolk Island	Currency is that of Australia	$A 2.0714	$A 1.9754
Northern Mariana Islands	Currency is that of USA	US$ 1.5525	US$ 1.5630
Norway	Krone of 100 øre	Kroner 9.9360	Kroner 10.0138
Oman	Rial Omani (OR) of 1,000 baiza	OR 0.5978	OR 0.6019
Pakistan	Pakistan rupee of 100 paisa	Rs 48.5758	Rs 55.6184
Palau	Currency is that of USA	US$ 1.5525	US$ 1.5630
Panama	Balboa of 100 centésimos (US notes are also in circulation)	Balboa 1.5525	Balboa 1.5630
Papua New Guinea	Kina (K) of 100 toea	K 2.1209	K 2.0512
Paraguay	Guaraní (Gs) of 100 céntimos	Gs 3046.78	Gs 3243.23
Peru	New Sol of 100 cénts	New Sol 3.5009	New Sol 3.8607
Philippines	Philippine peso (P) of 100 centavos	P 40.3185	P 40.9428
Poland	Złoty of 100 groszy	Złotys 3.8393	Złotys 4.2803
Portugal	Escudo (Esc) of 100 centavos	Esc 236.570	Esc 236.873
Puerto Rico	Currency is that of USA	US$ 1.5525	US$ 1.5630
Qatar	Qatar riyal of 100 dirhams	Riyals 5.6527	Riyals 5.6909
Réunion	Currency is that of France	Francs 7.8444	Francs 7.9027
Romania	Leu (Lei) of 100 bani	Lei 3221.44	Lei 4798.41
Russia	Rouble of 100 kopeks	Roubles 0.9717	Roubles 8384.71
Rwanda	Rwanda franc of 100 centimes	Francs 496.490	Francs 507.037
St Christopher and Nevis	East Caribbean dollar (EC$) of 100 cents	EC$ 4.1918	EC$ 4.2201
St Helena	St Helena pound (£) of 100 pence	*at parity with £ sterling*	

COUNTRY/TERRITORY	MONETARY UNIT	AVERAGE RATE TO £ 1 September 1995	AVERAGE RATE TO £ 30 August 1996
St Lucia	East Caribbean dollar (EC$) of 100 cents	EC$ 4.1918	EC$ 4.2201
St Pierre and Miquelon	Currency is that of France	Francs 7.8444	Francs 7.9027
St Vincent and the Grenadines	East Caribbean dollar (EC$) of 100 cents	EC$ 4.1918	EC$ 4.2201
El Salvador	El Salvador colón (₡) of 100 centavos	₡ 13.5999	₡ 13.6841
San Marino	Italian currency is in circulation	Lire 2523.90	Lire 2358.53
São Tomé and Príncipe	Dobra of 100 centavos	Dobra 1953.56	Dobra 3727.96
Saudi Arabia	Saudi riyal (SR) of 20 qursh or 100 halala	SR 5.8229	SR 5.8621
Senegal	Franc CFA	Francs 784.440	Francs 790.270
Seychelles	Seychelles rupee of 100 cents	Rs 7.5110	Rs 7.7916
Sierra Leone	Leone (Le) of 100 cents	Le 1133.33	Le 1359.81
Singapore	Singapore dollar (S$) of 100 cents	S$ 2.2061	S$ 2.1995
Slovakia	Koruna (Kčs) of 100 haléru	Kčs 47.2737	Kčs 47.8356
Slovenia	Tolar (SIT) of 100 stotin	Tolars 190.849	Tolars 205.460
Solomon Islands	Solomon Islands dollar (SI$) of 100 cents	SI$ 4.6488	SI$ 5.5526
Somalia	Somali shilling of 100 cents	Shillings 4067.55	Shillings 4095.06
South Africa	Rand (R) of 100 cents	R 5.6802	R 7.0140
Spain	Peseta of 100 céntimos	Pesetas 194.893	Pesetas 195.445
Sri Lanka	Sri Lankan rupee of 100 cents	Rs 78.4323	Rs 86.9029
Sudan	Sudanese dinar (SD) of 10 pounds	SD 80.8543	SD 225.072
Suriname	Suriname guilder of 100 cents	Guilders 763.831	Guilders 640.830
Swaziland	Lilangeni (E) of 100 cents (South African currency also in circulation)	E 5.6802	E 7.0140
Sweden	Swedish krona of 100 öre	Kronor 11.3549	Kronor 10.3397
Switzerland	Swiss franc of 100 rappen (or centimes)	Francs 1.8588	Francs 1.8718
Syria	Syrian pound (S$) of 100 piastres	S£ 65.1274	S£ 65.5679
Taiwan	New Taiwan dollar (NT$) of 100 cents	NT$ 42.6914	NT$ 42.9317
Tajikistan	Tajik rouble (TJR) of 100 tanga	—	TJR 83.8471
Tanzania	Tanzanian shilling of 100 cents	Shillings 939.263	Shillings 906.540
Thailand	Baht of 100 satang	Baht 38.8747	Baht 39.5518
Togo	Franc CFA	Francs 784.440	Francs 790.270
Tokelau	Currency is that of New Zealand	NZ$ 2.3755	NZ$ 2.2644
Tonga	Pa'anga (T$) of 100 seniti	T$ 2.0714	T$ 1.9754
Trinidad and Tobago	Trinidad and Tobago dollar (TT$) of 100 cents	TT$ 8.8570	TT$ 9.2860
Tunisia	Tunisian dinar of 1,000 millimes	Dinars 1.4746	Dinars 1.4974
Turkey	Turkish lira (TL) of 100 kurus	TL 74892.7	TL 135613.7
Turkmenistan	Manat	—	—
Turks and Caicos Islands	US dollar (US$)	US$ 1.5525	US$ 1.5630
Tuvalu	Australian dollar ($A) of 100 cents	$A 2.0714	$A 1.9754
Uganda	Uganda shilling of 100 cents	Shillings 1490.40	Shillings 1667.72
Ukraine	Karbovanets (Ka)	Ka 253057.7	Ka 275869.6
United Arab Emirates	UAE dirham of 100 fils	Dirham 5.7024	Dirham 5.7407
United Kingdom	Pound sterling (£) of 100 pence	£ 1.00	£ 1.00
United States of America	US dollar (US$) of 100 cents	US$ 1.5525	US$ 1.5630
Uruguay	New Uruguayan peso of 100 centésimos	Pesos 10.1223	Pesos 12.9651
Uzbekistan	Sum	—	—
Vanuatu	Vatu of 100 centimes	Vatu 174.269	Vatu 173.313
Vatican City State	Italian currency is legal tender	Lire 2523.90	Lire 2358.53
Venezuela	Bolívar (Bs) of 100 céntimos	Bs 263.591	Bs 742.425
Vietnam	Dông of 10 hào or 100 xu	Dông 17105.5	Dông 17223.5
Virgin Islands (US)	Currency is that of USA	US$ 1.5525	US$ 1.5630
Wallis and Futuna Islands	Franc CFP	Francs 142.661	Francs 143.981
Western Samoa	Tala (WS$) of 100 sene	WS$ 3.8968	WS$ 3.8069
Republic of Yemen	Riyal of 100 fils	Riyals 78.0132	Riyals 218.820
Yugoslavia, Federal Rep.	New dinar of 100 paras	—	New Dinars 7.6879
Zaïre	Zaïre (Z) of 100 makuta	Zaïre 8419.52	Zaïre 77999.2
Zambia	Kwacha (K) of 100 ngwee	K 1459.23	K 1985.01
Zimbabwe	Zimbabwe dollar (Z$) of 100 cents	Z$ 13.4408	Z$ 16.1615

Time Zones

Standard time differences from the Greenwich meridian

+ hours ahead of GMT
− hours behind GMT
* may vary from standard time at some part of the year (Summer Time or Daylight Saving Time)
h hours
m minutes

	h	m
Afghanistan	+ 4	30
*Albania	+ 1	
Algeria	+ 1	
*Andorra	+ 1	
Angola	+ 1	
Anguilla	− 4	
Antigua and Barbuda	− 4	
Argentina	− 3	
Armenia	+ 4	
Aruba	− 4	
Ascension Island	0	
*Australia	+10	
Broken Hill area (NSW)	+ 9	30
Lord Howe Island	+10	30
Northern Territory	+ 9	30
*South Australia	+ 9	30
Western Australia	+ 8	
*Austria	+ 1	
Azerbaijan	+ 4	
*Azores	− 1	
*Bahamas	− 5	
Bahrain	+ 3	
Bangladesh	+ 6	
Barbados	− 4	
*Belarus	+ 2	
*Belgium	+ 1	
Belize	− 6	
Benin	+ 1	
*Bermuda	− 4	
Bhutan	+ 6	
Bolivia	− 4	
*Bosnia-Hercegovina	+ 1	
Botswana	+ 2	
Brazil		
Acre	− 5	
*eastern, including all coast and Brasilia	− 3	
Fernando de Norouha Island	− 2	
*western	− 4	
British Antarctic Territory	− 3	
British Indian Ocean Territory	+ 5	
Diego Garcia	+ 6	
British Virgin Islands	− 4	
Brunei	+ 8	
*Bulgaria	+ 2	
Burkina Faso	0	
Burundi	+ 2	
Cambodia	+ 7	
Cameroon	+ 1	
Canada		
*Alberta	− 7	
*British Columbia	− 8	
British Columbia NE	− 7	
*Labrador	− 4	

	h	m
*Manitoba	− 6	
*New Brunswick	− 4	
*Newfoundland	− 3	30
*Northwest Territories		
east of 68° W.	− 4	
68° W.–85° W.	5	
85° W.–102° W.	− 6	
west of 102° W.	− 7	
*Nova Scotia	− 4	
Ontario		
*east of 90° W.	− 5	
west of 90° W.	− 5	
*Prince Edward Island	− 4	
*Quebec		
east of 63° W.	− 4	
west of 63° W.	− 5	
*Saskatchewan	− 6	
*Yukon	− 8	
*Canary Islands	0	
Cape Verde	− 1	
Cayman Islands	− 5	
Central African Republic	+ 1	
Chad	+ 1	
*Chatham Island	+12	45
*Chile	− 4	
China	+ 8	
Christmas Island (Indian Ocean)	+ 7	
Cocos Keeling Islands	+ 6	30
Colombia	− 5	
Comoros	+ 3	
Congo	+ 1	
Cook Islands	− 10	
Costa Rica	− 6	
Côte d'Ivoire	0	
*Croatia	+ 1	
*Cuba	− 5	
*Cyprus	+ 2	
*Czech Republic	+ 1	
*Denmark	+ 1	
Djibouti	+ 3	
Dominica	− 4	
Dominican Republic	− 4	
Ecuador	− 5	
Galápagos Islands	− 6	
*Egypt	+ 2	
Equatorial Guinea	+ 1	
Eritrea	+ 3	
*Estonia	+ 2	
*Ethiopia	+ 3	
*Falkland Islands	− 4	
*Faröe Islands	0	
Fiji	+12	
*Finland	+ 2	
*France	+ 1	
French Guiana	− 3	
French Polynesia	−10	
Marquesas Islands	− 9	30
Gabon	+ 1	
The Gambia	0	
*Georgia	+ 4	
*Germany	+ 1	
Ghana	0	
*Gibraltar	+ 1	
*Greece	+ 2	
Greenland	− 3	

	h	m
Danmarkshavn	0	
Mesters Vig		
*Scoresby Sound	− 1	
*Thule area	− 4	
Grenada	− 4	
Guadeloupe	− 4	
Guam	+10	
Guatemala	− 6	
Guinea	0	
Guinea-Bissau	0	
Guyana	− 4	
*Haiti	− 5	
Honduras	− 6	
Hong Kong	+ 8	
*Hungary	+ 1	
Iceland	0	
India	+ 5	30
Indonesia		
Bali	+ 8	
Flores	+ 8	
Irian Jaya	+ 9	
Java	+ 7	
Kalimantan (south and east)	+ 8	
Kalimantan (west and central)	+ 7	
Molucca Islands	+ 9	
Sulawesi	+ 8	
Sumatra	+ 7	
Sumbawa	+ 8	
Tanimbar	+ 9	
Timor	+ 8	
*Iran	+ 3	30
*Iraq	+ 3	
*Ireland, Republic of	0	
*Israel	+ 2	
*Italy	+ 1	
Jamaica	− 5	
Japan	+ 9	
*Jordan	+ 2	
*Kazakhstan	+ 6	
Kenya	+ 3	
Kiribati		
Banaba	+12	
Gilbert Islands	+12	
Kiritimati Island	−10	
Line Islands	+14	
Phoenix Islands	−13	
Korea, North	+ 9	
Korea, South	+ 9	
Kuwait	+ 3	
*Kyrgyzstan	+ 5	
Laos	+ 7	
*Latvia	+ 2	
*Lebanon	+ 2	
Lesotho	+ 2	
Liberia	0	
Libya	+ 2	
*Liechtenstein	+ 1	
*Lithuania	+ 2	
*Luxembourg	+ 1	
Macao	+ 8	
*Macedonia (Former Yug. Rep. of)	+ 1	
Madagascar	+ 3	
*Madeira	0	

	h	m
Malawi	+ 2	
Malaysia	+ 8	
Maldives	+ 5	
Mali	0	
*Malta	+ 1	
Marshall Islands	+12	
Ebon Atoll	−12	
Martinique	− 4	
Mauritania	0	
Mauritius	+ 4	
Mexico	− 6	
central	− 7	
western	− 8	
Micronesia		
Caroline Islands	+10	
Kosrae	+11	
Pingelap	+11	
Pohnpei	+11	
*Moldova	+ 2	
*Monaco	+ 1	
*Mongolia	+ 8	
Montserrat	− 4	
Morocco	0	
Mozambique	+ 2	
Myanmar	+ 6	30
*Namibia	+ 1	
Nauru	+12	
Nepal	+ 5	45
*Netherlands	+ 1	
Netherlands Antilles	− 4	
New Caledonia	+11	
*New Zealand	+12	
Nicaragua	− 6	
Niger	+ 1	
Nigeria	+ 1	
Niue	−11	
Norfolk Island	+11	30
Northern Mariana Islands	+10	
*Norway	+ 1	
Oman	+ 4	
Pakistan	+ 5	
Palau	+ 9	
Panama	− 5	
Papua New Guinea	+10	
*Paraguay	− 4	
Peru	− 5	
Philippines	+ 8	
*Poland	+ 1	
*Portugal	+ 1	
Puerto Rico	− 4	
Qatar	+ 3	
Réunion	+ 4	
*Romania	+ 2	
*Russia		
Zone 1	+ 2	
Zone 2	+ 3	
Zone 3	+ 4	
Zone 4	+ 5	
Zone 5	+ 6	
Zone 6	+ 7	
Zone 7	+ 8	
Zone 8	+ 9	
Zone 9	+10	
Zone 10	+11	
Zone 11	+12	
Rwanda	+ 2	
St Helena	0	
St Kitts and Nevis	− 4	

	h	m
St Lucia	− 4	
*St Pierre and Miquelon	− 3	
St Vincent and the Grenadines	− 4	
El Salvador	− 6	
Samoa, American	−11	
*San Marino	+ 1	
São Tomé and Príncipe	0	
Saudi Arabia	+ 3	
Senegal	0	
Seychelles	+ 4	
Sierra Leone	0	
Singapore	+ 8	
*Slovakia	+ 1	
*Slovenia	+ 1	
Solomon Islands	+11	
Somalia	+ 3	
South Africa	+ 2	
South Georgia	− 2	
*Spain	+ 1	
Sri Lanka	+ 5	30
Sudan	+ 2	
Suriname	− 3	
Swaziland	+ 2	
*Sweden	+ 1	
*Switzerland	+ 1	
*Syria	+ 2	
Taiwan	+ 8	
Tajikistan	+ 5	
Tanzania	+ 3	
Thailand	+ 7	
Togo	0	
Tonga	+13	
Trinidad and Tobago	− 4	
Tristan da Cunha	0	
Tunisia	+ 1	
*Turkey	+ 2	
Turkmenistan	+ 5	
*Turks and Caicos Islands	− 5	
Tuvalu	+12	
Uganda	+ 3	
*Ukraine	+ 2	
*Simferopol	+ 3	
United Arab Emirates	+ 4	
United States		
*Alaska, east of 169° 30′ W.	− 9	
*Aleutian Islands, west of 169° 30′ W.	−10	
eastern time	− 5	
*central time	− 6	
Hawaii	−10	
*mountain time	− 7	
*Pacific time	− 8	
Uruguay	− 3	
Uzbekistan	+ 5	
Vanuatu	+11	
*Vatican City State	+ 1	
Venezuela	− 4	
Vietnam	+ 7	
Virgin Islands (US)	− 4	
Western Samoa	−11	
Yemen	+ 3	
*Yugoslavia (Fed. Rep. of)	+ 1	
Zaïre		
East	+ 2	
West	+ 1	

	h	m
Zambia	+ 2	
Zimbabwe	+ 2	

Source: reproduced with permission from data produced by HM Nautical Almanac Office

The Olympic Games

Atlanta, USA, 19 July to 4 August 1996

ARCHERY (MEN)
Individual: Justin Huish (USA)
Team: USA

ARCHERY (WOMEN)
Individual: Kim Kyung-Wook (S. Korea)
Team: S. Korea

ATHLETICS (MEN)

	hr.	min.	sec.
100 *metres:* Donovan Bailey (Canada)			9.94
200 *metres:* Michael Johnson (USA)			19.32
400 *metres:* Michael Johnson (USA)			43.49
800 *metres:* Vebjorn Rodal (Norway)		1	42.58
1,500 *metres:* Noureddine Morceli (Algeria)		3	35.78
5,000 *metres:* Venuste Nyongabo (Burundi)		13	07.96
10,000 *metres:* Haile Gebrsilassie (Ethiopia)		27	07.34
Marathon: Josiah Thugwane (S. Africa)	2	12	36
3,000 *metres steeplechase:* Joseph Keter (Kenya)		8	07.12
110 *metres hurdles:* Allen Johnson (USA)			12.95
400 *metres hurdles:* Derrick Adkins (USA)			47.55
20 *km walk:* Jefferson Perez (Ecuador)	1	20	07
50 *km walk:* Robert Korzeniowski (Poland)	3	43	30
4 x 100 *metres relay:* Canada			37.69
4 x 400 *metres relay:* USA		2	55.99

	metres
High jump: Charles Austin (USA)	2.39
Pole vault: Jean Galfione (France)	5.92
Long jump: Carl Lewis (USA)	8.50
Triple jump: Kenny Harrison (USA)	18.09
Shot: Randy Barnes (USA)	21.62
Discus: Lars Riedel (Germany)	69.40
Hammer: Balazs Kiss (Hungary)	81.24
Javelin: Jan Zelezny (Czech Republic)	88.16
Decathlon: Dan O'Brien (USA)	8,824 points

ATHLETICS (WOMEN)

	hr.	min.	sec.
100 *metres:* Gail Devers (USA)			10.94
200 *metres:* Marie-José Pérec (France)			22.12
400 *metres:* Marie-José Pérec (France)			48.25
800 *metres:* Svetlana Masterkova (Russia)		1	57.73
1,500 *metres:* Svetlana Masterkova (Russia)		4	00.83
5,000 *metres:* Wang Junxia (China)		14	59.88
10,000 *metres:* Fernanda Ribeiro (Portugal)		31	01.63
Marathon: Fatuma Roba (Ethiopia)	2	26	05
100 *metres hurdles:* Lyudmila Engquist (Sweden)			12.58
400 *metres hurdles:* Deon Hemmings (Jamaica)			52.82
10 *km walk:* Yelena Nikolayeva (Russia)		41	49
4 x 100 *metres relay:* USA			41.95
4 x 400 *metres relay:* USA		3	20.91

	metres
High jump: Stefka Kostadinova (Bulgaria)	2.05
Long jump: Chioma Ajunwa (Nigeria)	7.12
Triple jump: Inessa Kravets (Ukraine)	15.33
Shot: Astrid Kumbernuss (Germany)	20.56
Discus: Ilke Wyludda (Germany)	69.66
Javelin: Heli Rantanen (Norway)	67.94
Heptathlon: Ghada Shouaa (Syria)	6,780 points

BADMINTON (MEN)
Singles: Poul-Erik Hoyer-Larsen (Denmark)
Doubles: Indonesia

BADMINTON (WOMEN)
Singles: Bang Soo-Hyun (S. Korea)
Doubles: China

BADMINTON (MIXED)
Doubles: S. Korea

BASEBALL
Team: Cuba

BASKETBALL
Men: USA
Women: USA

BEACH VOLLEYBALL
Men's Pairs: USA
Women's Pairs: Brazil

BOXING
Up to 48 *kg:* Daniel Petrov (Bulgaria)
Up to 51 *kg:* Maikro Romero (Cuba)
Up to 54 *kg:* Istvan Kovacs (Hungary)
Up to 57 *kg:* Somluck Kamsing (Thailand)
Up to 60 *kg:* Hocine Soltani (Algeria)
Up to 63.5 *kg:* Hector Vinent (Cuba)
Up to 67 *kg:* Oleg Saitov (Russia)
Up to 71 *kg:* David Reid (USA)
Up to 75 *kg:* Ariel Hernandez (Cuba)
Up to 81 *kg:* Vasili Jirov (Kazakhstan)
Up to 91 *kg:* Felix Savon (Cuba)
Over 91 *kg:* Vladimir Klichko (Ukraine)

CANOEING (MEN)
K1 500 *metres:* Antonio Rossi (Italy)
K1 1,000 *metres:* Knut Holmann (Norway)
K2 500 *metres:* Germany
K2 1,000 *metres:* Italy
K4 1,000 *metres:* Germany
C1 500 *metres:* Martin Doktor (Czech Republic)
C1 1,000 *metres:* Martin Doktor (Czech Republic)
C2 500 *metres:* Hungary
C2 1,000 *metres:* Germany
Slalom
K1: Oliver Fix (Germany)
C1: Michal Martikan (Slovakia)
C2: France

CANOEING (WOMEN)
K1 500 *metres:* Rita Koban (Hungary)
K2 500 *metres:* Sweden
K4 500 *metres:* Germany

Slalom
K1: Stepanka Hilgertova (Czech Republic)

CYCLING (MEN)

	hr.	min.	sec.
1 km time trial: Florian Rousseau (France)		1	02.712
Sprint: Jens Fiedler (Germany)			
4,000 metres individual pursuit: Andrea Collinelli (Italy)		4	20.893
4,000 metres team pursuit: France		4	05.930
Points race: Silvio Martinello (Italy)			
Individual road race: Pascal Richard (Switzerland)	4	53	56
Road time trial: Miguel Indurain (Spain)	1	04	05
Cross-country (mountain bike): Bart Brentjens (Netherlands)	2	17	38

CYCLING (WOMEN)

	hr.	min.	sec.
Sprint: Felicia Ballanger (France)			
3,000 metres individual pursuit: Antonella Bellutti (Italy)		3	33.595
Points race: Nathalie Lancien (France)			
Individual road race: Jeannie Longo-Ciprelli (France)	2	36	13
Individual time trial: Zulfia Zabirova (Russia)		36	40
Cross-country (mountain bike): Paola Pezzo (Italy)	1	50	51

DIVING (MEN)
Springboard: Ni Xiong (China), 701.46 points
Platform: Dimitri Sautin (Russia), 692.34 points

DIVING (WOMEN)
Springboard: Fu Mingxia (China), 547.68 points
Platform: Fu Mingxia (China), 521.58 points

EQUESTRIANISM
Three-Day Eventing
Individual: Blyth Tait (New Zealand) on Ready Teddy
Team: Australia
Dressage
Individual: Isabel Werth (Germany) on Gigolo
Team: Germany
Jumping
Individual: Ulrich Kirchhoff (Germany) on Jus de Pommes
Team: Germany

FENCING (MEN)
Foil
Individual: Alessandro Puccini (Italy)
Team: Russia
Sabre
Individual: Sergei Podnyakov (Russia)
Team: Russia
Epée
Individual: Alexander Beketov (Russia)
Team: Italy

FENCING (WOMEN)
Foil
Individual: Laura Badea (Romania)
Team: Italy
Epée
Individual: Laura Flessel (France)
Team: France

FOOTBALL
Men: Nigeria
Women: USA

GYMNASTICS (MEN)
Team: Russia
Individual all-round: Li Xiaoshuang (China)
Floor: Ioannis Melissanidis (Greece)
Pommel Horse: Lin Donghua (Switzerland)
Rings: Yuri Chechi (Italy)
Vault: Alexei Nemov (Russia)
Parallel Bars: Rustam Sharipov (Ukraine)
Horizontal Bar: Andreas Wecker (Germany)

GYMNASTICS (WOMEN)
Team: USA
Individual all-round: Lilia Podkopayeva (Ukraine)
Floor: Lilia Podkopayeva (Ukraine)
Beam: Shannon Miller (USA)
Vault: Simona Amanar (Romania)
Asymmetrical Bars: Svetlana Chorkina (Russia)
Rhythmic
Individual: Yekaterina Serebryanskaya (Ukraine)
Team: Spain

HANDBALL
Men: Croatia
Women: Denmark

HOCKEY
Men: Netherlands
Women: Australia

JUDO (MEN)
Up to 60 kg: Tadahiro Nomura (Japan)
Up to 65 kg: Udo Quellmalz (Germany)
Up to 71 kg: Kenzo Nakamura (Japan)
Up to 78 kg: Djamel Bouras (France)
Up to 86 kg: Jeon Ki-Young (S. Korea)
Up to 95 kg: Pawel Nastula (Poland)
Over 95 kg: David Douillet (France)

JUDO (WOMEN)
Up to 48 kg: Kye Sun (N. Korea)
Up to 52 kg: Marie-Claire Restoux (France)
Up to 56 kg: Driulis Gonzalez (Cuba)
Up to 61 kg: Yuko Emoto (Japan)
Up to 66 kg: Cho Min-Sun (S. Korea)
Up to 72 kg: Ulla Werbrouck (Hungary)
Over 72 kg: Sun Fu-Ming (China)

MODERN PENTATHLON
Individual: Alexander Parygin (Kazakhstan), 5,551 points

ROWING (MEN)
Single Sculls: Xeno Mueller (Switzerland)
Double Sculls: Italy
Quad Sculls: Germany
Coxless Pairs: Great Britain
Coxless Fours: Australia
Eights: Netherlands
Lightweight Double Sculls: Switzerland
Lightweight Coxless Fours: Denmark

ROWING (WOMEN)
Single Sculls: Yekaterina Khodotovich (Belarus)
Double Sculls: Canada
Quad Sculls: Germany
Coxless Pairs: Australia

Eights: Romania
Lightweight Double Sculls: Romania

SHOOTING (MEN)

Air Pistol: Roberto di Donna (Italy)
Rapid-Fire Pistol: Ralf Schumann (Germany)
Free Pistol: Boris Kokorev (Russia)
Small-Bore Rifle, 3 Positions: Jean-Pierre Amat (France)
Small-Bore Rifle, Prone: Christian Klees (Germany)
Air Rifle: Artem Khadzhibekov (Russia)
Running Target: Ling Yang (China)
Skeet: Ennio Falco (Italy)
Trap: Michael Diamond (Australia)
Double Trap: Russell Mark (Australia)

SHOOTING (WOMEN)

Air Pistol: Olga Klochneva (Russia)
Sport Pistol: Li Duihong (China)
Small-Bore Rifle, 3 Positions: Alexandra Ivosev (Yugoslavia)
Air Rifle: Renata Mauer (Poland)
Double Trap: Kim Rhode (USA)

SOFTBALL

Team: USA

SWIMMING (MEN)

	min.	sec.
50 *metres freestyle:* Aleksandr Popov (Russia)		22.13
100 *metres freestyle:* Aleksandr Popov (Russia)		48.74
200 *metres freestyle:* Danyon Loader (New Zealand)	1	47.63
400 *metres freestyle:* Danyon Loader (New Zealand)	3	47.97
1,500 *metres freestyle:* Kieren Perkins (Australia)	14	56.40
100 *metres backstroke:* Jeff Rouse (USA)		54.10
200 *metres backstroke:* Brad Bridgewater (USA)	1	58.54
100 *metres breaststroke:* Frederik Deburghgraeve (Belgium)	1	00.65
200 *metres breaststroke:* Norbert Rozsa (Hungary)	2	12.57
100 *metres butterfly:* Denis Pankratov (Russia)		52.27
200 *metres butterfly:* Denis Pankratov (Russia)	1	56.51
200 *metres individual medley:* Attila Czene (Hungary)	1	59.91
400 *metres individual medley:* Tom Dolan (USA)	4	14.90
4 x 100 *metres freestyle relay:* USA	3	15.41
4 x 200 *metres freestyle relay:* USA	7	14.84
4 x 100 *metres medley relay:* USA	3	34.84

SWIMMING (WOMEN)

	min.	sec.
50 *metres freestyle:* Amy van Dyken (USA)		24.87
100 *metres freestyle:* Le Jingyi (China)		54.50
200 *metres freestyle:* Claudia Poll (Costa Rica)	1	58.16
400 *metres freestyle:* Michelle Smith (Ireland)	4	07.25
800 *metres freestyle:* Brooke Bennett (USA)	8	27.89
100 *metres backstroke:* Beth Botsford (USA)	1	01.19
200 *metres backstroke:* Krysztina Egerszegi (Hungary)	2	07.83
100 *metres breaststroke:* Penelope Heyns (S. Africa)	1	07.73
200 *metres breaststroke:* Penelope Heyns (S. Africa)	2	25.41
100 *metres butterfly:* Amy van Dyken (USA)		59.10
200 *metres butterfly:* Susan O'Neill (Australia)	2	07.76

200 *metres individual medley:* Michelle Smith (Ireland)	2	13.93
400 *metres individual medley:* Michelle Smith (Ireland)	4	39.18
4 x 100 *metres freestyle relay:* USA	3	39.29
4 x 200 *metres freestyle relay:* USA	7	59.87
4 x 100 *metres medley relay:* USA	4	02.88

SYNCHRONIZED SWIMMING

Team: USA

TABLE TENNIS (MEN)

Singles: Liu Guoliang (China)
Doubles: China

TABLE TENNIS (WOMEN)

Singles: Deng Yaping (China)
Doubles: China

TENNIS (MEN)

Singles: Andre Agassi (USA)
Doubles: Australia

TENNIS (WOMEN)

Singles: Lindsay Davenport (USA)
Doubles: USA

VOLLEYBALL

Men: Netherlands
Women: Cuba

WATER POLO

Team: Spain

WEIGHTLIFTING

Up to 54 kg: Halil Mutlu (Turkey)
Up to 59 kg: Tang Ningsheng (China)
Up to 64 kg: Naim Suleymanoglu (Turkey)
Up to 70 kg: Zhang Xugang (China)
Up to 76 kg: Pablo Lara (Cuba)
Up to 83 kg: Pyrros Dimas (Greece)
Up to 91 kg: Alexei Petrov (Russia)
Under 99 kg: Akakidi Khakiashvilis (Greece)
Up to 108 kg: Timur Taimazov (Ukraine)
Over 108 kg: Andrei Chemerkin (Russia)

WRESTLING (FREESTYLE)

Up to 48 kg: Kim Il (N. Korea)
Up to 52 kg: Valentin Jordanov (Bulgaria)
Up to 57 kg: Kendall Cross (USA)
Up to 62 kg: Thomas Brands (USA)
Up to 68 kg: Vadim Bogiyev (Russia)
Up to 74 kg: Buvaisa Saityev (Russia)
Up to 82 kg: Khadshimurad Magomedov (Russia)
Up to 90 kg: Rasul Khadem Azghadi (Iran)
Up to 100 kg: Kurt Angle (USA)
Over 100 kg: Mahmut Demir (Turkey)

WRESTLING (GRECO-ROMAN)

Up to 48 kg: Sim Kwon-Ho (S. Korea)
Up to 52 kg: Arman Nazaryan (Armenia)
Up to 57 kg: Yovei Melnichenko (Kazakhstan)
Up to 62 kg: Wlodzimierz Zawadzki (Poland)
Up to 68 kg: Ryzsard Wolny (Poland)
Up to 74 kg: Feliberto Aguilera (Cuba)
Up to 82 kg: Hamza Yerlikaya (Turkey)
Up to 90 kg: Vyachetslav Oleynyk (Ukraine)
Up to 100 kg: Andreas Wronski (Poland)
Over 100 kg: Alexandr Karelin (Russia)

YACHTING (MEN)

Mistral Sailboard: Nikolas Kaklamanakis (Greece)
Finn: Mateusz Kusnierewicz (Poland)
470: Ukraine

YACHTING (WOMEN)

Mistral Sailboard: Lai-Shan Lee (Hong Kong)
Europe: Kristine Roug (Denmark)
470: Spain

YACHTING (MIXED)

Star: Brazil
Soling: Germany
Laser: Robert Scheidt (Brazil)
Tornado: Spain

MEDAL TABLE

	Gold	Silver	Bronze	Total
USA	44	32	25	101
Russia	26	21	16	63
Germany	20	18	27	65
China	16	22	12	50
France	15	7	15	37
Italy	13	10	12	35
Australia	9	9	23	41
Cuba	9	8	8	25
Ukraine	9	2	12	23
South Korea	7	15	5	27
Poland	7	5	5	17
Hungary	7	4	10	21
Spain	5	6	6	17
Romania	4	7	9	20
Netherlands	4	5	10	19
Greece	4	4	0	8
Czech Republic	4	3	4	11
Switzerland	4	3	0	7
Denmark	4	1	1	6
Turkey	4	1	1	6
Canada	3	11	8	22
Bulgaria	3	7	5	15
Japan	3	6	5	14
Kazakhstan	3	4	4	11
Brazil	3	3	9	15
New Zealand	3	2	1	6
South Africa	3	1	1	5
Ireland	3	0	1	4
Sweden	2	4	2	8
Norway	2	2	3	7
Belgium	2	2	2	6
Nigeria	2	1	3	6
North Korea	2	1	2	5
Algeria	2	0	1	3
Ethiopia	2	0	1	3
Great Britain	1	8	6	15
Belarus	1	6	8	15
Kenya	1	4	3	8
Jamaica	1	3	2	6
Finland	1	2	1	4
Indonesia	1	1	2	4
Yugoslavia	1	1	2	4
Iran	1	1	1	3
Slovakia	1	1	1	3
Armenia	1	1	0	2
Croatia	1	1	0	2
Portugal	1	0	1	2
Thailand	1	0	1	2
Burundi	1	0	0	1

	Gold	Silver	Bronze	Total
Costa Rica	1	0	0	1
Ecuador	1	0	0	1
Hong Kong	1	0	0	1
Syria	1	0	0	1
Argentina	0	2	1	3
Namibia	0	2	0	2
Slovenia	0	2	0	2
Austria	0	1	2	3
Malaysia	0	1	1	2
Moldova	0	1	1	2
Uzbekistan	0	1	1	2
Azerbaijan	0	1	0	1
Bahamas	0	1	0	1
Latvia	0	1	0	1
Philippines	0	1	0	1
Taiwan	0	1	0	1
Tonga	0	1	0	1
Zambia	0	1	0	1
Georgia	0	0	2	2
Morocco	0	0	2	2
Trinidad	0	0	2	2
India	0	0	1	1
Israel	0	0	1	1
Lithuania	0	0	1	1
Mexico	0	0	1	1
Mongolia	0	0	1	1
Mozambique	0	0	1	1
Puerto Rico	0	0	1	1
Tunisia	0	0	1	1
Uganda	0	0	1	1
	271	273	298	842

The Olympic Games

Venues of the modern Olympic Games

I	Athens, Greece	1896
II	Paris, France	1900
III	St Louis, USA	1904
*	Athens	1906
IV	London, Britain	1908
V	Stockholm, Sweden	1912
†VI	Berlin, Germany	1916
VII	Antwerp, Belgium	1920
VIII	Paris, France	1924
IX	Amsterdam, Netherlands	1928
X	Los Angeles, USA	1932
XI	Berlin, Germany	1936
†XII	Tokyo, Japan, then Helsinki, Finland	1940
†XIII	London, Britain	1944
XIV	London, Britain	1948
XV	Helsinki, Finland	1952
§XVI	Melbourne, Australia	1956
XVII	Rome, Italy	1960
XVIII	Tokyo, Japan	1964
XIX	Mexico City, Mexico	1968
XX	Munich, West Germany	1972
XXI	Montreal, Canada	1976
XXII	Moscow, USSR	1980
XXIII	Los Angeles, USA	1984
XXIV	Seoul, South Korea	1988
XXV	Barcelona, Spain	1992
XXVI	Atlanta, USA	1996
XXVII	Sydney, Australia	2000

WINTER OLYMPIC GAMES

I	Chamonix, France	1924
II	St Moritz, Switzerland	1928
III	Lake Placid, USA	1932
IV	Garmisch-Partenkirchen, Germany	1936
V	St Moritz, Switzerland	1948
VI	Oslo, Norway	1952
VII	Cortina d'Ampezzo, Italy	1956
VIII	Squaw Valley, USA	1960
IX	Innsbruck, Austria	1964
X	Grenoble, France	1968
XI	Sapporo, Japan	1972
XII	Innsbruck, Austria	1976
XIII	Lake Placid, USA	1980
XIV	Sarajevo, Yugoslavia	1984
XV	Calgary, Canada	1988
XVI	Albertville, France	1992
XVII	Lillehammer, Norway	1994
XVIII	Nagano, Japan	1998
XIX	Salt Lake City, USA	2002

* The 'Intercalated' Games
† These Games were scheduled but did not take place owing to World Wars
§ Equestrian events were held in Stockholm, Sweden

The Commonwealth Games

The Games were originally called the British Empire Games. From 1954 to 1966 the Games were known as the British Empire and Commonwealth Games, and from 1970 to 1974 as the British Commonwealth Games. Since 1978 the Games have been called the Commonwealth Games.

BRITISH EMPIRE GAMES

I	Hamilton, Canada	1930
II	London, England	1934
III	Sydney, Australia	1938
IV	Auckland, New Zealand	1950

BRITISH EMPIRE AND COMMONWEALTH GAMES

V	Vancouver, Canada	1954
VI	Cardiff, Wales	1958

VII	Perth, Australia	1962
VIII	Kingston, Jamaica	1966

BRITISH COMMONWEALTH GAMES

IX	Edinburgh, Scotland	1970
X	Christchurch, New Zealand	1974

COMMONWEALTH GAMES

XI	Edmonton, Canada	1978
XII	Brisbane, Australia	1982
XIII	Edinburgh, Scotland	1986
XIV	Auckland, New Zealand	1990
XV	Victoria, Canada	1994
XVI	Kuala Lumpur, Malaysia	1998
XVII	Manchester, England	2002

Events of the Year

1 September 1995 to 31 August 1996

SEPTEMBER 1995

8. David Trimble was elected leader of the Ulster Unionists. **11.** The TUC conference opened in Brighton; it was addressed by the President of the European Commission, Jacques Santer. **14.** Kevin McNamara resigned as Labour's Civil Service spokesman over the approach of the Labour leader (Tony Blair) to the Northern Ireland peace process and in particular Mr Blair's support for the Government over the decommissioning of IRA weapons. Nuclear Electric was fined £250,000 for serious lapses in safety procedures after an accident at the Wylfa power station in Anglesey in July 1993. **18.** The Liberal Democrat party conference opened in Glasgow. **20.** A commission headed by the Bishop of Durham recommended changes in the organization of the Church of England, including the establishment of a National Council. **27.** Britain and Argentina signed an agreement on the joint exploration for and exploitation of oil around the Falkland Islands.

OCTOBER 1995

1. Metrication became compulsory in the UK for the sale of pre-packed food, petrol and other goods. **2.** The Labour Party conference opened in Brighton. **7.** The Conservative MP and former minister Alan Howarth resigned from the Conservative Party and said that he would take the Labour whip in the House of Commons. **9.** The former Prime Minister Lord Home of the Hirsel died. The Conservative Party conference opened in Blackpool. Lloyds Bank and the TSB announced that they were to merge. **15.** A bridge linking the Isle of Skye to the mainland of Scotland was opened. **16.** Derek Lewis was sacked as director-general of the Prison Service after the publication of a highly critical report on security in the service following a review by Gen. Sir John Learmont. Mr Lewis later sued the Home Secretary (Michael Howard) for unfair dismissal. **17.** President Ahtisaari of Finland arrived in Britain for a four-day state visit. A junior minister at the Home Office, Nicholas Baker, resigned on health grounds. **19.** The Shadow Cabinet was reshuffled. **26.** A Canadian chat show host posing as the Canadian prime minister, Jean Chrétien, held a telephone conversation with The Queen about the independence referendum in Quebec; he then broadcast an edited tape of the conversation on a Montreal radio station. **29.** Anti-nuclear protesters clashed with police in the grounds of Chequers before a visit by the French President, Jacques Chirac. On 30 October Mr Major and M. Chirac reached agreement on defence, naval and nuclear issues. **31.** The education association appointed by the Government in July 1995 to run Hackney Downs school, London, recommended that the school should be closed down.

NOVEMBER 1995

1. The Queen arrived in New Zealand for a tour including the Commonwealth heads of government meeting in Auckland and signed her assent to an Act compensating a Maori tribe for lands confiscated by British colonists in 1863. **6.** The Prince of Wales, the Prime Minister (John Major), the Leader of the Opposition (Tony Blair) and the leader of the Liberal Democrats (Paddy Ashdown) attended the funeral of the assassinated Israeli Prime Minister Yitzhak Rabin in Jerusalem. In the House of Commons an Opposition amendment requiring MPs to disclose how much they earn from outside consultancies was passed by 322 votes to 271. **7.** The last Royal Navy ships left Rosyth naval base on the Firth of Forth. **10.** At the Commonwealth heads of government meeting in Auckland John Major attacked a statement condemning French nuclear tests which had been agreed by all the other heads of government. **11.** Nigeria was suspended from membership of the Commonwealth following the execution of the writer Ken Saro-Wiwa. Thousands of people observed an Armistice Day two-minute silence at 11 a.m. **13.** The Prince of Wales left Britain for a five-day official visit to Germany and Latvia. **15.** The state opening of Parliament took place. Demonstrators threw paint and flour at the Conservative Party chairman, Brian Mawhinney, at College Green, Westminster. **16.** Queen Elizabeth the Queen Mother underwent a hip replacement operation. **20.** The Princess of Wales was interviewed on the BBC1 programme *Panorama*; she talked frankly about her unhappiness during her marriage and her husband's affair with Camilla Parker Bowles, and admitted that she had also had an extra-marital affair. She said that members of the Royal Household had waged a campaign against her since her separation from the Prince of Wales, that she did not want a divorce and that she did not know if her husband would become King. She also said that she would like to be an ambassador for Britain and a 'queen in people's hearts'. Her press secretary, Geoffrey Crawford, resigned because the Princess had given the interview without his knowledge. **21.** Buckingham Palace officials said in a press statement that they would be talking to the Princess of Wales to see how they could help her define her future role and continue to support her as a member of the Royal Family. **28.** The Chancellor of the Exchequer (Kenneth Clarke) presented his Budget to the House of Commons (*see* page 1154). **29.** President Clinton started a three-day visit to the British Isles; he held talks with John Major at Downing Street and then addressed both Houses of Parliament. On 30 November he became the first serving US president to visit Northern Ireland, and on 1 December he visited Dublin and received the freedom of the city. **30.** The Queen became the first reigning monarch for more than 400 years to attend a Roman Catholic service in an official capacity when she attended a service at Westminster Cathedral to mark the centenary of its foundation.

DECEMBER 1995

7. Beef prices fell sharply because of public fears over conflicting reports of a link between bovine spongiform encephalopathy (BSE) in cattle and Creutzfeld-Jakob disease (CJD) in humans; the Prime Minister said in the House of Commons that there was no scientific evidence of a link. **8.** An official at the British embassy in Colombia who had been kidnapped by left-wing guerrillas on 26 August was released unharmed. **12.** The Defence Secretary (Michael Portillo) announced plans to send more than 13,000 British troops to join the NATO force implementing the peace settlement in Bosnia. **13.** Rioting broke out in Brixton, London, during a demonstration over the death of a man in police custody. Bank base rates were cut by a quarter of a per cent to 6.5 per cent. **16.** Eighteen-year-old Leah Betts died four days after taking an Ecstasy tablet at her birthday party; her parents warned other teenagers of the dangers of taking the drug. **15.** The Court of Appeal ruled that the rail franchising director (Roger Salmon) had acted illegally in setting minimum service requirements which were lower than those already in existence for five of the new companies set up as part of the privatization of British Rail. On 18 December the Transport Secretary (Sir George Young) said that the instructions to the franchising director would be clarified to ensure that franchise holders would be able to adjust commercial services while operating core services at a broadly similar level to those in operation immediately before franchising. **19.** A government motion on European fish quotas was defeated in the House of Commons; two Conservative MPs voted with the Opposition and 11 abstained. The first franchise to be awarded as part of the privatization of British Rail was won by the bus company Stagecoach. **20.** Buckingham Palace confirmed that The Queen had written to the Prince and Princess of Wales expressing her view that an early divorce was desirable. **21.** The Prince of Wales said that he had no intention of remarrying. **24-28.** Strong winds and heavy snow brought down power lines in many parts of Scotland; a state of emergency was declared in Shetland on 26 December. **29.** The Conservative MP Emma Nicholson resigned from the Conserva-

tive Party and said that she would take the Liberal Democrat whip in the House of Commons.

JANUARY 1996

1-2. Thousands of households in Wales, Scotland, Northern Ireland and northern England were left without water supplies when pipes burst in the rapid thaw following the cold snap. **3.** Eleven-year-old David Kearney, who had been savaged by two rottweilers near his home in Darwen, Lancs, on 23 December, died. **4.** The chief executive of the Stock Exchange, Michael Lawrence, was dismissed. **8.** An industrial tribunal ruled that the Labour Party's policy of women-only shortlists in marginal parliamentary seats was illegal. **11.** Baroness Thatcher gave a lecture in London in which she said that pro-European One-Nation Conservatives were 'No Nation Conservatives' and said that the Government was unpopular because it had let down its middle class supporters. **11.** The Prince of Wales, the Prime Minister and the Leader of the Opposition attended a requiem mass for François Mitterrand, the former President of France, in Paris. **17.** Sir Richard Body, MP, accepted the Conservative whip; he had resigned it in November 1994. **18.** Bank base rates were cut to 6.25 per cent. The Home Secretary said that the policy of chaining pregnant women prisoners in hospital would be discontinued. **22.** The private secretary to the Princess of Wales, Patrick Jephson, resigned. **23.** Forte shareholders voted to accept a £3,800 million hostile take-over bid from Granada. **25.** Results showed that more than 50 per cent of 11-year-olds failed to reach the expected standard in English and mathematics in the first national school tests taken in May 1995. **30.** The Princess Royal arrived in the Falkland Islands for a five-day official visit.

FEBRUARY 1996

1. The Hemsworth by-election took place (*see* page 235). **5.** The first privatized rail services began running on South West Trains and Great Western routes; the privatization of the London, Tilbury and Southend line was cancelled because of an alleged fraud relating to ticket revenue arrangements. **6.** British Gas announced that it would split into two companies, and that its chief executive, Cedric Brown, would retire in April 1996. **7.** Tony Blair said that a Labour government would remove the voting rights of hereditary peers in the House of Lords. **8.** The Prince of Wales arrived in Split for a two-day official visit to Croatia and Bosnia. **15.** The report of the Inquiry into Exports of Defence Equipment and Dual-Use Goods to Iraq headed by Sir Richard Scott and set up after the collapse of the Matrix Churchill trial in 1992 was published (*see* below). The Chief Secretary to the Treasury and former Foreign Office minister (William Waldegrave) and the Attorney-General (Sir Nicholas Lyell) rejected calls by Opposition MPs for their resignations. On 26 February the Government won a vote on the Scott report by one vote. **22.** The Conservative MP

Peter Thurnham resigned the party whip. **28.** The Princess of Wales said that she had agreed to a divorce from Prince Charles and announced the basic terms of the settlement; the Queen said that she was interested to hear that the princess had agreed to a divorce but that no settlement details had been discussed.

Main findings and recommendations of the Scott inquiry:
– there had been a deliberate failure to inform Parliament of a secret relaxation of the guidelines on sales of equipment to Iraq because ministers feared public opposition
– the Attorney-General had been wrong to advise ministers that it was their duty to sign public interest immunity certificates which could have affected the outcome of the Matrix Churchill trial
– the then Foreign Office minister (William Waldegrave) had known the facts that made untrue his statements to the effect that there had been no change in policy; however Mr Waldegrave had not intended to mislead Parliament
– there had been no organized conspiracy between ministers to affect the outcome of the trial or cover up the Government's actions
– new guidelines should be drawn up on the issuing of public interest immunity certificates, which should not be used again in criminal cases
– written procedures should be put in place to avoid systematic failures to pass on intelligence to relevant government departments
– ministers should never withhold information in order to avoid political embarrassment
– if the Government intends to use export controls to pursue foreign policy objectives, this should be stated in legislation and open to public debate
– a new export licensing system should be introduced
– the use of 'waivers' by HM Custom and Excise should cease

MARCH 1996

7. An earthquake registering 3.2 on the Richter scale hit Shropshire. **8.** Bank base rates were cut to 6 per cent. **12.** The Government published a White Paper on Europe (*see* pages 1168–9). **20.** The Health Secretary (Stephen Dorrell) said that the most likely cause of a new strain of CJD that had recently been identified was beef from cows with BSE eaten before some types of offal were banned in 1989. On 21 March five European countries banned the import of British beef and prices at cattle markets fell as consumers boycotted British beef and beef products. More European countries banned the import of British beef on 22 March, and on 23 March the fast food chain McDonald's suspended the sale of British beef products in all its outlets. **24.** The Queen with the Duke of Edinburgh arrived in Warsaw at the start of a week-long state visit to Poland and the Czech Republic. **25.** The Government's Spongiform Encephalopathy Advisory Committee (SEAC) said that children were no more susceptible

than adults to infection by BSE. **28.** The Agriculture Minister (Douglas Hogg) announced a ban on the sale of meat from newly-slaughtered cattle over 30 months old. **29.** The Home Office agreed to settle the unfair dismissal claim of the former director-general of the Prison Service, Derek Lewis, who was sacked in October 1995.

APRIL 1996

2–3. Emergency legislation introduced by the Government to strengthen anti-terrorism laws passed through all its parliamentary stages; the Liberal Democrats and some Labour MPs protested at the guillotine imposed to limit debate on the measure. **3.** EU agriculture ministers agreed to provide financial assistance for British measures to eradicate BSE in cattle but refused to lift the world-wide export ban. A British aid worker was shot dead in Angola. The Home Secretary (Michael Howard) published a White Paper on crime and criminal justice, including proposals for radical reforms to sentencing (*see* pages 1169–70). **11.** Labour won the Staffordshire South East by-election (*see* page 235). **16.** The Government said that it would challenge the EU ban on the export of British beef and beef products in the European Court of Justice. The Agriculture Minister (Douglas Hogg) announced a package of measures to help cattle farmers and the beef industry, including £550 million to slaughter and destroy cattle over 30 months old to prevent them from entering the food chain. **18.** Thousands of fishermen held a rally in central London and burned an EU flag in protest at Britain's participation in the common fisheries policy. **21.** The Queen celebrated her 70th birthday. **23.** The Prince of Wales arrived in Canada for an eight-day official visit. **24.** The Government announced plans to slaughter up to 40,000 cattle. The Home Secretary and the Scottish Secretary (Michael Forsyth) announced a firearms amnesty to run from 3 June to 30 June.

MAY 1996

2. The Conservative Party lost hundreds of council seats in local elections held in 150 authorities in England. **3.** Royal Insurance and Sun Alliance announced that they were to merge. **6.** An earthquake registering 2.8 on the Richter scale hit parts of Staffordshire and south Cheshire. **7.** The Register of MPs' Interests was published in the House of Commons; 12 Conservative and two Labour MPs had refused to disclose full details of their outside earnings resulting from their membership of Parliament as required by new rules introduced as a result of the Nolan inquiry. **9.** In a district auditor's report Dame Shirley Porter, the former leader of Westminster Council, and five other council officers were ordered to pay a total surcharge of £31.6 million for their wilful misconduct in attempting to gerrymander the allocation of council homes to increase the Conservative vote in marginal wards in the late 1980s. **14.** President Chirac of France arrived in Britain for a three-day state visit. **15.**

Nine hostages, including four British students, who were kidnapped in Indonesia on 8 January were freed in a rescue operation mounted by Indonesian special forces; two Indonesian hostages and eight kidnappers were killed. **17.** Four British diplomats were expelled by Russia for alleged espionage activities; Britain responded by expelling four Russian embassy staff on the same grounds. **20.** Trading in Railtrack shares began. **21.** In an emergency statement in the House of Commons the Prime Minister said that Britain would use its veto to block all further EU policy initiatives until progress was made on lifting the ban on British beef exports. Eleven-year-old Jaymee Bowen, who was refused experimental treatment for leukaemia on the NHS in 1995 and whose treatment was subsequently paid for by a private donor, died. **26.** The Ministry of Agriculture, Fisheries and Food said that phthalates, chemicals used to soften plastic, had been found in baby formula milk; the Ministry refused to name the brands containing higher levels on the grounds that there was no danger to babies' health. **30.** The Duke and Duchess of York were granted a divorce. **31.** A visit by the Queen to the University of Wales, Aberystwyth, was curtailed because of threatened protests by Welsh language activists.

JUNE 1996

2. Rod Richards, a junior Welsh Office minister, resigned after newspaper allegations of an extramarital affair. **4–7.** The President of the Republic of Ireland, Mary Robinson, made an official visit to Britain, the first Irish president to do so since the foundation of the Republic of Ireland. **7.** Two women were bitten by a rabid bat in Newhaven, E. Sussex. **11.** In the House of Commons, 78 Conservative MPs supported the introduction of a bill calling for a referendum on Britain's future in the EU. **19.** Britain accepted a framework plan drawn up by the European Commission that detailed the measures required from Britain, including an increased cattle cull, to lead to a gradual removal of the beef export ban; at an EU summit meeting in Florence on 21 June the framework was agreed by member states and Britain ended its policy of non-co-operation. **20.** The House of Commons trade and industry select committee cleared the former Cabinet minister Jonathan Aitken of involvement in the illegal export of arms to Iraq in the 1980s. **21.** Postal workers held a 24-hour strike over pay and conditions. **25.** The Prince of Wales began a three-day visit to Northern Ireland. The Government published an education White Paper including proposals for greater selection in schools (*see* page 1170). **26.** Violence broke out in central London, Bradford and other areas after England's defeat by Germany in the European football championships. **27–8.** Postal workers held another 24-hour strike.

JULY 1996

3. The Prime Minister said that the Stone of Scone would be returned to Scotland. **5.** In a speech in the House of Lords, the Archbishop of Canterbury (Dr George Carey) deplored the current tendency towards 'privatized morality' and called on schools to reinstate the daily act of worship. **8.** President Nelson Mandela of South Africa arrived in Britain at the start of a four-day state visit. On 9 July he was welcomed by crowds on Horse Guards parade and in the Mall, and a state banquet was held at Buckingham Palace. On 10 July he received eight honorary degrees in a ceremony at Buckingham Palace, held talks with Mr Major at Downing Street and addressed business executives in the City of London. On 11 July he addressed both Houses of Parliament and attended a concert at the Royal Albert Hall. On 12 July he visited Brixton and addressed crowds outside the South African embassy in Trafalgar Square. **10.** MPs voted in favour of awarding themselves a 26 per cent pay increase. **12.** The Prince and Princess of Wales reached agreement over a divorce settlement; a decree nisi was pronounced on 15 July. **15.** Shares in British Energy began trading on the Stock Exchange. **20.** Up to 45 British tourists were injured when a bomb planted by Basque separatists exploded at Reus airport, near Barcelona, Spain. **22.** The Paymaster-General, David Heathcoat-Amory, resigned from the Government in protest at its policy towards the European Union and in particular its failure to rule out British participation in a single European currency. **23.** The Prime Minister reshuffled some junior ministerial posts. **27.** A British aid worker was kidnapped in Chechnya; he was released unharmed on 21 August.

AUGUST 1996

1. The Central Veterinary Laboratory published evidence showing that BSE can be transmitted from cow to calf. **6.** The Government suspended the Post Office's monopoly on letter delivery for one month because of a series of one-day strikes over new working practices. **22.** The Home Secretary (Michael Howard) announced that a voluntary identity card would be introduced in Britain. The Prison Service released hundreds of prisoners affected by a change in the legal interpretation of sentencing guidelines relating to time spent on remand by prisoners subsequently given consecutive sentences; on 23 August the Home Secretary suspended further releases. After a legal challenge in the High Court the revised interpretation was deemed to be an 'absurdity' and the Home Secretary's decision was upheld. **28.** The Prince and Princess of Wales were divorced.

NORTHERN IRELAND AFFAIRS

SEPTEMBER 1995

5. A summit meeting between John Major and John Bruton planned for 6 September was postponed at the request of the Irish government on the grounds that agreement could not be reached on the terms of reference of an international commission to oversee the decommissioning of terrorist arms. **6.** John Adair was sentenced in Belfast to 16 years' imprisonment for directing the terrorist activities of the UFF. **7.** John Bruton called on the British government to invite Sinn Fein to join all-party talks. **10.** Rioting broke out between loyalists and nationalists in Dunloy, Co. Antrim. **19.** The new leader of the Ulster Unionists (David Trimble) met John Major at Downing Street. The leader of the Ulster Democratic Party (Gary McMichael) met John Bruton in Dublin, the first formal meeting between a loyalist leader and an Irish Prime Minister. **22.** David Trimble called for the setting-up of a directly-elected assembly for Northern Ireland. **29.** The IRA ruled out any decommissioning of weapons in advance of a political settlement.

OCTOBER 1995

2. David Trimble held talks with John Bruton in Dublin.

NOVEMBER 1995

2. The Secretary of State for Northern Ireland (Sir Patrick Mayhew) announced the departure of a third army unit from Northern Ireland. **6.** The Irish government sanctioned the early release of four IRA prisoners from Portlaoise prison, including Nessan Quinlivan and Pearse McCauley who escaped while on remand in London in 1991; the British government started proceedings for their extradition. **10.** A vehicle carrying a 1,000 lb bomb was intercepted by police near Carrickmacross, Co. Monaghan. **11.** John Bruton called on the British government to open all-party talks in advance of decommissioning of arms by the IRA; on 12 November John Major said that this would be a 'reckless short-term gesture'. **15.** Unionist leaders called on John Major to set a date for elections to a constituent assembly. **17.** Eighty-four republican and loyalist prisoners were released from prison under the Northern Ireland (Remission of Sentences) Act 1995. **28.** John Major and John Bruton agreed to set up a three-member international body chaired by a former US senator George Mitchell to advise both governments on suitable methods of arms decommissioning; they also set a target date of the end of February 1996 for the beginning of all-party talks. **30.** President Clinton became the first serving US president to visit Northern Ireland and was greeted by large crowds in Belfast and Londonderry; he met leading political figures and urged Northern Ireland to become 'a model of peace through tolerance'.

DECEMBER 1995

1. Sir Patrick Mayhew invited leaders of all the political parties to join preliminary talks on a separate basis to establish an agenda for full negotiations. On 5 December David Trimble refused to join talks involving the Irish government. **4.** The leader of the SDLP (John Hume) and David Trimble held their first formal talks since Mr Trimble's election. **8.** The IRA said there was no question of surrendering any weapons before the start of all-party talks. **15.** The international arms decommissioning body met for the first time. **21.** The Prime Minister visited Northern Ireland and attacked Sinn Fein for claiming that Sinn Fein and the IRA were totally separate organizations. He later met John Bruton in Dublin. The planned release of ten IRA prisoners in the Republic of Ireland was cancelled because of the alleged involvement of the IRA in the murders of three suspected drug dealers in Belfast during December by a group calling itself Direct Action Against Drugs. **27.** A man was shot dead in west Belfast.

JANUARY 1996

1. A man was shot in Lurgan, Co. Armagh; he died on 2 January. **2.** Sir Patrick Mayhew said that the murders carried out by Direct Action Against Drugs could put the planned all-party talks in jeopardy. **24.** The international advisory body on the decommissioning of paramilitary weapons said that no weapons would be decommissioned before the start of all-party talks and that a compromise agreement was necessary under which weapons would be decommissioned during negotiations. It set out proposals for the decommissioning process and six principles to which all parties should adhere (*see* below). John Major endorsed the principles and proposed that elections should be held in the spring to provide a pool of representatives to conduct all-party talks. **25.** John Bruton said that the question of elections should be resolved during, not before, all-party talks. Sir Patrick Mayhew proposed a Grand Committee for Northern Ireland pending a political settlement. **26.** Gerry Adams said that Sinn Fein was implacably opposed to elections. **30.** The alleged leader of the INLA, Gino Gallagher, was shot dead near the Falls Road, Belfast.

Principles set out by the disarmament body:

– democratic and exclusively peaceful means of resolving political issues
– the total disarmament of all paramilitary organizations
– agreement for the disarmament to be independently verified
– renunciation of the use of force to influence the outcome of all-party talks
– agreement to abide by the terms of any agreement reached in all-party talks
– the cessation of 'punishment' killings and beatings

FEBRUARY 1996

1. President Clinton met Gerry Adams at the White House. **2.** Shots were fired at the home of an RUC reserve officer in Moy, Co. Tyrone. **7.** The Irish foreign minister, Dick Spring, proposed a two-day summit meeting to help to bring about all-party talks. **9.** The IRA announced at 6 p.m. that it was calling off its cease-fire; at 7 p.m. two people were killed, more than 100 injured, and extensive damage was caused when a bomb exploded at South Quay in

London's docklands. **12.** In a televised broadcast, John Major said that the peace process would continue but that ministers would not meet Sinn Fein until IRA violence ended. Thousands of people attended a peace rally in Belfast. **15.** An IRA bomb was defused in central London. Five hundred troops were flown to Northern Ireland. **18.** An IRA member was killed and at least nine people were injured when a bomb exploded on a bus in central London; police said that the bus was not believed to have been the intended target. **21.** The Ulster Unionists issued proposals for an elected 'peace convention'; they were rejected by Sinn Fein. **23.** Security patrols resumed on the streets of Belfast. **26.** More troops were flown to Northern Ireland. **28.** John Major and John Bruton met at Downing Street and announced that intensive multilateral consultations would start on 4 March aimed at reaching agreement on the processes for elections to be held in May and the basis for all-party talks to begin on 10 June; they said that Sinn Fein would be admitted to the talks if the IRA resumed its cease-fire. They also agreed to consider whether parallel referendums on a peaceful political settlement should be held in Northern Ireland and the Republic.

MARCH 1996

9. A small IRA bomb exploded in west London. **12.** The Combined Loyalist Military Command said that if IRA bombing continued it would be matched 'blow for blow'. **15.** The British and Irish governments issued a consultative document on the framework for all-party talks. **21.** John Major outlined the processes for elections to a peace forum to be held on 30 May. **22.** The INLA said that its units had been placed on stand-by.

APRIL 1996

4. The IRA issued a statement in which it reaffirmed its commitment to 'the armed struggle' but said that it was ready to help to develop the conditions which would allow negotiations to proceed. **8.** Violence broke out in the Lower Ormeau Road, Belfast, when a crowd gathered to protest at the re-routing of an Apprentice Boys' march. **16.** A draft bill on the proposed elections in Northern Ireland was published. **17.** A small IRA bomb exploded in Kensington, London. **19.** Gerry Adams said that all the nationalist parties should ignore the forthcoming elections. **24.** The detonator of a 30 lb IRA bomb exploded under Hammersmith Bridge, London; it failed to ignite the bomb. **24.** Gerry Adams said that Sinn Fein would take part in the forthcoming elections but would not sit in the forum.

MAY 1996

16. John Major said that he would not let the issue of arms decommissioning block progress on political negotiations. **20.** Gerry Adams said that he was prepared to agree to the six principles set out by the Mitchell report (*see* above) within the context of all-party talks. **25.** A member of an INLA breakaway group was shot dead in Belfast. **30.** In elections to the peace forum the Ulster Unionist Party won 30 seats, the Democratic Unionist Party 24, the SDLP 21, Sinn Fein 17, the Alliance Party 7, the UK Unionist Party 3, the Progressive Unionist Party 2, the Ulster Democratic Party 2, the Women's Coalition 2 and Labour 2; the turnout was 64.52 per cent.

JUNE 1996

6. The framework for all-party talks was agreed by the British and Irish governments. **7.** An Irish special branch detective was shot dead in Adare, Co. Limerick; the IRA said that its members were responsible but that the murder had been unauthorized. **9.** A member of an INLA breakaway group was shot dead in Belfast. **10.** All-party talks opened at Stormont Castle, Belfast; Sinn Fein delegates were turned away because the IRA had failed to call a cease-fire. Unionist delegates objected to the appointment of the former US senator George Mitchell as chairman of the talks. Disputes over the chairmanship continued but Mr Mitchell was appointed temporary chairman on 12 June. **14.** The elected Northern Ireland forum opened in Belfast under the interim chairmanship of John Gorman, a Roman Catholic Unionist. Sinn Fein members boycotted the forum. **15.** More than 200 people were injured and extensive damage was caused when an IRA bomb exploded in central Manchester. **28.** Three IRA mortar bombs were fired at a British military base in Osnabrück, Germany; there were no injuries but several buildings were badly damaged.

JULY 1996

7. Thousands of Orangemen refused to accept a police ban on their marching through a predominantly Roman Catholic area of Portadown, Co. Armagh; a stand-off ensued. **8.** A Roman Catholic taxi driver was found murdered near Lurgan, Co. Armagh; loyalist demonstrators blocked major roads throughout Northern Ireland and sectarian incidents occurred in Belfast. **9–10.** Trouble continued and two extra infantry battalions were sent to Northern Ireland. **11.** The Orangemen were allowed to march through the disputed area; petrol bombs were thrown by nationalists and police fired plastic bullets to scatter them. **12.** Three RUC officers were shot and wounded in the Ardoyne area of Belfast. Rioting broke out in Belfast, Londonderry and Armagh, and shots were fired at a police station in west Belfast. John Bruton accused John Major of yielding to pressure and failing to treat the two communities in Northern Ireland impartially. **13.** A Roman Catholic man died after being crushed by a security vehicle during disturbances in Londonderry. Rioting continued and the SDLP withdrew from the Northern Ireland Forum. **14.** Seventeen people were injured when a bomb, believed to have been planted by a republican group, destroyed a hotel in Enniskillen, Co. Fermanagh. Disturbances continued in Belfast and Londonderry. **15.** Police raided houses in Peckham and Tooting, London, and discovered 36 bombs under construction. **29.** The all-party talks at Stormont Castle were suspended for six weeks after disagreements over the issue of decommissioning arms.

AUGUST 1996

7. Part of the city wall of Londonderry overlooking the Bogside was sealed off by police and troops to prevent an Apprentice Boys march using the route on 10 August.

ACCIDENTS AND DISASTERS

SEPTEMBER 1995

5–6. Twelve people were killed and widespread damage was caused when Hurricane Luis hit Antigua and St Martin in the Caribbean. **8.** One person was killed and at least five injured when the diesel tank fell off an inter-city train and set carriages on fire outside Maidenhead station, Berks. **17.** At least nine people were killed and widespread damage was caused when Hurricane Marilyn hit the US Virgin Islands and Puerto Rico. **19.** The cross-channel Sealink ferry *Stena Challenger* ran aground outside Calais; it was refloated on 20 September. **23.** Mount Ruapehu in New Zealand's North Island began erupting.

OCTOBER 1995

1. At least 68 people were killed and 200 injured when an earthquake registering 6.0 on the Richter scale hit western Turkey. Twenty-nine people were killed when a typhoon hit the Philippines. **5.** At least 11 people were killed and widespread damage was caused when Hurricane Opal hit Florida, USA. **7.** At least 20 people were killed when an earthquake registering 7.0 on the Richter scale hit central Sumatra. **9.** At least 48 people were killed when an earthquake registering 7.5 on the Richter scale hit western Mexico. Schools and offices were closed in Redcar, Cleveland, after a major fire at an ICI chemical plant. **24.** At least 29 people were killed when an earthquake registering 6.5 on the Richter scale hit Yunnan province, south-west China. **29.** At least 300 people were killed in a fire on an underground train in Baku, Azerbaijan. About 100 people were killed when a tropical storm hit the central Philippines.

NOVEMBER 1995

2–3. At least 66 people were killed and thousands of homes were destroyed when Typhoon Angela hit the Philippines. **12.** At least 50 people were killed in avalanches near Mount Everest.

DECEMBER 1995

21. At least 140 people were killed when an American Airlines plane crashed in the Andes near Cali, Colombia. **22.** Three men were killed in an explosion at a gas production platform in Howden, Tyne and Wear. **23.** At least 425 people, most of them children and teenagers, were killed in a fire at a school in Dabwali, northern India. **25.** At least 135 people were killed when the River Umsindusi burst its banks in Edendale township near Pietermaritzburg, South Africa. **28.** An 11-year-old girl and two men who tried to rescue her died after being trapped under ice on a frozen lake at Hemsworth park, W. Yorks.

JANUARY 1996

17. About 500 workmen were evacuated when the NatWest tower in the City of London caught fire; no-one was injured. **19.** At least 200 people died when a ferry capsized off the north coast of Indonesia.

FEBRUARY 1996

3. At least 240 people were killed when an earthquake registering 7.0 on the Richter scale hit Lijiang, south-west China.

MARCH 1996

8. One person was killed and at least 20 injured when a freight train and a mail train crashed head-on in Stafford. **18.** At least 150 people were killed in a fire in a disco in Manila, the Philippines. **29.** About 62 people were killed when an earthquake hit Pujili, central Ecuador.

APRIL 1996

3. Thirty-three people, including the US Commerce Secretary Ron Brown, were killed when their plane crashed outside Dubrovnik, Croatia. **11.** At least 16 people were killed when fire broke out in a flower shop at Düsseldorf airport, Germany. **18.** Sixty people were killed when two trains crashed head-on in northern India.

MAY 1996

11. A plane crashed in the Florida Everglades, USA, killing 109 people. **21.** About 600 people were presumed drowned when a ferry sank in Lake Victoria, Tanzania.

JULY 1996

18. All 230 people aboard a TWA jumbo jet were killed when it exploded soon after take-off from J. F. Kennedy airport, New York, *en route* to Paris. About 50 children were injured when the roof was torn off their double-decker school bus as it went under a low bridge in Murdishaw, Runcorn. **22.** The death toll from flooding in central and eastern China since early 1996 reached 800.

AUGUST 1996

8. A woman was killed and more than 60 people were injured when two trains crashed head-on near Watford Junction station, Herts. At least 83 people were killed when flash floods swept away a camp-site in the Spanish Pyrenees. **11.** Five teen-agers were killed in a car crash near Ingoldmells, Lincs. **19.** Two children disappeared from a beach at Holme next the Sea, Norfolk; they were later found drowned. **29.** All 141 people on board a Russian airliner were reported to have been killed when it crashed in Spitsbergen in the Arctic Circle. **31.** The death toll from flooding during the monsoon season in Nepal reached 244.

ARTS, SCIENCE AND MEDIA

SEPTEMBER 1995

20. The Jerwood Prize for modern art, worth £30,000, was awarded jointly to Patrick Caulfield and Maggi Hambling. **26.** Penguin, HarperCollins and Random House announced that they would pull out of the Net Book Agreement from 1 October; on 28 September the Publishers' Association announced that it could no longer enforce the terms of the agreement.

OCTOBER 1995

5. Seamus Heaney was awarded the Nobel Prize for Literature. **19.** The Department of Health warned that seven brands of contraceptive pill were more likely than others to cause thrombosis; the advice was described as premature by the doctor leading the research. **27.** The Independent Television Commission awarded the licence for Britain's fifth and final terrestrial television channel to Channel 5 Broadcasting, a consortium led by the Pearson and MAI media groups.

NOVEMBER 1995

7. Pat Barker was awarded the Booker Prize for *The Ghost Road.* **17.** *Today* newspaper was published for the last time. **20.** The Kirklees sports stadium in Huddersfield, W. Yorks, won the 1995 RIBA Building of the Year Award. **28.** Damien Hirst won the Turner Prize for modern art.

DECEMBER 1995

7. The Galileo spacecraft successfully launched a probe into Jupiter's atmosphere and transmitted data back to NASA. **13.** The managing director of the Royal Philharmonic Orchestra, Paul Findlay, was sacked. **22.** The Millennium Commission rejected an application for a £50 million grant for a new Cardiff Bay Opera House.

JANUARY 1996

9. Sir Christopher Bland was appointed chairman of the BBC from April 1996. **29.** La Fenice opera house in Venice was destroyed by fire.

FEBRUARY 1996

6. Sir Simon Rattle said that he would resign as music director of the City of Birmingham Sym-phony Orchestra in 1998. **13.** The pop group Take That split up. **19.** Oasis won the Brit awards for best band, best album and best video; Jarvis Cocker, the lead singer of Pulp, disrupted a performance by Michael Jackson during the awards ceremony in London. **26.** The actor Haing Ngor was shot dead in Los Angeles.

MARCH 1996

6. Trevor Nunn was appointed director of the National Theatre from October 1997. **25.** Emma Thompson became the first person to win Oscars for both acting and writing when she won the award for best adapted screenplay for *Sense and Sensibility.* **31.** Rafal Payne was named the BBC Young Musician of the Year.

APRIL 1996

24. The Press Complaints Commission upheld a complaint from The Queen over an article in the magazine *BusinessAge* that presented an inaccurate and speculative estimation of her wealth.

MAY 1996

15. Helen Dunmore won the first Orange prize for women's fiction, worth £30,000. **17.** The Victoria and Albert Museum unveiled plans for a glass extension seven storeys high.

JUNE 1996

2. More than 1 million people went to the cinema for £1 on National Cinema Day. **4.** The European Ariane 5 space rocket, which had taken more than ten years to develop and was carrying cargo worth £500 million, veered off course after take-off from French Guiana on its maiden flight and was blown up for safety reasons. **7.** The BBC announced a radical restructuring of its operations. **17.** London City Ballet went into liquidation. **23.** A farewell gala was held at Sadler's Wells Theatre, London, to mark its closure; in July 1996 work began on a new theatre on the site. **24.** Hundreds of people complained to the *Daily Mirror* over its use of Second World War imagery in its articles about the run-up to the European Championships semi-final between England and Germany.

JULY 1996

3. A 12th-century reliquary casket believed to have held the blood and bones of St Thomas à Becket was sold at Sotheby's to a private collector for £4.18 million. On 4 July the National Heritage Secretary (Virginia Bottomley) made an unprecedented intervention to prevent the casket from leaving the country without an export licence. On 11 July the collector withdrew and the bid from the National Heritage Memorial Fund was accepted.

AUGUST 1996

6. Scientists announced that a meteorite which was found in Antarctica and was believed to have been ejected from Mars millions of years ago, contained structures likely to be microfossils of bacteria, thus providing the first evidence of life on the planet. On 7 August President Clinton said that further missions to Mars would be launched to investigate the discovery. **9.** Doctors said that a woman in Birmingham who had received fertility treatment was pregnant with eight babies. **14.** NASA scientists said that images taken by the spacecraft Galileo of Europa, one of Jupiter's moons, showed that icy floes on its surface could be floating on slush or water. **21.** A re-creation of Shakespeare's Globe Theatre in Southwark, London, opened with a production of *Two Gentlemen of Verona*. **23.** Classic FM was taken over by the radio group GWR. **26.** The rock group R.E.M. signed a record £51.6 million deal with Warner Brothers Records. **28.** The Advertising Standards Authority ruled that a Conservative Party advertisement depicting the Labour leader, Tony Blair, with demonic eyes broke its code of practice and should be withdrawn.

CRIMES AND LEGAL AFFAIRS

SEPTEMBER 1995

10. Eighteen-year-old Rachel Lean was found stabbed to death near RAF Coltishall, Norfolk; a woman was charged with the murder. **11.** James Doyle was sentenced at the Central Criminal Court to 24 years' imprisonment for masterminding a series of armed robberies in London in 1991-2. **16.** Fifteen-year-old Naomi Smith was found murdered near her home in Nuneaton, Warks. **19.** In the first successful private prosecution for rape in England and Wales, Christopher Davies was sentenced in Maidstone to 14 years' imprisonment for raping two women in 1991 and 1992. **24.** Lee Tyson was sentenced in Winchester to life imprisonment for the murder in October 1994 of a woman manager in the company for which he worked. A 16-year-old boy killed 12 people and wounded eight others near Toulon, France; he then shot himself. **27.** The European Court of Human Rights ruled that Britain had breached the Human Rights Convention over the shooting of three IRA members in Gibraltar in 1988. Paul Hickson, a former Olympic swimming coach, was sentenced in Cardiff to 17 years' imprisonment for the rape and indecent assault of girls he trained between 1976 and 1991.

OCTOBER 1995

3. The former American footballer and actor O. J. Simpson was acquitted in Los Angeles of murdering his former wife and her friend in June 1994. **4.** The trial of Geoffrey Knights, the partner of the actress Gillian Taylforth, was halted because of what Judge Sanders called 'unlawful, misleading, scandalous and malicious' reporting of the case by eight tabloid newspapers. **12.** The Home Secretary (Michael Howard) announced plans to end the automatic early release of prisoners and ensure longer prison terms for habitual criminals; the Lord Chief Justice (Lord Taylor of Gosforth) said that longer sentences would not deter criminals and that mandatory minimum sentences were inconsistent with the interests of justice. An elderly couple and their daughter and granddaughter were found murdered at their home in London. **17.** Keith Moore, an accountant, was sentenced in Southwark to six years' imprisonment for stealing £6 million from the rock musician Sting for whom he worked. **21.** A stable-girl was found beaten to death at National Hunt stables at Buckfastleigh, Devon; on 22 October a man was charged with the murder. **27.** In a landmark judgment, the High Court ruled that the former owner of an asbestos factory near Leeds was liable to compensate people who had lived near the factory and developed cancer caused by asbestos dust. The Home Secretary banned the leader of the Moonies religious cult from entering Britain; on 1 November the High Court ruled that the Home Secretary had acted unlawfully because he had failed to follow rules of procedural fairness before taking the decision. **31.** Badrul Miah was sentenced at the Central Criminal Court to life imprisonment for the murder of 15-year-old Richard Everitt in a racial attack in north London in August 1994. Members of the insolvent Lloyds Syndicate 418, which made heavy losses in the 1980s and early 1990s, won a libel action in the High Court against the syndicate, its agents and its auditors.

NOVEMBER 1995

7. The convictions of four businessmen in 1992 for illegally exporting defence equipment to Iraq through their company Ordtec were ruled by the Court of Appeal to be 'unsafe and unsatisfactory' because of the failure of the Government to disclose documents vital to the defence case. Graeme Souness, the former Liverpool and Glasgow Rangers football manager, accepted £100,000 libel damages from Mirror Group Newspapers in place of the £750,000 he was awarded in the High Court in June 1995. **10.** At Southwark coroner's court an inquest jury found that Richard O'Brien, who died in April 1994 after being arrested and pinned to the ground by five police officers, was unlawfully killed. **19.** Four people died in a fire started deliberately in a block of flats in Shepherd's Bush, London. **20.** Sam Hill, who was sentenced in 1988 to life imprisonment for murder, was released after the Court of Appeal found that his conviction was unsafe and unsatisfactory. **21–22.** Rosemary West was convicted in Winchester of murdering ten young women and girls, including her daughter and step-daughter, between 1971 and 1987; she was sentenced to ten terms of life imprisonment. The Lord Chancellor (Lord Mackay of Clashfern) started an inquiry into payments which had been made or promised to newspapers to prosecution witnesses in the trial. **26.** The Liberal Democrat leader, Paddy Ashdown, was threatened at knifepoint in his constituency at

Yeovil, Somerset. **30.** The European Court of Justice ruled that Britain's procedures for implementing exclusion orders under the Prevention of Terrorism Act were unlawful because they infringed the right of free movement for EU nationals guaranteed by the Treaty of Rome.

DECEMBER 1995

1. Nick Leeson, the trader who precipitated the collapse of Barings Bank, pleaded guilty in Singapore to two charges of fraud and forgery in return for nine other charges being dropped; on 2 December he was sentenced to six and a half years' imprisonment. Two British women, Susan Hagan and Sally-Anne Croft, were each sentenced in Portland, Oregon, to five years' imprisonment for their part in a plot to murder the US Attorney for Oregon in 1985. **4.** A diamond necklace and bracelet belonging to the Duchess of York were stolen on a flight from the USA; they were recovered in New York on 5 December and a baggage handler was arrested. **7.** Three men believed to have been involved in drug dealing were shot dead in a country lane in Essex. **8.** Philip Lawrence, the headmaster of St George's Roman Catholic School in Maida Vale, London, was stabbed to death outside the school after going to the aid of one of his pupils who was being attacked by a gang; a 15-year-old boy was charged with the murder. **12.** Victor Willoughby was sentenced at the Central Criminal Court to five terms of life imprisonment for raping five women in 1993–4. The Court of Appeal reduced libel damages of £350,000 awarded to the rock star Elton John against the publishers of the *Sunday Mirror* in November 1993 to £75,000, and said that judge and counsel could in future give guidance to juries on the level of libel damages. **13.** The conviction of Sara Thornton, who was released on bail in July 1995 after serving five years of a life sentence for the murder of her husband, was quashed by the Court of Appeal; following a retrial Thornton was convicted on 30 May 1996 of manslaughter on the grounds of diminished responsibility and sentenced to five years' imprisonment; she did not return to prison as she had already served the period of the sentence. **14.** Stephen Wilkinson, a paranoid schizophrenic, was convicted in Leeds of the manslaughter of 12-year-old Nikki Conroy, who was stabbed to death at her school in Cleveland in March 1994; he was ordered to be detained indefinitely in a mental hospital. **15.** Dr Simon Heighes, an Oxford don, was sentenced in Oxford to two years' imprisonment for stealing rare books from university libraries and selling them. **19.** The Conservative MP David Ashby lost a libel action in the High Court against the *Sunday Times* over an article published in January 1994 that said that he was a homosexual, a liar and a hypocrite. **20.** Gordon Wardell was sentenced in Oxford to life imprisonment for the murder of his wife in September 1994; he had faked a robbery at the building society where she worked and claimed that she had been kidnapped by a gang

who had also attacked him. **23.** The bodies of 16 members of the Solar Temple cult were found near Grenoble, France. **29.** The body of 19-year-old Celine Figard, a French student who was last seen hitching a lift from a lorry driver on 19 December, was found in a lay-by near Hawford, Worcs. Ten people were stabbed by a shop assistant at a food store in Birmingham.

JANUARY 1996

3. Nineteen-year-old Anthony Erskine was kicked to death after going to the aid of his father who was being taunted by a gang of youths outside his home in Stratford-upon-Avon, Warks. Four people were stabbed by a woman at a Jobcentre in Bexleyheath, south-east London. **4.** A man was found tied to his bed at his home in north London after being burgled on 26 December; he died the next day. **14.** The body of a British tourist, Johanne Masheder, who had been missing since mid December 1995, was found in a ravine near Kanchanaburi, Thailand; a Thai monk was charged with murder and sentenced to death. **19.** Kevin and Ian Maxwell, the sons of the late publisher Robert Maxwell, were cleared at the Central Criminal Court of conspiring to defraud Mirror Group Newspapers pensioners of £122 million; on 26 January the Serious Fraud Office said that Kevin Maxwell and other former executives of the company would face further charges. **20.** A woman and four of her children were murdered in incidents in Birmingham and Bristol. **25.** An inquest jury found that a Nigerian asylum seeker who had died in a struggle with two police officers in east London in December 1994 was unlawfully killed. **29.** A man who suffered severe burns in the fire at King's Cross underground station in London in 1987 was awarded £650,000 damages in an out-of-court settlement with London Regional Transport.

FEBRUARY 1996

2. Paddy Ashdown's car was destroyed by a petrol bomb outside his home in Somerset. **9.** Lord Brocket was sentenced at Luton Crown Court to five years' imprisonment for a £4.5 million insurance fraud involving four classic cars. **17.** The body of 18-year-old Louise Smith, who went missing early on Christmas morning 1995, was found in a quarry near her home in Chipping Sodbury. **19.** Richard Whyte was sentenced at the Central Criminal Court to life imprisonment for the rape and murder of Caroline Williams in August 1994. **21.** The European Court of Human Rights ruled that the role of the Home Secretary and the Parole Board in reviewing the continued detention after completion of their minimum sentence of juveniles convicted of murder and detained 'at Her Majesty's pleasure' failed to meet the requirements of an independent assessment and therefore breached the human rights of the juvenile offenders. **28.** Steven Grieveson was sentenced at Leeds Crown Court to three terms of life imprisonment for the murders of three teenagers in Sunderland in 1993–4. A British woman,

Sandra Gregory, was sentenced at a court in Bangkok to 25 years' imprisonment for smuggling heroin out of Thailand in February 1993.

MARCH 1996

4. The body of five-year-old Rosemary McCann, who went missing on 14 January, was found in Oldham. A British woman, Caroline Beale, pleaded guilty in New York to the reckless manslaughter of her new-born baby in September 1994; she received permission to return to Britain for psychiatric treatment. 9. The body of a woman was found in the River Ely, Cardiff; she had been attacked while walking her dogs. 13. Sixteen children and their teacher were shot dead and a further 12 children and two teachers were injured at Dunblane primary school, Perthshire, by a gunman, Thomas Hamilton, who then shot himself. On 14 March a public inquiry into the killings, to be headed by Lord Cullen, was announced. On 15 March John Major and Tony Blair visited Dunblane. On 17 March a minute's silence was observed throughout Britain and the Queen and the Princess Royal visited the town. 29. Three British soldiers were sentenced in Cyprus to life imprisonment for the abduction, attempted rape and manslaughter of a Danish tour guide in September 1994.

APRIL 1996

2. Brendan O'Donnell was sentenced at the Central Criminal Court in Dublin to three terms of life imprisonment for the murders of a woman, her three-year-old son and a priest in Co. Clare in 1994. 3. A Greek businessman who had been kidnapped, drugged and locked in a cupboard for nine days in Maida Vale, London, was freed by police. A High Court judge gave doctors permission to switch off the life support machine of a three-month old baby girl with severe brain damage; he refused, however, to lay down guidelines for such decisions. 6. A 74-year-old man was beaten and robbed when he stopped his car to ask directions in Chapeltown, Leeds; he later died of a heart attack. 10. Scotland Yard disclosed that a blackmailer had been sending explosive devices to branches of Barclays Bank since December 1994; on 20 April a small bomb exploded outside a branch of the bank in west London. The Lord Advocate said that doctors in Scotland who stopped treating coma patients deemed to be incapable of recovery would be granted immunity from prosecution when the patient died. 17. Robin Pask was sent to a psychiatric hospital for an indefinite period for the manslaughter of an Open University lecturer, Elizabeth Howe, at a summer school in York in July 1992. 19. John Scripps, a Briton who had been convicted of murdering a tourist in Singapore in March 1995, was hanged at Changi jail, Singapore. 19. A rugby player who was paralysed after a scrum collapsed in a match in 1991 was awarded damages against the referee for his failure to exercise reasonable skill in preventing scrum collapses during the match. 25. Jonathan Jones, who

was sentenced in April 1995 to two terms of life imprisonment for the murder of his girlfriend's parents, was released when the Appeal Court found that his conviction was unsafe. A private murder prosecution at the Central Criminal Court brought by the parents of Stephen Lawrence, a black teenager who was murdered in London in April 1993, collapsed when the judge ruled that the evidence of a key witness was unsafe and could not be put before the jury. The Appeal Court ruled that Customs and Excise had wrongly charged retailers VAT on interest-free credit deals since the tax was introduced in 1973; Customs and Excise said it would contest the judgement in the House of Lords. 28. Thirty-two people were shot dead by a man at a tourist centre in Port Arthur, Tasmania. He then took three people hostage in a guest-house; the hostages died when the guest-house was destroyed by fire, but the man survived and was charged with the murders. 29. Darren Carr was convicted at Birmingham Crown Court of the manslaughter of a woman and her two daughters by setting their home on fire in Abingdon, Oxon, in June 1995. 30. Thirteen-year-old Louise Allen was kicked to death after trying to break up a fight in Corby, Northants; two girls aged 12 and 13 were charged with her manslaughter.

MAY 1996

1. A man was shot dead in Liverpool in what was believed to be the latest of a series of revenge attacks. 2. The High Court ruled that the Home Secretary (Michael Howard) had acted unlawfully in fixing a 15-year minimum sentence for the two boys who murdered two-year-old James Bulger in February 1993. Matthew Simmons was fined £500 at Croydon magistrates' court and banned from going to football matches for a year for using threatening words and behaviour towards the Manchester United footballer Eric Cantona at a match in January 1995; he was also sentenced to seven days' imprisonment for attacking the prosecuting solicitor. The Lord Chief Justice, Lord Taylor of Gosforth, announced his early retirement owing to ill-health. 5. Four children were killed in a house fire started deliberately in Southampton. 7. Steven Heaney was sentenced at Liverpool Crown Court to two terms of life imprisonment for the murders of two boys, Paul Barker and Robert Gee, at fishing ponds at Eastam Rake, Cheshire, in July 1995. 9. Eighteen-year-old Helen Martin was found beaten to death near Symonds Yat, Herefordshire. 14. The Home Secretary said in a written answer in the House of Commons that equipment used since 1989 to test for traces of explosives in evidence presented in terrorist trials had been contaminated with the explosive RDX, and that about 12 convictions would be reviewed. 16. Timothy Morss and Brett Tyler were sentenced at the Central Criminal Court to life imprisonment for sexually assaulting and murdering nine-year-old Daniel Handley in October 1994. 19. A man was stabbed to death by

another driver on a slip-road of the M25 in Kent. **22.** The businessman Owen Oyston was sentenced at Liverpool Crown Court to six years' imprisonment for raping a 16-year-old model in 1992. **23.** An 11-year-old boy was convicted at Leeds Crown Court of the manslaughter of an elderly woman who was hit by a concrete block he had pushed off the roof of a block of flats in Leeds in August 1995; he was freed under a three-year-supervision order. **28.** A German woman on holiday in Britain was shot dead in an attempted robbery at a hotel in Bedford. **30.** A man was shot dead during a row about a minor traffic accident in London.

JUNE 1996

3. In an out-of-court settlement 14 police officers accepted a total of £1.2 million in compensation for the psychological trauma they suffered attempting to rescue victims of the Hillsborough football stadium disaster in 1989. **24.** An elderly couple were found murdered at their home in Fulham, London. **26.** Ray Lee was sentenced at the Central Criminal Court to ten years' imprisonment for the manslaughter of PC Phillip Walters in April 1995.

JULY 1996

2. The Government published a White Paper proposing radical reforms to the legal aid system (*see* page 1170). **4.** Simon Smith was sentenced in Stafford to three terms of life imprisonment for suffocating three of his children in separate incidents between 1989 and 1994. **7.** Nine-year-old Jade Matthews was found beaten to death on a railway line near her home in Bootle, Merseyside; a 13-year-old boy was charged with the murder. **8.** Three children and four adults were injured when a man with a machete attacked them in the playground of an infants' school in Wolverhampton. **10.** A woman and her six-year-old daughter were found beaten to death in a field near Nonington, Kent; her nine-year-old daughter was seriously injured in the attack. **18.** Howard Hughes was sentenced in Chester to three terms of life imprisonment for the rape and murder of seven-year-old Sophie Hook in Llandudno in July 1995. **19.** Thirteen-year-old Caroline Dickinson, who was on a school trip to Brittany, was raped and murdered at a youth hostel in Pleine-Fougères. **26.** The Master of the Rolls (Lord Woolf) published proposals for a radical reform of the civil justice system in England and Wales. **27.** Two people were killed and about 110 injured when a bomb exploded in the Centennial Olympic Park in Atlanta, Georgia. **31.** Michael Brookes was sentenced at the Central Criminal Court to life imprisonment for the murder of 16-year-old Lynn Siddons in 1978. The former Test cricketers Ian Botham and Allan Lamb lost a High Court libel action in which they claimed that the former Pakistan captain Imran Khan had described them as racist and lower class and had accused Botham of ball-tampering.

AUGUST 1996

8. The fashion designer Ossie Clark was stabbed to death at his home in London; his former lover was charged with the murder. **13.** A vicar was stabbed to death outside his church in Anfield, Liverpool. **14.** Richard Humphrey was sentenced at the Central Criminal Court to four terms of life imprisonment for the murder in May 1995 of a woman in south London, three attempted murders, and robbery and firearms offences. **17.** Belgian police launched investigations into a suspected international paedophile ring after the bodies of two children were found in the garden of a house in Sars-la-Buissière, Belgium. **20.** Sixteen-year-old Lucy Burchell, who had been working as a prostitute, was found murdered in Ladywood, Birmingham. **22.** The Home Office said that it would be examining the trial of Ralston Edwards, who was convicted at the Central Criminal Court on two charges of rape; because he had elected to defend himself, he had cross-examined his victim over a period of six days during the trial. **26.** Fourteen-year-old Caroline Glachan was found murdered at Bonhill, Dumbarton. **27.** A hijacked Sudanese airliner with 200 people on board landed at Stansted airport, Essex. Over a period of eight hours all the passengers and crew were released; one person had been injured. The Iraqi hijackers surrendered and sought political asylum in Britain.

ENVIRONMENT

SEPTEMBER 1995

4. Foresters acting on the orders of the Duke of Edinburgh began to fell 28 ancient oak trees on Queen Anne's Ride, Windsor Great Park. After protests from conservationists the felling was halted, and on 9 October the Crown Estate Commissioners said that the remaining 20 oak trees would be preserved. Greenpeace apologized to Shell UK for miscalculating the pollution risk posed by the Brent Spar oil rig. **5.** France carried out the first of a series of underground nuclear tests at Mururoa atoll in the south Pacific. **13.** The Welsh Secretary (William Hague) rejected a scheme to build a barrage across the River Usk. **22.** The UN agreed formally to ban the export of toxic waste from developed to developing countries. **23.** A 30-mile slick formed off Flamborough Head; the oil was believed to have been discharged from a tanker. **24.** A leaked government report disclosed that more than half the wetland nature reserves in Britain had been damaged or seriously threatened in the past five years. The Ramblers' Association held a series of rallies to demand the 'right to roam' in the British countryside.

OCTOBER 1995

17. The Government published a White Paper on the English countryside (*see* page 1168). 20. The Secretary of State for Scotland (Michael Forsyth) announced proposals to sell 109,000 hectares of Crown land in the Scottish Highlands to crofters; he also encouraged lairds to sell their land to crofters. The National Trust for Scotland revoked the ban on fox-hunting on its land which had been imposed in February 1995.

DECEMBER 1995

11. British Energy abandoned plans to build two new nuclear power stations.

JANUARY 1996

9–11. Anti-road protesters prevented contractors from undertaking clearance work for the construction of the Newbury bypass; on 12 January 34 people were arrested for aggravated trespass.

FEBRUARY 1996

15. The Liberian-registered tanker *Sea Empress* ran aground at the entrance to Milford Haven harbour, south Wales. On 17 February the tanker's crew was lifted to safety by helicopter after a salvage attempt failed; nearby homes were evacuated and Milford Haven port was closed. On 20 February another salvage attempt failed. On 21 February the tanker was refloated; about 65,000 tons of crude oil had leaked into the sea. 21. Coalite Products was fined £150,000 and ordered to pay an estimated £300,000 costs for knowingly burning large quantities of chemical waste at a low temperature and emitting dioxins into the atmosphere in 1990 and 1991. 29. Bailiffs began to evict protesters from camps set up on the site of the Newbury bypass.

MARCH 1996

21. The European Court of Justice ruled that Britain had acted illegally in 1993 in excluding part of the Lappel Bank reserve on the River Medway, Kent, from Special Protection Area listing under the EU's Birds Directive, thereby favouring economic interests over the interests of the environment.

MAY 1996

15. The Government published a strategy for protecting the rarest and most threatened life forms in Britain.

JUNE 1996

5. The Prince of Wales opened the £330 million second Severn crossing. 19. Some of the prehistoric stones at Avebury were damaged by being daubed with painted symbols. 23–4. Greenpeace vessels clashed with Danish boats involved in the industrial fishing of sand eels in the Firth of Forth.

JULY 1996

2. The European Commission ordered an emergency 50 per cent cut in the North Sea herring catch.

13. The *Sunday Telegraph* published details of a leaked Ministry of Defence document concerning the contamination of parts of Berkshire by radioactive fall-out after a fire at the Greenham Common air base in 1958. 18. Chris Green resigned as chief executive of English Heritage over alleged administrative irregularities.

AUGUST 1996

5. Severn Trent Water Authority was fined £175,000 for leaking chemicals into the River Wye, killing 33,000 young salmon. 20. The Environment Secretary (John Gummer) announced a national air quality strategy, including new targets for reducing the level of eight hazardous pollutants in the atmosphere by 2005.

SPORT

SEPTEMBER 1995

2. Frank Bruno won the WBC world heavyweight boxing championship when he defeated Oliver McCall on points at Wembley. 7. The Rugby Football Union announced that the sport below international level would remain amateur for the 1995–6 season. The jockey Lester Piggott announced his retirement. 18. Eleven leading rugby union clubs passed a vote of no confidence in the RFU commission set up to establish guidelines in the open era; on 8 November the commission published proposals for the future structure and management of the sport. 21. The England rugby union player Rob Andrew joined Newcastle United Sporting Club as rugby development director; on 19 October he announced his retirement from international rugby after being dropped by his club Wasps. 24. Europe's golfers won the Ryder Cup for the first time since 1989.

OCTOBER 1995

7. Middlesbrough signed the Brazilian midfielder Juninho for £4.75 million. 11. The Scotland and Everton footballer Duncan Ferguson was jailed after losing his appeal against a three-month sentence imposed in May 1995 for head-butting a player while playing for Glasgow Rangers in April 1994. 12. Three players were sent home from the rugby league world cup after testing positive for drugs. 13. The boxer James Murray collapsed in the final round of a British bantamweight title fight against Drew Docherty in Glasgow; he died on 14 October. Rioting broke out in the hall at the end of the fight. 16. The former world boxing champion Chris Eubank announced his retirement. The England cricketer Devon Malcolm accepted substantial undisclosed damages in the High Court over an article in *Wisden Cricket Monthly* that questioned his commitment to the national team because he was born and brought up in the West Indies.

Phillip DeFreitas later won libel damages over the same article and Chris Lewis received an apology from the magazine. **18.** The three-times Grand National winner Red Rum died and was buried at Aintree racecourse. **25.** The British Boxing Board of Control proposed a 12-point plan to make the sport safer. **31.** After six years playing rugby league the former rugby union international Jonathan Davies signed for Cardiff rugby union club.

NOVEMBER 1995

10. The Formula 1 racing driver Mika Häkkinen was seriously injured after losing control of his car during the qualifying session for the Australian Grand Prix in Adelaide. **16.** The first cricket Test match between England and South Africa in South Africa since 1965 opened in Pretoria. **22.** Colin McRae became the first Briton to win the world motor rallying championship. **27.** Graeme Le Saux and David Batty of Blackburn Rovers were fined by the club after exchanging blows during a match on 22 November. **28.** The Football League agreed a £125 million five-year deal with Sky television to broadcast Endsleigh League and Coca Cola Cup matches.

DECEMBER 1995

1. Sarah Hardcastle won the 800 metres freestyle gold medal at the world short-course championships. **3.** The England wicketkeeper Jack Russell became the first cricketer to take 11 catches in a Test match in the game against South Africa in Johannesburg. **3–4.** The England cricket captain Mike Atherton was 185 not out after batting for 10¾ hours to force a draw in the second Test against South Africa. **8.** A former press officer of the International Amateur Athletic Federation (IAAF) claimed that the result of the 1994 female athlete of the year award had been rigged. **10.** Jonathan Edwards was named BBC Sports Personality of the Year. **13.** ITV bought the rights to screen all Formula One grand prix from 1997. **17.** The European Court of Justice ruled that football clubs of different EU member states should not be able to charge transfer fees for players whose contracts have expired, and that the limit of three foreign players in a team was illegal. On 22 December the Premier League abandoned its limit on the number of EU players clubs can field. **21.** Jack Charlton resigned as manager of the Republic of Ireland football team. **22.** The Norwegian adventurer Borge Ousland reached the South Pole and became the first person to ski alone and unaided to both Poles.

JANUARY 1996

4. St Helens beat Warrington 80–0 in the rugby league Regal Trophy semi-final; on 5 January Warrington's coach, Brian Johnson, resigned. **5.** David Hempleman-Adams became the first Briton to walk solo and unsupported to the South Pole. **6.** In Liverpool's 7–0 defeat of Rochdale at Anfield, Ian Rush scored a record 42nd goal in an FA Cup match.

10. The England football coach Terry Venables said that he would resign after the European Championships in June 1996 in order to concentrate on several pending legal cases. **12.** UEFA banned Tottenham Hotspur and Wimbledon from their European tournaments for one year, with the suspension active for five years, for fielding under-strength teams in the 1995 InterToto Cup; on 26 January the ban was rescinded and replaced by fines. **14.** At a special general meeting, members of the Rugby Football Union voted to hold a second meeting to decide whether rugby union in England should become open. **15.** The England cricketer Devon Malcolm strongly criticized his treatment by the chairman of selectors, Ray Illingworth. **16.** The British champion skier Kirsteen McGibbon was killed in a fall while training in Austria. Wigan won the Rugby League championship for the seventh successive season.

FEBRUARY 1996

1. The Leyton Orient footballer Roger Stanislaus was banned for one year by the FA for testing positive for a performance-enhancing drug in November 1995; on 6 February he was sacked by Leyton Orient. **5.** Mick McCarthy was appointed manager of the Republic of Ireland football team. **6.** The House of Lords passed an amendment to the Broadcasting Bill preventing satellite television from obtaining exclusive coverage of major sporting events. On 4 March the National Heritage Secretary (Virginia Bottomley) said that the right of terrestrial channels to show live coverage of eight major events would be safeguarded. **11.** The jockey Walter Swinburn was badly injured in a fall in Hong Kong. **12.** The World Boxing Organization heavyweight champion Tommy Morrison was suspended after confirmation that he is HIV positive. **29.** At the cricket world cup in India, the West Indies were beaten by the amateur Kenyan team. On 5 March the West Indies captain Richie Richardson announced that he would retire from international cricket after the world cup and a new captain, team coach and team manager were appointed.

MARCH 1996

6. At the cricket world cup in Kandy, Sri Lanka scored a record one-day total of 398 runs in their match against Kenya. **9.** Will Carling announced his resignation as England rugby union captain. **13.** The cricket world cup semi-final between India and Sri Lanka in Calcutta was halted by crowd rioting; Sri Lanka was awarded the match by default. **24.** The IAAF decided to allow prize money to be awarded at major championships. **25.** The British athlete Diane Modahl, who was suspended in August 1994 after a positive drugs test, was cleared by the IAAF. Ray Illingworth resigned as manager of the England cricket team; on 29 March David Lloyd was appointed its coach. **27.** Frans Botha was stripped of his IBF world heavyweight boxing title after testing positive for steroids.

APRIL 1996

2. The Sri Lankan cricketer Sanath Jayasuriya scored the fastest-ever century in a one-day international when he reached 100 in 48 balls against Pakistan in Singapore; he also hit a record 11 sixes in his innings and made a record 29 runs in one over. 9. The Rugby Football Union confirmed that there would be a ten-club first division in the 1996–7 season, and reasserted its right as a governing body to control the game in England. 11. The twenty leading rugby union clubs in England said that they would not take part in RFU competitions in the 1996–7 season and put forward their own proposals for a competition structure. 18. David Graveney and Graham Gooch were elected to the selection committee for the England cricket team, defeating six other candidates including Ian Botham. 26. Shaun Pollock took four wickets in four balls in his début for Warwickshire. 27. A football match between Brighton and York was abandoned after 16 minutes when Brighton fans invaded the pitch in protest at plans to sell the Goldstone Ground and ground-share with Portsmouth for a season; on 30 April the club announced that it would remain at the ground for one more season. 29. Ronnie O'Sullivan was fined £20,000 and banned from snooker tournaments for two years, the ban being suspended for two years, for assaulting a press offficer at the world championships in Sheffield. 30. The Newcastle United striker Faustino Asprilla was fined £20,000 and suspended for one match by the FA for elbowing and head-butting the Manchester City captain Keith Curle during a match in February.

MAY 1996

2. Glen Hoddle was appointed coach of the England football team from July 1996. 4. In the Pilkington Cup final at Twickenham the referee awarded a last-minute penalty try against Leicester which gave Bath victory. The Leicester flanker Neil Back pushed the referee over at the end of the match; he later said that he had mistaken him for a Bath player. On 13 May he was banned for six months by the RFU. 5. Manchester United won the Premiership for the third time in four years. 6. Stephen Hendry won the world snooker championship for the sixth time in seven years. 7. Rugby Union in England officially became professional. 8. In the first inter-code rugby match between club sides for more than 100 years, Wigan beat Bath 82–6 in a match played under league rules at Maine Road; on 25 May Bath beat Wigan 44–19 in a match played under union rules at Twickenham. 11. Manchester United became the first team to win the FA Cup and League championship in the same year for a second time when they beat Liverpool to win the FA Cup. The rugby league club Wigan won the rugby union Middlesex Sevens tournament at Twickenham. 24. The RFU and the leading clubs reached agreement on the future operation of the sport. 28. Cathay Pacific said that members of the England football squad had caused damage on the flight back from a tour to China and Hong Kong; on 3 June the England coach (Terry Venables) said that the squad took collective responsibility for the incident and that fines had been imposed.

JUNE 1996

6. Premier League football clubs agreed a £743 million four-year television deal with BSkyB and the BBC. 8. The European football championships opened at Wembley stadium, London. Alex Greaves became the first woman to ride in the Derby. 10. The RFU signed an exclusive five-year £87.5 million television deal with BSkyB which put the future of the Five Nations championship in jeopardy. 23. Michael Johnson broke the world 200 metres record, set in 1979, with a time of 19.66 seconds. 26. In the semi-finals of the European championships Germany beat England 6–5 on penalties at Wembley after sudden-death extra time. 28. At Wimbledon two British men (Tim Henman and Luke Milligan) met in a singles match on Centre Court for the first time since 1938. 30. In the final of the European Championships Germany beat the Czech Republic 2–1 at Wembley after sudden-death extra time.

JULY 1996

1. Tim Henman became the first British man to reach the quarter-finals at Wimbledon for 23 years when he beat Magnus Gustafsson in straight sets. On 4 July he was beaten in straight sets by Todd Martin, the only original seed to reach the semi-finals of the men's championship. 4. The Italian striker Fabrizio Ravanelli joined Middlesbrough for £7 million. 6. Steffi Graf won the ladies' singles championship at Wimbledon for the seventh time. 7. In the men's singles final at Wimbledon Richard Krajicek beat the unseeded MaliVai Washington in straight sets. 8. Fifteen-year-old Martina Hingis became the youngest-ever Wimbledon champion when she won the ladies' doubles championship with Helena Sukova. 13. England were excluded from the 1997 Five Nations' rugby union championship. 19. The Olympic Games opened in Atlanta, Georgia. The National Hunt jockey Richard Davis died after being crushed by his horse in a fall at Southwell racecourse. 21. Tom Lehman became the first American since 1926 to win the Open golf championship. 24. The Prime Minister said that a national Academy of Sport would be set up. 27. At the Olympic Games Donovan Bailey set a new world record of 9.84 seconds in the final of the 100 metres; Linford Christie was disqualified from the race after two false starts. Steve Redgrave won his fourth successive Olympic gold medal in his event when he won the coxless pairs with Matthew Pinsent. 29. The Blackburn Rovers striker Alan Shearer was transferred to Newcastle United for a world record fee of £15 million. 30. Carl Lewis won the Olympic long jump gold medal, his fourth successive Olympic gold medal in the event.

AUGUST 1996

1. Michael Johnson set a new world record of 19.32 for the 200 metres and became the first man to win Olympic gold medals for both the 200 metres and the 400 metres. 12. Bruce Rioch was sacked as manager of Arsenal FC. 15. The paralympics opened in Atlanta, Georgia. 20. The fast bowler Ed Giddins was banned from professional cricket until April 1998 by the TCCB for cocaine use. 21. Kenny Dalglish resigned as director of football at Blackburn Rovers. 26. St Helens won the inaugural rugby league Stones Super League championship. Alan Ball resigned as manager of Manchester City FC. 28. Chris Boardman set a new world record of 4 minutes 13.353 seconds when he won the 4,000 metres individual pursuit world cycling championship. 30. The former world boxing champion Frank Bruno announced his retirement.

APPOINTMENTS AND RESIGNATIONS

In addition to those mentioned above, the following appointments and resignations were announced:

1995

1 September: Phil Hall was appointed editor of the *News of the World*

29 September: Max Hastings, the editor of the *Daily Telegraph*, was appointed editor of the London *Evening Standard* from January 1996

18 October: Charles Moore was appointed editor of the *Daily Telegraph*; Dominic Lawson, the editor of *The Spectator*, was appointed editor of the *Sunday Telegraph* in his place

19 October: Frank Johnson was appointed editor of *The Spectator*

30 October: Bill Cockburn, the chief executive of the Post Office, was appointed chief executive of W. H. Smith

1 November: Sir Nicholas Lloyd resigned as editor of the *Daily Express*

3 November: Robert Ayling was appointed chief executive of British Airways

13 November: Ian Hargreaves resigned as editor of the *Independent*

15 November: Peter Middleton resigned as chief executive of Lloyd's of London; he was replaced by Ron Sandler

24 November: Richard Addis was appointed editor of the *Daily Express*; Peter Bonfield was appointed chief executive of British Telecom from January 1996

8 December: Steve Platt resigned as editor of the *New Statesman and Society*

1996

19 February: Liz Forgan resigned as managing director of BBC Network Radio

29 March: Will Hutton was appointed editor of the *Observer* in the place of Andrew Jaspan

26 April: Andrew Marr was appointed editor of the *Independent*

4 July: Genista McIntosh was appointed general director of the Royal Opera House from early 1997

29 July: Sir Peter Hall was appointed artistic director of the Old Vic theatre from January 1997

AFRICA

SEPTEMBER 1995

11. Rwandan government soldiers killed over 100 Hutu villagers in the north-west of the country in retaliation for attacks on army units by Hutu militias based in Zaire. 28. Mercenaries led by a former French colonel launched a coup d'état in the Comoros in which President Djohar was arrested and replaced by a Military Transition Council.

OCTOBER 1995

1. Islamic militants killed 18 people in an attack on a bus in southern Algeria. 4. French forces landed in the Comoros, releasing President Djohar and arresting the coup leaders. 15. The leader of Zimbabwe's only parliamentary opposition party, Revd Ndabaningi Sithole, was arrested in connection with an alleged assassination attempt on President Mugabe. 22. In the presidential election in Côte d'Ivoire, President Konan-Bédié was returned to office with an overwhelming majority following an opposition boycott. 29. A car bomb planted by Islamic fundamentalists exploded at a police barracks on the outskirts of Algiers, killing 11 people. 29. The first free democratic national election for the Tanzanian presidency was won by Benjamin Mkapa of the Chama Cha Mapinduzi ruling party.

NOVEMBER 1995

7. Rwandan government troops attacked a Hutu base on the Zaire border, killing 171. 10. Ken Saro-Wiwa and eight other human rights activists were executed in Nigeria despite Commonwealth pleas for clemency. 11. Nigeria's membership of the Commonwealth was suspended. 16. The Algerian presidential election was won by President Liamine Zeroual. 23. An Egyptian military court jailed 54 members of the Islamic fundamentalist Muslim Brotherhood for aiding the armed campaign against the government.

DECEMBER 1995

10–14. Algerian security forces killed 36 Islamic militants and captured caches of arms in a series of raids. 25. Fourteen people were killed in KwaZulu/Natal, South Africa, in continuing communal violence. 26. Ten people were killed in fighting between Inkatha and ANC supporters in KwaZulu/Natal.

JANUARY 1996

15. King Moshoeshoe II of Lesotho was killed in a car accident. 16. Sierra Leone's president, Capt. Valentine Strasser, was overthrown in a military coup led by his deputy, Capt. Julius Bio. 27. President Ousmane of Niger was overthrown in a coup by the armed forces, who established a National Salvation Committee. 29. Ten people were killed when seven unidentified gunmen opened fire on a queue of 2,000 people seeking employment outside a factory near Johannesburg, South Africa.

FEBRUARY 1996

7. King Letsie was sworn in as king of Lesotho. 11. Eighteen people were killed by two car bombs planted by Islamic fundamentalists in Algiers. 18. Twelve people were killed by two car bombs in Algiers.

MARCH 1996

4. The former South African defence minister Gen. Magnus Malan went on trial in Durban charged with collusion in the murders of 13 people massacred in Natal in 1987. 8. The mandate for the deployment of UN forces in Rwanda ended and the remaining troops began to leave. 17. Robert Mugabe was re-elected President of Zimbabwe in an election in which only 31 per cent of the electorate voted and the two opposition candidates, Bishop Abel Muzorewa and Revd Ndabaningi Sithole, withdrew, claiming the election was unfair. 21. Ten ANC sympathisers and one child were shot dead in KwaZulu/Natal on the first day of campaigning for local elections. 28. Thousands of Zaïrean-born Tutsis began crossing the border into Rwanda as a result of a pogrom by Hutu militia and Zaïrean soldiers. 29. The military government in Sierra Leone handed over power to President Kabbah. 30. Libyan government forces were sent to Benghazi to put down a fundamentalist uprising which had begun ten days earlier with the escape of 400 prisoners.

APRIL 1996

3. Five members of the South African neo-Nazi Afrikaner Resistance Movement (AWB) were each sentenced to 26 years' imprisonment for a bombing campaign which killed 20 people in April 1994. 6. Fighting broke out in Monrovia, Liberia, following the dismissal from the government of Roosevelt Johnson. 10. Warring factions in Liberia agreed to a cease-fire. 11. Forty-nine African countries signed the Treaty of Pelindaba which declared the continent a nuclear-free zone. 18. Islamic militants opened fire on a hotel in Cairo, Egypt, killing 17 Greek tourists and one Egyptian. 21. The US sent a diplomatic mission to Liberia in an attempt to negotiate peace; militia gunmen released 127 people, including 71 foreigners. 23. Seven people died in a shoot-out between Egyptian police and two men suspected of massacring Greek tourists.

MAY 1996

1. Fighting resumed in Liberia. 2–3. Sixteen people died in communal violence in KwaZulu/Natal. 3. Roosevelt Johnson was smuggled out of Liberia for peace talks in Ghana. 4–5. Nigerian and Cameroonian forces clashed in a struggle for control of the mineral-rich Bakassi peninsula. 8. The South African Constituent Assembly adopted a new constitution. 9. The National Party said it would withdraw from South Africa's Government of National Unity. 11. In the presidential election in Uganda, President Museveni was returned to power for a second five-year term. 14. A freighter carrying 3,500 Liberian refugees docked in Ghana, having spent ten days at sea. 19. Two hundred soldiers mutinied in the Central African Republic, killing three people and taking a minister and an Army Chief of Staff hostage; on 27 May the mutineers released their hostages and were returned to barracks by French troops. 28. France suspended military co-operation with Burundi after 51 Tutsi refugees were killed by Hutu rebels.

JUNE 1996

4. Kudirat Abiola, wife of the jailed Nigerian opposition leader, Chief Moshood Abiola, was murdered. 13. Nigeria agreed to receive a Commonwealth task force to discuss a return to democracy. Burundian soldiers massacred at least 70 Hutu civilians in central Burundi. 17. Nineteen people died in pre-election violence in KwaZulu/Natal, South Africa. 18. A Russian trawler carrying 400 refugees returned to Liberia after three weeks at sea. 20. The Rwandan government began issuing new passports, thereby invalidating those held by Hutu refugees in exile. 22. Eight people were killed in fighting between rival factions in Mogadishu, Somalia.

JULY 1996

4. Sixty people were reported to have been killed near Bujumbura, Burundi, bringing the total number of deaths to 1,060 during the week. Twelve people were killed in clashes between police and anti-government rebels in Benghazi, Libya. 14. Fifty people died when security forces opened fire on spectators at a football match in Libya after the crowd began chanting anti-Gadhafi slogans. 20–21. At least 300 Tutsis were massacred by Hutus at Bugendana, Burundi. 23. Tutsi mourners attacked the helicopter carrying President Ntibantaganya of Burundi, who was attempting to attend the funeral of the victims of the Bugendana massacre. 25. The army overthrew President Ntibantaganya of Burundi and installed a moderate Tutsi, Maj. Pierre Buyoya, as transitional head of state. 31. The leaders of six African nations, meeting in Tanzania, decided to impose economic sanctions against Burundi's

military government. Fifteen people were trampled to death in a South African railway station as security guards attempted to deter fare dodgers with electric cattle prods. The leaders of Liberia's warring factions agreed to an immediate cease-fire and withdrawal of troops.

AUGUST 1996

2. The Somali warlord Gen. Mohammed Aideed died from gunshot wounds. 10–11. Ethiopian forces attacked Muslim fundamentalist militia in northern Somalia.

THE AMERICAS

SEPTEMBER 1995

7. Senator Robert Packwood (Republican) resigned from the US Senate after the ethics committee voted to expel him for sexual harassment of women over a 20-year period. 19. The *Washington Post* in agreement with the *New York Times* published the 35,000-word manifesto of the 'Unabomber' so that he would end his terrorist campaign. 20. The US Senate approved an amended version of the House of Representatives' welfare reform bill. 29. Pete Wilson, the governor of California, withdrew from the campaign for the Republican Party nomination for the 1996 presidential election.

OCTOBER 1995

1. The Egyptian cleric Sheikh Omar Abderahman and nine co-defendants were convicted in New York of bombing the World Trade Centre in 1993; on 17 January the Sheik was sentenced to life imprisonment and his co-defendants to terms of between 25 and 35 years each. 6. The USA relaxed restrictions on travel to Cuba and ended the restrictions on US news organizations opening offices in Cuba. 9. A suspected terrorist bomb derailed a train in Arizona, killing one person and injuring 100. 16. An estimated 400,000 black men gathered in Washington DC to listen to an address by Louis Farrakhan, the extremist leader of the Nation of Islam. 31. A referendum on sovereignty for Quebec was defeated by 50.6 per cent to 49.4 per cent.

NOVEMBER 1995

8. Gen. Colin Powell announced that he would not run for the US presidency in 1996. 13. President Clinton vetoed a borrowing bill proposed by Congress because of the budget cuts it contained, leading to a partial closure of government agencies as the federal government ran out of funding. 15. The US Treasury borrowed US$61,000 million from two government pension schemes to pay US$25,000 million due to holders of US securities. 19. President Clinton and Congress reached a temporary budget compromise to allow federal

government operations to continue until 15 December.

DECEMBER 1995

6. President Clinton vetoed a bill which would have balanced the federal budget in seven years by reducing projected spending and cutting taxes. 12. The Senate committee investigating the Whitewater affair claimed a breakthrough when files relating to Hillary Clinton's involvement in the land and banking scandal were found in the basement of one of her associates. 13. President Clinton refused to comply with a Senate subpoena to release unconditionally documents relating to the Whitewater affair. 15. The Senate Whitewater committee rejected President Clinton's conditional offer to release Whitewater documents and voted to take the administration to court over the subpoena. 16. The US federal government laid off non-essential employees as government agencies were again closed down because of the budget stalemate between President Clinton and Congress. 17. Rene Préval won the Haitian presidential election. 21. President Clinton agreed to release unconditionally documents relating to the Whitewater affair after the Senate voted to take the administration to the Supreme Court to force it to hand over the documents. 22. The White House surrendered to the Senate Whitewater committee subpoenaed documents which showed that administration officials had tried to obtain confidential information about independent inquiries into the Whitewater affair.

JANUARY 1996

5. President Clinton and Congress reached a budget compromise which allowed federal government agencies to resume work until 26 January. Under congressional pressure the White House released two confidential memos which implicated Hillary Clinton in the decision in 1993 to dismiss seven White House travel staff and transfer the White House travel contract to a business partly-owned by a friend. 9. An appeal court in St Louis, Missouri ruled that President Clinton should face a civil trial while he was in office over an alleged sexual advance to a woman in 1991. 22. The special prosecutor investigating the Whitewater affair subpoenaed Hillary Clinton to appear before a federal grand jury to answer questions over the legal work that she had done for Madison Guaranty, the bank at the centre of the scandal; Mrs Clinton appeared before the jury four days later. 26. President Clinton and Congress agreed on a compromise short-term budget plan to keep the US federal government functioning until mid-March.

FEBRUARY 1996

6. President Clinton was subpoenaed by an Arkansas judge to appear as a defence witness in the trial of his former business partner Susan McDougal. 7. Patrick Buchanan won the Louisiana state primary vote fo

the Republican presidential nomination. Twenty-seven current and former officials of the Clinton administration were subpoenaed to testify to a House of Representatives' committee about the dismissal of White House travel office officials; the Justice Department was ordered to release all the documents on the affair that it possessed. **13.** Senator Robert Dole won the Iowa state primary vote for the Republican presidential nomination. **14.** The Colombian Attorney-General charged President Samper with using money from the Cali drugs cartel to finance his 1994 election campaign and also with obstruction of investigations into electoral fraud. **20.** Patrick Buchanan won the New Hampshire state primary vote. **24.** Cuban Air Force fighters shot down over international waters two US-based civilian light aircraft operated by Cuban exile organizations who were searching for Cuban refugees fleeing to Florida. Two days later President Clinton increased US sanctions against Cuba. **25.** Steve Forbes won the Delaware primary vote for the Republican presidential nomination. **27.** Senator Robert Dole won the North and South Dakota primary votes but lost the Arizona vote to Steve Forbes.

MARCH 1996

2. Senator Robert Dole won the South Carolina state primary vote. **5.** Senator Robert Dole won the state primary votes in Maine, Vermont, Connecticut, Rhode Island, Massachusetts, Maryland, Colorado and Georgia. **6.** Republican candidates Lamar Alexander and Senator Richard Lugar withdrew from the presidential campaign. **8.** Senator Robert Dole won the New York state primary vote. **12.** Senator Robert Dole won the primary votes in Texas, Florida, Mississippi, Tennessee, Louisiana, Oregon, and Oklahoma. **14.** The Republican candidate Steve Forbes withdrew from the presidential campaign. **19.** Senator Robert Dole won the state primary votes in Michigan, Ohio, Illinois and Wisconsin. **22.** The House of Representatives voted to lift a ban on the public ownership of assault weapons. **27.** Senator Robert Dole won the California, Washington and Nevada state primary votes, clinching the Republican presidential nomination. **28.** Congress approved a bill enabling the President to exercise a 'line-item veto' over legislation.

APRIL 1996

2. David Hale, a witness in the Whitewater trial, alleged that President Clinton had agreed to accept a covert loan of £98,684 while governor of Arkansas. **3.** Theodore Kaczynski, thought to be the Unabomber, was detained in Montana. **3.** Five thousand people were evacuated from the south of Montserrat as a volcano erupted on the island. **10.** President Clinton vetoed a bill that would have prohibited a form of late-term abortion. **23.** Gen. Lino Oviedo complied with a request from President Wasmosy of Chile to resign as head of the army, having refused the previous day. **24.** President Clinton reached

agreement with Congress on a spending bill which would end the dispute over the budget.

MAY 1996

1. President Clinton ordered the release of 12 million barrels of petroleum onto the market in an attempt to curb rising fuel prices. **3.** The Attorney-General of Columbia, Orlando Vasquez Velasqez, was arrested on drugs and corruption charges. **9.** President Clinton, giving evidence via videotape at the trial of his former business partners in Arkansas, denied involvement in procuring an illegal loan. **15.** Republican presidential nominee Robert Dole resigned his seat in the Senate. **16.** The top US naval officer Adm. Jeremy 'Mike' Boorda committed suicide, having allegedly worn medals he had not been awarded. **28.** President Clinton's former business partners Jim and Susan McDougal and the governor of Arkansas, Jim Guy Tucker, were found guilty of conspiracy and fraud. **30.** President Clinton surrendered documents relating to the dismissal of members of the White House travel office which had been subpoenaed by a congressional committee.

JUNE 1996

13. President Samper was cleared of drug corruption charges by Colombia's House of Representatives. An 81-day siege by the FBI of a white supremacist militia group at a ranch in Montana ended peacefully. **14.** An FBI report criticized President Clinton for obtaining 408 confidential files on Republican officials. **17.** Hillary Clinton sent an affidavit to the Senate Whitewater committee in an attempt to refute accusations of corruption. **18.** The Senate Whitewater committee issued a report accusing Hillary Clinton of involvement in a fraudulent land deal whilst her husband was governor of Arkansas. Theodore Kaczynski, the alleged Unabomber, was charged on ten counts, including four bombings. **24.** The US Supreme Court agreed to delay a sexual harassment lawsuit against President Clinton until after the November presidential election. **25.** President Clinton agreed to allow congressional investigators to view subpoenaed documents relating to the dismissal of members of the White House travel office. **26.** The director of President Clinton's personal security office, Craig Livingstone, resigned, accepting responsibility for ordering FBI files on Republican officials.

JULY 1996

8. Abdala Bucaram was elected President of Ecuador. **16.** President Clinton announced that any lawsuits relating to the Helms-Burton Act, penalizing foreign companies benefiting from American property seized by Cuba, would be delayed for six months. **23.** The US House of Representatives approved a bill designed to impose sanctions on foreign companies investing in oil and gas fields in Libya and Iran.

AUGUST 1996

1. Two Arkansas bankers were acquitted of concealing funds donated to President Clinton's 1990 gubernatorial campaign. 2. Coca farmers in Colombia staged violent protests against a government plan to destroy their crops. 5. Republican presidential candidate Robert Dole unveiled an election manifesto in which he called for tax cuts of 15 per cent. 9. Jack Kemp was chosen to be Robert Dole's presidential running mate. 11. The Republican Party convention to nominate formally the party's presidential candidate opened; Robert Dole was officially nominated on the 15th. 18. Ross Perot was nominated as the presidential candidate of the Reform Party. 22. President Clinton signed a bill ending the guarantee of federal aid to the poor. 23. President Clinton signed an executive order classifying nicotine as an addictive drug. 25. The Democratic Party convention to nominate formally the party's presidential candidate opened in Chicago; President Clinton embarked on a four-day train journey to the convention. 29. President Clinton delivered his key-note speech to the Democratic convention; Dick Morris, a senior aide to President Clinton, resigned amid allegations that he had had an affair with a prostitute.

ASIA

SEPTEMBER 1995

4. A car bomb in the Kashmiri capital Srinagar killed 15 people. Taliban, the fundamentalist Islamic students movement, captured Afghanistan's second city Herat and the surrounding province from government forces. 10. The Nepali Prime Minister Man Mohan Adhikari resigned after his government lost a parliamentary vote of confidence. 18. In elections to Hong Kong's Legislative Council, the Democratic Party and its allies won 29 seats, pro-China parties won seven seats, and independents and liberals won 24 seats.

OCTOBER 1995

2. Sri Lankan forces began an offensive to recapture the Jaffna peninsula from the Tamil Tiger guerrillas. 20. Tamil Tiger guerrillas blew up the two main oil storage depots in Colombo. 22–26. Tamil Tiger guerrillas killed 127 civilians in eastern Sri Lanka.

NOVEMBER 1995

14. Sri Lankan government forces advanced to within one mile of the centre of Jaffna and captured the Tamil Tigers' political headquarters. 19. Sixteen people were killed and the Egyptian embassy was destroyed by a car bomb planted by Islamic extremists in the Pakistani capital Islamabad. The annual meeting of heads of government of the Asia-Pacific Economic Co-operation (APEC) Forum

ended with agreement on a mutual opening of markets to each other's products by 2020. 20. Sri Lankan troops surrounded Jaffna and captured the nearby town of Nallur.

DECEMBER 1995

3. The Sri Lankan army captured Jaffna. The ruling Kuomintang party won Taiwan's legislative election. 13. After a closed trial, the Chinese pro-democracy activist Wei Jingsheng was jailed for 14 years for allegedly attempting to overthrow the government. 22. A car bomb exploded in Peshawar, Pakistan, killing 60 people. 28. The Chinese National People's Congress approved the establishment and membership of the 150-member Hong Kong Preparatory Committee to choose the territory's first post-1997 government.

JANUARY 1996

5. The Japanese coalition government resigned following the resignation of the Prime Minister, Tomiichi Murayama, who stated that the position was beyond his capability. 11. A new coalition government under Ryutaro Hashimoto was approved by the Japanese parliament. 17. Three Indian Cabinet ministers and the leader of the country's main opposition party resigned after police charged them with bribery and corruption. 31. A Tamil Tiger lorry bomb exploded in the centre of Colombo, killing 81 people.

FEBRUARY 1996

3. The International Committee of the Red Cross began an airlift of food and medicines into the Afghan capital Kabul after supplies in the besieged city had been exhausted. 20. Two more Indian Cabinet ministers resigned after being implicated in bribery and corruption.

MARCH 1996

7. During military manoeuvres, China began to test-fire surface-to-surface missiles off the coast of Taiwan. 10. China began naval and military exercises along the coast opposite Taiwan and in the Taiwan Strait. US battle groups were ordered to Taiwan. 15. The first direct talks between the Indian government and representatives of Kashmiri secessionist groups took place in New Delhi. 18. China began a second series of military and naval exercises in the Taiwan Strait and warned the USA not to send its carrier battle groups into the strait. 23. President Lee Teng-hui won the first democratic presidential elections in Taiwan. 24. China announced that Hong Kong's existing Legislative Council would be wound up 1 July 1997 and replaced by a Provisional Legislative Council. Kashmiri separatists killed 11 of the 2,000 troops besieging a mosque which they had seized. 25. China ended its military exercises in the Taiwan Strait. 30. Muhammad Habibur Rahman was installed as head of a caretaker government following the dissolution of Bangladesh's parliament. 30. Indian troops killed 22 Kashmiri rebels in

Srinagar. **31.** Tamil Tiger rebels attacked a military base in eastern Sri Lanka, killing 54 people.

APRIL 1996

1. Myanmar's Constitutional Convention decided guidelines for choosing the president, including a 20-year residency requirement, which would exclude the opposition leader Aung San Suu Kyi. **3.** The Hong Kong government released 207 Vietnamese boat people who had been detained illegally. Two Indian ministers resigned in protest at Congress (I)'s alliance with a small party led by an actress. **5–7.** North Korean soldiers made three incursions into the demilitarized zone on the border with South Korea. **8.** President Kumaratunga of Sri Lanka extended the 11-year-old state of emergency across the country, increasing police and military powers and curtailing civil liberties. **11.** The ruling New Korea Party won 139 of the 253 seats in the South Korean National Assembly, 11 short of a majority. **16.** A peace plan for the Korean peninsular, announced by US President Clinton, was rejected by North Korea. **17.** The USA and Japan issued a joint declaration reaffirming their commitment to a joint defence strategy in East Asia; the USA pledged to maintain 100,000 troops in the region, including 47,000 in Japan, but to close 11 military bases in Japan. **19.** Nearly 20,000 Sri Lankan troops embarked on a fresh offensive against Tamil Tiger rebels in the Jaffna peninsula. **20.** A bomb, jointly planted by Punjabi and Kashmiri separatists in a hotel in New Delhi, India, killed 17 people. **23.** Shoko Asahara, the leader of the Aum Shinrikyo cult in Japan, went on trial accused of mass murder. **28.** Fifty-two people were killed by a bomb planted on a bus in Lahore, Pakistan. **30.** Human rights activist Liu Gang escaped from China to the USA.

MAY 1996

6. Eleven people were shot dead during voting in Assam, India. **8.** North Korea requested 3,000 tonnes of rice from the USA to cope with expected food shortages. Eight people died in an explosion on a bus in Lahore, Pakistan. **10.** The Prime Minister of India, Narashima Rao, resigned as it became clear that his Congress (I) party had lost the general election. **13.** More than 500 people were killed by a tornado in Bangladesh. Hezb-i-Islami troops returned to Kabul following an accord with the Afghan government. **14.** Chinese troops clashed with monks in Tibet who had refused to remove pictures of the Dalai Lama. **15.** The Bharatiya Janata Party (BJP) was invited to form the next government after emerging as the largest party in India's general election. **16.** Atal Behari Vajpayee was appointed Prime Minister of India. The Sri Lankan army ousted Tamil Tiger rebels from their last remaining stronghold. **17.** Seven North Korean soldiers entered the demilitarized zone on the border with South Korea. **20.** Soldiers loyal to the sacked army chief Gen. Abu Saleh Muhammad Nasim mutinied in Bangladesh. **21.** A bomb planted by Kashmiri separatists exploded in Delhi, India, killing 25 people. **22.** Gen. Abu Saleh Muhammad Nasim was detained and charged with sedition. A bomb blast in Rajhastan, India, killed 14 people. **26–28.** The National League for Democracy, led by Aung San Suu Kyi, held a meeting of its members in Myanmar despite the arrest of 262 supporters. **28.** The Prime Minister of India, Atal Vajpayee, resigned. The Sri Lankan government offered an amnesty to Tamil Tiger rebels. **30.** Four people died during the second round of voting in Kashmir.

JUNE 1996

1. H. D. Deve Gowda became Prime Minister of India at the head of a United Front coalition government. **13.** Following the general election in Bangladesh, the opposition Awami League emerged as the largest party, but without an overall majority. **19.** The Indian government abandoned its austerity programme, which had threatened to split the 13-party coalition. **20.** Soldiers and police broke up a 5,000-strong demonstration by opposition party supporters in Jakarta, Indonesia. **23.** China invited President Lee Teng-hui of Taiwan to visit Beijing for talks on reunification, with the proviso that he would not be treated as a head of state.

JULY 1996

1. The Democratic Union coalition defeated the ruling Mongolian People's Revolutionary Party to win Mongolia's general election. **4.** A Tamil Tiger suicide bomber killed 21 people in Jaffna, Sri Lanka. **18.** More than 4,000 Tamil Tigers overran the Mullaitivu military garrison in northern Sri Lanka, killing 1,200 soldiers. **19.** A Tamil Tiger suicide boat sank a Sri Lankan government naval ship. **22.** A bomb exploded in Lahore, Pakistan, killing 20 people. **24.** Two bombs exploded on a train in Columbo, Sri Lanka, killing 70 people; Sri Lankan troops retook the military garrison in Mullaitivu. Opposition parties in Pakistan formed an alliance in an attempt to oust the government. A national emergency was declared in Japan following the outbreak of a food poisoning epidemic which had affected 8,230 people and killed seven. **26.** The Sri Lankan army launched an attack on the town of Killinochchi, held by the Tamil Tigers. **27–28.** Two people died during anti-government riots in Jakarta, Indonesia. **29.** China exploded a nuclear device underground and immediately declared a moratorium on nuclear tests.

AUGUST 1996

1. The attempt by Megawati Sukarnoputri, daughter of Indonesia's former President, to have her removal from the leadership of the opposition Indonesian Democracy Party by a rebel party conference in June 1995 ruled invalid, was postponed by an Indonesian court; pro-democracy demonstrations were broken up by riot police. **4–5.** Sri Lankan government troops attacked the Tamil Tiger headquarters in Killinochchi, killing 200 guerrillas. **8.** A Khmer Rouge commander, Ieng Sary, and two generals were reported to have defected to the Cambodian government. **9.** Megawati Sukarnoputri was interrogated by Indonesian police. **14.** Prime Minister Hashimoto of Japan apologized for the abuse of Asian 'comfort women' by Japanese soldiers during the Second World War. **19.** The Philippines government held talks with the Moro National Liberation Front on the creation of an autonomous state in the Muslim Mindanao region. **20.** South Korean riot police ended a nine-day demonstration by students demanding reunification with North Korea. **26.** Former South Korean president Chun Doo-hwan was sentenced to death and his successor, Roh Tae-woo, was imprisoned after both had been found guilty of mutiny and treason for seizing power in a coup in 1979 and ordering the military to attack pro-democracy demonstrators. **29.** British forces began withdrawing from Hong Kong.

AUSTRALASIA AND THE PACIFIC

SEPTEMBER 1995

1. French commandos seized two Greenpeace ships which had entered the exclusion zone around the nuclear test site at the Muroroa atoll in French Polynesia. **5.** France carried out the first of a series of underground nuclear tests at Muroroa. **6.** Anti-nuclear protesters set light to the terminal at Tahiti's international airport in a riot which was dispersed by French police. The following day the rioting escalated, with looting and burning of shops and offices in Papeete. **10.** French commandos seized the yacht *La Ribaude* after it sailed into the exclusion zone around Muroroa, arresting eight MPs from four countries who were on board. **22.** The International Court of Justice rejected on technical grounds New Zealand's attempt to reopen its 1973 legal action to stop France conducting nuclear tests in French Polynesia.

OCTOBER 1995

1. France carried out its second nuclear test at Fangataufa atoll. **27.** France carried out its third nuclear test at Muroroa.

NOVEMBER 1995

2. The Queen signed the Waikato-Raupatu Claims Settlement, which compensates the Tainui federation of Maori tribes in New Zealand's North Island for the confiscation of their land by British settlers in 1863. **21.** France carried out its fourth nuclear test at Muroroa.

DECEMBER 1995

27. France carried out its fifth nuclear test at Muroroa.

JANUARY 1996

27. France carried out its sixth nuclear test at Fangataufa. **29.** President Chirac announced that the series of nuclear tests was complete.

MARCH 1996

2. In Australia's general election the Labor party was defeated by the opposition Liberal-National coalition. **25.** The trial opened of Ivan Milat, accused of murdering seven backpackers in Australia; he was found guilty and sentenced to life imprisonment on 26 July.

APRIL 1996

28. A gunman killed 35 people in Tasmania, Australia (*see also* Crimes and Legal Affairs).

MAY 1996

10. Australian state and territory governments agreed to ban all automatic and semi-automatic weapons. **29.** The Australian government launched an inquiry into allegations that its diplomats had sexually abused Asian children.

JUNE 1996

19. Papua New Guinea security forces executed eight former secessionist guerrillas on the island of Bougainville. **20.** Papua New Guinea armed forces launched an offensive against Bougainville Revolutionary Army rebels.

JULY 1996

1. Euthanasia was legalized in Australia's Northern Territory.

AUGUST 1996

19. Students, Aborigines and trade unionists stormed Parliament House in protest at the Australian government's austerity budget.

EUROPE

SEPTEMBER 1995

3. Four people were slightly injured by a terrorist bomb, which failed to explode properly, in Paris. **6.** A bomb exploded in a Lyon suburb. **8.** France deployed armed troops at tourist sites, schools, public buildings, railway stations, airports and borders because of the bombings. **10.** The Catalan Nationalist Party withdrew its parliamentary support of the Spanish socialist government because of continuing allegations that the government had organized illegal anti-terrorist squads. **11.** French security forces arrested 40 suspected Islamic extremists and recovered armaments, forged documents and suspect vehicles in a series of raids around Paris and Grenoble. **13.** Greece and the Former Yugoslav Republic of Macedonia (FYROM) signed an agreement normalizing diplomatic relations under which

Greece would end its economic embargo and FYROM would change its flag. **20.** The Turkish Prime Minister Tansu Çiller resigned after the Republican People's Party withdrew from her coalition government; President Demirel asked her to form a new government the next day. **26.** The trial of the former Italian Prime Minister Giulio Andreotti on charges of collusion with the Mafia opened in Palermo, Sicily. **29.** French gendarmes shot dead Khaled Kelkal, a French-Algerian wanted for the attempted bombing of the Paris to Lyon railway in August, after he opened fire on them.

OCTOBER 1995

1. The Socialist Party won the Portuguese general election. **6.** A bomb exploded near a Paris Metro station, injuring 13 people. **10.** Public sector workers held a one-day nation-wide strike in France in protest at a public sector wage freeze and planned job cuts. **15.** A bomb exploded in a Paris suburb. The Turkish Prime Minister Tansu Çiller resigned after her new minority government lost a parliamentary vote of confidence. **17.** A bomb planted by the Algerian Armed Islamic Group exploded on a Paris Metro train, injuring 29 people; on 19 October the French government deployed an extra 2,500 troops in the country's major cities. **27.** The former Italian Prime Ministers Bettino Craxi and Arnaldo Forlani, former foreign minister Gianni de Michelis and the Northern League leader Umberto Bossi were sent to prison for terms of between six months and four years after being found guilty of corruption.

NOVEMBER 1995

2. French police and security forces arrested ten suspected Islamic terrorists and seized bomb-making equipment in raids in three cities. **5.** A new Turkish coalition government of the True Path and Republican People's Parties under Tansu Çiller was approved by the Turkish parliament. Giulio Andreotti was charged with ordering the murder in 1979 of an investigative journalist because of information that the journalist had obtained about the murder of Prime Minister Aldo Moro in 1978. **7.** The French Prime Minister Alain Juppé resigned and was immediately reappointed by President Chirac in a reshuffle which reduced the number of government ministers from 25 to 16. **13.** The trial began of six former leaders of the East German politburo, including former Communist Party leader Egon Krenz, on charges of manslaughter and attempted manslaughter arising from the East German government's policy of shooting to kill people attempting to cross the border to the west. **19.** A former Communist minister, Aleksander Kwasniewski, won the second round of the Polish presidential election, defeating the incumbent President Lech Walesa. **24.** A nation-wide strike by French public sector workers in protest at government measures to reform the social welfare system closed down most of the country's transport system. **25.** In a referendum the electorate of the Irish Republic voted to amend the constitution to legalize divorce.

DECEMBER 1995

5. More French public sector workers, and civil servants and students joined the two-week long transport strike. **7.** A strikers' march in France ended in violent clashes with the police. **11.** A car bomb planted by the Basque separatist group ETA exploded in Madrid, killing six people. **15.** French public sector and transport workers began to return to work after the government conceded some of the strikers' demands. **17.** The Austrian coalition government was returned to power in the general election. **19.** A public sector strike in Belgium affected the state-owned railways and airline; it was in protest at proposed government austerity measures. **21.** The outgoing President of Poland, Lech Walesa, accused Prime Minister Jozef Oleksy of supplying secrets to Russian secret services. **24.** The Islamic Refah (Welfare) Party won the most seats in the Turkish general election. **30.** The Italian President refused to accept the resignation of Prime Minister Lamberto Dini and his government of technocrats and ordered the government to remain in office until parliament could debate the formation of another government.

JANUARY 1996

8. The former French President François Mitterrand died. **11.** The Italian Prime Minister Lamberto Dini tendered his resignation for the second time in two weeks; the President reserved judgement on whether to accept it. **14.** Jorge Sampaio won the Portuguese presidential election. **15.** Andreas Papandreou resigned as Prime Minister of Greece after two months of serious illness; Constantine Simitis was elected Prime Minister on 18 January. **17.** The former Italian Prime Minister Silvio Berlusconi went on trial in Milan, charged with corruption. **18.** A hostel in Lubeck, northern Germany, was destroyed in a suspected arson attack which left ten people dead. **25.** The Spanish Supreme Court charged a former Interior minister, José Barrionuevo, with organizing illegal anti-terrorist squads in the 1980s. **26.** The Polish Prime Minister Jozef Oleksy resigned after an investigation was launched into allegations that he had passed national secrets to the KGB and its successors; Oleksy was succeeded five days later by Wlodzimierz Cimoszewicz. **30–31.** Greek and Turkish forces confronted each other over the uninhabited islet of Imia in the eastern Aegean Sea until the US government intervened to diffuse the situation.

FEBRUARY 1996

1. President Scalfaro appointed Antonio Maccanico as Italy's Prime Minister. **14.** A Spanish judge was assassinated by the ETA. **16.** President Scalfaro dissolved parliament and called parliamentary elections after Antonio Maccanico was unable to form a government. **19.** French police arrested 24 suspected Islamic extremists in the Paris region in a series of raids.

MARCH 1996

3. The Popular Party won the most votes in Spain's general election but failed to achieve a parliamentary majority. 6. President Demirel of Turkey approved the formation of a coalition government of the Motherland and True Path parties, with the premiership to rotate between the two party leaders. 15. The ruling Swedish Social Democratic Party elected finance minister Goran Persson as its new leader, and he became Prime Minister three days later. 22. Erik Asbrik was appointed finance minister of Sweden. 26. Slovakia ratified a treaty with Hungary recognizing their mutual border and the rights of Slovakia's ethnic Hungarian community. 28. The former Polish head of state, Wojciech Jaruzelski, was charged with ordering troops to fire on protesters, killing 44 people, in 1970.

APRIL 1996

2. The Belgian government's plan to cut 300 teaching jobs in Wallonia provoked violent clashes between demonstrators and the police. 6. Turkish troops launched a combined air and ground assault on Kurdish rebels in the south-east of Turkey. 11. The trial opened in Italy of former Prime Minister Giulio Andreotti. 16. Former Italian Prime Minister Bettino Craxi was fined £15 million and sentenced to eight years' imprisonment in absentia for corruption. 22. The left-wing Olive Tree alliance led by Romano Prodi won the Italian general election. 24. The Turkish parliament voted to investigate corruption charges against former Prime Minister Tansu Çiller. 26. The Catalan Nationalist Party in Spain agreed to support the Popular Party of José Maria Aznar, enabling him to form a government with a 16-seat majority.

MAY 1996

5. Voters in Brandenburg rejected unification of their state with Berlin. 6. Spain threatened to close its border with Gibraltar unless Britain cracked down on smuggling from the colony. 7. The new Spanish government announced spending cuts of £1 billion and a reorganization of the country's intelligence services. 8. Erich Priebke, a former SS captain, went on trial in Italy for his alleged role in the murder of 335 people in 1944. 13. The Belgian parliament passed a law giving Prime Minister Dehaene extensive powers to cut government spending. Corsican nationalists embarked on a terrorist campaign in response to a police crackdown on drug dealing and smuggling. 17. The Gibraltar Social Democrats, led by Peter Caruana, were elected to office. 18. President Demirel of Turkey survived an assassination attempt. 19. Turkish troops killed 60 Kurdish Workers Party (PKK) guerrillas. 20. A Spanish soldier was killed by a bomb believed to have been planted by the ETA. 20–21. More than 100,000 German public service

employees took strike action in protest at government austerity measures. 24. Turkey's True Parth party withdrew from the ruling coalition. 25. King Simeon II returned to Bulgaria after 50 years in exile. 26. The opposition Socialist Party withdrew from Albania's general election in protest at alleged ballot rigging and intimidation. 27. In Cyprus the Democrat Rally-Liberal Party coalition government won the general election with a majority of one. The ruling Democratic Party claimed to have won 100 of the 140 seats contested in Albania's parliamentary election. 28. Members of Albania's Socialist Party clashed with police while protesting against the May 26 election, which international observers declared unfair. President Chirac of France announced that military conscription would be phased out from January 1997. 31. The leaders of Albania's opposition Socialist Party went on hunger strike to demand fresh elections.

JUNE 1996

4. The ruling Civic Democratic Party won the Czech parliamentary election, but were two seats short of a majority. 6. Prime Minister Yilmaz of Turkey resigned a day before his government was due to face a vote of confidence. 15. More than 30,000 German trade unionists demonstrated against the government's austerity programme. 16. The ruling Democratic Party of Albania won the rerun of the disputed general election after opposition parties boycotted it. 18. President Ulmanis was elected for a second term by the Latvian parliament. 27. Turkish troops entered northern Iraq in an offensive against Kurdish guerrillas. 28. Necmettin Erbakan, leader of the Islamist Welfare Party, was sworn in as Prime Minister of Turkey at the head of a coalition government which included the True Path party, whose leader, Tansu Çiller, was appointed deputy prime minister. 30. Prime Minister Simitis of Greece was elected leader of the Panhellenic Socialist Party (PASOK), following the death of former leader Andreas Papandreou.

JULY 1996

3. The German Constitutional Court ruled that former slave labourers used by companies during the Nazi regime would be allowed to claim compensation. 17. France announced the disbanding of a quarter of its military regiments as part of a plan to create a purely professional army by 2002. 18. The president of the French state railway, Loïk Le Floch-Prigent, was remanded in custody on charges of corruption; Michel Mouillot, the mayor of Cannes, was also arrested. 20–21. The ETA planted five bombs in the Costa Dorada region of Spain. 23. French police arrested six ETA members, including Julián Atxurra Egurola, alias Pototo, believed to be a senior ETA leader; a further three members were arrested the following day. 25. The Belgian Senate passed three laws enabling Prime Minister Dehaene to rule by decree as a means of imposing austerity measures.

AUGUST 1996

1. Erich Priebke, a former SS officer, was found guilty of complicity in the murder of 335 civilians in 1944, but was released because he was following orders; he was rearrested the same day pending an application for extradition from Italy to Germany. **9.** French police began investigating corruption allegations against former directors of the state-owned bank Crédit Lyonnais. **10.** One man was killed when Greek Cypriot motor cyclists attempted to cross the buffer zone into Turkish-controlled northern Cyprus, in a protest at the division of the island. **14.** A Greek Cypriot was shot dead by Turkish troops while demonstrating in the Cyprus buffer zone. **23.** French police rounded up 300 African illegal immigrants who had occupied a church in Paris for seven weeks, including ten who had been on hunger strike for 50 days.

THE COMMONWEALTH OF INDEPENDENT STATES

SEPTEMBER 1995

10. Russian and Chechen negotiators agreed a schedule for the disarmament of Chechen guerrillas, a partial withdrawal of Russian forces and a prisoner exchange. **13.** A rocket-propelled grenade was fired at the US Embassy in Moscow. **21.** Russian commandos freed 18 hostages and captured two gunmen when they stormed a bus which had been hijacked in the Dagestan republic in southern Russia.

OCTOBER 1995

6. The commander of Russian forces in Chechenia, Gen. Anatoly Romanov was seriously wounded in a bomb attack in Grozny. **9.** The Russian government said that it was to stop observing the July cease-fire with Chechen rebels as the rebels had not disarmed and fighting was increasing. **15.** Russian special forces stormed a hijacked bus in central Moscow, killing the hijacker who had held South Korean tourists hostage. **26.** President Yeltsin suffered his second heart attack in three months.

NOVEMBER 1995

5. The incumbent, Eduard Shevardnadze, won the presidential election in Georgia.

DECEMBER 1995

4. A car bomb exploded in Grozny, killing 11 people. Russian aircraft bombed rebel positions in Chechenia in retaliation. **8.** The Russian government and the Russian-supported government in the Chechen republic signed an autonomy agreement allowing the republic its own consulates and trade missions abroad, an amnesty for guerrillas who laid down their arms, and the right of Chechen conscripts in the Russian armed forces to serve only in Chechenia. **11.** Chechen guerrillas attacked the Russian military headquarters in Grozny. **14–23.** Russian troops and Chechen guerrillas fought for control of the city of Gudermes, which the Russian forces eventually retook. **17.** In parliamentary elections to the State Duma in Russia, the Communist Party won the largest number of seats. **26.** President Yeltsin returned home after spending two months recovering from his heart attack in October.

JANUARY 1996

9. Chechen separatists broke through Russian positions on the Russian-Chechen border and took some 2,000 civilians hostage in the hospital in the Russian town of Kizlyar. **10.** The Chechen rebels left Kizlyar in a fleet of buses with over 100 Russian hostages and headed for Chechenia but were stopped at the border village of Pervomayskiy by Russian forces, who surrounded the convoy. **14.** The Russian government gave the Chechen rebels in Pervomayskiy a 24-hour deadline to free their hostages. **15.** After their ultimatums were ignored, Russian forces attacked the Chechen rebels in Pervomayskiy, capturing the village on the 18th and releasing 82 hostages; some Chechen rebels escaped to Chechenia with an unknown number of hostages. **16.** As fighting continued in Pervomayskiy, a group of armed Chechens seized Russian power workers in Grozny and another group seized a Turkish ferry with mainly Russian passengers in Trabzon. **19.** The Chechen gunmen on the Turkish ferry surrendered to Turkish police and released their hostages. **24.** Chechen rebels who had escaped from Pervomayskiy released 45 Russian hostages in exchange for the bodies of Chechens killed in the village.

FEBRUARY 1996

20. After five days of fighting, Russian forces captured the town of Novogroznensky from Chechen rebels. **22.** The IMF agreed to lend US$10,000 million to Russia to support economic reforms and cover part of the budget deficit.

MARCH 1996

6–10. Russian forces repulsed attacks by Chechen guerrillas attempting to infiltrate Grozny. **8.** Four Chechen gunmen hijacked a Turkish Cypriot aircraft with 109 passengers and crew on board and forced it to fly to Munich; the gunmen surrendered the next day. **29.** Russia, Belarus, Kazakhstan, and Kyrgyzstan signed an agreement to form a common market and customs union and to create an interstate council. **31.** President Yeltsin announced a cease-fire and partial troop withdrawal from Chechenia.

APRIL 1996

1. Chechen rebels killed 28 Russian soldiers. **2.** The presidents of Russia and Belarus signed a treaty to form a Commonwealth of Sovereign States; the treaty provided for co-operation on foreign and defence policy and a single currency by the end of 1997. **3.** Russian aircraft bombed Shalazhi, one of the 156 Chechen towns and villages which had signed a

peace agreement with the Russian military. **4.**
Chechen rebels shot down a Russian military
aircraft. **16.** More than 70 Russian soldiers died in
an ambush of their convoy by Chechen rebels. **23.**
The Chechen rebel leader Dzhokhar Dudayev was
reported to have been killed by a Russian missile on
the 21st.

MAY 1996

4. Chechen rebels attacked government offices in
Grozny. **5.** The rebel leader Zelimkhan Yandarbiyev rejected negotiations with Russia; a Russian
aircraft was shot down over southern Chechenia. **16.**
President Yeltsin vowed to abolish conscription in
the Russian army by 2000, including voluntary
service only in Chechenia to take immediate effect.
22. Forty Russian soldiers were killed attempting to
storm a Chechen stronghold at Bamut. **27.** President
Yeltsin met Zelimkhan Yandarbiyev; an immediate
three-day cease-fire was declared as a prelude to the
permanent cessation of hostilities on 1 June. President Kuchma of Ukraine sacked Prime Minister
Evgeny Marchuk, whom he blamed for the country's worsening economic situation. **28.** President
Yeltsin visited Grozny. **29.** President Yeltsin announced a power-sharing treaty under which Chechenia would become a sovereign state within the
Russian Federation.

JUNE 1996

1. Twenty-six Russian soldiers were captured by
Chechen rebels south-west of Grozny. **2.** Four
Russian soldiers were killed by a mine in Grozny.
10. Russia signed an agreement with Chechen rebels
agreeing to withdraw all forces, apart from two
brigades, by September. **16.** President Yeltsin won
the first round of voting in Russia's presidential
election. **18.** Gen. Aleksandr Lebed, the third-placed
candidate in the Russian presidential election, was
appointed National Security Adviser and secretary
of the presidential Security Council by President
Yeltsin; defence minister Gen. Pavel Grachev
resigned. **20.** President Yeltsin dismissed his security advisor, the head of the Federal Security Service
and the First Deputy Prime Minister, after they had
allegedly arranged for the arrest of two members of
Yeltsin's campaign team.

JULY 1996

4. Boris Yeltsin was re-elected President of Russia. **9.**
The Russian army attacked a village in Chechenia,
believed to be the location of the Chechen leader
Zelimkhan Yandarbiyev, in violation of the May
cease-fire. **11.** A bomb exploded in central Moscow;
a Russian general was killed in Chechenia. **12.** A
second bomb exploded in central Moscow. **15.**
Russian troops in Chechenia destroyed a base at
Mekhketi believed to be the headquarters of Zelimkhan Yandarbiyev. **16.** Prime Minister Lazarenko of
Ukraine survived an assassination attempt when a
bomb exploded beneath his car.

AUGUST 1996

6. Chechen rebels launched a counterattack against
Russian troops, seizing parts of Grozny and two
other towns. **22.** A cease-fire was agreed by Russian
troops and Chechen rebels. President Yeltsin returned to work at the Kremlin following two weeks'
recuperation from the demands of the presidential
election campaign. **25.** Russian troops began withdrawing from Grozny. **27.** Russian and Chechen
commanders signed a cease-fire agreement. **31.**
Gen. Aleksandr Lebed signed an agreement with
the Chechen leader Aslan Maskhadov designed to
end the conflict in Chechenia by delaying a decision
on the region's status until 2001.

THE FORMER YUGOSLAVIA

SEPTEMBER 1995

1. NATO aircraft ended their bombing operations
but UN artillery continued to bombard Bosnian
Serb artillery and missile sites around Sarajevo. **3.**
UN peacekeepers opened a road into Sarajevo for a
convoy of lorries bringing aid into the city and
breaking its siege. **5.** After the Bosnian Serbs failed to
comply with an ultimatum to withdraw all their
heavy weapons from within 12½ miles of Sarajevo,
halt attacks on safe areas, allow Sarajevo airport to
reopen, and allow UN forces freedom of movement,
NATO aircraft recommenced bombing Bosnian
Serb artillery positions, ammunition dumps, and
communication centres. Bosnian Serb forces shelled
Sarajevo in response. **8.** The foreign ministers of
Bosnia, Croatia and the rump Yugoslav state (negotiating on behalf of the Bosnian Serbs) reached
agreement in Geneva that Bosnia-Hercegovina
would be recognized as existing within its present
borders and comprising the Muslim-Croat Federation, holding 51 per cent of the land and the (Bosnian
Serb) Republica Srpska, holding the remaining 49
per cent. **10.** The USS *Normandy* destroyed Bosnian
Serb ground-to-air missile sites around Banja Luka
with cruise missiles after Bosnian Serb Gen. Mladic
rejected UN demands that the Bosnian Serbs withdraw heavy weapons from around Sarajevo. NATO
aircraft bombed Bosnian Serb positions around
Tuzla from which the Bosnian Serbs had been
shelling Tuzla airport. **11.** NATO aircraft bombed
Bosnian Serb military and communications installations throughout Bosnia and widened the range of
targets to include bridges and supply routes. **12.**
NATO aircraft destroyed the Bosnian Serbs' main
munitions dump at Vogosca near Sarajevo. Bosnian
government and Bosnian Croat forces began an
advance in western Bosnia. **14.** NATO suspended its
bombing campaign after US envoy Richard Holbrooke brokered an agreement between President
Milosevic of Serbia and Bosnian Serb leaders under
which the Bosnian Serbs would withdraw their
heavy weapons from around Sarajevo over a six-day
period. Bosnian government, Bosnian Croat and
Croatian army forces captured the towns of Donji
Vakuf, Drvar, Jajce and Sipovo in central and

western Bosnia from Bosnian Serb forces. **15.** Bosnian government and Bosnian Croat forces captured Bosanki Petrovac. Sarajevo airport reopened for the first time in five months. **17.** Bosnian Serb forces began to withdraw their heavy weapons from the exclusion zone around Sarajevo. Bosnian government, Bosnian Croat and Croatian forces captured Kljuc; 90,000 Bosnian Serb refugees fled to Banja Luka. **20.** NATO indefinitely suspended air strikes against the Bosnian Serbs after it had confirmed that most of the Bosnian Serbs' heavy weapons had been removed from the Sarajevo exclusion zone and that air and land routes into the city had been opened. **26.** Foreign ministers from Bosnia-Hercegovina, Croatia and the rump Yugoslav state reached agreement in New York on a set of constitutional principles for Bosnia-Hercegovina.

OCTOBER 1995

3. President Gligorov of the former Yugoslav Republic of Macedonia was seriously injured in a car bomb attack in Skopje. Bosnian government forces launched artillery attacks from within Sarajevo on Bosnian Serb positions around the city and were rebuked by the UN, which refused a Bosnian Serb request to be allowed to move their heavy weapons back into the exclusion zone around the city. **4.** NATO aircraft fired missiles at Bosnian Serb missile batteries in Bosnia after the batteries had 'locked on' to the aircraft. **5.** President Izetbegovic of Bosnia and the Bosnian Serb leaders Radovan Karadzic and Gen. Ratko Mladic signed a US-brokered nation-wide cease-fire agreement, to become effective five days later provided that gas and electricity supplies to Sarajevo had been restored. **8.** Bosnian Serb forces launched artillery attacks on a Muslim refugee camp near Tuzla, and an air attack on the government-held town of Tesanjika. **9.** The Bosnian government postponed the implementation of the cease-fire agreement because gas and electricity had yet to be restored to Sarajevo and Bosnian Serb artillery had shelled Tuzla airport. NATO aircraft bombed a Bosnian Serb command post near Tuzla in retaliation. **10.** Bosnian government forces captured the western Bosnian town of Mrkonjic Grad. **12.** The nation-wide Bosnian cease-fire came into effect. Bosnian government and Bosnian Croat forces captured the town of Sanski Most. Bosnian Serb forces forced 6,000 Muslims out of the Banja Luka region, the men being taken into concentration camps. UN troops were prevented from opening a road from Sarajevo to Gorazde by Bosnian Serb forces. **13.** In defiance of the cease-fire, Bosnian government and Bosnian Croat forces shelled Prijedor and advanced on Banja Luka. **15.** Bosnian government forces uncovered evidence of the massacre of Muslims by Bosnian Serb forces in Sanski Most. **22.** The fighting in northern Bosnia between government and Bosnian Serb forces ended. **29.** The Croatian Democratic Union (HDZ) won the Croatian parliamentary elections.

NOVEMBER 1995

1. Bosnian peace negotiations opened at Dayton, Ohio, USA between delegations led by President Izetbegovic of Bosnia, President Tudjman of Croatia and President Milosevic of Serbia. President Tudjman and President Milosevic signed a US-brokered agreement to resolve peacefully the dispute over the Croatian region of eastern Slavonia held by ethnic Serbs. **9.** The International War Crimes Tribunal for the former Yugoslavia issued its first indictments against three Yugoslav Army officers, charging them with the murder of 261 Croatian men in Vukovar in 1991. A report by the UN special investigator for human rights in the former Yugoslavia accused Croatian forces of carrying out attacks on Serb civilians during their Krajina offensive in August. **12.** The Croatian government and Croatian Serb leaders in the Serb-held region of eastern Slavonia signed an agreement providing for the return of the region to Croatian rule after a one-year transition period and the return of 100,000 refugees. **13.** The International War Crimes Tribunal issued indictments against six Bosnian Croat political, military and police leaders. **21.** President Izetbegovic, President Tudjman and President Milosevic initialled a peace settlement for Bosnia-Hercegovina in Dayton, Ohio. **22.** The UN Security Council voted to lift the sanctions imposed on the rump Yugoslav state and also voted to lift gradually the arms embargo on all the former Yugoslav states.

DECEMBER 1995

4. The first troops of NATO's Peace Implementation Force (IFOR) began arriving in Bosnia-Hercegovina to enforce the Dayton peace agreement. **8.** The Bosnian Peace Implementation Conference opened in London; it closed the following day having established a framework for civilian police and aid organizations to operate in Bosnia, and appointed the EU envoy Carl Bildt as High Representative in charge of all civilian operations. **12.** Two French airmen held by the Bosnian Serbs since 30 August were released. **14.** President Izetbegovic, President Tudjman and President Milosevic signed the Paris Peace Treaty ending the war in Bosnia and creating the Union of Bosnia-Hercegovina. **20.** The UNPROFOR peacekeeping operation in Bosnia-Hercegovina ended and responsibility for implementing the Dayton Peace Agreement was transferred to IFOR. **26.** The NATO commander in Bosnia-Hercegovina, Adm. Leighton Smith, refused a request by the Bosnian Serb leadership that their forces be allowed to remain in Bosnian Serb-held areas of Sarajevo until September 1996. **27.** Bosnian government and Bosnian Serb forces withdrew from their frontline positions in and around Sarajevo.

JANUARY 1996

2. The Bosnian government protested to IFOR after 17 Bosnian civilians travelling through Bosnian Serb-held suburbs of Sarajevo were abducted by

Bosnian Serb forces. **4.** Sixteen of the abducted civilians were freed after the intervention of IFOR commanders in Sarajevo, but the Bosnian government stated that three more civilians had been abducted. **9.** Bosnian Serbs fired a rocket-propelled grenade at a tram in Sarajevo, killing one person; NATO forces returned fire. **15.** The Bosnian government refused to participate in an exchange of prisoners until it received information from the Bosnian Serbs about 24,000 missing Muslims. The UN Security Council voted to send 5,000 peacekeepers to the Croatian region of eastern Slavonia held by Croatian Serbs. **19.** Bosnian government, Bosnian Serb and Bosnian Croat forces withdrew 2 km either side of cease-fire lines and transferred military authority in the 4 km-wide zones of separation to IFOR. **28.** Three British soldiers serving with IFOR were killed when their tank hit a mine near Gornji Vakuf. Bosnian government and Bosnian Serb forces released about 500 of 650 remaining prisoners.

FEBRUARY 1996

3. Five Bosnian Serb-held suburbs of Sarajevo and a land corridor from Sarajevo to Gorazde were transferred nominally to Bosnian government control, though Bosnian Serb police officers remained until the 19th; land around the western Bosnian town of Mrkonjic Grad was transferred to Bosnian Serb control. **5.** Bosnian government forces detained eight Bosnian Serb soldiers as suspected war criminals. **9.** Bosnian Serb military and civilian authorities severed all communications with IFOR until the eight detained Bosnian Serbs were released. **12.** The two senior Bosnian Serb officers detained by the Bosnian government, Gen. Djordje Djukic and Col. Aleksa Krsmanovic, were flown to the Hague to appear before the International War Crimes Tribunal. **17.** President Izetbegovic, President Tudjman and President Milosevic attended a two-day US-organized summit in Rome and agreed that communications with IFOR by the Bosnian Serbs would resume. **20.** At the instigation of the Bosnian Serb leadership, thousands of Bosnian Serbs began to leave the suburbs of Sarajevo which were being transferred to Bosnian government control. **23.** The Bosnian government took control of the first of five Bosnian Serb-held suburbs of Sarajevo. **27.** The UN suspended sanctions against the Bosnian Serbs after IFOR certified that the Bosnian Serbs had withdrawn from all zones of confrontation.

MARCH 1996

1. Gen. Djordje Djukic was charged with crimes against humanity and violation of the laws and customs of war by the International War Crimes Tribunal. **7.** The International War Crimes Tribunal requested that Serbia hand over two Bosnian Serb soldiers who had been arrested by Serbian police after admitting in an interview with a newspaper to participating in a massacre of Muslims from Srebrenica in July 1995. **12.** Bosnian government

forces took control of a second Sarajevo suburb; most of the buildings had been destroyed by Bosnian Serbs as they left. **19.** Land transfers throughout Bosnia were completed and Sarajevo was reunited under Bosnian government control. Three suspected war criminals were arrested in Germany and Austria. **22.** The UN confirmed that 3,000 Muslims had been killed by Bosnian Serb forces in Srebrenica in July 1995. **31.** Bosnian Muslims and Croats agreed on a joint flag and a customs union.

APRIL 1996

5. A *Los Angeles Times* report claimed that the US government had approved the covert shipment of Iranian arms to Bosnia in 1994 despite the arms embargo. The Bosnian government released 18 Serb prisoners of war. **7.** President Chirac of France admitted that he had approved the sale of weapons to the Bosnian Serbs in order to secure the release of two French pilots shot down over Pale in August 1995. **8.** The Federal Republic of Yugoslavia signed a treaty with the Former Yugoslav Republic of Macedonia normalizing relations. **10.** Bosnian Serbs released three prisoners of war and promised to send files on 16 others to the International War Crimes Tribunal, thereby becoming eligible to participate in the conference for reconstruction. **12–13.** Fifty-five states attended an international aid conference in Brussels and pledged £800 million for the reconstruction of Bosnia; Bosnian Serbs refused to attend as part of the Bosnian delegation and were told to expect little aid until their war leaders were banned from office. **24.** The International War Crimes Tribunal released Gen. Djordie Djukic because he was suffering from terminal cancer. **26.** The Pentagon confirmed that the USA would maintain peacekeeping troops in Bosnia beyond the 20 December deadline agreed at the Dayton peace talks. **29.** Three Muslims were killed attempting to return to their homes in a Serb-held area.

MAY 1996

7. Dusan Tadic, a Serb accused of killing 16 Bosnian Muslims, went on trial at the International War Crimes Tribunal. **8.** The International War Crimes Tribunal announced that it had detained Zejnil Delalic, a Bosnian Muslim officer accused of murder. **13.** An alleged war criminal, Goran Lajic, was handed over to the International War Crimes Tribunal by German authorities. **15.** Radovan Karadzic sacked the prime minister of the Republika Srpska, Rajko Kasagic. **22.** The Bosnian government threatened to boycott the general election set for September unless Bosnian Serb leaders were tried for war crimes. **23.** Elections due to be held in Mostar on 31 May were postponed until 31 June. **30.** Carl Bildt, the EU's mediator in Bosnia, said he would not co-operate with Biljana Plavsic, who had been appointed to represent the Republika Serpska in its dealings with the international community. **31.** Drazen Erdemovic, a Croat who served in the

Bosnian Serb army, pleaded guilty to murdering 70 Muslims after the fall of Srebrenica in July 1995.

JUNE 1996

2. The USA warned that sanctions might be reimposed on Serbia unless the Bosnian Serb leaders Radovan Karadzic and Gen. Ratko Mladic were removed from office. 6. The president of the International War Crimes Tribunal asked for sanctions to be reimposed on the Bosnian Serbs and Serbia, for failing to hand over Karadzic and Mladic. 13. An international conference to review the Dayton peace accord opened in Florence, Italy. NATO defence ministers endorsed a plan to give IFOR increased powers. 14. Delegates at the Florence summit agreed that elections should go ahead in Bosnia despite the absence of full democracy; an arms limitation agreement was also signed. 16. Separatist Croats in Bosnia announced a government for their breakaway state of Herceg-Bosna. 18. The UN arms embargo on the former Yugoslavia was lifted. 27. The International War Crimes Tribunal began preliminary hearings into the Karadzic and Mladic cases. 28. Gen. Mladic was reported to have suffered a stroke. 29. The Group of Seven (G7) nations threatened to reimpose trade sanctions on Bosnia unless Karadzic retired from political office. 30. Karadzic said that he was transferring his presidential powers to a deputy, Biljana Plavsic, but would retain the title of President of Republika Srpska; the Party for Social Democracy defeated the Croat Democratic Party in municipal elections in Mostar.

JULY 1996

7. War crimes investigators began exhuming the bodies of Muslims thought to have been massacred following the capture of Srebrenica by Bosnian Serbs in July 1995. 8. The Organization for Security and Co-operation in Europe warned that it would ban the Serb Democratic Party from contesting the election in September unless Radovan Karadzic resigned as party leader. 9. The Muslim-Croat Federation parliament in Bosnia passed a law unifying Muslim and Croat forces in a single Federation army. UN investigators unearthed the bodies of ten people believed to have been murdered by Bosnian Serbs as they fled the enclave of Srebrenica in July 1995. 11. The International War Crimes Tribunal issued arrest warrants for Radovan Karadzic and Gen. Ratko Mladic. 15. Former American chief negotiator Richard Holbrooke began a special mission to Serbia in an attempt to have Karadzic and Mladic removed from power in Republika Srpska. 19. Radovan Karadzic resigned as President of the Republika Srpska and as leader of the ruling Serb Democratic Party. 23. Bosnian Croats blocked the adoption of a new mandate for the EU administration in Mostar and boycotted the first sitting of the city council. 24. The EU threatened to withdraw from Mostar unless Bosnian Croats participated in the city council. 31. Bosnian

Muslims and Croats agreed a plan to dismantle the Croat breakaway state of Herceg-Bosna.

AUGUST 1996

6. Bosnian Croats in Mostar agreed to recognize the results of the municipal election pending a ruling from the Supreme Court. 12. A NATO inspection team was refused access to the Han Pijesak military complex east of Sarajevo where Gen. Ratko Mladic was thought to be. 13. NATO was permitted access to the Han Pijesak military complex. 23. Croatia and Yugoslavia formally established diplomatic relations. 27. Bosnia's municpal elections were postponed.

EUROPEAN UNION

SEPTEMBER 1995

3. The official in charge of the European Monetary System (EMS) unit of the European Commission denounced a future single currency as a dangerous confidence trick and a threat to peace between France and Germany. The EU Reflection Group of ministers and representatives of the European Parliament and Commission held their first meeting to draw up an agenda for the Intergovernmental Conference in 1996. 17. Sweden held its first election to the European Parliament. 30. EU finance ministers and central bank governors unanimously agreed that stage three of economic and monetary union would begin in 1999 with the introduction of a single currency.

OCTOBER 1995

13. Latvia applied for EU membership. 17. The European Court of Justice ruled in a test case that positive discrimination favouring women over men in employment matters was illegal.

NOVEMBER 1995

14. The president of the Court of Auditors refused to approve the accounts for the 1994 budget because expenditure of £4,200 million was not properly documented and at least £410 million had been lost through fraud and a failure to collect payments. 28. The EU and 12 Mediterranean states signed an agreement in Barcelona to create an economic and political partnership leading to a free trade zone by 2010.

DECEMBER 1995

4. Estonia applied for EU membership. 13. The European Parliament approved the creation from 1 January 1996 of a customs union between the EU and Turkey. 16. The European Council summit in Madrid approved the name 'euro' for the single currency and confirmed that it would come into operation on 1 January 1999.

FEBRUARY 1996

21. The Schengen Agreement signatory states agreed to increase co-operation over the extradition of terrorist suspects.

MARCH 1996

22. Following an announcement by the British government on 20 March that BSE in cattle might be the cause of a new strain of CJD in humans, the EU's Scientific Veterinary Committee recommended tighter safety measures for British beef, including a cull of older cattle. 25. The EU banned the export of British beef and beef products world-wide; the ban was officially confirmed on 27 March. France announced that it would open its borders with Germany and Spain in accordance with the Schengen Agreement but retain controls at borders with the Benelux countries because of concerns about drug trafficking. 29. The Intergovernmental Conference opened in Turin, Italy.

APRIL 1996

3. At an emergency meeting in Luxembourg EU agriculture ministers agreed to provide financial assistance for British measures to eradicate BSE in cattle but refused to lift the world-wide export ban. 13. EU finance ministers met in Verona, Italy, to discuss a new exchange rate mechanism (ERM) to link countries inside the single currency area to those outside it, obliging governments to enact legislation to cut their country's deficit should it exceed 3 per cent of GNP and establishing a two-year ERM-membership requirement for single currency entry. 14. The European agriculture commissioner (Franz Fischler) said that the ban on British beef and beef products had been imposed to ensure that the European beef market did not collapse.

MAY 1996

8. The European Commission reported that £880 million, 1.4 per cent of the EU budget, had been lost through crime in 1995. 9. Spain signed an informal agreement with France promising support in all EU negotiations in return for tougher action against terrorism. 20. EU veterinary experts voted to continue the total ban on British beef exports in opposition to a Commission recommendation that the ban on beef products should be lifted. 21. Britain said it would block all EU decisions until progress was made on lifting the beef ban. The EU struck a deal with Spain to waive a fine of £230 million for breaching agricultural regulations. 29. The European Commission announced a £52 million compensation package for farmers and a 40 per cent reduction in the EU fishing fleet. The President of the European Commission, Jacques Santer, lambasted Britain for its policy of non-co-operation.

JUNE 1996

3. EU finance ministers agreed to drop the two-year membership of ERM as a precondition for entry into

economic and monetary union in 1999. EU agricultural ministers voted in favour of lifting the ban on the export of British beef products, but by too small a majority for the ban to be lifted immediately. 5. The European Commission authorized the partial lifting of the ban on the export of British beef products and warned Britain to end its policy of non-co-operation. 18. The European Commission endorsed a plan for lifting the world-wide ban on British beef exports provided the UK government ended its policy of non-co-operation with the EU. 19. EU veterinary experts approved the phased lifting of the ban on British beef, but insisted on the slaughter of up to 67,000 cattle in addition to the 150,000 already being culled. 21. The UK ended its policy of non-co-operation after agreement was reached at the EU summit in Florence for a gradual lifting of the beef ban.

JULY 1996

12. The European Court of Justice rejected an attempt by the British government to obtain an interim injunction temporarily lifting the ban on British beef exports. 24. The EU authorized a £588 million subsidy to Air France by the French government. 30. The EU Commission threatened to fine European companies co-operating with the USA's Helms-Burton law punishing foreign companies which benefit from US property seized by Cuba.

AUGUST 1996

2. Germany called for the reimposition of a total ban on the export of British beef following the publication of a study suggesting that BSE might be transmitted from cow to calf.

THE MIDDLE EAST

SEPTEMBER 1995

28. Israel and the PLO signed an agreement extending Palestinian autonomy on the West Bank.

OCTOBER 1995

6. The Israeli Knesset voted by 61 votes to 59 to approve the agreement on the second stage of Palestinian autonomy. 10. Several hundred Palestinian prisoners refused to leave Israeli jails, as agreed under the Israeli-PLO autonomy agreement, in protest at the Israelis' refusal to release four female Palestinian prisoners. 11. The UN special commission overseeing Iraqi disarmament presented a report to the UN Security Council which stated that Iraq had manufactured more chemical and biological weapons material than it had previously admitted and had not destroyed most of it. 13. Three Israeli soldiers were killed in a bomb attack by the Hezbollah militia on an Israeli convoy in the South Lebanon Security Zone. 15. Six Israeli soldiers were

killed in a bomb attack by Hezbollah militia on their convoy in south Lebanon; Israel retaliated with artillery and air attacks. **15.** Saddam Hussein won 99.96 per cent of the vote in a referendum in Iraq nominating him for a seven-year presidential term. **25.** Israeli troops began their withdrawal from Palestinian towns in the West Bank. **29.** The leader of the militant Islamic Jihad movement, Fathi Shiqaqi, was assassinated in Malta, allegedly by agents of the Israeli secret service Mossad.

NOVEMBER 1995

2. Eleven Israeli settlers in the Gaza Strip were injured in two suicide car bomb attacks by Palestinian militants. **4.** The Israeli Prime Minister Yitzhak Rabin was assassinated at a peace rally in Tel Aviv by an extremist Jew opposed to the Palestinian peace process; the gunman, Yigal Amir, was arrested immediately. **9.** Israeli police arrested five suspects involved in a suspected conspiracy to murder Yitzhak Rabin and uncovered a cache of illegally-held arms. **13.** A car bomb exploded at a joint US-Saudi military base in Riyadh, killing six people. Israeli forces completed their withdrawal from the West Bank town of Jenin and control of the town was handed over to the Palestinian National Authority (PNA).

DECEMBER 1995

10. Israeli forces completed their withdrawal from the West Bank town of Tulkarm. **11.** Israeli forces withdrew from Nablus. **15–18.** Eritrean forces landed on the disputed island of Greater Hanish in the Red Sea and seized control from Yemeni forces after a three-day battle. **18.** Yemeni aircraft attacked Greater Hanish. **21.** Israeli forces completed their withdrawal from Bethlehem. **27.** Syrian and Israeli delegations began three days of preliminary peace negotiations at Wye Plantation, Maryland, USA. Israeli forces completed their withdrawal from the West Bank town of Ramallah.

JANUARY 1996

1. King Fahd of Saudi Arabia transferred the management of government affairs to Crown Prince Abdullah whilst he was recovering from illness. **5.** Yehiya Ayyash, believed to have masterminded the Hamas bombing campaign against Israel, was killed by the Israeli secret services in the Gaza Strip; on the 7th Israel imposed an indefinite ban on Palestinian workers entering Israel from the West Bank and Gaza Strip in an attempt to stop retaliatory bombings. **10.** King Hussein of Jordan made his first official visit to Israel; Israel released 800 Palestinian prisoners. **16.** Two Israeli soldiers were killed when their vehicle was attacked by suspected Islamic militants near Hebron. **19.** Three members of Hamas were shot dead at an Israeli checkpoint near Jenin. **20.** Elections were held in the West Bank, Gaza Strip and East Jerusalem for a Palestinian leader and a Palestinian Council; the leadership election was won by Yasser Arafat.

FEBRUARY 1996

12. Yasser Arafat was sworn in as the first elected Palestinian leader or president. **20.** Lt.-Gen. Hussein Hassan and Col. Saddam Kamel, two sons-in-law of President Saddam Hussein of Iraq who had defected to Jordan in August 1995, returned to Iraq after being pardoned by the President. They were killed on the 23rd after having been divorced by their wives. **21.** King Fahd of Saudi Arabia resumed full control of government affairs. **25.** Two Hamas suicide bombers killed 25 Israelis when they exploded bombs in Jerusalem and Ashkelon.

MARCH 1996

3. A Hamas suicide bomber killed 18 people with a bomb on a bus in Jerusalem; in response Yasser Arafat outlawed the military wings of Hamas and Islamic Jihad. **4.** A Hamas suicide bomber exploded a bomb in Tel Aviv, killing 14 people. The Israeli government responded by announcing that it would mount military operations against Hamas in Palestinian Autonomous Areas. **8.** Iraqi officials prevented UN weapons inspectors from searching a building in Baghdad which they suspected housed parts for ballistic missiles. **13.** Western and Middle Eastern heads of state and government held a one-day anti-terrorism summit in Egypt in support of the Israeli-Palestinian peace process. **24.** Iraqis elected 220 members to the 250-member National Assembly in a poll in which 93 per cent of the electorate allegedly participated. **26.** The execution of a man convicted of murdering a police officer sparked unrest among the Shi'ite community in Bahrain. **27.** Yigal Amir, who assassinated the Israeli Prime Minister Yitzhak Rabin, was sentenced life imprisonment.

APRIL 1996

11. Seven people died in Israeli air strikes on a Hezbollah base in Beirut which were launched in response to rocket attacks on northern Israel. **12.** Israel intensified its attacks on Hezbollah targets in Lebanon following further rocket attacks on Israel's northern cities; about 400,000 Lebanese and 11,000 Israelis fled the affected areas. **16.** The USA announced a peace plan designed to end the conflict between Hezbollah and Israel and revive Israeli negotiations with Syria and Lebanon. **17.** Hezbollah rejected the US peace plan. **18.** An Israeli shell fell on a UN base in Qana, south Lebanon, killing 109 people. **21.** The Society of Combatant Clergy won 120 of the 270 seats in Iran's consultative assembly, although no group won overall control. **24.** The PLO National Council voted to eliminate from its charter clauses calling for the destruction of the Israeli state. **25.** The Israeli Labour Party formally ended its opposition to a Palestinian state. **26.** Israel and Hezbollah agreed to a cease-fire, to come into effect the following day.

MAY 1996

5. Israel and the PLO began talks on a final peace settlement in Taba, Egypt. Nine bombs exploded in Bahrain. **9.** Fighting resumed in south Lebanon between Israel and Hezbollah. **13.** A gunman shot dead a Jewish settler north of Jerusalem. **15.** Israel imposed a total military blockade of the West Bank and Gaza Strip. **18.** Hassan Salameh, a leading member of Hamas, was shot and detained by Israeli soldiers. **19.** Two Hezbollah members were killed by Israeli soldiers in south Lebanon; a civilian was injured, prompting claims that Israel had broken the cease-fire. **20.** Iraq accepted a UN deal permitting the sale of oil to fund humanitarian aid. **31.** The Likud leader Binyamin Netanyahu was confirmed as Israel's prime minister having narrowly defeated the incumbent, Shimon Peres.

JUNE 1996

4. The government of Bahrain foiled an Iranian-backed coup attempt and arrested 44 people. **10.** Five soldiers and two settlers were killed in attacks by Hezbollah and a suspected Palestinian gunman in Israel. **13.** Iraq barred UN inspectors from visiting three military sites. **20.** The Israeli government rejected the offer of a conditional cease-fire by the military wing of Hamas. **21.** UN inspectors in Iraq destroyed a biological weapons factory. **22.** Iraq agreed to allow UN weapons inspectors unconditional access to military sites. **25.** Nineteen people died in a bomb explosion at a US air force base near Dhahran, Saudi Arabia.

JULY 1996

1. The USA objected to Iraq's attempts to resume oil exports under an agreement with the UN, claiming that Iraq would use the revenue to import unauthorized equipment. **12.** President Saddam Hussein of Iraq was reported to have foiled a coup attempt by 50 military officers. **16.** Israel announced the easing of the 19-week blockade of the West Bank and Gaza Strip, imposed following a spate of terrorist attacks. **17.** Public sector workers in Israel went on strike in protest at the government's proposed cuts in government spending. **19.** UN inspectors abandoned an attempt to inspect an Iraqi military installation after being refused unconditional access. In a deal with Hezbollah, Israel exchanged 45 Lebanese prisoners and the corpses of 123 Hezbollah fighters for the remains of two Israeli soldiers. **25.** Israel offered to withdraw from southern Lebanon in exchange for peace along the northern border and the disarming of Hezbollah. **26.** Israel sealed off the West Bank and Gaza Strip following the shooting of two Israelis. **28–29.** Iranian troops launched an offensive against Kurdish guerrillas in northern Iraq.

AUGUST 1996

2. Palestinians rioted in the West Bank, broke into a prison and released ten political prisoners; Israel submitted a secret peace proposal to Syria via the USA. **4.** Hamas called for Palestinians to launch an uprising against the Palestinian National Authority and its leader Yasser Arafat, amid continuing unrest. **7.** Syria rejected the Israeli peace proposal and demanded the return of the Golan Heights. **8.** Israeli jets bombed Hezbollah targets in southern Lebanon in response to the killing of an Israeli soldier in a shelling attack. **16.** Demonstrators in the city of Karak in southern Jordan clashed with police in a protest at an increase in the price of bread; rioting spread to other cities. **17.** King Hussein of Jordan dissolved the House of Representatives. **27.** The Israeli government approved the construction of 1,800 homes in the West Bank. **28.** Yasser Arafat urged Palestinians to rebel against Israeli authority. **29.** Palestinians staged a four-hour strike in protest at renewed Israeli settlement on the West Bank. **31.** Iraqi troops seized the Kurdish city of Arbil in the UN-designated safe haven in northern Iraq.

INTERNATIONAL RELATIONS

SEPTEMBER 1995

4. The fourth UN world conference on women opened in Beijing, China, with speeches by President Finnbogadóttir of Iceland, Prime Minister Benazir Bhutto of Pakistan and Prime Minister Khaleda Zia of Bangladesh. The conference closed on 15 September with the adoption of a non-binding conference paper which advocated sexual freedom and denounced violence against women; parts of this were rejected by several delegations and governments. **27.** The Council of Europe's European Court of Human Rights overturned the verdict of the Commission of Human Rights and declared that the killing of three IRA terrorists by the SAS in Gibraltar in 1988 was a breach of international conventions.

OCTOBER 1995

13. The NATO Secretary-General Willy Claes was questioned by a Belgian parliamentary committee about corruption charges involving two defence contracts signed in 1988 when he was Belgium's economics minister; the committee voted to agree to his legal indictment. **19.** The Belgian parliament voted to revoke Claes's immunity and send him for trial on corruption charges; Claes resigned his NATO post the next day.

NOVEMBER 1995

1. Cameroon became a member of the Commonwealth. **9.** The Commonwealth heads of government meeting began in Auckland, New Zealand. **10.** The Commonwealth heads of government meeting issued a communiqué condemning France's nuclear tests, despite British objections; the British delegation issued a separate statement supporting nuclear deterrence and nuclear tests. **11.** Nigeria's membership of the Commonwealth was suspended follow-

BRITISH BEEF CRISIS
Fears about BSE in British beef caused beef consumption to plummet across Europe in 1996, damaging
farmers' livelihoods (*Associated Press*)

NORTHERN IRELAND
Huge crowds greeted President Clinton on his visit to Ireland in November 1995, when he encouraged hopes of progress in the peace process (*PA News*)

NORTHERN IRELAND
Sinn Fein representatives were barred from the Northern Ireland peace talks at Stormont in June 1996 (above; *Pacemaker Press*) after the IRA broke, and failed to reinstate, their cease-fire with bombings in London and Manchester (*Rex Features*)

NORTHERN IRELAND
Tension rose in Northern Ireland in July and August 1996 as the Orange Order lodges held their traditional marches, some in nationalist areas (*PA News*)

ROYAL DIVORCE
Princess Diana gave an unprecedentedly frank interview on the BBC's *Panorama* programme in November 1995. The Prince and Princess of Wales were divorced in August 1996 (*BBC TV*)

DUNBLANE SHOOTING TRAGEDY
Sixteen children and a teacher were shot dead at a primary school in Dunblane in March 1996 (above; *Rex Features*). The Queen and the Princess Royal visited the injured and bereaved on 17 March, when a minute's silence was held nation-wide (*PA News*)

MANDELA STATE VISIT
President Mandela of South Africa attracted huge crowds wherever he went during his state visit to Britain in July 1996 (*PA News*)

PRIME MINISTER ASSASSINATED
The Israeli Prime Minister Yitzhak Rabin was assassinated in November 1995, raising fears for the future of the Middle East peace process (*Rex Features*)

TWA FLIGHT 800
A Paris-bound jumbo jet exploded shortly after take-off from New York in July 1996, killing all on board (*PA News*)

RUSSIA
Fighting in the separatist republic of Chechenia ended with a cease-fire agreement in August 1996 and Russian forces began to withdraw (*Associated Press*)

Boris Yeltsin was re-elected President of Russia in July 1996 despite ill-health but subsequently was hardly seen in public. He announced in September that he needed heart surgery, creating a power vacuum in Russia (*Rex Features*)

VOLCANIC ACTIVITY IN NEW ZEALAND
Mount Ruapehu began erupting in autumn 1995 (*Rex Features*)

THE GLOBE THEATRE
A reconstruction, complete with thatched roof, of the theatre at which many of Shakespeare's plays were first performed, was opened on London's Bankside in August 1996 (*Rex Features*)

Deaths included (left to right): (top) François Mitterrand, Yitzhak Rabin, Ella Fitzgerald, Sir Kingsley Amis; (bottom) Dean Martin, Andreas Papandreou, George Burns, Lord Home (Sir Alec Douglas-Home) (*Rex Features*)

Gene Kelly, dancer, actor, choreographer and film director, died in February 1996 (*Kobal*)

THE OLYMPIC GAMES
Michael Johnson achieved a unique 200 metre and 400 metre double at the Games, as well as setting a new world record in the 200 metres (*Richard Pelham / The Sun*)

Matthew Pinsent and Steve Redgrave won Britain's only gold medal, Redgrave achieving the rare feat of winning the gold medal in his event at four consecutive Olympic Games (*Allsport*)

EURO '96
Germany's football team celebrate their winning goal in the European Championship final (*Allsport*)

BRITISH TENNIS HOPE
Tim Henman reached the quarter-finals at Wimbledon in 1996, the first British man to do so for 23 years, and won Olympic silver in the men's doubles in August (*Allsport*)

ing the execution of Ken Saro-Wiwa and eight other human rights activists. **12.** Mozambique, a former Portuguese colony, became a member of the Commonwealth as 'a unique and special case'. **17.** Russia failed to meet the deadline for completion of its agreed reductions in military equipment under the Conventional Forces in Europe (CFE) Treaty 1989, refusing to reduce the forces on its northern and southern borders. **28.** The Czech Republic became a member of the OECD. **30.** The Eurocorps, comprising troops from Germany, France, Spain, Belgium and Luxembourg, became fully operational.

DECEMBER 1995

1. The Spanish foreign minister Javier Solana Madariaga was appointed Secretary-General of NATO. **5.** France announced that it was upgrading its involvement in NATO by rejoining the Military Committee. **12.** The International Criminal Tribunal for Rwanda charged eight Hutu leaders with genocide and crimes against humanity. **20.** Ukraine agreed to close down the Chernobyl nuclear power station by 2000 in exchange for financial help from the G7 nations.

JANUARY 1996

5. The UN set a deadline of 31 January for member states to pay their outstanding debts of £1,600 million, of which £774 million was owed by the USA.

FEBRUARY 1996

28. Russia was admitted by the Council of Europe as a member on condition that it reform its legal and penal systems, protect its ethnic minorities and abolish the death penalty.

MARCH 1996

10. The former Prime Minister Baroness Thatcher gave a speech at Fulton, Missouri, in which she warned of the growing threat to the West's security from the development of weapons of mass destruction and ballistic missiles by rogue states. **29.** Hungary became a member of the OECD.

APRIL 1996

1. The UN announced an 8 per cent cut in staff and a £168 million cut in its budget in 1996–7. **23.** A Commonwealth task force agreed measures to tighten sanctions against Nigeria. **24.** The Council of Europe voted to admit Croatia. **25.** President Yeltsin of Russia and President Jiang of China signed a strategic partnership accord. **26.** China, Kazakhstan, Kyrgyzstan, Russia and Tajikistan signed a security pact affirming their common borders. **30.** Israel and the USA signed a counterterrorism accord.

MAY 1996

3. A UN conference in Geneva ended, having failed to conclude a total ban on land mines. **5.** Talks aimed at concluding a comprehensive nuclear test ban opened in Geneva. **14.** Russia threatened to form a military alliance with Belarus if NATO pursued plans to admit former Communist countries. **15.** NATO's North Atlantic Council approved the formation of combined joint task forces under European control. The USA announced tariffs on Chinese imports in retaliation for alleged copyright infringements; China imposed retaliatory sanctions on American goods. The USA agreed to ban certain land mines in line with the UN conference in Geneva. **17.** Russia expelled four British diplomats accused of spying; Britain expelled four Russian diplomats in retaliation. **31.** The Council of Europe refused Croatia accession until its human rights record improved.

JUNE 1996

3. Habitat II, a UN conference on human settlements opened in Istanbul, Turkey. NATO members agreed a new alliance arrangement with a greater role for the Western European Union. **4.** Russia said it was willing to compromise on the enlargement of NATO. **17.** China closed down 15 pirate compact disc factories, narrowly averting a trade war with the USA over copyright violations. **20.** The USA said that it would use its veto to prevent UN Secretary-General Boutros Boutros Ghali from standing for a second term in office. **23.** Arab leaders issued a final communiqué at the end of their summit warning Israel not to renege on its existing agreements and demanding withdrawal from all territory seized since 1967. **25.** Following two days of talks with a Nigerian delegation in London, a Commonwealth ministerial action group on human rights decided not to impose sanctions on Nigeria for its human rights abuses. **28.** The UN-sponsored conference on disarmament ended without the conclusion of a comprehensive test ban treaty for nuclear weapons.

JULY 1996

17. Angola, Brazil, Cape Verde, Guinea-Bissau, Mozambique, Portugal and São Tomé and Príncipe formed the Community of Portuguese-Speaking Countries to preserve cultural links and foster political co-operation. **19.** Myanmar was given observer status in ASEAN. **30.** The G7 nations agreed 25 measures to counter terrorism. Turkey agreed to renew the mandate for the international military operation to protect the Kurds in northern Iraq.

AUGUST 1996

5. President Clinton signed legislation imposing sanctions on foreign companies that invest more than £25 million annually in the energy sectors in Libya and Iran. **7.** The USA approved the sale of £1.3 billion of Iraqi oil over six months, the revenue to be used to purchase food and humanitarian aid. China agreed to sign a comprehensive test ban treaty for nuclear weapons.

Obituaries

Adams, Charles, CMG, British ambassador to Thailand since 1992, aged 57 – 10 July 1996

Adams, Donald, opera and operetta singer, aged 67 – 8 April 1996

Aidid, Gen. Muhammad, leader of the Somali National Alliance, aged 59 – 1 August 1996

Airedale, 4th Baron, a Deputy Speaker of the House of Lords since 1962, aged 80 – 19 March 1996

Amis, Sir Kingsley, CBE, novelist and poet, aged 73 – 22 October 1995

Appleby, Barry, cartoonist, creator of the Gambols, aged 86 – 11 March 1996

Armstrong, Rt. Hon. Ernest, Labour MP for Durham North West 1964–87 and junior government minister 1974–9, aged 81 – 8 July 1996

Ashbrook, 10th Viscount, KCVO, MBE, aged 90 – 5 December 1995

Atholl, 10th Duke, aged 64 – 27 February 1996

Avonside, Lord (Ian Shearer), PC, QC, Senator of the College of Justice of Scotland 1964–84, aged 81 – 22 February 1996

Barrow, Dame Nita, GCMG, Governor-General of Barbados since 1990, aged 79 – 19 December 1995

Bearsted, 4th Viscount, MC, TD, merchant banker, aged 84 – 9 June 1996

Bebb, Dewi, Welsh rugby player and sports commentator, aged 57 – 14 March 1996

Berghaus, Ruth, German stage director and choreographer, aged 68 – 25 January 1996

Blackwood, Caroline, novelist, aged 64 – 14 February 1996

Bottomley, Lord (Arthur), OBE, PC, Labour MP for Chatham 1945–50, Rochester and Chatham 1950–9, and Middlesbrough East 1962, Secretary of State for Commonwealth Relations 1964–6, Minister of Overseas Development 1966–7, aged 88 – 3 November 1995

Boyne, 10th Viscount, KCVO, Lord Lieutenant of Shropshire since 1994 and a Lord-in-Waiting to The Queen since 1981, aged 64 – 14 December 1995

Brand, Lord, Solicitor-General for Scotland 1970–2, Senator of the College of Justice 1972–89, aged 72 – 14 April 1996

Brett, Jeremy, actor, aged 59 – 12 September 1995

Broccoli, Cubby, film producer, aged 87 – 27 June 1996

Brodkey, Harold, American author, aged 65 – 26 January 1996

Brodsky, Joseph, Russian Jewish poet, winner of the Nobel prize for literature in 1987, aged 55 – 28 January 1996

Broughshane, 2nd Baron, aged 92 – 22 September 1995

Brown, Ronald, US Secretary for Commerce, aged 54, in an air crash – 3 April 1996

Bruce, Brenda, OBE, actress, aged 76 – 19 February 1996

Burke, Admiral Arleigh, American naval commander in Second World War, aged 94 – 1 January 1996

Burns, George, American comedian, aged 100 – 9 March 1996

Burton, Beryl, OBE, British and international cycling champion, aged 58 – 5 May 1996

Cadell, Simon, actor, aged 45 – 6 March 1996

Caine, Marti, comedienne, aged 50 – 4 November 1995

Cairncross, John, Foreign Office and Treasury official dismissed in 1952 for passing information to Soviet spy Guy Burgess, aged 82 – 8 October 1995

Cameron, Sir John (Hon. Lord Cameron), KT, DSC, Senator of the College of Justice and Lord of Session 1955–85, aged 96 – 30 May 1996

Cargill, Patrick, actor and dramatist, aged 77 – 23 March 1996

Carlill, Vice-Adm. Sir Stephen, KBE, CB, DSO, last British commander of the Indian Navy, aged 93 – 9 February 1996

Cherkassky, Shura, Russian concert pianist, aged 84 – 27 December 1995

Chermayeff, Serge, architect, aged 95 – 8 May 1996

Chukovskaya, Lydia, Russian writer, aged 88 – 7 February 1996

Clark, Prof. Sir Grahame, CBE, FBA, archaeologist, aged 88 – 12 September 1995

Clark, Ossie, fashion designer, aged 54 – 7 August 1996

Clay-Jones, 'Clay', OBE, chairman of *Gardeners' Question Time* 1985–93, aged 71 – 3 July 1996

Clough, Gordon, radio journalist, aged 61 – 6 April 1996

Colbert, Claudette, American actress, aged 92 – 30 July 1996

Collison, Lord (Harold), CBE, trade unionist, and chairman of the Supplementary Benefits Commission 1969–75, aged 86 – 29 December 1995

Colyton, 1st Baron (Henry Hopkinson), CMG, PC, Conservative MP for Taunton 1950–6 and Minister of State for Colonial Affairs 1952–5, aged 94 – 6 January 1995

Condon, Richard, American thriller-writer, aged 81 – 9 April 1996

Courtenay, Margaret, actress, aged 72 – 15 February 1996

Davie, Prof. Donald, poet and critic, aged 73 – 18 September 1995

Davies, Robertson, Canadian author, aged 82 – 4 December 1995

Diamond, Harry, Republican Labour MP for Lower Falls, Belfast 1945–69 in the Parliament of Northern Ireland, aged 87 – May 1996

Dickson, Dorothy, actress and musical comedy star, aged 102 – 25 September 1995

Dormer, 16th Baron, aged 81 – 21 December 1995

Drew, Dame Jane, DBE, architect, aged 85 – 27 July 1996

Dudayev, Gen. Dzhokhar, president of Chechenia since 1991, aged 52 – 21 April 1996

Dunmore, 11th Earl, aged 82 – 28 September 1995

Duras, Marguerite, French novelist, aged 81 – 3 March 1996

Eddington, Paul, CBE, actor, aged 68 – 4 November 1995

Edwards, Percy, MBE, bird and animal impersonator, aged 88 – 7 June 1996

Effingham, 6th Earl, aged 90 – 22 February 1996

Ellis, Vivian, CBE, songwriter and composer, aged 91 – 19 June 1996

Enright, Derek, MP, Labour MP for Hemsworth since 1991 and MEP for Leeds 1979–84, aged 60 – 31 October 1995

Evans, Very Revd Eric, KCVO, Dean of St Paul's Cathedral since 1988, aged 68 – 17 August 1996

Ewart, Gavin, poet, aged 79 – 23 October 1995

Factor, Max, jun., make-up artist and cosmetics company executive, aged 91 – 7 June 1996

Faithfull, Baroness, OBE, organizer of childcare in local and central government from 1930s to 1974, President of the

National Children's Bureau since 1984, aged 85 –
13 March 1996

Fitzgerald, Ella, American jazz singer, aged 78 – 15 June
1996

Fleetwood, Susan, actress, aged 51 – 29 September 1995

Fraser of Kilmorack, Lord, CBE, director of the Conservative Research Department 1951–64, deputy chairman of
the Conservative Party Organization 1964–75, aged 80 –
1 July 1996

Garfield, Leon, writer, aged 74 – 2 June 1996

Garson, Greer, actress, aged 92 – 6 April 1996

Glendevon, 1st Baron (Lord John Hope), ERD, PC, Conservative MP for Northern Midlothian and Peebles
1945–64 and Minister for Works 1959–62, aged 83 –
18 January 1996

Goetz, Walter, cartoonist, aged 83 – 13 September 1995

Gould, Morton, American composer, conductor and
pianist, aged 82 – 21 February 1996

Gridley, 2nd Baron, colonial administrator, businessman,
conservationist, aged 90 – August 1996

Griffiths, Edward, Labour MP for Sheffield Brightside
1968–74, aged 66 – 18 October 1995

Grinkov, Sergei, Russian Olympic pairs figure skating
champion, aged 28 – 20 November 1995

Gryn, Hugo, CBE, rabbi and broadcaster, aged 66 –
18 August 1996

Guerin, Veronica, Irish journalist, aged 33 – assassinated
26 June 1996

Haden-Guest, 4th Baron, ballet dancer 1935–9, UN
administrator 1946–72, aged 82 – 8 April 1996

Haldane, Brodrick, society photographer, aged 83 –
3 February 1996

Hamilton, Geoff, gardening broadcaster and journalist,
aged 59 – 4 August 1996

Harris, 6th Baron, aged 75 – 17 September 1995

Harris, 7th Baron, aged 79 – 30 June 1996

Harrison, Kathleen, actress, aged 103 – 7 December 1995

Hawkes, Jacquetta, OBE, archaeologist and author, aged 85
– 18 March 1996

Hayward, Ron, CBE, general secretary of the Labour Party
1972–82, aged 78 – 22 March 1996

Hemingway, Margot, American actress and model, aged 41
– 1 July 1996

Heward, Air Chief Marshal Sir Anthony, KCB, OBE, DFC and
bar, AFC, aged 77 – 27 October 1995

Hills, Dick, comedy writer, aged 70 – 6 June 1996

Home of the Hirsel, Lord (former 14th Earl of Home), KT,
PC, Prime Minister (as Sir Alec Douglas-Home) 1963–4,
Foreign Secretary 1960–3 and 1970–4, a Conservative
MP 1931–51 and a Minister of State in the Lords
1951–60, aged 92 – 9 October 1995

Houghton of Sowerby, Lord (Douglas), CH, PC, Labour MP
for Sowerby 1949–74, Cabinet minister 1964–8, chairman of the Parliamentary Labour Party 1968–74, aged
97 – 2 May 1996

Hulme, Maj.-Gen. Jerrie, CB, Director-General of Ordnance Services 1988–90, senior logistics officer to UN
High Commissioner for Refugees in the former Yugoslavia since 1992, aged 60 – 20 September 1995

Hyson, Dorothy, film and stage actress, aged 81 – 23 May
1996

Iliffe, 2nd Baron, newspaper proprietor, aged 88 –
15 February 1996

Jacques, Lord, chairman of the Co-operative Union
1964–70, aged 90 – 20 December 1995

Jay, Lord (Douglas), PC, Labour MP for Battersea 1946–83,
President of the Board of Trade 1964–7, aged 88 –
6 March 1996

Jellicoe, Sir Geoffrey, CBE, RA, landscape architect, aged 95
– 17 July 1996

Jenco, Revd Lawrence, American hostage in Beirut
1985–6, aged 61 – 19 July 1996

Jewel, Jimmy, comedian and actor, aged 82 – 3 December
1995

Jones, Air Marshal Sir Laurence, KCB, AFC, Lieutenant
Governor of the Isle of Man since 1990, aged 62 –
23 September 1995

Kanyon, Prof. John, FBA, historian, aged 68 – 6 January
1996

Keane, Molly (M. J. Farrell), author, aged 91 – 22 April
1996

Kelly, Gene, American dancer, actor, choreographer and
film director, aged 83 – 2 February 1996

Kieslowski, Krzysztof, Polish film-maker, aged 54 –
12 March 1996

Killearn, 2nd Baron, businessman, aged 76 – 27 July 1996

Kirstein, Lincoln, founder and general director of New
York City Ballet, aged 88 – 5 January 1995

Lanigan, John, Australian-born opera singer, aged 75 –
1 August 1996

Lawrence, William, chief constable of South Wales
Constabulary since 1989, aged 53 – 21 May 1996

Laye, Evelyn, CBE, actress and singer, aged 95 – 17 February 1996

Learoyd, Wing Cdr Roderick, VC, aged 82 – 24 January
1996

Leary, Timothy, clinical psychologist and writer, 1960s
drugs proselytizer, aged 75 – 31 May 1996

Leathers, 2nd Viscount, shipping executive, aged 87 –
21 January 1996

Lenihan, Brian, Irish politician and Deputy Prime Minister
1987–90, aged 64 – 1 November 1995

Lightbown, Sir David, MP, Conservative MP for Staffordshire South East since 1983, aged 63 – 12 December 1995

Lindwall, Ray, MBE, Australian fast bowler, aged 74 –
23 June 1996

Luke, 2nd Baron, KCVO, businessman, aged 90 – 25 May
1996

MacCaig, Norman, OBE, poet, aged 85 – 23 January 1996

McCluskie, Sam, general secretary of the National Union
of Seamen 1986–90, aged 63 – 15 September 1995

McClymont, J. M., GC – 10 June 1996

MacDermot, Niall, CBE, QC, Labour MP for Lewisham
North 1957–9 and Derby North 1962–70, Financial
Secretary to the Treasury 1964–7, and secretary-
general, International Commission of Jurists 1970–90,
aged 79 – 22 February 1996

McFadzean, Lord, KT, chairman of BICC 1954–73 and
deputy chairman of Midland Bank 1968–77, aged 92 –
14 January 1996

McKaig, Adm. Sir John, KCB, CBE, UK Military Representative to NATO 1973–5, aged 73 – 7 January 1996

McKay, Margaret, Labour MP for Clapham 1964–70, aged
85 – 1 March 1996

Mackay Brown, George, OBE, poet and story-writer, aged
74 – 13 April 1996

Maclean of Duncconell, Sir Fitzroy, Bt., KT, CBE, diplomat,
soldier, traveller, author and historian, Conservative MP
for Lancaster 1941–59 and Argyll and North Bute
1959–74, aged 85 – 15 June 1996

Madge, Charles, poet, sociologist and co-founder of Mass
Observation, aged 83 – 17 January 1996

Malle, Louis, French film director, aged 63 – 23 November
1995

Mann, Jackie, CBE, DFM, Battle of Britain fighter pilot and
from 1989–91 a hostage in Beirut, aged 81 – 12 November 1995

Margadale, 1st Baron, TD, Conservative MP for Salisbury
1942–64, chairman of the 1922 committee 1955–64,
aged 89 – 25 May 1996

Marks, Alfred, OBE, comedian, actor and singer, aged 75 – 1 July 1996

Marshall of Goring, Lord, CBE, FRS, chairman of the Atomic Energy Authority 1981–2 and of the Central Electricity Generating Board 1982–9, aged 63 – 20 February 1996

Martin, Dean, American singer, comedian and actor, aged 78 – 25 December 1995

Matthews, Lord, former deputy chairman and group chief executive of Trafalgar House, aged 76 – 5 December 1995

Maxwell, James, actor, and an artistic director of the Royal Exchange Theatre, Manchester, aged 66 – 18 August 1995

Mazar, Prof. Benjamin, Israeli archaeologist, excavator of the Temple Mount in Jerusalem, aged 89 – 9 September 1995

Meade, Prof. James, CB, FBA, economist and Nobel laureate 1977, aged 88 – 22 December 1995

Mersey, Katherine, Dowager Viscountess, and Lady Nairne (12th in line), aged 83 – 20 October 1995

Milne, Christopher, the Christopher Robin of the Winnie the Pooh books, aged 75 – 20 April 1996

Mitchell, Colin ('Mad Mitch'), soldier and Conservative MP for West Aberdeenshire 1970–4, aged 70 – 20 July 1996

Mitford, Jessica, writer, aged 78 – 23 July 1996

Mitterrand, François, President of France 1981–95, aged 79 – 8 January 1996

Moshoeshoe II, King of Lesotho 1966–90 and since 1995, aged 57 – 15 January 1996

Mott, Prof. Sir Nevill, CH, FRS, physicist and Nobel laureate 1977, aged 90 – 8 August 1996

Mullard, Arthur, comic actor, aged 83 – 11 December 1995

Muskie, Edmund, US Senator 1959–80 and Secretary of State 1980–1, aged 81 – 26 March 1996

Niarchos, Stavros, Greek shipowner and financier, aged 86 – 15 April 1996

Nix, Frank, GC, aged 82 – 8 August 1996

Norfolk, Lavinia, Duchess of, LG, CBE, Lord Lieutenant of West Sussex 1975–90, aged 79 – 10 October 1995

Northumberland, 11th Duke, aged 42 – 31 October 1995

O'Brien of Lothbury, Lord, GBE, PC, Governor of the Bank of England 1966–73, aged 87 – 24 November 1995

Packard, David, co-founder of Hewlitt Packard in 1939, aged 83 – March 1996

Paisley, Bob, footballer, manager of Liverpool Football Club 1974–83, aged 77 – 14 February 1996

Papandreou, Andreas, prime minister of Greece 1981–9 and 1993–6, aged 77 – 23 June 1996

Pargeter, Edith (Ellis Peters), OBE, BEM, novelist, aged 82 – 14 October 1995

Parsons, Sir Anthony, GCMG, MVO, MC, diplomat, aged 73 – 12 August 1996

Patton, John, GC, OBE, aged 80 – 13 May 1996

Pearsall, Phyllis, MBE, founder of Geographer's A–Z Map Company, aged 89 – 28 August 1996

Peierls, Sir Rudolf, CBE, FRS, physicist, aged 88 – 19 September 1995

Pertwee, Jon, actor, aged 76 – 20 May 1996

Piratin, Philip, Communist MP for Stepney, Mile End 1945–50, aged 88 – 10 December 1995

Pritchard, Lord, businessman, aged 85 – 16 October 1995

Rabin, Yitzhak, Prime Minister of Israel 1974–7 and since 1992, Defence Minister 1984–90, Army Chief of Staff 1964–7, aged 73 – assassinated 4 November 1995

Rahi, Sultan, Pakistani film actor, aged 57 – 9 January 1996

Red Rum, winner of the Grand National 1973, 1974 and 1977, aged 30 – 18 October 1995

Rimmer, Reginald, GC, aged 93 – 21 February 1996

Robinson, Rt. Hon. Sir Kenneth, Labour MP for St Pancras North 1949–70, Minister of Health 1964–8, chairman of the Arts Council 1977–82 and of London Transport Executive 1975–8, aged 84 – 16 February 1996

Rotherwick, 2nd Baron, shipping magnate, aged 83 – 11 June 1996

Rudolph, Arthur, German rocket scientist, aged 89 – 1 January 1996

Saro-Wiwa, Ken, Nigerian novelist and playwright, aged 54 – executed 10 September 1995

Scott, Annie, Britain's oldest person, aged 113 – 21 April 1996

Shawe-Taylor, Desmond, CBE, chief music critic of the *Sunday Times* 1959–83, aged 88 – 1 November 1995

Shotter, Winifred, actress, aged 91 – 4 April 1996

Siegel, Jery, creator of Superman, aged 81 – 28 January 1996

Sinclair, Jean, founder of the Black Sash anti-apartheid movement in South Africa, aged 87 – 6 June 1996

Sinden, Jeremy, actor, aged 45 – 29 May 1996

Skelton, Barbara, writer, aged 79 – 27 January 1996

Smythe, Pat, OBE, international showjumper, aged 67 – 27 February 1996

Snagge, John, OBE, broadcaster, aged 91 – 25 March 1996

Stair, 13th Earl, KCVO, MBE, aged 89 – 26 February 1996

Stedman, Baroness, OBE, Labour councillor and a junior minister, leader of the SDP in the House of Lords 1988–91, aged 79 – 8 June 1996

Stephens, Sir Robert, actor, aged 64 – 12 November 1995

Sylvester, W. G., GC – 23 February 1996

Thirkettle, Joan, ITN news reporter, aged 48 – 11 May 1996

Tran Van Tra, Gen., Vietnamese army general in Vietnam War, aged 77 – 20 April 1996

Travers, P. L., OBE, author, creator of Mary Poppins, aged 96 – 23 April 1996

Tweedsmuir, 2nd Baron, CBE, CD, FRSE, soldier, explorer, writer and businessman, aged 84 – 20 June 1996

Walker, Patric, astrologer, aged 64 – 8 October 1995

Warner, Sir Frederick, GCVO, KCMG, former ambassador and Conservative MEP 1979–84, aged 77 – 30 September 1995

Warnock, Sir Geoffrey, philosopher, Principal of Hertford College, Oxford 1971–88 and Vice-Chancellor of the University of Oxford 1981–5, aged 72 – 8 October 1995

Warrell, Charles, creator of the I–Spy books, aged 106 – 26 November 1995

Warwick, 8th Earl, aged 61 – 20 January 1996

Watkinson, 1st Viscount, CH, PC, Conservative MP for Woking 1950–64, Minister of Transport 1955–9 and Minister of Defence 1959–62, aged 85 – 19 December 1995

Webb, Kaye, MBE, children's book publisher and founder of the Puffin Club, aged 81 – 16 January 1996

Weeks, Alan, sports commentator, aged 72 – 11 June 1996

White, Wilfred, OBE, show jumper, aged 91 – 21 November 1995

Whittle, Air Cdre Sir Frank, OM, KBE, CB, FRS, FEng., inventor of the jet engine, aged 89 – 8 August 1996

Wingate Gray, Brig. Michael, OBE, MC and bar, a former director of the SAS, aged 74 – 3 November 1995

Worlock, Most Revd Archbishop Derek, CH, Roman Catholic Archbishop of Liverpool since 1976, aged 76 – 8 February 1996

Worsnip, Glyn, television presenter and actor, aged 57 – 6 June 1996

The Queen's Awards

The Queen's Award for Export Achievement and The Queen's Award for Technological Achievement were instituted by royal warrant in 1976. The two separate awards took the place of The Queen's Award to Industry, which had been instituted in 1965. In 1992 the scheme was extended with the launch of a third award, The Queen's Award for Environmental Achievement.

The export and technological awards are designed to recognize and encourage outstanding achievements in exporting goods or services from the United Kingdom and in advancing process or product technology. The purpose of the environmental award is to recognize and encourage product and process development which has major benefits for the environment and which is commercially successful.

The awards differ from a personal royal honour in that they are given to a unit as a whole, management and employees working as a team. They may be applied for by any organization within the United Kingdom, the Channel Islands or the Isle of Man producing goods or services which meet the criteria for the awards. Eligibility is not influenced in any way by the particular activities of the unit applying, its location, or size. Units or agencies of central and local government with industrial functions, as well as research associations, educational institutions and bodies of a similar character, are also eligible, provided that they can show they have contributed to industrial efficiency.

Each award is formally conferred by a grant of appointment and is symbolized by a representation of its emblem cast in stainless steel and encapsulated in a transparent acrylic block.

Awards are held for five years and holders are entitled to fly the appropriate award flag and to display the emblem on the packaging of goods produced in this country, on the goods themselves, on the unit's stationery, in advertising and on certain articles used by employees. Units may also display the emblem of any previous current awards during the five years.

Awards are announced on 21 April (the birthday of The Queen) and published formally in a special supplement to the London Gazette.

Awards Office

All enquiries about the scheme and requests for application forms (completed forms must be returned by 31 October) should be made to: The Secretary, The Queen's Awards Office, Bridge Place, 88–89 Eccleston Square, London SW1V 1PT. Tel: 0171–222 2277.

EXPORT ACHIEVEMENT

The criterion upon which recommendations for an award for export achievement are based is a substantial and sustained increase in export earnings to a level which is outstanding for the products or services concerned and for the size of the applicant unit's operations. Account will be taken of any special market factors described in the application. Applicants for the award will be expected to explain the basis of the achievement (e.g. improved marketing organization or new initiative to cater for export markets) and this will be taken into consideration. Export earnings considered will include receipts by the applicant unit in this country from the export of goods produced in this country, and the provision of services to non-residents. Account will be taken of the overseas expenses incurred other than marketing expenses. Income from profits (after overseas tax) remitted to this country from the applicant unit's direct investments in its overseas branches, subsidiaries or associates in the same general line of business will be taken into account, but not receipts from profits on other overseas investments or by interest on overseas loans or credits.

In 1996, The Queen's Award for Export Achievement was conferred on the following concerns:

Anglo Beef Processors Ltd, Blisworth, Northants
Audience Systems Ltd, Westbury, Wilts
Autoflame Engineering Ltd, London SE6
Avesta Sheffield Ltd, Sheffield
Bartle Bogle Hegarty Ltd, London W1
Bass Beers Worldwide Ltd, Birmingham
Beamech Group Ltd, Manchester
Beck & Pollitzer Engineering Ltd, Dartford, Kent
Biotrace Ltd, Bridgend, Mid Glam
J. Blackledge & Son Ltd, Chorley, Lancs
Brett Martin Ltd, Newtownabbey, Co. Antrim
Bridge of Weir Leather Company Ltd, Bridge of Weir, Renfrewshire
British Chrome & Chemicals, Stockton-on-Tees, Cleveland
British Steel Special Sections (Skinningrove), Carlin How, Saltburn-by-the-Sea, Cleveland
Burberrys Ltd, Manufacturing and Export Division, London E9
Camlaw Ltd, Tamworth, Staffs
Chadwyck-Healey Ltd, Cambridge
The Chartered Association of Certified Accountants (ACCA), London WC2
Toby Churchill Ltd, Cambridge
Cincinnati Milacron (UK) Ltd, Machine Tool Division, Birmingham
Corsair Toiletries Ltd, St Albans, Herts
Dairy Produce Packers Ltd, Coleraine, Co. Londonderry
Designers Guild Ltd, London W11
Digi-Media Vision Ltd (trading as DMV), Eastleigh, Hants
Dunlop Hydraulic Hose Ltd, Gateshead
EBI Foods Ltd, Abingdon, Oxon
Edwards High Vacuum International, Crawley, W. Sussex
English Hop Products Ltd, Tonbridge, Kent
Epichem Ltd, Wirral, Merseyside
Eurostock Meat Marketing Ltd, Newry, Co. Down

Evans Medical Ltd, Leatherhead, Surrey
Fermec Holdings Ltd, Manchester
J. & S. Franklin Ltd, London WC2
GPT Public Networks Group, Coventry
Garigue, London SW5
Gates Power Transmission Ltd, Dumfries
Genesis Tilemates Ltd, Stokesley, N. Yorks
Glass Eels Ltd, Gloucester
Gossard, Leighton Buzzard, Beds
William Grant & Sons Ltd, Motherwell, Lanarkshire
Guinness Brewing Worldwide Ltd, London NW10
HSB Engineering Insurance Ltd, London EC3
Halcrow Holdings Ltd, London W6
Healey & Baker, London W1
International Diamalt Co Ltd, Newark, Notts
International Labmate Ltd, St Albans, Herts
IPTest Ltd, Guildford, Surrey
JCB Materials Handling Ltd, Rocester, Staffs
JCB Special Products Ltd, Stoke-on-Trent, Staffs
Laminar Medica Ltd, Tring, Herts
Lilly Industries Ltd, Basingstoke, Hants
Lombard Risk Systems Ltd, London EC4
Magneco Metrel (UK) Ltd, Shildon, Co. Durham
Maybridge Chemical Company Ltd, Tintagel, Cornwall
McCalls Special Products, Sheffield
McKechnie Vehicle Components, Extrusion Operation,
    Milton Keynes
Mechatherm International Ltd, Kingswinford,
    W. Midlands
Mivan Ltd, Antrim, Co. Antrim
Mobile Systems International PLC, London E14
Molypress Ltd, Calne, Wilts
Abraham Moon & Sons Ltd, Leeds
Morrisflex Ltd, Consumable Tools Division, Daventry,
    Northants
Morrison Bowmore Distillers Ltd, Glasgow
Motorola Ltd, European Cellular Infrastructure Division,
    Swindon
Motorola Ltd, Europe, Middle East and Africa Cellular
    Subscriber Division, Bathgate, West Lothian
Mott MacDonald Group Ltd, Croydon, Surrey
Mulberry Company (Design) Ltd, Home Division,
    Shepton Mallet, Somerset
New Holland (UK) Ltd, Basildon, Essex
Newbridge Networks Ltd, Newport, Gwent
Nikwax Ltd, Wadhurst, E. Sussex
Nortel Radio Infrastructure, GPS Unit, Paignton, Devon
Ocular Sciences Ltd, Southampton
Orb Electrical Steels Ltd, Newport, Gwent
Oxford Metrics Ltd, Oxford
Oxford University Press, Oxford
Pamarco Europe Ltd, Warrington, Cheshire
Paper Makers Export Ltd, Wellingborough, Northants
Paradise Datacom Ltd, Tiptree, Essex
Parkman Consultants Ltd, Sutton, Surrey
Percell Group Ltd, Newport, Gwent
Puretone Ltd, Rochester, Kent
Queensgate Instruments Ltd, Bracknell, Berks
Quick Controls Ltd, Manchester
RBR Armour Ltd, London SE1
Reilor Ltd, Preston, Lancs
Reynard Racing Cars Ltd, Bicester, Oxon
Robinson Special Packaging, Chesterfield, Derbys
Robobond Ltd (trading as Emafyl), London SE18
Segal Quince Wicksteed Ltd, Swavesey, Cambs
Sinclair International Ltd, Norwich
Smith's Environmental Products Ltd, Chelmsford, Essex
Speedibake Ltd, Northampton
Statestrong Ltd, Lytham, Lancs
Steel Wheels Ltd, Kidderminster, Worcs

Storehouse PLC, London NW1
Swiftpack Automation Ltd, Alcester, Warks
Syfer Technology Ltd, Norwich
Terex Equipment Ltd, Motherwell, Lanarkshire
Thermopol Ltd, Crawley, W. Sussex
TRAK Microwave Ltd, Dundee
Unipath Ltd, Consumer and Clinical Diagnostics, Bedford
Universal Bulk Handling Ltd, Burscough, Lancs
Van Leer Metallized Products Ltd, Caerphilly, Mid Glam
Visual Communications Group Ltd, London E14
Weetabix Ltd, Kettering, Northants
Willis Corroon Group PLC, Financial Risks and Specie
    Division, London EC3
Windsong International Ltd, Orpington, Kent

TECHNOLOGICAL ACHIEVEMENT

The criterion upon which recommendations for an award
for technological achievement are based is a significant
advance, leading to increased efficiency, in the application
of technology to a production or development process in
British industry or the production for sale of goods which
incorporate new and advanced technological qualities. An
award is only granted for production or development
processes which have achieved commercial success.

In 1996 The Queen's Award for Technological
Achievement was conferred on the following concerns:

Affinity Chromatography Ltd, Ballasalla, IOM –
    innovating means of separating protein pharmaceuticals
Amersham Healthcare, Little Chalfont, Bucks – *Metastron:
    a therapeutic option for treating metastatic bone pain*
Bede Scientific Instruments Ltd, Bowburn, Co.
    Durham – *direct drive x-ray diffractometer*
Chas A. Blatchford & Sons Ltd, Products Division,
    Basingstoke, Hants – *electro-mechanical computer controlled
    lower limb prostheses*
Digi-Media Vision Ltd (trading as DMV), Eastleigh,
    Hants – *professional digital video compression technology*
Glaxo Research and Development Ltd, Greenford,
    Middx – *Sumatriptan-Imigran: medicine for migraine and
    cluster headache*
Marks & Spencer PLC, London W1 – *'dry' discharge method for
    garment panel printing*
Oxford Magnet Technology Ltd, Witney, Oxon – *open C
    magnet system for magnetic resonance imaging scanner*
Philips Medical Systems (Radiotherapy), Crawley,
    W. Sussex – *multileaf collimator for radiotherapy treatment
    machine*
Rover Group Ltd, Electronics and Control Systems,
    Coventry – *microprocessor controlled engine management
    system*
Scimat Ltd, Swindon, Wilts – *membranes for the rechargeable
    battery industry*
Smith & Nephew PLC, Group Research Centre,
    York – *IV3000: materials innovation in infection control*
Ultra Electronics Ltd, Noise and Vibration Systems
    Division, Greenford, Middx – *system for reducing cabin
    noise in turboprop aircraft*
Institute of Biotechnology, University of Cambridge,
    Cambridge – *innovating means of separating protein
    pharmaceuticals*
Wace Screen, Wakefield, W. Yorks – *'dry' discharge method
    for garment panel printing*
Westwind Air Bearings Ltd, Poole, Dorset – *aerodynamic
    spindle for optical scanning*

ENVIRONMENTAL ACHIEVEMENT

The criterion upon which recommendations for an award for environmental achievement are based is a significant advance in the application by British industry of the development of products, technology or processes which offer major benefits in environmental terms compared to existing products, technology or processes. An award is only granted for products, technology or processes which have achieved commercial success.

In 1996 The Queen's Award for Environmental Achievement was conferred on the following concerns:

Brook Hansen, Huddersfield, W. Yorks – *energy efficient electric motors*

Hoover Ltd, Merthyr Tydfil, Mid Glam – *environmentally advanced washing machine range*

Hydro Chemicals Ltd (Hydrocare), Immingham, Lincs – *Nutriox process for elimination of odour and septicity in municipal sewer networks*

International Combustion Ltd, Derby – *EnviroNOx: low NOx burners for power stations*

Lucas Diesel Systems, Stonehouse, Glos – *electronic unit injector systems for diesel engines*

Ultra Hydraulics Ltd, Mobile Products Division, Cheltenham, Glos – *'Stealth' ultra quiet, high performance external gear pumps for off highway and mechanical handling vehicles*

Chemical Elements

Element	Symbol	Atomic Number	Element	Symbol	Atomic Number	Element	Symbol	Atomic Number
Actinium	Ac	89	Hafnium	Hf	72	Promethium	Pm	61
Aluminium	Al	13	Helium	He	2	Protactinium	Pa	91
Americium	Am	95	Holmium	Ho	67	Radium	Ra	88
Antimony	Sb	51	Hydrogen	H	1	Radon	Rn	86
Argon	Ar	18	Indium	In	49	Rhenium	Re	75
Arsenic	As	33	Iodine	I	53	Rhodium	Rh	45
Astatine	At	85	Iridium	Ir	77	Rubidium	Rb	37
Barium	Ba	56	Iron	Fe	26	Ruthenium	Ru	44
Berkelium	Bk	97	Krypton	Kr	36	Samarium	Sm	62
Beryllium	Be	4	Lanthanum	La	57	Scandium	Sc	21
Bismuth	Bi	83	Lawrencium	Lr	103	Selenium	Se	34
Boron	B	5	Lead	Pb	82	Silicon	Si	14
Bromine	Br	35	Lithium	Li	3	Silver	Ag	47
Cadmium	Cd	48	Lutetium	Lu	71	Sodium	Na	11
Caesium	Cs	55	Magnesium	Mg	12	Strontium	Sr	38
Calcium	Ca	20	Manganese	Mn	25	Sulphur	S	16
Californium	Cf	98	Mendelevium	Md	101	Tantalum	Ta	73
Carbon	C	6	Mercury	Hg	80	Technetium	Tc	43
Cerium	Ce	58	Molybdenum	Mo	42	Tellurium	Te	52
Chlorine	Cl	17	Neodymium	Nd	60	Terbium	Tb	65
Chromium	Cr	24	Neon	Ne	10	Thallium	Tl	81
Cobalt	Co	27	Neptunium	Np	93	Thorium	Th	90
Copper	Cu	29	Nickel	Ni	28	Thulium	Tm	69
Curium	Cm	96	Niobium	Nb	41	Tin	Sn	50
Dysprosium	Dy	66	Nitrogen	N	7	Titanium	Ti	22
Einsteinium	Es	99	Nobelium	No	102	Tungsten (Wolfram)	W	74
Erbium	Er	68	Osmium	Os	76	Uranium	U	92
Europium	Eu	63	Oxygen	O	8	Vanadium	V	23
Fermium	Fm	100	Palladium	Pd	46	Xenon	Xe	54
Fluorine	F	9	Phosphorus	P	15	Ytterbium	Yb	70
Francium	Fr	87	Platinum	Pt	78	Yttrium	Y	39
Gadolinium	Gd	64	Plutonium	Pu	94	Zinc	Zn	30
Gallium	Ga	31	Polonium	Po	84	Zirconium	Zr	40
Germanium	Ge	32	Potassium	K	19			
Gold	Au	79	Praseodymium	Pr	59			

Index

Stop-press

CHANGES SINCE PAGES WENT TO PRESS

ROYAL HOUSEHOLDS
Aide-de-Camp General – Gen. Sir John Wilsey relinquishes appointment

PEERAGE
2nd Viscount Hanworth died
3rd Baron Daresbury died
Lord Amery of Lustleigh, PC, died
Marmaduke Hussey gazetted Baron Hussey of North Bradley
Field Marshal Sir Richard Vincent gazetted Baron Vincent of Coleshill

BARONETAGE AND KNIGHTAGE
Daniel Charles Williams, Governor-General of Grenada, appointed GCMG
Died: Sir Dennis Titchener-Barrett; Sir Charles Dorman; Sir Anthony Harris; Air Marshal Sir Rochford Hughes; Sir Peter Lloyd; Sir Reginald Pullen; Sir Jeremy Rowe

EUROPEAN PARLIAMENT
Kenneth Stewart, Labour MEP for Merseyside, died

GOVERNMENT DEPARTMENTS AND PUBLIC OFFICES
Home Office – 1,500 staff in the Prison Service made redundant in September 1996, including over 100 governors
British Library – major restructuring announced in September 1996
British Museum – Sir Martin Rees appointed a trustee
Department of National Heritage – A. Honnor appointed special adviser to Secretary of State

LAW COURTS AND OFFICES
Lords of Appeal in Ordinary – Lord Keith of Kinkel retired 30 September
Timothy Lloyd appointed to High Court (Chancery Division)
Timothy Walker appointed to High Court (Queen's Bench Division)
David E. Neuberger appointed to High Court (Chancery Division)
J. C. Warner appointed to Midland and Oxford circuit

POLICE SERVICE
Northamptonshire – C. Fox appointed chief constable

DEFENCE
Ministry of Defence – Richard Spring, MP, appointed parliamentary private secretary to Nicholas Soames and James Arbuthnot
Navy – Vice-Adm. Dunt to be Chief of Fleet Support in place of Vice-Adm. Sir Toby Frere; Cmdre B. Perowne to be promoted Rear-Admiral and to be Director-General, Fleet Support (Operations and Plans) in place of Rear-Adm. P. Spencer
Army – Maj.-Gen. R. Cordy-Simpson to be Deputy Force Commander Operations, Operation Joint Endeavour (in Bosnia), phase V, in acting rank of Lieutenant-General; Maj.-Gen. K. Drewienkiewicz to be Chief of Staff Headquarters Landcent, Operation Joint Endeavour, phase V; Maj.-Gen. M. D. Regan, OBE, retires
RAF – Air Vice-Marshal D. H. Hull retires

THE CHURCHES

Church of England
London – Ven. S. J. Oliver to be Canon Residentiary, St
Paul's Cathedral
Winchester – Ven. J. M. Gledhill to be Suffragan Bishop
of Southampton
St Edmundsbury and Ipswich – Rt. Revd Richard Lewis
(Suffragan Bishop of Taunton, diocese of Bath and
Wells) to be Bishop of St Edmundsbury and Ipswich
Worcester – Revd P. J. Marshall (Canon Residentiary,
Ripon) to be Dean

Roman Catholic Church
Argyll and the Isles – Bishop Wright resigned
Burundi – Archbishop Ruhuna killed

LOCAL GOVERNMENT
Lord Mayor of London 1996–7: Alderman Roger Cork
Sheriffs of the City of London 1996–7: Clive Martin;
Keith Knowles
Lord Lieutenant of Orkney, Brig. M. G. Dennison, died

MUSEUMS AND GALLERIES
Exeter Maritime Museum closed

THE MEDIA
Broadcasting Complaints Commission – Ms J. Leighton
appointed chairman

TRADE UNIONS
Elizabeth Symons resigned as secretary-general of the
Association of First Division Civil Servants

COUNTRIES OF THE WORLD
Afghanistan – Taliban rebels seized Kabul on 26–27
September, driving out government forces; a six-
member interim ruling council was set up
Armenia – President Levon Ter-Petrosyan re-elected
on 23 September; ballot followed by accusations of
corruption and demonstrations
Bosnia – elections for a three-member presidency,
national House of Representatives and assemblies for
the Srpska Republika and Muslim-Croat Federation
on 14 September; President Izetbegovic won most
votes in presidential election, followed by Mladen
Ivanic (Serb) and Kresimir Zubak (Croat)
Gambia – Col. Yayah Jammeh elected president on 27
September in first ballot since 1994 coup
Greece – general election on 22 September won by
Pasok party; Costas Simitis reappointed Prime
Minister
Grenada – Governor-General now Sir Daniel Williams,
GCMG
Japan – Prime Minister Hashimoto dissolved the Diet
on 27 September and called a general election for 20
October
Madagascar – President Zafy resigned on 5 September
after his impeachment was confirmed; Prime Minister
Ratsirahonana assumed presidential responsibilities
Thailand – Prime Minister Banharn Silpa-Archa
resigned on 21 September and a general election was
called

EVENTS – SEPTEMBER 1996

3–4. US aircraft and warships launched cruise missiles
against Iraqi targets in southern Iraq. The air exclusion
zone was extended from the 32nd to the 33rd parallel. **5.**
The RFU reached an agreement with the other home
rugby unions which saved the Five Nations
Championship. **8.** Kurdish refugees fled to Iran following the capture of the towns of Degala and Koi Sanjak
by the Iraqi government-backed Kurdistan Democratic
Party (KDP). **9.** The KDP captured the city of
Sulaimaniya. **16.** Roderick Wright resigned as the
Roman Catholic bishop of Argyll and the Isles after
going into hiding with a woman from his diocese; he
was later revealed to be the father of a 15-year-old son
by another woman. **19.** The Government abandoned
plans to slaughter 147,000 cattle after the European
Commission agreed to examine new scientific evidence
which showed that BSE would die out naturally by
2001. **23.** Ten tons of explosives were found by police
in a storage unit in Hornsey, north London. An IRA
terrorist suspect was shot dead by police in a raid on a
guesthouse in Hammersmith, west London, and five
more suspects were detained in other raids in London.
Four gunmen killed 21 people in a mosque in Pakistan
in a wave of violence following the killing of Prime
Minister Bhutto's estranged brother. **24.** China, France,
Russia, the UK and the USA signed the Comprehensive
Test Ban Treaty banning nuclear tests, although the
treaty did not acquire legal status because of India's
refusal to sign. **25–27.** Sixty-seven people died in
clashes between Israeli security forces and Palestinians
protesting against the opening of a tunnel near the Al
Aqsa mosque in east Jerusalem. **28.** At Ascot, Frankie
Dettori became the first jockey to win all seven races at
a meeting.

OBITUARIES

September
  3. Lord (Julian) Amery of Lustleigh, PC, former
     Conservative MP, junior minister and Minister of
     State, aged 77
     Robert (Bob) Brown, former Labour MP and junior
     minister, aged 75
  5. Clem Thomas, rugby player and journalist, aged 67
 13. Jane Baxter, film and stage actress, aged 87
 14. Juliet Prowse, actress and dancer, aged 59
 17. Spiro Agnew, vice-president of the USA 1969–73,
     aged 77
 20. Paul Erdös, Hungarian-born mathematician, aged 83
 21. Julius Silverman, former Labour MP, aged 90
 23. Dorothy Lamour, American film actress, aged 81
 23. Muhammad Najibullah, president of Afghanistan
     1986–92, executed aged 49
 28. Leslie Crowther, CBE, actor and comedian, aged 63